COME VISIT OUR NEW YORK CITY SHOWROOM! (OPEN WEEKDAYS, BY APPT ONLY.)
FOUR COLOR COMICS
BUY
WHY YOU SHOULD CALL US BEFORE YOU SELL YOUR COLLECTION OF COMICS, ARTWORK OR MEMORABILIA:
SELL
We make it easy! No waiting for payment, No song and dance about grading. We'll come to you: Anywhere, Anytime! FOUR COLOR COMICS takes the risk out of selling. Treat yourself to an honest, straight-forward experience—Sell your collection to us and walk away with more money in your pocket and a smile on your face.
And if you're looking to buy comics, original artwork or memorabilia, give us a call first! We probably already have that elusive issue or object you've been searching for—and at a price you'll like!
CALL ROBERT ROGOVIN!
(212) 675-6990
S0-BOF-047
NEW YORK SHOWROOM: 115 W. 27th St, NY, NY 10001 TEL: (212) 675-6990, FAX (212) 675-6145
NEW!
Visit our on-line
SEARCHABLE DATABASE!
1000's of Golden and Silver Age comics available without scrolling thru endless listings!
www.fourcolorcomics.com
ORIGINAL COMIC ART
SEARCH COMICS!
MOVIE POSTERS

METROPOLIS
COLLECTIBLES, INC
873 Broadway, Suite 201
New York, NY 10003
BUYING
Absolutely no other comic dealer buys or sells more Golden and Silver age comic books than
Metropolis.
1. We pay more because we sell more!
2. We travel anywhere to buy your books!
3. We have millions of dollars to spend!
4. We offer a toll-free phone number!
5. Over 25 years experience
6. We offer immediate payment!
7. We offer a free appraisal service.
CALL TOLL-FREE
1-800-229-6387
tel 212-260-4147
fax 212-260-4304
email us at:
buying@metropoliscomics.com
visit us on the web at:
www.metropoliscomics.com
Action Comics
Batman
Fantastic Four
Showcase
COMICS GUARANTY, LLC
Charter
Member Dealer
© DC

31st Edition

COMICS FROM 1842-PRESENT INCLUDED
FULLY ILLUSTRATED CATALOGUE & EVALUATION GUIDE

BY ROBERT M. OVERSTREET

GEMSTONE PUBLISHING

J. C. Vaughn, **Executive Editor**
Arnold T. Blumberg, **Editor** • Brenda Busick, **Creative Director**
Mark Huesman, **Pricing Coordinator**
Kimberly Grover, **Administrative Assistant**

SPECIAL CONTRIBUTORS TO THIS EDITION

Robert L. Beerbohm • Arnold T. Blumberg • M. Thomas Inge
Matt Nelson • Charles S. Novinskie • Richard D. Olson, Ph.D. • J. C. Vaughn

SENIOR ADVISORS FOR OVER 25 YEARS

Dave Alexander • Landon Chesney • Bruce Hamilton • Paul Levitz • Michelle Nolan
Terry Stroud • Harry B. Thomas •Doug Sulipa • Raymond S. True

SENIOR ADVISORS FOR OVER 20 YEARS

Gary M. Carter • Bill Cole • Gene Seger • Steve Geppi • Stan Gold
M. Thomas Inge • Phil Levine • Richard Olson • Ron Pussell
David R. Smith • John K. Snyder

SPECIAL ADVISORS TO THIS EDITION

Dave Anderson • David J. Anderson, D.D.S. • Robert L. Beerbohm • Jon Berk • Steve Borock
John Chruscinski • Gary Colabuono • Larry Curcio • Gary Dolgoff • Joe Dungan • Conrad Eschenberg
Richard Evans • Stephen Fishler • Philip J. Gaudino • Steve Gentner • Michael Goldman • Jamie Graham
Daniel Greenhalgh • Eric Groves • Gary Guzzo • John Grasse • Mark Haspel • John Hauser • John Hone
George Huang • Bill Hughes • Rob Hughes • Ed Jaster • Joseph Koch • Joe Mannarino • Rick Manzella
Harry Matetsky • Jon McClure • Matt Nelson • Michael Naiman • Josh Nathanson • James Payette
Yolanda Ramirez • Todd Reznik • "Doc" Robinson • Robert Rogovin • Rory Root • Robert Roter
Chuck Rozanski • Matt Schiffman • Dave Smith • Laura Sperber • Tony Starks • Joel Thingvall
Joe Vereneault • Frank Verzyl • John Verzyl • Rose Verzyl • Jerry Weist • Harley Yee • Vincent Zurzolo, Jr.

The Crown Publishing Group
New York

Gemstone Publishing

Important Notice. All of the information, including valuations, in this book has been compiled from the most reliable sources, and every effort has been made to eliminate errors and questionable data. Nevertheless, the possibility of error always exists in a work of such immense scope. The publisher will not be held responsible for losses which may occur in the purchase, sale, or other transaction of items because of information contained herein. Readers who feel they have discovered errors are invited to *write* and inform us so that the errors may be corrected in subsequent editions.

Cover Illustrations: The Fantastic Four #1 re-created by John K. Snyder III and Detective Comics #31 re-created by Murphy Anderson; used with permission.

THE OFFICIAL OVERSTREET COMIC BOOK PRICE GUIDE (31st Edition) is an original publication of Gemstone Publishing, Inc. and House of Collectibles. Distributed by The Crown Publishing Group, a division of Random House, Inc., New York and simultaneously in Canada by Random House of Canada Limited, Toronto. This edition has never before appeared in book form.

House of Collectibles
The Crown Publishing Group
299 Park Ave.
New York, New York 10171

www.randomhouse.com

Published by arrangement with Gemstone Publishing.

ISBN: 0-609-80820-6
ISSN: 0891-8872

Printed in the United States of America

10 9 8 7 6 5 4 3 2 1

Thirty-First Edition: May 2001

COLLECTORS
ASSEMBLE!
BUYING and SELLING
COMICS PRE 1966
Collectors Assemble!
ComicCollectors.net
Marnin Rosenberg
P.O. Box 2047
Great Neck, NY 11022-2047
(516) 466-8147
www.ComicCollectors.net
for high grade quality rare vintage comic books!!!
SPECIALIZING IN RARE HIGH GRADE INVESTMENT COMICS

TABLE OF CONTENTS

ACKNOWLEDGEMENTS

Mark Arnold (Harvey data); Larry Bigman (Frazetta-Williamson data); Glenn Bray (Kurtzman data); Gary Carter (DC data); J. B. Clifford Jr. (EC data); Gary Coddington (Superman data); Wilt Conine (Fawcett data); Dr. S. M. Davidson (Cupples & Leon data); Al Dellinges (Kubert data); David Gerstein (Walt Disney Comics data); Kevin Hancer (Tarzan data); Charles Heffelfinger and Jim Ivey (March of Comics listing); R. C. Holland and Ron Pussell (Seduction and Parade of Pleasure data); Grant Irwin (Quality data); Richard Kravitz (Kelly data); Phil Levine (giveaway data); Dan Malan & Charles Heffelfinger (Classic Comics data); Fred Nardelli (Frazetta data); Michelle Nolan (love comics); Mike Nolan (MLJ, Timely, Nedor data); George Olshevsky (Timely data); Chris Pedrin (DC War data); Scott Pell ('50s data); Greg Robertson (National data); Don Rosa (Late 1940s to 1950s data); Matt Schiffman (Bronze Age data); Frank Scigliano (Little Lulu data); Gene Seger (Buck Rogers data); Rick Sloane (Archie data); David R. Smith, Archivist, Walt Disney Productions (Disney data); Tony Starks (Silver and Bronze Age data); Don and Maggie Thompson (Four Color listing); Mike Tiefenbacher & Jerry Sinkovec (Atlas and National data); Raymond True & Philip J. Gaudino (Classic Comics data); Jim Vadeboncoeur Jr. (Williamson and Atlas data); Kim Weston (Disney and Barks data); Cat Yronwode (Spirit data); Andrew Zerbe and Gary Behymer (M. E. data).

In celebration of the 40th anniversary of Fantastic Four, we are fortunate to present one of John K. Snyder's best efforts on the cover of this book. I would also like to thank Murphy Anderson for his recreation of Detective Comics #31, published as our alternate cover, and to his son Murphy III for his logo design for this cover. Credit is also due Arnie Sawyer for his improvements to both logo and spine designs.

The new 10 point grading system adopted in the 30th Edition of the Guide was the result of extensive input from my team of advisors. Although a similar system was considered years ago, the original concept of using .5 point increments was submitted by Stephen Fishler, which eventually evolved into the final version we are using today.

Credit is due my two grading advisors, Steve Borock and Mark Haspel of Comics Guaranty Corp., for reviewing the new grading changes in this edition.

Tribute is also given to Chuck Rozanski for his voluminous contribution of pricing data for this edition, which included internet sales.

My gratitude is given to Chris Pedrin, known for his extensive published research on DC war comics, for checking the accuracy of and providing needed data for this and previous editions of the guide. Thanks, Chris, from me and all of fandom for your excellent contribution to this area of research.

Thanks to Stephen Fishler and Marc Patten for "How to Sell Your Comic Collection;" to Dr. Richard Olson for grading and Yellow Kid information; to Tom Inge for his "Chronology of the American Comic Book;" to Matt Nelson for his rewriting the restored comics section; to Arnold T. Blumberg for his introduction to the Promotional Comics section; to Robert Beerbohm and Richard Olson for their introductions to the Platinum Age and Golden Age sections; to Bill Blackbeard of the San Francisco Academy of Comic Art for his Platinum Age cover photos; to Bill Spicer and Zetta DeVoe (Western Publishing Co.) for their contribution of data; and especially to Bill for his kind permission to reprint portions of his and Jerry Bails' America's Four Color Pastime.

Special recognition is due Bob Beerbohm who spent months researching the Platinum section in this edition. He organized a team of experts from around the world who sent him detailed data for updating this section. My hat is off to Bob and his colleagues for a job well done.

Thanks again to Doug Sulipa, Jon McClure and Tony Starks for continuing to provide detailed Bronze Age data! Harry Thomas, Stephen Fishler, Jim Payette, Rob Rogovin, Joe Vereneault, John Verzyl, Frank Verzyl, Josh Nathanson, Vincent Zurzolo Jr., Ed Jaster, Ron Pussell, Dave Alexander and Terry Stroud supplied detailed pricing data, market reviews or other material in this edition.

Acknowledgement is also due to the following people who generously contributed much needed data/photographs for this edition: Stephen Baer, Ron Ballard, Ken Barnes, Jonathan Bennett, Chris Boyko, Mike Bromberg, Mike Browning, Marshall Crist, Howard Leroy Davis, Tom Gordon, Marty Hay, Dennis Hernandez, David Kell, Robert Koopmans, Tony Kowalik, Ken Kwilinski, Joseph Latino, Paul Levitz, Dennis Lynch, William Mahan, Howard E. Michaels Jr., Al Mindy, John Mlachnik, David B. Morgan, Doug Ogle, Anthony Pearce, Dennis Petilli, Robert Quesinberry, Larry Reese, Tom Sodano, Jim Stangas, West Stephan, Jeff Tignor, Fiorello B. Ventresco, Jeff Walker, Kirk Wallace, Timothy M. Walters, Murray R. Ward, Bob Wayne, Doug Wheeler, and David Young.

Finally, special credit is due our talented production staff for their assistance with this edition; to Arnold T. Blumberg (Editor), Brenda Busick (Creative Director), and Mark Huesman (Pricing Coordinator), as well as to our Executive Editor, J. C. Vaughn, for their valuable contributions to this edition. Thanks to my wife, Caroline, for her encouragement and support on such a tremendous project, and to all who placed ads in this edition.

Detective
COMICS
10¢

BATMAN

ACTION
COMICS

WHIZ
COMICS
10¢
GANGWAY FOR CAPTAIN MARVEL!

MARVEL
COMICS

WHY THE FF M

BY ARNOLD T. BLUMBERG

By now we all know the story about the origin of the FF, either in the Marvel Universe with that storm of cosmic rays, or in the real world with Martin Goodman, Stan Lee and Jack Kirby. The Marvel Age of Comics was born that fateful day in 1961, and forty years later, "The World's Greatest Comic Magazine" is still going strong, albeit with different numbering.

So here without further ado are forty reasons why the Fantastic Four made it from 1961 to 2001—a brief alphabetical retrospective of their comic book odyssey.

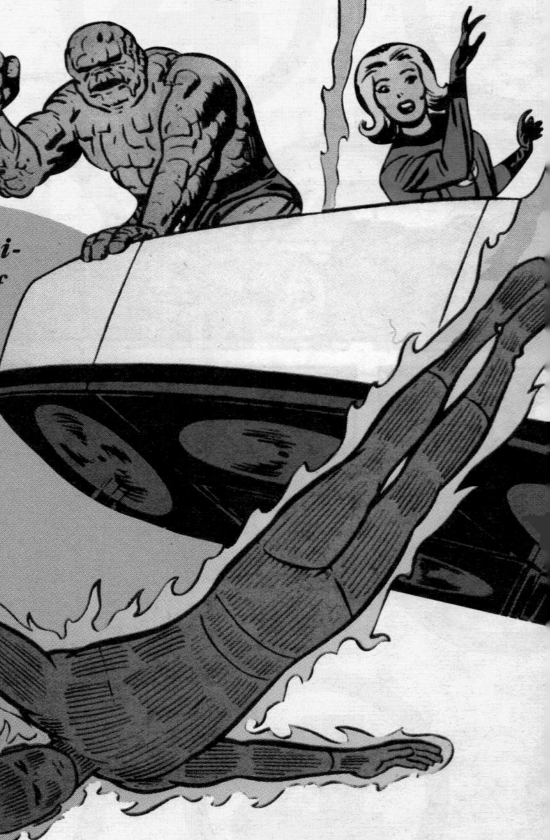

EATEST FAMILY:

DE IT TO FORTY

Agatha Harkness–There aren't many parents who would hire an honest-to-goodness witch as a nanny, but when the child is the mutant baby of two members of the Fantastic Four, Mary Poppins just ain't gonna cut it.

Alicia Masters–The blind sculptress captured the Thing's scaly heart and ours as well. Their tragic love affair went through some interesting twists, and there was the matter of her father being the evil Pupper Master, but no one's perfect.

Baxter Building, The–Even when it was replaced by Four Freedoms Plaza, this remained the one true home for the FF and one of Marvel New York's most recognizable landmarks.

Ben Grimm, aka The Thing–Truly a tragic figure, the monster with a heart of gold. Ben was just a cigar-chompin' flyboy until that fateful test flight, but now he provides the brute force that carries the FF through their many amazing adventures. Underneath his rocky exterior, he's a wide-eyed child, and a swell guy to boot.

Black Panther–At a time when African-American heroes were hard to find in comics, Marvel blazed the trail with King T'Challa of Wakanda. T'Challa had a habit of donning black spandex and fighting villains like Klaw, the Master of Sound. It's a comic book thing.

Changing cast–Although the true FF remains Reed, Sue, Johnny and Ben, there were a number of temporary teammates from the Inhumans' Crystal and Medusa to Luke Cage, Thundra, She-Hulk, Lyta, and even the "New" team of Spider-Man, Ghost Rider, the Hulk and Wolverine!

Cover of FF #1–The image of that gape-mouthed Kirby monster breaking through the sidewalk and surrounded by an assortment of characters who might be monsters themselves–this was the birth of a legend, and the perfect cover to introduce us to the Fantastic Four. It's also one of the most redrawn (and ripped off) cover layouts in comic book history, reused by the FF title itself on several occasions!

Death of Sue's second child, The–One of the most heart-wrenching moments in Marvel history. After a citywide slugfest between Reed and Doctor Octopus, Mr. Fantastic convinces Ock with words that he should help them combat the radiation affecting Sue's delivery of their second child...but they're too late. Even the Fantastic Four were not able to snatch victory from the hands of the Grim Reaper in this dark but moving installment.

Doctor Doom–Need more be said about this imposing monarch, this towering intellect, this superior force of nature that is Victor Von Doom? Kneel before the Ruler of Latveria, the single greatest villain in the history of the Marvel Universe, for none may match the power that is Doom! Forever hidden beneath a mask of iron and a cloak of regal green, he plans for the eventual destruction of the Fantastic Four. Doom will one day triumph, and then let the world tremble!

Family–The key to the FF's success. They are much more than another collection of brightly-garbed muscle-bound types. They are a family that cares as much about each other as they do about defeating injustice and protecting the weak. Despite all of their superhero trappings and extraordinary powers, they're human, and that's why we love them.

Fighting–Oh yes, families can fight, and this one is capable of some pretty strange bickering from time to time. How many families do you know that can hurl huge pieces of furniture, imprison each other in invisible force fields, wrap themselves around each other, or toss fireballs? But it's all in fun, even with the massive property damage.

Franklin Richards–A mutant with incredible psychic powers, Franklin's bizarre rate of aging and occasional reality-threatening episodes have been the fodder for plenty of stories. Franklin has been depowered by his own father (the catalyst for a temporary rift between Reed and Sue), rapidly aged into a Christ-like figure, and sent through time. All in a day's work.

Frightful Four, The–It was inevitable that the FF would spawn a rival team. The Wizard headed up the membership of the Frightful Four, which started out with the Trapster (aka Paste Pot Pete), the Inhumans' own Medusa in a brief brush with evil, and Spidey's old sparring partner, the Sandman.

Galactus Trilogy, The–The FF has long been associated with epic storytelling, and here's where it all began. This first cosmic trilogy, appearing in **FF** #48-50, introduced us to the Silver Surfer, another figure of tragic nobility, and his master, the space-faring Galactus, Destroyer of Worlds. Only by threatening the annihilation of all reality was the FF (with some help from the Watcher) able to turn this huge invader away.

H.E.R.B.I.E.–If a super-team can survive the introduction of a robotic annoyance like this little creep, then they truly are heroes. First created to take the place of the Human Torch in a cartoon version of the FF, H.E.R.B.I.E. wormed his way into the actual comic and was promptly dispatched (thank God). Rest in pieces, you freaky metal malcontent.

Impossible Man, The–While not quite as irredeemable a character as H.E.R.B.I.E., the Impossible Man was also rather annoying. An interfering imp from another planet, this pointy-headed green shape-shifter was Marvel's answer to Mr. Mxyzptlk and Bat-Mite, always popping up to aggravate the FF and cause trouble.

Inhumans, The–This fascinating group of outcasts are steadfast friends (for the most part) of our intrepid team and lived either in a mountain retreat under a sealed dome or in a secret location on the Moon over the years. Ruled by the strong but silent Black Bolt, the Inhumans all sport some pretty wild abnormalities, from cloven hoofs or wings to prehensile hair or the ability to teleport.

Invincible Man, The–The FF has a foe that has returned many times to plague them but has never been the same person twice. How is that possible? It's easy with the Invincible Man! Originally a disguise created for the Super-Skrull, the distinctive hooded suit would turn up again and again to confound the FF as to the true identity of the wearer.

"It's Clobberin' Time!" –One of comicdom's most memorable catch-phrases, second only to the Torch's own "Flame On!" and other Marvel excalamations like "Avengers Assemble!" The Thing's phrase perfectly captures his devil-may-care attitude and dedication to the belief that anything can be solved by pounding on someone with beefy three-fingered fists. He's usually right too.

John Byrne's reign–John Byrne's tenure on the series was one of the most consistent, sustained periods in the title's history, bringing the FF back to their roots and sending them off in a bewildering number of directions. A trip to a tiny town controlled by the Puppet Master in #236 was a memorable 20th anniversary highlight, but there are just too many to list.

Johnny Storm, aka The Human Torch–Not exactly the sharpest matchstick in town, Johnny was usually more concerned with picking up chicks and working on hot rods than anything else. He did some growing up over the years, but retained his free-wheeling attitude and willingness to indulge in playful banter and roughhousing with the Thing and Spider-Man.

"Milk" Annual, The–Well, that's how I remember it–actually it's **Fantastic Four Annual** #17. In one of the FF's most unforgettable forays into horror, the team discovers a small town that's been changed into a collection of shape-changing monsters. The key is the milk they've been drinking, which came from some cows Reed should remember well (hint: they're shape-shifting Skrulls!).

Negative Zone, The–Another dimension of adventure and excitement discovered by Reed and often explored by the team through a portal maintained in one of Reed's enormous labs. The Negative Zone introduced us to creatures like Annihilus and Blastaar and even hosted the conception of Reed and Sue's second child.

Reed and Sue's marriage–In a genre that rarely allows married superhero couples to live happily without heaping endless tragedy upon them, the marriage of Reed and Sue Richards is rock-steady. Their steadfast devotion to one another is the strength from which the team thrives. Now watch some upstart writer split them up.

Reed Richards, aka Mr. Fantastic–The driving force of the Fantastic Four and the intellectual center of the entire Marvel Universe. He is the quintessential scientist–an explorer, a seeker of truth. While occasionally aloof, he is a loving husband and father and the best team leader in the history of comics...and he can stretch like a rubber band!

Roberta–The FF are so up-to-date and cutting edge, even their secretary is the product of Reed's highly advanced technological know-how! Stationed on the ground floor of the Baxter Building, Roberta is a robot receptionist mounted on a pivot arm hidden beneath her desk. Must make it difficult for her to go off for a cigarette break.

Spider-Man/Torch friendship–If Reed and Sue represent Marvel's most stable marriage, then Spider-Man and the Human Torch have enjoyed the longest lasting friendship between heroes in the Marvel Universe. Starting as bitter rivals, they even made it through the horrific "Spider-Mobile" era! Their standard meeting place atop the head of the Statue of Liberty has given Marvel fans another reason to gaze in awe at the Lady whenever they visit New York.

Spin-offs–Although the FF never achieved the cult status of the X-Men or Spider-Man, the first Marvel stars have appeared in a variety of solo series and guest shots over the years. The Torch had his own run in **Strange Tales** and the Thing starred in **Marvel Two-in-One** and later **The Thing**. Add up the multitude of mini-series, cameos and **Marvel Team-Up** guest shots, and you have the hardest working family in comics.

Stan and Jack–the Gods of the Marvel Universe, world-builders extraordinaire. From their prolific fingertips did spring every element, every nuance, every divine spark that gave Marvel and its fans a reality in which to play for generations to come. The Fantastic Four were the first to explore this new universe, investigating its many wonders while encountering a veritable parade of the most exotic characters ever created for comics. The first 100 issues of the **Fantastic Four** are unrivaled classics of the medium, a perfect primer for constructing a successful comic book saga. While some would almost equal the scope and grandeur of what Stan and Jack have wrought, no one would ever top them. Even the dread Doom would bow to these legendary creators.

Sub-Mariner–Sub-Mariner was a villain with a noble heart, threatening the world as often as he'd help it, and completing a romantic triangle with Reed and Sue. Sometimes Sue wasn't sure who her heart belonged to, adding a welcome twist to the usual villain dynamic.

Sue Storm Richards, aka the Invisible Girl (later Woman)–The heart and spiritual center of the team. She keeps the peace between the Thing and the Torch, and even got a chance to strut her stuff in dominatrix garb as her darker side, Malice. During Reed's absence, Sue proved herself to be a capable leader in her own right. She's come a long way, baby.

Thing/Hulk Feud–What's a superhero story without two heroes fighting? The first encounter between these two turned into an ongoing rivalry that led to many other battles over the years. The original fight was evidently deemed so effective it was literally lifted, redrawn and repeated almost verbatim in another comic years later! "Wotta revoltin' development!"

"This Man, This Monster"–Most FF fans agree that this Stan Lee story, appearing in **FF** #51, is one of the most memorable tales of real heroism in comics. An imposter takes the Thing's place in the FF but learns the true meaning of friendship and sacrifice in a morality play that ranks with some of Stan's best work.

Truth behind the Thing's incurable condition, The–It was John Byrne who nailed down the reason why no cure ever worked on the behemoth. His fear of losing Alicia, who fell in love with him in his burlier guise, was so deep-seated that he physically rejected a cure. Now that's tragic.

Unstable molecules–Trust Reed Richards to finally provide a scientific explanation for all those seemingly indestructible skintight superhero suits. His invention of "unstable molecules" allowed the creation of clothing that could mimic the powers of its wearer and transform with them. Soon there was only one fashion choice for the discerning Marvel adventurer.

Vehicles and Gadgets–Who else but Jack Kirby could have drawn all of those gleaming metal structures that snaked their way through the Baxter Building? Kirby's gift for drawing gadgetry on a grand scale led to endless scenes of the Thing holding aloft some monstrous mechanism of Reed's. Jack also gave us the sleek lines of the Fantasti-Car and Pogo Plane.

Walt Simonson's run–Simonson's short tenure upped the ante on the SF elements, particularly with a time travel story arc that incorporated a number of in-joke references to **Doctor Who**. The style of illustration was distinctly different from what had come before, but it was undoubtedly still the Fantastic Four. No heroes being reborn here...ugh.

Watcher, The–Pledged to observe humanity but never interfere, the egg-headed alien violated his oath on numerous occasions, assisting in the defense of the Earth in the Galactus trilogy and transporting the team to another galaxy to witness the trial of Reed Richards years later. He's basically a "deus ex machina" in sandals, and his funky home on the Moon is another Marvel Universe landmark.

Weaving the universe tighter–The Fantastic Four often serve as the focal point for the Marvel Universe. The Avengers, the X-Men, Daredevil, Ka-Zar, and even Spider-Man himself would regularly drop by for a cameo or full-blown appearance, especially if the entire world faced imminent disaster. The FF were a popular family and knew how to socialize.

Yancy Street gang–How many of us would feel comfortable giving the Thing a raspberry? The Yancy streeters don't care that the Thing is a hero and an international idol adored by millions; to them, he's just another big ox who needs to be taken down a peg.

If the FF of the 21st century appear as little more than a shadow of the original team that revolutionized the genre five decades ago, it's a testament to the genius of Stan and Jack that they made it at all. This year, a 12 issue maxi-series celebrates the glory days of the team while underlining all of the elements that made them such an enduring success. After forty years, hundreds of epic tales and more cries of "It's Clobberin' Time" than one can count, the Fantastic Four remain unbowed by the wonders they've witnessed or the battles they have fought. They are a super-team without peer, and they symbolize the traits we all aspire to achieve while providing us with an exhilarating escape from the world's woes. First and foremost, they are a family, and we are privileged to have been a welcome visitor in their home for so many years.

FROM ALL STAR TO SE
60 YEARS OF

NSATION TO WONDER:

WONDER WOMAN

BY CHARLES S. NOVINSKIE

By today's standards, it's common to see women portrayed as lead characters and strong role models in everything from movies to, well, comic books. Back in the early 1940s there were very few female role models, however, especially in the testosterone-dominated world of comic books. When it comes to Wonder Woman, there was nothing common about her. In fact, the birth of Wonder Woman in 1941 was as radically different as her creator, William Moulton Marston.

William Moulton Marston, writing under the pen name of Charles Moulton, was as unique an individual as the characters he created. Already a noted psychologist, Marston was a published author and in 1915 created the systolic blood pressure test, claiming that changes in blood pressure could reveal if a person was lying. This discovery led to the invention of the first polygraph, or lie detector, in 1921. Marston was indeed an anomaly in the comics industry of the early 1940s. He was already in his late forties and serving as an educational consultant for Detective Comics when he pitched the idea for Wonder Woman.

The premise was a simple one for Moulton, who would be declared a feminist in today's terms. The face of America in 1941 was one in turmoil, and yet there was a sort of calm-before-the-storm demeanor as far as the United States involvement in World War II was concerned. Much like today, the comic book buying audience consisted of boys. Superman was indeed the comic that enthralled everyone, and it was Moulton that figured that a female "superman" would appeal in a similar way to girls and thus reach an untapped market. In the December 1941/January 1942 bimonthly issue of **All Star Comics** #8, Wonder Woman was born. While the dream of capturing the hearts of girls everywhere never really fully blossomed, the character did catch on, no doubt buoyed by the sale of Wonder Woman comics to boys that had their pulses more than a little raised by the exploits of scantily-clad Hippolyte, Queen of the Amazons, and her daughter, Princess Diana, as detailed by old-school cartoonist Harry Peter.

In January 1942, **Sensation Comics** #1 was launched, with Wonder Woman as the lead character. The story continued the origin of Princess Diana and her life on Paradise Island–a world free from men, and also free of war and all the ills created by man. Paradise Island was a place in which the Amazons, recently freed from slavery by Queen Hippolyte, could live eternally as long as they never left the island. All of this quickly changed when a plane crashed on the island and Princess Diana exclaimed, "A man! A man on Paradise Island!" This man, of course, was Steve Trevor, and he quickly became the focus of Princess

Diana's life. A smattering of feminism, a bevy of beautiful women, and a good dose of mythology and Wonder Woman was off and running, complete with a magic golden lasso (which forced those bound by it to tell the truth, Marston's own version of the lie detector), bullet-deflecting bracelets, and even an invisible plane. Moulton had created one of the most enduring and endearing characters to ever grace the pages of a comic book. By the summer of 1942, **Wonder Woman** #1 went on sale.

It was with issue #1 of **Wonder Woman** that Princess Diana removed herself from the self-proclaimed exile that was Paradise Island. Like all of the other comics of their time, Wonder Woman was enlisted to help fight the Axis powers. If nothing else, this gave Wonder Woman's alter ego, Diana Prince, the opportunity to share in the exploits of Steve Trevor. Formerly a nurse, Diana Prince was conveniently moved to a secretarial position with U.S. Army Intelligence. Wonder Woman was so successful that by the end of 1942 she triumphantly appeared quarterly in **Comic Cavalcade**. By early 1944, Wonder Woman, now appearing in three separate titles, was contracted by King Features Syndicate to appear daily in newspapers across the country.

There is no doubt that the success of Wonder Woman was due to the unconventional background of psychologist William Marston and the stylistic artwork of Harry Peter. It was with Moulton's death in 1947 and the exit of Harry Peter as artist that Wonder Woman's exploits were no longer, well, wonderful. Robert Kanigher, then writer of **Black Canary**, was offered the chance to not only edit but to write the adventures of the Amazon Princess. Now that the war was over, comics shifted towards romance. Kanigher, eager to guide Wonder Woman in a new direction, created Wonder Girl and Wonder Tot. Unfortunately, many of the stories produced in the 1950s had very little to do with DC continuity, or for that matter, Wonder Woman continuity. The same period did produce some wonderfully illustrated pieces by Mike Esposito and Ross Andru however.

The sixties saw a revamp for Wonder Woman after the character nearly failed to make it through the fifties, and what a revamp it was. Newly assigned editor Jack Miller named Denny O'Neil as writer and Mike Sekowsky as penciler. Adding his own distinctive flair to the inking was Dick Giordano. Diana Prince had been transformed from her former lackluster self to a modern, self-sufficient, confident woman of the late 1960s. Of course, she had to be a dynamic individual if she was ever going to clear the love of her life, Steve Trevor, of murder charges. In an effort to reinvent Diana Prince, O'Neil had her sacrifice her powers as an Amazon princess in order to stay on Earth. Even Steve Trevor, invincible during his war exploits, met the cruel fate of O'Neil's imagination. It is believed that Diana Prince's revamping (and new sleek look) was due to the popularity of Diana Rigg's Emma Peel, the beautiful but capable secret agent that fought opposite Patrick MacNee's John Steed on the popular British television show, *The Avengers*. By 1970, the new Wonder Woman was back in action and ready to tackle any adventure that was thrown her way.

1972 was perhaps a peak for feminist movements around the US. In fact, it was Gloria Steinem's debut of **Ms.** magazine that once again shaped the future of Diana Prince. *The* magazine for the feminist movement, **Ms.** featured none other than Wonder Woman on the cover in full Amazon garb with a headline declaring "Wonder Woman For President." The path was clear: **Ms.** had declared that the Wonder Woman of old be returned. By 1973, Wonder Woman did indeed return to her roots when she awoke from a trance on Paradise Island. Robert Kanigher was once again given editorial control over Wonder Woman. Kanigher's main emphasis seemed geared towards correcting discrepancies in continuity created during the past decade of storytelling. Eventually, Julius Schwartz took over as editor with **Wonder**

Woman #212 in 1974. Maybe it was a sign of the changing times, but the Wonder Woman of the '70s never seemed to fit in. Creative teams changed time and time again as different writers and artists tried to recapture the Amazon appeal that Wonder Woman possessed during the Moulton/Peter era.

It was writer Gerry Conway who scripted the final issue of **Wonder Woman**, #329, in February 1986. Ironically, this last issue featured the wedding of Princess Diana to Steve Trevor (hey, does anyone every really stay dead in comics?). The demise of **Wonder Woman** was directly related to a revamping of the DC universe known as **Crisis on Infinite Earths**. The premise was simple: to reorganize the entire DC universe in order to free many of its main characters from decades of unwanted baggage. Writer-editor Marv Wolfman was in charge of overseeing the 12-issue **Crisis**. With the help of Len Wein, George Perez, and the dimension-crunching Anti-Monitor, no fewer than twelve dimensions were boiled down into one easy-to-manage DC universe. It took all twelve issues before Wonder Woman met her demise as Princess Diana was reduced to the clay from which she was originally formed. This clay was then scattered over Paradise Island. And as any diehard comic book enthusiast knows, that demise had revival written all over it.

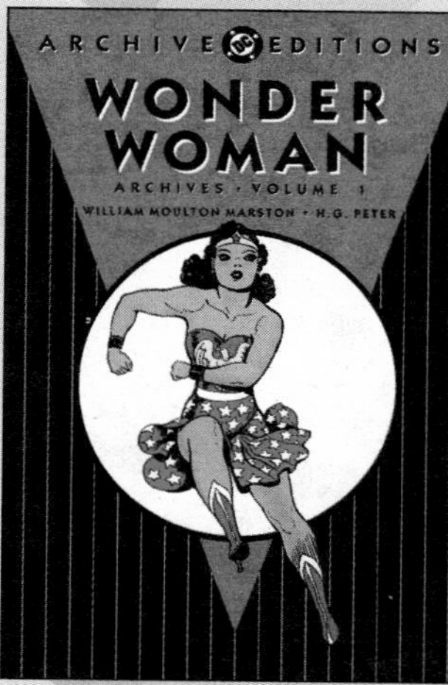

After wrapping up his **Crisis** chores, George Perez stepped in to reintroduce everyone's favorite Amazon princess. After nearly five decades since **Wonder Woman** #1 hit the stands, a new, revamped **Wonder Woman** #1 was released. Perez worked with Greg Potter, and later Len Wein, to present a Princess Diana that was born on Paradise Island and totally unaware of the outside world. Wonder Woman's exploits in the outside world presented her as an ambassador of the Amazons and did away with any need for an alter ego. Newcomers to the Wonder Woman mythos were Julia and Vanessa Kapatelis, a substitute family for Princess Diana, as well as long-time supporting cast members Etta Candy and Steve Trevor. Perez eventually left the book to turn his talents towards the **New Titans**. By 1990 Perez was back on board writing, following a short stay by writer Mindy Newell. Jill Thompson rendered the pencils until the "retirement" of Perez with **Wonder Woman** #62.

After a short hiatus, **Wonder Woman** #63 hit the stands in the summer of 1992. Bolstered by covers from talented British artist Brian Bolland, the book appeared to be picking up steam under the guidance of writer William Messner-Loebs. It was editor Paul Kupperberg that hired on the little-known Brazilian artist, Mike Deodato Jr. Deodato's "good girl art" style fit well for Princess Diana's return to Paradise Island. Messner-Loebs and Deodato's swan song was **Wonder Woman** #100 in July of 1995. With **Wonder Woman** #101, John Byrne was brought onboard to once again retool the Amazon princess. By issue #127, Byrne's plans for Princess Diana became apparent: death and ascension. Appearing dead after an epic battle, Princess Diana ascended to Olympus where she was reborn as Diana, Goddess of Truth. Byrne had indeed attained the unattainable, propelling Wonder Woman to the height of superhero status while staying true to her mythological origins.

The most recent redirection of Diana's life began in **Wonder Woman** #164 under the pen of writer-artist Phil Jimenez. While there are no doubt many more twists and turns to her future, one aspect is crystal clear: Wonder Woman has emerged as one of the greatest comic book superheroes and has indeed stood the test of time as befits her legendary status.

Charles S. Novinskie, a life-long comic book fan and former sales/promotions manager for Topps Comics, occasionally writes about comics and trading cards from his home in Grand Junction, Colorado. He can be contacted at Charlienovinskie@hotmail.com.

Brownie Points
THE STORY OF PALMER COX

BY ARNOLD T. BLUMBERG

While many of us in comics talk about the debut of the Brownies as a pop culture watershed–a moment when the twin phenomena of comic characters and character merchandising first met with such force, setting the stage for an entire industry to come–there are doubtless many collectors who don't know the full story behind the origin of one of the most important cartoon creations in entertainment history.

The story of the Brownies' beginnings are at once fanciful and factual, a dual origin of the man and his mini-creations, whose legacy would live on to the present day in unlikely descendents like the Smurfs and Pokémon. Palmer Cox, one of nine children born to Michael and Sarah Miller Cox on an unassuming farm near Quebec, would grow up to establish that legacy and become one of the towering figures in early American pop culture history.

Born April 28, 1840, Palmer Cox lived in a region filled with the Scottish folklore that would later inspire his most memorable creations. He graduated from the Granby Academy in 1858 and fell into a series of building and woodworking jobs, from the construction of railroad cars to working with his brother Edwin as a barn framer in Ontario. Legend has it that he drew on loose timbers, cultivating his skills as an illustrator.

In 1863 he arrived in Oakland, California after a trip west that took him across the Isthmus of Panama...on foot! He became a US citizen at this time, remaining in California for 13 years and initially continuing his building work on steamboats and railroad cars. When he relocated to San Francisco, then a burgeoning literary center, he began contributing poetry, prose, and cartoons to publications like **The Golden Era**, **The Alta California**, and **The San Francisco Examiner**. An active Mason who became Master of his lodge in 1874, Cox published his first book that year as well, titled **Squibs of California**, or **Everyday Life**. The book was based on his diary and contained almost 500 pages of written and illustrated work.

The east coast and the promise of a more illustrious literary career called to Cox, and in 1875 he left San Francisco for New York. Struggling for a while, he soon took the post as chief artist for **Uncle Sam: The American Journal of Wit and Humor**. He also published three more books with illustrated verse, and soon his work appeared in periodicals like **Scribner's Monthly**, **Harper's Young People**, and the children's magazines **Wide Awake** and **St. Nickolas**.

Wide Awake hosted the first appearance of the Brownies in February 1881 (although similar characters had previously debuted in three other Cox stories), "The Battle of the Types." Exactly two years later, "The Brownie's Ride" appeared in **St. Nickolas**, and twenty-four Brownie stories followed. In 1887, **The Brownies, Their Book** collected these features in one volume. A second collection was released in 1890, titled **Another**

Brownie Book.

The Brownies Through the Year was a series created by Cox to appear in **The Ladies Home Journal** (which also featured an essay titled "The Origin of the 'Brownies'" in November 1892; see at right). The series was collected in the third volume, **The Brownies at Home**, in 1893. Eventually, twelve books featuring the Brownies were published, and their popularity led to the earliest cross-promotional merchandising with comic characters in American history. Their success even extended to live theater. The first of two plays written by Cox, **The Brownies in Fairyland**, was adapted into book form in 1894, while **Palmer Cox's Brownies** was performed at the Fourteenth Street Theatre in New York. Opening on November 12, 1894, the show toured for five years following 100 performances at its original venue.

By 1905, Cox returned to Quebec and built a turreted, seventeen room house with a four-story tower based on his own plans. Dubbed "Brownie Castle," the estate was his home until his death on July 24, 1924. The inscription on Cox's tombstone stands as a reminder of the legacy he left behind: "In Creating the Brownies, He Bestowed a Priceless Heritage on Childhood."

Brownie-related books by Palmer Cox:

The Brownies, Their Book, 1887
Another Brownie Book, 1890
The Brownies at Home, 1893
The Brownies Around the World, 1894
The Brownies Through the Union, 1895
Brownie Year Book, 1895
The Brownies Abroad, 1899
The Brownies in the Philippines, 1904
Brownie Clown of Brownie Town, 1908
The Brownies' Latest Adventures, 1910
The Brownies Many More Nights, 1913
The Brownies and Prince Florimel
or *Brownieland, Fairyland and Demonland*, 1918

While the preceding brief biography sheds some light on the origins of the man behind the phenomenon, what of the Brownies themselves? At right we present the essay written by Palmer Cox for the November 1892 ***Ladies Home Journal*** *that tells the "true" story of the Brownies and sets the record straight once and for all...*

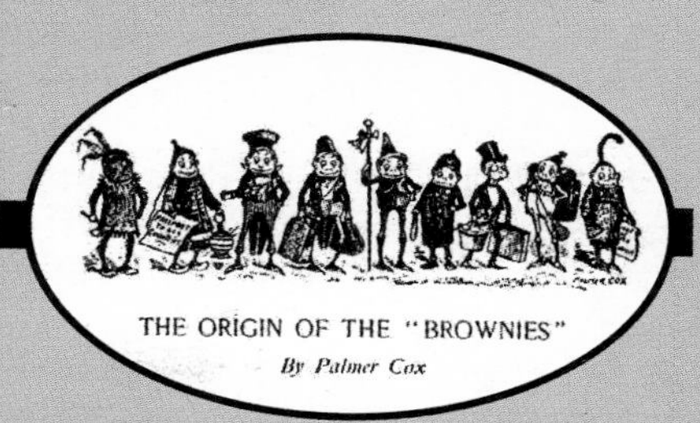

(originally published in ***The Ladies Home Journal****, November 1892)*

During the publication of the series of the "Brownies" just closed in The Ladies Home Journal, the question has often come to me "What is the origin of the Brownies?" And perhaps there is no better time to answer this question than now, before the next series of "Brownie" adventures shall begin on this page.

The "Brownie," as the cyclopeaedia informs us, springs from an old Scotch tradition, but it leaves us to follow up the tradition ourselves and learn how far back into the past it may be traced. Now a tradition, or legend, is about as difficult game to hunt to cover as your literary fowler can flush, but enough can be found to prove that the "Brownies" were good-natured little spirits or goblins of the fairy order. They were all little men, and appeared only at night to perform good and helpful deeds or enjoy harmless pranks while weary households slept, never allowing themselves to be seen by mortals. No person, except those gifted with second sight, could see the "Brownies;" but from the privileged few, principally old women, who were thus enabled to now and then catch a glimpse of their goblin guests, correct information regarding their size and color is said to have been gained.

They were called "Brownies" on account of their color, which was said to be brown owing to their constant exposure to all kinds of weather, and also because they had brown hair, something which was not common in the country where the "Brownie" was located, as the people generally had red or black hair. There are different stories about the origin of the name. One is that during the time the Covenanters in Scotland were persecuted because they were said to teach a false and pernicious doctrine, many of them were forced to conceal themselves in caves and secret places, and food was carried to them by friends. One band of Covenanters was led by a little hunchback named Brown, who being small and active could slip out at night with some of the lads and bring in the provisions left by friends in secret places. They dressed themselves in a fantastic manner, and if seen in the dusk of the evening they would be taken for fairies. Those who knew the truth named Brown and his band the "Brownies." This is very plausible, but we have too high an opinion of the "Brownies" to believe that they took their name from a mortal. We are inclined to believe that the well-deserving hunchback took his name from the "Brownies," instead of the "Brownies" deriving their name from him. Besides the story does not reach back far enough.

The "Brownies" were an ancient and well-organized band long before there was a Covenanter to flee to caves and caverns. Indeed, from what can be gathered from the writings of ancient authors, one is led to believe the "Brownie" idea is a very old one. It is fair to presume that the "Brownies" enjoyed their nightly pranks, or skipped over the dewy heather to aid deserving peasants even before the red-haired Dane crossed the border to be Caledonia's unwelcome guest. Every family seems to have been haunted by a spirit they called "Brownie" which did different sorts of work, and they in return gave him offerings of the various products of the place. The "Brownie" idea was woven into the affairs of everyday life. In fact it seemed to be part of their religion, and a large part at that. When they churned their milk, or brewed, they poured some milk or wort through a hole in a flat, thin stone called "Brownie's stone." In other cases they poured the offerings in the corner of the room, believing that good would surely come to their homes if "the Brownies" were remembered. On out of the way islands, where the people could neither read nor write, and were wholly ignorant of what was going on in other parts of the country, so much so that they looked upon a person that could understand black marks on paper as a supernatural being, the "Brownie" was regarded as their helper. The poet Milton had doubtless one of these "Brownies" in his mind when he penned the lines in "L'Allegro" to the "lubber fiend," who drudged and sweat "To earn his cream-bowl duly set."

But, strange to say, he was not as complimentary as the untarnished reputation of the "Brownies" might lead one to expect. In some villages, near their chapel, they had a large flat stone called "Brownie's stone," upon which the ancient inhabitants offered a cow's milk every Sunday to secure the good-will of the "Brownies." That the "Brownies were good eaters, and could out-do the cat in their love for cream, is well proven in many places.

It may be gratifying to some to know that even kings have not thought it beneath their dignity to dip the royal pen in the "Brownies" behalf. King James in his "Demonology" says:" The spirit called 'Brownie' appeared like a man and haunted divers houses without doing any evil, but doing as it were necessarie turnes up and down the house, yet some were so blinded as to believe that their house was all the sonsier, as they called it, that such spirits resorted there." Other writers say that the "Brownie" was a sturdy fairy, who, if he was fed well and treated kindly would do, as the people said, a great deal of work. He is said to have been obliging, and used to come into houses by night, and for a dish of cream perform lustily any piece of work that might remain to be done. The superstitious inhabitants had absolute faith in the "Brownies" wisdom or judgment. The "Brownie" spirit was said to reach over the table and make a mark where his favorite was to sit at a game if he wished to win, and this "tip" from the "Brownie" was never disregarded by the player.

The seeker after facts concerning the origin of the "Brownies" will find it difficult to gather them in. He may visit the largest libraries in the land and turn the leaves of old volumes that have been neglected for centuries, and fail to find more than that at one time in the long long ago, the "Brownie" was a power in the land that no well-regulated family could fail to do without. One thing is certain, however, the more we learn about the "Brownies" the more we like them. Theirs is a genealogy that one can trace back through the dusty centuries of the past without finding one blot on their scutcheon, or discovering that they descended from a race of robbers or evil doers. It is indeed refreshing to learn that at a time when the age was so dark that even Christianity could scarcely send a ray of light through it, and when every man's hand seemed to be against his brother, when poachers, moss-troopers and plundering men of might were denuding the land, the "Brownies" through rain and shine were found at their post every night, aiding the distressed, picking up the work that weary hands let fall, and in many ways winning the love and respect of the people.

See Next Page for Ordering Information ⟶

THE FINAL STEP IN COMIC BOOK PROTECTION!

Now Available R-Kival™ Quality Grey Acid-Free

Corrugated Boxes

Exclusively From Bill Cole Enterprises

Same Great Acid Free Properties as our Comic Book Cartons —
(minimum pH of 8.5 with a 3% Calcium Carbonate Buffer Throughout)

These corrugated boxes have a 200lb test bursting strength which means you can stack them as high as you want.

Since you only store your comics in protective sleeves made entirely from Mylar® D — and you only use genuine acid free backing boards to support your comics — Now, don't store them in anything but R-Kival™ quality acid free boxes

OVER TIME, ANY OTHER BOXES CAN RUIN YOUR COMICS

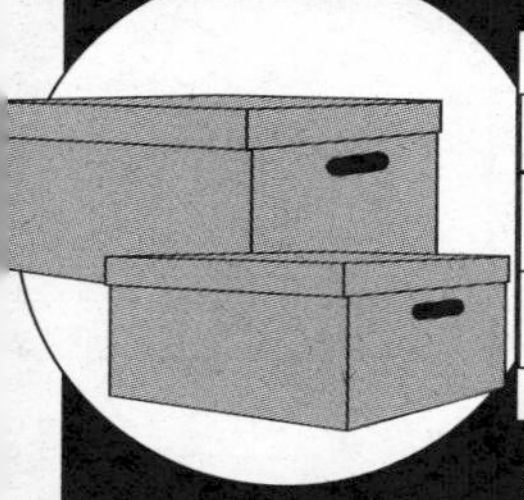

Acid Free Corrugated Cartons

CAT #	SIZE L x W x H	DESCRIPTION	PRICE PER 5	wt. lbs.	PRICE PER 10	wt. lbs.	PRICE PER 25	wt. lbs.	PRICE PER 50	wt. lbs.
C-13	15" x 8" x 11 1/2"	**Grey Acid free Corrugated Boxes** *fits Current through Silver/Golden Age comics, will hold approx. 120*	$ 57.50	8	$110.00	10	$ 262.50	38	$ 450.00	76
C-15	15" x 9" x 12 1/2"	**Grey Acid free Corrugated Boxes** *fits Super Golden Age Comics and Magazines will hold approx. 95*	63.75	9	120.00	11	287.50	39	540.00	78

Note: *Acid-Free Boxes may only be ordered in increments of 5. Sorry, no mix and match.*

Shipped flat! • Easy assembly does not require glue or tape!

GENERAL SHIPPING & HANDLING

TOTAL SHIPPING WEIGHT	IF YOUR ZIP CODE BEGINS WITH: 0,1	2,3 or 4	5,6 or 7	8,9	APO, FPO, AK, HI & ALL U.S. TER. via Parcel Post	ALL FOREIGN COUNTRIES via Parcel Post
0-2	6.75	7.75	8.25	9.00	8.00	13.75
3-5	8.25	9.00	9.50	10.25	10.50	16.00
6-10	10.25	11.50	12.00	13.25	18.50	32.25
11-15	11.50	13.25	14.00	16.50	24.00	41.50
16-20	13.25	15.75	16.75	20.50	28.00	53.75
21-25	15.75	17.50	20.50	22.25	31.50	72.00
26-30	17.50	19.75	22.75	26.00	32.00	82.50
31-35	20.25	22.75	25.50	30.00	33.00	93.00
36-40	21.50	23.50	27.00	30.50	36.50	104.00
41-45	22.50	26.00	30.00	34.00	37.50	114.00
46-50	24.00	28.75	32.00	37.50	38.50	128.00

Note: *If weight is above 50 lbs., add together additional amounts.*
(Example: 60 lbs. in Zip 1 would be $24.00 plus $10.25, or $34.25 total.)

PAYMENT MUST ACCOMPANY ORDERS

MA residents add 5% sales tax.

24 hour Toll Free Order Line for Mastercard, Visa, or Discover Orders Only

1-800-225-8249

This is a recorded tape and does not relay product information or messages.

24 hour Toll Free FAX Line for ordering only

1-800-FAX-BCE8
(1-800-329-2238)

Bill Cole Enterprises, Inc.

P.O. Box 60, DEPT. 01, Randolph, MA 02368-0060
(781) 986-2653 FAX (781) 986-2656
e-mail: bcemylar@cwbusiness.com web site: http://bcemylar.com

MURPHY ANDERSON

RE-CREATIONS IN A FLASH

BY ARNOLD T. BLUMBERG

Now that the hobby of comic book collecting has grown into a multi-million dollar industry, with some of the most active collecting pursued by adults with a plethora of memories and money to invest in them, there is a desire for more prestigious collectibles aside from just comics themselves. While original artwork from comic book interiors and covers has always been a popular category with a wide range of collectors, there aren't many people who can expect to hang a comic book masterpiece up on their wall.

Well, now there are at least a few more chances to showcase your fondest four-color memories in an ornate frame. For the last four years, Murphy Anderson has been painting re-creations of classic comic book covers from the annals of comic book history. Murphy is one of the living legends of comics, a celebrated artist whose work helped to define the DC Universe through titles like **The Justice League of America**, **Flash** and **Strange Adventures**. His distinctive characters and action-oriented style was an inspiration to generations of readers and future creators. Decades after his work established a definitive look for much of the DC universe, Murphy has returned to the heroes and stories that made him famous by painting highly detailed, exacting re-creations of those well-known covers. In fact, not only has Murphy tackled paintings that replicate his younger self's cover work, he has also flawlessly recreated Golden Age classics originally drawn by fellow comic book legend Lou Fine among others.

So how does Murphy Anderson manage to re-create a piece from forty, fifty, or even sixty years ago with such painstaking attention to detail, crafting a new piece of fine pop art while retaining the charm of the original comic book cover? And how did this bit of artistic time travel begin?

"It was when I was visiting John [Snyder] and Steve [Geppi] one day. They were buying cover re-creations from some other people. I told them how much I'd always admired Lou Fine's work and they suggested that I re-create some of Lou Fine's old covers as well as some that I had done personally. The first one was **Science Comics** #1, by Lou Fine. The first one I did that I had been involved with was the Justice League try-out [**Brave and the Bold** #28]."

Tackling re-creations of previously existing comic book art is certainly different than composing a new piece, but Murphy found the process very familiar. "That was fun for me because that was in effect how I learned to draw in the first place, copying stuff that I saw in the funnies or in comic books. I always tried to figure out why they need to have this brush stroke go this way, was it a brush, was it a pen. Originally, like many young kids of the day, we just thought it was all done with a pen, and it was a revelation to me to find out a little later that Lou Fine worked with a brush. Not that he didn't use a pen too occasionally, but most of his work was done with Japanese brushes, which accounted for those very thin lines."

Murphy had a newfound respect for Fine when he attempted to use the same tools. "It was later that I learned about the Japanese brushes, and it was funny because later when I talked to Will [Eisner], I learned they were using them in Will's shop. It was all a matter of economy; the Japanese brushes were very cheap. It took a special hand to work with them, and I must confess it was something that I wouldn't have had the patience for. The brush doesn't snap back; when you bend it you have to straighten it out on the next stroke."

While Fine's techniques may have required some care and precision, Murphy proved himself up to the task in recreating the Fine 'look.' "I tried to make it as close to his as possible, starting as a pencil drawing and then inking it. I had seen some of [Fine's] pencils and I was amazed how much [mine] turned out looking like his. I even tried to get down–when I could–the same number of brush strokes, not that I was able to do that. It was very time consuming, because I had to be constantly referring back to the original. I'd make two or three strokes and then look back to see where the next ones went."

Despite the difficulty, the experience was a worthwhile one for Murphy. "It was a learning process all over again, because I had such admiration for [Fine] and it all came back. I still admire the guy. I think he was one of the greatest, and that includes [Hal] Foster, [Milton] Caniff, and [Alex] Raymond. I think he was certainly on par with if not even a little better than those guys."

Doing my own work was different," Murphy continues. "I would pencil it and get them down, the same as with Lou Fine's, but in doing my own work, I had the latitude to fix things that bothered me. I never attempted to do that with [Fine's] stuff, and I didn't change shapes or anything, but if I felt an eye was not quite correct for instance, I would fix that."

At one point, Murphy had five or six re-creations in the works at one time. His most recent re-creation now graces one of the covers of this year's 31st edition Guide, but it also represents a bit of a departure for him. "The [**Detective Comics** #31] cover is one I would never have picked to do myself. In my book, Bob Kane did his best stuff when he was doing humor. When he did the straight stuff, I don't think he was very comfortable with it. It just looked to me like he was working very hard to try to do it while the other stuff seemed to be done very easily. He's one of the reasons why I never thought that an artist could be really good in both areas."

Murphy eventually learned differently. "I discovered a little later on that Will was doing the humorous stuff as well as he was doing the straight stuff. He could handle it, he still does, and actually that's what many of the better cartoonists were doing, like Roy Crane and Caniff. They had their feet in both camps. Hotshot Charlie comes to mind as one of Caniff's characters who's almost like a character out of Disney. But you never saw Alex Raymond doing that sort of thing, or Hal Foster. Anyhow, I thought you had to be one or the other, but that's not true. There are many of the straight artists who can do great cartooning."

Proving that even an accomplished artist can still learn new things, Murphy has been enjoying his run of re-creations, and there may be some others in the future. Although he doesn't seek out work any more, apart from the occasional call from DC to participate in a special project or two, Murphy is a living Silver Age legend who has recaptured the luster of that adventurous era and the Golden Age as well with his one-of-a-kind paintings. Now sought-after gems by a master illustrator, these works of art stand as a testament to the lasting influence of those fantasy epics and the man who helped bring them to life. But gaze upon them while you can, before they too are gone...in a flash.

Extra

John K. Snyder III, who provided the incredible re-creation of Fantastic Four #1 that serves as one of our covers, is an artist's artist. With a track record of highly resonant, evocative art that richly personifies each of the projects he's worked on, he moves from comic books to posters to trading cards, book covers and elsewhere with ease...and with purpose.

illustrations colored by Michael C. Malbrough

A fiery team of decidedly capable, dynamic and sexy women throw themselves into battle against the forces of a bombastic would-be tyrant. The threat is vanquished. These women succeed, and they look good doing it.

Danger Girl, you say? 1998, Cliffhanger Productions, you say? Nope.

Try the pages of Timothy Truman's **Scout**, Eclipse Comics, 1985. That's where John K. Snyder III's **Fashion in Action** debuted.

"To me it seemed like a natural, but when you take a good look at

ordinary!

BY J.C. VAUGHN

what was around at the time, there were hardly any female lead characters or groups other than, say, Wonder Woman and Elektra. Today you've got **Tomb Raider**, **Witchblade**, **Danger Girl**, and so many others," he says.

The comparisons with **Danger Girl**, though, don't have him crying foul. In fact, he enjoys the verve and energy of that title.

"It actually feels like a good bit of validation," he says.

The invigorating early days of creator-ownership in the 1980s brought with them an air of excitement. The independents, a loose term coined at the time for any publisher that wasn't Marvel or DC, brought out innovative new titles. Both established professionals and newcomers who felt constrained by the big two unleashed a wave of new talent. Snyder was a part of that wave.

While recent high profile undertakings like DC's **Doctor Mid-Nite** (1999) and an upcoming Green Lantern project have thrust him back into the spotlight, many may not realize the scope of his career since those early days at Eclipse.

In addition to writing and drawing **Fashion in Action**, he illustrated **The Prowler** at Eclipse, **Suicide Squad** (with writers John Ostrander and Kim Yale) and the pre-Vertigo **Books of Magic** spin-off

Mister E at DC, and he adapted both Robert Louis Stevenson's **Dr. Jekyll & Mr. Hyde** and Joseph Conrad's **The Secret Agent** for First Comics' Classics Illustrated line.

During that time, he also began his association with **Doctor Mid-Nite** writer Matt Wagner with a lengthy run as the artist on Wagner's **Grendel**, then published by Comico. He painted the top selling **Onslaught** poster for Marvel's X-Men line, and worked with **Earth X** writer Jim Krueger on his **Foot Soldiers** series, providing character design illustrations and covers.

"John's ability to capture shadow is my favorite part of his artwork. He works through symbols and design in such a way that he is one of my favorite painters," Krueger says. "He has been doing, for years, almost the definitive pinups of my characters."

Among the many specialty assignments he's taken on are the **Star Wars** card featuring Darth Vader and Boba Fett for Topps, a Captain America card for Fleer, and a **Jonny Quest** promotional comic for Dark Horse.

He also has numerous projects outside of comic book, including film development work and, very notably, the covers for the even-numbered volumes in Harlan Ellison's **Edgeworks** series.

"John is extraordinary. Let me put it differently: John is extraordinary. No, let me amend that: John is extraordinary," Ellison says.

Beau Smith, who worked with Snyder at Eclipse and who now heads up the marketing efforts of Todd McFarlane Productions, has had a chance to see Snyder's work develop over the years. He echoes Ellison's praise.

"I first met John back in the mid '80s and even though his attire was that of Chess King," says with a laugh. "His artwork was way ahead of time. It still is. It really stands up."

It was **Doctor Mid-Nite**, though, that brought Snyder back to the limelight. He had been looking for an opportunity to work with Wagner and the late DC Comics writer/editor Archie Goodwin.

"I've always liked the Golden Age characters. Dr. Mid-Nite was a longtime favorite of mine. He was one of the underdogs, the kind of second tier characters who you never hear much about. It was a perfect opportunity. I did some preliminary sketches, sent them off to Archie and Matt, we talked about it quite a bit, and Matt developed it from there," Snyder says.

"I really wanted to do a modern day pulp. So did Matt. We set out to do a story about somebody who actually was a good guy. When I would show the book in progress to people, the usual question would be 'Is this going to be a Vertigo book?' Because of the dark alleys, the city and the dark, creepy stuff, they would immediately assume this was going to be some dark interpretation of the character. That was just the world the character was in. He's a good guy in a bad world," he says.

"Over the many years that John and I have collaborated, his exacting and innovative approach to his art has never failed to amaze me," Wagner says. "A consumate perfectionist, John seemingly approaches each and every gig as if it were his last. The resultant works are always evocative and, most often, sublime. He's one of the few painters in the field with a design sense to rival his draftsmanship. A master visualist."

Now, Snyder says he's glad to see the reincarnated Doctor Mid-Nite as part of the Justice Society of America in the popular **JSA** series.

"I'd love to work with [series writer] David Goyer. His handling of our interpretation of Doctor Mid-Nite is really dead-on. I enjoy that he's kind of picked up where we left off and developed him even further from there," he says.

He anticipates working with Harlan Ellison again on the even-numbered **Edgeworks** series covers, (Snyder also worked on Ellison's **Dream Corridor**), and continues to collaborate further with Jim Krueger. He said he would also like to team up with writers Mark Millar and Brian Michael Bendis some day.

"From their work, I think they're creators I would enjoy working with. I've been checking out Millar's work on **The Authority** and it's fantastic. Bendis has a very healthy, open-minded approach to making superhero books fun, and most importantly, new again," he says.

With his upcoming Green Lantern project (with writer Steven T. Seagle) nearing completion, he's looking to the future with enthusiasm.

"One of the true benefits of working in this field is the opportunity to work with and get to know such a large, geographically separated group of people, artists, writers, editors, and the other people behind the scenes who are unified by a desire to tell stories," he says.

With that in mind, don't be surprised to see the return of **Fashion in Action** sometime soon.

BEN

BY J.C. VAUGHN

The conventional wisdom suggests that Brian Michael Bendis should have cut his professional teeth on company-owned titles for the "Big Two," Marvel and DC, before venturing out into the make-or-break world of creator owned projects. Now he's one of the hottest creators in the medium; the conventional wisdom was wrong.

He's the author – and in some cases, the artist – of **Torso**, **Fortune & Glory**, **Powers**, and **Ultimate Spider-Man** among others. He's written **Sam & Twitch** and **Hellspawn** for Todd McFarlane, a Batman story for DC, and seems to have found a home of sorts at Marvel Comics. His work has been favorably reviewed by **Spin**, **Entertainment Weekly**, and other publications outside the industry. The comics press just love him, too, but they're not the only ones calling; the guys from Hollywood want him as well. He's had four of his

works optioned for the silver screen and written two of the screenplays himself.

Suddenly he's an overnight sensation with an expanding cadre of die-hard fans, one of the hippest message boards on the Internet, and a name that is rapidly becoming the comic book equivalent of a household word.

Yes, the world is unfolding right at the feet of Brian Michael Bendis. It's been easy for him...except, of course, for all the hard work and the fact that "overnight" took the better part of a decade.

He broke in at Caliber with a group of talented newcomers including Marc Andreyko (**The Lost**), David Mack (**Kabuki**), Phil Hester (**The Wraith**), Mark Ricketts (**Nowheresville**), and Galen Showman (**Renfield**). There, in his gritty, crime-themed stories of characters on the edge, he found a distinctive voice, though it was in a niche market many so-called experts labeled as "dead" save for the likes of David Lapham and Frank Miller. It is that voice that appeals to many of his fans, including fellow professionals.

"The staccato verse, the half-finished sentences, usually one spoken over the other," says Jim Valentino, publisher of Image Comics. "Like any good writer there is an ear for the cadence of normal speech patterns, rather than an adherence to the 'rules' of proper English."

"As a development exec, I can't tell you how many scripts I read where the characters talk like they've seen too many movies themselves. It's not realistic. Bendis' characters and dialogue put a smile on my face because I can picture them actually having the conversation that I'm reading on the page," says Jason Pritchett, a film industry executive and frequent poster on the Bendis' internet message board. "His work is sometimes dark and gritty, but there's always a touch of light-heartedness and fun buried in there somewhere."

Challenged and inspired by his contemporaries, Bendis developed not only his voice, but a loyal fan following with **Fire**, **AKA Goldfish**, and **Jinx** at Caliber before moving on to the proverbial greener pastures at Image. He still counts the early experience at Caliber as vital though.

"At school they pitted us against each other, so that we would compete. But there was only one other guy who was into comics, so it didn't even make sense. When I met my Caliber friends, particularly David, I was thrilled to have peers with similar interests. We all sort of graduated around the same time and connected creatively. It's one of the greatest things I've had in my life. None of us

got left behind," he says.

Almost simultaneously Bendis and Mack made the move to Image Comics, successfully expanding their audiences. In recent months they have worked together at Marvel, where Bendis will succeed Mack as writer of **Daredevil**, with Mack then illustrating the Bendis-written story arc beginning with **Daredevil #16**.

"I can't tell you how great it is for this to be happening for David and me now," Bendis says. "There's no one else that either of us is more likely to turn for advice or inspiration. There's no jealousy at all. It's all positive. The topper is that we get to work on **Daredevil** together."

For his part, David Mack agrees. "We give each other a little bit more objective sense or criticism, yet still understand what the other is trying to do," he says. "It was great to finally get a chance to work on a high profile project together."

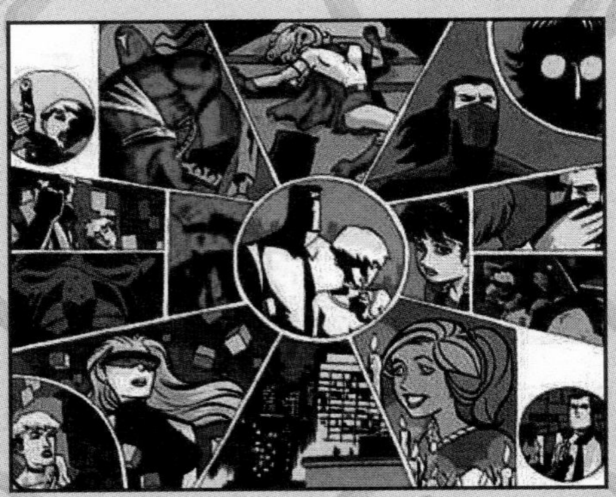

The gigs writing the **Daredevil** story arc, another **Daredevil** mini-series, **Ultimate Spider-Man**, and **Ultimate Marvel Team-Up** may seem at least superficially odd for a writer with such solid indy press credentials. What made Marvel, with the company battered by the tumult of bankruptcy, hand over the reigns of its chancy reboot of its premiere character to a creator whose comics – even the letter columns – were filled with swearing, sarcasm, and a tongue-in-cheek brand of happy cynicism? Storytelling, says Bill Jemas, President of Marvel Comics.

"Joe Quesada, then editor of Marvel Knights [now Marvel's Editor-in-Chief], gave me samples of **Torso** and **Powers**," he says. "From his prior work, it was clear that Brian had a great ear for dialogue and super storytelling skills."

Jemas, who in the last year with Quesada has engineered an astounding talent recruitment drive for Marvel's top comics, had roughed out many of the essentials of **Ultimate Spider-Man**. The goal was to make the classic character more accessible to potential younger readers. They gave Bendis a crack at developing the script.

"The Spidey scripts were so strong that we had no doubt that fans would enjoy the books," he says. "The characters come to life, and the reader has a truly immersive experience."

With **Ultimate Spider-Man** now a huge hit and other projects in the pipeline, Bendis continues to make time for daily interaction with fans, retailers and other professionals on his Jinxworld website at www.jinxworld.com. A survey of the subject lines found there might include "Questions for Bendis," "Big News Tomorrow!" (a teaser from Bendis himself), or "Your top 5 favorite non-lethal infections." The range covers the spectrum, and includes promoting the recently launched **Ultimate Marvel Team-Up** and its Who's Who list of collaborators. Matt Wagner (**Mage**), Bill Sienkiewicz (**Elektra: Assassin**), **Powers**' co-creator Mike Oeming, Terry Moore (**Strangers in Paradise**), Steve Rude (**Nexus**), and John Romita Sr. are among the talent who have already signed on. The website was the first place many heard about the project.

Michael Avon Oeming, who co-created **Powers** with Bendis, says he knows what draws these other creators to Bendis, and he says it's the same whether it's a Marvel project or a black & white comic from Oni Press. "The story structure and pacing. No exposition, no thought balloons. It just feels real and intelligent," he says.

WILL 2001 BE A COMIC BOOK ODYSSEY?

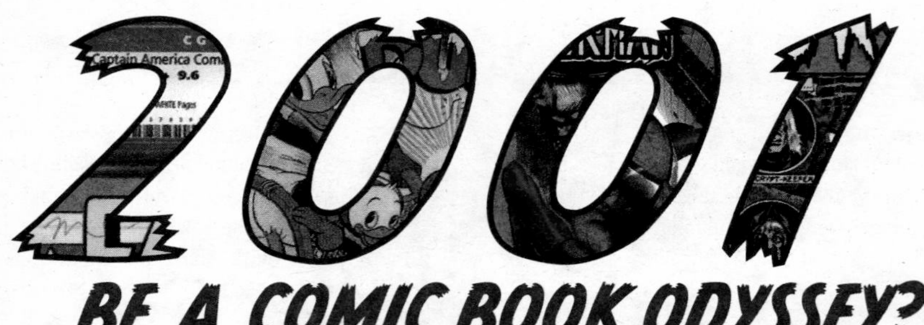

BY ROBERT M. OVERSTREET

Last year's guide was assembled on the heels of the feared Y2K debacle, which disappeared at the stroke of midnight. As we predicted, the year 2000 turned out to be quite a robust year for most collectible markets, including vintage comic books. The national economy was impacted by a lackluster stock market which went into a major decline in the fall, freeing up investment capital for other areas of interest.

Certified Comics: Arguably one of the most important events in the comic book market to date is the arrival of the professionally graded comic book via Comics Guaranty Corp. Internet and mail-order customers can buy these books with confidence. Certification not only makes it easier to sell on the Internet and through the mail, but has attracted newcomers to the market as well. We have heard few complaints about the work of their graders and the standards they have established.

Record sales occurred all year as slabbed comic books became the driving force of the market. The news of the year was made when a slabbed **Captain America Comics** #1 (Allentown copy), graded at NM+ 9.6, sold for **$265,000**. Hundreds of other record prices occurred last year, which are listed following this market report.

Internet Sales: Of course the Internet was already being widely used for buying and selling comic books before last year, but this venue became even stronger as the year 2000 progressed. Through numerous auctions either held at private websites or on the now famous eBay site, slabbed comics began appearing, and sold for multiples of Guide. Included in these sales were famous pedigree comics such as Mile High, Gaines file copies and others. Thousands of other comics were auctioned on the web all year long. Realized prices ranged from way below Guide to above Guide levels. More and more dealers either established new websites or improved the ones they had to make it even easier for their customers to use and buy, buy, buy.

Professional Auctions: The Greg Manning auction in April was the first to offer certified comics for sale to the general public. Prices realized for many of these certified books were profound, ranging from below Guide to as much as six times NM Guide. Of the certified books, there were 140 that brought Guide to six times Guide, and 104 that brought below Guide. There were 124 uncertified books that sold for Guide to as much as eight times Guide, and only 43 books that sold for below Guide. of course, a lot of the uncertified books were high grade and were from known pedigree collections, which increased the likelihood that they would bring high prices. High grade books have always been easy to sell, certified or not.

In June, Sotheby's held their auction, which also contained many certified comics. Most books that graded 9.0 and higher were selling for multiples of Guide. As the year went by, the demand for CGC graded comics increased. Obviously the advantage of getting high grade pedigree comics graded is that they might grade at 9.6 or even 9.8, and these grades command very high multiples of Guide. And of course, certified books sell much easier on the Internet or to new customers. As of this writing, only one Golden Age book has been graded 9.9, which is the Mile High copy of **Zip Comics** #7.

In October, Manning launched their second auction, with a full color 338 page catalog. More record prices were set on Golden and Silver Age books. An **All Select** #1 in CGC VF 8.0 sold for $11,500. A **Wonder Woman** #1 in CGC VF 8.0 brought $23,000. Horror comics remained hot, carrying over from 1999. A **Startling Terror Tales** #11 in CGC NM- 9.2 brought $7475 and a **Weird Tales Of The Future** #7 in CGC NM 9.4 fetched $9200. Key Silver Age books set more record prices. An **Amazing Fantasy** #15 in CGC VF/NM 9.0 got $40,250 while a **Fantastic Four** #1 in CGC NM- 9.2 brought $46,000. An **X-Men** #1 in CGC NM- 9.2 sold for $14,375 and an **Incredible Hulk** #1 in CGC VF/NM 9.0 brought $15,525.

Changes in this Guide: Questionaires were sent out last fall to our advisors about a possible change in the Guide's format concerning the pricing columns. Many of our advisors thought that we should drop the NM 9.4 listing to a lower grade such as NM- 9.2, VF/NM 9.0 or even VF+ 8.5. However, after giving this a lot of thought, we felt that it was too early to make such a radical change, especially since certified grading has only just begun. We adopted a more prudent "wait and see" attitude. Obviously we are paying close attention to the recent auctions, where books in the higher grades consistently bring multiples of Guide. We are also learning that Golden Age and Silver Age books that grade 9.4 or higher bring very high multiples as the market learns of the scarcity of these grades. However, newer comics do commonly reach these grades.

© MAR Captain America Comics #1 (Allentown copy) CGC graded NM+ 9.6 sold for $265,000.

While witnessing the seemingly insane prices that some books bring at auction, we should keep in mind that these certified books only represent a very small part of the total market. Some may think that the Guide should reflect these "top of the market" prices. However we have always felt that the Guide must be responsible in its evaluation of the market and show "weighted" prices that reflect the market as a whole.

Because high grade books are selling for way over last year's Guide, we have expanded our price spreads in this edition from Good to Near Mint to reflect this development. You will note that NM prices have gone up 20% or more in many cases while the Good and Fine prices are showing smaller increases overall. This increase in the NM prices also means an increase in all grades above Fine. We have also noted that prices realized from slabbed books can be higher than unslabbed books, but this is not a guaranteed result. Many of the slabbed books at auction have sold for under Guide while an equal number have brought over Guide prices (see Manning auction).

The comic book maket is very diverse, ranging from several thousand comic book stores to mail-order and convention dealers to flea markets and professional auction houses to collectors selling individual books on the Internet. In this kind of market, prices paid for back issue comic books vary tremendously. It is our job to reflect a "fair market" price that represents the market as a whole. Many comic book stores and small dealers may have trouble getting "Guide price" while the top dealers easily sell certain books for multiples of Guide.

One last note: The Platinum Age section has been completely overhauled thanks to our Platinum Age advisor, Bob Beerbohm. This section now includes dozens of brand new discoveries that have never been listed before. Many of the existing listings have also been expanded with new entries. Bob has worked very hard on this section and deserves our gratitude for a job well done.

Important: The following market reports were submitted by some of our many advisors and are published here for your information only. The opinions in these reports belong to each contributor and do not necessarily reflect the views of the publisher.

Dave Anderson

It's definitely been an interesting year. There seems to be no regard to Guide when it comes to high grade books, especially those that are graded 9.6 or better by CGC. That population is so small that the competition for them keeps driving prices to higher levels. This year also saw an influx into our hobby of more people who are exclusively investors and who do not have a real interest in comics. Across the board these investors insist on a book being CGC graded before buying. Many very desireable books could disappear for years only to resurface when the investors decide to cash out. If held for the long term, they will do well, but if in six months they all want to sell, it could be a problem as they paid very high prices. Meanwhile, as these books disappear, it makes those that remain within the hobby even more valuable and desireable. In addition, many of the best comic collections in the world have remained intact as their owners resisted temptations to sell.

© MAR

The X-Men movie debut made early Wolverine appearances like **Giant-Size X-Men** #1 a hot ticket.

Over all, if the books being sold are CGC graded and encapsulated, they sell very well at or above Guide. If they are not CGC graded, they consistently sell for about 25% less. The Internet has also opened up the market to a whole new audience, and many books (like VG Marvels for example) can now be sold much easier.

Stephen Barrington

The 2000 market showed strong gains in DC Silver Age, particularly among the Superman and Batman titles. Batman was especially popular with issues from Fair-Good to Fine+ selling quickly at Guide. For the most part, Marvel Silver Age collectors demand higher grades while many DC fans are content to buy issues in lower grades. Golden and Atom Age issues were hard to find, especially in Fine or better condition. Not so well-known titles don't sell well in our area. Timely's and DC's main hero books don't last long when priced right. On the Silver and Bronze Age markets, X-Men continue to lead the way with G-S #1 and #94-140 selling briskly in nice condition. Hulk #181 is also right up there. The X-Men movie generated a greater interest in Wolverine but not the X-Men titles themselves. DC's Vertigo titles (Preacher, Hellblazer, 100 Bullets and Transmetropolitan) cater to a select audience. They don't sell over Guide in south Alabama but were going for multiples of Guide at the San Diego Comicon.

EC reprints by Gemstone are solid sellers with new readers being created every day. Many are discovering how great these books are and are wanting more. Various horror titles from the '70s and '80s sell well when priced right. A fair number of non-collectors are picking these up just for the enjoyment of reading them.

New comics continue to sell well, with DC and Marvel at the head of the list. Back issues of recently cancelled titles from Marvel, DC and Image sell quickly in bargain bins. X-Men issues from #150 up, with few exceptions, don't command premium prices. Amazing Spider-Man (1st series) issues are still highly sought after in Fine or better but do sell well in Good to Very Good condition when the prices are low. The 1968 Marvel #1s (Hulk #102, Captain Marvel #1, Captain America #100, Iron Man #1, Sub-Mariner #1) seem to have peaked with few interested in the high prices listed in the Guide.

Summary: Over all, the market has been solid when books are priced right. 1970s issues in nice shape (DC and Marvel) sell well since more have not gotten too expensive. Marvel doesn't seem to be giving a lot of its new titles a chance, cancelling many after only a few issues. DC seems to be more patient and is more consistent with its books. Bargain bin comics seem to interest younger fans in an inexpensive way. They then graduate to buying more and more new releases. The comic market should continue to thrive in 2001 with these new collectors perpetuating the hobby.

Conrad Eschenberg

The market is alive and well and off to the races! After stellar performances at the San Diego and Chicago Comicons, the market is poised for an upward thrust in popularity, and with that comes an increase in sales and prices. Both conventions set records for fan attendance, and sales were very good for many dealers attending the show. Record prices were paid for CGC slabbed books both at Greg Manning's auction and especially on the Internet. People are paying stupid money for high grade books there, but this will not last. Once the supply of CGC comics catches up to demand, prices will stabilize. Nearly $3,000 for a recent Internet sale of Incredible Hulk #181NM is unheard of. In the interim, prices will continue to rise and break records.

© HOKE

Classic covers like **Power Comics** #3 show the timeless appeal of L.B. Cole.

Nearly all genres of comics are selling at stronger levels than last year. High grade comics at 9.0 (VF/NM) or better are blazing. Golden and Atom Age comics sell in all grades as supplies of any condition are low. Comics with origins, first appearances and especially noted artists–Ditko, Schomburg, L. B. Cole, Kirby, Steranko, Adams, –sell extremely well. Silver Age DC and Marvel books are slower, selling in grades below 9.0.

Original art is bringing record prices everywhere, on the net, at conventions, on the phone, etc. Some pieces are changing hands monthly and selling for more each time. There is not enough quality art to go around as dealers hold on to good pieces and buy and sell with other dealers more frequently. Comic covers from the '60s and '70s are bringing record prices. A 1970s Hulk cover selling for $300 in 1998 brings $1,200 to $2,000 or more today. This is not an isolated condition. Art by Ditko, Kirby, Miller, B. Smith, N. Adams, Steranko, Byrne, Frazetta, J. Jones, Kaluta, Wrightson, etc., continues to bring higher and higher prices.

Summary: We are entering a new era in the comic and original comic art market. The Internet is making the hobby more global and exposing it to many more buyers and sellers. More collectors are selling their own comics and art to other collectors. The slabbing of comics and grading by a third party, namely CGC, is bringing new buyers into the market who set record prices on a monthly basis. More comic collectors are buying original art, and more dealers are are getting into that area as well. There are fewer dealers at the major conventions; there are fewer conventions and comic stores. Prices for comics and art are on the rise. You will always profit when you buy what you really like and enjoy.

Dan Fogel & Jim Pitts (Comic Detectives)

There are basically two kinds of comic collectors today, albeit with sub-divisions. One camp still reads new comics, which, being so expensive today, takes up virtually all of their designated budget. Any back issues, if bought at all, are recent numbers of the current or near-current runs. They don't care about, nor can they afford to buy, Bronze, Silver or earlier books. Any extra money goes to cards, video games or videos.

The other camp of collectors is only interested in Silver or Gold, preferably at half-Guide for VF+ or better books. They don't care about the current books that contain storyline of the same characters, only the books of their youth or what they think is hot. Both kinds of collectors are demanding more value for their money in either quantity or quality.

High grade is still king, with high grade keys outperforming old sales records yearly. The advent of the Internet has made it possible for more collectors to sell directly to each other. In the case of on-line auctions, it's equally possible that a given group of books can sell for under Guide one day and double Guide the next.

So-called impartial third-party graders have a short-term influence when first introduced due to the novelty, but over time a book doesn't gain value due to a plastic wrapping that can't be unsealed without voiding the grade or value assigned to it. Comics are made to be read, which requires opening them, which also has to be done to verify the grade in the first place. Stamps and coins only have two sides and can therefore be "slabbed" with less taken on faith. This trend will ultimately have an adverse affect on comics as cards graded in similar fashion are looked down upon by graded card collectors.

© EC Publ.

There's a resurgence of interest in **MAD Magazines** between #50-100, like #69 shown.

There has also been a resurgence of interest in MADs between #50-100 and Warren horror. Bettie Page stays a strong seller. Sports comics of the '40s and '50s sell well too. Key underground comics like Zap Comix, The Fabulous Furry Freak Brothers and Cherry are growing increasingly popular and prices are rising due to low early print runs and relative unavailability.

Jef Hinos

The twin revolutionary forces of eBay and CGC have increasingly dominated the Market this past year. The effect has been greatly stimulating and will reshape the comic book market forever. We have probably entered a new "Age" but just haven't agreed on a name for it yet. Silicon anyone?

eBay has made all collectibles, including comic books, more liquid than ever before. It has enabled the average collector to cut out the middle man and turn some unwanted items into cash, thereby fueling more buying. It has also caused dealers to sell books faster than ever, also stimulating more purchasing of collections, and all of this at previously unheard of low prices. This is bringing people into the market, causing many books to go up in value.

CGC grading has broadened the confidence level of grading to collectors and the general public. It has made sight-unseen buying much easier and accepted. This has brought many people into the market who may have liked comics before but did not have the expertise to determine for themselves if a book was fairly graded and priced. These people now seem to be going after everything, but especially key books and high grades. We are seeing new records being set every day.

Another exciting thing about CGC is that the most profound change is yet to come. That's when they release their population figures of graded books and we finally have a rough but better than ever quantitative handle on which books are really rare, which are common, and which are the finest known copies for each issue. This will cause a dramatic realignment of values. What if, for example, we find out that Hulk #1, 2, 4, &6 have many high grade copies but #3 and #5 have only one third as many? Also, look for the spread between "raw" and "slabbed" books to widen and the greatest appreciation in the market to be in third party CGC graded books for some time to come.

The combination of CGC and eBay has produced something akin to a stock market for comic books. One has only to search completed auctions or use Honesty.com's price-finder to see what any particular book has been bringing. There has never been so much timely information available before. It also seems that the market is increasingly split between high-grade investor/collectors and reader/collectors who prefer inexpensive low-grade copies.

CGC Graded Comics: Having a book CGC certified and encapsulated is very worthwhile for key issues and high grades. They tend to sell faster and at higher prices. For books in those categories the

© L&S

Red Ryder Comics #1 shows the appeal of a cowboy... and a rifle with notable Yuletide popularity.

process is almost a must.

I have had about 200 books slabbed in the past seven months and every one has listed on eBay and sold for very close to or above Guide.

In grades of NM9.4 or better you can almost be assured of a price well above that in the 30th edition Guide. Every 9.6 or better seems to result in another jaw-dropping record price and this trend shows no signs of abating.

Internet Sales: Over the past year I've gone from traditional marketing to almost exclusively selling on the Internet, mainly through eBay. I was finding it increasingly difficult to handle both on- and off-line sales simultaneously, so I opted to go entirely Internet. Sales are great and getting stronger. I don't miss the print ads and direct mail catalogs.

It takes some strategy, some tweaking, and seeing what others have done to get it working efficiently. The combination of low overhead and great mass-market reach is hard to ignore. I have sold many books to people who are not even comic collectors but who collect certain characters or categories. These people will pay far over Guide and are not too concerned about high grade, only that it's complete.

Market 2000: I see strong demand for Roy Rogers, Little Lulu, Red Ryder and Wonder Woman, especially issues #90-120. Demand is also high for Amazing Spider-Man, Golden and Silver Age romance titles, Dick Tracy, and Kirby cover westerns. After being long dormant, Avengers #1-100 is alive and well with good demand. All Dell funny animal titles with the exception of high grade keys are down. Supply on WDC&S, Donald Duck, Mickey Mouse, etc. is huge, with collections surfacing regularly and demand weak to moderate. Especially slow are MAD Magazine issues, one of the few things that don't get bids on eBay, same as the Dells. Non-first edition Classics are also down, although Classics Junior issues do well. Mid-range Archies are slow. Tales to Astonish #60-101, Tales of Suspense #60-99, and Strange Tales #120-168 need to be discounted 25% in mid grades to sell.

Ed Jaster (Jaster Collectibles Inc.)

The market is very strong and continues to grow. New collectors are coming into the hobby, typically drawn in by eBay. CGC has also attracted investors and new collectors that were hesitant to buy expensive material before certification. These customers are starting to attend shows and buy from print advertising too. Lost in all the hysteria is the fact that CGC material is less than 1% of the total market. This is a broad-based "bull" market including all grades, publishers and genres.

Notable Issues: FF#1, AF#15 and Batman #1 sell repeatedly at 1.25 to 1.5 Guide in all grades. Wonder Woman sells well above Guide in all grades and eras. Burnley covers on Starman (Adventure) are moving, and all Neal Adams and Wrightson covers are hot. Superboy, Lois Lane, Jimmy Olsen and Adventure Comics with Superboy are also all in very high demand. Dell TV/movie/Disney titles are down and sell consistently under 50% of Guide on eBay.

© DC

Ted Knight met his final fate in 2000's **Starman** #72, but collectors can remember him through Jack Burnley's dynamic covers like **Adventure Comics #64.**

CGC Graded Comics: In grades under 9.0, CGC grading adds liquidity rather than price. Books that might sit in inventory move well when certified. Non-Marvels in 9.0 or better generally bring a premium but rarely much more than what was projected when unslabbed. Major keys (Cap #1, Batman #1, Detective #27, Action #1) all seem to do about

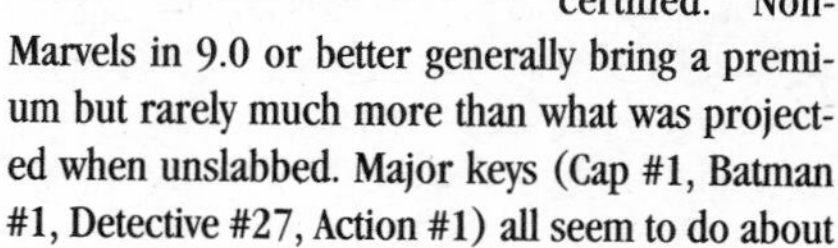

50% better when slabbed. DC and Timely Golden Age in 9.4 or better just about double in value over Guide, but nothing approaches the effect on Marvels and modern books in high grade.

All Marvels in 9.4 or better cannot be priced accurately. You just don't know what someone will pay, from three to ten times Guide! Supply of this material is much lower than thought and demand is intense. The trend will probably continue for some time as there are just not enough high grade Marvels to go around. Modern (1975 and up) results are even more uncanny.

Internet Sales: On eBay, westerns, Dells, Gold Keys, Charltons, damaged/incomplete GA, low and mid grade SA in groups, and funny animals typically get 40-70% of Guide. Little Lulus, Harvey "kids" comics, and Katy Keene do very well and there is strong demand. This demand, however, is coming from people who are not in the mainstream of the hobby. These buyers have little idea of what a price guide is and certainly don't travel to conventions or buy other comic publications. Marvels in 8.5 or better and certified keys in any grade do well. Any Marvel key will sell on eBay when it's in a "Universal Holder" at or above traditional price in any grade. Non-key Marvels in 8.5 or better will reach sticker price or better about 90% of the time. In 9.4 or better, amazing prices are always achieved.

© Lucasfilms

Star Wars #1, a key part of the Bronze Age boom.

Jason McKibben (Clarence Road)

Sales are still HOT for Golden Age books. Any grade goes for solid Guide, VF and higher goes from anywhere near 1.5 to four times Guide. Silver Age sales are strong, staying at solid Guide due to a lot of people selling off their stock. Once supply dries up (soon?) expect these prices to soar. As with all grades, if it's slabbed by CGC it's as good as sold. CGC books sell on average at four times Guide and higher for 9.0 and above. As far as eBay, this is my first year dealing on the Internet and I love it. Great for selling high grade keys and anything slabbed by CGC. It's like the biggest convention on Earth and it's open 24/7!

The REAL boom is happening in the Bronze Age. X-Men G-S #1 (NM) just sold on eBay for over $2,000! More copies are selling now for $1,400 to $1,750. I personally sold some of my Bronze books at four times Guide, including a CGC 9.6 Star Wars #1 for $122.50 at the beginning of the year. Even completely obscure titles from the '70s are receiving double Guide without hesitation. Try finding key '70s issues in FN or better for under Guide these days.

In general, westerns (any grade from Golden to Bronze), pre-Code horror, romance (Golden and Silver Age), and Bronze Age (keys at three times Guide and non-keys at two times Guide) are all up. Most early '90s to present are hard sells at cover price. Anything less than NM is almost impossible to sell, even early Spawn, which were a constant seller until just recently.

Terry O'Neill (Terry's Comics)

The year 2000 was "Very Good to Fine" for comic sales. There was high demand for high-grade Bronze and Silver Age comics. This was particularly true of most Marvel titles. I was fortunate to buy a few nice collections of early books from their original owners, which enabled me to get a better handle on what was selling and what was not.

Golden Age: With the exception of Timely, most Golden Age Superhero books were selling at or below Guide. I put some DC titles (Action #89, #101, and several Detectives in the #100-#200 range) in nice middle grade on eBay to test demand and was shocked to only get half Guide on them (I guess that's why they have reserve prices). On the other hand I placed a couple of coverless Captain Americas on auction and I was paid up to the VG price for them. Who can figure this out? Generally speaking, most Golden Age comics move within a year of purchase. I purchased a small low-grade collection of early Golden Age books and sold most of these at about 120% of Guide. This batch included Batman #1-12, Detective #37 and 38, Superman #2-26, most issues of Action #5-50, and many early Timely and Fawcett titles. It is getting harder to turn a profit on the early GA due to intense competition amongst dealers to acquire them. I wound up paying about 85% of Guide for everything. In addition I am unable to locate enough MLJ, Centaur and Harvey titles; they are on a lot of want lists and demand is very high.

Atom Age: It has been said many times but I will repeat it–this era is just plain scarce in almost any title. I rarely get a run of comics through this era and they are not showing up in collections. The pre-code horror craze is slowing down a little. So you can expect that many of these books will start to sit on dealers' walls unless they are priced at something a little closer to Guide than the stratosphere. Crime titles are hard to come by and are selling very well; perhaps some horror or war collectors are venturing into different genres. The western comics are not just selling, but selling well, especially photo cover titles like Roy Rogers and Gene Autry. Now that these old cowboys have passed away, there is a certain age group that has fond memories of growing up watching them in serials. Early DC war and sci-fi titles are still scarce as ever but have slowed down in sales. Most Atlas, especially the pre-code titles, are moving quite well. I try to keep a good inventory of Atlas and I have had to pay much higher percentages of Guide to keep up a good selection. They generally sell at 90% to 125% of Guide. Resistance is usually for middle grade books over $50. Romance and teen comics are real movers but that's probably because they're still such a bargain. The best sellers are Fox and St. John romance and teen titles such as Archie and Millie the Model. Most funny animal comics, even Barks and Kelly, are hard to move and often go as low as 25% of Guide just to turn them over. Other titles from this era, such as Tarzan, Lulu and Dick Tracy, are steady sellers at around Guide. The oddest group is the Dell photo cover books. These tend to be collected by non-comic collectors and sometimes they will pay really high and other times they won't pay hardly anything for them. There is no consistent pattern.

Silver Age: I am happy to say that this era of comics has made a comeback at full strength. The adjustment of prices on lower grade books along with the renewed interest in Bronze Age books has created a very strong market for almost every title of most publishers of Silver Age material. It's good when you can sell titles like Marvel's Captain Marvel and Brand Echh comics as well as DC titles like Metamorpho and Rip Hunter at Guide. The only trick here is finding enough of these books in high grade. Dealers that specialize in high grade usually buy the few I have found in better condition before I even get them up on my display board. I have been able to come across a few odd titles of Silver Age Charltons and was surprised to sell them at or over Guide. What a truly great market the year 2000 has been.

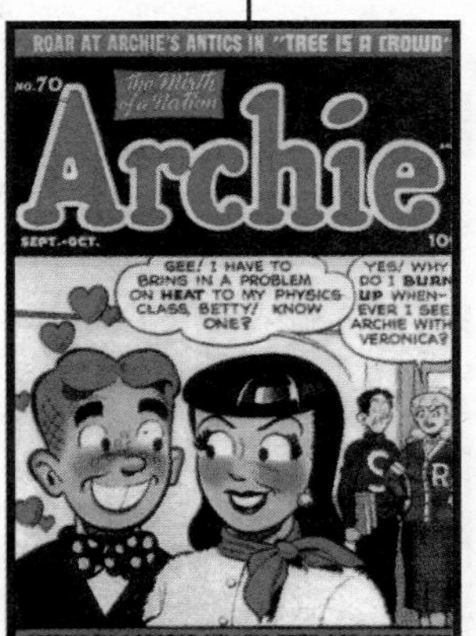

© AP

Early Archies continue to be best sellers. **Archie** #70 shown.

Bronze Age: This era of comics has become a respected collectible category. As these books are now in the 20-30 year old age group, I myself as well as other dealers of my age group must acknowledge that they are truly established as collectibles. I must dispel the notion of buying them off the local newsstand for cover price and stop thinking that most of them will wind up in my quarter box; old habits die hard. I have been selling middle to lower grade copies at or slightly above Guide, and higher grade copies above to far above Guide.

Magazines and Independents: The magazine market has cooled quite a bit since last year but it's definitely not dead. The main exception is the second rate horror publisher Eerie. These books have the grossest, most bizarre covers ever produced en masse. Typically there is a monster being bitten by a vampire that is being attacked by a werewolf, and there is always a severed head or limb somewhere in the picture. The independent market (1980s) is alive but few dealers could survive by only selling this group of comics.

Summary: Convention sales have been as good as or better than the same shows last year. Attendance for all conventions seems to be up. My last catalog was the best one yet and Internet sales are starting to become a significant percentage of my total sales.

Ron Pussell (Redbeard's Book Den)

Prices continued their upward movement during the past year, with strong demand fueling gains. Collections of older books that made their way to the marketplace in the face of this renewed demand were quickly consumed.

Internet trading has reached new heights in the comic book marketplace. Back issue sales remain very strong. Auction sales have become a significant factor in supplying collectors' needs. Although there can be reasonable prices at these auction areas, it is definitely caveat emptor in the auction arena.

Grading certification by CGC has also had a major impact. High grade certified books are setting record prices at a dizzying pace. Multiples of guide on top graded books are common. It may be quite a while before prices stabilize in this very volatile area of collecting.

Golden Age: The cornerstone of the hobby, with collections very difficult to obtain. Almost nothing of a significant nature has been offered. Demand far out-strips supply. CGC certified books have driven the high-grade copies to new record heights. Most of the mainline titles in less than Fine sell for 95%–215% of Guide. Sales were strong throughout the year at these prices.

© FAW

Captain Marvel Adventures #16 and other Fawcett titles are popular in lower grades.

1930s TITLES: Supply limitations once again governed the increases in this area. Demand far outweighs supply. DC titles were still the most requested.

1940s TITLES: Superhero titles still lead the way. DC is the hottest area, followed by Timely.

DC: In higher grade all mainline superhero titles were selling at 195%–400% of Guide; in lesser grade the books were selling for 110%–225% of Guide. Key scarcer issues were of course selling at even higher percentages. Best-selling titles are Batman, Superman, Flash, Green Lantern and related titles. Small gains by offbeat titles.

TIMELY: Still solid. High grade copies for most titles sell at 195%–400% of Guide, lesser condition copies sell for 105%–215% of Guide. Captain America related titles are still the most popular. Solid demand for Human Torch, Sub-Mariner and related titles. Small gains by offbeat titles.

FAWCETT: Led by Captain Marvel and related titles, sales were at 95%–185% of Guide in lesser condition, and 175%–350% of Guide for higher grade copies. Good sales for Spy Smasher and Captain Midnight. Small gains by offbeat titles.

CENTAUR: Demand has reached a temporary plateau. Still an interesting publisher that will gain further should Timely prices become too high in relation to Centaur levels. This publisher has become a poor man's Timely. Books are selling at 100%–200% of Guide in lesser condition, and sell at 180%–350% of Guide in higher grade.

FOX: Solid demand for this publisher. Superhero titles sold at 100%–200% above Guide in lesser grade, and 185%–375% in higher grade. Continued strong demand for early Lou Fine cover books.

GLEASON: Sales at 95%–175% above Guide in lesser condition, and 145%–300% in higher grade. Best sellers are still Silver Streak, Daredevil and early issues of Boy.

FICTION HOUSE: Demand from good girl art collectors continues to lead to good sales for this publisher. Planet is still the most popular, followed by Jumbo, Jungle, Fight, Rangers and Wings. These titles sell for 100%–190% over Guide in lesser condition, and 175%–315% in higher grade. Small gains by offbeat titles.

QUALITY: Led by all Lou Fine titles, demand remained solid for this publisher. Prices at 95%–185% in lesser condition, and 165% –300% in higher grade. Sales of Blackhawk and related titles are at 90%–165% over Guide in lesser grade, and 145%–275% of Guide in higher grade. Small gains by offbeat titles.

MLJ: Still strong demand for this publisher. Sales at 100%–200% of Guide in lesser condition, and 200%–385% in higher grade.

CLASSIC COMICS: Mediocre sales for #1-50 first editions in most grades. Slow sales on #51 up with a few exceptions.

FUNNY ANIMAL: Timely and DC are still the most requested publishers. Small gains for all publishers. Sales at 90%–175% of Guide in lesser condition, and 135%–250% of Guide in higher grade.

MISC. PUBLISHERS: Sales and demand still primarily for keys and first issues of superhero titles. Good gains across the board in higher grade.

Atomic Age: Still a hot area, with collector demand still exceeding current supply. Fox is the publisher that continues to lead the way. Demand is very strong in all grades due to their relative scarcity. Print runs were much lower during this time period for many publishers.

© WDC

Early high-grade **Walt Disney's Comics & Stories** with art by the legendary Carl Barks remain in private collections, rarely seen on the comics market.

DELL/GK: Strong sales on lesser condition titles. Most collections of older books have large amounts of lesser condition Dell/GK titles. Carl Barks Duck One-Shot and early Comics & Stories are currently unavailable in high grade at current price levels. Where are all those high-grade copies of prior years? The fact that all these high-grade copies remain in private collections says a lot about the collectiblity and desirability of Barks books.

ATLAS: There are many collectors for this publisher. Horror/science fiction titles still lead the way at 125%–250% of Guide in lesser condition, and 200%–400% in higher grade. Crime titles are selling well at 110%–175% of Guide in lesser condition, and 175%–335% in higher grade.

DC: Still a very strong following and demand for the number one publisher in the hearts of collectors.

TV/MOVIE TITLES: Good demand for both movie and TV related titles. Sales very strong for lesser condition titles at Guide. Medium grade titles are slower.

EC: Horror and SF titles are very popular with sales at 100%–190% of Guide in lesser condition, and 195%–395% in higher grade. MAD still leads the way, selling quickly at 105%–200% of Guide in lesser condition, and 200-400% in higher grade. Gaines file copies continue to sell for record prices.

WESTERNS: Average sales led yet again by the photo cover issues. Gene Autry titles sell well.

GIANTS: If reasonable, annuals sell well in lower grade. Sales in higher grades are quite brisk due to their scarcity at 135%–400% of Guide. Most collections of older books have large amounts of lesser condition Dell Giants that sell OK at 90% of Guide.

ROMANCE: Big demand, since one can still spend a few hundred dollars in this area and buy a sizable stack of books. I don't see this lasting much longer. Sales are at 125%–200% of Guide in lesser condition, and 175%–395% in higher grade. Fox romance titles are still very hot. Sales in lesser condition are at 165%–275% of Guide, and 225%–450% in higher grade.

HUMOR: Marginal sales at 95%–135% of Guide in lesser condition, and 125%–250% in higher grade.

STRIP REPRINTS: Small increase in demand for earlier issues.

GOOD GIRL ART: Higher prices have cooled demand, but still a very hot area. Phantom Lady remains the most popular. Atlas titles have a good following. Large demands for the recognized cover classics. Sales in the 145%–275% range in lesser condition, and 195%–395% in higher grade.

AVON: Strong demand for all horror/science fiction titles and crime titles. Sales at 135%–215% of Guide in lesser condition, and 185%–395% in higher grade. Western and war titles are a bit slower for this publisher. Sales in lesser condition at 95%–175% of Guide, and 145%–275% in higher grade.

HORROR/SCIENCE FICTION: This is the hottest area of the Atomic Age. Strong sales and demand at 150%–275% over Guide, and 215%–485% in higher grade. DC horror/science fiction titles still have a solid following, but higher prices have temporarily slowed sales.

SPORTS: Good sales at 100%–195% in lower grade, and 165%–395% in higher grade.

ART TITLES: Baker is still very hot with sales in the 140%–250% of Guide in lesser condition, and 195%–475% in higher grade. LB Cole continues to sell well at 135%–265% in lesser grade, and 175%–415% in higher grade. Good sales for Wolverton horror/science fiction titles. Sales at 145%–215% in lesser condition, and 180%–465% in higher grade. Ditko and Kirby books continue to sell well at 140%–215% in lesser condition, and 175%–450% in higher grade. Good demand for Kubert books, with sales in the 135%–200% range in lesser condition and 165%–425% in higher grade. Strong sales once again for Frazetta work. Sales for lesser condition at 145%–210% and 170%–435% in higher grade. Krigstein, Toth and Williamson are requested at a slower rate then the current biggies. Prices at around 130%–190% in lesser condition, and 160%–400% in higher grade. Katz and Torres demand slight in comparison to others. Prices at 125%–180% of Guide in lesser condition, and 155%–375% in higher grade.

© DC DC's Silver Age war titles show strong sales. **Our Army at War** #159 shown.

Silver Age: Still the most impacted area from Internet trading. with continued strong sales of lesser condition books. These same books continue to sell moderately from mail-order catalogues or at conventions. Most sales at prices over Guide are in the high-grade area. The hottest Marvel title continues to be Spider-Man, followed by Fantastic Four. There's good demand for offbeat Kirby western titles. The best-selling DC is still Showcase and key Brave And The Bold in high grade. Very strong sales for the DC war titles continue, led by Our Army At War.

Bronze Age: Sales in this area continue to be mixed. Record prices are still being realized for very high-grade copies of mid-70's books. Sales are much slower on lesser condition copies at conventions and mail-order catalogues. Demand is still solid via the Internet.

MARNIN ROSENBERG (COMICCOLLECTORS.NET/ COLLECTORSASSEMBLE.COM)

In my nearly thirty years in this wonderful hobby, I have never seen a year like 2000. What a way for the comics genre to begin a new century!

During February 1999, ComicCollectors.net acquired nearly 1,800 high grade comic books from the pedigree Bethlehem collection, a fantastic group of pre- and post-Code horror, sci-fi, war and crime comics ranging from 1949-1969. The first sales from this group began on October 10, 1999 and immediately record prices were realized. Bill Hughes of Greg Manning Auctions convinced me to consign over 400 lots, many of them from the cream of the Bethlehem collection, along with other Mile High books, to the Spring 2000 comic book auction. Mr. Hughes had the foresight to literally "force me" to certify all the most important books. Many record prices were realized.

There's never been a better time to become part of the comic book universe, whether you enjoy comics, strictly invest in comics, or both.

MATT SCHIFFMAN

Golden Age: HIGH GRADE: A very interesting trend further established itself this year in the Golden Age market. True high grade material under the Timely heading continued to bring higher multiples of Guide although many of these sales were kept very quiet. The usual Timely multiple in VF or better brought from 1.8 to three times Guide, at least until you reached $5,000 in Guide value, at which point the multiples dropped off. DC high grade also continued to bring multiples, but a blanket statement on all DC can't be made. Only Batman/Detective, Superman/Action and Wonder Woman in VF or better brought a multiple of 1.5 to 1.8 for those books. Keys brought slightly more in the high grades but not as much as in lower grades. Fox, Fiction House and Standard Nedor, and Centaurs established themselves as solid second tier publishers, bringing multiples in VF or better both on-line and in standard sales. Excusing a few Timelys, these books in high grade brought a higher multiple than the balance of the Timelys or the rest of the DCs. Fawcett, Harvey and the second and third tier DCs suffered in all grades, excluding a few off eBay exceptions here and there, but not nearly enough to establish a definite trend.

© MAR

An upswing in Golden Age sales can be seen with the solid second tier publishers like Fiction House. **Planet Comics** #3 shown.

MID GRADE: A tough sell for most books. Although DCs are a very hard sell except for keys, there is evidence that an entire Golden Age price movement upward is in the works and should be developing over the next nine months. Timely in mid grade sells well but there seems to be plenty to purchase minus keys. The balance of the publishers are a tough sell in the VG to FN/VF grade because of their high Guide values.

LOW GRADE: The real trend in Golden Age comics is the emergence of the low grade material from Timely, Fox, Standard, Nedor, Fiction House and DC keys breaking out of the usual mode of 8-10% of NM Guide. On-line sales have pushed the lower grade to 22-30% of Guide. This two year trend doesn't seem to be ending any time soon. Even books not yet broken out in the Guide are being singled out for high price escalation.

OVERVIEW: Golden Age is on the upswing but prices in mid grade are very stagnant. If the book is not deemed interesting or some type of a key/hot title or issue, it's lucky if it brings 50% of Guide.

Atom Age: HIGH GRADE: Almost as a rule, high grade books sell well above Guide with the exceptions of Four Color, Disney, westerns and other Dells. Even funny animals do well if they aren't in the Dell family. Fox and Good Girl lead the way with establishing high multiples of Guide in high grade. Two to three times Guide is not unheard of for many of these titles. Even the ultra-high grade Phantom Lady books sell for these multiples. Most do so well because of their perceived low Guide value vs. market scarcity and demand. All Fox romance titles sell for crazy multiples in high grade on-line, in private sales and noted at the Manning auctions. San Diego had a run of 20 books in VG sell for $150 each while averaging about $25 each in the Guide. High grade westerns sell well with this new trend, but come nowhere near Guide levels even on eBay. DC mainstream books do well and even publishers such as Timely, Fawcett and Fiction House do well in high grade.

Fox Romance titles like **My Love Life** #12 sell like crazy.

© FOX

MID GRADE: Mid grade books do well along the lines of high grade, but only certain crime, horror or Good Girl will make multiples of existing Guide prices. War comics are showing increased interest and higher prices, as are Atlas and Harvey (the more gruesome the better). The ultra-low prices in all grades fuel this growing demand and by next year we should see the emergence of the previously scarcer high grade books and the multiples that even now they are starting to bring. Mid grade war brings roughly 1.5 to 1.7 of Guide, while Fox books still bring 25% or more of Guide and will always bring a lot of interest on- and off-line.

LOW GRADE: Interest in low grade material is mainly in the Fox, Good Girl, horror, or Timely books. These continue to bring higher than Guide prices. Even the low grade Fox jungle and romance will often reflect the Golden Age Timely phenomenon in low grade books, whereas the value ratios get thrown out the window and GD can bring just a few percentage points under VG or VG/FN. Western keys sell well in low grade while they sit in mid grade.

Silver Age: HIGH GRADE:The point of true debate. Unfortunately, the release of the population study by CGC will change everything that we've seen to date in the high multiples of Guide. We've seen an abatement of really wild and totally unjustifiable bids, and incredibly huge warehouse finds and inventories of Iron Man #1, Cap #100s, etc. One problem is not to overstate the jump in NM prices on titles and issues that are truly reflective of the new market.

MID GRADE: Very difficult to sell unless it's a key, a Marvel before 1964, or a DC before 1962. eBay prices reflect that it's lucky to reach 45% of Guide if it sells at all. Key issues continue to move but even AF#15, TOS#39, FF#1 and others still have a tough time reaching Guide levels.

LOW GRADE: Low grade books sell very well but almost always below Guide. If it Guides for $15-25, it will probably bring $9-14. Keys are always the exception and even show a tendency to move above Guide prices if it's a DC book. Dells move very well in low grades, especially TV and movie stuff, but not too well in higher grades around Guide prices.

Bronze Age: HIGH GRADE: A revelation in the past year as the large mail order dealers have moved in and started to offer this stuff to their clients. Marvel Team-Up #1 in NM is now a $180 book. Hulk #181 in NM for $3,800? Yes, but after the population study comes out then we'll see. The same is true for X-Men #94 and G-S #1. High grade DC and Marvel sell for multiples of Guide, but variants are not bringing what they should in order to justify their high rankings and prices. Most are held by dealers that cannot move them. eBay does not support the NM prices either at this time. The novelty is over, much like the DC romance 100 pagers that now sell very well in the $75 range. House of Secrets in true NM can bring $750 but the lower grades are plentiful. Magazines are very popular and the Vampirella books are doing very well in high grade. Besides the variants, other novelty books like the DC 100PG SS #5 is down. #4 sells in NM for $500 and $280 in VF/VF+.

Marvel Team-Up #1 and other Bronze Age gems are finding an eager reception.

MID GRADE: Only the very scarce stuff has much of a chance to arrive at Guide prices and eBay is flooded with everything, even the variants. Detective #400, Green Lantern #76, DC 100PG SS #4—all do very well and sell above Guide, but Hulk #181, and X-Men G-S #1 and #94 cannot meet Guide or they have yet to do so this year.

LOW GRADE: Harder to move, but very popular at below Guide prices. A hard market to track as most dealers do not report or even recall sales. A few lower grade key books once in a while will hit a home run on eBay, but these are not so much the rule as the exception.

TONY STARKS (COMICS INA FLASH!)

What a year 2000 has turned out to be. Sales of back issue comic books have been great. Low grade books continue to sell well due to the lower prices instituted a few years ago. These lower prices rekindled interest and brought many former collectors back into the hobby. At the same time, interest in NM book is red hot and many collectors and investors view key issues in 9.2+ as severely undervalued. The hobby has diversified, and every genre and period of time–Platinum to Bronze, hero to horror, magazines to treasuries–has eager fans.

The CGC phenomenon has hit the hobby like a tidal wave. A close examination of all the record prices set reveals they are all virtually high grade, 9.4+ slabbed books. This is having an effect on the price of lower grade books however. Who wants to sell a NM G-S X-Men #1 for Guide or even double Guide when the same book might bring three or even four times Guide graded and slabbed? The key, as one colleague remarked, is to be able to grade at CGC's standard and to be able to spot restoration.

Even common and newer books are not immune. Sixty bucks for a 1977 Spider-Woman slabbed at 9.6 NM+? Wolverine #1 (mini) 9.6 NM+ selling for $200? Wizard's "Perfect 10" Spider-Man #1 (gold, 1990) at $550+?! The week after the Spider-Man sold, I was cleaned out of McFarlane's Spider-Man title–books which had sat unnoticed and unsold for years. Some participants seem to be just looking at the label and not at the book. Yes, the Spider-Man #1 in 10 may be perfect, but it sure isn't scarce, and somebody someday is going to be the last person holding it when supply catches up with demand.

Bronze Age: My specialty. The Bronze Age is HOT! Have we seen any books escalate in demand and price more than G-S X-Men #1, Incredible Hulk #181 or X-Men #94? The average '70s collector continues to be interested in the unusual and offbeat. Collectors still pay big bucks for books like Blitzkreig (#1NM $35, #2-5NM $20) and Ghosts (#1GD $8). But it's getting increasingly difficult to keep nice 15-20 cent cover price copies of most of the mainstream titles, like Action Comics (#432FN $4), Adventure Comics (#431NM $38, a NM run of #441-490 at or above Guide), Amazing Spider-Man (#90NM $30), and Defenders below #20 (multiple copies in all conditions at Guide or above, #10NM $30). Other super-hero sales of note include Captain America #193NM (Kirby's return) $10, #200 $7, Red Wolf #1NM $15, Super Friends #1NM $40 and #2NM $15, and a whole run of issues #3-41 at 1.5 to two times Guide. A lot of what were once slow titles have found new life. Kamandi, Demon, Plastic Man, Conan, Brave & the Bold, Marvel Team-Up, Marvel Two-in-One, Ghost Rider and many more are selling well again. Wonder Woman is scorching hot. I have sold out of issues below #230 in all grades at 1.25 to two times Guide.

Inexpensive #1s from DC and Marvel published during the '70s are increasing in demand. From Battlestar Galactica to Spider-Woman, Beowulf to Omega the Unknown, Eternals to Shogun Warriors, the interest is slowly building. These books are cheap and over 20 years old. The Atlas/Seaboard titles from 1975 are way up in demand. Any NM issue sells at $5 minimum, with #1s at $6. Better issues (Scorpion #1NM, Chaykin art and bondage cover $8) bring even more. I can't keep treasuries and digests in stock even at above Guide prices. Magazines have taken off again, with monster stuff leading the pack. Creepy (#1 FR/GD $5, #32VG $7.50, #40FN $6.50) and Eerie issues are in demand, as are Skywald titles like Psycho and Nightmare. Vampirella is now selling well again after a lot of overexposure in the comic book series. Marvel's Tales of the Zombie is hot (#1FN $6, #9NM $10). Deadly Hands of Kung-Fu and the Conan magazine have seen a marked increase in interest. What is interesting about magazine sales is that the majority of collectors seem to be looking for them in lower grades. It's actually easier to get over Guide for GD and VG books than it is for NM.

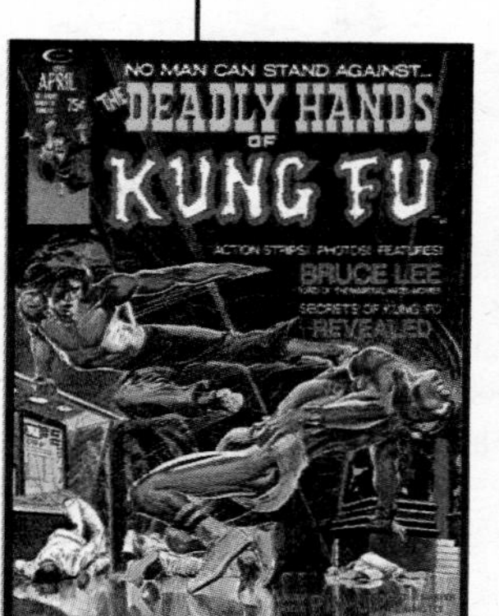

© CC

Deadly Heads of Kung Fu #1 and other magazines have a marked increase in interest, especially in lower grades.

Charlton's horror/mystery books and romance titles are much in demand. First issues of titles like Ghost Manor (#1FN $20), Scary Tales (#1NM $25), Midnight Tales (#1NM $30) and Ghostly Tales (#55VG $12) are way undervalued and go for 1.5 to two times Guide. There are a lot of collectors that would love to have a list of all the Charlton horror/mystery books that were done by the "good" artists–Ditko, first and foremost, but also Aparo, Newton, Howard and a few others. Charlton's TV titles, such as Emergency (#1NM $25, #2-4NM $15), Six Million Dollar Man and Space: 1999 are also starting to move up in demand.

At the zenith of romance comics about two years ago, any VG copy of any romance comic published in the last 35 years was a sure sell at over Guide. Now collectors are more picky. The giant size issues (particularly the 52 pagers) are still good sellers, but now collectors ask for non-giant size issues with "cool" covers. What's a cool cover? Girls in bikinis are cool; a girl getting a big kiss from some macho guy is cool, and really cool if she's in a bikini (Young Love #92NM $20, Summer Love #48VG $5). "Women's Lib" covers and stories are great (Young Love #106FN $3.50). "Hippie" and "swinger" issues are also cool, especially if they mention Woodstock. In short, guys are buying these books because the stories are ludicrous and the covers exploitative. Bad taste is just so much fun.

Silver Age: GD and VG are selling well, while NM is of course always welcome and now sells for Guide at minimum, bringing a premium for most key issues. I have sold thousands of issues of mainstream titles in various grades, from Action Comics (#376VG $4) to World's Finest Comics (#183 & #186VG $4). Hardly anything sells more than Guide and sometimes it's a little less. Stand-outs include Action, Brave & the Bold, and Wonder Woman (as mentioned earlier, this lady is HOT). Both Guide relatively low compared to other titles, which may explain the interest. Gold Key titles such as Doctor Solar, Magnus and Turok are once again steady sellers now that Acclaim has stopped destroying the characters. Slow titles include Strange Tales and Sgt. Fury. Strangely enough, Marvel's western titles are slow as Silver Age books but screaming hot as Bronze Age books. Maybe it's the great Gil Kane covers on the '70s books.

Silver Age issues of **The Brave and the Bold** are marketplace stand-outs.

Doug Sulipa (Doug Sulipa's Comic World)

eBay: eBay has been at the forefront of the attention of many people in the marketplace. It's a dumping ground for overstock material, so many items sell at low percentages of Guide. Much goes unsold, as even eBay is now over-saturated with overstock material. There is mistrust of grading, with good reason, which also often lowers values. Known dealers and sellers with high feedback get better prices, as people can bid with more confidence. Good items thru trusted sellers often bring well over Guide prices. Many scarcer but still cheaper oddball comics bring multiples of Guide with regularity. Mainstream titles in low grade do poorly. Record high and low prices are set daily. Although a good indicator of trends, eBay is not a good source for averaging prices. The results are often very erratic. Also, in spite of all the attention, less than 10% of back issues sold on the market are sold on eBay! The effects are beginning to level. Many people are still entering the market, but many are returning to more reliable markets. Much quality material is not being put on eBay due to risk of low prices. Customers tire of buying items one at a time. Still eBay has brought much great material back into the market and is an excellent way to study current trends. Many new, returning and foreign collectors have entered the market through eBay!

Professional Grading: Probably the biggest news on the market is the great success of CGC graded comics. World record prices are being set daily for certified high grade comics. This has also caused a flurry of requests to dealers for high grade copies not yet "slabbed." Contrary to the trends of the last 5 years, the most activity in "slabbed" comics is with the traditional well-known Key issues, mostly Marvel, but also DC! Many of these comics were dead sellers and now have new life. Many new "investors" are entering the market to buy these certified comics. New buyers in the market should consult knowledgable dealers before paying high multiples of Guide on these certified comics. Be warned, given 5 years or 100 times as many items certified comics, current pricing structures can change drastically. Many

'70s comics are scarcer than originally thought in strict high grades. Some long-time high grade collectors are resisting paying the "new" multiples. Professional grading is here to stay, but its long-term effects will not be known for years to come.

Silver Age: Low grade reading copies remain in very high demand and are getting scarcer on non-mainstream titles. There are a lot of superhero comics still on the market in reading copies, but a shortage on other genres. Many dealers have begun to put minimum prices of $2 to $5 range on "reading copies" regardless of Guide values and report they sell quite well. CGC graded comics in VFNM 9.0 or better regularly bring over Guide, and has greatly renewed interest in all the mainstream titles. The true scarcity of 9.0 or better copies, is slowly becoming apparent. Silver Age has been selling well for all companies and in all grades. SA inventories are getting depleted as more enter permanent collections. Also, many collectors are selling via eBay rather than to dealers. It is getting more difficult to replenish dealer stocks. It is now apparent that many SA titles are scarce in even VF, especially war, teen, cartoon, love and western. The "new" high prices on high grade have created a bigger audience for mid-grade nice copies in VG to FVF. There is a shortage of the many 1969-1973 superhero comics, the period when both Marvel and DC greatly expanded title counts and thereby diluted print runs. Consistant dealer shortages on these issues has caused rising prices and demand. Good Artist comics are again in heavy demand and due for more price increases! Most long-time and proven series were stong sellers. This includes renewed interest in comics that became famous from newspaper strips, such as Beetle Bailey, Blondie, Dennis the Menace, Dick Tracy, Phantom, Popeye, Sad Sack, Tarzan and others. Cartoon comics remained elusive in high grades, with the exception of the few file copies on the market. All Giants were very popular and are bringing over Guide in all grades.

© FAW

There's renewed interest in comic characters who debuted in newspaper strips. **Dennis the Menace** #1 shown

Bronze Age: Bronze Age comics remained extremely popular. There are more people trying to complete sets in this era than any other, while they're still affordable. Everything sells by every company and in any grade, but most popular are highest grade investment copies and lowest grade reading copies. People have realized that many traditionally non-collected titles are just not to be found in high grades and they now actively seek any grade, but are quite satisfied with nice mid-grade copies. Many people with new disposable incomes grew up on this era and are willing to spend there funds here. CGC awareness has made us all realize how scarce many of even the most common titles are now becoming in strict NM. 20-30 years of handling has made even most large original dealer new copies drop to FVF or lower average copies, many only in VGF! If demand for high grade continues, it will not be long before everything 1980 and older sells at $10 minimum in strict NM! Original-owner high grade collections are still not surfacing as expected. It is assumed that many consider current price levels too low. The shortage of 1969-1973 comics is growing more acute as dealers sell out and can not restock. There was a sales implosion in the late '70s to early '80s that saw the death of many publishers and genres. We saw Charlton, Harvey, Fawcett, Seaboard, Gold Key, and Warren all fold. Archie cut titles and frequency. We saw many genres disappear, including most cartoon, war, western, love, reprints, teen, horror, humor and others!

Many Bronze Age collectors have spilled over into the '80s to finish off titles that began in the '70s. Some might argue that the Bronze Age ended when Crisis and Secret Wars began. Even if not, demand for titles up to that point has grown. As people complete runs, new awareness of scarcer high numbers is arising and beginning to get reflected in prices. The last 10 or so issues of titles like Wonder Woman, Flash and JLA are in higher demand. Reprint titles have been selling quite well, especially the Marvel Horror titles. All non-regular format items continue to sell well, and often well over Guide, including magazines, fanzines, digests, treasuries, paperbacks, promo items, giveaways and all types of memorabilia. Traditionally non-collected titles remain in high demand and yet lower supply. All magazines remained in strong demand, especially all horror titles by every company. Mainstream titles have made a growing comeback, mainly due to the infleunce of certified graded copies. CGC 9.0 or better brings multiples of Guide. This has caused those who resist the new high prices to snap up nice non-certified VF copies at up to 100% of NM price with more regularity. Marvel price variants had some demand, most notably from completionists. Bronze Age collectors remain the biggest completionists! High demand for reprint titles of the '70s from both DC and Marvel continues with some of the teen, love and cartoon prices beginning to rival the '50s titles they reprint. But there are few completionists of the '50s titles, so it is feasible some might one day outprice the originals! There has been a notable increase in demand for the few remaining Bronze Age titles that still guide at the $2 to $4 range. This has made Atlas Seaboard the company most wanted to complete. All Giants were in large demand. DC's "Dollar Comics" have most notably been in demand. They had too many pages for a round-bound format and strict-NM copies are proving much scarcer than previously thought. Treasuries and Digests are also scarce in True NM, because they typically did not have readily available storage bags. The odd sizes also made them awkward for both collectors and dealers to store and handle. Both formats were considered peripheral items and have suffered both in condition and supply over these 15-28 years.

DC's "Dollar Comics" like **Superman Family** #195 have been in demand.

Modern Age: Many have thought of all Post-1980 comics as dead for several years now, but as prices continue to rise on Bronze and Silver age, more people have shifted to these low priced items. The biggest growing demand is for Bronze titles that spill over into the '80s. Most Marvel and DC titles up to and including Crisis and Secret Wars have experienced increased demand and sales. Most other newstand publishers were dying in this period and many people are looking to fill in runs. All 1984-86 Charltons had low print runs and remain elusive to collectors. There is an oversupply of the early issues of the first Direct-Only titles (like Dazzler #1-5)! Many last or last 10 issues of titles cancelled in this period are notabley scarcer than the few years previous. Most titles from genres that died in the early '80s had smaller print runs and may cause future problems for collectors as supplies dwindle. Variant collectors have noted that early Direct-Only copies are in shorter supply than newsstand copies of this period, especially on DC titles. Comics from the 1st Batman movie in 1989 to the end of the exhaustive Death of Superman 1993 titles seem to be the most overprinted period which currently glut the market.

But there were other boom and bust periods in the last 20 years, especially in the alternative comics market. In the last 5 years, mass hoarding of new comics, especially by dealers, has nearly come to a halt. High cover prices has been the main cause. Collectors have lost confidence that new comics can be good investments. Many longtime collectors report that new comics are now alien to them but buyers of new comics, on the other hand, have little interest in Pre-1990 comics. Many newer comics do bring good premiums, but prices are too volatile on most to firmly report. Collectors are now more interested in proven winners. All that said, there is a noticable shortage of oridinary back issues from 1995-2000 titles. Any non-key issue can fast become hard to find, as no one wants to risk investing in recent comics inventories. This is an area to watch for in the future. Low supplies of recent titles may lend itself to future health in the back issue markets. Many alternative titles have had increased demand. Currently the best sellers include all "good" artists issues, all TV/movie titles, all character and cartoon titles, many of the better manga titles, comic strip reprint titles, horror titles, most 3-D titles, sports/personality/rock titles, and titles resurrected from other publishers. Many were over-published, like early Pacific, but dumping has slowed or ended, and quanties have dissipated. Many alternates had original quantities of 1000 to 5000 published and are legitimately hard to find. Many high profile top alternates had relatively low print runs of 5000 to 20,000 copies and supply is diminishing. Collectors report many of these sets are hard to complete as dealers do not want to bother. Character driven titles are bringing premiums, such as "How to Draw" titles with GI Joe, Transformers and John Byrne, and 3-D titles with Robert E. Howard, GI Joe, Starwars, etc. High numbers are becoming scarce on popular titles like Dick Tracy weekly/monthly, Kitchen Sink Spirit, Zot, and ending issues of titles like Dreadstar. Marvel and DC character-driven titles are in bigger demand. Most Star titles by Marvel were in demand and most at over low Guide levels. Many of the '80s mini series have renewed demand. These finite little gems guarantee self-contained stories and many are above par for the period. This has caused many to take another look at them while they're still afforable. In very high demand, with little supply, are many high numbered issues before cancellation of long-running titles. Final issues and high numbered issues are consistently elusive. Some titles that can be filled in with a little legwork include Flash #340-350, Wonder Woman #321-329, Groo #87-120, all 1984-86 Charltons, Gold Key/Whitman final issues, Sgt Rock #400-422, Conan #251-275, Savage Sword #201-225, Dick Tracy monthly/weekly #81—99, Spirit (Kitchen Sink) #61-87, All Star Squadron #51-67 and others! Other titles had very low print runs and even lower survival rates, and are very difficult to find, bringing prices of $5 to $15 each. These are Transformers #71-79 and GI JOE #141 to 154 (The final issues vary widely: Transformers #80–$15-$40, GI JOE #155–$10 to $30). By the time these titles reached these high numbers, most collectors and dealers alike gave up on them. The big news is the record prices for Modern Age comics graded by CGC. It is becoming common to see exceptional examples bringing 10 to 100 times NM Guide prices. Buyers should take heed–it is too early to tell on most titles what is truely scarce and at what CGC grade level.

© DC

Final issues of long running titles, like **Flash** #350, can be elusive.

Artist Issues: Artist issues are again gaining in popularity. All traditionally highly collectible artists continue to be stable and sell well. Kirby remains the most widely collected artist. Many choose to collect Kirby through reprints to keep their costs down, thus demand is good for all such titles. Afforable never-reprinted titles remain in highest demand. There is a resurrgance in demand, and all bringing premiums over Guide in all grades, for Neal Adams, Wrightson, Toth, Eisner, Jeff Jones, Kirby, Wood, Baker and Wolverton. There is especilly a lot of interest and escalating prices on more recent vintage artists like J.Byrne, G.Perez, F.Miller, A.Ross, D.Rosa, W.Pini, D.Sim, and J.Starlin. All scarcer items are bringing good premiums due to heavy buyer competition.

© MAR

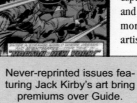

Never-reprinted issues featuring Jack Kirby's art bring premiums over Guide.

Comic Digests: Once ignored, but now firmly entrenched as desirable collectibles, digests continue to grow in demand and value as supply disappears. DC digests are still the most collected, with Best of DC #41 thru the last issue #71 remaining the scarcest issues due to low print runs. Many people consider them to be like mini-trade paperbacks because they are full of classic reprints at low cost. The original material and Comic Cavalcade reprint issues remain in high demand when identified. All the Gold Key digests remain in high demand. Golden Comics Digest #2,7,11–the Hanna Barbera issues–are in huge demand but are not to be found. They can command 200-300% current Guide. All issues of Mystery Comic digest are in big demand. Fast sellers include Fiction illustrated #3 (Steranko), Shocking Tales #1, Archie Superhero #1,2, all Archie titles #1-10 issues, all Archies with Adams or other artists, all 1970s digests in general, and Harvey #1-5 issues. Marvel digests have also grown strongly in demand, including; GI Joe, Spider-Man, Star and Transformers. Digest awareness has increased demand for the many British and other foreign comic digests. Those with classic USA reprint material sell best, but foreign digests are also selling better with all-new unseen in USA material, especially if they feature popular themes like war, sex and horror.

© DC

DC Digests, like the **Best of DC #45**, are both popular and scarce.

Canadian Editions: Canada had an embargo on US editions, several times, from the WWII years through the mid-'50s! During these periods, printing plates were sent to Canada and separate Canadian editions were printed. Most had "cereal box" type cover stock. This cover stock did not survive time well, and most are quite scarce in above VG condition. Most issues were from near the same vintage as US equivalents. In some issues, contents got switched around in comparison to the US equivalents. Some also dropped page counts or changed titles. Most of the direct reprints were in color. Publishers that had Golden Age editions in Canada include DC, Timely, Dell, Fawcett, Classics, EC, Archie, Toby, Quality, Avon, Fiction House, Lev Gleason and others. The survival rate on these comics is very low. Many may no longer exist and many others exist only in quantities of 1 to 10 copies. Due to scarcity, prices are beginning to approach US equivalent prices. The EC reprints still bring 25%-35% less than US edition due to poor printing quality, the exception being the much requested and rare Weird Suspense Stories #1! Superior put out several series of all-new material, mostly love and horror titles, and all are getting scarcer, especially in high grade!

Canada also had an industry of "Canadian Whites" which are all new charcaters with all new comics and stories for Canada in b&w! Most had newsprint covers. They also experimented, mainly with Fawcett titles, with taking US comics and having them re-drawn by Canadian artists for publication in designated Canadian White titles. All are scare to rare, and many likely no longer exist. May to August 1968 Canadian 15 cent cover price editions exist on all Gold Key titles. They are approximately 10 times scarcer than US editions and bring 100-150% guide values! Variant collectors are paying 150%-250% Guide for the Canadian newstand variant editions of the 1980s Marvel (10/82—8/86) and DC (10/82—9/88) issues.

Canada also had a fairly big French language edition industry from the '70s thru the '90s. A limited amount were also issued in the 1960s and all are quite scarce today. Since the audience was mainly French-speaking Canadians, which only comprises about 1% of North Americans, the print runs are quite small. The French Canadian comics, for the most part, are comprised of reprints of Marvel, DC and Archie comics. They also ventured into some Gold Key, King, original character and overseas reprint material. Artist and character collectors seek these Canadian comics the most. There was also the curious practice of taking unsold copies and rebinding them into Giant annuals with new wraparound outer covers. These are especially treasuered by collectors.

Humor and Parody Magazines: Sales have significantly increased. Many highly collectible characters, TV shows, movies and other items can easily bring far above Guide values, especially in the non-comic collectibles arena. Since many are hard to find, condition is less of a factor to buyers on any desirable parody. Most in fact now sell as character items more than for the title itself, with perhaps the exception of MAD. It seems only MAD exists in large enough quantities to satisfy most want lists.

© Skywald

Psycho #2, one of the Skywald horror magazines in high demand.

Horror Magazines: All b&w horror mags are strong sellers from every company. Warren leads the pack, mostly because they are best known and had the biggest output. Many people are trying to fill in sets. Middle number Creepy and Eerie, especially from #40-#70, are in shorter supply, as they were in low supply in the Warren warehouse which was dispersed in the early '80s. Also the high numbers of Creepy, Eerie and Vampirella are in lower supply, due to low final print runs as Warren was folding. Teen-age love mags from Warren are a hot commodity as a spillover from the love comic collecting craze. Marvel mags are consistent sellers, and are in shorter supply as more disappear into permanent collections. Most of the last two to four issues seem in shorter supply. Eerie Publication mags continued to sell well and '60s issues are getting more elusive. Stanley Publications mags were in even more demand, mainly because they had a much smaller total output and they reprinted more pre-code horror titles. All Skywald titles were in very high demand, including Psycho, Nightmare and Scream. Nightmare #20 is in huge demand and is beginning to break the $100 mark! Nightmare, Psycho #20 and up, and Scream #9—11 are low print, on most want lists and getting scarcer. Web of Horror is very much requested and due for a big price rise. All photo horror mags remained popular too, with Famous Monsters leading the way. Also popular were Charlton's Mad Monsters and Horror Monsters, plus Fangoria and all similar mags. Issues with popular characters on the cover brought premium prices with regularity.

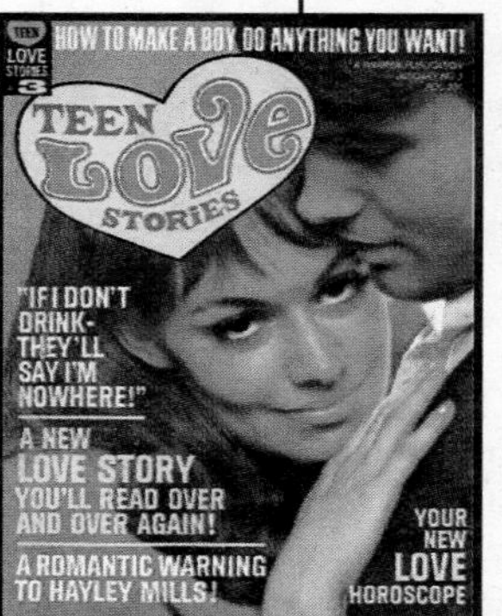

© WP

Teen-age love magazines from Warren are a hot commodity. **Teen Love Stories** #3 shown.

TV, Movie, Character, Cartoon and Personality Comics: This remains a very fast growing area of collecting, especially via the internet. Trends show although still strong, there's a slight cooling of pre-1970 titles in favor of 1975–1985 titles. TV Cartoons have a big following and condition is not a priority to many buyers. Demand is much higher on TV items as compared to movie items, but on movie items from 1980–1995, there are more buyers. Many Marvel, DC and alternative comics of the period had lower print runs and less direct market distribution than mainstream and superhero items of the period. Supply can and is beginning to disappear on these items. Prices are expected to rise as most have low Guide values.

Religious Comics: Buyers of religious comics, most especially Christian related comics, are serious buyers and typically want all the different items that they can afford. Low Guide values make Guide irrelevant to many buyers and sellers. All comics by Spire Christian comics are the most sought. Most Spire issues with a single printing, usually '80s titles, are scarce and sell at $5 to $10 each in any decent condition. Archie Spires are especially hot as two collecting groups want them. The Marvel titles are fast-sellers and getting harder to find. The DC Bible treasury is very popular. Treasure Chest sells best in low grade reading copies because of the huge size of the series. Crusaders had great art and many are attempting to complete the run but find that all the high numbers are scarce. Dennis the Menace and the Bible Kids is hot, but #7–10 are scarce and might have had only regional distribution. All the Catechetical Guild one-shots are in very high demand, but most are not to be found because of low Guide values. Most in VG bring $10-$15 or more. All the obscure publishers like Logos and Open Door are highly sought and difficult to obtain.

Romance: For several years running now, these have been strong sellers. Most people buy them for their scarcity. Most of the original print runs are destroyed because they were almost entirely held by non-collectors. There are some completionists, but due to quantity and scarcity, most choose to collect by titles, decades, publishers, or by key issues. Big demand and low supply of key issues is driving up prices, which have a while to go before peaking. Our Love Story #5, with the classic Steranko 'Mod' story, is by far the most requested and sells instantly in all grades, with NM copies in the $200 range! The reprints in My Love #23, Captain America Special #2 and Young Romance UK Comic Digest #3, are all bringing multiples of Guide! My Love and Our Love Story in all grades have constant unsatisfied demand with still escalating prices. Virtually all love comics are scarce in strict NM; most are in VG or less. All Marvels in NM bring multiples of Guide. DC titles sell strongly, but are diluted when compared to Marvel due to long runs. Giants, artists and key issues are hot! Charlton titles are still selling fast, as they remain the cheapest in this genre. Short runs of 30 or less are in high demand as many try to complete sets. Soap Opera Love and Soap Opera Romance both had low print runs and sell briskly when found. Outside of Marvel titles, high grade copies are not required by most buyers. Atlas/Seaboard's Gothic Romance is very scarce and high grade copies bring $100-$150. Vicki #3, 4 are very elusive and on many want lists. Marvel's Gothic Tales of Love #1,2 do exist, but are not to be found in any grade at any price. The strength of Post-1960 love comics has spilled into bigger demand for Atom to Silver Age romance. Especially popular are anything in the $5 to $20 range. Naturally artist issues remained very popular. All with Kirby art were bringing premiums from 20% to 100% over Guide.

© DELL

Demand for Dell titles has increased with the passing of our cowboy heroes.

War Comics: War comic collectors are serious collectors and avid readers as a whole. Virually all titles by all publishers in any condition sell well. This is one area where many people are always trying to fill in runs. DC is still the strongest, followed by Atlas, Marvel and Charlton. Many of the obscure '50s titles sell much faster than in many years. At Charlton, there is a growing respect for Sam Glanzman art issues. If identified as Glanzman, chance of sale virually doubles. Prices might be due for increases in the next few years. Interest has risen for the classic UK Weekly War comic digests of the '60s to '80s, as people discover they are getting scarcer. Our Army At War #83, 168, 242, GI Combat #68, 144-148,150, and Star Spangled War #94 are all red hot and selling in the double Guide range if you can find copies. Sgt. Rock prototypes and pre-Rock Easy Co. stories continue to be in demand.

Western Comics: Demand for Dell titles has increased with the passing of Gene Autry and Roy Rogers. Often requested and making a comeback in demand were Western Roundup, Lone Ranger, Red Ryder, and Sgt. Preston, King of The Royal Mounted. Dumping of Dells has ceased and prices have experienced a moderate rise. Charlton westerns that finished Fawcett titles are in short supply and often scarcer than their older counterparts. Most Charlton westerns are in demand due to low Guide values. Any key, Giant, or artist issue sells swiftly and at over Guide levels. The awareness of low Guide values of all oddball '50s publishers and titles has increased demand on same. Many collectors of pre-1960 titles are very loyal to their genre, are consistently reliable buyers, and prefer lower cost reading copies. Vintage western buyers seem to be grouped regionally and sales can be spectacular in one area and disappointing in the next. There is resistance to VF or better copies. Fastest selling were all Marvel western titles of the '70s as many try to complete runs. Kirby issues of the '50s through the '70s all sold swiftly. All Star/Weird Western #10-38 were hot and supply is getting smaller. Jonah Hex #1-20, 80 up and digests were in big demand. The oddball short DC and Marvel titles are finite, so they're easier to collect and hot, like Trigger Twins, Gunslinger, Western Team-Up, and '70s Marvel Wyatt Earp. The '80s Charlton reprints were good sellers, especially artist issues.

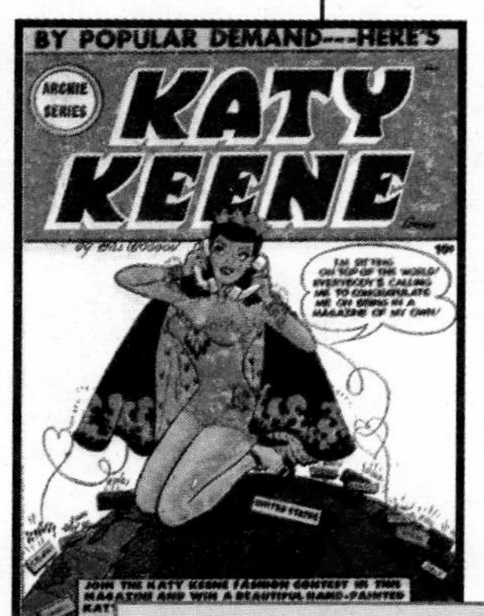

© AP

Katy Keene remains a popular title for collectors of comics and paper dolls.

Miscellaneous: People remain intrigued with anything and everything oddball. This started with Bronze Age, but is spilling more and more to Silver and Atom Age titles. Low Guide value seems to be the key ingredient. IW and Super Reprints titles are all up in demand. Teen comics from all publishers and years seem to have more and more buyers. Binky, Millie, Bunny, Teen-In, Vicki, Chili, Tippy Teen and all similar titles are now commonly heard requests and all still bring premiums. Charlton was the epitome of the oddball publisher and many are trying all types of titles and genres. ACG titles are all steady sellers, with Herbie and superhero issues most requested. Anything with crossover characters and odd appearances is getting more attention, like Real Life and True Comics. Any forgotten publishers and comics from 1960–1980 sells fast at over Guide, including Fatman, Capt Marvel (MF Ent), Henry Brewster, True Comics and Adventure Stories (1965 Parents), Fast Willie Jackson, Classics swipe titles, Golden Legacy, Star Reach and others. Tower has renewed demand, mostly because they were loaded with great artists.

Archie: Collectors remain loyal to this company. There is a strong reader base that just wants reading copies. Betty and Veronica, Josie, Sabrina, and Cheryl Blossom are all the strongest sellers. Suzie has picked up in demand, marking the trend toward female titles. Nice covers, especially with swimsuits, cheerleaders, UFOs, and DeCarlo art sell fast. Sabrina and Josie with Pussycats remained hot, with all key, early, giant and high number issues being nearly non-existent on the market. Josie #45-74, 91 up and Sabrina #1-20, 71 up brought 200% or more Guide when found. Covers and inside appearances in any other title of Josie, Sabrina, and Cheryl Blossom sold very fast. Archie's TV Laughout, and Little Archie's with Little Sabrina were again up in demand!. Archie Giant spot appearance issues are red hot. All giants from all years sold in every condition, especially '60s squarebound issues. Digests continue to be hotly pursued, particularilly all #1-10 issues and any pre-1980 issues. Final issues and last 5-10 issues of titles cancelled in the '80s had low print runs and are an obstacle to many trying to fill in these runs. The '60s Archie heroes are hot, including digests. The '60s superheroes titles are again selling, especially Mighty Comics and Mighty Crusaders, likely due to the many heroes. Fast on the move are all the Red Circle thru Archie Adventure series superhero and horror titles of the '70s and '80s. Sorcery and Madhouse #95-97 are hot and bringing double Guide and up, mostly due to great artists. The Red Circle superhero issues are way up in demand, mostly for good art like Toth and Steranko, but also for heroes like Black Hood. Katy Keene has regained some strong demand from paper doll and other collectors on the internet. Especially hot and getting much scarcer are the '80s Katy Keene comics and digests, many bringing 200-1000% of Guide #30. Still blazing hot are all Sonic the Hedgehog comics from 1993 to 1996, which consistantly bring $10 and up, with the mini #0,1 and regular #1,2 in the $20-$35 range. Spire titles remain hot, with scarce single print issues in very high demand. Many now want first printing Spire, while others want any reading copy. Christmas and

Archie treasuries are rare in any grade, with GD copies now bringing $20+. The Archie All-Star Specials, rebound Giants, remained rare and very elusive in any grade. Madhouse #22 was very much wanted, with all copies gone instantly from the market at multiples of Guide. All Sabrina issues sold quite well and over Guide.

Atlas/Seaboard: This is one company everyone seems to want to complete. Vickis remained scarce, with #3 and #4 almost never seen for sale. Gothic Romances #1 was in huge demand and has broken the $100 barrier, selling up to $150 or more. One shots and last issues were a bit more elusive. The four issue Movie Monsters series is tough to find. The war titles, Blazing Battle Tales and Savage Combat Tales, were bringing double Guide or more, especially SCT #2 with Toth art. The magazines, Devilina, Thrilling Adv. and Weird Tales of the Macabre sell very fast, with all the #2s in very low supply and bringing over Guide. Many great writers and artists appear in this short-lived company, which has led to the current big demand. Values continue to rise.

Charlton: It is amazing how popular many of these comics have become in the last five years. There is something for everyone in this company, with many undocumented artists, characters, appearences, themes and more yet to be discovered. As more people try them, more trends arise. Most of John Byrne's earliest pro work appears here, and he is one of the most collected artists. The text illos issues are getting tough to locate in any grade. Many Ditko issues are undocumented and most post-1960 issues have yet to break out at higher prices even though the majority is new material. Wally Wood new and reprint art issues are in high demand and very under-valued. Sam Glanzman, Pete Morisi, Don Newton, Sanho Kim, Tom Sutton, Boyette, Staton, and Wayne Howard are all names perhaps best known for their classic Charlton art and all are gaining a new respect, demand and have rising values. The TV tiltles are all in high and steady demand, including Space: 1999, Six Million Dollar Man, and Bionic Woman. The mags are all getting scarcer and all bring over Guide, esp. Neal Adams issues. The superhero titles have picked up in demand, especially the Ditko issues. The modern reprints sell very well on any title that lists at $10 or more in the Guide, and some are trying to make sets. Charlton Bullseye mag is hot and selling fast at over Guide. All 1984–86 issues had low print runs and are making completing these sets difficult. Attack #48 is red hot for the Kirby and Wood art, as is Gunfighters #85 for the Kirby art. Charlton Classics has had a big increase in demand for the Hercules by Glanzman reprints. The war titles have especially picked up in demand, particularly Glanzman, Navy related titles, and '60s issues. The Hot Rod comics were almost unique to Charlton and are steady sellers. The Surf N Wheels title is a strange mix of heroes of the surf and motorcycles and sells fast. All Hanna-Barbera and cartoon titles continue to have a strong following, with high demand for Bugaloos. Blondie, Beetle Bailey and Popeye are in short supply, due to low Guide values. Haunted Love was a high demand title. Space Adventures and Space War Ditko reprint issues sold very well as a thrifty alternative to the high-priced originals. Yang is gaining popularity as a strange western/martial arts title with GGA, slavery, drugs and more.

DC: Everything from Crisis and earlier sells in any grade. Superman and Batman titles haved increased in demand, as more people realize these titles will be solid sellers forever. Wonder Woman was in very high demand, especially #177-214 which were in very short supply. Artist issues were much requested, especially Wrightson, Kirby and Neal Adams. All heroines were in demand, including Supergirl, Isis, Huntress, and Power Girl. Many team titles were in constant demand, including JLA, JSA, Legion, Freedom Fighters, Doom Patrol and others. Many minor key issues with little or no

A high demand for Wonder Woman comes between issues #177-214. (#178 shown)

break-out prices in current Guide sold much better than surrounding issues. Many hunted down and paid premiums for their favorite characters in DC Comics Presents, Brave and Bold, and similar titles. Hunger Dogs and New Gods #6 (1984) were red hot. Many mini-series and short series from all years sold well because they're easier to collect. Shazam and Super Friends are still selling well. Amazing World of DC is hot, with #9 bringing $75-$100. All the oddball, teen, love, western, war, humor/cartoon, and horror titles were in constant demand, as many try to fill out runs. Still hot and often at over Guide were all treasuries, digests, magazines, paperbacks, and giveaways.

© DC

The Amazing World of DC Comics is hot, especially #9 featuring the Legion.

Dell: Demand has slowly picked up across the board as many prices are now falling behind other vintage comics. Dell had a great wealth of popular characters, so they have never stopped selling. They are perhaps generally more plentiful than other comics of there time because they sold a lot of product, but constant demand eats at the supply until prices must again rise. Animation related titles have their core buyers who tend to gravitate to sellers with better selections. Looney Tunes was a huge success in the animated film business and are finally gaining more respect in the comics. Hanna-Barbera has its serious fans. TV comics are much more popular than movie related titles with the exception of big stars like Annette Funicello and John Wayne! Universal monster movie titles are hot. 1962 Dells are in lower supply, as "old Dell" became Gold Key and "New Dell" emerged in 1963. The New Dell horror and war titles continue to gain demand, such as Combat, Ghost Stories, and Air War. The Post-1962 "New Dell" is like a different company to many and collecting trends and habits are different. The Dell file copies have spoiled buyers into thinking they can find any Dell in NM. If not in the File collection, they can all be scarce in NM, as collectors are finding out!

Dells were typically among the most well read and handed down comics, so most normal inventory copies are in G or VG. But this is a plus, as many buyers prefer reading copies. Tarzan is fast gaining renewed demand as one of the world's most recognizable charaters.

Dennis the Menace: Dennis has been one of the most popular newspaper comics for several generations. Add TV, movies, paperbacks, merchandising and long runs of comics, and you see why he is still constantly collected. Demand has continued to increase for several years now. All giants are undervalued and selling well. For many, condition is not a priority with these. The digests and Marvel issues sell swiftly.

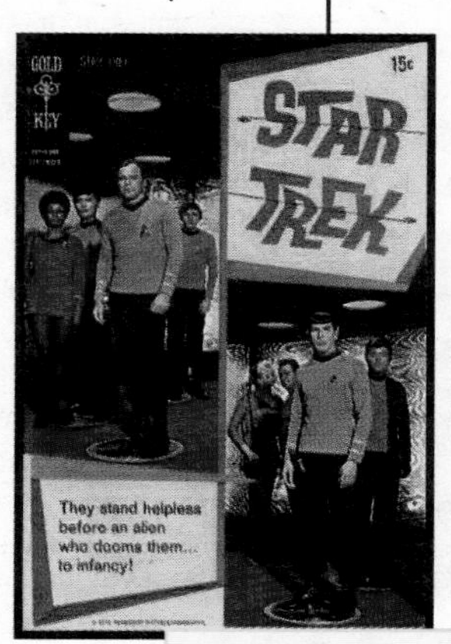

© Paramount

Gold Key issues like **Star Trek** #8 are scarce.

Gold Key: GKs from 1963 remained in short supply, especially with high grade keys. Gold Key is loaded with TV, character, cartoon, artist and genre titles that makes them steady sellers. They appeal more to a younger generation, as does the lower prices, thus they outsell their predecessor Dell. Hanna-Barbera titles remained very popular. TV titles are strong. Cartoon titles have slowly been gaining new popularity for 3+ years now. Horror titles have steady demand. There is a shortage of early issues of Tarzan, Turok, Magnus, Dr. Solar, Space Family Robinson, Star Trek and Phantom. Except for file copies, most pre-1970 issues are scarce in NM, especially cartoon titles! Occult Files of Dr. Spector is up in demand for monster, Dr. Solar and Owl appear-

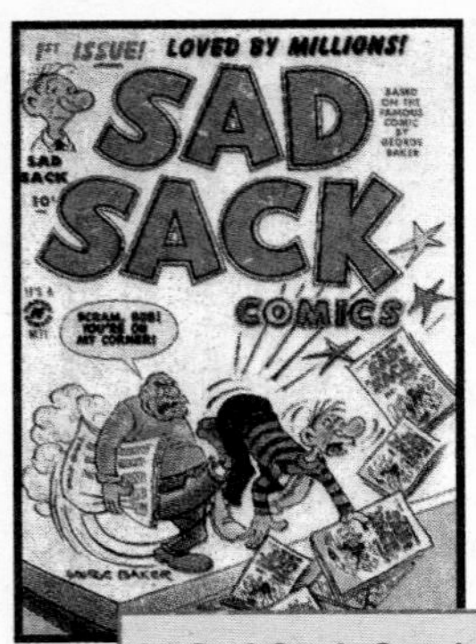

© HARV

All **Sad Sack Comics** are up in demand. (#1 shown)

ances.

Harvey: It turns out Harvey Pop and Rock Happening are the same tiltle, which explains endless want list problems for this hot title. Bunny is in big demand. Blondie and Dagwood are much requested and still very undervalued. All Sad Sack is up in demand, as a proven long-time character. All giants were hot again, with diminishing supplies. The square-bound issues often brought up to double Guide. Many are attempting to complete their 1970 thru early '80s runs, most starting with issues #1-10, which are now in lower supply. Some of the late '80s revival issues are tougher than '70s issues. The circa 1990 Hanna-Barbera titles are very good sellers, as few have them and they remain undervalued. All the digests sell well, especially all #1-10 issues. Little Dot's Aunts and Uncles and Wendy are much requested and seem to be in short supply. The '60s horror and superhero titles show some increased demand.

Marvel: Almost all Marvels are hot again, but once you pass Secret Wars-I, they slow again in sales. Of all companies, Marvel sports the most completionists, so oddball Bronze titles just keep selling. Silver Age issues have regained a lot of demand. CGC has brought out many great high grade copies and set countless record prices. Certified graded comics are still a tiny part of the market but growing fast. Even so, they have had a great influence on the market, especially on Marvel comics. This is where many of the most serious high grade collectors lurk and with deep pockets. Many long time collectors continue dealing with trusted sellers to avoid paying huge multiples needed to buy CGC copies. High grade Marvels are disappearing at an accelerated rate. CGC and high grade buyers seem to prefer mainstream and superhero titles, possibly because there is little hope of completing NM runs of oddball titles. Buyer resistance is low, on premium priced, non-CGC graded comics, still at resonable percentages of Guide. Many collectors are phoning dealers around the country trying to circumvent high CGC prices and "scoop" other collectors, only to be disappointed.

Hulk #181, GS X-Men #1 and X-Men #94 are on fire and NM 9.4+ copies consistantly bring $1500+ range prices each. Most strict graded VF Bronze keys will now bring near NM prices, as we realize how scarce true NM bronze comics are. All 1964 and earlier Marvels are hot in all grades. Most 1966–1968 Marvels are readily availiable and slower selling, with the exception of very high grade and low grade reading copies. Most 1969–1973 vintage Marvels had lower print runs and prices are far too low to keep up with demand, especially on Avengers #71-120, Hulk #131-170, Captain America #131-170, FF #112-130, Captain Marvel #17-27, Conan #25-50, Daredevil #81-120, Iron Man #31-70, Submariner #21-50, Thor #181-225, X-Men #67-93. Most 1975-1980 Marvels are in fairly good supply, but there is a shortage of copies in strictly graded VF or better. All western, war, teen, cartoon, love, and reprint titles remain in high demand and are selling in all grades. All odd formats are hot, including; treasuries, digests, mags, and paperbacks. Many TV, movie, character, and cartoon titles from the late '70s to the late '80s are all in higher demand, with less supply. The '70s mags are gaining as sellers have few in stock. Even the late '70s to early '80s mags are up in demand and price, such as Marvel Preview, Marvel Comics Super Special, Epic, Tomb of Dracula, Hulk mag and Bizarre Adventures. All giants pre-1980 are in demand, including Giant Size, Annuals and Marvel Tales and

© MAR

Fantastic Four #4, a vintage Marvel that is hot in all grades

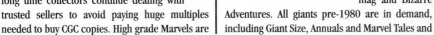

Superheroes. These are proving quite tough to find in high grades and many will pay premiums. Demand for reading copies is getting higher for most SA and Bronze issues, and they sell fast to eager readers worldwide. Planet of the Apes #21 up had small print runs and are sold out through most dealers, with issue #29 selling as high as $50-$75.

Walt Disney: Disney prices have been in a long slump, mostly due to over-reprinting of Mickey and Duck titles. Now most vintage issues remain undervalued as compared to their classic stature in the hobby, and have been slowly picking up demand again. Perhaps people now see the bargains. Uncle Scrooge #179, Donald Duck #222 and WDC&S #480 were red hot and bringing world record prices. All non-reprinted, and non-Duck/Mouse titles have made good gains. Animation titles sold best, especially with renewed demand for Winnie the Pooh, WD Showcase, Animation Movie Classics, Super Goof, Huey Dewey and Louie, Beagle Boys and Moby Duck. TV and movie titles were up in demand, especially Zorro, Annette, WD Presents, Scarecrow, and well known classic movies. Don Rosa art continues to be popular, as many want new great stories beyond the Barks classics and find them here. The WD Paint Books and Jungle Book treasury remain hot and scarce. The Gladstone digests sell well. Interest is gaining on foreign Disneys, especially if they feature new stories not in US editions.

© WHIT

Whitman's three-pack yielded some of today's most elusive rarities, like **Battle of the Planets #8.**

Warren: Warren has gained a lot of attention from fans and the fan press, and has become a renewed favorite. Many are now attempting to get complete runs and finding issue numbers troublesome. Many mid-series numbers are in smaller supply and with spines that damage easily. Many of the color inserts issues are missing the bonuses and posters. Wrightson, Corben and other artist issues have been in short supply. High numbers are in low supply. There is big demand for reading copies and they sell swiftly at reasonable minimum values, well above last year's Guide. In high demand were Blazing Combat #1, Creepy #9,146, Comix International #1, Spirit Special #1, Teen Love Stories #1-3, Warren Presents #13,14, Vampirella #101-113, Annual #1, Special #1, Famous Monster #81-120, anthologies, paperbacks and others.

Whitman: The scarce Whitman pre-pack or three-pack comics remained in high demand, with almost no supply. Uncle Scrooge #179 is the holy grail of post-Golden Age Disney comics, and several copies sold in the $1200.00+ range, plus a VG copy for $510.00. Donald Duck #222 and WDC&S #480 remain quite rare and sell in the $125-$200+ range. Buck Rogers #10 likely does not exist. Battle of the Planets #7-9 are in big demand, but remain elusive in any grade. The pre-1980 Whitmans are simply variants of the Gold Keys, but in smaller quantities. They now sell at the same price as Gold Keys, but anything of interest to completionists can easily bring 200-300% Guide. The 8-12/1980 Whitmans remain by far the scarcest issues. Others might be considered rare but do not command the attention of Scrooge #179. The second scarcest group is the un-dated, no code on cover issues from 1982. Now that the Guide indicates these as scarcer, collectors report they are even more difficult to find at current low price levels. For Whitman variants of DCs, there are 126 issues in 14 titles known to exist. Being a finite set, these have made many people begin to try for complete sets. They are scarcer but not impossible to find, and are therefore a popular challenge to collectors. They are selling at two to four times the regular format issues, about $10 average for VF or better copies.

HARRY B. THOMAS

The market is in the best shape I have ever seen. A large part of that has been the Internet in general and eBay in particular. The arrival of eBay a few years back allowed our comic book hobby to increase its numbers by literally thousands almost overnight. Folks who had no idea of the availability to collect and own comic books they remembered from their childhood are now a part of the hobby.

While I detest the idea of slabbed comic books, CGC has also been a "shot in the arm" for the hobby and helps keep dealers honest as to restoration of their offerings.

Dell comics in general and Disney and westerns in particular have shown real popularity and above Guide prices on eBay. I can't find a Tarzan or Roy Rogers comic in nice condition to complete my runs anymore at Guide! All Dells from the late '40s to the mid-'50s, especially Roy Rogers, Tarzan, Gene Autry and Disney (particularly Barks issues) are going up. In the late '40s, Dell experimented with a flat, matte-like finish cover stock. This paper did not age well. Chipping and browning inside the covers is common and unlike the glossy stock they generally used. It's tough to find Dells with this type of cover in high grade. Two key books that had this type of cover were Roy Rogers #1 and Four Color #178 with the first appearance of Uncle Scrooge.

Michael Tierney (The Comic Book Store)

The future of the industry looks more positive than it has for several years. Given time, I think future collectors will look back at the 1990s as the unique and volatile time that it was. DC anchored the industry and aggressively maintained their sales levels after the post-1992 leveling adjustments, while Marvel was a sleeping giant that slipped deeper into a coma every year.

This past era will probably be split into two categories: the early and later '90s. The early '90s will be desolate in collector demand. The late '90s will someday hopefully be recognized for the collecting opportunities that most people are overlooking today. Comics from the late '90s and the early part of the new millennium feature innovative new work in storytelling and artistry that was lacking in the early '90s, but with print runs that are the lowest in the entire history of the industry. When the first issue of the four-part Wolverine mini-series by Frank Miller came out in 1982, many said that it would never be collectible because of the then astounding print run that numbered in the hundreds of thousands. Time and increased demand has proven that opinion completely wrong. The print runs in recent years have been so low that when the gems buried in the gravel are recognized, the demand will overwhelm supply. This is where the future hot books will come from.

I'm seeing more activity from new customers than at any other time since the start of the '90s. The most interesting thing about this new activity is who is buying what. The number of women collectors has exploded, and the joke about token female collectors is no longer valid. From adolescents to adults, women are buying mainly a wide variety of manga. They are not interested in much from Marvel or DC, so any stores not already stocking a wide array of publishers in a family oriented atmosphere are probably not seeing the same results. These new customers have not had an impact on the sales of older comics yet, but they will soon.

The Platinum edition of **Spider-Man** #1 is a favorite of CGC and eBay connoisseurs.

© MAR

CGC Graded Comics: Putting aside the issue of archival storage for the moment, the encapsulation of any comic for resale at any grade other than 9.0 or higher is generally an unwise investment. Sales inside the store of CGC books graded below 9.0 have been at the same price range as those without CGC grading; sales on the Internet mirror this result. A Platinum edition of McFarlane's Spider-Man #1, CGC graded at 9.6, went at auction for $305, well over double Guide. On the flip side, a beautiful copy of Batman #38 that received a low CGC grade of 3.0 because of discoloration went for only $123.20, well below Guide. Another Golden Age book, Batman #166, CGC graded at 6.5, sold for $54, nearly double Guide. Which was the exception? Consider how a very nice Detective #327, featuring the first "New Look" Silver Age Batman, CGC graded at 7.0, went for a meager $38.70, slightly below Guide. Our experiences on other CGC books for less recognized characters like the Flash all sold well below Guide even when graded as high as 8.5. The results: books graded 9.0 or higher move at substantially increased values. For anything less on older books, you probably won't see a return on your investment in grading services.

For newer comics, scarcity is the key. The Platinum Spider-Man #1 had a limited print run of only 10,000. I have talked several customers out of the idea suggested by another publication to encapsulate runs of Watchmen. To invest $14 encasing any $5 comic that is readily available in high grade has to be the most foolish venture that I can envision. Wasting people's money by convincing them to make worthless investments is damaging to any industry. CGC is a service that has a need and a place in the comic industry that will be more fully appreciated if it can survive public misconceptions caused by the abuses of others.

Back to archival storage. The CGC slab is a nice stackable case that features a light UV barrier for protection against moderate light damage. The second layer of protection is a thin wrap of Mylar surrounding the book. The third form of protection is a deacidification sheet inserted inside the book itself. This is the belt and suspenders of archival storage. If your concern is long-term maintenance and not instant resale, then this is the other very overlooked use for CGC's services. This would be the only instance in which I could look a customer in the eye and tell them to encapsulate a $5 comic.

© DC

Action Comics is a perennial best selling title from the Golden Age. (#12 shown)

Vincent Zurzolo (Metropolis)

The year 2000 has been an extremely strong year for the hobby. Key Golden, Atom, Silver and Bronze have done increasingly better than in the past. '50s superhero books in high grade are in extremely high demand. Actions, Adventures, and Superboy are all doing well. High grade Marvels are setting tons of records in VF or better. The three key Bronze Age books that are doubling in value on an almost monthly basis are X-Men G-S #1, X-Men #94 and Hulk #181. Horror books continue to do well. With the exception of high grade or pedigree books the prices have stabilized. Disneys, Dells and Classics are slow. TV covers and Gold Keys are consistently collected.

High grade Bronze Age Marvels and DCs are red hot. I can't keep '70s FF, Detective, Batman, Avengers, Spider-Man, or Jimmy Olsen in stock. In the Golden Age, the best titles are Action, Cap, All-Select, Detective, Superman and Adventure. Barks stories continue to be extremely popular. Platinum and early Golden Age are also in demand. Non-superhero titles like King, Ace, Famous Funnies and the like are finding new homes.

Later issues of Tales of Suspense, Tales to Astonish, and Strange Tales are up. Cheap '70s horror, Marvel, DC and the indies of the time are also on the rise. Dells, Dell Giants, Mystery Men, Phantom Lady, non-Barks Disneys and non-key Four Colors are all down.

CGC Graded Comics: Prices on high grade comics have in many cases quintupled. Restored books don't sell well because of purple label. Mid and low grade books have not changed much. Modern books in high grade skyrocket in value. Look for this trend to continue.

Internet Sales: Internet business is steady. We find many customers will order through our website but others still like to call up on the phone. With about half of our inventory up at all times, customers find our site helpful in finding what they need.

KEY COMICS SOLD IN 2000

The following lists of sales were reported to Gemstone during the year and represent only a small portion of the total amount of important books that have sold.

GOLDEN-ATOM AGE SALES

Action #1 Fair $30,000
Action #54 (Mile High) NM $4,350
Action #59 (M.H.) VF/NM $4,000
Action #94 (M.H.) NM $2,100
Action #154 (M.H.) NM+ $1,800
Adventure #43 FN+ $1,000
Adventure #48 (Nova Scotia) VF $21,000
Adventures of the Fly #2 (Bethlehem) NM/NM+ $840
All-American #19 VG+ $1,625
All-American #90 FN $450
All-Flash #1 VG+ $1,900
All Star Comics #3 VF- $21,000
All Star Comics #8 FN- $6,000
All Star Comics #35 FN+ $500
All Star Comics #52 G+ $175
All Star Comics #57 VF+ $1,000
Amazing Mystery Funnies V2#12 (Mile High) VF+ $3,800
Amazing Mystery Funnies #23 (Larson) VF+ $950
Archie #1 G/VG $4,000
Archie #1 VG- $4,500
Batman #1 G+ $9,000
Batman #11 VF+(rest.) $1500
Batman #50 F $305
Batman #100 FN+ $635
Beware #9 (Northland) NM- $450
Big Shot #14 F+ $120
Big Shot #28 (Mile High) VF $600
Black Cat Comics #2 VF/NM $265
Black Knight(Atlas) #2 VG $80
Blue Beetle #4 VG+ $175
Blue Beetle #46 FN $70
Blue Beetle #54 FN $1000
Blue Ribbon #5 (Larson) VF/NM $1,100
Boy Commandos #1 VG+ $975
Brave and the Bold #3 (River City) F/VF $220
Buffalo Bill Picture Stories #1 VF $50
Bugs Bunny FC #142 VF $105
Bugs Bunny FC #250 ANM $110
Bugs Bunny FC #289 VF $60
Bugs Bunny FC #307 VF+ $55
Buster Crabbe #5 FN+ $800
Canteen Kate #1(M.H.) VF/NM $1450
Canteen Kate #1(Bethlehem) NM/NM+ $1440
Captain America #1 FN- $14,300
Captain America #1 VG/FN $12,000
Captain America #52 VG+ $300
Captain America #66 VG+ $400
Captain America #76 FN+ $500
Captain Marvel #10 VF/NM $950
Captain Marvel #21 FN $300
Captain Marvel #29 VG $90
Captain Marvel #31 VG $86
Captain Marvel #38 VG/FN $68
Captain Marvel Advs. #24 (Mile High) NM+ $1,935
Captain Marvel Jr. #4 FN+ $700
Captain Marvel Jr. #18 NM- $500
Captain Science #2 (Bethlehem) NM $900
Comic Cavalcade #21 G/VG $125
Comic Cavalcade #29 VG+ $175
Crypt of Terror #17 (Gaines file) NM+ $7,800
Danger Trail #1 NM $1,080
Daring Love #1 VG $600
Detective Comics #27 VG- $55,000
Detective Comics #151 (Mile High) NM+ $2,650
Detective Comics #167 VG $125
Detective Dan VF $1500
Detective Eye #2 (M.H.) NM $4,500
Dick Tracy FC #96 AVF $150
Exciting #37 AFN $120
Extra #1 (Bethlehem)VF $183
Famous Crimes #1 F/VF $350
Famous Funnies #209 NM $2,750
Famous Funnies #210 VF $1,000
Fight Comics #50 FN+ $100
Flash Comics #81 FN+ $400
Flash Comics #96 FN $350
Flash Comics #100 VG $540
Flash Comics #104 G+ $675
Four Color #92 VG $40
Four Color #324 (M.H.)NM+ $260
Gene Autry #84 FN/FN+ $76
Green Lantern #1 FN/VF $14,000
Green Lantern #1 VG+ $7,000
Green Lantern #14 FN/VF $850
Haunt of Fear #15 VF/NM $250
Human Torch #9 VG+ $450
JoJo #11 FN/VF $150
Jungle Comics #30 (Rockford) VF/NM $325
Junior #11 FN/VF $450
Lars of Mars #11 (Northford) VF+ $675
Little Lulu FC #74 G $320
Little Lulu FC #110 FN $110
Little Lulu FC #115 FN+ $125
Little Lulu FC #120 VG+ $65
Little Lulu FC #139 VG $60
Little Lulu FC #146 FN+ $100
Lone Ranger #1 VF $529
Mad #1 VF- $2,350
Mad #2 VF+ $895
March of Comics #20 F $1,350
Marvel Boy #1 FN $300
Marvel Comics #1 G+ $10,000
Marvel Family #80 VG $80
Marvel Mystery Comics #62 (Mile High) VF/NM $6,000
Miss Beverly Hills #1 VF/NM $450
Mister Mystery #1 (Bethlehem) VF $1,030
Mister Mystery #7 VG/F $380
More Fun Comics #52 VF- $36,500
Motion Picture Funnies #1 VF $15,000
Mystery in Space #3 FN $200
Mystery in Space #5 AVF $400
National Comics #27 (Mile High) NM+ $2,100
New York World's Fair 1939 VF $17,000
Phantom Lady #17 FN $2,000
Piracy #1-7 G-VG $160 (set)
Planet Comics #33 FN+ $340
Planet Comics #60 VG $110
Plastic Man #1 VF- $2700
Porky Pig FC #322 NM $50
Rawhide Kid #17 G/VG $250
Shield-Wizard #7 VF $550
Space Detective #3 VG $85
Sparkler #28 VF+$275
Sparkler #31 VF $250
Sparkler #39 FN $120
Spirit #22 VF- $600
Startling #51 VF+ $450
Strange Adventures #1 VF- $1,260
Strange Fantasy #9 G+ $75
Sub-Mariner Comics #1 Fair $1,500
Sub-Mariner Comics #36 VG $150
Superboy #1 NM- $9,200
Superman #14 VG/FN $775
Tales From the Crypt #20 (Gaines file) NM/M $5,700
Tales of Suspense #39 G $200
Tarzan #1 VG- $207
Teenage Dope Slaves VF/NM $1,900
Thun'da #1 FN $325
Tom Mix #3 VF/NM $175
Vault of Horror #26 FN $100
Vault of Horror #37 VG $45

Voodoo #1 (Bethlehem)NM- $1,200
War Against Crime #10 F/VF $1,200
Weird Fantasy #15 AVG $55
Weird Science-Fantasy #29 FN+$350
Whiz Comics #25 VF/NM (rest.) $3,200
Wonder Comics #17 VF+ $800
Wonder Woman #1 VG+ $4,200
Wonder Woman #11 VF/NM $800
World's Finest #2 VG- $495
Wow Comics #9(restored) $600

SILVER-BRONZE-MODERN AGE SALES

Silver Age Sales:

Action Comics #242 VG $190
Action Comics #252 G $75
Action Comics #252 VF- $680
Action Comics #297 NM- $90
Adventure Comics #247 VG $328
Adventure Comics #300 VF/NM $250
All-Amer. Men of War #108 NM $45
Amazing Advs.('61) #2 F+ $175
Amazing Advs.('61) #4 VF $400
Amazing Advs.('61) #5 F $140
Amazing Advs.('61) #6 F+ $275
Amazing Adult Fantasy #14 VF $400
Amazing Fantasy #15 G/VG $1,700
Amaz. Spider-Man #1 F+ $6,000
Amaz. Spider-Man #1 G+ $900
Amaz. Spider-Man #7 NM- $1,275
Amaz. Spider-Man #40 VF/NM $422
Amaz. Spider-Man #50 VF/NM $500
Amaz. Spider-Man #102 NM $225
Amaz. Spider-Man #120 NM $125
Amaz. Spider-Man #122 NM- $150
Atom #1 VF/NM $600
Atom #3 (Slobodian) NM $295
Avengers #1 NM $4,800
Avengers #4 NM- $2,450
Batman #155 (Northland) NM- $650
Batman #171 F+ $200
Batman Annual #1 FN $125
Brave and the Bold #17 VF/NM$360
Brave and the Bold #28 VG- $350
Brave and the Bold #34 FN $325
Brave and the Bold #54 (Pacific Coast)NM/M $1,725
Brave and the Bold #63 NM+ $100
Bullwinkle #1 NM- $125
Captain America #100 VF- $101
Daredevil #1 VF- $900
Daredevil #5 NM- $300
Daredevil #6 NM- $125
Daredevil #6 NM- $200
Daredevil #17 NM- $160
Doom Patrol #88 FN- $20
Fantastic Four #1 G $625
Fantastic Four #3 F/VF $925
Fantastic Four #15 NM- $525
Fantastic Four #48 NM- $900
Fantastic Four #48 NM- $1,750
Fantastic Four #58 NM $120
Fantastic Four Annual #3 F $60
Flash #105 G+ $305
Flash Annual #1 (White Mountain) VF $420
Four Color #1128 (Rocky & Friends) NM $400
Four Color #1152 (Rocky & Friends) NM $250
Ghost Rider('67) #1 (Northland) NM- $100
GI Combat #87 FN $475
Green Lantern #40 FN- $150
Incredible Hulk #1 G/VG $815
Incredible Hulk #6 VF/NM $2,200
Incredible Hulk #108 NM $135
Iron Man #1 VF/NM $440
Iron Man & Sub-Mariner #1 (Northland) NM $300
Journey Into Mystery #116 NM $124
Journey Into Mystery #124 (M.H. II) NM+ $150
Jughead's Folly #1 VG+ $73
Justice League of Amer. #1 VG $700
Justice League of America #39 (Northland) VF/NM $100
Magnus Robot Fighter #1 VF/NM $180
My Greatest Adventure #80 (Pacific Coast) NM++ $2,951
Our Army at War #83 G- $210
Peanuts #1 VF/NM $195
Plastic Man #1 VF $40
Sea Devils #1 (Mass.) VF $450
Sgt. Fury #1 VG/FN $215
Sgt. Fury #16 NM+ $125
Showcase #4 (Mohawk) $25,000
Showcase #9 G- $325
Showcase #55 NM $325
Showcase #61 NM $190
Showcase #75 F $35
Silver Surfer #1 FN- $150
Space Family Robinson #1 (Mohawk Valley) VF/NM $275
Spectre #2 (Oakland) NM $100
Star Trek #1 FN+ $153
Strange Tales #89 VG $113
Strange Tales #118 NM- $120
Strange Tales #126 NM- $80
Superman Ann. #1 FN $125
Tales of Suspense #40 NM- $2,160
Tales of Suspense #54 NM- $125
Tales to Astonish #45 NM- $250
Tales to Astonish #59 VG $35
Tales to Astonish #100 NM $90
Thor #126 VF-(7.5) $74
Uncle Scrooge #47 VF $75
X-Men #1 (Bethlehem) NM $22,645
X-Men #1 NM $10,000
X-Men #1 NM- $11,690
X-Men #13 NM- $210
X-Men #29 (Pacific Coast) NM++ $365
X-Men #30 (Pacific Coast) NM/M $335
X-Men #38 (Pacific Coast) NM/M $350
X-Men #49 (Oakland) NM $125
X-Men #50 (Oakland) NM- $125
X-Men #55 NM $125

Bronze Age Sales:

Adventure #436 NM $35
All-Star Western #10 VF- $103
Batman #251 VF $45
Batman Family #1 VF/NM $22
Dark Mansion of Forbidden Love #1 NM- $190
Defenders #1 NM $55
Giant-Size X-Men #1 FN $250
Giant-Size X-Men #1 FN- $225
Green Lantern #77 NM $120
Green Lantern #87 NM- $46
House of Mystery #185 NM $36
House of Secrets #88 NM $65
Incredible Hulk #181 NM $1500
Incredible Hulk #181 VF+ $300
Incredible Hulk #181 VG+ $150
Joker #1 NM $32
Justice League of Am. #100 NM- $27
Marvel Premiere #15 NM $65
Marvel Premiere #50 NM $16
Shazam! #1 NM $18
Sinister House of Secret Love #1 VF/NM $170
Strawberry Shortcake #1 NM $16
Superfriends #1 NM+ $45
Teenage Mutant N.T. #1 NM $185
Tomb of Dracula #1 VF/NM $70
Werewolf by Night #1 NM- $65
Werewolf by Night #32 NM $85
Wonder Woman #199 NM $60
Wonder Woman #201 NM $30
X-Men #94 FN+ $213
X-Men #94 FN $150
X-Men #100 VF $75

Modern Age Sales:

Batman:Dark Knight HC (S&N) $500
Elseworlds 80-Pg. Giant VF+ $400
Spider-Man #1 Platinum Ed. $300

Golden Age Sales:

Action #1 VG(4.0) $112,500
Action #2 VG/FN(5.0) $12,500
Action #3 VG(4.0) $7,300
Action #4 VG/FN(5.0) $5,600
Action #5 FN(6.0) $6,750
Action #6 FN(6.0) $6,750
Action #80 NM(9.4) $2,600
Action #112 (Mile High)NM+(9.6) $2,100
Adventure #61 G+(2.5) $1,100
All-American #16 VG(3.5) $15,000
All-Flash #5 VF(8.0) $2,850
America's Best #15 (Mile High) NM-(9.2) $1,000
America's Best #17 (Mile High) NM-(9.2) $1,000
Archie #24 VF(8.0) $310
Batman #1 G-(1.8) $7,000
Batman #49 VF+(8.5) $1,247
Captain America #1 FN+(6.5) $18,000
Captain America #17 FN+(6.5) $1,000
Detective #31 VG/FN(5.0) $9,300
Detective #33 VG+(4.5) $9,000
Detective #41 VF-(7.5) $1,550
Detective #122 VF/NM(9.0) $1,900
Fairy Tale Parade #5 VF/NM(9.0) $442
Feature Comics #61(San Francisco) NM+(9.6) $450
Flash Comics #57 FN+(6.5) $212
Four Color V1#16 GD(2.0) $945
Four Color #386 VF-(7.5) $510
Green Lantern #1 FN(6.0) $7,000
Green Lantern #1 VG-(3.5) $4,800
Human Torch #34 VF(8.0) $650
Mad #1 VF-(7.5) $2,500
New York World's Fair 1939 FN(6.0) $5,100
Plastic Man #1 NM-(9.2) $5,500
Police Comics #11 VF(8.0) $1,427
Speed Comics #42 (Mile High) NM(9.4) $1,350
Spy Smasher #7 (Rockford) NM-(9.2) $750
Star Spangled #91 VF(8.0) $436
Superman #9 FN/VF(7.0) $1,010
Superman #76 FN+(6.5) $462
Thing!, The #12 VG+(4.5) $366
Thrilling Comics #37 NM(9.4)$500
Voodoo Annual #1 VF(8.0) $2,200
Wonder Woman #22 FN+(6.5) $300

Silver Age Sales:

Adventure Comics #247 F/VF (7.0) $1,425
Amazing Fantasy #15 F/VF (7.0) $7,500
Amazing Fantasy #15 F/VF (7.0) $6,500
Amaz. Spider-Man #1 VF/NM(9.0) $17,000
Amaz. Spider-Man #1 VG(4.0) $1,400
Amaz. Spider-Man #1 Golden Records reprint set w/record NM(9.4) $311
Amaz. Spider-Man #3 NM(9.4)$5,800
Amaz. Spider-Man #3 VG+(4.5) $650
Amaz. Spider-Man #14 VF/NM(9.0) $760
Amaz. Spider-Man #101 NM (9.4) $250
Aquaman #1 VF+(8.5) $455
Avengers #4 VF/NM(9.0) $2,025
Brave and the Bold #28 VG/F(5.0) $585
Brave and the Bold #43 (White Mountain) NM(9.4) $800
Brave and the Bold #51 (White Mountain) NM(9.4) $405
Daredevil #3 VF/NM(9.0) $350
Detective #291 NM-(9.2) $203
Fantastic Four #1 VF(8.0) $1,526
Fantastic Four #4 F/VF(7.0) $695
Fantastic Four #48 NM/M(9.8) $8500
Flash #105 VF/NM(9.0) $6,000
Green Lantern #1 VF(8.0) $1,495
Incredible Hulk #6 VF-(7.5) $936
Iron Man #1 NM-(9.2) $485
Iron Man #1 VF/NM(9.0) $300
Iron Man #2 NM/M(9.8) $675
Justice League #1 VF-(7.0) $995
Justice League #76 NM-(9.2) $50
Nick Fury #1 NM+(9.6) $350
Our Army at War #83 F/VF(7.0) $1,000
Showcase #4 FN/VF-(7.0) $2,000
Showcase #7 (Bethlehem) NM-(9.2) $3,200
Showcase #43 VF/NM(9.0) $500
Showcase #22 F(6.0) $699
Silver Surfer #1 NM(9.4) $1,175
Silver Surfer #1 NM-(9.2) $510
Sub-Mariner #1 NM(9.6) $512
Sub-Mariner #1 NM(9.6) $587
Superman's G.F. Lois Lane #1 VG (4.0) $355
Tales of Suspense #39 VG+(4.5) $421
X-Men #1 VF+(8.5) $7,000
X-Men #1 FN/VF(7.0) $2,800
X-Men #4 NM(9.4) $1,700
X-Men #7 NM-(9.2) $400

Bronze Age Sales:

All Star Western #10 NM+(9.6) $1200
All Star Western #10 NM+(9.6) $2415
Amaz. Spider-Man #129 NM(9.5) $150
Amaz. Spider-Man #129 NM(9.6) $996
Batman #234 NM(9.4) $255
Defenders #1 NM(9.4) $277
Flaming Carrot #1 VF/NM(9.0) $66
Giant-Size X-Men #1 NM+(9.6) $1,825
Giant-Size X-Men #1 VF(8.0) $400
Iron Man #47 NM+(9.6) $203
Kamandi #1 NM(9.4) $76
Marvel Spotlight #5 NM+(9.6) $800
New Gods #1 NM+(9.6) $255
Star Wars #1(30¢-c) NM+(9.6) $122.50
Tomb of Dracula #1 NM (9.4) $205 Weird War Tales #1 NM(9.2) $345
Weird War Tales #1 VF+(8.5) $175
Werewolf By Night #1 NM-(9.2) $123
Wonder Woman #199 NM(9.4)$160
Wonder Woman #200 NM-(9.2)$52
Wonder Woman #212 NM(9.4)$61
X-Men #94 VF+(8.5) $333
X-Men #98 VF+(8.5) $51
X-Men #99 VF+(8.5) $51
X-Men #100 VF/NM(9.0) $77
X-Men #103 NM-(9.2) $76
X-Men #111 NM-(9.2) $51
X-Men #116 NM-(9.2) $51
X-Men #125 NM(9.4) $71
X-Men #140 NM-(9.2) $46

Modern Age Sales:

Amaz. Spider-Man #300 NM/M(9.8) $610
Batman: Killing Joke M(10) $416
Batman: The Dark Knight #1 NM+(9.6) $131
Danger Girl #1 Chromium NM+(9.6) $75
Harley Quinn #1 NM/M(9.8) $46
Spawn #1 M(10) $810
Superman #75 NM+(9.6) $22
Witchblade #1 NM+(9.6) $81

The following tables denote the rate of appreciation of the top Golden Age, Platinum Age, Silver Age and Bronze Age books, as well as selected genres over the past year. The retail value for a Near Mint copy of each book (or VF where a Near Mint copy is not known to exist) in 2001 is compared to its value in 2000. The rate of return for 2001 over 2000 is given. The place in rank is given for each comic by year, with its corresponding value in highest known grade. These tables can be very useful in forecasting trends in the market place. For instance, the investor might want to know which book is yielding the best dividend from one year to the next, or one might just be interested in seeing how the popularity of books changes from year to year. For instance, *All Star Comics* #8 was in 22nd place in 2000 and has increased to 19th place in 2001. Premium books are also included in these tables and are denoted with an asterisk(*).

The following tables are meant as a guide to the investor. However, it should be pointed out that trends may change at anytime and that some books can meet market resistance with a slowdown in price increases, while others can develop into real comers from a presently dormant state. In the long run, if the investor sticks to the books that are appreciating steadily each year, he shouldn't go very far wrong.

TOP GOLDEN AGE BOOKS

2001 OVER 2000 GUIDE VALUES

ISSUE NO.	2001 RANK	2001 NM PRICE	2000 RANK	2000 NM PRICE	$ INCR.	% INCR.
Action Comics #1	1	$285,000	1	$200,000	$85,000	43%
Detective Comics #27	2	$240,000	2	$175,000	$65,000	37%
Marvel Comics #1	3	$175,000	4	$125,000	$50,000	40%
Superman #1	4	$175,000	3	$140,000	$35,000	25%
All-American Comics #16	5	$100,000	5	$70,000	$30,000	43%
Batman #1	6	$85,000	6	$65,000	$20,000	31%
Captain America Comics #1	7	$80,000	9	$58,000	$22,000	38%
Flash Comics #1	8	$75,000	8	$60,000	$15,000	25%
Whiz Comics #2 (#1)	9	$72,000	7	$64,000	$8,000	13%
More Fun Comics #52	10	$62,000	11	$50,000	$12,000	24%
Detective Comics #1	11	VF $55,000	10	VF $50,000	$5,000	10%
Adventure Comics #40	12	$44,000	14	$34,000	$10,000	29%
Detective Comics #33	13	$44,000	13	$36,000	$8,000	22%
New Fun Comics #1	14	VF $42,000	12	VF $39,000	$3,000	8%
All Star Comics #3	15	$40,000	15	$31,500	$8,500	27%
Detective Comics #38	16	$38,000	16	$31,000	$7,000	23%
Green Lantern #1	17	$35,000	19	$28,000	$7,000	25%
More Fun Comics #53	18	$33,000	17	$30,000	$3,000	10%
All Star Comics #8	19	$32,000	22	$25,500	$6,500	25%
Captain Marvel Adventures #1	20	$32,000	18	$28,500	$3,500	12%
Detective Comics #29	21	$32,000	20	$26,000	$6,000	23%
Detective Comics #31	22	$32,000	21	$26,000	$6,000	23%
Action Comics #2	23	$30,000	27	$21,000	$9,000	43%
Human Torch #2 (#1)	24	$28,000	25	$22,000	$6,000	27%
Sensation Comics #1	25	$27,000	26	$22,000	$5,000	23%
Sub-Mariner Comics #1	26	$27,000	28	$21,000	$6,000	29%
New York World's Fair 1939	27	$26,000	23	$24,000	$2,000	8%
Adventure Comics #48	28	$25,000	29	$20,000	$5,000	25%
Famous Funnies-Series 1 #1	29	$25,000	24	$22,500	$2,500	11%
Marvel Mystery Comics #2	30	$25,000	31	$20,000	$5,000	25%
Marvel Mystery Comics #9	31	$23,000	34	$18,500	$4,500	24%
*** Century Of Comics nn**	32	VF $22,000	30	VF $20,000	$2,000	10%
*** Motion Picture Funnies Weekly #1**	33	$22,000	32	$20,000	$2,000	10%
Wonder Woman #1	34	$22,000	35	$18,000	$4,000	22%
Daring Mystery Comics #1	35	$21,000	36	$17,000	$4,000	24%
Action Comics #7	36	$20,000	48	$14,300	$5,700	40%
All Winners Comics #1	37	$20,000	44	$15,000	$5,000	33%
New Fun Comics #6	38	VF $20,000	33	VF $19,000	$1,000	5%
Marvel Mystery Comics #5	39	$19,500	43	$15,500	$4,000	26%
Action Comics #3	40	$19,000	46	$14,500	$4,500	31%

ISSUE NO.	2001 RANK	2001 NM PRICE	2000 RANK	2000 NM PRICE	$ INCR.	% INCR.
Detective Comics #28	41	$19,000	42	$15,500	$3,500	23%
Jumbo Comics #1	42	VF $19,000	37	VF $17,000	$2,000	12%
Walt Disney's Comics & Stories #1	43	$19,000	40	$16,500	$2,500	15%
New Comics #1	44	VF $18,500	38	VF $17,000	$1,500	9%
Famous Funnies #1	45	$18,000	41	$16,000	$2,000	13%
Marvel Mystery Comics 132 pg.	46	VF $18,000	-	VF $16,000	$2,000	13%
New Fun Comics #2	47	VF $18,000	39	VF $17,000	$1,000	6%
Amazing Man Comics #5	48	$17,000	45	$14,750	$2,250	15%
World's Best Comics #1	49	$17,000	47	$14,500	$2,500	17%
All-American Comics #19	50	$16,000	56	$12,500	$3,500	28%
All Flash #1	51	$16,000	51	$13,000	$3,000	23%
Captain America Comics 132 pg.	52	$16,000	-	$12,000	$4,000	33%
Wonder Comics #1	53	$16,000	50	$14,000	$2,000	14%
Detective Comics #2	54	VF $15,500	49	VF $14,300	$1,200	8%
All-American Comics #17	55	$15,000	55	$12,500	$2,500	20%
Mystic Comics #1	56	$15,000	60	$12,500	$2,500	20%
Wow Comics #1	57	$15,000	54	$13,000	$2,000	15%
All Star Comics #1	58	$14,500	62	$12,000	$2,500	21%
Archie Comics #1	59	$14,500	57	$12,500	$2,000	16%
* Funnies on Parade nn	60	$14,500	64	$11,500	$3,000	26%
Silver Streak #6	61	$14,500	53	$13,000	$1,500	12%
Action Comics #10	62	$14,000	76	$10,000	$4,000	40%
Batman #2	63	$14,000	63	$11,500	$2,500	22%
More Fun Comics #55	64	$14,000	66	$11,500	$2,500	22%
New York World's Fair 1940	65	$14,000	52	$13,000	$1,000	8%
Pep Comics #22	66	$14,000	70	$11,000	$3,000	27%
Suspense Comics #3	67	$14,000	72	$11,000	$3,000	27%
Big Book of Fun Comics #1	68	VF $13,500	58	VF $12,500	$1,000	8%
Double Action Comics #2	69	$13,000	59	$12,500	$500	4%
New Book of Comics #1	70	VF $13,000	61	VF $12,500	$500	4%
Superman #2	71	$12,750	83	$10,000	$2,750	28%
Adventure Comics #61	72	$12,500	77	$10,000	$2,500	25%
Adventure Comics #73	73	$12,500	79	$10,000	$2,500	25%
Captain America Comics #2	74	$12,500	80	$10,000	$2,500	25%
Daredevil Comics #1	75	$12,500	73	$10,500	$2,000	19%
More Fun Comics #73	76	$12,500	69	$11,000	$1,500	14%
Silver Streak #1	77	$12,500	71	$11,000	$1,500	14%
USA Comics #1	78	$12,500	84	$10,000	$2,500	25%
Young Allies Comics #1	79	$12,500	85	$10,000	$2,500	25%
Adventure Comics #72	80	$12,000	78	$10,000	$2,000	20%
Four Color Ser. 1 (Donald Duck) #4	81	$12,000	67	$11,000	$1,000	9%
Looney Tunes and Merrie Melodies #1	82	$12,000	74	$10,500	$1,500	14%
More Fun Comics #14	83	VF $12,000	65	VF $11,500	$500	4%
Red Raven Comics #1	84	$12,000	82	$10,000	$2,000	20%
Big All-American #1	85	$11,500	87	$9,500	$2,000	21%
Marvel Mystery Comics #3	86	$11,500	90	$9,000	$2,500	28%
Planet Comics #1	87	$11,500	89	$9,500	$2,000	21%
Action Comics #4	88	$11,000	95	$8,300	$2,700	33%
Action Comics #5	89	$11,000	96	$8,300	$2,700	33%
Action Comics #6	90	$11,000	97	$8,300	$2,700	33%
Detective Comics #3	91	VF $11,000	75	VF $10,200	$800	8%
Four Color Ser. 1 (Mickey Mouse) #16	92	VF $11,000	81	VF $10,000	$1,000	10%
Green Giant Comics #1	93	$11,000	91	$8,800	$2,200	25%
Mickey Mouse Magazine #1	94	$11,000	68	$11,000	$0	0%
More Fun Comics #54	95	$11,000	93	$8,400	$2,600	31%
Mystery Men Comics #1	96	$11,000	88	$9,500	$1,500	16%
Comics Magazine #1	97	VF $10,800	86	VF $9,600	1,200	13%
Famous Funnies Carnival of Comics nn	98	$10,500	92	$8,500	$2,000	24%
Captain America Comics #3	99	$10,000	98	$8,200	$1,800	22%
Detective Comics #35	100	$10,000	-	$8,000	$2,000	25%

TOP 10 PLATINUM AGE BOOKS

2001 OVER 2000 GUIDE VALUES

TITLE/ISSUE#	2001 RANK	2001 VF PRICE	2000 RANK	2000 VF PRICE	$ INCR.	% INCR.
Mickey Mouse Book (2nd printing)-variant	1	FN $12,000	1	FN $12,000	$0	0%
Mickey Mouse Book (1st printing)	2	VF $11,000	2	VF $11,000	$0	0%
Mickey Mouse Book (2nd printing)	3	VF $10,000	3	VF $10,000	$0	0%
Yellow Kid in McFadden Flats	4	FN $8,500	4	FN $8,500	$0	0%
Pore Li'l Mose	5	FN $5,000	9	FN $3,000	$2,000	67%
Buster Brown and His Resolutions 1903	6	FN $4,500	5	FN $4,000	$500	13%
* Buster Brown's Blue Ribbon #1 1904	7	VF $3,600	6	VF $3,600	$0	0%
Little Sammy Sneeze	8	FN $3,400	8	FN $3,000	$400	13%
Journey...Jeremiah Saddlebags	9	FN $3,000	-	-	-	-
Little Nemo 1906	10	FN $3,000	10	FN $2,800	$200	7%

TOP 10 SILVER AGE BOOKS

2001 OVER 2000 GUIDE VALUES

TITLE/ISSUE#	2001 RANK	2001 NM PRICE	2000 RANK	2000 NM PRICE	$ INCR.	% INCR.
Amazing Fantasy #15	1	$35,000	1	$25,000	$10,000	40%
Showcase #4 (The Flash)	2	$32,000	2	$25,000	$7,000	28%
Amazing Spider-Man #1	3	$25,000	4	$18,000	$7,000	39%
Fantastic Four #1	4	$24,000	3	$19,000	$5,000	26%
Incredible Hulk #1	5	$15,000	5	$12,000	$3,000	25%
Showcase #8 (The Flash)	6	$14,000	6	$12,000	$2,000	17%
X-Men #1	7	$9,500	8	$6,200	$3,300	53%
Showcase #9 (Lois Lane)	8	$8,400	7	$6,700	$1,700	25%
Brave and the Bold #28	9	$6,000	-	$5,100	$900	18%
Detective Comics #225	10	$6,000	9	$5,600	$400	7%

TOP 10 BRONZE AGE BOOKS

2001 OVER 2000 GUIDE VALUES

TITLE/ISSUE#	2001 RANK	2001 NM PRICE	2000 RANK	2000 NM PRICE	$ INCR.	% INCR.
Giant-Size X-Men #1	1	$900	2	$490	$410	84%
Incredible Hulk #181	2	$900	4	$480	$420	88%
X-Men #94	3	$750	5	$460	$290	63%
House of Secrets #92	4	$600	3	$490	$110	22%
Star Wars #1 (35¢ cover price variant)	5	$600	1	$530	$70	13%
DC 100 Page Super Spectacular #5	6	$475	6	$420	$55	13%
Vampirella Special HC	7	$400	-	$350	$50	14%
All-Star Western #10	8	$350	-	$200	$150	75%
Cerebus #1	9	$350	-	$230	$120	52%
Vampirella #113	10	$300	9	$270	$30	11%

TOP 10 CRIME BOOKS

2001 OVER 2000 GUIDE VALUES

TITLE/ISSUE#	2001 RANK	2001 NM PRICE	2000 RANK	2000 NM PRICE	$ INCR.	% INCR.
Crime Does Not Pay #22	1	$2,200	1	$1,700	$500	29%
True Crime Comics #2	2	$1,300	2	$1,050	$250	24%
Crime Does Not Pay #23	3	$1,200	3	$975	$225	23%
Crimes By Women #1	4	$1,190	4	$960	$230	24%
True Crime Comics #3	5	$975	6	$775	$200	26%
Crime Does Not Pay #24	6	$950	5	$775	$175	23%
The Killers #1	7	$950	7	$750	$200	27%
True Crime Comics #4	8	$875	8	$700	$175	25%
The Killers #2	9	$800	9	$650	$150	23%
True Crime Comics Vol. 2 #1	10	$775	10	$625	$150	24%

TOP 10 HORROR BOOKS

2001 OVER 2000 GUIDE VALUES

TITLE/ISSUE#	2001 RANK	2001 NM PRICE	2000 RANK	2000 NM PRICE	$ INCR.	% INCR.
Vault of Horror #12	1	$4,600	1	$4,000	$600	15%
Tales of Terror Annual #1	2	VF $3,400	2	VF $3,200	$200	6%
Eerie #1	3	$3,200	4	$2,600	$600	23%
Journey into Mystery #1	4	$3,100	3	$2,800	$300	11%
Strange Tales #1	5	$3,100	5	$2,600	$500	19%
Crypt of Terror #17	6	$2,800	6	$2,350	$450	19%
Haunt of Fear #15	7	$2,800	7	$2,350	$450	19%
Crime Patrol #15	8	$2,600	8	$2,000	$600	30%
House of Mystery #1	9	$2,000	9	$1,700	$300	18%
Tales to Astonish #1	10	$1,800	10	$1,500	$300	20%

TOP 10 ROMANCE BOOKS

2001 OVER 2000 GUIDE VALUES

TITLE/ISSUE#	2001 RANK	2001 NM PRICE	2000 RANK	2000 NM PRICE	$ INCR.	% INCR.
Giant Comics Edition #12	1	$975	1	$825	$150	18%
Intimate Confessions #1	2	$700	2	$560	$140	25%
Giant Comics Edition #15	3	$550	4	$450	$100	22%
Romance Trail #1	4	$550	5	$450	$100	22%
Young Lovers #18	5	$550	6	$440	$110	25%
Giant Comics Edition #9	6	$535	3	$480	$55	11%
DC 100 Page Super Spectacular #5	7	$475	7	$420	$55	13%
Secret Hearts #1	8	$475	9	$410	$65	16%
Giant Comics Edition #13	9	$470	8	$420	$50	12%
Women in Love - 1952	10	$465	-	$380	$85	22%

TOP 10 SCI-FI BOOKS

2001 OVER 2000 GUIDE VALUES

TITLE/ISSUE#	2001 RANK	2001 NM PRICE	2000 RANK	2000 NM PRICE	$ INCR.	% INCR.
Strange Adventures #1	1	$3,500	2	$2,600	$900	35%
Mystery In Space #1	2	$3,200	1	$2,600	$600	23%
Showcase #17 (Adam Strange)	3	$2,600	3	$2,100	$500	24%
Strange Adventures #9	4	$2,200	7	$1,600	$600	38%
Journey Into Unknown Worlds #36	5	$2,100	5	$1,700	$400	24%
Showcase #15 (Space Ranger)	6	$2,100	4	$1,750	$350	20%
Fawcett Movie #15 (Man From Planet X)	7	$2,000	6	$1,650	$350	21%
Weird Fantasy #13 (#1)	8	$2,000	8	$1,600	$400	25%
Weird Science #12 (#1)	9	$2,000	9	$1,600	$400	25%
Weird Science-Fantasy Annual 1952	10	$1,800	10	$1,500	$300	20%

TOP 10 WESTERN BOOKS

2001 OVER 2000 GUIDE VALUES

TITLE/ISSUE#	2001 RANK	2001 NM PRICE	2000 RANK	2000 NM PRICE	$ INCR.	% INCR.
Gene Autry Comics #1	1	$8,400	1	$7,200	$1,200	17%
*Lone Ranger Ice Cream 1939 2nd	2	VF $6,000	3	VF $5,500	$500	9%
*Lone Ranger Ice Cream 1939	3	VF $5,500	2	VF $5,500	$0	0%
Hopalong Cassidy #1	4	$5,200	4	$4,800	$400	8%
*Red Ryder Victory Patrol '42	5	$4,400	5	$4,000	$400	10%
*Red Ryder Victory Patrol '43	6	$4,000	6	$3,750	$250	7%
*Red Ryder Victory Patrol '44	7	$3,800	7	$3,550	$250	7%
*Tom Mix Ralston #1	8	$3,500	8	$3,000	$500	17%
Red Ryder Comics #1	9	$3,000	9	$2,600	$400	15%
Roy Rogers Four Color #38	10	$2,600	10	$2,200	$400	18%

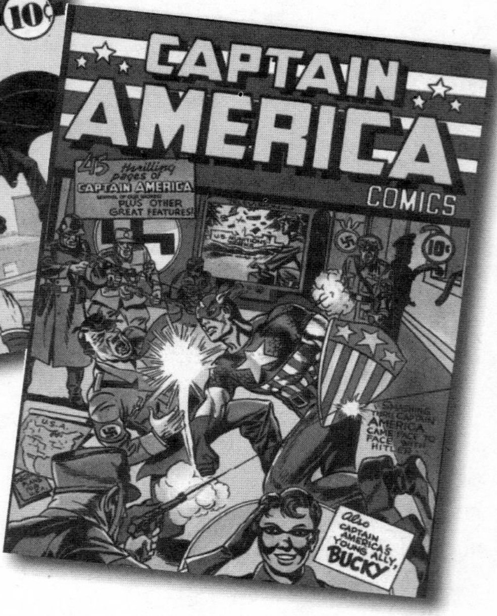

If you're looking to buy, you should know that we also offer a vast inventory of comics and related collectibles for purchase. Again, our volume trading and high-profile market presence work in your favor.

There's no funny business when you do business with Greg Manning's World's Finest Comics & Collectibles.

Call Bill Hughes at1-800-221-0243.

Visit www.gregmanning.com.

GREG MANNING AUCTIONS, INC.

GREG MANNING'S WORLDS FINEST COMICS & COLLECTIBLES

775 Passaic Avenue • West Caldwell, New Jersey 07006
TEL: 973-882-0004 • FAX: 973-882-3499 • www.gregmanning.com
NASDAQ symbol GMAI

Greg Manning Auctions, Inc. ("GMAI") has purchased certain assets of Mark Wilson, d/b/a "World's Finest Comics", including the name "World's Finest Comics. GMAI has not assumed any liabilities associated with these assets, and any claims relating thereto incurred prior to November 7, 2000, are the sole responsibility of Mark Wilson, d/b/a "World's Finest Comics".

CGC is the hobby's Official Stamp of Approval

With a large number of books from all eras and genres now certified, it increasingly obvious that CGC is th comic book hobby's Stamp of Approval.

- More liquidity.
- For the first time a grading standard accepted by both buyers and sellers.
- The industry's most thorough restoration check included in the grading fee.
- Safest way to buy and most effective way to sell online.
- The industry's only 3rd party impartial grading service.

When you also consider our t grading experts, and our proven reputation for integrity, impartiali and consistency, it's no wonder that CGC is grading more of the hobby's finest books, from Golde Age to Modern, every day.

The verdict is in. As a major figure in the hobby has put it, *"There is no doubt that CGC is t future of comic book collecting."*

CGC is an independent member of the Certified Collectibles Group, the world's leading group of impartial certification companies.

www.CGCcomics.com

www.CollectiblesGroup.com

Get your books CGC'd

Ready to submit books to CGC?
Call us for instructions and submission forms!

1-877-NM-COMIC
or visit our web site at
www.CGCcomics.com

P.O. Box 1938 • Parsippany, NJ 07054 • Phone (973) 984-0055 • Toll Free (877) NM-COMIC

PAPER ART RESTORATION

ASKS AN IMPORTANT QUESTION:

WHY HAVE THIS...

WHEN I CAN GIVE YOU THIS!

OUR SERVICES INCLUDE ALL PHASES OF PAPER ART RESTORATION, FROM THE SMALLEST TEAR TO MAJOR PIECE REPLACEMENT.
ASK ABOUT OUR OTHER RESTORATION SERVICES.

OUR RATE IS $55.00 PER HOUR. ESTIMATES ARE FREE & QUESTIONS ARE ALWAYS WELCOME.

P.O. Box 881 Kelso, WA 98626

Phone: (360) 577-0351
Fax: (360) 577-0351

www.fantasymasterpieces.com

10 YEARS PROVIDING THE ABSOLUTE BEST IN PAPER ART RESTORATION TO EVERYONE WHO LOVES COMICS!

Matthew Wilson, Conservator

COMIC BOOKS WANTED

The following prices represent a small sample of the prices that we will pay for your comic books. Other dealers say that they will pay top dollar, but when it really comes down to it, they simply do not. If you have comics to sell, we invite you to contact every comic dealer in the country to get their offers. Then come to us to get your best offer. We can afford to pay the highest price for your Golden and Silver Age comics because that is all we sell. If you wish to sell us your comic books, please either ship us the books securely via Registered U.S. Mail or UPS. However, if your collection is too large to ship, kindly send us a detailed list of what you have and we will travel directly to you. The prices below are for NM copies, but we are interested in all grades. Thank You.

Action #1	$275,000
Action #242	$2,500
Adventure #40	$45,000
Adventure #48	$23,000
Adventure #210	$3,500
All-American #16	$75,000
All-American #19	$14,000
All-Star #3	$30,000
Amazing Fantasy #15	$40,000
Amaz.Spiderman #1	$21,000
Arrow #1	$3,000
Batman #1	$75,000
Brave & the Bold #28	$5,800
Captain America #1	$65,000
Detective #1	$82,000
Detective #27	$230,000
Detective #38	$40,000
Detective #168	$4,500
Detective #225	$6,000
Detec. Picture Stories#1	$4,500
Donald Duck #9	$7,000
Fantastic Comics #3	$15,000
Fantastic Four #1	$30,000
Fantastic Four #5	$4,500
Flash Comics #1	$79,000
Green Hornet #1	$3,800
Green Lantern #1	(GA)$30,000
Green Lantern #1	(SA)$4,000
Human Torch #2(#1)	$25,000
Incredible Hulk #1	$14,000
Journey into Myst. #83	$6,500
Justice League #1	$4,000
Jumbo Comics #1	$17,000
Marvel Comics #1	$125,000
More Fun #52	$75,000
More Fun #54	$10,000
More Fun #55	$23,000
More Fun #73	$17,000
More Fun #101	$9,000
New Fun #6	$21,000
Pep Comics #22	$18,000
Showcase #4	$30,000
Showcase #8	$10,000
Superboy #1	$7,500
Superman #1	$185,000
Superman #14	$5,500
Suspense Comics #3	$20,000
Tales of Suspense #1	$2,300
Tales of Suspense #39	$4,750
Tales to Astonish #27	$4,000
Target Comics V1#7	$4,500
Walt Disney C&S #1	$16,500
Whiz #2 (#1)	$57,000
Wonder Woman #1	$20,000
Wow #1 (1936)	$9,500
Young Allies #1	$10,000
X-Men #1	$11,500

The following is a sample of the books we are purchasing:

Action Comics	#1-400
Adventure Comics	#32-400
Advs. Into Weird Worlds	all
All-American Comics	#1-102
All-Flash Quarterly	#1-32
All-Select	#1-11
All-Star Comics	#1-57
All-Winners	#1-21
Amazing Spiderman	#1-150
Amazing Man	#5-26
Amaz. Mystery Funnies	#1
Avengers	#1-100
Batman	#1-300
Blackhawk	#9-130
Boy Commandos	#1-32
Brave & the Bold	#1-100
Captain America	#1-78
Captain Marvel Advs.	#1-150
Challengers	#1-25
Classic Comics	#1-169
Comic Cavalcade	#1-63
Daredevil Comics	#1-60
Daredevil (MCG)	#1-50
Daring Mystery	#1-8
Detective Comics	#1-450
Donald Duck 4-Colors	#4-up
Fantastic Four	#1-100
Fight Comics	#1-86
Flash	#105-150
Flash Comics	#1-104
Funny Pages	#6-42
Green Lantern (GA)	#1-38
Green Lantern (SA)	#1-90
Hit Comics	#1-65
Human Torch	#2(#1)-38
Incredible Hulk	#1-6
Jimmy Olsen	1-150
Journey Into Mystery	#1-125
Jumbo Comics	#1-167
Jungle Comics	#1-163
Justice League	#1-110
Mad	#1-50
Marvel Mystery	#1-92
Military Comics	#1-43
More Fun Comics	#7-127
Mystery in Space	#1-75
Mystic Comics	#1-up
National Comics	#1-75
New Adventure	#12-31
New Comics	#1-11
New Fun Comics	#1-6
Our Army at War	#1-200
Our Fighting Forces	#1-180
Planet Comics	#1-73
Rangers Comics	#1-69
Reform School Girl	
Sensation Comics	#1-116
Shadow Comics	all
Showcase	#1-100
Star-Spangled Comics	#1-130
Strange Tales	#1-145
Sub-Mariner	#1-42
Superboy	#1-110
Superman	#1-250
Tales From The Crypt	#20-46
Tales of Suspense	#1-80
Tales to Astonish	#1-80
Terrific Comics	all
Thing	#1-17
USA Comics	#1-17
Weird Comics	#1-20
Weird Mysteries	#1-12
Weird Tales From The Future	all
Wings Comics	#1-124
Whiz Comics	#1-155
Wonder Comics	#1-20
Wonder Woman	#1-200
Wonderworld	#3-33
World's Finest	#1-200
X-Men	#1-30

METROPOLIS

COLLECTIBLES, INC
873 BROADWAY, SUITE 201
NEW YORK, NY 10003
Toll Free: 1-800-229-6387
Tel: 212-260-4147 Fax: 212-260-4304
Email: buyingl@metropoliscomics.com
Web: www.metropoliscomics.com

COME VISIT OUR NEW YORK CITY SHOWROOM! OPEN WEEKDAYS, BY APPOINTMENT ON

SILVER

WHY YOU SHOULD CALL US BEFORE YOU SELL YOUR COLLECTION OF COMICS, ARTWORK OR MEMORABILIA

We make it easy! No waiting for payment. No song and dance about grading. We'll come to you; anywhere, anytime! Four Color Comics takes the risk out of selling. Treat yourself to an honest, straight-forward experience—Sell your collection to us and walk away with more money in your pocket and a smile on your face.

www.fourcolorcomics.com

FOUR COLOR COMICS

115 West 27th Street, New York, NY 1000
TEL: (212) 675-6990 FAX: (212) 675-6145

DID YOU TURN INTO A
MONSTER
THE LAST TIME YOU RECEIVED
A MAIL ORDER?
If this looks familiar, treat yourself to honest grading and fair pricing by buying your Silver and Golden Age comics from us!
At FOUR COLOR COMICS, we specialize in treating the customer right and we unconditionally guarantee every book we sell!
Fantastic Four
10¢
FEATURING: "THE THING!" "MR. FANTASTIC!" "HUMAN TORCH!" "INVISIBLE GIRL!" TOGETHER FOR THE FIRST TIME IN ONE MIGHTY MAGAZINE!
DESIGN: ARNIE SAWYER All artwork: © DC COMICS, © MARVEL ENTERTAINMENT GROUP, INC
FOUR COLOR
COMICS
NY SHOWROOM (By Appointment Only): 115 West 27th St, New York, NY 10001 (212) 675-6990 Fax:(212) 675-6145
IF YOU'VE GOT BOOKS TO SELL, CALL IMMEDIATELY: (212) 675-6990

FOUR COLOR
COMICS
BUYING PRE-1955 POSTERS
I buy, sell, and collect movie posters and theater displays. I can and will pay you the highest price for your poster or collection of posters. Call me before you sell.
Of particular interest:
EARLY DISNEY
UNIVERSAL HORROR
1950'S SCIENCE-FICTION
1930'S POSTERS
115 West 27th St.
New York, NY 10001
Tel: (212) 675-6990
Fax: (212) 675-6145
Keybooks@aol.com
www.fourColorComics.com
D.W. GRIFFITH'S MIGHTY SPECTACLE
THE BIRTH OF A NATION
FOUNDED ON THOMAS DIXON'S THE CLANSMAN
THE DAY THE EARTH STOOD STILL
MICHAEL RENNIE · PATRICIA NEAL · HUGH MARLOWE
FRANKENSTEIN meets THE WOLF MAN
ILONA MASSEY
KING KONG
FAY WRAY · ROBT. ARMSTRONG
BRUCE CABOT
EDGAR WALLACE

The REDISTRIBUTOR

No. 1

HINDS FINDS ALL KINDS

Jef Hinds COMICS

JOE'S OLD COMIC BOOKS HAVE STOOD IN THE ATTIC FOR OVER FIFTY YEARS. I THINK IT'S TIME TO JUST BURN 'EM UP!

!! THINK AGAIN!

JEF TO THE RESCUE!

THE SUPERHEROES' SUPERHERO!

HE FINDS THEM! HE PRESERVES THEM! HE REDISTRIBUTES THEM!

Follow the Leader in Golden and Silver Age Comics with
BEDROCK CITY
COMIC COMPANY ™
6517 Westheimer
(at Hillcroft)
Houston, Texas 77057
(713) 780-0675
2204-D FM 1960 W.
(at Kuykendahl)
Houston, Texas 77090
(281) 444-9763
fax (713) 780-2366
www.bedrockcity.com
Shazam © 1997 D.C. Comics

OVER 50,000 DIFFERENT COMICS IN STOCK

I PAY BIG CASH FOR QUALITY COMICS

BIG CASH FOR ALL GOLDEN AGE (FR-MINT) AND SILVER AGE (VG-MINT) 1933 THRU 1963. THOUSANDS OF DOLLARS ALSO AVAILABLE FOR OLDER DISNEY CARTOON POSTERS, RARER COMIC ART AND PAINTINGS. SEND ME YOUR LIST FOR FAST CASH OFFER!!! WITH OVER 50,000 DIFFERENT COMICS I OFFER BULK COMICS (AS LOW AS 5¢ EACH) OR THAT MULTI-THOUSAND DOLLAR TREASURE YOU DESIRE. CREDIT CARDS AND LAYAWAYS ARE FINE.

SAMPLE BUYING PRICES (SUBJECT TO INCREASE)

BRAVE & BOLD #1-43,50,61 ....N-MINTS ARE WORTH 110%-300%
SHOWCASE #1-45,55,60. ....CHOICE ISSUES 110%-300% PAID
CAPT. AMERICA #1-78 ....VG OR BETTER 75%-125% OFFERED
MORE FUN #1-107 ....VG OR BETTER 70%-150% PAID
ACTION #1-252 ....VG OR BETTER 65%-150% PAID
DETECTIVE #1-233 ....VG OR BETTER 70%-150% PAID

"BIG CASH FOR OTHER DC, TIMELYS, OTHER GOLD OR SILVER AGE."

MULTIPLE GUIDE OFFERED FOR HIGH GRADE CGC!

SERVING FANDOM FOR OVER 30 YEARS

MARTY HAY

P.O. BOX 359 • 329 E. MAIN
mhay@cybertrails.com
SPRINGERVILLE, AZ 85938
WORK (520) 333-2222
HOME (520) 333-2255

SERVING FANDOM FOR OVER 30 YEARS

I WILL PAY MORE THAN ANY BUYING PRICES OFFERED IN THIS GUIDE!

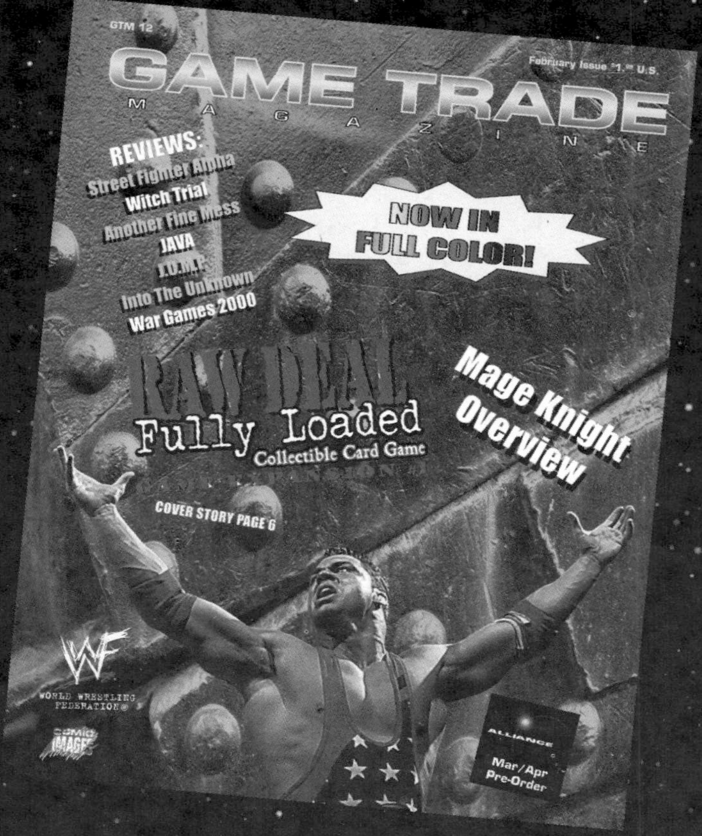

BELIEVE IT OR NOT!

Albuquerque
Indianapolis
Omaha
Dallas
Louisville
St. Louis

Houston
Nashville
Cincinnati
Little Rock
Sioux Falls
El Paso

New Orleans
Chicago
Kansas City
Shreveport
Des Moines
Minneapolis

Birmingham
Jackson
San Antonio
Denver
Memphis
Wichita

WE ARE **JUST A 1 DAY DRIVE** (OR LESS) FROM YOU!!

We are a one day drive from you and will **gladly** travel to you if have quality **PRE-1965** comic books to sell. Although many dealers "claim" they will fly to you, the simple truth is that most will ask you to **mail** some if not all of your books for their personal inspection and grading. We realize that many people are uncomfortable with this and so **we'll make it easy for you** by coming to your town and meeting you **personally**. We have actually driven to towns like **Jasper, AR, Lone Tree, IA** and **Grand Forks, ND** to purchase books and collections for our clients. We will pay you **CASH** on the spot, **no** time payments, **no** I.O.U.'s, **no** promises, **no** "cherry picking" books from your collection and **no** "we'll take it on consignment" options. All you need to do is **call us (preferred)**, FAX, or mail us a list of what you have and tell us **when** we can come to you. **It's just that simple!**

In the past few years, we have purchased books in **ALL** grades (some for **WORLD RECORD PRICES**) like **Action 1, Detective 27, Marvel 1, Superman 1, Captain America 1, All American 16, New Fun 2,** and **Batman 1** plus every "key" **Marvel** and **DC Silver Age** issue imaginable! Many of our purchases have come in **DIRECT COMPETITION** with other dealers who advertise in this guide. We don't mind the competition because we at WANT LIST COMICS can be **EXTREMELY COMPETITIVE** when we purchase individual books or collections. Often times, it's not who has **(or claims to have)** the most money that counts, it's who **has** the most established customers **looking anxiously** for comic books to buy. Because we have **many** want list customers waiting in line for books we purchase (*please note our other ads in this guide) we can usually expect a quick return on our money invested and therefore justify buying books at **very, very** high percentages of current Overstreet. We have purchased **some books at OVER 250% Guide** because of customer demand!

Give us a chance to make an offer **IN PERSON** before shipping your books to someplace you've never been before. **Don't** deal with a fast talking voice on the phone . . . **don't** spend money on postage and worry about your books arriving with damage or loss to their destination . . . **don't** let someone talk you into something you really don't want to do. **YOU DON'T HAVE TO!** If you need references of people we've bought books from in the past ·· **no problem** ·· we'll get you in contact with them and you can check us out. **We want to provide you with many good reasons for doing business with us. Please give us that opportunity!**

WE PAY GENEROUS FINDER'S FEES FOR ANY INFORMATION LEADING TO THE PURCHASE OF INDIVIDUAL BOOKS OR COLLECTIONS
FOR A QUICK REPLY CALL, FAX, OR WRITE US AT:

Our office/warehouse # is:

1-918-299-0440

Call us anytime between 1 pm and 8 pm, CST
Please ask for our private FAX #

WANT LIST COMICS

COMICS
GUARANTY, LLC
Charter
Member Dealer

BOX 701932
TULSA, OK 74170-1932

Senior Advisor to the Overstreet Comic Price Guide
CBG Customer Service Award
References gladly provided!

PACIFIC COMIC Exchange, Inc.
Buying & Selling 1933 - 1975 Comics
www.pcei.com
• Buying & Selling 1933-1975 Comics
• Consignments Accepted
• Certify your Comics
• Online Auctions
COMICS
Look! It's America's Greatest Comic Exchange!
Catalog
Rare Books
Certify
Auctions
PCE
GOLD + SILVER
COMIC
PCE Founded 1990
PCEI
PCE
PCE
PO Box 2629, Palos Verdes Peninsula, CA 90274 Ph: (310) 544-4936 FAX: (310) 544-4900
Toll-Free: (866) 500-7352 E-mail: sales@pcei.com See catalog at: www.pcei.com
Design: C.Hassett
VISA
Copyright © 2001 by PACIFIC COMIC EXCHANGE, INC. All rights reserved.

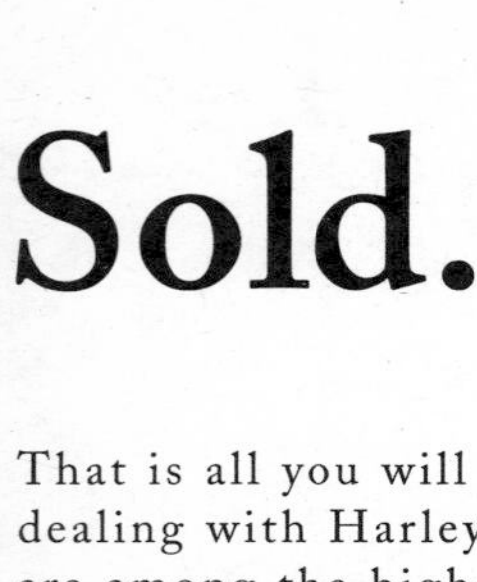

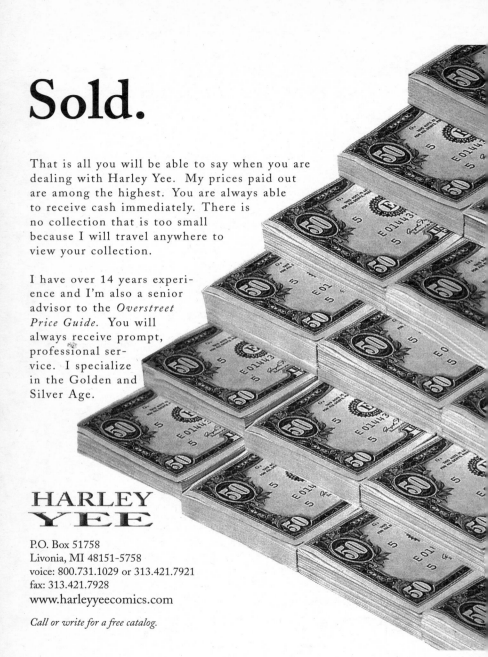

That is all you will be able to say when you are dealing with Harley Yee. My prices paid out are among the highest. You are always able to receive cash immediately. There is no collection that is too small because I will travel anywhere to view your collection.

I have over 14 years experience and I'm also a senior advisor to the *Overstreet Price Guide*. You will always receive prompt, professional service. I specialize in the Golden and Silver Age.

HARLEY YEE

P.O. Box 51758
Livonia, MI 48151-5758
voice: 800.731.1029 or 313.421.7921
fax: 313.421.7928
www.harleyyeecomics.com

Call or write for a free catalog.

Roy Rogers
comics
52 pages
ALL COMICS!

MERRILY WE MOP ALONG
WITH A CONGOLEUM RUG IT WON'T BE LONG

I HUFF AND I PUFF THROUGH THE WIDE OPEN DOOR
BUT I CAN'T BUDGE CONGOLEUM—IT LIES FLAT ON THE FLOOR

GENE AUTRY COMICS

No. 5
BATMAN

TARZAN'S REVENGE

ALWAYS look for the seal
Dell Comics are GOOD comics

Detective COMICS
FLASH
FUN COMICS

FRANKENSTEIN

Buster Brown

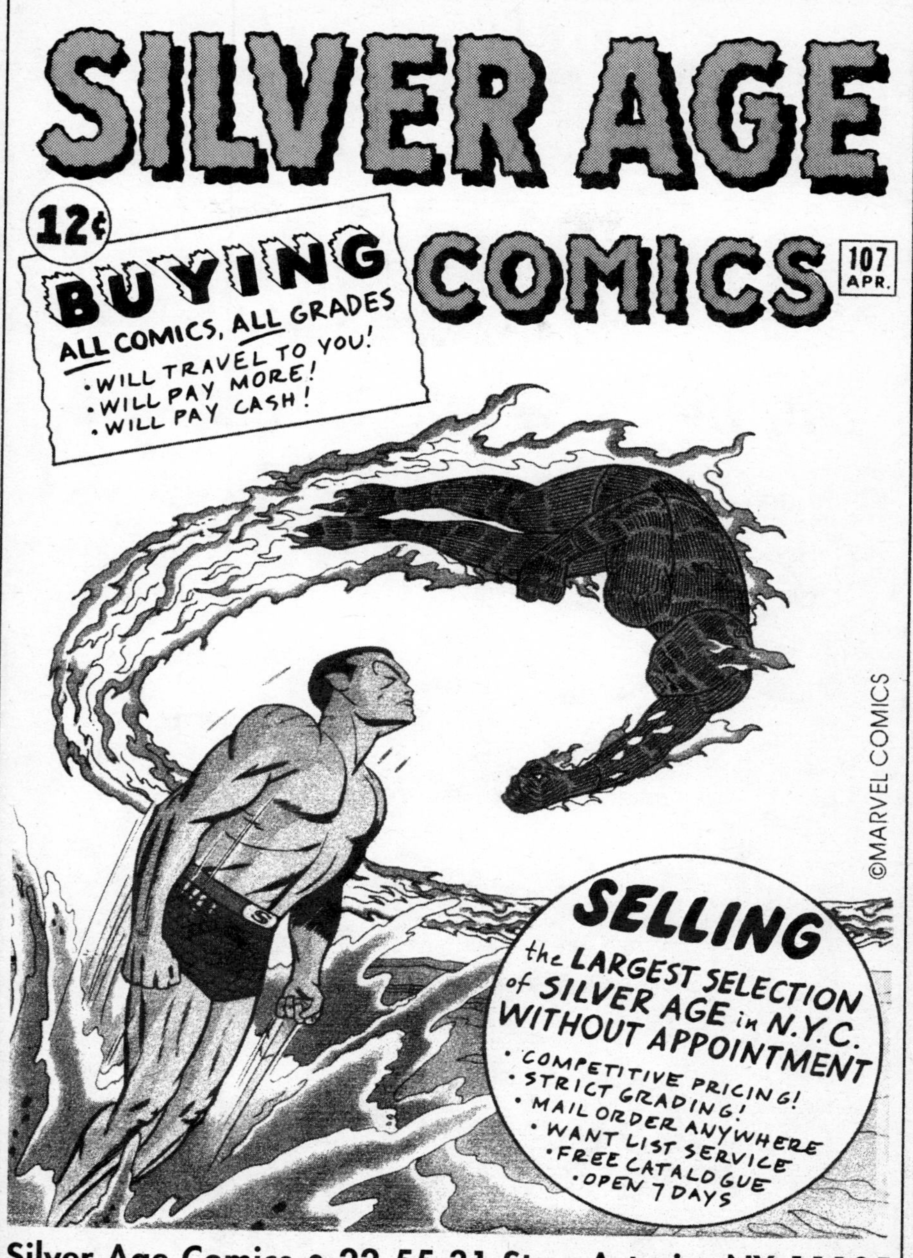
SILVER AGE
12¢
BUYING
COMICS
107
APR.
ALL COMICS, ALL GRADES
•WILL TRAVEL TO YOU!
•WILL PAY MORE!
•WILL PAY CASH!
©MARVEL COMICS
SELLING
the LARGEST SELECTION of SILVER AGE in N.Y.C. WITHOUT APPOINTMENT
•COMPETITIVE PRICING!
•STRICT GRADING!
•MAIL ORDER ANYWHERE
•WANT LIST SERVICE
•FREE CATALOGUE
•OPEN 7 DAYS

the GOBLIN'S DEN
7 Pinesmoke Cr.
issauga, Ontario, Canada
3L4
(905)848-0559 Fax#(416)622-0574
l:GOBLINSDEN@home.com
ALWAYS
Buying & Selling
Pre-1977
Comics
e also buy: Action Figures, Model Kits &
morabilia
ighest Prices Paid for quality pre-code Horror,
me & Good Girl
DAN ORGILL '98.
(AFTER ROMITA)

ARY DOLGOFF
COMICS
Buying ALL
COMICS 1933-1979
ALL GRADES
ALL TYPES
PAYING:
(FOR ALL 1933-1953 SUPERHERO COMICS)
50%-70% OF GUIDE
FINDER FEES PAID!!
NOT TOO LONG AGO, WE PAID A $5,000 FINDER'S FEE!
PLUS, MANY SMALLER (THAN $5,000) FEES HAVE BEEN PAID FOR OTHER DEALS!!
SPENDING:
$500 - $500,000
ON COLLECTIONS AND DEALERS' STOCK!
CAPTAIN AMERICA
FUN
TALES OF TERROR

APRIL
PHANTOM LADY
"The SODA MINT KILLER!"
A TRUE CRIME
MAY, 1939
10¢
SUB-MARIN
THE
HITLER'S
DEATH'S
BRIGHT FINGER

WANTED

COMICS

Golden Age • Silver Age • DC • Timely • EC • Disney • Early Marvel • Fox • Quality • Fiction House • Horror • Sci-Fi • Movie • TV • Romance • Western • Coverless and Incomplete Comics Too! (1933-1969)

Original Comic Art & Pulps

I will buy for **CASH** any books on the following list from poor to mint conditions.

Action	Comic Cavelcade	Little Lulu	Superman
Adventure	Crime Suspense	March of Comics	Tales from the Crypt
All American	Daring	Mad	Tales of Suspense
All Flash	Detective Comics	Marvel Mystery	Tales of Action
All Select	Donald Duck	Mickey Mouse	Tip Top
All Star	Fantastic Four	More Fun	USA
All Western	Feature Books	Mystic	Vault of Horror
All Winners	Flash	Pop	W.D. Comics & St.
Amazing Fantasy	Four Color	Planet	Weird Fantasy
Amazing Spiderman	Green Lantern	Plastic Man	Weird Science
Archie	Haunt of Fear	Pogo	Whiz
Avengers	Human Torch	Police	Wonder Woman
Batman	Hulk	Popular	World's Finest
Blue Beetle	Journey into Mystery	Sensation	Young Allies
Capt. America	Jimmy Olsen	Shadow	X-Men
Capt. Marvel	JLA	Showcase	
Classics	King	Super	

Procedure: Send a complete listing of all the books you have for sale. In case of large collections, I will make travel arrangements to meet you at your convenience.

or

Ship books insured, and upon arrival, I will respond with an immediate cash offer. If no mutual agreement is reached, then I will return books at my expense.

TOMORROWS TRESASURES
PO Box 925
Commack, NY 11725
Phone/Fax: 631-543-5737
Email: comics@tomorrowstreasures.com
Web Site: www.tomorrowstreasures.com

MOTOR CITY COMICS
Gold & Silver Age
NOW OPEN
Come Visit Our Warehouse
by appointment only
WE ALSO DEAL IN PULPS
& ORIGINAL ART
OCTOBER
Batman, Spectre, Green Lantern © DC Comics

NYC's BEST COMIC BOOK CONVENTIONS!
CELEBRITIES! ARTISTS! DEALERS!
BIG APPLE
Comic book, art & toy
SHOW
@ ST. PAUL CHURCH AUDITORIUM
9th AVE. & 60th ST., NYC
Adm. ONLY $6. EACH DAY
SAT. JULY 7th
FRI. & SAT. SEPT. 14th & 15th
2001
Over 50,000 FANS attended over the last 4 years!
See our website for 2002 dates
www.bigapplecon.com
AND THE
3RD
NATIONAL
COMIC BOOK, ART, TOY & SCI-FI
EXPO
the METROPOLITAN PAVILION
125 W. 18th ST., NYC
FRI.-SAT.-SUN
NOV. 9th-10th-11th
2001
McLAUGHLIN
SPURLOCK
For dealer tables or if you are a collector, contact
Michael Carbonaro or Chris McFarlane
Big Apple Conventions
74-05 Metropolitan Ave.
Middle Village, NY 11379
718-326-2713
www.bigapplecon.com

TOMORROWS
TREASURES
BUYING
Golden & Silver Age Comics:
DC • Timely • EC • Disney • Early Marvel
• Fox • Quality • Fiction House • Horror
• Sci -Fi • Movie • TV • Romance •
Western (1933-1969) • Coverless &
Incomplete Comics Too!
Original Comic Art & Pulps
P.O. Box 925
Commack, NY 11725
24 Hr. Phone/Fax: 631-543-5737
Email:
comics@tomorrowstreasures.com
Web Site:
www.tomorrowstreasures.com
Send $2.00 for a
100 page illustrated
comic catalog.
OUR 29th
CONSECUTIVE
YEAR IN
BUSINESS

That's Right!!

I will pay **LESS** for books I do not need. If you have books for sale that are common, chances are I have multiple copies currently in stock. (So do **ALL** of the larger Golden Age/Silver Age Dealers.)

If I buy these items, (with or without the books I need) I will **NOT** pay **MORE**, top dollar, etc. NO ONE will, despite all the high-flying rhetoric to the contrary.

FACT IS........

$ I **WILL** pay more, Top Dollar, Etc. for **ANY** (Pre-1969) books that I **DO NOT** currently have in stock. (There are thousands.)

$ At any given moment, you cannot possibly know which books I need **UNLESS** you contact me.

$ Regardless of ALL of the claims of Top $ Paid, the person with the **GREATEST NEED** at the time of sale, will usually pay you the most for your books. I am only one of many (not the only) dealer that **CAN** and **WILL** pay top dollar for what I need.

$ ***Conclusion***: If you have for sale any Golden/Silver Age books, Original comic art, or Pulps, then I invite you to seriously consider contacting Richard Muchin, a full time professional with almost 30 years of experience for details.

TOMORROWS TREASURES

Address: PO Box 925 Commack, NY 11725
24 hr. Phone/Fax: 631-543-5737
Email: comics@tomorrowstreasures.com
Web Site: www.tomorrowstreasures.com

Send $2.00 for our 100 page Illustrated comic catalog.

...we've worked on preserving and
restoring classic Golden Age and
Silver Age comics for over 17
years. From a simple cleaning
and pressing to a more
detailed intervention
we'll add value and life
to your collection
ACTION COMICS
SHOWCASE
AMAZING FANTASY
SPIDER MAN
The Restoration Lab
The experts in Comic Book conservation.

comicseller.com

Find It. *Buy It.* Bag It.

As the long-standing leader in high-quality archival supplies, we at E. Gerber Products offer serious protection for the serious collector creating the finest preservation and storage supply products on the market – affordable archival supplies that enable you to keep your collectibles pristine and resistant to the ravages of time.

We stock a full line of products designed to protect your collection. Try our products and see what a difference quality can make!

Why Mylar®? Why not plastic bags like Polyethylene or Polypropylene?

* Resistance to diffusion of gases like Oxygen, CO_2, and Sulphur Dioxide, is 100 times that of other plastics.
* Hundreds of times more stable than other plastics; no damaging "off-gassing."
* 50 times the strength of other plastics.
* Does not absorb harmful moisture like other plastics.

Mylar® by Dupont Co. or approved equivalent.

Archives are made from 4 mil thick Mylar D® and feature two flaps for easy use.

Item#	Size	Description	Price per: 50	200	100
700R	7 x 10 1/2	Current Comics- 1990's	19.25	63.00	276.00
725R	7 1/4 x 10 1/2	Standard Comics - 1970's-90's	19.50	64.00	282.00
775R	7 3/4 x 10 1/2	Silver/Golden Comics - 1950's-70's	20.00	66.00	288.00
800R	8 X 11	Golden Age Comics - 1940's-50's	21.25	70.00	306.00
825R	8 1/4 x 11	Super Golden Age Comics	22.25	73.00	318.00
Add Shipping & Handling			**$2.00**	**$7.00**	**$22.00**

Made from 2 mil thick Mylar D®, these sleeves offer collectors twice the thickness and 4 times the protection of 1 mil thick bags. Mylites 2 also feature a flap that can be folded over, tucked in, or taped closed.

Item#	Size	Description	Price per: 50	200	100
700M2	7 x 10 3/4	Current Comics- 1990's	10.75	36.00	155.00
725M2	7 1/4 x 10 3/4	Standard Comics - 1970's-90's	11.00	37.00	160.00
775M2	7 3/4 x 10 3/4	Silver/Gold Comics - 1950's-70's	11.50	38.00	165.00
800M2	8 x 10 3/4	Golden Age Comics - 1940's-50's	12.00	39.00	175.00
825M2	8 1/4 x 10 3/4	Super Golden Age Comics	12.50	42.00	180.00
Add Shipping & Handling			**$1.00**	**$4.00**	**$11.00**

Made from 1 mil thick Mylar D®, these sleeves offer are your least expensive permanent storage solution, outlasting polybags 500 to 1! Mylites also feature a flap that can be folded over, tucked in, or taped closed.

Item#	Size	Description	Price per: 100	100
700M	7 x 10 3/4	Current Comics - 1990's	$15.50	$118.00
725M	7 1/4 x 10 3/4	Standard Comics - 1970's-90's	15.75	119.00
775M	7 3/4 x 10 3/4	Silver/Gold Comics- 1950's-70's	16.75	122.00
Add Shipping & Handling			**$2.00**	**$9.00**

Satisfaction Guaranteed

All E. Gerber archival supply products carry our assurance of the highest quality standards in both material and manufacturing.

For a complete catalog of our affordable archival products, please call us toll-free a **1-800-79-MYLAR** from 8:00 a.m. to 5:00 p.m. Eastern Standard Time, or mail your catalog request to:

E. Gerber Products, Inc.
1720 Belmont Avenue, Suite C
Baltimore, MD 21244
Fax: 1-410-944-9363
e-mail: archival@egerber.com
Visit us on the Web at www.egerber.com!

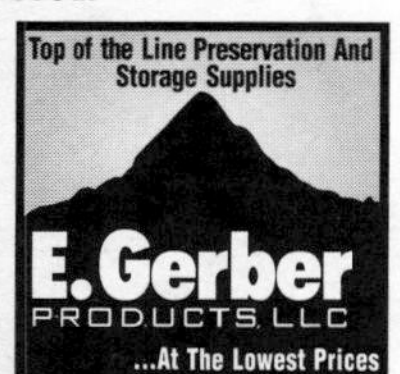

Top of the Line Preservation And Storage Supplies
E.Gerber
PRODUCTS, LLC
...At The Lowest Prices

THE BEST PROTECTION AT THE BEST PRICE!

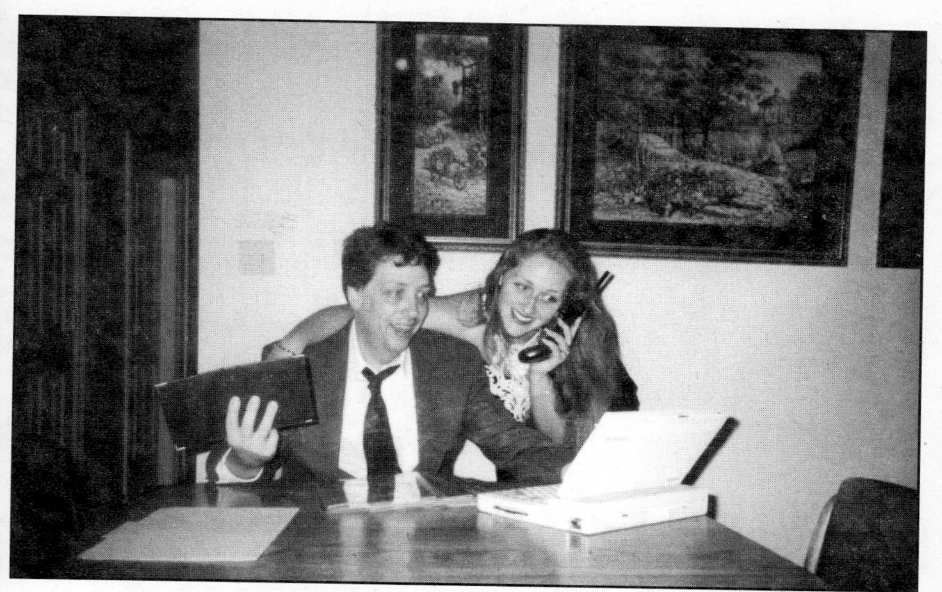

JOHN VERZYL AND DAUGHTER ROSE, "HARD AT WORK."

John Verzyl started collecting comic books in 1965, and within ten years he had amassed thousands of Golden and Silver Age comic books. In 1979, with his wife Nanette, he opened "COMIC HEAVEN," a retail store devoted entirely to the buying and selling of comic books.

Over the years, John Verzyl has come to be recognized as an authority in the field of comic books. He has served as a special advisor to the "Overstreet Comic Book Price Guide" for the last ten years. Thousands of his "mint" comics were photographed for Ernst Gerber's newly-released "Photo-Journal Guide To Comic Books." His tables and displays at the annual San Diego Comic Convention and the Chicago Comic Convention draw customers from all over the country.

The first COMIC HEAVEN AUCTION was held in 1987, and today his Auction Catalogs are mailed out to more than ten thousand interested collectors and dealers.

Comic Heaven
John and Nanette Verzyl
P.O. Box 900
Big Sandy, TX 75755
1-903-636-5555

Congratulations! We at Gemstone welcome you to the hobby of comic books. This book is the most comprehensive reference work available on comics. It is also respected and used by dealers and collectors everywhere. The Overstreet price is the accepted price around the world, and we have not earned this privilege easily. Through hard work, diligence and constant contact with the market for decades, Overstreet has become the most trusted name in comics.

HOW TO USE THIS BOOK

This volume is an accurate, detailed alphabetical list of comic books and their retail values. Comic books are listed by title, regardless of company. Prices listed are shown in Good, Fine and Near Mint condition with many key books priced in an additional Very Fine grade. Comic books that fall in between the grades listed can be priced simply with the following procedure: Very Good is half way between Good and Fine; Very Fine is half way between Fine and Near Mint (unless a VF price is already shown). The older true Mint books usually bring a premium over the Near Mint price. Books in Fair bring 50 to 70% of the Good price. Some books only show a Very Fine price as the highest grade. The author has not been able to determine if these particular books exist in better than Very Fine condition, thus the omission of a Near Mint price. Most comic books are listed in groups, i.e., 11-20, 21-30, 31-50, etc.

The prices listed opposite these groupings represent the value of each issue in that group. More detailed information is given for individual comic books. If you are looking for a particular character, consult the first appearance indexes which will help you locate the correct title and issue. This book also contains hundreds of ads covering all aspects of this hobby. Whether you are buying or selling, the advertising sections can be of tremendous benefit to you.

NEW COMIC BOOKS

This book lists all new comic books at cover price, regardless of their performance in the secondary market. In many cases, new comics are not worth their cover price in the secondary market, and collectors may pay pennies on the dollar for copies of these issues. Nevertheless, since these comics have yet to establish themselves as collectors' items, they are listed at full cover price. It should also be noted that regarding polybagged comics, it is the official policy of **The Overstreet Comic Book Price Guide** to grade comics regardless of whether they are still sealed in their polybag or not. If opened, the polybag and its contents should be preserved separately so that all components of the original package remain together.

COMIC BOOK VALUES

All values listed in this book are in U.S. currency and are retail prices based on (but not limited to) reports from our extensive network of experienced advisors which include convention sales, mail order, auctions, unpublished personal sales and stores. Overstreet, with several decades of market experience, has developed a unique and comprehensive system for gathering, documenting, averaging and pricing data on comic books. The end result is a true fair market value for your use. We have earned the reputation for our cautious, conservative approach to pricing comic books. You, the collector, can be assured that the prices listed in this volume are the most accurate and useful in print.

IMPORTANT NOTE: This book is not a dealer's price list, although some dealers may base their prices on the values listed. The true value of any comic book is what you are willing to pay. Prices listed herein are an indication of what collectors (not dealers) would probably pay. For one reason or another, these collectors might want certain books badly, or else need specific issues to complete their runs and so are willing to pay more.

DEALERS' POSITION: Dealers are not in a position to pay the full prices listed, but work on a percentage depending largely on the amount of investment required and the quality of material offered. Usually they will pay from 20 to 70% of the list price depending on how long it will take them to sell the collection after making the investment; the higher the demand and better the condition, the more the percentage. Most dealers are faced with expenses such as advertising, travel, telephone and mailing, rent, employee salaries, plus convention costs. These costs must all be factored in before the books are sold. The high demand books usually sell right away but there are many other titles that are difficult to sell due to low demand. Sometimes a dealer will have costs tied up in this types of books for several years before finally moving them. Remember, his position is that of handling, demand, and overhead. Most dealers are victims of these economics.

HOW COMICS ARE LISTED

Comic books are listed alphabetically by title. The true title of a comic book can usually be found listed with the publisher's information, or indicia, often found at the bottom of the first page. Titles that appear on the front cover can vary from the official title listed inside.

Comic book titles, sequence of issues, dates of first and last issues, publishing companies, origin and special issues are listed when known. Prominent and collectible artists are also pointed out (usually in footnotes). Page counts will always include covers. Most comic books began with a #1, but occasionally many titles began with an odd number. There is a reason for this. Publishers had to register new titles with the post office for 2nd class permits. The registration fee was expensive. To avoid this expense, many publishers would continue the numbering of new titles from old defunct titles. For instance, **Weird Science** #12 (1st issue) was continued from the defunct **Saddle Romances** #11 (the last issue). In doing this, the publishers hoped to avoid having to register new titles. However, the post office would soon discover the new title and force the publisher to pay the registration fee as well as to list the correct number. For instance, the previous title mentioned began with #12 (1st issue). Then #13 through #15 were published. The next issue became #5 after the Post Office correction. Now the sequence of published issues (see the listings) is #12-15, 5-on. This created a problem in early fandom for the collector because the numbers 12-15 in this title were duplicated.

WHAT COMICS ARE LISTED

The Guide lists primarily American comic books due to space limitations. The earliest comic books date back to 1897 and are included in their own section under The Platinum Age. These books basically reprinted newspaper strips and were published in varying sizes, usually with cardboard covers, but sometimes as hardbacks. The format of **Funnies On Parade**, published in 1933 (saddle-stitched), soon became the standard for the modern comic book, although squarebound versions were also published. Most of these formats that appeared on newsstands will be included.

NEW COMIC LISTINGS

The 1980s and '90s have experienced an explosion of publishers with hundreds of new titles appearing in black & white and color. Many of these comics are listed in this book, but not all due to space limitation. We will attempt to list complete information only on those titles that show some collector interest. The selection of titles to include is constantly being monitored by our board of advisors. Please do not contact us to list your new comic books. Listings are determined by the marketplace. However, we are interested in receiving review copies of all new comic books published.

GRADING

For complete, detailed information on grading and restoration, consult the **Overstreet Comic Book Grading Guide**. Copies are available through all normal distribution channels or can be ordered direct from the publisher by sending $12 plus $2 postage and handling. You can also call Gemstone toll free at 1-888-375-9800.

The Overstreet Comic Book Grading Card, known as the **ONE** and **OWL Card** is also available. This card has two functions. The **ONE Card** (**O**verstreet's **N**umerical **E**quivalent) is used to convert grading condition terms to the new numerical grading system. The **OWL Card** (**O**verstreet's **W**hiteness **L**evel) is used for grading the whiteness of paper. The color scale on the **OWL Card** is simply placed over the interior comic book paper. The paper color is matched with the color on the card to get the **OWL** number. The **ONE/OWL Card** may be ordered direct from the publisher by sending $1.30 per card.

HOW TO GRADE

Before a comic book's true value can be assessed, its condition or state of preservation must be determined. In all comic books, the better the condition the more desirable and valuable the book. Comic books in **MINT** condition will bring several times the price of the same book in **POOR** condition. Therefore it is very important to be able to properly grade your books. Comics should be graded from the inside out, so the following comic book areas should be examined before assigning a final grade.

Check inside pages, inside spine and covers and outside spine and covers for any tears, markings, brittleness, tape, soiling, chunks out or other defects that would affect the grade. After all the above steps have been taken, then the reader can begin to consider an overall grade for his or her book. The grading of a comic book is done by simply looking at the book and describing its condition, which may range from absolutely perfect newsstand condition **MINT** to extremely worn, dirty, and torn **POOR**.

Numerous variables influence the evaluation of a comic book's condition and all must be considered in the final evaluation. Although the grade of a comic book is based upon an accumulation of defects, some defects may be more extreme for a particular grade as long as other acceptable listed defects are almost non-existent. As grading is the most subjective aspect of determining a comic's value, it is very important that the grader be careful not to allow wishful thinking to influence what the eyes see. It is also very important to realize that older comics in **MINT** condition are extremely scarce and are rarely advertised for sale; most of the higher grade comics advertised range from **VERY FINE** to **NEAR MINT**.

GRADING DEFINITIONS

Note: This edition uses both the traditional grade abbreviations and the **ONE** number throughout the listings. The **O**verstreet **N**umerical **E**quivalent (**ONE**) spread range is given with each grade.

MINT (MT) (ONE 9.9-10.0): Near perfect in every way. Only the most subtle bindery or printing defects are allowed. Cover is flat with no surface wear. Cover inks are bright with high reflectivity and minimal fading. Corners are cut square and sharp. Staples are generally centered, clean with no rust. Cover is generally well centered and firmly secured to interior pages. Paper is supple and fresh. Spine is tight and flat.

NEAR MINT/MINT (NM/MT) (ONE 9.8): A comic book that has enough positive qualities to make it better than a NM+, but has enough detracting qualities to keep it from being a MT 9.9. In most cases the comic book has a better appearance than a NM+.

NEAR MINT (NM) (ONE 9.2-9.7): Nearly perfect with only minor imperfections allowed. This grade should have no corner or impact creases, stress marks should be almost invisible, and bindery tears must be less than 1/16 inch. A couple of very tiny color flecks, or a combination of the above that keeps the book from being perfect, where the overall eye appeal is less than Mint drops the book into this grade. Only the most subtle binding and/or printing defects allowed. Cover is flat with no surface wear. Cover inks are bright with high reflectivity and minimum of fading. Corners are cut square and sharp with ever so slight blunting permitted. Staples are generally centered, clean with no rust. Cover is well centered and firmly secured to interior pages. Paper is supple and like new. Spine is tight and flat.

VERY FINE/NEAR MINT (VF/NM) (ONE 9.0): A comic book that has enough positive qualities to make it better than a VF+, but has enough detracting qualities to keep it from being a NM-. In most cases the comic book has a better appearance than a VF+.

VERY FINE (VF) (ONE 7.5-8.5): An excellent copy with outstanding eye appeal. Sharp, bright and clean with supple pages. Cover is relatively flat with almost no surface wear. Cover inks are generally bright with moderate to high reflectivity. Staples may show some discoloration. Spine may have a couple of almost insignificant transverse stress lines and is almost completely flat. A barely unnoticeable 1/4 inch crease is acceptable, if color is not broken. Pages and covers can be yellowish/tannish (at the least, but not brown and will usually be off-white to white).

FINE/VERY FINE (FN/VF) (ONE 7.0): A comic

book that has enough positive qualities to make it better than a FN+, but has enough detracting qualities to keep it from being a VF-. In most cases the comic book has a better appearance than a FN+.

FINE (FN) (ONE 5.5-6.5): An above-average copy that shows minor wear but is still relatively flat and clean with no significant creasing or other serious defects. Eye appeal is somewhat reduced because of slight surface wear and possibly a small defect such as a few slight cross stress marks on spine or a very slight spine split (1/4"). A Fine condition comic book appears to have been read a few times and has been handled with moderate care. Compared to a VF, cover inks are beginning to show a significant reduction in reflectivity but it is still a highly collectible and desirable book.Pages and interior covers may be tan, but pages must still be fairly supple with no signs of brittleness.

VERY GOOD/FINE (VG/FN) (ONE 5.0): A comic book that has enough positive qualities to make it better than a VG+, but has enough detracting qualities to keep it from being a FN-. In most cases the comic book has a better appearance than a VG+.

VERY GOOD (VG) (ONE 3.5-4.5): The average used comic book. A comic in this grade shows some wear, can have a reading or center crease or a moderately rolled spine, but has not accumulated enough total defects to reduce eye appeal to the point that it is not a desirable copy. Some discoloration, fading and even minor soiling is allowed. As much as a 1/4" triangle can be missing out of the corner or edge. A missing square piece (1/8" by 1/8") is also acceptable. Store stamps, name stamps, arrival dates, initials, etc. have no effect on this grade. Cover and interior pages can have some minor tears and folds and the centerfold may be detached at one staple. The cover may also be loose, but not completely detached. Common bindery and printing defects do not affect grade. Pages and inside covers may be brown but not brittle. Tape should never be used for comic book repair; however many VG condition comics have minor tape repair.

GOOD/VERY GOOD (GD/VG) (ONE 3.0): A comic book that has enough positive qualities to keep it better than a GD+, but has enough detracting qualities to keep it from being a VG-. In most cases the comic book has a better appearance than a GD+.

NEW TEN POINT GRADING SYSTEM

10.0	Mint
9.9	Mint
9.8	Near Mint/Mint
9.6	Near Mint +
9.4	Near Mint
9.2	Near Mint -
9.0	Very Fine/Near Mint
8.5	Very Fine +
8.0	Very Fine
7.5	Very Fine -
7.0	Fine/Very Fine
6.5	Fine +
6.0	Fine
5.5	Fine -
5.0	Very Good/Fine
4.5	Very Good +
4.0	Very Good
3.5	Very Good -
3.0	Good/Very Good
2.5	Good +
2.0	Good
1.8	Good -
1.5	Fair/Good
1.0	Fair
0.5	Poor

GOOD (GD) (ONE 1.8-2.5): A copy in this grade has all pages and covers, although there may be small pieces missing inside; the largest piece allowed from front or back cover is a 1/2" triangle or a square 1/4" by 1/4". Books in this grade are commonly creased, scuffed, abraded, soiled and may have as much as a 2" spine split, but are still completely readable. Often paper quality is low but not brittle. Cover reflectivity is low and in some cases completely absent. This grade can have a moderate accumulation of defects but still maintains its basic structural integrity.

FAIR/GOOD (FR/GD) (ONE 1.5): A comic book that has enough positive qualities to keep it better than a FR+, but has enough detracting qualities to keep it from being a GD-. In most cases the comic book has a better appearance than a FR+.

FAIR (FR) (ONE 1.0): A copy in this grade is usually soiled, ragged and possibly unattactive. Creases, tears and/or folds are prevalent. Spine may be split up to 2/3rds its entire length. Staples may be gone. Up to 1/10th of the front cover may be missing. These books are readable although soiling, staining, tears, markings or chunks missing may moderately interfere with reading the complete story. Some collectors consider this the lowest collectible grade because comic books in lesser condition are usually defaced and/or brittle. Very often paper quality is low and may have slight brittleness around the edges but not in the central portions of the pages. Comic books in this grade may have a clipped coupon so long as it is noted along side of the nomenclature; ie: "Fair (1.0) Coupon Clipped." Valued at 50-70% of good.

POOR (PR) (ONE 0.5): Most comic books in this grade have been sufficiently degraded to the point that copies may have extremely severe stains, missing staples, brittleness, mildew or moderate to heavy cover abrasion to the point that some cover inks are indistinct/absent. Comic books in this grade can have small chunks missing and pieces out of pages. They may have been defaced with paints, varnishes, glues, oil, indelible markers or dyes. Covers may be split the entire length of the book, but both halves must be present and basically still there with some chunks missing. A page(s) may be missing as long as it is noted along side of the nomenclature; ie: " POOR (0.5) 2nd Page Missing." Value depends on extent of defects but would average about 1/3 of GOOD.

DUST JACKETS

Many of the early strip reprint comics were printed in hardback with dust jackets. Books with dust jackets are worth more. The value can increase from 20 to 50 percent depending on the rarity of book. Usually, the earlier the book, the greater the percentage. Unless noted, prices listed are without dust jackets. The condition of the dust jacket should be graded independently of the book itself.

RESTORED COMICS

When restoration of comics first began, it was a collection of crude, damaging attempts to preserve or fix comics exhibiting defects like tears or missing pieces. At first using tape, glue and color pens, restoration soon evolved, utilizing more advanced techniques like chemical baths and deacidification. Today, professional restorers work in a quickly maturing field using methods that have stood the test of time. There is still a stigma attached to restoration, however, often due to a lack of knowledge about how restored comics relate to the market.

Many restored comics are unnecessarily put through the process, begging the question 'when should I restore my comics?' If a comic is in VG or better, don't restore it. Restoration for preserving deteriorating comics, taking an ugly pile of loose pages and restoring them to an attractive form that can be handled and enjoyed. In the case of comics in VG or higher grades, the book is already an attractive item and restoration would be excessive.

The value of the comic should also be high enough to justify restoration. With prices of $30-$75 an hour to restore a comic, only very valuable books should be candidates. It's recommended to avoid restoring Silver Age comics, apart from key issues, due to their relative availability. Restored Silver Age comics also do not rise in value as much as a restored Golden Age comic.

Bindery chips, a common defect in Golden Age comics, are considered printing defects and are relatively acceptable in the market. Restoration on such a defect by itself would usually be considered excessive. Books with brown or brittle pages are usually not good candidates either. Even though the comic will look better, its page quality will still rate a lower grade. Bleaching and other treatments can be used, but are expensive, frowned upon and not very effective. Only the most expensive books should ever be considered for page treatment. Similarly, books missing covers and interior pages are poor candidates for restoration. A comic must be relatively complete to be successfully restored.

Preventative restoration, widely used and accepted by collectors, consists of "non-additive" restoration on a book with one or two major defects. A prime example would be a $2,000 book in Fine that has a 2" piece of tape on the cover. Removal of the tape improves the value and appearance of the book. The process is cheap and quick, and nothing is "added" to the comic, such as Japan paper or color touch (see the glossary for definitions). Although it's always imperative to disclose any and all restoration work on a book, some collectors don't even view these simple repairs as restoration. Other defects fixable by "preventative" techniques are water stains, warping, dirt or writing, rusty staples, and spine rolls.

These minor fixes work best with books above VG, the one exception to the rule noted earlier. Once restored, a comic's value depends upon several factors:

The amount of restoration: In general, the more restoration has been performed, the less the comic is worth compared to its apparent grade value. A lightly restored book will be valued higher than a book with heavy restoration in the same apparent grade.

The "before" and "restored" grades: As a rule of thumb, consider these formulae:

Golden Age key issues:
(guide value of comic before restoration)
+(guide value of comic's apparent grade)/2.5

Golden Age common issues:
(guide value of comic before restoration)
+(guide value of comic's apparent grade)/2.0

Silver Age issues:
(guide value of comic before restoration)
+(guide value of comic's apparent grade)/3.0

These formulae serve only as a benchmark. Each book is unique and may vary in pricing.

The market demand: This is highly subjective, but the higher the demand, the likelier your restored book will fetch its apparent grade price. Consequently, if the comic is slow on the market, a restored copy may be less than the value derived from the above formulae.

The market value: The market fluctuates widely on restored copies of expensive books. A small variance in perception of what a restored copy is worth can mean a difference of thousands of dollars on high end comics (see formulae above). Values tend to be more stable on common books.

Age of the comic: The younger a comic, the less likely the book will increase in value significantly from restoration. This applies mainly to Silver Age comics, as noted earlier.

Armed with this knowledge and a good understanding of the market, you should be able to make an informed decision about restoration. When in doubt, contact a reputable dealer or collector who is familiar with restored comics in the marketplace.

SCARCITY OF COMICS

1897-1933 Comics: Most of these books are bound with thick cardboard covers and are very rare to non-existent in VF or better condition. Due to their extreme age, paper browning is very common. Brittleness could be a problem.

1933-1940 Comics: There are many issues from this period that are very scarce in any condition, especially from the early to mid-1930s. Surviving copies of any particular issue range from a handful to several hundred. Near Mint to Mint copies are virtually non-existent with known examples of any particular issue limited to five or fewer copies. Most surviving copies are in FN-VF or less condition. Brittleness or browning of paper is fairly common and could be a problem.

1941-1952 Comics: Surviving comic books would number from less than 100 to several thousand copies of each issue. Near Mint to Mint copies are a little more common but are still relatively scarce with only a dozen or so copies in this grade existing of any particular issue. Exceptions would be recent warehouse finds of most Dell comics (6-100 copies, but usually 30 or less), and Harvey comics (1950s-1970s) surfacing. Due to low paper quality of the late 1940s and 1950s, many comics from this period are rare in Near Mint to Mint condition. Most remaining copies are VF or less. Browning of paper could be a problem.

1953-1959 Comics: As comic book sales continued to drop during the 1950s, production values were lowered resulting in cheaply printed comics. For this reason, high grade copies are extremely rare. Many Atlas and Marvel comics have chipping along the trimmed edges (Marvel chipping) which reduces even more the number of surviving high grade copies.

1960-1979 Comics: Early '60s comics are rare in Near Mint to Mint condition. Most copies of early '60s Marvels and DCs grade no higher than VF. Many early keys in NM or MT exist in numbers less than 10-20 of each. Mid-'60s to late-'70s books in high grade are more common due to the hoarding of comics that began in the mid-'60s.

1980-Present: Comics of today are common in high grade. VF to NM is the standard rather than the exception.

When you consider how few Golden and Silver Age books exist compared to the current market, you will begin to appreciate the true rarity of these early books. In many cases less than 5-10 copies exist of a particular issue in Near Mint to Mint condition, while most of the 1930s books do not exist in this grade at all.

The Ongoing Evolution in Grading

Special Commentary by Comics Guaranty, LLC

We see a lot of comic books at Comics Guaranty, LLC (CGC). At this writing, we've graded 25,000 comics since we opened our doors on January 4, 2000. That's an average of more than 2,500 a month that have received a page count, restoration check, the careful eye of three independent graders, and a final "QC" check once the book's in our protective holder before it's out the door and on its way back to the submitter.

As you can imagine, we get lots of feedback, like how to grade a certain defect such as a tear on the cover as opposed to a tear on a page. Or a bindery chip compared to a small piece torn off the cover. Or a crease on the front cover as opposed to one on the back cover. Or a sun/dust shadow on the cover as opposed to very light tanning on the edges of the interior cover. You get the idea.

One thing is for certain: everyone has a unique opinion. More importantly, everyone passionately believes his or her opinion to be the correct one. It's this diversity of opinion that makes the comic book industry so vibrant. It's also a diversity CGC took into account while establishing our grading standards. We believed it was essential to draw from the Overstreet grading guidelines, as well as to get a "reality check" from the day-to-day experience of the country's top dealers and collectors. So we put 50 of the hobby's top experts through a grueling, hours-long grading test to establish a median standard that would accurately reflect the standards our hobby would consider fair.

Considering the response we've had in just 10 months, it's fair to say we have a pretty good understanding of what collectors and dealers will and won't allow in a certain grade (one simple example: the hobby will not allow a 1" spine split in a 9.4 even if the comic looks 9.6!).

What is not so simple is the market's judgment of tape and restoration. According to this Guide, tape as a defect is allowed in 4.5 or lower and is not a form of restoration. At the same time, a 2" archivally-safe tear seal on a 4.5 is considered restoration. Something about this standard is troublesome. Putting five pieces of tape on a fully split spine might bring the grade up from 1.5 to 2.5 even though the tape application has initiated increased deterioration of the paper it is placed upon. Take the same comic, however, and seal its spine with an archivally-safe glue, which will not cause any paper deterioration, and to much of the market the comic is now somehow less desirable because it is "restored."

As we discuss this standard with experts in other collectibles fields (movie posters, fine art, vintage autos, antique furniture and others) we hear a different perspective. Their experience is that if performed expertly and responsibly, restoration is not only a form of enhancement, but an essential form of preservation. Equally puzzling is that a small amount of glue and color touch on a Golden Age comic book that would grade out 9.0 (even if the work wasn't done) is somehow less desirable than the next best existing copy that grades 7.0. How can this be? Put the two copies side by side and it's obvious there is a world of difference between them. Even so, too many people would shy away from the better copy. Why?

One of the reasons that comes to mind is disclosure or the lack thereof. Twenty-five years ago, touching up a comic was not considered wrong. The problem arose when these comics were offered for sale and the seller did not disclose what had been done. The buyer assumed he or she was purchasing a comic in 9.4–and by the standards of the day it was 9.4–but in today's reality the same comic now could be an 8.5 with some defects fixed or hidden. Worse, when the owner went to sell or trade the same comic years later and the previous work was discovered, he or she felt deceived. By not having a practice of full disclosure, legitimate and enhancing restoration has been painted with the same brush as undisclosed and deceptive restoration.

So here is something to consider: Would you rather own a comic book graded 4.5 with tape on the spine that makes it less attractive and initiates accelerated deterioration of the paper, or would you rather have a book graded 4.5 with archivally-safe glue on the spine that makes the comic more attractive? Since both tape and archivally-safe glue produce the same intended result of holding the spine together, we would suggest the glue for what it does not provide–namely, the ugly appearance and the accelerated deterioration of the comic.

Even with advent of CGC, a few issues concerning grading and the interpretation of restoration remain, and will no doubt only be resolved as part of the ongoing evolution in grading.

If you'd like to contact CGC concerning these issues, please write Comics Guaranty, LLC, P.O. Box 1938, Parsippany, NJ 07054-0237, fax (973) 721-9474, or visit them on the internet at www.CGCcomics.com.

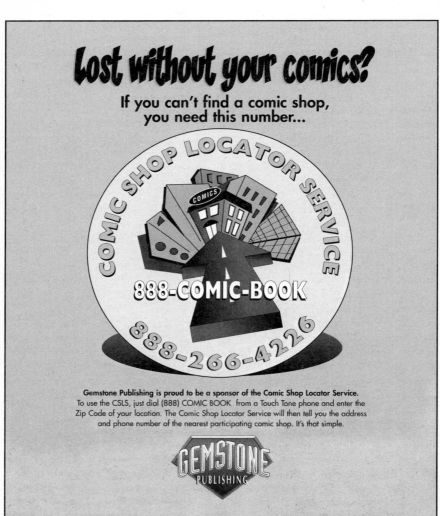

New comic books are available in many different kinds of stores. Grocery stores, drug stores, Wal-Mart, K-Mart, book stores, comic book stores and card and comics specialty shops are a few examples. Local flea markets and, of course, comic book conventions in your area are excellent sources for new and old comic books.

Most collectors begin by buying new issues in Mint condition directly off the newsstand or from their local comic store. (Subscription copies are available from several mail-order services, and often the publishers themselves.) Each week new comics appear on the stands that are destined to become true collectors' items. The trick is to locate a store that carries a complete line of comics. In several localities this may be difficult. Most collectors frequent several magazine stands in order not to miss something they want. Even then, it pays to keep in close contact with collectors in other areas. Sooner or later, nearly every collector has to rely upon a friend in Fandom or a dealer to obtain for him an item that is unavailable locally (see ads in this book).

Before you buy any comic to add to your collection, you should carefully inspect its condition. Unlike stamps and coins, defective comics are generally not highly prized. The cover should be properly cut and printed. Remember that every blemish or sign of wear depreciates the beauty and value of your comics.

The serious collector usually buys extra copies of popular titles. He may trade these multiples for items unavailable locally (for example, foreign comics), or he may store the multiples for resale at some future date. Such speculation is, of course, a gamble. Selecting the right investment books is tricky business that requires special knowledge. With experience, the beginner will improve his buying skills. Remember, if you play the new comics market, be prepared to buy and sell fast as values rise and fall rapidly.

Today's comic books offer a wide variety of subjects, art styles and writers to satisfy even the most discriminating fan. Whether it's the latest new hot title or company, or one of many popular titles that have been around for a long time, the comic book fan has a broad range from which to pick. Print runs of many popular titles have dropped over the past few years, creating the possibility of a true rarity occurring when demand outstrips supply. Less "gimmicky" covers are seen these days, but occasionally an eye-catching specialty cover will appear, such as the Superman new costume issue (#123) that glows-in-the-dark. Some cover variants continue to appear as well. "Bad Girl" and horror titles have been popular along with the standard superhero fare. The collector should always stay informed about the new trends developing in this fast-moving market. Since the market fluctuates greatly, and there is a vast array of comics to choose from, it's recommended first and foremost that you collect what you enjoy reading; that way, despite any value changes, you will always maintain a sense of personal satisfaction with your collection.

POLYBAGGED COMICS: It is the official policy of this Guide to grade comics regardless of whether they are still sealed in their polybag or not. Sealed comics in bags are not always in MINT condition and could even be damaged. The value should not suffer as long as the bag (opened) and all of its original manufactured contents are preserved and kept together.

COLLECTING ON A BUDGET: Collectors check out their local newsstand or comic specialty store for the latest arrivals. Hundreds of brand new comic books are displayed each week for the collector, much more than anyone can afford to purchase. Today's reader must be careful and budget his money wisely in choosing what to buy.

COLLECTING ARTISTS: Many collectors enjoy favorite artists and follow their work from issue to issue, title to title, company to company. In recent years, some artists have achieved "star" status. Autograph signings occur at all major comic conventions as well as special promotions with local stores. Fans line up by the hundreds at such events to meet these superstars. Some of the current top artists of new comics are: Todd McFarlane, Alex Ross, Jim Lee, Michael Turner, Marc Silvestri, Rob Liefeld, Chris Bachalo, J. Scott Campbell, Humberto Ramos, and Adam and Andy Kubert. Original artwork from these artists have been bringing record prices at auctions and from dealers' lists.

COLLECTING BY COMPANIES: Some collectors become loyal to a particular company and only collect its titles. It's another way to specialize and collect in a market that expands faster than your pocket book.

COLLECTING #1 ISSUES: For decades, comic enthusiasts have always collected first (#1) issues. This is yet another way to control spending and build an interesting collection for the future. #1 issues have everything going for them--some introduce new characters, while others are underprinted, creating a rarity factor. #1 issues cross many subjects as well as companies, and make for an intriguing collection.

BACK ISSUES

A back issue is any comic currently not available on the stands. Collectors of current titles often want to find the earlier issues in order to complete the run. Thus a back issue collector is born. Comic books have been published and collected for over 100 years. However, the earliest known comic book dealers didn't appear until the late 1930s. But today, there are hundreds of dealers that sell old comic books (See ads in this book).

LOCATING BACK ISSUES: The first place to begin, of course, is with your collector friends who may have unwanted back issues or duplicates for sale. Look in the yellow pages, or call the Comic Shop Locator Service at 1-888-COMIC-BOOK, to see if you have a comic book store available. If you do, they would know of other collectors in your area. Advertising in local papers could get good results. Go to regional markets and look for comic book dealers. There are many trade publications in the hobby that would put you in touch with out-of-town dealers. This Annual Guide has ads buying and selling old comic books. Some dealers publish regular price lists of old comic books for sale. Get on their mailing list.

Putting a quality collection of old comics together takes a lot of time, effort and money. Many old comics are not easy to find. Persistence and luck play a big part in acquiring needed issues. Most quality collections are put together over a long period of time by placing mail orders with dealers and other collectors.

Comics of early vintage are extremely expensive if they are purchased through a regular dealer or collector. Unless you have unlimited funds to invest in your hobby, you will find it necessary to restrict your collecting in certain ways. However you define your collection, you should be careful to set your goals well within affordable limits.

PRESERVATION & STORAGE

Comic books are fragile and easy to damage. Most dealers and collectors hesitate to let anyone personally handle their rare comics. It is common courtesy to ask permission before handling another person's comic book. Most dealers would prefer to remove the comic from its bag and show it to the customer themselves. In this way, if the book is damaged, it would be the dealer's responsibility–not the customer's. Remember, the slightest crease or chip could render an otherwise Mint book to Near Mint or even Very Fine.

Consult the **Overstreet Comic Book Grading Guide** and learn the proper way to hold a comic book. The following steps are provided to aid the novice in the proper handling of comic books: 1. Remove the comic from its protective sleeve or bag very carefully. 2. Gently lay the comic (unopened) in the palm of your hand so that it will stay relatively flat and secure. 3. You can now leaf through the book by carefully rolling or flipping the pages with the thumb and forefinger of your other hand. Caution: Be sure the book always remains relatively flat or slightly rolled. Avoid creating stress points on the covers with your fingers and be particularly cautious in bending covers back too far on Mint books. 4. After examining the book, carefully insert it back into the bag or protective sleeve. Watch corners and edges for folds or tears as you replace the book. Always keep tape completely away while inserting a comic in a bag.

Comic books should also be protected from the elements as well as the dangers of light, heat, and humidity. This can easily be achieved with proper storage. Improper storage methods will be detrimental to the "health" of your collection, and may even quicken its deterioration.

Store comic books away from direct light sources, especially florescent which contains high levels of ultraviolet (UV) radiation. UV lights are like sunlight, and will quickly fade the cover inks. Tungsten filament lighting is safer than florescent but should still be used at brief intervals. Remember, exposure to light accumulates damage, so store your collection in a cool, dark place away from windows.

Temperatures must also be carefully regulated. Fungus and mold thrives in higher temperatures, so the lower the temperature, the longer the life of your collection.

Atmospheric pollution is another problem associated with long term storage of paper. Sulfuric dioxide which can occur from automobile exhaust will cause paper to turn yellow over a period of time. For this reason, it is best not to store your valuable comics close to a garage. Some of the best preserved comic books known were protected from exposure to the air such as the Gaines EC collection. These books were carefully wrapped in paper at time of publication, and completely sealed from the air. Each package was then sealed in a box and stored in a closet in New York. After over 40 years of storage when the packages were opened, you could instantly catch the odor of fresh newsprint; the paper was snow white and supple, and the cover inks were as brilliant as the day they were printed. This illustrates how important it is to protect your comics from the atmosphere.

Like UV, high relative humidity (rh) can also be damaging to paper. Maintaining a low and stable relative humidity, around 50%, is crucial; varying humidity will only damage your collection.

Care must be taken when choosing materials for storing your comics. Many common items such as plastic bags, boards, and boxes may not be as safe as they seem. Some contain chemicals that will actually help to destroy your collection rather than save it. Always purchase materials designed for long-term storage, such as Mylar type "D" sleeves and acid-free boards and boxes. Polypropylene and polyethylene bags, while safe for temporary storage, should be changed every three to five years.

Comics are best stored vertically in boxes. For shelving, make sure that comics do not come into direct contact with the shelving surface. Use acid-free boards as a buffer between shelves comics. Also, never store comics directly on the floor; elevate them 6-10 inches to allow for flooding. Similarly, never store your collection directly against a wall, particularly an outside wall. Condensation and poor air circulation will encourage mold and fungus growth.

When handling your high grade comics, wash your hands first, eliminating harmful oils from the skin before coming into contact with the books. Lay the comic on a flat surface and slowly turn the pages. This will minimize the stress to the staples and spine. With these guidelines, your collection should enjoy a long life and maintain a reasonable condition and value.

BUYING & SELLING

Whether you're a new collector just starting to acquire comics or a long-time collector now interested in selling a collection, by purchasing this Guide, you have begun the long process necessary to successfully buy and sell comics.

SELLING YOUR COMICS

If you are planning to sell a collection, you must first decide what category listed below best describes your collection. As a rule of thumb, the lower categories will need less detail provided in your inventory list. A collection of key late '30s DCs will require you to list exact titles, numbers, and grades, as well as possible restoration information. If, however, you have 20,000 miscellaneous '80s and '90s comics for sale, a rough list of the number of books and publishers should be enough. The categories are:

1. PLATINUM AGE (1897-1932): The supply is very scarce. More people are becoming interested in these early books due to comics passing their 100th birthday. Moderate interest among average dealers, but high interest with dealers that specialize in this material. A detailed list will be necessary paying attention to brittleness, damage and pages missing. Dealers will pay up to a high percentage of Guide list for key titles.

2. GOLDEN AGE, All Grades (1933 - pre-1956): The most desirable. A detailed inventory will be necessary. Key higher grade books are easier to sell, but lower grades in most titles show the best selling potential, due to the fact that many collectors cannot afford a $20,000 VF book but may be able to afford a GD for only $2,000. Highest demand is for the superhero titles such as **Batman**, **Superman**, **Human Torch**, etc. The percentage of Guide that dealers will pay for your collection will vary depending on condition and contents. A collection of low demand titles will not bring the same percentage as a collection of prime titles.

3. High Grade SILVER AGE (1956-mid 1960s): A detailed inventory will be necessary. There are always investors looking for VF or better books from this period. Dealers will usually pay a high percentage of Guide list for these high grade books. Silver Age below VF will fall into category #4.

4. Low Grade SILVER AGE: Spanning books lower than VF from the late '50s to 1970, this category exhibits the average grade of most collections. Consequently, the supply of this material is much more common than category #2. This means that you could be competing with many other similar collections being offered at the same time. You will have to shop this type of collection to get the best price, and be prepared to sell at a significant discount if you find a willing buyer with good references.

5. MODERN AGE (post-1970): Certain titles from the early 1970s in high grade are showing increasing demand. However, many books from the 1980s to the 1990s are in low demand with the supply for the most part always being of high grade books. These collections are typified by long runs of certain titles and/or publishers. A detailed inventory will not be necessary. Contact local comic stores or buyers first to gauge their level of interest. Dealing with buyers outside your area should be avoided if possible.

IMPORTANT: Many of the 1980s and 1990s books are listed at cover price. This indicates that these books have not established a collector's value. When selling books of this type, the true market value could be 20-50% of cover price or less.

6. BULK (post-1980 in quantities greater than 5,000): These collections usually contain multiple copies of the same issues. It is advisable to price on a per-book basis (2¢ and 20¢ each). Do NOT attempt an inventory list, and only contact buyers who advertise buying in bulk quantity.

You should never deal with a buyer without fully checking their references. For additional verification, consult The Better Business Bureau; the local BBB may be able to help you in establishing a buyer's credibility, as well as assisting in resolving any disputes. **The Overstreet Comic Book Price Guide** and **Comic Book Marketplace** are also recognized authorities. Advertised dealers will likely have a more established reputation.

Potential buyers will be most concerned with the retail value of your entire collection, which may be more or less than Guide depending what you have and their current demand. Some rare early books in VF or NM may bring a price over Guide list while other titles in lower grade may sell for a price under Guide list. Most vintage books, however, will sell for around the Guide price. However, 1980s or 1990s books that list at cover price may only be worth a percentage of that price. You must then decide on what percentage you would be willing to accept for your collection, taking into account how the collection breaks down into fast, moderate and slow moving books. To expect someone to pay full retail is unrealistic. You will have to be flexible in order to close a deal.

Many buyers may want to purchase only certain key or high grade books from your collection, almost always favoring the buyer. While you may be paid a high percentage of retail, you will find that "cherry-picked" collections are much more difficult to sell. Furthermore, the percentage of retail that you will receive for a "cherry-picked" collection will be much lower than if the collection had been left intact. Remember, key issues and/or high grade issues make or break a collection. Selling on consignment, another popular option in today's market, could become a breeding ground for cherry-pickers, so again, always check a dealer's references thoroughly.

Some collectors may choose to sell their comic books on a piecemeal basis, requiring much greater care and detail in preparing an inventory list and grading comics for sale. You will be able to realize a higher percentage of retail by selling your collection this way, but the key books will certainly sell first, leaving a significant portion of the collection unsold. You will need to keep repricing and discounting your books to encourage buyers.

You can advertise your collection in trade publications or through mass mailings. If you sell books through the mail, you must also establish a reasonable return policy, as some books will unquestionably be returned. Check the local post office and/or UPS regarding the various rates and services available for shipping your books. Marketing your books at conventions is another option. As a dealer, you will also incur overhead expenses such as postage, mailing and display supplies, advertising costs, etc.

In all cases, be willing to establish trust with a prospective buyer. By following the procedures outlined here, you will be able to sell your collection successfully, for a fair price, with both parties walking away satisfied. After all, collecting comic books is supposed to be fun; it only becomes a chore if you let it.

WHERE TO BUY AND SELL

Throughout this book you will find the advertisements of many reputable dealers who sell back-issue comics magazines. If you are an inexperienced collector, be sure to compare prices before you buy. When a dealer is selected (ask for references), send him a small order (under $100) first to check out his grading accuracy, promptness in delivery, guarantees of condition advertised, and whether he will accept returns when dissatisfied. Never send cash through the mail. Send money orders or checks for your personal protection. Beware of bargains, as the items advertised sometimes do not exist but are only a fraud to get your money.

The Price Guide is indebted to everyone who placed ads in this volume. Your mentioning this book when dealing with the advertisers would be greatly appreciated.

COMIC CONVENTIONS

The first comic book conventions, or cons, were originally conceived as the comic book counterpart to science fiction fandom conventions. There were many attempts to form successful national cons, but they were all stillborn. It is interesting that after only three relatively organized years of existence, the first comic con was held. Of course, its magnitude was nowhere near as large as most established cons held today.

What is a comic con? Dealers, collectors, fans, publishers, distributors, manufacturers, whatever they call themselves can be found trading, selling, and buying the adventures of their favorite characters for hours on end. Additionally most cons have guests of honor, usually professionals in the field of comic art, either writers, artists, or editors. The committees put together panels for the con attendees in which the assembled pros talk about certain areas of comics, most of the time fielding questions from the assembled audience. At cons one can usually find displays of various and sundry things, usually toys, thousands of comic books, original art, and more. There can be the showing of movies or videos. Of course there is always the chance to get together with friends at cons and just talk about comics. One also has a good opportunity to make new friends who have similar interests and with whom one can correspond after the convention is over.

It is difficult to describe accurately what goes on at a con. The best way to find out is to go to one and see for yourself. The largest cons are WonderCon (April), Pittsburgh (April), San Diego (July), Chicago (July), and Atlanta (July). For accurate dates and addresses, consult ads in this edition as well as some of the adzines. Please remember when writing for convention information to include a self addressed, stamped envelope for reply.

It's possible to discern two distinct and largely unrelated movements in the history of Comics Fandom. The first began around 1953 as a response to the the trend-setting EC lines of comics. The first true comics fanzines of this movement were short-lived. Bob Stewart's **EC FAN BULLETIN** was a hectographed newsletter that ran two issues about six months apart; Jimmy Taurasi's **FANTASY COMICS**, a newsletter devoted to all science-fiction comics of the period, was a monthly that ran for about six months. These were followed by other newsletters such as Mike May's **EC FAN JOURNAL**, and George Jennings' **EC WORLD PRESS**. EC fanzines of a wider and more critical scope appeared somewhat later. Two of the finest were **POTRZEBIE**, from a number of fans, and Ron Parker's **HOOHAH**. Gauging from the response that **POTRZEBIE** received from an EC letter column plug, Ted White estimated the average age of EC fans at 9 to 13, while many were actually in their mid-teens. This was discouraging to many fanzine editors hoping to reach an older audience. Consequently, many gave up their efforts on behalf of Comics Fandom, especially with the demise of the EC groups, and turned to SF (science fiction) fandom with its longer tradition and older membership. While the flourish of fan activity in response to the EC comics was certainly noteworthy, it never developed into a full-fledged, independent, and self-sustaining movement.

The second movement began in 1960, largely as a response to (and later stimulus for) the reappearance of the costumed hero and the Second Heroic Age of Comics. Most historians date the Second Heroic Age from **Flash** #105, February 1959. The letter departments of Julius Schwartz (editor at National Periodicals), and later those of Stan Lee (Marvel Group) and Bill Harris (Gold Key) were influential in bringing comics readers into Fandom. Sparks were lit among SF fans first, when experienced fan writers, who were part of an established tradition, produced the first in a series of articles on '40s comics–ALL IN COLOR FOR A DIME. The series was introduced in **XERO** #1 (September 1960), a general SF fanzine edited and published by Dick Lupoff.

Meanwhile, outside SF fandom, Jerry Bails and Roy Thomas, two comics fans of long-standing, conceived the first true comics fanzine in response to the Second Heroic Age, **ALTER EGO**, appearing in March 1961. The first issues were widely circulated, and profoundly influenced the comics fan movement, attracting many fans in their twenties and thirties, unlike the earlier EC fan following. Many of these older fans had been collectors for years but were largely unknown to each other. Joined by scores of new, younger fans, this group formed the nucleus of a self-sustaining and still growing movement. Although it has borrowed a few appropriate SF terms, Comics Fandom of the '60s was an independent movement without the advantages and disadvantages of a longer tradition. What Comics Fandom did derive from SF fans was largely thanks to fanzines produced by so-called double fans, the most notable being **COMIC ART**, edited and published by Don and Maggie Thompson.

The **ROCKET'S BLAST COMIC COLLECTOR** by G.B. Love was the first sucessful adzine in the early 1960s and was instrumental in the development of the comics market. G.B. remembers beginning his fanzine **THE ROCKET'S BLAST** in late 1961. Only six copies of the first 4 page issue were printed. Soon after Mr. Love had a letter published in **MYSTERY IN SPACE**, telling all about his new fanzine. His circulation began to grow. Buddy Saunders, a well known comic book store owner, designed the first **ROCKET'S BLAST** logo and was an artist on the publication for many years thereafter. With issue #29 he took over **THE COMICOLLECTOR** fanzine from Biljo White and combined it with **ROCKET'S BLAST** to form the **RBCC**. He remembers that the **RBCC** hit its highest circulation of 2,500 around 1971. Many people who wrote, drew or otherwise contributed to the **RBCC** went on to become well known writers, artists, dealers and store-owners in the comics field.

FOREIGN EDITION COMICS

One interesting and relatively inexpensive source of early vintage comics is the foreign market. Many American newspaper and magazine strips are reprinted abroad (in English and in other languages) months and even years after they appear in the States. By arranging trades with foreign collectors, one can obtain substantial runs of American comic book reprints and newspaper strips dating back years. These reprints are often in black and white, and sometimes the reproduction is poor. Once interest in foreign-published comics has been piqued, a collector might become interested in original strips from these countries.

NEWSPAPER STRIPS

Collecting newspaper comic strips is somewhat different than collecting comic books, although it can be equally satisfying. Most strip collectors begin by clipping strips from their local paper, but soon branch out to out-of-town papers. Naturally this can become more expensive and more frustrating, as it is easy to miss out-of-town editions. Consequently, most strip collectors work out trade agreements with collectors in other cities. This usually means saving local strips for trade only.

Back issues of some newspaper comic strips are also occasionally available from dealers. Prices vary greatly depending on age, condition, and demand.

ORIGINAL ART

Some enthusiasts collect original comic book and strip art. These mostly black and white, inked drawings are usually done on illustration paper at about 30 percent larger than the original printed panels. Because original art is a one-of-a-kind article, it is highly prized and can be difficult to obtain.

Interest in original comic art has increased tremendously in the past few years because more current art is available now that companies return originals to the artists, who then either sell the work themselves at cons, or through agents and dealers. The best way to find the piece you want is to scour cons and get on as many art dealers' mailing lists as possible. Although the masters' works from the Golden and Silver Ages bring fine art prices, most current work is available at moderate prices, with something for everyone at various costs, from Kirby to McFarlane, Ditko to Bachalo.

TOYS AND MORE

In the past ten years or so, interest in collecting comic-related merchandise has soared. Comic book and toy shows are often dominated by toys and related products.

Action figures and limited edition statues based on comic characters are currently the most popular. Highly successful toy action figure lines based on Batman, Spawn, Spider-Man, and many others cram toy store shelves. Statues and figurines, either painted or in kit form, are very popular higher-end collectibles. Statues of characters like Witchblade, Sandman, Shi, and many more draw collector attention through print, web, and convention advertising.

Numerous other tie-in products based on comic characters are released every year and seem to represent a large percentage of the collectible market today. Books like **Hake's Price Guide to Character Toys**, and periodicals like **Collecting Figures** and **Toyfare** track the collectibility of these items.

COVER BAR CODES

Today's comic books are cover-coded for the direct sales (comic shop, newsstand, and foreign markets). They are all first printings, with the special coding being the only difference. The comics sold to the comic shops have to be coded differently, as they are sold on a no-return basis while newsstand comics are not. The Price Guide has not detected any price difference between these versions. Currently, the difference is easily detected by looking at the front cover bar code (a box located at the lower left). The bar code used to be filled in for newsstand sales and left blank or contain a character for comic shop sales. Now, as you can see here, direct sale editions are clearly marked, both versions containing the bar code.

Newsstand

Direct Sales (DC)

Direct Edition (Marvel)

MARVEL REPRINTS

In recent years Marvel has reprinted some of their comics. There has been confusion in identifying the reprints from the originals, but in 99% of the cases, the reprints have listed "reprint," or "2nd printing," etc. in the indicia, along with a later copyright date in some cases. Some Marvel 2nd printings have a gold logo. The only known exceptions are a few of the movie books such as **Star Wars**, the **Marvel Treasury Editions**, and tie-ins such as **G.I. Joe**. These books were reprinted and not identified as reprints. The **Star Wars** reprints have a large diamond with no date and a blank UPC symbol on the cover. Others had cover variations such as a date missing or different colors. Beginning in mid-1990, all Marvel 2nd printings have a gold logo.

Gold Key and other comics were also sold with a Whitman label. Even though collectors may prefer one label over the other, the Price Guide does not differentiate in the price. Beginning in 1980, all comics produced by Western carried the Whitman label.

PUBLISHERS' CODES

The following abbreviations are used with cover reproductions throughout the book for copyright purposes:

AC-(Americomics)
ACE-Ace Periodicals
ACG-American Comics Group
AJAX-Ajax-Farrell
AP-Archie Publications
ATLAS-Atlas Comics (see below)
AVON-Avon Periodicals
BP-Better Publications
C & L-Cupples & Leon
CC-Charlton Comics
CEN-Centaur Publications
CCG-Columbia Comics Group
CG-Catechetical Guild
CHES-Harry 'A' Chesler
CLDS-Classic Det. Stories
CM-Comics Magazine
CRO-Cross Generation
DC-DC Comics, Inc.
DEF-Defiant Comics
DELL-Dell Publishing Co.
DH-Dark Horse
DMP-David McKay Publishing
DS-D. S. Publishing Co.
EAS-Eastern Color Printing Co.
EC-E. C. Comics
ECL-Eclipse Comics
ENWIL-Enwil Associates
EP-Elliott Publications
ERB-Edgar Rice Burroughs
FAW-Fawcett Publications
FC-First Comics
FF-Famous Funnies
FH-Fiction House Magazines
FOX-Fox Features Syndicate
GIL-Gilberton
GK-Gold Key
GP-Great Publications
HARV-Harvey Publications
H-B-Hanna-Barbera
HILL-Hillman Periodicals
HOKE-Holyoke Publishing Co.
IM-Image Comics
KING-King Features Syndicate
LEV-Lev Gleason Publications
MAL-Malibu Comics
MAR-Marvel Characters, Inc.
ME-Magazine Enterprises
MLJ-MLJ Magazines
MS-Mirage Studios
NOVP-Novelty Press
PG-Premier Group
PINE-Pines
PMI-Parents' Magazine Institute
PRIZE-Prize Publications
QUA-Quality Comics Group
REAL-Realistic Comics
RH-Rural Home
S & S-Street and Smith Publishers
SKY-Skywald Publications
STAR-Star Publications
STD-Standard Comics
STJ-St. John Publishing Co.
SUPR-Superior Comics
TC-Tower Comics
TCOW-Top Cow Productions
TM-Trojan Magazines
TMP-Todd McFarlane Productions
TOBY-Toby Press
TOPS-Topps Comics
UFS-United Features Syndicate
VAL-Valiant
VITL-Vital Publications
WB-Warner Brothers
WDC-The Walt Disney Company
WEST-Western Publishing Co.
WHIT-Whitman Publishing Co.
WHW-William H. Wise
WMG-William M. Gaines (E. C.)
WP-Warren Publishing Co.
WSP-WildStorm Productions
YM-Youthful Magazines
Z-D-Ziff-Davis Publishing Co.

TIMELY/MARVEL/ATLAS

"A Marvel Magazine" and "Marvel Group" were the designations used between December 1946 and May 1947 for the Timely/Marvel/Atlas group of comics during that period, although these taglines were not used on all of the titles/issues during that time. The Timely Comics symbol was used between July 1942 and September 1942, although again not on all titles/issues during the period. The round "Marvel Comic" symbol was used between February 1949 and June 1950. An early Comics Code symbol (star and bar) was used between April 1952 and February 1955. The Atlas globe symbol was used between December 1951 and September 1957. The M over C symbol (signifying the beginning of Marvel Comics as we know it today) was introduced in July 1961 and remained until the price increased to 12 cents in February 1962. We present here the publishers' codes for the Timely/Marvel/Atlas group of comics:

ACI-Animirth Comics, Inc.
AMI-Atlas Magazines, Inc.
ANC-Atlas News Co., Inc.
BPC-Bard Publishing Corp.
BFP-Broadcast Features Pubs.
CBS-Crime Bureau Stories
CLDS-Classic Detective Stories
CCC-Comic Combine Corp.
CDS-Current Detective Stories
CFI-Crime Files, Inc.
CmPI-Comedy Publications, Inc.
CmPS-Complete Photo Story
CnPC-Cornell Publishing Corp.
CPC-Chipiden Publishing Corp.
CPI-Crime Publications, Inc.
CPS-Canam Publishing Sales Corp.
CSI-Classics Syndicate, Inc.
DCI-Daring Comics, Inc.
EPC-Euclid Publishing Co.
EPI-Emgee Publications, Inc.
FCI-Fantasy Comics, Inc.
FPI-Foto Parade, Inc.
GPI-Gem Publishing, Inc.
HPC-Hercules Publishing Corp.
IPS-Interstate Publishing Corp.
JPI-Jaygee Publications, Inc.
LBI-Lion Books, Inc.
LCC-Leading Comic Corp.
LMC-Leading Magazine Corp.
MALE-Male Publishing Corp.
MAP-Miss America Publishing Corp.
MCI-Marvel Comics, Inc.
MgPC-Margood Publishing Corp.
MjMC-Marjean Magazine Corp.
MMC-Mutual Magazine Corp.
MPC-Medalion Publishing Corp.
MPI-Manvis Publications, Inc.
NPI-Newsstand Publications, Inc.
NPP-Non-Pareil Publishing Corp.
OCI-Official Comics, Inc.
OMC-Official Magazine Corp.
OPI-Olympia Publications, Inc.
PPI-Postal Publications, Inc.
PrPI-Prime Publications, Inc.
RCM-Red Circle Magazines, Inc.
SAI-Sports Actions, Inc.
SePI-Select Publications, Inc.
SnPC-Snap Publishing Co.
SPC-Select Publishing Co.
SPI-Sphere Publications, Inc.
TCI-Timely Comics, Inc.
TP-Timely Publications
20 CC-20th Century Comics Corp.
USA-U.S.A. Publications, Inc.
VPI-Vista Publications, Inc.
WFP-Western Fiction Publishing
WPI-Warwick Publications, Inc.
YAI-Young Allies, Inc.
ZPC-Zenith Publishing Co., Inc.

COMIC BOOK ARTISTS

Many of the more popular artists in the business are specially noted in the listings. When more than one artist worked on a story, their names are separated by a (/). The first name did the pencil drawings and the second the inks. When two or more artists work on a story, only the most prominent will be noted in some cases. We wish all good artists could be listed, but due to space limitation, only the most popular can. The following list of artists are considered to be either the most collected in the comic field or are historically significant. Artists designated below with an (*) indicate that only their most noted work will be listed. The rest will eventually have all their work shown as the information becomes available. This list could change from year to year as new artists come into prominence:

Adams, Arthur
Adams, Neal
Aparo, Jim
Bachalo, Chris
Bagley, Mark
Baker, Matt
Barks, Carl
Beck, C. C.
*Brunner, Frank
*Buscema, John
Byrne, John
Campbell, J. Scott
Capullo, Greg
*Check, Sid
Colan, Gene
Cole, Jack
Cole, L. B.
Craig, Johnny
Crandall, Reed
Darrow, Geof
Davis, Jack
Disbrow, Jayson
*Ditko, Steve
Eisner, Will
*Elder, Bill
Evans, George
Everett, Bill
Feldstein, Al
Fine, Lou
Foster, Harold
Fox, Matt
Frazetta, Frank
Gibbons, Dave
*Giffen, Keith
Golden, Michael
Gottfredson, Floyd
*Guardineer, Fred
Gustavson, Paul
*Heath, Russ
Howard, Wayne
*Infantino, Carmine
Ingels, Graham
Jones, Jeff
Kamen, Jack
Kane, Bob
*Kane, Gil
Kelly, Walt
Kieth, Sam
Kinstler, E. R.
Kirby, Jack
Krenkel, Roy
Krigstein, Bernie
Kubert, Adam
Kubert, Andy
*Kubert, Joe
Kurtzman, Harvey
Lapham, Dave
Larsen, Erik
Lee, Jae
Lee, Jim
Liefeld, Rob
Madureira, Joe
Manning, Russ
McFarlane, Todd
McWilliams, Al
Meskin, Mort
Mignola, Mike
Miller, Frank
Moreira, Ruben
*Morisi, Pete
*Newton, Don
Nostrand, Howard
Orlando, Joe
Pakula, Mac
*Palais, Rudy
*Perez, George
Portacio, Whilce
Powell, Bob
Quesada, Joe
Raboy, Mac
Ramos, Humberto
Raymond, Alex
Ravielli, Louis
*Redondo, Nestor
Rogers, Marshall
Ross, Alex
Schomburg, Alex
Sears, Bart
Siegel & Shuster
Silvestri, Marc
Simon & Kirby (S&K)
*Simonson, Walt
Smith, Paul
Stanley, John
*Starlin, Jim
Steranko, Jim
Stevens, Dave
Texeira, Mark
Thibert, Art
Torres, Angelo
Toth, Alex
Turner, Michael
Tuska, George
Ward, Bill
Williamson, Al
Windsor-Smith, Barry
Woggon, Bill
Wolverton, Basil
Wood, Wallace
Wrightson, Bernie
Zeck, Mike

ARTISTS' FIRST WORK

Adams, Neal - (1 pg.) **Archie's Jokebook Mag.** #41, 9/59; (1st on Batman, cvr only) **Detective Comics** #370, 12/67; (1st Warren art) **Creepy** #14
Aparo, Jim - **Go-Go** #1, 6/66
Balent, Jim - **Sgt. Rock** #393, 10/84
Barks, Carl - (art only) **Donald Duck Four Color** #9, 8/42; (scripts only) **Large Feature Comic** #7, ca. Spring 1942
Broderick, Pat - (cover & art) **Planet of Vampires** #1, 2/75
Brunner, Frank - (fan club sketch) **Creepy** #10, 1965
Buckler, Rich - **Flash Gordon** #10, 11/67
Burnley, Jack - (cover & art) **NY World's Fair** nn, '40
Buscema, John - (1st at Marvel) **Strange Tales** #150, 11/66
Byrne, John - **Nightmare** #20, 8/74; (1st at DC) **Untold Legend of the Batman** #1, 7/80; (1st at Marvel) **Giant-Size Dracula** #5, 6/75
Capullo, Greg - (1st on X-Force) **X-Force Annual** #1, '92
Colan, Gene - **Wings Comics** #53, 1/45
Cole, Jack - (1 pg.) **Star Comics** #11, 4/38
Crandall, Reed - **Hit Comics** #10, 4/41
Davis, Jack - (cartoon) **Tip Top Comics** #32, 12/38
Ditko, Steve - (1st publ.) **Black Magic** V4#3, 11-12/53 (1st drawn story), **Fantastic Fears** #5, 1-2/54
Everett, Bill - **Amazing Mystery Funnies** V1#2, 9/38
Fine, Lou - (1st cvr) **Wonder Comics** #2, 6/39; **Jumbo Comics** #4, 12/38
Frazetta, Frank - **Tally-Ho Comics** nn, 12/44
Garney, Ron - **G. I. Joe, A Real American Hero** #110, 3/91
Giffen, Keith - (1 pg.) **Deadly Hands of Kung-Fu** #17, 11/75; (1st story) **Deadly Hands of Kung-Fu** #22, 4?/76; (tied w/Deadly Hands) **Amazing Adventures** #35, 3/76
Golden, Michael - **Marvel Classics Comics** #28, '77
Grell, Mike - **Adventure Comics** #435, 9-10/74
Hamner, Cully - **Green Lantern: Mosaic** #1, 6/92
Hughes, Adam - **Blood of Dracula** #1, 11/87
Ingels, Graham art at E.C. - **Saddle Justice** #4, Sum '48
Jurgens, Dan - **Warlord** #53, 1/82
Kaluta, Michael - **Teen Confessions** #59, 12/69
Kelly, Walt - **New Comics** #1, 12/35
Keown, Dale - **Samurai** #13, 1987; **Nth Man the Ultimate Ninja** #8, 1/90; (1st at Marvel); (1st on Hulk) **Incredible Hulk** #367, 3/90
Kieth, Sam - **Primer** #5, 11?/83
Kirby, Jack - **Jumbo Comics** #1, 9/38;
Kubert, Adam/Andy/Joe art - **Sgt. Rock** #422, 7/88
Kurtzman, Harvey - **Tip Top Comics** #36, 4/39; (1st at E.C.) **Lucky Fights It Through** nn, 1949
Larsen, Erik - **Megaton** #1, 11/83
Lee, Jae - **Marvel Comics Presents** #85, '91
Lee, Jim - (1st at Marvel) **Alpha Flight** #51, 10/87; (1st on X-Men) **X-Men** #248?, ?/89; (art on Punisher) **Punisher War Journal** #1, 11/88
Liefeld, Rob - (1st at DC) **Warlord** #131, 9/88; (1st at Marvel) **X-Factor** #40, 4?/89; (1st full story) **Megaton** #8, 8/87; (inside front cover only) **Megaton** #5, 6/86
Lim, Ron - (art on Silver Surfer) **Silver Surfer Ann.** #1, '88
Matsuda, Jeff - **Brigade** #0, 9/93
Mayer, Sheldon - **New Comics** #1, 12/35
McFarlane, Todd - **Coyote** #11, ?/85; (1st full story) **All Star Squadron** #47, 7/85; (1st on Hulk) **Incredible Hulk** #330, 4/87
Medina, Angel - (pin-up only) **Megaton** #3, 2/86
Mignola, Mike - **Marvel Fanfare** #15, 5/83
Miller, Frank - **Twilight Zone** #84, 6/78; (1st on Batman) **DC Special Series** #21, Spr '80; (1st on Daredevil) **Spect. Spider-Man** #27, 2/79
Newton, Don - **Many Ghosts of Dr. Graves** #45, 5/74
Perez, George - (1st at DC) **Flash** #289, 9/80; (2 pgs.); **Astonishing Tales** #25, 8/74
Portacio, Whilce - (1st on X-Men) **X-Men** #201, 1/86
Pulido, Brian - **Evil Ernie** #1, 12/91
Quesada, Joe - (1st on X-Factor) **X-Factor Ann.** #7, '92
Raboy, Mac - (1st cover for Fawcett) **Master Comics** #21, 12/41
Ramos, Humberto - (1st U.S. work) **Hardwire** #15, 6/94
Romita, John - **Strange Tales** #4, 12/51; (1st at Marvel) **Daredevil** #12, 1/66
Romita, John Jr. - (1st complete story) **Iron Man** #115, 10/78
Ross, Alex - **The Terminator: The Burning Earth** V2#1, 3/90
Shuster, Joe - (cover) **New Adv. Comics** #16, 6/37
Siegel & Shuster - **New Fun Comics** #6, 10/35
Simon & Kirby - **Blue Bolt** #2, 7/40
Simonson, Walter - **Magnus, Robot Fighter** #10, 5/65
Smith, Paul - (1 pg. pin-up) **King Conan** #7, 9/81; (1st full story) **Marvel Fanfare** #1, 3/82
Steranko, Jim - **Spyman** #1, Sep '66; (1st at Marvel) **Strange Tales** #151, 12/66
Swan, Curt - **Dick Cole** #1, 12-1/48-49
Talbot, Bryan - (1st U.S. work) **Hellblazer Annual** #1, Summer '89
Thomas, Roy - (scripts) **Son of Vulcan** #50, 1/66
Torres, Angelo - **Crime Mysteries** #13, 5/54
Turner, Mike - **Cyberforce Origins-Stryker**, 2/95
Weeks, Lee - **Tales of Terror** #5, 11/85
Weiss, Alan - (illo) **Blue Beetle** #5, 3-4/65
Williamson, Al - (1st at E.C.) **Tales From the Crypt** #31, 9/52; (text illos) **Famous Funnies** #169, 8/48
Windsor-Smith, Barry - **X-Men** #53, 2/69
Wood, Wally - (1st at E.C.) **Saddle Romances** #10, 1-2/50
Wrightson, Bernie - **House of Mystery** #179, 4/68; (1st at Marvel) **Chamber of Darkness** #7, 10/70; (1st cover) **Web of Horror** #3, 4/70; (fan club sketch) **Creepy** #9
Zeck, Mike - (illos) **Barney and Betty Rubble** #11, 2/75

The American Comic Book: 1842-2000

THE MARKETING OF A MEDIUM

by Arnold T. Blumberg

A very rare piece indeed, this represents one of the few existing examples of Palmer Cox's signature, as Cox always printed his name on his art. The character depicted in the upper left, "The Dude," represents a typical New Yorker and was Cox's favorite.

Starting with the 30th edition of ***The Overstreet Comic Book Price Guide****, we now list premium and giveaway comics (now collectively referred to as "promotional comics" in this edition) in their own section. This article first appeared in last year's edition and provides a brief introduction to this often overlooked corner of the comic book collecting universe. We hope that by setting promotional comics apart, we can draw attention to this fertile but as yet poorly represented area of comic book history.*

Everyone wants something for free. It's in our nature to look for the quick fix, the good deal, the complimentary gift. We long to hit the lottery and quit our job, to win the trip around the world, or find that pot of gold at the end of the proverbial rainbow. Collectors in particular are certainly built to appreciate the notion of the "free gift," since it not only means a new item to collect and enjoy, but no risk or obligation in order to acquire it.

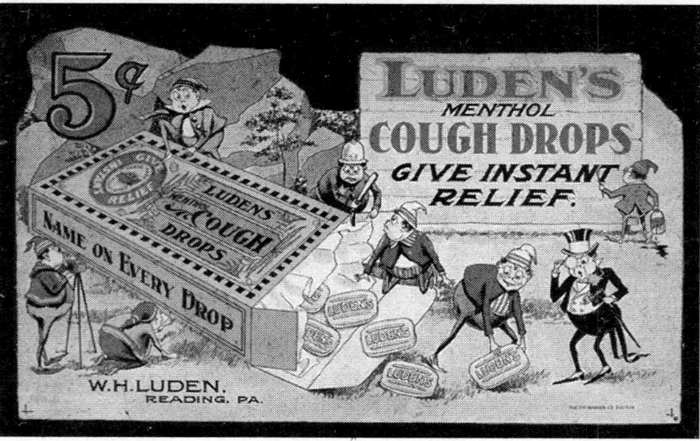

One of the best examples of the Brownies' proliferation into all kinds of merchandise. This rare Luden's Cough Drop ad (1890s) is the earliest known character die-cut sign.

Ah, but there's the rub, because things are not always what they seem, and "free gifts" usually come with a price. As the saying goes, "there's no such thing as a free lunch," so if it seems too good to be true, it probably is. This is the case even in the world of comics, where premiums and giveaways have a familiar agenda hidden behind the bright colors and fanciful stories. But where did it all begin?

EXTRA EXTRA

As we learn more about the early history of the comic book industry through continual investigation and the publishing of articles like those regularly featured in this book, we gain a much greater understanding of the financial and creative forces at work in shaping the medium, but perhaps one of the most intriguing and least recognized factors that influenced the dawn of comics is the concept of the premium or giveaway. (Note: Some of the historical information referenced in this article is derived from material also presented in Robert L. Beerbohm's introductory article to the Platinum Age and Modern Age sections.)

The birth of the comic book as we know it today is intimately connected with the development of the comic strip in American newspapers and their use as an advertising and marketing tool for staple products such as bread, milk, and cereal. From the very beginning, comic characters have played several roles in pop culture, entertaining the youth of the country while also (sometimes none too subtly) acting as hucksters for whatever corporation foots the bill. From important staples to frivolous material produced simply to make a buck, these products have utilized the comics medium to sell, sell, sell. And what better way to hook a prospective customer than to give them "something for nothing?"

Although comic characters were already being aggressively merchandised all around the world by the mid-1890s--as with, for example, Palmer Cox's **The Brownies**--the real starting point for the success of comics as a giveaway marketing mechanism can be traced to the introduction of **The Yellow Kid**, Richard Outcault's now legendary newspaper strip.

Newspaper publishers had already recognized that comic strips could boost circulation as well as please sponsors and advertisers by drawing more eyes to the page, so Sunday "supplements" were introduced to entice fans. Outcault's creation cemented the theory with proof of comic characters' marketing and merchandising power.

Soon after, Outcault (who had most likely been inspired by Cox's merchandising success with **The Brownies** in the first place) caught lightning in a bottle once more with **Buster Brown**, who has the distinction of being America's first nationally licensed comic strip character. Soon, comic strips proliferated throughout the nation's newspapers, offering companies the chance to license recognizable personas as their own personal pitchmen (or women or animals...). Comic character merchandise wasn't far behind, resulting in a boom of future collectibles now catalogued in volumes like **Hake's Price Guide to Character Toys**.

Comic books themselves were at the heart of this movement, and giveaway and premium collections of comic strips not only appealed to children and adults alike, but provided the impetus for the birth of the modern comic book format itself. It could be said that without the concept of the giveaway comic or the marketing push behind it, there would be no comic book industry as we have it today.

Thanks to men like Harry I. Wildenberg of Eastern Printing and companies like Gulf Oil (who liked Wildenberg's idea of an advertising-driven comics tabloid and produced **Gulf Comic Weekly**), the modern comic came into being around 1932-33.

What most people agree was the first modern format comic, **Funnies on Parade**, was released as a result of this growing merchandising movement, and sparked by the success of Wildenberg's and Gulf Oil's grand experiment. Through the auspices of Proctor & Gamble, **Funnies on Parade** was printed and given away in the Spring of 1933. A medium was born, and a marketing tool had completed its first step in the long road to maturity.

The impact of this new approach to advertising was not lost on the business world. Contrary to modern belief, comic books were hardly discounted by the adults of the time, at least not those who had the marketing savvy to recognize an opportunity--or a threat--when they saw one.

READ ALL ABOUT IT

In the April 1933 issue of **Fortune** magazine, an article titled "The Funny Papers" trumpeted the arrival of comics as a force to be reckoned with in the world of advertising and business, and what's more, a force to fear as well. At first providing a brief survey of the newspaper comic strip business (which for many of the magazine's readers must have seemed a foreign topic for serious discussion), the article goes on to examine the incredible financial draw of comics and their characters:

"Between 70 and 75 per cent {sic} of the readers of any newspaper follow its comic sections regularly...Even the advertiser has succumbed to the comic, and in 1932 spent well over $1,000,000 for comic-paper space."

"Comic Weekly is the comic section of seventeen Hearst Sunday papers...Advertisers who market their wares through balloon-speaking manikins {sic} may enjoy the proximity of Jiggs, Maggie, Barney Google, and other funny Hearst headliners."

Although the article continues to cast the notion of relying on comic strip material to sell product in a negative light, actually suggesting that advertisers who utilize comics are violating unspoken rules of "advertising decorum" and bringing themselves "down to the level" of comics (and since when have advertisers been stalwart preservers of good taste and high moral standards), there is no doubt that they are viewing comics in a new light. The comic characters have arrived by 1933...and they're ready to help sell your merchandise too.

THE MARCH OF WAR & BEYOND

Through the relentless currents of time, comic strips, books, and the characters that starred in them became more and more an intrinsic part of American culture. During the turmoil of the Great Depression and World War II, comic characters in print and celluloid form entertained while inform-

One of the earliest examples of the business world acknowledging the influence of the comic book on modern pop culture and American enterprise. FORTUNE Magazine, April 1933.

ing and selling at the same time, and premium and giveaway comics came well and truly into their own, pushing everything from loaves of bread to war bonds.

In the 1950s and '60s, there was a shift in focus as the power of giveaway and premium comics was applied to more altruistic endeavors than simply selling something. Comic book format pamphlets, fully illustrated and often inventively written, taught children about banking, money, the dangers of poison and other household products, and even chronicled moments in American history. The comic book as giveaway was now not only a marketing gimmick--it was a tool for educating as well.

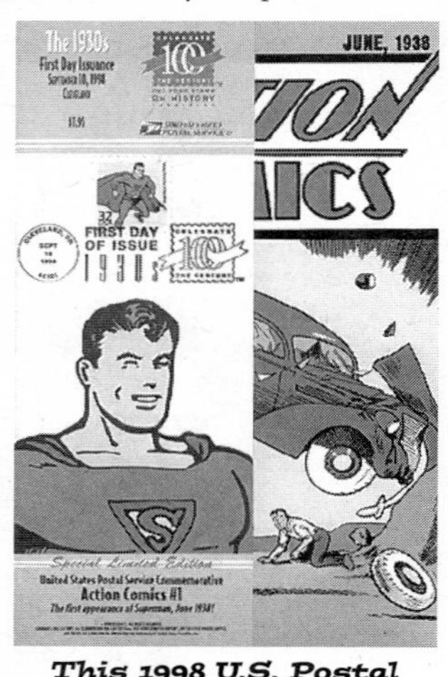

This 1998 U.S. Postal Service premium is one of the most recent examples of the continuing popularity of promotional comics.

The 1970s and '80s saw another boom in premium and giveaway comics. Every product imaginable seemed to have a licensing deal with a comic book character, usually one of the prominent flag bearers of the Big Two, Marvel or DC. Spider-Man fought bravely against the Beetle for the benefit of All Detergent; Captain America allied himself with the Campbell Kids; and Superman helped a class of computer students beat a disaster-conjuring foe at his own game with the help of Radio Shack Tandy computers.

Newspapers rediscovered the power of comics, not just with enlarged strip supplements but with actual comic books. Spider-Man, the Hulk, and others turned up as giveaway comic extras in various American newspapers (including Chicago and Dallas publications), while a whole series of public information comics like those produced decades earlier used superheroes to caution children about the dangers of smoking, drugs, and child abuse.

Comics also turned up in a plethora of other toy products as the 1980s introduced kids to the joy of electronic games and action figures. Supplementary comics provided "free" with action figure and video game packages told the backstory about the product, adding depth to the play experience while providing an extra incentive to buy. Comics became an intrinsic part of the Atari line of video cartridges, for example, eventually spawning its own full-blown newsstand series as well.

Today, premium comics continue to thrive and are still utilized as a valuable marketing and promotional tool. "Free" comics are still packaged with action figures and video games, and offered as mail-away premiums from a variety of product manufacturers. The comic industry itself has expanded its use of giveaway comics to self-promote as well, with "ashcan" and other giveaway editions turning up at conventions and comic shops to advertise upcoming series and special events. Many of these function as old-fashioned premiums, with a coupon or other response required from the reader to receive the comic.

As for the supplements and giveaways printed all those years ago, they have spawned a collectible fervor all their own, thanks to their atypical distribution and frequent rarity. For that and the desire to delve deeper into comics history, we hope that by focusing more directly on this genre, we can enhance our understanding of this vital component in the development and history of the modern comic book.

Whether you're a collector or not, we're all motivated by that desire to get something for nothing. For as long as consumers are enticed by the notion of the "free gift," promotional comics will remain a vital marketing component in many business models, but they will also continue to fight the stigma that has long been associated with the industry as a whole. "Respectable" sources like **Fortune** may have taken notice of the power of comic-related advertising 67 years ago, but after all this time comics still fight an uphill battle to establish some measure of dignity for the medium. It's a hard fight in an industry that still relies mostly on simplistic superheroes, but perhaps the higher visibility of promotional comics will eventually prove to be a deciding factor in that intellectual war.

See ya in the funny papers.

Adventures @ eBay #1 © eBay Inc.

Air Power
© Prudential Insurance Co.

Alice in Wonderland -Rexall
© H-B

GD2.0 FN6.0 NM9.4

ACTION COMICS
DC Comics: 1947 - 1998 (Giveaway)
1 (1976, 1983) paper cover w/10¢ price, 16pgs. in color; reprints complete Superman story from #1 ('38) 2.00 6.00 18.00
1 (1976) Safeguard Giveaway; paper cover w/"free", 16pgs. in color; reprints complete Superman story from #1 ('38) 2.30 7.00 20.00
1 (1987 Nestle Quik; 1988, 50¢) 1.00 3.00 7.50
1 (1998 U.S. Postal Service, $7.95) Reprints entire issue; extra outer half-cover contains First Day Issuance of 32¢ Superman stamp with Sept. 10, 1998 Cleveland, OH postmark 7.95
Theater (1947, 32 pgs., 6-1/2 x 8-1/4", nn)-Vigilante story based on Columbia Vigilante serial; no Superman-c or story 66.00 198.00 575.00

ADVENTURE COMICS
IGA: No date (early 1940s) (Paper-c, 32 pgs.)
Two diff. issues; Super-Mystery-r from 1941 26.00 79.00 210.00

ADVENTURE IN DISNEYLAND
Walt Disney Productions (Dist. by Richfield Oil): May, 1955 (Giveaway, soft-c., 16 pgs)
nn 10.00 30.00 80.00

ADVENTURES @ EBAY
eBay: 2000 (6 3/4" x 4 1/2", 16 pgs.)
1-Judd Winick-a/Rucka & Van Meter-s; intro to eBay comic buying 1.00

ADVENTURES OF G. I. JOE
1969 (3-1/4x7") (20 & 16 pgs.)
First Series: 1-Danger of the Depths. 2-Perilous Rescue. 3-Secret Mission to Spy Island. 4-Mysterious Explosion. 5-Fantastic Free Fall. 6-Eight Ropes of Danger. 7-Mouth of Doom. 8-Hidden Missile Discovery. 9-Space Walk Mystery. 10-Fight for Survival. 11-The Shark's Surprise.
Second Series: 2-Flying Space Adventure. 4-White Tiger Hunt. 7-Capture of the Pygmy Gorilla. 12-Secret of the Mummy's Tomb.
Third Series: Reprinted surviving titles of First Series. Fourth Series: 13-Adventure Team Headquarters. 14-Search For the Stolen Idol.
each.... 1.75 5.25 14.00

ADVENTURES OF KOOL-AID MAN
Marvel Comics: 1983; 1984 (Mail order giveaway)
1,2 2.00

ADVENTURES OF MARGARET O'BRIEN, THE
Bambury Fashions (Clothes): 1947 (20 pgs. in color, slick-c, regular size) (Premium)
nn "The Big City" movie adaptation (scarce) 20.00 60.00 160.00

ADVENTURES OF QUIK BUNNY
Nestle's Quik: 1984 (Giveaway, 32 pgs.)
nn-Spider-Man app. 1.50 4.50 12.00

ADVENTURES OF STUBBY, SANTA'S SMALLEST REINDEER, THE
W. T. Grant Co.: nd (early 1940s) (Giveaway, 12 pgs.)
nn 5.00 15.00 32.00

ADVENTURES OF THE BIG BOY
Timely Comics/Webs Adv. Corp./Illus. Features: 1956 - No. 466, 1996? (Giveaway) (East & West editions of early issues)
1-Everett-a 150.00 425.00 900.00
2-Everett-a 50.00 125.00 300.00
3-5: 4-Robot-c 25.00 75.00 140.00
6-10: 6-Sci/fic issue 10.00 30.00 110.00
11-20 5.00 15.00 55.00
21-30 3.00 10.00 30.00
31-50 2.00 6.00 18.00
51-100 1.10 3.30 9.00
101-150 2.40 7.00
151-240 6.00
241-265,267-269,271-300: 4.00
266-Superman x-over 2.50 7.50 25.00
270-TV's Buck Rogers-c/s 2.50 7.50 25.00
301-400 3.00
401-466 2.50
1-50 ('76-'84,Paragon Prod.) (...Shoney's Big Boy) 1.50
Summer, 1959 issue, large size 11.00 33.00 90.00
NOTE: No. 467 was completed but never published.

ADVENTURES WITH SANTA CLAUS
Promotional Publ. Co. (Murphy's Store): No date (early 50's) (9-3/4x 6-3/4", 24 pgs., giveaway, paper-c)
nn-Contains 8 pgs. ads 4.25 13.00 28.00
16 pg. version 4.25 13.00 28.00

AIR POWER (CBS TV & the U.S. Air Force Presents)
Prudential Insurance Co.: 1956 (5-1/4x7-1/4", 32 pgs., giveaway, soft-c)
nn-Toth-a? Based on 'You Are There' TV program by Walter Cronkite 11.00 33.00 80.00

ALICE IN BLUNDERLAND
Industrial Services: 1952 (Paper cover, 16 pgs. in color)
nn-Facts about big government waste and inefficiency 14.00 43.00 105.00

ALICE IN WONDERLAND
Western Printing Company/Whitman Publ. Co.: 1965; 1969; 1982
Meets Santa Claus(1950s), nd, 16 pgs. 4.65 14.00 28.00
Rexall Giveaway(1965, 16 pgs., 5x7-1/4) Western Printing (TV, Hanna-Barbera) 2.60 7.80 26.00
Wonder Bakery Giveaway(1969, 16 pgs, color, nn, nd) (Continental Baking Company) 2.50 7.50 25.00
1-(Whitman; 1982)-r/4-Color #331 4.00

ALICE IN WONDERLAND MEETS SANTA
No publisher: nd (6-5/8x9-11/16", 16 pgs., giveaway, paper-c)
nn 11.00 33.00 75.00

ALL ABOARD, MR. LINCOLN
Assoc. of American Railroads: Jan, 1959 (16 pgs.)
nn-Abraham Lincoln and the Railroads 6.00 18.00 42.00

ALL NEW COMICS
Harvey Comics: Oct, 1993 (Giveaway, no cover price, 16 pgs.)(Hanna-Barbera)
1-Flintstones, Scooby Doo, Jetsons, Yogi Bear & Wacky Races previews for upcoming Harvey's new Hanna-Barbera line-up 3.00
NOTE: Material previewed in Harvey giveaway was eventually published by Archie.

AMAZING SPIDER-MAN, THE
Marvel Comics Group
Aim Toothpaste Giveaway (36 pgs., reg. size)-1 pg. origin recap; Green Goblin-c/story 1.25 3.75 10.00
Aim Toothpaste Giveaway (16 pgs., reg. size)-Dr. Octopus app. 1.50 4.50 12.00
All Detergent Giveaway (1979, 36 pgs.), nn-Origin-r 2.00 6.00 15.00
Giveaway-Acme & Dingo Children's Boots (1980)-Spider-Woman app. 2.00 6.00 15.00
Amazing Spider-Man nn (1990, 6-1/8x9", 28 pgs.)-Shan-Lon giveaway; r/ Amazing Spider-Man #303 w/McFarlane-c/a 1.10 3.30 9.00
...& Power Pack (1984, nn)(Nat'l Committee for Prevention of Child Abuse (two versions, mail offer & store giveaway)-Mooney-a; Byrne-c
Mail offer 1.25 3.75 10.00
Store giveaway 3.00
...& The Hulk (Special Edition)(6/8/80; 20 pgs.)-Supplement to Chicago Tribune (giveaway) 2.00 6.00 15.00
...& The Incredible Hulk (1981, 1982; 36 pgs.)-Sanger Harris or May D&F supplement to Dallas Times, Dallas Herald, Denver Post, Kansas City Star, Tulsa World; Foley's supplement to Houston Chronicle (1982, 16 pgs.)-"Great Rodeo Robbery"; The Jones Store-giveaway (1983, 16 pgs.) 2.25 6.75 18.00
...and the New Mutants Featuring Skids nn (National Committee for Prevention of Child Abuse/K-Mart giveaway)-Williams-c(i) 5.00
...Captain America, The Incredible Hulk, & Spider-Woman (1981) (7-11 Stores giveaway; 36 pgs.) 1.50 4.50 12.00
...: Danger in Dallas (1983) (Supplement to Dallas Times Herald) giveaway 1.50 4.50 12.00
...: Danger in Denver (1983) (Supplement to Denver Post) giveaway for May D&F stores 1.50 4.50 12.00

Archie Comics -Fairmont Potato Chip © AP

Atari Force #1 © Atari

Back to the Future Special © Universal Studios

..., Fire-Star, And Ice-Man at the Dallas Ballet Nutcracker (1983; supplement to Dallas Times Herald)-Mooney-p 1.50 4.50 12.00
Giveaway-Esquire Magazine (2/69)-Miniature-Still attached 10.50 31.50 115.00
Giveaway-Eye Magazine (2/69)-Miniature-Still attached 10.50 31.50 115.00
..., Storm & Powerman (1982; 20 pgs.)(American Cancer Society) giveaway 2.40 6.00
...Vs. The Hulk (Special Edition; 1979, 20 pgs.)(Supplement to Columbus Dispatch)-Giveaway 1.50 4.50 15.00
...Vs. The Prodigy (Giveaway, 16 pgs. in color (1976, 5x6-1/2")-Sex education; (1 million printed; 35-50¢) 2.50 7.50 20.00

AMERICA MENACED!
Vital Publications: 1950 (Paper-c)

nn-Anti-communism 40.00 120.00 260.00

AMERICAN COMICS
Theatre Giveaways (Liberty Theatre, Grand Rapids, Mich. known): 1940's

Many possible combinations. "Golden Age" superhero comics with new cover added and given away at theaters. Following known: Superman #59, Capt. Marvel #20, Capt. Marvel Jr. #5, Action #33, Classics Comics #8, Whiz #39. Value would vary with book and should be 70-80 percent of the original.

ANDY HARDY COMICS
Western Printing Co.:
...& the New Automatic Gas Clothes Dryer (1952, 5x7-1/4", 16 pgs.) Bendix Giveaway (soft-c) 7.50 22.50 45.00

ANIMANIACS EMERGENCY WORLD
DC Comics: 1995

nn-American Red Cross 2.00

APACHE HUNTER
Creative Pictorials: 1954 (18 pgs. in color) (promo copy) (saddle stitched)

nn-Severin, Heath stories 17.00 51.00 130.00

AQUATEERS MEET THE SUPER FRIENDS
DC Comics: 1979

nn-American Red Cross 2.00

ARCHIE AND HIS GANG (Zeta Beta Tau Presents...)
Archie Publications: Dec. 1950 (St. Louis National Convention giveaway)

nn-Contains new cover stapled over Archie Comics #47 (11-12/50) on inside; produced for Zeta Beta Tau 15.00 45.00 120.00

ARCHIE COMICS
Archie Publications
...And His Friends Help Raise Literacy Awareness In Mississippi nn (3/94)-Giveaway 4.00
...And the History of Electronics nn (5/90, 36 pgs.)-Radio Shack giveaway; Howard Bender-c/a 5.00
Fairmont Potato Chips Giveaway-Mini comics 1970 (8 issues-nn's., 8 pgs. each) 2.50 7.50 22.00
Fairmont Potato Chips Giveaway-Mini comics 1970 (6 issues-nn's.,6 7/8" x 2 1/4" 8 pgs. each) 2.50 7.50 20.00
Fairmont Potato Chips Giveaway-Mini comics 1971 (4 issues-nn's.,6 7/8" x 5", 8 pgs. each) 2.50 7.50 20.00
Official Boy Scout Outfitter (1946, 9-1/2x6-1/2, 16 pgs.)-B. R. Baker Co. (Scarce) 47.00 141.00 425.00
Shoe Store giveaway (1948, Feb?) 17.00 51.00 135.00
...'s Weird Mysteries (9/99, 8 1/2"x 5 1/2") Diamond Comic Dist. 1.00

ARCHIE SHOE-STORE GIVEAWAY
Archie Publications: 1944-49 (12-15 pgs. of games, puzzles, stories like Superman-Tim books, No nos. - came out monthly)

(1944-47)-issues 13.00 33.00 105.00
2/48-Peggy Lee photo-c 11.00 33.00 90.00
3/48-Marylee Robb photo-c 10.50 32.00 85.00
4/48-Gloria De Haven photo-c 11.00 33.00 90.00
5/48,6/48,7/48 10.50 32.00 85.00
8/48-Story on Shirley Temple 12.50 37.50 100.00
10/48-Archie as Wolf on cover 12.50 37.50 100.00
5/49-Kathleen Hughes photo-c 9.30 28.00 65.00
7/49 9.30 28.00 65.00
8/49-Archie photo-c from radio show 15.00 45.00 120.0
10/49-Gloria Mann photo-c from radio show 11.00 33.00 90.0
11/49,12/49 8.65 26.00 60.0

ARCHIE'S JOKE BOOK MAGAZINE (See Joke Book ...)
Archie Publications

Drug Store Giveaway (No. 39 w/new-c) 4.30 13.00 26.0

ARCHIE'S TEN ISSUE COLLECTOR'S SET (Title inside of cover only)
Archie Publications: June, 1997 - No. 10, June, 1997 ($1.50, 20 pgs.)

1-10: 1,7-Archie. 2,8-Betty & Veronica. 3,9-Veronica. 4-Betty. 5-World of Arch 6-Jughead. 10-Archie and Friends 2.0

ASTRO COMICS
American Airlines (Harvey): 1968 - 1979 (Giveaway)

Reprints of Harvey comics. 1968-Hot Stuff. 1969-Casper, Spooky, Hot Stuff, Stumbo the Giant, Little Audrey, Little Lotta, & Richie Rich reprints.
1970-r/Richie Rich #97 (all scarce) 2.30 7.00 20.0
1973-r/Richie Rich #122. 1975-Wendy. 1975-Richie Rich & Casper. 1977-r/Richie Rich & Casper #20. 1978-r/Richie Rich & Casper #25. 1979-r/Richie Rich & Casper #30 (scarce) 2.30 7.00 20.0

ATARI FORCE
DC Comics: 1982 - No. 5, 1983

1-3 (1982, 5X7", 52 pgs.)-Given away with Atari games 5.0
4,5 (1982-1983, 52 pgs.)-Given away with Atari games (scarcer) 1.00 3.00 8.0

AURORA COMIC SCENES INSTRUCTION BOOKLET
Aurora Plastics Co.: 1974 (6-1/4x9-3/4," 8 pgs., slick paper) (Included with superhero model kits)

181-140-Tarzan; Neal Adams-a 5.00 10.00 28.0
182-140-Spider-Man. 7.00 20.00 38.0
183-140-Tonto(Gil Kane art). 184-140-Hulk. 185-140-Superman. 186-140-Superboy. 187-140-Batman. 188-140-The Lone Ranger(1974-by Gil Kane). 192-140-Captain America(1975). 193-140-Robin 3.00 8.00 24.0

BACK TO THE FUTURE
Harvey Comics
Special nn (1991, 20 pgs.)-Brunner-c; given away at Universal Studios in Florida 3.0

BALTIMORE COLTS
American Visuals Corp.: 1950 (Giveaway)

nn-Eisner-c 47.00 141.00 400.0

BAMBI (Disney)
K. K. Publications (Giveaways): 1941, 1942

1941-Horlick's Malted Milk & various toy stores; text & pictures; most copies mailed out with store stickers on-c 50.00 125.00 260.0
1942-Same as 4-Color #12, but no price (Same as '41 issue?) (Scarce) 75.00 200.00 420.0

BATMAN
DC Comics: 1966 - Present

Act II Popcorn mini-comic(1998) 2.0
Batman #121 Toys R Us edition (1997) r/1st Mr. Freeze 2.0
Batman #362 Mervyn's edition (1989) 2.0
Batman Adventures #25 Best Wesern edition (1997) 2.0
Batman and Other DC Classics 1 (1989, giveaway)-DC Comics/Diamond Comic Distributors; Batman origin-r/Batman #47, Camelot 3000-r by Bolland, Justice League-r('87), New Teen Titans-r by Perez. 2.0
Batman Beyond Six Flags edition 5.0
Batman: Canadian Multiculturalism Custom (1992) 2.0
Batman Claritan edition (1999) 2.0

Kellogg's Poptarts comics (1966, Set of 6, 16 pgs.); All were folded and placed i Poptarts boxes. Infantino art on Catwoman and Joker issues.
"The Man in the Iron Mask", "The Penguin's Fowl Play", "The Joker's Happy Victims", "The Catwoman's Catnapping Caper", "The Mad Hatter's Hat Crimes", "The Case of the Batman II" each.... 3.20 9.60 35.0

Mask of the Phantasm (1993) Mini-comic released w/video 5.0
Pizza Hut giveaway (12/77)-exact-r of #122,123; Joker-c/story 1.00 3.00 8.0
Prell Shampoo giveaway (1966, 16 pgs.)- "The Joker's Practical Jokes"

Blondie Comics -NY State Mental Health 1950 © HARV

Bob & Betty & Santa's Wishing Whistle © Sears

GD2.0 FN6.0 NM9.4

(6-7/8x3-3/8") 3.20 9.60 35.00
Revell in pack (1995) 2.00

BATMAN RECORD COMIC
National Periodical Publications: 1966 (one-shot)

1-With record (still sealed) 13.50 40.00 150.00
Comic only 7.00 21.00 75.00

BEETLE BAILEY
Charlton Comics: 1969-1970 (Giveaways)

Bold Detergent ('69)-same as regular issue (#67) 1.25 3.75 10.00
Cerebral Palsy Assn. V2#71('69) - V2#73(#1,1/70) 1.25 3.75 10.00
Red Cross (1969, 5x7", 16 pgs., paper-c) 1.25 3.75 10.00

BEST WESTERN GIVEAWAY
DC Comics: 1999

nn-Best Western hotels 2.00

BIG JIM'S P.A.C.K.
Mattel, Inc. (Marvel Comics): No date (1975) (16 pgs.)

nn-Giveaway with Big Jim doll; Buscema/Sinnott-c/a 2.50 7.50 25.00

"BILL AND TED'S EXCELLENT ADVENTURE" MOVIE ADAPTATION
DC Comics: 1989 (No cover price)

nn-Torres-a 2.00

BLACK GOLD
Esso Service Station (Giveaway): 1945? (8 pgs. in color)

nn-Reprints from True Comics 6.00 18.00 35.00

BLAZING FOREST, THE (See Forest Fire and Smokey The Bear)
Western Printing: 1962 (20 pgs., 5x7", slick-c)

nn-Smokey The Bear fire prevention 1.50 4.50 12.00

BLESSED PIUS X
Catechetical Guild (Giveaway): No date (Text/comics, 32 pgs., paper-c)

nn 4.15 12.50 25.00

BLIND JUSTICE (Also see Batman: Blind Justice)
DC Comics/Diamond Comic Distributors: 1989 (Giveaway, squarebound)

nn-Contains Detective #598-600 by Batman movie writer Sam Hamm, w/covers; published same time as originals? 2.40 6.00

BLONDIE COMICS
Harvey Publications: 1950-1964

1950 Giveaway 5.35 16.00 35.00
1962,1964 Giveaway 2.00 6.00 16.00
N. Y. State Dept. of Mental Hygiene Giveaway-(1950) Regular size; 16 pgs.; no # 2.50 7.50 24.00
N. Y. State Dept. of Mental Hygiene Giveaway-(1956) Regular size; 16 pgs.; no # 2.00 6.00 18.00
N. Y. State Dept. of Mental Hygiene Giveaway-(1961) Regular size; 16 pgs.; no # 2.00 6.00 16.00

BLOOD IS THE HARVEST
Catechetical Guild: 1950 (32 pgs., paper-c)

(Scarce)-Anti-communism (13 known copies) 106.00 320.00 900.00
Black & white version (5 known copies), saddle stitched 40.00 120.00 325.00
Untrimmed version (only one known copy); estimated value-$600

NOTE: *In 1979 nine copies of the color version surfaced from the old Guild's files plus the five black & white copies.*

BLUE BIRD CHILDREN'S MAGAZINE, THE
Graphic Information Service: V1#2, 1957 - No. 10 1958 (16 pgs., soft-c, regular size)

V1#2-10: Pat, Pete & Blue Bird app. 5.00

BLUE BIRD COMICS
Various Shoe Stores/Charlton Comics: Late 1940's - 1964 (Giveaway)

nn(1947-50)(36 pgs.)-Several issues; Human Torch, Sub-Mariner app. in some 20.00 60.00 140.00
1959-Li'l Genius, Timmy the Timid Ghost, Wild Bill Hickok (All #1) 2.40 7.35 22.00
1959-(6 titles; all #2) Black Fury #1,4,5, Freddy #4, Li'l Genius, Timmy the Timid Ghost #4, Masked Raider #4, Wild Bill Hickok (Charlton) 2.40 7.35 22.00
1959-(#5) Masked Raider #21 2.40 7.35 22.00
1960-(6 titles)(All #4) Black Fury #8,9, Masked Raider, Freddy #8,9, Timmy the Timid Ghost #9, Li'l Genius #7,9 (Charlt.) 2.00 6.00 18.00
1961,1962-(All #10's) Atomic Mouse #12,13,16, Black Fury #11,12, Freddy, Li'l Genius, Masked Raider, Six Gun Heroes, Texas Rangers in Action, Timmy the Ghost, Wild Bill Hickok, Wyatt Earp #3,11-13,16-18 (Charlton) 2.00 6.00 18.00
1963-Texas Rangers #17 (Charlton) 1.50 4.50 12.00
1964-Mysteries of Unexplored Worlds #18, Teenage Hotrodders #18, War Heroes #18 (Charlton) 1.50 4.50 12.00
1965-War Heroes #18 1.10 3.30 9.00

NOTE: *More than one issue of each character could have been published each year. Numbering is sporadic.*

BOB & BETTY & SANTA'S WISHING WHISTLE
Sears Roebuck & Co.: 1941 (Christmas giveaway, 12 pgs.)

nn 11.00 33.00 80.00

BOBBY BENSON'S B-BAR-B RIDERS (Radio)
Magazine Enterprises/AC Comics

...in the Tunnel of Gold-(1936, 5-1/4x8"; 100 pgs.) Radio giveaway by Hecker-H.O. Company(H.O. Oats); contains 22 color pgs. of comics, rest in novel form 10.00 30.00 65.00
...And The Lost Herd-same as above 10.00 30.00 65.00

BOBBY SHELBY COMICS
Shelby Cycle Co./Harvey Publications: 1949

nn 4.00 11.00 22.00

BOYS' RANCH
Harvey Publications: 1951

Shoe Store Giveaway #5,6 (Identical to regular issues except Simon & Kirby centerfold replaced with ad) 25.00 75.00 150.00

BOZO THE CLOWN (TV)
Dell Publishing Co.: 1961

Giveaway-1961, 16 pgs., 3-1/2x7-1/4", Apsco Products 4.10 12.30 45.00

BRER RABBIT IN "ICE CREAM FOR THE PARTY"
American Dairy Association: 1955 (5x7-1/4", 16 pgs., soft-c) (Walt Disney) (Premium)

nn-(Scarce) 50.00 150.00 350.00

BUCK ROGERS (In the 25th Century)
Kelloggs Corn Flakes Giveaway: 1933 (6x8", 36 pgs)

370A-By Phil Nowlan & Dick Calkins; 1st Buck Rogers radio premium & 1st app. in comics (tells origin) (Reissued in 1995) 100.00 350.00 550.00
with envelope 175.00 450.00 650.00

BUGS BUNNY (Puffed Rice Giveaway)
Quaker Cereals: 1949 (32 pgs. each, 3-1/8x6-7/8")

A1-Traps the Counterfeiters, A2-Aboard Mystery Submarine, A3- Rocket to the Moon, A4-Lion Tamer, A5-Rescues the Beautiful Princess, B1-Buried Treasure, B2-Outwits the Smugglers, B3-Joins the Marines, B4-Meets the Dwarf Ghost, B5-Finds Aladdin's Lamp, C1-Lost in the Frozen North, C2-Secret Agent, C3-Captured by Cannibals, C4-Fights the Man from Mars, C5-And the Haunted Cave

each.... 8.35 25.00 55.00
Mailing Envelope (has illo of Bugs on front)(Each envelope designates what set it contains, A,B or C on front) 8.35 25.00 55.00

BUGS BUNNY (3-D)
Cheerios Giveaway: 1953 (Pocket size) (15 titles)

each.... 10.00 30.00 65.00
Mailing Envelope (has bugs drawn on front) 10.00 30.00 65.00

BUGS BUNNY POSTAL COMIC
DC Comics: 1997 (64 pgs., 7.5" x 5")

nn-Mail Fan; Daffy Duck app. 4.00

BULLETMAN
Fawcett Publications

Well Known Comics (1942)-Paper-c, glued binding; printed in red (Bestmaid/Samuel Lowe giveaway) 20.00 65.00 140.00

BULLS-EYE (Cody of The Pony Express No. 8 on)

Buster Brown Comics #8 © Brown Shoe Co.

Captain America & the Campbell Kids © MAR

Captain Marvel and the Lts. of Safety #1 © FAW

Charlton: 1955

Great Scott Shoe Store giveaway-Reprints #2 with new cover 20.00 75.00 160.00

BUSTER BROWN COMICS (Radio)(Also see My Dog Tige in Promotional sec.)
Brown Shoe Co: 1945 - No. 43, 1959 (No. 5: paper-c)

	GD2.0	FN6.0	NM9.4
nn, nd (#1,scarce)-Featuring Smilin' Ed McConnell & the Buster Brown gang "Midnight" the cat, "Squeaky" the mouse & "Froggy" the Gremlin; covers mention diff. shoe stores. Contains adventure stories	62.00	187.00	560.00
2	19.00	58.00	150.00
3,5-10	10.00	30.00	80.00
4 (Rare)-Low print run due to paper shortage	16.00	48.00	125.00
11-20	7.50	22.50	50.00
21-24,26-28	5.35	16.00	35.00
25,33-37,40,41-Crandall-a in all	10.00	30.00	75.00
29-32-"Interplanetary Police Vs. the Space Siren" by Crandall (pencils only #29)	10.00	30.00	75.00
38,39,42,43	5.35	16.00	35.00

BUSTER BROWN COMICS (Radio)
Brown Shoe Co: 1950s

...Goes to Mars (2/58-Western Printing), slick-c, 20 pgs., reg. size 11.00 33.00 85.00
...In "Buster Makes the Team!" (1959-Custom Comics) 7.50 22.50 50.00
...In The Jet Age ('50s), slick-c, 20 pgs., 5x7-1/4" 10.00 30.00 80.00
...Of the Safety Patrol ('60-Custom Comics) 3.00 9.00 32.00
...Out of This World ('59-Custom Comics) 7.35 22.00 50.00
...Safety Coloring Book ('58, 16 pgs.)-Slick paper 6.70 20.00 45.00

CALL FROM CHRIST
Catechetical Educational Society: 1952 (Giveaway, 36 pgs.)

nn 4.00 11.00 22.00

CANCELLED COMIC CAVALCADE
DC Comics, Inc.: Summer, 1978 - No. 2, Fall, 1978 (8-1/2x11", B&W)
(Xeroxed pgs. on one side only w/blue cover and taped spine)

1-(412 pgs.) Contains xeroxed copies of art for: Black Lightning #12, cover to #13; Claw #13, 14; The Deserter #1; Doorway to Nightmare #6; Firestorm #6; The Green Team #2,3.
2-(532 pgs.) Contains xeroxed copies of art for: Kamandi #60 (including Omac), #61; Prez #5; Shade #9 (including The Odd Man); Showcase #105 (Deadman), 106 (The Creeper); Secret Society of Super Villains #16 & 17; The Vixen #1; and covers to Army at War #2, Battle Classics #3, Demand Classics #1 & 2, Dynamic Classics #3, Mr. Miracle #26, Ragman #6, Weird Mystery #25 & 26, & Western Classics #1 & 2. (Rare)
(One set sold in 1989 for $1,200.00)

NOTE: *In June, 1978, DC cancelled several of their titles. For copyright purposes, the unpublished original art for these titles was xeroxed, bound in the above books, published and distributed. Only 35 copies were made.*

CAP'N CRUNCH COMICS (See Quaker Oats)
Quaker Oats Co.: 1963; 1965 (16 pgs.; miniature giveaways; 2-1/2x6-1/2")

(1963 titles)- "The Picture Pirates", "The Fountain of Youth", "I'm Dreaming of a Wide Isthmus". (1965 titles)- "Bewitched, Betwitched, & Betweaked", "Seadog Meets the Witch Doctor", "A Witch in Time" 9.00 27.00 55.00

CAPTAIN ACTION (Toy)
National Periodical Publications

...& Action Boy('67)-Ideal Toy Co. giveaway (1st app. Captain Action) 25.00 75.00 150.00

CAPTAIN AMERICA
Marvel Comics Group

...& The Campbell Kids (1980, 36pg. giveaway, Campbell's Soup/U.S. Dept. of Energy) 1.25 3.75 10.00
...Goes To War Against Drugs(1990, no #, giveaway)-Distributed to direct sales shops; 2nd printing exists 5.00
...Meets The Asthma Monster (1987, no #, giveaway, Your Physician and Glaxo, Inc.) 2.40 6.00
...Vs. Asthma Monster (1990, no #, giveaway, Your Physician & Allen & Hanbury's) 5.00

CAPTAIN AMERICA COMICS
Timely/Marvel Comics: 1954

Shoestore Giveaway #77 56.00 170.00 500.00

CAPTAIN ATOM
Nationwide Publishers

...- Secret of the Columbian Jungle (16 pgs. in color, paper-c, 3-3/4x5-1/8")- Fireside Marshmallow giveaway 4.15 12.50 25.00

CAPTAIN BEN DIX IN ACTION WITH THE INVISIBLE CREW
Bendix Aviation Corp.: 1940s (nd), 20 pgs, 8-1/4"x11", heavy paper

nn-WWII bomber-c; Jap app. 5.00 15.00 30.00

CAPTAIN FORTUNE PRESENTS
Vital Publications: 1955 - 1959 (Giveaway, 3-1/4x6-7/8", 16 pgs.)

"Davy Crockett in Episodes of the Creek War", "Davy Crockett at the Alamo", "In Sherwood Forest Tells Strange Tales of Robin Hood" ('57), "Meets Bolivar the Liberator" ('59), "Tells How Buffalo Bill Fights the Dog Soldiers" ('57), "Young Davy Crockett" 2.40 6.00 12.00

CAPTAIN GALLANT (...of the Foreign Legion) (TV)
Charlton Comics

Heinz Foods Premium (#1?)(1955; regular size)-U.S. Pictorial; contains Buster Crabbe photos; Don Heck-a 1.00 3.00 8.00

CAPTAIN MARVEL ADVENTURES
Fawcett Publications

Bond Bread Giveaways-(24 pgs.; pocket size-7-1/4x3-1/2"; paper cover): "...& the Stolen City" ('48), "The Boy Who Never Heard of Capt. Marvel", "Meets the Weatherman" -(1950)(reprint) each.... 37.00 110.00 220.00
...Well Known Comics (1944; 12 pgs.; 8-1/2x10-1/2")-printed in red & in blue; soft-c; glued binding)-Bestmaid/Samuel Lowe Co. giveaway 25.00 75.00 165.00

CAPTAIN MARVEL ADVENTURES
Fawcett Publications (Wheaties Giveaway): 1945 (6x8", full color, paper-c)

nn- "Captain Marvel & the Threads of Life" plus 2 other stories (32 pgs.) 79.00 250.00 550.00

NOTE: *All copies were taped at each corner to a box of Wheaties and are never found in Fine or Mint condition. Prices listed for each grade include tape.*

CAPTAIN MARVEL AND THE LTS. OF SAFETY
Ebasco Services/Fawcett Publications: 1950 - 1951 (3 issues - no No.'s)

	GD2.0	FN6.0	VF8.0
nn (#1) "Danger Flies a Kite" ('50, scarce),	233.00	700.00	1400.00
nn (#2)"Danger Takes to Climbing" ('50),	183.00	550.00	1000.00
nn (#3)"Danger Smashes Street Lights" ('51)	183.00	550.00	1000.00

CAPTAIN MARVEL, JR.
Fawcett Publications: (1944; 12 pgs.; 8-1/2x10-1/2")

	GD2.0	FN6.0	NM9.4
...Well Known Comics (Printed in blue; paper-c, glued binding)-Bestmaid/Samuel Lowe Co. giveaway	12.50	37.50	100.00

CARDINAL MINDSZENTY (The Truth Behind the Trial of...)
Catechetical Guild Education Society: 1949 (24 pgs., paper cover)

nn-Anti-communism 6.70 20.00 45.00
Press Proof-(Very Rare)-(Full color, 7-1/2x11-3/4", untrimmed) Only two known copies 150.00
Preview Copy (B&W, stapled), 18 pgs.; contains first 13 pgs. of Cardinal Mindszenty and was sent out as an advance promotion. Only one known copy 150.00 - 200.00

NOTE: *Regular edition also printed in French. There was also a movie released in 1949 called "Guilty of Treason" which is a fact-based account of the trial and imprisonment of Cardinal Mindszenty by the Communist regime in Hungary.*

CARNIVAL OF COMICS
Fleet-Air Shoes: 1954 (Giveaway)

nn-Contains a comic bound with new cover; several combinations possible; Charlton's Eh! known 3.60 9.00 18.00

CARTOON NETWORK
DC Comics: 1997 (Giveaway)

nn-reprints Cow and Chicken, Scooby-Doo, & Flintstones stories 2.00

CARVEL COMICS (Amazing Advs. of Capt. Carvel)
Carvel Corp. (Ice Cream): 1975 - No. 5, 1976 (25¢; #3-5: 35¢) (#4,5: 3-1/4x5")

Casper's Dental Health Activity Book © Paramount

Cheerios Premium - Donald Duck & the Pirates © WDC

	GD2.0	FN6.0	NM9.4
-3		2.40	6.00
,5(1976)-Baseball theme	1.25	3.75	10.00

ASE OF THE WASTED WATER, THE
heem Water Heating: 1972? (Giveaway)

-Neal Adams-a	3.65	11.00	40.00

ASPER SPECIAL
rget Stores (Harvey): nd (Dec, 1990) (Giveaway with $1.00 cover)

ree issues-Given away with Casper video			4.00

ASPER, THE FRIENDLY GHOST (Paramount Picture Star…)(2nd Series)
rvey Publications
nerican Dental Association (Giveaways):

s Dental Health Activity Book-1977	1.00	2.80	7.00
Presents Space Age Dentistry-1972	1.10	3.30	9.00
His Den, & Their Dentist Fight the Tooth Demons-1974	1.10	3.30	9.00

LEBRATE THE CENTURY SUPERHEROES STAMP ALBUM
Comics: 1998 - No. 5, 2000 (32 pgs.)

-5: Historical stories hosted by DC heroes			3.00

NTIPEDE
Comics: 1983

Based on Atari video game			2.00

NTURY OF COMICS
stern Color Printing Co.: 1933 (100 pgs.) (Probably the 3rd comic book)
ight by Wheatena, Milk-O-Malt, John Wanamaker, Kinney Shoe Stores, & others to be used as premiums and radio giveaways. No publisher listed.

	GD2.0	FN6.0	VF8.2
Mutt & Jeff, Joe Palooka, etc. reprints	3670.00	11,000.00	22,000.00

EERIOS PREMIUMS (Disney)
lt Disney Productions: 1947 (16 titles, pocket size, 32 pgs.)

	GD2.0	FN6.0	NM9.4
ling Envelope for each set "W,X,Y & Z" (has Mickey illo on front)(each envelope designates the set it contains on the front)	10.00	30.00	65.00
et "W"			
-Donald Duck & the Pirates	10.00	30.00	65.00
-Bucky Bug & the Cannibal King	4.65	14.00	28.00
Pluto Joins the F.B.I.	4.65	14.00	28.00
-Mickey Mouse & the Haunted House	5.35	16.00	36.00
et "X"			
Donald Duck, Counter Spy	10.00	30.00	60.00
Goofy Lost in the Desert	4.65	14.00	28.00
Br'er Rabbit Outwits Br'er Fox	4.65	14.00	28.00
Mickey Mouse at the Rodeo	5.35	16.00	36.00
et "Y"			
Donald Duck's Atom Bomb by Carl Barks. Disney has banned reprinting this ook	90.00	270.00	800.00
Br'er Rabbit's Secret	4.65	14.00	28.00
Dumbo & the Circus Mystery	5.00	15.00	30.00
lickey Mouse Meets the Wizard	5.35	16.00	36.00
et "Z"			
Donald Duck Pilots a Jet Plane (not by Barks)	10.00	30.00	65.00
Pluto Turns Sleuth Hound	4.65	14.00	28.00
he Seven Dwarfs & the Enchanted Mtn.	5.35	16.00	36.00
lickey Mouse's Secret Room	5.35	16.00	36.00

ERIOS 3-D GIVEAWAYS (Disney)
Disney Productions: 1954 (24 titles, pocket size) (Glasses came in lopes)

ses only…	6.40	19.25	45.00
ng Envelope (no art on front)	10.00	30.00	65.00
(Set 1)			
onald Duck & Uncle Scrooge, the Firefighters	10.00	30.00	65.00
lickey Mouse & Goofy, Pirate Plunder	10.00	30.00	60.00
onald Duck's Nephews, the Fabulous Inventors	10.00	30.00	65.00
lickey Mouse, Secret of the Ming Vase	10.00	30.00	60.00
onald Duck with Huey, Dewey, & Louie; …the Seafarers (title on 2nd age)	10.00	30.00	65.00
lickey Mouse, Moaning Mountain	10.00	30.00	60.00
7-Donald Duck, Apache Gold	10.00	30.00	65.00
8-Mickey Mouse, Flight to Nowhere	10.00	30.00	60.00
(Set 2)			
1-Donald Duck, Treasure of Timbuktu	10.00	30.00	65.00
2-Mickey Mouse & Pluto, Operation China	10.00	30.00	60.00
3-Donald Duck in the Magic Cows	10.00	30.00	65.00
4-Mickey Mouse & Goofy, Kid Kokonut	10.00	30.00	60.00
5-Donald Duck, Mystery Ship	10.00	30.00	65.00
6-Mickey Mouse, Phantom Sheriff	10.00	30.00	60.00
7-Donald Duck, Circus Adventures	10.00	30.00	65.00
8-Mickey Mouse, Arctic Explorers	10.00	30.00	60.00
(Set 3)			
1-Donald Duck & Witch Hazel	10.00	30.00	65.00
2-Mickey Mouse in Darkest Africa	10.00	30.00	60.00
3-Donald Duck & Uncle Scrooge, Timber Trouble	10.00	30.00	70.00
4-Mickey Mouse, Rajah's Rescue	10.00	30.00	60.00
5-Donald Duck in Robot Reporter	10.00	30.00	65.00
6-Mickey Mouse, Slumbering Sleuth	10.00	30.00	60.00
7-Donald Duck in the Foreign Legion	10.00	30.00	65.00
8-Mickey Mouse, Airwalking Wonder	10.00	30.00	60.00

CHESTY AND COPTIE (Disney)
Los Angeles Community Chest: 1946 (Giveaway, 4pgs.)

nn-(One known copy) by Floyd Gottfredson	95.00	285.00	900.00

CHESTY AND HIS HELPERS (Disney)
Los Angeles War Chest: 1943 (Giveaway, 12 pgs., 5-1/2x7-1/4")

nn-Chesty & Coptie	62.00	185.00	600.00

CHRISTMAS ADVENTURE, THE
S. Rose (H. L. Green Giveaway): 1963 (16 pgs.)

nn	1.25	3.75	10.00

CHRISTMAS AT THE ROTUNDA (Titled Ford Rotunda Christmas Book 1957 on) (Regular size)
Ford Motor Co. (Western Printing): 1954 - 1961 (Given away every Christmas at one location)

1954-56 issues (nn's)	5.00	15.00	30.00
1957-61 issues (nn's)	4.00	12.00	24.00

CHRISTMAS CAROL, A
Sears Roebuck & Co.: No date (1942-43) (Giveaway, 32 pgs., 8-1/4x10-3/4", paper cover)

nn-Comics & coloring book	18.00	54.00	145.00

CHRISTMAS CAROL, A
Sears Roebuck & Co.: 1940s ? (Christmas giveaway, 20 pgs.)

nn-Comic book & animated coloring book	16.00	49.00	130.00

CHRISTMAS CAROLS
Hot Shoppes Giveaway: 1959? (16 pgs.)

nn	4.00	10.00	20.00

CHRISTMAS COLORING FUN
H. Burnside: 1964 (20 pgs., slick-c, B&W)

nn	1.75	5.25	14.00

CHRISTMAS DREAM, A
Promotional Publishing Co.: 1950 (Kinney Shoe Store Giveaway, 16 pgs.)

nn	4.00	12.00	24.00

CHRISTMAS DREAM, A
J. J. Newberry Co.: 1952? (Giveaway, paper cover, 16 pgs.)

nn	4.00	11.00	22.00

CHRISTMAS DREAM, A
Promotional Publ. Co.: 1952 (Giveaway, 16 pgs., paper cover)

nn	4.00	11.00	22.00

CHRISTMAS FUN AROUND THE WORLD
No publisher: No date (early 50's) (16 pgs., paper cover)

nn	4.00	12.00	24.00

CHRISTMAS IS COMING!
No publisher: No date (early 50's?) (Store giveaway, 16 pgs.)

Cinema Comics Herald - Thunder Birds © 20th Century Fox

Classics Giveaways - Robin Hood Flour © GIL

C-M-O Comics #1 © CEN

nn 4.00 10.00 20.00

CHRISTMAS JOURNEY THROUGH SPACE
Promotional Publishing Co.: 1960

nn-Reprints 1954 issue Jolly Christmas Book with new slick cover 2.80 8.40 28.00

CHRISTMAS ON THE MOON
W. T. Grant Co.: 1958 (Giveaway, 20 pgs., slick cover)

nn 8.65 26.00 60.00

CHRISTMAS PLAY BOOK
Gould-Stoner Co.: 1946 (Giveaway, 16 pgs., paper cover)

nn 8.35 25.00 55.00

CHRISTMAS ROUNDUP
Promotional Publishing Co.: 1960

nn-Marv Levy-c/a 1.50 4.50 12.00

CHRISTMAS STORY CUT-OUT BOOK, THE
Catechetical Guild: No. 393, 1951 (15¢, 36 pgs.)

393-Half text & half comics 5.50 16.50 38.00

CHRISTMAS USA (Through 300 Years) (Also see Uncle Sam's…)
Promotional Publ. Co.: 1956 (Giveaway)

nn-Marv Levy-c/a 2.40 6.00 12.00

CHRISTMAS WITH SNOW WHITE AND THE SEVEN DWARFS
Kobackers Giftstore of Buffalo, N.Y.: 1953 (16 pgs., paper-c)

nn 6.00 18.00 42.00

CHRISTOPHERS, THE
Catechetical Guild: 1951 (Giveaway, 36 pgs.) (Some copies have 15¢ sticker)

nn-Stalin as Satan in Hell 25.00 75.00 200.00

CINDERELLA IN "FAIREST OF THE FAIR"
American Dairy Association (Premium): 1955 (5x7-1/4", 16 pgs., soft-c) (Walt Disney)

nn 10.00 30.00 75.00

CINEMA COMICS HERALD
Paramount Pictures/Universal/RKO/20th Century Fox/Republic:
1941 - 1943 (4-pg. movie "trailers", paper-c, 7-1/2x10-1/2")(Giveaway)

"Mr. Bug Goes to Town" (1941) 10.00 30.00 75.00
"Bedtime Story" 6.00 18.00 42.00
"Lady For A Night", John Wayne, Joan Blondell ('42) 12.50 37.50 100.00
"Reap The Wild Wind" (1942) 8.70 26.00 60.00
"Thunder Birds" (1942) 8.00 24.00 56.00
"They All Kissed the Bride" 8.00 24.00 56.00
"Arabian Nights" (nd) 8.00 24.00 56.00
"Bombardie" (1943) 8.00 24.00 56.00
"Crash Dive" (1943)-Tyrone Power 8.00 24.00 56.00

NOTE: *The 1941-42 issues contain line art with color photos. 1943 issues are line art.*

CLASSICS GIVEAWAYS (Classic Comics reprints)

12/41–Walter Theatre Enterprises (Huntington, WV) giveaway containing #2 (orig.) w/new generic-c (only 1 known copy) 113.00 339.00 1000.00
1942–Double Comics containing CC#1 (orig.) (diff. cover) (not actually a giveaway) (very rare) (also see Double Comics) (only one known copy) 218.00 654.00 1950.00
12/42–Saks 34th St. Giveaway containing CC#7 (orig.) (diff. cover) (very rare; only 6 known copies) 714.00 2142.00 5000.00
2/43–American Comics containing CC#8 (orig.) (Liberty Theatre giveaway) (different cover) (only one known copy) (see American Comics) 163.00 490.00 1400.00
12/44–Robin Hood Flour Co. Giveaway - #7-CC(R) (diff. cover) (rare) (edition probably 5 [22]) 300.00 900.00 2400.00

NOTE: How are above editions determined without CC covers? 1942 is dated 1942, and CC#1-first reprint did not come out until 5/43. 12/42 and 2/43 are determined by blue note at bottom of first text page only in original edition. 12/44 is estimated from page width each reprint edition had progressively slightly smaller page width.

1951–Shelter Thru the Ages (C.I. Educational Series) (actually Giveaway by the Ruberoid Co.) (16 pgs.) (contains original artwork by H. C. Kiefer) (there are 5 diff. back cover ad variations: "Ranch" house ad, "Igloo" ad, "Doll House" ad, "Tree House" ad & blank)(scarce) 88.00 264.00 750.00
1952–George Daynor Biography Giveaway (CC logo) (partly comic book/pictures/newspaper articles) (story of man who built Palace Depression out of junkyard swamp in NJ) (64 pgs.)(very rare; only 3 known copies, one missing-bc) 857.00 2571.00 630
1953–Westinghouse/Dreams of a Man (C.I. Educational Series) (Westingho bio./Westinghouse Co. giveaway) (contains original artwork by H. C. Kief (16 pgs.) (also French/Spanish/Italian versions) (scarce) 84.00 252.00 70

NOTE: Reproductions of 1951, 1952, and 1953 exist with color photocopy covers and b white photocopy interior ("W.C.N. Reprint") 2.00 5.00 1

1951-53–Coward Shoe Giveaways (all editions very rare); 2 variations of back-c ad exist:
With back-c photo ad: 5 (87), 12 (89), 22 (85), 32 (85),49 (85), 69 (87), 72 (no HRN), 80 (0), 91 (0), 92 (0), 96 (0), 98 (0), 100 (0), 101 (0), 103-105 (all Os) 42.00 126.00 36
With back-c cartoon ad: 106-109 (all 0s), 110 (111), 112 (0) 47.00 141.00 40
1956–Ben Franklin 5-10 Store Giveaway (#65-PC with back cover ad) (scarce) 39.00 117.00 31
1956–Ben Franklin Insurance Co. Giveaway (#65-PC with diff. back cover a (very rare) 74.00 221.00 70
11/56–Sealtest Co. Edition - #4 (135) (identical to regular edition except for Sealtest logo printed, not stamped, on front cover) (only two copies know to exist) 43.00 129.00 37
1958–Get-Well Giveaway containing #15-CI (new cartoon-type cover) (Pressman Pharmacy) (only one copy known to exist) 40.00 120.00 32
1967-68–Twin Circle Giveaway Editions - all HRN 166, with back cover ad for National Catholic Press.
2(R68), 4(R67), 10(R68), 13(R68) 3.00 9.00 3
48(R67), 128(R68), 535(576-R68) 3.50 10.50 3
16(R68), 68(R67) 5.00 15.00 5
12/69–Christmas Giveaway ("A Christmas Adventure") (reprints Picture Parade #4-1953, new cover) (4 ad variations)
Stacy's Dept. Store 2.80 8.40 2
Anne & Hope Store 5.50 16.50 5
Gibson's Dept. Store (rare) 5.50 16.50 5
"Merry Christmas" & blank ad space 2.80 8.40 2

CLIFF MERRITT SETS THE RECORD STRAIGHT
Brotherhood of Railroad Trainsmen: Giveaway (2 different issues)

…and the Very Candid Candidate by Al Williamson
…Sets the Record Straight by Al Williamson (2 different-c: one by Williamson, the other by McWilliams)

CLYDE BEATTY COMICS (Also see Crackajack Funnies)
Commodore Productions & Artists, Inc.

…African Jungle Book('56)-Richfield Oil Co. 16 pg. giveaway, soft-c 11.00 33.00 8

C-M-O COMICS
Chicago Mail Order Co.(Centaur): 1942 - No. 2, 1942 (68 pgs., full color)

1-Invisible Terror, Super Ann, & Plymo the Rubber Man app. (all Centaur costume heroes) 84.00 253.00 80
2-Invisible Terror, Super Ann app. 55.00 165.00 50

COCOMALT BIG BOOK OF COMICS
Harry 'A' Chesler (Cocomalt Premium): 1938 (Reg. size, full color, 52 pgs

1-(Scarce)-Biro-c/a; Little Nemo by Winsor McCay Jr., Dan Hastings; Jack Cole, Guardineer, Gustavson, Bob Wood-a 225.00 675.00 200

COMIC BOOK (Also see Comics From Weatherbird)
American Juniors Shoe: 1954 (Giveaway)

Contains a comic rebound with new cover. Several combinations possible. Contents determines price.

COMIC BOOK MAGAZINE
Chicago Tribune & other newspapers: 1940 - 1943 (Similar to Spirit Secti (7-3/4x10-3/4"; full color; 16-24 pgs. ea.)

1940 issues 8.35 25.00 5
1941, 1942 issues 5.85 17.50 3
1943 issues 5.35 16.00 3

NOTE: *Published weekly. Texas Slim, Kit Carson, Spooky, Josie, Nuts & Jolts, Lew Brenda Starr, Daniel Boone, Captain Storm, Rocky, Smokey Stover, Tiny Tim, Little J Manchu appear among others. Early issues had photo stories with pictures from the movie*

Comic Books #1 - Green Jet © Met. Printing Co.

Daisy Comics © EAS

DC Spotlight #1 © DC

GD2.0 FN6.0 NM9.4

ssues had comic art.

OMIC BOOKS (Series 1)
etropolitan Printing Co. (Giveaway): 1950 (16 pgs.; 5-1/4x8-1/2"; full color; ound at top; paper cover)

-Boots and Saddles; intro The Masked Marshal 5.00 15.00 35.00
-The Green Jet; Green Lama by Raboy 30.00 90.00 240.00
-My Pal Dizzy (Teen-age) 3.60 9.00 18.00
-New World; origin Atomaster (costumed hero) 10.00 30.00 70.00
-Talullah (Teen-age) 3.60 9.00 18.00

OMIC CAVALCADE
l-American/National Periodical Publications

veaway (1944, 8 pgs., paper-c, in color)-One Hundred Years of Co-operation-r/Comic Cavalcade #9 75.00 225.00 700.00
veaway (1945, 16 pgs., paper-c, in color)-Movie "Tomorrow The World" (Nazi theme); r/Comic Cavalcade #10 100.00 300.00 900.00
veaway (c. 1944-45; 8 pgs, paper-c, in color)-The Twain Shall Meet-r/Comic Cavalcade #8 75.00 225.00 700.00

OMIC SELECTIONS (Shoe store giveaway)
rents' Magazine Press: 1944-46 (Reprints from Calling All Girls, True mics, True Aviation, & Real Heroes)

4.15 12.50 25.00
-5 3.60 9.00 18.00

MICS FROM WEATHER BIRD (Also see Comic Book, Edward's Shoes, ee Comics to You & Weather Bird)
eather Bird Shoes: 1954 - 1957 (Giveaway)
ntains a comic bound with new cover. Many combinations possible. Contents would determine e. Some issues do not contain complete comics, but only parts of comics.Value equals 40 to percent of contents.

MICS READING LIBRARIES (Educational Series)
ng Features (Charlton Publ.): 1973, 1977, 1979 (36 pgs. in color) veaways)

)1-Tiger, Quincy 1.00 3.00 8.00
)2-Beetle Bailey, Blondie & Popeye 1.50 4.50 12.00
)3-Blondie, Beetle Bailey 1.00 3.00 8.00
)4-Tim Tyler's Luck, Felix the Cat 2.30 7.00 20.00
)5-Quincy, Henry 1.00 3.00 8.00
)6-The Phantom, Mandrake 2.30 7.00 20.00
1977 reprint(R-04) 1.25 3.75 10.00
)7-Popeye, Little King 1.85 5.50 15.00
)8-Prince Valiant(Foster), Flash Gordon 2.50 7.50 25.00
1977 reprint 1.75 5.25 14.00
9-Hagar the Horrible, Boner's Ark 1.50 4.50 12.00
0-Redeye, Tiger 1.00 3.00 8.00
1-Blondie, Hi & Lois 1.00 3.00 8.00
2-Popeye-Swee'pea, Brutus 1.85 5.50 15.00
3-Beetle Bailey, Little King 1.00 3.00 8.00
4-Quincy-Hamlet 1.00 3.00 8.00
5-The Phantom, The Genius 1.85 5.50 15.00
6-Flash Gordon, Mandrake 2.50 7.50 25.00
1977 reprint 1.50 4.50 12.00
er 1977 editions.... 2.40 6.00
9 editions(68pgs.) 2.40 6.00
E: Above giveaways available with purchase of $45.00 in merchandise. Used as a reading aid for small children.

MMANDMENTS OF GOD
echetical Guild: 1954, 1958

-Same contents in both editions; diff-c 4.00 10.00 20.00

MPLIMENTARY COMICS
es Promotion Publ.: No date (1950's) (Giveaway)

Strongman by Powell, 3 stories 6.70 20.00 45.00

ACKAJACK FUNNIES (Giveaway)
o-Meal: 1937 (Full size, soft-c, full color, 32 pgs.)(Before No. 1?)

eatures Dan Dunn, G-Man, Speed Bolton, Buck Jones, The Nebbs, Clyde Beatty, Freckles, Major Hoople, Wash Tubbs 100.00 300.00 950.00

OSLEY'S HOUSE OF FUN (Also see Tee and Vee Crosley...)
sley Div. AVCO Mfg. Corp.: 1950 (Giveaway, paper cover, 32 pgs.)

GD2.0 FN6.0 NM9.4

nn-Strips revolve around Crosley appliances 4.25 13.00 26.00

DAGWOOD SPLITS THE ATOM (Also see Topix V8#4)
King Features Syndicate: 1949 (Science comic with King Features characters) (Giveaway)

nn-Half comic, half text; Popeye, Olive Oyl, Henry, Mandrake, Little King, Katzenjammer Kids app. 7.50 22.50 52.00

DAISY COMICS (Daisy Air Rifles)
Eastern Color Printing Co.: Dec, 1936 (5-1/4x7-1/2")

nn-Joe Palooka, Buck Rogers (2 pgs. from Famous Funnies No. 18, 1st full cover app.), Napoleon Flying to Fame, Butty & Fally 34.00 103.00 270.00

DAISY LOW OF THE GIRL SCOUTS
Girl Scouts of America: 1954, 1965 (16 pgs., paper-c)

1954-Story of Juliette Gordon Low 4.00 12.00 24.00
1965 1.50 4.50 12.00

DAN CURTIS GIVEAWAYS
Western Publishing Co.:1974 (3x6", 24 pgs., reprints)

1-Dark Shadows 1.50 4.50 12.00
2,6-Star Trek 1.85 5.50 15.00
3,4,7-9: 3-The Twilight Zone. 4-Ripley's Believe It or Not! 7-The Occult Files of Dr. Spektor. 8-Dagar the Invincible. 9-Grimm's Ghost Stories 1.00 3.00 8.00
5-Turok, Son of Stone (partial-r/Turok #78) 1.50 4.50 12.00

DANNY KAYE'S BAND FUN BOOK
H & A Selmer: 1959 (Giveaway)

nn 5.85 17.50 40.00

DAREDEVIL
Marvel Comics Group: 1993

...Vs. Vapora 1 (Engineering Show Giveaway, 16 pg.)–Intro Vapora 3.50

DAVY CROCKETT (TV)
Dell Publishing Co./Gold Key

...Christmas Book (no date, 16 pgs., paper-c)-Sears giveaway 5.85 17.50 40.00
...Safety Trails (1955, 16pgs, 3-1/4x7")-Cities Service giveaway 7.50 22.50 52.00

DAVY CROCKETT
Charlton Comics

Hunting With... nn ('55, 16 pgs.)-Ben Franklin Store giveaway (Publ.-S. Rose) 5.00 15.00 30.00

DAVY CROCKETT
Walt Disney Prod.: (1955, 16 pgs., 5x7-1/4", slick, photo-c)
...In the Raid at Piney Creek-American Motors giveaway 7.50 22.50 52.00

DC SAMPLER
DC Comics : nn (#1) 1983 - No. 3, 1984 (36 pgs.; 6 1/2" x 10", giveaway)

nn(#1) -3: nn-Wraparound-c, previews upcoming issues. 3-Kirby-a 5.00

DC SPOTLIGHT
DC Comics : 1985 (50th anniversary special) (giveaway)

1-Includes profiles on Batman:The Dark Knight & Watchmen 4.00

DENNIS THE MENACE
Hallden (Fawcett)

...& Dirt ('59,'68)-Soil Conservation giveaway; r-# 36; Wiseman-c/a 1.00 3.00 8.00
...Away We Go('70)-Caladayl giveaway 2.40 6.00
...Coping with Family Stress-giveaway 5.00
...Takes a Poke at Poison('61)-Food & Drug Admin. giveaway; Wiseman-c/a 1.00 3.00 8.00
...Takes a Poke at Poison-Revised 1/66, 11/70 4.00
...Takes a Poke at Poison-Revised 1972, 1974, 1977, 1981 4.00

DETECTIVE COMICS (Also see other Batman titles)
National Periodical Publications/DC Comics

27 (1984)-Oreo Cookies giveaway (32 pgs., paper-c) r-/Det. 27, 38 & Batman No. 1 (1st Joker) 6.00 18.00 40.00
38 (1995) Blockbuster Video edition; reprints 1st Robin app. 2.00

Dick Tracy Motorola Giveaway © KING

Dot and Dash and the Lucky Jingle Piggie © Sears

Evel Knievel © Ideal Toy Co.

38 (1997) Toys R Us edition 2.00
359 (1997) Toys R Us edition; reprints 1st Batgirl app. 2.00

DICK TRACY GIVEAWAYS
1939 - 1958; 1990

Buster Brown Shoes Giveaway (1940s?, 36 pgs. in color); 1938-39-r by Gould 36.00 107.00 290.00
Gillmore Giveaway (See Superbook)
...Hatful of Fun (No date, 1950-52, 32pgs.; 8-1/2x10")-Dick Tracy hat promotion; Dick Tracy games, magic tricks. Miller Bros. premium 18.00 54.00 140.00
Motorola Giveaway (1953)-Reprints Harvey Comics Library #2; "The Case of the Sparkle Plenty TV Mystery" 5.00 15.00 35.00
Original Dick Tracy by Chester Gould, The (Aug, 1990, 16 pgs., 5-1/2x8-1/2")-Gladstone Publ.; Bread Giveaway 3.00 9.00 30.00
Popped Wheat Giveaway (1947, 16 pgs. in color)-1940-r; Sig Feuchtwanger Publ.; Gould-a 3.00 7.50 15.00
...Presents the Family Fun Book; Tip Top Bread Giveaway, no date or number (1940, Fawcett Publ., 16 pgs. in color)-Spy Smasher, Ibis, Lance O'Casey app. 56.00 170.00 535.00
Same as above but without app. of heroes & Dick Tracy on cover only 14.00 43.00 115.00
Service Station Giveaway (1958, 16 pgs. in color)(regular size, slick cover)-Harvey Info. Press 4.00 10.00 20.00
Shoe Store Giveaway (Weatherbird)(1939, 16 pgs.)-Gould-a 13.50 41.00 105.00

DICK TRACY SHEDS LIGHT ON THE MOLE
Western Printing Co.: 1949 (16 pgs.) (Ray-O-Vac Flashlights giveaway)
nn-Not by Gould 7.15 21.50 50.00

DICK WINGATE OF THE U.S. NAVY
Superior Publ./Toby Press: 1951; 1953 (no month)
nn-U.S. Navy giveaway 4.00 11.00 22.00
1(1953, Toby)-Reprints nn issue? (same-c) 4.00 10.00 20.00

DIG 'EM
Kellogg's Sugar Smacks Giveaway: 1973 (2-3/8x6", 16 pgs.)
nn-4 different issues 1.00 2.80 7.00

DOC CARTER VD COMICS
Health Publications Institute, Raleigh, N. C. (Giveaway): 1949 (16 pgs. in color) (Paper-c)
nn 19.00 58.00 150.00

DONALD AND MICKEY MERRY CHRISTMAS (Formerly Famous Gang Book Of Comics)
K. K. Publ./Firestone Tire & Rubber Co.: 1943 - 1949 (Giveaway, 20 pgs.)
Put out each Christmas; 1943 issue titled "Firestone Presents Comics" (Disney)
1943-Donald Duck-r/WDC&S #32 by Carl Barks 73.00 219.00 800.00
1944-Donald Duck-r/WDC&S #35 by Barks 68.00 204.00 750.00
1945- "Donald Duck's Best Christmas", 8 pgs. Carl Barks; intro. & 1st app. Grandma Duck in comic books 100.00 300.00 1100.00
1946-Donald Duck in "Santa's Stormy Visit", 8 pgs. Carl Barks 70.00 210.00 775.00
1947-Donald Duck in "Three Good Little Ducks", 8 pgs. Carl Barks 70.00 210.00 775.00
1948-Donald Duck in "Toyland", 8 pgs. Carl Barks 70.00 210.00 775.00
1949-Donald Duck in "New Toys", 8 pgs. Barks 64.00 192.00 700.00

DONALD DUCK
K. K. Publications: 1944 (Christmas giveaway, paper-c, 16 pgs.)(2 versions)
nn-Kelly cover reprint 80.00 240.00 800.00

DONALD DUCK AND THE RED FEATHER
Red Feather Giveaway: 1948 (8-1/2x11", 4 pgs., B&W)
nn 16.50 49.50 165.00

DONALD DUCK IN "THE LITTERBUG"
Keep America Beautiful: 1963 (5x7-1/4", 16 pgs., soft-c) (Disney giveaway)
nn 3.50 10.50 35.00

DONALD DUCK "PLOTTING PICNICKERS" (See Frito-Lay Giveaway)

DONALD DUCK'S SURPRISE PARTY
Walt Disney Productions: 1948 (16 pgs.) (Giveaway for Icy Frost Twins Ice Cream Bars)
nn-(Rare)-Kelly-c/a 314.00 943.00 240

DOT AND DASH AND THE LUCKY JINGLE PIGGIE
Sears Roebuck Co.: 1942 (Christmas giveaway, 12 pgs.)
nn-Contains a war stamp album and a punch out Jingle Piggie bank 10.00 30.00 7

DOUBLE TALK (Also see Two-Faces)
Feature Publications: No date (1962?) (32 pgs., full color, slick-c)
Christian Anti-Communism Crusade (Giveaway)
nn-Sickle with blood-c 8.15 24.50 9

DUMBO (Walt Disney's..., The Flying Elephant)
Weatherbird Shoes/Ernest Kern Co.(Detroit)/ Wieboldt's (Chicago): 194
(K.K. Publ. Giveaway)
nn-16 pgs., 9x10" (Rare) 47.00 140.00 42
nn-52 pgs., 5-1/2x8-1/2", slick cover in color; B&W interior; half text, half reprints 4-Color No. 17 (Dept. store) 29.00 86.00 23

DUMBO WEEKLY
Walt Disney Prod.: 1942 (Premium supplied by Diamond D-X Gas Stations)
1 75.00 225.00 70
2-16 23.00 68.00 18
Binder only 42
NOTE: *A cover and binder came separate at gas stations. Came with membership card.*

EAT RIGHT TO WORK AND WIN
Swift & Company: 1942 (16 pgs.) (Giveaway)
Blondie, Henry, Flash Gordon by Alex Raymond, Toots & Casper, Thimble Theatre(Popeye), Tillie the Toiler, The Phantom, The Little King, & Bringing up Father - original strips just f book -(in daily strip form which shows what foods we should eat and why)
50.00 150.00 35

EDWARD'S SHOES GIVEAWAY
Edward's Shoe Store: 1954 (Has clown on cover)
Contains comic with new cover. Many combinations possible. Contents determines price, 50-60 percent of original. (Similar to Comics From Weatherbird & Free Comics to You)

ELSIE THE COW
D. S. Publishing Co.
Borden's cheese comic picture bk ("40, giveaway) 18.00 54.00 14
Borden Milk Giveaway-(16 pgs., nn) (3 ishs, 1957) 14.00 41.00 11
Elsie's Fun Book(1950; Borden Milk) 14.00 41.00 11
Everyday Birthday Fun With... (1957; 20 pgs.)(100th Anniversary); Kubert-a 14.00 41.00 11

ESCAPE FROM FEAR
Planned Parenthood of America: 1956, 1962, 1969 (Giveaway, 8 pgs. full color) (On birth control)
1956 edition 10.00 30.00 7
1962 edition 4.55 13.65 5
1969 edition 2.50 7.50 2

EVEL KNIEVEL
Marvel Comics Group (Ideal Toy Corp.): 1974 (Giveaway, 20 pgs.)
nn-Contains photo on inside back-c 2.80 8.40 2

FAMOUS COMICS (Also see Favorite Comics)
Zain-Eppy/United Features Syndicate: No date; Mid 1930's (24 pgs., pape
nn-Reprinted from 1933 & 1934 newspaper strips in color; Joe Palooka, Hairbreadth Harry, Napoleon, The Nebbs, etc. (Many different versions known) 50.00 250.00 45

FAMOUS FAIRY TALES
K. K. Publ. Co.: 1942; 1943 (32 pgs.); 1944 (16 pgs.) (Giveaway, soft-c)
1942-Kelly-a 42.00 125.00 37
1943-r-/Fairy Tale Parade No. 2,3; Kelly-a 34.00 101.00 27
1944-Kelly-a 30.00 90.00 24

FAMOUS FUNNIES -A CARNIVAL OF COMICS
Eastern Color: 1933 GD2.0 FN6.0 VF8.0 NM
(Probably the second comic book), 36 pgs., no date given, no publisher, no numbe tains strip reprints of The Bungle Family, Dixie Dugan, Hairbreadth Harry, Joe Palooka, Ke Up With the Jones, Mutt & Jeff, Reg'lar Fellers, S'Matter Pop, Strange As It Seems, and o This book was sold by M. C. Gaines to Wheatena, Milk-O-Malt, John Wanamaker, Kinney Stores, & others to be given away as premiums and radio giveaways (1933). Originally cam

Flash Gordon Gordon Bread © KING

Forest Ranger Handbook © Wrather Corp.

Future Cop: L.A.P.D © Electronic Arts

GD2.0 FN6.0 NM9.4

mailing envelope.
913.00 2740.00 5480.00 10,500.00

AMOUS GANG BOOK OF COMICS (Becomes Donald & Mickey Merry Christmas 1943 on)
irestone Tire & Rubber Co.: Dec, 1942 (Christmas giveaway, 32 pgs., paper-c)

	GD2.0	FN6.0	NM9.4
n-(Rare)-Porky Pig, Bugs Bunny, Mary Jane & Sniffles, Elmer Fudd; r/Looney Tunes	68.00	205.00	650.00

ANTASTIC FOUR
arvel Comics: 1981(32pgs., Young Model Builders Club)
n 2.40 6.00

ATHER OF CHARITY
atechetical Guild Giveaway: No date (32 pgs.; paper cover)
n 2.80 7.00 14.00

AVORITE COMICS (Also see Famous Comics)
rocery Store Giveaway (Diff. Corp.) (detergent): 1934 (36 pgs.)
ook 1-The Nebbs, Strange As It Seems, Napoleon, Joe Palooka, Dixie Dugan, S'Matter Pop, Hairbreadth Harry, etc. reprints 79.00 237.00 750.00
ook 2,3 55.00 165.00 500.00

AWCETT MINIATURES (See Mighty Midget)
awcett Publications: 1946 (3-3/4x5", 12-24 pgs.) (Wheaties giveaways)
aptain Marvel "And the Horn of Plenty"; Bulletman story 17.00 51.00 135.00
aptain Marvel "& the Raiders From Space"; Golden Arrow story 17.00 51.00 135.00
aptain Marvel Jr. "The Case of the Poison Press!" Bulletman story 17.00 51.00 135.00
electa of the Planets; C. C. Beck art; B&W inside; 12 pgs.; 3 printing variations (coloring) exist 25.00 75.00 200.00

GHT FOR FREEDOM
ational Assoc. of Mfgrs./General Comics: 1949, 1951 (Giveaway, 16 pgs.)

	GD2.0	FN6.0	NM9.4
-Dan Barry-c/a; used in **POP**, pg. 102	5.70	17.00	40.00

RE AND BLAST
ational Fire Protection Assoc.: 1952 (Giveaway, 16 pgs., paper-c)
-Mart Baily A-Bomb-c; about fire prevention 16.00 48.00 125.00

RE CHIEF AND THE SAFE OL' FIREFLY, THE
ational Board of Fire Underwriters: 1952 (16 pgs.) (Safety brochure given ay at schools) (produced by American Visuals Corp.)(Eisner)
-(Rare) Eisner-c/a 50.00 150.00 450.00

ASH
Comics: 1990
Brochure for CBS TV series 2.00

ASH COMICS
ational Periodical Publications: 1946 (6-1/2x8-1/4", 32 pgs.) heaties Giveaway)
Johnny Thunder, Ghost Patrol, The Flash & Kubert Hawkman app.; Irwin Hasen-c/a 325.00 1200.00 -
TE: All known copies were taped to Wheaties boxes and are never found in mint condition. ies with light tape residue bring the listed prices in all grades

ASH FORCE 2000
Comics: 1984
5 2.00

ASH GORDON
Publishing Co.: 1943 (20 pgs.)
y's Giveaway-(Rare); not by Raymond 59.00 176.00 550.00

ASH GORDON
vey Comics: 1951 (16 pgs. in color, regular size, paper-c)
rdon Bread giveaway)
: 1-r/strips 10/24/37 - 2/6/38. 2-r/strips 7/14/40 - 10/6/40; Reprints by Raymond each.... 1.50 4.50 10.00
E: Most copies have brittle edges.

REST FIRE (Also see The Blazing Forest and Smokey The Bear)
erican Forestry Assn.(Commerical Comics): 1949 (dated-1950) (16 pgs., paper-c)
nn-Intro/1st app. Smokey The Forest Fire Preventing Bear; created by Rudy Wendelein; Wendelein/Sparling-a; 'Carter Oil Co.' on back-c of original 17.00 51.00 135.00

FOREST RANGER HANDBOOK
Wrather Corp.: 1967 (5x7", 20 pgs., slick-c)
nn-WIth Corey Stuart & Lassie photo-c 2.30 7.00 20.00

FORGOTTEN STORY BEHIND NORTH BEACH, THE
Catechetical Guild: No date (8 pgs., paper-c)
nn 3.20 8.00 16.00

48 FAMOUS AMERICANS
J. C. Penney Co. (Cpr. Edwin H. Stroh): 1947 (Giveaway) (Half-size in color)
nn-Simon & Kirby-a 11.50 34.00 90.00

FRANKIE LUER'S SPACE ADVENTURES
Luer Packing Co.: 1955 (5x7", 36 pgs., slick-c)
nn- With Davey Rocket 3.60 9.00 18.00

FREDDY
Charlton Comics
Schiff's Shoes Presents... #1 (1959)-Giveaway 1.50 4.50 12.00

FREE COMICS TO YOU FROM... (name of shoe store) (Has clown on cover & another with a rabbit) (Like comics from Weather Bird & Edward's Shoes)
Shoe Store Giveaway: Circa 1956, 1960-61
Contains a comic bound with new cover - several combinations possible; some Harvey titles known. Contents determine price.

FREEDOM TRAIN
Street & Smith Publications: 1948 (Giveaway)
nn-Powell-c w/mailer 20.00 75.00 160.00

FRIENDLY GHOST, CASPER, THE (Becomes Casper... #254 on)
Harvey Publications
American Dental Assoc. giveaway-Small size (1967, 16 pgs.) 2.50 7.50 24.00

FRITO-LAY GIVEAWAY
Frito-Lay: 1962 (3-1/4x7", soft-c, 16 pgs.) (Disney)
nn-Donald Duck "Plotting Picnickers" 5.00 15.00 55.00
nn-Ludwig Von Drake "Fish Stampede" 3.20 9.60 35.00
nn- Mickey Mouse & Goofy "Bicep Bungle" 3.80 11.40 40.00

FRONTIER DAYS
Robin Hood Shoe Store (Brown Shoe): 1956 (Giveaway)
1 3.20 8.00 16.00

FUNNIES ON PARADE (Premium)(See Toy World Funnies)
Eastern Color Printing Co.: 1933 (Probably the 1st comic book) (36 pgs., slick cover) No date or publisher listed

	GD2.0	FN6.0	VF8.0	NM9.4
nn-Contains Sunday page reprints of Mutt & Jeff, Joe Palooka, Hairbreadth Harry, Reg'lar Fellers, Skippy, & others (10,000 print run). This book was printed for Proctor & Gamble to be given away & came out before Famous Funnies or Century of Comics.	1160.00	3480.00	6960.00	14,500.00

FUNNY PICTURE STORIES (Comic Pages V3#4 on)
Comics Magazine Co./Centaur Publications

	GD2.0	FN6.0	NM9.4
Laundry giveaway (16-20 pgs., 1930s)-slick-c	30.00	100.00	230.00

FUNNY STUFF
National Periodical Publications (Wheaties Giveaway): 1946 (6-1/2x8-1/4")
nn-(Scarce)-Dodo & the Frog, Three Mouseketeers, etc.; came taped to Wheaties box; never found in better than fine 170.00 450.00 –

FUTURE COP: L.A.P.D. (Electronic Arts video game)
DC Comics (WildStorm): 1998
nn-Ron Lim-a/Dave Johnson-c 2.00

GABBY HAYES WESTERN (Movie star)
Fawcett Publications
Quaker Oats Giveaway nn's(#1-5, 1951, 2-1/2x7") (Kagran Corp.)-...In Tracks of Guilt, ...In the Fence Post Mystery, ...In the Accidental Sherlock, ... In the Frame-Up, ...In the Double Cross Brand known

Gene Autry mailing envelope

Hoppy the Marvel Bunny (Well Known Comics) © FAW

11.00 33.00 80.00
Mailing Envelope (has illo of Gabby on front) 11.00 33.00 80.00

GARY GIBSON COMICS (Donut club membership)
National Dunking Association: 1950 (Included in donut box with pin and card)

1-Western soft-c, 16 pgs.; folded into the box 4.00 10.00 22.00

GENE AUTRY COMICS
Dell Publishing Co.

...Adventure Comics And Play-Fun Book ('47)-32 pgs., 8x6-1/2"; games, comics, magic (Pillsbury premium) 40.00 120.00 340.00
Quaker Oats Giveaway(1950)-2-1/2x6-3/4"; 5 different versions; "Death Card Gang", "Phantoms of the Cave", "Riddle of Laughing Mtn.", "Secret of Lost Valley", "Bond of the Broken Arrow" (came in wrapper) each... 15.00 45.00 120.00
Mailing Envelope (has illo. of Gene on front) 15.00 45.00 120.00
3-D Giveaway(1953)-Pocket-size; 5 different 15.00 45.00 120.00
Mailing Envelope (no art on front) 12.50 37.50 100.00

GENE AUTRY TIM (Formerly Tim) (Becomes Tim in Space)
Tim Stores: 1950 (Half-size) (B&W Giveaway)

nn-Several issues (All Scarce) 16.00 48.00 125.00

GENERAL FOODS SUPER-HEROES
DC Comics: 1979, 1980

1-4 (1979) 2.00
1-4 (1980) 2.00

G. I. COMICS (Also see Jeep & Overseas Comics)
Giveaways: 1945 - No. 73?, 1946 (Distributed to U. S. Armed Forces)

1-73-Contains Prince Valiant by Foster, Blondie, Smilin' Jack, Mickey Finn, Terry & the Pirates, Donald Duck, Alley Oop, Moon Mullins & Capt. Easy strip reprints (at least 73 issues known to exist) 8.35 25.00 55.00

GOLDEN ARROW
Fawcett Publications

...Well Known Comics (1944; 12 pgs.; 8-1/2x10-1/2"; paper-c; glued binding)-Bestmaid/Samuel Lowe giveaway; printed in green 9.30 28.00 65.00

GOLDILOCKS & THE THREE BEARS
K. K. Publications: 1943 (Giveaway)

nn 10.00 30.00 75.00

GREAT PEOPLE OF GENESIS, THE
David C. Cook Publ. Co.: No date (Religious giveaway, 64 pgs.)

nn-Reprint/Sunday Pix Weekly 3.60 9.00 18.00

GREAT SACRAMENT, THE
Catechetical Guild: 1953 (Giveaway, 36 pgs.)

nn 4.00 10.00 20.00

GRIT (YOU'VE GOT TO HAVE...)
GRIT Publishing Co.: 1959

nn-GRIT newspaper sales recruitment comic;Schaffenberger-a. Later version has altered artwork 4.00 10.00 20.00

GULF FUNNY WEEKLY (Gulf Comic Weekly No. 1-4)(See Standard Oil Comics)
Gulf Oil Company (Giveaway): 1933 - No. 422, 5/23/41 (in full color; 4 pgs.; tabloid size to 2/3/39; 2/10/39 on, regular comic book size)(early issues undated)

1 75.00 300.00 700.00
2-5 30.00 100.00 240.00
6-30 19.00 56.00 150.00
31-100 13.00 39.00 105.00
101-196 8.65 26.00 60.00
197-Wings Winfair begins(1/29/37); by Fred Meagher beginning in 1938 28.00 83.00 220.00
198-300 (Last tabloid size) 14.00 43.00 110.00
301-350 (Regular size) 8.35 25.00 55.00
351-422 6.00 18.00 42.00

GULLIVER'S TRAVELS
Macy's Department Store: 1939, small size

nn-Christmas giveaway 14.00 42.00 110.00

GUN THAT WON THE WEST, THE
Winchester-Western Division & Olin Mathieson Chemical Corp.: 1956 (Giveaway, 24 pgs.)

nn-Painted-c 5.00 15.00 32.

HAPPINESS AND HEALING FOR YOU (Also see Oral Roberts'...)
Commercial Comics: 1955 (36 pgs., slick cover) (Oral Roberts Giveaway)

nn 9.30 28.00 65.
NOTE: *The success of this book prompted Oral Roberts to go into the publishing business him self to produce his own material.*

HAPPY TOOTH
DC Comics: 1996

1 2.

HAWTHORN-MELODY FARMS DAIRY COMICS
Everybody's Publishing Co.: No date (1950's) (Giveaway)

nn-Cheerie Chick, Tuffy Turtle, Robin Koo Koo, Donald & Longhorn Legends 2.00 5.00 10.

HENRY ALDRICH COMICS (TV)
Dell Publishing Co.

Giveaway (16 pgs., soft-c, 1951)-Capehart radio 2.50 7.50 24.

HERE IS SANTA CLAUS
Goldsmith Publishing Co. (Kann's in Washington, D.C.): 1930s (16 pgs., 8 color) (stiff paper covers)

nn 10.00 30.00 75.

HERE'S HOW AMERICA'S CARTOONISTS HELP TO SELL U.S. SAVINGS BONDS
Harvey Comics: 1950? (16 pgs., giveaway, paper cover)

Contains: Joe Palooka, Donald Duck, Archie, Kerry Drake, Red Ryder, Blondie & Steve Canyon 18.00 53.00 140.

HISTORY OF GAS
American Gas Assoc.: Mar, 1947 (Giveaway, 16 pgs.)

nn-Miss Flame narrates 5.00 15.00 35.

HONEYBEE BIRDWHISTLE AND HER PET PEPI (Introducing...)
Newspaper Enterprise Assoc.: 1969 (Giveaway, 24 pgs., B&W, slick cover)

nn-Contains Freckles newspaper strips with a short biography of Henry Fornhals (artist) & Fred Fox (writer) of the strip 4.55 13.65 50.

HOPALONG CASSIDY
Fawcett Publications

Grape Nuts Flakes giveaway (1950,9x6") 15.00 45.00 120.
...& the Mad Barber (1951 Bond Bread giveaway)-7x5"; used in **SOTI**, pgs. 308,309 25.00 75.00 200.
...Meets the Brend Brothers Bandits (1951 Bond Bread giveaway, color, paper-c, 16pgs. 3-1/2x7")-Fawcett Publ. 12.00 36.00 95.
...Strange Legacy (1951 Bond Bread giveaway) 12.00 36.00 95.
White Tower Giveaway (1946, 16pgs., paper-c) 12.00 36.00 95.

HOPPY THE MARVEL BUNNY (WELL KNOWN COMICS)
Fawcett Publications: 1944 (8-1/2x10-1/2", paper-c)

Bestmaid/Samuel Lowe (printed in red or blue) 10.00 30.00 70.

HOT STUFF, THE LITTLE DEVIL
Harvey Publications (Illustrated Humor):1963

Shoestore Giveaway 2.00 6.00 18.

HOW STALIN HOPES WE WILL DESTROY AMERICA
Joe Lowe Co. (Pictorial Media): 1951 (Giveaway, 16 pgs.)

nn 50.00 150.00 450.

HURRICANE KIDS, THE (Also See Magic Morro, The Owl, Popular Comics #
R.S. Callender: 1941 (Giveaway, 7-1/2x5-1/4", soft-c)

nn-Will Ely-a. 10.00 30.00 70.

IF THE DEVIL WOULD TALK
Roman Catholic Catechetical Guild/Impact Publ.: 1950; 1958 (32 pgs.; pap cover; in full color)

nn-(Scarce)-About secularism (20-30 copies known to exist); very low distribution 81.00 245.00 770.
1958 Edition-(Impact Publ.); art & script changed to meet church criticism of earlier edition; 80 plus copies known to exist 25.00 75.00 200.

The Iron Horse Goes to War © AAR

Jackie Joyner Kersee in High Hurdles © DC

Joe Palooka Fights His Way Back © HARV

GD2.0 FN6.0 NM9.4

Black & White version of nn edition; small size; only 4 known copies exist 30.00 90.00 240.00

NOTE: *The original edition of this book was printed and killed by the Guild's board of directors. It is believed that a very limited number of copies were distributed. The 1958 version was a complete bomb with very limited, if any, circulation. In 1979, 11 original, 4 1958 reprints, and 4 B&W's surfaced from the Guild's old files in St. Paul, Minnesota.*

IN LOVE WITH JESUS
Catechetical Educational Society: 1952 (Giveaway, 36 pgs.)
nn 4.65 14.00 28.00

NTERSTATE THEATRES' FUN CLUB COMICS
nterstate Theatres: Mid 1940's (10¢ on cover) (B&W cover) (Premium)
Cover features MLJ characters looking at a copy of Top-Notch Comics, but contains an early Detective Comic on inside; many combinations possible 8.35 25.00 60.00

RON GIANT
DC Comics: 1999 (4 pages, theater giveaway)
1-Previews movie 2.00

RON HORSE GOES TO WAR, THE
Association of American Railroads: 1960 (Giveaway, 16 pgs.)
nn-Civil War & railroads 4.65 14.00 28.00

S THIS TOMORROW?
Catechetical Guild: 1947 (One Shot) (3 editions) (52 pgs.)
1-Theme of communists taking over the USA; (no price on cover) Used in **POP**, pg. 102 16.00 48.00 125.00
1-(10¢ on cover) 22.00 66.00 175.00
1-Has blank circle with no price on cover 23.00 69.00 185.00
Black & White advance copy titled "Confidential" (52 pgs.)-Contains script and art edited out of the color edition, including one page of extreme violence showing mob nailing a Cardinal to a door; (only two known copies) 50.00 200.00 450.00

NOTE: *The original color version first sold for 10 cents. Since sales were good, it was later printed as a giveaway. Approximately four million in total were printed. The two black and white copies listed plus two other versions as well as a full color untrimmed version surfaced in 1979 from the Guild's old files in St. Paul, Minnesota.*

IT'S FUN TO STAY ALIVE
National Automobile Dealers Association: 1948 (Giveaway, 16 pgs., heavy stock paper)
Featuring: Bugs Bunny, The Berrys, Dixie Dugan, Elmer, Henry, Tim Tyler, Bruce Gentry, Abbie an' Slats, Joe Jinks, The Toodles, & Cokey; all art copyright 1946-48 drawn especially for this book. 18.00 53.00 140.00

JACK & JILL VISIT TOYTOWN WITH ELMER THE ELF
Butler Brothers (Toytown Stores): 1949 (Giveaway, 16 pgs., paper cover) 4.00 12.00 24.00

JACK ARMSTRONG (Radio)(See True Comics)
Parents' Institute: 1949
?-Premium version(distr. in Chicago only); Free printed on upper right-c; no price (Rare) 21.00 64.00 165.00

JACKIE JOYNER KERSEE IN HIGH HURDLES (Kellogg's Tony's Sports Comics)
DC Comics: 1992 (Sports Illustrated)
2.00

JACKPOT OF FUN COMIC BOOK
DCA Food Ind.: 1957, giveaway
-Features Howdy Doody 10.00 30.00 75.00

JEEP COMICS
R. B. Leffingwell & Co.: 1945 - 1946
-46(Giveaways)-Strip reprints in all; Tarzan, Flash Gordon, Blondie, The Nebbs, Little Iodine, Red Ryder, Don Winslow, The Phantom, Johnny Hazard, Katzenjammer Kids; distr. to U.S. Armed Forces from 1945-1946 5.00 15.00 35.00

JINGLE BELLS CHRISTMAS BOOK
Montgomery Ward (Giveaway): 1971 (20 pgs., B&W inside, slick-c)
4.00

JOAN OF ARC
Catechetical Guild (Topix) (Giveaway): No date (28 pgs.)
10.00 30.00 70.00

GD2.0 FN6.0 NM9.4

NOTE: *Unpublished version exists which came from the Guild's files.*

JOE PALOOKA (2nd Series)
Harvey Publications
...Body Building Instruction Book (1958 B&M Sports Toy giveaway, 16pgs., 5-1/4x7")-Origin 10.00 30.00 65.00
...Fights His Way Back (1945 Giveaway, 24 pgs.) Family Comics 17.00 51.00 135.00
...in Hi There! (1949 Red Cross giveaway, 12 pgs., 4-3/4x6") 9.15 27.00 60.00
...in It's All in the Family (1945 Red Cross giveaway, 16 pgs., regular size) 10.00 30.00 75.00

JOE THE GENIE OF STEEL
U.S. Steel Corp., Pittsburgh, PA: 1950 (16 pgs.)
nn 4.00 11.00 22.00

JOHNNY JINGLE'S LUCKY DAY
American Dairy Assoc.: 1956 (16 pgs.; 7-1/4x5-1/8") (Giveaway) (Disney)
nn 4.65 14.00 28.00

JO-JOY (The Adventures of...)
W. T. Grant Dept. Stores: 1945 - 1953 (Christmas gift comic, 16 pgs., 7-1/16x10-1/4")
1945-53 issues 5.00 15.00 30.00

JOLLY CHRISTMAS BOOK (See Christmas Journey Through Space)
Promotional Publ. Co.: 1951; 1954; 1955 (36 pgs.; 24 pgs.)
1951-(Woolworth giveaway)-slightly oversized; no slick cover; Marv Levy-c/a 6.70 20.00 45.00
1954-(Hot Shoppes giveaway)-regular size-reprints 1951 issue; slick cover added; 24 pgs.; no ads 6.70 20.00 45.00
1955-(J. M. McDonald Co. giveaway)-reg. size 5.00 15.00 35.00

JOURNEY OF DISCOVERY WITH MARK STEEL (See Mark Steel)

JUMPING JACKS PRESENTS THE WHIZ KIDS
Jumping Jacks Stores giveaway: 1978 (In 3-D) with glasses (4 pgs.)
nn 4.00

JUNGLE BOOK FUN BOOK, THE (Disney)
Baskin Robbins: 1978
nn-Ice Cream giveaway 1.75 5.25 14.00

JUSTICE LEAGUE OF AMERICA
DC Comics: 1999 (included in Justice League of America Monopoly game)
nn-Reprints 1st app. in Brave and the Bold #28 2.00

KASCO KOMICS
Kasko Grainfeed (Giveaway): 1945; No. 2, 1949 (Regular size, paper-c)
1(1945)-Similar to Katy Keene; Bill Woggon-a; 28 pgs.; 6-7/8x9-7/8" 17.00 51.00 135.00
2(1949)-Woggon-c/a 13.00 39.00 105.00

KATY AND KEN VISIT SANTA WITH MISTER WISH
S. S. Kresge Co. : 1948 (Giveaway, 16 pgs., paper-c)
nn 5.00 15.00 30.00

KELLOGG'S CINNAMON MINI-BUNS SUPER-HEROES
DC Comics: 1993 (4 1/4" x 2 3/4")
4 editions: Flash, Justice League America, Superman, Wonder Woman and the Star Riders each..... 2.00

KERRY DRAKE DETECTIVE CASES
Publisher's Syndicate
...in the Case of the Sleeping City-(1951)-16 pg. giveaway for armed forces; paper cover 5.00 15.00 30.00

KEY COMICS
Key Clothing Co./Peterson Clothing: 1951 - 1956 (32 pgs.) (Giveaway)
Contains a comic from different publishers bound with new cover. Cover changed each year. Many combinations possible. Distributed in Nebraska, Iowa, & Kansas. Contents would determine price, 40-60 percent of original.

KIRBY'S SHOES COMICS
Kirby's Shoes: 1959 (8 pgs., soft-c)
nn-Features Kirby the Golden Bear 1.25 3.75 10.00

Kite Fun Book 1963 Top Cat
© H-B

Little Klinker
© L. K. Ventures

Loaded #1
© Gremlin Interactive Ltd.

KITE FUN BOOK
Pacific, Gas & Electric/Sou. California Edison/Florida Power & Light/ Missouri Public Service Co.: 1953 - 1981 (16pgs, 5x7-1/4", soft-c)

1953-Pinocchio Learns About Kites (Disney) 47.00 141.00 420.00
1954-Donald Duck Tells About Kites-Fla. Power, S.C.E. & version with label issues-Barks pencils-8 pgs.; inks-7 pgs. (Rare) 400.00 1200.00 3000.00
1954-Donald Duck Tells About Kites-P.G.&E. issue -7th page redrawn changing middle 3 panels to show P.G.&E. in story line; (All Barks; last page Barks pencils only) Scarce 247.00 741.00 2300.00
1955-Brer Rabbit in "A Kite Tail" (Disney) 34.00 103.00 270.00
1956-Woody Woodpecker (Lantz) 14.00 43.00 110.00
1957-?
1958-Tom And Jerry (M.G.M.) 10.00 30.00 65.00
1960-Porky Pig (Warner Bros.) 4.55 13.65 50.00
1960-Bugs Bunny (Warner Bros.) 4.55 13.65 50.00
1961-Huckleberry Hound (Hanna-Barbera) 5.50 16.50 60.00
1962-Yogi Bear (Hanna-Barbera) 3.65 11.00 40.00
1963-Rocky and Bullwinkle (TV)(Jay Ward) 10.00 30.00 110.00
1963-Top Cat (TV)(Hanna-Barbera) 4.55 13.65 50.00
1964-Magilla Gorilla (TV)(Hanna-Barbera) 4.10 12.30 45.00
1965-Jinks, Pixie and Dixie (TV)(Hanna-Barbera) 3.00 9.00 32.00
1965-Tweety and Sylvester (Warner); S.C.E. version with Reddy Kilowatt app. 2.00 6.00 16.00
1966-Secret Squirrel (Hanna-Barbera); S.C.E. version with Reddy Kilowatt app. 6.50 19.50 70.00
1967-Beep! Beep! The Road Runner (TV)(Warner) 2.50 7.50 22.00
1968-Bugs Bunny (Warner Bros.) 2.50 7.50 25.00
1969-Dastardly and Muttley (TV)(Hanna-Barbera) 4.10 12.30 45.00
1970-Rocky and Bullwinkle (TV)(Jay Ward) 7.00 21.00 75.00
1971-Beep! Beep! The Road Runner (TV)(Warner) 2.30 7.00 20.00
1972-The Pink Panther (TV) 2.00 6.00 16.00
1973-Lassie (TV) 3.00 9.00 32.00
1974-Underdog (TV) 2.40 7.35 22.00
1975-Ben Franklin 1.25 3.75 10.00
1976-The Brady Bunch (TV) 2.50 7.50 25.00
1977-Ben Franklin 1.25 3.75 10.00
1977-Popeye 2.00 6.00 18.00
1978-Happy Days (TV) 2.00 6.00 18.00
1979-Eight is Enough (TV) 2.00 6.00 18.00
1980-The Waltons (TV, released in 1981) 2.00 6.00 18.00

KNOW YOUR MASS
Catechetical Guild: No. 303, 1958 (35¢, 100 Pg. Giant) (Square binding)

303-In color 5.00 15.00 30.00

K. O. PUNCH, THE (Also see Lucky Fights It Through)
E. C. Comics: 1948 (Educational giveaway)

nn-Feldstein-splash; Kamen-a 94.00 282.00 800.00

KOREA MY HOME (Also see Yalta to Korea)
Johnstone and Cushing: nd (1950s)

nn-Anti-communist; Korean War 24.00 73.00 190.00

KRIM-KO KOMICS
Krim-ko Chocolate Drink: 5/18/35 - No. 6, 6/22/35; 1936 - 1939 (weekly)

1-(16 pgs., soft-c, Dairy giveaways)-Tom, Mary & Sparky Advs. by Russell Keaton, Jim Hawkins by Dick Moores, Mystery Island! by Rick Yager begin 14.00 43.00 110.00
2-6 (6/22/35) 10.00 30.00 75.00
Lola, Secret Agent; 184 issues, 4 pg. giveaways - all original stories each.... 7.00 21.00 45.00

LABOR IS A PARTNER
Catechetical Guild Educational Society: 1949 (32 pgs., paper-c)

nn-Anti-communism 19.00 58.00 150.00
Confidential Preview-(8-1/2x11", B&W, saddle stitched)-only one known copy; text varies from color version, advertises next book on secularism (If the Devil Would Talk) 22.00 66.00 175.00

LADY AND THE TRAMP IN "BUTTER LATE THAN NEVER"
American Dairy Assoc. (Premium): 1955 (16 pgs., 5x7-1/4", soft-c) (Disney)

nn 11.00 33.00 80.00

LASSIE (TV)
Dell Publ. Co

The Adventures of... nn-(Red Heart Dog Food giveaway, 1949)-16 pgs, soft-c; 1st app. Lassie in comics 34.00 125.00 270.(

LIFE OF THE BLESSED VIRGIN
Catechetical Guild (Giveaway): 1950 (68pgs.) (square binding)

nn-Contains "The Woman of the Promise" & "Mother of Us All" rebound 5.00 15.00 32.

LIGHTNING RACERS
DC Comics: 1989

1 2.(

LI'L ABNER (Al Capp's) (Also see Natural Disasters!)
Harvey Publ./Toby Press

...& the Creatures from Drop-Outer Space-nn (Job Corps giveaway; 36 pgs., in color)(entire book by Frank Frazetta) 29.00 88.00 220.(
...Joins the Navy (1950) (Toby Press Premium) 15.00 50.00 90.(
...by Al Capp Giveaway (Circa 1955, nd) 15.00 50.00 90.(

LITTLE ALONZO
Macy's Dept. Store: 1938 (B&W, 5-1/2x8-1/2")(Christmas giveaway)

nn-By Ferdinand the Bull's Munro Leaf 8.65 26.00 60.

LITTLE DOT
Harvey Publications

Shoe store giveaway 2 3.80 11.40 40.

LITTLE FIR TREE, THE
W. T. Grant Co. : nd (1942) (8-1/2x11") (12 pgs. with cover, color & B&W, hea paper) (Christmas giveaway)

nn-Story by Hans Christian Anderson; 8 pg. Kelly-r/Santa Claus Funnies (not signed); X-Mas-c
(One copy in Mint sold for $1750.00 in 1986 & another copy in VF sold for $1000.00 in 1991)

LITTLE KLINKER
Little Klinker Ventures: Nov, 1960 (20 pgs.) (slick cover) (Montgomery Ward Giveaway)

nn 1.75 5.25 14.

LITTLE MISS SUNBEAM COMICS
Magazine Enterprises/Quality Bakers of America

Bread Giveaway 1-4(Quality Bakers, 1949-50)-14 pgs. each 5.00 15.00 35.
Bread Giveaway (1957,61; 16pgs, reg. size) 5.00 15.00 30.

LITTLE ORPHAN ANNIE
David McKay Publ./Dell Publishing Co.

Junior Commandos Giveaway (same-c as 4-Color #18, K.K. Publ.)(Big Shoe Store); same back cover as '47 Popped Wheat giveaway; 16 pgs; flag-c; r/strips 9/7/42-10/10/42 34.00 125.00 270.(
Popped Wheat Giveaway ('47)-16 pgs. full color; reprints strips from 5/3/40 to 6/20/40 3.00 7.50 15.(
Quaker Sparkies Giveaway (1940) 21.00 64.00 165.(
Quaker Sparkies Giveaway (1941, full color, 20 pgs.); "LOA and the Rescue"; r/strips 4/13/39-6/21/39 & 7/6/39-7/17/39. "LOA and the Kidnappers"; r/strips 11/28/38-1/28/39 19.00 58.00 150.(
Quaker Sparkies Giveaway (1942, full color, 20 pgs.); "LOA and Mr. Gudge"; r/strips 2/13/38-3/21/38 & 4/18/37-5/30/37. "LOA and the Great Am" 17.00 51.00 135.(

LITTLE TREE THAT WASN'T WANTED, THE
W. T. Grant Co. (Giveaway): 1960, (Color, 28 pgs.)

nn-Christmas giveaway 2.50 7.50 25.(

LOADED (Also see Re-Loaded)
DC Comics: 1995 (Interplay Productions)

1-Garth Ennis-s; promotes video game 3.(

LONE RANGER, THE
Dell Publishing Co.

Cheerios Giveaways (1954, 16 pgs., 2-1/2x7", soft-c) #1- "The Lone Ranger, His Mask & How He Met Tonto". #2- "The Lone Ranger & the Story of

Major Inapak, The Space Ace #1 © ME

The Man Who Wouldn't Quit © HARV

March of Comics #20 © WDC

GD2.0 FN6.0 NM9.4

Silver" each.... 20.00 60.00 130.00
Doll Giveaways (Gabriel Ind.)(1973, 3-1/4x5")- "The Story of The Lone Ranger" & "The Carson City Bank Robbery" 1.85 5.50 15.00
How the Lone Ranger Captured Silver Book(1936)-Silvercup Bread giveaway 100.00 300.00 550.00
...In Milk for Big Mike (1955, Dairy Association giveaway), soft-c; 5x7-1/4", 16 pgs. 20.00 60.00 135.00
Legend of The Lone Ranger (1969, 16 pgs., giveaway)-Origin The Lone Ranger 3.00 9.00 32.00
Merita Bread giveaway (1954, 16 pgs., 5x7-1/4")- "How to Be a Lone Ranger Health & Safety Scout" 25.00 75.00 160.00

LONE RANGER COMICS, THE
Lone Ranger, Inc. : Book 1, 1939(inside) (shows 1938 on-c) (52 pgs. in color; regular size) (Ice cream mail order)

GD2.0 FN6.0 VF8.0

Book 1-(Scarce)-The first western comic devoted to a single character; not by Vallely 917.00 3000.00 5500.00
2nd version w/large full color promo poster pasted over centerfold & a smaller poster pasted over back cover; includes new additional premiums not originally offered (Rare) 1000.00 3200.00 6000.00

LOONEY TUNES
DC Comics: 1991, 1998
Claritan promotional issue (1998) 2.00
Colgate mini-comic (1998) 2.00
Tyson's 1-10 (1991) 2.00

LUCKY FIGHTS IT THROUGH (Also see The K. O. Punch)
Educational Comics: 1949 (Giveaway, 16 pgs. in color, paper-c)

GD2.0 FN6.0 NM9.4

nn-(Very Rare)-1st Kurtzman work for E. C.; V.D. prevention 125.00 375.00 1000.00
nn-Reprint in color (1977) 6.00
NOTE: *Subtitled "The Story of That Ignorant, Ignorant Cowboy". Prepared for Communications Materials Center, Columbia University.*

LUDWIG VON DRAKE (See Frito-Lay Giveaway)

MACO TOYS COMIC
Maco Toys/Charlton Comics: 1959 (Giveaway, 36 pgs.)
1-All military stories featuring Maco Toys 1.50 4.50 12.00

MAD MAGAZINE
DC Comics: 1997, 1999
Special Edition (1997, Tang giveaway) 2.00
Stocking Stuffer (1999) 2.00

MAGAZINELAND
DC Comics: 1977
nn 2.00

MAGIC MORRO (Also see Super Comics #21, The Owl, & The Hurricane Kids)
K. K. Publications: 1941 (7-1/2x5-1/4, giveaway, soft-c)
1-Ken Ernst-a. 12.00 36.00 95.00

MAGIC OF CHRISTMAS AT NEWBERRYS, THE
E. S. London: 1967 (Giveaway) (B&W, slick-c, 20 pgs.)
nn 1.00 3.00 8.00

MAJOR INAPAK THE SPACE ACE
Magazine Enterprises (Inapac Foods): 1951 (20 pgs.) (Giveaway)
1-Bob Powell-c/a 5.00
NOTE: *Many warehouse copies surfaced in 1973.*

MAMMY YOKUM & THE GREAT DOGPATCH MYSTERY
Toby Press: 1951 (Giveaway)
nn-Li'l Abner 18.00 54.00 140.00
nn-Reprint (1956) 5.00 15.00 30.00

MAN OF PEACE, POPE PIUS XII
Catechetical Guild: 1950 (See Pope Pius XII... & To V2#8)
nn-All Powell-a 5.00 15.00 32.00

MAN OF STEEL BEST WESTERN
DC Comics: 1997
nn-Best Western hotels 2.00

GD2.0 FN6.0 NM9.4

MAN WHO WOULDN'T QUIT, THE
Harvey Publications Inc.: 1952 (16 pgs., paper cover)
nn-The value of voting 20.00

MARCH OF COMICS (Boys' and Girls'...#3-353)
K. K. Publications/Western Publishing Co.: 1946 - No. 488, April, 1982 (#1-4 are not numbered) (K.K. Giveaway) (Founded by Sig Feuchtwanger)

Early issues were full size, 32 pages, and were printed with and without an extra cover of slick stock, just for the advertiser. The binding was stapled if the slick cover was added; otherwise, the pages were glued together at the spine. Most 1948 - 1951 issues were full size,24 pages, pulp covers. Starting in 1952 they were half-size and 32 pages with slick covers.1959 and later issues had only 16 pages plus covers. 1952 -1959 issues read oblong; 1960 and later issues read upright. All have new stories except where noted.

nn (#1, 1946)-Goldilocks; Kelly back-c (16 pgs., stapled) 36.00 107.00 250.00
nn (#2, 1946)-How Santa Got His Red Suit; Kelly-a (11 pgs., r/4-Color #61 from 1944) (16pgs., stapled) 36.00 107.00 250.00
nn (#3, 1947)-Our Gang (Walt Kelly) 46.00 137.00 340.00
nn (#4)-Donald Duck by Carl Barks, "Maharajah Donald", 28 pgs.; Kelly-c? (Disney) 857.00 2571.00 7000.00
5-Andy Panda (Walter Lantz) 21.50 64.00 150.00
6-Popular Fairy Tales; Kelly-c; Noonan-a(2) 25.00 75.00 175.00
7-Oswald the Rabbit 24.00 71.00 165.00
8-Mickey Mouse, 32 pgs. (Disney) 71.00 215.00 500.00
9(nn)-The Story of the Gloomy Bunny 11.00 33.00 90.00
10-Out of Santa's Bag 10.00 30.00 80.00
11-Fun With Santa Claus 9.30 28.00 65.00
12-Santa's Toys 9.30 28.00 65.00
13-Santa's Surprise 9.30 28.00 65.00
14-Santa's Candy Kitchen 9.30 28.00 65.00
15-Hip-It-Ty Hop & the Big Bass Viol 8.65 26.00 60.00
16-Woody Woodpecker (1947)(Walter Lantz) 16.00 47.00 110.00
17-Roy Rogers (1948) 29.00 86.00 225.00
18-Popular Fairy Tales 13.00 39.00 90.00
19-Uncle Wiggily 11.00 33.00 75.00
20-Donald Duck by Carl Barks, "Darkest Africa", 22 pgs.; Kelly-c (Disney) 500.00 1500.00 4000.00
21-Tom and Jerry 13.00 39.00 90.00
22-Andy Panda (Lantz) 11.50 34.00 80.00
23-Raggedy Ann & Andy; Kerr-a 17.00 49.00 115.00
24-Felix the Cat, 1932 daily strip reprints by Otto Messmer 27.00 81.00 210.00
25-Gene Autry 27.00 81.00 210.00
26-Our Gang; Walt Kelly 26.00 79.00 185.00
27-Mickey Mouse; r/in M. M. #240 (Disney) 50.00 150.00 350.00
28-Gene Autry 26.00 79.00 200.00
29-Easter Bonnet Shop 5.85 17.50 40.00
30-Here Comes Santa 5.50 16.50 38.00
31-Santa's Busy Corner 5.50 16.50 38.00
32-No book produced
33-A Christmas Carol (12/48) 5.50 16.50 38.00
34-Woody Woodpecker 11.50 34.00 80.00
35-Roy Rogers (1948) 29.00 86.00 220.00
36-Felix the Cat(1949); by Messmer; '34 strip-r 24.00 71.00 175.00
37-Popeye 18.00 54.00 125.00
38-Oswald the Rabbit 10.00 30.00 58.00
39-Gene Autry 26.00 79.00 200.00
40-Andy and Woody 10.00 30.00 58.00
41-Donald Duck by Carl Barks, "Race to the South Seas", 22 pgs.; Kelly-c 500.00 1500.00 3500.00
42-Porky Pig 10.00 30.00 65.00
43-Henry 8.00 24.00 55.00
44-Bugs Bunny 11.00 33.00 75.00
45-Mickey Mouse (Disney) 39.00 116.00 270.00
46-Tom and Jerry 11.00 33.00 75.00
47-Roy Rogers 25.00 75.00 190.00
48-Greetings from Santa 5.00 15.00 30.00
49-Santa Is Here 5.00 15.00 30.00
50-Santa Claus' Workshop (1949) 5.00 15.00 30.00
51-Felix the Cat (1950) by Messmer 19.00 58.00 150.00
52-Popeye 15.00 45.00 105.00
53-Oswald the Rabbit 10.00 30.00 58.00

March of Comics #70 © MGM

March of Comics #115 © WB

March of Comics #151 © Roy Rogers

	GD2.0	FN6.0	NM9.4
54-Gene Autry	23.00	69.00	175.00
55-Andy and Woody	8.70	26.00	52.00
56-Donald Duck; not by Barks; Barks art on back-c (Disney)	36.00	109.00	255.00
57-Porky Pig	8.70	26.00	60.00
58-Henry	6.35	19.00	38.00
59-Bugs Bunny	10.00	30.00	65.00
60-Mickey Mouse (Disney)	35.00	105.00	245.00
61-Tom and Jerry	8.70	26.00	52.00
62-Roy Rogers	24.00	71.00	180.00
63-Welcome Santa (1/2-size, oblong)	5.00	15.00	30.00
64(nn)-Santa's Helpers (1/2-size, oblong)	5.00	15.00	30.00
65(nn)-Jingle Bells (1950) (1/2-size, oblong)	5.00	15.00	30.00
66-Popeye (1951)	13.00	39.00	90.00
67-Oswald the Rabbit	8.50	25.50	52.00
68-Roy Rogers	22.00	66.00	175.00
69-Donald Duck; Barks-a on back-c (Disney)	31.00	94.00	220.00
70-Tom and Jerry	8.00	24.00	48.00
71-Porky Pig	8.50	25.50	52.00
72-Krazy Kat	10.00	30.00	65.00
73-Roy Rogers	19.00	56.00	150.00
74-Mickey Mouse (1951)(Disney)	29.00	86.00	200.00
75-Bugs Bunny	8.70	26.00	52.00
76-Andy and Woody	8.00	24.00	48.00
77-Roy Rogers	18.00	54.00	145.00
78-Gene Autry (1951); last regular size issue	18.00	53.00	140.00
Note: All pre #79 issues came with or without a slick protective wrap-around cover over the regular cover which advertised Poll Parrott Shoes, Sears, etc. This outer cover protects the inside pages making them in nicer condition. Issues with the outer cover are worth 10-20% more			
79-Andy Panda (1952, 5x7" size)	5.00	15.00	35.00
80-Popeye	11.50	34.00	80.00
81-Oswald the Rabbit	5.00	15.00	30.00
82-Tarzan; Lex Barker photo-c	20.00	60.00	160.00
83-Bugs Bunny	6.70	20.00	40.00
84-Henry	4.65	14.00	28.00
85-Woody Woodpecker	4.65	14.00	28.00
86-Roy Rogers	14.00	41.00	110.00
87-Krazy Kat	8.70	26.00	52.00
88-Tom and Jerry	5.70	17.00	34.00
89-Porky Pig	4.65	14.00	28.00
90-Gene Autry	13.00	39.00	105.00
91-Roy Rogers & Santa	14.00	41.00	110.00
92-Christmas with Santa	4.15	12.50	25.00
93-Woody Woodpecker (1953)	4.00	12.00	24.00
94-Indian Chief	10.00	30.00	70.00
95-Oswald the Rabbit	4.00	12.00	24.00
96-Popeye	10.00	30.00	68.00
97-Bugs Bunny	5.70	17.00	34.00
98-Tarzan; Lex Barker photo-c	21.00	62.00	150.00
99-Porky Pig	4.00	12.00	24.00
100-Roy Rogers	10.70	32.00	85.00
101-Henry	4.00	11.00	22.00
102-Tom Corbett (TV)('53, early app).; painted-c	17.00	49.00	115.00
103-Tom and Jerry	4.00	12.00	24.00
104-Gene Autry	11.00	33.00	85.00
105-Roy Rogers	11.00	33.00	85.00
106-Santa's Helpers	4.15	12.50	25.00
107-Santa's Christmas Book - not published			
108-Fun with Santa (1953)	4.15	12.50	25.00
109-Woody Woodpecker (1954)	4.15	12.50	25.00
110-Indian Chief	5.70	17.00	34.00
111-Oswald the Rabbit	4.00	11.00	22.00
112-Henry	4.00	10.00	20.00
113-Porky Pig	4.00	11.00	22.00
114-Tarzan; Russ Manning-a	21.00	62.00	150.00
115-Bugs Bunny	4.25	13.00	28.00
116-Roy Rogers	11.00	33.00	85.00
117-Popeye	10.00	30.00	68.00
118-Flash Gordon; painted-c	13.50	41.00	95.00
119-Tom and Jerry	4.00	11.00	22.00

	GD2.0	FN6.0	NM9.4
120-Gene Autry	11.00	33.00	85.
121-Roy Rogers	11.00	33.00	85.
122-Santa's Surprise (1954)	4.00	11.00	22.
123-Santa's Christmas Book	4.00	11.00	22.
124-Woody Woodpecker (1955)	4.00	10.00	20.
125-Tarzan; Lex Barker photo-c	19.00	58.00	140.
126-Oswald the Rabbit	4.00	10.00	20.
127-Indian Chief	5.70	17.00	40.
128-Tom and Jerry	4.00	10.00	20.
129-Henry	3.40	8.50	17.
130-Porky Pig	4.00	10.00	20.
131-Roy Rogers	11.00	33.00	85.
132-Bugs Bunny	4.00	12.00	24.
133-Flash Gordon; painted-c	12.00	36.00	85.
134-Popeye	8.00	24.00	48.0
135-Gene Autry	10.00	30.00	75.0
136-Roy Rogers	10.00	30.00	75.0
137-Gifts from Santa	2.80	7.00	14.0
138-Fun at Christmas (1955)	2.80	7.00	14.
139-Woody Woodpecker (1956)	4.00	10.00	20.0
140-Indian Chief	5.70	17.00	40.0
141-Oswald the Rabbit	4.00	10.00	20.0
142-Flash Gordon	12.00	36.00	85.0
143-Porky Pig	4.00	10.00	20.0
144-Tarzan; Russ Manning-a; painted-c	18.00	54.00	130.0
145-Tom and Jerry	4.00	10.00	20.0
146-Roy Rogers; photo-c	11.00	33.00	75.0
147-Henry	3.00	7.50	15.0
148-Popeye	8.00	24.00	48.0
149-Bugs Bunny	4.00	11.00	22.0
150-Gene Autry	10.00	30.00	75.0
151-Roy Rogers	10.00	30.00	75.0
152-The Night Before Christmas	3.20	8.00	16.0
153-Merry Christmas (1956)	3.20	8.00	16.0
154-Tom and Jerry (1957)	4.00	10.00	20.0
155-Tarzan; photo-c	18.00	54.00	125.0
156-Oswald the Rabbit	4.00	10.00	20.0
157-Popeye	6.70	20.00	40.0
158-Woody Woodpecker	4.00	10.00	20.0
159-Indian Chief	5.70	17.00	40.0
160-Bugs Bunny	4.00	11.00	22.0
161-Roy Rogers	10.00	30.00	65.0
162-Henry	3.00	7.50	15.0
163-Rin Tin Tin (TV)	7.50	22.50	50.0
164-Porky Pig	4.00	10.00	20.0
165-The Lone Ranger	10.00	30.00	70.0
166-Santa and His Reindeer	2.80	7.00	14.0
167-Roy Rogers and Santa	10.00	30.00	65.
168-Santa Claus' Workshop (1957)	3.20	8.00	16.
169-Popeye (1958)	6.70	20.00	40.
170-Indian Chief	5.70	17.00	40.
171-Oswald the Rabbit	3.60	9.00	18.
172-Tarzan	13.50	41.00	95.
173-Tom and Jerry	3.60	9.00	18.
174-The Lone Ranger	10.00	30.00	70.
175-Porky Pig	3.60	9.00	18.
176-Roy Rogers	9.15	27.00	60.
177-Woody Woodpecker	3.60	9.00	18.
178-Henry	3.00	7.50	15.
179-Bugs Bunny	3.60	9.00	18.0
180-Rin Tin Tin (TV)	6.50	19.50	45.0
181-Happy Holiday	2.40	6.00	12.0
182-Happi Tim	3.20	8.00	16.0
183-Welcome Santa (1958)	2.40	6.00	12.0
184-Woody Woodpecker (1959)	3.20	8.00	16.0
185-Tarzan; photo-c	13.00	39.00	90.0
186-Oswald the Rabbit	3.20	8.00	16.0
187-Indian Chief	5.35	16.00	32.0
188-Bugs Bunny	3.20	8.00	16.0
189-Henry	2.80	7.00	14.0
190-Tom and Jerry	3.20	8.00	16.0

March of Comics #271 © H-B

March of Comics #294 © KING

March of Comics #306 © WDC

	GD2.0	FN6.0	NM9.4
191-Roy Rogers	8.35	25.00	55.00
192-Porky Pig	3.20	8.00	16.00
193-The Lone Ranger	10.00	30.00	65.00
194-Popeye	5.85	17.50	35.00
195-Rin Tin Tin (TV)	6.00	18.00	40.00
196-Sears Special - not published			
197-Santa Is Coming	2.80	7.00	14.00
198-Santa's Helpers (1959)	2.80	7.00	14.00
199-Huckleberry Hound (TV)(1960, early app.)	7.15	21.50	50.00
200-Fury (TV)	5.35	16.00	32.00
201-Bugs Bunny	3.20	8.00	16.00
202-Space Explorer	9.15	27.50	55.00
203-Woody Woodpecker	2.80	7.00	14.00
204-Tarzan	10.00	30.00	70.00
205-Mighty Mouse	6.35	19.00	38.00
206-Roy Rogers; photo-c	8.35	25.00	55.00
207-Tom and Jerry	2.80	7.00	14.00
208-The Lone Ranger; Clayton Moore photo-c	12.00	36.00	90.00
209-Porky Pig	2.80	7.00	14.00
210-Lassie (TV)	6.35	19.00	38.00
211-Sears Special - not published			
212-Christmas Eve	2.80	7.00	14.00
213-Here Comes Santa (1960)	2.80	7.00	14.00
214-Huckleberry Hound (TV)(1961)	6.00	18.00	40.00
215-Hi Yo Silver	6.40	19.25	45.00
216-Rocky & His Friends (TV)(1961); predates Rocky and His Fiendish Friends #1 (see Four Color #1128)	10.00	30.00	75.00
217-Lassie (TV)	5.70	17.00	35.00
218-Porky Pig	2.80	7.00	14.00
219-Journey to the Sun	5.35	16.00	32.00
220-Bugs Bunny	3.20	8.00	16.00
221-Roy and Dale; photo-c	7.50	22.50	50.00
222-Woody Woodpecker	2.80	7.00	14.00
223-Tarzan	10.00	30.00	70.00
224-Tom and Jerry	2.80	7.00	14.00
225-The Lone Ranger	7.50	22.50	50.00
226-Christmas Treasury (1961)	2.80	7.00	14.00
227-Letters to Santa (1961)	2.80	7.00	14.00
228-Sears Special - not published?			
229-The Flintstones (TV)(1962); early app.; predates 1st Flintstones Gold Key issue (#7)	10.00	30.00	75.00
230-Lassie (TV)	5.00	15.00	30.00
231-Bugs Bunny	3.20	8.00	16.00
232-The Three Stooges	10.00	30.00	70.00
233-Bullwinkle (TV) (1962, very early app.)	11.00	32.00	80.00
34-Smokey the Bear	4.00	12.00	24.00
35-Huckleberry Hound (TV)	6.00	18.00	40.00
36-Roy and Dale	5.85	17.50	40.00
37-Mighty Mouse	5.00	15.00	30.00
38-The Lone Ranger	7.50	22.50	50.00
39-Woody Woodpecker	2.80	7.00	14.00
40-Tarzan	9.15	27.50	60.00
41-Santa Claus Around the World	2.40	6.00	12.00
42-Santa's Toyland (1962)	2.40	6.00	12.00
43-The Flintstones (TV)(1963)	9.15	27.50	55.00
44-Mister Ed (TV); early app.; photo-c	5.85	17.50	35.00
45-Bugs Bunny	3.20	8.00	16.00
46-Popeye	4.35	13.00	26.00
47-Mighty Mouse	4.70	14.00	28.00
48-The Three Stooges	10.00	30.00	70.00
49-Woody Woodpecker	2.80	7.00	14.00
50-Roy and Dale	5.85	17.50	40.00
51-Little Lulu & Witch Hazel	14.00	43.00	100.00
52-Tarzan; painted-c	9.15	27.50	55.00
53-Yogi Bear (TV)	7.15	21.50	50.00
54-Lassie (TV)	5.35	16.00	32.00
55-Santa's Christmas List	2.80	7.00	14.00
56-Christmas Party (1963)	2.80	7.00	14.00
57-Mighty Mouse	4.70	14.00	28.00
58-The Sword in the Stone (Disney)	9.15	27.50	55.00
59-Bugs Bunny	3.20	8.00	16.00

	GD2.0	FN6.0	NM9.4
260-Mister Ed (TV)	5.00	15.00	30.00
261-Woody Woodpecker	2.80	7.00	14.00
262-Tarzan	8.35	25.00	50.00
263-Donald Duck; not by Barks (Disney)	10.00	30.00	65.00
264-Popeye	4.35	13.00	26.00
265-Yogi Bear (TV)	5.70	17.00	35.00
266-Lassie (TV)	4.15	12.50	25.00
267-Little Lulu; Irving Tripp-a	11.50	34.00	80.00
268-The Three Stooges	10.00	30.00	60.00
269-A Jolly Christmas	2.00	5.00	10.00
270-Santa's Little Helpers	2.00	5.00	10.00
271-The Flintstones (TV)(1965)	9.15	27.50	60.00
272-Tarzan	8.35	25.00	50.00
273-Bugs Bunny	3.20	8.00	16.00
274-Popeye	4.35	13.00	26.00
275-Little Lulu; Irving Tripp-a	10.00	30.00	65.00
276-The Jetsons (TV)	16.00	47.00	120.00
277-Daffy Duck	3.20	8.00	16.00
278-Lassie (TV)	4.15	12.50	25.00
279-Yogi Bear (TV)	5.70	17.00	35.00
280-The Three Stooges; photo-c	10.00	30.00	60.00
281-Tom and Jerry	2.40	6.00	12.00
282-Mister Ed (TV)	5.00	15.00	30.00
283-Santa's Visit	2.80	7.00	14.00
284-Christmas Parade (1965)	2.80	7.00	14.00
285-Astro Boy (TV); 2nd app. Astro Boy	41.00	122.00	300.00
286-Tarzan	7.50	22.50	45.00
287-Bugs Bunny	3.20	8.00	16.00
288-Daffy Duck	2.80	7.00	14.00
289-The Flintstones (TV)	8.50	26.00	60.00
290-Mister Ed (TV); photo-c	4.00	12.00	24.00
291-Yogi Bear (TV)	5.00	15.00	30.00
292-The Three Stooges; photo-c	10.00	30.00	60.00
293-Little Lulu; Irving Tripp-a	9.15	27.50	55.00
294-Popeye	4.35	13.00	26.00
295-Tom and Jerry	2.40	6.00	12.00
296-Lassie (TV); photo-c	4.00	11.00	22.00
297-Christmas Bells	2.40	6.00	12.00
298-Santa's Sleigh (1966)	2.40	6.00	12.00
299-The Flintstones (TV)(1967)	8.50	26.00	60.00
300-Tarzan	7.50	22.50	45.00
301-Bugs Bunny	2.80	7.00	14.00
302-Laurel and Hardy (TV); photo-c	5.00	15.00	32.00
303-Daffy Duck	2.00	5.00	10.00
304-The Three Stooges; photo-c	9.15	27.50	55.00
305-Tom and Jerry	2.00	5.00	10.00
306-Daniel Boone (TV); Fess Parker photo-c	5.85	17.50	40.00
307-Little Lulu; Irving Tripp-a	7.50	22.50	45.00
308-Lassie (TV); photo-c	4.00	11.00	22.00
309-Yogi Bear (TV)	4.25	13.00	28.00
310-The Lone Ranger; Clayton Moore photo-c	12.00	36.00	90.00
311-Santa's Show	2.80	7.00	14.00
312-Christmas Album (1967)	2.80	7.00	14.00
313-Daffy Duck (1968)	2.00	5.00	10.00
314-Laurel and Hardy (TV)	5.00	15.00	30.00
315-Bugs Bunny	2.80	7.00	14.00
316-The Three Stooges	7.50	22.50	45.00
317-The Flintstones (TV)	7.15	21.50	50.00
318-Tarzan	6.70	20.00	40.00
319-Yogi Bear (TV)	4.25	13.00	28.00
320-Space Family Robinson (TV); Spiegle-a	14.00	43.00	110.00
321-Tom and Jerry	2.00	5.00	10.00
322-The Lone Ranger	6.70	20.00	45.00
323-Little Lulu; not by Stanley	4.35	13.00	26.00
324-Lassie (TV); photo-c	4.00	11.00	22.00
325-Fun with Santa	2.80	7.00	14.00
326-Christmas Story (1968)	2.80	7.00	14.00
327-The Flintstones (TV)(1969)	7.15	21.50	50.00
328-Space Family Robinson (TV); Spiegle-a	14.00	43.00	110.00
329-Bugs Bunny	2.80	7.00	14.00
330-The Jetsons (TV)	11.50	34.00	80.00

March of Comics #337 © H-B

March of Comics #435 © Terrytoons

March of Comics #487 © WB

	GD2.0	FN6.0	NM9.4
331-Daffy Duck	2.00	5.00	10.00
332-Tarzan	5.35	16.00	32.00
333-Tom and Jerry	2.00	5.00	10.00
334-Lassie (TV)	4.00	10.00	20.00
335-Little Lulu	4.35	13.00	26.00
336-The Three Stooges	7.50	22.50	45.00
337-Yogi Bear (TV)	4.25	13.00	28.00
338-The Lone Ranger	6.70	20.00	45.00
339-(Was not published)			
340-Here Comes Santa (1969)	2.40	6.00	12.00
341-The Flintstones (TV)	7.15	21.50	50.00
342-Tarzan	5.35	16.00	32.00
343-Bugs Bunny	2.40	6.00	12.00
344-Yogi Bear (TV)	4.15	12.50	25.00
345-Tom and Jerry	2.00	5.00	10.00
346-Lassie (TV)	4.00	10.00	20.00
347-Daffy Duck	2.00	5.00	10.00
348-The Jetsons (TV)	10.00	30.00	70.00
349-Little Lulu; not by Stanley	4.00	11.00	22.00
350-The Lone Ranger	5.00	15.00	30.00
351-Beep-Beep, the Road Runner (TV)	2.80	7.00	14.00
352-Space Family Robinson (TV); Spiegle-a	14.00	43.00	110.00
353-Beep-Beep, the Road Runner (1971) (TV)	2.80	7.00	14.00
354-Tarzan (1971)	4.70	14.00	28.00
355-Little Lulu; not by Stanley	4.00	11.00	22.00
356-Scooby Doo, Where Are You? (TV)	7.15	21.50	50.00
357-Daffy Duck & Porky Pig	2.00	5.00	10.00
358-Lassie (TV)	4.00	10.00	20.00
359-Baby Snoots	2.80	7.00	14.00
360-H. R. Pufnstuf (TV); photo-c	7.15	21.50	50.00
361-Tom and Jerry	2.00	5.00	10.00
362-Smokey the Bear (TV)	2.00	5.00	10.00
363-Bugs Bunny & Yosemite Sam	2.40	6.00	12.00
364-The Banana Splits (TV); photo-c	5.70	17.00	40.00
365-Tom and Jerry (1972)	2.00	5.00	10.00
366-Tarzan	4.35	13.00	26.00
367-Bugs Bunny & Porky Pig	2.40	6.00	12.00
368-Scooby Doo (TV)(4/72)	5.70	17.00	40.00
369-Little Lulu; not by Stanley	3.60	9.00	18.00
370-Lassie (TV); photo-c	4.00	10.00	20.00
371-Baby Snoots	2.40	6.00	12.00
372-Smokey the Bear (TV)	2.00	5.00	10.00
373-The Three Stooges	6.70	20.00	40.00
374-Wacky Witch	2.00	5.00	10.00
375-Beep-Beep & Daffy Duck (TV)	2.00	5.00	10.00
376-The Pink Panther (1972) (TV)	2.80	7.00	14.00
377-Baby Snoots (1973)	2.40	6.00	12.00
378-Turok, Son of Stone; new-a	16.00	47.00	115.00
379-Heckle & Jeckle New Terrytoons (TV)	2.00	5.00	10.00
380-Bugs Bunny & Yosemite Sam	2.00	5.00	10.00
381-Lassie (TV)	3.20	8.00	16.00
382-Scooby Doo, Where Are You? (TV)	5.00	15.00	30.00
383-Smokey the Bear (TV)	1.60	4.00	8.00
384-Pink Panther (TV)	2.00	5.00	10.00
385-Little Lulu	3.00	7.50	15.00
386-Wacky Witch	1.60	4.00	8.00
387-Beep-Beep & Daffy Duck (TV)	1.60	4.00	8.00
388-Tom and Jerry (1973)	1.60	4.00	8.00
389-Little Lulu; not by Stanley	3.00	7.50	15.00
390-Pink Panther (TV)	1.60	4.00	8.00
391-Scooby Doo (TV)	4.15	12.50	25.00
392-Bugs Bunny & Yosemite Sam	1.20	3.00	6.00
393-New Terrytoons (Heckle & Jeckle) (TV)	1.20	3.00	6.00
394-Lassie (TV)	2.40	6.00	12.00
395-Woodsy Owl	1.20	3.00	6.00
396-Baby Snoots	1.60	4.00	8.00
397-Beep-Beep & Daffy Duck (TV)	1.20	3.00	6.00
398-Wacky Witch	1.20	3.00	6.00
399-Turok, Son of Stone; new-a	13.00	39.00	100.00
400-Tom and Jerry	1.20	3.00	6.00
401-Baby Snoots (1975) (r/#371)	1.60	4.00	8.00

	GD2.0	FN6.0	NM9
402-Daffy Duck (r/#313)	1.00	2.50	5.0
403-Bugs Bunny (r/#343)	1.20	3.00	6.0
404-Space Family Robinson (TV)(r/#328)	10.00	30.00	75.0
405-Cracky	1.00	2.50	5.0
406-Little Lulu (r/#355)	2.80	7.00	14.0
407-Smokey the Bear (TV)(r/#362)	1.20	3.00	6.0
408-Turok, Son of Stone; c-r/Turok #20 w/changes; new-a	10.00	30.00	70.0
409-Pink Panther (TV)	1.00	2.50	5.0
410-Wacky Witch	.80	2.00	4.0
411-Lassie (TV)(r/#324)	2.40	6.00	12.0
412-New Terrytoons (1975) (TV)	.80	2.00	4.0
413-Daffy Duck (1976)(r/#331)	.80	2.00	4.0
414-Space Family Robinson (r/#328)	10.00	30.00	70.0
415-Bugs Bunny (r/#329)	.80	2.00	4.0
416-Beep-Beep, the Road Runner (r/#353)(TV)	.80	2.00	4.0
417-Little Lulu (r/#323)	2.80	7.00	14.0
418-Pink Panther (r/#384) (TV)	.80	2.00	4.0
419-Baby Snoots (r/#377)	1.00	2.50	5.0
420-Woody Woodpecker	.80	2.00	4.0
421-Tweety & Sylvester	.80	2.00	4.0
422-Wacky Witch (r/#386)	.80	2.00	4.0
423-Little Monsters	1.00	2.50	5.0
424-Cracky (12/76)	.80	2.00	4.0
425-Daffy Duck	.80	2.00	4.0
426-Underdog (TV)	5.00	15.00	30.0
427-Little Lulu (r/#335)	2.00	5.00	9.0
428-Bugs Bunny	.60	1.50	3.0
429-The Pink Panther (TV)	.60	1.50	3.0
430-Beep-Beep, the Road Runner (TV)	.60	1.50	3.0
431-Baby Snoots	.80	2.00	4.0
432-Lassie (TV)	1.20	3.00	6.0
433-437: 433-Tweety & Sylvester. 434-Wacky Witch. 435-New Terrytoons (TV) 436-Wacky Advs. of Cracky. 437-Daffy Duck	.60	1.50	3.0
438-Underdog (TV)	4.15	12.50	25.
439-Little Lulu (r/#349)	2.00	5.00	9.
440-442,444-446: 440-Bugs Bunny. 441-The Pink Panther (TV). 442-Beep-Beep, the Road Runner (TV). 444-Tom and Jerry. 445-Tweety and Sylvester. 446-Wacky Witch	.80	2.00	4.
443-Baby Snoots	.80	2.00	4.
447-Mighty Mouse	1.20	3.00	6.
448-455,457,458: 448-Cracky. 449-Pink Panther (TV). 450-Baby Snoots 451-Tom and Jerry. 452-Bugs Bunny. 453-Popeye. 454-Woody Woodpecker. 455-Beep-Beep, the Road Runner (TV). 457-Tweety & Sylvester. 458-Wacky Witch	.80	2.00	4.0
456-Little Lulu (r/#369)	1.20	3.50	7.0
459-Mighty Mouse	1.20	3.00	6.0
460-466: 460-Daffy Duck. 461-The Pink Panther (TV). 462-Baby Snoots. 463-Tom and Jerry. 464-Bugs Bunny. 465-Popeye. 466-Woody Woodpecker	.70	2.00	4.0
467-Underdog (TV)	4.00	10.00	20.0
468-Little Lulu (r/#385)	.85	2.50	5.0
469-Tweety & Sylvester	.70	2.00	4.0
470-Wacky Witch	.70	2.00	4.0
471-Mighty Mouse	.80	2.50	5.0
472-474,476-478: 472-Heckle & Jeckle(12/80). 473-Pink Panther(1/81)(TV). 474-Baby Snoots. 476-Bugs Bunny. 477-Popeye. 478-Woody Woodpecker	.70	2.00	4.0
475-Little Lulu (r/#323)	.85	2.50	5.0
479-Underdog (TV)	3.00	7.50	15.0
480-482: 480-Tom and Jerry. 481-Tweety and Sylvester. 482-Wacky Witch	.70	2.00	4.0
483-Mighty Mouse	.80	2.00	5.0
484-487: 484-Heckle & Jeckle. 485-Baby Snoots. 486-The Pink Panther (TV). 487-Bugs Bunny	.70	2.00	4.0
488-Little Lulu (4/82) (r/#335)	.85	2.50	5.0

MARGARET O'BRIEN (See The Adventures of...)

MARK STEEL

American Iron & Steel Institute: 1967, 1968, 1972 (Giveaway) (24 pgs.)

1967,1968- "Journey of Discovery with..."; Neal Adams art

Marvel Comics Present Spider-Man © MAR

Mickey Mouse Magazine #9 © WDC

Military Courtesy © U.S. Army

GD2.0 FN6.0 NM9.4

2.50 7.50 25.00
1972- "...Fights Pollution"; N. Adams-a 1.85 5.50 15.00

MARVEL COLLECTOR'S EDITION: X-MEN
Marvel Comics: 1993 (3-3/4x6-1/2")
1-4-Pizza Hut giveaways 3.00

MARVEL COMICS PRESENTS
Marvel Comics: 1987, 1988 (4 1/4 x 6 1/4, 20 pgs.)
...Mini Comic Giveaway

	GD2.0	FN6.0	NM9.4
nn-(1988) Alf	1.00	3.00	8.00
nn-(1987) Captain America r/ #250	1.00	2.80	7.00
nn-(1987) Care Bears (Star Comics...)	1.00	2.80	7.00
nn-(1988) Flintstone Kids	1.00	3.00	8.00
nn-(1987) Heathcliffe (Star Comics...)	1.00	2.80	7.00
nn-(1987) Spider-Man-r/Spect. Spider-Man #21	1.00	2.80	7.00
nn-(1988) Spider-Man-r/Amazing Spider-Man #1	1.00	2.80	7.00
nn-(1988) X-Men-reprints X-Men #53; B. Smith-a	1.00	2.80	7.00

MARVEL MINI-BOOKS
Marvel Comics Group: 1966 (50 pgs., B&W; 5/8x7/8") (6 different issues) (Smallest comics ever published) (Marvel Mania Giveaways)
Captain America, Millie the Model, Spider-Man, Sgt. Fury, Hulk, Thor 7.25 21.75 80.00
NOTE: *Each came in six different color covers, usually one color: Pink, yellow, green, etc.*

MARY'S GREATEST APOSTLE (St. Louis Grignion de Montfort)
Catechetical Guild (Topix) (Giveaway): No date (16 pgs.; paper cover)
nn 3.60 9.00 18.00

MASK
DC Comics: 1985
1-3 2.00

MASKED PILOT, THE (See Popular Comics #43)
R.S. Callender: 1939 (7-1/2x5-1/4", 16 pgs., premium, non-slick-c)
nn-Bob Jenney-a 10.00 30.00 75.00

MASTERS OF THE UNIVERSE (He-Man)
DC Comics: 1982
1-7 2.00

McCRORY'S CHRISTMAS BOOK
Western Printing Co: 1955 (36 pgs., slick-c) (McCrory Stores Corp. giveaway)
nn-Painted-c 4.00 10.00 20.00

McCRORY'S TOYLAND BRINGS YOU SANTA'S PRIVATE EYES
Promotional Publ. Co.: 1956 (16 pgs.) (Giveaway)
nn-Has 9 pg. story plus 7 pgs. toy ads 3.20 8.00 16.00

McCRORY'S WONDERFUL CHRISTMAS
Promotional Publ. Co.: 1954 (20 pgs., slick-c) (Giveaway)
nn 4.00 10.00 20.00

McDONALDS COMMANDRONS
DC Comics: 1985
nn-Four editions 2.00

MEET HIYA A FRIEND OF SANTA CLAUS
Julian J. Proskauer/Sundial Shoe Stores, etc.: 1949 (18 pgs.?, paper-c) (Giveaway)
nn 5.85 17.50 40.00

MEET THE NEW POST GAZETTE SUNDAY FUNNIES
Pittsburgh Post Gazette: 3/12/49 (7-1/4x10-1/4", 16 pgs., paper-c)
Commercial Comics (insert in newspaper)
Dick Tracy by Gould, Gasoline Alley, Terry & the Pirates, Brenda Starr, Buck Rogers by Yager, The Gumps, Peter Rabbit by Fago, Superman, Funnyman by Siegel & Shuster, The Saint, Archie, others done especially for this book. A fine copy sold at auction in 1985 for $276.00.
400.00 1200.00 2800.00

MEN OF COURAGE
Catechetical Guild: 1949
Bound Topix comics-V7#2,4,6,8,10,16,18,20 5.00 15.00 30.00

MEN WHO MOVE THE NATION
Publisher unknown: (Giveaway) (B&W)
nn-Neal Adams-a 5.00 15.00 32.00

MERRY CHRISTMAS, A
K. K. Publications (Child Life Shoes): 1948 (Giveaway)
nn 5.00 15.00 35.00

MERRY CHRISTMAS
K. K. Publications (Blue Bird Shoes Giveaway): 1956 (7-1/4x5-1/4")
nn 4.00 11.00 22.00

MERRY CHRISTMAS FROM MICKEY MOUSE
K. K. Publications: 1939 (16 pgs.) (Color & B&W) (Shoe store giveaway)
nn-Donald Duck & Pluto app.; text with art (Rare); c-reprint/Mickey Mouse Mag. V3#3 (12/37)(Rare) 315.00 1260.00 2600.00

MERRY CHRISTMAS FROM SEARS TOYLAND (See Santa's Christmas Comic)
Sears Roebuck Giveaway: 1939 (16 pgs.) (Color)
nn-Dick Tracy, Little Orphan Annie, The Gumps, Terry & the Pirates 105.00 525.00 1100.00

MICKEY MOUSE (Also see Frito-Lay Giveaway)
Dell Publ. Co
...& Goofy Explore Business(1978) 2.40 6.00
...& Goofy Explore Energy(1976-1978, 36 pgs.); Exxon giveaway in color; regular size 2.40 6.00
...& Goofy Explore Energy Conservation(1976-1978)-Exxon 2.40 6.00
...& Goofy Explore The Universe of Energy(1985, 20 pgs.); Exxon giveaway in color; regular size 5.00
The Perils of Mickey nn (1993, 5-1/4x7-1/4", 16 pgs.)-Nabisco giveaway w/ games, Nabisco coupons & 6 pgs. of stories; Phantom Blot app. 3.00

MICKEY MOUSE MAGAZINE
Walt Disney Productions: V1#1, Jan, 1933 - V1#9, Sept, 1933 (5-1/4x7-1/4")
No. 1-3 published by Kamen-Blair (Kay Kamen, Inc.)

	GD2.0	FN6.0	VF8.0
(Scarce)-Distributed by dairies and leading stores through their local theatres. First few issues had 5¢ listed on cover, later ones had no price.			
V1#1	533.00	2132.00	4800.00
2-9	218.00	545.00	1200.00

MICKEY MOUSE MAGAZINE
Walt Disney Productions: V1#1, 11/33 - V2#12, 10/35 (Mills giveaways issued by different dairies)

	GD2.0	FN6.0	NM9.4
V1#1	240.00	960.00	1800.00
2-12: 2-X-Mas issue	80.00	320.00	600.00
V2#1-12: 2-X-Mas issue. 4-St. Valentine-c	55.00	192.00	400.00
V4#1 (Giveaway)	55.00	192.00	400.00

MIGHTY ATOM, THE
Whitman
Giveaway (1959, '63, Whitman)-Evans-a 2.00 6.00 18.00
Giveaway ('64r, '65r, '66r, '67r, '68r)-Evans-r? 1.00 3.00 8.00
Giveaway ('73r, '76r) 2.40 6.00

MILITARY COURTESY
U.S. Army : (16 pgs.)
nn-Regulations and saluting instructions 20.00

MINUTE MAN
Sovereign Service Station giveaway: No date (16 pgs., B&W, paper-c blue & red)
nn-American history 2.40 6.00 12.00

MINUTE MAN ANSWERS THE CALL, THE
By M. C. Gaines: 1942 (4 pgs.) (Giveaway inserted in Jr. JSA Membership Kit)
nn-Sheldon Moldoff-a 22.00 66.00 175.00

MIRACLE ON BROADWAY
Broadway Comics: Dec, 1995 (Giveaway)
1-Ernie Colon-c/a; Jim Shooter &Co. story; 1st known digitally printed comic book; 1st app. Spire & Knights on Broadway (1150 print run) 20.00
NOTE: *Miracle on Broadway was a limited edition comic given to 1100 VIPs in the entertainment industry for the 1995 Holiday Season.*

MISS SUNBEAM (See Little Miss Sunbeam Comics)

MR. BUG GOES TO TOWN (See Cinema Comics Herald)
K.K. Publications: 1941 (Giveaway, 52 pgs.)

Motion Picture Funnies Weekly #1 © First Funnies Inc.

Natural Disasters! © Graphic Information Service

The Owl © WEST

nn-Cartoon movie (scarce) 75.00 300.00 700.00

MOTHER OF US ALL
Catechetical Guild Giveaway: 1950? (32 pgs.)
nn 3.60 9.00 18.00

MOTION PICTURE FUNNIES WEEKLY (Amazing Man #5 on?)
First Funnies, Inc.: 1939 (Giveaway)(B&W, 36 pgs.)
No month given; last panel in Sub-Mariner story dated 4/39
(Also see Colossus, Green Giant & Invaders No. 20)
1-Origin & 1st printed app. Sub-Mariner by Bill Everett (8 pgs.); Fred Schwab-c; reprinted in Marvel Mystery #1 with color added over the craft tint which was used to shade the black & white version; Spy Ring, American Ace (reprinted in Marvel Mystery #3) app. (Rare)-only eight (8) known copies,one near mint with white pages, the rest with brown pages. 4400.00 11,000.00 22,000.00
Covers only to #2-4 (set) 750.00
NOTE: The only eight known copies (with a ninth suspected) were discovered in 1974 in the estate of the deceased publisher. Covers only to issues No. 2-4 were also found which evidently were printed in advance along with #1. #1 was to be distributed only through motion picture movie houses. However, it is believed that only advanced copies were sent out and the motion picture houses not going for the idea. Possible distribution at local theaters in Boston suspected. The last panel of Sub-Mariner contains a rectangular box with "Continued Next Week" printed in it. When reprinted in Marvel Mystery, the box was left in with lettering omitted.

MY DOG TIGE (Buster Brown's Dog)
Buster Brown Shoes: 1957 (Giveaway)
nn 5.00 15.00 32.00

MY GREATEST THRILLS IN BASEBALL
Mission of California: Date? (16 pg. Giveaway)
nn-By Mickey Mantle 79.00 212.00 550.00

NATURAL DISASTERS!
Graphic Information Service/ Civil Defense: 1956 (16 pgs., soft-c)
nn-Al Capp Li'l Abner-c; Li'l Abner cameo (1 panel); narrated by Mr. Civil Defense 10.00 50.00 80.00

NAVY: HISTORY & TRADITION
Stokes Walesby Co./Dept. of Navy: 1958 - 1961 (nn) (Giveaway)
1772-1778, 1778-1782, 1782-1817, 1817-1865, 1865-1936, 1940-1945:
1772-1778-16 pg. in color 4.25 13.00 28.00
1861: Naval Actions of the Civil War: 1865-36 pg. in color; flag-c 4.25 13.00 28.00

NEW ADVENTURE OF WALT DISNEY'S SNOW WHITE AND THE SEVEN DWARFS, A (See Snow White Bendix Giveaway)

NEW ADVENTURES OF PETER PAN (Disney)
Western Publishing Co.: 1953 (5x7-1/4", 36 pgs.) (Admiral giveaway)
nn 14.00 41.00 110.00

NEW TEEN TITANS, THE
DC Comics: Nov. 1983
nn(11/83-Keebler Co. Giveaway)-In cooperation with "The President's Drug Awareness Campaign"; came in Presidential envelope w/letter from White House (Nancy Reagan) 3.00
nn-(re-issue of above on Mando paper for direct sales market); American Soft Drink Ind. version; I.B.M. Corp. version 3.00

NOLAN RYAN IN THE WINNING PITCH (Kellogg's Tony's Sports Comics)
DC Comics: 1992 (Sports Illustrated)
nn 2.00

OLD GLORY COMICS
Chesapeake & Ohio Railway: 1944 (Giveaway)
nn-Capt. Fearless reprint 6.00 18.00 42.00

ON THE AIR
NBC Network Comic: 1947 (Giveaway, paper-c)
nn-(Rare) 30.00 100.00 200.00

OUT OF THE PAST A CLUE TO THE FUTURE
E. C. Comics (Public Affairs Comm.): 1946? (16 pgs.) (paper cover)
nn-Based on public affairs pamphlet "What Foreign Trade Means to You" 24.00 71.00 180.00

OUTSTANDING AMERICAN WAR HEROES
The Parents' Institute: 1944 (16 pgs., paper-c)
nn-Reprints from True Comics 4.00 12.00 24.0

OVERSEAS COMICS (Also see G.I. Comics & Jeep Comics)
Giveaway (Distributed to U.S. Armed Forces): 1944 - No. 105?, 1946 (7-1/4x10-1/4"; 16 pgs. in color)
23-105-Bringing Up Father (by McManus), Popeye, Joe Palooka, Dick Tracy, Superman, Gasoline Alley, Buz Sawyer, Li'l Abner, Blondie, Terry & the Pirates, Out Our Way 6.00 18.00 42.0

OWL, THE (See Crackajack Funnies #25 & Popular Comics #72)(Also see The Hurricane Kids & Magic Morro
Western Pub. Co./R.S. Callender: 1940 (Giveaway)(7-1/2x5-1/4")(Soft-c, colo
nn-Frank Thomas-a 22.00 66.00 175.0

OXYDOL-DREFT
Oxydol-Dreft:1950 (Set of 6 pocket-size giveaways; distributed through the ma as a set) (Scarce)
1-3: 1-Li'l Abner. 2-Daisy Mae. 3-Shmoo 13.00 40.00 100.0
4-John Wayne; Williamson/Frazetta-c from John Wayne #3 17.00 51.00 135.0
5-Archie 15.00 45.00 120.0
6-Terrytoons Mighty Mouse 13.00 40.00 100.0
Mailing Envelope (has All Capp's Shmoo on front) 15.00 45.00 120.0

OZZIE SMITH IN THE KID WHO COULD (Kellogg's Tony's Sports Comics)
DC Comics: 1992 (Sports Illustrated)
nn-Ozzie Smith app. 2.0

PADRE OF THE POOR
Catechetical Guild: nd (Giveaway) (16 pgs., paper-c)
nn 4.00 10.00 20.0

PAUL TERRY'S HOW TO DRAW FUNNY CARTOONS
Terrytoons, Inc. (Giveaway): 1940's (14 pgs.) (Black & White)
nn-Heckle & Jeckle, Mighty Mouse, etc. 12.00 36.00 95.0

PETER PAN (See New Adventures of Peter Pan)

PETER PENNY AND HIS MAGIC DOLLAR
American Bankers Association, N. Y. (Giveaway): 1947 (16 pgs.; paper-c; regular size)
nn-(Scarce)-Used in **SOTI**, pg. 310, 311 17.00 51.00 135.0
Diff. version (7-1/4x11")-redrawn, 16 pgs., paper-c 10.00 30.00 70.0

PETER WHEAT (The Adventures of...)
Bakers Associates Giveaway: 1948 - 1956? (16 pgs. in color) (paper covers)
nn(No.1)-States on last page, end of 1st Adventure of...; Kelly-a 33.00 130.00 260.0
nn(4 issues)-Kelly-a 20.00 80.00 160.0
6-10-All Kelly-a 15.00 45.00 120.0
11-20-All Kelly-a 13.00 40.00 105.0
21-35-All Kelly-a 11.00 33.00 90.0
36-66 8.35 25.00 60.0
...Artist's Workbook ('54, digest size) 8.35 25.00 60.0
...Four-In-One Fun Pack (Vol. 2, '54), oblong, comics w/puzzles 10.00 30.00 70.0
...Fun Book ('52, 32 pgs., paper-c, B&W & color, 8-1/2x10-3/4")-Contains cut-outs, puzzles, games, magic & pages to color 12.00 36.00 95.0
NOTE: ***Al Hubbard** art #36 on; written by Del Connell.*

PETER WHEAT NEWS
Bakers Associates: 1948 - No. 30, 1950 (4 pgs. in color)
Vol. 1-All have 2 pgs. Peter Wheat by Kelly 27.00 110.00 220.0
2-10 18.00 54.00 140.0
11-20 11.00 33.00 90.0
21-30 8.35 25.00 60.0
NOTE: *Early issues have no date & **Kelly** art.*

PINOCCHIO
Cocomalt/Montgomery Ward Co.: 1940 (10 pgs.; giveaway, linen-like paper)
nn-Cocomalt edition 40.00 120.00 320.0
nn-store edition 31.00 94.00 250.0

PIUS XII MAN OF PEACE
Catechetical Guild: No date (12 pgs.; 5-1/2x8-1/2") (B&W)

Poll Parrot #2 © K.K. Pub.

Railroads Deliver the Goods © Assoc. of American R.R.

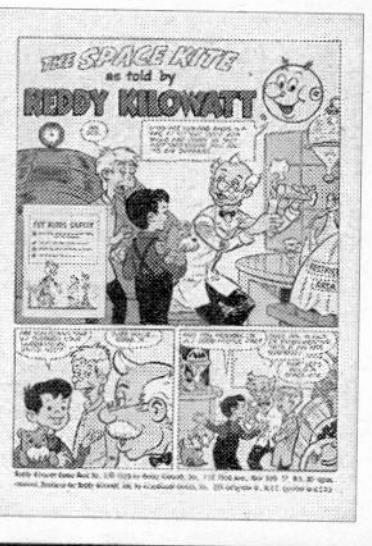

Reddy Kilowatt #3 (1960) © EC

GD2.0 FN6.0 NM9.4

nn-Catechetical Guild Giveaway 4.65 14.00 28.00

PLOT TO STEAL THE WORLD, THE
Work & Unity Group: 1948, 16pgs., paper-c
nn-Anti commumism 19.00 56.00 150.00

POCAHONTAS
Pocahontas Fuel Company (Coal): 1941 - No. 2, 1942
nn(#1), 2-Feat. life story of Indian princess Pocahontas & facts about Pocahontas coal, Pocahontas, VA. 16.00 49.00 130.00

POLL PARROT
Poll Parrot Shoe Store/International Shoe
K. K. Publications (Giveaway): 1950 - No. 4, 1951; No. 2, 1959 - No. 16, 1962
1 ('50)-Howdy Doody; small size 27.00 82.00 165.00
2-4('51)-Howdy Doody 22.00 68.00 135.00
2('59)-16('62): 2-The Secret of Crumbley Castle. 5-Bandit Busters. 7-The Make-Believe Mummy. 8-Mixed Up Mission('60). 10-The Frightful Flight. 11-Showdown at Sunup. 12-Maniac at Mubu Island. 13-...and the Runaway Genie. 14-Bully for You. 15-Trapped In Tall Timber. 16-...& the Rajah's Ruby('62) 2.30 7.00 20.00

POPEYE
Whitman
Bold Detergent giveaway (Same as regular issue #94)1.00 3.00 8.00
Quaker Cereal premium (1989, 16pp, small size,4 diff.)(Popeye & the Time Machine,--On Safari, --& Big Foot, --vs. Bluto) 1.85 5.50 15.00

POPEYE
Charlton (King Features) (Giveaway): 1972 - 1974 (36 pgs. in color)
E-1 to E-15 (Educational comics) 1.00 3.00 8.00
nn-Popeye Gettin' Better Grades-4 pgs. used as intro. to above giveaways (in color) 1.00 3.00 8.00

POPSICLE PETE FUN BOOK (See All-American Comics #6)
Joe Lowe Corp.: 1947, 1948
nn-36 pgs. in color; Sammy 'n' Claras, The King Who Couldn't Sleep & Popsicle Pete stories, games, cut-outs 11.00 33.00 85.00
Adventure Book ('48)-Has Classics ad with checklist to HRN #343 (Great Expectations #43) 10.00 30.00 75.00

PORKY'S BOOK OF TRICKS
K. K. Publications (Giveaway): 1942 (8-1/2x5-1/2", 48 pgs.)
nn-7 pg. comic story, text stories, plus games & puzzles 53.00 237.00 475.00

POST GAZETTE (See Meet the New...)

POWER RECORD COMICS
Marvel Comics/Power Records: 1974 - 1978 ($1.49, 7x10" comics, 20 pgs. with 45 R.P.M. record)
PR10-Spider-Man-r/from #124,125; Man-Wolf app. PR18-Planet of the Apes-r. PR19-Escape from the Planet of the Apes-r. PR20-Beneath the Planet of the Apes-r. PR21-Battle for the Planet of the Apes-r. PR24-Spider-Man II-New-a begins. PR27-Batman "Stacked Cards"; N. Adams-a(p). PR30-Batman; N. Adams-r/Det.(7 pgs.).
With record; each... 3.00 9.00 32.00
PR11-Hulk-r. PR12-Captain America-r/#168. PR13-Fantastic Four-r/#126. PR14-Frankenstein-Ploog-r/#1. PR15-Tomb of Dracula-Colan-r/#2. PR16-Man-Thing-Ploog-r/#5. PR17-Werewolf by Night-Ploog-r/Marvel Spotlight #2. PR28-Superman "Alien Creatures". PR29-Space: 1999 Breakaway". PR31-Conan-N. Adams-a; reprinted in Conan #116. PR32-Space: 1999 "Return to the Beginning". PR33-Superman-G.A. origin, Buckler-a(p). PR34-Superman. PR35-Wonder Woman-Buckler-a(p)
With record; each... 2.80 8.40 28.00
PR25-Star Trek "Passage to Moauv". PR26-Star Trek "Crier in Emptiness." PR36-Holo-Man. PR37-Robin Hood. PR39-Huckleberry Finn. PR40-Davy Crockett. PR41-Robinson Crusoe. PR42-20,000 Leagues Under the Sea. PR46-Star Trek "The Robot Masters". PR47-Little Women
With record; each... 2.50 7.50 24.00

PURE OIL COMICS (Also see Salerno Carnival of Comics, 24 Pages of Comics, & Vicks Comics)
Pure Oil Giveaway: Late 1930's (24 pgs., regular size, paper-c)
nn-Contains 1-2 pg. strips; i.e., Hairbreadth Harry, Skyroads, Buck Rogers by Calkins & Yager, Olly of the Movies, Napoleon, S'Matter Pop, etc.
Also a 16 pg. 1938 giveaway w/Buck Rogers 53.00 160.00 325.00

QUAKER OATS (Also see Cap'n Crunch)
Quaker Oats Co.: 1965 (Giveaway) (2-1/2x5-1/2") (16 pgs.)
"Plenty of Glutton", starring Quake & Quisp; 2.50 7.50 20.00
"Lava Come-Back", "Kite Tale" 2.40 6.00

RAILROADS DELIVER THE GOODS!
Assoc. of American Railroads: Dec, 1954; Sept, 1957 (16 pgs.)
nn-The story of railway freight 6.00 18.00 42.00

RAILS ACROSS AMERICA!
Assoc. of American Railroads: nd (16 pgs.)
nn 6.00 18.00 42.00

REAL FUN OF DRIVING!!, THE
Chrysler Corp.: 1965, 1966, 1967 (Regular size, 16 pgs.)
nn-Schaffenberger-a (12 pgs.) 5.00

REAL HIT
Fox Features Publications: 1944 (Savings Bond premium)
1-Blue Beetle-r 19.00 56.00 150.00
NOTE: *Two versions exist, with and without covers. The coverless version has the title, No. 1 and price printed at top of splash page.*

RED BALL COMIC BOOK
Parents' Magazine Institute: 1947 (Red Ball Shoes giveaway)
nn-Reprints from True Comics 3.00 7.50 15.00

REDDY GOOSE
International Shoe Co. (Western Printing): No #, 1958?; No. 2, Jan, 1959 - No. 16, July, 1962 (Giveaway)
nn (#1) 5.00 15.00 55.00
2-16 3.00 9.00 32.00

REDDY KILOWATT (5¢) (Also see Story of Edison)
Educational Comics (E. C.): 1946 - No. 2, 1947; 1956 - 1960 (no month) (16 pgs., paper-c)
nn-Reddy Made Magic (1946, 5¢) 12.00 36.00 95.00
nn-Reddy Made Magic (1958) 8.35 25.00 60.00
2-Edison, the Man Who Changed the World (3/4" smaller than #1) (1947, 5¢) 12.00 36.00 95.00
...Comic Book 2 (1954)- "Light's Diamond Jubilee" 9.00 27.00 65.00
...Comic Book 2 (1958, 16 pgs.)- "Wizard of Light" 8.35 25.00 60.00
...Comic Book 3 (1956, 8 pgs.)- "The Space Kite"; Orlando story; regular size 8.35 25.00 60.00
...Comic Book 3 (1960, 8 pgs.)- "The Space Kite"; Orlando story; regular size 4.60 13.80 50.00
NOTE: *Several copies surfaced in 1979.*

REDDY MADE MAGIC
Educational Comics (E. C.): 1956, 1958 (16 pgs., paper-c)
1-Reddy Kilowatt-r (splash panel changed) 11.00 33.00 85.00
1 (1958 edition) 6.70 20.00 42.00

RED ICEBERG, THE
Impact Publ. (Catechetical Guild): 1960 (10¢, 16 pgs., Communist propaganda)
nn-(Rare)- 'We The People' back-c 31.00 93.00 340.00
2nd version- 'Impact Press' back-c 31.00 93.00 350.00
3rd version-"Explains comic" back-c 31.00 93.00 350.00
NOTE: *This book was the Guild's last anti-communist propaganda book and had very limited circulation. 3 - 4 copies surfaced in 1979 from the defunct publisher's files. Other copies do turn up.*

RED RYDER COMICS
Dell Publ. Co.
Buster Brown Shoes Giveaway (1941, color, soft-c, 32 pgs.) 27.00 81.00 215.00
Red Ryder Super Book of Comics (1944, paper-c, 32 pgs.; blank back-c) Magic Morro app. 29.00 86.00 230.00
Red Ryder Victory Patrol-nn(1942, 32 pgs.)(Langendorf bread; includes cut-out membership card and certificate, order blank and "Slide-Up" decoder, and a Super Book of Comics in color (same content as Super Book #4 w/diff. cover (Pan-Am)) (Rare) 463.00 1621.00 4400.00
Red Ryder Victory Patrol-nn(1943, 32 pgs.)(Langendorf bread; includes cut-out "Rodeomatic" radio decoder, order coupon for "Magic V-Badge", cut-out membership card and certificate and a full color Super Book of comics comic book) (Rare) 421.00 1475.00 4000.00

Red Ryder Victory Patrol 1944 © DELL

RED RYDER
VICTORY PATROL
SUPER BOOK
OF COMICS
Langendorf Bread

Robin Hood - Ghosts of Waylea © WDC

Santa's Fun Book © Promotional Publ.

Red Ryder Victory Patrol-nn(1944, 32 pgs.)-r-/#43,44; comic has a paper-c & is stapled inside a triple cardboard fold-out-c; contains membership card, decoder, map of R.R. home range, etc. Herky app. (Langendorf Bread give-away; sub-titled 'Super Book of Comics')(Rare) 400.00 1400.00 3800.00

Wells Lamont Corp. giveaway (1950)-16 pgs. in color; regular size; paper-c; 1941-r 25.00 75.00 200.00

RE-LOADED (Also see Loaded)
DC Comics: 1996 (Interplay Productions)

1-Promotes video game 3.00

RICHIE RICH, CASPER & WENDY NATIONAL LEAGUE
Harvey Publications: June, 1976 (52 pgs.)

1 (Released-3/76 with 6/76 date) 1.75 5.25 14.00
1 (6/76)-2nd version w/San Francisco Giants & KTVU 2 logos; has "Compliments of Giants and Straw Hat Pizza" on-c 1.75 5.25 14.00
1-Variants for other 11 NL teams, similar to Giants version but with different ad on inside front-c 1.75 5.25 14.00

RIDE THE HIGH IRON!
Assoc. of American Railroads: Jan, 1957 (16 pgs.)

nn-The Story of modern passenger trains 6.00 18.00 42.00

RIPLEY'S BELIEVE IT OR NOT!
Harvey Publications

J. C. Penney giveaway (1948) 8.35 25.00 60.00

ROBIN HOOD (New Adventures of...)
Walt Disney Productions: 1952 (Flour giveaways, 5x7-1/4", 36 pgs.)

"New Adventures of Robin Hood", "Ghosts of Waylea Castle", & "The Miller's Ransom" each.... 4.25 13.00 26.00

ROBIN HOOD'S FRONTIER DAYS (...Western Tales, Adventures of... #1)
Shoe Store Giveaway (Robin Hood Stores): 1956 (20 pgs., slick-c)(7 issues?)

nn 5.00 15.00 30.00
nn-Issues with Crandall-a 7.70 23.00 52.00

ROCKETS AND RANGE RIDERS
Richfield Oil Corp.: May, 1957 (Giveaway, 16 pgs., soft-c)

nn-Toth-a 17.00 51.00 135.00

ROUND THE WORLD GIFT
National War Fund (Giveaway): No date (mid 1940's) (4 pgs.)

nn 12.00 36.00 95.00

ROY ROGERS COMICS
Dell Publishing Co.

...& the Man From Dodge City (Dodge giveaway, 16 pgs., 1954)-Frontier, Inc. (5x7-1/4") 14.00 43.00 115.00
Official Roy Rogers Riders Club Comics (1952; 16 pgs., reg. size, paper-c) 40.00 160.00 325.00

RUDOLPH, THE RED-NOSED REINDEER
Montgomery Ward: 1939 (2,400,000 copies printed); Dec, 1951 (Giveaway)

Paper cover-1st app. in print; written by Robert May; ill. by Denver Gillen 14.00 41.00 110.00
Hardcover version 19.00 56.00 150.00
1951 Edition (Has 1939 date)-36 pgs., slick-c printed in red & brown; pulp interior printed in four mixed-ink colors: red, green, blue & brown 8.65 26.00 60.00
1951 Edition with red-spiral promotional booklet printed on high quality stock, 8-1/2"x11", in red & brown, 25 pages composed of 4 fold outs, single sheets and the Rudolph comic book inserted (rare) 50.00 150.00 450.00

SAD CASE OF WAITING ROOM WILLIE, THE
American Visuals Corp. (For Baltimore Medical Society): (nd, 1950?) (14 pgs. in color; paper covers; regular size)

nn-By Will Eisner (Rare) 48.00 144.00 430.00

SAD SACK COMICS
Harvey Publications: 1957-1962

Armed Forces Complimentary copies, HD #1-40 (1957-1962) 1.50 4.50 12.00

SALERNO CARNIVAL OF COMICS (Also see Pure Oil Comics, 24 Pages of Comics, & Vicks Comics)
Salerno Cookie Co.: Late 1930s (Giveaway, 16 pgs, paper-c)

nn-Color reprints of Calkins' Buck Rogers & Skyroads, plus other strips from Famous Funnies 50.00 150.00 450.00

SALUTE TO THE BOY SCOUTS
Association of American Railroads: 1960 (16 pgs.)

nn-History of scouting and the railroad 2.30 7.00 20.00

SANTA AND POLLYANNA PLAY THE GLAD GAME
Sales Promotion: Aug, 1960 (16 pgs.) (Disney giveaway)

nn 2.00 6.00 18.00

SANTA & THE BUCCANEERS
Promotional Publ. Co.: 1959 (Giveaway)

nn-Reprints 1952 Santa & the Pirates 1.85 5.50 15.00

SANTA & THE CHRISTMAS CHICKADEE
Murphy's: 1974 (Giveaway, 20 pgs.)

nn 1.00 3.00 8.00

SANTA & THE PIRATES
Promotional Publ. Co.: 1952 (Giveaway)

nn-Marv Levy-c/a 3.60 9.00 18.00

SANTA CLAUS FUNNIES (Also see The Little Fir Tree)
W. T. Grant Co./Whitman Publishing: nd; 1940 (Giveaway, 8x10"; 12 pgs., color & B&W, heavy paper)

nn-(2 versions- no date and 1940) 14.00 41.00 110.00

SANTA ON THE JOLLY ROGER
Promotional Publ. Co. (Giveaway): 1965

nn-Marv Levy-c/a 1.00 3.00 8.00

SANTA! SANTA!
R. Jackson: 1974 (20 pgs.) (Montgomery Ward giveaway)

nn 2.40 6.00

SANTA'S CHRISTMAS COMIC VARIETY SHOW (See Merry Christmas From Sears Toyland)
Sears Roebuck & Co.: 1943 (24 pgs.)

Contains puzzles & new comics of Dick Tracy, Little Orphan Annie, Moon Mullins, Terry & the Pirates, etc. 81.00 325.00 650.00

SANTA'S CHRISTMAS TIME STORIES
Premium Sales, Inc.: nd (Late 1940s) (16 pgs., paper-c) (Giveaway)

nn 5.50 16.50 38.00

SANTA'S CIRCUS
Promotional Publ. Co.: 1964 (Giveaway, half-size)

nn-Marv Levy-c/a 1.25 3.75 10.00

SANTA'S FUN BOOK
Promotional Publ. Co.: 1951, 1952 (Regular size, 16 pgs., paper-c) (Murphy's giveaway)

nn 4.00 12.00 24.00

SANTA'S GIFT BOOK
No Publisher: No date (16 pgs.)

nn-Puzzles, games only 3.60 9.00 18.00

SANTA'S NEW STORY BOOK
Wallace Hamilton Campbell: 1949 (16 pgs., paper-c) (Giveaway)

nn 5.00 15.00 35.00

SANTA'S REAL STORY BOOK
Wallace Hamilton Campbell/W. W. Orris: 1948, 1952 (Giveaway, 16 pgs.)

nn 5.00 15.00 35.00

SANTA'S RIDE
W. T. Grant Co.: 1959 (Giveaway)

nn 2.30 7.00 20.00

SANTA'S RODEO
Promotional Publ. Co.: 1964 (Giveaway, half-size)

nn-Marv Levy-a 1.25 3.75 10.00

SANTA'S SECRET CAVE

Sergeant Preston of the Yukon © Quaker Cereals

Special Edition #4 © DC

GD2.0 FN6.0 NM9.4

W.T. Grant Co.: 1960 (Giveaway, half-size)
nn 2.00 6.00 16.00

SANTA'S SECRETS
Sam B. Anson Christmas giveaway: 1951, 1952? (16 pgs., paper-c)
nn-Has games, stories & pictures to color 4.00 10.00 20.00

SANTA'S STORIES
K. K. Publications (Klines Dept. Store): 1953 (Regular size, paper-c)
nn-Kelly-a 18.00 53.00 140.00
nn-Another version (1953, glossy-c, half-size, 7-1/4x5-1/4")-Kelly-a 11.50 34.00 90.00

SANTA'S SURPRISE
K. K. Publications: 1947 (Giveaway, 36 pgs., slick-c)
nn 6.40 19.25 45.00

SANTA'S TOYTOWN FUN BOOK
Promotional Publ. Co.: 1953 (Giveaway)
nn-Marv Levy-c 3.20 8.00 16.00

SANTA TAKES A TRIP TO MARS
Bradshaw-Diehl Co., Huntington, W.VA.: 1950S (nd) (Giveaway, 16 pgs.)
nn 3.20 8.00 16.00

SERGEANT PRESTON OF THE YUKON
Quaker Cereals: 1956 (4 comic booklets) (Soft-c, 16 pgs., 7x2-1/2" & 5x2-1/2") Giveaways
"How He Found Yukon King", "The Case That Made Him A Sergeant", "How Yukon King Saved Him From The Wolves", "How He Became A Mountie"
each... 10.00 40.00 80.00

SHAZAM! (Visits Portland Oregon in 1943)
DC Comics: 1989 (69¢ cover)
nn-Promotes Super-Heroes exhibit at Oregon Museum of Science and Industry; reprints Golden Age Captain Marvel story 5.00

SHERIFF OF COCHISE, THE (TV)
Mobil: 1957 (16 pgs.) Giveaway
nn-Schaffenberger-a 3.60 9.00 18.00

SILLY PUTTY MAN
DC Comics: 1978
1 2.00

SKATING SKILLS
Custom Comics, Inc./Chicago Roller Skates: 1957 (36 & 12 pgs.; 5x7", two versions) (10¢)
nn-Resembles old ACG cover plus interior art 3.20 8.00 16.00

SKIPPY'S OWN BOOK OF COMICS (See Popular Comics)
No publisher listed: 1934 (Giveaway, 52 pgs., strip reprints)
nn-(Scarce)-By Percy Crosby 450.00 1350.00 5000.00
Published by Max C. Gaines for Phillip's Dental Magnesia to be advertised on the Skippy Radio Show and given away with the purchase of a tube of Phillip's Tooth Paste. This is the first four-color comic book of reprints about one character.

SKY KING "RUNAWAY TRAIN" (TV)
National Biscuit Co.: 1964 (Regular size, 16 pgs.)
nn 20.00 50.00 80.00

SLAM BANG COMICS
Post Cereal Giveaway: No. 9, No date
9-Dynamic Man, Echo, Mr. E, Yankee Boy app. 8.65 26.00 60.00

SMILIN' JACK
Dell Publishing Co.
Popped Wheat Giveaway (1947)-1938 strip reprints; 16 pgs. in full color 2.00 5.00 8.00
Shoe Store Giveaway-1938 strip reprints; 16 pgs. 5.00 15.00 30.00
Sparked Wheat Giveaway (1942)-16 pgs. in full color 5.00 15.00 30.00

SMOKEY STOVER
Dell Publishing Co.
General Motors giveaway (1953) 6.40 19.25 45.00
National Fire Protection giveaway(1953 & 1954)-16 pgs., paper-c 6.40 19.25 45.00

SMOKEY THE BEAR (See Forest Fire for 1st app.)
Dell Publ. Co.: 1959
True Story of..., The -U.S. Forest Service giveaway-Publ. by Western Printing Co.; reprints 1st 16 pgs. of Four Color #932 4.00 11.00 22.00
1964,1969 reprints 3.60 9.00 18.00

SNOW FOR CHRISTMAS
W. T. Grant Co.: 1957 (16 pgs.) (Giveaway)
nn 4.00 11.00 22.00

SNOW WHITE AND THE SEVEN DWARFS
Bendix Washing Machines: 1952 (32 pgs., 5x7-1/4", soft-c) (Disney)
nn 11.00 33.00 90.00

SNOW WHITE AND THE SEVEN DWARFS
Promotional Publ. Co.: 1957 (Small size)
nn 4.15 12.50 25.00

SNOW WHITE AND THE SEVEN DWARFS
Western Printing Co.: 1958 (16 pgs, 5x7-1/4", soft-c) (Disney premium)
nn- "Mystery of the Missing Magic" 7.15 21.50 50.00

SNOW WHITE AND THE 7 DWARFS IN "MILKY WAY"
American Dairy Assoc.: 1955 (16 pgs., soft-c, 5x7-1/4") (Disney premium)
nn 11.00 33.00 90.00

SPACE GHOST COAST TO COAST
Cartoon Network: Apr, 1994 (giveaway to Turner Broadcasting employees)
1-(8 pgs.); origin of Space Ghost 5.00

SPACE PATROL (TV)
Ziff-Davis Publishing Co. (Approved Comics)
...'s Special Mission (8 pgs., B&W, Giveaway) 78.00 275.00 550.00

SPECIAL AGENT
Assoc. of American Railroads: Oct, 1959 (16 pgs.)
nn-The Story of the railroad police 8.30 25.00 58.00

SPECIAL DELIVERY
Post Hall Synd.: 1951 (32 pgs.; B&W) (Giveaway)
nn-Origin of Pogo, Swamp, etc.; 2 pg. biog. on Walt Kelly
(One copy sold in 1980 for $150.00)

SPECIAL EDITION (U. S. Navy Giveaways)
National Periodical Publications: 1944 - 1945 (Regular comic format with wording simplified, 52 pgs.)
1-Action (1944)-Reprints Action #80 59.00 177.00 550.00
2-Action (1944)-Reprints Action #81 59.00 177.00 550.00
3-Superman (1944)-Reprints Superman #33 59.00 177.00 550.00
4-Detective (1944)-Reprints Detective #97 59.00 177.00 550.00
5-Superman (1945)-Reprints Superman #34 59.00 177.00 550.00
6-Action (1945)-Reprints Action #84 59.00 177.00 550.00
NOTE: ***Wayne Boring*** *c-1, 2, 6.* ***Dick Sprang*** *c-4.*

SPIDER-MAN (See Amazing Spider-Man, The)

SPIRIT, THE (Weekly Comic Book)
Will Eisner: 6/2/40 - 10/5/52 (16 pgs.; 8 pgs.) (no cover) (in color)
(Distributed through various newspapers and other sources)
NOTE: **Eisner** script, pencils/inks for the most part from 6/2/40-4/26/42; a few stories assisted by Jack Cole, Fine, Powell and Kotsky.
6/2/40(#1)-Origin/1st app. The Spirit; reprinted in Police #11; Lady Luck (Brenda Banks)(1st app.) by Chuck Mazoujian & Mr. Mystic (1st. app.) by S. R. (Bob) Powell begin 65.00 195.00 550.00
6/9/40(#2) 31.00 92.00 225.00
6/16/40(#3)-Black Queen app. in Spirit 18.00 54.00 135.00
6/23/40(#4)-Mr. Mystic receives magical necklace 15.00 45.00 110.00
6/30/40(#5) 15.00 45.00 110.00
7/7/40(#6)-1st app.: Spirit carplane; Black Queen app. in Spirit 15.00 45.00 110.00
7/14/40(#7)-8/4/40(#10): 7/21/40-Spirit becomes fugitive wanted for murder 12.00 36.00 90.00
8/11/40-9/22/40 11.00 33.00 80.00
9/29/40-Ellen drops engagement with Homer Creep 10.00 30.00 70.00

The Spirit 6/23/40 © Will Eisner

The Spirit 7/7/40 © Will Eisner

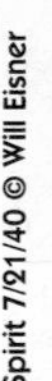

The Spirit 7/21/40 © Will Eisner

	GD2.0	FN6.0	NM9.4
10/6/40-11/3/40	10.00	30.00	70.00
11/10/40-The Black Queen app.	10.00	30.00	70.00
11/17/40, 11/24/40	10.00	30.00	70.00
12/1/40-Ellen spanking by Spirit on cover & inside; Eisner-1st 3 pgs., J. Cole rest	14.00	43.00	110.00
12/8/40-3/9/41	8.35	25.00	55.00
3/16/41-Intro. & 1st app. Silk Satin	13.00	39.00	95.00
3/23/41-6/1/41: 5/11/41-Last Lady Luck by Mazoujian; 5/18/41-Lady Luck by Nick Viscardi begins, ends 2/22/42	8.35	25.00	55.00
6/8/41-2nd app. Satin; Spirit learns Satin is also a British agent	10.00	30.00	75.00
6/15/41-1st app. Twilight	10.00	30.00	65.00
6/22/41-Hitler app. in Spirit	8.35	25.00	55.00
6/29/41-1/25/42,2/8/42	6.00	18.00	45.00
2/1/42-1st app. Duchess	10.00	30.00	65.00
2/15/42-4/26/42-Lady Luck by Klaus Nordling begins 3/1/42	6.70	20.00	50.00
5/3/42-8/16/42-Eisner/Fine/Quality staff assists on Spirit	4.30	13.00	32.00
8/23/42-Satin cover splash; Spirit by Eisner/Fine although signed by Fine	10.00	30.00	70.00
8/30/42,9/27/42-10/11/42,10/25/42-11/8/42-Eisner/Fine/Quality staff assists on Spirit	4.30	13.00	32.00
9/6/42-9/20/42,10/18/42-Fine/Belfi art on Spirit; scripts by Manly Wade Wellman	3.00	9.00	22.00
11/15/42-12/6/42,12/20/42,12/27/42,1/17/43-4/18/43,5/9/43-8/8/43-Wellman/Woolfolk scripts, Fine pencils, Quality staff inks	3.00	9.00	22.00
12/13/42,1/3/43,1/10/43,4/25/43,5/2/43-Eisner scripts/layouts; Fine pencils, Quality staff inks	3.75	11.25	28.00
8/15/43-Eisner script/layout; pencils/inks by Quality staff; Jack Cole-a	2.40	7.20	18.00
8/22/43-12/12/43-Wellman/Woolfolk scripts, Fine pencils, Quality staff inks; Mr. Mystic by Guardineer-10/10/43-10/24/43	2.40	7.20	18.00
12/19/43-8/13/44-Wellman/Woolfolk/Jack Cole scripts; Cole, Fine & Robin King-a; Last Mr. Mystic-5/14/44	2.20	6.50	16.00
8/20/44-12/16/45-Wellman/Woolfolk scripts; Fine art with unknown staff assists	2.20	6.50	16.00

NOTE: *Scripts/layouts by Eisner, or Eisner/Nordling, Eisner/Mercer or Spranger/Eisner; inks by Eisner or Eisner/Spranger in issues 12/23/45-2/2/47.*

	GD2.0	FN6.0	NM9.4
12/23/45-1/6/46: 12/23/45-Christmas-c	4.00	12.00	30.00
1/13/46-Origin Spirit retold	6.40	19.00	48.00
1/20/46-1st postwar Satin app.	5.30	16.00	40.00
1/27/46-3/10/46: 3/3/46-Last Lady Luck by Nordling	4.00	12.00	30.00
3/17/46-Intro. & 1st app. Nylon	5.30	16.00	40.00
3/24/46,3/31/46,4/14/46	4.00	12.00	30.00
4/7/46-2nd app. Nylon	4.70	14.00	35.00
4/21/46-Intro. & 1st app. Mr. Carrion & His Pet Buzzard Julia	6.40	19.00	48.00
4/28/46-5/12/46,5/26/46-6/30/46: Lady Luck by Fred Schwab in issues 5/5/46-11/3/46	4.00	12.00	30.00
5/19/46-2nd app. Mr. Carrion	4.70	14.00	35.00
7/7/46-Intro. & 1st app. Dulcet Tone & Skinny	5.60	17.00	42.00
7/14/46-9/29/46	4.00	12.00	30.00
10/6/46-Intro. & 1st app. P'Gell	6.40	19.00	48.00
10/13/46-11/3/46,11/16/46-11/24/46	4.00	12.00	30.00
11/10/46-2nd app. P'Gell	5.00	15.00	38.00
12/1/46-3rd app. P'Gell	4.70	14.00	35.00
12/8/46-2/2/47	3.50	10.50	26.00

NOTE: *Scripts, pencils/inks by Eisner except where noted in issues 2/9/47-12/19/48.*

	GD2.0	FN6.0	NM9.4
2/9/47-7/6/47: 6/8/47-Eisner self satire	3.50	10.50	26.00
7/13/47- "Hansel & Gretel" fairy tales	5.30	16.00	40.00
7/20/47-Li'L Abner, Daddy Warbucks, Dick Tracy, Fearless Fosdick parody; A-Bomb blast-c	5.60	17.00	42.00
7/27/47-9/14/47	3.50	10.50	26.00
9/21/47-Pearl Harbor flashback	4.30	13.00	32.00
9/28/47-1st mention of Flying Saucers in comics-3 months after 1st sighting in Idaho on 6/25/47	9.30	28.00	70.00
10/5/47- "Cinderella" fairy tales	5.30	16.00	40.00
10/12/47-11/30/47	3.50	10.50	26.00
12/7/47-Intro. & 1st app. Powder Pouf	6.40	19.00	48.00
12/14/47-12/28/47	3.50	10.50	26.00
1/4/48-2nd app. Powder Pouf	4.70	14.00	35.00
1/11/48-1st app. Sparrow Fallon; Powder Pouf app.	4.70	14.00	35.00
1/18/48-He-Man ad cover; satire issue	4.70	14.00	35.00
1/25/48-Intro. & 1st app. Castanet	5.60	17.00	42.00
2/1/48-2nd app. Castanet	4.00	12.00	30.00
2/8/48-3/7/48	3.50	10.50	26.00
3/14/48-Only app. Kretchma	4.00	12.00	30.00
3/21/48,3/28/48,4/11/48-4/25/48	3.50	10.50	26.00
4/4/48-Only app. Wild Rice	4.00	12.00	30.00
5/2/48-2nd app. Sparrow	3.50	10.50	26.00
5/9/48-6/27/48,7/11/48,7/18/48: 6/13/48-TV issue	3.50	10.50	26.00
7/4/48-Spirit by Andre Le Blanc	2.70	8.00	20.00
7/25/48-Ambrose Bierce's "The Thing" adaptation classic by Eisner/Grandenetti	9.30	28.00	70.00
8/1/48-8/15/48,8/29/48-9/12/48	3.50	10.50	26.00
8/22/48-Poe's "Fall of the House of Usher" classic by Eisner/Grandenetti	9.30	28.00	70.00
9/19/48-Only app. Lorelei	5.00	15.00	38.00
9/26/48-10/31/48	3.50	10.50	26.00
11/7/48-Only app. Plaster of Paris	5.00	15.00	38.00
11/14/48-12/19/48	3.50	10.50	26.00

NOTE: *Scripts by Eisner or Feiffer or Eisner/Feiffer or Nordling. Art by Eisner with backgrounds by Eisner, Grandenetti, Le Blanc, Stallman, Nordling, Dixon and/or others in issues 12/26/48-4/1/51 except where noted.*

	GD2.0	FN6.0	NM9.4
12/26/48-Reprints some covers of 1948 with flashbacks	3.50	10.50	26.00
1/2/49-1/16/49	3.50	10.50	26.00
1/23/49,1/30/49-1st & 2nd app. Thorne	5.00	15.00	38.00
2/6/49-8/14/49	3.50	10.50	26.00
8/21/49,8/28/49-1st & 2nd app. Monica Veto	5.00	15.00	38.00
9/4/49,9/11/49	3.50	10.50	26.00
9/18/49-Love comic cover; has gag love comic ads on inside	5.00	15.00	38.00
9/25/49-Only app. Ice	4.30	13.00	32.00
10/2/49,10/9/49-Autumn News appears & dies in 10/9 issue	4.30	13.00	32.00
10/16/49-11/27/49,12/18/49,12/25/49	3.50	10.50	26.00
12/4/49,12/11/49-1st & 2nd app. Flaxen	4.00	12.00	30.00
1/1/50-Flashbacks to all of the Spirit girls-Thorne, Ellen, Satin, & Monica	6.70	20.00	50.00
1/8/50-Intro. & 1st app. Sand Saref	9.30	28.00	70.00
1/15/50-2nd app. Saref	6.70	20.00	50.00
1/22/50-2/5/50	3.50	10.50	26.00
2/12/50-Roller Derby issue	4.70	14.00	35.00
2/19/50-Half Dead Mr. Lox - Classic horror	4.70	14.00	35.00
2/26/50-4/23/50,5/14/50,5/28/50,7/23/50-9/3/50	3.50	10.50	26.00
4/30/50-Script/art by Le Blanc with Eisner framing	1.85	5.60	14.00
5/7/50,6/4/50-7/16/50-Abe Kanegson-a	1.85	5.60	14.00
5/21/50-Script by Feiffer/Eisner, art by Blaisdell, Eisner framing	1.85	5.60	14.00
9/10/50-P'Gell returns	5.00	15.00	38.00
9/17/50-1/7/51	3.50	10.50	26.00
1/14/51-Life Magazine cover; brief biography of Comm. Dolan, Sand Saref, Silk Satin, P'Gell, Sammy & Willum, Darling O'Shea, & Mr. Carrion & His Pet Buzzard Julia, with pin-ups by Eisner	5.00	15.00	38.00
1/21/51,2/4/51-4/1/51	3.50	10.50	26.00
1/28/51- "The Meanest Man in the World" classic by Eisner	5.00	15.00	38.00
4/8/51-7/29/51,8/12/51-Last Eisner issue	3.50	10.50	26.00
8/5/51,8/19/51-7/20/52-Not Eisner	1.85	5.60	14.00
7/27/52-(Rare)-Denny Colt in Outer Space by Wally Wood; 7 pg. S/F story of E.C. vintage	32.00	95.00	235.00
8/3/52-(Rare)- "Mission...The Moon" by Wood	32.00	95.00	235.00
8/10/52-(Rare)- "A DP On The Moon" by Wood	32.00	95.00	235.00
8/17/52-(Rare)- "Heart" by Wood/Eisner	27.00	81.00	200.00
8/24/52-(Rare)- "Rescue" by Wood	32.00	95.00	235.00
8/31/52-(Rare)- "The Last Man" by Wood	32.00	95.00	235.00
9/7/52-(Rare)- "The Man in The Moon" by Wood	32.00	95.00	235.00
9/14/52-(Rare)-Eisner/Wenzel-a	8.75	27.00	70.00
9/21/52-(Rare)- "Denny Colt, Alias The Spirit/Space Report" by Eisner/Wenzel	11.50	34.00	85.00
9/28/52-(Rare)- "Return From The Moon" by Wood	32.00	95.00	235.00

Steve Canyon's Secret Mission © HARV

Super Book of Comics #4 - Red Ryder © WEST

Super-Book of Comics #14 © WB

GD2.0 FN6.0 NM9.4

10/5/52-(Rare)- "The Last Story" by Eisner 11.50 34.00 85.00
Large Tabloid pages from 1946 on (Eisner) - Price 200 percent over listed prices.
NOTE: *Spirit sections came out in both large and small format. Some newspapers went to the 8-pg. format months before others. Some printed the pages so they cannot be folded into a small comic book section; these are worth less. (Also see Three Comics & Spiritman).*

SPY SMASHER
Fawcett Publications

Well Known Comics (1944, 12 pgs., 8-1/2x10-1/2"), paper-c, glued binding, printed in green; Bestmaid/Samuel Lowe giveaway 16.00 48.00 125.00

STANDARD OIL COMICS (Also see Gulf Funny Weekly)
Standard Oil Co.: 1933 (Giveaway, tabloid size, 4 pgs. in color)

1-Series has original art 55.00 165.00 500.00
2-5 25.00 75.00 200.00
6-14: 14-Fred Opper strip, 1 pg. 12.50 37.50 100.00

STAR TEAM
Marvel Comics Group: 1977 (6-1/2x5", 20 pgs.) (Ideal Toy Giveaway)

nn 1.50 4.50 12.00

STEVE CANYON COMICS
Harvey Publications

Dept. Store giveaway #3(6/48, 36pp) 10.00 30.00 75.00
...'s Secret Mission (1951, 16 pgs., Armed Forces giveaway); Caniff-a 10.00 30.00 70.00
Strictly for the Smart Birds (1951, 16 pgs.)-Information Comics Div. (Harvey) Premium 9.35 28.00 65.00

STORIES OF CHRISTMAS
K. K. Publications: 1942 (Giveaway, 32 pgs., paper cover)

nn-Adaptation of "A Christmas Carol"; Kelly story "The Fir Tree"; Infinity-c 38.00 113.00 300.00

STORY HOUR SERIES (Disney)
Whitman Publ. Co.: 1948, 1949; 1951-1953 (36 pgs., paper-c) (4-3/4x6-1/2")
Given away with subscription to Walt Disney's Comics & Stories

nn(1948)-Mickey Mouse and the Boy Thursday 12.00 36.00 95.00
nn(1948)-Mickey Mouse the Miracle Master 12.00 36.00 95.00
nn(1948)-Minnie Mouse and Antique Chair 12.00 36.00 95.00
nn(1949)-The Three Orphan Kittens(B&W & color) 7.50 22.50 52.00
nn(1949)-Danny-The Little Black Lamb 7.50 22.50 52.00
800(1948)-Donald Duck in "Bringing Up the Boys" 18.00 54.00 140.00
1953 edition 11.00 33.00 90.00
801(1948)-Mickey Mouse's Summer Vacation 10.00 30.00 70.00
1951, 1952 editions 5.00 15.00 30.00
802(1948)-Bugs Bunny's Adventures 8.35 25.00 58.00
803(1948)-Bongo 5.70 17.00 40.00
804(1948)-Mickey and the Beanstalk 8.35 25.00 58.00
805-15(1949)-Andy Panda and His Friends 6.70 20.00 46.00
806-15(1949)-Tom and Jerry 7.50 22.50 52.00
808-15(1949)-Johnny Appleseed 5.70 17.00 40.00
1948, 1949 Hard Cover Edition of each.... 30% - 40% more.

STORY OF EDISON, THE
Educational Comics: 1956 (16 pgs.) (Reddy Killowatt)

nn-Reprint of Reddy Kilowatt #2(1947) 8.35 25.00 50.00

STORY OF HARRY S. TRUMAN, THE
Democratic National Committee: 1948 (Giveaway, regular size, soft-c, 16 pg.)

nn-Gives biography on career of Truman; used in **SOTI**, pg. 311 14.00 43.00 110.00

STRANGE AS IT SEEMS
McNaught Syndicate: 1936 (B&W, 5x7", 24 pgs.)

nn-Ex-Lax giveaway 7.15 21.50 50.00

SUGAR BEAR
Post Cereal Giveaway: No date, circa 1975? (2-1/2x4-1/2", 16 pgs.)

"The Almost Take Over of the Post Office", "The Race Across the Atlantic", "The Zoo Goes Wild" each... 2.40 6.00

SUNDAY WORLD'S EASTER EGG FULL OF EASTER MEAT FOR LITTLE PEOPLE
Supplement to the New York World: 3/27/1898 (soft-c, 16pg, 4"x8" approx., opens at top, color & B&W)(Giveaway)(shaped like an Easter egg)

nn-By R.F. Outcault 16.00 48.00 125.00

SUPER BOOK OF COMICS
Western Publishing Co.: nd (1942-1943?) (Soft-c, 32 pgs.) (Pan-Am/Gilmore Oil/Kelloggs premiums)

nn-Dick Tracy (Gilmore)-Magic Morro app. 44.00 132.00 400.00
1-Dick Tracy & The Smuggling Ring; Stratosphere Jim app. (Rare) (Pan-Am) 44.00 132.00 400.00
1-Smilin' Jack, Magic Morro (Pan-Am) 17.00 51.00 135.00
2-Smilin' Jack, Stratosphere Jim (Pan-Am) 17.00 51.00 135.00
2-Smitty, Magic Morro (Pan-Am) 17.00 51.00 135.00
3-Captain Midnight, Magic Morro (Pan-Am) 36.00 107.00 290.00
3-Moon Mullins? 17.00 51.00 135.00
4-Red Ryder, Magic Morro (Pan-Am). Same content as Red Ryder Victory Patrol comic w/diff. cover 21.00 64.00 165.00
4-Smitty, Stratosphere Jim (Pan-Am) 17.00 51.00 135.00
5-Don Winslow, Magic Morro (Gilmore) 21.00 64.00 165.00
5-Don Winslow, Stratosphere Jim (Pan-Am) 21.00 64.00 165.00
5-Terry & the Pirates 25.00 75.00 200.00
6-Don Winslow, Stratosphere Jim (Pan-Am)-McWilliams-a 21.00 64.00 165.00
6-King of the Royal Mounted, Magic Morro (Pan-Am) 21.00 64.00 165.00
7-Dick Tracy, Magic Morro (Pan-Am) 29.00 86.00 230.00
7-Little Orphan Annie 14.00 43.00 115.00
8-Dick Tracy, Stratosphere Jim (Pan-Am) 25.00 75.00 200.00
8-Dan Dunn, Magic Morro (Pan-Am) 14.00 43.00 115.00
9-Terry & the Pirates, Magic Morro (Pan-Am) 25.00 75.00 200.00
10-Red Ryder, Magic Morro (Pan-Am) 21.00 64.00 165.00

SUPER-BOOK OF COMICS
Western Publishing Co.: (Omar Bread & Hancock Oil Co. giveaways)
1944 - No. 30, 1947 (Omar); 1947 - 1948 (Hancock) (16 pgs.)

Note: The Hancock issues are all exact reprints of the earlier Omar issues. The issue numbers were removed in some of the reprints.

1-Dick Tracy (Omar, 1944) 24.00 73.00 195.00
1-Dick Tracy (Hancock, 1947) 18.00 54.00 145.00
2-Bugs Bunny (Omar, 1944) 8.35 25.00 60.00
2-Bugs Bunny (Hancock, 1947) 6.70 20.00 46.00
3-Terry & the Pirates (Omar, 1944) 13.00 39.00 105.00
3-Terry & the Pirates (Hancock, 1947) 11.50 34.00 90.00
4-Andy Panda (Omar, 1944) 8.35 25.00 60.00
4-Andy Panda (Hancock, 1947) 6.70 20.00 46.00
5-Smokey Stover (Omar, 1945) 6.70 20.00 46.00
5-Smokey Stover (Hancock, 1947) 5.00 15.00 35.00
6-Porky Pig (Omar, 1945) 8.35 25.00 60.00
6-Porky Pig (Hancock, 1947) 6.70 20.00 46.00
7-Smilin' Jack (Omar, 1945) 8.35 25.00 60.00
7-Smilin' Jack (Hancock, 1947) 6.70 20.00 46.00
8-Oswald the Rabbit (Omar, 1945) 6.70 20.00 46.00
8-Oswald the Rabbit (Hancock, 1947) 5.00 15.00 35.00
9-Alley Oop (Omar, 1945) 14.00 43.00 115.00
9-Alley Oop (Hancock, 1947) 13.00 39.00 105.00
10-Elmer Fudd (Omar, 1945) 6.70 20.00 46.00
10-Elmer Fudd (Hancock, 1947) 5.00 15.00 35.00
11-Little Orphan Annie (Omar, 1945) 9.15 27.00 64.00
11-Little Orphan Annie (Hancock, 1947) 7.50 22.50 54.00
12-Woody Woodpecker (Omar, 1945) 6.70 20.00 46.00
12-Woody Woodpecker (Hancock, 1947) 5.00 15.00 35.00
13-Dick Tracy (Omar, 1945) 14.00 43.00 115.00
13-Dick Tracy (Hancock, 1947) 13.00 39.00 105.00
14-Bugs Bunny (Omar, 1945) 6.70 20.00 46.00
14-Bugs Bunny (Hancock, 1947) 5.00 15.00 35.00
15-Andy Panda (Omar, 1945) 5.85 17.50 40.00
15-Andy Panda (Hancock, 1947) 5.00 15.00 35.00
16-Terry & the Pirates (Omar, 1945) 13.00 39.00 105.00
16-Terry & the Pirates (Hancock, 1947) 10.00 30.00 75.00
17-Smokey Stover (Omar, 1946) 6.70 20.00 46.00
17-Smokey Stover (Hancock, 1948?) 5.00 15.00 35.00

Supergirl 1986 © DC

Superman Miniature 1B © DC

Superman-Tim 1/48 © DC

	GD2.0	FN6.0	NM9.4
18-Porky Pig (Omar, 1946)	5.85	17.50	40.00
18-Porky Pig (Hancock, 1948?)	5.00	15.00	35.00
19-Smilin' Jack (Omar, 1946)	6.70	20.00	46.00
nn-Smilin' Jack (Hancock, 1948)	5.00	15.00	35.00
20-Oswald the Rabbit (Omar, 1946)	5.85	17.50	40.00
nn-Oswald the Rabbit (Hancock, 1948)	5.00	15.00	35.00
21-Gasoline Alley (Omar, 1946)	9.15	27.00	64.00
nn-Gasoline Alley (Hancock, 1948)	7.50	22.50	54.00
22-Elmer Fudd (Omar, 1946)	5.85	17.50	40.00
nn-Elmer Fudd (Hancock, 1948)	5.00	15.00	35.00
23-Little Orphan Annie (Omar, 1946)	8.35	25.00	60.00
nn-Little Orphan Annie (Hancock, 1948)	6.70	20.00	46.00
24-Woody Woodpecker (Omar, 1946)	5.85	17.50	40.00
nn-Woody Woodpecker (Hancock, 1948)	5.00	15.00	35.00
25-Dick Tracy (Omar, 1946)	13.00	39.00	105.00
nn-Dick Tracy (Hancock, 1948)	10.00	30.00	80.00
26-Bugs Bunny (Omar, 1946))	5.85	17.50	40.00
nn-Bugs Bunny (Hancock, 1948)	5.00	15.00	35.00
27-Andy Panda (Omar, 1946)	5.85	17.50	40.00
27-Andy Panda (Hancock, 1948)	5.00	15.00	35.00
28-Terry & the Pirates (Omar, 1946)	13.00	39.00	105.00
28-Terry & the Pirates (Hancock, 1948)	10.00	30.00	75.00
29-Smokey Stover (Omar, 1947)	5.85	17.50	40.00
29-Smokey Stover (Hancock, 1948)	5.00	15.00	35.00
30-Porky Pig (Omar, 1947)	5.85	17.50	40.00
30-Porky Pig (Hancock, 1948)	5.00	15.00	35.00
nn-Bugs Bunny (Hancock, 1948)-Does not match any Omar book	5.85	17.50	40.00

SUPER CIRCUS (TV)
Cross Publishing Co.

	GD2.0	FN6.0	NM9.4
1-(1951, Weather Bird Shoes giveaway)	6.70	20.00	46.00

SUPERGEAR COMICS
Jacobs Corp.: 1976 (Giveaway, 4 pgs. in color, slick paper)

	GD2.0	FN6.0	NM9.4
nn-(Rare)-Superman, Lois Lane; Steve Lombard app. (500 copies printed, over half destroyed?)	4.55	13.65	50.00

SUPERGIRL
DC Comics: 1984, 1986 (Giveaway, Baxter paper)

	GD2.0	FN6.0	NM9.4
nn-(American Honda/U.S. Dept. Transportation) Torres-c/a			2.00

SUPER HEROES PUZZLES AND GAMES
General Mills Giveaway (Marvel Comics Group): 1979 (32 pgs., regular size)

	GD2.0	FN6.0	NM9.4
nn-Four 2-pg. origin stories of Spider-Man, Captain America, The Hulk, & Spider-Woman	2.00	6.00	18.00

SUPERMAN
National Periodical Publ./DC Comics

	GD2.0	FN6.0	NM9.4
72-Giveaway(9-10/51)-(Rare)-Price blackened out; came with banner wrapped around book; without banner	74.00	221.00	700.00
72-Giveaway with banner	103.00	308.00	975.00
Bradman birthday custom (1988)			2.00
... For the Animals (2000, Doris Day Animal Foundation, 30 pgs.) polybagged with Gotham Adventures #22, Hourman #12, Impulse #58, Looney Tunes #62, Stars and S.T.R.I.P.E. #8 and Superman Adventures #41			2.00
Kelloggs Giveaway-(2/3 normal size, 1954)-r-two stories/Superman #55	34.00	103.00	270.00
Kenner: Man of Steel (Doomsday is Coming) (1995, 16 pgs.) packaged with set of Superman and Doomsday action figures			2.00
...Meets the Quik Bunny (1987, Nestles Quik premium, 36 pgs.)			4.00
Pizza Hut Premiums (12/77)-Exact reprints of 1950s comics except for paid ads (set of 6 exist?); Vol. 1-r#97 (#113-r also known)		2.40	6.00
Radio Shack Giveaway-36 pgs. (7/80) "The Computers That Saved Metropolis", Starlin/Giordano-a; advertising insert in Action #509, New Advs. of Superboy #7, Legion of Super-Heroes #265, & House of Mystery #282. (All comics were 68 pgs.) Cover of inserts printed on newsprint. Giveaway contains 4 extra pgs. of Radio Shack advertising that inserts do not have			4.00
Radio Shack Giveaway-(7/81) "Victory by Computer"			4.00
Radio Shack Giveaway-(7/82) "Computer Masters of Metropolis"			4.00

SUPERMAN ADVENTURES, THE (TV)
DC Comics: 1996 (Based on animated series)

	GD2.0	FN6.0	NM9
1-(1996) Preview issue distributed at Warner Bros. stores			3.0
Titus Game Edition (1998)			2.0

SUPERMAN AND THE GREAT CLEVELAND FIRE
National Periodical Publ.: 1948 (Giveaway, 4 pgs., no cover) (Hospital Fund)

	GD2.0	FN6.0	NM9
nn-In full color	90.00	300.00	600.0

SUPERMAN (Miniature)
National Periodical Publ.: 1942; 1955 - 1956 (3 issues, no #'s, 32 pgs.)
The pages are numbered in the 1st issue: 1-32; 2nd: 1A-32A, and 3rd: 1B-32B

	GD2.0	FN6.0	NM9
No date-Py-Co-Pay Tooth Powder giveaway (8 pgs.; circa 1942)	84.00	253.00	725.0
1-The Superman Time Capsule (Kellogg's Sugar Smacks)(1955)	56.00	169.00	475.0
1A-Duel in Space (1955)	50.00	150.00	420.0
1B-The Super Show of Metropolis (also #1-32, no B)(1955)	50.00	150.00	420.0

NOTE: *Numbering variations exist. Each title could have any combination-#1, 1A, or 1B.*

SUPERMAN RECORD COMIC
National Periodical Publications: 1966 (Golden Records)

	GD2.0	FN6.0	NM9
(With record)-Record reads origin of Superman from comic; came with iron-on patch, decoder, membership card & button; comic-r/Superman #125,146	22.00	66.00	175.0
Comic only	12.50	37.50	100.0

SUPERMAN'S BUDDY (Costume Comic)
National Periodical Publications: 1954 (4 pgs., slick paper-c; one-shot) (Came in box w/costume)

	GD2.0	FN6.0	NM9
1-w/box & costume	131.00	395.00	1250.0
Comic only	63.00	189.00	600.0
1-(1958 edition)-Printed in 2 colors	19.00	56.00	150.0

SUPERMAN'S CHRISTMAS ADVENTURE
National Periodical Publications: 1940, 1944 (Giveaway, 16 pgs.)
Distributed by Nehi drinks, Bailey Store, Ivey-Keith Co., Kennedy's Boys Shop, Macy's Store, Boston Store

	GD2.0	FN6.0	NM9
1(1940)-Burnley-a; F. Ray-c/r from Superman #6 (Scarce)-Superman saves Santa Claus. Santa makes real Superman Toys offered in 1940. 1st merchandising story	625.00	2500.00	5000.0
nn(1944) w/Santa Claus & X-mas tree-c	128.00	511.00	1150.0
nn(1944) w/Candy cane & Superman-c	117.00	467.00	1050.0

SUPERMAN-TIM (Becomes Tim)
Superman-Tim Stores/National Periodical Publ.: Aug, 1942 - May, 1950 (Half size) (B&W Giveaway w/2 color covers) (Publ. monthly 2/43 on)

	GD2.0	FN6.0	NM9
8/42 (#1)-All have Superman illos.	150.00	600.00	1200.0
1/43 (#2)	44.00	133.00	400.0
2/43 (#3)	42.00	125.00	375.0
3/43 (#4)	42.00	125.00	375.0
4/43, 5/43, 6/43, 7/43, 8/43	40.00	120.00	325.0
9/43, 10/43, 11/43, 12/43	35.00	105.00	280.0
1/44-12/44	28.00	83.00	220.0
1/45-5/45, 10-12/45, 1/46-8/46	25.00	75.00	200.0
6/45-Classic Superman-c	28.00	83.00	220.0
7/45-Classic Superman flag-c	28.00	837.00	220.0
9/45-1st stamp album issue	82.00	287.00	575.0
9/46-2nd stamp album issue	64.00	225.00	450.0
10/46-1st Superman story	35.00	105.00	280.0
11/46, 12/46, 1/47-8/47 issues-Superman story in each; 2/47-Infinity-c. All 36 pgs.	35.00	105.00	280.0
9/47-Stamp album issue & Superman story	60.00	210.00	420.0
10/47, 11/47, 12/47-Superman stories (24 pgs.)	35.00	105.00	280.0
1/48-7/48,10/48, 11/48, 2/49, 4/49-11/49	28.00	84.00	225.0
8/48-Contains full page ad for Superman-Tim watch giveaway	28.00	83.00	220.0
9/48-Stamp album issue	36.00	108.00	290.0
1/49-Full page Superman bank cut-out	28.00	83.00	220.0
3/49-Full page Superman boxing game cut-out	28.00	83.00	220.0
12/49-3/50, 5/50-Superman stories	31.00	94.00	250.0
4/50-Superman story, baseball stories; photo-c without Superman	31.00	94.00	250.0

NOTE: *All issues have Superman illustrations throughout. The page count varies depending on whether a Superman-Tim comic story is inserted. If it is, the page count is either 36 or 24 pages.*

Tastee-Freez Comics #2 © HARV

Time of Decision © HARV

Titans Beat © DC

Otherwise all issues are 16 pages. Each issue has a special place for inserting a full color Superman stamp. The stamp album issues had spaces for the stamps given away the past year. The books were mailed as a subscription premium. The stamps were given away free (or when you made a purchase) only when you physically came into the store.

SUPER SEAMAN SLOPPY
Allied Pristine Union Council, Buffalo, NY: 1940s, 8pg., reg. size (Soft-c)
nn 4.00 10.00 20.00

SWAMP FOX, THE
Walt Disney Productions: 1960 (14 pgs, small size) (Canada Dry Premiums)
Titles: (A)-Tory Masquerade, (B)-Turnabout Tactics, (C)-Rindau Rampage; each came in paper sleeve, books 1,2 & 3;
Set with sleeves 6.00 18.00 60.00
Comic only 2.00 6.00 18.00

SWORDQUEST
DC Comics/Atari Pub.: 1982, 52pg., 5"x7" (Giveaway with video games)
1-3-Roy Thomas & Gerry Conway-s; George Pérez & Dick Giordano-c/a 1.50 4.50 12.00

SYNDICATE FEATURES (Sci/fi)
Harry A. Chesler Syndicate: V1#3, 11/15/37 (Tabloid size, 3 colors, 4 pgs.) (Editors premium)(Came folded)
V1#3-Dan Hastings daily strips-Guardineer-a 560.00 1680.00 2800.00

TASTEE-FREEZ COMICS
Harvey Comics: 1957 (10¢, 36 pgs.)(6 different issues given away)
1,3: 1-Little Dot. 3-Casper 4.10 12.30 45.00
2,4,5: 2-Rags Rabbit. 4-Sad Sack. 5-Mazie 3.00 9.00 30.00
6-Dick Tracy 4.10 12.30 45.00

TAYLOR'S CHRISTMAS TABLOID
Dept. Store Giveaway: Mid 1930s, Cleveland, Ohio (Tabloid size; in color)
nn-(Very Rare)-Among the earliest pro work of Siegel & Shuster; one full color page called "The Battle in the Stratosphere", with a pre-Superman look; Shuster art thoughout. (Only 1 known copy)
Estimated value... 4000.00

TAZ'S 40TH BIRTHDAY BLOWOUT
DC Comics: 1994 (K-Mart giveaway, 16 pgs.)
nn-Six pg. story, games and puzzles 2.00

TEE AND VEE CROSLEY IN TELEVISION LAND COMICS
Also see Crosley's House of Fun)
Crosley Division, Avco Mfg. Corp. : 1951 (52 pgs.; 8x11"; paper cover; in color) (Giveaway)
Many stories, puzzles, cut-outs, games, etc. 5.00 15.00 35.00

TENNESSEE JED (Radio)
Fox Syndicate? (Wm. C. Popper & Co.): nd (1945) (16 pgs.; paper cover; regular size; giveaway)
nn 33.00 110.00 220.00

TENNIS (...For Speed, Stamina, Strength, Skill)
Tennis Educational Foundation: 1956 (16 pgs.; soft cover; 10¢)
Book 1-Endorsed by Gene Tunney, Ralph Kiner, etc. showing how tennis has helped them 5.00 15.00 32.00

TERRY AND THE PIRATES
Dell Publishing Co.: 1939 - 1953 (By Milton Caniff)
Buster Brown Shoes giveaway(1938)-32 pgs.; in color 29.00 86.00 220.00
Canada Dry Premiums-Books #1-3(1953, 36 pgs.; 2x5")-Harvey; #1-Hot Shot Charlie Flies Again; 2-In Forced Landing; 3-Dragon Lady in Distress) 17.00 51.00 135.00
Gambles Giveaway (1938, 16 pgs.) 10.00 30.00 65.00
Gillmore Giveaway (1938, 24 pgs.) 10.00 30.00 70.00
Popped Wheat Giveaway(1938)-Strip reprints in full color; Caniff-a 2.00 5.00 8.00
Shoe Store giveaway (Weatherbird)(1938, 16 pgs., soft-c)(2-diff.) 10.00 30.00 70.00
Sparked Wheat Giveaway(1942, 16 pgs.)-In color 10.00 30.00 70.00

TERRY AND THE PIRATES
Libby's Radio Premium: 1941 (16 pgs.; reg. size)(shipped folded in the mail)

GD2.0 FN6.0 VF8.0
"Adventure of the Ruby of Genghis Khan" - Each pg. is a puzzle that must be completed to read the story 400.00 1320.00 2400.00

THAT THE WORLD MAY BELIEVE
Catechetical Guild Giveaway: No date (16 pgs.) (Graymoor Friars distr.)
GD2.0 FN6.0 NM9.4
nn 2.00 5.00 12.00

3-D COLOR CLASSICS (Wendy's Kid's Club)
Wendy's Int'l Inc.: 1995 (5 1/2" x 8", comes with 3-D glasses)
The Elephant's Child, Gulliver's Travels, Peter Pan, The Time Machine, 20,000 Leagues Under the Sea: Neal Adams-a in all each.... 2.00

350 YEARS OF AMERICAN DAIRY FOODS
American Dairy Assoc.: 1957 (5x7", 16 pgs.)
nn-History of milk 3.00 7.50 15.00

THUMPER (Disney)
Grosset & Dunlap: 1942 (50¢, 32pgs., hardcover book, 7"x8-1/2" w/dust jacket)
nn-Given away (along with a copy of Bambi) for a $2.00, 2-year subscription to WDC&S in 1942. (Xmas offer). Book only 18.00 53.00 140.00
Dust jacket only 10.00 30.00 70.00

TILLY AND TED-TINKERTOTLAND
W. T. Grant Co.: 1945 (Giveaway, 20 pgs.)
nn-Christmas comic 6.40 19.25 45.00

TIM (Formerly Superman-Tim; becomes Gene Autry-Tim)
Tim Stores: June, 1950 - Oct, 1950 (B&W, half-size)
4 issues; 6/50, 9/50, 10/50 known 16.00 48.00 125.00

TIM AND SALLY'S ADVENTURES AT MARINELAND
Marineland Restaurant & Bar, Marineland, CA: 1957 (5x7", 16 pgs., soft-c)
nn-copyright Oceanarium, Inc. 2.40 6.00 12.00

TIME OF DECISION
Harvey Publications Inc.: (16 pgs., paper cover)
nn-ROTC recruitment 20.00

TIM IN SPACE (Formerly Gene Autry Tim; becomes Tim Tomorrow)
Tim Stores: 1950 (1/2 size giveaway) (B&W)
nn 10.00 30.00 80.00

TIM TOMORROW (Formerly Tim In Space)
Tim Stores: 8/51, 9/51, 10/51, Christmas, 1951 (5x7-3/4")
nn-Prof. Fumble & Captain Kit Comet in all 10.00 30.00 80.00

TITANS BEAT (Teen Titans)
DC Comics: Aug, 1996 (16 pgs., paper-c)
1-Intro./preview new Teen Titans members; Pérez-a 2.00

TOM MIX (...Commandos Comics #10-12)
Ralston-Purina Co.: Sept, 1940 - No. 12, Nov, 1942 (36 pgs.); 1983 (one-shot)
Given away for two Ralston box-tops; 1983 came in cereal box
1-Origin (life) Tom Mix; Fred Meagher-a 350.00 1750.00 3500.00
2 106.00 319.00 950.00
3-9 66.00 197.00 625.00
10-12: 10-Origin Tom Mix Commando Unit; Speed O'Dare begins; Japanese sub-c. 12-Sci/fi-c 55.00 165.00 500.00
1983- "Taking of Grizzly Grebb", Toth-a; 16 pg. miniature 1.85 5.50 15.00

TOM SAWYER COMICS
Giveaway: 1951? (Paper cover)
nn-Contains a coverless Hopalong Cassidy from 1951; other combinations known 4.00 12.00 24.00

TOPPS COMICS PRESENTS
Topps Comics: No. 0, 1993 (Giveaway, B&W, 36 pgs.)
0-Dracula vs. Zorro, Teenagents, Silver Star, & Bill the Galactic Hero 2.00

TOWN THAT FORGOT SANTA, THE
W. T. Grant Co.: 1961 (Giveaway, 24 pgs.)
nn 2.30 7.00 20.00

TOY WORLD FUNNIES (See Funnies On Parade)

Toy World Funnies © EAS

Untold Legend of the Batman #1 © DC

What's In It For You? © HARV

Eastern Color Printing Co.: 1933 (36 pgs., slick cover, Golden Eagle and Wanamaker giveaway)

nn-Contains contents from Funnies On Parade/Century Of Comics. A rare variation of Funnies On Parade; same format, similar contents, same cover except for large Santa placed in certer (value will be based on sale)

TRAPPED
Harvey Publications (Columbia Univ. Press): 1951 (Giveaway, soft-c, 16 pgs)

nn-Drug education comic (30,000 printed?) distributed to schools.; mentioned in **SOTI**, pgs. 256,350 — 2.00 — 5.00 — 10.00

NOTE: *Many copies surfaced in 1979 causing a setback in price; beware of trimmed edges, because many copies have a brittle edge.*

TRIP TO OUTER SPACE WITH SANTA
Sales Promotions, Inc/Peoria Dry Goods: 1950s (paper-c)

nn-Comics, games & puzzles — 4.00 — 11.00 — 22.00

TRIP WITH SANTA ON CHRISTMAS EVE, A
Rockford Dry Goods Co.: No date (Early 1950s) (Giveaway, 16 pgs., paper-c)

nn — 4.00 — 11.00 — 22.00

TRUTH BEHIND THE TRIAL OF CARDINAL MINDSZENTY, THE (See Cardinal Mindszenty)

24 PAGES OF COMICS (No title) (Also see Pure Oil Comics, Salerno Carnival of Comics, & Vicks Comics)
Giveaway by various outlets including Sears: Late 1930s

nn-Contains strip reprints-Buck Rogers, Napoleon, Sky Roads, War on Crime — 60.00 — 148.00 — 325.00

TWISTED METAL (Video game)
DC Comics: 1996

nn — 2.00

TWO FACES OF COMMUNISM (Also see Double Talk)
Christian Anti-Communism Crusade, Houston, Texas: 1961 (Giveaway, paper-c, 36 pgs.)

nn — 12.50 — 37.50 — 100.00

2001, A SPACE ODYSSEY (Movie)
Marvel Comics Group

Howard Johnson giveaway (1968, 8pp); 6 pg. movie adaptation, 2 pg. games, puzzles; McWilliams-a — 1.00 — 3.00 — 8.00

UNCLE SAM'S CHRISTMAS STORY
Promotional Publ. Co.: 1958 (Giveaway)

nn-Reprints 1956 Christmas USA — 1.75 — 5.25 — 14.00

UNKEPT PROMISE
Legion of Truth: 1949 (Giveaway, 24 pgs.)

nn-Anti-alcohol — 9.30 — 28.00 — 65.00

UNTOLD LEGEND OF THE BATMAN, THE
DC Comics: 1989 (28 pgs., 6X9", limited series)

1-3: Batman cereal premiums; 1st & 2nd printings known — 2.40 — 6.00

UNTOUCHABLES, THE (TV)
Leaf Brands, Inc.

Topps Bubblegum premiums produced by Leaf Brands, Inc.-2-1/2x4-1/2", 8 pgs. (3 diff. issues) "The Organization, Jamaica Ginger, The Otto Frick Story (drug), 3000 Suspects, The Antidote, Mexican Stakeout, Little Egypt, Purple Gang, Bugs Moran Story, & Lily Dallas Story" — 2.50 — 7.50 — 25.00

VICKS COMICS (See Pure Oil Comics, Salerno Carnival of Comics & 24 Pages of Comics)
Eastern Color Printing Co. (Vicks Chemical Co.): nd (circa 1938) (Giveaway, 68 pgs. in color)

nn-Famous Funnies-r (before #40); contains 5 pgs. Buck Rogers (4 pgs. from F.F. #15, & 1 pg. from #16) Joe Palooka, Napoleon, etc. app. — 69.00 — 206.00 — 650.00

nn-16 loose, untrimmed page giveaway; paper-c; r/Famous Funnies #14; Buck Rogers, Joe Palooka app. — 26.00 — 79.00 — 205.00

WALT DISNEY'S COMICS & STORIES
K.K. Publications: 1942-1963 known (7-1/3"x10-1/4", 4 pgs. in color, slick paper) (folded horizontally once or twice as mailers) (Xmas subscription offer)

1942 mailer-r/Kelly cover to WDC&S 25; 2-year subscription + two Grosset & Dunlap hardcover books (32-pages each), of Bambi and of Thumper, offere for $2.00; came in an illustrated C&S envelope with an enclosed postage paid envelope (Rare)
- Mailer only — 23.00 — 68.00 — 250.0
- with envelopes — 30.00 — 90.00 — 325.0

1947,1948 mailer — 16.00 — 48.00 — 175.0

1949 mailer-A rare Barks item: Same WDC&S cover as 1942 mailer, but with a changed so that nephew is handing teacher Donald a comic book rather than an apple, as originally drawn by Kelly. The tiny, 7/8"x1-1/4" cover show was a rejected cover by Barks that was intended for C&S 110, but was redrawn by Kelly for C&S 111. The original art has been lost and this is its only app. (Rare) — 41.00 — 123.00 — 450.0

1950 mailer-P.1 r/Kelly cover to Dell Xmas Parade 1 (without title); p.2 r/Kelly cover to C&S 101 (w/o title), but with the art altered to show Donald reading C&S 122 (by Kelly); hardcover book, "Donald Duck in Bringing Up the Boys" given with a $1.00 one-year subscription; P.4 r/full Kelly Xmas cover to C&S 99 (Rare) — 16.00 — 48.00 — 175.0

1953 mailer-P.1 r/cover Dell Xmas Parade 4 (w/o title); insides offer "Donald Duck Full Speed Ahead," a 28-page, color, 5-5/8"x6-5/8" book, not of the Story Hour series; P.4 r/full Barks C&S 148 cover (Rare) — 11.00 — 33.00 — 125.0

1963 mailer-Pgs. 1,2 & 4 r/GK Xmas art; P.3 r/a 1963 C&S cover (Scarce) — 6.85 — 20.00 — 75.0

NOTE: *It is assumed a different mailer was printed each Xmas for at least twenty years. A 1 mailer is known.*

WALT DISNEY'S COMICS & STORIES
Walt Disney Productions: 1943 (36 pgs.) (Dept. store Xmas giveaway)

nn-X-Mas-c with Donald & the Boys; Donald Duck by Jack Hannah; Thumper by Ken Hultgren — 45.00 — 136.00 — 500.0

WATCH OUT FOR BIG TALK
Giveaway: 1950

nn-Dan Barry-a; about crooked politicians — 5.00 — 15.00 — 35.0

WEATHER-BIRD (See Comics From..., Dick Tracy, Free Comics to You... Super Circus & Terry and the Pirates)
International Shoe Co./Western Printing Co.: 1958 - No. 16, July, 1962 (Sho store giveaway)

1 — 3.20 — 9.60 — 35.0
2-16 — 2.00 — 6.00 — 18.0

NOTE: *The numbers are located in the lower bottom panel, pg. 1. All feature a character called Weather-Bird.*

WEATHER BIRD COMICS (See Comics From Weather Bird)
Weather Bird Shoes: 1957 (Giveaway)

nn-Contains a comic bound with new cover. Several combinations possible; contents determines price (40 - 60 percent of contents).

WHAT DO YOU KNOW ABOUT THIS COMICS SEAL OF APPROVAL?
No publisher listed (DC Comics Giveaway): nd (1955) (4 pgs., slick paper-c)

nn-(Rare) — 68.00 — 205.00 — 650.0

WHAT'S BEHIND THESE HEADLINES
William C. Popper Co.: 1948 (16 pgs.)

nn-Comic insert "The Plot to Steal the World" — 5.35 — 16.00 — 37.0

WHAT'S IN IT FOR YOU?
Harvey Publications Inc.: (16 pgs., paper cover)

nn-National Guard recruitment — 20.0

WHEATIES (Premiums)
Walt Disney Productions: 1950 & 1951 (32 titles, pocket-size, 32 pgs.)

Mailing Envelope (no art on front)(Designates sets A,B,C or D on front) — 8.65 — 26.00 — 60.0

(Set A-1 to A-8, 1950)

A-1-Mickey Mouse & the Disappearing Island, A-5-Mickey Mouse, Roving Reporte each... — 5.00 — 15.00 — 35.0

A-2-Grandma Duck, Homespun Detective, A-6-Li'l Bad Wolf, Forest Ranger, A-7-Goofy, Tightrope Acrobat, A-8-Pluto & the Bogus Money each... — 5.00 — 15.00 — 30.0

A-3-Donald Duck & the Haunted Jewels, A-4-Donald Duck & the Giant Ape each... — 8.65 — 26.00 — 60.0

Whiz Comics - Wheaties Giveaways © FAW

Woody Woodpecker Meets Scotty MacTape © Walter Lantz

Your Vote Is Vital © HARV

GD2.0 FN6.0 NM9.4

(Set B-1 to B-8, 1950)

B-1-Mickey Mouse & the Pharoah's Curse, B-4-Mickey Mouse & the Mystery Sea Monster each... 5.00 15.00 35.00

B-2-Pluto, Canine Cowpoke, B-5-Li'l Bad Wolf in the Hollow Tree Hideout, B-7-Goofy & the Gangsters each... 5.00 15.00 30.00

B-3-Donald Duck & the Buccaneers, B-6-Donald Duck,Trail Blazer, B-8 Donald Duck, Klondike Kid each... 8.65 26.00 60.00

(Set C-1 to C-8, 1951)

C-1-Donald Duck & the Inca Idol, C-5-Donald Duck in the Lost Lakes, C-8-Donald Duck Deep-Sea Diver each... 8.65 26.00 60.00

C-2-Mickey Mouse & the Magic Mountain, C-6-Mickey Mouse & the Stagecoach Bandits each... 5.00 15.00 35.00

C-3-Li'l Bad Wolf, Fire Fighter, C-4-Gus & Jaq Save the Ship, C-7-Goofy, Big Game Hunter each... 5.00 15.00 30.00

(Set D-1 to D-8, 1951)

D-1-Donald Duck in Indian Country, D-5-Donald Duck, Mighty Mystic each... 8.65 26.00 60.00

D-2-Mickey Mouse and the Abandoned Mine, D-6-Mickey Mouse & the Medicine Man each... 5.00 15.00 35.00

D-3-Pluto & the Mysterious Package, D-4-Bre'r Rabbit's Sunken Treasure, D-7-Li'l Bad Wolf and the Secret of the Woods, D-8-Minnie Mouse, Girl Explorer each... 5.00 15.00 30.00

NOTE: *Some copies lack the Wheaties ad.*

WHIZ COMICS (Formerly Flash Comics & Thrill Comics #1)
Fawcett Publications

Wheaties Giveaway(1946, Miniature, 6-1/2x8-1/4", 32 pgs.); all copies were taped at each corner to a box of Wheaties and are never found in very fine or mint condition; "Capt. Marvel & the Water Thieves", plus Golden Arrow, Ibis, Crime Smasher stories 138.00 550.00 –

WILD KINGDOM (TV)
Western Printing Co.: 1965 (Giveaway, regular size, slick-c, 16 pgs.)

nn-Mutual of Omaha's... 1.75 5.25 14.00

WISCO/KLARER COMIC BOOK (Miniature)
Marvel Comics/Vital Publ./Fawcett Publ.: 1948 - 1964 (3-1/2x6-3/4", 24 pgs.)

Given away by Wisco "99" Service Stations, Carnation Malted Milk, Klarer Health Wieners, Fleers Dubble Bubble Gum, Rodeo All-Meat Wieners, Perfect Potato Chips, & others; see ad in Tom Mix #21

Blackstone & the Gold Medal Mystery (1948) 7.50 22.50 52.00
Blackstone "Solves the Sealed Vault Mystery" (1950) 7.50 22.50 52.00
Blaze Carson in "The Sheriff Shoots It Out" (1950) 7.50 22.50 52.00
Captain Marvel & Billy's Big Game (r/Capt. Marvel Adv. #76) 31.00 92.00 245.00
(Prices vary widely on this book)
China Boy in "A Trip to the Zoo" #10 (1948) 5.00 15.00 30.00
Indoors-Outdoors Game Book 3.00 7.50 15.00
Jim Solar Space Sheriff in "Battle for Mars", "Between Two Worlds", "Conquers Outer Space", "The Creatures on the Comet", "Defeats the Moon Missile Men", "Encounter Creatures on Comet", "Meet the Jupiter Jumpers", "Meets the Man From Mars", "On Traffic Duty", "Outlaws of the Spaceways", "Pirates of the Planet X", "Protects Space Lanes", "Raiders From the Sun", "Ring Around Saturn", "Robots of Rhea", "The Sky Ruby", "Spacetts of the Sky", "Spidermen of Venus", "Trouble on Mercury" 6.40 19.25 45.00
Johnny Starboard & the Underseas Pirates (1948) 4.15 12.50 25.00
Kid Colt in "He Lived by His Guns" (1950) 8.65 26.00 60.00
Little Aspirin as "Crook Catcher" #2 (1950) 3.00 7.50 15.00
Little Aspirin in "Naughty But Nice" #6 (1950) 3.00 7.50 15.00
Return of the Black Phantom (not M.E. character)(Roy Dare)(1948) 5.00 15.00 35.00
Secrets of Magic 3.60 9.00 18.00
Slim Morgan "Brings Justice to Mesa City" #3 3.60 9.00 18.00
Super Rabbit(1950)-Cuts Red Tape, Stops Crime Wave! 10.00 30.00 75.00
Tex Farnum, Frontiersman (1948) 4.00 11.00 22.00
Tex Taylor in "Draw or Die, Cowpoke!" (1950) 5.70 17.00 40.00
Tex Taylor in "An Exciting Adventure at the Gold Mine" (1950) 5.00 15.00 35.00
Wacky Quacky in "All-Aboard" 2.40 6.00 12.00
When School Is Out 2.40 6.00 12.00
Willie in a "Comic-Comic Book Fall" #1 3.00 7.50 15.00
Wonder Duck "An Adventure at the Rodeo of the Fearless Quacker!" (1950) 9.30 28.00 65.00
Rare uncut version of three; includes Capt. Marvel, Tex Farnum, Black Phantom Estimated value... $400.00
Rare uncut version of three; includes China Boy, Blackstone, Johnny Starboard & the Underseas Pirates Estimated value... $125.00

WOMAN OF THE PROMISE, THE
Catechetical Guild: 1950 (General Distr.) (Paper cover, 32 pgs.)

nn 4.15 12.50 25.00

WONDERFUL WORLD OF DUCKS (See Golden Picture Story Book)
Colgate Palmolive Co.: 1975

1-Mostly-r 2.40 6.00

WONDER WOMAN
DC Comics: 1977

Pizza Hut Giveaways (12/77)-Reprints #60,62 2.40 6.00

WONDER WORKER OF PERU
Catechetical Guild: No date (5x7", 16 pgs., B&W, giveaway)

nn 4.00 12.00 24.00

WOODY WOODPECKER
Dell Publishing Co.

Clover Stamp-Newspaper Boy Contest('56)-9 pg. story-(Giveaway) 5.00 15.00 35.00
In Chevrolet Wonderland(1954-Giveaway)(Western Publ.)-20 pgs., full story line; Chilly Willy app. 21.00 64.00 165.00
...Meets Scotty MacTape(1953-Scotch Tape giveaway)-16 pgs., full size 21.00 64.00 165.00

WOOLWORTH'S CHRISTMAS STORY BOOK
Promotional Publ. Co.(Western Printing Co.): 1952 - 1954 (16 pgs., paper-c) (See Jolly Christmas Book)

nn 5.00 15.00 35.00
NOTE: *1952 issue-Marv Levy c/a.*

WOOLWORTH'S HAPPY TIME CHRISTMAS BOOK
F. W. Woolworth Co.(Whitman Publ. Co.): 1952 (Christmas giveaway)

nn-36 pgs. 5.00 15.00 35.00

WORLD'S FINEST COMICS
National Periodical Publ./DC Comics

Giveaway (c. 1944-45, 8 pgs., in color, paper-c)-Johnny Everyman-r/World's Finest 25.00 80.00 200.00
Giveaway (c. 1949, 8 pgs., in color, paper-c)- "Make Way For Youth" r/World's Finest; based on film of same name 22.00 70.00 175.00
#176, #179- Best Western reprint edition (1997) 2.00

WORLD'S GREATEST SUPER HEROES
DC Comics (Nutra Comics) (Child Vitamins, Inc.): 1977 (Giveaway, 3-3/4x3-3/4", 24 pgs.)

nn-Batman & Robin app.; health tips 1.25 3.75 10.00

XMAS FUNNIES
Kinney Shoes: No date (Giveaway, paper cover, 36 pgs.?)

Contains 1933 color strip-r; Mutt & Jeff, etc. 53.00 213.00 320.00

YALTA TO KOREA (Also see Korea My Home)
M. Phillip Corp. (Republican National Committee): 1952 (Giveaway, paper-c)

nn-(8 pgs.)-Anti-communist propaganda book 20.00 60.00 160.00

YOGI BEAR (TV)
Dell Publishing Co.

Giveaway ('84, '86)-City of Los Angeles, "Creative First Aid" & "Earthquake Preparedness for Children" 4.00

YOUR TRIP TO NEWSPAPERLAND
Philadelphia Evening Bulletin (Printed by Harvey Press): June, 1955 (14x11-1/2", 12 pgs.)

nn-Joe Palooka takes kids on newspaper tour 5.00 15.00 30.00

YOUR VOTE IS VITAL!
Harvey Publications Inc.: 1952 (5" x 7", 16 pgs., paper cover)

nn-The importance of voting 20.00

The American Comic Book: 1842-1935

IN THE BEGINNING: PLATINUM AGE KNOWLEDGE IS GROWING BY LEAPS & BOUNDS!

by Robert L. Beerbohm & Richard D. Olson, PhD

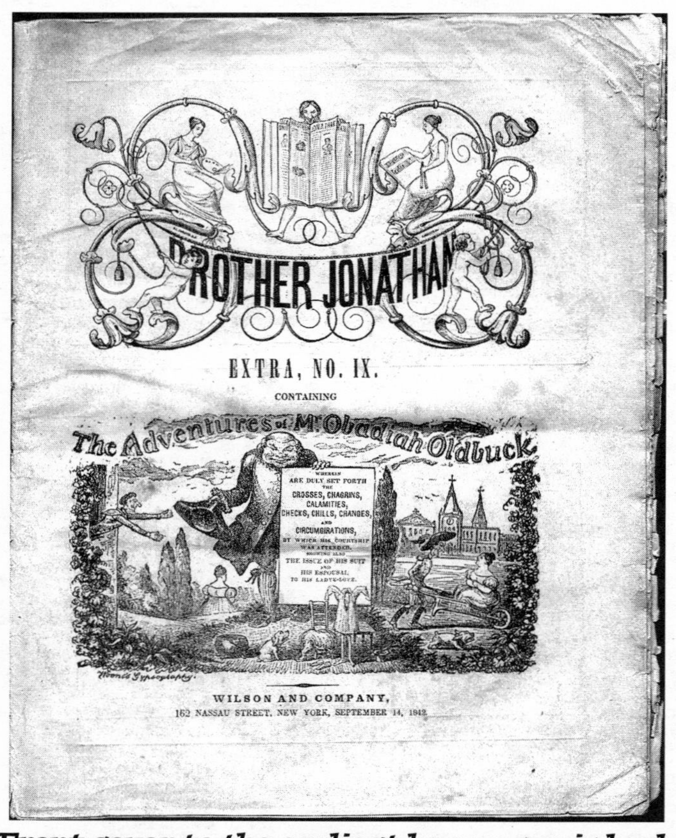

Front cover to the earliest known comic book published in America, "The Adventures of Mr. Obadiah Oldbuck" by Rodolphe Töpffer, Sept. 1842, Wilson & Co. NY.

Adventures of Mr. Obadiah Oldbuck, 1842. Page 8 of a 40 page graphic novel by Rodolphe Töpffer...the history books have to be rewritten.

This year the Platinum index section has been more than doubled in size with hundreds of new listings. The story of the success of the comic strip as we know it today is tied closely to the companies who sponsored them and paid licenses to the copyright holder for the purpose of advertising products. What mainly keeps the Platinum Age from being collected as much as later era comics is simply a general lack of awareness as well as the extreme rarity of many of these volumes, especially in any type of high grade. Many Platinum Age books are much rarer than so-called Golden Age comic books. Yet despite this rarity, **Mutt & Jeff**, **Bringing Up Father**, **The Katzenjammer Kids**, and many more were as popular, if not more so, than **Superman** and **Batman** when they were introduced. Recent research has come up with some more amazing rediscoveries. There is much that can be learned and applied to today's comics market by a simple historical examination of the medium's evolution.

The first known cartoon printed on paper in the **New World** was in a Puritan children's book first published in 1646. Titled simply "The Burning of Mr. John Rogers," it showed in flaming graphic detail what happens to those who stray from the flock and have to be burned at the stake. Wertham would have had a field day with this one! The first cartoon published in a newspaper in America is generally credited to Benjamin Franklin's "God Helps Those Who Help Themselves," in his periodical **Plain Truth** (1747). Other panel cartoons soon followed all over America, many utilizing word balloons. In 1753 his famous "Join Or Die" snake parts was published.

According to **The New York Times** (Sept. 3, 1904), the first American comic book was issued as a supplement to Brother Jonathan (New York, Sept. 14, 1842). It was a reprint of Rodolphe Töpffer's **The Adventures of Mr. Obadiah Oldbuck**, and it was 40 pages in length, side-stitched, printed on both sides of the paper with six to twelve panels per page, and measuring 8 1/2" x 11". One copy missing its outer wrap turned up in Oakland, California in late 1998, confirming its existence. You can take a look at the earliest known American comic book at www.reuben.org/evry/obadiah.html. Another whole complete copy turned up four months later in the Northeast, which is the copy pictured here for the first time in well over a century. This serves to push back the concept of what we think a comic book might be by well over 50 years. It bears further close scrutiny by the international comics scholar community.

Töpffer, who was Swiss, created at least seven widely published comic books which might also be called "graphic novels." Jerry Robinson, in his authoritative 1974 history book **The Comics**, wrote that "Töpffer is considered by some historians the inventor of the picture story, as he called it, and consequently the father of today's comics." Many other comics historians of equal stature have written just as eloquently about the man who invented the modern comic strip in 1827. By 1841, Töpffer's picture stories had been translated into over half a dozen languages including rare British editions; the American **Obadiah Oldbuck** is a reprint of this reprint. One more British reprint was printed in America by 1846 by

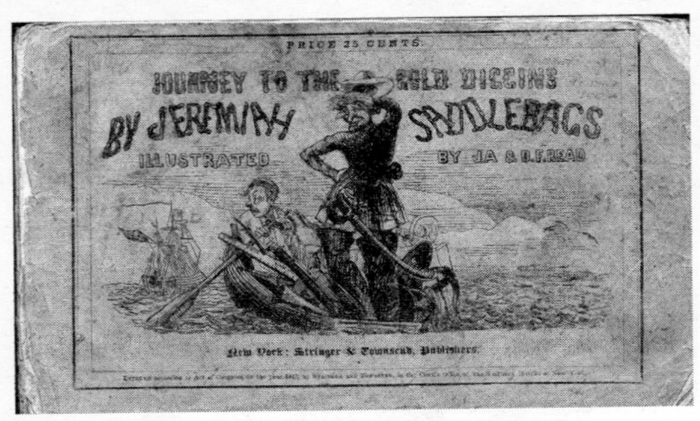

1849's *Journey to the Gold Diggins By Jeremiah Saddlebags*, the first sequential comic book by American creators, was recently rediscovered.

Wilson & Company, titled **Wonderful Adventures of Bachelor Butterfly**. In 1849 Wilson reprinted **Obadiah** with a new title, **Mishaps and Adventures of Obadiah Oldbuck**, this time strip-shaped, with certain panels deleted and some of the text altered to smooth over these deletions. Töpffer's comic books remained in print beginning in the 1860s through another publisher named Dick & Fitzgerald in the USA until at least 1877. Over 100 years later, even though he is widely acknowledged in Europe as the father of the comic book graphic novel, Töpffer remains relatively obscure on this side of the Atlantic.

With the third millennium now upon us this year, we keep rediscovering many other comic books printed, distributed and widely read in America throughout the 1800s which are little known today due to their extreme rarity. During the last decade, serious collectors have begun looking into the dim past and are steadily expanding their awareness of these earlier comic books. As knowledge grows in this area, we hope to report next year more about what we tentatively dub "Victorian Age" comic books.

Newly discovered for this year is the earliest known sequential comic book by an American creator was **Journey to the Gold Diggins By Jeremiah Saddlebags** by the brothers J.A. and D.F. Read - first published in 1849. Read more about this amazing item in the Plat index section.

The first graphic advertising utilizing fold-out comic strips appeared several years after the Civil War, initially sponsored by cereal and tobacco companies. At first these ads contained young kids, then animals of all kinds. With the immigrant influx of the 1870s and '80s, fairies soon dominated the scene. Palmer Cox's **The Brownies** were the first North American comics-type characters to be internationally merchandised. For over a quarter of a century, Cox deftly combined the popular advertising motifs of animals and fairies into a wonderful, whimsical world of society at its best and worst. Cox's (1840-1924) first work in **St. Nicholas**, a magazine for children, was in the March 1879 issue, titled "The Wasp and the Bee." He began his famous creation with his trademark verse and art with a creation entitled **The Brownies' Ride** in the February 1883 issue.

The Brownies' first book was issued by 1887, titled **The Brownies: Their Book**; many more followed. Cox also added a run of his hugely popular characters in **Ladies Home Journal** from October 1891 through February 1895, as well as a special on December 1910. With the 1892-93 World's Fair, the merchandising exploded with a host of products, including pianos, paper dolls and other figurines, chairs, stoves, puzzles, cough drops, coffee, soap, boots, candy, and many more. Brownies material was being produced in Europe as well as the United States.

Cox ran The Brownies as a newspaper strip in the **San Francisco Examiner** during 1898 and in the **New York World** in 1900. It was syndicated from 1903 through 1907. He seems to have retired from regularly drawing The Brownies with the January 1914 issue of **St. Nicholas** when he was 74. A wealthy man, he lived to the ripe old age of 84.

By the mid-1890s, while keeping careful track of quickly rising circulations of magazines with graphic humor such as **Harper's**, **Puck**, **St. Nicholas**, **Judge**, **Life** and **Truth**, New York based newspaper publishers began to recognize that illustrated humor would sell extra papers. Thus was born the Sunday "comic supplement." Most of the regular favorites were under contract with these magazines; however, there was an artist working for **Truth** who wasn't. Roy L McCardell, then a staffer at **Puck**, informed Morrill Goddard, Sunday editor of **The New**

York World, that he knew someone who could fit what was needed at the then largest newspaper in America.

Richard F. Outcault (1863-1928) first introduced his street children strip in the June 2, 1894 issue of **Truth**, somewhat inspired by Michael Angelo Woolf's slum kids single panel cartoons in Life which had begun in the mid 1880s. The interested collector should seek out a copy of Woolf's **Sketches of Lowly Life In A Great City** (1899) listed in the Guide for the first time. It's also possible that Outcault's **Hogan's Alley** cast, including the Yellow Kid, was inspired by Charles W. Saalburg's **The Ting Ling Kids** which began in the **Chicago Inter-Ocean** by May 1894. By 1895 Saalburg was Art Director in charge of coloring for the new color printing press at the **New York World**. Edward Harrigan's play "O'Reilly and the Four Hundred," which had a song beginning with the words "Down in Hogan's Alley..." likely provided direct inspiration.

By the November 18, 1894 issue of the **World**, Outcault was working for Goddard and Saalburg. Outcault produced a successful Sunday newspaper sequential comic strip in color with "The Origin of a New Species" on the back page in the World's first colored Sunday supplement. Long time pro Walt McDougall, a famous cartoonist reputed to have turned the 1884 Presidential race with a single cartoon that ran in the **World**, handled the cartoon art on the front page. Earlier, **The World** began running full page color single panels on May 21, 1893. McDougall did various other page panels during 1893, but it was January 28, 1894 when the first sequence of comic pictures in a newspaper appeared in panels in the same format as our comic strips today. It was a full page cut up into nine panels, and the sequence was drawn entirely in pantomime, with no words. This historic page was drawn by Mark Fenderson.

The second page to appear in panels was an eight panel strip from February 4, 1894, also lacking words except for the title. This page was a collaboration between Walt McDougall and Mark Fenderson titled "The Unfortunate Fate of a Well-Intentioned Dog." From then on, many full page color strips by McDougall and Fenderson appeared; they were the first cartoonists to draw for the Sunday newspaper comic section. It was Outcault, however, who soon became the most famous cartoonist featured. After first appearing in black and white in Pulitzer's **The New York World** on February 17, 1895 and again on March 10, 1895, **The Yellow Kid** was introduced to the public in color on May 5, 1895.

Some have erroneously reported in scholarly journals that perhaps it was Frank Ladendorf's "Uncle Reuben," first introduced May 26, 1895, which became the first regularly recurring comics character in newspapers. This is wrong, as even Outcault's "Yellow Kid" began in Pulitzer's paper a good three months before **Uncle Reuben**. Until firm evidence to the contrary comes to light, that honor will forever be enshrined with Jimmy Swinnerton's **Little Bears** cartoon characters, found all over inside Hearst's **San Francisco Examiner** as early as 1892. Though never actually a comic strip, they nonetheless were the earliest presently known recurring comics characters in American newspapers. There never was a strip titled **Little Bears and Tigers**, as the Tigers portion was strictly for New York consumption when Hearst ordered Swinnerton to move to the Big Apple to compete better in the brew-

THE BROWNIES' RIDE.

BY PALMER COX.

ONE night a cunning brownie band
Was roaming through a farmer's land,
And while the rogues went prying round,
The farmer's mare at rest they found;

And peeping through the stable-door,
They saw the harness that she wore:
The whip was hanging on the wall,
Old Mag was grinding in the stall;

The Brownies by Palmer Cox, 1883, were the earliest known recurring comic characters merchandised in North America.

ing comic strip wars.

The Yellow Kid is widely recognized today as the first newspaper comic strip to demonstrate without a doubt that the general public was ready for full color comics. **The Yellow Kid** was the first in the USA to show that (1) comics could increase newspaper sales, and that (2) comic characters could be merchandised. **The Yellow Kid** was the headlining spark of what soon became dubbed by Hearst as "eight pages of polychromatic effulgence that makes the rainbow look like a lead pipe."

Ongoing research suggests that Palmer Cox's fabulous success with **The Brownies** was a direct inspiration for Richard Outcault's future merchandising work. The ultimate proof lies in the fourth Yellow Kid cartoon, which appeared in the February 9, 1895 issue of **Truth**. It was reprinted in the **New York World** eight days later on February 17, 1895, becoming the first Yellow Kid cartoon in the newspapers. The caption read "FOURTH WARD BROWNIES. MICKEY, THE ARTIST (adding a finishing touch) Dere, Chimmy! If Palmer Cox wuz t' see yer, he'd git yer copyrighted in a minute." The Yellow Kid was widely licensed in the greater New York area for all kinds of products, including gum and cigarette cards, toys, pin backs, cookies, post cards, tobacco products, and appliances. There was also a short-lived humor magazine from Street & Smith named **The Yellow Kid**, featuring exquisite Outcault covers, plus a 196-page comic book from Dillingham & Co. known as **The Yellow Kid in McFadden's Flats**, dated to early 1897. In addition, there were several Yellow Kid plays produced, spawning other collectibles like show posters, programs and illustrated sheet music. (For those interested in more information regarding the Yellow Kid, it is available on the Internet at www.neponset.com/yellowkid.)

Mickey Dugan burned brightly for a few years as Outcault secured a copyright on the character with the United States Government by Sept. 1896. By the time he completed the necessary paper work, however, hundreds of business people nationwide had pirated the image of The Yellow Kid and plastered it all over every product imaginable; mothers were even dressing their newborns to look like Dugan. (Outcault, however, kept regularly utilizing images of **The Yellow Kid** in his comics style advertising work confirmed as late as 1915.) Outcault soon found himself in a maelstrom not of his choosing, which probably pushed him to eventually drop the character. Outcault's creation went back and forth between newspaper giants Pulitzer and Hearst until Bennett's New York Herald mercifully snatched the cartoonist away in 1900 to do what amounted to a few relatively short-run strips. Later, he did one particular strip for a year - a satire of rural black America titled **Pore Li'l Mose**, and then his newer creation, **Buster Brown**, debuted May 4, 1902. Mose had a very rare comic book collection published in 1902 by Cupples & Leon, now highly sought after by today's savvy collectors. Outcault continued drawing him in the background of occasional **Buster Brown** strips for many years to come.

"Fourth Ward Brownies," artwork by Richard F. Outcault, Feb. 17, 1895. First appearance in Pulitzer's NY World. Note the Yellow Kid, second from left.

William Randolph Hearst loved the comic strip medium ever since he was a little boy growing up on **Max & Moritz** by Wilhelm Busch in American collected book editions translated from the original German (these collections were first published in book form in 1871, serving as the influence for **The Katzenjammer Kids**). One of the ways Hearst responded to losing Outcault in 1900 was by purchasing the highly successful

STOKES' COMIC JUVENILES

Foxy Grandpa and the Boys
Foxy Grandpa's Triumphs
Foxy Grandpa's Frolics
Foxy Grandpa's Surprises
Foxy Grandpa Up-to-date
Jimmy and His Scrapes
Little Sammy Sneeze
The Trials of Lulu and Leander
Sam and His Laugh
Handy Happy Hooligan
Happy Hooligan Home Again
Happy Hooligan's Travels
Maud the Mirthful Mule
Maud the Matchless
Maud

HERE WE ARE AGAIN

Outcault's Buster, Mary Jane and Tige
Outcault's Buster Brown and Company
Buster Brown's Antics
Buster Brown's Pranks
Buster Brown, His Dog Tige and Their Troubles
Buster Brown and His Resolutions
Willie Westinghouse Edison Smith
The Komical Katzenjammers
The Cruise of the Katzenjammer Kids
The Tricks of the Katzenjammer Kids
The Three Funmakers: (Hooligan, Maud and the Katzenjammer Kids)

Each, oblong 4to, boards in colors, pictures in colors, 60 cents

Earliest known display ad for comic books found in The Three Fun Makers, 1908, with 27 titles then in print. Note cover price says 60 cents per copy.

23 year old humor magazine **Puck** from the heirs of founder Joseph Keppler. With **Puck** and its exclusive cartoonist contracts, he got, among others, the very popular F. M. Howarth and Frederick Burr Opper's undivided attention. Opper had first burst upon the comics scene in America back in 1880. Within a year Hearst had transformed this **National Lampoon** of its day into the colored Sunday comics section, **Puck-The Comic Weekly**. At first featuring Rudolph Dirk's **The Katzenjammer Kids** (1897), **Happy Hooligan** and other fine strips by the wildly popular Opper and a few others including Rudolph's brother Gus Dirks, the Hearst comic section steadily added more strips; for decades to come, there wasn't anything else that could compete with **Puck**. Hearst hired the best of the best and transformed **Puck** into the most popular comics section anywhere.

Outcault, meanwhile, followed in Palmer Cox's footprints a decade later by using the nexus of a World's Fair as a jumping off venue. **Buster Brown** was an instant sensation when he debuted as the new merchandising mascot of the Brown Shoe Company at the 1904 St. Louis World's Fair in a special Buster Brown Shoes pavilion. The character has the honor of being the first nationally licensed comic strip character in America. Many hundreds of different **Buster Brown** premiums have been issued. Comic books by Frederick A. Stokes Company featuring **Buster Brown & His Dog Tige** began as early as 1903 with **Buster Brown and His Resolutions**, simultaneously published in several different languages throughout the world.

After a few years, Buster and Outcault returned to Hearst in late 1905, joining what soon became the flagship of the comics world. Buster's popularity quickly spread all over the United States and then the world as he single-handedly spawned the first great comics licensing dynasty. For years, there were little people traveling from town to town performing as **Buster Brown** and selling shoes while accompanied by small dogs named Tige. Many other highly competitive licensed strips would soon follow. We suggest checking out **Hake's Price Guide to Character Toys** for information on several hundred **Buster Brown** competitors, as well as several pages of the more fascinating **Buster Brown** material.

Soon there were many comic strip syndicates not only offering hundreds of various comic strips but also offering to license the characters for any company interested in paying the fee. The history of the comic strips with wide popularity since **The Yellow Kid** has been intertwined with give-

Top, The Katzenjammer Kids by Rudolph Dirks, WR Hearst (86 pages), 1902. Bottom, Happy Hooligan and His Brother... by F. Opper, also Hearst (86 pages), 1902.

away premiums and character-based, store-bought merchandise of all kinds. Since its infancy as a profitable art form unto itself with **The Yellow Kid**, the comic strip world has profited from selling all sorts of "stuff" to the public featuring their favorite character or strip as its motif. American business gladly responded to the desire for comic character memorabilia with thousands of fun items to enjoy and collect. Most of the early comics were not aimed specifically at kids, though children understandably enjoyed them as well.

The comic book has generally been associated with almost all of the licensed merchandise in this century. In the Platinum Age section beginning right after this essay, you will find a great many comic books in varied formats and sizes published before the advent of the first successful monthly newsstand comic book, **Famous Funnies**. What drove each of these evolutionary format changes was the need by their producers to make money. Following are some "new" highlights recently rediscovered. Space precludes mentioning others.

In 1892, Charles Scribner's Sons published A. B. Frost's **Bull Calf and Other Tales**, measuring 8 1/2 x 6 3/4. It contains sequential comic strip art on quite a few pages as well as single panel cartoons. By 1898, Charles Scribner's Sons also issued E.W. Kemble's **The Billy Goat and Other Comicalities** as a 112 page hardcover measuring 8 1/2 x 6 3/4, which also has sequential comic strip pages.

Another very significant format was F. M. Howarth's **Funny Folks**, published in 1899 by E. P. Dutton and drawn from color as well as black and white pages of **Puck**. This rather large hardcover volume measured 16 1/2 wide by 12 tall. It contains numerous sequential comic strip pages as well as single gag illustrations. Howarth's art was a joy to behold and deserves wider recognition.

By October 1900, Hearst had already caused F. Opper's **Folks In Funnyville** to be collected by publisher R. H. Russell, NY in a 12 x 9 hard cover format from his **New York Journal American Humorist** section. At the end of 1900, Carl Shultze's **Vaudevilles and Other Things** had its first edition published by Isaac H. Blanchard Co., NY. It measures 10 1/2 wide x 13 tall with 22 pages including covers. Each interior page is a 2 to 7 panel comic strip with lots of color.

There was also a recently unearthed 2nd and 3rd printings of **Vaudevilles** with the inscription "From the Originator of the 'Foxy Grandpa' Series" at the bottom of its front cover of the 3rd printing. This note is lacking on the earlier first two editions, and it also switches format size to 11 tall and 13 inches wide.

E. W. Kemble's **The Blackberries** had a color collection by 1901, also published by R. H. Russell, NY, as well as a few other comic-related volumes by Kemble still to be unearthed and properly identified. If you have information you wish to share, please send it to the authors of this essay for future updates.

Confirmed is the exact format of Hearst's 1902 **The Katzenjammer Kids** and **Happy**

Hooligan And His Brother Gloomy Gus. They both measure 15 5/16 wide x 10 inches tall and contain 88 pages including covers. Confirmed this year also is the fact that there are two separate editions with different covers for the pictured 1902 first edition and a 1903 Frederick Stokes edition of **Katzenjammer Kids** and **Happy Hooligan** with differing contents. They both are two different books entirely, and what confuses many collectors is that they have identical indicia title pages, as does an entirely different **KK** from 1905.

Settling on a popular size of 17" wide by 11" tall, comic books were soon available that featured Charles "Bunny" Shultze's **Foxy Grandpa**, Rudolph Dirk's **The Katzenjammer Kids**, Winsor McCay's **Little Sammy Sneeze**, **Rarebit Fiend** and **Little Nemo**, and Fred Opper's **Happy Hooligan** and **Maud**, in addition to dozens of **Buster Brown** comic books. For well over a decade, these large-size, full-color volumes were the norm, retailing for 60 cents. These collections offered Sunday comics at full-size with only one side printed on a page.

Unearthed this year is the very rare **Brainy Bowers and Drowsy Dugan** by R. W. Taylor which is now crowned the first collection of daily newspaper strip reprints published in America.

The Outbursts of Everett True by A. D. Condo and J. W. Raper was first published by Saalfield in 1907 in a 88 page hardcover collection. It qualifies as the 2nd daily comic strip collection as it predates first **Mutt & Jeff** collection by 3 years. Condo & Raper's creation began a regular run several times a week in daily newspapers in 1905 and lasted until 1927, when Condo got too sick to continue. This same **Everett True** collection was later truncated a bit by Saalfield in 1921 to 56 strips in just 32 pages measuring the 10x10 Cupples & Leon size.

By 1908 Stokes had a large backlist of full color comic books for sale at 60 cents each. Some of these titles date back to 1903 and were reprinted over and over as demanded warranted. Note the number of titles in the advertisement pulled from the back of **The Three Fun Makers**

With the ever-increasing popularity of Bud Fisher's new daily strip sensation, **Mutt & Jeff**, a new format was created for reprinting daily strips in black and white, a hardcover book about 15" wide by 5" tall, published by Ball starting in 1910, for five volumes. In 1912 Ball also branched out to at least the just unearthed **Doings of the Van Loons** by Fred. I. Leipziger. This rare comic book is the same exact format as the Ball **Mutt & Jeff** books and is listed for the first time this year. Cartoons Magazine also began in 1912 and ran thru 1921 before undergoing a radical format change. It is notable as a wonder source for information on early comics & their creators.

The next significant evolutionary change occurred in 1919, when Cupples & Leon began issuing their black and white daily strip reprint books in a new aforementioned format, about 10" wide by 10" tall, with four panels reprinted per page in a two by two matrix. These books were 52 pages for 25 cents, and the first editions featured

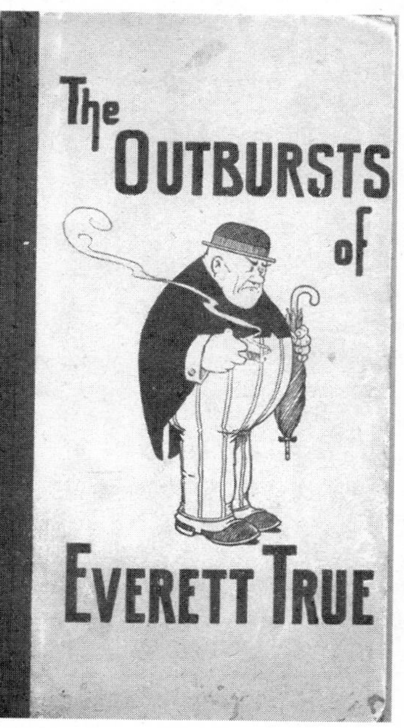

Above, Vaudevilles and Other Things by Carl "Bunny" Schultze, 1900. Right, The Outbursts of Everett True, 1907. Very scarce first edition.

Reg'lar Fellers by Gene Byrne, 1921, one of the last 3 oblong large size comic books.

issued tons of **Little Orphan Annie** material. Merchandising pioneers Sam Gold and Kay Kamen spearheaded this transformation.

Upwards of a thousand of these **Funnies On Parade** precursors, in all formats, were published through 1935 and were very popular. Toward the end of this era, beautiful collections of **Popeye**, **Mickey Mouse**, **Dick Tracy**, and many others were published which today command ever higher prices on the open market as they are rediscovered by the advanced collector.

Each year, this Platinum Age section grows as advanced collectors continue to report in with new finds. We encourage readers to help with this section of the book, as each new data entry is very important. For further information on this earlier fascinating era of American comic books, check out Robert L. Beerbohm's "The American Comic Book 1897-1932," originally printed in the 27th edition of **The Overstreet Comic Book Price Guide** and on Gemstone's web site at www.gemstonepub. com. Robert may be contacted at beerbohm@teknetwork.com.

Bringing Up Father and **Mutt & Jeff**. By 1921 the last of the oblong (11x15 approx. size) color comic books were issued, with Cupples & Leon's **Jimmie Dugan** And **The Reg'lar Fellers** by Gene Byrne and EmBee's **The Trouble Of Bringing Up Father** by self publisher George McManus. Of special historical interest, Embee issued the first 10 cent monthly comic book, **Comic Monthly**, with a first issue dated January 1922. A dozen 8 1/2" by 9" issues were published, each featuring solo adventures of popular King Features strips. The monthly 10 cent comic book concept had finally arrived, though it would be more than a decade before it became successful.

In 1926, Cupples & Leon added a new 7" wide by 9" tall format with **Little Orphan Annie**, **Smitty**, and others. These books were issued in both soft cover and hardcover editions with dust jackets, and became extremely popular at 60 cents per copy. Dell began publishing all original material in **The Funnies** in late 1929 in a larger tabloid format. At least three dozen issues were published before Delacorte threw in the towel. Even the extremely popular **Big Little Book**, introduced in 1932, can be viewed as a smaller version of the existing formats. The competition amongst publishers now included Dell, McKay, Sonnet. Saalfield and Whitman. The 1930s saw a definite shift in merchandising comic strip material from adults to children. This was the decade when Kellogg's placed **Buck Rogers** on the map, and when Ovaltine

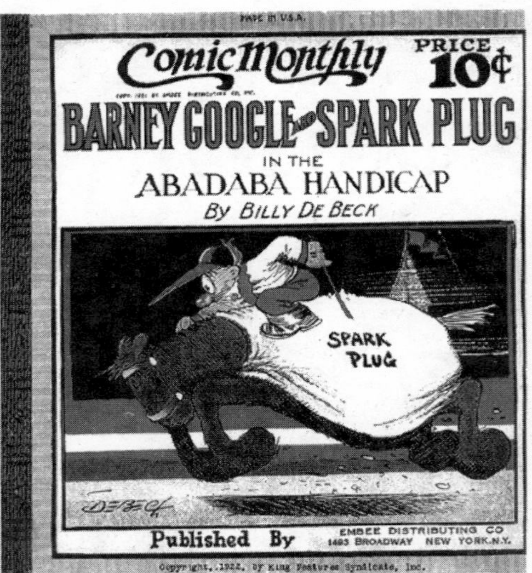

Comic Monthly #11, Nov. 1922, EmBee Publishing Co., is the first monthly newsstand comic book series.

The Adventures of Willie Green
© Frank M. Acton

Alphonse and Gaston 1902
© Hearst's NY American & Journal

American-Journal-Examiner Joke Book
Special Supplement #2
© New York American

GD2.0 FN6.0 VF8.0

LLECTOR'S NOTE: The books listed in this section were published decades
fore organized comics fandom began archiving and helping to preserve these
gile popular culture artifacts. Consequently, copies of most all of these comics
nost never surface in Fine+ or better shape. Most are in the Fair to VG range.
ou want to collect these only in high grade, your collection will be very small.
e prices given for G, F and VF categories are for strictly graded editions. If you
ed help grading your item, we refer you to the grading section in this book.
For ease of ascertaining the contents of each item of this expanded listing, we
er the following list of categories found immediately following each title:

REPRINTS OF EUROPEAN COMICS
EARLY AMERICAN GRAPHIC STORIES
REPRINTS OF NEWSPAPER COMIC STRIPS
REPRINTS OF SINGLE PANELS AND CARTOONS
REPRINTS OF MAGAZINE COMICS AND CARTOONS
BOOKS ILLUSTRATED BY POPULAR CARTOONISTS
ILLUSTRATED TEXT NOVELIZATIONS OF COMIC SERIES
BOOKS FEATURING ORIGINAL COMICS MATERIAL
OTHER
LLUSTRATED BOOKS THAT INSPIRED COMICS SERIES
"HOW TO DRAW CARTOONS" BOOKS

first dimension given is Height and the 2nd one is Width. Some original British
ions are included in the section, as to better explain their American counter-
s. This section expanded and completely revised by Robert Beerbohm & Doug
eeler with able assistance from Bill Blackbeard, Ray Bottorff Jr, Alfredo Castelli,
nardo De Sá, Joe Evans, Tom Gordon, Bruce Hamilton, Andy Konkykru, Don
tz, Richard Olson, Robert Quesinberry, Steve Rowe, Randy Scott, John Snyder,
Spiegelman, Steve Thompson, Craig Yoe.

/ENTURES OF EVA, PORA AND TED (E)
porated Milk Association: 1932 (5x15", 16 pgs, B&W)

By Steve 10.00 30.00 60.00
E: Appears to have had green, blue or white paper cover versions.

/ENTURES OF HAWKSHAW (C) (See Hawkshaw The Detective)
Saalfield Publishing Co.: 1917 (9-3/4x13-1/2", 48 pgs., color & two-tone)

y Gus Mager (only 24 pgs. of strips, reverse of each pg. is blank)
50.00 175.00 300.00
927 Reprints 1917 issue 43.00 152.00 260.00

/ENTURES OF MR. OBADIAH OLDBUCK, THE (A)
& Bogue, London: nd (1841) (9-3/16x5-15/16, 176 pgs, B&W, gilted
dcover)

by Rodolphe Töpffer (Very Rare) ??? ??? ???
E: This is the British edition, translating the unauthorized redrawn 1839 edition, from Parisian sher Aubert, adapted from Töpffer's original "Les Amours de Mr. Vieux Bois" (aka "Histoire de ieux Bois") originally published in French in Switzerland, in 1837 (2nd ed. 1839). Early 19th ry books are often found rebound, with original cover and/or title page gone. To distinguish ns having no cover or title page: the British oblong editions (published by Tilt & Bogue) use an Numerals to number pages. American oblong shaped editions use Arabic Numerals. British inted on one side only. It is the earliest known English language sequential comic book.

ENTURES OF MR. OBADIAH OLDBUCK, THE (A)
on and Company, New York: September 14, 1842 (11-3/4x9", 40 pgs,
', hemp paper cover & interior)

her Jonathan Extra, No. IX - by Rodolphe Töpffer
xtremely Rare) ??? ??? ???
: Only three copies known to exist, one with outer wrap missing, two are in private hands. st known sequential American comic book, reprinting the 1841 British edition. Pages are ered via Roman numerals. States "BROTHER JONATHAN EXTRA -- ADVENTURES OF BADIAH OLDBUCK." at the top of each page. Printed 2 to 3 tiers of panels on both sides of page. Copies could be had for ten cents according to adverts in Brother Jonathan.

ENTURES OF MR. OBADIAH OLDBUCK, THE (A)
on & Co, New York: nd (1849) (5-11/16x8-3/8", 92 pgs, B&W, paper
?)

y Rodolphe Töpffer (Very Rare) ??? ??? ???
: 2nd Wilson & Co printing, reformatted into a small oblong format, with nine panels edited nd text modified to smooth out this removal. Results in four less printed tiers/strips. Pages mbered via Arabic numerals. Every panel on Pages 11, 14, 19, 21, 24, 34, 35 has one line Reformatted to conform with British first edition.

GD2.0 FN6.0 VF8.0

ADVENTURES OF MR. OBADIAH OLDBUCK, THE (A)
Dick & Fitzgerald, New York: nd (various printings; est. late 1860's to 1876+) (Thirty Cents, 84 pgs, B&W, paper cover) (all versions Rare)

nn-black print on green cover (5-11/16x8-15/16"); string bound ??? ???
nn-black print on blue cover suspected to exist, same format as green cover
nn-black print on white cover (5-13/16x9-3/16"); staple bound beneath cover);
this is a later printing than the blue or green cover ??? ??? ???
NOTE: *Reprints the abbreviated 1849 Wilson & Co. 2nd printing. Pages are numbered via Arabic numerals. Many of the panels on Pages 11, 14, 19, 21, 24, 34, 35 take two lines to print the same words found in the Wilson & Co version, which used only one text line for the same panels. Unknown whether the blue or green cover is earlier. White cover version has "thirty cents" line blackened out on the two copies known to exist.*

ADVENTURES OF SLIM AND SPUD, THE (E)
Prairie Farmer Publ. Co.: 1924 (3-3/4x 9-3/4", 104 pgs., B&W strip reprints)

nn 29.00 114.00 200.00
NOTE: *Illustrated mailing envelope exists postmarked out of Chicago, add 50%.*

ADVENTURES OF WILLIE WINTERS, THE
Kelloggs Toasted Corn Flake Co.: 1912 (6-7/8x9-1/2", 20 pgs, full color)

nn-By Byron Williams & Dearborn Melvill 42.00 146.00 250.00

ADVENTURES OF WILLIE GREEN, THE (C)
Frank M. Acton Co.: 1915 (50¢, 52 pgs, 8-1/2X16", B&W, soft-c)

Book 1-By Harris Brown; strip-r 54.00 189.00 325.00

A. E. F. IN CARTOONS BY WALLY, THE (C)
Don Sowers & Co.: 1933 (12x10-1/8", 88 pgs, hardcover B&W)

nn-By Wally Wallgren (WW One Stars & Stripes-r) 20.00 60.00 120.00

AFTER THE TOWN GOES DRY (F)
The Howell Publishing Co, Chicago: 1919 (48 pgs, hardbound two color cover)

nn-By Henry C. Taylor; illus by Frank King 20.00 70.00 140.00

AIN'T IT A GRAND & GLORIOUS FEELING? (D) (Also see Mr. & Mrs.)
Whitman Publishing Co.: 1922 (9x9-3/4", 52 pgs., stiff cardboard-c)

nn-1921 daily strip-r; B&W, color-c; Briggs-a 43.00 172.00 300.00
nn-(9x9-1/2", 28pgs., stiff cardboard-c)-Sunday strip-r in color (inside front-c
says "More of the Married Life of Mr. & Mrs".) 36.00 143.00 250.00
NOTE: *This is the 2nd Whitman comic book, after Brigg's MR. & MRS.*

ALL THE FUNNY FOLKS (G)
World Press Today, Inc.: 1926 (11-1/2x8-1/2", 112 pgs., color, hard-c)

nn-Barney Google, Spark Plug, Jiggs & Maggie, Tillie The Toiler, Happy
Hooligan, Hans & Fritz, Toots & Casper, etc. 100.00 400.00 700.00
With Dust Jacket 143.00 571.00 1000.00

ALPHONSE AND GASTON AND THEIR FRIEND LEON (C)
Hearst's New York American & Journal: 1902,1903 (10x15-1/4", Sunday strip reprints in color)

nn-(1902)- By Fred Opper 371.00 1300.00 -
nn-(1903) - By Frederick Opper 279.00 975.00 -

AMERICAN-JOURNAL-EXAMINER JOKE BOOK SPECIAL SUPPLEMENT (H)
New York American: 1911-12 (12x9 3/4", 16 pgs) (known issues) (Very Rare)

1 Tom Powers Joke Book(12/10/11) 80.00 280.00 -
2 Mutt & Jeff Joke Book (Bud Fisher 12/17/11) 100.00 350.00 -
3 TAD's Joke Book (Thomas Dorgan 12/24/11) 80.00 280.00 -
4 F. Opper's Joke Book (Frederick Burr Opper 12/31/11)
(contains Happy Hooligan) 100.00 350.00 -
5 ??? (01/07/12) ??? ??? ???
6 Swinnerton's Joke Book (Jimmy Swinnerton 01/14/12)
(contains Mr. Jack) 100.00 350.00 -
7 The Monkey's Joke Book (Gus Mager 01/21/12)
(contains Sherlocko the Monk) 100.00 350.00 -
8 Joys And Glooms Joke Book (T. E. Powers 01/28/12)
80.00 280.00 -
9 The Dingbat Family's Joke Book (George Herriman 02/04/12)
(contains early Krazy Kat & Ignatz) 200.00 700.00 -
10 Valentine Joke Book, A (Opper,Howarth,Mager, T. E. Powers 02/11/12)

The Strange and Wonderful Adventures
of Bachelor Butterfly
© Dick & Fitzgerald, New York

Barker's "Komic" Picture Souvenir
© Leonhart & Son

Barney Google and Spark Plug #
© C&L

GD2.0 FN6.0 VF8.0

80.00 280.00 -
11 Little Hatchet Joke Book (T. E. Powers 02/18/12)
80.00 280.00 -
12 Jungle Joke Book (Rudolph Dirks 02/25/12) 100.00 350.00 -
13 The Hayseeds Joke Book (03/03/12) 80.00 280.00 -
14 Married Life Joke Book (T.E. Powers 03/10/12) 80.00 280.00 -
NOTE: *These were insert newspaper supplements similar to Eisner's later Spirit sections. A Valentine Joke Book recently surfaced from Hearst's Boston Sunday American proving that other cities besides New York City had these special supplements. Each issue also contains work by other cartoonists besides the cover featured creator and those already listed above such as Sidney Smith, Winsor McCay, Hy Mayer, Grace Weiderseim (later Drayton), others.*

AMERICA'S BLACK & WHITE BOOK
100 Pictured Reasons Why We Are At War
Cupples & Leon: 1917 (10-3/4x8", 216 pgs)
nn-W. A. Rogers (New York Herald-r) 32.00 114.00 195.00

ANGELIC ANGELINA
Cupples & Leon Company: 1909 (11-1/2x17", 30 pgs., 2 colors)
nn-By Munson Paddock 67.00 233.00 400.00

ANDY GUMP, HIS LIFE STORY (G)
The Reilly & Lee Co, Chicago: 1924 (192 pgs, hardbound)
nn-By Sidney Smith (over 100 illustrations) 20.00 80.00 140.00

AT THE BOTTOM OF THE LADDER (E)
J.P. Lippincott Company: 1926 (11x8-1/4", 296 pgs, hardcover, B&W)
nn-By Camillus Kessler 32.00 128.00 225.00
NOTE: *Hilarious single panel cartoons showing first jobs of then important "captains of industry."*

BACHELOR BUTTERFLY, THE VERITABLE HISTORY OF MR. (A)
D. Bogue, London: 1845 (5-1/2x10-1/4", 74 pgs, B&W, gilted hardcover)
nn- by Rodolphe Töpffer (Very Rare) ??? ??? ???
NOTE: This is the British Edition from the serialization in L'Illustration from Paris publisher Dubochet which was engraved by Cham. Predates the first French collected edition. The first story page is numbered Page 3. Page 17 shows Bachelor Butterfly being swallowed by a whale.

BACHELOR BUTTERFLY, THE STRANGE ADVENTURES OF (A)
Wilson & Co., New York: 1846 (5-3/8x10-1/8", 68 pgs, B&W, soft cover?)
nn- by Rodolphe Töpffer (Very Rare) ??? ??? ???
NOTE: *2nd earliest known sequential comic book printed in the USA. From the British D. Bogue 1845 edition, itself from the earlier French language "Histoire de Mr. Cryptogame". Released the same year as the French Dubochet first collected edition. Two variations known, the earlier printing with Page number 17 placed on the inside (left) bottom corner in error, with slightly later printings corrected to place page number 17 on the outside (right) bottom corner of that page. For both printings: the first story page is numbered 2. Page 17 shows Bachelor Butterfly already in the whale. In "most" panels with 3 lines of text, the third line is indented further than the second, which is in turn indented further than the first.*

BACHELOR BUTTERFLY,THE STRANGE & WONDERFUL ADVENTURES OF
Dick & Fitzgerald, New York: nd (various printings; est. late 1860's to 1877+) (30 Cents, 68 pgs, B&W, paper cover string bound) (all versions Rare) (A)
nn-black print on blue cover (5-1/2x10-1/2") ??? ??? ???
nn-black print on green cover (5-1/2x10-1/2") ??? ??? ???
NOTE: *Reprints the earlier Wilson & Co. edition. Page 2 is the first story page. Page 17 shows Bachelor Butterfly already in the whale. In most panels with 3 lines of text, the second and third lines are equally indented in from the first. Unknown which cover (blue or green) is earlier.*

BAD BOY'S FIRST READER
G.W. Carleton & Co.: 1881 (5-3/4 x 4-1/8, 44 pages, paper cover, B&W)
nn-By Frank Bellew (Senior) 100.00 200.00 300.00
NOTE: *Parody of a children's ABC primer, one cartoon illustration plus text per page. Includes one panel of Boss Tweed.*

BANANA OIL (C)
MS Publ. Co.: 1924 (9-7/8x10", 52 pgs., B&W)
nn-Milt Gross-a; not reprints 61.00 244.00 425.00

BARKER'S "KOMIC" PICTURE SOUVENIR
Leonhart & Son: 1893 (7x10, color cover, B&W; 1904, 6x9 - four different issues known to exist issued by The Barker, Moore & Mein Medicine Co.)
nn-artist unknown (1893) (first edition150 pgs) 100.00 300.00 -
nn-artist unknown (1893) (2nd edition ??? pgs) 100.00 300.00 -

GD2.0 FN6.0 V

nn-artist unknown (1893) (3rd edition 175 pgs) 100.00 300.00
nn-artist unknown (1893) (4th edition 125 pgs) 100.00 300.00
1-4 -artist unknown (1904) (52 pgs each) 40.00 120.00
NOTE: *These are all premium comic books, predating Buster Brown.*

BARNEY GOOGLE AND SPARK PLUG (C) (See Comic Monthly)
Cupples & Leon Co.: 1923 - No. 6, 1928 (52 pgs., B&W, daily strip-r)
1 (nn)-By Billy DeBeck 57.00 229.00 40
2-4 46.00 186.00 32
NOTE: *Started June 17, 1919 as newspaper strip; Spark Plug introduced July 17, 1922.*

BART'S CARTOONS FOR 1902 FROM THE MINNEAPOLIS JOURNAL
MINNEAPOLIS JOURNAL: 1903 (11x9", 102 pgs, paperback, B&W)
nn-By Charles L. Bartholomew 28.00 99.00 17

BELIEVE IT OR NOT! by Ripley (D)
Simon & Schuster: 1929 (8x 5-1/4", 68 pgs, red, B&W cover, B&W interior)
nn-By Robert Ripley (strip-r text & art) 40.00 120.00 24
NOTE: *There are many reprintings of this, 1929 was the first print.*

BEN WEBSTER (C)
Standard Printing Company: 1928-1931 (13-3/4x4-7/16", 768 pgs, soft-c)
1 - "Bound to Win" 40.00 120.00 24
2 - "...in old Mexico 40.00 120.00 24
3 - "...At Wilderness Lake 40.00 120.00 24
4 - "...in the Oil Fields 40.00 120.00 24
NOTE: *Self Published by Edwin Alger, also contains fan's letter pages.*

BILLY BOUNCE (G)
Donohue & Co.: 1906 (288 pgs, hardbound)
nn-By W.W. Denslow & Dudley Bragdon 100.00 350.00 60
NOTE: *Billy Bounce was created in 1901 as a comic strip by W. W. Denslow (strip ran from 1901 NOV 11 to 1905 DEC 3), but the series is best remembered in the C. W. Kahles versi (from 1902 SEP 28). Denslow resumed his character in the above illustrated book.*

BILLY GOAT AND OTHER COMICALITIES, THE
Charles Scribner's Sons: 1898 (6-3/4x8-1/2", 116 pgs., Hardcover)
nn - By E. W. Kemble 133.00 400.00

BILLY HON'S FAMOUS CARTOON BOOK (K)
Wasley Publishing Co.: 1927 (7-1/2x10", 68 pgs, softbound wraparound)
nn-By Billy Hon 12.00 48.00 8

BILLY THE BOY ARTIST'S BOOK OF FUNNY PICTURES (C)
C.M.Clark Publishing Co.: 1910 (9x12", hardcover-c, Boston Globe strip-r)
nn-By Ed Payne 79.00 277.00 47
NOTE: *This long lived strip ran in The Boston Globe from Nov 5 1899-Jan 7 1955.*

BIRD CENTER CARTOONS: A Chronicle of Social Happenings
A. C. McClurg & Co.: 1904 (12-3/8x9-1/2", 216 pgs, hardcover, B&W)
nn-By John McCutcheon 40.00 140.00 24
NOTE: *Satirical cartoons and text concerning a mythical town.*

BLACKBERRIES, THE
R. H. Russell: 1901 (9"x12", color, hard-c)
nn-By E. W. Kemble 279.00 975.00

BOBBY THATCHER & TREASURE CAVE (C)
Altemus Co.: 1932 (9x7", 86 pgs., B&W, hard-c)
nn-Reprints; Storm-a 24.00 96.00 17

BOBBY THATCHER'S ROMANCE (C)
The Bell Syndicate/Henry Altemus Co.: 1931 (8-3/4x7", color cover, B&W)
nn-By Storm 24.00 96.00 17

BOOK OF CARTOONS, A
Edward T. Miller: 1903 (12-1/4x9-1/4", 120 pgs, hardcover, B&W)
nn-By Harry J. Westerman (Ohio State Journal-r) 20.00 70.00 12

BOY'S & GIRLS' BIG PAINTING BOOK OF INTERESTING COMIC PICTU
M. A. Donohue & Co.: 1914-16 (9x15, 70 pgs)
nn-By Carl "Bunny" Schultze (Foxy Grandpa-r) 81.00 284.00

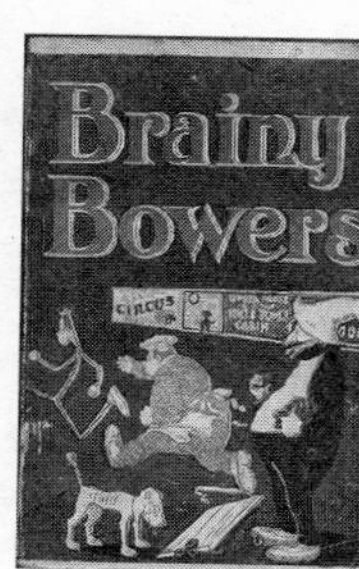

Brainy Bowers and Drowsy Duggan
© STAR

Bringing Up Father #2
© C&L

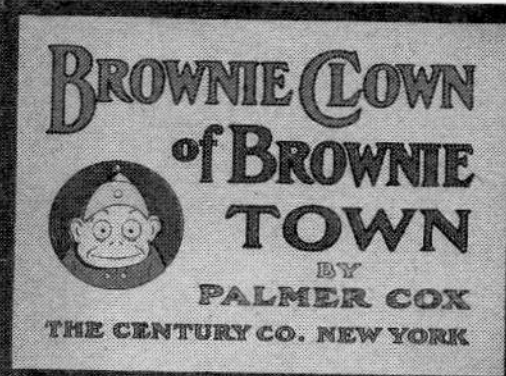

Brownie Clown of Brownie Town
© The Century Co.

GD2.0 FN6.0 VF8.0

2 (1914) 81.00 284.00 -
337 (1914) (sez "Big Painting & Drawing Book") 81.00 284.00 -
n-(1916) (sez "Big Painting Book")(9-1/4x15") 81.00 284.00 -

RAIN LEAKS: Dialogues of Mutt & Flea (C)
K. Printing Co. (Rochester Evening Times): 1911 (76 pgs, 6-5/8x4-5/8, ardcover, B&W)
n-By Leo Edward O'Melia; newspaper strip-r 29.00 100.00 171.00

RAINY BOWERS AND DROWSY DUGGAN (C)
ar Publishing: 1905 (7-1/4 x 4-9/16", 98 pgs, blue, brown & white color cover, &W interior, 25¢) (daily strip-r 1902-04 Chicago Daily News)
- By R. W. Taylor (Very Rare) 200.00 700.00 -

RAINY BOWERS AND DROWSY DUGGAN GETTING ON IN THE WORLD ITH NO VISIBLE MEANS OF SUPPORT (STORIES TOLD IN PICTURES TO AKE THEIR TELLING SHORT) (C)
ax Stein/Star Publishing: 1905 (7-3/8x5 1/8", 164 pgs, slick black, red & tan lor cover, interior newsprint) (daily strip-r 1902-04 Chicago Daily News)
-By R. W. Taylor (Very Rare) 200.00 700.00 -
-possible hard cover edition also? ??? ??? ???
TE: *Brainy Bowers is the earliest known daily strip reprint book.*

RINGING UP FATHER (C)
ar Co. (King Features): 1917 (5-1/2x16-1/2", 100 pgs., B&W, cardboard-c)
-(Rare)-Daily strip- by George McManus 158.00 553.00 950.00

RINGING UP FATHER (C)
pples & Leon Co.: 1919 - No. 26, 1934 (10x10", 52 pgs., B&W, f cardboard-c) (No. 22 is 9-1/4x9-1/2")
Daily strip-r by George McManus in all 32.00 128.00 225.00
10 32.00 128.00 225.00
-20 (Scarcer) 50.00 200.00 350.00
-26 (Rare) 100.00 300.00 500.00
Big Book 1 (1926)-Thick book (hardcover; 10-1/4x10-1/4", 142 pgs.) 121.00 484.00 850.00
w/dust jacket (rare) 183.00 732.00 1275.00
Big Book 2 (1929) 96.00 384.00 675.00
w/dust jacket (rare) 183.00 732.00 1275.00
TE: *The Big Books contain 3 regular issues rebound.*

NGING UP FATHER, THE TROUBLE OF (C)
bee Publ. Co.: 1921 (9x15", Sunday-r in color)
(Rare) 75.00 300.00 525.00
E: *Ties with Mutt & Jeff (EmBee) and Jimmie Dugan And The Reg'lar Fellers (C&L) as the of the oblong size era.*

OWNIE CLOWN OF BROWNIE TOWN (C)
Century Co.: 1908 (6-7/8 x 9-3/8", 112 pgs, color hardcover & interior)
By Palmer Cox (rare; 1907 newspaper strip-r) 200.00 700.00 1200.00

DDY TUCKER & HIS FRIENDS (C) (Also see Buster Brown Nuggets)
pples & Leon Co.: 1906 (11 1/4 x17 1/2", color)
1905 Sunday strip-r by R. F. Outcault 271.00 950.00 -

FFALO BILL'S PICTURE STORIES
eet & Smith Publications: 1909 (Soft cardboard cover)
67.00 233.00 400.00

GHOUSE FABLES (C) (see also Comic Monthly)
bee Distributing Co. (King Features): 1921 (10¢, 4x4-1/2", 48 pgs.)
By Barney Google (Billy DeBeck) 43.00 171.00 300.00

G MOVIES (H)
Publishing Co.: 1931 (9-13/16x9-7/8", 52 pgs., B&W)
Original material; Stookie Allen-a 32.00 128.00 225.00

L CALF AND OTHER TALES (E)
rles Scribner's Sons: 1892 (116 pgs., 7"x9", hardcover, B&W)
y Arthur Burdett Frost 150.00 450.00 -

GD2.0 FN6.0 VF8.0

BUNNY'S BLUE BOOK (see also Foxy Grandpa) (C)
Frederick A. Stokes Co.: 1911 (10x15, 60¢)
nn-By Carl "Bunny" Shultze strip-r 100.00 350.00 -

BUNNY'S RED BOOK (see also Foxy Grandpa) (C)
Frederick A. Stokes Co.: 1912 (10x15)
nn-By Carl "Bunny" Schultze strip-r 100.00 350.00 -

BUNNY'S GREEN BOOK (see also Foxy Grandpa) (C)
Frederick A. Stokes Co.: 1913 (10x15")
nn-By Carl "Bunny" Schultze 100.00 350.00 -

BUSHEL OF MERRY THOUGHTS, A (see Mischief Book, The) (A)
Samson Low Son & Marsten: 1868 (68 pgs, handcolored hardcover, B&W)
nn- (6-1/4 x 9-7/8, 138 pgs) red binding, publisher's name on title page only. 300.00 600.00 -
nn- (6-1/2 x 10, 134 pgs) green binding, publisher's name on cover & title page. 300.00 600.00 -
NOTE: *Cover plus story title pages designed by Leighton Brothers, based on Busch art. Translated by Harry Rogers (who is credited instead of Busch). This is a British publication, notable as the earliest known English language anthology collection of Wilhelm Busch comic strips. Page 13 of second story missing from all editions (panel dropped). Unknown which of the two editions was published first. Had a modern reprint, by Dover in 1971.*

BUSTER BROWN (C) (Also see Brown's Blue Ribbon Book of Jokes and Jingles & Buddy Tucker & His Friends)
Frederick A. Stokes Co.: 1903 - 1916 (Daily strip-r in color)
1903...& His Resolutions (11-1/4x16", 66 pgs.) by R. F. Outcault (Rare)-1st nationally distributed comic. Distr. through Sears & Roebuck(Rare) 1285.00 4500.00 -
1904...His Dog Tige & Their Troubles (11-1/4x16-1/4", 66 pgs.)(Rare) 429.00 1500.00 -
1905...Pranks (11-1/4x16-3/8", 66 pgs.) 371.00 1300.00 -
1906...Antics (11x16-3/8", 66 pgs.) 371.00 1300.00 -
1906...And Company (11x16-1/2", 66 pgs.) 271.00 950.00 -
1906...Mary Jane & Tige (11-1/4x16, 66 pgs.) 271.00 950.00 -
1908 Collection of Buster Brown Comics 214.00 750.00 -
1909 Outcault's Real Buster and The Only Mary Jane (11x16, 66 pgs, Stokes) 208.00 729.00 -
1910...Up to Date (10-1/8x15-3/4", 66 pgs.) 208.00 729.00 1250.00
1911...Fun And Nonsense (10-1/8x15-3/4", 66 pgs.) 183.00 642.00 1100.00
1912...The Fun Maker (10-1/8x15-3/4", 66 pgs.) -Yellow Kid (4 pgs.) 183.00 642.00 1100.00
1913...At Home (10-1/8x15-3/4", 56 pgs.) 167.00 583.00 1000.00
1914...And Tige Here Again (10x16, 62 pgs, Stokes) 150.00 525.00 900.00
1915...And His Chum Tige (10x16, Stokes) 150.00 525.00 900.00
1916...The Little Rogue (10-1/8x15-3/4", 62 pgs.) 162.00 567.00 975.00
1917...And the Cat (5-1/2x 6-1/2, 26 pgs, Stokes) 112.00 392.00 675.00
1917...Disturbs the Family (5-1/2x 6 1/2, 26 pgs, Stokes
NOTE: *Story featuring statue of "the Chinese Yellow Kid"* 112.00 392.00 675.00
1917...The Real Buster Brown (5-1/2x 6 -/2, 26 pgs, Stokes 112.00 392.00 675.00

Frederick A. Stokes Co. Hard Cover Series (G)
...Abroad (1904, 10-1/4x8", 86 pgs., B&W, hard-c)-R. F. Outcault-a (Rare) 200.00 700.00 1200.00
...Abroad (1904, B&W, 67 pgs.)-R. F. Outcault-a 200.00 700.00 1200.00
NOTE: *Not an actual comic book, but prose with illustrations.*
..."Tige" His Story 1905 (10x8", 63 pgs., B&W) (63 illos.)
nn-By RF Outcault 143.00 500.00 -
...My Resolutions 1906 (10x8", B&W, 68 pgs.)-R.F. Outcault-a (Rare) 233.00 817.00 1400.00
...Autobiography 1907 (10x8", B&W, 71 pgs.) (16 color plates & 36 B&W illos) 67.00 233.00 400.00
...And Mary Jane's Painting Book 1907 (10x13-1/4", 60 pgs, both card & hardcover versions exist
nn-RFO (first printing blank on top of cover) 67.00 233.00 400.00
First Series- this is a reprint if it says First Series 67.00 233.00 400.00

Buster Brown 1909 - The Busy Body
© C&L

Buster Brown Nuggets -Buster Brown Plays Cowboy © C&L

Buster Brown Drawing Book
© C&L

Volume Two - By RFO 67.00 233.00 400.00
... My Resolutions by Buster Brown (1907, 68 pgs, small size, cardboard covers) scarce 43.00 150.00 260.00

NOTE: *Not actual comic book per se, but a compilation of the Resolutions found at the end of Outcault's Buster Brown newspaper strips.*

BUSTER BROWN (C)
Cupples & Leon Co./N. Y. Herald Co.: 1906 - 1917 (11x17", color, strip-r)
NOTE: *Early issues by R. F. Outcault; most C&L editions are not by Outcault.*

1906...His Dog Tige And Their Jolly Times (11-3/8x16-5/8", 68 pgs.) 283.00 992.00 1700.00
1906...His Dog Tige & Their Jolly Times (11x16, 46 pgs.) 158.00 554.00 950.00
1907...Latest Frolics (11-3/8x16-5/8", 66 pgs., reprints 1905-06 strips) 158.00 554.00 950.00
1908...Amusing Capers (58 pgs.) 125.00 438.00 750.00
1909...The Busy Body (11-3/8x16-5/8", 62 pgs.) 125.00 438.00 750.00
1910...On His Travels (11x16", 58 pgs.) 112.00 392.00 675.00
1911...Happy Days (11-3/8x16-5/8", 58 pgs.) 112.00 392.00 675.00
1912...In Foreign Lands (10x16", 58 pgs) 112.00 392.00 675.00
1913...And His Pets (11x16", 58 pgs.) 112.00 392.00 675.00
1914...Funny Tricks (11-3/8x16-5/8", 58 pgs.) 112.00 392.00 675.00
1916...At Play (10x16, 58 pgs) 112.00 392.00 675.00

BUSTER BROWN NUGGETS (C)
Cupples & Leon Co./N.Y.Herald Co.: 1907 (1905, 7-1/2x6-1/2", 36 pgs., color, strip-r, hard-c)(By R. F. Outcault) (NOTE: books are all unnumbered)

Buster Brown Goes Fishing 39.00 137.00 235.00
Buster Brown Goes Swimming 39.00 137.00 235.00
Buster Brown Plays Indian 39.00 137.00 235.00
Buster Brown Goes Shooting 39.00 137.00 235.00
Buster Brown Plays Cowboy 39.00 137.00 235.00
Buster Brown On Uncle Jack's Farm 39.00 137.00 235.00
Buster Brown Tige And The Bull 39.00 137.00 235.00
Buster Brown And Uncle Buster 39.00 137.00 235.00
Buddy Tucker Meets Alice in Wonderland 50.00 175.00 300.00
Buddy Tucker Visits The House That Jack Built 39.00 137.00 235.00

BUSTER BROWN MUSLIN SERIES (C)
Saalfield: 1907 (also contain copyright Cupples & Leon)

...Goes Fishing (1907, 6-7/8x6-1/8", 24 pgs., color)-r/1905 Sunday comics page by Outcault(Rare) 50.00 175.00 300.00
...Plays Indian (1907, 6-7/8x6-1/8", 24 pgs., color)-r/1905 Sunday comics page by Outcault(Rare) 42.00 146.00 250.00
...Plays Cowboy (1907, 6-3/4x6", 10 pgs., color)-r/1905 Sunday comics page by Outcault(Rare) 42.00 146.00 250.00
...And The Donkey (1907, 6-7/8x6-1/8", 24 pgs., color)-r/1905 Sunday comics page by Outcault (Rare) 42.00 146.00 250.00

NOTE: *These are muslin versions of the C&L BB Nugget series.*
NOTE: *Muslin books are all cloth books, made to be washable so as not easily stained/destroyed by very young children. The Muslin books contain one strip each (the title strip), to the more common NUGGET's three strips.*

BUSTER BROWN PREMIUMS (Advertising premium booklets)
Various Publishers: 1904 - 1912 (3x5" to 5x7"; sizes vary)

The Brown Shoe Company, St. Louis, USA
Set of five books (5x7", 16 pgs., color)

Brown's Blue Ribbon Book of Jokes and Jingles Book 1 (nn, 1904)-By R. F. Outcault; Buster Brown & Tige, Little Tommy Tucker, Jack & Jill, Little Boy Blue, Dainty Jane; The Yellow Kid app. on back-c (1st BB comic book premium) 600.00 2100.00 3600.00
Buster Brown's Blue Ribbon Book of Jokes and Jingles Book 2 (1905)-Original color art by Outcault 267.00 933.00 1600.00
Buster's Book of Jokes & Jingles Book 3 (1909) not signed by R.F. Outcault 267.00 933.00 1600.00
NOTE: *Reprinted from the Blue Ribbon post cards with advert jingles added.*
Buster's Book of Instructive Jokes and Jingles Book 4 (1910)-Original color art not signed by R.F. Outcault 267.00 933.00 1600.00
...Book of Travels nn (1912, 3x5")-Original color art not signed by Outcault 117.00 408.00 70

NOTE: *Estimated 5 or 6 known copies exist of books #1-4.*

The Buster Brown Bread Company

"Buster Brown" Bread Book of Rhymes, The (1904, 4x6", 12 pgs., half color, B&W)- Original color art not signed by RFO 158.00 553.00 95

Buster Brown's Hosiery Mills

"How Buster Brown Got The Pie" nn (nd, 7x5-1/4". 16 pgs, color paper cover color interior By R.F. Outcault 83.00 292.00 50
"The Autobiography of Buster Brown" nn (nd,9x6-1/8", 36 pgs, text story & ar R.F. Outcault 83.00 292.00 50
NOTE: *Similar to, but a distinctly different item than "Buster Brown's Autobiography."*

The Buster Brown Stocking Company

Buster Brown Drawing Book, The nn (nd, 5x6", 20 pgs.)-B&W reproductions of 1903 R.F. Outcault art to trace 100.00 350.00 60
NOTE: *Reprints a comic strip from Burr McIntosh Magazine, which includes Buster, Yellov and Pore Li'l Mose (only known story involving all three.)*

Collins Baking Company

Buster Brown Drawing Book nn (1904, 5x3", 12 pgs.)-Original B&W art to trace not signed by R.F. Outcault 100.00 350.00 60

C. H. Morton, St. Albans, VT

Merry Antics of Buster Brown, Buddy Tucker & Tige nn (nd, 3-1/2x5-1/2", 16 pgs.)-Original B&W art by R.F. Outcault 83.00 292.00 50

Ivan Frank & Company

Buster Brown nn (1904, 3x5", 12 pgs.)-B&W repros of R. F. Outcault Sunday pages (First premium to actually reproduce Sunday comic pages – may b first premium comic strip-r book?) 125.00 438.00 75
Buster Brown's Pranks (1904, 3-1/2x5-1/8", 12 pgs.)-reprints intro of Buddy Tucker into the BB newspaper strip before he was spun off into his own s lived newspaper strip 125.00 438.00 75

Pond's Extract

Buster Brown's Experiences With Pond's Extract nn (1904, 6-3/4x4-1/2", 28 pgs.)-Original color art by R.F. Outcault (may be the first BB premium comic book with original art) 200.00 700.00 120

Ringen Stove Company

Quick Meal Steel Ranges nn (nd, 5x3", 16 pgs.)-Original B&W art not signed by R.F. Outcault 83.00 292.00 50

Steinwender Stoffregen Coffee Co.

"Buster Brown Coffee" (1905, 4-7/8x3", color paper cover, B&W interior, 12 ed pages, plus 1 tracing paper page above each interior image (total of sheets) (Very Rare) 83.00 292.00 50
NOTE: *Part of a BB drawing contest. If instructions had been followed, most copies would ended up destroyed.*

No Publisher Listed

The Drawing Book nn (1906, 3-9/16x5", 8 pgs.)-Original B&W art to trace no signed by R.F. Outcault 83.00 292.00 50

BUTLER BOOK A Series of Clever Cartoons of Yale Undergraduate Life
Yale Record: June 16, 1913 (10-3/4 x 17", 34 pgs, paper cover B&W)

nn-By Alban Bernard Butler 20.00 70.00 12
NOTE: *Cartoons and strips reprinted from The Yale Record student newspaper.*

BUTTONS & FATTY IN THE FUNNIES
Whitman Publishing Co.: nd 1927 (10-1/4x15-1/2", 28pg., color)

W936-Signed "M.E.B.", probably Merrill Blosser; strips in color copyright The Brooklyn Daily Eagle; (very rare) 61.00 244.00 42

CAMION CARTOONS
Marshall Jones Company: 1919 (7-1/2x5", 136 pgs, B&W)

nn-By Kirkland H. Day (W.W.One occupation) 20.00 70.00 12

CARLO (H)
Doubleday, Page & Co.: 1913 (8 x 9-5/8, 120 pgs, hardcover, B&W)

nn - by A.B. Frost 40.00 140.00 24
NOTE: *Original sequential strips about a dog. Became short lived newspaper comic strip in*

CARTOON BOOK, THE
Bureau of Publicity, War Loan Organization, Treasury Department,

Charlie Chaplin in the Army
© Essaney

Comic Monthly #2
© Embee Dist. Co.

Comic Monthly #7
© Embee Dist. Co.

GD2.0 FN6.0 VF8.0 | GD2.0 FN6.0 VF8.0

…hington, D.C.: 1918 (6-1/2x4-7/8", 48 pgs, paper cover, B&W)

	GD2.0	FN6.0	VF8.0
…y various artists	31.00	108.00	185.00

…: *U.S. government issued booklet of WW I propaganda cartoons by 46 artists promoting the sale of Liberty Loan bonds. The artists include: Berryman, Clare Briggs, Cesare, J. N. …" Darling, Rube Goldberg, Kemble, McCutcheon, George McManus, F. Opper, T. E. Powers, …y, Satterfield, H. T. Webster, Gaar Williams.*

…TOONS BY BRADLEY: CARTOONIST OF THE CHICAGO DAILY NEWS
…d McNally & Company: 1917 (11-1/4x8-3/4", 112 pgs, hardcover, B&W)

…y Luther D. Bradley (editorial)	20.00	70.00	120.00

…TOONS BY FONTAINE FOX (Toonerville Trolley) (D)
…per & Brothers Publishers: nd early '20s (9x7-7/8",102 pgs.,hardcover,B&W)

…ond Book- By Fontaine Fox (Toonerville-r)	54.00	189.00	325.00

…TOONS BY McCUTCHEON (D)
…. McClurg & Co.: 1903 (12-3/8x9-3/4", 212 pgs, hardcover, B&W)

…y John McCutcheon	20.00	70.00	120.00

…TOONS BY W. A. IRELAND (D)
Columbus-Evening Dispatch: 1907 (13-3/4 x 10-1/2", 66 pgs, hardcover)

…y W. A. Ireland (strip-r)	20.00	70.00	120.00

…TOONS MAGAZINE (I)
…. Windsor, Publisher: Jan 1912-June 1921 (1912-June 1913 issues 12x9-68-76 pgs; 1913-1921 issues 10x7", average 112 to 188 pgs, color covers)

…2-Jan-Dec	15.00	51.00	90.00
…3-1915	15.00	51.00	90.00
…6-1917	15.00	51.00	90.00
…7-(Apr) "How Comickers Regard Their Characters"	30.00	105.00	150.00
…7-(June) "A Genius of the Comic Page" - long article on George Herriman, …razy Kat, etc with lots of Herriman art; "Cartoonists and Their Cars"	58.00	204.00	350.00
…3-1919	20.00	70.00	120.00
…0-1921	15.00	53.00	90.00

…: *Many issues contain a wealth of historical background on then current cartoonists of the …with an international slant; each issue profusely illustrated with many cartoons.*

…TOONS OF OUR WAR WITH SPAIN (D)
…derick A. Stokes Company: 1898 (11-1/2x10", 72 pgs, hardcover, B&W)

…y Charles Nelan (r-New York Herald)	20.00	70.00	120.00
…2nd printing noted on copyright page	20.00	70.00	120.00

…RLIE CHAPLIN (C)
…anay/M. A. Donohue & Co.: 1917 (9x16", B&W, large size soft-c)

…es 1, #315-Comic Capers (9-3/4x15-3/4")-18 pgs. by Segar; Series 1, …316-In the Movies	233.00	817.00	1400.00
…es 1, #317-Up in the Air, #318-In the Army	233.00	817.00	1400.00
…ny Stunts-(12-1/2x16-3/8", color)	233.00	817.00	1400.00

…: *All contain pre-Thimble Theatre Segar art.*

…SING THE BLUES
…bleday Page: 1912 (7-1/2x10", 52 pgs., B&W, hard-c)

…y Rube Goldberg	150.00	525.00	900.00

…LDREN'S CHRISTMAS BOOK, THE
New York Sunday World: 1897 (10-1/4x8-3/4", 16 pgs, full color)

…12, 1897 - By George Luks, G.H. Grant, Will Crawford, others) (Rare)	80.00	280.00	-

…P'S DOGS (E)
Russell and Son Publishers: 1895 (hardcover, B&W)

…y Frank P. W. "Chip" Bellew early printing 80 pgs, 8-7/8x11-7/8"; …dark green border of hardcover surrounds all four sides of pasted on …over image; pages arranged in error -- see NOTE below. (more scarce)	100.00	350.00	-
…y Frank P. W. "Chip" Bellew later printing, 72 pgs, 11-3/4x8-7/8; …green border only on the binding side (one side) of the cover image.	50.00	175.00	-

…: *Strip reprints from LIFE MAGAZINE. The difference in page count is due to more blank pages in the first printing -- all printings have the same comics contents, but with the pages in the first printing arranged differently. This is noticeable particularly in the 2-page strip "Getting a Pointer", which appears on the 2nd & 3rd to last pages of the later printings, but in the early printing the first half of this strip is near the middle of the book, while the last half appears on the 2nd to last story page.*

CHIP'S OLD WOOD CUTS (D)
R.H. Russell & Son: 1895 (8-7/8x11-3/4", 72 pgs, hardcover, B&W)

nn-By Frank P. W. ("Chip") Bellew	100.00	350.00	-

CHIP'S UNNATURAL HISTORY (D)
Frederick A. Stokes & Brother: 1888 (7x5-1/4", 64 pgs, hardcover, B&W)

nn-By Frank P. W. ("Chip") Bellew	50.00	175.00	-

NOTE: *Title page lists publisher as "Successors to White, Stokes & Allen."*

CLANCY THE COP (H)
Dell Publishing Co.: 1930 - No. 2, 1931 (10x10", 52 pgs., B&W, cardboard-c)

1, 2- By Vep (original material; not reprints)	57.00	229.00	400.00

CLIFFORD MCBRIDE'S IMMORTAL NAPOLEON & UNCLE ELBY
The Castle Press: 1932 (12x17"; soft-c cartoon book)

nn-Intro. by Don Herod	36.00	144.00	250.00

COLLECTED DRAWINGS OF BRUCE BAIRNSFATHER, THE
W. Colston Leigh: 1931 (11-1/4x8-1/4 ", 168 pages, hardcover, B&W)

nn-By Bruce Bairnsfather	24.00	96.00	165.00

COLLEGE EXPERIENCES OF ICHABOD ACADEMIUS, THE (B)
unknown, New Haven: 1847? (extremely little is known of this comic book)

nn-By William T. Peters (Extremely Rare)	???	???	???

COMICAL COONS
R.H. Russell: 1898 (8-7/8 x 11-7/8, 68 pgs, hardcover, B&W)

nn - By E. W. Kemble	???	???	???

NOTE: *Collection of racist 2-panel stories of African Americans.*

COMIC ANIMALS
Charles E. Graham & Co.: 1903 (9-3/4x7-1/4", 90 pgs, color cover)

nn-By Walt McDougall (not comic strips)	43.00	150.00	260.00

COMIC CUTS
H. L. Baker Co., Inc.: 5/19/34-7/28/34 (Tabloid size 10-1/2x15-1/2", 24 pgs., 5¢) (full color, not reprints; published weekly; created for news stand sales)

V1#1 - V1#7(6/30/34), V1#8(7/14/34), V1#9(7/28/34)-Idle Jack strips	50.00	150.00	300.00

NOTE: *According to a 1958 Lloyd Jacquet interview, this short-lived comics magazine was the direct inspiration for Major Malcolm Wheeler-Nicholson's New Fun Comics, not Famous Funnies.*

COMIC MONTHLY (C)
Embee Dist. Co.: Jan, 1922 - No. 12, Dec, 1922 (10¢, 8-1/2"x9", 28 pgs., 2-color covers) (1st monthly newsstand comic publication) (Reprints 1921 B&W dailies)

1-Polly & Her Pals by Cliff Sterrett	193.00	772.00	1350.00
2-Mike & Ike by Rube Goldberg	114.00	456.00	800.00
3-S'Matter, Pop?	114.00	456.00	800.00
4-Barney Google by Billy DeBeck	114.00	456.00	800.00
5-Tillie the Toiler by Russ Westover	114.00	456.00	800.00
6-Indoor Sports by Tad Dorgan	114.00	456.00	800.00
NOTE: #6 contains more Judge Rummy than Indoor Sports			
7-Little Jimmy by James Swinnerton	114.00	456.00	800.00
8-Toots and Casper by Jimmy Murphy	114.00	456.00	800.00
9-New Bughouse Fables by Barney Google	114.00	456.00	800.00
10-Foolish Questions by Rube Goldberg	114.00	456.00	800.00
11-Barney Google & Spark Plug by Billy DeBeck	114.00	456.00	800.00
12-Polly & Her Pals by Cliff Sterrett	193.00	772.00	1350.00

COMIC PAINTING AND CRAYONING BOOK (H)
Saalfield Publ. Co.: 1917 (13-1/2x10", 32 pgs.) (No price on-c)

nn-Tidy Teddy by F. M. Follett, Clarence the Cop, Mr. & Mrs. Butt-In; regular comic stories to read or color	50.00	175.00	300.00

COMPLETE TRIBUNE PRIMER, THE (F)
Mutual Book Company: 1901 (7 1/4 x 5", 152 pgs, red hardcover)

Daffydils
© C&L

Felix the Cat Book 260
© McLoughlin Bros.

Foolish Questions
Embee Publ.

nn-By Frederick Opper; has 75 Opper cartoons 25.00 88.00 150.00

COURTSHIP OF TAGS, THE (C)
McCormick Press: pre-1910 (9x4", 88 pgs, red & B&W cover, B&W interior)
nn-By O. E. Wertz (strip-r Wichita Daily Beacon) 25.00 88.00 150.00

DAFFYDILS
Cupples & Leon Co.: 1911 (6x8", 52 pgs., B&W, hard-c)
nn-By "Tad" Dorgan 58.00 204.00 350.00

DEADWOOD GULCH (H) (See The Funnies 1929)
Dell Publishing Co.: 1931 (10x10", 52 pgs., B&W, color covers, B&W interior)
nn-By Charles "Boody" Rogers (original material) 50.00 175.00 300.00

DESTINY A Novel In Pictures (H)
Farrar & Rinehart: 1930 (8x7", 424 pgs, B&W hardcover, dust jacket?)
nn-By Otto Nuckel (original graphic novel) 25.00 100.00 175.00

DICK TRACY & DICK TRACY JR. CAUGHT THE RACKETEERS, HOW
Cupples & Leon Co.: 1933 (8-1/2x7", 88 pgs., hard-c) (See Treasure Box of Famous Comics) (C)
2-(Numbered on pg. 84)-Continuation of Stooge Viller book (daily strip reprints from 8/3/33 thru 11/8/33)(Rarer than #1) 79.00 316.00 550.00
With dust jacket... 118.00 472.00 825.00

DICK TRACY & DICK TRACY JR. AND HOW THEY CAPTURED "STOOGE" VILLER (C)
Cupples & Leon Co.: 1933 (8-1/2x7", 100 pgs., hard-c, one-shot)
Reprints 1932 & 1933 Dick Tracy daily strips
nn(No.1)-1st app. of "Stooge" Viller 79.00 316.00 550.00
with dust jacket... 118.00 472.00 825.00

DIMPLES By Grace Drayton (See Dolly Dimples)
Hearst's International Library Co.: 1915 (6 1/4 x 5 1/4, 12 pgs) (5 known)
nn-Puppy and Pussy; nn-She Goes For a Walk; nn-She Had A Sneeze; nn-She Has a Naughty Play Husband; nn-Wait Till Fido Comes Home 20.00 70.00 140.00

DOINGS OF THE DOO DADS, THE (C)
Detroit News (Universal Feat. & Specialty Co.): 1922 (50¢, 7-3/4x7-3/4", 34 pgs, B&W, red & white-c, square binding)
nn-Reprints 1921 newspaper strip "Text & Pictures" given away as prize in the Detroit News Doo Dads contest; by Arch Dale 43.00 173.00 300.00

DOINGS OF THE VAN-LOONS (C)
Ball Publications: 1912 (5-3/4X15-1/2", 68pg., B&W, hard-c)
nn-By Fred I. Leipziger 88.00 306.00 525.00

DOLLY DIMPLES & BOBBY BOUNCE (See Dimples)
Cupples & Leon Co.: 1933 (8-3/4x7")
nn-Grace Drayton-a 24.00 96.00 165.00

DREAMS OF THE RAREBIT FIEND (C)
Frederick A. Stokes Co.:1905 (10-1/4x7-1/2", 68 pgs, thin paper cover all B&W) newspaper reprints from the New York Evening Telegram
nn-By Winsor "Silas" McCay (Very Rare) (Four copies known to exist)
Estimated value.... 571.00 2000.00 -

DRISCOLL'S BOOK OF PIRATES (H)
David McKay Publ.: 1934 (9x7", 124 pgs, B&W hardcover)
nn-By Montford Amory (original material) 21.00 64.00 150.00

DUCKY DADDLES
Frederick A. Stokes Co: July 1911 (15x10")
nn-by Grace Weiderseim (later Drayton) strip-r 50.00 175.00 300.00

DUMBUNNIES AND THEIR FRIENDS IN RABBITBORO, THE (H)
Albertine Randall Wheelan: 1931 (8-3/4x7-1/8", 82 pgs, color hardcover, B&W)
nn-By Albertine Randall Wheelan (self-pub) 34.00 103.00 240.00

EDISON - INSPIRATION TO YOUTH (C)
Thomas A. Edison, Incorporated: 1939 (9-1/2 x 6-1/2, paper cover, B&W)

nn - photo-c 40.00 120.00 24
NOTE: *Reprints strip material found in the 1928 Life of Thomas A. Edison in Word and Pict*

EXPANSION BEING BART'S BEST CARTOONS FOR 1899
Minneapolis Journal: 1900 (10-1/4x8-1/4", 124 pgs, paperback, B&W)
v2#1 - By Charles L. Bartholomew 24.00 84.00 14

FAMOUS COMICS (C)
King Features Synd. (Whitman Pub. Co.): 1934 (100 pgs., daily newspape (3-1/2x8-1/2"; paper cover)(came in an illustrated box)
684 (#1) - Little Jimmy, Katz Kids & Barney Google 34.00 103.00 24
684 (#2) - Polly, Little Jimmy, Katzenjammer Kids 34.00 103.00 24
684 (#3) - Little Annie Rooney, Polly and Her Pals, Katzenjammer Kids 34.00 103.00 24
Box price... 32.00 96.00 22

FAMOUS COMICS CARTOON BOOKS (C)
Whitman Publishing Co.: 1934 (8x7-1/4", 72 pgs, B&W hard-c, daily strip-r
1200-The Captain & the Kids; Dirks reprints credited to Bernard Dibble 29.00 86.00 20
1202-Captain Easy & Wash Tubbs by Roy Crane; 2 slightly different versions of cover exist 34.00 103.00 24
1203-Ella Cinders By Conselman & Plumb 28.00 84.00 19
1204-Freckles & His Friends 25.00 75.00 17
NOTE: *Called Famous Funnies Cartoon Books inside back area sales advertisement.*

FANTASIES IN HA-HA
Meyer Bros & Co.: 1900 (14 x 11-7/8", 64 pgs, color cover hardcover, B&W
nn-By Hy Mayer 40.00 140.00 24

FELIX (C)
Henry Altemus Company: 1931 (6-1/2"x8-1/4", 52 pgs., color, hard-c w/dus jacket)
1-3-Sunday strip reprints of Felix the Cat by Otto Messmer. Book No. 2 r/19 Sunday panels mostly two to a page in a continuity format oddly arrange each tier of panels reads across two pages, then drops to the next tier. (Books 1 & 3 have not been documented.)(Rare)
Each 104.00 416.00 72
With dust jacket 150.00 600.00 105

FELIX THE CAT BOOK (C)
McLoughlin Bros.: 1927 (8"x15-3/4", 52 pgs, half in color-half in B&W)
nn-Reprints 23 Sunday strips by Otto Messmer from 1926 & 1927, every oth one in color, two pages per strip. (Rare) 200.00 800.00 140
260-Reissued (1931), reformatted to 9-1/2"x10-1/4" (same color plates, but strip per every three pages), retitled ("Book" dropped from title) and abridg (only eight strips repeated from first issue, 28 pgs.).(Rare) 79.00 316.00 55

F. FOX'S FUNNY FOLK (see Toonerville Trolley; Cartoons by Fontaine Fo
George H. Doran Company: 1917 (10-1/4x8-1/4", 228 pgs, red, B&W cove B&W interior, hardcover; dust jacket?)
nn-By Fontaine Fox (Toonerville Trolley strip-r) 54.00 190.00 32

FOLKS IN FUNNYVILLE (D)
R.H. Russell: 1900 (12"Tx9"w)(cardboard-c)
nn-By Frederick Opper 271.00 950.00
NOTE: *Reprinted from Hearst's NY Journal American Humorist supplements.*

FOOLISH QUESTIONS (D)
Small, Maynard & Co.: 1909 (6-7/8 x 5-1/2", 174 pgs, hardcover, B&W)
nn-By Rube Goldberg (first Goldberg item) 75.00 263.00 45

FOOLISH QUESTIONS (Boxed card set) (D)
Wallie Dorr Co., N.Y.: 1919 (5-1/4x3-3/4")(box & card backs are red)
nn-Boxed set w/52 B&W comics on cards; each a single panel gag complete set w/box 75.00 263.00 45

FOOLISH QUESTIONS (D)
EmBee Distributing Co.: 1921 (10¢, 4x5 1/2; 52 pgs, 3 color covers; B&W)

The Latest Adventures of Foxy Grandpa 1905
© Bunny Publ.

Giggles
© Pratt Food Co.

The Gumps #4
© C&L

GD2.0 FN6.0 VF8.0

1-By Rube Goldberg 46.00 160.00 275.00

FOXY GRANDPA (Also see The Funnies, 1st series) (C)
N. Y. Herald/Frederick A. Stokes Co./M. A. Donahue & Co./Bunny Publ. L. R. Hammersly Co.): 1901 - 1916 (Strip-r in color, hard-c)

1901-9x15" in color-N. Y. Herald 271.00 950.00 -
1902- "Latest Larks of...", 32 pgs., 9-1/2x15-1/2" 164.00 575.00 -
1902- "The Many Advs. of...", 9x12", 148 pgs., Hammersly Co. 179.00 625.00 -
1903- "Latest Advs.", 9x15", 24 pgs., Hammersly Co. 164.00 575.00 -
1903- "...'s New Advs.", 11x15", 66 pgs., Stokes 164.00 575.00 -
1904- "Up to Date", 10x15", 66 pgs., Stokes 146.00 510.00 875.00
1904- "The Many Adventures of...", 9x15, 144pgs, Donohue 146.00 510.00 875.00
1905- "& Flip Flaps", 9-1/2x15-1/2", 52 pgs. 146.00 510.00 875.00
1905- "The Latest Advs. of...", 9x15", 28, 52, & 66 pgs, M.A. Donohue Co.; re-issue of 1902 issue 104.00 365.00 625.00
1905- "Latest Larks of...", 9-1/2x15-1/2", 52 pgs., Donahue; re-issue of 1902 issue 104.00 365.00 625.00
1905- "Latest Larks of...", 9-1/2x15-1/2", 24 pgs. edition, Donahue; re-issue of 1902 issue 104.00 365.00 625.00
1905- "Merry Pranks of...", 9-1/2x15-1/2", 52 pgs., Donahue 104.00 365.00 625.00
1905-"...Surprises",10x15", color, 64 pg,Stokes, 60¢ 104.00 365.00 625.00
1906- "Frolics", 10x15", 30 pgs., Stokes 104.00 365.00 625.00
1907?-"...& His Boys",10x15", 64 color pgs, Stokes 104.00 365.00 625.00
1907- "Triumphs", 10x15", 62 pgs, Stokes 104.00 365.00 625.00
1908-"...Mother Goose", Stokes 104.00 365.00 625.00
1909- "...& Little Brother", 10x15, 58 pgs, Stokes 104.00 365.00 625.00
1911- "Latest Tricks", r-1910,1911 Sundays-Stokes Co. 104.00 365.00 625.00
1914-(9-1/2x15-1/2", 24 pgs.)-6 color cartoons/page, Bunny Publ. Co. 88.00 306.00 525.00
1915 - ...Always Jolly (10x16, Stokes) 88.00 306.00 525.00
1916- "Merry Book", (10x15", 64 pgs, Stokes) 88.00 306.00 525.00
1917-"...Adventures (5 1/2 x 6 1/2, 26 pgs, Stokes) 52.00 184.00 315.00
1917-"...Frolics (5 1/2 x 6 1/2, 26 pgs, Stokes) 52.00 184.00 315.00
1917-"...Triumphs (5 1/2 x 6 1/2, 26 pgs, Stokes) 52.00 184.00 315.00

FOXY GRANDPA SPARKLETS SERIES (C)
M. A. Donahue & Co.: 1908 (7-3/4x6-1/2"; 24 pgs., color)

"...Rides the Goat", "...& His Boys", "...Playing Ball", "...Fun on the Farm", "...Fancy Shooting", "...Show His Boys Up-To-Date Sports", "...Plays Santa Claus" each.... 88.00 306.00 525.00
1910- "Playing Ball"; Bunny illos; 8 pgs., linen like pgs., no date 73.00 254.00 435.00

FRAGMENTS FROM FRANCE (D)
G. P. Putnam & Sons: 1917 (9x6-1/4", 168 pgs, hardcover, $1.75)

nn - By Bruce Bairnsfather 25.00 88.00 150.00
NOTE: *WW 1 trench warfare cartoons; color dust jacket.*

FUNNIES, THE (H) (See Clancy the Cop, Deadwood Gulch, Bug Movies)
Dell Publishing Co.: 1929 - No. 36, 10/18/30 (10¢; 5¢ No. 22 on) (16 pgs.)
Full tabloid size in color; not reprints; published every Saturday

1-My Big Brudder, Jonathan, Jazzbo & Jim, Foxy Grandpa, Sniffy, Jimmy Jams & other strips begin; first four-color comic newsstand publication; also contains magic, puzzles & stories 186.00 684.00 1300.00
2-21 (1930, 10¢) 54.00 214.00 375.00
22(nn-7/12/30-5¢) 43.00 171.00 300.00
23(nn-7/19/30-5¢), 24(nn-7/26/30-5¢), 25(nn-8/2/30), 26(nn-8/9/30), 27(nn-8/16/30), 28(nn-8/23/30), 29(nn-8/30/30), 30(nn-9/6/30), 31(nn-9/13/30), 32(nn-9/20/30), 33(nn-9/27/30), 34(nn-10/4/30), 35(nn-10/11/30), 36(nn, no date-10/18/30) each.... 43.00 171.00 300.00

FUNNY FOLK (E)
E. P. Dutton: 1899 (12"x16-1/2", 90 pgs., 14 strips in color-rest in B&W, hard-c)

GD2.0 FN6.0 VF8.0

(Reprints many sequential strips & single panel cartoons from Puck)
nn-By Franklin Morris Howarth 400.00 1400.00 -
NOTE: *This might be considered a "missing link" between Victorian & Platinum Age comic books.*

GASOLINE ALLEY (Also see Popular Comics & Super Comics) (C)
Reilly & Lee Publishers: 1929 (8-3/4x7", B&W daily strip-r, hard-c)

nn-By King (96 pgs.) 50.00 200.00 350.00
NOTE: *Of all the Frank King reprint books, this is the only one to reprint actual complete newspaper strips - all others are illustrated prose text stories.*

GIGGLES
Pratt Food Co.: 1908-09? (12x9", 8 pgs, color)

1-6 By Walt McDougall (#6 dated Jan 1909) 40.00 140.00 -

GOD'S MAN (H)
Jonathan cape and Harrison Smith Inc.: 1929 (8-1/4x6", 298 pgs, B&W hardcover w/dust jacket) (original graphic novel in wood cuts)

nn-By Lynd Ward - - -

GOOD THINGS OF LIFE, THE (E)
White, Stokes, & Allen, NY: 1884 (8-3/8x10-1/2", 74 pgs, B&W hardcover)

nn-First printing 150.00 300.00 -
nn-1886 reprint 100.00 200.00 300.00
NOTE: *Contains lots of sequential comic strips by Palmer Cox, E. W. Kemble, Walt H. McDougall.*

GUMPS, THE (C)
Landfield-Kupfer/Cupples & Leon No. 2: No. 1, 1918 - No. 6, 1921;

Book No. 1(1918)(Rare)-cardboard-c, 5-1/4x13-1/3", 64 pgs., daily strip-r by Sidney Smith 67.00 233.00 400.00
Book No.2(1918)-(Rare); 5-1/4x13-1/3"; paper cover; 36 pgs. daily strip reprints by Sidney Smith 67.00 233.00 400.00
Book No. 3-6 (Rare) 121.00 423.00 725.00

GUMPS, ANDY AND MIN, THE (C)
Landfield-Kupfer Printing Co., Chicago/Morrison Hotel: nd (1920s) (Giveaway, 5-1/2"x14", 20 pgs., B&W, soft-c)

nn-Strip-r by Sidney Smith; art & logo embossed on cover w/hotel restaurant menu on back-c or a hotel promo ad; 4 different contents of issues known 50.00 175.00 300.00

GUMPS, THE (C)
Cupples & Leon: 1924-1930 (10x10, 52 pgs, B&W)

nn(1924)-By Sidney Smith 61.00 244.00 425.00
2,3 39.00 154.00 270.00
4-7 33.00 131.00 230.00

GUMP'S CARTOON BOOK, THE (C)
The National Arts Company: 1931 (13-7/8x10", 36 pgs, color covers, B&W)

nn-By Sidney Smith 57.00 228.00 400.00

GUMPS PAINTING BOOK, THE (C)
The National Arts Company: 1931 (11 x 15 1/4", 20 pgs, half in full color)

nn-By Sidney Smith 57.00 228.00 400.00

HAMBONE'S MEDITATIONS
Jahl & Co.: no date 1920 (6-1/8 x 7-1/2, 108 pgs, paper cover, B&W)

nn - By J. P. Alley 33.00 132.00 230.00
NOTE: *Reprint of racist single panel newspaper series, 2 cartoons per page.*

HAN OLA OG PER (C)
Anundsen Publishing Co, Decorah, Iowa: 1927 (10-3/8 x 15-3/4", 54 pgs, paper cover, B&W)

nn-American origin Norwegian language strips-r 33.00 131.00 230.00
NOTE: *1940s and modern reprints exist.*

HANS UND FRITZ (C)
The Saalfield Publishing Co.: 1917, 1927-29 (10x13-1/2", 28 pgs., B&W)

nn-By R. Dirks (1917, r-1916 strips) 96.00 335.00 575.00
The Funny Larks Of... By R. Dirks (©1917 outside cover; ©1916 inside indica) 96.00 335.00 575.00

Happy Hooligan Book 1 1902
© Frederick A. Stokes

Images d'Epinal
© Humoristic Pub. Co.

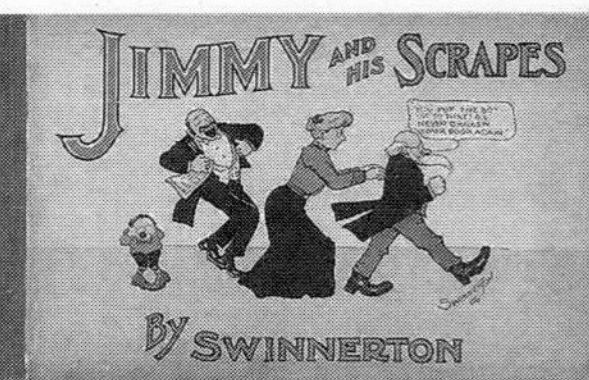

Jimmy and His Scrapes
© Frederick A. Stokes

The Funny Larks Of... (1927) reprints 1917 edition of 1916 strips Halloween-c 58.00 204.00 350.00
The Funny Larks Of... 2 (1929) 58.00 204.00 350.00
193 - By R. Dirks; contains 1916 Sunday strip reprints of Katzenjammer Kids & Hawkshaw the Detective - reprint of 1917 nn edition (1929) this edition is not rare 58.00 204.00 350.00

HAPPY DAYS (D)
Coward-McCann Inc.: 1929 (12-1/2x9-5/8", 110 pgs, hardcover B&W)
nn-By Alban Butler (WW 1 cartoons) 20.00 60.00 120.00

HAPPY HOOLIGAN (See Alphonse…) (C)
Hearst's New York American & Journal: 1902,1903
Book 1-(1902)-"And His Brother Gloomy Gus", By Fred Opper; has 1901-02-r; (yellow & black)(86 pgs.)(10x15-1/4") 371.00 1300.00 -
New Edition, 1903 -10x15" 82 pgs. in color 279.00 975.00 -

HAPPY HOOLIGAN (C)
Frederick A. Stokes Co.: 1906-08 (10x15", cardboard color-c)
1906-:Travels of...), 32 pgs,10-1/4x15-3/4", 1905-r 200.00 700.00 -
1908-"Handy--", 68 pgs, color 200.00 700.00 -
1908?-"--Home Again", 68 pgs., 60¢; by F. Opper; full color-c 200.00 700.00 -

HAPPY HOOLIGAN (Story of…) (G)
McLoughlin Bros.: No. 281, 1932 (12x9-1/2", 16 pgs., soft-c)
281-Three-color text, pictures on heavy paper 64.00 193.00 450.00

HAROLD TEEN (C)
Cupples & Leon Co.: 1929 (9-7/8x9-7/8", 52 pgs, cardboard covers)
nn-By Carl Ed 41.00 164.00 290.00
nn-(1931, 8-11/16x6-7/8", 96 pgs, hardcover w/dj) 41.00 164.00 290.00
NOTE: *Title 2nd book:* ***HAROLD TEEN AND HIS OLD SIDE-KICK– POP JENKINS,*** *(Adv. of...)*

HAROLD TEEN PAINT AND COLOR BOOK
McLoughlin Bros Inc.: 1932 (13x9-3/4, 28 pgs, B&W and color)
#2054 25.00 100.00 175.00

HAWKSHAW THE DETECTIVE (See Advs. of…, Hans Und Fritz & Okay) (C)
The Saalfield Publishing Co.: 1917 (10-1/2x13-1/2", 24 pgs., B&W)
nn-By Gus Mager (Sunday strip-r) 54.00 190.00 325.00

HEALTH GUYED
Frederick A. Stokes Company: 1890 (5-3/8 x 8-3/8, 56 pgs, hardcover, B&W)
nn - by Frank P.W. ("Chip") Bellew (Junior) 50.00 175.00 -
NOTE: *Text & cartoon illustration parody of a health guide.*

HE DONE HER WRONG (H)
Doubleday, Doran & Company: 1930 (8-1/4x 7-1/4", 276pgs, hardcover with dust jacket, B&W interiors)
nn-By Milt Gross 50.00 200.00 350.00
NOTE: *A seminal original material wordless graphic novel, not reprints. Several modern reprints.*

HENRY (C)
David McKay Co.: 1935 (25¢, soft-c)
Book 1-By Carl Anderson 50.00 200.00 350.00
NOTE: *Ties with Popeye (David McKay) and Little Annie Rooney (David McKay) as the last of the 10x10" Platinum Age comic books.*

HENRY (E)
Greenberg Publishers Inc.: 1935 (11-1/4x 8 5/8", 72 pgs, red & blue color hardcover,dust jacket, B&W interiors) (strip-r from Saturday Evening Post)
nn-By Carl Anderson 50.00 200.00 350.00

HIGH KICKING KELLYS, THE
Vaudeville News Corporation, NY: 1926 (5x11", B&W, two color soft-c)
nn-By Jack A. Ward (scarce) 40.00 160.00 280.00

HIGHLIGHTS OF HISTORY (C)
World Syndicate Publishing Co.: 1933-34 (4-1/2x4", 288 pgs)
nn-5 different unnumbered issues; daily strip-r 10.00 40.00 70.00
NOTE: *Titles include Buffalo Bill, Daniel Boone, Kit Carson, Pioneers of the Old West, Winning of the Old Northwest. There are line drawing color covers and embossed hardcover versions. It unknown which came out first.*

HOMER HOLCOMB AND MAY (C)
no publisher listed: 1920s (4 x 9-1/2", 40 pgs, paper cover, B&W)
nn-By Doc Bird Finch (strip-r) 10.00 40.00 70.0

HOME, SWEET HOME (C)
M.S. Publishing Co.: 1925 (10-1/4x10")
nn-By Tuthill 33.00 134.00 235.

HOW THEY DRAW PROHIBITION (D)
Association Against Prohibition: 1930 (10x9", 100 pgs.)
nn-Single panel and multi-panel comics (rare) 71.00 285.00 500.0
NOTE: *Contains art by J.N. "Ding" Darling, James Flagg, Rollin Kirby, Winsor McCay, T.E. Powers, H.T. Webster, others. Also comes with a loose sheet listing all the newspapers where cartoons originally appeared.*

HOW TO DRAW: A PRACTICAL BOOK OF INSTRUCTION (K)
Harper & Brothers: 1904 (9-1/4x12-3/8", 128 pgs, hardcover, B&W)
nn-Edited By Leon Barritt 57.00 228.00 400.
NOTE: *Strips reprinted include: "Buster Brown" by Outcault, "Foxy Grandpa" by Bunny, "Happ Hooligan" by Opper, "Katzenjammer Kids" by Dirks, "Lady Bountiful" by Gene Carr, "Mr. Jack" Swinnerton, "Panhandle Pete" by George McManus, "Mr E.Z. Mark" by F.M. Howarth others; n character strips by Hy Mayer, Winsor McCay, T.E. Powers, others; single panel cartoons by Davenport, Frost, McDougall, Nast, W.A. Rogers, Sullivant, others.*

HOW TO DRAW CARTOONS (K)
Garden City Publishing Co.: 1926, 1937 (10 1/4 x 7 1/2, 150 pgs)
1926 first edition By Clare Briggs 25.00 75.00 150.0
1937 2nd edition By Clare Briggs 20.00 60.00 120.0
NOTE: *Seminal "how to" break into the comics syndicates with art by Briggs, Fisher, Goldberg, King, Webster, Opper, Tad, Hershfield, McCay, Ding, others. Came with Dust Jacket -add 50*

HOW TO DRAW FUNNY PICTURES: A Complete Course in Cartooning (K)
Frederick J. Drake & Co.: 1936 (10-1/4x6-3/4", 168 pgs, hardcover, B&W)
nn-By E.C. Matthews (200 illus by Zimmerman) 20.00 60.00 120.0

HY MAYER (E)
Puck Publishing: 1915 (13-1/2 x 20-3/4", 52 pgs, hardcover cover, color & B&W interiors) (reprints from Puck)
nn-By Hy Mayer 40.00 140.00 240.

IMAGES d'EPINAL (A)
Humoristic Publishing Co., Kansas City. Mo: 1888? (15-1/2x11-1/2",108 pg plus hardcover color-c)
nn-Various French artists (rare) 800.00 1600.00 -
NOTE: Printed and hand colored by stencils in France expressly for the Humoristic Publishing Company . Printed on one side only. This is supposedly a collection of sixty broadsheets, origi nally sold separately. All copies known only have fifty of these broadsheets (slightly bigger, be binding). There are three slightly different covers, with or without the indication in French "Text en Anglais" ("Texts in English"), with or without the general title "Contes de Fées" ("Fairy Tales

IT HAPPENS IN THE BEST FAMILIES (C)
Powers Photo Engraving Co.: 1920 (52 pgs.)(9-1/2x10-3/4")
nn-By Briggs; B&W Sunday strips-r 29.00 114.00 200.
Special Railroad Edition (30¢)-r/strips from 1914-1920 26.00 103.00 180.

JIMMIE DUGAN AND THE REG'LAR FELLERS (C)
Cupples & Leon: 1921, 46 pgs. (11"x16")
nn-By Gene Byrne 71.00 284.00 500.0
NOTE: *Ties with EmBee's Mutt & Jeff and Trouble of Bringing Up Father as the last of this siz*

JIMMY (C)
N. Y. American & Journal: 1905 (10x15", 40 pgs., color)
nn-By Jimmy Swinnerton 179.00 625.00 1075.0

JIMMY AND HIS SCRAPES (C)
Frederick A. Stokes: 1906, (10-1/4x15-1/4", 66 pgs, cardboard-c, color)
nn-By Jimmy Swinnerton 67.00 233.00 400.

JIMMY, STORY OF (G)
McLoughlin Bros.:1932 (9-1/2"X12", 16 pgs., soft cover)

Journey to the Gold Diggins By Jeremiah Saddlebags
© Stringer & Townsend

The Cruise of the Katzenjammer Kids
© NY American & Journal

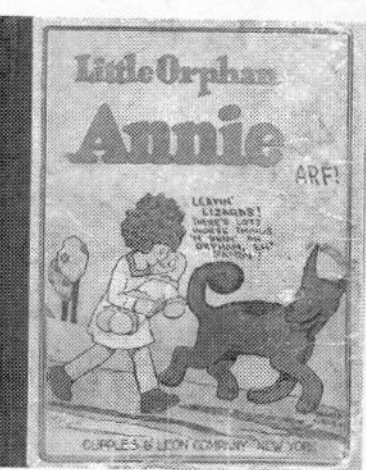

Little Orphan Annie 1926
© C&L

GD2.0 FN6.0 VF8.0

nn-By Jimmy Swinnerton and Mary Kinnaird 64.00 193.00 450.00

JOE PALOOKA (C)
Cupples & Leon Co.: 1933 (9-13/16x10", 52 pgs., B&W daily strip-r)
nn-by Ham Fisher (scarce) 114.00 456.00 800.00

JOLLY POLLY'S BOOK OF ENGLISH AND ETIQUETTE (D)
Jos. J. Frisch: 1931 (60 cents, 8 x 5-1/8, 88 pgs, paper cover, B&W)
nn-By Jos. J. Frisch 20.00 60.00 120.00
NOTE: *Reprint of single panel newspaper series, 4 per page, of English and etiquette lessons taught by a flapper.*

JOURNEY TO THE GOLD DIGGINS BY JEREMIAH SADDLEBAGS (B)
Various publishers: 1849 (25 cents, 5-5/8 x 8-3/4, 68 pgs, green & black paper cover, B&W interior)
nn-New York edition, Stringer & Townsend, Publishers
(Extremely Rare) 1500.00 3000.00 -
nn-Cincinnati, Ohio edition, published by U.P. James (Extremely Rare);
(a GVG (1 pg. missing) sold for $2000 in 2000) 1500.00 3000.00 -
nn-1950 reprint, with introduction, published by William P. Wreden, Burlingame, California: 1950 (5-7/8 x 9, 92 pgs, hardcover, color interior)
(390 copies printed) 33.00 100.00 200.00
NOTE: *By J.A. and D.F. Read. Earliest known sequential comic book by an American creator with the format of the picture story directly inspired by Töpffer's Obadiah Oldbuck and Bachelor Butterfly. The New York and Cincinnati editions were both published in 1849, one soon after the other. Antiquarian Book sources have traditionally cited that the Cincinnati edition preceded the New York, but without referencing their evidence. Conflicting with this, the Cincinnati edition lists the New York publishers' 1849 copyright, while the New York edition makes no reference to the Cincinnati publishers. Such would indicate that the New York edition was first. Both are extremely rare, and until resolved both will be regarded as published simultaneously.*

JOYS AND GLOOMS (C)
Reilly & Britton Co.: 1912 (11x8", 68 pgs, hardcover, B&W interior)
nn-By T. E. Powers (newspaper strip-r) 42.00 146.00 250.00

JUST KIDS, THE STORY OF (G)
McLoughlin Bros.: No. 283, 1932 (12x9-1/2", 16 pgs., paper-c)
283-Three-color text, pictures on heavy paper 29.00 114.00 200.00

KAPTAIN KIDDO AND PUPPO
Frederick A. Stokes Co.: 1910-1913 (11x16-1/2", 62 pgs)
1910-By Grace Wiederseim (later Drayton) 40.00 140.00 240.00
1910-Turr-ble Tales of... By Grace Wiederseim). 40.00 140.00 240.00
Edward Stern & Co.: 1910 (11x16-1/2", 64 pgs)
1913- ...'Speriences By Grace Drayton 40.00 140.00 240.00

KATZENJAMMER KIDS, THE (Also see Hans Und Fritz) (C)
New York American & Journal: 1902,1903 (10x15-1/4", 86 pgs., color)
By Rudolph Dirks; strip first appeared in 1897) © W.R. Hearst
NOTE: *All KK books 1902-1905 all have the same exact title page with a 1902 copyright by W.R. Hearst; almost always look instead on the front cover.*
1902 (Rare) (red & black); has 1901-02 strips 457.00 1600.00 -
1903- **A New Edition** (Rare), 86 pgs 400.00 1400.00 -
1904- 10x15", 84 pgs 214.00 750.00 -
1905?-The Cruise of the, 10x15", 60¢, in color 214.00 750.00 -
1905-A Series of Comic Pictures, 10x15", 84 pgs. in color, possible reprint of 1904 edition 214.00 750.00 -
1905-Tricks of... (10x15", 66 pgs, Stokes) 214.00 750.00 -
1906-Stokes (10x16", 32 pgs. in color) 186.00 650.00 -
1907- The Cruise of the, 10x15", 62 pgs 1905-r? 186.00 650.00 -
1910-The Komical...(10x15) 108.00 379.00 650.00
1921-Embee Dist. Co., 10x16", 20 pgs. in color 100.00 350.00 600.00

KATZENJAMMER KIDS MAGIC DRAWING AND COLORING BOOK (C)
Sam L Gabriel Sons And Company: 1931 (8 1/2 x 12", 36 pages, stiff-c
838 By Knerr 50.00 200.00 350.00

KEEPING UP WITH THE JONESES (C)
Cupples & Leon Co.: 1920 - No. 2, 1921 (9-1/4x9-1/4",52 pgs.,B&W daily strip-r)
1,2-By Pop Momand 39.00 154.00 270.00

LADY BOUNTIFUL (C)

GD2.0 FN6.0 VF8.0

Saalfield Publ. Co./Press Publ. Co.: 1917 (13-13/8x10", 36 pgs, color cardboard-c, B&W interiors)
nn-By Gene Carr; 2 panels per page 50.00 175.00 300.00
193S - 2nd printing (13-1/8x10",28 pgs color-c,B&W) 33.00 117.00 200.00

LAUGHS YOU MIGHT HAVE HAD From The Comic Pages of Six Week Day Issues of the Post-Dispatch (C)
St. Louis Post-Dispatch: 1921 (9 x 10 1/2", 28 pgs, B&W, red ink cover)
nn-Various comic strips 39.00 154.00 270.00

LIFE OF DAVY CROCKETT IN PICTURE AND STORY, THE
Cupples & Leon: 1935 (8-3/4x7", 64 pgs, B&W hardcover, dust jacket?)
nn-By C. Richard Schaare 28.00 112.00 195.00

LIFE OF THOMAS A. EDISON IN WORD AND PICTURE, THE (C)
Thomas A. Edison Industries: 1928 (10x8", 52 pgs, paper cover, B&W)
nn-Photo-c 50.00 200.00 350.00
NOTE: *Reprints newspaper strip which ran August to November 1927.*

LIFE'S LITTLE JOKES (D)
M.S. Publ. Co.: No date (1924)(10-1/16x10", 52 pgs., B&W)
nn-By Rube Goldberg 64.00 257.00 450.00

LILY OF THE ALLEY IN THE FUNNIES
Whitman Publishing Co.: No date (1927) (10-1/4x15-1/2"; 28 pgs., color)
W936-By T. Burke (Rare) 57.00 228.00 400.00

LITTLE ANNIE ROONEY (C)
David McKay Co.: 1935 (25¢, soft-c)
Book 1 43.00 172.00 300.00
NOTE: *Ties with Henry & Popeye (David McKay) as the last of the 10x10" size Plat comic books.*

LITTLE BIRD TOLD ME, A (E)
Life Publishing Co.: 1905? (96 pgs, hardbound)
nn-By Walt Kuhn (Life-r) 38.00 134.00 230.00

LITTLE FOLKS PAINTING BOOK (C)
The National Arts Company: 1931 (10-7/8 x 15-1/4", 20 pgs, half in full color)
nn-By "Tack" Knight (strip-r) 33.00 132.00 230.00

LITTLE JOHNNY & THE TEDDY BEARS (reprints from Judge) (E)
Reilly & Britton Co.: 1907 (10x14", 32 pgs.; green, red, black interior color)
nn-By J. R. Bray-a/Robert D. Towne-s 67.00 233.00 400.00

LITTLE JOURNEY TO THE HOME OF BRIGGS THE SKY-ROCKET, THE
Lockhart Art School: 1917 (10-3/4x7-7/8", 20 pgs, B&W) (I)
nn-About Clare Briggs (bio & lots of early art) 38.00 134.00 230.00

LITTLE KING, THE (see New Yorker Cartoon Albums for 1st appearance) (E)
Farrar & Reinhart, Inc: 1933 (10 1/4 x 8 3/4, 80 pgs, hardcover w/dust jacket
nn- By Otto Soglow (strip-r The New Yorker) 40.00 120.00 280.00
NOTE: *Copies with dust jacket are worth 50% more.*

LITTLE NEMO (...in Slumberland) (C)
Doffield & Co.(1906)/Cupples & Leon Co.(1909): 1906, 1909 (Sunday strip-r in color, cardboard covers)
1906-11x16-1/2" by Winsor McCay; 30 pgs. (Rare) 857.00 3000.00 -
1909-10x14" by Winsor McCay (Rare) 714.00 2500.00 -

LITTLE ORPHAN ANNIE (See Treasure Box of Famous Comics) (C)
Cupples & Leon Co.: 1926 - 1934 (8-3/4x7", 100 pgs., B&W daily strip-r, hard-c)
1(1926)-Little Orphan Annie 50.00 200.00 350.00
1(1926)-softback (see Treasure Box...)
2('27)-In the Circus 36.00 144.00 250.00
3('28)-The Haunted House 36.00 144.00 250.00
4('29)-Bucking the World 36.00 144.00 250.00
5('30)-Never Say Die 30.00 120.00 210.00
6('31)-Shipwrecked 30.00 120.00 210.00
7('32)-A Willing Helper 24.00 96.00 170.00
8('33)-In Cosmic City 24.00 96.00 170.00

The Trials of Lulu and Leander
© NY American & Journal

Maud the Mirthful Mule
© Frederick A. Stokes

Mickey Mouse Book
© WDC

GD2.0 FN6.0 VF8.0

9('34)-Uncle Dan (Rare) 43.00 172.00 300.00
NOTE: *Each book reprints dailies from the previous year. Each hardcover came with a dust jacket. Books with dust jackets are worth 50% more.*

LITTLE SAMMY SNEEZE (C)
New York Herald Co.: Dec 1905 (11x16-1/2", 72 pgs., color)

nn-By Winsor McCay (Very Rare) 971.00 3400.00 -
NOTE: *Rarely found in fine to mint condition.*

LITTLE SKEEZIX BOOKS (Also see Skeezix) (G)
Reilly & Lee Co.: No date (1927-28?) Boxed set of three Skeezix books)

nn-Box with 3 issues of Skeezix (possibly remainders). Skeezix & Pal, Skeezix at the Circus, Skeezix & Uncle Walt known. Set... 80.00 320.00 550.00

LULU AND LEANDER (C)
New York American & Journal: 1904 (76 pgs); **William A Stokes & Co:** 1906

nn-By F.M. Howarth 143.00 500.00 860.00
nn-The Trials of...(1906, 10x16", 68 pgs. in color) 143.00 500.00 860.00

MADMAN'S DRUM (H)
Jonathan Cape and Harrison Smith Inc.: 1930 (8-1/4x6", 274 pgs, B&W hardcover w/dust jacket) (original graphic novel in wood cuts)

nn-By Lynd Ward - - -

MAMA'S ANGEL CHILD IN TOYLAND (G)
Rand McNally, Chicago: 1915 (128 pgs, hardbound)

nn-By M.T. "Penny" Ross & Marie C, Sadler 40.00 140.00 240.00
NOTE: *Mamma's Angel Child published as a comic strip by the "Chicago Tribune" 1908 Mar 1 to 1920 Oct 17.This novel dedicated to Esther Starring Richartz, "the original Mamma's Angel Kid."*

MAUD (C)
Frederick A. Stokes Co.: 1906 - 1908? (10x15-1/2", cardboard-c)

1906-By Fred Opper (Scarce), 66 pgs. color 243.00 850.00 -
1907-The Matchless, 10x15" 70 pgs in color 186.00 650.00 -
1908-The Mirthful Mule, 10x15", 64 pgs in color 186.00 650.00 -

MAX AND MAURICE: A Juvenile History in Seven Tricks (A)
Roberts Bros: 1871 first edition (8-1/8 x 5-5/8", 74 pgs, hardcover, B&W)

nn-By Wilhelm Busch 300.00 600.00 -
nn-1882 reprint (76 pgs, entire book in color) 200.00 400.00 -
nn-1902 (64 pages, Little,Brown-r , same size) 10.00 30.00 90.00
NOTE: Each of the above contains 56 pages of art and text in a transitional format between a regular children's book and a comic book (the page count difference is ad pages in back). Seminal inspiration for William Randolph Hearst to acquire as a "new comic" (following the wild success of Outcault's Yellow Kid) to license M&M from Busch and hire Rudolph Dirks in late 1897 to create a New York American newspaper incarnation. In Hearst's English language newspapers it was called The Katzenjammer Kids and in his German language NYC newspaper it was titled Max & Moritz, Busch's original title. An unknown number of other reprints exist.

MEMORIAL EDITION The Drawings of Clare Briggs (D)
Wm H. Wise & Company: 1930 (7-1/2x8-3/4", 284 pgs, pebbled false black leather, B&W) posthumous boxed set of 7 books by Clare Briggs

nn-The Days of Real Sport; nn-Golf; nn-Real Folks at Home; nn-Ain't it a Grand and Glorious Feeling?; nn-That Guiltiest Feeling; nn-Somebody's Always Taking the Joy Out of Life; nn-When a Feller Needs a Friend
Each book 30.00 120.00 210.00
NOTE: *Also exists in a whitish cream colored paper back edition; first edition unknown presently.*

MEN OF DARING
Cupples & Leon Co.: 1933 (8-3/4x7", 100 pgs)

nn-By Stookie Allen, intro by Lowell Thomas 30.00 90.00 180.00

MICKEY MOUSE BOOK
Bibo & Lang: 1930-1931 (12x9", stapled-c, 20 pgs., 4 printings)

nn-First Disney licensed publication (a magazine, not a book–see first book, Adventures of Mickey Mouse). Contains story of how Mickey met Walt and got his name; games, cartoons & song "Mickey Mouse (You Cute Little Feller)," written by Irving Bibo; Minnie, Clarabelle Cow, Horace Horsecollar & caricature of Walt shaking hands with Mickey. The changes made with the 2nd printing have been verified by billing affidavits in the Walt Disney Archives and include:Two Win Smith Mickey strips from 4/15/30 and 4/17/30 added to page 8 & back-c; "Printed in U.S.A." added to front cover; Bobette Bibo's age of 11 years added t title page; faulty type on the word "tail" corrected top of page 3; the word "start" added to bottom of page 7, removing the words "start 1 2 3 4" from the top of page 7; music and lyrics were rewritten on pages 12-14. A green ink border was added beginning with 2nd printing and some covers have inking variations. Art b Albert Barbelle, drawn in an Ub Iwerks style. Total circulation : 97,938 copies varying from 21,000 to 26,000 per printing.

1st printing. Contains the song lyrics **censored** in later printings, "When little Minnie's pursued by a big bad villain we feel so bad then we're glad when yo up and kill him." Attached to the Nov. 15, 1930 issue of the Official Bulletin of the Mickey Mouse Club notes: "Attached to this Bulletin is a new Mickey Mouse Book that has just been published." This is thought to be the reason why a slightly disproportionate larger number of copies of the first printing stil exist 1200.00 5400.00 11,000.0
2nd printing with a theater/advertising. Christmas greeting added to inside front cover (1 copy known with Dec. 27, 1930 date) ---- 12,000.00 ----
2nd-4th printings 1100.00 5000.00 10,000.0
NOTE: Theater/advertising copies do not qualify as separate printings. Most copies are missing pages 9 & 10 which had a puzzle to be cut out. *Puzzle (pages 9 and 10) cut out or missing, sub tract 60% to 75%.*

MICKEY MOUSE COLORING BOOK (D)
Saalfield Publishing Company:1931 (15-1/4x10-3/4", 32 pgs, color soft cover, half printed in full color interior, rest B&W, only Saalfield MM item known)

871 - By Ub Iwerks & Floyd Gottfredson (rare) 400.00 1200.00 2400.0
NOTE: *Contains reprints of first MM daily strip ever, including the "missing" speck the chicken is after found only on the original daily strip art by Iwerks plus other very early MM art.*

MICKEY MOUSE, THE ADVENTURES OF (G)
David McKay Co., Inc.: Book I, 1931 - Book II, 1932 (5-1/2"x8-1/2", 32 pgs.)

Book I-First Disney book, by strict definition (1st printing-50,000 copies)(see Mickey Mouse Book by Bibo & Lang). Illustrated text refers to Clarabelle Cow as "Carolyn" and Horace Horsecollar as "Henry". The name "Donald Duck" appears with a non-costumed generic duck on back cover & inside, not in the context of the character that later debuted in the Wise Little Hen.
Hardback w/characters on back-c 75.00 300.00 525.0
Softcover w/characters on back-c 38.00 151.00 265.0
Version without characters on back-c 45.00 180.00 315.0
Book II-Less common than Book I. Character development brought into conformity with the Mickey Mouse cartoon shorts and syndicated strips. Captain Church Mouse, Tanglefoot, Peg-Leg Pete and Pluto appear with Mickey & Minnie 46.00 186.00 325.0

MICKEY MOUSE COMIC (C)
David McKay Co.: 1931 - No. 4, 1934 (10"x9-3/4", 52 pgs., cardboard-c) (Later reprints exist)

1 (1931)-Reprints Floyd Gottfredson daily strips in black & white from 1930 & 1931, including the famous two week sequence in which Mickey tries to commit suicide 229.00 914.00 1600.0
2 (1932)-1st app. of Pluto reprinted from 7/8/31 daily. All pgs. from 1931 164.00 656.00 1150.0
3 (1933)-Reprints 1932 & 1933 Sunday pages in color, one strip per page, including the "Lair of Wolf Barker" continuity pencilled by Gottfredson and inked by Al Taliaferro & Ted Thwaites. First app. Mickey's nephews, Morty & Ferdie, one identified by name of Mortimer Fieldmouse, not to be confused with Uncle Mortimer Mouse who is introduced in the Wolf Barker story 214.00 856.00 1500.0
4 (1934)-1931 dailies, include the only known reprint of the infamous strip of 2/4/31 where the villainous Kat Nipp snips off the end of Mickey's tail with pair of scissors 129.00 514.00 900.0

MICKEY MOUSE (C)
Whitman Publishing Co.: 1933-34 (10x8-3/4", 34 pgs, cardboard-c)

948-1932 & 1933 Sunday strips in color, printed from the same plates as Micke Mouse Book #3 by David McKay, but only pages 5-17 & 32-48 (including all of the "Wolf Barker" continuity) 157.00 629.00 1100.0
NOTE: *Some copies bound with back cover upside down. Variance doesn't affect value. Sam art appears on front and back covers of all copies. Height of Whitman reissue of McKay book*

Museum of Wonders
© Routledge & Sons

Mutt & Jeff #17
© C&L

The Nebbs
© C&L

	GD2.0	FN6.0	VF8.0

trimmed 1/2 inch.

MILITARY WILLIE
J. I. Austen Co.: 1907 (7x9-1/2", 14 pgs., every other page in color, stapled)

nn-By F. R. Morgan	70.00	245.00	400.00

MINNEAPOLIS JOURNAL WAR CARTOONS
Minneapolis Journal: 1899 (9x8", 160 pgs, paperback, punched & string bound)

nn-By Charles L. Bartholomew	28.00	99.00	170.00

MINNEAPOLIS TRIBUNE CARTOON BOOK (D)
Minneapolis Tribune: 1899-1903 (11-3/8x9-3/8", B&W, paper cover)

nn (#1) (1899)	28.00	99.00	170.00
nn (#2) (1900)	28.00	99.00	170.00
nn (#3) (1901) (published Jan 01, 1901)	28.00	99.00	170.00
nn (#4) (1902) (114 pgs)	28.00	99.00	170.00
nn (#5) (1903 (9x10-3/4",110 pgs, B&W; color-c)	28.00	99.00	170.00

NOTE: *All by Roland C. Bowman (editorial-r)*

MINUTE BIOGRAPHIES: INTIMATE GLIMPSES INTO THE LIVES OF 150 FAMOUS MEN AND WOMEN
Grossett & Dunlap: 1931, 1933 (10-1/4x7-3/4", 168 pgs, hardcover, B&W)

nn-By Nisenson (art) & Parker(text)	20.00	60.00	120.00
More.... (1933)	20.00	60.00	120.00

MISCHIEF BOOK, THE (A)
R. Worthington: 1880 (7-1/8 x 10-3/4, 176 pgs, hardcover, B&W)

nn - By Wilhelm Busch	300.00	600.00	-

NOTE: *Cover designed by R. Lewis, based on Busch art. Translated by Abby Langdon Alger. American published anthology collection of Wilhelm Busch comic strips. Includes two of the strips found in the British "Bushel of Merry-Thoughts" collection, translated better, along with the dropped panel restored.*

MISCHIEVOUS MONKS OF CROCODILE ISLE, THE (C)
J. I. Austen Co., Chicago: 1908 (8-1/2x11-1/2", 12 pgs., 4 pgs. in color)

nn-By F. R. Morgan; reads longwise	96.00	335.00	575.00

MR. & MRS. (Also see Ain't It A Grand and Glorious Feeling?) (C)
Whitman Publishing Co.: 1922 (9x9-1/2", 52 & 28 pgs., cardboard-c)

nn-By Briggs (B&W, 52 pgs.)	37.00	149.00	260.00
nn-28 pgs.-(9x9-1/2")-Sunday strips-r in color	41.00	163.00	285.00

NOTE: *The earliest presently known Whitman comic books were published in 1922.*

MR. BLOCK (C)
Industrial Workers of the World (IWW): 1913, 1919

nn-By Ernest Riebe (C)	50.00	150.00	-
...And The Profiteers (original material) (H)	50.00	150.00	

NOTE: *Mr Block was a daily strip published from 1912 NOV 7 to 1913 SEP ? by the socialist newspaper "Industrial Worker"; Mr Block was a "square" guy (his head was in fact a block) who enthusiastically supported the same system that exploited him. The noted Joe Hill wrote a song about him (Mr Block,1913, on the air of "It loooks me like a big time tonight") for the Industrial Worker Songbook".*

MR. TWEE-DEEDLE (C)
Cupples & Leon: 1913, 1917 (10 x 16, color strips-r from NY Herald)

nn-By John B. Gruelle (later of Raggedy Ann fame)	114.00	400.00	-
nn-"Further Adventures of..." By Gruelle	114.00	400.00	-

MONKEY SHINES OF MARSELEEN AND SOME OF HIS ADVENTURES (C)
McLaughlin Bros. New York: 1906 (10 x 12-3/8", 36 pgs, full color hardcover)

nn-By Norman E. Jennett strip-r NY Evening Telegram	67.00	233.00	400.00

MONKEY SHINES OF MARSELEEN (C)
Cupples & Leon Co.: 1909 (11-1/2 x 17", 28 pgs. in two colors)

nn-By Norman E. Jennett	63.00	219.00	375.00

MOON MULLINS (C)
Cupples & Leon Co.: 1927 - 1933 (52 pgs., B&W daily strip-r)

Series 1('27)-By Willard	57.00	228.00	400.00
Series 2('28), Series 3('29), Series 4('30)	39.00	156.00	275.00
Series 5('31), 6('32), 7('33)	36.00	144.00	250.00
Big Book 1('30)-B&W (scarce)	100.00	400.00	700.00
w/dust jacket (rare)	183.00	732.00	1275.00

MUSEUM OF WONDERS, A (F)
Routledge & Sons: 1894 (13x10", 64 pgs, color cover, B&W)

nn-By Frederick Opper	50.00	175.00	300.00

MUTT & JEFF (...Cartoon, The) (C)
Ball Publications: 1911 - No. 5, 1916 (5-3/4 x 15-1/2", 68 pgs, B&W, hard-c)

1(1910)(50¢) very common	71.00	286.00	500.00
2,3: 2 (1911)-Opium den panels; Jeff smokes opium (pipe dreams). 3 (1912) both very common	71.00	286.00	500.00
2 -Reprint of 1913 edition with black ink cover	50.00	175.00	300.00
4 (1915) (50¢) (Scarce)	111.00	443.00	775.00
5 (1916) (Rare) -Photos of Fisher, 1st pg.	171.00	685.00	1200.00

NOTE: *Mutt & Jeff first appeared in newspapers in 1907. Cover variations exist showing Mutt & Jeff reading various newspapers; i.e., The Oregon Journal, The American, and The Detroit News. Reprinting of each issue began soon after publication. No. 4 and 5 may not have been reprinted. Values listed include the reprints. Mutt & Jeff was the first successful American daily newspaper comic strip and as such remains one of the seminal strips of all time.*

MUTT & JEFF (C)
Cupples & Leon Co.: No. 6, 1919 - No. 22, 1933? (9-1/2x9-1/2", 52 pgs., B&W dailies, stiff-c)

6, 7 - By Bud Fisher (very common)	32.00	128.00	225.00
8-10	46.00	186.00	325.00
11-18 (Somewhat Scarcer)	60.00	240.00	420.00
19-22 (Rare)	71.00	286.00	500.00
nn (1920)-(Advs. of...) 11x16"; 44 pgs.; full color reprints of 1919 Sunday strips	93.00	372.00	650.00
Big Book nn (1926, 144 pgs., hardcovers)	114.00	456.00	800.00
w/dust jacket	193.00	772.00	1350.00
Big Book 1 (1928) - Thick book (hardcovers)	114.00	456.00	800.00
w/dust jacket (rare)	182.00	729.00	1275.00
Big Book 2 (1929) - Thick book (hardcovers)	114.00	456.00	800.00
w/dust jacket (rare)	182.00	729.00	1275.00

NOTE: *The Big Books contain three previous issues rebound.*

MUTT & JEFF (C)
Embee Publ. Co.: 1921 (9x15", color cardboard-c & interior)

nn-Sunday strips in color (Rare)- BY Bud Fisher	143.00	572.00	1000.00

NOTE: *Ties with The Trouble of Bringing Up Father (EmBee) and Jimmie Dugan & The Reg'lar Fellers (C&L) as the last of this size.*

MYSTERIOUS STRANGER AND OTHER CARTOONS, THE
McClure, Phillips & Co.: 1905 (12-3/8x9-3/4", 338 pgs, hardcover, B&W)

nn-By John McCutcheon	32.00	128.00	225.00

NEBBS, THE (C)
Cupples & Leon Co.: 1928 (52 pgs., B&W daily strip-r)

nn-By Sol Hess; Carlson-a	40.00	160.00	280.00

NERVY NAT'S ADVENTURES (E)
Leslie-Judge Co.: 1911 (90 pgs, 85¢, 1903 strip reprints from **Judge**)

nn-By James Montgomery Flagg	75.00	263.00	450.00

NEWLYWEDS (C)
Saalfield Publ. Co.: 1907 (13x10, 52 pg hardcover); 1917 (cardboard-c)

...& Their Baby' by McManus; daily strips 50% color	200.00	700.00	-
...& Their Baby's Comic Pictures, The, by McManus, Saalfield, (1917, 10x14", 22 pgs, oblong, cardboard-c); reprints 'Newlyweds' (Baby Snookums strips) mainly from 1916; blue cover; says for painting & crayoning, but 50% of the pages in full color. (Scarce)	82.00	286.00	490.00

NEW YORKER CARTOON ALBUM, THE (E)
Doubleday, Doran& Company Inc.: (1928-1931); **Harper & Brothers.:** (1931-1933); **Random House** (1935-1937), 12x9", various pg counts, hardcovers w/dust jackets)

1928: nn-114 pgs Arno, Held, Soglow, Williams, etc	20.00	60.00	120.00
1928: SECOND-114 pgs Arno, Bairnsfather, Gross, Held, Soglow, Williams	10.00	30.00	60.00

Oh Skin-nay!
© P.F. Volland

The Adventures of Peck's Bad Boy With the Teddy Bear Show
© Charles C. Thompson, Co.

Pictures of Life and Character
© G.P. Putnam's Sons

GD2.0 FN6.0 VF8.0

1930: THIRD-172 pgs Arno, Bairnsfather, Held, Soglow, Art Young 10.00 30.00 60.00
1931: FOURTH-154 pgs Arno, Held, Soglow, Steig, Thurber, Williams, Art Young, "Little King" by Soglow begins 10.00 30.00 60.00
1932: FIFTH-156 pgs Arno, Bairnsfather, Held, Hoff, Soglow, Steig, Thurber, Williams 10.00 30.00 60.00
1933: SIXTH-156 pgs same as above 10.00 30.00 60.00
1935: SEVENTH-164 pgs 10.00 30.00 60.00
1937: 168 pgs; Charles Addams plus same as above but no Little King, two page "Gone With The Wind" parody strip 10.00 30.00 60.00
NOTE: *Some sequential strips but mostly single panel cartoons.*

NIPPY'S POP (C)
The Saalfield Publishing Co.: 1917 (10-1/2x13-1/2", B&W, Sunday strip-r)
nn-32 pgs. 43.00 152.00 260.00

OH, MAN (A Bully Collection of Those Inimitable Humor Cartoons) (D)
P.F. Volland & Co.: 1919 (8-1/2x13")
nn-By Briggs 43.00 152.00 260.00
NOTE: *Originally came in illustrated box with Briggs art (box is Rare - worth 50% more with box).*

OH SKIN-NAY! (D)
P.F. Volland & Co.: 1913 (8-1/2x13", 125 pgs)
nn-The Days Of Real Sport by Briggs 43.00 152.00 260.00
NOTE: *Originally came in illustrated box with Briggs art (box is Rare - worth 50% more with box).*

ON AND OFF MOUNT ARARAT (also see **Tigers**) (C)
Hearst's New York American & Journal: 1902, 86pgs. 10x15-1/4"
nn-Noah's Ark satire by Jimmy Swinnerton (rare) 286.00 1000.00 -

ON THE LINKS (C)
Associated Feature Service: Dec, 1926 (9x10", 48 pgs.)
nn-Daily strip-r 25.00 100.00 175.00

ONE HUNDRED WAR CARTOONS (D)
Idaho Daily Statesman: 1918 (7-3/4x10", 102 pgs, paperback, B&W)
nn-By Villeneuve (WW I cartoons) 20.00 60.00 120.00

OUTBURSTS OF EVERETT TRUE, THE (C)
Saalfield Publ. Co.(Werner Co.): 1907 (92 pgs, 9-7/16x5-1/4")
1907 (2-4 panel strips-r)-By Condo & Raper 83.00 292.00 500.00
1921-Full color-c; reprints 56 of 88 cartoons from1907 ed. (10x10", 32 pgs B&W) 40.00 140.00 240.00

OVER THERE COMEDY FROM FRANCE
Observer House Printing: nd (WW 1 era) (6x14", 60 pgs, paper cover
nn-artist(s) unknown 15.00 53.00 90.00

PECKS BAD BOY (C)
Charles C. Thompson Co, Chicago (by Walt McDougal): 1906-1908 (strip-r)
...& His Country Cousin Cynthia (1907)-12x16-1/2," 34 pgs In color 100.00 350.00 600.00
Advs. of...And His Country Cousins (1907) 5-1/2x10 1/2", 18 pgs In color 50.00 175.00 300.00
...& Their Advs With The Teddy Bear (1907) 5-1/2x10-1/2", 18 pgs in color 50.00 175.00 300.00
...& Their Balloon Trip To the Country (1907) 5-1/2x 10-1/2, 18 pgs in color 50.00 175.00 300.00
...With the Teddy Bear Show (1907) 5-1/2x 10-1/2 50.00 175.00 300.00
...With The Billy Whiskers Goats (1907) 5-1/2 x 10-1/2, 18 pgs in color 50.00 175.00 300.00
...& His Chums (1908) - 11x16-1/4, 34 pgs Stanton & Van Vliet Co 100.00 350.00 600.00
...& His Chums (1908)-Hardcover; full color;16 pgs. 100.00 350.00 600.00
Advs. of...in Pictures (1908) (11x17, 36 pgs)-In color; Stanton & Van V. Liet Co. 100.00 350.00 600.00

PERCY & FERDIE (C)
Cupples & Leon Co.: 1921 (10x10", 52 pgs., B&W dailies, cardboard-c)
nn-By H. A. MacGill (Rare) 61.00 244.00 425.00

GD2.0 FN6.0 VF8

PETER RABBIT (C)
John H. Eggers Co. The House of Little Books Publishers: 1922 - 1923
B1-B4-(Rare)-(Set of 4 books which came in a cardboard box)-Each book reprints half of a Sunday page per page and contains 8 B&W and 2 color pages; by Harrison Cady (9-1/4x6-1/4", paper-c)
each.... 43.00 172.00 300.0
Box only 57.00 228.00 400.0

PICTORIAL HISTORY OF THE DEPARTMENT OF COMMERCE UNDER HERBERT HOOVER (see Picture Life of a Great American) (H)
Hoover-Curtis Campaign Committee of New York State: no date, 1928 (3-1 x 5-1/4, 32 pgs, paper cover, B&W)
nn - by Satterfield (scarce) 40.00 120.00 240.0
NOTE: *1928 Presidential Campaign giveaway. Original material, contents completely different from Picture Life of a Great American.*

PICTURE LIFE OF A GREAT AMERICAN (see Pictorial History of the Department of Commerce under Herbert Hoover) (H)
Hoover-Curtis Campaign Committee of New York State: no date, 1928 paper cover, B&W)
nn- (8-3/4 x 7, 20 pgs) Text cover, 2 page text introduction, 18 pgs of comics (scarcer first print) 40.00 120.00 240.
nn- (9 x 6-3/4,24 pgs) Illustrated cover,5 page text introduction, 18 pgs of comics (scarce) 40.00 120.00 240.
NOTE: *1928 Presidential Campaign giveaway. Unknown which above version was published f Both contain the same original comics material by Satterfield.*

PICTURES OF LIFE AND CHARACTER (A)
G.P. Putnam's Sons: 1880s (8-5/8x6-1/4,218 pgs, hardcover, color cover,B&W
nn- John Leech (single panel cartoon-r from Punch) 40.00 120.00 240.0

PICTURES OF LIFE AND CHARACTER (Parchment-Paper Series) (A)
D. Appleton & Co.: 1884 (30 cents, 5-3/4 x 4-1/2, 104 pgs, paper cover, B&W)
nn-John Leech (single panel cartoon-r from Punch) 40.00 120.00 240.0
NOTE: *An advertisment in the back refers to a cloth-bound edition for 50 cents.*

PINK LAFFIN
Whitman Publishing Co.: 1922 (9x12")(Strip-r)
...the Lighter Side of Life, ...He Tells 'Em, ...and His Family, ...Knockouts; Ray Gleason-a (All rare) each... 26.00 104.00 185.0

POPEYE CARTOON BOOK (C)
The Saalfield Co.: 1934 (8-1/2x13", 40 pgs, cardboard-c)
2095-(Rare)-1933 strip reprints in color by Segar. Each page contains a vertica half of a Sunday strip, so the continuity reads row by row completely across each double page spread. If each page is read by itself, the continuity mak no sense. Each double page spread reprints one complete Sunday page from 1933 250.00 750.00 2000.0
12 Page Version 100.00 300.00 800.0

POPEYE (See Thimble Theatre for earlier Popeye) (C)
David McKay Publications: 1935 (25¢; 52 pgs, B&W) (By Segar)
1-Daily strip reprints- "The Gold Mine Thieves" 107.00 321.00 750.0
2-Daily strip-r (scarce) 100.00 300.00 700.0
NOTE: *Ties with Henry & Little Annie Rooney (David McKay) as the last of the 10x10" size boo*

PORE LI'L MOSE (C)
New York Herald Publ. by Grand Union Tea
Cupples & Leon Co.: 1902 (10-1/2x15", 78 pgs., color)
nn-By R. F. Outcault; Earliest known C&L comic book (Rare in high grade - high demand) 1429.00 5000.00 -
NOTE: *One page racist strips about turn of the century African-Americans.*

PRETTY PICTURES (E)
Farrar & Rinehart: 1931 (12 x 8-7/8", 104 pgs, color hardcover w/dust jacket, B&W; reprints from New Yorker, Judge, Life, Collier's Weekly)
nn-By Otto Soglow (contains "The Little King") 33.00 134.00 235.0

RAMBILICUS BOOK, THE (F)
Jacobs & Co.: 1903 (10x7", 240 pgs, hardcover)

Roger Bean, R.G. #4
© C&L

Seaman Si
© Pierce Publ. Co.

Stuff and Nonsense
© Charles Scribner's Sons

GD2.0 FN6.0 VF8.0

nn-By Walt McDougall (not a true comic book) 34.00 120.00 -

RED CARTOONS (D)
Daily Worker Publishing Company: 1926 (12 x 9,68 pgs,cardboard cover,B&W)
nn-By Various (scarce) 40.00 160.00 280.00
NOTE: *Reprint of American Communist Party editorial cartoons, from The Daily Worker, The Workers Monthly, and the Liberator. Art by Fred Ellis, William Gropper, Clive Weed, Art Young.*

REG'LAR FELLERS (See All-American Comics, Jimmie Dugan & The..., Popular Comics & Treasure Box of Famous Comics) (C)
Cupples & Leon Co./MS Publishing Co.: 1921-1929
1(1921)-52 pgs. B&W dailies (Cupples & Leon, 10x10") 43.00 171.00 300.00
1925, 48 pgs. B&W dailies (MS Publ.) 39.00 157.00 275.00
Hardcover (1929, 96 pgs.)-B&W reprints 54.00 214.00 375.00

RIPLEY (See Believe It Or Not)

ROGER BEAN, R. G. (Regular Guy)(C)
The Indiana News Co, Distributers.: 1915 - No. 2, 191 (5-3/8x17", 68 pgs., B&W,hardcovers); #3-#5 published by **Chas. B. Jackson:** 1916-1919
(No. 1 2 4 & 5 bound on side, No. 3 bound at top)
1-By Chas B. Jackson (68pgs.)(Scarce) 60.00 210.00 360.00
2- 5-5/8x17-1/8", 66 pgs (says 1913 inside - an obvious printing error) (red or green binding) 60.00 210.00 360.00
3-Along the Firing Line... (1916 62 pgs, 6x17") 60.00 210.00 360.00
4-Into the Trenches and Out Again with... (68 pgs) 60.00 210.00 360.00
5 ...And The Reconstruction Period (5-3/8x15-1/2", 84 pgs) (Scarce) (has $1 printed on cover) 60.00 210.00 360.00
Baby Grand Editions 1-5 (10x10", cardboard-c) 60.00 210.00 360.00

SAM AND HIS LAUGH (C)
Frederick A. Stokes: 1906 (10x15", cardboard-c, Sunday strip-r in color)
nn-By Jimmy Swinnerton (Very Rare) 200.00 700.00 1200.00

SCHOOL DAYS (C)
Harper & Bros.: 1919 (9x8", 104 pgs.)
nn-By Clare Victor Dwiggins 42.00 144.00 250.00

SEAMAN SI - A Book of Cartoons About the Funniest "Gob" in the Navy (C)
Pierce Publishing Co.: 1916 (4 x 8 1/2, 200 pgs, hardcover, B&W)
nn-By Perce Pearce (The American Sailor strip-r) 43.00 150.00 260.00
nn- 1918 reprint (4-1/8x8-1/4")(Reilly & Britton Co.) 26.00 90.00 156.00

SECRET AGENT X-9 (C)
David McKay Pbll.: 1934 (Book 1: 84 pgs; Book 2: 124 pgs.) (8x7-1/2")
Book 1-Contains reprints of the first 13 weeks of the strip by Dashiell Hammett & Alex Raymond, complete except for 2 dailies 83.00 250.00 500.00
Book 2-Contains reprints immediately following contents of Book 1, for 20 weeks by Dashiell Hammett & Alex Raymond; complete except for two dailies. 83.00 250.00 500.00
NOTE: *Raymond misdated the last 5 strips from 6/34, and while the dating sequence is confusing, the continuity is correct.*

SILK HAT HARRY'S DIVORCE SUIT (C)
. A. Donoghue & Co.: 1912 (5-3/4x15-1/2", B&W)
nn-Newspaper-r by Tad (Thomas A. Dorgan) 33.00 117.00 200.00

SKEEZIX (Also see Gasoline Alley & Little Skeezix Books) (G)
Reilly & Lee Co.: 1925 - 1928 (Strip-r, soft covers) (pictures & text)
and Uncle Walt (1924)-Origin 26.00 104.00 180.00
and Pal (1925) 21.00 84.00 150.00
at the Circus (1926) 21.00 84.00 150.00
& Uncle Walt (1927) 21.00 84.00 150.00
Out West (1928) 21.00 84.00 150.00
Hardback Editions... 34.00 136.00 235.00

SKETCHES OF LOWLY LIFE IN A GREAT CITY (E)
. P. Puntam's Sons: 1899 (8-5/8x11-1/4", 200 pgs, hardcover, B&W)
Reprints from Life and Judge of Woolf's cartoons of NYC slum children)
nn-By Michael Angelo Woolf 150.00 300.00 600.00

GD2.0 FN6.0 VF8.0

NOTE: *Woolf's cartoons are regarded as the primary influence on R.F. Outcault in the later development of The Yellow Kid newspaper strip.*

SKIPPY
No publisher listed: Circa 1920s (10x8", 16 pgs., color/B&W cartoons)
nn-By Percy Crosby 81.00 322.00 565.00

SKIPPY (F)
Grossett & Dunlap: 1929 (7-3/8x6, 370 pgs, hardcover text with some art)
nn-By Percy Crosby (issued with a dust jacket) 21.00 84.00 150.00

SLOVENLY PETER; or, Cheerful Stories and Funny Pictures, For Good Little People. (A & D)
Porter & Coates, Philadelphia: 1880 (4to, 100 pgs. handcolored hardcover)
nn-By Heinrich Hoffman 200.00 400.00 -
NOTE: *Translation of the German "Der Struwwelpeter". The John C. Winston Co. did a number of reprints from at least 1901-1940 which range in price from $95 to $350 plus The Limited Editions Club, New York, published 1500 copies of a Samuel ("Mark Twain") Clemens translated version done in 1891 in Berlin but not printed until 1935 ranges in price from $285 to $450.*

S'MATTER POP? (C)
Saalfield Publ. Co.: 1917 (10x14", 44 pgs., B&W, cardboard-c)
nn-By Charlie Payne; in full color; pages printed on one side 48.00 169.00 290.00

SMITTY (See Treasure Box of Famous Comics) (C)
Cupples & Leon Co.: 1928 - 1933 (9x7", 96 pgs., B&W strip-r, hardcover)
1928-(96 pgs. 7x8-3/4") 41.00 166.00 290.00
1929-At the Ball Game (Babe Ruth on cover) 57.00 229.00 400.00
1930-The Flying Office Boy, 1931-The Jockey, 1932-In the North Woods each... 31.00 126.00 220.00
1933-At Military School 31.00 126.00 220.00
NOTE: *Each hardbound was published with a dust jacket; worth 50% more with dust jacket.*

SOCIAL HELL, THE (H)
Rich Hill: 1902
nn-By Ryan Walker 20.00 70.00 120.00
NOTE: *"The conditions of workers and the corruption of a political system beholden to corporate interests have been a major focus of human rights concerns since the 19th century. This early graphic novel depicts the social evils of unreformed capitalism. Ryan Walker was a syndicate cartoonist for many mainstream newspapers as well as for the communist Daily Worker." This description comes from <http://www.lib.uconn.edu/DoddCenter/ascexh3.html>, where you can find also a reproduction of the cover. I add that Ryan Walker was the editor of "The Saint Louis Republic" comic section since its inception in 1897; the supplement published "Alma and Oliver", George McManus's first series.*

SPORT AND THE KID (see The Umbrella Man)
Lowman & Hanford Co.: 1913 (6-1/4x6-5/8",114 pgs, hardcover, B&W&orange)
nn-By J.R. "Dok" Hager 20.00 70.00 120.00

STRANGE AS IT SEEMS (D)
Blue-Star Publishing Co.: 1932 (64 pgs., B&W, square binding)
1-Newspaper-r 32.00 128.00 225.00
NOTE: Published with and without No. 1 and price on cover.
Ex-Lax giveaway(1936, B&W, 24 pgs., 5x7")-McNaught Synd. 13.00 52.00 90.00

STUFF AND NONSENSE (Harper's Monthly strip-r) (E)
Charles Scribner's Sons: 1884 (10-1/4x7-3/4 ", 100 pgs, hardcover)
nn-By Arthur Burdett Frost 80.00 160.00 -

TAILSPIN TOMMY STORY & PICTURE BOOK (C)
McLoughlin Bros.: No. 266, 1931? (nd) (10x10-1/2", color strip-r)
266-By Forrest 38.00 151.00 265.00

TAILSPIN TOMMY (Also see Famous Feature Stories & The Funnies)(C)
Cupples & Leon Co.: 1932 (100 pgs., hard-c)
nn-(Scarce)-B&W strip reprints from 1930 by Hal Forrest & Glenn Claffin 100.00 300.00 -

TALES OF DEMON DICK AND BUNKER BILL
Whitman Publishing Co.: 1934 (5-1/4x10-1/2", 80 pgs, color hardcover, B&W)
793 - By Spencer 33.00 100.00 200.00

THIMBLE THEATRE
Starring
POPEYE
BY SEGAR
SERIES
No. ONE
25

Thimble Theater #1
© KING

Tillie the Toiler #7
© C&L

Tim McCoy, Police Car 17
© Whitman Publ. Co.

GD2.0 FN6.0 VF8.0

TARZAN BOOK (The Illustrated...) (C)
Grosset & Dunlap: 1929 (9x7", 80 pgs.)

1(Rare)-Contains 1st B&W Tarzan newspaper comics from 1929. By Hal Foster Cloth reinforced spine & dust jacket (50¢); Foster-c
With dust jacket... 82.00 328.00 575.00
Without dust jacket... 33.00 132.00 230.00
2nd Printing(1934, 25¢, 76 pgs.)-4 Foster pgs. dropped; paper spine, circle in lower right cover with 25¢ price. The 25¢ is barely visible on some copies 31.00 124.00 220.00
1967-House of Greystoke reprint-7x10", using the complete 300 illustrations/ text from the 1929 edition minus the original indicia, foreword, etc. Initial version bound in gold paper & sold for $5.00. Officially titled **Burroughs Bibliophile #2**. A very few additional copies were bound in heavier blue paper. Gold binding... 2.25 6.75 18.00
Blue binding... 2.50 7.50 24.00

TARZAN OF THE APES TO COLOR (C)
Saalfield Publishing Co.: No. 988, 1933 (15-1/4x10-3/4", 24 pgs) (Coloring book)

988-(Very Rare)-Contains 1929 daily reprints with some new art by Hal Foster. Two panels blown up large on each page with one at the top of opposing pages on every other double-page spread. Believed to be the only time these panels appeared in color. Most color panels are reproduced a second time in B&W to be colored 257.00 1028.00 1800.00

TARZAN OF THE APES The Big Little Cartoon Book (C)
Whitman Publishing Company: 1933 (4-1/2x3 5/8", 320 pgs, color-c, B&W)

744 - By Hal Foster (comics on every page) 36.00 144.00 250.00

TECK HASKINS AT OHIO STATE (D)
Lea-Mar Press: 1908 (7-1/4x5-3/8", 84 pgs, B&W hardcover)

nn-By W.A. Ireland; football cartoons-r from Columbus Ohio Evening Dispatch 28.00 99.00 170.00
NOTE: *Small blue & white patch of cover art pasted atop a color cloth quilt patter; pasted patch can easily peel off some copies.*

TECK 1909 (D)
Lea-Mar Press: 1909 (8-5/8 x 8-1/8", 124 pgs., B&W hardcover, 25¢)

nn-By W.A. Ireland; Ohio State University baseball cartoons-r from Columbus Evening Dispatch 28.00 99.00 170.00

TEXAS HISTORY MOVIES (C)
various editions, 1928 to 1986 (B&W)

Book I -1928 Southwest Press (7-1/4 x 5-3/8, 56 pgs, cardboard cover) for the Magnolia Petroleum Company 30.00 90.00 180.00
nn-1928 Southwest Press (12-3/8 x 9-1/4, 232 pgs, hardcover) 50.00 150.00 300.00
nn-1935 Magnolia Petroleum Company (6 x 9, 132 pgs, paper cover) 20.00 60.00 120.00
NOTE: *Exists with either Wagon Train or Texas Flag & Lafitte/pirate covers.*
nn-1943 Magnolia Petroleum Company (132 pgs, paper cover) 15.00 45.00 90.00
nn-1963 Graphic Ideas Inc (11 x 8-1/2, softcover) 10.00 30.00 60.00
NOTE: *Reprints daily newspaper strips from the Dallas News, on Texas history. 1935 editions onward distributed within the Texas Public School System. Prior to that they appear to be give-away comic books for the Magnolia Petroleum Company. There are many more editions than the ones pointed out above.*

THAT ROOKIE FROM THE 13TH SQUAD (C)
Harper & Brothers Publishers: Feb 1918 (8x9-1/4", 72 pgs, hardcover, B&W)

nn-By Lieut. P(ercy) L. Crosby 58.00 204.00 350.00

THIMBLE THEATRE STARRING POPEYE (See also Popeye) (C)
Sonnet Publishing Co.: 1931 - No. 2, 1932 (25¢, B&W, 52 pgs.)(Rare)

1-Daily strip serial-r in both by Segar 157.00 628.00 1100.00
2 136.00 544.00 950.00
NOTE: *The very first Popeye reprint book. Popeye first entered Thimble Theatre in 1929.*

THREE FUN MAKERS, THE (C)
Stokes and Company: 1908 (10x15", 64 pgs., color) (1904-06 Sunday strip-r)

nn-Maud, Katzenjammer Kids, Happy Hooligan 314.00 1100.00 -
NOTE: *This is the first comic book to compile more than one strip together.*

TIGERS (Also see On and Off Mount Ararat) (C)
Hearst's New York American & Journal: 1902, 86pgs. 10x15-1/4"

nn-Funny animal strip-r by Jimmy Swinnerton 286.00 1000.00 -

TILLIE THE TOILER (C)
Cupples & Leon Co.: 1925 - No. 8, 1933 (52 pgs., B&W, daily strip-r)

nn (#1) 50.00 200.00 350.0
2-8 37.00 149.00 260.0
NOTE: *First strip appearance was January, 1921.*

TIMID SOUL, THE (C)
Simon & Schuster: 1931 (12-1/4x9", 136 pgs, B&W hardcover, dust jacket?)

nn- By H. T. Webster (newspaper strip-r) 40.00 120.00 240.0

TIM McCOY, POLICE CAR 17
Whitman Publishing Co.: 1934 (14-3/4x11", 32 pgs, stiff color covers)

674-1933 movie illustrated; first movie adaptation in comic books original material? 46.00 186.00 325.0

TOAST BOOK
John C. Winston Co: 1905 (7-1/4 x 6,104 pgs,skull-shaped book, feltcover, B&W

nn-by Clare Dwiggins 50.00 175.00 300.0
NOTE: *Cartoon illustrations accompanying toasts/poems, most involving alcohol.*

TOM SAWYER & HUCK FINN (C)
Stoll & Edwards Co.:1925 (10x10-3/4", 52 pgs, stiff covers)

nn-By Dwiggins; 1923, 1924-r color Sunday strips 35.00 140.00 245.0

TOONERVILLE TROLLEY AND OTHER CARTOONS (C) (See Cartoons by Fontaine Fox)
Cupples & Leon Co.: 1921 (10 x10", 52 pgs., B&W, daily strip-r)

1-By Fontaine Fox 64.00 257.00 450.0

TREASURE BOX OF FAMOUS COMICS (C)
Cupples & Leon Co.: 1934 8-1/2x(6-7/8", 36 pgs, soft covers) (Boxed set of 5 books)

Little Orphan Annie (1926) 21.00 84.00 150.0
Reg'lar Fellers (1928) 19.00 76.00 130.0
Smitty (1928) 19.00 76.00 130.0
Harold Teen (1931) 19.00 76.00 130.0
How Dick Tracy & Dick Tracy Jr. Caught The Racketeers (1933) 26.00 104.00 185.0
Softcover set of five books in box 160.00 640.00 1125.0
Box only 57.00 228.00 400.0
NOTE: *Dates shown are copyright dates; all books actually came out in 1934 or later. The soft-covers are abbreviated versions of the hardcover editions listed under each character.*

TRUTH SAVE IT FROM ABUSE & OVERWORK BEING THE EPISODE OF THE HIRED HAND & MRS. STIX PLASTER, CONCERTIST (C)
Radio Truth Society of WBAP: no date, 1924 (6-3/8 x 4-7/8, 40 pgs, paper cover, B&W)

nn - by V.T. Hamlin (Very Rare) 100.00 400.00 700.0
NOTE: *Radio station WBAP giveaway reprints strips from the Ft. Worth Texas Star-Telegram s at local radio station. 1st collected work by V.T. Hamlin, pre-Alley Oop.*

TWENTY FIVE YEARS AGO (see At The Bottom Of The Ladder) (D)
Coward-McCann: 1931 (5-3/4x8-1/4, 328 pgs, hardcover, B&W)

nn - By Camillus Kessler 32.00 128.00 225.0
NOTE: Multi-image panel cartoons showing historical events for dates during the year

UMBRELLA MAN, THE (See Sport And The Kid)
Lowman & Hanford Co.: 1911 (8-7/8x5-1/8",112 pgs, paperback, B&W&orang

nn - By J.R. "Dok" Hager (Seattle Times-r) 20.00 70.00 120.0

UNCLE BANTAM'S FUNNY BOOKS, FOR THE AMUSEMENT OF HIS LITTL NEPHEWS AND NIECES. WITH SEVENTY-FIVE ILLUSTRATIONS. (A & D)
Philadelphia: Davis Porter & Co.: 1865 (Quarto, 54 pgs, col. ill. ; pictorial paper covered boards) (See also Slovenly Peter)

When a Feller Needs a Friend
© P.F. Volland & Co.

Willie and His Papa and the Rest of the Family
© G&D

The Yellow Kid #4
© Howard Ainslee & Co.

GD2.0 FN6.0 VF8.0

nn-By Heinrich Hoffman 500.00 1000.00 -
NOTE: *Translation of "Der Struwwelpeter", first published in Germany in 1844. Hand-colored illustrations with lines of verse. This is a complete collection of six of the "Uncle Bantam's Funny Books" in one volume, each with 8 pgs.*

UNCLE REMUS AND BRER RABBIT (C)
Frederick A. Stokes Co.: 1907 (64 pgs, hardbound, color)
nn - By Joel C Harris & J.M. Conde 50.00 175.00 300.00

UPSIDE DOWNS OF LITTLE LADY LOVEKINS AND OLD MAN MUFFAROO
New York Herald: 1905 (?) (C)
nn- by Gustav Verbeck 100.00 350.00 600.00

VAUDEVILLES AND OTHER THINGS (C)
Isaac H. Blandiard Co.: 1900 (13x10-1/2", 22 pgs., color) plus two reprints
nn-By Bunny (Scarce) 229.00 800.00 -
nn-2nd print "By the Creator of Foxy Grandpa" on-c but only has copyright info of 1900 (10-1/2x15 1/2, 28 pgs, color) 171.00 600.00
nn-3rd print. "By the creator of Foxy Grandpa" on-c; has both 1900 and 1901 copyright info (11x13") 171.00 600.00 -

VIGNETTES OF LIFE
The Reilly & Lee Co.: 1930 (9x12-1/4", 104 pgs, hardcover w/dust jacket, B&W)
nn-By Norman J. Lynd (intro by C.D. Gibson) 20.00 60.00 90.00

WALLY - HIS CARTOONS OF THE A.E.F. (C)
Stars & Stripes: 1917 (7x18; 96 pgs, B&W)
nn-By Wally Wallgeen 20.00 70.00 120.00
NOTE: *World War One cartoons reprints from Stars & Stripes; sold to U.S. servicemen with profits to go to French War Orphans Fund.*

WAR CARTOONS (D)
Dallas News: 1918 (11x9", 112 pgs, hardcover, B&W)
nn-By John Knott (WWOne cartoons) 20.00 70.00 120.00

WHEN A FELLER NEEDS A FRIEND (D)
P. F. Volland & Co.: 1914 (11-11/16x8-7/8)
nn-By Clare Briggs 37.00 131.00 225.00
NOTE: *Originally came in box with Briggs art (box is Rare - worth more with box. There are also numerous more modern reprints)*

WILD PILGRIMAGE (H)
Harrison Smith & Robert Haas: 1932 (9-7/8x7", 210 pgs, B&W hardcover w/dust jacket) (original wordless graphic novel in woodcuts)
nn-By Lynd Ward - - -

WILLIE AND HIS PAPA AND THE REST OF THE FAMILY (D)
Grossett & Dunlap: 1901 (9-1/2x8", 200 pgs, hardcover from N.Y. Evening Journal by Permission of W. R. Hearst) (pictures & text)
nn-By Frederick Opper 50.00 175.00 300.00
NOTE: *Political satire series of single panel cartoons, involving whiny child Willie (President William McKinley), his rambunctious and uncontrollable cousin Teddy (Vice President Roosevelt), and Willie's Papa (trusts/monopolies) and their Maid (Senator) Hanna.*

WILLIE GREEN COMICS, THE (C)
Frank M. Acton Co./Harris Brown: 1915 (8x15, 36 pgs); 1921 (6x10-1/8", 52 pgs, color paper cover, B&W interior, 25¢)
Book No. 1 By Harris Brown 45.00 158.00 270.00
Book 2 (#2 sold via mail order directly from the artist)(rare) 45.00 158.00 270.00
NOTE: *Book No. 1 possible reprint of Adv. of Willie Green.*

WILLIE WESTINGHOUSE EDISON SMITH THE BOY INVENTOR (C)
William A. Stokes Co.: 1906 (10x16", 36 pgs. in color)
nn-By Frank Crane (Scarce) 214.00 750.00 -

WINNIE WINKLE (C)
Cupples & Leon Co.: 1930 - No. 4, 1933 (52 pgs., B&W daily strip-r)
1 39.00 157.00 275.00
2-4 26.00 106.00 185.00

WISDOM OF CHING CHOW, THE (see also The Gumps)
R. J. Jefferson Printing Co.: 1928 (4x3", 100 pgs, red & B&W cardboard cover) (newspaper strip-r The Chicago Tribune)
nn-By Sidney Smith (scarce) 20.00 80.00 120.00

WORLD OF TROUBLE, A (D)
Minneapolis Journal: 1901 (10x8-3/4", 100 pgs, 40 pgs full color)
v3#1 - By Charles L. Bartholomew (editorial-r) 28.00 99.00 170.00

WORLD OVER, THE (F)
G. W. Dillingham Company, New York: 1897 (192 pgs, hardbound)
nn-By Joe Kerr; 80 illus by R.F. Outcault 200.00 700.00 -

YELLOW KID, THE (Magazine)(E)(becomes The Yellow Book #10 on)
Howard Ainslee & Co., N.Y.: Mar. 20, 1897 - #9, July 17, 1897 (5¢, B&W w/color covers, 52p., stapled) (not a comic book)
1-R.F. Outcault Yellow kid on-c only #1-6. The same Yellow Kid color ad app. on back-c #1-6 (advertising the New York Sunday Journal) 857.00 3000.00 -
2-6 (#2 4/3/97, #5 5/22/97, #6, 6/5/97) 743.00 2600.00 -
7-9 (Yellow Kid not on-c) 121.00 425.00 -
NOTE: *Richard Outcault's Yellow Kid from the Hearst New York American represents the very first successful newspaper comic strip in America. Listed here due to historical importance.*

YELLOW KID IN MCFADDEN'S FLATS, THE (C)
G. W. Dillingham Company, New York: 1897 (50¢, 7-1/2x5-1/2", 196 pgs., B&W, squarebound)
nn-The first "comic" book featuring The Yellow Kid; E. W. Townsend narrative w/R. F. Outcault Sunday comic page art-r & some original drawings 5000.00 8500.00 -

A VERY SHORT LIST OF RECOMMENDED REFERENCE TOOLS:

A HISTORY OF AMERICAN GRAPHIC HUMOR by William Murrell
Vol. 1: 1747-1865 (Whitney Museum of Art, New York: 1933)
Vol 2: 1865-1938 (Whitney Museum of Art, New York: 1938)
CARTOON CAVALCADE By Thomas Craven (Simon & Schuster, 1943)
THE COMICS By Coulton Waugh (Macmillian, 1947)
FROM CAVE PAINTING TO COMIC STRIPS By L. Hogben (Chanticleer, 1949)
COMIC ART IN AMERICA By Stephen Becker (Simon & Schuster, 1959)
THE HISTORY OF THE COMIC STRIP by David Kunzle
Vol 1: THE EARLY COMIC STRIP c1450-1825 (Univ of Calif Press, 1973)
Vol 2: THE NINETEENTH CENTURY (Univ of Calif. Press, 1991)
THE COMICS By Jerry Robinson (G Putnam's Sons, 1974)
NEMO MAGAZINE edited by Richard Marschall (FBI, 1983-1991)
THE INTERNATIONAL BOOK OF COMICS By Denis Gifford (Crescent, 1984)
HISTORY OF THE COMIC BOOK:1899-1936 By Charles Wooley (Wooley,1986)
AMERICA'S GREAT COMIC-STRIP ARTISTS By Richard Marschall (1989, 97)
A REJECTION OF ORDER, THE DEVELOPMENT OF THE NEWSPAPER COMIC STRIP IN AMERICA, 1830-1920 By Elsa Ann Nystrom (UMI, 1989)
THE AMERICAN COMIC BOOK CATALOGUE: THE EVOLUTIONARY ERA, 1884-1939 By Denis Gifford (Mansell Publishing, London: 1990)
THE ART OF THE FUNNIES By RC Harvey (Univ of Mississippi Press, 1994)
INKS CARTOON & COMIC ART STUDIES ed. by Lucy Caswell (OSU, 1994-97)
THE COMIC STRIP CENTURY By Bill Blackbeard Two volume set (KSP, 1995)
THE FUNNIES:100 Years of American Comic Strips By Ron Goulart(Adams,1995)
THE YELLOW KID edited by Bill Blackbeard (KSP, 1995)
COMIC STRIPS & CONSUMER CULTURE By Ian Gordon (Smithsonian, 1998)
FORGING A NEW MEDIUM edited by Lefevre& Dierick (VUB University, 1998)
WEIRD BUT TRUE TOON FACTOIDS By Craig Yoe (Random House, 1999)

For a free, lively e-mail discussion group of Platinum Age comics collectors, fans, enthusiasts, dealers, and scholars you can join to look, listen, learn, and share by going to PlatinumAgeComics@eGroups.com as well as The Grand Comics Database at www.comics.org. Also go www.bugpowder.com/andy/early and www.geocities.com/~quesinberry/comics/comllst for more great resources.

The American Comic Book: 1933-PRESENT

THE GOLDEN AGE AND BEYOND: ORIGINS OF THE MODERN COMIC BOOK

by Robert L. Beerbohm & Richard D. Olson, PhD
©2000

***Standard Oil Comics Weekly* #14, 1933. Newly discovered comics tabloid, same size as *Gulf Funny Weekly*. But where are the earlier issues that supposedly exist?**

The formats that comic publishing pioneer Cupples & Leon popularized in 1919, although similar in appearance to comics of the Golden Age, are quite different in appearance from today's comics. Even so, the books and those formats were consistently successful until 1929, when they had to compete against The Great Depression; the Depression eventually won. One major reason for a format change was that at a cost of 25¢ per book for the 10" x 10" cardboard style and 60¢ for the 7" x 8 1/2" dustjacketed hardcovers, the price became increasingly prohibitive for most consumers already stifled by the crushed economy. As a result, all Cupples & Leon style books published between 1929-1935 are much rarer than their earlier counterparts because most Americans had little money to spend after paying for necessities like food and shelter.

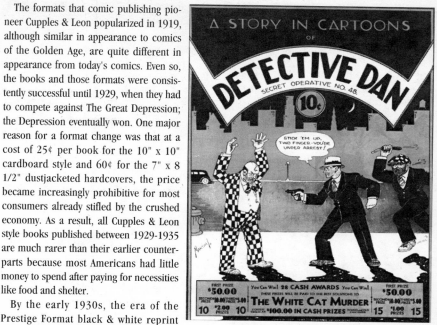

Detective Dan, early 1933, Humor Publishing Co. The first original newsstand comic book and direct inspiration for Siegel and Shuster to convert Superman into a comic book.

By the early 1930s, the era of the Prestige Format black & white reprint comic book was over. In 1932-33 a lot of format variations arose, collecting such newspaper strips as **Bobby Thatcher**, **Bringing Up Father**, **Buck Rogers**, **Dick Tracy**, **Happy Hooligan**, **Joe Palooka**, **Just Kids**, **The Little King**, **Little Orphan Annie**, **Men of Daring**, **Mickey Mouse**, **Moon Mullins**, **Mutt & Jeff**, **Smitty**, **Tailspin Tommy**, **Tarzan**, **Thimble Theater starring Popeye**, **Tillie the Toiler**, **Winnie Winkle**, and the **Highlights of History** series. With the 1933 newsstand appearance of Humor's **Detective Dan**, **Adventures of Detective Ace King**, **Bob Scully**, **Two Fisted Hick Detective**, and others, these little understood original material comic books were the direct inspiration for Jerry Siegel and Joe Shuster to transform their fanzine character **The Superman** from **Science Fiction** #3 (January 1933) into a comic strip that would stand as a watershed mark in American pop culture. The stage was set for a new frontier.

Prior to Humor's very rare output, there was Embee's **Comic Monthly**'s dozen issues in 1922, and several dozen of Dell's **The Funnies** tabloid in 1929-30. All except **Comic Monthly** contained only original material and still failed. With another format change, however, including four colors, double page counts and a hefty price reduction (starting for free as promotional premiums due to the nationwide numbing effects of worldwide deflation), the birthing pangs of the modern American comic book occurred in late 1932. Created out of desperation, to keep the printing presses rolling, the modern American comic book was born when a 45-year-old sales manager for Eastern Color Printing Company of New York reinvented the format.

Harry I. Wildenberg's job was to come up with ideas that would sell color printing for Eastern, a company which also printed the comic sections for a score of newspapers, including the **Boston Globe**, the **Brooklyn Times**, the **Providence Journal**, and the **Newark Ledger**. Down-time meant less take-home pay, so Wildenberg was always racking his brains for something to fit the color presses. He was fascinated by the miles of funny sheets which rolled off Eastern's presses

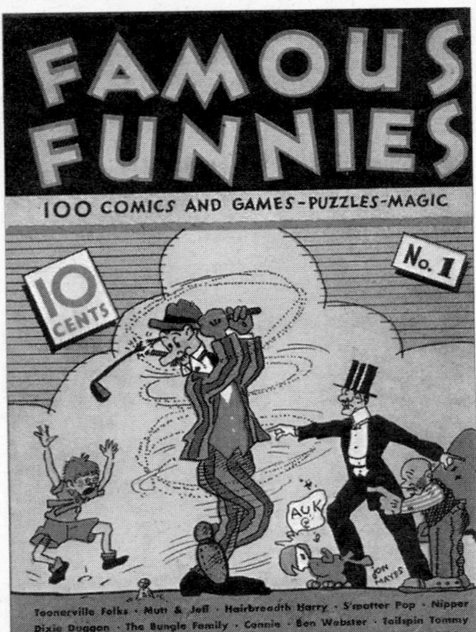

Famous Funnies #1, July 1934, was the first successful newsstand comic book, and it ran until 1955.

each week, and he constantly sought new ways to exploit their commercial possibilities. If the funny papers were this popular, he reasoned, they should prove a good advertising medium. He decided to suggest a comics tabloid to one of his clients.

That client, Gulf Oil Company, liked the idea, and hired a few artists to create an original comic called **Gulf Comic Weekly**. The comic was dated April 1933 and was 10 1/2" x 15". It was the first comic to be advertised nationally on the radio beginning April 30th. Its first artists were Stan Schendel doing **The Uncovered Wagon**, Victor doing **Curly and the Kids**, and Svess on a strip named **Smileage**. All were full page, full color comic strips. Wildenberg promptly had Eastern print this four page comic, making it probably the first tabloid newsprint comic published for American distribution outside of a newspaper in the 20th Century. Wildenberg and Gulf were astonished when the tabloids were grabbed up as fast as Gulf service stations could offer them. Distribution shot up to 3,000,000 copies a week after Gulf changed the name to **Gulf Funny Weekly**. The series remained a tabloid until early 1939 and ran for 422 issues until May 23, 1941.

Recent research has also turned up "new" unrediscovered comics material from other oil companies from this same time span of 1933-34. Perhaps spurred by the runaway success of **Gulf Funny Weekly**, these other oil companies found they had to compete with licensed comic strip material of their own in order to remain profitable. The authors of this essay are actively soliciting help in uncovering more information regarding the following:

There are at least 14 issues (and possibly many more) of a four page tabloid-size full color comics giveaway titled **Standard Oil Comics**, dating from 1933. The issues seen so far contain Fred Opper's **Si and Mirandi**, an older couple who interact with perennial favorites, **Happy Hooligan** and **Maud the Mule**. Other strips include **Pesty And His Pop** and **Smiling Slim** by Sid Hicks. Considering the concept of **Gulf Funny Weekly** has been well known for decades while **Standard Oil Comics** remains virtually unknown, our guess is **Gulf Comic Weekly** began first and ran many years longer than Rockefeller's version.

Beginning with the March-April 1934 issue of **Shell Globe** (V4 #2), characters from Bud Fisher (**Mutt & Jeff**) and Fontaine Fox (**Toonerville Folks**) were licensed to sell gas & oil for this company. 52,000 eight foot standees were made for Fisher's **Mutt and Jeff** and Fox's **Powerful Katrinka and the Skipper** for placement around 13,000 Shell gas stations. Augmenting them was an army of 250,000 miniature figures of the same characters. In addition, more than 1,000,000 play masks were given away to children along with more than 285,000 window stickers. If that wasn't enough, hundreds of thousands of 3x5 foot posters featuring these characterswere released in conjunction with twenty-four sheet outdoor billboards. Radio announcements of this promotion began running April 7th, 1934. It is presently unknown if Shell had a comics tabloid created to give away to customers.

The idea for creating an actual comic book, however, did not occur to Wildenberg until later in 1933, when he was idly folding a newspaper in halves then in quarters. As he looked at the twice-folded paper, it occurred to him that it was a convenient book size (actually it was late stage "Dime Novel" size, which companies like Street & Smith were pumping out). The format had its heyday from the 1880s through the 1910s, having been invented by the firm of Beadle and Adam in 1860 in more of a digest format. According to a 1942 article by Max Gaines, another contributing factor in the development of the format was an inspection of a promotional folder published by the Ledger Syndicate, in which four-color Sunday comic pages were printed in 7" x 9".

According to a 1949 interview with Wildenberg, he thought "why not a comic book? It would have 32 or 64 pages and make a fine item for concerns which distribute premiums." Wildenberg obtained publishing rights to certain Associated, Bell, Fisher, McNaught and Public Ledger Syndicate comics, had an artist make up a few dummies by hand, and then had his sales staff walk them around to his biggest advertisers. Wildenberg received a telegram from Proctor & Gamble for an order of a million copies for a 32-page color comic magazine called **Funnies on Parade**. The entire print run was given away in just a few weeks in the Spring of 1933.

Also working for Eastern Color at this same time were quite a few future legends of the comics business, such as Max Gaines, Lev Gleason and a fellow named Harold Moore (all sales staff directly underneath the supervision of Wildenberg), Sol Harrison as a color separator, and George Dougherty Sr. as a printer. All of them worked on the **Funnies on Parade** project. Morris Margolis was brought in from Charlton

Publications in Derby, Connecticut to solve binding problems centered on getting the pages in proper numerical sequence on that last fold to "modern" comic book size. All were infected with the comics bug for mostof the rest of their lives.

The success of **Funnies on Parade** quickly led to Eastern publishing additional giveaway books in the same format by late 1933, including the 32 page **Famous Funnies A Carnival of Comics**, the 100 page **A Century of Comics** and **Skippy's Own Book of Comics**; the latter became the first "new" format comic book about a single character. These thicker issues had press runs of up to 500,000 per title. The idea that anyone would pay for them seemed fantastic to Wildenberg, so Max Gaines stickered ten cents on several dozen of the latest premium, **Famous Funnies A Carnival of Comics**, as a test, and talked a couple newsstands into participating in this experiment. The copies sold out over the weekend and newsies asked for more.

Not to be outdone, Shell Oil began a huge comics promotion in March 1934 to compete with Gulf and Standard Oil.

Eastern sales staffers then approached Woolworth's. The late Oscar Fitz-Alan Douglas, sales brains of Woolworth, showed some interest, but after several months of deliberation decided the book would not give enough value for ten cents. Kress, Kresge, McCrory, and several other dime stores turned them down even more abruptly. Wildenberg next went to George Hecht, editor of **Parents Magazine**, and tried to persuade him to run a comic supplement or publish a "higher level" comic magazine. Hecht also frowned on the idea.

In Wildenberg's 1949 interview, he

noted that "even the comic syndicates couldn't see it. 'Who's going to read old comics?' they asked." With the failures of **Comic Monthly** and **The Funnies** still fresh in some minds, no one could see why children would pay ten cents for a comic magazine when they could get all they want for free in a Sunday newspaper. But Wildenberg had become convinced that children as well as grown-ups were not getting all the comics they wanted in the Sunday papers; otherwise, the **Gulf Comic Weekly** and the premium comics would not have met with such success. Wildenberg said, "I decided that if boys and girls were willing to work for premium coupons to obtain comic books, they might be willing to pay ten cents on the newsstands." This conviction was also strengthened by Max Gaines' ten cent sticker experiment.

George Janosik, the president of Eastern Color, then called on George Delacorte to form a 50-50 joint venture to publish and market a comic book "magazine" for retail sales, but American News turned them down cold. The magazine monopoly also remembered Delacorte's abortive **The Funnies** from just a few years before. After much discussion on how to proceed, Delacorte finally agreed to publish it and a partnership was formed. They printed 40,000 copies for distribution to a few chain stores. Known today as **Famous Funnies Series One**, half of its pages came from reprints of the reprints in **Funnies on Parade** and **Famous Funnies A Carnival of Comics**.

With 68 full-color pages at only ten cents a piece, it sold out in thirty days with not a single returned copy. Delacorte refused to print a second edition. "Advertisers won't use it," he complained. "They say it's not dignified enough." The profit, however, was approximately $2,000. This particular edition is the rarest of all these early Eastern comic book experiments.

In early 1934, while riding the train, another Eastern Color employee named Harold A. Moore read an account from a prominent New York newspaper that indicated they owed much of their circulation success to their comics section. Mr. Moore went back to Harry Gold, President of American News, with the article in hand. He succeeded in acquiring a print order for 250,000 copies for a proposed monthly comics magazine. In May 1934, **Famous Funnies** #1 (with a July cover date) hit the newsstands with Steven O. Douglass as its only editor (even though Harold Moore was listed as such in #1) until it ceased publication some twenty years later. It was a 64-page version of the 32-page giveaways, and more importantly, it still sold for a dime! The first issue lost $4,150.60. Ninety percent of the copies sold out and a second issue dated September debuted in July. From then on, the comic book was published monthly. **Famous Funnies** also began carrying original material, apparently as early as the second issue. With #3, **Buck Rogers** took center stage and stayed there for the next twenty years, with covers by Frank Frazetta -- some of his best comics work ever.

Delacorte got cold feet and sold back his interest to Eastern, even though the seventh issue cleared a profit of $2,664.25. Wildenberg emphasized that Eastern could make a manufacturer's

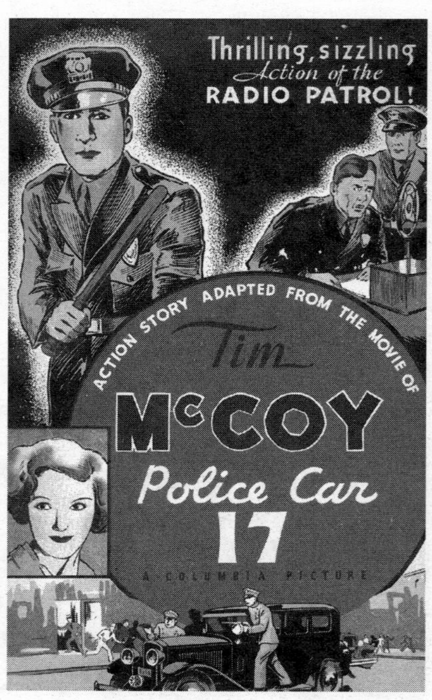

Tim McCoy Police Car 17, Whitman's first comic (1934), and also the first movie adaptation comic book. This has been a sleeper for too long.

King Comics #1, April 1936, marking King Features Syndicate's entry into the new 64 page color comic market and featuring the first appearances of Flash Gordon, Popeye, and Mandrake the Magician.

profit by printing its own books as well as the publishing profits once it was distributed. Every issue showed greater sales than the preceding one, until within a year, close to a million 64-page books were being sold monthly at ten cents apiece; Eastern received the lion's share of the receipts, and soon found it was netting $30,000 per issue. The comic syndicates received $640 ($10 a page) for publishing rights. Original material could be obtained from budding professionals for just $5 a page. According to Will Eisner in R. C. Harvey's **The Art of the Comic Book**, the prices then paid for original material had a long range effect of keeping creator wages low for years.

Initially, Eastern's experiment was eyed with skepticism by the publishing world, but within a year or so after **Famous Funnies** was nonchalantly placed on sale alongside slicker magazines like **Atlantic Monthly** or **Harper's**, at least five other competitors entered the field. In late 1934, pulp writer turned publisher Major Wheeler-Nicholson introduced **New Fun** #1 at almost tabloid-size containing all original material. Around this same time, Whitman brought out the first original material movie adaptation, **Tim McCoy Police Car 17**, in the tabloid New Fun format with stiff card covers. A few years before, they had introduced the new comics formats known as the **Big Little Book** and the **Big Big Book**. The **BLB** and **BBB** formats would go toe-to-toe with Eastern's creation throughout the 1930s, but Eastern would win out.

The very last 10" x 10" comic books pioneered by Cupples & Leon were published in mid-1935 by the David McKay Company. In late 1935, Max Gaines (with his youthful assistant Sheldon Mayer) reached an agreement with George Delacorte (who was reentering the comic book business a third time) and McClure Syndicate (a growing newspaper comic strip enterprise) to reprint newspaper comic strips in **Popular Comics**. Also by late 1935, Lev Gleason, another pioneer who participated in **Funnies on Parade**, had become the first editor of United Feature's own **Tip Top Comics**. In 1939 he would begin publishing his own titles, creating the crime comic book as a separate popular genre by 1942 with **Crime Does Not Pay**.

Industry giant King Features introduced **King Comics** #1 (April 1936) through publisher David McKay, with Ruth Plumly Thompson as editor. McKay had already been issuing various format comic books with King Feature characters for a few years, including **Mickey Mouse**, **Henry**, **Popeye** and **Secret Agent X-9**, wherein Dashiell Hammett received cover billing and Alex Raymond was listed simply as "illustrator." McKay readily adapted to this format. Soon most young comic book illustrators were copying Raymond's style.

The following month, William Cook and John Mahon, former disgruntled employees of Wheeler-Nicholson, brought out **The Comics Magazine** #1 (May 1936). This was followed by

In the early 1950s, Carl Barks increased the circulation of WDCS to over 4 million per issue, and in 1952 his creation, Uncle Scrooge, got his own comic book, selling over a million an issue while the superhero slumbered.

Henle Publishing issuing **Wow**, which contained the earliest comics work of Will Eisner, Bob Kane, Dick Briefer and others. By the end of 1936, Cook and Mahon pioneered the first single theme comic books: **Funny Picture Stories** (adventure), **Detective Picture Stories** (crime), and **Western Picture Stories** (the Western). The company would eventually be known historically as Centaur Comics, and serve as the subject of endless debate among fan historians regarding their earliest origins.

Almost forty years after the first newspaper strip comic book compilations were issued at the dawn of international popularity for American comic strips, the race was on to get out of the starting block. In late 1937 Major Wheeler-Nicholson stumbled when he couldn't pay his printing bill to Harry Donenfeld. In a recent intervew, Harry's son, Irwin, said "in 1932 my father and Paul Sampliner started Independent News with Jack Liebowitz as the accountant. The company was begun with Paul Sampliner's mother's money. If it hadn't been for her investments into building the distribution as well as purchasing color printing presses, there might never have been a DC Comics."

Soon after the Major lost control of his company, **Action Comics** #1 was published with a cover date of June 1938, and the Golden Age of superhero comics had begun. Early in 1938 at McClure Syndicate, Max Gaines and Shelly Mayer showed editor Vin Sullivan a many times rejected sample strip. Sullivan then talked Harry Donenfeld, Paul Sampliner and Jack Liebowitz into publishing Jerry Siegel and Joe Shuster's creation, **The Last Son of Krypton**. This was followed in 1939 by a lucrative partnership for Gaines with the Detective Comics people in the All-American Comics Group.

While there's a great deal of controversy surrounding such labeling, the Golden Age is often viewed these days as beginning with **Action Comics** #1 and continuing through the end of World War II. There was a time not that long ago that the newspaper reprint comic book was collected with more fervor than the heroic comics of the '40s. **Feature Book** #26, **Four Color** #10 and **Single Series** #20 were the holy grails of collecting.

The Atom Age began in early 1946, revamping the industry once again as circulations soon hit their all-time highs with over a billion issues sold a year. By the early 1950s one in three periodicals sold in the USA was a comic book. This continued until the advent of the self-censoring, industry-stifling Comics Code, created in response to a public outcry spearheaded by Dr. Frederic Wertham's tirade against the American comics industry, published in book form as **Seduction of the Innocent**.

It took a year or two to recover from that moralistic assault, with many historians concluding that the Silver Age of Superheroes began with the publication of **Showcase** #4 in 1956, continuing through those turbulent times until Jack Kirby left Marvel for DC in 1969. Others point to the 1952 releases of Kurtzman's **MAD** #1 and Bark's **Uncle Scrooge Four Color** #386 (#1) as true Silver, since those titles soon broke the "million sold per issue" mark when the rest of the comic book industry was reeling from the effects of the public uproar fueled by Wertham.

The Bronze Age has been generally stated to begin when the Code approved newsstand comic book industry raised its standard cover price from 12 to 15 cents. As circulations plummeted after the **Batman** TV craze wore off by 1968 and the superhero glut withered on the stands, out in San Francisco cartoonist Robert Crumb's creator-owned **Zap Comics** #1 appeared, printed by Charles Plymell. Soon thereafter, Jay Lynch and Skip Williamson brought out **Bijou Funnies**, Gilbert Shelton self-published **Feds N Heads** and Crumb let S. Clay Wilson, Victor Moscoso and Rick Griffin into **Zap**.

As originally published by the Print Mint beginning with #2, **Zap Comics** almost single-handedly spawned an industry with tremendous growth in alternative comix running through the 1970s. During this decade the San Francisco Bay Area was an intense hotbed of comix being issued without a comics code "seal of approval" from companies such as Rip Off Press, Last Gasp, San Francisco Comic Book Company, Cpmpany & Sons, Weirdom Publications, Star*Reach, and Comics & Comix. Kitchen Sink prospered for many years in Wisconsin and many small press comix publishers scattered across the USA and Canada issued single titles.

With the advent of the Direct Market by 1979, the last 20 years have generally been called The Modern Age, although there are hints of a new age emerging since the mid-1990s. In each of the above Ages, however, the secret for consumers and collectors has remained the same: buy what you enjoy. We did, and we're still collectors today!

Zap Comics #1, Feb. 1968, paved the way for the introduction of the Direct Market and has sold over a million copies, continuously in print for over 30 years. Last Gasp's first comic was Slow Death #1 (1970), below left, with a cover by Greg Irons. Bijou Funnies #8 (1973) by Kitchen Sink sports a cover by Harvey Kurtzman!

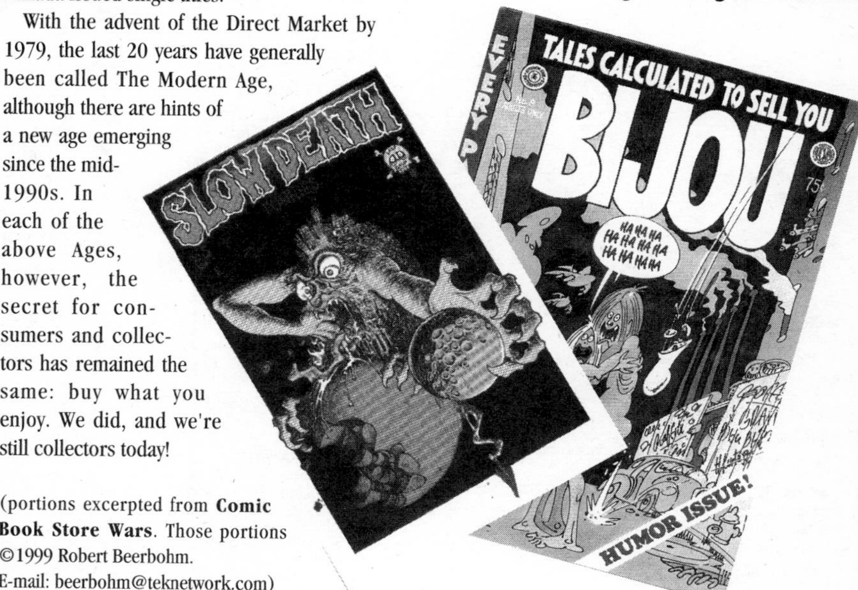

(portions excerpted from **Comic Book Store Wars**. Those portions ©1999 Robert Beerbohm. E-mail: beerbohm@teknetwork.com)

Abbott & Costello #15 © STJ

Ace Comics #63 © DMP

Acme Novelty Library #1 © Chris Ware

The correct title listing for each comic book can be determined by consulting the indicia (publication data) on the beginning interior pages of the comic. The official title is determined by those words of the title in capital letters only, and not by what is on the cover.

Titles are listed in this book as if they were one word, ignoring spaces, hyphens, and apostrophes, to make finding titles easier. Comic books listed should be assumed to be in color unless noted "B&W".

Comic publishers are invited to send us sample copies for possible inclusion in future guides.

Near Mint is the highest value listed in this price guide. True mint books from the 1970s through the present do exist, so the Near Mint value listed should be interpreted as a Mint value for those books.

A-1 (See A-One)

AARON STRIPS
Image Comics: Apr, 1997 - No. 4, Oct, 1997;
Amazing Aaron Prod.: No. 5, Jan, 1999 - Present ($2.95, B&W)

1-6-Reprints Adventures of Aaron newspaper strips 3.00

ABBIE AN' SLATS (...With Becky No. 1-4) (See Comics On Parade, Fight for Love, Giant Comics Edition 2, Giant Comics Editions #1, Sparkler Comics, Tip Topper, Treasury of Comics, & United Comics)
United Features Syndicate: 1940; March, 1948 - No. 4, Aug, 1948 (Reprints)

Single Series 25 ('40) 38.00 113.00 300.00
Single Series 28 32.00 96.00 255.00
1 (1948) 17.00 51.00 135.00
2-4: 3-r/Sparkler #68-72 9.30 28.00 65.00

ABBOTT AND COSTELLO (...Comics)(See Giant Comics Editions #1 & Treasury of Comics)
St. John Publishing Co.: Feb, 1948 - No. 40, Sept, 1956 (Mort Drucker-a in most issues)

1 55.00 165.00 500.00
2 29.00 87.00 235.00
3-9 (#8, 8/49; #9, 2/50) 18.00 54.00 140.00
10-Son of Sinbad story by Kubert (new) 22.00 66.00 175.00
11,13-20 (#11, 10/50; #13, 8/51; #15, 12/52) 13.00 39.00 105.00
12-Movie issue 14.00 41.00 110.00
21-30: 28-r/#8. 30-Painted-c 10.00 30.00 75.00
31-40: 33,38-Reprints 7.85 23.50 55.00
3-D #1 (11/53, 25¢)-Infinity-c 35.00 105.00 280.00

ABBOTT AND COSTELLO (TV)
Charlton Comics: Feb, 1968 - No. 22, Aug, 1971 (Hanna-Barbera)

1 7.25 21.75 80.00
2 3.45 10.35 38.00
3-10 3.00 9.00 32.00
11-22 2.50 7.50 24.00

ABC (See America's Best TV Comics)

ABE SAPIEN: DRUMS OF THE DEAD
Dark Horse Comics: Mar, 1998 ($2.95, one-shot)

1-McDonald-s/Thompson-a. Hellboy back-up; Mignola-s/a/c 3.00

A. BIZARRO
DC Comics: Jul, 1999 - No. 4, Oct, 1999 (2.50, limited series)

1-4-Gerber-s/Bright-a 2.50

ABOMINATIONS (See Hulk)
Marvel Comics: Dec, 1996 - No. 3, Feb, 1997 (1.50, limited series)

1-3-Future Hulk stoyline 2.00

ABRAHAM LINCOLN LIFE STORY (See Dell Giants)

ABRAHAM STONE
Marvel Comics (Epic): July, 1995 - No. 2, Aug, 1995 ($6.95, limited series)

1,2-Joe Kubert-s/a 7.00

ABSENT-MINDED PROFESSOR, THE
Dell Publishing Co.: Apr, 1961 (Disney)

Four Color #1199-Movie, photo-c 6.70 20.00 80.00

ABSOLUTE VERTIGO
DC Comics (Vertigo): Winter, 1995 (99¢, mature)

nn-1st app. Preacher. Previews upcoming titles including Jonah Hex: Riders of the Worm, The Invisibles (King Mob), The Eaters, Ghostdancing & Preacher 1.00 3.00 8.00

ABYSS, THE (Movie)
Dark Horse Comics: June, 1989 - No. 2, July, 1989 ($2.25, limited series)

1,2-Adaptation of film; Kaluta & Moebius-a 2.50

ACCELERATE
DC Comics (Vertigo): Aug, 2000 - No. 4, Nov, 2000 ($2.95, limited series)

1-4-Pander Bros.-a/Kadrey-s 3.00

ACCLAIM ADVENTURE ZONE
Acclaim Books: 1997 ($4.50, digest size)

1-Short stories of Turok, Troublemakers, Ninjak and others 4.50

ACE COMICS
David McKay Publications: Apr, 1937 - No. 151, Oct-Nov, 1949 (All contain some newspaper strip reprints)

1-Jungle Jim by Alex Raymond, Blondie, Ripley's Believe It Or Not, Krazy Kat begin (1st app. of each) 310.00 930.00 3250.00
2 95.00 285.00 900.00
3-5 63.00 189.00 600.00
6-10 47.00 141.00 420.00
11-The Phantom begins (1st app., 2/38) (in brown costume) 74.00 222.00 700.00
12-20 40.00 120.00 325.00
21-25,27-30 35.00 105.00 280.00
26-Origin & 1st app. Prince Valiant (5/39); begins series? 95.00 285.00 900.00
31-40: 37-Krazy Kat ends 25.00 75.00 200.00
41-60 18.00 54.00 145.00
61-64,66-76-(7/43; last 68 pgs.) 16.00 49.00 130.00
65-(8/42)-Flag-c 18.00 54.00 145.00
77-84 (3/44; all 60 pgs.) 13.00 39.00 105.00
85-99 (52 pgs.) 11.00 33.00 90.00
100 (7/45; last 52 pgs.) 12.50 37.50 100.00
101-134: 128-(11/47)-Brick Bradford begins. 134-Last Prince Valiant (all 36 pgs.) 9.30 28.00 65.00
135-151: 135-(6/48)-Lone Ranger begins 8.35 25.00 58.00

ACE KELLY (See Tops Comics & Tops In Humor)

ACE KING (See Adventures of Detective...)

ACES
Acme Press (Eclipse): Apr, 1988 - No. 5, Dec, 1988 ($2.95, B&W, magazine)

1-5 3.00

ACES HIGH
E.C. Comics: Mar-Apr, 1955 - No. 5, Nov-Dec, 1955

1-Not approved by code 17.50 52.00 190.00
2 10.00 30.00 110.00
3-5 9.00 27.00 100.00

NOTE: *All have stories by **Davis**, **Evans**, **Krigstein**, and **Wood**. **Evans** c-1-5.*

ACES HIGH
Gemstone Publishing: Apr, 1999 - No. 5, Aug, 1999 ($2.50)

1-5-Reprints E.C. issues 2.50
Annual 1 ($13.50) r/#1-5 13.50

ACME NOVELTY LIBRARY, THE
Fantagraphics Books: Winter 1993-94 - Present (quarterly, various sizes)

1-Introduces Jimmy Corrigan; Chris Ware-s/a in all 7.00
1-2nd and later printings 4.00
2,3: 2-Quimby 5.00
4-Sparky's Best Comics & Stories 6.00
5-12: Jimmy Corrigan in all 5.00
13-($10.95-c) 11.00
14-($12.95-c) Concludes Jimmy Corrigan saga 13.00

Action Comics #30 © DC

Action Comics #80 © DC

Action Comics #285 © DC

GD2.0 FN6.0 NM9.4 GD2.0 FN6.0 NM9.4

Jimmy Corrigan, The Smartest Kid on Earth (2000, Pantheon Books, Hardcover, $27.50, 380 pgs.) Collects Jimmy Corrigan stories; folded dust jacket 27.50
NOTE: *Multiple printings exist for most issues.*

ACTION ADVENTURE (War) (Formerly Real Adventure)
Gillmor Magazines: V1#2, June, 1955 - No. 4, Oct, 1955
V1#2-4 4.65 14.00 28.00

ACTION COMICS (...Weekly #601-642) (Also see The Comics Magazine #1, More Fun #14-17 & Special Edition) (Also see Promotional Comics section)
National Periodical Publ./Detective Comics/DC Comics: 6/38 - No. 583, 9/86; No. 584, 1/87 - Present

GD2.0 FN6.0 VF8.0 NM9.4

1-Origin & 1st app. Superman by Siegel & Shuster, Marco Polo, Tex Thompson, Pep Morgan, Chuck Dawson & Scoop Scanlon; 1st app. Zatara & Lois Lane; Superman story missing 4 pgs. which were included when reprinted in Superman #1; Clark Kent works for Daily Star; story continued in #2 35,000.00 90,000.00 150,000.00 285,000.00
1-Reprint, Oversize 13-1/2x10". **WARNING:** This comic is an exact reprint of the original except for its size. DC published it in 1974 with a second cover titling it as a Famous First Edition. There have been many reported cases of the outer cover being removed and the interior sold as the original edition. The reprint with the new outer cover removed is practically worthless. See Famous First Edition for value.

GD2.0 FN6.0 NM9.4

1(1993)-Came w/Reign of Superman packs 1.50
2-O'Mealia non-Superman covers thru #6 2857.00 8570.00 30,000.00
3 (Scarce)-Superman apps. in costume in only one panel 1800.00 5400.00 19,000.00
4-6: 6-1st Jimmy Olsen (called office boy) 1050.00 3150.00 11,000.00
7-2nd Superman cover 1900.00 5700.00 20,000.00
8,9 770.00 2300.00 8000.00
10-3rd Superman cover by Siegel & Shuster 1333.00 4000.00 14,000.00
11,14: 14-Clip Carson begins, ends #41; Zatara-c 400.00 1200.00 4200.00
12-Has 1 pg. Batman ad for Det. #27 (5/39); Zatara sci-fi cover 420.00 1260.00 4400.00
13-Shuster Superman-c; last Scoop Scanlon 652.00 1956.00 7500.00
15-Guardineer Superman-c; Detective Comics ad 539.00 1617.00 6200.00
16 300.00 900.00 3000.00
17-Superman cover; last Marco Polo 420.00 1260.00 4800.00
18-Origin 3 Aces; 1st X-Ray Vision? 300.00 900.00 3000.00
19-Superman covers begin; has full pg. ad for New York World's Fair 1939 420.00 1260.00 4400.00
20-The 'S' left off Superman's chest; Clark Kent works at 'Daily Star' 400.00 1200.00 4200.00
21-Has 2 ads for More Fun #52 (1st Spectre) 274.00 822.00 2600.00
22,24,25: 24-Kent at Daily Planet. 25-Last app. Gargantua T. Potts, Tex Thompson's sidekick 263.00 789.00 2500.00
23-1st app. Luthor (w/red hair) & Black Pirate; Black Pirate by Moldoff; 1st mention of The Daily Planet (4/40)-Has 1 panel ad for Spectre in More Fun 626.00 1878.00 7200.00
26-28,30 221.00 663.00 2100.00
29-1st Lois Lane-c (10/40) 263.00 789.00 2500.00
31,32: 32-Intro/1st app. Krypto Ray Gun in Superman story by Burnley 137.00 410.00 1300.00
33-Origin Mr. America; Superman by Burnley; has half page ad for All Star Comics #3 168.00 505.00 1600.00
34,35,38,39 131.00 395.00 1250.00
36,37: 36-Classic robot-c. 37-Origin Congo Bill 142.00 426.00 1350.00
40-(9/41)-Intro/1st app. Star Spangled Kid & Stripesy; Jerry Siegel photo 147.00 442.00 1400.00
41 116.00 348.00 1100.00
42-1st app./origin Vigilante; Bob Daley becomes Fat Man; origin Mr. America's magic flying carpet; The Queen Bee & Luthor app; Black Pirate ends; not in #41 168.00 505.00 1600.00
43-46,48-50: 44-Fat Man's i.d. revealed to Mr. America. 45-1st app. Stuff (Vigilante's oriental sidekick) 116.00 348.00 1100.00
47-1st Luthor cover in comics (4/42) 179.00 537.00 1700.00
51-1st app. The Prankster 126.00 379.00 1200.00
52-Fat Man & Mr. America become the Ameri-commandos; origin Vigilante retold; classic Superman and back-ups-c 131.00 395.00 1250.00
53-60: 56-Last Fat Man. 57-2nd Lois Lane-c in Action (3rd anywhere, 2/43). 59-Kubert Vigilante begins?, ends #70. 60-First app. Lois Lane as Superwoman 84.00 253.00 800.00
61-Historic Atomic Radiation-c (6/43) 89.00 268.00 850.00
62,63-Japan war-c: 63-Last 3 Aces 84.00 253.00 800.00
64-Intro Toyman 87.00 261.00 825.00
65-70 76.00 229.00 725.00
71-79: 74-Last Mr. America 71.00 213.00 675.00
80-2nd app. & 1st Mr. Mxyztplk-c (1/45) 95.00 285.00 900.00
81-88,90: 83-Intro Hocus & Pocus 68.00 205.00 650.00
89-Classic rainbow cover 74.00 221.00 700.00
91-99: 93-X-Mas-c. 99-1st small logo (8/46) 66.00 197.00 625.00
100 126.00 379.00 1200.00
101-Nuclear explosion-c (10/46) 131.00 395.00 1250.00
102-120: 102-Mxyztplk-c. 105,117-X-Mas-c 61.00 182.00 575.00
121-126,128-140: 135,136,138-Zatara by Kubert 55.00 165.00 525.00
127-Vigilante by Kubert; Tommy Tomorrow begins (12/48, see Real Fact #6) 61.00 183.00 580.00
141-157,159-161: 151-Luthor/Mr. Mxyztplk/Prankster team-up. 156-Lois Lane as Super Woman. 160- Last 52 pgs. 53.00 158.00 475.00
158-Origin Superman retold 116.00 348.00 1100.00
162-180: 168,176-Used in **POP**, pg. 90. 173-Robot-c 44.00 133.00 400.00
181-201: 191-Intro. Janu in Congo Bill. 198-Last Vigilante. 201-Last pre-code issue 42.00 125.00 375.00
202-220,232: 212-(1/56)-Includes 1956 Superman calendar that is part of story. 232-1st Curt Swan-c in Action 40.00 120.00 325.00
221-231,233-240: 221-1st S.A. issue. 224-1st Golden Gorilla story. 228-(5/57)-Kongorilla in Congo Bill story (Congorilla try-out) 34.00 103.00 275.00
241,243-251: 241-Batman x-over. 248-Origin/1st app. Congorilla; Congo Bill renamed Congorilla. 251-Last Tommy Tomorrow 28.00 84.00 225.00
242-Origin & 1st app. Brainiac (7/58); 1st mention of Shrunken City of Kandor 125.00 375.00 1750.00
252-Origin & 1st app. Supergirl (5/59); intro new Metallo 125.00 375.00 1750.00
253-2nd app. Supergirl 47.00 142.00 425.00
254-1st meeting of Bizarro & Superman-c/story 36.00 107.00 285.00
255-1st Bizarro Lois Lane-c/story & both Bizarros leave Earth to make Bizarro World 28.00 84.00 225.00
256-260: 259-Red Kryptonite used 18.00 53.00 140.00
261-1st X-Kryptonite which gave Streaky his powers; last Congorilla in Action; origin & 1st app. Streaky The Super Cat 19.00 56.00 150.00
262,264-266,268-270 16.00 48.00 125.00
263-Origin Bizarro World 21.00 62.00 165.00
267(8/60)-3rd Legion app; 1st app. Chameleon Boy, Colossal Boy, & Invisible Kid, 1st app. of Supergirl as Superwoman. 44.00 133.00 400.00
271-275,277-282: 274-Lois Lane as Superwoman; 282-Last 10¢ issue 12.00 36.00 95.00
276(5/61)-6th Legion app; 1st app. Brainiac 5, Phantom Girl, Triplicate Girl, Bouncing Boy, Sun Boy, & Shrinking Violet; Supergirl joins Legion 21.00 64.00 200.00
283(12/61)-Legion of Super-Villains app. 1st 12¢ 10.00 30.00 110.00
284(1/62)-Mon-el app. 10.00 30.00 110.00
285(2/62)-12th Legion app; Brainiac 5 cameo; Supergirl's existence revealed to world; JFK & Jackie cameos 11.50 34.00 125.00
286-292,294-299: 286(3/62)-Legion of Super Villains app. 287(4/62)-15th Legion app.(cameo). 288-Mon-el app.; r-origin Supergirl. 289(6/62)-16th Legion app. (Adult); Lightning Man & Saturn Woman's marriage 1st revealed. 290(7/62)-17th Legion app. (cameo); Phantom Girl app. 1st Supergirl emergency squad 291,292,294-299: 291-1st meeting Supergirl & Mr. Mxyzptlk. 292-2nd app. Superhorse (see Adv. #293). 297-Mon-el app. 298-Legion cameo 7.25 21.75 80.00
293-Origin Comet (Superhorse) 10.00 30.00 110.00
300-(5/63) 8.15 24.50 90.00
301-308,310-320: 304-Origin & 1st app. Black Flame (9/63). 306-Brainiac 5, Mon-el app. 307-Saturn Girl app. 313-Batman app. 314-retells origin Supergirl; J.L.A. x-over. 317-Death of Nor-Kan of Kandor. 319-Shrinking Violet app. 3.65 11.00 40.00
309-(2/64)-Legion app.; Batman & Robin-c & cameo; JFK app. (he died 11/22/63; on stands same time as death) 4.10 12.30 45.00

Action Comics #591 © DC

Action Comics #1,000,000 © DC

Action Comics Annual #6 © DC

GD2.0 FN6.0 NM9.4

321-333,335-339: 336-Origin Akvar (Flamebird) 3.00 9.00 32.00
334-Giant G-20; origin Supergirl, Streaky, Superhorse & Legion (all-r) 6.80 20.50 75.00
340-Origin, 1st app. of the Parasite 3.45 10.35 38.00
341-346,348-359: 341-Batman app. in Supergirl back-up story. 342-UFO story. 344-Batman x-over. 345-Allen Funt/Candid Camera story. 350-Batman, Green Arrow & Green Lantern app. in Supergirl back-up story. 358-Superboy meets Supergirl 2.50 7.50 25.00
347,360-Giant Supergirl G-33,G-45; 347-Origin Comet-r plus Bizarro story. 360-Legion-r; r/origin Supergirl 4.55 13.65 50.00
361-372,374-378: 361-2nd app. Parasite. 363-366-Leper/Death story. 365-JLA & Legion app. 366-JLA app. 370-New facts about Superman's origin. 376-Last Supergirl in Action. 377-Legion begins (thru #392). 378-Last 12¢ issue 2.30 7.00 20.00
373-Giant Supergirl G-57; Legion-r 4.10 12.30 45.00
379-399,401: 388-Sgt. Rock app. 392-Batman-c/app.; last Legion in Action; Saturn Girl gets new costume. 393-401-All Superman issues. 1.85 5.50 15.00
400 2.50 7.50 24.00
402-Last 15¢ issue; Superman vs. Supergirl duel 2.40 7.35 22.00
403-413: All 52 pg. issues. 411-Origin Eclipso-(r). 413-Metamorpho begins, ends #418 2.40 7.35 22.00
414-424: 419-Intro. Human Target. 421-Intro Capt. Strong; Green Arrow begins. 422,423-Origin Human Target 1.25 3.75 10.00
425-Neal Adams-a(p); The Atom begins 2.00 6.00 18.00
426-431,433-436,438,439 1.00 2.80 7.00
432-1st S.A. Toyman app (2/74). 2.00 6.00 18.00
437,443-(100 pg. Giants) 2.50 7.50 25.00
440-1st Grell-a on Green Arrow 1.50 4.50 12.00
441,442,444-448: 441-Grell-a on Green Arrow continues 2.40 6.00
449-(68 pgs.) 1.00 3.00 8.00
450-483,485-499: 454-Last Atom. 456-Grell Jaws-c. 458-Last Green Arrow. 466-Batman, Flash app. 485-Adams-c. 487,488-(44 pgs.). 487-Origin & 1st app. Microwave Man; origin Atom retold 4.50
482,487-492,495,496,498-Whitman variants (no cover price) 4.50
484-Earth II Superman & Lois Lane wed; 40th anniversary issue(6/78) 2.40 6.00
484-Variant includes 3-D Superman punchout doll in cello. pack; 4 different inserts; Canadian promo?) 1.25 3.75 10.00
500-($1.00, 68 pgs.)-Infinity-c; Superman life story; shows Legion statues in museum 2.40 6.00
501-543,545-551,554-582: 511-514-Airwave II solo stories. 513-The Atom begins. 517-Aquaman begins; ends #541. 521-1st app. The Vixen. 532,536-New Teen Titans cameo. 535,536-Omega Men app. 546-J.L.A., New Teen Titans app. 551-Starfire becomes Red-Star 2.50
504,505,507,508-Whitman variants (no cover price) 2.50
544-(6/83, Mando paper, 68 pgs.)-45th Anniversary issue; origins new Luthor & Brainiac; Omega Men cameo; Shuster-a (pin-up); article by Siegel 5.00
552,553-Animal Man-c & app. (2/84 & 3/84) 4.50
583-Alan Moore scripts; last Earth 1 Superman story (cont'd from Superman #423) 2.40 6.00
584-599: 584-Byrne-a begins; New Teen Titans app. 586-Legends x-over. 596-Millennium x-over; Spectre app. 598-1st app. Checkmate 3.00
600-($2.50, 84 pgs., 5/88) 2.40 6.00
601-642-Weekly issues ($1.50, 52 pgs.): 601-Re-intro The Secret Six. 611-614-: Catwoman stories (new costume in #611). 613-618-Nightwing stories 2.50
643-Superman & monthly issues begin again; Perez-c/a/scripts begin; swipes cover to Superman #1 3.00
644-649,651-661,663-673,675-683: 645-1st app. Maxima. 654-Part 3 of Batman storyline. 655-Free extra 8 pgs. 660-Death of Lex Luthor. 661-Begin $1.00-c. 667-($1.75, 52 pgs.). 675-Deathstroke cameo. 679-Last $1.00 issue. 683-Doomsday cameo 2.50
650-($1.50, 52 pgs.)-Lobo cameo (last panel) 3.00
662-Clark Kent reveals i.d. to Lois Lane; story cont'd in Superman #53 4.00
674-Supergirl logo & c/story (reintro) 5.00
683,685-2nd & 3rd printings 2.00
684-Doomsday battle issue 3.00
685,686-Funeral for a Friend issues; Supergirl app. 2.50
687-($1.95)-Collector's Ed.w/die-cut-c 2.50

GD2.0 FN6.0 NM9

687-($1.50)-Newsstand Edition with mini-poster 2.0
688-699,701-703-($1.50): 688-Guy Gardner-c/story. 697-Bizarro-c/story. 703-(9/94)-Zero Hour 2.0
695-($2.50)-Collector's Edition w/embossed foil-c 2.5
700-($2.95, 68 pgs.)-Fall of Metropolis Pt 1; Pete Ross marries Lana Lang; Curt Swan & Murphy Anderson inks 3.0
700-Platinum 15.0
700-Gold 18.0
0(10/94), 704(11/94)-710-719,721-731: 710-Begin $1.95-c. 714-Joker app. 719-Batman-c/app. 721-Mr. Mxyzptlk app. 723-Brainiac as Superman; Dave Johnson-c. 727-Final Night x-over. 2.0
720-Lois breaks off engagement w/Clark 3.0
720-2nd print. 2.0
732-749,751-767: 732-New powers. 733-New costume, Ray app. 738-Immoner s/a(p) begins. 741-Legion app. 744-Millennium Giants x-over. 745-747-70's-style Superman vs. Prankster. 753-JLA-c/app. 757-Hawkman-c. 760-1st Encantadora. 761-Wonder Woman app. 765-Joker & Harley-c/app. 766-Batman-c/app. 2.0
750-($2.95) 3.0
768,769,771-774: 768-Begin $2.25-c; Marvel Family-c/app. 771-Nightwing-c/ap 772,773-Ra's al Ghul app. 2.2
770-($3.50) Conclusion of Emperor Joker x-over 3.5
775-($3.75) Bradstreet-c 3.7
#1,000,000 (11/98) Gene Ha-c; 853rd Century x-over 2.0
Annual 1-6('87-'94, $2.95)-1-Art Adams-c/a(p); Batman app. 2-Perez-c/a(i) 3-Armageddon 2001. 4-Eclipso vs. Shazam. 5-Bloodlines; 1st app. Loose Cannon. 6-Elseworlds story 3.0
Annual 7,9 ('95, '97, $3.95)-7-Year One story. 9-Pulp Heroes sty 4.0
Annual 8 (1996, $2.95)-Legends of the Dead Earth story 3.0

NOTE:***Supergirl's*** *origin in 262, 280, 285, 291, 305, 309.* ***N. Adams*** *c-356, 358, 359, 361-3 366, 367, 370-374, 377-379i, 398-400, 402, 404,405, 419p, 466, 468, 469, 473i, 485.* ***Aparo*** *642.* ***Austin*** *c/a-682i.* ***Baily*** *a-24, 25.* ***Boring*** *a-164, 194, 211, 223, 233, 241, 250, 261, 266-2 346, 348, 352, 356, 357.* ***Burnley*** *a-28-33; c-48?, 53-55, 58, 59?, 60-63, 65, 66p, 67p, 70p, 7 79p, 82p, 84-86p, 90-92p, 93p?, 94p, 107p, 108p.* ***Byrne*** *a-584-598p, 599i, 600p; c-584-5 596-600.* ***Ditko*** *a-642.* ***Giffen*** *a-560, 563, 565, 577, 579; c-539, 560, 563, 565, 577, 579.* ***Grell*** *440-442, 444-446, 450-452, 456-458; c-456.* ***Guardineer*** *a-24, 25; c-8, 11, 12, 14-16, 18.* ***Guice*** *a(p)-676-681, 683-698, 700; c-683, 685, 686, 687(direct), 688-693i, 694-696, 697i, 6 700.* ***Infantino*** *a-642.* ***Kaluta*** *c-613.* ***Bob Kane's*** *Clip Carson-14-41.* ***Gil Kane*** *a-443r, 493r, 5 541, 544-546, 551-554, 601-605, 642; c-535p, 540, 541, 544p, 545-549, 551-554, 580, 6* ***Kirby*** *c-638.* ***Meskin*** *a-42-121(most).* ***Mignola*** *a-600, Annual 2; c-c-614.* ***Moldoff*** *a-23-25, 44* ***Mooney*** *a-667p.* ***Mortimer*** *c-153, 154, 159-172, 174, 178-181, 184, 186-189, 191-193, 196, 2 206.* ***Orlando*** *a-617p; c-621.* ***Perez*** *a-600i, 643-652p, Annual 2p; c-529p, 602, 643-651, Ann 2p.* ***Quesada*** *c-Annual 4p.* ***Fred Ray*** *c-34, 36-46, 50-52.* ***Siegel & Shuster*** *a-1-27.* ***Paul Sm*** *c-608.* ***Starlin*** *a-509; c-631.* ***Leonard Starr*** *a-597i(part),* ***Staton*** *a-525p, 526p, 531p, 535p, 53* ***Swan/Moldoff*** *c-281, 286, 287, 293, 298, 334.* ***Thibert*** *c-676, 677p, 678-681, 684.* ***Toth*** *a-4 407, 413, 431; c-616.* ***Tuska*** *a-486p, 550.* ***Williamson*** *a-568i.* ***Zeck*** *c-Annual 5*

ACTION FORCE (Also see G.I. Joe European Missions)
Marvel Comics Ltd. (British): Mar, 1987 - No. 50, 1988 ($1.00, weekly, magazine)

1,3: British G.I. Joe series. 3-w/poster insert 6.0
2,4 4.0
5-10 3.0
11-30 2.5
31-50 2.0
...Special 1 (7/87) Summer holiday special; Snake Eyes-c/app. 6.0
...Special 2 (10/87) Winter special; 4.0

ACTION GIRL
Slave Labor Graphics: Oct, 1994 - Present ($2.50/$2.75, B&W)

1-18: 4-Begin $2.75-c 2.7
1-6 ($2.75, 2nd printings): All read 2nd Print in indicia. 1-(2/96). 2-(10/95). 3-(2/96). 4-(7/96). 5-(2/97). 6-(9/97) 2.7
1-4 ($2.75, 3rd printings): All read 3rd Print in indicia. 2.7

ACTION PLANET COMICS
Action Planet: 1996 - No. 3, Sept, 1997 ($3.95, B&W, 44 pgs.)

1-3: 1-Intro Monster Man by Mike Manley & other stories 4.0
Giant Size Action Planet Halloween Special (1998, $5.95, oversized) 6.0

ACTUAL CONFESSIONS (Formerly Love Adventures)
Atlas Comics (MPI): No. 13, Oct, 1952 - No. 14, Dec, 1952

13,14 5.70 17.00 40.0

Adrenalynn #1 © Tony Daniel

Adventure Comics #46 © DC

Adventure Comics #195 © DC

GD2.0 FN6.0 NM9.4

ACTUAL ROMANCES (Becomes True Secrets #3 on?)
Marvel Comics (IPS): Oct, 1949 - No. 2, Jan, 1950 (52 pgs.)
1 10.00 30.00 75.00
2-Photo-c 7.00 21.00 48.00

ADAM AND EVE
Spire Christian Comics (Fleming H. Revell Co.): 1975,1978 (35¢/49¢)
nn-By Al Hartley 1.00 2.80 7.00

ADAM STRANGE (Also see Green Lantern #132, Mystery In Space #53 & Showcase #17)
DC Comics: 1990 - No. 3, 1990 ($3.95, 52 pgs, limited series, squarebound)
Book One - Three: Andy & Adam Kubert-c/a 4.00

ADAM-12 (TV)
Gold Key: Dec, 1973 - No. 10, Feb, 1976 (Photo-c)
1 5.85 17.50 70.00
2-10 2.80 8.40 28.00

ADDAM OMEGA
Antarctic Press: Feb, 1997 - No. 4, Aug, 1997 ($2.95, B&W)
1-4 3.00

ADDAMS FAMILY (TV cartoon)
Gold Key: Oct, 1974 - No. 3, Apr, 1975 (Hanna-Barbera)
1 8.35 25.00 100.00
2,3 5.35 16.00 65.00

ADLAI STEVENSON
Dell Publishing Co.: Dec, 1966
12-007-612-Life story; photo-c 3.00 9.00 30.00

ADOLESCENT RADIOACTIVE BLACK BELT HAMSTERS (See Clint)
Comic Castle/Eclipse Comics: 1986 - No. 9, Jan, 1988 ($1.50, B&W)
1-9: 1st & 2nd printings exist 2.00
1-Limited Edition 3.00
1-In 3-D (7/86) 2.50
2-4 ($2.50) 2.50
Massacre The Japanese Invasion #1 (8/89, $2.00) 2.00

ADRENALYNN (See The Tenth)
Image Comics: Aug, 1999 - No. 4, Feb, 2000 ($2.50)
1-4-Tony Daniel-s/Marty Egeland-a; origin of Adrenalynn 2.50

ADULT TALES OF TERROR ILLUSTRATED (See Terror Illustrated)

ADVANCED DUNGEONS & DRAGONS (Also see TSR Worlds)
DC Comics: Dec, 1988 - No. 36, Dec, 1991 (Newsstand #1 is Holiday, 1988-89) ($1.25/$1.50/$1.75)
1-Based on TSR role playing game 3.50
2-36: 25-$1.75-c begins 2.00
Annual 1 (1990, $3.95, 68 pgs.) 4.00

ADVENTURE BOUND
Dell Publishing Co.: Aug, 1949
Four Color 239 4.60 13.75 55.00

ADVENTURE COMICS (Formerly New Adventure)(...Presents Dial H For Hero #479-490)
National Periodical Publications/DC Comics: No. 32, 11/38 - No. 490, 2/82; No. 491, 9/82 - No. 503, 9/83
32-Anchors Aweigh (ends #52), Barry O'Neil (ends #60, not in #33), Captain Desmo (ends #47), Dale Daring (ends #47), Federal Men (ends #70), The Golden Dragon (ends #36), Rusty & His Pals (ends #52) by Bob Kane, Todd Hunter (ends #38) and Tom Brent (ends #39) begin
466.00 1400.00 3400.00
33-38: 37-Cover used on Double Action #2 216.00 650.00 1600.00
39(6/39):-Jack Wood begins, ends #42; 1st mention of Marijuana in comics
216.00 650.00 1600.00
GD2.0 FN6.0 VF8.0 NM9.4
40-(Rare, 7/39, on stands 6/10/39)-The Sandman begins by Bert Christman (who died in WWII); believed to be 1st conceived story (see N.Y. World's Fair for 1st published app.); Socko Strong begins, ends #54
3833.00 11,500.00 24,000.00 44,000.00
GD2.0 FN6.0 NM9.4
41-O'Mealia shark-c 478.00 1435.00 5500.00
42,44-Sandman-c by Flessel. 44-Opium story 608.00 1826.00 7000.00
43,45 300.00 900.00 3000.00
46,47-Sandman covers by Flessel. 47-Steve Conrad Adventurer begins, ends #76
438.00 1314.00 4600.00
GD2.0 FN6.0 VF8.0 NM9.4
48-Intro & 1st app. The Hourman by Bernard Baily; Baily-c (Hourman c-48,50,52-59) 2000.00 6000.00 13,000.00 25,000.00
GD2.0 FN6.0 NM9.4
49,50: 50-Cotton Carver by Jack Lehti begins, ends #64
232.00 695.00 2200.00
51,60-Sandman-c: 51-Sandman-c by Flessel. 300.00 900.00 3000.00
52-59: 53-1st app. Jimmy "Minuteman" Martin & the Minutemen of America in Hourman; ends #78. 58-Paul Kirk Manhunter begins (1st app.), ends #72
211.00 633.00 2000.00
GD2.0 FN6.0 VF8.0 NM9.4
61-1st app. Starman by Jack Burnley (4/41); Starman c-61-72; Starman by Burnley in #61-80 1000.00 3000.00 6500.00 12,500.00
GD2.0 FN6.0 NM9.4
62-65,67,68,70: 67-Origin & 1st app. The Mist; classic Burnley-c 70-Last Federal Men 179.00 537.00 1700.00
66-Origin/1st app. Shining Knight (9/41) 221.00 663.00 2100.00
69-1st app. Sandy the Golden Boy (Sandman's sidekick) by Paul Norris (in a Bob Kane style); Sandman dons new costume 190.00 570.00 1800.00
71-Jimmy Martin becomes costumed aide to the Hourman; 1st app. Hourman's Miracle Ray machine 168.00 505.00 1600.00
GD2.0 FN6.0 VF8.0 NM9.4
72-1st Simon & Kirby Sandman (3/42, 1st DC work)
1000.00 3000.00 6250.00 12,000.00
73-Origin Manhunter by Simon & Kirby; begin new series; Manhunter-c
1000.00 3000.00 6500.00 12,500.00
GD2.0 FN6.0 NM9.4
74-78,80: 74-Thorndyke replaces Jimmy, Hourman's assistant; new Sandman-c begin by S&K. 75-Thor app. by Kirby; 1st Kirby Thor (see Tales of the Unexpected #16). 77-Origin Genius Jones; Mist story. 80-Last S&K Manhunter & Burnley Starman 179.00 537.00 1700.00
79-Classic Manhunter-c 211.00 633.00 2000.00
81-90: 83-Last Hourman. 84-Mike Gibbs begins, ends #102
116.00 348.00 1100.00
91-Last Simon & Kirby Sandman 100.00 300.00 950.00
92-99,101,102: 92-Last Manhunter. 101-Shining Knight origin retold. 102-Last Starman, Sandman, & Genius Jones; most-S&K-c (Genius Jones cont'd in More Fun #108) 92.00 276.00 875.00
100-S&K-c 121.00 363.00 1150.00
103-Aquaman, Green Arrow, Johnny Quick & Superboy all move over from More Fun Comics #107; 8th app. Superboy; Superboy-c begin; 1st small logo (4/46) 284.00 853.00 2700.00
104 100.00 300.00 950.00
105-110 71.00 213.00 675.00
111-120: 113-X-Mas-c 63.00 189.00 600.00
121-126,128-130: 128-1st meeting Superboy & Lois Lane
55.00 165.00 525.00
127-Brief origin Shining Knight retold 58.00 174.00 550.00
131-141,143-149: 132-Shining Knight 1st return to King Arthur time; origin aide Sir Butch 47.00 140.00 420.00
142-Origin Shining Knight & Johnny Quick retold 53.00 158.00 475.00
150,151,153,155,157,159,161,163-All have 6 pg. Shining Knight stories by Frank Frazetta. 159-Origin Johnny Quick 55.00 165.00 500.00
152,154,156,158,160,162,164-169: 166-Last Shining Knight. 168-Last 52 pg. issue 41.00 123.00 370.00
170-180 40.00 120.00 340.00
181-199: 189-B&W and color illo in **POP** 40.00 120.00 330.00
200 (5/54) 53.00 158.00 475.00
201-208: 207-Last Johnny Quick (not in 205) 36.00 107.00 320.00
209-Last pre-code issue; origin Speedy 38.00 113.00 340.00
GD2.0 FN6.0 VF8.0 NM9.4
210-1st app. Krypto (Superdog)-c/story (3/55)

Adventure Comics #226 © DC

Adventure Comics #427 © DC

Adventure Comics #452 © DC

GD2.0 FN6.0 NM9.4

250.00 750.00 1800.00 3600.00

GD2.0 FN6.0 NM9.4

211-213,215-219 33.00 100.00 300.00
214-2nd app. Krypto 50.00 150.00 500.00
220-Krypto-c/sty 36.00 108.00 325.00
221-246: 229-1st S.A. issue. 237-1st Intergalactic Vigilante Squadron (6/57) 28.00 83.00 250.00

GD2.0 FN6.0 VF8.0 NM9.4

247(4/58)-1st Legion of Super Heroes app.; 1st app. Cosmic Boy, Lightning Boy (later Lightning Lad in #267), & Saturn Girl (origin) 325.00 975.00 2600.00 5500.00

GD2.0 FN6.0 NM9.4

248-252,254,255-Green Arrow in all: 255-Intro. Red Kryptonite in Superboy (used in #252 but with no effect) 21.00 63.00 190.00
253-1st meeting of Superboy & Robin; Green Arrow by Kirby in #250-255 (also see World's Finest #96-99) 28.00 83.00 250.00
256-Origin Green Arrow by Kirby 59.00 177.00 650.00
257-259: 258-Green Arrow x-over in Superboy 18.00 53.00 160.00
260-1st Silver-Age origin Aquaman (5/59) 68.00 205.00 750.00
261-265,268,270: 262-Origin Speedy in Green Arrow. 270-Congorilla begins, ends #281,283 14.00 43.00 130.00
266-(11/59)-Origin & 1st app. Aquagirl (tryout, not same as later character) 16.00 47.00 140.00
267(12/59)-2nd Legion of Super Heroes; Lightning Boy now called Lightning Lad; new costumes for Legion 82.00 245.00 900.00
269-Intro. Aqualad (2/60); last Green Arrow (not in #206) 27.00 80.00 240.00
271-Origin Luthor retold 30.00 90.00 270.00
272-274,277-280: 279-Intro White Kryptonite in Superboy. 280-1st meeting Superboy-Lori Lemaris 13.00 38.00 115.00
275-Origin Superman-Batman team retold (see World's Finest #94) 23.00 70.00 210.00
276-(9/60) Re-intro Metallo (3rd app?); story similar to Superboy #49 14.00 42.00 125.00
281,284,287-289: 281-Last Congorilla. 284-Last Aquaman in Adv. 287,288-Intro Dev-Em, the Knave from Krypton. 287-1st Bizarro Perry White & J. Olsen. 288-Bizarro-c. 289-Legion cameo (statues) 12.00 35.00 105.00
282(3/61)-5th Legion app; intro/origin Star Boy 21.00 63.00 190.00
283-Intro. The Phantom Zone 21.00 63.00 190.00
285-1st Tales of the Bizarro World-c/story (ends #299) in Adv. (see Action #255) 18.00 53.00 160.00
286-1st Bizarro Mxyzptlk; Bizarro-c 16.00 47.00 140.00
290(11/61)-9th Legion app; origin Sunboy in Legion (last 10¢ issue) 21.00 63.00 190.00
291,292,295-298: 291-1st 12¢ ish, (12/61). 292-1st Bizarro Lana Lang & Lucy Lane. 295-Bizarro-c; 1st Bizarro Titano 8.15 24.50 90.00
293(2/62)-13th Legion app; Mon-el & Legion Super Pets (1st app./origin) app. (1st Superhorse). 1st Bizarro Luthor & Kandor 13.50 40.00 150.00
294-1st Bizarro Marilyn Monroe, Pres. Kennedy. 10.50 31.50 115.00
299-1st Gold Kryptonite (8/62) 8.65 26.00 95.00
300-Tales of the Legion of Super-Heroes series begins (9/62); Mon-el leaves Phantom Zone (temporarily), joins Legion 35.00 105.00 420.00
301-Origin Bouncing Boy 13.50 40.00 150.00
302-305: 303-1st app. Matter-Eater Lad. 304-Death of Lightning Lad in Legion 9.00 27.00 100.00
306-310: 306-Intro. Legion of Substitute Heroes. 307-1st app. Element Lad in Legion. 308-1st app. Lightning Lass in Legion 8.15 24.50 90.00
311-320: 312-Lightning Lad back in Legion. 315-Last new Superboy story; Colossal Boy app. 316-Origins & powers of Legion given. 317-Intro. Dream Girl in Legion; Lightning Lass becomes Light Lass; Hall of Fame series begins. 320-Dev-Em 2nd app. 6.80 20.50 75.00
321-Intro Time Trapper 5.90 17.75 65.00
322-330: 327-Intro/1st app. Lone Wolf in Legion. 329-Intro The Bizarro Legionnaires; intro Legion flight rings 5.00 15.00 55.00
331-340: 337-Chlorophyll Kid & Night Girl app. 340-Intro Computo in Legion 4.10 12.30 45.00
341-Triplicate Girl becomes Duo Damsel 3.20 9.60 35.00
342-345,347-351: 345-Last Hall of Fame; returns in 356,371. 348-Origin Sunboy; intro Dr. Regulus in Legion. 349-Intro Universo & Rond Vidar. 351-1st app. White Witch. 3.00 9.00 30.0

GD2.0 FN6.0 NM9.

346-1st app. Karate Kid, Princess Projectra, Ferro Lad, & Nemesis Kid. 3.65 11.00 40.0
352,354-360: 354,355-Superman meets the Adult Legion. 355-Insect Queen joins Legion (4/67) 2.80 8.40 28.0
353-Death of Ferro Lad in Legion 3.20 9.60 35.0
361-364,366,368-370: 369-Intro Mordru in Legion 2.50 7.50 25.0
365,367: 365-Intro Shadow Lass (memorial to Shadow Woman app. in #354's Adult Legion-s); lists origins & powers of L.S.H. 367-New Legion headquarters 2.80 8.40 28.0
371,372: 371-Intro. Chemical King (mentioned in #354's Adult Legion-s). 372-Timber Wolf & Chemical King join 2.80 8.40 28.0
373,374,376-380: 372-Intro. Tornado Twins (Flash descendants). 374-Article on comics fandom. 380-Last Legion in Adventure; last 12¢-c 2.50 7.50 25.0
375-Intro Quantum Queen & The Wanderers 2.80 8.40 28.0
381-Supergirl begins; 1st full length Supergirl story & her 1st solo book (6/69) 6.80 20.50 75.0
382-389,391-396,398 2.30 7.00 20.0
390-Giant Supergirl G-69 3.65 11.00 40.0
397-1st app. new Supergirl 2.50 7.50 25.0
399-Unpubbed G.A. Black Canary story 2.50 7.50 25.0
400-New costume for Supergirl (12/70) 3.00 9.00 30.0
401,402: 402-Last 15¢-c 1.85 5.50 15.0
403-68 pg. Giant G-81; Legion-r/#304,305,308,312 3.65 11.00 40.0
404-408-(20¢-c) 1.50 4.50 12.0
409-411,413-415,417-420-(52 pgs.): 413-Hawkman by Kubert r/B&B #44; G.A. Robotman-r/Det. #178; Zatanna by Morrow. 414-r-2nd Animal Man/Str. Advs #184. 415-Animal Man-r/Str. Adv.#190 (origin recap). 417-Morrow Vigilante; Frazetta Shining Knight-r/Adv. #161; origin The Enchantress; no Zatanna. 418-Prev. unpub. Dr. Mid-Nite story from 1948; no Zatanna. 420-Animal Man-r/Str. Adv. #195 2.00 6.00 18.0
412-(52 pgs.) Reprints origin & 1st app. of Animal Man from Strange Adventures #180 2.30 7.00 20.0
416-Also listed as DC 100 Pg. Super Spectacular #10; Golden Age-r; r/1st app. Black Canary from Flash #86; no Zatanna
(see DC 100 Pg. Super Spectacular #10 for price)
421-424,427: Last Supergirl in Adventure. 427-Last Vigilante 1.25 3.75 10.0
425-New look, content change to adventure; Kaluta-c; Toth-a, origin Capt. Fear 2.30 7.00 20.0
426-1st Adventurers Club. 1.50 4.50 12.0
428-Origin/1st app. Black Orchid (c/story, 6-7/73) 3.80 11.40 42.0
429,430-Black Orchid-c/stories 2.30 7.00 20.0
431-Spectre by Aparo begins, ends #440. 4.10 12.30 45.0
432-439-Spectre app. 433-437-Cover title is Weird Adv. Comics. 436-Last 20¢ issue. 2.40 7.35 22.0
440-New Spectre origin. 3.00 9.00 30.0
441-458: 441-452-Aquaman app. 443-Fisherman app. 445-447-The Creeper app. 446-Flag-c. 449-451-Martian Manhunter app. 450-Weather Wizard app. in Aquaman story. 453-458-Superboy app. 453-Intro. Mighty Girl. 457,458-Eclipso app. 2.40 6.0
459,460 (68 pgs.): 459-New Gods/Darkseid storyline concludes from New Gods #19 (#459 is dated 9-10/78) without missing a month. 459-Flash (ends #466), Deadman (ends #466), Wonder Woman (ends #464), Green Lantern (ends #460). 460-Aquaman (ends #478) 2.00 6.00 16.0
461,462 ($1.00, 68 pgs.): 461-Justice Society begins; ends 466. 461,462-Death Earth II Batman 2.00 6.00 18.0
463-466 ($1.00 size, 68 pgs.) 1.25 3.75 10.0
467-Starman by Ditko & Plastic Man begins; 1st app. Prince Gavyn (Starman). 1.50 4.50 12.0
468-490: 470-Origin Starman. 479-Dial 'H' For Hero begins, ends #490. 478-Last Starman & Plastic Man. 480-490: Dial 'H' For Hero 4.0
491-503: 491-100pg. Digest size begins; r/Legion of Super Heroes/Adv. #247, 267; Spectre, Aquaman, Superboy, S&K Sandman, Black Canary-r & new Shazam by Newton begin. 492,495,496,499-S&K Sandman-r/Adventure in all. 493-Challengers of the Unknown begins by Tuska w/brief origin. 493-495, 497-499-G.A. Captain Marvel-r. 494-499-Spectre-r/Spectre 1-3, 5-7. 496-Capt. Marvel Jr. new-s, Cockrum-a. 498-Mary Marvel new-s; Plastic Man-r

Adventures #1 © STJ

Adventures In The DC Universe #11 © DC

Adventures Into The Unknown #13 © ACG

begin; origin Bouncing Boy-r/ #301. 500-Legion-r (Digest size, 148 pgs.).
501-503: G.A.-r 1.75 5.25 14.00
... 80 Page Giant (10/98, $4.95) Wonder Woman, Shazam, Superboy, Supergirl Green Arrow, Legion, Bizarro World stories 5.00

NOTE: *Bizarro covers-285, 286, 288, 294, 295, 329. Vigilante app.-420, 426, 427.* **N. Adams** *a(r)-495i-498i; c-365-369, 371-373, 375-379, 381-383.* **Aparo** *a-431-433, 434i, 435, 436, 437i, 438i, 439-452, 503r; c-431-452.* **Austin** *a-449i 451i.* **Bernard Baily** *c-48, 50, 52-59.* **Bolland** *c-475.* **Burnley** *c-61-72, 116-120p.* **Chaykin** *a-438.* **Ditko** *a-467-478p; c-467p.* **Creig Flessel** *c-32, 33, 40, 42, 44, 46, 47, 51, 60.* **Giffen** *c-491p-494p, 500p.* **Grell** *a-435-437, 440.* **Guardineer** *c-34, 35, 45.* **Infantino** *a-416r.* **Kaluta** *c-425.* **Bob Kane** *a-38.* **G. Kane** *a-414r, 425; c-496-499, 537.* **Kirby** *a-250-256.* **Kubert** *a-413.* **Meskin** *a-81,127.* **Moldoff** *a-494i; c-49.* **Morrow** *a-413-415, 417, 422, 502r, 503r.* **Netzer/Nasser** *a-449-451.* **Newton** *a-459-461, 464-466, 491p, 492p.* **Paul Norris** *a-69.* **Orlando** *a-457p, 458p.* **Perez** *c-484-486, 490p.* **Simon/Kirby** *a-503r; c-73-97, 100-102.* **Starlin** *c-471.* **Staton** *a-445-447i, 456-458p, 459, 460, 461p-465p, 466,467p-478p, 502p(r); c-458, 461(back).* **Toth** *a-418, 419, 425, 431, 495p-497p.* **Tuska** *a-494p.*

ADVENTURE COMICS (Also see All Star Comics 1999 crossover titles)
DC Comics: May, 1999 ($1.99, one-shot)

1-Golden Age Starman and the Atom; Snejbjerg-a 2.00

ADVENTURE INTO MYSTERY
Atlas Comics (BFP No. 1/OPI No. 2-8): May, 1956 - No. 8, July, 1957

1-Powell s/f-a; Forte-a; Everett-c 30.00 90.00 335.00
2-Flying Saucer story 17.00 51.00 185.00
3,6-Everett-c 14.00 42.00 155.00
4-7: 4-Williamson-a, 4 pgs; Powell-a. 5-Everett-c/a, Orlando-a. 7-Torres-a; Everett-c 16.00 48.00 175.00
8-Moriera, Sale, Torres, Woodbridge-a, Severin-c 14.00 42.00 155.00

ADVENTURE IS MY CAREER
U.S. Coast Guard Academy/Street & Smith: 1945 (44 pgs.)

nn-Simon, Milt Gross-a 19.00 56.00 150.00

ADVENTURERS, THE
Aircel Comics/Adventure Publ.: Aug, 1986 - No. 10, 1987? ($1.50, B&W) V2#1, 1987 - V2#9, 1988; V3#1, Oct, 1989 - V3#6, 1990

1-Peter Hsu-a 3.00
1-Cover variant, limited ed. 5.00
1-2nd print (1986); 1st app. Elf Warrior 2.25
2,3, 0 (#4, 12/86)-Origin, 5-10, Book II, reg. & Limited Ed. #1 2.25
Book II, #2,3,0,4-7 2.25
Book III, #1 (10/89, $2.25)-Reg. & limited-c, Book III, #2-6 2.25

ADVENTURES (No. 2 Spectacular... on cover)
St. John Publishing Co.: Nov, 1949 - No. 2, Feb, 1950 (No. 1 ...in Romance on cover) (Slightly larger size)

1(Scarce); Bolle, Starr-a(2) 26.00 77.00 205.00
2(Scarce)-Slave Girl; China Bombshell app.; Bolle, L. Starr-a 40.00 120.00 340.00

ADVENTURES FOR BOYS
Bailey Enterprises: Dec, 1954

nn-Comics, text, & photos 5.70 17.00 40.00

ADVENTURES IN PARADISE (TV)
Dell Publishing Co.: Feb-Apr, 1962

Four Color#1301 4.10 12.30 45.00

ADVENTURES IN ROMANCE (See Adventures)

ADVENTURES IN SCIENCE (See Classics Illustrated Special Issue)

ADVENTURES IN THE DC UNIVERSE
DC Comics: Apr, 1997 - No. 19, Oct, 1998 ($1.75/$1.95/$1.99)

1-Animated style in all: JLA-c/app 4.00
2-11,13-17,19: 2-Flash app. 3-Wonder Woman. 4-Green Lantern. 6-Aquaman. 7-Shazam Family. 8-Blue Beetle & Booster Gold. 9-Flash. 10-Legion. 11-Green Lantern & Wonder Woman. 13-Impulse & Martian Manhunter. 14-Superboy/Flash race 3.00
12,18-JLA-c/app 3.50
Annual 1(1997, $3.95)-Dr. Fate, Impulse, Rose & Thorn, Superboy, Mister Miracle app. 4.00

ADVENTURES IN THE RIFLE BRIGADE
DC Comics (Vertigo): Oct, 2000 - No. 3, Dec, 1999 ($2.50, limited series)

1-3-Ennis-s/Ezquerra-a/Bolland-c 2.50

ADVENTURES IN 3-D (With glasses)
Harvey Publications: Nov, 1953 - No. 2, Jan, 1954 (25¢)

1-Nostrand, Powell-a, 2-Powell-a 18.00 53.00 140.00

ADVENTURES INTO DARKNESS (See Seduction of the Innocent 3-D)
Better-Standard Publications/Visual Editions: No. 5, Aug, 1952- No. 14, 1954

5-Katz-c/a; Toth-a(p) 38.00 113.00 300.00
6-Tuska, Katz-a 22.00 66.00 175.00
7-9: 7-Katz-c/a. 8,9-Toth-a(p) 23.00 69.00 185.00
10-12: 10,11-Jack Katz-a. 12-Toth-a; lingerie panel 20.00 60.00 160.00
13-Toth-a(p); Cannibalism story cited by T. E. Murphy articles 23.00 69.00 185.00
14 16.00 48.00 125.00

NOTE: **Fawcette** *a-13.* **Moriera** *a-5.* **Sekowsky** *a-10, 11, 13(2).*

ADVENTURES INTO TERROR (Formerly Joker Comics)
Marvel/Atlas Comics (CDS): No. 43, Nov, 1950 - No. 31, May, 1954

43(#1) 63.00 189.00 600.00
44(#2, 2/51)-Sol Brodsky-c 42.00 125.00 375.00
3(4/51), 4 28.00 83.00 220.00
5-Wolverton-c panel/Mystic #6; Rico-c panel also; Atom Bomb story 33.00 98.00 260.00
6,8: 8-Wolverton text illo r-/Marvel Tales #104 26.00 77.00 205.00
7-Wolverton-a "Where Monsters Dwell", 6 pgs.; Tuska-c; Maneely-c panels 55.00 165.00 500.00
9,10,12-Krigstein-a. 9-Decapitation panels 23.00 68.00 180.00
11,13-20 20.00 60.00 160.00
21-24,26-31 18.00 53.00 140.00
25-Matt Fox-a 23.00 68.00 180.00

NOTE: **Ayers** *a-21.* **Colan** *a-3, 5, 14, 21, 24, 25, 28, 29; c-27.* **Colletta** *a-30.* **Everett** *c-13, 21, 25.* **Fass** *a-28, 29.* **Forte** *a-28.* **Heath** *a-43, 44, 4-6, 22, 24, 26; c-43, 9, 11.* **Lazarus** *a-7.* **Maneely** *a-7(3 pg.), 10, 11, 21., 22 c-15, 29.* **Don Rico** *a-4, 5(3 pg.).* **Sekowsky** *a-43, 3, 4.* **Sinnott** *a-8, 9, 11, 28.* **Tuska** *a-14; c-7.*

ADVENTURES INTO THE UNKNOWN
American Comics Group: Fall, 1948 - No. 174, Aug, 1967 (No. 1-33: 52 pgs.)
(1st continuous series Supernatural comic; see Eerie #1)

1-Guardineer-a; adapt. of 'Castle of Otranto' by Horace Walpole 190.00 570.00 1800.00
2,3: 3-Feldstein-a (9 pgs) 74.00 221.00 700.00
4,5: 5-'Spirit Of Frankenstein' series begins, ends #12 (except #11) 40.00 120.00 325.00
6-10 33.00 98.00 260.00
11-16,18-20: 13-Starr-a 26.00 79.00 210.00
17-Story similar to movie 'The Thing' 31.00 94.00 250.00
21-26,28-30 21.00 62.00 165.00
27-Williamson/Krenkel-a (8 pgs.) 28.00 84.00 225.00
31-50: 38-Atom bomb panels 17.00 51.00 135.00
51-(1/54)-(3-D effect-c/story)-Only white cover 35.00 105.00 280.00
52-58: (3-D effect-c/stories with black covers). 52-E.C. swipe/Haunt Of Fear #14 33.00 98.00 260.00
59-3-D effect story only; new logo 26.00 79.00 210.00
60-Woodesque-a by Landau 11.00 33.00 90.00
61-Last pre-code issue (1-2/55) 11.00 33.00 90.00
62-70 6.35 19.00 70.00
71-90 5.00 15.00 55.00
91,96(#95 on inside),107,116-All have Williamson-a 6.35 19.00 70.00
92-95,97-99,101-106,108-115,117-128: 109-113,118-Whitney painted-c. 128-Williamson/Krenkel/Torres-a(r)/Forbidden Worlds #63; last 10¢ issue 4.10 12.30 45.00
100 4.55 13.65 50.00
129-153,157: 153,157-Magic Agent app. 3.20 9.60 35.00
154-Nemesis series begins (origin), ends #170 4.10 12.30 45.00
155,156,158-167,170-174 3.00 9.00 32.00
168-Ditko-a(p) 3.65 11.00 40.00
169-Nemesis battles Hitler 3.45 10.35 38.00

NOTE: *"Spirit of Frankenstein" series in 5, 6, 8-10, 12, 16.* **Buscema** *a-100, 106, 108-110, 158r, 165r.* **Cameron** *a-34.* **Craig** *a-152, 160.* **Goode** *a-45, 47, 60.* **Landau** *a-51, 59-63.* **Lazarus** *a-34, 48, 51, 52, 56, 58, 79, 87; c-31-56, 58.* **Reinman** *a-102, 111, 112, 115-118, 124, 130, 137, 141, 145, 164.* **Whitney** *c-12-30, 57, 59-on (most.)* **Torres/Williamson** *a-116.*

Adventures Into Weird Worlds #26 © MAR

The Adventures of Bob Hope #13 © DC

The Adventures of Evil and Malice #3 © Jimmie Robinson

 GD2.0 FN6.0 NM9.4

ADVENTURES INTO WEIRD WORLDS
Marvel/Atlas Comics (ACI): Jan, 1952 - No. 30, June, 1954

	GD2.0	FN6.0	NM9.4
1-Atom bomb panels	55.00	165.00	500.00
2-Sci/fic stories (2); one by Maneely	38.00	113.00	300.00
3-10: 7-Tongue ripped out. 10-Krigstein, Everett-a	26.00	77.00	205.00
11-21: 21-Hitler in Hell story	21.00	62.00	165.00
22-26: 24-Man holds hypo & splits in two	19.00	56.00	150.00
27-Matt Fox end of world story-a; severed head-c	36.00	108.00	290.00
28-Atom bomb story; decapitation panels	21.00	64.00	170.00
29,30	15.00	45.00	120.00

NOTE: *Ayers a-8, 26. **Everett** a-4, 5; c-6, 8, 10-13, 18, 19, 22, 24, 25; a-4, 25. **Fass** a-7. **Forte** a-21, 24. **Al Hartley** a-2. **Heath** a-1, 4, 17, 22; c-7, 9, 20. **Maneely** a-2, 3, 11, 20, 22, 23, 25; c-1, 3, 22, 25-27, 29. **Reinman** a-24, 28. **Rico** a-13. **Robinson** a-13. **Sinnott** a-25, 30. **Tuska** a-1, 2, 12, 15. **Whitney** a-7. **Wildey** a-28. Bondage c-22.*

ADVENTURES IN WONDERLAND
Lev Gleason Publications: April, 1955 - No. 5, Feb, 1956 (Jr. Readers Guild)

	GD2.0	FN6.0	NM9.4
1-Maurer-a	10.00	30.00	70.00
2-4	6.00	18.00	42.00
5-Christmas issue	7.00	21.00	48.00

ADVENTURES OF AARON
Image Comics: Mar, 1997 - No. 3, Sept, 1997 (2.95, B&W)

1,2,100(#3),3(#4) 3.00

ADVENTURES OF ALAN LADD, THE
National Periodical Publ.: Oct-Nov, 1949 - No. 9, Feb-Mar, 1951 (All 52 pgs.)

	GD2.0	FN6.0	NM9.4
1-Photo-c	92.00	276.00	875.00
2-Photo-c	49.00	147.00	440.00
3-6: Last photo-c	40.00	120.00	325.00
7-9	33.00	98.00	260.00

NOTE: ***Dan Barry** a-1. **Moreira** a-3-7.*

ADVENTURES OF ALICE (Also see Alice in Wonderland & ...at Monkey Island)
Civil Service Publ./Pentagon Publishing Co.: 1945

	GD2.0	FN6.0	NM9.4
1	10.50	32.00	85.00
2-Through the Magic Looking Glass	10.00	30.00	70.00

ADVENTURES OF BARON MUNCHAUSEN, THE
Now Comics: July, 1989 - No. 4, Oct, 1989 ($1.75, limited series)

1-4: Movie adaptation 2.00

ADVENTURES OF BARRY WEEN, BOY GENIUS, THE
Image Comics: Mar, 1999 - No. 3, May, 1999 ($2.95, B&W, limited series)

1-3-Judd Winick-s/a 3.00
TPB (Oni Press, 11/99, $8.95) 8.95

ADVENTURES OF BAYOU BILLY, THE
Archie Comics: Sept, 1989 - No. 5, June, 1990 ($1.00)

1-5: Esposito-c/a(i). 5-Kelley Jones-c 2.50

ADVENTURES OF BOB HOPE, THE (Also see True Comics #59)
National Per. Publ.: Feb-Mar, 1950 - No. 109, Feb-Mar, 1968 (#1-10: 52pgs.)

	GD2.0	FN6.0	NM9.4
1-Photo-c	168.00	505.00	1600.00
2-Photo-c	76.00	229.00	725.00
3,4-Photo-c	47.00	140.00	420.00
5-10	40.00	120.00	350.00
11-20	24.00	71.00	190.00
21-31 (2-3/55; last precode)	16.00	48.00	125.00
32-40	8.65	26.00	95.00
41-50	7.25	21.75	80.00
51-70	5.00	15.00	55.00
71-93	3.20	9.60	35.00
94-Aquaman cameo	3.65	11.00	40.00
95-1st app. Super-Hip & 1st monster issue (11/65)	4.55	13.65	50.00
96-105: Super-Hip and monster stories in all. 103-Batman, Robin, Ringo Starr cameos	3.20	9.60	35.00
106-109-All monster-c/stories by N. Adams-c/a	5.00	15.00	55.00

NOTE: *Buzzy in #34. Kitty Karr of Hollywood in #15, 17-20, 23, 28. Liz in #26, 109. Miss Beverly Hills of Hollywood in #7, 8, 10, 13, 14. Miss Melody Lane of Broadway in #15. Rusty in #23, 25. Tommy in #24. No 2nd feature in #2-4, 6, 8, 11, 12, 28-108.*

ADVENTURES OF CAPTAIN AMERICA
Marvel Comics: Sept, 1991 - No. 4, Jan, 1992 ($4.95, 52 pgs., squarebound, limited series)

1-4: 1-Origin in WW2; embossed-c; Nicieza scripts; Maguire-c/a(p) begins, ends #3. 2-4-Austin-c/a(i). 3,4-Red Skull app. 5.00

ADVENTURES OF CYCLOPS AND PHOENIX (Also See Askani'son & The Further Adventures of Cyclops And Phoenix)
Marvel Comics: May, 1994 - No. 4, Aug, 1994 ($2.95, limited series)

1-4-Characters from X-Men; origin of Cable 4.00
Trade paperback ($14.95)-reprints #1-4 15.00

ADVENTURES OF DEAN MARTIN AND JERRY LEWIS, THE
(The Adventures of Jerry Lewis #41 on) (See Movie Love #12)
National Periodical Publications: July-Aug, 1952 - No. 40, Oct, 1957

	GD2.0	FN6.0	NM9.4
1	89.00	268.00	850.00
2-3 pg origin on how they became a team	44.00	133.00	400.00
3-10: 3- I Love Lucy text featurette	24.00	71.00	190.00
11-19: Last precode (2/55)	15.00	45.00	120.00
20-30	12.50	37.50	100.00
31-40	10.00	30.00	75.00

ADVENTURES OF DETECTIVE ACE KING, THE (Also see Bob Scully-- & Detective Dan)
Humor Publ. Corp.: No date (1933) (36 pgs., 9-1/2x12") (10¢, B&W, one-shot) (paper-c)

	GD2.0	FN6.0	VF8.0
Book 1-Along with Detective Dan, the first comic w/original art & the first of a single theme.; Not reprints; Ace King by Martin Nadle (The American Sherlock Holmes). A Dick Tracy look-alike	300.00	900.00	2100.00

ADVENTURES OF EVIL AND MALICE, THE
Image Comics: June, 1999 - No. 3, Nov, 1999 ($3.50/$3.95, limited series)

	GD2.0	FN6.0	NM9.4
1,2-Jimmie Robinson-s/a			3.50
3-(3.95)			3.95

ADVENTURES OF FELIX THE CAT, THE
Harvey Comics: May, 1992 ($1.25)

1-Messmer-r 3.00

ADVENTURES OF FORD FAIRLANE, THE
DC Comics: May, 1990 - No. 4, Aug, 1990 ($1.50, limited series, mature)

1-4: Andrew Dice Clay movie tie-in; Don Heck inks 2.00

ADVENTURES OF HOMER COBB, THE
Say/Bart Prod. : Sept, 1947 (Oversized)
(Published in the U.S., but printed in Canada)

	GD2.0	FN6.0	NM9.4
1-(Scarce)-Feldstein-c/a	28.00	84.00	225.00

ADVENTURES OF HOMER GHOST (See Homer The Happy Ghost)
Atlas Comics: June, 1957 - No. 2, Aug, 1957

	GD2.0	FN6.0	NM9.4
V1#1,2: 2-Robot-c	7.15	21.50	50.00

ADVENTURES OF JERRY LEWIS, THE (Adventures of Dean Martin & Jerry Lewis No. 1-40)(See Super DC Giant)
National Periodical Publ.: No. 41, Nov, 1957 - No. 124, May-June, 1971

	GD2.0	FN6.0	NM9.4
41	6.80	20.50	75.00
42-60	5.45	16.35	60.00
61-67,69-73,75-80	4.10	12.30	45.00
68,74-Photo-c (movie)	5.00	15.00	55.00
81,82,85-87,90,91,93,94,96,98,99: 93-Beatles parody as babies	3.00	9.00	32.00
83,84,88: 83-1st Monsters-c/s. 84-Jerry as a Super-hero-c/s. 88-1st Witch, Miss Kraft	3.20	9.60	35.00
89-Bob Hope app.; Wizard of Oz & Alfred E. Neuman in MAD parody	3.20	9.60	35.00
92-Superman cameo	4.10	12.30	45.00
95-1st Uncle Hal Wack-A-Buy Camp-c/s	3.20	9.60	35.00
97-Batman/Robin/Joker-c/story; Riddler & Penguin app; Dick Sprang-c.	6.35	19.00	70.00
100	3.45	10.35	38.00
101,103,104-Neal Adams-c/a	5.00	15.00	55.00
102-Beatles app.; Neal Adams c/a	6.80	20.50	75.00

Adventures of Mighty Mouse #12 © Paul Terry

The Adventures of Pinky Lee #2 © MAR

Adventures of Superman #573 © DC

	GD2.0	FN6.0	NM9.4
105-Superman x-over	4.10	12.30	45.00
106-111,113-116	2.50	7.50	24.00
112,117: 112-Flash x-over. 117-W. Woman x-over	4.10	12.30	45.00
118-124	2.00	6.00	18.00

NOTE: *Monster-c/s-90,93,96,98,101. Wack-A-Buy Camp-c/s-96,99,102,107,108.*

ADVENTURES OF JO-JOY, THE (See Jo-Joy)

ADVENTURES OF LASSIE, THE (See Lassie)

ADVENTURES OF LUTHER ARKWRIGHT, THE
Valkyrie Press/Dark Horse Comics: Oct, 1987 - No. 9, Jan, 1989 ($2.00, B&W)
V2, #1, Mar, 1990 - V2#9, 1990 ($1.95, B&W)

	GD2.0	FN6.0	NM9.4
1-9: 1-Alan Moore intro., V2#1-9 (Dark Horse): r-1st series; new-c			4.00
TPB (1997, $14.95) r/#1-9 w/Michael Moorcock intro.			15.00

ADVENTURES OF MIGHTY MOUSE (Mighty Mouse Adventures No. 1)
St. John Publishing Co.: No. 2, Jan, 1952 - No. 18, May, 1955

	GD2.0	FN6.0	NM9.4
2	24.00	73.00	195.00
3-5	12.50	37.50	100.00
6-18	10.00	30.00	70.00

ADVENTURES OF MIGHTY MOUSE (2nd Series)
(Two No. 144's; formerly Paul Terry's Comics; No. 129-137 have nn's)
(Becomes Mighty Mouse No. 161 on)
St. John/Pines/Dell/Gold Key: No. 126, Aug, 1955 - No. 160, Oct, 1963

	GD2.0	FN6.0	NM9.4
126(8/55), 127(10/55), 128(11/55)-St. John	8.65	26.00	60.00
nn(129, 4/56)-144(8/59)-Pines	4.55	13.65	50.00
144(10-12/59)-155(7-9/62) Dell	3.65	11.00	40.00
156(10/62)-160(10/63) Gold Key	4.10	12.30	45.00

NOTE: *Early issues titled "Paul Terry's Adventures of ...."*

ADVENTURES OF MIGHTY MOUSE (Formerly Mighty Mouse)
Gold Key: No. 166, Mar, 1979 - No. 172, Jan, 1980

	GD2.0	FN6.0	NM9.4
166-172			5.00

ADVS. OF MR. FROG & MISS MOUSE (See Dell Junior Treasury No. 4)

ADVENTURES OF OZZIE & HARRIET, THE (See Ozzie & Harriet)

ADVENTURES OF PATORUZU
Green Publishing Co.: Aug, 1946 - Winter, 1946

	GD2.0	FN6.0	NM9.4
nn's-Contains Animal Crackers reprints	5.00	15.00	30.00

ADVENTURES OF PINKY LEE, THE (TV)
Atlas Comics: July, 1955 - No. 5, Dec, 1955

	GD2.0	FN6.0	NM9.4
1	26.00	79.00	210.00
2-5	16.00	48.00	125.00

ADVENTURES OF PIPSQUEAK, THE (Formerly Pat the Brat)
Archie Publications (Radio Comics): No. 34, Sept, 1959 - No. 39, July, 1960

	GD2.0	FN6.0	NM9.4
34	3.20	9.60	35.00
35-39	2.50	7.50	25.00

ADVENTURES OF QUAKE & QUISP, THE (See Quaker Oats "Plenty of Glutton")

ADVENTURES OF REX THE WONDER DOG, THE (Rex...No. 1)
National Periodical Publications: Jan-Feb, 1952 - No. 45, May-June, 1959; No. 46, Nov-Dec, 1959

	GD2.0	FN6.0	NM9.4
1-(Scarce)-Toth-c/a	111.00	332.00	1050.00
2-(Scarce)-Toth-c/a	55.00	165.00	525.00
3-(Scarce)-Toth-a	44.00	133.00	400.00
4,5	38.00	113.00	300.00
6-10	28.00	84.00	225.00
11-Atom bomb-c/story; dinosaur-c/sty	33.00	98.00	260.00
12-19: 19-Last precode (1-2/55)	16.00	49.00	130.00
20-46	12.00	36.00	95.00

NOTE: ***Infantino, Gil Kane** art in 5-19 (most)*

ADVENTURES OF RHEUMY PEEPERS AND CHUNKY HIGHLIGHTS, THE
Oni Press: Feb, 1999 ($2.95, B&W, one-shot)

	GD2.0	FN6.0	NM9.4
nn-Penn Jillette-s/Renée French-a			3.00

ADVENTURES OF ROBIN HOOD, THE (Formerly Robin Hood)
Magazine Enterprises (Sussex Publ. Co.): No. 7, 9/57 - No. 8, 11/57
(Based on Richard Greene TV Show)

	GD2.0	FN6.0	NM9.4
7,8-Richard Greene photo-c. 7-Powell-a	15.00	45.00	120.00

ADVENTURES OF ROBIN HOOD, THE
Gold Key: Mar, 1974 - No. 7, Jan, 1975 (Disney cartoon) (36 pgs.)

	GD2.0	FN6.0	NM9.4
1(90291-403)-Part-r of $1.50 editions	1.75	5.25	14.00
2-7: 1-7 are part-r	1.00	3.00	8.00

ADVENTURES OF SNAKE PLISSKEN
Marvel Comics: Jan, 1997 ($2.50, one-shot)

	GD2.0	FN6.0	NM9.4
1-Based on Escape From L.A. movie; Brereton-c			2.50

ADVENTURES OF SPIDER-MAN, THE (Based on animated TV series)
Marvel Comics: Apr, 1996 - No. 12, Mar, 1997 (99¢)

	GD2.0	FN6.0	NM9.4
1-12: 1-Punisher app. 2-Venom cameo. 3-X-Men. 6-Fantastic Four			2.00

ADVENTURES OF SUPERBOY, THE (See Superboy, 2nd Series)

ADVENTURES OF SUPERMAN (Formerly Superman)
DC Comics: No. 424, Jan, 1987 - No. 499, Feb, 1993;
No. 500, Early June, 1993 - Present

	GD2.0	FN6.0	NM9.4
424-Ordway-c/a/Wolfman-s begin following Byrne's Superman revamp			2.50
425-435,437-462: 426-Legends x-over. 432-1st app. Jose Delgado who becomes Gangbuster in #434. 437-Millennium x-over. 438-New Brainiac app. 440-Batman app. 449-Invasion			2.50
436-Byrne scripts begin; Millennium x-over			3.00
463-Superman/Flash race; cover swipe/Superman #199			4.00
464-Lobo-c & app. (pre-dates Lobo #1)			4.00
465-495: 467-Part 2 of Batman story. 473-Hal Jordan, Guy Gardner x-over. 477-Legion app. 491-Last $1.00-c. 480-($1.75, 52 pgs.). 495-Forever People-c/story; Darkseid app.			2.00
496,497: 496-Doomsday cameo. 497-Doomsday battle issue			3.00
496,497-2nd printings			2.00
498,499-Funeral for a Friend; Supergirl app.			2.50
498-2nd & 3rd printings			2.00
500-($2.95, 68 pgs.)-Collector's edition w/card			3.50
500-($2.50, 68 pgs.)-Regular edition w/different-c			2.50
500-Platinum edition			20.00
501-($1.95)-Collector's edition with die-cut-c			2.00
501-($1.50)-Regular edition w/mini-poster & diff.-c			2.00
502-516: 502-Supergirl-c/story. 508-Challengers of the Unknown app. 510-Bizarro-c/story. 516-(9/94)-Zero Hour			2.00
505-($2.50)-Holo-grafx foil-c edition			2.50
0,517-523: 0-(10/94). 517-(11/94)			2.00
524-549,551-580: 524-Begin $1.95-c. 527-Return of Alpha Centurion (Zero Hour) 533-Impulse c/app. 535-Luthor-c/app. 536-Brainiac app. 537-Parasite app. 540-Final Night x-over. 541 Superboy-c/app.; Lois & Clark honeymoon. 545-New powers. 546-New costume. 551-Cyborg app. 555-Red & Blue Supermen battle. 557-Millennium Giants x-over, 558-560: Superman Silver Age-style story; Krypto app. 561-Begin $1.99-c. 565-JLA app.			2.00
550-($3.50)-Double sized			3.50
581-588: 581-Begin $2.25-c. 583-Emperor Joker. 588-Casey-s			2.25
#1,000,000 (11/98) Gene Ha-c; 853rd Century x-over			3.00
Annual 1 (1987, $1.25, 52 pgs.)-Starlin-c & scripts			4.00
Annual 2,3 (1990, 1991, $2.00, 68 pgs.): 2-Byrne-c/a(i); Legion '90 (Lobo) app. 3-Armageddon 2001 x-over			3.00
Annual 4-6 ('92-'94, $2.50, 68 pgs.): 4-Guy Gardner/Lobo-c/story; Eclipso storyline; Quesada-c(p). 5-Bloodlines storyline. 6-Elseworlds sty.			3.00
Annual 7,9('95, '97, $3.95)-7-Year One story. 9-Pulp Heroes sty			4.00
Annual 8 (1996, $2.95)-Legends of the Dead Earth story			3.00

NOTE: ***Erik Larsen** a-431.*

ADVENTURES OF THE DOVER BOYS
Archie Comics (Close-up): September, 1950 - No. 2, 1950 (No month given)

	GD2.0	FN6.0	NM9.4
1,2	8.65	26.00	60.00

ADVENTURES OF THE FLY (The Fly #1-6; Fly Man No. 32-39; See The Double Life of Private Strong, The Fly, Laugh Comics & Mighty Crusaders)
Archie Publications/Radio Comics: Aug, 1959 - No. 30, Oct, 1964; No. 31, May, 1965

	GD2.0	FN6.0	NM9.4
1-Shield app.; origin The Fly; S&K-c/a	46.00	138.00	600.00
2-Williamson, S&K-a	28.00	85.00	310.00
3-Origin retold; Davis, Powell-a	22.50	67.00	245.00

Adventures of the Jaguar #2 © AP

Aftermath #1 © Chaos! Comics

Age of Bronze #7 © Eric Shanower

	GD2.0	FN6.0	NM9.4
4-Neal Adams-a(p)(1 panel); S&K-c; Powell-a; 2 pg. Shield story	12.50	37.00	135.00
5-10: 7-1st S.A. app. Black Hood (7/60). 8-1st S.A. app. Shield (9/60). 9-Shield app. 9-1st app. Cat Girl. 10-Black Hood app.	8.15	24.50	90.00
11-13,15-20: 13-1st app. Fly Girl w/o costume. 16-Last 10¢ issue. 20-Origin Fly Girl retold	5.00	15.00	55.00
14-Origin & 1st app. Fly Girl in costume	6.80	20.50	75.00
21-30: 23-Jaguar cameo. 27-29-Black Hood 1 pg. strips. 30-Comet x-over (1st S.A. app.) in Fly Girl	3.20	9.60	35.00
31-Black Hood, Shield, Comet app.	3.65	11.00	40.00

NOTE: ***Simon*** *c-2-4.* ***Tuska*** *a-1. Cover title to #31 is Flyman; Advs. of the Fly inside.*

ADVENTURES OF THE JAGUAR, THE (See Blue Ribbon Comics, Laugh Comics & Mighty Crusaders)
Archie Publications (Radio Comics): Sept, 1961 - No. 15, Nov, 1963

	GD2.0	FN6.0	NM9.4
1-Origin Jaguar (1st app?) by J. Rosenberger	17.50	52.00	190.00
2,3: 3-Last 10¢ issue	8.65	26.00	95.00
4-6-Catgirl app. (#4's-c is same as splash pg.)	6.80	20.50	75.00
7-10	5.00	15.00	55.00
11-15:13,14-Catgirl, Black Hood app. in both	4.10	12.30	45.00

ADVENTURES OF THE MASK (TV cartoon)
Dark Horse Comics: Jan, 1996 - No. 12, Dec, 1996 ($2.50)

1-12: Based on animated series 2.50

ADVENTURES OF THE NEW MEN (Formerly Newmen #1-21)
Maximum Press: No. 22, Nov, 1996; No. 23, March, 1997 ($2.50)

22,23-Sprouse-c/a 2.50

ADVENTURES OF THE OUTSIDERS, THE (Formerly Batman & The Outsiders; also see The Outsiders)
DC Comics: No. 33, May, 1986 - No. 46, June, 1987

33-46: 39-45-r/Outsiders #1-7 by Aparo 2.00

ADVENTURES OF THE SUPER MARIO BROTHERS (See Super Mario Bros.)
Valiant: 1990 - No. 9, Oct, 1991 ($1.50)

V2#1-9 4.00

ADVENTURES OF THE THING, THE (Also see The Thing)
Marvel Comics: Apr, 1992 - No. 4, July, 1992, ($1.25, limited series)

1-4: 1-r/Marvel Two-In-One #50 by Byrne; Kieth-c. 2-4-r/Marvel Two-In-One #80,51 & 77; 2-Ghost Rider-c/story; Quesada-c. 3-Miller-r/Quesada-c; new Perez-a (4 pgs.) 2.00

ADVENTURES OF THE X-MEN, THE (Based on animated TV series)
Marvel Comics: Apr, 1996 - No. 12, Mar, 1997 (99¢)

1-6: 1-Wolverine/Hulk battle. 3-Spider-Man-c. 5,6-Magneto-c/app. 3.00
7-12 2.00

ADVENTURES OF TINKER BELL (See Tinker Bell, 4-Color No. 896 & 982)

ADVENTURES OF TOM SAWYER (See Dell Junior Treasury No. 10)

ADVENTURES OF YOUNG DR. MASTERS, THE
Archie Comics (Radio Comics): Aug, 1964 - No. 2, Nov, 1964

	GD2.0	FN6.0	NM9.4
1	2.40	7.35	22.00
2	2.00	6.00	16.00

ADVENTURES ON OTHER WORLDS (See Showcase #17 & 18)

ADVENTURES ON THE PLANET OF THE APES (Also see Planet of the Apes)
Marvel Comics Group: Oct, 1975 - No. 11, Dec, 1976

	GD2.0	FN6.0	NM9.4
1-Planet of the Apes magazine-r in color; Starlin-c; adapts movie thru #6	2.00	6.00	16.00
2-11: 5-7-(25¢-c edition). 7-Adapts 2nd movie (thru #11)	1.00	3.00	8.00
5-7-(30¢-c variants, limited distribution)	2.00	6.00	16.00

NOTE: ***Alcala*** *a-6-11r.* ***Buckler*** *c-2p.* ***Nasser*** *c-7.* ***Ploog*** *a-1-9.* ***Starlin*** *c-6.* ***Tuska*** *a-1-5r.*

AFRICA
Magazine Enterprises: 1955

	GD2.0	FN6.0	NM9.4
1(A-1#137)-Cave Girl, Thun'da; Powell-c/a(4)	24.00	71.00	190.00

AFRICAN LION (Disney movie)
Dell Publishing Co.: Nov, 1955

	GD2.0	FN6.0	NM9.4
Four Color #665	5.00	15.00	60.0

AFTER DARK
Sterling Comics: No. 6, May, 1955 - No. 8, Sept, 1955

	GD2.0	FN6.0	NM9.4
6-8-Sekowsky-a in all	8.65	26.00	60.0

AFTERMATH (Leads into Lady Death: Dark Millennium)
Chaos! Comics: Feb, 2000 ($2.95, one-shot)

1-Pulido & Kaminski-s/Luke Ross-a; Reis-c 3.0
1-($6.95) DF Edition; Brereton painted-c 7.0

AGAINST BLACKSHARD 3-D (Also see SoulQuest)
Sirius Comics: August, 1986 ($2.25)

1 3.0

AGENT LIBERTY SPECIAL (See Superman, 2nd Series)
DC Comics: 1992 ($2.00, 52 pgs, one-shot)

1-1st solo adventure; Guice-c/a(i) 2.0

AGENT THREE-ZERO
Galaxinovels, Inc.: Sept, 1993 ($3.95, 52 pgs.)

1-Polybagged with card & mini-poster; Platt-c/a(1st work) 4.0

AGENT THREE-ZERO: THE BLUE SULTANS QUEST/ BLUE SULTAN–GALAXI FACT FILES
Galaxi Novels: 1994 ($2.95, color w/text-no comics, limited series)

1-($2.95)-Flip book w/Blue Sultan 3.0
1-($3.95)-Polybagged w/trading card; flip book w/Blue Sultan 4.0
1-($5.95)-Platinum embossed edition; flip book w/ Blue Sultan 6.0

AGENTS OF LAW (Also see Comic's Greatest World)
Dark Horse Comics: Mar, 1995 - No.6, Sept, 1995 ($2.50)

1-6: 5-Predator app. 6-Predator app.; death of Law 2.5

AGE OF APOCALYPSE: THE CHOSEN
Marvel Comics: Apr, 1995 ($2.50, one-shot)

1-Wraparound-c 3.0

AGE OF BRONZE
Image Comics: Nov, 1998 - Present ($2.95/$3.50, B&W, limited series)

1-6-Eric Shanower-c/s/a 3.0
7-9-($3.50) 3.5
...Special (6/99, $2.95) Story of Agamemnon and Menelaus 3.0

AGE OF HEROES, THE
Halloween Comics/Image Comics #3 on: 1996 - Present ($2.95, B&W)

1-5: James Hudnall scripts; John Ridgway-c/a 3.0
...Special ($4.95) r/#1,2 5.0
...Special 2 ($6.95) r/#3,4 7.0
...Wex 1 ('98, $2.95) Hudnall-s/Angel Fernandez-a 3.0

AGE OF INNOCENCE: THE REBIRTH OF IRON MAN
Marvel Comics: Feb, 1996 ($2.50, one-shot)

1-New origin of Tony Stark 3.0

AGE OF REPTILES
Dark Horse Comics: Nov, 1993 - No. 4, Feb, 1994 ($2.50, limited series)

1-4: Delgado-c/a/scripts in all 3.0

AGE OF REPTILES: THE HUNT
Dark Horse Comics: May, 1996 - No. 5, Sept, 1996 ($2.95, limited series)

1-5: Delgado-c/a/scripts in all; wraparound-c 3.0

AGGIE MACK
Four Star Comics Corp./Superior Comics Ltd.: Jan, 1948 - No. 8, Aug, 1949

	GD2.0	FN6.0	NM9.4
1-Feldstein-a, "Johnny Prep"	33.00	98.00	260.00
2,3-Kamen-c	17.00	51.00	135.00
4-Feldstein "Johnny Prep"; Kamen-c	23.00	68.00	180.00
5-8-Kamen-c/a	18.00	53.00	140.0

AGGIE MACK
Dell Publishing Co.: Apr - Jun, 1962

	GD2.0	FN6.0	NM9.4
Four Color #1335	3.20	9.60	35.0

AIR ACE (Formerly Bill Barnes No. 1-12)

Air Ace V2 #1 © Condé Nast

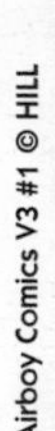

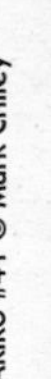

	GD2.0	FN6.0	NM9.4

ɜt & Smith Publications: V2#1, Jan, 1944 - V3#8(No. 20), Feb-Mar, 1947

	30.00	90.00	240.00
·-Classic-c	25.00	75.00	200.00
·-12: 7-Powell-a	13.00	39.00	105.00
·-6	10.50	32.00	85.00
·-Powell bondage-c/a; all atomic issue	22.00	66.00	175.00
·(V5#8 on-c)-Powell-c/a	12.00	36.00	95.00

ʒOY (Also see Airmaidens, Skywolf, Target: Airboy & Valkyrie)
ɘse Comics: July, 1986 - No. 50, Oct, 1989 (#1-8, 50¢, 20 pgs., bi-weekly; ı, 36pgs.; #34-on monthly)

ɜ: 2-1st Marisa; Skywolf gets new costume. 3-The Heap begins. 5-Valkyrie ɜturns; Dave Stevens-c. 9-Begin $1.25-c; Skywolf begins. 11-Origin of G.A. ɾboy & his plane Birdie. 28-Mr. Monster vs. The Heap. 33-Begin $1.75-c. ·-40-The Heap by Infantino. 41-r/1st app. Valkyrie from Air Fighters.

·-Begin $1.95-c. 46,47-part-r/Air Fighters. 48-Black Angel-r/A.F			2.00
$4.95, 52 pgs.)-Kubert-c			5.00

: Evans c-21. Gulacy c-7, 20. Spiegle a-34, 35, 37. Ken Steacy painted c-17, 33.

ɜOY COMICS (Air Fighters Comics No. 1-22)
ıan Periodicals: V2#11, Dec, 1945 - V10#4, May, 1953 (No V3#3)

1	68.00	205.00	650.00
2-Valkyrie app.	44.00	133.00	400.00
,2(no #3)	38.00	113.00	300.00
·-The Heap app. in Skywolf	34.00	101.00	270.00
·,7,8,10,11	28.00	84.00	225.00
·-Valkyrie-c/app.	31.00	94.00	250.00
·-Origin The Heap	34.00	101.00	270.00
·-Skywolf & Airboy x-over; Valkyrie app.	38.00	113.00	300.00
-Iron Lady app.	33.00	98.00	260.00
,3,12: 2-Rackman begins	23.00	69.00	185.00
·-Simon & Kirby-c	26.00	79.00	210.00
·-11-All S&K-a	25.00	75.00	200.00
-4,6-11: 4-Infantino Heap. 10-Origin The Heap	16.00	49.00	130.00
·-Skull-c.	19.00	57.00	150.00
2-Krigstein-a(p)	19.00	57.00	150.00
-3,5-12: 6,8-Origin The Heap	16.00	49.00	130.00
·-Origin retold	21.00	62.00	165.00
-12: 7,8,10-Origin The Heap	16.00	49.00	130.00
-3,5-12	15.00	45.00	120.00
-Krigstein-a	16.00	48.00	125.00
-4,6-12: 2-Valkyrie app. 7-One pg. Frazetta ad	12.00	36.00	95.00
(#100)	13.00	39.00	105.00
·1-4	11.00	33.00	90.00

: Barry a-V2#3, 7. Bolle a-V4#12. McWilliams a-V3#7, 9. Powell a-V7#2, 3, V8#1, 6. a-V5#1, 12. Dick Wood a-V4#12. Bondage-c V5#8.

ɜOY MEETS THE PROWLER
ɘse Comics: Aug, 1987 ($1.95, one-shot)

ɔhn Snyder, III-c/a			2.00

ɜOY-MR. MONSTER SPECIAL
ɘse Comics: Aug, 1987 ($1.75, one-shot)

			3.00

ɜOY VERSUS THE AIR MAIDENS
ɘse Comics: July, 1988 ($1.95)

			3.00

ꟻIGHTERS CLASSICS
ɘse Comics: Nov, 1987 - No. 6, May, 1989 ($3.95, 68 pgs., B&W)

Reprints G.A. Air Fighters #2-7. 1-Origin Airboy			4.00

ꟻIGHTERS COMICS (Airboy Comics #23 (V2#11) on)
an Periodicals: Nov, 1941; No. 2, Nov, 1942 - V2#10, Fall, 1945

-(Produced by Funnies, Inc.); Black Commander only app.	211.00	633.00	2000.00
(11/42)-(Produced by Quality artists & Biro for Hillman); Origin & 1st app. ʌirboy & Iron Ace; Black Angel (1st app.), Flying Dutchman & Skywolf 1st app.) begin; Fuje-a; Biro-c/a	314.00	943.00	3300.00
-Origin/1st app. The Heap; origin Skywolf; 2nd Airboy app./c	158.00	474.00	1500.00

	GD2.0	FN6.0	NM9.4
4-Japan war-c	110.00	330.00	1045.00
5,6: 6-Japanese soldiers as rats-c	84.00	252.00	800.00
7-12: 7,10,11-War covers	70.00	210.00	665.00
V2#1,3-9: 5-Flag-c; Fuje-a. 7-Valkyrie app.	63.00	189.00	600.00
2-Skywolf by Giunta; Flying Dutchman by Fuje; 1st meeting Valkyrie & Airboy (she worked for the Nazis in beginning); 1st app. Valkyrie (11/43); Valkyrie-c	100.00	300.00	950.00
10-Origin The Heap & Skywolf	70.00	210.00	665.00

NOTE: *Fuje a-V1#2, 5, 7, V2#2, 3, 5, 7-9. Giunta a-V2#2, 3, 7, 9.*

AIRFIGHTERS MEET SGT. STRIKE SPECIAL, THE
Eclipse Comics: Jan, 1988 ($1.95, one-shot, stiff-c)

1-Airboy, Valkyrie, Skywolf app.			2.00

AIR FORCES (See American Air Forces)

AIRMAIDENS SPECIAL
Eclipse Comics: August, 1987 ($1.75, one-shot, Baxter paper)

1-Marisa becomes La Lupina (origin)			2.00

AIR RAIDERS
Marvel Comics (Star Comics)/Marvel #3 on: Nov, 1987- No. 5, Mar, 1988 ($1.00)

1,5: Kelley Jones-a in all			3.50
2-4: 2-Thunderhammer app.			2.50

AIRTIGHT GARAGE, THE (Also see Elsewhere Prince)
Marvel Comics (Epic Comics): July, 1993 - No. 4, Oct, 1993 ($2.50, limited series, Baxter paper)

1-4: Moebius-c/a/scripts			2.50

AIR WAR STORIES
Dell Publishing Co.: Sept-Nov, 1964 - No. 8, Aug, 1966

1-Painted-c; Glanzman-c/a begins	3.20	9.60	35.00
2-8: 2-Painted-c (all painted?)	2.40	7.35	22.00

AKIKO
Sirius: Mar, 1996 - Present ($2.50/$2.95, B&W)

1-Crilley-c/a/scripts in all			5.00
2			4.00
3-24 ($2.50), 25-($2.95, 32 pgs.)-w/Asala back-up pages			3.00
26-39			2.50
40,41: 40-Begin $2.95-c			2.95
TPB Volume 1,4 ('97, 2/00, $14.95) 1-r/#1-7. 4-r/#19-25			15.00
TPB Volume 2,3 ('98, '99, $11.95) 2-r/#8-13. 3- r/#14-18			12.00

AKIKO ON THE PLANET SMOO
Sirius: Dec, 1995 ($3.95, B&W)

V1#1-($3.95)-Crilley-c/a/scripts; gatefold-c	1.00	2.80	7.00
Ashcan ('95, mail offer)			2.00
Hardcover V1#1 (12/95, $19.95, B&W, 40 pgs.)			20.00
The Color Edition(2/00,$4.95)			5.00

AKIRA
Marvel Comics (Epic Comics): Sept, 1988 - No. 38, Dec, 1995 ($3.50/$3.95/$6.95, deluxe, 68 pgs.)

1-Manga by Katsuhiro Otomo	2.50	7.50	23.00
1,2-2nd printings (1989, $3.95)			5.00
2	1.50	4.50	12.00
3-5	1.10	3.30	9.00
6-16	1.00	3.00	7.00
17-33: 17-$3.95-c begins		2.40	6.00
34-38: 34-(1994)-$6.95-c begins. 35-37: 35-(1995). 37-Texieira back-up, Gibbons, Williams pin-ups. 38-Moebius, Allred, Pratt, Toth, Romita, Van Fleet, O'Neill, Madureira pin-ups.	1.10	3.30	9.00

ALADDIN & HIS WONDERFUL LAMP (See Dell Jr Treasury #2)

ALAN LADD (See The Adventures of...)

ALAN MOORE'S AWESOME UNIVERSE HANDBOOK
Awesome Entertainment: Apr, 1999 - Present ($2.95, B&W)

1-Alan Moore-text/ Alex Ross-sketch pages and 2 covers			3.00

ALAN MOORE'S SONGBOOK
Caliber Comics: 1998 ($5.95, B&W)

Alarming Tales #2 © HARV

Alf #1 © MAR

Alien Encounters #10 © ECL

GD2.0 FN6.0 NM9.4

1-Alan Moore song lyrics w/illust. by various 6.00

ALARMING ADVENTURES
Harvey Publications: Oct, 1962 - No. 3, Feb, 1963

	GD2.0	FN6.0	NM9.4
1-Crandall/Williamson-a	7.65	23.00	85.00
2-Williamson/Crandall-a	5.00	15.00	55.00
3	4.10	12.30	45.00

NOTE: **Bailey** a-1, 3. **Crandall** a-1p, 2i. **Powell** a-2(2). **Severin** c-1-3. **Torres** a-2? **Tuska** a-1. **Williamson** a-1i, 2p.

ALARMING TALES
Harvey Publications (Western Tales): Sept, 1957 - No. 6, Nov, 1958

	GD2.0	FN6.0	NM9.4
1-Kirby-c/a(4); Kamandi prototype story by Kirby	23.00	69.00	185.00
2-Kirby-a(4)	18.00	53.00	140.00
3,4-Kirby-a. 4-Powell, Wildey-a	12.50	37.50	100.00
5-Kirby/Williamson-a; Wildey-a; Severin-c	14.00	41.00	110.00
6-Williamson-a?; Severin-c	11.00	33.00	90.00

ALBEDO
Thoughts And Images: Apr, 1985 - No. 14, Spring, 1989 (B&W)
Antarctic Press: (Vol. 2) Jun, 1991 - No. 10 ($2.50)

	GD2.0	FN6.0	NM9.4
0-Yellow cover; 50 copies	5.45	16.35	60.00
0-White cover, 450 copies	2.40	7.35	22.00
0-Blue, 1st printing, 500 copies	2.40	7.35	22.00
0-Blue, 2nd printing, 1000 copies	1.50	4.50	12.00
0-3rd & 4th printing			4.00
1-Dark red	1.50	4.50	12.00
1-Bright red		2.40	6.00
2-1st app. Usagi Yojimbo by Stan Sakai; 2000 copies - no 2nd printing	1.50	4.50	12.00
3			4.00
4-Usagi Yojimbo-c			5.00
5-14			3.00
(Vol. 2) 1-10			2.50
Color Special			3.00

ALBEDO ANTHROPOMORPHICS
Antarctic Press: (Vol. 3) Spring, 1994 - No. 4, Jan, 1996 ($2.95, color); (Vol. 4) Dec, 1999 - No. 2, Jan, 1999 ($2.95/$2.99, B&W)

V3#1-4-Steve Gallacci-c/a 3.00
V4#1,2 3.00

ALBERTO (See The Crusaders)

ALBERT THE ALLIGATOR & POGO POSSUM (See Pogo Possum)

ALBUM OF CRIME (See Fox Giants)

ALBUM OF LOVE (See Fox Giants)

AL CAPP'S DOGPATCH (Also see Mammy Yokum)
Toby Press: No. 71, June, 1949 - No. 4, Dec, 1949

	GD2.0	FN6.0	NM9.4
71(#1)-Reprints from Tip Top #112-114	24.00	71.00	190.00
2-4: 4-Reprints from Li'l Abner #73	16.00	48.00	125.00

AL CAPP'S SHMOO (Also see Oxydol-Dreft & Washable Jones & Shmoo)
Toby Press: July, 1949 - No. 5, Apr, 1950 (None by Al Capp)

	GD2.0	FN6.0	NM9.4
1	40.00	120.00	320.00
2-5: 3-Sci-fi trip to moon. 4-X-Mas-c; origin/1st app. Super-Shmoo	28.00	83.00	220.00

AL CAPP'S WOLF GAL
Toby Press: 1951 - No. 2, 1952

1,2-Edited-r from Li'l Abner #63,64 34.00 101.00 270.00

ALEXANDER THE GREAT (Movie)
Dell Publishing Co.: No. 688, May, 1956

Four Color 688-Buscema-a; photo-c 6.30 19.00 75.00

ALF (TV) (See Star Comics Digest)
Marvel Comics: Mar, 1988 - No. 50, Feb, 1992 ($1.00)

	GD2.0	FN6.0	NM9.4
1-(Giant) Photo-c			4.00
1-2nd printing			2.50
2-19: 6-Photo-c			2.50
20-22: 20-Conan parody. 21-Marx Brothers. 22-X-Men parody			3.00

23-30: 24-Rhonda-c/app. 29-3-D cover
31-49: 44-X-Men parody. 45-Wolverine, Punisher, Capt. America-c
50-($1.75, 52 pgs.)-Final issue; photo-c
Annual 1-3: 1-Rocky & Bullwinkle app. 2-Sienkiewicz-c. 3-TMNT parody
...Comics Digest 1,2: 1-(1988)-Reprints Alf #1,2 1.00 3.00
Holiday Special 1,2 ('88, Wint. '89, 68 pgs.): 2-X-Men parody-c
Spring Special 1 (Spr/89, $1.75, 68 pgs.) Invisible Man parody
TPB (68 pgs.) r/#1-3; photo-c

ALFRED HARVEY'S BLACK CAT
Lorne-Harvey Productions: 1995 ($3.50, B&W/color)

1-Origin by Mark Evanier & Murphy Anderson; contains history of Alfred Ha & Harvey Publications; 5 pg. B&W Sad Sack story; Hildebrandts-c

ALGIE
Timor Publ. Co.: Dec, 1953 - No. 3, 1954

	GD2.0	FN6.0	NM
1-Teenage	5.00	15.00	3.
1-Misprint exists w/Secret Mysteries #19 inside	6.40	19.25	4
2,3	4.00	11.00	2.
Accepted Reprint #2(nd)	3.00	7.50	1
Super Reprint #15	1.50	4.50	1

ALIAS:
Now Comics: July, 1990 - No. 5, Nov, 1990 ($1.75)

1-5: 1-Sienkiewicz-c

ALICE (New Adventures in Wonderland)
Ziff-Davis Publ. Co.: No. 10, 7-8/51 - No. 11(#2), 11-12/51

	GD2.0	FN6.0	NM
10-Painted-c; Berg-a	22.00	66.00	17
11-(#2 on inside) Dave Berg-a	12.00	36.00	9

ALICE AT MONKEY ISLAND (See The Adventures of Alice)
Pentagon Publ. Co. (Civil Service): No. 3, 1946

3 8.65 26.00 6

ALICE IN WONDERLAND (Disney; see Advs. of Alice, Dell Jr. Treasury #1 The Dreamery, Movie Comics, Walt Disney Showcase #22, and World's Greatest Stories)
Dell Publishing Co.: No. 24, 1940; No. 331, 1951; No. 341, July, 1951

	GD2.0	FN6.0	NM
Single Series 24 (#1)(1940)	42.00	125.00	37
Four Color 331, 341-"Unbirthday Party w/...	14.00	42.00	17

ALIEN ENCOUNTERS (Replaces Alien Worlds)
Eclipse Comics: June, 1985 - No. 14, Aug, 1987 ($1.75, Baxter paper, mat

1-14: Nudity, strong language in all. 9-Snyder-a

ALIEN LEGION (See Epic & Marvel Graphic Novel #25)
Marvel Comics (Epic Comics): Apr, 1984 - No. 20, Sept, 1987

nn-With bound-in trading card; Austin-i
2-20: 2-$1.50-c. 7,8-Portacio-i

ALIEN LEGION (2nd Series)
Marvel Comics (Epic): Aug, 1987(indicia)(10/87 on-c) - No. 18, Aug, 1990

V2#1-18-Stroman-a in all. 7-18-Farmer-i

ALIEN LEGION: (Series of titles; all Marvel/Epic Comics)
--BINARY DEEP, 1993 ($3.50, one-shot, 52 pgs.), nn-With bound-in trading

--JUGGER GRIMROD, 8/92 ($5.95, one-shot, 52 pgs.) Book 1 2.40

--ONE PLANET AT A TIME, 5/93 - Book 3, 7/93 ($4.95, squarebound, 52 p
Book 1-3: Hoang Nguyen-a

--ON THE EDGE (The... #2 & 3), 11/90 - No. 3, 1/91 ($4.50, 52 pgs.)
1-3-Stroman & Farmer-a

--TENANTS OF HELL, '91 - No. 2, '1 ($4.50, squarebound, 52 pgs.)
Book 1,2-Stroman-c/a(p)

ALIEN NATION (Movie)
DC Comics: Dec, 1988 ($2.50; 68 pgs.)

1-Adaptation of film; painted-c

ALIEN RESURRECTION (Movie)
Dark Horse Comics: Oct, 1997 - No. 2, Nov, 1997 ($2.50; limited series)

1,2-Adaptation of film; Dave McKean-c

Aliens: Earth War #3 © 20th Century Fox

Aliens/Predator: The Deadliest of the Species #10 © 20th Century Fox

Alison Dare, Little Miss Adventures #1 © J. Torres & J. Bone

GD2.0 FN6.0 NM9.4

ENS, THE (Captain Johner and...)(Also see Magnus Robot Fighter...)
d Key: Sept-Dec, 1967; No. 2, May, 1982
Reprints from Magnus #1,3,4,6-10; Russ Manning-a in all 2.50 7.50 25.00
Same contents as #1 2.40 6.00

ENS (Movie) (See Alien: The Illustrated..., Dark Horse Comics & Dark Horse
sents #24)
k Horse Comics: May, 1988 - No. 6, July, 1989 ($1.95, B&W, limited series)
Based on movie sequel;1st app. Aliens in comics 1.75 5.25 14.00
nd - 6th printings; 4th w/new inside front-c 2.50
1.00 2.80 7.00
nd & 3rd printing, 3-6-2nd printings 2.50
5.00
3.50
Comic #1 (2/89, 4x6")-Was included with Aliens Portfolio 4.00
ection 1 ($10.95,)-r/#1-6 plus Dark Horse Presents #24 plus new-a 12.00
ection 1-2nd printing (1991, $11.95)-On higher quality paper than 1st print;
Dorman painted-c 12.00
dcover ('90, $24.95, B&W)-r/1-6, DHP #24 25.00
num Edition - (See Dark Horse Presents: Aliens Platinum Edition) -

ENS
k Horse Comics: V2#1, Aug, 1989 - No. 4, 1990 ($2.25, limited series)
1-Painted art by Denis Beauvais 5.00
1-2nd printing (1990), 2-4 2.50

ENS: (Series of titles, all Dark Horse)
CHEMY, 10/97 - No. 3, 11/97 ($2.95),1-3-Corben-c/a, Arcudi-s 3.00
OCALYPSE - THE DESTROYING ANGELS, 1/99 - No. 4, 4/99 ($2.95)
-Doug Wheatly-a/Schultz-s 3.00
RSERKERS, 1/95 - No. 4, 4/95 ($2.50) 1-4 2.50
LONIAL MARINES, 1/93 - No. 10, 7/94 ($2.50) 1-10 2.50
RTH ANGEL. 8/94 ($2.95) 1-Byrne-a/story; wraparound-c 3.00
RTH WAR, 6/90 - No. 4, 10/90 ($2.50) 1-All have Sam Kieth-a & Bolton
painted-c 4.50
nd printing, 3,4 2.50
3.50
NOCIDE, 11/91 - No. 4, 2/92 ($2.50) 1-4-Arthur Suydam painted-c. 4-
raparound-c, poster 2.50
ASS CORRIDOR, 6/98 ($2.95) 1-David Lloyd-s/a 3.00
RVEST (See Aliens: Hive)
VOC, 6/97 - No. 2, 7/97 ($2.95) 1,2: Schultz-s, Kent Williams-c, 40 artists
ncluding Art Adams, Kelley Jones, Duncan Fegredo, Kevin Nowlan 3.00
VE, 2/92 - No. 4,5/92 ($2.50) 1-4: Kelley Jones-c/a in all 3.00
arvest TPB ('98, $16.95) r/series; Bolton-c 17.00
NAPPED, 12/97 - No. 3, 2/98 ($2.50) 1-3 2.50
BYRINTH, 9/93 - No. 4, 1/94 ($2.50)1-4: 1-Painted-c 2.50
VESICK, 12/96 ($2.95) 1 3.00
NDO HEAT, 2/96 ($2.50) nn-Sequel to Mondo Pest 2.50
NDO PEST, 4/95 ($2.95, 44 pgs.)nn-r/Dark Horse Comics #22-24 3.00
SIC OF THE SPEARS, 1/94 - No. 4, 4/94 ($2.50) 1-4 2.50
WT'S TALE, 6/92 - No. 2, 7/92 ($4.95) 1,2-Bolton-c 5.00
, 3/97 ($2.95)1 3.00
EDATOR: THE DEADLIEST OF SPECIES, 7/93 - No. 12,8/95 ($2.50)
olton painted-c; Guice-a(p) 4.50
mbossed foil platinum edition 10.00
2: Bolton painted-c. 2,3-Guice-a(p) 3.00
RGE, 8/97 ($2.95) nn-Hester-a 3.00
GUE, 4/993 - No. 4, 7/93 ($2.50)1-4: Painted-c 2.50
CRIFICE, 5/93 ($4.95, 52 pgs.) nn-P. Milligan scripts; painted-c/a 5.00
LVATION, 11/93 ($4.95, 52 pgs.)nn-Mignola-c/a(p); Gibbons script 5.00

GD2.0 FN6.0 NM9.4

--SPECIAL, 6/97 ($2.50) 1 2.50
--STALKER, 6/98 ($2.50)1-David Wenzel-s/a 2.50
--STRONGHOLD, 5/94 - No. 4, 9/94 ($2.50) 1-4 2.50
--SURVIVAL, 2/98 - No. 3, 4/98 ($2.95)1-3-Tony Harris-c 3.00

ALIENS VS. PREDATOR (See Dark Horse Presents #36)
Dark Horse Comics: June, 1990 - No. 4, Dec, 1990 ($2.50, limited series)
1-Painted-c 1.00 3.00 7.00
1-2nd printing 3.00
0-(7/90, $1.95, B&W)-r/Dark Horse Pres. #34-36 1.10 3.30 9.00
2,3 5.00
4-Dave Dorman painted-c 4.00
Annual (7/99, $4.95) Jae Lee-c 5.00
--VS. PREDATOR: BOOTY, 1/96 ($2.50) nn-painted-c 2.50
--VS. PREDATOR: DUEL, 3/95 - No. 2, 4/95 ($2.50) 1,2 2.50
--VS. PREDATOR: ETERNAL, 6/98 - No. 4, 9/98 ($2.50)1-4: Edginton-s/Maleev-a; Fabry-c 2.50
--VS. PREDATOR VS. THE TERMINATOR, 4/00 - No. 4, 7/00 ($2.95)
1-4: Ripley app.; Dwayne Turner-c 2.95
--VS. PREDATOR: WAR, No. 0, 5/95 - No. 4, 8/95 ($2.50) 0-4: Corben painted-c 2.50
--VS. PREDATOR: XENOGENESIS, 12/99 - No. 4, 3/00 ($2.95) 1-4: Watson-s/ Mel Rubi-a 3.00
--WRAITH, 7/98 ($2.95)1-Jay Stephens-s 3.00
--XENOGENESIS, 8/99 - No. 4, 11/99 ($2.95) 1-4: T&M Bierbaum-s 3.00

ALIEN TERROR (See 3-D Alien Terror)

ALIEN: THE ILLUSTRATED STORY (Also see Aliens)
Heavy Metal Books: 1980 ($3.95, soft-c, 8x11")
nn-Movie adaptation; Simonson-a 2.00 6.00 18.00

ALIEN^3 (Movie)
Dark Horse Comics: June, 1992 - No. 3, July, 1992 ($2.50, limited series)
1-3: Adapts 3rd movie; Suydam painted-c 2.50

ALIEN WORLDS (Also see Eclipse Graphic Album #22)
Pacific Comics/Eclipse: Dec, 1982 - No. 9, Jan, 1985
1,2,4: 2,4-Dave Stevens-c/a 2.40 6.00
3,5-9: 3.00
3-D No. 1-Art Adams 1st published art 2.40 6.00

ALISON DARE, LITTLE MISS ADVENTURES
Oni Press: Sept, 2000 ($4.50, B&W, one-shot)
1-J. Torres-s/J.Bone-c/a 4.50

ALISTER THE SLAYER
Midnight Press: Oct, 1995 ($2.50)
1-Boris-c 2.50

ALL-AMERICAN COMICS (...Western #103-126, ...Men of War #127 on; also see The Big All-American Comic Book)
All-American/National Periodical Publ.: April, 1939 - No. 102, Oct, 1948
1-Hop Harrigan (1st app.), Scribbly by Mayer (1st DC app.), Toonerville Folks, Ben Webster, Spot Savage, Mutt & Jeff, Red White & Blue (1st app.), Adv. in the Unknown, Tippie, Reg'lar Fellers, Skippy, Bobby Thatcher, Mystery Men of Mars, Daiseybelle, Wiley of West Point begin 832.00 2500.00 6200.00
2-Ripley's Believe It or Not begins, ends #24 232.00 700.00 1700.00
3-5: 5-The American Way begins, ends #10 168.00 505.00 1250.00
6,7: 6-Last Spot Savage; Popsicle Pete begins, ends #26, 28. 7-Last Bobby Thatcher 140.00 425.00 1025.00
8-The Ultra Man begins & 1st-c app. 210.00 625.00 1500.00
9,10: 10-X-Mas-c 130.00 400.00 950.00
11-15: 11-Ultra Man-c. 12-Last Toonerville Folks. 15-Last Tippie & Reg'lar Fellars; Ultra Man-c 125.00 375.00 900.00

GD2.0 FN6.0 VF8.0 NM9.4

16-(Rare)-Origin/1st app. Green Lantern by Sheldon Moldoff (c/a)(7/40) & begin series; appears in costume on-c & only one panel inside; created by Martin Nodell. Inspired in 1940 by a switchman's green lantern that would

All-American Comics #17 © DC

All-American Men of War #5 © DC

Alley Cat #6
© Alley Baggett & Action Toys

give trains the go ahead to proceed.
8000.00 24,000.00 52,000.00 100,000.00

GD2.0 FN6.0 NM9.4

17-2nd Green Lantern 1200.00 3600.00 15,000.00
18-N.Y. World's Fair-c/story 826.00 2478.00 9,500.00

GD2.0 FN6.0 VF8.0 NM9.4

19-Origin/1st app. The Atom (10/40); last Ultra Man
1280.00 3840.00 8320.00 16,000.00

GD2.0 FN6.0 NM9.4

20-Atom dons costume; Ma Hunkle becomes Red Tornado (1st app.)(1st DC costumed heroine, before Wonder Woman, 11/40); Rescue on Mars begins, ends #25; 1 pg. origin Green Lantern 429.00 1287.00 4500.00
21-23: 21-Last Wiley of West Point & Skippy. 23-Last Daiseybelle; 3 Idiots begin, end #82 263.00 790.00 2500.00
24-Sisty & Dinky become the Cyclone Kids; Ben Webster ends; origin Dr. Mid-Nite & Sargon, The Sorcerer in text with app. 300.00 900.00 3000.00

GD2.0 FN6.0 VF8.0 NM9.4

25-Origin & 1st story app. Dr. Mid-Nite by Stan Asch; Hop Harrigan becomes Guardian Angel; last Adventure in the Unknown
833.00 2500.00 5200.00 9500.00

GD2.0 FN6.0 NM9.4

26-Origin/1st story app. Sargon, the Sorcerer 343.00 1030.00 3600.00
27: #27-32 are misnumbered in indicia with correct No. appearing on-c. Intro. Doiby Dickles, Green Lantern's sidekick 362.00 1086.00 3800.00
28-Hop Harrigan gives up costumed i.d. 168.00 505.00 1600.00
29,30 168.00 505.00 1600.00
31-40: 35-Doiby learns Green Lantern's i.d. 121.00 363.00 1150.00
41-50: 50-Sargon ends 100.00 300.00 950.00
51-60: 59-Scribbly & the Red Tornado ends 87.00 261.00 825.00
61-Origin/1st app. Solomon Grundy (11/44) 435.00 1305.00 5000.00
62-70: 70-Kubert Sargon; intro Sargon's helper, Maximillian O'Leary
82.00 245.00 775.00
71-88: 71-Last Red White & Blue. 72-Black Pirate begins (not in #74-82); last Atom. 73-Winky, Blinky & Noddy begins, ends #82. 79,83-Mutt & Jeff-c.
68.00 205.00 650.00
89-Origin & 1st app. Harlequin 103.00 308.00 975.00
90-99: 90-Origin/1st app. Icicle. 99-Last Hop Harrigan
95.00 285.00 900.00
100-1st app. Johnny Thunder by Alex Toth (8/48); western theme begins (Scarce) 190.00 570.00 1800.00
101-Last Mutt & Jeff (Scarce) 126.00 379.00 1200.00
102-Last Green Lantern, Black Pirate & Dr. Mid-Nite (Scarce)
263.00 789.00 2500.00

NOTE: *No Atom in 47, 62-69.* ***Kinstler*** *Black Pirate-89.* ***Stan Aschmeier*** *a (Dr. Mid-Nite) 25-84; c-7.* ***Mayer*** *c-1, 2(part), 6, 10.* ***Moldoff*** *c-16-23.* ***Nodell*** *c-31.* ***Paul Reinman*** *a (Green Lantern)-53-55p, 56-84, 87; (Black Pirate)-83-88, 90; c-52, 55-76, 78, 80, 81, 87.* ***Toth*** *a-88, 92, 96, 98-102; c(p)-92, 96-102. Scribbly by* ***Mayer*** *in #1-59. Ultra Man by* ***Mayer*** *in #8-19.*

ALL-AMERICAN COMICS (Also see All Star Comics 1999 crossover titles)
DC Comics: May, 1999 ($1.99, one-shot)

1-Golden Age Green Lantern and Johnny Thunder; Barreto-a 2.00

ALL-AMERICAN MEN OF WAR (Previously All-American Western)
National Periodical Publ.: No. 127, Aug-Sept, 1952 - No. 117, Sept-Oct, 1966

127 (#1, 1952) 75.00 225.00 1050.00
128 (1952) 50.00 150.00 650.00
2(12-1/'52-53)-5 43.00 129.00 555.00
6-Devil Dog story; Ghost Squadron story 33.00 99.00 400.00
7-10: 8-Sgt. Storm Cloud-s 33.00 99.00 400.00
11-16,18: 18-Last precode (2/55) 31.00 93.00 350.00
17-1st Frogman-s in this title 31.00 93.00 350.00
19,20,22-27 21.00 63.00 230.00
21-Easy Co. prototype 23.00 68.00 250.00
28 (12/55)-1st Sgt. Rock prototype; Kubert-a 29.00 88.00 325.00
29,30,32-Wood-a 22.50 67.00 245.00
31,33-38,40: 34-Gunner prototype-s. 35-Greytone-c. 36-Little Sure Shot prototype-s. 38-1st S.A. issue 17.00 51.00 185.00
39 (11/56)-2nd Sgt. Rock prototype; 1st Easy Co.? 25.00 75.00 275.00
41,43-47,49,50: 46-Tankbusters-c/s 14.00 42.00 155.00
42-Pre-Sgt. Rock Easy Co.-c/s 15.00 45.00 165.00
48-Easy Co.-c/s; Nick app.; Kubert-a 15.00 45.00 165.00
51-56,58-62,65,66: 61-Gunner-c/s 10.50 31.50 11
57(5/58),63,64 -Pre-Sgt. Rock Easy Co.-c/s 14.50 43.50 16
67-1st Gunner & Sarge by Andru & Esposito 31.00 93.00 34
68,69: 68-2nd app. Gunner & Sarge. 69-1st Tank Killer-c/s
13.50 40.00 15
70 10.00 30.00 11
71-80: 71,72,76-Tank Killer-c/s. 74-Minute Commandos-c/s
7.25 21.75 8
81,84-88: 88-Last 10¢ issue 6.80 20.50 7
82-Johnny Cloud begins(1st app.), ends #117 12.50 37.00 13
83-2nd Johnny Cloud 7.25 21.75 8
89-100: 89-Battle Aces of 3 Wars begins, ends #98 4.55 13.65 5
101-111,113-117: 111,114,115-Johnny Cloud. 117-Johnny Cloud-c & 3-part story 3.25 9.75 3
112-Balloon Buster series begins, ends #114,116 3.65 11.00 4

NOTE: *Frogman stories in 17, 38, 44, 45, 50, 51, 53, 55-58, 63, 65, 66, 72, 76, 77.* ***Colan*** ***Drucker*** *a-47, 58, 61, 63, 65, 69, 71, 74, 77.* ***Grandenetti*** *c(p)-127, 128, 2-17(most).* ***Heath*** *27, 32, 38, 41, 45, 47, 50, 51, 55-58, 62, 64, 71, 75, 76, 78, 95, 111-117; c-85, 91, 94-96 101, 110-112, others?* ***Infantino*** *a-8.* ***Kirby*** *a-29.* ***Krigstein*** *a-128('52), 2, 3, 5.* ***Kubert*** *a-2 28, 29, 33, 34, 36, 38, 39, 41-43, 47-50, 52, 53, 55, 56, 59, 60, 63-65, 69, 71-73, 76, 102 105, 106, 108, 114; c-41, 44, 52, 54, 55, 58, 64, 69, 76, 77, 79, 102-106, 108, 113-117, o Tank Killer in 69, 71, 76 by* ***Kubert.*** ***P. Reinman*** *c-55, 57, 61, 62, 71, 72, 74-76, 80.* ***J. Seve*** *58.*

ALL-AMERICAN SPORTS
Charlton Comics: Oct, 1967

1 2.50 7.50 2

ALL-AMERICAN WESTERN (Formerly All-American Comics; Becomes All-American Men of War)
National Periodical Publications: No. 103, Nov, 1948 - No. 126, June-July, 1952 (103-121: 52 pgs.)

103-Johnny Thunder & his horse Black Lightning continues by Toth, ends #1 Foley of The Fighting 5th, Minstrel Maverick, & Overland Coach begin; Captain Tootsie by Beck; mentioned in Love and Death
50.00 150.00 45
104-Kubert-a 39.00 116.00 31
105,107-Kubert-a 33.00 98.00 26
106,108-110,112: 112-Kurtzman's "Pot-Shot Pete" (1 pg.)
26.00 79.00 21
111,114-116-Kubert-a 28.00 84.00 22
113-Intro. Swift Deer, J. Thunder's new sidekick (4-5/50); classic Toth-c; Kubert-a 30.00 90.00 24
117-126: 121-Kubert-a; bondage-c 19.00 57.00 15

NOTE: ***G. Kane*** *c(p)-119, 120, 123.* ***Kubert*** *a-103-105, 107, 111, 112(1 pg.), 113-116, 121 a 103-126; c(p)-103-116, 121, 122, 124-126. Some copies of #125 have #12 on-c.*

ALL COMICS
Chicago Nite Life News: 1945

1 12.50 37.50 10

ALLEGRA
Image Comics (WildStorm): Aug, 1996 - No. 4, Dec, 1996 ($2.50)

1-4

ALLEY CAT (Alley Baggett)
Image Comics: July, 1999 - Present ($2.50)

Preview Edition -Diamond Dateline supplement
Prelude
Prelude w/variant-c
1-Photo-c
1-Painted-c by Dorian
1-Another Universe Edition, 1-Wizard World Edition
2-6
Lingerie Edition (10/99, $4.95) Photos, pin-ups, cover gallery
...Vs. Lady Pendragon ('99, $3.00) Stinsman-c

ALLEY OOP (See The Comics, The Funnies, Red Ryder and Super Book #
Dell Publishing Co.: No. 3, 1942

Four Color 3 (#1) 48.00 144.00 57

ALLEY OOP
Argo Publ.: Nov, 1955 - No. 3, Mar, 1956 (Newspaper reprints)

All Famous Police Cases #13 © STJ

All-Flash #13 © DC

All Humor Comics #7 © QUA

GD2.0 FN6.0 NM9.4 — GD2.0 FN6.0 NM9.4

16.00 48.00 125.00
11.00 33.00 90.00

EY OOP
Publishing Co.: 12-2/62-63 - No. 2, 9-11/63
5.90 17.75 65.00
5.00 15.00 55.00

EY OOP
dard Comics: No. 10, Sept, 1947 - No. 18, Oct, 1949
23.00 69.00 185.00
8: 17,18-Schomburg-c 18.00 53.00 140.00

EY OOP ADVENTURES
rctic Press: Aug, 1998 - No. 3, Dec, 1998 ($2.95)
-Jack Bender-s/a 3.00

EY OOP ADVENTURES (Alley Oop Quarterly in indicia)
rctic Press: Sept, 1999 - No. 3, Mar, 2000 ($2.50/$2.99, B&W)
-Jack Bender-s/a 3.00

-FAMOUS CRIME (Formerly Law Against Crime #1-3; becomes All-ous Police Cases #6 on)
Publications: No. 4, 2/50 - No. 5, 5/50; No. 8, 5/51 - No. 10, 11/51
#1-1st series)-Formerly Law-Crime 28.00 83.00 220.00
#2) 18.00 53.00 140.00
#3-2nd series) 17.00 51.00 135.00
#4)-Used in **SOTI**, illo- "The wish to hurt or kill couples in lovers' lanes is a ot uncommon perversion;" L.B. Cole-c/a(r)/Law-Crime #3
34.00 103.00 275.00
#5)-Becomes All-Famous Police Cases #6 16.00 48.00 125.00
:: *All have **L.B. Cole** covers.*

FAMOUS CRIME STORIES (See Fox Giants)

-FAMOUS POLICE CASES (Formerly All Famous Crime #10 [#5])
Publications: No. 6, Feb, 1952 - No. 16, Sept, 1954
17.00 51.00 135.00
: 7-Baker story; . 8-Marijuana story 16.00 48.00 125.00
6 14.00 41.00 110.00
:: ***L. B. Cole** c-all; a-15, 1pg. **Hollingsworth** a-15.*

-FLASH (...Quarterly No. 1-5)
onal Per. Publ./All-American: Summer, 1941 - No. 32, Dec-Jan, 1947-48
GD2.0 FN6.0 VF8.0 NM9.4
rigin The Flash retold by E. E. Hibbard; Hibbard c-1-10,12-14,16,31p.
1280.00 3840.00 8320.00 16,000.00
GD2.0 FN6.0 NM9.4
rigin recap 314.00 943.00 3300.00
168.00 505.00 1600.00
/inky, Blinky & Noddy begins (1st app.), ends #32
126.00 379.00 1200.00
0 103.00 308.00 975.00
3: 12-Origin/1st The Thinker. 13-The King app. 89.00 268.00 850.00
reen Lantern cameo 103.00 308.00 975.00
0: 18-Mutt & Jeff begins, ends #22 74.00 221.00 700.00
1 58.00 174.00 550.00
)rigin/1st app. The Fiddler; 1st Star Sapphire 105.00 316.00 1000.00
:: *Book length stories in 2-13, 16. Bondage c-31, 32. **Martin Nodell** c-15, 17-28.*

FOR LOVE (Young Love V3#5-on)
Publications: Apr-May, 1957 - V3#4, Dec-Jan, 1959-60
6.35 19.00 70.00
-6: 5-Orlando-c 3.65 11.00 40.00
-5(1/59), 5(3/59) 2.80 8.40 28.00
(5/59), 1(7/59)-4: 2-Powell-a 2.00 6.00 18.00

FUNNY COMICS
m Publ./National Periodical Publications (Detective): Winter, 1943-44 - 3, May-June, 1948
enius Jones (1st app.), Buzzy (1st app., ends #4), Dover & Clover (see ore Fun #93) begin; Bailey-a 47.00 141.00 425.00
23.00 69.00 185.00
3-10 14.00 41.00 110.00
11-13,15,18,19-Genius Jones app. 13.00 39.00 105.00
14,17,20-23 10.00 30.00 70.00
16-DC Super Heroes app. 31.00 94.00 250.00

ALL GOOD
St. John Publishing Co.: Oct, 1949 (50¢, 260 pgs.)
nn-(8 St. John comics bound together) 61.00 182.00 575.00
NOTE: *Also see Li'l Audrey Yearbook & Treasury of Comics.*

ALL GOOD COMICS (See Fox Giants)
Fox Features Syndicate: No.1, Spring, 1946 (36 pgs.)
1-Joy Family, Dick Transom, Rick Evans, One Round Hogan
24.00 71.00 190.00

ALL GREAT (See Fox Giants)
Fox Feature Syndicate: 1946 (36 pgs.)
1-Crazy House, Bertie Benson Boy Detective, Gussie the Gob
24.00 71.00 190.00

ALL GREAT
William H. Wise & Co.: nd (1945?) (132 pgs.)
nn-Capt. Jack Terry, Joan Mason, Girl Reporter, Baron Doomsday; Torture scenes 40.00 120.00 320.00

ALL GREAT COMICS (Formerly Phantom Lady #13? Dagar, Desert Hawk No. 14 on)
Fox Features Syndicate: No. 14, Oct, 1947 - No. 13, Dec, 1947 (Newspaper strip reprints)
14(#12)-Brenda Starr & Texas Slim-r (Scarce) 55.00 165.00 500.00
13-Origin Dagar, Desert Hawk; Brenda Starr (all-r); Kamen-c; Dagar covers begin 52.00 157.00 470.00

ALL-GREAT CONFESSIONS (See Fox Giants)

ALL GREAT CRIME STORIES (See Fox Giants)

ALL GREAT JUNGLE ADVENTURES (See Fox Giants)

ALL HALLOW'S EVE
Innovation Publishing: 1991 ($4.95, 52 pgs.)
1-Painted-c/a 5.00

ALL HERO COMICS
Fawcett Publications: Mar, 1943 (100 pgs., cardboard-c)
1-Capt. Marvel Jr., Capt. Midnight, Golden Arrow, Ibis the Invincible, Spy Smasher, Lance O'Casey; 1st Banshee O'Brien; Raboy-c
158.00 474.00 1500.00

ALL HUMOR COMICS
Quality Comics Group: Spring, 1946 - No. 17, December, 1949
1 19.00 56.00 150.00
2-Atomic Tot story; Gustavson-a 10.00 30.00 75.00
3-9: 3-Intro Kelly Poole who is cover feature #3 on. 5-1st app. Hickory? 8-Gustavson-a 6.00 18.00 42.00
10-17 5.00 15.00 30.00

ALLIANCE, THE
Image Comics (Shadowline Ink): Aug, 1995 - No. 3, Nov, 1995 ($2.50)
1-3: 2-(9/95) 2.50

ALL LOVE (...Romances No. 26)(Formerly Ernie Comics)
Ace Periodicals (Current Books): No. 26, May, 1949 - No. 32, May, 1950
26 (No. 1)-Ernie, Lily Belle app. 8.65 26.00 60.00
27-L. B. Cole-a 12.00 36.00 95.00
28-32 5.00 15.00 35.00

ALL-NEGRO COMICS
All-Negro Comics: June, 1947 (15¢)
1 (Rare) 600.00 1800.00 4200.00
NOTE: *Seldom found in fine or mint condition; many copies have brown pages.*

ALL-NEW COLLECTORS' EDITION (Formerly Limited ...)
DC Comics, Inc.: Jan, 1978 - Vol. 8, No. C-62, 1979 (No. 54-58: 76 pgs.)
C-53-Rudolph the Red-Nosed Reindeer 3.65 14.60 40.00
C-54-Superman Vs. Wonder Woman 3.00 12.00 30.00
C-55-Superboy & the Legion of Super-Heroes; Wedding of Lightning Lad &

All-New Comics #5 © HARV

All-Select Comics #7 © MAR

All Star Comics #3 © DC

GD2.0 FN6.0 NM9.4 GD2.0 FN6.0 NM

Saturn Girl; Grell-c/a 3.00 12.00 32.00
C-56-Superman Vs. Muhammad Ali: story & wraparound N. Adams-c/a 4.10 16.40 45.00
C-58-Superman Vs. Shazam 2.80 11.20 28.00
C-60-Rudolph's Summer Fun(8/78) 3.20 12.80 35.00
C-61-(See Famous First Edition-Superman #1)
C-62-Superman the Movie (68 pgs.; 1979)-Photo-c from movie plus photos inside (also see DC Special Series #25) 2.00 8.00 18.00
NOTE: ***Buckler** a-C-58; c-C-58*

ALL-NEW COMICS (...Short Story Comics No. 1-3)
Family Comics (Harvey Publications): Jan, 1943 - No. 14, Nov, 1946; No. 15, Mar-Apr, 1947 (10 x 13-1/2")

1-Steve Case, Crime Rover, Johnny Rebel, Kayo Kane, The Echo, Night Hawk, Ray O'Light, Detective Shane begin (all 1st app.?); Red Blazer on cover only; Sultan-a 284.00 853.00 2700.00
2-Origin Scarlet Phantom by Kubert 100.00 300.00 950.00
3 74.00 221.00 700.00
4 61.00 182.00 575.00
5-11: 5-Schomburg-c thru #11. 6-The Boy Heroes & Red Blazer (text story) begin, end #12; Black Cat app.; intro. Sparky in Red Blazer. 7-Kubert, Powell-a; Black Cat & Zebra app. 8,9: 8-Shock Gibson app.; Kubert, Powell-a; Schomburg-c. 9-Black Cat app.; Kubert-a. 10-The Zebra app. (from Green Hornet Comics); Kubert-a(3). 11-Girl Commandos, Man In Black app. 68.00 205.00 650.00
12,13: 12-Kubert-a. 13-Stuntman by Simon & Kirby; Green Hornet, Joe Palooka, Flying Fool app.; Green Hornet-c 58.00 174.00 550.00
14-The Green Hornet & The Man in Black Called Fate by Powell, Joe Palooka app.; J. Palooka-c by Ham Fisher 55.00 165.00 500.00
15-(Rare)-Small size (5-1/2x8-1/2"; B&W; 32 pgs.). Distributed to mail subscribers only. Black Cat and Joe Palooka app. 63.00 190.00 600.00
NOTE: *Also see Boy Explorers No. 2, Flash Gordon No. 5, and Stuntman No. 3. **Powell** a-11. **Schomburg** c-5-11. Captain Red Blazer & Spark on c-5-11 (w/Boy Heroes #12).*

ALL-OUT WAR
DC Comics: Sept-Oct, 1979 - No. 6, Aug, 1980 ($1.00, 68 pgs.)

1-The Viking Commando(origin), Force Three(origin), & Black Eagle Squadron begin 1.00 2.80 7.00
2-6 4.00
NOTE: ***Ayers** a(p)-1-6. **Elias** r-2. **Evans** a-1-6. **Kubert** c-16.*

ALL PICTURE ADVENTURE MAGAZINE
St. John Publishing Co.: Oct, 1952 - No. 2, Nov, 1952 (100 pg. Giants, 25¢, squarebound)

1-War comics 28.00 84.00 225.00
2-Horror-crime comics 42.00 125.00 375.00
NOTE: *Above books contain three St. John comics rebound; variations possible. **Baker** art known in both.*

ALL PICTURE ALL TRUE LOVE STORY
St. John Publishing Co.: Oct., 1952 - No. 2, Nov., 1952 (100 pgs., 25¢)

1-Canteen Kate by Matt Baker 47.00 140.00 420.00
2-Baker-c/a 31.00 94.00 250.00

ALL-PICTURE COMEDY CARNIVAL
St. John Publishing Co.: October, 1952 (100 pgs., 25¢)(Contains 4 rebound comics)

1-Contents can vary; Baker-a 40.00 120.00 360.00

ALL REAL CONFESSION MAGAZINE (See Fox Giants)

ALL ROMANCES (Mr. Risk No. 7 on)
A. A. Wyn (Ace Periodicals): Aug, 1949 - No. 6, June, 1950

1 9.30 28.00 65.00
2 5.00 15.00 30.00
3-6 4.15 12.50 25.00

ALL-SELECT COMICS (Blonde Phantom No. 12 on)
Timely Comics (Daring Comics): Fall, 1943 - No. 11, Fall, 1946

1-Capt. America (by Rico #1), Human Torch, Sub-Mariner begin; Black Widow story (4 pgs.); Classic Schomburg-c 957.00 2745.00 11,000.00
2-Red Skull app. 314.00 943.00 3300.00
3-The Whizzer begins 211.00 633.00 2000.00
4,5-Last Sub-Mariner 147.00 442.00 1400.
6-9: 6-The Destroyer app. 8-No Whizzer 116.00 348.00 1100.
10-The Destroyer & Sub-Mariner app.; last Capt. America & Human Torch issue 116.00 348.00 1100.
11-1st app. Blonde Phantom; Miss America app.; all Blonde Phantom-c by Shores 253.00 758.00 2400.
NOTE: ***Schomburg** c-1-10. **Sekowsky** a-7. #7 & 8 show 1944 in indicia, but should be 1945.*

ALL SPORTS COMICS (Formerly Real Sports Comics; becomes All Time Sports Comics No. 4 on)
Hillman Periodicals: No. 2, Dec-Jan, 1948-49; No. 3, Feb-Mar, 1949

2-Krigstein-a(p), Powell, Starr-a 35.00 105.00 280.
3-Mort Lawrence-a 24.00 71.00 190.

ALL STAR COMICS (All Star Western No. 58 on)
National Periodical Publ./All-American/DC Comics: Sum, '40 - No. 57, Feb Mar, '51; No. 58, Jan-Feb, '76 -No. 74, Sept-Oct, '78

GD2.0 FN6.0 VF8.0 NM

1-The Flash (#1 by E.E. Hibbard), Hawkman(by Shelly), Hourman(by Bernar Baily), The Sandman(by Creig Flessel), The Spectre(by Baily), Biff Bronsor Red White & Blue(ends #2) begin; Ultra Man's only app. (#1-3 are quarterly #4 begins bi-monthly issues) 1160.00 3480.00 7540.00 14,500

GD2.0 FN6.0 NM

2-Green Lantern (by Martin Nodell), Johnny Thunder begin; Green Lantern figure swipe from the cover of All-American Comics #16; Flash figure swipe from the cover of Flash Comics #8; Moldoff/Bailey-c (cut & paste-c.) 504.00 1513.00 5800

GD2.0 FN6.0 VF8.0 NM

3-Origin & 1st app. The Justice Society of America (Win/40); Dr. Fate & The Atom begin, Red Tornado cameo 3200.00 9600.00 19,200.00 40,000
3-Reprint, Oversize 13-1/2x10". **WARNING:** This comic is an exact reprint of the orig inal except for its size. DC published it in 1974 with a second cover titling it as a Famous Edition. There have been many reported cases of the outer cover being removed and the in sold as the original edition. The reprint with the new outer cover removed is practically worth See Famous First Edition for value.

GD2.0 FN6.0 NM

4-1st adventure for J.S.A. 504.00 1513.00 5800
5-1st app. Shiera Sanders as Hawkgirl (1st costumed super-heroine, 6-7/41) 435.00 1305.00 5000
6-Johnny Thunder joins JSA 300.00 900.00 3000
7-Batman, Superman, Flash cameo; last Hourman; Doiby Dickles app. 333.00 1000.00 3500

GD2.0 FN6.0 VF8.0 NM

8-Origin & 1st app. Wonder Woman (12-1/41-42)(added as 9 pgs. making bc 76 pgs.; origin cont'd in Sensation #1; see W.W. #1 for more detailed origin Dr. Fate dons new helmet; Hop Harrigan text stories & Starman begin; Shie app.; Hop Harrigan JSA guest; Starman & Dr. Mid-Nite become members 2560.00 7680.00 15,360.00 32,000

GD2.0 FN6.0 NM

9-11: 9-JSA's girlfriends cameo; Shiera app.; J. Edgar Hoover of FBI made associate member of JSA. 10-Flash, Green Lantern cameo; Sandman new costume. 11-Wonder Woman begins; Spectre cameo; Shiera app.; Moldoff Hawkman-c 295.00 885.00 2800
12-Wonder Woman becomes JSA Secretary 263.00 790.00 2500
13,15: Sandman w/Sandy in #14 & 15. 15-Origin & 1st app. Brain Wave; Shie app. 242.00 726.00 2300
14-(12/42) Junior JSA Club begins; w/membership offer & premiums 247.00 742.00 2350
16-20: 19-Sandman w/Sandy. 20-Dr. Fate & Sandman cameo 179.00 537.00 1700
21-23: 21-Spectre & Atom cameo; Dr. Fate by Kubert; Dr. Fate, Sandman en 22-Last Hop Harrigan; Flag-c. 23-Origin/1st app. Psycho Pirate; last Spect & Starman 158.00 474.00 1500
24-Flash & Green Lantern cameo; Mr. Terrific only app.; Wildcat, JSA guest; Kubert Hawkman begins; Hitler-c 158.00 474.00 1500
25-27: 25-Flash & Green Lantern start again. 26-Robot-c. 27-Wildcat, JSA guest (#24-26: only All-American imprint) 132.00 395.00 1250
28-32 121.00 363.00 1150
33-Solomon Grundy & Doiby Dickles app; classic Solomon Grundy cover. La Solomon Grundy G.A. app. 300.00 900.00 3000
34,35-Johnny Thunder cameo in both 116.00 347.00 1100

All Star Comics #38 © DC

All Star Western #87 © DC

All Top Comics #6 © FOX

GD2.0 FN6.0 NM9.4

-Batman & Superman JSA guests 279.00 837.00 2650.00
-Johnny Thunder cameo; origin & 1st app. Injustice Society; last Kubert Hawkman 153.00 458.00 1450.00
-Black Canary begins; JSA Death issue 179.00 537.00 1700.00
,40: 39-Last Johnny Thunder 111.00 332.00 1050.00
-Black Canary joins JSA; Injustice Society app. (2nd app.?) 111.00 332.00 1050.00
-Atom & the Hawkman don new costumes 111.00 332.00 1050.00
-49,51-56: 43-New logo; Robot-c. 55-Sci/Fi story. 56-Robot-c 111.00 332.00 1050.00
-Frazetta art, 3 pgs. 121.00 363.00 1150.00
-Kubert-a, 6 pgs. (Scarce); last app. G.A. Green Lantern, Flash & Dr.Mid-Nite 158.00 474.00 1500.00
2 #58-(1976) JSA (Flash, Hawkman, Dr. Mid-Nite, Wildcat, Dr. Fate, Green Lantern, Star Spangled Kid, & Robin) app.; intro Power Girl. 2.00 6.00 18.00
2 #59-68,70-74(1976-78) 1.10 3.30 9.00
2 #69-1st Earth-2 Huntress (Helena Wayne) 2.00 6.00 18.00

TE: *No Atom-27, 36; no Dr. Fate-13; no Flash-8, 9, 11-23; no Green Lantern-8, 9,11-23; vkman in 1-57 (only one to app. in all 57 issues); no Johnny Thunder-5, 36; no Wonder man-9, 10, 23. Book length stories in 4-9, 11-14, 18-22, 25, 26, 29, 30, 32-36, 42, 43. Johnny l in #42-46, 48, 49, 51, 52,54-57.* ***Baily*** *a-1-10, 12, 13, 14i, 15-20.* ***Burnley*** *Starman-8-13; c-13.* ***Grell*** *c-58.* ***E.E. Hibbard*** *c-3, 4, 6-10.* ***Infantino*** *c-40.* ***Kubert*** *Hawkman-24-30, 33-37.* ***npert/Baily/Flessel*** *c-1, 2.* ***Moldoff*** *Hawkman-3-23; c-11.* ***Mart Nodell*** *c-25i, 26i, 27-32.* ***cell*** *c-5.* ***Simon & Kirby*** *Sandman 14-17, 19.* ***Staton*** *a-66-74p. c-74p.* ***Toth*** *a-37(2), 38(2), 41; c-38, 41.* ***Wood*** *a-58i-63i, 64, 65; c-63i, 64, 65. Issues 1-7, 9-16 are 68 pgs.; #8 is 76 .; #17-19 are 60 pgs.; #20-57 are 52 pgs.*

L STAR COMICS (Also see crossover 1999 editions of Adventure, American, National, Sensation, Smash, Star Spangled and Thrilling Comics)
Comics: May, 1999 - No. 2, May, 1999 ($2.95, bookends for JSA x-over)

2-Justice Society in World War 2; Robinson-s/Johnson-c 3.00
0-Page Giant (9/99, $4.95) Phantom Lady app. 5.00

L STAR INDEX, THE
ependent Comics Group (Eclipse): Feb, 1987 ($2.00, Baxter paper)

2.40 6.00

L-STAR SQUADRON (See Justice League of America #193)
Comics: Sept, 1981 - No. 67, Mar, 1987

Original Atom, Hawkman, Dr. Mid-Nite, Robotman (origin), Plastic Man, Johnny Quick, Liberty Belle, Shining Knight begin 4.00
46,48,49: 4, 7-Spectre app. 5-Danette Reilly becomes new Firebrand. 8-Re-ntro Steel, the Indestructable Man. 12-Origin G.A. Hawkman retold. 23-Origin/1st app. The Amazing Man. 24-Batman app. 25-1st app. Infinity, Inc. (9/83), 26-Origin Infinity, Inc. (2nd app.); Robin app. 27-Dr. Fate vs. The Spectre. 30-35-Spectre app. 33-Origin Freedom Fighters of Earth-X. 36,37-Superman vs. Capt. Marvel; Ordway-c. 41-Origin Starman 3.00
-Origin Dr. Fate; McFarlane-a (1st full story)/part-c (7/85) 2.40 6.00
Double size; Crisis x-over 4.50
-67: 51-56-Crisis x-over. 61-Origin Liberty Belle. 62-Origin The Shining Knight. 63-Origin Robotman. 65-Origin Johnny Quick. 66-Origin Tarantula 3.50
nual 1-3: 1(11/82)-Retells origin of G.A. Atom, Guardian & Wildcat; Jerry Ordway's 1st pencils for DC.(1st work was inking Carmine Infantino in House of Mystery #94) 2(11/83)-Infinity, Inc. app. 3(9/84) 3.50

E: ***Buckler*** *a-1-5; c-1, 3-5, 51.* ***Kubert*** *c-2, 7-18. JLA app. in 14, 15. JSA app. in 4, 14, 15, 27, 28.*

L-STAR STORY OF THE DODGERS, THE
dium Communications: Apr, 1979 ($1.00)

1.25 3.75 10.00

L STAR WESTERN (Formerly All Star Comics No. 1-57)
ional Periodical Publ.: No. 58, Apr-May, 1951 - No. 119, June-July, 1961

Trigger Twins (ends #116), Strong Bow, The Roving Ranger & Don Caballero begin 43.00 130.00 390.00
60: Last 52 pgs. 24.00 71.00 190.00
66: 61-64-Toth-a 20.00 60.00 160.00
Johnny Thunder begins; Gil Kane-a 24.00 71.00 190.00
81: Last precode (2-3/55) 10.00 30.00 80.00
98: 97-1st S.A. issue 10.00 30.00 75.00
Frazetta-r/Jimmy Wakely #4 10.00 30.00 80.00

GD2.0 FN6.0 NM9.4

100 10.00 30.00 80.00
101-107,109-116,118,119 8.65 26.00 60.00
108-Origin J. Thunder; J. Thunder logo begins 20.00 60.00 160.00
117-Origin Super Chie 12.00 36.00 95.00

NOTE: ***Gil Kane*** *c(p)-58, 59, 61, 63, 64, 68, 69, 70-95(most), 97-199(most).* ***Infantino*** *art in most issues. Madame .44 app.-#117-119.*

ALL-STAR WESTERN (Weird Western Tales No. 12 on)
National Periodical Publications: Aug-Sept, 1970 - No. 11, Apr-May, 1972

1-Pow-Wow Smith-r; Infantino-a 3.20 9.60 35.00
2-6: 2-Outlaw begins; El Diablo by Morrow begins; has cameos by Williamson, Torres, Kane, Giordano & Phil Seuling. 3-Origin El Diablo. 5-Last Outlaw issue. 6-Billy the Kid begins, ends #8 2.00 6.00 18.00
7-9-(52 pgs.) 9-Frazetta-a, 3pgs.(r) 2.40 7.35 22.00
10-(52 pgs.) Jonah Hex begins (1st app., 2-3/72) 25.00 75.00 350.00
11-(52 pgs.) 2nd app. Jonah Hex 13.50 40.00 150.00

NOTE: ***Neal Adams*** *c-2-5;* ***Aparo*** *a-5.* ***G. Kane a****-3, 4, 6, 8.* ***Kubert*** *a-4r, 7-9r.* ***Morrow*** *a-2-4, 10, 11. No. 7-11 have 52 pgs..*

ALL SURPRISE (Becomes Jeanie #13 on) (Funny animal)
Timely/Marvel (CPC): Fall, 1943 - No. 12, Winter, 1946-47

1-Super Rabbit, Gandy & Sourpuss begin 30.00 90.00 240.00
2 14.00 41.00 110.00
3-10,12 10.50 32.00 85.00
11-Kurtzman "Pigtales" art 12.00 36.00 95.00

ALL TEEN (Formerly All Winners; All Winners & Teen Comics No. 21 on)
Marvel Comics (WFP): No. 20, January, 1947

20-Georgie, Mitzi, Patsy Walker, Willie app.; Syd Shores-c 10.00 30.00 70.00

ALL-TIME SPORTS COMICS (Formerly All Sports Comics)
Hillman Per.: V2No. 4, Apr-May, 1949 - V2No. 7, Oct-Nov, 1949 (All 52 pgs.)

V2#4 22.00 66.00 175.00
5-7: 5-(V1#5 inside)-Powell-a; Ty Cobb sty. 7-Krigstein-p; Walter Johnson & Knute Rockne sty 16.00 49.00 130.00

ALL TOP
William H. Wise Co.: 1944 (132 pgs.)

Capt. V, Merciless the Sorceress, Red Robbins, One Round Hogan, Mike the M.P., Snooky, Pussy Katnip app. 29.00 86.00 230.00

ALL TOP COMICS (My Experience No. 19 on)
Fox Features Synd./Green Publ./Norlen Mag.: 1945; No. 2, Sum, 1946 - No. 18, Mar, 1949; 1957 - 1959

1-Cosmo Cat & Flash Rabbit begin (1st app.) 23.00 68.00 180.00
2 (#1-7 are funny animal) 10.00 30.00 80.00
3-7 8.65 26.00 60.00
8-Blue Beetle, Phantom Lady, & Rulah, Jungle Goddess begin (11/47); Kamen-c 232.00 695.00 2200.00
9-Kamen-c 121.00 363.00 1150.00
10-Kamen bondage-c 132.00 395.00 1250.00
11-13,15-17: 11-Rulah-c. 15-No Blue Beetle 105.00 316.00 1000.00
14-No Blue Beetle; used in **SOTI**, illo- "Corpses of colored people strung up by their wrists" 137.00 411.00 1300.00
18-Dagar, Jo-Jo app; no Phantom Lady or Blue Beetle 68.00 205.00 650.00
6(1957-Green Publ.)-Patoruzu the Indian; Cosmo Cat on cover only. 6(1958-Literary Ent.)-Muggy Doo; Cosmo Cat on cover only. 6(1959-Norlen)-Atomic Mouse; Cosmo Cat on cover only. 6(1959)-Little Eva. 6(Cornell)-Supermouse on-c 4.15 12.50 25.00

NOTE: *Jo-Jo by* ***Kamen****-12,18.*

ALL TRUE ALL PICTURE POLICE CASES
St. John Publishing Co.: Oct, 1952 - No. 2, Nov, 1952 (100 pgs.)

1-Three rebound St. John crime comics 40.00 120.00 340.00
2-Three comics rebound 30.00 90.00 240.00

NOTE: *Contents may vary.*

ALL-TRUE CRIME (...Cases No. 26-35; formerly Official True Crime Cases)
Marvel/Atlas Comics: No. 26, Feb, 1948 - No. 52, Sept, 1952
(OFI #26,27/CFI #28,29/LCC #30-46/LMC #47-52)

26(#1)-Syd Shores-c 33.00 99.00 265.00

All True Crime Cases #27 © MAR

All Winners Comics #4 © MAR

Alpha Flight V2 #8 © MAR

GD2.0 FN6.0 NM9.4

27(4/48)-Electric chair-c 24.00 71.00 190.00
28-41,43-48,50-52: 35-37-Photo-c 10.00 30.00 80.00
42,49-Krigstein-a. 49-Used in **POP**, Pg 79 10.50 32.00 85.00
NOTE: ***Robinson** a-47, 50. **Shores** c-26. **Tuska** a-48(3).*

ALL-TRUE DETECTIVE CASES (Kit Carson No. 5 on)
Avon Periodicals: #2, Apr-May, 1954 - No. 4, Aug-Sept, 1954
2(#1)-Wood-a 21.00 62.00 165.00
3-Kinstler-c 10.50 32.00 85.00
4-r/Gangsters And Gun Molls #2; Kamen-a 18.00 53.00 140.00
nn(100 pgs.)-7 pg. Kubert-a, Kinstler back-c 38.00 113.00 300.00

ALL TRUE ROMANCE (...Illustrated No. 3)
Artful Publ. #1-3/Harwell(Comic Media) #4-20?/Ajax-Farrell(Excellent Publ.) No. 22 on/Four Star Comic Corp.: 3/51 - No. 20, 12/54; No. 22, 3/55 - No. 30?, 7/57; No. 3(#31), 9/57;No. 4(#32), 11/57; No. 33, 2/58 - No. 34, 6/58
1 (3/51) 15.00 45.00 120.00
2 (10/51; 11/51 on-c) 7.85 23.50 55.00
3(12/51) - #5(5/52) 6.40 19.25 45.00
6-Wood-a, 9 pgs. (exceptional) 15.00 45.00 120.00
7-10 (2-#7s: #7(11/52, 9/52 inside, #7(11/52, 11/52 inside)) 5.00 15.00 35.00
11-13,16-19(9/54),20(12/54) (no #21) 4.65 14.00 28.00
14-Marijuana story 5.00 15.00 32.00
22: Last precode issue (1st Ajax, 3/55) 4.00 12.00 24.00
23-27,29,30(7/57) 4.00 10.00 20.00
28 (9/56)-L. B. Cole, Disbrow-a 9.30 28.00 65.00
3(#31, 9/57),4(#32, 11/57),33,34 (Farrell, '57- '58) 3.60 9.00 18.00

ALL WESTERN WINNERS (Formerly All Winners; becomes Western Winners with No. 5; see Two-Gun Kid No. 5)
Marvel Comics(CDS): No. 2, Winter, 1948-49 - No. 4, April, 1949
2-Black Rider (origin & 1st app.) & his horse Satan, Kid Colt & his horse Steel, & Two-Gun Kid & his horse Cyclone begin; Shores c-2-4 79.00 237.00 750.00
3-Anti-Wertham editorial 40.00 120.00 340.00
4-Black Rider i.d. revealed; Heath, Shores-a 40.00 120.00 340.00

ALL WINNERS COMICS (All Teen #20) (Also see Timely Presents: ...)
USA No. 1-7/WFP No. 10-19/YAI No. 21: Summer, 1941 - No. 19, Fall, 1946; No. 21, Winter, 1946-47; (No #20) (No. 21 continued from Young Allies No. 20)
GD2.0 FN6.0 VF8.0 NM9.4
1-The Angel & Black Marvel only app.; Capt. America by Simon & Kirby, Human Torch & Sub-Mariner begin (#1 was advertised as All Aces); 1st app. All-Winners Squad in text story by Stan Lee 1600.00 4800.00 10,400.00 20,000.00
GD2.0 FN6.0 NM9.4
2-The Destroyer & The Whizzer begin; Simon & Kirby Captain America 435.00 1305.00 5000.00
3 295.00 885.00 2800.00
4-Classic War-c by Al Avison 305.00 915.00 3200.00
5 195.00 584.00 1850.00
6-The Black Avenger only app.; no Whizzer story; Hitler, Hirohito & Mussolini-c 232.00 695.00 2200.00
7-10 168.00 505.00 1600.00
11,13-18: 11-1st Atlas globe on-c (Winter, 1943-44; also see Human Torch #14). 14-16-No Human Torch 122.00 367.00 1200.00
12-Red Skull story; last Destroyer; no Whizzer story 152.00 458.00 1450.00
19-(Scarce)-1st story app. & origin All Winners Squad (Capt. America & Bucky, Human Torch & Toro, Sub-Mariner, Whizzer, & Miss America; r-in Fantasy Masterpieces #10 400.00 1200.00 4200.00
21-(Scarce)-All Winners Squad; bondage-c 343.00 1030.00 3600.00
NOTE: ***Everett** Sub-Mariner-1, 3, 4; **Burgos** Torch-1, 3, 4. **Schomburg** c-1, 7-18. **Shores** c-19p, 21.*

(2nd Series - August, 1948, Marvel Comics (CDS))
(Becomes All Western Winners with No. 2)
1-The Blonde Phantom, Capt. America, Human Torch, & Sub-Mariner app. 274.00 822.00 2600.00

ALL YOUR COMICS (See Fox Giants)
Fox Feature Syndicate (R. W. Voight): Spring, 1946 (36 pgs.)
1-Red Robbins, Merciless the Sorceress app. 19.00 56.00 150.

ALMANAC OF CRIME (See Fox Giants)

AL OF FBI (See Little Al of the FBI)

ALPHA AND OMEGA
Spire Christian Comics (Fleming H. Revell): 1978 (49¢)
nn 2.40 6.

ALPHA CENTURION (See Superman, 2nd Series & Zero Hour)
DC Comics: 1996 ($2.95, one-shot)
1 3.

ALPHA FLIGHT (See X-Men #120,121 & X-Men/Alpha Flight)
Marvel Comics: Aug, 1983 - No. 130, Mar, 1994 (#52-on are direct sales only
1-Byrne-a begins (52pgs.)-Wolverine & Nightcrawler cameo 3.
2-12,14-16,18-32,35-50: 2-Vindicator becomes Guardian; origin Marrina & Alpha Flight. 3-Concludes origin Alpha Flight. 6-Origin Shaman. 7-Origin Snowbird. 10,11-Origin Sasquatch. 12-(52 pgs.)-Death of Guardian. 16-Wolverine cameo. 20-New headquarters. 25-Return of Guardian. 28-Last Byrne issue. 39-47,49-Portacio-a(i). 50-Double size; Portacio-a(i) 2.
13,17,33,34: 13-Wolverine app. 17-X-Men x-over (70% r-/X-Men #109); Wolverine cameo. 33-X-Men (Wolverine) app. 34-Origin Wolverine 3.
51-Jim Lee's 1st work at Marvel (10/87); Wolverine cameo; 1st Jim Lee Wolverine; Portacio-a(i) 5.
52,53-Wolverine app.; Lee-a on Wolverine; Portacio-a(i); 53-Lee/Portacio-a 2.
54-105: 54,63,64-No Jim Lee-a. 54-Portacio-a(i). 55-62-Jim Lee-a(p). 71-Intro The Sorcerer (villain). 74-Wolverine, Spider-Man & The Avengers app. 89-Original Guardian returns. 75-Double size ($1.95, 52 pgs.). 87-90-Wolverin 4 part story w/Jim Lee-c. 91-Dr. Doom app. 94-F.F. x-over. 99-Galactus, Avengers app. 100-($2.00, 52 pgs.)-Avengers & Galactus app. 102-Intro Weapon Omega. 104-Last $1.50-c 2.
106-Northstar revelation issue 2.
106-2nd printing (direct sale only) 2.
107-119,121-129: 107-X-Factor x-over. 110-112-Infinity War x-overs. 110, 111 Wolverine app. (brief). 111-Thanos cameo 2.
120-($2.25)-Polybagged w/Paranormal Registration Act poster 2.
130-($2.25, 52 pgs.) 2.
Annual 1,2 (9/86, 12/87) 2.
Special V2#1(6/92, $2.50, 52 pgs.)-Wolverine-c/story 2.
NOTE: ***Austin** c-1i, 2i, 53i. **Byrne** c-81, 82. **Guice** c-85, 91-99. **Jim Lee** a(p)-51, 53, 55-62, 6 53, 87-90. **Mignola** a-29-31p. **Whilce Portacio** a(i)-39-47, 49-54.*

ALPHA FLIGHT (2nd Series)
Marvel Comics: Aug, 1997 - No. 20, Mar, 1999 ($2.99/$1.99)
1-($2.99)-Wraparound cover 2.40 6.
2,3: 2-Variant-c 4.
4-11,13-20: 8,9-Wolverine-c/app. 3.
12-($2.99) Death of Sasquatch; wraparound-c 4.
.../Inhumans '98 Annual ($3.50) Raney-a 3.

ALPHA FLIGHT: IN THE BEGINNING
Marvel Comics: July, 1997 ($1.95, one-shot)
(-1)-Flashback w/Wolverine 2.

ALPHA FLIGHT SPECIAL
Marvel Comics: July, 1991 - No. 4, Oct, 1991 ($1.50, limited series)
1-4: 1-3-r-A. Flight #97-99 w/covers. 4-r-A.Flight #100 2.

ALPHA KORPS
Diversity Comics: Sept, 1996 ($2.50)
1-Origin/1st app. Alpha Korps 2.

ALPHA WAVE
Darkline Comics: Mar, 1987 ($1.75, 36 pgs.)
1 2.

ALTERED IMAGE
Image Comics: Apr, 1998 - No. 3, Sept, 1998 ($2.50, limited series)
1-3-Spawn, Witchblade, Savage Dragon; Valentino-s/a 3.

ALTER EGO
First Comics: May, 1986 - No. 4, Nov, 1986 (Mini-series)

Amazing Adult Fantasy #11 © MAR

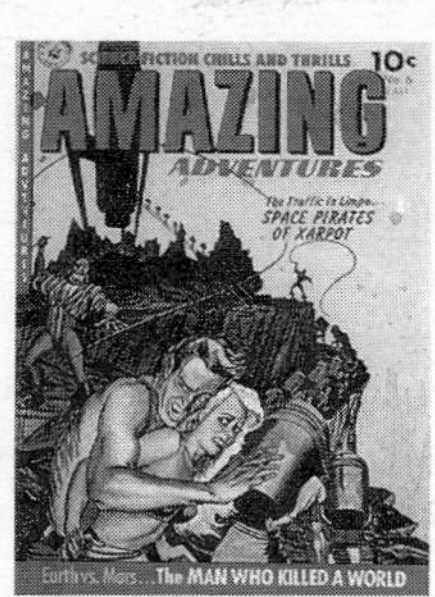

Amazing Adventures #6 © Z-D

Amazing Detective Cases #14 © MAR

GD2.0 FN6.0 NM9.4

4 2.00

VIN (TV) (See Four Color Comics No. 1042)
l Publishing Co.: Oct-Dec, 1962 - No. 28, Oct, 1973

021-212 (#1) 8.35 25.00 100.00
4.60 13.75 55.00
10 4.10 12.30 45.00
-28 3.20 9.60 35.00
in For President (10/64) 3.45 10.35 38.00
His Pals in Merry Christmas with Clyde Crashcup & Leonardo 1
(02-120-402)-(12-2/64) 7.00 21.00 84.00
printed in 1966 (12-023-604 4.50 13.50 55.00

VIN & THE CHIPMUNKS
rvey Comics: July, 1992 - No. 5, May, 1994

5 2.50

ALGAM AGE OF COMICS, THE: THE DC COMICS COLLECTION
Comics: 1996 ($12.95, trade paperback)

r/Amazon, Assassins, Doctor Strangefate, JLX, Legends of the Dark Claw, & Super Soldier 13.00

ANDA AND GUNN
age Comics: Apr, 1997 - No. 4, Oct, 1997 ($2.95, B&W, limited series)

4 3.00

AZING ADULT FANTASY (Formerly Amazing Adventures #1-6; becomes azing Fantasy #15)
rvel Comics Group (AMI): No. 7, Dec, 1961 - No. 14, July, 1962

Ditko-c/a begins, ends #14 50.00 150.00 650.00
Last 10¢ issue 41.00 123.00 500.00
13: 12-1st app. Mailbag. 13-Anti-communist sty 39.00 118.00 470.00
-Prototype issue (Professor X) 41.00 123.00 525.00

AZING ADVENTURE FUNNIES (Fantoman No. 2 on)
ntaur Publications: June, 1940 - No. 2, Sept. 1940

The Fantom of the Fair by Gustavson (r/Amaz. Mystery Funnies V2#7,V2#8), The Arrow, Skyrocket Steele From the Year X by Everett (r/AMF #2); Burgos-a 179.00 537.00 1700.00
Reprints; Published after Fantoman #2 116.00 348.00 1100.00
TE: ***Burgos** a-1(2). **Everett** a-1(3). **Gustavson** a-1(5), 2(3). **Pinajian** a-2.*

AZING ADVENTURES (Also see Boy Cowboy & Science Comics)
-Davis Publ. Co.: 1950; No. 1, Nov, 1950 - No. 6, Fall, 1952 (Painted covers)

50 (no month given) (8-1/2x11) (8 pgs.) Has the front & back cover plus Schomburg story used in Amazing Advs. #1 (Sent to subscribers of Z-D s/f magazines & ordered through mail for 10¢. Used to test market)
44.00 133.00 400.00
Wood, Schomburg, Anderson, Whitney-a 71.00 213.00 675.00
5: 2-Schomburg-a. 2,4,5-Anderson-a. 3,5-Starr-a 36.00 108.00 290.00
Krigstein-a 38.00 113.00 300.00

AZING ADVENTURES (Becomes Amazing Adult Fantasy #7 on)
as Comics (AMI)/Marvel Comics No. 3 on: June, 1961 - No. 6, Nov, 1961

Origin Dr. Droom (1st Marvel-Age Superhero) by Kirby; Kirby/Ditko-a (5 pgs.) Ditko & Kirby-a in all; Kirby monster c-1-6 107.00 321.00 1500.00
46.00 138.00 600.00
6: 6-Last Dr. Droom 41.00 123.00 525.00

AZING ADVENTURES
rvel Comics Group: Aug, 1970 - No. 39, Nov, 1976

Inhumans by Kirby(p) & Black Widow (1st app. in Tales of Suspense #52) double feature begins 4.10 12.30 45.00
4: 2-F.F. brief app. 4-Last Inhumans by Kirby 2.30 7.00 20.00
8: Adams-a(p); 8-Last Black Widow; last 15¢-c 2.80 8.40 28.00
10: Magneto app. 10-Last Inhumans (origin-r by Kirby)
2.00 6.00 16.00
-New Beast begins(1st app. in mutated form; origin in flashback); X-Men cameo in flashback (#11-17 are X-Men tie-ins) 8.15 24.50 90.00
-17: 12-Beast battles Iron Man. 13-Brotherhood of Evil Mutants x-over from X-Men. 15-X-Men app. 16-Juggernaut app. 17-Last Beast (origin); X-Men app.
2.50 7.50 25.00

GD2.0 FN6.0 NM9.4

18-War of the Worlds begins (5/73); 1st app. Killraven; Neal Adams-a(p)
2.00 6.00 18.00
19-35,38,39: 19-Chaykin-a. 25-Buckler-a. 35-Giffen's first published story (art), along with Deadly Hands of Kung-Fu #22 (3/76) 1.00 2.80 7.00
36,37-(Regular 25¢ edition)(7-8/76) 1.00 2.80 7.00
36,37-(30¢-c variants, limited distribution) 1.75 5.25 14.00
NOTE: ***N. Adams** c-6-8. **Buscema** a-1p, 2p. **Colan** a-3-5p, 26p. **Ditko** a-24r. **Everett** a(i)3-5, 7-9. **Giffen** a-35i, 38p. **G. Kane** c-11, 25p, 29p. **Ploog** a-12i. **Russell** a-27-32, 34-37, 39; c-28, 30-32, 33i, 34, 35, 37, 39i. **Starliing** a-17. **Starlin** c-15p, 16, 17, 27. **Sutton** a-11-15p.*

AMAZING ADVENTURES
Marvel Comics Group: Dec, 1979 - No. 14, Jan, 1981

V2#1-Reprints story/X-Men #1 & 38 (origins) 5.00
2-14: 2-6-Early X-Men-r. 7,8-Origin Iceman 4.00
NOTE: ***Byrne** c-6p, 9p. **Kirby** a-1-14r; c-7, 9. **Steranko** a-12r. **Tuska** a-7-9.*

AMAZING ADVENTURES
Marvel Comics: July, 1988 ($4.95, squarebound, one-shot, 80 pgs.)

1-Anthology; Austin, Golden-a 5.00

AMAZING ADVENTURES OF CAPTAIN CARVEL AND HIS CARVEL CRUSADERS, THE (See Carvel Comics)

AMAZING CHAN & THE CHAN CLAN, THE (TV)
Gold Key: May, 1973 - No. 4, Feb, 1974 (Hanna-Barbera)

1-Warren Tufts-a in all 2.50 7.50 25.00
2-4 2.00 6.00 16.00

AMAZING COMICS (Complete Comics No. 2)
Timely Comics (EPC): Fall, 1944

1-The Destroyer, The Whizzer, The Young Allies (by Sekowsky), Sergeant Dix; Schomburg-c 190.00 570.00 1800.00

AMAZING DETECTIVE CASES (Formerly Suspense No. 2?)
Marvel/Atlas Comics (CCC): No. 3, Nov, 1950 - No. 14, Sept, 1952

3 26.00 79.00 210.00
4-6 15.00 45.00 120.00
7-10 13.00 39.00 105.00
11,12,14: 11-(3/52)-Change to horror 23.00 68.00 180.00
12-Krigstein-a 23.00 68.00 180.00
13-(Scarce)-Everett-a; electrocution-c/story 28.00 84.00 225.00
NOTE: ***Colan** a-9. **Maneely** c-13. **Sekowsky** a-12. **Sinnott** a-13. **Tuska** a-10.*

AMAZING FANTASY (Formerly Amazing Adult Fantasy #7-14)
Atlas Magazines/Marvel: #15, Aug, 1962 (Sept, 1962 shown in indicia); #16, Dec, 1995 - #18, Feb, 1996

GD2.0 FN6.0 VF8.0 NM9.4

15-Origin/1st app. of Spider-Man by Ditko (11 pgs.); 1st app. Aunt May & Uncle Ben; Kirby/Ditko-c 1167.00 3500.00 12,825.00 35,000.00

GD2.0 FN6.0 NM9.4

16-18 ('95-'96, $3.95): Kurt Busiek scripts; painted-c/a by Paul Lee 4.00

AMAZING GHOST STORIES (Formerly Nightmare)
St. John Publishing Co.: No. 14, Oct, 1954 - No. 16, Feb, 1955

14-Pit & the Pendulum story by Kinstler; Baker-c 31.00 94.00 250.00
15-r/Weird Thrillers #5; Baker-c, Powell-a 22.00 66.00 175.00
16-Kubert reprints of Weird Thrillers #4; Baker-c; Roussos, Tuska-a; Kinstler-a (1 pg.) 23.00 68.00 180.00

AMAZING HIGH ADVENTURE
Marvel Comics: 8/84; No. 2, 10/85; No. 3, 10/86 - No. 5, 1986 ($2.00)

1-5: Painted-c on all. 3,4-Baxter paper. 4-Bolton-c/a. 5-Bolton-a 3.00
NOTE: ***Bissette** a-4. **Severin** a-1, 3. **Sienkiewicz** a-1,2. **Paul Smith** a-2. **Williamson** a-2i.*

AMAZING-MAN COMICS (Formerly Motion Picture Funnies Weekly?) (Also see Stars And Stripes Comics)
Centaur Publications: No. 5, Sept, 1939 - No. 26, Jan, 1942

GD2.0 FN6.0 VF8.0 NM9.4

5(#1)(Rare)-Origin/1st app. A-Man the Amazing Man by Bill Everett; The Cat-Man by Tarpe Mills (also #8), Mighty Man by Filchock, Minimidget & sidekick Ritty, & The Iron Skull by Burgos begins
1360.00 4080.00 8840.00 17,000.00

GD2.0 FN6.0 NM9.4

6-Origin The Amazing Man retold; The Shark begins; Ivy Menace by Tarpe

Amazing-Man Comics #15 © CEN

Amazing Mystery Funnies #23 © CEN

Amazing Spider-Man #2 © MAR

GD2.0 FN6.0 NM9.4 | **GD2.0 FN6.0 NM9**

Mills app. 300.00 900.00 3000.00
7-Magician From Mars begins; ends #11 211.00 633.00 2000.00
8-Cat-Man dresses as woman 137.00 411.00 1300.00
9-Magician From Mars battles the 'Elemental Monster,' swiped into The Spectre in More Fun #54 & 55. Ties w/Marvel Mystery #4 for 1st Nazi War-c on a comic (2/40) 147.00 442.00 1400.00
10,11: 11-Zardi, the Eternal Man begins; ends #16; Amazing Man dons costume; last Everett issue 121.00 363.00 1150.00
12,13 105.00 316.00 1000.00
14-Reef Kinkaid, Rocke Wayburn (ends #20), & Dr. Hypno (ends #21) begin; no Zardi or Chuck Hardy 89.00 268.00 850.00
15,17-20: 15-Zardi returns; no Rocke Wayburn. 17-Dr. Hypno returns; no Zardi 76.00 229.00 725.00
16-Mighty Man's powers of super strength & ability to shrink & grow explained; Rocke Wayburn returns; no Dr. Hypno; Al Avison (a character) begins, ends #18 (a tribute to the famed artist) 82.00 245.00 775.00
21-Origin Dash Dartwell (drug-use story); origin & only app. T.N.T. 82.00 245.00 775.00
22-Dash Dartwell, the Human Meteor & The Voice app; last Iron Skull & The Shark; Silver Streak app. (classic-c) 89.00 268.00 850.00
23-Two Amazing Man stories; intro/origin Tommy the Amazing Kid; The Marksman only app. 74.00 221.00 700.00
24-King of Darkness, Nightshade, & Blue Lady begin; end #26; 1st app. Super-Ann 74.00 221.00 700.00
25,26 (Scarce): Meteor Martin by Wolverton in both; 26-Electric Ray app. 111.00 332.00 1050.00

NOTE: ***Everett*** *a-5-11; c-5-11.* ***Gilman*** *a-14-20.* ***Giunta/Mirando*** *a-7-10.* ***Sam Glanzman*** *a-14-16, 18-21, 23.* ***Louis Glanzman*** *a-6, 9-11, 14-21; c-13-19, 21.* ***Robert Golden*** *a-9.* ***Gustavson*** *a-6; c-22, 23.* ***Lubbers*** *a-14-21.* ***Simon*** *a-10.* ***Frank Thomas*** *a-6, 9-11, 14, 15, 17-21.*

AMAZING MYSTERIES (Formerly Sub-Mariner Comics No. 31)
Marvel Comics (CCC): No. 32, May, 1949 - No. 35, Jan, 1950 (1st Marvel Horror Comic)

32-The Witness app. 79.00 237.00 750.00
33-Horror format 38.00 113.00 300.00
34,35: Changes to Crime. 34,35-Photo-c 19.00 56.00 150.00

AMAZING MYSTERY FUNNIES
Centaur Publications: Aug, 1938 - No. 24, Sept, 1940 (All 52 pgs.)

V1#1-Everett-c(1st); Dick Kent Adv. story; Skyrocket Steele in the Year X on cover only 333.00 1000.00 3500.00
2-Everett 1st-a (Skyrocket Steele) 179.00 537.00 1700.00
3 89.00 268.00 850.00
3(#4, 12/38)-nn on cover, #3 on inside; bondage-c 79.00 237.00 750.00
V2#1-4,6: 2-Drug use story. 3-Air-Sub DX begins by Burgos. 4-Dan Hastings, Hastings, Sand Hog begins (ends #5). 6-Last Skyrocket Steele 74.00 221.00 700.00
5-Classic Everett-c 103.00 308.00 975.00
7 (Scarce)-Intro. The Fantom of the Fair & begins; Everett, Gustavson, Burgos-a 333.00 1000.00 3500.00
8-Origin & 1st app. Speed Centaur 126.00 379.00 1200.00
9-11: 11-Self portrait and biog. of Everett; Jon Linton begins; early Robot cover (11/39) 74.00 221.00 700.00
12 (Scarce)-1st Space Patrol; Wolverton-a (12/39); new costume Phantom of the Fair 190.00 570.00 1800.00
V3#1(#17, 1/40)-Intro. Bullet; Tippy Taylor serial begins, ends #24 (continued in The Arrow #2) 74.00 221.00 700.00
18,20: 18-Fantom of the Fair by Gustavson 71.00 213.00 675.00
19,21-24: Space Patrol by Wolverton in all 89.00 268.00 850.00

NOTE: ***Burgos*** *a-V2#3-9.* ***Eisner*** *a-V1#2, 3(2).* ***Everett*** *a-V1#2-4, V2#1, 3-6; c-V1#1-4, V2#3, 5, 18.* ***Filchock*** *a-V2#9.* ***Flessel*** *a-V2#6.* ***Guardineer*** *a-V1#4, V2#4-6;* ***Gustavson*** *a-V2#4, 5, 9-12, V3#1, 18, 19; c-V2#7, 9, 12, V3#1, 21, 22;* ***McWilliams*** *a-V2#9, 10.* ***TarpeMills*** *a-V2#2, 4-6, 9-12, V3#1.* ***Leo Morey****(Pulp artist) c-V2#10; text illo-V2#11.* ***FrankThomas*** *a-6-V2#11.* ***Webster*** *a-V2#4.*

AMAZING SAINTS
Logos International: 1974 (39¢)

nn-True story of Phil Saint 5.00

AMAZING SCARLET SPIDER
Marvel Comics: Nov, 1995 - No. 2, Dec, 1995 ($1.95, limited series)

1,2: Replaces "Amazing Spider-Man" for two issues. 1-Venom/Carnage cameos. 2-Green Goblin & Joystick-c/app. 2.0

AMAZING SPIDER-MAN, THE (See All Detergent Comics, Amazing Fantasy, America's Best TV Comics, Aurora, Deadly Foes of Spider-Man, Fireside Book Series, Giant-Size Spider-Man, Giant Size Super-Heroes Featuring..., Marvel Collectors Item Classics, Marvel Fanfare, Marvel Graphic Novel, Marvel Spec. Ed., Marvel Tales, Marvel Team-Up, Marvel Treasury Ed., Nothing Can Stop the Juggernaut, Official Marvel Index To..., Peter Parker, Power Record Comics, Spectacular..., Spider-Man, Spider-Man Digest, Spider-Man Saga, Spider-Man 2099, Spider-Man Vs. Wolverine, Spidey Super Stories, Strange Tales Annual, Superman Vs. ..., Try-Out Winner Book, Web of Spider- Man & Within Our Reach)

AMAZING SPIDER-MAN, THE
Marvel Comics Group: March, 1963 - No. 441, Nov, 1998

GD2.0 FN6.0 VF8.0 NM9.

1-Retells origin by Steve Ditko; 1st Fantastic Four x-over (ties w/F.F. #12 as first Marvel x-over); intro. John Jameson & The Chameleon; Spider-Man's 2nd app.; Kirby/Ditko-c; Ditko-c/a #1-38
800.00 2400.00 8800.00 25,000.0

GD2.0 FN6.0 NM9.

1-Reprint from the Golden Record Comic set 11.00 33.00 120.0
with record (1966) 16.50 49.00 180.0
2-1st app. the Vulture & the Terrible Tinkerer 238.00 712.00 3800.0
3-1st full-length story; Human Torch cameo; intro. & 1st app. Doc Octopus; Spider-Man pin-up by Ditko 180.00 540.00 2700.0
4-Origin & 1st app. The Sandman (see Strange Tales #115 for 2nd app.); Intro. Betty Brant & Liz Allen 154.00 462.00 2200.0
5-Dr. Doom app. 132.00 396.00 1850.0
6-1st app. Lizard 114.00 343.00 1600.0
7,8,10: 7-Vs. The Vulture; 1st monthly issue. 8-Fantastic Four app. in back-up story by Kirby/Ditko. 10-1st app. Big Man & The Enforcers 79.00 236.00 1050.0
9-Origin & 1st app. Electro (2/64) 82.00 246.00 1150.0
11,12: 11-1st app. Bennett Brant. 12-Doc Octopus unmasks Spider-Man-c/sto 46.00 138.00 600.0
13-1st app. Mysterio 61.00 182.00 850.0
14-(7/64)-1st app. The Green Goblin (c/story)(Norman Osborn); Hulk x-over 150.00 450.00 2100.0
15-1st app. Kraven the Hunter; 1st mention of Mary Jane Watson (not shown) 54.00 161.00 750.0
16-Spider-Man battles Daredevil (1st x-over 9/64); still in old yellow costume 41.00 123.00 500.0
17-2nd app. Green Goblin (c/story); Human Torch x-over (also in #18 & #21) 54.00 161.00 750.0
18-1st app. Ned Leeds who later becomes Hobgoblin; Fantastic Four cameo; 3rd app. Sandman 40.00 119.00 475.0
19-Sandman app. 33.00 100.00 400.0
20-Origin & 1st app. The Scorpion 41.00 123.00 500.0
21-2nd app. The Beetle (see Strange Tales #123) 29.00 88.00 325.0
22-1st app. Princess Python 27.50 82.00 300.0
23-3rd app. The Green Goblin-c/story; Norman Osborn app. 37.00 112.00 450.0
24 23.50 71.00 260.0
25-(6/65)-1st app. Mary Jane Watson (cameo; face not shown); 1st app. Spencer Smythe; Norman Osborn app. 29.00 87.00 320.0
26-4th app. The Green Goblin-c/story; 1st app. Crime Master; dies in #27 31.00 93.00 360.0
27-5th app. The Green Goblin-c/story; Norman Osborn app. 29.00 88.00 325.0
28-Origin & 1st app. Molten Man (9/65, scarcer in high grade) 41.00 123.00 500.0
29,30 19.00 57.00 210.0
31-38: 31-1st app. Harry Osborn who later becomes 2nd Green Goblin, Gwen Stacy & Prof. Warren. 34-4th app. Kraven the Hunter. 36-1st app. Looter. 37-Intro. Norman Osborn. 38-(7/66)-2nd app. Mary Jane Watson (cameo; face not shown); last Ditko issue 19.00 57.00 210.0
39-The Green Goblin-c/story; Green Goblin's i.d. revealed as Norman Osborn Romita-a begins (8/66; see Daredevil #16 for 1st Romita-a on Spider-Man) 25.00 75.00 275.0
40-1st told origin The Green Goblin-c/story 33.00 100.00 400.0
41-1st app. Rhino 23.00 68.00 250.0

Amazing Spider-Man #42 © MAR

Amazing Spider-Man #225 © MAR

Amazing Spider-Man #276 © MAR

GD2.0 FN6.0 NM9.4

42-(11/66)-3rd app. Mary Jane Watson (cameo in last 2 panels); 1st time face is shown 16.00 48.00 175.00
43-49: 44,45-2nd & 3rd app. The Lizard. 46-Intro. Shocker. 47-M. J. Watson & Peter Parker 1st date. 47-Green Goblin cameo; Harry & Norman Osborn app. 47,49-5th & 6th app. Kraven the Hunter 11.50 34.00 125.00
50-1st app. Kingpin (7/67) 41.00 123.00 500.00
51-2nd app. Kingpin 18.00 54.00 200.00
52-60: 52-1st app. Joe Robertson & 3rd app. Kingpin. 56-1st app. Capt. George Stacy. 57,58-Ka-Zar app. 59-1st app. Brainwasher (alias Kingpin); 1st-c app. M. J. Watson 8.15 24.50 90.00
61-74: 67-1st app. Randy Robertson. 69-Kingpin-c. 69,70-Kingpin app. 73-1st app. Silvermane. 74-Last 12¢ issue 5.90 17.75 65.00
75-89,91-93,95,99: 78,79-1st app. The Prowler. 83-1st app. Schemer & Vanessa (Kingpin's wife). 84,85-Kingpin-c/story. 86-Re-intro & origin Black Widow in new costume. 93-1st app. Arthur Stacy 4.55 13.65 50.00
90-Death of Capt. Stacy 6.35 19.00 70.00
94-Origin retold 8.15 24.50 90.00
96-98-Green Goblin app. (97,98-Green Goblin-c); drug books not approved by CCA 10.00 30.00 110.00
100-Anniversary issue (9/71); Green Goblin cameo (2 pgs.) 20.00 60.00 220.00
101-1st app. Morbius the Living Vampire; Wizard cameo; last 15¢ issue (10/71) 13.50 40.00 150.00
101-Silver ink 2nd printing (9/92, $1.75) 2.00
102-Origin & 2nd app. Morbius (25¢, 52 pgs.) 9.00 27.00 100.00
103-118: 104,111-Kraven the Hunter-c/stories. 108-1st app. Sha-Shan. 109-Dr. Strange-c/story (6/72). 110-1st app. Gibbon. 113-1st app. Hammerhead. 116-118-reprints story from Spectacular Spider-Man Mag. in color with some changes 3.20 9.60 35.00
119,120-Spider-Man vs. Hulk (4 & 5/73) 5.00 15.00 55.00
121-Death of Gwen Stacy (6/73) (killed by Green Goblin) (reprinted in Marvel Tales #98 & 192) 13.50 40.00 150.00
122-Death of The Green Goblin-c/story (7/73) (reprinted in Marvel Tales #99 & 192) 15.00 45.00 165.00
123,125-128: 123-Cage app. 125-Man-Wolf origin. 127-1st mention of Harry Osborn becoming Green Goblin 3.00 9.00 30.00
124-1st app. Man-Wolf (9/73) 4.10 12.30 45.00
129-1st app. Jackal & The Punisher (2/74) 17.50 52.00 190.00
130-133,138-141,152-154,160: 131-Last 20¢ issue. 139-1st app. Grizzly. 140-1st app. Glory Grant. 2.00 6.00 16.00
134-(7/74); 1st app. Tarantula; Harry Osborn discovers Spider-Man's ID; Punisher cameo 3.20 9.60 35.00
135-2nd full Punisher app. (8/74) 5.00 15.00 55.00
136-Reappearance of The Green Goblin (Harry Osborn; Norman Osborn's son) 4.35 13.00 48.00
137-Green Goblin-c/story (2nd Harry Osborn) 3.80 11.40 42.00
142,143-Gwen Stacy clone cameos: 143-1st app. Cyclone 2.50 7.50 25.00
144-147: 144-Full app. of Gwen Stacy clone. 145,146-Gwen Stacy clone story line continues. 147-Spider-Man learns Gwen Stacy is clone 2.00 6.00 18.00
148-Jackal revealed 2.80 8.40 28.00
149-Spider-Man clone story begins, clone dies (?); origin of Jackal 4.10 12.30 45.00
150-Spider-Man decides he is not the clone 2.00 6.00 18.00
151-Spider-Man disposes of clone body 2.00 6.00 18.00
155-159-(Regular 25¢ editions). 159- Last 25¢ issue(8/76) 2.00 6.00 18.00
155-159-(30¢-c variants, limited distribution) 2.50 7.50 24.00
161-Nightcrawler app. from X-Men; Punisher cameo; Wolverine & Colossus app. 2.00 6.00 18.00
162-Punisher, Nightcrawler app.; 1st Jigsaw 2.00 6.00 18.00
163-168,181-190: 167-1st app. Will O' The Wisp. 181-Origin retold; gives life history of Spidey; Punisher cameo in flashback (1 panel). 182-(7/78)-Peter 's first proposal to Mary Jane, but she refuses 1.25 3.75 10.00
169-173-(Regular 30¢ edition). 169-Clone story recapped. 171-Nova app. 1.25 3.75 10.00
169-173-(35¢-c variants, limited dist.)(6-10/77) 1.85 5.50 15.00
174,175-Punisher app. 1.75 5.25 14.00

GD2.0 FN6.0 NM9.4

176-180-Green Goblin app 2.00 6.00 18.00
191-193,195-199,203-208,210-219: 193-Peter & Mary Jane break up. 196-Faked death of Aunt May. 203-2nd app. Dazzler. 209-1st app. Calypso (Kraven's girlfriend). 210-1st app. Madame Web. 212-1st app. Hydro Man; origin Sandman 1.00 3.00 8.00
194-1st app. Black Cat 2.00 6.00 16.00
200-Giant origin issue (1/80) 2.40 7.35 22.00
201,202-Punisher app. 1.25 3.75 10.00
209-Origin & 1st app. Calypso (10/80) 1.25 3.75 10.00
220-237: 225-(2/82)-Foolkiller-c/story. 226,227-Black Cat returns. 236-Tarantula dies. 234-Free 16 pg. insert "Marvel Guide to Collecting Comics". 235-Origin Will-'O-The-Wisp 1.00 2.80 7.00
238-(3/83)-1st app. Hobgoblin (Ned Leeds); came with skin "Tattooz" decal. **Note:** The same decal appears in the more common Fantastic Four #252 which is being removed & placed in this issue as incentive to increase value (Value listed is with or without tattooz) 5.45 16.35 60.00
239-2nd app. Hobgoblin & 1st battle w/Spidey 3.20 9.60 35.00
240-243,246-248: 241-Origin The Vulture. 243-Reintro Mary Jane Watson after 4 year absence 2.40 6.00
244-3rd app. Hobgoblin (cameo) 1.10 3.30 9.00
245-(10/83)-4th app. Hobgoblin (cameo); Lefty Donovan gains powers of Hobgoblin & battles Spider-Man 1.50 4.50 12.00
249-251: 3 part Hobgoblin/Spider-Man battle. 249-Retells origin & death of 1st Green Goblin. 251-Last old costume 1.50 4.50 12.00
252-Spider-Man dons new black costume (5/84); ties with Marvel Team-Up #141 & Spectacular Spider-Man #90 for 1st new costume (See Marvel S-H Secret Wars #8) 2.80 8.40 28.00
253-1st app. The Rose 1.00 2.80 7.00
254-258: 256-1st app. Puma. 257-Hobgoblin cameo; 2nd app. Puma; M. J. Watson reveals she knows Spidey's i.d. 258-Hobgoblin app. (minor) 2.40 6.00
259-Full Hobgoblin app.; Spidey back to old costume; origin Mary Jane Watson 1.10 3.30 9.00
260-Hobgoblin app. 1.00 2.80 7.00
261-Hobgoblin-c/story; painted-c by Vess 1.00 3.00 8.00
262-Spider-Man unmasked; photo-c 2.40 6.00
263,264,266-274,277-280,282,283: 274-Zarathos (The Spirit of Vengeance) app. 277-Vess back-up art. 279-Jack O'Lantern-c/story. 282-X-Factor x-over 5.00
265-1st app. Silver Sable (6/85) 1.00 3.00 8.00
265-Silver ink 2nd printing ($1.25) 2.00
275-($1.25, 52 pgs.)-Hobgoblin-c/story; origin-r by Ditko 1.50 4.50 12.00
276-Hobgoblin app. 1.00 2.80 7.00
281-Hobgoblin battles Jack O'Lantern 1.00 2.80 7.00
284,285: 284-Punisher cameo; Gang War story begins; Hobgoblin-c/story. 285-Punisher app.; minor Hobgoblin app. 1.00 2.80 7.00
286-288: 286-Hobgoblin-c & app. (minor). 287-Hobgoblin app. (minor). 288-Full Hobgoblin app.; last Gang War 1.00 2.80 7.00
289-(6/87, $1.25, 52 pgs.)-Hobgoblin's i.d. revealed as Ned Leeds; death of Ned Leeds; Macendale (Jack O'Lantern) becomes new Hobgoblin (1st app.) 2.00 6.00 18.00
290-292,295-297: 290-Peter proposes to Mary Jane. 292-She accepts; leads into Amazing Spider-Man Annual #21 5.00
293,294-Part 2 & 5 of Kraven story from Web of Spider-Man. 294-Death of Kraven 1.00 2.80 7.00
298-Todd McFarlane-c/a begins (3/88); 1st app. Eddie Brock who becomes Venom; (cameo on last pg.) 3.00 9.00 30.00
299-1st app. Venom with costume (cameo) 2.30 7.00 20.00
300 ($1.50, 52 pgs.; 25th Anniversary)-1st full Venom app.; last black costume (5/88) 6.35 19.00 70.00
301-305: 301 ($1.00 issues begin). 304-1st bi-weekly issue 1.25 3.75 10.00
306-311,313,314: 306-Swipes-c from Action #1. 315-317-Venom app. 1.00 3.00 8.00
312-Hobgoblin battles Green Goblin 1.50 4.50 12.00
315-317-Venom app. 1.50 4.50 12.00
318-323,325: 319-Bi-weekly begins again 2.40 6.00
324-Sabretooth app.; McFarlane cover only 2.40 6.00

Amazing Spider-Man #396 © MAR

Amazing Spider-Man #432 © MAR

Amazing Spider-Man Annual #17 © MAR

GD2.0 FN6.0 NM9.4

326,327,329: 327-Cosmic Spidey continues from Spectacular Spider-Man (no McFarlane-c/a) 4.00
328-Hulk x-over; last McFarlane issue 1.00 3.00 8.00
330,331-Punisher app. 331-Minor Venom app. 3.00
332,333-Venom-c/story 2.40 6.00
334-336,338-343: 341-Tarantula app. 3.00
337-Hobgoblin app. 3.50
344-1st app. Cletus Kasady (Carnage) 1.10 3.30 9.00
345-1st full app. Cletus Kasady; Venom cameo on last pg. 1.25 3.37 10.00
346,347-Venom app. 2.40 6.00
348,349,351-359: 348-Avengers x-over. 351,352-Nova of New Warriors app. 353-Darkhawk app.; brief Punisher app. 354-Punisher cameo & Nova, Night Thrasher (New Warriors), Darkhawk & Moon Knight app. 357,358-Punisher, Darkhawk, Moon Knight, Night Thrasher, Nova x-over. 358-3 part gatefold-c; last $1.00-c. 360-Carnage cameo 2.50
350-($1.50, 52pgs.)-Origin retold; Spidey vs. Dr. Doom; pin-ups; Uncle Ben app. 4.00
360-Carnage cameo 3.00
361-Intro Carnage (the Spawn of Venom); begin 3 part story; recap of how Spidey's alien costume became Venom 1.10 3.30 9.00
361-($1.25)-2nd printing; silver-c 2.50
362,363-Carnage & Venom-c/story 2.40 6.00
362-2nd printing 2.00
364,366-374,376-387: 364-The Shocker app. (old villain). 366-Peter's parents-c/story. 369-Harry Osborn back-up (Gr. Goblin II). 373-Venom back-up. 374-Venom-c/story. 376-Cardiac app. 378-Maximum Carnage part 3. 381,382-Hulk app. 383-The Jury app. 384-Venom/carnage app. 387-New costume Vulture 2.50
365-($3.95, 84 pgs.)-30th anniversary issue w/silver hologram on-c; Spidey/ Venom/Carnage pull-out poster; contains 5 pg. preview of Spider-Man 2099 (1st app.); Spidey's origin retold; Lizard app.; reintro Peter's parents in Stan Lee 3 pg. text w/illo (story continues thru #370). 5.00
365-Second printing; gold hologram on-c 4.00
375-($3.95, 68 pgs.)-Holo-grafx foil-c; vs. Venom story; ties into Venom: Lethal Protector #1; Pat Olliffe-a. 5.00
388-($2.25, 68 pgs.)-Newsstand edition; Venom back-up & Cardiac & chance back-up 2.25
388-($2.95, 68 pgs.)-Collector's edition w/foil-c 3.00
389-396,398,399,401-420: 389-$1.50-c begins; bound-in trading card sheet; Green Goblin app. 394-Power & Responsibility Pt. 2. 396-Daredevil-c & app. 403-Carnage app. 406-1st New Doc Octopus. 407-Human Torch, Silver Sable, Sandman app. 409-Kaine, Rhino app. 410-Carnage app. 414-The Rose app. 415-Onslaught story; Spidey vs. Sentinels. 416-Epilogue to Onslaught; Garney-a(p); Williamson-a(i) 2.00
390-($2.95)-Collector's edition polybagged w/16 pg. insert of new animated Spidey TV show plus animation cel 3.00
394-($2.95, 48 pgs.)-Deluxe edition; flip book w/Birth of a Spider-Man Pt. 2; silver foil both-c 3.00
397-($2.25)-Flip book w/Ultimate Spider-Man 2.25
400-($2.95)-Death of Aunt May 3.00
400-($3.95)-Death of Aunt May; embossed double-c 5.00
400-Collector's Edition; white-c 1.10 3.30 9.00
408-($2.95) Polybagged version with TV theme song cassette 8.00
421-424, -1 (7/97)($1.95-c) 2.00
425-($2.99)-48 pgs., wraparound-c 3.00
426,428-433: 426-Begin $1.99-c. 432-Spiderhunt pt. 2 2.00
427-($2.25) Return of Dr. Octopus; double gatefold-c 2.25
434-440: 434-Double cover with "Amazing Ricochet #1". 438-Daredevil app. 439-Avengers-c/app. 440-Byrne-s 2.00
441-Final issue; Byrne-s 3.00
Annual 1 (1964, 72 pgs.)-Origin Spider-Man; 1st app. Sinister Six (Dr. Octopus, Electro, Kraven the Hunter, Mysterio, Sandman, Vulture) (41 pg. story); plus gallery of Spidey foes; early X-Men app. 62.00 188.00 875.00
Annual 2 (1965, 25¢, 72 pgs.)-Reprints from #1,2,5 plus new Doctor Strange story 27.50 82.00 300.00
Special 3 (11/66, 25¢, 72 pgs.)-Avengers & Hulk x-over; Doctor Octopus-r from #11,12; Romita-a 10.50 31.50 115.00
Special 4 (11/67, 25¢, 68 pgs.)-Spidey battles Human Torch (new 41 pg. story) 9.50 28.50 105.0
Special 5 (11/68, 25¢, 68 pgs.)-New 40 pg. Red Skull story; 1st app. Peter Parker's parents; last annual with new-a 8.65 26.00 95.0
Special 6 (11/69, 25¢, 68 pgs.)-Reprints 41 pg. Sinister Six story from annual #1 plus 2 Kirby/Ditko stories (r) 3.80 11.40 42.0
Special 7 (12/70, 25¢, 68 pgs.)-All-r(#1,2) new Vulture-c 3.80 11.40 42.0
Special 8 (12/71)-All-r 3.80 11.40 42.0
King Size 9 ('73)-Reprints Spectacular Spider-Man (mag.) #2; 40 pg. Green Goblin-c/story (re-edited from 58 pgs.) 3.80 11.40 42.0
Annual 10 (1976)-Origin Human Fly (vs. Spidey); new-a begins 2.00 6.00 18.0
Annual 11-13 ('77-'79):12-Spidey vs. Hulk-r/#119,120. 13-New Byrne/Austin-a; Dr. Octopus x-over w/Spectacular S-M Ann. #1 1.50 4.50 12.0
Annual 14 (1980)-Miller-c/a(p); Dr. Strange app. 1.75 5.25 14.0
Annual 15 (1981)-Miller-c/a(p); Punisher app. 1.75 5.25 14.0
Annual 16-20: 16 ('82)-Origin/1st app. new Capt. Marvel (female heroine). 17 ('83)-Kingpin app. 18 ('84)-Scorpion app.; JJJ weds. 19 ('85). 20 ('86)-Origin Iron Man of 2020 2.40 6.0
Annual 21 (1987)-Special wedding issue; newsstand & direct sale versions exist & are worth same 1.25 3.75 10.0
Annual 22 (1988, $1.75, 68 pgs.)-1st app. Speedball; Evolutionary War x-over; Daredevil app. 2.40 6.0
Annual 23 (1989, $2.00, 68 pgs.)-Atlantis Attacks; origin Spider-Man retold; She-Hulk app.; Byrne-c; Liefeld-a(p), 23 pgs. 4.0
Annual 24 (1990, $2.00, 68 pgs.)-Ant-Man app. 3.0
Annual 25 (1991, $2.00, 68 pgs.)-3 pg. origin recap; Iron Man app.; 1st Venom solo story; Ditko-a (6 pgs.) 5.0
Annual 26 (1992, $2.25, 68 pgs.)-New Warriors-c/story; Venom solo story cont'd in Spectacular Spider-Man Annual #12 4.0
Annual 27,28 ('93, '94, $2.95, 68 pgs.)-27-Bagged w/card; 1st app. Annex. 28-Carnage-c/story; Rhino & Cloak and Dagger back-ups 3.0
'96 Special-($2.95, 64 pgs.)-"Blast From The Past" 4.0
'97 Special-($2.99)-Wraparound-c,Sundown app. 4.0
Marvel Graphic Novel - Parallel Lives (3/89, $8.95) 1.25 3.75 10.0
Marvel Graphic Novel - Spirits of the Earth (1990, $18.95, HC) 2.50 7.50 25.0
Super Special 1 (4/95, $3.95)-Flip Book 4.0
...: Skating on Thin Ice 1(1990, $1.25, Canadian)-McFarlane-c; anti-drug issue; Electro app. 1.10 3.30 9.0
...: Skating on Thin Ice 1 (2/93, $1.50, American) 3.0
...: Double Trouble 2 (1990, $1.25, Canadian) 2.40 6.0
...: Double Trouble 2 (2/93, $1.50, American) 2.0
...: Hit and Run 3 (1990, $1.25, Canadian)-Ghost Rider-c/story 1.10 3.30 9.0
...: Hit and Run 3 (2/93. $1.50, American) 2.0
...: Carnage (6/93, $6.95)-r/ASM #344,345,359-363 1.00 2.80 7.0
...: Chaos in Calgary 4 (Canadian; part of 5 part series)-Turbine,Night Rider, Frightful app. 1.75 5.25 14.0
...: Chaos in Calgary 4 (2/93, $1.50, American) 2.0
...: Deadball 5 (1993, $1.60, Canadian)-Green Goblin-c/story; features Montreal Expos 2.00 6.00 18.0

Note: Prices listed above are for English Canadian editions. French editions are worth double.

...: Soul of the Hunter nn (8/92, $5.95, 52 pgs.)-Zeck-c/a(p) 2.40 6.0

NOTE: ***Austin*** *a(i)-248, 335, 337, Annual 13; c(i)-188, 241, 242, 248, 331, 334, 343, Annual 2* ***J. Buscema*** *a(p)-72, 73, 76-81, 84, 85.* ***Byrne*** *a-189p, 190p, 206p, Annual 3r, 6r, 7r, 13p; 189p, 268, 296, Annual 12.* ***Ditko*** *a-1-38, Annual 1, Special 3(r), 2, 24(2); c-1i, 2-38.* ***Guice*** *c Annual 18i.* ***Gil Kane*** *a(p)-89-105, 120-124, 150, Annual 10, 12i, 24p; c-90p, 96, 98, 99, 10 105p, 129p, 131p, 132p, 137-140p, 143p, 148p, 149p, 151p, 153p, 160p, 161p, Annual 10p,* ***Kirby*** *a-8.* ***Erik Larsen*** *a-324, 327, 329-350; c-327, 329-350, 354i, Annual 25.* ***McFarlane*** *298p, 299p, 300-303, 304-323p, 325p, 328; c-298-325, 328.* ***Miller*** *c-218, 219.* ***Mooney*** *a-6 67-82i, 84-88i, 173i, 178i, 189i, 190i, 192i, 193i, 196-202i, 207i, 211-219i, 221i, 222i, 226i, 22 229-233i, Annual 11i, 17i.* ***Nasser*** *c-228p.* ***Nebres*** *a-Annual 24i.* ***Russell*** *c-357i.* ***Simonson*** *222, 337i.* ***Starlin*** *a-113i, 114i, 187p.* ***Williamson*** *a-365i.*

AMAZING SPIDER-MAN (Volume 2)
Marvel Comics: Jan, 1998 - Present ($2.99/$1.99/$2.25)

1-($2.99)-Byrne-a 4.0
1-($6.95) Dynamic Forces variant-c by the Romitas 1.25 3.75 10.0
2-($1.99) Two covers -by John Byrne and Andy Kubert 3.0

Amazing Spider-Man V2 #9 © MAR

Amazing World of DC Comics #1 © DC

American Library #6 © DMP

3-11: 4-Fantastic Four app. 5-Spider-Woman-c 2.00
12-($2.99) Sinister Six return (cont. in Peter Parker #12) 3.00
13-17: 13-MJ's plane explodes 1.99
18,19,21-24,26: 18-Begin $2.25-c. 19-Venom-c. 24-Maximum Security 2.25
20-($2.99, 100 pgs.) Spider-Slayer issue; new story and reprints 3.00
25-($2.99) Regular cover; Peter Parker becomes the Green Goblin 3.00
25-($3.99) Holo-foil enhanced cover 4.00
1999, 2000 Annual (6/99, '00, $3.50) 1999-Buscema-a 3.50

AMAZING WILLIE MAYS, THE
Famous Funnies Publ.: No date (Sept, 1954)
nn 71.00 284.00 675.00

AMAZING WORLD OF DC COMICS
DC Comics: Jul, 1974 - No. 17, 1978 ($1.50, B&W, mail-order DC Pro-zine)
1-Kubert interview; unpublished Kirby-a; Infantino-c 5.00 15.00 55.00
2-4: 3-Julie Schwartz profile. 4-Batman; Robinson-c 3.60 10.80 40.00
5-Sheldon Mayer 3.00 9.00 30.00
6,8,13: 6-Joe Orlando; EC-r; Wrightson pin-up. 8-Infantino; Batman-r from Pop Tart giveaway. 13-Humor; Aragonés-c; Wood/Ditko-a; photos from serials of Superman, Batman, Captain Marvel 2.00 6.00 16.00
7,10-12: 7-Superman; r/1955 Pep comic giveaway. 10-Behind the scenes at DC; Showcase article. 11-Super-Villains; unpubl. Secret Society of S.V. story. 12-Legion; Grell-c/interview; 2.50 7.50 23.00
9-Legion of Super-Heroes; lengthy bios and history; Cockrum-c 6.00 18.00 66.00
14-Justice League 2.50 7.50 25.00
15-Wonder Woman; Nasser-c 3.60 10.80 36.00
16-Golden Age heroes 3.00 9.00 30.00
17-Shazam; G.A., 70s, TV and Fawcett heroes 2.50 7.50 25.00

AMAZING WORLD OF SUPERMAN (See Superman)

AMAZING X-MEN
Marvel Comics: Mar, 1995 - No. 4, July, 1995 ($1.95, limited series)
1-Age of Apocalypse; Andy Kubert-c/a 3.50
2-4 2.50

AMAZON
Comico: Mar, 1989 - No. 3, May, 1989 ($1.95, limited series)
1-3: Ecological theme 2.00

AMAZON (Also see Marvel Versus DC #3 & DC Versus Marvel #4)
DC Comics (Amalgam): Apr, 1996 ($1.95, one-shot)
1-John Byrne-c/a/scripts 2.00

AMAZON ATTACK 3-D
The 3-D Zone: Sept, 1990 ($3.95, 28 pgs.)
1-Chaykin-a 4.50

AMAZON WOMAN (1st Series)
FantaCo: Summer, 1994 - No. 2, Fall, 1994 ($2.95, B&W, limited series, mature)
1,2: Tom Simonton-c/a/scripts 3.00

AMAZON WOMAN (2nd Series)
FantaCo: Feb, 1996 - No. 4, May, 1996 ($2.95, B&W, limited series, mature)
1-4: Tom Simonton-a/scripts 3.00
Invaders of Terror ('96, $5.95) Simonton-a/s 2.40 6.00

AMBUSH (See Zane Grey, Four Color 314)

AMBUSH BUG (Also see Son of...)
DC Comics: June, 1985 - No. 4, Sept, 1985 (75¢, limited series)
1-4: Giffen-c/a in all 2.00
Nothing Special 1 (9/92, $2.50, 68pg.)-Giffen-c/a 3.00
Stocking Stuffer (2/86, $1.25)-Giffen-c/a 3.00

AMERICA AT WAR - THE BEST OF DC WAR COMICS (See Fireside Book Series)

AMERICA IN ACTION
Dell(Imp. Publ. Co.)/Mayflower House Publ.: 1942; Winter, 1945 (36 pgs.)
1942-Dell-(68 pgs.) 16.00 49.00 130.00
1-(1945)-Has 3 adaptations from American history; Kiefer, Schrotter & Webb-a 11.00 33.00 90.00

GD2.0 FN6.0 NM9.4

AMERICAN, THE
Dark Horse Comics: July, 1987 - No. 8, 1989 ($1.50/$1.75, B&W)
1-8: ($1.50) 2.00
Collection ($5.95, B&W)-Reprints 2.40 6.00
Special 1 (1990, $2.25, B&W) 2.25

AMERICAN AIR FORCES, THE (See A-1 Comics)
William H. Wise(Flying Cadet Publ. Co./Hasan(No.1)/Life's Romances/ Magazine Ent. No. 5 on): Sept-Oct, 1944-No. 4, 1945; No. 5, 1951-No. 12, 1954
1-Article by Zack Mosley, creator of Smilin' Jack 15.00 45.00 120.00
2-Classic-c 20.00 60.00 160.00
3,4 9.30 28.00 65.00
NOTE: *All part comic, part magazine. Art by* **Whitney, Chas. Quinlan, H. C. Kiefer,** *and* **Tony Dipreta**.
5(A-1 45)(Formerly Jet Powers), 6(A-1 54), 7(A-1 58), 8(A-1 65), 9(A-1 67), 10(A-1 74), 11(A-1 79), 12(A-1 91) 6.00 18.00 42.00
NOTE: **Powell** *c/a-5-12.*

AMERICAN FLAGG! (See First Comics Graphic Novel 3,9,12,21 & Howard Chaykin's..)
First Comics: Oct, 1983 - No. 50, Mar, 1988
1,21-27,50: 1-Chaykin-c/a begins. 21-27-Alan Moore scripts 4.00
2-20,28-49: 31-Origin Bob Violence 3.00
Special 1 (11/86)-Introduces Chaykin's Time[2] 4.00

AMERICAN FREAK: A TALE OF THE UN-MEN
DC Comics (Vertigo): Feb, 1994 - No. 5, Jun, 1994 ($1.95, mini-series, mature)
1-5 2.00

AMERICAN GRAPHICS
Henry Stewart: No. 1, 1954; No. 2, 1957 (25¢)
1-The Maid of the Mist, The Last of the Eries (Indian Legends of Niagara) (sold at Niagara Falls) 10.00 30.00 75.00
2-Victory at Niagara & Laura Secord (Heroine of the War of 1812) 6.40 19.25 45.00

AMERICAN INDIAN, THE (See Picture Progress)

AMERICAN LIBRARY
David McKay Publ.: 1943 - No. 6, 1944 (15¢, 68 pgs., B&W, text & pictures)
nn (#1)-Thirty Seconds Over Tokyo (movie) 35.00 105.00 280.00
nn (#2)-Guadalcanal Diary; painted-c (only 10¢) 26.00 79.00 210.00
3-6: 3-Look to the Mountain. 4-Case of the Crooked Candle (Perry Mason). 5-Duel in the Sun. 6-Wingate's Raiders 12.00 36.00 95.00

AMERICAN: LOST IN AMERICA, THE
Dark Horse Comics: July, 1992 - No. 4, Oct, 1992 ($2.50, limited series)
1-4: 1-Dorman painted-c. 2-Phillips painted-c. 3-Mignola-c. 4-Jim Lee-c 2.50

AMERICAN SPLENDOR: (Series of titles)
Dark Horse Comics: Aug, 1996 - Present (B&W, all one-shots)
--**COMIC-CON COMICS** (8/96) 1-H. Pekar script. --**MUSIC COMICS** (11/97) nn-H. Pekar-s/Sacco-a; r/Village Voice jazz strips. --**ODDS AND ENDS** (12/97) 1-Pekar-s. --**ON THE JOB** (5/97) 1-Pekar-s. --**A STEP OUT OF THE NEST** (8/94) 1-Pekar-s. --**TERMINAL** (9/99) 1-Pekar-s. --**TRANSATLANTIC** (7/98) 1-"American Splendour" on cover; Pekar-s 3.00
--**BEDTIME STORIES** (6/00, $3.95) 4.00

AMERICAN SPLENDOR: WINDFALL
Dark Horse Comics: Sept, 1995 - No. 2, Oct,1995 ($3.95, B&W, limited series)
1,2-Pekar script 4.00

AMERICAN TAIL: FIEVEL GOES WEST, AN
Marvel Comics: Early Jan, 1992 - No. 3, Early Feb, 1992 ($1.00, limited series)
1-3-Adapts Universal animated movie; Wildman-a 2.50
1-($2.95-c, 69 pgs.) Deluxe squarebound edition 4.00

AMERICAN WOMAN
Antarctic Press (Barrage Studios): Jun, 1998 - No. 2 ($2.95)
1,2: 1-Denham-s/a. 2-Stockton-s 3.00

AMERICA'S BEST COMICS
Nedor/Better/Standard Publications: Feb, 1942; No. 2, Sept, 1942 - No. 31, July, 1949 (New logo with #9)

America's Best Comics #28 © STD

America's Greatest Comics #5 © FAW

Anarky #3 © DC

1-The Woman in Red, Black Terror, Captain Future, Doc Strange, The Liberator, & Don Davis, Secret Ace begin 242.00 726.00 2300.00
2-Origin The American Eagle; The Woman in Red ends 95.00 285.00 900.00
3-Pyroman begins (11/42, 1st app.; also see Startling Comics #18, 12/42) 71.00 213.00 675.00
4-6: 5-Last Capt. Future (not in #4); Lone Eagle app. 6-American Crusader app. 55.00 165.00 525.00
7-Hitler, Mussolini & Hirohito-c 79.00 237.00 750.00
8-Last Liberator 53.00 158.00 475.00
9-The Fighting Yank begins; The Ghost app. 61.00 182.00 575.00
10,12-17,19-21: 10-Flag-c. 14-American Eagle ends. 21-Infinity-c. 50.00 150.00 450.00
11-Hirohito & Tojo-c. (10/44) 55.00 165.00 525.00
18-Classic-c 55.00 165.00 500.00
22-Capt. Future app. 44.00 133.00 400.00
23-Miss Masque begins; last Doc Strange 53.00 158.00 475.00
24-Miss Masque bondage-c 51.00 153.00 460.00
25-Last Fighting Yank; Sea Eagle app. 40.00 120.00 350.00
26-31: 26-The Phantom Detective & The Silver Knight app.; Frazetta text illo & some panels in Miss Masque. 27,28-Commando Cubs. 27-Doc Strange. 28-Tuska Black Terror. 29-Last Pyroman 40.00 120.00 350.00
NOTE: *American Eagle not in 3, 8, 9, 13. Fighting Yank not in 10, 12. Liberator not in 2, 6, 7. Pyroman not in 9, 11, 14-16, 23, 25-27.* ***Schomburg (Xela)*** *c-5, 7-31. Bondage c-18, 24.*

AMERICA'S BEST COMICS PREVIEW
Wizard: 1999 (Magazine supplement)
1-Previews Tom Strong, Top Ten, Promethea, Tomorrow Stories 1.00

AMERICA'S BEST TV COMICS (TV)
American Broadcasting Co. (Prod. by Marvel Comics): 1967 (25¢, 68 pgs.)
1-Spider-Man, Fantastic Four (by Kirby/Ayers), Casper, King Kong, George of the Jungle, Journey to the Center of the Earth stories (promotes new TV cartoon show) 13.50 40.00 150.00

AMERICA'S BIGGEST COMICS BOOK
William H. Wise: 1944 (196 pgs., one-shot)
1-The Grim Reaper, The Silver Knight, Zudo, the Jungle Boy, Commando Cubs, Thunderhoof app. 40.00 120.00 360.00

AMERICA'S FUNNIEST COMICS
William H. Wise: 1944 - No. 2, 1944 (15¢, 80 pgs.)
nn(#1), 2 28.00 84.00 225.00

AMERICA'S GREATEST COMICS
Fawcett Publications: May?, 1941 - No. 8, Summer, 1943 (15¢, 100 pgs., soft cardboard-c)
1-Bulletman, Spy Smasher, Capt. Marvel, Minute Man & Mr. Scarlet begin; Classic Mac Raboy-c. 1st time that Fawcett's major super-heroes appear together as a group on a cover. Fawcett's 1st squarebound comic. 284.00 853.00 2700.00
2 137.00 411.00 1300.00
3 97.00 291.00 925.00
4,5: 4-Commando Yank begins; Golden Arrow, Ibis the Invincible & Spy Smasher cameo in Captain Marvel 74.00 221.00 700.00
6,7: 7-Balbo the Boy Magician app.; Captain Marvel, Bulletman cameo in Mr. Scarlet 68.00 205.00 650.00
8-Capt. Marvel Jr. & Golden Arrow app.; Spy Smasher x-over in Capt. Midnight; no Minute Man or Commando Yank 68.00 205.00 650.00

AMERICA'S SWEETHEART SUNNY (See Sunny, ...)

AMERICA VS. THE JUSTICE SOCIETY
DC Comics: Jan, 1985 - No. 4, Apr, 1985 ($1.00, limited series)
1-Double size; Alcala-a(i) in all 2.40 6.00
2-4: 3,4-Spectre cameo 4.50

AMERICOMICS
Americomics: April, 1983 - No. 6, Mar, 1984 ($2.00, Baxter paper/slick paper)
1-Intro/origin The Shade; Intro. The Slayer, Captain Freedom and The Liberty Corps; Perez-c 5.00
1,2-2nd printings ($2.00) 2.00
2-6: 2-Messenger app. & 1st app. Tara on Jungle Island. 3-New & old Blue Beetle battle. 4-Origin Dragonfly & Shade. 5-Origin Commando D. 6-Origin the Scarlet Scorpion 3.0
Special 1 (8/83, $2.00)-Sentinels of Justice (Blue Beetle, Captain Atom, Nightshade & The Question) 4.0

AMETHYST
DC Comics: Jan, 1985 - No. 16, Aug, 1986 (75¢)
1-16: 8-Fire Jade's i.d. revealed 2.0
Special 1 (10/86, $1.25), 1-4 (11/87 - 2/88)(Limited series) 2.0

AMETHYST, PRINCESS OF GEMWORLD (See Legion of Super-Heroes #298)
DC Comics: May, 1983 - No. 12, Apr, 1984 (Maxi-series)
1-(60¢) 2.0
1,2-(35¢): tested in Austin & Kansas City 2.50 7.50 20.0
2-12: Perez-c(p) #6-11, Annual 1(9/84) 2.0
NOTE: ***Perez*** *c-4i, 5-11p.*

AMY RACECAR COLOR SPECIAL (See Stray Bullets)
El Capitán Books: July, 1997; Oct, 1999 ($2.95/$3.50)
1-David Laphan-a/scripts 3.0
2-($3.50) 3.5

ANARCHO DICTATOR OF DEATH (See Comics Novel)

ANARKY (See Batman titles)
DC Comics: May, 1997 - No. 4, Aug, 1997 ($2.50, limited series)
1 3.5
2-4 2.5

ANARKY (See Batman titles)
DC Comics: May, 1999 - No. 8, Dec, 1999 ($2.50)
1-8: 1-JLA app.; Grant-s/Breyfogle-a. 3-Green Lantern app. 7-Day of Judgmen Haunted Tank app. 8-Joker-c/app. 2.5

ANCHORS ANDREWS (The Saltwater Daffy)
St. John Publishing Co.: Jan, 1953 - No. 4, July, 1953
(Anchors the Saltwater... No. 4)
1-Canteen Kate by Matt Baker (9 pgs.) 19.00 56.00 150.0
2-4 6.00 18.00 42.0

ANDY & WOODY (See March of Comics No. 40, 55, 76)

ANDY BURNETT (TV, Disney)
Dell Publishing Co.: Dec, 1957
Four Color 865-Photo-c 9.00 27.00 110.0

ANDY COMICS (Formerly Scream Comics; becomes Ernie Comics)
Current Publications (Ace Magazines): No. 20, June, 1948-No. 21, Aug, 194
20,21: Archie-type comic 6.00 18.00 42.0

ANDY DEVINE WESTERN
Fawcett Publications: Dec, 1950 - No. 2, 1951
1 55.00 165.00 500.0
2 40.00 120.00 360.0

ANDY GRIFFITH SHOW, THE (TV)(1st show aired 10/3/60)
Dell Publishing Co.: #1252, Jan-Mar, 1962; #1341, Apr-Jun, 1962
Four Color 1252(#1), Four Color 1341-Photo-c 33.00 100.00 400.0

ANDY HARDY COMICS (See Movie Comics #3 by Fiction House)
Dell Publishing Co.: April, 1952 - No. 6, Sept-Nov, 1954
Four Color 389(#1) 3.20 9.60 35.0
Four Color 447,480,515, #5,#6 2.80 8.40 28.0

ANDY PANDA (Also see Crackajack Funnies #39, The Funnies, New Funnies & Walter Lantz...)
Dell Publishing Co.: 1943 - No. 56, Nov-Jan, 1961-62 (Walter Lantz)
Four Color 25(#1, 1943) 50.00 150.00 600.0
Four Color 54(1944) 30.00 90.00 360.0
Four Color 85(1945) 16.00 48.00 190.0
Four Color 130(1946),154,198 9.50 29.00 115.0
Four Color 216,240,258,280,297 6.25 18.50 75.0
Four Color 326,345,358 4.10 12.30 45.0
Four Color 383,409 3.20 9.60 35.0
16(11-1/52-53) - 30 2.30 7.00 20.0

Angel #12 © 20th Century Fox

Animal Comics #15 © DELL

Animal Man #30 © DC

	GD2.0	FN6.0	NM9.4
31-56	1.75	5.25	14.00

(See March of Comics #5, 22, 79, & Super Book #4, 15, 27.)

A-NEXT (See Avengers)
Marvel Comics: Oct, 1998 - No. 12, Sept, 1999 ($1.99)

	GD2.0	FN6.0	NM9.4
1-Next generation of Avengers; Frenz-a			2.50
2-12: 2-Two covers. 3-Defenders app.			2.00

ANGEL
Dell Publishing Co.: Aug, 1954 - No. 16, Nov-Jan, 1958-59

	GD2.0	FN6.0	NM9.4
Four Color 576(#1, 8/54)	2.50	7.50	25.00
2(5-7/55) - 16	2.00	6.00	16.00

ANGEL (TV) (Also see Buffy the Vampire Slayer)
Dark Horse Comics: Nov, 1999 - Present ($2.95)

	GD2.0	FN6.0	NM9.4
1-12: 1-3,5-7,10,11-Zanier-a. 1-4,7,10-Matsuda and photo-c			3.00

ANGELA
Image Comics (Todd McFarlane Productions): Dec, 1994 - No. 3, Feb, 1995 ($2.95, limited series)

	GD2.0	FN6.0	NM9.4
1-Gaiman scripts & Capullo-c/a in all; Spawn app.	1.25	3.75	10.00
2	1.00	3.00	8.00
3	1.00	2.80	7.00
Special Edition (1995)-Pirate Spawn-c	3.00	9.00	30.00
Special Edition (1995)-Angela-c	3.00	9.00	30.00
TPB ($9.95, 1995) reprints #1-3 & Special Ed. w/additional pin-ups			10.00

ANGELA/GLORY: RAGE OF ANGELS (See Glory/Angela: Rage of Angels)
Image Comics (Todd McFarlane Productions): Mar, 1996 ($2.50, one-shot)

	GD2.0	FN6.0	NM9.4
1-Liefeld-c/Cruz-a(p); Darkchylde preview flip book			4.00
1-Variant-c			4.00

ANGEL AND THE APE (Meet Angel No. 7) (See Limited Collector's Edition C-34 & Showcase No. 77)
National Periodical Publications: Nov-Dec, 1968 - No. 6, Sept-Oct, 1969

	GD2.0	FN6.0	NM9.4
1-(11-12/68)-Not Wood-a	3.65	11.00	40.00
2-6-Wood inks in all. 4-Last 12¢ issue	2.80	8.40	28.00

ANGEL AND THE APE (2nd Series)
DC Comics: Mar, 1991 - No. 4, June, 1991 ($1.00, limited series)

	GD2.0	FN6.0	NM9.4
1-4			2.50

ANGEL FIRE
Crusade Comics: June, 1997 - No. 3, Oct, 1997 ($2.95, limited series)

	GD2.0	FN6.0	NM9.4
1-3: 1-(3 variant covers). 3-B&W			3.00

ANGEL LOVE
DC Comics: Aug, 1986 - No. 8, Mar, 1987 (75¢, limited series)

	GD2.0	FN6.0	NM9.4
1-8, Special 1 (1987, $1.25, 52 pgs.)			2.00

ANGEL OF LIGHT, THE (See The Crusaders)

ANIMA
DC Comics: Mar, 1994 - No. 15, July, 1995 ($1.75/$1.95/$2.25)

	GD2.0	FN6.0	NM9.4
1-7,0,8-15: 7-(9/94)-Begin $1.95-c; Zero Hour x-over			2.50

ANIMAL ADVENTURES
Timor Publications/Accepted Publ. (reprints): Dec, 1953 - No. 3, May?, 1954

	GD2.0	FN6.0	NM9.4
1-Funny animal	5.70	17.00	40.00
2,3: 2-Featuring Soopermutt (2/54)	4.15	12.50	25.00
1-3 (reprints, nd)	2.40	6.00	12.00

ANIMAL ANTICS (Movie Town... No. 24 on)
National Periodical Publ: Mar-Apr, 1946 - No. 23, Nov-Dec, 1949 (All 52 pgs.?)

	GD2.0	FN6.0	NM9.4
1-Raccoon Kids begins by Otto Feur; some-c by Grossman; Seaman Sy Wheeler by Kelly in some issues	44.00	133.00	400.00
2	25.00	75.00	200.00
3-10: 10-Post-c/a	15.00	45.00	120.00
11-23: 14,15,18,19-Post-a	10.00	30.00	80.00

ANIMAL COMICS
Dell Publishing Co.: Dec-Jan, 1941-42 - No. 30, Dec-Jan, 1947-48

	GD2.0	FN6.0	NM9.4
1-1st Pogo app. by Walt Kelly (Dan Noonan art in most issues)	95.00	285.00	1000.00
2-Uncle Wiggily begins	48.00	144.00	500.00
3,5	35.00	105.00	360.00
4,6,7-No Pogo	20.00	60.00	210.00
8-10	24.00	72.00	260.00
11-15	15.00	45.00	155.00
16-20	10.00	30.00	105.00
21-30: 24-30- "Jigger" by John Stanley	7.50	22.50	80.00

NOTE: ***Dan Noonan** a-18-30. **Gollub** art in most later issues; c-29, 30. **Kelly** c-7-26.*

ANIMAL CRACKERS (Also see Adventures of Patoruzu)
Green Publ. Co./Norlen/Fox Feat.(Hero Books): 1946; No. 31, July, 1950; No. 9, 1959

	GD2.0	FN6.0	NM9.4
1-Super Cat begins (1st app.)	16.00	49.00	130.00
2	9.30	28.00	65.00
31(Fox)-Formerly My Love Secret	6.00	18.00	42.00
9(1959-Norlen)-Infinity-c	4.00	11.00	22.00
nn, nd ('50s), no publ.; infinity-c	4.00	11.00	22.00

ANIMAL FABLES
E. C. Comics (Fables Publ. Co.): July-Aug, 1946 - No. 7, Nov-Dec, 1947

	GD2.0	FN6.0	NM9.4
1-Freddy Firefly (clone of Human Torch), Korky Kangaroo, Petey Pig, Danny Demon begin	40.00	120.00	340.00
2-Aesop Fables begin	26.00	79.00	210.00
3-6	21.00	64.00	170.00
7-Origin Moon Girl	58.00	174.00	550.00

ANIMAL FAIR (Fawcett's...)
Fawcett Publications: Mar, 1946 - No. 11, Feb, 1947

	GD2.0	FN6.0	NM9.4
1	25.00	75.00	200.00
2	12.00	36.00	95.00
3-6	9.30	28.00	65.00
7-11	7.15	21.50	50.00

ANIMAL FUN
Premier Magazines: 1953 (25¢, came w/glasses)

	GD2.0	FN6.0	NM9.4
1-(3-D)-Ziggy Pig, Silly Seal, Billy & Buggy Bear	35.00	105.00	280.00

ANIMAL MAN (See Action Comics #552, 553, DC Comics Presents #77, 78, Secret Origins #39, Strange Adventures #180 & Wonder Woman #267, 268)
DC Comics (Vertigo imprint #57 on): Sept, 1988 - No. 89, Nov, 1995 ($1.25/$1.50/$1.75/$1.95/$2.25, mature)

	GD2.0	FN6.0	NM9.4
1-Grant Morrison scripts begin, ends #26		2.40	6.00
2-Superman cameo			3.00
3-49,51-55,57-89: 6-Invasion tie-in. 9-Manhunter-c/story. 24-Arkham Asylum story; Bizarro Superman app. 25-Inferior Five app. 26-Morrison apps. in story; part photo-c (of Morrison?). 68-Photo-c			2.50
50-($2.95, 52 pgs.)-Last issue w/Veitch scripts			4.00
56-($3.50, 68 pgs.)			4.50
Annual 1 (1993, $3.95, 68 pgs.)-Bolland-c; Children's Crusade Pt. 3			5.00

NOTE: ***Bolland** c-1-63. 71-**Sutton**-a(i)*

ANIMAL MYSTIC (See Dark One...)
Cry For Dawn/Sirius: 1993 - No. 4, 1995 ($2.95?/$3.50, B&W)

	GD2.0	FN6.0	NM9.4
1	2.50	7.50	25.00
1-Alternate	4.55	13.65	50.00
1-2nd printing		2.40	6.00
2	2.30	7.00	20.00
2,3-2nd prints (Sirius)			4.00
3,4: 4-Color poster insert, Linsner-s	1.25	3.75	10.00
TPB ($14.95) r/			15.00

ANIMAL MYSTIC WATER WARS
Sirius: 1996 - Present ($2.95, limited series)

	GD2.0	FN6.0	NM9.4
1-6-Dark One-c/a/scripts			5.00

ANIMAL WORLD, THE (Movie)
Dell Publishing Co.: No. 713, Aug, 1956

	GD2.0	FN6.0	NM9.4
Four Color 713	3.20	9.60	35.00

ANIMANIACS (TV)
DC Comics: May, 1995 - No. 59, Apr, 2000 ($1.50/$1.75/$1.95/$1.99)

	GD2.0	FN6.0	NM9.4
1		2.40	6.00
2-20: 13-Manga issue. 19-X-Files parody; Miran Kim-c; Adlard-a (4 pgs.)			4.00

Animaniacs #34 © WB

Annie Oakley #4 © MAR

A-1 Comics #48 © ME

21-59: 26-E.C. parody-c. 34-Xena parody. 43-Pinky & the Brain take over 2.50
A Christmas Special (12/94, $1.50, "1" on-c) 3.00

ANIMATED COMICS
E. C. Comics: No date given (Summer, 1947?)

1 (Rare) 68.00 205.00 650.00

ANIMATED FUNNY COMIC TUNES (See Funny Tunes)

ANIMATED MOVIE-TUNES (Movie Tunes No. 3)
Margood Publishing Corp. (Timely): Fall, 1945 - No. 2, Sum, 1946

1,2-Super Rabbit, Ziggy Pig & Silly Seal 23.00 68.00 180.00

ANIMAX
Marvel Comics (Star Comics): Dec, 1986 - No. 4, June, 1987

1-4: Based on toys; Simonson-a 3.00

ANNE RICE'S INTERVIEW WITH THE VAMPIRE
Innovation Books: 1991 - No. 12, Jan, 1994 ($2.50, limited series)

1-12: Adapts novel; Moeller-a 3.00

ANNE RICE'S THE MASTER OF RAMPLING GATE
Innovation Books: 1991 ($6.95, one-shot)

1-Bolton painted-c; Colleen Doran painted-a 7.00

ANNE RICE'S THE MUMMY OR RAMSES THE DAMNED
Millennium Publications: Oct, 1990 - No. 12, Feb, 1992 ($2.50, limited series)

1-12: Adapts novel; Mooney-p in all 3.00

ANNE RICE'S THE WITCHING HOUR
Millennium Publ./Comico: 1992 - No. 13, Jan, 1993 ($2.50, limited series)

1-13 3.00

ANNETTE (Disney, TV)
Dell Publishing Co.: No. 905, May, 1958; No. 1100, May, 1960
(Mickey Mouse Club)

Four Color 905-Annette Funicello photo-c 27.00 80.00 320.00
Four Color 1100-...'s Life Story (Movie); A. Funicello photo-c
22.00 65.00 260.00

ANNEX (See Amazing Spider-Man Annual #27 for 1st app.)
Marvel Comics: Aug, 1994 - No. 4, Nov, 1994 ($1.75)

1-4: 1,4-Spider-Man app. 2.00

ANNIE
Marvel Comics Group: Oct, 1982 - No. 2, Nov, 1982 (60¢)

1,2-Movie adaptation 3.00
Treasury Edition ($2.00, tabloid size) 2.30 7.00 20.00

ANNIE OAKLEY (See Tessie The Typist #19, Two-Gun Kid & Wild Western)
Marvel/Atlas Comics(MPI No. 1-4/CDS No. 5 on): Spring, 1948 - No. 4, 11/48; No. 5, 6/55 - No. 11, 6/56

1 (1st Series, 1948)-Hedy Devine app. 42.00 125.00 375.00
2 (7/48, 52 pgs.)-Kurtzman-a, "Hey Look", 1 pg; Intro. Lana; Hedy Devine app; Captain Tootsie by Beck 26.00 79.00 210.00
3,4 22.00 66.00 175.00
5 (2nd Series, 1955)-Reinman-a ; Maneely-c 16.00 48.00 125.00
6-9: 6,8-Woodbridge-a. 9-Williamson-a (4 pgs.) 12.00 36.00 95.00
10,11: 11-Severin-c 10.50 32.00 85.00

ANNIE OAKLEY AND TAGG (TV)
Dell Publishing Co./Gold Key: 1953 - No. 18, Jan-Mar, 1959; July, 1965
(Gail Davis photo-c #3 on)

Four Color 438 (#1) 14.00 42.00 170.00
Four Color 481,575 (#2,3) 8.00 24.00 95.00
4(7-9/55)-10 7.65 23.00 85.00
11-18(1-3/59) 5.85 17.50 70.00
1(7/65-Gold Key)-Photo-c (c-r/#6) 4.60 13.75 55.00
NOTE: *Manning a-13. Photo back c-4, 9, 11.*

ANOTHER WORLD (See Strange Stories From...)

ANTARCTIC PRESS JAM 1996
Antarctic Press: Dec, 1996 ($2.95, one-shot)

1 3.00

ANTHRO (See Showcase #74)
National Periodical Publications: July-Aug, 1968 - No. 6, July-Aug, 1969

1-(7-8/68)-Howie Post-a in all 4.55 13.65 50.00
2-6: 5-Last 12¢ issue. 6-Wood-c/a (inks) 3.00 9.00 30.00

ANT-MAN'S BIG CHRISTMAS
Marvel Comics: Feb, 2000 ($5.95, square-bound, one-shot)

1-Bob Gale-s/Phil Winslade-a; Avengers app. 5.95

ANTONY AND CLEOPATRA (See Ideal, a Classical Comic)

ANYTHING GOES
Fantagraphics Books: Oct, 1986 - No. 6, 1987 ($2.00, #1-5 color & B&W/#6 B&W, limited series)

1-6: 1-Flaming Carrot app. (1st in color?); G. Kane-c. 2-6: 2-Miller-c(p); Alan Moore scripts; Kirby-a; early Sam Kieth-a (2 pgs.). 3-Capt. Jack, Cerebus app.; Cerebus-c by N. Adams. 4-Perez-c. 5-3rd color Teenage Mutant Ninja Turtles app. 3.50

A-1
Marvel Comics (Epic Comics): 1992 - No. 4, 1993 ($5.95, limited ser., mature)

1-4: 1-Fabry-c/a, Russell-a, S. Hampton-a. 3-Bisley-c; Kent Williams-a. 4-McKean-a; Dorman-s/a. 6.00

A-1 COMICS (A-1 appears on covers No. 1-17 only)(See individual title listings.) (1st two issues not numbered.)
Life's Romances Publ.-No. 1/Compix/Magazine Ent.: 1944 - No. 139, Sept-Oct, 1955 (No #2)

(See Individual Alphabetical listings for prices)

nn-Kerry Drake, Johnny Devildog, Rocky, Streamer Kelly (slightly large size)
9-Texas Slim (all)
11-Teena; Ogden Whitney-c
12,15-Teena
13-Guns of Fact & Fiction (1948). Used in **SOTI**, pg. 19; Ingels & Johnny Craig-a
16-Vacation Comics; The Pixies, Tom Tom, Flying Fredd, & Koko & Kola
18,20-Jimmy Durante; photo covers
19-Tim Holt #3; photo-c
22-Dick Powell (1949)-Photo-c
23-Cowboys and Indians #6; Doc Holiday-c/story
25-Fibber McGee & Molly (1949) (Radio)
26-Trail Colt #2-Ingels-c
28-Christmas-(Koko & Kola #6) ("50)
30-Jet Powers #1-Powell-a
32-Jet Powers #2
33-Muggsy Mouse #1('51)
35-Jet Powers #3-Williamson/Evans-a
37-Ghost Rider #5-Frazetta-c (1951)
39-Muggsy Mouse #3
41-Cowboys 'N' Indians #7 (1951)
43-Dogface Dooley #2
45-American Air Forces #5-Powell-c/a
47-Thun'da, King of the Congo #1-Frazetta-c/a('52)
50-Danger Is Their Business #11 ('52)-Powell-a
53-Dogface Dooley #4
55-U.S. Marines #5-Powell-a
56-Thun'da #2-Powell-c/a
58-American Air Forces #7-Powell-a
60-The U.S. Marines #6-Powell-a
62-Starr Flagg, Undercover Girl #5 (#1) reprinted from A-1 #24
65-American Air Forces #8-Powell-a
67-American Air Forces #9-Powell-a
69-Ghost Rider #9(10/52)
1-Dotty Dripple (1 pg.), Mr. Ex, Bush Berry, Rocky, Lew Loyal (20 pgs.)
2-8,10-Texas Slim & Dirty Dalton, The Corsair, Teddy Rich, Dotty Dripple, Inca Dinca, Tommy Tinker Little Mexico & Tugboat Tim, The Masquerader & others. 7-Corsair-c/s. 8-Intro. Rodeo Ryan
14-Tim Holt Western Adventures #1 (1948)
17-Tim Holt #2; photo-c; last issue to carry A-1 on cover (9-10/48)
21-Joan of Arc (1949)-Movie adaptation; Ingrid Bergman photo-covers & interior photos; Whitney-a
24-Trail Colt #1-Frazetta-r in-Manhunt #13; Ingels-c; L. B. Cole-a
27-Ghost Rider #1(1950)-Origin
29-Ghost Rider #2-Frazetta-c (1950)
31-Ghost Rider #3-Frazetta-c & origin ('51)
34-Ghost Rider #4-Frazetta-c (1951)
36-Muggsy Mouse #2; Racist-c
38-Jet Powers #4-Williamson/Wood-a
40-Dogface Dooley #1('51)
42-Best of the West #1-Powell-a
44-Ghost Rider #6
46-Best of the West #2
48-Cowboys 'N' Indians #8
49-Dogface Dooley #3
51-Ghost Rider #7 ('52)
52-Best of the West #3
54-American Air Forces #6(8/52)-Powell-a
57-Ghost Rider #8
59-Best of the West #4
61-Space Ace #5(1953)-Guardineer-
63-Manhunt #13-Frazetta
64-Dogface Dooley #5
66-Best of the West #5
68-U.S. Marines #7-Powell-a
70-Best of the West #6

A-1 Comics #126 © ME

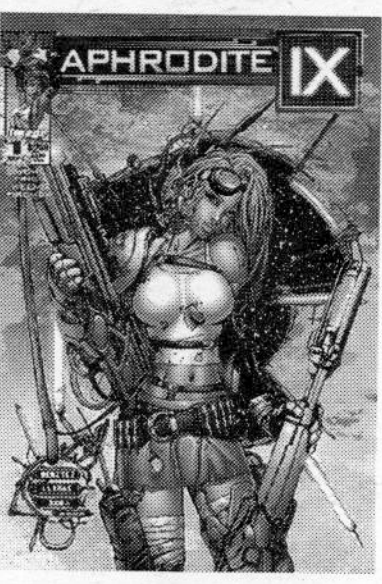

Aphrodite IX #1 © Top Cow

Approved Comics #8 © STJ

71-Ghost Rider #10(12/52)-
Vs. Frankenstein
74-American Air Forces #10-Powell-a
76-Best of the West #7
78-Thun'da #4-Powell-c/a
80-Ghost Rider #12(6/52)-
One-eyed Devil-c
83-Thun'da #5-Powell-c/a
84-Ghost Rider #13(7-8/53)
86-Thun'da #6-Powell-c/a
88-Bobby Benson's B-Bar-B Riders #20
90-Red Hawk #11(1953)-Powell-c/a
91-American Air Forces #12-Powell-a
93-Great Western #8('54)-Origin
The Ghost Rider; Powell-a
95-Muggsy Mouse #4
96-Cave Girl #12, with Thun'da;
Powell-c/a
99-Muggsy Mouse #5
101-White Indian #12-Frazetta-a(r)
101-Dream Book of Romance #6
(4-6/54); Marlon Brando photo-c;
Powell, Bolle, Guardineer-a
105-Great Western #9-Ghost Rider
app.; Powell-a, 6 pgs.; Bolle-c
107-Hot Dog #1
108-Red Fox #15 (1954)-L.B. Cole
c/a; Powell-a
110-Dream Book of Romance #8
(10/54)-Movie photo-c
112-Ghost Rider #14 ('54)
114-Dream Book of Love #2-
Guardineer, Bolle-a; Piper Laurie,
Victor Mature photo-c
118-Undercover Girl #7-Powell-c
120-Badmen of the West #2
121-Mysteries of Scotland Yard #1;
reprinted from Manhunt (5 stories)
124-Dream Book of Romance #8
(10-11/54)
126-I'm a Cop #2-Powell-a
128-I'm a Cop #3-Powell-a
130-Strongman #1-Powell-a (2-3/55)
132-Strongman #2
134-Strongman #3
136-Hot Dog #4
138-The Avenger #4-Powell-c/a
72-U.S. Marines #8-Powell-a(3)
73-Thun'da #3-Powell-c/a
75-Ghost Rider #11(3/52)
77-Manhunt #14
79-American Air Forces #11-Powell-a
81-Best of the West #8
82-Cave Girl #11(1953)-Powell-c/a;
origin (#1)
85-Best of the West #9
87-Best of the West #10(9-10/53)
89-Home Run #3-Powell-a;
Stan Musial photo-c
92-Dream Book of Romance #5-
Photo-c; Guardineer-a
94-White Indian #11-Frazetta-a(r);
Powell-c
97-Best of the West #11
98-Undercover Girl #6-Powell-c
100-Badmen of the West #1-
Meskin-a(?)
103-Best of the West #12-Powell-a
104-White Indian #13-Frazetta-a(r)
('54)
106-Dream Book of Love #1 (6-7/54)
-Powell, Bolle-a; Montgomery Clift,
Donna Reed photo-c
109-Dream Book of Romance #7
(7-8/54). Powell-a; movie photo-c
111-I'm a Cop #1 ('54); drug
mention story; Powell-a
113-Great Western #10; Powell-a
115-Hot Dog #3
116-Cave Girl #13-Powell-c/a
117-White Indian #14
119-Straight Arrow's Fury #1 (origin);
Fred Meagher-c/a
122-Black Phantom #1 (11/54)
123-Dream Book of Love #3
(10-11/54)-Movie photo-c
125-Cave Girl #14-Powell-c/a
127-Great Western #11('54)-Powell-a
129-The Avenger #1('55)-Powell-c
131-The Avenger #2('55)-Powell-c/a
133-The Avenger #3-Powell-c/a
135-White Indian #15
137-Africa #1-Powell-c/a(4)
139-Strongman #4-Powell-a

NOTE: *Bolle a-110. Photo-c-17-22, 89, 92, 101, 106, 109, 110, 114, 123, 124.*

APACHE
Fiction House Magazines: 1951

1 — 21.00 62.00 165.00
I.W. Reprint No. 1-r/#1 above — 2.80 8.40 28.00

APACHE KID (Formerly Reno Browne; Western Gunfighters #20 on)
(Also see Two-Gun Western & Wild Western)
Marvel/Atlas Comics(MPC No. 53-10/CPS No. 11 on): No. 53, 12/50 - No. 10, 1/52; No. 11, 12/54 - No. 19, 4/56

53(#1)-Apache Kid & his horse Nightwind (origin), Red Hawkins by Syd Shores begins — 34.00 103.00 275.00
2(2/51) — 16.00 49.00 130.00
3-5 — 11.00 33.00 90.00
6-10 (1951-52): 7-Russ Heath-a — 10.00 30.00 75.00
11-19 (1954-56) — 7.85 23.50 55.00

NOTE: ***Heath** a-7. c-11, 13. **Maneely** a-53; c-53(#1), 12, 14-16. **Powell** a-14. **Severin** c-17.*

APACHE MASSACRE (See Chief Victorio's...)

APACHE TRAIL
Steinway/America's Best: Sept, 1957 - No. 4, June, 1958

1 — 10.00 30.00 80.00
2-4: 2-Tuska-a — 7.00 21.00 48.00

APE (Magazine)
Dell Publishing Co.: 1961 (52 pgs., B&W)

1-Comics and humor — 3.00 9.00 32.00

APHRODITE IX
Image Comics (Top Cow): Sept, 2000 - Present ($2.50)

1-Four covers by Finch, Turner, Silvestri, Benitez — 2.50
1-Tower Record Ed.; Finch-c — 2.50
1-DF Chrome ($14.99) — 15.00
Convention Preview — 10.00
Wizard #0 (4/00, bagged w/Tomb Raider magazine) Preview & sketchbook — 5.00

APOLLO SMILE
Eagle Wing Press: July, 1998 - Present ($2.95)

1,2-Manga — 3.00

APPARITION
Caliber Comics: 1995 ($3.95, 52 pgs., B&W)

1 ($3.95) — 4.00
V2#1-6 ($2.95) — 3.00
Visitations — 4.00

APPLESEED
Eclipse Comics: Sept, 1988 - Book 4, Vol. 4, Aug, 1991 ($2.50/$2.75/$3.50, 52/68 pgs, B&W)

Book One, Vol. 1-5: 5-(1/89), Book Two, Vol. 1(2/89) -5(7/89): Art Adams-c, Book Three, Vol. 1(8/89) -4 ($2.75), Book Three, Vol. 5 ($3.50), Book Four, Vol. 1 (1/91) - 4 (8/91) ($3.50, 68 pgs.) — 4.00

APPLESEED DATABOOK
Dark Horse Comics: Apr, 1994 - No. 2, May, 1994 ($3.50, B&W, limited series)

1,2: 1-Flip book format — 3.50

APPROVED COMICS (Also see Blue Ribbon Comics)
St. John Publishing Co. (Most have no c-price): March, 1954 - No. 12, Aug, 1954 (Painted-c on #1-5,7,8,10)

1-The Hawk #5-r — 10.00 30.00 75.00
2-Invisible Boy (3/54)-Origin; Saunders-c — 16.00 49.00 130.00
3-Wild Boy of the Congo #11-r (4/54) — 10.00 30.00 75.00
4,5: 4-Kid Cowboy-r. 5-Fly Boy-r — 10.00 30.00 75.00
6-Daring Adv.-r (5/54); Krigstein-a(2); Baker-c — 12.00 36.00 95.00
7-The Hawk #6-r — 10.00 30.00 75.00
8-Crime on the Run (6/54); Powell-a; Saunders-c — 10.00 30.00 75.00
9-Western Bandit Trails #3-r, with new-c; Baker-c/a — 12.00 36.00 95.00
10-Dinky Duck (Terrytoons) — 4.00 12.00 24.00
11-Fightin' Marines #3-r (8/54); Canteen Kate app; Baker-c/a — 12.50 37.50 100.00
12-Northwest Mounties #4-r(8/54); new Baker-c — 12.50 37.50 100.00

AQUAMAN (See Adventure #260, Brave & the Bold, DC Comics Presents #5, DC Special #28, DC Special Series #1, DC Super Stars #7, Detective, JLA, Justice League of America, More Fun #73, Showcase #30-33, Super DC Giant, Super Friends, and World's Finest Comics)

AQUAMAN (1st Series)
National Periodical Publications/DC Comics: Jan-Feb, 1962 - #56, Mar-Apr, 1971; #57, Aug-Sept,1977 - #63, Aug-Sept, 1978

1-(1-2/62)-Intro. Quisp — 61.00 182.00 850.00
2 — 30.00 90.00 330.00
3-5 — 17.00 51.00 185.00
6-10 — 11.00 33.00 120.00
11-20: 11-1st app. Mera. 18-Aquaman weds Mera; JLA cameo — 9.00 27.00 100.00
21-32: 23-Birth of Aquababy. 26-Huntress app.(3-4/66). 29-1st app. Ocean Master, Aquaman's step-brother. 30-Batman & Superman-c & cameo — 5.00 15.00 55.00
33-1st app. Aqua-Girl (see Adventure #266) — 5.45 16.35 60.00
34-40: 40-Jim Aparo's 1st DC work (8/68) — 3.45 10.35 38.00
41-46,47,49: 45-Last 12¢-c — 2.80 8.40 28.00
48-Origin reprinted — 3.00 9.00 30.00
50-52-Deadman by Neal Adams — 5.00 15.00 55.00
53-56('71): 56-1st app. Crusader; last 15¢-c — 1.25 3.75 10.00

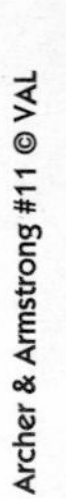
Aquaman (3rd series) #75 © DC

Archer & Armstrong #11 © VAL

Archie & Friends #40 © AP

57('77)-63: 58-Origin retold 1.00 2.80 7.00
NOTE: ***Aparo*** *a-40-45, 46p, 47-59; c-58-63.* ***Nick Cardy*** *c-1-39.* ***Newton*** *a-60-63.*

AQUAMAN (1st limited series)
DC Comics: Feb, 1986 - No. 4, May, 1986 (75¢, limited series)

1-New costume; 1st app. Nuada of Thierna Na Oge. 5.00
2-4: 3-Retelling of Aquaman & Ocean Master's origins. 3.50
Special 1 (1988, $1.50, 52 pgs.) 3.50
NOTE: ***Craig Hamilton*** *c/a-1-4p.* ***Russell*** *c-2-4i.*

AQUAMAN (2nd limited series)
DC Comics: June, 1989 - No. 5, Oct, 1989 ($1.00, limited series)

1-5: Giffen plots/breakdowns; Swan-a(p). 2.50
Special 1 (Legend of..., $2.00, 1989, 52 pgs.)-Giffen plots/breakdowns; Swan-a(p). 2.50

AQUAMAN (2nd Series)
DC Comics: Dec, 1991 - No. 13, Dec, 1992 ($1.00/$1.25)

1-5 2.00
6-13: 6-Begin $1.25-c. 9-Sea Devils app. 2.00

AQUAMAN (3rd Series)(Also see Atlantis Chronicles)
DC Comics: Aug, 1994 - No. 75, Jan, 2001 ($1.50/$1.75/$1.95/$1.99/$2.50)

1-(8/94)-Peter David scripts begin; reintro Dolphin 5.00
2-(9/94)-Aquaman loses hand 2.40 6.00
0-(10/94)-Aquaman replaces lost hand w/hook. 2.40 6.00
3-8: 3-(11/94)-Superboy-c/app. 4-Lobo app. 6-Deep Six app. 3.00
9-42,44-69: 9-Begin $1.75-c. 10-Green Lantern app. 11-Reintro Mera. 15-Reintro Kordax. 16-vs. JLA. 18-Reintro Ocean Master & Atlan (Aquaman's father). 19-Reintro Garth (Aqualad). 23-1st app. Deep Blue (Neptune Perkins & Tsunami's daughter). 23,24-Neptune Perkins, Nuada, Tsunami, Arion, Power Girl, & The Sea Devils app. 26-Final Night. 28-Martian Manhunter-c/app. 29-Black Manta-c/app. 32-Swamp Thing-c/app. 37-Genesis x-over 41-Maxima-c/app. 44-G.A. Flash & Sentinel app. 50-Larsen-s begins. 53-Superman app. 60-Tempest marries Dolphin; Teen Titans app. 63-Kaluta covers begin. 66-JLA app. 2.00
43-Millennium Giants x-over; Superman-c/app. 3.00
70-75: 70-Begin $2.50-c. 71-73-Warlord-c/app. 75-Final issue 2.50
#1,000,000 (11/98) 853rd Century x-over 3.00
Annual 1 (1995, $3.50)-Year One story 3.50
Annual 2 (1996, $2.95)-Legends of the Dead Earth story 3.00
Annual 3 (1997, $3.95)-Pulp Heroes story 4.00
Annual 4,5 ('98, ''99, $2.95)-4-Ghosts; Wrightson-c. 5-JLApe 3.00
...Secret Files 1 (12/98, $4.95) Origin-s and pin-ups 5.00
NOTE: ***Art Adams****-c, Annual 5.* ***Mignola*** *c-6.* ***Simonson*** *c-15.*

AQUAMAN: TIME & TIDE (3rd limited series) (Also see Atlantis Chronicles)
DC Comics: Dec, 1993 - No. 4, Mar, 1994 ($1.50, limited series)

1-4: Peter David scripts; origin retold. 3.00
Trade paperback ($9.95) 10.00

AQUANAUTS (TV)
Dell Publishing Co.: May - July, 1961

Four Color 1197-Photo-c 6.70 20.00 80.00

ARABIAN NIGHTS (See Cinema Comics Herald)

ARACHNOPHOBIA (Movie)
Hollywood Comics (Disney Comics): 1990 ($5.95, 68 pg. graphic novel)

nn-Adaptation of film; Spiegle-a 6.00
Comic edition ($2.95, 68 pgs.) 3.00

ARAK/SON OF THUNDER (See Warlord #48)
DC Comics: Sept, 1981 - No. 50, Nov, 1985

1,24,50: 1-1st app. Angelica, Princess of White Cathay. 24,50-(52 pgs.) 3.00
2-23,25-49: 3-Intro Valda. 12-Origin Valda. 20-Origin Angelica 2.00
Annual 1(10/84) 3.00

ARCANA (Also see Books of Magic limited & ongoing series and Mister E)
DC Comics (Vertigo): 1994 ($3.95, 68 pgs., annual)

1-Bolton painted-c; Children's Crusade/Tim Hunter story 4.00

ARCANUM
Image Comics (Top Cow Productions): Apr, 1997 - No. 8, Feb, 1998 ($2.50)

1/2 Gold Edition 15.0
1-Brandon Peterson-s/a(p), 1-Variant-c, 4-American Ent. Ed. 4.0
2-8 3.0
3-Variant-c 2.40 6.0

ARCHANGEL (See Uncanny X-Men, X-Factor & X-Men)
Marvel Comics: Feb, 1996 ($2.50, B&W, one-shot)

1-Milligan story 2.5

ARCHER & ARMSTRONG
Valiant: July (June inside), 1992 - No. 26, Oct, 1994 ($2.50)

0-(7/92)-B. Smith-c/a; Reese-i assists 3.0
0-(Gold Logo) 6.0
1-7,9-26: 1-(8/92)-Origin & 1st app. Archer; Miller-c; B. Smith/Layton-a. 2-2nd app Turok(c/story); Smith/Layton-a; Simonson-c. 3,4-Smith-c&a(p) & scripts. 10-2nd app. Ivar. 10,11-B. Smith-c. 21,22-Shadowman app. 22-w/bound-in trading card. 25-Eternal Warrior app. 26-Flip book w/Eternal Warrior #26 2.5
8-($4.50, 52 pgs.)-Combined with Eternal Warrior #8; B. Smith-c/a & scripts; 1st app. Ivar the Time Walker 4.5

ARCHIE (See Archie Comics) (Also see Christmas & Archie, Everything's..., Explorers of the Unknown, Jackpot, Little..., Oxydol-Dreft, Pep, Riverdale High, Teenage Mutant Ninja Turtles Adventures & To Riverdale and Back Again)

ARCHIE AMERICANA SERIES, BEST OF THE FORTIES
Archie Publications: 1991 ($10.95, trade paperback)

V1-r/early strips from 1940's; intro. by Steven King. 1.85 5.50 15.0

ARCHIE AMERICANA SERIES, BEST OF THE FIFTIES
Archie Publications: 1991 ($8.95, trade paperback)

V2-r/strips from 1950's; 1.75 5.25 14.0
2nd printing (1998, $9.95) 10.0

ARCHIE AMERICANA SERIES, BEST OF THE SIXTIES
Archie Publications: 1995 ($9.95, trade paperback)

V3-r/strips from 1960's; intro. by Frankie Avalon. 12.0

ARCHIE AMERICANA SERIES, BEST OF THE SEVENTIES
Archie Publications: 1997 ($9.95, trade paperback)

V4-r/strips from 1970's 12.0

ARCHIE AND BIG ETHEL
Spire Christian Comics (Fleming H. Revell Co.): 1982 (69¢)

nn-(Low print run) 1.25 3.75 10.0

ARCHIE & FRIENDS
Archie Comics: Dec, 1992 - Present ($1.25/$1.50/$1.75/$1.79/$1.99, bi-monthly)

1 5.0
2,4,10-14,17,18,20-Sabrina app. 20-Archie's Band-c 4.0
3,5-9,16 2.5
15-Babewatch-s with Sabrina app. 2.40 6.0
19-Josie and the Pussycats app.; E.T. parody-c/s 5.0
21-46 2.0

ARCHIE AND ME (See Archie Giant Series Mag. #578, 591, 603, 616, 626)
Archie Publications: Oct, 1964 - No. 161, Feb, 1987

1 15.50 46.50 170.0
2 7.65 23.00 85.0
3-5 4.10 12.30 45.0
6-10 2.50 7.50 25.0
11-20 2.00 6.00 18.0
21(6/68)-26,28-30: 21-UFO story. 26-X-Mas-c 1.85 5.50 15.0
27-Groovyman & Knowman superhero-s; UFO-sty 2.30 7.00 20.0
31-42: 37-Japan Expo '70-c/s 1.10 3.30 9.0
43-48,50-63-(All Giants): 43-(8/71) Mummy-s. 44-Mermaid-s. 62-Elvis cameo-c. 63-(2/74) 1.85 5.50 15.00
49-(Giant) Josie & the Pussycats-c/app. 2.00 6.00 18.00
64-66,68-99-(Regular size): 85-Bicentennial-s. 98-Collectors Comics 1.00 2.80 7.00
67-Sabrina app.(8/74) 1.50 4.50 12.00
100-(4/78) 1.10 3.30 9.00
101-120: 107-UFO-s 5.00

Archie...Archie Andrews, Where Are You? #112 © AP

Archie Comics #40 © AP

Archie Comics #500 © AP

GD2.0 FN6.0 NM9.4

121(8/80)-159: 134-Riverdale 2001 4.00
160,161: 160-Origin Mr. Weatherbee. 161-Last issue 5.00

ARCHIE AND MR. WEATHERBEE
Spire Christian Comics (Fleming H. Revell Co.): 1980 (59¢)
nn-(Low print run) 1.00 3.00 8.00

ARCHIE...ARCHIE ANDREWS, WHERE ARE YOU? (...Comics Digest #9, 10; ...Comics Digest Mag. No. 11 on)
Archie Publications: Feb, 1977 - Present (Digest size, 160-128 pgs., quarterly)
1 2.50 7.50 23.00
2,3,5,7-9-N. Adams-a; 8-r-/origin The Fly by S&K. 9-Steel Sterling-r 1.75 5.25 14.00
4,6,10 ($1.00/$1.50): 17-Katy Keene story 1.25 3.75 10.00
11-20 1.00 3.00 8.00
21-50,100 2.40 6.00
51-70 4.00
71-117: 113-Begin $1.95-c 3.00

ARCHIE AS PUREHEART THE POWERFUL (Also see Archie Giant Series #142, Jughead as Captain Hero, Life With Archie & Little Archie)
Archie Publications (Radio Comics): Sept, 1966 - No. 6, Nov, 1967
1-Super hero parody 8.15 24.50 90.00
2 5.00 15.00 55.00
3-6 3.65 11.00 40.00
NOTE: *Evilheart cameos in all. Title: Archie As Pureheart the Powerful #1-3; ...As Capt. Pureheart-#4-6.*

ARCHIE AT RIVERDALE HIGH (See Archie Giant Series Magazine #573, 586, 604 & Riverdale High)
Archie Publications: Aug, 1972 - No. 113, Feb, 1987
1 5.00 15.00 55.00
2 2.80 8.40 28.00
3-5 2.30 7.00 20.00
6-10 1.75 5.25 14.00
11-30 1.10 3.30 9.00
31(12/75)-46,48-50(12/77): 47-Betty mud wrestling-s 1.00 2.80 7.00
47-Archie in drag-s 1.10 3.30 9.00
51-80,100 (12/84) 5.00
81(8/81)-88, 91,93-95,97,98: 96-Anti-smoking issue 4.00
89,90-Early Cheryl Blossom app. 90-Archies Band app. 1.00 3.30 9.00
92,96,99-Cheryl Blossom app. 2.40 6.00
101,102,104-109,111,112: 102-Ghost-c 3.00
103-Archie dates Cheryl Blossom-s 1.10 3.30 9.00
110,113: 110-Godzilla-s. 113-Last issue 5.00

ARCHIE COMICS (Archie #114 on; 1st Teen-age comic; Radio show aired 6/2/45 by NBC)
MLJ Magazines No. 1-19/Archie Publ.No. 20 on: Winter, 1942-43 - No. 19, 3-4/46; No. 20, 5-6/46 - Present

	GD2.0	FN6.0	VF8.0	NM9.4
1 (Scarce)-Jughead, Veronica app.; 1st app. Mrs. Andrews	1160.00	3480.00	7540.00	14,500.00

	GD2.0	FN6.0	NM9.4
2	295.00	885.00	2800.00
3 (60 pgs.)(scarce)	232.00	695.00	2200.00
4,5: 4-Article about Archie radio series	121.00	363.00	1150.00
6,8-10: 6-X-Mas-c.	87.00	261.00	825.00
7-1st definitive love triangle story	91.00	272.00	860.00
11-20: 15,17,18-Dotty & Ditto by Woggon. 16-Woggon-a	57.00	171.00	540.00
21-30: 23-Betty & Veronica by Woggon. 25-Woggon-a. 30-Coach Piffle app., a Coach Kleets prototype. 34-Pre-Dilton try-out (named Dilbert)	40.00	120.00	340.00
31-40	24.00	71.00	190.00
41-50	16.00	49.00	130.00
51-60: (1954) 51-Katy Keene app.	7.65	23.00	85.00
61-70 (1954): 65-70, Katy Keene app.	6.35	19.00	70.00
71-80: 72-74-Katy Keene app.	5.00	15.00	55.00
81-99: 94-1st Coach Kleets	3.80	11.40	42.00
100	5.00	15.00	55.00
101-122,124-130 (1962)	2.80	8.40	28.00
123-UFO-c/s; Vampire-s	3.00	9.00	30.00
131-157,159,160	2.00	6.00	17.00
158-Archie in drag story	2.30	7.00	20.00
161(2/66)-182,184,186-195,197-199: 168-Superhero gag-c. 176,178-Twiggy-c	1.50	4.50	12.00
183-1st Caveman Archie gang story	2.00	6.00	16.00
185-1st "The Archies" Band story	2.00	6.00	18.00
196 (12/69)-1st Cricket O'Dell	2.50	7.50	24.00
200 (6/70)	2.00	6.00	16.00
201-230(11/73): 213-Sabrina/Josie-c cameos. 229-Lost Child issue	1.00	3.00	8.00
231-260(3/77): 253-Tarzan parody	1.00	2.80	7.00
261-282, 284-299		2.40	6.00
283(8/79)-Cover/story plugs "International Children's Appeal" which was a fraudulent charity, according to TV's 20/20 news program broadcast July 20, 1979	1.00	2.80	7.00
300(1/81)-Anniversary issue	1.00	2.80	7.00
301-321,323-325,327-335,337-350: 323-Cheryl Blossom pin-up			4.00
322-E.T. story			5.00
326-Early Cheryl Blossom story	1.75	5.25	14.00
336-Michael Jackson/Boy George parody			5.00
351-399: 356-Calgary Olympics Special. 393-Infinity-c; 1st comic book printed on recycled paper			3.00
400 (6/92)-Shows 1st meeting of Little Archie and Veronica		2.40	6.00
401-428			2.50
429-Love Showdown part 1			5.00
430-505: 467- "A Storm Over Uniforms" x-over parts 3,4			2.00
Annual 1 ('50)-116 pgs. (Scarce)	163.00	490.00	1550.00
Annual 2 ('51)	82.00	245.00	775.00
Annual 3 ('52)	50.00	150.00	450.00
Annual 4,5 (1953-54)	38.00	113.00	300.00
Annual 6-10 (1955-59): 8-(100 pgs.). 10-(84 pgs.) Elvis record on-c	14.00	42.00	155.00
Annual 11-15 (1960-65): 12,13-(84 pgs.) 14,15-(68 pgs.)	6.35	19.00	70.00
Annual 16-20 (1966-70)(all 68 pgs.): 20-Archie's band-c	3.00	9.00	30.00
Annual 21-26 (1971-75): 21,22 (68 pgs.). 22,23-Archie's band-s. 23-Archie's band/Josie/Sabrina-c. 23-26-(52 pgs.). 25-Cavemen-s	2.00	6.00	16.00
Annual Digest 27 ('75)	3.00	9.00	30.00
...28-30	2.00	6.00	18.00
...31-34	1.75	5.25	14.00
...35-40 (...Magazine #35 on)	1.25	3.75	10.00
...41-65 ('94)			4.00
...66-69			2.00
...All-Star Specials(Winter '75, $1.25)-6 remaindered Archie comics rebound in each; titles: "The World of Giant Comics", "Giant Grab Bag of Comics", "Triple Giant Comics" & "Giant Spec. Comics	3.00	9.00	32.00
Special Edition-Christmas With Archie 1(1/75)-Treasury (rare)	4.10	12.30	45.00

NOTE: *Archies Band-s-185, 188-192, 197, 198, 201, 204, 205, 208, 209, 215, 329, 330; Band-c-191, 330. Cavemen Archie Gang-s-183, 192, 197, 208, 210, 220, 223, 282, 333, 335, 338, 340.* ***Al Fagly*** *c-17-35.* ***Bob Montana*** *c-38, 41-50, 58, Annual 1-4.* ***Bill Woggon*** *c-53, 54.*

ARCHIE COMICS DIGEST (...Magazine No. 37-95)
Archie Publications: Aug, 1973 - Present (Small size, 160-128 pgs.)

	GD2.0	FN6.0	NM9.4
1	8.15	24.50	90.00
2	4.10	12.30	45.00
3-5	3.20	9.60	35.00
6-10	2.30	7.00	20.00
11-33: 32,33-The Fly-r by S&K	1.50	4.50	12.00
34-60	1.10	3.30	9.00
61-80,100	1.00	2.80	7.00
81-99			5.00
101-140: 36-Katy Keene story			4.00
141-165			3.00
166-169			2.25
170-177			2.19

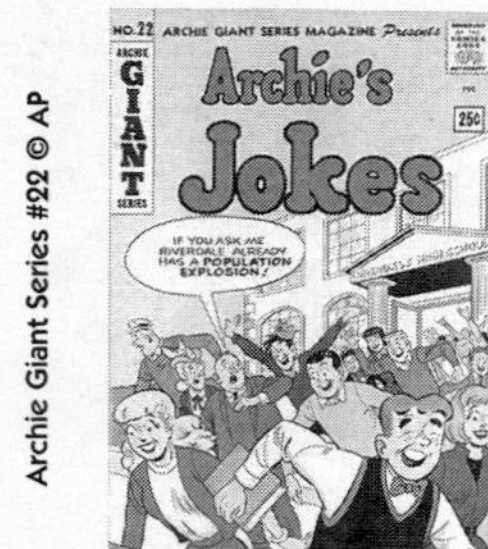

Archie Giant Series #22 © AP

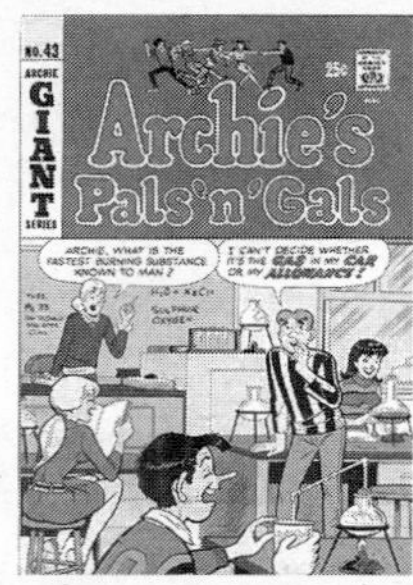

Archie Giant Series #43 © AP

Archie Giant Series #187 © AP

GD2.0 FN6.0 NM9.4

NOTE: ***Neal Adams*** *a-1, 2, 4, 5, 19-21, 24, 25, 27, 29, 31, 33. X-mas c-88, 94, 100, 106.*

ARCHIE COMICS PRESENTS: THE LOVE SHOWDOWN COLLECTION
Archie Publications: 1994 ($4.95, squarebound)
nn-r/Archie #429, Betty #19, Betty & Veronica #82, & Veronica #39 6.00

ARCHIE GETS A JOB
Spire Christian Comics (Fleming H. Revell Co.): 1977
nn 1.00 2.80 7.00

ARCHIE GIANT SERIES MAGAZINE
Archie Publications: 1954 - No. 632, July, 1992 (No #36-135, no #252-451) (#1 not code approved) (#1-233 are Giants; #12-184 are 68 pgs.,#185-194,197-233 are 52 pgs.; #195,196 are 84 pgs.; #234-up are 36 pgs.)

1-Archie's Christmas Stocking 116.00 348.00 1100.00
2-Archie's Christmas Stocking('55) 68.00 205.00 650.00
3-6-Archie's Christmas Stocking('56- '59) 47.00 141.00 425.00
7-10: 7-Katy Keene Holiday Fun(9/60); Bill Woggon-c. 8-Betty & Veronica Summer Fun(10/60); baseball story w/Babe Ruth & Lou Gehrig. 9-The World of Jughead (12/60). 10-Archie's Christmas Stocking(1/61) 36.00 107.00 285.00
11,13,16,18: 11-Betty & Veronica Spectacular (6/61). 13-Betty & Veronica Summer Fun (10/61). 16-Betty & Veronica Spectacular (6/62). 18-Betty & Veronica Summer Fun (10/62) 23.00 69.00 205.00
12,14,15,17,19,20: 12-Katy Keene Holiday Fun (9/61). 14-The World of Jughead (12/61); Vampire-s. 15-Archie's Christmas Stocking (1/62). 17-Archie's Jokes (9/62); Katy Keene app. 19-The World of Jughead (12/62). 20-Archie's Christmas Stocking (1/63) 12.50 37.00 135.00
21,23,26,28: 21-Betty & Veronica Spectacular (6/63). 23-Betty & Veronica Summer Fun (10/63). 26-Betty & Veronica Spectacular (6/64). 28-Betty & Veronica Summer Fun (9/64) 9.00 27.00 100.00
22,24,25,27,29,30: 22-Archie's Jokes (9/63). 24-The World of Jughead (12/63). 25-Archie's Christmas Stocking (1/64). 27-Archie's Jokes (8/64). 29-Around the World with Archie (10/64); Doris Day-s. 30-The World of Jughead (12/64) 7.25 21.75 80.00
31-35,136-141: 31-Archie's Christmas Stocking (1/65). 32-Betty & Veronica Spectacular (6/65). 33-Archie's Jokes (8/65). 34-Betty & Veronica Summer Fun (9/65). 35-Around the World with Archie (10/65). 136-The World of Jughead (12/65). 137-Archie's Christmas Stocking (1/66). 138-Betty & Veronica Spectacular (6/66). 139-Archie's Jokes (6/66). 140-Betty & Veronica Summer Fun (8/66). 141-Around the World with Archie (9/66) 5.90 17.75 65.00
36-135-Do not exist
142-Archie's Super-Hero Special (10/66)-Origin Capt. Pureheart, Capt. Hero, and Evilheart 6.35 19.00 70.00
143-The World of Jughead(12/66); Capt. Hero-c/s; Man From R.I.V.E.R.D.A.L.E., Pureheart, Superteen app. 4.55 13.65 50.00
144-160: 144-Archie's Christmas Stocking (1/67). 145-Betty & Veronica Spectacular (6/67). 146-Archie's Jokes (6/67). 147-Betty & Veronica Summer Fun (8/67) 148-World of Archie (9/67). 149-World of Jughead (10/67). 150-Archie's Christmas Stocking (1/68). 151-World of Archie (2/68). 152-World of Jughead (2/68). 153-Betty & Veronica Spectacular (6/68). 154-Archie Jokes (6/68). 155-Betty & VeronicaSummer Fun (8/68). 156-World of Archie (10/68). 157-World of Jughead (12/68). 158-Archie's Christmas Stocking (1/69). 159-Betty & Veronica Christmas Spectacular (1/69). 160-World of Archie (2/69); Frankenstein-s each... 3.00 9.00 30.00
161-World of Jughead (2/69); Super-Jughead-s; 11 pg.early Cricket O'Dell-s 3.00 9.00 32.00
162-183: 162-Betty & Veronica Spectacular (6/69). 163-Archie's Jokes(8/69). 164-Betty & Veronica Summer Fun (9/69). 165-World of Archie (9/69). 166-World of Jughead (9/69). 167-Archie's Christmas Stocking (1/70). 168-Betty & Veronica Christmas Spect. (1/70). 169-Archie's Christmas Love-In (1/70). 170-Jughead's Eat-Out Comic Book Mag. (12/69). 171-World of Archie (2/70). 172-World of Jughead (2/70). 173-Betty & Veronica Spectacular (6/70). 174-Archie's Jokes (8/70). 175-Betty & Veronica Summer Fun (9/70). 176-Li'l Jinx Giant Laugh-Out (8/70). 177-World of Archie (9/70). 178-World of Jughead (9/70). 179-Archie's Christmas Stocking(1/71). 180-Betty & Veronica Christmas Spect. (1/71). 181-Archie's Christmas Love-In (1/71). 182-World of Archie (2/71). 183-World of Jughead (2/71)-Last squarebound
each... 2.30 7.00 20.00
184-189,193,194,197-199 (52 pgs.): 184-Betty & Veronica Spectacular (6/71). 185-Li'l Jinx Giant Laugh-Out (6/71). 186-Archie's Jokes (8/71). 187-Betty & Veronica Summer Fun (9/71). 188-World of Archie (9/71). 189-World of Jughead (9/71). 193-World of Archie (3/72).194-World of Jughead (4/72). 197-Betty & Veronica Spectacular (6/72). 198-Archie's Jokes (8/72). 199-Betty & Veronica Summer Fun (9/72)
each... 2.00 6.00 18.00
190-192: 190-Archie's Christmas Stocking (12/71); Sabrina on-c. 191-Betty & Veronica Christmas Spect.(2/72); Sabrina app.. 192-Archie's Christmas Love-In (1/72); Archie Band-c/s 2.50 7.50 25.00
195-(84 pgs.)-Li'l Jinx Christmas Bag (1/72). 3.00 9.00 30.00
196-(84 pgs.)-Sabrina's Christmas Magic (1/72) 4.10 12.30 45.00
200-(52 pgs.)-World of Archie (10/72) 2.50 7.50 25.00
201-206,208-219,221-230,232,233 (All 52 pgs.): 201-Betty & Veronica Spectacular (10/72). 202-World of Jughead (11/72). 203-Archie's Christmas Stocking (12/72). 204-Betty & Veronica Christmas Spectacular (2/73). 205-Archie's Christmas Love-In (1/73). 206-Li'l Jinx Christmas Bag (12/72). 208-World of Archie (3/73). 209-World of Jughead (4/73). 210-Betty & Veronica Spectacular (6/73). 211-Archie's Jokes (8/73). 212-Betty & Veronica Summer Fun (9/73). 213-World of Archie (10/73). 214-Betty & Veronica Spectacular (10/73). 215-World of Jughead (11/73). 216-Archie's Christmas Stocking (12/73). 217-Betty & Veronica Christmas Spectacular (2/74). 218-Archie's Christmas Love-In (1/74). 219-Li'l Jinx Christmas Bag (12/73). 221-Betty & Veronica Spectacular (Advertised as World of Archie) (6/74). 222-Archie's Jokes (advertised as World of Jughead) (8/74). 223-Li'l Jinx (8/74). 224-Betty & Veronica Summer Fun (9/74). 225-World of Archie (9/74). 226-Betty & Veronica Spectacular (10/74). 227-World of Jughead (10/74). 228-Archie's Christmas Stocking (12/74). 229-Betty & Veronica Christmas Spectacular (12/74). 230-Archie's Christmas Love-In (1/75). 232-World of Archie (3/75). 233-World of Jughead (4/75)
each... 1.25 3.75 10.00
207,220,231,243: Sabrina's Christmas Magic. 207-(12/72). 220-(12/73). 231-(1/75). 243-(1/76)
each... 2.00 6.00 18.00
234-242,244-251 (36 pgs.): 234-Betty & Veronica Spectacular (6/75). 235-Archie's Jokes (8/75). 236-Betty & Veronica Summer Fun (9/75). 237-World of Archie (9/75) 238-Betty & Veronica Spectacular (10/75). 239-World of Jughead (10/75). 240-Archie's Christmas Stocking (12/75). 241-Betty & Veronica Christmas Spectacular (12/75). 242-Archie's Christmas Love-In (1/76). 244-World of Archie (3/76). 245-World of Jughead (4/76). 246-Betty & Veronica Spectacular (6/76). 247-Archie's Jokes (8/76). 248-Betty & Veronica Summer Fun (9/76). 249-World of Archie (9/76). 250-Betty & Veronica Spectacular (10/76). 251-World of Jughead
each.... 1.10 3.30 9.00
252-451-Do not exist
452-454,456-466,468-478, 480-490,492-499: 452-Archie's Christmas Stocking (12/76). 453-Betty & Veronica Christmas Spectacular (12/76). 454-Archie's Christmas Love-In (1/77). 456-World of Archie (3/77). 457-World of Jughead (4/77). 458-Betty & Veronica Spectacular (6/77). 459-Archie's Jokes (8/77)-Shows 8/76 in error. 460-Betty & Veronica Summer Fun (9/77). 461-World of Archie (9/77). 462-Betty & Veronica Spectacular (10/77). 463-World of Jughead (10/77). 464-Archie's Christmas Stocking (12/77). 465-Betty & Veronica Christmas Spectacular (12/77). 466-Archie's Christmas Love-In (1/78). 468-World of Archie (2/78). 469-World of Jughead (2/78). 470-Betty & Veronica Spectacular(6/78). 471-Archie's Jokes (8/78). 472-Betty & Veronica Summer Fun (9/78). 473-World of Archie (9/78). 474-Betty & Veronica Spectacular (10/78). 475-World of Jughead (10/78). 476-Archie's Christmas Stocking (12/78). 477-Betty & Veronica Christmas Spectacular (12/78). 478-Archie's Christmas Love-In (1/79). 480-The World of Archie (3/79). 481-World of Jughead (4/79). 482-Betty & Veronica Spectacular (6/79). 483-Archie's Jokes (8/79). 484-Betty & Veronica Summer Fun(9/79). 485-The World of Archie (9/79). 486-Betty & Veronica Spectacular(10/79). 487-The World of Jughead (10/79). 488-Archie's Christmas Stocking (12/79). 489-Betty & Veronica Christmas Spectacular (1/80). 490-Archie's Christmas Love-in (1/80). 492-The World of Archie (2/80). 493-The World of Jughead (4/80). 494-Betty & Veronica Spectacular (6/80). 495-Archie's Jokes (8/80). 496-Betty & Veronica Summer Fun (9/80). 497-The World of Archie (9/80). 498-Betty & Veronica Spectacular (10/80). 499-The World of Jughead (10/80).
each... 1.00 3.00 8.00
455,467,479,491,503-Sabrina's Christmas Magic: 455-(1/77). 467-(1/78).

Archie Giant Series #454 © AP

Archie's Double Digest #89 © AP

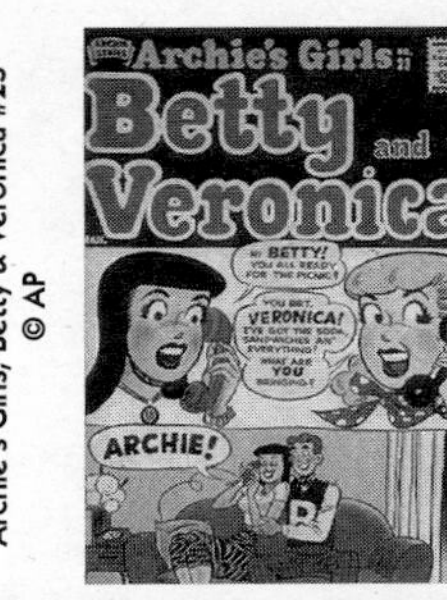

Archie's Girls, Betty & Veronica #23 © AP

GD2.0 FN6.0 NM9.4

479-(1/79) Dracula/Werewolf-s. 491-(1/80), 503(1/81) 1.85 5.50 15.00

0-Archie's Christmas Stocking (12/80) 1.25 3.75 10.00

1-514,516-527,529-532,534-539,541-543,545-550: 501-Betty & Veronica Christmas Spectacular (12/80). 502-Archie's Christmas Love-in (1/81). 504-The World of Archie (3/81). 505-The World of Jughead (4/81). 506-Betty & Veronica Spectacular (6/81). 507-Archie's Jokes (8/81). 508-Betty & Veronica Summer Fun (9/81). 509-The World of Archie (9/81). 510-Betty & Vernonica Spectacular (9/81). 511-The World of Jughead (10/81). 512-Archie's Christmas Stocking (12/81). 513-Betty & Veronica Christmas Spectacular (12/81). 514-Archie's Christmas Love-in (1/82). 516-The World of Archie (3/82). 517-The World of Jughead (4/82). 518-Betty & Veronica Spectacular (6/82). 519-Archie's Jokes (8/82). 520-Betty & Veronica Summer Fun (9/82). 521-The World of Archie (9/82). 522-Betty & Veronica Spectacular (10/82). 523-The World of Jughead (10/82).524-Archie's Christmas Stocking (1/83). 525-Betty and Veronica Christmas Spectacular (1/83). 526-Betty and Veronica Spectacular (5/83). 527-Little Archie (8/83). 529-Betty and Veronica Summer Fun (8/83). 530-Betty and Veronica Spectacular (9/83). 531-The World of Jughead (9/83). 532-The World of Archie (10/83). 534-Little Archie (1/84). 535-Archie's Christmas Stocking (1/84). 536-Betty and Veronica Christmas Spectacular (1/84). 537-Betty and Veronica Spectacular (6/84). 538-Little Archie (8/84). 539-Betty and Veronica Summer Fun (8/84). 541-Betty and Veronica Spectacular (9/84). 542-The World of Jughead (9/84). 543-The World of Archie (10/84). 545-Little Archie (12/84). 546-Archie's Christmas Stocking (12/84). 547-Betty and Veronica Christmas Spectacular (12/84). 548-?. 549-Little Archie. 550-Betty and Veronica Summer Fun
each... 2.40 6.00

5,528,533,540,544: 515-Sabrina's Christmas Magic (1/82). 528-Josie and the Pussycats (8/83). 533-Sabrina; Space Pirates by Frank Bolling (10/83). 540-Josie and the Pussycats (8/84). 544-Sabrina the Teen-Age Witch (10/84).
each... 1.50 4.50 12.00

1,562,571,584,597-Josie and the Pussycats 1.00 3.00 8.00

2-561,563-570,572-583,585-596,598-600: 552-Betty & Veronica Spectacular. 553-The World of Jughead. 554-The World of Archie. 555-Betty's Diary. 556-Little Archie (1/86). 557-Archie's Christmas Stocking (1/86). 558-Betty & Veronica Christmas Spectacular (1/86). 559-Betty & Veronica Spectacular. 560-Little Archie. 561-Betty & Veronica Summer Fun. 563-Betty & Veronica Spectacular. 564-World of Jughead. 565-World of Archie. 566-Little Archie. 567-Archie's Christmas Stocking. 568-Betty & Veronica Christmas Spectacular. 569-Betty & Veronica Spring Spectacular. 570-Little Archie. 571-Dracula-c/s. 572-Betty & Veronica Summer Fun. 573-Archie At Riverdale High. 574-World of Archie. 575-Betty & Veronica Spectacular. 576-Pep. 577-World of Jughead. 578-Archie And Me. 579-Archie's Christmas Stocking. 580-Betty and Veronica Christmas Spectacular. 581-Little Archie Christmas Special. 582-Betty & Veronica Spring Spectacular. 583-Little Archie. 585-Betty & Veronica Summer Fun. 586-Archie At Riverdale High. 587-The World of Archie (10/88); 1st app. Explorers of the Unknown. 588-Betty & Veronica Spectacular. 589-Pep (10/88). 590-The World of Jughead. 591-Archie & Me. 592-Archie's Christmas Stocking. 593-Betty & Veronica Christmas Spectacular. 594-Little Archie. 595-Betty & Veronica Spring Spectacular. 596-Little Archie. 598-Betty & Veronica Summer Fun. 599-The World of Archie (10/89); 2nd app. Explorers of the Unknown. 600-Betty and Veronica Spectacular each.... 4.00

)1,602,604-609,611-629: 601-Pep. 602-The World of Jughead. 604-Archie at Riverdale High. 605-Archie's Christmas Stocking. 606-Betty and Veronica Christmas Spectacular. 607-Little Archie. 608-Betty and Veronica Spectacular. 609-Little Archie. 611-Betty and Veronica Summer Fun. 612-The World of Archie. 613-Betty and Veronica Spectacular. 614-Pep (10/90). 615-Veronica's Summer Special. 616-Archie and Me. 617-Archie's Christmas Stocking. 618-Betty & Veronica Christmas Spectacular. 619-Little Archie. 620-Betty and Veronica Spectacular. 621-Betty and Veronica Summer Fun. 622-Josie & the Pussycats; not published. 623-Betty and Veronica Spectacular. 624-Pep Comics. 625-Veronica's Summer Special. 626-Archie and Me. 627-World of Archie. 628-Archie's Pals 'n' Gals Holiday Special. 629-Betty & Veronica Christmas Spectacular.
each.... 2.50

)3-Archie and Me; Titanic app. 4.00

0-Josie and the Pussycats 5.00

30-632: 630-Archie's Christmas Stocking. 631-Archie's Pals 'n' Gals. 632-Betty & Veronica Spectacular 2.50

NOTE: *Archies Band-c-173,180,192; s-189,192. Archie Cavemen-165,225,232,244,249. Little Sabrina-527,534,538,545,556,566. UFO-s-178,487,594.*

ARCHIE MEETS THE PUNISHER (Same contents as The Punisher Meets Archie)
Marvel Comics & Archie Comics Publ.: Aug, 1994 ($2.95, 52 pgs., one-shot)

1-Batton Lash story, J. Buscema-a on Punisher, S. Goldberg-a on Archie 4.00

ARCHIE'S ACTIVITY COMICS DIGEST MAGAZINE
Archie Enterprises: 1985 - No. 4? (Annual, 128 pgs., digest size)

	GD2.0	FN6.0	NM9.4
1	1.10	3.30	9.00
2-4		2.40	6.00

ARCHIE'S CAR
Spire Christian Comics (Fleming H. Revell co.): 1979 (49¢)

nn 2.40 6.00

ARCHIE'S CHRISTMAS LOVE-IN (See Archie Giant Series Mag. No. 169, 181,192, 205, 218, 230, 242, 454, 466, 478, 490, 502, 514)

ARCHIE'S CHRISTMAS STOCKING (See Archie Giant Series Mag. No. 1-6,10, 15, 20, 25, 31, 137, 144, 150, 158, 167, 179, 190, 203, 216, 228, 240, 452, 464, 476, 488, 500, 512, 524, 535, 546, 557, 567, 579, 592, 605, 617, 630)

ARCHIE'S CHRISTMAS STOCKING
Archie Comics: 1993 -Present ($2.00, 52 pgs.)(Bound-in calendar poster in all)

1-5: 1-Dan DeCarlo-c/a 3.00
6,7: 6-(1998, $2.25). 7-(1999, $2.29) 2.50

ARCHIE'S CLEAN SLATE
Spire Christian Comics (Fleming H. Revell Co.): 1973 (35/49¢)

	GD2.0	FN6.0	NM9.4
1-(35¢-c edition)(Some issues have nn)	1.10	3.30	9.00
1-(49¢-c edition)	1.00	2.80	7.00

ARCHIE'S DATE BOOK
Spire Christian comics (Fleming H. Revell Co.): 1981

nn 1.00 2.80 7.00

ARCHIE'S DOUBLE DIGEST QUARTERLY MAGAZINE
Archie Comics: 1981 - Present ($1.95/$2.75/$2.95/$3.19, 256 pgs.) (A.D.D. Magazine No. 10 on)

	GD2.0	FN6.0	NM9.4
1	2.30	7.00	20.00
2-10; 6-Katy Keene story.	1.50	4.50	12.00
11-30: 29-Pureheart story	1.10	3.30	9.00
31-50		2.40	6.00
51-70,100			4.50
71-99,101-114			3.25
115-122: 115-Begin $3.19-c			3.19

ARCHIE'S FAMILY ALBUM
Spire Christian Comics (Fleming H. Revell Co.): 1978 (39¢, 36 pgs.)

nn 2.40 6.00

ARCHIE'S FESTIVAL
Spire Christian Comics (Fleming H. Revell Co.): 1980 (49¢)

nn 1.00 2.80 7.00

ARCHIE'S GIRLS, BETTY AND VERONICA (Becomes Betty & Veronica)(Also see Veronica)
Archie Publications (Close-Up): 1950 - No. 347, Apr, 1987

	GD2.0	FN6.0	NM9.4
1	158.00	474.00	1500.00
2	74.00	221.00	700.00
3-5	45.00	135.00	405.00
6-10: 6-Dan DeCarlo's 1st Archie work; Betty's 1st ponytail. 10-Katy Keene app. (2 pgs.)	40.00	120.00	325.00
11-20: 11,13,14,17-19-Katy Keene app. 17-Last pre-code issue (3/55). 20-Debbie's Diary (2 pgs.)	28.00	84.00	225.00
21-30: 27,30-Katy Keene app. 29-Tarzan	20.00	60.00	160.00
31-43,45-50: 41-Marilyn Monroe and BrigitteBardot mentioned. 45-Fabian 1 pg. photo & bio. 46-Bobby Darin 1 pg. photo & bio	12.50	37.50	100.00
44-Elvis Presley 1 pg. photo & bio	15.00	45.00	120.00
51-55,57-74: 73-Sci-fi-c	6.80	20.50	75.00
56-Elvis and Bobby Darin records parody	7.65	23.00	85.00

Archie's Girls, Betty & Veronica #320 © AP

Archie's Joke Book #26 © AP

Archie's Pal, Jughead #8 © AP

75-Betty & Veronica sell souls to Devil 12.75 38.00 140.00
76-99: 82-Bobby Rydell 1 pg. illustrated bio; Elvis mentioned on-c.
84-Connie Francis 1 pg. illustrated bio 3.65 11.00 40.00
100 4.55 13.65 50.00
101-117,120 (12/65): 113-Monsters-s 2.60 7.80 26.00
118-(10/65) 1st app./origin Superteen (also see Betty & Me #3)
4.10 12.30 45.00
119-2nd app./last Superteen story 3.00 9.00 30.00
121,122,124-126,128-140 (8/67): 135,140-Mod-c. 136-Slave Girl-s
2.00 6.00 18.00
123-"Jingo"-Ringo parody-c 2.00 6.00 18.00
127-Beatles Fan Club-s 3.00 9.00 30.00
141-156,158-163,165-180 (12/70) 1.75 5.25 14.00
157,164-Archies Band 2.30 7.00 20.00
181-193,195-199 1.25 3.75 10.00
194-Sabrina-c/s 2.00 6.00 18.00
200-(8/72) 1.75 5.25 14.00
201-205,207,209,211-215,217-240 1.10 3.30 9.00
206,208,216-Sabrina c/app. 206-Josie-c. 210-Sabrina app.
1.85 5.50 15.00
241 (1/76)-270 (6/78) 1.00 2.80 7.00
271-299: 281-UFO-s 2.40 6.00
300 (12/80)-Anniversary issue 1.00 2.80 7.00
301-309,311-319 4.00
310-John Travolta parody story 2.40 6.00
320 (10/82)-Intro. of Cheryl Blossom on cover and inside story (she also appears, but not on the cover, in Jughead #325 with same 10/82 publication date)
3.00 9.00 30.00
321,322-Cheryl Blossom app. 1.75 5.25 14.00
323,326,327,330,331,333-347: 333-Monsters-s 3.00
324,325-Crickett O'Dell app. 5.00
328-Cheryl Blossom app. 1.10 3.30 9.00
329,332: 329-Betty dressed as Madonna. 332-Superhero costume party 5.00
Annual 1 (1953) 84.00 253.00 800.00
Annual 2(1954) 40.00 120.00 360.00
Annual 3-5 (1955-1957) 34.00 101.00 270.00
Annual 6-8 (1958-1960) 22.00 66.00 175.00

ARCHIE'S HOLIDAY FUN DIGEST
Archie Comics: 1997 - Present ($1.75/$1.95/$1.99/$2.19, annual)
1-5-Christmas stories 2.25

ARCHIE'S JOKEBOOK COMICS DIGEST ANNUAL (See Jokebook...)

ARCHIE'S JOKE BOOK MAGAZINE (See Joke Book ...)
Archie Publ: 1953 - No. 3, Sum, 1954; No. 15, Fall, 1954 - No. 288, 11/82 (subtitled...Laugh-In #127-140; ...Laugh-Out #141-194)
1953-One Shot (#1) 84.00 253.00 800.00
2 44.00 133.00 400.00
3 (no #4-14) 38.00 113.00 300.00
15-20: 15-Formerly Archie's Rival Reggie #14; last pre-code issue (Fall/54).
15-17-Katy Keene app. 22.00 66.00 175.00
21-30 13.00 39.00 105.00
31-40,42,43: 42-Bio of Ed "Kookie" Byrnes. 43-story about guitarist Duane Eddy
10.00 30.00 70.00
41-1st professional comic work by Neal Adams (9/59), 1 pg.
22.00 66.00 175.00
44-47-N. Adams-a in all, 1-3 pgs. 12.00 36.00 95.00
48-Four pgs. N. Adams-a 12.50 37.50 100.00
49-56,58-60 (1962) 3.00 9.00 30.00
57-Elvis mentioned; Marilyn Monroe cameo 3.45 10.35 38.00
61-80 (8/64): 66-(12¢ cover) 2.00 6.00 18.00
66-(15¢ cover variant) 2.50 7.50 25.00
81-89,91,92,94-99 1.75 5.25 14.00
90,93: 90-Beatles gag. 93-Beatles cameo 2.30 7.00 20.00
100 (5/66) 2.00 6.00 18.00
101,103-117,119-123,127,129,131-140 (9/69): 105-Superhero gag-c. 108-110-Archies Archers Band-s. 116-Beatles/Monkees/Bob Dylan cameos (posters) 1.50 4.50 12.00
102 (7/66) Archie Band prototype-c; Elvis parody panel, Rolling Stones mention
2.00 6.00 18.00
118,124,125,126,128,130: 118-ArchieBand-c; Veronica & Groovers band-s. 124-Archies Band-c/app. 125-Beatles cameo (poster). 126,130-Monkees cameo. 128-Veronica/Archies Band app. 2.00 6.00 18.0
141-173,175-181,183-199 1.10 3.30 9.0
174-Sabrina-c. 182-Sabrina cameo 1.50 4.50 12.0
200 (9/74) 1.50 4.50 12.0
201-230 (3/77) 2.40 6.0
231-239,241-288 4.0
240-Elvis record-c 2.40 6.0
NOTE: *Archies Band-c-118,124,147,172; 1 pg.-s-127,128,138,140,143,147,167; 2 pg.-s-124,1 155. Sabrina app.-247,248,252-259,261,262,264,266-270,274,277,284-286.*

ARCHIE'S JOKES (See Archie Giant Series Mag. No. 17, 22, 27, 33, 139, 146, 154, 163, 174, 186, 198, 211, 222, 235, 247, 459, 471, 483, 495, 519)

ARCHIE'S LOVE SCENE
Spire Christian Comics (Fleming H. Revell Co.): 1973 (35¢/49¢/no price)
1-(35¢ Edition) 1.25 3.75 10.0
1-(49¢ Edition/no price) (Some copies have nn) 1.00 2.80 7.0

ARCHIE'S MADHOUSE (Madhouse Ma-ad No. 67 on)
Archie Publications: Sept, 1959 - No. 66, Feb, 1969
1-Archie begins 23.00 68.00 250.0
2 11.50 34.00 125.0
3-5 7.65 23.00 85.0
6-10 5.00 15.00 55.0
11-17 (Last w/regular characters) 3.80 11.40 42.0
18-21,29: 18-New format begins 2.80 8.40 28.0
22-1st app. Sabrina, the Teen-age Witch (10/62) 20.50 61.00 225.0
23,24-Sabrina app. 6.80 20.50 75.0
25,26,28-Sabrina app. 25-1st app. Captain Sprocket (4/63)
5.00 15.00 55.0
27-Sabrina-c; no story 4.10 12.30 45.0
30,34,38-40: No Sabrina. 34-Bordered-c begin. 2.00 6.00 18.0
31,32-Sabrina app.? 2.00 6.00 18.0
33,37-Sabrina app. 3.65 11.00 40.0
35-Beatles cameo. No Sabrina 2.50 7.50 25.0
36-1st Salem the Cat w/Sabrina story 4.55 13.65 50.0
41-48,51-57,60-62,64-66; No Sabrina 43-Mighty Crusaders cameo. 44-Swipes Mad #4 (Super-Duperman) in "Bird Monsters From Outer Space"
1.85 5.50 15.0
49,50,58,59,63-Sabrina stories 3.00 9.00 30.0
Annual 1 (1962-63) no Sabrina 6.80 20.50 75.0
Annual 2 (1964) no Sabrina 4.10 12.30 45.0
Annual 3 (1965)-Origin Sabrina the Teen-Age Witch 7.65 23.00 85.0
Annual 4,5('66-68)(Becomes Madhouse Ma-ad Annual #7 on);
no Sabrina 2.30 7.00 20.0
Annual 6 (1969)-Sabrina the Teen-Age Witch-sty 4.10 12.30 45.0
NOTE: *Cover title to #61-65 is "Madhouse" and to #66 is "Madhouse Ma-ad Jokes".*

ARCHIE'S MECHANICS
Archie Publications: Sept, 1954 - No. 3, 1955
1-(15¢; 52 pgs.) 76.00 229.00 725.0
2-(10¢)-Last pre-code issue 47.00 140.00 420.0
3-(10¢) 40.00 120.00 350.0

ARCHIE'S ONE WAY
Spire Christian Comics (Fleming H. Revell Co.): 1972 (35¢/39¢/49¢, 36 pgs.)
nn-(35¢ Edition) 1.10 3.30 9.00
nn-(39¢, 49¢, no price editions) 1.00 2.80 7.00

ARCHIE'S PAL, JUGHEAD (Jughead No. 127 on)
Archie Publications: 1949 - No. 126, Nov, 1965
1 (1949)-1st app. Moose (see Pep #33) 126.00 379.00 1200.00
2 (1950) 61.00 182.00 575.0
3-5 40.00 120.00 340.0
6-10: 7-Suzie app. 28.00 84.00 225.00
11-20 18.00 53.00 140.00
21-30: 23-25,28-30-Katy Keene app. 23-Early Dilton-s. 28-Debbie's Diary app.
12.00 36.00 95.00
31-50: 49-Archies Rock 'N' Rollers band-c 5.00 15.00 55.00
51-70: 67-Betty seducing Jughead-c. 68-Early Archie Gang Cavemen-s

Archie's Pals 'n' Gals #1 © AP

Archie's Rival Reggie #4 © AP

Archie's TV Laugh-Out #1 © AP

GD2.0 FN6.0 NM9.4

	GD2.0	FN6.0	NM9.4
	3.20	9.60	35.00
71-76,81-84,87,89-99: 72-Jughead dates Betty & Veronica	2.30	7.00	20.00
77,78,80,85,86,88-Horror/Sci-Fi-c	2.50	7.50	25.00
79-Creature From the Black Lagoon-c	3.20	9.60	35.00
100	2.50	7.50	25.00
101-Return of Big Ethyl	2.50	7.50	25.00
102-126	2.00	6.00	18.00
Annual 1 (1953, 25¢)	53.00	158.00	475.00
Annual 2 (1954, 25¢)-Last pre-code issue	38.00	113.00	300.00
Annual 3-5 (1955-57, 25¢)	26.00	79.00	210.00
Annual 6-8 (1958-60, 25¢)	16.00	49.00	130.00

ARCHIE'S PAL JUGHEAD COMICS (Formerly Jughead #1-45)
Archie Comic Publ.: No. 46, June, 1993 - Present ($1.25/$1.50/$1.75/$1.79)

	GD2.0	FN6.0	NM9.4
46-60			3.00
61-133: 100-"A Storm Over Uniforms" x-over part 1,2			2.00

ARCHIE'S PALS 'N' GALS (Also see Archie Giant Series Magazine #628)
Archie Publ: 1952-53 - No. 6, 1957-58; No. 7, 1958 - No. 224, Sept, 1991
(...All News Stories on-c #49-59)

	GD2.0	FN6.0	NM9.4
1-(116 pgs., 25¢)	71.00	213.00	675.00
2(Annual)('54, 25¢)	40.00	120.00	340.00
3-5(Annual, '55-57, 25¢): 3-Last pre-code issue	29.00	87.00	235.00
6-10('58-'60)	17.00	51.00	135.00
11-18,20 (84 pgs.): 12-Harry Belafonte 2 pg. photos & bio 17-B&V paper dolls	10.00	30.00	70.00
19-Marilyn Monroe app.	11.00	33.00	90.00
21,22,24-28,30 (68 pgs.)	4.10	12.30	45.00
23-(Wint./62) 6 pg. Josie-s with Pepper and Melody (1st app.?); Betty in towel pin-up	7.25	21.75	80.00
29-Beatles satire (68 pgs.)	6.35	19.00	70.00
31(Wint. 64/65)-39 -(68 pgs.)	3.65	11.00	40.00
40-Early Superteen-s; with Pureheart	5.00	15.00	55.00
41(8/67)-43,45-50(2/69) (68 pgs.)	2.80	8.40	28.00
44-Archies Band-s; WEB cameo	3.20	9.60	35.00
51(4/69),52,55-64(6/71): 62-Last squarebound	2.40	7.35	22.00
53-Archies Band-c/s	2.80	8.40	28.00
54-Satan meets Veronica-s	3.00	9.00	32.00
65(8/70),67-70,73-81,83(6/74) (52 pgs.)	2.00	6.00	16.00
66,82-Sabrina-c	2.50	7.50	25.00
71,72-Two part drug story (8/72,9/72)	2.40	7.35	22.00
75-Archies Band-s	2.40	7.35	22.00
84-99	1.10	3.30	9.00
100 (12/75)	1.50	4.50	12.00
101-130(3/79): 125,126-Riverdale 2001-s	1.00	2.80	7.00
131-160,162-170 (7/84)			5.00
161 (11/82) 3rd app./1st solo Cheryl Blossom-s and pin-up; 2nd Jason Blossom	2.50	7.50	24.00
171-173,175,177-197,199: 197-G. Colan-a			3.00
174,176,198: 174-New Archies Band-s. 176-Cyndi Lauper-c. 198-Archie gang on strike at Archie Ent. offices			5.00
200(9/88)-Illiteracy-s			5.00
201,203-224: Later issues $1.00 cover			2.00
202-Explains end of Archie's jalopy; Dezerland-c/s; James Dean cameo			5.00

NOTE: *Archies Band-c-45,47,49,53,56; s-44,53,75,174. UFO-s-50,63,209,220.*

ARCHIE'S PALS 'N' GALS DOUBLE DIGEST MAGAZINE
Archie Comic Publications: Nov, 1992 - Present ($2.50/$2.75/$2.95/$2.99)

	GD2.0	FN6.0	NM9.4
1-3: 1-Capt. Hero story; Pureheart app. 2-Superduck story; Little Jinx in all		2.40	6.00
4-29: 4-Begin $2.75-c.			4.00
30-47: 40-Begin $2.99-c			3.00
48-55: 48-Begin $3.19-c			3.19

ARCHIE'S PARABLES
Spire Christian Comics (Fleming H. Revell Co.): 1973,1975 (39/49¢, 36 pgs.)

	GD2.0	FN6.0	NM9.4
nn-By Al Hartley; 39¢ Edition	1.10	3.30	9.00
49¢, no price editions	1.00	2.80	7.00

ARCHIE'S R/C RACERS (Radio controlled cars)
Archie Comics: Sept, 1989 - No. 10, Mar, 1991 (95¢/$1)

	GD2.0	FN6.0	NM9.4
1,2,5-7,10: 5-Elvis parody. 7-Supervillain-c/s. 10-UFO-c/s			4.00
3,4,8,9			3.00

ARCHIE'S RIVAL REGGIE (Reggie & Archie's Joke Book #15 on)
Archie Publications: 1950 - No. 14, Aug, 1954

	GD2.0	FN6.0	NM9.4
1-Reggie 1st app. in Jackpot Comics #5	74.00	221.00	700.00
2	40.00	120.00	325.00
3-5	28.00	84.00	225.00
6-10	20.00	60.00	160.00
11-14: Katy Keene in No. 10-14, 1-2 pgs.	14.00	38.00	115.00

ARCHIE'S RIVERDALE HIGH (See Riverdale High)

ARCHIE'S ROLLER COASTER
Spire Christian Comics (Fleming H. Revell Co.): 1981 (69¢)

	GD2.0	FN6.0	NM9.4
nn	1.00	3.00	8.00

ARCHIE'S SOMETHING ELSE
Spire Christian Comics (Fleming H. Revell Co.): 1975 (39/49¢, 36 pgs.)

	GD2.0	FN6.0	NM9.4
nn-(39¢-c) Hell's Angels Biker on motorcycle-c	1.25	3.75	10.00
nn-(49¢-c)	1.00	2.80	7.00
Barbour Christian Comics Edition (1986, no price listed)	1.10	3.30	9.00

ARCHIE'S SONSHINE
Spire Christian Comics (Fleming H. Revell Co.): 1973, 1974 (39/49¢, 36 pgs.)

	GD2.0	FN6.0	NM9.4
39¢ Edition	1.10	3.30	9.00
49¢, no price editions	1.00	2.80	7.00

ARCHIE'S SPORTS SCENE
Spire Christian Comics (Fleming H. Revell Co.): 1983 (no cover price)

	GD2.0	FN6.0	NM9.4
nn	1.00	3.00	8.00

ARCHIE'S SPRING BREAK
Archie Comics: 1996 - Present ($2.00, 48 pgs., annual)

	GD2.0	FN6.0	NM9.4
1-4: 1,2-Dan DeCarlo-c			2.25

ARCHIE'S STORY & GAME COMICS DIGEST MAGAZINE
Archie Enterprises: Nov, 1986 - Present ($1.25/$1.35/$1.50/$1.95, 128 pgs., digest-size)

	GD2.0	FN6.0	NM9.4
1: Many copies were marked-up in print run	1.75	5.25	14.00
2-10	1.10	3.30	9.00
11-20		2.40	6.00
21-38			3.00
39-42-($1.95)			2.00

ARCHIE'S SUPER HERO SPECIAL (See Archie Giant Series Mag. No. 142)

ARCHIE'S SUPER HERO SPECIAL (...Comics Digest Mag. 2)
Archie Publications (Red Circle): Jan, 1979 - No. 2, Aug, 1979(95¢, 148 pgs.)

	GD2.0	FN6.0	NM9.4
1-Simon & Kirby r-/Double Life of Pvt. Strong #1,2; Black Hood, The Fly, Jaguar, The Web app.	1.85	5.50	15.00
2-Contains contents to the never published Black Hood #1; origin Black Hood; N. Adams, Wood, McWilliams, Morrow, S&K-a(r); N. Adams-c. The Shield, The Fly, Jaguar, Hangman, Steel Sterling, The Web, The Fox-r	1.75	5.25	14.00

ARCHIE'S SUPER TEENS
Archie Comic Publications, Inc.: 1994 - No. 4, 1996 ($2.00, 52 pgs.)

	GD2.0	FN6.0	NM9.4
1-4: 1-Staton/Esposito-c/a; pull-out poster. 2-Fred Hembeck script; Bret Blevins/Terry Austin-a			2.00

ARCHIE'S TV LAUGH-OUT ("...Starring Sabrina" on-c #1-50)
Archie Publications: Dec, 1969 - No. 106, Apr, 1986 (#1-7: 68 pgs.)

	GD2.0	FN6.0	NM9.4
1-Sabrina begins, thru #106	9.00	27.00	100.00
2 (68 pgs.)	4.55	13.65	50.00
3-6 (68 pgs.)	3.00	9.00	30.00
7-Josie begins, thru #105; Archie's & Josie's Bands cover logos begin	5.45	16.35	60.00
8-23 (52 pgs.): 10-1st Josie on-c. 12-1st Josie and Pussycats on-c. 14-Beatles cameo on poster	2.80	8.40	28.00
24-40: 37,39,40-Bicenntennial-c	1.85	5.50	15.00
41,47,56: 41-Alexandra rejoins J&P band. 47-Fonz cameo; voodoo-s. 56-Fonz parody; B&V with Farrah hair-c	2.00	6.00	16.00

Archie's Weird Mysteries #1 © AP

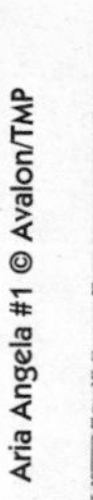
Aria Angela #1 © Avalon/TMP

Armageddon #1 © Chaos! Comics

GD2.0 FN6.0 NM9.4

42-46,48-55,57-60 1.25 3.75 10.00
61-68,70-80: 63-UFO-s. 79-Mummy-s 1.00 2.80 7.00
69-Sherlock Holmes parody 1.00 2.80 7.00
81-90,94,95,97-99: 84 Voodoo-s 2.40 6.00
91-Early Cheryl Blossom-s; Sabrina/Archies Band-c 1.85 5.50 15.00
92-A-Team parody 1.00 2.80 7.00
93-(2/84) Archie in drag-s; Hill Street Blues-s; Groucho Marx parody; cameo parody app. of Batman, Spider-Man, Wonder Woman and others 1.25 3.75 10.00
96-MASH parody-s; Jughead in drag; Archies Band-c 1.00 3.00 8.00
100-(4/85) Michael Jackson parody-c/s; J&P band and Archie band on-c 1.50 4.50 12.00
101-104-Lower print run. 104-Miami Vice parody-c 1.00 2.80 7.00
105-Wrestling/Hulk Hogan parody-c; J&P band-s 1.25 3.75 10.00
106-Last issue; low print run (scarce) 1.25 3.75 10.00

NOTE: ***Dan DeCarlo-a** 78-up(most), **c**-89-up(most). **Archies Band-s** 2,7,9-11,15,20,25, 37,64,65,67,68,70,73,76,78,79,83,84,86,90,96,100,101; **Archies Band-c** 2,17,20,91,94,96,99-103. **Josie-s** 12,21,26,35,52,78,80,90. **Josie-c** 10,91,94. **Josie and the Pussycats (as a band in costume)-s** 7,9,10,37,38,41,42,66,84,99-101,105. **Josie w/Pussycats member Valerie &/or Melody-s** 17,20,22,25,27-29,31,33,36,39,40,43-51,53-65,67-77,79,81-83,85-89,92-94,102-104. **Josie w/Pussycats band-c** 12,14,17,18,22,24. **Sabrina-s** 1-9,11-86,88-106. **Sabrina-c** 1-18,21,23,27,49,91,94.*

ARCHIE'S VACATION SPECIAL
Archie Publications: Winter, 1994 - Present ($2.00/$2.25/$2.29/$2.49, annual)
1-8: 8-(2000, $2.49) 2.50

ARCHIE'S WEIRD MYSTERIES (TV)
Archie Comics: Feb, 2000 - Present ($1.79/$1.99)
1-8 2.00

ARCHIE'S WORLD
Spire Christian Comics (Fleming H. Revell Co.): 1973, 1976 (39/49¢)
39¢ Edition 1.10 3.30 9.00
49¢ Edition, no price editions 1.00 2.80 7.00

ARCHIE 3000
Archie Comics: May, 1989 - No. 16, July, 1991 (75¢/95¢/$1.00)
1,16: 16-Aliens-c/s 3.50
2-15: 6-Begin $1.00-c; X-Mas-c 2.50

ARCOMICS PREMIERE
Arcomics: July, 1993 ($2.95)
1-1st lenticular-c on a comic (flicker-c) 3.00

AREA 88
Eclipse Comics/VIZ Comics #37 on: May 26, 1987 - No. 42, 1989 ($1.50/$1.75, B&W)
1-42: 1,2-2nd printings exist 2.00

AREALA: ANGEL OF WAR (See Warrior Nun titles)
Antarctic Press: Sept, 1998 - No. 4, June, 1999 ($2.95/$2.99, color/B&W)
1-4: 3,4-B&W. 4-($2.99-c) 3.00

ARENA
Alchemy Studios: Jan, 1990 ($1.50, 7x10-1/8", 20 pgs.)
1-Science fiction 2.00
1-Signed & numbered ed. (500 copies) 3.00

ARGUS (See Flash, 2nd Series) (Also see Showcase '95 #1,2)
DC Comics: Apr, 1995 - No. 6, Oct, 1995 ($1.50, limited series)
1-6: 4-Begin $1.75-c 2.00

ARIA
Image Comics (Avalon Studios): Jan, 1999 - Present ($2.50)
Preview (11/98, $2.95) 5.00
1-Anacleto-c/a 1.00 2.80 7.00
1-Variant-c by Michael Turner 1.00 2.80 7.00
1-($10.00) Alternate-c by Turner 1.25 3.75 10.00
1,2-(Blanc & Noir) Black and white printing of pencil art 3.00
1-(Blanc & Noir) DF Edition 5.00
2-4: 2,4-Anacleto-c/a. 3-Martinez-a 2.50
4-($6.95) Glow in the Dark-c 1.25 3.75 10.00
Aria Angela 1 (2/00, $2.95) Anacleto-a; 4 covers by Anacleto, JG Jones, Portacio and Quesada 2.95
Aria Angela Blanc & Noir 1 (4/00, $2.95) Anacleto-c 2.95
Aria Angela European Ashcan 10.00
Aria Angela 2 (10/00, $2.95) Anacleto-a/c 2.95

GD2.0 FN6.0 NM9.4

ARIANE AND BLUEBEARD (See Night Music #8)

ARIEL & SEBASTIAN (See Cartoon Tales & The Little Mermaid)

ARION, LORD OF ATLANTIS (Also see Warlord #55)
DC Comics: Nov, 1982 - No. 35, Sept, 1985
1-35: 1-Story cont'd from Warlord #62, Special #1 (11/85) 2.00

ARION THE IMMORTAL (Also see Showcase '95 #7)
DC Comics: July, 1992 - No. 6, Dec, 1992 ($1.50, limited series)
1 3.00
2-6: 4-Gustovich-a(i) 2.00

ARISTOCATS (See Movie Comics & Walt Disney Showcase No. 16)

ARISTOKITTENS, THE (...Meet Jiminy Cricket No. 1)(Disney)
Gold Key: Oct, 1971 - No. 9, Oct, 1975
1 2.50 7.50 24.00
2-5,7-9 2.00 6.00 16.00
6-(52 pgs.) 2.00 6.00 18.00

ARIZONA KID, THE (Also see The Comics & Wild Western)
Marvel/Atlas Comics(CSI): Mar, 1951 - No. 6, Jan, 1952
1 23.00 68.00 180.00
2-4: 2-Heath-a(3) 11.00 33.00 90.00
5,6 10.00 30.00 75.00

NOTE: ***Heath** a-1-3; c-1-3. **Maneely** c-4-6. **Morisi** a-4-6. **Sinnott** a-6.*

ARK, THE (See The Crusaders)

ARKAGA
Image Comics: Sept, 1997 ($2.95, one-shot)
1-Jorgensen-s/a 3.00

ARMAGEDDON
Chaos! Comics: Oct, 1999 - No. 4, Jan, 2000 ($2.95, limited series)
Preview 5.00
1-4-Lady Death, Evil Ernie, Purgatori app. 2.95

ARMAGEDDON: ALIEN AGENDA
DC Comics: Nov, 1991 - No. 4, Feb, 1992 ($1.00, limited series)
1-4 2.00

ARMAGEDDON FACTOR, THE
AC Comics: 1987 - No. 2, 1987; No. 3, 1990 ($1.95)
1,2: Sentinels of Justice, Dragonfly, Femforce 2.00
3-($3.95, color)-Almost all AC characters app. 4.00

ARMAGEDDON: INFERNO
DC Comics: Apr, 1992 - No. 4, July, 1992 ($1.00, limited series)
1-4: Many DC heroes app. 3-A. Adams/Austin-a 2.50

ARMAGEDDON 2001
DC Comics: May, 1991 - No. 2, Oct, 1991 ($2.00, squarebound, 68 pgs.)
1-Features many DC heroes; intro Waverider 3.00
1-2nd & 3rd printings; 3rd has silver ink-c 2.00
2 2.50

ARMATURE
Olyoptics: Nov, 1996 - No. 2, ($2.95, limited series)
1,2-Steve Oliff-c/s/a; Maxx app. 3.00

ARMED & DANGEROUS
Acclaim Comics (Armada): Apr, 1996 - No.4, July, 1996 ($2.95, B&W)
1-4-Bob Hall-c/a & scripts 3.00
Special 1 (8/96, $2.95, B&W)-Hall-c/a & scripts. 3.00

ARMED & DANGEROUS HELL'S SLAUGHTERHOUSE
Acclaim Comics (Armada): Oct, 1996 - No. 4, Jan, 1997 ($2.95, B&W)
1-4: Hall-c/a/scripts. 3.00

ARMOR (AND THE SILVER STREAK) (Revengers Featuring... in indicia for #1-3)

Army and Navy Comics #3 © Condé Nast

Arrowhead #2 © MAR

Art of Zen #1 © Entity

	GD2.0	FN6.0	NM9.4

ontinuity Comics: Sept, 1985 - No.13, Apr, 1992 ($2.00)
-13: 1-Intro/origin Armor & the Silver Streak; Neal Adams-c/a. 7-Origin Armor; Nebres-i 3.00

RMOR (DEATHWATCH 2000)
ontinuity Comics: Apr, 1993 - No.6, Nov, 1993 ($2.50)
-6: 1-3-Deathwatch 2000 x-over 2.50

RMORED TROOPER VOTOMS (Manga)
M Comics: July, 1996 ($2.95)
3.00

RMORINES (See X-O Manowar #25)
liant: June, 1994 - No. 12, June, 1995 ($2.25)
-12: 7-Wraparound-c. 12-Byrne-c/swipe (X-Men, 1st Series #138) 2.25

RMORINES (Volume 2)
claim Comics: Oct, 1999 - No. 4 ($3.95/$2.50, limited series)
-($3.95) Calafiore & P. Palmiotti-a 3.95
,3-($2.50) 2.50

RMY AND NAVY COMICS (Supersnipe No. 6 on)
reet & Smith Publications: May, 1941 - No. 5, July, 1942

-Cap Fury & Nick Carter	50.00	150.00	450.00
-Cap Fury & Nick Carter	30.00	90.00	240.00
,4: 4-Jack Farr-c/a	21.00	64.00	170.00
-Supersnipe app.; see Shadow V2#3 for 1st app.; Story of Douglas MacArthur; George Marcoux-c/a	50.00	150.00	450.00

RMY ATTACK
harlton Comics: July, 1964 - No. 4, Feb, 1965; V2#38, July, 1965 - No. 47, b, 1967

#1	3.20	9.60	35.00
2-4(2/65)	2.30	7.00	20.00
2#38(7/65)-47 (formerly U.S. Air Force #1-37)	2.00	6.00	18.00

TE: *Glanzman a-1-3. Montes/Bache a-44.*

RMY AT WAR (Also see Our Army at War & Cancelled Comic Cavalcade)
C Comics: Oct-Nov, 1978
-Kubert-c; all new story and art 2.40 6.00

RMY OF DARKNESS (Movie)
ark Horse Comics: Nov, 1992 - No. 2, Dec, 1992; No. 3, Oct, 1993 ($2.50, limited series)
-3-Bolton painted-c/a 4.00

RMY SURPLUS KOMIKZ FEATURING CUTEY BUNNY
rmy Surplus Komikz/Eclipse Comics: 1982 - No. 5, 1985 ($1.50, B&W)
-Cutey Bunny begins 2.40 6.00
2-5: 5-(Eclipse)-JLA/X-Men/Batman parody 4.00

RMY WAR HEROES (Also see Iron Corporal)
harlton Comics: Dec, 1963 - No. 38, June, 1970

	3.45	10.35	38.00
2-10	2.50	7.50	25.00
1-21,23-30: 24-Intro. Archer & Corp. Jack series	2.00	6.00	18.00
2-Origin/1st app. Iron Corporal series by Glanzman	2.50	7.50	25.00
1-38	1.50	4.50	12.00
odern Comics Reprint 36 ('78)			4.00

TE: *Montes/Bache a-1, 16, 17, 21, 23-25, 27-30.*

ROUND THE BLOCK WITH DUNC & LOO (See Dunc and Loo)

ROUND THE WORLD IN 80 DAYS (Movie) (See A Golden Picture Classic)
ell Publishing Co.: Feb, 1957
our Color 784-Photo-c 5.85 17.50 70.00

ROUND THE WORLD UNDER THE SEA (See Movie Classics)

ROUND THE WORLD WITH ARCHIE (See Archie Giant Series Mag. #29, 35, 141)

ROUND THE WORLD WITH HUCKLEBERRY & HIS FRIENDS (See Dell Giant No. 44)

RRGH! (Satire)
arvel Comics Group: Dec, 1974 - No. 5, Sept, 1975 (25¢)

1-Dracula story; Sekowsky-a(p)	2.30	7.00	20.00
2-5: 2-Frankenstein. 3-Mummy. 4-Nightstalker(TV); Dracula-c/app., Hunchback. 5-Invisible Man, Dracula	1.75	5.25	14.00

NOTE *Alcala a-2; c-3. Everett a-1r, 2r. Grandenetti a-4. Maneely a-4r. Sutton a-1-3.*

ARROW (See Protectors)
Malibu Comics: Oct, 1992 ($1.95, one-shot)
1-Moder-a(p) 2.00

ARROW, THE (See Funny Pages)
Centaur Publications: Oct, 1940 - No. 2, Nov, 1940; No. 3, Oct, 1941

1-The Arrow begins(r/Funny Pages)	295.00	885.00	2800.00
2,3: 2-Tippy Taylor serial continues from Amazing Mystery Funnies #24. 3-Origin Dash Dartwell, the Human Meteor; origin The Rainbow-r; bondage-c	126.00	379.00	1200.00

NOTE: *Gustavson a-1, 2; c-3.*

ARROWHEAD (See Black Rider and Wild Western)
Atlas Comics (CPS): April, 1954 - No. 4, Nov, 1954

1-Arrowhead & his horse Eagle begin	16.00	48.00	125.00
2-4: 4-Forte-a	10.00	30.00	75.00

NOTE: *Heath c-3. Jack Katz a-3. Maneely c-2. Pakula a-2. Sinnott a-1-4; c-1.*

ARSENAL (Teen Titans' Speedy)
DC Comics: Oct, 1998 - No. 4, Jan, 1999 ($2.50, limited series)
1-4: Grayson-s. 1-Black Canary app. 2-Green Arrow app. 2.50

ARSENAL SPECIAL (See New Titans, Showcase '94 #7 & Showcase '95 #8)
DC Comics: 1996 ($2.95, one-shot)
1 3.00

ARTBABE
Fantagraphics Books: May, 1996 - Apr, 1999 ($2.50/$2.95/$3.50, B&W)
V1 #5, V2 #1-3 3.00
#4-($3.50) 3.50

ARTEMIS: REQUIEM (Also see Wonder Woman, 2nd Series #90)
DC Comics: June, 1996 - No. 6, Nov, 1996 ($1.75, limited series)
1-6: Messner-Loebs scripts & Ed Benes-c/a in all. 1,2-Wonder Woman app. 3.00

ARTESIA
Sirius Entertainment: Jan, 1999 - No. 6, June, 1999 ($2.95, limited series)
1-6-Mark Smylie-s/a 3.00
Annual 1 (1999, $3.50) 3.50

ARTESIA AFIELD
Sirius Entertainment: Jul, 2000 - No. 6 ($2.95, limited series)
1-4-Mark Smylie-s/a 3.00

ART OF ZEN INTERGALACTIC NINJA, THE
Entity Comics: 1994 - No. 2, 1994 ($2.95)
1,2 3.00

ARZACH (See Moebius...)
Dark Horse Comics: 1996 ($6.95, one-shot)
nn-Moebius-c/a/scripts 1.00 2.80 7.00

ASCENSION
Image Comics (Top Cow Productions): Oct, 1997 - No. 22, Mar, 2000 ($2.50)

Preview	1.00	2.80	7.00
Preview Gold Edition			10.00
Preview San Diego Edition	1.85	5.50	15.00
0			5.00
1/2	1.00	3.00	8.00
1-David Finch-s/a(p)/Batt-s/a(i)			5.00
1-Variant-c w/Image logo at lower right	1.00	3.00	8.00
2-6			4.00
7-22			3.00
Fan Club Edition		2.40	6.00

...COLLECTED EDITION
1998 - No. 2 ($4.95, squarebound) 1,2: 1-r/#1,2. 2-r/#3,4 5.00

ASH

Ash: Cinder & Smoke #2 © Quesada & Palmiotti

Astonishing #5 © MAR

Astonishing X-Men #1 © MAR

Event Comics: Nov, 1994 - No. 6, Dec, 1995; No. 0, May, 1996 ($2.50/$3.00)
0-Present & Future (Both 5/96, $3.00, foil logo-c)-w/pin-ups 3.00
0-Blue Foil logo-c (Present and Future) (1000 each) 5.00
0-Silver Prism logo-c (Present and Future) (500 each) 12.00
0-Red Prism logo-c (Present and Future) (250 each) 20.00
0-Gold Hologram logo-c (Present and Future) (1000 each) 10.00
1-Quesada-p/story; Palmiotti-i/story: Barry Windsor-Smith pin-up 1.85 5.50 15.00
2-Mignola Hellboy pin-up 1.00 3.30 9.00
3,4: 3-Big Guy pin-up by Geoff Darrow. 4-Jim Lee pin-up 6.00
4-Fahrenheit Gold 9.00
4-6-Fahrenheit Red (5,6-1000) 10.00
4-6-Fahrenheit White 15.00
5, 6-Double-c w/Hildebrandt Bros.-a, Quesada & Palmiotti. 6-Texiera-c 4.00
5,6-Fahrenheit Gold (2000) 5.00
6-Fahrenheit White (500)-Texiera-c 15.00
Volume 1 (1996, $14.95, TPB)-r/#1-5, intro by James Robinson 15.00
Wizard Mini-Comic (1996, magazine supplement) 1.00
Wizard #1/2 (1997, mail order) 5.00

ASH: CINDER & SMOKE
Event Comics: May, 1997 - No. 6, Oct, 1997 ($2.95, limited series)
1-6:Ramos-a/Waid, Augustyn-s in all
2-6-variant covers by Ramos and Quesada 3.00

ASH: FILES
Event Comics: Mar, 1997 ($2.95, one-shot)
1-Comics w/text 3.00

ASH: FIRE AND CROSSFIRE
Event Comics: Jan, 1999 - No. 5 ($2.95, limited series)
1,2-Robinson-s/Quesada & Palmiotti-c/a 3.00

ASH: FIRE WITHIN, THE
Event Comics: Sept, 1996 - No. 2, Jan, 1997 ($2.95, unfinished limited series)
1,2:Quesada & Palmiotti-c/s/a 3.00

ASH/ 22 BRIDES
Event Comics: Dec, 1996 - No. 2, Apr, 1997 ($2.95, limited series)
1,2:Nicieza-s/Ramos-c/a 3.00

ASKANI'SON (See Adventures of Cyclops & Phoenix limited series)
Marvel Comics: Jan, 1996 - No. 4, May, 1996 ($2.95, limited series)
1-4: Story cont'd from Advs. of Cyclops & Phoenix; Lobdell/Loeb story; Gene Ha-c/a(p) 3.00
TPB (1997, $12.99) r/#1-4; Gene Ha painted-c 13.00

ASSASSINETTE
Pocket Change Comics: 1994 - No.7, 1995? ($2.50, B&W)
1-7: 1-Silver foil-c 2.50

ASSASSINETTE HARDCORE
Pocket Change Comics: 1995 - No.2, 1995 ($2.50, B&W, limited series)
1,2 2.50

ASSASSINS
DC Comics (Amalgam): Apr, 1996 ($1.95)
1 2.00

ASSASSINS, INC.
Silverline Comics: 1987 - No. 2, 1987 ($1.95)
1,2 2.00

ASTER
Entity Comics: Oct, 1994 - No. 4, 1995 ($2.95)
0-4: 1,3,4-Foil Logo. 2-Foil-c. 3-Variant-c exists. 3.00

ASTER: THE LAST CELESTIAL KNIGHT
Entity Comics: 1995 - No. 3, 1996 ($2.50)
1-3 2.50

ASTONISHING (Formerly Marvel Boy No. 1, 2)
Marvel/Atlas Comics(20CC): No. 3, Apr, 1951 - No. 63, Aug, 1957
3-Marvel Boy continues; 3-5-Marvel Boy-c 90.00 268.00 850.00
4-6-Last Marvel Boy; 4-Stan Lee app. 63.00 189.00 600.00
7-10: 7-Maneely s/f story. 10-Sinnott s/f story 31.00 94.00 250.00
11,12,15,17,20 28.00 83.00 220.00
13,14,16,18,19-Krigstein-a. 18-Jack The Ripper sty 28.00 84.00 225.00
21,22,24 24.00 73.00 195.00
23-E.C. swipe "The Hole In The Wall" from Vault Of Horror #16 24.00 73.00 195.00
25,29: 25-Crandall-a. 29-Decapitation-c 22.00 66.00 175.00
26-28 20.00 60.00 160.00
30-Tentacled eyeball-c/story; classic-c 28.00 84.00 225.00
31-37-Last pre-code issue 18.00 54.00 145.00
38-43,46,48-52,56,58,59,61 13.00 39.00 105.00
44,45,47,53-55,57,60: 44-Crandall swipe/Weird Fantasy #22. 45,47-Krigstein-a. 53-Ditko-a. 54-Torres-a, 55-Crandall, Torres-a. 57-Williamson/Krenkel-a (4 pgs.). 60-Williamson/Mayo-a (4 pgs.) 14.00 43.00 115.00
62,63: 62-Torres, Powell-a. 63-Woodbridge-a 14.00 41.00 110.00
NOTE: ***Ayers*** *a-16.* ***Berg*** *a-36, 53, 56.* ***Cameron*** *a-50.* ***Gene Colan*** *a-12, 20, 29, 56.* ***Ditko*** *a-5* ***Drucker*** *a-41, 62.* ***Everett*** *a-3-6(3), 6, 10, 12, 37, 47, 48, 58; c-3-5, 13,15, 16, 18, 29, 47, 49, 5 53-55, 57, 59-63.* ***Fass*** *a-11, 34.* ***Forte*** *a-53, 58, 60.* ***Fuje*** *a-11.* ***Heath*** *a-8, 29; c-8, 9, 19, 22, 2 26.* ***Kirby*** *a-56.* ***Lawrence*** *a-28, 37, 38, 42.* ***Maneely*** *a-7(2); c-7, 31, 33, 34, 56.* ***Moldoff*** *a-3* ***Morisi*** *a-10, 60.* ***Morrow*** *a-52, 61.* ***Orlando*** *a-47, 58, 61.* ***Pakula*** *a-10.* ***Powell*** *a-43, 44, 4* ***Ravielli*** *a-28.* ***Reinman*** *a-32, 34, 38.* ***Robinson*** *a-20.* ***J. Romita*** *a-7, 18, 24, 43, 57,6* ***Roussos*** *a-55.* ***Sale*** *a-28, 38, 59; c-32.* ***Sekowsky*** *a-13.* ***Severin*** *c-46.* ***Shores*** *a-16, 60.* ***Sinno*** *a-11, 30.* ***Whitney*** *a-13.* ***Ed Win*** *a-20. Canadian reprints exist.*

ASTONISHING TALES (See Ka-Zar)
Marvel Comics Group: Aug, 1970 - No. 36, July, 1976 (#1-7: 15¢; #8: 25¢)
1-Ka-Zar (by Kirby(p) #1,2; by B. Smith #3-6) & Dr. Doom (by Wood #1-4; by Tuska #5,6; by Colan #7,8; 1st Marvel villain solo series) double feature begins; Kraven the Hunter-c/story; Nixon cameo 3.65 11.00 40.00
2-Kraven the Hunter-c/story; Kirby, Wood-a 2.30 7.00 20.00
3-6: B. Smith-p; Wood-a-#3,4. 5,6-Red Skull 2-part story 2.80 8.40 28.00
7-Last 15¢ issue; Black Panther app. 2.00 6.00 16.00
8-(25¢, 52 pgs.)-Last Dr. Doom of series 2.50 7.50 23.00
9-All Ka-Zar issues begin; Lorna-r/Lorna #14 1.75 5.25 14.00
10-B. Smith/Sal Buscema-a. 2.00 6.00 18.00
11-Origin Ka-Zar & Zabu; death of Ka-Zar's father 2.00 6.00 16.00
12-2nd app.Man-Thing; by Neal Adams (see Savage Tales #1 for 1st app.) 2.50 7.50 23.00
13-3rd app.Man-Thing 2.00 6.00 18.00
14-20: 14-Jann of the Jungle-r (1950s); reprints censored Ka-Zar-s from Savage Tales #1. 17-S.H.I.E.L.D. begins. 19-Starlin-a(p). 20-Last Ka-Zar (continues into 1974 Ka-Zar series) 1.00 3.00 8.00
21-(12/73)-It! the Living Colossus begins, ends #24 (see Supernatural Thrillers #1) 2.30 7.00 20.00
22-24: 23,24-IT vs. Fin Fang Foom 1.75 5.25 14.00
25-1st app. Deathlok the Demolisher; full length stories begin, end #36; Perez's 1st work, 2 pgs. (8/74) 3.00 9.00 30.00
26-28,30 1.00 3.00 8.00
29-r/origin/1st app. Guardians of the Galaxy from Marvel Super-Heroes #18 plus-c w/4 pgs. omitted; no Deathlok story 1.00 3.00 8.00
31-34: 31-Watcher-r/Silver Surfer #3 1.00 2.80 7.00
35,36-(Regular 25¢ edition)(5,7/76) 1.00 2.80 7.00
35,36-(30¢-c, low distribution) 1.50 4.50 12.00
NOTE: ***Buckler*** *a-13i, 16p, 25, 26p, 27p, 28, 29p-36p; c-13, 25p, 26-30, 32-35p, 36.* ***Joh Buscema*** *a-9, 12p-14p, 16p; c-4-6p, 12p.* ***Colan*** *a-7p, 8p.* ***Ditko*** *a-21r.* ***Everett*** *a-6i.* ***G. Kane*** *a 11p, 15p; c-9, 10p, 11p, 14, 15p, 21p.* ***McWilliams*** *a-30i.* ***Starlin*** *a-19p; c-16p.* ***Sutton & Trimp*** *a-8.* ***Tuska*** *a-5p, 6p, 8p.* ***Wood*** *a-1-4.* ***Wrightson*** *c-31i.*

ASTONISHING X-MEN
Marvel Comics: Mar, 1995 - No.4, July, 1995 ($1.95, limited series)
1-Age of Apocalypse; Magneto-c 4.00
2-4 3.00

ASTONISHING X-MEN
Marvel Comics: Sept, 1999 - No.3, Nov, 1999 ($2.50, limited series)
1-3-New team, Cable & X-Man app.; Peterson-a 2.50
TPB (11/00, $15.95) r/#1-3, X-Men #92 & #95, Uncanny X-Men #375 15.95

ASTOUNDING SPACE THRILLS: THE COMIC BOOK
Image Comics: Apr, 2000 - Present ($2.95, limited series)

The Atom #7 © DC

Atom-Age Combat #3 © Fago Magazines

Atomic Comics #4 © Green Publ. Co.

GD2.0 FN6.0 NM9.4

1-3-Steve Conley-s/a. 2,3-Flip book w/Crater Kid — 2.95

ASTRO BOY (TV) (See March of Comics #285 & The Original...)
Gold Key: August, 1965 (12¢)
1(10151-508)-Scarce;1st app. Astro Boy in comics 43.00 — 130.00 — 520.00

ASTRO CITY (See Kurt Busiek's Astro City)

ASYLUM
Millennium Publications: 1993 ($2.50)
1-3: 1-Bolton-c/a; Russell 2-pg. illos — 2.50

ASYLUM
Maximum Press: Dec, 1995 - No. 11, Jan, 1997 ($2.95/$2.99, anthology) (#1-6 are flip books)
1-10: 1-Warchild by Art Adams, Beanworld, Avengelyne, Battlestar Galactica. 2-Intro Mike Deodato's Deathkiss; Cybrid story begins, ends #5. 4-1st app.Christian; painted Battlestar Galactica story begins. 5-Intro Black Seed (formerly Black Flag) by Dan Fraga; B&W Christian story. 6-Intro Bionix (Six Million Dollar Man & the Bionic Woman). 7-Begin $2.99-c; Don Simpson's Megaton Man; Black Seed pinup. 8-B&W-a. 9- Foot Soldiers & Kid Supreme. 10-Lady Supreme by Terry Moore-c/app. — 4.00

ATARI FORCE (Also see Promotional comics section)
DC Comics: Jan, 1984 - No. 20, Aug, 1985 (Mando paper)
1-20: 1-(1/84)-Intro Tempest, Packrat, Babe, Morphea, & Dart — 2.00
Special 1 (4/86) — 2.00
NOTE: ***Byrne*** *c-Special 1i.* ***Giffen*** *a-12p, 13i.* ***Rogers*** *a-18p, Special 1p.*

A-TEAM, THE (TV) (Also see Marvel Graphic Novel)
Marvel Comics Group: Mar, 1984 - No. 3, May, 1984
1-3 — 3.00
1,2-(Whitman bagged set) w/75¢-c — 1.00 — 3.00 — 8.00
3-(Whitman, no bag) w/75¢-c — 1.00 — 2.80 — 7.00

ATLANTIS CHRONICLES, THE (Also see Aquaman, 3rd Series & Aquaman: Time & Tide)
DC Comics: Mar, 1990 - No. 7, Sept, 1990 ($2.95, limited series, 52 pgs.)
1-7: 1-Peter David scripts. 7-True origin of Aquaman; nudity panels — 3.25

ATLANTIS, THE LOST CONTINENT
Dell Publishing Co.: May, 1961
Four Color #1188-Movie, photo-c — 10.00 — 30.00 — 120.00

ATLAS (See 1st Issue Special)

ATLAS
Dark Horse Comics: Feb, 1994 - No. 4, 1994 ($2.50, limited series)
1-4 — 2.50

ATOM, THE (See Action #425, All-American #19, Brave & the Bold, D.C. Special Series #1, Detective, Flash Comics #80, Power Of The Atom, Showcase #34 -36 , Super Friends, Sword of The Atom, Teen Titans & World's Finest)

ATOM, THE (...& the Hawkman No. 39 on)
National Periodical Publ.: June-July, 1962 - No. 38, Aug-Sept, 1968
1-(6-7/62)-Intro Plant-Master; 1st app. Maya — 68.00 — 204.00 — 950.00
2 — 31.00 — 93.00 — 350.00
3-1st Time Pool story; 1st app. Chronos (origin) — 20.50 — 61.00 — 225.00
4,5: 4-Snapper Carr x-over — 16.00 — 48.00 — 175.00
6,9,10 — 11.00 — 33.00 — 120.00
7-Hawkman x-over (6-7/63; 1st Atom & Hawkman team-up); 1st app. Hawkman since Brave & the Bold tryouts — 27.50 — 82.00 — 300.00
8-Justice League, Dr. Light app. — 12.00 — 36.00 — 130.00
11-15: 13-Chronos-c/story — 7.25 — 21.75 — 80.00
16-20: 19-Zatanna x-over — 5.45 — 16.35 — 60.00
21-28,30: 28-Chronos-c/story — 4.35 — 13.00 — 48.00
29-1st solo Golden Age Atom x-over in S.A. — 14.50 — 43.50 — 160.00
31-35,37,38: 31-Hawkman x-over. 37-Intro. Major Mynah; Hawkman cameo — 4.35 — 13.00 — 48.00
36-G.A. Atom x-over — 5.45 — 16.35 — 60.00
NOTE: ***Anderson*** *a-1-11i, 13i; c-inks-1-25, 31-35, 37.* ***Sid Greene*** *a-8i-37i.* ***Gil Kane*** *a-1p-37p; c-1p-28p, 29, 33p, 34.* ***George Roussos*** *38i* ***Mike Sekowsky*** *38p Time Pool stories also in 6, 9,12, 17, 21, 27, 35.*

ATOM, THE (See Tangent Comics/ The Atom)

ATOM AGE (See Classics Illustrated Special Issue)

ATOM-AGE COMBAT
St. John Publishing Co.: June, 1952 - No. 5, Apr, 1953; Feb, 1958
1-Buck Vinson in all — 44.00 — 133.00 — 400.00
2-Flying saucer story — 28.00 — 83.00 — 220.00
3,5: 3-Mayo-a (6 pgs.). 5-Flying saucer-c/story — 23.00 — 68.00 — 180.00
4 (Scarce) — 28.00 — 83.00 — 220.00
1(2/58-St. John) — 19.00 — 56.00 — 150.00

ATOM-AGE COMBAT
Fago Magazines: No. 2, Jan, 1959 - No. 3, Mar, 1959
2-A-Bomb explosion-c; — 25.00 — 75.00 — 200.00
3 — 19.00 — 56.00 — 150.00

ATOMAN
Spark Publications: Feb, 1946 - No. 2, April, 1946
1-Origin & 1st app. Atoman; Robinson/Meskin-a; Kidcrusaders, Wild Bill Hickok, Marvin the Great app. — 59.00 — 177.00 — 560.00
2-Robinson/Meskin-a; Robinson c-1,2 — 42.00 — 125.00 — 375.00

ATOM & HAWKMAN, THE (Formerly The Atom)
National Periodical Publ: No. 39, Oct-Nov, 1968 - No. 45, Oct-Nov, 1969
39-43: 40-41-Kubert/Anderson-a. 43-(7/69)-Last 12¢ issue; 1st app. Gentleman Ghost — 3.80 — 11.40 — 42.00
44,45: 44-(9/69)-1st 15¢-c; origin Gentleman Ghost — 3.80 — 11.40 — 42.00
NOTE: ***M. Anderson*** *a-39, 40i, 41i, 43, 44.* ***Sid Greene*** *a-40i-45i.* ***Kubert*** *a-40p, 41p; c-39-45.*

ATOM ANT (TV) (See Golden Comics Digest #2) (Hanna-Barbera)
Gold Key: January, 1966 (12¢)
1(10170-601)-1st app. Atom Ant, Precious Pup, and Hillbilly Bears — 29.00 — 87.00 — 350.00

ATOM ANT & SECRET SQUIRREL
Archie Publications: Nov, 1995 - No. 12 ($1.50, bi-monthly)
1-12-Hanna-Barbera characters — 2.50

ATOMIC AGE
Marvel Comics (Epic Comics): Nov, 1990 - No. 4, Feb, 1991 ($4.50, limited series, squarebound, 52 pgs.)
1-4: Williamson-a(i); sci-fi story set in 1957 — 4.50

ATOMIC ATTACK (True War Stories; formerly Attack, first series)
Youthful Magazines: No. 5, Jan, 1953 - No. 8, Oct, 1953 (1st story is sci/fi in all issues)
5-Atomic bomb-c; science fiction stories in all — 40.00 — 120.00 — 325.00
6-8 — 25.00 — 75.00 — 200.00

ATOMIC BOMB
Jay Burtis Publications: 1945 (36 pgs.)
1-Airmale & Stampy (scarce) — 58.00 — 174.00 — 550.00

ATOMIC BUNNY (Formerly Atomic Rabbit)
Charlton Comics: No. 12, Aug, 1958 - No. 19, Dec, 1959
12 — 11.00 — 33.00 — 90.00
13-19 — 7.00 — 21.00 — 48.00

ATOMIC COMICS
Daniels Publications (Canadian): Jan, 1946 (Reprints, one-shot)
1-Rocketman, Yankee Boy, Master Key app. — 36.00 — 108.00 — 290.00

ATOMIC COMICS
Green Publishing Co.: Jan, 1946 - No. 4, July-Aug, 1946 (#1-4 were printed w/o cover gloss)
1-Radio Squad by Siegel & Shuster; Barry O'Neal app.; Fang Gow cover-r/ Detective Comics (Classic-c) — 134.00 — 400.00 — 1275.00
2-Inspector Dayton; Kid Kane by Matt Baker; Lucky Wings, Congo King, Prop Powers (only app.) begin — 62.00 — 186.00 — 590.00
3,4: 3-Zero Ghost Detective app.; Baker-a(2) each; 4-Baker-c — 42.00 — 126.00 — 375.00

ATOMIC KNIGHTS (See Strange Adventures #117)

ATOMIC MOUSE (TV, Movies) (See Blue Bird, Funny Animals, Giant Comics Edition & Wotalife Comics)

Atomic Rabbit #4 © CC

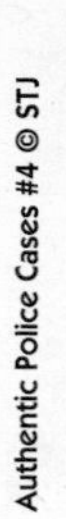

Authentic Police Cases #4 © STJ

The Authority #11 © WSP

Capitol Stories/Charlton Comics: 3/53 - No. 54, 6/63; No. 1, 12/84; V2#10, 19/85 - No. 12, 1/86

1-Origin & 1st app.; Al Fago-c/a in all? 31.00 94.00 250.00
2 12.00 36.00 95.00
3-10: 5-Timmy The Timid Ghost app.; see Zoo Funnies 10.00 30.00 75.00
11-13,16-25 5.50 16.50 38.00
14,15-Hoppy The Marvel Bunny app. 7.85 23.50 55.00
26-(68 pgs.) 10.00 30.00 80.00
27-40: 36,37-Atom The Cat app. 5.00 15.00 32.00
41-54 3.60 9.00 18.00
1 (1984)-Low print run 2.40 6.00
V2#10 (9/85) -12(1/86)-Low print run 5.00

ATOMIC RABBIT (Atomic Bunny #12 on; see Giant Comics #3 & Wotalife)
Charlton Comics: Aug, 1955 - No. 11, Mar, 1958

1-Origin & 1st app.; Al Fago-c/a in all? 28.00 83.00 220.00
2 11.00 33.00 90.00
3-10 7.85 23.50 55.00
11-(68 pgs.) 11.00 33.00 90.00

ATOMICS, THE
AAA Pop Comics: Jan, 2000 - Present ($2.95)

1-11-Mike Allred-s/a; 1-Madman-c/app. 2.95
...King-Size Giant Spectacular: Jigsaw (2000, $10.00) r/#1-4 10.00

ATOMIC SPY CASES
Avon Periodicals: Mar-Apr, 1950 (Painted-c)

1-No Wood-a; A-bomb blast panels; Fass-a 32.00 96.00 255.00

ATOMIC THUNDERBOLT, THE
Regor Company: Feb, 1946 (one-shot)

1-Intro. Atomic Thunderbolt & Mr. Murdo 58.00 174.00 550.00

ATOMIC TOYBOX
Image Comics: Dec, 1999 - Present ($2.95)

1- Aaron Lopresti-c/s/a 2.95

ATOMIC WAR!
Ace Periodicals (Junior Books): Nov, 1952 - No. 4, Apr, 1953

1-Atomic bomb-c 87.00 261.00 825.00
2,3: 3-Atomic bomb-c 57.00 171.00 540.00
4-Used in **POP**, pg. 96 & illo. 57.00 171.00 540.00

ATOMIK ANGELS
Crusade Comics: May, 1996 - No. 4, Nov. 1996 ($2.50)

1-4: 1-Freefall from Gen 13 app. 3.00
1-Variant-c 4.00
Intrep-Edition (2/96, B&W, giveaway at launch party)-Previews Atomik Angels #1; includes Billy Tucci interview. 4.00

ATOM SPECIAL (See Atom & Justice League of America)
DC Comics: 1993/1995 ($2.50/$2.95)(68pgs.)

1,2: 1-Dillon-c/a. 2-McDonnell-a/Bolland-c/Peyer-s 3.00

ATOM THE CAT (Formerly Tom Cat; see Giant Comics #3)
Charlton Comics: No. 9, Oct, 1957 - No. 17, Aug, 1959

9 9.30 28.00 65.00
10,13-17 5.00 15.00 35.00
11,12: 11(64 pgs)-Atomic Mouse app. 12(100 pgs.) 10.50 32.00 85.00

ATTACK
Youthful Mag./Trojan No. 5 on: May, 1952 - No. 4, Nov, 1952; No. 5, Jan, 1953 - No. 5, Sept, 1953

1-(1st series)-Extreme violence 30.00 90.00 240.00
2,3-Both Harrison-c/a; bondage, whipping 15.00 45.00 120.00
4-Krenkel-a (7 pgs.); Harrison-a (becomes Atomic Attack #5 on) 15.00 45.00 120.00
5-(#1, Trojan, 2nd series) 12.00 36.00 95.00
6-8 (#2-4), 5 9.30 28.00 65.00

ATTACK
Charlton Comics: No. 54, 1958 - No. 60, Nov, 1959

54 (25¢, 100 pgs.) 10.00 30.00 80.00
55-60 4.65 14.00 28.00

ATTACK!
Charlton Comics: 1962 - No. 15, 3/75; No. 16, 8/79 - No. 48, 10/84

nn(#1)-('62) Special Edition 3.45 10.35 38.00
2('63), 3(Fall, '64) 2.50 7.50 25.00
V4#3(10/66), 4(10/67)-(Formerly Special War Series #2; becomes Attack At Sea V4#5) 2.30 7.00 20.00
1(9/71) 2.30 7.00 20.00
2-5: 4-American Eagle app. 1.50 4.50 12.00
6-15(3/75): 1.10 3.30 9.00
16(8/79) - 40 3.00
41-47 Low print run 4.00
48(10/84)-Wood-r; S&K-c 2.40 6.00
Modern Comics 13('78)-r 3.00
NOTE: ***Sutton** a-9,10,13.*

ATTACK!
Spire Christian Comics (Fleming H. Revell Co.): 1975 (39¢/49¢, 36 pgs.)

nn 2.40 6.00

ATTACK AT SEA (Formerly Attack!, 1967)
Charlton Comics: V4#5, Oct, 1968

V4#5 2.30 7.00 20.00

ATTACK ON PLANET MARS (See Strange Worlds #18)
Avon Periodicals: 1951

nn-Infantino, Fawcette, Kubert & Wood-a; adaptation of Tarrano the Conqueror by Ray Cummings 74.00 221.00 700.00

ATTITUDE LAD
Slave Labor Graphics: Apr, 1994 - No. 3, Nov, 1994 ($2.95, B&W)

1-3 3.00

AUDREY & MELVIN (Formerly Little...)(See Little Audrey & Melvin)
Harvey Publications: No. 62, Sept, 1974

62 1.25 3.75 10.00

AUGIE DOGGIE (TV) (See Hanna-Barbera Band Wagon, Quick-Draw McGraw, Spotlight #2, Top Cat & Whitman Comic Books)
Gold Key: October, 1963 (12¢)

1-Hanna-Barbera character 17.50 52.00 210.00

AUTHENTIC POLICE CASES
St. John Publishing Co.: 2/48 - No. 6, 11/48; No. 7, 5/50 - No. 38, 3/55

1-Hale the Magician by Tuska begins 42.00 125.00 375.00
2-Lady Satan, Johnny Rebel app. 26.00 77.00 205.00
3-Veiled Avenger app.; blood drainage story plus 2 Lucky Coyne stories; used in **SOTI**, illo. from Red Seal #16 44.00 133.00 400.00
4,5: 4-Masked Black Jack app. 5-Late 1930s Jack Cole-a(r); transvestism story 26.00 79.00 210.00
6-Matt Baker-c; used in **SOTI**, illo- "An invitation to learning", r-in Fugitives From Justice #3; Jack Cole-a; also used by the N.Y. Legis. Comm. 47.00 140.00 420.00
7,8,10-14: 7-Jack Cole-a; Matt Baker-a begins #8, ends #?; Vic Flint in #10-14. 10-12-Baker-a(2 each) 22.00 66.00 175.00
9-No Vic Flint 17.00 51.00 135.00
15-Drug-c/story; Vic Flint app.; Baker-c 21.00 62.00 165.00
16,18,20,21,23: Baker-a(i) 13.00 39.00 105.00
17,19,22-Baker-c 15.00 43.00 115.00
24-28 (All 100 pgs.): 26-Transvestism 28.00 83.00 220.00
29-32 8.65 26.00 60.00
33-38: 33-Transvestism; Baker-c. 34-Baker-c; r/#9. 35-Baker-c/a(2); r/#10 36-r/#11; Vic Flint strip-r; Baker-c/a(2) unsigned. 37-Baker-c; r/#17. 38-Baker-c/a; r/#18 12.00 36.00 95.00
NOTE: ***Matt Baker** c-6-16, 17, 19, 22, 27, 29, 31-38; a-13, 16. Bondage c-1, 3.*

AUTHORITY, THE (See Stormwatch and Jenny Sparks: The Secret History of...)
DC Comics (WildStorm): May, 1999 - Present ($2.50)

1-Wraparound-c; Warren Ellis-s/Bryan Hitch and Paul Neary-a 6.00
2-4 5.00
5-12: 12-Death of Jenny Sparks 4.00

Avataars: Covenant of the Shield #1 © MAR

The Avengers #1 © GK

The Avengers #11 © MAR

13-16: Millar-s begins;Quitely & Scott-a; Authority vs. Marvel-esque villains 3.00
17-22: 17,18-Weston-a. 19,20,22-Quitely-a. 21-McCrea-a 2.50
Annual 2000 ($3.50) Devil's Night x-over; Hamner-a/Bermejo-c 3.50
... :Relentless TPB (2000, $17.95) r/#1-8 17.95
... :Under New Management TPB (2000, $17.95) r/#9-16; new Quitely-c 17.95

AUTOMATON
Image Comics (Flypaper Press): Sept, 1998 - No. 3, 1998 ($2.95, lim. series)
1-3-R.A. Jones-s/Peter Vale-a 3.00

AUTUMN
Caliber Comics: 1995 - No. 3, 1995 ($2.95, B&W)
1-3 3.00

AUTUMN ADVENTURES (Walt Disney's...)
Disney Comics: Autumn, 1990; No. 2, Autumn, 1991 ($2.95, 68 pgs.)
1-Donald Duck-r(2) by Barks, Pluto-r, & new-a 4.00
2-D. Duck-r by Barks; new Super Goof story 4.00

AVATAARS: COVENANT OF THE SHIELD
Marvel Comics: Sept, 2000 - No. 3, Nov, 2000 ($2.99, limited series)
1-3-Kaminski-s/Oscar Jimenez-a 3.00

AVATAR
DC Comics: Feb, 1991 - No. 3, Apr, 1991 ($5.95, limited series, 100 pgs.)
1-3: Based on TSR's Forgotten Realms 2.40 6.00

AVENGEBLADE
Maximum Press: July, 1996 - No. 2, Aug, 1996 ($2.99, limited series)
1,2: Bad Girls parody 3.00

AVENGELYNE
Maximum Press: May, 1995 - No. 3, July, 1995 ($2.50/$3.50, limited series)
1/2 1.85 5.50 15.00
1/2 Platinum 20.00
1-Newstand ($2.50)-Photo-c; poster insert 1.00 3.00 8.00
1-Direct Market ($3.50)-Chromium-c; poster 1.10 3.30 9.00
1-Glossy edition 3.00 9.00 30.00
1-Gold 15.00
2-3: 2-Polybagged w/card 4.00
3-Variant-c; Deodato pin-up 2.40 6.00
..Swimsuit (8/95, $2.95)-Pin-ups/photos. 3-Variant-c exist (2 photo, 1 Liefeld-a) 5.00
..Swimsuit (1/96, $3.50, 2nd printing)-photo-c 5.00
Trade paperback (12/95, $9.95) 10.00

AVENGELYNE
Maximum Press: V2#1, Apr, 1996 - No. 14, Apr, 1997 ($2.95/$2.50)
V2#1-Four covers exist (2 photo-c). 5.00
V2#2-Three covers exist (1 photo-c); flip book w/Darkchylde 2.25 6.75 18.00
V2#0, 3-14: 0-(10/96).3-Flip book w/Priest preview. 4-Cybrid app; w/Darkchylde/Avengelyne poster. 5-Flip book w/Blindside. 6-Divinity-c/app. 4.00
..Bible (10/96, $3.50) 3.50

AVENGELYNE (Volume 3)
Awesome Comics: Mar, 1999 ($2.50)
1-Fraga & Liefeld-a 2.50

AVENGELYNE: ARMAGEDDON
Maximum Press: Dec, 1996 - No. 3, Feb, 1997 ($2.99, limited series)
1-3-Scott Clark-a(p) 4.00

AVENGELYNE: DEADLY SINS
Maximum Press: Feb, 1996 - No. 2, Mar, 1996 ($2.95, limited series)
1,2: 1-Two-c exist (1 photo, 1 Liefeld-a). 2-Liefeld-c; Pop Mhan-a(p). 3.00

AVENGELYNE/GLORY
Maximum Press: Sept, 1995 ($3.95, one-shot)
1-Chromium-c 5.00
1-Variant-c 2.40 6.00

AVENGELYNE/GLORY: GODYSSEY, THE (See Glory/...)
Maximum Press: Sept, 1996 ($2.99, one-shot)
1-Two covers (1 photo) 3.00

AVENGELYNE/GLORY SWIMSUIT SPECIAL
Maximum Press: June, 1996 ($2.95)
1-Pin-ups & photos of Avengelyne and Glory; photo-c (variant illos-c. also exists) 4.00

AVENGELYNE/POWER
Maximum Press: Nov, 1995 - No.3, Jan, 1996 ($2.95, limited series)
1-3: 1,2-Liefeld-c. 3-Three variant-c. exist (1 photo-c) 3.00
1-Variant-c 3.50

AVENGELYNE • PROPHET
Maximum Press: May, 1996; No. 2, Feb. 1997 ($2.95, unfinished lim. series)
1,2-Liefeld-c/a(p) 3.00

AVENGELYNE/ WARRIOR NUN AREALA (See Warrior Nun/...)
Maximum Press: Nov, 1996 ($2.99, one-shot)
1 4.00

AVENGER, THE (See A-1 Comics)
Magazine Enterprises: Feb-Mar, 1955 - No. 4, Aug-Sept, 1955
1(A-1 #129)-Origin 40.00 129.00 320.00
2(A-1 #131), 3(A-1 #133) Robot-c, 4(A-1 #138) 26.00 79.00 210.00
IW Reprint #9('64)-Reprints #1 (new cover) 2.80 8.40 28.00
NOTE: ***Powell** a-2-4; c-1-4.*

AVENGERS, THE (TV)(Also see Steed and Mrs. Peel)
Gold Key: Nov, 1968 ("John Steed & Emma Peel" cover title) (15¢)
1-Photo-c 23.00 68.00 270.00
1-(rare variant with photo back-c) 28.00 85.00 340.00

AVENGERS, THE (See Essential..., Giant-Size..., Kree/Skrull War Starring..., Marvel Graphic Novel #27, Marvel Super Action, Marvel Super Heroes('66), Marvel Treasury Ed., Marvel Triple Action, Solo Avengers, Tales Of Suspense #49, West Coast Avengers & X-Men Vs....)

AVENGERS, THE (The Mighty Avengers on cover only #63-69)
Marvel Comics Group: Sept, 1963 - No. 402, Sept, 1996
1-Origin & 1st app. The Avengers (Thor, Iron Man, Hulk, Ant-Man, Wasp); Loki app. 214.00 642.00 3200.00
2-Hulk leaves Avengers 54.00 161.00 750.00
3-1st Sub-Mariner x-over (outside the F.F.); Hulk & Sub-Mariner team-up & battle Avengers; Spider-Man cameo (1/64) 37.00 112.00 450.00
4-Revival of Captain America who joins the Avengers; 1st Silver Age app. of Captain America & Bucky (3/64) 143.00 429.00 2000.00
4-Reprint from the Golden Record Comic set 9.00 27.00 100.00
With Record (1966) 13.50 40.00 150.00
5-Hulk app. 24.50 74.00 270.00
6-8: 6-Intro/1st app. original Zemo & his Masters of Evil. 8-Intro Kang 19.50 58.00 215.00
9-Intro Wonder Man who dies in same story 20.50 61.00 225.00
10-Intro/1st app. Immortus; early Hercules app. (11/64) 17.50 52.00 190.00
11-Spider-Man-c & x-over (12/64) 20.50 61.00 225.00
12-15: 15-Death of original Zemo 12.50 37.00 135.00
16-New Avengers line-up (Hawkeye, Quicksilver, Scarlet Witch join; Thor, Iron Man, Giant-Man, Wasp leave) 13.00 39.00 145.00
17-19: 19-Intro/1st app. Swordsman; origin Hawkeye (8/65) 9.00 27.00 100.00
20-22: Wood inks 5.90 17.75 65.00
23-30: 23-Romita Sr. inks (1st Silver Age Marvel work). 25-Dr. Doom-c/story. 28-Giant-Man becomes Goliath (5/66) 4.35 13.00 48.00
31-40 3.20 9.60 35.00
41-46,49-52,54-56: 43,44-1st app. Red Guardian. 46-Ant-Man returns (re-intro, 11/67). 52-Black Panther joins; 1st app. The Grim Reaper. 54-1st app. new Masters of Evil. 56-Zemo app; story explains how Capt. America became imprisoned in ice during WWII, only to be rescued in Avengers #4 3.00 9.00 30.00
47-Magneto-c/story 3.20 9.60 35.00
48-Origin/1st app. new Black Knight (1/68) 3.00 9.00 32.00
53-X-Men app. 3.80 11.40 42.00

The Avengers #160 © MAR

The Avengers #200 © MAR

The Avengers #267 © MAR

GD2.0 FN6.0 NM9.4

57-1st app. S.A. Vision (10/68) 7.65 23.00 85.00
58-Origin The Vision 5.00 15.00 55.00
59-65: 59-Intro. Yellowjacket. 60-Wasp & Yellowjacket wed. 63-Goliath becomes Yellowjacket; Hawkeye becomes the new Goliath. 65-Last 12¢ issue 2.60 7.80 26.00
66,67-B. Smith-a 3.00 9.00 30.00
68-70: 70-Nighthawk on cover 2.40 7.35 22.00
71-1st app. The Invaders (12/69); 1st app. Nighthawk; Black Knight joins 3.65 11.00 40.00
72-79,81,82,84-86,89-91: 82-Daredevil app 2.30 7.00 20.00
80-Intro. Red Wolf (9/70) 2.60 7.80 26.00
83-Intro. The Liberators (Wasp, Valkyrie, Scarlet Witch, Medusa & the Black Widow) 2.80 8.40 28.00
87-Origin The Black Panther 3.00 9.00 32.00
88-Written by Harlan Ellison 2.40 7.35 22.00
92-Last 15¢ issue; Neal Adams-c 2.50 7.50 24.00
93-(52 pgs.)-Neal Adams-c/a 5.90 17.75 65.00
94-96-Neal Adams-c/a 3.65 11.00 40.00
97-G.A. Capt. America, Sub-Mariner, Human Torch, Patriot, Vision, Blazing Skull, Fin, Angel, & new Capt. Marvel x-over 2.50 7.50 24.00
98,99: 98-Goliath becomes Hawkeye; Smith c/a(i). 99-Smith-c, Smith/Sutton-a 2.60 7.80 26.00
100-(6/72)-Smith-c/a; featuring everyone who was an Avenger 7.25 21.75 80.00
101-Harlan Ellison scripts 2.00 6.00 16.00
102-106,108,109 1.75 5.25 14.00
107-Starlin-a(p) 2.00 6.00 16.00
110,111-X-Men app. 2.50 7.50 25.00
112-1st app. Mantis 2.00 6.00 18.00
113-115,119-124,126-130: 123-Origin Mantis 1.50 4.50 12.00
116-118-Defenders/Silver Surfer app. 2.30 7.00 20.00
125-Thanos-c & brief app. 2.00 6.00 18.00
131-133,136-140: 136-Ploog-r/Amazing Advs. #12 1.10 3.30 9.00
134,135-True origin Vision 1.50 4.50 12.00
141-143,145,152-163 1.00 2.80 7.00
144-Origin & 1st app. Hellcat 1.50 4.50 12.00
146-149-(Reg.25¢ editions)(4-7/76) 1.00 2.80 7.00
146-149-(30¢-c variants, limited distribution) 1.75 5.25 14.00
150-Kirby-a(r); new line-up: Capt. America, Scarlet Witch, Iron Man, Wasp, Yellowjacket, Vision & The Beast 1.10 3.30 9.00
150-(30¢-c variant, limited distribution) 2.00 6.00 18.00
151-Wonder Man returns w/new costume 1.10 3.30 9.00
160-164-(35¢-c variants, limited dist.)(6-10/77) 1.75 5.25 14.00
164-166: Byrne-a 1.00 3.00 8.00
167-180: 168-Guardians of the Galaxy app. 174-Thanos cameo. 176-Starhawk app. 5.00
181-191-Byrne-a: 181-New line-up: Capt. America, Scarlet Witch, Iron Man, Wasp, Vision, Beast & The Falcon. 183-Ms. Marvel joins. 185-Origin Quicksilver & Scarlet Witch 2.40 6.00
192-199,201-213,217-238,241-249, 251-262: 195-1st Taskmaster. 211-New line-up: Capt. America, Iron Man, Tigra, Thor, Wasp & Yellowjacket. 213-Yellowjacket leaves. 217-Yellowjacket & Wasp return. 221-Hawkeye & She-Hulk join. 227-Capt. Marvel (female) joins; origins of Ant-Man, Wasp, Giant-Man, Goliath, Yellowjacket, & Avengers. 230-Yellowjacket quits. 231-Iron Man leaves. 232-Starfox (Eros) joins. 234-Origin Quicksilver, Scarlet Witch. 236-New logo. 238-Origin Blackout 3.00
200-(10/80, 52 pgs.)-Ms. Marvel leaves. 5.00
214-Ghost Rider-c/story 2.40 6.00
215,216,239,240,250: 215,216-Silver Surfer app. 216-Tigra leaves. 239-(1/84) Avengers app. on David Letterman show. 240-Spider-Woman revived. 250-($1.00, 52 pgs.) 4.00
263-1st app. X-Factor (1/86)(story continues in Fant. Four #286) 2.40 6.00
264-299: 272-Alpha Flight app. 291-$1.00 issues begin. 297-Black Knight, She-Hulk & Thor resign. 298-Inferno tie-in 3.00
300 (2/89, $1.75, 68 pgs.)-Thor joins; Simonson-a 4.00
301-304,306-313,319-325,327,329-343: 302-Re-intro Quasar. 320-324-Alpha Flight app. (320-cameo). 327-2nd app. Rage. 341,342-New Warriors app. 343-Last $1.00-c 2.50
305,314-318: 305-Byrne scripts begin. 314-318-Spider-Man x-over 3.00

GD2.0 FN6.0 NM9

326-1st app. Rage (11/90) 4.0
328,344-349,351-359,361,362,364,365,367: 328-Origin Rage. 365-Contains coupon for Hunt for Magneto contest 2.0
350-($2.50, 68 pgs.)-Double gatefold-c showing-c to #1; r/#53 w/cover in flip book format; vs. The Starjammers 3.0
360-($2.95, 52 pgs.)-Embossed all-foil-c; 30th ann. 4.0
363-($2.95, 52 pgs.)-All silver foil-c 3.0
366-($3.95, 68 pgs.)-Embossed all gold foil-c 4.0
368,370-374,376-399: 368-Bloodties part 1; Avengers/X-Men x-over. 374-boun in trading card sheet. 380-Deodato-a. 390,391-"The Crossing." 395-Death of "old" Tony Stark; wraparound-c. 3.0
369-($2.95)-Foil embossed-c; Bloodties part 5 3.0
375-($2.00, 52 pgs.)-Regular ed.; Thunderstrike returns; leads into Malibu Comics' Black September. 2.5
375-($2.50, 52 pgs.)-Collector's ed. w/bound-in poster; leads into Malibu Comics' Black September. 3.0
400-402: Waid-s; 402-Deodato breakdowns; cont'd in X-Men #56 & Onslaught: Marvel Universe. 4.0
Special 1 (9/67, 25¢, 68 pgs.)-New-a; original & new Avengers team-up 6.80 20.50 75.0
Special 2 (9/68, 25¢, 68 pgs.)-New-a; original vs. new Avengers 3.65 11.00 40.0
Special 3 (9/69, 25¢, 68 pgs.)-r/Avengers #4 plus 3 Capt. America stories by Kirby (art); origin Red Skull 2.80 8.40 28.0
Special 4 (1/71, 25¢, 68 pgs.)-Kirby-r/Avengers #5,6 2.00 6.00 18.0
Special 5 (1/72, 52 pgs.)-Spider-Man x-over 2.00 6.00 18.0
Annual 6 (11/76) 1.10 3.30 9.0
Annual 7 (11/77)-Starlin-c/a; Warlock dies; Thanos app. 2.40 7.35 22.0
Annual 8 (1978)-Dr. Strange, Ms. Marvel app. 1.00 2.80 7.0
Annual 9 (1979)-Newton-a(p) 5.0
Annual 10 (1981)-Golden-p; X-Men cameo; 1st app. Rogue & Madelyne Pryor 2.50 7.50 25.0
Annual 11-18: 11(1982)-Vs. The Defenders. 12('83), 13('84), 14('85),15('86), 16('87), 17 ('88)-Evolutionary War x-over, 18('89)-Atlantis Attacks 3.5
Annual 19-23 (90-'94, 68 pgs.). 22-Bagged/card 3.0
...Kree-Skrull War ('00, $24.95, TPB) new Neal Adams-c 24.9
Marvel Double Feature...Avengers/Giant-Man #379 ($2.50, 52 pgs.)-Same as Avengers #379 w/Giant-Man flip book 2.5
Marvel Graphic Novel - Deathtrap The Vault (1991, $9.95) Venom-c/app. 1.50 4.50 12.0
The Yesterday Quest ($6.95)-r/#181,182,185-187 1.00 2.80 7.0
Under Siege ('98, $16.95, TPB) r/#270,271,273-277 17.0
...: Visionaries ('99, $16.95)-r/early George Perez art 17.0

NOTE: ***Austin*** *c(i)-157, 167, 168, 170-177, 181, 183-188, 198-201, Annual 8.* ***John Buscema*** *41-44p, 46p, 47p, 49, 50, 51-62p, 74-77, 79-85, 87-91, 97, 105p, 121p, 124p,125p, 152, 153 255-279p, 281-302p; c-41-66, 68-71, 73-91, 97-99, 178, 256-259p, 261-279p, 281-302p.* ***Byr*** *a-164-166p, 181-191p, 233p, Annual 13i, 14p; c-186-190p, 233p, 260, 305p; scripts-305-31* ***Colan*** *a(p)-63-65, 111, 206-208, 210, 211; c(p)-65, 206-208, 210, 211.* ***Ditko*** *a-Annual 13.* ***Gui*** *a-Annual 12p.* ***Don Heck*** *a-9-15, 17-40, 157.* ***Kane*** *c-37p, 159p.* ***Kane/Everett*** *c-97.* ***Kirby*** *a- 8p, Special 3r, 4r(p); c-1-30, 148, 151-158; layouts-14-16.* ***Ron Lim*** *c(p)-335-341.* ***Miller*** *c-193* ***Mooney*** *a-86i, 179p, 180p.* ***Nebres*** *a-178i; c-179i.* ***Newton*** *a-204p, Annual 9p.* ***Perez*** *a(p)-14 143, 144, 148, 150, 154, 155, 160, 161, 162, 167,168, 170, 171, 194-196, 198-202, Annual 6, c(p)-160-162, 164-166, 170-174, 181,183-185, 191, 192, 194-201, 379-382, Annual 8.* ***Starlin*** *121, 135.* ***Staton*** *a-127-134i.* ***Tuska*** *a-47i,48i, 51i, 53i, 54i, 106p, 107p, 135p, 137-140p, 163 Guardians of the Galaxy app. in #167, 168, 170, 173, 175, 181.*

AVENGERS, THE (Volume Two)
Marvel Comics: V2#1, Nov, 1996 - No. 13, Nov, 1997 ($2.95/$1.95/$1.99) (Produced by Extreme Studios)

1-($2.95)-Heroes Reborn begins; intro new team (Captain America, Swordsman, Scarlet Witch, Vision, Thor, Hellcat & Hawkeye); 1st app. Avengers Island; Loki & Enchantress app.; Rob Liefeld-p & plot; Chap Yaep-p; Jim Valentino scripts; variant-c exists 5.00
1-($1.95)-Variant-c 2.40 6.00
2-13: 2,3-Jeph Loeb scripts begin, Kang app. 4-Hulk-c/app. 5-Thor/Hulk battle; 2 covers. 10,11,13-"World War 3"-pt. 2, x-over w/Image characters. 12-($2.99) "Heroes Reunited"-pt. 2 4.00

AVENGERS, THE (Volume Three)
Marvel Comics: Feb, 1998 - Present ($2.99/$1.99)

1-($2.99, 48 pgs.) Busiek-s/Perez-a/wraparound-c; Avengers reassemble

The Avengers V3 #25 © MAR

Avengers Forever #12 © MAR

Avengers United They Stand #1 © MAR

GD2.0 FN6.0 NM9.4

after Heroes Return 5.00
1-Variant Heroes Return cover 1.00 2.80 7.00
1-Rough Cut-Features original script and pencil pages 3.00
2-($1.99)Perez-c, 2-Lago painted-c 4.00
3,4: 3-Wonder Man-c/app. 4-Final roster chosen; Perez poster 3.00
5-11: 5,6-Squadron Supreme-c/app. 8-Triathlon-c/app. 2.50
12-($2.99) Thunderbolts app. 3.00
13-24,26,28: 13-New Warriors app. 16-18-Ordway-s/a. 19-Ultron returns. 26-Immonen-a 2.00
25,27-($2.99) 25-vs. the Exemplars; Spider-Man app. 27-100 pgs. 3.00
29-33,35-37: 29-Begin $2.25-c. 35-Maximum Security x-over; Romita Jr.-a. 36-Epting-a; poster by Alan Davis 2.25
34-($2.99) Last Pérez-a; Thunderbirds app. 3.00
#11/2 (12/99, $2.50) Timm-c/a/Stern-s; 1963-style issue 2.50
.../ Squadron Supreme '98 Annual ($2.99) 3.00
1999, 2000 Annual (7/99, '00, $3.50) 1999-Manco-a. 2000-Breyfogle-a 3.50
The Morgan Conquest TPB ('00, $14.95) r/#1-4 14.95
Ultron Unleashed TPB (8/99, $3.50) reprints early app. 3.50
Wizard #0-Ultron Unlimited prelude 1.00

AVENGERS COLLECTOR'S EDITION, THE
Marvel Comics: 1993 (Ordered through mail w/candy wrapper, 20 pgs.)
1-Contains 4 bound-in trading cards 5.00

AVENGERS FOREVER
Marvel Comics: Dec, 1998 - No. 12, Feb, 2000 ($2.99)
1-Busiek-s/Pacheco-a in all 4.00
2-12: 4-Four covers. 6-Two covers. 12-Rick Jones becomes Capt. Marvel 3.00

AVENGERS INFINITY
Marvel Comics: Sept, 2000 - No. 4, Dec, 2000 ($2.99, limited series)
1-4-Stern-s/Chen-a 3.00

AVENGERS LOG, THE
Marvel Comics: Feb, 1994 ($1.95)
1-Gives history of all members; Perez-c 2.00

AVENGERS SPOTLIGHT (Formerly Solo Avengers #1-20)
Marvel Comics: No. 21, Aug, 1989 - No. 40, Jan, 1991 (75¢/$1.00)
21-Byrne-c/a 3.00
22-40: 26-Acts of Vengeance story. 31-34-U.S. Agent series. 36-Heck-i. 37-Mortimer-i. 40-The Black Knight app. 2.00

AVENGERS STRIKEFILE
Marvel Comics: Jan, 1994 ($1.75, one-shot)
1 2.00

AVENGERS: THE CROSSING
Marvel Comics: July, 1995 ($4.95, one-shot)
1-Deodato-c/a; 1st app. Thor's new costume 5.00

AVENGERS: THE LEGEND
Marvel Comics: Oct, 1996 ($3.95, one-shot)
1-Tribute issue 4.00

AVENGERS: THE TERMINATRIX OBJECTIVE
Marvel Comics: Sept, 1993 - No. 4, Dec, 1993 ($1.25, limited series)
1 ($2.50)-Holo-grafx foil-c 2.50
2-4-Old vs. current Avengers 2.00

AVENGERS: TIMESLIDE
Marvel Comics: Feb, 1996 ($4.95, one-shot)
1-Foil-c 5.00

AVENGERS TWO: WONDER MAN & BEAST
Marvel Comics: May, 2000 - No. 3, July, 2000 ($2.99, limited series)
1-3: Stern-s/Bagley-c/a 3.00

AVENGERS/ULTRAFORCE (See Ultraforce/Avengers)
Marvel Comics: Oct, 1995 ($3.95, one-shot)
1-Wraparound foil-c by Perez 4.00

AVENGERS UNITED THEY STAND
Marvel Comics: Nov, 1999 - No. 7, June, 2000 ($2.99/$1.99)

GD2.0 FN6.0 NM9.4

1-Based on the animated series 2.99
2-6-($1.99) 2-Avengers battle Hydra 1.99
7-($2.99) Devil Dinosaur-c/app.; reprints Avengers Action Figure Comic 2.99

AVENGERS UNIVERSE
Marvel Comics: Jun, 2000 - Present ($3.99)
1-3-Reprints recent stories 4.00

AVENGERS UNPLUGGED
Marvel Comics: Oct, 1995 - No. 6, Aug, 1996 (99¢, bi-monthly)
1-6 2.00

AVENGERS WEST COAST (Formerly West Coast Avengers)
Marvel Comics: No. 48, Sept, 1989 - No. 102, Jan, 1994 ($1.00/$1.25)
48,49: 48-Byrne-c/a & scripts continue thru #57 3.00
50-Re-intro original Human Torch 4.00
51-69,71-74,76-83,85,86,89-99: 54-Cover swipe/F.F. #1. 78-Last $1.00-c. 79-Dr. Strange x-over. 93-95-Darkhawk app. 2.00
70,75,84,87,88: 70-Spider-Woman app. 75 (52 pgs.)-Fantastic Four x-over. 84-Origin Spider-Woman retold; Spider-Man app. (also in #85,86). 87,88-Wolverine-c/story 3.00
100-($3.95, 68 pgs.)-Embossed all red foil-c 4.00
101,102: 101-X-Men x-over 4.00
Annual 5-8 ('90- '93, 68 pgs.)-5,6-West Coast Avengers in indicia. 7-Darkhawk app. 8-Polybagged w/card 3.00

AVIATION ADVENTURES AND MODEL BUILDING
Parents' Magazine Institute: No. 16, Dec, 1946 - No. 17, Feb, 1947 (True Aviation Advs. ...No. 15)
16,17-Half comics and half pictures 7.00 21.00 48.00

AVIATION CADETS
Street & Smith Publications: 1943
nn 17.00 51.00 135.00

A-V IN 3-D
Aardvark-Vanaheim: Dec, 1984 ($2.00, 28 pgs. w/glasses)
1-Cerebus, Flaming Carrot, Normalman & Ms. Tree 3.00

AWAKENING, THE
Image Comics: Oct, 1997 - No. 4, Apr, 1998 ($2.95, B&W, limited series)
1-4-Stephen Blue-s/c/a 3.00

AWESOME ADVENTURES
Awesome Entertainment: Aug, 1999 ($2.50)
1-Alan Moore-s/ Steve Skroce-a; Youngblood story 2.50

AWESOME HOLIDAY SPECIAL
Awesome Entertainment: Dec, 1997 ($2.50, one-shot)
1-Flip book w/covers of Fighting American & Coven. Holiday stories also featuring Kaboom and Shaft by regular creators. 3.00
1-Gold Edition 5.00

AWFUL OSCAR (Formerly & becomes Oscar Comics with No. 13)
Marvel Comics: No. 11, June, 1949 - No. 12, Aug, 1949
11,12 8.65 26.00 60.00

AWKWARD UNIVERSE
Slave Labor Graphics: 12/95 ($9.95, graphic novel)
nn 10.00

AXA
Eclipse Comics: Apr, 1987 - No. 2, Aug, 1987 ($1.75)
1,2 2.00

AXEL PRESSBUTTON (Pressbutton No. 5; see Laser Eraser &...)
Eclipse Comics: Nov, 1984 - No. 6, July, 1985 ($1.50/$1.75, Baxter paper)
1-6: Reprints Warrior (British mag.). 1-Bolland-c; origin Laser Eraser & Pressbutton 3.00

AXIS ALPHA
Axis Comics: Feb, 1994 ($2.50, one-shot)
V1-Previews Axis titles including, Tribe, Dethgrip, B.E.A.S.T.I.E.S. & more; Pitt app. in Tribe story. 3.00

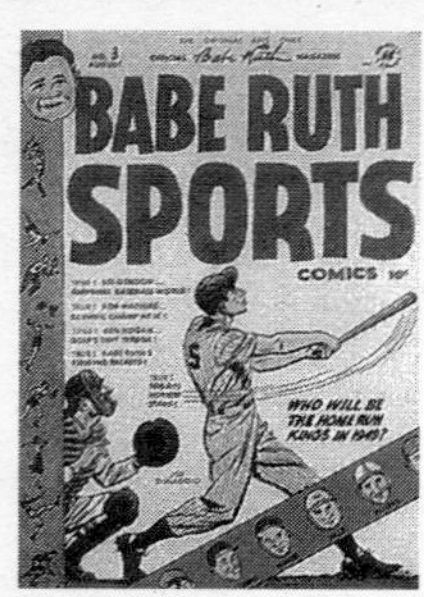

Babe Ruth Sports Comics #3 © HARV

Baby Huey & Papa #10 © HARV

Bachelor's Diary #1 © AVON

AZRAEL (...Agent of the Bat #47 on)(Also see Batman: Sword of Azrael)
DC Comics: Feb, 1995 - Present ($1.95/$2.25/$2.50)

1-Dennis O'Neil scripts begin 5.00
2,3 3.00
4-46,48-62: 5,6-Ras Al Ghul app. 13-Nightwing-c/app. 15-Contagion Pt. 5 (Pt. 4 on-c). 16-Contagion Pt. 10. 22-Batman-c/app. 23, 27-Batman app. 27,28-Joker app. 35-Hitman app. 36-39-Batman, Bane app. 50-New costume. 53-Joker-c/app. 56,57,60-New Batgirl app. 2.50
47-($3.95) Flip book with Batman: Shadow of the Bat #80 4.00
63-66: 63-Huntress-c/app.; returns to old costume 2.25
67-74: 67-Begin $2.50-c. 70-74-Harris-c 2.50
75-($3.95) New costume; Harris-c 3.95
#1,000,000 (11/98) Giarrano-a 2.25
Annual 1 (1995, $3.95)-Year One story 4.00
Annual 2 (1996, $2.95)-Legends of the Dead Earth story 3.00
Annual 3 (1997, $3.95)-Pulp Heroes story; Orbik-c 4.00
Plus (12/96, $2.95)-Question-c/app. 3.00

AZRAEL/ ASH
DC Comics: 1997 ($4.95, one-shot)

1-O'Neil-s/Quesada, Palmiotti-a 5.00

AZTEC ACE
Eclipse Comics: Mar, 1984 - No. 15, Sept, 1985 ($2.25/$1.50/$1.75, Baxter paper)

1-$2.25-c (52 pgs.) 2.50
2-15: 2-Begin 36 pgs. 2.00
NOTE: ***N. Redondo** a-1i-8i, 10i. c-6-8i.*

AZTEK: THE ULTIMATE MAN
DC Comics: Aug, 1996 - No. 10, May 1997 ($1.75)

1-1st app. Aztek & Synth; Grant Morrison & Mark Millar scripts in all 4.00
2-9: 2-Green Lantern app. 3-1st app. Death-Doll. 4-Intro The Lizard King. 5-Origin. 6-Joker app.; Batman cameo. 7-Batman app. 8-Luthor app. 9-vs. Parasite-c/app. 3.00
10-JLA-c/app. 1.25 3.75 10.00
NOTE: ***Breyfogle** c-5p. **N. Steven Harris** a-1-5p. **Porter** c-1p. **Wieringo** c-2p.*

BABE (...Darling of the Hills, later issues)(See Big Shot and Sparky Watts)
Prize/Headline/Feature: June-July, 1948 - No. 11, Apr-May, 1950

1-Boody Rogers-a 22.00 66.00 175.00
2-Boody Rogers-a 12.50 37.50 100.00
3-11-All by Boody Rogers 11.00 33.00 90.00

BABE
Dark Horse Comics (Legend): July, 1994 - No. 4, Jan, 1994 ($2.50, lim. series)

1-4: John Byrne-c/a/scripts; ProtoTykes back-up story 2.50

BABE RUTH SPORTS COMICS (Becomes Rags Rabbit #11 on?)
Harvey Publications: April, 1949 - No. 11, Feb, 1951

1-Powell-a 40.00 120.00 320.00
2-Powell-a 27.00 81.00 215.00
3-11: Powell-a in most 22.00 66.00 175.00
NOTE: *Baseball c-2-4, 9. Basketball c-1, 6. Football c-5. Yogi Berra c/story-8. Joe DiMaggio c/story-3. Bob Feller c/story-4. Stan Musial c-9.*

BABES IN TOYLAND (Disney, Movie) (See Golden Pix Story Book ST-3)
Dell Publishing Co.: No. 1282, Feb-Apr, 1962

Four Color 1282-Annette Funicello photo-c 11.70 35.00 140.00

BABES OF BROADWAY
Broadway Comics: May, 1996 ($2.95, one-shot)

1-Pin-ups of Broadway Comics' female characters; Alan Davis, Michael Kaluta, J. G. Jones, Alan Weiss, Guy Davis & others-a; Giordano-c. 3.00

BABE 2
Dark Horse Comics (Legend): Mar, 1995 - No. 2, May, 1995 ($2.50, lim. series)

1,2: John Byrne-c/a/scripts 2.50

BABY HUEY
Harvey Comics: No. 100, Oct, 1990 - No. 101, Nov, 1990; No. 1, Oct, 1991 - No. 9, June, 1994 ($1.00/$1.25/$1.50, quarterly)

100,101,1,2 ($1.00): 1-Cover says "Big Baby Huey" 4.50
3-9 ($1.25-$1.50) 3.00

BABY HUEY AND PAPA (See Paramount Animated...)
Harvey Publications: May, 1962 - No. 33, Jan, 1968 (Also see Casper The Friendly Ghost)

1 16.50 49.00 180.00
2 7.65 23.00 85.00
3-5 5.00 15.00 55.00
6-10 2.80 8.40 28.00
11-20 2.30 7.00 20.00
21-33 2.00 6.00 16.00

BABY HUEY DIGEST
Harvey Publications: June, 1992 (Digest-size, one-shot)

1-Reprints 2.40 6.00

BABY HUEY DUCKLAND
Harvey Publications: Nov, 1962 - No. 15, Nov, 1966 (25¢ Giants, 68 pgs.)

1 12.50 37.00 135.00
2-5 5.00 15.00 55.00
6-15 2.80 8.40 28.00

BABY HUEY, THE BABY GIANT (Also see Big Baby Huey, Casper, Harvey Hits #22, Harvey Comics Hits #60, & Paramount Animated Comics)
Harvey Publ: 9/56 - #97, 10/71; #98, 10/72; #99, 10/80; #100, 10/90 - #102?

1-Infinity-c 39.00 118.00 470.00
2 19.50 58.00 215.00
3-Baby Huey takes anti-pep pills 12.50 37.00 135.00
4,5 9.00 27.00 100.00
6-10 5.00 15.00 55.00
11-20 3.65 11.00 40.00
21-40 2.80 8.40 28.00
41-60 2.30 7.00 20.00
61-79 (12/67) 2.00 6.00 16.00
80(12/68) - 95-All 68 pg. Giants 2.50 7.50 23.00
96,97-Both 52 pg. Giants 2.00 6.00 16.00
98-Regular size 1.25 3.75 10.00
99-Regular size 2.40 6.00
100-102 ($1.00) 3.00

BABYLON 5 (TV)
DC Comics: Jan, 1995 - No. 11, Dec, 1995 ($1.95/$2.50)

1 1.50 4.50 12.00
2-5 1.00 3.00 8.00
6-11: 7-Begin $2.50-c 2.40 6.00
... The Price of Peace (1998, $9.95, TPB) r/#1-4,11 10.00

BABYLON 5: IN VALEN'S NAME
DC Comics: Mar, 1998 - No. 3, May, 1998 ($2.50, limited series)

1-3 4.00

BABY SNOOTS (Also see March of Comics #359, 371, 396, 401, 419, 431,443, 450, 462, 474, 485)
Gold Key: Aug, 1970 - No. 22, Nov, 1975

1 2.50 7.50 24.00
2-11 1.50 4.50 12.00
12-22: 22-Titled Snoots, the Forgetful Elefink 1.00 2.80 7.00

BACCHUS (Also see Eddie Campbell's ...)
Harrier Comics (New Wave): 1988 - No. 2, Aug, 1988 ($1.95, B&W)

1,2: Eddie Campbell-c/a/scripts. 2.00

BACHELOR FATHER (TV)
Dell Publishing Co.: No. 1332, 4-6/62 - No. 2, 1962

Four Color 1332 (#1), 2-Written by Stanley 7.50 22.50 90.00

BACHELOR'S DIARY
Avon Periodicals: 1949 (15¢)

1(Scarce)-King Features panel cartoons & text-r; pin-up, girl wrestling photos; similar to Sideshow 40.00 120.00 340.00

BACKPACK MARVELS (B&W backpack-sized reprint collections)
Marvel Comics: Nov, 2000 - Present ($6.95, B&W, digest-size)

Avengers 1 -r/Avengers #181-189; profile pages 6.95

Backlash #7 © WSP

Badmen of Tombstone #1 © AVON

Baffling Mysteries #14 © ACE

GD2.0 FN6.0 NM9.4

r-Man 1-r/ASM #234-240 6.95
ı 1-r/Uncanny X-Men #167-173 6.95
ı 2-r/Uncanny X-Men #174-179; new painted-c by Greg Horn 6.95

(DOWN THE LINE
se Books: 1991 (Mature adults, 8-1/2 x 11", 52 pgs.)
oft-c, $8.95)-Bolton-c/a 9.00
mited Hard-c, $29.95) 30.00

(LASH (Also see The Kindred)
e Comics (WildStorm Prod.): Nov,1994 - No. 32, May, 1997 ($1.95/$2.50)
ouble-c; variant-double-c 3.00
)-32: 5-Intro Mindscape; 2 pinups. 19-Fire From Heaven Pt 2. 20-Fire From
eaven Pt 10. 31-WildC.A.T.S app. 2.50
1.95, newsstand)-Wildstorm Rising Pt. 8 2.50
2.50, direct market)-Wildstorm Rising Pt. 8 2.50
3.95)-Double-size 4.00
aboo's African Holiday (9/99, $5.95) Booth-s/a(p) 6.00

(LASH/SPIDER-MAN
e Comics (WildStorm Productions): Aug, 1996 - No. 2, Sept, 1996
), limited series)
Pike (villain from WildC.A.T.S) & Venom app. 3.00

(TO THE FUTURE (Movie, TV cartoon)
ey Comics: Nov, 1991 - No. 4, June, 1992 ($1.25)
,2-Gil Kane-c; based on animated cartoon 3.00

(TO THE FUTURE: FORWARD TO THE FUTURE
ey Comics: Oct, 1992 - No. 3, Feb, 1993 ($1.50, limited series)
3.00

BOY
ress: Dec, 1997 ($4.95, one-shot)
ank Miller-s/Simon Bisley-a/painted-c 5.00

COMPANY
ty Comics/Fleetway Quality #15 on: Aug, 1988 - No. 19?, 1990
)/$1.75, high quality paper)
: 5,6-Guice-c 2.00

EGGS, THE
im Comics (Armada): June, 1995 - No. 8, Jan, 1997 ($2.95)
Layton scripts; Perlin-a. 5-8-"That Dirty Yellow Mustard."
William Shatner app. 3.00

GE OF JUSTICE (Formerly Crime And Justice #21)
ton Comics: No. 22, 1/55 - No. 2, 4/55 - No. 4, 10/55
)(1/55) 10.00 30.00 75.00
5.00 15.00 35.00

GER, THE
al Comics(#1-4)/First Comics: Dec, 1983 - No. 70, Apr, 1991; V2#1,
g, 1991
4.00
: 52-54-Tim Vigil-c/a 2.50
3.95, 52 pgs.) 4.00
(Spring, 1991, $4.95) 5.00

GER, THE
e Comics: V3#78, May, 1997 - Present ($2.95, B&W)
over lists #1, Baron-s 3.00
2, 80/#3, 81(indicia lists #80)/#4,82-88/#5-11 3.00

GER GOES BERSERK
Comics: Sept, 1989 - No. 4, Dec, 1989 ($1.95, lim. series, Baxter paper)
2-Paul Chadwick-c/a(2pgs.) 2.50

GER: SHATTERED MIRROR
Horse Comics: July, 1994 - No. Oct, 1994 ($2.50, limited series)
2.50

GER: ZEN POP FUNNY-ANIMAL VERSION
Horse Comics: July, 1994 - No. 2, Aug, 1994 ($2.50, limited series)

GD2.0 FN6.0 NM9.4

1,2 2.50

BADLANDS
Vortex Comics: May, 1990 ($3.00, glossy stock, mature)
1-Chaykin-c 3.00

BADLANDS
Dark Horse Comics: July, 1991 - No. 6, Dec, 1991 ($2.25, B&W, limited series)
1-6: 1-John F. Kennedy-c; reprints Vortex Comics issue 2.25

BADMEN OF THE WEST
Avon Periodicals: 1951 (Giant) (132 pgs., painted-c)
1-Contains rebound copies of Jesse James, King of the Bad Men of Deadwood, Badmen of Tombstone; other combinations possible.
Issues with Kubert-a... 40.00 120.00 325.00

BADMEN OF THE WEST! (See A-1 Comics)
Magazine Enterprises: 1953 - No. 3, 1954
1(A-1 100)-Meskin-a? 24.00 71.00 190.00
2(A-1 120), 3: 2-Larsen-a 15.00 45.00 120.00

BADMEN OF TOMBSTONE
Avon Periodicals: 1950
nn 15.00 45.00 120.00

BADROCK (Also see Youngblood)
Image Comics (Extreme Studios): Mar, 1995 - No. 2, Jan, 1996 ($1.75/$2.50)
1-Variant-c (3) 3.00
2-Liefeld-c/a & story; Savage Dragon app, flipbook w/Grifter/Badrock #2; variant-c exist 2.50
Annual 1(1995,$2.95)-Arthur Adams-c 3.00
Annual 1 Commemorative ($9.95)-3,000 printed 10.00
.../Wolverine (6/96, $4.95, squarebound)-Sauron app; pin-ups; variant-c exists 5.00
.../Wolverine (6/96)-Special Comicon Edition 5.00

BADROCK AND COMPANY (Also see Youngblood)
Image Comics (Extreme Studios): Sept, 1994 - No.6, Feb, 1995 ($2.50)
1-6 : 6-Indicia reads "October 1994"; story cont'd in Shadowhawk #17 2.50

BAFFLING MYSTERIES (Formerly Indian Braves No. 1-4; Heroes of the Wild Frontier No. 26-on)
Periodical House (Ace Magazines): No. 5, Nov, 1951 - No. 26, Oct, 1955
5 36.00 108.00 290.00
6-19,21-24: 8-Woodish-a by Cameron. 10-E.C. Crypt Keeper swipe on-c.
24-Last pre-code issue 22.00 66.00 170.00
20-Classic-c 26.00 79.00 210.00
25-Reprints; surrealistic-c 18.00 54.00 145.00
26-Reprints 15.00 45.00 120.00
NOTE: ***Cameron*** *a-8, 10, 16-18, 20-22.* ***Colan*** *a-5, 11, 25r/5.* ***Sekowsky*** *a-5, 6, 22. Bondage c-20, 23. Reprints in 18(1), 19(1), 24(3).*

BALBO (See Master Comics #33 & Mighty Midget Comics)

BALDER THE BRAVE
Marvel Comics Group: Nov, 1985 - No. 4, 1986 (Limited series)
1-4: Simonson-c/a; character from Thor 2.00

BALLAD OF HALO JONES, THE
Quality Comics: Sept, 1987 - No. 12, Aug, 1988 ($1.25/$1.50)
1-12: Alan Moore scripts in all 2.00

BALL AND CHAIN
DC Comics (Homage): Nov, 1999 - No. 4, Feb, 2000 ($2.50, limited series)
1-4-Lobdell-s/Garza-a 2.50

BALLISTIC (Also See Cyberforce)
Image Comics (Top Cow Productions): Sept, 1995 - No. 3, Dec, 1995 ($2.50, limited series)
1-3: Wetworks app, Turner-c/a 3.00

BALLISTIC ACTION
Image Comics (Top Cow Productions): May, 1996 ($2.95, one-shot)
1-Pin-ups of Top Cow characters participating in outdoor sports 3.00

Bang-Up Comics #1 © Progressive Publishers

Barbie #16 © Mattel

Barb Wire #4 © DH

BALLISTIC IMAGERY
Image Comics (Top Cow Productions): Jan, 1996 ($2.50, anthology, one-shot)
1-Cyberforce app. 2.50

BALLISTIC/ WOLVERINE
Image Comics (Top Cow Productions): Feb, 1997 ($2.95, one-shot)
1-Devil's Reign pt. 4; Witchblade cameo (1 page) 4.00

BALOO & LITTLE BRITCHES (Disney)
Gold Key: Apr, 1968
1-From the Jungle Book 3.00 9.00 30.00

BAMBI (Disney) (See Movie Classics, Movie Comics, and Walt Disney Showcase No. 31)
Dell Publishing Co.: No. 12, 1942; No. 30, 1943; No. 186, Apr, 1948; 1984
Four Color 12-Walt Disney's... 58.00 175.00 700.00
Four Color 30-Bambi's Children (1943) 54.00 163.00 650.00
Four Color 186-Walt Disney's...; reprinted as Movie Classic Bambi #3 (1956) 16.00 48.00 195.00
1-(Whitman, 1984; 60¢)-r/Four Color #186 2.40 6.00

BAMBI (Disney)
Grosset & Dunlap: 1942 (50¢, 7"x8-1/2", 32pg, hard-c w/dust jacket)
nn-Given away w/a copy of Thumper for a $2.00, 2-yr. subscription to WDC&S in 1942 (Xmas offer). Book only 19.00 56.00 150.00
w/dust jacket 34.00 101.00 270.00

BAMM BAMM & PEBBLES FLINTSTONE (TV)
Gold Key: Oct, 1964 (Hanna-Barbera)
1 8.35 25.00 100.00

BANANA SPLITS, THE (TV) (See Golden Comics Digest & March of Comics No. 364)
Gold Key: June, 1969 - No. 8, Oct, 1971 (Hanna-Barbera)
1-Photo-c on all 10.00 30.00 120.00
2-8 6.30 19.00 75.00

BAND WAGON (See Hanna-Barbera Band Wagon)

BANDY MAN, THE
Caliber: 1996 - No. 3, ($2.95, B&W, limited series)
1-3-Stephan Petrucha scripts; 1-Jill Thompson-a; Miran Kim-c 3.00

BANG-UP COMICS
Progressive Publishers: Dec, 1941 - No. 3, June, 1942
1-Cosmo Mann & Lady Fairplay begin; Buzz Balmer by Rick Yager in all (origin #1) 95.00 285.00 900.00
2,3 50.00 150.00 450.00

BANNER COMICS (Becomes Captain Courageous No. 6)
Ace Magazines: No. 3, Sept, 1941 - No. 5, Jan, 1942
3-Captain Courageous (1st app.) & Lone Warrior & Sidekick Dicky begin; Jim Mooney-c 103.00 308.00 975.00
4,5: 4-Flag-c 63.00 189.00 600.00

BARABBAS
Slave Labor Graphics: Aug, 1986 - No. 2, Nov, 1986 ($1.50, B&W, lim. series)
1,2 2.00

BARBARIANS, THE
Atlas Comics/Seaboard Periodicals: June, 1975
1-Origin, only app. Andrax; Iron Jaw app.; Marcos-a 5.00

BARBIE
Marvel Comics: Jan, 1991 - No. 66, Apr, 1996 ($1.00/$1.25/$1.50)
1-Polybagged w/Barbie Pink Card; Romita-c 1.25 3.75 10.00
2-49,51-66 2.40 6.00
50-(Giant) 1.00 3.00 8.00

BARBIE & KEN
Dell Publishing Co.: May-July, 1962 - No. 5, Nov-Jan, 1963-64
01-053-207(#1)-Based on Mattel toy dolls 37.00 112.00 450.00
2-4 29.00 87.00 320.00
5 (Rare) 32.00 95.00 380.00

BARBIE FASHION
Marvel Comics: Jan, 1991 - No. 63, Jan, 1996 ($1.00/$1.25/$1.50)
1-Polybagged w/doorknob hanger 1.25 3.75 1
2-49,51-63: 4-Contains preview to Sweet XVI. 14-Begin $1.25-c 2.40
50-(Giant) 1.00 3.00

BARBI TWINS, THE
Topps Comics: 1995 ($2.50/$5.00)
1-Razor app.
Swimsuit Art Calendar ($5.00)-art by Linsner, Bradstreet, Hughes; Julie Bell-

BARB WIRE (See Comics' Greatest World)
Dark Horse Comics: Apr, 1994 - No. 9, Feb, 1995 ($2.00/$2.50)
1-9: 1-Foil logo
Trade paperback (1996, $8.95)-r/#2,3,5,6 w/Pamela Anderson bio

BARB WIRE: ACE OF SPADES
Dark Horse Comics: May, 1996 - No. 4, Sept, 1996 ($2.95, limited series)
1-4: Chris Warner-c/a(p)/scripts; Tim Bradstreet-c/a(i) in all

BARB WIRE COMICS MAGAZINE SPECIAL
Dark Horse Comics: May, 1996 ($3.50, B&W, magazine, one-shot)
nn-Adaptation of film; photo-c; poster insert.

BARB WIRE MOVIE SPECIAL
Dark Horse Comics: May, 1996 ($3.95, one-shot)
nn-Adaptation of film; photo-c; 1st app. new look

BARKER, THE (Also see National Comics #42)
Quality Comics Group/Comic Magazine: Autumn, 1946 - No. 15, Dec, 194
1 20.00 60.00 16
2 10.00 30.00 8
3-10 7.85 23.50 5
11-14 5.00 15.00 3
15-Jack Cole-a(p) 6.00 18.00 4
NOTE: ***Jack Cole*** *art in some issues.*

BARNABY
Civil Service Publications Inc.: 1945 (25¢,102 pgs., digest size)
V1#1-r/Crocket Johnson strips from 1942 3.60 9.00 1

BARNEY AND BETTY RUBBLE (TV) (Flintstones' Neighbors)
Charlton Comics: Jan, 1973 - No. 23, Dec, 1976 (Hanna-Barbera)
1 3.20 9.60 3
2-11: 11(2/75)-1st Mike Zeck-a (illos) 2.00 6.00 1
12-23 1.50 4.50 1

BARNEY BAXTER (Also see Magic Comics)
David McKay/Dell Publishing Co./Argo: 1938 - No. 2, 1956
Feature Books 15(McKay-1938) 28.00 85.00 34
Four Color 20(1942) 27.00 80.00 32
1,2 (1956-Argo) 8.65 26.00 6

BARNEY BEAR ...
Spire Christian Comics (Fleming H. Revell Co.): 1977-1981
...Home Plate nn-(1979, 49¢), ...Lost and Found nn-(1979, 49¢), Out of The Woods nn-(1980, 49¢), Sunday School Picnic nn-(1981, 69¢, The Swamp Gang!-(1977, 39¢) 2.40

BARNEY GOOGLE & SNUFFY SMITH
Dell Publishing Co./Gold Key: 1942 - 1943; April, 1964
Four Color 19(1942) 38.00 115.00 46
Four Color 40(1944) 22.00 66.00 26
Large Feature Comic 11(1943) 25.00 75.00 30
1(10113-404)-Gold Key (4/64) 3.65 11.00 4

BARNEY GOOGLE & SNUFFY SMITH
Toby Press: June, 1951 - No. 4, Feb, 1952 (Reprints)
1 12.00 36.00 9
2,3 7.85 23.50 5
4-Kurtzman-a "Pot Shot Pete", 5 pgs.; reprints John Wayne #5 12.00 36.00 9

Barnyard Comics #8 © Nedor

Baseball Thrills #3 © Z-D

Batgirl #1 © DC

GD2.0 FN6.0 NM9.4

NEY GOOGLE AND SNUFFY SMITH
ʼlton Comics: Mar, 1970 - No. 6, Jan, 1971

	GD2.0	FN6.0	NM9.4
	2.50	7.50	23.00
	1.75	5.25	14.00

NYARD COMICS (Dizzy Duck No. 32 on)
ɔr/Polo Mag./Standard(Animated Cartoons): June, 1944 - No. 31, Sept, ; No. 10, 1957

	GD2.0	FN6.0	NM9.4
ın, 52 pgs.)-Funny animal	19.00	56.00	150.00
·2 pgs.)	10.00	30.00	75.00
	7.00	21.00	48.00
2,16	5.50	16.50	38.00
5,17,21,23,26,27,29-All contain Frazetta text illos	7.85	23.50	55.00
:0,22,24,25-All contain Frazetta-a & text illos	10.00	30.00	80.00
·0,31	4.00	12.00	24.00
957)(Exist?)	2.40	6.00	12.00

RY M. GOLDWATER
Publishing Co.: Mar, 1965 (Complete life story)

55-503-Photo-c 3.20 9.60 35.00

RY WINDSOR-SMITH: STORYTELLER
Horse Comics: Oct, 1996 - No. 9, July, 1997 ($4.95, oversize)

1-Intro Young Gods, Paradox Man & the Freebooters; Barry nith-c/a/scripts 5.00
iew 4.00

SINISTER (Also see Shaman's Tears)
aim Comics (Windjammer): Jun, 1995 - No. 4, Sept, 1995 ($2.50, lim. series)

Mike Grell-c/a/scripts 2.50

TMAN (Also see Simpson's Comics & Radioactive Man)
ʒo Comics: 1993 - No. 6, 1994 ($1.95/$2.25)

؛2.95)-Foil-c; bound-in jumbo Bartman poster 5.00
. 3-w/trading card 3.00

T SIMPSON (See Simpsons Comics Presents Bart Simpson)

EBALL COMICS
Eisner Productions: Spring, 1949 (Reprinted later as a Spirit section)

ʼill Eisner-c/a 68.00 205.00 650.00

EBALL COMICS
ıen Sink Press: 1991 ($3.95, coated stock)

1949 ish. by Eisner; contains trading cards 6.00

EBALL HEROES
ɔett Publications: 1952 (one-shot)

ɔcarce)-Babe Ruth photo-c; baseball's Hall of Fame biographies 79.00 237.00 750.00

EBALL'S GREATEST HEROES
ıum Comics: Dec, 1991 - No. 2, May, 1992 ($1.75)

ickey Mantle #1; photo-c; Sinnott-a(p) 4.00
rooks Robinson #1; photo-c; Sinnott-a(i) 3.00

EBALL THRILLS
Davis Publ. Co.: No. 10, Sum, 1951 - No. 3, Sum, 1952
nders painted-c No.1,2)

	GD2.0	FN6.0	NM9.4
·1)-Bob Feller, Musial, Newcombe & Boudreau stories	40.00	120.00	360.00
owell-a(2)(Late Sum, '51); Feller, Berra & Mathewson stories	30.00	90.00	240.00
instler-c/a; Joe DiMaggio story	30.00	90.00	240.00

EBALL THRILLS 3-D
3-D Zone: May, 1990 ($2.95, w/glasses)

ew L.B. Cole-c; life stories of Ty Cobb & Ted Williams 5.00

ICALLY STRANGE (Magazine)
C. Comics (Archie Comics Group): Dec, 1982 ($1.95, B&W)

ʼ1,000 printed; all but 1,000 destroyed; pgs. out of sequence) 2.00 6.00 16.00

GD2.0 FN6.0 NM9.4

1-Wood, Toth-a; Corben-c; reprints & new art 1.50 4.50 12.00

BASIC HISTORY OF AMERICA ILLUSTRATED
Pendulum Press: 1976 (B&W) (Soft-c $1.50; Hard-c $4.50)

07-1999-America Becomes a World Power 1890-1920. 07-2251-The Industrial Era 1865-1915. 07-226x-Before the Civil War 1830-1860. 07-2278-Americans Move Westward 1800-1850. 07-2286-The Civil War 1850-1876; Redondo-a. 07-2294-The Fight for Freedom 1750-1783. 07-2308-The New World 1500-1750. 07-2316-Problems of the New Nation 1800-1830. 07-2324-Roaring Twenties and the Great Depression 1920-1940. 07-2332-The United States Emerges 1783-1800. 07-2340-America Today 1945-1976. 07-2359-World War II 1940-1945

Softcover editions each 5.00
Hardcover editions each 10.00

BASIL (...the Royal Cat)
St. John Publishing Co.: Jan, 1953 - No. 4, Sept, 1953

	GD2.0	FN6.0	NM9.4
1-Funny animal	5.50	16.50	38.00
2-4	4.00	10.00	20.00
I.W. Reprint 1	1.25	3.75	10.00

BASIL WOLVERTON'S FANTASTIC FABLES
Dark Horse Comics: Oct, 1993 - No. 2, Dec, 1993 ($2.50, B&W, limited series)

1,2-Wolverton-c/a(r) 5.00

BASIL WOLVERTON'S GATEWAY TO HORROR
Dark Horse Comics: June, 1988 ($1.75, B&W, one-shot)

1-Wolverton-r 5.00

BASIL WOLVERTON'S PLANET OF TERROR
Dark Horse Comics: Oct, 1987 ($1.75, B&W, one-shot)

1-Wolverton-r; Alan Moore-c 5.00

BATGIRL (See Batman: No Man's Land stories)
DC Comics: Apr, 2000 - Present ($2.50)

1-Scott & Campanella-a 4.00
1-(2nd printing) 2.50
2-13: 12-"Officer Down" x-over 2.50
Annual 1 ('00, $3.50) Planet DC; intro. Aruna 3.50

BATGIRL ADVENTURES (See Batman Adventures, The)
DC Comics: Feb, 1998 ($2.95, one-shot) (Based on animated series)

1-Harley Quinn and Poison Ivy app.; Timm-c 5.00

BATGIRL SPECIAL
DC Comics: 1988 ($1.50, one-shot, 52 pgs)

1-Kitson-a/Mignola-c 1.00 2.80 7.00

BAT LASH (See DC Special Series #16, Showcase #76, Weird Western Tales)
National Periodical Publications: Oct-Nov, 1968 - No. 7, Oct-Nov, 1969 (All 12¢ issues)

	GD2.0	FN6.0	NM9.4
1-(10-11/68)-2nd app. Bat Lash	3.20	9.60	35.00
2-7	2.40	7.35	22.00

BATMAN (See Anarky, Aurora, The Best of DC #2, Blind Justice, The Brave & the Bold, Cosmic Odyssey, DC 100-Page Super Spec. #14,20, DC Special, DC Special Series, Detective, Dynamic Classics, 80-Page Giants, Gotham By Gaslight, Gotham Nights, Greatest Batman Stories Ever Told, Greatest Joker Stories Ever Told, Heroes Against Hunger, JLA,The Joker, Justice League of America, Justice League Int., Legends of the Dark Knight, Limited Coll. Ed., Man-Bat, Nightwing, Power Record Comics, Real Fact #5, Robin, Saga of Ra's Al Ghul, Shadow of the..., Star Spangled, Super Friends, 3-D Batman, Untold Legend of..., Wanted... & World's Finest Comics)

BATMAN
National Per. Publ./Detective Comics/DC Comics: Spring, 1940 - Present (#1-5 were quarterly)

	GD2.0	FN6.0	VF8.0	NM9.4
1-Origin The Batman reprinted (2 pgs.) from Det. #33 w/splash from #34 by Bob Kane; see Detective #33 for 1st origin; 1st app. Joker (2 stories intended for 2 separate issues of Det. Comics which would have been 1st & 2nd app.); splash pg. to 2nd Joker story is similar to cover of Det. #40 (story intended for #40); 1st app. The Cat (Catwoman)(1st villainess in comics); has Batman story (w/Hugo Strange) without Robin originally planned for Det. #38; mentions location (Manhattan) where Batman lives (see Det. #31). This book was created entirely from the inventory of Det. Comics; 1st Batman/Robin pin-up on back-c; has text piece & photo of Bob Kane	6067.00	18,200.00	42,500.00	85,000.00

Batman #8 © DC

Batman #97 © DC

Batman #133 © DC

1-Reprint, oversize 13-1/2x10". **WARNING**: This comic is an exact duplicate reprint of the original except for its size. DC published it in 1974 with a second cover titling it as a Famous First Edition. There have been many reported cases of the outer cover being removed and the interior sold as the original edition. The reprint with the new outer cover removed is practically worthless. See Famous First Edition for value.

GD2.0 FN6.0 NM9.4

2-2nd app. The Joker; 2nd app. Catwoman (out of costume) in Joker story; 1st time called Catwoman
NOTE: A 15¢-c for Canadian distr. exists.
1120.00 3360.00 14,000.00
3-3rd app Catwoman (1st in costume & 1st costumed villainess); 1st Puppet Master app.; classic Kane & Moldoff-c 783.00 2350.00 9000.00
4-3rd app. The Joker (see Det. #45 for 4th); 1st mention of Gotham City in a Batman comic (on newspaper)(Win/40) 626.00 1878.00 7200.00
5-1st app. the Batmobile with its bat-head front 452.00 1357.00 5200.00
6,7: 7-Bullseye-c 420.00 1260.00 4400.00
8-Infinity-c. 343.00 1030.00 3600.00
9-10:9-1st Batman x-mas story; Burnley-c. 10-Catwoman story (gets new costume) 324.00 971.00 3400.00
11-Classic Joker-c by Ray/Robinson (3rd Joker-c, 6-7/42); Joker & Penguin app. 609.00 1826.00 7000.00
12,15: 15-New costume Catwoman 284.00 853.00 2700.00
13-Jerry Siegel (Superman's co-creator) appears in a Batman story. 300.00 900.00 2850.00
14-2nd Penguin-c; Penguin app. (12-1/42-43) 311.00 933.00 2950.00
16-Intro/origin Alfred (4-5/43); cover is a reverse of #9 cover by Burnley; 1st small logo 478.00 1435.00 5500.00
17,20: 17-Classic war-c; Penguin app. 20-1st Batmobile-c (12-1/43-44); Joker app. 200.00 600.00 1900.00
18-Hitler, Hirohito, Mussolini-c. 263.00 790.00 2500.00
19-Joker app. 190.00 570.00 1800.00
21,22,24,26,28-30: 21-1st skinny Alfred in Batman (2-3/44). 21,30-Penguin app. 22-1st Alfred solo-c/story (Alfred solo stories in 22-32,36); Catwoman & The Cavalier app. 28-Joker story 147.00 442.00 1400.00
23-Joker-c/story 211.00 633.00 2000.00
25-Only Joker/Penguin team-up; 1st team-up between two major villains 216.00 647.00 2050.00
27-Classic Burnley Christmas-c; Penguin app. 195.00 584.00 1850.00
31,32,34-36,39: 32-Origin Robin retold. 35-Catwoman story (in new costume w/o cat head mask). 36-Penguin app. 111.00 332.00 1050.00
33-Christmas-c 118.00 355.00 1125.00
37,40,44-Joker-c/stories 147.00 442.00 1400.00
38-Penguin-c/story 121.00 363.00 1150.00
41,45,46: 41-1st Sci-fi cover/story in Batman; Penguin app.(6-7/47). 45-Christmas-c/story; Catwoman story; Vicki Vale app. (1st app?) 79.00 237.00 750.00
42-2nd Catwoman-c (1st in Batman)(8-9/47); Catwoman story also. 121.00 363.00 1150.00
43-Penguin-c/story 105.00 316.00 1000.00
47-1st detailed origin The Batman (6-7/48); 1st Bat-signal-c this title (see Detective #108); Batman tracks down his parent's killer and reveals i.d. to him 305.00 915.00 3200.00
48-1000 Secrets of the Batcave; r-in #203; Penguin story 105.00 316.00 1000.00
49-Joker-c/story; 1st app. Mad Hatter; Vicki Vale app. 168.00 505.00 1600.00
50-Two-Face impostor app. 90.00 270.00 850.00
51,53,54,56,57,59,60: 57-Centerfold is a 1950 calendar. 59-1st app. Deadshot; Batman in the future-c/story 76.00 229.00 725.00
52,55-Joker-c/stories 100.00 300.00 950.00
58,61: 58-Penguin-c. 61-Origin Batman Plane II 84.00 253.00 800.00
62-Origin Catwoman; Catwoman-c 116.00 348.00 1100.00
63,80-Joker stories. 63-Flying saucer story(2-3/51) 71.00 213.00 675.00
64,67,70-72,74-77,79: 70-Robot-c. 72-Last 52 pg. issue. 74-Used in **POP**, Pg. 90. 79-Vicki Vale in "The Bride of Batman" 61.00 182.00 575.00
65,69,84-Catwoman-c/stories. 84-Two-Face app. 70.00 210.00 660.00
66,73-Joker-c/stories. 66-Pre-2nd Batman & Robin team try-out. 73-Vicki Vale story 82.00 245.00 775.00
68,81-Two-Face-c/stories 63.00 189.00 600.00
78-(8-9/53)-Roh Kar, The Man Hunter from Mars story-the 1st lawman of Mars to come to Earth (green skinned) 76.00 229.00 725.00
82,83,85-89: 86-Intro Batmarine (Batman's submarine). 89-Last pre-code issue 57.00 171.00 540
90,91,93-99: 97-2nd app. Bat-Hound-c/story; Joker app. 99-(4/56)-Last G.A. Penguin app. 49.00 147.00 440
92-1st app. Bat-Hound-c/story 63.00 189.00 600
100-(6/56) 247.00 742.00 2350
101-(8/56)-Clark Kent x-over who protects Batman's i.d. (3rd story) 51.00 153.00 460
102-104,106-109: 103-1st S.A. issue; 3rd Bat-Hound-c/story 42.00 126.00 400
105-1st Batwoman in Batman (2nd anywhere) 55.00 165.00 520
110-Joker story 43.00 129.00 410
111-120: 112-1st app. Signalman (super villain). 113-1st app. Fatman; Batma meets his counterpart on Planet X w/a chest plate similar to S.A. Batman's design (yellow oval w/black design inside). 36.00 108.00 340
121- Origin/1st app. of Mr. Zero (Mr. Freeze). 43.00 129.00 410
122,124-126,128,130: 124-2nd app. Signal Man. 126-Batwoman-c/story. 128-Batwoman cameo. 130-Lex Luthor app. 24.00 72.00 230
123,127: 123-Joker story; Bat-Hound app. 127-(10/59)-Batman vs. Thor the Thunder God-c/story; Joker story; Superman cameo 27.00 81.00 260
129-Origin Robin retold; bondage-c; Batwoman-c/story (reprinted in Batman Family #8) 29.00 87.00 275
131-135,137-139,141-143: 131-Intro 2nd Batman & Robin series (see #66; als in #135,145,154,159,163). 133-1st Bat-Mite in Batman (3rd app. anywhere 134-Origin The Dummy (not Vigilante's villain). 139-Intro 1st original Bat-G only app. Signalman as the Blue Bowman. 141-2nd app. original Bat-Girl. 143-(10/61)-Last 10¢ issue 19.00 57.00 180
136-Joker-c/story 22.00 66.00 210
140,144-Joker stories. 140-Batwoman-c/story; Superman cameo. 144-(12/61)-1st 12¢ issue 16.50 49.00 180
145,148-Joker-c/stories 18.00 53.00 195
146,147,149,150 12.00 36.00 130
151-154,156-158,160-162,164-168,170: 152-Joker story. 156-Ant-Man/Robin team-up(6/63). 164-New Batmobile(6/64) new look & Mystery Analysts series begins 9.00 27.00 100
155-1st S.A. app. The Penguin (5/63) 31.00 93.00 340
159,163-Joker-c/stories. 159-Bat-Girl app. 11.50 34.00 125
169-2nd SA Penguin app. 12.50 37.00 135
171-1st Riddler app.(5/65) since Dec. 1948 37.00 112.00 450
172-175,177,178,180,184 5.90 17.75 65
176-(80-Pg. Giant G-17); Joker-c/story; Penguin app. in strip-r; Catwoman reprint 8.15 24.50 90
179-2nd app. Silver Age Riddler 12.75 38.00 140
181-Batman & Robin poster insert; intro. Poison Ivy 15.50 46.50 170
182,187-(80 Pg. Giants G-24, G-30); Joker-c/stories 6.80 20.50 75
183-2nd app. Poison Ivy 9.00 27.00 100
185-(80 Pg. Giant G-27) 6.80 20.50 75
186-Joker-c/story 6.35 19.00 70
188,191,192,194-196,199 3.45 10.35 38
189-1st S.A. app. Scarecrow; retells origin of G.A. Scarecrow from World's Finest #3(1st app.) 8.15 24.50 90
190-Penguin app. 3.80 11.40 42
193-(80-Pg. Giant G-37) 5.90 17.75 65
197-4th S.A. Catwoman app. cont'd from Det. #369; 1st new Batgirl app. in Batman (5th anywhere) 5.90 17.75 65
198-(80-Pg. Giant G-43); Joker-c/story-r/World's Finest #61; Catwoman-r/ Det. #211; Penguin-r; origin-r/#47 6.80 20.50 75
200-(3/68)-Joker cameo; retells origin of Batman & Robin; 1st Neal Adams work this title (cover only) 12.75 38.00 140
201-Joker story 3.65 11.00 40
202,204-207,209-212,: 212-Last 12¢ issue 2.80 8.40 28
203-(80 Pg. Giant G-49); r/#48, 61, & Det. 185; Batcave Blueprints 4.55 13.65 50
208-(80 Pg. Giant G-55); New origin Batman by Gil Kane plus 3 G.A. Batman reprints w/Catwoman, Vicki Vale & Batwoman 4.55 13.65 50
213-(80-Pg. Giant G-61); 30th anniversary issue (7-8/69); origin Alfred (r/Batman #16), Joker(r/Det. #168), Clayface; new origin Robin with new facts 6.80 20.50 75

Batman #334 © DC

Batman #454 © DC

Batman #461 © DC

GD2.0 FN6.0 NM9.4

-217: 214-Alfred given a new last name- "Pennyworth" (see Detective #96)
2.50 7.50 25.00
-(80-Pg. Giant G-67) 4.55 13.65 50.00
-Neal Adams-a 4.10 12.30 45.00
,221,224-226,229-231 2.50 7.50 23.00
-Beatles take-off; art lesson by Joe Kubert 3.65 11.00 40.00
,228,233-(80-Pg. Giants G-73,G-79,G-85) 4.10 12.30 45.00
-Neal Adams cover swipe of Detective #31 3.00 9.00 30.00
-N. Adams-a. Intro/1st app. Ras Al Ghul; origin Batman & Robin retold; ast 15¢ issue 8.65 26.00 95.00
-(9/71)-1st modern app. of Harvey Dent/Two-Face; (see World's Finest #173 or Batman as Two-Face; only S.A. mention of character); N. Adams-a; 52 pg. issues begin, end #242 12.50 37.00 135.00
,236,239-242: 239-XMas-c. 241-Reprint/#5 2.80 8.40 28.00
-N. Adams-a. G.A. Batman-r/Det. #37; 1st app. The Reaper; Wrightson/Ellison plots 5.45 16.35 60.00
-Also listed as DC 100 Page Super Spectacular #8; Batman, Legion, Aquaman-r; G.A. Atom, Sargon (r/Sensation #57), Plastic Man (r/Police #14) stories; Doom Patrol origin-r; N. Adams wraparound-c (see DC 100 Pg. Super Spectacular #8 for price)
-245-Neal Adams-a 3.65 11.00 40.00
-250,252,253: 246-Scarecrow app. 253-Shadow-c & app.
2.50 7.50 23.00
-(9/73)-N. Adams-c/a; Joker-c/story 5.90 17.75 65.00
,256-259,261-All 100 pg. editions; part-r: 254-(2/74)-Man-Bat-c & app. 256-Catwoman app. 257-Joker & Penguin app. 258-The Cavalier-r. 259-Shadow-c/app. 3.00 9.00 30.00
-(100 pgs.)-N. Adams-c/a; tells of Bruce Wayne's father who wore bat costume & fought crime (r/Det. #235); r/story Batman #22
4.35 13.00 48.00
-Joker-c/story (100 pgs.) 4.35 13.00 48.00
(68pgs.) 2.50 7.50 25.00
,264,266-285,287-290,292,293,295-299: 266-Catwoman back to old costume 1.75 5.25 14.00
-Wrightson-a(i) 2.00 6.00 16.00
,291,294: 294-Joker-c/stories 2.00 6.00 17.00
-Double-size 2.30 7.00 20.00
-(7/78)-310,312-315,317-320,325-331,333-352: 304-(44 pgs.). 306-3rd app. Black Spider. 308-Mr. Freeze app. 310-1st modern app. The Gentleman Ghost in Batman; Kubert-c. 312,314,346-Two-Face-c/stories. 313-2nd app. Calendar Man. 318-Intro Firebug. 319-2nd modern age app. The Gentleman Ghost; Kubert-c. 344-Poison Ivy app. 345-1st app. new Dr. Death. 345,346,351-7 pg. Catwoman back-ups 1.25 3.75 10.00
,316,322-324: 311-Batgirl-c/story; Batgirl reteams w/Batman. 316-Robin returns. 322-324-Catwoman (Selina Kyle) app. 322,323-Cat-Man cameos (1st in Batman, 1 panel each). 323-1st meeting Catwoman & Cat-Man. 324-1st full app. Cat-Man this title 1.50 4.50 12.00
,353,359-Joker-c/stories. 1.50 4.50 12.00
-Catwoman's 1st solo. 1.50 4.50 12.00
-356,358,360-365,369,370: 361-1st app Harvey Bullock
1.00 2.80 7.00
-1st app. Jason Todd (3/83); see Det. #524; 1st app. Croc (cameo)
1.25 3.75 10.00
-Jason Todd 1st in Robin costume; Joker-c/story 1.50 4.50 12.00
-Jason in red & green costume (not as Robin) 1.00 3.00 8.00
-1st new Robin in costume (Jason Todd) 1.10 3.30 9.00
-399,401-403: 371-Cat-Man-c/story; brief origin Cat-Man (cont'd in Det. #538). 386,387-Intro Black Mask (villain). 380-391-Catwoman app. 398-Catwoman & Two-Face app. 401-2nd app. Magpie (see Man of Steel #3 for 1st). 403-Joker cameo 4.50

E: Most issues between 397 & 432 were reprinted in 1989 and sold in multi-packs. Some not identified as reprints but have newer ads copyrighted after cover dates. 2nd and 3rd print-exist.

($1.50, 68pgs.)-Dark Knight special; intro by Stephen King; Art Adams/Austin-a 2.25 6.75 19.00
-Miller scripts begin (end 407); Year 1; 1st modern app. Catwoman (2/87)
1.25 3.75 10.00
-407: 407-Year 1 ends (See Det. Comics for Year 2)
1.00 2.80 7.00

408-410: New Origin Jason Todd (Robin) 5.00
411-416,421-425: 411-Two-face app. 412-Origin/1st app. Mime. 414-Starlin scripts begin, end #429. 416-Nightwing-c/story. 423-McFarlane-c 4.00
417-420: "Ten Nights of the Beast" storyline 5.00
426-($1.50, 52 pgs.)- "A Death In The Family" storyline begins, ends #429
1.50 4.50 12.00
427- "A Death In The Family" part 2. 1.25 3.75 10.00
428-Death of Robin (Jason Todd) 1.00 3.00 8.00
429-Joker-c/story; Superman app. 5.00
430-432 3.00
433-435-Many Deaths of the Batman story by John Byrne-c/scripts 3.00
436-Year 3 begins (ends #439); origin original Robin retold by Nightwing (Dick Grayson); 1st app. Timothy Drake (8/89) 3.00
436-441: 436-2nd printing. 437-Origin Robin cont. 440,441: "A Lonely Place of Dying" Parts 1 & 3 2.50
442-1st app. Timothy Drake in Robin costume 3.00
443-456,458,459,462-464: 445-447-Batman goes to Russia. 448,449-The Penguin Affair Pts 1 & 3. 450-Origin Joker. 450,451-Joker-c/stories. 452-454-Dark Knight Dark City storyline; Riddler app. 455-Alan Grant scripts begin, ends #466, 470. 464-Last solo Batman story; free 16 pg. preview of Impact Comics line 2.50
457-Timothy Drake officially becomes Robin & dons new costume 3.00
457-Direct sale edition (has #000 in indicia) 3.00
460,461,465-487: 460,461-Two part Catwoman story. 465-Robin returns to action with Batman. 470-War of the Gods x-over. 475,476-Return of Scarface-c/story. 476-Last $1.00-c.477,478-Photo-c 2.50
488-Cont'd from Batman: Sword of Azrael #4; Azrael-c & app.
1.00 2.80 7.00
489-Bane-c/story; 1st app. Azrael in Bat-costume 4.00
490-Riddler-c/story; Azrael & Bane app. 5.00
491,492: 491-Knightfall lead-in; Joker-c/story; Azrael & Bane app.; Kelley Jones-c begin. 492-Knightfall part 1; Bane app. 4.00
492-Platinum edition (promo copy) 10.00
493-496: 493-Knightfall Pt. 3. 494-Knightfall Pt. 5; Joker-c & app. 495-Knightfall Pt. 7; brief Bane & Joker apps. 496-Knightfall Pt. 9, Joker-c/story; Bane cameo. 3.00
497-(Late 7/93)-Knightfall Pt. 11; Bane breaks Batman's back; B&W outer-c; Aparo-a(p); Giordano-a(i) 4.00
497-499: 497-2nd printing. 497-Newsstand edition w/o outer cover. 498-Knightfall part 15; Bane & Catwoman-c & app. (see Showcase 93 #7 & 8) 499-Knightfall Pt. 17; Bane app. 2.50
500-($2.50, 68 pgs.)-Knightfall Pt. 19; Azrael in new Bat-costume; Bane-c/story 2.50
500-($3.95, 68 pgs.)-Collector's Edition w/die-cut double-c w/foil by Joe Quesada & 2 bound-in post cards 4.50
501-508,510,511: 501-Begin $1.50-c. 501-508-Knightquest. 503,504-Catwoman app. 507-Ballistic app.; Jim Balent-a(p). 510-KnightsEnd Pt. 7. 511-(9/94)-Zero Hour; Batgirl-c/story 2.50
509-($2.50, 52 pgs.)-KnightsEnd Pt. 1 3.00
512-514,516-518: 512-(11/94)-Dick Grayson assumes Batman role 2.50
515-Special Ed.($2.50)-Kelley Jones-a begins; all black embossed-c; Troika Pt. 1 3.00
515-Regular Edition 2.50
519-534,536-549: 519-Begin $1.95-c. 521-Return of Alfred, 522-Swamp Thing app. 525-Mr. Freeze app. 527,528-Two Face app. 529-Contagion Pt. 6. 530-532-Deadman app. 533-Legacy prelude. 534-Legacy Pt. 5. 536-Final Night x-over; Man-Bat-c/app. 540,541-Spectre-c-app. 544-546-Joker & The Demon. 548,549-Penguin-c/app. 2.50
530-532 ($2.50)-Enhanced edition; glow-in-the-dark-c. 3.00
535-(10/96, $2.95)-1st app. The Ogre 3.00
535-(10/96, $3.95)-1st app. The Ogre; variant, cardboard, foldout-c 4.00
550-($3.50)-Collector's Ed., includes 4 collector cards; intro. Chase, return of Clayface; Kelley Jones-c 3.50
550-($2.95)-Standard Ed.; Williams & Gray-c 3.00
551,552,554-562: 551,552-Ragman c/app. 554-Cataclysm pt. 12. 2.00
553-Cataclysm pt.3 4.00
563-No Man's Land; Joker-c by Campbell; Bob Gale-s 2.40 6.00
564-569: 569-New Batgirl-c/app. 2.00
570-574: 572-Joker and Harley app. 2.00

Batman #581 © DC

Batman Special #1 © DC

Batman: The Chalice HC © DC

GD2.0 FN6.0 NM9.4

575-579: 575-New look Batman begins; McDaniel-a 2.00
580-587: 580-Begin $2.25-c. 587-Gordon shot 2.25
#0 (10/94)-Zero Hour issue released between #511 & #512; Origin retold 2.50
#1,000,000 (11/98) 853rd Century x-over 2.00
Annual 1 (8-10/61)-Swan-c 55.00 166.00 775.00
Annual 2 29.00 87.00 320.00
Annual 3 (Summer, '62)-Joker-c/story 30.00 90.00 330.00
Annual 4,5 13.00 39.00 145.00
Annual 6,7 (7/64, 25¢, 80 pgs.) 10.00 30.00 110.00
Annual V5#8 (1982)-Painted-c 1.00 2.80 7.00
Annual 9,10,12: 9(7/85). 10(1986). 12(1988, $1.50) 5.00
Annual 11 (1987, $1.25)-Penguin-c/story; Alan Moore-s 1.00 2.80 7.00
Annual 13 (1989, $1.75, 68 pgs.)-Gives history of Bruce Wayne, Dick Grayson, Jason Todd, Alfred, Comm. Gordon, Barbara Gordon (Batgirl) & Vicki Vale; Morrow-i 4.00
Annual 14-17 ('90-'93, 68 pgs.)-14-Origin Two-Face. 15-Armageddon 2001 x-over; Joker app. 15 (2nd printing). 16-Joker-c/s; Kieth-c. 17 (1993, $2.50, 68 pgs.)-Azrael in Bat-costume; intro Ballistic 4.00
Annual 18 (1994, $2.95) 3.00
Annual 19 (1995, $3.95)-Year One story; retells Scarecrow's origin 4.00
Annual 20 (1996, $2.95)-Legends of the Dead Earth story; Giarrano-a 3.00
Annual 21 (1997, $3.95)-Pulp Heroes story 4.00
Annual 22,23 ('98, '99, $2.95)-22-Ghosts; Wrightson-c. 23-JLApe; Art Adams-c 3.00
Annual 24 ('00, $3.50) Planet DC; intro. The Boggart; Aparo-a 3.50
Special 1 (4/84)-Mike W. Barr story; Golden-c/a 2.40 6.00

NOTE: ***Art Adams** a-400p. **Neal Adams** c-200, 203, 210, 217, 219-222, 224-227, 229, 230, 232, 234, 236-241, 243-246, 251, 255, Annual 14. **Aparo** a-414-420, 426-435, 440-448, 450, 451, 480-483, 486-491, 494-500; c-414-416, 481, 482, 463i, 486, 487i. **Bolland** a-400; c-445-447. **Burnley** a-10, 12-18, 20, 22, 25, 27; c-9, 15, 16, 27, 28p, 40p, 42p. **Byrne** c-401, 433-435, 533-535, Annual 11. **Travis Charest** c-488-490p. **Colan** a-340p, 343-345p, 348-351p, 373p, 383p; c-343p, 345p, 350p. **J. Cole** a-238r. **Cowan** a-Annual 10p. **Golden** a-295p, 303p, 484, 485. **Alan Grant** scripts-455-466, 470, 474-476, 479, 480, Annual 16(part). **Grell** a-287, 288p, 289p, 290; c-287-290. **Infantino/Anderson** c-167, 173, 175, 181, 186, 191, 192, 194, 195, 198, 199. **Kelley Jones** a-513-519, 521-525, 527; c-491-499, 500(newsstand), 501-510, 513. **Kaluta** c-242, 248, 253, Annual 12. **G. Kane/Anderson** c-178-180. **Bob Kane** a-1, 2, 5; c-1-5, 7, 17. **G. Kane** a-(r)-254, 255, 259, 261, 353i. **Kubert** a-238r, 400; c-310, 319p, 327, 328, 344. **McFarlane** c-423. **Mignola** c-426-429, 452-454, Annual 18. **Moldoff** c-101-140. **Moldoff/Giella** a-164-175, 177-181, 183, 184, 186. **Moldoff/Greene** a-169, 172-174, 177-179, 181, 184. **Mooney** a-255r. **Morrow** a-Annual 13i. **Newton** a-305, 306, 328p, 331p, 332p, 337p, 338p, 346p, 352-357p, 360-372p, 374-378p; c-374p, 378p. **Nino** a-Annual 9. **Irv Novick** c-201, 202. **Perez** a-400; c-436-442. **Fred Ray** c-8, 10; w/**Robinson**-11. **Robinson/Roussos** a-12-17, 20, 22, 24, 25, 27, 28, 31, 33, 37. **Robinson** a-12, 14, 18, 22-32,34, 36, 37, 255r, 260r, 261r; c-6, 8, 10, 12-15, 18, 21, 24, 26, 30, 37, 39. **Simonson** a-300p, 312p, 321p; c-300p, 312p, 366, 413i. **P. Smith** a-Annual 9. **Dick Sprang** c-19, 20, 22, 23, 25, 29, 31-36, 38, 51, 55, 66, 73, 76. **Starlin** c/a-402. **Staton** a-334. **Sutton** a-400. **Wrightson** a-265i, 400; c-320r. Bat-Hound app. in 92, 97, 103, 123, 125, 133, 156, 158. Bat-Mite app. in 133, 136, 144, 146, 158, 161. Batwoman app. in 105, 116, 122, 125, 128, 129, 131, 133, 139, 140, 141, 144, 145, 150, 151, 153, 154, 157, 159, 162, 163. **Zeck** c-417-420. Catwoman back-ups in 332, 345, 346, 348-351. Joker app. in 1, 2, 4, 5, 7-9, 11-13, 19, 20, 23, 25, 28, 32 & many more. Robin solo back-up stories in 337-339, 341-343.*

BATMAN (Hardcover books and trade paperbacks)
...: A LONELY PLACE OF DYING (1990, $3.95, 132 pgs.)-r/Batman #440-442 & New Titans #60,61; Perez-c 4.00
...: ANARKY TPB (1999, $12.95) r/early appearances 13.00
...AND DRACULA: RED RAIN nn (1991, $24.95)-Hard-c.; Elseworlds storyline 32.00
...AND DRACULA: Red Rain nn (1992, $9.95)-SC 12.00
ARKHAM ASYLUM Hard-c (1989, $24.95) 30.00
ARKHAM ASYLUM Soft-c ($14.95) 15.00
BIRTH OF THE DEMON Hard-c (1992, $24.95)-Origin of Ras al Ghul 25.00
BIRTH OF THE DEMON Soft-c (1993, $12.95) 13.00
BLIND JUSTICE nn (1992, $7.50)-r/Det. #598-600 7.50
BLOODSTORM (1994, $24.95,HC) Kelley Jones-c/a 28.00
BRIDE OF THE DEMON Hard-c (1990, $19.95) 20.00
BRIDE OF THE DEMON Soft-c ($12.95) 13.00
...: CASTLE OF THE BAT ($5.95)-Elseworlds story 6.00
...: CATACLYSM ('99, $17.95)-r/ story arc 18.00
...: COLLECTED LEGENDS OF THE DARK KNIGHT nn (1994, $12.95)-r/Legends of the Dark Knight #32-34,38,42,43 13.00
...: CRIMSON MIST (1999, $24.95,HC)-Elseworlds story Doug Moench-s/Kelley Jones-c/a 25.00
...: DARK JOKER-THE WILD (1993, $24.95,HC)-Elseworlds story Doug Moench-s/Kelley Jones-c/a 25
...: DARK JOKER-THE WILD (1993, $9.95,SC) 10
...DARK KNIGHT DYNASTY nn (1997, $24.95)-Hard-c.; 3 Elseworlds stories; Barr-s/ S. Hampton painted-a, Gary Frank, McDaniel-a(p) 25
...DARK KNIGHT DYNASTY Softcover (2000, $14.95) Hampton-c 15
...DEADMAN: DEATH AND GLORY nn (1996, $24.95)-Hard-c.; Robinson-s/ Estes-c/a 25
...DEADMAN: DEATH AND GLORY ($12.95)-SC 13
DEATH IN THE FAMILY (1988, $3.95, trade paperback)-r/Batman #426-429 b Aparo 5
DEATH IN THE FAMILY: (2nd - 5th printings) 4
DIGITAL JUSTICE nn (1990, $24.95, Hard-c.)-Computer generated art 25
... FACES (1995, $9.95, TPB) 10
...: FORTUNATE SON HC (1999, $24.95) Gene Ha-a 24
...: FORTUNATE SON SC (2000, $14.95) Gene Ha-a 14
FOUR OF A KIND TPB (1998, $14.95)-r/1995 Year One Annuals featuring Poison Ivy, Riddler, Scarecrow, & Man-Bat 15
...GOTHIC (1992, $12.95, TPB)-r/Legends of the Dark Knight #6-10 13
...: HAUNTED KNIGHT-(1997,12.95) r/ Halloween sp.. 13
... IN THE SEVENTIES TPB ($19.95) Intro. by Dennis O'Neil 20.
... IN THE SIXTIES TPB ($19.95) Intro. by Adam West 20
... LEGACY-(1996,17.95) reprints Legacy 18
...: THE MANY DEATHS OF THE BATMAN (1992, $3.95, 84 pgs.)-r/Batman #433-435 w/new Byrne-c 4
...: THE MOVIES (1997, $19.95)-r/movie adaptions of Batman, Batman Retur Batman Forever, Batman and Robin 20.
...: PREY (1992, $12.95)-Gulacy/Austin-a 13.
...: PRODIGAL (1997, $14.95)-Gulacy/Austin-a 15.
SHAMAN (1993, $12.95)-r/Legends/D.K. #1-5 13.
...: SON OF THE DEMON Hard-c (9/87, $14.95) 30.
...: SON OF THE DEMON limited signed & numbered Hard-c (1,700) 45.
...: SON OF THE DEMON Soft-c w/new-c ($8.95) 10.
...: SON OF THE DEMON Soft-c (1989, $9.95, 2nd printing - 4th printing) 10.
... : STRANGE APPARITIONS ($12.95) r/'77-'78 Englehart/Rogers stories fror Detective #469-479; also Simonson-a 12.
...: TALES OF THE DEMON (1991, $17.95, 212 pgs.)-Intro by Sam Hamm; reprints by N. Adams(3) & Golden; contains Saga of Ra's Al Ghul #1 18.
...: TEN NIGHTS OF THE BEAST (1994, $5.95)-r/Batman #417-420 6.
...: THE CHALICE (HC, '99, $24.95) Van Fleet painted-a 25.
...: THE CHALICE (SC, '00, $14.95) Van Fleet painted-a 15.
...: THE LAST ANGEL (1994, $12.95, TPB) 13.
...: THRILLKILLER (1998, $12.95, TPB)-r/series & Thrillkiller '62 13.
...: VENOM (1993, $9.95, TPB)-r/Legends of the Dark Knight #16-20; embossed-c 10.
YEAR ONE Hard-c (1988, $12.95) 18.
YEAR ONE (1988, $9.95, TPB)-r/Batman #404-407 by Miller; intro by Miller 10
YEAR ONE (TPB, 2nd & 3rd printings) 10.
YEAR TWO (1990, $9.95, TPB)-r/Det. 575-578 by McFarlane; wraparound-c 10.

BATMAN (one-shots)
... ABDUCTION, THE (1998, $5.95) 6
... & ROBIN (1997, $5.95)-Movie adaption 6
...: ARKHAM ASYLUM - TALES OF MADNESS (5/98, $2.95) Cataclysm x-over pt. 16; Grant-s/Taylor-a 3.
... : BANE (1997, $4.95)-Dixon-s/Burchett-a; Stelfreeze-c; cover interlocks w/Batman:(Batgirl, Mr. Freeze, Poison Ivy) 5.
... : BATGIRL (1997, $4.95)-Puckett-s/Haley,Kesel-a; Stelfreeze-c; cover interlocks w/Batman:(Bane, Mr. Freeze, Poison Ivy) 5.
... : BATGIRL (6/98, $1.95)-Girlfrenzy; Balent-a 2.
... : BLACKGATE (1/97, $3.95) Dixon-s 4.
... : BLACKGATE - ISLE OF MEN (4/98, $2.95) Cataclysm x-over pt. 8; Moench-s/Aparo-a 3.
... BOOK OF SHADOWS, THE (1999, $5.95) 6.
BROTHERHOOD OF THE BAT (1995, $5.95)-Elseworlds-s 6.
... BULLOCK'S LAW (8/99, $4.95) Dixon-s 5.
.../CAPTAIN AMERICA (1996, $5.95, DC/Marvel) Elseworlds story;

Batman: Mask of the Phantasm © DC

Batman and Robin Adventures: Sub-Zero © DC

Batman Adventures: The Lost Years #4 © DC

GD2.0 FN6.0 NM9.4 GD2.0 FN6.0 NM9.4

Byrne-c/s/a 6.00
.. : CATWOMAN DEFIANT nn (1992, $4.95, prestige format)-Milligan scripts; cover interlocks w/Batman: Penguin Triumphant; special foil logo. 5.00
.. /DAREDEVIL (2000, $5.95)-Barreto-a 6.00
.. : DARK ALLEGIANCES (1996, $5.95)-Elseworlds story, Chaykin-c/a. 6.00
.. : DARK KNIGHT GALLERY (1/96, $3.50)-Pin-ups by Pratt, Balent, & others. 3.50
.:DAY OF JUDGMENT (11/99, $3.95) 4.00
.:DEATH OF INNOCENTS (12/96, $3.95)-O'Neil-s/ Staton-a(p) 4.00
./DEMON (1996, $4.95)-Alan Grant scripts 5.00
./DEMON: A TRAGEDY (2000, $5.95)-Grant-s/Murray painted-a 6.00
.:D.O.A. (1999, $6.95)-Bob Hall-s/a 6.95
.:DREAMLAND (2000, $5.95)-Grant-s/Breyfogle-a 6.00
. : EGO (2000, $6.95)-Darwyn Cooke-s/a 7.00
. 80-PAGE GIANT (8/98, $4.95) Stelfreeze-c 5.00
. 80-PAGE GIANT 2 (10/99, $4.95) Luck of the Draw 5.00
. 80-PAGE GIANT 3 (7/00, $5.95) Calendar Man 5.00
. FOREVER (1995, $5.95, direct market) 6.00
. FOREVER (1995, $3.95, newsstand) 4.00
ULL CIRCLE nn (1991, $5.95, 68 pgs.)-Sequel to Batman: Year Two 6.00
.GALLERY, The 1 (1992, $2.95)-Pin-ups by Miller, N. Adams & others 3.00
.GOTHAM BY GASLIGHT (1989, $3.95) 4.00
.GOTHAM CITY SECRET FILES 1 (4/00, $4.95) Batgirl app. 4.95
./GREEN ARROW: THE POISON TOMORROW nn (1992, $5.95, square-bound, 68 pgs.)-Netzer-c/a 6.00
OLY TERROR nn (1991, $4.95, 52 pgs.)-Elseworlds story 5.00
./HOUDINI: THE DEVIL'S WORKSHOP (1993, $5.95) 6.00
. :HUNTRESS/SPOILER - BLUNT TRAUMA (5/98, $2.95) Cataclysm pt. 13 Dixon-s/Barreto & Sienkiewicz-a 3.00
: I, JOKER nn (1998, $4.95)-Elseworlds story;Bob Hall-s/a 5.00
: IN DARKEST KNIGHT nn (1994, $4.95, 52 pgs.)-Elseworlds story; Batman w/Green Lantern's ring. 5.00
:JOKER'S APPRENTICE (5/99, $3.95) Von Eeden-a 4.00
:JUDGE DREDD: JUDGEMENT ON GOTHAM nn (1991, $5.95, 68 pgs.) Grant/Wagner scripts; Simon Bisley-c/a 6.00
:JUDGE DREDD: JUDGEMENT ON GOTHAM nn (2nd printing) 6.00
JUDGE DREDD: THE ULTIMATE RIDDLE (1995, $4.95) 5.00
:JUDGE DREDD: VENDETTA IN GOTHAM (1993, $5.95) 6.00
: KNIGHTGALLERY (1995, $3.50)-Elseworlds sketchbook. 3.50
/ LOBO (2000, $5.95)-Elseworlds; Joker app.; Bisley-a 5.95
: MASK OF THE PHANTASM (1994, $2.95)-Movie adapt. 3.00
: MASK OF THE PHANTASM (1994, $4.95)-Movie adapt. 5.00
: MASQUE (1997, $6.95)-Elseworlds; Grell-c/s/a 7.00
: MASTER OF THE FUTURE nn (1991, $5.95, 68 pgs.)-Elseworlds storyline; sequel to Gotham By Gaslight; embossed-c 6.00
: MITEFALL (1995, $4.95)-Alan Grant script, Kevin O'Neill-a 5.00
: MR. FREEZE (1997, $4.95)-Dini-s/Buckingham-a; Stelfreeze-c; cover interlocks w/Batman:(Bane, Batgirl, Poison Ivy) 5.00
NOSFERATU (1999, $5.95) McKeever-a 6.00
OF ARKHAM (2000, $5.95)-Elseworlds; Grant-s/Alcatena-a 6.00
PENGUIN TRIUMPHANT nn (1992, $4.95)-Staton-a(p); special foil logo 5.00
PHANTOM STRANGER nn (1997, $4.95) nn-Grant-s/Ransom-a 5.00
: PLUS (2/97, $2.95) Arsenal-c/app. 3.00
: POISON IVY (1997, $4.95)-J.F. Moore-s/Apthorp-a; Stelfreeze-c; cover interlocks w/Batman:(Bane, Batgirl, Mr. Freeze) 5.00
PUNISHER: LAKE OF FIRE (1994, $4.95, DC/Marvel) 5.00
:REIGN OF TERROR ('99, $4.95) Elseworlds 5.00
RETURNS MOVIE SPECIAL (1992, $3.95) 4.00
RETURNS MOVIE PRESTIGE (1992, $5.95, squarebound)-Dorman painted-c 6.00
RIDDLER-THE RIDDLE FACTORY (1995, $4.95)-Wagner script 5.00
SCARECROW 3-D (12/98, $3.95) w/glasses 4.00
SCAR OF THE BAT nn (1996, $4.95)-Elseworlds story; Max Allan Collins script; Barreto-a. 5.00
SCOTTISH CONNECTION (1998, $5.95) Quitely-a 6.00
SEDUCTION OF THE GUN nn (1992, $2.50, 68 pgs.) 2.50

.../SPAWN: WAR DEVIL nn (1994, $4.95, 52 pgs.) 5.00
.../SPIDER-MAN (1997, $4.95) Dematteis-s/Nolan & Kesel-a 5.00
... : THE ABDUCTION ('98, $5.95) 6.00
... :THE BLUE, THE GREY, & THE BAT (1992, $5.95)-Weiss/Lopez-a 6.00
... :THE HILL (5/00, $2.95)-Priest-s/Martinbrough-a 3.00
... :THE KILLING JOKE (1988, deluxe 52 pgs., mature readers)-Bolland-c/a; Alan Moore scripts; Joker cripples Barbara Gordon 12.00
...: THE KILLING JOKE (2nd thru 8th printings) 3.50
...: THE OFFICIAL COMIC ADAPTATION OF THE WARNER BROS. MOTION PICTURE (1989, $2.50, regular format, 68 pgs.)-Ordway-c. 3.00
...: THE OFFICIAL COMIC ADAPTATION OF THE WARNER BROS. MOTION PICTURE (1989, $4.95, prestige format, 68 pgs.)-same interiors but different-c than regular format. 5.00
...: TWO-FACE-CRIME AND PUNISHMENT-(1995, $4.95)-Scott McDaniel-a 5.00
... : TWO FACES (11/98, $4.95) Elseworlds 5.00
...: VENGEANCE OF BANE SPECIAL 1 (1992, $2.50, 68 pgs.)-Origin & 1st app. Bane (see Batman #491) 1.00 3.00 10.00
...: VENGEANCE OF BANE SPECIAL 1 (2nd printing) 2.50
....:VENGEANCE OF BANE II nn (1995, $3.95)-sequel 4.00
...Vs. THE INCREDIBLE HULK (1995, $3.95)-r/DC Special Series #27 4.00
...: VILLAINS SECRET FILES (10/98, $4.95) Origin-s 5.00

BATMAN ADVENTURES, THE (Based on animated series)
DC Comics: Oct, 1992 - No. 36, Oct, 1995 ($1.25/$1.50)

1-Penguin-c/story 4.00
1 ($1.95, Silver Edition)-2nd printing 2.00
2-6,8-19: 2,12-Catwoman-c/story. 3-Joker-c/story. 5-Scarecrow-c/story. 10-Riddler-c/story. 11-Man-Bat-c/story. 12-Batgirl & Catwoman-c/story. 16-Joker-c/story; begin $1.50-c. 18-Batgirl-c/story. 19-Scarecrow-c/story. 3.00
7-Special edition polybagged with Man-Bat trading card 5.00
20-24,26-32: 26-Batgirl app. 2.50
25-($2.50, 52 pgs.)-Superman app. 3.00
33-36: 33-Begin $1.75-c 2.00
Annual 1,2 ('94, '95): 2-Demon-c/story; Ra's al Ghul app. 3.50
Holiday Special 1 (1995, $2.95) 4.00
The Collected Adventures Vol. 1,2 ('93, '95, $5.95) 6.00
TPB ('98, $7.95) r/#1-6; painted wraparound-c 8.00

BATMAN ADVENTURES, THE: MAD LOVE
DC Comics: Feb, 1994 ($3.95/$4.95)

1-Origin of Harley Quinn; Dini-s/Timm-c/a 1.50 4.50 12.00
1-($4.95, Prestige format) new Timm painted-c 2.40 6.00

BATMAN ADVENTURES, THE: THE LOST YEARS (TV)
DC Comics: Jan, 1998 - No. 5, May, 1998 ($1.95) (Based on animated series)

1-5-Leads into Fall '97's new animated episodes. 4-Tim Drake becomes Robin. 5-Dick becomes Nightwing 2.00
TPB-(1999, $9.95) r/series 9.95

BATMAN/ALIENS
DC Comics/Dark Horse: Mar, 1997 - No. 2, Apr, 1997 ($4.95, lim. series)

1,2: Wrightson-c/a. 5.00
TPB-(1997, $14.95) w/prequel from DHP #101,102 15.00

BATMAN AND ROBIN ADVENTURES (TV)
DC Comics: Nov, 1995 - No. 25, Dec, 1997 ($1.75) (Based on animated series)

1-Dini-s. 2.00
2-24: 2-4-Dini script. 4-Penguin-c/story. 5-Joker-c/story; Poison Ivy, Harley Quinn-c/app. 9-Batgirl & Talia-c/story. 10-Ra's Al Ghul-c/story 11-Man-Bat app. 12-Bane-c/app. 13-Scarecrow-c/app. 15 Deadman-c/app. 16-Catwoman-c/app. 18-Joker-c/app. 24-Poison Ivy app. 1.75
25-($2.95, 48 pgs.) 3.00
Annual 1,2 (11/96, 11/97): 1-Phantasm-c/app. 2-Zatara and Zatanna-c/app. 4.00
...: Sub-Zero(1998, $3.95) Adaption of animated video 4.00

BATMAN AND SUPERMAN ADVENTURES: WORLD'S FINEST
DC Comics: 1997 ($6.95, square-bound, one-shot) (Based on animated series)

1-Adaption of animated crossover episode; Dini-s/Timm-c. 7.00

Batman and Superman: World's Finest #10 © DC

Batman Beyond #4 © DC

Batman: Harley Quinn #1 © DC

BATMAN AND SUPERMAN: WORLD'S FINEST
DC Comics: Apr, 1999 - No. 10, Jan, 2000 ($4.95/$1.99, limited series)

1,10-($4.95, squarebound) Taylor-a 5.00
2-9-($1.99) 5-Batgirl app. 8-Catwoman-c/app. 2.00

BATMAN AND THE OUTSIDERS (The Adventures of the Outsiders#33 on) (Also see Brave & The Bold #200 & The Outsiders) (Replaces The Brave and the Bold)
DC Comics: Aug, 1983 - No. 32, Apr, 1986 (Mando paper #5 on)

1,5: 1-Batman, Halo, Geo-Force, Katana, Metamorpho & Black Lightning begin. 5-New Teen Titans x-over 3.00
2-4,6-32: 9-Halo begins. 11,12-Origin Katana. 18-More info on Metamorpho's origin. 28-31-Lookers origin. 32-Team disbands 2.00
Annual 1,2 (9/84, 9/85): 2-Metamorpho & Sapphire Stagg wed 3.00

NOTE: ***Aparo*** *a-1-9, 11-13p, 16-20; c-1-4, 5i, 6-21, Annual 1, 2.* ***B. Kane*** *a-3r.* ***Layton*** *a-19i, 20i.* ***Lopez*** *a-3p.* ***Miller*** *c-Annual 1.* ***Perez*** *c-5p.* ***B. Willingham*** *a-14p.*

BATMAN: BANE OF THE DEMON
DC Comics: Mar, 1998 - No. 4, June, 1998 ($1.95, limited series)

1-4-Dixon-s/Nolan-a; prelude to Legacy x-over 2.00

BATMAN BEYOND (Based on animated series)(Mini-series)
DC Comics: Mar, 1999 - No. 6, Aug, 1999 ($1.99)

1-6: 1,2-Adaption of pilot episode, Timm-c 2.00
TPB (1999, $9.95) r/#1-6 9.95

BATMAN BEYOND (Based on animated series)(Continuing series)
DC Comics: Nov, 1999 - Present ($1.99)

1-17: 1-Rousseau-a; Batman vs. Batman. 14-Demon-c/app. 2.00

BATMAN: BLACK & WHITE
DC Comics: June, 1996 - No. 4, Sept, 1996 ($2.95, B&W, limited series)

1-Stories by McKeever, Timm, Kubert, Chaykin, Goodwin; Jim Lee-c; Allred inside front-c; Moebius inside back-c 4.00
2-4: 2-Stories by Simonson, Corben, Bisley & Gaiman; Miller-c. 3-Stories by M. Wagner, Janson, Sienkiewicz, O'Neil & Kristiansen; B. Smith-c; Russell inside front-c; Silvestri inside back-c. 4-Stories by Bolland, Goodwin & Gianni, Strnad & Nowlan, O'Neil & Stelfreeze; Toth-c; pin-ups by Neal Adams & Alex Ross 3.00
Hardcover ('97, $39.95) r/series w/new art & cover plate 40.00
Softcover ('00, $19.95) r/series 20.00

BATMAN: BOOK OF THE DEAD
DC Comics: Jun, 1999 - No. 2, July, 1999 ($4.95, limited series, prestige format)

1,2-Elseworlds; Kitson-a 5.00

BATMAN: CATWOMAN DEFIANT (See Batman one-shots)

BATMAN CHRONICLES, THE
DC Comics: Summer, 1995 - No. 23, Winter, 2001 ($2.95, quarterly)

1-3,5-19: 1-Dixon/Grant/Moench script. 3-Bolland-c. 5-Oracle Year One story, Richard Dragon app.,Chaykin-c. 6-Kaluta-c; Ra's Al Ghul story. 7-Superman-c /app.11-Paul Pope-s/a. 12-Cataclysm pt. 10. 18-No Man's Land 3.50
4-Hitman story by Ennis, Contagion tie-in; Balent-c 1.10 3.30 12.00
20-23: 20-Catwoman and Relative Heroes-c/app. 21-Pander Bros.-a 2.95
...Gallery (3/97, $3.50) Pin-ups 3.50
...Gauntlet, The (1997, $4.95, one-shot) 5.00

BATMAN: DARK KNIGHT OF THE ROUND TABLE
DC Comics: 1999 - No. 2, 1999 ($4.95, limited series, prestige format)

1,2-Elseworlds; Giordano-a 5.00

BATMAN: DARK VICTORY
DC Comics: 1999 - No. 13, 2000 ($4.95/$2.95, limited series)

Wizard #0 Preview 1.00
1-($4.95) Loeb-s/Sale-c/a 5.00
2-12-($2.95) 3.00
13-($4.95) 5.00

BATMAN FAMILY, THE
National Periodical Pub./DC Comics: Sept-Oct, 1975 - No. 20, Oct-Nov, 1978 (#1-4, 17-on: 68 pgs.) (Combined with Detective Comics with No. 481)

1-Origin/2nd app. Batgirl-Robin team-up (The Dynamite Duo); reprints plus one new story begins; N. Adams-a(r); r/1st app. Man-Bat from Det. #400 2.30 7.00 20.
2-5: 2-r/Det. #369. 3-Batgirl & Robin learn each's i.d.; r/Batwoman app. from Batman #105. 4-r/1st Fatman app. from Batman #113. 5-r/1st Bat-Hound app. from Batman #92 1.50 4.50 12.
6,9-Joker's daughter on cover (1st app?) 2.00 6.00 16.
7,8,14-16: 8-r/Batwoman app.14-Batwoman app. 15-3rd app. Killer Moth. 16-Bat-Girl cameo (last app. in costume until New Teen Titans #47) 1.25 3.75 10.
10-1st revival Batwoman; Cavalier app.; Killer Moth app. 2.00 6.00 18.
11-20: 11-13-Rogers-a(p): 11-New stories begin; Man-Bat begins. 13-Batwom cameo. 17-($1.00 size)-Batman, Huntress begin; Batwoman & Catwoman 1 meet. 18-20: Huntress by Staton in all. 20-Origin Ragman retold 1.75 5.25 14.

NOTE: ***Aparo*** *a-17; c-11-16.* ***Austin*** *a-12i.* ***Chaykin*** *a-14p.* ***Michael Golden*** *a-15-17,18-2* ***Grell*** *a-1; c-1.* ***Gil Kane*** *a-2r.* ***Kaluta*** *c-17, 19.* ***Newton*** *a-13.* ***Robinson*** *a-1r, 3i(r), 9r.* ***Russe*** *18i, 19i.* ***Starlin*** *a-17; c-18, 20.*

BATMAN: GCPD
DC Comics: Aug, 1996 - No. 4, Nov, 1996 ($2.25, limited series)

1-4: Features Jim Gordon; Aparo/Sienkiewicz-a 2.2

BATMAN: GORDON OF GOTHAM
DC Comics: June, 1998 - No. 4, Sept, 1998 ($1.95, limited series)

1-4: Gordon's early days in Chicago 2.2

BATMAN: GORDON'S LAW
DC Comics: Dec, 1996 - No. 3, Feb, 1997 ($1.95, limited series)

1-3: Dixon-s/Janson-c/a 2.

BATMAN: GOTHAM ADVENTURES (TV)
DC Comics: June, 1998 - Present ($2.95/$1.95)

1-($2.95) Based on Kids WB Batman animated series 3.
2-3-($1.95): 2-Two-Face-c/app. 2.
4-22: 4-Begin $1.99-c. 5-Deadman-c. 13-MAD #1 cover swipe 2.
23-34: 31-Joker-c/app. 2.
TPB (2000, $9.95) r/#1-6 10.

BATMAN: GOTHAM KNIGHTS
DC Comics: Mar, 2000 - Present ($2.50)

1-10-Grayson-s; B&W back-ups by various 2.
11-($3.25) Bolland-c; Kyle Baker back-up story 3.2

BATMAN: GOTHAM NIGHTS II (First series listed under Gotham Nights)
DC Comics: Mar, 1995 - No. 4, June, 1995 ($1.95, limited series)

1-4 2.

BATMAN/GRENDEL (1st limited series)
DC Comics: 1993 - No. 2, 1993 ($4.95, limited series, squarebound; 52 pgs.)

1,2: Batman vs. Hunter Rose. 1-Devil's Riddle; Matt Wagner-c/a/scripts. 2-Devil's Masque; Matt Wagner-c/a/scripts 2.40 6.

BATMAN/GRENDEL (2nd limited series)
DC Comics: June, 1996 - No. 2, July, 1996 ($4.95, limited series, squareboun

1,2: Batman vs. Grendel Prime. 1-Devil's Bones. 2-Devil's Dance; Wagner-c/a 5.

BATMAN: HARLEY QUINN
DC Comics: 1999 ($5.95, prestige format)

1-Intro. of Harley Quinn into regular DC continuity; Dini-s/Alex Ross-c 9.
1-(2nd printing) 6.

BATMAN: HAUNTED GOTHAM
DC Comics: 2000 - No. 4, 2000 ($4.95, limited series, squarebound)

1-4-Moench-s/Kelley Jones-c/a 4.

BATMAN/ HELLBOY/STARMAN
DC Comics/Dark Horse: Jan, 1999 - No. 2, Feb, 1999 ($2.50, limited series)

1,2: Robinson-s/Mignola-a. 2-Harris-c 2.

BATMAN/ HUNTRESS: CRY FOR BLOOD
DC Comics: Jun, 2000 - No. 6, Nov, 2000 ($2.50, limited series)

1-6: Rucka-s/Burchett-a 2.

Batman: Legends of the Dark Knight #125 © DC

Batman: No Man's Land TPB © DC

Batman: Shadow of the Bat #76 © DC

	GD2.0	FN6.0	NM9.4

TMAN: JOKER TIME (...: It's Joker Time! on cover)
Comics: 2000 - No. 3 ($4.95, limited series, squarebound)

-3-Bob Hall-s/a			4.95

TMAN/ JUDGE DREDD "DIE LAUGHING"
Comics: 1998 - No. 2, 1999 ($4.95, limited series, squarebound)

2: 1-Fabry-c/a. 2-Jim Murray-c/a			5.00

TMAN: KNIGHTGALLERY (See Batman one-shots)

TMAN: LEGENDS OF THE DARK KNIGHT (Legends of the Dark...#1-36)
Comics: Nov, 1989 - Present ($1.50/$1.75/$1.95/$1.99/$2.25)

"Shaman" begins, ends #5; outer cover has four different color variations, all worth same			4.00
-10- "Gothic" by Grant Morrison (scripts)			3.00
-15: 11-15-Gulacy/Austin-a. 13-Catwoman app.			3.00
-Intro drug Bane uses; begin Venom story			5.00
-20			4.00
-49,51-63: 38-Bat-Mite-c/story. 46-49-Catwoman app. w/Heath-c/a. 51-Ragman app.; Joe Kubert-c. 59,60,61-Knightquest x-over. 62,63-KnightsEnd Pt. 4 & 10			3.00
-($3.95, 68 pgs.)-Bolland embossed gold foil-c; Joker-c/story; pin-ups by Chaykin, Simonson, Williamson, Kaluta, Russell, others			5.00
-99: 64-(9/94)-Begin $1.95-c. 71-73-James Robinson-s, J. Watkiss-c/a. 74,75-Ted McKeever-c/a/s. 76-78-Scott Hampton-c/a/s. 81-Card insert. 83,84-Ellis-s. 85-Robinson-s. 91-93-Ennis-s. 94-Michael T. Gilbert-s/a.			3.00
)-($3.95) Alex Ross painted-c; gallery by various			5.00
-115: 101-Ezquerra-a. 102-104-Robinson-s			2.50
6-No Man's Land stories begin; Huntress-c			4.00
7-119,121-126: 122-Harris-c			2.50
)-ID of new Batgirl revealed			4.00
7-131: Return to Legends stories; Green Arrow app.			2.00
2-139: 132-136 ($2.25-c) Archie Goodwin-s/Rogers-a. 137-139-Gulacy-a			2.25
(10/94)-Zero Hour; Quesada/Palmiotti-c; released between #64&65			3.00
nual 1-7 ('91-'97, $3.50-$3.95, 68 pgs.): 1-Joker app. 2-Netzer-c/a. 3-New Batman (Azrael) app. 4-Elseworlds story. 5-Year One; Man-Bat app. 6-Legend of the Dead Earth story. 7-Pulp Heroes story			4.00
lloween Special 1 (12/93, $6.95, 84 pgs.)-Embossed & foil stamped-c	1.00	2.80	7.00
tman Madness-...Halloween Special (1994, $4.95)			5.00
tman Ghosts-...Halloween Special (1995, $4.95)			5.00

TE: ***Aparo*** *a-Annual 1.* ***Chaykin*** *scripts-24-26.* ***Giffen*** *a-Annual 1.* ***Golden*** *a-Annual 1.* ***Alan nt*** *scripts-38, 52, 53.* ***Gil Kane*** *c/a-24-26.* ***Mignola*** *a-54; c-54, 62.* ***Morrow*** *a-Annual 3i.* ***esada*** *a-Annual 1.* ***James Robinson*** *scripts- 71-73.* ***Russell*** *c/a-42, 43.* ***Sears*** *a-21, 23; c-21,* ***Zeck*** *a-69, 70; c-69, 70.*

TMAN-LEGENDS OF THE DARK KNIGHT: JAZZ
Comics: Apr, 1995 - No. 3, June, 1995 ($2.50, limited series)

3			2.50

TMAN: MANBAT
Comics: Oct, 1995 - No. 3, Dec, 1995 ($4.95, limited series)

-3-Elseworlds-Delano-script; Bolton-a.			5.00
B-(1997, $14.95) r/#1-3			15.00

TMAN: MITEFALL (See Batman one-shots)

TMAN MINIATURE (See Batman Kellogg's)

TMAN: NO MAN'S LAND (Also see 1999 Batman titles)
Comics: (one shots)

(3/99, $2.95) Alex Ross-c; Bob Gale-s; begins year-long story arc			3.00
llector's Ed. (3/99, $3.95) Ross lenticular-c			5.00
(: Ground Zero on cover) (12/99, $4.95) Orbik-c			5.00
Gallery (7/99, $3.95) Jim Lee-c			4.00
Secret Files (12/99, $4.95) Maleev-c			5.00
B ('99, $12.95) r/early No Man's Land stories; new Batgirl early app.			13.00
Law and a New Order TPB(1999, $5.95) Ross-c			6.00
lume 2 ('00, $12.95) r/later No Man's Land stories; Batgirl(Huntress) app.; Deodato-c			13.00
lume 3 ('00, $12.95) Intro. new Batgirl; Cariello-c			13.00

TMAN: OUTLAWS
Comics: 2000 - No. 3, 2000 ($4.95, limited series)

1-3-Moench-s/Gulacy-a			5.00

BATMAN: PENGUIN TRIUMPHANT (See Batman one-shots)

BATMAN/PREDATOR III: BLOOD TIES
DC Comics/Dark Horse Comics: Nov, 1997 - No. 4, Feb, 1998 ($1.95, lim. series)

1-4: Dixon-s/Damaggio-c/a			2.00
TPB-(1998, $7.95) r/#1-4			8.00

BATMAN RETURNS MOVIE SPECIAL (See Batman one-shots)

BATMAN: RIDDLER-THE RIDDLE FACTORY (See Batman one-shots)

BATMAN: RUN, RIDDLER, RUN
DC Comics: 1992 - Book 3, 1992 ($4.95, limited series)

Book 1-3: Mark Badger-a & plot			5.00

BATMAN: SECRET FILES
DC Comics: Oct, 1997 ($4.95)

1-New origin-s and profiles			5.00

BATMAN: SHADOW OF THE BAT
DC Comics: June, 1992 - No. 94, Feb, 2000 ($1.50/$1.75/$1.95/$1.99)

1-The Last Arkham-c/story begins; Alan Grant scripts in all			4.00
1-($2.50)-Deluxe edition polybagged w/poster, pop-up & book mark			5.00
2-7: 4-The Last Arkham ends. 7-Last $1.50-c			3.00
8-28: 14,15-Staton-a(p). 16-18-Knightfall tie-ins. 19-28-Knightquest tie-ins w/Azrael as Batman. 25-Silver ink-c; anniversary issue			2.50
29-($2.95, 52 pgs.)-KnightsEnd Pt. 2			3.00
30-72: 30-KnightsEnd Pt. 8. 31-(9.94)-Begin $1.95-c; Zero Hour. 32-(11/94). 33-Robin-c. 35-Troika-Pt.2. 43,44-Cat-Man & Catwoman-c. 48-Contagion Pt. 1; card insert. 49-Contagion Pt.7. 56,57,58-Poison Ivy-c/app. 62-Two-Face app. 69,70-Fate app.			2.50
35-($2.95)-Variant embossed-c			3.00
73,74,76-78: Cataclysm x-over pts. 1,9. 76-78-Orbik-c			2.00
75-($2.95) Mr. Freeze & Clayface app.; Orbik-c			3.00
79,81,82: 79-Begin $1.99-c; Orbik-c			2.00
80-($3.95) Flip book with Azrael #47			4.00
83-No Man's Land; intro. new Batgirl (Huntress)			12.00
84,85-No Man's Land			4.00
86-94: 87-Deodato-a. 90-Harris-c. 92-Superman app. 93-Joker and Harley app. 94-No Man's Land ends			3.00
#0 (10/94) Zero Hour; released between #31&32			2.50
#1,000,000 (11/98) 853rd Century x-over; Orbik-c			2.00
Annual 1-5 ('93-'97 $2.95-$3.95, 68 pgs.): 3-Year One story; Poison Ivy app. 4-Legends of the Dead Earth story; Starman cameo. 5-Pulp Heroes story; Poison Ivy app.			4.00

BATMAN-SPAWN: WAR DEVIL (See Batman one-shots)

BATMAN SPECTACULAR (See DC Special Series No. 15)

BATMAN: SWORD OF AZRAEL (Also see Azrael & Batman #488,489)
DC Comics: Oct, 1992 - No. 4, Jan, 1993 ($1.75, limited series)

1-Wraparound gatefold-c; Quesada-c/a(p) in all; 1st app. Azrael	1.10	3.30	9.00
2-4: 4-Cont'd in Batman #488		2.40	6.00
Silver Edition 1-4 (1993, $1.95)-Reprints #1-4			2.00
Trade Paperback (1993, $9.95)-Reprints #1-4			10.00
Trade Paperback Gold Edition			15.00

BATMAN/ TARZAN: CLAWS OF THE CAT-WOMAN
Dark Horse Comics/DC Comics: Sept, 1999 - No. 4, Dec, 1999 ($2.95, limited series)

1-4: Marz-s/Kordey-a			2.95

BATMAN: THE CULT
DC Comics: 1988 - No. 4, Nov, 1988 ($3.50, deluxe limited series)

1-Wrightson-a/painted-c in all		2.40	6.00
2-4			5.00
Trade Paperback ('91, $14.95)-New Wrightson-c			15.00

BATMAN: THE DARK KNIGHT RETURNS
DC Comics: Mar, 1986 - No. 4, 1986 ($2.95, squarebound, limited series)

Batman: The Long Halloween #8 © DC

Battle #6 © MAR

Battle Action #5 © ATLAS

1-Miller story & c/a(p); set in the future 3.20 9.60 35.00
1,2-2nd & 3rd printings, 3-2nd printing 2.40 6.00
2-Carrie Kelly becomes 1st female Robin 2.00 6.00 18.00
3-Death of Joker; Superman app. 1.50 4.50 12.00
4-Death of Alfred; Superman app. 1.10 3.30 9.00
Hard-c, signed & numbered edition ($40.00)(4000 copies) 250.00
Hard-c, trade edition 50.00
Soft-c, trade edition (1st printing only) 2.00 6.00 18.00
Soft-c, trade edition (2nd thru 8th printings) 1.10 3.30 9.00
10th Anniv. Slipcase set ('96, $100.00): Signed & numbered hard-c edition (10,000 copies), sketchbook, copy of script for #1, 2 colorprints 100.00
10th Anniv. Hard-c ('96, $45.00) 45.00
10th Anniv. Soft-c ('97, $14.95) 15.00

NOTE: *The #2 second printings can be identified by matching the grey background colors on the inside front cover and facing page. The inside front cover of the second printing has a dark grey background which does not match the lighter grey of the facing page. On the true 1st printings, the backgrounds are both light grey. All other issues are clearly marked.*

BATMAN: THE DOOM THAT CAME TO GOTHAM
DC Comics: 2000 - No. 3, 2001 ($4.95, limited series)
1-3-Elseworlds; Mignola-c/s; Nixey-a; Etrigan app. 4.95

BATMAN: THE KILLING JOKE (See Batman one-shots)

BATMAN: THE LONG HALLOWEEN
DC Comics: Oct, 1996 - No. 13, Oct, 1997 ($2.95/$4.95, limited series)
1-($4.95)-Loeb-s/Sale-c/a in all 1.00 3.00 8.00
2-5($2.95): 2-Solomon Grundy-c/app. 3-Joker-c/app., Catwoman, Poison Ivy app. 2.40 6.00
6-10: 6-Poison Ivy-c. 7-Riddler-c/app. 5.00
11,12 4.00
13-($4.95, 48 pgs.)-Killer revelations 5.00
HC-($29.95) r/series 30.00
SC-($19.95) 20.00

BATMAN: THE OFFICIAL COMIC ADAPTATION OF THE WARNER BROS. MOTION PICTURE (See Batman one-shots)

BATMAN: THE ULTIMATE EVIL
DC Comics: 1995 ($5.95, limited series, prestige format)
1,2-Barrett, Jr. adaptation of Vachss novel. 6.00

BATMAN 3-D (Also see 3-D Batman)
DC Comics: 1990 ($9.95, w/glasses, 8-1/8x10-3/4")
nn-Byrne-a/scripts; Riddler, Joker, Penguin & Two-Face app. plus r/1953 3-D Batman; pin-ups by many artists 1.50 4.50 12.00

BATMAN: TOYMAN
DC Comics: Nov, 1998 - No. 4, Feb, 1999 ($2.25, limited series)
1-4-Hama-s 2.25

BATMAN: TURNING POINTS
DC Comics: Jan, 2001 - No. 5, Jan, 2001 ($2.50, weekly limited series)
1-5: 2-Giella-a. 3-Kubert-c/ Giordano-a. 4-Chaykin-c. 5-Pope-c/a 2.50

BATMAN: TWO-FACE-CRIME AND PUNISHMENT (See Batman one-shots)

BATMAN: TWO-FACE STRIKES TWICE
DC Comics: 1993 - No. 2, 1993 ($4.95, 52 pgs.)
1,2-Flip book format w/Staton-a (G.A. side) 5.00

BATMAN VERSUS PREDATOR
DC Comics/Dark Horse Comics: 1991 - No. 3, 1992 ($4.95/$1.95, limited series) (1st DC/Dark Horse x-over)
1 (Prestige format, $4.95)-1 & 3 contain 8 Batman/Predator trading cards; Andy & Adam Kubert-a; Suydam painted-c 6.00
1-3 (Regular format, $1.95)-No trading cards 4.00
2,3-(Prestige)-2-Extra pin-ups inside; Suydam-c 5.00
TPB (1993, $5.95, 132 pgs.)-r/#1-3 w/new introductions & forward plus new wraparound-c by Gibbons 6.00

BATMAN VERSUS PREDATOR II: BLOODMATCH
DC Comics: Late 1994 - No. 4, 1995 ($2.50, limited series)
1-4-Huntress app.; Moench scripts; Gulacy-a 2.50
TPB (1995, $6.95)-r/#1-4 7.00

BATMAN VS. THE INCREDIBLE HULK (See DC Special Series No. 27)

BATMAN: WAR ON CRIME
DC Comics: Nov, 1999 ($9.95, treasury size, one-shot)
nn-Painted art by Alex Ross; story by Alex Ross and Paul Dini 10.0

BATMAN/ WILDCAT
DC Comics: Apr, 1997 - No.3, June, 1997 ($2.25, mini-series)
1-3: Dixon/Smith-s: 1-Killer Croc app. 2.2

BAT MASTERSON (TV) (Also see Tim Holt #28)
Dell Publishing Co.: Aug-Oct, 1959; Feb-Apr, 1960 - No. 9, Nov-Jan, 1961-62
Four Color 1013 (#1) (8-10/59) 11.70 35.00 140.0
2-9: Gene Barry photo-c on all. 2-Two different back-c exist 5.85 17.50 70.0

BATS (See Tales Calculated to Drive You Bats)

BATS, CATS & CADILLACS
Now Comics: Oct, 1990 - No. 2, Nov, 1990 ($1.75)
1,2: 1-Gustovich-a(i); Snyder-c 2.0

BAT-THING
DC Comics (Amalgam): June, 1997 ($1.95, one-shot)
1-Hama-s/Damaggio & Sienkiewicz-a 2.0

BATTLE
Marvel/Atlas Comics(FPI #1-62/ Male #63 on): Mar, 1951 - No. 70, Jun, 1960
1 30.00 90.00 240.0
2 14.00 41.00 110.0
3-10: 4-1st Buck Pvt. O'Toole. 10-Pakula-a 10.00 30.00 80.0
11-20: 11-Check-a 8.65 26.00 60.0
21,23-Krigstein-a 10.00 30.00 70.0
22,24-36: 32-Tuska-a. 36-Everett-a 7.00 21.00 48.0
37-Kubert-a (Last precode, 2/55) 7.85 23.50 55.0
38-40,42-48 5.70 17.00 40.0
41,49: 41-Kubert/Moskowitz-a. 49-Davis-a 7.15 21.50 50.0
50-54,56-58 5.50 16.50 38.0
55-Williamson-a (5 pgs.) 7.85 23.50 55.0
59-Torres-a 6.00 18.00 42.0
60-62: 60,62-Combat Kelly app. 61-Combat Casey app. 5.50 16.50 38.0
63-Ditko-a 10.00 30.00 75.0
64-66-Kirby-a. 66-Davis-a; has story of Fidel Castro in pre-Communism days (an admiring profile) 11.00 33.00 90.0
67,68: 67-Williamson/Crandall-a (4 pgs.); Kirby, Davis-a. 68-Kirby/ Williamson-a (4 pgs.); Kirby/Ditko-a 12.00 36.00 95.0
69,70: 69-Kirby-a. 70-Kirby/Ditko-a 10.50 32.00 85.0

NOTE: ***Andru** a-37. **Berg** a-38, 14, 60-62. **Colan** a-33, 55. **Everett** a-36, 50, 70; c-56, 57. **Hea** a-6, 9, 13, 31, 69; c-6, 9, 12, 26, 35, 37. **Kirby** c-64-69. **Maneely** a-4, 6, 31, 61; c-4, 33, 59, **Orlando** a-47. **Powell** a-53; 55. **Reinman** a-8, 9, 26, 32. **Robinson** a-9, 39. **Romita** a- **Severin** a-28, 32-34, 66-69; c-36, 55. **Sinnott** a-33, 37. **Woodbridge** a-52, 55.*

BATTLE ACTION
Atlas Comics (NPI): Feb, 1952 - No. 12, 5/53; No. 13, 11/54 - No. 30, 8/57
1-Pakula-a 24.00 71.00 190.0
2 12.00 36.00 95.0
3,4,6,7,9,10: 6-Robinson-c/a. 7-Partial nudity 7.15 21.50 50.0
5-Used in **POP**, pg. 93,94 7.85 23.50 55.0
8-Krigstein-a 8.65 26.00 60.0
11-15 (Last precode, 2/55) 7.15 21.50 50.0
16-29: 27,30-Torres-a 6.40 19.25 45.0

NOTE: *Battle Brady app. 5-7, 10-12. **Berg** a-3. **Check** a-11. **Everett** a-7; c-13, 25. **Heath** a-3, 18; c-3,15, 18, 21. **Maneely** a-1; c-5. **Reinman** a-1. **Robinson** a-6, 7; c-6. **Shores** a-7(2). **Sinn** a-3. **Woodbridge** a-28, 30.*

BATTLE ATTACK
Stanmor Publications: Oct, 1952 - No. 8, Dec, 1955
1 10.00 30.00 75.0
2 6.00 18.00 42.0
3-8: 3-Hollingsworth-a 5.00 15.00 30.0

BATTLEAXES
DC Comics (Vertigo): May, 2000 - No. 4, Aug, 2000 ($2.50, limited series)

Battle Brady #10 © MAR

Battle Chasers #3 © Joe Madureira

Battle Cry #3 © Stanmor

1-4: Terry LaBan-s/Alex Horley-a 2.50

BATTLE BEASTS
Blackthorne Publishing: Feb, 1988 - No. 4, 1988 ($1.50/$1.75, B&W/color)
1-4: 1-3- (B&W)-Based on Hasbro toys. 4-Color 2.00

BATTLE BRADY (Formerly Men in Action No. 1-9; see 3-D Action)
Atlas Comics (IPC): No. 10, Jan, 1953 - No. 14, June, 1953
10: 10-12-Syd Shores-c 14.00 41.00 110.00
11-Used in **POP**, pg. 95 plus B&W & color illos 9.30 28.00 65.00
12-14 7.85 23.50 55.00

BATTLE CHASERS
Image Comics (Cliffhanger): Apr, 1998 - No. 4, Dec, 1998;
DC Comics (Cliffhanger): No. 5, May, 1999 - Present ($2.50)
Prelude (2/98) 1.25 3.75 10.00
Prelude Gold Ed. 10.00
1-Madureira & Sharrieff-s/Madureira-a(p)/Charest-c 1.10 3.30 9.00
1-American Ent. Ed. w/"racy" cover 1.25 3.75 10.00
1-Gold Edition 9.00
1-Chromium cover 40.00
1-2nd printing 3.00
2 5.00
2-Dynamic Forces BattleChrome cover 1.50 4.50 12.00
3-Red Monika cover by Madureira 3.00
4-7: 4-Four covers. 6-Back-up by Warren-s/a. 7-3 covers (Madureira, Ramos, Campbell) 2.50
...: A Gathering of Heroes HC ('99, $24.95) r/#1-5, Prelude, Frank Frazetta Fantasy Ill.; cover gallery 24.95
...: A Gathering of Heroes SC ('99, $14.95) 14.95
..Collected Edition 1,2 (11/98, 5/99, $5.95) 1-r/#1,2. 2-r/#3,4 6.00

3ATTLE CLASSICS (See Cancelled Comic Cavalcade)
)C Comics: Sept-Oct, 1978 (44 pgs.)
1-Kubert-r; new Kubert-c 2.40 6.00

3ATTLE CRY
;tanmor Publications: 1952 (May) - No. 20, Sept, 1955
1 12.00 36.00 95.00
2 7.00 21.00 48.00
3,5-10: 8-Pvt. Ike begins, ends #13,17 5.00 15.00 30.00
4-Classic E.C. swipe 6.40 19.25 45.00
11-20 4.15 12.50 25.00
IOTE: *Hollingsworth a-9; c-20.*

ATTLEFIELD (War Adventures on the...)
tlas Comics (ACI): April, 1952 - No. 11, May, 1953
1-Pakula, Reinman-a 20.00 60.00 160.00
2-5: 2-Heath, Maneely, Pakula, Reinman-a 10.00 30.00 80.00
6-11 7.15 21.50 50.00
OTE: *Colan a-11. Everett a-8. Heath a-1, 2, 5p; c-2, 8, 9, 11. Ravielli a-11.*

ATTLEFIELD ACTION (Formerly Foreign Intrigues)
harlton Comics: No. 16, Nov, 1957 - No. 62, 2-3/66; No. 63, 7/80 - No. 89, 1/84
2#16 5.50 16.50 38.00
17,20-30 4.00 11.00 22.00
18,19-Check-a (2 stories in #18) 2.50 7.50 25.00
31-62(1966) 2.00 6.00 18.00
63-80(1983-84) 4.00
81-83,85-89 (Low print run) 5.00
84-Kirby reprints; 3 stories 1.10 3.30 9.00
)TE: *Montes/Bache a-43, 55, 62. Glanzman a-87r.*

ATTLE FIRE
ragon Magazine/Stanmor Publications: Apr, 1955 - No. 7, 1955
9.30 28.00 65.00
2 5.00 15.00 32.00
3-7 4.00 11.00 22.00

ATTLE FOR A THREE DIMENSIONAL WORLD
) Cosmic Publications: May, 1983 (20 pgs., slick paper w/stiff-c, $3.00)
-Kirby c/a in 3-D; shows history of 3-D 1.00 3.00 8.00

BATTLEFORCE
Blackthorne Publishing: Nov, 1987 - No. 2, 1988 ($1.75, color/B&W)
1,2: Based on game. 1-In color. 2-B&W 2.00

BATTLE FOR INDEPENDENTS, THE (Also See Cyblade/Shi & Shi/Cyblade: The Battle For Independents)
Image Comics (Top Cow Productions)/Crusade Comics: 1995 ($29.95)
nn-boxed set of all editions of Shi/Cyblade & Cyblade/Shi plus new variant. 3.65 11.00 40.00

BATTLE FOR THE PLANET OF THE APES (See Power Record Comics)

BATTLEFRONT
Atlas Comics (PPI): June, 1952 - No. 48, Aug, 1957
1-Heath-c 28.00 83.00 220.00
2-Robinson-a(4) 13.00 39.00 105.00
3-5 10.50 32.00 85.00
6-10: Combat Kelly in No. 6-10 10.00 30.00 75.00
11-22,24-28: 14,16-Battle Brady app. 22-Teddy Roosevelt & His Rough Riders story. 28-Last pre-code (2/55) 7.15 21.50 50.00
23,43-Check-a 7.85 23.50 55.00
29-39,41,44-47 5.70 17.00 40.00
40,42-Williamson-a 8.65 26.00 60.00
48-Crandall-a 7.15 21.50 50.00
NOTE: *Ayers a-19, 32. Berg a-44. Colan a-21, 22, 32, 33, 40. Drucker a-28, 29. Everett a-44. Heath c-23, 26, 27, 29, 32. Maneely a-22, 23; c-2, 13, 22, 35. Morisi a-42. Morrow a-41.Orlando a-47. Powell a-19, 21, 25, 29, 32, 40, 47. Robinson a-1-4, 5(4); c-4, 5. Robert Sale a-19. Severin a-32; c-40. Woodbridge a-45, 46.*

BATTLEFRONT
Standard Comics: No. 5, June, 1952
5-Toth-a 14.00 41.00 110.00

BATTLE GODS: WARRIORS OF THE CHAAK
Dark Horse Comics: Apr, 2000 - Present ($2.95)
1-4-Francisco Ruiz Velasco-s/a 2.95

BATTLE GROUND
Atlas Comics (OMC): Sept, 1954 - No. 20, Aug, 1957
1 20.00 60.00 160.00
2-Jack Katz-a 10.00 30.00 80.00
3,4-Last precode (3/55) 7.85 23.50 55.00
5-8,10 7.15 21.50 50.00
9,11,13,18: 9-Krigstein-a. 11,13,18-Williamson-a in each 9.30 28.00 65.00
12,15-17,19,20 6.40 19.25 45.00
14-Kirby-a 10.00 30.00 75.00
NOTE: *Ayers a-13. Colan a-11, 13. Drucker a-7, 12, 13, 20. Heath c-2, 5, 13. Maneely a-19; c-1, 19. Orlando a-17.Pakula a-11. Severin a-5, 12, 19. c-20. Tuska a-11.*

BATTLE HEROES
Stanley Publications: Sept, 1966 - No. 2, Nov, 1966 (25¢)
1 2.50 7.50 25.00
2 2.00 6.00 18.00

BATTLE OF THE BULGE (See Movie Classics)

BATTLE OF THE PLANETS (TV)
Gold Key/Whitman No. 6 on: 6/79 - No. 10, 12/80
(Based on syndicated cartoon by Sandy Frank)
1: Mortimer a-1-4,7-10 1.50 4.50 12.00
2-6,10 1.00 3.00 8.00
7,8(11/80),9 (3-pack only?) 2.00 6.00 18.00

BATTLE REPORT
Ajax/Farrell Publications: Aug, 1952 - No. 6, June, 1953
1 9.30 28.00 65.00
2-6 5.50 16.50 38.00

BATTLE SQUADRON
Stanmor Publications: April, 1955 - No. 5, Dec, 1955
1 8.65 26.00 60.00
2-5: 3-Iwo Jima & flag-c 5.00 15.00 30.00

BATTLESTAR GALACTICA (TV) (Also see Marvel Comics Super Special #8)

Battlestar Galactica: Season III #1 © Universal Studios

Beanbags #2 © Z-D

Beast Boy #1 © DC

Marvel Comics Group: Mar, 1979 - No. 23, Jan, 1981

1: 1-5 adapt TV episodes 1.00 2.80 7.00
2-23: 1-3-Partial-r 5.00

NOTE: ***Austin*** *c-9i, 10i.* ***Golden*** *c-18.* ***Simonson*** *a(p)-4, 5, 11-13, 15-20, 22, 23; c(p)-4, 5,11-17, 19, 20, 22, 23.*

BATTLESTAR GALACTICA (TV) (Also see Asylum)
Maximum Press: July, 1995 - No.4, Nov, 1995 ($2.50, limited series)

1-4: Continuation of TV series 4.00
Trade paperback (12/95, $12.95)-reprints series 13.00

BATTLESTAR GALACTICA (TV)
Realm Press: Dec, 1997 - No. 5, July, 1998 ($2.99)

1-5-Chris Scalf-s/painted-a/c 3.00
...Search For Sanctuary (9/98, $2.99) Scalf & Kuhoric-s 3.00
...Search For Sanctuary Special (4/00, $3.99) Kuhoric-s/Scalf & Scott-a 4.00

BATTLESTAR GALACTICA: APOLLO'S JOURNEY (TV)
Maximum Press: Apr, 1996 - No. 3, June, 1996 ($2.95, limited series)

1-3: Richard Hatch scripts 4.00

BATTLESTAR GALACTICA: JOURNEY'S END (TV)
Maximum Press: Aug, 1996 - No. 4, Nov, 1996 ($2.99, limited series)

1-4-Continuation of the T.V. series 4.00

BATTLESTAR GALACTICA: SEASON III
Realm Press: June/July, 1999 - Present ($2.99)

1-3: 1-Kuhoric-s/Scalf & Scott-a; Scalf-c. 2-Covers by Scalf and Stinsman. 3-Two covers 3.00
1-Variant-c by Jae Lee 3.00
Gallery (4/00, $3.99) short story and pin-ups 4.00
1999 Tour Book (5/99, $2.99) 3.00
1999 Tour Book Convention Edition (6.99) 7.00
...Special: Centurion Prime (12/99, $3.99) Kuhoric-s 4.00

BATTLESTAR GALACTICA: SPECIAL EDITION (TV)
Maximum Press: Jan, 1997 ($2.99, one-shot)

1-Fully painted; Scalf-c/s/a; r/Asylum 3.00

BATTLESTAR GALACTICA: STARBUCK (TV)
Maximum Press: Dec, 1995 - No. 3, Mar, 1996 ($2.50, limited series)

1-3 3.00

BATTLESTAR GALACTICA: THE COMPENDIUM (TV)
Maximum Press: Feb, 1997 ($2.99, one-shot)

1 3.00

BATTLESTAR GALACTICA: THE ENEMY WITHIN (TV)
Maximum Press: Nov, 1995 - No. 3, Feb, 1996 ($2.50, limited series)

1-3: 3-Indicia reads Feb, 1995 in error. 3.00

BATTLESTONE (Also see Brigade & Youngblood)
Image Comics (Extreme): Nov, 1994 - No. 2, Dec, 1994 ($2.50, limited series)

1,2-Liefeld plots 2.50

BATTLE STORIES (See XMas Comics)
Fawcett Publications: Jan, 1952 - No. 11, Sept, 1953

1-Evans-a 14.00 41.00 110.00
2 7.85 23.50 55.00
3-11 6.00 18.00 42.00

BATTLE STORIES
Super Comics: 1963 - 1964

Reprints #10-12,15-18: 10-r/U.S Tank Commandos #? 11-r/? 11, 12,17-r/Monty Hall #?; 13-Kintsler-a (1pg).15-r/American Air Forces #7 by Powell; Bolle-r. 18-U.S. Fighting Air Force #? 1.50 4.50 12.00

BATTLETECH (See Blackthorne 3-D Series #41 for 3-D issue)
Blackthorne Publishing: Oct, 1987 - No. 6, 1988 ($1.75/$2.00)

1-6: Based on game. 1-Color. 2-Begin B&W 3.00
Annual 1 ($4.50, B&W) 5.00

BATTLETECH
Malibu Comics: Feb, 1995 ($2.95)

0 3.0

BATTLETECH FALLOUT
Malibu Comics: Dec, 1994 - No. 4, Mar, 1995 ($2.95)

1-4-Two edi. exist #1; normal logo 3.0
1-Gold version w/foil logo stamped "Gold Limited Edition 8.0
1-Full-c holographic limited edition 2.40 6.0

BATTLETIDE (Death's Head II & Killpower...)
Marvel Comics UK, Ltd.: Dec, 1992 - No. 4, Mar, 1993 ($1.75, mini-series)

1-4: Wolverine, Psylocke, Dark Angel app. 2.0

BATTLETIDE II (Death's Head II & Killpower...)
Marvel Comics UK, Ltd.: Aug, 1993 - No. 4, Nov, 1993 ($1.75, mini-series)

1-($2.95)-Foil embossed logo 3.0
2-4: 2-Hulk-c/story 2.0

BATTLEZONES: DREAM TEAM 2 (See Dream Team)
Malibu Comics (Ultraverse): Mar, 1996 ($3.95)

1-pin-ups between Marvel & Malibu characters by Mike Wieringo, Phil Jimene Mike McKone, Cully Hamner, Gary Frank & others 4.0

BAYWATCH COMIC STORIES (TV) (Magazine)
Acclaim Comics (Armada): May, 1996 - No. 4, 1997 ($4.95) (Photo-c on all)

1-4: Photo comics based on TV show 5.0

BEACH BLANKET BINGO (See Movie Classics)

BEAGLE BOYS, THE (Walt Disney)(See The Phantom Blot)
Gold Key: 11/64; No. 2, 11/65; No. 3, 8/66 - No. 47, 2/79 (See WDC&S #134)

1 3.45 10.35 38.0
2-5 2.30 7.00 20.0
6-10 1.85 5.50 15.0
11-20: 11,14,19-r 1.50 4.50 12.0
21-30: 27-r 1.00 3.00 8.0
31-47 2.40 6.0

BEAGLE BOYS VERSUS UNCLE SCROOGE
Gold Key: Mar, 1979 - No. 12, Feb, 1980

1 1.50 4.50 12.0
2-12: 9-r 2.40 6.0

BEANBAGS
Ziff-Davis Publ. Co. (Approved Comics): Winter, 1951 - No. 2, Spring, 1952

1,2 10.00 30.00 80.0

BEANIE THE MEANIE
Fago Publications: No. 3, May, 1959

3 4.65 14.00 28.0

BEANY AND CECIL (TV) (Bob Clampett's...)
Dell Publishing Co.: Jan, 1952 - 1955; July-Sept, 1962 - No. 5, July-Sept, 196

Four Color 368 25.00 75.00 300.0
Four Color 414,448,477,530,570,635(1/55) 16.00 48.00 190.0
01-057-209 (#1) 15.00 45.00 180.0
2-5 10.00 30.00 120.0

BEAR COUNTRY (Disney)
Dell Publishing Co.: No. 758, Dec, 1956

Four Color 758-Movie 4.60 13.75 55.0

BEAST (See X-Men)
Marvel Comics: May, 1997 - No. 3, 1997 ($2.50, mini-series)

1-3-Giffen-s/Nocon-a 3.0

BEAST BOY (See Titans)
DC Comics: Jan, 2000 - No. 4, Apr, 2000 ($2.95, mini-series)

1-4-Justiano-c/a; Raab & Johns-s 2.9

B.E.A.S.T.I.E.S. (Also see Axis Alpha)
Axis Comics: Apr, 1994 ($1.95)

1-Javier Saltares-c/a/scripts 2.0

BEATLES, THE (See Girls' Romances #109, Go-Go, Heart Throbs #101, Herbie #5, Howard the Duck Mag. #4, Laugh #166, Marvel Comics Super Special #4, My LittleMargie # Not Brand Echh, Strange Tales #130, Summer Love, Superman's Pal Jimmy Olsen #79, Te

Beep Beep, The Road Runner #11 © WB

Bee 29, The Bombardier #1 © Neal Publications

Before the Fantastic Four: Reed Richards #1 © MAR

GD2.0 FN6.0 NM9.4

nfessions #37, Tippy's Friends & Tippy Teen)

EATLES, THE (Life Story)
ll Publishing Co.: Sept-Nov, 1964 (35¢)
-(Scarce)-Stories with color photo pin-ups; Paul S. Newman-s 42.00 126.00 550.00

EATLES EXPERIENCE, THE
volutionary Comics: Mar, 1991 - No. 8, 1991 ($2.50, B&W, limited series)
-8: 1-Gold logo 4.00

EATLES YELLOW SUBMARINE (See Movie Comics under Yellow...)

EAUTIFUL PEOPLE
ave Labor Graphics: Apr, 1994 ($4.95, 8-1/2x11", one-shot)
5.00

AUTIFUL STORIES FOR UGLY CHILDREN
Comics (Piranha Press): 1989 - No. 30, 1991 ($2.00/$2.50, B&W, mature)
l. 1-20: 12-$2.50-c begins 3.00
-30 4.00
Cotton Candy Autopsy ($12.95, B&W)-Reprints 1st two volumes 13.00

EAUTY AND THE BEAST, THE
arvel Comics Group: Jan, 1985 - No. 4, Apr, 1985 (limited series)
-4: Dazzler & the Beast from X-Men; Sienkiewicz-c on all 3.00

EAUTY AND THE BEAST (Graphic novel)(Also see Cartoon Tales & sney's New Adventures of...)
sney Comics: 1992
-($4.95, prestige edition)-Adapts animated film 2.40 6.00
-($2.50, newsstand edition) 3.00

AUTY AND THE BEAST
sney Comics: Sept., 1992 - No. 2, 1992 ($1.50, limited series)
,2 3.00

AUTY AND THE BEAST: PORTRAIT OF LOVE (TV)
st Comics: May, 1989 - No. 2, Mar, 1990 ($5.95, 60 pgs., squarebound)
,2: 1-Based on TV show, Wendy Pini-a/scripts. 2-...: Night of Beauty; by Wendy Pini 2.40 6.00

AVER VALLEY (Movie)(Disney)
ll Publishing Co.: No. 625, Apr, 1955
ur Color 625 5.85 17.50 70.00

EAVIS AND BUTTHEAD (MTV's...)(TV cartoon)
arvel Comics: Mar, 1994 - No. 28, June, 1996 ($1.95)
-Silver ink-c. 1, 2-Punisher & Devil Dinosaur app. 4.00
-2nd printing 2.00
,3: 2-Wolverine app. 3-Man-Thing, Spider-Man, Venom, Carnage, Mary Jane & Stan Lee cameos; John Romita, Sr. art (2 pgs.) 2.50
-28: 5-War Machine, Thor, Loki, Hulk, Captain America & Rhino cameos. 6-Psylocke, Polaris, Daredevil & Bullseye app. 7-Ghost Rider & Sub-Mariner app. 8-Quasar & Eon app.9-Prowler & Nightwatch app. 11-Black Widow app. 12-Thunderstrike & Bloodaxe app. 13-Night Thrasher app. 14-Spider-Man 2099 app. 15-Warlock app. 16-X-Factor app. 25-Juggernaut app. 2.50

ECK & CAUL INVESTIGATIONS
untlet Comics (Caliber): Jan, 1994 - No. 5, 1995? ($2.95, B&W)
-5 3.00
ecial 1 ($4.95) 5.00

DKNOBS AND BROOMSTICKS (See Walt Disney Showcase No. 6 & 50)

EDLAM
aos! Comics: Sept, 2000 ($2.95, one-shot)
-Steven Grant-s/David Brewer-a 2.95

EDLAM!
lipse Comics: Sept, 1985 - No. 2, Sept, 1985 (B&W-r in color)
,2: Bissette-a 2.00

DTIME STORY (See Cinema Comics Herald)

EELZELVIS
ave Labor Graphics: Feb, 1994 ($2.95, B&W, one-shot)

GD2.0 FN6.0 NM9.4

1 3.00

BEEP BEEP, THE ROAD RUNNER (TV)(See Daffy & Kite Fun Book)
Dell Publishing Co./Gold Key No. 1-88/Whitman No. 89 on: July, 1958 - No. 14, Aug-Oct, 1962; Oct, 1966 - No. 105, 1983

	GD2.0	FN6.0	NM9.4
Four Color 918 (#1, 7/58)	8.75	26.25	105.00
Four Color 1008,1046 (11-1/59-60)	4.60	13.75	55.00
4(2-4/60)-14(Dell)	3.80	11.40	42.00
1(10/66, Gold Key)	4.35	13.00	48.00
2-5	3.00	9.00	32.00
6-14	2.50	7.50	23.00
15-18,20-40	2.00	6.00	16.00
19-With pull-out poster	3.00	9.00	32.00
41-50	1.50	4.50	12.00
51-70	1.00	3.00	8.00
71-88			5.00
89,90,94-101		2.40	6.00
91(8/80), 92(9/80), 93 (3-pack?) (low printing)	1.75	5.25	14.00
102-105 (All #90189 on-c; nd or date code; pre-pack?)	1.25	3.75	10.00

NOTE: *See March of Comics #351, 353, 375, 387, 397, 416, 430, 442, 455. #5, 8-10, 35, 53, 59-62, 68-r; 96-102, 104 are 1/3-r.*

BEETLE BAILEY (See Comics Reading Library, Giant Comic Album & Sarge Snorkel)
Dell Publishing Co./Gold Key #39-53/King #54-66/Charlton #67-119/ Gold Key #120-131/Whitman #132: #459, 5/53 - #38, 5-7/62; #39, 11/62 - #53, 5/66; #54, 8/66 - #65, 12/67;#67, 2/69 - #119, 11/76; #120, 4/78 - #132, 4/80

	GD2.0	FN6.0	NM9.4
Four Color 469 (#1)-By Mort Walker	9.00	27.00	110.00
Four Color 521,552,622	4.60	13.75	55.00
5(2-4/56)-10(5-7/57)	4.10	12.30	45.00
11-20(4-5/59)	3.00	9.00	32.00
21-38(5-7/62)	2.50	7.50	23.00
39-53(5/66)	2.00	6.00	18.00
54-65 (No. 66 publ. overseas only?)	1.85	5.50	15.00
67-69: 69-Last 12¢ issue	1.75	5.25	14.00
70-99	1.40	4.15	11.00
100	1.75	5.25	14.00
101-119	1.00	3.00	8.00
120-132			5.00

BEETLE BAILEY
Harvey Comics: V2#1, Sept, 1992 - V2#9, Aug, 1994 ($1.25/$1.50)
V2#1-4 3.00
5-9-($1.50) 2.00
Big Book 1(11/92),2(5/93)(Both $1.95, 52 pgs.) 3.50
Giant Size V2#1(10/92),2(3/93)(Both $2.25,68 pgs.) 3.50

BEETLEJUICE (TV)
Harvey Comics: Oct, 1991 ($1.25)
1 2.50

BEETLEJUICE CRIMEBUSTERS ON THE HAUNT
Harvey Comics: Sept, 1992 - No. 3, Jan, 1993 ($1.50, limited series)
1-3 2.50

BEE 29, THE BOMBARDIER
Neal Publications: Feb, 1945
1-(Funny animal) 26.00 79.00 210.00

BEFORE THE FANTASTIC FOUR: BEN GRIMM AND LOGAN
Marvel Comics: July, 2000 - No. 3, Sept, 2000 ($2.99, limited series)
1-3-The Thing and Wolverine app.; Hama-s 3.00

BEFORE THE FANTASTIC FOUR: REED RICHARDS
Marvel Comics: Sept, 2000 - No. 3, Dec, 2000 ($2.99, limited series)
1-3-Peter David-s/Duncan Fegredo-c/a 3.00

BEFORE THE FANTASTIC FOUR: THE STORMS
Marvel Comics: Dec, 2000 - No. 3, Feb, 2001 ($2.99, limited series)
1-3-Adlard-a 3.00

BEHIND PRISON BARS
Realistic Comics (Avon): 1952

Behind Prison Bars #1 © AVON

Ben Casey #2 © DELL

The Best of DC #10 © DC

GD2.0 FN6.0 NM9.4

1-Kinstler-c 30.00 90.00 240.00

BEHOLD THE HANDMAID
George Pflaum: 1954 (Religious) (25¢ with a 20¢ sticker price)

nn 4.00 12.00 24.00

BELIEVE IT OR NOT (See Ripley's…)

BEN AND ME (Disney)
Dell Publishing Co.: No. 539, Mar, 1954

Four Color 539 3.25 9.60 36.00

BEN BOWIE AND HIS MOUNTAIN MEN
Dell Publishing Co.: 1952 - No. 17, Nov-Jan, 1958-59

Four Color 443 (#1) 5.85 17.50 70.00
Four Color 513,557,599,626,657 3.20 9.60 35.00
7(5-7/56)-11: 11-Intro/origin Yellow Hair 3.20 9.60 35.00
12-17 2.80 8.40 28.00

BEN CASEY (TV)
Dell Publishing Co.: June-July, 1962 - No. 10, June-Aug, 1965 (Photo-c)

12-063-207 (#1) 4.60 13.75 55.00
2(10/62),3,5-10 3.45 10.35 38.00
4-Marijuana & heroin use story 4.10 12.30 45.00

BEN CASEY FILM STORY (TV)
Gold Key: Nov, 1962 (25¢) (Photo-c)

30009-211-All photos 7.00 21.00 85.00

BENEATH THE PLANET OF THE APES (See Movie Comics & Power Record Comics)

BEN FRANKLIN (See Kite Fun Book)

BEN HUR
Dell Publishing Co.: No. 1052, Nov, 1959

Four Color 1052-Movie, Manning-a 9.00 27.00 110.00

BEN ISRAEL
Logos International: 1974 (39¢)

nn-Christian religious 1.00 3.00 8.00

BEOWULF (Also see First Comics Graphic Novel #1)
National Periodical Publications: Apr-May, 1975 - No. 6, Feb-Mar, 1976

1 1.00 2.80 7.00
2-6: 4-Dracula-c/s. 5-Flying saucer-c/story 5.00

BERLIN
Black Eye Productions: Apr, 1996 - Present ($2.50/$2.95, B&W)

1-8: Jason Lutes-c/a/scripts. 5-7-($2.95) 3.00

BERNI WRIGHTSON, MASTER OF THE MACABRE
Pacific Comics/Eclipse Comics No. 5: July, 1983 - No. 5, Nov, 1984 ($1.50, Baxter paper)

1-5: Wrightson-c/a(r). 4-Jeff Jones-r (11 pgs.) 5.00

BERRYS, THE (Also see Funny World)
Argo Publ.: May, 1956

1-Reprints daily & Sunday strips & daily Animal Antics by Ed Nofziger 5.00 15.00 35.00

BERZERKERS (See Youngblood V1#2)
Image Comics (Extreme Studios): Aug, 1995 - No. 3, Oct, 1995 ($2.50, limited series)

1-3: Beau Smith scripts, Fraga-a 2.50

BEST COMICS
Better Publications: Nov, 1939 - No. 4, Feb, 1940(Large size, reads sideways)

1-(Scarce)-Red Mask begins(1st app.) & c/s-all. Contains 6 pg. Boston Celtics photo story 79.00 237.00 750.00
2-4: 4-Cannibalism story 50.00 150.00 450.00

BEST FROM BOY'S LIFE, THE
Gilberton Company: Oct, 1957 - No. 5, Oct, 1958 (35¢)

1-Space Conquerors & Kam of the Ancient Ones begin, end #5; Bob Cousy photo/story 10.50 32.00 85.00
2,3,5 6.40 19.25 45.00

4-L.B. Cole-a 7.85 23.50 55.00

BEST LOVE (Formerly Sub-Mariner Comics No. 32)
Marvel Comics (MPI): No. 33, Aug, 1949 - No. 36, April, 1950 (Photo-c 33-36)

33-Kubert-a 11.00 33.00 90.00
34 6.40 19.25 45.00
35,36-Everett-a 8.65 26.00 60.00

BEST OF BUGS BUNNY, THE
Gold Key: Oct, 1966 - No. 2, Oct, 1968

1,2-Giants 4.55 13.65 50.00

BEST OF DC, THE (Blue Ribbon Digest) (See Limited Coll. Ed. C-52)
DC Comics: Sept-Oct, 1979 - No. 71, Apr, 1986 (100-148 pgs; mostly reprints)

1,2,5-9: 1-Superman, w/"Death of Superman"-r. 2-Batman 40th Ann. Special. 5-Best of 1979. 6,8-Superman. 7-Superboy. 9-Batman, Creeper app. 1.00 3.00 8.00
3-Superfriends 1.50 4.50 12.00
4-Rudolph the Red Nosed Reindeer 1.85 5.50 15.00
10-Secret Origins of Super Villains; 1st ever Penguin origin-s 2.00 6.00 18.00
11-16,18-20: 11-The Year's Best Stories. 12-Superman Time and Space Stories. 13-Best of DC Comics Presents. 14-New origin stories of Batman villains. 15-Superboy. 16-Superman Anniv. 18-Teen Titans new-s., Adams, Kane-a; Perez-c. 19-Superman. 20-World's Finest 1.00 3.00 8.00
17-Supergirl 1.50 4.50 12.00
21-Justice Society 1.75 5.25 14.00
22-27: 22-Christmas; unpublished Sandman story w/Kirby-a. 23-(148 pgs.)-Best of 1981. 24 Legion, new story and 16 pgs. new costumes. 25-Superman. 26-Brave & Bold. 27-Superman vs. Luthor 1.25 3.75 10.00
28,29: 28-Binky, Sugar & Spike app. 29-Sugar & Spike, 3 new stories; new Stanley & his Monster story 1.75 5.25 14.00
30,32-36,38,40: 30-Detective Comics. 32-Superman. 33-Secret origins of Legion Heroes and Villains. 34-Metal Men; has #497 on-c from Adv. Comics. 35-The Year's Best Comics Stories(148 pgs.). 36-Superman vs. Kryptonite. 38-Superman. 40-World of Krypton 1.25 3.75 10.00
31-JLA 1.75 5.25 14.00
37,39: 37-"Funny Stuff", Mayer-a. 39-Binky 1.75 5.25 14.00
41,43,45,47,49,53,55,58,60,63,65,68,70: 41-Sugar & Spike new stories with Mayer-a. 43,49,55-Funny Stuff. 45,53,70-Binky. 47,58,65,68-Sugar & Spike. 60-Plop!; Wood-c(r) & Aragonés-r (5/85). 63-Plop!; Wrightson-a(r) 1.85 5.50 16.00
42,44,46,48,50-52,54,56,57,59,61,62,64,66,67,69,71: 42,56-Superman vs. Aliens. 44,57,67-Superboy & LSH. 46-Jimmy Olsen. 48-Superman Team-ups. 50-Year's best Superman. 51-Batman Family. 52 Best of 1984. 54,56,59-Superman. 61-(148 pgs.)Year's best. 62-Best of Batman 1985. 69-Year's best Team stories. 71-Year's best 1.50 4.50 12.00

NOTE: ***N. Adams*** *a-2r, 14r, 18r, 26, 51.* ***Aparo*** *a-9, 14, 26, 30; c-9, 14, 26.* ***Austin*** *a-51i.* ***Buckler*** *a-40p; c-16, 22.* ***Giffen*** *a-50, 52; c-33p.* ***Grell*** *a-33p.* ***Grossman*** *a-37.* ***Heath*** *a-26.* ***Infantino*** *a-10r, 18.* ***Kaluta*** *a-40.* ***G. Kane*** *a-10r, 18r; c-40, 44.* ***Kubert*** *a-10r, 21, 26.* ***Layton*** *a-21.* ***S. Mayer*** *c-29, 37, 41, 43, 47; a-28, 29, 37, 41, 43, 47, 58, 65, 68.* ***Moldoff*** *c-64p.* ***Morrow*** *a-40; c-40.* ***W. Mortimer*** *a-39p.* ***Newton*** *a-5, 51.* ***Perez*** *a-24, 50p; c-18, 21, 23.* ***Rogers*** *a-14, 51p.* ***Simonson*** *a-11r.* ***Spiegle*** *a-52.* ***Starlin*** *a-51.* ***Staton*** *a-5, 21.* ***Tuska*** *a-24.* ***Wolverton*** *a-60.* ***Wood*** *a-60, 63; c-60, 63.* ***Wrightson*** *a-60. New art in #14, 18, 24.*

BEST OF DENNIS THE MENACE, THE
Hallden/Fawcett Publications: Summer, 1959 - No. 5, Spring, 1961 (100 pgs.)

1-All reprints; Wiseman-a 6.80 20.50 75.00
2-5 4.55 13.65 50.00

BEST OF DONALD DUCK, THE
Gold Key: Nov, 1965 (12¢, 36 pgs.)(Lists 2nd printing in indicia)

1-Reprints Four Color #223 by Barks 6.70 20.00 80.00

BEST OF DONALD DUCK & UNCLE SCROOGE, THE
Gold Key: Nov, 1964 - No. 2, Sept, 1967 (25¢ Giants)

1(30022-411)('64)-Reprints 4-Color #189 & 408 by Carl Barks; cover of F.C. #189 redrawn by Barks 6.70 20.00 80.00
2(30022-709)('67)-Reprints 4-Color #256 & "Seven Cities of Cibola" & U.S. #8 by Barks 6.70 20.00 80.00

BEST OF HORROR AND SCIENCE FICTION COMICS
Bruce Webster: 1987 ($2.00)

Best of the West #1 © ME

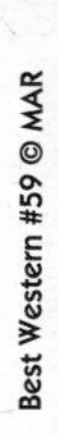
Best Western #59 © MAR

Betty and Her Steady #2 © AVON

GD2.0 FN6.0 NM9.4

1-Wolverton, Frazetta, Powell, Ditko-r 5.00

EST OF MARMADUKE, THE
harlton Comics: 1960

1-Brad Anderson's strip reprints 2.80 8.40 28.00

EST OF MS. TREE, THE
yramid Comics: 1987 - No. 4, 1988 ($2.00, B&W, limited series)

1-4 2.00

EST OF THE BRAVE AND THE BOLD, THE (See Super DC Giant)
C Comics: Oct, 1988 - No. 6, Jan, 1989 ($2.50, limited series)

1-6: Neal Adams-r, Kubert-r & Heath-r in all 4.00

EST OF THE WEST (See A-1 Comics)
agazine Enterprises: 1951 - No. 12, April-June, 1954

1(A-1 42)-Ghost Rider, Durango Kid, Straight Arrow, Bobby Benson begin 40.00 120.00 360.00
2(A-1 46) 22.00 66.00 175.00
3(A-1 52), 4(A-1 59), 5(A-1 66) 18.00 54.00 145.00
6(A-1 70), 7(A-1 76), 8(A-1 81), 9(A-1 85), 10(A-1 87), 11(A-1 97), 12(A-1 103) 13.00 39.00 105.00

OTE: *Bolle a-9. Borth a-12. Guardineer a-5, 12. Powell a-1, 12.*

EST OF UNCLE SCROOGE & DONALD DUCK, THE
old Key: Nov, 1966 (25¢)

1(30030-611)-Reprints part 4-Color #159 & 456 & Uncle Scrooge #6,7 by Carl Barks 6.70 20.00 80.00

EST OF WALT DISNEY COMICS, THE
estern Publishing Co.: 1974 ($1.50, 52 pgs.) (Walt Disney)
-1/2x11" cardboard covers; 32,000 printed of each)

6170-Reprints 1st two stories less 1 pg. each from 4-Color #62 3.20 9.60 35.00
6171-Reprints Mickey Mouse and the Bat Bandit of Inferno Gulch from 1934 (strips) by Gottfredson 3.20 9.60 35.00
6172-r/Uncle Scrooge #386 & two other stories 3.20 9.60 35.00
6173-Reprints "Ghost of the Grotto" (from 4-Color #159) & "Christmas on Bear Mountain" (from 4-Color #178) 3.20 9.60 35.00

EST ROMANCE
tandard Comics (Visual Editions): No. 5, Feb-Mar, 1952 - No. 7, Aug, 1952

5-Toth-a; photo-c 12.00 36.00 95.00
6,7-Photo-c 5.00 15.00 35.00

EST SELLER COMICS (See Tailspin Tommy)

EST WESTERN (Formerly Terry Toons? or Miss America Magazine
arvel Comics (IPC): V7#24(#57)?; Western Outlaws & Sheriffs No. 60 on)
o. 58, June, 1949 - No. 59, Aug, 1949

8,59-Black Rider, Kid Colt, Two-Gun Kid app.; both have Syd Shores-c 21.00 62.00 165.00

ETTIE PAGE COMICS
ark Horse Comics: Mar, 1996 ($3.95)

1-Dave Stevens-c; Blevins & Heath-a; Jaime Hernandez pin-up 5.00

ETTIE PAGE COMICS: QUEEN OF THE NILE
ark Horse Comics: Dec, 1999 - No. 3, Apr, 2000 ($2.95, limited series)

-3-Silke-s/a; Stevens-c 3.00

ETTIE PAGE COMICS: SPICY ADVENTURE
ark Horse Comics: Jan, 1997 ($2.95, one-shot, mature)

n-Silke-c/s/a 3.50

ETTY (See Pep Comics #22 for 1st app.)
chie Comics: Sept, 1992 - Present ($1.25/$1.50/$1.75/$1.79)

4.00
-18,20-24: 20-1st Super Sleuther-s 3.00
9-Love Showdown part 2 5.00
5-Pin-up page of Betty as Marilyn Monroe, Madonna, Lady Di 4.50
6-95: 57- "A Storm Over Uniforms" x-over part 5,6 2.00

ETTY AND HER STEADY (Going Steady with Betty No. 1)
von Periodicals: No. 2, Mar-Apr, 1950

2 9.30 28.00 65.00

BETTY AND ME
Archie Publications: Aug, 1965 - No. 200, Aug, 1992

1 9.00 27.00 100.00
2,3: 3-Origin Superteen 4.55 13.65 50.00
4,5,7,8: Superteen in new costume #4-7; dons new helmet in #5, ends #8. 3.20 9.60 35.00
6,10: Girl from R.I.V.E.R.D.A.L.E. 2.50 7.50 25.00
9,11-15,17-20(4/69): 9-UFO-s 2.30 7.00 20.00
16-Classic cover; w/risqué cover dialogue 2.50 7.50 25.00
21,24-35: 33-Paper doll page 1.50 4.50 12.00
22-Archies Band-s 1.75 5.25 14.00
23-I Dream of Jeannie parody 2.00 6.00 18.00
36(8/71),37,41-55 (52 pgs.) : 42-Betty as vamp-s 2.00 6.00 16.00
38-Sabrina app. 2.50 7.50 25.00
39-Josie and Sabrina cover cameos 2.30 7.00 20.00
40-Archie & Betty share a cabin 2.00 6.00 18.00
56(4/71)-80(12/76): 79 Betty Cooper mysteries thru #86. 79-81-Drago the Vampire-s 1.00 3.00 8.00
81-99: 83-Harem-c. 84-Jekyll & Hyde-c/s 2.40 6.00
100(3/79) 1.00 3.00 8.00
101,118: 101-Elvis mentioned. 118-Tarzan mentioned 4.50
102-117,119-130(9/82): 103,104-Space-s. 124-DeCarlo-c begins 4.00
131-138,140,142-147,149-154,156-158: 135,136-Jason Blossom app. 136-Cheryl Blossom cameo. 137-Space-s. 138-Tarzan parody 3.00
139,141,148: 139-Katy Keene collecting-s; Archie in drag-s. 141-Tarzan parody-s. 148-Cyndi Lauper parody-s 4.00
155,159,160(8/87): 155-Archie in drag-s. 159-Superhero gag-c. 160-Wheel of Fortune parody 3.00
161-169,171-199 2.00
170-New Archie Superhero-s 3.00
200 4.00

BETTY AND VERONICA (Also see Archie's Girls...)
Archie Enterprises: June, 1987 - Present (75¢ /$1.25/$1.50/$1.75/$1.79/$1.99)

1,82: 82-Love Showdown part 3 5.00
2-10 4.00
11-81,83-157 2.50
Summer Fun 1 (1994, $2.00, 52 pgs. plus poster) 2.00

BETTY & VERONICA ANNUAL DIGEST (...Digest Magazine #1-4, 44 on; ...Comics Digest Mag. #5-43)
Archie Publications: Nov, 1980 - Present ($1.00/$1.50/$1.75/$1.95/$1.99, digest size)

1 2.30 7.00 20.00
2-10: 2(11/81-Katy Keene story), 3(8/82) 1.50 4.50 12.00
11-30 1.00 3.00 8.00
31-50 2.40 6.00
51-70 3.50
71-118: 110-Begin $2.19-c 2.20

BETTY & VERONICA ANNUAL DIGEST MAGAZINE
Archie Comics: Sept, 1989 - Present ($1.50/$1.75/$1.79, 128 pgs.)

1 2.40 6.00
2-10: 9-Neon ink logo 5.00
11-17: 16-Begin $1.79-c 3.00

BETTY & VERONICA CHRISTMAS SPECTACULAR (See Archie Giant Series Magazine #159, 168, 180, 191, 204, 217, 229, 241, 453, 465, 477, 489, 501, 513, 525, 536, 547, 558, 568, 580, 593, 606, 618)

BETTY & VERONICA DOUBLE DIGEST MAGAZINE
Archie Enterprises: 1987 - Present ($2.25/$2.75/$1.50/$2.79/$2.95/$2.99, digest size, 256 pgs.)(...Digest #12 on)

1 1.25 3.75 10.00
2-10 2.40 6.00
11-25: 5,17-Xmas-c. 16-Capt. Hero story 4.00
26-94: 87-Begin $3.19-c 3.20

BETTY & VERONICA SPECTACULAR (See Archie Giant Series Mag. #11, 16, 21, 26, 32, 138, 145, 153, 162, 173, 184, 197, 201, 210, 214, 221, 226, 234, 238, 246, 250, 458, 462, 470, 482, 486, 494, 498, 506, 510, 518, 522, 526, 530, 537, 552, 559, 563, 569, 575, 582, 588,

Beware #9 © TM

The Beyond #9 © ACE

Big All-American Comic Book #1 © DC

600, 608, 613, 620, 623, and Betty & Veronica)

BETTY AND VERONICA SPECTACULAR
Archie Comics: Oct, 1992 - Present ($1.25/$1.50/$1.75/$1.99)

1-Dan DeCarlo-c/a 4.00
2-20 3.00
21-45 2.00

BETTY & VERONICA SPRING SPECTACULAR (See Archie Giant Series Magazine #569, 582, 595)

BETTY & VERONICA SUMMER FUN (See Archie Giant Series Mag. #8, 13, 18, 23, 28, 34, 140, 147, 155, 164, 175, 187, 199, 212, 224, 236, 248, 460, 484, 496, 508, 520, 529, 539, 550, 561, 572, 585, 598, 611, 621)
Archie Comics: 1994 - Present ($2.00/$2.25/$2.29)

1-6: 5-($2.25-c). 6-($2.29-c) 2.50

BETTY BOOP'S BIG BREAK
First Publishing: 1990 ($5.95, 52 pgs.)

nn-By Joshua Quagmire; 60th anniversary ish. 6.00

BETTY PAGE 3-D COMICS
The 3-D Zone: 1991 ($3.95, "7-1/2x10-1/4," 28 pgs., no glasses)

1-Photo inside covers; back-c nudity 2.40 6.00

BETTY'S DIARY (See Archie Giant Series Magazine No. 555)
Archie Enterprises: April, 1986 - No. 40, Apr, 1991 (#1:65¢; 75¢/95¢)

1 5.00
2-10 4.00
11-40 2.50

BETTY'S DIGEST
Archie Enterprises: Nov, 1996 - Present ($1.75/$1.79)

1,2 3.00

BEVERLY HILLBILLIES (TV)
Dell Publishing Co.: 4-6/63 - No. 18, 8/67; No. 19, 10/69; No. 20, 10/70; No. 21, Oct, 1971

1-Photo-c 16.00 48.00 190.00
2-Photo-c 8.35 25.00 100.00
3-9: All have photo covers 5.85 17.50 70.00
10: No photo cover 4.10 12.30 45.00
11-21: All have photo covers. 18-Last 12¢ issue. 19-21-Reprint #1-3 (covers and insides) 4.60 13.75 55.00

NOTE: *#1-9, 11-21 are photo covers.*

BEWARE (Formerly Fantastic; Chilling Tales No. 13 on)
Youthful Magazines: No. 10, June, 1952 - No. 12, Oct, 1952

10-E.A. Poe's Pit & the Pendulum adaptation by Wildey; Harrison/Bache-a; atom bomb and shrunken head-c 50.00 150.00 450.00
11-Harrison-a; Ambrose Bierce adapt. 34.00 103.00 275.00
12-Used in **SOTI**, pg. 388; Harrison-a 34.00 103.00 275.00

BEWARE
Trojan Magazines/Merit Publ. No. ?: No. 13, 1/53 - No. 16, 7/53; No. 5, 9/53 - No. 15, 5/55

13(#1)-Harrison-a 50.00 150.00 450.00
14(#2, 3/53)-Krenkel/Harrison-c; dismemberment, severed head panels 34.00 103.00 275.00
15,16(#3, 5/53; #4, 7/53)-Harrison-a 28.00 83.00 220.00
5,9,12,13 28.00 83.00 220.00
6-Ill. in **SOTI**- "Children are first shocked and then desensitized by all this brutality." Corpse on cover swipe/V.O.H. #26; girl on cover swipe/Advs. Into Darkness #10 53.00 158.00 475.00
7,8-Check-a 28.00 83.00 220.00
10-Frazetta/Check-c; Disbrow, Check-a 58.00 174.00 550.00
11-Disbrow-a; heart torn out, blood drainage 33.00 98.00 260.00
14,15: 14-Myron Fass-c. 15-Harrison-a 24.00 73.00 195.00

NOTE: ***Fass** a-5, 6, 8; c-6, 11, 14. **Forte** a-8. **Hollingsworth** a-15(#3), 16(#4), 9; c-16(#4), 8, 9. **Kiefer** a-16(#4), 5, 6, 10.*

BEWARE (Becomes Tomb of Darkness No. 9 on)
Marvel Comics Group: Mar, 1973 - No. 8, May, 1974 (All reprints)

1-Everett-c; Kirby & Sinnott-r ('54) 2.00 6.00 18.00
2-8: 2-Forte, Colan-r. 6-Tuska-a. 7-Torres-r/Mystical Tales #7 1.50 4.50 12.00

NOTE: ***Infantino** a-4r. **Gil Kane** c-4. **Wildey** a-7r.*

BEWARE TERROR TALES
Fawcett Publications: May, 1952 - No. 8, July, 1953

1-E.C. art swipe/Haunt of Fear #5 & Vault of Horror #26 44.00 133.00 400.00
2 30.00 90.00 240.00
3-7 24.00 71.00 190.00
8-Tothish-a; people being cooked-c 28.00 84.00 225.00

NOTE: ***Andru** a-2. **Bernard Bailey** a-1; c-1-5. **Powell** a-1, 2, 8. **Sekowsky** a-2.*

BEWARE THE CREEPER (See Adventure, Best of the Brave & the Bold, Brave & the Bold, 1st Issue Special, Flash #318-323, Showcase #73, World's Finest #249)
National Periodical Publications: May-June, 1968 - No. 6, Mar-Apr, 1969 (All 12¢ issues)

1-(5-6/68)-Classic Ditko-c; Ditko-a in all 7.65 23.00 85.00
2-6: 2-5-Ditko-c. 2-Intro. Proteus. 6-Gil Kane-c 4.55 13.65 50.00

BEWITCHED (TV)
Dell Publishing Co.: 4-6/65 - No. 11, 10/67; No. 12, 10/68 - No. 13, 1/69; No. 14, 10/69

1-Photo-c 15.00 45.00 175.00
2-No photo-c 7.00 20.00 85.00
3-13-All have photo-c. 12-Reprints #1 5.00 15.00 60.00
14-No photo-c; reprints #2 3.65 11.00 40.00

BEYOND, THE
Ace Magazines: Nov, 1950 - No. 30, Jan, 1955

1-Bakerish-a(p) 40.00 120.00 350.00
2-Bakerish-a(p) 26.00 79.00 210.00
3-10: 10-Woodish-a by Cameron 17.00 51.00 135.00
11-20: 18-Used in **POP**, pgs. 81,82 14.00 41.00 110.00
21-26,28-30 13.00 39.00 105.00
27-Used in **SOTI**, pg. 111 14.00 41.00 110.00

NOTE: ***Cameron** a-10, 11p, 12p, 15, 16, 21-27, 30; c-20. **Colan** a-6, 13, 17. **Sekowsky** a-2, 3, 4, 7, 11, 14, 27r. No. 1 was to appear as Challenge of the Unknown No. 7.*

BEYOND THE GRAVE
Charlton Comics: July, 1975 - No. 6, June, 1976; No. 7, Jan, 1983 - No. 17, Oct, 1984

1-Ditko-a (6 pgs.); Sutton painted-c 2.30 7.00 20.00
2-6: 2-5-Ditko-a; Ditko c-2,3,6 1.50 4.50 12.00
7-17: ('83-'84) Reprints. 13-Aparo-c(r). 15-Sutton-c (low print run) 2.40 6.00
Modern Comics Reprint 2('78) 3.00

NOTE: ***Howard** a-4. **Kim** a-1. **Larson** a-4, 6.*

BIBLE TALES FOR YOUNG FOLK (...Young People No. 3-5)
Atlas Comics (OMC): Aug, 1953 - No. 5, Mar, 1954

1 25.00 75.00 200.00
2-Everett, Krigstein-a 18.00 53.00 140.00
3-5: 4-Robinson-c 14.00 41.00 110.00

BIG (Movie)
Hit Comics (Dark Horse Comics): Mar, 1989 ($2.00)

1-Adaptation of film; Paul Chadwick-c 2.00

BIG ALL-AMERICAN COMIC BOOK, THE (See All-American Comics)
All-American/National Per. Publ.: 1944 (132 pgs., one-shot) (Early DC Annual)

1-Wonder Woman, Green Lantern, Flash, The Atom, Wildcat, Scribbly, The Whip, Ghost Patrol, Hawkman by Kubert (1st on Hawkman), Hop Harrigan, Johnny Thunder, Little Boy Blue, Mr. Terrific, Mutt & Jeff app.; Sargon on cover only; cover by Kubert/Hibbard/Mayer/others 820.00 2460.00 11,500.00

BIG BABY HUEY (Also see Baby Huey)
Harvey Comics: Oct, 1991 - No. 4, Mar, 1992 ($1.00, quarterly)

1-4 3.00

BIG BANG COMICS (Becomes Big Bang #4)
Caliber Press: Spring, 1994 - No. 4, Feb, 1995; No. 0, May, 1995 ($1.95, lim. series)

Big Book of Vice © Paradox Press

Big Chief Wahoo #2 © EAS

Big Shot Comics #14 © CCG

1-4-($1.95-c) 2.00
0-(5/95, $2.95) Alex Ross-c; color and B&W pages 3.00
Your Big Book of Big Bang Comics TPB ('98, $11.00) r/#0-2 11.00

BIG BANG COMICS (Volume 2)
Image Comics (Highbrow Entertainment): V2#1, May, 1996 - Present ($1.95/$2.50/$2.95/$3.95)

1-23,26: 1-Mighty Man app. 2-4-S.A. Shadowhawk app.5-Begin $2.95-c. 6-Curt Swan/Murphy Anderson-c. 7-Begin B&W. 12-Savage Dragon-c/app. 15-Bissette-c. 16,17,21-Shadow Lady 3.00
24,25,27-34-($3.95): 24,27-History of Big Bang Comics Vol. 1,2 4.00

BIG BLACK KISS
Vortex Comics: Sep, 1989 - No, 3, Nov, 1989 ($3.75, B&W, lim. series, mature)

1-3-Chaykin-s/a 4.00

BIG BLOWN BABY (Also see Dark Horse Presents)
Dark Horse Comics: Aug, 1996 - No. 4, Nov, 1996 ($2.95, lim. series, mature)

1-4: Bill Wray-c/a/scripts 3.00

BIG BOOK OF ..., THE
DC Comics (Paradox Press): 1994 - Present (B&W)($12.95 - $14.95)

nn-...**BAD**,1998 ($14.95),...**CONSPIRACIES,** 1995 ($12.95), ...**DEATH**,1994 ($12.95), ...**FREAKS,** 1996 ($14.95), ...**GRIMM,** 1999 ($14.95), ...**HOAXES,** 1996 ($14.95), ...**LITTLE CRIMINALS,** 1996 ($14.95), ...**LOSERS,**1997 ($14.95), **MARTYRS,** 1997 ($14.95), ...**SCANDAL,**1997 ($14.95), ...**THE WEIRD WILD WEST,**1998 ($14.95), ...**THUGS,** 1997 ($14.95), ...**UNEXPLAINED,** 1997 ($14.95), ...**URBAN LEGENDS,** 1994 ($12.95), ...**VICE,** 1999 ($14.95), ...**WEIRDOS,** 1995 ($12.95) 12.95 - 14.95 ea.

BIG BOOK OF FUN COMICS (See New Book of Comics)
National Periodical Publications: Spring, 1936 (Large size, 52 pgs.)
(1st comic book annual & DC annual)

	GD2.0	FN6.0	VF8.0
1 (Very rare)-r/New Fun #1-5	2250.00	6750.00	13,500.00

BIG BOOK ROMANCES
Fawcett Publications: Feb, 1950 (no date given) (148 pgs.)

	GD2.0	FN6.0	NM9.4
1-Contains remaindered Fawcett romance comics - several combinations possible	38.00	113.00	300.00

BIG BOY (See Adventures of the Big Boy)

BIG BRUISERS
Image Comics (WildStorm Productions): July, 1996 ($3.50, one-shot)

1-Features Maul from WildC.A.T.S, Impact from Cyberforce & Badrock from Youngblood; wraparound-c 3.50

BIG CHIEF WAHOO
Eastern Color Printing/George Dougherty (distr. by Fawcett): July, 1942 - No. 7, Wint., 1943/44?(no year given)(Quarterly)

1-Newspaper-r (on sale 6/15/42)	40.00	120.00	360.00
2-Steve Roper app.	23.00	68.00	180.00
3-5: 4-Chief is holding a Katy Keene comic	17.00	51.00	135.00
6-7	12.00	36.00	95.00

NOTE: *Kerry Drake in some issues.*

BIG CIRCUS, THE (Movie)
Dell Publishing Co.: No. 1036, Sept-Nov, 1959

Four Color 1036-Photo-c 5.85 17.50 70.00

BIG COUNTRY, THE (Movie)
Dell Publishing Co.: No. 946, Oct, 1958

Four Color 946-Photo-c 6.70 20.00 80.00

BIG DADDY ROTH (Magazine)
Millar Publications: Oct-Nov, 1964 - No. 4, Apr-May, 1965 (35¢)

1-Toth-a	16.50	49.00	180.00
2-4-Toth-a	12.00	36.00	130.00

BIG GUY AND RUSTY THE BOY ROBOT, THE (Also See Madman Comics #6,7 & Martha Washington Stranded In Space)
Dark Horse (Legend): July, 1995 - No. 2, Aug, 1995 ($4.95, oversize, lim. series)

1,2-Frank Miller scripts & Geoff Darrow-c/a 1.10 3.30 9.00
Trade paperback (10/96, $14.95)-r/1,2 w/cover gallery 15.00

BIG HERO ADVENTURES (See Jigsaw)

BIG HAIR PRODUCTIONS
Image Comics: Feb, 2000 - Present ($3.50, B&W)

1,2 3.50

BIG JON & SPARKIE (Radio)(Formerly Sparkie, Radio Pixie)
Ziff-Davis Publ. Co.: No. 4, Sept-Oct, 1952 (Painted-c)

4-Based on children's radio program 19.00 56.00 150.00

BIG LAND, THE (Movie)
Dell Publishing Co.: No. 812, July, 1957

Four Color 812-Alan Ladd photo-c 9.00 27.00 110.00

BIG RED (See Movie Comics)

BIG SHOT COMICS
Columbia Comics Group: May, 1940 - No. 104, Aug, 1949

1-Intro. Skyman; The Face (1st app.; Tony Trent), The Cloak (Spy Master), Marvelo, Monarch of Magicians, Joe Palooka, Charlie Chan, Tom Kerry, Dixie Dugan, Rocky Ryan begin; Charlie Chan moves over from Feature Comics #31 (4/40).	211.00	633.00	2000.00
2	79.00	237.00	750.00
3-The Cloak called Spy Chief; Skyman-c	73.00	219.00	690.00
4,5	53.00	158.00	475.00
6-10: 8-Christmas-c	42.00	125.00	375.00
11-13	40.00	120.00	340.00
14-Origin & 1st app. Sparky Watts (6/41)	41.00	122.00	365.00
15-Origin The Cloak	42.00	125.00	375.00
16-20	33.00	98.00	260.00
21-23,26,27,29,30: 29-Intro. Capt. Yank; Bo (a dog) newspaper strip-r by Frank Beck begin, ends #104. 30-X-Mas-c	26.00	79.00	210.00
24-Tojo-c.	38.00	113.00	300.00
25-Hitler-c	31.00	94.00	250.00
28-Hitler, Tojo & Mussolini-c	40.00	120.00	350.00
31,33-40	20.00	60.00	160.00
32-Vic Jordan newspaper strip reprints begin, ends #52; Hitler, Tojo & Mussolini-c	34.00	103.00	275.00
41,42,44,45,47-50: 42-No Skyman. 50-Origin The Face retold	16.00	49.00	130.00
43-Hitler-c	25.00	75.00	200.00
46-Hitler, Tojo-c	22.00	66.00	175.00
51-56,58-60	14.00	41.00	110.00
57-Hitler, Tojo Halloween mask-c	19.00	56.00	150.00
61-70: 63 on-Tony Trent, the Face	10.50	32.00	85.00
71-80: 73-The Face cameo. 74-(2/47)-Mickey Finn begins. 74,80-The Face app. in Tony Trent. 78-Last Charlie Chan strip-r	10.00	30.00	80.00
81-90: 85-Tony Trent marries Babs Walsh. 86-Valentines-c	9.30	28.00	65.00
91-99,101-104: 69-94-Skyman in Outer Space. 96-Xmas-c	7.85	23.50	55.00
100	10.00	30.00	75.00

NOTE: ***Mart Bailey** art on "The Face" No. 1-104. **Guardineer** a-5. Sparky Watts by **Boody Rogers**-No. 14-42, 77-104, (by others No. 43-76). Others than Tony Trent wear "The Face" mask in No. 46-63, 93. Skyman by **Ogden Whitney**-No. 1, 2, 4, 12-37, 49, 70-101. Skyman covers-No. 1, 3, 7-12, 14, 16, 20, 27, 89, 95, 100.*

BIG TEX
Toby Press: June, 1953

1-Contains (3) John Wayne stories-r with name changed to Big Tex 10.00 30.00 70.00

BIG-3
Fox Features Syndicate: Fall, 1940 - No. 7, Jan, 1942

1-Blue Beetle, The Flame, & Samson begin	211.00	633.00	2000.00
2	87.00	261.00	825.00
3-5	61.00	182.00	575.00
6,7: 6-Last Samson. 7-V-Man app.	51.00	153.00	460.00

BIG TOP COMICS, THE (TV's Great Circus Show)
Toby Press: 1951 - No. 2, 1951 (No month)

Bill Battle, The One Man Army #1 © FAW

Bill Boyd Western #10 © FAW

Billy the Kid #9 © TOBY

GD2.0 FN6.0 NM9.4

1,2 8.65 26.00 60.00

BIG TOWN (Radio/TV) (Also see Movie Comics, 1946)
National Periodical Publ: Jan, 1951 - No. 50, Mar-Apr, 1958 (No. 1-9: 52pgs.)
1-Dan Barry-a begins 63.00 189.00 600.00
2 35.00 105.00 280.00
3-10 20.00 60.00 160.00
11-20 14.00 41.00 110.00
21-31: Last pre-code (1-2/55) 10.50 32.00 85.00
32-50 8.65 26.00 60.00

BIG VALLEY, THE (TV)
Dell Publishing Co.: June, 1966 - No. 5, Oct, 1967; No. 6, Oct, 1969
1: Photo-c #1-5 4.55 13.65 50.00
2-6: 6-Reprints #1 3.00 9.00 30.00

BIKER MICE FROM MARS (TV)
Marvel Comics: Nov, 1993 - No. 3, Jan, 1994 ($1.50, limited series)
1-3: 1-Intro Vinnie, Modo & Throttle. 2-Origin 3.00

BILL & TED'S BOGUS JOURNEY
Marvel Comics: Sept, 1991 ($2.95, squarebound, 84 pgs.)
1-Adapts movie sequel 3.00

BILL & TED'S EXCELLENT COMIC BOOK (Movie)
Marvel Comics: Dec, 1991 - No. 12, 1992 ($1.00/$1.25)
1-12: 3-Begin $1.25-c 2.00

BILL BARNES COMICS (...America's Air Ace Comics No. 2 on)
(Becomes Air Ace V2#1 on; also see Shadow Comics)
Street & Smith Publications: Oct, 1940(No. month given) - No. 12, Oct, 1943
1-23 pgs.-comics; Rocket Rooney begins 79.00 237.00 750.00
2-Barnes as The Phantom Flyer app.; Tuska-a 42.00 125.00 375.00
3-5 35.00 1035.00 280.00
6-12 30.00 90.00 240.00

BILL BATTLE, THE ONE MAN ARMY (Also see Master Comics No. 133)
Fawcett Publications: Oct, 1952 - No. 4, Apr, 1953 (All photo-c)
1 11.00 33.00 90.00
2 7.15 21.50 50.00
3,4 6.00 18.00 42.00

BILL BLACK'S FUN COMICS
Paragon #1-3/Americomics #4: Dec, 1982 - No. 4, Mar, 1983 ($1.75, Baxter paper)(1st AC comic)
1-Intro. Capt. Paragon, Phantom Lady & Commando D (#1-3 are B&W fanzines; 8-1/2x11") 3.00
2-4: 4-($2.00, color)-Origin Nightfall (formerly Phantom Lady); Nightveil app. 3-Kirby-c. 4-Kirby-a 3.00

BILL BOYD WESTERN (Movie star; see Hopalong Cassidy & Western Hero)
Fawcett Publ: Feb, 1950 - No. 23, June, 1952 (1-3,7,11,14-on: 36 pgs.)
1-Bill Boyd & his horse Midnite begin; photo front/back-c 49.00 146.00 440.00
2-Painted-c 28.00 84.00 225.00
3-Photo-c begin, end #23; last photo back-c 21.00 64.00 170.00
4-6(52 pgs.) 17.00 51.00 135.00
7,11(36 pgs.) 13.50 41.00 110.00
8-10,12,13(52 pgs.) 14.00 43.00 115.00
14-22 13.00 39.00 105.00
23-Last issue 14.00 43.00 115.00

BILL BUMLIN (See Treasury of Comics No. 3)

BILL ELLIOTT (See Wild Bill Elliott)

BILLI 99
Dark Horse Comics: Sept, 1991 - No. 4, 1991 ($3.50, B&W, lim. series, 52 pgs.)
1-4: Tim Sale-c/a 3.50

BILL STERN'S SPORTS BOOK
Ziff-Davis Publ. Co.(Approved Comics): Spring-Sum, 1951 - V2#2, Win, 1952
V1#10-(1951) 20.00 60.00 160.00
2-(Sum/52; reg. size) 15.00 45.00 120.00
V2#2-(1952, 96 pgs.)-Krigstein, Kinstler-a 20.00 60.00 160.00

BILL THE BULL: ONE SHOT, ONE BOURBON, ONE BEER
Boneyard Press: Dec, 1994 ($2.95, B&W, mature)
1 3.00

BILL THE CLOWN
Slave Labor Graphics: Feb, 1992 ($2.50, one-shot)
1,1-(2nd printing, 4/93, $2.95) 3.00
Comedy Isn't Pretty 1 (11/92, $2.50) 3.00
Death & Clown White 1 (9/93, $2.95) 3.00

BILLY AND BUGGY BEAR (See Animal Fun)
I.W. Enterprises/Super: 1958; 1964
I.W. Reprint #1, #7('58)-All Surprise Comics #?(Same issue-r for both) 1.50 4.50 12.00
Super Reprint #10(1964) 1.50 4.50 12.00

BILLY BUCKSKIN WESTERN (2-Gun Western No. 4)
Atlas Comics (IMC No. 1/MgPC No. 2,3): Nov, 1955 - No. 3, Mar, 1956
1-Mort Drucker-a; Maneely-c/a 14.00 41.00 110.00
2-Mort Drucker-a 10.00 30.00 80.00
3-Williamson, Drucker-a 11.00 33.00 90.00

BILLY BUNNY (Black Cobra No. 6 on)
Excellent Publications: Feb-Mar, 1954 - No. 5, Oct-Nov, 1954
1 7.15 21.50 50.00
2 4.65 14.00 28.00
3-5 4.00 11.00 22.00

BILLY BUNNY'S CHRISTMAS FROLICS
Farrell Publications: 1952 (25¢ Giant, 100 pgs.)
1 19.00 56.00 150.00

BILLY COLE
Cult Press: May, 1994 - No. 4, Aug, 1994 ($2.75, B&W, limited series)
1-4 2.75

BILLY MAKE BELIEVE
United Features Syndicate: No. 14, 1939
Single Series 14 30.00 90.00 240.00

BILLY NGUYEN, PRIVATE EYE
Caliber Press: V2#1, 1990 ($2.50)
V2#1 2.50

BILLY THE KID (Formerly The Masked Raider; also see Doc Savage Comics & Return of the Outlaw)
No. 9, Nov, 1957 - No. 121, Dec, 1976; No. 122, Sept, 1977 - No. 123,
Charlton Publ. Co.: Oct, 1977; No. 124, Feb, 1978 - No. 153, Mar, 1983
9 10.00 30.00 70.00
10,12,14,17-19: 12-2 pg Check-sty 6.00 18.00 42.00
11-(68 pgs.)-Origin & 1st app. The Ghost Train 8.65 26.00 60.00
13-Williamson/Torres-a 7.15 21.50 50.00
15-Origin; 2 pgs. Williamson-a 7.15 21.50 50.00
16-Williamson-a, 2 pgs. 7.00 21.00 48.00
20-26-Severin-a(3-4 each) 7.15 21.50 50.00
27-30: 30-Masked Rider app. 2.80 8.40 28.00
31-40 2.30 7.00 20.00
41-60 2.00 6.00 17.00
61-65 1.50 4.50 12.00
66-Bounty Hunter series begins. 1.85 5.50 15.00
67-80: Bounty Hunter series; not in #79,82,84-86 1.50 4.50 12.00
81-90: 87-Last Bounty Hunter 1.50 3.00 8.00
91-123: 110-Dr. Young of Boothill app. 111-Origin The Ghost Train. 117-Gunsmith & Co., The Cheyenne Kid app. 2.40 6.00
124(2/78)-153 4.00
Modern Comics 109 (1977 reprint) 3.00
NOTE: ***Boyette*** *a-91-110.* ***Kim*** *a-73.* ***Morsi*** *a-12,14.* ***Sattler*** *a-118-123.* ***Severin*** *a(r)-121-129, 134; c-23, 25.* ***Sutton*** *a-111.*

BILLY THE KID ADVENTURE MAGAZINE
Toby Press: Oct, 1950 - No. 29, 1955

Billy West #3 © STD

Birds of Prey #15 © DC

Bishop The Last X-Man #4 © MAR

GD2.0 FN6.0 NM9.4

1-Williamson/Frazetta-a (2 pgs) r/from John Wayne Adventure Comics #2; photo-c 30.00 90.00 240.00
2-Photo-c 10.00 30.00 70.00
3-Williamson/Frazetta "The Claws of Death", 4 pgs. plus Williamson art 34.00 101.00 270.00
4,5,7,8,10: 4,7-Photo-c 7.15 21.50 50.00
6-Frazetta assist on "Nightmare"; photo-c 14.00 41.00 110.00
9-Kurtzman Pot-Shot Pete; photo-c 11.00 33.00 90.00
11,12,15-20: 11-Photo-c 6.40 19.25 45.00
13-Kurtzman-r/John Wayne #12 (Genius) 7.15 21.50 50.00
14-Williamson/Frazetta; r-of #1 (2 pgs.) 10.00 30.00 75.00
21,23-29 5.00 15.00 35.00
22-Williamson/Frazetta-r(1pg.)/#1; photo-c 6.40 19.25 45.00

BILLY THE KID AND OSCAR (Also see Fawcett's Funny Animals)
Fawcett Publications: Winter, 1945 - No. 3, Summer, 1946 (Funny animal)

1 14.00 41.00 110.00
2,3 10.00 30.00 75.00

BILLY WEST (Bill West No. 9,10)
Standard Comics (Visual Editions): 1949-No. 9, Feb, 1951; No. 10, Feb, 1952

1 11.00 33.00 90.00
2 6.40 19.25 45.00
3-6,9,10 5.00 15.00 32.00
7,8-Schomburg-c 5.70 17.00 40.00
NOTE: *Celardo a-1-6, 9; c-1-3.* ***Moreira*** *a-3.* ***Roussos*** *a-2.*

BING CROSBY (See Feature Films)

BINGO (...Comics) (H. C. Blackerby)
Howard Publ.: 1945 (Reprints National material)

1-L. B. Cole opium-c 34.00 101.00 270.00

BINGO, THE MONKEY DOODLE BOY
St. John Publishing Co.: Aug, 1951; Oct, 1953

1(8/51)-By Eric Peters 5.70 17.00 40.00
1(10/53) 4.65 14.00 28.00

BINKY (Formerly Leave It to...)
National Periodical Publ./DC Comics: No. 72, 4-5/70 - No. 81, 10-11/71; No. 82, Summer/77

72-76 2.00 6.00 18.00
77-79: (68pgs.). 77-Bobby Sherman 1pg. story w/photo. 78-1 pg. sty on Barry Williams of Brady Bunch. 79-Osmonds 1pg. story 3.20 9.60 35.00
80,81 (52pgs.)-Sweat Pain story 2.80 8.40 28.00
82 (1977, one-shot) 1.75 5.25 14.00

BINKY'S BUDDIES
National Periodical Publications: Jan-Feb, 1969 - No. 12, Nov-Dec, 1970

1 3.65 11.00 40.00
2-12: 3-Last 12¢ issue 2.00 6.00 18.00

BIONEERS
Mirage Publishing: Aug, 1994 ($2.75)

1-w/bound-in trading card 2.75

BIONIC WOMAN, THE (TV)
Charlton Publications: Oct, 1977 - No. 5, June, 1978

1 1.25 3.75 10.00
2-5 2.40 6.00

BIRDS OF PREY (Also see Black Canary/Oracle: Birds of Prey)
DC Comics: Jan,1999 - Present ($1.99/$2.50)

1-Dixon-s/Land-c/a 4.00
2-27: 6-Nightwing-c/app. 15-Guice-a begins. 23-Grodd-c/app. 26-Bane 2.50
TPB (1999, $17.95) r/ previous series and one-shots 18.00

BIRDS OF PREY: BATGIRL
DC Comics: Feb,1998 ($2.95, one-shot)

1-Dixon-s/Frank-c 4.00

BIRDS OF PREY: MANHUNT
DC Comics: Sept, 1996 - No. 4, Dec, 1996 ($1.95, limited series)

1-4: Features Black Canary, Oracle, Huntress, & Catwoman; Chuck Dixon scripts; Gary Frank-c on all. 1-Catwoman cameo only 5.00
NOTE: ***Gary Frank*** *c-1-4.* ***Matt Haley*** *a-1-4p.* ***Wade Von Grawbadger*** *a-1i.*

BIRDS OF PREY: REVOLUTION
DC Comics: 1997 ($2.95, one-shot)

1-Frank-c/Dixon-s 3.50

BIRDS OF PREY: THE RAVENS
DC Comics: June,1998 ($1.95, one-shot)

1-Dixon-s; Girlfrenzy issue 3.00

BIRDS OF PREY: WOLVES
DC Comics: Oct, 1997 ($2.95, one-shot)

1-Dixon-s/Giordano & Faucher-a 3.50

BIRTH CAUL, THE
Eddie Campbell Comics: 1999 ($5.95, B&W, one-shot)

1-Alan Moore-s/Eddie Campbell-a 6.00

BIRTH OF THE DEFIANT UNIVERSE, THE
Defiant Comics: May, 1993

nn-contains promotional artwork & text; limited print run of 1000 copies. 1.25 3.75 10.00

BISHOP (See Uncanny X-Men & X-Men)
Marvel Comics: Dec, 1994 - No.4, Mar, 1995 ($2.95, limited series)

1-4: Foil-c; Shard & Mountjoy in all. 1-Storm app. 3.00

BISHOP THE LAST X-MAN
Marvel Comics: Oct, 1999 - No. 16, Jan, 2001 ($2.99/$1.99/$2.25)

1-($2.99)-Jeanty-a 3.00
2-8-($1.99): 2-Two covers 2.00
9-11,13-16: 9-Begin $2.25-c. 15-Maximum Security x-over; Xavier app. 2.25
12-($2.99) 2.99

BISHOP: XAVIER SECURITY ENFORCER
Marvel Comics: Jan, 1998 - No.3, Mar, 1998 ($2.50, limited series)

1-3: Ostrander-s 3.00

BIZARRE ADVENTURES (Formerly Marvel Preview)
Marvel Comics Group: No. 25, 3/81 - No. 34, 2/83 (#25-33: Magazine-$1.50)

25,26: 25-Lethal Ladies. 26-King Kull; Bolton-c/a 1.00 2.80 7.00
27,28: 27-Phoenix, Iceman & Nightcrawler app. 28-The Unlikely Heroes; Elektra by Miller; Neal Adams-a 1.10 3.30 9.00
29,30,32,33: 29-Stephen King's Lawnmower Man. 30-Tomorrow; 1st app. Silhouette. 32-Gods; Thor-c/s. 33-Horror; Dracula app.; photo-c 2.40 6.00
31-After The Violence Stops; new Hangman story; Miller-a 1.00 3.00 8.00
34 ($2.00, Baxter paper, comic size)-Son of Santa; Christmas special; Howard the Duck by Paul Smith 5.00
NOTE: ***Alcala*** *a-27i.* ***Austin*** *a-25i, 28i.* ***Bolton*** *a-26, 32.* ***J. Buscema*** *a-27p, 29, 30p; c-26.* ***Byrne*** *a-31 (2 pg.).* ***Golden*** *a-25p, 28p.* ***Perez*** *a-27p.* ***Rogers*** *a-25p.* ***Simonson*** *a-29; c-29.* ***Paul Smith*** *a-34.*

BLACK AND WHITE (See Large Feature Comic, Series I)

BLACK & WHITE (Also see Codename: Black & White)
Image Comics (Extreme): Oct,1994 - No. 3, Jan,1995 ($1.95, limited series)

1-3: Thibert-c/story 2.00

BLACK & WHITE MAGIC
Innovation Publishing: 1991 ($2.95, 98 pgs., B&W w/30 pgs. color, squarebound)

1-Contains rebound comics w/covers removed; contents may vary 3.00

BLACK AXE
Marvel Comics (UK): Apr, 1993 - No. 7, Oct, 1993 ($1.75)

1-4: 1-Romita Jr.-c. 2-Sunfire-c/s 2.00
5-7: 5-Janson-c; Black Panther app. 6,7-Black Panther-c/s 3.00

BLACKBALL COMICS
Blackball Comics: Mar, 1994 ($3.00)

1-Trencher-c/story by Giffen; John Pain by O'Neill 3.00

BLACKBEARD'S GHOST (See Movie Comics)

Black Cat Comics #3 © HARV

Black Cobra #3 © Farrell Pub.

Black Diamond Western #13 © LEV

BLACK BEAUTY (See Son of Black Beauty)
Dell Publishing Co.: No. 440, Dec, 1952

Four Color 440 3.20 9.60 35.00

BLACK CANARY (See All Star Comics #38, Flash Comics #86, Justice League of America #75 & World's Finest #244)
DC Comics: Nov, 1991 - No. 4, Feb, 1992 ($1.75, limited series)

1-4 2.00

BLACK CANARY
DC Comics: Jan, 1993 - No. 12, Dec, 1993 ($1.75)

1-12: 8-The Ray-c/story. 9,10-Huntress-c/story 2.00

BLACK CANARY/ORACLE: BIRDS OF PREY (Also see Showcase '96 #3)
DC Comics: 1996 ($3.95, one-shot)

1-Chuck Dixon scripts & Gary Frank-c/a. 1.00 2.80 7.00

BLACK CAT COMICS (...Western #16-19; ...Mystery #30 on)
(See All-New #7,9, The Original Black Cat, Pocket & Speed Comics)
Harvey Publications (Home Comics): June-July, 1946 - No. 29, June, 1951

1-Kubert-a; Joe Simon c-1-3 66.00 197.00 625.00
2-Kubert-a 38.00 113.00 300.00
3,4: 4-The Red Demons begin (The Demon #4 & 5)
30.00 90.00 240.00
5,6,7: 5,6-The Scarlet Arrow app. in ea. by Powell; S&K-a in both. 6-Origin Red Demon. 7-Vagabond Prince by S&K plus 1 more story
38.00 113.00 300.00
8-S&K-a; Kerry Drake begins, ends #13 33.00 98.00 260.00
9-Origin Stuntman (r/Stuntman #1) 38.00 113.00 300.00
10-20: 14,15,17-Mary Worth app. plus Invisible Scarlet O'Neil-#15,20,24
25.00 75.00 200.00
21-26 20.00 60.00 160.00
27,28: 27-Used in **SOTI**, pg. 193; X-Mas-c; 2 pg. John Wayne story. 28-Intro. Kit, Black Cat's new sidekick 21.00 64.00 170.00
29-Black Cat bondage-c; Black Cat stories 21.00 62.00 165.00

BLACK CAT MYSTERY (Formerly Black Cat; ...Western Mystery #54; ...Western #55,56;...Mystery #57; ...Mystic #58-62; Black Cat #63-65)
Harvey Publications: No. 30, Aug, 1951 - No. 65, Apr, 1963

30-Black Cat on cover only 28.00 83.00 220.00
31,32,34,37,38,40 21.00 64.00 170.00
33-Used in **POP**, pg. 89; electrocution-c 23.00 69.00 185.00
35-Atomic disaster cover/story 24.00 73.00 195.00
36,39-Used in **SOTI**: #36-Pgs. 270,271; #39-Pgs. 386-388
26.00 79.00 210.00
41-43 21.00 64.00 170.00
44-Eyes, ears, tongue cut out; Nostrand-a 22.00 66.00 175.00
45-Classic "Colorama" by Powell; Nostrand-a 38.00 113.00 300.00
46-49,51-Nostrand-a in all 22.00 66.00 175.00
50-Check-a; classic Warren Kremer-c showing a man's face & hands burning away 63.00 189.00 600.00
52,53 (r/#34 & 35) 14.00 41.00 110.00
54-Two Black Cat stories (2/55, last pre-code) 18.00 53.00 140.00
55,56-Black Cat app. 14.00 41.00 110.00
57(7/56)-Kirby-c 12.50 37.50 100.00
58-60-Kirby-a(4). 58,59-Kirby-c. 60,61-Simon-c 18.00 53.00 140.00
61-Nostrand-a; "Colorama" r/#45 18.00 53.00 140.00
62 (3/58)-E.C. story swipe 12.50 37.50 100.00
63-65: Giants(10/62,1/63, 4/63); Reprints; Black Cat app. 63-origin Black Kitten. 65-1 pg. Powell-a 16.00 48.00 125.00

NOTE: ***Kremer** a-37, 39, 43; c-36, 37, 47. **Meskin** a-51. **Palais** a-30, 31(2), 32(2), 33-35, 37-40. **Powell** a-32-35, 36(2), 40, 41, 43-53, 57. **Simon** c-63-65. **Sparling** a-44. Bondage c-32, 34, 43.*

BLACK COBRA (Bride's Diary No. 4 on) (See Captain Flight #8)
Ajax/Farrell Publications(Excellent Publ.): No. 1, 10-11/54; No. 6(No. 2), 12-1/54-55; No. 3, 2-3/55

1-Re-intro Black Cobra & The Cobra Kid (costumed heroes)
30.00 90.00 240.00
6(#2)-Formerly Billy Bunny 18.00 53.00 140.00
3-(Pre-code)-Torpedoman app. 16.00 49.00 130.00

BLACK CONDOR (Also see Crack Comics, Freedom Fighters & Showcase '94 #10,11)
DC Comics: June, 1992 - No. 12, May, 1993 ($1.25)

1-12: 1-10,12-Heath-c. 9,10-The Ray app. 12-Batman-c/scripts 2.00

BLACK CROSS SPECIAL (See Dark Horse Presents)
Dark Horse Comics: Jan, 1988 ($1.75, B&W, one-shot)(Reprints & new-a)

1-1st & 2nd print; 2nd has 2pgs new-a 2.00

BLACK CROSS: DIRTY WORK (See Dark Horse Presents)
Dark Horse Comics: Apr, 1997 ($2.95, one-shot)

1-Chris Warner-c/s/a 3.00

BLACK DIAMOND
Americomics: May, 1983 - No. 5, 1984 (no month)($2.00-$1.75, Baxter paper)

1-3-Movie adapt.; 1-Colt back-up begins 3.00
4,5 2.50

NOTE: ***Bill Black** a-1i; c-1. **Gulacy** c-2-5. Sybil Danning photo back-c-1.*

BLACK DIAMOND WESTERN (Formerly Desperado No. 1-8)
Lev Gleason Publ: No. 9, Mar, 1949 - No. 60, Feb, 1956 (No. 9-28: 52 pgs.)

9-Black Diamond & his horse Reliapon begin; origin & 1st app. Black Diamond 20.00 60.00 160.00
10 10.00 30.00 75.00
11-15 7.85 23.50 55.00
16-28(11/49-11/51)-Wolverton's Bing Bang Buster 10.00 30.00 80.00
29-40: 31-One pg. Frazetta anti-drug ad 5.50 16.50 38.00
41-50,53-59 5.00 15.00 30.00
51-3-D effect-c/story 12.50 37.50 100.00
52-3-D effect story 12.00 36.00 95.00
60-Last issue 5.50 16.50 38.00

NOTE: ***Biro** c-9-35?. **Fass** a-58, c-54-56, 58. **Guardineer** a-9, 15, 18. **Kida** a-9. **Maurer** a-10. **E** **Moore** a-16. **Morisi** a-55. **Tuska** a-10, 48.*

BLACK DRAGON, THE
Marvel Comics (Epic Comics): 5/85 - No. 6, 10/85 (Baxter paper, mature)

1-6: 1-Chris Claremont story & John Bolton painted-c/a in all 3.00

BLACK DRAGON, THE
Dark Horse Comics: Apr, 1996 ($17.95, B&W, trade paperback)

nn-Reprints Epic Comics limited series; intro by Anne McCaffrey 18.00

BLACK FLAG (See Asylum #5)
Maximum Press: Jan, 1995 - No.4, 1995; No. 0, July, 1995 ($2.50, B&W) (No. 0 in color)

Preview Edition (6/94, $1.95, B&W)-Fraga/McFarlane-c. 2.00
0-4: 0-(7/95)-Liefeld/Fraga-c. 1-(1/95). 3.00
1-Variant cover 5.00
2,4-Variant covers 3.00

NOTE: ***Fraga** a-0-4, Preview Edition; c-1-4. **Liefeld/Fraga** c-0. **McFarlane/Fraga** c-Preview Edition.*

BLACK FURY (Becomes Wild West No. 58) (See Blue Bird)
Charlton Comics Group: May, 1955 - No. 57, Mar-Apr, 1966 (Horse stories)

1 7.00 21.00 48.00
2 4.00 12.00 24.00
3-10 3.60 9.00 18.00
11-15,19,20 2.40 6.00 12.00
16-18-Ditko-a 7.00 21.00 48.00
21-30 1.00 3.00 8.00
31-57 2.40 6.00

BLACK GOLIATH (See Avengers #32-35,41,54)
Marvel Comics Group: Feb, 1976 - No. 5, Nov, 1976

1-Tuska-a(p) thru #3 1.00 3.00 8.00
2-5: 2-4-(Regular 25¢ editions). 4-Kirby-c/Buckler-a 5.00
2-4-(30¢-c variants, limited distribution)(4,6,8/76) 1.00 3.00 8.00

BLACKHAWK (Formerly Uncle Sam #1-8; see Military & Modern Comics)
Comic Magazines(Quality)No. 9-107(12/56); National Periodical PublicationsNo. 108(1/57)-250; DC Comics No. 251 on: No. 9, Winter, 1944 - No. 243, 10-11/68; No. 244, 1-2/76 - No. 250, 1-2/77; No. 251, 10/82 - No. 273, 11/84

9 (1944) 305.00 915.00 3200.00

Blackhawk #30 © QUA

Blackhawk #122 © DC

Black Knight #4 © MAR

GD2.0 FN6.0 NM9.4

10 (1946) 111.00 332.00 1050.00
11-15: 14-Ward-a; 13,14-Fear app. 71.00 213.00 675.00
16-20: 20-Ward Blackhawk 58.00 174.00 550.00
21-30 (1950) 44.00 133.00 400.00
31-40: 31-Chop Chop by Jack Cole 38.00 113.00 300.00
41-49,51-60: 42-Robot-c 30.00 90.00 240.00
50-1st Killer Shark; origin in text 33.00 98.00 260.00
61,62: 61-Used in **POP**, pg. 91. 62-Used in **POP**, pg. 92 & color illo
26.00 79.00 210.00
63-70,72-80: 65-H-Bomb explosion panel. 66-B&W & color illos **POP**. 70-Return of Killer Shark; atomic explosion panel. 75-Intro. Blackie the Hawk
24.00 71.00 190.00
71-Origin retold; flying saucer-c; A-Bomb panels 28.00 83.00 220.00
81-86: Last precode (3/55) 22.00 66.00 175.00
87-92,94-99,101-107: 91-Robot-c. 105-1st S.A. 18.00 53.00 140.00
93-Origin in text 18.00 54.00 145.00
100 22.00 66.00 175.00
108-1st DC issue (1/57); re-intro. Blackie, the Hawk, their mascot; not in #115
41.00 123.00 500.00
109-117: 117-(10/57)-Mr. Freeze app. 15.50 46.50 170.00
118-(11/57)-Frazetta-r/Jimmy Wakely #4 (3 pgs.) 16.50 49.00 180.00
119-130 (11/58): 120-Robot-c 11.00 33.00 120.00
131-140 (9/59): 133-Intro. Lady Blackhawk 8.15 24.50 90.00
141-150,152-163,165,166: 141-Cat-Man returns-c/s. 143-Kurtzman-r/Jimmy Wakely #4. 150-(7/60)-King Condor returns. 166-Last 10¢ issue
5.90 17.75 65.00
151-Lady Blackhawk receives & loses super powers 6.35 19.00 70.00
164-Origin retold 6.80 20.50 75.00
167-180 3.45 10.35 38.00
181-190 2.80 8.40 28.00
191-196,199,201,202,204-210: 196-Combat Diary series begins.
2.40 7.35 22.00
197-New look for Blackhawks 2.80 8.40 28.00
198,200: 198-Origin retold 2.80 8.40 28.00
203-Origin Chop Chop (12/64) 2.80 8.40 28.00
211-227,229-243(1968): 230-Blackhawks become superheroes; JLA cameo
242-Return to old costumes 2.00 6.00 16.00
228-Batman, Green Lantern, Superman, The Flash cameos.
2.30 7.00 20.00
244 ('76) -250: 250-Chuck dies 5.00
251-273: 251-Origin retold; Black Knights return. 252-Intro Domino. 253-Part origin Hendrickson. 258-Blackhawk's Island destroyed. 259-Part origin Chop-Chop. 265-273 (75¢ cover price) 2.00

NOTE: ***Chaykin** a-260; c-257-260, 262. **Crandall** a-10, 11, 13, 16?, 18-20, 22-26, 30-33, 35p, 36(2), 37, 38?, 39-44, 46-50, 52-58, 60, 63, 64, 66, 67; c-14-20, 22-63(most except #28-33, 36, 37, 39). **Evans** a-244, 245,246i, 248-250i. **G. Kane** c-263, 264. **Kubert** c-244, 245. **Newton** a-266p. **Severin** a-257.**Spiegle** a-261-267, 269-273; c-265-272. **Toth** a-260p. **Ward** a-16-27(Chop Chop, 8pgs. ea.); pencilled stories-No. 17-63(approx.). **Wildey** a-268. Chop Chop solo stories in #10-95?*

BLACKHAWK
DC Comics: Mar, 1988 - No. 3, May, 1988 ($2.95, limited series, mature)

1-3: Chaykin painted-c/a/scripts 3.00

BLACKHAWK (Also see Action Comics #601)
DC Comics: Mar, 1989 - No. 16, Aug, 1990 ($1.50, mature)

1-6,8-16: 16-Crandall-c swipe 2.00
7-($2.50, 52 pgs.)-Story-r/Military #1 2.50
Annual 1 (1989, $2.95, 68 pgs.)-Recaps origin of Blackhawk, Lady Blackhawk, and others 3.00
Special 1 (1992, $3.50, 68 pgs.)-Mature readers 3.50

BLACKHAWK INDIAN TOMAHAWK WAR, THE
Avon Periodicals: 1951 (Also see Fighting Indians of the Wild West)

nn-Kinstler-c; Kit West story 19.00 56.00 150.00

BLACK HEART ASSASSIN
Iguana Comics: Jan, 1994 ($2.95)

1 3.00

BLACK HOLE (See Walt Disney Showcase #54) (Disney, movie)
Whitman Publishing Co.: Mar, 1980 - No. 4, Sept, 1980

GD2.0 FN6.0 NM9.4

11295(#1) (1979, Golden, $1.50-c, 52 pgs., graphic novel; 8 1/2x11") Photo-c; Spiegle-a. 2.00 6.00 18.00
1-4: 1,2-Movie adaptation. 2-4-Spiegle-a. 3-McWilliams-a; photo-c.
3,4-New stories 1.00 2.80 7.00

BLACK HOOD, THE (See Blue Ribbon, Flyman & Mighty Comics)
Red Circle Comics (Archie): June, 1983 - No. 3, Oct, 1983 (Mandell paper)

1-Morrow, McWilliams, Wildey-a; Toth-c 4.00
2,3: The Fox by Toth-c/a; Boyette-a. 3-Morrow-a; Toth wraparound-c 3.00
(Also see Archie's Super-Hero Special Digest #2)

BLACK HOOD
DC Comics (Impact Comics): Dec, 1991 - No. 12, Dec, 1992 ($1.00)

1-12: 11-Intro The Fox. 12-Origin Black Hood 2.00
Annual 1 (1992, $2.50, 68 pgs.)-w/Trading card 2.50

BLACK HOOD COMICS (Formerly Hangman #2-8; Laugh Comics #20 on; also see Black Swan, Jackpot, Roly Poly & Top-Notch #9)
MLJ Magazines: No. 9, Wint., 1943-44 - No. 19, Sum., 1946 (on radio in 1943)

9-The Hangman & The Boy Buddies cont'd 104.00 312.00 985.00
10-Hangman & Dusty, the Boy Detective app. 59.00 177.00 560.00
11-Dusty app.; no Hangman 46.00 138.00 410.00
12-18: 14-Kinstler blood-c. 17-Hal Foster swipe from Prince Valiant; 1st issue with "An Archie Magazine" on-c 40.00 120.00 360.00
19-I.D. exposed; last issue 52.00 157.00 470.00

NOTE: *Hangman by **Fuje** in 9, 10. **Kinstler** a-15, c-14-16.*

BLACK JACK (Rocky Lane's...; formerly Jim Bowie)
Charlton Comics: No. 20, Nov, 1957 - No. 30, Nov, 1959

20 8.65 26.00 60.00
21,27,29,30 5.00 15.00 35.00
22-(68 pgs.) 7.85 23.50 55.00
23-Williamson/Torres-a 7.15 21.50 50.00
24-26,28-Ditko-a 9.30 28.00 65.00

BLACK KNIGHT, THE
Toby Press: May, 1953; 1963

1-Bondage-c 24.00 71.00 190.00
Super Reprint No. 11 (1963)-Reprints 1953 issue 2.50 7.50 25.00

BLACK KNIGHT, THE (Also see The Avengers #48, Marvel Super Heroes & Tales To Astonish #52)
Atlas Comics (MgPC): May, 1955 - No. 5, April, 1956

1-Origin Crusader; Maneely-c/a 86.00 257.00 815.00
2-Maneely-c/a(4) 60.00 180.00 570.00
3-5: 4-Maneely-c/a. 5-Maneely-c, Shores-a 48.00 145.00 435.00

BLACK KNIGHT (Also see Avengers & Ultraforce)
Marvel Comics: June, 1990 - No. 4, Sept, 1990 ($1.50, limited series)

1-4: 1-Original Black Knight returns. 3,4-Dr. Strange app. 2.00
NOTE: ***Buckler** c-1-4p*

BLACK KNIGHT: EXODUS
Marvel Comics: Dec, 1996 ($2.50, one-shot)

1-Raab-s; Apocalypse-c/app. 2.50

BLACK LAMB, THE
DC Comics (Helix): Nov, 1996 - No, 6, Apr, 1997 ($2.50, limited series)

1-6: Tim Truman-c/a/scripts 2.50

BLACK LIGHTNING (See The Brave & The Bold, Cancelled Comic Cavalcade, DC Comics Presents #16, Detective #490 and World's Finest #257)
National Periodical Publ./DC Comics: Apr, 1977 - No. 11, Sept-Oct, 1978

1,11: 1-Origin Black Lightning. 11-The Ray new solo story 2.40 6.00
2,3,6-10: 4.00
4,5-Superman-c/s. 4-Intro Cyclotronic Man 5.00
NOTE: ***Buckler** c-1-3p, 6-11p. #11 is 44 pgs.*

BLACK LIGHTNING (2nd Series)
DC Comics: Feb, 1995 - No. 13, Feb, 1996 ($1.95/$2.25)

1-5-Tony Isabella scripts begin, ends #8 3.00
6-13: 6-Begin $2.25-c. 13-Batman-c/app. 3.00

BLACK MAGIC (...Magazine) (Becomes Cool Cat V8#6 on)

Black Magic #33 © Headline

Black Orchid (series) #2 © DC

Black Panther V2 #2 © MAR

Crestwood Publ. V1#1-4,V6#1-V7#5/Headline V1#5-V5#3,V7#6-V8#5: 10-11/50 - V4#1, 6-7/53: V4#2, 9-10/53 - V5#3, 11-12/54; V6#1, 9-10/57 - V7#2, 11-12/58: V7#3, 7-8/60 - V8#5, 11-12/61
(V1#1-5, 52pgs.; V1#6-V3#3, 44pgs.)

	GD2.0	FN6.0	NM9.4
V1#1-S&K-a, 10 pgs.; Meskin-a(2)	97.00	292.00	925.00
2-S&K-a, 17 pgs.; Meskin-a	47.00	142.00	425.00
3-6(8-9/51)-S&K, Roussos, Meskin-a	42.00	125.00	375.00
V2#1(10-11/51),4,5,7(#13),9(#15),12(#18)-S&K-a	32.00	96.00	255.00
2,3,6,8,10,11(#17)	23.00	68.00	180.00
V3#1(#19, 12/52) - 6(#24, 5/53)-S&K-a	25.00	75.00	200.00
V4#1(#25, 6-7/53), 2(#26, 9-10/53)-S&K-a(3-4)	26.00	79.00	210.00
3(#27, 11-12/53)-S&K-a; Ditko-a (2nd published-a); also see Captain 3-D, Daring Love #1, Strange Fantasy #9, & Fantastic Fears #5 (Fant. Fears was 1st drawn, but not 1st publ.)	41.00	133.00	400.00
4(#28)-Eyes ripped out/story-S&K, Ditko-a	36.00	108.00	290.00
5(#29, 3-4/54)-S&K, Ditko-a	27.00	81.00	215.00
6(#30, 5-6/54)-S&K, Powell?-a	21.00	64.00	170.00
V5#1(#31, 7-8/54 - 3(#33, 11-12/54)-S&K-a	16.00	49.00	130.00
V6#1(#34, 9-10/57), 2(#35, 11-12/57)	10.00	30.00	70.00
3(1-2/58) - 6(7-8/58)	10.00	30.00	70.00
V7#1(9-10/58) - 3(7-8/60)	8.65	26.00	60.00
4(9-10/60), 5(11-12/60)-Torres-a	10.00	30.00	70.00
6(1-2/61)-Powell-a(2)	8.65	26.00	60.00
V8#1(3-4/61)-Powell-c/a	8.65	26.00	60.00
2(5-6/61)-E.C. story swipe/W.F. #22; Ditko, Powell-a	10.00	30.00	70.00
3(7-8/61)-E.C. story swipe/W.F. #22; Powell-a(2)	10.00	30.00	70.00
4(9-10/61)-Powell-a(5)	8.65	26.00	60.00
5-E.C. story swipe/W.S.F. #28; Powell-a(3)	10.00	30.00	70.00

NOTE: ***Bernard Baily*** *a-V4#6?, V5#3(2).* ***Grandenetti*** *a-V2#3, 11.* ***Kirby*** *c-V1#1-6, V2#1-12, V3#1-6, V4#1, 2, 4-6, V5#1-3.* ***McWilliams*** *a-V3#2i.* ***Meskin*** *a-V1#1(2), 2, 3, 4(2), 5(2), 6, V2/1, 2, 3(2), 4(3), 5, 6(2), 7-9, 11, 12i, V3#1(2), 5, 6, V5#1(2), 2.* ***Orlando*** *a-V6#1, 4, V7#2; c-V6/1-6.* ***Powell*** *a-V5#1?.* ***Roussos*** *a-V1#3-5, 6(2), V2#3(2), 4, 5(2), 6, 8, 9, 10(2), 11, 12p, V3#1(2), 2i, 5, V5#2.* ***Simon*** *a-V2#12, V3#2, V7#5? c-V4#3?, V7#3?, 4, 5?, 6?, V8#1-5.* ***Simon & Kirby*** *a-V1#1, 2(2), 3-6, V2#1, 4, 5, 7, 9, 12, V3#1-6, V4#1(3), 2(4), 3(2), 4(2), 5, 6, V5#1-3; c-V2#1.* ***Leonard Starr*** *a-V1#1.* ***Tuska*** *a-V6#3, 4.* ***Woodbridge*** *a-V7#4.*

BLACK MAGIC
National Periodical Publications: Oct-Nov, 1973 - No. 9, Apr-May, 1975

	GD2.0	FN6.0	NM9.4
1-S&K reprints	2.50	7.50	24.00
2-8-S&K reprints	1.75	5.25	14.00
9-S&K reprints	2.00	6.00	16.00

BLACK MAGIC
Eclipse International: Apr, 1990 - No. 4, Oct, 1990 ($2.75, B&W, mini-series)

	GD2.0	FN6.0	NM9.4
1-($3.50, 68pgs.)-Japanese manga			3.50
2-4 ($2.75, 52 pgs.)			3.00

BLACKMAIL TERROR (See Harvey Comics Library)

BLACK MASK
DC Comics: 1993 - No. 3, 1994 ($4.95, limited series, 52 pgs.)

	GD2.0	FN6.0	NM9.4
1-3			5.00

BLACK OPS
Image Comics (WildStorm): Jan, 1996 - No. 5, May, 1996 ($2.50, lim. series)

	GD2.0	FN6.0	NM9.4
1-5			2.50

BLACK ORCHID (See Adventure Comics #428 & Phantom Stranger)
DC Comics: Holiday, 1988-89 - No. 3, 1989 ($3.50, lim. series, prestige format)

	GD2.0	FN6.0	NM9.4
Book 1,3: Gaiman scripts & McKean painted-a in all		2.40	6.00
Book 2-Arkham Asylum story; Batman app.	1.00	3.00	8.00
TPB (1991, $19.95) r/#1-3; new McKean-c			20.00

BLACK ORCHID
DC Comics: Sept, 1993 - No. 22, June, 1995 ($1.95/$2.25)

	GD2.0	FN6.0	NM9.4
1-22: Dave McKean-c all issues			2.25
1-Platinum Edition			12.00
Annual 1 (1993, $3.95, 68 pgs.)-Children's Crusade			4.00

BLACKOUTS (See Broadway Hollywood...)

BLACK PANTHER, THE (Also see Avengers #52, Fantastic Four #52, Jungle Action & Marvel Premiere #51-53)
Marvel Comics Group: Jan, 1977 - No. 15, May, 1979

	GD2.0	FN6.0	NM9.4
1	2.00	6.00	16.00
2-13: 4,5-(Regular 30¢ editions). 8-Origin	1.00	3.00	8.00
4,5-(35¢-c variants, limited dist.)(7,9/77)	1.75	5.25	14.00
14,15-Avengers x-over. 14-Origin	1.25	3.75	10.00

NOTE: ***J. Buscema*** *c-15p.* ***Kirby*** *c/a & scripts-1-12.* ***Layton*** *c-13i.*

BLACK PANTHER
Marvel Comics Group: July, 1988 - No. 4, Oct, 1988 ($1.25)

	GD2.0	FN6.0	NM9.4
1-4-Gillis-s/Cowan & Delarosa-a			2.00

BLACK PANTHER (Marvel Knights)
Marvel Comics: Nov, 1998 - Present ($2.50)

	GD2.0	FN6.0	NM9.4
1-Texeira-a/c; Priest-s			5.00
1-($6.95) DF edition w/Quesada & Palmiotti-c			7.00
2-4: 2-Two covers by Texeira and Timm. 3-Fantastic Four app.			3.00
5-27: 5-Evans-a. 6-8-Jusko-a. 8-Avengers-c/app. 15-Hulk app. 22-Moon Knight app. 23-Avengers app. 25-Maximum Security x-over. 26-Storm-c/app.			2.50

BLACK PANTHER: PANTHER'S PREY
Marvel Comics: May, 1991 - No. 4, Oct, 1991 ($4.95, squarebound, lim. series, 52 pgs.)

	GD2.0	FN6.0	NM9.4
1-4: McGregor-s/Turner-a			5.00

BLACK PEARL, THE
Dark Horse Comics: Sept, 1996 - No. 5, Jan, 1997 ($2.95, limited series)

	GD2.0	FN6.0	NM9.4
1-5: Mark Hamill scripts			3.00

BLACK PHANTOM (See Tim Holt #25, 38)
Magazine Enterprises: Nov, 1954 (one-shot) (Female outlaw)

	GD2.0	FN6.0	NM9.4
1 (A-1 #122)-The Ghost Rider story plus 3 Black Phantom stories; Headlight-c/a	39.00	116.00	310.00

BLACK PHANTOM
AC Comics: 1989 - No. 3, 1990 ($2.50, B&W; #2 color)(Reprints & new-a)

	GD2.0	FN6.0	NM9.4
1-3: 1-Ayers-r, Bolle-r/B.P. #1-3-Redmask-r			2.75

BLACK PHANTOM, RETURN OF THE (See Wisco)

BLACK RIDER (Western Winners #1-7; Western Tales of Black Rider #28-31; Gunsmoke Western #32 on)(See All Western Winners, Best Western, Kid Colt, Outlaw Kid, Rex Hart, Two-Gun Kid, Two-Gun Western, Western Gunfighters, Western Winners, & Wild Western)
Marvel/Atlas Comics(CDS No. 8-17/CPS No. 19 on): No. 8, 3/50 - No. 18, 1/52; No. 19, 11/53 - No. 27, 3/55

	GD2.0	FN6.0	NM9.4
8 (#1)-Black Rider & his horse Satan begin; 36 pgs; Stan Lee photo-c as Black Rider)	42.00	125.00	375.00
9-52 pgs. begin, end #14	23.00	69.00	185.00
10-Origin Black Rider	28.00	84.00	225.00
11-14: 14-Last 52pgs.	17.00	51.00	135.00
15-19: 19-Two-Gun Kid app.	14.00	43.00	115.00
20-Classic-c; Two-Gun Kid app.	16.00	48.00	125.00
21-27: 21-23-Two-Gun Kid app. 24,25-Arrowhead app. 26-Kid Colt app. 27-Last issue; last precode. Kid Colt app. The Spider (a villain) burns to death	12.50	37.50	100.00

NOTE: ***Ayers*** *c-22.* ***Jack Keller*** *a-15, 26, 27.* ***Maneely*** *a-14; c-16, 17, 25, 27.* ***Syd Shores*** *a-19, 21, 22, 23(3), 24(3), 25-27; c-19, 21, 23.* ***Sinnott*** *a-24, 25.* ***Tuska*** *a-12, 19-21.*

BLACK RIDER RIDES AGAIN!, THE
Atlas Comics (CPS): Sept, 1957

	GD2.0	FN6.0	NM9.4
1-Kirby-a(3); Powell-a; Severin-c	25.00	75.00	200.00

BLACK SEPTEMBER (Also see Avengers/Ultraforce, Ultraforce (1st series) #10 & Ultraforce/Avengers)
Malibu Comics (Ultraverse): 1995 ($1.50, one-shot)

	GD2.0	FN6.0	NM9.4
Infinity-Intro to the newUltraverse; variant-c exists.			2.00

BLACKSTONE (See Super Magician Comics & Wisco Giveaways)

BLACKSTONE, MASTER MAGICIAN COMICS
Vital Publ./Street & Smith Publ.: Mar-Apr, 1946 - No. 3, July-Aug, 1946

	GD2.0	FN6.0	NM9.4
1	28.00	84.00	225.00
2,3	19.00	56.00	150.00

BLACKSTONE, THE MAGICIAN (...Detective on cover only #3 & 4)

Black Terror #14 © BP

Black Widow #3 © MAR

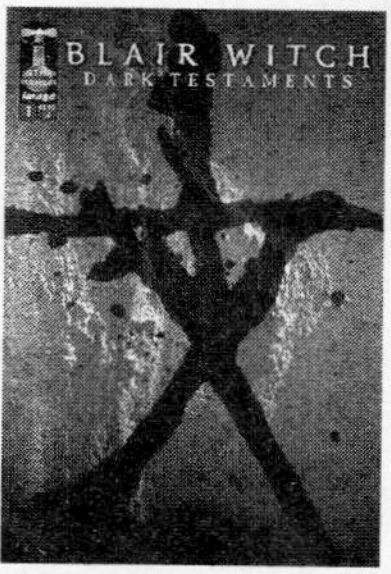

Blair Witch: Dark Testaments #1 © Oni Press

GD2.0 FN6.0 NM9.4

Marvel Comics (CnPC): No. 2, May, 1948 - No. 4, Sept, 1948 (No #1) (Cont'd from E.C. #1?)

	GD2.0	FN6.0	NM9.4
2-The Blonde Phantom begins, ends #4	58.00	174.00	550.00
3,4: 3-Blonde Phantom by Sekowsky	40.00	120.00	350.00

BLACKSTONE, THE MAGICIAN DETECTIVE FIGHTS CRIME
E. C. Comics: Fall, 1947

	GD2.0	FN6.0	NM9.4
1-1st app. Happy Houlihans	47.00	142.00	425.00

BLACK SUN (X-Men Black Sun on cover)
Marvel Comics: Nov, 2000 - No. 5, Nov, 2000 ($2.99, weekly limited series)

1-(...: X-Men), 2-(...: Storm), 3-(...: Banshee and Sunfire), 4-(...: Colossus and Nightcrawler), 5-(...: Wolverine and Thunderbird); Claremont-s in all; Evans interlocking painted covers; Magik returns 3.00

BLACK SWAN COMICS
MLJ Magazines (Pershing Square Publ. Co.): 1945

	GD2.0	FN6.0	NM9.4
1-The Black Hood reprints from Black Hood No. 14; Bill Woggon-a; Suzie app.	23.00	68.00	180.00

BLACK TARANTULA (See Feature Presentations No. 5)

BLACK TERROR (See America's Best Comics & Exciting Comics)
Better Publications/Standard: Winter, 1942-43 - No. 27, June, 1949

	GD2.0	FN6.0	NM9.4
1-Black Terror, Crime Crusader begin	284.00	853.00	2700.00
2	105.00	316.00	1000.00
3	74.00	221.00	700.00
4,5	63.00	189.00	600.00
6-10: 7-The Ghost app.	55.00	165.00	525.00
11-20: 20-The Scarab app.	47.00	140.00	420.00
21-Miss Masque app.	51.00	153.00	460.00
22-Part Frazetta-a on one Black Terror story	47.00	140.00	420.00
23,25-27	43.00	130.00	390.00
24-Frazetta-a (1/4 pg.)	44.00	133.00	400.00

NOTE: ***Schomburg (Xela)** c-2-27; bondage c-2, 17, 24. **Meskin** a-27. **Moreira** a-27. **Robinson/Meskin** a-23, 24(3), 25, 26. **Roussos/Mayo** a-24. **Tuska** a-26, 27.*

BLACK TERROR, THE (Also see Total Eclipse)
Eclipse Comics: Oct, 1989 - No. 3, June, 1990 ($4.95, 52 pgs., squarebound, limited series)

1-3: Beau Smith & Chuck Dixon scripts; Dan Brereton painted-c/a 5.00

BLACKTHORNE 3-D SERIES
Blackthorne Publishing Co.: May, 1985 - No. 80, 1989 ($2.25/$2.50)

	GD2.0	FN6.0	NM9.4
1-Sheena in 3-D #1. D. Stevens-c/retouched-a			5.00
2-10: 2-MerlinRealm in 3-D #1. 3-3-D Heroes #1. Goldyn in 3-D #1. 5-Bizarre 3-D Zone #1. 6-Salimba in 3-D #1. 7-Twisted Tales in 3-D #1. 8-Dick Tracy in 3-D #1. 9-Salimba in 3-D #2. 10-Gumby in 3-D #1			5.00
11-19: 11-Betty Boop in 3-D #1. 12-Hamster Vice in 3-D #1. 13-Little Nemo in 3-D #1. 14-Gumby in 3-D #2. 15-Hamster Vice #6 in 3-D. 16-Laffin' Gas #6 in 3-D. 17-Gumby in 3-D #3. 18-Bullwinkle and Rocky in 3-D #1. 19-The Flintstones in 3-D #1.			5.00
20,26,35,39,52,62-G.I. Joe in 3-D. 62-G.I. Joe Annual		2.40	6.00
21-24,27-28: 21-Gumby in 3-D #4. 22-The Flintstones in 3-D #2. 23-Laurel & Hardy in 3-D #1. 24-Bozothe Clown in 3-D #1. 27-Bravestarr in 3-D #1. 28- Gumby in 3-D #5.			5.00
25,29,37-The Transformers in 3-D	1.00	2.80	7.00
30-Star Wars in 3-D #1	1.50	4.50	12.00
31-34,36,38,40: 31-The California Raisins in 3-D #1. 32-Richie Rich & Casper in 3-D #1. 33-Gumby in 3-D #6. 34-Laurel & Hardy in 3-D #2. 36-The Flintstones in 3-D #3. 38-Gumby in 3-D #7. 40-Bravestarr in 3-D #2			5.00
41-46,49,50: 41-Battletech in 3-D #1. 42-The Flintstones in 3-D #4. 43-Underdog in 3-D #1 44-The California Raisins in 3-D #2. 45-Red Heat in 3-D #1 (movie adapt.). 46-The California Raisins in 3-D #3. 49-Rambo in 3-D #1. 49-Sad Sack in 3-D #1. 50-Bullwinkle For President in 3-D #1			5.00
47,48-Star Wars in 3-D #2,3	1.10	3.30	9.00
51,53-60: 51-Kull in 3-D #1. 53-Red Sonja in 3-D #1. 54-Bozo in 3-D #2. 55-Waxwork in 3-D #1 (movie adapt.). 56. 57-Casper in 3-D #1. 58-Baby Huey in 3-D #1. 59-Little Dot in 3-D #1. 60-Solomon Kane in 3-D #1			5.00
61,63-80: 61-Werewolf in 3-D #1. 63-The California Raisins in 3-D #4. 64-To Die For in 3-D #1. 65-Capt. Holo in 3-D #1. 66-Playful Little Audrey in 3-D #1. 67-Kull in 3-D #2. 68. 69-The California Raisins in 3-D #5. 70-Wendy in 3-D #1. 71. 72-Sports Hall of Shame #1. 73. 74-The Noid in 3-D #1. 75-Moonwalker in 3-D #1 (Michael Jackson movie adapt.). 76-79. 80-The Noid in 3-D #2			5.00

BLACK WIDOW (Marvel Knights) (Also see Marvel Graphic Novel)
Marvel Comics: May, 1999 - No. 3, Aug, 1999 ($2.99, limited series)

	GD2.0	FN6.0	NM9.4
1-(June on-c) Devin Grayson-s/J.G. Jones-c/a; Daredevil app.			4.00
1-Variant-c by J.G. Jones			5.00
2,3			4.00
...Web of Intrigue (6/99, $3.50) r/origin & early appearances			3.50

BLACK WIDOW (Marvel Knights) (Volume 2)
Marvel Comics: Jan, 2001 - No. 3, Mar, 2001 ($2.99, limited series)

1-3-Grayson & Rucka-s/Scott Hampton-c/a; Daredevil app. 3.00

BLACKWULF
Marvel Comics: June, 1994 - No. 10, Mar, 1995 ($1.50)

	GD2.0	FN6.0	NM9.4
1-($2.50)-Embossed-c; Angel Medina-a			2.50
2-10			2.00

BLADE (The Vampire Hunter)
Marvel Comics: Mar, 1998 ($3.50, one-shot)

1-Colan-a(p)/Christopher Golden-s 3.50

BLADE (The Vampire Hunter)
Marvel Comics: Nov, 1998 - No. 3, Jan, 1999 ($3.50/$2.99)

	GD2.0	FN6.0	NM9.4
1-($3.50) Contains Movie insider pages; McKean-a			3.50
2,3-($2.99): 2-Two covers			3.00
...Sins of the Father (10/98, $5.99) Sears-a; movie adaption			6.00

BLADE OF THE IMMORTAL (Manga)
Dark Horse Comics: June, 1996 - Present ($2.95/$3.95, B&W)

	GD2.0	FN6.0	NM9.4
1	1.25	3.75	10.00
2-5: 2-#1 on cover in error		2.40	6.00
6-10			5.00
11,19,20,34-($3.95, 48 pgs.): 34-Food one-shot			4.00
12-18,21-33,35-41,43-46: 12-20- Dreamsong. 21-28-On Silent Wings. 29-33-Dark Shadow. 35-42-Heart of Darkness. 43-46-The Gathering			3.00
42-($3.50) Ends Heart of Darkness			3.50

BLADE RUNNER (Movie)
Marvel Comics Group: Oct, 1982 - No. 2, Nov, 1982

1,2-r/Marvel Super Special #22; 1-Williamson-c/a. 2-Williamson-a 3.00

BLADESMEN UNDERSEA
Blue Comet Press: 1994 ($3.50, B&W)

1-Polybagged w/trading card 3.50

BLADE: THE VAMPIRE-HUNTER
Marvel Comics: July, 1994 - No. 10, Apr, 1995 ($1.95)

	GD2.0	FN6.0	NM9.4
1-($2.95)-Foil-c; Dracula returns; Wheatley-c/a			3.00
2-10: 2,3,10-Dracula-c/app. 8-Morbius app.			2.50

BLADE: VAMPIRE-HUNTER
Marvel Comics: Dec, 1999 - Present ($3.50/$2.50)

	GD2.0	FN6.0	NM9.4
1-($3.50)-Bart Sears-s; Sears and Smith-a			3.50
2-6-($2.50): 2-Regular & Wesley Snipes photo-c			2.50

BLAIR WITCH CHRONICLES, THE
Oni Press: Mar, 2000 - No. 4, July, 2000 ($2.95, B&W, limited series)

	GD2.0	FN6.0	NM9.4
1-4-Van Meter-s.1-Guy Davis-a. 2-Mireault-a			3.00
1-DF Alternate-c by John Estes			6.95
TPB (9/00, $15.95) r/#1-4 & Blair Witch Project one-shot			16.00

BLAIR WITCH: DARK TESTAMENTS
Image Comics: Oct, 2000 ($2.95, one-shot)

1-Edington-s/Adlard-a; story of murderer Rustin Parr 3.00

BLAIR WITCH PROJECT, THE (Movie companion, not adaption)
Oni Press: July, 1999 ($2.95, B&W, one-shot)

	GD2.0	FN6.0	NM9.4
1-(1st printing) History of the Blair Witch, art by Edwards, Mireault, and Davis; Van Meter-s; only the stick figure is red on the cover			12.00
1-(2nd printing) Stick figure and title lettering are red on cover			4.00
1-(3rd printing) Stick figure, title, and creator credits are red on cover			3.00

Blaze of Glory #1 © MAR

Blazing Sixguns #1 © AVON

Blazing West #1 © ACG

DF Glow in the Dark variant-c ($10.00) 10.00

BLAST (Satire Magazine)
G & D Publications: Feb, 1971 - No. 2, May, 1971

1-Wrightson & Kaluta-a/Everette-c 5.90 17.75 65.00
2-Kaluta-c/a 4.10 12.30 45.00

BLAST CORPS
Dark Horse Comics: Oct, 1998 ($2.50, one-shot, based on Nintendo game)

1-Reprints from Nintendo Power magazine; Mahn-a 2.50

BLASTERS SPECIAL
DC Comics: 1989 ($2.00, one-shot)

1-Peter David scripts; Invasion spin-off 2.00

BLAST-OFF (Three Rocketeers)
Harvey Publications (Fun Day Funnies): Oct, 1965 (12¢)

1-Kirby/Williamson-a(2); Williamson/Crandall-a; Williamson/Torres/Krenkel-a; Kirby/Simon-c 4.55 13.65 50.00

BLAZE
Marvel Comics: Aug, 1994 - No. 12, July, 1995 ($1.95)

1-($2.95)-Foil embossed-c 3.00
2-12: 2-Man-Thing-c/story. 11,12-Punisher app. 2.00

BLAZE CARSON (Rex Hart #6 on)(See Kid Colt, Tex Taylor, Wild Western, Wisco)
Marvel Comics (USA): Sept, 1948 - No. 5, June, 1949

1: 1,2-Shores-c 26.00 79.00 210.00
2,4,5: 4-Two-Gun Kid app. 5-Tex Taylor app. 19.00 56.00 150.00
3-Used by N.Y. State Legis. Comm. (injury to eye splash); Tex Morgan app. 20.00 60.00 160.00

BLAZE: LEGACY OF BLOOD (See Ghost Rider & Ghost Rider/Blaze)
Marvel Comics (Midnight Sons imprint): Dec, 1993 - No. 4, Mar, 1994 ($1.75, limited series)

1-4 2.00

BLAZE OF GLORY
Marvel Comics: Feb, 2000 - No. 4, Mar, 2000 ($2.99, limited series)

1-4-Ostrander-s/Manco-a; Two-Gun Kid, Rawhide Kid, Red Wolf and Ghost Rider app. 3.00

BLAZE THE WONDER COLLIE (Formerly Molly Manton's Romances #1?)
Marvel Comics(SePI): No. 2, Oct, 1949 - No. 3, Feb, 1950 (Both have photo-c)

2(#1), 3-(Scarce) 23.00 68.00 180.00

BLAZING BATTLE TALES
Seaboard Periodicals (Atlas): July, 1975

1-Intro. Sgt. Hawk & the Sky Demon; Severin, McWilliams, Sparling-a; Nazi-c by Thorne 1.00 3.00 8.00

BLAZING COMBAT (Magazine)
Warren Publishing Co.: Oct, 1965 - No. 4, July, 1966 (35¢, B&W)

1-Frazetta painted-c on all 16.00 48.00 175.00
2 4.10 12.30 45.00
3,4: 4-Frazetta half pg. ad 3.20 9.60 35.00
...Anthology (reprints from No. 1-4) 4.35 13.00 48.00

NOTE: *Above has art by* ***Colan, Crandall, Evans, Morrow, Orlando, Severin, Torres, Toth, Williamson,*** *and* ***Wood.***

BLAZING COMBAT: WORLD WAR I AND WORLD WAR II
Apple Press: Mar, 1994 ($3.75, B&W)

1,2: 1-r/Colan, Toth, Goodwin, Severin, Wood-a. 2-r/Crandall, Evans, Severin, Torres, Williamson-a 4.00

BLAZING COMICS (Also see Blue Circle Comics and Red Circle Comics)
Enwil Associates/Rural Home: 6/44 - #3, 9/44; #4, 2/45; #5, 3/45; #5(V2#2), 3/55 - #6(V2#3), 1955?

1-The Green Turtle, Red Hawk, Black Buccaneer begin; origin Jun-Gal 50.00 150.00 450.00
2-5: 3-Briefer-a. 5-(V2#2 inside) 34.00 103.00 275.00
5(3/55, V2#2-inside)-Black Buccaneer-c, 6(V2#3-inside, 1955)-Indian/Japanese-c; cover is from Apr. 1945 15.00 45.00 120.00

NOTE: *No. 5 & 6 contain remaindered comics rebound and the contents can vary. Cloak & Daggar, Will Rogers, Superman 64, Star Spangled 130, Kaanga known. Value would be half of contents.*

BLAZING SIXGUNS
Avon Periodicals: Dec, 1952

1-Kinstler-c/a; Larsen/Alascia-a(2), Tuska?-a; Jesse James, Kit Carson, Wild Bill Hickok app. 15.00 45.00 120.00

BLAZING SIXGUNS
I.W./Super Comics: 1964

I.W. Reprint #1,8,9: 1-r/Wild Bill Hickok #26, Western True Crime #? & Blazing Sixguns #1 by Avon; Kinstler-c. 8-r/Blazing Western #?; Kinstler-c. 9-r/Blazing Western #1; Ditko-r; Kintsler-c reprinted from Dalton Boys #1. 1.85 5.50 15.00
Super Reprint #10,11,15,16: 10,11-r/The Rider #2,1. 15-r/Silver Kid Western #?. 16-r/Buffalo Bill #?; Wildey-r; Severin-c. 17(1964)-r/Western True Crime #? 1.85 5.50 15.00
12-Reprints Bullseye #3; S&K-a 3.20 9.60 35.00
18-r/Straight Arrow #? by Powell; Severin-c 1.85 5.50 15.00

BLAZING SIX-GUNS (Also see Sundance Kid)
Skywald Comics: Feb, 1971 - No. 2, Apr, 1971 (52 pgs.)

1-The Red Mask, Sundance Kid begin, Avon's Geronimo reprint by Kinstler; Wyatt Earp app. 1.85 5.50 15.00
2-Wild Bill Hickok, Jesse James, Kit Carson-r plus M.E. Red Mask-r 1.25 3.75 10.00

BLAZING WEST (The Hooded Horseman #21 on)
American Comics Group (B&I Publ./Michel Publ.): Fall, 1948 - No. 20, Nov-Dec, 1951

1-Origin & 1st app. Injun Jones, Tenderfoot & Buffalo Belle; Texas Tim & Ranger begins, ends #13 20.00 60.00 160.00
2,3 (1-2/49) 10.00 30.00 75.00
4-Origin & 1st app. Little Lobo; Starr-a (3-4/49) 8.65 26.00 60.00
5-10: 5-Starr-a 7.15 21.50 50.00
11-13 5.50 16.50 38.00
14(11-12/50)-Origin/1st app. The Hooded Horseman 10.50 32.00 85.00
15-20: 15,16,18,19-Starr-a 7.85 23.50 55.00

BLAZING WESTERN
Timor Publications: Jan, 1954 - No. 5, Sept, 1954

1-Ditko-a (1st Western-a?); text story by Bruce Hamilton 15.00 45.00 120.00
2-4 6.40 19.25 45.00
5-Disbrow-a 7.15 21.50 50.00

BLEAT
Slave Labor Graphics: Aug, 1995 ($2.95)

1 3.00

BLINDSIDE
Image Comics (Extreme Studios): Aug, 1996 ($2.50)

1-Variant-c exists 2.50

BLINK (See X-Men Age of Apocalypse storyline)
Marvel Comics: March, 2001 - No. 4, June, 2001 ($2.99, limited series)

1-Adam Kubert-c/Lobdell-s 3.00

BLIP
Marvel Comics Group: 2/1983 - 1983 (Video game mag. in comic format)

1-1st app. Donkey Kong & Mario Bros. in comics, 6pgs. comics; photo-c 1.00 2.80 7.00
2-Spider-Man photo-c; 6pgs. Spider-Man comics w/Green Goblin 1.00 3.00 8.00
3,4,6 4.00
5-E.T., Indiana Jones; Rocky-c 5.00
7-6pgs. Hulk comics; Pac-Man & Donkey Kong Jr. Hints 2.40 6.00

BLISS ALLEY
Image Comics: July, 1997 - No. 2($2.95, B&W)

1,2-Messner-Loebs-s/a 3.00

BLITZKRIEG

Blonde Phantom #16 © MAR

Blood Legacy #1 © Top Cow

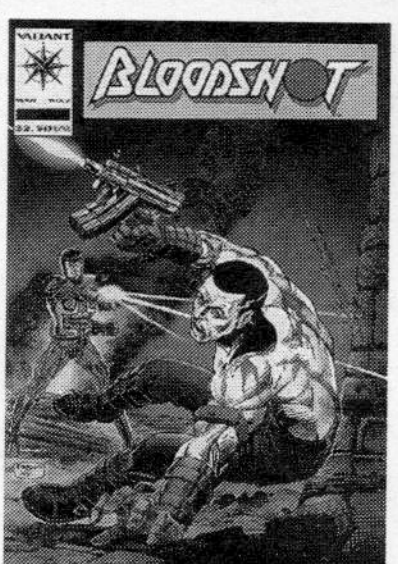

Bloodshot #2 © VAL

GD2.0 FN6.0 NM9.4

National Periodical Publications: Jan-Feb, 1976 - No. 5, Sept-Oct, 1976

	GD2.0	FN6.0	NM9.4
1-Kubert-c on all	3.20	9.60	35.00
2-5	2.30	7.00	20.00

BLONDE PHANTOM (Formerly All-Select #1-11; Lovers #23 on)(Also see Blackstone, Marvel Mystery, Millie The Model #2, Sub-Mariner Comics #25 & Sun Girl)
Marvel Comics (MPC): No. 12, Winter, 1946-47 - No. 22, Mar, 1949

	GD2.0	FN6.0	NM9.4
12-Miss America begins, ends #14	147.00	442.00	1400.00
13-Sub-Mariner begins (not in #16)	92.00	276.00	875.00
14,15: 15-Kurtzman's "Hey Look"	84.00	253.00	800.00
16-Captain America with Bucky story by Rico(p), 6 pgs.; Kurtzman's "Hey Look" (1 pg.)	116.00	348.00	1100.00
17-22: 22-Anti Wertham editorial	74.00	221.00	700.00

NOTE: ***Shores** c-12-18.*

BLONDIE (See Ace Comics, Comics Reading Libraries, Dagwood, Daisy & Her Pups, Eat Right to Work…, King & Magic Comics)
David McKay Publications: 1942 - 1946

	GD2.0	FN6.0	NM9.4
Feature Books 12 (Rare)	76.00	228.00	725.00
Feature Books 27-29,31,34(1940)	20.00	60.00	160.00
Feature Books 36,38,40,42,43,45,47	19.00	56.00	150.00
…1944 (Hard-c, 1938, B&W, 128 pgs.)-1944 daily strip-r	15.00	45.00	120.00

BLONDIE & DAGWOOD FAMILY
Harvey Publ. (King Features Synd.): Oct, 1963 - No. 4, Dec, 1965 (68 pgs.)

	GD2.0	FN6.0	NM9.4
1	2.80	8.40	28.00
2-4	2.00	6.00	16.00

BLONDIE COMICS (…Monthly No. 16-141)
David McKay #1-15/Harvey #16-163/King #164-175/Charlton #177 on: Spring, 1947 - No. 163, Nov, 1965; No. 164, Aug, 1966 - No. 175, Dec, 1967; No. 177, Feb, 1969 - No. 222, Nov, 1976

	GD2.0	FN6.0	NM9.4
1	25.00	75.00	200.00
2	12.50	37.50	100.00
3-5	10.00	30.00	80.00
6-10	8.65	26.00	60.00
11-15	6.00	18.00	42.00
16-(3/50; 1st Harvey issue)	7.85	23.50	55.00
17-20: 20-(3/51)-Becomes Daisy & Her Pups #21 & Chamber of Chills #21	3.45	10.35	38.00
21-30	2.80	8.40	28.00
31-50	2.40	7.35	22.00
51-80	2.30	7.00	20.00
81-99	2.00	6.00	18.00
00	2.40	7.35	22.00
01-124,126-130	2.00	6.00	16.00
25 (80 pgs.)	3.00	9.00	30.00
31-136,138,139	1.50	4.50	12.00
37,140-(80 pgs.)	2.80	8.40	28.00
41-147,149-154,156,160,164-167	2.00	6.00	16.00
48,155,157-159,161-163 are 68 pgs.	2.60	7.80	26.00
68-175	1.25	3.75	10.00
77-199 (no #176)	1.10	3.30	9.00
00	1.50	4.50	12.00
01-210,213-222	1.00	3.00	8.00
11,212-1st & 2nd app. Super Dagwood	1.25	3.75	10.00

BLOOD
Marvel Comics (Epic Comics): Feb, 1988 - No. 4, Apr, 1988 ($3.25, mature)
1-4: DeMatteis scripts & Kent Williams-c/a 3.50

BLOOD AND GLORY (Punisher & Captain America)
Marvel Comics: Oct, 1992 - No. 3, Dec, 1992 ($5.95, limited series)
1-3: 1-Embossed wraparound-c by Janson; Chichester & Clarke-s 6.00

BLOOD & ROSES: FUTURE PAST TENSE (Bob Hickey's…)
Sky Comics: Dec, 1993 ($2.25)
1-Silver ink logo 2.25

BLOOD & ROSES: SEARCH FOR THE TIME-STONE (Bob Hickey's…)
Sky Comics: Apr, 1994 ($2.50)
1 2.50

BLOOD AND SHADOWS
DC Comics (Vertigo): 1996 - Book 4, 1996 ($5.95, squarebound, mature)
Books 1-4: Joe R. Lansdale scripts; Mark A. Nelson-c/a. 6.00

BLOOD: A TALE
DC Comics (Vertigo): Nov, 1996 - No. 4, Feb, 1997 ($2.95, limited series)
1-4: Reprints Epic series w/new-c; DeMatteis scripts; Kent Williams-c/a 3.00

BLOODBATH
DC Comics: Early Dec, 1993 - No. 2, Late Dec, 1993 ($3.50, 68 pgs.)
1-Neon ink-c; Superman app.; new Batman-c /app. 3.50
2-Hitman 2nd app. 1.00 2.80 7.00

BLOODFIRE
Lightning Comics: June, 1993 - No. 12, May, 1994 ($2.95)
1-($3.50)-Foil-c; 1st app. Bloodfire 3.50
2-12: 2-Origin; contracts HIV virus via transfusion. 5-Polybagged w/card & collectors warning on bag. 12-(5/94) 3.00
0-(Indicia reads June 1994, May on-c, $3.50) 3.50
…/Hellina 1 (7/95, $3.00) 3.00
…/Hellina 1 (7/95, $9.95)-Nude edition; Deodato-c 10.00
…/Hellina (8/95, $9.95)-Commemorative edition 10.00

BLOOD LEGACY: THE STORY OF RYAN
Image Comics (Top Cow): May, 2000 - No. 4, Nov, 2000 ($2.50)
1-4-Kerri Hawkins-s. 1-Andy Park-a(p); 3 covers 2.50
Preview Special ('00, $4.95) B&W flip-book w/The Magdalena Preview 4.95

BLOODLINES: A TALE FROM THE HEART OF AFRICA (See Tales From the Heart of Africa)
Marvel Comics (Epic Comics): 1992 ($5.95, 52 pgs.)
1-Story cont'd from Tales From… 6.00

BLOOD OF DRACULA
Apple Comics: Nov, 1987 - No. 20?, 1990 ($1.75/$1.95, B&W)($2.25 #14,16 on)
1-3,5-14,20: 1-10-Chadwick-c 3.00
4,16-19-Lost Frankenstein pgs. by Wrightson 5.00
15-Contains stereo flexidisc ($3.75) 4.00

BLOOD OF THE INNOCENT (See Warp Graphics Annual)
WaRP Graphics: 1/7/86 - No. 4, 1/28/86 (Weekly mini-series, mature)
1-4 2.00

BLOODPACK
DC Comics: Mar, 1995 - No. 4, June,1995 ($1.50, limited series)
1-4 2.00

BLOODPOOL
Image Comics (Extreme): Aug, 1995 - No. 4, Nov, 1995 ($2.50, limited series)
1-4: Jo Duffy scripts in all 2.50
Special (3/96, $2.50)-Jo Duffy scripts 2.50
Trade Paperback (1996, $12.95)-r/#1-4 13.00

BLOOD REIGN SAGA
London Night Studios: 1996 ($3.00, B&W, mature)
1-"Encore Edition" 3.00

BLOODSCENT
Comico: Oct, 1988 ($2.00, one-shot, Baxter paper)
1-Colan-p 2.00

BLOODSEED
Marvel Comics (Frontier Comics): Oct, 1993 - No. 2, Nov, 1993 ($1.95)
1,2: Sharp/Cam Smith-a 3.00

BLOODSHOT (See Eternal Warrior #4 & Rai #0)
Valiant/Acclaim Comics (Valiant): Feb, 1993 - No. 51, Aug, 1996 ($2.25/$2.50)
1-($3.50)-Chromium embossed-c by B. Smith w/poster 4.00
2-5,8-14: 3-$2.25-c begins; cont'd in Hard Corps #5. 4-Eternal Warrior-c/story. 5-Rai & Eternal Warrior app. 14-(3/94)-Reese-c(i) 2.50
6,7-1st app. Ninjak (out of costume). 7-In costume 3.00

Blood Syndicate #18 © Milestone Media

The Blue Beetle #5 © FOX

Blue Beetle #1 © DC

GD2.0 FN6.0 NM9.4

0-(3/94, $3.50)-Wraparound chromium-c by Quesada(p); origin 3.50
0-Gold variant 6.00
15(4/94)-51: 16-w/bound-in trading card. 51-Bloodshot dies? 2.50
Yearbook 1 (1994, $3.95) 4.00
Special 1 (3/94, $5.95)-Zeck-c/a(p) 6.00

BLOODSHOT (Volume Two)
Acclaim Comics (Valiant): July, 1997 - No. 16, Oct, 1998 ($2.50)

1-16: 1-Two covers. 5-Copycat-c. X-O Manowar-c/app 3.00

BLOODSTRIKE (See Supreme V2#3)
Image Comics (Extreme Studios): 1993 - No. 22, May, 1995; No. 25, May, 1994 ($1.95/$2.50)

1-22, 25: Liefeld layouts in early issues. 1-Blood Brothers prelude. 2-1st app. Lethal. 5-1st app. Noble. 9-Black and White part 6 by Art Thibert; Liefeld pin-up. 9,10-Have coupon #3 & 7 for Extreme Prejudice #0. 10-(4/94). 11-(7/94). 16:Platt-c; Prophet app. 17-19-polybagged w/card . 25-(5/94)-Liefeld/Fraga-c 3.00

NOTE: ***Giffen** story/layouts-4-6. **Jae Lee** c-7, 8. **Rob Liefeld** layouts-1-3. **Art Thibert** c-6i.*

BLOODSTRIKE ASSASSIN
Image Comics (Extreme Studios): June, 1995 - No. 3, Aug, 1995; No. 0, Oct, 1995 ($2.50, limited series)

0-3: 3-(8/95)-Quesada-c. 0-(10/95)-Battlestone app. 3.00

BLOOD SWORD, THE
Jademan Comics: Aug, 1988 - No. 53, Dec, 1992 ($1.50/$1.95, 68 pgs.)

1-53: Kung Fu stories 2.50

BLOOD SWORD DYNASTY
Jademan Comics: 1989 -No. 41, Jan, 1993 ($1.25, 36 pgs.)

1-41: Ties into Blood Sword 2.50

BLOOD SYNDICATE
DC Comics (Milestone): Apr, 1993 - No. 35, Feb, 1996 ($1.50/-$3.50)

1-($2.95)-Collector's Edition; polybagged with poster, trading card, & acid-free backing board (direct sale only) 3.50
1-9,11-24,26,27,29,33-34: 8-Intro Kwai. 15-Byrne-c. 16-Worlds Collide Pt. 6; Superman-c/app.17-Worlds Collide Pt. 13. 29-(99¢); Long Hot Summer x-over 2.00
10,28,30-32: 10-Simonson-c. 30-Long Hot Summer x-over 2.50
25-($2.95, 52 pgs.) 3.00
35-Kwai disappears; last issue 3.50

BLOODWULF
Image Comics (Extreme): Feb, 1995 - No. 4, May, 1995 ($2.50, limited series)

1-4: 1-Liefeld-c w/4 diferent captions & alternate-c. 2.50
Summer Special (8/95, $2.50)-Jeff Johnson-c/a; Supreme app; story takes place between Legend of Supreme #3 & Supreme #23. 2.50

BLOODY MARY
DC Comics (Helix): Oct, 1996 - No. 4, Jan, 1997 ($2.25, limited series)

1-4: Garth Ennis scripts; Ezquerra-c/a in all 3.50

BLOODY MARY: LADY LIBERTY
DC Comics (Helix): Sept, 1997 - No. 4, Dec, 1997 ($2.50, limited series)

1-4: Garth Ennis scripts; Ezquerra-c/a in all 3.00

BLUE
Image Comics (Action Toys): Aug, 1999 - Present ($2.50)

1,2-Aronowitz-s/Struzan-c 2.50

BLUEBEARD
Slave Labor Graphics: Nov, 1993 - No. 3, Mar, 1994 ($2.95, B&W, lim. series)

1-3: James Robinson scripts. 2-(12/93) 3.00
Trade paperback (6/94, $9.95) 13.00
Trade paperback (2nd printing, 7/96, $12.95)-New-c 13.00

BLUE BEETLE, THE (Also see All Top, Big-3, Mystery Men & Weekly Comic Magazine)
Fox Publ. No. 1-11, 31-60; Holyoke No. 12-30: Winter, 1939-40 - No. 57, 7/48; No. 58, 4/50 - No. 60, 8/50

1-Reprints from Mystery Men #1-5; Blue Beetle origin; Yarko the Great-r/from Wonder/Wonderworld 2-5 all by Eisner; Master Magician app.; (Blue Beetle in 4 different costumes) 429.00 1286.00 4500.00
2-K-51-r by Powell/Wonderworld 8,9 147.00 442.00 1400.00
3-Simon-c 105.00 316.00 1000.00
4-Marijuana drug mention story 71.00 213.00 675.00
5-Zanzibar The Magician by Tuska 63.00 189.00 600.00
6-Dynamite Thor begins (1st); origin Blue Beetle 59.00 177.00 560.00
7,8-Dynamo app. in both. 8-Last Thor 55.00 165.00 525.00
9-12: 9,10-The Blackbird & The Gorilla app. in both. 10-Bondage/hypo-c 11(2/42)-The Gladiator app. 12(6/42)-The Black Fury app. 50.00 150.00 450.00
13-V-Man begins (1st app.), ends #18; Kubert-a; centerfold spread 59.00 177.00 560.00
14,15-Kubert-a in both. 14-Intro. side-kick (c/text only), Sparky (called Spunky #17-19) 52.00 157.00 470.00
16-18: 17-Brodsky-c 41.00 122.00 365.00
19-Kubert-a 42.00 125.00 375.00
20-Origin/1st app. Tiger Squadron; Arabian Nights begin 46.00 137.00 410.00
21-26: 24-Intro. & only app. The Halo. 26-General Patton story & photo 34.00 101.00 270.00
27-Tamaa, Jungle Prince app. 31.00 94.00 250.00
28-30(2/44) 28.00 84.00 225.00
31(6/44), 33,34,36-40: 34-38-"The Threat from Saturn" serial. 26.00 79.00 210.00
32-Hitler-c 40.00 120.00 325.00
35-Extreme violence 31.00 94.00 250.00
41-45 24.00 71.00 190.00
46-The Puppeteer app. 27.00 81.00 215.00
47-Kamen & Baker-a begin 116.00 348.00 1100.00
48-50 95.00 285.00 900.00
51,53 79.00 237.00 750.00
52-Kamen bondage-c; true crime stories begin 118.00 355.00 1125.00
54-Used in **SOTI**. Illo, "Children call these 'headlights' comics" 126.00 379.00 1200.00
55-57: 56-Used in **SOTI**, pg. 145. 57(7/48)-Last Kamen issue; becomes Western Killers? 76.00 229.00 725.00
58(4/50)-60-No Kamen-a 16.00 49.00 130.00

NOTE: ***Kamen** a-47-51, 53, 55-57; c-47, 49-52. **Powell** a-4(2). Bondage-c 9-12, 46, 52.*

BLUE BEETLE (Formerly The Thing; becomes Mr. Muscles No. 22 on) (See Charlton Bullseye & Space Adventures)
Charlton Comics: No. 18, Feb, 1955 - No. 21, Aug, 1955

18,19-(Pre-1944-r). 18-Last pre-code issue. 19-Bouncer, Rocket Kelly-r 20.00 60.00 160.00
20-Joan Mason by Kamen 25.00 75.00 200.00
21-New material 18.00 53.00 140.00

BLUE BEETLE (Unusual Tales #1-49; Ghostly Tales #55 on)(See Captain Atom #83 & Charlton Bullseye)
Charlton Comics: V2#1, June, 1964 - V2#5, Mar-Apr, 1965; V3#50, July, 1965 V3#54, Feb-Mar, 1966; #1, June, 1967 - #5, Nov, 1968

V2#1-Origin/1st S.A. app. Dan Garrett-Blue Beetle 7.25 21.75 80.00
2-5: 5-Weiss illo; 1st published-a? 5.00 15.00 55.00
V3#50-54-Formerly Unusual Tales 4.55 13.65 50.00
1(1967)-Question series begins by Ditko 10.00 30.00 110.00
2-Origin Ted Kord-Blue Beetle (see Capt. Atom #83 for 1st Ted Kord Blue Beetle); Dan Garrett x-over 4.55 13.65 50.00
3-5 (All Ditko-c/a in #1-5) 3.65 11.00 40.00
1,3(Modern Comics-1977)-Reprints 5.00

NOTE: *#6 only appeared in the fanzine 'The Charlton Portfolio.'*

BLUE BEETLE (Also see Americomics, Crisis On Infinite Earths, Justice League & Showcase '94 #2-4)
DC Comics: June, 1986 - No. 24, May, 1988

1-Origin retold; intro. Firefist 3.00
2-19,21-24: 2-Origin Firefist. 5-7-The Question app. 11-14-New Teen Titans x-over. 21-Millennium tie-in 2.00
20-Justice League app.; Millennium tie-in 2.50

BLUEBERRY (See Lt. Blueberry & Marshal Blueberry)

Blue Bolt V2 #2 © Premium Service Co.

Blue Monday: The Kids Are Alright #2 © Chynna Clugston-Major

Blue Ribbon Comics #3 © MLJ

Marvel Comics (Epic Comics): 1989 - No. 5, 1990 ($12.95/$14.95, graphic novel)
1,3,4,5-($12.95)-Moebius-a in all 15.00
2-($14.95) 17.00

BLUE BOLT
Funnies, Inc. No. 1/Novelty Press/Premium Group of Comics: June, 1940 - No. 101 (V10#2), Sept-Oct, 1949
V1#1-Origin Blue Bolt by Joe Simon, Sub-Zero Man, White Rider & Super Horse, Dick Cole, Wonder Boy & Sgt. Spook (1st app. of each) 300.00 900.00 3000.00
2-Simon & Kirby's 1st art & 1st super-hero (Blue Bolt) 158.00 474.00 1500.00
3-1 pg. Space Hawk by Wolverton; 2nd S&K-a on Blue Bolt (same cover date as Red Raven #1); 1st time S&K names app. in a comic; Simon-c 132.00 395.00 1250.00
4,5-S&K-a in each; 5-Everett-a begins on Sub-Zero 121.00 363.00 1150.00
6,8-10-S&K-a 111.00 332.00 1050.00
7-S&K-c/a 126.00 379.00 1200.00
11,12: 11-Robot-c 108.00 324.00 1025.00
V2#1-Origin Dick Cole & The Twister; Twister x-over in Dick Cole, Sub-Zero, & Blue Bolt; origin Simba Karno who battles Dick Cole thru V2#5 & becomes main supporting character V2#6 on; battle-c 38.00 113.00 300.00
2-Origin The Twister retold in text 30.00 90.00 240.00
3-5: 5-Intro. Freezum 27.00 81.00 215.00
6-Origin Sgt. Spook retold 22.00 66.00 175.00
7-12: 7-Lois Blake becomes Blue Bolt's costume aide; last Twister. 12-Text-sty by Mickey Spillaine 19.00 56.00 150.00
V3#1-3 15.00 45.00 120.00
4-12: 4-Blue Bolt abandons costume 11.00 33.00 90.00
V4#1-Hitler, Tojo, Mussolini-c 28.00 84.00 225.00
V4#2-12: 3-Shows V4#3 on-c, V4#4 inside (9-10/43). 5-Infinity-c. 8-Last Sub-Zero 10.00 30.00 75.00
V5#1-8, V6#1-3,5-10, V7#1-12 10.00 30.00 70.00
V6#4-Racist cover 10.50 32.00 85.00
V8#1-6,8-12, V9#1-5,7,8, V10#1(#100),V10#2(#101)-Last Dick Cole, Blue Bolt 9.30 28.00 65.00
V8#7,V9#6,9-L. B. Cole-c 19.00 56.00 150.00
NOTE: *Everett c-V1#4, 11, V2#1, 2.* ***Gustavson*** *a-V1#1-12, V2#1-7.* ***Kiefer*** *c-V3#1.* ***Rico*** *a-V6#10, V7#4. Blue Bolt not in V9#8.*

BLUE BOLT (Becomes Ghostly Weird Stories #120 on; continuation of Novelty Blue Bolt) (...Weird Tales of Terror #111,...Weird Tales #112-119)
Star Publications: No. 102, Nov-Dec, 1949 - No. 119, May-June, 1953
102-The Chameleon, & Target app. 34.00 101.00 270.00
103,104-The Chameleon app. 104-Last Target 31.00 94.00 250.00
105-Origin Blue Bolt (from #1) retold by Simon; Chameleon & Target app.; opium den story 50.00 150.00 450.00
106-Blue Bolt by S&K begins; Spacehawk reprints from Target by Wolverton begin, ends #110; Sub-Zero begins; ends #109 47.00 142.00 425.00
107-110: 108-Last S&K Blue Bolt reprint. 109-Wolverton-c(r)/inside Spacehawk splash. 110-Target app. 44.00 133.00 400.00
111,112: 111-Red Rocket & The Mask-r; last Blue Bolt; 1pg. L. B. Cole-a 112-Last Torpedo Man app. 41.00 123.00 370.00
113-Wolverton's Spacehawk-r/Target V3#7 43.00 130.00 390.00
114,116: 116-Jungle Jo-r 41.00 123.00 370.00
115-Sgt. Spook app. 43.00 130.00 390.00
117-Jo-Jo & Blue Bolt-r 42.00 125.00 375.00
118-"White Spirit" by Wood 43.00 130.00 390.00
119-Disbrow/Cole-c; Jungle Jo-r 42.00 125.00 375.00
Accepted Reprint #103(1957?, nd) 10.00 30.00 80.00
NOTE: ***L. B. Cole*** *c-102-108, 110 on.* ***Disbrow*** *a-112(2), 113(3), 114(2), 115(2), 116-118.* ***Hollingsworth*** *a-117.* ***Palais*** *a-112r. Sci/Fi c-105-110. Horror c-111.*

BLUE BULLETEER, THE (Also see Femforce Special)
AC Comics: 1989 ($2.25, B&W, one-shot)
1-Origin by Bill Black; Bill Ward-a 4.00

BLUE BULLETEER (Also see Femforce Special)
AC Comics: 1996 ($5.95, B&W, one-shot)
1-Photo-c 2.40 6.00

BLUE CIRCLE COMICS (Also see Red Circle Comics, Blazing Comics & Roly Poly Comic Book)
Enwil Associates/Rural Home: June, 1944 - No. 6, Apr, 1945
1-The Blue Circle begins (1st app.); origin & 1st app. Steel Fist 28.00 84.00 225.00
2 19.00 56.00 150.00
3-Hitler parody-c 23.00 68.00 180.00
4-6: 5-Last Steel Fist. 15.00 45.00 120.00
6-(Dated 4/45, Vol. 2#3 inside)-Leftover covers to #6 were later restapled over early 1950's coverless comics; variations of the coverless comics exist. Colossal Features known. 15.00 45.00 120.00

BLUE DEVIL (See Fury of Firestorm #24, Underworld Unleashed, Starman #38)
DC Comics: June, 1984 - No. 31, Dec, 1986 (75¢/$1.25)
1 3.00
2-16,19-31: 4-Origin Nebiros. 7-Gil Kane-a. 8-Giffen-a 2.00
17,18-Crisis x-over 3.00
Annual 1 (11/85)-Team-ups w/Black Orchid, Creeper, Demon, Madame Xanadu, Man-Bat & Phantom Stranger 2.00

BLUE MONDAY: THE KIDS ARE ALRIGHT
Oni Press: Feb, 2000 - No. 3, May, 2000 ($2.95, B&W)
1-3-Chynna Clugston-Major-s/a/c. 1-Variant-c by Warren. 2-Dorkin-c 3.00
3-Variant cover by J. Scott Campbell 3.00
TPB (12/00, $10.95, digest-sized) r/#1-3 & earlier short stories 11.00

BLUE PHANTOM, THE
Dell Publishing Co.: June-Aug, 1962
1(01-066-208)-by Fred Fredericks 3.00 9.00 30.00

BLUE RIBBON COMICS (...Mystery Comics No. 9-18)
MLJ Magazines: Nov, 1939 - No. 22, Mar, 1942 (1st MLJ series)
1-Dan Hastings, Richy the Amazing Boy, Rang-A-Tang the Wonder Dog begin (1st app. of each); Little Nemo app. (not by W. McCay); Jack Cole-a(3) 305.00 915.00 3200.00
2-Bob Phantom, Silver Fox (both in #3), Rang-A-Tang Club & Cpl. Collins begin (1st app. of each); Jack Cole-a 126.00 379.00 1200.00
3-J. Cole-a 84.00 253.00 800.00
4-Doc Strong, The Green Falcon, & Hercules begin (1st app. each); origin & 1st app. The Fox & Ty-Gor, Son of the Tiger 92.00 276.00 875.00
5-8: 8-Last Hercules; 6,7-Biro, Meskin-a. 7-Fox app. on-c 63.00 189.00 600.00
9-(Scarce)-Origin & 1st app. Mr. Justice (2/41) 284.00 853.00 2700.00
10-13: 12-Last Doc Strong. 13-Inferno, the Flame Breather begins, ends #19; Devil-c 100.00 300.00 950.00
14,15,17,18: 15-Last Green Falcon 84.00 253.00 800.00
16-Origin & 1st app. Captain Flag (9/41) 163.00 490.00 1550.00
19-22: 20-Last Ty-Gor. 22-Origin Mr. Justice retold 84.00 253.00 800.00
NOTE: ***Biro*** *c-3-5; a-2 (Cpl. Collins & Scoop Cody).* ***S. Cooper*** *c-9-17. 20-22 contain "Tales From the Witch's Cauldron" (same strip as "Stories of the Black Witch" in Zip Comics). Mr. Justice c-9-18. Captain Flag c-16(w/Mr. Justice), 19-22.*

BLUE RIBBON COMICS (Becomes Teen-Age Diary Secrets #4)
(Also see Approved Comics, Blue Ribbon Comics and Heckle &Jeckle)
Blue Ribbon (St. John): Feb, 1949 - No. 6, Aug, 1949
1,3-Heckle & Jeckle (Terrytoons) 9.30 28.00 65.00
2(4/49)-Diary Secrets; Baker-c 20.00 60.00 160.00
4(6/49)-Teen-Age Diary Secrets; Baker c/a(2) 20.00 60.00 160.00
5(8/49)-Teen-Age Diary Secrets; Oversize; photo-c; Baker-a(2)- Continues as Teen-Age Diary Secrets 26.00 79.00 210.00
6-Dinky Duck(8/49)(Terrytoons) 5.00 15.00 30.00

BLUE RIBBON COMICS
Red Circle Prod./Archie Ent. No. 5 on: Nov, 1983 - No. 14, Dec, 1984
1-S&K-r/Advs. of the Fly #1,2; Williamson/Torres-r/Fly #2; Ditko-c 5.00
2-7,9-14: 3-Origin Steel Sterling. 5-S&K Shield-r; new Kirby-c. 6,7-The Fox app. 11-Black Hood. 12-Thunder Agents; Noman new Ditko-a. 13-Thunder Bunny. 14-Web & Jaguar 4.00
8-Toth centerspread; Black Hood app. 5.00
NOTE: ***N. Adams*** *a(r)-8.* ***Buckler*** *a-4i.* ***Nino*** *a-2i.* ***McWilliams*** *a-8.* ***Morrow*** *a-8.*

Bobby Benson B-Bar-B #7 © ME

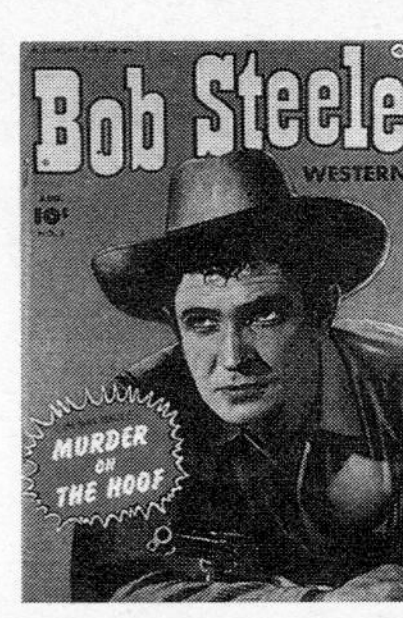

Bob Steele Western #5 © FAW

Body Doubles #4 © DC

BLUE STREAK (See Holyoke One-Shot No. 8)

BLYTHE (Marge's)
Dell Publishing Co.: No. 1072, Jan-Mar, 1960
Four Color 1072 4.60 13.75 55.00

B-MAN (See Double-Dare Adventures)

BO (Tom Cat #4 on) (Also see Big Shot #29 & Dixie Dugan)
Charlton Comics Group: June, 1955 - No. 3, Oct, 1955 (A dog)
1-3: Newspaper reprints by Frank Beck 7.15 21.50 50.00

BOATNIKS, THE (See Walt Disney Showcase No. 1)

BOB BURDEN'S ORIGINAL MYSTERYMEN PRESENTS
Dark Horse Comics: 1999 - Present ($2.95/$3.50)
1-3-Bob Burden-s/Sadowski-a(p) 3.00
4-($3.50) All Villain issue 3.50

BOBBY BENSON'S B-BAR-B RIDERS (Radio) (See Best of The West, The Lemonade Kid & Model Fun)
Magazine Enterprises/AC Comics: May-June, 1950 - No. 20, May-June, 1953
1-The Lemonade Kid begins; Powell-a (Scarce) 43.00 130.00 390.00
2 17.00 51.00 135.00
3-5: 4,5-Lemonade Kid-c (#4-Spider-c) 13.00 39.00 105.00
6-8,10 12.00 36.00 95.00
9,11,13-Frazetta-c; Ghost Rider in #13-15 by Ayers-a. 13-Ghost Rider-c 34.00 103.00 275.00
12,17-20: 20-(A-1 #88) 11.00 33.00 90.00
14-Decapitation/Bondage-c & story; classic horror-c 25.00 75.00 200.00
15-Ghost Rider-c 17.00 51.00 135.00
16-Photo-c 13.00 39.00 105.00
1 (1990, $2.75, B&W)-Reprints; photo-c & inside covers 2.75
NOTE: ***Ayers** a-13-15, 20. **Powell** a-1-12(4 ea.), 13(3), 14-16(Red Hawk only); c-1-8,1 0, 12. Lemonade Kid in most 1-13.*

BOBBY COMICS
Universal Phoenix Features: May, 1946
1-By S. M. Iger 7.85 23.50 55.00

BOBBY SHERMAN (TV)
Charlton Comics: Feb, 1972 - No. 7, Oct, 1972
1-Based on TV show "Getting Together" 3.65 11.00 40.00
2-7: 4-Photo-c 2.80 8.40 28.00

BOB COLT (Movie star)(See XMas Comics)
Fawcett Publications: Nov, 1950 - No. 10, May, 1952
1-Bob Colt, his horse Buckskin & sidekick Pablo begin; photo front/back-c begin 40.00 120.00 345.00
2 26.00 79.00 210.00
3-5 21.00 62.00 165.00
6-Flying Saucer story 18.00 53.00 140.00
7-10: 9-Last photo back-c 16.00 49.00 130.00

BOB HOPE (See Adventures of... & Calling All Boys #12)

BOB MARLEY, TALE OF THE TUFF GONG (Music star)
Marvel Comics: Aug, 1994 - No, 3, Nov, 1994 ($5.95, limited series)
1-3 2.40 6.00

BOB POWELL'S TIMELESS TALES
Eclipse Comics: March, 1989 ($2.00, B&W)
1-Powell-r/Black Cat #5 (Scarlet Arrow), 9 & Race for the Moon #1 3.00

BOB SCULLY, THE TWO-FISTED HICK DETECTIVE (Also see Advs. of Detective Ace King and Detective Dan)
Humor Publ. Co.: No date (1933) (36 pgs., 9-1/2x11", B&W, paper-c; 10¢-c)
nn-By Howard Dell; not reprints 84.00 253.00 800.00

BOB SON OF BATTLE
Dell Publishing Co.: No. 729, Nov, 1956
Four Color 729 3.20 9.60 35.00

BOB STEELE WESTERN (Movie star)
Fawcett Publications/AC Comics: Dec, 1950 - No. 10, June, 1952; 1990
1-Bob Steele & his horse Bullet begin; photo front/back-c begin 58.00 174.00 550.00
2 33.00 98.00 260.00
3-5: 4-Last photo back-c 24.00 73.00 195.00
6-10: 10-Last photo-c 19.00 56.00 150.00
1 (1990, $2.75, B&W)-Bob Steele & Rocky Lane reprints; photo-c & inside covers 2.75

BOB SWIFT (Boy Sportsman)
Fawcett Publications: May, 1951 - No. 5, Jan, 1952
1 10.00 30.00 70.00
2-5: Saunders painted-c #1-5 5.00 15.00 35.00

BOB, THE GALACTIC BUM
DC Comics: Feb, 1995 - No. 4, June, 1995 ($1.95, limited series)
1-4: 1-Lobo app. 2.50

BODY BAGS
Dark Horse Comics (Blanc Noir): Sept, 1996 - No. 4, Jan, 1997 ($2.95, mini-series, mature)(1st Blanc Noir series)
1-Jason Pearson-c/a/scripts in all. 1-Intro Clownface & Panda. 1.00 3.00 8.00
2 1.25 3.75 10.00
3,4 2.40 6.00

BODYCOUNT (Also see Casey Jones & Raphael)
Image Comics (Highbrow Entertainment): Mar, 1996 - No. 4, July, 1996 ($2.50, limited series)
1-4: Kevin Eastman-a(p)/scripts; Simon Bisley-c/a(i); Turtles app. 2.50

BODY DOUBLES (See Resurrection Man)
DC Comics: Oct, 1999 - No. 4, Jan, 2000 ($2.50, limited series)
1,2-Lanning & Abnett-s. 2-Black Canary app. 4-Wonder Woman app. 2.50
...(Villains) (2/98, $1.95, one-shot) 1-Pearson-c; Deadshot app. 2.00

BOFFO LAFFS
Paragraphics: 1986 - No. 5 ($2.50/$1.95)
1-($2.50) First comic cover with hologram 2.50
2-5 2.00

BOHOS
Image Comics (Flypaper Press): June, 1998 - Present ($2.95)
1-3-Whorf-s/Penaranda-a 3.00

BOLD ADVENTURES
Pacific Comics: Oct, 1983 - No. 3, June, 1984 ($1.50)
1-Time Force, Anaconda, & The Weirdling begin 3.00
2,3: 2-Soldiers of Fortune begins. 3-Spitfire 3.00
NOTE: ***Kaluta** c-3. **Nebres** a-1-3. **Nino** a-2, 3. **Severin** a-3.*

BOLD STORIES (Also see Candid Tales & It Rhymes With Lust)
Kirby Publishing Co.: Mar, 1950 - July, 1950 (Digest size, 144 pgs.)
March issue (Very Rare) - Contains "The Ogre of Paris" by Wood 121.00 363.00 1150.00
May issue (Very Rare) - Contains "The Cobra's Kiss" by Graham Ingels (21 pgs.) 105.00 316.00 1000.00
July issue (Very Rare) - Contains "The Ogre of Paris" by Wood 95.00 285.00 900.00

BOLT AND STAR FORCE SIX
Americomics: 1984 ($1.75)
1-Origin Bolt & Star Force Six 3.00
Special 1 (1984, $2.00, 52pgs., B&W) 3.00

BOMBARDIER (See Bee 29, the Bombardier & Cinema Comics Herald)

BOMBAST
Topps Comics: 1993 ($2.95, one-shot) (Created by Jack Kirby)
1-Polybagged w/Kirbychrome trading card; Savage Dragon app.; Kirby-c; has coupon for Amberchrome Secret City Saga #0 3.00

BOMBA THE JUNGLE BOY (TV)
National Periodical Publ.: Sept-Oct, 1967 - No. 7, Sept-Oct, 1968 (12¢)
1-Intro. Bomba; Infantino/Anderson-c 2.80 8.40 28.00

Bomber Comics #4 © EP

Bone #3 © Jeff Smith

Books of Magic #74 © DC

GD2.0 FN6.0 NM9.4

2-7 2.30 7.00 20.00

BOMBER COMICS
Elliot Publ. Co./Melverne Herald/Farrell/Sunrise Times: Mar, 1944 - No. 4, Winter, 1944-45

1-Wonder Boy, & Kismet, Man of Fate begin 66.00 197.00 625.00
2-Hitler-c 44.00 133.00 400.00
3: 2-4-Have Classics Comics ad to HRN 20 40.00 120.00 340.00
4-Hitler, Tojo & Mussolini-c; Sensation Comics #13-c/swipe; has Classics Comics ad to HRN 20. 55.00 165.00 525.00

BONANZA (TV)
Dell/Gold Key: June-Aug, 1960 - No. 37, Aug, 1970 (All Photo-c)

Four Color 1110 (6-8/60) 35.00 105.00 420.00
Four Color 1221,1283, & #01070-207, 01070-210 17.00 50.00 200.00
1(12/62-Gold Key) 17.50 52.50 210.00
2 8.75 26.50 105.00
3-10 7.00 20.00 85.00
11-20 5.85 17.50 70.00
21-37: 29-Reprints 4.60 13.75 55.00

BONE
Cartoon Books #1-20, 28 on/Image Comics #21-27: July, 1991 - Present ($2.95, B&W)

1-Jeff Smith-c/a in all 8.15 24.50 90.00
1-2nd printing 1.50 4.50 12.00
1-3rd thru 5th printings 4.00
2-1st printing 4.00 12.25 45.00
2-2nd & 3rd printings 4.00
3-1st printing 3.50 10.50 35.00
3-2nd thru 4th printings 4.00
4,5 1.85 5.50 15.00
6-10 1.00 3.00 8.00
11-37: 21-1st Image issue 4.00
13 1/2 (1/95, Wizard) 1.25 3.75 10.00
13 1/2 (Gold) 1.50 4.50 12.00
38-($4.95) Three covers by Miller, Ross, Smith 5.00
39,40-($2.95) 3.00
1-27-($2.95): 1-Image reprints begin w/new-c. 2-Allred pin-up. 3.00
... Holiday Special (1993, giveaway) 3.00
... Reader -($9.95) Behind the scenes info 10.00
... Sourcebook-San Diego Edition 3.00
Complete Bone Adventures Vol 1,2 ('93, '94, $12.95, r/#1-6 & #7-12) 13.00
Volume 1-($19.95, hard-c)-"Out From Boneville" 20.00
Volume 1-($12.95, soft-c) 13.00
Volume 2,5-($22.95, hard-c)-"The Great Cow Race" & "Rock Jdaw" 23.00
Volume 2,5-($14.95, soft-c) 15.00
Volume 3,4-($24.95, hard-c)-"Eyes of the Storm" & "The Dragonslayer" 25.00
Volume 3,4-($16.95, soft-c) 17.00
Volume 6-($15.95, soft-c)-"Old Man's Cave" 16.00
NOTE: *Printings not listed sell for cover price.*

BONGO (See Story Hour Series)

BONGO & LUMPJAW (Disney, see Walt Disney Showcase #3)
Dell Publishing Co.: No. 706, June, 1956; No. 886, Mar, 1958

Four Color 706 (#1) 5.00 15.00 60.00
Four Color 886 4.10 12.30 45.00

BON VOYAGE (See Movie Classics)

BOOF
Image Comics (Todd McFarlane Prod.): July, 1994 - No. 6, Dec, 1994 ($1.95)

1-6 2.00

BOOF AND THE BRUISE CREW
Image Comics (Todd McFarlane Prod.): July, 1994 - No. 6, Dec, 1994 ($1.95)

1-6 2.00

BOOK AND RECORD SET (See Power Record Comics)

BOOK OF ALL COMICS
William H. Wise: 1945 (196 pgs.)(Inside f/c has Green Publ. blacked out)

GD2.0 FN6.0 NM9.4

nn-Green Mask, Puppeteer & The Bouncer 40.00 120.00 320.00

BOOK OF ANTS, THE
Artisan Entertainment: 1998 ($2.95, B&W)

1-Based on the movie Pi; Aronofsky-s 3.00

BOOK OF BALLADS AND SAGAS, THE
Green Man Press: Oct, 1995 - Present ($2.95/$3.50/$3.25, B&W)

1-4: 1-Vess-c/a; Gaiman story. 3.50

BOOK OF COMICS, THE
William H. Wise: No date (1944) (25¢, 132 pgs.)

nn-Captain V app. 40.00 120.00 320.00

BOOK OF FATE, THE (See Fate)
DC Comics: Feb, 1997 - No. 12, Jan, 1998 ($2.25/$2.50)

1-12: 4-Two-Face-c/app. 6-Convergence. 11-Sentinel app. 3.00

BOOK OF LOVE (See Fox Giants)

BOOK OF NIGHT, THE
Dark Horse Comics: July, 1987 - No. 3, 1987 ($1.75, B&W)

1-3: Reprints from Epic Illustrated; Vess-a 2.25
TPB-r/#1-3 15.00
Hardcover-Black-c with red crest 100.00
Hardcover w/slipcase (1991) signed and numbered 50.00

BOOK OF THE DEAD
Marvel Comics: Dec, 1993 - No. 4, Mar, 1994 ($1.75, limited series, 52 pgs.)

1-4: 1-Ploog Frankenstein & Morrow Man-Thing-r begin; Wrightson-r/Chamber of Darkness #7. 2-Morrow new painted-c; Chaykin/Morrow Man-Thing; Krigstein-r/Uncanny Tales #54; r/Fear #10. 3-r/Astonishing Tales #10 & Starlin Man-Thing. 3,4-Painted-c 3.00

BOOKS OF FAERIE, THE
DC Comics (Vertigo): Mar, 1997 - No. 3, May,1997 ($2.50, limited series)

1-3-Gross-a 2.50
TPB (1998, $14.95) r/#1-3 & Arcana Annual #1 15.00

BOOKS OF FAERIE, THE : AUBERON'S TALE
DC Comics (Vertigo): Aug, 1998 - No. 3, Oct,1998 ($2.50, limited series)

1-3-Gross-a 3.00

BOOKS OF FAERIE, THE : MOLLY'S STORY
DC Comics (Vertigo): Sept, 1999 - No. 4, Dec,1999 ($2.50, limited series)

1-4-Ney Rieber-s/Mejia-a 3.00

BOOKS OF MAGIC
DC Comics: 1990 - No. 4, 1991 ($3.95, 52 pgs., limited series, mature)

1-Bolton painted-c/a; Phantom Stranger app.; Gaiman scripts in all 1.10 3.30 9.00
2,3: 2-John Constantine, Dr. Fate, Spectre, Deadman app. 3-Dr. Occult app.; minor Sandman app. 2.40 6.00
4-Early Death-c/app. (early 1991) 1.00 2.80 7.00
Trade paperback-($19.95)-Reprints limited series 20.00

BOOKS OF MAGIC (Also see Names of Magic, The)
DC Comics (Vertigo): May, 1994 - No. 75, Aug, 2000 ($1.95/$2.50, mature)

1-Charles Vess-c 1.50 4.50 12.00
1-Platinum 2.50 7.50 20.00
2,3 1.00 2.80 7.00
4-Death app. 1.00 2.80 7.00
5-14; Charles Vess-c 4.00
15-50: 15-$2.50-c begins. 22-Kaluta-c. 25-Death-c/app; Bachalo-c 3.00
51-75: 51-Peter Gross-s/a begins. 55-Medley-a 2.50
Annual 1,2 (2/97, 2/98, $3.95) 4.00
Bindings (1995, $12.95, TPB)-r/#1-4 13.00
Girl in the Box (1999, $14.95, TPB)-r/#26-32 15.00
Reckonings (1997, $12.95, TPB)-r/#14-20 13.00
Summonings (1996, $17.50, TPB)-r/#5-13, Vertigo Rave #1 17.50
The Burning Girl (2000, $17.95, TPB)-r/#33-41 18.00
Transformations (1998, $12.95, TPB)-r/#21-25 13.00

BOONDOGGLE

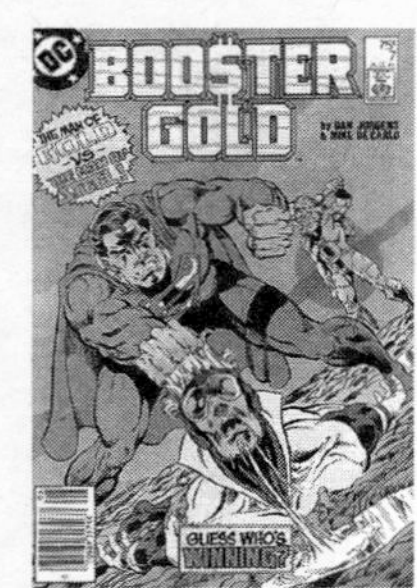

Booster Gold #7 © DC

The Bouncer #14 © FOX

Boy Comics #6 © LEV

Knight Press: Mar, 1995 - No. 4 ($2.95, B&W)

	GD2.0	FN6.0	NM9.4
1-4: Stegelin-c/a/scripts			3.00

BOONDOGGLE
Caliber Press: Jan, 1997 - No. 2 ($2.95, B&W)

	GD2.0	FN6.0	NM9.4
1,2: Stegelin-c/a/scripts			3.00

BOOSTER GOLD (See Justice League #4)
DC Comics: Feb, 1986 - No. 25, Feb, 1988 (75¢)

	GD2.0	FN6.0	NM9.4
1			3.00
2-25: 4-Rose & Thorn app. 6-Origin. 6,7,23-Superman app. 8,9-LSH app. 22-JLI app. 24,25-Millennium tie-ins			2.00

NOTE: ***Austin** c-22i. **Byrne** c-23i.*

BOOTS AND HER BUDDIES
Standard Comics/Visual Editions/Argo (NEA Service): No. 5, 9/48 - No. 9, 9/49; 12/55 - No. 3, 1956

	GD2.0	FN6.0	NM9.4
5-Strip-r	15.00	45.00	120.00
6,8	10.00	30.00	80.00
7-(Scarce)-Spanking panels(3)	12.00	36.00	95.00
9-(Scarce)-Frazetta-a (2 pgs.)	25.00	75.00	200.00
1-3(Argo-1955-56)-Reprints	5.00	15.00	35.00

BOOTS & SADDLES (TV)
Dell Publ. Co.: No. 919, July, 1958; No. 1029, Sept, 1959; No. 1116, Aug, 1960

	GD2.0	FN6.0	NM9.4
Four Color 919 (#1)-Photo-c	7.50	22.50	90.00
Four Color 1029, 1116-Photo-c	4.60	13.75	55.00

BORDERLINE
Friction Press: June, 1992 ($2.25, B&W)

	GD2.0	FN6.0	NM9.4
0-Ashcan edition; 1st app. of Cliff Broadway			2.00
1-Painted-c			3.00
1-Special Edition (bagged w/ photo, S&N)			4.00

BORDER PATROL
P. L. Publishing Co.: May-June, 1951 - No. 3, Sept-Oct, 1951

	GD2.0	FN6.0	NM9.4
1	11.00	33.00	90.00
2,3	8.65	26.00	60.00

BORDER WORLDS (Also see Megaton Man)
Kitchen Sink Press: 7/86 - No. 7, 1987; V2#1, 1990 - No. 4, 1990 ($1.95-$2.00, B&W, mature)

	GD2.0	FN6.0	NM9.4
1-7, V2#1-4: Donald Simpson-c/a/scripts			3.00

BORIS KARLOFF TALES OF MYSTERY (TV) (...Thriller No. 1,2)
Gold Key: No. 3, April, 1963 - No. 97, Feb, 1980

	GD2.0	FN6.0	NM9.4
3-5-(Two #5's, 10/63,11/63): 5-(10/63)-11 pgs. Toth-a.	3.20	9.60	35.00
6-8,10: 10-Orlando-a	2.80	8.40	28.00
9-Wood-a	3.00	9.00	32.00
11-Williamson-a, 8 pgs.; Orlando-a, 5 pgs.	3.00	9.00	32.00
12-Torres, McWilliams-a; Orlando-a(2)	2.50	7.50	25.00
13,14,16-20	2.30	7.00	20.00
15-Crandall	2.50	7.50	23.00
21-Jeff Jones-a(3 pgs.) "The Screaming Skull"	2.50	7.50	23.00
22-Last 12¢ issue	2.00	6.00	16.00
23-30: 23-Reprint; photo-c	1.75	5.25	12.00
31-50: 36-Weiss-a	1.25	3.75	10.00
51-74: 74-Origin & 1st app. Taurus	1.00	3.00	8.00
75-79,87-97: 90-r/Torres, McWilliams-a/#12; Morrow-c		2.40	6.00
80-86-(52 pgs.)	1.10	3.30	9.00
Story Digest 1(7/70-Gold Key)-All text/illos.; 148pp.	3.20	9.60	35.00

(See Mystery Comics Digest No. 2, 5, 8, 11, 14, 17, 20, 23, 26)
NOTE: ***Bolle** a-51-54, 56, 58, 59. **McWilliams** a-12, 14, 18, 19, 72, 80, 81, 93. **Orlando** a-11-15, 21. Reprints: 78, 81-86, 88, 90, 92, 95, 97.*

BORIS KARLOFF THRILLER (TV) (Becomes Boris Karloff Tales...)
Gold Key: Oct, 1962 - No. 2, Jan, 1963 (84 pgs.)

	GD2.0	FN6.0	NM9.4
1-Photo-c	6.65	20.00	80.00
2	4.55	13.65	50.00

BORIS THE BEAR
Dark Horse Comics/Nicotat Comics #13 on: Aug, 1986 - No. 34, 1990 ($1.50/$1.75/$1.95, B&W)

	GD2.0	FN6.0	NM9.4
1, Annual 1 (1988, $2.50)			3.00
1 (2nd printing),2,3,4A,4B,5-12, 14-34: 8-(44 pgs.)			2.00
13-1st Nicotat Comics issue			3.00

BORIS THE BEAR INSTANT COLOR CLASSICS
Dark Horse Comics: July, 1987 - No. 3, 1987 ($1.75/$1.95)

	GD2.0	FN6.0	NM9.4
1-3			2.00

BORN AGAIN
Spire Christian Comics (Fleming H. Revell Co.): 1978 (39¢)

	GD2.0	FN6.0	NM9.4
nn-Watergate, Nixon, etc.		2.40	6.00

BOUNCER, THE (Formerly Green Mask #9)
Fox Features Syndicate: 1944 - No. 14, Jan, 1945

	GD2.0	FN6.0	NM9.4
nn(1944, #10?)	28.00	83.00	220.00
11(#1)(9/44)-Origin; Rocket Kelly, One Round Hogan app.	23.00	68.00	180.00
12-14: 14-Reprints no # issue	18.00	53.00	140.00

BOUNTY GUNS (See Luke Short's..., Four Color 739)

BOX OFFICE POISON
Antarctic Press: 1996 - No. 21, Sept, 2000 ($2.95, B&W)

	GD2.0	FN6.0	NM9.4
1-Alex Robinson-s/a in all	1.00	2.80	7.00
2-5			4.00
6-21, ...Kolor Karnival 1 (5/99, $2.99)			3.00
...Super Special 0 (5/97, $4.95)			5.00
Sherman's March: Collected BOP Vol. 1 (9/98, $14.95) r/#0-4			15.00

BOY AND HIS 'BOT, A
Now Comics: Jan, 1987 ($1.95)

	GD2.0	FN6.0	NM9.4
1-A Holiday Special			2.00

BOY AND THE PIRATES, THE (Movie)
Dell Publishing Co.: No. 1117, Aug, 1960

	GD2.0	FN6.0	NM9.4
Four Color 1117-Photo-c	5.85	17.50	70.00

BOY COMICS (Captain Battle No. 1 & 2; Boy Illustories No. 43-108) (Stories by Charles Biro)(Also see Squeeks)
Lev Gleason Publ. (Comic House): No. 3, Apr, 1942 - No. 119, Mar, 1956

	GD2.0	FN6.0	NM9.4
3(No.1)-Origin Crimebuster, Bombshell & Young Robin Hood; Yankee Longago, Case 1001-1008, Swoop Storm, & Boy Movies begin; 1st app. Iron Jaw; Crimebuster's pet monkey Squeeks begins	295.00	885.00	2800.00
4-Hitler, Tojo, Mussolini-c	126.00	379.00	1200.00
5	89.00	268.00	850.00
6-Origin Iron Jaw; origin & death of Iron Jaw's son; Little Dynamite begins, ends #39; 1st Iron Jaw-c	253.00	758.00	2400.00
7-Flag & Hitler, Tojo, Mussolini-c	84.00	253.00	800.00
8-Death of Iron Jaw; Iron Jaw-c	89.00	268.00	850.00
9-Iron Jaw-c	79.00	237.00	750.00
10-Return of Iron Jaw; classic Biro-c; Iron Jaw-c	121.00	363.00	1150.00
11-Classic Iron Jaw-c	79.00	237.00	750.00
12,13	55.00	165.00	500.00
14-Iron Jaw-c	59.00	177.00	560.00
15-Death of Iron Jaw	71.00	213.00	675.00
16,18-20	38.00	113.00	300.00
17-Flag-c	40.00	120.00	325.00
21-29,31,32-(All 68 pgs.). 28-Yankee Longago ends. 32-Swoop Storm & Young Robin Hood end	25.00	75.00	200.00
30-(68 pgs.)-Origin Crimebuster retold	36.00	108.00	290.00
33-40: 34-Crimebuster story(2); suicide-c/story	19.00	56.00	150.00
41-50	17.00	51.00	135.00
51-59: 57-Dilly Duncan begins, ends #71	15.00	45.00	120.00
60-Iron Jaw returns	17.00	51.00	135.00
61-Origin Crimebuster & Iron Jaw retold	19.00	56.00	150.00
62-Death of Iron Jaw explained	18.00	53.00	140.00
63-73: 63-McWilliams-a. 73-Frazetta 1-pg. ad	12.50	37.50	100.00
74-88: 80-1st app. Rocky X of the Rocketeers; becomes "Rocky X" #101; Iron Jaw, Sniffer & the Deadly Dozen in 80-118	10.00	30.00	75.00
89-92-The Claw serial app. in all	10.00	30.00	80.00

Boy Commandos #10 © DC

Boy Loves Girl #30 © LEV

The Bradleys #5 © Peter Bagge

GD2.0 FN6.0 NM9.4

93-Claw cameo; Rocky X by Sid Check 10.00 30.00 75.00
94-97,99 10.00 30.00 70.00
98,100: 98-Rocky X by Sid Check 10.00 30.00 75.00
101-107,109,111,119: 111-Crimebuster becomes Chuck Chandler. 119-Last Crimebuster 8.65 26.00 60.00
108,110,112-118-Kubert-a 10.00 30.00 70.00
(See Giant Boy Book of Comics)
NOTE: *Boy Movies in 3-5,40,41. Iron Jaw app.-3, 4, 6, 8, 10, 11, 13-15; returns-60-62, 68, 69, 72-79, 81-118.* ***Biro*** *c-all.* ***Briefer*** *a-5, 13, 14, 16-20 among others.* ***Fuje*** *a-55, 18 pgs.* ***Palais*** *a-14, 16, 17, 19, 20 among others.*

BOY COMMANDOS (See Detective #64 & World's Finest Comics #8)
National Periodical Publications: Winter, 1942-43 - No. 36, Nov-Dec, 1949
1-Origin Liberty Belle; The Sandman & The Newsboy Legion x-over in Boy Commandos; S&K-a, 48 pgs.; S&K cameo? (classic WWII-c) 478.00 1435.00 5500.00
2-Last Liberty Belle; Hitler-c; S&K-a, 46 pgs.; WWII-c 158.00 474.00 1500.00
3-S&K-a, 45 pgs.; WWII-c 105.00 316.00 1000.00
4-6: All WWII-c. 6-S&K-a 74.00 221.00 700.00
7-10: All WWII-c 53.00 158.00 475.00
11-13: All WWII-c. 11-Infinity-c 40.00 120.00 320.00
14,16,18-19-All have S&K-a. 18-2nd Crazy Quilt-c 30.00 90.00 240.00
15-1st app. Crazy Quilt, their arch nemesis 40.00 120.00 350.00
17,20-Sci/fi-c/stories 34.00 101.00 270.00
21,22,25: 22-3rd Crazy Quilt-c; Judy Canova x-over 23.00 69.00 185.00
23-S&K-c/a(all) 30.00 90.00 240.00
24-1st costumed superhero satire-c (11-12/47). 28.00 83.00 220.00
26-Flying Saucer story (3-4/48)-4th of this theme; see The Spirit 9/28/47(1st), Shadow Comics V7#10 (2nd, 1/48) & Captain Midnight #60 (3rd, 2/48) 26.00 79.00 210.00
27,28,30: 30-Cleveland Indians story 22.00 66.00 175.00
29-S&K story (1) 24.00 73.00 195.00
31-35: 32-Dale Evans app. on-c & in story. 33-Last Crazy Quilt-c. 34-Intro. Wolf, their mascot 21.00 64.00 170.00
36-Intro The Atomobile c/sci-fi story (Scarce) 38.00 113.00 300.00
NOTE: *Most issues signed by* ***Simon & Kirby*** *are not by them.* ***S&K*** *c-1-9, 13, 14, 17, 21, 23, 24, 30-32.* ***Feller*** *c-30.*

BOY COMMANDOS
National Per. Publ.: Sept-Oct, 1973 - No. 2, Nov-Dec, 1973 (G.A. S&K reprints)
1,2: 1-Reprints story from Boy Commandos #1 plus-c & Detective #66 by S&K. 2-Infantino/Orlando-c 1.25 3.75 10.00

BOY COWBOY (Also see Amazing Adventures & Science Comics)
Ziff-Davis Publ. Co.: 1950 (8 pgs. in color)
nn-Sent to subscribers of Ziff-Davis mags. & ordered through mail for 10¢; used to test market for Kid Cowboy 25.00 75.00 200.00

BOY DETECTIVE
Avon Periodicals: May-June, 1951 - No. 4, May, 1952
1 19.00 56.00 125.00
2,3: 3-Kinstler-c 11.00 33.00 90.00
4-Kinstler-c 14.00 41.00 110.00

BOY EXPLORERS COMICS (Terry and The Pirates No. 3 on)
Family Comics (Harvey Publ.): May-June, 1946 - No. 2, Sept-Oct, 1946
1-Intro The Explorers, Duke of Broadway, Calamity Jane & Danny Dixon... Cadet; S&K-c/a, 24 pgs. 63.00 189.00 600.00
2-(Scarce)-Small size (5-1/2x8-1/2"; B&W; 32 pgs.) Distributed to mail subscribers only; S&K-a 63.00 189.00 600.00
(Also see All New No. 15, Flash Gordon No. 5, and Stuntman No. 3)

BOY ILLUSTORIES (See Boy Comics)

BOY LOVES GIRL (Boy Meets Girl No. 1-24)
Lev Gleason Publications: No. 25, July, 1952 - No. 57, June, 1956
25(#1) 6.40 19.25 45.00
26,27,29-33: 30-33-Serial, 'Loves of My Life 4.65 14.00 28.00
34-42: 39-Lingerie panels 4.00 11.00 22.00
28-Drug propaganda story 5.00 15.00 30.00
43-Toth-a 6.00 18.00 42.00
44-50: 50-Last pre-code (2/55) 3.60 9.00 18.00
51-57: 57-Ann Brewster-a 2.80 7.00 14.00

BOY MEETS GIRL (Boy Loves Girl No. 25 on)
Lev Gleason Publications: Feb, 1950 - No. 24, June, 1952 (No. 1-17: 52 pgs.)
1-Guardineer-a 9.30 28.00 65.00
2 5.00 15.00 35.00
3-10 5.00 15.00 30.00
11-24 4.15 12.50 25.00
NOTE: ***Briefer*** *a-24.* ***Fuje*** *c-3,7. Painted-c 1-17. Photo-c 19-21, 23.*

BOYS' AND GIRLS' MARCH OF COMICS (See March of Comics)

BOYS' RANCH (Also see Western Tales & Witches' Western Tales)
Harvey Publ.: Oct, 1950 - No. 6, Aug, 1951 (No.1-3, 52 pgs.; No. 4-6, 36 pgs.)
1-S&K-c/a(3) 61.00 182.00 575.00
2-S&K-c/a(3) 42.00 125.00 375.00
3-S&K-c/a(2); Meskin-a 40.00 120.00 340.00
4-S&K-c/a, 5 pgs. 36.00 108.00 290.00
5,6-S&K-c, splashes & centerspread only; Meskin-a 20.00 60.00 160.00

BOZO (Larry Harmon's Bozo, the World's Most Famous Clown)
Innovation Publishing: 1992 ($6.95, 68 pgs.)
1-Reprints Four Color #285(#1) 1.00 2.80 7.00

BOZO THE CLOWN (TV) (Bozo No. 7 on)
Dell Publishing Co.: July, 1950 - No. 4, Oct-Dec, 1963
Four Color 285(#1) 19.00 57.00 225.00
2(7-9/51)-7(10-12/52) 10.50 31.00 125.00
Four Color 464,508,551,594(10/54) 8.35 25.00 100.00
1(nn, 5-7/62) 5.85 17.50 70.00
2 - 4(1963) 4.60 13.75 55.00

BOZZ CHRONICLES, THE
Marvel Comics (Epic Comics): Dec, 1985 - No. 6, 1986 (Lim. series, mature)
1-6-Logan/Wolverine look alike in 19th century. 1,3,5- Blevins-a 3.00

BRADLEYS, THE (Also see Hate)
Fantagraphics Books: Apr, 1999 - No. 6, Jan, 2000 ($2.95, B&W, limited series)
1-6-Reprints Peter Bagge's-s/a 3.00

BRADY BUNCH, THE (TV)(See Kite Fun Book and Binky #78)
Dell Publishing Co.: Feb, 1970 - No. 2, May, 1970
1 10.00 30.00 120.00
2 6.70 20.00 80.00

BRAIN, THE
Sussex Publ. Co./Magazine Enterprises: Sept, 1956 - No. 7, 1958
1-Dan DeCarlo-a in all including reprints 8.65 26.00 60.00
2,3 5.00 15.00 32.00
4-7 4.00 12.00 24.00
I.W. Reprints #1-4,8-10('63),14: 2-Reprints Sussex #2 with new cover added 1.50 4.50 12.00
Super Reprint #17,18(nd) 1.50 4.50 12.00

BRAINBANX
DC Comics (Helix): Mar, 1997 - No. 6, Aug, 1997 ($2.50, limited series)
1-6: Elaine Lee-s/Temujin-a 2.50

BRAIN BOY
Dell Publishing Co.: Apr-June, 1962 - No. 6, Sept-Nov, 1963 (Painted c-#1-6)
Four Color 1330(#1)-Gil Kane-a; origin 12.50 37.50 150.00
2(7-9/62),3-6: 4-Origin retold 7.00 21.00 85.00

BRAM STOKER'S BURIAL OF THE RATS (Movie)
Roger Corman's Cosmic Comics: Apr, 1995 - No.3, June, 1995 ($2.50)
1-3: Adaptation of film; Jerry Prosser scripts 2.50

BRAM STOKER'S DRACULA (Movie)(Also see Dracula: Vlad the Impaler)
Topps Comics: Oct, 1992 - No. 4, Jan, 1993 ($2.95, limited series, polybagged)
1-(1st & 2nd printing)-Adaptation of film begins; Mignola-c/a in all; 4 trading cards & poster;photo scenes of movie 3.00
1-Crimson foil edition (limited to 500) 10.00
2-Bound-in poster & cards 3.00

Brass (2nd series) #1 © WSP

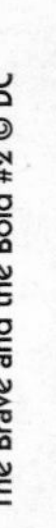
The Brave and the Bold #2 © DC

The Brave and the Bold #56 © DC

2-4: 2-Bound-in poster & cards. 4 trading cards in both. 3-Contains coupon to win 1 of 500 crimson foil-cedition of #1. 4-Contains coupon to win 1 of 500 uncut sheets of all 16 trading cards 3.00

BRAND ECHH (See Not Brand Echh)

BRAND NEW YORK: WHAT JUSTICE
Comic Box Inc.: July, 1997 ($3.95, B&W&Red)

1-Zoltan-s/a, Peter Avanti-s 4.00

BRAND OF EMPIRE (See Luke Short's...Four Color 771)

BRASS
Image Comics (WildStorm Productions): Aug, 1996 - No. 3, May, 1997 ($2.50, limited series)

1-($4.50) Folio Ed.; oversized 4.50
1-3: Wiesenfeld-s/Bennett-a. 3-Grunge & Roxy(Gen 13) cameo 2.50

BRASS
DC Comics (WildStorm): Aug, 2000 - No. 6 ($2.50, limited series)

1-5-Arcudi-s 2.50

BRATPACK/MAXIMORTAL SUPER SPECIAL
King Hell Press: 1996 ($2.95, B&W, limited series)

1,2: Veitch-s/a 3.00

BRATS BIZARRE
Marvel Comics (Epic/Heavy Hitters): 1994 - No. 4, 1994 ($2.50, limited series)

1-4: All w/bound-in trading cards 2.50

BRAVADOS, THE (See Wild Western Action)
Skywald Publ. Corp.: Aug, 1971 (52 pgs., one-shot)

1-Red Mask, The Durango Kid, Billy Nevada-r; Bolle-a; 3-D effect story 1.25 3.75 14.00

BRAVE AND THE BOLD, THE (See Best Of... & Super DC Giant) (Replaced by Batman & The Outsiders)
National Periodical Publ./DC Comics: Aug-Sept, 1955 - No. 200, July, 1983

1-Viking Prince by Kubert, Silent Knight, Golden Gladiator begin; part Kubert-c 219.00 656.00 3500.00
2 100.00 300.00 1400.00
3,4 54.00 161.00 750.00
5-Robin Hood begins (4-5/56, 1st DC app.), ends #15; see Robin Hood Tales #7 57.00 171.00 800.00
6-10: 6-Robin Hood by Kubert; last Golden Gladiator app.; Silent Knight; no Viking Prince. 8-1st S.A. issue 41.00 123.00 525.00
11-22,24: 12,14-Robin Hood-c. 18,21-23-Grey tone-c. 22-Last Silent Knight. 24-Last Viking Prince by Kubert (2nd solo book) 33.00 100.00 400.00
23-Viking Prince origin by Kubert; 1st B&B single theme issue & 1st Viking Prince solo book 41.00 123.00 525.00
25-1st app. Suicide Squad (8-9/59) 40.00 120.00 475.00
26,27-Suicide Squad 30.00 90.00 330.00

GD2.0 FN6.0 VF8.0 NM9.4

28-(2-3/60)-Justice League intro./1st app.; origin/1st app. Snapper Carr 353.00 1060.00 2825.00 6000.00

GD2.0 FN6.0 NM9.4

29-Justice League (4-5/60)-2nd app. battle the Weapons Master; robot-c 160.00 480.00 2400.00
30-Justice League (6-7/60)-3rd app.; vs. Amazo 136.00 407.00 1900.00
31-1st app. Cave Carson (8-9/60); scarce in high grade; 1st try-out series 33.00 100.00 400.00
32,33-Cave Carson 22.00 65.00 240.00
34-Origin/1st app. Silver-Age Hawkman, Hawkgirl & Byth (2-3/61); Gardner Fox story, Kubert-c/a ; 1st S.A. Hawkman tryout series; 2nd in #42-44; both series predate Hawkman #1 (4-5/64) 160.00 480.00 2400.00
35-Hawkman by Kubert (4-5/61)-2nd app. 44.00 133.00 575.00
36-Hawkman by Kubert; origin & 1st app. Shadow Thief (6-7/61)-3rd app. 40.00 120.00 475.00
37-Suicide Squad (2nd tryout series) 23.00 68.00 250.00
38,39-Suicide Squad. 38-Last 10¢ issue 20.00 60.00 220.00
40,41-Cave Carson Inside Earth (2nd try-out series). 40-Kubert-a. 41-Meskin-a 14.50 43.50 160.00
42-Hawkman by Kubert (2nd tryout series); Hawkman earns helmet wings; Byth app. 29.00 88.00 325.00
43-Hawkman by Kubert; more detailed origin 33.00 100.00 400.00
44-Hawkman by Kubert; grey-tone-c 25.00 75.00 275.00
45-49-Strange Sports Stories by Infantino 6.80 20.50 75.00
50-The Green Arrow & Manhunter From Mars (10-11/63); 1st Manhunter x-over outside of Detective (pre-dates House of Mystery #143); team-ups begin 17.50 52.00 190.00
51-Aquaman & Hawkman (12-1/63-64); pre-dates Hawkman #1 23.00 68.00 250.00
52-(2-3/64)-3 Battle Stars; Sgt. Rock, Haunted Tank, Johnny Cloud, & Mlle. Marie team-up for 1st time by Kubert (c/a) 16.50 49.00 180.00
53-Atom & The Flash by Toth 6.80 20.50 75.00
54-Kid Flash, Robin & Aqualad; 1st app./origin Teen Titans (6-7/64) 27.50 82.00 300.00
55-Metal Men & The Atom 5.45 16.35 60.00
56-The Flash & Manhunter From Mars 5.45 16.35 60.00
57-Origin & 1st app. Metamorpho (12-1/64-65) 15.50 46.50 170.00
58-2nd app. Metamorpho by Fradon 7.65 23.00 85.00
59-Batman & Green Lantern; 1st Batman team-up in Brave and the Bold 10.00 30.00 110.00
60-Teen Titans (2nd app.)-1st app. new Wonder Girl (Donna Troy), who joins Titans (6-7/65) 9.00 27.00 100.00
61-Origin Starman & Black Canary by Anderson 12.50 37.00 135.00
62-Origin Starman & Black Canary cont'd. 62-1st S.A. app. Wildcat (10-11/65); 1st S.A. app. of G.A. Huntress (W.W. villain) 10.00 30.00 110.00
63-Supergirl & Wonder Woman 5.45 16.35 60.00
64-Batman Versus Eclipso (see H.O.S. #61) 6.35 19.00 70.00
65-Flash & Doom Patrol (4-5/66) 3.20 9.60 35.00
66-Metamorpho & Metal Men (6-7/66) 3.20 9.60 35.00
67-Batman & The Flash by Infantino; Batman team-ups begin, end #200 (8-9/66) 5.00 15.00 55.00
68-Batman/Metamorpho/Joker/Riddler/Penguin-c/story; Batman as Bat-Hulk (Hulk parody) 7.25 21.75 80.00
69-Batman & Green Lantern 3.65 11.00 40.00
70-Batman & Hawkman; Craig-a(p) 3.65 11.00 40.00
71-Batman & Green Arrow 3.65 11.00 40.00
72-Spectre & Flash (6-7/67); 4th app. The Spectre; predates Spectre #1 4.10 12.30 45.00
73-Aquaman & The Atom 3.20 9.60 35.00
74-Batman & Metal Men 3.20 9.60 35.00
75-Batman & The Spectre (12-1/67-68); 6th app. Spectre; came out between Spectre #1 & #2 3.65 11.00 40.00
76-Batman & Plastic Man (2-3/68); came out between Plastic Man #8 & #9 3.20 9.60 35.00
77-Batman & The Atom 3.20 9.60 35.00
78-Batman, Wonder Woman & Batgirl 3.20 9.60 35.00
79-Batman & Deadman by Neal Adams (8-9/68); early Deadman app. 5.90 17.75 65.00
80-Batman & Creeper (10-11/68); N. Adams-a; early app. The Creeper; came out between Creeper #3 & #4 4.35 13.00 48.00
81-Batman & Flash; N. Adams-a 4.35 13.00 48.00
82-Batman & Aquaman; N. Adams-a; origin Ocean Master retold (2-3/69) 4.35 13.00 48.00
83-Batman & Teen Titans; N. Adams-a (4-5/69) 4.35 13.00 48.00
84-Batman (G.A., 1st S.A. app.) & Sgt. Rock; N. Adams-a; last 12¢ issue (6-7/69) 4.35 13.00 48.00
85-Batman & Green Arrow; 1st new costume for Green Arrow by Neal Adams (8-9/69) 4.55 13.65 50.00
86-Batman & Deadman (10-11/69); N. Adams-a; story concludes from Strange Adventures #216 (1-2/69) 4.35 13.00 48.00
87-Batman & Wonder Woman 3.00 9.00 30.00
88-Batman & Wildcat 3.00 9.00 30.00
89-Batman & Phantom Stranger (4-5/70); early Phantom Stranger app. (came out between Phantom Stranger #6 & 7 2.80 8.40 28.00
90-Batman & Adam Strange 2.80 8.40 28.00
91-Batman & Black Canary (8-9/70) 2.80 8.40 28.00
92-Batman; intro the Bat Squad 2.80 8.40 28.00
93-Batman-House of Mystery; N. Adams-a 3.65 11.00 40.00

Breakfast After Noon #1 © Andi Watson

Brenda Starr #14 © SUPR

The Brave and the Bold #136 © DC

GD2.0 FN6.0 NM9.4

3atman-Teen Titans 2.50 7.50 23.00
3atman & Plastic Man 2.50 7.50 23.00
3atman & Sgt. Rock; last 15¢ issue 2.60 7.80 26.00
3atman & Wildcat; 52 pg. issues begin, end #102; reprints origin & 1st app.
)eadman from Strange Advs. #205 2.50 7.50 25.00
3atman & Phantom Stranger; 1st Jim Aparo Batman-a?
2.50 7.50 25.00
3atman & Flash 2.50 7.50 25.00
(2-3/72, 25¢, 52 pgs.)-Batman-Gr. Lantern-Gr. Arrow-Black Canary-
Robin; Deadman-r by Adams/Str. Advs. #210 4.35 13.00 48.00
Batman & Metamorpho; Kubert Viking Prince 2.00 6.00 18.00
Batman-Teen Titans; N. Adams-a(p) 2.50 7.50 23.00
107,109,110: Batman team-ups: 103-Metal Men. 104-Deadman. 105-
Vonder Woman. 106-Green Arrow. 107-Black Canary. 109-Demon.
10-Wildcat 1.50 4.50 12.00
Sgt. Rock 2.00 6.00 16.00
Batman/Joker-c/story 2.00 6.00 16.00
117: All 100 pgs.; Batman team-ups: 112-Mr. Miracle. 113-Metal Men;
eprints origin/1st Hawkman from Brave and the Bold #34; r/origin Multi-Man/
;hallengers #14. 114-Aquaman. 115-Atom; r/origin Viking Prince from #23;
'Dr. Fate/Hourman/Solomon Grundy/Green Lantern from Showcase #55.
16-Spectre. 117-Sgt. Rock; last 100 pg. issue 2.50 7.50 25.00
Batman/Wildcat/Joker-c/story 2.00 6.00 16.00
121-123,125-128,132-140: Batman team-ups: 119-Man-Bat. 121-Metal
Aen. 122-Swamp Thing. 123-Plastic Man/Metamorpho. 125-Flash.
26-Aquaman. 127-Wildcat. 128-Mr. Miracle. 132-Kung-Fu Fighter.
33-Deadman. 134-Green Lantern. 135-Metal Men. 136-Metal Men/Green
Arrow. 137-Demon. 138-Mr. Miracle. 139-Hawkman. 140-Wonder Woman
1.00 3.00 8.00
Kamandi(68 pgs.) 1.50 4.50 12.00
Sgt. Rock 1.50 4.50 12.00
130-Batman/Green Arrow/Atom parts 1 & 2; Joker & Two Face-c/stories
1.75 5.25 14.00
Batman & Wonder Woman vs. Catwoman-c/sty 1.25 3.75 10.00
Batman/Black Canary vs. Joker-c/story 1.75 5.25 14.00
160: Batman team-ups: 142-Aquaman. 143-Creeper; origin Human Target
44 pgs.). 144-Green Arrow; origin Human Target part 2 (44 pgs.).
45-Phantom Stranger. 146-G.A. Batman/Unknown Soldier. 147-Supergirl.
48-Plastic Man; X-Mas-c. 149-Teen Titans. 150-Anniversary issue;
Superman. 151-Flash. 152-Atom. 153-Red Tornado. 154-Metamorpho.
55-Green Lantern. 156-Dr. Fate. 157-Batman vs. Kamandi (ties into
Kamandi #59). 158-Wonder Woman. 159-Ra's Al Ghul. 160-Supergirl.
2.40 6.00
181,183-190,192-195,198,199: Batman team-ups: 161-Adam Strange.
62-G.A. Batman/Sgt. Rock. 163-Black Lightning. 164-Hawkman.
65-Man-Bat. 166-Black Canary; Nemesis (intro) back-up story begins,
nds #192; Penguin-c/story. 167-G.A. Batman/Blackhawk; origin Nemesis.
68-Green Arrow. 169-Zatanna. 170-Nemesis. 171-Scalphunter.172-
Firestorm. 173-Guardians of the Universe. 174-Green Lantern. 175-Lois Lane.
76-Swamp Thing. 177-Elongated Man. 178-Creeper. 179-Legion. 180-
Spectre. 181-Hawk & Dove. 183-Riddler. 184-Huntress. 185-Green Arrow.
86-Hawkman. 187-Metal Men. 188,189-Rose & the Thorn. 190-Adam
Strange. 192-Superboy vs. Mr. I.Q. 193-Nemesis. 194-Flash. 195-I...Vampire.
98-Karate Kid. 199-Batman vs. The Spectre 4.00
G.A. Robin; G.A. Starman app.; 1st modern app. G.A. Batwoman 5.00
Batman/Joker-c/story; Nemesis app. 1.00 3.00 8.00
Ragman; origin Ragman retold. 2.40 6.00
Catwoman; Earth II Batman & Catwoman marry; 2nd modern app. of G.A.
Batwoman 1.00 3.00 8.00
Double-sized (64 pgs.); printed on Mando paper; Earth One & Earth Two
Batman app. in separate stories; intro/1st app. Batman & The Outsiders
1.10 3.30 9.00

E: ***Neal Adams*** *a-79-86, 93, 100r, 102; c-75, 76, 79-86, 88-90, 93, 95, 99, 100r.* ***M. erson*** *a-115r; c-72i, 96i.* ***Andru/Esposito*** *c-25-27.* ***Aparo*** *a-98, 100-102, 104-125, 126i, 136, 138-145, 147, 148i, 149-152, 154, 155, 157-162, 168-170, 173-178, 180-182, 184, 186i-191i-193i, 195, 196, 200; c-105-109, 111-136, 137i, 138-175, 177, 180-184, 186-200.* ***in*** *a-166i.* ***Bernard Baily*** *c-32, 33, 58.* ***Buckler*** *a-185, 186p; c-137, 178p, 185p, 186p.* ***dano*** *a-143, 144.* ***Infantino*** *a-67p, 72p, 97r, 98r, 115r, 172p, 183p, 190p, 194p; c-45-49, 69p, 70p, 72p, 96p, 98r.* ***Kaluta*** *c-176.* ***Kane*** *a-115r; c-59, 64.* ***Kubert*** *&/or* ***Heath*** *a-1-24; nts-101, 113, 115, 117.* ***Kubert*** *a-99r; c-22-24, 34-36, 40, 42-44, 52.* ***Mooney*** *a-114r.* ***imer*** *a-64, 69.* ***Newton*** *a-153p, 156p, 165p.* ***Irv Novick*** *c-1(part), 2-21.* ***Fred Ray*** *a-78r.* ***Roussos*** *a-50, 76i, 114r.* ***Staton*** *148p. 52 pgs.-97, 100; 68 pgs.-120; 100 pgs.-112-117.*

GD2.0 FN6.0 NM9.4

BRAVE AND THE BOLD, THE
DC Comics: Dec, 1991 - No. 6, June, 1992 ($1.75, limited series)

1-6: Green Arrow, The Butcher, The Question in all; Grell scripts in all 2.00
NOTE: ***Grell*** *c-3, 4-6.*

BRAVE AND THE BOLD SPECIAL, THE (See DC Special Series No. 8)

BRAVE EAGLE (TV)
Dell Publishing Co.: No. 705, June, 1956 - No. 929, July, 1958

Four Color 705 (#1)-Photo-c 5.85 17.50 70.00
Four Color 770, 816, 879 (2/58), 929-All photo-c 3.20 9.60 35.00

BRAVE OLD WORLD (V2K)
DC Comics (Vertigo): Feb, 2000 - No. 4, May, 2000 ($2.50, mini-series)

1-4-Messner-Loeb-s/Guy Davis & Phil Hester-a 2.50

BRAVE ONE, THE (Movie)
Dell Publishing Co.: No. 773, Mar, 1957

Four Color 773-Photo-c 4.60 13.75 55.00

BRAVURA
Malibu Comics (Bravura): 1995 (mail-in offer)

0-wraparound holographic-c; short stories and promo pin-ups of Chaykin's Power &Glory, Gil Kane's & Steven Grant's Edge, Starlin's Breed, & Simonson's Star Slammers. 5.00
1 1/2 7.00

BREAKFAST AFTER NOON
Oni Press: May, 2000 - No. 6, ($2.95, B&W, limited series)

1-5-Andi Watson-s/a 3.00

BREAKNECK BLVD.
MotioN Comics/Slave Labor Graphics Vol. 2: No. 0, Feb, 1994 - No. 2, Nov, 1994; Vol. 2#1, Jul, 1995 - #6, Dec., 1996 ($2.50/$2.95, B&W)

0-2, V2#1-6: 0-Perez/Giordano-c 3.00

BREAK-THRU (Also see Exiles V1#4)
Malibu Comics (Ultraverse): Dec, 1993 - No. 2, Jan, 1994 ($2.50, 44 pgs.)

1,2-Perez-c/a(p); has x-overs in Ultraverse titles 2.50

BREATHTAKER
DC Comics: 1990 - No. 4, 1990 ($4.95, 52 pgs., prestige format, mature)

Book 1-4: Mark Wheatley-painted-c/a & scripts; Marc Hempel-a 5.00
TPB (1994, $14.95) r/#1-4; intro by Neil Gaiman 15.00

'BREED
Malibu Comics (Bravura): Jan, 1994 - No. 6, 1994 ($2.50, limited series)

1-6: 1-(48 pgs.)-Origin & 1st app. of 'Breed by Starlin; contains Bravura stamps; spot varnish-c. 2-5-contains Bravura stamps. 6-Death of Rachel 3.00
...:Book of Genesis (1994, $12.95)-reprints #1-6 13.00

'BREED II
Malibu Comics (Bravura): Nov, 1994 - No. 6, Apr, 1995 ($2.95, limited series)

1-6: Starlin-c/a/scripts in all. 1-Gold edition 3.00

BREEZE LAWSON, SKY SHERIFF (See Sky Sheriff)

BRENDA LEE STORY, THE
Dell Publishing Co.: Sept, 1962

01-078-209 8.00 23.00 95.00

BRENDA STARR (Also see All Great)
Four Star Comics Corp./Superior Comics Ltd.: No. 13, 9/47; No. 14, 3/48; V2#3, 6/48 - V2#12, 12/49

V1#13-By Dale Messick 78.00 234.00 740.00
14-Kamen bondage-c 80.00 240.00 760.00
V2#3-Baker-a? 66.00 198.00 625.00
4-Used in **SOTI**, pg. 21; Kamen bondage-c 78.00 234.00 740.00
5-10 64.00 192.00 610.00
11,12 (Scarce) 65.00 195.00 620.00
NOTE: *Newspaper reprints plus original material through #6. All original #7 on.*

BRENDA STARR (...Reporter)(Young Lovers No. 16 on?)
Charlton Comics: No. 13, June, 1955 - No. 15, Oct, 1955

Brick Bradford #7 © STD

Brigade #7 © Rob Liefeld

Broadway Romances #2 © QUA

	GD2.0	FN6.0	NM9.4
13-15-Newspaper-r	38.00	113.00	300.00

BRENDA STARR REPORTER
Dell Publishing Co.: Oct, 1963

1	16.50	49.00	180.00

BRER RABBIT (See Kite Fun Book, Walt Disney Showcase #28 and Wheaties)
Dell Publishing Co.: No. 129, 1946; No. 208, Jan, 1949; No. 693, 1956 (Disney)

Four Color 129 (#1)-Adapted from Disney movie "Song of the South"	27.50	82.50	330.00
Four Color 208 (1/49)	11.30	34.00	135.00
Four Color 693-Part-r 129	8.35	25.00	100.00

BRIAN BOLLAND'S BLACK BOOK
Eclipse Comics: July, 1985 (one-shot)

1-British B&W-r in color			3.00

BRICK BRADFORD (Also see Ace Comics & King Comics)
King Features Syndicate/Standard: No. 5, July, 1948 - No. 8, July, 1949 (Ritt & Grey reprints)

5	19.00	56.00	150.00
6-Robot-c (by Schomburg?).	28.00	83.00	220.00
7-Schomburg-c. 8-Says #7 inside, #8 on-c	14.00	41.00	110.00

BRIDE'S DIARY (Formerly Black Cobra No. 3)
Ajax/Farrell Publ.: No. 4, May, 1955 - No. 10, Aug, 1956

4 (#1)	6.40	19.25	45.00
5-8	4.65	14.00	28.00
9,10-Disbrow-a	6.00	18.00	42.00

BRIDES IN LOVE (Hollywood Romances & Summer Love No. 46 on)
Charlton Comics: Aug, 1956 - No. 45, Feb, 1965

1	9.30	28.00	65.00
2	5.00	15.00	35.00
3-6,8-10	2.80	8.40	28.00
7-(68 pgs.)	3.20	9.60	35.00
11-20	2.00	6.00	18.00
21-45	1.25	3.75	10.00

BRIDES ROMANCES
Quality Comics Group: Nov, 1953 - No. 23, Dec, 1956

1	11.00	33.00	90.00
2	6.00	18.00	42.00
3-10: Last precode (3/55)	5.00	15.00	32.00
11-17,19-22: 15-Baker-a(p)?; Colan-a	4.00	12.00	24.00
18-Baker-a	5.50	16.50	38.00
23-Baker-c/a	8.65	26.00	60.00

BRIDE'S SECRETS
Ajax/Farrell(Excellent Publ.)/Four-Star: Apr-May, 1954 - No. 19, May, 1958

1	10.00	30.00	75.00
2	5.50	16.50	38.00
3-6: Last precode (3/55)	4.65	14.00	28.00
7-11,13-19: 18-Hollingsworth-a	4.15	12.50	25.00
12-Disbrow-a	5.00	15.00	30.00

BRIDE-TO-BE ROMANCES (See True...)

BRIGADE
Image Comics (Extreme Studios): Aug, 1992 - No. 4, 1993 ($1.95, lim. series)

1-Liefeld part plots/scripts in all, Liefeld-c(p); contains 2 Brigade trading cards; 1st app. Genocide			3.00
1-Gold foil stamped logo edition			8.00
2-Contains coupon for Image Comics #0 & 2 trading cards			3.00
2-With coupon missing			2.00
3-Contains 2 bound-in trading cards; 1st Birds of Prey			2.50
4-Flip book format featuring Youngblood #5			2.50

BRIGADE
Image Comics (Extreme): V2#1, May, 1993 - V2#22, July, 1995, V2#25, May, 1996 ($1.95/$2.50)

V2#1-22,25: 1-Gatefold-c; Liefeld co-plots; Blood Brothers part 1; Bloodstrike app.; 1st app. Boone & Hacker. 2-(6/93, V2#1 on inside)-Foil merricote-c (news stand ed. w/out foil-c exists). 3-1st app. Roman; Perez-c(i); Liefeld scripts. 1st app. Coral & Worlok. 6-8-Thibert-c(i). 8-Liefeld scripts; Black and White part 5 by Art Thibert. 8,9-Coupons #2 & 6 for Extreme Prejudice #0 bound- 11-(8/94, $2.50) WildC.A.T.S app. 16-Polybagged w/ trading card. 19-Glor app. 20 (Regular-c.)-Troll, Supreme, Shadowhawk, Glory,Vanguard, & Roman form new team. 22-"Supreme Apocalypse" Pt. 4; Marv Wolfman scripts; polybagged w/ trading card. 25-Images of Tomorrow			2
0-(9/93)-Liefeld scripts; 1st app. Warcry; Youngblood & Wildcats app.;			2
20-(Variant-c. by Quesada & Palmiotti)-Troll, Supreme, Shadowhawk, Glory, Vanguard, & Roman form new team.			2
Sourcebook 1 (8/94, $2.95)			3

BRIGADE
Awesome Entertainment: July, 2000 ($2.99)

1-Flip book w/Century preview			3

BRIGAND, THE (See Fawcett Movie Comics No. 18)

BRINGING UP FATHER
Dell Publishing Co.: No. 9, 1942 - No. 37, 1944

Large Feature Comic 9	20.00	60.00	240
Four Color 37	19.00	57.00	230

BRING BACK THE BAD GUYS
Marvel Comics: 1998($24.95, TPB)

1-Reprints stories of Marvel villains' secrets			25

BRING ON THE BAD GUYS (See Fireside Book Series)

BRINKE OF DESTRUCTION
High-Top and Brinke Stevens: Dec, 1995 - Jan, 1997($2.95)

1-3: 1-Boris-c. 2-Julie Bell-c. 3-Garris-c			3.
Holiday Special ($6.99)-Comic w/audio tape	1.00	2.80	7.

BRINKE OF DISASTER
Revenge Entertainment Group: 1996 ($2.25, B&W, one-shot)

nn-Photo-c			2.

BRINKE OF ETERNITY
Chaos! Comics: Apr, 1994 ($2.75, one-shot)

1			3.
1-Signed Edition			4.

BROADWAY HOLLYWOOD BLACKOUTS
Stanhall: Mar-Apr, 1954 - No. 3, July-Aug, 1954

1	10.50	32.00	85.
2,3	7.85	23.50	55.

BROADWAY ROMANCES
Quality Comics Group: January, 1950 - No. 5, Sept, 1950

1-Ward-c/a (9 pgs.); Gustavson-a	34.00	101.00	270.
2-Ward-a (9 pgs.); photo-c	24.00	73.00	195.
3-5: All-Photo-c	11.00	33.00	90.

BROKEN ARROW (TV)
Dell Publishing Co.: No. 855, Oct, 1957 - No. 947, Nov, 1958

Four Color 855 (#1)-Photo-c	5.00	15.00	60.
Four Color 947-Photo-c	4.55	13.65	50.

BROKEN CROSS, THE (See The Crusaders)

BRONCHO BILL (See Comics On Parade, Sparkler & Tip Top Comics)
United Features Syndicate/Standard(Visual Editions) No. 5-on: 1939 - 194 No. 5, 1?/48 - No. 16, 8?/50

Single Series 2 ('39)	49.00	147.00	440
Single Series 19 ('40)(#2 on cvr)	41.00	123.00	370
5	12.50	37.50	100
6(4/48)-10(4/49)	7.85	23.50	55
11(6/49)-16	6.00	18.00	42

NOTE: *Schomburg c-6, 7, 9-13, 16.*

BROOKLYN DREAMS
DC Comics (Paradox Press): 1994, ($4.95, B&W, limited series, mature)

1-4			5

BROOKS ROBINSON (See Baseball's Greatest Heroes #2)

Bruce Gentry #1 © BP

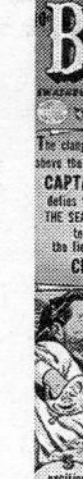
Buccaneers #25 © QUA

Buck Rogers #5 © KFS

GD2.0 FN6.0 NM9.4

OTHER BILLY THE PAIN FROM PLAINS
rvel Comics Group: 1979 (68pgs.)

B&W comics, satire, Jimmy Carter-c & x-over w/Brother Billy peanut jokes.
Joey Adams-a (scarce) 2.40 7.35 22.00

OTHER POWER, THE GEEK (See Saga of Swamp Thing Annual & Vertigo ions)
tional Periodical Publications: Sept-Oct, 1968 - No. 2, Nov-Dec, 1968

Origin; Simon-c(i?) 4.55 13.65 50.00
2.50 7.50 25.00

OTHERS, HANG IN THERE, THE
re Christian Comics (Fleming H. Revell Co.): 1979 (49¢)

1.00 2.80 7.00

OTHERS OF THE SPEAR (Also see Tarzan)
d Key/Whitman No. 18: June, 1972 - No. 17, Feb, 1976; No. 18, May, 1982

3.20 9.60 35.00
Painted-c begin, end #17 2.00 6.00 18.00
10 1.50 4.50 12.00
-18: 12-Line drawn-c. 13-17-Spiegle-a. 18-r/#2; Leopard Girl-r
1.00 2.80 7.00

OTHERS, THE CULT ESCAPE, THE
re Christian Comics (Fleming H. Revell Co.): 1980 (49¢)

5.00

OWNIES (See New Funnies)
l Publishing Co.: No. 192, July, 1948 - No. 605, Dec, 1954

ır Color 192(#1)-Kelly-a 12.50 37.50 150.00
ır Color 244(9/49), 293 (9/50)-Last Kelly c/a 10.00 30.00 120.00
ır Color 337(7-8/51), 365(12-1/51-52), 398(5/52) 3.65 11.00 40.00
ır Color 436(11/52), 482(7/53), 522(12/53), 605 3.20 9.60 35.00

UCE GENTRY
tter/Standard/Four Star Publ./Superior No. 3: Jan, 1948 - No. 8, Jul, 1949

Ray Bailey strip reprints begin, end #3; E. C. emblem appears as a monogram on stationery in story; negligee panels 47.00 140.00 420.00
3 35.00 105.00 280.00
8 24.00 73.00 195.00
TE: *Kamenish a-2-7; c-1-8.*

UCE LEE (Also see Deadly Hands of Kung Fu)
libu Comics: July, 1994 - No. 6, Dec, 1994 ($2.95, 36 pgs.)

6: 1-(44 pgs.)-Mortal Kombat prev., 1st app. in comics. 2,6-(36 pgs.) 5.00

UCE JONES' OUTER EDGE
ovation: 1993 ($2.50, B&W, one-shot)

Bruce Jones-c/a/script 2.50

UCE WAYNE: AGENT OF S.H.I.E.L.D. (Also see Marvel Versus DC #3 & Versus Marvel #4)
rvel Comics (Amalgam): Apr, 1996 ($1.95, one-shot)

Chuck Dixon scripts & Cary Nord-c/a. 2.00

UISER
them Publications: Feb, 1994 ($2.45)

2.45

UTE, THE
aboard Publ. (Atlas): Feb, 1975 - No. 3, July, 1975

Origin & 1st app; Sekowsky-a(p) 2.40 6.00
Sekowsky-a(p); Fleisher-s 5.00
Brunner/Starlin/Weiss-a(p) 2.40 6.00

UTE & BABE
inous Press: July, 1994 - No. 2, Aug, 1994

($3.95, 8 tablets plus-c)-"...It Begins..."; tablet format 4.00
($2.50, 36 pgs.)-"Mael's Rage", 2-(40 pgs.)-Stiff additional variant-c 2.50

UTE FORCE
rvel Comics: Aug, 1990 - No. 4, Nov, 1990 ($1.00, limited series)

4: Animal super-heroes; Delbo & DeCarlo-a 2.50

GD2.0 FN6.0 NM9.4

BUBBLEGUM CRISIS: GRAND MAL
Dark Horse Comics: Mar, 1994 - No. 4, June, 1994 ($2.50, limited series)

1-4-Japanese manga 2.50

BUCCANEER
I. W. Enterprises: No date (1963)

I.W. Reprint #1(r-/Quality #20), #8(r-/#23): Crandall-a in each
2.50 7.50 25.00

BUCCANEERS (Formerly Kid Eternity)
Quality Comics: No. 19, Jan, 1950 - No. 27, May, 1951 (No. 24-27: 52 pgs.)

19-Captain Daring, Black Roger, Eric Falcon & Spanish Main begin;
Crandall-a 50.00 150.00 450.00
20,23-Crandall-a 38.00 113.00 300.00
21-Crandall-c/a 40.00 120.00 360.00
22-Bondage-c 30.00 90.00 240.00
24-26: 24-Adam Peril, U.S.N. begins. 25-Origin & 1st app. Corsair Queen.
26-last Spanish Main 26.00 79.00 210.00
27-Crandall-c/a 38.00 113.00 300.00
Super Reprint #12 (1964)-Crandall-r/#21 3.00 9.00 30.00

BUCCANEERS, THE (TV)
Dell Publishing Co.: No. 800, 1957

Four Color 800-Photo-c 6.70 20.00 80.00

BUCKAROO BANZAI (Movie)
Marvel Comics Group: Dec, 1984 - No. 2, Feb, 1985

1,2-Movie adaptation; r/Marvel Super Special #33; Texiera-c/a 2.00

BUCK DUCK
Atlas Comics (ANC): June, 1953 - No. 4, Dec, 1953

1-Funny animal stories in all 13.00 39.00 105.00
2-4: 2-Ed Win-a(5) 7.00 21.00 48.00

BUCK JONES (Also see Crackajack Funnies, Famous Feature Stories, Master Comics #7 & Wow Comics #1, 1936)
Dell Publishing Co.: No. 299, Oct, 1950 - No. 850, Oct, 1957 (All Painted-c)

Four Color 299(#1)-Buck Jones & his horse Silver-B begin; painted back-c
begins, ends #5 11.70 35.00 140.00
2(4-6/51) 6.30 19.00 75.00
3-8(10-12/52) 5.00 15.00 60.00
Four Color 460,500,546,589 4.60 13.75 55.00
Four Color 652,733,850 3.20 9.60 35.00

BUCK ROGERS (Also see Famous Funnies, Pure Oil Comics, Salerno Carnival of Comics, 24 Pages of Comics, & Vicks Comics)
Famous Funnies: Winter, 1940-41 - No. 6, Sept, 1943

1-Sunday strip reprints by Rick Yager; begins with strip #190; Calkins-c
300.00 900.00 3000.00
2 (7/41)-Calkins-c 126.00 379.00 1200.00
3 (12/41), 4 (7/42) 108.00 324.00 1025.00
5,6: 5-Story continues with Famous Funnies No. 80; Buck Rogers, Sky Roads.
6-Reprints of 1939 dailies; contains B.R. story "Crater of Doom" (2 pgs.)
by Calkins not-r from Famous Funnies 95.00 285.00 900.00

BUCK ROGERS
Toby Press: No. 100, Jan, 1951 - No. 9, May-June, 1951

100(#7)-All strip-r begin 28.00 84.00 225.00
101(#8), 9-All Anderson-a(1947-49-r/dailies) 22.00 66.00 175.00

BUCK ROGERS (...in the 25th Century No. 5 on) (TV)
Gold Key/Whitman No. 7 on: Oct, 1964; No. 2, July, 1979 - No. 16, May, 1982 (No #10)

1(10128-410, 12¢)-1st S.A. app. Buck Rogers & 1st new B. R. in comics
since 1933 giveaway; painted-c; back-c pin-up 6.70 20.00 80.00
2(7/79)-6: 3,4,6-Movie adaptation; painted-c 1.00 2.80 7.00
7,11 (Whitman) 1.00 3.00 8.00
8,9 (prepack)(scarce) 2.00 6.00 18.00
12-16 5.00
Giant Movie Edition 11296(64pp, Whitman, $1.50), reprints GK #2-4 minus
cover; tabloid size; photo-c (See Marvel Treasury) 2.30 7.00 20.00
Giant Movie Edition 02489(Western/Marvel, $1.50), reprints GK #2-4 minus

Buffalo Bill #2 © YM

Buffy the Vampire Slayer #4 © 20th Century Fox

Bugs Bunny #62 © WB

cover 2.00 6.00 18.00
NOTE: ***Bolle** a-2p,3p, Movie Ed.(p). **McWilliams** a-2i,3i, 5-11, Movie Ed.(i). Painted c-1-9,11-13.*

BUCK ROGERS (Comics Module)
TSR, Inc.: 1990 - No. 10, 1991 ($2.95, 44 pgs.)

1-10 (1990): 1-Begin origin in 3 parts. 2-Indicia says #1. 2,3-Black Barney back-up story. 4-All Black Barney issue; B. B.-c. 5-Indicia says #6; Black Barney-c & lead story; Buck Rogers back-up story. 10-Flip book (72pgs.) 3.00

BUCKSKIN (TV)
Dell Publishing Co.: No. 1011, July, 1959 - No. 1107, June-Aug, 1960

	GD2.0	FN6.0	NM9.4
Four Color 1011 (#1)-Photo-c	6.70	20.00	80.00
Four Color 1107-Photo-c	5.85	17.50	70.00

BUCKY O'HARE (Funny Animal)
Continuity Comics: 1988 ($5.95, graphic novel)

	GD2.0	FN6.0	NM9.4
1-Michael Golden-c/a(r); r/serial-Echo of Futurepast #1-6.		2.40	6.00
Deluxe Hardcover ($40, 52pg, 8x11")			40.00

BUCKY O'HARE
Continuity Comics: Jan, 1991 - No. 5, 1991 ($2.00)

1-6: 1-Michael Golden-c/a 2.50

BUDDIES IN THE U.S. ARMY
Avon Periodicals: Nov, 1952 - No. 2, 1953

	GD2.0	FN6.0	NM9.4
1-Lawrence-c	12.00	36.00	95.00
2-Mort Lawrence-c/a	8.65	26.00	60.00

BUFFALO BEE (TV)
Dell Publishing Co.: No. 957, Nov, 1958 - No. 1061, Dec-Feb, 1959-60

	GD2.0	FN6.0	NM9.4
Four Color 957 (#1)	9.00	27.00	110.00
Four Color 1002 (8-10/59), 1061	6.30	19.00	75.00

BUFFALO BILL (See Frontier Fighters, Super Western Comics & Western Action Thrillers)
Youthful Magazines: No. 2, Oct, 1950 - No. 9, Dec, 1951

	GD2.0	FN6.0	NM9.4
2-Annie Oakley story	12.00	36.00	95.00
3-9: 2-4-Walter Johnson-c/a. 9-Wildey-a	8.65	26.00	60.00

BUFFALO BILL CODY (See Cody of the Pony Express)

BUFFALO BILL, JR. (TV) (See Western Roundup)
Dell/Gold Key: Jan, 1956 - No. 13, Aug-Oct, 1959; 1965 (All photo-c)

	GD2.0	FN6.0	NM9.4
Four Color 673 (#1)	6.30	19.00	75.00
Four Color 742,766,798,828,856(11/57)	4.55	13.65	50.00
7(2-4/58)-13	3.65	11.00	40.00
1(6/65, Gold Key)-Photo-c(r/F.C. #798); photo-b/c	3.65	11.00	40.00

BUFFALO BILL PICTURE STORIES
Street & Smith Publications: June-July, 1949 - No. 2, Aug-Sept, 1949

	GD2.0	FN6.0	NM9.4
1,2-Wildey, Powell-a in each	13.00	39.00	105.00

BUFFY THE VAMPIRE SLAYER (Based on the TV series)
Dark Horse Comics: 1998 - Present ($2.95)

	NM9.4
1-Bennett-a/Watson-s; Art Adams-c	5.00
1-Variant photo-c	5.00
1-Gold foil logo Art Adams-c	15.00
1-Gold foil logo photo-c	20.00
2-15-Regular and photo-c. 4-7-Gomez-a. 5,8-Green-c	4.00
16-26	2.95
Annual '99 ($4.95)-Two stories and pin-ups	4.95
Wizard #1/2	12.00

BUFFY THE VAMPIRE SLAYER: ANGEL
Dark Horse Comics: May, 1999 - No. 3, July, 1999 ($2.95, limited series)

1-3-Gomez-a; Matsuda-c & photo-c for each 3.00

BUFFY THE VAMPIRE SLAYER: GILES
Dark Horse Comics: Oct, 2000 ($2.95, one-shot)

1Powell & photo-c 3.00

BUFFY THE VAMPIRE SLAYER: SPIKE AND DRU
Dark Horse Comics: Apr, 1999; No. 2, Oct, 1999 ($2.95)

1,2-Photo-c 3.00

BUFFY THE VAMPIRE SLAYER: THE ORIGIN (Adapts movie screenplay)
Dark Horse Comics: Jan, 1999 - No. 3, Mar, 1999 ($2.95, limited series)

1-3-Brereton-s/Bennett-a; reg & photo-c for each 3.

BUG
Marvel Comics: Mar, 1997 ($2.99, one-shot)

1-Micronauts character 3.

BUGALOOS (TV)
Charlton Comics: Sept, 1971 - No. 4, Feb, 1972

	GD2.0	FN6.0	NM9.4
1	3.20	9.60	35.
2-4	2.40	7.35	22.

NOTE: *No. 3(1/72) went on sale late in 1972 (after No. 4) with the 1/73 issues.*

BUGBOY
Image Comics: June, 1998 ($3.95, B&W, one-shot)

1-Mark Lewis-s/a 4.

BUGHOUSE (Satire)
Ajax/Farrell (Excellent Publ.): Mar-Apr, 1954 - No. 4, Sept-Oct, 1954

	GD2.0	FN6.0	NM9.4
V1#1	19.00	56.00	150.
2-4	11.00	33.00	90.

BUGS BUNNY (See The Best of..., Camp Comics, Comic Album #2, 6, 10, 14, Dell Giant #28, 32, 46, Dynabrite, Golden Comics Digest #1, 3, 5, 6, 8, 10, 14, 15, 17, 21, 26, 30, 34, 39, 47, Kite Fun Book, Large Feature Comic #8, Looney Tunes and Merry Melodies, March of Comics #44, 59, 75, 83, 97, 115, 132, 149, 160, 179, 188, 201, 220, 231, 245, 259, 273, 287, 301, 315, 329, 343, 363, 367, 380, 392, 403, 415, 428, 440, 452, 464, 476, 487, Porky Pig, Puffed Wheat, Story Hour Series #802, Super Book #14, 26 and Whitman Comic Books)

BUGS BUNNY (See Dell Giants for annuals)
Dell Publishing Co./Gold Key No. 86-218/Whitman No. 219 on: 1942 - No. 245, 1983

	GD2.0	FN6.0	NM9.4
Large Feature Comic 8(1942)-(Rarely found in fine-mint condition)	117.00	350.00	1400.
Four Color 33 ('43)	112.00	337.00	1350.
Four Color 51	35.00	106.00	425.
Four Color 88	20.00	61.00	245.
Four Color 123('46),142,164	15.50	46.00	185.
Four Color 187,200,217,233	10.50	31.00	125.
Four Color 250-Used in **SOTI**, pg. 309	11.00	33.00	135.
Four Color 266,274,281,289,298('50)	8.35	25.00	100.
Four Color 307,317(#1),327(#2),338,347,355,366,376,393	7.00	21.00	85.
Four Color 407,420,432(10/52)	5.85	17.50	70.
Four Color 498(9/53),585(9/54), 647(9/55)	4.60	13.75	55.
Four Color 724(9/56),838(9/57),1064(12/59)	4.10	12.30	45.
28(12-1/52-53)-30	4.10	12.30	45.
31-50	3.20	9.60	35.
51-85(7-9/62)	2.50	7.50	24.
86(10/62)-88-Bugs Bunny's Showtime-(25¢, 80pgs.)	5.90	17.75	65.
89-99	2.00	6.00	18.
100	2.40	7.35	22.
101-118: 118-Last 12¢ issue	1.75	5.25	14.
119-140	1.25	3.75	10.
141-170	1.00	3.00	8.
171-218			5.
219,220,225-237: 229-Swipe of Barks story/WDC&S #223		2.40	6.
221(9/80),222(11/80)-Pre-pack? (Scarce)	1.75	5.25	14.
223 (1/81),224 (3/81)-Low distr.	1.10	3.30	9.
238-245 (#90070 on-c, nd, nd code; pre-pack?	1.50	4.50	12.

NOTE: *Reprints-100, 102, 104, 123, 143, 144, 147, 167, 173, 175-177, 179-185, 187, 190.*

	GD2.0	FN6.0	NM9.4
...Comic-Go-Round 11196-(224 pgs.)($1.95)(Golden Press, 1979)	2.50	7.50	25.
...Winter Fun 1(12/67-Gold Key)-Giant	3.65	11.00	40.

BUGS BUNNY
DC Comics: June, 1990 - No. 3, Aug, 1990 ($1.00, limited series)

1-3: Daffy Duck, Elmer Fudd, others app. 2.

BUGS BUNNY (...Monthly on-c)
DC Comics: 1993 - No. 3, 1994? ($1.95)

1-3-Bugs, Porky Pig, Daffy, Road Runner 3.

Bulletman #11 © FAW

Bulls-Eye #2 © PRIZE

Buster Crabbe #8 © FF

GD2.0 FN6.0 NM9.4

IGS BUNNY & PORKY PIG
ıld Key: Sept, 1965 (Paper-c, giant, 100 pgs.)
(30025-509) 7.50 22.50 90.00

IGS BUNNY'S ALBUM (See Bugs Bunny, Four Color No. 498,585,647,724)

IGS BUNNY LIFE STORY ALBUM (See Bugs Bunny, Four Color No. 838)

JGS BUNNY MERRY CHRISTMAS (See Bugs Bunny, Four Color No. 1064)

ILDING, THE
tchen Sink Press: 1987; 2000 (8 1/2" x 11" sepia toned graphic novel)
-Will Eisner-s/c/a 10.00
-(DC Comics, 9/00, $9.95) reprints 1987 edition 10.00

JLLET CROW, FOWL OF FORTUNE
lipse Comics: Mar, 1987 - No. 2, Apr, 1987 ($2.00, B&W, limited series)
,2-The Comic Reader-r & new-a 2.00

JLLETMAN (See Fawcett Miniatures, Master Comics, Mighty Midget Comics, ckel Comics & XMas Comics)
wcett Publications: Sum, 1941 - #12, 2/12/43; #14, Spr, 1946 - #16, Fall, 46 (No #13)
-Silver metallic-c 333.00 1000.00 3500.00
-Raboy-c 147.00 442.00 1400.00
,5-Raboy-c each 105.00 316.00 1000.00
92.00 276.00 875.00
-10: 7-Ghost Stories told by night watchman of cemetery begins; Eisnerish-a; hidden message "Chic Stone is a jerk" 76.00 229.00 725.00
,12,14-16 (nn 13): 12-Robot-c 58.00 174.00 550.00
TE: *Mac Raboy c-1-3, 5, 6, 10. "Bulletman the Flying Detective" on cover #8 on.*

JLLETPROOF MONK
age Comics (Flypaper Press): 1998 - No. 3, 1999 ($2.95, limited series)
-3-Oeming-a 3.00

JLLETS AND BRACELETS (Also see Marvel Versus DC #3 & DC Versus arvel #4)
arvel Comics (Amalgam): Apr, 1996 ($1.95)
-John Ostrander script & Gary Frank-c/a 2.00

JLLS-EYE (Cody of The Pony Express No. 8 on)
ainline No. 1-5/Charlton No. 6,7: 7-8/54-No. 5, 3-4/55; No. 6, 6/55; No. 7, 8/55
-S&K-c, 2 pgs.-a 53.00 160.00 480.00
-S&K-c/a 44.00 133.00 400.00
-5-S&K-c/a(2 each). 4-Last pre-code issue (1-2/55). 5-Censored issue with tomahawks removed in battle scene 39.00 116.00 310.00
-S&K-c/a 31.00 94.00 250.00
-S&K-c/a(3) 39.00 116.00 310.00

JLLS-EYE COMICS (Formerly Komik Pages #10; becomes Kayo #12)
arry 'A' Chesler: No. 11, 1944
-Origin K-9, Green Knight's sidekick, Lance; The Green Knight, Lady Satan, Yankee Doodle Jones app. 40.00 120.00 350.00

JLLWHIP GRIFFIN (See Movie Comics)

JLLWINKLE (...and Rocky No. 20 on; See March of Comics #233 and Rocky Bullwinkle)(TV) (Jay Ward)
ell/Gold Key: 3-5/62 - #11, 4/74; #12, 6/76 - #19, 3/78; #20, 4/79 - #25, 2/80
ur Color 1270 (3-5/62) 18.75 56.00 225.00
-090-209 (Dell, 7-9/62) 15.00 45.00 175.00
(11/62, Gold Key) 13.35 40.00 160.00
(2/63) 8.00 24.00 95.00
(4/72)-11(4/74-Gold Key) 4.55 13.65 50.00
2-14: 12(6/76)-Reprints. 13(9/76), 14-New stories 2.30 7.00 20.00
5-25 1.50 4.50 12.00
other Moose Nursery Pomes 01-530-207 (5-7/62, Dell) 18.35 55.00 220.00
TE: *Reprints: 6, 7, 20-24.*

JLLWINKLE (...& Rocky No. 2 on)(TV)
harlton Comics: July, 1970 - No. 7, July, 1971
5.00 15.00 55.00
-7 4.10 12.30 45.00

GD2.0 FN6.0 NM9.4

BULLWINKLE AND ROCKY
Star Comics/Marvel Comics No. 3 on: Nov, 1987 - No. 9, Mar, 1989
1-9: Boris & Natasha in all. 3,5,8-Dudley Do-Right app. 4-Reagan-c 4.00

BUMMER
Fantagraphics Books: June, 1995 ($3.50, B&W, mature)
1 3.50

BUNNY (Also see Harvey Pop Comics)
Harvey Publications: Dec, 1966 - No. 20, Dec, 1971; No. 21, Nov, 1976
1-68 pg. Giants begin 5.90 17.75 65.00
2-10 3.20 9.60 35.00
11-18: 18-Last 68 pg. Giant 3.00 9.00 30.00
19-21-52 pg. Giants: 21-Fruitman app. 2.50 7.50 25.00

BURKE'S LAW (TV)
Dell Publ.: 1-3/64; No. 2, 5-7/64; No. 3, 3-5/65 (All have Gene Barry photo-c)
1-Photo-c 4.55 13.65 50.00
2,3-Photo-c 3.45 10.35 38.00

BURNING ROMANCES (See Fox Giants)

BUSTER BEAR
Quality Comics Group (Arnold Publ.): Dec, 1953 - No. 10, June, 1955
1-Funny animal 9.30 28.00 65.00
2 5.00 15.00 32.00
3-10 4.15 12.50 25.00
I.W. Reprint #9,10 (Super on inside) 2.40 6.00 12.00

BUSTER BROWN COMICS (See Promotional Comics section)

BUSTER BUNNY
Standard Comics(Animated Cartoons)/Pines: Nov, 1949 - No. 16, Oct, 1953
1-Frazetta 1 pg. text illo. 9.30 28.00 65.00
2 5.00 15.00 32.00
3-16: 15-Racist-c 4.00 12.00 24.00

BUSTER CRABBE (TV)
Famous Funnies Publ.: Nov, 1951 - No. 12, 1953
1-1st app.(?) Frazetta anti-drug ad; text story about Buster Crabbe & Billy the Kid 36.00 108.00 285.00
2-Williamson/Evans-c; text story about Wild Bill Hickok & Pecos Bill 38.00 114.00 300.00
3-Williamson/Evans-c/a 40.00 120.00 320.00
4-Frazetta-c/a, 1pg.; bondage-c 47.00 140.00 420.00
5-Frazetta-c; Williamson/Krenkel/Orlando-a, 11pgs. (per Mr. Williamson) 116.00 348.00 1100.00
6,8 18.00 53.00 140.00
7-Frazetta one pg. ad 19.00 56.00 150.00
9-One pg. Frazetta Boy Scouts ad (1st?) 16.00 49.00 130.00
10-12 11.00 33.00 90.00
NOTE: Eastern Color sold 3 dozen each NM file copies of #s 9-12 a few years ago.

BUSTER CRABBE (The Amazing Adventures of...)(Movie star)
Lev Gleason Publications: Dec, 1953 - No. 4, June, 1954
1,4: 1-Photo-c. 4-Flash Gordon-c 21.00 64.00 170.00
2,3-Toth-a 20.00 60.00 160.00

BUTCH CASSIDY
Skywald Comics: June, 1971 - No. 3, Oct, 1971 (52 pgs.)
1-Red Mask reprint, retitled Maverick; Bolle-a; Sutton-a 2.00 6.00 16.00
2,3: 2-Whip Wilson-r. 3-Dead Canyon Days reprint/Crack Western No. 63; Sundance Kid app.; Crandall-a 1.50 4.50 12.00

BUTCH CASSIDY (...& the Wild Bunch)
Avon Periodicals: 1951
1-Kinstler-c/a 18.00 53.00 140.00
NOTE: *Reinman story; Issue number on inside spine.*

BUTCH CASSIDY (See Fun-In No. 11 & Western Adventure Comics)

BUTCHER, THE (Also see Brave and the Bold, 2nd Series))
DC Comics: May, 1990 - No. 5, Sept, 1990 ($1.50, mature)
1-5: 1-No indicia inside 2.00

Buz Sawyer #3 © STD

Cable #71 © MAR

Cadillacs & Dinosaurs #2 © MAR

BUTCHER KNIGHT
Image Comics (Top Cow): 2000
Preview (B&W, 16 pgs.) Dwayne Turner-c/a 1.00

BUZ SAWYER (Sweeney No. 4 on)
Standard Comics: June, 1948 - No. 3, 1949
1-Roy Crane-a 22.00 66.00 175.00
2-Intro his pal Sweeney 12.50 37.50 100.00
3 10.00 30.00 80.00

BUZ SAWYER'S PAL, ROSCOE SWEENEY (See Sweeney)

BUZZ, THE (Also see Spider-Girl)
Marvel Comics: July, 2000 - No. 3, Sept, 2000 ($2.99, limited series)
1-3-Buscema-a/DeFalco & Frenz-s 3.00

BUZZ BUZZ COMICS MAGAZINE
Horse Press: May, 1996 ($4.95, B&W, over-sized magazine)
1-Paul Pope-c/a/scripts; Moebius-a 5.00

BUZZY (See All Funny Comics)
National Periodical Publications/Detective Comics: Winter, 1944-45 - No. 75, 1-2/57; No. 76, 10/57; No. 77, 10/58
1 (52 pgs. begin); "America's favorite teenster" 28.00 84.00 225.00
2 (Spr, 1945) 13.00 39.00 105.00
3-5 10.00 30.00 70.00
6-10 6.40 19.25 45.00
11-20 5.50 16.50 38.00
21-30 4.65 14.00 28.00
31,35-38 4.00 12.00 24.00
32-34,39-Last 52 pgs. Scribbly story by Mayer in each (these four stories were done for Scribbly #14 which was delayed for a year) 5.00 15.00 30.00
40-77: 62-Last precode (2/55) 4.00 11.00 22.00

BUZZY THE CROW (See Harvey Comics Hits #60 & 62, Harvey Hits #18 & Paramount Animated Comics #1)

BY BIZARRE HANDS
Dark Horse Comics: Apr, 1994 - No. 3, June, 1994 ($2.50, B&W, mature)
1-3: Lansdale stories 2.50

CABBOT: BLOODHUNTER (Also see Bloodstrike & Bloodstrike: Assassin)
Maximum Press: Jan, 1997 ($2.50, one-shot)
1-Rick Veitch-a/script; Platt-c; Thor, Chapel & Prophet cameos 2.50

CABLE (See Ghost Rider &..., & New Mutants #87)
Marvel Comics: May, 1993 - Present ($3.50/$1.95/$1.50/$1.99/$2.25)
1-($3.50, 52 pgs.)-Gold foil & embossed-c; Thibert a-1-4p; c-1-3 3.50
2-15: 3-Extra 16 pg. X-Men/Avengers ann. preview. 4-Liefeld-a assist; last Thibert-a(p). 6-8-Reveals that Baby Nathan is Cable; gives background on Stryfe. 9-Omega Red-c/story. 11-Bound-in trading card sheet 2.50
16-Newsstand edition 2.50
16-Enhanced edition 5.00
17-20-($1.95)-Deluxe edition, 20-w/bound in '95 Fleer Ultra cards 3.00
17-20-($1.50)-Standard edition 2.50
21-24, 26-44, -1(7/97): 21-Begin $1.95-c; return from Age of Apocalyse. 24-Grizzly dies. 28-vs. Sugarman; Mr. Sinister app. 30-X-Man-c/app.; Exodus app. 31-vs. X-Man. 32-Post app. 33-Post-c/app; Mandarin app (flashback); includes "Onslaught Update". 34-Onslaught x-over; Hulk-c/app.; Apocalypse app (cont'd in Hulk #444). 35-Onslaught x-over; Apocalypse vs. Cable. 36-w/card insert. 38-Weapon X-c/app; Psycho Man & Micronauts app. 40-Scott Clark-a(p). 41-Bishop-c/app. 2.50
25 ($3.95)-Foil gatefold-c 4.00
45-49,51-74: 45-Operation Zero Tolerance. 51-1st Casey-s. 54-Black Panther. 55-Domino-c/app. 62-Nick Fury-c/app.63-Stryfe-c/app. 67,68-Avengers-c/app. 71,73-Liefeld-a 2.50
50-($2.99) Double sized w/wraparound-c 3.00
75 -($2.99) Liefeld-c/a; Apocalypse: The Twelve x-over 3.00
76-79: 76-Apocalypse: The Twelve x-over 2.00
80-88: 80-Begin $2.25-c. 87-Mystique-c/app. 2.25
.../Machine Man '98 Annual ($2.99) Wraparound-c 3.00
.../X-Force '96 Annual ($2.95) Wraparound-c 3.00
...'99 Annual ($3.50) vs. Sinister; computer photo-c 3.5
...Second Genesis 1 (9/99, $3.99) r/New Mutants #99, 100 and X-Force #1; Liefeld-c 4.0

CABLE - BLOOD AND METAL (Also see New Mutants #87 & X-Force #8)
Marvel Comics: Oct, 1992 - No. 2, Nov, 1992 ($2.50, limited series, 52 pgs.)
1-Fabian Nicieza scripts; John Romita, Jr.-c/a in both; Cable vs. Stryfe; 2nd app. of The Wild Pack (becomes The Six Pack); wraparound-c. 3.5
2-Prelude to X-Cutioner's Song 2.5

CADET GRAY OF WEST POINT (See Dell Giants)

CADILLACS & DINOSAURS (TV)
Marvel Comics (Epic Comics): Nov, 1990 - No. 6, Apr, 1991 ($2.50, limited series, coated paper)
1-6: r/Xenozoic Tales in color w/new-c 3.0
...In 3-D #1 (7/92, $3.95, Kitchen Sink)-With glasses 5.5

CADILLACS AND DINOSAURS (TV)
Topps Comics: V2#1, Feb, 1994 - V2#9, 1995 ($2.50, limited series)
V2#1-($2.95)-Collector's edition w/Stout-c & bound-in poster; Buckler-a; foil stamped logo; Giordano-a in all 2.40 6.0
V2#1-9: 1-Newsstand edition w/Giordano-c. 2,3-Collector's editions w/Stout-c & posters. 2,3-Newsstand ed. w/Giordano-c; w/o posters. 4-6-Collectors & Newsstand editions; Kieth-c. 7-9-Linsner-c 3.0

CAFFEINE
Slave Labor Graphics: Jan, 1996 - No. 10, 1999 ($2.95/$3.95, B&W)
1-9 3.0
10-($3.95) 3.9

CAGE (Also see Hero for Hire, Power Man & Punisher)
Marvel Comics: Apr, 1992 - No. 20, Nov, 1993 ($1.25)
1,3,10,12: 3-Punisher-c & minor app. 10-Rhino & Hulk-c/story. 12-(52 pgs.)-Iron Fist app. 3.0
2,4-9,11,13-20: 9-Rhino-c/story; Hulk cameo 2.0

CAGED HEAT 3000 (Movie)
Roger Corman's Cosmic Comics: Nov, 1995 - No. 3, Jan, 1996 ($2.50)
1-3: Adaptation of film 2.5

CAGES
Tundra Publ.: 1991 - No. 10, May, 1996 ($3.50/$3.95/$4.95, limited series)
1-Dave McKean-c/a in all 1.50 4.50 12.0
2-Misprint exists 1.00 3.00 8.0
3-9: 5-$3.95-c begins 4.0
10-($4.95) 5.0

CAIN'S HUNDRED (TV)
Dell Publishing Co.: May-July, 1962 - No. 2, Sept-Nov, 1962
nn(01-094-207) 2.60 7.80 26.0
2 2.00 6.00 18.0

CAIN/VAMPIRELLA FLIP BOOK
Harris Comics: Oct, 1994 ($6.95, one-shot, squarebound)
nn-contains Cain #3 & #4; flip book is r/Vampirella story from 1993 Creepy Fearbook. 1.05 3.15 8.5

CALIBER PRESENTS
Caliber Press: Jan, 1989 - No. 24, 1991 ($1.95/$2.50, B&W, 52 pgs.)
1-Anthology; 1st app. The Crow; Tim Vigil-c/a 4.50 13.65 50.0
2-Deadworld story; Tim Vigil-a 1.00 2.80 7.0
3-24: 15-24 ($3.50, 68 pgs.) 3.5

CALIBER PRESENTS: CINDERELLA ON FIRE
Caliber Press: 1994 ($2.95, B&W, mature)
1 3.0

CALIBER SPOTLIGHT
Caliber Press: May, 1995 ($2.95, B&W)
1-Kabuki app 3.5

CALIBRATIONS
Caliber: 1996 - No. 5 (99¢, anthology)

Calling All Boys #1 © PMI

Campus Loves #4 © QUA

Candy Comics #3 © WHW

GD2.0 FN6.0 NM9.4

1-5: 1-Jill Thompson-c/a. 1,2-Atmospherics by Warren Ellis 2.50

CALIFORNIA GIRLS
Eclipse Comics: June, 1987 - No. 8, May, 1988 ($2.00, 40 pgs, B&W)

1-8: All contain color paper dolls 2.50

CALLING ALL BOYS (Tex Granger No. 18 on)
Parents' Magazine Institute: Jan, 1946 - No. 17, May, 1948 (Photo c-1-5,7,8)

1 11.00 33.00 90.00
2-Contains Roy Rogers article 6.00 18.00 42.00
3-7,9,11,14-17: 6-Painted-c. 11-Rin Tin Tin photo on-c; Tex Granger begins. 14-J. Edgar Hoover photo on-c. 15-Tex Granger-c begin 4.65 14.00 28.00
8-Milton Caniff story 7.00 21.00 48.00
10-Gary Cooper photo on-c 6.40 19.25 45.00
12-Bob Hope photo on-c 10.00 30.00 75.00
13-Bing Crosby photo on-c 9.30 28.00 65.00

CALLING ALL GIRLS
Parents' Magazine Institute: Sept, 1941 - No. 89, Sept, 1949 (Part magazine, part comic)

1 14.00 41.00 110.00
2-Photo-c 7.85 23.50 55.00
3-Shirley Temple photo-c 10.00 30.00 70.00
4-10: 4,5,7,9-Photo-c. 9-Flag-c 5.00 15.00 35.00
11-Tina Thayer photo-c; Mickey Rooney photo-b/c; B&W photo inside of Gary Cooper as Lou Gehrig in "Pride of Yankees" 5.70 17.00 40.00
12-20 4.65 14.00 28.00
21-39,41-43(10-11/45)-Last issue with comics 4.00 11.00 22.00
40-Liz Taylor photo-c 12.00 36.00 95.00
44-51(7/46)-Last comic book size issue 4.00 10.00 20.00
52-89 3.60 9.00 18.00
NOTE: ***Jack Sparling*** *art in many issues; becomes a girls' magazine "Senior Prom" with #90.*

CALLING ALL KIDS (Also see True Comics)
Parents' Magazine Institute: Dec-Jan, 1945-46 - No. 26, Aug, 1949

1-Funny animal 10.50 32.00 85.00
2 5.70 17.00 40.00
3-10 4.15 12.50 25.00
11-26 4.00 10.00 20.00

CALVIN (See Li'l Kids)

CALVIN & THE COLONEL (TV)
Dell Publishing Co.: No. 1354, Apr-June, 1962 - No. 2, July-Sept, 1962

Four Color 1354(#1) 7.50 22.50 90.00
2 4.60 13.75 55.00

CAMBION
Slave Labor Graphics: Dec, 1995 - No. 2, Feb, 1996 ($2.95, B&W)

1,2 3.00

CAMELOT 3000
DC Comics: Dec, 1982 - No. 11, July, 1984; No. 12, Apr, 1985 (Direct sales, maxi series, Mando paper)

1-12: 1-Mike Barr scripts & Brian Bolland-c/a begin. 5-Intro Knights of New Camelot 3.00
TPB (1988, $12.95) r/#1-12 15.00
NOTE: ***Austin*** *a-7i-12i.* ***Bolland*** *a-1-12p; c-1-12.*

CAMERA COMICS
U.S. Camera Publishing Corp./ME: July, 1944 - No. 9, Summer, 1946

nn (7/44) 24.00 71.00 190.00
nn (9/44) 19.00 58.00 155.00
1(10/44)-The Grey Comet 19.00 58.00 155.00
2 13.00 39.00 105.00
3-Nazi WW II-c; photos 12.00 36.00 95.00
4-9: All half photos 11.00 33.00 90.00

CAMP CANDY (TV)
Marvel Comics: May, 1990 - No. 6, Oct, 1990 ($1.00, limited series)

1-6: Post-c/a(p); featuring John Candy 3.00

CAMP COMICS

GD2.0 FN6.0 NM9.4

Dell Publishing Co.: Feb, 1942 - No. 3, April, 1942 (All have photo-c)

1- "Seaman Sy Wheeler" by Kelly, 7 pgs.; Bugs Bunny app.; Mark Twain adaptation 63.00 189.00 600.00
2-Kelly-a, 12 pgs.; Bugs Bunny app.; classic-c 58.00 174.00 550.00
3-(Scarce)-Dave Berg & Walt Kelly-a 55.00 165.00 525.00

CAMP RUNAMUCK (TV)
Dell Publishing Co.: Apr, 1966

1-Photo-c 3.00 9.00 32.00

CAMPUS LOVES
Quality Comics Group (Comic Magazines): Dec, 1949 - No. 5, Aug, 1950

1-Ward-c/a (9 pgs.) 31.00 94.00 250.00
2-Ward-c/a 24.00 71.00 190.00
3-5: 5-Spanking panels (2) 12.00 36.00 95.00
NOTE: ***Gustavson*** *a-1-5. Photo c-3-5.*

CAMPUS ROMANCE (...Romances on cover)
Avon Periodicals/Realistic: Sept-Oct, 1949 - No. 3, Feb-Mar, 1950

1-Walter Johnson-a; c-/Avon paperback #348 22.00 66.00 175.00
2-Grandenetti-a; c-/Avon paperback #151; spanking panel 16.00 49.00 130.00
3-c-/Avon paperback #201 16.00 49.00 130.00
Realistic reprint 7.15 21.50 50.00

CANADA DRY PREMIUMS (See Swamp Fox, The & Terry & The Pirates)

CANDID TALES (Also see Bold Stories & It Rhymes With Lust)
Kirby Publ. Co.: April, 1950; June, 1950 (Digest size) (144 pgs.) (Full color)

nn-(Scarce) Contains Wood female pirate story, 15 pgs., and 14 pgs. in June issue; Powell-a 95.00 285.00 900.00
NOTE: *Another version exists with Dr. Kilmore by Wood; no female pirate story.*

CANDY
William H. Wise & Co.: Fall, 1944 - No. 3, Spring, 1945

1-Two Scoop Scuttle stories by Wolverton 39.00 116.00 310.00
2,3-Scoop Scuttle by Wolverton, 2-4 pgs. 28.00 84.00 225.00

CANDY (Teen-age)(Also see Police Comics #37)
Quality Comics Group (Comic Magazines): Autumn, 1947 - No. 64, Jul, 1956

1-Gustavson-a 22.00 66.00 175.00
2-Gustavson-a 11.00 33.00 90.00
3-10 7.85 23.50 55.00
11-30 5.00 15.00 35.00
31-63 5.00 15.00 32.00
64-Ward-c(p)? 5.00 15.00 32.00
Super Reprint No. 2,10,12,16,17,18('63- '64):17-Candy #12 1.85 5.50 15.00
NOTE: ***Jack Cole*** *1-2 pg. art in many issues.*

CANNON (See Heroes, Inc. Presents Cannon)

CANNONBALL COMICS
Rural Home Publishing Co.: Feb, 1945 - No. 2, Mar, 1945

1-The Crash Kid, Thunderbrand, The Captive Prince & Crime Crusader begin; skull-c 79.00 237.00 750.00
2-Devil-c 63.00 189.00 600.00

CANTEEN KATE (See All Picture All True Love Story & Fightin' Marines)
St. John Publishing Co.: June, 1952 - No. 3, Nov, 1952

1-Matt Baker-c/a 55.00 165.00 500.00
2-Matt Baker-c/a 42.00 125.00 375.00
3-(Rare)-Used in **POP**, pg. 75; Baker-c/a 50.00 150.00 450.00

CAP'N QUICK & A FOOZLE (Also see Eclipse Mag. & Monthly)
Eclipse Comics: July, 1984 - No. 3, Nov, 1985 ($1.50, color, Baxter paper)

1-3-Rogers-c/a 3.00

CAPTAIN ACTION (Toy)
National Periodical Publications: Oct-Nov, 1968 - No. 5, June-July, 1969 (Based on Ideal toy)

1-Origin; Wood-a; Superman-c app. 10.00 30.00 110.00
2,3,5-Kane/Wood-a 6.35 19.00 70.00
4 4.55 13.65 50.00

Captain Aero Comics V3 #11 © HOKE

Captain America #110 © MAR

Captain America #200 © MAR

GD2.0 FN6.0 NM9.

CAPTAIN AERO COMICS (Samson No. 1-6; also see Veri Best Sure Fire &Veri Best Sure Shot Comics)
Holyoke Publishing Co.: V1#7(#1), Dec, 1941 - V2#4(#10), Jan, 1943; V3#9(#11), Sept, 1943 -V4#3(#17), Oct, 1944; #21, Dec, 1944 - #26, Aug, 1946 (No #18-20)

V1#7(#1)-Flag-Man & Solar, Master of Magic, Captain Aero, Cap Stone, Adventurer begin 158.00 474.00 1500.00
8-10: 8(#2)-Pals of Freedom app. 9(#3)-Alias X begins; Pals of Freedom app. 10(#4)-Origin The Gargoyle; Kubert-a 76.00 229.00 725.00
11,12(#5,6)-Kubert-a; Miss Victory in #6 63.00 189.00 600.00
V2#1,2(#7,8): 8-Origin The Red Cross; Miss Victory app.; Brodsky-c(i) 40.00 120.00 360.00
3(#9)-Miss Victory app. 36.00 107.00 285.00
4(#10)-Miss Victory app. 28.00 84.00 225.00
V3#9 - V3#13(#11-15): 11,15-Miss Victory app. 23.00 69.00 185.00
V4#2(#16) 22.00 66.00 175.00
V4#3(#17), 21-25-L. B. Cole covers. 22-Intro/origin Mighty Mite. 42.00 125.00 375.00
26-L. B. Cole S/F-c; Palais-a(2) (scarce) 84.00 253.00 800.00
NOTE: ***L.B. Cole** c-17. **Hollingsworth** a-23. **Infantino** a-23, 26. **Schomburg** c-15, 16.*

CAPTAIN AMERICA (See Adventures of..., All-Select, All Winners, Aurora, Avengers #4, Blood and Glory, Captain Britain 16-20, Giant-Size..., The Invaders, Marvel Double Feature, Marvel Fanfare, Marvel Mystery, Marvel Super-Action, Marvel Super Heroes V2#3, Marvel Team-Up, Marvel Treasury Special, Power Record Comics, USA Comics, Young Allies & Young Men)

CAPTAIN AMERICA (Formerly Tales of Suspense #1-99) (Captain America and the Falcon #134-223 & Steve Rogers: Captain America #444-454 appears on cover only)
Marvel Comics Group: No. 100, Apr, 1968 - No. 454, Aug, 1996

100-Flashback on Cap's revival with Avengers & Sub-Mariner; story continued from Tales of Suspense #99; Kirby-c/a begins 33.00 100.00 400.00
101-The Sleeper-c/story; Red Skull app. 5.90 17.75 65.00
102-108: 102-Sleeper-c/s. 103,104-Red Skull-c/sty 3.65 11.00 40.00
109-Origin Capt. America retold 5.90 17.75 65.00
110,111,113-Classic Steranko-c/a: 110-Rick becomes Cap's partner; Hulk x-over; 1st app. Viper. 111-Death of Steve Rogers. 113-Cap's funeral 5.90 17.75 65.00
112-Origin retold; last Kirby-c/a 3.25 9.75 36.00
114,115: 115-Last 12¢ issue 2.50 7.50 25.00
116,118-120 2.30 7.00 20.00
117-1st app. The Falcon (9/69) 5.00 15.00 55.00
121-136,139,140: 121-Retells origin. 133-The Falcon becomes Cap's partner; origin Modok. 140-Origin Grey Gargoyle retold 1.50 4.50 12.00
137,138-Spider-Man x-over 1.85 5.50 15.00
141,142: 142-Last 15¢ issue 1.25 3.75 10.00
143-(52 pgs). 1.75 5.25 14.00
144-153: 144-New costume Falcon. 153-1st app. (cameo) Jack Monroe 1.25 3.75 10.00
156-171,176-179: 155-158-Cap's strength increased. 160-1st app. Solarr. 164-1st app. Nightshade. 176-End of Capt. America 1.00 3.00 8.00
154-1st full app. Jack Monroe (Nomad)(10/72) 1.50 4.50 12.00
155-Origin; redrawn w/Falcon added; origin Jack Monroe 1.50 4.50 12.00
172-175: X-Men x-over 1.50 4.50 12.00
180-Intro/origin of Nomad (Steve Rogers) 1.25 3.75 10.00
181-Intro/origin new Cap. 1.25 3.75 10.00
182,184-192: 186-True origin The Falcon 5.00
183-Death of new Cap; Nomad becomes Cap 1.00 2.80 7.00
193-Kirby-c/a begins 1.50 4.50 12.00
194-199-(Regular 25¢ edition)(4-7/76) 1.00 3.00 8.00
196-199-(30¢-c variants, limited distribution) 1.50 4.50 12.00
200-(Regular 25¢ edition)(8/76) 1.25 3.75 10.00
200-(30¢-c variant, limited distribution) 1.85 5.50 15.00
201-214-Kirby-c/a 1.00 2.80 7.00
215-240,242-246: 215-Retells Cap's origin. 216-r/story from Strange Tales #114. 217-1st app. Marvel Man (later Quasar). 229-Marvel Man app. 230-Battles Hulk-c/story cont'd in Hulk #232. 233-Death of Sharon Carter. 234,235-Daredevil x-over; 235(7/79)-Miller-a(p). 244,245-Miller-c. 3.00
210-214-(35¢-c variants, limited dist.)(6-10/77) 2.40 6.00
241-Punisher app.; Miller-c. 1.25 3.75 10.00
241-2nd print 2.0
247-255-Byrne-a. 255-Origin; Miller-c. 5.0
256-281,284,285,289-322,324-326,328-331: 264-Old X-Men cameo in flash-back. 265,266-Nick Fury & Spider-Man app. 267-1st app. Everyman. 269-1st Team America. 279-(3/83)-Contains Tattooz skin decals. 281-1950s Bucky returns. 284-Patriot (Jack Mace) app. 285-Death of Patriot. 298-Origin Red Skull. 328-Origin & 1st app. D-Man 2.0
282-Bucky becomes new Nomad (Jack Monroe) 4.0
282-Silver ink 2nd print ($1.75) w/original date (6/83) 2.0
283,327,333-340: 283-2nd app. Nomad. 327-Capt. Amer. battles Super Patriot. 333-Intro & origin new Captain (Super Patriot). 339-Fall of the Mutants tie-in 3.0
286-288-Deathlok app. 2.5
323-1st app. new Super Patriot (see Nick Fury) 4.0
332-Old Cap resigns 5.0
341-343,345-349 2.0
344-($1.50, 52 pgs.)-Ronald Reagan cameo 2.5
350-($1.75, 68 pgs.)-Return of Steve Rogers (original Cap) to original costume 3.0
351-382,384-396: 351-Nick Fury app. 354-1st app. U.S. Agent (6/89, see Avengers West Coast)373-Bullseye app. 375-Daredevil app. 386-U.S. Agen app. 387-389-Red Skull back-up stories. 396-Last $1.00-c. 396,397-1st app. all new Jack O'Lantern 2.0
383-($2.00, 68 pgs.)-50th anniversary issue; Red Skull story; Jim Lee-c(i) 3.0
397-399,401-424,425: 402-Begin 6 part Man-Wolf story w/Wolverine in #403-407. 405-410-New Jack O'Lantern app. in back-up story. 406-Cable & Shatterstar cameo. 407-Capwolf vs. Cable-c/story. 408-Infinity War x-over; Falcon solo back-up. 423-Vs. Namor-c/story 2.0
400-($2.25, 84 pgs.)-Flip book format w/double gatefold-c; r/Avengers #4 plus-c; contains cover pin-ups. 2.5
425-($2.95, 52 pgs.)-Embossed Foil-c ed.n; Fighting Chance Pt. 1 3.0
425-($1.75, 52 pgs.)-Regular edition 2.0
426-443,446,447,449-453: 427-Begin $1.50-c; bound-in trading card sheet. 449-Thor app. 450-"Man Without A Country" storyline begins, ends #453; Bill Clinton app; variant-c exists. 451-1st app.Cap's new costume. 452-Machinesmith app. 453-Cap gets old costume back; Bill Clinton app. 2.0
444-Mark Waid scripts & Ron Garney-c/a(p) begins, ends #454; Avengers app. 5.0
445,454: 445-Sharon Carter & Red Skull return. 3.0
448-($2.95, double-sized issue)-Waid script & Garney-c/a; Red Skull dies? 3.5
Special 1(1/71)-Origin retold 3.00 9.00 30.0
Special 2(1/72, 52 pgs.)-Colan-r/Not Brand Echh; all-r 2.00 6.00 16.0
Annual 3('76, 52 pgs.)-Kirby-c/a(new) 1.50 4.50 12.0
Annual 4('77, 34 pgs.)-Magneto-c/story 1.50 4.50 12.0
Annual 5-7: (52 pgs.)('81-'83) 4.0
Annual 8(9/86)-Wolverine-c/story 2.00 6.00 18.0
Annual 9-13('90-'94, 68 pgs.)-9-Nomad back-up. 10-Origin retold (2 pgs.). 11-Falcon solo story. 12-Bagged w/card. 13-Red Skull-c/story 3.0
...Ashcan Edition ('95, 75¢) 2.0
...: Deathlok Lives! nn(10/93, $4.95)-r/#286-288 5.0
...Drug War 1-(1994, $2.00, 52 pgs.)-New Warriors app. 2.0
...Man Without a Country(1998, $12.99, TPB)-r/#450-453 13.0
...Medusa Effect 1 (1994, $2.95, 68 pgs.)-Origin Baron Zemo 3.0
...Operation Rebirth (1996, $9.95)-r/#445-448 10.0
...Streets of Poison ($15.95)-r/#372-378 16.0
...: The Movie Special nn (5/92, $3.50, 52 pgs.)-Adapts movie; printed on coated stock; The Red Skull app. 3.5
NOTE: ***Austin** c-225i, 239i, 246i. **Buscema** a-115p, 217p; c-136p, 217, 297. **Byrne** c-223(part), 238, 239, 247p-254p, 290, 291, 313p; a-247-254p, 255, 313p, 350. **Colan** a(p)-116-137, 256, Annual 5; c(p)-116-123, 126, 129. **Everett** a-136i, 137i; c-126i. **Garney** a(p)-444-454. **Gil Kane** 145p; c-147p, 149p, 150p, 170p, 172-174, 180, 181p, 183-190p, 215, 216, 220, 221. **Kirby** a(p)-100-109, 112, 193-214, 216, Special 1, 2(layouts), Annual 3, 4; c-100-109, 112, 126p, 193-214. **Ron Lim** a(p)-366, 368-378, 380-386; c-366p, 368-378p, 379, 380-393p. **Miller** c-241p, 244p, 245p, 255p, Annual 5. **Mooney** a-149i. **Morrow** a-144. **Perez** c-243p, 246p. **Robbins** c(p)-183-187, 189-192, 225. **Roussos** a-140i, 168i. **Starlin/Sinnott** c-162. **Sutton** a-244i. **Tuska** a-112i, 215p, Special 2. **Waid** scripts-444-454. **Williamson** a-313i. **Wood** a-127i. **Zeck** a-263-289; c-300.*

CAPTAIN AMERICA (Volume Two)
Marvel Comics: V2#1, Nov, 1996 - No. 13, Nov, 1997($2.95/$1.95/$1.99) (Produced by Extreme Studios)

Captain America V3 #32 © MAR

Captain America Comics #2 © MAR

Captain America: Sentinel of Liberty #1 © MAR

GD2.0 FN6.0 NM9.4

-($2.95)-Heroes Reborn begins; Rob Liefeld-c/a; Jeph Loeb scripts; reintro Nick Fury 5.00
-($2.95)-(Variant-c)-Liefeld-c/a 5.00
-(7/96, $2.95)-(Exclusive Comicon Ed.)-Liefeld-c/a 1.00 2.80 7.00
-11,13: 5-Two-c. 6-Cable-c/app. 13-"World War 3"-pt. 4, x-over w/Image 2.50
2-($2.99) "Heroes Reunited"-pt. 4 3.50

APTAIN AMERICA (Vol. Three) (Also see Capt. America: Sentinel of Liberty)
arvel Comics: Jan, 1998 - Present ($2.99/$1.99/$2.25)

-($2.99) Mark Waid-s/Ron Garney-a 4.00
-Variant cover 2.40 6.00
-($1.99): 2-Two covers 3.00
-11: 3-Returns to old shield. 4-Hawkeye app. 5-Thor-c/app. 7-Andy Kubert-c/a begin. 9-New shield 2.50
2-($2.99) Battles Nightmare; Red Skull back-up story 3.50
3-17,19-Red Skull returns 2.00
8-($2.99) Cap vs. Korvac in the Future 3.00
0-24,26-29: 20,21-Sgt. Fury back-up story painted by Evans 2.00
5-($2.99) Cap & Falcon vs. Hatemonger 3.00
0-38: 30-Begin $2.25-c. 32-Ordway-a. 33-35-Jurgens-a; U.S. Agent app. 36-Maximum Security x-over 2.25
/Citizen V '98 Annual ($3.50) Busiek & Kesel-s 3.50
99 Annual ($3.50) Flag Smasher app. 3.50
'00 Annual ($3.50) Continued from #35 vs. Protocide; Jurgens-s 3.50

APTAIN AMERICA COMICS
mely/Marvel Comics (TCI 1-20/CmPS 21-68/MjMC 69-75/Atlas Comics rPI 76-78): Mar, 1941 - No. 75, Feb, 1950; No. 76, 5/54 - No. 78, 9/54
o. 74 & 75 titled Capt. America's Weird Tales)

GD2.0 FN6.0 VF8.2 NM9.4

-Origin & 1st app. Captain America & Bucky by S&K; Hurricane, Tuk the Caveboy begin by S&K; 1st app. Red Skull; Hitler-c (by Simon?); intro of the "Capt. America Sentinels of Liberty Club" (advertised on inside front-c.); indicia reads Vol. 2, Number 1 5,700.00 17,100.00 39,900.00 80,000.00

GD2.0 FN6.0 NM9.4

-S&K Hurricane; Tuk by Avison (Kirby splash); classic Hitler-c 1000.00 3000.00 12,500.00
-Classic Red Skull-c & app; Stan Lee's 1st text (1st work for Marvel) 870.00 2610.00 10,000.00
-1st full pg. panel in comics 583.00 1748.00 6700.00
 504.00 1513.00 5800.00
-Origin Father Time; Tuk the Caveboy ends 452.00 1357.00 5200.00
-Red Skull app.; classic-c 522.00 1565.00 6000.00
-10-Last S&K issue, (S&K centerfold #6-10) 400.00 1200.00 4200.00
1-Last Hurricane, Headline Hunter; Al Avison Captain America begins, ends #20; Avison-c(p) 333.00 1000.00 3500.00
2-The Imp begins, ends #16; last Father Time 314.00 943.00 3300.00
3-Origin The Secret Stamp; classic-c 343.00 1030.00 3600.00
4,15 314.00 942.00 3300.00
6-Red Skull unmasks Cap; Red Skull-c 381.00 1143.00 4000.00
7-The Fighting Fool only app. 284.00 853.00 2700.00
8-Classic-c 284.00 853.00 2700.00
9-Human Torch begins #19 232.00 695.00 2200.00
0-Sub-Mariner app.; no H. Torch 232.00 695.00 2200.00
1-25: 25-Cap drinks liquid opium 210.00 663.00 2100.00
6-30: 27-Last Secret Stamp; last 68 pg. issue. 28-60 pg. issues begin. 205.00 615.00 1950.00
1-35,38-40: 34-Centerfold poster of Cap 179.00 537.00 1700.00
6-Classic Hitler-c 274.00 821.00 2600.00
7-Red Skull app. 221.00 663.00 2100.00
1-45,47: 41-Last Jap War-c. 47-Last German War-c 158.00 474.00 1500.00
6-German Holocaust-c; classic 190.00 570.00 1800.00
8-58,60 121.00 363.00 1150.00
9-Origin retold 295.00 885.00 2800.00
1-Red Skull-c/story 242.00 726.00 2300.00
2,64,65: 65-Kurtzman's "Hey Look" 163.00 490.00 1550.00
3-Intro/origin Asbestos Lady 168.00 505.00 1600.00
6-Bucky is shot; Golden Girl teams up with Captain America & learns his i.d; origin Golden Girl 174.00 521.00 1650.00

GD2.0 FN6.0 NM9.4

67-73: 67-Captain America/Golden Girl team-up; Mxyztplk swipe; last Toro in Human Torch. 68,70-Sub-Mariner/Namora, and Captain America/Golden Girl team-up in each. 69-Human Torch/Sun Girl team-up. 70-Science fiction-c/story. 71-Anti Wertham editorial; The Witness, Bucky app. 168.00 505.00 1600.00
74-(Scarce)(10/49)-Titled "Captain America's Weird Tales"; Red Skull-c & app.; classic-c 435.00 1305.00 5000.00
75(2/50)-Titled "C.A.'s Weird Tales"; no C.A. app.; horror cover/stories 168.00 505.00 1600.00
76-78(1954): Human Torch/Toro stories; all have communist-c/stories 100.00 300.00 950.00
132-Pg. Issue (B&W-1942)(Canadian)-Very rare. Has blank inside-c and back-c; contains Marvel Mystery #33 & Captain America #18 w/cover from Captain America #22; same contents as Marvel Mystery annual 2666.00 8000.00 16,000.00

NOTE: ***Crandall** a-2i, 3i, 9i, 10i. **Kirby** c-1, 2, 5-8p. **Rico** c-69-71. **Romita** c-77, 78. **Schomburg** c-3, 4, 26-29, 31, 33, 37-39, 41, 42, 45-54, 58. **Sekowsky** c-55, 56. **Shores** c-1i, 2i, 5-7i, 11i, 20-25, 30, 32, 34, 35, 40, 57, 59-67. **S&K** c-9, 10. Bondage c-3, 7, 15, 16, 34, 38.*

CAPTAIN AMERICA/NICK FURY: BLOOD TRUCE
Marvel Comics: Feb, 1995 ($5.95, one-shot, squarebound)

nn-Chaykin story 2.40 6.00

CAPTAIN AMERICA, SENTINEL OF LIBERTY (See Fireside Book Series)

CAPTAIN AMERICA: SENTINEL OF LIBERTY
Marvel Comics: Sept, 1998 - No. 12, Aug, 1999 ($1.99)

1-Waid-s/Garney-a 3.00
1-Rough Cut ($2.99) Features original script and pencil pages 3.00
2-5: 2-Two-c; Invaders WW2 story 2.00
6-($2.99) Iron Man-c/app. 3.00
7-11: 8-Falcon-c/app. 9-Falcon poses as Cap 2.00
12-($2.99) Final issue; Bucky-c/app. 3.00

CAPTAIN AMERICA SPECIAL EDITION
Marvel Comics Group: Feb, 1984 - No. 2, Mar, 1984 ($2.00, Baxter paper)

1-Steranko-c/a(r) in both; r/ Captain America #110,111 4.00
2-Reprints the scarce Our Love Story #5, and C.A. #113 2.40 6.00

CAPTAIN AMERICA: THE CLASSIC YEARS
Marvel Comics: Jun, 1998 - Present (trade paperbacks)

1-($19.95) Reprints Captain America Comics #1-5 20.00
2-($24.95) Reprints Captain America Comics #6-10 25.00

CAPTAIN AMERICA: THE LEGEND
Marvel Comics: Sept, 1996 ($3.95, one-shot)

1-Tribute issue; wraparound-c 4.00

CAPTAIN AND THE KIDS, THE (See Famous Comics Cartoon Books)

CAPTAIN AND THE KIDS, THE (See Comics on Parade, Katzenjammer Kids, Okay Comics & Sparkler Comics)
United Features Syndicate/Dell Publ. Co.: 1938 -12/39; Sum, 1947 - No. 32, 1955; Four Color No. 881, Feb, 1958

Single Series 1(1938) 89.00 268.00 850.00
Single Series 1(Reprint)(12/39- "Reprint" on-c) 47.00 141.00 425.00
1(Summer, 1947-UFS)-Katzenjammer Kids 14.00 41.00 110.00
2 8.65 26.50 60.00
3-10 7.00 21.00 48.00
11-20 5.00 15.00 32.00
21-32 (1955) 4.65 14.00 28.00
50th Anniversary issue-(1948)-Contains a 2 pg. history of the strip, including an account of the famous Supreme Court decision allowing both Pulitzer & Hearst to run the same strip under different names 10.00 30.00 75.00
Special Summer issue, Fall issue (1948) 6.40 19.25 45.00
Four Color 881 (Dell) 3.20 9.60 35.00

CAPTAIN ATOM
Nationwide Publishers: 1950 - No. 7, 1951 (5¢, 5x7-1/4", 52 pgs.)

1-Science fiction 40.00 120.00 325.00
2-7 21.00 64.00 170.00

CAPTAIN ATOM (Formerly Strange Sus. Stories #77)(Also see Space Adv.)

Captain Battle #5 © LEV

Captain Carrot and His Amazing Zoo Crew #1 © DC

Captain Easy #12 © NEA

Charlton Comics: V2#78, Dec, 1965 - V2#89, Dec, 1967

V2#78-Origin retold; Bache-a (3 pgs.) 8.15 24.50 90.00
79-82: 79-1st app. Dr. Spectro; 3 pg. Ditko cut & paste /Space Adventures #24. 82-Intro. Nightshade (9/66) 5.00 15.00 55.00
83-86: Ted Kord Blue Beetle in all. 83-(11/66)-1st app. Ted Kord. 84-1st app. new Captain Atom 4.35 13.00 48.00
87-89: Nightshade by Aparo in all 4.35 13.00 48.00
83-85(Modern Comics-1977)-reprints 5.00
NOTE: ***Aparo** a-87-89. **Ditko** c/a(p) 78-89. #90 only published in fanzine 'The Charlton Bullseye' #1, 2.*

CAPTAIN ATOM (Also see Americomics & Crisis On Infinite Earths)
DC Comics: Mar, 1987 - No. 57, Sept, 1991 (Direct sales only #35 on)

1-(44 pgs.)-Origin/1st app. with new costume 3.00
2-49: 5-Firestorm x-over. 6-Intro. new Dr. Spectro. 11-Millennium tie-in 14-Nightshade app. 16-Justice League app. 17-$1.00-c begins; Swamp Thing app. 20-Blue Beetle x-over. 24,25-Invasion tie-in 2.00
51-57: 50-($2.00, 52 pgs.). 57-War of the Gods x-over 2.50
Annual 1,2 ('88, '89)-1-Intro Major Force 2.50

CAPTAIN BATTLE (Boy Comics #3 on) (See Silver Streak Comics)
New Friday Publ./Comic House: Summer, 1941 - No. 2, Fall, 1941

1-Origin Blackout by Rico; Captain Battle begins (1st appeared in Silver Streak #10, 5/41) 126.00 379.00 1200.00
2 79.00 237.00 750.00

CAPTAIN BATTLE (2nd Series)
Magazine Press/Picture Scoop No. 5: No. 3, Wint, 1942-43; No. 5, Sum, 1943 (No #4)

3-Origin Silver Streak-r/SS#3; origin Lance Hale-r/Silver Streak; Simon-a(r) (52 pgs., nd) 68.00 205.00 650.00
5-Origin Blackout retold (68 pgs.) 50.00 150.00 450.00

CAPTAIN BATTLE, JR.
Comic House (Lev Gleason): Fall, 1943 - No. 2, Winter, 1943-44

1-The Claw vs. The Ghost 100.00 300.00 950.00
2-Wolverton's Scoop Scuttle; Don Rico-c/a; The Green Claw story is reprinted from Silver Streak #6 79.00 237.00 750.00

CAPTAIN BEN DIX
Bendix Aviation Corporation: 1943 (Small size)

nn 7.15 21.50 50.00

CAPTAIN BRITAIN (Also see Marvel Team-Up No. 65, 66)
Marvel Comics International: Oct. 13, 1976 - No. 39, July 6, 1977 (Weekly)

1-Origin; with Capt. Britain's face mask inside 1.75 5.25 14.00
2-Origin, part II; Capt. Britain's Boomerang inside 1.00 3.00 8.00
3-11: 3,8-Vs. Bank Robbers. 4-7-Vs. Hurricane. 9-11: Vs. Dr. Synne 4.00
12-27: (scarce)-12,13-Vs. Dr. Synne. 14,15-Vs. Mastermind. 16-20-With Capt. America; 17 misprinted & color section reprinted in #18. 21-23,25,26-With Capt. America. 24-With C.B.'s Jet Plane inside. 27-Origin retold 1.50 4.50 12.00
28-32,36-39: 28-32-Vs. Lord Hawk. 36-Star Sceptre. 37-39-Vs. Highwayman & Munipulator 3.50
33-35-More on origin 4.00
Annual (1978, Hardback, 64 pgs.)-Reprints #1-7 with pin-ups of Marvel characters 1.50 4.50 12.00
Summer Special (1980, 52 pgs.)-Reprints 4.00
NOTE: *No. 1, 2, & 24 are rarer in mint due to inserts. Distributed in Great Britain only. Nick Fury-r by **Steranko** in 1-20, 24-31, 35-37. Fantastic Four-r by **J. Buscema** in all. New **Buscema**-a in 24-30. Story from No. 39 continues in Super Spider-Man (British weekly) No. 231-247. Following cancellation of his series, new Captain Britain stories appeared in "Super Spider-Man" (British weekly) No. 231-247. Captain Britain stories which appear in Super-Spider-Man No 248-253 are reprints of Marvel Team-Up No. 65&66. Capt. Britain strips also appeared in Hulk Comic (weekly) 1, 3-30, 42-55, 57-60, in Marvel Superheroes (monthly) 377-388, in Daredevils (monthly) 1-11, Mighty World of Marvel (monthly) 7-16 & Captain Britain (monthly) 1-14. Issues 1-23 have B&W & color, paper-c, & are 32 pgs. Issues 24 on are all B&W w/glossy-c & are 36 pgs.*

CAPTAIN CANUCK
Comely Comix (Canada) (All distr. in U. S.): 7/75 - No. 4, 7/77; No. 4, 7-8/79 - No. 14, 3-4/81

1-1st app. Bluefox 5.00
2,3(5-7/76)-2-1st app. Dr. Walker, Redcoat & Kebec. 3-1st app. Heather 4.00
4(1st printing-2/77)-10x14-1/2"; (5.00); B&W; 300 copies serially numbered and signed with one certificate of authenticity 8.15 24.50 90.0
4(2nd printing-7/77)-11x17", B&W; only 15 copies printed; signed by creator Richard Comely, serially #'d and two certificates of authenticity inserted; orange cardboard covers (Very Rare) 11.00 33.00 120.0
4-14: 4(7-8/79)-1st app. Tom Evans & Mr. Gold; origin The Catman. 5-Origin Capt. Canuck's powers; 1st app. Earth Patrol & Chaos Corps. 8-Jonn 'The Final Chapter'. 9-1st World Beyond. 11-1st 'Chariots of Fire' story 3.0
Special Collectors Pack (polybagged) 1.10 3.30 9.0
Summer Special 1(7-9/80, 95¢, 64 pgs.) 3.0
NOTE: *30,000 copies of No. 2 were destroyed in Winnipeg.*

CAPTAIN CARROT AND HIS AMAZING ZOO CREW (Also see New Teen Titans & Oz-Wonderland War)
DC Comics: Mar, 1982 - No. 20, Nov, 1983

1-20: 1-Superman app. 3-Re-intro Dodo & The Frog. 9-Re-intro Three Mouseketeers, the Terrific Whatzit. 10,11- Pig Iron reverts back to Peter Porkchops. 20-The Changeling app. 3.0

CAPTAIN CARVEL AND HIS CARVEL CRUSADERS (See Carvel Comics)

CAPTAIN CONFEDERACY
Marvel Comics (Epic Comics): Nov, 1991 - No. 4, Feb, 1992 ($1.95)

1-4: All new stories 2.0

CAPTAIN COURAGEOUS COMICS (Banner #3-5; see Four Favorites #5)
Periodical House (Ace Magazines): No. 6, March, 1942

6-Origin & 1st app. The Sword; Lone Warrior, Capt. Courageous app.; Capt. moves to Four Favorites #5 in May 76.00 229.00 725.0

CAPT'N CRUNCH COMICS (See Cap'n...)

CAPTAIN DAVY JONES
Dell Publishing Co.: No. 598, Nov, 1954

Four Color 598 4.10 12.30 45.0

CAPTAIN EASY (See The Funnies & Red Ryder #3-32)
Hawley/Dell Publ./Standard(Visual Editions)/Argo: 1939 - No. 17, Sept, 194 April, 1956

nn-Hawley(1939)-Contains reprints from The Funnies & 1938 Sunday strips by Roy Crane 87.00 260.00 825.0
Four Color 24 (1943) 42.00 125.00 500.0
Four Color 111(6/46) 14.00 42.00 170.0
10(Standard-10/47) 11.00 33.00 90.0
11,12,14,15,17: 11-17 all contain 1930s & '40s strip-r 9.30 28.00 65.0
13,16: Schomburg-c 10.00 30.00 75.0
Argo 1(4/56)-Reprints 7.00 21.00 48.0

CAPTAIN EASY & WASH TUBBS (See Famous Comics Cartoon Books)

CAPTAIN ELECTRON
Brick Computer Science Institute: Aug, 1986 ($2.25)

1-Disbrow-a 2.2

CAPTAIN EO 3-D (Disney)
Eclipse Comics: July, 1987 (Eclipse 3-D Special #18, $3.50, Baxter)

1-Adapts 3-D movie 4.0
1-2-D limited edition 2.40 6.0
1-Large size (11x17", 8/87)-Sold only at Disney Theme parks ($6.95) 1.75 5.25 14.0

CAPTAIN FEARLESS COMICS (Also see Holyoke One-Shot #6, Old Glory Comics & Silver Streak #1)
Helnit Publishing Co. (Holyoke Publ. Co.): Aug, 1941 - No. 2, Sept, 1941

1-Origin Mr. Miracle, Alias X, Captain Fearless, Citizen Smith Son of the Unknown Soldier; Miss Victory (1st app.) begins (1st patriotic heroine? before Wonder Woman) 84.00 253.00 800.0
2-Grit Grady, Captain Stone app. 53.00 158.00 475.0

CAPTAIN FLAG (See Blue Ribbon Comics #16)

CAPTAIN FLASH
Sterling Comics: Nov, 1954 - No. 4, July, 1955

1-Origin; Sekowsky-a; Tomboy (female super hero) begins; only pre-code issue; atomic rocket-c 40.00 120.00 350.0

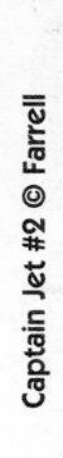
Captain Flight Comics #11 © Four Star Pub.

Captain Jet #2 © Farrell

Captain Marvel ('68) #2 © MAR

GD2.0 FN6.0 NM9.4 GD2.0 FN6.0 NM9.4

2-4: 4-Flying saucer invasion-c 23.00 68.00 180.00

APTAIN FLEET (Action Packed Tales of the Sea)
ff-Davis Publishing Co.: Fall, 1952

-Painted-c 15.00 45.00 120.00

APTAIN FLIGHT COMICS
our Star Publications: Mar, 1944 - No. 10, Dec, 1945; No. 11, Feb-Mar, 1947

1 40.00 120.00 350.00
2-4: 4-Rock Raymond begins, ends #7 24.00 71.00 190.00
5-Bondage, classic torture-c; Red Rocket begins; the Grenade app. (scarce) 89.00 268.00 850.00
6 22.00 66.00 175.00
7-10: 7-L. B. Cole covers begin, end #11. 8-Yankee Girl begins; intro. Black Cobra & Cobra Kid & begins. 9-Torpedoman app.; last Yankee Girl; Kinstler-a. 10-Deep Sea Dawson, Zoom of the Jungle, Rock Raymond, Red Rocket, & Black Cobra app; bondage-c 47.00 142.00 425.00
1-Torpedoman, Blue Flame (Human Torch clone) app.; last Black Cobra, Red Rocket; classic L. B. Cole robot-c (scarce) 89.00 268.00 850.00

APTAIN GALLANT (...of the Foreign Legion) (TV) (Texas Rangers in Action o. 5 on?)
harlton Comics: 1955; No. 2, Jan, 1956 - No. 4, Sept, 1956

on-Heinz version (#1)-Buster Crabbe photo on-c; full page Buster Crabbe photo inside front-c 10.00 30.00 70.00
2-4: Buster Crabbe in all 8.65 26.00 60.00

APTAIN GLORY
opps Comics: Apr, 1993 ($2.95) (Created by Jack Kirby)

-Polybagged w/Kirbychrome trading card; Ditko-a & Kirby-c; has coupon for Amberchrome Secret City Saga #0 3.00

APTAIN HERO (See Jughead as...)

APTAIN HERO COMICS DIGEST MAGAZINE
rchie Publications: Sept, 1981

-Reprints of Jughead as Super-Guy 1.25 3.75 10.00

APTAIN HOBBY COMICS
xport Publication Ent. Ltd. (Dist. in U.S. by Kable News Co.): Feb, 1948 anadian)

7.00 21.00 48.00

APT. HOLO IN 3-D (See Blackthorne 3-D Series #65)

APTAIN HOOK & PETER PAN (Movie)(Disney)
ell Publishing Co.: No. 446, Jan, 1953

our Color 446 8.35 25.00 100.00

APTAIN JET (Fantastic Fears No. 7 on)
our Star Publ./Farrell/Comic Media: May, 1952 - No. 5, Jan, 1953

-Bakerish-a 20.00 60.00 160.00
2 11.00 33.00 90.00
3-5,6(?) 10.00 30.00 75.00

APTAIN JOHNER & THE ALIENS
aliant: May, 1995 - No. 2, May, 1995 ($2.95, shipped in same month)

,2: Reprints Magnus Robot Fighter 4000 A.D. back-up stories; new Paul Smith-c 3.00

APTAIN JUSTICE (TV)
arvel Comics: Mar, 1988 - No. 2, Apr, 1988 (limited series)

,2-Based on True Colors television series. 2.00

APTAIN KANGAROO (TV)
ell Publishing Co.: No. 721, Aug, 1956 - No. 872, Jan, 1958

our Color 721 (#1)-Photo-c 14.00 42.00 170.00
our Color 780, 872-Photo-c 11.70 35.00 140.00

APTAIN KIDD (Formerly Dagar; My Secret Story #26 on)(Also see Comic omics & Fantastic Comics)
ox Feature Syndicate: No. 24, June, 1949 - No. 25, Aug, 1949

4,25: 24-Features Blackbeard the Pirate 14.00 41.00 110.00

APTAIN MARVEL (See All Hero, All-New Collectors' Ed., America's Greatest, Fawcett Miniature, Gift, Legends, Limited Collectors' Ed., Marvel Family, Master No. 21, Mighty Midget Comics, Shazam, Special Edition Comics, Whiz, Wisco, World's Finest #253 and XMas Comics)

CAPTAIN MARVEL (Becomes ...Presents the Terrible 5 No. 5)
M. F. Enterprises: April, 1966 - No. 4, Nov, 1966 (25¢ Giants)

nn-(#1 on pg. 5)-Origin; created by Carl Burgos 3.00 9.00 30.00
2-4: 3-(#3 on pg. 4)-Fights the Bat 2.30 7.00 20.00

CAPTAIN MARVEL (Marvel's Space-Born Super-Hero! Captain Marvel #1-6; see Giant-Size..., Life Of..., Marvel Graphic Novel #1, Marvel Spotlight V2#1 & Marvel Super-Heroes #12)
Marvel Comics Group: May, 1968 - No. 19, Dec, 1969; No. 20, June, 1970 - No. 21, Aug, 1970; No. 22, Sept, 1972 - No. 62, May, 1979

1 9.00 27.00 100.00
2-Super Skrull-c/story 3.00 9.00 30.00
3-5: 4-Captain Marvel battles Sub-Mariner 2.00 6.00 18.00
6-11: 11-Capt. Marvel given great power by Zo the Ruler; Smith/Trimpe-c; Death of Una 1.50 4.50 12.00
12,13,15-20: 16,17-New costume 1.00 3.00 8.00
14,21: 14-Capt. Marvel vs. Iron Man; last 12¢ issue. 21-Capt. Marvel battles Hulk; last 15¢ issue 1.75 5.25 14.00
22-24 1.00 3.00 8.00
25,26: 25-Starlin-c/a begins; Starlin's 1st Thanos saga begins (3/73), ends #34; Thanos cameo (5 panels). 26-Minor Thanos app. (see Iron Man #55); 1st Thanos-c 2.00 6.00 18.00
27,28-1st & 2nd full app. Thanos. 28-Thanos-c/s 1.75 5.25 14.00
29,30-Thanos cameos. 29-C.M. gains more powers 1.25 3.75 10.00
31,32: Thanos app. 31-Last 20¢ issue. 32-Thanos-c 1.50 4.50 12.00
33-Thanos-c & app.; Capt. Marvel battles Thanos; 1st origin Thanos 1.85 5.50 15.00
34-1st app. Nitro; C.M. contracts cancer which eventually kills him; last Starlin-c/a 1.25 3.75 10.00
35,37-40,42,46-48,50,53-56,58-62: 39-Origin Watcher. 58-Thanos cameo 4.00
36,41,43,49: 36-R-origin/1st app. Capt. Marvel from Marvel Super-Heroes #12. 41,43-Wrightson part inks; #43-c(i). 49-Starlin & Weiss-p assists 5.00
44,45-(Regular 25¢ editions)(5,7/76) 4.00
44,45-(30¢-c variants, limited distribution) 2.40 6.00
51,52-(Regular 30¢ editions)(7,9/77) 4.00
51,52-(35¢-c variants, limited distribution) 2.40 6.00
57-Thanos appears in flashback 1.00 2.80 7.00

NOTE: ***Alcala** a-35. **Austin** a-46i, 49-53i; c-52i. **Buscema** a-18p-21p. **Colan** a(p)-1-4; c(p)-1-4, 8, 9. **Heck** a-5-10p, 16p. **Gil Kane** a-17-21p; c-17-24p, 37p, 53. **Starlin** a-36. **McWilliams** a-40i. #25-34 were reprinted in The Life of Captain Marvel.*

CAPTAIN MARVEL
Marvel Comics: Nov, 1989 ($1.50, one-shot, 52 pgs.)

1-Super-hero from Avengers; new powers 3.00

CAPTAIN MARVEL
Marvel Comics: Feb, 1994 ($1.75, 52 pgs.)

1-(Indicia reads Vol 2 #2)-Minor Captain America app. 2.00

CAPTAIN MARVEL
Marvel Comics: Dec, 1995 - No. 6, May, 1996 ($2.95/$1.95)

1 ($2.95)-Advs. of Mar-Vell's son begins; Fabian Nicieza scripts; foil-c 3.00
2-6: 2-Begin $1.95-c 2.00

CAPTAIN MARVEL (Vol. 3) (See Avengers Forever)
Marvel Comics: Jan, 2000 - Present ($2.50)

1-14: 1-Peter David-s. 2-Two covers; Hulk app. 9-Silver Surfer app. 12-Maximum Security x-over 2.50
Wizard #0-Preview and history of Rick Jones 1.00

CAPTAIN MARVEL ADVENTURES (See Special Edition Comics for pre #1)
Fawcett Publications: 1941 (March) - No. 150, Nov, 1953
(#1 on stands 1/16/41)

GD2.0 FN6.0 VF8.2 NM9.4

nn(#1)-Captain Marvel & Sivana by Jack Kirby. The cover was printed on unstable paper stock and is rarely found in Fine or Mint condition; blank back inside-c 2560.00 7680.00 16,650.00 32,000.00

GD2.0 FN6.0 NM9.4

2-(Advertised as #3, which was counting Special Edition Comics as the real #1); Tuska-a 400.00 1200.00 4200.00

Captain Marvel Adventures #19 © FAW

NO. 1 NOV. 18
CAPTAIN MARVEL JR.
10¢
CAPTAIN MARVEL JR. SINKS THE JAPS!

Captain Marvel, Jr. #1 © FAW

MARCH
CAPTAIN MIDNIGHT
10¢
CAPTAIN MIDNIGHT SPRAYS DEATH FROM THE SKIES!

Captain Midnight #18 © FAW

	GD2.0	FN6.0	NM9.4
3-Metallic silver-c	268.00	805.00	2550.00
4-Three Lt. Marvels app.	190.00	570.00	1800.00
5	147.00	442.00	1400.00
6-10: 9-1st Otto Binder scripts on Capt. Marvel	111.00	332.00	1050.00
11-15: 12-Capt. Marvel joins the Army. 13-Two pg. Capt. Marvel pin-up. 15-Comic cards on back-c begin, end #26	87.00	260.00	825.00
16,17: 17-Painted-c	82.00	245.00	775.00
18-Origin & 1st app. Mary Marvel & Marvel Family (12/11/42); painted-c; Mary Marvel by Marcus Swayze	200.00	600.00	1900.00
19-Mary Marvel x-over; Christmas-c	68.00	205.00	650.00
20,21-Attached to the cover, each has a miniature comic just like the Mighty Midget Comics #11, except that each has a full color promo ad on the back cover. Most copies were circulated without the miniature comic. These issues with miniatures attached are very rare, and should not be mistaken for copies with the similar Mighty Midget glued in its place. The Mighty Midgets had blank back covers except for a small victory stamp seal. Only the Capt. Marvel, Captain Marvel Jr. and Golden Arrow No. 11 miniatures have been positively documented as having been affixed to these covers. Each miniature was only partially glued by its back cover to the Captain Marvel comic making it easy to see if it's the genuine miniature rather than a Mighty Midget. with comic attached....	343.00	1029.00	3600.00
20-Without miniature	63.00	189.00	600.00
21-Without miniature; Hitler-c	84.00	253.00	800.00
22-Mr. Mind serial begins; 1st app. Mr. Mind	90.00	270.00	850.00
23-25	61.00	182.00	575.00
26-30: 26-Flag-c. 29-1st Mr. Mind-c & 1st app. (his voice was heard over the radio before now)(11/43)	53.00	160.00	480.00
31-35: 35-Origin Radar (5/44, see Master #50)	49.00	147.00	440.00
36-40: 37-Mary Marvel x-over	42.00	125.00	375.00
41-46: 42-Christmas-c. 43-Capt. Marvel 1st meets Uncle Marvel; Mary Batson cameo. 46-Mr. Mind serial ends	38.00	113.00	300.00
47-50	35.00	105.00	280.00
51-53,55-60: 51-63-Bi-weekly issues. 52-Origin & 1st app. Sivana Jr.; Capt. Marvel Jr. x-over	30.00	90.00	240.00
54-Special oversize 68 pg. issue	31.00	94.00	250.00
61-The Cult of the Curse serial begins	35.00	105.00	280.00
62-65-Serial cont.; Mary Marvel x-over in #65	30.00	90.00	240.00
66-Serial ends; Atomic War-c	34.00	101.00	270.00
67-77,79: 69-Billy Batson's Christmas; Uncle Marvel, Mary Marvel, Capt. Marvel Jr. x-over. 71-Three Lt. Marvels app. 79-Origin Mr. Tawny	26.00	79.00	210.00
78-Origin Mr. Atom	30.00	90.00	240.00
80-Origin Capt. Marvel retold	58.00	174.00	550.00
81-84,86-90: 81,90-Mr. Atom app. 82-Infinity-c. 86-Mr. Tawny app.	25.00	75.00	200.00
85-Freedom Train issue	30.00	90.00	240.00
91-99: 96-Mr. Tawny app.	24.00	73.00	195.00
100-Origin retold; silver metallic-c	44.00	133.00	400.00
101-115,117-120	23.00	69.00	185.00
116-Flying Saucer issue (1/51)	26.00	79.00	210.00
121-Origin retold	31.00	94.00	250.00
122-137,139-149: 141-Pre-code horror story "The Hideous Head-Hunter". 142-used in **POP**, pgs. 92,96	22.00	66.00	175.00
138-Flying Saucer issue (11/52)	26.00	79.00	210.00
150-(Low distribution)	40.00	120.00	350.00

NOTE: ***Swayze** a-12, 14, 15, 18, 19, 40; c-12, 15, 19.*

CAPTAIN MARVEL AND THE GOOD HUMOR MAN (Movie)
Fawcett Publications: 1950

nn-Partial photo-c w/Jack Carson & the Captain Marvel Club Boys	47.00	142.00	425.00

CAPTAIN MARVEL COMIC STORY PAINT BOOK (See Comic Story...)

CAPTAIN MARVEL, JR. (See Fawcett Miniatures, Marvel Family, Master Comics, Mighty Midget Comics, Shazam & Whiz Comics)

CAPTAIN MARVEL, JR.
Fawcett Publications: Nov, 1942 - No. 119, June, 1953 (No #34)

1-Origin Capt. Marvel Jr. retold (Whiz #25); Capt. Nazi app. Classic Raboy-c	478.00	1435.00	5500.00
2-Vs. Capt. Nazi; origin Capt. Nippon	190.00	570.00	1800.00
3	105.00	316.00	1000.00
4-Classic Raboy-c	113.00	340.00	1075.00

	GD2.0	FN6.0	NM9.
5-Vs. Capt. Nazi	95.00	285.00	900.0
6-8: 8-Vs. Capt. Nazi	74.00	221.00	700.0
9-Classic flag-c	79.00	237.00	750.0
10-Hitler-c	84.00	253.00	800.0
11,12,15-Capt. Nazi app.	63.00	189.00	600.0
13-Hitler-c	74.00	221.00	700.0
14,16-20: 14-X-Mas-c. 16-Capt. Marvel & Sivana x-over. 19-Capt. Nazi & Capt. Nippon app.	55.00	165.00	525.0
21-30: 25-Flag-c	44.00	133.00	400.0
31-33,36-40: 37-Infinity-c	31.00	94.00	250.0
35-#34 on inside; cover shows origin of Sivana Jr. which is not on inside. Evidently the cover to #35 was printed out of sequence and bound with contents to #34	31.00	94.00	250.0
41-70: 42-Robot-c. 53-Atomic Bomb-c/story	24.00	71.00	190.0
71-99,101-104: 104-Used in **POP**, pg. 89	17.00	51.00	135.0
100	20.00	60.00	160.0
105-114,116-118: 116-Vampira, Queen of Terror app. 119-Electric chair-c	15.00	45.00	120.0
115-Injury to eye-c; Eyeball story w/injury-to-eye panels	31.00	94.00	250.0
119-Electric chair-c (scarce)	35.00	105.00	280.0

NOTE: ***Mac Raboy** c-1-28, 30-32, 57, 59 among others.*

CAPTAIN MARVEL PRESENTS THE TERRIBLE FIVE
M. F. Enterprises: Aug, 1966; V2#5, Sept, 1967 (No #2-4) (25¢)

1	3.00	9.00	30.0
V2#5-(Formerly Captain Marvel)	2.00	6.00	18.0

CAPTAIN MARVEL'S FUN BOOK
Samuel Lowe Co.: 1944 (1/2" thick) (cardboard covers)(25¢)

nn-Puzzles, games, magic, etc.; infinity-c	35.00	105.00	280.0

CAPTAIN MARVEL SPECIAL EDITION (See Special Edition)

CAPTAIN MARVEL STORY BOOK
Fawcett Publications: Summer, 1946 - No. 4, Summer?, 1948

1-Half text	55.00	165.00	500.0
2-4	40.00	120.00	340.0

CAPTAIN MARVEL THRILL BOOK (Large-Size)
Fawcett Publications: 1941 (B&W w/color-c)

	GD2.0	FN6.0	VF8.2
1-Reprints from Whiz #8,10, & Special Edition #1 (Rare)	270.00	810.00	2700.0

NOTE: *Rarely found in Fine or Mint condition.*

CAPTAIN MIDNIGHT (TV, radio, films) (See The Funnies, Popular Comics & Super Book of Comics)(Becomes Sweethearts No. 68 on)
Fawcett Publications: Sept, 1942 - No. 67, Fall, 1948 (#1-14: 68 pgs.)

	GD2.0	FN6.0	NM9.4
1-Origin Captain Midnight, star of radio and movies; Captain Marvel cameo on cover	295.00	885.00	2800.0
2-Smashes the Jap Juggarnaut	134.00	403.00	1275.0
3-5: Grapples the Gremlins	97.00	292.00	925.0
6-10: 9-Raboy-c. 10-Raboy Flag-c	71.00	213.00	675.0
11-20: 11,17,18-Raboy-c. 16 (1/44)	53.00	158.00	475.0
21-30: 22-War savings stamp-c. 24-Jap flag sunburst-c.	42.00	125.00	375.0
31-40	32.00	96.00	255.0
41-59,61-67: 50-Sci/fi theme begins?	26.00	77.00	205.0
60-Flying Saucer issue (2/48)-3rd of this theme; see The Spirit 9/28/47(1st), Shadow Comics V7#10 (2nd, 1/48) & Boy Commandos #26 (4th, 3-4/48)	33.00	98.00	260.0

CAPTAIN NICE (TV)
Gold Key: Nov, 1967 (one-shot)

1(10211-711)-Photo-c	6.30	19.00	75.0

CAPTAIN N: THE GAME MASTER (TV)
Valiant Comics: 1990 - No. 6? ($1.95, thick stock, coated-c)

1-6: 4-6-Layton-c			2.0

CAPTAIN PARAGON (See Bill Black's Fun Comics)
Americomics: Dec, 1983 - No. 4, 1985

Captain Science #2 © YM

Captain Steve Savage #4 © AVON

Captain Video #4 © FAW

GD2.0 FN6.0 NM9.4

1-Intro/1st app. Ms. Victory 3.00
2-4 2.00

CAPTAIN PARAGON AND THE SENTINELS OF JUSTICE
AC Comics: April, 1985 - No. 6, 1986 ($1.75)

1-6: 1-Capt. Paragon, Commando D., Nightveil, Scarlet Scorpion, Stardust & Atoman begin 3.00

CAPTAIN PLANET AND THE PLANETEERS (TV cartoon)
Marvel Comics: Oct, 1991 - No. 12, Oct, 1992 ($1.00/$1.25)

1-N. Adams painted-c 4.00
2-12: 3-Romita-c 3.00

CAPTAIN POWER AND THE SOLDIERS OF THE FUTURE (TV)
Continuity Comics: Aug, 1988 - No. 2, 1988 ($2.00)

1,2: 1-Neal Adams-c/layouts/inks; variant-c exists. 3.00

CAPTAIN PUREHEART (See Archie as...)

CAPTAIN ROCKET
P. L. Publ. (Canada): Nov, 1951

1 42.00 125.00 375.00

CAPT. SAVAGE AND HIS LEATHERNECK RAIDERS (...And His Battlefield Raiders #9 on)
Marvel Comics Group (Animated Timely Features): Jan, 1968 - No. 19, Mar, 1970 (See Sgt. Fury No. 10)

1-Sgt. Fury & Howlers cameo 3.00 9.00 30.00
2,7,11: 2-Origin Hydra. 1-5,7-Ayers/Shores-a. 7-Pre-"Thing" Ben Grimm story. 11-Sgt. Fury app. 2.00 6.00 18.00
3-6,8-10,12-14: 14-Last 12¢ issue 1.85 5.50 15.00
15-19 1.50 4.50 12.00

CAPTAIN SCIENCE (Fantastic No. 8 on)
Youthful Magazines: Nov, 1950 - No. 7, Dec, 1951

1-Wood-a; origin; 2 pg. text w/ photos of George Pal's "Destination Moon." 82.00 246.00 780.00
2 42.00 125.00 375.00
3,6,7; 3,6-Bondage c-swipes/Wings #94,91 40.00 120.00 325.00
4,5-Wood/Orlando-c/a(2) each 78.00 235.00 740.00
NOTE: *Fass a-4. Bondage c-3, 6, 7.*

CAPTAIN SILVER'S LOG OF SEA HOUND (See Sea Hound)

CAPTAIN SINBAD (Movie Adaptation) (See Fantastic Voyages of... & Movie Comics)

CAPTAIN STERNN: RUNNING OUT OF TIME
Kitchen Sink Press: Sept, 1993 - No. 5, 1994 ($4.95, limited series, coated stock, 52 pgs.)

1-5: Berni Wrightson-c/a/scripts 6.00
1-Gold ink variant 10.00

CAPTAIN STEVE SAVAGE (...& His Jet Fighters, No. 2-13)
Avon Periodicals: 1950 - No. 8, 1/53; No. 5, 9-10/54 - No. 13, 5-6/56

nn(1st series)-Wood art, 22 pgs. (titled "...Over Korea") 38.00 113.00 300.00
1(4/51)-Reprints nn issue (Canadian) 15.00 45.00 120.00
2-Kamen-a 10.00 30.00 80.00
3-11 (#6, 9-10/54, last precode) 7.15 21.50 50.00
12-Wood-a (6 pgs.) 11.00 33.00 90.00
13-Check, Lawrence-a 7.85 23.50 55.00
NOTE: ***Kinstler** c-2-5, 7-9, 11. **Lawrence** a-8. **Ravielli** a-5, 9.*
5(9-10/54-2nd series)(Formerly Sensational Police Cases) 7.15 21.50 50.00
6-Reprints nn issue; Wood-a 10.00 30.00 75.00
7-13: 9,10-Kinstler-c. 10-r/cover #2 (1st series). 13-r/cover #8 (1st series) 5.00 15.00 35.00

CAPTAIN STONE (See Holyoke One-Shot No. 10)

CAPT. STORM (Also see G. I. Combat #138)
National Periodical Publications: May-June, 1964 - No. 18, Mar-Apr, 1967 (Grey tone c-8)

1-Origin 4.10 12.30 45.00
2-18: 3,6,13-Kubert-a. 4-Colan-a. 12-Kubert-c 3.00 9.00 32.00

GD2.0 FN6.0 NM9.4

CAPTAIN 3-D (Super hero)
Harvey Publications: December, 1953 (25¢, came with 2 pairs of glasses)

1-Kirby/Ditko-a (Ditko's 3rd published work tied with Strange Fantasy #9, see also Daring Love #1 & Black Magic V4 #3); shows cover in 3-D on inside; Kirby/Meskin-c 10.50 32.00 85.00
NOTE: *Half price without glasses*

CAPTAIN THUNDER AND BLUE BOLT
Hero Comics: Sept, 1987 - No. 10, 1988 ($1.95)

1-10: 1-Origin Blue Bolt. 3-Origin Capt. Thunder. 6-1st app. Wicket. 8-Champions x-over 2.00

CAPTAIN TOOTSIE & THE SECRET LEGION (Advs. of...)(Also see Monte Hale #30,39 & Real Western Hero)
Toby Press: Oct, 1950 - No. 2, Dec, 1950

1-Not Beck-a; both have sci/fi covers 30.00 90.00 240.00
2-The Rocketeer Patrol app.; not Beck-a 19.00 56.00 150.00

CAPTAIN TRIUMPH (See Crack Comics #27)

CAPTAIN VENTURE & THE LAND BENEATH THE SEA (See Space Family Robinson)
Gold Key: Oct, 1968 - No. 2, Oct, 1969

1-r/Space Family Robinson serial; Spiegle-a 4.10 12.30 45.00
2-Spiegle-a 3.65 11.00 40.00

CAPTAIN VICTORY AND THE GALACTIC RANGERS
Pacific Comics: Nov, 1981 - No. 13, Jan, 1984 ($1.00, direct sales, 36-48 pgs.) (Created by Jack Kirby)

1-13: 1-1st app. Mr. Mind. 3-N. Adams-a 3.00
Special 1-(10/83)-Kirby c/a(p) 4.00
NOTE: ***Conrad** a-10, 11. **Ditko** a-6. **Kirby** a-1-3p; c-1-13.*

CAPTAIN VICTORY AND THE GALACTIC RANGERS
Jack Kirby Comics: July, 2000 - No. 3 ($2.95, B&W, limited series)

1-New Jeremy Kirby-s with reprinted Jack Kirby-a; Liefeld pin-up art 2.95

CAPTAIN VIDEO (TV) (See XMas Comics)
Fawcett Publications: Feb, 1951 - No. 6, Dec, 1951 (No. 1,5,6-36pgs.; 2-4, 52pgs.) (All photo-c)

1-George Evans-a(2) 111.00 332.00 1050.00
2-Used in **SOTI**, pg. 382 73.00 220.00 695.00
3-6-All Evans-a except #5 mostly Evans 62.00 186.00 590.00
NOTE: *Minor **Williamson** assists on most issues. Photo c-1, 5, 6; painted c-2-4.*

CAPTAIN WILLIE SCHULTZ (Also see Fightin' Army)
Charlton Comics: No. 76, Oct, 1985 - No. 77, Jan, 1986

76,77-Low print run 4.00

CAPTAIN WIZARD COMICS (See Meteor, Red Band & Three Ring Comics)
Rural Home: 1946

1-Capt. Wizard dons new costume; Impossible Man, Race Wilkins app. 30.00 90.00 240.00

CARE BEARS (TV, Movie)(See Star Comics Magazine)
Star Comics/Marvel Comics No. 15 on: Nov, 1985 - No. 20, Jan, 1989

1-20: Post-a begins. 11-$1.00-c begins. 13-Madballs app. 3.00

CAREER GIRL ROMANCES (Formerly Three Nurses)
Charlton Comics: June, 1964 - No. 78, Dec, 1973

V4#24-31 2.00 6.00 16.00
32-Elvis Presley, Herman's Hermits, Johnny Rivers line drawn-c 9.00 27.00 100.00
33-50 1.75 5.25 14.00
51-78 1.25 3.75 10.00

CAR 54, WHERE ARE YOU? (TV)
Dell Publishing Co.: Mar-May, 1962 - No. 7, Sept-Nov, 1963; 1964 - 1965 (All photo-c)

Four Color 1257(#1, 3-5/62) 6.70 20.00 80.00
2(6-8/62)-7 4.35 13.00 48.00
2,3(10-12/64), 4(1-3/65)-Reprints #2,3,&4 of 1st series 2.80 8.40 28.00

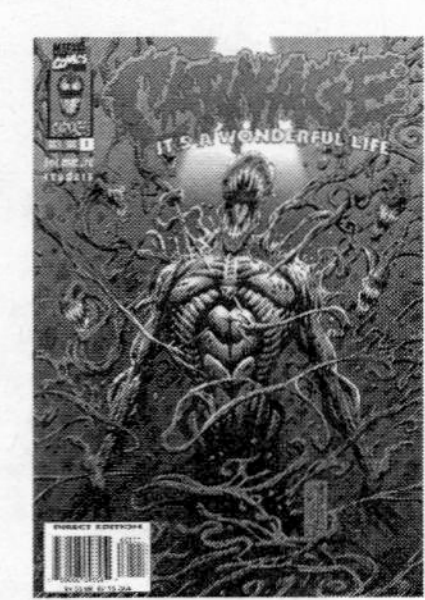

Carnage: It's a Wonderful Life #1 © MAR

Cartoon Network Starring #2 © H-B

Casey Jones #2 © MS

GD2.0 FN6.0 NM9.4

CARL BARKS LIBRARY OF WALT DISNEY'S GYRO GEARLOOSE COMICS AND FILLERS IN COLOR, THE
Gladstone: 1993 ($7.95, 8-1/2x11", limited series, 52 pgs.)
1-6: Carl Barks reprints 1.25 3.75 10.00

CARL BARKS LIBRARY OF WALT DISNEY'S COMICS AND STORIES IN COLOR, THE
Gladstone: Jan, 1992 - No. 51, Mar, 1996 ($8.95, 8-1/2x11", 60 pgs.)
1,2,6,8-51: 1-Barks Donald Duck-r/WDC&S #31-35; 2-r/#36,38-41; 6-r/#57-61; 8-r/#67-71; 9-r/#72-76; 10-r/#77-81; 11-r/#82-86; 12-r/#87-91; 13-r/#92-96; 14-r/#97-101; 15-r/#102-106; 16-r/#107-111; 17-r/#112,114,117,124,125; 18-r/#126-130; 19-r/#131,132(2),133,134; 20-r/#135-139; 21-r/#140-144; 22-r/#145-149; 23-r/#150-154; 24-r/#155-159; 25-r/#160-164; 26-r/#165-169; 27-r/#170-174;28-r/#175-179; 29-r/#180-184; 30-r/#185-189; 31-r/#190-194; 32-r/#195-199;33-r/#200-204; 34-r/#205-209; 35-r/#210-214; 36-r/#215-219; 37-r/#220-224; 38-r/#225-229; 39-r/#230-234; 40-r/#235-239; 41-r/#240-244; 42r/#245-249; 43-r/#250-254; 44-50; All contain one Heroes & Villains trading card each 1.25 3.75 10.00
3,4,7: 3-r/#42-46. 4-r/#47-51. 7-r/#62-66. 1.85 5.50 15.00
5-r/#52-56 2.30 7.00 20.00

CARL BARKS LIBRARY OF WALT DISNEY'S DONALD DUCK ADVENTURES IN COLOR, THE
Gladstone: Jan, 1994 - No. 25, Jan, 1996 ($7.95-$9.95, 44-68 pgs., 8-1/2"x11") (all contain one Donald Duck trading card each)
1-5,7-25-Carl Barks-r: 1-r/FC #9; 2-r/FC #29; 3-r/FC #62; 4-r/FC #108; 5-r/FC #147 & #79(Mickey Mouse); 7-r/FC #159. 8-r/FC #178 & 189. 9-r/FC #199 & 203; 10-r/FC 223 & 238; 11-r/Christmas Parade #1 & 2; 12-r/FC #296; 13-r/FC #263; 14-r/MOC #20 & 41; 15-r/FC 275 & 282; 16-r/FC #291&300; 17-r/FC #308 & 318; 18-r/Vac. Parade #1 & Summer Fun #2; 19-r/FC #328 & 367 1.50 4.50 12.00
6-r/MOC #4, Cheerios "Atom Bomb," D.D. Tells About Kites 2.30 7.00 20.00

CARL BARKS LIBRARY OF WALT DISNEY'S DONALD DUCK CHRISTMAS STORIES IN COLOR, THE
Gladstone: 1992 ($7.95, 44pgs., one-shot)
nn-Reprints Firestone giveaways 1945-1949 1.85 5.50 15.00

CARL BARKS LIBRARY OF WALT DISNEY'S UNCLE SCROOGE COMICS ONE PAGERS IN COLOR, THE
Gladstone: 1992 - No. 2, 1993 ($8.95, limited series, 60 pgs., 8-1/2x11")
1-Carl Barks one pg. reprints 2.50 7.50 25.00
2-Carl Barks one pg. reprints 1.85 5.50 15.00

CARNAGE: IT'S A WONDERFUL LIFE
Marvel Comics: Oct, 1996 ($1.95, one-shot)
1-David Quinn scripts 3.00

CARNAGE: MIND BOMB
Marvel Comics: Feb, 1996 ($2.95, one-shot)
1-Warren Ellis script; Kyle Hotz-a 3.00

CARNATION MALTED MILK GIVEAWAYS (See Wisco)

CARNEYS, THE
Archie Comics: Summer, 1994 ($2.00, 52 pgs)
1-Bound-in pull-out poster 2.50

CARNIVAL COMICS (Formerly Kayo #12; becomes Red Seal Comics #14)
Harry 'A' Chesler/Pershing Square Publ. Co.: 1945
nn (#13)-Guardineer-a 16.00 49.00 130.00

CAROLINE KENNEDY
Charlton Comics: 1961 (one-shot)
nn-Interior photo covers of Kennedy family 8.65 26.00 95.00

CAROUSEL COMICS
F. E. Howard, Toronto: V1#8, April, 1948
V1#8 5.75 17.00 40.00

CARTOON KIDS
Atlas Comics (CPS): 1957 (no month)
1-Maneely-c/a; Dexter The Demon, Willie The Wise-Guy, Little Zelda app. 10.00 30.00 75.00

GD2.0 FN6.0 NM9.4

CARTOON NETWORK PRESENTS
DC Comics: Aug, 1997 - No. 24, Aug, 1999 ($1.75-$1.99, anthology)
1-24: 1-Dexter's Lab. 2-Space Ghost. 12-Bizarro World 2.00
1-Platinum Edition 2.00

CARTOON NETWORK PRESENTS SPACE GHOST
Archie Comics: Mar, 1997 ($1.50)
1-Scott Rosema-p 2.00

CARTOON NETWORK STARRING... (Anthology)
DC Comics: Sept, 1999 - No. 18, Feb, 2001 ($1.99)
1-Powerpuff Girls 4.00
2-18: 2,8,11,14,17-Johnny Bravo. 12,15,18-Space Ghost 2.00

CARTOON TALES (Disney's...)
W.D. Publications (Disney): nd, nn (1992) ($2.95, 6-5/8x9-1/2", 52 pgs.)
nn-Ariel & Sebastian-Serpent Teen; Beauty and the Beast; A Tale of Enchantment; Darkwing Duck - Just Us Justice Ducks; 101 Dalmatians - Canine Classics; Tale Spin - Surprise in the Skies; Uncle Scrooge - Blast to the Past 4.00

CARVERS
Image Comics (Flypaper Press): 1998 - No. 3, 1999 ($2.95)
1-3-Pander Bros.-a/Fleming-s 3.00

CAR WARRIORS
Marvel Comics (Epic): June, 1991 - No. 4, Sept, 1991 ($2.25, lim. series)
1-4: 1-Says April in indicia 2.25

CASE OF THE SHOPLIFTER'S SHOE (See Perry Mason, Feature Book No.50)

CASE OF THE WINKING BUDDHA, THE
St. John Publ. Co.: 1950 (132 pgs.; 25¢; B&W; 5-1/2x7-5-1/2x8")
nn-Charles Raab-a; reprinted in Authentic Police Cases No. 25 28.00 83.00 220.00

CASEY-CRIME PHOTOGRAPHER (Two-Gun Western No. 5 on)(Radio)
Marvel Comics (BFP): Aug, 1949 - No. 4, Feb, 1950
1-Photo-c; 52 pgs. 23.00 68.00 180.00
2-4: Photo-c 15.00 45.00 120.00

CASEY JONES (TV)
Dell Publishing Co.: No. 915, July, 1958
Four Color 915-Alan Hale photo-c 4.60 13.75 55.00

CASEY JONES & RAPHAEL (See Bodycount)
Mirage Studios: Oct, 1994 ($2.75, unfinished limited series)
1-Bisley-c; Eastman story & pencils 2.75

CASEY JONES: NORTH BY DOWNEAST
Mirage Studios: May, 1994 - No. 2, July, 1994 ($2.75, limited series)
1,2-Rick Veitch script & pencils; Kevin Eastman story & inks 2.75

CASPER ADVENTURE DIGEST
Harvey Comics: V2#1, Oct, 1992 - V2#8, Apr, 1994 ($1.75/$1.95, digest-size)
V2#1: Casper, Richie Rich, Spooky, Wendy 5.00
2-8 3.50

CASPER AND...
Harvey Comics: Nov, 1987 - No. 12, June, 1990 (.75/$1.00, all reprints)
1-Ghostly Trio 4.00
2-12: 2-Spooky; begin $1.00-c. 3-Wendy. 4-Nightmare. 5-Ghostly Trio. 6-Spooky. 7-Wendy. 8-Hot Stuff. 9-Baby Huey. 10-Wendy.11-Ghostly Trio. 12-Spooky 3.00

CASPER AND FRIENDS
Harvey Comics: Oct, 1991 - No. 5, July, 1992 ($1.00/$1.25)
1-Nightmare, Ghostly Trio, Wendy, Spooky 4.00
2-5 3.00

CASPER AND FRIENDS MAGAZINE: Mar, 1997 - No. 3, July, 1997 ($3.99)
1-3 4.00

CASPER AND NIGHTMARE (See Harvey Hits# 37, 45, 52, 56, 59, 62, 65, 68,71, 75)

Casper and Nightmare #23 © Paramount

Casper Spaceship #1 © Paramount

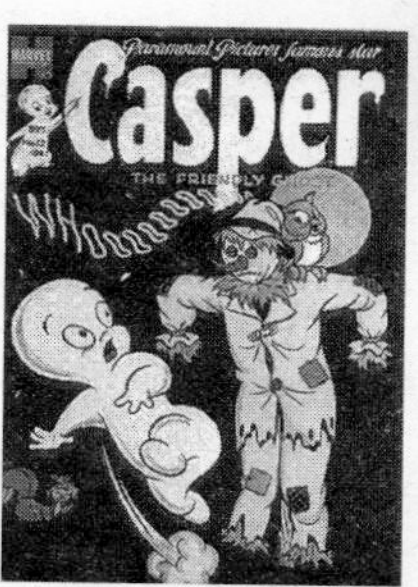

Casper, The Friendly Ghost #12 © Paramount

CASPER AND NIGHTMARE (Nightmare & Casper No. 1-5)
Harvey Publications: No. 6, 11/64 - No. 44, 10/73; No. 45, 6/74 - No. 46, 8/74 (25¢)

	GD2.0	FN6.0	NM9.4
6: 68 pg. Giants begin, ends #32	3.80	11.40	42.00
7-10	2.80	8.40	28.00
11-20	2.30	7.00	20.00
21-37: 33-37-(52 pg. Giants)	2.00	6.00	16.00
38-46	1.10	3.30	9.00

NOTE: *Many issues contain reprints.*

CASPER AND SPOOKY (See Harvey Hits No. 20)
Harvey Publications: Oct, 1972 - No. 7, Oct, 1973

	GD2.0	FN6.0	NM9.4
1	2.50	7.50	24.00
2-7	1.50	4.50	12.00

CASPER AND THE GHOSTLY TRIO
Harvey Pub.: Nov, 1972 - No. 7, Nov, 1973; No. 8, Aug, 1990 - No. 10, Dec, 1990

	GD2.0	FN6.0	NM9.4
1	2.50	7.50	24.00
2-7	1.50	4.50	12.00
8-10			4.00

CASPER AND WENDY
Harvey Publications: Sept, 1972 - No. 8, Nov, 1973

	GD2.0	FN6.0	NM9.4
1: 52 pg. Giant	2.50	7.50	24.00
2-8	1.50	4.50	12.00

CASPER BIG BOOK
Harvey Comics: V2#1, Aug, 1992 - No. 3, May, 1993 ($1.95, 52 pgs.)

	GD2.0	FN6.0	NM9.4
V2#1-Spooky app.			4.00
2,3			3.00

CASPER CAT (See Dopey Duck)
I. W. Enterprises/Super: 1958; 1963

	GD2.0	FN6.0	NM9.4
1,7:1-Wacky Duck #?.7-Reprint, Super No. 14('63)	1.50	4.50	12.00

CASPER DIGEST (...Magazine #?; ...Halloween Digest #8, 10)
Harvey Publications: Oct, 1986 - No. 18, Jan, 1991 ($1.25/$1.75, digest-size)

	GD2.0	FN6.0	NM9.4
1	1.10	3.30	9.00
2-18: 11-Valentine-c. 18-Halloween-c		2.40	6.00

CASPER DIGEST (...Magazine #? on)
Harvey Comics: V2#1, Sept, 1991 - V2#14, Nov, 1994 ($1.75/$1.95, digest-size)

	GD2.0	FN6.0	NM9.4
V2#1			4.00
2-14			3.00

CASPER DIGEST STORIES
Harvey Publications: Feb, 1980 - No. 4, Nov, 1980 (95¢, 132 pgs., digest size)

	GD2.0	FN6.0	NM9.4
1	1.75	5.25	14.00
2-4	1.00	3.00	8.00

CASPER DIGEST WINNERS
Harvey Publications: Apr, 1980 - No. 3, Sept, 1980 (95¢, 132 pgs., digest size)

	GD2.0	FN6.0	NM9.4
1	1.75	5.25	14.00
2,3	1.00	3.00	8.00

CASPER ENCHANTED TALES DIGEST
Harvey Comics: May, 1992 - No. 10, Oct, 1994 ($1.75, digest-size, 98 pgs.)

	GD2.0	FN6.0	NM9.4
1-Casper, Spooky, Wendy stories			5.00
2-10			3.50

CASPER GHOSTLAND
Harvey Comics: May, 1992 ($1.25)

	GD2.0	FN6.0	NM9.4
1			3.00

CASPER GIANT SIZE
Harvey Comics: Oct, 1992 - No. 4, Nov, 1993 ($2.25, 68 pgs.)

	GD2.0	FN6.0	NM9.4
V2#1-4-Casper, Wendy, Spooky stories			4.00

CASPER HALLOWEEN TRICK OR TREAT
Harvey Publications: Jan, 1976 (52 pgs.)

	GD2.0	FN6.0	NM9.4
1	2.50	7.50	24.00

CASPER IN SPACE (Formerly Casper Spaceship)
Harvey Publications: No. 6, June, 1973 - No. 8, Oct, 1973

	GD2.0	FN6.0	NM9.4
6-8	1.50	4.50	12.00

CASPER'S GHOSTLAND
Harvey Publications: Winter, 1958-59 - No. 97, 12/77; No. 98, 12/79 (25¢)

	GD2.0	FN6.0	NM9.4
1-84 pgs. begin, ends #10	16.50	49.00	180.00
2	8.65	26.60	95.00
3-10	6.35	19.00	70.00
11-20: 11-68 pgs. begin, ends #61. 13-X-Mas-c	4.55	13.65	50.00
21-40	3.45	10.35	38.00
41-61	2.30	7.00	20.00
62-77: 62-52 pgs. begin	1.50	4.50	12.00
78-98: 94-X-Mas-c	1.00	2.80	7.00

NOTE: *Most issues contain reprints w/new stories.*

CASPER SPACESHIP (Casper in Space No. 6 on)
Harvey Publications: Aug, 1972 - No. 5, April, 1973

	GD2.0	FN6.0	NM9.4
1: 52 pg. Giant	2.60	7.80	26.00
2-5	1.75	5.25	14.00

CASPER STRANGE GHOST STORIES
Harvey Publications: October, 1974 - No. 14, Jan, 1977 (All 52 pgs.)

	GD2.0	FN6.0	NM9.4
1	2.50	7.50	24.00
2-14	1.75	5.25	14.00

CASPER, THE FRIENDLY GHOST (See America's Best TV Comics, Famous TV Funday Funnies, The Friendly Ghost..., Nightmare &..., Richie Rich and..., Tastee-Freez, Treasury of Comics, Wendy the Good Little Witch & Wendy Witch World)

CASPER, THE FRIENDLY GHOST (Becomes Harvey Comics Hits No. 61 (No. 6), and then continued with Harvey issue No. 7)(1st Series)
St. John Publishing Co.: Sept, 1949 - No. 5, Aug, 1951

	GD2.0	FN6.0	NM9.4
1(1949)-Origin & 1st app. Baby Huey & Herman the Mouse (1st time the name Casper app. in any media, even films)	158.00	474.00	1500.00
2,3 (2/50 & 8/50)	68.00	205.00	650.00
4,5 (3/51 & 8/51)	53.00	158.00	475.00

CASPER, THE FRIENDLY GHOST (Paramount Picture Star...)(2nd Series)
Harvey Publications (Family Comics): No. 7, Dec, 1952 - No. 70, July, 1958
Note: No. 6 is Harvey Comics Hits No. 61 (10/52)

	GD2.0	FN6.0	NM9.4
7-Baby Huey begins, ends #9	31.00	93.00	350.00
8,9	18.00	53.00	195.00
10-Spooky begins (1st app., 6/53), ends #70?	20.00	60.00	220.00
11-18: Alfred Harvey app. in story	11.00	33.00	120.00
19-1st app. Nightmare (4/54)	15.50	46.50	170.00
20-Wendy the Witch begins (1st app., 5/54)	20.50	61.00	225.00
21-30: 24-Infinity-c	8.15	24.50	90.00
31-40	5.90	17.75	65.00
41-50	4.55	13.65	50.00
51-70 (Continues as Friendly Ghost... 8/58)	4.10	12.30	45.00

CASPER THE FRIENDLY GHOST (Formerly The Friendly Ghost...)(3rd Series)
Harvey Comics: No. 254, July, 1990 - No. 260, Jan, 1991 ($1.00)

	GD2.0	FN6.0	NM9.4
254-260			3.00

CASPER THE FRIENDLY GHOST (4th Series)
Harvey Comics: Mar, 1991 - No. 28, Nov, 1994 ($1.00/$1.25/$1.50)

	GD2.0	FN6.0	NM9.4
1-Casper becomes Mighty Ghost; Spooky & Wendy app.			4.00
2-10: 7,8-Post-a			3.00
11-28-($1.50)			2.00

CASPER T.V. SHOWTIME
Harvey Comics: Jan, 1980 - No. 5, Oct, 1980

	GD2.0	FN6.0	NM9.4
1	1.10	3.30	9.00
2-5			5.00

CASSETTE BOOKS (Classics Illustrated)
Cassette Book Co./I.P.S. Publ.: 1984 (48 pgs, b&w comic with cassette tape)

NOTE: *This series was illegal. The artwork was illegally obtained, and the Classics Illustrated copyright owner, Twin Circle Publ. sued to get an injunction to prevent the continued sale of this series. Many C.I. collectors obtained copies before the 1987 injunction, but now they are already scarce. Here again the market is just developing, but sealed mint copies of com ic and tape should be worth at least $25.*

1001 (CI#1-A2)New-PC 1002(CI#3-A2)CI-PC 1003(CI#13-A2)CI-PC
1004(CI#25)CI-LDC 1005(CI#10-A2)New-PC 1006(CI#64)CI-LDC

Castle Waiting V2 #3 © Linda Medley

Catman Comics #7 © HOKE

Catwoman #65 © DC

GD2.0 FN6.0 NM9.4

CASTILIAN (See Movie Classics)

CASTLE WAITING
Olio: 1997 - No. 7, 1999 ($2.95, B&W)
Cartoon Books: Vol. 2, Aug, 2000 - Present ($2.95, B&W)

1-Linda Medley-s/a in all 1.00 3.00 8.00
2 4.00
3-7 3.00
The Lucky Road TPB r/#1-7 16.95
Hiatus Issue (1999) Crilley-c; short stories and previews 3.00
Vol. 2 #1-3 2.95

CASUAL HEROES
Image Comics (Motown Machineworks): Apr, 1996 ($2.25, unfinished lim. series

1-Steve Rude-c 2.25

CAT, T.H.E. (TV) (See T.H.E. Cat)

CAT, THE (See Movie Classics)

CAT, THE (Female hero)
Marvel Comics Group: Nov, 1972 - No. 4, June, 1973

1-Origin & 1st app. The Cat (who later becomes Tigra); Mooney-a(i); Wood-c(i)/a(i) 2.50 7.50 24.00
2,3: 2-Marie Severin/Mooney-a. 3-Everett inks 1.75 5.25 14.00
4-Starlin/Weiss-a(p) 2.00 6.00 16.00

CATALYST: AGENTS OF CHANGE (Also see Comics' Greatest World)
Dark Horse Comics: Feb, 1994 - No.7, Nov, 1994 ($2.00, limited series)

1-7: 1-Foil stamped logo 2.00

CAT & MOUSE
EF Graphics (Silverline): Dec, 1988 ($1.75, color w/part B&W)

1-1st printing (12/88, 32 pgs.), 1-2nd printing (5/89, 36 pgs.) 2.00

CAT FROM OUTER SPACE (See Walt Disney Showcase #46)

CATHOLIC COMICS (See Heroes All Catholic...)
Catholic Publications: June, 1946 - V3#10, July, 1949

1 30.00 90.00 240.00
2 15.00 45.00 120.00
3-13(7/47) 13.00 39.00 15.00
V2#1-10 10.00 30.00 75.00
V3#1-10: Reprints 10-part Treasure Island serial from Target V2#2-11 (see Key Comics #5) 10.00 30.00 80.00

CATHOLIC PICTORIAL
Catholic Guild: 1947

1-Toth-a(2) (Rare) 40.00 120.00 320.00

CATMAN COMICS (Formerly Crash Comics No. 1-5)
Holyoke Publishing Co./Continental Magazines V2#12, 7/44 on: 5/41 - No. 17, 1/43; No. 18, 7/43 - No. 22, 12/43; No. 23, 3/44 - No. 26, 11/44; No. 27, 4/45 - No. 30, 12/45; No. 31, 6/46 - No. 32, 8/46

1(V1#6)-Origin The Deacon & Sidekick Mickey, Dr. Diamond & Rag-Man; The Black Widow app.; The Catman by Chas. Quinlan & Blaze Baylor begin 333.00 1000.00 3500.00
2(V1#7) 121.00 363.00 1150.00
3(V1#8)-The Pied Piper begins; classic Hitler, Stalin & Mussolini-c 100.00 300.00 950.00
4(V1#9) 90.00 270.00 855.00
5(V2#10)-Origin Kitten; The Hood begins (c-redated), 6,7(V2#11,12) 73.00 219.00 695.00
8(V2#13,3/42)-Origin Little Leaders; Volton by Kubert begins (his 1st comic book work) 90.00 270.00 855.00
9,10(V2#14,15): 10-Origin Blackout retold; Phantom Falcon begins 60.00 180.00 570.00
11 (V3#1)-Kubert-a 60.00 180.00 570.00
12 (V3#2), 14, 15, 17, 18(V3#8, 7/43) 53.00 159.00 475.00
13-(scarce) 73.00 219.00 695.00
16 (V3#5)-Hitler, Tojo, Mussolini, Stalin-c 68.00 205.00 650.00
19,20: 19 (V2#6)-Hitler, Tojo, Mussolini-c. 20 (V2#7): Classic Hitler-c 74.00 221.00 700.00
21-23 (V2#10, 3/44) 47.00 141.00 420.00
nn(V3#13, 5/44)-Rico-a; Schomburg bondage-c 47.00 141.00 420.0
nn(V2#12, 7/44, nn(V3#1, 9/44)-Origin The Golden Archer; Leatherface app. 43.00 129.00 390.0
nn(V3#2, 11/44)-L. B. Cole-c 76.00 228.00 720.0
27-Origins Catman & Kitten retold; L. B. Cole Flag-c; Infantino-a 84.00 252.00 790.0
28-Catman learns Kitten's I.D.; Dr. Macabre, Deacon app.; L. B. Cole c/a 87.00 261.00 825.0
29-32-L. B. Cole-c; bondage-#30 77.00 221.00 730.0
NOTE: ***Fuje*** *a-11, 29(3), 30.* ***Palais*** *a-11, 29(2), 30(2), 32; c-25(7/44).* ***Rico*** *a-11(2).*

CATSEYE
Hyperwerks Comics: Dec, 1998 - No. 4, June, 1999 ($2.95)

1-4-Altstaetter-s/a 3.0

CAT TALES (3-D)
Eternity Comics: Apr, 1989 ($2.95)

1-Felix the Cat-r in 3-D 5.0

CATWOMAN (Also see Action Comics Weekly #611, Batman #404-407, Detective Comics, & Superman's Girlfriend Lois Lane #70, 71)
DC Comics: Feb, 1989 - No. 4, May, 1989 ($1.50, limited series, mature)

1 1.25 3.75 10.0
2-4: 3-Batman cameo. 4-Batman app. 1.10 3.30 9.0
Her Sister's Keeper (1991, $9.95, trade paperback)-r/#1-4 10.0

CATWOMAN (Also see Showcase '93, Showcase '95 #4, & Batman #404-407)
DC Comics: Aug, 1993 - Present ($1.50-$2.25)

0-(10/94)-Zero Hour; origin retold. Released between #14&15 3.0
1-($1.95)-Embossed-c; Bane app.; Balent c-1-10; a-1-10p 4.0
2-20: 3-Bane flashback cameo. 4-Brief Bane app. 6,7-Knightquest tie-ins; Batman (Azrael) app. 8-1st app. Zephyr. 12-KnightsEnd pt. 6. 13-new Knigh End Aftermath.14-(9/94)-Zero Hour 3.0
21-24, 26-30, 33-49: 21-$1.95-c begins. 28,29-Penguin cameo app. 36-Legacy pt. 2. 38-40-Year Two; Batman, Joker, Penguin & Two-Face app. 46-Two-Face app. 2.5
25,31,32: 25-($2.95)-Robin app. 31-Contagion pt. 4 (Reads pt. 5 on-c). 32-Contagion pt. 9. 3.0
50-($2.95, 48 pgs.)-New armored costume 3.0
50-($2.95, 48 pgs.)-Collector's Ed.w/metallic ink-c 3.0
51-77: 51-Huntress-c/app. 54-Grayson-s begins. 56-Cataclysm pt.6. 57-Poison Ivy-c/app.63-65-Joker-c/app. 72-No Man's Land; Ostrander-s begins 2.5
78-82: 80-Catwoman goes to jail 2.0
83-90: 83-Begin $2.25-c. 83,84,89-Harley Quinn-c/app. 2.2
#1,000,000 (11/98) 853rd Century x-over 2.0
Annual 1 (1994, $2.95, 68 pgs.)-Elseworlds story; Batman app.; no Balent-a 3.0
Annual 2,4 ('95, '97, $3.95)-2-Year One story. 4-Pulp Heroes 4.0
Annual 3 (1996, $2.95)-Legends of the Dead Earth story 3.0
...Plus 1 (11/97, $2.95) Screamqueen (Scare Tactics) app. 3.0
TPB ($9.95) r/#15-19, Balent-c 10.0

CATWOMAN/ GUARDIAN OF GOTHAM
DC Comics: 1999 - No. 2, 1999 ($5.95, limited series)

1,2-Elseworlds; Moench-s/Balent-a 6.0

CATWOMAN/VAMPIRELLA: THE FURIES
DC Comics/Harris Publ.: Feb, 1997 ($4.95, squarebound, one-shot, 46 pgs.) (1st DC/Harris x-over)

nn-Reintro Pantha; Chuck Dixon scripts; Jim Balent-c/a 5.0

CATWOMAN/WILDCAT
DC Comics: Aug, 1998 - No. 4, Nov, 1998 ($2.50, limited series)

1-4-Chuck Dixon & Beau Smith-s; Stelfreeze-c 3.0

CAUGHT
Atlas Comics (VPI): Aug, 1956 - No. 5, Apr, 1957

1 21.00 62.00 165.0
2-4: 3-Maneely, Pakula, Torres-a. 4-Maneely-a 10.50 32.00 85.0
5-Crandall, Krigstein-a 12.00 36.00 95.0
NOTE: ***Drucker*** *a-2.* ***Heck*** *a-4.* ***Severin*** *c-1, 2, 4, 5.* ***Shores*** *a-4.*

CAVALIER COMICS

Cavewoman: Pangean Sea Prelude © Budd Root

Celestine #1 © Alan Moore

Cerebus #171 © Dave Sim

GD2.0 FN6.0 NM9.4

A. W. Nugent Publ. Co.: 1945; 1952 (Early DC reprints)
2(1945)-Speed Saunders, Fang Gow 21.00 64.00 170.00
2(1952) 10.50 32.00 85.00

CAVE GIRL (Also see Africa)
Magazine Enterprises: No. 11, 1953 - No. 14, 1954
11(A-1 82)-Origin; all Cave Girl stories 44.00 133.00 400.00
12(A-1 96), 13(A-1 116), 14(A-1 125)-Thunda by Powell in each
35.00 105.00 280.00
NOTE: ***Powell*** *c/a in all.*

CAVE GIRL
AC Comics: 1988 ($2.95, 44 pgs.) (16 pgs. of color, rest B&W)
1-Powell-r/Cave Girl #11; Nyoka photo back-c from movie; Powell/Bill Black-c; Special Limited Edition on-c 4.00

CAVE KIDS (TV) (See Comic Album #16)
Gold Key: Feb, 1963 - No. 16, Mar, 1967 (Hanna-Barbera)
1 6.30 19.00 75.00
2-5 3.20 9.60 35.00
6-16: 7,12-Pebbles & Bamm Bamm app. 16-1st Space Kidettes
2.50 7.50 25.00

CAVEWOMAN
Basement Comics: Jan, 1994 - No. 6, 1995 ($2.95)
1 3.00 9.00 30.00
2 1.85 5.50 15.00
3-6 1.00 3.00 8.00
...: Meets Explorers ('97, $2.95) 3.00
...: One-Shot Special (7/00, $2.95) Massey-s/a 3.00

CAVEWOMAN: MISSING LINK
Basement Comics: 1997 - No. 4, 1998 ($2.95, B&W, limited series)
1-4 3.00

CAVEWOMAN: ODYSSEY
Caliber: 1999 - No. 5 ($2.95, limited series)
1 2.95

CAVEWOMAN: PANGAEAN SEA
Basement Comics: Oct, 1999 ($4.95, B&W, limited series)
Prelude-Budd Root-s/a 4.95
1-(6/00, $2.95) Budd Root-s/a 2.95

CAVEWOMAN: RAIN
Caliber: 1996 - No. 8, 1998 ($2.95, limited series)
1-8, 8-Alternate cover 4.00
8-Green foil cover 5.00

CELESTINE (See Violator Vs. Badrock #1)
Image Comics (Extreme): May, 1996 - No. 2, June, 1996 ($2.50, limited series)
1,2: Warren Ellis scripts 2.50

CENTURION OF ANCIENT ROME, THE
Zondervan Publishing House: 1958 (no month listed) (B&W, 36 pgs.)
(Rare) All by Jay Disbrow 33.00 98.00 260.00

CENTURIONS (TV)
DC Comics: June, 1987 - No. 4, Sept, 1987 (75¢, limited series)
1-4 2.00

CENTURY: DISTANT SONS
Marvel Comics: Feb, 1996 ($2.95, one-shot)
1-Wraparound-c 3.00

CENTURY OF COMICS (See Promotional Comics section)

CEREBUS BI-WEEKLY
Aardvark-Vanaheim: Dec. 2, 1988 - No. 26, Nov. 11, 1989 ($1.25, B&W)
Reprints Cerebus The Aardvark#1-26
1-16, 18, 19, 21-26: 2.50
17-Hepcats app. 1.50 4.50 12.00
20-Milk & Cheese app. 1.85 5.50 15.00

CEREBUS: CHURCH & STATE
Aardvark-Vanaheim: Feb, 1991 - No. 30, Apr, 1992 ($2.00, B&W, bi-weekly)
1-30: r/Cerebus #51-80 3.00

CEREBUS: HIGH SOCIETY
Aardvark-Vanaheim: Feb, 1990 - No. 25, 1991 ($1.70, B&W)
1-25: r/Cerebus #26-50 3.00

CEREBUS JAM
Aardvark-Vanaheim: Apr, 1985
1-Eisner, Austin, Dave Sim-a (Cerebus vs. Spirit) 2.40 6.00

CEREBUS THE AARDVARK (See A-V in 3-D, Nucleus, Power Comics)
Aardvark-Vanaheim: Dec, 1977 - Present ($1.70/$2.00/$2.25, B&W)
0 3.00
0-Gold 20.00
1-1st app. Cerebus; 2000 print run; most copies poorly printed
31.00 93.00 350.00
Note: *There is a counterfeit version known to exist. It can be distinguished from the original in the following ways: inside cover is glossy instead of flat, black background on the front cover is blotted or spotty. Reports show that a counterfeit #2 also exists.*
2-Dave Sim art in all 9.00 27.00 100.00
3-Origin Red Sophia 8.15 24.50 90.00
4-Origin Elrod the Albino 5.45 16.35 60.00
5,6 4.55 13.65 50.00
7-10 3.20 9.60 35.00
11,12: 11-Origin The Cockroach 2.50 7.50 24.00
13-15: 14-Origin Lord Julius 1.85 5.50 15.00
16-20, 23-30: 23-Preview of Wandering Star by Teri S. Wood. 26-High Society begins,ends #50 1.00 3.00 8.00
21-B. Smith letter in letter column 3.20 9.60 35.00
22-Low distribution; no cover price 2.00 6.00 16.00
31-Origin Moonroach 1.25 3.75 10.00
32-40, 53-Intro. Wolveroach (cameo) 2.40 6.00
41-50,52: 52-Church & State begins, ends #111; Cutey Bunny app. 5.00
51,54: 51-Cutey Bunny app. 54-1st full Wolveroach story 1.00 3.00 8.00
55,56-Wolveroach app.; Normalman back-ups by Valentino 5.00
57-100: 61,62: Flaming Carrot app. 65-Gerhard begins 4.00
101-160: 104-Flaming Carrot app. 112/113-Double issue. 114-Jaka's Story begins, ends #136. 139-Melmoth begins, ends #150. 151-Mothers & Daughters begins, ends #200 3.00
161-Bone app. 1.00 3.00 8.00
162-231: 175-($2.25, 44 pgs). 201-Guys storyline begins; Eddie Campbell's Bacchus app. 220-231-Rick's Story 2.50
232-261: 232-Going Home begins 2.25
Free Cerebus (Giveaway, 1991-92?, 36 pgs.)-All-r 2.00

CHAIN GANG WAR
DC Comics: July, 1993 - No. 12, June, 1994 ($1.75)
1-($2.50)-Embossed silver foil-c, Dave Johnson-c/a 2.50
2-4,6-12: 3-Deathstroke app. 4-Brief Deathstroke app. 6-New Batman (Azrael) cameo. 11-New Batman-c/story. 12-New Batman app. 2.00
5-($2.50)-Foil-c; Deathstroke app; new Batman cameo (1 panel) 2.50

CHAINS OF CHAOS
Harris Comics: Nov, 1994 - No. 3, Jan, 1995 ($2.95, limited series)
1-3-Re-Intro of The Rook w/ Vampirella 3.00

CHALLENGE OF THE UNKNOWN (Formerly Love Experiences)
Ace Magazines: No. 6, Sept, 1950 (See Web Of Mystery No. 19)
6- "Villa of the Vampire" used in N.Y. Joint Legislative Comm. Publ; Sekowsky-a 30.00 90.00 240.00

CHALLENGER, THE
Interfaith Publications/T.C. Comics: 1945 - No. 4, Oct-Dec, 1946
nn; nd; 32 pgs.; Origin the Challenger Club; Anti-Fascist with funny animal filler 40.00 120.00 320.00
2-4: Kubert-a; 4-Fuje-a 30.00 90.00 240.00

CHALLENGERS OF THE FANTASTIC
Marvel Comics (Amalgam): June 1997 ($1.95, one-shot)
1-Karl Kesel-s/Tom Grummett-a 2.00

CHALLENGERS OF THE UNKNOWN (See Showcase #6, 7, 11, 12, Super

Challengers of the Unknown (3rd series) #8 © DC

Chamber of Chills #24 © HARV

Champion Comics #4 © HARV

DC Giant, and Super Team Family)
National Per. Publ./DC Comics: 4-5/58 - No. 77, 12-1/70-71; No. 78, 2/73 - No. 80, 6-7/73; No. 81, 6-7/77 - No. 87, 6-7/78

1-(4-5/58)-Kirby/Stein-a(2); Kirby-c 167.00 500.00 2500.00
2-Kirby/Stein-a(2) 64.00 193.00 900.00
3-Kirby/Stein-a(2) 55.00 165.00 775.00
4-8-Kirby/Wood-a plus cover to #8 44.00 133.00 575.00
9,10 26.50 79.00 290.00
11-15: 11-Grey tone-c. 14-Origin/1st app. Multi-Man (villain) 18.00 53.00 195.00
16-22: 18-Intro. Cosmo, the Challengers Spacepet. 22-Last 10¢ issue 12.50 37.00 135.00
23-30 6.35 19.00 70.00
31-Retells origin of the Challengers 6.80 20.50 75.00
32-40 3.20 9.60 35.00
41-47,49,50,52-60: 43-New look begins. 49-Intro. Challenger Corps. 55-Death of Red Ryan. 60-Red Ryan returns 2.40 7.35 22.00
48,51: 48-Doom Patrol app. 51-Sea Devils app. 2.50 7.50 24.00
61-68: 64,65-Kirby origin-r, parts 1 & 2. 66-New logo. 68-Last 12¢ issue. 1.50 4.50 12.00
69-73,75-80: 69-1st app. Corinna. 77-Last 15¢ issue 1.00 3.00 8.00
74-Deadman by Tuska/Adams; 1 pg. Wrightson-a 2.30 7.00 20.00
81,83-87: 81-(6-7/77). 83-87-Swamp Thing app. 1.00 2.80 7.00
82-Swamp Thing begins, c/s 1.25 3.75 10.00

NOTE: ***N. Adams*** *c-67, 68, 70, 72, 74i, 81i.* ***Buckler*** *c-83-86p.* ***Giffen*** *a-83-87p.* ***Kirby*** *a-75-80r; c-75, 77, 78.* ***Kubert*** *c-64, 66, 69, 76, 79.* ***Nasser*** *c/a-81p, 82p.* ***Tuska*** *a-73.* ***Wood*** *r-76.*

CHALLENGERS OF THE UNKNOWN
DC Comics: Mar, 1991 - No. 8, Oct, 1991 ($1.75, limited series)

1-Jeph Loeb scripts & Tim Sale-a in all (1st work together); Bolland-c 2.50
2-8: 2-Superman app. 3-Dr. Fate app. 6-G. Kane-c(p). 7-Steranko-c/swipe by Art Adams 2.50

NOTE: ***Art Adams*** *c-7.* ***Hempel*** *c-5.* ***Gil Kane*** *c-6p.* ***Sale*** *a-1-8; c-3, 8.* ***Wagner*** *c-4.*

CHALLENGERS OF THE UNKNOWN
DC Comics: Feb, 1997 - No. 18, July, 1998 ($2.25)

1-18: 1-Intro new team; Leon-c/a(p) begins. 4-Origin of new team. 11,12-Batman app. 15-Millennium Giants x-over; Superman-c/app. 2.50

CHALLENGE TO THE WORLD
Catechetical Guild: 1951 (10¢, 36 pgs.)

nn 4.00 12.00 24.00

CHAMBER OF CHILLS (Formerly Blondie Comics #20; ...of Clues No. 27 on)
Harvey Publications/Witches Tales: No. 21, June, 1951 - No. 26, Dec, 1954

21 (#1) 42.00 126.00 375.00
22,24 (#2,4) 28.00 84.00 225.00
23 (#3)-Excessive violence; eyes torn out 31.00 94.00 250.00
5(2/52)-Decapitation, acid in face scene 31.00 94.00 250.00
6-Woman melted alive 30.00 90.00 240.00
7-Used in **SOTI**, pg. 389; decapitation/severed head panels 28.00 84.00 225.00
8-10: 8-Decapitation panels 24.00 71.00 190.00
11,12,14 18.00 53.00 140.00
13,15-24-Nostrand-a in all. 13,21-Decapitation panels. 18-Atom bomb panels. 20-Nostrand-c 25.00 75.00 200.00
25,26 15.00 45.00 120.00

NOTE: *About half the issues contain bondage, torture, sadism, perversion, gore, cannabalism, eyes ripped out, acid in face, etc.* ***Elias*** *c-4-11, 14-19, 21-26.* ***Kremer*** *a-12, 17.* ***Palais*** *a-21(1), 23.* ***Nostrand/Powell*** *a-13, 15, 16.* ***Powell*** *a-21, 23, 24('51), 5-8, 11, 13, 18-21, 23-25. Bondage-c-21, 24('51), 7. 25-r/#5; 26-r/#9.*

CHAMBER OF CHILLS
Marvel Comics Group: Nov, 1972 - No. 25, Nov, 1976

1-Harlan Ellison adaptation 2.30 7.00 20.00
2-5: 2-1st app. John Jakes (Brak the Barbarian) 1.50 4.50 12.00
6-25: 22,23-(Regular 25¢ editions) 1.25 3.75 10.00
22,23-(30¢-c variants, limited distribution)(5,7/76) 1.85 5.50 15.00

NOTE: ***Adkins*** *a-1i, 2i.* ***Brunner*** *a-2-4; c-4.* ***Chaykin*** *a-4.* ***Ditko*** *r-14, 16, 19, 23, 24.* ***Everett*** *a-3i, 11r,21r.* ***Heath*** *a-1r.* ***Gil Kane*** *c-2p.* ***Kirby*** *r-11, 18, 19, 22.* ***Powell*** *a-13r.* ***Russell*** *a-1p, 2p.* ***Williamson/Mayo*** *a-13r.* ***Robert E. Howard*** *horror story adaptation-2, 3.*

CHAMBER OF CLUES (Formerly Chamber of Chills)
Harvey Publications: No. 27, Feb, 1955 - No. 28, April, 1955

27-Kerry Drake-r/#19; Powell-a; last pre-code 10.50 32.00 85.00
28-Kerry Drake 7.85 23.50 55.00

CHAMBER OF DARKNESS (Monsters on the Prowl #9 on)
Marvel Comics Group: Oct, 1969 - No. 8, Dec, 1970

1-Buscema-a(p) 5.00 15.00 55.00
2,3: 2-Neal Adams scripts. 3-Smith, Buscema-a 2.80 8.40 28.00
4-A Conan-esque tryout by Smith (4/70); reprinted in Conan #16; Marie Severin/Everett-c 4.55 13.65 50.00
5,8: 5-H.P. Lovecraft adaptation. 8-Wrightson-c 2.30 7.00 20.00
6 2.00 6.00 16.00
7-Wrightson-c/a, 7pgs. (his 1st work at Marvel); Wrightson draws himself in 1st & last panels; Kirby/Ditko-r; last 15¢-c 2.50 7.50 25.00
1-(1/72; 25¢ Special, 52 pgs.) 2.50 7.50 25.00

NOTE: ***Adkins/Everett*** *a-8.* ***Buscema*** *a-Special 1r.* ***Craig*** *a-5.* ***Ditko*** *a-6-8r.* ***Heck*** *a-1, 2, 8, Special 1r.* ***Kirby*** *a(p)-4, 5, 7r.* ***Kirby/Everett*** *c-5.* ***Severin/Everett*** *c-6.* ***Shores*** *a-2, 3i, Special 1r.* ***Sutton*** *a-1, 2i, 4, 7, Special 1r.* ***Wrightson*** *c-7, 8.*

CHAMP COMICS (Formerly Champion No. 1-10)
Worth Publ. Co./Champ Publ./Family Comics(Harvey Publ.): No. 11, Oct, 1940 No. 24, Dec, 1942; No. 25, April, 1943

11-Human Meteor cont'd. from Champion 84.00 261.00 825.00
12-17,20: 14,15-Crandall-c. 20-The Green Ghost app. 65.00 195.00 620.00
18,19-Simon-c. 19-The Wasp app. 82.00 245.00 780.00
21-23,25: 22-The White Mask app. 23-Flag-c 52.00 156.00 470.00
24-Hitler, Tojo & Mussolini-c 55.00 165.00 500.00

CHAMPION (See Gene Autry's...)

CHAMPION COMICS (Formerly Speed Comics #1?; Champ Comics No. 11 on)
Worth Publ. Co.(Harvey Publications): No. 2, Dec, 1939 - No. 10, Aug, 1940 (no No.1)

2-The Champ, The Blazing Scarab, Neptina, Liberty Lads, Jungleman, Bill Handy, Swingtime Sweetie begin 168.00 505.00 1600.00
3-7: 7-The Human Meteor begins? 76.00 229.00 725.00
8-10: 8-Simon-c. 9-1st S&K-c (1st collaboration together). 10-Bondage-c by Kirby 135.00 405.00 1280.00

CHAMPIONS, THE
Marvel Comics Group: Oct, 1975 - No. 17, Jan, 1978

1-Origin & 1st app. The Champions (The Angel, Black Widow, Ghost Rider, Hercules, Iceman); Venus x-over 2.00 6.00 18.00
2-4,8-14,16,17: 2,3-Venus x-over. 11-14,17-Byrne-a 1.10 3.30 9.00
5-7-(Regular 25¢ edition)(4-8/76) 6-Kirby-c 1.10 3.30 9.00
5-7-(30¢-c variants, limited distribution) 1.75 5.25 14.00
15-(Regular 30¢ edition)(9/77)-Byrne-a 1.10 3.30 9.00
15-(35¢-c variant, limited distribution) 1.75 5.25 14.00

NOTE: ***Buckler/Adkins*** *c-3.* ***Byrne*** *a-11-15, 17.* ***Kane/Adkins*** *c-1.* ***Kane/Layton*** *c-11.* ***Tuska*** *a-3p, 4p, 6p, 7p. Ghost Rider c-1-4, 7, 8, 10, 14, 16, 17 (4, 10, 14 are more prominent).*

CHAMPIONS (Game)
Eclipse Comics: June, 1986 - No. 6, Feb, 1987 (limited series)

1-6: 1-Intro Flare; based on game. 5-Origin Flare 2.00

CHAMPIONS (Also see The League of Champions)
Hero Comics: Sept, 1987 - No. 12, 1989 ($1.95)

1-12: 1-Intro The Marksman & The Rose. 14-Origin Malice 2.00
Annual 1(1988, $2.75, 52pgs.)-Origin of Giant 2.75

CHAMPION SPORTS
National Periodical Publications: Oct-Nov, 1973 - No. 3, Feb-Mar, 1974

1 2.50 7.50 23.00
2,3 1.50 4.50 12.00

CHANNEL ZERO
Image Comics: Feb, 1998 - No. 5 ($2.95, B&W, limited series)

1-5, ...Dupe (1/99) -Brian Wood-s/a 3.00

CHAOS (See The Crusaders)

CHAOS! BIBLE
Chaos! Comics: Nov, 1995 ($3.30, one-shot)

Charlie Chan #4 © PRIZE

Charm School #1 © Elizabeth Watasin

Chase #4 © DC

GD2.0 FN6.0 NM9.4

1-Profiles of characters & creators 3.50

CHAOS! CHRONICLES
Chaos! Comics: Feb, 2000 ($3.50, one-shot)
1-Profiles of characters, checklist of Chaos! comics and products 3.50

CHAOS EFFECT, THE
Valiant: 1994
Alpha (Giveaway w/trading card checklist) 2.00
Alpha-Gold variant, Omega-Gold variant 5.00
Omega (11/94, $2.25); Epilogue Pt. 1, 2 (12/94, 1/95; $2.95) 3.00

CHAOS! GALLERY
Chaos! Comics: Aug, 1997 ($2.95, one-shot)
1-Pin-ups of characters 3.00

CHAOS! QUARTERLY
Chaos! Comics: Oct, 1995 -No. 3, May, 1996 ($4.95, quarterly)
1-3: 1-anthology; Lady Death-c by Julie Bell. 2-Boris "Lady Demon"-c 5.00
1-Premium Edition (7,500) 25.00

CHAPEL (Also see Youngblood & Youngblood Strikefile #1-3)
Image Comics (Extreme Studios): No. 1 Feb, 1995 - No. 2, Mar, 1995 ($2.50, limited series)
1,2 2.50

CHAPEL (Also see Youngblood & Youngblood Strikefile #1-3)
Image Comics (Extreme Studios): V2 #1, Aug, 1995 - No. 7, Apr, 1996 ($2.50)
V2#1-7: 4-Babewatch x-over. 5-vs. Spawn. 7-Shadowhawk-c/app; Shadowhunt x-over 2.50
#1-Quesada & Palmiotti variant-c 2.50

CHAPEL (Also see Youngblood & Youngblood Strikefile #1-3)
Awesome Entertainment: Sept, 1997 ($2.99, one-shot)
1 (Reg. & alternate covers) 3.00

CHARLEMAGNE (Also see War Dancer)
Defiant Comics: Mar, 1994 - No. 5, July, 1994 ($2.50)
1/2 (Hero Illustrated giveaway)-Adam Pollina-c/a.
1-(3/94, $3.50, 52 pgs.)-Adam Pollina-c/a. 3.50
2,3,5: Adam Pollina-c/a. 2-War Dancer app. 5-Pre-Schism issue. 2.50
4-($3.25, 52 pgs.) 3.25

CHARLIE CHAN (See Big Shot Comics, Columbia Comics, Feature Comics & The New Advs. of...)

CHARLIE CHAN (The Adventures of...) (Zaza The Mystic No. 10 on) (TV)
Crestwood(Prize) No. 1-5; Charlton No. 6(6/55) on: 6-7/48 - No. 5, 2-3/49; No.6, 6/55 - No. 9, 3/56

	GD2.0	FN6.0	NM9.4
1-S&K-c, 2 pgs.; Infantino-a	76.00	229.00	725.00
2-5-S&K-c: 3-S&K-c/a	50.00	150.00	450.00
6 (6/55-Charlton)-S&K-c	36.00	107.00	285.00
7-9	18.00	53.00	140.00

CHARLIE CHAN
Dell Publishing Co.: Oct-Dec, 1965 - No. 2, Mar, 1966

	GD2.0	FN6.0	NM9.4
1-Springer-a	4.10	12.30	45.00
2	2.80	8.40	28.00

CHARLIE McCARTHY (See Edgar Bergen Presents...)
Dell Publishing Co.: No. 171, Nov, 1947 - No. 571, July, 1954 (See True Comics #14)

	GD2.0	FN6.0	NM9.4
Four Color 171	25.00	75.00	300.00
Four Color 196-Part photo-c; photo back-c	17.00	50.00	200.00
1(3-5/49)-Part photo-c; photo back-c	15.00	45.00	175.00
2-9(7/52; #5,6-52 pgs.)	6.70	20.00	80.00
Four Color 445,478,527,571	4.60	13.75	55.00

CHARLTON BULLSEYE
CPL/Gang Publications: 1975 - No. 5, 1976 ($1.50, B&W, bi-monthly, magazine format)

	GD2.0	FN6.0	NM9.4
1: 1 & 2 are last Capt. Atom by Ditko/Byrne intended for the never published Capt. Atom #90; Nightshade app.; Jeff Jones-a	4.10	12.30	45.00
2-Part 2 Capt. Atom story by Ditko/Byrne	2.50	7.50	25.00
3-Wrong Country by Sanho Kim	1.85	5.50	15.00
4-Doomsday + 1 by John Byrne	2.00	6.00	18.00
5-Doomsday + 1 by Byrne, The Question by Toth; Neal Adams back-c; Toth-c	3.00	9.00	30.00

CHARLTON BULLSEYE
Charlton Publications: June, 1981 - No. 10, Dec, 1982; Nov, 1986
1-Blue Beetle, The Question app.; 1st app. Rocket Rabbit 5.00
2-10: 2-1st app. Neil The Horse; Rocket Rabbit app. 4-Vanguards. 6-Origin & 1st app. Thunderbunny 4.00
Special 1,2: 1(11/86) (Half in B&W). 2-Atomic Mouse app. (1987) 5.00

CHARLTON CLASSICS
Charlton Comics: Apr, 1980 - No. 9, Aug, 1981

	GD2.0	FN6.0	NM9.4
1		2.40	6.00
2-9			4.00

CHARLTON CLASSICS LIBRARY (1776)
Charlton Comics: V10 No.1, Mar, 1973 (one-shot)

	GD2.0	FN6.0	NM9.4
1776 (title) - Adaptation of the film musical "1776"; given away at movie theatres	1.75	5.25	14.00

CHARLTON PREMIERE (Formerly Marine War Heroes)
Charlton Comics: V1#19, July, 1967; V2#1, Sept, 1967 - No. 4, May, 1968

	GD2.0	FN6.0	NM9.4
V1#19, V2#1,2,4: V1#19-Marine War Heroes. V2#1-Trio; intro. Shape, Tyro Team & Spookman. 2-Children of Doom. 4-Unlikely Tales; Aparo, Ditko-a	2.30	7.00	20.00
V2#3-Sinistro Boy Fiend; Blue Beetle & Peacemaker x-over	2.50	7.50	24.00

CHARLTON SPORT LIBRARY - PROFESSIONAL FOOTBALL
Charlton Comics: Winter, 1969-70 (Jan. on cover) (68 pgs.)

	GD2.0	FN6.0	NM9.4
1	3.00	9.00	30.00

CHARM SCHOOL: MAGICAL WITCH BUNNY (See Action Girl Comics #13)
Slave Labor Graphics: Apr, 2000 - Present ($2.95, B&W)
1-3-Elizabeth Watasin-s/a 2.95

CHASE (See Batman #550 for 1st app.)
DC Comics: Feb, 1998 - No. 9, Oct, 1998; #1,000,000 Nov, 1998 ($2.50)
1-9: Williams III & Gray-a. 1-Includes 4 Chase cards. 4-Teen Titans app. 7,8-Batman app. 9-GL Hal Jordan-c/app. 2.50
#1,000,000 (11/98) Final issue; 853rd Century x-over 2.50

CHASSIS
Millenium Publications: 1996 - No. 3 ($2.95)
1-3: 1-Adam Hughes-c. 2-Conner var-c. 3.00

CHASSIS
Hurricane Entertainment: 1998 - No. 3 ($2.95)
0,1-3: 1-Adam Hughes-c. 0-Green var-c. 3.00

CHASSIS (Vol. 3)
Image Comics: Nov, 1999 - Present ($2.95, limited series)
1-4: 1-Two covers by O'Neil and Green. 2-Busch var-c. 3.00
1-($6.95) DF Edition alternate-c by Wieringo 6.95

CHASTITY
Chaos! Comics: (one-shots)
#1/2 (1/01, $2.95) Batista-a 3.00
Reign of Terror 1 (10/00, $2.95) Grant-s/Ross-a/Rio-c 3.00

CHASTITY: LUST FOR LIFE
Chaos! Comics: May, 1999 - No. 3, July, 1999 ($2.95, limited series)
1-3-Nutman-s/Benes-c/a 3.00

CHASTITY: ROCKED
Chaos! Comics: Nov, 1998 - No. 4, Feb, 1999 ($2.95, limited series)
1-4-Nutman-s/Justiniano-c/a 3.00

CHASTITY: THEATER OF PAIN
Chaos! Comics: Feb, 1997 - No. 3, June, 1997 ($2.95, limited series)
1-3-Pulido-s/Justiniano-c/a 3.00
TPB (1997, $9.95) r/#1-3 10.00

Cheryl Blossom #25 © AP

Cheval Noir #17 © DH

Chief Crazy Horse nn © AVON

GD2.0 FN6.0 NM9.4

CHECKMATE (TV)
Gold Key: Oct, 1962 - No. 2, Dec, 1962
1-Photo-c on both 4.60 13.75 55.00
2 4.55 13.65 50.00

CHECKMATE! (See Action Comics #598)
DC Comics: Apr, 1988 - No. 33, Jan, 1991 ($1.25)
1-33: 13: New format begins 2.00
NOTE: ***Gil Kane** c-2, 4, 7, 8, 10, 11, 15-19.*

CHERYL BLOSSOM (See Archie's Girls, Betty and Veronica #320 for 1st app.)
Archie Publications: Sept, 1995 - No. 3, Nov, 1995 ($1.50, limited series)
1-3 4.00
Special 1-4 ('95, '96, $2.00) 4.00

CHERYL BLOSSOM (Cheryl's Summer Job)
Archie Publications: July, 1996 - No. 3, Sept, 1996 ($1.50, limited series)
1-3 3.00

CHERYL BLOSSOM (...Goes Hollywood)
Archie Publications: Dec, 1996 - No. 3, Feb, 1997 ($1.50, limited series)
1-3 2.50

CHERYL BLOSSOM
Archie Publications: Apr, 1997 - Present ($1.50/$1.75/$1.79/$1.99)
1-34: 1-7-Dan DeCarlo-c/a. 32-Begin $1.99-c. 34-Sabrina app. 2.00

CHESTY SANCHEZ
Antarctic Press: Nov, 1995 - No. 2, Mar, 1996 ($2.95, B&W)
1,2 3.00
...Super Special (2/99, $5.99) 6.00

CHEVAL NOIR
Dark Horse Comics: 1989 - No. 48, Nov, 1993 ($3.50, B&W, 68 pgs.)
1-8,10 ($3.50): 6-Moebius poster insert 3.50
9,11,13,15,17,20,22 ($4.50, 84 pgs.) 4.50
12,18,19,21,23,25,26 ($3.95): 12-Geary-a; Mignola-c. 26-Moebius-a begins 4.00
14 ($4.95, 76 pgs.)(7 pgs. color) 5.00
16,24 ($3.75): 16-19-Contain trading cards 3.75
27-48 ($2.95): 33-Snyder III-c 3.00
NOTE: ***Bolland** a-2, 6, 7, 13, 14. **Bolton** a-2, 4, 45; c-4, 20. **Chadwick** c-13. **Dorman** painted c-16. **Geary** a-13, 14. **Kelley Jones** c-27. **Kaluta** a-6; c-6, 18. **Moebius** c-5, 9, 26. **Dave Stevens** c-1, 7. **Sutton** painted c-36.*

CHEYENNE (TV)
Dell Publishing Co.: No. 734, Oct, 1956 - No. 25, Dec-Jan, 1961-62
Four Color 734(#1)-Clint Walker photo-c 16.00 48.00 190.00
Four Color 772,803: Clint Walker photo-c 7.00 21.00 85.00
4(8-10/57) - 25: 4-9,13-25-Clint Walker photo-c. 10-12-Ty Hardin photo-c 4.60 13.75 55.00

CHEYENNE AUTUMN (See Movie Classics)

CHEYENNE KID (Formerly Wild Frontier No. 1-7)
Charlton Comics: No. 8, July, 1957 - No. 99, Nov, 1973
8 (#1) 6.00 18.00 42.00
9,15-19 4.65 14.00 28.00
10-Williamson/Torres-a(3); Ditko-c 9.30 28.00 65.00
11-(68 pgs.)-Cheyenne Kid meets Geronimo 10.00 30.00 80.00
12-Williamson/Torres-a(2) 10.00 30.00 80.00
13-Williamson/Torres-a (5 pgs.) 6.40 19.25 45.00
14-Williamson-a (5 pgs.?) 6.40 19.25 45.00
20-22,24,25-Severin c/a(3) each 3.00 9.00 30.00
23,27-29 2.00 6.00 16.00
26,30-Severin-a 2.40 7.35 22.00
31-59 1.85 5.50 15.00
60-65,67-80 1.25 3.75 10.00
66-Wander by Aparo begins, ends #87 1.50 4.50 12.00
81-99: Apache Red begins #88, origin in #89 1.00 3.00 8.00
Modern Comics Reprint 87,89(1978) 3.00

CHIAROSCURO (THE PRIVATE LIVES OF LEONARDO DA VINCI)
DC Comics (Vertigo): July, 1995 - No. 10, Apr, 1996 ($2.50/$2.95, limited series, mature)
1-9 2.50
10-($2.95) 3.00

CHICAGO MAIL ORDER (See C-M-O Comics)

CHI-CHIAN
Sirius Entertainment: 1997 - No. 6, 1998 ($2.95, limited series)
1-6-Voltaire-s/a 3.00

CHIEF, THE (Indian Chief No. 3 on)
Dell Publishing Co.: No. 290, Aug, 1950 - No. 2, Apr-June, 1951
Four Color 290(#1) 5.45 16.25 65.00
2 4.60 13.75 55.00

CHIEF CRAZY HORSE (See Wild Bill Hickok #21)
Avon Periodicals: 1950 (Also see Fighting Indians of the Wild West!)
nn-Fawcette-c 20.00 60.00 160.00

CHIEF VICTORIO'S APACHE MASSACRE (See Fight Indians of/Wild West!)
Avon Periodicals: 1951
nn-Williamson/Frazetta-a (7 pgs.); Larsen-a; Kinstler-c 42.00 125.00 375.00

CHILDHOOD'S END
Image Comics: Oct, 1997 ($2.95, B&W)
1-Bourne-s/Calafiore-a 3.00

CHILDREN OF FIRE
Fantagor Press: Nov, 1987 - No. 3, 1988 ($2.00, limited series)
1-3: by Richard Corben 3.00

CHILDREN OF THE VOYAGER (See Marvel Frontier Comics Unlimited)
Marvel Frontier Comics: Sept, 1993 - No. 4, Dec, 1993 ($1.95, limited series)
1-($2.95)-Embossed glow-in-the-dark-c; Paul Johnson-c/a 3.00
2-4 2.00

CHILDREN'S BIG BOOK
Dorene Publ. Co.: 1945 (25¢, stiff-c, 68 pgs.)
nn-Comics & fairy tales; David Icove-a 10.50 32.00 85.00

CHILDREN'S CRUSADE, THE
DC Comics (Vertigo): Dec, 1993 - No. 2, Jan, 1994 ($3.95, limited series)
1,2-Neil Gaiman scripts & Chris Bachalo-a; framing issues for Children's Crusade x-over 4.00

CHILD'S PLAY: THE SERIES (Movie)
Innovation Publishing: May, 1991 - #3, 1991 ($2.50, 28pgs.)
1-3 2.50

CHILD'S PLAY 2 THE OFFICIAL MOVIE ADAPTATION (Movie)
Innovation Publishing: 1990 - No. 3, 1990 ($2.50, bi-weekly limited series)
1-3: Adapts movie sequel 2.50

CHILI (Millie's Rival)
Marvel Comics Group: 5/69 - No. 17, 9/70; No. 18, 8/72 - No. 26, 12/73
1 5.45 16.35 60.00
2-5 2.80 8.40 28.00
6-17 2.00 6.00 18.00
18-26 1.50 4.50 12.00
Special 1(12/71, 52 pgs.) 3.20 9.60 35.00

CHILLER
Marvel Comics (Epic): Nov, 1993 - No. 2, Dec, 1993 ($7.95, lim. series)
1,2-(68 pgs.) 1.00 3.00 8.00

CHILLING ADVENTURES IN SORCERY (...as Told by Sabrina #1, 2) (Red Circle Sorcery No. 6 on)
Archie Publications (Red Circle Productions): 9/72 - No. 2, 10/72; No. 3, 10/73 - No. 5, 2/74
1-Sabrina cameo as narrator 3.20 9.60 35.00
2-Sabrina cameo as narrator 2.00 6.00 18.00
3-5: Morrow-c/a, all. 4,5-Alcazar-a 1.25 3.75 10.00

CHILLING TALES (Formerly Beware)

Chip 'n' Dale Rescue Rangers #1 © WDC

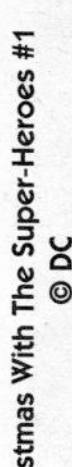
Christmas With The Super-Heroes #1 © DC

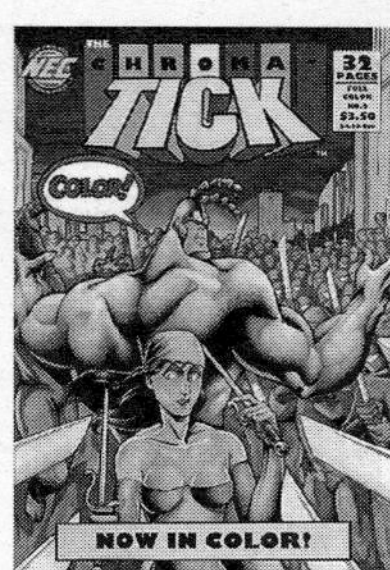

Chroma-Tick #3 © Ben Edlund

GD2.0 FN6.0 NM9.4

'outhful Magazines: No. 13, Dec, 1952 - No. 17, Oct, 1953
13(No.1)-Harrison-a; Matt Fox-c/a 53.00 158.00 475.00
14-Harrison-a 38.00 113.00 300.00
15-Has #14 on-c; Matt Fox-c; Harrison-a 42.00 126.00 375.00
16-Poe adapt.-`Metzengerstein'; Rudyard Kipling adapt.- 'Mark of the Beast,' by Kiefer; bondage-c 31.00 94.00 250.00
17-Matt Fox-c; Sir Walter Scott & Poe adapt. 40.00 120.00 325.00

:HILLING TALES OF HORROR (Magazine)
;tanley Publications: V1#1, 6/69 - V1#7, 12/70; V2#2, 2/71 - V2#5, 10/71 (50¢, 3&W, 52 pgs.)
'1#1 4.55 13.65 50.00
2-7: 7-Cameron-a 3.20 9.60 35.00
'2#2,3,5: 2-Spirit of Frankenstein-r/Adventures into the Unknown #16 3.00 9.00 30.00
'2#4-r/9 pg. Feldstein-a from Adventures into the Unknown #3 3.20 9.60 35.00
IOTE: *Two issues of V2#2 exist, Feb, 1971 and April, 1971.*

:HILLY WILLY
Dell Publ. Co.: No. 740, Oct, 1956 - No. 1281, Apr-June, 1962 (Walter Lantz)
'our Color 740 (#1) 4.55 13.65 50.00
'our Color 852 (2/58),967 (2/59),1017 (9/59), 1074 (2-4/60),1122 (8/60), 1177 (4-6/61), 1212 (7-9/61), 1281 3.20 9.60 35.00

:HINA BOY (See Wisco)

:HIP 'N' DALE (Walt Disney)(See Walt Disney's C&S #204)
Dell Publishing Co./Gold Key/Whitman No. 65 on: Nov, 1953 - No. 30, June-Aug, 1962; Sept, 1967 - No. 83, 1982
'our Color 517(#1) 8.00 24.00 95.00
'our Color 581,636 4.60 13.75 55.00
4(12/55-2/56)-10 4.35 13.00 48.00
11-30 3.20 9.60 35.00
1(Gold Key, 1967)-Reprints 2.50 7.50 24.00
2-10 1.50 4.50 12.00
11-20 1.00 2.80 7.00
21-40 2.40 6.00
41-64,70-77 5.00
65,66 (Whitman) 4.00
67-69 (3-pack? 1980)(scarce) 1.25 3.75 10.00
78-83 (All #90214; 3-pack?, nd, dn code 1.00 3.00 8.00
IOTE: *All Gold Key/Whitman issues have reprints except No. 32-35, 38-41, 45-47. No. 23-28, 0-42, 45-47, 49 have new covers.*

:HIP 'N DALE RESCUE RANGERS
Disney Comics: June, 1990 - No. 19, Dec, 1991 ($1.50)
1-19: New stories; 1,2-Origin 2.00

:HITTY CHITTY BANG BANG (See Movie Comics)

:.H.I.X.
nage Comics (Studiosaurus): Jan, 1998 ($2.50)
1-Dodson, Haley, Lopresti, Randall, and Warren-s/c/a 3.00
1-($5.00) "X-Ray Variant" cover 5.00
:.H.I.X. That Time Forgot 1 (8/98, $2.95) 3.00

:HOICE COMICS
;reat Publications: Dec, 1941 - No. 3, Feb, 1942
1-Origin Secret Circle; Atlas the Mighty app.; Zomba, Jungle Fight, Kangaroo Man, & Fire Eater begin 158.00 474.00 1500.00
2 83.00 250.00 790.00
3-Double feature; Features movie "The Lost City" (classic cover); continued from Great Comics #3 116.00 348.00 1100.00

:HOO CHOO CHARLIE
;old Key: Dec, 1969
1-John Stanley-a (scarce) 9.50 28.50 105.00

:HRISTIAN (See Asylum)
laximum Press: Jan, 1996 ($2.99, one-shot)
1-Pop Mhan-a 3.00

:HRISTIAN HEROES OF TODAY
David C. Cook: 1964 (36 pgs.)
nn 1.75 5.25 14.00

CHRISTMAS (Also see A-1 Comics)
Magazine Enterprises: No. 28, 1950
A-1 28 5.00 15.00 35.00

CHRISTMAS ADVENTURE, A (See Classics Comics Giveaways, 12/69)

CHRISTMAS ALBUM (See March of Comics No. 312)

CHRISTMAS ANNUAL
Golden Special: 1975 ($1.95, 100 pgs., stiff-c)
nn-Reprints Mother Goose stories with Walt Kelly-a 3.20 9.60 35.00

CHRISTMAS & ARCHIE
Archie Comics: Jan, 1975 ($1.00, 68 pgs., 10-1/4x13-1/4" treasury-sized)
1 4.10 12.30 45.00

CHRISTMAS BELLS (See March of Comics No. 297)

CHRISTMAS CARNIVAL
Ziff-Davis Publ. Co./St. John Publ. Co. No. 2: 1952 (25¢, one-shot, 100 pgs.)
nn 30.00 90.00 240.00
2-Reprints Ziff-Davis issue plus-c 16.00 49.00 130.00

CHRISTMAS CAROL, A (See March of Comics No. 33)

CHRISTMAS EVE, A (See March of Comics No. 212)

CHRISTMAS IN DISNEYLAND (See Dell Giants)

CHRISTMAS PARADE (See Dell Giant No. 26, Dell Giants, March of Comics No. 284, Walt Disney Christmas Parade & Walt Disney's...)

CHRISTMAS PARADE (Walt Disney's)
Gold Key: Jan, 1963 (no month listed) - No. 9, Jan, 1972 (#1,5: 80 pgs.; #2-4,7-9: 36 pgs.)
1 (30018-301)-Giant 8.00 24.00 95.00
2-6: 2-r/F.C. #367 by Barks. 3-r/F.C. #178 by Barks. 4-r/F.C. #203 by Barks. 5-r/Christ. Parade #1 (Dell) by Barks; giant. 6-r/Christmas Parade #2 (Dell) by Barks (64 pgs.); giant 5.85 17.50 70.00
7-Pull-out poster (half price w/o poster) 4.10 12.30 45.00
8-r/F.C. #367 by Barks; pull-out poster 5.85 17.50 70.00
9 3.20 9.60 35.00

CHRISTMAS PARTY (See March of Comics No. 256)

CHRISTMAS STORIES (See Little People No. 959, 1062)

CHRISTMAS STORY (See March of Comics No. 326)

CHRISTMAS STORY BOOK (See Woolworth's Christmas Story Book)

CHRISTMAS TREASURY, A (See Dell Giants & March of Comics No. 227)

CHRISTMAS WITH ARCHIE
Spire Christian Comics (Fleming H. Revell Co.): 1973, 1974 (49¢, 52 pgs.)
nn-Low print run 1.50 4.50 12.00

CHRISTMAS WITH MOTHER GOOSE
Dell Publishing Co.: No. 90, Nov, 1945 - No. 253, Nov, 1949
Four Color 90 (#1)-Kelly-a 17.50 52.50 210.00
Four Color 126 ('46), 172 (11/47)-By Walt Kelly 13.00 40.00 160.00
Four Color 201 (10/48), 253-By Walt Kelly 11.70 35.00 140.00

CHRISTMAS WITH SANTA (See March of Comics No. 92)

CHRISTMAS WITH THE SUPER-HEROES (See Limited Collectors' Edition)
DC Comics: 1988; No. 2, 1989 ($2.95)
1,2: 1-(100 pgs.)-All reprints; N. Adams-r, Byrne-c; Batman, Superman, JLA, LSH Christmas stories; r-Miller's 1st Batman/DC Special Series #21. 2-(68 pgs.)-Superman by Chadwick; Batman, Wonder Woman, Deadman, Gr. Lantern, Flash app.; Morrow-a; Enemy Ace by Byrne; all new-a 4.00

CHROMA-TICK, THE (...Special Edition, #1,2) (Also see The Tick)
New England Comics Press: Feb, 1992 - No. 8, Nov, 1993 ($3.95/$3.50, 44 pgs.)
1,2-Includes serially numbered trading card set 4.00
3-8 ($3.50, 36 pgs.): 6-Bound-in card 3.50

CHROME

Chronos #1 © DC

Chyna #1 © Chaos! Comics

City of Silence #3
© Warren Ellis & Gary Erskine

GD2.0 FN6.0 NM9.4

Hot Comics: 1986 - No. 3, 1986 ($1.50, limited series)

1-3 — 2.00

CHROMIUM MAN, THE
Triumphant Comics: Aug, 1993 - No.10, May, 1994 ($2.50)

1-1st app. Mr. Death; all serially numbered — 2.50
2-10: 2-1st app. Prince Vandal. 3-1st app. Candi, Breaker & Coil. 4,5-Triumphant Unleashed x-over. 8,9-(3/94). 10-(5/94) — 2.50
0-(4/94)-Four color-c, 0-All pink-c & all blue-c; no cover price — 2.50

CHROMIUM MAN: VIOLENT PAST, THE
Triumphant Comics: Jan, 1994 - No. 2, Jan, 1994 ($2.50, limited series)

1,2-Serially numbered to 22,000 each — 2.50

CHRONICLES OF CORUM, THE (Also see Corum...)
First Comics: Jan, 1987 - No. 12, Nov, 1988 ($1.75/$1.95, deluxe series)

1-12: Adapts Michael Moorcock's novel — 2.00

CHRONOS
DC Comics: Mar, 1998 - No. 11, Feb. 1999 ($2.50)

1-11-J.F. Moore-s/Guinan-a — 2.50
#1,000,000 (11/98) 853rd Century x-over — 2.50

CHRONOWAR (Manga)
Dark Horse Comics: Aug, 1996 - No. 9, Apr, 1997 ($2.95, limited series)

1-9 — 3.00

CHUCKLE, THE GIGGLY BOOK OF COMIC ANIMALS
R. B. Leffingwell Co.: 1945 (132 pgs., one-shot)

	GD2.0	FN6.0	NM9.4
1-Funny animal	20.00	60.00	160.00

CHUCK NORRIS (TV)
Marvel Comics (Star Comics): Jan, 1987 - No. 4, July, 1987

1-3: Ditko-a — 3.00
4-No Ditko-a (low print run) — 5.00

CHUCK WAGON (See Sheriff Bob Dixon's...)

CHYNA (WWF Wrestling)
Chaos! Comics: Sept, 2000 ($2.95, one-shot)

1-Grant-s/Barrows-a; photo-c — 2.95
1-($9.95) Premium Edition; Cleavenger-c — 9.95

CICERO'S CAT
Dell Publishing Co.: July-Aug, 1959 - No. 2, Sept-Oct, 1959

	GD2.0	FN6.0	NM9.4
1,2-Cat from Mutt & Jeff	3.45	10.35	38.00

CIMARRON STRIP (TV)
Dell Publishing Co.: Jan, 1968

	GD2.0	FN6.0	NM9.4
1-Stuart Whitman photo-c	3.45	10.35	38.00

CINDER AND ASHE
DC Comics: May, 1988 - No. 4, Aug, 1988 ($1.75, limited series)

1-4: Mature readers — 2.00

CINDERELLA (Disney) (See Movie Comics)
Dell Publishing Co.: No. 272, Apr, 1950 - No. 786, Apr, 1957

	GD2.0	FN6.0	NM9.4
Four Color 272	10.00	30.00	120.00
Four Color 786-Partial-r 272	5.85	17.50	70.00

CINDERELLA
Whitman Publishing Co.: Apr, 1982

nn-Reprints 4-Color #272 — 4.00

CINDERELLA LOVE
Ziff-Davis/St. John Publ. Co. No. 12 on: No. 10, 1950; No. 11, 4-5/51; No. 12, 9/51; No. 4, 10-11/51 - No. 11, Fall, 1952; No. 12, 10/53 - No. 15, 8/54; No. 25, 12/54 - No. 29, 10/55 (No #16-24)

	GD2.0	FN6.0	NM9.4
10(#1)(1st Series, 1950)-Painted-c	14.00	41.00	110.00
11(#2, 4-5/51)-Crandall-a; Saunders painted-c	10.00	30.00	70.00
12(#3, 9/51)-Photo-c	7.15	21.50	50.00
4-8: 4,6,7-Photo-c	6.00	18.00	42.00
9-Kinstler-a; photo-c	7.85	23.50	55.00
10,11(Fall/'52), 14: 10,11-Photo-c. 14-Baker-a	7.15	21.50	50.00
12(St. John-10/53)-#13:13-Painted-c.	5.50	16.50	38.00
15(8/54)-Matt Baker-c	8.65	26.00	60.00
25(2nd Series)(Formerly Romantic Marriage)	5.50	16.50	38.00
26-Baker-c; last precode (2/55)	8.65	26.00	60.00
27,29: Both Matt Baker-c	8.65	26.00	60.00
28	4.65	14.00	28.00

CINDY COMICS (...Smith No. 39, 40; Crime Can't Win No. 41 on)(Formerly Krazy Komics) (See Junior Miss & Teen Comics)
Timely Comics: No. 27, Fall, 1947 - No. 40, July, 1950

	GD2.0	FN6.0	NM9.4
27-Kurtzman-a, 3 pgs: Margie, Oscar begin	20.00	60.00	160.00
28-31-Kurtzman-a	12.00	36.00	95.00
32-40: 33-Georgie story; anti-Wertham editorial	8.65	26.00	60.00

NOTE: *Kurtzman's "Hey Look"-#27(3), 29(2), 30(2), 31; "Giggles 'n' Grins"-28.*

CIRCUS (...the Comic Riot)
Globe Syndicate: June, 1938 - No. 3, Aug, 1938

	GD2.0	FN6.0	NM9.4
1-(Scarce)-Spacehawks (2 pgs.), & Disk Eyes by Wolverton (2 pgs.), Pewee Throttle by Cole (2nd comic book work; see Star Comics V1#11), Beau Gus, Ken Craig & The Lords of Crillon, Jack Hinton by Eisner, Van Bragger by Kane	800.00	2400.00	6400.00
2,3-(Scarce)-Eisner, Cole, Wolverton, Bob Kane-a in each	400.00	1200.00	3200.00

CIRCUS BOY (TV) (See Movie Classics)
Dell Publishing Co.: No. 759, Dec, 1956 - No. 813, July, 1957

	GD2.0	FN6.0	NM9.4
Four Color 759 (#1)-The Monkees' Mickey Dolenz photo-c	11.00	33.00	130.00
Four Color 785 (4/57),813-Mickey Dolenz photo-c	10.00	30.00	120.00

CIRCUS COMICS
Farm Women's Pub. Co./D. S. Publ.: 1945 - No. 2, Jun, 1945; Wint., 1948-49

	GD2.0	FN6.0	NM9.4
1-Funny animal	12.00	36.00	95.00
2	8.65	26.00	60.00
1(1948)-D.S. Publ.; 2 pgs. Frazetta	24.00	73.00	195.00

CIRCUS OF FUN COMICS
A. W. Nugent Publ. Co.: 1945 - No. 3, Dec, 1947 (A book of games & puzzles)

	GD2.0	FN6.0	NM9.4
1	13.00	39.00	105.00
2,3	8.65	26.00	60.00

CISCO KID, THE (TV)
Dell Publishing Co.: July, 1950 - No. 41, Oct-Dec, 1958

	GD2.0	FN6.0	NM9.4
Four Color 292(#1)-Cisco Kid, his horse Diablo, & sidekick Pancho & his horse Loco begin; painted-c begin	22.00	66.00	265.00
2(1/51)-5	10.00	30.00	120.00
6-10	7.50	22.50	90.00
11-20	6.70	20.00	80.00
21-36-Last painted-c	5.00	15.00	60.00
37-41: All photo-c	9.15	27.50	110.00

NOTE: ***Buscema** a-40. **Ernest Nordli** painted c-5-16, 20, 35.*

CISCO KID COMICS
Bernard Bailey/Swappers Quarterly: Winter, 1944 (one-shot)

	GD2.0	FN6.0	NM9.4
1-Illustrated Stories of the Operas: Faust; Funnyman by Giunta; Cisco Kid (1st app.) & Superbaby begin; Giunta-c	40.00	120.00	360.00

CITIZEN SMITH (See Holyoke One-Shot No. 9)

CITY OF SILENCE
Image Comics: May, 2000 - No. 3, July, 2000 ($2.50)

1-3-Ellis-s/Erskine-a — 2.50

CITY OF THE LIVING DEAD (See Fantastic Tales No. 1)
Avon Periodicals: 1952

	GD2.0	FN6.0	NM9.4
nn-Hollingsworth-c/a	43.00	129.00	390.00

CITY PEOPLE NOTEBOOK
Kitchen Sink Press: 1989 ($9.95, B&W, magazine sized)

nn-Will Eisner-s/a — 10.00
nn-(DC Comics, 2000) Reprint — 10.00

CITY SURGEON (Blake Harper...)
Gold Key: August, 1963

Claire Voyant nn © STD

Clandestine #3 © MAR

Classic Comics #1 © GIL

	GD2.0	FN6.0	NM9.4
1(10075-308)-Painted-c	3.20	9.60	35.00

CIVIL WAR MUSKET, THE (Kadets of America Handbook)
Custom Comics, Inc.: 1960 (25¢, half-size, 36 pgs.)

	GD2.0	FN6.0	NM9.4
nn	2.50	7.50	25.00

CLAIRE VOYANT (Also see Keen Teens)
Leader Publ./Standard/Pentagon Publ.: 1946 - No. 4, 1947 (Sparling strip reprints)

	GD2.0	FN6.0	NM9.4
nn	59.00	177.00	560.00
2,4: 2-Kamen-c. 4-Kamen bondage-c	47.00	142.00	425.00
3-Kamen bridal-c; contents mentioned in Love and Death, a book by Gershom Legman(1949) referenced by Dr. Wertham in **SOTI**	55.00	165.00	500.00

CLANDESTINE (Also see Marvel Comics Presents & X-Men: ClanDestine)
Marvel Comics: Oct, 1994 - No.12, Sept, 1995 ($2.95/$2.50)

1-($2.95)-Alan Davis-c/a(p)/scripts & Mark Farmer-c/a(i) begin, ends #8; Modok app.; Silver Surfer cameo; gold foil-c 3.00
2-12: 2-Wraparound-c. 2,3-Silver Surfer app. 5-Origin of ClanDestine. 6-Capt. America, Hulk, Spider-Man, Thing & Thor-c; Spider-Man cameo. 7-Spider-Man-c/app; Punisher cameo. 8-Invaders & Dr. Strange app. 9-12-Modok app. 10-Captain Britain-c/app. 11-Sub-Mariner app 2.50
Preview (10/94, $1.50) 2.00

CLASH
DC Comics: 1991 - No. 3, 1991 ($4.95, limited series, 52 pgs.)

Book One - Three: Adam Kubert-c/a 5.00

CLASSIC COMICS/ILLUSTRATED - INTRODUCTION
by Dan Malan

Further revisions have been made to help in understanding the **Classics** section. **Classics** reprint editions prior to 1963 had either incorrect dates or no dates listed. Those reprint editions should be identified only by the highest number on the reorder list (HRN). Past price guides listed what were calculated to be approximately correct dates, but many people found it confusing for the price guide to list a date not listed in the comic itself.

We have also attempted to clear up confusion about edition variations, such as color, printer, etc. Such variations will be identified by letters. Editions will now be determined by three categories. Original edition variations will be Edition 1A, 1B, etc. All reprint editions prior to 1963 will be identified by HRN only. All reprint editions from 9/63 on will be identified by the correct date listed in the comic.

We have also included new information on four recent reprintings of **Classics** not previously listed. From 1968-1976 Twin Circle, the Catholic newspaper, serialized over 100 **Classics** titles. That list can be found under non-series items at the end of this section. In 1972 twelve **Classics** were reissued as **Now Age Books Illustrated**. They are listed under **Pendulum Illustrated Classics**. In 1982, 20 **Classics** were reissued, adapted for teaching English as a second language. They are listed under **Regents Illustrated Classics**. Then in 1984, six **Classics** were reissued with cassette tapes. See the listing under **Cassette Books**.

UNDERSTANDING CLASSICS ILLUSTRATED
by Dan Malan

Since **Classics Illustrated** is the most complicated comic book series, with all its reprint editions and variations, with changes in covers and artwork, with a variety of means of identifying editions, and with the most extensive worldwide distribution of any comic-book series; therefore this introductory section is provided to assist you in gaining expertise about this series.

THE HISTORY OF CLASSICS

The **Classics** series was the brain child of Albert L. Kanter, who saw in the new comic-book medium a means of introducing children to the great classics of literature. In October of 1941 his Gilberton Co. began the **Classic Comics** series with **The Three Musketeers**, with 64 pages of storyline. In those early years, the struggling series saw irregular schedules and numerous printers, not to mention variable art quality and liberal story adaptations. With No.13 the page total was reduced to 56 (except for No. 33, originally scheduled to be No. 9), and with No. 15 the coming-next ad on the outside back cover moved inside. In 1945 the Jerry Iger Shop began producing all new CC titles, beginning with No. 23. In 1947 the search for a classier logo resulted in **Classics Illustrated**, beginning with No. 35, **Last Days of Pompeii**. With No. 45 the page total dropped again to 48, which was to become the standard.

Two new developments in 1951 had a profound effect upon the success of the series. One was the introduction of painted covers, instead of the old line drawn covers, beginning with No. 81, **The Odyssey**. The second was the switch to the major national distributor Curtis. They raised the cover price from 10 to 15 cents, making it the highest priced comic-book, but it did not slow the growth of the series, because they were marketed as books, not comics. Because of this higher quality image, **Classics** flourished during the fifties while other comic series were reeling from outside attacks. They diversified with their new **Juniors**, **Specials**, and **World Around Us** series.

Classics artwork can be divided into three distinct periods. The pre-Iger era (1941-44) was mentioned above for its variable art quality. The Iger era (1945-53) was a major improvement in art quality and adaptations. It came to be dominated by artists Henry Kiefer and Alex Blum, together accounting for some 50 titles. Their styles gave the first real personality to the series. The EC era (1954-62) resulted from the demise of the EC horror series, when many of their artists made the major switch to classical art.

But several factors brought the production of new CI titles to a complete halt in 1962. Gilberton lost its 2nd class mailing permit. External factors like television, cheap paperback books, and Cliff Notes were all eating away at their market. Production halted with No.167, **Faust**, even though many more titles were already in the works. Many of those found their way into foreign series, and are very desirable to collectors. In 1967, **Classics Illustrated** was sold to Patrick Frawley and his Catholic publication, Twin Circle. They issued two new titles in 1969 as part of an attempted revival, but succumbed to major distribution problems in 1971. In 1988, the trio: First Publishing, Berkley Press, and Classics Media Group acquired the use rights for the old CI series art, logo, and name from the Frawley Group. So far they have used only the name in the new series, but do have plans to reprint the old CI.

One of the unique aspects of the **Classics Illustrated** (CI) series was the proliferation of reprint variations. Some titles had as many as 25 editions. Reprinting began in 1943. Some **Classic Comics** (CC) reprints (r) had the logo format revised to a banner logo, and added a motto under the banner. In 1947 CC titles changed to the CI logo, but kept their line drawn covers (LDC). In 1948, Nos. 13, 18, 29 and 41 received second covers (LDC2), replacing covers considered too violent, and reprints of Nos. 13-44 had pages reduced to 48, except for No. 26, which had 48 pages to begin with.

Starting in the mid-1950s, 70 of the 80 LDC titles were reissued with new painted covers (PC). Thirty of them also received new interior artwork (A2). The new artwork was generally higher quality with larger art panels and more faithful but abbreviated storylines. Later on, there were 29 second painted covers (PC2), mostly by Twin Circle. Altogether there were 199 interior art variations (169 (O)s and 30 A2 editions) and 272 different covers (169 (O)s, four LDC2s, 70 new PCs of LDC (O)s, and 29 PC2s). It is mildly astounding to realize that there are nearly 1400 different editions in the U.S. CI series.

FOREIGN CLASSICS ILLUSTRATED

If U.S. Classics variations are mildly astounding, the veritable plethora of foreign CI variations will boggle your imagination. While we still anticipate additional discoveries, we presently know about series in 25 languages and 27 countries. There were 250 new CI titles in foreign series, and nearly 400 new foreign covers of U.S. titles. The 1400 U.S. CI editions pale in comparison to the 4000 plus foreign editions. The very nature of CI lent itself to flourishing as an international series. Worldwide, they published over one billion copies! The first foreign CI series consisted of six Canadian Classic Comic reprints in 1946.

The following chart shows when CI series first began in each country:
1946: Canada. 1947: Australia. 1948: Brazil/The Netherlands. 1950: Italy. 1951: Greece/Japan/Hong Kong(?)/England/Argentina/Mexico. 1952: West Germany. 1954: Norway. 1955: New Zealand/South Africa. 1956: Denmark/Sweden/Iceland. 1957: Finland/France. 1962: Singapore(?). 1964: India (8 languages). 1971: Ireland (Gaelic). 1973: Belgium(?) /Philippines(?) & Malaysia(?).

Significant among the early series were Brazil and Greece. In 1950, Brazil was the first country to begin doing its own new titles. They issued nearly 80 new CI titles by Brazilian authors. In Greece in 1951 they actually had debates in parliament about the effects of Classics Illustrated on Greek culture, leading to the inclusion of 88 new Greek History & Mythology titles in the CI series.

But by far the most important foreign CI development was the joint European

Classic Comics #2 © GIL

Classic Comics #3 © GIL

Classic Comics #4 © GIL

series which began in 1956 in 10 countries simultaneously. By 1960, CI had the largest European distribution of any American publication, not just comics! So when all the problems came up with U.S. distribution, they literally moved the CI operation to Europe in 1962, and continued producing new titles in all four CI series. Many of them were adapted and drawn in the U.S., the most famous of which was the British CI #158A. Dr. No, drawn by Norman Nodel. Unfortunately, the British CI series ended in late 1963, which limited the European CI titles available in English to 15. Altogether there were 82 new CI art titles in the joint European series, which ran until 1976.

IDENTIFYING CLASSICS EDITIONS

HRN: This is the highest number on the reorder list. It should be listed in ( ) after the title number. It is crucial to understanding various CI editions.

ORIGINALS (O): This is the all-important First Edition. To determine (O)s,there is one primary rule and two secondary rules (with exceptions):

Rule No. 1: All (O)s and only (O)s have coming-next ads for the next number. **Exceptions**: No. 14(15) (reprint) has an ad on the last inside text page only. No. 14(0) also has a full-page outside back cover ad (also rule 2). Nos.55(75) and 57(75) have coming-next ads. (Rules 2 and 3 apply here). Nos. 168(0) and 169(0) do not have coming-next ads. No.168 was never reprinted; No. 169(0) has HRN (166). No. 169(169) is the only reprint.

Rule No. 2: On nos.1-80, all (O)s and only (O)s list 10c on the front cover. **Exceptions**: Reprint variations of Nos. 37(62), 39(71), and 46(62) list 10c on the front cover. (Rules 1 and 3 apply here.)

Rule No. 3: All (O)s have HRN close to that title No. **Exceptions**: Some reprints also have HRNs close to that title number: a few CC(r)s, 58(62), 60(62), 149(149), 152(149) 153(149), and title nos. in the 160's. (Rules 1 and 2 apply here.)

DATES: Many reprint editions list either an incorrect date or no date. Since Gilberton apparently kept track of CI editions by HRN, they often left the (O) date on reprints. Often, someone with a CI collection for sale will swear that all their copies are originals. That is why we are so detailed in pointing out how to identify original editions. Except for original editions, which should have a coming-next ad, etc., all CI dates prior to 1963 are incorrect! So you want to go by HRN only if it is (165) or below, and go by listed date if it is 1963 or later. There are a few (167) editions with incorrect dates. They could be listed either as (167) or (62/3), which is meant to indicate that they were issued sometime between late 1962 and early 1963.

COVERS: A change from CC to LDC indicates a logo change, not a cover change; while a change from LDC to LDC2, LDC to PC, or from PC to PC2 does indicate a new cover. New PCs can be identified by HRN, and PC2s can be identified by HRN and date. Several covers had color changes, particularly from purple to blue.

Notes: If you see 15 cents in Canada on a front cover, it does not necessarily indicate a Canadian edition. Editions with an HRN between 44 and 75, with 15 cents on the cover are Canadian. Check the publisher's address. An HRN listing two numbers with a / between them indicates that there are two different reorder lists in the front and back covers. Official Twin Circle editions have a full-page back cover ad for their TC magazine, with no CI reorder list. Any CI with just a Twin Circle sticker on the front is not an official TC edition.

TIPS ON LISTING CLASSICS FOR SALE

It may be easy to just list Edition 17, but Classics collectors keep track of CI editions in terms of HRN and/or date, (O) or (r), CC or LDC, PC or PC2, A1 or A2, soft or stiff cover, etc. Try to help them out. For originals, just list (0), unless there are variations such as color (Nos. 10 and 61), printer (Nos. 18-22), HRN (Nos. 95, 108, 160), etc. For reprints, just list HRN if it's (165) or below. Above that, list HRN and date. Also, please list type of logo/cover/art for the convenience of buyers. They will appreciate it.

CLASSIC COMICS (Also see Best from Boys Life, Cassette Books, Famous Stories, Fast Fiction, Golden Picture Classics, King Classics, Marvel Classics Comics, Pendulum Illustrated Classics, Picture Parade, Picture Progress, Regents Ill. Classics, Spitfire, Stories by Famous Authors, Superior Stories, and World Around Us.)

CLASSIC COMICS (Classics Illustrated No. 35 on)
Elliot Publishing #1-3 (1941-1942)/Gilberton Publications #4-167 (1942-1967) /Twin Circle Pub. (Frawley) #168-169 (1968-1971):
10/41 - No. 34, 2/47; No. 35, 3/47 - No. 169, Spring 1969
(Reprint Editions of almost all titles 5/43 - Spring 1971)
(Painted Covers (0)s No. 81 on, and (r)s of most Nos. 1-80)

Abbreviations:
A–Art; C or c–Cover; CC–Classic Comics; CI–Classics Ill.; Ed–Edition; LDC–Line Drawn Cover; PC–Painted Cover; r–Reprint

1. The Three Musketeers

Ed	HRN	Date	Details	A	C			
1	–	10/41	Date listed-1941; Elliot Pub; 68 pgs.	1	1	435.00	1305.00	5000.00
2	10	–	10¢ price removed on all (r)s; Elliot Pub; CC-r	1	1	36.00	107.00	285.00
3	15	–	Long Isl. Ind. Ed.; CC-r	1	1	26.00	79.00	210.00
4	18/20		Sunrise Times Ed.; CC-r	1	1	18.00	53.00	140.00
5	21	–	Richmond Courier Ed.; CC-r	1	1	16.00	48.00	125.00
6	28	1946	CC-r	1	1	13.00	39.00	105.00
7	36	–	LDC-r	1	1	7.85	23.50	55.00
8	60	–	LDC-r	1	1	5.00	15.00	35.00
9	64	–	LDC-r	1	1	4.65	14.00	28.00
10	78	–	C-price 15¢;LDC-r	1	1	4.00	12.00	24.00
11	93	–	LDC-r	1	1	4.00	12.00	24.00
12	114	–	Last LDC-r	1	1	4.00	10.00	20.00
13	134	–	New-c; old-a; 64 pg. PC-r	1	2	4.00	11.00	22.00
14	143	–	Old-a; PC-r; 64 pg.	1	2	3.60	9.00	18.00
15	150	–	New-a; PC-r; Evans/Crandall-a	2	2	4.00	10.00	20.00
16	149	–	PC-r	2	2	2.00	5.00	10.00
17	167	–	PC-r	2	2	2.00	5.00	10.00
18	167	4/64	PC-r	2	2	2.00	5.00	10.00
19	167	1/65	PC-r	2	2	2.00	5.00	10.00
20	167	3/66	PC-r	2	2	2.00	5.00	10.00
21	166	11/67	PC-r	2	2	2.00	5.00	10.00
22	166	Spr/69	C-price 25¢ ; stiff-c; PC-r	2	2	2.00	5.00	10.00
23	169	Spr/71	PC-r; stiff-c	2	2	2.00	5.00	10.00

2. Ivanhoe

Ed	HRN	Date	Details	A	C			
1	(O)	12/41?	Date listed-1941; Elliot Pub; 68 pgs.	1	1	221.00	663.00	2100.00
2	10	–	Price & 'Presents' removed; Elliot Pub; CC-r	1	1	31.00	94.00	250.00
3	15	–	Long Isl. Ind. ed.; CC-r	1	1	20.00	60.00	160.00
4	18/20		Sunrise Times ed.; CC-r	1	1	18.00	53.00	140.00
5	21	–	Richmond Courier ed.; CC-r	1	1	16.00	48.00	125.00
6	28	1946	Last 'Comics'-r	1	1	13.00	39.00	105.00
7	36	–	1st LDC-r	1	1	8.65	26.00	60.00
8	60	–	LDC-r	1	1	5.00	15.00	35.00
9	64	–	LDC-r	1	1	4.65	14.00	28.00
10	78	–	C-price 15¢; LDC-r	1	1	4.00	12.00	24.00
11	89	–	LDC-r	1	1	4.00	11.00	22.00
12	106	–	LDC-r	1	1	3.60	9.00	18.00
13	121	–	Last LDC-r	1	1	3.60	9.00	18.00
14	136	–	New-c&a; PC-r	2	2	4.00	12.00	24.00
15	142	–	PC-r	2	2	2.20	5.50	11.00
16	153	–	PC-r	2	2	2.20	5.50	11.00
17	149	–	PC-r	2	2	2.20	5.50	11.00
18	167	–	PC-r	2	2	2.00	5.00	10.00
19	167	5/64	PC-r	2	2	2.00	5.00	10.00
20	167	1/65	PC-r	2	2	2.00	5.00	10.00
21	167	3/66	PC-r	2	2	2.00	5.00	10.00
22A	166	9/67	PC-r	2	2	2.00	5.00	10.00

GD2.0 FN6.0 NM9.4

Classic Comics #5 © GIL

Classic Comics #6 © GIL

Classic Comics #7 © GIL

Ed	HRN	Date	Details	A	C	GD2.0	FN6.0	NM9.4
22B	166	–	Center ad for Children's Digest & Young Miss; rare; PC-r	2	2	10.50	32.00	85.00
23	166	R/68	C-Price 25¢; PC-r	2	2	2.00	5.00	10.00
24	169	Win/69	Stiff-c	2	2	2.00	5.00	10.00
25	169	Win/71	PC-r; stiff-c	2	2	2.00	5.00	10.00

3. The Count of Monte Cristo

Ed	HRN	Date	Details	A	C	GD2.0	FN6.0	NM9.4
1	(O)	3/42	Elliot Pub; 68 pgs.	1	1	137.00	411.00	1300.00
2	10	–	Conray Prods; CC-r	1	1	27.00	81.00	215.00
3	15	–	Long Isl. Ind. ed.; CC-r	1	1	21.00	64.00	170.00
4	18/20		Sunrise Times ed.; CC-r	1	1	19.00	56.00	150.00
5	20	–	Sunrise Times ed.; CC-r	1	1	16.00	49.00	130.00
6	21	–	Richmond Courier ed.; CC-r	1	1	16.00	48.00	125.00
7	28	1946	CC-r; new Banner logo	1	1	12.50	37.50	100.00
8	36	–	1st LDC-r	1	1	8.65	26.00	60.00
9	60	–	LDC-r	1	1	5.00	15.00	35.00
10	62	–	LDC-r	1	1	5.70	17.00	40.00
11	71	–	LDC-r	1	1	4.30	13.00	26.00
12	87	–	C-price 15¢; LDC-r	1	1	4.00	12.00	24.00
13	113	–	LDC-r	1	1	3.60	9.00	18.00
14	135	–	New-c&a; PC-r; Cameron-a	2	2	4.00	11.00	22.00
15	143	–	PC-r	2	2	2.20	5.50	11.00
16	153	–	PC-r	2	2	2.20	5.50	11.00
17	161	–	PC-r	2	2	2.20	5.50	11.00
18	167	–	PC-r	2	2	2.00	5.00	10.00
19	167	7/64	PC-r	2	2	2.00	5.00	10.00
20	167	7/65	PC-r	2	2	2.00	5.00	10.00
21	167	7/66	PC-r	2	2	2.00	5.00	10.00
22	166	R/68	C-price 25¢; PC-r	2	2	2.00	5.00	10.00
23	169	–	Win/69 Stiff-c; PC-r	2	2	2.00	5.00	10.00

4. The Last of the Mohicans

Ed	HRN	Date	Details	A	C	GD2.0	FN6.0	NM9.4
1	(O)	8/42	Date listed-1942; Gilberton #4(0) on; 68 pgs.	1	1	116.00	348.00	1100.00
2	12	–	Elliot Pub; CC-r	1	1	27.00	81.00	215.00
3	15	–	Long Isl. Ind. ed.; CC-r	1	1	21.00	64.00	170.00
4	20	–	Long Isl. Ind. ed.; CC-r; banner logo	1	1	18.00	54.00	145.00
5	21	–	Queens Home News ed.; CC-r	1	1	16.00	49.00	130.00
6	28	1946	Last CC-r; new	1	1	13.00	39.00	105.00
7	36	–	1st LDC-r	1	1	8.65	26.00	60.00
8	60	–	LDC-r	1	1	5.00	15.00	35.00
9	64	–	LDC-r	1	1	4.30	13.00	26.00
10	78	–	C-price 15¢; LDC-r	1	1	4.00	12.00	24.00
11	89	–	LDC-r	1	1	4.00	11.00	22.00
12	117	–	Last LDC-r	1	1	3.60	9.00	18.00
13	135	–	New-c; PC-r	1	2	4.00	11.00	22.00
14	141	–	PC-r	1	2	2.80	7.00	14.00
15	150	–	New-a; PC-r; Severin, L.B. Cole-a	2	2	4.00	12.00	24.00
16	161	–	PC-r	2	2	2.00	5.00	10.00
17	167	–	PC-r	2	2	2.00	5.00	10.00
18	167	6/64	PC-r	2	2	2.00	5.00	10.00
19	167	8/65	PC-r	2	2	2.00	5.00	10.00
20	167	8/66	PC-r	2	2	2.00	5.00	10.00
21	166	R/67	C-price 25¢; PC-r	2	2	2.00	5.00	10.00
22	169	Spr/69	Stiff-c; PC-r	2	2	2.00	5.00	10.00

5. Moby Dick

Ed	HRN	Date	Details	A	C	GD2.0	FN6.0	NM9.4
1A	(O)	9/42	Date listed-1942; Gilberton; 68 pgs.	1	1	147.00	442.00	1400.00
1B			inside-c, rare free promo			221.00	663.00	2100.00
2	10	–	Conray Prods; Pg. 64 changed from 105 title list to letter from Editor; CC-r	1	1	29.00	86.00	230.00
3	15	–	Long Isl. Ind. ed.; Pg. 64 changed from Letter to the Editor to Ill. poem-Concord Hymn; CC-r	1	1	24.00	73.00	195.00
4	18/20	–	Sunrise Times ed.; CC-r	1	1	19.00	56.00	150.00
5	20	–	Sunrise Times ed.; CC-r	1	1	18.00	54.00	145.00
6	21	–	Sunrise Times ed.; CC-r	1	1	16.00	49.00	130.00
7	28	1946	CC-r; new banner logo	1	1	14.00	43.00	115.00
8	36	–	1st LDC-r	1	1	8.65	26.00	60.00
9	60	–	LDC-r	1	1	5.00	15.00	35.00
10	62	–	LDC-r	1	1	5.70	17.00	40.00
11	71	–	LDC-r	1	1	4.65	14.00	28.00
12	87	–	C-price 15¢; LDC-r	1	1	4.30	13.00	26.00
13	118	–	LDC-r	1	1	4.00	11.00	22.00
14	131	–	New c&a; PC-r	2	2	4.00	12.00	24.00
15	138	–	PC-r	2	2	2.20	5.50	11.00
16	148	–	PC-r	2	2	2.20	5.50	11.00
17	158	–	PC-r	2	2	2.20	5.50	11.00
18	167	–	PC-r	2	2	2.00	5.00	10.00
19	167	6/64	PC-r	2	2	2.00	5.00	10.00
20	167	7/65	PC-r	2	2	2.00	5.00	10.00
21	167	3/66	PC-r	2	2	2.00	5.00	10.00
22	166	9/67	PC-r	2	2	2.00	5.00	10.00
23	166	Win/69	New-c & c-price 25¢; Stiff-c; PC-r	2	3	3.60	9.00	18.00
24	169	Win/71	PC-r	2	3	3.40	8.50	17.00

6. A Tale of Two Cities

Ed	HRN	Date	Details	A	C	GD2.0	FN6.0	NM9.4
1	(O)	10/42	Date listed-1942; 68 pgs. Zeckerberg c/a	1	1	116.00	348.00	1100.00
2	14	–	Elliot Pub; CC-r	1	1	26.00	77.00	205.00
3	18	–	Long Isl. Ind. ed.; CC-r	1	1	20.00	60.00	160.00
4	20	–	Sunrise Times ed.; CC-r	1	1	18.00	54.00	145.00
5	28	1946	Last CC-r; new banner logo	1	1	13.00	39.00	105.00
6	51	–	1st LDC-r	1	1	7.85	23.50	55.00
7	64	–	LDC-r	1	1	5.00	15.00	30.00
8	78	–	C-price 15¢; LDC-r	1	1	4.30	13.00	26.00
9	89	–	LDC-r	1	1	3.60	9.00	18.00
10	117	–	LDC-r	1	1	3.60	9.00	18.00
11	132	–	New-c&a; PC-r; Joe Orlando-a	2	2	4.00	12.00	24.00
12	140	–	PC-r	2	2	2.00	5.00	10.00
13	147	–	PC-r	2	2	2.00	5.00	10.00
14	152	–	PC-r; very rare	2	2	19.00	56.00	150.00
15	153	–	PC-r	2	2	2.20	5.50	11.00
16	149	–	PC-r	2	2	2.20	5.50	11.00
17	167	–	PC-r	2	2	2.00	5.00	10.00
18	167	6/64	PC-r	2	2	2.00	5.00	10.00
19	167	8/65	PC-r	2	2	2.00	5.00	10.00
20	166	5/67	PC-r	2	2	2.00	5.00	10.00

Classic Comics #8 © GIL

Classic Comics #9 © GIL

Classic Comics #11 © GIL

Ed	HRN	Date	Details	A	C	GD2.0	FN6.0	NM9.4
21	166	Fall/68	New-c & 25¢; PC-r	2	3	4.00	11.00	22.00
22	169	Sum/70	Stiff-c; PC-r	2	3	3.40	8.50	17.00

7. Robin Hood

Ed	HRN	Date	Details	A	C	GD2.0	FN6.0	NM9.4
1	(O)	12/42	Date listed-1942; first Gift Box ad-bc; 68 pgs.	1	1	84.00	253.00	800.00
2	12	–	Elliot Pub; CC-r	1	1	25.00	75.00	200.00
3	18	–	Long Isl. Ind. ed.; CC-r	1	1	19.00	56.00	150.00
4	20	–	Nassau Bulletin ed.; CC-r	1	1	18.00	53.00	140.00
5	22	–	Queens Cty. Times ed.; CC-r	1	1	16.00	48.00	125.00
6	28	–	CC-r	1	1	14.00	41.00	110.00
7	51	–	LDC-r	1	1	7.85	23.50	55.00
8	64	–	LDC-r	1	1	5.00	15.00	32.00
9	78	–	LDC-r	1	1	4.00	12.00	24.00
10	97	–	LDC-r	1	1	4.00	11.00	22.00
11	106	–	LDC-r	1	1	3.00	7.50	18.00
12	121	–	LDC-r	1	1	3.00	7.50	18.00
13	129	–	New-c; PC-r	1	2	4.00	12.00	24.00
14	136	–	New-a; PC-r	2	2	4.00	12.00	24.00
15	143	–	PC-r	2	2	2.20	5.50	11.00
16	153	–	PC-r	2	2	2.20	5.50	11.00
17	164	–	PC-r	2	2	2.00	5.00	10.00
18	167	–	PC-r	2	2	2.00	5.00	10.00
19	167	6/64	PC-r	2	2	2.00	5.00	10.00
20	167	5/65	PC-r	2	2	2.00	5.00	10.00
21	167	7/66	PC-r	2	2	2.00	5.00	10.00
22	166	12/67	PC-r	2	2	2.00	5.00	10.00
23	169	Sum/69	Stiff-c; c-price 25¢; PC-r	2	2	2.00	5.00	10.00

8. Arabian Nights

Ed	HRN	Date	Details	A	C	GD2.0	FN6.0	NM9.4
1	(O)	2/43	Original; 68 pgs. Lilian Chestney-c/a	1	1	147.00	442.00	1400.00
2	17	–	Long Isl. ed.; pg. 64 changed from Gift Box ad to Letter from British Medical Worker; CC-r	1	1	55.00	165.00	500.00
3	20	–	Nassau Bulletin; Pg. 64 changed from letter to article-Three Men Named Smith; CC-r	1	1	44.00	133.00	400.00
4A	28	1946	CC-r; new banner logo, slick-c	1	1	33.00	99.00	265.00
4B	28	1946	Same, but w/stiff-c	1	1	33.00	99.00	265.00
5	51	–	LDC-r	1	1	23.00	69.00	185.00
6	64	–	LDC-r	1	1	19.00	56.00	150.00
7	78	–	LDC-r	1	1	18.00	53.00	140.00
8	164	–	New-c&a; PC-r	2	2	16.00	48.00	125.00

9. Les Miserables

Ed	HRN	Date	Details	A	C	GD2.0	FN6.0	NM9.4
1A	(O)	3/43	Original; slick paper cover; 68 pgs.	1	1	84.00	253.00	800.00
1B	(O)	3/43	Original; rough, pulp type-c; 68 pgs.	1	1	105.00	316.00	1000.00
2	14	–	Elliot Pub; CC-r	1	1	27.00	81.00	215.00
3	18	3/44	Nassau Bul. Pg. 64 changed from Gift Box ad to Bill of Rights article; CC-r	1	1	23.00	68.00	180.00
4	20	–	Richmond Courier ed.; CC-r	1	1	19.00	56.00	150.00
5	28	1946	Gilberton; pgs. 60-64 rearranged/ illos added; CC-r	1	1	14.00	41.00	110.00
6	51	–	LDC-r	1	1	8.65	26.00	60.00
7	71	–	LDC-r	1	1	5.70	17.00	40.00
8	87	–	C-price 15¢; LDC-r	1	1	5.00	15.00	35.00
9	161	–	New-c&a; PC-r	2	2	5.00	15.00	35.00
10	167	9/63	PC-r	2	2	3.40	8.50	17.00
11	167	12/65	PC-r	2	2	3.40	8.50	17.00
12	166	R/1968	New-c & price 25¢; PC-r	2	3	4.00	12.00	24.00

10. Robinson Crusoe (Used in **SOTI**, pg. 142)

Ed	HRN	Date	Details	A	C	GD2.0	FN6.0	NM9.4
1A	(O)	4/43	Original; Violet-c; 68 pgs; Zuckerberg c/a	1	1	71.00	213.00	675.00
1B	(O)	4/43	Original; blue-grey-c, 68 pgs.	1	1	80.00	240.00	760.00
2A	14	–	Elliot Pub; violet-c; 68 pgs; CC-r	1	1	29.00	86.00	230.00
2B	14	–	Elliot Pub; blue-grey-c; CC-r	1	1	26.00	77.00	205.00
3	18	–	Nassau Bul. Pg. 64 changed from Gift Box ad to Bill of Rights article; CC-r	1	1	19.00	56.00	150.00
4	20	–	Queens Home News ed.; CC-r	1	1	16.00	49.00	130.00
5	28	1946	Gilberton; pg. 64 changes from Bill of Rights to WWII article-One Leg Shot Away; last CC-r	1	1	13.00	39.00	105.00
6	51	–	LDC-r	1	1	7.85	23.50	55.00
7	64	–	LDC-r	1	1	5.00	15.00	35.00
8	78	–	C-price 15¢; LDC-r	1	1	4.30	13.00	26.00
9	97	–	LDC-r	1	1	4.00	12.00	24.00
10	114	–	LDC-r	1	1	3.60	9.00	18.00
11	130	–	New-c; PC-r	1	2	4.00	12.00	24.00
12	140	–	New-a; PC-r	2	2	4.00	12.00	24.00
13	153	–	PC-r	2	2	2.00	5.00	10.00
14	164	–	PC-r	2	2	2.00	5.00	10.00
15	167	–	PC-r	2	2	2.00	5.00	10.00
16	167	7/64	PC-r	2	2	2.80	7.00	14.00
17	167	5/65	PC-r	2	2	2.80	7.00	14.00
18	167	6/66	PC-r	2	2	2.00	5.00	10.00
19	166	Fall/68	C-price 25¢; PC-r	2	2	2.00	5.00	10.00
20	166	R/68	(No Twin Circle ad)	2	2	2.20	5.50	11.00
21	169	Sm/70	Stiff-c; PC-r	2	2	2.20	5.50	11.00

11. Don Quixote

Ed	HRN	Date	Details	A	C	GD2.0	FN6.0	NM9.4
1	10	5/43	First (O) with HRN list; 68 pgs.	1	1	79.00	237.00	750.00
2	18	–	Nassau Bulletin ed.; CC-r	1	1	24.00	73.00	195.00
3	21	–	Queens Home News ed.; CC-r	1	1	19.00	56.00	150.00
4	28	–	CC-r	1	1	14.00	41.00	110.00
5	110	–	New-PC; PC-r	1	2	5.00	15.00	35.00
6	156	–	Pgs. reduced 68 to 52; PC-r	1	2	3.60	9.00	18.00
7	165	–	PC-r	1	2	2.40	6.00	12.00
8	167	1/64	PC-r	1	2	2.40	6.00	12.00
9	167	11/65	PC-r	1	2	2.40	6.00	12.00
10	166	R/1968	New-c & price 25¢; PC-r	1	3	4.30	13.00	26.00

12. Rip Van Winkle and the Headless Horseman

Ed	HRN	Date	Details	A	C	GD2.0	FN6.0	NM9.4
1	11	6/43	Original; 68 pgs.	1	1	79.00	237.00	750.00
2	15	–	Long Isl. Ind. ed.;	1	1	24.00	71.00	190.00

Classic Comics #12 © GIL

Classic Comics #14 © GIL

Classic Comics #16 © GIL

Ed	HRN	Date	Details	A	C	GD2.0	FN6.0	NM9.4
			CC-r					
3	20	–	Long Isl. Ind. ed.;	1	1	19.00	56.00	150.00
4	22	–	Queens Cty. Times ed.; CC-r	1	1	16.00	48.00	125.00
5	28	–	CC-r	1	1	13.00	39.00	105.00
6	60	–	1st LDC-r	1	1	7.00	21.00	48.00
7	62	–	LDC-r	1	1	5.00	15.00	30.00
8	71	–	LDC-r	1	1	4.00	12.00	24.00
9	89	–	C-price 15¢; LDC-r	1	1	4.00	11.00	22.00
10	118	–	LDC-r	1	1	3.60	9.00	18.00
11	132	–	New-c; PC-r	1	2	4.00	12.00	24.00
12	150	–	New-a; PC-r	2	2	4.00	12.00	24.00
13	158	–	PC-r	2	2	2.20	5.50	11.00
14	167	–	PC-r	2	2	2.20	5.50	11.00
15	167	12/63	PC-r	2	2	2.00	5.00	10.00
16	167	4/65	PC-r	2	2	2.00	5.00	10.00
17	167	4/66	PC-r	2	2	2.00	5.00	10.00
18	166	R/1968	New-c&price 25¢; PC-r; stiff-c	2	3	3.40	8.50	17.00
19	169	Sm/70	PC-r; stiff-c	2	3	2.80	7.00	14.00

13. Dr. Jekyll and Mr. Hyde (Used in **SOTI**, pg. 143)(1st horror comic?)

Ed	HRN	Date	Details	A	C	GD2.0	FN6.0	NM9.4
1	12	8/43	Original 60 pgs.	1	1	116.00	348.00	1100.00
2	15	–	Long Isl. Ind. ed.; CC-r	1	1	34.00	103.00	275.00
3	20	–	Long Isl. Ind. ed.; CC-r	1	1	24.00	71.00	190.00
4	28	–	No c-price; CC-r	1	1	18.00	54.00	145.00
5	60	–	New-c; Pgs. reduced from 60 to 52; H.C. Kiefer-c; LDC-r	1	2	7.00	21.00	48.00
6	62	–	LDC-r	1	2	5.00	15.00	35.00
7	71	–	LDC-r	1	2	4.65	14.00	28.00
8	87	–	Date returns (erroneous); LDC-r	1	2	4.30	13.00	26.00
9	112	–	New-c&a; PC-r; Cameron-a	2	3	5.00	15.00	32.00
10	153	–	PC-r	2	3	2.20	5.50	11.00
11	161	–	PC-r	2	3	2.20	5.50	11.00
12	167	–	PC-r	2	3	2.00	5.00	10.00
13	167	8/64	PC-r	2	3	2.00	5.00	10.00
14	167	11/65	PC-r	2	3	2.00	5.00	10.00
15	166	R/68	C-price 25¢; PC-r	2	3	2.00	5.00	10.00
16	169	Wn/69	PC-r; stiff-c	2	3	2.00	5.00	10.00

14. Westward Ho!

Ed	HRN	Date	Details	A	C	GD2.0	FN6.0	NM9.4
1	13	9/43	Original; last outside bc coming-next ad; 60 pgs.	1	1	190.00	570.00	1800.00
2	15	–	Long Isl. Ind. ed.; CC-r	1	1	55.00	165.00	525.00
3	21	–	Queens Home News; Pg. 56 changed from coming-next ad to Three Men Named Smith; CC-r	1	1	42.00	126.00	380.00
4	28	1946	Gilberton; Pg. 56 changed again to WWII article-Speaking for America; last CC-r	1	1	38.00	113.00	300.00
5	53	–	Pgs. reduced from 60 to 52; LDC-r	1	1	34.00	103.00	275.00

15. Uncle Tom's Cabin (Used in **SOTI**, pgs. 102, 103)

Ed	HRN	Date	Details	A	C	GD2.0	FN6.0	NM9.4
1	14	11/43	Original; Outside-bc ad: 2 Gift Boxes; 60 pgs.; color var. on-c; green trunk,root on left & brown trunk, root on left	1	1	66.00	197.00	625.00
2	15	–	Long Isl. Ind. listed- bottom inside-fc; also Gilberton listed bottom-pg. 1; CC-r; green root vs. brown root var. occurs again	1	1	26.00	77.00	205.00
3	21	–	Nassau Bulletin ed.; CC-r	1	1	20.00	60.00	160.00
4	28	–	No c-price; CC-r	1	1	14.00	41.00	110.00
5	53	–	Pgs. reduced 60 to 52; LDC-r	1	1	7.85	23.50	55.00
6	71	–	LDC-r	1	1	5.00	15.00	35.00
7	89	–	C-price 15¢; LDC-r	1	1	5.00	15.00	32.00
8	117	–	New-c/lettering changes; PC-r	1	2	4.00	12.00	24.00
9	128	–	'Picture Progress' promo; PC-r	1	2	2.80	7.00	14.00
10	137	–	PC-r	1	2	2.20	5.50	11.00
11	146	–	PC-r	1	2	2.20	5.50	11.00
12	154	–	PC-r	1	2	2.20	5.50	11.00
13	161	–	PC-r	1	2	2.00	5.00	10.00
14	167	–	PC-r	1	2	2.00	5.00	10.00
15	167	6/64	PC-r	1	2	2.00	5.00	10.00
16	167	5/65	PC-r	1	2	2.00	5.00	10.00
17	166	5/67	PC-r	1	2	2.00	5.00	10.00
18	166	Wn/69	New-stiff-c; PC-r	1	3	3.40	8.50	17.00
19	169	Sm/70	PC-r; stiff-c	1	3	2.80	7.00	14.00

16. Gullivers Travels

Ed	HRN	Date	Details	A	C	GD2.0	FN6.0	NM9.4
1	15	12/43	Original-Lilian Chestney c/a; 60 pgs.	1	1	68.00	205.00	650.00
2	18/20	–	Price deleted; Queens Home News ed; CC-r	1	1	23.00	69.00	185.00
3	22	–	Queens Cty. Times ed.; CC-r	1	1	18.00	54.00	145.00
4	28	–	CC-r	1	1	13.00	39.00	105.00
5	60	–	Pgs. reduced to 48; LDC-r	1	1	6.00	18.00	42.00
6	62	–	LDC-r	1	1	5.00	15.00	30.00
7	78	–	C-price 15¢; LDC-r	1	1	4.30	13.00	26.00
8	89	–	LDC-r	1	1	4.00	11.00	22.00
9	155	–	New-c; PC-r	1	2	4.00	12.00	24.00
10	165	–	PC-r	1	2	2.00	5.00	10.00
11	167	5/64	PC-r	1	2	2.00	5.00	10.00
12	167	11/65	PC-r	1	2	2.00	5.00	10.00
13	166	R/1968	C-price 25¢; PC-r	1	2	2.00	5.00	10.00
14	169	Wn/69	PC-r; stiff-c	1	2	2.00	5.00	10.00

17. The Deerslayer

Ed	HRN	Date	Details	A	C	GD2.0	FN6.0	NM9.4
1	16	1/44	Original; Outside-bc ad: 3 Gift Boxes; 60 pgs.	1	1	58.00	174.00	550.00
2A	18	–	Queens Cty Times (inside-fc); CC-r	1	1	24.00	71.00	190.00
2B	18	–	Gilberton (bottom-pg. 1); CC-r; Scarce	1	1	34.00	103.00	275.00
3	22	–	Queens Cty. Times ed.; CC-r	1	1	19.00	56.00	150.00
4	28	–	CC-r	1	1	14.00	41.00	110.00
5	60	–	Pgs.reduced to 52; LDC-r	1	1	7.00	21.00	48.00
6	64	–	LDC-r	1	1	4.65	14.00	28.00
7	85	–	C-price 15¢; LDC-r	1	1	4.00	11.00	22.00
8	118	–	LDC-r	1	1	3.60	9.00	18.00
9	132	–	LDC-r	1	1	3.60	9.00	18.00
10	167	11/66	Last LDC-r	1	1	3.40	8.50	17.00

Classic Comics #18 © GIL

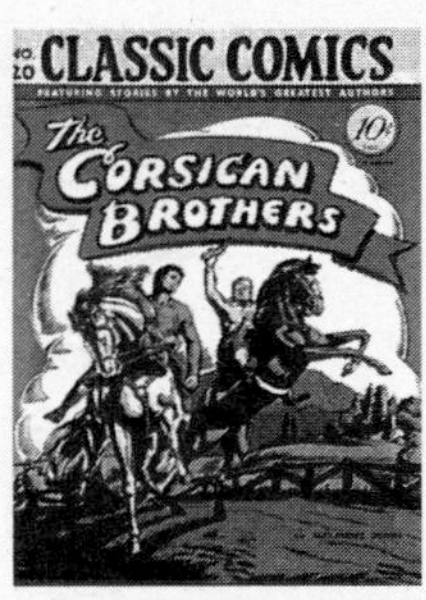

Classic Comics #20 © GIL

Classic Comics #22 © GIL

Ed	HRN	Date	Details	A	C	GD2.0	FN6.0	NM9.4
11	166	R/1968	New-c & price 25¢; PC-r	1	2	4.00	12.00	24.00
12	169	Spr/71	Stiff-c; letters from parents & educators; PC-r	1	2	3.40	8.50	17.00

18. The Hunchback of Notre Dame

Ed	HRN	Date	Details	A	C	GD2.0	FN6.0	NM9.4
1A	17	3/44	Orig.; Gilberton ed; 60 pgs.	1	1	76.00	229.00	725.00
1B	17	3/44	Orig.; Island Pub. Ed.; 60 pgs.	1	1	68.00	205.00	650.00
2	18/20	–	Queens Home News ed.; CC-r	1	1	26.00	77.00	205.00
3	22	–	Queens Cty. Times ed.; CC-r	1	1	19.00	58.00	155.00
4	28	–	CC-r	1	1	16.00	49.00	130.00
5	60	–	New-c; 8pgs. deleted; Kiefer-c; LDC-r	1	2	6.40	19.25	45.00
6	62	–	LDC-r	1	2	4.65	14.00	28.00
7	78	–	C-price 15¢; LDC-r	1	2	4.30	13.00	26.00
8A	89	–	H.C.Kiefer on bottom right-fc; LDC-r	1	2	4.00	12.00	24.00
8B	89	–	Name omitted; LDC-r	1	2	5.00	15.00	32.00
9	118	–	LDC-r	1	2	4.00	11.00	22.00
10	140	–	New-c; PC-r	1	3	5.00	15.00	32.00
11	146	–	PC-r	1	3	4.00	12.00	24.00
12	158	–	New-c&a; PC-r; Evans/Crandall-a	2	4	4.30	13.00	26.00
13	165	–	PC-r	2	4	2.20	5.50	11.00
14	167	9/63	PC-r	2	4	2.20	5.50	11.00
15	167	10/64	PC-r	2	4	2.20	5.50	11.00
16	167	4/66	PC-r	2	4	2.00	5.00	10.00
17	166	R/1968	New price 25¢; PC-r	2	4	2.00	5.00	10.00
18	169	Sp/70	Stiff-c; PC-r	2	4	2.00	5.00	10.00

19. Huckleberry Finn

Ed	HRN	Date	Details	A	C	GD2.0	FN6.0	NM9.4
1A	18	4/44	Orig.; Gilberton ed.; 60 pgs.	1	1	50.00	150.00	450.00
1B	18	4/44	Orig.; Island Pub.; 60 pgs.	1	1	55.00	165.00	500.00
2	18	–	Nassau Bulletin ed.; fc-price 15¢-Canada; no coming-next ad; CC-r	1	1	24.00	73.00	195.00
3	22	–	Queens City Times ed.; CC-r	1	1	19.00	56.00	150.00
4	28	–	CC-r	1	1	13.00	39.00	105.00
5	60	–	Pgs. reduced to 48; LDC-r	1	1	6.00	18.00	42.00
6	62	–	LDC-r	1	1	5.00	15.00	30.00
7	78	–	LDC-r	1	1	4.00	12.00	24.00
8	89	–	LDC-r	1	1	4.00	11.00	22.00
9	117	–	LDC-r	1	1	3.60	9.00	18.00
10	131	–	New-c&a; PC-r	2	2	4.00	11.00	22.00
11	140	–	PC-r	2	2	2.20	5.50	11.00
12	150	–	PC-r	2	2	2.20	5.50	11.00
13	158	–	PC-r	2	2	2.20	5.50	11.00
14	165	–	PC-r (scarce)	2	2	4.00	11.00	22.00
15	167	–	PC-r	2	2	2.00	5.00	10.00
16	167	6/64	PC-r	2	2	2.00	5.00	10.00
17	167	6/65	PC-r	2	2	2.00	5.00	10.00
18	167	10/65	PC-r	2	2	2.00	5.00	10.00
19	166	9/67	PC-r	2	2	2.00	5.00	10.00
20	166	Win/69	C-price 25¢; PC-r; stiff-c	2	2	2.00	5.00	10.00
21	169	Sm/70	PC-r; stiff-c	2	2	2.00	5.00	10.00

20. The Corsican Brothers

Ed	HRN	Date	Details	A	C	GD2.0	FN6.0	NM9.4
1A	20	6/44	Orig.; Gilberton ed.; bc-ad: 4 Gift Boxes; 60 pgs.	1	1	42.00	125.00	375.0
1B	20	6/44	Orig.; Courier ed.; 60 pgs.	1	1	40.00	120.00	340.0
1C	20	6/44	Orig.; Long Island Ind. ed.; 60 pgs.	1	1	40.00	120.00	340.0
2	22	–	Queens Cty. Times ed.; white logo banner; CC-r	1	1	20.00	60.00	160.0
3	28	–	CC-r	1	1	19.00	56.00	150.0
4	60	–	Cl logo; no price; 48 pgs.; LDC-r	1	1	16.00	49.00	130.0
5A	62	–	LDC-r; Classics Ill. logo at top of pgs.	1	1	14.00	41.00	110.0
5B	62	–	w/o logo at top of pg. (scarcer)	1	1	15.00	45.00	120.0
6	78	–	C-price 15¢; LDC-r	1	1	13.00	39.00	105.0
7	97	–	LDC-r	1	1	12.00	36.00	95.0

21. 3 Famous Mysteries ("The Sign of the 4", "The Murders in the Rue Morgue", "The Flayed Hand")

Ed	HRN	Date	Details	A	C	GD2.0	FN6.0	NM9.4
1A	21	7/44	Orig.; Gilberton ed.; 60 pgs.	1	1	89.00	268.00	850.0
1B	21	7/44	Orig. Island Pub. Co.; 60 pgs.	1	1	92.00	276.00	875.0
1C	21	7/44	Original; Courier Ed.; 60 pgs.	1	1	76.00	229.00	725.0
2	22	–	Nassau Bulletin ed.; CC-r	1	1	38.00	113.00	300.0
3	30	–	CC-r	1	1	29.00	87.00	235.0
4	62	–	LDC-r; 8 pgs. deleted; LDC-r	1	1	23.00	69.00	185.0
5	70	–	LDC-r	1	1	21.00	62.00	165.0
6	85	–	C-price 15¢; LDC-r	1	1	18.00	54.00	145.0
7	114	–	New-c; PC-r	1	2	18.00	54.00	145.0

22. The Pathfinder

Ed	HRN	Date	Details	A	C	GD2.0	FN6.0	NM9.4
1A	22	10/44	Orig.; No printer listed; ownership statement inside fc lists Gilberton & date; 60 pgs.	1	1	43.00	128.00	385.0
1B	22	10/44	Orig.; Island Pub. ed.; 60 pgs.	1	1	40.00	120.00	330.0
1C	22	10/44	Orig.; Queens Cty Times ed. 60 pgs.	1	1	40.00	120.00	330.0
2	30	–	C-price removed; CC-r	1	1	14.00	41.00	110.0
3	60	–	Pgs. reduced to 52; LDC-r	1	1	5.00	15.00	35.0
4	70	–	LDC-r	1	1	4.00	12.00	28.0
5	85	–	C-price 15¢; LDC-r	1	1	4.00	12.00	24.0
6	118	–	LDC-r	1	1	4.00	11.00	22.0
7	132	–	LDC-r	1	1	3.60	9.00	18.0
8	146	–	LDC-r	1	1	3.60	9.00	18.0
9	167	11/63	New-c; PC-r	1	2	5.00	15.00	32.0
10	167	12/65	PC-r	1	2	3.60	9.00	18.0
11	166	8/67	PC-r	1	2	3.60	9.00	18.0

23. Oliver Twist (1st Classic produced by the Iger Shop)

Ed	HRN	Date	Details	A	C	GD2.0	FN6.0	NM9.4
1	23	7/45	Original; 60 pgs.	1	1	40.00	120.00	360.0
2A	30	–	Printers Union logo on bottom left-fc same as 23(Orig.) (very rare); CC-r	1	1	31.00	94.00	250.0

Classic Comics #24 © GIL

Classic Comics #26 © GIL

Classic Comics #28 © GIL

Ed	HRN	Date	Details	A	C	GD2.0	FN6.0	NM9.4
2B	30	–	Union logo omitted; CC-r	1	1	13.00	39.00	105.00
3	60	–	Pgs. reduced to 48; LDC-r	1	1	5.50	16.50	38.00
4	62	–	LDC-r	1	1	5.00	15.00	30.00
5	71	–	LDC-r	1	1	4.30	13.00	26.00
6	85	–	C-price 15¢; LDC-r	1	1	4.00	12.00	24.00
7	94	–	LDC-r	1	1	3.60	9.00	18.00
8	118	–	LDC-r	1	1	3.60	9.00	18.00
9	136	–	New-PC, old-a; PC-r	1	2	4.00	11.00	22.00
10	150	–	Old-a; PC-r	1	2	3.40	8.50	17.00
11	164	–	Old-a; PC-r	1	2	4.00	10.00	20.00
12	164	–	New-a; PC-r; Evans/Crandall-a	2	2	5.00	15.00	32.00
13	167	–	PC-r	2	2	3.60	9.00	18.00
14	167	8/64	PC-r	2	2	2.00	5.00	10.00
15	167	12/65	PC-r	2	2	2.00	5.00	10.00
16	166	R/1968	New 25¢; PC-r	2	2	2.00	5.00	10.00
17	169	Win/69	Stiff-c; PC-r	2	2	2.00	5.00	10.00

24. A Connecticut Yankee in King Arthur's Court

Ed	HRN	Date	Details	A	C	GD2.0	FN6.0	NM9.4
1	–	9/45	Original	1	1	40.00	120.00	320.00
2	30	–	No price circle; CC-r	1	1	12.50	37.50	100.00
3	60	–	8 pgs. deleted; LDC-r	1	1	5.00	15.00	35.00
4	62	–	LDC-r	1	1	5.00	15.00	30.00
5	71	–	LDC-r	1	1	4.65	14.00	28.00
6	87	–	C-price 15¢; LDC-r	1	1	4.00	12.00	24.00
7	121	–	LDC-r	1	1	4.00	11.00	22.00
8	140	–	New-c&a; PC-r	2	2	4.00	12.00	24.00
9	153	–	PC-r	2	2	2.20	5.50	11.00
10	164	–	PC-r	2	2	2.00	5.00	10.00
11	167	–	PC-r	2	2	2.00	5.00	10.00
12	167	7/64	PC-r	2	2	2.00	5.00	10.00
13	167	6/66	PC-r	2	2	2.00	5.00	10.00
14	166	R/1968	C-price 25¢; PC-r	2	2	2.00	5.00	10.00
15	169	Spr/71	PC-r; stiff-c	2	2	2.00	5.00	10.00

25. Two Years Before the Mast

Ed	HRN	Date	Details	A	C	GD2.0	FN6.0	NM9.4
1	–	10/45	Original; Webb/Heames-a&c	1	1	40.00	120.00	320.00
2	30	–	Price circle blank; CC-r	1	1	12.50	37.50	100.00
3	60	–	8 pgs. deleted; LDC-r	1	1	5.00	15.00	35.00
4	62	–	LDC-r	1	1	5.00	15.00	30.00
5	71	–	LDC-r	1	1	4.00	12.00	24.00
6	85	–	C-price 15¢; LDC-r	1	1	4.00	11.00	22.00
7	114	–	LDC-r	1	1	3.60	9.00	18.00
8	156	–	3 pgs. replaced by fillers; new-c; PC-r	1	2	4.00	12.00	24.00
9	167	12/63	PC-r	1	2	2.00	5.00	10.00
10	167	12/65	PC-r	1	2	2.00	5.00	10.00
11	166	9/67	PC-r	1	2	2.00	5.00	10.00
12	169	Win/69	C-price 25¢; stiff-c PC-r	1	2	2.00	5.00	10.00

26. Frankenstein (2nd horror comic?)

Ed	HRN	Date	Details	A	C	GD2.0	FN6.0	NM9.4
1	26	12/45	Orig.; Webb/Brewster a&c; 52 pgs.	1	1	95.00	285.00	900.00
2A	30	–	Price circle blank; no indicia; CC-r	1	1	29.00	87.00	235.00
2B	30	–	With indicia; scarce; CC-r	1	1	34.00	103.00	275.00
3	60	–	LDC-r	1	1	16.00	49.00	130.00
4	62	–	LDC-r	1	1	14.00	41.00	110.00
5	71	–	LDC-r	1	1	6.40	19.25	45.00
6A	82	–	C-price 15¢; soft-c LDC-r	1	1	5.00	15.00	35.00
6B	82	–	Stiff-c; LDC-r	1	1	6.40	19.25	45.00
7	117	–	LDC-r	1	1	4.00	11.00	22.00
8	146	–	New Saunders-c; PC-r	1	2	4.30	13.00	26.00
9	152	–	Scarce; PC-r	1	2	7.00	21.00	48.00
10	153	–	PC-r	1	2	2.20	5.50	11.00
11	160	–	PC-r	1	2	2.20	5.50	11.00
12	165	–	PC-r	1	2	2.00	5.00	10.00
13	167	–	PC-r	1	2	2.00	5.00	10.00
14	167	6/64	PC-r	1	2	2.00	5.00	10.00
15	167	6/65	PC-r	1	2	2.00	5.00	10.00
16	167	10/65	PC-r	1	2	2.00	5.00	10.00
17	166	9/67	PC-r	1	2	2.00	5.00	10.00
18	169	Fall/69	C-price 25¢; stiff-c PC-r	1	2	2.00	5.00	10.00
19	169	Spr/71	PC-r; stiff-c	1	2	2.00	5.00	10.00

27. The Adventures of Marco Polo

Ed	HRN	Date	Details	A	C	GD2.0	FN6.0	NM9.4
1	–	4/46	Original	1	1	40.00	120.00	340.00
2	30	–	Last 'Comics' reprint; CC-r	1	1	13.00	39.00	105.00
3	70	–	8 pgs. deleted; no c-price; LDC-r	1	1	5.00	15.00	32.00
4	87	–	C-price 15¢; LDC-r	1	1	4.00	12.00	24.00
5	117	–	LDC-r	1	1	3.40	8.50	17.00
6	154	–	New-c; PC-r	1	2	4.00	11.00	22.00
7	165	–	PC-r	1	2	2.00	5.00	10.00
8	167	4/64	PC-r	1	2	2.00	5.00	10.00
9	167	6/66	PC-r	1	2	2.00	5.00	10.00
10	169	Spr/69	New price 25¢; stiff-c; PC-r	1	2	2.00	5.00	10.00

28. Michael Strogoff

Ed	HRN	Date	Details	A	C	GD2.0	FN6.0	NM9.4
1	–	6/46	Original	1	1	40.00	120.00	350.00
2	51	–	8 pgs. cut; LDC-r	1	1	13.00	39.00	105.00
3	115	–	New-c; PC-r	1	2	5.00	15.00	30.00
4	155	–	PC-r	1	2	3.40	8.50	17.00
5	167	11/63	PC-r	1	2	2.80	7.00	14.00
6	167	7/66	PC-r	1	2	2.80	7.00	14.00
7	169	Sm/69	C-price 25¢; stiff-c PC-r	1	3	3.40	8.50	17.00

29. The Prince and the Pauper

Ed	HRN	Date	Details	A	C	GD2.0	FN6.0	NM9.4
1	–	7/46	Orig.; "Horror"-c	1	1	55.00	165.00	525.00
2	60	–	8 pgs. cut; new-c by Kiefer; LDC-r	1	2	6.00	18.00	42.00
3	62	–	LDC-r	1	2	5.00	15.00	32.00
4	71	–	LDC-r	1	2	4.00	12.00	24.00
5	93	–	LDC-r	1	2	4.00	11.00	22.00
6	114	–	LDC-r	1	2	3.60	9.00	18.00
7	128	–	New-c; PC-r	1	3	4.00	11.00	22.00
8	138	–	PC-r	1	3	2.20	5.50	11.00
9	150	–	PC-r	1	3	2.20	5.50	11.00
10	164	–	PC-r	1	3	2.00	5.00	10.00
11	167	–	PC-r	1	3	2.00	5.00	10.00
12	167	7/64	PC-r	1	3	2.00	5.00	10.00
13	167	11/65	PC-r	1	3	2.00	5.00	10.00
14	166	R/68	C-price 25¢; PC-r	1	3	2.00	5.00	10.00
15	169	Sm/70	PC-r; stiff-c	1	3	2.00	5.00	10.00

30. The Moonstone

Ed	HRN	Date	Details	A	C	GD2.0	FN6.0	NM9.4
1	–	9/46	Original; Rico-c/a	1	1	40.00	120.00	340.00
2	60	–	LDC-r; 8pgs. cut	1	1	7.00	21.00	48.00
3	70	–	LDC-r	1	1	6.00	18.00	42.00
4	155	–	New L.B. Cole-c;	1	2	6.40	19.25	45.00

Classic Comics #32 © GIL

Classics Illustrated #36 © GIL

Classics Illustrated #40 © GIL

Ed	HRN	Date	Details	A	C	GD2.0	FN6.0	NM9.4
			PC-r					
5	165	–	PC-r; L.B. Cole-c	1	2	4.00	12.00	24.00
6	167	1/64	PC-r; L.B. Cole-c	1	2	2.40	6.00	12.00
7	167	9/65	PC-r; L.B. Cole-c	1	2	2.20	5.50	11.00
8	166	R/1968	C-price 25¢; PC-r	1	2	2.00	5.00	10.00

31. The Black Arrow

Ed	HRN	Date	Details	A	C	GD2.0	FN6.0	NM9.4
1	–	10/46	Original	1	1	31.00	94.00	250.00
2	51	–	CI logo; LDC-r 8pgs. deleted	1	1	5.50	16.50	38.00
3	64	–	LDC-r	1	1	4.00	12.00	24.00
4	87	–	C-price 15¢; LDC-r	1	1	4.00	11.00	22.00
5	108	–	LDC-r	1	1	3.60	9.00	18.00
6	125	–	LDC-r	1	1	3.40	8.50	17.00
7	131	–	New-c; PC-r	1	2	4.00	11.00	22.00
8	140	–	PC-r	1	2	2.20	5.50	11.00
9	148	–	PC-r	1	2	2.20	5.50	11.00
10	161	–	PC-r	1	2	2.00	5.00	10.00
11	167	–	PC-r	1	2	2.00	5.00	10.00
12	167	7/64	PC-r	1	2	2.00	5.00	10.00
13	167	11/65	PC-r	1	2	2.00	5.00	10.00
14	166	R/1968	C-price 25¢; PC-r	1	2	2.00	5.00	10.00

32. Lorna Doone

Ed	HRN	Date	Details	A	C	GD2.0	FN6.0	NM9.4
1	–	12/46	Original; Matt Baker c&a	1	1	40.00	120.00	320.00
2	53/64	–	8 pgs. deleted; LDC-r	1	1	7.85	23.50	55.00
3	85	1951	C-price 15¢; LDC-r; Baker c&a	1	1	6.00	18.00	42.00
4	118	–	LDC-r	1	1	4.00	12.00	24.00
5	138	–	New-c; old-c becomes new title pg.; PC-r	1	2	4.00	12.00	24.00
6	150	–	PC-r	1	2	2.00	5.00	10.00
7	165	–	PC-r	1	2	2.00	5.00	10.00
8	167	1/64	PC-r	1	2	2.40	6.00	12.00
9	167	11/65	PC-r	1	2	2.40	6.00	12.00
10	166	R/1968	New-c; PC-r	1	3	4.00	12.00	24.00

33. The Adventures of Sherlock Holmes

Ed	HRN	Date	Details	A	C	GD2.0	FN6.0	NM9.4
1	33	1/47	Original; Kiefer-c; contains Study in Scarlet & Hound of the Baskervilles; 68 pgs.	1	1	116.00	348.00	1100.00
2	53	–	"A Study in Scarlet" (17 pgs.) deleted; LDC-r	1	1	43.00	128.00	385.00
3	71	–	LDC-r	1	1	36.00	107.00	285.00
4A	89	–	C-price 15¢; LDC-r	1	1	29.00	86.00	230.00
4B	89	–	Kiefer's name omitted from-c	1	1	30.00	90.00	240.00

34. Mysterious Island (Last "Classic Comic")

Ed	HRN	Date	Details	A	C	GD2.0	FN6.0	NM9.4
1	–	2/47	Original; Webb/ Heames-c/a	1	1	40.00	120.00	340.00
2	60	–	8 pgs. deleted; LDC-r	1	1	6.00	18.00	42.00
3	62	–	LDC-r	1	1	5.00	15.00	30.00
4	71	–	LDC-r	1	1	6.00	18.00	42.00
5	78	–	C-price 15¢ in circle; LDC-r	1	1	4.30	13.00	26.00
6	92	–	LDC-r	1	1	4.00	12.00	24.00
7	117	–	LDC-r	1	1	3.60	9.00	18.00
8	140	–	New-c; PC-r	1	2	4.00	11.00	22.00
9	156	–	PC-r	1	2	2.20	5.50	11.00
10	167	10/63	PC-r	1	2	2.00	5.00	10.00
11	167	5/64	PC-r	1	2	2.00	5.00	10.00
12	167	6/66	PC-r	1	2	2.00	5.00	10.00
13	166	R/1968	C-price 25¢; PC-r	1	2	2.00	5.00	10.00

35. Last Days of Pompeii (First "Classics Illustrated")

Ed	HRN	Date	Details	A	C	GD2.0	FN6.0	NM9.4
1	–	3/47	Original; LDC; Kiefer-c/a	1	1	40.00	120.00	340.00
2	161	–	New c&a; 15¢; PC-r; Kirby/Ayers-a	2	2	5.00	15.00	35.00
3	167	1/64	PC-r	2	2	4.00	10.00	20.00
4	167	7/66	PC-r	2	2	4.00	10.00	20.00
5	169	Spr/70	New price 25¢; stiff-c; PC-r	2	2	4.00	10.00	20.00

36. Typee

Ed	HRN	Date	Details	A	C	GD2.0	FN6.0	NM9.4
1	–	4/47	Original	1	1	23.00	68.00	180.00
2	64	–	No c-price; 8 pg. ed.; LDC-r	1	1	6.40	19.25	45.00
3	155	–	New-c; PC-r	1	2	4.00	11.00	22.00
4	167	9/63	PC-r	1	2	2.40	6.00	12.00
5	167	7/65	PC-r	1	2	2.40	6.00	12.00
6	169	Sm/69	C-price 25¢; stiff-c PC-r	1	2	2.40	6.00	12.00

37. The Pioneers

Ed	HRN	Date	Details	A	C	GD2.0	FN6.0	NM9.4
1	37	5/47	Original; Palais-c/a	1	1	16.00	48.00	125.00
2A	62	–	8 pgs. cut; LDC-r; price circle blank	1	1	5.00	15.00	30.00
2B	62	–	10¢; LDC-r;	1	1	25.00	75.00	200.00
3	70	–	LDC-r	1	1	4.00	11.00	22.00
4	92	–	15¢; LDC-r	1	1	3.60	9.00	18.00
5	118	–	LDC-r	1	1	3.40	8.50	17.00
6	131	–	LDC-r	1	1	3.40	8.50	17.00
7	132	–	LDC-r	1	1	3.40	8.50	17.00
8	153	–	LDC-r	1	1	3.40	8.50	17.00
9	167	5/64	LDC-r	1	1	2.40	6.00	12.00
10	167	6/66	LDC-r	1	1	2.40	6.00	12.00
11	166	R/1968	New-c; 25¢; PC-r	1	2	4.00	12.00	24.00

38. Adventures of Cellini

Ed	HRN	Date	Details	A	C	GD2.0	FN6.0	NM9.4
1	–	6/47	Original; Froehlich c/a	1	1	29.00	86.00	230.00
2	164	–	New-c&a; PC-r	2	2	4.00	11.00	22.00
3	167	12/63	PC-r	2	2	2.40	6.00	12.00
4	167	7/66	PC-r	2	2	2.40	6.00	12.00
5	169	Spr/70	Stiff-c; new price 25¢; PC-r	2	2	2.80	7.00	14.00

39. Jane Eyre

Ed	HRN	Date	Details	A	C	GD2.0	FN6.0	NM9.4
1	–	7/47	Original	1	1	28.00	84.00	225.00
2	60	–	No c-price; 8 pgs. cut; LDC-r	1	1	5.50	16.50	38.00
3	62	–	LDC-r	1	1	5.00	15.00	32.00
4	71	–	LDC-r; c-price 10¢	1	1	4.65	14.00	28.00
5	92	–	C-price 15¢; LDC-r	1	1	4.00	12.00	24.00
6	118	–	LDC-r	1	1	4.00	11.00	22.00
7	142	–	New-c; old-a; PC-r	1	2	4.30	13.00	26.00
8	154	–	Old-a; PC-r	1	2	4.00	11.00	22.00
9	165	–	New-a; PC-r	2	2	4.30	13.00	26.00
10	167	12/63	PC-r	2	2	4.00	11.00	22.00
11	167	4/65	PC-r	2	2	4.00	10.00	20.00
12	167	8/66	PC-r	2	2	4.00	10.00	20.00
13	166	R/1968	New-c; PC-r	2	3	7.85	23.50	55.00

40. Mysteries ("The Pit and the Pendulum", "The Advs. of Hans Pfall" & "The Fall of the House of Usher")

Ed	HRN	Date	Details	A	C	GD2.0	FN6.0	NM9.4
1	–	8/47	Original; Kiefer-	1	1	58.00	174.00	550.00

Classics Illustrated #42 © GIL

Classics Illustrated #46 © GIL

Classics Illustrated #49 © GIL

Ed	HRN	Date	Details	A	C	GD2.0	FN6.0	NM9.4
			c/a, Froehlich, Griffiths-a					
2	62	–	LDC-r; 8pgs. cut	1	1	25.00	75.00	200.00
3	75	–	LDC-r	1	1	21.00	64.00	170.00
4	92	–	C-price 15¢; LDC-r	1	1	18.00	53.00	140.00

41. Twenty Years After

Ed	HRN	Date	Details	A	C	GD2.0	FN6.0	NM9.4
1	–	9/47	Original; 'horror'-c	1	1	40.00	120.00	340.00
2	62	–	New-c; no c-price 8 pgs. cut; LDC-r; Kiefer-c	1	2	6.00	18.00	42.00
3	78	–	C-price 15¢; LDC-r	1	2	5.00	15.00	30.00
4	156	–	New-c; PC-r	1	3	4.00	11.00	22.00
5	167	12/63	PC-r	1	3	2.00	5.00	10.00
6	167	11/66	PC-r	1	3	2.00	5.00	10.00
7	169	Spr/70	New price 25¢; stiff-c; PC-r	1	3	2.00	5.00	10.00

42. Swiss Family Robinson

Ed	HRN	Date	Details	A	C	GD2.0	FN6.0	NM9.4
1	42	10/47	Orig.; Kiefer-c&a;	1	1	21.00	62.00	165.00
2A	62	–	8 pgs. cut; outside bc: Gift Box ad; LDC-r	1	1	5.50	16.50	38.00
2B	62	–	8 pgs. cut; outside-bc: Reorder list; scarce; LDC-r	1	1	10.00	30.00	70.00
3	75	–	LDC-r	1	1	4.30	13.00	26.00
4	93	–	LDC-r	1	1	4.00	12.00	24.00
5	117	–	LDC-r	1	1	4.00	11.00	22.00
6	131	–	New-c; old-a; PC-r	1	2	4.00	11.00	22.00
7	137	–	Old-a; PC-r	1	2	3.20	8.00	16.00
8	141	–	Old-a; PC-r	1	2	3.20	8.00	16.00
9	152	–	New-a; PC-r	2	2	4.00	11.00	22.00
10	158	–	PC-r	2	2	2.00	5.00	10.00
11	165	–	PC-r	2	2	3.20	8.00	16.00
12	167	12/63	PC-r	2	2	2.40	6.00	12.00
13	167	4/65	PC-r	2	2	2.00	5.00	10.00
14	167	5/66	PC-r	2	2	2.00	5.00	10.00
15	166	11/67	PC-r	2	2	2.00	5.00	10.00
16	169	Spr/69	PC-r; stiff-c	2	2	2.00	5.00	10.00

3. Great Expectations (Used in **SOTI**, pg. 311)

Ed	HRN	Date	Details	A	C	GD2.0	FN6.0	NM9.4
1	–	11/47	Original; Kiefer-a/c	1	1	82.00	245.00	775.00
2	62	–	No c-price; 8 pgs. cut; LDC-r	1	1	53.00	160.00	480.00

4. Mysteries of Paris (Used in **SOTI**, pg. 323)

Ed	HRN	Date	Details	A	C	GD2.0	FN6.0	NM9.4
1A	44	12/47	Original; 56 pgs.; Kiefer-c/a	1	1	63.00	189.00	600.00
1B	44	12/47	Orig.; printed on white/heavier paper; (rare)	1	1	68.00	205.00	650.00
2A	62	–	8 pgs. cut; outside-bc: Gift Box ad; LDC-r	1	1	29.00	86.00	230.00
2B	62	–	8 pgs. cut; outside-bc: reorder list; LDC-r	1	1	29.00	86.00	230.00
3	78	–	C-price 15¢; LDC-r	1	1	24.00	73.00	195.00

5. Tom Brown's School Days

Ed	HRN	Date	Details	A	C	GD2.0	FN6.0	NM9.4
1	44	1/48	Original; 1st 48pg. issue	1	1	14.00	41.00	110.00
2	64	–	No c-price; LDC-r	1	1	6.00	18.00	42.00
3	161	–	New-c&a; PC-r	2	2	3.60	9.00	18.00
4	167	2/64	PC-r	2	2	2.40	6.00	12.00
5	167	8/66	PC-r	2	2	2.40	6.00	12.00
6	166	R/1968	C-price 25¢; PC-r	2	2	2.40	6.00	12.00

46. Kidnapped

Ed	HRN	Date	Details	A	C	GD2.0	FN6.0	NM9.4
1	47	4/48	Original; Webb-c/a	1	1	13.00	39.00	105.00
2A	62	–	Price circle blank; LDC-r	1	1	5.00	15.00	32.00
2B	62	–	C-price 10¢; rare; LDC-r	1	1	29.00	87.00	235.00
3	78	–	C-price 15¢; LDC-r	1	1	4.30	13.00	26.00
4	87	–	LDC-r	1	1	4.00	11.00	22.00
5	118	–	LDC-r	1	1	3.60	9.00	18.00
6	131	–	New-c; PC-r	1	2	4.00	11.00	22.00
7	140	–	PC-r	1	2	2.20	5.50	11.00
8	150	–	PC-r	1	2	2.20	5.50	11.00
9	164	–	Reduced pg.width; PC-r	1	2	2.00	5.00	10.00
10	167	–	PC-r	1	2	2.00	5.00	10.00
11	167	3/64	PC-r	1	2	2.00	5.00	10.00
12	167	6/65	PC-r	1	2	2.00	5.00	10.00
13	167	12/65	PC-r	1	2	2.00	5.00	10.00
14	166	9/67	PC-r	1	2	2.00	5.00	10.00
15	166	Win/69	New price 25¢; PC-r; stiff-c	1	2	2.00	5.00	10.00
16	169	Sm/70	PC-r; stiff-c	1	2	2.00	5.00	10.00

47. Twenty Thousand Leagues Under the Sea

Ed	HRN	Date	Details	A	C	GD2.0	FN6.0	NM9.4
1	47	5/48	Orig.; Kiefer-a&c;	1	1	13.00	39.00	105.00
2	64	–	No c-price; LDC-r	1	1	5.00	15.00	32.00
3	78	–	C-price 15¢; LDC-r	1	1	4.00	12.00	24.00
4	94	–	LDC-r	1	1	4.00	11.00	22.00
5	118	–	LDC-r	1	1	3.60	9.00	18.00
6	128	–	New-c; PC-r	1	2	4.00	11.00	22.00
7	133	–	PC-r	1	2	2.80	7.00	14.00
8	140	–	PC-r	1	2	2.20	5.50	11.00
9	148	–	PC-r	1	2	2.20	5.50	11.00
10	156	–	PC-r	1	2	2.20	5.50	11.00
11	165	–	PC-r	1	2	2.20	5.50	11.00
12	167	–	PC-r	1	2	2.20	5.50	11.00
13	167	3/64	PC-r	1	2	2.20	5.50	11.00
14	167	8/65	PC-r	1	2	2.20	5.50	11.00
15	167	10/66	PC-r	1	2	2.20	5.50	11.00
16	166	R/1968	C-price 25¢; new-c PC-r	1	3	2.80	7.00	14.00
17	169	Spr/70	Stiff-c; PC-r	1	3	3.40	8.50	17.00

48. David Copperfield

Ed	HRN	Date	Details	A	C	GD2.0	FN6.0	NM9.4
1	47	6/48	Original; Kiefer-c/a	1	1	14.00	41.00	110.00
2	64	–	Price circle replaced by motif of boy reading; LDC-r	1	1	5.00	15.00	32.00
3	87	–	C-price 15¢; LDC-r	1	1	4.00	11.00	22.00
4	121	–	New-c; PC-r	1	2	3.60	9.00	18.00
5	130	–	PC-r	1	2	2.20	5.50	11.00
6	140	–	PC-r	1	2	2.20	5.50	11.00
7	148	–	PC-r	1	2	2.20	5.50	11.00
8	156	–	PC-r	1	2	2.20	5.50	11.00
9	167	–	PC-r	1	2	2.00	5.00	10.00
10	167	4/64	PC-r	1	2	2.00	5.00	10.00
11	167	6/65	PC-r	1	2	2.00	5.00	10.00
12	166	5/67	PC-r	1	2	2.00	5.00	10.00
13	166	R/67	PC-r; C-price 25¢	1	2	2.80	7.00	14.00
14	166	Spr/69	C-price 25¢; stiff-c PC-r	1	2	2.00	5.00	10.00
15	169	Win/69	Stiff-c; PC-r	1	2	2.00	5.00	10.00

49. Alice in Wonderland

Ed	HRN	Date	Details	A	C	GD2.0	FN6.0	NM9.4
1	47	7/48	Original; 1st Blum a & c	1	1	19.00	56.00	150.00
2	64	–	No c-price; LDC-r	1	1	6.40	19.25	45.00

Classics Illustrated #51 © GIL

Classics Illustrated #55 © GIL

Classics Illustrated #57 © GIL

Ed	HRN	Date	Details	A	C	GD2.0	FN6.0	NM9.4
3A	85	–	C-price 15¢; soft-c LDC-r	1	1	5.00	15.00	35.00
3B	85	–	Stiff-c; LDC-r	1	1	6.00	18.00	42.00
4	155	–	New PC, similar to orig.; PC-r	1	2	5.00	15.00	35.00
5	165	–	PC-r	1	2	4.30	13.00	26.00
6	167	3/64	PC-r	1	2	4.00	11.00	22.00
7	167	6/66	PC-r	1	2	4.00	11.00	22.00
8A	166	Fall/68	New-c; soft-c; 25¢ c-price; PC-r	1	3	5.00	15.00	35.00
8B	166	Fall/68	New-c; stiff-c; 25¢ c-price; PC-r	1	3	9.30	28.00	65.00

50. Adventures of Tom Sawyer (Used in **SOTI**, pg. 37)

Ed	HRN	Date	Details	A	C	GD2.0	FN6.0	NM9.4
1A	51	8/48	Orig.; Aldo Rubano a&c	1	1	14.00	41.00	110.00
1B	51	9/48	Orig.; Rubano c&a	1	1	14.00	41.00	110.00
1C	51	9/48	Orig.; outside-bc: blue & yellow only; rare	1	1	21.00	62.00	165.00
2	64	–	No c-price; LDC-r	1	1	4.65	14.00	28.00
3	78	–	C-price 15¢; LDC-r	1	1	4.00	11.00	22.00
4	94	–	LDC-r	1	1	3.60	9.00	18.00
5	117	–	LDC-r	1	1	3.40	8.50	17.00
6	132	–	LDC-r	1	1	3.40	8.50	17.00
7	140	–	New-c; PC-r	1	2	4.00	11.00	22.00
8	150	–	PC-r	1	2	2.40	6.00	12.00
9	164	–	New-a; PC-r	2	2	4.00	11.00	22.00
10	167	–	PC-r	2	2	2.40	6.00	12.00
11	167	1/65	PC-r	2	2	2.00	5.00	10.00
12	167	5/66	PC-r	2	2	2.00	5.00	10.00
13	166	12/67	PC-r	2	2	2.00	5.00	10.00
14	169	Fall/69	C-price 25¢; stiff-c; PC-r	2	2	2.00	5.00	10.00
15	169	Win/71	PC-r	2	2	2.00	5.00	10.00

51. The Spy

Ed	HRN	Date	Details	A	C	GD2.0	FN6.0	NM9.4
1A	51	9/48	Original; inside-bc illo: Christmas Carol	1	1	12.50	37.50	100.00
1B	51	9/48	Original; inside-bc illo: Man in Iron Mask	1	1	12.50	37.50	100.00
1C	51	8/48	Original; outside-bc: full color	1	1	12.50	37.50	100.00
1D	51	8/48	Original; outside-bc: blue & yellow only; scarce	1	1	16.00	49.00	130.00
2	89	–	C-price 15¢; LDC-r	1	1	4.30	13.00	26.00
3	121	–	LDC-r	1	1	4.00	11.00	22.00
4	139	–	New-c; PC-r	1	2	4.00	11.00	22.00
5	156	–	PC-r	1	2	2.20	5.50	11.00
6	167	11/63	PC-r	1	2	2.00	5.00	10.00
7	167	7/66	PC-r	1	2	2.00	5.00	10.00
8A	166	Win/69	C-price 25¢; soft-c; scarce; PC-r	1	2	4.00	12.00	24.00
8B	166	Win/69	C-price 25¢; stiff-c; PC-r	1	2	2.00	5.00	10.00

52. The House of the Seven Gables

Ed	HRN	Date	Details	A	C	GD2.0	FN6.0	NM9.4
1	53	10/48	Orig.; Griffiths a&c	1	1	12.50	37.50	100.00
2	89	–	C-price 15¢; LDC-r	1	1	4.30	13.00	26.00
3	121	–	LDC-r	1	1	4.00	11.00	22.00
4	142	–	New-c&a; PC-r; Woodbridge-a	2	2	4.00	12.00	24.00
5	156	–	PC-r	2	2	2.20	5.50	11.00
6	165	–	PC-r	2	2	2.00	5.00	10.00
7	167	5/64	PC-r	2	2	2.40	6.00	12.00
8	167	3/66	PC-r	2	2	2.00	5.00	10.00
9	166	R/1968	C-price 25¢; PC-r	2	2	2.00	5.00	10.00
10	169	Spr/70	Stiff-c; PC-r	2	2	2.00	5.00	10.00

53. A Christmas Carol

Ed	HRN	Date	Details	A	C	GD2.0	FN6.0	NM9.4
1	53	11/48	Original & only ed; Kiefer-c/a	1	1	19.00	56.00	150.00

54. Man in the Iron Mask

Ed	HRN	Date	Details	A	C	GD2.0	FN6.0	NM9.4
1	55	12/48	Original; Froehlich-a, Kiefer-c	1	1	12.50	37.50	100.00
2	93	–	C-price 15¢; LDC-r	1	1	5.00	15.00	30.00
3A	111	–	(O) logo lettering; scarce; LDC-r	1	1	6.00	18.00	42.00
3B	111	–	New logo as PC; LDC-r	1	1	4.65	14.00	28.00
4	142	–	New-c&a; PC-r	2	2	4.00	12.00	24.00
5	154	–	PC-r	2	2	2.20	5.50	11.00
6	165	–	PC-r	2	2	2.00	5.00	10.00
7	167	5/64	PC-r	2	2	2.00	5.00	10.00
8	167	4/66	PC-r	2	2	2.00	5.00	10.00
9A	166	Win/69	C-price 25¢; soft-c PC-r	2	2	4.00	12.00	24.00
9B	166	Win/69	Stiff-c	2	2	2.00	5.00	10.00

55. Silas Marner (Used in **SOTI**, pgs. 311, 312)

Ed	HRN	Date	Details	A	C	GD2.0	FN6.0	NM9.4
1	55	1/49	Original-Kiefer-c	1	1	12.50	37.50	100.00
2	75	–	Price circle blank; 'Coming Next' ad; LDC-r	1	1	5.00	15.00	32.00
3	97	–	LDC-r	1	1	4.00	11.00	22.00
4	121	–	New-c; PC-r	1	2	4.00	11.00	22.00
5	130	–	PC-r	1	2	2.20	5.50	11.00
6	140	–	PC-r	1	2	2.20	5.50	11.00
7	154	–	PC-r	1	2	2.20	5.50	11.00
8	165	–	PC-r	1	2	2.00	5.00	10.00
9	167	2/64	PC-r	1	2	2.00	5.00	10.00
10	167	6/65	PC-r	1	2	2.00	5.00	10.00
11	166	5/67	PC-r	1	2	2.00	5.00	10.00
12A	166	Win/69	C-price 25¢; soft-c PC-r	1	2	4.00	12.00	24.00
12B	166	Win/69	C-price 25¢; stiff-c PC-r	1	2	2.00	5.00	10.00

56. The Toilers of the Sea

Ed	HRN	Date	Details	A	C	GD2.0	FN6.0	NM9.4
1	55	2/49	Original; A.M. Froehlich-c/a	1	1	23.00	68.00	180.00
2	165	–	New-c&a; PC-r; Angelo Torres-a	2	2	6.00	18.00	42.00
3	167	3/64	PC-r	2	2	4.00	12.00	24.00
4	167	10/66	PC-r	2	2	4.00	12.00	24.00

57. The Song of Hiawatha

Ed	HRN	Date	Details	A	C	GD2.0	FN6.0	NM9.4
1	55	3/49	Original; Alex Blum-c/a	1	1	12.50	37.50	100.00
2	75	–	No c-price w/15¢ sticker; 'Coming Next' ad; LDC-r	1	1	5.00	15.00	32.00
3	94	–	C-price 15¢; LDC-r	1	1	4.30	13.00	26.00
4	118	–	LDC-r	1	1	4.00	11.00	22.00
5	134	–	New-c; PC-r	1	2	4.00	11.00	22.00
6	139	–	PC-r	1	2	2.20	5.50	11.00
7	154	–	PC-r	1	2	2.20	5.50	11.00
8	167	–	Has orig.date; PC-r	1	2	2.00	5.00	10.00
9	167	9/64	PC-r	1	2	2.00	5.00	10.00
10	167	10/65	PC-r	1	2	2.00	5.00	10.00
11	166	F/1968	C-price 25¢; PC-r	1	2	2.00	5.00	10.00

58. The Prairie

Classics Illustrated #61 © GIL

Classics Illustrated #65 © GIL

Classics Illustrated #66 © GIL

HRN	Date	Details	A	C	GD2.0	FN6.0	NM9.4
60	4/49	Original; Palais c/a	1	1	12.50	37.50	100.00
62	–	No c-price; no coming-next ad; LDC-r	1	1	7.85	23.50	55.00
62		10¢ (rare)	1	1	16.00	49.00	130.00
78	–	C-price 15¢ in dbl. circle; LDC-r	1	1	4.30	13.00	26.00
114	–	LDC-r	1	1	4.00	11.00	22.00
131	–	LDC-r	1	1	3.60	9.00	18.00
132	–	LDC-r	1	1	3.60	9.00	18.00
146	–	New-c; PC-r	1	2	4.00	11.00	22.00
155	–	PC-r	1	2	2.20	5.50	11.00
167	5/64	PC-r	1	2	2.00	5.00	10.00
167	4/66	PC-r	1	2	2.00	5.00	10.00
169	Sm/69	New price 25¢; stiff-c; PC-r	1	2	2.00	5.00	10.00

Wuthering Heights

HRN	Date	Details	A	C	GD2.0	FN6.0	NM9.4
60	5/49	Original; Kiefer-c/a	1	1	14.00	41.00	110.00
85	–	C-price 15¢; LDC-r	1	1	5.50	16.50	38.00
156	–	New-c; PC-r	1	2	4.00	12.00	24.00
167	1/64	PC-r	1	2	2.40	6.00	12.00
167	10/66	PC-r	1	2	2.40	6.00	12.00
169	Sm/69	C-price 25¢; stiff-c; PC-r	1	2	2.40	6.00	12.00

Black Beauty

HRN	Date	Details	A	C	GD2.0	FN6.0	NM9.4
62	6/49	Original; Froehlich-c/a	1	1	12.50	37.50	100.00
62	–	No c-price; no coming-next ad; LDC-r (rare)	1	1	15.00	45.00	120.00
85	–	C-price 15¢; LDC-r	1	1	5.00	15.00	30.00
158	–	New L.B. Cole-c/a; PC-r	2	2	5.00	15.00	35.00
167	2/64	PC-r	2	2	3.40	8.50	17.00
167	3/66	PC-r	2	2	3.40	8.50	17.00
166	R/1968	New-c&price, 25¢; PC-r	2	3	7.85	23.50	55.00

The Woman in White

HRN	Date	Details	A	C	GD2.0	FN6.0	NM9.4
62	7/49	Original; Blum-c/a fc-purple; bc: top illos light blue	1	1	14.00	41.00	110.00
62	7/49	Original; Blum-c/a fc-pink; bc: top illos light violet	1	1	14.00	41.00	110.00
156	–	New-c; PC-r	1	2	4.65	14.00	28.00
167	1/64	PC-r	1	2	3.60	9.00	18.00
166	R/1968	C-price 25¢; PC-r	1	2	3.60	9.00	18.00

Western Stories ("The Luck of Roaring Camp" and "The Outcasts of Poker Flat")

HRN	Date	Details	A	C	GD2.0	FN6.0	NM9.4
62	8/49	Original; Kiefer-c/a	1	1	12.00	36.00	95.00
89	–	C-price 15¢; LDC-r	1	1	5.00	15.00	30.00
121	–	LDC-r	1	1	4.00	12.00	24.00
137	–	New-c; PC-r	1	2	4.00	11.00	22.00
152	–	PC-r	1	2	2.00	5.00	10.00
167	10/63	PC-r	1	2	2.00	5.00	10.00
167	6/64	PC-r	1	2	2.00	5.00	10.00
167	11/66	PC-r	1	2	2.00	5.00	10.00
166	R/1968	New-c&price 25¢; PC-r	1	3	4.00	11.00	22.00

The Man Without a Country

Ed	HRN	Date	Details	A	C	GD2.0	FN6.0	NM9.4
	62	9/49	Original; Kiefer-c/a	1	1	12.50	37.50	100.00
	78	–	C-price 15¢ in double circle; LDC-r	1	1	5.00	15.00	30.00
3	156	–	New-c, old-a; PC-r	1	2	4.30	13.00	26.00
4	165	–	New-a & text pgs.; PC-r; A. Torres-a	2	2	4.00	12.00	24.00
5	167	3/64	PC-r	2	2	2.00	5.00	10.00
6	167	8/66	PC-r	2	2	2.00	5.00	10.00
7	169	Sm/69	New price 25¢; stiff-c; PC-r	2	2	2.00	5.00	10.00

64. Treasure Island

Ed	HRN	Date	Details	A	C	GD2.0	FN6.0	NM9.4
1	62	10/49	Original; Blum-c/a	1	1	12.50	37.50	100.00
2A	82	–	C-price 15¢; soft-c LDC-r	1	1	4.65	14.00	28.00
2B	82	–	Stiff-c; LDC-r	1	1	5.00	15.00	30.00
3	117	–	LDC-r	1	1	4.00	12.00	24.00
4	131	–	New-c; PC-r	1	2	4.00	11.00	22.00
5	138	–	PC-r	1	2	2.20	5.50	11.00
6	146	–	PC-r	1	2	2.20	5.50	11.00
7	158	–	PC-r	1	2	2.20	5.50	11.00
8	165	–	PC-r	1	2	2.00	5.00	10.00
9	167	–	PC-r	1	2	2.00	5.00	10.00
10	167	6/64	PC-r	1	2	2.00	5.00	10.00
11	167	12/65	PC-r	1	2	2.00	5.00	10.00
12A	166	10/67	PC-r	1	2	2.00	5.00	10.00
12B	166	10/67	w/Grit ad stapled in book	1	2	12.50	37.50	100.00
13	169	Spr/69	New price 25¢; stiff-c; PC-r	1	2	2.20	5.50	11.00
14	–	1989	Long John Silver's Seafood Shoppes; $1.95, First/Berkley Publ.; Blum-r	1	2			4.00

65. Benjamin Franklin

Ed	HRN	Date	Details	A	C	GD2.0	FN6.0	NM9.4
1	64	11/49	Original; Kiefer-c; Iger Shop-a	1	1	12.50	37.50	100.00
2	131	–	New-c; PC-r	1	2	4.00	12.00	24.00
3	154	–	PC-r	1	2	2.40	6.00	12.00
4	167	2/64	PC-r	1	2	2.20	5.50	11.00
5	167	4/66	PC-r	1	2	2.20	5.50	11.00
6	169	Fall/69	New price 25¢; stiff-c; PC-r	1	2	2.20	5.50	11.00

66. The Cloister and the Hearth

Ed	HRN	Date	Details	A	C	GD2.0	FN6.0	NM9.4
1	67	12/49	Original & only ed; Kiefer-a & c	1	1	28.00	83.00	220.00

67. The Scottish Chiefs

Ed	HRN	Date	Details	A	C	GD2.0	FN6.0	NM9.4
1	67	1/50	Original; Blum-a&c	1	1	10.50	32.00	85.00
2	85	–	C-price 15¢; LDC-r	1	1	5.00	15.00	30.00
3	118	–	LDC-r	1	1	4.00	12.00	24.00
4	136	–	New-c; PC-r	1	2	4.00	12.00	24.00
5	154	–	PC-r	1	2	2.40	6.00	12.00
6	167	11/63	PC-r	1	2	2.80	7.00	14.00
7	167	8/65	PC-r	1	2	2.40	6.00	12.00

68. Julius Caesar (Used in **SOTI**, pgs. 36, 37)

Ed	HRN	Date	Details	A	C	GD2.0	FN6.0	NM9.4
1	70	2/50	Original; Kiefer-c/a	1	1	10.00	30.00	80.00
2	85	–	C-price 15¢; LDC-r	1	1	4.65	14.00	28.00
3	108	–	LDC-r	1	1	4.00	12.00	24.00
4	156	–	New L.B. Cole-c; PC-r	1	2	4.30	13.00	26.00
5	165	–	New-a by Evans, Crandall; PC-r	2	2	4.30	13.00	26.00
6	167	2/64	PC-r	2	2	2.00	5.00	10.00
7	167	10/65	Tarzan books inside cover; PC-r	2	2	2.00	5.00	10.00

Classics Illustrated #71 © GIL

Classics Illustrated #76 © GIL

Classics Illustrated #79 © GIL

Ed	HRN	Date	Details	A	C	GD2.0	FN6.0	NM9.4
8	166	R/1967	PC-r	2	2	2.00	5.00	10.00
9	169	Win/69	PC-r; stiff-c	2	2	2.00	5.00	10.00

69. Around the World in 80 Days

Ed	HRN	Date	Details	A	C	GD2.0	FN6.0	NM9.4
1	70	3/50	Original; Kiefer-c/a	1	1	10.00	30.00	80.00
2	87	–	C-price 15¢; LDC-r	1	1	4.65	14.00	28.00
3	125	–	LDC-r	1	1	4.00	12.00	24.00
4	136	–	New-c; PC-r	1	2	4.00	12.00	24.00
5	146	–	PC-r	1	2	2.20	5.50	11.00
6	152	–	PC-r	1	2	2.20	5.50	11.00
7	164	–	PC-r	1	2	2.00	5.00	10.00
8	167	–	PC-r	1	2	2.00	5.00	10.00
9	167	7/64	PC-r	1	2	2.00	5.00	10.00
10	167	11/65	PC-r	1	2	2.00	5.00	10.00
11	166	7/67	PC-r	1	2	2.00	5.00	10.00
12	169	Spr/69	C-price 25¢; stiff-c; PC-r	1	2	2.00	5.00	10.00

70. The Pilot

Ed	HRN	Date	Details	A	C	GD2.0	FN6.0	NM9.4
1	71	4/50	Original; Blum-c/a	1	1	10.00	30.00	75.00
2	92	–	C-price 15¢; LDC-r	1	1	5.00	15.00	30.00
3	125	–	LDC-r	1	1	4.00	12.00	24.00
4	156	–	New-c; PC-r	1	2	4.30	13.00	26.00
5	167	2/64	PC-r	1	2	3.40	8.50	17.00
6	167	5/66	PC-r	1	2	2.80	7.00	14.00

71. The Man Who Laughs

Ed	HRN	Date	Details	A	C	GD2.0	FN6.0	NM9.4
1	71	5/50	Original; Blum-c/a	1	1	16.00	49.00	130.00
2	165	–	New-c&a; PC-r	2	2	10.00	30.00	75.00
3	167	4/64	PC-r	2	2	9.30	28.00	65.00

72. The Oregon Trail

Ed	HRN	Date	Details	A	C	GD2.0	FN6.0	NM9.4
1	73	6/50	Original; Kiefer-c/a	1	1	10.00	30.00	75.00
2	89	–	C-price 15¢; LDC-r	1	1	5.00	15.00	30.00
3	121	–	LDC-r	1	1	4.00	12.00	24.00
4	131	–	New-c; PC-r	1	2	4.00	12.00	24.00
5	140	–	PC-r	1	2	2.20	5.50	11.00
6	150	–	PC-r	1	2	2.20	5.50	11.00
7	164	–	PC-r	1	2	2.00	5.00	10.00
8	167	–	PC-r	1	2	2.00	5.00	10.00
9	167	8/64	PC-r	1	2	2.00	5.00	10.00
10	167	10/65	PC-r	1	2	2.00	5.00	10.00
11	166	R/1968	C-price 25¢; PC-r	1	2	2.00	5.00	10.00

73. The Black Tulip

Ed	HRN	Date	Details	A	C	GD2.0	FN6.0	NM9.4
1	75	7/50	1st & only ed.; Alex Blum-c/a	1	1	34.00	103.00	275.00

74. Mr. Midshipman Easy

Ed	HRN	Date	Details	A	C	GD2.0	FN6.0	NM9.4
1	75	8/50	1st & only edition	1	1	34.00	103.00	275.00

75. The Lady of the Lake

Ed	HRN	Date	Details	A	C	GD2.0	FN6.0	NM9.4
1	75	9/50	Original; Kiefer-c/a	1	1	10.00	30.00	75.00
2	85	–	C-price 15¢; LDC-r	1	1	5.00	15.00	32.00
3	118	–	LDC-r	1	1	4.30	13.00	26.00
4	139	–	New-c; PC-r	1	2	4.00	12.00	24.00
5	154	–	PC-r	1	2	2.20	5.50	11.00
6	165	–	PC-r	1	2	2.00	5.00	10.00
7	167	4/64	PC-r	1	2	2.00	5.00	10.00
8	167	5/66	PC-r	1	2	2.00	5.00	10.00
9	169	Spr/69	New price 25¢; stiff-c; PC-r	1	2	2.00	5.00	10.00

76. The Prisoner of Zenda

Ed	HRN	Date	Details	A	C	GD2.0	FN6.0	NM9.4
1	75	10/50	Original; Kiefer-c/a	1	1	10.00	30.00	70.00
2	85	–	C-price 15¢; LDC-r	1	1	5.00	15.00	30.00
3	111	–	LDC-r	1	1	4.00	12.00	24.00
4	128	–	New-c; PC-r	1	2	4.00	12.00	24.
5	152	–	PC-r	1	2	2.20	5.50	11.
6	165	–	PC-r	1	2	2.00	5.00	10.
7	167	4/64	PC-r	1	2	2.00	5.00	10.
8	167	9/66	PC-r	1	2	2.00	5.00	10.
9	169	Fall/69	New price 25¢; stiff-c; PC-r	1	2	2.00	5.00	10.

77. The Iliad

Ed	HRN	Date	Details	A	C	GD2.0	FN6.0	NM9.4
1	78	11/50	Original; Blum-c/a	1	1	10.00	30.00	70.
2	87	–	C-price 15¢; LDC-r	1	1	5.00	15.00	32.
3	121	–	LDC-r	1	1	4.00	12.00	24.
4	139	–	New-c; PC-r	1	2	4.00	11.00	22.
5	150	–	PC-r	1	2	2.20	5.50	11.
6	165	–	PC-r	1	2	2.00	5.00	10.
7	167	10/63	PC-r	1	2	2.00	5.00	10.
8	167	7/64	PC-r	1	2	2.00	5.00	10.
9	167	5/66	PC-r	1	2	2.00	5.00	10.
10	166	R/1968	C-price 25¢; PC-r	1	2	2.00	5.00	10.

78. Joan of Arc

Ed	HRN	Date	Details	A	C	GD2.0	FN6.0	NM9.4
1	78	12/50	Original; Kiefer-c/a	1	1	10.00	30.00	70
2	87	–	C-price 15¢; LDC-r	1	1	5.00	15.00	30.
3	113	–	LDC-r	1	1	4.00	12.00	24.
4	128	–	New-c; PC-r	1	2	4.00	12.00	24.
5	140	–	PC-r	1	2	2.20	5.50	11.
6	150	–	PC-r	1	2	2.20	5.50	11
7	159	–	PC-r	1	2	2.20	5.50	11
8	167	–	PC-r	1	2	2.00	5.00	10
9	167	12/63	PC-r	1	2	2.00	5.00	10
10	167	6/65	PC-r	1	2	2.00	5.00	10.
11	166	6/67	PC-r	1	2	2.00	5.00	10
12	166	Win/69	New-c&price, 25¢; PC-r; stiff-c	1	3	4.30	13.00	26.

79. Cyrano de Bergerac

Ed	HRN	Date	Details	A	C	GD2.0	FN6.0	NM9.4
1	78	1/51	Orig.; movie promo inside front-c; Blum-c/a	1	1	10.00	30.00	70.
2	85	–	C-price 15¢; LDC-r	1	1	5.00	15.00	30.
3	118	–	LDC-r	1	1	4.00	12.00	24.
4	133	–	New-c; PC-r	1	2	4.00	12.00	24.
5	156	–	PC-r	1	2	3.40	8.50	17.
6	167	8/64	PC-r	1	2	3.40	8.50	17.

80. White Fang (Last line drawn cover)

Ed	HRN	Date	Details	A	C	GD2.0	FN6.0	NM9.4
1	79	2/51	Orig.; Blum-c/a	1	1	10.00	30.00	70.
2	87	–	C-price 15¢; LDC-r	1	1	5.00	15.00	32.
3	125	–	LDC-r	1	1	4.00	12.00	24.
4	132	–	New-c; PC-r	1	2	4.00	11.00	22.
5	140	–	PC-r	1	2	2.20	5.50	11.
6	153	–	PC-r	1	2	2.20	5.50	11.
7	167	–	PC-r	1	2	2.00	5.00	10.
8	167	9/64	PC-r	1	2	2.00	5.00	10.
9	167	7/65	PC-r	1	2	2.00	5.00	10.
10	166	6/67	PC-r	1	2	2.00	5.00	10.
11	169	Fall/69	New price 25¢; PC-r; stiff-c	1	2	2.00	5.00	10.

81. The Odyssey (1st painted cover)

Ed	HRN	Date	Details	A	C	GD2.0	FN6.0	NM9.4
1	82	3/51	First 15¢ Original; Blum-c	1	1	10.00	30.00	70.
2	167	8/64	PC-r	1	1	3.40	8.50	17
3	167	10/66	PC-r	1	1	3.40	8.50	17
4	169	Spr/69	New, stiff-c; PC-r	1	2	4.00	12.00	24

82. The Master of Ballantrae

Ed	HRN	Date	Details	A	C

Classics Illustrated #83 © GIL

Classics Illustrated #84 © GIL

Classics Illustrated #90 © GIL

Ed	HRN	Date	Details	A	C	GD2.0	FN6.0	NM9.4
	82	4/51	Original; Blum-c	1	1	7.15	21.50	50.00
	167	8/64	PC-r	1	1	4.00	11.00	22.00
	166	Fall/68	New, stiff-c; PC-r	1	2	4.00	12.00	24.00

. The Jungle Book

Ed	HRN	Date	Details	A	C	GD2.0	FN6.0	NM9.4
	85	5/51	Original; Blum-c Bossert/Blum-a	1	1	7.15	21.50	50.00
	110	–	PC-r	1	1	2.80	7.00	14.00
	125	–	PC-r	1	1	2.20	5.50	11.00
	134	–	PC-r	1	1	2.20	5.50	11.00
	142	–	PC-r	1	1	2.20	5.50	11.00
	150	–	PC-r	1	1	2.20	5.50	11.00
	159	–	PC-r	1	1	2.20	5.50	11.00
	167	–	PC-r	1	1	2.00	5.00	10.00
	167	3/65	PC-r	1	1	2.00	5.00	10.00
	167	11/65	PC-r	1	1	2.00	5.00	10.00
	167	5/66	PC-r	1	1	2.00	5.00	10.00
	166	R/1968	New c&a; stiff-c; PC-r	2	2	4.00	12.00	24.00

. The Gold Bug and Other Stories ("The Gold Bug", "The Tell-Tale Heart", "The Cask of Amontillado")

Ed	HRN	Date	Details	A	C	GD2.0	FN6.0	NM9.4
	85	6/51	Original; Blum-c/a; Palais, Laverly-a	1	1	11.00	33.00	90.00
	167	7/64	PC-r	1	1	10.00	30.00	75.00

. The Sea Wolf

Ed	HRN	Date	Details	A	C	GD2.0	FN6.0	NM9.4
	85	7/51	Original; Blum-c/a	1	1	5.70	17.00	40.00
	121	–	PC-r	1	1	2.20	5.50	11.00
	132	–	PC-r	1	1	2.20	5.50	11.00
	141	–	PC-r	1	1	2.20	5.50	11.00
	161	–	PC-r	1	1	2.00	5.00	10.00
	167	2/64	PC-r	1	1	2.00	5.00	10.00
	167	11/65	PC-r	1	1	2.00	5.00	10.00
	169	Fall/69	New price 25¢; stiff-c; PC-r	1	1	2.00	5.00	10.00

Under Two Flags

Ed	HRN	Date	Details	A	C	GD2.0	FN6.0	NM9.4
	87	8/51	Original; first delBourgo-a	1	1	5.00	15.00	35.00
	117	–	PC-r	1	1	2.80	7.00	14.00
	139	–	PC-r	1	1	2.40	6.00	12.00
	158	–	PC-r	1	1	2.40	6.00	12.00
	167	2/64	PC-r	1	1	2.00	5.00	10.00
	167	8/66	PC-r	1	1	2.00	5.00	10.00
	169	Sm/69	New price 25¢; stiff-c; PC-r	1	1	2.00	5.00	10.00

A Midsummer Nights Dream

Ed	HRN	Date	Details	A	C	GD2.0	FN6.0	NM9.4
	87	9/51	Original; Blum c/a	1	1	5.50	16.50	38.00
	161	–	PC-r	1	1	2.20	5.50	11.00
	167	4/64	PC-r	1	1	2.00	5.00	10.00
	167	5/66	PC-r	1	1	2.00	5.00	10.00
	169	Sm/69	New price 25¢; stiff-c; PC-r	1	1	2.00	5.00	10.00

Men of Iron

Ed	HRN	Date	Details	A	C	GD2.0	FN6.0	NM9.4
	89	10/51	Original	1	1	5.50	16.50	38.00
	154	–	PC-r	1	1	2.40	6.00	12.00
	167	1/64	PC-r	1	1	2.00	5.00	10.00
	166	R/1968	C-price 25¢; PC-r	1	1	2.00	5.00	10.00

Crime and Punishment (Cover illo. in **POP**)

Ed	HRN	Date	Details	A	C	GD2.0	FN6.0	NM9.4
	89	11/51	Original; Palais-a	1	1	5.70	17.00	40.00
	152	–	PC-r	1	1	2.40	6.00	12.00
	167	4/64	PC-r	1	1	2.00	5.00	10.00
	167	5/66	PC-r	1	1	2.00	5.00	10.00

Ed	HRN	Date	Details	A	C	GD2.0	FN6.0	NM9.4
5	169	Fall/69	New price 25¢ stiff-c; PC-r	1	1	2.00	5.00	10.00

90. Green Mansions

Ed	HRN	Date	Details	A	C	GD2.0	FN6.0	NM9.4
1	89	12/51	Original; Blum-c/a	1	1	5.50	16.50	38.00
2	148	–	New L.B. Cole-c; PC-r	1	2	3.60	9.00	18.00
3	165	–	PC-r	1	2	2.00	5.00	10.00
4	167	4/64	PC-r	1	2	2.00	5.00	10.00
5	167	9/66	PC-r	1	2	2.00	5.00	10.00
6	169	Sm/69	New price 25¢; stiff-c; PC-r	1	2	2.00	5.00	10.00

91. The Call of the Wild

Ed	HRN	Date	Details	A	C	GD2.0	FN6.0	NM9.4
1	92	1/52	Orig.; delBourgo-a	1	1	5.50	16.50	38.00
2	112	–	PC-r	1	1	2.40	6.00	12.00
3	125	–	'Picture Progress' on back-c; PC-r	1	1	2.40	6.00	12.00
4	134	–	PC-r	1	1	2.40	6.00	12.00
5	143	–	PC-r	1	1	2.40	6.00	12.00
6	165	–	PC-r	1	1	2.40	6.00	12.00
7	167	–	PC-r	1	1	2.00	5.00	10.00
8	167	4/65	PC-r	1	1	2.00	5.00	10.00
9	167	3/66	PC-r	1	1	2.00	5.00	10.00
10	166	11/67	PC-r	1	1	2.00	5.00	10.00
11	169	Spr/70	New price 25¢; stiff-c; PC-r	1	1	2.00	5.00	10.00

92. The Courtship of Miles Standish

Ed	HRN	Date	Details	A	C	GD2.0	FN6.0	NM9.4
1	92	2/52	Original; Blum-c/a	1	1	5.00	15.00	35.00
2	165	–	PC-r	1	1	2.20	5.50	11.00
3	167	3/64	PC-r	1	1	2.20	5.50	11.00
4	166	5/67	PC-r	1	1	2.20	5.50	11.00
5	169	Win/69	New price 25¢ stiff-c; PC-r	1	1	2.20	5.50	11.00

93. Pudd'nhead Wilson

Ed	HRN	Date	Details	A	C	GD2.0	FN6.0	NM9.4
1	94	3/52	Orig.; Kiefer-c/a;	1	1	5.50	16.50	38.00
2	165	–	New-c; PC-r	1	2	2.80	7.00	14.00
3	167	3/64	PC-r	1	2	2.40	6.00	12.00
4	166	R/1968	New price 25¢; soft-c; PC-r	1	2	2.40	6.00	12.00

94. David Balfour

Ed	HRN	Date	Details	A	C	GD2.0	FN6.0	NM9.4
1	94	4/52	Original; Palais-a	1	1	5.50	16.50	38.00
2	167	5/64	PC-r	1	1	3.40	8.50	17.00
3	166	R/1968	C-price 25¢; PC-r	1	1	3.40	8.50	17.00

95. All Quiet on the Western Front

Ed	HRN	Date	Details	A	C	GD2.0	FN6.0	NM9.4
1A	96	5/52	Orig.; del Bourgo-a	1	1	10.00	30.00	80.00
1B	99	5/52	Orig.; del Bourgo-a	1	1	8.65	26.00	60.00
2	167	10/64	PC-r	1	1	4.00	12.00	24.00
3	167	11/66	PC-r	1	1	4.00	12.00	24.00

96. Daniel Boone

Ed	HRN	Date	Details	A	C	GD2.0	FN6.0	NM9.4
1	97	6/52	Original; Blum-a	1	1	5.00	15.00	32.00
2	117	–	PC-r	1	1	2.20	5.50	11.00
3	128	–	PC-r	1	1	2.20	5.50	11.00
4	132	–	PC-r	1	1	2.20	5.50	11.00
5	134	–	"Story of Jesus" on back-c; PC-r	1	1	2.20	5.50	11.00
6	158	–	PC-r	1	1	2.20	5.50	11.00
7	167	1/64	PC-r	1	1	2.00	5.00	10.00
8	167	5/65	PC-r	1	1	2.00	5.00	10.00
9	167	11/66	PC-r	1	1	2.00	5.00	10.00
10	166	Win/69	New-c; price 25¢; PC-r; stiff-c	1	2	3.40	8.50	17.00

Classics Illustrated #101 © GIL

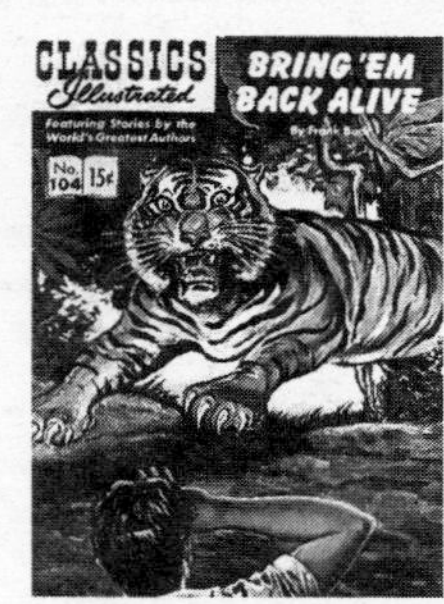

Classics Illustrated #104 © GIL

Classics Illustrated #108 © GIL

97. King Solomon's Mines

Ed	HRN	Date	Details	A	C	GD2.0	FN6.0	NM9.4
1	96	7/52	Orig.; Kiefer-a	1	1	5.00	15.00	32.00
2	118	–	PC-r	1	1	2.40	6.00	12.00
3	131	–	PC-r	1	1	2.40	6.00	12.00
4	141	–	PC-r	1	1	2.40	6.00	12.00
5	158	–	PC-r	1	1	2.40	6.00	12.00
6	167	2/64	PC-r	1	1	2.00	5.00	10.00
7	167	9/65	PC-r	1	1	2.00	5.00	10.00
8	169	Sm/69	New price 25¢; stiff-c; PC-r	1	1	2.00	5.00	10.00

98. The Red Badge of Courage

Ed	HRN	Date	Details	A	C	GD2.0	FN6.0	NM9.4
1	98	8/52	Original	1	1	5.00	15.00	35.00
2	118	–	PC-r	1	1	2.40	6.00	12.00
3	132	–	PC-r	1	1	2.40	6.00	12.00
4	142	–	PC-r	1	1	2.40	6.00	12.00
5	152	–	PC-r	1	1	2.40	6.00	12.00
6	161	–	PC-r	1	1	2.40	6.00	12.00
7	167	–	Has orig.date; PC-r	1	1	2.40	6.00	12.00
8	167	9/64	PC-r	1	1	2.40	6.00	12.00
9	167	10/65	PC-r	1	1	2.40	6.00	12.00
10	166	R/1968	New-c&price 25¢; PC-r; stiff-c	1	2	4.00	11.00	22.00

99. Hamlet (Used in **POP**, pg. 102)

Ed	HRN	Date	Details	A	C	GD2.0	FN6.0	NM9.4
1	98	9/52	Original; Blum-a	1	1	5.50	16.50	38.00
2	121	–	PC-r	1	1	2.40	6.00	12.00
3	141	–	PC-r	1	1	2.40	6.00	12.00
4	158	–	PC-r	1	1	2.40	6.00	12.00
5	167	–	Has orig.date; PC-r	1	1	2.00	5.00	10.00
6	167	7/65	PC-r	1	1	2.00	5.00	10.00
7	166	4/67	PC-r	1	1	2.00	5.00	10.00
8	169	Spr/69	New-c&price 25¢; PC-r; stiff-c	1	2	4.00	11.00	22.00

100. Mutiny on the Bounty

Ed	HRN	Date	Details	A	C	GD2.0	FN6.0	NM9.4
1	100	10/52	Original	1	1	5.00	15.00	32.00
2	117	–	PC-r	1	1	2.40	6.00	12.00
3	132	–	PC-r	1	1	2.40	6.00	12.00
4	142	–	PC-r	1	1	2.40	6.00	12.00
5	155	–	PC-r	1	1	2.40	6.00	12.00
6	167	–	Has orig. date;PC-r	1	1	2.00	5.00	10.00
7	167	5/64	PC-r	1	1	2.00	5.00	10.00
8	167	3/66	PC-r	1	1	2.00	5.00	10.00
9	169	Spr/70	PC-r; stiff-c	1	1	2.00	5.00	10.00

101. William Tell

Ed	HRN	Date	Details	A	C	GD2.0	FN6.0	NM9.4
1	101	11/52	Original; Kiefer-c delBourgo-a	1	1	5.00	15.00	32.00
2	118	–	PC-r	1	1	2.40	6.00	12.00
3	141	–	PC-r	1	1	2.40	6.00	12.00
4	158	–	PC-r	1	1	2.40	6.00	12.00
5	167	–	Has orig.date; PC-r	1	1	2.00	5.00	10.00
6	167	11/64	PC-r	1	1	2.00	5.00	10.00
7	166	4/67	PC-r	1	1	2.00	5.00	10.00
8	169	Win/69	New price 25¢; stiff-c; PC-r	1	1	2.00	5.00	10.00

102. The White Company

Ed	HRN	Date	Details	A	C	GD2.0	FN6.0	NM9.4
1	101	12/52	Original; Blum-a	1	1	9.30	28.00	65.00
2	165	–	PC-r	1	1	4.30	13.00	26.00
3	167	4/64	PC-r	1	1	4.30	13.00	26.00

103. Men Against the Sea

Ed	HRN	Date	Details	A	C	GD2.0	FN6.0	NM9.4
1	104	1/53	Original; Kiefer-c; Palais-a	1	1	5.50	16.50	38.00
2	114	–	PC-r	1	1	4.00	10.00	20.
3	131	–	New-c; PC-r	1	2	4.00	12.00	24.
4	158	–	PC-r	1	2	3.40	8.50	17.
5	149	–	White reorder list; came after HRN-158; PC-r	1	2	4.65	14.00	28.
6	167	3/64	PC-r	1	2	2.40	6.00	12.

104. Bring 'Em Back Alive

Ed	HRN	Date	Details	A	C	GD2.0	FN6.0	NM
1	105	2/53	Original; Kiefer-c/a	1	1	5.00	15.00	32.
2	118	–	PC-r	1	1	2.20	5.50	11.
3	133	–	PC-r	1	1	2.20	5.50	11.
4	150	–	PC-r	1	1	2.20	5.50	11.
5	158	–	PC-r	1	1	2.20	5.50	11.
6	167	10/63	PC-r	1	1	2.00	5.00	10.
7	167	9/65	PC-r	1	1	2.00	5.00	10.
8	169	Win/69	New price 25¢; stiff-c; PC-r	1	1	2.00	5.00	10.

105. From the Earth to the Moon

Ed	HRN	Date	Details	A	C	GD2.0	FN6.0	NM
1	106	3/53	Original; Blum-a	1	1	5.00	15.00	32.
2	118	–	PC-r	1	1	2.20	5.50	11.
3	132	–	PC-r	1	1	2.20	5.50	11.
4	141	–	PC-r	1	1	2.20	5.50	11.
5	146	–	PC-r	1	1	2.20	5.50	11.
6	156	–	PC-r	1	1	2.20	5.50	11.
7	167	–	Has orig. date; PC-r	1	1	2.00	5.00	10.
8	167	5/64	PC-r	1	1	2.00	5.00	10.
9	167	5/65	PC-r	1	1	2.00	5.00	10.
10A	166	10/67	PC-r	1	1	2.00	5.00	10.
10B	166	10/67	w/Grit ad stapled in book	1	1	10.50	32.00	85.
11	169	Sm/69	New price 25¢; stiff-c; PC-r	1	1	2.00	5.00	10.
12	169	Spr/71	PC-r	1	1	2.00	5.00	10.

106. Buffalo Bill

Ed	HRN	Date	Details	A	C	GD2.0	FN6.0	NM
1	107	4/53	Orig.; delBourgo-a	1	1	5.00	15.00	30.
2	118	–	PC-r	1	1	2.20	5.50	11.
3	132	–	PC-r	1	1	2.20	5.50	11.
4	142	–	PC-r	1	1	2.20	5.50	11.
5	161	–	PC-r	1	1	2.00	5.00	10.
6	167	3/64	PC-r	1	1	2.00	5.00	10.
7	166	7/67	PC-r	1	1	2.00	5.00	10.
8	169	Fall/69	PC-r; stiff-c	1	1	2.00	5.00	10.

107. King of the Khyber Rifles

Ed	HRN	Date	Details	A	C	GD2.0	FN6.0	NM
1	108	5/53	Original	1	1	5.00	15.00	32.
2	118	–	PC-r	1	1	2.20	5.50	11.
3	146	–	PC-r	1	1	2.20	5.50	11.
4	158	–	PC-r	1	1	2.20	5.50	11.
5	167	–	Has orig.date; PC-r	1	1	2.00	5.00	10.
6	167	–	PC-r	1	1	2.00	5.00	10.
7	167	10/66	PC-r	1	1	2.00	5.00	10.

108. Knights of the Round Table

Ed	HRN	Date	Details	A	C	GD2.0	FN6.0	NM
1A	108	6/53	Original; Blum-a	1	1	5.50	16.50	38.
1B	109	6/53	Original; scarce	1	1	6.40	19.25	45.
2	117	–	PC-r	1	1	2.20	5.50	11.
3	165	–	PC-r	1	1	2.00	5.00	10.
4	167	4/64	PC-r	1	1	2.00	5.00	10.
5	166	4/67	PC-r	1	1	2.00	5.00	10.
6	169	Sm/69	New price 25¢; stiff-c; PC-r	1	1	2.00	5.00	10.

109. Pitcairn's Island

Classics Illustrated #115 © GIL

Classics Illustrated #127 © GIL

HRN	Date	Details	A	C	GD2.0	FN6.0	NM9.4
110	7/53	Original; Palais-a	1	1	5.50	16.50	38.00
165	–	PC-r	1	1	2.40	6.00	12.00
167	3/64	PC-r	1	1	2.40	6.00	12.00
166	6/67	PC-r	1	1	2.40	6.00	12.00

A Study in Scarlet

HRN	Date	Details	A	C	GD2.0	FN6.0	NM9.4
111	8/53	Original	1	1	11.00	33.00	90.00
165	–	PC-r	1	1	10.00	30.00	70.00

The Talisman

HRN	Date	Details	A	C	GD2.0	FN6.0	NM9.4
112	9/53	Original; last H.C. Kiefer-a	1	1	5.50	16.50	38.00
165	–	PC-r	1	1	2.20	5.50	11.00
167	5/64	PC-r	1	1	2.20	5.50	11.00
166	Fall/68	C-price 25¢; PC-r	1	1	2.20	5.50	11.00

Adventures of Kit Carson

HRN	Date	Details	A	C	GD2.0	FN6.0	NM9.4
113	10/53	Original; Palais-a	1	1	5.00	15.00	35.00
129	–	PC-r	1	1	2.20	5.50	11.00
141	–	PC-r	1	1	2.20	5.50	11.00
152	–	PC-r	1	1	2.20	5.50	11.00
161	–	PC-r	1	1	2.00	5.00	10.00
167	–	PC-r	1	1	2.00	5.00	10.00
167	2/65	PC-r	1	1	2.00	5.00	10.00
167	5/66	PC-r	1	1	2.00	5.00	10.00
166	Win/69	New-c&price 25¢; PC-r; stiff-c	1	2	3.40	8.50	17.00

The Forty-Five Guardsmen

HRN	Date	Details	A	C	GD2.0	FN6.0	NM9.4
114	11/53	Orig.; delBourgo-a	1	1	8.65	26.00	60.00
166	7/67	PC-r	1	1	3.00	9.00	30.00

The Red Rover

HRN	Date	Details	A	C	GD2.0	FN6.0	NM9.4
115	12/53	Original	1	1	8.65	26.00	60.00
166	7/67	PC-r	1	1	3.00	9.00	30.00

How I Found Livingstone

HRN	Date	Details	A	C	GD2.0	FN6.0	NM9.4
116	1/54	Original	1	1	10.00	30.00	70.00
167	1/67	PC-r	1	1	3.80	11.40	42.00

The Bottle Imp

HRN	Date	Details	A	C	GD2.0	FN6.0	NM9.4
117	2/54	Orig.; Cameron-a	1	1	10.00	30.00	70.00
167	1/67	PC-r	1	1	3.80	11.40	42.00

Captains Courageous

HRN	Date	Details	A	C	GD2.0	FN6.0	NM9.4
118	3/54	Orig.; Costanza-a	1	1	8.65	26.00	60.00
167	2/67	PC-r	1	1	2.40	7.35	22.00
169	Fall/69	New price 25¢; stiff-c; PC-r	1	1	2.40	7.35	22.00

Rob Roy

HRN	Date	Details	A	C	GD2.0	FN6.0	NM9.4
119	4/54	Original; Rudy & Walter Palais-a	1	1	10.00	30.00	70.00
167	2/67	PC-r	1	1	3.80	11.40	42.00

Soldiers of Fortune

HRN	Date	Details	A	C	GD2.0	FN6.0	NM9.4
120	5/54	Schaffenberger-a	1	1	7.85	23.50	55.00
166	3/67	PC-r	1	1	2.40	7.35	22.00
169	Spr/70	New price 25¢; stiff-c; PC-r	1	1	2.40	7.35	22.00

The Hurricane

HRN	Date	Details	A	C	GD2.0	FN6.0	NM9.4
121	6/54	Orig.; Cameron-a	1	1	7.85	23.50	55.00
166	3/67	PC-r	1	1	3.00	9.00	30.00

121. Wild Bill Hickok

Ed	HRN	Date	Details	A	C	GD2.0	FN6.0	NM9.4
1	122	7/54	Original	1	1	4.65	14.00	28.00
2	132	–	PC-r	1	1	2.20	5.50	11.00
3	141	–	PC-r	1	1	2.20	5.50	11.00
4	154	–	PC-r	1	1	2.20	5.50	11.00
5	167	–	PC-r	1	1	2.00	5.00	10.00
6	167	8/64	PC-r	1	1	2.00	5.00	10.00
7	166	4/67	PC-r	1	1	2.00	5.00	10.00
8	169	Win/69	PC-r; stiff-c	1	1	2.00	5.00	10.00

122. The Mutineers

Ed	HRN	Date	Details	A	C	GD2.0	FN6.0	NM9.4
1	123	9/54	Original	1	1	5.50	16.50	38.00
2	136	–	PC-r	1	1	2.20	5.50	11.00
3	146	–	PC-r	1	1	2.20	5.50	11.00
4	158	–	PC-r	1	1	2.20	5.50	11.00
5	167	11/63	PC-r	1	1	2.00	5.00	10.00
6	167	3/65	PC-r	1	1	2.00	5.00	10.00
7	166	8/67	PC-r	1	1	2.00	5.00	10.00

123. Fang and Claw

Ed	HRN	Date	Details	A	C	GD2.0	FN6.0	NM9.4
1	124	11/54	Original	1	1	5.50	16.50	38.00
2	133	–	PC-r	1	1	2.20	5.50	11.00
3	143	–	PC-r	1	1	2.20	5.50	11.00
4	154	–	PC-r	1	1	2.20	5.50	11.00
5	167	–	Has orig.date; PC-r	1	1	2.00	5.00	10.00
6	167	9/65	PC-r	1	1	2.00	5.00	10.00

124. The War of the Worlds

Ed	HRN	Date	Details	A	C	GD2.0	FN6.0	NM9.4
1	125	1/55	Original; Cameron-c/a	1	1	7.85	23.50	55.00
2	131	–	PC-r	1	1	2.80	7.00	14.00
3	141	–	PC-r	1	1	2.80	7.00	14.00
4	148	–	PC-r	1	1	2.80	7.00	14.00
5	156	–	PC-r	1	1	2.80	7.00	14.00
6	165	–	PC-r	1	1	3.20	8.00	16.00
7	167	–	PC-r	1	1	2.40	6.00	12.00
8	167	11/64	PC-r	1	1	2.80	7.00	14.00
9	167	11/65	PC-r	1	1	2.40	6.00	12.00
10	166	R/1968	C-price 25¢; PC-r	1	1	2.40	6.00	12.00
11	169	Sm/70	PC-r; stiff-c	1	1	2.40	6.00	12.00

125. The Ox Bow Incident

Ed	HRN	Date	Details	A	C	GD2.0	FN6.0	NM9.4
1	–	3/55	Original; Picture Progress replaces reorder list	1	1	4.65	14.00	28.00
2	143	–	PC-r	1	1	2.20	5.50	11.00
3	152	–	PC-r	1	1	2.20	5.50	11.00
4	149	–	PC-r	1	1	2.20	5.50	11.00
5	167	–	PC-r	1	1	2.00	5.00	10.00
6	167	11/64	PC-r	1	1	2.00	5.00	10.00
7	166	4/67	PC-r	1	1	2.00	5.00	10.00
8	169	Win/69	New price 25¢; stiff-c; PC-r	1	1	2.00	5.00	10.00

126. The Downfall

Ed	HRN	Date	Details	A	C	GD2.0	FN6.0	NM9.4
1	5/55	–	Orig.; 'Picture Progress' replaces reorder list; Cameron-c/a	1	1	5.50	16.50	38.00
2	167	8/64	PC-r	1	1	3.20	8.00	16.00
3	166	R/1968	C-price 25¢; PC-r	1	1	3.20	8.00	16.00

127. The King of the Mountains

Ed	HRN	Date	Details	A	C	GD2.0	FN6.0	NM9.4
1	128	7/55	Original	1	1	5.50	16.50	38.00
2	167	6/64	PC-r	1	1	2.80	7.00	14.00
3	166	F/1968	C-price 25¢; PC-r	1	1	2.80	7.00	14.00

Classics Illustrated #128 © GIL

Classics Illustrated #130 © GIL

Classics Illustrated #132 © GIL

128. Macbeth (Used in **POP**, pg. 102)

Ed	HRN	Date	Details	A	C	GD2.0	FN6.0	NM9.4
1	128	9/55	Orig.; last Blum-a	1	1	5.50	16.50	38.00
2	143	–	PC-r	1	1	2.20	5.50	11.00
3	158	–	PC-r	1	1	2.20	5.50	11.00
4	167	–	PC-r	1	1	2.00	5.00	10.00
5	167	6/64	PC-r	1	1	2.00	5.00	10.00
6	166	4/67	PC-r	1	1	2.00	5.00	10.00
7	166	R/1968	C-Price 25¢; PC-r	1	1	2.00	5.00	10.00
8	169	Spr/70	Stiff-c; PC-r	1	1	2.00	5.00	10.00

129. Davy Crockett

Ed	HRN	Date	Details	A	C	GD2.0	FN6.0	NM9.4
1	129	11/55	Orig.; Cameron-a	1	1	11.00	33.00	90.00
2	167	9/66	PC-r	1	1	10.00	30.00	70.00

130. Caesar's Conquests

Ed	HRN	Date	Details	A	C	GD2.0	FN6.0	NM9.4
1	130	1/56	Original; Orlando-a	1	1	6.00	18.00	42.00
2	142	–	PC-r	1	1	2.20	5.50	11.00
3	152	–	PC-r	1	1	2.20	5.50	11.00
4	149	–	PC-r	1	1	2.20	5.50	11.00
5	167	–	PC-r	1	1	2.00	5.00	10.00
6	167	10/64	PC-r	1	1	2.00	5.00	10.00
7	167	4/66	PC-r	1	1	2.00	5.00	10.00

131. The Covered Wagon

Ed	HRN	Date	Details	A	C	GD2.0	FN6.0	NM9.4
1	131	3/56	Original	1	1	4.65	14.00	28.00
2	143	–	PC-r	1	1	2.20	5.50	11.00
3	152	–	PC-r	1	1	2.20	5.50	11.00
4	158	–	PC-r	1	1	2.20	5.50	11.00
5	167	–	PC-r	1	1	2.00	5.00	10.00
6	167	11/64	PC-r	1	1	2.00	5.00	10.00
7	167	4/66	PC-r	1	1	2.00	5.00	10.00
8	169	Win/69	New price 25¢; stiff-c; PC-r	1	1	2.00	5.00	10.00

132. The Dark Frigate

Ed	HRN	Date	Details	A	C	GD2.0	FN6.0	NM9.4
1	132	5/56	Original	1	1	5.50	16.50	38.00
2	150	–	PC-r	1	1	2.40	6.00	12.00
3	167	1/64	PC-r	1	1	2.20	5.50	11.00
4	166	5/67	PC-r	1	1	2.20	5.50	11.00

133. The Time Machine

Ed	HRN	Date	Details	A	C	GD2.0	FN6.0	NM9.4
1	132	7/56	Orig.; Cameron-a	1	1	6.00	18.00	42.00
2	142	–	PC-r	1	1	2.80	7.00	14.00
3	152	–	PC-r	1	1	2.80	7.00	14.00
4	158	–	PC-r	1	1	2.80	7.00	14.00
5	167	–	PC-r	1	1	2.40	6.00	12.00
6	167	6/64	PC-r	1	1	3.00	7.50	15.00
7	167	3/66	PC-r	1	1	2.40	6.00	12.00
8	166	12/67	PC-r	1	1	2.40	6.00	12.00
9	169	Win/71	New price 25¢; stiff-c; PC-r	1	1	2.20	5.50	11.00

134. Romeo and Juliet

Ed	HRN	Date	Details	A	C	GD2.0	FN6.0	NM9.4
1	134	9/56	Original; Evans-a	1	1	5.50	16.50	38.00
2	161	–	PC-r	1	1	2.20	5.50	11.00
3	167	9/63	PC-r	1	1	2.00	5.00	10.00
4	167	5/65	PC-r	1	1	2.00	5.00	10.00
5	166	6/67	PC-r	1	1	2.00	5.00	10.00
6	166	Win/69	New c&price 25¢; stiff-c; PC-r	1	2	4.00	12.00	24.00

135. Waterloo

Ed	HRN	Date	Details	A	C	GD2.0	FN6.0	NM9.4
1	135	11/56	Orig.; G. Ingels-a	1	1	5.50	16.50	38.00
2	153	–	PC-r	1	1	2.20	5.50	11.00
3	167	–	PC-r	1	1	2.00	5.00	10.00
4	167	9/64	PC-r	1	1	2.00	5.00	10.00
5	166	R/1968	C-price 25¢; PC-r	1	1	2.00	5.00	10.

136. Lord Jim

Ed	HRN	Date	Details	A	C	GD2.0	FN6.0	NM
1	136	1/57	Original; Evans-a	1	1	5.50	16.50	38.
2	165	–	PC-r	1	1	2.00	5.00	10.
3	167	3/64	PC-r	1	1	2.00	5.00	10.
4	167	9/66	PC-r	1	1	2.00	5.00	10
5	169	Sm/69	New price 25 ¢; stiff-c; PC-r	1	1	2.00	5.00	10.

137. The Little Savage

Ed	HRN	Date	Details	A	C	GD2.0	FN6.0	NM
1	136	3/57	Original; Evans-a	1	1	5.50	16.50	38.
2	148	–	PC-r	1	1	2.20	5.50	11
3	156	–	PC-r	1	1	2.20	5.50	11.
4	167	–	PC-r	1	1	2.00	5.00	10.
5	167	10/64	PC-r	1	1	2.00	5.00	10.
6	166	8/67	PC-r	1	1	2.00	5.00	10.
7	169	Spr/70	New price 25¢; stiff-c; PC-r	1	1	2.00	5.00	10

138. A Journey to the Center of the Earth

Ed	HRN	Date	Details	A	C	GD2.0	FN6.0	NM
1	136	5/57	Original	1	1	7.85	23.50	55.
2	146	–	PC-r	1	1	2.80	7.00	14.
3	156	–	PC-r	1	1	2.80	7.00	14.
4	158	–	PC-r	1	1	2.80	7.00	14.
5	167	–	PC-r	1	1	2.40	6.00	12.
6	167	6/64	PC-r	1	1	3.20	8.00	16
7	167	4/66	PC-r	1	1	3.20	8.00	16
8	166	R/68	C-price 25¢; PC-r	1	1	2.40	6.00	12.

139. In the Reign of Terror

Ed	HRN	Date	Details	A	C	GD2.0	FN6.0	NM
1	139	7/57	Original; Evans-a	1	1	4.65	14.00	28.
2	154	–	PC-r	1	1	2.40	6.00	12.
3	167	–	Has orig.date; PC-r	1	1	2.00	5.00	10.
4	167	7/64	PC-r	1	1	2.00	5.00	10.
5	166	R/1968	C-price 25¢; PC-r	1	1	2.00	5.00	10.

140. On Jungle Trails

Ed	HRN	Date	Details	A	C	GD2.0	FN6.0	NM
1	140	9/57	Original	1	1	4.65	14.00	28.
2	150	–	PC-r	1	1	2.20	5.50	11.
3	160	–	PC-r	1	1	2.20	5.50	11.
4	167	9/63	PC-r	1	1	2.00	5.00	10.
5	167	9/65	PC-r	1	1	2.00	5.00	10.

141. Castle Dangerous

Ed	HRN	Date	Details	A	C	GD2.0	FN6.0	NM
1	141	11/57	Original	1	1	6.40	19.25	45.
2	152	–	PC-r	1	1	2.20	5.50	11.
3	167	–	PC-r	1	1	2.20	5.50	11.
4	166	7/67	PC-r	1	1	2.20	5.50	11.

142. Abraham Lincoln

Ed	HRN	Date	Details	A	C	GD2.0	FN6.0	NM
1	142	1/58	Original	1	1	6.00	18.00	42.
2	154	–	PC-r	1	1	2.20	5.50	11.
3	158	–	PC-r	1	1	2.20	5.50	11.
4	167	10/63	PC-r	1	1	2.00	5.00	10.
5	167	7/65	PC-r	1	1	2.00	5.00	10.
6	166	11/67	PC-r	1	1	2.00	5.00	10.
7	169	Fall/69	New price 25¢; stiff-c; PC-r	1	1	2.00	5.00	10.

143. Kim

Ed	HRN	Date	Details	A	C	GD2.0	FN6.0	NM
1	143	3/58	Original; Orlando-a	1	1	5.00	15.00	32.
2	165	–	PC-r	1	1	2.00	5.00	10.
3	167	11/63	PC-r	1	1	2.00	5.00	10.
4	167	8/65	PC-r	1	1	2.00	5.00	10.
5	169	Win/69	New price 25¢; stiff-c; PC-r	1	1	2.00	5.00	10.

Classics Illustrated #145 © GIL

Classics Illustrated #147 © GIL

Classics Illustrated #149 © GIL

GD2.0 FN6.0 NM9.4

144. The First Men in the Moon

Ed	HRN	Date	Details	A	C	GD2.0	FN6.0	NM9.4
1	143	5/58	Original; Woodbridge/Williamson/Torres-a	1	1	5.70	17.00	40.00
2	152	–	(Rare)-PC-r	1	1	7.85	23.50	55.00
3	153	–	PC-r	1	1	2.20	5.50	11.00
4	161	–	PC-r	1	1	2.00	5.00	10.00
5	167	–	PC-r	1	1	2.00	5.00	10.00
6	167	12/65	PC-r	1	1	2.00	5.00	10.00
7	166	Fall/68	New-c&price 25¢; PC-r; stiff-c	1	2	4.00	10.00	20.00
8	169	Win/69	Stiff-c; PC-r	1	2	3.00	7.50	15.00

145. The Crisis

Ed	HRN	Date	Details	A	C	GD2.0	FN6.0	NM9.4
1	143	7/58	Original; Evans-a	1	1	5.50	16.50	38.00
2	156	–	PC-r	1	1	2.20	5.50	11.00
3	167	10/63	PC-r	1	1	2.00	5.00	10.00
4	167	3/65	PC-r	1	1	2.00	5.00	10.00
5	166	R/68	C-price 25¢; PC-r	1	1	2.00	5.00	10.00

146. With Fire and Sword

Ed	HRN	Date	Details	A	C	GD2.0	FN6.0	NM9.4
1	143	9/58	Original; Woodbridge-a	1	1	6.00	18.00	42.00
2	156	–	PC-r	1	1	2.80	7.00	14.00
3	167	11/63	PC-r	1	1	2.40	6.00	12.00
4	167	3/65	PC-r	1	1	2.40	6.00	12.00

147. Ben-Hur

Ed	HRN	Date	Details	A	C	GD2.0	FN6.0	NM9.4
1	147	11/58	Original; Orlando-a	1	1	5.00	15.00	32.00
2	152	–	Scarce; PC-r	1	1	5.70	17.00	40.00
3	153	–	PC-r	1	1	2.20	5.50	11.00
4	158	–	PC-r	1	1	2.20	5.50	11.00
5	167	–	Orig.date; but PC-r	1	1	2.00	5.00	10.00
6	167	2/65	PC-r	1	1	2.00	5.00	10.00
7	167	9/66	PC-r	1	1	2.00	5.00	10.00
8A	166	Fall/68	New-c&price 25¢; PC-r; soft-c	1	2	4.00	12.00	24.00
8B	166	Fall/68	New-c&price 25¢; PC-r; stiff-c; scarce	1	2	5.70	17.00	40.00

148. The Buccaneer

Ed	HRN	Date	Details	A	C	GD2.0	FN6.0	NM9.4
1	148	1/59	Orig.; Evans/Jenny-a; Saunders-c	1	1	5.00	15.00	32.00
2	568	–	Juniors list only PC-r	1	1	2.40	6.00	12.00
3	167	–	PC-r	1	1	2.00	5.00	10.00
4	167	9/65	PC-r	1	1	2.00	5.00	10.00
5	169	Sm/69	New price 25¢; PC-r; stiff-c	1	1	2.00	5.00	10.00

149. Off on a Comet

Ed	HRN	Date	Details	A	C	GD2.0	FN6.0	NM9.4
1	149	3/59	Orig.;G.McCann-a; blue reorder list	1	1	5.50	16.50	38.00
2	155	–	PC-r	1	1	2.20	5.50	11.00
3	149	–	PC-r; white reorder list; no coming-next ad	1	1	2.20	5.50	11.00
4	167	12/63	PC-r	1	1	2.00	5.00	10.00
5	167	2/65	PC-r	1	1	2.00	5.00	10.00
6	167	10/66	PC-r	1	1	2.00	5.00	10.00
7	166	Fall/68	New-c & price 25¢; PC-r	1	2	4.00	11.00	22.00

150. The Virginian

Ed	HRN	Date	Details	A	C	GD2.0	FN6.0	NM9.4
1	150	5/59	Original	1	1	6.40	19.25	45.00
2	164	–	PC-r	1	1	3.60	9.00	18.00
3	167	10/63	PC-r	1	1	4.00	12.00	24.00
4	167	12/65	PC-r	1	1	3.60	9.00	18.00

151. Won By the Sword

Ed	HRN	Date	Details	A	C	GD2.0	FN6.0	NM9.4
1	150	7/59	Original	1	1	6.00	18.00	42.00
2	164	–	PC-r	1	1	3.00	7.50	15.00
3	167	10/63	PC-r	1	1	3.00	7.50	15.00
4	166	7/67	PC-r	1	1	3.00	7.50	15.00

152. Wild Animals I Have Known

Ed	HRN	Date	Details	A	C	GD2.0	FN6.0	NM9.4
1	152	9/59	Orig.; L.B. Cole c/a	1	1	7.15	21.50	50.00
2A	149	–	PC-r; white reorder list; no coming-next ad; IBC: Jr. list #572	1	1	2.20	5.50	11.00
2B	149	–	PC-r; inside-bc: Jr. list to #555	1	1	2.40	6.00	12.00
2C	149	–	PC-r; inside-bc: has World Around Us ad; scarce	1	1	4.00	12.00	24.00
3	167	9/63	PC-r	1	1	2.00	5.00	10.00
4	167	8/65	PC-r	1	1	2.00	5.00	10.00
5	169	Fall/69	New price 25¢; stiff-c; PC-r	1	1	2.00	5.00	10.00

153. The Invisible Man

Ed	HRN	Date	Details	A	C	GD2.0	FN6.0	NM9.4
1	153	11/59	Original	1	1	7.85	23.50	55.00
2A	149	–	PC-r; white reorder list; no coming-next ad; inside-bc: Jr. list to #572	1	1	3.00	7.50	15.00
2B	149	–	PC-r; inside-bc: Jr. list to #555	1	1	3.20	8.00	16.00
3	167	–	PC-r	1	1	2.40	6.00	12.00
4	167	2/65	PC-r	1	1	2.40	6.00	12.00
5	167	9/66	PC-r	1	1	2.40	6.00	12.00
6	166	Win/69	New price 25¢; PC-r; stiff-c	1	1	2.40	6.00	12.00
7	169	Spr/71	Stiff-c; letters spelling 'Invisible Man' are 'solid' not 'invisible;' PC-r	1	1	2.40	6.00	12.00

154. The Conspiracy of Pontiac

Ed	HRN	Date	Details	A	C	GD2.0	FN6.0	NM9.4
1	154	1/60	Original	1	1	7.00	21.00	48.00
2	167	11/63	PC-r	1	1	3.40	8.50	17.00
3	167	7/64	PC-r	1	1	3.40	8.50	17.00
4	166	12/67	PC-r	1	1	3.40	8.50	17.00

155. The Lion of the North

Ed	HRN	Date	Details	A	C	GD2.0	FN6.0	NM9.4
1	154	3/60	Original	1	1	6.00	18.00	42.00
2	167	1/64	PC-r	1	1	3.00	7.50	15.00
3	166	R/1967	C-price 25¢; PC-r	1	1	2.40	6.00	12.00

156. The Conquest of Mexico

Ed	HRN	Date	Details	A	C	GD2.0	FN6.0	NM9.4
1	156	5/60	Orig.; Bruno Premiani-c/a	1	1	6.00	18.00	42.00
2	167	1/64	PC-r	1	1	2.40	6.00	12.00
3	166	8/67	PC-r	1	1	2.40	6.00	12.00
4	169	Spr/70	New price 25¢; stiff-c; PC-r	1	1	2.00	5.00	10.00

157. Lives of the Hunted

Ed	HRN	Date	Details	A	C	GD2.0	FN6.0	NM9.4
1	156	7/60	Orig.; L.B. Cole-c	1	1	7.00	21.00	48.00
2	167	2/64	PC-r	1	1	3.60	9.00	18.00
3	166	10/67	PC-r	1	1	3.60	9.00	18.00

158. The Conspirators

Ed	HRN	Date	Details	A	C

Classics Illustrated #160 © GIL

Classics Illustrated #161 © GIL

Classics Illustrated - Hamlet © Acclaim

Ed	HRN	Date	Details	A	C	GD2.0	FN6.0	NM9.4
1	156	9/60	Original	1	1	6.40	19.25	45.00
2	167	7/64	PC-r	1	1	3.60	9.00	18.00
3	166	10/67	PC-r	1	1	3.60	9.00	18.00

159. The Octopus

Ed	HRN	Date	Details	A	C	GD2.0	FN6.0	NM9.4
1	159	11/60	Orig.; Gray Morrow-a; L.B. Cole-c	1	1	7.00	21.00	48.00
2	167	2/64	PC-r	1	1	3.20	8.00	16.00
3	166	R/1967	C-price 25¢; PC-r	1	1	3.20	8.00	16.00

160. The Food of the Gods

Ed	HRN	Date	Details	A	C	GD2.0	FN6.0	NM9.4
1A	159	1/61	Original	1	1	7.00	21.00	48.00
1B	160	1/61	Original; same, except for HRN	1	1	6.40	19.25	45.00
2	167	1/64	PC-r	1	1	3.20	8.00	16.00
3	166	6/67	PC-r	1	1	3.20	8.00	16.00

161. Cleopatra

Ed	HRN	Date	Details	A	C	GD2.0	FN6.0	NM9.4
1	161	3/61	Original	1	1	7.00	21.00	48.00
2	167	1/64	PC-r	1	1	4.00	10.00	20.00
3	166	8/67	PC-r	1	1	4.00	10.00	20.00

162. Robur the Conqueror

Ed	HRN	Date	Details	A	C	GD2.0	FN6.0	NM9.4
1	162	5/61	Original	1	1	7.00	21.00	48.00
2	167	7/64	PC-r	1	1	3.60	9.00	18.00
3	166	8/67	PC-r	1	1	3.60	9.00	18.00

163. Master of the World

Ed	HRN	Date	Details	A	C	GD2.0	FN6.0	NM9.4
1	163	7/61	Original; Gray Morrow-a	1	1	6.40	19.25	45.00
2	167	1/65	PC-r	1	1	3.60	9.00	18.00
3	166	R/1968	C-price 25¢; PC-r	1	1	3.60	9.00	18.00

164. The Cossack Chief

Ed	HRN	Date	Details	A	C	GD2.0	FN6.0	NM9.4
1	164	(1961)	Orig.; nd(10/61?)	1	1	6.40	19.25	45.00
2	167	4/65	PC-r	1	1	3.60	9.00	18.00
3	166	Fall/68	C-price 25¢; PC-r	1	1	3.60	9.00	18.00

165. The Queen's Necklace

Ed	HRN	Date	Details	A	C	GD2.0	FN6.0	NM9.4
1	164	1/62	Original; Morrow-a	1	1	6.40	19.25	45.00
2	167	4/65	PC-r	1	1	3.60	9.00	18.00
3	166	Fall/68	C-price 25¢; PC-r	1	1	3.60	9.00	18.00

166. Tigers and Traitors

Ed	HRN	Date	Details	A	C	GD2.0	FN6.0	NM9.4
1	165	5/62	Original	1	1	10.00	30.00	75.00
2	167	2/64	PC-r	1	1	4.65	14.00	28.00
3	167	11/66	PC-r	1	1	4.65	14.00	28.00

167. Faust

Ed	HRN	Date	Details	A	C	GD2.0	FN6.0	NM9.4
1	165	8/62	Original	1	1	14.00	41.00	110.00
2	167	2/64	PC-r	1	1	7.00	21.00	48.00
3	166	6/67	PC-r	1	1	7.00	21.00	48.00

168. In Freedom's Cause

Ed	HRN	Date	Details	A	C	GD2.0	FN6.0	NM9.4
1	169	Win/69	Original; Evans/ Crandall-a; stiff-c; 25¢; no coming-next ad;	1	1	18.00	53.00	140.00

169. Negro Americans The Early Years

Ed	HRN	Date	Details	A	C	GD2.0	FN6.0	NM9.4
1	166	Spr/69	Orig. & last issue; 25¢; Stiff-c; no coming-next ad; other sources indicate publication date of 5/69	1	1	14.00	41.00	110.00
2	169	Spr/69	Stiff-c	1	1	7.85	23.50	55.00

NOTE: *Many other titles were prepared or planned but were only issued in British/European series.*

CLASSIC PUNISHER (Also see Punisher)
Marvel Comics: Dec, 1989 ($4.95, B&W, deluxe format, 68 pgs.)

1-Reprints Marvel Super Action #1 & Marvel Preview #2 plus new story 5.0(

CLASSICS ILLUSTRATED
First Publishing/Berkley Publishing: Feb, 1990 - No. 27, July, 1991 ($3.75/$3.95, 52 pgs.)

1-27: 1-Gahan Wilson-c/a. 4-Sienkiewicz painted-c/a. 6-Russell scripts/layouts. 7-Spiegle-a. 9-Ploog-c/a. 16-Staton-a. 18-Gahan Wilson-c/a; 20-Geary-a. 26-Aesop's Fables (6/91). 26,27-Direct sale only 4.0(

CLASSICS ILLUSTRATED
Acclaim Books/Twin Circle PublishingCo.: Feb, 1997 - Present ($4.99, diges size) (Each book contains study notes)

A Christmas Carol-(12/97), A Connecticut Yankee in King Arthur's Court-(5/97), All Quiet on the Western Front-(1/98), A Midsummer's Night Dream-(4/97) Around the World in 80 Days-(1/98), A Tale of Two Cities-(2/97)Joe Orlando-r, Captains Courageous-(11/97), Crime and Punishment-(3/97), Dr. Jekyll and Mr. Hyde-(10/97), Don Quixote-(12/97), Frankenstein-(10/97), Great Expectations-(4/97), Hamlet-(3/97), Huckleberry Finn-(3/97), Jane Eyre-(2/97), Kidnapped-(1/98), Les Miserables-(5/97), Lord Jim-(9/97), Macbeth-(5/97), Moby Dick-(4/97), Oliver Twist-(5/97), Robinson Crusoe-(9/97, Romeo & Juliet-(2/97), Silas Marner-(11/97), The Call of the Wild-(9/97), The Count of Monte Cristo-(1/98), The House of the Seven Gables-(9/97), The Iliad-(12/97), The Invisible Man-(10/97), The Last of the Mohicans-(12/97), The Master of Ballantrae-(11/97), The Odyssey-(3/97), The Prince and the Pauper-(4/97), The Red Badge Of Courage-(9/97), Tom Sawyer-(2/97) Wuthering Heights-(11/97) 5.0(

NOTE: *Stories reprinted from the original Gilberton Classic Comics and Classics Illustrated.*

CLASSICS ILLUSTRATED GIANTS
Gilberton Publications: Oct, 1949 (One-Shots - "OS")
These Giant Editions, all with new Kiefer front and back covers, were advertised from 10/49 to 2/52. They were 50¢ on the newsstand and 60¢ by mail. They are actually four Classics in one volume. All the stories are reprints of the Classics Illustrated Series. NOTE: There were also British hardback Adventure & Indian Giants in 1952, with the same covers but different contents: Adventure - 2, 7, 10 Indian - 17, 22, 37, 58. They are also rare.

"An Illustrated Library of Great Adventure Stories" - reprints of No. 6,7,8,10 (Rare); Kiefer-c 132.00 395.00 1250.0(
"An Illustrated Library of Exciting Mystery Stories" - reprints of No. 30,21,40, 13 (Rare) 147.00 442.00 1400.0(
"An Illustrated Library of Great Indian Stories" - reprints of No. 4,17,22,37 (Rare) 132.00 395.00 1250.0(

INTRODUCTION TO CLASSICS ILLUSTRATED JUNIOR

Collectors of Juniors can be put into one of two categories: those wh want any copy of each title, and those who want all the originals. Those seekir every original and reprint edition are a limited group, primarily because Junio have no changes in art or covers to spark interest, and because reprints are s low in value it is difficult to get dealers to look for specific reprint editions.

In recent years it has become apparent that most serious Classics colle tors seek Junior originals. Those seeking reprints seek them for low cost. Th has made the previous note about the comparative market value of reprints ina equate. Three particular reprint editions are worth even more. For the 535-Tw Circle edition, see Giveaways. There are also reprint editions of 501 and 5C which have a full-page bc ad for the very rare Junior record. Those may sell a high as $10-$15 in mint. Original editions of 557 and 558 also have that ad.

There are no reprint editions of 577. The only edition, from 1969, is a 25 ce stiff-cover edition with no ad for the next issue. All other original editions hav coming-next ad. But 577, like C.I. #168, was prepared in 1962 but not issue Copies of 577 can be found in 1963 British/European series, which then conti ued with dozens of additional new Junior titles.

PRICES LISTED BELOW ARE FOR ORIGINAL EDITIONS, WHICH HAVE AN AD FOR THE NEXT ISSUE.

NOTE: *Non HRN 576 copies- many are written on or colored . Reprints with 576 HRN are worth about 1/3 original prices. All other HRN #'s are 1/2 original price*

Classics Illustrated Junior #504 © GIL

Classics Illustrated Special Issue #141A © GIL

Classic Star Wars #3 © Lucasfilm Ltd.

GD2.0 FN6.0 NM9.4

CLASSICS ILLUSTRATED JUNIOR
Famous Authors Ltd. (Gilberton Publications): Oct, 1953 - Spring, 1971
501-Snow White & the Seven Dwarfs; Alex Blum-a 10.00 30.00 80.00
502-The Ugly Duckling 7.85 23.50 55.00
503-Cinderella 5.00 15.00 35.00
504-512: 504-The Pied Piper. 505-The Sleeping Beauty. 506-The Three Little Pigs. 507-Jack & the Beanstalk. 508-Goldilocks & the Three Bears. 509-Beauty and the Beast. 510-Little Red Riding Hood. 511-Puss-N Boots. 512-Rumpelstiltskin 4.00 12.00 24.00
513-Pinocchio 5.00 15.00 35.00
514-The Steadfast Tin Soldier 7.15 21.50 50.00
515-Johnny Appleseed 4.00 12.00 24.00
516-Aladdin and His Lamp 5.00 15.00 30.00
517-519: 517-The Emperor's New Clothes. 518-The Golden Goose. 519-Paul Bunyan 4.00 12.00 24.00
520-Thumbelina 5.00 15.00 32.00
521-King of the Golden River 4.00 12.00 24.00
522,523,530: 522-The Nightingale. 523-The Gallant Tailor. 530-The Golden Bird 4.00 11.00 22.00
524-The Wild Swans 5.00 15.00 30.00
525,526: 525-The Little Mermaid. 526-The Frog Prince 5.00 15.00 30.00
527-The Golden-Haired Giant 4.00 12.00 24.00
528-The Penny Prince 4.00 12.00 24.00
529-The Magic Servants 4.00 12.00 24.00
531-Rapunzel 4.00 12.00 24.00
532-534: 532-The Dancing Princesses. 533-The Magic Fountain. 534-The Golden Touch 4.00 10.00 20.00
535-The Wizard of Oz 6.40 19.25 45.00
536-The Chimney Sweep 4.00 12.00 24.00
537-The Three Fairies 4.65 14.00 28.00
538-Silly Hans 4.00 10.00 20.00
539-The Enchanted Fish 5.00 15.00 32.00
540-The Tinder-Box 5.00 15.00 32.00
541-Snow White & Rose Red 4.00 11.00 22.00
542-The Donkey's Tale 4.00 11.00 22.00
543-The House in the Woods 4.00 12.00 24.00
544-The Golden Fleece 5.00 15.00 35.00
545-The Glass Mountain 4.00 11.00 22.00
546-The Elves & the Shoemaker 4.00 11.00 22.00
547-The Wishing Table 4.00 12.00 24.00
548-551: 548-The Magic Pitcher. 549-Simple Kate. 550-The Singing Donkey. 551-The Queen Bee 4.00 10.00 20.00
552-The Three Little Dwarfs 4.00 12.00 24.00
553,556: 553-King Thrushbeard. 556-The Elf Mound 4.00 10.00 20.00
554-The Enchanted Deer 5.00 15.00 30.00
555-The Three Golden Apples 4.00 11.00 22.00
557-Silly Willy 4.65 14.00 28.00
558-The Magic Dish; L.B. Cole-c; soft and stiff-c exist on original 5.70 17.00 40.00
559-The Japanese Lantern; 1 pg. Ingels-a; L.B. Cole-c 5.70 17.00 40.00
560-The Doll Princess; L.B. Cole-c 5.70 17.00 40.00
561-Hans Humdrum; L.B. Cole-c 5.00 15.00 30.00
562-The Enchanted Pony; L.B. Cole-c 5.70 17.00 40.00
563,565-567,570: 563-The Wishing Well; L.B. Cole-c. 565-The Silly Princess; L.B. Cole-c. 566-Clumsy Hans; L.B. Cole-c. 567-The Bearskin Soldier; L.B. Cole-c. 570-The Pearl Princess 4.00 12.00 24.00
564-The Salt Mountain; L.B.Cole-c. 568-The Happy Hedgehog; L.B. Cole-c. 4.65 14.00 28.00
569,573: 569-The Three Giants.573-The Crystal Ball 4.00 11.00 22.00
571,572: 571-How Fire Came to the Indians. 572-The Drummer Boy 5.00 15.00 32.00
574-Brightboots 4.00 11.00 22.00
575-The Fearless Prince 4.65 14.00 28.00
576-The Princess Who Saw Everything 5.00 15.00 35.00
577-The Runaway Dumpling 6.40 19.25 45.00
NOTE: *Prices are for original editions. Last reprint - Spring, 1971.* ***Costanza*** *&* ***Schaffenberger*** *art in many issues.*

CLASSICS ILLUSTRATED SPECIAL ISSUE
Gilberton Co.: (Came out semi-annually) Dec, 1955 - Jul, 1962 (35¢, 100 pgs.)
129-The Story of Jesus (titled ...Special Edition) "Jesus on Mountain" cover 9.30 28.00 65.00
"Three Camels" cover (12/58) 10.50 32.00 85.00
"Mountain" cover (no date)-Has checklist on inside b/c to HRN #161 & different testimonial on back-c 7.15 21.50 50.00
"Mountain" cover (1968 re-issue; has white 50¢ circle) 7.00 21.00 48.00
132A-The Story of America (6/56); Cameron-a 7.85 23.50 55.00
135A-The Ten Commandments(12/56) 7.00 21.00 48.00
138A-Adventures in Science(6/57); HRN to 137 6.00 18.00 42.00
138A-(6/57)-2nd version w/HRN to 149 5.00 15.00 32.00
138A-(12/61)-3rd version w/HRN to 149 6.00 18.00 42.00
141A-The Rough Rider (Teddy Roosevelt)(12/57); Evans-a 7.00 21.00 48.00
144A-Blazing the Trails West(6/58)- 73 pgs. of Crandall/Evans plus Severin-a 6.40 19.25 45.00
147A-Crossing the Rockies(12/58)-Crandall/Evans-a 7.00 21.00 48.00
150A-Royal Canadian Police(6/59)-Ingels, Sid Check-a 7.00 21.00 48.00
153A-Men, Guns & Cattle(12/59)-Evans-a (26 pgs.); Kinstler-a 7.00 21.00 48.00
156A-The Atomic Age(6/60)-Crandall/Evans, Torres-a 7.00 21.00 48.00
159A-Rockets, Jets and Missiles(12/60)-Evans, Morrow-a 7.00 21.00 48.00
162A-War Between the States(6/61)-Kirby & Crandall/Evans-a; Ingels-a 13.00 39.00 105.00
165A-To the Stars(12/61)-Torres, Crandall/Evans, Kirby-a 7.85 23.50 55.00
166A-World War II('62)-Torres, Crandall/Evans, Kirby-a 10.00 30.00 75.00
167A-Prehistoric World(7/62)-Torres & Crandall/Evans-a; two versions exist (HRN to 165 & HRN to 167) 10.00 30.00 75.00
nn Special Issue-The United Nations (1964; 50¢; scarce); this is actually part of the European Special Series, which cont'd on after the U.S. series stopped issuing new titles in 1962. This English edition was prepared specifically for sale at the U.N. It was printed in Norway 31.00 94.00 250.00
NOTE: *There was another U.S. Special Issue prepared in 1962 with artwork by* ***Torres*** *entitled World War I. Unfortunately, it was never issued in any English-language edition. It was issued in 1964 in West Germany, The Netherlands, and some Scandanavian countries, with another edition in 1974 with a new cover.*

CLASSICS LIBRARY (See King Classics)

CLASSIC STAR WARS (Also see Star Wars)
Dark Horse Comics: Aug, 1992 - No. 20, June, 1994 ($2.50)
1-Begin Star Wars strip-r by Williamson; Williamson redrew portions of the panels to fit comic book format 2.40 6.00
2-10: 8-Polybagged w/Star Wars Galaxy trading card. 8-M. Schultz-c 4.00
11-19: 13-Yeates-c. 17-M. Schultz-c. 19-Evans-c 3.00
20-($3.50, 52 pgs.)-Polybagged w/trading card 3.50
Escape To Hoth TPB ($16.95) r/#15-20 17.00
The Rebel Storm TPB - r/#8-14 17.00
Trade paperback ($29.95, slip-cased)-Reprints all movie adaptations 30.00
NOTE: *Williamson c-1-5,7,9,10,14,15,20.*

CLASSIC STAR WARS: (Title series). **Dark Horse Comics**
--A NEW HOPE, 6/94 - No. 2, 7/94 ($3.95)
1,2: 1-r/Star Wars #1-3, 7-9 publ; 2-r/Star Wars #4-6, 10-12 publ. by Marvel Comics 4.00
--DEVILWORLDS, 8/96 - No.2, 9/96 ($2.50s)1,2: r/Alan Moore-s 2.50
--HAN SOLO AT STARS' END, 3/97 - No.3, 5/97 ($2.95s)
1-3: r/strips by Alfredo Alcala 3.00
--RETURN OF THE JEDI, 10/94 - No.2, 11/94 ($3.50)
1,2: 1-r/1983-84 Marvel series; polybagged with w/trading card 3.50
--THE EARLY ADVENTURES, 8/94 - No. 9, 4/95 ($2.50)1-9 2.50
--THE EMPIRE STRIKES BACK, 8/94 - No. 2, 9/94 ($3.95)
1-r/Star Wars #39-44 published by Marvel Comics 4.00

Clay Cody, Gunslinger #1 © BP

Clerks: The Lost Scene #1 © View Askew

Clue Comics #5 © HILL

CLASSIC X-MEN (Becomes X-Men Classic #46 on)
Marvel Comics Group: Sept, 1986 - No. 45, Mar, 1990

1-Begins-r of New X-Men 3.50
2-10: 10-Sabretooth app. 3.00
11-45: 11-1st origin of Magneto in back-up story. 17-Wolverine-c. 27-r/X-Men #121. 26-r/X-Men #120; Wolverine-c/app. 35-r/X-Men #129. 39-New Jim Lee back-up story (2nd-a on X-Men). 43-Byrne-c/a(r); $1.75, double-size 2.50

NOTE: ***Art Adams** c(p)-1-10, 12-16, 18-23. **Austin** c-10,15-21,24-28i. **Bolton** back up stories in 1-28,30-35. **Williamson** c-12-14i.*

CLAW (See Capt. Battle, Jr. Daredevil Comics & Silver Streak Comics)

CLAW THE UNCONQUERED (See Cancelled Comic Cavalcade)
National Periodical Publications/DC Comics: 5-6/75 - No. 9, 9-10/76; No. 10, 4-5/78 - No. 12, 8-9/78

1-1st app. Claw 1.00 3.00 8.00
2-12: 3-Nudity panel. 9-Origin 5.00

NOTE: ***Giffen** a-8-12p. **Kubert** c-10-12. **Layton** a-9i, 12i.*

CLAY CODY, GUNSLINGER
Pines Comics: Fall, 1957

1-Painted-c 5.00 15.00 35.00

CLEAN FUN, STARRING "SHOOGAFOOTS JONES"
Specialty Book Co.: 1944 (10¢, B&W, oversized covers, 24 pgs.)

nn-Humorous situations involving Negroes in the Deep South
White cover issue... 9.30 28.00 65.00
Dark grey cover issue... 10.00 30.00 75.00

CLEMENTINA THE FLYING PIG (See Dell Jr. Treasury)

CLEOPATRA (See Ideal, a Classical Comic No. 1)

CLERKS: THE COMIC BOOK (Also see Oni Double Feature #1)
Oni Press: Feb, 1998 ($2.95, B&W, one-shot)

1-Kevin Smith-s 1.50 4.50 12.00
1-Second printing 4.00
...Holiday Special (12/98, $2.95) Smith-s 4.00
...The Lost Scene (12/99, $2.95) Smith-s/Hester-a 4.00

CLIFFHANGER (See Battle Chasers, Crimson, and Danger Girl)
WildStorm Prod./Wizard Press: 1997 (Wizard supplement)

0-Sketchbook preview of Cliffhanger titles 2.40 6.00

CLIMAX! (Mystery)
Gillmor Magazines: July, 1955 - No. 2, Sept, 1955

1,2 12.50 37.50 100.00

CLINT (Also see Adolescent Radioactive Black Belt Hamsters)
Eclipse Comics: Sept, 1986 - No. 2, Jan, 1987 ($1.50, B&W)

1,2 2.00

CLINT & MAC (TV, Disney)
Dell Publishing Co.: No. 889, Mar, 1958

Four Color 889-Alex Toth-a, photo-c 12.50 37.50 150.00

CLIVE BARKER'S BOOK OF THE DAMNED: A HELLRAISER COMPANION
Marvel Comics (Epic): Oct, 1991 - No. 3, Nov, 1992 ($4.95, semi-annual)

Volume 1-3-(52 pgs.): 1-Simon Bisley-c. 2-(4/92). 3-(11/92)-McKean-a (1 pg.) 5.00

CLIVE BARKER'S HELLRAISER (Also see Epic, Hellraiser Nightbreed –Jihad, Revelations, Son of Celluloid, Tapping the Vein & Weaveworld)
Marvel Comics (Epic Comics): 1989 - No. 20, 1993 ($4.50-6.95, mature readers, quarterly, 68 pgs.)

Book 1-4,10-16,18,19: Based on Hellraiser & Hellbound movies; Bolton-c/a; Spiegle & Wrightson-a (graphic album). 10-Foil-c. 12-Sam Kieth-a 5.00
Book 5-9 ($5.95): 7-Bolton-a. 8-Morrow-a 6.00
Book 17-Alex Ross-a, 34 pgs. 1.50 4.50 12.00
Book 20-By Gaiman/McKean 1.00 3.00 8.00
...Dark Holiday Special ('92, $4.95)-Conrad-a 5.00
...Spring Slaughter 1 ('94, $6.95, 52 pgs.)-Painted-c 7.00
...Summer Special 1 ('92, $5.95, 68 pgs.) 6.00

CLIVE BARKER'S NIGHTBREED (Also see Epic)
Marvel Comics (Epic Comics): Apr, 1990 - No. 25, Mar, 1993 ($1.95/$2.25/$2.50, mature readers)

1-25: 1-4-Adapt horror movie. 5-New stories; Guice-a(p) 2.50

CLIVE BARKER'S THE HARROWERS
Marvel Comics (Epic Comics): Dec, 1993 - No. 6, May, 1994 ($2.50)

1-($2.95)-Glow-in-the-dark-c; Colan-c/a in all 3.00
2-6 2.50

NOTE: ***Colan** a(p)-1-6; c-1-3, 4p, 5p. **Williamson** a(i)-2, 4, 5(part).*

CLOAK AND DAGGER
Ziff-Davis Publishing Co.: Fall, 1952

1-Saunders painted-c 26.00 77.00 205.00

CLOAK AND DAGGER (Also see Marvel Fanfare)
Marvel Comics Group: Oct, 1983 - No. 4, Jan, 1984 (Mini-series) (See Spectacular Spider-Man #64)

1-4-Austin-c/a(i) in all. 4-Origin 2.00

CLOAK AND DAGGER (2nd Series)(Also see Marvel Graphic Novel #34 & Strange Tales)
Marvel Comics Group: July, 1985 - No. 11, Jan, 1987

1-11: 9-Art Adams-p 2.00
...And Power Pack (1990, $7.95, 68 pgs.) 8.00

NOTE: ***Mignola** c-7, 8.*

CLOAK AND DAGGER (3rd Series listed as Mutant Misadventures Of...)

CLOBBERIN' TIME
Marvel Comics: Sept, 1995 ($1.95) (Based on card game)

nn-Overpower game guide; Ben Grimm story 2.00

CLONEZONE SPECIAL
Dark Horse Comics/First Comics: 1989 ($2.00, B&W)

1-Back-up series from Badger & Nexus 2.00

CLOSE ENCOUNTERS (See Marvel Comics Super Special & Marvel Special Edition)

CLOSE SHAVES OF PAULINE PERIL, THE (TV cartoon)
Gold Key: June, 1970 - No. 4, March, 1971

1 2.50 7.50 25.00
2-4 2.00 6.00 18.00

CLOWN COMICS (No. 1 titled Clown Comic Book)
Clown Comics/Home Comics/Harvey Publ.: 1945 - No. 3, Win, 1946

nn (#1) 10.50 32.00 85.00
2,3 7.15 21.50 50.00

CLOWNS, THE (I Pagliacci)
Dark Horse Comics: 1998 ($2.95, B&W, one-shot)

1-Adaption of the opera; P. Craig Russell-script 3.00

CLUBHOUSE RASCALS (#1 titled ...Presents?) (Also see Three Rascals)
Sussex Publ. Co. (Magazine Enterprises): June, 1956 - No. 2, Oct, 1956

1,2: The Brain app. 5.50 16.50 38.00

CLUB "16"
Famous Funnies: June, 1948 - No. 4, Dec, 1948

1-Teen-age humor 11.00 33.00 90.00
2-4 7.00 21.00 48.00

CLUE COMICS (Real Clue Crime V2#4 on)
Hillman Periodicals: Jan, 1943 - No. 15(V2#3), May, 1947

1-Origin The Boy King, Nightmare, Micro-Face, Twilight, & Zippo 105.00 316.00 1000.00
2 50.00 150.00 450.00
3-5 38.00 113.00 300.00
6,8,9: 8-Palais-c/a(2) 28.00 84.00 225.00
7-Classic torture-c 42.00 125.00 375.00
10-Origin/1st app. The Gun Master & begin series; content changes to crime 28.00 84.00 225.00
11 21.00 62.00 165.00
12-Origin Rackman; McWilliams-a, Guardineer-a(2) 27.00 81.00 215.00

Codename: Firearm #2 © MAL

Code of Honor #2 © MAR

Colossal Features Magazine #33 © FOX

	GD2.0	FN6.0	NM9.4
V2#1-Nightmare new origin; Iron Lady app.; Simon & Kirby-a	47.00	140.00	420.00
V2#2-S&K-a(2)-Bondage/torture-c; man attacks & kills people with electric iron. Infantino-a	48.00	145.00	435.00
V2#3-S&K-a(3)	48.00	145.00	435.00

CLUELESS SPRING SPECIAL (TV)
Marvel Comics: May, 1997 ($3.99, magazine sized, one-shot)

1-Photo-c from TV show 4.00

CLUTCHING HAND, THE
American Comics Group: July-Aug, 1954

1 36.00 108.00 290.00

CLYDE BEATTY COMICS (Also see Crackajack Funnies)
Commodore Productions & Artists, Inc.: October, 1953 (84 pgs.)

1-Photo front/back-c; movie scenes and comics 27.00 81.00 215.00

CLYDE CRASHCUP (TV)
Dell Publishing Co.: Aug-Oct, 1963 - No. 5, Sept-Nov, 1964

1-All written by John Stanley 12.50 37.50 150.00
2-5 11.30 34.00 135.00

COBALT BLUE (Also see Power Comics)
Innovation Publishing: Sept, 1989 - No. 2, Oct, 1989 ($1.95, 28 pgs.)

1,2-Gustovich-c/a/scripts 2.00
The Graphic Novel ($6.95, color, 52 pgs.)-r/1,2 7.00

CODE BLUE
Image Comics (Jet-Black): Apr, 1998 ($2.95, B&W)

1-Jimmie Robinson-s/a 3.00

CODE NAME: ASSASSIN (See 1st Issue Special)

CODENAME: DANGER
Lodestone Publishing: Aug, 1985 - No. 4, May, 1986 ($1.50)

1-4 2.00

CODENAME DOUBLE IMPACT
High Impact Entertainment: 1997 ($2.95, B&W)

1,2 3.00

CODENAME: FIREARM (Also see Firearm)
Malibu Comics (Ultraverse): June, 1995 - No. 5, Sept, 1995 ($2.95, bimonthly limited series)

0-5: 0-2-Alec Swan back-up story by James Robinson 3.00
NOTE: *Perez c-0.*

CODENAME: GENETIX
Marvel Comics UK: Jan, 1993 - No. 4, May, 1993 ($1.75, limited series)

1-4: Wolverine in all 2.50

CODENAME SPITFIRE (Formerly Spitfire And The Troubleshooters)
Marvel Comics Group: No. 10, July, 1987 - No. 13, Oct, 1987

10-13: 10-Rogers-c/a 2.50

CODENAME: STRYKE FORCE (Also See Cyberforce V1#4 & Cyberforce/Stryke Force: Opposing Forces ($1.95-$2.25)
Image Comics (Top Cow Productions): Jan, 1994 - No. 14, Sept, 1995

0,1-14: 1-12-Silvestri stories, Peterson-a. 4-Stormwatch app. 14-Story continues in Cyberforce/Stryke Force: Opposing Forces; Turner-a 2.25
1-Gold, 1-Blue 4.00

CODE NAME: TOMAHAWK
Fantasy General Comics: Sept, 1986 ($1.75, high quality paper)

1-Sci/fi 2.00

CODE OF HONOR
Marvel Comics: Feb, 1997 - No. 4, May, 1997 ($5.95, limited series)

1-4-Fully painted by various; Dixon-s 6.00

CODY OF THE PONY EXPRESS (See Colossal Features Magazine)
Fox Features Syndicate: Sept, 1950 (See Women Outlaws)(One shot)

1-Painted-c 12.50 37.50 100.00

CODY OF THE PONY EXPRESS (Buffalo Bill...) (Outlaws of the West #11 on; Formerly Bullseye)
Charlton Comics: No. 8, Oct, 1955; No. 9, Jan, 1956; No. 10, June, 1956

8-Bullseye on splash pg; not S&K-a 7.00 21.00 48.00
9,10: Buffalo Bill app. in all 5.00 15.00 32.00

CODY STARBUCK (1st app. in Star Reach #1)
Star Reach Productions: July, 1978

nn-Howard Chaykin-c/a 1.00 2.80 7.00
2nd printing 5.00
NOTE: *Both printings say First Printing. True first printing is on lower-grade paper, somewhat off-register, and snow in snow sequence has green tint.*

CO-ED ROMANCES
P. L. Publishing Co.: November, 1951

1 6.40 19.25 45.00

COFFEE WORLD
World Comics: Oct, 1995 ($1.50, B&W, anthology)

1-Shannon Wheeler's Too Much Coffee Man story 2.00

COFFIN, THE
Oni Press: Sept, 2000 - No. 4 ($2.95, B&W, limited series)

1,2-Hester-s/Huddleston-a 2.95

COLLECTORS DRACULA, THE
Millennium Publications: 1994 - No. 2, 1994 ($3.95, color/B&W, 52 pgs., limited series)

1,2-Bolton-a (7 pgs.) 4.00

COLLECTORS ITEM CLASSICS (See Marvel Collectors Item Classics)

COLONIA
Colonia Press: 1998 ($2.95, B&W)

1-5-Jeff Nicholson-s/a 3.00

COLORS IN BLACK
Dark Horse Comics: Mar, 1995 - No. 4, June, 1995 ($2.95, limited series)

1-4 3.00

COLOSSAL FEATURES MAGAZINE (Formerly I Loved) (See Cody of the Pony Express)
Fox Features Syndicate: No. 33, 5/50 - No. 34, 7/50; No. 3, 9/50 (Based on Columbia serial)

33,34: Cody of the Pony Express begins. 33-Painted-c. 34-Photo-c 13.00 39.00 105.00
3-Authentic criminal cases 12.50 37.50 100.00

COLOSSAL SHOW, THE (TV)
Gold Key: Oct, 1969

1 4.35 13.00 48.00

COLOSSUS (See X-Men)
Marvel Comics: Oct, 1997 ($2.99, 48 pgs., one-shot)

1-Raab-s/Hitch & Nealy-a, wraparound-c 3.00

COLOSSUS COMICS (See Green Giant & Motion Picture Funnies Weekly)
Sun Publications (Funnies, Inc.?): March, 1940

1-(Scarce)-Tulpa of Tsang(hero); Colossus app. 429.00 1286.00 4500.00
NOTE: *Cover by artist that drew Colossus in Green Giant Comics.*

COLOUR OF MAGIC, THE (Terry Pratchett's...)
Innovation Publishing: 1991 - No. 4, 1991 ($2.50, limited series)

1-4: Adapts 1st novel of the Discworld series 3.00

COLT .45 (TV)
Dell Publishing Co.: No. 924, 8/58 - No. 1058, 11-1/59-60; No. 4, 2-4/60 - No. 9, 5-7/61

Four Color 924(#1)-Wayde Preston photo-c on all 9.00 27.00 110.00
Four Color 1004,1058, #4,5,7-9: 1004-Photo-b/c 7.00 21.00 85.00
6-Toth-a 8.00 24.00 95.00

COLUMBIA COMICS
William H. Wise Co.: 1943

1-Joe Palooka, Charlie Chan, Capt. Yank, Sparky Watts, Dixie Dugan app. 28.00 84.00 225.00

Combat Kelly #8 © MAR

Comedy Comics #14 © MAR

Comic Capers #6 © MAR

GD2.0 FN6.0 NM9.4 GD2.0 FN6.0 NM9.4

COLUMBUS
Dark Horse Comics: Sept, 1992 ($2.50, B&W, one-shot)

1-Yeates painted-c 2.50

COMANCHE (See Four Color No. 1350)

COMANCHEROS, THE
Dell Publishing Co.: No. 1300, Mar-May, 1962

Four Color 1300-Movie, John Wayne photo-c 15.00 45.00 180.00

COMBAT
Atlas Comics (ANC): June, 1952 - No. 11, April, 1953

1 23.00 68.00 180.00
2-Heath-c/a 11.00 33.00 90.00
3,5-9,11: 9-Robert Q. Sale-a 9.30 28.00 65.00
4-Krigstein-a 10.00 30.00 70.00
10-B&W and color illos. in **POP** 9.30 28.00 65.00
NOTE: *Combat Casey in 7-11.* ***Heath*** *c-1, 2, 9.* ***Maneely*** *a-1; c-3.* ***Pakula*** *a-1.* ***Reinman*** *a-1.*

COMBAT
Dell Publishing Co.: Oct-Nov, 1961 - No. 40, Oct, 1973 (No #9)

1 4.55 13.65 50.00
2,3,5: 2.80 8.40 28.00
4-John F. Kennedy c/story (P.T. 109) 3.45 10.35 38.00
6,7,8(4-6/63), 8(7-9/63) 2.50 7.50 24.00
10-26: 26-Last 12¢ issue 2.00 6.00 18.00
27-40(reprints #1-14). 30-r/#4 1.75 5.25 14.00
NOTE: ***Glanzman*** *c/a-1-27, 28-40r.*

COMBAT CASEY (Formerly War Combat)
Atlas Comics (SAI): No. 6, Jan, 1953 - No. 34, July, 1957

6 (Indicia shows 1/52 in error) 14.00 41.00 110.00
7-Spanking panel 8.65 26.00 60.00
8-Used in **POP**, pg. 94 7.15 21.50 50.00
9 6.40 19.25 45.00
10,13-19-Violent art by R. Q. Sale; Battle Brady x-over #10 10.00 30.00 80.00
11,12,20-Last Precode (2/55) 6.40 19.25 45.00
21-34 5.70 17.00 40.00
NOTE: ***Everett*** *a-6.* ***Heath*** *c-10, 17, 19, 30.* ***Maneely*** *c-6, 8.* ***Powell*** *a-29(5), 30(5), 34.* ***Severin*** *c-26, 33.*

COMBAT KELLY
Atlas Comics (SPI): Nov, 1951 - No. 44, Aug, 1957

1-1st app. Combat Kelly; Heath-a 28.00 83.00 220.00
2 12.50 37.50 100.00
3-10 10.00 30.00 75.00
11-Used in **POP**, pgs. 94,95 plus color illo. 8.65 26.00 60.00
12-Color illo. in **POP** 8.65 26.00 60.00
13-16 7.15 21.50 50.00
17-Violent art by R. Q. Sale; Combat Casey app. 10.00 30.00 80.00
18-20,22-44: 18-Battle Brady app. 28-Last precode (1/55). 38-Green Berets story (8/56) 6.40 19.25 45.00
21-Transvestism-c 7.00 21.00 48.00
NOTE: ***Berg*** *a-8, 12-14, 16, 17, 19-23, 25, 26, 28, 31-36, 42-44; c-2.* ***Colan*** *a-42.* ***Heath*** *a-4; c-31.* ***Lawrence*** *a-23.* ***Maneely*** *a-4(2), 6, 7(3), 8; c-4, 5, 7, 8, 10, 25.* ***R.Q. Sale*** *a-17, 25.* ***Severin*** *c-41, 42.* ***Whitney*** *a-5.*

COMBAT KELLY (...and the Deadly Dozen)
Marvel Comics Group: June, 1972 - No. 9, Oct, 1973

1-Intro & origin new Combat Kelly; Ayers/Mooney-a; Severin-c (20¢) 2.00 6.00 18.00
2,5-8 1.25 3.75 10.00
3,4: 3-Origin. 4-Sgt. Fury-c/s 1.75 5.25 14.00
9-Death of the Deadly Dozen 2.00 6.00 16.00

COMBINED OPERATIONS (See The Story of the Commandos)

COMEBACK (See Zane Grey 4-Color 357)

COMEDY CARNIVAL
St. John Publishing Co.: no date (1950's) (100 pgs.)

nn-Contains rebound St. John comics 34.00 103.00 275.00

COMEDY COMICS (1st Series) (Daring Mystery #1-8) (Becomes Margie Comics #35 on)
Timely Comics (TCI 9,10): No. 9, April, 1942 - No. 34, Fall, 1946

9-(Scarce)-The Fin by Everett, Capt. Dash, Citizen V, & The Silver Scorpion app.; Wolverton-a; 1st app. Comedy Kid; satire on Hitler & Stalin; The Fin, Citizen V & Silver Scorpion cont. from Daring Mystery 247.00 741.00 2350.00
10-(Scarce)-Origin The Fourth Musketeer, Victory Boys; Monstro, the Mighty app. 176.00 529.00 1675.00
11-Vagabond, Stuporman app. 50.00 150.00 450.00
12,13 14.00 41.00 110.00
14-Origin/1st app. Super Rabbit (3/43) plus-c 50.00 150.00 450.00
15-20 12.50 37.50 100.00
21-32 10.00 30.00 75.00
33-Kurtzman-a (5 pgs.) 12.00 36.00 95.00
34-Intro Margie; Wolverton-a (5 pgs.) 19.00 56.00 150.00

COMEDY COMICS (2nd Series)
Marvel Comics (ACI): May, 1948 - No. 10, Jan, 1950

1-Hedy, Tessie, Millie begin; Kurtzman's "Hey Look" (he draws himself) 33.00 99.00 265.00
2 12.50 37.50 100.00
3,4-Kurtzman's "Hey Look" (?&3) 14.00 41.00 110.00
5-10 7.85 23.50 55.00

COMET, THE (See The Mighty Crusaders & Pep Comics #1)
Red Circle Comics (Archie): Oct, 1983 - No. 2, Dec, 1983

1,2: 1-Re-intro & origin The Comet; The American Shield begins. 2-Origin continues. Nino & Infantino art in both. Hangman in both 3.00

COMET, THE
DC Comics (Impact Comics): July, 1991 - No. 18, Dec, 1992 ($1.00/$1.25)

1 2.50
2-18: 4-Black Hood app. 6-Re-intro Hangman. 8-Web x-over. 10-Contains Crusaders trading card. 4-Origin. Netzer(Nasser) c(p)-11,14-17 2.00
Annual 1 (1992, $2.50, 68 pgs.)-Contains Impact trading card; Shield back-up story 2.50

COMET MAN, THE (Movie)
Marvel Comics Group: Feb, 1987 - No. 6, July, 1987 (limited series)

1-6: 3-Hulk app. 4-She-Hulk shower scene c/s. Fantastic 4 app. 5-Fantastic 4 app. 2.00
NOTE: ***Kelley Jones*** *a-1-6p.*

COMIC ALBUM (Also see Disney Comic Album)
Dell Publishing Co.: Mar-May, 1958 - No. 18, June-Aug, 1962

1-Donald Duck 7.50 22.50 90.00
2-Bugs Bunny 4.10 12.30 45.00
3-Donald Duck 5.85 17.50 70.00
4-6,8-10: 4-Tom & Jerry. 5-Woody Woodpecker. 6,10-Bugs Bunny. 8-Tom & Jerry. 9-Woody Woodpecker 3.20 9.60 35.00
7,11,15: Popeye. 11-(9-11/60) 4.10 12.30 45.00
12-14: 12-Tom & Jerry. 13-Woody Woodpecker. 14-Bugs Bunny 3.20 9.60 35.00
16-Flintstones (12-2/61-62)-3rd app. Early Cave Kids app. 6.70 20.00 80.00
17-Space Mouse (3rd app.) 4.10 12.30 45.00
18-Three Stooges; photo-c 6.70 20.00 80.00

COMIC BOOK
Marvel Comics-#1/Dark Horse Comics-#2: 1995 ($5.95, oversize)

1-Spumco characters by John K. 1.00 2.80 7.00
2-(Dark Horse) 2.40 6.00

COMIC CAPERS
Red Circle Mag./Marvel Comics: Fall, 1944 - No. 6, Summer, 1946

1-Super Rabbit, The Creeper, Silly Seal, Ziggy Pig, Sharpy Fox begin 25.00 75.00 200.00
2 12.50 37.50 100.00
3-6 10.00 30.00 80.00

COMIC CAVALCADE
All-American/National Periodical Publications: Winter, 1942-43 - No. 63,

Comic Cavalcade #3 © DC

Comic Comics #3 © FAW

Comics' Greatest World: Hero Zero © DH

June-July, 1954 (Contents change with No. 30, Dec-Jan, 1948-49 on)

	GD2.0	FN6.0	VF8.0	NM9.4
1-The Flash, Green Lantern, Wonder Woman, Wildcat, The Black Pirate by Moldoff (also #2), Ghost Patrol, and Red White & Blue begin; Scribbly app.; Minute Movie	825.00	2475.00	5150.00	9500.00

	GD2.0	FN6.0	NM9.4
2-Mutt & Jeff begin; last Ghost Patrol & Black Pirate; Minute Movies	232.00	695.00	2200.00
3-Hop Harrigan & Sargon, the Sorcerer begin; The King app.	163.00	490.00	1550.00
4,5: 4-The Gay Ghost, The King, Scribbly, & Red Tornado app. 5-Christmas-c. 5-Prints ad for Jr. JSA membership kit that includes "The Minute Man Answers The Call"	142.00	426.00	1350.00
6-10: 7-Red Tornado & Black Pirate app.; last Scribbly. 9-Fat & Slat app.; X-Mas-c	105.00	316.00	1000.00
11,12,14,16-20: 12-Last Red White & Blue. 19-Christmas-c	90.00	269.00	850.00
13-Solomon Grundy app.; X-Mas-c	147.00	442.00	1400.00
15-Johnny Peril begins (1st app.,6-7/46), ends #29 (See Danger Trail & Sensation Mystery)	97.00	291.00	925.00
21-23: 23-Harry Lampert-c (Toth swipes)	84.00	253.00	800.00
24-Solomon Grundy x-over in Green Lantern	105.00	316.00	1000.00
25-28: 25-Black Canary app.; X-Mas-c. 26-28-Johnny Peril app. 28-Last Mutt & Jeff	74.00	221.00	700.00
29-(10-11/48)-Last Flash, Wonder Woman, Green Lantern & Johnny Peril; Wonder Woman invents "Thinking Machine"; 2nd computer in comics (after Flash Comics #52); Leave It to Binky story (early app.)	84.00	253.00	800.00
30-(12-1/48-49)-The Fox & the Crow, Dodo & the Frog & Nutsy Squirrel begin	40.00	120.00	360.00
31-35	23.00	69.00	185.00
36-49	16.00	49.00	130.00
50-62(Scarce)	20.00	60.00	160.00
63(Rare)	33.00	99.00	265.00

NOTE: **Grossman** *a-30-63.* **E.E. Hibbard** *c-(Flash only)-1-4, 7-14, 16-19, 21.* **Sheldon Mayer** *a(2-3)-40-63.* **Moulson** *c(G.L.)-7, 15.* **Nodell** *c(G.L.)-9.* **H.G. Peter** *c(W. Woman only)-1, 3-21, 24.* **Post** *a-31, 36.* **Purcell** *c(G.L.)-2-5, 10.* **Reinman** *a(Green Lantern)-4-6, 8, 9, 13, 15-21; c(Gr. Lantern)-6, 8, 19.* **Toth** *a(Green Lantern)-26-28; c-27. Atom app.-22, 23.*

COMIC COMICS
Fawcett Publications: Apr, 1946 - No. 10, Feb, 1947

1-Captain Kidd; Nutty Comics #1 in indicia	12.50	37.50	100.00
2-10-Wolverton-a, 4 pgs. each. 5-Captain Kidd app. Mystic Moot by Wolverton in #2-10?	14.00	41.00	110.00

COMIC CUTS (Also see The Funnies)
H. L. Baker Co., Inc.: 5/19/34 - 7/28/34 (5¢, 24 pgs.) (Tabloid size in full color) (Not reprints; published weekly; created for newsstand sale)

V1#1 - V1#7(6/30/34), V1#8(7/14/34), V1#9(7/28/34)-Idle Jack strips	10.00	30.00	70.00

COMIC LAND
Fact and Fiction Publ.: March, 1946

1-Sandusky & the Senator, Sam Stupor, Sleuth, Marvin the Great, Sir Passer, Phineas Gruff app.; Irv Tirman & Perry Williams art	14.00	41.00	110.00

COMICO CHRISTMAS SPECIAL
Comico: Dec, 1988 ($2.50, 44pgs.)

1-Rude/Williamson-a; Dave Stevens-c 4.00

COMICO COLLECTION (Also see Grendel)
Comico: 1987 ($9.95, slipcased collection)

nn-Contains exclusive Grendel: Devil's Vagary, 9 random Comico comics, a poster and newsletter in black slipcase w/silver ink 25.00

COMICO PRIMER (See Primer)

COMIC PAGES (Formerly Funny Picture Stories)
Centaur Publications: V3#4, July, 1939 - V3#6, Dec, 1939

V3#4-Bob Wood-a	70.00	210.00	660.00
5,6: 6-Schwab-c	53.00	158.00	475.00

COMICS (See All Good)

COMICS, THE
Dell Publ. Co.: Mar, 1937 - No. 11, Nov, 1938 (Newspaper strip-r; bi-monthly)

1-1st app. Tom Mix in comics; Wash Tubbs, Tom Beatty, Myra North, Arizona Kid, Erik Noble & International Spy w/Doctor Doom begin	179.00	537.00	1700.00
2	82.00	245.00	775.00
3-11: 3-Alley Oop begins	68.00	205.00	650.00

COMICS AND STORIES (See Walt Disney's Comics and Stories)

COMICS & STORIES (Also see Wolf & Red)
Dark Horse Comics: Apr, 1996 - No. 4, July, 1996 ($2.95, limited series) (Created by Tex Avery)

1-4: Wolf & Red app; reads Comics and Stories on-c. 1-Terry Moore-a. 2-Reed Waller-a. 3.00

COMICS CALENDAR, THE (The 1946...)
True Comics Press (ordered through the mail): 1946 (25¢, 116 pgs.) (Stapled at top)

nn-(Rare) Has a "strip" story for every day of the year in color	40.00	120.00	340.00

COMICS DIGEST (Pocket size)
Parents' Magazine Institute: Winter, 1942-43 (B&W, 100 pgs)

1-Reprints from True Comics (non-fiction World War II stories)	9.30	28.00	65.00

COMICS EXPRESS
Eclipse Comics: Nov, 1989 - No. 2, Jan, 1990 ($2.95, B&W, 68pgs.)

1,2: Collection of strip-r; 2(12/89-c, 1/90 inside) 3.00

COMICS FOR KIDS
London Publ. Co./Timely: 1945 (no month); No. 2, Sum, 1945 (Funny animal)

1,2-Puffy Pig, Sharpy Fox	14.00	41.00	110.00

COMICS' GREATEST WORLD
Dark Horse Comics: Jun, 1993 - V4#4, Sept, 1993 ($1.00, weekly, lim. series)

Arcadia (Wk 1): V1#1,2,4: 1-X: Frank Miller-c. 2-Pit Bulls. 4-Monster.			2.00
1-B&W Press Proof Edition (1500 copies)	1.25	3.75	10.00
1-Silver-c; distr. retailer bonus w/print & cards	1.00	3.00	8.00
3-Ghost, Dorman-c; Hughes-a			4.00
Retailer's Prem. Emb. Silver Foil Logo-r/V1#1-4	1.25	3.75	10.00
Golden City (Wk 2: V2#1-4: 1-Rebel; Ordway-c. 2-Mecha; Dave Johnson-c. 3-Titan; Walt Simonson-c. 4-Catalyst; Perez-c.			2.00
1-Gold-c; distr. retailer bonus w/print & cards.		2.40	6.00
Retailer's Prem. Embos. Gold Foil Logo-r/V2#1-4	1.00	3.00	8.00
Steel Harbor (Week 3): V3#1-Barb Wire; Dorman-c; Gulacy-a(p)			4.00
2-4: 2-The Machine. 3-Wolfgang. 4-Motorhead			2.00
1-Silver-c; distr. retailer bonus w/print & cards	1.00	3.00	8.00
Retailer's Prem. Emb. Red Foil Logo-r/V3#1-4.	1.25	3.75	10.00
Vortex (Week 4): V4#1-4: 1-Division 13; Dorman-c. 2-Hero Zero; Art Adams-c. 3-King Tiger; Chadwick-a(p); Darrow-c. 4-Vortex; Miller-c.			2.00
1-Gold-c; distr. retailer bonus w/print & cards.		2.40	6.00
Retailer's Prem. Emb. Blue Foil Logo-r/V4#1-4.	1.00	3.00	8.00

COMICS' GREATEST WORLD: OUT OF THE VORTEX (See Out of The Vortex)

COMICS HITS (See Harvey Comics Hits)

COMICS MAGAZINE, THE (...Funny Pages #3)(Funny Pages #6 on)
Comics Magazine Co. (1st Comics Mag./Centaur Publ.): May, 1936 - No. 5, Sept, 1936 (Paper covers)

	GD2.0	FN6.0	VF8.0
1-1st app. Dr. Mystic (a.k.a. Dr. Occult) by Siegel & Shuster (the 1st app. of a Superman prototype in comics). Dr. Mystic is not in costume but later appears in costume as a more pronounced prototype in More Fun #14-17. (1st episode of "The Koth and the Seven"; continues in More Fun #14; originally scheduled for publication at DC). 1 pg. Kelly-a; Sheldon Mayer-a	1350.00	4050.00	10,800.00

	GD2.0	FN6.0	NM9.4
2-Federal Agent (a.k.a. Federal Men) by Siegel & Shuster; 1 pg. Kelly-a	275.00	825.00	2200.00
3-5	225.00	675.00	1800.00

Comics on Parade #12 © UFS

Commander Battle and the Atomic Sub #6 © ACG

Complete Book of Comics & Funnies #1 © WHW

COMICS NOVEL (Anarcho, Dictator of Death)
Fawcett Publications: 1947

1-All Radar; 51 pg anti-fascism story 30.00 90.00 240.00

COMICS ON PARADE (No. 30 on are a continuation of Single Series)
United Features Syndicate: Apr, 1938 - No. 104, Feb, 1955

1-Tarzan by Foster; Captain & the Kids, Little Mary Mixup, Abbie & Slats, Ella Cinders, Broncho Bill, Li'l Abner begin 333.00 1000.00 3500.00
2 (Tarzan & others app. on-c of #1-3,17) 121.00 363.00 1150.00
3 95.00 285.00 900.00
4,5 74.00 221.00 700.00
6-10 53.00 158.00 475.00
11-16,18-20 42.00 125.00 375.00
17-Tarzan-c 50.00 150.00 450.00
21-29: 22-Son of Tarzan begins. 22,24,28-Tailspin Tommy-c. 29-Last Tarzan issue 38.00 113.00 300.00
30-Li'l Abner 23.00 69.00 185.00
31-The Captain & the Kids 16.00 48.00 125.00
32-Nancy & Fritzi Ritz 13.00 39.00 105.00
33,36,39,42-Li'l Abner 19.00 56.00 150.00
34,37,40-The Captain & the Kids (10/41,6/42,3/43) 16.00 48.00 125.00
35,38-Nancy & Fritzi Ritz. 38-Infinity-c 13.00 39.00 105.00
41-Nancy & Fritzi Ritz 10.00 30.00 80.00
43-The Captain & the Kids 16.00 48.00 125.00
44)3/44),47,50: Nancy & Fritzi Ritz 10.00 30.00 80.00
45-Li'l Abner 16.00 48.00 125.00
46,49-The Captain & the Kids 13.00 39.00 105.00
48-Li'l Abner (3/45) 16.00 48.00 125.00
51,54-Li'l Abner 13.00 39.00 105.00
52-The Captain & the Kids (3/46) 10.00 30.00 70.00
53,55,57-Nancy & Fritzi Ritz 10.00 30.00 70.00
56-The Captain & the Kids (r/Sparkler) 10.00 30.00 70.00
58-Li'l Abner; continues as Li'l Abner #61? 13.00 39.00 105.00
59-The Captain & the Kids 7.85 21.00 48.00
60-70-Nancy & Fritzi Ritz 6.85 21.00 48.00
71-99,101-104-Nancy & Sluggo: 71-76-Nancy only 6.00 18.00 42.00
100-Nancy & Sluggo 7.85 23.50 55.00
Special Issue, 7/46; Summer, 1948 - The Captain & the Kids app. 6.00 18.00 42.00

NOTE: Bound Volume (Very Rare) includes No. 1-12; bound by publisher in pictorial comic boards & distributed at the 1939 World's Fair and through mail order from ads in comic books (also see Tip Top) 253.00 758.00 2400.00
NOTE: *Li'l Abner reprinted from Tip Top.*

COMICS REVUE
St. John Publ. Co. (United Features Synd.): June, 1947 - No. 5, Jan, 1948

1-Ella Cinders & Blackie 10.00 30.00 75.00
2,4: 2-Hap Hopper (7/47). 4-Ella Cinders (9/47) 7.85 23.50 55.00
3,5: 3-Iron Vic (8/47). 5-Gordo No. 1 (1/48) 7.15 21.50 50.00

COMIC STORY PAINT BOOK
Samuel Lowe Co.: 1943 (Large size, 68 pgs.)

1055-Captain Marvel & a Captain Marvel Jr. story to read & color; 3 panels in color per pg. (reprints) 74.00 221.00 700.00

COMIX BOOK
Marvel Comics Group/Krupp Comics Works No. 4,5: 1974 - No. 5, 1976 ($1.00, B&W, magazine)

1-Underground comic artists; 2 pgs. Wolverton-a 2.50 7.50 24.00
2,3: 2-Wolverton-a (1 pg.) 2.30 7.00 20.00
4(2/76), 4(5/76), 5 (Low distribution) 2.50 7.50 23.00
NOTE: *Print run No. 1-3: 200-250M; No. 4&5: 10M each.*

COMIX INTERNATIONAL
Warren Magazines: Jul, 1974 - No. 5, Spring, 1977 (Full color, stiff-c, mail only)

1-Low distribution; all Corben story remainders from Warren 7.65 23.00 85.00
2,4: 2-Wood, Wrightson-r. 4-printing w/Corben sty 3.00 9.00 30.00
3-5: 4-(printing without Corben story). 4-Crandall-a. 5-Spirit story 2.50 7.50 24.00
NOTE: *No. 4 had two printings with extra **Corben** story in one. No. 3 may also have a variation. No. 3 has two Jeff Jones reprints from Vampirella.*

GD2.0 FN6.0 NM9.4

COMMANDER BATTLE AND THE ATOMIC SUB
Amer. Comics Group (Titan Publ. Co.): Jul-Aug, 1954 - No. 7, Aug-Sep, 1955

1 (3-D effect)-Moldoff flying saucer-c 47.00 140.00 420.00
2,4-7: 2-Moldoff-c. 4-(1-2/55)-Last pre-code; Landau-a. 5-3-D effect story (2 pgs.). 6,7-Landau-a. 7-Flying saucer-c 31.00 94.00 250.00
3-H-Bomb-c; Atomic Sub becomes Atomic Spaceship 33.00 98.00 260.00

COMMANDO ADVENTURES
Atlas Comics (MMC): June, 1957 - No. 2, Aug, 1957

1,2-Severin-c. 2-Drucker-a? 10.00 30.00 70.00

COMMANDO YANK (See The Mighty Midget Comics & Wow Comics)

COMPLETE BOOK OF COMICS AND FUNNIES
William H. Wise & Co.: 1944 (25¢, one-shot, 196 pgs.)

1-Origin Brad Spencer, Wonderman; The Magnet, The Silver Knight by Kinstler, & Zudo the Jungle Boy app. 40.00 120.00 340.00

COMPLETE BOOK OF TRUE CRIME COMICS
William H. Wise & Co.: No date (Mid 1940's) (25¢, 132 pgs.)

nn-Contains Crime Does Not Pay rebound (includes #22) 105.00 316.00 1000.00

COMPLETE COMICS (Formerly Amazing Comics No. 1)
Timely Comics (EPC): No. 2, Winter, 1944-45

2-The Destroyer, The Whizzer, The Young Allies & Sergeant Dix; Schomburg-c 147.00 442.00 1400.00

COMPLETE GUIDE TO THE DEADLY ARTS OF KUNG FU AND KARATE
Marvel Comics: 1974 (68 pgs., B&W magazine)

V1#1-Bruce Lee-c and 5 pg. story (scarce) 3.20 9.60 35.00

COMPLETE LOVE MAGAZINE (Formerly a pulp with same title)
Ace Periodicals (Periodical House): V26#2, May-June, 1951 - V32#4(#191), Sept, 1956

V26#2-Painted-c (52 pgs.) 6.00 18.00 42.00
V26#3-6(2/52), V27#1(4/52)-6(1/53) 5.00 15.00 30.00
V28#1(3/53), V28#2(5/53), V29#3(7/53)-6(12/53) 4.00 12.00 24.00
V30#1(2/54), V30#1(#176, 4/54),2,4-6(#181, 1/55) 4.00 12.00 24.00
V30#3(#178)-Rock Hudson photo-c 5.00 15.00 30.00
V31#1(#182, 3/55)-Last precode 4.00 12.00 24.00
V31#2(5/55)-6(#187, 1/56) 4.00 10.00 20.00
V32#1(#188, 3/56)-4(#191, 9/56) 4.00 10.00 20.00
NOTE: *(34 total issues). Photo-c V27#5-on. Painted-c V26#3.*

COMPLETE MYSTERY (True Complete Mystery No. 5 on)
Marvel Comics (PrPI): Aug, 1948 - No. 4, Feb, 1949 (Full length stories)

1-Seven Dead Men 44.00 133.00 400.00
2-4: 2-Jigsaw of Doom! 3-Fear in the Night; Burgos-c/a (28 pgs.). 4-A Squealer Dies Fast 40.00 120.00 340.00

COMPLETE ROMANCE
Avon Periodicals: 1949

1-(Scarce)-Reprinted as Women to Love 40.00 120.00 320.00

CONAN (See Chamber of Darkness #4, Giant-Size..., Handbook of..., King Conan, Marvel Graphic Novel #19, 28, Marvel Treasury Ed., Power Record Comics, Robert E. Howard's..., Savage Sword of Conan, and Savage Tales)

CONAN: (Title Series): Marvel Comics

CONAN, 8/95 - No. 11, 6/96 ($2.95), 1-11: 4-Malibu Comic's Rune app. 3.00

...CLASSIC, 6/94 - No. 11, 4/95 ($1.50), 1-11: 1-r/Conan #1 by B. Smith, r/covers w/changes. 2-11-r/Conan #2-11 by Smith. 2-Bound w/cover to Conan The Adventurer #2 by mistake 2.00

...DEATH COVERED IN GOLD, 9/99 - No. 3, 11/99 ($2.99), 1-3-Roy Thomas-s/John Buscema-a 3.00

...FLAME AND THE FIEND, 8/00 - No. 3, 10/00 ($2.99), 1-3-Thomas-s 3.00

...RETURN OF STYRM, 9/98 - No. 3, 11/98 ($2.99), 1-3-Parente & Soresina-a; painted-c 3.00

...RIVER OF BLOOD, 6/98 - No. 3, 8/98 ($2.50), 1-3 2.50

...SCARLET SWORD, 12/98 - No. 3, 2/99 ($2.99), 1-3-Thomas-s/Raffaele-a

Conan Saga #57 © Conan Properties

Conan the Barbarian #100 © Conan Properties

Condorman #1 © WDC

3.00

CONAN SAGA, THE
Marvel Comics: June, 1987 - No. 97, Apr, 1995 ($2.00/$2.25, B&W, magazine)

1-Barry Smith-r; new Smith-c 5.00
2-27: 2-9,11-new Barry Smith-c. 13,15-Boris-c. 17-Adams-r.18,25-Chaykin-r. 22-r/Giant-Size Conan 1,2 4.00
28-97: 28-Begin $2.25-c. 31-Red Sonja-r by N. Adams/SSOC #1; 1 pg. Jeff Jones-r. 32-Newspaper strip-r begin by Buscema. 33-Smith/Conrad-a. 39-r/Kull #1('71) by Andru/Wood. 44-Swipes-c/Savage Tales #1. 57-Brunner-r/SSOC #30. 66-r/Conan Annual #2 by Buscema. 79-r/Conan #43-45 w/Red Sonja. 85-Based on Conan #57-63 2.50

NOTE: ***J. Buscema*** *r-32-on; c-86.* ***Chaykin*** *r-34.* ***Chiodo*** *painted c-63, 65, 66, 82.* ***G. Colan*** *a-47p.* ***Jusko*** *painted c-64, 83.* ***Kaluta*** *c-84.* ***Nino*** *a-37.* ***Ploog*** *a-50.* ***N. Redondo*** *painted c-48, 50, 51, 53, 57, 62.* ***Simonson*** *r-50-54, 56.* ***B. Smith*** *r-51.* ***Starlin*** *c-34.* ***Williamson*** *r-50i.*

CONAN THE ADVENTURER
Marvel Comics: June, 1994 - No. 14, July, 1995 ($1.50)

1-($2.50)-Embossed foil-c; Kayaran-a 2.50
2-14 2.00
2-Contents are Conan Classics #2 by mistake 2.00

CONAN THE BARBARIAN
Marvel Comics: Oct, 1970 - No. 275, Dec, 1993

1-Origin/1st app. Conan (in comics) by Barry Smith; 1st app. Kull (cameo); #1-9 are 15¢ issues 22.00 65.00 240.00
2 7.65 23.00 85.00
3-(Low distribution in some areas) 13.50 40.00 150.00
4,5 5.45 16.35 60.00
6-9: 8-Hidden panel message, pg. 14. 9-Last 15¢-c 3.65 11.00 40.00
10,11 (25¢ 52 pg. giants): 10-Black Knight-r; Kull story by Severin 5.00 15.00 55.00
12,13: 12-Wrightson-c(i) 3.00 9.00 30.00
14,15-Elric app. 3.65 11.00 40.00
16,19,20: 16-Conan-r/Savage Tales #1 2.50 7.50 25.00
17,18-No Barry Smith-a 1.85 5.50 15.00
21,22: 22-Has reprint from #1 2.30 7.00 20.00
23-1st app. Red Sonja (2/73) 3.00 9.00 30.00
24-1st full Red Sonja story; last Smith-a 2.50 7.50 25.00
25-John Buscema-c/a begins 1.75 5.25 14.00
26-30 1.50 4.50 12.00
31-36,38-40 1.00 3.00 9.00
37-Neal Adams-c/a; last 20¢ issue; contains pull-out subscription form 1.75 5.25 14.00
41-43,46-50: 48-Origin retold 1.00 2.80 7.00
44,45-N. Adams-i(Crusty Bunkers). 45-Adams-c 1.10 3.30 9.00
51-57,59,60: 59-Origin Belit 5.00
58-2nd Belit app. (see Giant-Size Conan #1) 2.40 6.00
61-65-(Regular 25¢ editions)(4-8/76) 4.00
61-65-(30¢-c variants, limited distribution) 2.40 6.00
66-99: 68-Red Sonja story cont'd from Marvel Feature #7. 84-Intro. Zula. 85-Origin Zula. 87-r/Savage Sword of Conan #3 in color 3.50
100-(52 pg. Giant)-Death of Belit 5.00
101-114,116-249: 116-r/Power Record Comic PR31. 200-(52 pgs.). 232-Young Conan storyline begins; Conan is born. 244-Return of Zula. 2.00
115-Double size 3.00
250-(60 pgs.) 4.00
251-274: 262-Adapted from R.E. Howard story 3.00
275-($2.50, 68 pgs.)-Final issue; painted-c 4.00
King Size 1(1973, 35¢)-Smith-r/#2,4; Smith-c 2.00 6.00 16.00
Annual 2(1976, 50¢)-New full length story 2.40 6.00
Annual 3,4: 3('78)-Chaykin/N. Adams-r/SSOC #2. 4('78)-New full length story 1.00 2.80 7.00
Annual 5,6: 5(1979)-New full length Buscema story & part-c, 6(1981)-Kane-c/a 4.00
Annual 7-12: 7('82)-Based on novel "Conan of the Isles" (new-a). 8(1984). 9(1984). 10(1986). 11(1986). 12(1987) 3.00
Special Edition 1 (Red Nails) 4.00

NOTE: ***Arthur Adams*** *c-248, 249.* ***Neal Adams*** *a-116r(i); c-49i.* ***Austin*** *a-125, 126; c-125i, 126i.* ***Brunner*** *c-17i. c-40.* ***Buscema*** *a-25-36p, 38, 39, 41-56p, 58-63p, 65-67p, 68, 70-78p, 84-86p, 88-91p, 93-126p, 136p, 140, 141-144p, 146-158p, 159, 161, 162, 163p, 165-185p, 187-190p, Annual 2(3pgs.). 3-5p, 7p; c(p)-26, 36, 44, 46, 52, 56, 58, 59, 64, 65, 72, 78-80, 83-91, 93-103, 105-126, 136-151, 155-159, 161, 162, 168, 169, 171, 172, 174, 175, 178-185, 188, 189, Annual 4, 5, 7.* ***Chaykin*** *a-79-83.* ***Golden*** *c-152.* ***Kaluta*** *c-167.* ***Gil Kane*** *a-12p, 17p, 18p, 127-130, 131-134p; c-12p, 17p, 18p, 23, 25, 27-32, 34, 35, 38, 39, 41-43, 45-51, 53-55, 57, 60-63, 65-71, 73p, 76p, 127-134.* ***Jim Lee*** *c-242.* ***McFarlane*** *c-241p.* ***Ploog*** *a-57.* ***Russell*** *a-21; c-251i.* ***Simonson*** *c-135.* ***B. Smith*** *a-1-11p, 12, 13-15p, 16, 19-21, 23, 24; c-1-11, 13-16, 19-24p.* ***Starlin*** *a-64.* ***Wood*** *a-47r. Issue Nos. 3-5, 7-9, 11, 16-18, 21, 23, 25, 27-30, 35, 37, 38, 42, 45, 52, 57, 58, 65, 69-71, 73, 79-83, 99, 100, 104, 114, Annual 2 have original Robert E. Howard stories adapted. Issues #32-34 adapted from Norvell Page's novel* ***Flame Winds****.*

GD2.0 FN6.0 NM9.4

CONAN THE BARBARIAN (Volume 2)
Marvel Comics: July, 1997 - No. 3, Oct, 1997 ($2.50, limited series)

1-3-Castellini-a 2.50

CONAN THE BARBARIAN MOVIE SPECIAL (Movie)
Marvel Comics Group: Oct, 1982 - No. 2, Nov, 1982

1,2-Movie adaptation; Buscema-a 2.50

CONAN THE BARBARIAN: THE USURPER
Marvel Comics: Dec, 1997 - No. 3, Feb, 1998 ($2.50, limited series)

1-3-Dixon-s 2.50

CONAN THE DESTROYER (Movie)
Marvel Comics Group: Jan, 1985 - No. 2, Mar, 1985

1,2-r/Marvel Super Special 2.50

CONAN THE KING (Formerly King Conan)
Marvel Comics Group: No. 20, Jan, 1984 - No. 55, Nov, 1989

20-47 2.00
48-55 ($1.50) 3.00

NOTE: ***Kaluta*** *c-20-23, 24i, 26, 27, 30, 50, 52.* ***Williamson*** *a-37i; c-37i, 38i.*

CONAN: THE LORD OF THE SPIDERS
Marvel Comics: Mar, 1998 - No. 3, May, 1998 ($2.50, limited series)

1-3-Roy Thomas-s/Raffaele-a 2.50

CONAN THE SAVAGE
Marvel Comics: Aug, 1995 - No. 10, May, 1996 ($2.95, B&W, Magazine)

1-10: 1-Bisley-c. 4-vs. Malibu Comic's Rune. 5,10-Brereton-c 3.00

CONAN VS. RUNE (Also See Conan #4)
Marvel Comics: Nov, 1995 ($2.95, one-shot)

1-Barry Smith-c/a/scripts 3.00

CONCRETE (Also see Dark Horse Presents & Within Our Reach)
Dark Horse Comics: March, 1987 - No. 10, Nov, 1988 ($1.50, B&W)

1-Paul Chadwick-c/a in all 1.25 3.75 10.00
1-2nd print 3.00
2 2.40 6.00
3-Origin 5.00
4-10 4.00
A New Life 1 (1989, $2.95, B&W)-r/#3,4 plus new-a (11 pgs.) 3.00
Celebrates Earth Day 1990 ($3.50, 52 pgs.) 2.40 6.00
Color Special 1 (2/89, $2.95, 44 pgs.)-r/1st two Concrete apps. from Dark Horse Presents #1,2 plus new-a 2.40 6.00
Land And Sea 1 (2/89, $2.95, B&W)-r/#1,2 2.40 6.00
Odd Jobs 1 (7/90, $3.50)-r/5,6 plus new-a 3.50

CONCRETE: (Title series), **Dark Horse Comics**

--ECLECTICA, 4/93 - No. 2, 5/93 ($2.95) 1,2 3.00
--FRAGILE CREATURE, 6/91 - No. 4, 2/92 ($2.50) 1-4 2.50
--KILLER SMILE, (Legend), 7/94 - No. 4, 10/94 ($2.9) 1-4 3.00
--STRANGE ARMOR, 12/97 - No. 5, 5/98 ($2.95, color) 1-5-Chadwick-s/c/a; retells origin 3.00
--THINK LIKE A MOUNTAIN, (Legend), 3/96 - No. 6, 8/96 ($2.95)
1-6: Chadwick-a/scripts & Darrow-c in all 3.00

CONDORMAN (Walt Disney)
Whitman Publishing: Oct, 1981 - No. 3, Jan, 1982

1-3: 1,2-Movie adaptation; photo-c 2.40 6.00

CONEHEADS
Marvel Comics: June, 1994 - No. 4, 1994 ($1.75, limited series)

1-4 2.00

Confessions of Romance #8 © STAR

Congo Bill #3 © DC

Contest of Champions II #1 © MAR

GD2.0 FN6.0 NM9.4

CONFESSIONS ILLUSTRATED (Magazine)
E. C. Comics: Jan-Feb, 1956 - No. 2, Spring, 1956

1-Craig, Kamen, Wood, Orlando-a 16.00 49.00 130.00
2-Craig, Crandall, Kamen, Orlando-a 14.00 41.00 110.00

CONFESSIONS OF LOVE
Artful Publ.: Apr, 1950 - No. 2, July, 1950 (25¢, 7-1/4x5-1/4", 132 pgs.)

1-Bakerish-a 27.00 81.00 215.00
2-Art & text; Bakerish-a 15.00 45.00 120.00

CONFESSIONS OF LOVE (Formerly Startling Terror Tales #10; becomes Confessions of Romance No. 7 on)
Star Publications: No. 11, 7/52 - No. 14, 1/53; No. 4, 3/53- No. 6, 8/53

11-13: 12,13-Disbrow-a 15.00 45.00 120.00
14,5,6 10.50 32.00 85.00
4-Disbrow-a 12.00 36.00 95.00
NOTE: *All have* ***L. B. Cole*** *covers.*

CONFESSIONS OF ROMANCE (Formerly Confessions of Love)
Star Publications: No. 7, Nov, 1953 - No. 11, Nov, 1954

7 15.00 45.00 120.00
8 10.50 32.00 85.00
9-Wood-a 13.00 39.00 105.00
10,11-Disbrow-a 12.00 36.00 95.00
NOTE: *All have* ***L. B. Cole*** *covers.*

CONFESSIONS OF THE LOVELORN (Formerly Lovelorn)
American Comics Group (Regis Publ./Best Synd. Features): No. 52, Aug, 1954 - No. 114, June-July, 1960

52 (3-D effect) 28.00 84.00 225.00
53,55 8.65 26.00 60.00
54 (3-D effect) 28.00 84.00 225.00
56-Anti-communist propaganda story, 10 pgs; last pre-code (2/55) 10.00 30.00 80.00
57-90,100 5.00 15.00 35.00
91-Williamson-a 8.65 26.00 60.00
92-99,101-114 4.65 14.00 28.00
NOTE: ***Whitney*** *a-most issues; c-52, 53. Painted c-106, 107.*

CONFIDENTIAL DIARY (Formerly High School Confidential Diary; Three Nurses #18 on)
Charlton Comics: No. 12, May, 1962 - No. 17, Mar, 1963

12-17 2.00 6.00 18.00

CONGO BILL (See Action Comics & More Fun Comics #56)
National Periodical Publication: Aug-Sept, 1954 - No. 7, Aug-Sept, 1955

GD2.0 FN6.0 VF8.0
1 (Scarce) 112.00 338.00 900.00
2,7 (Scarce) 87.00 262.00 700.00
3-6 (Scarce). 4-Last pre-code issue 69.00 206.00 550.00
NOTE: *(Rarely found in fine to mint condition.)* ***Nick Cardy*** *c-1-7.*

CONGO BILL
DC Comics (Vertigo): Oct, 1999 - No. 4, Jan, 2000 ($2.95, limited series)

GD2.0 FN6.0 NM9.4
1-4-Corben-c 3.00

CONGORILLA (Also see Actions Comics #224)
DC Comics: Nov, 1992 - No. 4, Feb, 1993 ($1.75, limited series)

1-4: 1,2-Brian Bolland-c 2.00

CONJURORS
DC Comics: Apr, 1999 - No. 3, Jun, 1999 ($2.95, limited series)

1-3-Elseworlds; Phantom Stranger app.; Barreto-c/a 3.00

CONNECTICUT YANKEE, A (See King Classics)

CONQUEROR, THE
Dell Publishing Co.: No., 690, Mar, 1956

Four Color 690-Movie, John Wayne photo-c 16.00 48.00 190.00

CONQUEROR COMICS
Albrecht Publishing Co.: Winter, 1945

nn 19.00 56.00 150.00

GD2.0 FN6.0 NM9.4

CONQUEROR OF THE BARREN EARTH (See The Warlord #63)
DC Comics: Feb, 1985 - No. 4, May, 1985 (Limited series)

1-4: Back-up series from Warlord 2.00

CONQUEST
Store Comics: 1953 (6¢)

1-Richard the Lion Hearted, Beowulf, Swamp Fox 5.00 15.00 35.00

CONQUEST
Famous Funnies: Spring, 1955

1-Crandall-a, 1 pg.; contains contents of 1953 ish. 4.00 11.00 22.00

CONSPIRACY
Marvel Comics: Feb, 1998 - No. 2, Mar, 1998 ($2.99, limited series)

1,2-Painted art by Korday/Abnett-s 3.00

CONSTRUCT
Caliber (New Worlds): 1996 - No. 6, 1997 ($2.95, B&W, limited series)

1-6: Paul Jenkins scripts 3.00

CONTACT COMICS
Aviation Press: July, 1944 - No. 12, May, 1946

nn-Black Venus, Flamingo, Golden Eagle, Tommy Tomahawk begin 50.00 150.00 450.00
2-5: 3-Last Flamingo. 3,4-Black Venus by L. B. Cole. 5-The Phantom Flyer app. 40.00 120.00 340.00
6,11-Kurtzman's Black Venus; 11-Last Golden Eagle, last Tommy Tomahawk; Feldstein-a 42.00 125.00 375.00
7-10 38.00 113.00 300.00
12-Sky Rangers, Air Kids, Ace Diamond app.; L.B. Cole sci-fi cover 68.00 205.00 650.00
NOTE: ***L. B. Cole*** *a-3, 9; c-1-12.* ***Giunta*** *a-3.* ***Hollingsworth*** *a-5, 7, 10.* ***Palais*** *a-11, 12.*

CONTEMPORARY MOTIVATORS
Pendelum Press: 1977 - 1978 ($1.45, 5-3/8x8", 31 pgs., B&W)

14-3002 The Caine Mutiny; 14-3010 Banner in the Sky; 14-3029 God Is My Co-Pilot; 14-3037 Guadalcanal Diary; 14-3045 Hiroshima; 14-3053 Hot Rod; 14-3061 Just Dial a Number; 14-3088 The Diary of Anne Frank; 14-3096 Lost Horizon 1.00 2.80 7.00
NOTE: *Also see Pendulum Illustrated Classics. Above may have been distributed the same.*

CONTEST OF CHAMPIONS (See Marvel Super-Hero...)

CONTEST OF CHAMPIONS II
Marvel Comics: Sept, 1999 - No. 5 ($2.50, limited series)

1-5-Claremont-s/Jimenez-a 2.50

CONTRACTORS
Eclipse Comics: June, 1987 ($2.00, B&W, one-shot)

1-Funny animal 2.00

CONTRACT WITH GOD, A
Baronet Publishing Co./Kitchen Sink Press: 1978 ($7.95, B&W, graphic novel)

nn-Will Eisner-s/a 8.00
Reprint (DC Comics, 2000, $12.95) 13.00

CONVOCATIONS: A MAGIC THE GATHERING GALLERY
Acclaim Comics (Armada): Jan, 1996 ($2.50, one-shot)

1-pin-ups by various artists including Kaluta, Vess, and Dringenberg 2.50

COO COO COMICS (...the Bird Brain No. 57 on)
Nedor Publ. Co./Standard (Animated Cartoons): Oct, 1942 - No. 62, Apr, 1952

1-Origin/1st app. Super Mouse & begin series (cloned from Superman); the first funny animal super hero series (see Looney Tunes #5 for 1st funny animal super hero) 30.00 90.00 240.00
2 13.00 39.00 105.00
3-10: 10-(3/44) 8.65 26.00 60.00
11-33: 33-1 pg. Ingels-a 6.00 18.00 42.00
34-40,43-46,48-Text illos by Frazetta in all. 36-Super Mouse covers begin 10.00 30.00 75.00
41-Frazetta-a (6-pg. story & 3 text illos) 18.00 53.00 140.00
42,47-Frazetta-a & text illos. 12.50 37.50 100.00
49-(1/50)-3-D effect story; Frazetta text illo 10.00 30.00 80.00
50,51-3-D effect-c only. 50-Frazetta text illo 10.00 30.00 75.00

Cookie #8 © ACG

Cosmic Slam #1 © Ultimate Sports Ent. Inc.

Cosmo Cat #1 © FOX

	GD2.0	FN6.0	NM9.4
52-62: 56-Last Supermouse?	5.00	15.00	35.00

"COOKIE" (Also see Topsy-Turvy)
Michel Publ./American Comics Group(Regis Publ.): Apr, 1946 - No. 55, Aug-Sept, 1955

1-Teen-age humor	20.00	60.00	160.00
2	10.00	30.00	80.00
3-10	7.85	23.50	55.00
11-20	6.00	18.00	42.00
21-23,26,28-30	5.00	15.00	30.00
24,25,27-Starlett O'Hara stories	5.00	15.00	35.00
31-34,37-50,52-55	4.65	14.00	28.00
35,36-Starlett O'Hara stories	5.00	15.00	32.00
51-(10-11/54) 8pg. TrueVision 3-D effect story	8.65	26.00	60.00

COOL CAT (Formerly Black Magic)
Prize Publications: V8#6, Mar-Apr, 1962 - V9#2, July-Aug, 1962

V8#6, nn(V9#1, 5-6/62), V9#2 2.80 8.40 28.00

COOL WORLD (Movie)
DC Comics: Apr, 1992 - No. 4, Sept, 1992 ($1.75, limited series)

1-4: Prequel to animated/live action movie by Ralph Bakshi. 1-Bakshi-c. Bill Wray inks in all 2.00
Movie Adaptation nn ('92, $3.50, 68pg.)-Bakshi-c 3.50

COPPER CANYON (See Fawcett Movie Comics)

COPS (TV)
DC Comics: Aug, 1988 - No. 15, Aug, 1989 ($1.00)

1 ($1.50, 52 pgs.)-Based on Hasbro Toys 2.50
2-15: 14-Orlando-c(p) 2.00

COPS: THE JOB
Marvel Comics: June, 1992 - No. 4, Sept, 1992 ($1.25, limited series)

1-4: All have Jusko scripts & Golden-c 2.00

CORBEN SPECIAL, A
Pacific Comics: May, 1984 (one-shot)

1-Corben-c/a; E.A. Poe adaptation 5.00

CORKY & WHITE SHADOW (Disney, TV)
Dell Publishing Co.: No. 707, May, 1956 (Mickey Mouse Club)

Four Color 707-Photo-c 6.70 20.00 80.00

CORLISS ARCHER (See Meet Corliss Archer)

CORMAC MAC ART (Robert E. Howard's...)
Dark Horse Comics: 1990 - No. 4, 1990 ($1.95, B&W, mini-series)

1-4: All have Bolton painted-c; Howard adapts. 3.00

CORNY'S FETISH
Dark Horse Comics: Apr, 1998 ($4.95, B&W, one-shot)

1-Renée French-s/a; Bolland-c 5.00

CORPORAL RUSTY DUGAN (See Holyoke One-Shot #2)

CORPSES OF DR. SACOTTI, THE (See Ideal a Classical Comic)

CORSAIR, THE (See A-1 Comics No. 5, 7, 10)

CORTEZ AND THE FALL OF THE AZTECS
Tome Press: 1993 ($2.95, B&W, limited series)

1,2 3.00

CORUM: THE BULL AND THE SPEAR (See Chronicles Of Corum)
First Comics: Jan, 1989 - No. 4, July, 1989 ($1.95)

1-4: Adapts Michael Moorcock's novel 2.00

COSMIC BOOK, THE
Ace Comics: Dec, 1986 - No. 1, 1987 ($1.95)

1,2: 1-(44pgs.)-Wood, Toth-a. 2-(B&W) 2.00

COSMIC BOY (Also see The Legion of Super-Heroes)
DC Comics: Dec, 1986 - No. 4, Mar, 1987 (limited series)

1-4: Legends tie-ins all issues 2.00

COSMIC ODYSSEY
DC Comics: 1988 - No. 4, 1988 ($3.50, limited series, squarebound)

1-4: Reintro. New Gods into DC continuity; Superman, Batman, Green Lantern (John Stewart) app; Starlin scripts, Mignola-c/a in all. 2-Darkseid merges Demon & Jason Blood (separated in Demon limited series #4); John Stewart responsible for the death of a star system. 4.00
Trade paperback-r/#1-4. 20.00

COSMIC POWERS
Marvel Comics: Mar, 1994 - No. 6, Aug, 1994 ($2.50, limited series)

1-6: 1-Ron Lim-c/a(p). 1,2-Thanos app. 2-Terrax. 3-Ganymede & Jack of Hearts app. 2.50

COSMIC POWERS UNLIMITED
Marvel Comics: May, 1995 - No. 5, May, 1996 ($3.95, quarterly)

1-5 4.00

COSMIC RAY
Image Comics: June, 1999 - No. 2 ($2.95, B&W)

1,2-Steven Blue-s/a 3.00

COSMIC SLAM
Ultimate Sports Entertainment: 1999 ($3.95, one-shot)

1-McGwire, Sosa, Bagwell, Justice battle aliens; Sienkiewicz-c 3.95

COSMO CAT (Becomes Sunny #11 on; also see All Top & Wotalife Comics)
Fox Publications/Green Publ. Co./Norlen Mag.: July-Aug, 1946 - No. 10, Oct, 1947; 1957; 1959

	GD2.0	FN6.0	NM9.4
1	28.00	84.00	225.00
2	14.00	41.00	110.00
3-Origin (11-12/46)	19.00	56.00	150.00
4-10: 4-Robot-c	9.30	28.00	65.00
2-4(1957-Green Publ. Co.)	5.00	15.00	32.00
2-4(1959-Norlen Mag.)	4.65	14.00	28.00
I.W. Reprint #1	2.00	6.00	16.00

COSMO THE MERRY MARTIAN
Archie Publications (Radio Comics): Sept, 1958 - No. 6, Oct, 1959

1-Bob White-a in all	14.00	41.00	110.00
2-6	10.00	30.00	75.00

COTTON WOODS
Dell Publishing Co.: No. 837, Sept, 1957

Four Color 837 3.20 9.60 35.00

COUGAR, THE (Cougar No. 2)
Seaboard Periodicals (Atlas): April, 1975 - No. 2, July, 1975

1,2: 1-Vampire; Adkins-a(p). 2-Cougar origin; werewolf-s; Buckler-c(p) 5.00

COUNTDOWN (See Movie Classics)

COUNTDOWN
DC Comics (WildStorm): June, 2000 - No. 8, Jan, 2001 ($2.95)

1-8-Mariotte-s/Lopresti-a 3.00

COUNT DUCKULA (TV)
Marvel Comics: Nov, 1988 - No. 15, Jan, 1991 ($1.00)

1-7,9-15: Dangermouse back-ups. 4.00
8-Geraldo Rivera photo-c/& app.; Sienkiewicz-a(i) 5.00

COUNT OF MONTE CRISTO, THE
Dell Publishing Co.: No. 794, May, 1957

Four Color 794-Movie, Buscema-a 8.35 25.00 100.00

COURAGE COMICS
J. Edward Slavin: 1945

1,2,77 9.30 28.00 65.00

COURTSHIP OF EDDIE'S FATHER (TV)
Dell Publishing Co.: Jan, 1970 - No. 2, May, 1970

1-Bill Bixby photo-c on both	4.10	12.30	45.00
2	3.20	9.60	35.00

COVEN
Awesome Entertainment: Aug, 1997 - No. 5, Mar, 1998 ($2.50)

Preview	1.00	3.00	8.00
1-Loeb-s/Churchill-a; Churchill-c	1.00	3.00	8.00

Coven #4 © Awesome Ent.

Cowboy Love #3 © FAW

Cowgirl Romances #7 © FH

	GD2.0	FN6.0	NM9.4
1-Liefeld variant-c	1.00	2.80	7.00
1-Pollina variant-c	1.00	3.00	8.00
1-American Entertainment Ed.	1.00	3.00	8.00
1-American Entertainment Gold Ed.			10.00
1-Fan Appreciation Ed.(3/98); new Churchill-c			3.00
1-Fan Appreciation Gold Ed.			10.00
1+ :Includes B&W art from Kaboom	1.25	3.75	10.00
1+ :Gold Ed.			7.50
1+ :Red Foil cover			12.00
2-Regular-c w/leaping Fantom		2.40	6.00
2-Variant-c w/circle of candles	1.00	3.00	8.00
2-American Entertainment Gold Ed.			8.00
2-Dynamic Forces Gold Ed.			10.00
3-6-Contains flip book preview of ReGex			3.00
3-White variant-c	1.00	2.80	7.00
3,4: 3-Halloween wraparound-c. 4-Purple variant-c			3.00
4-Dynamic Forces Ed.			5.00
4,5-Dynamic Forces Gold Ed.	1.00	3.00	8.00
5-Dynamic Forces Ed.			4.00
...Black & White (9/98) Short stories			3.00
...Fantom Special (2/98) w/sketch pages			5.00
...Fantom Special Gold Ed.			10.00

COVEN
Awesome Entertainment: Jan, 1999 - Present ($2.50)

	GD2.0	FN6.0	NM9.4
1-3: 1-Loeb-s/Churchill-a; 6 covers by various. 2-Supreme-c/app. 3-Flip book w/Kaboom preview			2.50
... Dark Origins (7/99, 2.50) w/Lionheart gallery			2.50

COVERED WAGONS, HO (Disney, TV)
Dell Publishing Co.: No. 814, June, 1957 (Donald Duck)

	GD2.0	FN6.0	NM9.4
Four Color 814-Mickey Mouse app.	4.60	13.75	55.00

COWBOY ACTION (Formerly Western Thrillers No. 1-4; Becomes Quick-Trigger Western No. 12 on)
Atlas Comics (ACI): No. 5, March, 1955 - No. 11, March, 1956

	GD2.0	FN6.0	NM9.4
5	12.50	37.50	100.00
6-10: 6-8-Heath-c	10.00	30.00	70.00
11-Williamson-a (4 pgs.); Baker-a	10.00	30.00	80.00

NOTE: ***Ayers** a-8. **Drucker** a-6. **Maneely** c/a-5, 6. **Severin** c-10. **Shores** a-7.*

COWBOY COMICS (Star Ranger #12, Stories #14)(Star Ranger Funnies #15)
Centaur Publishing Co.: No. 13, July, 1938 - No. 14, Aug, 1938

	GD2.0	FN6.0	NM9.4
13-(Rare)-Ace and Deuce, Lyin Lou, Air Patrol, Aces High, Lee Trent, Trouble Hunters begin	121.00	363.00	1150.00
14-Filchock-c	84.00	253.00	800.00

NOTE: ***Guardineer** a-13, 14. **Gustavson** a-13, 14.*

COWBOY IN AFRICA (TV)
Gold Key: Mar, 1968

	GD2.0	FN6.0	NM9.4
1(10219-803)-Chuck Connors photo-c	4.10	12.30	45.00

COWBOY LOVE (Becomes Range Busters?)
Fawcett Publications/Charlton Comics No. 28 on: 7/49 - V2#10, 6/50; No. 11, 1951; No. 28, 2/55 - No. 31, 8/55

	GD2.0	FN6.0	NM9.4
V1#1-Rocky Lane photo back-c	19.00	56.00	150.00
2	7.15	21.50	50.00
V1#3,4,6 (12/49)	6.40	19.25	45.00
5-Bill Boyd photo back-c (11/49)	7.85	23.50	55.00
V2#7-Williamson/Evans-a	10.00	30.00	70.00
V2#8-11	5.00	15.00	35.00
V1#28 (Charlton)-Last precode (2/55) (Formerly Romantic Story?)	5.00	15.00	35.00
V1#29-31 (Charlton; becomes Sweetheart Diary #32 on)	5.00	15.00	30.00

NOTE: ***Powell** a-10. **Marcus Swayze** a-2, 3. Photo c-1-11. No. 1-3, 5-7, 9, 10 are 52 pgs.*

COWBOY ROMANCES (Young Men No. 4 on)
Marvel Comics (IPC): Oct, 1949 - No. 3, Mar, 1950 (All photo-c & 52 pgs.)

	GD2.0	FN6.0	NM9.4
1-Photo-c	23.00	69.00	185.00
2-William Holden, Mona Freeman "Streets of Laredo" photo-c	15.00	45.00	120.00
3-Photo-c	12.50	37.50	100.00

COWBOYS 'N' INJUNS (...and Indians No. 6 on)
Com No. 1-5/Magazine Enterprises No. 6 on: 1946 - No. 5, 1947; No. 6, 1949 - No. 8, 1952

	GD2.0	FN6.0	NM9.4
1	11.00	33.00	90.00
2-5-All funny animal western	8.65	26.00	60.00
6(A-1 23)-Half violent, half funny; Ayers-a	10.00	30.00	75.00
7(A-1 41, 1950), 8(A-1 48)-All funny	7.85	23.50	55.00
I.W. Reprint No. 1,7 (Reprinted in Canada by Superior, No. 7)	2.00	6.00	16.00
Super Reprint #10 (1963)	2.00	6.00	16.00

COWBOY WESTERN COMICS (TV)(Formerly Jack In The Box; Becomes Space Western No. 40-45 & Wild Bill Hickok & Jingles No. 68 on; title:Cowboy Western Heroes No. 47 & 48; Cowboy Western No. 49 on)
Charlton (Capitol Stories): No. 17, 7/48 - No. 39, 8/52; No. 46, 10/53; No. 47, 12/53; No. 48, Spr, '54;
No. 49, 5-6/54 - No. 67, 3/58 (nn 40-45)

	GD2.0	FN6.0	NM9.4
17-Jesse James, Annie Oakley, Wild Bill Hickok begin; Texas Rangers app.	19.00	56.00	150.00
18,19-Orlando-c/a. 18-Paul Bunyan begins. 19-Wyatt Earp story	11.00	33.00	90.00
20-25: 21-Buffalo Bill story. 22-Texas Rangers-c/story. 24-Joel McCrea photo-c & adaptation from movie "Three Faces West". 25-James Craig photo-c & adaptation from movie "Northwest Stampede"	10.00	30.00	75.00
26-George Montgomery photo-c and adaptation from movie "Indian Scout"; 1 pg. bio on Will Rogers	12.00	36.00	95.00
27-Sunset Carson photo-c & adapts movie "Sunset Carson Rides Again" plus 1 other Sunset Carson story	58.00	174.00	550.00
28-Sunset Carson line drawn-c; adapts movies "Battling Marshal" & "Fighting Mustangs" starring Sunset Carson	33.00	99.00	265.00
29-Sunset Carson line drawn-c; adapts movies "Rio Grande" with Sunset Carson & "Winchester '73" w/James Stewart plus 5 pg. life history of Sunset Carson featuring Tom Mix	33.00	99.00	265.00
30-Sunset Carson photo-c; adapts movie "Deadline" starring Sunset Carson plus 1 other Sunset Carson story	58.00	174.00	550.00
31-34,38,39,47-50 (no #40-45): 50-Golden Arrow, Rocky Lane & Blackjack (r?) stories	8.65	26.00	60.00
35,36-Sunset Carson-c/stories (2 in each). 35-Inside front-c photo of Sunset Carson plus photo on-c	33.00	99.00	265.00
37-Sunset Carson stories (2)	21.00	64.00	170.00
46-(Formerly Space Western)-Space western story	20.00	60.00	160.00
51-57,59-66: 51-Golden Arrow(r?) & Monte Hale-r renamed Rusty Hall. 53,54-Tom Mix-r. 55-Monte Hale story(r?). 66-Young Eagle story. 67-Wild Bill Hickok and Jingles-c/story	6.00	18.00	42.00
58-(1/56, 15¢, 68 pgs.)-Wild Bill Hickok, Annie Oakley & Jesse James stories; Forgione-a	8.65	26.00	60.00
67-(15¢, 68 pgs.)-Williamson/Torres-a, 5 pgs.	10.00	30.00	75.00

NOTE: *Many issues trimmed 1" shorter. **Maneely** a-67(5). Inside front/back photo c-29.*

COWGIRL ROMANCES (Young Men No. 4 on)
Marvel Comics (CCC): No. 28, Jan, 1950 (52 pgs.)

	GD2.0	FN6.0	NM9.4
28(#1)-Photo-c	20.00	60.00	160.00

COWGIRL ROMANCES
Fiction House Magazines: 1950 - No. 12, Winter, 1952-53 (No. 1-3: 52 pgs.)

	GD2.0	FN6.0	NM9.4
1-Kamen-a	34.00	101.00	270.00
2	17.00	51.00	135.00
3-5: 5-12-Whitman-c (most)	15.00	45.00	120.00
6-9,11,12	14.00	41.00	110.00
10-Frazetta?/Williamson?-a; Kamen?/Baker-a; r/Mitzi story from Movie Comics #4 w/all new dialogue	31.00	94.00	250.00

COW PUNCHER (...Comics)
Avon Periodicals: Jan, 1947; No. 2, Sept, 1947 - No. 7, 1949

	GD2.0	FN6.0	NM9.4
1-Clint Cortland, Texas Ranger, Kit West, Pioneer Queen begin; Kubert-a; Alabam stories begin	40.00	120.00	350.00
2-Kubert, Kamen/Feldstein-a; Kamen-c	35.00	105.00	280.00
3-5,7: 3-Kiefer story	25.00	75.00	195.00
6-Opium drug mention story; bondage, headlight-c; Reinman-a			

Crackajack Funnies #32 © DELL

Crack Comics #33 © QUA

Cracked #20 © Major Magazines

GD2.0 FN6.0 NM9.4

32.00 96.00 255.00

COWPUNCHER
Realistic Publications: 1953 (nn) (Reprints Avon's No. 2)
nn-Kubert-a 10.00 30.00 80.00

COWSILLS, THE (See Harvey Pop Comics)

COW SPECIAL, THE
Image Comics (Top Cow): Spring-Summer 2000 ($2.95)
1-Previews upcoming Top Cow projects; Yancy Butler photo-c 3.00

COYOTE
Marvel Comics (Epic Comics): June, 1983 - No. 16, Mar, 1986
1-10,15: 7-10-Ditko-a 2.00
11-1st McFarlane-a. 2.40 6.00
12-14,16: 12-14-McFarlane-a. 14-Badger x-over. 16-Reagan c/app. 4.00

CRACKAJACK FUNNIES (Also see The Owl)
Dell Publishing Co.: June, 1938 - No. 43, Jan, 1942
1-Dan Dunn, Freckles, Myra North, Wash Tubbs, Apple Mary, The Nebbs, Don Winslow, Tom Mix, Buck Jones, Major Hoople, Clyde Beatty, Boots begin 242.00 726.00 2300.00
2 97.00 291.00 925.00
3 71.00 213.00 675.00
4 53.00 158.00 475.00
5-Nude woman on cover 55.00 165.00 500.00
6-8,10: 8-Speed Bolton begins (1st app.) 42.00 125.00 375.00
9-(3/39)-Red Ryder strip-r begin by Harman; 1st app. in comics & 1st cover app. 126.00 379.00 1200.00
11-14 40.00 120.00 360.00
15-Tarzan text feature begins by Burroughs (9/39); not in #26,35 43.00 130.00 390.00
16-24: 18-Stratosphere Jim begins (1st app., 12/39). 23-Ellery Queen begins plus-c (1st comic book app., 5/40) 34.00 101.00 270.00
25-The Owl begins (1st app., 7/40); in new costume #26 by Frank Thomas (also see Popular Comics #72) 76.00 229.00 725.00
26-30: 28-Part Owl-c 53.00 158.00 475.00
31-Owl covers begin, end #42 55.00 165.00 500.00
32-Origin Owl Girl 58.00 174.00 550.00
33-38: 36-Last Tarzan issue. 37-Cyclone & Midge begin (1st app.) 47.00 140.00 420.00
39-Andy Panda begins (intro/1st app., 9/41) 55.00 165.00 500.00
40-42: 42-Last Owl-c. 40.00 120.00 350.00
43-Terry & the Pirates-r 36.00 108.00 290.00
NOTE: *McWilliams art in most issues.*

CRACK COMICS (Crack Western No. 63 on)
Quality Comics Group: May, 1940 - No. 62, Sept, 1949
1-Origin & 1st app. The Black Condor by Lou Fine, Madame Fatal, Red Torpedo, Rock Bradden & The Space Legion; The Clock, Alias the Spider (by Gustavson), Wizard Wells, & Ned Brant begin; Powell-a; Note: Madame Fatal is a man dressed as a woman 452.00 1357.00 5200.00
2 232.00 695.00 2200.00
3 158.00 474.00 1500.00
4 132.00 395.00 1250.00
5-10: 5-Molly The Model begins. 10-Tor, the Magic Master begins 103.00 308.00 975.00
11-20: 13-1 pg. J. Cole-a. 15-1st app. Spitfire 89.00 268.00 850.00
21-24: 23-Pen Miller begins; continued from National Comics #22. 24-Last Fine Black Condor 68.00 205.00 650.00
25,26: 26-Flag-c 55.00 165.00 525.00
27-(1/43)-Intro & origin Captain Triumph by Alfred Andriola (Kerry Drake artist) & begin series 103.00 308.00 975.00
28-30 47.00 140.00 420.00
31-39: 31-Last Black Condor 29.00 87.00 235.00
40-46 21.00 64.00 170.00
47-57,59,60-Capt. Triumph by Crandall 23.00 68.00 180.00
58,61,62-Last Captain Triumph 15.00 45.00 120.00
NOTE: *Black Condor by* **Fine**: *No. 1, 2, 4-6, 8, 10-24; by* **Sultan**: *No. 3, 7; by* **Fugitani**: *No. 9.* **Cole** *a-34.* **Crandall** *a-61(unsigned); c-48, 49, 51-61.* **Guardineer** *a-17.* **Gustavson** *a-1, 13, 17.* **McWilliams** *a-15-27. Black Condor c-2, 4, 6, 8, 10, 12, 14, 16, 18, 20-26. Capt. Triumph c-27-62. The Clock c-1, 3, 5, 7, 9, 11, 13, 15, 17, 19.*

CRACKED (Magazine) (Satire) (Also see The 3-D Zone #19)
Major Magazines(#1-212)/Globe Communications(#213-346/American Media #347 on): Feb-Mar, 1958 - Present
1-One pg. Williamson-a; Gunsmoke-s 13.50 40.00 150.00
2-1st Shut-Ups & Bonus Cut-Outs; Frankenstein-s 6.80 20.50 75.00
3-5 5.00 15.00 55.00
6-10: 7-Reprints 1st 6 covers on-c. 8-Frankenstein-c. 10-Wolverton-a 4.10 12.30 45.00
11-12, 13(nn,3/60), 3.25 9.75 36.00
14-17, 18(nn,2/61), 19,20: 14-Kirby-a 3.10 9.30 34.00
21-27(11/62), 27(No.28, 2/63; mis-#d), 29(5/63) 3.00 9.00 32.00
30-40(11/64): 37-Beatles and Superman cameos 3.00 9.00 30.00
41-45,47-56,59,60: 47,49,52-Munsters. 51-Beatles inside-c 59-Laurel and Hardy photos 2.80 8.40 28.00
46,57,58: 46,58-Man From U.N.C.L.E. 46-Beatles. 57-Rolling Stones 2.80 8.40 28.00
61-80: 62-Beatles cameo. 69-Batman, Superman app. 70-(8/68) Elvis cameo. 71-Garrison's Gorillas; W.C. Fields photos 2.00 6.00 18.00
81-99: 99-Alfred E. Neuman on-c 2.00 6.00 18.00
100 2.80 8.40 28.00
101-119: 104-Godfather-c/s. 108-Archie Bunker-s. 112,119-Kung Fu (TV) 113-Tarzan-s. 115-MASH. 117-Cannon. 118-The Sting-c/s 1.50 4.50 12.00
120(12/74) Six Million Dollar Man-c/s; Ward-a 2.00 6.00 16.00
121,122,124-126,128-133,136-140: 121-American Graffiti. 122-Korak-c/s. 124,131-Godfather-c/s. 128-Capone-c. 129,131-Jaws. 132-Baretta-c/s. 133-Space 1999. 136-Laverne and Shirley/Fonz-c. 137-Travolta/Kotter-c/s. 138-Travolta/Laverne and Shirley/Fonz-c. 139-Barney Miller-c/s. 140-King Kong-c/s; Fonz-s 1.50 4.50 12.00
123-Planet of the Apes-c/s; Six Million Dollar Man 2.00 6.00 16.00
127,134,135: 127-Star Trek-c/s; Ward-a. 134-Fonz-c/s; Starsky and Hutch. 135-Bionic Woman-c/s; Ward-a 1.75 5.25 14.00
141,151-Charlie's Angels-c/s. 151-Frankenstein 1.75 5.25 14.00
142,143,150,152-155,157: 142-MASH-c/s. 143-Rocky-c/s; King Kong-s. 150-(5/78) Close Encounters-c/s. 152-Close Enc./Star Wars-c/s. 153-Close Enc./Fonz-c/s. 154-Jaws II-c/s; Star Wars-s. 155-Star Wars/Fonz-c 1.50 4.50 12.00
144,149,156,158-160: 144-Fonz/Happy Days-c. 149-Star Wars/Six Mil.$ Man-c/s. 156-Grease/Travolta-c. 158-Mork & Mindy. 159-Battlestar Galactica-c/s; MASH-s. 160-Superman-c/s 1.60 4.85 13.00
145,147-Both have insert postcards: 145-Fonz/Rocky/L&S-c/s. 147-Star Wars-s; Farrah photo page (missing postcards-1/2 price) 2.30 7.00 20.00
146,148: 46-Star Wars-c/s with stickers insert (missing stickers-1/2 price). 148-Star Wars-c/s with inside-c color poster 2.50 7.50 23.00
161,170-Ward-a: 161-Mork & Mindy-c/s. 170-Dukes of Hazzard-c/s 1.10 3.30 9.00
162,165-168,171,172,175-178,180-Ward-a: 162-Sherlock Holmes-s. 165-Dracula-c/s. 167-Mork-c/s. 168,175-MASH-c/s. 168-Mork-s. 172-Dukes of Hazzard/CHiPs-c/s. 176-Barney Miller-c/s 1.00 3.00 8.00
163,179:163-Postcard insert; Mork & Mindy-c/s. 179-Insult cards insert; Popeye, Dukes of Hazzard-c/s 2.00 6.00 18.00
164,169,173,174: 164-Alien movie-c/s; Mork & Mindy-s. 169-Star Trek. 173,174-Star Wars-Empire Strikes Back. 173-SW poster 1.50 4.50 12.00
181,182,185-191,193,194,196-198-most Ward-a: 182-MASH-c/s. 185-Dukes of Hazzard-c/s; Jefferson-s. 187-Love Boat. 188-Fall Guy-s. 189-Fonz/Happy Days-c. 190,194-MASH-c/s. 191-Magnum P.I./Rocky-c; Magnum-s. 193-Knight Rider-s. 196-Dukes of Hazzard/Knight Rider-c/s. 198-Jaws III-c/s; Fall Guy-s 1.00 2.80 7.00
183,184,192,195,199,200-Ward-a in all: 183-Superman-c/s. 184-Star Trek-c/s. 192-E.T.-c/s; Rocky-s. 195-E.T.-c/s. 199-Jabba-c; Star Wars-s. 200-(12/83) 1.00 3.00 8.00
201,203,210-A-Team-c/s 2.40 6.00
202,204-206,211-224,226,227,230-233: 202-Knight Rider-s. 204-Magnum P.I.; A-Team-s. 206-Michael Jackson/Mr. T-c/s. 212-Prince-s; Cosby-s. 213-Monsters issue-c/s. 215-Hulk Hogan/Mr. T-c/s. 216-Miami Vice-s; James Bond-s. 217-Rambo-s; Cosby-s; A-Team-s. 218-Rocky-c/s. 219-Arnold/Commando-c/s; Rocky-s; Godzilla. 220-Rocky-c/s. 221-Stephen King app. 223-Miami Vice-s. 224-Cosby-s. 226-29th Anniv.; Tarzan-s; Aliens-s; Family

Cracked #265 © Globe Communications Corp.

Crack Western #83 © QUA

Crash Comics #5 © Tem Publishing Co.

Ties-s. 227-Cosby, Family Ties, Miami Vice-s. 230-Monkees-c/s; Elvis on-c; Gumby-s. 232-Alf, Cheers, StarTrek-s. 233-Superman/James Bond-c/s; Robocop, Predator-s 4.50
207-209,225,234: 207-Michael Jackson-c/s. 208-Indiana Jones-c/s. 209-Michael Jackson/Gremlins-c/s; Star Trek III-s. 225-Schwarzenegger/Stallone/G.I. Joe-c/s. 234-Don Martin-a begins; Batman/Robocop/Clint Eastwood-c/s 2.40 6.00
228,229: 228-Star Trek-c/s; Alf, Pee Wee Herman-s. 229-Monsters issue-c/s; centerfold with many superheroes 2.40 6.00
235,239,243,249: 235-1st Martin-c; Star Trek:TNG-s; Alf-s. 239-Beetlejuice-c/s; Mike Tyson-s. 243-X-Men and other heroes app. 249-Batman/Indiana Jones/ Ghostbusters-c/s 2.40 6.00
236,244,245,248: 236-Madonna/Stallone-c/s; Twilight Zone-s. 244-Elvis-c/s; Martin-c. 245-Roger Rabbit-c/s. 248-Batman issue 2.40 6.00
237,238,240-242,246,247,250: 237-Robocop-s. 238-Rambo-c/s; Star Trek-s. 242-Dirty Harry-s, Ward-a. 246-Alf-s; Star Trek-s., Ward-a. 247-Star Trek-s. 250-Batman/Ghostbusters-s 4.00
251-253,255,256,259,261-265,275-278,281,284,286-297,299: 252-Star Trek-s. 253-Back to the Future-c/s. 255-TMNT-c/s. 256-TMNT-c/s; Batman, Bart Simpson on-c. 259-Die Hard II, Robocop-s. 261-TMNT, Twin Peaks-s. 262-Rocky-c/s; Rocky Horror-s. 265-TMNT-s. 276-Aliens III, Batman-s. 277-Clinton-c. 284-Bart Simpson-c; 90210-s. 297-Van Damme-s/photo-c. 299-Dumb & Dumber-c/s 4.00
254,257,266,267,272,280,282,285,298,300: 254-Back to the Future, Punisher-s; Wolverton-a, Batman-s, Ward-a. 257-Batman, Simpsons-s; Spider-Man and other heroes app. 266-Terminator-c/s. 267-Toons-c/s. 272-Star Trek VI-s. 280-Swimsuit issue. 282-Cheers-c/s. 285-Jurassic Park-c/s. 298-Swimsuit issue; Martin-c. 300-(8/95) Brady Bunch-c/s 5.00
258,260,274,279,283: 258-Simpsons-c/s; Back to the Future-s. 260-Spider-Man -c/s; Simpsons-s. 274-Batman-c/s. 279-Madonna-c/s. 283-Jurassic Park-c/s; Wolverine app. inside back-c 5.00

	GD2.0	FN6.0	NM9.4
301-305,307-348			2.50
306-Toy Story-c/s			4.00
Biggest... (Winter, 1977)	2.00	6.00	16.00
Biggest, Greatest... nn('65)	3.20	9.60	35.00
Biggest, Greatest... 2('66) - #5('69)	2.50	7.50	23.00
Biggest, Greatest... 6('70) - #12('76)	2.00	6.00	18.00
...Blockbuster 1,2 ('88)	1.00	2.80	7.00
...Digest 1(Fall, '86, 148 pgs.) - #5	1.00	2.80	7.00
...Collectors' Edition 4 ('73; formerly ...Special)	1.75	5.25	14.00
5-10	1.75	5.25	14.00
11-30: 23-Ward-a	1.25	3.75	10.00
31-50	1.00	3.00	8.00
51-70		2.40	6.00
71-84: 83-Elvis, Batman parodies			4.00
...Party Pack 1,2('88)			4.00
...Shut-Ups (2/72-'72; Cracked Spec. #3) 1	2.50	7.50	23.00
2	1.75	5.25	14.00
...Special 3('73; formerly Cracked Shut-Ups; ...Collectors' Edition#4 on)	1.50	4.50	12.00
Extra Special... 1('76)	1.85	5.50	15.00
Extra Special... 2('76)	1.50	4.50	12.00
Giant... nn('65)	4.00	12.00	44.00
Giant... 2('66)-5('69)	2.80	8.40	28.00
Giant...6('70)-12('76)	2.50	7.50	23.00
Giant...nn(9/77)-24	2.00	6.00	16.00
Giant...25-35	1.50	4.50	12.00
Giant...36-48('87)	1.00	3.00	8.00
King Sized... 1('67)	3.80	11.40	42.00
King Sized... 2('68)-5('71)	2.80	8.40	28.00
King Sized... 6('72)-11('77)	2.50	7.50	22.00
King Sized... 12-17	1.50	4.50	12.00
King Sized... 18-22 (Sum/'86)	1.00	3.00	8.00
Super... 1('68)	3.20	9.60	35.00
Super... 2('69)-5	2.80	8.40	28.00
Super... 6-10	2.50	7.50	23.00
Super... 11-16	2.00	6.00	16.00
Super... 17-24('88)	1.50	4.50	12.00
Super... 1('87, 100 pgs.)-Severin & Elder-a	1.00	3.00	8.00

NOTE: ***Burgos*** *a-1-10.* ***Colan*** *a-257.* ***Davis*** *a-5, 11-17, 24, 40, 80; c-12-14, 16.* ***Elder*** *a-5, 6, 13; c-10.* ***Everett*** *a-1-10, 23-25, 61; c-1.* ***Heath*** *a-1-3, 6, 13, 14, 17, 110; c-6.* ***Jaffee*** *a-5, 6.* ***D Martin*** *c-235, 244, 247, 259, 261, 264.* ***Morrow*** *a-8-10.* ***Reinman*** *a-1-4.* ***Severin*** *c/a-in most issues.* ***Shores*** *a-3-7.* ***Torres*** *a-7-10.* ***Ward*** *a-22-24, 27, 35, 40, 120-193, 195, 197-205, 24 244, 246, 247, 250, 252-257.* ***Williamson*** *a-1 (1 pg.).* ***Wolverton*** *a-10 (2 pgs.), Giant nn('6* ***Wood*** *a-27, 35, 40. Alfred E. Neuman c-177, 200, 202. Batman c-234, 248, 249, 256, 27 Captain America c-256. Christmas c-234, 243. Spider-Man c-260. Star Trek c-127, 169, 207, 22 Star Wars c-145, 146, 148, 149, 152, 155, 173, 174, 199. Superman c-183, 233. #144, 146 ha free full-color pre-glued stickers. #145, 147, 155, 163 have free full-color postcards. #123, 13 154, 157 have free iron-ons.*

CRACKED MONSTER PARTY
Globe Communications: July, 1988 - No. 26, 1990?

1	1.50	4.50	12.0
2-10	1.00	3.00	8.0
11-26			5.0

CRACKED'S FOR MONSTERS ONLY
Major Magazines: Sept, 1969 - No. 9, Sept, 1969

1	3.20	9.60	35.0
2-9	2.00	6.00	18.0

CRACKED SPACED OUT
Globe Communications: Fall, 1993 - No. 4, 1994?

1-4			3.0

CRACK WESTERN (Formerly Crack Comics; Jonesy No. 85 on)
Quality Comics Group: No. 63, Nov, 1949 - No. 84, May, 1953
(36 pgs., 63-68,74-on)

63(#1)-Ward-c; Two-Gun Lil (origin & 1st app.)(ends #84), Arizona Ames, his horse Thunder (with sidekick Spurs & his horse Calico), Frontier Marshal (ends #70), & Dead Canyon Days (ends #69) begin; Crandall-a	22.00	66.00	175.0
64,65: 64-Ward-c. Crandall-a in both.	16.00	49.00	130.0
66,68-Photo-c. 66-Arizona Ames becomes A. Raines (ends #84)	14.00	41.00	110.0
67-Randolph Scott photo-c; Crandall-a	16.00	49.00	130.0
69(52pgs.)-Crandall-a	14.00	41.00	110.0
70(52pgs.)-The Whip (origin & 1st app.) & his horse Diablo begin (ends #84); Crandall-a	14.00	41.00	110.0
71(52pgs.)-Frontier Marshal becomes Bob Allen F. Marshal (ends #84); Crandall-c/a	16.00	49.00	130.0
72(52pgs.)-Tim Holt photo-c	13.00	39.00	105.0
73(52pgs.)-Photo-c	10.00	30.00	70.0
74-76,78,79,81,83-Crandall-c. 83-Crandall-a(p)	12.00	36.00	95.0
77,80,82	8.65	26.00	60.0
84-Crandall-c/a	13.00	39.00	105.0

NOTE: ***Crandall*** *c-71p, 74-81, 83p(w/****Cuidera****-i).*

CRASH COMICS (Catman Comics No. 6 on)
Tem Publishing Co.: May, 1940 - No. 5, Nov, 1940

1-The Blue Streak, Strongman (origin), The Perfect Human, Shangra begin (1st app. of each); Kirby-a	295.00	885.00	2800.0
2-Simon & Kirby-a	147.00	442.00	1400.0
3,5-Simon & Kirby-a	126.00	379.00	1200.0
4-Origin & 1st app. The Catman; S&K-a	295.00	885.00	2800.0

NOTE: *Solar Legion by* ***Kirby*** *No. 1-5 (5 pgs. each). Strongman c-1-4. Catman c-5.*

CRASH DIVE (See Cinema Comics Herald)

CRASH METRO AND THE STAR SQUAD
Oni Press: May, 1999 ($2.95, B&W, one-shot)

1-Allred-s/Ontiveros-a			3.0

CRASH RYAN (Also see Dark Horse Presents #44)
Marvel Comics (Epic): Oct, 1984 - No. 4, Jan, 1985 (Baxter paper, lim. series)

1-4			2.0

CRAZY (Also see This Magazine is Crazy)
Atlas Comics (CSI): Dec, 1953 - No. 7, July, 1954

1-Everett-c/a	26.00	79.00	210.0
2	19.00	56.00	150.0
3-7: 4-I Love Lucy satire. 5-Satire on censorship	15.00	45.00	120.0

NOTE: ***Ayers*** *a-5.* ***Berg*** *a-1, 2.* ***Burgos*** *c-5, 6.* ***Drucker*** *a-6.* ***Everett*** *a-1-4.* ***Al Hartley*** *a-4.* ***Hea*** *a-3, 7; c-7.* ***Maneely*** *a-1-7, c-3, 4.* ***Post*** *a-3-6. Funny monster c-1-4.*

Crazy #2 © MAR

Crazy Magazine #45 © MAR

Crazy Magazine #57 © MAR

GD2.0 FN6.0 NM9.4

CRAZY (Satire)
Marvel Comics Group: Feb, 1973 - No. 3, June, 1973

1-Not Brand Echh-r; Beatles cameo (r) 2.30 7.00 20.00
2,3-Not Brand Echh-r; Kirby-a 1.75 5.25 14.00

CRAZY MAGAZINE (Satire)
Oct, 1973 - No. 94, Apr, 1983 (40-90¢, B&W magazine)
Marvel Comics: (#1, 44 pgs; #2-90, reg. issues, 52 pgs; #92-95, 68 pgs)'

1-Wolverton(1 pg.), Bode-a; 3 pg. photo story of Neal Adams & Dick Giordano; Harlan Ellison story; TV Kung Fu sty. 3.00 9.00 32.00
2-"Live & Let Die" c/s; 8pgs; Adams/Buscema-a; McCloud w5 pgs. Adams-a; Kurtzman's "Hey Look" 2 pg.-r 2.50 7.50 23.00
3-5: 3-"High Plains Drifter" w/Clint Eastwood c/s; Waltons app; Drucker, Reese-a. 4-Shaft-c/s; Ploog-a; Nixon 3 pg. app; Freas-a. 5-Michael Crichton's "Westworld" c/s; Nixon app. 2.00 6.00 18.00
6,7,18: 6-Exorcist c/s; Nixon app. 7-TV's Kung Fu c/s; Nixon app.; Ploog & Freas-a. 18-Six Million Dollar Man/Bionic Woman c/s; Welcome Back Kotter story 1.85 5.50 15.00
8-10: 8-Serpico c/s; Casper parody; TV's Police Story. 9-Joker cameo; Chinatown story; Eisner s/a begins; Has 1st 8 covers on-c. 10-Playboy Bunny-c; M. Severin-a; Lee Marrs-a begins; "Deathwish" story 1.50 4.50 12.00
11-17,19: 11-Towering Inferno. 12-Rhoda. 13-"Tommy" the Who Rock Opera. 14-Mandingo. 15-Jaws story. 16-Santa/Xmas-c; "Good Times" TV story; Jaws. 17-Bi-Centennial ish; Baretta; Woody Allen. 19-King Kong c/s; Reagan, J. Carter, Howard the Duck cameos, "Laverne & Shirley" 1.10 3.30 9.00
20,24,27: 20-Bi-Centennial-c; Space 1999 sty; Superheroes song sheet, 4pgs. 24-Charlies Angels. 27-Charlies Angels/Travolta/Fonz-c; Bionic Woman sty 1.75 5.25 14.00
21-23,25,26,28-30: 21-Starskey & Hutch. 22-Mount Rushmore/J. Carter-c; TV's Barney Miller; Superheroes spoof. 23-Santa/Xmas-c; "Happy Days" sty; "Omen" sty. 25-J. Carter-c/s; Grandenetti-a begins; TV's Alice; Logan's Run. 26-TV Stars-c; Mary Hartman, King Kong. 28-Donny & Marie Osmond-c/s; Marathon Man. 29-Travolta/Kotter-c; "One Day at a Time", Gong Show. 30-1977, 84 pgs. w/bonus; Jaws, Baretta, King Kong, Happy Days 1.10 3.30 9.00
31,33-35,38,40: 31-"Rocky"-c/s; TV game shows. 33-Peter Benchley's "Deep". 34-J. Carter-c; TV's "Fish". 35-Xmas-c with Fonz/Six Million Dollar Man/ Wonder Woman/Darth Vader/Travolta, TV's "Mash" & "Family Matters". 38-Close Encounters of the Third Kind-c/s. 40-"Three's Company-c/s 1.00 2.80 7.00
32-Star Wars/Darth Vader-c/s; "Black Sunday" 2.00 6.00 16.00
36,42,47,49: 36-Farrah Fawcett/Six Million Dollar Man-c; TV's Nancy Drew & Hardy Boys; 1st app. Howard The Duck in Crazy, 2 pgs. 42-84 pgs. w/bonus; TV Hulk/Spider-Man-c; Mash, Gong Show, One Day at a Time, Disco, Alice. 47-Battlestar Galactica xmas-c; movie "Foul Play". 49-1979, 84 pgs. w/bonus; Mork & Mindy-c; Jaws, Saturday Night Fever, Three's Company 1.10 3.30 9.00
37-1978, 84 pgs. w/bonus. Darth Vader-c; Barney Miller, Laverne & Shirley, Good Times, Rocky, Donny & Marie Osmond, Bionic Woman 1.75 5.25 14.00
39,44: 39-Saturday Night Fever-c/s. 44-"Grease"-c w/Travolta/O. Newton-John 1.50 4.50 12.00
41-Kiss-c & 1pg. photos; Disaster movies, TV's "Family", Annie Hall 3.00 9.00 30.00
43,45,46,48,51: 43-Jaws-c; Saturday Night Fever; Stallone's "Fist".43-E.C. swipe from Mad #131 45-Travolta/O. Newton-John/J. Carter-c; Eight is Enough. 46-TV Hulk-c/s; Punk Rock. 48-"Wiz"-c, Battlestar Galactica-s. 51-Grease/Mork & Mindy/D&M Osmond-c, Mork & Mindy-sty. "Boys from Brazil" 1.00 2.80 7.00
50,58: 50-Superman movie-c/sty, Playboy Mag., TV Hulk, Fonz; Howard the Duck, 1 pg. 58-1980, 84 pgs. w/32 pg. color comic bonus insert-Full reprint of Crazy Comic #1, Battlestar Galactica, Charlie's Angels, Starsky & Hutch 1.75 5.25 14.00
52,59,60,64: 52-1979, 84 pgs. w/bonus. Marlon Brando-c; TV Hulk, Grease. Kiss, 1 pg. photos. 59-Santa Ptd-c by Larkin; "Alien", "Moonraker", Rocky-2, Howard the Duck, 1 pg. 60-Star Trek w/Muppets-c; Star Trek sty; 1st app/origin Teen Hulk; Severin-a. 64-84 pgs. w/bonus Monopoly game satire. "Empire Strikes Back", 8 pgs,.One Day at a Time. 1.75 5.25 14.00

GD2.0 FN6.0 NM9.4

53,54,65,67-70: 53-"Animal House"-c/sty; TV's "Vegas", Howard the Duck, 1 pg. 54-Love at First Bite-c/sty, Fantasy Island sty, Howard the Duck 1 pg. 65-(Has #66 on-c, Aug/'80). "Black Hole" w/Janson-a; Kirby,Wood/Severin-a(r), 5 pgs. Howard the Duck, 3 pgs.; Broderick-a; Buck Rogers, Mr. Rogers. 67-84 pgs. w/bonus; TV's Kung Fu, Excorcist; Ploog-a(r). 68-American Gigalo, Dukes of Hazzard, Teen Hulk; Howard the Duck, 3 pgs. Broderick-a; Monster sty/5 pg. Ditko-a(r). 69-Obnoxio the Clown-c/sty; Stephen King's "Shining", Teen Hulk, Richie Rich, Howard the Duck, 3pgs; Broderick-a. 70-84 pgs. Towering Inferno, Daytime TV; Trina Robbins-a 1.00 2.80 7.00
55-57,61,63: 55-84 pgs. w/bonus; Love Boat, Mork & Mindy, Fonz, TV Hulk. 56-Mork/Rocky/J. Carter-c; China Syndrome. 57-TV Hulk with Miss Piggy-c, Dracula, Taxi, Muppets. 61-1980, 84 pgs. Adams-a(r), McCloud, Pro wrestling, Casper, TV's Police Story. 63-Apocalypse Now-Coppola's cult movie; 3rd app. Teen Hulk, Howard the Duck, 3 pgs. 1.10 3.30 9.00
62-Kiss Ptd-c & 2 pg. app; Quincy, 2nd app. Teen Hulk 2.60 7.80 26.00
66-Sept/'80, Empire Strikes Back-c/sty; Teen Hulk by Severin, Howard the Duck, 3pgs. by Broderick 1.50 4.50 12.00
71,72,75-77,79: 71-Blues Brothers parody, Teen Hulk, Superheroes parody, WKRP in Cincinnati, Howard the Duck, 3pgs. by Broderick. 72-Jackie Gleason/Smokey & the Bandit II-c/sty, Shogun, Teen Hulk. Howard the Duck, 3pgs. by Broderick. 75-Flash Gordon movie c/sty; Teen Hulk, Cat in the Hat, Howard the Duck 3pgs. by Broderick. 76-84 pgs. w/bonus; Monster-sty w/ Crandall-a(r), Monster-stys(2) w/Kirby-a(r), 5pgs. ea; Mash, TV Hulk, Chinatown. 77-Popeye movie/R. Williams-c/sty; Teen Hulk, Love Boat, Howard the Duck 3 pgs. 79-84 pgs. w/bonus color stickers; has new material; "9 to 5" w/Dolly Parton, Teen Hulk, Magnum P.I., Monster-sty w/5pgs, Ditko-a(r), "Rat" w/Sutton-a(r), Everett-a, 4 pgs.(r) 1.00 2.80 7.00
73,74,78,80: 73-84 pgs. w/bonus Hulk/Spiderman Finger Puppets-c & bonus; "Live & Let Die, Jaws, Fantasy Island. 74-Dallas/"Who Shot J.R."-c/sty; Elephant Man, Howard the Duck 3pgs. by Broderick. 78-Clint Eastwood-c/sty; Teen Hulk, Superheroes parody, Lou Grant. 80-Star Wars, 2 pg. app; "Howling", TV's "Greatest American Hero" 1.10 3.30 9.00
81,84,86,87,89: 81-.Superman Movie II-c/sty; Wolverine cameo, Mash, Teen Hulk. 84-American Werewolf in London, Johnny Carson app; Teen Hulk. 86-Time Bandits-c/sty; Private Benjamin. 87-Rubix Cube-c; Hill Street Blues, "Ragtime", Origin Obnoxio the Clown; Teen Hulk. 89-Burt Reynolds "Sharkeys Machine", Teen Hulk 1.00 2.80 7.00
82-X-Men-c w/new Byrne-a, 84 pgs. w/new material; Fantasy Island, Teen Hulk, "For Your Eyes Only", Spiderman/Human Torch-r by Kirby/Ditko; Sutton-a(r); Rogers-a; Hunchback of Notre Dame, 5 pgs. 2.00 6.00 16.00
83-Raiders of the Lost Ark-c/sty; Hart to Hart; Reese-a; Teen Hulk 1.50 4.50 12.00
85,88: 85-84 pgs; Escape from New York, Teen Hulk; Kirby-a(r), 5 pgs, Posiedon Adventure, Flintstones, Sesame Street. 88-84 pgs. w/bonus Dr. Strange Game; some new material; Jeffersons, X-Men/Wolverine, 10 pgs.; Byrne-a; Apocalypse Now, Teen Hulk 1.10 3.30 9.00
90-94: 90-Conan-c/sty; M. Severin-a; Teen Hulk. 91-84 pgs, some new material; Bladerunner-c/sty, "Deathwish-II, Teen Hulk, Black Knight, 10 pgs.-'50s-r w/Maneely-a. 92-Wrath of Khan Star Trek-c/sty; Joanie & Chachi, Teen Hulk. 93-"E.T."-c/sty, Teen Hulk, Archie Bunkers Place, Dr. Doom Game. 94-Poltergeist, Smurfs, Teen Hulk, Casper, Avengers parody-8pgs. Adams-a. 1.75 5.25 14.00
Crazy Summer Special #1 (Sum, '75, 100 pgs.)-Nixon, TV Kung Fu, Babe Ruth, Joe Namath, Waltons, McCloud, Chariots of the Gods 2.00 6.00 16.00

NOTE: ***N. Adams** a-2, 61r, 94p. **Austin** a-82i. **Buscema** a-2, 82. **Byrne** c-82p. **Nick Cardy** c-7, 8, 10, 12-16, Super Special 1. **Crandall** a-76r. **Ditko** a-68r, 79r, 82r. **Drucker** a-3. **Eisner** a-9-16. **Kelly Freas** c-1-6, 9, 11; a-7. **Kirby/Wood** a-66r. **Ploog** a-1, 4, 7, 67r, 73r. **Rogers** a-82. **Sparling** a-92. **Wood** a-65r. Howard the Duck in 36, 50, 51, 53, 54, 59, 63, 65, 66, 68, 69, 71, 72, 74, 75, 77. Hulk in 46, c-42, 46, 57, 73. Star Wars in 32, 66; c-37.*

CRAZYMAN
Continuity Comics: Apr, 1992 - No. 3, 1992 ($2.50, high quality paper)

1-($3.95, 52 pgs.)-Embossed-c; N. Adams part-i 4.00
2,3 ($2.50): 2-N. Adams/Bolland-c 2.50

CRAZYMAN
Continuity Comics: V2#1, 5/93 - No. 4, 1/94 ($2.50, high quality paper)

V2#1-4: 1-Entire book is die-cut. 2-(12/93)-Adams-c(p) & part scripts. 3-(12/93).

Creed: Cranial Disorder #3 © Trent Kaniuga

The Creeper #4 © DC

Creepy #111 © WP

GD2.0 FN6.0 NM9.4

4-Indicia says #3, Jan. 1993 — 2.50

CRAZY, MAN, CRAZY (Magazine) (Becomes This Magazine is...?) (Formerly From Here to Insanity)
Humor Magazines (Charlton): V2#1, Dec, 1955 - V2#2, June, 1956

V2#1,V2#2-Satire; Wolverton-a, 3 pgs. — 12.50 37.50 100.00

CREATURE, THE (See Movie Classics)

CREATURE
Antarctic Press: Oct, 1997 - No. 2 ($2.95, B&W)

1,2-Don Walker-s/a — 3.00

CREATURE COMMANDOS
DC Comics: May, 2000 - No. 8, Dec, 2000 ($2.50, limited series)

1-8: Truman-s/Eaton-a — 2.50

CREATURES OF THE ID
Caliber Press: 1990 ($2.95, B&W)

1-Frank Einstein (Madman) app.; Allred-a — 3.00 9.00 30.00

CREATURES ON THE LOOSE (Formerly Tower of Shadows No. 1-9)(See Kull)
Marvel Comics: No. 10, March, 1971 - No. 37, Sept, 1975 (New-a & reprints)

10-(15¢)-1st full app. King Kull; see Kull the Conqueror; Wrightson-a — 3.65 11.00 40.00
11-15: 15-Last 15¢ issue — 2.00 6.00 16.00
16-Origin Warrior of Mars (begins, ends #21) — 1.50 4.50 12.00
17-20 — 1.00 3.00 8.00
21-Steranko-c — 1.25 3.75 10.00
22-Steranko-c; Thongor stories begin — 1.50 4.50 12.00
23-29-Thongor-c/stories — 5.00
30-Manwolf begins — 1.75 5.25 14.00
31-33 — 1.25 3.75 10.00
34-37 — 1.00 3.00 8.00

NOTE: ***Crandall** a-13. **Ditko** r-15, 17, 18, 20, 22, 24, 27, 28. **Everett** a-16i(new). **Matt Fox** r-21i. **Howard** a-26i. **Gil Kane** a-16p, 17p, 19i; c-16, 17, 19, 20, 25, 29, 33p, 35p, 36p. **Kirby** a-10-15r, 16(2)r, 17r, 19r. **Morrow** a-20, 21. **Perez** a-33-37; c-34p. **Shores** a-11. **innott** r-21. **Sutton** c-10. **Tuska** a-31p, 32p.*

CREECH, THE
Image Comics: Oct, 1997 - No. 3, Dec, 1997 ($1.95/$2.50, limited series)

1-3: 1-Capullo-s/c/a(p) — 2.50
TPB (1999, $9.95) r/#1-3, McFarlane intro. — 10.00

CREED
Hall of Heroes Comics: Dec, 1994 - No. 2, Jan, 1995 ($2.50, B&W)

1 — 1.85 5.50 15.00
2 — 1.50 4.50 12.00

CREED
Lightning Comics: June, 1995 - Present ($2.75/$3.00, B&W/color)

1-($2.75) — 4.00
1-($3.00, color) — 4.50
1-($9.95)-Commemorative Edition — 10.00
1-TwinVariant Edition (1250? print run) — 10.00
1-Special Edition; polybagged w/certificate — 4.00
1 Gold Collectors Edition; polybagged w/certificate — 3.00
2,3-($3.00, color)-Butt Naked Edition & regular-c — 3.00
3-($9.95)-Commemorative Edition; polybagged w/certificate & card — 10.00

CREED: APPLE TREE
Gearbox Press: Dec, 2000 - No. 2 ($2.95, B&W)

1,2-Kaniuga-s/c/a — 3.00

CREED: CRANIAL DISORDER
Lightning Comics: Oct, 1996 ($3.00, one-shot)

1-3-Two covers — 3.00
1-($5.95)-Platinum Edition — 6.00
2,3-($9.95)Ltd.l Edition — 10.00

CREED: MECHANICAL EVOLUTION
Gearbox Press: Sept, 2000 - No. 2, Oct, 2000 ($2.95, B&W)

1,2-Kaniuga-s/c/a — 3.00

CREED/TEENAGE MUTANT NINJA TURTLES

GD2.0 FN6.0 NM9.

Lightning Comics: May, 1996 ($3.00, one-shot)

1-Kaniuga-a(p)/scripts; Laird-c; variant-c exists — 3.0
1-($9.95)-Platinum Edition — 10.0
1-Special Edition; polybagged w/certificate — 5.0

CREED: USE YOUR DELUSION
Avatar Press: Jan, 1998 - No. 2, Feb, 1998 ($3.00, B&W)

1,2-Kaniuga-s/c/a — 3.0
1,2-($4.95) Foil cover — 5.0

CREEPER, THE (See Beware... , Showcase #73 & 1st Issue Special #7)
DC Comics: Dec, 1997 - No. 11; #1,000,000 Nov, 1998 ($2.50)

1-11-Kaminski-s/Martinbrough-a(p). 7,8-Joker-c/app. — 3.0
#1,000,000 (11/98) 853rd Century x-over — 2.5

CREEPSVILLE
Laughing Reindeer Press: V2#1, Winter, 1995 ($4.95)

V2#1-Comics w/text — 5.0

CREEPY (See Warren Presents)
Warren Publishing Co./Harris Publ. #146: 1964 - No. 145, Feb, 1983; No. 146 1985 (B&W, magazine)

1-Frazetta-a (his last story in comics?); Jack Davis-c; 1st Warren all comics magazine; 1st app. Uncle Creepy — 9.50 28.50 105.0
2-Frazetta-c & 1 pg. strip — 5.50 16.50 55.0
3-8,11-13,15-17: 3-7,9-11,15-17-Frazetta-c. 7-Frazetta 1 pg. strip. 15,16-Adams-a. 16-Jeff Jones-a — 3.50 10.50 28.0
9-Creepy fan club sketch by Wrightson (1st published-a); has 1/2 pg. anti-smoking strip by Frazetta; Frazetta-c; 1st Wood and Ditko art on this title; Toth-a — 5.00 15.00 50.0
10-Brunner fan club sketch (1st published work) — 4.35 13.00 35.0
14-Neal Adams 1st Warren work — 4.00 12.00 32.0
18-28,30,31: 27-Frazetta-c — 3.00 9.00 24.0
29,34: 29-Jones-a — 3.50 10.50 28.0
32-(scarce) Frazetta-c; Harlan Ellison sty — 5.60 17.00 45.0
33,35,37,39,40,42-47,49: 35-Hitler/Nazi-s. 39-1st Uncle Creepy solo-s, Cousin Eerie app.; early Brunner-a. 42-1st San Julian-c. 44-1st Ploog-a. 46-Corben-a — 2.75 8.25 22.0
36-(11/70)1st Corben art at Warren — 3.50 10.50 28.0
38,41-(scarce): 38-1st Kelly-c. 41-Corben-a — 4.35 13.00 35.0
48,55,65-(1972, 1973, 1974 Annuals) #55 & 65 contain an 8 pg. slick comic insert. 48-(84 pgs.). 55-Color poster bonus (1/2 price if missing). 65-(100 pgs.) Summer Giant — 3.75 11.25 30.0
50-Vampirella/Eerie/Creepy-c — 4.00 12.00 32.0
51,54,56-61,64: All contain an 8 pg. slick comic insert in middle. 59-Xmas horror. 54,64-Chaykin-a — 3.00 9.00 24.0
52,53,66,71,72,75,76,78-80: 71-All Bermejo-a; Space & Time issue. 72-Gual-a. 78-Fantasy issue. 79,80-Monsters issue — 2.00 6.00 14.0
62,63-1st & 2nd full Wrightson story art; Corben-a; 8 pg. color comic insert — 3.15 9.45 25.0
67,68,73 — 2.85 8.50 20.0
69,70-Edgar Allan Poe issues; Corben-a — 2.60 7.00 18.0
74,77: 74-All Crandell-a. 77-Xmas Horror issue; Corben-a,Wrightson-a — 3.15 9.45 22.0
81,84,85,88-90,92-94,96-99,102,104-112,114-118,120,122-130: 84,93-Sports issue. 85,97,102-Monster issue. 89-All war issue; Nino-a. 94-Weird Children issue. 96,109-Aliens issue. 99-Disasters. 103-Corben-a. 104-Robots issue. 106-Sword & Sorcery.107-Sci-fi. 116-End of Man. 125-Xmas Horror — 1.50 4.50 9.0
82,100,101: 82-All Maroto issue. 100-(8/78) Anniversary. 101-Corben-a — 2.15 6.45 15.0
83,95-Wrightson-a. 83-Corben-a. 95-Gorilla/Apes. — 2.00 6.00 12.0
86,87,91,103-Wrightson-a. 86-Xmas Horror — 2.00 6.00 12.0
113-All Wrightson-r issue — 2.85 8.50 20.0
119,121: 119-All Nino issue.121-All Severin-r issue — 2.00 6.00 12.0
131,133-136,138,140: 135-Xmas issue — 2.00 6.00 12.0
132,137,139: 132-Corben. 137-All Williamson-r issue. 139-All Toth-r issue — 2.15 6.45 15.0
141,143,144 (low dist.): 144-Giant, $2.25; Frazetta-c — 2.60 7.00 18.0
142,145 (low dist.): 142-(10/82, 100 pgs.) All Torres issue. 145-(2/83) last

Crime and Justice #7 © CC

Crime Clinic #4 © Z-D

Crime Does Not Pay #43 © LEV

Warren issue 2.60 7.00 18.00

146 ($2.95)-1st from Harris; resurrection issue 5.00 15.00 75.00

Year Book '68-'70: '70-Neal Adams, Ditko-a(r) 4.35 13.00 35.00

Annual 1971,1972 4.35 13.00 35.00

1993 Fearbook ($3.95)-Harris Publ.; Brereton-c; Vampirella by Busiek-s/Art Adams-a; David-s; Paquette-a 4.35 13.00 35.00

...:The Classic Years TPB (Harris/Dark Horse,'91, $12.95) Kaluta-c; art by Frazetta,Torres, Crandall, Ditko, Morrow, Williamson, Wrightson 25.00

NOTE: *All issues contain many good artists works:* ***Neal Adams, Brunner, Corben, Craig (Taycee), Crandall, Ditko, Evans, Frazetta, Heath, Jeff Jones, Krenkel, McWilliams, Morrow, Nino, Orlando, Ploog, Severin, Torres, Toth, Williamson, Wood, & Wrightson****; covers by* ***Crandall, Davis, Frazetta, Morrow, San Julian, Todd/Bode****; Otto Binder's "Adam Link" stories in No. 2, 4, 6, 8, 9, 12, 13, 15 with* ***Orlando*** *art.* ***Frazetta*** *c-2-7, 9-11, 15-17, 27, 32, 83r, 89r, 91r.* ***E.A. Poe*** *adaptations in 66, 69, 70.*

CREEPY (Mini-series)
Harris Comics/Dark Horse: 1992 - Book 4, 1992 (48 pgs, B&W, squarebound)

Book 1-4: Brereton painted-c on all. Stories and art by various incl. David (all), Busiek(2), Infantino(2), Guice(3), Colan(1) 1.50 4.50 12.00

CREEPY THINGS
Charlton Comics: July, 1975 - No. 6, June, 1976

1 1.75 5.25 14.00

2-6: Ditko-a in 3,5. Sutton c-3,4 1.00 3.00 8.00

Modern Comics Reprint 2-6(1977) 4.00

NOTE: ***Larson*** *a-2,6.* ***Sutton*** *a-1,2,4,6.* ***Zeck*** *a-2.*

CREMATOR
Chaos! Comics: Dec, 1998 - No. 5, May, 1999 ($2.95, limited series)

1-5-Leonardo Jimenez-s/a 3.00

CRIME AND JUSTICE (Badge Of Justice #22 on; Rookie Cop? No. 27 on)
Capitol Stories/Charlton Comics: March, 1951 - No. 21; No. 23 - No. 26, Sept, 1955 (No #22)

1 31.00 94.00 250.00

2 10.00 30.00 80.00

3-8,10-13: 6-Negligee panels 10.00 30.00 70.00

9-Classic story "Comics Vs. Crime" 23.00 69.00 185.00

14-Color illos in **POP**; gory story of man who beheads women 18.00 53.00 140.00

15-17,19-21,23-26; 15-Negligee panels. 23-26 (exist?) 6.40 19.25 45.00

18-Ditko-a 24.00 71.00 190.00

NOTE: ***Alascia*** *c-20.* ***Ayers*** *a-17.* ***Shuster*** *a-19-21; c-19. Bondage c-11, 12.*

CRIME AND PUNISHMENT (Title inspired by 1935 film)
Lev Gleason Publications: April, 1948 - No. 74, Aug, 1955

1-Mr. Crime app. on-c 31.00 94.00 250.00

2 16.00 49.00 130.00

3-Used in **SOTI**, pg. 112; injury-to-eye panel; Fuje-a 19.00 56.00 150.00

4,5 12.00 36.00 95.00

6-10 10.00 30.00 75.00

11-20 9.30 28.00 65.00

21-30 7.15 21.50 50.00

31-38,40-44,46: 46-One pg. Frazetta-a 6.00 18.00 42.00

39-Drug mention story "The 5 Dopes" 10.00 30.00 70.00

45- "Hophead Killer" drug story 10.00 30.00 70.00

47-57,60-65,70-74: 6.00 18.00 42.00

58-Used in **POP**, pg. 79 6.40 19.25 45.00

59-Used in **SOTI**, illo "What comic-book America stands for" 28.00 83.00 220.00

66-Toth-c/a(4); 3-D effect issue (3/54); 1st "Deep Dimension" process 36.00 108.00 290.00

67- "Monkey on His Back" heroin story; 3-D effect issue 31.00 94.00 250.00

68-3-D effect issue; Toth-c (7/54) 27.00 81.00 215.00

69- "The Hot Rod Gang" dope crazy kids 10.00 30.00 75.00

NOTE: ***Biro*** *c-most.* ***Everett*** *a-31.* ***Fuje*** *a-3, 4, 12, 13, 17, 18, 20, 26, 27.* ***Guardineer*** *a-2-4, 10, 14, 17, 18, 20, 26-28, 32, 38-44,54.* ***Kinstler*** *c-69.* ***McWilliams*** *a-41, 48, 49.* ***Tuska*** *a-28, 30, 51, 64, 70.*

CRIME AND PUNISHMENT: MARSHALL LAW TAKES MANHATTAN
Marvel Comics (Epic Comics): 1989 ($4.95, 52 pgs., direct sales only, mature)

nn-Graphic album featuring Marshall Law 5.00

CRIME CAN'T WIN (Formerly Cindy Smith)
Marvel/Atlas Comics (TCI 41/CCC 42,43,4-12): No. 41, 9/50 - No. 43, 2/51; No. 4, 4/51 - No. 12, 9/53

41(#1) 25.00 75.00 200.00

42(#2) 14.00 41.00 110.00

43(#3)-Horror story 17.00 51.00 135.00

4(4/51),5-12: 10-Possible use in **SOTI**, pg. 161 10.50 32.00 85.00

NOTE: ***Robinson*** *a-9-11.* ***Tuska*** *a-43.*

CRIME CASES COMICS (Formerly Willie Comics)
Marvel/Atlas Comics(CnPC No.24-8/MJMC No.9-12): No. 24, 8/50 - No. 27, 3/51; No. 5, 5/51 - No. 12, 7/52

24 (#1, 52 pgs.)-True police cases 16.00 49.00 130.00

25-27(#2-4): 27-Morisi-a 10.50 32.00 85.00

5-12: 11-Robinson-a. 12-Tuska-a 10.00 30.00 75.00

CRIME CLINIC
Ziff-Davis Publishing Co.: No. 10, July-Aug, 1951 - No. 5, Summer, 1952

10(#1)-Painted-c; origin Dr. Tom Rogers 27.00 81.00 215.00

11(#2),4,5: 4,5-Painted-c 19.00 56.00 150.00

3-Used in **SOTI**, pg. 18 20.00 60.00 160.00

NOTE: *All have painted covers by* ***Saunders. Starr*** *a-10.*

CRIME CLINIC
Slave Labor Graphics: May, 1995 - No. 2, Oct, 1995 ($2.95, B&W, limited series)

1,2 3.00

CRIME DETECTIVE COMICS
Hillman Periodicals: Mar-Apr, 1948 - V3#8, May-June, 1953

V1#1-The Invisible 6, costumed villains app; Fuje-c/a, 15 pgs. 26.00 79.00 210.00

2,5: 5-Krigstein-a 10.50 32.00 85.00

3,4,6,7,10-12: 6-McWilliams-a 10.00 30.00 75.00

8-Kirbyish-a by McCann 10.00 30.00 75.00

9-Used in **SOTI**, pg. 16 & "Caricature of the author in a position comic book publishers wish he were in permanently" illo. 35.00 105.00 280.00

V2#1,4,7-Krigstein-a: 1-Tuska-a 10.00 30.00 80.00

2,3,5,6,8-12 (1-2/52) 7.15 21.50 50.00

V3#1-Drug use-c 7.85 23.50 55.00

2-8 5.70 17.00 40.00

NOTE: ***Briefer*** *a-11, V3#1.* ***Kinstlerish-a*** *by* ***McCann****-V2#7, V3#2.* ***Powell*** *a-10, 11.* ***Starr*** *a-10.*

CRIME DETECTOR
Timor Publications: Jan, 1954 - No. 5, Sept, 1954

1 19.00 56.00 150.00

2 10.00 30.00 80.00

3,4 10.00 30.00 75.00

5-Disbrow-a (classic) 21.00 64.00 170.00

CRIME DOES NOT PAY (Formerly Silver Streak Comics No. 1-21)
Comic House/Lev Gleason/Golfing (Title inspired by film): No. 22, June, 1942 - No. 147, July, 1955 (1st crime comic)

22 (23 on cover, 22 on indicia)-Origin The War Eagle & only app.; Chip Gardner begins; #22 was rebound in Complete Book of True Crime (Scarce) 232.00 695.00 2200.00

23 (Scarce) 126.00 379.00 1200.00

24-Intro. & 1st app. Mr. Crime (Scarce). 100.00 300.00 950.00

25,26,28-30: 30-Wood and Biro app. 55.00 165.00 525.00

27-Classic Biro-c 60.00 180.00 575.00

31,32,34-40 38.00 113.00 300.00

33-Classic Biro Hanging & hatchet-c 40.00 120.00 350.00

41-Origin & 1st app. Officer Common Sense 28.00 83.00 220.00

42-Electrocution-c 34.00 101.00 270.00

43-46,48-50: 44,45,50 are 68 pg. issues 18.00 53.00 140.00

47-Electric chair-c 31.00 94.00 250.00

51-70: 63,64-Possible use in **SOTI**, pg. 306. 63-Contains Biro & Gleason's self censorship code of 12 listed restrictions (5/48) 16.00 48.00 125.00

71-99: 87-Chip Gardner begins, ends #100 12.50 37.50 100.00

Crime Exposed #10 © MAR

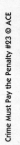

Crime Must Pay the Penalty #23 © ACE

Crime Patrol #13 © WMG

	GD2.0	FN6.0	NM9.4
100	13.00	39.00	105.00
101-104,107-110: 102-Chip Gardner app	10.00	30.00	75.00
105-Used in **POP**, pg. 84	10.50	32.00	85.00
106,114-Frazetta-a, 1 pg.	10.00	30.00	75.00
111-Used in **POP**, pgs. 80 & 81; injury-to-eye sty illo	10.00	30.00	75.00
112,113,115-130	7.85	23.50	55.00
131-140	5.70	17.00	40.00
141,142-Last pre-code issue; Kubert-a(1)	9.30	28.00	65.00
143-Kubert-a in one story	9.30	28.00	65.00
144-146	5.70	17.00	40.00
147-Last issue (scarce); Kubert-a	12.50	37.50	100.00
1(Golfing-1945)	6.00	18.00	42.00
The Best of...(1944, 128 pgs.)-Series contains 4 rebound issues	76.00	229.00	725.00
...1945 issue	58.00	174.00	550.00
...1946-48 issues	42.00	125.00	375.00
...1949-50 issues	40.00	120.00	325.00
...1951-53 issues	33.00	98.00	260.00

NOTE: *Many issues contain violent covers and stories. Who Dunnit by* ***Guardineer****-39-42, 44-105, 108-110; Chip Gardner by* ***Bob Fujitani (Fuje)****-88-103.* ***Alderman*** *a-29, 41-44, 49.* ***Dan Barry*** *a-75.* ***Biro*** *c-1-76, 122, 142.* ***Briefer*** *a-29(2), 30, 31, 33, 37, 39.* ***G. Colan*** *a-105.* ***Fuje*** *c-88, 89, 91-94, 96, 98, 99, 102, 103.* ***Guardineer*** *a-57, 71.* ***Kubert*** *c-143.* ***Landau*** *a-118.* ***Maurer*** *a-29, 39, 41, 42.* ***McWilliams*** *a-91, 93, 95, 100-103.* ***Palais*** *a-30, 33, 37, 39, 41-43, 44(2), 46, 49.* ***Powell*** *a-146, 147.* ***Tuska*** *a-48, 50(2), 51, 52, 56, 57(2), 60-64, 66, 67, 71. Painted c-87-102. Bondage c-43, 62, 98.*

CRIME EXPOSED
Marvel Comics (PPI)/Marvel Atlas Comics (PrPI): June, 1948; Dec, 1950 - No. 14, June, 1952

	GD2.0	FN6.0	NM9.4
1(6/48)	31.00	92.00	245.00
1(12/50)	19.00	56.00	150.00
2	13.00	39.00	105.00
3-9,11,14	10.00	30.00	80.00
10-Used in **POP**, pg. 81	10.50	32.00	85.00
12-Krigstein & Robinson-a	10.50	32.00	85.00
13-Used in **POP**, pg. 81; Krigstein-a	11.00	33.00	90.00

NOTE: ***Maneely*** *c-8.* ***Robinson*** *a-11, 12.* ***Tuska*** *a-3, 4.*

CRIMEFIGHTERS
Marvel Comics (CmPS 1-3/CCC 4-10): Apr, 1948 - No. 10, Nov, 1949

	GD2.0	FN6.0	NM9.4
1-Some copies are undated & could be reprints	24.00	73.00	195.00
2,3: 3-Morphine addict story	13.00	39.00	105.00
4-10: 6-Anti-Wertham editorial. 9,10-Photo-c	10.50	32.00	85.00

CRIME FIGHTERS (...Always Win)
Atlas Comics (CnPC): No. 11, Sept, 1954 - No. 13, Jan, 1955

	GD2.0	FN6.0	NM9.4
11-13: 11-Maneely-a,13-Pakula, Reinman, Severin-a	10.50	32.00	85.00

CRIME-FIGHTING DETECTIVE (Shock Detective Cases No. 20 on; formerly Criminals on the Run)
Star Publications: No. 11, Apr-May, 1950 - No. 19, June, 1952 (Based on true crime cases)

	GD2.0	FN6.0	NM9.4
11-L. B. Cole-c/a (2 pgs.); L. B. Cole-c on all	19.00	58.00	155.00
12,13,15-19: 17-Young King Cole & Dr. Doom app.	14.00	43.00	115.00
14-L. B. Cole-c/a, r/Law-Crime #2	16.00	49.00	130.00

CRIME FILES
Standard Comics: No. 5, Sept, 1952 - No. 6, Nov, 1952

	GD2.0	FN6.0	NM9.4
5-1pg. Alex Toth-a; used in **SOTI**, pg. 4 (text)	24.00	71.00	190.00
6-Sekowsky-a	12.00	36.00	95.00

CRIME ILLUSTRATED (Magazine)
E. C. Comics: Nov-Dec, 1955 - No. 2, Spring, 1956 (25¢, Adult Suspense Stories on-c)

	GD2.0	FN6.0	NM9.4
1-Ingels & Crandall-a	14.00	41.00	110.00
2-Ingels & Crandall-a	12.00	36.00	95.00

NOTE: ***Craig*** *a-2.* ***Crandall*** *a-1, 2; c-2.* ***Evans*** *a-1.* ***Davis*** *a-2.* ***Ingels*** *a-1, 2.* ***Krigstein/ Crandall*** *a-1.* ***Orlando*** *a-1, 2; c-1.*

CRIME INCORPORATED (Formerly Crimes Incorporated)
Fox Features Syndicate: No. 2, Aug, 1950; No. 3, Aug, 1951

	GD2.0	FN6.0	NM9.4
2	26.00	79.00	210.00
3(1951)-Hollingsworth-a	19.00	56.00	150.00

CRIME MACHINE (Magazine)
Skywald Publications: Feb, 1971 - No. 2, May, 1971 (B&W)

	GD2.0	FN6.0	NM9.4
1-Kubert-a(2)(r)(Avon)	5.00	15.00	55.00
2-Torres, Wildey-a; violent-c/a	3.20	9.60	35.00

CRIME MUST LOSE! (Formerly Sports Action?)
Sports Action (Atlas Comics): No. 4, Oct, 1950 - No. 12, April, 1952

	GD2.0	FN6.0	NM9.4
4-Ann Brewster-a in all; c-used in N.Y. Legis. Comm. documents	18.00	54.00	145.00
5-12: 9-Robinson-a. 11-Used in **POP**, pg. 89	12.00	36.00	95.00

CRIME MUST PAY THE PENALTY (Formerly Four Favorites; Penalty #47, 48)
Ace Magazines (Current Books): No. 33, Feb, 1948; No. 2, Jun, 1948 - No. 48, Jan, 1956

	GD2.0	FN6.0	NM9.4
33(#1, 2/48)-Becomes Four Teeners #34?	31.00	94.00	250.00
2(6/48)-Extreme violence; Palais-a?	20.00	60.00	160.00
3,4,8: 3- "Frisco Mary" story used in Senate Investigation report, pg. 7. 4,8-Transvestism stories	14.00	43.00	115.00
5-7,9,10	10.00	30.00	80.00
11-20-Drug story "Dealers in White Death"	10.00	30.00	70.00
21-32,34-40,42-48	6.40	19.25	45.00
33(7/53)- "Dell Fabry-Junk King" drug story; mentioned in Love and Death	10.00	30.00	70.00
41-reprints "Dealers in White Death"	7.15	21.50	50.00

NOTE: ***Cameron*** *a-29-31, 34, 35, 39-41.* ***Colan*** *a-20, 31.* ***Kremer*** *a-3, 37r.* ***Larsen*** *a-32.* ***Pala*** *a-5?,37.*

CRIME MUST STOP
Hillman Periodicals: October, 1952 (52 pgs.)

	GD2.0	FN6.0	NM9.4
V1#1(Scarce)-Similar to Monster Crime; Mort Lawrence, Krigstein-a	63.00	189.00	600.00

CRIME MYSTERIES (Secret Mysteries #16 on; combined with Crime Smashers #7 on)
Ribage Publ. Corp. (Trojan Magazines): May, 1952 - No. 15, Sept, 1954

	GD2.0	FN6.0	NM9.4
1-Transvestism story; crime & terror stories begin	54.00	162.00	485.00
2-Marijuana story (7/52)	40.00	120.00	325.00
3-One pg. Frazetta-a	35.00	105.00	280.00
4-Cover shows girl in bondage having her blood drained; 1 pg. Frazetta-a	54.00	162.00	485.00
5-10	29.00	87.00	235.00
11,12,14	27.00	81.00	215.00
13-(5/54)-Angelo Torres 1st comic work (inks over Check's pencils); Check-a	33.00	98.00	260.00
15-Acid in face-c	40.00	120.00	340.00

NOTE: ***Fass*** *a-13; c-4, 10.* ***Hollingsworth*** *a-10-13, 15; c-2, 12, 13, 15.* ***Kiefer*** *a-4.* ***Woodbridg*** *a-13? Bondage-c-1, 8, 12.*

CRIME ON THE RUN (See Approved Comics #8)

CRIME ON THE WATERFRONT (Formerly Famous Gangsters)
Realistic Publications: No. 4, May, 1952 (Painted cover)

	GD2.0	FN6.0	NM9.4
4	29.00	86.00	230.00

CRIME PATROL (Formerly International #1-5; International Crime Patrol #6; becomes Crypt of Terror #17 on)
E. C. Comics: No. 7, Summer, 1948 - No. 16, Feb-Mar, 1950

	GD2.0	FN6.0	NM9.4
7-Intro. Captain Crime	63.00	189.00	600.00
8-14: 12-Ingels-a	55.00	165.00	520.00
15-Intro. of Crypt Keeper (inspired by Witches Tales radio show) & Crypt of Terror (see Tales From the Crypt #33 for origin); used by N.Y. Legis. Comm.; last pg. Feldstein-a	236.00	709.00	2600.00
16-2nd Crypt Keeper app.; Roussos-a	155.00	465.00	1700.00

NOTE: ***Craig*** *c/a in most issues.* ***Feldstein*** *a-9-16.* ***Kiefer*** *a-8, 10, 11.* ***Moldoff*** *a-7.*

CRIME PATROL
Gemstone Publishing: Apr, 2000 - No. 10, Jan, 2001 ($2.50)

	GD2.0	FN6.0	NM9.4
1-10: E.C. reprints			2.50
Volume 1,2 (2000, $13.50) 1-r/#1-5. 2-r/#6-10			13.50

CRIME PHOTOGRAPHER (See Casey...)

CRIME REPORTER

Crime Smashers #5 © TM

Crimson #1 © Humberto Ramos

Crisis on Infinite Earths TPB © DC

GD2.0 FN6.0 NM9.4 **GD2.0 FN6.0 NM9.4**

St. John Publ. Co.: Aug, 1948 - No. 3, Dec, 1948 (Indicia shows Oct.)

1-Drug club story 49.00 147.00 440.00
2-Used in **SOTI**: illo- "Children told me what the man was going to do with the red-hot poker;" r/Dynamic #17 with editing; Baker-c; Tuska-a 68.00 205.00 650.00
3-Baker-c; Tuska-a 40.00 120.00 325.00

CRIMES BY WOMEN
Fox Features Syndicate: June, 1948 - No. 15, Aug, 1951; 1954
(True crime cases)

1-True story of Bonnie Parker 125.00 375.00 1190.00
2,3: 3-Used in **SOTI**, pg. 234 66.00 197.00 625.00
4,5,7-9,11-15: 8-Used in **POP**.14-Spanking panel r/from All Famous Crime Stories (1949) (Fox Giant) 58.00 174.00 550.00
6-Classic girl fight-c; acid-in-face panel 63.00 189.00 600.00
10-Used in **SOTI**, pg. 72; girl fight-c 59.00 177.00 560.00
54(M.S. Publ.-'54)-Reprint; (formerly My Love Secret) 26.00 79.00 210.00

CRIMES INCORPORATED (Formerly My Past)
Fox Features Syndicate: No. 12, June, 1950 (Crime Incorporated No. 2 on)

12 14.00 43.00 115.00

CRIMES INCORPORATED (See Fox Giants)

CRIME SMASHER (See Whiz #76)
Fawcett Publications: Summer, 1948 (one-shot)

1-Formerly Spy Smasher 43.00 130.00 390.00

CRIME SMASHERS (Becomes Secret Mysteries No. 16 on)
Ribage Publishing Corp.(Trojan Magazines): Oct, 1950 - No. 15, Mar, 1953

1-Used in **SOTI**, pg. 19,20, & illo "A girl raped and murdered;" Sally the Sleuth begins 80.00 240.00 760.00
2-Kubert-c 44.00 133.00 400.00
3,4 36.00 108.00 290.00
5-Wood-a 42.00 125.00 375.00
6,8-11: 8-Lingerie panel 28.00 83.00 220.00
7-Female heroin junkie story 29.00 86.00 230.00
12-Injury to eye panel; 1 pg. Frazetta-a 30.00 90.00 240.00
13-Used in **POP**, pgs. 79,80; 1 pg. Frazetta-a 30.00 90.00 240.00
14,15 24.00 73.00 195.00
NOTE: ***Hollingsworth*** *a-14.* ***Kiefer*** *a-15. Bondage c-7, 9.*

CRIME SUSPENSTORIES (Formerly Vault of Horror No. 12-14)
E. C. Comics: No. 15, Oct-Nov, 1950 - No. 27, Feb-Mar, 1955

15-Identical to #1 in content; #1 printed on outside front cover. #15 (formerly "The Vault of Horror") printed and blackened out on inside front cover with Vol. 1, No. 1 printed over it. Evidently, several of No. 15 were printed before a decision was made not to drop the Vault of Horror and Haunt of Fear series. The print run was stopped on No. 15 and continued on No. 1. All of No. 15 were changed as described above. 127.00 38.00 1400.00
1 96.00 286.00 1050.00
2 51.00 153.00 560.00
3-5: 3-Poe adaptation. 3-Old Witch stories begin 36.00 108.00 400.00
6-10 29.00 87.00 320.00
11,12,14,15: 15-The Old Witch guest stars 22.00 66.00 240.00
13,16-Williamson-a 25.00 75.00 275.00
17-Williamson/Frazetta-a (6 pgs.) 27.00 81.00 300.00
18,19: 19-Used in **SOTI**, pg. 235 19.00 57.00 210.00
20-Cover used in **SOTI**, illo "Cover of a children's comic book" 24.00 72.00 260.00
21,24-27: 24- "Food For Thought" similar to "Cave In" in Amazing Detective Cases #13 (1952) 12.00 36.00 135.00
22,23-Used in Senate investigation on juvenile delinquency. 22-Ax decapitation-c 19.00 57.00 210.00
NOTE: ***Craig*** *a-1-21; c-1-18, 20-22.* ***Crandall*** *a-18-26.* ***Davis*** *a-4, 5, 7, 9-12, 20.* ***Elder*** *a-17,18.* ***Evans*** *a-15, 19, 21, 23, 25, 27; c-23, 24.* ***Feldstein*** *c-19.* ***Ingels*** *a-1-12, 14, 15, 27.* ***Kamen*** *a-2, 18, 20-27; c-25-27.* ***Krigstein*** *a-22, 24, 25, 27.* ***Kurtzman*** *a-1, 3.* ***Orlando*** *a-16, 22, 24, 26.* ***Wood*** *a-1, 3. Issues No. 11-15 have E. C. "quickie" stories. No. 25 contains the famous "Are You a Red Dupe?" editorial. Ray Bradbury adaptations-15, 17.*

CRIME SUSPENSTORIES
Russ Cochran/Gemstone Publ.: Nov, 1992 - Present ($1.50/$2.00/$2.50)

1-24:Reprints Crime SuspenStories series 2.50

CRIMINALS ON THE RUN (Formerly Young King Cole)
(Crime Fighting Detective No. 11 on)
Premium Group (Novelty Press): V4#1, Aug-Sep, 1948-#10, Dec-Jan, 1949-50

V4#1-Young King Cole continues 30.00 90.00 240.00
2-6: 6-Dr. Doom app. 26.00 77.00 205.00
7-Classic "Fish in the Face" c by L. B. Cole 52.00 157.00 470.00
V5#1,2 (#8,9),10: 9,10-L. B. Cole-c 24.00 71.00 190.00
NOTE: *Most issues have* ***L. B. Cole*** *covers.* ***McWilliams*** *a-V4#6, 7, V5#2; c-V4#5.*

CRIMSON (Also see Cliffhanger #0)
Image Comics (Cliffhanger Productions): May, 1998 - No. 7, Dec, 1998;
DC Comics (Cliffhanger Prod.): No. 8, Mar, 1999 - No. 24, Apr, 2001 ($2.50)

1-Humberto Ramos-a/Augustyn-s 5.00
1-Variant-c by Warren 8.00
1-Chromium-c 30.00
2-Ramos-c with street crowd, 2-Variant-c by Art Adams 3.00
2-Dynamic Forces CrimsonChrome cover 12.00
3-7: 3-Ramos Moon background-c. 7-3-covers by Ramos, Madureira, & Campbell 3.00
8-22: 8-First DC issue 2.50
DF Premiere Ed. 1998 ($6.95) covers by Ramos and Jae Lee 7.00
Crimson: Scarlet X Blood on the Moon (10/99, $3.95) 4.00
Crimson Sourcebook (11/99, $2.95) Pin-ups and info 3.00
Heaven and Earth TPB (1/00, $14.95) r/#7-12 15.00
Loyalty and Loss TPB ('99, $12.95) r/#1-6 13.00

CRIMSON AVENGER, THE (See Detective Comics #20 for 1st app.)(Also see Leading Comics #1 & World's Best/Finest Comics)
DC Comics: June, 1988 - No. 4, Sept, 1988 ($1.00, limited series)

1-4 2.00

CRIMSON NUN
Antarctic Press: May, 1997 - No. 4, Nov, 1997 ($2.95, limited series)

1-4 3.00

CRIMSON PLAGUE
Event Comics: June, 1997 ($2.95, unfinished mini-series)

1-George Perez-a 3.00

CRIMSON PLAGUE (George Pérez's...)
Image Comics (Gorilla): June, 2000 - Present ($2.95, mini-series)

1-George Perez-a; reprints 6/97 issue with 16 new pages 3.00
2-($2.50) 2.50

CRISIS ON INFINITE EARTHS (Also see Official... Index and Legends of the DC Universe)
DC Comics: Apr, 1985 - No. 12, Mar, 1986 (maxi-series)

1-1st DC app. Blue Beetle & Detective Karp from Charlton; Pérez-c on all 1.50 4.50 12.00
2-6: 6-Intro Charlton's Capt. Atom, Nightshade, Question, Judomaster, Peacemaker & Thunderbolt into DC Universe 1.10 3.30 9.00
7-Double size; death of Supergirl 1.50 4.50 12.00
8-Death of the Flash (Barry Allen) 1.85 5.50 15.00
9-11: 9-Intro. Charlton's Ghost into DC Universe. 10-Intro. Charlton's Banshee, Dr. Spectro, Image, Punch & Jewellee into DC Universe; Starman (Prince Gavyn) dies. 1.10 3.30 9.00
12-(52 pgs.)-Deaths of Dove, Kole, Lori Lemaris, Sunburst, G.A. Robin & Huntress; Kid Flash becomes new Flash; 3rd & final DC app. of the 3 Lt. Marvels; Green Fury gets new look (becomes Green Flame in Infinity, Inc. #32) 1.25 3.75 10.00
Slipcased Hardcover (1998, $99.95) Wraparound dust-jacket cover by Pérez and Alex Ross; sketch pages by Pérez; intro by Wolfman 125.00
TPB (2000, $29.95) Wraparound-c by Pérez and Ross 30.00
NOTE: *Crossover issues: All Star Squadron 50-56,60; Amethyst 13; Blue Devil 17,18; DC Comics Presents 78,86-88,95; Detective Comics 558; Fury of Firestorm 41,42; G.I. Combat 274; Green Lantern 194-196,198; Infinity, Inc. 18-25 & Annual 1, Justice League of America 244,245 & Annual 3; Legion of Super-Heroes 16,18; Losers Special 1; New Teen Titans 13,14; Omega Men 31,33; Superman 413-415; Swamp Thing 44,46; Wonder Woman 327-329.*

CRITICAL MASS (See A Shadowline Saga: Critical Mass)

CRITTERS (Also see Usagi Yojimbo Summer Special)
Fantagraphics Books: 1986 - No. 50, 1990 ($1.70/$2.00, B&W)

CrossGen Primer © CRO

The Crow #2 © TMP

Crown Comics #15 © Golfing/McCombs

1-Cutey Bunny, Usagi Yojimbo app. 5.00
2-10: 3,6,7,10-Usagi Yojimbo app. 4.00
11-22,24-37,39-49: 11,14-Usagi Yojimbo app. 11-Christmas Special (68 pgs.); Usagi Yojimbo. 22-Watchmen parody; two diff. covers exist 2.00
23-With Alan Moore Flexi-disc ($3.95) 5.00
38-($2.75-c) Usagi Yojimbo app. 3.00
50 ($4.95, 84 pgs.)-Neil the Horse, Capt. Jack, Sam & Max & Usagi Yojimbo app.; Quagmire, Shaw-a 5.00
Special 1 (1/88, $2.00) 2.00

CROSS
Dark Horse Comics: No. 0, Oct, 1995 - No. 6, Apr, 1995 ($2.95, limited series, mature)

0-6: Darrow-c & Vachss scripts in all 3.00

CROSS AND THE SWITCHBLADE, THE
Spire Christian Comics (Fleming H. Revell Co.): 1972 (35-49¢)

1-Some issues have nn 2.40 6.00

CROSSFIRE
Spire Christian Comics (Fleming H. Revell Co.): 1973 (39/49¢)

nn 2.40 6.00

CROSSFIRE (Also see DNAgents)
Eclipse Comics: 5/84 - No. 17, 3/86; No. 18, 1/87 - No. 26, 2/88 ($1.50, Baxter paper)(#18-26 (B&W)

1-11,14-26: 1-DNAgents x-over; Spiegle-c/a begins 2.00
12,13-Death of Marilyn Monroe. 12-Dave Stevens-c 3.00

CROSSFIRE AND RAINBOW (Also see DNAgents)
Eclipse Comics: June, 1986 - No. 4, Sept, 1986 ($1.25, deluxe format)

1-3: Spiegle-a. 4-Dave Stevens-c 2.00

CROSSGEN...
CrossGeneration Comics

...Chronicles (6/00, $3.95) Intro. to CrossGen characters & company 4.00
...Chronicles (6/00, no cover price) same contents, customer preview 4.00
CrossGenesis (1/00) Previews CrossGen universe; cover gallery 3.00
...Primer (1/00) Wizard supplement; intro. to the CrossGen universe 1.00
...Sampler (2/00) Retailer preview book 3.00

CROSSING THE ROCKIES (See Classics Illustrated Special Issue)

CROSSROADS
First Comics: July, 1988 - No. 5, Nov, 1988 ($3.25, lim. series, deluxe format)

1-5 3.25

CROW, THE (Also see Caliber Presents)
Caliber Press: Feb, 1989 - No. 4, 1989 ($1.95, B&W, limited series)

1-James O'Barr-c/a/scripts 3.65 11.00 40.00
1-3-2nd printing 5.00
2-4 2.30 7.00 20.00
2-3rd printing 3.00

CROW, THE
Tundra Publishing, Ltd.: Jan, 1992 - No. 3, 1992 ($4.95, B&W, 68 pgs.)

1-3: 1-r/#1,2 of Caliber series. 2-r/#3 of Caliber series w/new material. 3-All new material 1.00 3.00 8.00

CROW, THE
Kitchen Sink Press: 1/96 - No. 3, 3/96 ($2.95, B&W)

1-3: James O'Barr-c/scripts 3.00
#0-A Cycle of Shattered Lives (12/98, $3.50) new story by O'Barr 3.50

CROW, THE
Image Comics (Todd McFarlane Prod.): Feb, 1999 - No. 10, Nov, 1999 ($2.50)

1-10: 1-Two covers by McFarlane and Kent Williams; Muth-s in all. 2-6,10-Paul Lee-a. 9-Tollagson-a 2.50
Book 1 - Vengeance (2000, $10.95, TPB) r/#1-3,5,6 10.95
Book 2 - Evil Beyond Reach (2000, $10.95, TPB) r/#4,7-10 10.95
Todd McFarlane Presents The Crow Magazine 1 (3/00, $4.95) 4.95

CROW, THE: CITY OF ANGELS (Movie)
Kitchen Sink Press: July, 1996 - No. 3, Sept, 1996 ($2.95, limited series)

1-3: Adaptation of film; two-c (photo & illos.). 1-Vincent Perez interview 3.0

CROW, THE: FLESH AND BLOOD
Kitchen Sink Press: May, 1996 - No. 3, July, 1996 ($2.95, limited series)

1-3: O'Barr-c 3.0

CROW, THE: RAZOR - KILL THE PAIN
London Night Studios: Apr, 1998 - No.3, July, 1998 ($2.95, B&W, lim. series)

1-3-Hartsoe-s/O'Barr-painted-c 3.0
0(10/98) Dorien painted-c, Finale (2/99) 3.0
The Lost Chapter (2/99, $4.95), Tour Book-(12/97) pin-ups; 4 diff.-c 5.0

CROW, THE: WAKING NIGHTMARES
Kitchen Sink Press: Jan, 1997 - No.4, 1998 ($2.95, B&W, limited series)

1-4-Miran Kim-c 3.0

CROW, THE: WILD JUSTICE
Kitchen Sink Press: Oct, 1996 - No. 3, Dec, 1996 ($2.95, B&W, limited series)

1-3-Prosser-s/Adlard-a 3.0

CROWN COMICS
Golfing/McCombs Publ.: Wint, 1944-45; No. 2, Sum, 1945 - No. 19, July, 1949

1- "The Oblong Box" E.A. Poe adaptation 35.00 105.00 280.0
2,3-Baker-a; 3-Voodah by Baker 24.00 73.00 195.0
4-6-Baker-c/a; Voodah app. #4,5 27.00 81.00 215.0
7-Feldstein, Baker, Kamen-a; Baker-c 24.00 73.00 195.0
8-Baker-a; Voodah app. 23.00 68.00 180.0
9-11,13-19: Voodah in #10-19. 13-New logo 14.00 41.00 110.0
12-Master Marvin by Feldstein, Starr-a; Voodah-c 14.00 43.00 115.0
NOTE: *Bolle a-11, 13-16, 18, 19; c-11p, 15.* ***Powell*** *a-19.* ***Starr*** *a-11-13; c-11i.*

CRUCIBLE
DC Comics (Impact): Feb, 1993 - No. 6, July, 1993 ($1.25, limited series)

1-6:1-(99¢)-Neon ink-c. 1,2-Quesada-c(p). 1-4-Quesada layouts 2.0

CRUEL AND UNUSUAL
DC Comics (Vertigo): June, 1999 - No. 4, Sept, 1999 ($2.95, limited series)

1-4-Delano & Peyer-s/McCrea-c/a 3.0

CRUSADER FROM MARS (See Tops in Adventure)
Ziff-Davis Publ. Co.: Jan-Mar, 1952 - No. 2, Fall, 1952 (Painted-c)

1-Cover is dated Spring 71.00 213.00 675.0
2-Bondage-c 55.00 165.00 500.0

CRUSADER RABBIT (TV)
Dell Publishing Co.: No. 735, Oct, 1956 - No. 805, May, 1957

Four Color 735 (#1) 31.00 93.00 375.0
Four Color 805 24.00 70.00 285.0

CRUSADERS, THE (Religious)
Chick Publications: 1974 - Vol. 17, 1988 (39/69¢, 36 pgs.)

Vol.1-Operation Bucharest ('74). Vol.2-The Broken Cross ('74). Vol.3-Scarface ('74). Vol.4-Exorcists ('75). Vol.5-Chaos ('75) 1.00 2.80 7.0
Vol.6-Primal Man? ('76)-(Disputes evolution theory). Vol.7-The Ark-(claims proof of existence, destroyed by Bolsheviks). Vol.8-The Gift-(Life story of Christ). Vol.9-Angel of Light-(Story of the Devil). Vol.10-Spellbound?-(Tells how rock music is Satanic & produced by witches). 11-Sabotage?. 12-Alberto 13-Double Cross. 14-The Godfathers. (No. 6-14 low in distribution; loaded in religious propaganda.). 15-The Force. 16-The Four Horsemen 1.00 2.80 7.0
Vol. 17-The Prophet (low print run) 1.00 3.00 8.0

CRUSADERS (Southern Knights No. 2 on)
Guild Publications: 1982 (B&W, magazine size)

1-1st app. Southern Knights 1.00 2.80 7.0

CRUSADERS, THE (Also see Black Hood, The Jaguar, The Comet, The Fly, Legend of the Shield, The Mighty... & The Web)
DC Comics (Impact): May, 1992 - No. 8, Dec, 1992 ($1.00/$1.25)

1-8-Contains 3 Impact trading cards 2.0

CRUSH, THE
Image Comics (Motown Machineworks): Jan, 1996 - No. 5, July, 1996 ($2.25, limited series)

Crypt of Dawn #3 © J.M. Linsner

Crypt of Terror #19 © WMG

Custer's Last Fight nn © AVON

	GD2.0	FN6.0	NM9.4
1-5: Baron scripts			3.00

CRY FOR DAWN
Cry For Dawn Pub.: 1989 - No. 9 ($2.25, B&W, mature)

	GD2.0	FN6.0	NM9.4
1	9.00	27.00	100.00
1-2nd printing	3.00	9.00	30.00
1-3rd printing	2.50	7.50	20.00
2	4.50	13.50	45.00
2-2nd printing	1.10	3.30	9.00
3	3.00	9.00	30.00
4-6	2.25	6.75	18.00
5-2nd printing			5.00
7-9	1.75	5.25	14.00
4-9-Signed & numbered editions	2.50	7.50	25.00
...Calendar (1993)			35.00

CRYIN' LION COMICS
William H. Wise Co.: Fall, 1944 - No. 3, Spring, 1945

	GD2.0	FN6.0	NM9.4
1-Funny animal	14.00	41.00	110.00
2-Hitler app.	11.00	33.00	90.00
3	10.00	30.00	70.00

CRYPT
Image Comics (Extreme): Aug, 1995 - No.2, Oct. 1995 ($2.50, limited series)

	GD2.0	FN6.0	NM9.4
1,2-Prophet app.			2.50

CRYPTIC WRITINGS OF MEGADETH
Chaos! Comics: Sept, 1997 - Present ($2.95, quarterly)

	GD2.0	FN6.0	NM9.4
1-4-Stories based on song lyrics by Dave Mustaine			3.00

CRYPT OF DAWN (see Dawn)
Sirius: 1996 ($2.95, B&W, limited series)

	GD2.0	FN6.0	NM9.4
1-Linsner-c/s; anthology.			5.00
2, 3 (2/98)			4.00
4,5: 4- (6/98), 5-(11/98)			3.00
Ltd. Edition			20.00

CRYPT OF SHADOWS
Marvel Comics Group: Jan, 1973 - No. 21, Nov, 1975 (#1-9 are 20¢)

	GD2.0	FN6.0	NM9.4
1-Wolverton-r/Advs. Into Terror #7	2.00	6.00	18.00
2-10: 2-Starlin/Everett-c	1.75	5.25	14.00
11-21: 18,20-Kirby-a	1.10	3.30	9.00

NOTE: ***Briefer** a-2r. **Ditko** a-13r, 18-20r. **Everett** a-6, 14r; c-2i. **Heath** a-1r. **Gil Kane** c-1, 6. **Mort Lawrence** a-1r, 8r. **Maneely** a-2r. **Moldoff** a-8. **Powell** a-12r, 14r. **Tuska** a-2r.*

CRYPT OF TERROR (Formerly Crime Patrol; Tales From the Crypt No. 20 on)
E. C. Comics: No. 17, Apr-May, 1950 - No. 19, Aug-Sept, 1950

	GD2.0	FN6.0	NM9.4
17-1st New Trend to hit stands	255.00	765.00	2800.00
18,19	145.00	435.00	1600.00

NOTE: ***Craig** c/a-17-19. **Feldstein** a-17-19. **Ingels** a-19. **Kurtzman** a-18. **Wood** a-18. Canadian reprints known; see Table of Contents.*

C•23 (Jim Lee's...) (Based on Wizards of the Coast card game)
Image Comics: Apr, 1998 - No. 8, Nov, 1998 ($2.50)

1-8: 1,2-Choi & Mariotte-s/ Charest-c. 2-Variant-c by Jim Lee. 4-Ryan Benjamin-c. 5,8-Corben var-c. 6-Flip book with Planetary preview; Corben-c 3.00

CUD
Fantagraphics Books: 8/92 - No. 8, 12/94 ($2.25-$2.75, B&W, mature)

	GD2.0	FN6.0	NM9.4
1-8: Terry LaBan scripts & art in all. 6-1st Eno & Plum			3.00

CUD COMICS
Dark Horse Comics: Jan, 1995 - Present ($2.95, B&W)

	GD2.0	FN6.0	NM9.4
1-8: Terry LaBan-c/a/scripts. 5-Nudity; marijuana story			3.00
Eno and Plum TPB (1997, $12.95) r/#1-4, DHP #93-95			13.00

CUPID
Marvel Comics (U.S.A.): Dec, 1949 - No. 2, Mar, 1950

	GD2.0	FN6.0	NM9.4
1-Photo-c	13.00	39.00	105.00
2-Bettie Page ('50s pin-up queen) photo-c; Powell-a (see My Love #4)	31.00	94.00	250.00

CURIO
Harry 'A' Chesler: 1930's(?) (Tabloid size, 16-20 pgs.)

	GD2.0	FN6.0	NM9.4
nn	20.00	60.00	160.00

CURLY KAYOE COMICS (Boxing)
United Features Syndicate/Dell Publ. Co.: 1946 - No. 8, 1950; Jan, 1958

	GD2.0	FN6.0	NM9.4
1 (1946)-Strip-r (Fritzi Ritz); biography of Sam Leff, Kayoe's artist	16.00	49.00	130.00
2	9.30	28.00	65.00
3-8	7.15	21.50	50.00
United Presents...(Fall, 1948)	7.15	21.50	50.00
Four Color 871 (Dell, 1/58)	2.50	7.50	25.00

CURSE OF DRACULA, THE
Dark Horse Comics: July, 1998 - No. 3, Sept, 1998 ($2.95, limited series)

	GD2.0	FN6.0	NM9.4
1-3-Wolfman-s/Colan-a			3.00

CURSE OF DREADWOLF
Lightning Comics: Sept, 1994 ($2.75, B&W)

	GD2.0	FN6.0	NM9.4
1			2.75

CURSE OF RUNE (Becomes Rune, 2nd Series)
Malibu Comics (Ultraverse): May, 1995 - No. 4, Aug, 1995 ($2.50, lim. series)

	GD2.0	FN6.0	NM9.4
1-4: 1-Two covers form one image			2.50

CURSE OF THE SPAWN
Image Comics (Todd McFarlane Prod.): Sept, 1996 - No. 29, Mar, 1999 ($1.95)

	GD2.0	FN6.0	NM9.4
1-Dwayne Turner-a(p)	1.00	2.80	7.00
1-B&W Edition	2.00	6.00	18.00
2-3			5.00
4-10			3.00
11-13: 12-Movie photo-c of Melinda Clarke (Priest)			2.50
14-26			2.00
Blood and Sutures ('99, $9.95, TPB) r/#5-8			10.00
Lost Values ('00, $10.95, TPB) r/#12-14,22; Ashley Wood-c			11.00
Sacrifice of the Soul ('99, $9.95, TPB) r/#1-4			10.00
Shades of Gray ('00, $9.95, TPB) r/#9-11,29			10.00

CURSE OF THE WEIRD
Marvel Comics: Dec, 1993 - No. 4, Mar, 1994 ($1.25, limited series)
(Pre-code horror-r)

1-4: 1,3,4-Wolverton-r(1-Eye of Doom; 3-Where Monsters Dwell; 4-The End of the World). 2-Orlando-r. 4-Zombie-r by Everett; painted-c 3.00

NOTE: ***Briefer** r-2. **Jack Davis** a-4r. **Ditko** a-1r, 2r, 4r; c-1r. **Everett** r-1. **Heath** r-1-3. **Kubert** r-3. **Wolverton** a-1r, 3r, 4r.*

CUSTER'S LAST FIGHT
Avon Periodicals: 1950

	GD2.0	FN6.0	NM9.4
nn-Partial reprint of Cowpuncher #1	17.00	51.00	135.00

CUTEY BUNNY (See Army Surplus Komikz Featuring...)

CUTIE PIE
Junior Reader's Guild (Lev Gleason): May, 1955 - No. 3, Dec, 1955; No. 4, Feb, 1956; No. 5, Aug, 1956

	GD2.0	FN6.0	NM9.4
1	6.00	18.00	42.00
2-5: 4-Misdated 2/55	4.00	12.00	24.00

CUTTING EDGE
Marvel Comics: Dec, 1995 ($2.95)

	GD2.0	FN6.0	NM9.4
1-Hulk-c/story; Messner-Loebs scripts			3.00

CYBERCITY
CPM Comics: Sept, 1995- Present ($2.95, bi-monthly)

	GD2.0	FN6.0	NM9.4
Part One #1,2; Part Two #1,2; Part Three #1,2			3.00

CYBERELLA
DC Comics (Helix): Sept, 1996 - No. 12, Aug, 1997 ($2.25/$2.50)
(1st Helix series)

	GD2.0	FN6.0	NM9.4
1-12: 1-5-Chaykin & Cameron-a. 1,2-Chaykin-c. 3-5-Cameron-c			2.50

CYBERFORCE
Image Comics (Top Cow Productions): Oct, 1992 - No. 4, 1993; No. 0, Sept, 1993 ($1.95, limited series)

1-Silvestri-c/a in all; coupon for Image Comics #0; 1st Top Cow Productions

Cyberforce V2 #3 © Top Cow

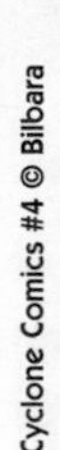

Cyclone Comics #4 © Bilbara

Daffy Four Color #457 © WB

title. 2.40 6.00
1-With coupon missing 2.00
2-4,0: 2-(3/93). 3-Pitt-c/story. 4-Codename: Stryke Force back-up (1st app.); foil-c. 0-(9/93)-Walt Simonson-c/a/scripts 3.00

CYBERFORCE
Image Comics (Top Cow Productions)/Top Cow Comics No. 28 on: V2#1, Nov, 1993 - No. 35, Sept. 1997 ($1.95)

V2#1-24: 1-7-Marc Silvestri/Keith Williams-c/a. 8-McFarlane-c/a. 10-Painted variant-c exists. 18-Variant-c exists. 23-Velocity-c. 2.50
1-3: 1-Gold Logo-c. 2-Silver embossed-c. 3-Gold embossed-c 10.00
1-(99¢, 3/96, 2nd printing) 2.00
25-($3.95)-Wraparound, foil-c 4.00
26-35: 28-(11/96)-1st Top Cow Comics iss. Quesada & Palmiotti's Gabriel app. 27-Quesada & Palmiotti's Ash app. 2.50
Annual 1,2 (3/95, 8/96, $2.50, $2.95) 3.00
NOTE: *Annuals read Volume One in the indica.*

CYBERFORCE ORIGINS
Image Comics (Top Cow Productions): Jan, 1995 - No. 3, Nov, 1995 ($2.50)

1-Cyblade (1/95) 5.00
1-Cyblade (3/96, 99¢, 2nd printing) 2.00
1A-Exclusive Ed.; Tucci-c 4.00
2,3: 2-Stryker (2/95)-1st Mike Turner-a. 3-Impact 2.50
(#4) Misery (12/95, $2.95) 3.00

CYBERFORCE/STRYKEFORCE: OPPOSING FORCES (See Codename: Stryke Force #15)
Image Comics (Top Cow Productions): Sept, 1995 - No.2, Oct, 1995 ($2.50, limited series)

1,2: 2-Stryker disbands Strykeforce. 2.50

CYBERFORCE UNIVERSE SOURCEBOOK
Image Comics (Top Cow Productions): Aug, 1994/Feb, 1995 ($2.50)

1,2-Silvestri-c 2.50

CYBERFROG
Hall of Heroes: June, 1994 - No. 2, Dec, 1994 ($2.50, B&W, limited series)

1,2 2.50

CYBERFROG
Harris Comics: Feb, 1996 - No. 3, Apr, 1996 ($2.95)

0-3: Van Sciver-c/a/scripts. 2-Variant-c exists 5.00

CYBERFROG: (Title series), **Harris Comics**

--RESERVOIR FROG, 9/96 - No. 2, 10/96 ($2.95) 1,2: Van Sciver-c/a/scripts; wraparound-c 3.00

--RD ANNIVERSARY SPECIAL, 1/97 - #2, ($2.50, B&W) 1,2 2.50

--VS. CREED, 7/97 ($2.95, B&W)1 3.00

CYBERNARY (See Deathblow #1)
Image Comics (WildStorm Productions): Nov, 1995 - No.5, Mar, 1996 ($2.50)

1-5 2.50

CYBERPUNK
Innovation Publishing: Sept, 1989 - No. 2, Oct, 1989 ($1.95, 28 pgs.) Book 2, #1, May, 1990 - No. 2, 1990 ($2.25, 28 pgs.)

1,2, Book 2 #1,2:1,2-Ken Steacy painted-covers (Adults) 2.25

CYBERPUNK: THE SERAPHIM FILES
Innovation Publishing: Nov, 1990 - No. 2, Dec, 1990 ($2.50, 28 pgs., mature)

1,2: 1-Painted-c; story cont'd from Seraphim 2.50

CYBERPUNX
Image Comics (Extreme Studios): Mar, 1996 ($2.50)

1 3.00

CYBERRAD
Continuity Comics: 1991 - No. 7, 1992 ($2.00)(Direct sale & newsstand-c variations)
V2#1, 1993 ($2.50)

1-7: 5-Glow-in-the-dark-c by N. Adams (direct sale only). 6-Contains 4 pg. fold-out poster; N. Adams layouts 2.00
V2#1-($2.95, direct sale ed.)-Die-cut-c w/B&W hologram on-c; Neal Adams sketches 3.00
V2#1-($2.50, newsstand ed.)-Without sketches 2.50

CYBERRAD DEATHWATCH 2000 (Becomes CyberRad w/#2, 7/93)
Continuity Comics: Apr, 1993 - No. 2, 1993 ($2.50)

1,2: 1-Bagged w/2 cards; Adams-c & layouts & plots. 2-Bagged w/card; Adams scripts 2.50

CYBER 7
Eclipse Comics: Mar, 1989 - #7, Sept, 1989; V2#1, Oct, 1989 - #10, 1990 ($2.00, B&W)

1-7, Book 2 #1-10: Stories translated from Japanese 2.00

CYBLADE/ GHOST RIDER
Marvel Comics /Top Cow Productions: Jan 1997 ($2.95, one-shot)

1-Devil's Reign pt. 2 4.00

CYBLADE/SHI (Also see Battle For The Independents & Shi/Cyblade: The Battle For The Independents)
Image Comics (Top Cow Productions): 1995 ($2.95, one-shot)

	GD2.0	FN6.0	NM9.4
San Diego Preview	2.30	7.00	20.00
1-($2.95)-1st app. Witchblade	2.50	4.50	12.00
1-($2.95)-variant-c; Tucci-a	1.00	3.00	8.00

CYBRID
Maximum Press: July, 1995; No. 0, Jan, 1997 ($2.95/$3.50)

1-(7/95) 3.00
0-(1/97)-Liefeld-a/script; story cont'd in Avengelyne #4 3.50

CYCLONE COMICS (Also see Whirlwind Comics)
Bilbara Publishing Co.: June, 1940 - No. 5, Nov, 1940

	GD2.0	FN6.0	NM9.4
1-Origin Tornado Tom; Volton (the human generator), Tornado Tom, Kingdom of the Moon, Mister Q begin (1st app. of each)	147.00	442.00	1400.00
2,3	74.00	221.00	700.00
4,5	58.00	174.00	550.00

CYCLOPS: RETRIBUTION
Marvel Comics: 1994 ($5.95, trade paperback)

nn-r/Marvel Comics Presents #17-24 2.40 6.00

CY-GOR (See Spawn #38 for 1st app.)
Image Comics (Todd McFarlane Prod.): July, 1999 - No. 6, Dec, 1999 ($2.50)

1-6-Veitch-s 2.50

CYNTHIA DOYLE, NURSE IN LOVE (Formerly Sweetheart Diary)
Charlton Publications: No. 66, Oct, 1962 - No. 74, Feb, 1964

66-74 2.00 6.00 16.00

DAEMONSTORM
Caliber Comics: 1997 ($3.95, one-shot)

1-McFarlane-c 4.00

DAEMONSTORM: STORMWALKER
Caliber Comics: 1997 ($3.95, B&W, one-shot)
nn 4.00

DAFFY (Daffy Duck No. 18 on)(See Looney Tunes)
Dell Publishing Co./Gold Key No. 31-127/Whitman No. 128 on: #457, 3/53 - #30, 7-9/62; #31, 10-12/62 - #145, 1983 (No #132,133)

	GD2.0	FN6.0	NM9.4
Four Color 457(#1)-Elmer Fudd x-overs begin	8.35	25.00	100.00
Four Color 536,615('55)	4.55	13.65	50.00
4(1-3/56)-11('57)	3.20	9.60	35.00
12-19(1958-59)	2.50	7.50	24.00
20-40(1960-64)	2.00	6.00	18.00
41-60(1964-68)	2.00	6.00	16.00
61-90(1969-74)-Road Runner in most	1.00	2.80	7.00
91-110	1.00	2.80	7.00
111-127			5.00
128,134-141		2.40	6.00
129(8/80), 130,131 (pre-pack?) (scarce)	1.50	4.50	12.00
142-145(#90029 on-c; nd, nd code, pre-pack?)	1.10	3.30	9.00
Mini-Comic 1 (1976; 3-1/4x6-1/2")		2.40	6.00

NOTE: *Reprint issues-No.41-46, 48, 50, 53-55, 58, 59, 65, 67, 69, 73, 81, 96, 103-108; 136-142*

Dagar Desert Hawk #15 © FOX

Dagwood #3 © KFS

Dale Evans Comics #11 © DC

144, 145(1/3-2/3-r). (See March of Comics No. 277, 288, 303, 313, 331, 347, 357,375, 387, 397, 402, 413, 425, 437, 460).

DAFFY TUNES COMICS
Four-Star Publications: June, 1947; No. 12, Aug, 1947

nn 7.85 23.50 55.00
12-Al Fago-c/a; funny animal 6.40 19.25 45.00

DAGAR, DESERT HAWK (Captain Kidd No. 24 on; formerly All Great)
Fox Features Syndicate: No. 14, Feb, 1948 - No. 23, Apr, 1949 (No #17,18)

14-Tangi & Safari Cary begin; Good bondage-c/a 76.00 229.00 725.00
15,16-E. Good-a; 15-Bondage-c 47.00 142.00 425.00
19,20,22: 19-Used in **SOTI**, pg. 180 (Tangi) 40.00 120.00 350.00
21,23: 21- "Bombs & Bums Away" panel in "Flood of Death" story used in **SOTI.** 23-Bondage-c 44.00 133.00 400.00
NOTE: *Tangi by **Kamen**-14-16, 19, 20; c-20, 21.*

DAGAR THE INVINCIBLE (Tales of Sword & Sorcery...) (Also see Dan Curtis Giveaways & Gold Key Spotlight)
Gold Key: Oct, 1972 - No. 18, Dec, 1976; No. 19, Apr, 1982

1-Origin; intro. Villains Olstellon & Scor 2.50 7.50 25.00
2-5: 3-Intro. Graylin, Dagar's woman; Jarn x-over 1.25 3.75 10.00
6-1st Dark Gods story 1.00 3.00 8.00
7-10: 9-Intro. Torgus. 10-1st Three Witches story 1.00 3.00 8.00
11-18: 13-Durak & Torgus x-over; story continues in Dr. Spektor #15. 14-Dagar's origin retold. 18-Origin retold 2.40 6.00
19-Origin-r/#18 5.00
NOTE: *Durak app. in 7, 12, 13. Tragg app. in 5, 11.*

DAGWOOD (Chic Young's) (Also see Blondie Comics)
Harvey Publications: Sept, 1950 - No. 140, Nov, 1965

1 12.75 38.00 140.00
2 6.80 20.50 75.00
3-10 5.00 15.00 55.00
11-20 4.10 12.30 45.00
21-30 3.65 11.00 40.00
31-50 3.20 9.60 35.00
51-70 2.50 7.50 25.00
71-100 2.00 6.00 18.00
101-128,130,135 1.75 5.25 14.00
129,131-134,136-140-All are 68-pg. issues 2.50 7.50 24.00
NOTE: *Popeye and other one page strips appeared in early issues.*

DAI KAMIKAZE!
Now Comics: June, 1987 - No. 12, Aug, 1988 ($1.75)

1-12: 1-1st app. Speed Racer; 2nd print exists 2.00

DAILY BUGLE (See Spider-Man)
Marvel Comics: Dec, 1996 - No. 3, Feb, 1997 ($2.50, B&W, limited series)

1-3-Paul Grist-s 2.50

DAISY AND DONALD (See Walt Disney Showcase No. 8)
Gold Key/Whitman No. 42 on: May, 1973 - No. 59, 1984 (no No. 48)

1-Barks-r/WDC&S #280,308 2.50 7.50 25.00
2-5: 4-Barks-r/WDC&S #224 1.75 5.25 14.00
6-10 1.25 3.75 10.00
11-20 1.00 3.00 8.00
21-41: 32-r/WDC&S #308 2.40 6.00
42-44 (Whitman) 1.00 3.00 8.00
45 (8/80),46-(pre-pack?)(scarce) 2.30 7.00 20.00
47-(12/80)-Only distr. in Whitman 3-pack (scarce) 3.65 11.00 40.00
48(3/81)-50(8/81): 50-r/#3 1.50 4.50 12.00
51-54: 51-Barks-r/4-Color #1150. 52-r/#2 1.10 3.30 9.00
55-59-(all #90284 on-c, nd, nd code, pre-pack?) 1.75 5.25 14.00

DAISY & HER PUPS (Blondie's Dogs)(Formerly Blondie Comics #20)
Harvey Publications: No. 21, 7/51 - No. 27, 7/52; No. 8, 9/52 - No. 18, 5/54

21 (#1)-Blondie's dog Daisy and her 5 pups led by Elmer begin. Rags Rabbit app 4.10 12.30 45.00
22-27 (#2-7): 26,27 have No. 6 & 7 on cover but No. 26 & 27 on inside. 23,25-The Little King app. 24-Bringing Up Father by McManus app. 25-27-Rags Rabbit app. 3.00 9.00 30.00
8-18: 8,9-Rags Rabbit app. 8,17-The Little King app. 11-The Flop Family Swan begins. 22-Cookie app. 11-Felix The Cat app. by 17,18-Popeye app. 2.40 7.35 22.00

DAISY DUCK & UNCLE SCROOGE PICNIC TIME (See Dell Giant #33)

DAISY DUCK & UNCLE SCROOGE SHOW BOAT (See Dell Giant #55)

DAISY DUCK'S DIARY (See Dynabrite Comics, & Walt Disney's C&S #298)
Dell Publishing Co.: No. 600, Nov, 1954 - No. 1247, Dec-Fef, 1961-62 (Disney)

Four Color 600 (#1) 6.30 19.00 75.00
Four Color 659, 743 (11/56) 5.00 15.00 60.00
Four Color 858 (11/57), 948 (11/58), 1247 (12-2/61-62) 4.55 13.65 50.00
Four Color 1055 (11-1/59-60), 1150 (12-1/60-61)-By Carl Barks) 9.00 27.00 110.00

DAISY HANDBOOK
Daisy Manufacturing Co.: 1946; No. 2, 1948 (10¢, pocket-size, 132 pgs.)

1-Buck Rogers, Red Ryder; Wolverton-a(2 pgs.) 40.00 120.00 320.00
2-Captain Marvel & Ibis the Invincible, Red Ryder, Boy Commandos & Robotman; Wolverton-a (2 pgs.); contains 8 pg. color catalog 40.00 120.00 320.00

DAISY MAE (See Oxydol-Dreft)

DAISY'S RED RYDER GUN BOOK
Daisy Manufacturing Co.: 1955 (25¢, pocket-size, 132 pgs.)

nn-Boy Commandos, Red Ryder; 1pg. Wolverton-a 26.00 79.00 210.00

DAKKON BLACKBLADE ON THE WORLD OF MAGIC: THE GATHERING
Acclaim Comics (Armada): June, 1996 ($5.95, one-shot)

1-Jerry Prosser scripts; Rags Morales-c/a. 2.40 6.00

DAKOTA LIL (See Fawcett Movie Comics)

DAKOTA NORTH
Marvel Comics Group: June, 1986 - No. 5, Feb, 1987

1-5 2.00

DAKTARI (Ivan Tors) (TV)
Dell Publishing Co.: July, 1967 - No. 3, Oct, 1968; No. 4, Sept, 1969 (All have photo-c)

1 3.00 9.00 32.00
2-4 2.50 7.50 24.00

DALE EVANS COMICS (Also see Queen of the West...)(See Boy Commandos #32)
National Periodical Publications: Sept-Oct, 1948 - No. 24, July-Aug, 1952 (No. 1-19: 52 pgs.)

1-Dale Evans & her horse Buttermilk begin; Sierra Smith begins by Alex Toth 100.00 300.00 950.00
2-Alex Toth-a 47.00 142.00 425.00
3-11-Alex Toth-a 33.00 98.00 260.00
12-20: 12-Target-c 16.00 48.00 125.00
21-24 17.00 51.00 135.00
NOTE: *Photo-c-1, 2, 4-14.*

DALGODA
Fantagraphics Books: Aug, 1984 - No. 8, Feb, 1986 (High quality paper)

1- Fujitake-c/a in all 2.50
2-7: 2,3-Debut Grimwood's Daughter. 8-Alan Moore story 2.00

DALTON BOYS, THE
Avon Periodicals: 1951

1-(Number on spine)-Kinstler-c 16.00 49.00 130.00

DAMAGE
DC Comics: Apr, 1994 - No. 20, Jan, 1996 ($1.75/$1.95)

1-20: 6-(9/94)-Zero Hour. 0-(10/94). 7-(11/94). 14-Ray app. 3.00

DAMAGE CONTROL (See Marvel Comics Presents #19)
Marvel Comics: 5/89 - No. 4, 8/89; V2#1, 12/89 - No. 4, 2/90 ($1.00) V3#1, 6/91 - No. 4, 9/91 ($1.25, all are limited series)

V1#1-4,V2#1-4,V3#1-4: V1#4-Wolverine app. V2#2,4-Punisher app. 1-Spider-Man app. 2-New Warriors app. 3,4-Silver Surfer app. 4-Infinity Gauntlet parody 2.00

Damned #3 © Steven Grant & Mike Zeck

Danger Girl #3 © J. Scott Campbell

Danger Trail #1 © DC

DAMNED
Image Comics (Homage Comics): June, 1997 - No. 4, Sept, 1997 ($2.50, limited series)
1-4-Steven Grant-s/Mike Zeck-c/a in all 2.50

DANCES WITH DEMONS (See Marvel Frontier Comics Unlimited)
Marvel Frontier Comics: Sept, 1993 - No. 4, Dec, 1993 ($1.95, limited series)
1-($2.95)-Foil embossed-c; Charlie Adlard & Rod Ramos-a 3.00
2-4 2.00

DANDEE: Four Star Publications: 1947 (Advertised, not published)

DAN DUNN (See Crackajack Funnies, Detective Dan, Famous Feature Stories & Red Ryder)

DANDY COMICS (Also see Happy Jack Howard)
E. C. Comics: Spring, 1947 - No. 7, Spring, 1948

	GD2.0	FN6.0	NM9.4
1-Funny animal; Vince Fago-a in all; Dandy in all	35.00	105.00	280.00
2	25.00	75.00	200.00
3-7: 3-Intro Handy Andy who is c-feature #3 on	19.00	56.00	150.00

DANGER
Comic Media/Allen Hardy Assoc.: Jan, 1953 - No. 11, Aug, 1954

	GD2.0	FN6.0	NM9.4
1-Heck-c/a	19.00	56.00	150.00
2,3,5,7,9-11:	10.00	30.00	80.00
6- "Narcotics" story; begin spy theme	10.50	32.00	85.00
4-Marijuana cover/story	12.50	37.50	100.00
8-Bondage/torture/headlights panels	14.00	41.00	110.00

NOTE: ***Morisi** a-2, 5, 6(3), 10; c-2. Contains some reprints from Danger & Dynamite.*

DANGER (Formerly Comic Media title)
Charlton Comics Group: No. 12, June, 1955 - No. 14, Oct, 1955

	GD2.0	FN6.0	NM9.4
12(#1)	9.30	28.00	65.00
13,14: 14-r/#12	7.15	21.50	50.00

DANGER
Super Comics: 1964
Super Reprint #10-12 (Black Dwarf; #10-r/Great Comics #1 by Novack. #11-r/Johnny Danger #1. #12-r/Red Seal #14), #15-r/Spy Cases #26. #16-Unpublished Chesler material (Yankee Girl), #17-r/Scoop #8 (Capt. Courage & Enchanted Dagger), #18(nd)-r/Guns Against Gangsters #5 (Gun-Master, Annie Oakley, The Chameleon; L.B. Cole-r) 2.00 6.00 16.00

DANGER AND ADVENTURE (Formerly This Magazine Is Haunted; Robin Hood and His Merry Men No. 28 on)
Charlton Comics: No. 22, Feb, 1955 - No. 27, Feb, 1956

	GD2.0	FN6.0	NM9.4
22-Ibis the Invincible-c/story; Nyoka app.; last pre-code issue	10.00	30.00	75.00
23-Lance O'Casey-c/sty; Nyoka app.; Ditko-a thru #27	12.00	36.00	95.00
24-27: 24-Mike Danger & Johnny Adventure begin	8.65	26.00	60.00

DANGER GIRL (Also see Cliffhanger #0)
Image Comics (Cliffhanger Productions): Mar, 1998 - No. 4, Dec, 1998;
DC Comics (Cliffhanger Prod.): No. 5, July, 1999 - No. 7, Feb, 2001

	GD2.0	FN6.0	NM9.4
Preview-Bagged in DV8 #14 Voyager Pack			4.00
Preview Gold Edition			8.00
1-($2.95) Hartnell & Campbell-s/Campbell/Garner-a	1.00	3.00	8.00
1-($4.95) Chromium cover			45.00
1-American Entertainment Ed.			8.00
1-American Entertainment Gold Ed., 1-Tourbook edition			10.00
1-"Danger-sized" ed.; over-sized format	3.00	9.00	30.00
2-($2.50)			4.00
2-Smoking Gun variant cover, 2-Platinum Ed., 2-Dynamic Forces Omnichrome variant-c	1.85	5.50	15.00
2-Gold foil cover			9.00
2-Ruby red foil cover			50.00
3,4: 3-c by Campbell, Charest and Adam Hughes. 4-Big knife variant-c			3.00
3,5: 3-Gold foil cover. 5-DF Bikini variant-c			10.00
4-6			2.50
7-($5.95) Wraparound gatefold-c; Last issue			5.95
San Diego Preview (8/98, B&W) flip book w/Wildcats preview			5.00
...Special (2/00, $3.50) art by Campbell, Chiodo, and Art Adams			3.50
... :The Dangerous Collection nn(8/98; r-#1)			6.00
... :The Dangerous Collection 2,3: 2-(11/98, $5.95) r/#2,3. 3-('99) r/#4,5			6.00
... :The Dangerous Collection nn, 2-($10.00) Gold foil logo			10.00

DANGER IS OUR BUSINESS!
Toby Press: 1953(Dec.) - No. 10, June, 1955

	GD2.0	FN6.0	NM9.4
1-Captain Comet by Williamson/Frazetta-a, 6 pgs. (science fiction)	43.00	128.00	385.00
2	12.00	36.00	95.00
3-10	10.00	30.00	80.00
I.W. Reprint #9('64)-Williamson/Frazetta-r/#1; Kinstler-c	8.15	24.50	90.00

DANGER IS THEIR BUSINESS (Also see A-1 Comic)
Magazine Enterprises: No. 50, 1952
A-1 50-Powell-a 13.00 39.00 105.00

DANGER MAN (TV)
Dell Publishing Co.: No. 1231, Sept-Nov, 1961
Four Color 1231-Patrick McGoohan photo-c 10.00 30.00 120.00

DANGER TRAIL (Also see Showcase #50, 51)
National Periodical Publ.: July-Aug, 1950 - No. 5, Mar-Apr, 1951 (52 pgs.)

	GD2.0	FN6.0	NM9.4
1-King Faraday begins, ends #4; Toth-a in all	116.00	348.00	1100.00
2	82.00	245.00	775.00
3-(Rare) one of the rarest early '50s DCs	116.00	348.00	1100.00
4,5: 5-Johnny Peril-c/story (moves to Sensation Comics #107); new logo (also see Comic Cavalcade #15-29)	68.00	205.00	650.00

DANGER TRAIL
DC Comics: Apr, 1993 - No. 4, July, 1993 ($1.50, limited series)
1-4: Gulacy-c on all 2.00

DANGER UNLIMITED (See San Diego Comic Con Comics #2 & Torch of Liberty Special)
Dark Horse (Legend): Feb, 1994 - No. 4, May, 1994 ($2.00, limited series)
1-4: Byrne-c/a/scripts in all; origin stories of both original team (Doc Danger, Thermal, Miss Mirage, & Hunk) & future team (Thermal, Belebet, & Caucus). 1-Intro Torch of Liberty & Golgotha (cameo) in back-up story. 4-Hellboy & Torch of Liberty cameo in lead story 2.00
Trade paperback (1995, $14.95)-r/#1-4; includes last pg. originally cut from #4 15.00

DAN HASTINGS (See Syndicate Features)

DANIEL BOONE (See The Exploits of..., Fighting... Frontier Scout...,The Legends of... & March of Comics No. 306)
Dell Publishing Co.: No. 1163, Mar-May, 1961
Four Color 1163-Marsh-a 4.60 13.75 55.00

DANIEL BOONE (TV) (See March of Comics No. 306)
Gold Key: Jan, 1965 - No. 15, Apr, 1969 (All have Fess Parker photo-c)

	GD2.0	FN6.0	NM9.4
1	8.35	25.00	100.00
2	4.55	13.65	50.00
3-5	3.65	11.00	40.00
6-15	2.50	7.50	25.00

DAN'L BOONE
Sussex Publ. Co.: Sept, 1955 - No. 8, Sept, 1957

	GD2.0	FN6.0	NM9.4
1	14.00	43.00	115.00
2	9.30	28.00	65.00
3-8	7.00	21.00	48.00

DANNY BLAZE (...Firefighter) (Nature Boy No. 3 on)
Charlton Comics: Aug, 1955 - No. 2, Oct, 1955

	GD2.0	FN6.0	NM9.4
1	10.00	30.00	75.00
2	8.65	26.00	60.00

DANNY DINGLE (See Sparkler Comics)
United Features Syndicate: No. 17, 1940
Single Series 17 25.00 75.00 200.00

DANNY THOMAS SHOW, THE (TV)
Dell Publishing Co.: No. 1180, Apr-June, 1961 - No. 1249, Dec-Feb, 1961-62

	GD2.0	FN6.0	NM9.4
Four Color 1180-Toth-a, photo-c	15.00	45.00	180.00
Four Color 1249-Manning-a, photo-c	15.00	45.00	180.00

Daredevil #7 © MAR

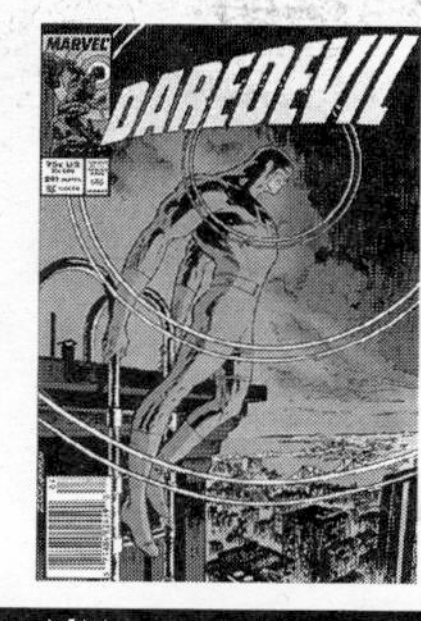

Daredevil #241 © MAR

Daredevil #373 © MAR

GD2.0 FN6.0 NM9.4

DARBY O'GILL & THE LITTLE PEOPLE (Movie)(See Movie Comics)
Dell Publishing Co.: 1959 (Disney)

Four Color 1024-Toth-a; photo-c. 9.00 27.00 110.00

DAREDEVIL (...& the Black Widow #92-107 on-c only; see Giant-Size...,Marvel Advs., Marvel Graphic Novel #24, Marvel Super Heroes, '66 & Spider-Man &...)
Marvel Comics Group: Apr, 1964 - No. 380, Oct, 1998

1-Origin/1st app. Daredevil; reprinted in Marvel Super Heroes #1 (1966); death of Battling Murdock; intro Foggy Nelson & Karen Page; Everett-c/a 154.00 462.00 2300.00
2-Fantastic Four cameo; 2nd app. Electro (Spidey villain); Thing guest star 42.00 126.00 550.00
3-Origin & 1st app. The Owl (villain) 31.00 93.00 360.00
4-The Purple Man app. 29.00 87.00 320.00
5-Minor costume change; Wood-a begins 20.00 60.00 220.00
6,8-10: 8-Origin/1st app. Stilt-Man 13.50 40.00 150.00
7-Daredevil battles Sub-Mariner & dons new red costume (4/65) 27.50 82.00 300.00
11-15: 12-1st app. Plunderer; Ka-Zar app. 13-Facts about Ka-Zar's origin; Kirby-a 6.80 20.50 75.00
16,17-Spider-Man x-over. 16-1st Romita-a on Spider-Man (5/66) 9.50 28.50 105.00
18-Origin & 1st app. Gladiator 5.45 16.35 60.00
19,20 4.55 13.65 50.00
21-26,28-30: 24-Ka-Zar app. 3.20 9.60 35.00
27-Spider-Man x-over 3.45 10.35 38.00
31-40: 38-Fantastic Four x-over; cont'd in F.F. #73. 39-1st Exterminator (later becomes Death-Stalker) 2.80 8.40 28.00
41,42,44-49: 41-Death Mike Murdock. 42-1st app. Jester. 45-Statue of Liberty photo-c 2.30 7.00 20.00
43,50-53: 43-Daredevil battles Captain America; origin partially retold. 50-52-B. Smith-a. 53-Origin retold; last 12¢ issue 2.50 7.50 25.00
54-56,58-60: 54-Spider-Man cameo. 56-1st app. Death's Head (9/69); story cont'd in #57 (not same as new Death's Head) 2.00 6.00 16.00
57-Reveals i.d. to Karen Page; Death's Head app. 2.00 6.00 18.00
61-76,78-80: 79-Stan Lee cameo. 80-Last 15¢ issue 1.75 5.25 14.00
77-Spider-Man x-over 2.00 6.00 18.00
81-(52 pgs.) Black Widow begins (11/71). 2.50 7.50 24.00
82,84-99: 87-Electro-c/story 1.50 4.50 12.00
83-B. Smith layouts/Weiss-p 2.00 6.00 16.00
100-Origin retold 2.50 7.50 23.00
101-104,106-120: 107-Starlin-c; Thanos cameo. 113-1st app. Deathstalker (cameo). 114-1st full app. Deathstalker 1.10 3.30 9.00
105-Origin Moondragon by Starlin (12/73); Thanos cameo in flashback (early app.) 1.50 4.50 12.00
121-130,137: 124-1st app. Copperhead; Black Widow leaves. 126-1st new Torpedo 2.40 6.00
131-Origin/1st app. new Bullseye (see Nick Fury #15) 2.30 7.00 20.00
132-136-(Regular 25¢ editions). 132-Bullseye app. 2.40 6.00
132-136-(30¢-c variants, limited distribution)(4-8/76) 1.10 3.30 9.00
138-Ghost Rider-c/story; Death's Head is reincarnated; Byrne-a 1.00 3.00 8.00
139-147,149-157: 142-Nova cameo. 146-Bullseye app. 150-1st app. Paladin. 151-Reveals i.d. to Heather Glenn. 155-Black Widow returns. 156-The 1960s Daredevil app. 5.00
148-(Regular 30¢ edition)(9/77) 5.00
148-(35¢-c, limited distribution) 1.00 2.80 7.00
158-Frank Miller art begins (5/79); origin/death of Deathstalker (see Captain America #235 & Spectacular Spider-Man #27 3.65 11.00 40.00
159 2.50 7.50 24.00
160,161,163,164,169: 163-Hulk cameo. 164-Origin retold. 169-Electra app. 1.50 4.50 15.00
162-Ditko-a; no Miller-a 2.40 6.00
165-167,170 1.25 3.75 10.00
168-Origin/1st app. Elektra 4.10 12.30 45.00
171-175: 174,175-Elektra app. 1.00 2.80 7.00
176-180-Elektra app. 178-Cage app. 179-Anti-smoking issue mentioned in the Congressional Record 2.40 6.00

GD2.0 FN6.0 NM9.4

181-(52 pgs.)-Death of Elektra; Punisher cameo out of costume 1.50 4.50 12.00
182-184-Punisher app. by Miller (drug issues) 5.00
185-191: 187-New Black Widow. 189-Death of Stick. 190-($1.00, 52 pgs.)-Elektra returns, part origin. 191-Last Miller Daredevil 4.00
192-195,197-199,201-207,209-218,220-226,234-237: 197-Bullseye app. 226-Frank Miller plots begin 2.50
196-Wolverine app. 1.10 3.30 9.00
200,208,219,228-233: 200-Bullseye app. 208-Harlan Ellison scripts borrowed from Avengers TV episode "House that Jack Built". 219-Miller-c/script. 228-233-Last Miller scripts 4.00
227-Miller scripts begin 3.00
238,248,249: 238-Mutant Massacre; Sabretooth app. 248,249-Wolverine app. 4.00
239,240,242-247 3.00
241-Todd McFarlane-a(p) 4.00
250,251,253,258: 250-1st app. Bullet. 258-Intro The Bengal (a villain) 2.50
252,260 (52 pgs.): 252-Fall of the Mutants. 260-Typhoid Mary app. 4.00
254-Origin & 1st app. Typhoid Mary (5/88) 2.40 6.00
255,256,258: 255,256-2nd/3rd app. Typhoid Mary. 259-Typhoid Mary app. 3.00
257-Punisher app. (x-over w/Punisher #10) 5.00
261-281,283-294,296-299,301-304,307-318: 270-1st app. Black Heart. 272-Intro Shotgun (villain). 281-Silver Surfer cameo. 283-Capt. America app. 297-Typhoid Mary app.; Kingpin storyline begins. 292-D.G. Chichester scripts begin. 293-Punisher app. 303-Re-intro the Owl. 304-Garney-c/a. 309-Punisher-c.; Terror app. 310-Calypso-c. 2.00
282,295,300,305,306: 282-Silver Surfer app. 295-Ghost Rider app. 300-($2.00, 52 pgs.)-Kingpin story ends. 305,306-Spider-Man-c 3.00
319-Prologue to Fall From Grace; Elektra returns 4.00
319-2nd printing w/black-c 2.00
320-Fall From Grace Pt 1 4.00
321-Fall From Grace regular ed.; Pt 2; new costume; Venom app. 3.00
321-($2.00)-Wraparound Glow-in-the-dark-c ed. 4.00
322-Fall From Grace Pt 3; Eddie Brock app. 3.50
323,324-Fall From Grace Pt. 4 & 5: 323-Vs. Venom-c/story. 324-Morbius-c/story 2.50
325-($2.50, 52 pgs.)-Fall From Grace ends; contains bound-in poster 3.00
326-349,351-353: 326-New logo. 328-Bound-in trading card sheet. 330-Gambit app. 348-1st Cary Nord art in DD (1/96);"Dec" on-c. 353-Karl Kesel scripts; Nord-c/a begins; Mr. Hyde-c/app. 2.00
350-($2.95)-Double-sized 3.00
350-($3.50)-Double-sized; gold ink-c 3.50
354-374,376-379: Kesel scripts, Nord-c/a in all. 354-$1.50-c begins. 355-Larry Hama layouts; Pyro app. 358-Mysterio-c/app. 359-Absorbing Man cameo. 360-Absorbing Man-c/app. 361-Black Widow-c/app. 363-Gene Colan-a(p) begins. 368-Omega Red-c/app. 372-Ghost Rider-c/app. 376-379-"Flying Blind", DD goes undercover for S.H.I.E.L.D. 2.00
375-($2.99) Wraparound-c; Mr. Fear-c/app. 3.00
380-($2.99) Final issue; flashback story 4.00
Special 1(9/67, 25¢, 68 pgs.)-New art/story 3.65 11.00 40.00
Special 2,3: 2(2/71, 25¢, 52 pgs.)-Entire book has Powell/Wood-r; Wood-c. 3(1/72, 52 pgs.)-Reprints 2.00 6.00 16.00
Annual 4(10/76) 2.40 6.00
Annual 4(#5)-10: ('89-94 68 pgs.)-5-Atlantis Attacks. 6-Sutton-a. 7-Guice-a (7 pgs.). 8-Deathlok-c/story. 9-Polybagged w/card. 10 3.00
.../Deadpool- (Annual '97, $2.99)-Wraparound-c 3.00
....:Fall From Grace TPB ($19.95)-r #319-325 20.00
....:Gang War TPB ($15.95)-r #169-172,180; Miller-s/a(p) 16.00
.../Punisher TPB (1988, $4.95)-r/D.D. #182-184 (all printings) 5.00
...Visionaries: Frank Miller Vol. 1 TPB ($17.95) r/#158-161,163-167 18.00

NOTE: ***Art Adams*** *c-238p, 239.* ***Austin*** *a-191i; c-151i, 200i.* ***John Buscema*** *a-136, 137p, 234p, 235p; c-86p, 136i, 137p, 142, 219.* ***Byrne*** *c-200p, 201, 203, 223.* ***Capullo*** *a-286p.* ***Colan*** *a(p)-20-49, 53-82, 84-98, 100, 110, 112, 124, 153, 154, 156, 157, Spec. 1p; c(p)-20-42, 44-49, 53-60, 71, 92, 98, 138, 153, 154, 156, 157, Annual 1.* ***Craig*** *a-50i, 52i.* ***Ditko*** *a-162, 234p, 235p, 264p; c-162.* ***Everett*** *c/a-1; inks-21, 83.* ***Garney*** *c/a-304.* ***Gil Kane*** *a-141p, 146-148p, 151p; c(p)-85, 90, 91, 93, 94, 115, 116, 119, 120, 125-128, 133, 139, 147, 152.* ***Kirby*** *c-2-4, 5p, 12p, 13p, 43, 136p.* ***Layton*** *c-202.* ***Miller*** *scripts-168-182, 183(part), 184-191, 219, 227-233; a-158-161p, 163-184p, 191p; c-158-161p, 163-184p, 185-189, 190p, 191.* ***Orlando*** *a-2-4p.* ***Powell*** *a-9p, 11p, Special 1r, 2r.* ***Simonson*** *c-199, 236p.* ***B. Smith*** *a-236p; c-51p, 52p, 217.* ***Starlin*** *a-105p.* ***Steranko*** *c-44i.* ***Tuska*** *a-39i, 145p.* ***Williamson*** *a(i)-237, 239, 240, 243, 248-257, 259-282, 283(part), 284, 285, 287, 288(part), 289(part), 293-300; c(i)-237, 243, 244, 248-257, 259-263, 265-278, 280-289,*

Daredevil V2 #9 © MAR

Daredevil Comics #3 © LEV

Daring Love #1 © Gilmore

GD2.0 FN6.0 NM9.4

Annual 8. ***Wood*** *a-5-8, 9i, 10, 11i, Spec. 2i; c-5i, 6-11, 164i.*

DAREDEVIL (Volume 2) (Marvel Knights)
Marvel Comics: Nov, 1998 - Present ($2.50)

1-Kevin Smith-s/Quesada & Palmiotti-a 4.00
1-($6.95) DF Edition w/Quesada & Palmiotti var.-c 7.00
1-($6.00) DF Sketch Ed. w/B&W-c 6.00
2-Two covers by Campbell and Quesada/Palmiotti 5.00
3-8: 4,5-Bullseye app. 8-Spider-Man-c/app. 2.50
9-11-David Mack-s; intro Echo 2.50
12,13: 12-Begin $2.99-c; Haynes-a. 13-Quesada-a 3.00
TPB ($9.95) r/#1-3 10.00
Visionaries TPB ($19.95) r/#1-8; Ben Affleck intro. 20.00

DAREDEVIL/ BATMAN (Also see Batman/Daredevil)
Marvel Comics/ DC Comics: 1997 ($5.99, one-shot)

nn-McDaniel-c/a 2.40 6.00

DAREDEVIL: NINJA
Marvel Comics: Dec, 2000 - No. 3, Feb, 2001 ($2.99, limited series)

1-3: Bendis-s/Haynes-a 3.00

DAREDEVIL/ SHI (See Shi/ Daredevil)
Marvel Comics/ Crusade Comics: Feb,1997 ($2.95, limited series)

1 3.00

DAREDEVIL/ SPIDER-MAN
Marvel Comics: Jan, 2001 - No. 4 ($2.99, limited series)

1,2-Jenkins-s/Winslade-a/Alex Ross-c; Stilt Man app. 3.00

DAREDEVIL THE MAN WITHOUT FEAR
Marvel Comics: Oct, 1993 - No. 5, Feb, 1994 ($2.95, limited series) (foil embossed covers)

1-5: Miller scripts; Romita, Jr./Williamson-c/a 4.00
Hardcover 100.00
Trade paperback 20.00

DAREDEVIL COMICS (See Silver Streak Comics)
Lev Gleason Publications (Funnies, Inc. No. 1): July, 1941 - No. 134, Sept, 1956 (Charles Biro stories)

GD2.0 FN6.0 VF8.0 NM9.4

1-No. 1 titled "Daredevil Battles Hitler"; The Silver Streak, Lance Hale, Cloud Curtis, Dickey Dean, Pirate Prince team up w/Daredevil and battle Hitler; Daredevil battles the Claw; Origin of Hitler feature story. Hitler photo app. on-c 1000.00 3000.00 6500.00 12,500.00

GD2.0 FN6.0 NM9.4

2-London, Pat Patriot (by Reed Crandall), Nightro, Real American No. 1 (by Briefer #2-11), Dickie Dean, Pirate Prince, & Times Square begin; intro. & only app. The Pioneer, Champion of America 300.00 900.00 3000.00
3-Origin of 13 190.00 570.00 1800.00
4 158.00 474.00 1500.00
5-Intro. Sniffer & Jinx; Ghost vs. Claw begins by Bob Wood, ends #20 126.00 379.00 1200.00
6-(#7 in indicia) 105.00 316.00 1000.00
7-10: 8-Nightro ends 89.00 268.00 850.00
11-London, Pat Patriot end; classic bondage/torture-c 105.00 316.00 1000.00
12-Origin of The Claw; Scoop Scuttle by Wolverton begins (2-4 pgs.), ends #22, not in #21 140.00 420.00 1325.00
13-Intro. of Little Wise Guys (10/42) 118.00 354.00 1125.00
14 63.00 189.00 600.00
15-Death of Meatball 92.00 276.00 875.00
16,17 58.00 174.00 550.00
18-New origin of Daredevil (not same as Silver Streak #6). Hitler, Mussolini Tojo and Mickey Mouse app. on-c 124.00 371.00 1175.00
19,20 50.00 150.00 450.00
21-Reprints cover of Silver Streak #6 (on inside) plus intro. of The Claw from Silver Streak #1 87.00 261.00 825.00
22-30: 27-Bondage/torture-c 40.00 120.00 340.00
31-Death of The Claw 79.00 237.00 750.00
32-37,39,41: 35-Two Daredevil stories begin, end #68 (35-41 are 64 pgs.) 30.00 90.00 240.00
38-Origin Daredevil retold from #18 42.00 125.00 375.00
42-50: 42-Intro. Kilroy in Daredevil; 1 panel Steranko-a 24.00 71.00 190.00
51-69-Last Daredevil issue (12/50) 17.00 51.00 135.00
70-Little Wise Guys take over book; McWilliams-a; Hot Rock Flanagan begins, ends #80 11.00 33.00 90.00
71-79,81: 79-Daredevil returns 10.00 30.00 70.00
80-Daredevil x-over 10.00 30.00 75.00
82,90,100: 82,90-One pg. Frazetta ad in both 10.00 30.00 70.00
83-89,91-99,101-134 8.65 26.00 60.00

NOTE: ***Biro*** *c/a-all?* ***Bolle*** *a-125.* ***Maurer*** *a-75.* ***McWilliams*** *a-73, 75, 79, 80.*

DARING ADVENTURES (Also see Approved Comics)
St. John Publishing Co.: Nov, 1953 (25¢, 3-D, came w/glasses)

1 (3-D)-Reprints lead story from Son of Sinbad #1 by Kubert 35.00 105.00 280.00

DARING ADVENTURES
I.W. Enterprises/Super Comics: 1963 - 1964

I. W. Reprint #8-r/Fight Comics #53; Matt Baker-a 5.00 15.00 55.00
I.W. Reprint #9-r/Blue Bolt #115; Disbrow-a(3) 5.45 16.35 60.00
Super Reprint #10,11('63)-r/Dynamic #24,16; 11-Marijuana story; Yankee Boy app.; Mac Raboy-a 3.20 9.60 35.00
Super Reprint #12('64)-Phantom Lady from Fox (r/#14 only? w/splash pg. omitted); Matt Baker-a 12.75 38.00 140.00
Super Reprint #15('64)-r/Hooded Menace #1 7.25 21.75 80.00
Super Reprint #16('64)-r/Dynamic #12 2.80 8.40 28.00
Super Reprint #17('64)-r/Green Lama #3 by Raboy 4.10 12.30 45.00
Super Reprint #18-Origin Atlas from unpublished Atlas Comics #1 3.65 11.00 40.00

DARING COMICS (Formerly Daring Mystery) (Jeanie Comics No. 13 on)
Timely Comics (HPC): No. 9, Fall, 1944 - No. 12, Fall, 1945

9-Human Torch, Toro & Sub-Mariner begin 116.00 348.00 1100.00
10-12: 10-The Angel only app. 11,12-The Destroyer app. 95.00 285.00 900.00

NOTE: ***Schomburg*** *c-9-11.* ***Sekowsky*** *c-12? Human Torch, Toro & Sub-Mariner c-9-12.*

DARING CONFESSIONS (Formerly Youthful Hearts)
Youthful Magazines: No. 4, 11/52 - No. 7, 5/53; No. 8, 10/53

4-Doug Wildey-a; Tony Curtis story 15.00 45.00 120.00
5-8: 5-Ray Anthony photo on-c. 6,8-Wildey-a 10.50 32.00 85.00

DARING ESCAPES
Image Comics: Sept, 1998 - No. 4, Mar, 1999 ($2.95/$2.50, mini-series)

1-Houdini; following app. in Spawn #19,20 3.00
2-4-($2.50) 2.50

DARING LOVE (Radiant Love No. 2 on)
Gilmor Magazines: Sept-Oct, 1953

1-Steve Ditko's 1st published work (1st drawn was Fantastic Fears #5)(Also See Black Magic #27)(scarce) 42.00 125.00 375.00

DARING LOVE (Formerly Youthful Romances)
Ribage/Pix: No. 15, 12/52; No. 16, 2/53-c, 4/53-Indicia; No. 17-4/53-c & indicia

15 10.00 30.00 80.00
16,17: 17-Photo-c 9.30 28.00 65.00

NOTE: ***Colletta*** *a-15.* ***Wildey*** *a-17.*

DARING LOVE STORIES (See Fox Giants)

DARING MYSTERY COMICS (Comedy Comics No. 9 on; title changed to Daring Comics with No. 9)
Timely Comics (TPI 1-6/TCI 7,8): 1/40 - No. 5, 6/40; No. 6, 9/40; No. 7, 4/41 - No. 8, 1/42

GD2.0 FN6.0 VF8.0 NM9.4

1-Origin The Fiery Mask (1st app.) by Joe Simon; Monako, Prince of Magic (1st app.), John Steele, Soldier of Fortune (1st app.), Doc Denton (1st app.) begin; Flash Foster & Barney Mullen, Sea Rover only app; bondage-c 1500.00 4500.00 10,500.00 21,000.00

GD2.0 FN6.0 NM9.4

2-(Rare)-Origin The Phantom Bullet (1st & only app.); The Laughing Mask & Mr. E only app.; Trojak the Tiger Man begins, ends #6; Zephyr Jones & K-4 & His Sky Devils app., also #4 652.00 1957.00 7500.00

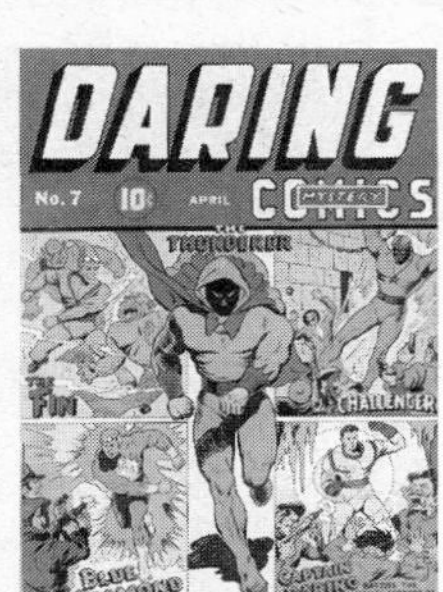

Daring Mystery Comics #7 © MAR

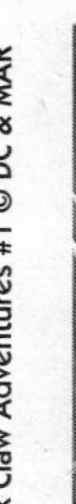
Darkchylde #0 © Randy Queen

Dark Claw Adventures #1 © DC & MAR

GD2.0 FN6.0 NM9.4

ne Phantom Reporter, Dale of FBI, Captain Strong only app.; Breeze Barton, arvex the Super-Robot, The Purple Mask begin 429.00 1286.00 4500.00
4-Last Purple Mask; Whirlwind Carter begins; Dan Gorman, G-Man app.
-The Falcon begins (1st app.); The Fiery Mask, Little Hercules app. by agendorf in the Segar style; bondage-c 300.00 900.00 3000.00
rigin & only app. Marvel Boy by S&K; Flying Flame, Dynaman, & Stupor-an only app.; The Fiery Mask by S&K; S&K-c 381.00 1143.00 4000.00
rigin The Blue Diamond, Captain Daring by S&K, The Fin by Everett, The hallenger, The Silver Scorpion & The Thunderer by Burgos; Mr. Millions app 305.00 915.00 3200.00
rigin Citizen V; Last Fin, Silver Scorpion, Capt. Daring by Borth, Blue iamond & The Thunderer; Kirby & part solo Simon-c; Rudy the Robot only pp.; Citizen V, Fin & Silver Scorpion continue in Comedy #9 253.00 758.00 2400.00
*: **Schomburg** c-1-4, 7. **Simon** a-2, 3, 5. Cover features: 1-Fiery Mask; 2-Phantom Bullet; 3- Mask; 4-G-Man; 5-The Falcon; 6-Marvel Boy; 7, 8-Multiple characters.*

ING NEW ADVENTURES OF SUPERGIRL, THE
:omics: Nov, 1982 - No. 13, Nov, 1983 (Supergirl No. 14 on)

rigin retold; Lois Lane back-ups in #2-12 5.00
3: 8,9-Doom Patrol app. 13-New costume; flag-c 3.00
*: **Buckler** c-1p, 2p. **Giffen** c-3p, 4p. **Gil Kane** c-6, ,8, 9, 11-13.*

K, THE
inum Comics: Nov, 1990 - No. 4, Feb, 1993; V2#1, May, 1993 - V2#7, 1994 ($1.95)

1-Bright-p; Panosian, Hanna-i; Stroman-c. 2-(1/92)-Stroman-c/a(p). Perez-c & part-i 3.00
,V2#2-6: V2#1-Red foil Bart Sears-c. V2#1-Red non-foil variant-c. 2#1-2nd printing w/blue foil Bart Sears-c. V2#2-Stroman/Bryant-a. 3-Perez-i). 3-6-Foil-c. 4-Perez-c & part-i;bound-in trading cards. 5,6-(2,3/94)-Perez-i). 7-(B&W)-Perez-c(i) 2.00
ention Book 1 ,2(Fall/94, 10/94)-Perez-c 2.00

K ANGEL (Formerly Hell's Angel)
el Comics UK, Ltd.: No. 6, Dec, 1992 - No. 16, Dec, 1993 ($1.75)

13-16: 6-Excalibur-c/story. 8-Psylocke app. 2.00
2-Wolverine/X-Men app. 3.00

K ANGEL: PHOENIX RESURRECTION (Kia Asamiya's...)
e Comics: May, 2000 - Present ($2.95)

Kia Asamiya-s/a 2.95

KCHYLDE (Also see Dreams of the Darkchylde)
mum Press #1-3/ Image Comics #4 on: June, 1996 - No. 5, Sept, 1997 5/ $2.50)

andy Queen-c/a/scripts; "Roses" cover 2.40 6.00
merican Entertainment Edition-wraparound-c 2.40 6.00
ashion magazine-style" variant-c 1.00 2.80 7.00
pecial Comicon Edition (contents of #1) Winged devil variant-c 5.00
2.50)-Remastered Ed.-wraparound-c 4.00
eg-c),2-Spiderweb and Moon variant-c 2.40 6.00
eg-c),3-"Kalvin Clein" variant-c by Drew 3.00
eg-c), 4-Variant-c 4.00
4.00
&W Edition, 5-Dynamic Forces Gold Ed. 8.00
/98, $2.50) 2.50
merican Entertainment Ed. 4.00
ynamic Forces Ed. 5.00
ynamic Forces Gold Ed. 7.00
Wizard offer 4.00
/ariant-c 6.00
Gold Ed. 9.00
e Descent TPB ('98, $19.95) r/#1-5; bagged with Darkchylde The Legacy review Special 1998; listed price is for TPB only 20.00

KCHYLDE SKETCH BOOK
e Comics (Dynamic Forces): 1998

egular-c 8.00
arkChrome cover 16.00

GD2.0 FN6.0 NM9.4

DARKCHYLDE SUMMER SWIMSUIT SPECTACULAR
DC Comics (WildStorm): Aug, 1999 ($3.95, one-shot)

1-Pin-up art by various 4.00

DARKCHYLDE SWIMSUIT ILLUSTRATED
Image Comics: 1998 ($2.50, one-shot)

1-Pin-up art by various 2.50
1-(6.95) Variant cover 7.00
1-American Entertainment Ed. 3.00
1-Dynamic Forces Ed. 4.00
1-Dynamic Forces Gold Ed. 6.00
1-Chromium cover 15.00

DARKCHYLDE THE DIARY
Image Comics: June, 1997 ($2.50, one-shot)

1-Queen-c/s/ art by various 2.50
1-Variant-c 5.00
1-Holochrome variant-c 8.00

DARKCHYLDE THE LEGACY
Image Comics/DC (WildStorm) #3 on: Aug, 1998 - No. 3 ($2.50)

1-3: 1-Queen-c. 2-Two covers by Queen and Art Adams 2.50

DARK CLAW ADVENTURES
DC Comics (Amalgam): June, 1997 ($1.95, one-shot)

1-Templeton-c/s/a & Burchett-a 2.00

DARK CROSSINGS: DARK CLOUDS RISING
Image Comics (Top Cow): June, 2000; Oct, 2000 ($5.95, limited series)

1-Witchblade, Darkness, Tomb Raider crossover; Dwayne Turner-a 5.95
1-(Dark Clouds Overhead) 5.95

DARK CRYSTAL, THE (Movie)
Marvel Comics Group: April, 1983 - No. 2, May, 1983

1,2-Adaptation of film 3.00

DARKDEVIL (See Spider-Girl)
Marvel Comics: Nov, 2000 - No. 3, Jan, 2001 ($2.99, limited series)

1-3: 1-Origin of Darkdevil; Kingpin-c/app. 3.00

DARK DOMINION
Defiant: Oct, 1993 - No. 10, July, 1994 ($2.50)

1-10-Len Wein scripts begin. 4-Free extra 16 pgs. 7-9-J.G. Jones-c/a. 10-Pre-Schism issue; Shooter/Wein script; John Ridgway-a 2.50

DARKER IMAGE (Also see Deathblow, The Maxx, & Bloodwulf)
Image Comics: Mar, 1993 ($1.95, one-shot)

1-The Maxx by Sam Kieth begins; Bloodwulf by Rob Liefeld & Deathblow by Jim Lee begin (both 1st app.); polybagged w/1 of 3 cards by Kieth, Lee or Liefeld 2.50
1-B&W interior pgs. w/silver foil logo 6.00

DARKEWOOD
Aircel Publishing: 1987 - No. 5, 1988 ($2.00, 28pgs, limited series)

1-5 2.00

DARK FANTASIES
Dark Fantasy: 1994 - No. 8, 1995 ($2.95)

1-Test print Run (3,000)-Linsner-c 1.00 3.00 8.00
1-Linsner-c 5.00
2-9: 2-4 (Deluxe), 2-4 (Regular), 5-8 (Deluxe; $3.95) 4.00
5-8 (Regular; $3.50) 3.50

DARK GUARD
Marvel Comics UK: Oct, 1993 - No. 4, Jan, 1994 ($1.75)

1-($2.95)-Foil stamped-c 3.00
2-4 2.00

DARKHAWK
Marvel Comics: Mar, 1991 - No. 50, Apr, 1995 ($1.00/$1.25/$1.50)

1-Origin/1st app. Darkhawk; Hobgoblin cameo 3.00
2,3,13,14: 2-Spider-Man & Hobgoblin app. 3-Spider-Man & Hobgoblin app. 13,14-Venom-c/story 2.50

Darkhold #14 © MAR

Dark Horse Presents #56 © DH

Dark Horse Presents #132 © DH

4-12,15-24,26-49: 6-Capt. America & Daredevil x-over. 9-Punisher app. 11,12-Tombstone app. 19-Spider-Man & Brotherhood of Evil Mutants-c/story. 20-Spider-Man app. 22-Ghost Rider-c/story. 23-Origin begins, ends #25. 27-New Warriors-c/story. 35-Begin 3 part Venom story. 39-Bound-in trading card sheet 2.00
25,50: (52 pgs.)-Red holo-grafx foil-c w/double gatefold poster; origin of Darkhawk armor revealed. 3.00
Annual 1-3 ('92-'94,68 pgs.)-1-Vs. Iron Man. 2 -Polybagged w/card 3.00

DARKHOLD: PAGES FROM THE BOOK OF SINS (See Midnight Sons Unltd)
Marvel Comics (Midnight Sons imprint #15 on): Oct, 1992 - No. 16, Jan, 1994

1-($2.75, 52 pgs.)-Polybagged w/poster by Andy & Adam Kubert; part 4 of Rise of the Midnight Sons storyline 2.75
2-10,12-16: 3-Reintro Modred the Mystic (see Marvel Chillers #1). 4-Sabertooth-c/sty. 5-Punisher & Ghost Rider app. 15-Spot varnish-c. 15,16-Siege of Darkness part 4&12 2.00
11-($2.25)-Outer-c is a Darkhold envelope made of black parchment w/gold ink 2.25

DARK HORSE CLASSICS (Title series), **Dark Horse Comics**
1992 ($3.95, B&W, 52 pgs. nn's: The Last of the Mohicans. 20,000 Leagues Under the Sea 4.00

DARK HORSE CLASSICS, 5/96 ($2.95) 1-r/Predator: Jungle Tales 3.00

--ALIENS VERSUS PREDATOR, 2/97 - No. 6, 7/97 ($2.95,) 1-6: r/Aliens Versus Predator 3.00

--GODZILLA: KING OF THE MONSTERS, 4/98 ($2.95) 1-6: 1-r/Godzilla: Color Special; Art Adams-a 3.00

--STAR WARS: DARK EMPIRE, 3/97 - No. 6, 8/97 ($2.95) 1-6: r/Star Wars: Dark Empire 3.00

--TERROR OF GODZILLA, 8/98 - No. 6, 1/99 ($2.95) 1-6-r/manga Godzilla in color; Art Adams-c 3.00

DARK HORSE COMICS
Dark Horse Comics: Aug, 1992 - No. 25, Sept, 1994 ($2.50)

1-Dorman double gategold painted-c; Predator, Robocop, Timecop (3-part) & Renegade stories begin 3.00
2-6,11-25: 2-Mignola-c. 3-Begin 3-part Aliens story; Aliens-c. 4-Predator-c. 6-Begin 4 part Robocop story. 12-Begin 2-part Aliens & 3-part Predator stories. 13-Thing From Another World begins w/Nino-a(i). 15-Begin 2-part Aliens: Cargo story. 16-Begin 3-part Predator story. 17-Begin 3-part Star Wars: Droids story & 3-part Aliens: Alien story; Droids-c. 19-Begin 2-part X story; X cover 2.50
7-Begin Star Wars: Tales of the Jedi 3-part story 1.00 2.80 7.00
8-1st app. X and begins; begin 4-part James Bond 2.40 6.00
9,10: 9-Star Wars ends. 10-X ends; Begin 3-part Predator & Godzilla stories 4.00

NOTE: ***Art Adams** c-11.*

DARK HORSE DOWN UNDER
Dark Horse Comics: June, 1994 - No. 3, Oct, 1994 ($2.50, B&W, limited series)

1-3 2.50

DARK HORSE MAVERICK 2000
Dark Horse Comics: July, 2000 ($3.95, B&W, one-shot)

nn-Short stories by Miller, Chadwick, Sakai, Pearson 4.00

DARK HORSE MONSTERS
Dark Horse Comics: Feb, 1997 ($2.95, one-shot)

1-reprints 3.00

DARK HORSE PRESENTS
Dark Horse Comics: July, 1986 - No. 157, Sept, 2000 ($1.50-$2.95, B&W)

1-1st app. Concrete by Paul Chadwick 1.25 3.75 10.00
1-2nd printing (1988, $1.50) 2.25
1-Silver ink 3rd printing (1992, $2.25)-Says 2nd printing inside 2.25
2-9: 2-6,9-Concrete app. 4.00
10-1st app. The Mask; Concrete app. 1.25 3.75 10.00
11-19,21-23: 11-19,21-Mask stories. 12,14,16,18,22-Concrete app. 15(2/88). 17-All Roachmill issue 3.00
20-(68 pgs.)-Concrete, Flaming Carrot, Mask 1.25 3.75 10.00
24-Origin Aliens-c/story (11/88); Mr. Monster app. 2.00 6.00 18
25-31,33,37-41,44,45,47-50: 28-(52 pgs.)-Concrete app.; Mr. Monster story (homage to Graham Ingels). 33-(44 pgs.). 38-Concrete. 40-(52 pgs.)-1st Argosy story. 44-Crash Ryan. 48-50-Contain 2 trading cards. 50-S/F story Perez
32,34,35: 32-(68 pgs.)-Annual; Concrete, American. 34-Aliens-c/story. 35-Predator-c/story
36-1st Aliens Vs. Predator story; painted-c, 36-Variant line drawn-c
42,43,46,51-53: 42,43-Aliens-c/stories. 46-Prequel to new Predator II mini-s 51-53-Sin City by Frank Miller, parts 2-4; 51,53-Miller-c (see D.H.P. Fifth Anniv. Special for pt. 1)
54-62: 54-(9/91) The Next Men begins (1st app.) by Byrne; Miller-a/Morrow- Homocide by Morrow (also in #55). 55-2nd app. The Next Men; parts 5 & Sin City by Miller; Miller-c. 56-(68 pg. annual)-part 7 of Sin City by Miller; prologue to Aliens: Genocide; Next Men by Byrne. 57-(52 pgs.)-Part 8 of City by Miller; Next Men by Byrne; Byrne & Miller-c; Alien Fire story; swipe cover to Daredevil #1. 58,59-Part 9,10 Sin City by Miller; Alien Fire stories 60,61-Part 11,12 Sin City by Miller. 62-Last Sin City (entire book by Miller, c/a;52 pgs.)
63-66,68-79,81-84-($2.25): 64-Dr. Giggles begins (1st app.), ends #66; Bor the Bear story. 66-New Concrete-c/story by Chadwick. 71-Begin 3 part Dominque story by Jim Balent; Balent-c. 72-(3/93)-Begin 3-part Eudaemo (1st app.) story by Nelson
67-($3.95, 68 pgs.)-Begin 3-part prelude to Predator: Race War mini-series; Oscar Wilde adapt. by Russell
80-Art Adams-c/a (Monkeyman & O'Brien)
85-87,92-99: 85-Begin $2.50-c. 92, 93, 95-Too Much Coffee Man
88-91-Hellboy by Mignola.
NOTE: *There are 5 different Dark Horse Presents #100 issues*
100-1-Intro Lance Blastoff by Miller; Milk & Cheese by Evan Dorkin
100-2-100-5: 100-2-Hellboy-c by Wrightson; Hellboy story by Mignola; includ Roberta Gregory & Paul Pope stories. 100-3-Darrow-c, Concrete by Chadwick; Pekar story. 100-4-Gibbons-c: Miller story, Geary story/a. 100 Allred-c, Adams, Dorkin, Pope
101-125: 101-Aliens c/a by Wrightson, story by Paul Pope. 103-Kirby gatefol 106-Big Blown Baby by Bill Wray. 107-Mignola-c/a . 109-Begin $2.95-c; Pope-c. 110-Ed Brubaker-a/scripts. 114-Flip books begin; Lance Blastoff Miller; Star Slammers by Simonson. 115-Miller-c. 117-Aliens-c/app. 118- Dorkin-c/a. 119-Monkeyman & O'Brien. 124-Predator. 125-Nocturnals
126-($3.95, 48 pgs.)-Flip book: Nocturnals, Starship Troopers
127-134,136-140: 127-Nocturnals. 129-The Hammer. 132-134-Warren-a
135-($3.50) The Mark
141-All Buffy the Vampire Slayer issue
142-149: 142-Mignola-c. 143-Tarzan. 146,147-Aliens vs. Predator. 148-Xena
150-($4.50) Buffy-c by Green; Buffy, Concrete, Fish Police app.
151-155: 151-Hellboy-c/app. 153-155-Angel flip-c
Annual 1997 ($4.95, 64 pgs.)-Flip book; Body Bags, Aliens. Pearson-c; storie by Allred & Stephens, Pope, Smith & Morrow 1.00 3.00
Annual 1998 ($4.95, 64 pgs.) 1st Buffy the Vampire Slayer comic app.; Hellboy story and cover by Mignola 1.00 2.80
Annual 1999 (7/99, $4.95) Stories of Xena, Hellboy, Ghost, Luke Skywalker, Groo, Concrete, the Mask and Usagi Yojimbo in their youth.
Annual 2000 ($4.95) Girl sidekicks; Chiodo-c and flip photo Buffy-c
...Aliens Platinum Edition (1992)-r/DHP #24,43,43,56 & Special
...Fifth Anniversary Special nn (4/91, $9.95)-Part 1 of Sin City by Frank Mille (c/a); Aliens, Aliens vs. Predator, Concrete, Roachmill, Give Me Liberty & The American stories
The One Trick Rip-off (1997, $12.95, TPB)-r/stories from #101-112
NOTE: ***Geary** a-59, 60. **Miller** a-Special, 51-53, 55-62; c-59-62, 100-1; c-51, 53, 55, 59-62, 100-1. **Moebius** a-63; c-63, 70. **Vess** a-78; c-75, 78.*

DARK KNIGHT (See Batman: The Dark Knight Returns & Legends of the...)

DARKLON THE MYSTIC (Also see Eerie Magazine #79,80)
Pacific Comics: Oct, 1983 (one-shot)

1-Starlin-c/a(r)

DARKMAN (Movie)
Marvel Comics: Sept, 1990; Oct, 1990 - No. 3, Dec, 1990 ($1.50)

1 (9/90, $2.25, B&W mag., 68 pgs.)-Adaptation of film

Dark Mysteries #19 © Merit Pub.

Darkness/Batman #1 © Top Cow & DC

Dark Shadows #35 © GK

GD2.0 FN6.0 NM9.4

3: Reprints B&W magazine 2.00

RKMAN
rvel Comics: V2#1, Apr, 1993 -No. 6, Sept, 1993 ($2.95, limited series)

1 ($3.95, 52 pgs.) 4.00
2-6 3.00

RK MANSION OF FORBIDDEN LOVE, THE (Becomes Forbidden Tales of k Mansion No. 5 on)
ional Periodical Publ.: Sept-Oct, 1971 - No. 4, Mar-Apr, 1972 (52 pgs.)

13.50 40.00 150.00
4: 2-Adams-c. 3-Jeff Jones-c 5.00 15.00 55.00

RKMINDS
ge Comics (Dreamwave Prod.): July, 1998 - No. 8, Apr, 1999 ($2.50)

Manga; Pat Lee-s/a; 2 covers 1.25 3.75 10.00
2nd printing 2.50
0-(1/99, $5.00) Story and sketch pages 5.00
3, 1/2-(5/99, $2.50) Story and sketch pages 2.50
Collected 1,2 (1/99,3/99; $7.95) 1-r/#1-3. 2-r/#4-6 8.00
Collected 3 (5/99; $5.95) r/#7,8 6.00

RKMINDS (Volume 2)
ge Comics (Dreamwave Prod.): Feb, 2000 - Present ($2.50)

3-Pat Lee-c 2.50
7/00) Origin of Mai Murasaki; sketchbook 2.50

RKMINDS / WITCHBLADE
ge Comics (Top Cow/Dreamwave Prod.): Aug, 2000 ($5.95, one-shot)

Wohl-s/Pat Lee-a; two covers by Silvestri and Lee 6.00

RK MYSTERIES (Thrilling Tales of Horror & Suspense)
ster" - "Merit" Publications: June-July, 1951 - No. 24, July, 1955

Wood-c/a (8 pgs.) 103.00 308.00 975.00
Wood/Harrison-c/a (8 pgs.) 70.00 210.00 665.00
9: 7-Dismemberment, hypo blood drainage stys 40.00 120.00 335.00
Cannibalism story; witch burning-c 42.00 125.00 375.00
13,15-18: 11-Severed head panels. 13-Dismemberment-c/story. 17-The Old Gravedigger host 31.00 94.00 250.00
Several E.C. Craig swipes 33.00 98.00 260.00
Injury-to-eye panel; E.C. swipe; torture-c 40.00 120.00 345.00
Female bondage, blood drainage story 39.00 118.00 315.00
22: 21-Devil-c. 22-Last pre-code issue, misdated 3/54 instead of 3/55
24.00 71.00 190.00
24 19.00 56.00 150.00

*E: **Cameron** a-1, 2. **Myron Fass** c/a-21. **Harrison** a-3, 7; c-3. **Hollingsworth** a-7-17, 20, 21, Wildey a-5. Woodish art by **Fleishman**-9; c-10, 14-17. Bondage c-10, 18, 19.*

RK NEMESIS (VILLAINS) (See Teen Titans)
Comics: Feb, 1998 ($1.95, one-shot)

Jurgens-s/Pearson-c 2.00

RKNESS, THE (See Witchblade #10)
ge Comics (Top Cow Productions): Dec, 1996 - Present ($2.50)

cial Preview Edition-(7/96, B&W)-Ennis script; Silvestri-a(p)
2.00 6.00 16.00
1.50 4.50 12.00
Gold Edition 16.00
1.25 3.75 10.00
2-Christmas-c 2.50 7.50 24.00
Ennis-s/Silvestri-a, 1-Black variant-c 1.50 4.50 12.00
Platinum variant-c 25.00
2: 1-Fan Club Ed. 1.00 2.80 7.00
4.00
10: 9,10-Witchblade "Family Ties" x-over pt. 2,3 3.50
Variant-c w/concubine 1.10 3.30 9.00
American Entertainment 2.40 6.00
American Entertainment Gold Ed. 12.00
American Entertainment Gold Ed. 7.00
American Entertainment Gold Ed. 7.00
Regular Ed.; Ennis-s/Silverstri & D-Tron-c 3.00
Nine (non-chromium) variant-c (Benitez, Cabrera, the Hildebrandts, Finch, Keown, Peterson, Portacio, Tan, Turner 5.00
11-Chromium-c by Silvestri & Batt 20.00
12-19: 13-Begin Benitez-a(p) 2.50
20-24,26-36: 34-Ripclaw app. 2.50
25-($3.99) Two covers (Benitez, Silvestri) 2.50
25-Chromium-c variant by Silvestri 6.00
Holiday Pin-up-American Entertainment 5.00
Holiday Pin-up Gold Ed.-American Entertainment 7.00
Infinity #1 (8/99, $3.50) Lobdell-s 3.50
Prelude-American Entertainment 4.00
Prelude Gold Ed.-American Entertainment 7.00
Wizard ACE Ed.- Reprints #1 1.10 3.30 9.00
...Collected Editions #1-4 ($4.95,TPB) 1-r/#1,2. 2-r/#3,4. 3- r/#5,6. 4- r/#7,8 5.00
...Collected Editions #5,6 ($5.95, TPB)5- r/#11,12. 6-r/#13,14 6.00
Deluxe Collected Editions #1 (12/98, $14.95, TPB) r/#1-6 & Preview 15.00

DARKNESS/ BATMAN
Image Comics (Top Cow Productions): Aug, 1999 ($5.95, one-shot)

1-Silvestri, Finch, Lansing-a(p) 6.00

DARK ONE'S THIRD EYE
Sirius Entertainment: 1996; Dec, 1998 ($4.95, B&W)

nn-Dark One-a; squarebound; pinups, Vol. 2-(12/98) 5.00

DARK OZ
Arrow Comics: 1997 - No. 5 ($2.75, B&W, limited series)

1-5-Bill Bryan-a 2.75

DARK REALM
Image Comics: Oct, 2000 - Present ($2.95, limited series)

1-Taeson Chang-a 2.95

DARKSEID (VILLAINS) (See Jack Kirby's New Gods and New Gods)
DC Comics: Feb, 1998 ($1.95, one-shot)

1-Byrne-s/Pearson-c 2.00

DARKSEID VS. GALACTUS: THE HUNGER
DC Comics: 1995 ($4.95, one-shot) (1st DC/Marvel x-over by John Byrne)

nn-John Byrne-c/a/script 5.00

DARK SHADOWS
Steinway Comic Publ. (Ajax)(America's Best): Oct, 1957 - No. 3, May, 1958

1 18.00 53.00 140.00
2,3 13.00 39.00 105.00

DARK SHADOWS (TV) (See Dan Curtis Giveaways)
Gold Key: Mar, 1969 - No. 35, Feb, 1976 (Photo-c: 1-7)

1(30039-903)-With pull-out poster (25¢) 30.00 90.00 300.00
1-With poster missing 9.15 27.50 110.00
2 7.50 22.50 90.00
3-With pull-out poster 15.00 45.00 150.00
3-With poster missing 5.85 17.50 70.00
4-7: 7-Last photo-c 6.65 20.00 80.00
8-10 5.00 15.00 60.00
11-20 4.55 13.65 50.00
21-35: 30-Last painted-c 3.65 11.00 40.00
Story Digest 1 (6/70, 148pp.)-Photo-c 8.35 25.00 100.00

DARK SHADOWS (TV) (See Nightmare on Elm Street)
Innovation Publishing: June, 1992 - No. 4, Spring, 1993 ($2.50, limited series, coated stock)

1-Based on 1991 NBC TV mini-series; painted-c 4.00
2-4 3.00

DARK SHADOWS: BOOK TWO
Innovation Publishing: 1993 - No. 4, July, 1993 ($2.50, limited series)

1-4-Painted-c. 4-Maggie Thompson scripts 3.00

DARK SHADOWS: BOOK THREE
Innovation Publishing: Nov, 1993 ($2.50)

1-(Whole #9) 3.00

DARKSIDE
Maximum Press: Oct, 1996 ($2.99, one-shot)

Darling Love #2 © AP

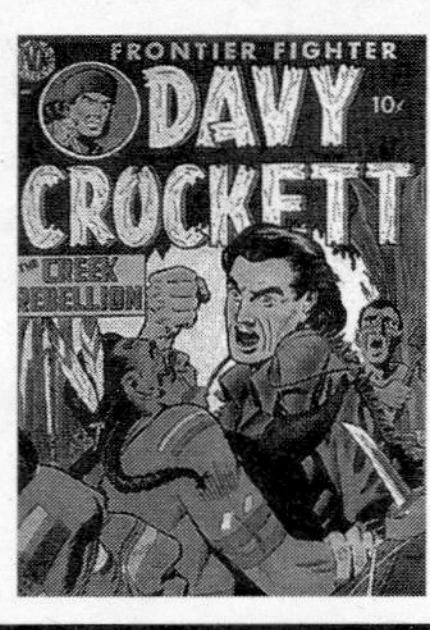

Davy Crockett nn © AVON

Dawn #2 © J.M. Linsner

1-Avengelyne-c/app. 3.00

DARKSTARS, THE
DC Comics: Oct, 1992 - No. 38, Jan, 1996 ($1.75/$1.95)

1-1st app. The Darkstars 3.00
2-24,0,25-38: 5-Hawkman & Hawkwoman app. 18-20-Flash app.. 24-(9/94)-Zero Hour. 0-(10/94). 25-(11/94). 30-Green Lantern app. 31-...vs. Darkseid. 32-Green Lantern app. 2.50
NOTE: ***Travis Charest** a(p)-4-7; c(p)-2-5; c-6-11. **Stroman** a-1-3; c-1.*

DARK TOWN
Mad Monkey Press: 1995 ($3.95, magazine-size, quarterly)

1-Kaja Blackley scripts; Vanessa Chong-a 4.00

DARKWING DUCK (TV cartoon) (Also see Cartoon Tales)
Disney Comics: Nov, 1991 - No. 4, Feb, 1992 ($1.50, limited series)

1-4: Adapts hour-long premiere TV episode 2.00

DARLING LOVE
Close Up/Archie Publ. (A Darling Magazine): Oct-Nov, 1949 - No. 11, 1952 (no month) (52 pgs.)(All photo-c?)

	GD2.0	FN6.0	NM9.4
1-Photo-c	17.00	51.00	135.00
2-Photo-c	10.00	30.00	80.00
3-8,10,11: 3-6-photo-c	8.65	26.00	60.00
9-Krigstein-a	10.00	30.00	70.00

DARLING ROMANCE
Close Up (MLJ Publications): Sept-Oct, 1949 - No. 7, 1951 (All photo-c)

	GD2.0	FN6.0	NM9.4
1-(52 pgs.)-Photo-c	23.00	68.00	180.00
2	10.00	30.00	75.00
3-7	9.30	28.00	65.00

DARQUE PASSAGES (See Master Darque)
Acclaim (Valiant): April, 1998 ($2.50)

1-Christina Z.-s/Manco-c/a 2.50

DART (Also see Freak Force & Savage Dragon)
Image Comics (Highbrow Entertainment): Feb, 1996 - No. 3, May, 1996 ($2.50, limited series)

1-3 3.00

DASTARDLY & MUTTLEY (See Fun-In No. 1-4, 6 and Kite Fun Book)

DATE WITH DANGER
Standard Comics: No. 5, Dec, 1952 - No. 6, Feb, 1953

	GD2.0	FN6.0	NM9.4
5,6-Secret agent stories: 6-Atom bomb story	8.65	26.00	60.00

DATE WITH DEBBI (Also see Debbi's Dates)
National Periodical Publ.: Jan-Feb, 1969 - No. 17, Sept-Oct, 1971; No. 18, Oct-Nov, 1972

	GD2.0	FN6.0	NM9.4
1-Teenage	4.10	12.30	45.00
2-5,17-(52 pgs) James Taylor sty.	2.30	7.00	20.00
6-12,18-Last issue	2.00	6.00	18.00
13-16-(68 pgs.): 14-1 pg. story on Jack Wild. 15-Marlo Thomas/"That Girl" sty	2.50	7.50	24.00

DATE WITH JUDY, A (Radio/TV, and 1948 movie)
National Periodical Publications: Oct-Nov, 1947 - No. 79, Oct-Nov, 1960 (No. 1-25: 52 pgs.)

	GD2.0	FN6.0	NM9.4
1-Teenage	28.00	83.00	220.00
2	13.00	39.00	105.00
3-10	10.00	30.00	80.00
11-20	7.00	21.00	48.00
21-40	5.50	16.50	38.00
41-45: 45-Last pre-code (2-3/55)	5.00	15.00	32.00
46-79: 79-Drucker-c/a	4.30	13.00	26.00

DATE WITH MILLIE, A (Life With Millie No. 8 on)(Teenage)
Atlas/Marvel Comics (MPC): Oct, 1956 - No. 7, Aug, 1957; Oct, 1959 - No. 7, Oct, 1960

	GD2.0	FN6.0	NM9.4
1(10/56)-(1st Series)-Dan DeCarlo-a in #1-7	25.00	75.00	200.00
2	12.50	37.50	100.00
3-7	10.00	30.00	70.00
1(10/59)-(2nd Series)	13.00	39.00	105.
2-7	10.00	30.00	70.

DATE WITH PATSY, A (Also see Patsy Walker)
Atlas Comics: Sept, 1957 (One-shot)

	GD2.0	FN6.0	NM9.4
1-Starring Patsy Walker	10.00	30.00	80.(

DAVID AND GOLIATH (Movie)
Dell Publishing Co.: No. 1205, July, 1961

	GD2.0	FN6.0	NM9.4
Four Color 1205-Photo-c	5.85	17.50	70.(

DAVID BORING (See Eightball)
Pantheon Books: 2000 ($24.95, hardcover w/dust jacket)

Hardcover - reprints David Boring stories from Eightball; Clowes-s/a 24.9

DAVID CASSIDY (TV)(See Partridge Family, Swing With Scooter #33 & Time For Love #30)
Charlton Comics: Feb, 1972 - No. 14, Sept, 1973

	GD2.0	FN6.0	NM9.4
1-Most have photo covers	4.55	13.65	50.
2-5	3.00	9.00	32.
6-14	2.80	8.40	28.

DAVID LADD'S LIFE STORY (See Movie Classics)

DAVY CROCKETT (See Dell Giants, Fightin..., Frontier Fighters, It's Game Time, Power Record Comics, Western Tales & Wild Frontier)

DAVY CROCKETT (Frontier Fighter...)
Avon Periodicals: 1951

	GD2.0	FN6.0	NM9.4
nn-Tuska?, Reinman-a; Fawcette-c	18.00	53.00	140.

DAVY CROCKETT (...King of the Wild Frontier No. 1,2)(TV)
Dell Publishing Co./Gold Key: 5/55 - No. 671, 12/55; No. 1, 12/63; No. 2, 11/ (Walt Disney)

	GD2.0	FN6.0	NM9.4
Four Color 631(#1)-Fess Parker photo-c	17.50	52.50	210.
Four Color 639-Photo-c	14.00	41.00	165.
Four Color 664,671(Marsh-a)-Photo-c	12.50	37.50	150.
1(12/63-Gold Key)-Fess Parker photo-c; reprints	12.50	37.50	150.
2(11/69)-Fess Parker photo-c; reprints	4.10	12.30	45.

DAVY CROCKETT (...Frontier Fighter #1,2; Kid Montana #9 on)
Charlton Comics: Aug, 1955 - No. 8, Jan, 1957

	GD2.0	FN6.0	NM9.4
1	9.30	28.00	65.(
2	6.00	18.00	42.(
3-8	5.00	15.00	30.(

DAWN
Sirius Entertainment: June, 1995 - No. 6, 1996 ($2.95)

	GD2.0	FN6.0	NM9.4
1/2-w/certificate		2.40	6.
1/2-Variant-c	1.85	5.50	15.
1-Linsner-c/a	1.00	2.80	7.
1-Black Light Edition	1.25	3.75	10.
1-White Trash Edition	1.85	5.50	15.
1-Look Sharp Edition	3.00	9.00	30.(
2-4: Linsner-c/a			4.
2-Variant-c, 3-Limited Edition	1.85	5.50	15.
4-6-Vibrato-c			3.
4, 5-Limited Edition	1.25	3.75	10.
6-Limited Edition	1.50	4.50	12.

Genesis Edition ('99, Wizard supplement) previews Return of the Goddess 1.
Lucifer's Halo TPB (11/97, $19.95) r/Drama, Dawn #1-6 plus 12 pages of new artwork 20.(
...: Tenth Anniversary Special(9/99, $2.95) Interviews 2.
The Portable Dawn ($9.95, 5"x4", 64 pgs.) Pocket-sized cover gallery 10.

DAWN: THE RETURN OF THE GODDESS
Sirius Entertainment: Apr, 1999 - No. 4, July, 2000 ($2.95, limited series)

1-4-Linsner-s/a 3.

DAYDREAMERS (See Generation X)
Marvel Comics: Aug, 1997 - No. 3, Oct, 1997 ($2.50, limited series)

1-3-Franklin Richards, Howard the Duck, Man-Thing app. 2.

DAY OF JUDGMENT

Day of Judgment #5 © DC

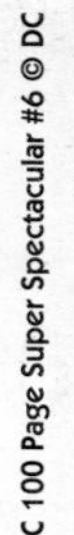

DC 100 Page Super Spectacular #6 © DC

GD2.0 FN6.0 NM9.4

: **Comics:** Nov, 1999 - No. 5, Nov, 1999 ($2.95/$2.50, limited series)
($2.95)Spectre possessed; Matt Smith-a 2.95
5: Parallax returns. 5-Hal Jordan becomes the Spectre 2.50
ecret Files 1 (11/99, $4.95) Harris-c 4.95

YS OF THE MOB (See In the Days of the Mob)

ZEY'S DIARY
l Publishing Co.: June-Aug, 1962
174-208: Bill Woggon-c/a 3.45 10.35 38.00

ZZLER, THE (Also see Marvel Graphic Novel & X-Men #130)
rvel Comics Group: Mar, 1981 - No. 42, Mar, 1986
22,24,27,28,38: 1-X-Men app. 22 (12/82)-vs. Rogue Battle-c/sty. 24-Full app. Rogue w/Powerman (Iron Fist). 27-Rogue app. 28-Full app. Rogue; Mystique app. 38-Wolverine-c/app.; X-Men app. 4.00
21,23,25,26,29-37,39-41: 2-X-Men app. 10,11-Galactus app. 21-Double size; photo-c. 23-Rogue/Mystique 1 pg. app. 26-Jusko-c. 33-Michael Jackson thriller swipe-c/sty. 40-Secret Wars II 3.00
-Beast-c/sty 4.00
TE: *No. 1 distributed only through comic shops.* ***Alcala*** *a-1i, 2i.* ***Chadwick*** *a-38-42p; c(p)-39, 42.* ***Guice*** *a-38i, 42i; c-38, 40.*

CHALLENGE
Comics: Nov, 1985 - No. 12, Oct, 1986 ($1.25, maxi-series)
12: 1-Colan-a. 2,8-Batman-c/app. 4-Gil Kane-c/a 2.00
TE: *Batman app. in 1-4, 6-12. Joker app. in 7.* ***nfantino*** *a-3.* ***Ordway*** *c-12.* ***Swan/Austin*** *c-*

COMICS PRESENTS
Comics: July-Aug, 1978 - No. 97, Sept, 1986 (Superman team-ups in all)
4th & final Superman/Flash race 1.25 3.75 10.00
Part 2 of Superman/Flash race 1.00 2.80 7.00
10: 4-Metal Men. 6-Green Lantern. 8-Swamp Thing. 9-Wonder Woman 5.00
-25,27-40,42-46,48-50,52-71,73-76,79-83: 13,43,80-Legion of Super-Heroes. 19-Batgirl. 31,58-Robin. 35-Man-Bat. 42-Sandman. 52-Doom Patrol. 82-Adam Strange. 83-Batman & Outsiders. 3.50
-(10/80)-Green Lantern; intro Cyborg, Starfire, Raven (1st app. New Teen Titans in 16 pg. preview); Starlin-c/a; Sargon the Sorcerer back-up 2.00 6.00 16.00
,72,77,78,97: 41-Superman/Joker-c/story. 72-Joker/Phantom Stranger-c/story.77,78-Animal Man app. (77-c also). 97-Phantom Zone 4.50
-He-Man-c/s (1st app. in comics) 1.00 2.80 7.00
,84,85: 51-Preview insert (16 pgs.) of He-Man (2nd app.). 84-Challengers of the Unknown; Kirby-c/s. 85-Swamp Thing; Alan Moore scripts 2.40 6.00
-96: 86-88-Crisis x-over. 88-Creeper 3.00
ıual 1,4: 1(9/82)-G.A. Superman. 4(10/85)-Superwoman 3.00
ıual 2,3: 2(7/83)-Intro/origin Superwoman. 3(9/84)-Shazam. 3.00
TE: ***Adkins*** *a-2, 54; c-2.* ***Buckler*** *a-33, 34; c-30, 33, 34.* ***Giffen*** *a-39; c-59.* ***Gil Kane*** *a-28, 35, ual 3; c-48p, 56, 58, 60, 62, 64, 68, Annual 2, 3.* ***Kirby*** *c/a-84.* ***Kubert*** *c/a-66.* ***Morrow*** *c/a-65.* ***vton*** *c/a-54p.* ***Orlando*** *c-53i.* ***Perez*** *a-26p, 61p; c-38, 61, 94.* ***Starlin*** *a-26-29p, 36p, 37p; c-29, 36, 37, 93.* ***Toth*** *a-84.* ***Williamson*** *i-79, 85, 87.*

GRAPHIC NOVEL (Also see DC Science Fiction…)
Comics: Nov, 1983 - No. 7, 1986 ($5.95, 68 pgs.)
3,5,7: 1-Star Raiders. 2-Warlords; not from regular Warlord series. 3-The Medusa Chain; Ernie Colon story/a. 5-Me and Joe Priest; Chaykin-c. 7-Space Clusters; Nino-c/a. 1.50 4.50 12.00
The Hunger Dogs by Kirby; Darkseid kills Himon from Mister Miracle & destroys New Genesis 3.00 9.00 30.00
Metalzoic; Sienkiewicz-c ($6.95) 1.50 4.50 12.00

/MARVEL: ALL ACCESS (Also see DC Versus Marvel & Marvel Versus DC)
Comics: 1996 - No. 4, 1997 ($2.95, limited series)
4: 1-Superman & Spider-Man app. 2-Robin & Jubilee app. 3-Dr. Strange & Batman-c/app., X-Men , JLA app. 4-X-Men vs. JLA-c/app. rebirth of Amalgam 3.00

/MARVEL: CROSSOVER CLASSICS II
Comics: 1998 ($14.95, TPB)
Reprints Batman/Punisher: Lake of Fire, Punisher/Batman: Deadly Knights, Silver Surfer/Superman, Batman & Capt. America 15.00

100 PAGE SUPER SPECTACULAR

GD2.0 FN6.0 NM9.4

(Title is 100 Page… No. 14 on)(Square bound) (Reprints, 50¢)
National Periodical Publications: No. 4, Summer, 1971 - No. 13, 6/72; No. 14, 2/73 - No. 22, 11/73 (No #1-3)
4-Weird Mystery Tales; Johnny Peril & Phantom Stranger; cover & splashes by Wrightson; origin Jungle Boy of Jupiter 13.50 40.00 150.00
5-Love Stories; Wood inks (7 pgs.)(scarcer) 40.00 120.00 475.00
6- "World's Greatest Super-Heroes"; JLA, JSA, Spectre, Johnny Quick, Vigilante & Hawkman; contains unpublished Wildcat story; N. Adams wrap-around-c; r/JLA #21,22 13.50 40.00 150.00
7-(Also listed as Superman #245) Air Wave, Kid Eternity, Hawkman-r; Atom-r/Atom #3 4.55 13.65 50.00
8-(Also listed as Batman #238) Batman, Legion, Aquaman-r; G.A. Atom, Sargon (r/Sensation #57), Plastic Man (r/Police #14) stories; Doom Patrol origin-r; N. Adams wraparound-c 8.15 24.50 90.00
9-(Also listed as Our Army at War #242) Kubert-c 7.25 21.75 80.00
10-(Also listed as Adventure Comics #416) Golden Age-reprints; r/1st app. Black Canary from Flash #86; no Zatanna 5.45 16.35 60.00
11-(Also listed as Flash #214) origin Metal Men-r/Showcase #37; never before pubbed G.A. Flash story. 5.00 15.00 55.00
12-14: 12-(Also listed as Superboy #185) Legion-c/story; Teen Titans, Kid Eternity (r/Hit #46), Star Spangled Kid-r(S.S. #55). 13-(Also listed as Superman #252) Ray(r/Smash #17), Black Condor, (r/Crack #18), Hawkman(r/Flash #24); Starman-r/Adv. #67; Dr. Fate & Spectre-r/More Fun #57; N. Adams-c. 14-Batman-r/Detective #31,32,156; Atom-r/Showcase #34 3.80 11.40 42.00
15,16,18,19,21,22: 15-r/2nd Boy Commandos/Det. #64. 21-Superboy; r/Brave & the Bold #54. 22-r/All-Flash #13. 2.80 8.40 28.00
17,20: 17-JSA-r/All Star #37 (10-11/47, 38 pgs.), Sandman-r/Adv. #65 (8/41), JLA #23 (11/63) & JLA #43 (3/66). 20-Batman-r/Det. #66,68, Spectre; origin Two-Face 3.20 9.50 35.00
NOTE: ***Anderson*** *r-11, 14, 18i, 22.* ***B. Baily*** *r-18, 20.* ***Burnley*** *r-18, 20.* ***Crandall*** *r-14p, 20.* ***Drucker*** *r-4.* ***Grandenetti*** *a-22(2)r.* ***Heath*** *a-22r.* ***Infantino*** *r-17, 20, 22.* ***G. Kane*** *r-18.* ***Kirby*** *r-15.* ***Kubert*** *r-6, 7, 16, 17; c-16, 19.* ***Manning*** *a-19r.* ***Meskin*** *r-4, 22.* ***Mooney*** *r-15, 21.* ***Toth*** *r-17, 20.*

DC ONE MILLION (Also see crossover #1,000,000 issues)
DC Comics: Nov, 1998 - No. 4, Nov, 1998 ($2.95/$1.99, weekly lim. series)
1-($2.95) JLA travels to the 853rd century; Morrison-s 3.00
2-4-($1.99) 2.00
... Eighty-Page Giant (8/99, $4.95) 5.00
TPB ('99, $14.95) r/#1-4 and several x-over stories 15.00

DC SCIENCE FICTION GRAPHIC NOVEL
DC Comics: 1985 - No. 7, 1987 ($5.95)
SF1-SF7: SF1-Hell on Earth by Robert Bloch; Giffen-p. SF2-Nightwings by Robert Silverberg; G. Colan-p. SF3-Frost & Fire by Bradbury. SF4-Merchants of Venus. SF5-Demon With A Glass Hand by Ellison; M. Rogers-a. SF6-The Magic Goes Away by Niven. SF7-Sandkings by George R.R. Martin 1.50 4.50 12.00

DC SILVER AGE CLASSICS
DC Comics: 1992 ($1.00, all reprints)
…Action Comics #252-r/1st Supergirl. Adventure Comics #247-r/1st Legion of S.H. The Brave and the Bold #28-r/1st JLA. Detective Comics #225-r/1st Martian Manhunter. Detective Comics #327-r/1st new look Batman. Green Lantern #76-r/Green Lantern/Gr. Arrow. House of Secrets #92-r/1st Swamp Thing. Showcase #4-r/1st S.A. Flash. Showcase #22-r/1st S.A. Green Lantern 2.00
...Sugar and Spike #99; 2 unpublished stories 4.00

DC SPECIAL (Also see Super DC Giant)
National Per. Publ.: 10-12/68 - No. 15, 11-12/71; No. 16, Spr/75 - No. 29, 8-9/77
1-All Infantino issue; Flash, Batman, Adam Strange-r; begin 68 pg. issues, end #21 4.55 13.65 50.00
2-Teen humor; Binky, Buzzy, Harvey app. 7.25 21.75 80.00
3-All-Girl issue; unpubl. GA Wonder Woman story 4.55 13.65 50.00
4-15: 4-Horror (1st Abel cameo). 5-All Kubert issue; Viking Prince, Sgt. Rock-r. 6-Western. 7,9,13-Strangest Sports. 11-Monsters. 12-Viking Prince; Kubert-c/a (r/B&B almost entirely). 15-G.A. Plastic Man origin-r/Police #1; origin Woozy by Cole; 14,15-(52 pgs.) 3.00 9.00 30.00
16-27: 16-Super Heroes Battle Super Gorillas; r/Capt. Storm #1, 1st Johnny Cloud/All-Amer. Men of War #82. 17-Early S.A. Green Lantern-r. 22-Origin

DC Special Series #18 © DC

DC Super-Stars #1 © DC

DC 2000 #1 © DC

Robin Hood. 26-Enemy Ace on-c only. 27-Captain Comet story
1.50 4.50 12.00
28,29: 28-Earth Shattering Disaster Stories; Legion of Super-Heroes story. 29-New "The Untold Origin of the Justice Society"; Staton-a
2.00 6.00 16.00

NOTE: ***N. Adams*** *c-3, 4, 6, 11, 29.* ***Grell*** *a-20; c-17, 20.* ***Heath*** *a-12r.* ***G. Kane*** *a-6p, 13r, 17r, 19-21r.* ***Kirby*** *a-4,11.* ***Kubert*** *a-6r, 12r, 22.* ***Meskin*** *a-10.* ***Moreira*** *a-10.* ***Staton*** *a-29p.* ***Toth*** *a-13, 20r. #1-15: 25¢; 16-27: 50¢; 28, 29: 60¢. #1-13, 16-21: 68 pgs.; 14, 15: 52 pgs.; 25-27: oversized.*

DC SPECIAL BLUE RIBBON DIGEST
DC Comics: Mar-Apr, 1980 - No. 24, Aug, 1982

1,2,4,5: 1-Legion reprints. 2-Flash. 4-Green Lantern. 5-Secret Origins; new Zatara and Zatanna 1.25 3.75 10.00
3-Justice Society 1.85 5.50 15.00
6-10: 6-Ghosts. 7-Sgt. Rock's Prize Battle Tales. 8-Legion. 9-Secret Origins. 10-Warlord-"The Deimos Saga"-Grell-s/c/a 1.25 3.75 10.00
11,16: 11-Justice League. 16-Green Lantern/Green Arrow-r; all Adams-a.
12-15,17-19: 12-Haunted Tank; reprints 1st app. 13-Strange Sports Stories. 14-UFO Invaders; Adam Strange app. 15-Secret Origins of Super Villains; JLA app. 17-Ghosts. 18-Sgt. Rock; Kubert front & back-c. 19-Doom Patrol; new Perez-c 1.75 5.25 14.00
20-Dark Mansion of Forbidden Love (scarce) 4.10 12.30 45.00
21-24: 21-Our Army at War. 22-Secret Origins. 23-Green Arrow, w/new 7 pg. story. 24-House of Mystery; new Kubert wraparound-c 2.00 6.00 18.00

NOTE: ***N. Adams*** *a-16(6)r, 17r, 23r; c-16.* ***Aparo*** *a-6r, 24r; c-23.* ***Grell*** *a-8, 10; c-10.* ***Heath*** *a-14.* ***Infantino*** *a-15r.* ***Kaluta*** *a-17r.* ***Gil Kane*** *a-15r, 22r.* ***Kirby*** *a-5, 9, 23r.* ***Kubert*** *a-3, 18r, 21r; c-7, 12, 14, 17, 18, 21, 24.* ***Morrow*** *a-24r.* ***Orlando*** *a-17r, 22r; c-1, 20.* ***Toth*** *a-21r, 24r.* ***Wood*** *a-3, 17r, 24r.* ***Wrightson*** *a-16r, 17r, 24r.*

DC SPECIAL SERIES
National Periodical Publications/DC Comics: 9/77 - No. 16, Fall, 1978; No. 17, 8/79 - No. 27, Fall, 1981 (No. 18, 19, 23, 24 - digest size, 100 pgs.; No. 25-27 - Treasury sized)

1-"5-Star Super-Hero Spectacular 1977"; Batman, Atom, Flash, Green Lantern, Aquaman, in solo stories, Kobra app.; N. Adams-c
1.85 5.50 15.00
2(#1)-"The Original Swamp Thing Saga 1977"-r/Swamp Thing #1&2 by Wrightson; new Wrightson wraparound-c. 1.10 3.30 9.00
3,4,6-8: 3-Sgt Rock. 4-Unexpected. 6-Secret Society of Super Villains, Jones-a. 7-Ghosts Special. 8-Brave and Bold w/ new Batman, Deadman & Sgt Rock team-up 1.50 4.50 12.00
5-"Superman Spectacular 1977"-(84 pg, $1.00)-Superman vs. Brainiac & Lex Luthor, new 63 pg. story 1.85 5.50 15.00
9-Wonder Woman; Ditko-a (11 pgs.) 1.85 5.50 15.00
10-"Secret Origins of Superheroes Special 1978"-(52 pgs.)-Dr. Fate, Lightray & Black Canary-c/new origin stories; Staton, Newton-a 1.50 4.50 12.00
11-"Flash Spectacular 1978"-(84 pgs.) Flash, Kid Flash, GA Flash & Johnny Quick vs. Grodd; Wood-i on Kid Flash chapter 1.50 4.50 12.00
12-"Secrets of Haunted House Special Spring 1978" 1.50 4.50 12.00
13-"Sgt. Rock Special Spring 1978", 50 pg new story 1.50 4.50 12.00
14,17,20-"Original Swamp Thing Saga", Wrightson-a: 14-Sum '78, r/#3,4. 17-Sum '79 r/#5-7. 20-Jan/Feb '80, r/#8-10 1.10 3.30 9.00
15-"Batman Spectacular Summer 1978", Ra's Al Ghul-app.; Golden-a. Rogers-a/front & back-c 1.75 5.25 14.00
16-"Jonah Hex Spectacular Fall 1978"; death of Jonah Hex, Heath-a; Bat Lash and Scalphunter stories 3.65 11.00 40.00
18,19-Digest size: 18-"Sgt. Rock's Prize Battle Tales Fall 1979". 19-"Secret Origins of Super-Heroes Fall 1979"; origins Wonder Woman (new-a),r/Robin, Batman-Superman team, Aquaman, Hawkman and others
1.50 4.50 12.00
21-"Super-Star Holiday Special Spring 1980", Frank Miller-a in "Batman--Wanted Dead or Alive" (1st Batman story); Jonah Hex, Sgt. Rock, Superboy &LSH and House of Mystery/Witching Hour-c/stories 2.40 7.35 22.00
22-"G.I. Combat Sept. 1980", Kubert-c. Haunted Tank-s 1.50 4.50 12.00
23,24-Digest size: 23-World's Finest-r. 24-Flash 1.75 5.25 14.00
V5#25-($2.95)-"Superman II, the Adventure Continues Summer 1981"; photos from movie & photo-c (see All-New Coll. Ed. C-62) 1.75 5.25 14.00
26-($2.50)-"Superman and His Incredible Fortress of Solitude Summer 1981"
1.75 5.25 14.00
27-($2.50)-"Batman vs. The Incredible Hulk Fall 1981" 2.50 7.50 23.00

NOTE: ***Aparo*** *c-8.* ***Heath*** *a-12i, 16.* ***Infantino*** *a-19r.* ***Kirby*** *a-23, 19r.* ***Kubert*** *c-13, 19r.* ***Nasser/Netzer*** *a-1, 10i, 15.* ***Newton*** *a-10.* ***Nino*** *a-4, 7.* ***Starlin*** *c-12.* ***Staton*** *a-1.* ***Tuska*** *a-*
#25 & 26. were advertised as All-New Collectors' Edition C-63, C-64. #26 was originally plan
as All-New Collectors' Ed. C-30?; has C-630 & A.N.C.E. on cover.

DC SUPER-STARS
National Periodical Publications/DC Comics: March, 1976 - No. 18, Winter, 1978 (No.3-18: 52 pgs.)

1-(68 pgs.)-Re-intro Teen Titans (predates T. T. #44 (11/76); tryout iss.) plus r/Teen Titans; W.W. as girl was original Wonder Girl
2.00 6.00 16.
2-7,9,11,12,16: 2,4,6,8-Adam Strange; 2-(68 pgs.)-r/1st Adam Strange/ Hawkman team-up from Mystery in Space #90 plus Atomic Knights origin-r. 3-Legion issue. 4-r/Tales/Unexpected #45 1.25 3.75 10.
8-r/1st Space Ranger from Showcase #15, Adam Strange-r/Mystery in Space #89 & Star Rovers-r/M.I.S. #80 1.50 4.50 12.
10-Strange Sports Stories; Batman/Joker-c/story 1.50 4.50 12.
13-Sergio Aragonés Special 2.00 6.00 16.
14,15,18: 15-Sgt. Rock 1.50 4.50 12.
17-Secret Origins of Super-Heroes (origin of The Huntress); origin Green Arrow by Grell; Legion app.; Earth II Batman & Catwoman marry (1st revealed; also see B&B #197 & Superman Family #211)
2.00 6.00 18.

NOTE: ***M. Anderson*** *r-2, 4, 6.* ***Aparo*** *c-7, 14, 18.* ***Austin*** *a-11i.* ***Buckler*** *a-14p; c-10.* ***Grell*** *a-*
G. Kane *a-1r, 10r.* ***Kubert*** *c-15.* ***Layton*** *c/a-16i, 17i.* ***Mooney*** *a-4r, 6r.* ***Morrow*** *c/a-11r.* ***Nas***
a-11. ***Newton*** *c/a-16p.* ***Staton*** *a-17; c-17. No. 10, 12-18 contain all new material; the rest reprints. #1 contains new and reprint material.*

DC 2000
DC Comics: 2000 - No. 2, 2000 ($6.95, limited series)

1,2-JLA visit 1941 JSA; Semeiks-a 6.

DCU HEROES SECRET FILES
DC Comics: Feb, 1999 ($4.95, one-shot)

1-Origin-s and pin-ups; new Star Spangled Kid app. 5.

DC UNIVERSE CHRISTMAS, A
DC Comics: 2000 ($19.95)

TPB-Reprints DC Christmas stories by various 20.

DC UNIVERSE HOLIDAY BASH
DC Comics: 1997- 1999 ($3.95)

I,II-(X-mas '96,'97) Christmas stories by various 4.
III (1999, for Christmas '98, $4.95) 5.

DC UNIVERSE: TRINITY
DC Comics: Aug, 1993 - No. 2, Sept, 1993 ($2.95, 52 pgs, limited series)

1,2-Foil-c; Green Lantern, Darkstars, Legion app. 3.

DCU VILLAINS SECRET FILES
DC Comics: Apr, 1999 ($4.95, one-shot)

1-Origin-s and profile pages 5.

DC VERSUS MARVEL
(See Marvel Versus DC) (Also see Amazon, Assassins Bruce Wayne: Agent of S.H.I. E. L.D., Bullets & Bracelets, Doctor Strangefate, JLX, Legend of the Dark Claw, Magneto & The Magnetic Men, Speed Demon, Spider-Boy, Super Soldier, X-Patrol)
DC Comics: No. 1, 1996, No. 4, 1996 ($3.95, limited series)

1,4: 1-Marz script, Jurgens-a(p); 1st app. of Access. 4.
.../Marvel Versus DC ($12.95, trade paperback) r/1-4 13.

D-DAY
(Also see Special War Series)
Charlton Comics (no No. 3): Sum/63; No. 2, Fall/64; No. 4, 9/66; No. 5, 10/67 No. 6, 11/68

1,2: 1(1963)-Montes/Bache-c. 2(Fall '64)-Wood-a(4) 3.20 9.60 35.
4-6('66-'68)-Montes/Bache-a #5 2.30 7.00 20.

DEAD AIR
Slave Labor Graphics: July, 1989 ($5.95, graphic novel)

nn-Mike Allred's 1st published work 6.

DEAD CORPSE
DC Comics (Helix): Sept, 1998 - No. 4, Dec, 1998 ($2.50, limited series)

1-4-Pugh-a/Hinz-s 2.

DEAD END CRIME STORIES

Dead Enders #8 © Brubaker & Pleece

Dead-Eye Western Comics #9 © HILL

Deadly Hands of Kung-Fu #16 © MAR

GD2.0 FN6.0 NM9.4

rby Publishing Co.: April, 1949 (52 pgs.)
-(Scarce)-Powell, Roussos-a; painted-c 50.00 150.00 450.00

EAD ENDERS
C Comics (Vertigo): Mar, 2000 - No. 16, June, 2001 ($2.50)
-14-Brubaker-s/Pleece & Case-a 2.50
ealing the Sun (2000, $9.95, TPB) r/#1-4, Vertigo Winter's Edge #3 10.00

EAD-EYE WESTERN COMICS
llman Periodicals: Nov-Dec, 1948 - V3#1, Apr-May, 1953
#1-(52 pgs.)-Krigstein, Roussos-a 18.00 53.00 140.00
#2,3-(52 pgs.) 10.00 30.00 70.00
#4-12-(52 pgs.) 6.00 18.00 42.00
?#1,2,5-8,10-12: 1-7-(52 pgs.) 5.00 15.00 32.00
3,4-Krigstein-a 7.00 21.00 48.00
9-One pg. Frazetta ad 5.00 15.00 32.00
3#1 5.00 15.00 30.00
)TE: *Briefer a-V1#8. Kinstleresque stories by* ***McCann****-12, V2#1, 2, V3#1.* ***McWilliams*** *a-#5.* ***Ed Moore*** *a-V1#4.*

EADFACE: DOING THE ISLANDS WITH BACCHUS
rk Horse Comics: July, 1991 - No. 3, Sept, 1991 ($2.95, B&W, lim. series)
-3: By Eddie Campbell 3.00

EADFACE: EARTH, WATER, AIR, AND FIRE
rk Horse Comics: July, 1992 - No. 4, Oct, 1992 ($2.50, B&W, limited series; itish-r)
-4: By Eddie Campbell 2.50

EAD IN THE WEST
rk Horse Comics: Oct, 1993 - No. 2, Mar, 1994 ($3.95, B&W, 52 pgs.)
,2-Timothy Truman-c 4.00

EAD KING (See Evil Ernie)
aos! Comics: May, 1998 - No. 4, Aug, 1998, ($2.95, limited series)
-4-Fisher-s 3.00

EADLIEST HEROES OF KUNG FU (Magazine)
rvel Comics Group: Summer, 1975 (B&W)(76 pgs.)
-Bruce Lee vs. Carradine painted-c; TV Kung Fu, 4pgs. photos/article; Enter the Dragon, 24 pgs. photos/article w/ Bruce Lee; Bruce Lee photo pinup 2.30 7.00 20.00

EADLINE USA
rk Horse Comics: Apr, 1992 - No. 8, Nov, 1992 ($3.95, B&W, 52 pgs.)
-8: Johnny Nemo w/Milligan scripts in all 4.00

EADLY DUO, THE
age Comics (Highbrow Entertainment): Nov, 1994 - No. 3, Jan, 1995 2.50, limited series)
3: 1-lst app. of Kill Cat 2.50

EADLY DUO, THE
age Comics (Highbrow Entertainment): June, 1995 - No. 4, Oct, 1995 2.50, limited series)
4: 1-Spawn app. 2-Savage Dragon app. 3-Gen 13 app. 2.50

EADLY FOES OF SPIDER-MAN (See Lethal Foes of...)
rvel Comics: May, 1991 - No. 4, Aug, 1991 ($1.00, limited series)
-4: 1-Punisher, Kingpin, Rhino app. 2.00

EADLY HANDS OF KUNG FU, THE (See Master of Kung Fu)
rvel Comics Group: April, 1974 - No. 33, Feb, 1977 (75¢) (B&W, magazine)
(V1#4 listed in error)-Origin Sons of the Tiger; Shang-Chi, Master of Kung Fu begins (ties w/Master of Kung Fu #17 as 3rd app. Shang-Chi); Bruce Lee painted-c by Neal Adams; 2pg. memorial photo pinup w/8 pgs. photos/articles; TV Kung Fu, 9 pgs. photos/articles; 15 pgs. Starlin-a. 3.00 9.00 30.00
:-Adams painted-c; 1st time origin of Shang-Chi, 34 pgs. by Starlin. TV Kung Fu, 6 pgs. ph/a w/2 pg. pinup. Bruce Lee, 11 pgs. ph/a 2.50 7.50 25.00
,4,7,10: 3-Adams painted-c; Gulacy-a. Enter the Dragon, photos/articles, 8 pgs. 4-TV Kung Fu painted-c by Neal Adams; TV Kung Fu 7 pg. article/art; Fu Manchu; Enter the Dragon, 10 pg. photos/article w/Bruce Lee. 7-Bruce Lee painted-c & 9 pgs. photos/articles-Return of Dragon plus 1 pg. photo pinup. 10-(3/75)-Iron Fist painted-c & 34 pg. sty-Early app. 2.00 6.00 18.00
5,6: 5-1st app. Manchurian, 6 pgs. Gulacy-a. TV Kung Fu, 4 pg. article; re books w/Barry Smith-a. Capt. America-sty, 10 pgs. Kirby-a(r). 6-Bruce Lee photos/article, 6 pgs.; 15 pgs. early Perez-a 2.00 6.00 16.00
8,9,11: 9-Iron Fist, 2 pg. Preview pinup; Nebres-a. 11-Billy Jack painted-c by Adams; 17 pgs. photos/article 1.75 5.25 14.00
12,13: 12-James Bond painted-c by Adams; 14 pg. photos/article. 13-16 pgs. early Perez-a; Piers Anthony, 7 pgs. photos/article 1.50 4.50 12.00
14-Classic Bruce Lee painted-c by Adams. Lee pinup by Chaykin. Lee 16 pg. photos/article w/2 pgs. Green Hornet TV 3.45 10.35 38.00
15,19: 15-Sum, '75 Giant Annual #1. 20pgs. Starlin-a. Bruce Lee photo pinup & 3 pg photos/article re book; Man-Thing app. Iron Fist-c/sty; Gulacy-a 18pgs. 19-Iron Fist painted-c & series begins; 1st White Tiger 1.75 5.25 14.00
16,18,20: 16-1st app. Corpse Rider, a Samurai w/Sanho Kim-a. 20-Chuck Norris painted-c & 16 pgs. interview w/photos/article; Bruce Lee vs. C. Norris pinup by Ken Barr. Origin The White Tiger, Perez-a 1.50 4.50 12.00
17-Bruce Lee painted-c by Adams; interview w/R. Clouse, director Enter Dragon 7 pgs. w/B. Lee app. 1st Giffen-a (1pg. 11/75) 2.50 7.50 25.00
21-Bruce Lee 1pg. photos/article 1.25 3.75 10.00
22,30-32: 22-1st app. Jack of Hearts (cameo). 1st Giffen sty-a (along w/Amazing Adv. #35, 3/76). 30-Swordquest-c/sty & conclusion; Jack of Hearts app. 31-Jack of Hearts app; Staton-a. 32-1st Daughters of the Dragon -c/sty, 21 pgs. M. Rogers-a/Claremont-sty; Iron Fist pinup 1.50 4.50 12.00
23-26,29: 23-1st full app. Jack of Hearts. 24-Iron Fist-c & centerfold pinup. early Zeck-a; Shang Chi pinup; 6 pgs. Piers Anthony text sty w/Perez/Austin-a; Jack of Hearts app. early Giffen-a. 25-1st app. Shimuru, "Samurai", 20 pgs. Mantlo-sty/Broderick-a; "Swordquest"-c & begins 17 pg. sty by Sanho Kim; 11 pg. photos/article; partly Bruce Lee. 26-Bruce Lee painted-c & pinup; 16 pgs. interviews w/Kwon & Clouse; talk about B. Lee re-filming of B. Lee legend. 29-Ironfist vs. Shang Chi battle-c/sty; Jack of Hearts app. 2.00 6.00 16.00
27 1.25 3.75 10.00
28-All Bruce Lee Special Issue; (1st time in comics). Bruce Lee painted-c by Ken Barr & pinup. 36 pgs. comics chronicaling Bruce Lee's life; 15 pgs. B. Lee photos/article (Rare in high grade) 4.35 13.00 48.00
33-Shang Chi-c/sty; Classic Daughters of the Dragon, 21 pgs. M. Rogers-a/Claremont-sty with Nudity; Bob Wall interview, photos/article, 14 pgs. 2.00 6.00 16.00
...Special Album Edition 1(Summer, '74)-Iron Fist-c/story (early app., 3rd?); 10 pgs. Adams-i; Shang Chi/Fu Manchu, 10 pgs.; Sons of Tiger, 11 pgs.; TV Kung Fu, 6 pgs. photos/article 2.30 7.00 20.00
NOTE: ***Bruce Lee:*** *1-7, 14, 15, 17, 25, 26, 28.* ***Kung Fu (TV):*** *1, 2, 4.* ***Jack of Hearts:*** *22, 23, 29-33.* ***Shang Chi Master of Kung Fu:*** *1-9, 11-18, 29, 31, 33.* ***Sons of Tiger:*** *1, 3, 4, 6-14, 16-19.* ***Swordquest:*** *25-27, 29-33.* ***White Tiger:*** *19-24, 26, 27, 29-33.* ***N. Adams*** *a-1i(part), 27i; c-1, 2-4, 11, 12, 14, 17.* ***Giffen*** *a-22p, 24p.* ***G. Kane*** *a-23p.* ***Kirby*** *a-5r.* ***Nasser*** *a-27p, 28.* ***Perez*** *a(p)-6-14, 16, 17, 19, 21.* ***Rogers*** *a-26, 32, 33.* ***Starlin*** *a-1, 2r, 15r.* ***Staton*** *a-28p, 31, 32.*

DEADMAN (See The Brave and the Bold & Phantom Stranger #39)
DC Comics: May, 1985 - No. 7, Nov, 1985 ($1.75, Baxter paper)
1-7: 1-Deadman-r by Infantino, N. Adams in all. 5-Batman-c/story-r/Str. Advs. 7-Batman-r 3.00

DEADMAN
DC Comics: Mar, 1986 - No. 4, June, 1986 (75¢, limited series)
1-4: Lopez-c/a. 4-Byrne-c(p) 2.00

DEADMAN: EXORCISM
DC Comics: 1992 - No. 2, 1992 ($4.95, limited series, 52 pgs.)
1,2: Kelley Jones-c/a in both 5.00

DEADMAN: LOVE AFTER DEATH
DC Comics: 1989 - No. 2, 1990 ($3.95, 52 pgs., limited series, mature)
Book One, Two: Kelley Jones-c/a in both. 1-contains nudity 4.00

DEAD OF NIGHT
Marvel Comics Group: Dec, 1973 - No. 11, Aug, 1975

Deadpool #46 © MAR

The Dead Who Walk nn © AVON

Dear Lonely Heart #1 © Artful Pub.

GD2.0 FN6.0 NM9.4

1-Horror reprints 2.00 6.00 16.00
2-10: 10-Kirby-a 1.25 3.75 10.00
11-Intro Scarecrow; Kane/Wrightson-c 2.30 7.00 20.00
NOTE: *Ditko r-7, 10. Everett c-2. Sinnott r-1.*

DEAD OR ALIVE - A CYBERPUNK WESTERN
Image Comics (Shok Studio): Apr, 1998 - No. 4, July, 1998 ($2.50, lim. series)
1-4 3.00

DEADPOOL (See New Mutants #98)
Marvel Comics: Aug, 1994 - No. 4, Nov, 1994 ($2.50, limited series)
1-4: Mark Waid's 1st Marvel work; Ian Churchill-c/a 2.50

DEADPOOL
Marvel Comics: Jan, 1997 - Present ($2.95/$1.95/$1.99)
1-($2.95)-Wraparound-c 4.00
2-Begin-$1.95-c. 3.00
3-10,12-22,24: 4-Hulk-c/app. 12-Variant-c. 14-Begin McDaniel-a. 22-Cable app. 2.00
11-($3.99)-Deadpool replaces Spider-Man from Amazing Spider-Man #47; Kraven, Gwen Stacy app. 5.00
23,25-($2.99); 23-Dead Reckoning pt. 1; wraparound-c 3.00
26-40: 27-Wolverine-c/app. 37-Thor app. 2.00
41-49: 41-Begin $2.25-c. 44-Black Panther-c/app. 46-49-Chadwick-a 2.25
#(-1) Flashback (7/97) Lopresti-a; Wade Wilson's early days 2.00
.../Death '98 Annual ($2.99) Kelly-s, ... Team-Up (12/98, $2.99) Widdle Wade-c/app., Baby's First Deadpool Book (12/98, $2.99), Encyclopædia Deadpoolica (12/98, $2.99) Synopses 3.00
Mission Improbable TPB (9/98, $14.95) r/#1-5 15.00
Wizard #0 ('98, bagged with Wizard #87) 2.00

DEADPOOL: THE CIRCLE CHASE (See New Mutants #98)
Marvel Comics: Aug, 1993 - No. 4, Nov, 1993 ($2.00, limited series)
1-($2.50)-Embossed-c 3.50
2-4 2.50

DEADSHOT (See Batman #59, Detective Comics #474, & Showcase '93 #8)
DC Comics: Nov, 1988 - No. 4, Feb, 1989 ($1.00, limited series)
1-4 2.00

DEADSIDE (See Shadowman)
Acclaim Comics: Feb, 1999 - No. 4, ($2.50, limited series)
1-3-Jenkins-s/Haselden-Wood-a 2.50

DEAD WHO WALK, THE (See Strange Mysteries, Super Reprint #15, 16)
Realistic Comics: 1952 (one-shot)
nn 50.00 150.00 450.00

DEADWORLD (Also see The Realm)
Arrow Comics/Caliber Comics: Dec, 1986 - No. 26 ($1.50/$1.95/#15-28: $2.50, B&W, mature)
1-26: 5-26-Graphic covers, 5-26: Tame covers 2.50
...Archives 1-3 (1992, $2.50) 2.50

DEAN MARTIN & JERRY LEWIS (See Adventures of...)

DEAR BEATRICE FAIRFAX
Best/Standard Comics (King Features): No. 5, Nov, 1950 - No. 9, Sept, 1951 (Vern Greene art)
5-All have Schomburg air brush-c 9.30 28.00 65.00
6-9 6.00 18.00 42.00

DEAR HEART (Formerly Lonely Heart)
Ajax: No. 15, July, 1956 - No. 16, Sept, 1956
15,16 5.50 16.50 38.00

DEAR LONELY HEART (...Illustrated No. 1-6)
Artful Publications: Mar, 1951; No. 2, Oct, 1951 - No. 8, Oct, 1952
1 16.00 49.00 130.00
2 7.85 23.50 55.00
3-Matt Baker Jungle Girl story 19.00 56.00 150.00
4-8 7.00 21.00 48.00

DEAR LONELY HEARTS (Lonely Heart #9 on)

GD2.0 FN6.0 NM9

Harwell Publ./Mystery Publ. Co. (Comic Media): Aug, 1953 -No. 8, Oct, 1954
1 10.00 30.00 75.0
2-8 6.40 19.25 45.0

DEARLY BELOVED
Ziff-Davis Publishing Co.: Fall, 1952
1-Photo-c 16.00 48.00 125.0

DEAR NANCY PARKER
Gold Key: June, 1963 - No. 2, Sept, 1963
1-Painted-c on both 3.00 9.00 30.0
2 2.50 7.50 23.0

DEATHBLOW (Also see Darker Image)
Image Comics (WildStorm Productions): May (Apr. inside), 1993 - No. 29, Aug, 1996 ($1.75/$1.95/$2.50)
0-(8/96, $2.95, 32 pgs.)-r/Darker Image w/new story & art; Jim Lee & Trevor Scott-a; new Jim Lee-c 3.0
1-($2.50)-Red foil stamped logo on black varnish-c; Jim Lee-c/a; flip-book side has Cybernary -c/story (#2 also) 2.5
1-($1.95)-Newsstand version w/o foil-c & varnish 2.0
2-29: 2-(8/93)-Lee-a; with bound-in poster. 2-($1.75)-Newsstand version w/o poster. 4-Jim Lee-c/Tim Sale-a begin. 13-W/pinup poster by Tim Sale & Jim Lee. 16 ($1.95, Newsstand)-Wildstorm Rising Pt. 6. 16. ($2.50, Direct Market)-Wildstorm Rising Pt. 617-Variant "Chicago Comicon" edition exists. 20,21-Gen 13 app. 23-Backlash-c/app. 24,25-Grifter-c/app; Gen 13 Dane from Wetworks app. 28-Deathblow dies. 29-Memorial issue 2.5
5-Alternate Portacio-c (Forms larger picture when combined with alternate-c f Gen 13 #5, Kindred #3, Stormwatch #10, Team 7 #1, Union #0, Wetworks # & WildC.A.T.S # 11) 2.40 6.0
...:Sinners and Saints TPB ('99, $19.95) r/#1-12; Sale-c 19.9

DEATHBLOW BYBLOWS
DC Comics (WildStorm): Nov, 1999 - No. 3, Jan, 2000 ($2.95, limited series)
1-3-Alan Moore-s/Jim Baikie-a 2.9

DEATHBLOW/WOLVERINE
Image Comics (WildStorm Productions)/ Marvel Comics: Sept, 1996 - No. 2 Feb, 1997 ($2.50, limited series)
1,2: Wiesenfeld-s/Bennett-a 2.5
TPB (1997, $8.95) r/#1,2 9.0

DEATHDEALER
Verotik: July, 1995 - No. 4, July, 1997 ($5.95)
1-Frazetta-c; Bisley-a 1.00 3.00 8.0
1-2nd print, 2-4-($6.95)-Frazetta-c; embossed logo 1.00 2.80 7.0

DEATHLOK (Also see Astonishing Tales #25)
Marvel Comics: July, 1990 - No. 4, Oct, 1990 ($3.95, limited series, 52 pgs.)
1-4: 1,2-Guice-a(p). 3,4-Denys Cowan-a, c-4 4.0

DEATHLOK
Marvel Comics: July, 1991 - No. 34, Apr, 1994 ($1.75)
1-Silver ink cover; Denys Cowan-c/a(p) begins 2.5
2-18,20-24,26-34: 2-Forge (X-Men) app. 3-Vs. Dr. Doom. 5-X-Men & F.F. x-over. 6,7-Punisher x-over. 9,10-Ghost Rider-c/story. 16-Infinity War x-ove 17-Jae Lee-c. 22-Black Panther app. 27-Siege app. 2.0
19-($2.25)-Foil-c 2.2
25-($2.95, 52 pgs.)-Holo-grafx foil-c 3.0
Annual 1 (1992, $2.25, 68 pgs.)-Guice-p; Quesada-c(p) 3.0
Annual 2 (1993, $2.95, 68 pgs.)-Bagged w/card; intro Tracer 3.0
NOTE: ***Denys Cowan** a(p)-9-13, 15, Annual 1; c-9-12, 13p, 14. **Guice/Cowan** c-8.*

DEATHLOK
Marvel Comics: Sept, 1999 - No. 11, June, 2000 ($1.99)
1-11: 1-Casey-s/Manco-a. 2-Two covers. 4-Canete-a 2.0

DEATHLOK SPECIAL
Marvel Comics: May, 1991 - No. 4, June, 1991 ($2.00, bi-weekly lim. series)
1-4: r/1-4(1990) w/new Guice-c #1,2; Cowan c-3,4 2.0
1-2nd printing w/white-c 2.0

DEATHMARK

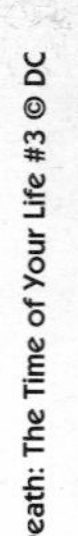
Deathmate Black © Image

Death: The Time of Your Life #3 © DC

Death Valley #2 © Comic Media

GD2.0 FN6.0 NM9.4

ightning Comics: Dec, 1994 ($2.95, B&W)

1 — 3.00

EATHMATE
aliant (Prologue/Yellow/Blue)/Image Comics (Black/Red/Epilogue): ept, 1993 - Epilogue (#6), Feb, 1994 ($2.95/$4.95, limited series)

review-(7/93, 8 pgs.) — 2.00
rologue (#1)–Silver foil; Jim Lee/Layton-c; B. Smith/Lee-a; Liefeld-a(p) — 3.00
rologue–Special gold foil ed. of silver ed. — 4.00
lack (#2)-(9/93, $4.95, 52 pgs.)-Silvestri/Jim Lee-c; pencils by Peterson/Silvestri/Capullo/Jim Lee/Portacio; 1st story app. Gen 13 telling their rebellion against the Troika (see WildC.A.T.S. Trilogy) — 4.00
lack-Special gold foil edition — 5.00
ellow (#3)-(10/93, $4.95, 52 pgs)-Yellow foil-c; Indicia says Prologue Sept 1993 by mistake; 3rd app. Ninjak; Thibert-c(i) — 5.00
ellow-Special gold foil edition — 4.00
lue (#4)-(10/93, $4.95, 52 pgs.)-Thibert blue foil-c(i); Reese-a(i) — 3.00
lue-Special gold foil edition — 4.00
ed (#5), Epilogue (#6)-(2/94, $2.95)-Silver foil Quesada/Silvestri-c; Silvestri-a(p) — 3.00

EATH METAL
larvel Comics UK: Jan, 1994 - No. 4, Apr, 1994 ($1.95, limited series)

1-4: 1-Silver ink-c. Alpha Flight app. — 2.00

EATH METAL VS. GENETIX
larvel Comics UK: Dec, 1993 - No. 2, Jan, 1994 (Limited series)

1-($2.95)-Polybagged w/2 trading cards — 3.00
2-($2.50)-Polybagged w/2 trading cards — 2.50

EATH OF CAPTAIN MARVEL (See Marvel Graphic Novel #1)

EATH OF MR. MONSTER, THE (See Mr. Monster #8)

EATH OF SUPERMAN (See Superman, 2nd Series)

EATH RACE 2020
oger Corman's Cosmic Comics: Apr, 1995 - No. 8, Nov, 1995 ($2.50)

1-8: Sequel to the Movie — 2.50

EATH RATTLE (Formerly an Underground)
itchen Sink Press: V2#1, 10/85 - No. 18, 1988, 1994 ($1.95, Baxter paper, ature); V3#1, 11/95 - No. 5, 6/96 ($2.95, B&W)

2#1-7,9-18: 1-Corben-c. 2-Unpubbed Spirit story by Eisner. 5-Robot Woman-r by Wolverton. 6-B&W issues begin. 10-Savage World-r by by Williamson/ Torres/ Krenkel/Frazetta from Witzend #1. 16-Wolverton Spacehawk-r — 3.00
8-(12/86)-1st app. Mark Schultz's Xenozoic Tales/Cadillacs & Dinosaurs — 4.00
8-(1994)-r plus interview w/Mark Schultz — 3.00
3#1-5 ($2.95-c) — 3.00

EATH'S HEAD (See Daredevil #56, Dragon's Claws #5 & Incomplete…)
larvel Comics: Dec, 1988 - No. 10, Sept, 1989 ($1.75)

1-Dragon's Claws spin-off — 2.00
2-Fantastic Four app.; Dragon's Claws x-over — 1.75
3-10: 8-Dr. Who app. 9-F. F. x-over; Simonson-c(p) — 1.75

EATH'S HEAD II (Also see Battletide)
larvel Comics UK, Ltd.: Mar, 1992 - No. 4, June (May inside), 1992 ($1.75, olor, limited series)

1-4: 2-Fantastic Four app. 4-Punisher, Spider-Man , Daredevil, Dr. Strange, Capt. America & Wolverine in the year 2020 — 2.00
1,2-Silver ink 2nd printiings — 2.00

EATH'S HEAD II (Also see Battletide)
larvel Comics UK, Ltd.: Dec, 1992 - No. 16, Mar, 1994 ($1.75/$1.95)

2#1-13,15,16: 1-Gatefold-c. 1-4-X-Men app.15-Capt. America & Wolverine app. — 2.00
14-($2.95)-Foil flip-c w/Death's Head II Gold #0 — 3.00
.Gold 1 (1/94, $3.95, 68 pgs.)-Gold foil-c — 4.00

EATH'S HEAD II & THE ORIGIN OF DIE CUT
larvel Comics UK, Ltd.: Aug, 1993 - No. 2, Sept, 1993 (limited series)

1-($2.95)-Embossed-c — 3.00

2 ($1.75) — 1.75

DEATHSTROKE: THE TERMINATOR (Deathstroke: The Hunted #0-47; Deathstroke #48-60) (Also see Marvel & DC Present, New Teen Titans #2, New Titans, Showcase '93 #7,9 & Tales of the Teen Titans #42-44)
DC Comics: Aug, 1991 - No. 60, June, 1996 ($1.75-$2.25)

1-New Titans spin-off; Mike Zeck c-1-28 — 3.00
1-Gold ink 2nd printing ($1.75) — 2.00
2 — 2.00
3-40,0(10/94),41(11/94)-49,51-60: 6,8-Batman cameo. 7,9-Batman-c/story. 9-1st new Vigilante (female) in cameo. 10-1st full app. new Vigilante; Perez-i. 13-Vs. Justice League; TeamTitans cameo on last pg. 14-Total Chaos, part 1; TeamTitans-c/story cont'd in New Titans #90. 15-Total Chaos, part 4. 40-(9/94). 0-(10/94)-Begin Deathstroke, The Hunted, ends #47. — 2.50
50 ($3.50) — 3.50
Annual 1-4 ('92-'95, 68 pgs.): 1-Nightwing & Vigilante app.; minor Eclipso app. 2-Bloodlines Deathstorm; 1st app. Gunfire. 3-Elseworlds story. 4-Year One story — 4.00

NOTE: ***Golden** a-12. **Perez** a-11i. **Zeck** c-Annual 1, 2.*

DEATH: THE HIGH COST OF LIVING (See Sandman #8) (Also see the Books of Magic limited & ongoing series)
DC Comics (Vertigo): Mar, 1993 - No. 3, May, 1993 ($1.95, limited series)

1-Bachalo/Buckingham-a; Dave McKean-c; Neil Gaiman scripts in all — 2.40 — 6.00
1-Platinum edition — 20.00
2 — 3.50
3-Pgs. 19 & 20 had wrong placement — 3.00
3-Corrected version w/pgs. 19 & 20 facing each other; has no-c & ads for Sebastion O & The Geek added — 4.00
Death Talks About Life-giveaway about AIDS prevention — 4.00
Hardcover (1994, $19.95)-r/#1-3 & Death Talks About Life; intro. by Tori Amos. — 20.00
Trade paperback (6/94, $12.95, Titan Books)-r/#1-3 & Death Talks About Life; prism-c — 13.00

DEATH: THE TIME OF YOUR LIFE (See Sandman #8)
DC Comics (Vertigo): Apr, 1996 - No. 3, July, 1996 ($2.95, limited series)

1-3: Neil Gaiman story & Bachalo/Buckingham-a; Dave McKean-c. 2-(5/96). — 3.00
Hardcover (1997, $19.95)-r/#1-3 w/3 new pages & gallery art by various artists — 20.00
Trade paperback (1997, $12.95)-r/#1-3 & Visions of Death gallery; Intro. by Claire Danes — 13.00

DEATH 3
Marvel Comics UK: Sept, 1993 - No. 4, Dec, 1993 ($1.75, limited series)

1-($2.95)-Embossed-c — 3.00
2-4 — 2.00

DEATH VALLEY (Cowboys and Indians)
Comic Media: Oct, 1953 - No. 6, Aug, 1954

	GD2.0	FN6.0	NM9.4
1-Billy the Kid; Morisi-a; Andru/Esposito-c/a	10.00	30.00	70.00
2-Don Heck-c	6.00	18.00	42.00
3-6: 3,5-Morisi-a. 5-Discount-a	5.00	15.00	35.00

DEATH VALLEY (Becomes Frontier Scout, Daniel Boone No.10-13)
Charlton Comics: No. 7, 6/55 - No. 9, 10/55 (Cont'd from Comic Media series)

	GD2.0	FN6.0	NM9.4
7-9: 8-Wolverton-a (half pg.)	5.00	15.00	35.00

DEATHWISH
DC Comics (Milestone Media): Dec, 1994 - No. 4, Mar, 1995 (2.50, lim. series)

1-4 — 2.50

DEATH WRECK
Marvel Comics UK: Jan, 1994 - No. 4, Apr, 1994 ($1.95, limited series)

1-4: 1-Metallic ink logo; Death's Head II app. — 2.00

DEBBIE DEAN, CAREER GIRL
Civil Service Publ.: April, 1945 - No. 2, July, 1945

	GD2.0	FN6.0	NM9.4
1,2-Newspaper reprints by Bert Whitman	12.50	37.50	100.00

DEBBI'S DATES (Also see Date With Debbi)

Defcon 4 #2 © Aegis Ent.

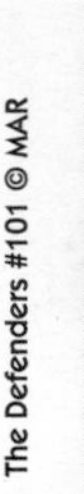

The Defenders #101 © MAR

Deity V2 #4 © Hyperwerks

National Periodical Publications: Apr-May, 1969 - No. 11, Dec-Jan, 1970-71

	GD2.0	FN6.0	NM9.4
1	3.80	11.40	42.00
2,3,5,7-11: 2-Last 12¢ issue	2.00	6.00	18.00
4-Neal Adams text illo	3.00	9.00	32.00
6-Superman cameo	4.10	12.30	45.00

DECADE OF DARK HORSE, A
Dark Horse Comics: Jul, 1996 - No. 4, Oct, 1996 ($2.95, B&W/color, lim. series)

1-4: 1-Sin City-c/story by Miller; Grendel by Wagner; Predator. 2-Star Wars wraparound-c. 3-Aliens-c/story; Nexus, Mask stories 3.00

DECAPITATOR (Randy Bowen's...)
Dark Horse Comics: Jun, 1998 - No. 4, ($2.95)

1-4-Bowen-s/art by various. 1-Mahnke-c. 3-Jones-c 4.00

DECEPTION, THE
Image Comics (Flypaper Press): 1999 - No. 3, 1999 ($2.95, B&W, mini-series)

1-3-Horley painted-c 3.00

DEEP, THE (Movie)
Marvel Comics Group: Nov, 1977 (Giant)

1-Infantino-c/a 5.00

DEEP DARK FANTASIES
Dark Fantasy Productions: Oct, 1995 ($4.50/$4.95, B&W)

1-($4.50)-Clive Barker-c, anthology 4.50
1-($4.95)-Red foil logo-c 5.00

DEFCON 4
Image Comics (WildStorm Productions): Feb, 1996 - No. 4, Sept, 1996 ($2.50, limited series)

	GD2.0	FN6.0	NM9.4
1/2	1.10	3.30	9.00
1/2 Gold-(1000 printed)			14.00
1-Main Cover by Mat Broome & Edwin Rosell			3.00
1-Hordes of Cymulants variant-c by Michael Golden			5.00
1-Backs to the Wall variant-c by Humberto Ramos & Alex Garner			5.00
1-Defcon 4-Way variant-c by Jim Lee	1.00	2.80	7.00
2-4			2.50

DEFENDERS, THE (TV)
Dell Publishing Co.: Sept-Nov, 1962 - No. 2, Feb-Apr, 1963

	GD2.0	FN6.0	NM9.4
12-176-211(#1)	3.45	10.35	38.00
12-176-304(#2)	3.00	9.00	30.00

DEFENDERS, THE (Also see Giant-Size..., Marvel Feature, Marvel Treasury Edition, Secret Defenders & Sub-Mariner #34, 35; The New...#140-on)
Marvel Comics Group: Aug, 1972 - No. 152, Feb, 1986

	GD2.0	FN6.0	NM9.4
1-The Hulk, Doctor Strange, Sub-Mariner begin	7.65	23.00	85.00
2-Silver Surfer x-over	3.20	9.60	35.00
3-5: 3-Silver Surfer x-over. 4-Valkyrie joins	2.50	7.50	25.00
6,7: 6-Silver Surfer x-over	2.00	6.00	18.00
8,9,11: 8-11-Defenders vs. the Avengers (Crossover with Avengers #115-118) 8,11-Silver Surfer x-over	2.50	7.50	25.00
10-Hulk vs. Thor battle	3.20	9.60	35.00
12-14: 12-Last 20¢ issue	1.25	3.75	10.00
15,16-Magneto & Brotherhood of Evil Mutants app. from X-Men	1.50	4.50	12.00
17-20: 17-Power Man x-over (11/74)	1.00	2.80	7.00
21-25: 24,25-Son of Satan app.			5.00
26-29-Guardians of the Galaxy app. (#26 is 8/75; pre-dates Marvel Presents #3): 28-1st full app. Starhawk (cameo #27). 29-Starhawk joins Guardians	1.00	2.80	7.00
30-33,39-50: 31,32-Origin Nighthawk. 44-Hellcat joins. 45-Dr. Strange leaves. 47-49-Early Moon Knight app. (5/77)			4.00
34-38-(Regular 25¢ editions): 35-Intro New Red Guardian			4.00
34-38-(30¢-c variants, limited distribution)(4-8/76)		2.40	6.00
51-60: 53-1st app. Lunatik (cameo, Lobo lookalike). 55-Origin Red Guardian; Lunatik cameo. 56-1st full Lunatik story			3.00
61-75: 61-Lunatik & Spider-Man app. 70-73-Lunatik (origin #71). 73-75-Foolkiller II app. (Greg Salinger). 74-Nighthawk resigns			2.50
76-95,97-99,101-124,126-149,151: 77-Origin Omega. 78-Original Defenders return thru #101. 94-1st Gargoyle. 101-Silver Surfer-c & app. 104-The Beast joins. 105-Son of Satan joins. 106-Death of Nighthawk. 120,121-Son of Satan-c/stories. 122-Final app. Son of Satan (2 pgs.). 129-New Mutants cameo (3/84, early x-over)			2.00
96-Ghost Rider app.			4.00
100-(52 pgs.)-Hellcat (Patsy Walker) revealed as Satan's daughter			5.00
125,150: 125-(52 pgs.)-Intro new Defenders. 150-(52 pgs.)-Origin Cloud			4.00
152-(52 pgs.)-Ties in with X-Factor & Secret Wars II			3.00
Annual 1 (1976, 52 pgs.)-New book-length story	1.50	4.50	12.00

NOTE: ***Art Adams*** *c-142p.* ***Austin*** *a-53i; c-65i, 119i, 145i.* ***Frank Bolle*** *a-7i, 10i, 11i.* ***Buckle*** *c(p)-34, 38, 76, 77, 79-86, 90, 91.* ***J. Buscema*** *c-66.* ***Giffen*** *a-42-49p, 50, 51-54p.* ***Golden*** *a-53, 54p; c-94, 96.* ***Guice*** *c-129.* ***G. Kane*** *c(p)-13, 16, 18, 19, 21-26, 31-33, 35-37, 40, 41, 52, 5* ***Kirby*** *c-42-45.* ***Mooney*** *a-3i, 31-34i, 62i, 63i, 85i.* ***Nasser*** *c-88p.* ***Perez*** *c(p)-51, 53, 54.* ***Roger*** *c-98.* ***Starlin*** *c-110.* ***Tuska*** *a-57p. Silver Surfer in No. 2, 3, 6, 8-11, 92, 98-101, 107, 112-11 122-125.*

DEFENDERS OF DYNATRON CITY
Marvel Comics: Feb, 1992 - No. 6, July, 1992 ($1.25, limited series)

1-6-Lucasarts characters. 2-Origin 3.00

DEFENDERS OF THE EARTH (TV)
Marvel Comics (Star Comics): Jan, 1987 - No. 4, July, 1987

1-4: The Phantom, Mandrake The Magician, Flash Gordon begin. 3-Origin Phantom. 4-Origin Mandrake 4.00

DEFINITIVE DIRECTORY OF THE DC UNIVERSE, THE (See Who's Who...)

DEITY (Also see Kosmic Kat)
Hyperwerks Comics: Sept, 1997 - No. 6, Apr, 1998, ($2.95, limited series)

1-6, 0(5/98) 4.00
1-Variant-c 5.00
2-6,0-Variant covers 3.00
0-NDC Edition 4.00
0-NDC Silver Ed. 8.00
0-NDC Gold Ed. 12.00

DEITY (Volume 2)
Hyperwerks Comics: Sept, 1998 - No. 5 ($2.95)

Preview (6/98) Flip book with Lady Pendragon preview 3.00
1-5: 1-Flip book w/Catseye preview 3.00

DEITY:REVELATIONS (Volume 3)
Hyperwerks Comics: July, 1999 - No. 4, Dec, 1999 ($2.95)

1-4-Alstaetter and Napton-s/a 3.00

DELECTA OF THE PLANETS (See Don Fortune & Fawcett Miniatures)

DELLA VISION (...The Television Queen) (Patty Powers #4 on)
Atlas Comics: April, 1955 - No. 3, Aug, 1955

	GD2.0	FN6.0	NM9.4
1-Al Hartley-c	15.00	45.00	120.00
2,3	10.00	30.00	80.00

DELL GIANT COMICS

Dell Publishing began to release square bound comics in 1949 with a 132 page issue called Christmas Parade #1. The covers were of a heavier stock t accommodate the increased number of pages. The books proved profitable at 2 cents, but the average number of pages was quickly reduced to 100. Ten year later they were converted to a numbering system similar to the Four Colc Comics, for greater ease in distribution and the page counts cut back to most 84 pages. The label "Dell Giant" began to appear on the covers in 1954. Becaus of the size of the books and the heavier, less pliant cover stock, they are rare found in high grade condition, and with the exception of a small quantity of copie released from Western Publishing's warehouse–are almost never found in nea mint.

	GD2.0	FN6.0	VF8.0	NM9.4
Abraham Lincoln Life Story 1(3/58)	5.00	15.00	40.00	100.00
Bugs Bunny Christmas Funnies 1(11/50, 116pp)	13.50	40.50	108.00	270.00
...Christmas Funnies 2(11/51, 116pp)	9.00	27.00	72.00	180.00
...Christmas Funnies 3-5(11/52-11/54,)-Becomes Christmas Party #6	8.00	24.00	64.00	160.00
...Christmas Funnies 7-9(12/56-12/58)	7.00	21.00	56.00	140.00
...Christmas Party 6(11/55)-Formerly Bugs Bunny Christmas Funnies	6.00	18.00	48.00	120.00

Dell Giant Comics - Bugs Bunny Vacation Funnies #8 © WB

Dell Giant Comics - Donald Duck Beach Party © WDC

Dell Giant Comics - Raggedy Ann & Andy © DELL

GD2.0 FN6.0 NM9.4

...County Fair 1(9/57) 9.00 27.00 72.00 180.00
...Halloween Parade 1(10/53) 8.50 25.50 68.00 170.00
...Halloween Parade 2(10/54)-Trick 'N' Treat Halloween Fun #3 on 7.00 21.00 36.00 140.00
...Trick 'N' Treat Halloween Fun 3,4(10/55-10/56)-Formerly Halloween Parade #2 8.00 24.00 64.00 160.00
...Vacation Funnies 1(7/51, 112pp) 13.50 40.50 108.00 270.00
...Vacation Funnies 2('52) 10.50 31.50 84.00 210.00
...Vacation Funnies 3-5('53-'55) 8.00 24.00 64.00 160.00
...Vacation Funnies 6-9('54-6/59) 7.00 21.00 56.00 140.00
Cadet Gray of West Point 1(4/58)-Williamson-a, 10pgs.; Buscema-a; photo-c 5.00 15.00 40.00 100.00
Christmas In Disneyland 1(12/57)-Barks-a, 18 pgs. 21.00 63.00 168.00 420.00
Christmas Parade 1(11/49)(132 pgs.)(1st Dell Giant)-Donald Duck (25pgs. by Barks, r-in G.K. Christmas Parade #5); Mickey Mouse & other film oriented stories; Cinderella (prior to movie), 7 Dwarfs, Bambi & Thumper, So Dear To My Heart, Flying Mouse, Dumbo, Cookieland & others 47.00 141.00 376.00 940.00
Christmas Parade 2('50)-Donald Duck (132 pgs.)(25 pgs. by Barks, r-in G.K. Christmas Parade #6). Mickey, Pluto, Chip & Dale, etc. Contents shift to a holiday expansion of W.D. C&S type format 36.00 108.00 288.00 720.00
Christmas Parade 3-7('51-'55, #3-116pgs; #4-7, 100 pgs.) 10.00 30.00 80.00 200.00
Christmas Parade 8(12/56)-Barks-a, 8 pgs. 18.00 54.00 144.00 360.00
Christmas Parade 9(12/58)-Barks-a, 20 pgs. 21.00 63.00 168.00 420.00
Christmas Treasury, A 1(11/54) 6.50 19.50 52.00 130.00
Davy Crockett, King Of The Wild Frontier 1(9/55)-Fess Parker photo-c; Marsh-a 14.50 43.50 116.00 290.00
Disneyland Birthday Party 1(10/58)-Barks-a, 16 pgs. r-by Gladstone 21.00 63.00 168.00 420.00
Donald and Mickey In Disneyland 1(5/58) 9.00 27.00 72.00 180.00
Donald Duck Beach Party 1(7/54)-Has an Uncle Scrooge story (not by Barks) that prefigures the later rivalry with Flintheart Glomgold and tells of Scrooge's wild rivalry with another millionaire 11.00 33.00 88.00 220.00
...Beach Party 2(1955)-Lady & Tramp 8.50 25.50 68.00 170.00
...Beach Party 3-5(1956-58) 8.50 25.50 68.00 170.00
...Beach Party 6(8/59, 84pp)-Stapled 5.50 16.50 44.00 110.00
Donald Duck Fun Book 1,2(1953 & 10/54)-Games, puzzles, comics & cut-outs (very rare in unused condition)(most copies commonly have defaced interior pgs.) 35.00 105.00 280.00 700.00
Donald Duck In Disneyland 1(9/55)-1st Disneyland Dell Giant 11.00 33.00 88.00 220.00
Golden West Rodeo Treasury 1(10/57) 7.00 21.00 56.00 140.00
Huey, Dewey and Louie Back To School 1(9/58) 7.00 21.00 56.00 140.00
Lady and The Tramp 1(6/55) 14.00 42.00 112.00 280.00
Life Stories of American Presidents 1(11/57)-Buscema-a 4.00 12.00 32.00 80.00
Lone Ranger Golden West 3(8/55)-Formerly Lone Ranger Western Treasury 14.50 43.50 116.00 290.00
Lone Ranger Movie Story nn(3/56)-Origin Lone Ranger in text; Clayton Moore photo-c 28.00 85.00 228.00 570.00
...Western Treasury 1(9/53)-Origin Lone Ranger, Silver, & Tonto; painted cover 16.00 48.00 128.00 320.00
...Western Treasury 2(8/54)-Becomes Lone Ranger Golden West #3 10.50 31.50 84.00 210.00
Marge's Little Lulu & Alvin Story Telling Time 1(3/59)-r/#2,5,3,11,30,10,21,17,8,14,16; Stanley-a 11.00 33.00 88.00 220.00
...& Her Friends 4(3/56)-Tripp-a 9.00 27.00 72.00 180.00
...& Her Special Friends 3(3/55)-Tripp-a 11.00 33.00 88.00 220.00
...& Tubby At Summer Camp 5,2: 5(10/57)-Tripp-a. 2(10/58)-Tripp-a 9.00 27.00 72.00 180.00
...& Tubby Halloween Fun 6,2: 6(10/57)-Tripp-a. 2(10/58)-Tripp-a 9.00 27.00 72.00 180.00
...& Tubby In Alaska 1(7/59)-Tripp-a 9.00 27.00 72.00 180.00

GD2.0 FN6.0 NM9.4

...On Vacation 1(7/54)-r/4C-110,14,4C-146,5,4C-97,4,4C-158,3,1;Stanley-a 20.00 60.00 160.00 400.00
...& Tubby Annual 1(3/53)-r/4C-165,4C-74,4C-146,4C-97,4C-158, 4C-139, 4C-131; Stanley-a (1st Lulu Dell Gnt) 24.50 73.50 196.00 490.00
...& Tubby Annual 2('54)-r/4C-139,6,4C-115,4C-74,5,4C-97,3,4C-146,18; Stanley-a 21.50 64.50 172.00 430.00
Marge's Tubby & His Clubhouse Pals 1(10/56)-1st app. Gran'pa Feeb;1st app. Janie; written by Stanley; Tripp-a 10.50 31.50 84.00 210.00
Mickey Mouse Almanac 1(12/57)-Barks-a, 8pgs. 21.50 64.50 172.00 430.00
...Birthday Party 1(9/53)-r/entire 48pgs. of Gottfredson's "Mickey Mouse in Love Trouble" from WDC&S 36-39. Quality equal to original. Also reprints one story each from 4-Color 27, 29, & 181 plus 6 panels of highlights in the career of Mickey Mouse 26.00 78.00 208.00 520.00
...Club Parade 1(12/55)-r/4-Color 16 with some death trap scenes redrawn by Paul Murry & recolored with night turned into day; quality less than original 20.00 60.00 160.00 400.00
...In Fantasy Land 1(5/57) 10.00 30.00 80.00 200.00
...In Frontier Land 1(5/56)-Mickey Mouse Club issue 10.00 30.00 80.00 200.00
...Summer Fun 1(8/58)-Mobile cut-outs on back-c; becomes Summer Fun with #2 10.00 30.00 80.00 200.00
Moses & The Ten Commandments 1(8/57)-Not based on movie; Dell's adaptation; Sekowsky-a 4.00 12.00 32.00 80.00
Nancy & Sluggo Travel Time 1(9/58) 5.50 16.50 44.00 110.00
Peter Pan Treasure Chest 1(1/53, 212pp)-Disney; contains 54-page movie adaptation & other P. Pan stories; plus Donald & Mickey stories w/P. Pan; a 32-page retelling of the Buried Treasure" ... "D. Duck Finds Pirate Gold" with yellow beak, called "Capt. Hook & the Buried Treasure" 85.00 255.00 680.00 1700.00
Picnic Party 6,7(7/55-6/56)(Formerly Vacation Parade)-Uncle Scrooge, Mickey & Donald 8.50 25.50 68.00 170.00
Picnic Party 8(7/57)-Barks-a, 6pgs 18.00 54.00 144.00 360.00
Pogo Parade 1(9/53)-Kelly-a(r-/Pogo from Animal Comics in this order: #11,13,21,14,27,16,23,9,18,15,17) 23.50 70.50 188.00 470.00
Raggedy Ann & Andy 1(2/55) 12.00 36.00 96.00 240.00
Santa Claus Funnies 1(11/52)-Dan Noonan -A Christmas Carol adaptation 6.50 19.50 52.00 130.00
Silly Symphonies 1(9/52)-Redrawing of Gotfredson's Mickey Mouse strip of "The Brave Little Tailor;" 2 Good Housekeeping pages (from 1943); Lady and the Two Siamese Cats, three years before "Lady & the Tramp;" a retelling of Donald Duck's first app. in "The Wise Little Hen" & other stories based on 1930's Silly Symphony cartoons 23.50 70.50 188.00 470.00
Silly Symphonies 2(9/53)-M. Mouse in "The Sorcerer's Apprentice", 2 Good Housekeeping pages (from 1944); The Pelican & the Snipe, Elmer Elephant, Peculiar Penguins, Little Hiawatha, & others 21.00 63.00 168.00 420.00
Silly Symphonies 3(2/54)-r/Mickey & The Beanstalk (4-Color #157, 39pgs.), Little Minnehaha, Pablo, The Flying Gauchito, Pluto, & Bongo, & 2 Good Housekeeping pages (1944) 18.00 54.00 144.00 360.00
Silly Symphonies 4(8/54)-r/Dumbo (4-Color 234), Morris The Midget Moose, The Country Cousin, Bongo, & Clara Cluck 18.00 54.00 144.00 360.00
Silly Symphonies 5-8: 5(2/55)-r/Cinderella (4-Color 272), Bucky Bug, Pluto, Little Hiawatha, The 7 Dwarfs & Dumbo, Pinocchio. 6(8/55)-r/Pinocchio (WDC&S 63), The 7 Dwarfs & Thumper (WDC&S 45), M. Mouse "Adventures With Robin Hood" (40 pgs.), Johnny Appleseed, Pluto & Peter Pan, & Bucky Bug; Cut-out on back-c. 7(2/57)-r/Reluctant Dragon, Ugly Duckling, M. Mouse & Peter Pan, Jiminy Cricket, Peter & The Wolf, Brer Rabbit, Bucky Bug; Cut-out on back-c. 8(2/58)-r/Thumper Meets The 7 Dwarfs (4-Color #19), Jiminy Cricket, Niok, Brer Rabbit; Cut-out on back-c 15.00 45.00 120.00 300.00
Silly Symphonies 9(2/59)-r/Paul Bunyan, Humphrey Bear, Jiminy Cricket, The Social Lion, Goliath II; cut-out on back-c 14.00 42.00 112.00 280.00
Sleeping Beauty 1(4/59) 23.50 70.50 188.00 470.00
Summer Fun 2(8/59, 84pp, stapled binding)(Formerly Mickey Mouse...)-Barks-a(2), 24 pgs. 21.00 63.00 168.00 420.00
Tarzan's Jungle Annual 1(8/52)-Lex Barker photo on-c of #1,2 11.00 33.00 88.00 220.00

Dell Giant Comics - Tarzan Jungle Annual #4 © ERB

Dell Giant #27 © WDC

Dell Giant #49 © WDC

GD2.0 FN6.0 NM9.4

...Annual 2(8/53) 8.50 25.50 68.00 170.00
...Annual 3-7('54-9/58)(two No. 5s)-Manning-a-No. 3,5-7; Marsh-a in No. 1-7 plus painted-c 1-7 7.00 21.00 56.00 140.00
Tom And Jerry Back To School 1(9/56) 10.50 31.50 84.00 210.00
...Picnic Time 1(7/58) 8.00 24.00 64.00 160.00
...Summer Fun 1(7/54)-Droopy written by Barks 13.00 39.00 104.00 260.00
...Summer Fun 2-4(7/55-7/57) 5.50 16.50 44.00 110.00
...Toy Fair 1(6/58) 8.00 24.00 64.00 160.00
...Winter Carnival 1(12/52)-Droopy written by Barks 18.00 54.00 144.00 360.00
...Winter Carnival 2(12/53)-Droopy written by Barks 15.00 45.00 120.00 300.00
...Winter Fun 3(12/54) 5.50 16.50 44.00 110.00
...Winter Fun 4-7(12/55-11/58) 4.50 13.50 36.00 90.00
Treasury of Dogs, A 1(10/56) 4.50 13.50 36.00 90.00
Treasury of Horses, A (9/55) 4.50 13.50 36.00 90.00
Uncle Scrooge Goes To Disneyland 1(8/57p)-Barks-a, 20pgs.r-by Gladstone 21.00 63.00 168.00 420.00
Vacation In Disneyland 1(8/58) 9.00 27.00 72.00 180.00
Vacation Parade 1(7/50, 132pp)-Donald Duck & Mickey Mouse; Barks-a, 55 pgs. 70.00 210.00 560.00 1400.00
Vacation Parade 2(7/51,116pp) 22.00 66.00 176.00 440.00
Vacation Parade 3-5(7/52-7/54)-Becomes Picnic Party No. 6 on. #4-Robin Hood Advs. 10.50 31.50 84.00 210.00
Western Roundup 1(6/52)-Photo-c; Gene Autry, Roy Rogers, Johnny Mack Brown, Rex Allen, & Bill Elliott begin; photo back-c begin, end No. 14,16,18 19.50 58.50 156.00 390.00
Western Roundup 2(2/53)-Photo-c 10.50 31.00 84.00 210.00
Western Roundup 3-5(7-9/53 - 1-3/54)-Photo-c 8.50 25.50 68.00 170.00
Western Roundup 6-10(4-6/54 - 4-6/55)-Photo-c 8.00 24.00 64.00 160.00
Western Roundup 11-17,25-Photo-c; 11-13,16,17-Manning-a. 11-Flying A's Range Rider, Dale Evans begin 7.00 21.00 56.00 140.00
Western Roundup 18-Toth-a; last photo-c; Gene Autry ends 7.50 22.50 60.00 150.00
Western Roundup 19-24-Manning-a. 19-Buffalo Bill Jr. begins (7-9/57; early app.). 19,20,22-Toth-a. 21-Rex Allen, Johnny Mack Brown end. 22-Jace Pearson's Texas Rangers, Rin Tin Tin, Tales of Wells Fargo (2nd app., 4-6/58) & Wagon Train (2nd app.) begin 6.50 19.00 52.00 130.00
Woody Woodpecker Back To School 1(10/52) 8.00 24.00 64.00 160.00
...Back To School 2-4,6('53-10/57)-County Fair No. 5 5.50 16.50 44.00 110.00
...County Fair 5(9/56)-Formerly Back To School 5.50 16.50 44.00 110.00
...County Fair 2(11/58) 4.50 13.50 36.00 90.00

DELL GIANTS (Consecutive numbering)
Dell Publishing Co.: No. 21, Sept, 1959 - No. 55, Sept, 1961 (Most 84 pgs., 25¢)

21-(#1)-M.G.M.'s Tom & Jerry Picnic Time (84pp, stapled binding)-Painted-c 9.00 27.00 72.00 180.00
22-Huey, Dewey & Louie Back to School (Disney; 10/59, 84pp, square binding begins) 6.50 19.50 52.00 130.00
23-Marge's Little Lulu & Tubby Halloween Fun (10/59)-Tripp-a 9.00 27.00 72.00 180.00
24-Woody Woodpecker's Family Fun (11/59)(Walter Lantz) 6.50 19.50 52.00 130.00
25-Tarzan's Jungle World(11/59)-Marsh-a; painted-c 8.50 25.50 68.00 170.00
26-Christmas Parade(Disney; 12/59)-Barks-a, 16pgs.; Barks draws himself on wanted poster pg. 13 18.00 54.00 144.00 360.00
27-Walt Disney's Man in Space (10/59) r-/4-Color 716,866, & 954 (100 pgs., 35¢)(TV) 8.00 24.00 64.00 160.00
28-Bugs Bunny's Winter Fun (2/60) 8.00 24.00 64.00 160.00
29-Marge's Little Lulu & Tubby in Hawaii (4/60)-Tripp-a 8.50 25.50 68.00 170.00
30-Disneyland USA(Disney; 6/60) 7.00 21.00 56.00 140.00
31-Huckleberry Hound Summer Fun (7/60)(TV)(HannaBarbera)-Yogi Bear & Pixie & Dixie app. 10.50 31.50 84.00 210.00
32-Bugs Bunny Beach Party 4.50 13.50 36.00 90.00
33-Daisy Duck & Uncle Scrooge Picnic Time (Disney; 9/60) 7.00 21.00 56.00 140.00
34-Nancy & Sluggo Summer Camp (8/60) 5.50 16.50 44.00 110.00
35-Huey, Dewey & Louie Back to School (Disney; 10/60)-1st app. Daisy Duck's Nieces, April, May & June 8.50 25.50 68.00 170.00
36-Marge's Little Lulu & Witch Hazel Halloween Fun (10/60)-Tripp-a 8.50 25.50 68.00 170.00
37-Tarzan, King of the Jungle (11/60)-Marsh-a; painted-c 8.00 24.00 64.00 160.00
38-Uncle Donald & His Nephews Family Fun (Disney; 11/60)-Cover painting based on a pencil sketch by Barks 10.50 31.50 84.00 210.00
39-Walt Disney's Merry Christmas (Disney; 12/60)-Cover painting based on a pencil sketch by Barks 10.50 31.50 84.00 210.00
40-Woody Woodpecker Christmas Parade (12/60)(Walter Lantz) 4.50 13.50 36.00 90.00
41-Yogi Bear's Winter Sports (12/60)(TV)(Hanna-Barbera)-Huckleberry Hound, Pixie & Dixie, Augie Doggie app. 10.50 31.50 84.00 210.00
42-Marge's Little Lulu & Tubby in Australia (4/61) 9.00 27.00 72.00 180.00
43-Mighty Mouse in Outer Space (5/61) 17.00 51.00 136.00 340.00
44-Around the World with Huckleberry and His Friends (7/61)(TV)(Hanna-Barbera)-Yogi Bear, Pixie & Dixie, Quick Draw McGraw, Augie Doggie app., 1st app. Yakky Doodle 10.50 31.50 84.00 210.00
45-Nancy & Sluggo Summer Camp (8/61) 4.50 13.50 36.00 90.00
46-Bugs Bunny Beach Party (8/61) 4.50 13.50 36.00 90.00
47-Mickey & Donald in Vacationland (Disney; 8/61) 6.50 19.50 52.00 130.00
48-The Flintstones (No. 1)(Bedrock Bedlam)(7/61)(TV)(Hanna-Barbera) 1st app. in comics 16.00 48.00 128.00 320.00
49-Huey, Dewey & Louie Back to School (Disney; 9/61) 6.50 19.50 52.00 130.00
50-Marge's Little Lulu & Witch Hazel Trick 'N' Treat (10/61) 8.50 25.50 68.00 170.00
51-Tarzan, King of the Jungle by Jesse Marsh (11/61)-Painted-c 6.00 18.00 48.00 120.00
52-Uncle Donald & His Nephews Dude Ranch (Disney; 11/61) 5.50 16.50 44.00 110.00
53-Donald Duck Merry Christmas (Disney; 12/61) 5.50 16.50 44.00 110.00
54-Woody Woodpecker's Christmas Party (12/61)-Issued after No. 55 5.50 16.50 44.00 110.00
55-Daisy Duck & Uncle Scrooge Showboat (Disney; 9/61) 6.50 19.50 52.00 130.00
NOTE: All issues printed with & without ad on back cover.

DELL JUNIOR TREASURY
Dell Publishing Co.: June, 1955 - No. 10, Oct, 1957 (15¢) (All painted-c)

	GD2.0	FN6.0	NM9.4
1-Alice in Wonderland; r/4-Color #331 (52 pgs.)	9.50	29.00	115.00
2-Aladdin & the Wonderful Lamp	6.65	20.00	80.00
3-Gulliver's Travels (1/56)	5.85	17.50	70.00
4-Adventures of Mr. Frog & Miss Mouse	6.30	19.00	75.00
5-The Wizard of Oz (7/56)	6.65	20.00	80.00
6-10: 6-Heidi (10/56). 7-Santa and the Angel. 8-Raggedy Ann and the Camel with the Wrinkled Knees. 9-Clementina the Flying Pig. 10-Adventures of Tom Sawyer	5.85	17.50	70.00

DEMOLITION MAN
DC Comics: Nov, 1993 - No. 4, Feb, 1994 ($1.75, color, limited series)

1-4-Movie adaptation 2.00

DEMON, THE (See Detective Comics No. 482-485)
National Periodical Publications: Aug-Sept, 1972 - V3#16, Jan, 1974

1-Origin; Kirby-c/a in all 2.80 8.40 28.00
2-5 1.75 5.25 14.00

The Demon (2nd series) #3 © DC

Dennis the Menace #5 © FAW

Dennis the Menace (Marvel) #4 © Field Ent. Inc.

	GD2.0	FN6.0	NM9.4
6-16	1.00	3.30	9.00

DEMON, THE (1st limited series)(Also see Cosmic Odyssey #2)
DC Comics: Nov, 1986 - No. 4, Feb, 1987 (75¢, limited series)
(#2 has #4 of 4 on-c)

	GD2.0	FN6.0	NM9.4
1-4: Matt Wagner-a(p) & scripts in all. 4-Demon & Jason Blood become separate entities.			2.50

DEMON, THE (2nd Series)
DC Comics: July, 1990 - No. 57, May, 1995 ($1.50/$1.75/$1.95)

	GD2.0	FN6.0	NM9.4
1-Grant scripts begin, ends #39: 1-4-Painted-c			4.00
2-18,20-27,29-39,41,42,46,47: 3,8-Batman app. (cameo #4). 12-Bisley painted-c. 12-15,21-Lobo app. (1 pg. cameo #11). 23-Robin app. 29-Superman app. 31,33-39-Lobo app.			2.50
19,28,40: 19-($2.50, 44 pgs.)-Lobo poster stapled inside. 28-Superman-c/story; begin $1.75-c. 40-Garth Ennis scripts begin			4.00
43-45-Hitman app.	1.00	3.00	8.00
46-48 Return of The Haunted Tank-c/s. 48-Begin $1.95-c.			5.00
49,51,0-(10/94),55-57: 51-(9/94)			2.50
50 ($2.95, 52 pgs.)			3.00
52-54-Hitman-s			4.00
Annual 1 (1992, $3.00, 68 pgs.)-Eclipso-c/story			3.00
Annual 2 (1993, $3.50, 68 pgs.)-1st app. of Hitman	2.00	6.00	16.00

NOTE: ***Alan Grant*** *scripts in #1-16, 20, 21, 23-25, 30-39, Annual 1.* ***Wagner*** *a/scripts-22.*

DEMON DREAMS
Pacific Comics: Feb, 1984 - No. 2, May, 1984

	GD2.0	FN6.0	NM9.4
1,2-Mostly r-/Heavy Metal			2.00

DEMONGATE
Sirius Entertainment: May, 1996 - No. 10 ($2.50, B&W)

	GD2.0	FN6.0	NM9.4
1-10-Bao Lin Hum/Steve Blevins-s/a			2.50

DEMON GUN
Crusade Ent.: June, 1996 - No. 3, Jan, 1997 ($2.95, B&W, limited series)

	GD2.0	FN6.0	NM9.4
1-3: Gary Cohn scripts in all. 2-(10/96)			3.00

DEMON-HUNTER
Seaboard Periodicals (Atlas): Sept, 1975

	GD2.0	FN6.0	NM9.4
1-Origin/1st app. Demon-Hunter; Buckler-c/a			5.00

DEMON KNIGHT: A GRIMJACK GRAPHIC NOVEL
First Publishing: 1990 ($8.95, 52 pgs.)

	GD2.0	FN6.0	NM9.4
nn-Flint Henry-a			9.00

DEMONSLAYER
Image Comics: Nov, 1999 - No. 3, Jan, 2000 ($2.95)

	GD2.0	FN6.0	NM9.4
1-3-Story & art by Mychaels & Mendoza			3.00

DEMONSLAYER: INTO HELL (Volume 2)
Image Comics: Apr, 2000 - No. 3, Aug, 2000 ($2.95)

	GD2.0	FN6.0	NM9.4
1-3-Story & art by Mychaels			3.00
1-3 ($5.00) Variant cover editions			5.00

DENNIS THE MENACE (TV with 1959 issues) (Becomes ...Fun Fest Series; See The Best of... & The Very Best of...)(...Fun Fest on-c only to #156-166)
Standard Comics/Pines No.15-31/Hallden (Fawcett) No.32 on: 8/53 - #14, 1/56; #15, 3/56 - #31, 11/58; #32, 1/59 - #166, 11/79

	GD2.0	FN6.0	NM9.4
1-1st app. Dennis, Mr. & Mrs. Wilson, Ruff & Dennis' mom & dad; Wiseman-a, written by Fred Toole-most issues	47.00	142.00	425.00
2	24.00	73.00	195.00
3-10: 8-Last pre-code issue	14.00	43.00	115.00
11-20	10.50	32.00	85.00
21-30: 22-1st app. Margaret w/blonde hair	8.00	24.00	56.00
31-1st app. Joey	6.00	18.00	42.00
32-40(1/60): 37-A-Bomb blast panel. 39-1st app. Gina (11/59)	5.00	15.00	34.00
41-60(7/62)	2.50	7.50	24.00
61-80(9/65),100(1/69)	2.00	6.00	16.00
81-99	1.75	5.25	14.00
101-117: 102-Last 12¢ issue	1.10	3.30	9.00
118(1/72)-131 (All 52 pages)	1.25	3.75	10.00
132(1/74)-166		2.40	6.00

NOTE: ***Wiseman*** *c/a-1-46, 53, 68, 69.*

DENNIS THE MENACE (Giants) (No. 1 titled Giant Vacation Special; becomes Dennis the Menace Bonus Magazine No. 76 on)
(#1-8,18,23,25,30,38: 100 pgs.; rest to #41: 84 pgs.; #42-75: 68 pgs.)
Standard/Pines/Hallden(Fawcett): Summer, 1955 - No. 75, Dec, 1969

	GD2.0	FN6.0	NM9.4
nn-Giant Vacation Special(Summ/55-Standard)	17.00	51.00	135.00
nn-Christmas issue (Winter '55)	15.00	45.00	120.00
2-Giant Vacation Special (Summer '56-Pines)	13.00	39.00	105.00
3-Giant Christmas issue (Winter '56-Pines)	12.00	36.00	95.00
4-Giant Vacation Special (Summer '57-Pines)	11.00	33.00	90.00
5-Giant Christmas issue (Winter '57-Pines)	11.00	33.00	90.00
6-In Hawaii (Giant Vacation Special)(Summer '58-Pines)	10.00	30.00	80.00
6-In Hawaii (Summer '59-Hallden)-2nd printing; says 3rd large printing on-c			
6-In Hawaii (Summer '60)-3rd printing; says 4th large printing on-c			
6-In Hawaii (Summer '62)-4th printing; says 5th large printing on-c each....	7.85	23.50	55.00
6-Giant Christmas issue (Winter '58)	10.00	30.00	80.00
7-In Hollywood (Winter '59-Hallden)	4.75	14.25	52.00
7-In Hollywood (Summer '61)-2nd printing	3.35	10.00	37.00
8-In Mexico (Winter '60, 100 pgs.-Hallden/Fawcett)	4.75	14.25	52.00
8-In Mexico (Summer '62, 2nd printing)	3.25	9.75	36.00
9-Goes to Camp (Summer '61, 84 pgs.)-1st CCA approved issue	4.75	14.25	52.00
9-Goes to Camp (Summer '62)-2nd printing	3.25	9.75	36.00
10-12: 10-X-Mas issue (Winter '61), 11-Giant Christmas issue (Winter '62), 12-Triple Feature (Winter '62)	5.45	16.35	60.00
13-17: 13-Best of Dennis the Menace (Spring '63)-Reprints, 14-And His Dog Ruff (Summer '63), 15-In Washington, D.C. (Summer '63), 16-Goes to Camp (Summer '63)-Reprints No. 9, 17-& His Pal Joey (Winter '63)	3.00	9.00	32.00
18-In Hawaii (Reprints No. 6)	2.50	7.50	25.00
19-Giant Christmas issue (Winter '63)	3.25	9.75	36.00
20-Spring Special (Spring '64)	3.25	9.75	36.00
21-40 (Summer '66): 30-r/#6. #35-Xmas spec.Wint,'65	2.50	7.50	24.00
41-60 (Fall '68)	2.00	6.00	16.00
61-75 (12/69): 68-Partial-r/#6	1.75	5.25	14.00

NOTE: ***Wiseman*** *c/a-1-8, 12, 14, 15, 17, 20, 22, 27, 28, 31, 35, 36, 41, 49.*

DENNIS THE MENACE
Marvel Comics Group: Nov, 1981 - No. 13, Nov, 1982

	GD2.0	FN6.0	NM9.4
1-New-a	1.00	2.80	7.00
2-13: 2-New art. 3-Part-r. 4,5-r. 5-X-Mas-c & issue, 7-Spider Kid-c/sty			5.00

NOTE: ***Hank Ketcham*** *c-most; a-3, 12.* ***Wiseman*** *a-4, 5.*

DENNIS THE MENACE AND HIS DOG RUFF
Hallden/Fawcett: Summer, 1961

	GD2.0	FN6.0	NM9.4
1-Wiseman-c/a	5.00	15.00	55.00

DENNIS THE MENACE AND HIS FRIENDS
Fawcett Publ.: 1969; No. 5, Jan, 1970 - No. 46, April, 1980 (All reprints)

	GD2.0	FN6.0	NM9.4
Dennis the Menace & Joey No. 2 (7/69)	2.00	6.00	18.00
Dennis the Menace & Ruff No. 2 (9/69)	2.00	6.00	18.00
Dennis the Menace & Mr. Wilson No. 1 (10/69)	2.50	7.50	24.00
Dennis & Margaret No. 1 (Winter '69)	2.50	7.50	24.00
5-20: 5-Dennis the Menace & Margaret. 6-...& Joey. 7-...& Ruff. 8-...& Mr. Wilson	1.25	3.75	10.00
21-37	1.00	3.00	8.00
38-46 (Digest size, 148 pgs., 4/78, 95¢)	1.25	3.75	10.00

NOTE: *Titles rotate every four issues, beginning with No. 5.*

DENNIS THE MENACE AND HIS PAL JOEY
Fawcett Publ.: Summer, 1961 (10¢) (See Dennis the Menace Giants No. 45)

	GD2.0	FN6.0	NM9.4
1-Wiseman-c/a	5.00	15.00	55.00

DENNIS THE MENACE AND THE BIBLE KIDS
Word Books: 1977 (36 pgs.)

	GD2.0	FN6.0	NM9.4
1-6: 1-Jesus. 2-Joseph. 3-David. 4-The Bible Girls. 5-Moses. 6-More About Jesus	1.00	2.80	7.00
7-10: 7-The Lord's Prayer. 8-Stories Jesus told. 9-Paul, God's Traveller.			

Dennis the Menace Bonus Magazine #86 © FAW

Desperados #1 © WSP

The Destructor #1 © Seaboard Per.

GD2.0 FN6.0 NM9.4

10-In the Beginning 1.10 3.30 9.00
NOTE: *Ketcham c/a in all.*

DENNIS THE MENACE BIG BONUS SERIES
Fawcett Publications: No. 10, Feb, 1980 - No. 11, Apr, 1980
10,11 2.40 6.00

DENNIS THE MENACE BONUS MAGAZINE (Formerly Dennis the Menace Giants Nos. 1-75)(...Big Bonus Series on-c for #174-194)
Fawcett Publications: No. 76, 1/70 - No. 95, 7/71; No. 95, 7/71; No. 97, '71; No. 194, 10/79; (No. 76-124: 68 pgs.; No. 125-163: 52 pgs.; No. 164 on: 36 pgs.)
76-90(3/71) 1.50 4.50 12.00
91-95, 97-110(10/72): Two #95's with same date(7/71) A-Summer Games, and B-That's Our Boy. No #96 1.25 3.75 10.00
111-124 1.00 3.00 8.00
125-163-(52 pgs.) 7.00
164-194: 166-Indicia printed backwards 5.00

DENNIS THE MENACE COMICS DIGEST
Marvel Comics Group: April, 1982 - No. 3, Aug, 1982 ($1.25, digest-size)
1-3-Reprints 1.10 3.30 9.00
1-Mistakenly printed with DC emblem on cover 1.75 5.25 14.00
NOTE: ***Ketcham** c-all. **Wiseman** a-all. A few thousand #1's were published with a DC emblem on cover.*

DENNIS THE MENACE FUN BOOK
Fawcett Publications/Standard Comics: 1960 (100 pgs.)
1-Part Wiseman-a 6.00 18.00 66.00

DENNIS THE MENACE FUN FEST SERIES (Formerly Dennis the Menace #166)
Hallden (Fawcett): No. 16, Jan, 1980 - No. 17, Mar, 1980 (40¢)
16,17-By Hank Ketcham 4.00

DENNIS THE MENACE POCKET FULL OF FUN!
Fawcett Publications (Hallden): Spring, 1969 - No. 50, March, 1980 (196 pgs.) (Digest size)(Scarce in VF or better)
1-Reprints in all issues 4.00 12.00 44.00
2-10 2.80 8.40 28.00
11-20 2.00 6.00 18.00
21-28 1.50 4.50 12.00
29-50: 35,40,46-Sunday strip-r 1.00 3.00 8.00
NOTE: *No. 1-28 are 196 pgs.; No. 29-36: 164 pgs.; No. 37: 148 pgs.; No. 38 on: 132 pgs. No. 8, 11, 15, 21, 25, 29 all contain strip reprints.*

DENNIS THE MENACE TELEVISION SPECIAL
Fawcett Publ. (Hallden Div.): Summer, 1961 - No. 2, Spring, 1962 (Giant)
1 5.50 16.50 60.00
2 3.00 9.00 33.00

DENNIS THE MENACE TRIPLE FEATURE
Fawcett Publications: Winter, 1961 (Giant)
1-Wiseman-c/a 5.50 16.50 60.00

DEPUTY, THE (TV)
Dell Publishing Co.: No. 1077, Feb-Apr, 1960 - No. 1225, Oct-Dec, 1961 (all-Henry Fonda photo-c)
Four Color 1077 (#1)-Buscema-a 12.00 35.00 145.00
Four Color 1130 (9-11/60)-Buscema-a,1225 9.00 27.00 110.00

DEPUTY DAWG (TV) (Also see New Terrytoons)
Dell Publishing Co./Gold Key: Oct-Dec, 1961 - No. 1299, 1962; No. 1, Aug, 1965
Four Color 1238,1299 11.00 33.00 130.00
1(10164-508)(8/65)-Gold Key 11.00 33.00 130.00

DEPUTY DAWG PRESENTS DINKY DUCK AND HASHIMOTO-SAN (TV)
Gold Key: August, 1965
1(10159-508) 9.50 28.50 115.00

DESERT GOLD (See Zane Grey 4-Color 467)

DESIGN FOR SURVIVAL (Gen. Thomas S. Power's...)
American Security Council Press: 1968 (36 pgs. in color) (25¢)
nn-Propaganda against the Threat of Communism-Aircraft cover; H-Bomb panel 2.50 7.50 23.00
Twin Circle Edition-Cover shows panels from inside 1.75 5.25 14.00

DESPERADO (Becomes Black Diamond Western No. 9 on)
Lev Gleason Publications: June, 1948 - No. 8, Feb, 1949 (All 52 pgs.)
1-Biro-c on all; contains inside photo-c of Charles Biro, Lev Gleason & Bob Wood 14.00 41.00 110.00
2 7.85 23.50 55.00
3-Story with over 20 killings 8.65 26.00 60.00
4-8 6.00 18.00 42.00
NOTE: ***Barry** a-2. **Fuje** a-4, 8. **Guardineer** a-5-7. **Kida** a-3-7. **Ed Moore** a-4, 6.*

DESPERADOES
Image Comics (Homage): Sept, 1997 - No. 5, June, 1998 ($2.50/$2.95)
1-5-Mariotte-s/Cassaday-c/a: 1-($2.50-c). 2-5-($2.95) 3.00
...: A Moment's Sunlight TPB ('98, $16.95) r/#1-5 17.00
...: Epidemic! (11/99, $5.95) Mariotte-s 5.95

DESPERATE TIMES (See Savage Dragon)
Image Comics: Jun, 1998 - No. 4, Dec, 1998 ($2.95, B&W)
1-4-Chris Eliopoulos-s/a 3.00

DESTINATION MOON (See Fawcett Movie Comics, Space Adventures #20, 23, & Strange Adventures #1)

DESTINY: A CHRONICLE OF DEATHS FORETOLD (See Sandman)
DC Comics (Vertigo): 1997 - No.3, 1998 ($5.95, limited series)
1-3-Kwitney-s in all: 1-Williams & Zulli-a, Williams painted-c. 2-Williams & Scott Hampton-painted-c/a. 3-Williams & Guay-a 2.40 6.00
TPB (2000, $14.95) r/series 14.95

DESTROY!!
Eclipse Comics: 1986 ($4.95, B&W, magazine-size, one-shot)
1 5.00
3-D Special 1-r-/#1 ($2.50) 5.00

DESTROYER, THE
Marvel Comics: Nov, 1989 - No. 9, Jun, 1990 ($2.25, B&W, magazine, 52 pgs.)
1-Based on Remo Williams movie, paperbacks 3.00
2-9: 2-Williamson part inks. 4-Ditko-a 3.00

DESTROYER, THE
Marvel Comics: V2#1, March, 1991 ($1.95, 52 pgs.)
V3#1, Dec, 1991 - No. 4, Mar, 1992 ($1.95, mini-series)
V2#1,V3#1-4: Based on Remo Williams paperbacks. V3#1-4-Simonson-c. 3-Morrow-a 2.00

DESTROYER, THE (Also see Solar, Man of the Atom)
Valiant: Apr, 1995 ($2.95, color, one-shot)
0-Indicia indicates #1 3.00

DESTROYER DUCK
Eclipse Comics: Feb, 1982 - No. 7, May, 1984 (#2-7: Baxter paper) ($1.50)
1-Origin Destroyer Duck; 1st app. Groo; Kirby-c/a(p) 1.00 3.00 8.00
2-5: 2-Starling back-up begins; Kirby-c/a(p) thru #5 4.00
6,7 3.00
NOTE: ***Neal Adams** c-1i. **Kirby** c/a-1-5p. **Miller** c-7.*

DESTRUCTOR, THE
Atlas/Seaboard: February, 1975 - No. 4, Aug, 1975
1-Origin/1st app.; Ditko/Wood-a; Wood-c(i) 2.40 6.00
2-4: 2-Ditko/Wood-a. 3,4-Ditko-a(p) 5.00

DETECTIVE COMICS (Also see other Batman titles)
National Periodical Publications/DC Comics: Mar, 1937 - Present
GD2.0 FN6.0 VF8.0
1-(Scarce)-Slam Bradley & Spy by Siegel & Shuster, Speed Saunders by Guardineer, Flat Foot Flannigan by Gustavson, Cosmo, the Phantom of Disguise, Buck Marshall, Bruce Nelson begin; Chin Lung in 'Claws of the Red Dragon' serial begins; Vincent Sullivan-c. 8,333.00 25,000.00 55,000.00
2 (Rare)-Creig Flessel-c begin; new logo 2333.00 6999.00 15,500.00
3 (Rare) 1666.00 5000.00 11,000.00
GD2.0 FN6.0 NM9.4

Detective Comics #9 © DC

Detective Comics #31 © DC

Detective Comics #116 © DC

GD2.0 FN6.0 NM9.4

4,5: 5-Larry Steele begins 1033.00 3099.00 6800.00
6,7,9,10 750.00 2250.00 5000.00
8-Mister Chang-c; classic-c 1133.00 3399.00 7500.00
11-17,19: 17-1st app. Fu Manchu in Det. 566.00 1700.00 3800.00
18-Fu Manchu-c; last Flessel-c 950.00 2850.00 6200.00
20-The Crimson Avenger begins (1st app.) 866.00 2600.00 5700.00
21,23-25 450.00 1350.00 3000.00
22-1st Crimson Avenger-c by Chambers (12/38) 583.00 1749.00 4000.00
26 400.00 1200.00 2600.00

GD2.0 FN6.0 VF8.0 NM9.4

27-The Bat-Man & Commissioner Gordon begin (1st app.), created by Bill Finger & Bob Kane (5/39); Batman-c (1st)(by Kane). Bat-Man's secret identity revealed as Bruce Wayne in 6pg. sty. Signed Rob't Kane (also see Det. PIcture Stories #5 & Funny Pages V3#1)
28,000.00 75,000.00 135,000.00 240,000.00

27-Reprint, Oversize 13-1/2x10". WARNING: This comic is an exact duplicate reprint of the original except for its size. DC published it in 1974 with a second cover titling it as Famous First Edition. There have been many reported cases of the outer cover being removed and the interior sold as the original edition. The reprint with the new outer cover removed is practically worthless; see Famous First Edition for value.

GD2.0 FN6.0 NM9.4

28-2nd app. The Batman (6 pg. story); non-Bat-Man-c; signed Rob't Kane
1520.00 4560.00 19,000.00

GD2.0 FN6.0 VF8.0 NM9.4

29-1st app. Doctor Death-c/story, Batman's 1st name villain. 1st 2 part story (10 pgs.). 2nd Batman-c by Kane 2560.00 7680.00 16,650.00 32,000.00

GD2.0 FN6.0 NM9.4

30-Dr. Death app. Story concludes from issue #29. Classic Batman splash panel by Kane. 609.00 1826.00 7000.00

GD2.0 FN6.0 VF8.0 NM9.4

31-Classic Batman over castle cover; 1st app. The Monk & 1st Julie Madison (Bruce Wayne's 1st love interest); 1st Batplane (Bat-Gyro) and Batarang; 2nd 2-part Batman adventure. Gardner Fox takes over script from Bill Finger. 1st mention of locale (New York City) where Batman lives
2560.00 7680.00 16,650.00 32,000.00

GD2.0 FN6.0 NM9.4

32-Batman story concludes from issue #31. 1st app. Dala (Monk's assistant). Batman uses gun for 1st time to slay The Monk and Dala. This was the 1st time a costumed hero used a gun in comic books. 1st Batman head logo on cover 557.00 1670.00 6400.00

GD2.0 FN6.0 VF8.0 NM9.4

33-Origin The Batman (2 pgs.)(1st told origin); Batman gun holster-c; Batman w/smoking gun panel at end of story. Batman story now 12 pgs. Classic Batman-c 3520.00 10,560.00 22,880.00 44,000.00

GD2.0 FN6.0 NM9.4

34-2nd Crimson Avenger-c by Creig Flessel and last non Batman-c. Story from issue #32 x-over as Bruce Wayne sees Julie Madison off to America from Paris. Classic Batman splash panel used later in Batman #1 for origin story. Steve Malone begins 435.00 1305.00 5000.00
35-Classic Batman hypodermic needle-c that reflects story in issue #34. Classic Batman with smoking .45 automatic splash panel. Batman-c begin
870.00 2610.00 10,000.00
36-Batman-c that reflects adventure in issue #35. Origin/1st app. of Dr. Hugo Strange (1st major villain, 2/40). 1st finned-gloves worn by Batman
626.00 1878.00 7200.00
37-Last solo Golden-Age Batman adventure in Detective Comics. Panel at end of story reflects solo Batman adventure in Batman #1 that was originally planned for Detective #38. Cliff Crosby begins
591.00 1774.00 6800.00

GD2.0 FN6.0 VF8.0 NM9.4

38-Origin/1st app. Robin the Boy Wonder (4/40); Batman and Robin-c begin; cover by Kane & Robinson taken from splash pg.
3040.00 9120.00 19,760.00 38,000.00

GD2.0 FN6.0 NM9.4

39-Opium story 522.00 1565.00 6000.00
40-Origin & 1st app. Clay Face (Basil Karlo); 1st Joker cover app. (6/40); Joker story intended for this issue was used in Batman #1 instead; cover is similar to splash pg. in 2nd Joker story in Batman #1 626.00 1878.00 7200.00
41-Robin's 1st solo 324.00 971.00 3400.00
42-44: 44-Crimson Avenger-new costume 232.00 695.00 2200.00
45-1st Joker story in Det. (3rd book app. & 4th story app. over all, 11/40)
324.00 971.00 3400.00
46-50: 46-Death of Hugo Strange. 48-1st time car called Batmobile (2/41); Gotham City 1st mention in Det. (1st mentioned in Wow #1; also see Batman #4). 49-Last Clay Face 211.00 633.00 2000.00
51-57 142.00 426.00 1350.00
58-1st Penguin app. (12/41); last Speed Saunders; Fred Ray-c
400.00 1200.00 4200.00
59,60: 59-Last Steve Malone; 2nd Penguin; Wing becomes Crimson Avenger's aide. 60-Intro. Air Wave; Joker app. (2nd in Det.)
163.00 490.00 1550.00
61,63: 63-Last Cliff Crosby; 1st app. Mr. Baffle 142.00 426.00 1350.00
62-Joker-c/story (2nd Joker-c, 4/42) 232.00 695.00 2200.00
64-Origin & 1st app. Boy Commandos by Simon & Kirby (6/42); Joker app.
381.00 1143.00 4000.00
65-1st Boy Commandos-c (S&K-a on Boy Commandos & Ray/Robinson-a on Batman & Robin on-c; 4 artists on one-c) 295.00 885.00 2800.00
66-Origin & 1st app. Two-Face 333.00 1000.00 3500.00
67-1st Penguin-c (9/42) 221.00 663.00 2100.00
68-Two-Face-c/story; 1st Two-Face-c 163.00 490.00 1550.00
69-Joker-c/story 163.00 490.00 1550.00
70 116.00 348.00 1100.00
71-Joker-c/story 137.00 411.00 1300.00
72,74,75: 74-1st Tweedledum & Tweedledee plus-c; S&K-a
103.00 308.00 975.00
73-Scarecrow-c/story (1st Scarecrow-c) 126.00 379.00 1200.00
76-Newsboy Legion & The Sandman x-over in Boy Commandos; S&K-a; Joker-c/story 163.00 490.00 1550.00
77-79: All S&K-a 111.00 332.00 1050.00
80-Two-Face app.; S&K-a 121.00 363.00 1150.00
81,82,84,86-90: 81-1st Cavalier-c & app. 89-Last Crimson Avenger; 2nd Cavalier-c & app. 89.00 269.00 850.00
83-1st "skinny" Alfred (2/44)(see Batman #21; last S&K Boy Commandos. (also #92,128); most issues #84 on signed S&K are not by them
100.00 300.00 950.00
85-Joker-c/story; last Spy; Kirby/Klech Boy Commandos
116.00 348.00 1100.00
91,102-Joker-c/story 111.00 332.00 1050.00
92-98: 96-Alfred's last name 'Beagle' revealed, later changed to 'Pennyworth' in #214 74.00 221.00 700.00
99-Penguin-c 113.00 340.00 1075.00
100 (6/45) 121.00 363.00 1150.00
101,103-108,110-113,115-117,119: 108-1st Bat-signal-c (2/46). 114-1st small logo (8/46) 71.00 213.00 675.00
109,114,118-Joker-c/stories 97.00 292.00 925.00
120-Penguin-c (white-c, rare above fine) 150.00 450.00 1650.00
121,123,125,127,129,130 68.00 205.00 650.00
122-1st Catwoman-c (4/47) 132.00 395.00 1250.00
124,128-Joker-c/stories 92.00 276.00 875.00
126-Penguin-c 92.00 276.00 875.00
131-134,136,139 58.00 174.00 550.00
135-Frankenstein-c/story 63.00 189.00 600.00
137-Joker-c/story; last Air Wave 76.00 229.00 725.00
138-Origin Robotman (see Star Spangled #7 for 1st app.); series ends #202
111.00 332.00 1050.00
140-The Riddler-c/story (1st app., 10/48) 429.00 1286.00 4500.00
141,143-148,150: 150-Last Boy Commandos 58.00 174.00 550.00
142-2nd Riddler-c/story 113.00 339.00 1075.00
149-Joker-c/story 79.00 237.00 750.00
151-Origin & 1st app. Pow Wow Smith, Indian lawman (9/49) & begins series
71.00 213.00 675.00
152,154,155,157-160: 152-Last Slam Bradley 58.00 174.00 550.00
153-1st app. Roy Raymond TV Detective (11/49) ; origin The Human Fly
66.00 197.00 625.00
156(2/50)-The new classic Batmobile 82.00 245.00 775.00
161-167,169,170,172-176: Last 52 pg. issue 55.00 165.00 500.00
168-Origin the Joker 333.00 1000.00 3500.00
171-Penguin-c 84.00 253.00 800.00
177-179,181-186,188,189,191,192,194-199,201,202,204,206-210,212,214-216: 184-1st app. Fire Fly. 185-Secret of Batman's utility belt. 187-Two-Face app.

Detective Comics #437 © DC

Detective Comics #546 © DC

Detective Comics #554 © DC

	GD2.0	FN6.0	NM9.4
202-Last Robotman & Pow Wow Smith. 215-1st app. of Batmen of all Nations. 216-Last precode (2/55)	49.00	147.00	440.00
180,193-Joker-c/story	55.00	165.00	500.00
187-Two-Face-c/story	54.00	162.00	485.00
190-Origin Batman retold	71.00	213.00	675.00
200(1/53),205: 205-Origin Batcave)	66.00	197.00	625.00
203,211-Catwoman-c/stories	55.00	165.00	500.00
213-Origin & 1st app. Mirror Man	58.00	174.00	550.00
217-224: 218-Batman Jr. & Robin Sr. app.	42.00	125.00	375.00

	GD2.0	FN6.0	VF8.0	NM9.4
225-(11/55)-1st app. Martian Manhunter, John Jones; later changed to J'onn J'onzz; origin begins; also see Batman #78	353.00	1060.00	2825.00	6000.00

	GD2.0	FN6.0	NM9.4
226-Origin Martian Manhunter cont'd (2nd app.)	133.00	400.00	1400.00
227-229: Martian Manhunter stories in all	52.50	158.00	525.00
230-1st app. Mad Hatter; brief recap origin of Martian Manhunter	55.00	165.00	550.00
231-Brief origin recap Martian Manhunter	38.00	114.00	360.00
232,234,237-240: 232-Batwoman app. 239-Early DC grey tone-c	36.00	107.00	340.00
233-Origin & 1st app. Batwoman (7/56)	127.00	381.00	1275.00
235-Origin Batman & his costume; tells how Bruce Wayne's father (Thomas Wayne) wore Bat costume & fought crime (reprinted in Batman #255)	62.00	186.00	625.00
236-1st S.A. issue; J'onn J'onzz talks to parents and Mars-1st since being stranded on Earth; 1st app. Bat-Tank?	41.00	123.00	390.00
241-260: 246-Intro. Diane Meade, John Jones' girl. 249-Batwoman-c/app. 253-1st app. The Terrible Trio. 254-Bat-Hound-c/story. 257-Intro. & 1st app. Whirly Bats. 259-1st app. The Calendar Man	31.00	93.00	280.00
261-264,266,268-271: 261-J. Jones tie-in to sci/fi movie "Incredible Shrinking Man"; 1st app. Dr. Double X. 262-Origin Jackal. 268,271-Manhunter origin recap	23.00	69.00	210.00
265-Batman's origin retold with new facts	36.00	107.00	340.00
267-Origin & 1st app. Bat-Mite (5/59)	37.00	110.00	350.00
272,274,275,277-280	19.00	57.00	170.00
273-J'onn J'onzz i.d. revealed for 1st time	19.50	58.00	175.00
276-2nd app. Bat-Mite	21.00	63.00	190.00
281-292, 294-297: 285,286,292-Batwoman-c/app. 287-Origin J'onn J'onzz retold. 289-Bat-Mite-c/story. 292-Last Roy Raymond. 297-Last 10¢ issue (11/61)	15.00	45.00	135.00
293-(7/61)-Aquaman begins (pre #1); ends #300	15.50	47.00	140.00
298-(12/61)-1st modern Clayface (Matt Hagen)	23.50	71.00	260.00
299,300: 300-(2/62)-Aquaman ends	10.00	30.00	110.00
301-(3/62)-J'onn J'onzz returns to Mars (1st time since stranded on Earth six years before)	8.65	26.00	95.00
302-326,329,330: 302,307,311,318,321,325-Batwoman-c/app. 311-Intro. Zook in John Jones; 1st app. Cat-Man. 318,325-Cat-Man-c/story (2nd & 3rd app.); also 1st & 2nd app. Batwoman as the Cat-Woman. 321-2nd Terrible Trio. 322-Bat-Girl's 1st/only app. in Det. (6th in all); Batman cameo in J'onn J'onzz (only hero to app. in series). 326-Last J'onn J'onzz, story cont'd in H.O.M. #143; intro. Idol-Head of Diabolu	6.80	20.50	75.00
327-(5/64)-Elongated Man begins, ends #383; 1st new look Batman with new costume; Infantino/Giella new look-a begins; Batman with gun	11.00	33.00	120.00
328-Death of Alfred; Bob Kane biog, 2 pgs.	9.50	28.50	105.00
331,333-340,342-358,360-364,366-368,370: 334-1st app. The Outsider. 345-Intro Block Buster. 347-"What If" theme story (1/66). 351-Elongated Man new costume. 355-Zatanna x-over in Elongated Man. 356-Alfred brought back in Batman, 1st SA app.? 362,364-S.A. Riddler app. (early). 363-2nd app. new Batgirl. 370-1st Neal Adams-a on Batman (cover only, 12/67)	4.10	12.30	45.00
332,341,365-Joker-c/stories	5.45	16.35	60.00
359-Intro/origin Batgirl (Barbara Gordon)-c/story (1/67); 1st app. Killer Moth.	11.00	33.00	120.00
369(11/67)-N. Adams-a (Elongated Man); 3rd app. S.A. Catwoman (cameo; leads into Batman #197); 4th app. new Batgirl	5.90	17.75	65.00
371-1st new Batmobile from TV show (1/68)	4.55	13.65	50.00
372-386,389,390: 375-New Batmobile-c. 377-S.A. Riddler app.	3.65	11.00	40.00
387-r/1st Batman story from #27 (30th anniversary, 5/69); Joker-c;	4.55	13.65	50.00
388-Joker-c/story; last 12¢ issue	4.10	12.30	45.00
391-394,396,398,399,401,403,405,406,409: 392-1st app. Jason Bard. 401-2nd Batgirl/Robin team-up	3.00	9.00	30.00
395,397,402,404,407,408,410-Neal Adams-a. 404-Tribute to Enemy Ace	3.45	10.35	38.00
400-(6/70)-Origin & 1st app. Man-Bat; 1st Batgirl/Robin team-up (cont'd in #401); Neal Adams-a	6.80	20.50	75.00
411-413: 413-Last 15¢ issue	2.50	7.50	25.00
414-424: All-25¢, 52 pgs. 418-Creeper x-over. 424-Last Batgirl.	3.00	9.00	30.00
425-436: 426,430,436-Elongated Man app. 428,434-Hawkman begins, ends #467	2.00	6.00	16.00
437-New Manhunter begins (10-11/73, 1st app.) by Simonson, ends #443	3.00	9.00	30.00
438-445 (All 100 Page Super Spectaculars): 438-Kubert Hawkman-r. 439-Origin Manhunter. 440-G.A. Manhunter(Adv. #79) by S&K, Hawkman, Dollman, Gr. Lantern; Toth-a. 441-G.A. Plastic Man, Batman, Ibis-r. 442-G.A. Newsboy Legion, Bl. Canary, Elongated Man, Dr. Fate-r. 443-Origin The Creeper-r; death of Manhunter; G.A. Green Lantern, Spectre-r; Batman-r/Batman #18. 444-G.A. Kid Eternity-r. 445-G.A. Dr. Midnite-r	4.10	12.30	45.00
446-460: 457-Origin retold & updated	1.75	5.25	14.00
461-465,469,470,480: 480-(44 pgs.). 463-1st app. Black Spider. 464-2nd app. Black Spider	1.50	4.50	12.00
466-468,471-474,478,479-Rogers-a in all: 466-1st app. Signalman since Batman #139. 469-Intro/origin Dr. Phosphorous. 470,471-1st modern app. Hugo Strange. 474-1st app. new Deadshot. 478-1st app. 3rd Clayface (Preston Payne). 479-(44 pgs.)-Clayface app.	2.40	7.35	22.00
475,476-Joker-c/stories; Rogers-a	3.45	10.35	38.00
477-Neal Adams-a(r); Rogers-a (3 pgs.)	2.40	7.35	22.00
481-(Combined with Batman Family, 12-1/78-79, begin $1.00, 68 pg. issues, ends #495); 481-495-Batgirl, Robin solo stories	1.85	5.50	15.00
482-Starlin/Russell, Golden-a; The Demon begins (origin-r), ends #485 (by Ditko #483-485)	1.25	3.75	10.00
483-40th Anniversary issue; origin retold; Newton Batman begins	1.85	5.50	15.00
484-495 (68 pgs): 484-Origin Robin. 485-Death of Batwoman. 487-The Odd Man by Ditko. 489-Robin/Batgirl team-up. 490-Black Lightning begins. 491-(#492 on inside)	1.10	3.30	9.00
496-499	1.00	2.80	7.00
500-($1.50, 52 pgs.)-Batman/Deadman team-up; new Hawkman story by Joe Kubert; incorrectly says 500th anniv. of Det.	1.50	4.50	12.00
501-503,505-523: 512-2nd app. new Dr. Death. 519-Last Batgirl. 521-Green Arrow series begins. 523-Solomon Grundy app.		2.40	6.00
504-Joker-c/story	1.10	3.30	9.00
524-2nd app. Jason Todd (cameo)(3/83)	1.00	2.80	7.00
525-3rd app. Jason Todd (See Batman #357)	1.00	2.80	7.00
526-Batman's 500th app. in Detective Comics ($1.50, 68 pgs.); Death of Jason Todd's parents, Joker-c/story (55 pgs.); Bob Kane pin-up	1.85	5.50	15.00
527-531,533,534,536-568,571,573: 538-Cat-Man-c/story cont'd from Batman #371. 542-Jason Todd quits as Robin (becomes Robin again #547). 549, 550-Alan Moore scripts (Green Arrow). 554-1st new Black Canary (9/85). 566-Batman villains profiled. 567-Harlan Ellison scripts.			4.00
532,569,570-Joker-c/stories	1.00	2.80	7.00
535-Intro new Robin (JasonTodd)-1st appeared in Batman.			5.00
572-(3/87, $1.25, 60 pgs.)-50th Anniv. of Det. Comics			5.00
574-Origin Batman & Jason Todd retold			4.00
575-Year 2 begins, ends #578	1.50	4.50	12.00
576-578: McFarlane-c/a. 578-Clay Face app.	1.25	3.75	10.00
579-597,601-610: 579-New bat wing logo. 583-1st app. villains Scarface & Ventriloquist. 589-595-(52 pgs.)-Each contain free 16 pg. Batman stories. 604-607-Mudpack storyline; 604,607-Contain Batman mini-posters. 610-Faked death of Penguin; artists names app. on tombstone on-c			3.00
598-($2.95, 84 pgs.)- "Blind Justice" storyline begins by Batman movie writer Sam Hamm, ends #600			4.00
599			3.00

Detective Comics #745 © DC

Detention Comics #1 © DC

Devil Dinosaur #4 © MAR

GD2.0 FN6.0 NM9.4

600-(5/89, $2.95, 84 pgs.)-50th Anniv. of Batman in Det.; 1 pg. Neal Adams pin-up, among other artists 4.00
611-626,628-658: 612-1st new look Cat-Man; Catwoman app. 615- "The Penguin Affair" part 2 (See Batman #448,449). 617-Joker-c/story. 624-1st new Catwoman (w/death) & 1st new Batwoman. 626-Batman's 600th app. in Det. 642-Return of Scarface, part 2. 644-Last $1.00-c. 652,653-Huntress-c/story w/new costume plus Travis Charest-c on both 3.00
627-($2.95, 84 pgs.)-Batman's 601st app. in Det.; reprints 1st story/#27 plus 3 versions (2 new) of same story 4.00
659-664: 659-Knightfall part 2; Kelley Jones-c. 660-Knightfall part 4; Bane-c by Sam Kieth. 661-Knightfall part 6; brief Joker & Riddler app. 662-Knightfall part 8; Riddler app.; Sam Kieth-c. 663-Knightfall part 10; Kelley Jones-c. 664-Knightfall part 12; Bane-c/story; Joker app.; continued in Showcase 93 #7 & 8; Jones-c 3.00
665-675: 665,666-Knightfall parts 16 & 18; 666-Bane-c/story. 667-Knightquest: The Crusade & new Batman begins (1st app. inBatman #500). 669-Begin $1.50-c; Knightquest, cont'd in Robin #1. 671,673-Joker app. 2.00
675-($2.95)-Collectors edition w/foil-c 3.50
676-($2.50, 52 pgs.)-KnightsEnd Pt. 3 3.00
677,678: 677-KnightsEnd Pt. 9. 678-(9/94)-Zero Hour tie-in. 2.00
679-685: 679-(11/94). 682-Troika Pt. 3 2.00
682-($2.50) Embossed-c Troika Pt. 3 2.50
686-699,701-719: 686-Begin $1.95-c. 693,694-Poison Ivy-c/app. 695-Contagion Pt. 2; Catwoman, Penguin app. 696-Contagion Pt. 8. 698-Two-Face-c/app. 701-Legacy Pt. 6; Batman vs. Bane-c/app. 702-Legacy Epilogue. 703-Final Night x-over. 705-707-Riddler-app. 714,715-Martian Manhunter-app. 2.00
700-($4.95, Collectors Edition)-Legacy Pt. 1; Ra's Al Ghul-c/app; Talia & Bane app; book displayed at shops in envelope 5.00
700-($2.95, Regular Edition)-Different-c 3.00
720-740: 720,721-Cataclysm pts. 5,14. 723-Green Arrow app. 730-740-No Man's Land stories 2.00
741-($2.50) Endgame; Joker-c/app. 2.50
742-749,751-754: 742-New look Batman begins. 751,752-Poison Ivy app. 2.50
750-($4.95, 64 pgs.) Ra's al Ghul-c 5.00
#0-(10/94) Zero Hour tie-in 2.00
#1,000,000 (11/98) 853rd Century x-over 2.00
Annual 1 (1988, $1.50) 5.00
Annual 2-7,9 ('89-'94, '96, 68 pgs.)-4-Painted-c. 5-Joker-c/story (54 pgs.) continued in Robin Annual #1; Sam Kieth-c; Eclipso app. 6-Azrael as Batman in new costume; intro Geist the Twilight Man; Bloodlines storyline. 7-Elseworlds story. 9-Legends of the Dead Earth story 3.00
Annual 8 (1995, $3.95, 68 pgs.)-Year One story 4.00
Annual 10 (1997, $3.95)-Pulp Heroes story 4.00

NOTE: ***Neal Adams*** *c-370, 372, 383, 385, 389, 391, 392, 394-422, 439.* ***Aparo*** *a-437, 438, 444-446, 500, 625-632p, 638-643p; c-430, 437, 440-446, 448, 468-470, 480, 484(back), 492-502,508, 509, 515, 518-522, 641, 716, 719, 722, 724.* ***Austin*** *a(i)-450, 451, 463-468, 471-476; c(i)-474-476, 478.* ***Baily*** *a-443r.* ***Buckler*** *a-434, 446p, 479p; c(p)-467, 482, 505-507, 511, 513-516, 518.* ***Burnley*** *a(Batman)-65, 75, 78, 83, 100, 103, 125; c-62i, 63i, 64, 73i, 78, 83p, 96p, 103p, 105p, 106, 108, 121p, 123p, 125p.* ***Chaykin*** *a-441.* ***Colan*** *a(p)-510, 512, 517, 523, 528-538, 540-546, 555-567; c(p)-510, 512, 528, 530-535, 537, 538, 540, 541, 543-545, 556-558, 560-564.* ***J. Craig*** *a-488.* ***Ditko*** *a-443r, 483-485, 487.* ***Golden*** *a-482p; c-625, 626, 628-631, 633, 644-646.* ***Alan Grant*** *scripts-584-597, 601-621, 641, 642, Annual 5.* ***Grell*** *a-445, 455, 463p, 464p; c-455.* ***Guardineer*** *c-23, 24, 26, 28, 30, 32.* ***Gustavson*** *a-441r.* ***Infantino*** *a-442(2)r, 500, 572.* ***Infantino/Anderson*** *c-333, 337-340, 343, 344, 347, 351, 352, 359, 361-368, 371.* ***Kelley Jones*** *c-651, 657i, 658i, 659, 661, 663-675.* ***Kaluta*** *c-423, 424, 426-428, 431, 434, 438, 484, 486, 572.* ***Bob Kane*** *a-Most early issues #27 on, 297r, 356r, 438-440r, 442r, 443r.* ***Kane/Robinson*** *c-33.* ***Gil Kane*** *a(p)-368, 370-374, 384, 385, 388-407, 438r, 439r, 520.* ***Kane/Anderson*** *c-369.* ***Sam Kieth*** *c-654-656 (657, 658 w/**Kelley Jones**), 660, 662, Annual #5.* ***Kubert*** *a-438r, 439r, 500; c-348, 350.* ***McFarlane*** *c/a(p)-576-578.* ***Meskin*** *a-420r.* ***Mignola*** *c-583.* ***Moldoff*** *c-233-354, 259, 266, 267, 275, 287, 289, 290, 297, 300.* ***Moldoff/Giella*** *a-328, 330, 332, 334, 336, 338, 340, 342, 344, 346, 348, 350, 352, 354, 356.* ***Mooney*** *a-444r.* ***Moreira*** *a-153-300, 419r, 444r, 445r.* ***Nasser/Netzer*** *a-654, 655, 657, 658.* ***Newton*** *a(p)-480, 481, 483-499, 501-509, 511, 513-516, 518-520, 524, 526, 539; c-526p.* ***Irv Novick*** *c-375-377.* ***Robbins*** *a-426p, 429p.* ***Robinson*** *a-part: 66, 68, 71-73; all: 74-76, 79, 80; c-62, 64, 66, 68-74, 76, 79, 82, 86, 88, 442r, 443r.* ***Rogers*** *a-466-468, 471-479p, 481p; c-471p, 472p, 473, 474-479p.* ***Roussos*** *Airwave-76-105(most); c(i)-71, 72, 74-76, 79, 107.* ***Russell*** *a-481i, 482i.* ***Simon/Kirby*** *a-440r, 442r.* ***Simonson*** *a-437-443, 450, 469, 470, 500.* ***Dick Sprang*** *c-77, 82, 84, 85, 87, 89-93, 95-100, 102, 103i, 104i, 106, 108, 114, 117, 118, 122, 123, 128, 129, 131, 133, 135, 141, 148, 149, 168, 622-624.* ***Starlin*** *a-481p, 482p; c-503, 504, 567p.* ***Starr*** *a-444r.* ***Toth*** *a-442; r-414, 416, 418, 424, 440-441, 443, 444.* ***Tuska*** *a-486p, 490p.* ***Matt Wagner*** *c-647-649.* ***Wrightson*** *c-425.*

DETECTIVE DAN, SECRET OP. 48 (Also see Adventures of Detective Ace King and Bob Scully, The Two-Fisted Hick Detective)

Humor Publ. Co. (Norman Marsh): 1933 (10¢, 10x13", 36 pgs., B&W, one-shot) (3 color, cardboard-c)

	GD2.0	FN6.0	VF8.0
nn-By Norman Marsh, 1st comic w/ original-a; 1st newsstand-c; Dick Tracy look-alike; forerunner of Dan Dunn. (Title and Wu Fang character inspired Detective #1 four years later.) (1st comic of a single theme)	1500.00	4500.00	7500.00

DETECTIVE EYE (See Keen Detective Funnies)
Centaur Publications: Nov, 1940 - No. 2, Dec, 1940

	GD2.0	FN6.0	NM9.4
1-Air Man (see Keen Detective) & The Eye Sees begins; The Masked Marvel & Dean Denton app.	211.00	633.00	2000.00
2-Origin Don Rance and the Mysticape; Binder-a; Frank Thomas-c	126.00	379.00	1200.00

DETECTIVE PICTURE STORIES (Keen Detective Funnies No. 8 on?)
Comics Magazine Company: Dec, 1936 - No. 5, Apr, 1937
(1st comic of a single theme)

	GD2.0	FN6.0	NM9.4
1 (all issues are very scarce)	550.00	1650.00	4200.00
2-The Clock app. (1/37, early app.)	233.00	699.00	1800.00
3,4: 4-Eisner-a	150.00	450.00	1100.00
5-The Clock-c/story (4/37); 1st detective/adventure art by Bob Kane; Bruce Wayne prototype app.(see Funny Pages V3/1)	166.00	500.00	1200.00

DETECTIVES, THE (TV)
Dell Publishing Co.: No. 1168, Mar-May, 1961 - No. 1240, Oct-Dec, 1961

	GD2.0	FN6.0	NM9.4
Four Color 1168 (#1)-Robert Taylor photo-c	9.00	27.00	110.00
Four Color 1219-Robert Taylor, Adam West photo-c	7.50	22.50	90.00
Four Color 1240-Tufts-a; Robert Taylor photo-c	7.50	22.50	90.00

DETECTIVES, INC. (See Eclipse Graphic Album Series)
Eclipse Comics: Apr, 1985 - No. 2, Apr, 1985 ($1.75, both w/April dates)

1,2: 2-Nudity 2.00

DETECTIVES, INC.: A TERROR OF DYING DREAMS
Eclipse Comics: Jun, 1987 - No. 3, Dec, 1987 ($1.75, B&W& sepia)

1-3: Colan-a 2.00
TPB ('99, $19.95) r/series 20.00

DETENTION COMICS
DC Comics: Oct, 1996 ($3.50, 56 pgs., one-shot)

1-Robin story by Dennis O'Neil & Norm Breyfogle; Superboy story by Ron Marz & Ron Lim; Warrior story by Ruben Diaz & Joe Phillips; Phillips-c 5.00

DETONATOR
Chaos! Comics: Dec, 1994 - No. 2, 1995 ($2.95, limited series)

1,2-Brian Pulido scripts; Steven Hughes-a 3.00

DEVASTATOR
Image Comics/Halloween: 1998 - No. 3 ($2.95, B&W, limited series)

1,2-Hudnall-s/Horn-c/a 3.00

DEVIL CHEF
Dark Horse Comics: July, 1994 ($2.50, B&W, one-shot)

nn 2.50

DEVIL DINOSAUR
Marvel Comics Group: Apr, 1978 - No. 9, Dec, 1978

	GD2.0	FN6.0	NM9.4
1-Kirby/Royer-a in all; all have Kirby-c	1.25	3.75	10.00
2-9: 4-7-UFO/sci. fic. 8-Dinoriders-c/sty		2.40	6.00

DEVIL DINOSAUR SPRING FLING
Marvel Comics: June, 1997 ($2.99. one-shot)

1-(48pgs.) Moon-Boy-c/app. 3.00

DEVIL-DOG DUGAN (Tales of the Marines No. 4 on)
Atlas Comics (OPI): July, 1956 - No. 3, Nov, 1956

	GD2.0	FN6.0	NM9.4
1-Severin-c	11.00	33.00	90.00
2-Iron Mike McGraw x-over; Severin-c	7.85	23.50	55.00
3	6.00	18.00	42.00

DEVIL DOGS
Street & Smith Publishers: 1942

	GD2.0	FN6.0	NM9.4
1-Boy Rangers, U.S. Marines	28.00	83.00	220.00

Dexter's Laboratory #14 © Cartoon Network

Diary Loves #10 © QUA

Dick Cole #10 © STAR

	GD2.0	FN6.0	NM9.4

DEVLIN (See Avengelyne/Glory)
Maximum Press: Apr, 1996 ($2.50, one-shot)

	GD2.0	FN6.0	NM9.4
1-Avengelyne app.			2.50

DEVILINA (Magazine)
Atlas/Seaboard: Feb, 1975 - No. 2, May, 1975 (B&W)

	GD2.0	FN6.0	NM9.4
1-Art by Reese, Marcos; "The Tempest" adapt.	2.00	6.00	16.00
2 (Low printing)	2.50	7.50	24.00

DEVIL KIDS STARRING HOT STUFF
Harvey Publications (Illustrated Humor): July, 1962 - No. 107, Oct, 1981 (Giant-Size #41-55)

	GD2.0	FN6.0	NM9.4
1 (12¢ cover price #1-#41-9/69)	14.50	43.50	160.00
2	7.25	21.75	80.00
3-10 (1/64)	5.00	15.00	55.00
11-20	3.00	9.00	30.00
21-30	2.50	7.50	23.00
31-40: 40-(6/69)	2.00	6.00	18.00
41-50: All 68 pg. Giants	2.50	7.50	23.00
51-55: All 52 pg. Giants	2.00	6.00	18.00
56-70	1.25	3.75	10.00
71-90		2.40	6.00
91-107			4.00

DEVILMAN
Verotik: June, 1995 -No. 3 ($2.95, mature)

	GD2.0	FN6.0	NM9.4
1-3: Go Nagai story and art. 3-Bisley-c			3.00

DEXTER COMICS
Dearfield Publ.: Summer, 1948 - No. 5, July, 1949

	GD2.0	FN6.0	NM9.4
1-Teen-age humor	8.65	26.00	60.00
2-Junie Prom app.	6.00	18.00	42.00
3-5	5.00	15.00	30.00

DEXTER'S LABORATORY (Cartoon Network)
DC Comics: Sept, 1999 - Present ($1.99)

	GD2.0	FN6.0	NM9.4
1-19: 2-McCracken-s			2.00

DEXTER THE DEMON (Formerly Melvin The Monster)(See Cartoon Kids & Peter the Little Pest)
Atlas Comics (HPC): No. 7, Sept, 1957

	GD2.0	FN6.0	NM9.4
7	5.00	15.00	35.00

DHAMPIRE: STILLBORN
DC Comics (Vertigo): 1996 ($5.95, one-shot, mature)

	GD2.0	FN6.0	NM9.4
1-Nancy Collins script; Paul Lee-c/a		2.40	6.00

DIARY CONFESSIONS (Formerly Ideal Romance)
Stanmor/Key Publ.(Medal Comics): No. 9, May, 1955 - No. 14, Apr, 1955

	GD2.0	FN6.0	NM9.4
9	6.40	19.25	45.00
10-14	5.00	15.00	32.00

DIARY LOVES (Formerly Love Diary #1; G. I. Sweethearts #32 on)
Quality Comics Group: No. 2, Nov, 1949 - No. 31, April, 1953

	GD2.0	FN6.0	NM9.4
2-Ward-c/a, 9 pgs.	16.00	49.00	130.00
3 (1/50)-Photo-c begin, end #27?	6.00	18.00	42.00
4-Crandall-a	8.65	26.00	60.00
5-7,10	5.00	15.00	32.00
8,9-Ward-a 6,8 pgs. 8-Gustavson-a; Esther Williams photo-c	10.00	30.00	80.00
11,13,14,17-20	5.00	15.00	30.00
12,15,16-Ward-a 9,7,8 pgs.	10.00	30.00	75.00
21-Ward-a, 7 pgs.	8.65	26.00	60.00
22-31: 31-Whitney-a	4.00	11.00	22.00

NOTE: *Photo c-3-10, 12-27.*

DIARY OF HORROR
Avon Periodicals: December, 1952

	GD2.0	FN6.0	NM9.4
1-Hollingsworth-c/a; bondage-c	40.00	120.00	320.00

DIARY SECRETS (Formerly Teen-Age Diary Secrets)(See Giant Comics Ed.)
St. John Publishing Co.: No. 10, Feb, 1952 - No. 30, Sept, 1955

	GD2.0	FN6.0	NM9.4
10-Baker-c/a most issues	18.00	51.00	140.00
11-16,18,19	12.50	37.50	100.00
17,20: Kubert-r/Hollywood Confessions #1. 17-r/Teen Age Romances #9	12.50	37.50	100.00
21-30: 22,27-Signed stories by Estrada. 28-Last precode (3/55)	9.30	28.00	65.00
nn-(25¢ giant, nd (1950?)-Baker-c & rebound St. John comics	47.00	140.00	420.00

DIATOM
Photographics: Apr, 1995 ($4.95, unfinished limited series)

	GD2.0	FN6.0	NM9.4
1-Photo/computer-a			5.00

DICK COLE (Sport Thrills No. 11 on)(See Blue Bolt & Four Most #1)
Curtis Publ./Star Publications: Dec-Jan, 1948-49 - No. 10, June-July, 1950

	GD2.0	FN6.0	NM9.4
1-Sgt. Spook; L. B. Cole-c; McWilliams-a; Curt Swan's 1st work	33.00	98.00	260.00
2,5	15.00	45.00	120.00
3,4,6-10: All-L.B. Cole-c. 10-Joe Louis story	22.00	66.00	175.00
Accepted Reprint #7(V1#6 on-c)(1950's)-Reprints #7; L.B. Cole-c	7.85	23.50	55.00
Accepted Reprint #9(nd)-(Reprints #9 & #8-c)	7.85	23.50	55.00

NOTE: ***L. B. Cole** c-1, 3, 4, 6-10. **Al McWilliams** a-6. Dick Cole in 1-9. Baseball c-10. Basketball c-9. Football c-8.*

DICKIE DARE
Eastern Color Printing Co.: 1941 - No. 4, 1942 (#3 on sale 6/15/42)

	GD2.0	FN6.0	NM9.4
1-Caniff-a, Everett-c	44.00	133.00	400.00
2	26.00	79.00	210.00
3,4-Half Scorchy Smith by Noel Sickles who was very influential in Milton Caniff's development	30.00	90.00	240.00

DICK POWELL (Also see A-1 Comics)
Magazine Enterprises: No. 22, 1949 (one shot)

	GD2.0	FN6.0	NM9.4
A-1 22-Photo-c	25.00	75.00	200.00

DICK QUICK, ACE REPORTER (See Picture News #10)

DICKS
Caliber Comics: 1997 - No. 4, 1998 ($2.95, B&W)

	GD2.0	FN6.0	NM9.4
1-4-Ennis-s/McCrea-c/a; r/Fleetway			3.00
TPB ('98, $12.95) r/series			13.00

DICK'S ADVENTURES
Dell Publishing Co.: No. 245, Sept, 1949

	GD2.0	FN6.0	NM9.4
Four Color 245	4.60	13.75	55.00

DICK TRACY (See Famous Feature Stories, Harvey Comics Library, Limited Collectors' Ed., Mammoth Comics, Merry Christmas, The Original..., Popular Comics, Super Book No. 1, 7, 13, 25, Super Comics & Tastee-Freez)

DICK TRACY
David McKay Publications: May, 1937 - Jan, 1938

	GD2.0	FN6.0	NM9.4
Feature Books nn - 100 pgs., partially reprinted as 4-Color No. 1 (appeared before Large Feature Comics, 1st Dick Tracy comic book) (Very Rare-five known copies; two incomplete)	625.00	1875.00	7500.00
Feature Books 4 - Reprints nn ish. w/new-c	114.00	341.00	1250.00
Feature Books 6,9	82.00	245.00	900.00

DICK TRACY (...Monthly #1-24)
Dell Publishing Co.: 1939 - No. 24, Dec, 1949

	GD2.0	FN6.0	NM9.4
Large Feature Comic 1 (1939) -Dick Tracy Meets The Blank	145.00	435.00	1600.00
Large Feature Comic 4,8	82.00	245.00	900.00
Large Feature Comic 11,13,15	75.00	225.00	825.00

	GD2.0	FN6.0	VF8.0	NM9.4
Four Color 1(1939)('35-r)	600.00	1800.00	3600.00	7200.00

	GD2.0	FN6.0	NM9.4
Four Color 6(1940)('37-r)-(Scarce)	146.00	438.00	1750.00
Four Color 8(1940)('38-'39-r)	73.00	219.00	875.00
Large Feature Comic 3(1941, Series II)	62.00	187.00	750.00
Four Color 21('41)('38-r)	60.00	180.00	725.00
Four Color 34('43)('39-'40-r)	42.00	125.00	500.00
Four Color 56('44)('40-r)	33.00	100.00	400.00
Four Color 96('46)('40-r)	24.00	72.00	290.00

Dick Tracy #32 © NY News Syndicate

Digimon Digital Monsters #9 © Toei

Dilton's Strange Science #1 © AP

	GD2.0	FN6.0	NM9.4
Four Color 133('47)('40-'41-r)	20.00	60.00	240.00
Four Color 163('47)('41-r)	17.00	50.00	200.00
Four Color 215('48)-Titled "Sparkle Plenty", Tracy-r	10.00	30.00	120.00
1(1/48)('34-r)	39.00	118.00	475.00
2,3	22.00	65.00	260.00
4-10	20.00	60.00	240.00
11-18: 13-Bondage-c	14.00	42.00	170.00
19-1st app. Sparkle Plenty, B.O. Plenty & Gravel Gertie in a 3-pg. strip not by Gould	15.00	45.00	180.00
20-1st app. Sam Catchem; c/a not by Gould	11.70	35.00	140.00
21-24-Only 2 pg. Gould-a in each	11.70	35.00	140.00

NOTE: *No. 19-24 have a 2 pg. biography of a famous villain illustrated by* ***Gould****: 19-Little Face; 20-Flattop; 21-Breathless Mahoney; 22-Measles; 23-Itchy; 24-The Brow.*

DICK TRACY (Continued from Dell series)(...Comics Monthly #25-140)
Harvey Publications: No. 25, Mar, 1950 - No. 145, April, 1961

	GD2.0	FN6.0	NM9.4
25-Flat Top-c/story (also #26,27)	18.00	54.00	200.00
26-28,30: 28-Bondage-c. 28,29-The Brow-c/stories	14.00	41.00	150.00
29-1st app. Gravel Gertie in a Gould-r	17.00	51.00	190.00
31,32,34,35,37-40: 40-Intro/origin 2-way wrist radio (6/51)	12.00	37.00	135.00
33- "Measles the Teen-Age Dope Pusher"	14.00	41.00	150.00
36-1st app. B.O. Plenty in a Gould-r	14.00	41.00	150.00
41-50	10.00	30.00	110.00
51-56,58-80: 51-2pgs Powell-a	8.50	25.50	95.00
57-1st app. Sam Catchem in a Gould-r	11.00	33.00	120.00
81-99,101-140	7.00	21.00	80.00
100, 141-145 (25¢)(titled "Dick Tracy")	8.00	23.00	85.00

NOTE: ***Powell*** *a(1-2pgs.)-43, 44, 104, 108, 109, 145. No. 110-120, 141-145 are all reprints from earlier issues.*

DICK TRACY
Blackthorne Publishing: 12/84 - No. 24, 6/89 (1-12: $5.95; 13-24: $6.95, B&W, 76 pgs.)

	GD2.0	FN6.0	NM9.4
1-8-1st printings; hard-c ed. ($14.95)			15.00
1-3-2nd printings, 1986; hard-c ed.			15.00
1-12-1st & 2nd printings; squarebound. thick-c			7.00
13-24 ($6.95): 21,22-Regular-c & stapled			7.00

NOTE: **Gould** daily & Sunday strip-r in all. 1-12 r-12/31/45-4/5/49; 13-24 r-7/13/41-2/20/44.

DICK TRACY (Disney)
WD Publications: 1990 - No. 3, 1990 (color) (Book 3 adapts 1990 movie)

	GD2.0	FN6.0	NM9.4
Book One ($3.95, 52pgs.)-Kyle Baker-c/a			4.00
Book Two, Three ($5.95, 68pgs.)-Direct sale			6.00
Book Two, Three ($2.95, 68pgs.)-Newsstand			3.00

DICK TRACY ADVENTURES
Gladstone Publishing: May, 1991 ($4.95, 76 pgs.)

	GD2.0	FN6.0	NM9.4
1-Reprints strips 2/1/42-4/18/42			5.00

DICK TRACY, EXPLOITS OF
Rosdon Books, Inc.: 1946 ($1.00, hard-c strip reprints)

	GD2.0	FN6.0	NM9.4
1-Reprints the near complete case of "The Brow" from 6/12/44 to 9/24/44 (story starts a few weeks late)	25.00	75.00	200.00
with dust jacket...	40.00	120.00	340.00

DICK TRACY MONTHLY/WEEKLY
Blackthorne Publishing: May, 1986 - No. 99, 1989 ($2.00, B&W)
(Becomes Weekly #26 on)

	GD2.0	FN6.0	NM9.4
1-60: Gould-r. 30,31-Mr. Crime app.			3.00
61-90			4.00
91-99			5.00

NOTE: *#1-10 reprint strips 3/10/40-7/13/41; #10(pg.8)-51 reprint strips 4/6/49-12/31/55; #52-99 reprint strips 12/26/56-4/26/64.*

DICK TRACY SPECIAL
Blackthorne Publ.: Jan, 1988 - No. 3, Aug. (no month), 1989 ($2.95, B&W)

	GD2.0	FN6.0	NM9.4
1-3: 1-Origin D. Tracy; 4/strips 10/12/31-3/30/32			3.00

DICK TRACY: THE EARLY YEARS
Blackthorne Publishing: Aug, 1987 - No. 4, Aug (no month) 1989 ($6.95, B&W, 76 pgs.)

	GD2.0	FN6.0	NM9.4
1-3: 1-4-r/strips 10/12/31(1st daily)-8/31/32 & Sunday strips 6/12/32-8/28/32; Big Boy apps. in #1-3	1.00	2.80	7.00
4 ($2.95, 52pgs.)			3.00

DICK TRACY UNPRINTED STORIES
Blackthorne Publishing: Sept, 1987 - No. 4, June, 1988 ($2.95, B&W)

	GD2.0	FN6.0	NM9.4
1-4: Reprints strips 1/1/56-12/25/56			3.00

DICK TURPIN (See Legend of Young...)

DIE-CUT
Marvel Comics UK, Ltd: Nov, 1993 - No. 4, Feb, 1994 ($1.75, limited series)

	GD2.0	FN6.0	NM9.4
1-4: 1-Die-cut-c; The Beast app.			2.00

DIE-CUT VS. G-FORCE
Marvel Comics UK, Ltd: Nov, 1993 - No. 2, Dec, 1993 ($2.75, limited series)

	GD2.0	FN6.0	NM9.4
1,2-($2.75)-Gold foil-c on both			2.75

DIE, MONSTER, DIE (See Movie Classics)

DIGIMON DIGITAL MONSTERS (TV)
Dark Horse Comics: May, 2000 - Present ($2.95)

	GD2.0	FN6.0	NM9.4
1-9			2.95

DIGITEK
Marvel UK, Ltd: Dec, 1992 - No. 4, Mar, 1993 ($1.95/$2.25, mini-series)

	GD2.0	FN6.0	NM9.4
1-4: 3-Deathlock-c/story			2.25

DILLY (Dilly Duncan from Daredevil Comics; see Boy Comics #57)
Lev Gleason Publications: May, 1953 - No. 3, Sept, 1953

	GD2.0	FN6.0	NM9.4
1-Teenage; Biro-c	5.00	15.00	35.00
2,3-Biro-c	4.00	12.00	24.00

DILTON'S STRANGE SCIENCE (See Pep Comics #78)
Archie Comics: May, 1989 - No. 5, May, 1990 (75¢/$1.00)

	GD2.0	FN6.0	NM9.4
1-5			3.00

DIME COMICS
Newsbook Publ. Corp.: 1945; 1951

	GD2.0	FN6.0	NM9.4
1-Silver Streak-c/story; L. B. Cole-c	58.00	174.00	550.00
1(1951)	5.00	15.00	35.00

DINGBATS (See 1st Issue Special)

DING DONG
Compix/Magazine Enterprises: Summer?, 1946 - No. 5, 1947 (52 pgs.)

	GD2.0	FN6.0	NM9.4
1-Funny animal	24.00	71.00	190.00
2 (9/46)	11.00	33.00	90.00
3 (Wint '46-'47) - 5	10.00	30.00	70.00

DINKY DUCK (Paul Terry's...) (See Approved Comics, Blue Ribbon, Giant Comics Edition #5A & New Terrytoons)
St. John Publishing Co./Pines No. 16 on: Nov, 1951 - No. 16, Sept, 1955; No. 16, Fall, 1956; No. 17, May, 1957 - No. 19, Summer, 1958

	GD2.0	FN6.0	NM9.4
1-Funny animal	11.00	33.00	90.00
2	6.40	19.25	45.00
3-10	4.65	14.00	28.00
11-16(9/55)	4.00	11.00	22.00
16(Fall,'56) - 19	3.60	9.00	18.00

DINKY DUCK & HASHIMOTO-SAN (See Deputy Dawg Presents...)

DINO (TV)(The Flintstones)
Charlton Publications: Aug, 1973 - No. 20, Jan, 1977 (Hanna-Barbera)

	GD2.0	FN6.0	NM9.4
1	2.50	7.50	25.00
2-10	2.00	6.00	16.00
11-20	1.25	3.75	10.00

DINO ISLAND
Mirage Studios: Feb, 1994 - No. 2, Mar, 1994 ($2.75, limited series)

	GD2.0	FN6.0	NM9.4
1,2-By Jim Lawson			2.75

DINO RIDERS
Marvel Comics: Feb, 1989 - No. 3, 1989 ($1.00)

	GD2.0	FN6.0	NM9.4
1-3: Based on toys			3.00

DINOSAUR REX
Upshot Graphics (Fantagraphics): 1986 - No. 3, 1986 ($2.00, limited series)

Dinosaurs For Hire #5 © Tom Mason

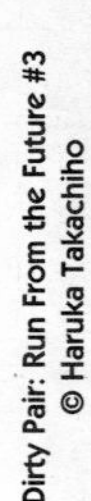
Dirty Pair: Run From the Future #3 © Haruka Takachiho

Disney's Aladdin #4 © WDC

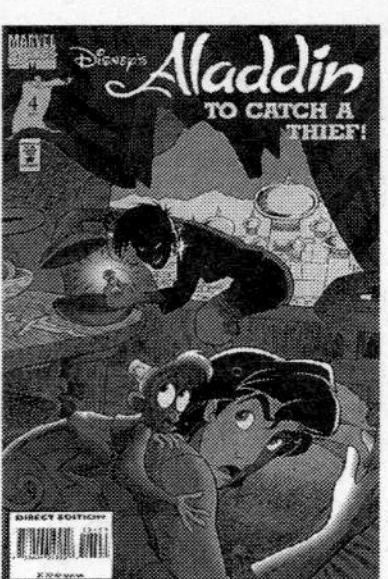

1-3 2.00

DINOSAURS, A CELEBRATION
Marvel Comics (Epic): Oct, 1992 - No. 4, Oct, 1992 ($4.95, lim. series, 52 pgs.)
1-4: 2-Bolton painted-c 5.00

DINOSAURS ATTACK! THE GRAPHIC NOVEL
Eclipse Comics: 1991 ($3.95, coated stock, stiff-c)
Book One- Based on Topps trading cards 4.00

DINOSAURS FOR HIRE
Malibu Comics: Feb, 1993 - No. 12, Feb, 1994 ($1.95/$2.50)
1-12: 1,10-Flip bk. 8-Bagged w/Skycap; Staton-c. 10-Flip book 2.50

DINOSAURS GRAPHIC NOVEL (TV)
Disney Comics: 1992 - No. 2, 1993 ($2.95, 52 pgs.)
1,2-Staton-a; based on Dinosaurs TV show 3.00

DINOSAURUS
Dell Publishing Co.: No. 1120, Aug, 1960
Four Color 1120-Movie, painted-c 6.70 20.00 80.00

DIPPY DUCK
Atlas Comics (OPI): October, 1957
1-Maneely-a; code approved 8.65 26.00 60.00

DIRECTORY TO A NONEXISTENT UNIVERSE
Eclipse Comics: Dec, 1987 ($2.00, B&W)
1 2.00

DIRTY DOZEN (See Movie Classics)

DIRTY PAIR (Manga)
Eclipse Comics: Dec, 1988 - No. 4, Apr, 1989 ($2.00, B&W, limited series)
1-4: Japanese manga with original stories 3.00
...: Start the Violence (Dark Horse, 9/99, $2.95) r/B&W stories in color from Dark Horse Presents #132-134; covers by Warren & Pearson 2.95

DIRTY PAIR: FATAL BUT NOT SERIOUS (Manga)
Dark Horse Comics: July, 1995 - No. 5, Nov, 1995 ($2.95, limited series)
1-5 3.00

DIRTY PAIR: RUN FROM THE FUTURE (Manga)
Dark Horse Comics: Jan, 2000 - No. 4, Mar, 2000 ($2.95, limited series)
1-4-Warren-s/c/a. Var.-c by Hughes(1), Stelfreeze(2), Timm(3), Ramos(4) 3.00

DIRTY PAIR: SIM HELL (Manga)
Dark Horse Comics: May, 1993 - No. 4, Aug, 1993 ($2.50, B&W, limited series)
1-4 3.00

DIRTY PAIR II (Manga)
Eclipse Comics: June, 1989 - No. 5, Mar, 1990 ($2.00, B&W, limited series)
1-5: 3-Cover is misnumbered as #1 3.00

DIRTY PAIR III, THE (A Plague of Angels) (Manga)
Eclipse Comics: Aug, 1990 - No. 5, Aug, 1991 ($2.00, B&W, limited series)
1,2 3.00
3-5: ($2.25) 2.25

DISAVOWED
DC Comics (Homage): Mar, 2000 - Present ($2.50)
1-6: 1-3-Choi&Heisler-s/Edwards-a. 4,5-Lucas-a 2.50

DISHMAN
Eclipse Comics: Sept, 1988 ($2.50, B&W, 52 pgs.)
1 2.50

DISNEY AFTERNOON, THE (TV)
Marvel Comics: Nov, 1994 - No. 10?, Aug, 1995 ($1.50)
1-10: 3-w/bound-in Power Ranger Barcode Card 3.00

DISNEY COMIC ALBUM
Disney Comics: 1990(no month, year) - No. 8, 1991 ($6.95/$7.95)
1,2 ($6.95): 1-Donald Duck and Gyro Gearloose by Barks(r). 2-Uncle Scrooge by Barks(r); Jr. Woodchucks app. 9.00
3-8: 3-Donald Duck-r/F.C. 308 by Barks; begin $7.95-c. 4-Mickey Mouse Meets the Phantom Blot; r/M.M Club Parade(censored 1956 version of story) 5-Chip `n' Dale Rescue Rangers; new-a. 6-Uncle Scrooge. 7-Donald Duck in Too Many Pets; Barks-r(4) including F.C. #29. 8-Super Goof; r/S.G. #1, D.D. #102 9.00

DISNEY COMIC HITS
Marvel Comics: Oct, 1995 - Present ($1.50/$2.50)
1-15: 4-Toy Story. 6-Aladdin. 7-Pocahontas. 10-The Hunchback of Notre Dame (Same story in Disney's The Hunchback of Notre Dame) 13-Aladdin and the Forty Thieves 4.00

DISNEY COMICS
Disney Comics: June, 1990
Boxed set of #1 issues includes Donald Duck Advs., Ducktales, Chip 'n Dale Rescue Rangers, Roger Rabbit, Mickey Mouse Advs. & Goofy Advs.; limited to 10,000 sets 1.85 5.50 15.00

DISNEYLAND BIRTHDAY PARTY (Also see Dell Giants)
Gladstone Publishing Co.: Aug, 1985 ($2.50)
1-Reprints Dell Giant with new-photo-c 1.50 4.50 12.00
...Comics Digest #1-(Digest) 1.75 5.25 14.00

DISNEYLAND MAGAZINE
Fawcett Publications: Feb. 15, 1972 - ? (10-1/4"x12-5/8", 20 pgs, weekly)
1-One or two page painted art features on Dumbo, Snow White, Lady & the Tramp, the Aristocats, Brer Rabbit, Peter Pan, Cinderella, Jungle Book, Alice & Pinocchio. Most standard characters app. 2.50 7.50 23.00

DISNEYLAND, USA (See Dell Giant No. 30)

DISNEY MOVIE BOOK
Walt Disney Productions (Gladstone): 1990 ($7.95, 8-1/2"x11", 52 pgs.) (w/pull-out poster)
1-Roger Rabbit in Tummy Trouble; from the cartoon film strips adapted to the comic format. Ron Dias-c 1.50 4.50 12.00

DISNEY'S ACTION CLUB
Acclaim Books: 1997 - No. 4 ($4.50, digest size)
1-4: 1-Hercules. 4-Mighty Ducks 4.50

DISNEY'S ALADDIN (Movie)
Marvel Comics: Oct, 1994 - No. 11, 1995 ($1.50)
1-11 3.00

DISNEY'S BEAUTY AND THE BEAST (Movie)
Marvel Comics: Sept, 1994 - No. 13, 1995 ($1.50)
1-13 3.00

DISNEY'S BEAUTY AND THE BEAST HOLIDAY SPECIAL
Acclaim Books: 1997 ($4.50, digest size, one-shot)
1-Based on The Enchanted Christmas video 4.50

DISNEY'S COLOSSAL COMICS COLLECTION
Disney Comics: 1991 - No. 10, 1993 ($1.95, digest-size, 96/132 pgs.)
1-10: Ducktales, Talespin, Chip 'n Dale's Rescue Rangers. 4-r/Darkwing Duck #1-4. 6-Goofy begins. 8-Little Mermaid 5.00

DISNEY'S COMICS IN 3-D
Disney Comics: 1992 ($2.95, w/glasses, polybagged)
1-Infinity-c; Barks, Rosa, Gottfredson-r 5.00

DISNEY'S ENCHANTING STORIES
Acclaim Books: 1997 - Present ($4.50, digest size)
1-5: 1-Hercules. 2-Pocahontas 4.50

DISNEY'S NEW ADVENTURES OF BEAUTY AND THE BEAST (Also see Beauty and the Beast & Disney's Beauty and the Beast)
Disney Comics: 1992 - No. 2, 1992 ($1.50, limited series)
1,2-New stories based on movie 3.00

DISNEY'S POCAHONTAS (Movie)
Marvel Comics: 1995 ($4.95, one-shot)
1-Movie adaptation 1.00 2.80 7.00

DISNEY'S TALESPIN LIMITED SERIES: "TAKE OFF" (TV) (See Talespin)

Distant Soil #16 © Colleen Doran

Divine Right #6 © WSP

Dixie Dugan #3 © McNaught Syndicate

GD2.0 FN6.0 NM9.4

W. D. Publications (Disney Comics): Jan, 1991 - No. 4, Apr, 1991 ($1.50, limited series, 52 pgs.)

1-4: Based on animated series; 4 part origin 2.50

DISNEY'S TARZAN (Movie)
Dark Horse Comics: June, 1999 - No. 2, July, 1999 ($2.95, limited series)

1,2: Movie adaptation 3.00

DISNEY'S THE LION KING (Movie)
Marvel Comics: July, 1994 - No. 2, July, 1994 ($1.50, limited series)

1,2: 2-part movie adaptation 3.00
1-($2.50, 52 pgs.)-Complete story 5.00

DISNEY'S THE LITTLE MERMAID (Movie)
Marvel Comics: Sept, 1994 - No. 12, 1995 ($1.50)

1-12 4.00

DISNEY'S THE LITTLE MERMAID LIMITED SERIES (Movie)
Disney Comics: Feb, 1992 - No. 4, May, 1992 ($1.50, limited series)

1-4: Peter David scripts 3.00

DISNEY'S THE LITTLE MERMAID: UNDERWATER ENGAGEMENTS
Acclaim Books: 1997 ($4.50, digest size)

1-Flip book 4.50

DISNEY'S THE HUNCHBACK OF NOTRE DAME (Movie)(See Disney's Comic Hits #10)
Marvel Comics: July, 1996 ($4.95, squarebound, one-shot)

1-Movie adaptation. 1.00 2.80 7.00

NOTE: A different edition of this series was sold at Wal-Mart stores with new covers depicting scenes from the 1989 feature film. Inside contents and price were identical.

DISNEY'S THE THREE MUSKETEERS (Movie)
Marvel Comics: Jan, 1994 - No. 2, Feb, 1994 ($1.50, limited series)

1,2-Morrow-c; Spiegle-a; Movie adaptation 2.00

DISNEY'S TOY STORY (Movie)
Marvel Comics: Dec, 1995 ($4.95, one-shot)

nn-Adaptation of film 1.00 2.80 7.00

DISTANT SOIL, A (1st Series)
WaRP Graphics: Dec, 1983 - No. 9, Mar 1986 ($1.50, B&W)

1-9: 1-4 are magazine size 3.00

NOTE: Second printings exist of #1, 2, 3 & 6.

DISTANT SOIL, A
Donning (Star Blaze): Mar, 1989 ($12.95, trade paperback)

nn-new material 13.00

DISTANT SOIL, A (2nd Series)
Aria Press/Image Comics (Highbrow Entertainment) #15 on: June, 1991 - Present ($1.75/$2.50/$2.95/$3.95, B&W)

1-27: 13-$2.95-c begins. 14-Sketchbook. 15-(8/96)-1st Image issue 3.00
29,30-($3.95) 3.95
The Ascendant ('98, $18.95,TPB) r/#13-25 19.00
The Gathering ('97, $18.95,TPB) r/#1-13; intro. Neil Gaiman 19.00

NOTE: Four separate printings exist for #1 and are clearly marked. Second printings exist of #2-4 and are also clearly marked.

DISTANT SOIL, A: IMMIGRANT SONG
Donning (Star Blaze): Aug, 1987 ($6.95, trade paperback)

nn-new material 7.00

DIVER DAN (TV)
Dell Publishing Co.: Feb-Apr, 1962 - No. 2, June-Aug, 1962

Four Color 1254(#1), 2 4.60 13.75 55.00

DIVINE RIGHT
Image Comics (WildStorm Prod.): Sept, 1997 - No. 12, Nov, 1999 ($2.50)

Preview 5.00
1,2: 1-Jim Lee-s/a(p)/c, 1-Variant-c by Charest 4.00
1-($3.50)-Voyager Pack w/Stormwatch preview 3.50
1-American Entertainment Ed. 6.00
2-Variant-c of Exotica & Blaze 5.00
3-5-Fairchild & Lynch app. 3.00
3-Chromium-c by Jim Lee 5.00
4,6-12: 4-American Entertainment Ed. 8-Two covers. 9-1st DC issue. 11,12-Divine Intervention pt. 1,4 3.00
5-Pacific Comicon Ed. 6.00
6-Glow in the dark variant-c, European Tour Edition 20.00
...Collected Edition #1-3 ($5.95, TPB) 1-r/#1,2. 2-r/#3,4. 3-r/#5,6 6.00
Divine Intervention/Gen 13 (11/99, $2.50) Part 3; D'Anda-a 2.50
Divine Intervention/Wildcats (11/99, $2.50) Part 2; D'Anda-a 2.50

DIVISION 13 (See Comic's Greatest World)
Dark Horse Comics: Sept, 1994 - Jan, 1995 ($2.50, color)

1-4: Giffen story in all. 1-Art Adams-c 2.50

DIXIE DUGAN (See Big Shot, Columbia Comics & Feature Funnies)
McNaught Syndicate/Columbia/Publication Ent.: July, 1942 - No. 13, 1949 (Strip reprints in all)

1-Joe Palooka x-over by Ham Fisher 28.00 84.00 225.00
2 15.00 45.00 120.00
3 11.00 33.00 90.00
4,5(1945-46)-Bo strip-r 8.65 26.00 60.00
6-13(1/47-49): 6-Paperdoll cut-outs 7.00 21.00 48.00

DIXIE DUGAN
Prize Publications (Headline): V3#1, Nov, 1951 - V4#4, Feb, 1954

V3#1 8.65 26.00 60.00
2-4 5.50 16.50 38.00
V4#1-4(#5-8) 5.00 15.00 30.00

DIZZY DAMES
American Comics Group (B&M Distr. Co.): Sept-Oct, 1952 - No. 6, Jul-Aug, 1953

1-Whitney-c 12.50 37.50 100.00
2 8.65 26.00 60.00
3-6 6.40 19.25 45.00

DIZZY DON COMICS
F. E. Howard Publications/Dizzy Don Ent. Ltd (Canada): 1942 - No. 22, Oct, 1946; No. 3, Apr, 1947 (Most B&W)

1 (B&W) 11.00 33.00 90.00
2 (B&W) 6.40 19.25 45.00
4-21 (B&W) 6.00 18.00 42.00
22-Full color, 52 pgs. 12.00 36.00 95.00
3 (4/47)-Full color, 52 pgs. 10.00 30.00 80.00

DIZZY DUCK (Formerly Barnyard Comics)
Standard Comics: No. 32, Nov, 1950 - No. 39, Mar, 1952

32-Funny animal 9.30 28.00 65.00
33-39 5.00 15.00 32.00

DNAGENTS (The New DNAgents V2/1 on)(Also see Surge)
Eclipse Comics: March, 1983 - No. 24, July, 1985 ($1.50, Baxter paper)

1,24: 1-Origin. 4-Amber app. 24-Dave Stevens-c 3.00
2-23: 8-Infinity-c 2.00

DOBERMAN (See Sgt. Bilko's Private...)

DOBIE GILLIS (See The Many Loves of...)

DOC CHAOS: THE STRANGE ATTRACTOR
Vortex Comics: Apr, 1990 - #3, 1990 ($3.00, 32 pgs.)

1-3: The Lust For Order 3.00

DOC SAMSON (Also see Incredible Hulk)
Marvel Comics: Jan, 1996 - No. 4, Apr, 1996 ($1.95, limited series)

1-4: 1-Hulk c/app. 2-She-Hulk-c/app. 3-Punisher-c/app. 4-Polaris-c/app. 2.00

DOC SAVAGE
Gold Key: Nov, 1966

1-Adaptation of the Thousand-Headed Man; James Bama c-r/1964 Doc Savage paperback 9.00 27.00 110.00

DOC SAVAGE (Also see Giant-Size...)
Marvel Comics Group: Oct, 1972 - No. 8, Jan, 1974

1 2.00 6.00 16.00

Doc Savage Comics #10 © Condé Nast

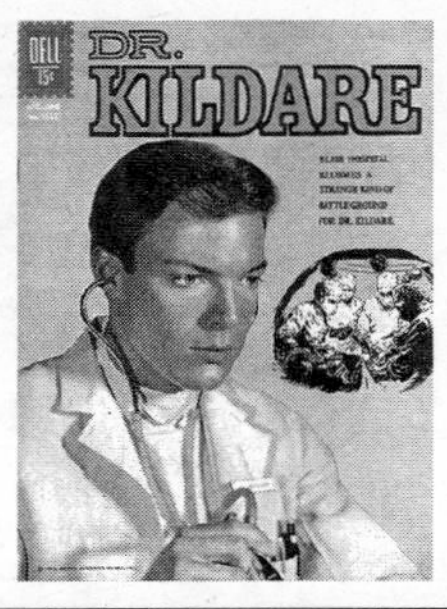

Dr. Kildare #1 © MGM

Doctor Mid-Nite #3 © DC

GD2.0 FN6.0 NM9.4

2,3-Steranko-c 1.25 3.75 10.00
4-8 1.00 3.00 8.00

NOTE: *Gil Kane* c-5, 6. *Mooney* a-1i. No. 1, 2 adapts pulp story "The Man of Bronze"; No. 3, 4 adapts "Death in Silver"; No. 5, 6 adapts "The Monsters"; No. 7, 8 adapts "The Brand of The Werewolf".

DOC SAVAGE (Magazine)
Marvel Comics Group: Aug, 1975 - No. 8, Spring, 1977 ($1.00, B&W)

1-Cover from movie poster; Ron Ely photo-c 1.50 4.75 12.00
2-5: 3-Buscema-a. 5-Adams-a(1 pg.), Rogers-a(1 pg) 1.00 2.80 7.00
6-8 1.00 3.00 8.00

DOC SAVAGE
DC Comics: Nov, 1987 - No. 4, Feb, 1988 ($1.75, limited series)

1-4 3.00

DOC SAVAGE
DC Comics: Nov, 1988 - No. 24, Oct, 1990 ($1.75/$2.00: #13-24)

1-24 3.00
Annual 1 (1989, $3.50, 68 pgs.) 4.00

DOC SAVAGE COMICS (Also see Shadow Comics)
Street & Smith Publications: May, 1940 - No. 20, Oct, 1943 (1st app. in Doc Savage pulp, 3/33)

1-Doc Savage, Cap Fury, Danny Garrett, Mark Mallory, The Whisperer, Captain Death, Billy the Kid, Sheriff Pete & Treasure Island begin; Norgil, the Magician app. 435.00 1305.00 5000.00
2-Origin & 1st app. Ajax, the Sun Man; Danny Garrett, The Whisperer end 158.00 474.00 1500.00
3 121.00 363.00 1150.00
4-Treasure Island ends; Tuska-a 97.00 292.00 925.00
5-Origin & 1st app. Astron, the Crocodile Queen, not in #9 & 11; Norgi the Magician app. 76.00 229.00 725.00
6-10: 6-Cap Fury ends; origin & only app. Red Falcon in Astron story. 8-Mark Mallory ends; Charlie McCarthy app. on-c plus true life story. 9-Supersnipe app. 10-Origin & only app. The Thunderbolt 61.00 182.00 575.00
11,12 51.00 153.00 460.00
V2#1-8(#13-20): 15-Origin of Ajax the Sun Man; Jack Benny on-c; Hitler app. 16-The Pulp Hero, The Avenger app.; Fanny Brice story. 17-Sun Man ends; Nick Carter begins; Duffy's Tavern part photo-c & story. 18-Huckleberry Finn part-c/story. 19-Henny Youngman part photo-c & life story. 20-Only all funny-c w/Huckleberry Finn 51.00 153.00 460.00

DOC SAVAGE: CURSE OF THE FIRE GOD
Dark Horse Comics: Sept, 1995 - No, 4, Dec, 1995 ($2.95, limited series)

1-4 3.00

DOC SAVAGE: THE MAN OF BRONZE
Skylark Pub: Mar, 1979, 68pgs. (B&W comic digest, 5-1/4x7-5/8")

15406-0: Whitman-a, 60 pgs., new comics 3.00 9.00 30.00

DOC SAVAGE: THE MAN OF BRONZE
Millennium Publications: 1991 - No. 4, 1991 ($2.50, limited series)

1-4: 1-Bronze logo 2.50
...: The Manual of Bronze 1 ($2.50, B&W, color, one-shot)-Unpublished proposed Doc Savage strip in color, B&W strip-r 2.50

DOC SAVAGE: THE MAN OF BRONZE, DOOM DYNASTY
Millennium Publ.: 1992 (Says 1991) - No. 2, 1992 ($2.50, limited series)

1,2 2.50

DOC SAVAGE: THE MAN OF BRONZE - REPEL
Innovation Publishing: 1992 ($2.50)

1-Dave Dorman painted-c 2.50

DOC SAVAGE: THE MAN OF BRONZE THE DEVIL'S THOUGHTS
Millennium Publ.: 1992 (Says 1991) - No. 3, 1992 ($2.50, limited series)

1-3 2.50

DOC STEARN...MR. MONSTER (See Mr. Monster)

DR. ANTHONY KING, HOLLYWOOD LOVE DOCTOR
Minoan Publishing Corp./Harvey Publications No. 4: 1952(Jan) - No. 3, May, 1953; No. 4, May, 1954

GD2.0 FN6.0 NM9.4

1 12.00 36.00 95.00
2-4: 4-Powell-a 7.85 23.50 55.00

DR. ANTHONY'S LOVE CLINIC (See Mr. Anthony's...)

DR. BOBBS
Dell Publishing Co.: No. 212, Jan, 1949

Four Color 212 4.10 12.30 45.00

DOCTOR BOOGIE
Media Arts Publishing: 1987 ($1.75)

1-Airbrush wraparound-c; Nick Cuti-i 2.00

DOCTOR CHAOS
Triumphant Comics: Nov, 1993 - No. 6, Mar, 1994 ($2.50)

1-6: 1,2-Triumphant Unleashed x-over. 2-1st app. War Dancer in pin-up. 3-Intro The Cry 2.50

DOCTOR CYBORG
Attention! Publishing: 1996 - No. 5 ($2.95, B&W)

1-5 3.00
The Clone Conspiracy TPB (1998, $14.95) r/#1-5 15.00

DR. DOOM'S REVENGE
Marvel Comics: 1989 (Came w/computer game from Paragon Software)

V1#1-Spider-Man & Captain America fight Dr. Doom 3.00

DR. FATE (See 1st Issue Special, The Immortal..., Justice League, More Fun #55, & Showcase)

DOCTOR FATE
DC Comics: July, 1987 - No. 4, Oct, 1987 ($1.50, limited series, Baxter paper)

1-4: Giffen-c/a in all 2.50

DOCTOR FATE
DC Comics: Winter, 1988-`89 - No. 41, June, 1992 ($1.25/$1.50 #5 on)

1-41: 15-Justice League app. 25-1st new Dr. Fate. 36-Original Dr. Fate returns 2.00
Annual 1(1989, $2.95, 68 pgs.)-Sutton-a 3.50

DR. FU MANCHU (See The Mask of...)
I.W. Enterprises: 1964

1-r/Avon's "Mask of Dr. Fu Manchu"; Wood-a 8.15 24.50 90.00

DR. GIGGLES (See Dark Horse Presents #64-66)
Dark Horse Comics: Oct, 1992 - No. 2, Oct, 1992 ($2.50, limited series)

1,2-Based on movie 2.50

DOCTOR GRAVES (Formerly The Many Ghosts of...)
Charlton Comics: No. 73, Sept, 1985 - No. 75, Jan, 1986

73-75-Low print run 5.00

DR. JEKYLL AND MR. HYDE (See A Star Presentation & Supernatural Thrillers #4)

DR. KILDARE (TV)
Dell Publishing Co.: No. 1337, 4-6/62 - No. 9, 4-6/65 (All Richard Chamberlain photo-c)

Four Color 1337(#1, 1962) 8.35 25.00 100.00
2-9 5.85 17.50 70.00

DR. MASTERS (See The Adventures of Young...)

DOCTOR MID-NITE (Also see All-American #25)
DC Comics: 1999 - No. 3, 1999 ($5.95, square-bound, limited series)

1-3-Matt Wagner-s/John K. Snyder III-painted art 6.00
TPB (2000, $19.95) r/series 19.95

DR. ROBOT SPECIAL
Dark Horse Comics: Apr, 2000 ($2.95, one-shot)

1-Bernie Mireault-s/a; some reprints from Madman Comics #12-15 2.95

DOCTOR SOLAR, MAN OF THE ATOM (Also see The Occult Files of Dr. Spektor #14 & Solar)
Gold Key/Whitman No. 28 on: 10/62 - No. 27, 4/69; No. 28, 4/81 - No. 31, 3/82 (1-27 have painted-c)

1-(#10000-210)-Origin/1st app. Dr. Solar (1st original Gold Key character) 18.35 55.00 220.00

Doctor Strange #37 © MAR

Doctor Strange Sorceror Supreme #69 © MAR

Dr. Tomorrow #4 © Acclaim

GD2.0 FN6.0 NM9.4

2-Prof. Harbinger begins 7.00 20.00 85.00
3,4 4.60 13.75 55.00
5-Intro. Man of the Atom in costume 5.00 15.00 60.00
6-10 3.20 9.60 35.00
1-14,16-20 2.80 8.40 28.00
5-Origin retold 3.00 9.00 32.00
!1-23: 23-Last 12¢ issue 2.40 7.35 22.00
!4-27 2.30 7.00 20.00
!8-31: 29-Magnus Robot Fighter begins. 31-The Sentinel app. 1.25 3.75 10.00

OTE: ***Frank Bolle*** *a-6-19, 29-31; c-29i, 30i.* ***Bob Fugitani*** *a-1-5.* ***Spiegle*** *a-29-31.* ***Al 'cWilliams*** *a-20-23.*

OCTOR SOLAR, MAN OF THE ATOM
aliant Comics: 1990 - No. 2, 1991 ($7.95, card stock-c, high quality, 96 pgs.)

1,2: Reprints Gold Key series 1.00 3.00 8.00

OCTOR SPEKTOR (See The Occult Files of..., & Spine-Tingling Tales)

OCTOR STRANGE (Formerly Strange Tales #1-168) (Also see The efenders, Giant-Size..., Marvel Fanfare, Marvel Graphic Novel, Marvel remiere, Marvel Treasury Edition & Strange Tales, 2nd Series)
larvel Comics Group: No. 169, 6/68 - No. 183, 11/69; 6/74 - No. 81, 2/87

69(#1)-Origin retold; panel swipe/M.D. #1-c 14.50 43.50 160.00
70-177: 177-New costume 3.45 10.35 38.00
78-183: 178-Black Knight app. 179-Spider-Man story-r. 180-Photo montage-c. 181-Brunner-c(part-i), last 12¢ issue 3.20 9.60 35.00
1(6/74, 2nd series)-Brunner-c/a 4.10 12.30 45.00
2 2.00 6.00 18.00
3-5 1.25 3.75 10.00
6-10 2.40 6.00
1-13,15-20: 13,15-17-(Regular 25¢ editions) 4.00
3-17-(30¢-c variants, limited distribution) 2.40 6.00
4-(5/76) Dracula app.; (regular 25¢ edition) 5.00
!1-40: 21-Origin-r/Doctor Strange #169. 31-Sub-Mariner-c/story 3.00
1-58,63-77,79-81: 56-Origin retold. 58-Re-intro Hannibal King (cameo) 2.00
i9-62: 59-Hannibal King full app. 59-62-Dracula app. (Darkhold storyline). 61,62-Doctor Strange, Blade, Hannibal King & Frank Drake team-up to battle Dracula. 62-Death of Dracula & Lilith 4.00
'8-New costume 2.50
nnual 1(1976, 52 pgs.)-New Russell-a (35 pgs.) 2.40 6.00
./Silver Dagger Special Edition 1 (3/83, $2.50)-r/#1,2,4,5; Wrightson-c 3.00
.What Is It That Disturbs You, Stephen? #1 (10/97, $5.99, 48 pgs.) Russell-a/Andreyko & Russell-s, retelling of Annual #1 story 2.40 6.00

OTE: ***Adkins*** *a-169, 170, 171i; c-169-171, 172i, 173.* ***Adams*** *a-4i.* ***Austin*** *a(i)-48-60, 66, 68,), 73; c(i)-38, 47-53, 55, 58-60, 70.* ***Brunner*** *a-1-5p; c-1-6, 22, 28-30, 33.* ***Colan*** *a(p)-172-178, 90-183, 6-18, 36-45, 47; c(p)-172, 174-183, 11-21, 23, 27, 35, 36, 47.* ***Ditko*** *a-179r, 3r.* ***Everett*** *-183i.* ***Golden*** *a-46p, 55p; c-42-44, 46, 55p.* ***G. Kane*** *c(p)-8-10.* ***Miller*** *c-46p.* ***Nebres*** *a-20, 22, 3, 24i, 26i, 32i; c-32i, 34.* ***Rogers*** *a-48-53p; c-47p-53p.* ***Russell*** *a-34i, 46i, Annual 1.* ***B. Smith*** *c-79.* ***Paul Smith*** *a-54p, 56p, 65, 66p, 68p, 69, 71-73; c-56, 65, 66, 68, 71.* ***Starlin*** *a-23p, 26; c-5, 26.* ***Sutton*** *a-27-29p, 31i, 33, 34p. Painted c-62, 63.*

OCTOR STRANGE (Volume 2)
larvel Comics: Feb, 1999 - No. 4, May, 1999 ($2.99, limited series)

1-4: 1,2-Tony Harris-a/painted cover. 3,4-Chadwick-a 3.00

OCTOR STRANGE CLASSICS
larvel Comics Group: Mar, 1984 - No. 4, June, 1984 ($1.50, Baxter paper)

1-4: Ditko-r; Byrne-c. 4-New Golden pin-up 3.00
OTE: ***Byrne*** *c-1i, 2-4.*

OCTOR STRANGEFATE (See Marvel Versus DC #3 & DC Versus Marvel #4)
C Comics (Amalgam): Apr, 1996 ($1.95)

1-Ron Marz script w/Jose Garcia-Lopez-(p) & Kevin Nowlan-(i). Access & Charles Xavier app. 2.00

OCTOR STRANGE MASTER OF THE MYSTIC ARTS (See Fireside Book Series)

OCTOR STRANGE, SORCERER SUPREME
larvel Comics (Midnight Sons imprint #60 on): Nov, 1988 - No. 90, June, 996 ($1.25/$1.50/$1.75/$1.95, direct sales only, Mando paper)

1 ($1.25) 3.00
2-9,12-14,16-25,27,29-40,42-49,51-64: 3-New Defenders app. 5-Guice-c/a begins. 14-18-Morbius story line. 31-36-Infinity Gauntlet x-overs. 31-Silver Surfer app. 33-Thanos-c & cameo. 36-Warlock app. 37-Silver Surfer app. 40-Daredevil x-over. 41-Wolverine-c/story. 42-47-Infinity War x-overs. 47-Gamora app. 52,53-Morbius-c/stories. 60,61-Siege of Darkness pt. 7 & 15. 60-Spot varnish-c. 61-New Doctor Strange begins (cameo, 1st app.). 62-Dr. Doom & Morbius app. 2.00
10,11,26,28,41: 10-Re-intro Morbius w/new costume (11/89). 11-Hobgoblin app. 26-Werewolf by Night app. 28-Ghost Rider-s cont'd from G.R. #12; published at same time as Doctor Strange/Ghost Rider Special #1(4/91) 3.00
15-Unauthorized Amy Grant photo-c 4.00
50-($2.95, 52 pgs.)-Holo-grafx foil-c; Hulk, Ghost Rider & Silver Surfer app.; leads into new Secret Defenders series 3.00
65-74, 76-90: 65-Begin $1.95-c; bound-in card sheet. 72-Silver ink-c. 80-82-Ellis-s. 84-DeMatteis story begins. 87-Death of Baron Mordo. 2.00
75 ($2.50) 2.50
75 ($3.50)-Foil-c 4.00
Annual 2-4 ('92-'94, 68 pgs.)-2-Defenders app. 3-Polybagged w/card 3.00
Ashcan (1995, 75¢) 2.00
.../Ghost Rider Special 1 (4/91, $1.50)-Same book as D.S.S.S. #28 2.00
...Vs. Dracula 1 (3/94, $1.75, 52 pgs.)-r/Tomb of Dracula #44 & Dr. Strange #14 2.00

NOTE: ***Colan*** *c/a-19.* ***Golden*** *c-28.* ***Guice*** *a-5-16, 18, 20-24; c-5-12, 20-24. See 1st series for Annual #1.*

DR. TOM BRENT, YOUNG INTERN
Charlton Publications: Feb, 1963 - No. 5, Oct, 1963

1 2.00 6.00 18.00
2-5 1.50 4.50 12.00

DR. TOMORROW
Acclaim Comics (Valiant): Sept, 1997 - No. 12 ($2.50)

1-12: 1-Mignola-c 2.50

DR. VOLTZ (See Mighty Midget Comics)

DR. WEIRD
Big Bang Comics: 1994 ($2.95, B&W)

1,2: 1-Frank Brunner-c 4.00

DR. WEIRD SPECIAL
Big Bang Comics: Feb, 1994 ($3.95, B&W, 68 pgs.)

1-Origin-r by Starlin; Starlin-c. 4.00

DOCTOR WHO (Also see Marvel Premiere #57-60)
Marvel Comics Group: Oct, 1984 - No. 23, Aug, 1986 ($1.50, color, direct sales, Baxter paper)

1-23-British-r. 4.00
Graphic Novel Voyager (1985, $8.95) color reprints of B&W comic pages from Doctor Who Magazine #88-99; Colin Baker afterword 12.00

DR. WHO & THE DALEKS (See Movie Classics)

DR. WONDER
Old Town Publishing: June, 1996 - Present ($2.95, B&W)

1-5: 1-Intro & origin of Dr. Wonder; Dick Ayers-c/a; Irwin Hasen-a; contains profiles of the artists 3.00

DOCTOR ZERO
Marvel Comics (Epic Comics): Apr, 1988 - No. 8, Aug, 1989 ($1.25/$1.50)

1-8: 1-Sienkiewicz-c. 6,7-Spiegle-a 2.00
NOTE: ***Sienkiewicz*** *a-3i, 4i; c-1.* ***Spiegle*** *a-6, 7.*

DO-DO (Funny Animal Circus Stories)
Nation-Wide Publishers: 1950 - No. 7, 1951 (5¢, 5x7-1/4" Miniature)

1 (52 pgs.) 25.00 75.00 200.00
2-7 12.50 37.50 100.00

DODO & THE FROG, THE (Formerly Funny Stuff; also see It's Game Time #2)
National Periodical Publications: No. 80, 9-10/54 - No. 88, 1-2/56; No. 89, 8-9/56; No. 90, 10-11/56; No. 91, 9/57; No. 92, 11/57 (See Comic Cavalcade)

80-1st app. Doodles Duck by Sheldon Mayer 20.00 60.00 160.00
81-91: Doodles Duck by Mayer in #81,83-90 13.00 39.00 105.00
92-(Scarce)-Doodles Duck by S. Mayer 18.00 53.00 140.00

DOGFACE DOOLEY
Magazine Enterprises: 1951 - No. 5, 1953

Doll Man Quarterly #10 © QUA

Domination Factor #2.3 © MAR

Domino #1 © MAR

1(A-1 40) 6.00 18.00 42.00
2(A-1 43), 3(A-1 49), 4(A-1 53), 5(A-1 64) 5.00 15.00 30.00
I.W. Reprint #1('64), Super Reprint #17 3.00 7.50 15.00

DOG MOON
DC Comics (Vertigo): 1996 ($6.95, one-shot)
1-Robert Hunter-scripts; Tim Truman-c/a. 7.00

DOG OF FLANDERS, A
Dell Publishing Co.: No. 1088, Mar, 1960
Four Color 1088-Movie, photo-c 4.10 12.30 45.00

DOGPATCH (See Al Capp's... & Mammy Yokum)

DOGS OF WAR (Also see Warriors of Plasm)
Defiant: Apr, 1994 - No. 5, Aug, 1994 ($2.50)
1-5 2.50

DOGS-O-WAR
Crusade Comics: June, 1996 - No. 3, Jan, 1997 ($2.95, B&W, limited series)
1-3: 1,2-Photo-c 3.00

DOLLFACE & HER GANG (Betty Betz'...)
Dell Publishing Co.: No. 309, Jan, 1951
Four Color 309 4.60 13.75 55.00

DOLLMAN (Movie)
Eternity Comics: Sept, 1991 - No. 4, Dec, 1991 ($2.50, limited series)
1-4: Adaptation of film 2.50

DOLL MAN QUARTERLY, THE (Doll Man #17 on; also see Feature Comics #27 & Freedom Fighters)
Quality Comics: Fall, 1941 - No. 7, Fall, '43; No. 8, Spr, '46 - No. 47, Oct, 1953
1-Dollman (by Cassone), Justin Wright begin 305.00 915.00 3200.00
2-The Dragon begins; Crandall-a(5) 132.00 395.00 1250.00
3,4 90.00 270.00 850.00
5-Crandall-a 74.00 221.00 700.00
6,7(1943) 55.00 165.00 500.00
8(1946)-1st app. Torchy by Bill Ward 155.00 465.00 1475.00
9 55.00 165.00 500.00
10-20 42.00 125.00 375.00
21-30: 28-Vs. The Flame 38.00 113.00 300.00
31-36,38,40: 31-(12/50)-Intro Elmo, the wonder dog (Dollman's faithful dog). 32-34-Jeb Rivers app.; 34 by Crandall(p) 31.00 92.00 245.00
37-Origin & 1st app. Dollgirl; Dollgirl bondage-c 42.00 125.00 375.00
39- "Narcotics...the Death Drug" c-/story 33.00 98.00 260.00
41-47 22.00 66.00 175.00
Super Reprint #11('64, r/#20),15(r/#23),17(r/#28): 15,17-Torchy app.; Andru/Esposito-c 3.20 9.60 35.00

NOTE: ***Ward** Torchy in 8, 9, 11, 12, 14-24, 26, 27; by Fox-#30, 35-47.* ***Crandall** a-2, 5, 10, 13 & Super #11, 17, 18.* ***Crandall/Cuidera** c-40-42.* ***Guardineer** a-3. Bondage c-27, 37, 38, 39.*

DOLLS
Sirius: June, 1996 ($2.95, B&W, one-shot)
1 3.00

DOLLY
Ziff-Davis Publ. Co.: No. 10, July-Aug, 1951 (Funny animal)
10-Painted-c 6.0 18.00 42.00

DOLLY DILL
Marvel Comics/Newsstand Publ.: 1945
1 15.00 45.00 120.00

DOMINATION FACTOR
Marvel Comics: Nov, 1999 - 4.8, Feb, 2000 ($2.50, interconnected mini- series)
1.1, 2.3, 3.5, 4.7-Fantastic Four; Jurgens-s/a 2.50
1.2, 2.4, 3.6, 4.8-Avengers; Ordway-s/a 2.50

DOMINION (Manga)
Eclipse Comics: Dec, 1990 - No. 6., July, 1990 ($2.00, B&W, limited series)
1-6 3.00

DOMINION: CONFLICT 1 (Manga)
Dark Horse Comics: Mar, 1996 - No. 6, Aug, 1996 ($2.95, B&W, limited series)
1-6: Shirow-c/a/scripts 3.00

DOMINIQUE: KILLZONE
Caliber Comics: May, 1995 ($2.95, B&W)
1 3.00

DOMINO (See X-Force)
Marvel Comics: Jan, 1997 - No. 3, Mar, 1997 ($1.95, limited series)
1-3: 2-Deathstrike-c/app. 2.00

DOMINO CHANCE
Chance Enterprises: May-June, 1982 - No. 9, May, 1985 (B&W)
1-9: 7-1st app. Gizmo, 2 pgs. 8-1st full Gizmo story, 1-Reprint, May, 1985 2.50

DONALD AND MICKEY IN DISNEYLAND (See Dell Giants)

DONALD AND SCROOGE
Disney Comics: 1992 ($8.95, squarebound, 100 pgs.)
nn-Don Rosa reprint special; r/U.S., D.D. Advs. 1.25 3.75 10.00
1-3 (1992, $1.50)-r/D.D. Advs. (Disney) #1,22,24 & U.S. #261-263,269 2.00

DONALD AND THE WHEEL (Disney)
Dell Publishing Co.: No. 1190, Nov, 1961
Four Color 1190-Movie, Barks-c 6.70 20.00 80.00

DONALD DUCK (See Adventures of Mickey Mouse, Cheerios, Donald & Mickey, Ducktales, Dynabrite Comics, Gladstone Comic Album, Mickey & Donald, Mickey Mouse Mag., Story Hour Series, Uncle Scrooge, Walt Disney's Comics & Stories, W. D.'s Donald Duck, Wheaties & Whitman Comic Books, Wise Little Hen, The)

DONALD DUCK
Whitman Publishing Co./Grosset & Dunlap/K.K.: 1935, 1936 (All pages on heavy linen-like finish cover stock in color;1st book ever devoted to Donald Duck; see Advs. of Mickey Mouse for 1st app.) (9-1/2x13")
978(1935)-16 pgs.; Illustrated text story book 350.00 1050.00 3000.00
nn(1936)-36 pgs.plus hard cover & dust jacket. Story completely rewritten with B&W illos added. Mickey appears and his nephews are named Morty & Monty
Book only 350.00 1050.00 2800.00
Dust jacket only.... 87.00 262.00 700.00

DONALD DUCK (Walt Disney's) (10¢)
Whitman/K.K. Publications: 1938 (8-1/2x11-1/2", B&W, cardboard-c)
(Has D. Duck with bubble pipe on-c)
GD2.0 FN6.0 VF8.0 NM9.4
nn-The first Donald Duck & Walt Disney comic book; 1936 & 1937 Sunday strip-r(in B&W); same format as the Feature Books; 1st strips with Huey, Dewey & Louie from 10/17/37 311.00 933.00 1866.00 2800.00

DONALD DUCK (Walt Disney's...#262 on; see 4-Color listings for titles & Four Color No. 1109 for origin story)
Dell Publ. Co./Gold Key #85-216/Whitman #217-245/Gladstone #246 on: 1940 - No. 84, Sept-Nov, 1962; No. 85, Dec, 1962 - No. 245, 1984; No. 246, Oct, 1986 - No. 279, May, 1990; No. 280, Sept, 1993 - No. 304
GD2.0 FN6.0 VF8.0 NM9.4
Four Color 4(1940)-Daily 1939 strip-r by Al Taliaferro 857.00 2571.00 6000.00 12,000.00
Large Feature Comic 16(1/41?)-1940 Sunday strips-r in B&W 393.00 1179.00 2750.00 5500.00
Large Feature Comic 20('41)-Comic Paint Book, r-single panels from Large Feature #16 at top of each pg. to color; daily strip-r across bottom of each pg. 443.00 1329.00 3100.00 6200.00
Four Color 9('42)- "Finds Pirate Gold"; 64 pgs. by Carl Barks & Jack Hannah (pgs. 1,2,5,12-40 are by Barks, his 1st Donald Duck comic book art work; © 8/17/42) 643.00 1929.00 4500.00 9000.00
Four Color 29(9/43)- "Mummy's Ring" by Barks; reprinted in Uncle Scrooge & Donald Duck #1('65), W. D. Comics Digest #44('73) & Donald Duck Advs. #14 500.00 1500.00 3500.00 7000.00
GD2.0 FN6.0 NM9.4
Four Color 62(1/45)- "Frozen Gold"; 52 pgs. by Barks, reprinted in The Best of W.D. Comics & Donald Duck Advs. #4 157.00 471.00 2200.00
Four Color 108(1946)- "Terror of the River"; 52 pgs. by Carl Barks; reprinted in Gladstone Comic Album #2 114.00 342.00 1600.00
Four Color 147(5/47)-in "Volcano Valley" by Barks 78.00 236.00 1100.00

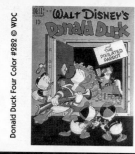

Donald Duck Four Color #282 © WDC

Donald Duck #27 © WDC

Donald Duck #263 © WDC

GD2.0 FN6.0 NM9.4

Four Color 159(8/47)-in "The Ghost of the Grotto";52 pgs. by Carl Barks; reprinted in Best of Uncle Scrooge & Donald Duck #1 ('66) & The Best of W.D. Comics & D.D. Advs. #9; two Barks stories 64.00 193.00 900.00
Four Color 178(12/47)-1st app. Uncle Scrooge by Carl Barks; reprinted in Gold Key Christmas Parade #3 & The Best of Walt Disney Comics 93.00 279.00 1300.00
Four Color 189(6/48)-by Carl Barks; reprinted in Best of Donald Duck & Uncle Scrooge #1('64) & D.D. Advs. #19 59.00 177.00 825.00
Four Color 199(10/48)-by Carl Barks; mentioned in Love and Death; r/in Gladstone Comic Album #5 64.00 193.00 900.00
Four Color 203(12/48)-by Barks; reprinted as Gold Key Christmas Parade #4 45.00 134.00 625.00
Four Color 223(4/49)-by Barks; reprinted as Best of Donald Duck #1 & Donald Duck Advs. #3 63.00 188.00 875.00
Four Color 238(8/49)-in "Voodoo Hoodoo" by Barks 45.00 134.00 625.00
Four Color 256(12/49)-by Barks; reprinted in Best of Donald Duck & Uncle Scrooge #2('67), Gladstone Comic Album #16 & W.D. Comics Digest 44('73) 33.00 99.00 460.00
Four Color 263(2/50)-Two Barks stories; r-in D.D. #278 31.00 92.00 440.00
Four Color 275(5/50), 282(7/50), 291(9/50), 300(11/50)-All by Carl Barks; 275, 282 reprinted in W.D. Comics Digest #44('73). #275 r/in Gladstone Comic Album #10. #291 r/in D. Duck Advs. #16 29.00 87.00 410.00
Four Color 308(1/51), 318(3/51)-by Barks; #318-reprinted in W.D. Comics Digest #34 & D.D. Advs. #2,19 25.00 75.00 350.00
Four Color 328(5/51)-by Carl Barks 27.00 81.00 380.00
Four Color 339(7-8/51), 379-2nd Uncle Scrooge-c; art not by Barks. 6.30 19.00 75.00
Four Color 348(9-10/51), 356,394-Barks-c only 15.00 45.00 180.00
Four Color 367(1-2/52)-by Barks; reprinted as Gold Key Christmas Parade #2 & #8 25.00 75.00 350.00
Four Color 408(7-8/52), 422(9-10/52)-All by Carl Barks. #408-r-in Best of Donald Duck & Uncle Scrooge #1('64) & Gladstone Comic Album #13 25.00 75.00 350.00
26(11-12/52)-In "Trick or Treat" (Barks-a, 36pgs.) 1st story r-in Walt Disney Digest #16 & Gladstone C.A. #23 25.00 76.00 360.00
27-30-Barks-c only 10.50 31.00 125.00
31-44,47-50 4.60 13.75 55.00
45-Barks-a (6 pgs.) 11.65 35.00 140.00
46- "Secret of Hondorica" by Barks, 24 pgs.; reprinted in Donald Duck #98 & 154 18.00 55.00 220.00
51-Barks-a,1/2 pg. 5.00 15.00 60.00
52- "Lost Peg-Leg Mine" by Barks, 10 pgs. 12.50 37.50 150.00
53,55-59 4.00 12.00 50.00
54- "Forbidden Valley" by Barks, 26 pgs. (10¢ & 15¢ versions exist) 13.00 38.00 155.00
60- "Donald Duck & the Titanic Ants" by Barks, 20 pgs. plus 6 more pgs. 13.00 38.00 155.00
61-67,69,70 3.30 10.00 40.00
68-Barks-a, 5 pgs. 9.50 29.00 115.00
71-Barks-r, 1/2 pg. 3.30 10.00 40.00
72-78,80,82-97,99,100: 96-Donald Duck Album 3.30 10.00 40.00
79,81-Barks-a, 1pg. 3.30 10.00 40.00
98-Reprints #46 (Barks) 3.30 10.00 40.00
01,103-111,113-135: 120-Last 12¢ issue. 134-Barks-r/#52 & WDC&S 194. 135-Barks-r/WDC&S 198, 19 pgs. 2.30 7.00 28.00
02-Super Goof. 112-1st Moby Duck 2.50 7.50 30.00
36-153,155,156,158 1.45 4.35 16.00
54-Barks-r(#46) 1.80 5.40 20.00
57,159,160,164: 157-Barks-r(#45). 159-Reprints/WDC&S #192 (10 pgs.). 160-Barks-r(#26). 164-Barks-r(#79) 1.45 4.35 16.00
61-163,165-173,175-187,189-191: 187-Barks r/#68. 1.10 3.30 12.00
74,188: 174-r/4-Color #394. 1.25 3.75 14.00
92-Barks-r(40 pgs.) from Donald Duck #60 & WDC&S #226,234 (52 pgs.) 1.65 4.90 18.00
93-200,202-207,209-211,213-216 1.00 3.00 8.00
01,208,212: 201-Barks-r/Christmas Parade #26, 16pgs. 208-Barks-r/#60 (6 pgs.). 212-Barks-r/WDC&S #130 1.00 3.00 8.00
217-219: 217 has 216 on-c. 219-Barks-r/WDC&S #106,107, 10 pgs. ea. 1.25 3.75 10.00
220,221,223,224 2.00 6.00 22.00
222-(8-12/80)-(Very low distribution) 9.00 27.00 175.00
225-228: 228-Barks-r/F.C. #275. 1.25 3.75 14.00
229-240: 229-Barks-r/F.C. #282. 230-Barks-r/ #52 & WDC&S #194 1.10 3.30 9.00
241-245 1.45 4.35 16.00
246-(1st Gladstone issue)-Barks-r/FC #422 1.65 4.90 18.00
247-249,251: 248,249-Barks-r/DD #54 & 26. 251-Barks-r/1945 Firestone 1.10 3.30 12.00
250-($1.50, 68 pgs.)-Barks-r/4-Color #9 1.25 3.75 14.00
252-277,280: 254-Barks-r/FC #328. 256-Barks-r/FC #147. 257-($1.50, 52 pgs.)-Barks-r/Vacaction Parade #1. 261-Barks-r/FC #300. 275-Kelly-r/FC #92. 280 (#1, 2nd Series) 2.40 6.00
278,279,286: 278,279 ($1.95, 68 pgs.): 278-Rosa-a; Barks-r/FC #263. 279-Rosa-c; Barks-r/MOC #4. 286-Rosa-a 1.00 2.80 7.00
281,282,284 5.00
283-Don Rosa-a, part-c & scripts 2.40 6.00
285,287-304 3.00
286 ($2.95, 68 pgs.)-Happy Birthday, Donald 4.00
Mini-Comic #1(1976)-(3-1/4x6-1/2"); r/D.D. #150 1.00 3.00 8.00

NOTE: *Carl Barks wrote all issues he illustrated, but #117, 126, 138 contain his script only. Issues 4-Color #189, 199, 203, 223, 238, 256, 263, 275, 282, 308, 348, 356, 367, 394, 408, 422, 26-30, 35, 44, 46, 52, 55, 57, 60, 65, 70-73, 77-80, 83, 101, 103, 105, 106, 111, 126, 246r, 266r, 268r, 271r, 275r, 278r(F.C. 263) all have* ***Barks*** *covers.* ***Barks*** *r-263-267, 269-278-282, 284, 285. #96 titled "Comic Album", #99-"Christmas Album". New art issues (not reprints)-106-46, 148-63, 167, 169, 170, 172, 173, 175, 178, 179, 196, 209, 223, 225, 236.* ***Taliaferro*** *daily newspaper strips #258-260, 264, 284, 285; Sunday strips #247, 280-283.*

DONALD DUCK ALBUM (See Comic Album No. 1,3 & Duck Album)
Dell Publishing Co./Gold Key: 5-7/59 - F.C. No. 1239, 10-12/61; 1962; 8/63 - No. 2, Oct, 1963

Four Color 995 (#1) 5.00 15.00 60.00
Four Color 1182, 01204-207 (1962-Dell) 4.10 12.30 45.00
Four Color 1099,1140,1239-Barks-c 5.85 17.50 70.00
1(8/63-Gold Key)-Barks-c 5.00 15.00 60.00
2(10/63) 4.10 12.30 45.00

DONALD DUCK AND THE BOYS (Also see Story Hour Series)
Whitman Publishing Co.: 1948 (5-1/4x5-1/2", 100pgs., hard-c; art & text)

845-(49) new illos by Barks based on his Donald Duck 10-pager in WDC&S #74, Expanded text not written by Barks; Cover not by Barks 50.00 150.00 600.00
(Prices vary widely on this book)

DONALD DUCK AND THE CHRISTMAS CAROL
Whitman Publishing Co.: 1960 (A Little Golden Book, 6-3/8"x7-5/8", 28 pgs.)

nn-Story book pencilled by Carl Barks with the intended title "Uncle Scrooge's Christmas Carol." Finished art adapted by Norman McGary. (Rare)-Reprinted in Uncle Scrooge in Color. 30.00 90.00 150.00

DONALD DUCK BEACH PARTY (Also see Dell Giants)
Gold Key: Sept, 1965 (12¢)

1(#10158-509)-Barks-r/WDC&S #45; painted-c 5.85 17.50 70.00

DONALD DUCK BOOK (See Story Hour Series)

DONALD DUCK COMICS DIGEST
Gladstone Publishing: Nov, 1986 - No. 5, July, 1987 ($1.25/$1.50, 96 pgs.)

1,3: 1-Barks-c/a-r 1.10 3.30 9.00
2,4,5: 4,5-$1.50-c 2.40 6.00

DONALD DUCK FUN BOOK (See Dell Giants)

DONALD DUCK IN DISNEYLAND (See Dell Giants)

DONALD DUCK MARCH OF COMICS (See March of Comics #4,20,41,56,69,263)

DONALD DUCK MERRY CHRISTMAS (See Dell Giant No. 53)

DONALD DUCK PICNIC PARTY (See Picnic Party listed under Dell Giants)

DONALD DUCK TELLS ABOUT KITES (See Kite Fun Book)

DONALD DUCK, THIS IS YOUR LIFE (Disney, TV)
Dell Publishing Co.: No. 1109, Aug-Oct, 1960

Don Fortune Magazine #6 © Don Fortune Publ.

Don Rosa's Comics & Stories #1 © Don Rosa

Doom Patrol (2nd series) #41 © DC

Four Color 1109-Gyro flashback to WDC&S #141; origin Donald Duck (1st told) 14.00 41.00 165.00

DONALD DUCK XMAS ALBUM (See regular Donald Duck No. 99)

DONALD IN MATHMAGIC LAND (Disney)
Dell Publishing Co.: No. 1051, Oct-Dec, 1959 - No. 1198, May-July, 1961

Four Color 1051 (#1)-Movie 8.35 25.00 100.00
Four Color 1198-Reprint of above 5.85 17.50 70.00

DONATELLO, TEENAGE MUTANT NINJA TURTLE
Mirage Studios: Aug, 1986 ($1.50, B&W, one-shot, 44 pgs.)

1 4.00

DONDI
Dell Publishing Co.: No. 1176, Mar-May, 1961 - No. 1276, Dec, 1961

Four Color 1176 (#1)-Movie; origin, photo-c 4.10 12.30 45.00
Four Color 1276 2.40 7.35 22.00

DON FORTUNE MAGAZINE
Don Fortune Publishing Co.: Aug, 1946 - No. 6, Feb, 1947

1-Delecta of the Planets by C. C. Beck in all 23.00 68.00 180.00
2 12.50 37.50 100.00
3-6: 3-Bondage-c 10.50 32.00 85.00

DONKEY KONG (See Blip #1)

DONNA MATRIX
Reactor, Inc.: Aug, 1993 ($2.95, 52 pgs.)

1-Computer generated-c/a by Mike Saenz; 3-D effects 3.00

DONNA MIA
Dark Fantasy Productions: Oct, 1995 -No. 2, Sept, 1996 ($3.95/$4.95, limited series, mature)

1,2-($4.95): 1-Kaluta-c-red foil; fold-out centerfold. 2-Kaluta blue foil-c; nudity 5.00
1,2-($3.95): Kaluta-c on both. 2-Nudity 4.00

DON NEWCOMBE
Fawcett Publications: 1950 (Baseball)

nn-Photo-c 40.00 120.00 350.00

DON ROSA'S COMICS AND STORIES
Fantagraphics Books (CX Comics): 1983 ($2.95)

1,2: 1-(68 pgs.) Reprints Rosa's The Pertwillaby Papers episodes #128-133. 2-(60 pgs.) Reprints episodes #134-138 1.50 4.50 12.00

DON SIMPSON'S BIZARRE HEROES (Also see Megaton Man)
Fiasco Comics: May, 1990 - Present ($2.50/$2.95, B&W)

1-10,0,11-17: 0-Begin $2.95-c; r/Bizarre Heroes #1. 17-(9/96)-Indicia also reads Megaton Man #0; intro Megaton Man and the Fiascoverse to new readers 3.00

DON'T GIVE UP THE SHIP
Dell Publishing Co.: No. 1049, Aug, 1959

Four Color 1049-Movie, Jerry Lewis photo-c 7.00 20.00 85.00

DON WINSLOW OF THE NAVY
Merwil Publishing Co.: Apr, 1937 - No. 2, May, 1937 (96 pgs.)(A pulp/comic book cross; stapled spine)

GD2.0 FN6.0 VF8.0

V1#1-Has 16 pgs. comics in color. Captain Colorful & Jupiter Jones by Sheldon Mayer; complete Don Winslow novel 575.00 1725.00 4000.00
2-Sheldon Mayer-a 150.00 450.00 1050.00

DON WINSLOW OF THE NAVY (See Crackajack Funnies, Famous Feature Stories, Popular Comics & Super Book #5,6)
Dell Publishing Co.: No. 2, Nov, 1939 - No. 22, 1941

Four Color 2 (#1)-Rare 133.00 400.00 1600.00
Four Color 22 30.00 90.00 360.00

DON WINSLOW OF THE NAVY (See TV Teens; Movie, Radio, TV) (Fightin' Navy No. 74 on)
Fawcett Publications/Charlton No. 70 on: 2/43 - #64, 12/48; #65, 1/51 - #69, 9/51; #70, 3/55 - #73, 9/55

GD2.0 FN6.0 NM9.4

1-(68 pgs.)-Captain Marvel on cover 105.00 316.00 1000.00
2 51.00 153.00 460.00
3 40.00 120.00 340.00
4-6: 6-Flag-c 33.00 98.00 260.00
7-10: 8-Last 68 pg. issue? 24.00 71.00 190.00
11-20 19.00 56.00 150.00
21-40 12.00 36.00 95.00
41-64: 51,60-Singapore Sal (villain) app. 64-(12/48) 10.00 30.00 80.00
65(1/51)-Flying Saucer attack; photo-c 14.00 41.00 110.00
66 - 69(9/51): All photo-c. 66-sci-fi story 13.00 39.00 105.00
70(3/55)-73: 70-73 r-/#26,58 & 59 10.00 30.00 70.00

DOOM
Marvel Comics: Oct, 2000 - No. 3, Dec, 2000 ($2.99, limited series)

1-3-Dr. Doom; Dixon-s/Manco-a 3.00

DOOM FORCE SPECIAL
DC Comics: July, 1992 ($2.95, 68 pgs., one-shot, mature) (X-Force parody)

1-Morrison scripts; Simonson, Steacy, & others-a; Giffen/Mignola-c 3.00

DOOM PATROL, THE (Formerly My Greatest Adventure No. 1-85; see Brave and the Bold, DC Special Blue Ribbon Digest 19, Official... Index & Showcase No. 94-96)
National Periodical Publications: No. 86, 3/64 - No. 121, 9-10/68; No. 122, 2/73 - No. 124, 6-7/73

86-1 pg. origin (#86-121 are 12¢ issues) 9.00 27.00 100.00
87-98: 88-Origin The Chief. 91-Intro. Mento 6.80 20.50 75.00
99-Intro. Beast Boy (later becomes the Changeling in New Teen Titans 7.25 21.75 80.00
100-Origin Beast Boy; Robot-Maniac series begins (12/65) 7.25 21.75 80.00
101-110: 102-Challengers of the Unknown app. 105-Robot-Maniac series ends. 106-Negative Man begins (origin) 3.65 11.00 40.00
111-120 3.00 9.00 30.00
121-Death of Doom Patrol; Orlando-c. 8.15 24.50 90.00
122-124: All reprints 1.10 3.30 9.00

DOOM PATROL
DC Comics (Vertigo imprint #64 on): Oct, 1987 - No, 87, Feb, 1995 (75¢-$1.95, new format)

1 4.00
2-18: 3-1st app. Lodestone. 4-1st app. Karma. 8,15,16-Art Adams-c(i). 18-Invasion tie-in. 3.00
19-(2/89)-Grant Morrison scripts begin, ends #63; 1st app Crazy Jane; $1.50-c & new format begins. 6.00
20-30: 29-Superman app. 30-Night Breed fold-out 3.50
31-49,51-56,58-60: 35-1st app. of Flex Mentallo (cameo). 36-1st full app. of Flex Mentallo. 39-World Without End preview.42-Origin of Flex Mentallo 2.50
50,57 ($2.50, 52 pgs.) 2.50
61-87: 61,70-Photo-c. 73-Death cameo (2 panels) 2.00
...And Suicide Squad 1 (3/88, $1.50, 52 pgs.)-Wraparound-c 2.00
Annual 1 (1988, $1.50, 52 pgs.) 2.00
Annual 2 (1994, $3.95, 68 pgs.)-Children's Crusade tie-in. 4.00

NOTE: ***Bisley*** *painted c-26-48, 55-58.* ***Bolland*** *c-64, 75.* ***Dringenberg*** *a-42(p).* ***Steacy*** *a-53.*

DOOM PATROL (See Tangent Comics/ Doom Patrol)

DOOMSDAY
DC Comics: 1995 ($3.95, one-shot)

1-Year One story by Jurgens, L. Simonson, Ordway, and Gil Kane; Darkseid, Superman app. 4.00

DOOMSDAY + 1 (Also see Charlton Bullseye)
Charlton Comics: July, 1975 - No. 6, June, 1976; No. 7, June, 1978 - No. 12, May, 1979

1: #1-5 are 25¢ issues 1.85 5.50 15.00
2-6: 4-Intro Lor. 5-Ditko-a(1 pg.) 6-Begin 30¢ issues 1.10 3.30 9.00
V3#7-12 (reprints #1-6) 4.00
5 (Modern Comics reprint, 1977) 3.00

NOTE: ***Byrne*** *c/a-1-12; Painted covers-2-7.*

DOOMSDAY SQUAD, THE
Fantagraphics Books: Aug, 1986 - No. 7, 1987 ($2.00)

1-7: Byrne-a in all. 1-3-New Byrne-c. 3-Usagi Yojimbo app. (1st in color).4-N

Doom 2099 #11 © MAR

Dork #3 © Evan Dorkin

Down With Crime #5 © FAW

GD2.0 FN6.0 NM9.4

Adams-c. 5-7-Gil Kane-c 3.00

DOOM'S IV
Image Comics (Extreme): July, 1994 - No.4, Oct, 1994 ($2.50, limited series)
1-4-Liefeld story 2.50
1,2-Two alternate Liefeld-c each, 4 covers form 1 picture 5.00

DOOM 2099 (See Marvel Comics Presents #118 & 2099: World of Tomorrow)
Marvel Comics: Jan, 1993 - No. 44, Aug, 1996 ($1.25/$1.50/$1.95)
1-24,26-44: 1-Metallic foil stamped-c. 4-Ron Lim-c(p). 17-bound-in trading card sheet. 40-Namor & Doctor Strange app. 41-Daredevil app., Namor-c/app. 44-Intro The Emissary; story contin'd in 2099: World of Tomorrow 2.00
1-2nd printing 2.00
25 ($2.25, 52 pgs.) 2.25
25 ($2.95, 52pgs.) Foil embossed cover 3.00
29 ($3.50)-acetate-c. 3.50

DOORWAY TO NIGHTMARE (See Cancelled Comic Cavalcade)
DC Comics: Jan-Feb, 1978 - No. 5, Sept-Oct, 1978
1-5-Madame Xanadu in all. 4-Craig-a 2.40 6.00
NOTE: *Kaluta covers on all. Merged into The Unexpected with No. 190.*

DOPEY DUCK COMICS (Wacky Duck No. 3) (See Super Funnies)
Timely Comics (NPP): Fall, 1945 - No. 2, Apr, 1946
1,2-Casper Cat, Krazy Krow 20.00 60.00 160.00

DORK
Slave Labor: June, 1993 - Present ($2.50-$2.95, B&W, mature)
1-7: Evan Dorkin-c/a/scripts in all. 1(8/95),2(1/96)-(2nd printing): Reads 2nd Print on bottom inside-c 3.00
8-($3.50) 3.50

DOROTHY LAMOUR (Formerly Jungle Lil)(Stage, screen, radio)
Fox Features Syndicate: No. 2, June, 1950 - No. 3, Aug, 1950
2,3-Wood-a(3) each, photo-c 26.00 79.00 210.00

DOT DOTLAND (Formerly Little Dot Dotland)
Harvey Publications: No. 62, Sept, 1974 - No. 63, Nov, 1974
62,63 1.00 3.00 8.00

DOTTY (...& Her Boy Friends)(Formerly Four Teeners; Glamorous Romances No. 41 on)
Ace Magazines (A. A. Wyn): No. 35, June, 1948 - No. 40, May, 1949
35-Teen-age 6.40 19.25 45.00
36-40: 37-Transvestism story 4.00 12.00 24.00

DOTTY DRIPPLE (Horace & Dotty Dripple No. 25 on)
Magazine Ent.(Life's Romances)/Harvey No. 3 on: 1946 - No. 24, June, 1952 (Also see A-1 No. 3-8, 10)
A-1 #1 (1pg. D. Dripple; Mr. Ex, Bush Berry, Rocky, Lew Loyal (20 pgs.) 10.00 30.00 80.00
1 (nd) (10¢) 7.85 23.50 55.00
2 4.30 13.00 26.00
3-10: 3,4-Powell-a 3.60 9.00 18.00
11-24 2.40 6.00 12.00

DOTTY DRIPPLE AND TAFFY
Dell Publishing Co.: No. 646, Sept, 1955 - No. 903, May, 1958
Four Color 646 (#1) 3.20 9.60 35.00
Four Color 691,718,746,801,903 2.40 7.35 22.00

DOUBLE ACTION COMICS
National Periodical Publications: No. 2, Jan, 1940 (68 pgs., B&W)
2-Contains original stories(?); pre-hero DC contents; same cover as Adventure No. 37. (seven known copies, five in high grade) (not an ashcan) 1445.00 4335.00 13,000.00
NOTE: *The cover to this book was probably reprinted from Adventure #37. #1 exists as an ash can copy with B&W cover; contains a coverless comic on inside with 1st & last page missing. Two copies exist in fair & fine condition proving at least limited newsstand distribution.*

DOUBLE COMICS
Elliot Publications: 1940 - 1944 (132 pgs.)
1940 issues; Masked Marvel-c & The Mad Mong vs. The White Flash covers known 221.00 663.00 2100.00
1941 issues; Tornado Tim-c, Nordac-c, & Green Light covers known 153.00 458.00 1450.00
1942 issues 113.00 340.00 1075.00
1943,1944 issues 92.00 276.00 875.00
NOTE: *Double Comics consisted of an almost endless combination of pairs of remaindered, unsold issues of comics representing most publishers and usually mixed publishers in the same book; e.g., a Captain America with a Silver Streak, or a Feature with a Detective, etc., could appear inside the same cover. The actual contents would have to determine its price. Prices listed are for average contents. Any containing rare origin or first issues are worth much more. Covers also vary in same year. Value would be approximately 50 percent of contents.*

DOUBLE-CROSS (See The Crusaders)

DOUBLE-DARE ADVENTURES
Harvey Publications: Dec, 1966 - No. 2, Mar, 1967 (35¢/25¢, 68 pgs.)
1-Origin Bee-Man, Glowing Gladiator, & Magic-Master; Simon/Kirby-a (last S&K art as a team?) 5.45 16.35 60.00
2-Williamson/Crandall-a; r/Alarming Adv. #3('63) 4.10 12.30 45.00
NOTE: ***Powell** a-1. **Simon/Sparling** c-1, 2.*

DOUBLE DRAGON
Marvel Comics: July, 1991 - No. 6, Dec, 1991 ($1.00, limited series)
1-6: Based on video game. 2-Art Adams-c 2.00

DOUBLE EDGE
Marvel Comics: Alpha, 1995; Omega, 1995 ($4.95, limited series)
Alpha ($4.95)- Punisher story, Nick Fury app. 5.00
Omega ($4.95)-Punisher, Daredevil, Ghost Rider app. Death of Nick Fury 5.00

DOUBLE LIFE OF PRIVATE STRONG, THE
Archie Publications/Radio Comics: June, 1959 - No. 2, Aug, 1959
1-Origin & re-intro The Shield; Simon & Kirby-c/a, their re-entry into the super-hero genre; intro./1st app. The Fly; 1st S.A. super-hero for Archie Publ. 50.00 150.00 650.00
2-S&K-c/a; Tuska-a; The Fly app. (2nd or 3rd?) 32.00 97.00 390.00

DOUBLE TROUBLE
St. John Publishing Co.: Nov, 1957 - No. 2, Jan-Feb, 1958
1,2: Tuffy & Snuffy by Frank Johnson; dubbed "World's Funniest Kids" 5.00 15.00 35.00

DOUBLE TROUBLE WITH GOOBER
Dell Publishing Co.: No. 417, Aug, 1952 - No. 556, May, 1954
Four Color 417 3.00 9.00 30.00
Four Color 471,516,556 2.00 6.00 18.00

DOUBLE UP
Elliott Publications: 1941 (Pocket size, 200 pgs.)
1-Contains rebound copies of digest sized issues of Pocket Comics, Speed Comics, & Spitfire Comics 76.00 229.00 725.00

DOVER & CLOVER (See All Funny & More Fun Comics #93)

DOVER BOYS (See Adventures of the...)

DOVER THE BIRD
Famous Funnies Publishing Co.: Spring, 1955
1-Funny animal; code approved 5.70 17.00 40.00

DOWN WITH CRIME
Fawcett Publications: Nov, 1952 - No. 7, Nov, 1953
1 31.00 94.00 250.00
2,4,5: 2,4-Powell-a in each. 5-Bondage-c 16.00 49.00 130.00
3-Used in **POP**, pg. 106; "H is for Heroin" drug story 18.00 53.00 140.00
6,7: 6-Used in **POP**, pg. 80 13.00 39.00 105.00

DO YOU BELIEVE IN NIGHTMARES?
St. John Publishing Co.: Nov, 1957 - No. 2, Jan, 1958
1-Mostly Ditko-c/a 48.00 145.00 435.00
2-Ayers-a 29.00 87.00 235.00

D.P. 7
Marvel Comics Group (New Universe): Nov, 1986 - No. 32, June, 1989
1-32, Annual #1 (11/87)-Intro. The Witness 2.00
NOTE: ***Williamson** a-9i, 11i; c-9i.*

The Dragon #2 © Erik Larsen

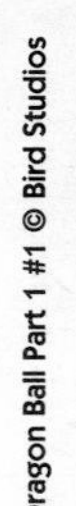

Dragon Ball Part 1 #1 © Bird Studios

Dragonheart #2 © Universal Studios

DRACULA (See Bram Stoker's Dracula, Giant-Size..., Little Dracula, Marvel Graphic Novel, Requiem for Dracula, Spider-Man Vs...., Tomb of... & Wedding of...; also see Movie Classics under Universal Presents as well as Dracula)

DRACULA (See Movie Classics for #1)(Also see Frankenstein & Werewolf)
Dell Publ. Co.: No. 2, 11/66 - No. 4, 3/67; No. 6, 7/72 - No. 8, 7/73 (No #5)

2-Origin & 1st app. Dracula (11/66) (super hero) 3.00 9.00 32.00
3,4: 4-Intro. Fleeta ('67) 2.30 7.00 20.00
6-('72)-r/#2 w/origin 2.00 6.00 18.00
7,8-r/#3, #4 1.75 5.25 14.00

DRACULA (Magazine)
Warren Publishing Co.: 1979 (120 pgs., full color)

Book 1-Maroto art; Spanish material translated into English 4.35 13.00 48.00

DRACULA CHRONICLES
Topps Comics: Apr, 1995 - No. 3, June, 1995 ($2.50, limited series)

1-3-Linsner-c 2.50

DRACULA LIVES! (Magazine)(Also see Tomb of Dracula)
Marvel Comics Group: 1973(no month) - No. 13, July, 1975 (75¢, B&W) (76 pgs.)

1-Boris painted-c 3.80 11.40 42.00
2 (7/73)-1st time origin Dracula; Adams, Starlin-a 3.00 9.00 30.00
3-1st app. Robert E. Howard's Soloman Kane; Adams-c/a 3.00 9.00 30.00
4,5: 4-Ploog-a. 5(V2#1)-Bram Stoker's Classic Dracula adapt. begins 2.30 7.00 20.00
6-9: 6-8-Bram Stoker adapt. 9-Bondage-c 2.50 7.50 23.00
10 (1/75)-16 pg. Lilith solo (1st?) 3.00 9.00 30.00
11-13: 11-21 pg. Lilith solo sty. 12-31 pg. Dracula sty 2.50 7.50 23.00
Annual 1(Summer, 1975, $1.25, 92 pgs.)-Morrow painted-c; 6 Dracula stys. 25 pgs. Adams-a(r) 2.60 7.80 26.00

NOTE: ***N. Adams** a-2, 3i, 10i, Annual 1r(2, 3i). **Alcala** a-9. **Buscema** a-3p, 6p, Annual 1p. **Colan** a(p)-1, 2, 5, 6, 8. **Evans** a-7. **Gulacy** a-9. **Heath** a-1r, 13. **Pakula** a-6r. Sutton a-13. **Weiss** r-Annual 1p. 4 **Dracula** stories each in 1, 609; 3 **Dracula** stories each in 2, 4, 5,, 13.*

DRACULA: LORD OF THE UNDEAD
Marvel Comics: Dec, 1998 - No. 3, Dec, 1998 ($2.99, limited series)

1-3-Olliffe & Palmer-a 3.00

DRACULA: RETURN OF THE IMPALER
Slave Labor Graphics: July, 1993 - No. 4, Oct, 1994 ($2.95, limited series)

1-4 3.00

DRACULA VERSUS ZORRO
Topps Comics: Oct, 1993 - No. 2, Nov, 1993 ($2.95, limited series)

1,2: 1-Spot varnish & red foil-c. 2-Polybagged w/16 pg. Zorro #0 3.00

DRACULA VERSUS ZORRO
Dark Horse Comics: Sept, 1998 - No. 2, Oct, 1998 ($2.95, limited series)

1,2 3.00

DRACULA: VLAD THE IMPALER (Also see Bram Stoker's Dracula)
Topps Comics: Feb, 1993 - No. 3, Apr, 1993 ($2.95, limited series)

1-3-Polybagged with 3 trading cards each; Maroto-c/a 3.00

DRAFT, THE
Marvel Comics: 1988 ($3.50, one-shot, squarebound)

1-Sequel to "The Pitt" 3.50

DRAG 'N' WHEELS (Formerly Top Eliminator)
Charlton Comics: No. 30, Sept, 1968 - No. 59, May, 1973

30 3.65 11.00 40.00
31-40-Scot Jackson begins 2.80 8.40 28.00
41-50 2.50 7.50 23.00
51-59: Scot Jackson 1.75 5.25 14.00
Modern Comics Reprint 58('78) 4.00

DRAGON, THE (Also see The Savage Dragon)
Image Comics (Highbrow Ent.): Mar, 1996 - No. 5, July, 1996 (99¢, lim. series)

1-5: Reprints Savage Dragon limited series w/new story & art. 5-Youngblood app; includes 5 pg. Savage Dragon story from 1984 2.00

DRAGON ARCHIVES, THE (Also see The Savage Dragon)
Image Comics: Jun, 1998 - No. 4, Jan, 1999 ($2.95, B&W)

1-4: Reprints early Savage Dragon app. 3.00

DRAGON, THE: BLOOD & GUTS (Also see The Savage Dragon)
Image Comics (Highbrow Entertainment): Mar, 1995 - No. 3, May, 1995 ($2.50, limited series)

1-3: Jason Pearson-c/a/scripts 2.50

DRAGON BALL
Viz Comics: 1998 - Present ($2.95, B&W, Manga reprints read right to left)

Part 1: 1-Akira Toriyama-s/a 1.00 2.80 7.00
2-12 4.00
1-12 (2nd & 3rd printings) 3.00
Part 2: 1-15: 15-($3.50-c) 3.50
Part 3: 1-14 2.95

DRAGON BALL Z
Viz Comics: 1998 - Present ($2.95, B&W, Manga reprints read right to left)

Part 1: 1-Akira Toriyama-s/a 1.50 4.50 12.00
2-9 5.00
1-9 (2nd & 3rd printings) 3.00
Part 2: 1-14 3.50
Part 3: 1-10 2.95
Part 4: 1-5 2.95

DRAGON CHIANG
Eclipse Books: 1991 ($3.95, B&W, squarebound, 52 pgs.)

nn -Timothy Truman-c/a(p) 4.00

DRAGONFLIGHT
Eclipse Books: Feb, 1991 - No. 3, 1991 ($4.95, 52 pgs.)

Book One - Three: Adapts 1968 novel 5.00

DRAGONFLY (See Americomics #4)
Americomics: Sum, 1985 - No. 8, 1986 ($1.75/$1.95)

1 3.00
2-8 2.00

DRAGONFORCE
Aircel Publishing: 1988 - No. 13, 1989 ($2.00)

1-Dale Keown-c/a/scripts in #1-12 3.00
2-13: 13-No Keown-a 2.00
...Chronicles Book 1-5 ($2.95, B&W, 60 pgs.): Dale Keown-r/Dragonring & Dragonforce 3.00

DRAGONHEART (Movie)
Topps Comics: May, 1996 - No. 2, June, 1996 ($2.95/$4.95, limited series)

1-($2.95, 24 pgs.)-Adaptation of the film; Hildebrandt Bros-c; Lim-a. 3.00
2-($4.95, 64 pgs.) 5.00

DRAGONLANCE (Also see TSR Worlds)
DC Comics: Dec, 1988 - No. 34, Sept, 1991 ($1.25/$1.50, Mando paper)

1, Annual 1 (1990, $2.95, 68 pgs.) 3.00
2-34: Based on TSR game. 30-32-Kaluta-c 2.00

DRAGON LINES
Marvel Comics (Epic Comics/Heavy Hitters): May, 1993 - No. 4, Aug, 1993 ($1.95, limited series)

1-($2.50)-Embossed-c; Ron Lim-c/a in all 2.50
2-4 2.00

DRAGON LINES: WAY OF THE WARRIOR
Marvel Comics (Epic Comics/ Heavy Hitters): Nov, 1993 - No. 2, Jan, 1994 ($2.25, limited series)

1,2-Ron Lim-c/a(p) 2.25

DRAGONQUEST
Silverwolf Comics: Dec, 1986 - No. 2, 1987 ($1.50, B&W, 28 pgs.)

1,2-Tim Vigil-c/a in all 3.00

DRAGONRING

Drakuun #19 © Johji Manabe

The Dreaming #56 © DC

Dreams of the Darkchylde #1 © Randy Queen

GD2.0 FN6.0 NM9.4

Aircel Publishing: 1986 - V2#15, 1988 ($1.70/$2.00, B&W/color)
1-6: 6-Last B&W issue, V2#1-15($2.00, color) 2.00

DRAGON'S CLAWS
Marvel UK, Ltd.: July, 1988 - No. 10, Apr, 1989 ($1.25/$1.50/$1.75, British)
1-10: 3-Death's Head 1 pg. strip on back-c (1st app.). 4-Silhouette of Death's Head on last pg. 5-1st full app. new Death's Head 2.00

DRAGONSLAYER (Movie)
Marvel Comics Group: October, 1981 - No. 2, Nov, 1981
1,2-Paramount Disney movie adaptation 3.00

DRAGON'S STAR 2
Caliber Press: 1994 ($2.95, B&W)
1 3.00

DRAGON STRIKE
Marvel Comics: Feb, 1994 ($1.25)
1-Based on TSR role playing game 2.00

DRAGOON WELLS MASSACRE
Dell Publishing Co.: No. 815, June, 1957
Four Color 815-Movie, photo-c 7.50 22.50 90.00

DRAGSTRIP HOTRODDERS (World of Wheels No. 17 on)
Charlton Comics: Sum, 1963; No. 2, Jan, 1965 - No. 16, Aug, 1967
1 5.45 16.35 60.00
2-5 3.20 9.60 35.00
6-16 2.80 8.40 28.00

DRAKUUN
Dark Horse Comics: Feb, 1997 - Present ($2.95, B&W, manga)
1-25; 1-6- Johji Manabe-s/a in all. Rise of the Dragon Princess series. 7-12-Revenge of Gustav. 13-18-Shadow of the Warlock. 19-25-The Hidden War 3.00

DRAMA
Sirius: June, 1994 ($2.95, mature)
1-1st full color Dawn app. in comics 2.50 7.50 20.00
1-Limited edition (1400 copies); signed & numbered; fingerprint authenticity 4.50 13.50 50.00
NOTE: *Dawn's 1st full color app. was a pin-up in Amazing Heroes' Swimsuit Special #5.*

DRAMA OF AMERICA, THE
Action Text: 1973 ($1.95, 224 pgs.)
1- "Students' Supplement to History" 5.00

DREADLANDS (Also see Epic)
Marvel Comics (Epic Comics): 1992 - No. 4, 1992 ($3.95, lim. series, 52 pgs.)
1-4: Stiff-c 4.00

DREADSTAR
Marvel Comics (Epic Comics)/First Comics No. 27 on: Nov, 1982 - No. 64, Mar, 1991
1-5,8-49 3.00
6,7,51-64: 6,7-1st app. Interstellar Toybox; 8pgs. ea.; Wrightson-a 4.00
50 5.00
Annual 1 (12/83)-r/The Price 4.00

DREADSTAR
Malibu Comics (Bravura): Apr, 1994 - No.6, Jan, 1995 ($2.50, limited series)
1-6-Peter David scripts: 1,2-Starlin-c 2.50
NOTE: *Issues 1-6 contain Bravura stamps.*

DREADSTAR AND COMPANY
Marvel Comics (Epic Comics): July, 1985 - No. 6, Dec, 1985
1-6: 1,3,6-New Starlin-a: 2-New Wrightson-c; reprints of Dreadstar series. 2.00

DREAM BOOK OF LOVE (Also see A-1 Comics)
Magazine Enterprises: No. 106, June-July, 1954 - No. 123, Oct-Nov, 1954
A-1 106 (#1)-Powell, Bolle-a; Montgomery Clift, Donna Reed photo-c 11.00 33.00 90.00
A-1-114 (#2)-Guardineer, Bolle-a; Piper Laurie, Victor Mature photo-c 10.00 30.00 70.00
A-1 123 (#3)-Movie photo-c 8.65 26.00 60.00

DREAM BOOK OF ROMANCE (Also see A-1 Comics)
Magazine Enterprises: No. 92, 1954 - No. 124, Oct-Nov, 1954
A-1 92 (#5)-Guardineer-a; photo-c 10.00 30.00 75.00
A-1 101 (#6)(4-6/54)-Marlon Brando photo-c; Powell, Bolle, Guardineer-a 18.00 53.00 140.00
A-1 109,110,124: 109 (#7)(7-8/54)-Powell-a; movie photo-c. 110 (#8)(1/54)-Movie photo-c. 124 (#8)(10-11/54) 8.65 26.00 60.00

DREAMER, THE
Kitchen Sink Press: 1986 ($6.95, B&W, graphic novel)
nn-Will Eisner-s/a 8.00
DC Comics Reprint ($7.95, 6/00) 7.95

DREAMERY, THE
Eclipse Comics: Dec, 1986 - No. 14, Feb, 1989 ($2.00, B&W, Baxter paper)
1-14: 2-7-Alice In Wonderland adapt. 2.00

DREAMING, THE (See Sandman, 2nd Series)
DC Comics (Vertigo): June, 1996 - No. 60, May, 2001 ($2.50)
1-McKean-c on all.; LaBan scripts & Snejbjerg-a 4.00
2-30,32-60: 2,3-LaBan scripts & Snejbjerg-a. 4-7-Hogan scripts; Parkhouse-a. 8-Zulli-a. 9-11-Talbot-s/Taylor-a(p). 41-Previews Sandman: The Dream Hunters. 50-Hempel, Fegredo, McManus, Totleben-a 2.50
31-($3.95) Art by various 4.00
...Beyond The Shores of Night TPB ('97, $19.95) r/#1-8 20.00
...Special (7/98, $5.95, one-shot) Trial of Cain 6.00
...Through The Gates of Horn and Ivory TPB ('99, $19.95) r/#15-19,22-25 20.00

DREAM OF LOVE
I. W. Enterprises: 1958 (Reprints)
1,2,8: 1-r/Dream Book of Love #1; Bob Powell-a. 2-r/Great Lover's Romances #10. 8-Great Lover's Romances #1; also contains 2 Jon Juan stories by Siegel & Schomburg; Kinstler-c. 1.85 5.50 15.00
9-Kinstler-c; 1pg. John Wayne interview & Frazetta illo from John Wayne Adv. Comics #2 1.85 5.50 15.00

DREAMS OF THE DARKCHYLDE
Darkchylde Entertainment: Oct, 2000 - Present ($2.95)
1-3-Randy Queen-s/Brandon Peterson-c/a 3.00

DREAM TEAM (See Battlezones: Dream Team 2)
Malibu Comics (Ultraverse): July, 1995 ($4.95, one-shot)
1-Pin-ups teaming up Marvel & Ultraverse characters by various artists including Allred, Romita, Darrow, Balent, Quesada & Palmiotti 5.00

DREAMWALKER
Dreamwalker Press: 1996 - No. 5, 1996 ($2.95, B&W)
1-5-Jenni Gregory-c/s/a 3.00

DREAMWALKER (Volume 2)
Caliber Comics (Tapestry): Dec, 1996 - No. 6, Jul, 1998 ($2.95, B&W)
1-6-Jenni Gregory-c/s/a 3.00

DREAMWALKER
Avatar Press: Jenni Gregory-c/s/a in all
#0 (11/98, $3.00) 3.00
--AUTUMN LEAVES, 9/99 - No. 2, 10/99 ($3.00) 1,2-wraparound-c 3.00
--CAROUSEL, 3/99 - No. 2, 4/99 ($3.00) 1,2 3.00
--SUMMER RAIN, 7/99 ($3.00, one-shot) 1 3.00

DRIFT FENCE (See Zane Grey 4-Color 270)

DRIFT MARLO
Dell Publishing Co.: May-July, 1962 - No. 2, Oct-Dec, 1962
01-232-207 (#1) 3.65 11.00 40.00
2 (12-232-212) 3.65 11.00 40.00

DRISCOLL'S BOOK OF PIRATES
David McKay Publ. (Not reprints): 1934 (B&W, hardcover; 124 pgs, 7x9")
nn-By Montford Amory 22.00 66.00 175.00

DROIDS (Also see Dark Horse Comics)

Ducktales #7 © WDC

Duncan's Kingdom #1 © Gene Yang & Derek Kirk

The Durango Kid #5 © ME

GD2.0 FN6.0 NM9.4

Marvel Comics (Star Comics): April, 1986 - No. 8, June, 1987
(Based on Saturday morning cartoon)
1-R2D2 & C-3PO from Star Wars app. in all 2.00 6.00 18.00
2-8: 2,5,7,8-Williamson-a(i) 1.40 4.15 11.00
NOTE: ***Romita** a-3p. **Sinnott** a-3i.*

DROOPY (see Tom & Jerry #60)

DROOPY (Tex Avery's...)
Dark Horse Comics: Oct, 1995 - No. 3, Dec, 1995 ($2.50, limited series)
1-3: Characters created by Tex Avery; painted-c 2.50

DROPSIE AVENUE: THE NEIGHBORHOOD
Kitchen Sink Press: June, 1995 ($15.95/$24.95, B&W)
nn-Will Eisner (softcover) 16.00
nn-Will Eisner (hardcover) 25.00

DROWNED GIRL, THE
DC Comics (Piranha Press): 1990 ($5.95, 52 pgs, mature)
nn 6.00

DRUG WARS
Pioneer Comics: 1989 ($1.95)
1-Grell-c 2.00

DRUID
Marvel Comics: May, 1995 - No. 4, Aug, 1995 ($2.50, limited series)
1-4: Warren Ellis scripts. 2.50

DRUM BEAT
Dell Publishing Co.: No. 610, Jan, 1955
Four Color 610-Movie, Alan Ladd photo-c 9.00 27.00 100.00

DRUMS OF DOOM
United Features Syndicate: 1937 (25¢)(Indian)(Text w/color illos.)
nn-By Lt. F.A. Methot; Golden Thunder app.; Tip Top Comics ad in comic; nice-c
34.00 101.00 270.00

DRUNKEN FIST
Jademan Comics: Aug, 1988 - No. 54, Jan, 1993 ($1.50/$1.95, 68 pgs.)
1-54 2.00

DUCK ALBUM (See Donald Duck Album)
Dell Publishing Co.: No. 353, Oct, 1951 - No. 840, Sept, 1957
Four Color 353 (#1)-Barks-c; 1st Uncle Scrooge-c (also appears on back-c).
8.35 25.00 100.00
Four Color 450-Barks-c 5.85 17.50 70.00
Four Color 492,531,560,586,611,649,686, 4.60 13.75 55.00
Four Color 726,782,840 4.60 13.75 55.00

DUCKMAN
Dark Horse Comics: Sept, 1990 ($1.95, B&W, one-shot)
1-Story & art by Everett Peck 2.00

DUCKMAN
Topps Comics: Nov, 1994 - No. 5, May, 1995; No. 0, Feb, 1996 ($2.50)
0 (2/96, $2.95, B&W)-r/Duckman #1 from Dark Horse Comics 4.00
1-5: 1-w/ coupon #A for Duckman trading card. 2-w/Duckman 1st season episode guide 3.00

DUCKMAN: THE MOB FROG SAGA
Topps Comics: Nov, 1994 - No. 3, Feb, 1995 ($2.50, limited series)
1-3: 1-w/coupon #B for Duckman tradiing card, S. Shaw!-c 2.50

DUCKTALES
Gladstone Publ.: Oct, 1988 - No. 13, May, 1990 (1,2,9-11: $1.50; 3-8: 95¢)
1-Barks-r 2.40 6.00
2-11: Barks-r 4.00
12,13 ($1.95, 68 pgs.)-Barks-r; 12-r/F.C. #495 5.00

DUCKTALES (TV)
Disney Comics: June, 1990 - No. 18, Nov, 1991 ($1.50)
1-All new stories 3.00
2-18 2.00

GD2.0 FN6.0 NM9.4

The Movie nn (1990, $7.95, 68 pgs.)-Graphic novel adapting animated movie 9.00

DUDLEY (Teen-age)
Feature/Prize Publications: Nov-Dec, 1949 - No. 3, Mar-Apr, 1950
1-By Boody Rogers 14.00 43.00 115.00
2,3 10.00 30.00 75.00

DUDLEY DO-RIGHT (TV)
Charlton Comics: Aug, 1970 - No. 7, Aug, 1971 (Jay Ward)
1 8.65 26.00 95.00
2-7 6.35 19.00 70.00

DUKE OF THE K-9 PATROL
Gold Key: Apr, 1963
1 (10052-304) 3.20 9.60 35.00

DUMBO (Disney; see Movie Comics, & Walt Disney Showcase #12)
Dell Publishing Co.: No. 17, 1941 - No. 668, Jan, 1958
Four Color 17 (#1)-Mickey Mouse, Donald Duck, Pluto app.
183.00 550.00 2200.00
Large Feature Comic 19 ('41)-Part-r 4-Color 17 250.00 750.00 3000.00
Four Color 234 ('49) 10.00 30.00 120.00
Four Color 668 (12/55)-1st of two printings. Dumbo on-c with starry sky. Reprints Four Color 234? same-c as 234 8.35 25.00 100.00
Four Color 668 (1/58)-2nd printing. Same cover altered with Timothy Mouse added. Same contents as above 5.85 17.50 70.00

DUMBO COMIC PAINT BOOK (See Dumbo, Large Feature Comic No. 19)

DUNC AND LOO (#1-3 titled "Around the Block with Dunc and Loo")
Dell Publishing Co.: Oct-Dec, 1961 - No. 8, Oct-Dec, 1963
1 9.00 27.00 110.00
2 5.85 17.50 70.00
3-8 4.55 13.65 50.00
NOTE: *Written by **John Stanley; Bill Williams** art.*

DUNCAN'S KINGDOM
Image Comics: 1999 - No. 2, 1999 ($2.95, B&W, limited series)
1,2-Gene Yang-s/Derek Kirk-a 2.95

DUNE (Movie)
Marvel Comics: Apr, 1985 - No. 3, June, 1985
1-3-r/Marvel Super Special; movie adaptation 3.00

DUNG BOYS, THE
Kitchen Sink Press: 1996 - No. 3, 1996 ($2.95, B&W, limited series)
1-3 3.00

DURANGO KID, THE (Also see Best of the West, Great Western & White Indian) (Charles Starrett starred in Columbia's Durango Kid movies)
Magazine Enterprises: Oct-Nov, 1949 - No. 41, Oct-Nov, 1955 (All 36 pgs.)
1-Charles Starrett photo-c; Durango Kid & his horse Raider begin; Dan Brand & Tipi (origin) begin by Frazetta & continue through #16
71.00 212.00 675.00
2-Starrett photo-c. 38.00 113.00 300.00
3-5-All have Starrett photo-c. 35.00 105.00 280.00
6-10: 7-Atomic weapon-c/story 19.00 56.00 150.00
11-16-Last Frazetta issue 13.00 39.00 105.00
17-Origin Durango Kid 19.00 56.00 150.00
18-30: 18-Fred Meagher-a on Dan Brand begins.19-Guardineer-c/a(3) begins, end #41. 23-Intro. The Red Scorpion 10.00 30.00 80.00
31-Red Scorpion returns 10.00 30.00 75.00
32-41-Bolle/Frazettaish-a (Dan Brand; true in later issues?)
10.00 30.00 75.00
NOTE: *#6, 8, 14, 15 contain **Frazetta** art not reprinted in White Indian. **Ayers** c-18. **Guardineer** a(3)-19-41; c-19-41. **Fred Meagher** a-18-29 at least.*

DURANGO KID, THE
AC Comics: 1990 - #2, 1990 ($2.50,$2.75, half-color)
1,2: 1-Starrett photo front/back-c; Guardineer-r. 2-B&W)-Starrett photo-c; White Indian-r by Frazetta; Guardineer-r (50th anniversary of films) 2.75

DUSTCOVERS: THE COLLECTED SANDMAN COVERS 1989-1997

DV8 #3 © WSP

Dynamic Comics #11 © CHES

Earth Man on Venus nn © AVON

GD2.0 FN6.0 NM9.4

DC Comics (Vertigo): 1997 ($39.95, Hardcover)

Reprints Dave McKean's Sandman covers with Gaiman text 40.00
Softcover (1998, $24.95) 30.00

DUSTY STAR
Image Comics (Desperado Studios): Apr, 1997 - Present ($2.95, B&W)

0,1-Pruett-s/Robinson-a 3.00

DV8 (See Gen 13)
Image Comics (WildStorm Productions): Aug, 1996 - No. 25, Dec, 1998; **DC Comics (WildStorm Prod.):** No. 0, Apr, 1999 - No. 32, Nov, 1999 ($2.50)

1/2 2.40 6.00
1-Warren Ellis scripts & Humberto Ramos-c/a(p) 4.00
1-(7-variant covers, w/1 by Jim Lee...each 4.00
2-4: 3-No Ramos-a 3.00
5-32: 14-Regular-c, 14-Variant-c by Charest. 26-(5/99)-McGuinness-c 2.50
14-($3.50) Voyager Pack w/Danger Girl preview 5.00
0-(4/99, $2.95) Two covers (Rio and McGuinness) 3.00
Annual 1 (1/98, $2.95) 3.00
Annual 1999 ($3.50) Slipstream x-over with Gen13 3.50
Rave-(7/96, $1.75)-Ramos-c; pinups & interviews 3.00

DV8 VS. BLACK OPS
Image Comics (WildStorm): Oct, 1997 - No. 3, Dec, 1997 ($2.50, lim. series)

1-3-Bury-s/Norton-a 3.00

DWIGHT D. EISENHOWER
Dell Publishing Co.: December, 1969

01-237-912 - Life story 2.50 7.50 24.00

DYLAN DOG
Dark Horse (Bonelli Comics): Mar, 1999 - No. 6, Aug, 1999 ($4.95, B&W, digest size)

1-6-Reprints Italian series in English; Mignola-c 5.00

DYNABRITE COMICS
Whitman Publishing Co.: 1978 - 1979 (69¢, 10x7-1/8", 48 pgs., cardboard-c) (Blank inside covers)

11350 - Walt Disney's Mickey Mouse & the Beanstalk (4-C 157). 11350-1 - Mickey Mouse Album (4-C 1057,1151,1246). 11351 - Mickey Mouse & His Sky Adventure (4-C 214, 343). 11352 - Donald Duck (4-C 408, Donald Duck 45,52)-Barks-a. 11352-1 - Donald Duck (4-C 318, 10 pg. Barks/WDC&S 125,128)-Barks-c(r). 11353 - Daisy Duck's Diary (4-C 1055,1150) Barks-a. 11354 - Goofy: A Gaggle of Giggles. 11354-1 - Super Goof Meets Super Thief. 11355 - Uncle Scrooge (Barks-a/U.S. 12,33). 11355-1 - Uncle Scrooge (Barks-a/U.S. 13,16) - Barks-c(r). 11356 - (?). 11357 - Star Trek (r/-Star Trek 33,41). 11358 - Star Trek (r/-Star Trek 34,36). 11359 - Bugs Bunny-r. 11360 - Winnie the Pooh Fun and Fantasy (Disney-r). 11361 - Gyro Gearloose & the Disney Ducks (r/4-C 1047,1184)-Barks-c(r)
each.... 6.00

DYNAMIC ADVENTURES
I. W. Enterprises: No. 8, 1964 - No. 9, 1964

8-Kayo Kirby-r by Baker?/Fight Comics 53. 2.50 7.50 24.00
9-Reprints Avon's "Escape From Devil's Island"; Kinstler-c
2.50 7.50 25.00
nn (no date)-Reprints Risks Unlimited with Rip Carson, Senorita Rio; r/Fight #53
2.50 7.50 24.00

DYNAMIC CLASSICS (See Cancelled Comic Cavalcade)
DC Comics: Sept-Oct, 1978 (44 pgs.)

1-Neal Adams Batman, Simonson Manhunter-r 6.00

DYNAMIC COMICS (No #4-7)
Harry 'A' Chesler: Oct, 1941 - No. 3, Feb, 1942; No. 8, Mar, 1944 - No. 25, May, 1948

1-Origin Major Victory by Charles Sultan (reprinted in Major Victory #1), Dynamic Man & Hale the Magician; The Black Cobra only app.; Major Victory & Dynamic Man begin 168.00 505.00 1600.00
2-Origin Dynamic Boy & Lady Satan; intro. The Green Knight & sidekick Lance Cooper 79.00 237.00 750.00
3-1st small logo, resumes with #10 66.00 197.00 625.00
8-Classic-c; Dan Hastings, The Echo, The Master Key, Yankee Boy begin; Yankee Doodle Jones app.; hypo story 74.00 221.00 700.00
9-Mr. E begins; Mac Raboy-c 68.00 205.00 650.00

GD2.0 FN6.0 NM9.4

10-Small logo begins 53.00 158.00 475.00
11-16: 15-The Sky Chief app. 16-Marijuana story 44.00 133.00 400.00
17(1/46)-Illustrated in **SOTI**, "The children told me what the man was going to do with the hot poker," but Wertham saw this in Crime Reporter #2
61.00 182.00 575.00
18,19,21,22,25: 21-Dinosaur-c; new logo 39.00 118.00 315.00
20-Bare-breasted woman-c 63.00 189.00 600.00
23,24-(68 pgs.): 23-Yankee Girl app. 40.00 120.00 340.00
I.W. Reprint #1,8('64): 1-r/#23. 8-Exist? 3.00 9.00 30.00
NOTE: ***Kinstler*** *c-IW #1.* ***Tuska*** *art in many issues, #3, 9, 11, 12, 16, 19. Bondage c-16.*

DYNAMITE (Becomes Johnny Dynamite No. 10 on)
Comic Media/Allen Hardy Publ.: May, 1953 - No. 9, Sept, 1954

1-Pete Morisi-a; Don Heck-c; r-as Danger #6 21.00 64.00 170.00
2 12.00 36.00 95.00
3-Marijuana story; Johnny Dynamite (1st app.) begins by Pete Morisi(c/a); Heck text-a; man shot in face at close range 15.00 45.00 120.00
4-Injury-to-eye, prostitution; Morisi-c/a 16.00 49.00 130.00
5-9-Morisi-c/a in all. 7-Prostitute story plus reprints 10.50 32.00 85.00

DYNAMO (Also see Tales of Thunder & T.H.U.N.D.E.R. Agents)
Tower Comics: Aug, 1966 - No. 4, June, 1967 (25¢)

1-Crandall/Wood, Ditko/Wood-a; Weed series begins; NoMan & Lightning cameos; Wood-c/a 6.80 20.50 75.00
2-4: Wood-c/a in all 4.10 12.30 45.00
NOTE: ***Adkins/Wood*** *a-2.* ***Ditko*** *a-4?.* ***Tuska*** *a-2, 3.*

DYNAMO JOE (Also see First Adventures & Mars)
First Comics: May, 1986 - No. 15, Jan, 1988 (#12-15: $1.75)

1-15: 4-Cargonauts begin, Special 1(1/87)-Mostly-r/Mars 2.00

DYNOMUTT (TV)(See Scooby-Doo (3rd series))
Marvel Comics Group: Nov, 1977 - No. 6, Sept, 1978 (Hanna-Barbera)

1-The Blue Falcon, Scooby Doo in all 2.30 7.00 20.00
2-6-All newsstand only 1.85 5.50 15.00

EAGLE, THE (1st Series) (See Science Comics & Weird Comics #8)
Fox Features Syndicate: July, 1941 - No. 4, Jan, 1942

1-The Eagle begins; Rex Dexter of Mars app. by Briefer; all issues feature German war covers 179.00 537.00 1700.00
2-The Spider Queen begins (origin) 84.00 253.00 800.00
3,4: 3-Joe Spook begins (origin) 68.00 205.00 650.00

EAGLE (2nd Series)
Rural Home Publ.: Feb-Mar, 1945 - No. 2, Apr-May, 1945

1-Aviation stories 42.00 125.00 375.00
2-Lucky Aces 25.00 75.00 200.00
NOTE: ***L. B. Cole*** *c/a in each.*

EAGLE
Crystal Comics/Apple Comics #17 on: Sept, 1986 - No. 23, 1989 ($1.50/1.75/1.95, B&W)

1-23: 12-Double size origin issue ($2.50) 2.00
1-Signed and limited 3.00

EAGLES DARE
Aager comics, Inc.: Aug, 1994 - Present? ($1.95, B&W, limited series)

1,2 2.00

EARTH 4 (Also see Urth 4)
Continuity Comics: Dec, 1993 - No. 4, Jan, 1994 ($2.50)

1-4: 1-3 all listed as Dec, 1993 in indicia 2.50

EARTH 4 DEATHWATCH 2000
Continuity Comics: Apr, 1993 - No. 3, Aug, 1993 ($2.50)

1-3 2.50

EARTH MAN ON VENUS (An...) (Also see Strange Planets)
Avon Periodicals: 1951

nn-Wood-a (26 pgs.); Fawcette-c 124.00 373.00 1180.00

EARTHWORM JIM (TV, cartoon)
Marvel Comics: Dec, 1995 - No. 3, Feb, 1996 ($2.25)

1-3: Based on video game and toys 2.25

Earth X #9 © MAR

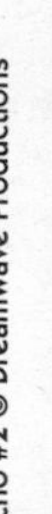
Echo #2 © Dreamwave Productions

Eddie Campbell's Bacchus #48 © Eddie Campbell

EARTH X
Marvel Comics: No. 0, Mar, 1999 - No. 12, Apr, 2000 ($3.99/$2.99, lim. series)

nn- (Wizard supplement) Alex Ross sketchbook; painted-c 5.00
Sketchbook (2/99) New sketches and previews 5.00
0-(3/99)-Prelude; Leon-a(p)/Ross-c 5.00
1-(4/99)-Leon-a(p)/Ross-c 6.00
1-2nd printing 3.00
2-12 3.00
#X (6/00, $3.99) 4.00
TPB (12/00, $24.95) r/#0,1-12, X; foreward by Joss Whedon 25.00

EASTER BONNET SHOP (See March of Comics No. 29)

EASTER WITH MOTHER GOOSE
Dell Publishing Co.: No. 103, 1946 - No. 220, Mar, 1949

Four Color 103 (#1)-Walt Kelly-a 18.35 55.00 220.00
Four Color 140 ('47)-Kelly-a 15.00 45.00 175.00
Four Color 185 ('48),220-Kelly-a 12.50 37.50 150.00

EAST MEETS WEST
Innovation Publishing: Apr, 1990 - No. 2, 1990 ($2.50, limited series, mature)

1,2: 1-Stevens part-i; Redondo-c(i). 2-Stevens-c(i); 1st app. Cheech & Chong in comics 2.50

E. C. CLASSIC REPRINTS
East Coast Comix Co.: May, 1973 - No. 12, 1976 (E. C. Comics reprinted in color minus ads)

1-The Crypt of Terror #1 (Tales from the Crypt #46) 1.75 5.25 14.00
2-12: 2-Weird Science #15('52). 3-Shock SuspenStories #12. 4-Haunt of Fear #12. 5-Weird Fantasy #13('52). 6-Crime SuspenStories #25. 7-Vault of Horror #26. 8-Shock SuspenStories #6. 9-Two-Fisted Tales #34. 10-Haunt of Fear #23. 11-Weird Science #12(#1). 12-Shock SuspenStories #2 1.10 3.30 9.00

EC CLASSICS
Russ Cochran: Aug, 1985 - No. 12, 1986? (High quality paper; each-r 8 stories in color) (#2-12 were resolicited in 1990)($4.95, 56 pgs., 8x11")

1-12: 1-Tales From the Crypt. 2-Weird Science. 3-Two-Fisted Tales (r/31); Frontline Combat (r/9). 4-Shock SuspenStories. 5-Weird Fantasy. 6-Vault of Horror. 7-Weird Science-Fantasy(r/23,24). 8-Crime SuspenStories (r/17,18). 9-Haunt of Fear (r/14,15). 10-Panic (r/1,2). 11-Tales From the Crypt (r/23,24). 12-Weird Science (r/20,22) 2.40 6.00

ECHO
Image Comics (Dreamwave Prod.): Mar, 2000 - Present ($2.50)

1-5: 1-3-Pat Lee-c 2.50
0-(7/00) 2.50

ECHO OF FUTUREPAST
Pacific Comics/Continuity Com.: May, 1984 - No. 9, Jan, 1986 ($2.95, 52 pgs.)

1-9: Neal Adams-c/a in all? 5.00
NOTE: ***N. Adams*** *a-1-6,7i,9i; c-1-3, 5p,7i,8,9i.* ***Golden*** *a-1-6 (Bucky O'Hare); c-6.* ***Toth*** *a-6,7.*

ECLIPSE GRAPHIC ALBUM SERIES
Eclipse Comics: Oct, 1978 - 1989 (8-1/2x11") (B&W #1-5)

1-Sabre (10/78, B&W, 1st print.); Gulacy-a; 1st direct sale graphic novel 14.00
1-Sabre (2nd printing, 1/79) 8.00
1-Sabre (3rd printing, $5.95) 6.00
3,4: 3-Detectives, Inc. (5/80, B&W, $6.95)-Rogers-a. 4-Stewart The Rat (1980, B&W)-G. Colan-a 9.00
5-The Price (10/81, B&W)-Starlin-a 15.00
2,6,7,13: 2-Night Music (11/79, B&W)-Russell-a. 6-I Am Coyote (11/84, color)-Rogers-c/a. 7-The Rocketeer (2nd print, $7.95). 7-The Rocketeer (3rd print, 1991, $8.95). 13-The Sisterhood of Steel ('87, $8.95, color) 10.00
7-The Rocketeer (9/85, color)-Dave Stevens-a (r/chapters 1-5)(see Pacific Presents & Starslayer); has 7 pgs. new-a 13.00
7-The Rocketeer, signed & limited HC 60.00
7-The Rocketeer, hardcover (1986, $19.95) 20.00
7-The Rocketeer, unsigned HC (3rd, $32.95) 33.00
8-Zorro In Old California ('86, color) 12.00
8,12-Hardcover 16.00
9,10: 9-Sacred And The Profane ('86)-Steacy-a. 10-Somerset Holmes ('86, $15.95)-Adults, soft-c 16.00
9,10,12-Hardcover ($24.95). 12-signed & #'d 25.00
11,14,16,18,20,23,24: 11-Floyd Farland, Citizen of the Future ('87, $3.95, B&W) 14-Samurai, Son of Death ('87, $4.95, B&W). 16,18,20,23-See Airfighters Classics #1-4. 24-Heartbreak ($4.95, B&W) 6.00
12,28,31,35: 12-Silverheels ('87, $7.95, color). 28-Miracleman Book I ($5.95) 31-Pigeons From Hell by R. E. Howard (11/88). 35-Rael: Into The Shadow of the Sun ('88, $7.95) 9.00
14,17,21,14-Samurai, Son of Death ($3.95, 2nd printing). 17-Valkyrie, Prisoner of the Past SC ('88, $3.95, color). 21-XYR-Multiple ending comic ('88, $3.95, B&W) 5.00
15,22,27: 15-Twisted Tales (11/87, color)-Dave Stevens-c. 22-Alien Worlds #1 (5/88, $3.95, 52 pgs.)-Nudity. 27-Fast Fiction (She) ($5.95, B&W) 7.00
17-Valkyrie, Prisoner of the Past S&N Hardcover ('88, $19.95) 20.00
19-Scout: The Four Monsters ('88, $14.95, color)-r/Scout #1-7; soft-c 15.00
25,30,32-34: 25-Alex Toth's Zorro Vol. 1 ,2($10.95, B&W). 30-Brought To Light; Alan Moore scripts ('89). 32-Teenaged Dope Slaves and Reform School Girls. 33-Bogie. 34-Air Fighters Classics #5 12.00
29-Real Love: Best of Simon & Kirby Romance Comics(10/88, $12.95) 14.00
30,31: Limited hardcover ed. ($29.95). 31-signed 30.00
36-Dr. Watchstop: Adventures in Time and Space ('89, $8.95) 9.00

ECLIPSE MAGAZINE (Becomes Eclipse Monthly)
Eclipse Publishing: May, 1981 - No. 8, Jan, 1983 ($2.95, B&W, magazine)

1-8: 1-1st app. Cap'n Quick and a Foozle by Rogers, Ms. Tree by Beatty, and Dope by Trina Robbins. 2-1st app. I Am Coyote by Rogers. 7-1st app. Masked Man by Boyer 5.00
NOTE: ***Colan*** *a-3, 5, 8.* ***Golden*** *c/a-2.* ***Gulacy*** *a-6, c-1, 6.* ***Kaluta*** *c/a-5.* ***Mayerik*** *a-2, 3.* ***Rogers*** *a-1-8.* ***Starlin*** *a-1.* ***Sutton*** *a-6.*

ECLIPSE MONTHLY
Eclipse Comics: Aug, 1983 - No. 10, Jul, 1984 (Baxter paper, $2.00/$1.50/$1.75)

1-10: ($2.00, 52 pgs.)-Cap'n Quick and a Foozle by Rogers, Static by Ditko, Dope by Trina Robbins, Rio by Doug Wildey, The Masked Man by Boyer begin. 3-Ragamuffins begins 3.00
NOTE: ***Boyer*** *c-6.* ***Ditko*** *a-1-3.* ***Rogers*** *a-1-4; c-2, 4, 7.* ***Wildey*** *a-1, 2, 5, 9, 10; c-5, 10.*

ECLIPSO (See Brave and the Bold #64, House of Secrets #61 & Phantom Stranger, 1987)
DC Comics: Nov, 1992 - No. 18, Apr, 1994 ($1.25)

1-18: 1-Giffen plots/breakdowns begin. 10-Darkseid app. Creeper in #3-6,9,11-13. 18-Spectre-c/s 2.00
Annual 1 (1993, $2.50, 68 pgs.)-Intro Prism 2.50

ECLIPSO: THE DARKNESS WITHIN
DC Comics: July, 1992 - No. 2, Oct, 1992 ($2.50, 68 pgs.)

1,2: 1-With purple gem attached to-c, 1-Without gem; Superman, Creeper app., 2-Concludes Eclipso storyline from annuals 2.50

E. C. 3-D CLASSICS (See Three Dimensional...)

ECTOKID (See Razorline)
Marvel Comics: Sept, 1993 - No. 9, May, 1994 ($1.75/$1.95)

1-($2.50)-Foil embossed-c; created by C. Barker 2.50
2-9: 2-Origin. 5-Saint Sinner x-over 2.00
...: Unleashed! 1 (10/94, $2.95, 52 pgs.) 3.00

ED "BIG DADDY" ROTH'S RATFINK COMIX (Also see Ratfink)
World of Fandom/ Ed Roth: 1991 - No. 3, 1991 ($2.50)

1-3: Regular Ed., 1-Limited double cover 1.25 3.75 10.00

EDDIE CAMPBELL'S BACCHUS
Eddie Campbell Comics: May, 1995 - Present ($2.95, B&W)

1-Cerebus app. 4.00
1-2nd printing (5/97) 3.00
2-56: 9-Alex Ross back-c 3.00
Doing The Islands With Bacchus ('97, $17.95) 18.00
Earth, Water, Air & Fire ('98, $9.95) 10.00
King Bacchus ('99, $12.95) 13.00
The Eyeball Kid ('98, $8.50) 8.50

EDDIE STANKY (Baseball Hero)

Edgar Rice Burroughs' Tarzan: The Return of Tarzan #1 © ERB

Eerie #10 © AVON

Eerie #84 © WP

GD2.0 FN6.0 NM9.4

vcett Publications: 1951 (New York Giants)
Photo-c 34.00 101.00 270.00

EN MATRIX, THE
nesive Comics: 1994 ($2.95)
2-Two variant-c; alternate-c on inside back-c 3.00

GAR BERGEN PRESENTS CHARLIE McCARTHY
itman Publishing Co. (Charlie McCarthy Co.): No. 764, 1938
pgs.; 15x10-1/2"; in color)
71.00 213.00 675.00

GAR RICE BURROUGHS' TARZAN: A TALE OF MUGAMBI
'k Horse Comics: 1995 ($2.95, one-shot)
3.00

GAR RICE BURROUGHS' TARZAN: IN THE LAND THAT TIME FORGOT D THE POOL OF TIME
'k Horse Comics: 1996 ($12.95, trade paperback)
r/Russ Manning-a 13.00

GAR RICE BURROUGHS' TARZAN OF THE APES
'k Horse Comics: May, 1999 ($12.95, trade paperback)
reprints 13.00

GAR RICE BURROUGHS' TARZAN: THE LOST ADVENTURE
'k Horse Comics: Jan, 1995 - No. 4, Apr, 1995 ($2.95, B&W, limited series)
4: ERB's last Tarzan story, adapted by Joe Lansdale 3.00
'dcover (12/95, $19.95) 20.00
ited Edition Hardcover ($99.95)-signed & numbered 100.00

GAR RICE BURROUGHS' TARZAN: THE RETURN OF TARZAN
'k Horse Comics: May, 1997 - No. 3, July, 1997 ($2.95, limited series)
3: 3.00

GAR RICE BURROUGHS' TARZAN: THE RIVERS OF BLOOD
'k Horse Comics: Nov, 1999 - No. 8 ($2.95, limited series)
3-Kordey-c/a 3.00

GE
ibu Comics (Bravura): July, 1994 - No. 3, Apr, 1995 ($2.50/$2.95, unfin-ed limited series)
2-S. Grant-story & Gil Kane-c/a; w/Bravura stamp 2.50
($2.95-c) 3.00

GE OF CHAOS
:ific Comics: July, 1983 - No. 3, Jan, 1984 (Limited series)
3-Morrow c/a; all contain nudity 2.00

WHEELAN'S JOKE BOOK STARRING FAT & SLAT (See Fat & Slat)

RIE (Strange Worlds No. 18 on)
on Per.: No. 1, Jan, 1947; No. 1, May-June, 1951 - No. 17, Aug-Sept, 1954
1947)-1st supernatural comic; Kubert, Fugitani-a; bondage-c
305.00 915.00 3200.00
1951)-Reprints story from 1947 #1 60.00 180.00 570.00
Wood-c/a; bondage-c 65.00 195.00 620.00
Wood-c; Kubert, Wood/Orlando-a 65.00 195.00 620.00
5-Wood-c 55.00 165.00 500.00
8,13,14: 8-Kinstler-a; bondage-c; Phantom Witch Doctor story
30.00 90.00 240.00
Wood/Orlando-c; Kubert-a 43.00 130.00 390.00
Kubert-a; Check-c 35.00 105.00 280.00
,11: 10-Kinstler-a. 11-Kinstlerish-a by McCann 29.00 86.00 230.00
-Dracula story from novel, 25 pgs. 36.00 107.00 285.00
-Reprints No. 1('51) minus-c(bondage) 23.00 68.00 180.00
-Wood-a r-/No. 2 23.00 68.00 180.00
-Wood/Orlando & Kubert-a; reprints #3 minus inside & outside Wood-c
28.00 83.00 220.00

TE: Hollingsworth a-9-11; c-10, 11.

RIE
'. Enterprises: 1964
. Reprint #1('64)-Wood-c(r); r-story/Spook #1 3.45 10.35 38.00

GD2.0 FN6.0 NM9.4

I.W. Reprint #2,6,8: 8-Dr. Drew by Grandenetti from Ghost #9
3.00 9.00 32.00
I.W. Reprint #9-r/Tales of Terror #1(Toby); Wood-c 3.80 11.40 42.00

EERIE (Magazine)(See Warren Presents)
Warren Publ. Co.: No. 1, Sept, 1965; No. 2, Mar, 1966 - No. 139, Feb, 1983

1-24 pgs., black & white, small size (5-1/4x7-1/4"), low distribution; cover from inside back cover of Creepy No. 2; stories reprinted from Creepy No. 7, 8. At least three different versions exist.

First Printing - B&W, 5-1/4" wide x 7-1/4" high, evenly trimmed. On page 18, panel 5, in the upper left-hand corner, the large rear view of a bald headed man blends into solid black and is unrecognizable. Overall printing quality is poor. 27.50 82.00 300.00

Second Printing - B&W, 5-1/4x7-1/4", with uneven, untrimmed edges (if one of these were trimmed evenly, the size would be less than as indicated). The figure of the bald headed man on page 18, panel 5 is clear and discernible. The staples have a 1/4" blue stripe.
12.75 38.00 140.00

Other unauthorized reproductions for comparison's sake would be practically worthless. One known version was probably shot off a first printing copy with some loss of detail; the finer lines tend to disappear in this version which can be determined by looking at the lower right-hand corner of page one, first story. The roof of the house is shaded with straight lines. These lines are sharp and distinct on original, but broken on this version.

NOTE: ***The Overstreet Comic Book Price Guide*** *recommends that, before buying a 1st issue, you consult an expert.*

2-Frazetta-c; Toth-a; 1st app. host Cousin Eerie 9.35 28.00 75.00
3-Frazetta-c & half pg. ad (rerun in #4); Toth, Williamson, Ditko-a
7.00 21.00 55.00
4-8: 4-Frazetta-a (1/2 pg. ad). 5,7,8-Frazetta-c. Ditko-a in all.
3.75 11.25 30.00
9-11,25: 9,10-Neal Adams-a, Ditko-a. 11-Karloff Mummy adapt.-Wood-s/a. 25-Steranko-c 4.00 12.00 32.00
12-16,18-22,24,32-35,40,45: 12,13,20-Poe-s. 12-Bloch-s. 12,15-Jones-a. 13-Lovecraft-s. 14,16-Toth-a. 16,19,24-Stoker-s. 16,32,33,43-Corben-a. 34-Early Boris-c. 35-Early Brunner-a. 35,40-Early Ploog-a. 40-Frankestein; Ploog-a (6/72, 6 months before Marvel's series) 3.00 9.00 24.00
17 (scarce) 10.00 30.00 85.00
23-Frazetta-c; Adams-a(reprint) 5.00 15.00 40.00
26-31,36-38,43,44 2.85 8.50 20.00
39,41: 39-1st Dax the Warrior; Maroto-a. 41 (scarce) 4.25 12.75 34.00
42,51: 42-('73 Annual, 84 pgs.) Spooktacular; Williamson-a. 51-('74 Annual, 76 pgs.) Color poster insert; Toth-a 4.00 12.00 32.00
46,48: 46-Dracula series by Sutton begins; 2pgs. Vampirella. 48-Begin "Mummy Walks" and "Curse of the Werewolf" series (both continue in #49,50,52,53)
3.15 9.45 22.00
47,49,50,52,53: 47-Lilith. 49-Marvin the Dead Thing. 50-Satanna, Daughter of Satan. 52-Hunter by Neary begins. 53-Adams-a 2.85 8.50 20.00
54,55-Color insert Spirit story by Eisner, reprints sections 12/21/47 & 6/16/46 54-Dr. Archaeus series begins 2.60 7.00 18.00
56,57,59,63,69,77,78: All have 8 pg. slick color insert. 56,57,77-Corben-a. 59-(100 pgs.) Summer Special, all Dax issue. 69-Summer Special, all Hunter issue, Neary-a. 78-All Mummy issue 2.60 7.00 18.00
58,60,62,68,72,: 8 pg. slick color insert & Wrightson-a in all. 58,60,62-Corben-a. 60-Summer Giant (9/74, $1.25) 1st Exterminator One; Wood-a. 62-Mummies Walk. 68-Summer Special (84 pgs.) 3.00 9.00 24.00
61,64-67,71: 61-Mummies Walk-s, Wood-a. 64-Corben-a. 64,65,67-Toth-a. 65,66-El Cid. 67-Hunter II. 71-Goblin-c/1st app. 2.30 7.00 16.00
70,73-75 2.00 6.00 12.00
76-1st app. Darklon the Mystic by Starlin-s/a 3.15 9.45 22.00
79,80-Origin Darklon the Mystic by Starlin 2.60 7.00 18.00
81,86,97: 81-Frazetta-c, King Kong; Corben-a. 86-(92 pgs.) All Corben issue. 97-Time Travel/Dinosaur issue; Corben,Adams-a 2.30 7.00 16.00
82-Origin/1st app. The Rook 2.85 8.50 20.00
83,85,88,89,91-93,98,99: 98-Rook (31 pgs.). 99-1st Horizon Seekers.
1.67 5.00 10.00
84,87,90,96,100: 84,100-Starlin-a. 87-Hunter 3; Nino-a. 87,90-Corben-a. 96-Summer Special (92 pgs.). 100-(92 pgs.) Anniverary issue; Rook (30 pgs.)
2.00 6.00 14.00
94,95-The Rook & Vampirella team-up. 95-Vampirella-c; 1st MacTavish
2.85 8.50 20.00
101,106,112,115,118,120,121,128: 101-Return of Hunter II, Starlin-a. 106-Hard John Nuclear Hit Parade Special, Corben-a. 112-All Maroto issue, Luana-s. 115-All José Ortiz issues. 118-1st Haggarth. 120-1st Zud Kamish.

Egypt #7 © Peter Milligan & Glyn Dillon

Eightball #21 © Daniel G. Clowes

Elektra #19 © MAR

121-Hunter/Darklon. 128-Starlin-a, Hsu-a 2.00 6.00 12.00
102-105,107-111,113,114,116,117,119,122-124,126,127,129: 104-Beast World. 103-105,109-111-Gulacy-a 1.67 5.00 10.00
125-(10/81, 84 pgs.) all Neal Adams issue 2.60 7.70 18.00
130-(76 pgs.) Vampirella-c/sty (54 pgs.); Pantha, Van Helsing, Huntress, Dax, Schreck, Hunter, Exterminator One, Rook app. 2.85 8.50 20.00
131,135,137-139 (lower distr.): 131-All Wood issue. 135-(10/82, 100 pgs.) All Ditko issue. 137-All Super-Hero issue. 138-Sherlock Holmes. 138,139-Color comic insert 2.30 7.00 16.00
132-134,136: 132-Rook returns. 133-All Ramon Torrents-a issue. 134,136-Color comic insert 2.00 6.00 12.00
Yearbook '70-Frazetta-c 5.00 15.00 40.00
Annual '71, '72-Reprints in both 4.30 13.00 35.00

NOTE: *The above books contain art by many good artists:* ***N. Adams, Brunner, Corben, Craig (Taycee), Crandall, Ditko, Eisner, Evans, Jeff Jones, Krenkel, McWilliams, Morrow, Orlando, Ploog, Severin, Starlin, Torres, Toth, Williamson, Wood,*** *and* ***Wrightson****; covers by* ***Bode', Corben, Davis, Frazetta, Morrow****, and* ***Orlando. Frazetta*** *c-2, 3, 7, 8, 23. Annuals from 1973-on are included in regular numbering. 1970-74 Annuals are complete reprints. Annuals from 1975-on are in the format of the regular issues.*

EERIE ADVENTURES (Also see Weird Adventures)
Ziff-Davis Publ. Co.: Winter, 1951 (Painted-c)

1-Powell-a(2), McCann-a; used in **SOTI;** bondage-c; Krigstein back-c 40.00 120.00 325.00

NOTE: *Title dropped due to similarity to Avon's Eerie & legal action.*

EERIE TALES (Magazine)
Hastings Associates: 1959 (Black & White)

1-Williamson, Torres, Tuska-a, Powell(2), & Morrow(2)-a 10.50 32.00 85.00

EERIE TALES
Super Comics: 1963-1964

Super Reprint No. 10,11,12,18: 10('63)-r/Spook #27. Purple Claw in #11,12 ('63); #12-r/Avon's Eerie #1('51)-Kida-r 2.50 7.50 25.00
15-Wolverton-a, Spacehawk-r/Blue Bolt Weird Tales #113; Disbrow-a 5.00 15.00 55.00

EGBERT
Arnold Publications/Quality Comics Group: Spring, 1946 - No. 20, 1950

	GD2.0	FN6.0	NM9.4
1-Funny animal; intro Egbert & The Count	19.00	56.00	150.00
2	10.00	30.00	75.00
3-10	6.00	18.00	42.00
11-20	4.65	14.00	28.00

EGON
Dark Horse Comics: Jan, 1998 - No.2, Feb, 1998 ($2.95, limited series)

1,2-Horley-painted-c 3.00

EGYPT
DC Comics (Vertigo): Aug, 1995 - No.7, Feb, 1996 ($2.50, lim. series, mature)

1-7: Milligan scripts in all. 3.00

EH! (...Dig This Crazy Comic) (From Here to Insanity No. 8 on)
Charlton Comics: Dec, 1953 - No. 7, Nov-Dec, 1954 (Satire)

1-Davis-*ish*-c/a by Ayers, Wood-*ish*-a by Giordano; Atomic Mouse app. 33.00 98.00 260.00

	GD2.0	FN6.0	NM9.4
2-Ayers-c/a	20.00	60.00	160.00
3,5,7	18.00	53.00	140.00
4,6: Sexual innuendo-c. 6-Ayers-a	19.00	56.00	150.00

EIGHTBALL (Also see David Boring)
Fantagraphics Books: Oct, 1989 - Present ($2.75/$2.95/$3.95, semi-annually, mature)

	GD2.0	FN6.0	NM9.4
1 (1st printing)	1.25	3.75	10.00
2,3		2.40	6.00
4-8			5.00
9-19: 17-(8/96)			4.00
20-($4.50)			4.50
21-($4.95) Concludes David Boring 3-parter			4.95

EIGHTH WONDER, THE
Dark Horse Comics: Nov, 1997 ($2.95, one-shot)

nn-Reprints stories from Dark Horse Presents #85-87 3.

EIGHT IS ENOUGH KITE FUN BOOK (See Kite Fun Book)

80 PAGE GIANT (...Magazine No. 2-15)
National Periodical Publications: 8/64 - No. 15, 10/65; No. 16, 11/65 - No. 8 7/71 (25¢)(All reprints) (#1-56: 84 pgs.; #57-89: 68 pgs.)

1-Superman Annual; originally planned as Superman Annual #9 (8/64) 36.00 108.00 540.

	GD2.0	FN6.0	NM
2-Jimmy Olsen	21.00	63.00	315.
3,4: 3-Lois Lane. 4-Flash-G.A.-r; Infantino-a	16.00	48.00	240.

5-Batman; has Sunday newspaper strip; Catwoman-r; Batman's Life Story-r (25th anniversary special) 16.00 48.00 240.
6-Superman 14.00 42.00 210.
7-Sgt. Rock's Prize Battle Tales; Kubert-c/a 17.00 51.00 255.
8-More Secret Origins-origins of JLA, Aquaman, Robin, Atom, & Superman; Infantino-a 30.00 90.00 450.
9-15: 9-Flash (r/Flash #106,117,123 & Showcase #14); Infantino-a. 10-Superboy. 11-Superman; all Luthor issue. 12-Batman; has Sunday newspa per strip. 13-Jimmy Olsen. 14-Lois Lane. 15-Superman and Batman; Joker c/story 13.00 39.00 195.

Continued as part of regular series under each title in which that particular book came out, a Giant being published instead of the regular size. Issues No. 16 to No. 89 are listed for your i mation. See individual titles for prices.
16-JLA #39 (11/65), 17-Batman #176, 18-Superman #183, 19-Our Army at War #164, 20-A #334, 21-Flash #160, 22-Superboy #129, 23-Superman #187, 24-Batman #182, 25-Jimmy O #95, 26-Lois Lane #68, 27-Batman #185, 28-World's Finest #161, 29-JLA #48, 30-Batman # 31-Superman #193, 32-Our Army at War #177, 33-Action #347, 34-Flash #169, 35-Supe #138, 36-Superman #197, 37-Batman #193, 38-Jimmy Olsen #104, 39-Lois Lane #77, 40-Wo Finest #170, 41-JLA #58, 42-Superman #202, 43-Batman #198, 44-Our Army at War #190, Action #360, 46-Flash #178, 47-Superboy #147, 48-Superman #207, 49-Batman #203, 50-Ji Olsen #113, 51-Lois Lane #86, 52-World's Finest #179, 53-JLA #67, 54-Superman #212, Batman #208, 56-Our Army at War #203, 57-Action #373, 58-Flash #187, 59-Superboy #156, Superman #217, 61-Batman #213, 62-Jimmy Olsen #122, 63-Lois Lane #95, 64-World's Fi #188, 65-JLA #76, 66-Superman #222, 67-Batman #218, 68-Our Army at War #216, Adventure #390, 70-Flash #196, 71-Superboy #165, 72-Superman #227, 73-Batman #223, Jimmy Olsen #131, 75-Lois Lane #104, 76-World's Finest #197, 77-JLA #85, 78-Superman # 79-Batman #228, 80-Our Army at War #229, 81-Adventure #403, 82-Flash #205, 83-Supe #174, 84-Superman #239, 85-Batman #233, 86-Jimmy Olsen #140, 87-Lois Lane #113, World's Finest #206, 89-JLA #93.

87TH PRECINCT (TV)
Dell Publishing Co.: Apr-June, 1962 - No. 2, July-Sept, 1962

	GD2.0	FN6.0	NM
Four Color 1309(#1)-Krigstein-a	9.00	27.00	110.
2	7.50	22.50	90.

EL BOMBO COMICS
Standard Comics/Frances M. McQueeny: 1946

nn(1946), 1(no date) 10.00 30.00 80.

EL CID
Dell Publishing Co.: No. 1259, 1961

Four Color 1259-Movie, photo-c 6.70 20.00 80.

EL DIABLO (See All-Star Western #2 & Weird Western Tales #12)
DC Comics: Aug, 1989 - No. 16, Jan, 1991 ($1.50-$1.75, color)

1 ($2.50, 52pgs.)-Masked hero 2.
2-16 2.

EL DORADO (See Movie Classics)

ELECTRIC UNDERTOW (See Strikeforce Morituri: Electric Undertow)

ELECTRIC WARRIOR
DC Comics: May, 1986 - No. 18, Oct, 1987 ($1.50, Baxter paper)

1-18 2.

ELEKTRA (Also see Daredevil #319-325)
Marvel Comics: Mar, 1995 - No. 4, June, 1995 ($2.95, limited series)

1-4-Embossed-c; Scott McDaniel-a 3.

ELEKTRA (Also see Daredevil)
Marvel Comics: Nov, 1996 - No. 19, Jun, 1998 ($1.95)

1-Peter Milligan scripts; Deodato-c/a 3.
1-Variant-c 5.
2-19: 4-Dr. Strange-c/app. 10-Logan-c/app. 2.
#(-1) Flashback (7/97) Matt Murdock-c/app.; Deodato-c/a 2.

Elementals #20 © Bill Willingham

Elflord V2 #5 © Aircel Publ.

Elfquest #14 © Richard & Wendy Pini

GD2.0 FN6.0 NM9.4

:yblade (Image, 3/97,$2.95) Devil's Reign pt. 7 3.00

:EKTRA: ASSASSIN (Also see Daredevil)
rvel Comics (Epic Comics): Aug, 1986 - No. 8, June, 1987 (Limited series, :ure)

Miller scripts in all; Sienkiewicz-c/a. 2.40 6.00
8 5.00
ned & numbered hardcover (Graphitti Designs, $39.95, 2000 print run)-
reprints 1-8 50.00
3 (2000, $24.95)

:EKTRA LIVES AGAIN (Also see Daredevil)
rvel Comics (Epic Comics): 1990 ($24.95, oversize, hardcover, 76 pgs.)
oduced by Graphitti Designs)

Frank Miller-c/a/scripts; Lynn Varley painted-a; Matt Murdock & Bullseye app.; Elektra dies 30.00

:EKTRA MEGAZINE
rvel Comics: Nov, 1996 - No. 2, Dec, 1996 ($3.95, 96 pgs., reprints, limited es)

2: Reprints Frank Miller's Elektra stories in Daredevil 4.00

:EKTRA SAGA, THE
rvel Comics Group: Feb, 1984 - No. 4, June, 1984 ($2.00, limited series, :ter paper)

4-r/Daredevil 168-190; Miller-c/a 3.00

:EMENTALS, THE (See The Justice Machine & Morningstar Spec.)
nico The Comic Co. : June, 1984 - No. 29, Sept, 1988; V2#1, Mar, 1989 - 28, 1994? ($1.50/$2.50, Baxter paper); V3#1, Dec, 1995 - No. 3 ($2.95)

Willingham-c/a, 1-8 4.00
29, V2#1-28: 9-Bissette-a(p). 10-Photo-c. V2#6-1st app. Strike Force America 18-Prelude to Avalon mini-series. 27-Prequel to Strike Force America series 3.00
#1-3: 1-Daniel-a(p), bagged w/gaming card 3.00
jerie (5/96, $2.95) 3.00
ecial 1,2 (3/86, 1/89)-1-Willingham-a(p) 3.00

:EMENTALS: (Title series), **Comico**

HOST OF A CHANCE, 12/95 ($5.95)-graphic nove, nn-Ross-c. 6.00

OW THE WAR WAS WON, 6/996 - No. 2, 8/96 ($2.95) 1,2-Tony Daniel-a, & 1-Variant-c; no logo 3.00

EX SPECIAL, 5/97 - No. 2, 6/97 ($2.95 1-Tony Daniel, Jeff Moy-a, 2-Robb Phipps, Adam McDaniel-a 3.00

WIMSUIT SPECTACULAR 1996, 6/96 ($2.95), 1-pin-ups, 1-Variant-c; no logo 3.00

HE VAMPIRE'S REVENGE, 6/96 - No. 2 8/96 ($2.95) 1,2-Willingham-s, 1-Variant-c; no logo 3.00

1 (ELEVEN ELEVEN)
isade Entertainment: Oct, 1996 ($2.95, B&W, one-shot)

Wrightson-c/a 3.00

:EVEN OR ONE
us: Apr, 1995 ($2.95)

Linsner-c/a 1.00 3.00 8.00
'6/96) 2nd printing 3.00

:LORD
:el Publ.: 1986 - No. 6, Oct, 1989 ($1.70, B&W); V2#1- V2#31, 1995 ($2.00)

3.00
4,V2#1-20,22-30: 4-6: Last B&W issue. V2#1-Color-a begin. 22-New cast. 25-Begin B&W 2.00
2-2nd printings 2.00
Double size ($4.95) 5.00

:LORD
rp Graphics: Jan, 1997-No.4, Apr, 1997 ($2.95, B&W, mini-series)

4 3.00

:LORD (CUTS LOOSE) (Vol. 2)
rp Graphics: Sept, 1997 - Present ($2.95, B&W, mini-series)

GD2.0 FN6.0 NM9.4

1-7 3.00

ELFLORD: DRAGON'S EYE
Night Wynd Enterprises: 1993 ($2.50, B&W)

1 2.50

ELFLORD: THE RETURN
Mad Monkey Press: 1996 ($6.95, magazine size)

1 7.00

ELFQUEST (Also see Fantasy Quarterly & Warp Graphics Annual)
Warp Graphics, Inc.: No. 2, Aug, 1978 - No. 21, Feb, 1985 (All magazine size)
No. 1, Apr, 1979

NOTE: ***Elfquest*** was originally published as one of the stories in **Fantasy Quarterly** #1. When the publisher went out of business, the creative team, Wendy and Richard Pini, formed WaRP Graphics and continued the series, beginning with **Elfquest** #2. **Elfquest** #1, which reprinted the story from **Fantasy Quarterly**, was published about the same time **Elfquest** #4 was released. Thereafter, most issues were reprinted as demand warranted, until Marvel announced it would reprint the entire series under its Epic imprint (Aug., 1985).

1(4/79)-Reprints Elfquest story from Fantasy Quarterly No. 1
1st printing ($1.00-c) 2.50 7.50 23.00
2nd printing ($1.25-c) 1.10 3.30 9.00
3rd printings ($1.50-c) 3.00
4th printing; different-c ($1.50-c) 2.00
2(8/78)-5: 1st printings ($1.00-c) 1.75 5.25 14.00
2nd printings ($1.25-c) 4.00
3rd & 4th printings ($1.50-c)(all 4th prints 1989) 2.50
6-9: 1st printings ($1.25-c) 2.40 6.00
2nd printings ($1.50-c) 3.50
3rd printings ($1.50-c) 2.00
10-21: ($1.50-c); 16-8pg. preview of A Distant Soil 4.00
10-14: 2nd printings ($1.50) 2.00

ELFQUEST
Marvel Comics (Epic Comics): Aug, 1985 - No. 32, Mar, 1988

1-Reprints in color the Elfquest epic by Warp Graphics 3.00
2-32 2.00

ELFQUEST (Title series), Warp Graphics
'89 - No. 4, '89 ($1.50, B&W) 1-4: R-original Elfquest series 2.00

ELFQUEST (Volume 2),**Warp Graphics:** V2#1, 5/96 - No. 33, 2/99 ($4.95/$2.95, B&W)
V2#1-31: 1,3,5,8,10,12,13,18,21,23,25-Wendy Pini-c 5.00
32,33-($2.95-c) 3.00

--BLOOD OF TEN CHIEFS, 7/93 - No. 20, 9/95 ($2.00/$2.50) 1-20-By Richard & Wendy Pini 2.50

--HIDDEN YEARS, 5/92 - No. 29, 3/96 ($2.00/$2.25)1-9,9 1/2, 10-29 2.50

--JINK, 11/94 - No. 12, 2/6 ($2.25/$2.50) 1-12-W. Pini/John Byrn-back-c 2.50

--KAHVI, 10/95 - No. 6,3/96 ($2.25, B&W) 1-6 2.50

--KINGS CROSS, 11/97 - No. 2, 12/97 ($2.95, B&W) 1,2 3.00

--KINGS OF THE BROKEN WHEEL, 6/90 - No. 9, 2/92 ($2.00, B&W) (3rd Elfquest saga) 1-9: By R. & W. Pini; 1-Color insert, 1-2nd printing 2.50

--METAMORPHOSIS, 4/96 ($2.95, B&W) 1 3.00

--NEW BLOOD (...Summer Special on-c #1 only), 8/92 - No. 35, 1/96 ($2.00-$2.50, color/B&W)
1-($3.95, 68 pgs.,...Summer Special on-c)-Byrne-a/scripts (16 pgs.) 4.00
2-34: Barry Blair-a in all 2.50
1993 Summer Special ($3.95) Byrne-a/scripts 4.00

--SHARDS, 8/94 - No. 16, 3/96 ($2.25/$2.50) 1-16 2.50

--SIEGE AT BLUE MOUNTAIN, WaRP Graphics/Apple 3/87 - No. 8, 12/88
(1.75/ $1.95, B&W) 1-Staton-a(i) in all; 2nd Elfquest saga 4.00
1-3-2nd printing, 3-8 2.50
2 3.00

--THE REBELS, 11/94 - No. 12, 3/96 ($2.25/$2.50, B&W/color) 1-12 2.50

--TWO-SPEAR, 10/95 - No. 5, 2/96 ($2.25, B&W) 1-5 2.50

--WAVE DANCERS, 12/93 - No. 6, 3/96, 1-6: 1-Foil-c & poster 2.50
Special 1 ($2.95) 3.00

Ella Cinders #3 © STJ

Ellery Queen #2 © Z-D

Elvira #54 © Queen "B" Productions

GD2.0 FN6.0 NM9.4

--WORLDPOOL, 7/97 ($2.95, B&W) 1-Richard Pini-s/Barry Blair-a 3.00

ELF-THING
Eclipse Comics: March, 1987 ($1.50, B&W, one-shot)
1 2.00

ELIMINATOR (Also see The Solution #16 & The Night Man #16)
Malibu Comics (Ultraverse): Apr, 1995 - No. 3, Jul, 1995 ($2.95/$2.50, lim. series)
0-Mike Zeck-a in all 3.00
1-3-($2.50): 1-1st app. Siren 2.50
1-($3.95)-Black cover edition 4.00

ELIMINATOR FULL COLOR SPECIAL
Eternity Comics: Oct, 1991 ($2.95, one-shot)
1-Dave Dorman painted-c 3.00

ELLA CINDERS (See Comics On Parade, Comics Revue #1,4, Famous Comics Cartoon Book, Giant Comics Editions, Sparkler Comics, Tip Top & Treasury of Comics)

ELLA CINDERS
United Features Syndicate: 1938 - 1940
Single Series 3(1938) 40.00 120.00 350.00
Single Series 21(#2 on-c, #21 on inside), 28('40) 35.00 105.00 280.00

ELLA CINDERS
United Features Syndicate: Mar, 1948 - No. 5, Mar, 1949
1-(#2 on cover) 12.50 37.50 100.00
2 8.65 26.00 60.00
3-5 6.00 18.00 42.00

ELLERY QUEEN
Superior Comics Ltd.: May, 1949 - No. 4, Nov, 1949
1-Kamen-c; L.B. Cole-a; r-in Haunted Thrills 49.00 148.00 445.00
2-4: 3-Drug use stories(2) 39.00 116.00 310.00
NOTE: *Iger shop art in all issues.*

ELLERY QUEEN (TV)
Ziff-Davis Publishing Co.: 1-3/52 (Spring on-c) - No. 2, Summer/52 (Saunders painted-c)
1-Saunders-c 43.00 129.00 390.00
2-Saunders bondage, torture-c 39.00 116.00 310.00

ELLERY QUEEN (Also see Crackajack Funnies No. 23)
Dell Publishing Co.: No. 1165, Mar-May, 1961 - No.1289, Apr, 1962
Four Color 1165 (#1)- 11.00 33.00 130.00
Four Color 1243 (11-1/61-61), 1289 8.75 26.50 105.00

ELMER FUDD (Also see Camp Comics, Daffy, Looney Tunes #1 & Super Book #10, 22)
Dell Publishing Co.: No. 470, May, 1953 - No. 1293, Mar-May, 1962
Four Color 470 (#1) 4.60 13.75 55.00
Four Color 558,628,689('56) 3.45 10.35 38.00
Four Color 725,783,841,888,938,977,1032,1081,1131,1171,1222,1293('62) 2.80 8.40 28.00

ELMO COMICS
St. John Publishing Co.: Jan, 1948 (Daily strip-r)
1-By Cecil Jensen 10.00 30.00 70.00

ELONGATED MAN (See Flash #112 & Justice League of America #105)
DC Comics: Jan, 1992 - No. 4, Apr, 1992 ($1.00, limited series)
1-4: 3-The Flash app. 2.00

ELRIC (Of Melnibone)(See First Comics Graphic Novel #6 & Marvel Graphic Novel #2)
Pacific Comics: Apr, 1983 - No. 6, Apr, 1984 ($1.50, Baxter paper)
1-6: Russell-c/a(i) in all 3.00

ELRIC
Topps Comics: 1996 ($2.95, one-shot)
0--One Life: Russell-c/a; adapts Neil Gaiman's short story "One Life--Furnished in Early Moorcock." 3.00

ELRIC, SAILOR ON THE SEAS OF FATE
First Comics: June, 1985 - No. 7, June, 1986 ($1.75, limited series)
1-7: Adapts Michael Moorcock's novel 3.

ELRIC, STORMBRINGER
Dark Horse Comics/Topps Comics: 1997 - No. 7, 1997($2.95, limited series)
1-7: Russell-c/s/a; adapts Michael Moorcock's novel 3.

ELRIC: THE BANE OF THE BLACK SWORD
First Comics: Aug, 1988 - No. 6, June, 1989 ($1.75/$1.95, limited series)
1-6: Adapts Michael Moorcock's novel 3.

ELRIC: THE VANISHING TOWER
First Comics: Aug, 1987 - No. 6, June, 1988 ($1.75, limited series)
1-6: Adapts Michael Moorcock's novel 3.

ELRIC: WEIRD OF THE WHITE WOLF
First Comics: Oct, 1986 - No. 5, June, 1987 ($1.75, limited series)
1-5: Adapts Michael Moorcock's novel 3.

EL SALVADOR - A HOUSE DIVIDED
Eclipse Comics: March, 1989 ($2.50, B&W, Baxter paper, stiff-c, 52 pgs.)
1-Gives history of El Salvador 2.

ELSEWHERE PRINCE, THE (Moebius' Airtight Garage)
Marvel Comics (Epic): May, 1990 - No. 6, Oct, 1990 ($1.95, limited series)
1-6: Moebius scripts & back-up-a in all 3.

ELSEWORLDS 80-PAGE GIANT
DC Comics: Aug, 1999 ($5.95, one-shot)
1-Most copies destroyed by DC over content of the "Superman's Babysitter" story; some UK shipments sold before recall 150.

ELSEWORLD'S FINEST
DC Comics: 1997 - No. 2, 1997 ($4.95, limited series)
1,2: Elseworld's story-Superman & Batman in the 1920's 5.

ELSEWORLD'S FINEST: SUPERGIRL & BATGIRL
DC Comics: 1998 ($5.95, one-shot)
1-Haley-a 6.

ELSIE THE COW
D. S. Publishing Co.: Oct-Nov, 1949 - No. 3, July-Aug, 1950
1-(36 pgs.) 23.00 69.00 185.
2,3 18.00 53.00 140.

ELSON'S PRESENTS
DC Comics: 1981 (100 pgs., no cover price)
Series 1-6: Repackaged 1981 DC comics; 1-DC Comics Presents #29, Flash #303, Batman #331. 2-Superman #335, Ghosts #96, Justice League of America #186. 3-New Teen Titans #3, Secrets of Haunted House #32, Wonder Woman #275. 4-Secrets of the LSH #1, Brave & the Bold #170, New Adv. of Superboy #13. 5-LSH #271, Green Lantern #136, Super Frien #40. 6-Action #515, Mystery in Space #115, Detective #498 1.50 4.50 12.

ELVEN (Also see Prime)
Malibu Comics (Ultraverse): Oct, 1994 - No. 4, Feb, 1995 ($2.50, lim. series)
0 ($2.95)-Prime app. 3.
1-4: 2,4-Prime app. 3-Primevil app. 2.
1-Limited Foil Edition- no price on cover 3.

ELVIRA MISTRESS OF THE DARK
Marvel Comics: Oct, 1988 ($2.00, B&W, magazine size)
1-Movie adaptation 5.

ELVIRA MISTRESS OF THE DARK
Claypool Comics (Eclipse): May, 1993 - Present ($2.50, B&W)
1-Austin-a(i). Spiegle-a 2.40 6.
2-6: Spiegle-a 4.
7-89-Photo-c: 2.
TPB ($12.95) 13.

ELVIRA'S HOUSE OF MYSTERY
DC Comics: Jan, 1986 - No. 11, Jan, 1987
1,11: 11-Dave Stevens-c 5.

E-Man #3 © FC

Empire #1 © Mark Waid & Barry Kitson

Enchanting Love #3 © Kirby Publ.

-10: 9-Photo-c, Special 1 (3/87, $1.25) 3.00

.VIS MANDIBLE, THE
: Comics (Piranha Press): 1990 ($3.50, 52 pgs., B&W, mature)
3.50

.VIS PRESLEY (See Career Girl Romances #32, Go-Go, Howard Chaykin's American .gg #10, Humbug #8, I Love You #60 & Young Lovers #18)

MAN
arlton Comics: Oct, 1973 - No. 10, Sept, 1975 (Painted-c No. 7-10)
-Origin & 1st app. E-Man; Staton c/a in all 2.00 6.00 18.00
-4: 2,4-Ditko-a. 3-Howard-a 1.00 3.00 8.00
-Miss Liberty Belle app. by Ditko 1.00 2.80 7.00
-10: 6,7,9,10-Early Byrne-a (#6 is 1/75). 6-Disney parody. 8-Full-length story; Nova begins as E-Man's partner 1.25 3.75 10.00
-4,9,10(Modern Comics reprints, '77) 4.00
TE: Killjoy app.-No. 2, 4. Liberty Belle app.-No. 5. Rog 2000 app.-No. 6, 7, 9, 10. Travis app.- . 3. ***Tom Sutton*** *a-1.*

MAN
mico: Sept, 1989 ($2.75, one-shot, no ads, high quality paper)
-Staton-c/a; Michael Mauser story 2.75

MAN
mico: V4#1, Jan, 1990 - No. 3, Mar, 1990 ($2.50, limited series)
-3: Staton-c/a 2.50

MAN
pha Productions: Oct, 1993 ($2.75)
#1-Staton-c/a; 20th anniversary issue 2.75

MAN COMICS (Also see Michael Mauser & The Original E-Man)
'st Comics: Apr, 1983 - No. 25, Aug, 1985 ($1.00/$1.25, direct sales only)
-25: 2-X-Men satire. 3-X-Men/Phoenix satire. 6-Origin retold. 8-Cutey Bunny app. 10-Origin Nova Kane. 24-Origin Michael Mauser 2.00
TE: ***Staton*** *a-1-5, 6-25p; c-1-25.*

MAN RETURNS
pha Productions: 1994 ($2.75, B&W)
-Joe Staton-c/a(p) 2.75

IBRACE
ndon Night Studios: Nov, 1996 ($3.00)
-Photo-c(Carmen Electra) 3.00
-($5.00)-NC-17 Edition 5.00

IBRACE: HUNGER OF THE FLESH
ndon Night Studios: July, 1997 - No. 3 ($3.00, limited series)
-3 3.00
-3-($6.00)-Nude Edition 6.00

IERALD DAWN
: Comics: 1991 ($4.95, trade paperback)
-Reprints Green Lantern: Emerald Dawn #1-6 5.00

IERALD DAWN II (See Green Lantern...)

IERGENCY (Magazine)
arlton Comics: June, 1976 - No. 4, Jan, 1977 (B&W)
-Neal Adams-c/a; Heath, Austin-a 2.80 8.40 28.00
,3: 2-N. Adams-c. 3-N. Adams-a. 2.50 7.50 23.00
-Alcala-a 2.00 6.00 16.00

IERGENCY (TV)
arlton Comics: June, 1976 - No. 4, Dec, 1976
-Staton-c; early Byrne-a (22 pages) 2.50 7.50 23.00
-4: 2-Staton-c. 2,3-Byrne text illos. 1.75 5.25 14.00

IERGENCY DOCTOR
arlton Comics: Summer, 1963 (one-shot)
2.80 8.40 28.00

IIL & THE DETECTIVES (See Movie Comics)

IMA PEEL & JOHN STEED (See The Avengers)

EMPEROR'S NEW CLOTHES, THE
Dell Publishing Co.: 1950 (10¢, 68 pgs., 1/2 size, oblong)
nn - (Surprise Books series) 4.00 11.00 22.00

EMPIRE
Image Comics (Gorilla): May, 2000 - Present ($2.50)
1,2: 1-Waid-s/Kitson-a; w/Crimson Plague prologue 2.50

EMPIRE STRIKES BACK, THE (See Marvel Comics Super Special #16 & Marvel Special Edition)

EMPTY LOVE STORIES
Slave Labor #1 & 2/Funny Valentine Press: Nov, 1994 - Present ($2.95, B&W)
1,2: Steve Darnall scripts in all. 1-Alex Ross-c. 2-(8/96)-Mike Allred-c 4.00
1,2-2nd printing (Funny Valentine Press) 3.00
... 1999-Jeff Smith-c; Doran-a 3.00
..."Special" (2.95) Ty Templeton-c 3.00

ENCHANTED
Sirius Entertainment: 1997 - No. 3 ($2.50, B&W, limited series)
1-3-Robert Chang-s/a 2.50

ENCHANTED (Volume 2)
Sirius Entertainment: 1998 - No. 3 ($2.95, limited series)
1-Robert Chang-s/a 3.00

ENCHANTED APPLES OF OZ, THE (See First Comics Graphic Novel #5)

ENCHANTER
Eclipse Comics: Apr, 1987 - No. 3, Aug. 1987 ($2.00, B&W, limited series)
1-3 2.00

ENCHANTING LOVE
Kirby Publishing Co.: Oct, 1949 - No. 6, July, 1950 (All 52 pgs.)
1-Photo-c 12.50 37.50 100.00
2-Photo-c; Powell-a 7.85 23.50 55.00
3,4,6: 3-Jimmy Stewart photo-c 7.00 21.00 48.00
5-Ingels-a, 9 pgs.; photo-c 14.00 41.00 110.00

ENCHANTMENT VISUALETTES (Magazine)
World Editions: Dec, 1949 - No. 5, Apr, 1950 (Painted c-1)
1-Contains two romance comic strips each 14.00 41.00 110.00
2 10.00 30.00 80.00
3-5 10.00 30.00 70.00

ENEMY
Dark Horse Comics: May, 1994 - No. 5, Sept, 1994 ($2.50, limited series)
1-5 2.50

ENEMY ACE SPECIAL (Also see Our Army at War #151, Showcase #57, 58 & Star Spangled War Stories #138)
DC Comics: 1990 ($1.00, one-shot)
1-Kubert-r/Our Army #151,153; c-r/Showcase 57 4.00

ENEMY ACE: WAR IDYLL
DC Comics: 1990 (Graphic novel)
Hardcover-George Pratt-s/painted-a/c 30.00
Softcover (1991, $14.95) 15.00

ENIGMA
DC Comics (Vertigo): Mar, 1993 - No. 8, Oct, 1993 ($2.50, limited series)
1-8: Milligan scripts 2.50
Trade paperback ($19.95)-reprints 20.00

ENO AND PLUM (Also see Cud Comics)
Oni Press: Mar, 1998 ($2.95, B&W)
1-Terry LaBan-s/c/a 3.00

ENSIGN O'TOOLE (TV)
Dell Publishing Co.: Aug-Oct, 1963 - No. 2, 1964
1 2.50 7.50 25.00
2 2.40 7.35 22.00

ENSIGN PULVER (See Movie Classics)

EPIC

Epic Illustrated #19 © MAR

ESPers #6 © James D. Hudnall

The Eternals #6 © MAR

Marvel Comics (Epic Comics): 1992 - Book 4, 1992 ($4.95, lim. series, 52 pgs.)

Book One-Four: 2-Dorman painted-c 5.00

NOTE: *Alien Legion in #3. Cholly & Flytrap by* ***Burden****(scripts) &* ***Suydam****(art) in 3, 4. Dinosaurs in #4. Dreadlands in #1. Hellraiser in #1. Nightbreed in #2. Sleeze Brothers in #2. Stalkers in #1-4. Wild Cards in #1-4.*

EPIC ILLUSTRATED (Magazine)
Marvel Comics Group: Spring, 1980 - No. 34, Feb, 1986 ($2.00/$2.50, B&W/color, mature)

1-10: 1-Frazetta-c; Silver Surfer/Galactus-sty; Wendy Pini-s/a; Suydam-s/a; Metamorphosis Odyssey begins (thru #9) Starlin-a. 2-Bissette/Veitch-a; Goodwin-s. 3-Goodwin-s. 4-Ellison 15 pg. story w/art by Steacy; Hempel-s/a; Veitch-s/a. 5-Hildebrandts-c/interview; Jusko-a; Vess-s/a. 6-Ellison-s (26 pgs). 7-Adams-s/a(16 pgs.); BWS interview. 8-Suydam-s/a; Vess-s/a. 9-Conrad-c. 10-Marada the She-Wolf-c/sty(21 pgs.) by Claremont and Bolton 5.00
11-20: 11-Wood-a; Jusko-a. 12-Wolverton Spacehawk-r edited & recolored w/article on him; Muth-a. 13-Blade Runner preview by Williamson. 14-Elric of Melnibone by Russell; Revenge of the Jedi preview. 15-Vallejo-c & interview; 1st Dreadstar story (cont'd in Dreadstar #1). 16-B. Smith-c/a(2); Sim-s/a. 17-Starslammers preview. 18-Go Nagai; Williams-a. 19-Jabberwocky w/Hampton-a; Cheech Wizard-s. 20-The Sacred & the Profane begins by Ken Steacy; Elric by Gould; Williams-a 6.00
21-30: 21-Vess-s/a. 22-Frankenstein w/Wrightson-a. 26-Galactus series begins (thru #34); Cerebus the Aardvark story by Dave Sim. 27-Groo. 28-Cerebus. 29-1st Sheeva. 30-Cerebus; History of Dreadstar, Starlin-s/a; Williams-a; Vess-a 1.00 2.80 7.00
31-33: 31-Bolton-c/a. 32-Cerebus portfolio. 1.25 3.75 10.00
34-R.E.Howard tribute by Thomas-s/Plunkett-a; Moore-s/Veitch-a; Cerebus; Cholly & Flytrap w/Suydam-a; BWS-a 2.00 6.00 16.00

NOTE: ***N. Adams*** *a-7; c-6.* ***Austin*** *a-15-20i.* ***Bode*** *a-19, 23, 27r.* ***Bolton*** *a-7, 10-12, 15, 18, 22-25; c-10, 18, 22, 23.* ***Boris*** *c/a-15.* ***Brunner*** *c-12.* ***Buscema*** *a-1p, 9p, 11-13p.* ***Byrne/Austin*** *a-26-34.* ***Chaykin*** *a-2; c-8.* ***Conrad*** *a-2-5, 7-9, 25-34; c-17.* ***Corben*** *a-15; c-2.* ***Frazetta*** *c-1.* ***Golden*** *a-3r.* ***Gulacy*** *c/a-3.* ***Jeff Jones*** *c-25.* ***Kaluta*** *a-17r, 21, 24r, 26; c-4, 28.* ***Nebres*** *a-1.* ***Reese*** *a-12.* ***Russell*** *a-2-4, 9, 14, 33; c-14.* ***Simonson*** *a-17.* ***B. Smith*** *c/a-7, 16.* ***Starlin*** *a-1-9, 14, 15, 34.* ***Steranko*** *c-19.* ***Williamson*** *a-13, 27, 34.* ***Wrightson*** *a-13p, 22, 25, 27, 34; c-30.*

EPIC LITE
Marvel Comics (Epic Comics): Sept, 1991 ($3.95, 52 pgs., one-shot)

1-Bob the Alien, Normalman by Valentino 4.00

EPICURUS THE SAGE
DC Comics (Piranha Press): Vol. 1, 1991 - Vol. 2, 1991 ($9.95, 8-1/8x10-7/8")

Volume 1,2-Sam Kieth-c/a 10.00

EPSILON WAVE
Independent Comics/Elite Comics No. 5 on: Oct, 1985 - V2#2, 1987 ($1.50/$1.25/$1.75)

1-8,V2#1,2: 1-3,6-Seadragon app. V2 (B&W) 2.00

ERADICATOR
DC Comics: Aug, 1996 - No. 3, Oct, 1996 ($1.75, limited series)

1-3: Superman app. 3.00

ERNIE COMICS (Formerly Andy Comics #21; All Love Romances #26 on)
Current Books/Ace Periodicals: No. 22, Sept, 1948 - No. 25, Mar, 1949

nn (9/48,11/48; #22,23)-Teenage humor 6.00 18.00 42.00
24,25 5.00 15.00 30.00

ESCAPADE IN FLORENCE (See Movie Comics)

ESCAPE FROM DEVIL'S ISLAND
Avon Periodicals: 1952

1-Kinstler-c; r/as Dynamic Adventures #9 38.00 113.00 300.00

ESCAPE FROM THE PLANET OF THE APES (See Power Record Comics)

ESCAPE TO WITCH MOUNTAIN (See Walt Disney Showcase No. 29)

ESPERS (Also see Interface)
Eclipse Comics: July, 1986 - No. 5, Apr, 1987 ($1.25/$1.75, Mando paper)

1-5-James Hudnall story & David Lloyd-a. 2.00

ESPERS
Halloween Comics: V2#1, 1996 - No. 6, 1997 ($2.95, B&W) (1st Halloween Comics series)

V2#1-6: James D. Hudnall scripts 3.0
Undertow TPB ('98, $14.95) r/#1-6 15.0

ESPERS
Image Comics: V3#1, 1997 - Present ($2.95, B&W, limited series)

V3#1-7: James D. Hudnall scripts 3.0
Black Magic TPB ('98, $14.95) r/#1-4 15.0

ESPIONAGE (TV)
Dell Publishing Co.: May-July, 1964 - No. 2, Aug-Oct, 1964

1,2 2.80 8.40 28.0

ESSENTIAL (Title series), **Marvel Comics**

--AVENGERS, '98 (B&W- r) V1-R-Avengers #1-24; new Immonen-c 15.0
V2(6/00)-Reprints Avengers #25-46, King-Size Special #1; Immonen-c 15.0

--CAPTAIN AMERICA, '00 (B&W- r) V1-Reprints stories from Tales of Suspens #59-99, Captain America #100-102; new Romita & Milgrom-c 15.0

--CONAN, '00 (B&W- r) V1-R-Conan the Barbarian#1-25; new Buscema-c 15.0

--FANTASTIC FOUR, '98 - Present (B&W-r)
V1-Reprints FF #1-20, Annual #1; new Alan Davis-c 15.0
V2-Reprints FF #21-40, Annual #2; Davis and Farmer-c 15.0

--HULK, '99 (B&W-r) V1-R-Incred. Hulk #1-6, Tales to Astonish stories; new Bruce Timm-c 15.0

--IRON MAN, '00 (B&W-r) V1-Tales Of Suspense #39-72; new Timm-c and back-c 15.0

--SILVER SURFER, '98 (B&W-r) V1-R-material from SS#1-18 and Fantastic Fo Annual #5 15.0

--SPIDER-MAN, '96 - Present (B&W-r)
V1-R-AF #15, Amaz. S-M #1-20, Ann. #1 (2 printings) 15.0
V2-R-Amaz. Spider-Man #21-43, Annual #2,3 15.0
V3-R-Amaz. Spider-Man #44-68 15.0

ESSENTIAL VERTIGO: THE SANDMAN
DC Comics (Vertigo): Aug, 1996 - No. 32, Mar, 1999 ($1.95/$2.25, reprints)

1-13,15-31: Reprints Sandman, 2nd series 3.0
14-($2.95) 3.5
32-($4.50) Reprints Sandman Special #1 4.5

ESSENTIAL UNCANNY X-MEN
Marvel Comics: 1999 - Present (B&W reprints)

V1-Reprints X-Men (1st series) #1-24; Timm-c 15.0

ESSENTIAL VERTIGO: SWAMP THING
DC Comics: Nov, 1996 - No. 24, Oct, 1998 ($1.95/$2.25,B&W, reprints)

1-11,13-24: 1-9-Reprints Alan Moore's Swamp Thing stories 3.0
12-($3.50) r/Annual #2 3.5

ESSENTIAL X-MEN
Marvel Comics: 1996 - Present (B&W reprints)

V1, V2-Reprints, V3--R-Uncanny X-Men #145-161, Ann. #3-5 15.0

ETC
DC Comics (Piranha Press): 1989 - No. 5, 1990 ($4.50, 60 pgs., mature)

Book 1-5: Conrad scripts/layouts in all 4.5

ETERNAL BIBLE, THE
Authentic Publications: 1946 (Large size) (16 pgs. in color)

1 14.00 41.00 110.0

ETERNALS, THE
Marvel Comics Group: July, 1976 - No. 19, Jan, 1978

1-(Regular 25¢ edition)-Origin & 1st app. Eternals 1.50 4.50 12.0
1-(30¢-c, limited distribution) 2.00 6.00 18.0
2-(Regular 25¢ edition)-1st app. Ajak & The Celestials 2.40 6.0
2-(30¢-c, limited distr.) 1.10 3.30 9.0
3-19: 14,15-Cosmic powered Hulk-c/story 2.40 6.0
Annual 1(10/77) 2.40 6.0

NOTE: ***Kirby*** *c/a(p) in all.*

ETERNALS, THE
Marvel Comics: Oct, 1985 - No. 12, Sept, 1986 (Maxi-series, mando paper)

Eternal Warrior #16 © VAL

E.V.E. Protomecha #1 © Lusen & Lichtner

Everything Happens to Harvey #5 © DC

GD2.0 FN6.0 NM9.4

1,12 (52 pgs.): 12-Williamson-a(i) 2.50
2-11 2.00

:TERNALS: THE HEROD FACTOR
Marvel Comics: Nov, 1991 ($2.50, 68 pgs.)

1 2.50

:TERNAL WARRIOR (See Solar #10 & 11)
/aliant/Acclaim Comics (Valiant): Aug, 1992 - No. 50, Mar, 1996 ($2.25/$2.50)

1-Unity x-over; Miller-c; origin Eternal Warrior & Aram (Armstrong) 3.00
1-Gold logo 5.00
1-Gold foil logo 2.40 6.00
2-8: 2-Unity x-over; Simonson-c. 3-Archer & Armstrong x-over. 4-1st app. Bloodshot (last pg. cameo); see Rai #0 for 1st full app.; Cowan-c. 5-2nd full app. Bloodshot (12/92; see Rai #0). 6,7: 6-2nd app. Master Darque. 8-Flip book w/Archer & Armstrong #8 3.00
9-25,27-37: 9-1st Book of Geomancer. 14-16-Bloodshot app. 18-Doctor Mirage cameo. 19-Doctor Mirage app. 22-W/bound-in trading card. 25-Archer & Armstrong app.; cont'd from A&A #25 2.50
26-($2.75, 44 pgs.)-Flip book w/Archer & Armstrong 2.75
35-50: 35-Double-c; $2.50-c begins. 50-Geomancer app. 2.50
Special 1 (2/96, $2.50)-Art Holcomb script 2.50
Yearbook 1 (1993, $3.95), 2(1994, $3.95) 4.00

:TERNAL WARRIORS: BLACKWORKS
Acclaim Comics (Valiant Heroes): Mar, 1998 ($3.50, one-shot)

1 3.50

:TERNAL WARRIORS: DIGITAL ALCHEMY
Acclaim Comics (Valiant Heroes): Vol. 2, Sep, 1997 ($3.95, one-shot, 64 pgs.)

Vol. 2-Holcomb-s/Eaglesham-a(p) 4.00

:TERNAL WARRIORS: FIST AND STEEL
Acclaim Comics (Valiant): May, 1996 - No. 2, June, 1996 ($2.50, lim. series)

1,2: Geomancer app. in both. 1-Indicia reads "June." 2-Bo Hampton-a 2.50

:TERNAL WARRIORS: TIME AND TREACHERY
Acclaim Comics (Valiant Heroes): Vol. 1, Jun, 1997 ($3.95, one-shot, 48 pgs.)

Vol. 1-Reintro Aram, Archer, Ivar the Timewalker, & Gilad the Warmaster; 1st app. Shalla Redburn; Art Holcomb script 4.00

:TERNITY SMITH
Renegade Press: Sept, 1986 - No. 5, May, 1987 ($1.25/$1.50, 36 pgs.)

1-5: 1st app. Eternity Smith. 5-Death of Jasmine 2.00

:TERNITY SMITH
Hero Comics: Sept, 1987 - No. 9, 1988 ($1.95)

V2#1-9: 8-Indigo begins 2.00

:TTA KETT
King Features Syndicate/Standard: No. 11, Dec, 1948 - No. 14, Sept, 1949

11-Teenage 8.65 26.00 60.00
12-14 5.70 17.00 40.00

:UDAEMON, THE (See Dark Horse Presents #72-74)
Dark Horse Comics: Aug, 1993 - No. 3, Nov, 1993 ($2.50, limited series)

1-3: Nelson-a, painted-c & scripts 2.50

:UROPA AND THE PIRATE TWINS
Powder Monkey Productions: Oct, 1996 - No. 2, ($2.50, B&W, limited series)

1,2: Two covers 2.50

:VANGELINE (Also see Primer)
Comico/First Comics V2#1 on/Lodestone Publ.:
1984 - #2, 6/84; V2#1, 5/87 - V2#12, Mar, 1989 (Baxter paper)

1,2, V2#1 (5/87) - 12, Special #1 (1986, $2.00)-Lodestone Publ. 2.00

:VA THE IMP
Red Top Comic/Decker: 1957 - No. 2, Nov, 1957

1,2 4.00 11.00 22.00

:.V.E. PROTOMECHA
Image Comics (Top Cow): Mar, 2000 - No. 6, Sept, 2000 ($2.50)

Preview ($5.95) Flip book w/Soul Saga preview 1.50 4.50 12.00
1-6: 1-Covers by Finch, Madureira, Garza. 2-Turner var-c 3.00
1-Another Universe variant-c 5.00

EVERYBODY'S COMICS (See Fox Giants)

EVERYMAN, THE
Marvel Comics (Epic Comics): Nov, 1991 ($4.50, one-shot, 52 pgs.)

1-Mike Allred-a 1.00 2.80 7.00

EVERYTHING HAPPENS TO HARVEY
National Periodical Publications: Sept-Oct, 1953 - No. 7, Sept-Oct, 1954

1 25.00 75.00 200.00
2 14.00 41.00 110.00
3-7 11.00 33.00 90.00

EVERYTHING'S ARCHIE
Archie Publications: May, 1969 - No. 157, Sept, 1991 (Giant issues No. 1-20)

1-(68 pages) 7.25 21.75 80.00
2-(68 pages) 5.00 15.00 55.00
3-5-(68 pages) 3.65 11.00 40.00
6-13-(68 pages) 2.80 8.40 28.00
14-31-(52 pages) 2.00 6.00 18.00
32 (7/74)-50 (8/76) 1.25 3.75 10.00
51-80 (12/79),100 (4/82) 1.00 3.00 8.00
81-99 2.40 6.00
101-120 5.00
121-157: 142,148-Gene Colan-a 3.00

EVERYTHING'S DUCKY (Movie)
Dell Publishing Co.: No. 1251, 1961

Four Color 1251 4.10 12.30 45.00

EVIL ERNIE
Eternity Comics: Dec, 1991 - No. 5, 1992 ($2.50, B&W, limited series)

1-1st app. Lady Death by Steven Hughes (12,000 print run); Lady Death app. in all issues 4.55 13.65 50.00
2,3: 2-1st Lady Death-c. 2,3-(7,000 print run) 2.50 7.50 25.00
4-(8,000 print run) 2.30 7.00 20.00
5 2.00 6.00 16.00
Special Edition 1 2.50 7.50 25.00
Youth Gone Wild! ($9.95, trade paperback)-r/#1-5 1.25 3.75 10.00
Youth Gone Wild! Director's Cut ($4.95)-Limited to 15,000 copies, shows the making of the comic 5.00

EVIL ERNIE (Monthly series)
Chaos! Comics: July, 1998 - No. 10, Apr, 1999 ($2.95)

1-10-Pulido & Nutman-s/Brewer-a 3.00
1-($10.00) Premium Ed. 10.00

EVIL ERNIE: BADDEST BATTLES
Chaos! Comics: Jan, 1997 ($1.50, one-shot)

1-Pin-ups, 1-Variant-c 2.00

EVIL ERNIE: DEPRAVED
Chaos! Comics: Jul, 1999 - No. 3, Sept, 1999 ($2.95, limited series)

1-3-Pulido-s/Brewer-a 3.00

EVIL ERNIE: DESTROYER
Chaos! Comics: Oct, 1997 - No. 9, Jun, 1998 ($2.95, limited series)

Preview ($2.50), 1-9-Flip cover 3.00

EVIL ERNIE: PIECES OF ME
Chaos! Comics: Nov, 2000 ($2.95, B&W, one-shot)

1-Flashback story; Pulido-s/Beck-a 2.95

EVIL ERNIE: REVENGE
Chaos! Comics: Oct, 1994 - No.4, Feb, 1995 ($2.95, limited series)

1: 1-Glow-in-the-dark-c; Lady Death app. 1-3-flip book w. Kilzone Preview (series of 3) 5.00
1-Commemorative-(4000 print run) 1.25 3.75 10.00
2-4 4.00
Trade paperback (10/95, $12.95) 13.00

EVIL ERNIE: STRAIGHT TO HELL

Evil Ernie Straight to Hell #4 © Chaos!

Excalibur #122 © MAR

Exciting Comics #7 © STD

GD2.0 FN6.0 NM9.4

Chaos! Comics: Oct, 1995 - No. 5, May, 1996 ($2.95, limited series)

1-5: 1-fold-out-c 3.00
1,3:1-($19.95) Chromium Ed. 3-Chastity Chase-c-(4000 printed) 20.00
Special Edition (10,000) 20.00

EVIL ERNIE: THE RESURRECTION
Chaos! Comics: 1993 - No. 4, 1994 (Limited series)

0 5.00
1 1.50 4.50 12.00
1A-Gold 3.00 9.00 30.00
2-4 1.00 3.00 8.00

EVIL ERNIE VS. THE MOVIE MONSTERS
Chaos! Comics: Mar, 1997 ($2.95, one-shot)

1 3.00
1-Variant-"Chaos-Scope•Terror Vision" card stock-c 5.00

EVIL ERNIE VS. THE SUPER HEROES
Chaos! Comics: Aug, 1995; Sept, 1998 ($2.95)

1-Lady Death poster 3.00
1-Foil-c variant (limited to 10,000) 2.50 7.50 20.00
1-Limited Edition (1000) 2.50 7.50 20.00
2-(9/98) Ernie vs. JLA and Marvel parodies 3.00

EVIL ERNIE: WAR OF THE DEAD
Chaos! Comics: Nov, 1999 - No. 3, Jan, 2000 ($2.95, limited series)

1-3-Pulido & Kaminski-s/Brewer-a. 3-End of Evil Ernie 2.95

EVIL EYE
Fantagraphics Books: June, 1998 - Present ($2.95, B&W)

1-6-Richard Sala-s/a 3.00

EWOKS (Star Wars) (TV) (See Star Comics Magazine)
Marvel Comics (Star Comics): June, 1985 - No. 14, Jul, 1987 (75¢/$1.00)

1,10: 10-Williamson-a (From Star Wars) 1.85 5.50 15.00
2-9 1.50 4.50 12.00
11-14: 14-($1.00-c) 1.75 5.25 14.00

EXCALIBUR (Also see Marvel Comics Presents #31)
Marvel Comics: Apr, 1988; Oct, 1988 - No. 125, Oct, 1998 ($1.50/$1.75/$1.99)

Special Edition nn (The Sword is Drawn)(4/88, $3.25)-1st Excalibur comic 2.40 6.00
Special Edition nn (4/88)-no price on-c (scarce) 1.25 3.75 10.00
Special Edition nn (2nd & print, 10/88, 12/89) 3.00
...The Sword is Drawn (Apr, 1992, $4.95) 4.00
1($1.50, 10/88)-X-Men spin-off; Nightcrawler, Shadowcat(Kitty Pryde), Capt. Britain, Phoenix & Meggan begin 5.00
2-4 3.00
5-10 2.50
11-49,51-70,72-74,76: 10,11-Rogers/Austin-a; Austin-i. 21-Intro Crusader X. 22-Iron Man x-over. 24-John Byrne app. in story. 26-Ron Lim-c/a. 27-B. Smith-a(p). 37-Dr. Doom & Iron Man app. 41-X-Men (Wolverine) app.; Cable cameo 49-Neal Adams c-swipe. 52,57-X-Men(Cyclops, Wolverine) app. 53-Spider-Man-c/story. 58-X-Men (Wolverine, Gambit, Cyclops, etc.)-c/story. 61-Phoenix returns. 68-Starjammers-c/story 2.00
50-($2.75, 56 pgs.)-New logo 2.75
71-($3.95, 52 pgs.)-Hologram on-c; 30th anniversary 4.00
75-($3.50, 52 pgs.)-Holo-grafx foil-c 4.00
75-($2.25, 52 pgs.)-Regular edition 2.25
77-81,83-86: 77-Begin $1.95-c; bound-in trading card sheet. 83-86-Deluxe Editions and Standard Editions. 86-1st app. Pete Wisdom 2.00
82-($2.50)-Newsstand edition 2.50
82-($3.50)-Enhanced edition 3.50
87-89,91-99,101-110: 87-Return from Age of Apocalypse. 92-Colossus-c/app. 94-Days of Future Tense 95-X-Man-c/app. 96-Sebastian Shaw & the Hellfire Club app. 99-Onslaught app. 101-Onslaught tie-in. 102-w/card insert. 103-Last Warren Ellis scripts; Belasco app. 104,105-Hitch & Neary-c/a. 109-Spiral-c/app. 2.00
90,100-($2.95)-double-sized. 100-Onslaught tie-in; wraparound-c 3.50
111-124: 111-Begin $1.99-c, wraparound-c. 119-Calafiore-a 2.00
125-($2.99) Wedding of Capt. Britain and Meggan 3.00

GD2.0 FN6.0 NM9.4

Annual 1,2 ('93, '94, 68 pgs.)-1st app. Khaos. 2-X-Men & Psylocke app. 3.00
#(-1) Flashback (7/97) 2.00
...Air Apparent nn (12/91, $4.95)-Simonson-c 5.00
...Mojo Mayhem nn (12/89, $4.50)-Art Adams/Austin-c/a 4.50
...: The Possession nn (7/91, $2.95, 52 pgs.) 3.00
...: XX Crossing (7/92, 5/92-inside, $2.50)-vs. The X-Men 2.50

EXCALIBUR
Marvel Comics: Feb, 2001 - No. 4, May, 2001 ($2.99)

1-Return of Captain Britain; Raimondi-a 3.00

EXCITING COMICS
Nedor/Better Publications/Standard Comics: Apr, 1940 - No. 69, Sept, 1949

1-Origin & 1st app. The Mask, Jim Hatfield, Sgt. Bill King, Dan Williams begin; early Robot-c (see Smash #1) 362.00 1086.00 3800.00
2-The Sphinx begins; The Masked Rider app.; Son of the Gods begins, ends #8 158.00 474.00 1500.00
3-Robot-c 105.00 316.00 1000.00
4-6 71.00 213.00 675.00
7,8 58.00 174.00 550.00
9-Origin/1st app. of The Black Terror & sidekick Tim, begin series (5/41) (Black Terror c-9-52,54,55) 783.00 2348.00 9000.00
10-2nd app. Black Terror 263.00 790.00 2500.00
11 132.00 395.00 1250.00
12,13 87.00 261.00 825.00
14-Last Sphinx, Dan Williams 61.00 182.00 575.00
15-The Liberator begins (origin) 63.00 189.00 600.00
16-20: 20-The Mask ends 53.00 158.00 475.00
21,23-25: 25-Robot-c 44.00 133.00 400.00
22-Origin The Eaglet; The American Eagle begins 53.00 158.00 475.00
26,27,29,30: 26-Schomburg-c begin 55.00 165.00 525.00
28-(Scarce) Crime Crusader begins, ends #58 66.00 197.00 625.00
31-38: 35-Liberator ends, not in 31-33 50.00 150.00 450.00
39-Origin Kara, Jungle Princess 61.00 182.00 575.00
40-50: 42-The Scarab begins. 45-Schomburg Robot-c. 49-Last Kara, Jungle Princess. 50-Last American Eagle 55.00 165.00 525.00
51-Miss Masque begins (1st app.) 61.00 182.00 575.00
52-54: Miss Masque ends. 53-Miss Masque-c 53.00 158.00 475.00
55-58: 55-Judy of the Jungle begins (origin), ends #69; 1 pg. Ingels-a; Judy of the Jungle c-56-66. 57,58-Airbrush-c 55.00 165.00 525.00
59-Frazetta art in Caniff style; signed Frank Frazeta (one t), 9 pgs. 55.00 165.00 525.00
60-66: 60-Rick Howard, the Mystery Rider begins. 66-Robinson/Meskin-a 50.00 150.00 450.00
67-69-All western covers 20.00 60.00 160.00

NOTE: ***Schomburg (Xela)** c-26-68; airbrush c-57-66. Black Terror by **R. Moreira**-#65. **Rousso** a-62. Bondage-c 9, 12, 13, 20, 23, 25, 30, 59.*

EXCITING ROMANCES
Fawcett Publications: 1949 (nd); No. 2, Spring, 1950 - No. 5, 10/50; No. 6 (1951, nd); No. 7, 9/51 -No. 12, 1/53

1,3: 1(1949). 3-Wood-a 13.00 39.00 105.00
2,4,5-(1950) 8.65 26.00 60.00
6-12 7.00 21.00 48.00

NOTE: ***Powell** a-8-10. **Marcus Swayze** a-5, 6, 9. Photo c-1-7, 10-12.*

EXCITING ROMANCE STORIES (See Fox Giants)

EXCITING WAR (Korean War)
Standard Comics (Better Publ.): No. 5, Sept, 1952 - No. 8, May, 1953; No. 9, Nov, 1953

5 8.65 26.00 60.00
6,7,9 5.00 15.00 35.00
8-Toth-a 7.85 23.50 55.00

EXCITING X-PATROL
Marvel Comics (Amalgam): June, 1997 ($1.95, one-shot)

1-Barbara Kesel-s/ Bryan Hitch-a 2.00

EXILES (Also see Break-Thru)
Malibu Comics (Ultraverse): Aug, 1993 - No. 4, Nov, 1993 ($1.95)

1,2,4: 1,2-Bagged copies of each exist. 2-Gustovich-c. 4-Team dies; story

Explorer Joe #2 © Z-D

Exposed #9 © DS

Factor X #2 © MAR

GD2.0 FN6.0 NM9.4

cont'd in Break-Thru #1 — 2.00
-($2.50, 40 pgs.)-Rune flip-c/story by B. Smith (3 pgs.) — 2.50
-Holographic-c edition — 1.00 — 3.00 — 8.00

:ILES (All New, The) (2nd Series) (Also see Black September)
alibu Comics (Ultraverse): Sept, 1995 - V2#11, Aug, 1996 ($1.50)

inity (9/95, $1.50)-Intro new team including Marvel's Juggernaut & Reaper. — 2.00
inity (2000 signed), V2#1 (2000 signed) — 1.25 — 3.75 — 10.00
#1-4,6-11: 1-(10/95, 64 pgs.)-Reprint of Ultraforce V2#1 follows lead story. 2-1st app. Hellblade. 8-Intro Maxis. 11-Vs. Maxis; Ripfire app.; cont'd in Ultraforce #12 — 2.00
#5-($2.50) Juggernaut returns to the Marvel Universe. — 2.50

:ILES VS THE X-MEN
alibu Comics (Ultraverse): Oct, 1995 (one-shot)

-Limited Super Premium Edition; signed w/certificate; gold foil logo,
-Limited Premium Edition — 1.25 — 3.75 — 10.00

:-MUTANTS
alibu Comics: Nov, 1992 - No. 18, Apr, 1994 ($1.95/$2.25/$2.50)

-18: 1-Polybagged w/Skycap — 2.50

:ORCISTS (See The Crusaders)

:OSQUAD (TV)
pps Comics: No. 0, Jan, 1994 ($1.25)

-($1.00, 20 pgs.)-1st app.; Staton-a(p); wraparound-c — 2.00

:OTIC ROMANCES (Formerly True War Romances)
ality Comics Group (Comic Magazines): No. 22, Oct, 1955-No. 31, Nov, 1956

: — 10.00 — 30.00 — 70.00
-26,29 — 5.00 — 15.00 — 35.00
',31-Baker-c/a — 12.50 — 37.50 — 100.00
,30-Baker-a — 10.00 — 30.00 — 80.00

PLOITS OF DANIEL BOONE
ality Comics Group: Nov, 1955 - No. 6, Oct, 1956

-All have Cuidera-c(i) — 28.00 — 83.00 — 220.00
 — 18.00 — 53.00 — 140.00
-6 — 15.00 — 45.00 — 120.00

PLOITS OF DICK TRACY (See Dick Tracy)

:PLORER JOE
f-Davis Comic Group (Approved Comics): Win, 1951 - No. 2, Oct-Nov, 1952

-2: Saunders painted covers; 2-Krigstein-a — 12.50 — 37.50 — 100.00

PLORERS OF THE UNKNOWN (See Archie Giant Series #587, 599)
chie Comics: June, 1990 - No. 6, Apr, 1991 ($1.00)

-6: Featuring Archie and the gang — 3.00

'POSED (...True Crime Cases; ...Cases in the Crusade Against Crime #5-9)
S. Publishing Co.: Mar-Apr, 1948 - No. 9, July-Aug, 1949

 — 23.00 — 68.00 — 180.00
-Giggling killer story with excessive blood; two injury-to-eye panels; electrocution panel — 28.00 — 84.00 — 225.00
8,9 — 11.00 — 33.00 — 90.00
Orlando-a — 12.00 — 36.00 — 95.00
-Breeze Lawson, Sky Sheriff by E. Good — 12.00 — 36.00 — 95.00
7: 6-Ingels-a; used in **SOTI**, illo. "How to prepare an alibi" 7-Illo. in **SOTI**, "Diagram for housebreakers;" used by N.Y. Legis. Committee — 39.00 — 118.00 — 315.00

POSURE
age Comics: 1999 - Present ($2.50)

-4: Al Rio-a/David Campiti-s. 1-Wraparound & photo covers — 2.50
-Variant-c — 10.00
elude ($5.00) — 5.00

POSURE SECOND COMING
atar Press: Sept, 2000 - Present ($3.50)

-Al Rio-a/David Campiti-s; wraparound & photo covers — 3.50

TRA!
E. C. Comics: Mar-Apr, 1955 - No. 5, Nov-Dec, 1955

1-Not code approved — 18.00 — 54.00 — 160.00
2-5 — 12.00 — 36.00 — 110.00
NOTE: ***Craig, Crandall, Severin*** *art in all.*

EXTRA!
Gemstone Publishing: Jan, 2000 - No. 5 ($2.50)

1,2-Reprints E.C. series — 2.50

EXTRA COMICS
Magazine Enterprises: 1948 (25¢, 3 comics in one)

1-Giant; consisting of rebound ME comics. Two versions known; (1)-Funnyman by Siegel & Shuster, Space Ace, Undercover Girl, Red Fox by L.B. Cole, Trail Colt & (2)-All Funnyman — 53.00 — 158.00 — 475.00

EXTREME
Image Comics (Extreme Studios): Aug, 1993 (Giveaway)

0 — 3.00

EXTREME DESTROYER
Image Comics (Extreme Studios): Jan, 1996 ($2.50)

Prologue 1-Polybagged w/card; Liefeld-c, Epilogue 1-Liefeld-c — 2.50

EXTREME JUSTICE
DC Comics: No. 0, Jan, 1995 - No. 18, July, 1996 ($1.50/$1.75)

0-18 — 3.00

EXTREMELY YOUNGBLOOD
Image Comics (Extreme Studios): Sept, 1996 ($3.50, one-shot)

1 — 3.50

EXTREME SACRIFICE
Image Comics (Extreme Studios): Jan, 1995 ($2.50, limited series)

Prelude (#1)-Liefeld wraparound-c; polybagged w/ trading card — 2.50
Epilogue (#2)-Liefeld wraparound-c; polybagged w/trading card — 2.50
Trade paperback (6/95, $16.95)-Platt-a — 17.00

EXTREME SUPER CHRISTMAS SPECIAL
Image Comics (Extreme Studios): Dec, 1994 ($2.95, one-shot)

1 — 3.00

EXTREMIST, THE
DC Comics (Vertigo): Sept, 1993 - No. 4, Dec, 1993 ($1.95, limited series)

1-4-Peter Milligan scripts; McKeever-c/a — 2.00
1-Platinum Edition — 5.00

EYE OF THE STORM
Rival Productions: Dec, 1994 - No. 7, June, 1995? ($2.95)

1-7: Computer generated comic — 3.00

FACE
DC Comics (Vertigo): Jan, 1995 ($4.95, one-shot)

1 — 5.00

FACE, THE (Tony Trent, the Face No. 3 on) (See Big Shot Comics)
Columbia Comics Group: 1941 - No. 2, 1943

1-The Face; Mart Bailey-c — 90.00 — 270.00 — 850.00
2-Bailey-c — 53.00 — 158.00 — 475.00

FACTOR X
Marvel Comics: Mar, 1995 - No. 4, July, 1995 ($1.95, limited series)

1-Age of Apocalypse — 3.00
2-4 — 2.00

FACULTY FUNNIES
Archie Comics: June, 1989 - No. 5, May, 1990 (75¢/95¢ #2 on)

1-5: 1,2-The Awesome Four app. — 3.00

FAFHRD AND THE GREY MOUSER (Also see Sword of Sorcery & Wonder Woman #202)
Marvel Comics: Oct, 1990 - No. 4, 1991 ($4.50, 52 pgs., squarebound)

1-4: Mignola/Williamson-a; Chaykin scripts — 4.50

FAIRY TALE PARADE (See Famous Fairy Tales)
Dell Publishing Co.: June-July, 1942 - No. 121, Oct, 1946 (Most by Walt Kelly)

Fairy Tales #11 © Z-D

Famous Crimes #14 © FOX

Famous First Edition F-4 © DC

	GD2.0	FN6.0	NM9.4
1-Kelly-a begins	121.00	363.00	1450.00
2(8-9/42)	50.00	150.00	600.00
3-5 (10-11/42 - 2-4/43)	35.00	105.00	420.00
6-9 (5-7/43 - 11-1/43-44)	27.00	80.00	320.00
Four Color 50('44),69('45), 87('45)	25.00	75.00	300.00
Four Color 104,114('46)-Last Kelly issue	18.00	55.00	220.00
Four Color 121('46)-Not by Kelly	11.00	33.00	130.00

NOTE: *#1-9, 4-Color #50, 69 have* ***Kelly*** *c/a; 4-Color #87, 104, 114-***Kelly** *art only. #9 has a redrawn version of The Reluctant Dragon. This series contains all the classic fairy tales from Jack In The Beanstalk to Cinderella.*

FAIRY TALES
Ziff-Davis Publ. Co. (Approved Comics): No. 10, Apr-May, 1951 - No. 11, June-July, 1951

	GD2.0	FN6.0	NM9.4
10,11-Painted-c	19.00	56.00	150.00

FAITH
DC Comics (Vertigo): Nov, 1999 - No. 5, Mar, 2000 ($2.50, limited series)

	GD2.0	FN6.0	NM9.4
1-5-Ted McKeever-s/c/a			2.50

FAITHFUL
Marvel Comics/Lovers' Magazine: Nov, 1949 - No. 2, Feb, 1950 (52 pgs.)

	GD2.0	FN6.0	NM9.4
1,2-Photo-c	10.00	30.00	70.00

FALCON (See Marvel Premiere #49)(Also see Avengers #181 & Captain America #117 & 133)
Marvel Comics Group: Nov, 1983 - No. 4, Feb, 1984 (Mini-series)

	GD2.0	FN6.0	NM9.4
1-4: 1-Paul Smith-c/a(p). 2-Paul Smith-c			2.00

FALLEN ANGEL ON THE WORLD OF MAGIC: THE GATHERING
Acclaim (Armada): May, 1996 ($5.95, one-shot)

	GD2.0	FN6.0	NM9.4
1-Nancy Collins story.			6.00

FALLEN ANGELS
Marvel Comics Group: April, 1987 - No. 8, Nov, 1987 (Limited series)

	GD2.0	FN6.0	NM9.4
1-8			2.00

FALLING IN LOVE
Arleigh Pub. Co./National Per. Pub.: Sept-Oct, 1955 - No. 143, Oct-Nov, 1973

	GD2.0	FN6.0	NM9.4
1	38.00	113.00	300.00
2	19.00	56.00	150.00
3-10	11.00	33.00	90.00
11-20	9.30	28.00	65.00
21-40	6.40	19.25	45.00
41-47: 47-Last 10¢ issue?	5.00	15.00	32.00
48-70	2.50	7.50	24.00
71-99,108: 108-Wood-a (4 pgs., 7/69)	2.00	6.00	18.00
100	3.00	9.00	32.00
101-107,109-124	1.75	5.25	14.00
134-143	1.50	4.50	12.00
125-133: 52 pgs.	2.50	7.50	25.00

NOTE: ***Colan*** *c/a-75, 81. 52 pgs.-#125-133.*

FALLING MAN, THE
Image Comics: Feb, 1998 ($2.95)

	GD2.0	FN6.0	NM9.4
1-McCorkindale-s/Hester-a			3.00

FALL OF THE HOUSE OF USHER, THE (See A Corben Special & Spirit section 8/22/48)

FALL OF THE ROMAN EMPIRE (See Movie Comics)

FAMILY AFFAIR (TV)
Gold Key: Feb, 1970 - No. 4, Oct, 1970 (25¢)

	GD2.0	FN6.0	NM9.4
1-With pull-out poster; photo-c	5.00	15.00	60.00
1-With poster missing	2.50	7.50	25.00
2-4: 3,4-Photo-c	3.00	9.00	30.00

FAMILY FUNNIES
Parents' Magazine Institute: No. 9, Aug-Sept, 1946

	GD2.0	FN6.0	NM9.4
9	4.65	14.00	28.00

FAMILY FUNNIES (Tiny Tot Funnies No. 9)
Harvey Publications: Sept, 1950 - No. 8, Apr, 1951

	GD2.0	FN6.0	NM9.4
1-Mandrake (has over 30 King Feature strips)	9.30	28.00	65.00
2-Flash Gordon, 1 pg.	6.40	19.25	45.0
3-8: 4,5,7-Flash Gordon, 1 pg.	5.50	16.50	38.0

FAMILY MAN
DC Comics (Paradox Press): 1995 - No. 3, 1995 ($4.95, B&W, digest-size, limited series)

	GD2.0	FN6.0	NM9
1-3			5.0

FAMILY MATTER
Kitchen Sink Press: 1998 ($24.95/$15.95, graphic novel)

	GD2.0	FN6.0	NM9
Hardcover ($24.95) Will Eisner-s/a			25.0
Softcover ($15.95)			16.0

FAMOUS AUTHORS ILLUSTRATED (See Stories by...)

FAMOUS CRIMES
Fox Features Syndicate/M.S. Dist. No. 51,52: June, 1948 - No. 19, Sept, 195 No. 20, Aug, 1951; No. 51, 52, 1953

	GD2.0	FN6.0	NM9
1-Blue Beetle app. & crime story-r/Phantom Lady #16	50.00	150.00	450.0
2-Has woman dissolved in acid; lingerie-c/panels	40.00	120.00	340.0
3-Injury-to-eye story used in **SOTI**, pg. 112; has two electrocution stories	47.00	142.00	425.0
4-6	22.00	66.00	175.0
7- "Tarzan, the Wyoming Killer" used in **SOTI**, pg. 44; drug trial/ possession story	40.00	120.00	340.0
8-20: 17-Morisi-a. 20-Same cover as #15	17.00	51.00	135.0
51(nd, 1953)	15.00	45.00	120.0
52	10.00	30.00	70.0

FAMOUS FEATURE STORIES
Dell Publishing Co.: 1938 (7-1/2x11", 68 pgs.)

	GD2.0	FN6.0	NM9
1-Tarzan, Terry & the Pirates, King of the Royal Mtd., Buck Jones, Dick Tracy Smilin' Jack, Dan Dunn, Don Winslow, G-Man, Tailspin Tommy, Mutt & Jeff Little Orphan Annie reprints - all illustrated text	68.00	205.00	650.0

FAMOUS FIRST EDITION (See Limited Collectors' Edition)
National Periodical Publications/DC Comics: ($1.00, 10x13-1/2", 72 pgs.) (No.6-8, 68 pgs.) 1974 - No. 8, Aug-Sept, 1975; C-61, 1979
(Hardbound editions with dust jackets are from Lyle Stuart, Inc.)

	GD2.0	FN6.0	NM9
C-26-Action Comics #1; gold ink outer-c	3.20	9.60	35.0
C-26-Hardbound edition w/dust jacket	16.50	49.00	180.0
C-28-Detective #27; silver ink outer-c	5.45	16.35	60.0
C-28-Hardbound edition w/dust jacket	21.50	64.00	235.0
C-30-Sensation #1(1974); bronze ink outer-c	3.20	9.60	35.0
C-30-Hardbound edition w/dust jacket	16.50	49.00	180.0
F-4-Whiz Comics #2(#1)(10-11/74)-Cover not identical to original (dropped "Gangway for Captain Marvel" from cover); gold ink on outer-c	3.20	9.60	35.0
F-4-Hardbound edition w/dust jacket	16.50	49.00	180.0
F-5-Batman #1(F-6 inside); silver ink on outer-c	4.55	13.65	50.0
F-5-Hardbound edition w/dust jacket	16.50	49.00	180.0
V2#F-6-Wonder Woman #1	3.20	9.60	35.0
F-7-All-Star Comics #3	2.80	8.40	28.0
F-8-Flash Comics #1(8-9/75)	2.80	8.40	28.0
V8#C-61-Superman #1(1979, $2.00)	2.50	7.50	24.0

Warning: The above books are almost **exact** reprints of the originals that they represent exc for the Giant-Size format. None of the originals are Giant-Size. The first five issues and C-61 w printed with two covers. Reprint information can be found on the outside cover, but not on inside cover which was reprinted exactly like the original (inside and out).

FAMOUS FUNNIES
Eastern Color: 1934; July, 1934 - No. 218, July, 1955

A Carnival of Comics (See Promotional Comics section)

	GD2.0	FN6.0	VF8.
Series 1-(Very rare)(nd-early 1934)(68 pgs.) No publisher given (Eastern Color PrintingCo.); sold in chain stores for 10¢. 35,000 print run. Contains Sunday strip reprints of Mutt & J Reg'lar Fellers, Nipper, Hairbreadth Harry, Strange As It Seems, Joe Palooka, Dixie Dugan, Nebbs, Keeping Up With the Jones, and others. Inside front and back covers and pages 1-1 Famous Funnies Series 1, #s 49-64 reprinted from **Famous Funnies**, **A Carnival of Com** and most of pages 17-48 reprinted from **Funnies on Parade**. This was the first comic book sol	4000.00	12,000.00	25,000.

No. 1 (Rare)(7/34-on stands 5/34) - Eastern Color Printing Co. First monthly newsstand comic book. Contains Sunday strip reprints of Toonerville Folks, Mutt & Jeff, Hairbreadth Harry, S'Ma

Famous Funnies #6 © EAS

Famous Funnies #124 © EAS

Fanboy #5 © DC

GD2.0 FN6.0 NM9.4

Pop, Nipper, Dixie Dugan, The Bungle Family, Connie, Ben Webster, Tailspin Tommy, The Nebbs, Joe Palooka, & others. 3000.00 9000.00 18,000.00

2 (Rare, 9/34) 525.00 1575.00 3400.00

3-Buck Rogers Sunday strip-r by Rick Yager begins, ends #218; not in #191-208; 1st comic book app. of Buck Rogers; the number of the 1st strip reprinted is pg. 190, Series No. 1 680.00 2040.00 4400.00

4 215.00 645.00 1400.00

5-1st Christmas-c on a newsstand comic 185.00 555.00 1200.00

6-10 123.00 370.00 800.00

GD2.0 FN6.0 NM9.4

11,12,18-Four pgs. of Buck Rogers in each issue, completes stories in Buck Rogers #1 which lacks these pages. 18-Two pgs. of Buck Rogers reprinted in Daisy Comics #1 97.00 291.00 775.00

13-17,19,20: 14-Has two Buck Rogers panels missing. 17-2nd Christmas-c on a newsstand comic (12/35) 75.00 225.00 600.00

21,23-30: 27-(10/36)-War on Crime begins (4 pgs.); 1st true crime in comics (reprints); part photo-c. 29-X-Mas-c (12/36) 53.00 160.00 425.00

22-Four pgs. of Buck Rogers needed to complete stories in Buck Rogers #1 58.00 173.00 460.00

31,33,34,36,37,39,40: 33-Careers of Baby Face Nelson & John Dillinger traced 40.00 120.00 320.00

32-(3/37) 1st app. the Phantom Magician (costume hero) in Advs. of Patsy 43.00 130.00 340.00

35-Two pgs. Buck Rogers omitted in Buck Rogers #2 43.00 130.00 340.00

38-Full color portrait of Buck Rogers 41.00 122.00 325.00

41-60: 41,53-X-Mas-c. 55-Last bottom panel, pg. 4 in Buck Rogers redrawn in Buck Rogers #3 28.00 84.00 225.00

61,63,64,66,67,69,70 22.00 66.00 175.00

62,65,68,73-78-Two pgs. Kirby-a "Lightnin' & the Lone Rider". 65,77-X-Mas-c 25.00 75.00 200.00

71,79,80: 80-(3/41)-Buck Rogers story continues from Buck Rogers #5 16.00 49.00 130.00

72-Speed Spaulding begins by Marvin Bradley (artist), ends #88. This series was written by Edwin Balmer & Philip Wylie (later appeared as film & book "When Worlds Collide") 18.00 53.00 140.00

81-Origin & 1st app. Invisible Scarlet O'Neil (4/41); strip begins #82, ends #167; 1st non-funny-c (Scarlet O'Neil) 17.00 51.00 135.00

82-Buck Rogers-c 18.00 53.00 140.00

83-87,90: 86-Connie vs. Monsters on the Moon-c (sci/fi). 87 has last Buck Rogers full page-r. 90-Bondage-c 13.00 39.00 105.00

88,89: 88-Buck Rogers in "Moon's End" by Calkins, 2 pgs.(not reprints). Beginning with #88, all Buck Rogers pgs. have rearranged panels. 89-Origin & 1st app. Fearless Flint, the Flint Man 14.00 41.00 110.00

91-93,95,96,98-99,101,103-110: 105-Series 2 begins (Strip Page #1) 12.00 36.00 95.00

94-Buck Rogers in "Solar Holocaust" by Calkins, 3 pgs.(not reprints) 12.50 37.50 100.00

97-War Bond promotion, Buck Rogers by Calkins, 2 pgs.(not reprints) 12.50 37.50 100.00

00-1st comic to reach #100; 100th Anniversary cover features 11 major Famous Funnies characters, including Buck Rogers 14.00 41.00 110.00

02-Chief Wahoo vs. Hitler,Tojo & Mussolini-c (1/43) 40.00 120.00 320.00

11-130 (5/45): 113-X-Mas-c 10.00 30.00 70.00

31-150 (1/47): 137-Strip page No. 110 omitted 7.85 23.50 55.00

51-162,164-168 6.40 19.25 45.00

63-St. Valentine's Day-c 7.15 21.50 50.00

69,170-Two text illos. by Williamson, his 1st comic book work 10.00 30.00 80.00

71-190: 171-Strip pgs. 227,229,230, Series 2 omitted. 172-Strip Pg. 232 omitted. 190-Buck Rogers ends with start of strip pg. 302, Series 2; Oaky Doaks-c/story 5.70 17.00 40.00

91-197,199,201,203,206-208: No Buck Rogers. 191-Barney Carr, Space detective begins, ends #192. 5.00 15.00 35.00

98,200,202,205-One pg. Frazetta ads; no B. Rogers 5.70 17.00 40.00

04-Used in **POP**, pg. 79,99; war-c begin, end #208 6.40 19.25 45.00

09-216: Frazetta-c. 209-Buck Rogers begins (12/53) with strip pg. 480, Series 2; 211-Buck Rogers ads by Anderson begins, ends #217. #215-Contains B. Rogers strip pg. 515-518, series 2 followed by pgs.179-181, Series 3 103.00 309.00 975.00

217,218-B. Rogers ends with pg. 199, Series 3. 218-Wee Three-c/story 5.70 17.00 40.00

NOTE: ***Rick Yager*** *did the Buck Rogers Sunday strips reprinted in Famous Funnies. The Sundays were formerly done by Russ Keaton and Lt. Dick Calkins did the dailies, but would sometimes assist Yager on a panel or two from time to time. Strip No. 169 is Yager's first full Buck Rogers page. Yager did the strip until 1958 when* ***Murphy Anderson*** *took over.* ***Tuska*** *art from 4/26/59 - 1965. Virtually every panel was rewritten for Famous Funnies. Not identical to the original Sunday page. The Buck Rogers reprints run continuously through Famous Funnies issue No. 190 (Strip No. 302) with no break in story line. The story line has no continuity after No. 190. The Buck Rogers newspaper strips came out in four series: Series 1, 3/30/30 - 9/21/41 (No. 1 - 600); Series 2, 9/28/41 -10/21/51 (No. 1 -525)(Strip No. 110-1/2 (1/2 pg.) published in only a few newspapers); Series 3, 10/28/51 -2/9/58 (No. 100-428)(No No.1-99); Series 4, 2/16/58 - 6/13/65 (No numbers, dates only).* ***Everett*** *c-85, 86.* ***Moulton*** *a-100. Chief Wahoo c-93, 97, 102, 116, 136, 139, 151. Dickie Dare c-83, 88. Fearless Flint c-89. Invisible Scarlet O'Neil c-81, 87, 95, 121(part), 132. Scorchy Smith c-84, 90.*

FAMOUS FUNNIES
Super Comics: 1964

Super Reprint Nos. 15-18:17-r/Double Trouble #1. 18-Space Comics #? 2.00 6.00 16.00

FAMOUS GANGSTERS (Crime on the Waterfront No. 4)
Avon Periodicals/Realistic No. 3: Apr, 1951 - No. 3, Feb, 1952

1-3: 1-Capone, Dillinger; c-/Avon paperback #329. 2-Dillinger Machine Gun Killer; Wood-c/a (1 pg.); r/Saint #7 & retitled "Mike Strong". 3-Lucky Luciano & Murder, Inc; c-/Avon paperback #66 38.00 113.00 300.00

FAMOUS INDIAN TRIBES
Dell Publishing Co.: July-Sept, 1962; No. 2, July, 1972

12-264-209(#1) (The Sioux) 2.00 6.00 18.00

2(7/72)-Reprints above 2.40 6.00

FAMOUS STARS
Ziff-Davis Publ. Co.: Nov-Dec, 1950 - No. 6, Spring, 1952 (All have photo-c)

1-Shelley Winters, Susan Peters, Ava Gardner, Shirley Temple; Jimmy Stewart & Shelley Winters photo-c; Whitney-a 33.00 98.00 260.00

2-Betty Hutton, Bing Crosby, Colleen Townsend, Gloria Swanson; Betty Hutton photo-c; Everett-a(2) 22.00 66.00 175.00

3-Farley Granger, Judy Garland's ordeal, Alan Ladd; Farley Granger & Judy Garland photo-c; Whitney-a 23.00 68.00 180.00

4-Al Jolson, Bob Mitchum, Ella Raines, Richard Conte, Vic Damone; Bob Mitchum photo-c; Crandall-a, 6pgs. 19.00 56.00 150.00

5-Liz Taylor, Betty Grable, Esther Williams, George Brent, Mario Lanza; Liz Taylor photo-c; Krigstein-a 28.00 83.00 220.00

6-Gene Kelly, Hedy Lamarr, June Allyson, William Boyd, Janet Leigh, Gary Cooper; Gene Kelly photo-c 16.00 49.00 130.00

FAMOUS STORIES (...Book No. 2)
Dell Publishing Co.: 1942 - No. 2, 1942

1,2: 1-Treasure Island. 2-Tom Sawyer 30.00 90.00 240.00

FAMOUS TV FUNDAY FUNNIES
Harvey Publications: Sept, 1961 (25¢ Giant)

1-Casper the Ghost, Baby Huey, Little Audrey 4.55 13.65 50.00

FAMOUS WESTERN BADMEN (Formerly Redskin)
Youthful Magazines: No. 13, Dec, 1952 - No. 15, Apr, 1953

13-Redskin story 12.00 36.00 95.00

14,15: 15-The Dalton Boys story 9.30 28.00 65.00

FAN BOY
DC Comics: Mar, 1999 - No. 6, Aug, 1999 ($2.50, limited series)

1-6: 1-Art by Aragonés and various in all. 2-Green Lantern-c/a by Gil Kane. 3-JLA. 4-Sgt. Rock. 5-Batman art by Sprang, Adams, Miller, Timm. 6-Wonder Woman; art by Rude, Grell 2.50

FANTASTIC (Formerly Captain Science; Beware No. 10 on)
Youthful Magazines: No. 8, Feb, 1952 - No. 9, Apr, 1952

8-Capt. Science by Harrison; decapitation, shrunken head panels 40.00 120.00 325.00

9-Harrison-a 30.00 90.00 240.00

FANTASTIC ADVENTURES
Super Comics: 1963 - 1964 (Reprints)

Fantastic Comics #6 © FOX

Fantastic Fears #5 © AJAX

Fantastic Four #1 © MAR

GD2.0 FN6.0 NM9.4

9,10,12,15,16,18: 9-r/? 10-r/He-Man #2(Toby). 11-Disbrow-a. 12-Unpublished Chesler material? 15-r/Spook #23. 16-r/Dark Shadows #2(Steinway); Briefer-a.18-r/Superior Stories #1 3.00 9.00 30.00
11-Wood-a; r/Blue Bolt #118 4.10 12.30 45.00
17-Baker-a(2) r/Seven Seas #6 4.10 12.30 45.00

FANTASTIC COMICS
Fox Features Syndicate: Dec, 1939 - No. 23, Nov, 1941

1-Intro/origin Samson; Stardust, The Super Wizard, Sub Saunders (by Kiefer), Space Smith, Capt. Kidd begin 435.00 1305.00 5000.00
2-Powell text illos 232.00 695.00 2200.00
3-Classic Lou Fine Robot-c; Powell text illos 1015.00 3045.00 6600.00
4,5: Last Lou Fine-c 179.00 537.00 1700.00
6,7-Simon-c 132.00 395.00 1250.00
8-10: 10-Intro/origin David, Samson's aide 92.00 276.00 875.00
11-17,19,20: 16-Stardust ends 76.00 229.00 725.00
18,23: 18-1st app. Black Fury & sidekick Chuck; ends #23. 23-Origin The Gladiator 79.00 237.00 750.00
21-The Banshee begins(origin); ends #23; Hitler-c 84.00 253.00 800.00
22-Hitler-c (likeness of Hitler as furnace on cover) 89.00 268.00 850.00
NOTE: ***Lou Fine** c-1-5. **Tuska** a-3-5, 8. Bondage c-6, 8, 9. Issue #11 has indicia to Mystery Men Comics #15. All issues feature Samson covers.*

FANTASTIC COMICS (Fantastic Fears #1-9; Becomes Samson #12)
Ajax/Farrell Publ.: No. 10, Nov-Dec, 1954 - No. 11, Jan-Feb, 1955

10 (#1) 19.00 56.00 150.00
11-Robot-c 22.00 66.00 175.00

FANTASTIC FABLES
Silverwolf Comics: Feb, 1987 - No. 2, 1987 ($1.50, 28 pgs., B&W)

1,2: 1-Tim Vigil-a (6 pgs.). 2-Tim Vigil-a (7 pgs.) 4.00

FANTASTIC FEARS (Formerly Captain Jet) (Fantastic Comics #10 on)
Ajax/Farrell Publ.: No. 7, May, 1953 - No. 9, Sept-Oct, 1954

7(#1, 5/53)-Tales of Stalking Terror 42.00 125.00 375.00
8(#2, 7/53) 31.00 94.00 250.00
3,4 23.00 69.00 185.00
5-(1-2/54)-Ditko story (1st drawn) is written by Bruce Hamilton; r-in Weird V2#8 (1st pro work for Ditko but Daring Love #1 was published 1st) 79.00 237.00 750.00
6-Decapitation-girl's head w/paper cutter (classic) 52.00 155.00 465.00
7(5-6/54), 9(9-10/54) 23.00 69.00 185.00
8(7-8/54)-Contains story intended for Jo-Jo; name changed to Kaza; decapitation story 28.00 84.00 225.00

FANTASTIC FIVE
Marvel Comics: Oct, 1999 - No. 5, Feb, 2000 ($1.99)

1-5: 1-M2 Universe; recaps origin; Ryan-a. 2-Two covers 2.00

FANTASTIC FORCE
Marvel Comics: Nov, 1994 - No. 18, Apr, 1996 ($1.75)

1-($2.50)-Foil wraparound-c; intro Fantastic Force w/Huntara, Delvor, Psi-Lord & Vibraxas 2.50
2-18: 13-She-Hulk app. 2.00

FANTASTIC FOUR (See America's Best TV..., Fireside Book Series, Giant-Size..., Giant Size Super-Stars, Marvel Collectors Item Classics, Marvel Milestone Edition, Marvel's Greatest, Marvel Treasury Edition, Marvel Triple Action, Official Marvel Index to... & Power Record Comics)

FANTASTIC FOUR
Marvel Comics Group: Nov, 1961 - No. 416, Sept, 1996 (Created by Stan Lee & Jack Kirby)

GD2.0 FN6.0 VF8.0 NM9.4

1-Origin & 1st app. The Fantastic Four (Reed Richards: Mr. Fantastic, Johnny Storm: The Human Torch, Sue Storm: The Invisible Girl, & Ben Grimm: The Thing–Marvel's 1st super-hero group since the G.A.; 1st app. S.A. Human Torch); origin/1st app. The Mole Man. 800.00 2400.00 8800.00 24,000.00

GD2.0 FN6.0 NM9.4

1-Golden Record Comic Set Reprint (1966)-cover not identical to original 14.50 43.50 160.00
with Golden Record 22.00 65.00 240.00
2-Vs. The Skrulls (last 10¢ issue) 263.00 788.00 4200.00

GD2.0 FN6.0 NM9.

3-Fantastic Four don costumes & establish Headquarters; brief 1pg. origin; intro The Fantasti-Car; Human Torch drawn w/two left hands on-c 180.00 540.00 2700.0
4-1st S. A. Sub-Mariner app. (5/62) 214.00 642.00 3300.0
5-Origin & 1st app. Doctor Doom 219.00 657.00 3500.0
6-Sub-Mariner, Dr. Doom team up; 1st Marvel villain team-up (2nd S.A. Sub-Mariner app. 129.00 386.00 1800.0
7-10: 7-1st app. Kurrgo. 8-1st app. Puppet-Master & Alicia Masters. 9-3rd Sub-Mariner app. 10-Stan Lee & Jack Kirby app. in story 69.00 206.00 960.0
11-Origin/1st app. The Impossible Man (2/63) 55.00 166.00 775.0
12-Fantantic Four Vs. The Hulk (1st meeting); 1st Hulk x-over & ties w/Amazing Spider-Man #1 as 1st Marvel x-over; (3/63) 104.00 311.00 1450.0
13-Intro. The Watcher; 1st app. The Red Ghost 41.00 123.00 525.0
14-19: 14-Sub-Mariner x-over. 15-1st app. Mad Thinker. 16-1st Ant-Man x-over (7/63); Wasp cameo. 18-Origin/1st app. The Super Skrull. 19-Intro. Rama-Tut; Stan Lee & Jack Kirby cameo 29.00 88.00 325.0
20-Origin/1st app. The Molecule Man 31.00 93.00 350.0
21-Intro. The Hate Monger; 1st Sgt. Fury x-over (12/63) 22.00 65.00 240.0
22-24: 22-Sue Storm gains more powers 15.50 46.50 170.0
25,26-The Hulk vs. The Thing (their 1st battle). 25-3rd Avengers x-over (1st time w/Capt. America)(cameo, 4/64); 2nd S.A. app. Cap (takes place between Avengers #4 & 5. 26-4th Avengers x-over 37.00 110.00 440.0
27-1st Doctor Strange x-over (6/64) 16.50 49.00 180.0
28-Early X-Men x-over (7/64); same date as X-Men #6 26.50 79.00 290.0
29,30: 30-Intro. Diablo 12.00 36.00 130.0
31-40: 31-Early Avengers x-over (10/64). 33-1st app. Attuma; part photo-c. 35-Intro/1st app. Dragon Man. 36-Intro/1st app. Madam Medusa & the Frightful Four (Sandman, Wizard, Paste Pot Pete). 39-Wood inks on Daredevil (early x-over) 10.00 30.00 110.0
41-44,47: 41-43-Frightful Four app. 44-Intro. Gorgon 7.25 21.75 80.0
45,46: 45-Intro/1st app. The Inhumans (c/story, 12/65); also see Incredible Hulk Special #1 & Thor #146, & 147. 46-1st Black Bolt-c (Kirby) & 1st full app. 8.65 26.00 95.0
48-Partial origin/1st app. The Silver Surfer & Galactus (3/66) by Lee & Kirby; Galactus cameo in last panel; 1st of 3 part story 75.00 225.00 1050.0
49-2nd app./1st cover Silver Surfer & Galactus 25.50 76.00 280.0
50-Silver Surfer battles Galactus; full S.S.-c 27.50 82.00 300.0
51,54: 54-Inhumans cameo 5.45 16.35 60.0
52-1st app. The Black Panther (7/66) 13.50 40.00 150.0
53-Origin & 2nd app. The Black Panther 9.50 28.50 105.0
55-Thing battles Silver Surfer; 4th app. Silver Surfer 9.00 27.00 100.0
56-Silver Surfer cameo 6.35 19.00 70.0
57-60: Dr. Doom steals Silver Surfer's powers (See Silver Surfer: Loftier Than Mortals) 59,60-Inhumans cameos 6.35 19.00 70.0
61-65,68-70: 61-Silver Surfer cameo; Sandman-c/s 4.55 13.65 50.0
66-Begin 2 part origin of Him (Warlock); does not app. (9/67) 9.50 28.50 105.0
67-Origin/1st app. Him (Warlock); 1 pg. cameo; see Thor #165,166 for 1st full app. 11.00 33.00 120.0
71,78-80 3.80 11.40 42.0
72-Silver Surfer-c/story (pre-dates Silver Surfer #1) 4.55 13.65 50.0
73-Spider-Man, D.D., Thor x-over; cont'd from Daredevil #38 4.10 12.30 45.0
74-77: Silver Surfer app.(#77 is same date/S.S. #1) 4.35 13.00 48.0
81-88: 81-Crystal joins & dons costume. 82,83-Inhumans app. 84-87-Dr. Doom app. 88-Last 12¢ issue 3.20 9.60 35.0
89-99,101: 94-Intro. Agatha Harkness. 3.00 9.00 30.0
100 (7/70) 8.15 24.50 90.0
102-104: F.F. vs. Sub-Mariner. 104-Magneto-c/story 3.00 9.00 32.0
105-109,111: 108-Last Kirby issue (not in #103-107) 2.30 7.00 20.0
110-Initial version w/green faces 3.20 9.60 35.0
110-Corrected-c w/flesh color faces and orange Thing. Initial version showed green faces. 3.00 9.00 30.0
112-Hulk Vs. Thing (7/71) 7.25 21.75 80.0
113-115: 115-Last 15¢ issue 2.00 6.00 18.0

Fantastic Four #201 © MAR

Fantastic Four V2 #4 © MAR

Fantastic Four V3 #26 © MAR

GD2.0 FN6.0 NM9.4

116 (52 pgs.) 2.50 7.50 24.00
117-120 1.75 5.25 14.00
121-123-Silver Surfer-c/stories. 122,123-Galactus 2.00 6.00 18.00
124,125,127,129-149: 129-Intro. Thundra. 130-Sue leaves F.F. 131-Quicksilver app. 132-Medusa joins. 133-Thundra Vs. Thing. 142-Kirbyish-a by Buckler begins. 143-Dr. Doom-c/story. 147-Sub-Mariner 1.50 4.50 12.00
126-Origin F.F. retold; cover swipe of F.F. #1 1.75 5.25 14.00
128-Four pg. insert of F.F. Friends & Foes 1.75 5.25 14.00
150-Crystal & Quicksilver's wedding 1.85 5.50 15.00
151-154,158-160: 151-Origin Thundra. 159-Medusa leaves; Sue rejoins 1.00 3.00 8.00
155-157: Silver Surfer in all 1.25 3.75 10.00
161-165,168,174-180: 164-The Crusader (old Marvel Boy) revived (origin #165); 1st app.Frankie Raye. 168-170-Cage app. 176-Re-intro Impossible Man; Marvel artists app. 180-r/#101 by Kirby 2.40 6.00
166,167-vs. Hulk 1.00 3.00 8.00
169-173-(Regular 25¢ edition)(4-8/75) 2.40 6.00
169-173-(30¢-c, limited distribution) 1.10 3.30 9.00
181-199: 189-G.A. Human Torch app. & origin retold. 190,191-Fantastic Four break up 5.00
184-(35¢-c variant, limited dist.)(7/77) 1.00 2.80 7.00
200-(11/78, 52 pgs.)-F.F. re-united vs. Dr. Doom 1.00 2.80 7.00
201-208,219,222-231: 207-Human Torch vs. Spider-Man-c/story. 211-1st app. Terrax. 224-Contains unused alternate-c for FF #3 and pin-ups 4.00
209-216,218,220,221-Byrne-a. 209-1st Herbie the Robot. 220-Brief origin 5.00
217-Dazzler app. by Byrne 5.00
232-Byrne-a begins 5.00
233-235,237-249,251-260: All Byrne-a. 238-Origin Frankie Raye. 244-Frankie Raye becomes Nova, Herald of Galactus. 252-Reads sideways; Annihilus app.; contains skin "Tattooz" decals 4.00
236-20th Anniversary issue(11/81, 68 pgs., $1.00)-Brief origin F.F.; Byrne-c/a(p); new Kirby-a(p) 5.00
250-(52 pgs)-Spider-Man x-over; Byrne-a; Skrulls impersonate New X-Men 5.00
261-285: 261-Silver Surfer. 262-Origin Galactus; Byrne writes & draws himself into story. 264-Swipes-c of F.F. #1. 274-Spider-Man's alien costume app. (4th app., 1/85, 2 pgs.) 3.00
286-2nd app. X-Factor continued from Avengers #263; story continues in X-Factor #1 4.00
287-295: 292-Nick Fury app. 293-Last Byrne-a 3.00
296-($1.50)-Barry Smith-c/a; Thing rejoins 4.00
297-318,321-330: 300-Johnny Storm & Alicia Masters wed. 306-New team begins (9/87). 311-Re-intro The Black Panther. 312-X-Factor x-over. 327-Mr. Fantastic & Invisible Girl return 2.50
319,320: 319-Double size. 320-Thing vs. Hulk 4.00
331-346,351-357,359,360: 334-Simonson-c/scripts begin. 337-Simonson-a begins. 342-Spider-Man cameo. 356-F.F. vs. The New Warriors; Paul Ryan-c/a begins. 360-Last $1.00-c 2.00
347-Ghost Rider, Wolverine, Spider-Man, Hulk-c/stories thru #349; Arthur Adams-c/a(p) in each 3.00
347,348-Gold 2nd printing 2.00
348,349 2.50
350-($1.50, 52 pgs.)-Dr. Doom app. 3.00
358-(11/91, $2.25, 88 pgs.)-30th anniversary issue; gives history of F.F.; die cut-c; Art Adams back-up story-a 2.50
361-368,370,372-374,376-380,382-386: 362-Spider-Man app. 367-Wolverine app. (brief). 370-Infinity War x-over; Thanos & Magus app. 374-Secret Defenders (Ghost Rider, Hulk, Wolverine) x-over 2.00
369-Infinity War x-over; Thanos app. 2.50
371-All white embossed-c ($2.00) 4.00
371-All red 2nd printing ($2.00) 2.50
375-($2.95, 52 pgs.)-Holo-grafx foil-c; ann. issue 3.00
381-Death of Reed Richards (Mister Fantastic) & Dr. Doom 4.00
387-Newsstand ed. ($1.25) 2.00
387-($2.95)-Collector's Ed. w/Die-cut foil-c 3.00
388-393,395-397: 388-bound-in trading card sheet. 394-($1.50-c) 2.00
394,398,399: 394 ($2.95)-Collector's Edition-polybagged w/16 pg. Marvel Action Hour book and acetate print; pink logo. 398,399-Rainbow Foil-c 3.00

GD2.0 FN6.0 NM9.4

400-Rainbow-Foil-c 3.50
401-415: 401,402-Atlantis Rising. 407,408-Return of Reed Richards. 411-Inhumans app. 414-Galactus vs. Hyperstorm. 415-Onslaught tie-in; X-Men app. 2.00
416-($2.50)-Onslaught tie-in; Dr. Doom app.; wraparound-c 3.00
Annual 1('63)-Origin F.F.; Ditko-i; early Spidey app. 57.00 171.00 800.00
Annual 2('64)-Dr. Doom origin & c/story 33.00 100.00 400.00
Annual 3('65)-Reed & Sue wed; r/#6,11 13.50 40.00 150.00
Special 4(11/66)-G.A. Torch x-over (1st S.A. app.) & origin retold; r/#25,26 (Hulk vs. Thing); Torch vs. Torch battle 8.65 26.00 95.00
Special 5(11/67)-New art; Intro. Psycho-Man; early Black Panther, Inhumans & Silver Surfer (1st solo story) app. 9.00 27.00 100.00
Special 6(11/68)-Intro. Annihilus; birth of Franklin Richards; new 48 pg. movie length epic; last non-reprint annual 5.00 15.00 55.00
Special 7(11/69)-r/F.F. #1-5; Marvel staff photos 2.80 8.40 28.00
Special 8-10: All reprints. 8(12/70)-F.F. vs. Sub-Mariner plus gallery of F.F. foes. 9(12/71). 10('73) 2.00 6.00 18.00
Annual 11-14: 11(1976)-New art begins again. 12(1978). 13(1978). 14(1979) 1.00 2.80 7.00
Annual 15-17: 15('80-'94, 68 pgs.).17(1983)-Byrne-c/a 5.00
Annual 18-27: 21(1988)-Evolutionary War x-over. 22-Atlantis Attacks x-over; Sub-Mariner & The Avengers app.; Buckler-a. 23-Byrne-c; Guice-p. 24-2 pg. origin recap of Fantastic Four; Guardians of the Galaxy x-over. 25-Moondragon story. 26-Bagged w/card 3.00
Special Edition 1(5/84)-r/Annual #1; Byrne-c/a 3.00
...: Monsters Unleashed nn (1992, $5.95)-r/F.F. #347-349 w/new Arthur Adams-c 2.40 6.00
...: Nobody Gets Out Alive (1994, $15.95) TPB r/ #387-392 16.00

NOTE: ***Arthur Adams*** *c/a-347-349p.* ***Austin*** *c(i)-232-236, 238, 240-242, 250i, 286i.* ***Buckler*** *c-151, 168.* ***John Buscema*** *a(p)-107, 108(w/**Kirby, Sinnott** & **Romita**),109-130, 132, 134-141, 160, 173-175, 202, 296-309p, Annual 11, 13; c(p)-107-122, 124-129, 133-139, 202, Annual 12p, Special 10.* ***Byrne*** *a-209-218p, 220p, 221p, 232-265, 266i, 267-273, 274-293p, Annual 17, 19; c-211-214p, 220p, 232-236p, 237, 238p, 239, 240-242p, 243-249, 250p, 251-267, 269-277, 278-281p, 283p, 284, 285, 286p, 288-293, Annual 17, 18.* ***Ditko*** *a-13i, 14i(w/**Kirby**-p), Annual 16.* ***G. Kane*** *c-145p, 146p, 150p, 160p.* ***Kirby*** *a-1-102p, 108p, 180r, 189r, 236p, Special 1-10; c-1-101, 164, 167, 171-177, 180, 181, 190, 200, Annual 11, Special 1-7, 9.* ***Marcos*** *a-Annual 14i.* ***Mooney*** *a-118i, 152i.* ***Perez*** *a(p)-164-167, 170-172, 176-178, 184-188, 191p, 192p. Annual 14p, 15p; c(p)-183-188, 191, 192, 194-197.* ***Simonson*** *a-337-341, 343, 344p, 345p, 346, 350p, 352-354; c-212, 334-341, 342p, 343-346, 350, 353, 354.* ***Steranko*** *c-130-132p.* ***Williamson*** *c-357i.*

FANTASTIC FOUR (Volume Two)
Marvel Comics: V2#1, Nov, 1996 - No. 13, Nov, 1997 ($2.95/$1.95/$1.99) (Produced by WildStorm Productions)

1-($2.95)-Reintro Fantastic Four; Jim Lee-c/a; Brandon Choi scripts; Mole Man app. 5.00
1-($2.95)-Variant-c 1.00 2.80 7.00
2-9: 2-Namor-c/app. 3-Avengers-c/app. 4-Two covers; Dr. Doom cameo 3.00
10,11,13: All $1.99-c. 13-"World War 3"-pt. 1, x-over w/Image 3.00
12-($2.99) "Heroes Reunited"-pt. 1 4.00
...: Heroes Reborn (7/00, $17.95, TPB) r/#1-6 17.95

FANTASTIC FOUR (Volume Three)
Marvel Comics: V3#1, Jan, 1998 - Present ($2.99/$1.99/$2.25)

1-($2.99)-Heroes Return; Lobdell-s/Davis & Farmer-a 5.00
1-Alternate Heroes Return-c 1.00 2.80 7.00
2-4,12: 2-2-covers. 4-Claremont-s/Larroca-a begin; Silver Surfer c/app.12-($2.99) Wraparound-c by Larroca 4.00
5-11: 6-Heroes For Hire app. 9-Spider-Man-c/app. 3.00
13-24: 13,14-Ronan-c/app. 2.00
25-($2.99) Dr. Doom returns 3.00
26-29: 27-Dr. Doom marries Sue 2.00
30-39: 30-Begin $2.25-c. 32-Namor-c/app. 35-Regular cover; Pacheco-s/a begins 37-Super-Skrull-c/app. 38-New Baxter Building 2.25
35-($3.25) Foil enhanced-c; Pacheco-s/a begins 3.25
...'98 Annual ($3.50) Immonen-a 3.50
...'99 Annual ($3.50) Ladronn-a 3.50
...'00 Annual ($3.50) Larocca-a; Marvel Girl back-up story 3.50
Wizard 1/2 -Lim-a 10.00

FANTASTIC FOUR: ATLANTIS RISING
Marvel Comics: June, 1995 - No. 2, July, 1995 ($3.95, limited series)

1,2: Acetate-c 4.00

Fantastic Four Unlimited #10 © MAR

Fantastic Worlds #6 © STD

Fast Fiction #5 © Seaboard Publ.

Collector's Preview (5/95, $2.25, 52 pgs.) 2.50

FANTASTIC FOUR: BIG TOWN
Marvel Comics: Jan, 2000 - No. 4, Apr, 2000 ($2.99, limited series)
1-2:"What If?" story; McKone-a 3.00

FANTASTIC FOUR: FIREWORKS
Marvel Comics: Jan, 1999 - No. 3, Mar, 1999 ($2.99, limited series)
1-3-Remix; Jeff Johnson-a 3.00

FANTASTIC FOUR INDEX (See Official...)

FANTASTIC FOUR ROAST
Marvel Comics Group: May, 1982 (75¢, one-shot, direct sales)
1-Celebrates 20th anniversary of F.F.#1; X-Men, Ghost Rider & many others cameo; Golden, Miller, Buscema, Rogers, Byrne, Anderson art; Hembeck/Austin-c 4.00

FANTASTIC FOUR: THE LEGEND
Marvel Comics: Oct, 1996 ($3.95, one-shot)
1-Tribute issue 4.00

FANTASTIC FOUR 2099
Marvel Comics: Jan, 1996 - No. 8, Aug, 1996 ($3.95/$1.95)
1-($3.95)-Chromium-c; X-Nation preview 4.00
2-8: 4-Spider-Man 2099-c/app. 5-Doctor Strange app. 7-Thibert-c 2.00
NOTE: ***Williamson*** *a-1i; c-1i.*

FANTASTIC FOUR UNLIMITED
Marvel Comics: Mar, 1993 - No. 12, Dec, 1995 ($3.95, 68 pgs.)
1-12: 1-Black Panther app. 4-Thing vs. Hulk. 5-Vs. The Frightful Four. 6-Vs. Namor. 7, 9-12-Wraparound-c 4.00

FANTASTIC FOUR UNPLUGGED
Marvel Comics: Sept, 1995 - No. 6, Aug 1996 (99¢, bi-monthly)
1-6 2.00

FANTASTIC FOUR VS. X-MEN
Marvel Comics: Feb, 1987 - No. 4, June, 1987 (Limited series)
1-4: 4-Austin-a(i) 3.00

FANTASTIC GIANTS (Formerly Konga #1-23)
Charlton Comics: V2#24, Sept, 1966 (25¢, 68 pgs.)
V2#24-Special Ditko issue; origin Konga & Gorgo reprinted plus two new Ditko stories 6.35 19.00 70.00

FANTASTIC TALES
I. W. Enterprises: 1958 (no date) (Reprint, one-shot)
1-Reprints Avon's "City of the Living Dead" 3.20 9.60 35.00

FANTASTIC VOYAGE (See Movie Comics)
Gold Key: Aug, 1969 - No. 2, Dec, 1969
1 (TV) 4.55 13.65 50.00
2 3.65 11.00 40.00

FANTASTIC VOYAGES OF SINDBAD, THE
Gold Key: Oct, 1965 - No. 2, June, 1967
1-Painted-c on both 5.00 15.00 60.00
2 4.55 13.65 50.00

FANTASTIC WORLDS
Standard Comics: No. 5, Sept, 1952 - No. 7, Jan, 1953
5-Toth, Anderson-a 35.00 105.00 280.00
6-Toth-c/a 30.00 90.00 240.00
7 19.00 56.00 150.00

FANTASY FEATURES
Americomics: 1987 - No. 2, 1987 ($1.75)
1,2 3.00

FANTASY ILLUSTRATED
New Media Publ.: Spring 1982 ($2.95, B&W magazine)
1-P. Craig Russell-c/a; art by Ditko, Sekowsky, Sutton; Englehart-s 1.00 2.80 7.00

FANTASY MASTERPIECES (Marvel Super Heroes No. 12 on)
Marvel Comics Group: Feb, 1966 - No. 11, Oct, 1967; V2#1, Dec, 1979 - No. 14, Jan, 1981
1-Photo of Stan Lee (12¢-c #1,2) 5.45 16.35 60.00
2-r/1st Fin Fang Foom from Strange Tales #89 3.00 9.00 30.00
3-8: 3-G.A. Capt. America-r begin, end #11; 1st 25¢ Giant; Colan-r. 3-6-Kirby-c (p). 4-Kirby-c(p)(i). 7-Begin G.A. Sub-Mariner, Torch-r/M. Mystery. 8-Torch battles the Sub-Mariner-r/Marvel Mystery #9 3.00 9.00 30.00
9-Origin Human Torch-r/Marvel Comics #1 3.20 9.60 35.00
10,11: 10-r/origin & 1st app. All Winners Squad from All Winners #19. 11-r/origin of Toro (H.T. #1) & Black Knight #1 3.00 9.00 30.00
V2#1(12/79, 75¢, 52 pgs.)-r/origin Silver Surfer from Silver Surfer #1 with editing plus reprints cover; J. Buscema-a 4.00
2-14-Reprints Silver Surfer #2-14 w/covers 2.50
NOTE: ***Buscema*** *c-V2#7-9(in part).* ***Ditko*** *r-1-3, 7, 9.* ***Everett*** *r-1,7-9.* ***Matt Fox*** *r-9i.* ***Kirby*** *r-1-1 c(p)-3, 4i, 5, 6.* ***Starlin*** *r-8-13. Some direct sale V2#14's had a 50¢ cover price. #3-11 contai Capt. America-r/Capt. America #3-10. #7-11 contain G.A.Human Torch & Sub-Mariner-r.*

FANTASY QUARTERLY (Also see Elfquest)
Independent Publishers Syndicate: Spring, 1978 (B&W) (2nd printing exist?)
1-1st app. Elfquest; Dave Sim-a (6 pgs.) 5.45 16.35 60.00

FANTOMAN (Formerly Amazing Adventure Funnies)
Centaur Publications: No. 2, Aug, 1940 - No. 4, Dec, 1940
2-The Fantom of the Fair, The Arrow, Little Dynamite-r begin; origin The Ermine by Filchock; Fantoman app. in 2-4; Burgos, J. Cole, Ernst, Gustavson-a 121.00 363.00 1150.00
3,4: Gustavson-r. 4-Red Blaze story 100.00 300.00 950.00

FAREWELL MOONSHADOW (See Moonshadow)
DC Comics (Vertigo): Jan, 1997 ($7.95, one-shot)
nn-DeMatteis-s/Muth-c/a 8.00

FARGO KID (Formerly Justice Traps the Guilty)(See Feature Comics #47
Prize Publications: V11#3(#1), June-July, 1958 - V11#5, Oct-Nov, 1958
V11#3(#1)-Origin Fargo Kid, Severin-c/a; Williamson-a(2); Heath-a 19.00 56.00 150.00
V11#4,5-Severin-c/a 12.00 36.00 95.00

FARMER'S DAUGHTER, THE
Stanhall Publ./Trojan Magazines: Feb-Mar, 1954 - No. 3, June-July, 1954; No. 4, Oct, 1954
1-Lingerie, nudity panel 21.00 62.00 165.00
2-4(Stanhall) 12.50 37.50 100.00

FASHION IN ACTION
Eclipse Comics: Aug, 1986 - Feb, 1987 (Baxter paper)
Summer Special 1 , Winter Special 1, each Snyder III-c/a 2.00

FASTBALL EXPRESS (Major League Baseball)
Ultimate Sports Force: 2000 ($3.95, one-shot)
1-Polybagged with poster; Johnson, Maddux, Park, Nomo, Clemens app. 4.00

FASTEST GUN ALIVE, THE (Movie)
Dell Publishing Co.: No. 741, Sept, 1956 (one-shot)
Four Color 741-Photo-c 6.70 20.00 80.00

FAST FICTION (...Action) (Stories by Famous Authors Illustrated #6 on)
Seaboard Publ./Famous Authors Ill.: Oct, 1949 - No. 5, Mar, 1950 (All have Kiefer-c)(48 pgs.)
1-Scarlet Pimpernel; Jim Lavery-c/a 38.00 113.00 300.00
2-Captain Blood; H. C. Kiefer-c/a 34.00 103.00 275.00
3-She, by Rider Haggard; Vincent Napoli-a 40.00 120.00 360.00
4-(1/50, 52 pgs.)-The 39 Steps; Lavery-c/a 26.00 79.00 210.00
5-Beau Geste; Kiefer-c/a 26.00 79.00 210.00
NOTE: ***Kiefer*** *a-2, 5; c-2, 3,5.* ***Lavery*** *c/a-1, 4.* ***Napoli*** *a-3.*

FAST FORWARD
DC Comics (Piranha Press): 1992 - No. 3, 1993 ($4.95, 68 pgs.)
1-3: 1-Morrison scripts; McKean-c/a. 3-Sam Kieth-a 5.00

FAST WILLIE JACKSON
Fitzgerald Periodicals, Inc.: Oct, 1976 - No. 7, 1977
1 1.75 5.25 14.00

Fathom #12 © Michael Turner

Fawcett Movie Comic #20 © FAW

Fawcett's Funny Animals #4 © FAW

GD2.0 FN6.0 NM9.4

2-7 1.00 3.00 8.00

FAT ALBERT (...& the Cosby Kids) (TV)
Gold Key: Mar, 1974 - No. 29, Feb, 1979

1 2.80 8.40 28.00
2-10 1.75 5.25 14.00
11-29 1.25 3.75 10.00

FATALE (Also see Powers That Be #1 & Shadow State #1,2)
Broadway Comics: Jan, 1996 - No. 6, Aug, 1996 ($2.50)

1-6: J.G. Jones-c/a in all, Preview Edition 1 (11/95, B&W) 2.50

FAT AND SLAT (Ed Wheelan) (Becomes Gunfighter No. 5 on)
E. C. Comics: Summer, 1947 - No. 4, Spring, 1948

1-Intro/origin Voltage, Man of Lightning; "Comics" McCormick, the World's No. 1 Comic Book Fan begins, ends #4 33.00 98.00 260.00
2-4: 4-Comics McCormick-c feature 23.00 69.00 185.00

FAT AND SLAT JOKE BOOK
All-American Comics (William H. Wise): Summer, 1944 (52 pgs., one-shot)

nn-by Ed Wheelan 25.00 75.00 200.00

FATE (See Hand of Fate & Thrill-O-Rama)

FATE
DC Comics: Oct, 1994 - No. 22, Sept, 1996 ($1.95/$2.25)

0,1-22: 8-Begin $2.25-c. 11-14-Alan Scott (Sentinel) app. 10,14-Zatanna app. 21-Phantom Stranger app. 22-Spectre app. 2.25

FATHOM
Comico: May, 1987 - No. 3, July, 1987 ($1.50, limited series)

1-3 2.00

FATHOM
Image Comics (Top Cow Prod.): Aug, 1998 - Present ($2.50)

Preview 10.00
0-Wizard supplement 8.00
0-($6.95) DF Alternate 6.95
1-Turner-s/a; three covers; alternate story pages 5.00
1-Wizard World Ed. 30.00
2-12: 12-Witchblade-c/app. 2.50
. Collected Edition 1 (3/99, $5.95) r/Preview & all three #1's 6.00
. Collected Edition 2-4 (3-12/99, $5.95) 2-r/#2,3. 3-r/#4,5. 4-r/#6,7 6.00
. Collected Edition 5 (4/00, $5.95) 5-r/#8,9 6.00
. Swimsuit Special (5/99, $2.95) Pin-ups by various 3.00
. Swimsuit Special 2000 (12/00, $2.95) Pin-ups by various; Turner-c 3.00

ATIMA...CHALLENGE TO THE WORLD
atechetical Guild: 1951, 36 pgs. (15¢)

n (not same as 'Challenge to the World') 3.60 9.00 18.00

ATMAN, THE HUMAN FLYING SAUCER
ghtning Comics(Milson Publ. Co.): April, 1967 - No. 3, Aug-Sept, 1967
8 pgs.) (Written by Otto Binder)

1-Origin/1st app. Fatman & Tinman by Beck 5.00 15.00 55.00
2-C. C. Beck-a 3.65 11.00 40.00
3-(Scarce)-Beck-a 5.90 17.75 65.00

AULTLINES
C Comics (Vertigo): May, 1997 - No. 6, Oct, 1997 ($2.50, limited series)

1-6-Lee Marrs-s/Bill Koeb-a in all 2.50

AUNTLEROY COMICS (Super Duck Presents...)
ose-Up/Archie Publications: 1950; No. 2, 1951; No. 3, 1952

-Super Duck-c/stories by Al Fagaly in all 8.65 26.00 60.00
,3 5.00 15.00 35.00

AUST
orthstar Publishing/Rebel Studios #7 on: 1989 - No 11, 1997 ($2.00/$2.25, &W, mature themes)

-Decapitation-c; Tim Vigil-c/a in all; Begin $2.00-c 2.30 7.00 20.00
-2nd printing 3.00
-3rd & 4th printing 3.00
1.50 4.50 12.00

GD2.0 FN6.0 NM9.4

2-2nd & 3rd printings, 3,5-2nd printing 3.00
3-Begin $2.25-c 1.00 3.00 8.00
4-10: 7-Begin Rebel Studios series 4.00
11-($2.25) 2.25

FAWCETT MOTION PICTURE COMICS (See Motion Picture Comics)

FAWCETT MOVIE COMIC
Fawcett Publications: 1949 - No. 20, Dec, 1952 (All photo-c)

nn- "Dakota Lil"; George Montgomery & Rod Cameron (1949) 31.00 94.00 250.00
nn- "Copper Canyon"; Ray Milland & Hedy Lamarr (1950) 24.00 71.00 190.00
nn- "Destination Moon" (1950) 76.00 229.00 725.00
nn- "Montana"; Errol Flynn & Alexis Smith (1950) 24.00 71.00 190.00
nn- "Pioneer Marshal"; Monte Hale (1950) 24.00 71.00 190.00
nn- "Powder River Rustlers"; Rocky Lane (1950) 36.00 108.00 290.00
nn- "Singing Guns"; Vaughn Monroe, Ella Raines & Walter Brennan (1950) 21.00 64.00 170.00
7- "Gunmen of Abilene"; Rocky Lane; Bob Powell-a (1950) 26.00 79.00 210.00
8- "King of the Bullwhip"; Lash LaRue; Bob Powell-a (1950) 40.00 120.00 320.00
9- "The Old Frontier"; Monte Hale; Bob Powell-a(2/51; mis-dated 2/50) 25.00 75.00 200.00
10- "The Missourians"; Monte Hale (4/51) 25.00 75.00 200.00
11- "The Thundering Trail"; Lash LaRue (6/51) 33.00 99.00 265.00
12- "Rustlers on Horseback"; Rocky Lane (8/51) 26.00 79.00 210.00
13- "Warpath"; Edmond O'Brien & Forrest Tucker (10/51) 18.00 53.00 140.00
14- "Last Outpost"; Ronald Reagan (12/51) 40.00 120.00 330.00
15-(Scarce)- "The Man From Planet X"; Robert Clark; Schaffenberger-a (2/52) 211.00 633.00 2000.00
16- "10 Tall Men"; Burt Lancaster 14.00 41.00 110.00
17- "Rose of Cimarron"; Jack Buetel & Mala Powers 11.00 33.00 90.00
18- "The Brigand"; Anthony Dexter & Anthony Quinn; Schaffenberger-a 11.00 33.00 90.00
19- "Carbine Williams"; James Stewart; Costanza-a; James Stewart photo-c 12.50 37.50 100.00
20- "Ivanhoe"; Robert Taylor & Liz Taylor photo-c 20.00 60.00 160.00

FAWCETT'S FUNNY ANIMALS (No. 1-26, 80-on titled "Funny Animals"; becomes Li'l Tomboy No. 92 on?)
Fawcett Publications/Charlton Comics No. 84 on: 12/42 - #79, 4/53; #80, 6/53 - #83, 12?/53; #84, 4/54 - #91, 2/56

1-Capt. Marvel on cover; intro. Hoppy The Captain Marvel Bunny, cloned from Capt. Marvel; Billy the Kid & Willie the Worm begin 55.00 165.00 500.00
2-Xmas-c 33.00 98.00 260.00
3-5: 3(2/43)-Spirit of '43-c 19.00 58.00 155.00
6,7,9,10 13.00 39.00 105.00
8-Flag-c 14.00 41.00 110.00
11-20: 14-Cover is a 1944 calendar 10.00 30.00 80.00
21-40: 25-Xmas-c. 26-St. Valentines Day-c 7.15 21.50 50.00
41-86,90,91 5.50 16.50 38.00
87-89(10-54-2/55)-Merry Mailman ish (TV/Radio)-part photo-c 7.15 21.50 50.00

NOTE: *Marvel Bunny in all issues to at least No. 68 (not in 49-54).*

FAZE ONE FAZERS
Americomics (AC Comics): 1986 - No. 4, Sept, 1986 (Limited series)

1-4 2.00

F.B.I., THE
Dell Publishing Co.: Apr-June, 1965

1-Sinnott-a 2.50 7.50 24.00

F.B.I. STORY, THE (Movie)
Dell Publishing Co.: No. 1069, Jan-Mar, 1960

Four Color 1069-Toth-a; James Stewart photo-c 10.00 30.00 120.00

FEAR (Adventure into...)

Fear Effect Special #1 © Eidos

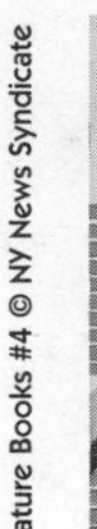
Feature Books #4 © NY News Syndicate

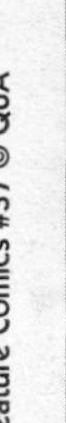
Feature Comics #37 © QUA

Marvel Comics Group: Nov, 1970 - No. 31, Dec, 1975

1-Fantasy & Sci-Fi-r in early issues; 68 pg. Giant size; Kirby-a(r) 3.20 9.60 35.00
2-6: 2-4-(68 pgs.). 5,6-(52 pgs.) Kirby-a(r) 2.30 7.00 20.00
7-9-Kirby-a(r) 1.50 4.50 12.00
10-Man-Thing begins (10/72, 4th app.), ends #19; see Savage Tales #1 for 1st app.; 1st solo series; Chaykin/Morrow-c/a; 2.50 7.50 25.00
11,12: 11-N. Adams-c. 12-Starlin/Buckler-a 1.25 3.75 10.00
13,14,16-18: 17-Origin/1st app. Wundarr 1.00 3.00 8.00
15-1st full-length Man-Thing story (8/73) 1.25 3.75 10.00
19-Intro. Howard the Duck; Val Mayerik-a (12/73) 2.50 7.50 25.00
20-Morbius, the Living Vampire begins, ends #31; has history recap of Morbius with X-Men & Spider-Man 2.50 7.50 25.00
21-23,25 1.00 3.00 8.00
24-Blade-c/sty 2.00 6.00 18.00
26-31 2.40 6.00

NOTE: ***Bolle** a-13i. **Brunner** c-15-17. **Buckler** a-11p, 12i. **Chaykin** a-10i. **Colan** a-23r. **Craig** a-10p. **Ditko** a-6-8r. **Evans** a-30. **Everett** a-9, 10i, 21r. **Gulacy** a-20p. **Heath** a-12r. **Heck** a-8r, 13r. **Gil Kane** a-21p; c(p)-20, 21, 23-28, 31. **Kirby** a-1-9r. **Maneely** a-24r. **Mooney** a-11i, 26r. **Morrow** a-11i. **Paul Reinman** a-14r. **Robbins** a(p)-25-27, 31. **Russell** a-23p, 24p. **Severin** c-8. **Starlin** c-12p.*

FEARBOOK
Eclipse Comics: April, 1986 ($1.75, one-shot, mature)

1-Scholastic Mag- r; Bissette-a 2.00

FEAR EFFECT SPECIAL
Image Comics (Top Cow): May, 2000 ($2.95)

1-Based on the video game 3.00

FEAR IN THE NIGHT (See Complete Mystery No. 3)

FEARLESS FAGAN
Dell Publishing Co.: No. 441, Dec, 1952 (one-shot)

Four Color 441 3.45 10.35 38.00

FEATURE BOOK (Dell) (See Large Feature Comic)

FEATURE BOOKS (Newspaper-r, early issues)
David McKay Publications: May, 1937 - No. 57, 1948 (B&W)
(Full color, 68 pgs. begin #26 on)

Note: See individual alphabetical listings for prices

nn-Popeye & the Jeep (#1, 100 pgs.); reprinted as Feature Books #3(Very Rare; only 3 known copies, 1-VF, 2-in low grade)
nn-Dick Tracy (#1)-Reprinted as Feature Book #4 (100 pgs.) & in part as 4-Color #1 (Rare, less than 10 known copies)

NOTE: *Above books were advertised together with different covers from Feat. Books #3 & 4.*

1-King of the Royal Mtd. (#1)
3-Popeye (7/37) by Segar;
4-Dick Tracy (8/37)-Same as nn issue but a new cover added
6-Dick Tracy (10/37)
8-Secret Agent X-9 (12/37) -Not by Raymond
9-Dick Tracy (1/38)
11-Little Annie Rooney (#1, 3/38)
13-Inspector Wade (5/38)
15-Barney Baxter (#1) (7/38)
17-Gangbusters (#1, 9/38) (1st app.)
20-Phantom (#1, 12/38)
22-Phantom
24-Lone Ranger (1941)
26-Prince Valiant (1941)-Hal Foster -c/a; newspaper strips reprinted, pgs. 1-28,30-63; color & 68 pg. issues begin; Foster cover is only original comic book artwork by him
36('43),38,40('44),42,43, 45,47-Blondie
39-Phantom
46-Mandrake in the Fire World-(58 pgs.)
48-Maltese Falcon by Dashiell Hammett('46)
51,54-Rip Kirby; Raymond-c/s; origin-#51
53,56,57-Phantom

2-Popeye (6/37) by Segar same as nn issue but a new cover added
5-Popeye (9/37) by Segar
7-Little Orphan Annie (#1, 11/37) (Rare)-Reprints strips from 12/31/34 to 7/17/35
10-Popeye (2/38)
12-Blondie (#1) (4/38) (Rare)
14-Popeye (6/38) by Segar
16-Red Eagle (8/38)
18,19-Mandrake
21-Lone Ranger
23-Mandrake
25-Flash Gordon (#1)-Reprints not by Raymond
27-29,31,34-Blondie
30-Katzenjammer Kids (#1, 1942)
32,35,41,44-Katzenjammer Kids
33(nn)-Romance of Flying; World War II photos
37-Katzenjammer Kids; has photo & biog. of Harold H.Knerr(1883-1949) who took over strip from Rudolph Dirks in 1914
49,50-Perry Mason; based on Gardner novels
52,55-Mandrake

NOTE: *All Feature Books through #25 are over-sized 8-1/2x11-3/8" comics with color covers a black and white interiors. The covers are rough, heavy stock. The page counts, including cove are as follows: nn, #3, 4-100 pgs.; #1, 2-52 pgs.; #5-25 are all 76 pgs. #33 was found in bou set from publisher.*

FEATURE COMICS (Formerly Feature Funnies)
Quality Comics Group: No. 21, June, 1939 - No. 144, May, 1950

21-The Clock, Jane Arden & Mickey Finn continue from Feature Funnies 59.00 177.00 560.0
22-26: 23-Charlie Chan begins (8/39, 1st app.) 42.00 125.00 375.0
26-(nn, nd)-Cover in one color, (10¢, 36 pgs.; issue No. blanked out. Two varia tions exist, each contain half of the regular #26) 31.00 94.00 250.0
27-(Rare)-Origin/1st app. Doll Man by Eisner (scripts) & Lou Fine (art); Doll Man begins, ends #139 381.00 1143.00 4000.0
28-2nd app. Doll Man by Lou Fine 158.00 474.00 1500.0
29 92.00 276.00 875.0
30-1st Doll Man-c 105.00 316.00 1000.0
31-Last Clock & Charlie Chan issue (4/40); Charlie Chan moves to Big Shot #1 following month (5/40) 74.00 221.00 700.0
32-37: 32-Rusty Ryan & Samar begin. 34-Captain Fortune app. 37-Last Fine Doll Man 55.00 165.00 500.0

Note: *A 15¢ Canadian version of Feature Comics #37, made in the US, exists.*

38-41: 38-Origin the Ace of Space. 39-Origin The Destroying Demon, ends #40; X-Mas-c. 40-Bruce Blackburn in costume 42.00 125.00 375.0
42,43,45-50: 42-USA, the Spirit of Old Glory begins. 46-Intro. Boyville Brigadiers in Rusty Ryan. 47-Fargo Kid begins. 48-USA ends 33.00 98.00 260.0
44-Doll Man by Crandall begins, ends #63; Crandall-a(2) 44.00 133.00 400.0
51-60: 56-Marijuana story in Swing Sisson strip. 57-Spider Widow begins. 60-Raven begins, ends #71 25.00 75.00 200.0
61-68 (5/43) 23.00 68.00 180.0
69,70-Phantom Lady x-over in Spider Widow 25.00 75.00 200.0
71-80,100: 71-Phantom Lady x-over. 72-Spider Widow ends 18.00 53.00 140.0
81-99 14.00 41.00 110.0
101-144: 139-Last Doll Man & last Doll Man-c. 140-Intro. Stuntman Stetson (Stuntman Stetson c-140-144) 12.00 36.00 95.0

NOTE: ***Celardo** a-37-43. **Crandall** a-44-60, 62, 63-on(most). **Gustavson** a-(Rusty Ryan)- 32-134. **Powell** a-34, 64-73. The Clock c-25, 28, 29. Doll Man c-30, 32, 34, 36, 38, 40, 42, 44, 46, 48, 50, 52, 54, 56, 58, 60, 62, 64, 66, 68, 70, 72, 74, 77-139. Joe Palooka c-21, 24, 27.*

FEATURE FILMS
National Periodical Publ.: Mar-Apr, 1950 - No. 4, Sept-Oct, 1950 (All photo-c)

1- "Captain China" with John Payne, Gail Russell, Lon Chaney & Edgar Bergen 63.00 189.00 600.0
2- "Riding High" with Bing Crosby 68.00 205.00 650.0
3- "The Eagle & the Hawk" with John Payne, Rhonda Fleming & D. O'Keefe 63.00 189.00 600.0
4- "Fancy Pants"; Bob Hope & Lucille Ball 71.00 213.00 675.0

FEATURE FUNNIES (Feature Comics No. 21 on)
Harry 'A' Chesler: Oct, 1937 - No. 20, May, 1939

1(V9#1-indicia)-Joe Palooka, Mickey Finn (1st app.), The Bungles, Jane Arden, Dixie Dugan (1st app.), Big Top, Ned Brant, Strange As It Seems, & Off the Record strip reprints begin 316.00 950.00 2400.0
2-The Hawk app. (11/37); Goldberg-c 145.00 437.00 1075.0
3-Hawks of Seas begins by Eisner, ends #12; The Clock begins; Christmas-c 112.00 337.00 825.0
4,5 83.00 250.00 625.0
6-12: 11-Archie O'Toole by Bud Thomas begins, ends #22 62.00 187.00 460.0
13-Espionage, Starring Black X begins by Eisner, ends #20 70.00 210.00 525.0
14-20 50.00 150.00 380.0

NOTE: *Joe Palooka covers 1, 6, 9, 12, 15, 18.*

FEATURE PRESENTATION, A (Feature Presentations Magazine #6)

Feeders #1 © Shane Hawks & Mike Allred

Felix the Cat #22 © KING

Femforce #96 © AC

(Formerly Women in Love) (Also see Startling Terror Tales #11)
Fox Features Syndicate: No. 5, April, 1950

5(#1)-Black Tarantula 40.00 120.00 360.00

FEATURE PRESENTATIONS MAGAZINE (Formerly A Feature Presentation #5; becomes Feature Stories Magazine #3 on)
Fox Features Syndicate: No. 6, July, 1950

6(#2)-Moby Dick; Wood-c 31.00 94.00 250.00

FEATURE STORIES MAGAZINE (Formerly Feature Presentations Mag. #6)
Fox Features Syndicate: No. 3, Aug, 1950

3-Jungle Lil, Zegra stories; bondage-c 34.00 101.00 270.00

FEDERAL MEN COMICS (See Adventure Comics #32, The Comics Magazine, New Adventure Comics, New Book of Comics, New Comics & Star Spangled Comics #91)
Gerard Publ. Co.: No. 2, 1945 (DC reprints from 1930's)

2-Siegel/Shuster-a; cover redrawn from Det. #9 40.00 120.00 320.00

FEEDERS
Dark Horse Comics: Oct, 1999 ($2.95, one-shot)

1-Mike Allred-c/a/Shane Hawks-s 2.95

FELICIA HARDY: THE BLACK CAT
Marvel Comics: July, 1994 - No. 4, Oct, 1994 ($1.50, limited series)

1-4: 1,4-Spider-Man app. 2.00

FELIX'S NEPHEWS INKY & DINKY
Harvey Publications: Sept, 1957 - No. 7, Oct, 1958

1-Cover shows Inky's left eye with 2 pupils 10.00 30.00 70.00
2-7 5.00 15.00 35.00
NOTE: ***Messmer*** *art in 1-6.* ***Oriolo*** *a-1-7.*

FELIX THE CAT (See Cat Tales 3-D, The Funnies, March of Comics #24,36, 51, New Funnies & Popular Comics)
Dell Publ. No. 1-19/Toby No. 20-61/Harvey No. 62-118/Dell No. 1-12:
1943 - No. 118, Nov, 1961; Sept-Nov, 1962 - No. 12, July-Sept, 1965

Four Color 15 71.00 213.00 850.00
Four Color 46('44) 40.00 120.00 480.00
Four Color 77('45) 38.00 113.00 450.00
Four Color 119('46)-All new stories begin 31.00 91.00 370.00
Four Color 135('46) 23.00 68.00 275.00
Four Color 162(9/47) 18.00 53.00 210.00
1(2-3/48)(Dell) 25.00 75.00 300.00
2 14.00 42.00 165.00
3-5 11.30 34.00 135.00
6-19(2-3/51-Dell) 8.00 24.00 95.00
20-30,32,33,36,38-61(6/55)-All Messmer issues.(Toby): 28-(2/52)-Some copies have #29 on cover, #28 on inside (Rare in high grade) 22.00 66.00 260.00
31,34,35-No Messmer-a; Messmer-c only 31,34 8.35 25.00 100.00
37-(100 pgs., 25 ¢, 1/15/53, X-Mas-c, Toby; daily & Sunday-r (rare) 44.00 131.00 525.00
62(8/55)-80,100 (Harvey) 4.10 12.30 45.00
81-99 3.45 10.35 38.00
101-118(11/61): 101-117-Reprints. 118-All new-a 2.80 8.40 28.00
12-269-211(#1, 9-11/62)(Dell)-No Messmer 3.80 11.40 42.00
2-12(7-9/65)(Dell, TV)-No Messmer 3.00 9.00 32.00
3-D Comic Book 1(1953-One Shot, 25¢)-w/glasses 40.00 120.00 325.00
Summer Annual nn ('53, 25¢, 100 pgs., Toby)-Daily & Sunday-r 40.00 120.00 440.00
Winter Annual 2 ('54, 25¢, 100 pgs., Toby)-Daily & Sunday-r 40.00 120.00 440.00
(Special note: Despite the covers on Toby 37 and the Summer Annual above proclaiming "all new stories," they were actually reformatted newspaper strips)
NOTE: ***Otto Messmer*** *went to work for Universal Film as an animator in 1915 and then worked for the Pat Sullivan animation studio in 1916. He created a black cat in the cartoon short, Feline Follies in 1919 that became known as Felix in the early 1920s. The Felix Sunday strip began Aug. 14, 1923 and continued until Sept. 19, 1943 whjen* ***Messmer*** *took the character to Dell (Western Publishing) and began doing Felix comic books, first adapting strips to the comic format. The first all new Felix comic was Four Color #119 in 1946 (#4 in the Dell run). The daily Felix was begun on May 9, 1927 by another artist, but by the following year,* ***Messmer*** *did it too. King Features took the daily away from* ***Messmer*** *in 1954 and he began to do some of his most dynamic art for Toby Press. The daily was continued by* ***Joe Oriolo*** *who drew it until it was discontinued Jan. 9, 1967.* ***Oriolo*** *was* ***Messmer's*** *assistant for many years and inked some of* ***Messmer's*** *pencils through the Toby run, as well as doing some of the stories by himself. Though* ***Messmer*** *continued to work for Harvey, his contirubitons were limited, and no all* ***Messmer*** *stories appeared after the Toby run until some early Toby reprints were published in the 1990s Harvey revival of the title. 4-Color No. 15, 46, 77 and the Toby Annuals are all daily or Sunday newspaper reprints from the 1930's-1940's drawn by* ***Otto Messmer****. #101-r/#64; 102-r/#65; 103-r/#67; 104-117-r/#68-81.* ***Messmer****-a in all Dell/Toby/Harvey issues except #31, 34, 35, 97, 98, 100, 118.* ***Oriolo*** *a-20, 31-on.*

FELIX THE CAT (Also see The Nine Lives of...)
Harvey Comics/Gladstone: Sept, 1991 - No. 7, Jan, 1993 ($1.25/$1.50, bi-monthly)

1: 1950s-r/Toby issues by Messmer begins. 1-Inky and Dinky back-up story (produced by Gladstone) 3.00
2-7, Big Book , V2#1 (9/92, $1.95, 52 pgs.) 3.00

FELIX THE CAT AND FRIENDS
Felix Comics: 1992 - No. 4, 1992 ($1.95)

1-4: 1-Contains Felix trading cards 3.00

FELIX THE CAT & HIS FRIENDS (Pat Sullivan's...)
Toby Press: Dec, 1953 - No. 3, 1954 (Indicia title for #2&3 as listed)

1 (Indicia title, "Felix and His Friends," #1 only) 30.00 90.00 240.00
2-3 19.00 56.00 150.00

FELIX THE CAT DIGEST MAGAZINE
Harvey Comics: July, 1992 ($1.75, digest-size, 98 pgs.)

1-Felix, Richie Rich stories 5.00

FELIX THE CAT KEEPS ON WALKIN'
Hamilton Comics: 1991 ($15.95, 8-1/2"x11", 132 pgs.)

nn-Reprints 15 Toby Press Felix the Cat and Felix and His Friends stories in new computer color 16.00

FEM FANTASTIQUE
AC Comics: Aug, 1988 ($1.95, B&W)

V2#1-By Bill Black; Betty Page pin-up 4.00

FEMFORCE (Also see Untold Origin of the Femforce)
Americomics: Apr, 1985 - No. 109 (1.75-/2.95, B&W #16-56)

1-Black-a in most; Nightveil, Ms. Victory begin 1.10 3.30 9.00
2 4.00
3-43,45-63,65-99: 25-Origin/1st app. new Ms. Victory. 28-Colt leaves. 29,30-Camilla-r by Mayo from Jungle Comics. 36-(2.95, 52 pgs.). 50 (2.95, 52 pgs.)-Contains flexi-disc; origin retold; most AC characters app. 51-Photo-c from movie. 57-Begin color issues. 95-Photo-c 3.00
44,64: 44-W/mini-comic, Catman & Kitten #0. 64-Re-intro Black Phantom 5.00
100-($3.95) 5.00
100-($6.90)-Polybagged 1.00 3.00 8.00
101-109-($4.95) 5.00
Special 1 (Fall, '84)(B&W, 52pgs.)-1st app. Ms. Victory, She-Cat, Blue Bulleteer, Rio Rita & Lady Luger 4.00
Bad Girl Backlash-(12/95, $5.00) 5.00
Frightbook 1 ('92, $2.95, B&W)-Halloween special, In the House of Horror 1 ('89, 2.50, B&W), Night of the Demon 1 ('90, 2.75, B&W), Out of the Asylum Special 1 ('87, B&W, $1.95), Pin-Up Portfolio 3.50
Pin-Up Portfolio (5 issues) 4.00

FEMFORCE UP CLOSE
AC Comics: Apr, 1992 - No. 11, 1995 ($2.75, quarterly)

1-11: 1-Stars Nightveil; inside f/c photo from Femforce movie. 2-Stars Stardust. 3-Stars Dragonfly. 4-Stars She-Cat 3.50

FERDINAND THE BULL (See Mickey Mouse Magazine V4#3)
Dell Publishing Co.: 1938 (10¢, large size, some color w/rest B&W)

nn 19.00 56.00 150.00

FERRET
Malibu Comics: Sept, 1992; May, 1993 - No. 10, Feb, 1994 ($1.95)

1-(1992, one-shot) 2.50
1-10: 1-Die-cut-c. 2-4-Collector's Ed. w/poster. 5-Polybagged w/Skycap 2.50
2-4-($1.95)-Newsstand Edition w/different-c 2.00

FEUD

F5 #1 © F5 Entertainment

Fight Against Crime #15 © Story Comics

Fight Comics #29 © FH

Marvel Comics (Epic Comics/Heavy Hitters): July, 1993 - No. 4, Oct, 1993 ($1.95, limited series)

	GD2.0	FN6.0	NM9.4
1-($2.50)-Embossed-c			2.50
2-4			2.00

F5
Image Comics: Jan, 2000 - No. 4, Oct, 2000 ($2.50/$2.95)

	GD2.0	FN6.0	NM9.4
Preview (1/00, $2.50) Character bios and b&w pages; Daniel-s/a			2.50
1-($2.95, 48 pages) Tony Daniel-s/a			3.00
1-($20.00) Variant bikini-c			20.00
2-4-($2.50)			2.50

FIBBER McGEE & MOLLY (Radio)(Also see A-1 Comics)
Magazine Enterprises: No. 25, 1949 (one-shot)

	GD2.0	FN6.0	NM9.4
A-1 25	10.00	30.00	75.00

55 DAYS AT PEKING (See Movie Comics)

FICTION ILLUSTRATED
Byron Press Publ.: 1976

	GD2.0	FN6.0	NM9.4
1,2: 1-Schlomo Raven; Sutton-a. 2-(128 pgs.)-Starfawn; Stephen Fabian-a.	1.75	5.25	14.00
3-Chandler; new Steranko-a	2.00	6.00	18.00

FIGHT AGAINST CRIME (Fight Against the Guilty #22, 23)
Story Comics: May, 1951 - No. 21, Sept, 1954

	GD2.0	FN6.0	NM9.4
1-True crime stories #1-4	36.00	107.00	285.00
2	19.00	56.00	150.00
3,5: 5-Frazetta-a, 1 pg.; content change to horror & suspense	16.00	48.00	125.00
4-Drug story "Hopped Up Killers"	17.00	51.00	135.00
6,7: 6-Used in **POP**, pgs. 83,84	13.00	39.00	105.00
8-Last crime format issue	12.00	36.00	95.00

NOTE: *No. 9-21 contain violent, gruesome stories with blood, dismemberment, decapitation, E.C. style plot twists and several E.C. swipes. Bondage c-4, 6, 18, 19.*

	GD2.0	FN6.0	NM9.4
9-11,13	36.00	107.00	285.00
12-Morphine drug story "The Big Dope"	39.00	118.00	315.00
14-Tothish art by Ross Andru; electrocution-c	38.00	113.00	300.00
15-B&W & color illos in **POP**	34.00	101.00	270.00
16-E.C. story swipe/Haunt of Fear #19; Tothish-a by Ross Andru; bondage-c	39.00	118.00	315.00
17-Wildey E.C. swipe/Shock SuspenStories #9; knife through neck-c (1/54)	36.00	107.00	285.00
18,19: 19-Bondage/torture-c	33.00	98.00	260.00
20-Decapitation cover; contains hanging, ax murder, blood & violence	55.00	165.00	500.00
21-E.C. swipe	28.00	84.00	225.00

NOTE: ***Cameron*** *a-4, 5, 8.* ***Hollingsworth*** *a-3-7, 9, 10, 13.* ***Wildey*** *a-6, 15, 16.*

FIGHT AGAINST THE GUILTY (Formerly Fight Against Crime)
Story Comics: No. 22, Dec, 1954 - No. 23, Mar, 1955

	GD2.0	FN6.0	NM9.4
22-Tothish-a by Ross Andru; Ditko-a; E.C. story swipe; electrocution-c (Last pre-code)	28.00	84.00	225.00
23-Hollingsworth-a	20.00	60.00	160.00

FIGHT COMICS
Fiction House Magazines: Jan, 1940 - No. 83, 11/52; No. 84, Wint, 1952-53; No. 85, Spring, 1953; No. 86, Summer, 1954

	GD2.0	FN6.0	NM9.4
1-Origin Spy Fighter, Starring Saber; Jack Dempsey life story; Shark Brodie & Chip Collins begin; Fine-c; Eisner-a	295.00	885.00	2800.00
2-Joe Louis life story; Fine/Eisner-c	111.00	332.00	1050.00
3-Rip Regan, the Power Man begins (3/40)	84.00	253.00	800.00
4,5: 4-Fine-c	63.00	189.00	600.00
6-10: 6,7-Powell-c	50.00	150.00	450.00
11-14: Rip Regan ends	42.00	125.00	375.00
15-1st app. Super American plus-c (10/41)	58.00	174.00	550.00
16-Captain Fight begins (12/41); Spy Fighter ends	58.00	174.00	550.00
17,18: Super American ends	44.00	133.00	400.00
19-Captain Fight ends; Senorita Rio begins (6/42, origin & 1st app.); Rip Carson, Chute Trooper begins	44.00	133.00	400.00
20	40.00	120.00	325.00
21-31: 31-Decapitation-c	30.00	90.00	240.00
32-Tiger Girl begins (6/44, 1st app.?)	40.00	120.00	320.00
33-50: 44-Capt. Fight returns. 48-Used in Love and Death by Legman. 49-Jungle-c begin, end #81	23.00	69.00	185.00
51-Origin Tiger Girl; Patsy Pin-Up app.	39.00	116.00	310.00
52-60,62-64-Last Baker issue	20.00	60.00	160.00
61-Origin Tiger Girl retold	23.00	69.00	185.00
65-78: 78-Used in **POP**, pg. 99	18.00	53.00	140.00
79-The Space Rangers app.	18.00	53.00	140.00
80-85: 81-Last jungle-c. 82-85-War-c/stories	15.00	45.00	120.00
86-Two Tigerman stories by Evans-r/Rangers Comics #40,41; Moreira-r/ Rangers Comics #45	15.00	45.00	120.00

NOTE: *Bondage covers, Lingerie, headlights panels are common. Captain Fight by* ***Kamen****-51-66. Kayo Kirby by* ***Baker****-#43-64, 67(not by Baker). Senorita Rio by* ***Kamen****-#57-64; by* ***Grandenetti****-#65, 66. Tiger Girl by* ***Baker****-#36-60, 62-64;* ***Eisner*** *c-1-3, 5, 10, 11.* ***Kamen*** *a-54?, 57?* ***Tuska*** *a-1, 5, 8, 10, 21, 29, 34.* ***Whitman*** *c-73-84.* ***Zolnerwich*** *c-16, 17, 22. Power Man c-5, 6, 9. Super American c-15-17. Tiger Girl c-49-81.*

FIGHT FOR LOVE
United Features Syndicate: 1952 (no month)

	GD2.0	FN6.0	NM9.4
nn-Abbie & Slats newspaper-r	10.00	30.00	70.00

FIGHTING AIR FORCE (See United States Fighting Air Force)

FIGHTIN' AIR FORCE (Formerly Sherlock Holmes?; Never Again? War and Attack #54 on)
Charlton Comics: No. 3, Feb, 1956 - No. 53, Feb-Mar, 1966

	GD2.0	FN6.0	NM9.4
V1#3	7.15	21.50	50.00
4-10	5.00	15.00	30.00
11(3/58, 68 pgs.)	6.40	19.25	45.00
12 (100 pgs.)	9.30	28.00	65.00
13-30: 13,24-Glanzman-a. 24-Glanzman-c	2.50	7.50	24.00
31-50: 50-American Eagle begins	2.00	6.00	18.00
51-53	1.75	5.25	14.00

FIGHTING AMERICAN
Headline Publ./Prize (Crestwood): Apr-May, 1954 - No. 7, Apr-May, 1955

	GD2.0	FN6.0	NM9.4
1-Origin & 1st app. Fighting American & Speedboy (Capt. America & Bucky clones); S&K-c/a(3); 1st super hero satire series	168.00	505.00	1600.00
2-S&K-a(3)	79.00	237.00	750.00
3-5: 3,4-S&K-a(3). 5-S&K-a(2); Kirby/?-a	63.00	189.00	600.00
6-Origin-r (4 pgs.) plus 2 pgs. by S&K	61.00	182.00	575.00
7-Kirby-a	53.00	160.00	480.00

NOTE: ***Simon*** *&* ***Kirby*** *covers on all. 6 is last pre-code issue.*

FIGHTING AMERICAN
Harvey Publications: Oct, 1966 (25¢)

	GD2.0	FN6.0	NM9.4
1-Origin Fighting American & Speedboy by S&K-r; S&K-c/a(3); 1 pg. Neal Adams ad	4.55	13.65	50.00

FIGHTING AMERICAN
DC Comics: Feb, 1994 - No. 6, 1994 ($1.50, limited series)

	GD2.0	FN6.0	NM9.4
1-6			2.00

FIGHTING AMERICAN (Vol. 3)
Awesome Entertainment: Aug, 1997 - No. 2, Oct, 1997 ($2.50)

	GD2.0	FN6.0	NM9.4
Preview-Agent America (pre-lawsuit)	1.00	2.80	7.00
1-Four covers by Liefeld, Churchill, Platt, McGuiness			2.50
1-Platinum Edition, 1-Gold foil Edition			10.00
1-Comic Cavalcade Edition, 2-American Ent. Spice Ed.			4.00
2-Platt-c, 2-Liefeld variant-c			2.50

FIGHTING AMERICAN: DOGS OF WAR
Awesome-Hyperwerks: Sept, 1998 - No. 3, May, 1999 ($2.50)

	GD2.0	FN6.0	NM9.4
Limited Convention Special (7/98, B&W) Platt-a			2.50
1-3-Starlin-s/Platt-a/c			2.50

FIGHTING AMERICAN: RULES OF THE GAME
Awesome Entertainment: Nov, 1997 - No. 3, Mar, 1998 ($2.50, lim. series)

	GD2.0	FN6.0	NM9.4
1-3: 1-Loeb-s/McGuinness-a/c. 2-Flip book with Swat! preview			2.50
1-Liefeld SPICE variant-c, 1-Dynamic Forces Ed.; McGuinness-c			2.50
1-Liefeld Fighting American & cast variant-c			2.50

FIGHTIN' ARMY (Formerly Soldier and Marine Comics) (See Captain Willy Schultz)

Fighting Daniel Boone nn © AVON

Fightin' Marines #2 © STJ

Fighting Yank #18 © Nedor

Charlton Comics: No. 16, 1/56 - No. 127, 12/76; No. 128, 9/77 - No. 172, 11/84

	GD2.0	FN6.0	NM9.4
16	7.85	23.50	55.00
17-19,21-23,25-30	5.00	15.00	30.00
20-Ditko-a	7.15	21.50	50.00
24 (3/58, 68 pgs.)	6.00	18.00	42.00
31-45	2.30	7.00	20.00
46-60	2.00	6.00	18.00
61-74	1.75	5.25	14.00
75-1st The Lonely War of Willy Schultz	2.00	6.00	16.00
76-80: 76-92-The Lonely War of Willy Schultz. 79-Devil Brigade	1.50	4.50	12.00
81-88,91,93-99: 82,83-Devil Brigade	1.25	3.75	10.00
89,90,92-Ditko-a	1.75	5.25	14.00
100	1.75	5.25	14.00
101-127	1.00	3.00	8.00
128-140		2.40	6.00
141-165			4.00
166-172-Low print run			5.00
108(Modern Comics-1977)-Reprint			4.00

NOTE: *Aparo c-154.* ***Glanzman*** *a-77-88.* ***Montes/Bache*** *a-48, 49, 51, 69, 75, 76, 170r.*

FIGHTING CARAVANS (See Zane Grey 4-Color 632)

FIGHTING DANIEL BOONE
Avon Periodicals: 1953

	GD2.0	FN6.0	NM9.4
nn-Kinstler-c/a, 22 pgs.	19.00	56.00	150.00
I.W. Reprint #1-Reprints #1 above; Kinstler-c/a; Lawrence/Alascia-a	2.30	7.00	20.00

FIGHTING DAVY CROCKETT (Formerly Kit Carson)
Avon Periodicals: No. 9, Oct-Nov, 1955

	GD2.0	FN6.0	NM9.4
9-Kinstler-c	10.00	30.00	75.00

FIGHTIN' FIVE, THE (Formerly Space War) (Also see The Peacemaker)
Charlton Comics: July, 1964 - No. 41, Jan, 1967; No. 42, Oct, 1981 - No. 49, Dec, 1982

	GD2.0	FN6.0	NM9.4
V2#28-Origin/1st app. Fightin' Five; Montes/Bache-a	4.55	13.65	50.00
29-39,41-Montes/Bache-a in all	2.50	7.50	24.00
40-Peacemaker begins (1st app.)	4.55	13.65	50.00
41-Peacemaker (2nd app.)	3.00	9.00	32.00
42-49: Reprints			4.00

FIGHTING FRONTS!
Harvey Publications: Aug, 1952 - No. 5, Jan, 1953

	GD2.0	FN6.0	NM9.4
1	8.65	26.00	60.00
2-Extreme violence; Nostrand/Powell-a	10.00	30.00	75.00
3-5: 3-Powell-a	5.00	15.00	35.00

FIGHTING INDIAN STORIES (See Midget Comics)

FIGHTING INDIANS OF THE WILD WEST!
Avon Periodicals: Mar, 1952 - No. 2, Nov, 1952

	GD2.0	FN6.0	NM9.4
1-Geronimo, Chief Crazy Horse, Chief Victorio, Black Hawk begin; Larsen-a; McCann-a(2)	16.00	48.00	125.00
2-Kinstler-c & inside-c only; Larsen, McCann-a	10.00	30.00	80.00
100 Pg. Annual (1952, 25¢)-Contains three comics rebound; Geronimo, Chief Crazy Horse, Chief Victorio; Kinstler-c	31.00	94.00	250.00

FIGHTING LEATHERNECKS
Toby Press: Feb, 1952 - No. 6, Dec, 1952

	GD2.0	FN6.0	NM9.4
1- "Duke's Diary"; full pg. pin-ups by Sparling	13.00	39.00	105.00
2-5: 2- "Duke's Diary". 3-5- "Gil's Gals"; full pg. pin-ups	10.00	30.00	65.00
6-(Same as No. 3-5?)	8.65	26.00	60.00

FIGHTING MAN, THE (War)
Ajax/Farrell Publications(Excellent Publ.): May, 1952 - No. 8, July, 1953

	GD2.0	FN6.0	NM9.4
1	12.50	37.50	100.00
2	6.40	19.25	45.00
3-8	5.00	15.00	35.00
Annual 1 (1952, 25¢, 100 pgs.)	23.00	68.00	180.00

FIGHTIN' MARINES (Formerly The Texan; also see Approved Comics)
St. John(Approved Comics)/Charlton Comics No. 14 on:
No. 15, 8/51 - No. 12, 3/53; No. 14, 5/55 - No. 132, 11/76; No. 133, 10/77 - No. 176, 9/84 (No #13?) (Korean War #1-3)

	GD2.0	FN6.0	NM9.4
15(#1)-Matt Baker c/a "Leatherneck Jack"; slightly large size; Fightin' Texan No. 16 & 17?	40.00	120.00	340.00
2-1st Canteen Kate by Baker; slightly large size; partial Baker-c	42.00	125.00	375.00
3-9,11-Canteen Kate by Baker; Baker c-#2,3,5-11; 4-Partial Baker-c	24.00	71.00	190.00
10-Matt Baker-c	10.00	30.00	70.00
12-No Baker-a; Last St. John issue?	5.00	15.00	32.00
14 (5/55; 1st Charlton issue; formerly?)-Canteen Kate by Baker; all stories reprinted from #2	18.00	53.00	140.00
15-Baker-c	8.65	26.00	60.00
16,18-20-Not Baker-c	5.00	15.00	30.00
17-Canteen Kate by Baker	12.50	37.50	100.00
21-24	4.65	14.00	28.00
25-(68 pgs.)(3/58)-Check-a?	7.85	23.50	55.00
26-(100 pgs.)(8/58)-Check-a(5)	10.50	32.00	85.00
27-50	2.30	7.00	20.00
51-81: 78-Shotgun Harker & the Chicken series begin	2.00	6.00	16.00
82-(100 pgs.)	3.25	9.75	36.00
83-85: 85-Last 12¢ issue	1.75	5.25	14.00
86-94: 94-Last 15¢ issue	1.50	4.50	12.00
95-100,122: 122-(1975) Pilot issue for "War" title (Fightin' Marines Presents War)	1.25	3.75	10.00
101-121	1.00	2.80	7.00
123-140			5.00
141-170			4.00
171-176-Low print run			5.00
120(Modern Comics reprint, 1977)			4.00

NOTE: *No. 14 & 16 (CC) reprint St. John issues; No. 16 reprints St. John insignia on cover.* ***Colan*** *a-3, 7.* ***Glanzman*** *c/a-92, 94.* ***Montes/Bache*** *a-48, 53, 55, 64, 65, 72-74, 77-83, 176r.*

FIGHTING MARSHAL OF THE WILD WEST (See The Hawk)

FIGHTIN' NAVY (Formerly Don Winslow)
Charlton Comics: No. 74, 1/56 - No. 125, 4-5/66; No. 126, 8/83 - No. 133, 10/84

	GD2.0	FN6.0	NM9.4
74	4.10	12.30	45.00
75-81	2.80	8.40	28.00
82-Sam Glanzman-a	3.00	9.00	30.00
83-(100 pgs.)	3.80	11.40	42.00
84-99,101: 101-UFO story	2.00	6.00	18.00
100	2.30	7.00	20.00
102-105,106-125('66)	1.75	5.25	14.00
126-133 (1984)-Low print run			5.00

NOTE: ***Montes/Bache*** *a-109.* ***Glanzman*** *a-82, 92, 96, 98, 100, 131r.*

FIGHTING PRINCE OF DONEGAL, THE (See Movie Comics)

FIGHTIN' TEXAN (Formerly The Texan & Fightin' Marines?)
St. John Publishing Co.: No. 16, Sept, 1952 - No. 17, Dec, 1952

	GD2.0	FN6.0	NM9.4
16,17: Tuska-a each. 17-Cameron-c/a	7.85	23.50	55.00

FIGHTING UNDERSEA COMMANDOS (See Undersea Fighting…)
Avon Periodicals: May, 1952 - No. 5, April, 1953 (U.S. Navy frogmen)

	GD2.0	FN6.0	NM9.4
1-Cover title is Undersea Fighting… #1 only	12.50	37.50	100.00
2	9.30	28.00	65.00
3-5: 1,3-Ravielli-c. 4-Kinstler-c	8.65	26.00	60.00

FIGHTING WAR STORIES
Men's Publications/Story Comics: Aug, 1952 - No. 5, 1953

	GD2.0	FN6.0	NM9.4
1	9.30	28.00	65.00
2-5	5.00	15.00	35.00

FIGHTING YANK (See America's Best Comics & Startling Comics)
Nedor/Better Publ./Standard: Sept, 1942 - No. 29, Aug, 1949

	GD2.0	FN6.0	NM9.4
1-The Fighting Yank begins; Mystico, the Wonder Man app; bondage-c	232.00	695.00	2200.00
2	100.00	300.00	950.00
3,4: 4-Schomburg-c begin	74.00	221.00	700.00

Firearm #8 © MAL

Firehair Comics #10 © FH

Fireside Books - Silver Surfer © MAR

5-10: 7-Grim Reaper app. 8,10-Bondage/torture-c 58.00 174.00 550.00
11,13-20: 11-The Oracle app. 15-Bondage/torture-c. 18-The American Eagle app. 50.00 150.00 450.00
12-Hirohito bondage-c 55.00 165.00 500.00
21,24: 21-Kara, Jungle Princess app. 24-Miss Masque app. 44.00 133.00 400.00
22-Miss Masque-c/story 53.00 159.00 475.00
23-Classic Schomburg hooded vigilante-c 55.00 165.00 500.00
25-Robinson/Meskin-a; strangulation, lingerie panel; The Cavalier app. 53.00 159.00 475.00
26-29: All-Robinson/Meskin-a. 28-One pg. Williamson-a 43.00 129.00 385.00
NOTE: ***Schomburg (Xela)*** *c-4-29; airbrush-c 28, 29. Bondage c-1, 4, 8, 10, 11, 12, 15, 17.*

FIGHTMAN
Marvel Comics: June, 1993 ($2.00, one-shot, 52 pgs.)
1 2.00

FIGHT THE ENEMY
Tower Comics: Aug, 1966 - No. 3, Mar, 1967 (25¢, 68 pgs.)
1-Lucky 7 & Mike Manly begin 3.20 9.60 35.00
2-Boris Vallejo, McWilliams-a 2.80 8.40 28.00
3-Wood-a (1/2 pg.); McWilliams, Bolle-a 2.80 8.40 28.00

FILM FUNNIES
Marvel Comics (CPC): Nov, 1949 - No. 2, Feb, 1950 (52 pgs.)
1-Krazy Krow, Wacky Duck 18.00 53.00 140.00
2-Wacky Duck 13.00 39.00 105.00

FILM STARS ROMANCES
Star Publications: Jan-Feb, 1950 - No. 3, May-June, 1950 (True life stories of movie stars)
1-Rudy Valentino & Gregory Peck stories; L. B. Cole-c; lingerie panels 42.00 125.00 375.00
2-Liz Taylor/Robert Taylor photo-c & true life story 40.00 120.00 325.00
3-Douglas Fairbanks story; photo-c 25.00 75.00 200.00

FINAL CYCLE, THE
Dragon's Teeth Productions: July, 1987 - No. 4, 1988 (Limited series)
1-4 2.00

FINAL NIGHT, THE (See DC related titles and Parallax: Emerald Night)
DC Comics: Nov, 1996 - No. 4, Nov, 1996 ($1.95, weekly limited series)
1-4: Kesel-s/Immonen-a(p) in all. 4-Parallax's final acts 3.50
Preview 2.00
TPB-(1998, $12.95) r/#1-4, Parallax: Emerald Night #1, and preview 13.00

FINALS
DC Comics (Vertigo): Sept, 1999 - No. 4, Dec, 1999 ($2.95, limited series)
1-4-Will Pfeifer-s/Jill Thompson-a 3.00

FIRE
Caliber Press: 1993 - No. 2, 1993 ($2.95, B&W, limited series, 52 pgs.)
1,2-Brian Michael Bendis-s/a 3.00
TPB (1999, $9.95) Restored reprint of series 10.00

FIREARM (Also see Codename: Firearm, Freex #15, Night Man #4 & Prime #10)
Malibu Comics (Ultraverse): Sept, 1993 - No. 18, Mar, 1995 ($1.95/$2.50)
0 ($14.95)-Came w/ video containing 1st half of story (comic contains 2nd half); 1st app. Duet 15.00
1,3-6: 1-James Robinson scripts begin; Cully Hamner-a; Howard Chaykin-c; 1st app Alec Swan. 3-Intro The Sportsmen; Chaykin-c. 4-Break-Thru x-over; Chaykin-c. 5-1st app. Ellen (Swan's girlfriend);2 pg. origin of Prime. 6-Prime app. (story cont'd in Prime #10);Brereton-c 2.00
1-($2.50)-Newsstand edition polybagged w/card 2.50
1-Ultra Limited silver foil-c 5.00
2 ($2.50, 44 pgs.)-Hardcase app.;Chaykin-c; Rune flip-c/story by B. Smith (3 pgs.) 2.50
7-10,12-17: 12-The Rafferty Saga begins, ends #18; 1st app. Rafferty 15-Night Man & Freex app. 17-Swan marries Ellen 2.00
11-($3.50, 68 pgs.)-Flip book w/Ultraverse Premiere #5 3.50
18-Death of Rafferty; Chaykin-c 2.50
NOTE: ***Brereton*** *c-6.* ***Chaykin*** *c-1-4, 14, 16, 18.* ***Hamner*** *a-1-4.* ***Herrera*** *a-12.* ***James Robinson*** *scripts-0-18.*

FIRE BALL XL5 (See Steve Zodiac & The ...)

FIREBRAND (Also see Showcase '96 #4)
DC Comics: Feb, 1996 - No. 9, Oct, 1996 ($1.75)
1-9: Brian Augustyn scripts; Velluto-c/a in all. 9-Daredevil #319-c/swipe 2.00

FIRE FROM HEAVEN
Image Comics (WildStorm Productions): Mar, 1996 ($2.50)
1,2-Moore-s 2.50

FIREHAIR COMICS (Formerly Pioneer West Romances #3-6; also see Rangers Comics)
Fiction House Magazines (Flying Stories): Winter/48-49; No. 2, Wint/49-50; No. 7, Spr/51 - No. 11, Spr/52
1-Origin Firehair 55.00 165.00 500.00
2-Continues as Pioneer West Romances for #3-6 28.00 84.00 225.00
7-11 19.00 56.00 150.00
I.W. Reprint 8-(nd)-Kinstler-c; reprints Rangers #57; Dr. Drew story by Grandenetti 2.80 8.40 28.00

FIRESIDE BOOK SERIES (Hard and soft cover editions)
Simon and Schuster: 1974 - 1980 (130-260 pgs.), Square bound, color
Amazing Spider-Man, The, 1979, 130 pgs., $3.95, Bob Larkin-c HC 8.15 24.50 90.00 / SC 5.00 15.00 55.00
America At War–The Best of DC War Comics, 1979, $6.95, 260 pgs, Kubert-c HC 12.50 37.00 135.00 / SC 7.65 23.00 85.00
Best of Spidey Super Stories (Electric Company) 1978, $3.95, SC 5.90 17.75 65.00
Bring On The Bad Guys (Origins of the Marvel Comics Villains) 1976, $6.95, 260 pgs.; Romita-c HC 7.65 23.00 85.00 / SC 4.55 13.65 50.00
Captain America, Sentinel of Liberty,1979, 130 pgs., $12.95, Cockrum-c HC 8.15 24.50 90.00 / SC 4.55 13.65 50.00
Doctor Strange Master of the Mystic Arts, 1980, 130 pgs. HC 8.15 24.50 90.00 / SC 4.55 13.65 50.00
Fantastic Four, The, 1979, 130 pgs. HC 7.25 21.75 80.00 / SC 4.10 12.30 45.00
Heart Throbs–The Best of DC Romance Comics, 1979, 260 pgs., $6.,95 HC 18.00 53.00 195.00 / SC 11.00 33.00 120.00
Incredible Hulk, The, 1978, 260 pgs. (8 1/4" x 11") HC 6.80 20.50 75.00 / SC 4.10 12.30 45.00
Marvel's Greatest Superhero Battles, 1978, 260 pgs., $6.95, Romita-c HC 10.50 31.50 115.00 / SC 5.90 17.75 65.00
Mysteries in Space, 1980, $7,95, Anderson-c. r-DC sci/fi stories HC 10.00 30.00 110.00 / SC 5.45 16.35 60.00
Origins of Marvel Comics, 1974, 260 pgs., $5.95. r-covers & origins of Fantastic Four, Hulk, Spider-Man, Thor, & Doctor Strange HC 7.65 23.00 85.00 / SC 4.55 13.65 50.00
Silver Surfer, The, 1978, 130 pgs., $4.95, Norem-c HC 9.00 27.00 100.00 / SC 5.45 16.35 60.00
Son of Origins of Marvel Comics, 1975, 260 pgs., $6.95, Romita-c. Reprints covers & origins of X-Men, Iron Man, Avengers, Daredevil, Silver Surfer HC 7.25 21.75 80.00 / SC 4.10 12.30 45.00
Superhero Women, The–Featuring the Fabulous Females of Marvel Comics, 1977, 260 pgs., $6.95, Romita-c HC 10.50 31.50 115.00 / SC 5.90 17.75 65.00
Note: Prices listed are for 1st printings. Later printings are worth 30% less.

FIRESTAR
Marvel Comics Group: Mar, 1986 - No. 4, June, 1986 (75¢)(From Spider-Man TV series)
1,2: 1-X-Men & New Mutants app. 2-Wolverine-c (not real Wolverine?); Art Adams-a(p) 4.00

Firestorm, The Nuclear Man #85 © DC

First Love Illustrated #2 © HARV

Fish Police #18 © Apple Press Inc.

3,4: 3-Art Adams/Sienkiewicz-c. 4-B. Smith-c 2.50

FIRESTONE (See Donald And Mickey Merry Christmas)

FIRESTORM (See Cancelled Comic Cavalcade, DC Comics Presents, Flash #289, The Fury of... & Justice League of America #179)
DC Comics: March, 1978 - No. 5, Oct-Nov, 1978

1,5: 1-Origin & 1st app. 1.00 3.00 8.00
2-4: 2-Origin Multiplex. 3-Origin & 1st app. Killer Frost. 4-1st app. Hyena 5.00

FIRESTORM, THE NUCLEAR MAN (Formerly Fury of Firestorm)
DC Comics: No. 65, Nov, 1987 - No. 100, Aug, 1990

65-99: 66-1st app. Zuggernaut; Firestorm vs. Green Lantern. 71-Death of Capt. X. 67,68-Millennium tie-ins. 83-1st new look 2.00
100-($2.95, 68 pgs.) 3.00
Annual 5 (10/87)-1st app. new Firestorm 2.00

FIRST, THE
CrossGeneration Comics: Jan, 2001 - Present ($2.95)

1-4: Barbara Kesel-s/Bart Sears & Andy Smith-a 3.00
Preview (11/00, free) 8 pg. intro 1.00

FIRST ADVENTURES
First Comics: Dec, 1985 - No. 5, Apr, 1986 ($1.25)

1-5: Blaze Barlow, Whisper & Dynamo Joe in all 2.00

FIRST AMERICANS, THE
Dell Publishing Co.: No. 843, Sept, 1957

Four Color 843-Marsh-a 8.35 25.00 100.00

FIRST CHRISTMAS, THE (3-D)
Fiction House Magazines (Real Adv. Publ. Co.): 1953 (25¢, 8-1/4x10-1/4", oversize)(Came w/glasses)

nn-(Scarce)-Kelly Freas painted-c; Biblical theme, birth of Christ; Nativity-c 33.00 98.00 260.00

FIRST COMICS GRAPHIC NOVEL
First Comics: Jan, 1984 - No. 21? (52pgs./176 pgs., high quality paper)

1,2: 1-Beowulf ($5.95)(both printings). 2-Time Beavers 8.00
3($11.95, 100 pgs.)-American Flagg! Hard Times (2nd printing exists) 14.00
4-Nexus ($6.95)-r/B&W 1-3 11.00
5,7: 5-The Enchanted Apples of Oz ($7.95, 52 pgs.)-Intro by Harlan Ellison (1986). 7-The Secret Island Of Oz ($7.95) 9.00
6-Elric of Melnibone ($14.95, 176 pgs.)-Reprints with new color 17.00
8,10,14,18: Teenage Mutant Ninja Turtles Book I -IV ($9.95, 132 pgs.)-8-r/TMNT #1-3 in color w/12 pgs. new-a; origin. 10-r/TMNT #4-6 in color. 14-r/TMNT #7,8 in color plus new 12 pg. story. 18-r/TMNT #10,11 plus 3 pg. fold-out 11.00
9-Time 2: The Epiphany by Chaykin (11/86, $7.95, 52pgs. - indicia says #8) 9.00
11-Sailor On The Sea of Fate ($14.95) 16.00
nn-Time 2: The Satisfaction of Black Mariah (9/87) 9.00
12-American Flagg! Southern Comfort (10/87, $11.95) 14.00
13,15-17,19,21: 13-The Ice King Of Oz. 15-Hex Breaker: Badger ($7.95). 16-The Forgotten Forest of Oz ($8.95). 17-Mazinger (68 pgs., $8.95).19-The Original Nexus Graphic Novel ($7.95, 104 pgs.)-Reprints First Comics Graphic Novel #4 ($7.95). 21-Elric, The Weird of the White Wolf; r/#1-5 10.00
20-American Flagg!: State of the Union ($11.95, 96 pgs.); r/A.F. 7-9 15.00
NOTE: *Most or all issues have been reprinted.*

1ST FOLIO (The Joe Kubert School Presents...)
Pacific Comics: Mar, 1984 ($1.50, one-shot)

1-Joe Kubert-c/a(2 pgs.); Adam & Andy Kubert-a 3.00

1ST ISSUE SPECIAL
National Periodical Publications: Apr, 1975 - No. 13, Apr, 1976 (Tryout series)

1,5,6: 1-Intro. Atlas; Kirby-c/a/script. 5-Manhunter; Kirby-c/a/script. 6-Dingbats 1.00 3.00 8.00
2,7,9,12: 2-Green Team (see Cancelled.Comic Cavalcade). 7-The Creeper by Ditko (c/a). 9-Dr. Fate; Kubert-c. 12-Origin/1st app. "Blue" Starman (2nd app. in Starman, 2nd Series #3); Kubert-c. 1.00 2.80 7.00
3,4,10,11: 3-Metamorpho by Ramona Fradon. 4-Lady Cop. 10-The Outsiders. 11-Code Name: Assassin; Grell-c. 2.40 6.00
8,13: 8-Origin/1st app. The Warlord; Grell-c/a (11/75). 13-Return of the New Gods; Darkseid app.; 1st new costume Orion; predates New Gods #12 by more than a year 2.00 6.00 16.00

FIRST KISS
Charlton Comics: Dec, 1957 - No. 40, Jan, 1965

V1#1 3.65 11.00 40.00
V1#2-10 2.50 7.50 25.00
11-40 1.75 5.25 14.00

FIRST LOVE ILLUSTRATED
Harvey Publications(Home Comics)(True Love): 2/49 - No. 9, 6/50; No. 10, 1/51 - No. 86, 3/58; No. 87, 9/58 - No. 88, 11/58; No. 89, 11/62, No. 90, 2/63

1-Powell-a(2) 18.00 53.00 140.00
2-Powell-a 10.00 30.00 70.00
3-"Was I Too Fat To Be Loved" story 10.00 30.00 70.00
4-10 6.00 18.00 42.00
11-30: 13-"I Joined a Teen-age Sex Club" story. 30-Lingerie panel 5.00 15.00 30.00
31-34,37,39-49: 49-Last pre-code (2/55) 4.00 12.00 24.00
35-Used in **SOTI**, illo "The title of this comic book is First Love" 19.00 56.00 150.00
36-Communism story, "Love Slaves" 6.00 18.00 42.00
38-Nostrand-a 6.00 18.00 42.00
50-66,71-90 4.00 11.00 22.00
67-70-Kirby-c 5.00 15.00 30.00
NOTE: ***Disbrow** a-13. **Orlando** c-87. **Powell** a-1, 3-5, 7, 10, 11, 13-17, 19-24, 26-29, 33,35-41, 43, 45, 46, 50, 54, 55, 57, 58, 61-63, 65, 71-73, 76, 79r, 82, 84, 88.*

FIRSTMAN
Image Comics: June, 1997 ($2.50)

1 Snyder-s/ Andy Smith-a 2.50

FIRST MEN IN THE MOON (See Movie Comics)

FIRST ROMANCE MAGAZINE
Home Comics(Harvey Publ.)/True Love: 8/49 - #6, 6/50; #7, 6/51 - #50, 2/58; #51, 9/58 - #52, 11/58

1 15.00 45.00 120.00
2 8.65 26.00 60.00
3-5 7.15 21.50 50.00
6-10,28: 28-Nostrand-a(Powell swipe) 5.50 16.50 38.00
11-20 5.00 15.00 30.00
21-27,29-32: 32-Last pre-code issue (2/55) 4.00 12.00 24.00
33-40,44-52 4.00 10.00 20.00
41-43-Kirby-c 4.65 14.00 28.00
NOTE: ***Powell** a-1-5, 8-10, 14, 18, 20-22, 24, 25, 28, 36, 46, 48, 51.*

FIRST TRIP TO THE MOON (See Space Adventures No. 20)

FIRST WAVE (Based on Sci-Fi Channel TV series)
Andromeda Entertainment: Dec, 2000 - Present ($2.99)

1-Kuhoric-s/Parsons-a/Busch-c 3.00

FISH POLICE (Inspector Gill of the...#2, 3)
Fishwrap Productions/Comico V2#5-17/Apple Comics #18 on: Dec, 1985 - No. 11, Nov, 1987 ($1.50, B&W); V2#5, April, 1988 - V2#17, May, 1989 ($1.75, color) No. 18, Aug, 1989 - No. 26, Dec, 1990 ($2.25, B&W)

1-11, 1(5/86),2-2nd print, V2#5-17-(Color): V2#5-11. 12-17, new-a, 18-26 ($2.25-c, B&W) 18-Origin Inspector Gill 2.50
Special 1($2.50, 7/87, Comico) 2.50
Graphic Novel: Hairballs (1987, $9.95, TPB) r/#1-4 in color 10.00

FISH POLICE
Marvel Comics: V2#1, Oct, 1992 - No. 6, Mar, 1993 ($1.25)

V2#1-6: 1-Hairballs Saga begins; r/#1 (1985) 2.00

5 CENT COMICS (Also see Whiz Comics)
Fawcett Publ.: Feb, 1940 (8 pgs., reg. size, B&W)

1 (nn-on c) 1st app. Dan Dare 522.00 1565.00 6000.00
NOTE: Only 2 known copies, in GD and NM condition. The NM copy sold in 1995 for $3000 and again in 1999 for $4800. A promo comic, same as ***Flash*** & ***Thrill Comics***.

5-STAR SUPER-HERO SPECTACULAR (See DC Special Series No. 1)

The Flame #4 © FOX

Flaming Love #4 © QUA

The Flash #176 © DC

FLAME, THE (See Big 3 & Wonderworld Comics)
Fox Features Synd.: Sum, 1940 - No. 8, Jan, 1942 (#1,2: 68 pgs; #3-8: 44 pgs.)

1-Flame stories reprinted from Wonderworld #5-9; origin The Flame; Lou Fine-a (36 pgs.), r/Wonderworld #3,10 314.00 943.00 3300.00
2-Fine-a(2); Wing Turner by Tuska 134.00 403.00 1275.00
3-8: 3-Powell-a 90.00 270.00 850.00

FLAME, THE (Formerly Lone Eagle)
Ajax/Farrell Publications (Excellent Publ.): No. 5, Dec-Jan, 1954-55 - No. 3, April-May, 1955

5(#1)-1st app. new Flame 44.00 133.00 400.00
2,3 30.00 90.00 240.00

FLAMING CARROT (...Comics #6? on; see Anything Goes, Cerebus, Teenage Mutant Ninja Turtles/Flaming Carrot Crossover & Visions)
Aardvark-Vanaheim/Renegade Press #6-17/Dark Horse #18 on: 5/84 - No. 5, 1/85; No. 6, 3/85 - Present? ($1.70/$2.00, B&W)

1-Bob Burden story/art 4.10 12.30 45.00
2 2.50 7.50 23.00
3 2.00 6.00 16.00
4-6 1.50 4.50 12.00
7-9 1.10 3.30 9.00
10-12 2.40 6.00
13-15 4.00
15-Variant without cover price 2.40 6.00
16-(6/87) 1st app. Mystery Men 1.00 2.80 7.00
17-20: 18-1st Dark Horse issue 4.00
21-23,25: 25-Contains trading cards; TMNT app. 3.00
24-(2.50, 52 pgs.)-10th anniversary issue 4.00
26-28: 26-Begin $2.25-c. 26,27-Teenage Mutant Ninja Turtles x-over. 27-Todd McFarlane-c 2.50
29-31-(2.50-c) 2.50
Annual 1(1/97, $5.00) 5.00
... :Fortune Favors the Bold (1998, $16.95, TPB) r/#19-24 17.00
... :Men of Mystery (7/97, $12.95, TPB) r/#1-3, + new material 13.00
... 's Greatest Hits (4/98, $17.95, TPB) r/#12-18, + new material 18.00
... :The Wild Shall Wild Remain (1997, $17.95, TPB) r/#4-11, + new s/a 18.00

FLAMING CARROT COMICS (Also see Junior Carrot Patrol)
Killian Barracks Press: Summer-Fall, 1981 ($1.95, one shot) (Lg size, 8-1/2x11")

1-Bob Burden-c/a/scripts; serially numbered to 6500 5.90 17.75 65.00

FLAMING LOVE
Quality Comics Group (Comic Magazines): Dec, 1949 - No. 6, Oct, 1950 (Photo covers #2-6) (52 pgs.)

1-Ward-c/a (9 pgs.) 38.00 113.00 300.00
2 17.00 51.00 135.00
3-Ward-a (9 pgs.); Crandall-a 26.00 77.00 205.00
4-6: 4-Gustavson-a 14.00 43.00 115.00

FLAMING WESTERN ROMANCES (Formerly Target Western Romances)
Star Publications: No. 3, Mar-Apr, 1950

3-Robert Taylor, Arlene Dahl photo on-c with biographies inside; L. B. Cole-c 40.00 120.00 325.00

FLARE (Also see Champions for 1st app. & League of Champions)
Hero Comics/Hero Graphics Vol. 2 on: Nov, 1988 - No. 3, Jan, 1989 ($2.75, color, 52 pgs); V2#1, Nov, 1990 - No. 7, Nov, 1991 ($2.95/$3.50, color, mature, 52 pgs.);V2#8, Oct, 1992 - No. 16, Feb, 1994 ($3.50/$3.95, B&W, 36 pgs.)

V1#1-3, V2#1-16: 5-Eternity Smith returns. 6-Intro The Tigress 4.00
Annual 1(1992, $4.50, B&W, 52 pgs.)-Champions-r 4.50

FLARE ADVENTURES
Hero Graphics: Feb, 1992 - No. 12, 1993? ($3.50/$3.95)

1 (90¢, color, 20 pgs.) 2.00
2-12-Flip books w/Champions Classics 4.00

FLASH, THE (See Adventure Comics, The Brave and the Bold, Crisis On Infinite Earths, DC Comics Presents, DC Special, DC Special Series, DC Super-Stars, The Greatest Flash Stories Ever Told, Green Lantern, Impulse, JLA, Justice League of America, Showcase, Speed Force, Super Team Family, Titans & World's Finest)

FLASH, THE (1st Series)(Formerly Flash Comics)(See Showcase #4,8,13,14)
National Periodical Publ./DC: No. 105, Feb-Mar, 1959 - No. 350, Oct, 1985

GD2.0 FN6.0 VF8.0 NM9.4
105-(2-3/59)-Origin Flash(retold), & Mirror Master (1st app.) 353.00 1060.00 2825.00 6000.00

GD2.0 FN6.0 NM9.4
106-Origin Grodd & Pied Piper; Flash's 1st visit to Gorilla City; begin Grodd the Super Gorilla trilogy (Scarce) 129.00 386.00 1800.00
107-Grodd trilogy, part 2 68.00 204.00 950.00
108-Grodd trilogy ends 57.00 171.00 800.00
109-2nd app. Mirror Master 42.00 126.00 550.00
110-Intro/origin The Weather Wizard & Kid Flash who later becomes Flash in Crisis On Infinite Earths #12; begin Kid Flash trilogy, ends #112 (also in #114,116,118) 107.00 321.00 1500.00
111-2nd Kid Flash tryout; Cloud Creatures 33.00 100.00 400.00
112-Origin & 1st app. Elongated Man (4-5/60); also apps. in #115,119,130 40.00 120.00 475.00
113-Origin & 1st app. Trickster 33.00 100.00 400.00
114-Captain Cold app. (see Showcase #8) 27.50 82.00 300.00
115,116,118-120: 119-Elongated Man marries Sue Dearborn. 120-Flash & Kid Flash team-up for 1st time 22.00 65.00 240.00
117-Origin & 1st app. Capt. Boomerang; 1st & only S.A. app. Winky Blinky & Noddy 28.00 85.00 310.00
121,122: 122-Origin & 1st app. The Top 16.50 49.00 180.00
123-(9/61)-Re-intro. Golden Age Flash; origins of both Flashes; 1st mention of an Earth II where DC G. A. heroes live 100.00 300.00 1400.00
124-Last 10¢ issue 13.50 40.00 150.00
125-128,130: 127-Return of Grodd-c/story. 128-Origin & 1st app. Abra Kadabra 13.00 39.00 145.00
129-2nd G.A. Flash x-over; J.S.A. cameo in flashback (1st S.A. app. G.A. Green Lantern, Hawkman, Atom, Black Canary & Dr. Mid-Nite) 29.00 87.00 320.00
131-136,138,140: 130-(7/62)-1st Gauntlet of Super-Villains (Mirror Master, Capt. Cold, The Top, Capt. Boomerang & Trickster). 131-Early Green Lantern x-over (9/62). 135-1st app. of Kid Flash's yellow costume (3/63). 136-1st Dexter Miles. 140-Origin & 1st app. Heat Wave 11.00 33.00 120.00
137-G.A. Flash x-over; J.S.A. cameo (1st S.A. app.)(1st real app. since 2-3/51); 1st S.A. app. Vandal Savage & Johnny Thunder; JSA team decides to re-form 40.00 120.00 480.00
139-Origin & 1st app. Prof. Zoom 12.00 36.00 130.00
141-150: 142-Trickster app. 9.00 27.00 100.00
151-Engagement of Barry Allen & Iris West; G.A. Flash vs. The Shade. 12.00 36.00 130.00
152-159 7.25 21.75 80.00
160-(80-Pg. Giant G-21); G.A. Flash & Johnny Quick-r 10.00 30.00 110.00
161-168,170: 165-Barry Allen weds Iris West. 167-New facts about Flash's origin. 168-Green Lantern-c/story. 170-Dr. Mid-Nite, Dr. Fate, G.A. Flash x-over 6.35 19.00 70.00
169-(80-Pg. Giant G-34)-New facts about origin 9.00 27.00 100.00
171-174,176,177,179,180: 171-JLA, Green Lantern, Atom flashbacks. 173-G.A. Flash x-over. 174-Barry Allen reveals I.D. to wife. 179-(5/68)-Flash travels to Earth-Prime and meets DC editor Julie Schwartz; 1st unnamed app. Earth-Prime (See Justice League of America #123 for 1st named app. & 3rd app. overall) 5.90 17.75 65.00
175-2nd Superman/Flash race (12/67) (See Superman #199 & World's Finest #198,199); JLA cameo; gold kryptonite used (on J'onn J'onzz impersonating Superman) 16.00 48.00 175.00
178-(80-Pg. Giant G-46) 7.65 23.00 85.00
181-186,188,189: 186-Re-intro. Sargon. 189-Last 12¢-c 3.65 11.00 40.00
187,196: (68-Pg. Giants G-58, G-70) 5.00 15.00 55.00
190-195,197-199 3.20 9.60 35.00
200 3.80 11.40 42.00
201-204,206,207: 201-New G.A. Flash story. 206-Elongated Man begins 207-Last 15¢ issue 2.50 7.50 24.00

The Flash #243 © DC

The Flash (2nd series) #104 © DC

The Flash (2nd series) #149 © DC

GD2.0 FN6.0 NM9.4

205-(68-Pg. Giant G-82) 4.10 12.30 45.00
208-213-(52 pg.): 211-G.A. Flash origin-r/#104. 213-Reprints #137 2.80 8.40 28.00
214-DC 100 Page Super Spectacular DC-11; origin Metal Men-r/Showcase #37; never before published G.A. Flash story.
(see DC 100 pg. Super Spec. #11 for price)
215 (52 pgs.)-Flash-r/Showcase #4; G.A. Flash x-over, continued in #216 3.20 9.60 35.00
216,220: 220-1st app. Turtle since Showcase #4 2.30 7.00 20.00
217-219: Neal Adams-a in all. 217-Green Lantern/Green Arrow series begins (9/72); 2nd G.L. & G.A. team-up series (see Green Lantern #76). 219-Last Green Arrow 3.00 9.00 30.00
221-225,227,228,230,231,233: 222-G. Lantern x-over. 228-(7-8/74)-Flash writer Cary Bates travels to Earth-One & meets Flash, Iris Allen & Trickster; 2nd unnamed app. Earth-Prime (See Justice League of America #123 for 1st named app. & 3rd app. overall) 1.75 5.25 14.00
226-Neal Adams-p 2.00 6.00 16.00
229,232-(100 pg. issues)-G.A. Flash-r & new-a 3.20 9.60 35.00
234-250: 235-Green Lantern x-over. 243-Death of The Top. 245-Origin The Floronic Man in Green Lantern back-up, ends #246. 246-Last Green Lantern. 250-Intro Golden Glider 1.10 3.30 9.00
251-288,290: 256-Death of The Top retold. 265-267-(44 pgs.). 267-Origin of Flash's uniform. 270-Intro The Clown. 275,276-Iris West Allen dies. 286-Intro/origin Rainbow Raider 2.40 6.00
289-1st Perez DC art (Firestorm); new Firestorm back-up series begins (9/80), ends #304 1.00 2.80 7.00
291-299,301-305: 291-1st app. Saber-Tooth (villain). 295-Gorilla Grodd-c/story. 298-Intro/origin new Shade. 301-Atomic bomb-c. 303-The Top returns. 304-Intro/origin Colonel Computron; 305-G.A. Flash x-over 4.00
300-(52 pgs.)-Origin Flash retold; 25th ann. issue 5.00
306-349: 306-313-Dr. Fate by Giffen. 309-Origin Flash retold. 318-323-Creeper back-ups. 323,324-Two part Flash vs. Flash story. 324-Death of Reverse Flash (Professor Zoom). 328-Iris West Allen's death retold. 344-Origin Kid Flash 3.00
350-Double size ($1.25) Final issue 5.00
Annual 1(10-12/63, 84 pgs.)-Origin Elongated Man & Kid Flash-r; origin Grodd; G.A. Flash-r 37.00 112.00 450.00
The Flash Spectacular (See DC Special Series No. 11)
The Life Story of the Flash (1997, $19.95, Hardcover) "Iris Allen's" chronicle of Barry Allen's life; comic panels w/additional text; Waid & Augustyn-s/ Kane & Staton-a/Orbik painted-c 20.00
The Life Story of the Flash (1998, $12.95, Softcover) New Orbik-c 13.00

NOTE: ***N. Adams*** *c-194, 195, 203, 204, 206-208, 211, 213, 215, 226p, 246.* ***M. Anderson*** *c-165, a(i)-195, 200-204, 206-208.* ***Austin*** *a-233i, 234i, 246i.* ***Buckler*** *a-271p, 272p; c(p)-247-250, 252, 253p, 255, 256p, 258, 262, 265-267, 269-271.* ***Giffen*** *a-306-313p; c-310p, 315.* ***Giordano*** *a-226i.* ***Sid Greene*** *a-167-174i, 229i(r).* ***Grell*** *a-237p, 238p, 240-243p; c-236.* ***Heck*** *a-198p.* ***Infantino/Anderson*** *a-135. c-135, 170-174, 192, 200, 201, 328-330.* ***Infantino/Giella*** *c-105-112, 163, 164, 166-168.* ***G. Kane*** *a-195p, 197-199p, 229r, 232r; c-197-199, 312p.* ***Kubert*** *a-108p, 215i(r); c-189-191.* ***Lopez*** *c-272.* ***Meskin*** *a-229r, 232r.* ***Perez*** *a-289-293p; c-293.* ***Starlin*** *a-294-296p.* ***Staton*** *c-263p, 264p. Green Lantern x-over-131, 143, 168, 171, 191.*

FLASH (2nd Series)(See Crisis on Infinite Earths #12 and Justice League Europe)
DC Comics: June, 1987 - Present (75¢-$1.99)

1-Guice-c/a begins; New Teen Titans app. 1.25 3.75 10.00
2-10: 3-Intro. Kilgore. 5-Intro. Speed McGee. 7-1st app. Blue Trinity. 8,9-Millennium tie-ins. 9-1st app. The Chunk 4.00
11-61: 12-Free extra 16 pg. Dr. Light story. 19-Free extra 16 pg. Flash story. 28-Capt. Cold app. 29-New Phantom Lady app. 40-Dr. Alchemy app. 50-($1.75, 52 pgs.) 2.50
62-78,80: 62-Flash: Year One begins, ends #65. 65-Last $1.00-c. 66-Aquaman app. 69,70-Green Lantern app. 70-Gorilla Grodd story ends. 73-Re-intro Barry Allen & begin saga ("Barry Allen's" true ID revealed in #78). 76-Re-intro of Max Mercury (Quality Comics' Quicksilver), not in uniform until #77. 80-($1.25-c) Regular Edition 4.00
79,80 ($2.50): 79-(68 pgs.) Barry Allen saga ends. 80-Foil-c 5.00
81-91,93,94,0,95-99,101: 81,82-Nightwing & Starfire app. 84-Razer app. 94-Zero Hour. 0-(10/94). 95-"Terminal Velocity" begins, ends #100. 96,98,99-Kobra app. 97-Origin Max Mercury; Chillblaine app. 4.00
92-1st Impulse 1.25 3.75 10.00
100 ($2.50)-Newstand edition; Kobra & JLA app. 4.00
100 ($3.50)-Foil-c edition; Kobra & JLA app. 5.00

GD2.0 FN6.0 NM9.4

102-131: 102-Mongul app.; begin-$1.75-c. 105-Mirror Master app. 107-Shazam app. 108-"Dead Heat" begins; 1st app. Savitar. 109-"Dead Heat" Pt. 2 (cont'd in Impulse #10). 110-"Dead Heat" Pt. 4 (cont'd in Impulse #11). 111-"Dead Heat" finale; Savitar disappears into the Speed Force; John Fox cameo (2nd app.). 112-"Race Against Time" begins, ends #118; re-intro John Fox; intro new Chillblaine. 113-Tornado Twins app. 119-Final Night x-over 127-129-Rogue's Gallery & Neron. 128,129-JLA-app.130-Morrison & Millar-s begin 2.00
132-150: 135-GL & GA app. 142-Wally marries Linda; Waid-s return. 144-Cobalt Blue origin. 145-Chain Lightning begins.147-Professor Zoom-c/app. 149-Barry Allen app. 150-($2.95) Final showdown with Cobalt Blue 3.00
151-162: 151-Casey-s. 152-New Flash-c. 154-New Flash ID revealed. 159-Wally marries Linda. 162-Last Waid-s. 2.00
163-170: 163-Begin $2.25-c. 164-170-Bolland-c 2.25
#1,000,000 (11/98) 853rd Century x-over 2.00
Annual 1-7,9: 2-('87-'94,'96, 68 pgs), 3-Gives history of G.A.,S.A., & Modern Age Flash in text. 4-Armaggedon 2001. 5-Eclipso-c/story. 7-Elseworlds story. 9-Legends of the Dead Earth story; J.H. Williams-a(p); Mick Gray-a(i) 3.00
Annual 8 (1995, $3.50)-Year One story 3.50
Annual 10 (1997, $3.95)-Pulp Heroes stories 4.00
Annual 11,12 ('98, '99)-11-Ghosts; Wrightson-c. 12-JLApe; Art Adams-c 3.00
Annual 13 ('00, $3.50) Planet DC; Alcatena-c/a 3.50
Dead Heat (2000, $14.95, TPB)-r/#108-111, Impulse #10,11 15.00
...80-Page Giant (8/98, $4.95) Flash family stories by Waid, Byrne, Millar, and others; Mhan-c 5.00
...80-Page Giant 2 (4/99, $4.95) Stories of Flash family, future Kid Flash, original Teen Titans, XS 5.00
...Plus 1 (1/1997, $2.95)-Nightwing-c/app. 3.00
...Secret Files 1 (11/97, $4.95) Origin-s & pin-ups 5.00
...Secret Files 2 (11/99, $4.95) Origin of Replicant 5.00
Special 1 (1990, $2.95, 84 pgs.)-50th anniversary issue; Kubert-c; 1st Flash story by Mark Waid; 1st app. John Fox (27th Century Flash) 3.00
TV Special 1 (1991, $3.95, 76 pgs.)-Photo-c plus behind the scenes photos of TV show; Saltares-a, Byrne scripts 4.00
Terminal Velocity (1996, $12.95, TPB)-r/#95-100. 13.00
The Return of Barry Allen (1996, $12.95, TPB)-r/#74-79. 13.00

NOTE: ***Guice*** *a-1-9p, 11p, Annual 1p; c-1-9p, Annual 1p.* ***Perez*** *c-15-17, Annual 2i.* ***Travest Charest*** *c/a-Annual 5p.*

FLASH, THE (See Tangent Comics/ The Flash)

FLASH AND GREEN LANTERN: THE BRAVE AND THE BOLD
DC Comics: Oct, 1999 - No. 6, Mar, 2000 ($2.50, limited series)

1-6-Waid & Peyer-s/Kitson-a. 4-Green Arrow app. 2.50

FLASH/ GREEN LANTERN: FASTER FRIENDS (See Green Lantern/Flash...)
DC Comics: No. 2, 1997 ($4.95, continuation of Green Lantern/Flash: Faster Friends #1)

2-Waid/Augustyn-s 5.00

FLASH COMICS (Whiz Comics No. 2 on)
Fawcett Publications: Jan, 1940 (12 pgs., B&W, regular size)
(Not distributed to newsstands; printed for in-house use)

NOTE: ***Whiz Comics*** *#2 was preceded by two books,* ***Flash Comics*** *and* ***Thrill Comics****, both dated Jan, 1940, (12 pgs, B&W, regular size) and were not distributed. These two books are identical except for the title, and were sent out to major distributors as ad copies to promote sales. It is believed that the complete 68 page issue of Fawcett's* ***Flash*** *and* ***Thrill Comics*** *#1 was finished and ready for publication with the January date. Since DC Comics was also about to publish a book with the same date and title, Fawcett hurriedly printed up the black and white version of* ***Flash Comics*** *to secure copyright before DC. The inside covers are blank, with the covers and inside pages printed on a high quality uncoated paper stock.The eight page origin story of Captain Thunder is composed of pages 1-7 and 13 of the Captain Marvel story essentially as they appeared in the first issue of* ***Whiz Comics****. The balloon dialogue on page thirteen was relettered to tie the story into the end of page seven in* ***Flash*** *and* ***Thrill Comics*** *to produce a shorter version of the origin story for copyright purposes. Obviously, DC acquired the copyright and Fawcett dropped* ***Flash*** *as well as* ***Thrill*** *and came out with* ***Whiz Comics*** *a month later. Fawcett never used the cover to* ***Flash*** *and* ***Thrill*** *#1, designing a new cover for* ***Whiz Comics****. Fawcett also must have discovered that Captain Thunder had already been used by another publisher (Captain Terry Thunder by Fiction House). All references to Captain Thunder were relettered to Captain Marvel before appearing in* ***Whiz****.*

1 (nn on-c, #1 on inside)-Origin & 1st app. Captain Thunder. Eight copies of Flash and three copies of Thrill exist. All 3 copies of Thrill sold in 1986 for between $4,000-$10,000 each. A NM copy of Thrill sold in 1987 for

Flash Comics #10 © DC

Flash Gordon #2 © KFS

Flashpoint #1 © DC

GD2.0 FN6.0 NM9.4

$12,000. A vg copy of Thrill sold in 1987 for $9000 cash; another copy sold in 1987 for $2000 cash, $10,000 trade; cover by Leo O'Mealia

FLASH COMICS (The Flash No. 105 on) (Also see All-Flash)
National Periodical Publ./All-American: Jan, 1940 - No. 104, Feb, 1949

	GD2.0	FN6.0	VF8.0	NM9.4
1-The Flash (origin/1st app.) by Harry Lampert, Hawkman (origin/1st app.) by Gardner Fox, The Whip, & Johnny Thunder (origin/1st app.) by Stan Asch; Cliff Cornwall by Moldoff, Flash Picture Novelets (later Minute Movies w/#12) begin; Moldoff (Shelly) cover; 1st app. Shiera Sanders who later becomes Hawkgirl, #24; reprinted in Famous First Edition (on sale 11/10/39); The Flash-c	6000.00	18,000.00	39,000.00	75,000.00

1-Reprint, Oversize 13-1/2x10". **WARNING:** This comic is an exact reprint of the original except for its size. DC published it in 1974 with a second cover titling it as a Famous First Edition. There have been many reported cases of the outer cover being removed and the interior sold as the original edition. The reprint with the new outer cover removed is practically worthless. See Famous First Edition for value.

	GD2.0	FN6.0	NM9.4
2-Rod Rian begins, ends #11; Hawkman-c	697.00	2090.00	8000.00
3-King Standish begins (1st app.), ends #41 (called The King #16-37,39-41); E.E. Hibbard-a begins on Flash	496.00	1487.00	5700.00
4-Moldoff (Shelly) Hawkman begins; The Whip-c	410.00	1230.00	4300.00
5-The King-c	333.00	1000.00	3500.00
6-2nd Flash-c (alternates w/Hawkman #6 on)	452.00	1357.00	5200.00
7-2nd Hawkman-c; 1st Moldoff Hawkman-c	429.00	1286.00	4500.00
8-New logo begins; classic Moldoff Flash-c	295.00	885.00	2800.00
9,10: 9-Moldoff Hawkman-c; 10-Classic Moldoff Flash-c	305.00	915.00	3200.00
11-13,15-20: 12-Les Watts begins; "Sparks" #16 on. 17-Last Cliff Cornwall	195.00	585.00	1850.00
14-World War II cover	232.00	695.00	2200.00
21-Classic Hawkman-c	190.00	570.00	1800.00
22,23	168.00	505.00	1600.00
24-Shiera becomes Hawkgirl (12/41); see All-Star Comics #5 for 1st app.	200.00	600.00	1900.00
25-28,30: 28-Last Les Sparks.	113.00	340.00	1075.00
29-Ghost Patrol begins (origin/1st app.), ends #104.	129.00	387.00	1225.00
31,33-Classic Hawkman-c. 33-Origin Shade	111.00	332.00	1050.00
32,34-40	103.00	309.00	975.00
41-50	92.00	276.00	875.00
51-61: 52-1st computer in comics, c/s (4/44). 59-Last Minute Movies. 61-Last Moldoff Hawkman	82.00	245.00	775.00
62-Hawkman by Kubert begins	100.00	300.00	945.00
63-85: 66-68-Hop Harrigan in all. 70-Mutt & Jeff app. 80-Atom begins, ends #104	74.00	221.00	700.00
86-Intro. The Black Canary in Johnny Thunder (8/47); see All-Star #38.	263.00	790.00	2500.00
87,88,90: 87-Intro. The Foil. 88-Origin Ghost.	114.00	342.00	1085.00
89-Intro villain The Thorn	158.00	474.00	1500.00
91,93-99: 98-Atom & Hawkman don new costumes	129.00	387.00	1225.00
92-1st solo Black Canary plus-c; rare in Mint due to black ink smearing on white-c	333.00	1000.00	3500.00
100 (10/48),103(Scarce)-52 pgs. each	295.00	885.00	2800.00
101,102(Scarce)	242.00	726.00	2300.00
104-Origin The Flash retold (Scarce)	626.00	1878.00	7200.00

NOTE: ***Irwin Hasen** a-Wheaties Giveaway. c-97, Wheaties Giveaway. **E.E. Hibbard** c-6, 12, 20, 24, 26, 28, 30, 44, 46, 48, 50, 62, 66, 68, 69, 72, 74, 76, 78, 80, 82. **Infantino** a-86p, 90, 93-95, 99-104; c-90, 92, 93, 97, 99, 101, 103. **Kinstler** a-87, 89(Hawkman); c-87. **Chet Kozlak** c-77, 79, 81. **Krigstein** a-94. **Kubert** a-62-76, 83, 85, 86, 88-104; c-63, 65, 67, 70, 71, 73, 75, 83, 85, 86, 88, 89, 91, 94, 96, 98, 100, 104. **Moldoff** a-3; c-3, 7-11, 13-17, plus odd #'s 19-61. **Martin Naydell** c-52, 54, 56, 58, 60, 64, 84.*

FLASH DIGEST, THE (See DC Special Series #24)

FLASH GORDON (See Defenders Of The Earth, Eat Right to Work..., Giant Comic Album, King Classics, King Comics, March of Comics #118, 133, 142, The Phantom #18, Street Comix & Wow Comics, 1st series)

FLASH GORDON
Dell Publishing Co.: No. 25, 1941; No. 10, 1943 - No. 512, Nov, 1953

	GD2.0	FN6.0	NM9.4
Feature Books 25 (#1)(1941))-r-not by Raymond	88.00	263.00	1050.00
Four Color 10(1943)-by Alex Raymond; reprints "The Ice Kingdom"	90.00	270.00	1075.00
Four Color 84(1945)-by Alex Raymond; reprints "The Fiery Desert"	42.00	125.00	500.00
Four Color 173	15.00	44.00	175.00
Four Color 190-Bondage-c; "The Adventures of the Flying Saucers"; 5th Flying Saucer story (6/48)- see The Spirit 9/28/47(1st), Shadow Comics V7#10 (2nd, 1/48), Captain Midnight #60 (3rd, 2/48) & Boy Commandos #26 (4th, 3-4/48)	17.00	50.00	200.00
Four Color 204,247	11.70	35.00	140.00
Four Color 424-Painted-c	9.00	27.00	110.00
2(5-7/53-Dell)-Painted-c; Evans-a?	5.35	16.00	65.00
Four Color 512-Painted-c	5.35	16.00	65.00

FLASH GORDON (See Tiny Tot Funnies)
Harvey Publications: Oct, 1950 - No. 4, April, 1951

	GD2.0	FN6.0	NM9.4
1-Alex Raymond-a; bondage-c; reprints strips from 7/14/40 to 12/8/40	33.00	98.00	260.00
2-Alex Raymond-a; r/strips 12/15/40-4/27/41	22.00	66.00	175.00
3,4-Alex Raymond-a; 3-bondage-c; r/strips 5/4/41-9/21/41. 4-r/strips 10/24/37-3/27/38	21.00	62.00	165.00
5-(Rare)-Small size-5-1/2x8-1/2"; B&W; 32 pgs.; Distributed to some mail subscribers only. Estimated value	50.00	150.00	450.00

(Also see All-New No. 15, Boy Explorers No. 2, and Stuntman No. 3)

FLASH GORDON
Gold Key: June, 1965

	GD2.0	FN6.0	NM9.4
1 (1947 reprint)-Painted-c	4.55	13.65	50.00

FLASH GORDON (Also see Comics Reading Libraries)
King #1-11/Charlton #12-18/Gold Key #19-23/Whitman #28 on: 9/66 - #11, 12/67; #12, 2/69 - #18, 1/70; #19, 9/78 - #37, 3/82
(Painted covers No. 19-30, 34)

	GD2.0	FN6.0	NM9.4
1-1st S.A. app Flash Gordon; Williamson c/a(2); E.C. swipe/Incredible S.F. #32; Mandrake story	4.55	13.65	50.00
1-Army giveaway(1968)("Complimentary" on cover)(Same as regular #1 minus Mandrake story & back-c)	3.65	11.00	40.00
2-8: 2-Bolle, Gil Kane-c; Mandrake story. 3-Williamson-c. 4-Secret Agent X-9 begins, Williamson-c/a(3). 5-Williamson-c/a(2). 6,8-Crandall-a. 7-Raboy-a (last in comics?). 8-Secret Agent X-9-r	3.00	9.00	30.00
9-13: 9,10-Raymond-r. 10-Buckler's 1st pro work (11/67). 1-Crandall-a. 12-Crandall-c/a. 13-Jeff Jones-a (15 pgs.)	2.50	7.50	25.00
14,15: 15-Last 12¢ issue	2.00	6.00	18.00
16,17: 17-Brick Bradford story	1.85	5.50	15.00
18-Kaluta-a (3rd pro work?)(see Teen Confessions)	2.30	7.00	20.00
19(9/78, G.K.), 20-26		2.40	6.00
27-29.34-37: 34-37-Movie adaptation	1.00	3.00	8.00
30 (10/80) (scarce)	2.00	6.00	16.00
30 (7/81; re-issue), 31-33-single issues		2.40	6.00
31-33 (Bagged 3-pack): Movie adaptation; Williamson-a.			18.00

NOTE: ***Aparo** a-8. **Bolle** a-21, 22. **Boyette** a-14-18. **Briggs** c-10. **Buckler** a-10. **Crandall** c-6. **Estrada** a-3. **Gene Fawcette** a-29, 30, 34, 37. **McWilliams** a-31-33, 36.*

FLASH GORDON
DC Comics: June, 1988 - No. 9, Holiday, 1988-'89 ($1.25, mini-series)

1-9: 1,5-Painted-c — 3.00

FLASH GORDON
Marvel Comics: June, 1995 - No. 2, July, 1995 ($2.95, limited series)

1,2: Schultz scripts; Williamson-a — 3.00

FLASH GORDON THE MOVIE
Western Publishing Co.: 1980 (8-1/4 x 11", $1.95, 68 pgs.)

	GD2.0	FN6.0	NM9.4
11294-Williamson-c/a; adapts movie	1.50	4.50	12.00
13743-Hardback edition	2.00	6.00	16.00

FLASHPOINT (Elseworlds Flash)
DC Comics: Dec, 1999 - No. 3, Feb, 2000 ($2.95, limited series)

1-3-Paralyzed Barry Allen; Breyfogle-a/McGreal-s — 3.00

FLAT-TOP
Mazie Comics/Harvey Publ.(Magazine Publ.) No. 4 on: 11/53 - No. 3, 5/54; No. 4, 3/55 - No. 7, 9/55

Flinch #9 © DC

Flintstones #4 © H-B

Flippity & Flop #7 © DC

GD2.0 FN6.0 NM9.4

1-Teenage; Flat-Top, Mazie, Mortie & Stevie begin 6.40 19.25 45.00
2,3 4.00 12.00 24.00
4-7 4.00 10.00 20.00

FLESH & BLOOD
Brainstorm Comics: Dec, 1995 ($2.95, B&W, mature)
1-Balent-c; foil-c. 3.00

FLESH AND BONES
Upshot Graphics (Fantagraphics Books): June, 1986 - No. 4, Dec, 1986 (Limited series)
1-4: Alan Moore scripts (r) & Dalgoda by Fujitake 3.00

FLESH CRAWLERS
Kitchen Sink Press: Aug, 1993 - No. 3, 1995 ($2.50, B&W, limited series, mature)
1-3 2.50

FLEX MENTALLO (Man of Muscle Mystery) (See Doom Patrol, 2nd Series)
DC Comics (Vertigo): Jun, 1996 - No. 4, Sept, 1996 ($2.50, lim. series, mature)
1-4: Grant Morrison scripts & Frank Quitely-c/a in all 3.00

FLINCH (Horror anthology)
DC Comics (Vertigo): Jun, 1999 - No. 16, Jan, 2001 ($2.50)
1-16: 1-Art by Jim Lee, Quitely, and Corben. 5-Sale-c. 11-Timm-a 2.50

FLINTSTONE KIDS, THE (TV) (See Star Comics Digest)
Star Comics/Marvel Comics #5 on: Aug, 1987 - No. 11, Apr, 1989
1-11 3.00

FLINTSTONES, THE (TV)(See Dell Giant #48 for No. 1)
Dell Publ. Co./Gold Key No. 7 (10/62) on: No. 2, Nov-Dec, 1961 - No. 60, Sept, 1970 (Hanna-Barbera)
2-2nd app. (TV show debuted on 9/30/60); 1st app. of Cave Kids; 15¢-c thru #5 11.00 33.00 120.00
3-6(7-8/62): 3-Perry Gunnite begins. 6-1st 12¢-c 6.80 20.50 75.00
7 (10/62; 1st GK) 6.80 20.50 75.00
8-10 5.00 15.00 55.00
11-1st app. Pebbles (6/63) 8.65 26.00 95.00
12-15,17-20 3.80 11.40 42.00
16-1st app. Bamm-Bamm (1/64) 7.65 23.00 85.00
21-23,25-30,33: 33-Meet Frankenstein & Dracula 3.45 10.35 38.00
24-1st app. The Grusomes 5.45 16.35 60.00
31,32,35-40: 31-Xmas-c. 39-Reprints 3.20 9.60 35.00
34-1st app. The Great Gazoo 5.45 16.35 60.00
41-60: 45-Last 12¢ issue 3.00 9.00 32.00
At N. Y. World's Fair ('64)-J.W. Books(25¢)-1st printing; no date on-c (29¢ version exists, 2nd print?) Most H-B characters app.; including Yogi Bear, Top Cat, Snagglepuss and the Jetsons 4.55 13.65 50.00
At N. Y. World's Fair (1965 on-c; re-issue). NOTE: Warehouse find in 1984 1.50 4.50 12.00
Bigger & Boulder 1(#30013-211) (Gold Key Giant, 11/62, 25¢, 84 pgs.) 8.15 24.50 90.00
Bigger & Boulder 2-(1966, 25¢)-Reprints B&B No. 1 6.80 20.50 75.00
...On the Rocks (9/61, $1.00, 6-1/4x9", cardboard-c, high quality paper,116 pgs.) B&W new material 9.00 27.00 100.00
...With Pebbles & Bamm Bamm (100 pgs., G.K.)-30028-511 (paper-c, 25¢) (11/65) 8.15 24.50 90.00
NOTE: *(See Comic Album #16, Bamm-Bamm & Pebbles Flintstone, Dell Giant 48, Golden Comics Digest, March of Comics #229, 243, 271, 289, 299, 317, 327, 341, Pebbles Flintstone, Top Comics #2-4, and Whitman Comic Book.)*

FLINTSTONES, THE (TV)(...& Pebbles)
Charlton Comics: Nov, 1970 - No. 50, Feb, 1977 (Hanna-Barbera)
1 7.65 23.00 85.00
2 3.65 11.00 40.00
3-7,9,10 2.50 7.50 25.00
8- "Flintstones Summer Vacation" (Summer, 1971, 52 pgs.) 5.45 16.35 60.00
11-20,36: 36-Mike Zeck illos (early work) 2.50 7.50 23.00
21-35,38-41,43-45 2.00 6.00 18.00
37-Byrne text illos (early work; see Nightmare #20) 2.50 7.50 25.00
42-Byrne-a (2 pgs.) 2.50 7.50 25.00
46-50 2.00 6.00 18.00
(Also see Barney & Betty Rubble, Dino, The Great Gazoo, & Pebbles & Bamm-Bamm)

FLINTSTONES, THE (TV)(See Yogi Bear, 3rd series) (Newsstand sales only)
Marvel Comics Group: October, 1977 - No. 9, Feb, 1979 (Hanna-Barbera)
1,7-9: 7-9-Yogi Bear app. 2.30 7.00 20.00
2,3,5,6: Yogi Bear app. 1.85 5.50 15.00
4-The Jetsons app. 2.30 7.00 20.00

FLINTSTONES, THE (TV)
Harvey Comics: Sept, 1992 - No. 13, Jun, 1994 ($1.25/$1.50) (Hanna-Barbera)
V2#1-13 3.00
...Big Book 1,2 (11/92, 3/93; both $1.95, 52 pgs.) 3.50
...Giant Size 1-3 (10/92, 4/93, 11/93; $2.25, 68 pgs.) 3.50

FLINTSTONES, THE (TV)
Archie Publications: Sept, 1995 - No. 22, June, 1997 ($1.50)
1-22 2.00

FLINTSTONES AND THE JETSONS, THE (TV)
DC Comics: Aug, 1997 - No. 21, May, 1999 ($1.75/$1.95)
1-21-($1.99): 19-Bizarro Elroy-c 2.00

FLINTSTONES CHRISTMAS PARTY, THE (See The Funtastic World of Hanna-Barbera No. 1)

FLIP
Harvey Publications: April, 1954 - No. 2, June, 1954 (Satire)
1,2-Nostrand-a each. 2-Powell-a 22.00 66.00 175.00

FLIPPER (TV)
Gold Key: Apr, 1966 - No. 3, Nov, 1967 (All have photo-c)
1 5.35 16.00 65.00
2,3 3.80 11.40 42.00

FLIPPITY & FLOP
National Per. Publ. (Signal Publ. Co.): 12-1/51-52 - No. 46, 8-10/59; No. 47, 9-11/60
1-Sam dog & his pets Flippity The Bird and Flop The Cat begin; Twiddle and Twaddle begin 26.00 79.00 210.00
2 14.00 43.00 115.00
3-5 12.00 36.00 95.00
6-10 10.00 30.00 80.00
11-20: 20-Last precode (3/55) 10.00 30.00 70.00
21-47 8.65 26.00 60.00

FLOATERS
Dark Horse Comics: Sept, 1993 - No. 5, Jan, 1994 ($2.50, B&W, lim. series)
1-5 2.50

FLOOD RELIEF
Malibu Comics (Ultraverse): Jan, 1994 (36 pgs.)(Ordered thru mail w/$5.00 to Red Cross)
1-Hardcase, Prime & Prototype app. 5.00

FLOYD FARLAND (See Eclipse Graphic Album Series #11)

FLY, THE (Also see Adventures of..., Blue Ribbon Comics & Flyman)
Archie Enterprises, Inc.: May, 1983 - No. 9, Oct, 1984
1-Mr. Justice app; origin Shield; Kirby-a; Steranko-c 4.00
2-9: Ditko-a in all. 2-Flygirl app. 4-8-Ditko-c(p) 3.00
NOTE: ***Ayers** c-9. **Buckler** a-1, 2. **Kirby** a-1. **Nebres** c-3, 4, 5i, 6, 7i. **Steranko** c-1, 2.*

FLY, THE
Impact Comics (DC): Aug, 1991 - No. 17, Dec, 1992 ($1.00)
1-17: 4-Vs. The Black Hood. 9-Trading card inside 2.00
Annual 1 ('92, $2.50, 68 pgs.)-Impact trading card 2.50

FLYBOY (Flying Cadets)(Also see Approved Comics #5)
Ziff-Davis Publ. Co. (Approved): Spring, 1952 - No. 2, Oct-Nov, 1952
1-Saunders painted-c 19.00 56.00 150.00
2-(10-11/52)-Saunders painted-c 13.00 39.00 105.00

FLYING ACES (Aviation stories)
Key Publications: July, 1955 - No. 5, Mar, 1956

Flying Saucers #1 © AVON

FOOM #17 © MAR

Forbidden Love #4 © QUA

1 5.70 17.00 40.00
2-5: 2-Trapani-a 4.00 12.00 24.00

FLYING A'S RANGE RIDER, THE (TV)(See Western Roundup under Dell Giants)
Dell Publishing Co.: #404, 6-7/52; #2, June-Aug, 1953 - #24, Aug, 1959 (All photo-c)

Four Color 404(#1)-Titled "The Range Rider" 10.00 30.00 120.00
2 6.30 19.00 75.00
3-10 4.60 13.75 55.00
11-16,18-24 4.55 13.65 50.00
17-Toth-a 5.35 16.00 65.00

FLYING CADET (WW II Plane Photos)
Flying Cadet Publ. Co.; Jan, 1943 - V2#8, 1947 (Half photos, half comics)

V1#1-Painted-c 14.00 41.00 110.00
2 7.85 23.50 55.00
3-9 (Two #6's, Sept. & Oct.): 5,6a,6b-Photo-c 7.00 21.00 48.00
V2#1-7(#10-16) 5.50 16.50 38.00
8(#17)-Bare-breasted woman-c 18.00 53.00 140.00

FLYING COLORS 10th ANNIVERSARY SPECIAL
Flying Colors Comics: Fall 1998 ($2.95, one-shot)

1-Dan Brereton-c; pin-ups by Jim Lee and Jeff Johnson 3.00

FLYIN' JENNY
Pentagon Publ. Co./Leader Enterprises #2: 1946 - No. 2, 1947 (1945 strip-r)

nn-Marcus Swayze strip-r (entire insides) 13.00 39.00 105.00
2-Baker-c; Swayze strip reprints 15.00 45.00 120.00

FLYING MODELS
H-K Publ. (Health-Knowledge Publs.): V61#3, May, 1954 (5¢, 16 pgs.)

V61#3 (Rare) 8.65 26.00 60.00

FLYING NUN (TV)
Dell Publishing Co.: Feb, 1968 - No. 4, Nov, 1968

1-Sally Field photo-c 4.60 13.75 55.00
2-4: 2-Sally Field photo-c 3.20 9.60 35.00

FLYING NURSES (See Sue & Sally Smith...)

FLYING SAUCERS (See The Spirit 9/28/47(1st app.), Shadow Comics V7#10 (2nd, 1/48), Captain Midnight #60 (3rd, 2/48), Boy Commandos #26 (4th, 3-4/48) & Flash Gordon Four Color 190 (5th, 6/48))

FLYING SAUCERS
Avon Periodicals/Realistic: 1950; 1952; 1953

1(1950)-Wood-a, 21 pgs.; Fawcette-c 76.00 229.00 725.00
nn(1952)-Cover altered plus 2 pgs. of Wood-a not in original 44.00 133.00 400.00
nn(1953)-Reprints above 35.00 105.00 280.00

FLYING SAUCERS (Comics)
Dell Publishing Co.: April, 1967 - No. 4, Nov, 1967; No. 5, Oct, 1969

1 3.20 9.60 35.00
2-5 2.50 7.50 24.00

FLY MAN (Formerly Adventures of The Fly; Mighty Comics #40 on)
Mighty Comics Group (Radio Comics) (Archie):
No. 32, July, 1965 - No. 39, Sept, 1966 (Also see Mighty Crusaders)

32,33-Comet, Shield, Black Hood, The Fly & Flygirl x-over. 33-Re-intro Wizard, Hangman (1st S.A. appearances) 3.65 11.00 40.00
34-39: 34-Shield begins. 35-Origin Black Hood. 36-Hangman x-over in Shield; re-intro. & origin of Web (1st S.A. app.). 37-Hangman, Wizard x-over in Flyman; last Shield issue. 38-Web story. 39-Steel Sterling story (1st S.A. app.) 2.80 8.40 28.00

FOES
Ram Comics: 1989 - No. 3, 1989 ($1.95, limited series)

1-3 2.00

FOLLOW THE SUN (TV)
Dell Publishing Co.: May-July, 1962 - No. 2, Sept-Nov, 1962 (Photo-c)

01-280-207(No.1) 4.10 12.30 45.00
12-280-211(No.2) 3.65 11.00 40.00

FOODANG
Continum Comics: July, 1994 ($1.95, B&W, bi-monthly)

1 2.00

FOODINI (TV)(The Great...; see Jingle Dingle & Pinhead &...)
Continental Publ. (Holyoke): March, 1950 - No. 4, Aug, 1950 (All have 52 pgs.)

1-Based on TV puppet show (very early TV comic) 20.00 60.00 160.00
2-Jingle Dingle begins 10.50 32.00 85.00
3,4 9.30 28.00 65.00

FOOEY (Magazine) (Satire)
Scoff Publishing Co.: Feb, 1961 - No. 4, May, 1961

1 4.55 13.65 50.00
2-4 3.00 9.00 32.00

FOOFUR (TV)
Marvel Comics (Star Comics)/Marvel No. 5 on: Aug, 1987 - No. 6, Jun, 1988

1-6 3.00

FOOLKILLER (Also see The Amazing Spider-Man #225, The Defenders #73 Man-Thing #3 & Omega the Unknown #8)
Marvel Comics: Oct, 1990 - No. 10, Oct, 1991 ($1.75, limited series)

1-10: 1-Origin 3rd Foolkiller; Greg Salinger app; DeZuniga-a(i) in 1-4. 8-Spider-Man x-over 2.00

FOOM (Friends Of Ol' Marvel)
Marvel Comics: 1973 - No. 22, 1979 (Marvel fan magazine)

1 3.65 11.00 40.00
2-Hulk-c by Steranko 3.00 9.00 30.00
3,4 2.50 7.50 25.00
5-11: 11-Kirby-a and interview 2.30 7.00 20.00
12-15: 12-Vision-c. 13-Daredevil-c. 14-Conan. 15-Howard the Duck 2.00 6.00 16.00
16,18-20: 16-Marvel bullpen. 19-Defenders 1.50 4.50 12.00
17, 21: 17-Stan Lee issue. 21-Star Wars 2.00 6.00 16.00
22-Spider-Man-c; low print run final issue 3.25 9.75 36.00

FOOTBALL THRILLS (See Tops In Adventure)
Ziff-Davis Publ. Co.: Fall-Winter, 1951-52 - No. 2, Fall, 1952 (Edited by "Red" Grange)

1-Powell a(2); Saunders painted-c; Red Grange, Jim Thorpe stories 28.00 84.00 225.00
2-Saunders painted-c 19.00 56.00 150.00

FOOT SOLDIERS, THE
Dark Horse Comics: Jan, 1996 - No. 4, Apr, 1996 ($2.95, limited series)

1-4: Jim Krueger story & Michael Avon Oeming-a. in all. 1-Alex Ross-c. 4-John K. Snyder, III-c. 3.00

FOOT SOLDIERS, THE (Volume Two)
Image Comics: Sept, 1997 - No. 5, May, 1998 ($2.95, limited series)

1-5: 1-Yeowell-a. 2-McDaniel, Hester, Sienkiewicz, Giffen-a 3.00

FOR A NIGHT OF LOVE
Avon Periodicals: 1951

nn-Two stories adapted from the works of Emile Zola; Astarita, Ravielli-a; Kinstler-c 30.00 90.00 240.00

FORBIDDEN KNOWLEDGE: ADVENTURE BEYOND THE DOORWAY TO SOULS WITH RADICAL DREAMER (Also see Radical Dreamer)
Mark's Giant Economy Size Comics: 1996 ($3.50, B&W, one-shot, 48 pgs.)

nn-Max Wrighter app.; Wheatley-c/a/script; painted infinity-c 3.50

FORBIDDEN LOVE
Quality Comics Group: Mar, 1950 - No. 4, Sept, 1950 (52 pgs.)

1-(Scarce)-Classic photo-c; Crandall-a 71.00 213.00 675.00
2-(Scarce)-Classic photo-c 53.00 158.00 475.00
3-(Scarce)-Photo-c 40.00 120.00 325.00
4-(Scarce)-Ward/Cuidera-a; photo-c 40.00 120.00 350.00

FORBIDDEN LOVE (See Dark Mansion of...)

FORBIDDEN PLANET
Innovation Publishing: May, 1992 - No. 4, 1992 ($2.50, limited series)

Forbidden Worlds #12 © ACG

Force Works #15 © MAR

Forever People #8 © DC

GD2.0 FN6.0 NM9.4

1-4: Adapts movie; painted-c 2.50

FORBIDDEN TALES OF DARK MANSION (Formerly Dark Mansion of Forbidden Love #1-4)
National Periodical Publ.: No. 5, May-June, 1972 - No. 15, Feb-Mar, 1974

5-(52 pgs.) 3.20 9.60 35.00
6-15: 13-Kane/Howard-a 2.00 6.00 16.00

NOTE: ***N. Adams*** *c-9.* ***Alcala*** *a-9-11, 13.* ***Chaykin*** *a-7,15.* ***Evans*** *a-14.* ***Heck*** *a-5.* ***Kaluta*** *a-7i, 8-12; c-7, 8, 13.* ***G. Kane*** *a-13.* ***Kirby*** *a-6.* ***Nino*** *a-8, 12, 15.* ***Redondo*** *a-14.*

FORBIDDEN WORLDS
American Comics Group: 7-8/51 - No. 34, 10-11/54; No. 35, 8/55 - No. 145, 8/67 (No. 1-5: 52 pgs.; No. 6-8: 44 pgs.)

1-Williamson/Frazetta-a (10 pgs.) 147.00 442.00 1400.00
2 66.00 197.00 625.00
3-Williamson/Orlando-a (7 pgs.); Wood (2 panels); Frazetta (1 panel) 68.00 205.00 650.00
4 40.00 120.00 350.00
5-Krenkel/Williamson-a (8 pgs.) 55.00 165.00 500.00
6-Harrison/Williamson-a (8 pgs.) 47.00 142.00 425.00
7,8,10: 7-1st monthly issue 30.00 90.00 240.00
9-A-Bomb explosion story 33.00 99.00 265.00
11-20 21.00 64.00 170.00
21-33: 24-E.C. swipe by Landau 15.00 45.00 120.00
34(10-11/54)(Scarce)(becomes Young Heroes #35 on)-Last pre-code issue; A-Bomb explosion story 16.00 49.00 130.00
35(8/55)-Scarce 15.00 45.00 120.00
36-62 10.00 30.00 75.00
63,69,76,78-Williamson-a in all; w/Krenkel #69 10.00 30.00 80.00
64,66-68,70-72,74,75,77,79-85,87-90 8.65 26.00 60.00
65- "There's a New Moon Tonight" listed in #114 as holding 1st record fan mail response 10.00 30.00 80.00
73-1st app. Herbie by Ogden Whitney 38.00 113.00 300.00
86-Flying saucer-c by Schaffenberger 9.30 28.00 65.00
91-93,95-100 4.10 12.30 45.00
94-Herbie (2nd app.) 7.65 23.00 85.00
101-109,111-113,115,117-120 3.20 9.60 35.00
110,114,116-Herbie app. 114-1st Herbie-c; contains list of editor's top 20 ACG stories. 116-Herbie goes to Hell 5.40 16.35 60.00
121-123 3.00 9.00 30.00
124,126-130: 24-Magic Agent app. 3.20 9.60 35.00
125-Magic Agent app.; intro. & origin Magicman series, ends #141 4.55 13.65 50.00
131-139: 133-Origin/1st app. Dragonia in Magicman (1-2/66); returns in #138. 136-Nemesis x-over in Magicman 3.00 9.00 30.00
140-Mark Midnight app. by Ditko 3.20 9.60 35.00
141-145 2.50 7.50 25.00

NOTE: ***Buscema*** *a-75, 79, 81, 82, 140r.* ***Cameron*** *a-5.* ***Disbrow*** *a-10.* ***Ditko*** *a-137p, 138, 140.* ***Landau*** *a-24, 27-29, 31-34, 48, 86r, 96, 143-45.* ***Lazarus*** *a-18, 23, 24, 57.* ***Moldoff*** *a-27, 31, 139r.* ***Reinman*** *a-93.* ***Whitney*** *a-115, 116, 137; c-40, 46, 57, 60, 68, 78, 79, 90, 93, 94, 100, 102, 103, 106-108, 114, 129.*

FORCE, THE (See The Crusaders)

FORCE OF BUDDHA'S PALM THE
Jademan Comics: Aug, 1988 - No. 55, Feb, 1993 ($1.50/$1.95, 68 pgs.)

1-55-Kung Fu stories 2.00

FORCE WORKS
Marvel Comics: July, 1994 - No. 22, Apr, 1996 ($1.50)

1-($3.95)-Fold-out pop-up-c; Iron Man, Wonder Man, Spider-Woman,U.S. Agent & Scarlet Witch (new costume) 4.00
2-11, 13-22: 5-Blue logo version & pink logo version. 9-Intro Dreamguard. 13-Avengers app. 2.00
5-Pink logo ($2.95)-polybagged w/ 16pg. Marvel Action Hour Preview & acetate print 3.00
12 ($2.50)-Flip book w/War Machine. 2.50

FORD ROTUNDA CHRISTMAS BOOK (See Christmas at the Rotunda)

FOREIGN INTRIGUES (Formerly Johnny Dynamite; becomes Battlefield Action #16 on)
Charlton Comics: No. 14, 1956 - No. 15, Aug, 1956

GD2.0 FN6.0 NM9.4

14,15-Johnny Dynamite continues 5.70 17.00 40.00

FOREMOST BOYS (See 4Most)

FOR ETERNITY
Antarctic Press: July, 1997 - No. 4, Jan, 1998 ($2.95, B&W)

1-4 3.00

FOREVER AMBER
Image Comics: July, 1999 - Oct, 1999 ($2.95, B&W)

1-4-Don Hudson-s/a 3.00

FOREVER DARLING (Movie)
Dell Publishing Co.: No. 681, Feb, 1956

Four Color 681-w/Lucille Ball & Desi Arnaz; photo-c 10.50 31.00 125.00

FOREVER PEOPLE, THE
National Periodical Publications: Feb-Mar, 1971 - No. 11, Oct-Nov, 1972 (Fourth World) (#1-3, 10-11 are 36 pgs; #4-9 are 52 pgs.)

1-1st app. Forever People; Superman x-over; Kirby-c/a begins; 1st full app. Darkseid (3rd anywhere, 3 weeks before New Gods #1); Darkseid storyline begins, ends #8(app. in 1-4,6,8; cameos in 5,11) 4.55 13.65 50.00
2-9: 4-G.A. reprints thru #9. 9,10-Deadman app. 2.80 8.40 28.00
10,11: 2.00 6.00 18.00
Jack Kirby's Forever People TPB ('99, $14.95, B&W&Grey) r/#1-11 plus cover gallery of original series 15.00

NOTE: ***Kirby*** *c/a(p)-1-11; #4-9 contain Sandman reprints from Adventure #85, 84, 75, 80, 77, 74 in that order.*

FOREVER PEOPLE
DC Comics: Feb, 1988 - No. 6, July, 1988 ($1.25, limited series)

1-6 2.00

FOR GIRLS ONLY
Bernard Baily Enterprises: 11/53 - No. 2, 6/54 (100 pgs., digest size, 25¢)

1-25% comic book, 75% articles, illos, games 12.50 37.50 100.00
2-Eddie Fisher photo & story. 10.00 30.00 70.00

FORGOTTEN FOREST OF OZ, THE (See First Comics Graphic Novel #16)

FORGOTTEN REALMS (Also see Avatar & TSR Worlds)
DC Comics: Sept, 1989 - No. 25, Sept, 1991 ($1.50/$1.75)

1, Annual 1 (1990, $2.95, 68 pgs.) 3.00
2-25: Based on TSR role-playing game. 18-Avatar story 2.00

FORLORN RIVER (See Zane Grey Four Color 395)

FOR LOVERS ONLY (Formerly Hollywood Romances)
Charlton Comics: No. 60, Aug, 1971 - No. 87, Nov, 1976

60 3.00 9.00 32.00
61-72,74-87 1.75 5.25 14.00
73-Spanking scene-c/story 2.00 6.00 18.00

FORTUNE AND GLORY
Oni Press: Dec, 1999 - No. 3, Apr, 2000 ($4.95, B&W, limited series)

1-3-Brian Michael Bendis in Hollywood 4.95
TPB ($14.95) 14.95

40 BIG PAGES OF MICKEY MOUSE
Whitman Publ. Co.: No. 945, Jan, 1936 (10-1/4x12-1/2", 44 pgs., cardboard-c)

945-Reprints Mickey Mouse Magazine #1, but with a different cover; ads were eliminated and some illustrated stories had expanded text. The book is 3/4" shorter than Mickey Mouse Mag. #1, but the reprints are the same size (Rare) 150.00 450.00 1425.00

FOR YOUR EYES ONLY (See James Bond...)

FOUR COLOR
Dell Publishing Co.: Sept?, 1939 - No. 1354, Apr-June, 1962 (Series I are all 68 pgs.)

NOTE: *Four Color only appears on issues #19-25, 1-99,101. Dell Publishing Co. filed these as Series I, #1-25, and Series II, #1-1354. Issues beginning with #710? were printed with and without ads on back cover. Issues without ads are worth more.*

SERIES I:	GD2.0	FN6.0	VF8.0	NM9.4
1(nn)-Dick Tracy	600.00	1800.00	3600.00	7200.00

Four Color (Series 1) #8 © NY News Syndicate

Four Color #30 © WDC

Four Color #68 © Oskar Lebeck

	GD2.0	FN6.0	VF8.0	NM9.4
2(nn)-Don Winslow of the Navy (#1) (Rare) (11/39?)	133.00	400.00		1600.00
3(nn)-Myra North (1/40?)	75.00	225.00		900.00
4-Donald Duck by Al Taliaferro (1940)(Disney)(3/40?)	857.00	2571.00		12,000.00
(Prices vary widely on this book)				
5-Smilin' Jack (#1) (5/40?)	58.00	175.00		700.00
6-Dick Tracy (Scarce)	146.00	438.00		1750.00
7-Gang Busters	35.00	105.00		420.00
8-Dick Tracy	73.00	219.00		875.00
9-Terry and the Pirates-r/Super #9-29	58.00	175.00		700.00
10-Smilin' Jack	50.00	150.00		600.00
11-Smitty (#1)	35.00	105.00		425.00
12-Little Orphan Annie; reprints strips from 12/19/37 to 6/4/38	48.00	144.00		575.00
13-Walt Disney's Reluctant Dragon('41)-Contains 2 pgs. of photos from film; 2 pg. foreword to Fantasia by Leopold Stokowski; Donald Duck, Goofy, Baby Weems & Mickey Mouse (as the Sorcerer's Apprentice) app. (Disney)	158.00	475.00		1900.00
14-Moon Mullins (#1)	35.00	105.00		420.00
15-Tillie the Toiler (#1)	34.00	102.00		410.00
16-Mickey Mouse (#1) (Disney) by Gottfredson	1000.00	3000.00	11,000.00	
17-Walt Disney's Dumbo, the Flying Elephant (#1)(1941)-Mickey Mouse, Donald Duck, & Pluto app. (Disney)	183.00	550.00		2200.00
18-Jiggs and Maggie (#1)(1936-38-r)	38.00	115.00		460.00
19-Barney Google and Snuffy Smith (#1)-(1st issue with Four Color on the cover)	38.00	115.00		460.00
20-Tiny Tim	28.00	85.00		340.00
21-Dick Tracy	60.00	180.00		725.00
22-Don Winslow	30.00	90.00		360.00
23-Gang Busters	27.00	80.00		320.00
24-Captain Easy	42.00	125.00		500.00
25-Popeye (1942)	69.00	206.00		825.00

SERIES II:

	GD2.0	FN6.0	VF8.0	NM9.4
1-Little Joe (1942)	50.00	150.00		600.00
2-Harold Teen	27.00	80.00		320.00
3-Alley Oop (#1)	48.00	144.00		575.00
4-Smilin' Jack	43.00	128.00		510.00
5-Raggedy Ann and Andy (#1)	50.00	150.00		600.00
6-Smitty	22.00	65.00		260.00
7-Smokey Stover (#1)	32.00	95.00		380.00
8-Tillie the Toiler	23.00	68.00		270.00
9-Donald Duck Finds Pirate Gold, by Carl Barks & Jack Hannah (Disney) (© 8/17/42)	643.00	1929.00	4500.00	9000.00
10-Flash Gordon by Alex Raymond; reprinted from "The Ice Kingdom"	88.00	263.00		1050.00
11-Wash Tubbs	29.00	88.00		350.00
12-Walt Disney's Bambi (#1)	58.00	175.00		700.00
13-Mr. District Attorney (#1)-See The Funnies #35 for 1st app.	29.00	87.00		350.00
14-Smilin' Jack	34.00	102.00		410.00
15-Felix the Cat (#1)	71.00	213.00		850.00
16-Porky Pig (#1)(1942)- "Secret of the Haunted House"	83.00	250.00		1000.00
17-Popeye	50.00	150.00		600.00
18-Little Orphan Annie's Junior Commandos; Flag-c; reprints strips from 6/14/42 to 11/21/42	38.00	113.00		450.00
19-Walt Disney's Thumper Meets the Seven Dwarfs (Disney); reprinted in Silly Symphonies	54.00	163.00		650.00
20-Barney Baxter	27.00	80.00		320.00
21-Oswald the Rabbit (#1)(1943)	50.00	150.00		600.00
22-Tillie the Toiler	17.50	52.50		210.00
23-Raggedy Ann and Andy	37.00	110.00		440.00
24-Gang Busters	27.00	80.00		320.00
25-Andy Panda (#1) (Walter Lantz)	50.00	150.00		600.00
26-Popeye	50.00	150.00		600.00
27-Walt Disney's Mickey Mouse and the Seven Colored Terror	83.00	250.00		1000.00
28-Wash Tubbs	21.00	63.00		250.00
29-Donald Duck and the Mummy's Ring, by Carl Barks (Disney) (9/43)	500.00	1500.00	3500.00	7000.00
30-Bambi's Children (1943)-Disney	54.00	163.00		650.00
31-Moon Mullins	18.35	55.00		220.00
32-Smitty	16.00	48.00		190.00
33-Bugs Bunny "Public Nuisance #1"	112.00	337.00		1350.00
34-Dick Tracy	42.00	125.00		500.00
35-Smokey Stover	17.00	50.00		200.00
36-Smilin' Jack	23.00	70.00		280.00
37-Bringing Up Father	19.00	57.00		230.00
38-Roy Rogers (#1, © 4/44)-1st western comic with photo-c (see Movie Comics #3)	217.00	650.00		2600.00
39-Oswald the Rabbit (1944)	35.00	105.00		420.00
40-Barney Google and Snuffy Smith	22.00	66.00		265.00
41-Mother Goose and Nursery Rhyme Comics (#1)-All by Walt Kelly	22.00	65.00		260.00
42-Tiny Tim (1934-r)	17.00	50.00		200.00
43-Popeye (1938-'42-r)	31.00	93.00		375.00
44-Terry and the Pirates (1938-r)	40.00	119.00		475.00
45-Raggedy Ann	30.00	90.00		360.00
46-Felix the Cat and the Haunted Castle	40.00	120.00		480.00
47-Gene Autry (copyright 6/16/44)	42.00	125.00		500.00
48-Porky Pig of the Mounties by Carl Barks (7/44)	96.00	288.00		1150.00
49-Snow White and the Seven Dwarfs (Disney)	60.00	181.00		725.00
50-Fairy Tale Parade-Walt Kelly art (1944)	25.00	75.00		300.00
51-Bugs Bunny Finds the Lost Treasure	35.00	106.00		425.00
52-Little Orphan Annie; reprints strips from 6/18/38 to 11/19/38	29.00	87.00		350.00
53-Wash Tubbs	15.00	46.00		185.00
54-Andy Panda	30.00	90.00		360.00
55-Tillie the Toiler	13.00	40.00		160.00
56-Dick Tracy	33.00	100.00		400.00
57-Gene Autry	40.00	119.00		475.00
58-Smilin' Jack	23.00	70.00		280.00
59-Mother Goose and Nursery Rhyme Comics-Kelly-c/a	19.00	57.00		225.00
60-Tiny Folks Funnies	15.00	45.00		180.00
61-Santa Claus Funnies(11/44)-Kelly art	23.00	70.00		280.00
62-Donald Duck in Frozen Gold, by Carl Barks (Disney) (1/45)	157.00	471.00		2200.00
63-Roy Rogers; color photo-all 4 covers	48.00	144.00		575.00
64-Smokey Stover	12.50	37.50		150.00
65-Smitty	12.50	37.50		150.00
66-Gene Autry	40.00	119.00		475.00
67-Oswald the Rabbit	17.50	52.50		210.00
68-Mother Goose and Nursery Rhyme Comics, by Walt Kelly	19.00	57.00		225.00
69-Fairy Tale Parade, by Walt Kelly	25.00	75.00		300.00
70-Popeye and Wimpy	25.00	75.00		300.00
71-Walt Disney's Three Caballeros, by Walt Kelly (© 4/45)-(Disney)	79.00	238.00		950.00
72-Raggedy Ann	25.00	75.00		300.00
73-The Gumps (#1)	11.70	35.00		140.00
74-Marge's Little Lulu (#1)	104.00	313.00		1250.00
75-Gene Autry and the Wildcat	30.00	90.00		360.00
76-Little Orphan Annie; reprints strips from 2/28/40 to 6/24/40	24.00	72.00		290.00
77-Felix the Cat	38.00	113.00		450.00
78-Porky Pig and the Bandit Twins	23.00	68.00		280.00
79-Walt Disney's Mickey Mouse in The Riddle of the Red Hat by Carl Barks (8/45)	104.00	313.00		1250.00
80-Smilin' Jack	15.00	45.00		180.00

Four Color #111 © NEA Services

Four Color #187 © WB

Four Color #191 © WB

	GD2.0	FN6.0	NM9.4
81-Moon Mullins	10.00	30.00	120.00
82-Lone Ranger	42.00	125.00	500.00
83-Gene Autry in Outlaw Trail	30.00	90.00	360.00
84-Flash Gordon by Alex Raymond-Reprints from "The Fiery Desert"	42.00	125.00	500.00
85-Andy Panda and the Mad Dog Mystery	16.00	48.00	190.00
86-Roy Rogers; photo-c	35.00	106.00	425.00
87-Fairy Tale Parade by Walt Kelly; Dan Noonan-c	25.00	75.00	300.00
88-Bugs Bunny's Great Adventure (Sci/fi)	20.00	61.00	245.00
89-Tillie the Toiler	13.00	40.00	150.00
90-Christmas with Mother Goose by Walt Kelly (11/45)	17.50	52.50	210.00
91-Santa Claus Funnies by Walt Kelly (11/45)	17.50	52.50	210.00
92-Walt Disney's The Wonderful Adventures Of Pinocchio (1945); Donald Duck by Kelly, 16 pgs. (Disney)	58.00	175.00	700.00
93-Gene Autry in The Bandit of Black Rock	27.00	80.00	320.00
94-Winnie Winkle (1945)	11.70	35.00	140.00
95-Roy Rogers Comics; photo-c	35.00	106.00	425.00
96-Dick Tracy	24.00	72.00	290.00
97-Marge's Little Lulu (1946)	48.00	144.00	575.00
98-Lone Ranger, The	31.00	94.00	375.00
99-Smitty	10.50	31.00	125.00
100-Gene Autry Comics; photo-c	27.00	80.00	320.00
101-Terry and the Pirates	26.00	78.00	310.00

NOTE: *No. 101 is last issue to carry "Four Color" logo on cover; all issues beginning with No. 100 are marked "...O. S." (One Shot) which can be found in the bottom left-hand panel on the first page; the numbers following "O. S." relate to the year/month issued.*

	GD2.0	FN6.0	NM9.4
102-Oswald the Rabbit-Walt Kelly art, 1 pg.	15.00	45.00	180.00
103-Easter with Mother Goose by Walt Kelly	18.35	55.00	220.00
104-Fairy Tale Parade by Walt Kelly	18.00	55.00	220.00
105-Albert the Alligator and Pogo Possum (#1) by Kelly (4/46)	71.00	213.00	850.00
106-Tillie the Toiler (5/46)	9.50	29.00	115.00
107-Little Orphan Annie; reprints strips from 11/16/42 to 3/24/43	21.00	63.00	250.00
108-Donald Duck in The Terror of the River, by Carl Barks (Disney) (© 4/16/46)	114.00	342.00	1600.00
109-Roy Rogers Comics; photo-c	27.00	80.00	320.00
110-Marge's Little Lulu	33.00	100.00	400.00
111-Captain Easy	14.00	42.00	170.00
112-Porky Pig's Adventure in Gopher Gulch	14.00	42.00	170.00
113-Popeye; all new Popeye stories begin	12.50	37.50	150.00
114-Fairy Tale Parade by Walt Kelly	18.00	55.00	220.00
115-Marge's Little Lulu	33.00	100.00	400.00
116-Mickey Mouse and the House of Many Mysteries (Disney)	23.00	69.00	275.00
117-Roy Rogers Comics; photo-c	21.00	63.00	250.00
118-Lone Ranger, The	31.00	94.00	375.00
119-Felix the Cat; all new Felix stories begin	31.00	91.00	370.00
120-Marge's Little Lulu	29.00	88.00	350.00
121-Fairy Tale Parade-(not Kelly)	11.00	33.00	130.00
122-Henry (#1) (10/46)	13.00	40.00	160.00
123-Bugs Bunny's Dangerous Venture	15.50	46.00	185.00
124-Roy Rogers Comics; photo-c	21.00	63.00	250.00
125-Lone Ranger, The	21.00	63.00	250.00
126-Christmas with Mother Goose by Walt Kelly (1946)	13.00	40.00	160.00
127-Popeye	12.50	37.50	150.00
128-Santa Claus Funnies- "Santa & the Angel" by Gollub; "A Mouse in the House" by Kelly	14.00	41.00	165.00
129-Walt Disney's Uncle Remus and His Tales of Brer Rabbit (#1) (1946)-Adapted from Disney movie "Song of the South"	27.50	82.50	330.00
130-Andy Panda (Walter Lantz)	9.50	29.00	115.00
131-Marge's Little Lulu	29.00	88.00	350.00
132-Tillie the Toiler (1947)	9.50	29.00	115.00
133-Dick Tracy	20.00	60.00	240.00
134-Tarzan and the Devil Ogre; Marsh-c/a	63.00	188.00	750.00
135-Felix the Cat	23.00	68.00	275.00
136-Lone Ranger, The	21.00	63.00	250.00

	GD2.0	FN6.0	NM9.4
137-Roy Rogers Comics; photo-c	21.00	63.00	250.00
138-Smitty	9.00	27.00	110.00
139-Marge's Little Lulu (1947)	27.00	81.00	325.00
140-Easter with Mother Goose by Walt Kelly	15.00	45.00	175.00
141-Mickey Mouse and the Submarine Pirates (Disney)	20.00	60.00	240.00
142-Bugs Bunny and the Haunted Mountain	15.50	46.00	185.00
143-Oswald the Rabbit & the Prehistoric Egg	9.00	27.00	110.00
144-Roy Rogers Comics (1947)-Photo-c	21.00	63.00	250.00
145-Popeye	12.50	37.50	150.00
146-Marge's Little Lulu	27.00	81.00	325.00
147-Donald Duck in Volcano Valley, by Carl Barks (Disney) (5/47)	78.00	236.00	1100.00
148-Albert the Alligator and Pogo Possum by Walt Kelly (5/47)	58.00	175.00	700.00
149-Smilin' Jack	10.00	30.00	120.00
150-Tillie the Toiler (6/47)	8.75	26.25	105.00
151-Lone Ranger, The	17.50	52.50	210.00
152-Little Orphan Annie; reprints strips from 1/2/44 to 5/6/44	13.00	40.00	160.00
153-Roy Rogers Comics; photo-c	19.00	57.00	225.00
154-Walter Lantz Andy Panda	9.50	29.00	115.00
155-Henry (7/47)	8.00	24.00	95.00
156-Porky Pig and the Phantom	10.00	30.00	120.00
157-Mickey Mouse & the Beanstalk (Disney)	20.00	60.00	240.00
158-Marge's Little Lulu	27.00	81.00	325.00
159-Donald Duck in the Ghost of the Grotto, by Carl Barks (Disney) (8/47)	64.00	193.00	900.00
160-Roy Rogers Comics; photo-c	19.00	57.00	225.00
161-Tarzan and the Fires Of Tohr; Marsh-c/a	54.00	163.00	650.00
162-Felix the Cat (9/47)	18.00	53.00	210.00
163-Dick Tracy	17.00	50.00	200.00
164-Bugs Bunny Finds the Frozen Kingdom	15.50	46.00	185.00
165-Marge's Little Lulu	27.00	81.00	325.00
166-Roy Rogers Comics (52 pgs.)-Photo-c	19.00	57.00	225.00
167-Lone Ranger, The	17.50	52.50	210.00
168-Popeye (10/47)	12.50	37.50	150.00
169-Woody Woodpecker (#1)- "Manhunter in the North"; drug use story	15.00	45.00	180.00
170-Mickey Mouse on Spook's Island (11/47)(Disney)-reprinted in Mickey Mouse #103	17.00	50.00	200.00
171-Charlie McCarthy (#1) and the Twenty Thieves	25.00	75.00	300.00
172-Christmas with Mother Goose by Walt Kelly (11/47)	13.00	40.00	160.00
173-Flash Gordon	15.00	44.00	175.00
174-Winnie Winkle	7.00	21.00	85.00
175-Santa Claus Funnies by Walt Kelly (1947)	14.00	41.00	165.00
176-Tillie the Toiler (12/47)	8.75	26.25	105.00
177-Roy Rogers Comics-(36 pgs.); Photo-c	19.00	57.00	225.00
178-Donald Duck "Christmas on Bear Mountain" by Carl Barks; 1st app. Uncle Scrooge (Disney)(12/47)	93.00	279.00	1300.00
179-Uncle Wiggily (#1)-Walt Kelly-c	15.00	45.00	180.00
180-Ozark Ike (#1)	10.00	30.00	120.00
181-Walt Disney's Mickey Mouse in Jungle Magic	17.00	50.00	200.00
182-Porky Pig in Never-Never Land (2/48)	10.00	30.00	120.00
183-Oswald the Rabbit (Lantz)	9.00	27.00	110.00
184-Tillie the Toiler	8.75	26.25	105.00
185-Easter with Mother Goose by Walt Kelly (1948)	12.50	37.50	150.00
186-Walt Disney's Bambi (4/48)-Reprinted as Movie Classic Bambi #3 (1956)	16.00	48.00	195.00
187-Bugs Bunny and the Dreadful Dragon	10.50	31.00	125.00
188-Woody Woodpecker (Lantz, 5/48)	10.00	30.00	120.00
189-Donald Duck in The Old Castle's Secret, by Carl Barks (Disney) (6/48)	59.00	177.00	825.00
190-Flash Gordon (6/48); bondage-c; "The Adventures of the Flying Saucers"; 5th Flying Saucer story- see The Spirit 9/28/47(1st), Shadow Comics V7#10 (2nd, 1/48),Captain Midnight #60 (3rd, 2/48) & Boy Commandos #26 (4th, 3-4/48)	17.00	50.00	200.00
191-Porky Pig to the Rescue	10.00	30.00	120.00

Four Color #231 © WDC

Four Color #235 © WDC

Four Color #275 © WDC

	GD2.0	FN6.0	NM9.4
192-The Brownies (#1)-by Walt Kelly (7/48)	12.50	37.50	150.00
193-M.G.M. Presents Tom and Jerry (#1)(1948)	15.00	45.00	180.00
194-Mickey Mouse in The World Under the Sea (Disney)-Reprinted in Mickey Mouse #101	17.00	50.00	200.00
195-Tillie the Toiler	6.30	19.00	75.00
196-Charlie McCarthy in The Haunted Hide-Out; part photo-c	17.00	50.00	200.00
197-Spirit of the Border (#1) (Zane Grey) (1948)	11.00	33.00	130.00
198-Andy Panda	9.50	29.00	115.00
199-Donald Duck in Sheriff of Bullet Valley, by Carl Barks; Barks draws himself on wanted poster, last page; used in Love & Death (Disney) (10/48)	64.00	193.00	900.00
200-Bugs Bunny, Super Sleuth (10/48)	10.50	31.00	125.00
201-Christmas with Mother Goose by W. Kelly	11.70	35.00	140.00
202-Woody Woodpecker	6.30	19.00	75.00
203-Donald Duck in the Golden Christmas Tree, by Carl Barks (Disney) (12/48)	45.00	134.00	625.00
204-Flash Gordon (12/48)	11.70	35.00	140.00
205-Santa Claus Funnies by Walt Kelly	12.50	37.50	150.00
206-Little Orphan Annie; reprints strips from 11/10/40 to 1/11/41	7.00	21.00	85.00
207-King of the Royal Mounted (#1) (12/48)	14.00	42.00	170.00
208-Brer Rabbit Does It Again (Disney) (1/49)	11.30	34.00	135.00
209-Harold Teen	4.55	13.65	50.00
210-Tippie and Cap Stubbs	4.10	12.30	45.00
211-Little Beaver (#1)	7.50	22.50	90.00
212-Dr. Bobbs	4.10	12.30	45.00
213-Tillie the Toiler	6.30	19.00	75.00
214-Mickey Mouse and His Sky Adventure (2/49)(Disney)-Reprinted in Mickey Mouse #105	13.00	40.00	160.00
215-Sparkle Plenty (Dick Tracy-r by Gould)	10.00	30.00	120.00
216-Andy Panda and the Police Pup (Lantz)	6.25	18.50	75.00
217-Bugs Bunny in Court Jester	10.50	31.00	125.00
218-Three Little Pigs and the Wonderful Magic Lamp (Disney) (3/49)(#1)	11.30	34.00	135.00
219-Swee'pe	8.35	25.00	100.00
220-Easter with Mother Goose by Walt Kelly	12.50	37.50	150.00
221-Uncle Wiggily-Walt Kelly cover in part	9.00	27.00	110.00
222-West of the Pecos (Zane Grey)	5.85	17.50	70.00
223-Donald Duck "Lost in the Andes" by Carl Barks (Disney-4/49) (square egg story)	63.00	188.00	875.00
224-Little Iodine (#1), by Hatlo (4/49)	9.00	27.00	110.00
225-Oswald the Rabbit (Lantz)	5.00	15.00	60.00
226-Porky Pig and Spoofy, the Spook	7.50	22.50	90.00
227-Seven Dwarfs (Disney)	10.00	30.00	120.00
228-Mark of Zorro, The (#1) (1949)	21.00	63.00	250.00
229-Smokey Stover	4.60	13.75	55.00
230-Sunset Pass (Zane Grey)	5.85	17.50	70.00
231-Mickey Mouse and the Rajah's Treasure (Disney)	13.00	40.00	160.00
232-Woody Woodpecker (Lantz, 6/49)	6.30	19.00	75.00
233-Bugs Bunny, Sleepwalking Sleuth	10.50	31.00	125.00
234-Dumbo in Sky Voyage (Disney)	10.00	30.00	120.00
235-Tiny Tim	4.10	12.30	45.00
236-Heritage of the Desert (Zane Grey) (1949)	5.85	17.50	70.00
237-Tillie the Toiler	6.30	19.00	75.00
238-Donald Duck in Voodoo Hoodoo, by Carl Barks (Disney) (8/49)	45.00	134.00	625.00
239-Adventure Bound (8/49)	4.60	13.75	55.00
240-Andy Panda (Lantz)	6.25	18.50	75.00
241-Porky Pig, Mighty Hunter	7.50	22.50	90.00
242-Tippie and Cap Stubbs	3.20	9.60	35.00
243-Thumper Follows His Nose (Disney)	10.00	30.00	120.00
244-The Brownies by Walt Kelly	10.00	30.00	120.00
245-Dick's Adventures (9/49)	4.60	13.75	55.00
246-Thunder Mountain (Zane Grey)	4.10	12.30	45.00
247-Flash Gordon	11.70	35.00	140.00
248-Mickey Mouse and the Black Sorcerer (Disney)	13.00	40.00	160.00
249-Woody Woodpecker in the "Globetrotter" (10/49)	6.30	19.00	75.00
250-Bugs Bunny in Diamond Daze; used in **SOTI**, pg. 309	11.00	33.00	135.00
251-Hubert at Camp Moonbeam	4.10	12.30	45.00
252-Pinocchio (Disney)-not by Kelly; origin	10.00	30.00	120.00
253-Christmas with Mother Goose by W. Kelly	11.70	35.00	140.00
254-Santa Claus Funnies by Walt Kelly; Pogo & Albert story by Kelly (11/49)	12.50	37.50	150.00
255-The Ranger (Zane Grey) (1949)	4.10	12.30	45.00
256-Donald Duck in "Luck of the North" by Carl Barks (Disney) (12/49)-Shows #257 on inside	33.00	99.00	460.00
257-Little Iodine	6.70	20.00	80.00
258-Andy Panda and the Balloon Race (Lantz)	6.25	18.50	75.00
259-Santa and the Angel (Gollub art-condensed from #128) & Santa at the Zoo (12/49)-two books in one	4.10	12.30	45.00
260-Porky Pig, Hero of the Wild West (12/49)	7.50	22.50	90.00
261-Mickey Mouse and the Missing Key (Disney)	13.00	40.00	160.00
262-Raggedy Ann and Andy	6.70	20.00	80.00
263-Donald Duck in "Land of the Totem Poles" by Carl Barks (Disney) (2/50)-Has two Barks stories	31.00	92.00	440.00
264-Woody Woodpecker in the Magic Lantern (Lantz)	6.30	19.00	75.00
265-King of the Royal Mounted (Zane Grey)	7.50	22.50	90.00
266-Bugs Bunny on the "Isle of Hercules" (2/50)-Reprinted in Best of Bugs Bunny #1	8.35	25.00	100.00
267-Little Beaver; Harmon-c/a	4.10	12.30	45.00
268-Mickey Mouse's Surprise Visitor (1950) (Disney)	12.50	37.50	150.00
269-Johnny Mack Brown (#1)-Photo-c	23.00	69.00	275.00
270-Drift Fence (Zane Grey) (3/50)	4.10	12.30	45.00
271-Porky Pig in Phantom of the Plains	7.50	22.50	90.00
272-Cinderella (Disney) (4/50)	10.00	30.00	120.00
273-Oswald the Rabbit (Lantz)	5.00	15.00	60.00
274-Bugs Bunny, Hare-brained Reporter	8.35	25.00	100.00
275-Donald Duck in "Ancient Persia" by Carl Barks (Disney) (5/50)	29.00	87.00	410.00
276-Uncle Wiggily	7.50	22.50	90.00
277-Porky Pig in Desert Adventure (5/50)	7.50	22.50	90.00
278-Bill Elliott Comics (#1)-Photo-c	12.50	37.50	150.00
279-Mickey Mouse and Pluto Battle the Giant Ants (Disney); reprinted in Mickey Mouse #102 & 245	9.00	27.00	110.00
280-Andy Panda in The Isle Of Mechanical Men (Lantz)	6.25	18.50	75.00
281-Bugs Bunny in The Great Circus Mystery	8.35	25.00	100.00
282-Donald Duck and the Pixilated Parrot by Carl Barks (Disney) (© 5/23/50)	29.00	87.00	410.00
283-King of the Royal Mounted (7/50)	7.50	22.50	90.00
284-Porky Pig in The Kingdom of Nowhere	7.50	22.50	90.00
285-Bozo the Clown & His Minikin Circus (#1) (TV)	19.00	57.00	225.00
286-Mickey Mouse in The Uninvited Guest (Disney	9.00	27.00	110.00
287-Gene Autry's Champion in The Ghost Of Black Mountain; photo-c	10.00	30.00	120.00
288-Woody Woodpecker in Klondike Gold (Lantz)	6.30	19.00	75.00
289-Bugs Bunny in "Indian Trouble"	8.35	25.00	100.00
290-The Chief (#1) (8/50)	5.45	16.00	65.00
291-Donald Duck in "The Magic Hourglass" by Carl Barks (Disney) (9/50)	29.00	87.00	410.00
292-The Cisco Kid Comics (#1)	22.00	66.00	265.00
293-The Brownies-Kelly-c/a	10.00	30.00	120.00
294-Little Beaver	4.10	12.30	45.00
295-Porky Pig in President Porky (9/50)	7.50	22.50	90.00
296-Mickey Mouse in Private Eye for Hire (Disney)	9.00	27.00	110.00
297-Andy Panda in The Haunted Inn (Lantz, 10/50)	6.25	18.50	75.00
298-Bugs Bunny in Sheik for a Day	8.35	25.00	100.00
299-Buck Jones & the Iron Horse Trail (#1)	11.70	35.00	140.00
300-Donald Duck in "Big-Top Bedlam" by Carl Barks (Disney) (11/50)	29.00	87.00	410.00
301-The Mysterious Rider (Zane Grey)	4.10	12.30	45.00
302-Santa Claus Funnies (11/50)	4.55	13.65	50.00

Four Color #302 © WEST

Four Color #336 © Walter Lantz

Four Color #362 © WDC

	GD2.0	FN6.0	NM9.4
303-Porky Pig in The Land of the Monstrous Flies	5.00	15.00	60.00
304-Mickey Mouse in Tom-Tom Island (Disney) (12/50)	7.50	25.00	90.00
305-Woody Woodpecker (Lantz)	4.10	12.30	45.00
306-Raggedy Ann	4.60	13.75	55.00
307-Bugs Bunny in Lumber Jack Rabbit	7.00	21.00	85.00
308-Donald Duck in "Dangerous Disguise" by Carl Barks (Disney) (1/51)	25.00	75.00	350.00
309-Betty Betz' Dollface and Her Gang (1951)	4.60	13.75	55.00
310-King of the Royal Mounted (1/51)	5.85	17.50	70.00
311-Porky Pig in Midget Horses of Hidden Valley	5.00	15.00	60.00
312-Tonto (#1)	9.00	27.00	110.00
313-Mickey Mouse in The Mystery of the Double-Cross Ranch (#1) (Disney) (2/51)	7.50	22.50	90.00

Note: Beginning with the above comic in 1951 Dell/Western began adding #1 in small print on the covers of several long running titles with the evident intention of switching these titles to their own monthly numbers, but when the conversions were made, there was no connection. It is thought that the post office may have stepped in and decreed the sequences should commence as though the first four colors printed had each begun with number one, or the first issues sold by subscription. Since the regular series' numbers don't correctly match to the numbers of earlier issues published, it's not known whether or not the numbering was in error.

	GD2.0	FN6.0	NM9.4
314-Ambush (Zane Grey)	4.10	12.30	45.00
315-Oswald the Rabbit (Lantz)	4.60	13.75	55.00
316-Rex Allen (#1)-Photo-c; Marsh-a	13.00	40.00	160.00
317-Bugs Bunny in Hair Today Gone Tomorrow (#1)	7.00	21.00	85.00
318-Donald Duck in "No Such Varmint" by Carl Barks (#1)-Indicia shows #317 (Disney, © 1/23/51)	25.00	75.00	350.00
319-Gene Autry's Champion; painted-c	4.55	13.65	50.00
320-Uncle Wiggily (#1)	7.50	22.50	90.00
321-Little Scouts (#1) (3/51)	3.20	9.60	35.00
322-Porky Pig in Roaring Rockets (#1 on-c)	5.00	15.00	60.00
323-Susie Q. Smith (#1) (3/51)	3.65	11.00	40.00
324-I Met a Handsome Cowboy (3/51)	8.35	25.00	100.00
325-Mickey Mouse in The Haunted Castle (#2) (Disney) (4/51)	7.50	22.50	90.00
326-Andy Panda (#1) (Lantz)	4.10	12.30	45.00
327-Bugs Bunny and the Rajah's Treasure (#2)	7.00	21.00	85.00
328-Donald Duck in Old California (#2) by Carl Barks-Peyote drug use issue (Disney) (5/51)	27.00	81.00	380.00
329-Roy Roger's Trigger (#1)(5/51)-Painted-c	12.50	37.50	150.00
330-Porky Pig Meets the Bristled Bruiser (#2)	5.00	15.00	60.00
331-Alice in Wonderland (Disney) (1951)	14.00	42.00	170.00
332-Little Beaver	4.10	12.30	45.00
333-Wilderness Trek (Zane Grey) (5/51)	4.10	12.30	45.00
334-Mickey Mouse and Yukon Gold (Disney) (6/51)	7.50	22.50	90.00
335-Francis the Famous Talking Mule (#1, 6/51)-1st Dell non animated movie comic (all issues based on movie)	7.50	22.50	90.00
336-Woody Woodpecker (Lantz)	4.10	12.30	45.00
337-The Brownies-not by Walt Kelly	3.65	11.00	40.00
338-Bugs Bunny and the Rocking Horse Thieves	7.00	21.00	85.00
339-Donald Duck and the Magic Fountain-not by Carl Barks (Disney) (7-8/51)	6.30	19.00	75.00
340-King of the Royal Mounted (7/51)	5.85	17.50	70.00
341-Unbirthday Party with Alice in Wonderland (Disney) (7/51)	14.00	42.00	170.00
342-Porky Pig the Lucky Peppermint Mine; r/in Porky Pig #3	4.10	12.30	45.00
343-Mickey Mouse in The Ruby Eye of Homar-Guy-Am (Disney)-Reprinted in Mickey Mouse #104	5.85	17.50	70.00
344-Sergeant Preston from Challenge of The Yukon (#1) (TV)	11.30	34.00	135.00
345-Andy Panda in Scotland Yard (8-10/51) (Lantz)	4.10	12.30	45.00
346-Hideout (Zane Grey)	4.10	12.30	45.00
347-Bugs Bunny the Frigid Hare (8-9/51)	7.00	21.00	85.00
348-Donald Duck "The Crocodile Collector"; Barks-c only (Disney) (9-10/51)	15.00	45.00	180.00
349-Uncle Wiggily	5.85	17.50	70.00

	GD2.0	FN6.0	NM9.4
350-Woody Woodpecker (Lantz)	4.10	12.30	45.00
351-Porky Pig & the Grand Canyon Giant (9-10/51)	4.10	12.30	45.00
352-Mickey Mouse in The Mystery of Painted Valley (Disney)	5.85	17.50	70.00
353-Duck Album (#1)-Barks-c (Disney)	8.35	25.00	100.00
354-Raggedy Ann & Andy	4.60	13.75	55.00
355-Bugs Bunny Hot-Rod Hare	7.00	21.00	85.00
356-Donald Duck in "Rags to Riches"; Barks-c only	15.00	45.00	180.00
357-Comeback (Zane Grey)	3.20	9.60	35.00
358-Andy Panda (Lantz) (11-1/52)	4.10	12.30	45.00
359-Frosty the Snowman (#1)	8.00	24.00	95.00
360-Porky Pig in Tree of Fortune (11-12/51)	4.10	12.30	45.00
361-Santa Claus Funnies	4.55	13.65	50.00
362-Mickey Mouse and the Smuggled Diamonds (Disney)	5.85	17.50	70.00
363-King of the Royal Mounted	5.00	15.00	60.00
364-Woody Woodpecker (Lantz)	3.65	11.00	40.00
365-The Brownies-not by Kelly	3.65	11.00	40.00
366-Bugs Bunny Uncle Buckskin Comes to Town (12-1/52)	7.00	21.00	85.00
367-Donald Duck in "A Christmas for Shacktown" by Carl Barks (Disney) (1-2/52)	25.00	75.00	350.00
368-Bob Clampett's Beany and Cecil (#1)	25.00	75.00	300.00
369-The Lone Ranger's Famous Horse Hi-Yo Silver (#1); Silver's origin	8.35	25.00	100.00
370-Porky Pig in Trouble in the Big Trees	4.10	12.30	45.00
371-Mickey Mouse in The Inca Idol Case (1952) (Disney)	5.85	17.50	70.00
372-Riders of the Purple Sage (Zane Grey)	3.20	9.60	35.00
373-Sergeant Preston (TV)	6.70	20.00	80.00
374-Woody Woodpecker (Lantz)	3.65	11.00	40.00
375-John Carter of Mars (E. R. Burroughs)-Jesse Marsh-a; origin	24.00	73.00	290.00
376-Bugs Bunny, "The Magic Sneeze"	7.00	21.00	85.00
377-Susie Q. Smith	3.20	9.60	35.00
378-Tom Corbett, Space Cadet (#1) (TV)-McWilliams-a	17.00	50.00	200.00
379-Donald Duck in "Southern Hospitality"; Not by Barks (Disney)	6.30	19.00	75.00
380-Raggedy Ann & Andy	4.60	13.75	55.00
381-Marge's Tubby (#1)	20.00	60.00	240.00
382-Snow White and the Seven Dwarfs (Disney)-origin; partial reprint of 4-Color #49 (Movie)	10.00	30.00	120.00
383-Andy Panda (Lantz)	3.20	9.60	35.00
384-King of the Royal Mounted (3/52)(Zane Grey)	5.00	15.00	60.00
385-Porky Pig in The Isle of Missing Ships (3-4/52)	4.10	12.30	45.00
386-Uncle Scrooge (#1)-by Carl Barks (Disney) in "Only a Poor Old Man" (3/52)	92.00	275.00	1100.00
387-Mickey Mouse in High Tibet (Disney) (4-5/52)	5.85	17.50	70.00
388-Oswald the Rabbit (Lantz)	4.60	13.75	55.00
389-Andy Hardy Comics (#1)	3.20	9.60	35.00
390-Woody Woodpecker (Lantz)	3.65	11.00	40.00
391-Uncle Wiggily	5.85	17.50	70.00
392-Hi-Yo Silver	4.55	13.65	50.00
393-Bugs Bunny	7.00	21.00	85.00
394-Donald Duck in Malayalaya-Barks-c only (Disney)	15.00	45.00	180.00
395-Forlorn River(Zane Grey)-First Nevada (5/52)	3.20	9.60	35.00
396-Tales of the Texas Rangers(#1)(TV)-Photo-c	10.50	31.00	125.00
397-Sergeant Preston of the Yukon (TV) (5/52)	6.70	20.00	80.00
398-The Brownies-not by Kelly	3.65	11.00	40.00
399-Porky Pig in The Lost Gold Mine	4.10	12.30	45.00
400-Tom Corbett, Space Cadet (TV)-McWilliams-c/a	9.00	27.00	110.00
401-Mickey Mouse and Goofy's Mechanical Wizard (Disney) (6-7/52)	4.10	12.30	45.00
402-Mary Jane and Sniffles	7.50	22.50	90.00
403-Li'l Bad Wolf (Disney) (6/52)(#1)	6.70	20.00	80.00
404-The Range Rider (#1) (TV)-Photo-c	10.00	30.00	120.00

Four Color #468 © WDC

Four Color #470 © WB

Four Color #505 © WDC

	GD2.0	FN6.0	NM9.4
405-Woody Woodpecker (Lantz) (6-7/52)	3.65	11.00	40.00
406-Tweety and Sylvester (#1)	8.00	24.00	95.00
407-Bugs Bunny, Foreign-Legion Hare	5.85	17.50	70.00
408-Donald Duck and the Golden Helmet by Carl Barks (Disney) (7-8/52)	25.00	75.00	350.00
409-Andy Panda (7-9/52)	3.20	9.60	35.00
410-Porky Pig in The Water Wizard (7/52)	4.00	12.30	45.00
411-Mickey Mouse and the Old Sea Dog (Disney) (8-9/52)	4.10	12.30	45.00
412-Nevada (Zane Grey)	3.20	9.60	35.00
413-Robin Hood (Disney-Movie) (8/52)-Photo-c (1st Disney movie four color book)	10.00	30.00	120.00
414-Bob Clampett's Beany and Cecil (TV)	16.00	48.00	190.00
415-Rootie Kazootie (#1) (TV)	10.00	30.00	120.00
416-Woody Woodpecker (Lantz)	3.65	11.00	40.00
417-Double Trouble with Goober (#1) (8/52)	3.00	9.00	30.00
418-Rusty Riley, a Boy, a Horse, and a Dog (#1)-Frank Godwin-a (strip reprints) (8/52)	4.10	12.30	45.00
419-Sergeant Preston (TV)	6.70	20.00	80.00
420-Bugs Bunny in The Mysterious Buckaroo (8-9/52)	5.85	17.50	70.00
421-Tom Corbett, Space Cadet(TV)-McWilliams-a	9.00	27.00	110.00
422-Donald Duck and the Gilded Man, by Carl Barks (Disney) (9-10/52) (#423 on inside)	25.00	75.00	350.00
423-Rhubarb, Owner of the Brooklyn Ball Club (The Millionaire Cat) (#1)-Painted cover	4.60	13.75	55.00
424-Flash Gordon-Test Flight in Space (9/52)	9.00	27.00	110.00
425-Zorro, the Return of	11.70	35.00	140.00
426-Porky Pig in The Scalawag Leprechaun	4.10	12.30	45.00
427-Mickey Mouse and the Wonderful Whizzix (Disney) (10-11/52)-Reprinted in Mickey Mouse #100	4.10	12.30	45.00
428-Uncle Wiggily	4.55	13.65	50.00
429-Pluto in "Why Dogs Leave Home" (Disney) (10/52)(#1)	8.35	25.00	100.00
430-Marge's Tubby, the Shadow of a Man-Eater	11.30	34.00	135.00
431-Woody Woodpecker (10/52) (Lantz)	3.65	11.00	40.00
432-Bugs Bunny and the Rabbit Olympics	5.85	17.50	70.00
433-Wildfire (Zane Grey) (11-1/52-53)	3.20	9.60	35.00
434-Rin Tin Tin "In Dark Danger" (#1) (TV) (11/52)-Photo-c	15.00	45.00	175.00
435-Frosty the Snowman (11/52)	4.10	12.30	45.00
436-The Brownies-not by Kelly (11/52)	3.20	9.60	35.00
437-John Carter of Mars (E. R. Burroughs)-Marsh-a	15.00	45.00	180.00
438-Annie Oakley (#1) (TV)	14.00	42.00	170.00
439-Little Hiawatha (Disney) (12/52)j(#1)	5.00	15.00	60.00
440-Black Beauty (12/52)	3.20	9.60	35.00
441-Fearless Fagan	3.45	10.35	38.00
442-Peter Pan (Disney) (Movie)	9.00	27.00	110.00
443-Ben Bowie and His Mountain Men (#1)	5.85	17.50	70.00
444-Marge's Tubby	11.30	34.00	135.00
445-Charlie McCarthy	4.60	13.75	55.00
446-Captain Hook and Peter Pan (Disney)(Movie)(1/53)	8.35	25.00	100.00
447-Andy Hardy Comics	2.80	8.40	28.00
448-Bob Clampett's Beany and Cecil (TV)	16.00	48.00	190.00
449-Tappan's Burro (Zane Grey) (2-4/53)	3.20	9.60	35.00
450-Duck Album; Barks-c (Disney)	5.85	17.50	70.00
451-Rusty Riley-Frank Godwin-a (strip-r) (2/53)	3.20	9.60	35.00
452-Raggedy Ann & Andy (1953)	4.60	13.75	55.00
453-Susie Q. Smith (2/53)	3.20	9.60	35.00
454-Krazy Kat Comics; not by Herriman	3.65	11.00	40.00
455-Johnny Mack Brown Comics(3/53)-Photo-c	5.85	17.50	70.00
456-Uncle Scrooge Back to the Klondike (#2) by Barks (3/53) (Disney)	58.00	175.00	700.00
457-Daffy (#1)	8.35	25.00	100.00
458-Oswald the Rabbit (Lantz)	3.20	9.60	35.00
459-Rootie Kazootie (TV)	6.70	20.00	80.00
460-Buck Jones (4/53)	4.60	13.75	55.00
461-Marge's Tubby	10.00	30.00	120.00

	GD2.0	FN6.0	NM9.4
462-Little Scouts	2.30	7.00	20.00
463-Petunia (4/53)	3.65	11.00	40.00
464-Bozo (4/53)	8.35	25.00	100.00
465-Francis the Famous Talking Mule	4.60	13.75	55.00
466-Rhubarb, the Millionaire Cat; painted-c	4.10	12.30	45.00
467-Desert Gold (Zane Grey) (5-7/53)	3.20	9.60	35.00
468-Goofy (#1) (Disney)	11.70	35.00	140.00
469-Beetle Bailey (#1) (5/53	9.00	27.00	110.00
470-Elmer Fudd	4.60	13.75	55.00
471-Double Trouble with Goober	2.00	6.00	18.00
472-Wild Bill Elliott (6/53)-Photo-c	4.10	12.30	45.00
473-Li'l Bad Wolf (Disney) (6/53)(#2)	4.10	12.30	45.00
474-Mary Jane and Sniffles	6.70	20.00	80.00
475-M.G.M.'s The Two Mouseketeers (#1)	6.70	20.00	80.00
476-Rin Tin Tin (TV)-Photo-c	7.50	22.50	90.00
477-Bob Clampett's Beany and Cecil (TV)	16.00	48.00	190.00
478-Charlie McCarthy	4.60	13.75	55.00
479-Queen of the West Dale Evans (#1)-Photo-c	22.00	65.00	260.00
480-Andy Hardy Comics	2.80	8.40	28.00
481-Annie Oakley And Tagg (TV)	8.00	24.00	95.00
482-Brownies-not by Kelly	3.20	9.60	35.00
483-Little Beaver (7/53)	3.20	9.60	35.00
484-River Feud (Zane Grey) (8-10/53)	3.20	9.60	35.00
485-The Little People-Walt Scott (#1)	5.85	17.50	70.00
486-Rusty Riley-Frank Godwin strip-r	3.20	9.60	35.00
487-Mowgli, the Jungle Book (Rudyard Kipling's)	5.00	15.00	60.00
488-John Carter of Mars (Burroughs)-Marsh-a; painted-c	15.00	45.00	180.00
489-Tweety and Sylvester	4.10	12.30	45.00
490-Jungle Jim (#1)	5.85	17.50	70.00
491-Silvertip (#1) (Max Brand)-Kinstler-a (8/53)	7.50	22.50	90.00
492-Duck Album (Disney)	4.60	13.75	55.00
493-Johnny Mack Brown; photo-c	5.85	17.50	70.00
494-The Little King (#1)	9.00	27.00	110.00
495-Uncle Scrooge (#3) (Disney)-by Carl Barks (9/53)	44.00	131.00	525.00
496-The Green Hornet; painted-c	23.00	70.00	280.00
497-Zorro (Sword of...)-Kinstler-a	12.50	37.50	150.00
498-Bugs Bunny's Album (9/53)	4.60	13.75	55.00
499-M.G.M.'s Spike and Tyke (#1) (9/53)	3.65	11.00	40.00
500-Buck Jones	4.60	13.75	55.00
501-Francis the Famous Talking Mule	4.10	12.30	45.00
502-Rootie Kazootie (TV)	6.70	20.00	80.00
503-Uncle Wiggily (10/53)	4.55	13.65	50.00
504-Krazy Kat; not by Herriman	3.65	11.00	40.00
505-The Sword and the Rose (Disney) (10/53)(Movie)-Photo-c	8.35	25.00	100.00
506-The Little Scouts	2.30	7.00	20.00
507-Oswald the Rabbit (Lantz)	3.20	9.60	35.00
508-Bozo (10/53)	8.35	25.00	100.00
509-Pluto (Disney) (10/53)	5.00	15.00	60.00
510-Son of Black Beauty	3.20	9.60	35.00
511-Outlaw Trail (Zane Grey)-Kinstler-a	4.10	12.30	45.00
512-Flash Gordon (11/53)	5.35	16.00	65.00
513-Ben Bowie and His Mountain Men	3.20	9.60	35.00
514-Frosty the Snowman (11/53)	4.10	12.30	45.00
515-Andy Hardy	2.80	8.40	28.00
516-Double Trouble With Goober	2.00	6.00	18.00
517-Chip 'N' Dale (#1) (Disney)	8.00	24.00	95.00
518-Rivets (11/53)	3.00	9.00	30.00
519-Steve Canyon (#1)-Not by Milton Caniff	8.35	25.00	100.00
520-Wild Bill Elliott-Photo-c	4.10	12.30	45.00
521-Beetle Bailey (12/53)	4.60	13.75	55.00
522-The Brownies	3.20	9.60	35.00
523-Rin Tin Tin (TV)-Photo-c (12/53)	7.50	22.50	90.00
524-Tweety and Sylvester	4.10	12.30	45.00
525-Santa Claus Funnies	4.55	13.65	50.00
526-Napoleon	2.50	7.50	25.00
527-Charlie McCarthy	4.60	13.75	55.00

Four Color #534 © Jill Marie Haycox

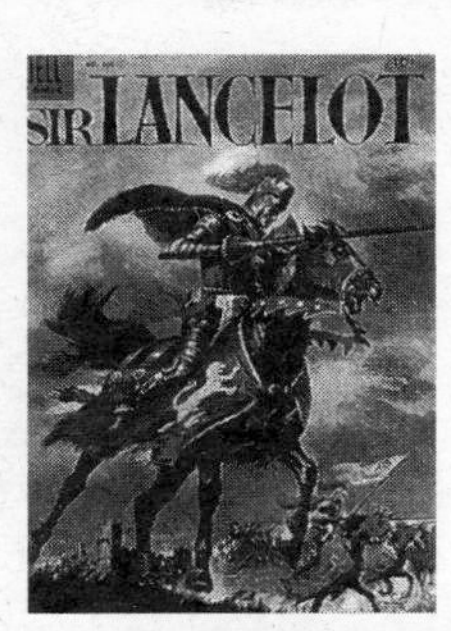

Four Color #606 © DELL

Four Color #631 © WDC

	GD2.0	FN6.0	NM9.4
28-Queen of the West Dale Evans; photo-c	10.00	30.00	120.00
29-Little Beaver	3.20	9.60	35.00
30-Bob Clampett's Beany and Cecil (TV) (1/54)	16.00	48.00	190.00
31-Duck Album (Disney)	4.60	13.75	55.00
32-The Rustlers (Zane Grey) (2-4/54)	3.20	9.60	35.00
33-Raggedy Ann and Andy	4.60	13.75	55.00
34-Western Marshal(Ernest Haycox's)-Kinstler-a	5.00	15.00	60.00
35-I Love Lucy (#1) (TV) (2/54)-Photo-c	50.00	150.00	600.00
36-Daffy (3/54)	4.50	13.65	50.00
37-Stormy, the Thoroughbred... (Disney-Movie) on top 2/3 of each page; Pluto story on bottom 1/3 of each page (2/54)	3.20	9.60	35.00
38-The Mask of Zorro; Kinstler-a	12.50	37.50	150.00
39-Ben and Me (Disney) (3/54)	3.25	9.60	36.00
40-Knights of the Round Table (3/54) (Movie)-Photo-c	6.70	20.00	80.00
41-Johnny Mack Brown; photo-c	5.85	17.50	70.00
42-Super Circus Featuring Mary Hartline (TV) (3/54)	6.70	20.00	80.00
43-Uncle Wiggily (3/54)	4.55	13.65	50.00
44-Rob Roy (Disney-Movie)-Manning-a; photo-c	7.50	22.50	90.00
45-The Wonderful Adventures of Pinocchio-Partial reprint of 4-Color #92 (Disney-Movie)	6.70	20.00	80.00
46-Buck Jones	4.60	13.75	55.00
47-Francis the Famous Talking Mule	4.10	12.30	45.00
48-Krazy Kat; not by Herriman (4/54)	3.20	9.60	35.00
49-Oswald the Rabbit (Lantz)	3.20	9.60	35.00
50-The Little Scouts	2.30	7.00	20.00
51-Bozo (4/54)	8.35	25.00	100.00
52-Beetle Bailey	4.60	13.75	55.00
53-Susie Q. Smith	3.20	9.60	35.00
54-Rusty Riley (Frank Godwin strip-r)	3.20	9.60	35.00
55-Range War (Zane Grey)	3.20	9.60	35.00
56-Double Trouble With Goober (5/54)	2.00	6.00	18.00
57-Ben Bowie and His Mountain Men	3.20	9.60	35.00
58-Elmer Fudd (5/54)	3.45	10.35	38.00
59-I Love Lucy (#2) (TV)-Photo-c	30.00	90.00	360.00
60-Duck Album (Disney) (5/54)	4.60	13.75	55.00
61-Mr. Magoo (5/54)	11.00	33.00	120.00
62-Goofy (Disney)(#2)	6.70	20.00	80.00
63-Rhubarb, the Millionaire Cat (6/54)	4.10	12.30	45.00
64-Li'l Bad Wolf (Disney)(#3)	4.10	12.30	45.00
65-Jungle Jim	3.20	9.60	35.00
66-Son of Black Beauty	3.20	9.60	35.00
67-Prince Valiant (#1)-By Bob Fuje (Movie)-Photo-c	11.00	33.00	130.00
68-Gypsy Colt (Movie) (6/54)	4.10	12.30	45.00
69-Priscilla's Pop	3.20	9.60	35.00
70-Bob Clampett's Beany and Cecil (TV)	16.00	48.00	190.00
71-Charlie McCarthy	4.60	13.75	55.00
72-Silvertip (Max Brand) (7/54); Kinstler-a	4.10	12.30	45.00
73-The Little People by Walt Scott	3.65	11.00	40.00
74-The Hand of Zorro; Kinstler-a	12.50	37.50	150.00
75-Annie Oakley and Tagg (TV)-Photo-c	8.00	24.00	95.00
76-Angel (#1) (8/54)	2.50	7.50	25.00
77-M.G.M.'s Spike and Tyke	2.50	7.50	25.00
78-Steve Canyon (8/54)	4.60	13.75	55.00
79-Francis the Famous Talking Mule	4.10	12.30	45.00
80-Six Gun Ranch (Luke Short-8/54)	3.20	9.60	35.00
81-Chip 'N' Dale (#2) (Disney)	4.60	13.75	55.00
82-Mowgli Jungle Book (Kipling) (8/54)	4.10	12.30	45.00
83-The Lost Wagon Train (Zane Grey)	3.20	9.60	35.00
84-Johnny Mack Brown-Photo-c	5.85	17.50	70.00
85-Bugs Bunny's Album	4.60	13.75	55.00
86-Duck Album (Disney)	4.60	13.75	55.00
87-The Little Scouts	2.30	7.00	20.00
88-King Richard and the Crusaders (Movie) (10/54) Matt Baker-a; photo-c	10.00	30.00	120.00
89-Buck Jones	4.60	13.75	55.00
90-Hansel and Gretel; partial photo-c	5.85	17.50	70.00

	GD2.0	FN6.0	NM9.4
591-Western Marshal(Ernest Haycox's)-Kinstler-a	4.60	13.75	55.00
592-Super Circus (TV)	5.85	17.50	70.00
593-Oswald the Rabbit (Lantz)	3.20	9.60	35.00
594-Bozo (10/54)	8.35	25.00	100.00
595-Pluto (Disney)	3.20	9.60	35.00
596-Turok, Son of Stone (#1)	58.00	175.00	700.00
597-The Little King	4.60	13.75	55.00
598-Captain Davy Jones	4.10	12.30	45.00
599-Ben Bowie and His Mountain Men	3.20	9.60	35.00
600-Daisy Duck's Diary (#1) (Disney) (11/54)	6.30	19.00	75.00
601-Frosty the Snowman	4.10	12.30	45.00
602-Mr. Magoo and Gerald McBoing-Boing	11.00	33.00	120.00
603-M.G.M.'s The Two Mouseketeers	4.10	12.30	45.00
604-Shadow on the Trail (Zane Grey)	3.20	9.60	35.00
605-The Brownies-not by Kelly (12/54)	3.20	9.60	35.00
606-Sir Lancelot (not TV)	6.70	20.00	80.00
607-Santa Claus Funnies	4.55	13.65	50.00
608-Silvertip- "Valley of Vanishing Men" (Max Brand)-Kinstler-a	4.10	12.30	45.00
609-The Littlest Outlaw (Disney-Movie) (1/55)-Photo-c	5.85	17.50	70.00
610-Drum Beat (Movie); Alan Ladd photo-c	9.00	27.00	110.00
611-Duck Album (Disney)	4.60	13.75	55.00
612-Little Beaver (1/55)	3.20	9.60	35.00
613-Western Marshal (Ernest Haycox's) (2/55)-Kinstler-a	4.60	13.75	55.00
614-20,000 Leagues Under the Sea (Disney) (Movie) (2/55)-Painted-c	9.00	27.00	110.00
615-Daffy	4.55	13.65	50.00
616-To the Last Man (Zane Grey)	3.20	9.60	35.00
617-The Quest of Zorro	11.70	35.00	140.00
618-Johnny Mack Brown; photo-c	5.85	17.50	70.00
619-Krazy Kat; not by Herriman	3.20	9.60	35.00
620-Mowgli Jungle Book (Kipling)	4.10	12.30	45.00
621-Francis the Famous Talking Mule (4/55)	3.20	9.60	35.00
622-Beetle Bailey	4.60	13.75	55.00
623-Oswald the Rabbit (Lantz)	3.00	9.00	30.00
624-Treasure Island(Disney-Movie)(4/55)-Photo-c	8.35	25.00	100.00
625-Beaver Valley (Disney-Movie)	5.85	17.50	70.00
626-Ben Bowie and His Mountain Men	3.20	9.60	35.00
627-Goofy (Disney) (5/55)	6.70	20.00	80.00
628-Elmer Fudd	3.45	10.35	38.00
629-Lady and the Tramp with Jock (Disney)	6.70	20.00	80.00
630-Priscilla's Pop	3.20	9.60	35.00
631-Davy Crockett, Indian Fighter (#1) (Disney) (5/55) (TV)-Fess Parker photo-c	17.50	52.50	210.00
632-Fighting Caravans (Zane Grey)	3.20	9.60	35.00
633-The Little People by Walt Scott (6/55)	3.65	11.00	40.00
634-Lady and the Tramp Album (Disney) (6/55)	4.55	13.65	50.00
635-Bob Clampett's Beany and Cecil (TV)	16.00	48.00	190.00
636-Chip 'N' Dale (Disney)	4.60	13.75	55.00
637-Silvertip (Max Brand)-Kinstler-a	4.10	12.30	45.00
638-M.G.M.'s Spike and Tyke (8/55)	2.50	7.50	25.00
639-Davy Crockett at the Alamo (Disney) (7/55) (TV)-Fess Parker photo-c	14.00	41.00	165.00
640-Western Marshal(Ernest Haycox's)-Kinstler-a	4.60	13.75	55.00
641-Steve Canyon (1955)-by Caniff	4.60	13.75	55.00
642-M.G.M.'s The Two Mouseketeers	4.10	12.30	45.00
643-Wild Bill Elliott; photo-c	3.20	9.60	35.00
644-Sir Walter Raleigh (5/55)-Based on movie "The Virgin Queen"; photo-c	6.30	19.00	75.00
645-Johnny Mack Brown; photo-c	5.85	17.50	70.00
646-Dotty Dripple and Taffy (#1)	3.20	9.60	35.00
647-Bugs Bunny's Album (9/55)	4.60	13.75	55.00
648-Jace Pearson of the Texas Rangers (TV)-Photo-c	4.60	13.75	55.00
649-Duck Album (Disney)	4.60	13.75	55.00
650-Prince Valiant; by Bob Fuje	6.30	19.00	75.00
651-King Colt (Luke Short) (9/55)-Kinstler-a	3.20	9.60	35.00

Four Color #684 © WB

Four Color #717 © WB

Four Color #721 © Keeshan & Miller

	GD2.0	FN6.0	NM9.4
652-Buck Jones	3.20	9.60	35.00
653-Smokey the Bear (#1) (10/55)	10.00	30.00	120.00
654-Pluto (Disney)	3.20	9.60	35.00
655-Francis the Famous Talking Mule	3.20	9.60	35.00
656-Turok, Son of Stone (#2) (10/55)	33.00	100.00	400.00
657-Ben Bowie and His Mountain Men	3.20	9.60	35.00
658-Goofy (Disney)	6.70	20.00	80.00
659-Daisy Duck's Diary (Disney)(#2)	5.00	15.00	60.00
660-Little Beaver	3.20	9.60	35.00
661-Frosty the Snowman	4.10	12.30	45.00
662-Zoo Parade (TV)-Marlin Perkins (11/55)	4.55	13.65	50.00
663-Winky Dink (TV)	7.50	22.50	90.00
664-Davy Crockett in the Great Keelboat Race (TV) (Disney) (11/55)-Fess Parker photo-c	12.50	37.50	150.00
665-The African Lion (Disney-Movie) (11/55)	5.00	15.00	60.00
666-Santa Claus Funnies	4.55	13.65	50.00
667-Silvertip and the Stolen Stallion (Max Brand) (12/55)-Kinstler-a	4.10	12.30	45.00
668-Dumbo (Disney) (12/55)-First of two printings. Dumbo on cover with starry sky. Reprints 4-Color #234?; same-c as #234	8.35	25.00	100.00
668-Dumbo (Disney) (1/58)-Second printing. Same cover altered, with Timothy Mouse added. Same contents as above	5.85	17.50	70.00
669-Robin Hood (Disney-Movie) (12/55)-Reprints #413 plus-c; photo-c	4.60	13.75	55.00
670-M.G.M's Mouse Musketeers (#1) (1/56)-Formerly the Two Mouseketeers	3.65	11.00	40.00
671-Davy Crockett and the River Pirates (TV) (Disney) (12/55)-Jesse Marsh-a; Fess Parker photo-c	12.50	37.50	150.00
672-Quentin Durward (1/56) (Movie)-Photo-c	6.30	19.00	75.00
673-Buffalo Bill, Jr. (#1) (TV)-James Arness photo-c	6.30	19.00	75.00
674-The Little Rascals (#1) (TV)	6.70	20.00	80.00
675-Steve Donovan, Western Marshal (#1) (TV)-Kinstler-a; photo-c	7.50	22.50	90.00
676-Will-Yum!	2.50	7.50	25.00
677-Little King	4.60	13.75	55.00
678-The Last Hunt (Movie)-Photo-c	7.50	22.50	90.00
679-Gunsmoke (#1) (TV)-Photo-c	16.00	48.00	190.00
680-Out Our Way with the Worry Wart (2/56)	2.50	7.50	25.00
681-Forever Darling (Movie) with Lucille Ball & Desi Arnaz (2/56)-; photo-c	10.50	31.00	125.00
682-The Sword & the Rose (Disney-Movie)-Reprint of #505; Renamed When Knighthood Was in Flower for the novel; photo-c	6.70	20.00	80.00
683-Hi and Lois (3/56)	3.00	9.00	32.00
684-Helen of Troy (Movie)-Buscema-a; photo-c	10.00	30.00	120.00
685-Johnny Mack Brown; photo-c	5.85	17.50	70.00
686-Duck Album (Disney)	4.60	13.75	55.00
687-The Indian Fighter (Movie)-Kirk Douglas photo-c	7.50	22.50	90.00
688-Alexander the Great (Movie) (5/56)-Buscema-a; photo-c	6.30	19.00	75.00
689-Elmer Fudd (3/56)	3.45	10.35	38.00
690-The Conqueror (Movie) - John Wayne photo-c	16.00	48.00	190.00
691-Dotty Dripple and Taffy	2.40	7.35	22.00
692-The Little People-Walt Scott	3.65	11.00	40.00
693-Song of the South (Disney) (1956)-Partial reprint of #129	8.35	25.00	100.00
694-Super Circus (TV)-Photo-c	5.85	17.50	70.00
695-Little Beaver	3.20	9.60	35.00
696-Krazy Kat; not by Herriman (4/56)	3.20	9.60	35.00
697-Oswald the Rabbit (Lantz)	3.00	9.00	30.00
698-Francis the Famous Talking Mule (4/56)	3.20	9.60	35.00
699-Prince Valiant-by Bob Fuje	6.30	19.00	75.00
700-Water Birds and the Olympic Elk (Disney-Movie) (4/56)	4.60	13.75	55.00
701-Jiminy Cricket (#1) (Disney) (5/56)	8.35	25.00	100.00
702-The Goofy Success Story (Disney)	6.70	20.00	80.00
703-Scamp (#1) (Disney)	8.35	25.00	100.00
704-Priscilla's Pop (5/56)	3.20	9.60	35.00
705-Brave Eagle (#1) (TV)-Photo-c	5.85	17.50	70.00
706-Bongo and Lumpjaw (Disney) (6/56)	5.00	15.00	60.00

	GD2.0	FN6.0	NM9.4
707-Corky and White Shadow (Disney) (5/56)-Mickey Mouse Club (TV); photo-c	6.70	20.00	80.00
708-Smokey the Bear	5.00	15.00	60.00
709-The Searchers (Movie) - John Wayne photo-c	24.00	73.00	290.00
710-Francis the Famous Talking Mule	3.20	9.60	35.00
711-M.G.M's Mouse Musketeers	2.50	7.50	25.00
712-The Great Locomotive Chase (Disney-Movie) (9/56)-Photo-c	6.70	20.00	80.00
713-The Animal World (Movie) (8/56)	3.20	9.60	35.00
714-Spin and Marty (#1) (TV) (Disney)-Mickey Mouse Club (6/56); photo-c	11.70	35.00	140.00
715-Timmy (8/56)	3.20	9.60	35.00
716-Man in Space (Disney)(A science feature from Tomorrowland)	8.35	25.00	100.00
717-Moby Dick (Movie)-Gregory Peck photo-c	8.35	25.00	100.00
718-Dotty Dripple and Taffy	2.40	7.35	22.00
719-Prince Valiant; by Bob Fuje (8/56)	6.30	19.00	75.00
720-Gunsmoke (TV)-James Arness photo-c	7.50	22.50	90.00
721-Captain Kangaroo (TV)-Photo-c	14.00	42.00	170.00
722-Johnny Mack Brown-Photo-c	5.85	17.50	70.00
723-Santiago (Movie)-Kinstler-a (9/56); Alan Ladd photo-c	10.00	30.00	120.00
724-Bugs Bunny's Album	4.10	12.30	45.00
725-Elmer Fudd (9/56)	2.80	8.40	28.00
726-Duck Album (Disney) (9/56)	4.60	13.75	55.00
727-The Nature of Things (TV) (Disney)-Jesse Marsh-a	4.60	13.75	55.00
728-M.G.M's Mouse Musketeers	2.50	7.50	25.00
729-Bob Son of Battle (11/56)	3.20	9.60	35.00
730-Smokey Stover	3.80	11.40	42.00
731-Silvertip and The Fighting Four (Max Brand)-Kinstler-a	4.10	12.30	45.00
732-Zorro, the Challenge of (10/56)	11.70	35.00	140.00
733-Buck Jones	3.20	9.60	35.00
734-Cheyenne (#1) (TV) (10/56)-Clint Walker photo-c	16.00	48.00	190.00
735-Crusader Rabbit (#1) (TV)	31.00	93.00	375.00
736-Pluto (Disney)	3.20	9.60	35.00
737-Steve Canyon-Caniff-a	4.60	13.75	55.00
738-Westward Ho, the Wagons (Disney-Movie)-Fess Parker photo-c	8.35	25.00	100.00
739-Bounty Guns (Luke Short)-Drucker-a	3.20	9.60	35.00
740-Chilly Willy (#1) (Walter Lantz)	4.55	13.65	50.00
741-The Fastest Gun Alive (Movie)(9/56)-Photo-c	6.70	20.00	80.00
742-Buffalo Bill, Jr. (TV)-Photo-c	4.55	13.65	50.00
743-Daisy Duck's Diary (Disney) (11/56)	5.00	15.00	60.00
744-Little Beaver	3.20	9.60	35.00
745-Francis the Famous Talking Mule	3.20	9.60	35.00
746-Dotty Dripple and Taffy	2.40	7.35	22.00
747-Goofy (Disney)	6.70	20.00	80.00
748-Frosty the Snowman (11/56)	3.65	11.00	40.00
749-Secrets of Life (Disney-Movie)-Photo-c	4.55	13.65	50.00
750-The Great Cat Family (Disney-TV/Movie)-Pinocchio & Alice app.	5.85	17.50	70.00
751-Our Miss Brooks (TV)-Photo-c	7.50	22.50	70.00
752-Mandrake, the Magician	10.00	30.00	120.00
753-Walt Scott's Little People (11/56)	3.65	11.00	40.00
754-Smokey the Bear	5.00	15.00	60.00
755-The Littlest Snowman (12/56)	4.10	12.30	45.00
756-Santa Claus Funnies	4.55	13.65	50.00
757-The True Story of Jesse James (Movie)-Photo-c	9.00	27.00	110.00
758-Bear Country (Disney-Movie)	4.60	13.75	55.00
759-Circus Boy (TV)-The Monkees' Mickey Dolenz photo-c (12/56)	11.00	33.00	130.00
760-The Hardy Boys (#1) (TV) (Disney)-Mickey Mouse Club; photo-c	10.50	31.00	125.00
761-Howdy Doody (TV) (1/57)	9.00	27.00	110.00
762-The Sharkfighters (Movie) (1/57); Buscema-a; photo-c			

Four Color #790 © MGM

Four Color #800 © Official Films

Four Color #845 © Universal

	GD2.0	FN6.0	NM9.4
	7.50	22.50	90.00
763-Grandma Duck's Farm Friends (#1) (Disney)	6.70	20.00	80.00
764-M.G.M's Mouse Musketeers	2.50	7.50	25.00
765-Will-Yum!	2.50	7.50	25.00
766-Buffalo Bill, Jr. (TV)-Photo-c	4.55	13.65	50.00
767-Spin and Marty (TV) (Disney)-Mickey Mouse Club (2/57)	9.00	27.00	110.00
768-Steve Donovan, Western Marshal (TV)-Kinstler-a; photo-c	5.85	17.50	70.00
769-Gunsmoke (TV)-James Arness photo-c	7.50	22.50	90.00
770-Brave Eagle (TV)-Photo-c	3.20	9.60	35.00
771-Brand of Empire (Luke Short)(3/57)-Drucker-a	3.20	9.60	35.00
772-Cheyenne (TV)-Clint Walker photo-c	7.00	21.00	85.00
773-The Brave One (Movie)-Photo-c	4.60	13.75	55.00
774-Hi and Lois (3/57)	2.40	7.35	22.00
775-Sir Lancelot and Brian (TV)-Buscema-a; photo-c	8.35	25.00	100.00
776-Johnny Mack Brown; photo-c	5.85	17.50	70.00
777-Scamp (Disney) (3/57)	5.85	17.50	70.00
778-The Little Rascals (TV)	4.35	13.00	48.00
779-Lee Hunter, Indian Fighter (3/57)	4.10	12.30	45.00
780-Captain Kangaroo (TV)-Photo-c	11.70	35.00	140.00
781-Fury (#1) (TV) (3/57)-Photo-c	7.50	22.50	90.00
782-Duck Album (Disney)	4.60	13.75	55.00
783-Elmer Fudd	2.80	8.40	28.00
784-Around the World in 80 Days (Movie) (2/57)-Photo-c	5.85	17.50	70.00
785-Circus Boy (TV) (4/57)-The Monkees' Mickey Dolenz photo-c	10.00	30.00	120.00
786-Cinderella (Disney) (3/57)-Partial-r of #272	5.85	17.50	70.00
787-Little Hiawatha (Disney) (4/57)(#2)	4.10	12.30	45.00
788-Prince Valiant; by Bob Fuje	6.30	19.00	75.00
789-Silvertip-Valley Thieves (Max Brand) (4/57)-Kinstler-a	4.10	12.30	45.00
790-The Wings of Eagles (Movie) (John Wayne)-Toth-a; John Wayne photo-c; 10¢ & 15¢ editions exist	15.00	45.00	170.00
791-The 77th Bengal Lancers (TV)-Photo-c	6.70	20.00	80.00
792-Oswald the Rabbit (Lantz)	3.00	9.00	30.00
793-Morty Meekle	2.50	7.50	25.00
794-The Count of Monte Cristo (5/57) (Movie)-Buscema-a	8.35	25.00	100.00
795-Jiminy Cricket (Disney)(#2)	5.85	17.50	70.00
796-Ludwig Bemelman's Madeleine and Genevieve	2.75	8.00	30.00
797-Gunsmoke (TV)-Photo-c	7.50	22.50	90.00
798-Buffalo Bill, Jr. (TV)-Photo-c	4.55	13.65	50.00
799-Priscilla's Pop	3.20	9.60	35.00
800-The Buccaneers (TV)-Photo-c	6.70	20.00	80.00
801-Dotty Dripple and Taffy	2.40	7.35	22.00
802-Goofy (Disney) (5/57)	6.70	20.00	80.00
803-Cheyenne (TV)-Clint Walker photo-c	7.00	21.00	85.00
804-Steve Canyon-Caniff-a (1957)	4.60	13.75	55.00
805-Crusader Rabbit (TV)	24.00	70.00	285.00
806-Scamp (Disney) (6/57)	5.85	17.50	70.00
807-Savage Range (Luke Short)-Drucker-a	3.20	9.60	35.00
808-Spin and Marty (TV)(Disney)-Mickey Mouse Club; photo-c	9.00	27.00	110.00
809-The Little People (Walt Scott)	3.65	11.00	40.00
810-Francis the Famous Talking Mule	3.00	9.00	30.00
811-Howdy Doody (TV) (7/57)	9.00	27.00	110.00
812-The Big Land (Movie); Alan Ladd photo-c	9.00	27.00	110.00
813-Circus Boy (TV)-The Monkees' Mickey Dolenz photo-c	10.00	30.00	120.00
814-Covered Wagons, Ho! (Disney)-Donald Duck (TV) (6/57); Mickey Mouse app.	4.60	13.75	55.00
815-Dragoon Wells Massacre (Movie)-photo-c	7.50	22.50	90.00
816-Brave Eagle (TV)-photo-c	3.20	9.60	35.00
817-Little Beaver	3.20	9.60	35.00
818-Smokey the Bear (6/57)	5.00	15.00	60.00
819-Mickey Mouse in Magicland (Disney) (7/57)	3.65	11.00	45.00

	GD2.0	FN6.0	NM9.4
820-The Oklahoman (Movie)-Photo-c	9.00	27.00	110.00
821-Wringle Wrangle (Disney)-Based on movie "Westward Ho, the Wagons"; Marsh-a; Fess Parker photo-c	7.50	22.50	90.00
822-Paul Revere's Ride with Johnny Tremain (TV) (Disney)-Toth-a	9.00	27.00	110.00
823-Timmy	2.50	7.50	24.00
824-The Pride and the Passion (Movie) (8/57)-Frank Sinatra & Cary Grant photo-c	8.35	25.00	100.00
825-The Little Rascals (TV)	4.35	13.00	48.00
826-Spin and Marty and Annette (TV) (Disney)-Mickey Mouse Club; Annette Funicello photo-c	23.00	70.00	280.00
827-Smokey Stover (8/57)	3.80	11.40	42.00
828-Buffalo Bill, Jr. (TV)-Photo-c	4.55	13.65	50.00
829-Tales of the Pony Express (TV) (8/57)-Painted-c	4.10	12.30	45.00
830-The Hardy Boys (TV) (Disney)-Mickey Mouse Club (8/57); photo-c	9.00	27.00	110.00
831-No Sleep 'Til Dawn (Movie)-Karl Malden photo-c	5.85	17.50	70.00
832-Lolly and Pepper (#1)	3.20	9.60	35.00
833-Scamp (Disney) (9/57)	5.85	17.50	70.00
834-Johnny Mack Brown; photo-c	5.85	17.50	70.00
835-Silvertip-The False Rider (Max Brand)	4.10	12.30	45.00
836-Man in Flight (Disney) (TV) (9/57)	6.70	20.00	80.00
837-All-American Athlete Cotton Woods	3.20	9.60	35.00
838-Bugs Bunny's Life Story Album (9/57)	4.10	12.30	45.00
839-The Vigilantes (Movie)	6.70	20.00	80.00
840-Duck Album (Disney) (9/57)	4.60	13.75	55.00
841-Elmer Fudd	2.80	8.40	28.00
842-The Nature of Things (Disney-Movie) ('57)-Jesse Marsh-a (TV series)	4.60	13.75	55.00
843-The First Americans (Disney) (TV)-Marsh-a	8.35	25.00	100.00
844-Gunsmoke (TV)-Photo-c	7.50	22.50	90.00
845-The Land Unknown (Movie)-Alex Toth-a	11.70	35.00	140.00
846-Gun Glory (Movie)-by Alex Toth; photo-c	9.00	27.00	110.00
847-Perri (squirrels) (Disney-Movie)-Two different covers published	4.60	13.75	55.00
848-Marauder's Moon (Luke Short)	3.20	9.60	35.00
849-Prince Valiant; by Bob Fuje	6.30	19.00	75.00
850-Buck Jones	3.20	9.60	35.00
851-The Story of Mankind (Movie) (1/58)-Hedy Lamarr & Vincent Price photo-c	6.70	20.00	80.00
852-Chilly Willy (2/58) (Lantz)	3.20	9.60	35.00
853-Pluto (Disney) (10/57)	3.20	9.60	35.00
854-The Hunchback of Notre Dame (Movie)-Photo-c	12.50	37.50	150.00
855-Broken Arrow (TV)-Photo-c	5.00	15.00	60.00
856-Buffalo Bill, Jr. (TV)-Photo-c	4.55	13.65	50.00
857-The Goofy Adventure Story (Disney) (11/57)	6.70	20.00	80.00
858-Daisy Duck's Diary (Disney) (11/57)	4.55	13.65	50.00
859-Topper and Neil (TV) (11/57)	4.10	12.30	45.00
860-Wyatt Earp (#1) (TV)-Manning-a; photo-c	10.00	30.00	120.00
861-Frosty the Snowman	3.65	11.00	40.00
862-The Truth About Mother Goose (Disney-Movie) (11/57)	6.70	20.00	80.00
863-Francis the Famous Talking Mule	3.00	9.00	30.00
864-The Littlest Snowman	4.10	12.30	45.00
865-Andy Burnett (TV) (Disney) (12/57)-Photo-c	9.00	27.00	110.00
866-Mars and Beyond (Disney-TV)(A science feature from Tomorrowland)	8.35	25.00	100.00
867-Santa Claus Funnies	4.55	13.65	50.00
868-The Little People (12/57)	3.65	11.00	40.00
869-Old Yeller (Disney-Movie)-Photo-c	4.60	13.75	55.00
870-Little Beaver (1/58)	3.20	9.60	35.00
871-Curly Kayoe	2.50	7.50	25.00
872-Captain Kangaroo (TV)-Photo-c	11.70	35.00	140.00
873-Grandma Duck's Farm Friends (Disney)	4.60	13.75	55.00
874-Old Ironsides (Disney-Movie with Johnny Tremain) (1/58)	5.85	17.50	70.00
875-Trumpets West (Luke Short) (2/58)	3.20	9.60	35.00
876-Tales of Wells Fargo (#1)(TV)(2/58)-Photo-c	9.00	27.00	110.00
877-Frontier Doctor with Rex Allen (TV)-Alex Toth-a; Rex Allen photo-c			

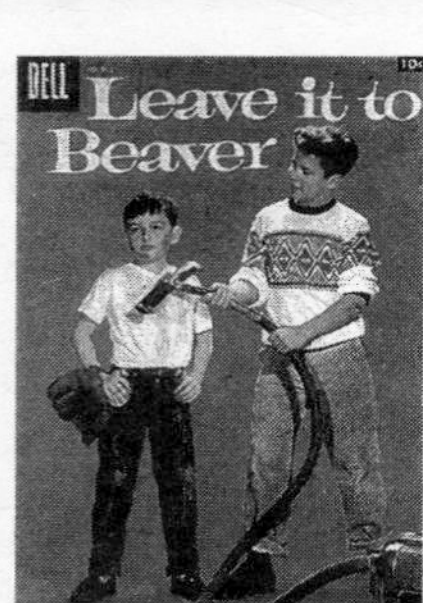

Four Color #912 © Gomalco Prod.

Four Color #919 © California National

Four Color #944 © Columbia Pictures

	GD2.0	FN6.0	NM9.4
	9.00	27.00	110.00
878-Peanuts (#1)-Schulz-c only (2/58)	14.00	42.00	170.00
879-Brave Eagle (TV) (2/58)-Photo-c	3.20	9.60	35.00
880-Steve Donovan, Western Marshal-Drucker-a (TV)-Photo-c	4.10	12.30	45.00
881-The Captain and the Kids (2/58)	3.20	9.60	35.00
882-Zorro (Disney)-1st Disney issue; by Alex Toth (TV) (2/58); photo-c	17.00	50.00	200.00
883-The Little Rascals (TV)	4.35	13.00	48.00
884-Hawkeye and the Last of the Mohicans (TV) (3/58); photo-c	6.70	20.00	80.00
885-Fury (TV) (3/58)-Photo-c	5.85	17.50	70.00
886-Bongo and Lumpjaw (Disney) (3/58)	4.10	12.30	45.00
887-The Hardy Boys (Disney) (TV)-Mickey Mouse Club (1/58)-Photo-c	9.00	27.00	110.00
888-Elmer Fudd (3/58)	2.80	8.40	28.00
889-Clint and Mac (Disney) (TV) (3/58)-Alex Toth-a; photo-c	12.50	37.50	150.00
890-Wyatt Earp (TV)-by Russ Manning; photo-c	7.00	21.00	85.00
891-Light in the Forest (Disney-Movie) (3/58)-Fess Parker photo-c	7.50	22.50	90.00
892-Maverick (#1) (TV) (4/58)-James Garner photo-c	25.00	75.00	300.00
893-Jim Bowie (TV)-Photo-c	4.60	13.75	55.00
894-Oswald the Rabbit (Lantz)	3.00	9.00	30.00
895-Wagon Train (#1) (TV) (3/58)-Photo-c	11.30	34.00	135.00
896-The Adventures of Tinker Bell (Disney)	8.00	24.00	95.00
897-Jiminy Cricket (Disney)	5.85	17.50	70.00
898-Silvertip (Max Brand)-Kinstler-a (5/58)	4.10	12.30	45.00
899-Goofy (Disney) (5/58)	4.10	12.30	45.00
900-Prince Valiant; by Bob Fuje	6.30	19.00	75.00
901-Little Hiawatha (Disney)	4.10	12.30	45.00
902-Will-Yum!	2.50	7.50	25.00
903-Dotty Dripple and Taffy	2.40	7.35	22.00
904-Lee Hunter, Indian Fighter	3.20	9.60	35.00
905-Annette (Disney) (TV) (5/58)-Mickey Mouse Club; Annette Funicello photo-c	27.00	80.00	320.00
906-Francis the Famous Talking Mule	3.00	9.00	30.00
907-Sugarfoot (#1) (TV)Toth-a; photo-c	12.50	37.50	150.00
908-The Little People and the Giant-Walt Scott (5/58)	3.65	11.00	40.00
909-Smitty	3.00	9.00	30.00
910-The Vikings (Movie)-Buscema-a; Kirk Douglas photo-c	8.35	25.00	100.00
911-The Gray Ghost (TV)-Photo-c	8.35	25.00	100.00
912-Leave It to Beaver (#1) (TV)-Photo-c	17.50	52.50	210.00
913-The Left-Handed Gun (Movie) (7/58); Paul Newman photo-c	10.00	30.00	120.00
914-No Time for Sergeants (Movie)-Andy Griffith photo-c; Toth-a	9.00	27.00	110.00
915-Casey Jones (TV)-Alan Hale photo-c	4.60	13.75	55.00
916-Red Ryder Ranch Comics (7/58)	3.45	10.35	38.00
917-The Life of Riley (TV)-Photo-c	11.30	34.00	135.00
918-Beep Beep, the Roadrunner (#1) (7/58)-Published with two different back covers	8.75	26.25	105.00
919-Boots and Saddles (#1) (TV)-Photo-c	7.50	22.50	90.00
920-Zorro (Disney) (TV) (6/58)Toth-a; photo-c	11.70	35.00	140.00
921-Wyatt Earp (TV)-Manning-a; photo-c	7.00	21.00	85.00
922-Johnny Mack Brown by Russ Manning; photo-c	6.30	19.00	75.00
923-Timmy	2.50	7.50	24.00
924-Colt .45 (#1) (TV) (8/58)-W. Preston photo-c	9.00	27.00	110.00
925-Last of the Fast Guns (Movie) (8/58)-Photo-c	6.70	20.00	80.00
926-Peter Pan (Disney)-Reprint of #442	4.10	12.30	45.00
927-Top Gun (Luke Short) Buscema-a	3.20	9.60	35.00
928-Sea Hunt (#1) (9/58) (TV)-Lloyd Bridges photo-c	11.70	35.00	140.00
929-Brave Eagle (TV)-Photo-c	3.20	9.60	35.00
930-Maverick (TV) (7/58)-James Garner photo-c	10.00	30.00	120.00
931-Have Gun, Will Travel (#1) (TV)-Photo-c	14.00	41.00	165.00

	GD2.0	FN6.0	NM9.4
932-Smokey the Bear (His Life Story)	5.00	15.00	60.00
933-Zorro (Disney, 9/58) (TV)-Alex Toth-a; photo-c	11.70	35.00	140.00
934-Restless Gun (#1) (TV)-Photo-c	11.30	34.00	135.00
935-King of the Royal Mounted	3.45	10.35	38.00
936-The Little Rascals (TV)	4.35	13.00	48.00
937-Ruff and Reddy (#1) (9/58) (TV) (1st Hanna-Barbera comic book)	12.50	37.50	150.00
938-Elmer Fudd (9/58)	2.80	8.40	28.00
939-Steve Canyon - not by Caniff	4.60	13.75	55.00
940-Lolly and Pepper (10/58)	2.50	7.50	25.00
941-Pluto (Disney) (10/58)	3.20	9.60	35.00
942-Pony Express (TV)	4.10	12.30	45.00
943-White Wilderness (Disney-Movie) (10/58)	5.85	17.50	70.00
944-The 7th Voyage of Sinbad (Movie) (9/58)-Buscema-a; photo-c	12.50	37.50	150.00
945-Maverick (TV)-James Garner/Jack Kelly photo-c	10.00	30.00	120.00
946-The Big Country (Movie)-Photo-c	6.70	20.00	80.00
947-Broken Arrow (TV)-Photo-c (11/58)	4.55	13.65	50.00
948-Daisy Duck's Diary (Disney) (11/58)	4.55	13.65	50.00
949-High Adventure(Lowell Thomas')(TV)-Photo-c	5.00	15.00	60.00
950-Frosty the Snowman	3.65	11.00	40.00
951-The Lennon Sisters Life Story (TV)-Toth-a, 32 pgs.; photo-c	14.00	42.00	170.00
952-Goofy (Disney) (11/58)	4.10	12.30	45.00
953-Francis the Famous Talking Mule	3.00	9.00	30.00
954-Man in Space-Satellites (TV)	6.70	20.00	80.00
955-Hi and Lois (11/58)	2.40	7.35	22.00
956-Ricky Nelson (#1) (TV)-Photo-c	18.35	55.00	220.00
957-Buffalo Bee (#1) (TV)	9.00	27.00	110.00
958-Santa Claus Funnies	4.10	12.30	45.00
959-Christmas Stories-(Walt Scott's Little People) (1951-56 strip reprints)	3.65	11.00	40.00
960-Zorro (Disney) (TV) (12/58)-Toth art; photo-c	11.70	35.00	140.00
961-Jace Pearson's Tales of the Texas Rangers (TV)-Spiegle-a; photo-c	4.55	13.65	50.00
962-Maverick (TV) (1/59)-James Garner/Jack Kelly photo-c	10.00	30.00	120.00
963-Johnny Mack Brown; photo-c	5.85	17.50	70.00
964-The Hardy Boys (TV) (Disney) (1/59)-Mickey Mouse Club; photo-c	9.00	27.00	110.00
965-Grandma Duck's Farm Friends (Disney)(1/59)	4.10	12.30	45.00
966-Tonka (starring Sal Mineo; Disney-Movie)-Photo-c	7.50	22.50	90.00
967-Chilly Willy (2/59) (Lantz)	3.20	9.60	35.00
968-Tales of Wells Fargo (TV)-Photo-c	8.35	25.00	100.00
969-Peanuts (2/59)	10.00	30.00	120.00
970-Lawman (#1) (TV)-Photo-c	12.50	37.50	150.00
971-Wagon Train (TV)-Photo-c	6.30	19.00	75.00
972-Tom Thumb (Movie)-George Pal (1/59)	9.00	27.00	110.00
973-Sleeping Beauty and the Prince(Disney)(5/59)	11.30	34.00	135.00
974-The Little Rascals (TV) (3/59)	4.35	13.00	48.00
975-Fury (TV)-Photo-c	5.85	17.50	70.00
976-Zorro (Disney) (TV)-Toth-a; photo-c	11.70	35.00	140.00
977-Elmer Fudd (3/59)	2.80	8.40	28.00
978-Lolly and Pepper	2.50	7.50	25.00
979-Oswald the Rabbit (Lantz)	3.00	9.00	30.00
980-Maverick (TV) (4-6/59)-James Garner/Jack Kelly photo-c	10.00	30.00	120.00
981-Ruff and Reddy (TV) (Hanna-Barbera)	8.00	24.00	95.00
982-The New Adventures of Tinker Bell (TV) (Disney)	7.50	22.50	90.00
983-Have Gun, Will Travel (TV) (4-6/59)-Photo-c	8.75	26.25	105.00
984-Sleeping Beauty's Fairy Godmothers (Disney)	8.35	25.00	100.00
985-Shaggy Dog (Disney-Movie)-Photo-all four covers; Annette on back-c(5/59)	6.70	20.00	80.00
986-Restless Gun (TV)-Photo-c	8.00	24.00	95.00
987-Goofy (Disney) (7/59)	4.10	12.30	45.00
988-Little Hiawatha (Disney)	4.10	12.30	45.00

Four Color #1006 © Oscar Films

Four Color #1047 © WDC

Four Color #1076 © Rebel Co.

	GD2.0	FN6.0	NM9.4
989-Jiminy Cricket (Disney) (5-7/59)	5.85	17.50	70.00
990-Huckleberry Hound (#1)(TV)(Hanna-Barbera); 1st app. Huck, Yogi Bear, & Pixie & Dixie & Mr. Jinks	11.70	35.00	140.00
991-Francis the Famous Talking Mule	3.00	9.00	30.00
992-Sugarfoot (TV)-Toth-a; photo-c	11.70	35.00	140.00
993-Jim Bowie (TV)-Photo-c	4.60	13.75	55.00
994-Sea Hunt (TV)-Lloyd Bridges photo-c	8.00	24.00	95.00
995-Donald Duck Album (Disney) (5-7/59)(#1)	5.00	15.00	60.00
996-Nevada (Zane Grey)	3.20	9.60	35.00
997-Walt Disney Presents-Tales of Texas John Slaughter (#1) (TV) (Disney)-Photo-c; photo of W. Disney inside-c	6.70	20.00	80.00
998-Ricky Nelson (TV)-Photo-c	18.35	55.00	220.00
999-Leave It to Beaver (TV)-Photo-c	15.00	45.00	175.00
1000-The Gray Ghost (TV) (6-8/59)-Photo-c	8.35	25.00	100.00
1001-Lowell Thomas' High Adventure (TV) (8-10/59)-Photo-c	4.60	13.75	55.00
1002-Buffalo Bee (TV)	6.30	19.00	75.00
1003-Zorro (TV) (Disney)-Toth-a; photo-c	11.70	35.00	140.00
1004-Colt .45 (TV) (6-8/59)-Photo-c	7.00	21.00	85.00
1005-Maverick (TV)-James Garner/Jack Kelly photo-c	10.00	30.00	120.00
1006-Hercules (Movie)-Buscema-a; photo-c	9.00	27.00	110.00
1007-John Paul Jones (Movie)-Robert Stack photo-c	4.60	13.75	55.00
1008-Beep Beep, the Road Runner (7-9/59)	4.60	13.75	55.00
1009-The Rifleman (#1) (TV)-Photo-c	23.00	70.00	280.00
1010-Grandma Duck's Farm Friends (Disney)-by Carl Barks	12.50	37.50	150.00
1011-Buckskin (#1) (TV)-Photo-c	6.70	20.00	80.00
1012-Last Train from Gun Hill (Movie) (7/59)-Photo-c	8.35	25.00	100.00
1013-Bat Masterson (#1) (TV) (8/59)-Gene Barry photo-c	11.70	35.00	140.00
1014-The Lennon Sisters (TV)-Toth-a; photo-c	13.00	40.00	160.00
1015-Peanuts-Schulz-c	10.00	30.00	120.00
1016-Smokey the Bear Nature Stories	3.20	9.60	35.00
1017-Chilly Willy (Lantz)	3.20	9.60	35.00
1018-Rio Bravo (Movie)(6/59)-John Wayne; Toth-a; John Wayne, Dean Martin & Ricky Nelson photo-c	20.00	60.00	240.00
1019-Wagon Train (TV)-Photo-c	6.30	19.00	75.00
1020-Jungle Jim-McWilliams-a	3.00	9.00	30.00
1021-Jace Pearson's Tales of the Texas Rangers (TV)-Photo-c	4.55	13.65	50.00
1022-Timmy	2.50	7.50	24.00
1023-Tales of Wells Fargo (TV)-Photo-c	8.35	25.00	100.00
1024-Darby O'Gill and the Little People (Disney-Movie)-Toth-a; photo-c	9.00	27.00	110.00
1025-Vacation in Disneyland (8-10/59)-Carl Barks-a(24pgs.) (Disney)	18.35	55.00	220.00
1026-Spin and Marty (TV) (Disney) (9-11/59)-Mickey Mouse Club; photo-c	7.50	22.50	90.00
1027-The Texan (#1)(TV)-Photo-c	8.35	25.00	100.00
1028-Rawhide (#1) (TV) (9-11/59)-Clint Eastwood photo-c; Tufts-a	23.00	68.00	270.00
1029-Boots and Saddles (TV) (9/59)-Photo-c	4.60	13.75	55.00
1030-Spanky and Alfalfa, the Little Rascals (TV)	4.35	13.00	48.00
1031-Fury (TV)-Photo-c	5.85	17.50	70.00
1032-Elmer Fudd	2.80	8.40	28.00
1033-Steve Canyon-not by Caniff; photo-c	4.60	13.75	55.00
1034-Nancy and Sluggo Summer Camp (9-11/59)	3.65	11.00	40.00
1035-Lawman (TV)-Photo-c	6.70	20.00	80.00
1036-The Big Circus (Movie)-Photo-c	5.85	17.50	70.00
1037-Zorro (Disney) (TV)-Tufts-a; Annette Funicello photo-c	15.00	45.00	175.00
1038-Ruff and Reddy (TV)(Hanna-Barbera)(1959)	8.00	24.00	95.00
1039-Pluto (Disney) (11-1/60)	3.20	9.60	35.00
1040-Quick Draw McGraw (#1) (TV) (Hanna-Barbera) (12-2/60)	13.00	40.00	160.00
1041-Sea Hunt (TV) (10-12/59)-Toth-a; Lloyd Bridges photo-c	8.35	25.00	100.00
1042-The Three Chipmunks (Alvin, Simon & Theodore) (#1) (TV) (10-12/59)	5.35	16.00	65.00
1043-The Three Stooges (#1)-Photo-c	19.00	56.00	225.00
1044-Have Gun, Will Travel (TV)-Photo-c	8.75	26.25	105.00
1045-Restless Gun (TV)-Photo-c	8.00	24.00	95.00
1046-Beep Beep, the Road Runner (11-1/60)	4.60	13.75	55.00
1047-Gyro Gearloose (#1) (Disney)-All Barks-c/a	18.35	55.00	220.00
1048-The Horse Soldiers (Movie) (John Wayne)-Sekowsky-a; painted cover featuring John Wayne	13.00	40.00	160.00
1049-Don't Give Up the Ship (Movie) (8/59)-Jerry Lewis photo-c	7.00	20.00	85.00
1050-Huckleberry Hound (TV) (Hanna-Barbera) (10-12/59)	8.00	24.00	95.00
1051-Donald in Mathmagic Land (Disney-Movie)	8.35	25.00	100.00
1052-Ben-Hur (Movie) (11/59)-Manning-a	9.00	27.00	110.00
1053-Goofy (Disney) (11-1/60)	4.10	12.30	45.00
1054-Huckleberry Hound Winter Fun (TV) (Hanna-Barbera) (12/59)	8.00	24.00	95.00
1055-Daisy Duck's Diary (Disney)-by Carl Barks (11-1/60)	9.00	27.00	110.00
1056-Yellowstone Kelly (Movie)-Clint Walker photo-c	5.00	15.00	60.00
1057-Mickey Mouse Album (Disney)	3.45	10.35	38.00
1058-Colt .45 (TV)-Photo-c	7.00	21.00	85.00
1059-Sugarfoot (TV)-Photo-c	8.35	25.00	100.00
1060-Journey to the Center of the Earth (Movie)-Pat Boone & James Mason photo-c	11.30	34.00	135.00
1061-Buffalo Bee (TV)	6.30	19.00	75.00
1062-Christmas Stories (Walt Scott's Little People strip-r)	3.65	11.00	40.00
1063-Santa Claus Funnies	4.10	12.30	45.00
1064-Bugs Bunny's Merry Christmas (12/59)	4.10	12.30	45.00
1065-Frosty the Snowman	3.65	11.00	45.00
1066-77 Sunset Strip (#1) (TV)-Toth-a (1-3/60)-Efrem Zimbalist, Jr. & Edd "Kookie" Byrnes photo-c	11.30	34.00	135.00
1067-Yogi Bear (#1) (TV) (Hanna-Barbera)	11.00	33.00	130.00
1068-Francis the Famous Talking Mule	3.00	9.00	30.00
1069-The FBI Story (Movie)-Toth-a; James Stewart photo on-c	10.00	30.00	120.00
1070-Solomon and Sheba (Movie)-Sekowsky-a; photo-c	9.00	27.00	110.00
1071-The Real McCoys (#1) (TV) (1-3/60)-Toth-a; Walter Brennan photo-c	9.00	27.00	110.00
1072-Blythe (Marge's)	4.60	13.75	55.00
1073-Grandma Duck's Farm Friends-Barks-c/a (Disney)	12.50	37.50	150.00
1074-Chilly Willy (Lantz)	3.20	9.60	35.00
1075-Tales of Wells Fargo (TV)-Photo-c	8.35	25.00	100.00
1076-The Rebel (#1) (TV)-Sekowsky-a; photo-c	10.00	30.00	120.00
1077-The Deputy (#1) (TV)-Buscema-a; Henry Fonda photo-c	12.00	35.00	145.00
1078-The Three Stooges (2-4/60)-Photo-c	10.00	30.00	120.00
1079-The Little Rascals (TV) (Spanky & Alfalfa)	4.35	13.00	48.00
1080-Fury (TV) (2-4/60)-Photo-c	5.85	17.50	70.00
1081-Elmer Fudd	2.80	8.40	28.00
1082-Spin and Marty (Disney) (TV)-Photo-c	7.50	22.50	90.00
1083-Men into Space (TV)-Anderson-a; photo-c	4.60	13.75	55.00
1084-Speedy Gonzales	4.55	13.65	50.00
1085-The Time Machine (H.G. Wells) (Movie) (3/60)-Alex Toth-a; Rod Taylor photo-c	15.00	45.00	175.00
1086-Lolly and Pepper	2.50	7.50	25.00
1087-Peter Gunn (TV)-Photo-c	9.00	27.00	110.00
1088-A Dog of Flanders (Movie)-Photo-c	4.10	12.30	45.00
1089-Restless Gun (TV)-Photo-c	8.00	24.00	95.00
1090-Francis the Famous Talking Mule	3.00	9.00	30.00
1091-Jacky's Diary (4-6/60)	4.10	12.30	45.00
1092-Toby Tyler (Disney-Movie)-Photo-c	5.85	17.50	70.00
1093-MacKenzie's Raiders (Movie/TV)-Richard Carlson photo-c from TV show	5.85	17.50	70.00
1094-Goofy (Disney)	4.10	12.30	45.00
1095-Gyro Gearloose (Disney)-All Barks-c/a	10.00	30.00	120.00

Four Color #1102 © Four Star

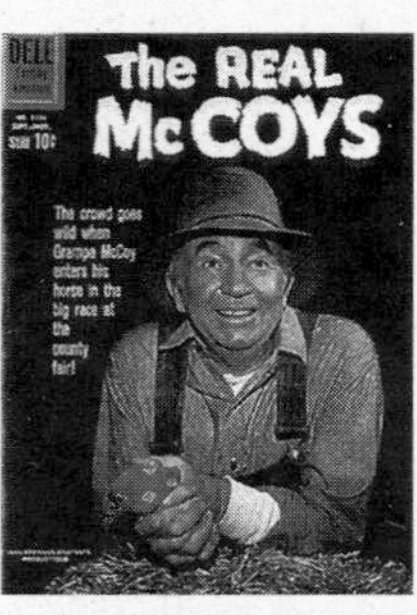

Four Color #1134 © Brennon-Westgate

Four Color #1141 © H-B

	GD2.0	FN6.0	NM9.4
1096-The Texan (TV)-Rory Calhoun photo-c	7.50	22.50	90.00
1097-Rawhide (TV)-Manning-a; Clint Eastwood photo-c	14.00	41.00	165.00
1098-Sugarfoot (TV)-Photo-c	8.35	25.00	100.00
1099-Donald Duck Album (Disney) (5-7/60)-Barks-c	5.85	17.50	70.00
1100-Annette's Life Story (Disney-Movie) (5/60)-Annette Funicello photo-c	22.00	65.00	260.00
1101-Robert Louis Stevenson's Kidnapped (Disney-Movie) (5/60); photo-c	5.85	17.50	70.00
1102-Wanted: Dead or Alive (#1) (TV) (5-7/60); Steve McQueen photo-c	12.00	35.00	145.00
1103-Leave It to Beaver (TV)-Photo-c	15.00	45.00	175.00
1104-Yogi Bear Goes to College (TV) (Hanna-Barbera) (6-8/60)	7.00	21.00	85.00
1105-Gale Storm (Oh! Susanna) (TV)-Toth-a; photo-c	12.50	37.50	150.00
1106-77 Sunset Strip(TV)(6-8/60)-Toth-a; photo-c	9.00	27.00	110.00
1107-Buckskin (TV)-Photo-c	5.85	17.50	70.00
1108-The Troubleshooters (TV)-Keenan Wynn photo-c	4.60	13.75	55.00
1109-This Is Your Life, Donald Duck (Disney) (TV) (8-10/60)-Gyro flashback to WDC&S #141; origin Donald Duck (1st told)	14.00	41.00	165.00
1110-Bonanza (#1) (TV) (6-8/60)-Photo-c	35.00	105.00	420.00
1111-Shotgun Slade (TV)-Photo-c	5.85	17.50	70.00
1112-Pixie and Dixie and Mr. Jinks (#1) (TV) (Hanna-Barbera) (7-9/60)	7.00	21.00	85.00
1113-Tales of Wells Fargo (TV)-Photo-c	8.35	25.00	100.00
1114-Huckleberry Finn (Movie) (7/60)-Photo-c	4.60	13.75	55.00
1115-Ricky Nelson (TV)-Manning-a; photo-c	14.00	41.00	165.00
1116-Boots and Saddles (TV) (8/60)-Photo-c	4.60	13.75	55.00
1117-Boy and the Pirates (Movie)-Photo-c	5.85	17.50	70.00
1118-The Sword and the Dragon (Movie) (6/60)-Photo-c	7.50	22.50	90.00
1119-Smokey the Bear Nature Stories	3.20	9.60	35.00
1120-Dinosaurus (Movie)-Painted-c	6.70	20.00	80.00
1121-Hercules Unchained (Movie) (8/60)-Crandall/Evans-a	9.00	27.00	110.00
1122-Chilly Willy (Lantz)	3.20	9.60	35.00
1123-Tombstone Territory (TV)-Photo-c	9.00	27.00	110.00
1124-Whirlybirds (#1) (TV)-Photo-c	8.35	25.00	100.00
1125-Laramie (#1) (TV)-Photo-c; G. Kane/Heath-a	9.00	27.00	110.00
1126-Sundance (TV) (8-10/60)-Earl Holliman photo-c	5.85	17.50	70.00
1127-The Three Stooges-Photo-c (8-10/60)	10.00	30.00	120.00
1128-Rocky and His Friends (#1) (TV) (Jay Ward) (8-10/60)	37.00	110.00	440.00
1129-Pollyanna (Disney-Movie)-Hayley Mills photo-c	7.50	22.50	90.00
1130-The Deputy (TV)-Buscema-a; Henry Fonda photo-c	9.00	27.00	110.00
1131-Elmer Fudd (9-11/60)	2.80	8.40	28.00
1132-Space Mouse (Lantz) (8-10/60)	4.10	12.30	45.00
1133-Fury (TV)-Photo-c	5.85	17.50	70.00
1134-Real McCoys (TV)-Toth-a; photo-c	9.00	27.00	110.00
1135-M.G.M.'s Mouse Musketeers (9-11/60)	2.50	7.50	25.00
1136-Jungle Cat (Disney-Movie)-Photo-c	5.85	17.50	70.00
1137-The Little Rascals (TV)	4.35	13.00	48.00
1138-The Rebel (TV)-Photo-c	8.35	25.00	100.00
1139-Spartacus (Movie) (11/60)-Buscema-a; Kirk Douglas photo-c	12.50	37.50	150.00
1140-Donald Duck Album (Disney)-Barks-c	5.85	17.50	70.00
1141-Huckleberry Hound for President (TV) (Hanna-Barbera) (10/60)	7.50	22.50	90.00
1142-Johnny Ringo (TV)-Photo-c	6.70	20.00	80.00
1143-Pluto (Disney) (11-1/61)	3.20	9.60	35.00
1144-The Story of Ruth (Movie)-Photo-c	9.00	27.00	110.00
1145-The Lost World (Movie)-Gil Kane-a; photo-c; 1 pg. Conan Doyle biography by Torres	10.00	30.00	120.00
1146-Restless Gun (TV)-Photo-c; Wildey-a	8.00	24.00	95.00

	GD2.0	FN6.0	NM9.4
1147-Sugarfoot (TV)-Photo-c	8.35	25.00	100.00
1148-I Aim at the Stars-the Wernher Von Braun Story (Movie) (11-1/61)-Photo-c	6.70	20.00	80.00
1149-Goofy (Disney) (11-1/61)	4.10	12.30	45.00
1150-Daisy Duck's Diary (Disney) (12-1/61) by Carl Barks	9.00	27.00	110.00
1151-Mickey Mouse Album (Disney) (11-1/61)	3.45	10.35	38.00
1152-Rocky and His Friends (TV) (Jay Ward) (12-2/61)	23.00	69.00	275.00
1153-Frosty the Snowman	3.65	11.00	40.00
1154-Santa Claus Funnies	4.10	12.30	45.00
1155-North to Alaska (Movie)-John Wayne photo-c	16.00	48.00	190.00
1156-Walt Disney Swiss Family Robinson (Movie) (12/60)-Photo-c	6.70	20.00	80.00
1157-Master of the World (Movie) (7/61)	4.60	13.75	55.00
1158-Three Worlds of Gulliver (2 issues exist with different covers) (Movie)-Photo-c	6.30	19.00	75.00
1159-77 Sunset Strip (TV)-Toth-a; photo-c	9.00	27.00	110.00
1160-Rawhide (TV)-Clint Eastwood photo-c	14.00	41.00	165.00
1161-Grandma Duck's Farm Friends (Disney) by Carl Barks (2-4/61)	12.50	37.50	150.00
1162-Yogi Bear Joins the Marines (TV) (Hanna-Barbera) (5-7/61)	7.00	21.00	85.00
1163-Daniel Boone (3-5/61); Marsh-a	4.60	13.75	55.00
1164-Wanted: Dead or Alive (TV)-Steve McQueen photo-c	9.00	27.00	110.00
1165-Ellery Queen (#1) (3-5/61)	11.00	33.00	130.00
1166-Rocky and His Friends (TV) (Jay Ward)	23.00	69.00	275.00
1167-Tales of Wells Fargo (TV)-Photo-c	7.50	22.50	90.00
1168-The Detectives (TV)-Robert Taylor photo-c	9.00	27.00	110.00
1169-New Adventures of Sherlock Holmes	16.00	48.00	190.00
1170-The Three Stooges (3-5/61)-Photo-c	10.00	30.00	120.00
1171-Elmer Fudd	2.80	8.40	28.00
1172-Fury (TV)-Photo-c	5.85	17.50	70.00
1173-The Twilight Zone (#1) (TV) (5/61)-Crandall/Evans-c/a; Crandall tribute to Ingles	20.00	60.00	240.00
1174-The Little Rascals (TV)	3.45	10.35	38.00
1175-M.G.M.'s Mouse Musketeers (3-5/61)	2.50	7.50	25.00
1176-Dondi (Movie)-Origin; photo-c	4.10	12.30	45.00
1177-Chilly Willy (Lantz) (4-6/61)	3.20	9.60	35.00
1178-Ten Who Dared (Disney-Movie) (12/60)-Painted-c; cast member photo on back-c	6.70	20.00	80.00
1179-The Swamp Fox (TV) (Disney)-Leslie Nielson photo-c	8.35	25.00	100.00
1180-The Danny Thomas Show (TV)-Toth-a; photo-c	15.00	45.00	180.00
1181-Texas John Slaughter (TV) (Disney) (4-6/61)-Photo-c	6.70	20.00	80.00
1182-Donald Duck Album (Disney) (5-7/61)	4.10	12.30	45.00
1183-101 Dalmatians (Disney-Movie) (3/61)	10.00	30.00	120.00
1184-Gyro Gearloose; All Barks-c/a (Disney) (5-7/61) Two variations exist	10.00	30.00	120.00
1185-Sweetie Pie	3.45	10.35	38.00
1186-Yak Yak (#1) by Jack Davis (2 versions - one minus 3-pg. Davis-c/a)	7.50	22.50	90.00
1187-The Three Stooges (6-8/61)-Photo-c	10.00	30.00	120.00
1188-Atlantis, the Lost Continent (Movie) (5/61)-Photo-c	10.00	30.00	120.00
1189-Greyfriars Bobby (Disney-Movie) (11/61)-Photo-c (scarce)	6.70	20.00	80.00
1190-Donald and the Wheel (Disney-Movie) (11/61); Barks-c	6.70	20.00	80.00
1191-Leave It to Beaver (TV)-Photo-c	15.00	45.00	175.00
1192-Ricky Nelson (TV)-Manning-a; photo-c	14.00	41.00	165.00
1193-The Real McCoys (TV) (6-8/61)-Photo-c	8.35	25.00	100.00
1194-Pepe (Movie) (4/61)-Photo-c	2.40	7.35	22.00
1195-National Velvet (#1) (TV)-Photo-c	5.85	17.50	70.00
1196-Pixie and Dixie and Mr. Jinks (TV) (Hanna-Barbera) (7-9/61)	5.00	15.00	60.00

Four Color #1199 © WDC

Four Color #1218 © DELL

Four Color #1221 © CBS

	GD2.0	FN6.0	NM9.4
1197-The Aquanauts (TV) (5-7/61)-Photo-c	6.70	20.00	80.00
1198-Donald in Mathmagic Land (Disney-Movie)-Reprint of #1051	5.85	17.50	70.00
1199-The Absent-Minded Professor (Disney-Movie) (4/61)-Photo-c	6.70	20.00	80.00
1200-Hennessey (TV) (8-10/61)-Gil Kane-a; photo-c	6.70	20.00	80.00
1201-Goofy (Disney) (8-10/61)	4.10	12.30	45.00
1202-Rawhide (TV)-Clint Eastwood photo-c	14.00	41.00	165.00
1203-Pinocchio (Disney) (3/62)	4.60	13.75	55.00
1204-Scamp (Disney)	3.65	11.00	40.00
1205-David and Goliath (Movie) (7/61)-Photo-c	5.85	17.50	70.00
1206-Lolly and Pepper (9-11/61)	2.50	7.50	25.00
1207-The Rebel (TV)-Sekowsky-a; photo-c	8.35	25.00	100.00
1208-Rocky and His Friends (Jay Ward) (TV)	23.00	69.00	275.00
1209-Sugarfoot (TV)-Photo-c (10-12/61)	8.35	25.00	100.00
1210-The Parent Trap (Disney-Movie) (8/61)-Hayley Mills photo-c	9.00	27.00	110.00
1211-77 Sunset Strip (TV)-Manning-a; photo-c	8.35	25.00	100.00
1212-Chilly Willy (Lantz) (7-9/61)	3.20	9.60	35.00
1213-Mysterious Island (Movie)-Photo-c	8.35	25.00	100.00
1214-Smokey the Bear	3.20	9.60	35.00
1215-Tales of Wells Fargo (TV) (10-12/61)-Photo-c	7.50	22.50	90.00
1216-Whirlybirds (TV)-Photo-c	7.50	22.50	90.00
1218-Fury (TV)-Photo-c	5.85	17.50	70.00
1219-The Detectives (TV)-Robert Taylor & Adam West photo-c	7.50	22.50	90.00
1220-Gunslinger (TV)-Photo-c	8.35	25.00	100.00
1221-Bonanza (TV) (9-11/61)-Photo-c	17.00	50.00	200.00
1222-Elmer Fudd (9-11/61)	2.80	8.40	28.00
1223-Laramie (TV)-Gil Kane-a; photo-c	5.85	17.50	70.00
1224-The Little Rascals (TV) (10-12/61)	3.45	10.35	38.00
1225-The Deputy (TV)-Henry Fonda photo-c	9.00	27.00	110.00
1226-Nikki, Wild Dog of the North (Disney-Movie) (9/61)-Photo-c	4.60	13.75	55.00
1227-Morgan the Pirate (Movie)-Photo-c	7.50	22.50	90.00
1229-Thief of Baghdad (Movie)-Crandall/Evans-a; photo-c	6.30	19.00	75.00
1230-Voyage to the Bottom of the Sea (#1) (Movie)-Photo insert on-c	10.00	30.00	120.00
1231-Danger Man (TV) (9-11/61)-Patrick McGoohan photo-c	10.00	30.00	120.00
1232-On the Double (Movie)	4.10	12.30	45.00
1233-Tammy Tell Me True (Movie) (1961)	5.85	17.50	70.00
1234-The Phantom Planet (Movie) (1961)	6.70	20.00	80.00
1235-Mister Magoo (#1) (12-2/62)	9.00	27.00	100.00
1235-Mister Magoo (3-5/65) 2nd printing; reprint of 12-2/62 issue	5.50	16.50	60.00
1236-King of Kings (Movie)-Photo-c	7.50	22.50	90.00
1237-The Untouchables (#1) (TV)-Not by Toth; photo-c	23.00	68.00	270.00
1238-Deputy Dawg (TV)	11.00	33.00	130.00
1239-Donald Duck Album (Disney) (10-12/61)-Barks-c	5.85	17.50	70.00
1240-The Detectives (TV)-Tufts-a; Robert Taylor photo-c	7.50	22.50	90.00
1241-Sweetie Pie	3.00	9.00	32.00
1242-King Leonardo and His Short Subjects (#1) (TV) (11-1/62)	13.00	40.00	160.00
1243-Ellery Queen	8.75	26.50	105.00
1244-Space Mouse (Lantz) (11-1/62)	4.10	12.30	45.00
1245-New Adventures of Sherlock Holmes	15.00	45.00	175.00
1246-Mickey Mouse Album (Disney)	3.45	10.35	38.00
1247-Daisy Duck's Diary (Disney) (12-2/62)	4.55	13.65	50.00
1248-Pluto (Disney)	3.20	9.60	35.00
1249-The Danny Thomas Show (TV)-Manning-a; photo-c	15.00	45.00	180.00
1250-The Four Horsemen of the Apocalypse (Movie)-Photo-c	6.70	20.00	80.00
1251-Everything's Ducky (Movie) (1961)	4.10	12.30	45.00
1252-The Andy Griffith Show (TV)-Photo-c; 1st show aired 10/3/60	33.00	100.00	400.00
1253-Space Man (#1) (1-3/62)	6.70	20.00	80.00
1254- "Diver Dan" (#1) (TV) (2-4/62)-Photo-c	4.60	13.75	55.00
1255-The Wonders of Aladdin (Movie) (1961)	5.85	17.50	70.00
1256-Kona, Monarch of Monster Isle (#1) (2-4/62)-Glanzman-a	6.80	20.50	75.00
1257-Car 54, Where Are You? (#1) (TV) (3-5/62)-Photo-c	6.70	20.00	80.00
1258-The Frogmen (#1)-Evans-a	6.70	20.00	80.00
1259-El Cid (Movie) (1961)-Photo-c	6.70	20.00	80.00
1260-The Horsemasters (TV, Movie) (Disney) (12-2/62)-Annette Funicello photo-c	11.70	35.00	140.00
1261-Rawhide (TV)-Clint Eastwood photo-c	14.00	41.00	165.00
1262-The Rebel (TV)-Photo-c	8.35	25.00	100.00
1263-77 Sunset Strip (TV) (12-2/62)-Manning-a; photo-c	8.35	25.00	100.00
1264-Pixie and Dixie and Mr. Jinks (TV) (Hanna-Barbera)	5.00	15.00	60.00
1265-The Real McCoys (TV)-Photo-c	8.35	25.00	100.00
1266-M.G.M.'s Spike and Tyke (12-2/62)	2.40	7.35	22.00
1267-Gyro Gearloose; Barks-c/a, 4 pgs. (Disney) (12-2/62)	7.00	21.00	85.00
1268-Oswald the Rabbit (Lantz)	3.00	9.00	30.00
1269-Rawhide (TV)-Clint Eastwood photo-c	14.00	41.00	165.00
1270-Bullwinkle and Rocky (#1) (TV) (Jay Ward) (3-5/62)	18.75	56.00	225.00
1271-Yogi Bear Birthday Party (TV) (Hanna-Barbera) (11/61) (Given away for 1 box top from Kellogg's Corn Flakes)	4.60	13.75	55.00
1272-Frosty the Snowman	3.65	11.00	40.00
1273-Hans Brinker (Disney-Movie)-Photo-c (2/62)	5.80	17.50	70.00
1274-Santa Claus Funnies (12/61)	4.10	12.30	45.00
1275-Rocky and His Friends (TV) (Jay Ward)	23.00	69.00	275.00
1276-Dondi	2.40	7.35	22.00
1278-King Leonardo and His Short Subjects (TV)	13.00	40.00	160.00
1279-Grandma Duck's Farm Friends (Disney)	4.10	12.30	45.00
1280-Hennessey (TV)-Photo-c	5.85	17.50	70.00
1281-Chilly Willy (Lantz) (4-6/62)	3.20	9.60	35.00
1282-Babes in Toyland (Disney-Movie) (1/62); Annette Funicello photo-c	11.70	35.00	140.00
1283-Bonanza (TV) (2-4/62)-Photo-c	17.00	50.00	200.00
1284-Laramie (TV)-Heath-a; photo-c	5.85	17.50	70.00
1285-Leave It to Beaver (TV)-Photo-c	15.00	45.00	175.00
1286-The Untouchables (TV)-Photo-c	16.00	48.00	190.00
1287-Man from Wells Fargo (TV)-Photo-c	5.00	15.00	60.00
1288-Twilight Zone (TV) (4/62)-Crandall/Evans-c/a	11.00	33.00	130.00
1289-Ellery Queen	8.75	26.50	105.00
1290-M.G.M.'s Mouse Musketeers	2.50	7.50	25.00
1291-77 Sunset Strip (TV)-Manning-a; photo-c	8.35	25.00	100.00
1293-Elmer Fudd (3-5/62)	2.80	8.40	28.00
1294-Ripcord (TV)	6.70	20.00	80.00
1295-Mister Ed, the Talking Horse (#1) (TV) (3-5/62)-Photo-c	12.50	37.50	150.00
1296-Fury (TV) (3-5/62)-Photo-c	5.85	17.50	70.00
1297-Spanky, Alfalfa and the Little Rascals (TV)	3.45	10.35	38.00
1298-The Hathaways (TV)-Photo-c	4.10	12.30	45.00
1299-Deputy Dawg (TV)	11.00	33.00	130.00
1300-The Comancheros (Movie) (1961)-John Wayne photo-c	15.00	45.00	180.00
1301-Adventures in Paradise (TV) (2-4/62)	4.10	12.30	45.00
1302-Johnny Jason, Teen Reporter (2-4/62)	3.20	9.60	35.00
1303-Lad: A Dog (Movie)-Photo-c	3.65	11.00	40.00
1304-Nellie the Nurse (3-5/62)-Stanley-a	6.70	20.00	80.00
1305-Mister Magoo (3-5/62)	9.00	27.00	100.00
1306-Target: The Corruptors (#1) (TV) (3-5/62)-Photo-c	5.00	15.00	60.00
1307-Margie (TV) (3-5/62)	5.00	15.00	60.00
1308-Tales of the Wizard of Oz (TV) (3-5/62)	11.00	33.00	130.00
1309-87th Precinct (#1) (TV) (4-6/62)-Krigstein-a; photo-c			

Four Favorites #14 © ACE

4Most V2 #2 © Premium Services

Fox and the Crow #5 © DC

GD2.0 FN6.0 NM9.4 | GD2.0 FN6.0 NM9.4

9.00 27.00 110.00
1310-Huck and Yogi Winter Sports (TV) (Hanna-Barbera) (3/62)
8.75 26.25 105.00
1311-Rocky and His Friends (TV) (Jay Ward) 23.00 69.00 275.00
1312-National Velvet (TV)-Photo-c 3.20 9.60 35.00
1313-Moon Pilot (Disney-Movie)-Photo-c 6.70 20.00 80.00
1328-The Underwater City (Movie) (1961)-Evans-a; photo-c
6.70 20.00 80.00
1329-See Gyro Gearloose #01329-207
1330-Brain Boy (#1)-Gil Kane-a 12.50 37.50 150.00
1332-Bachelor Father (TV) 7.50 22.50 90.00
1333-Short Ribs (4-6/62) 4.60 13.75 55.00
1335-Aggie Mack (4-6/62) 3.20 9.60 35.00
1336-On Stage; not by Leonard Starr 4.10 12.30 45.00
1337-Dr. Kildare (#1) (TV) (4-6/62)-Photo-c 8.35 25.00 100.00
1341-The Andy Griffith Show (TV) (4-6/62)-Photo-c 33.00 100.00 400.00
1348-Yak Yak (#2)-Jack Davis-c/a 7.50 22.50 90.00
1349-Yogi Bear Visits the U.N. (TV) (Hanna-Barbera) (1/62)-Photo-c
9.00 27.00 110.00
1350-Comanche (Disney-Movie)(1962)-Reprints 4-Color #966 (title change from "Tonka" to "Comanche") (4-6/62)-Sal Mineo photo-c
4.60 13.75 55.00
1354-Calvin & the Colonel (#1) (TV) (4-6/62) 7.50 22.50 90.00
NOTE: *Missing numbers probably do not exist.*

4-D MONKEY, THE (Adventures of... #? on)
Leung's Publications: 1988 - No. 11, 1990 ($1.80/$2.00, 52 pgs.)
1-11: 1-Karate Pig, Ninja Flounder & 4-D Monkey (48 pgs., centerfold is a Christmas card). 2-4 (52pgs.) 2.00

FOUR FAVORITES (Crime Must Pay the Penalty No. 33 on)
Ace Magazines: Sept, 1941 - No. 32, Dec, 1947
1-Vulcan, Lash Lightning (formerly Flash Lightning in Sure-Fire), Magno the Magnetic Man & The Raven begin; flag-c 147.00 442.00 1400.00
2-The Black Ace only app. 55.00 165.00 525.00
3-Last Vulcan 47.00 142.00 425.00
4,5: 4-The Raven & Vulcan end; Unknown Soldier begins (see Our Flag), ends #28. 5-Captain Courageous begins (5/42), ends #28 (moves over from Captain Courageous #6); not in #6 42.00 125.00 375.00
6-8: 6-The Flag app.; Mr. Risk begins (7/42) 40.00 120.00 325.00
9-Kurtzman-a (Lash Lightning); robot-c 42.00 125.00 375.00
10-Classic Kurtzman-c/a (Magno & Davey) 49.00 147.00 440.00
11-Kurtzman-a; Hitler, Mussolini, Hirohito-c; L.B. Cole-a; Unknown Soldier by Kurtzman 53.00 158.00 475.00
12-L.B. Cole-a 34.00 103.00 275.00
13-20: 18,20-Palais-c/a 28.00 84.00 225.00
21-No Unknown Soldier; The Unknown app. 21.00 64.00 170.00
22-26: 22-Captain Courageous drops costume. 23-Unknown Soldier drops costume. 25-29-Hap Hazard app. 26-Last Magno 21.00 64.00 170.00
27-29: Hap Hazard app. in all 16.00 49.00 130.00
30-32: 30-Funny-c begin (teen humor), end #32 13.00 39.00 105.00
NOTE: ***Dave Berg** c-5. **Jim Mooney** a-6; c-1-3. **Palais** a-18-20; c-18-25. Torture chamber c-5.*

FOUR HORSEMEN, THE (See The Crusaders)

FOUR HORSEMEN
DC Comics (Vertigo): Feb, 2000 - No. 4, May, 2000 ($2.50, limited series)
1-4-Essad Ribic-c/a; Robert Rodi-s 2.50

FOUR HORSEMEN OF THE APOCALYPSE, THE (Movie)
Dell Publishing Co.: No. 1250, Jan-Mar, 1962 (one-shot)
Four Color 1250-Photo-c 6.40 19.00 70.00

4MOST (Foremost Boys No. 32-40; becomes Thrilling Crime Cases #41 on)
Novelty Publications/Star Publications No. 37-on:
Winter, 1941-42 - V8#5(#36), 9-10/49; #37, 11-12/49 - #40, 4-5/50
V1#1-The Target by Sid Greene, The Cadet & Dick Cole begin with origins retold; produced by Funnies Inc.; quarterly issues begin, end V6#3
126.00 379.00 1200.00
2-Last Target (Spr/42) 50.00 150.00 450.00
3-Dan'l Flannel begins; flag-c 40.00 120.00 360.00
4-1pg. Dr. Seuss (signed) (Aut/42) 38.00 113.00 300.00
V2#1-3 14.00 41.00 110.00
4-Hitler, Tojo & Mussolini app. as pumpkins on-c 22.00 66.00 175.00
V3#1-4 12.00 36.00 95.00
V4#1-4: 2-Walter Johnson-c 10.00 30.00 70.00
V5#1-4: 1-The Target & Targeteers app. 9.30 28.00 65.00
V6#1-4 8.65 26.00 60.00
5-L. B. Cole-c 19.00 56.00 150.00
V7#1,3,5, V8#1, 37 8.65 26.00 60.00
2,4,6-L. B. Cole-c. 6-Last Dick Cole 19.00 56.00 150.00
V8#2,3,5-L. B. Cole-c/a 22.00 66.00 175.00
4-L. B. Cole-a 13.00 39.00 105.00
38-40: 38-Johnny Weismuller (Tarzan) life story & Jim Braddock (boxer) life story. 38-40-L.B. Cole-c. 40-Last White Rider 16.00 49.00 130.00
Accepted Reprint 38-40 (nd): 40-r/Johnny Weismuller life story; all have L.B. Cole-c 9.30 28.00 65.00

FOUR-STAR BATTLE TALES
National Periodical Publications: Feb-Mar, 1973 - No. 5, Nov-Dec, 1973
1-reprints begin 2.50 7.50 25.00
2-5 1.75 5.25 14.00
NOTE: ***Drucker** r-1, 3-5. **Heath** r-2, 5; c-1. **Krigstein** r-5. **Kubert** r-4; c-2.*

FOUR STAR SPECTACULAR
National Periodical Publications: Mar-Apr, 1976 - No. 6, Jan-Feb, 1977
1 1.25 3.75 10.00
2-6: Reprints in all. 2-Infinity cover 2.40 6.00
NOTE: *All contain DC Superhero reprints. #1 has 68 pgs.; #2-6, 52 pgs.. #1, 4-Hawkman app.; #2-Kid Flash app.; #3-Green Lantern app; #2, 4, 5-Wonder Woman, Superboy app; #5-Green Arrow, Vigilante app; #6-Blackhawk G.A.-r.*

FOUR TEENERS (Formerly Crime Must Pay The Penalty; Dotty No. 35 on)
A. A. Wyn: No. 34, April, 1948 (52 pgs.)
34-Teen-age comic; Dotty app.; Curly & Jerry continue from Four Favorites
5.00 15.00 35.00

FOURTH WORLD GALLERY, THE (Jack Kirby's...)
DC Comics: 1996 (9/96) ($3.50, one-shot)
nn-Pin-ups of Jack Kirby's Fourth World characters (New Gods, Forever People & Mister Miracle) by John Byrne, Rick Burchett, Dan Jurgens, Walt Simonson & others 3.50

FOX AND THE CROW (Stanley & His Monster No. 109 on) (See Comic Cavalcade & Real Screen Comics)
National Periodical Publications: Dec-Jan, 1951-52 - No. 108, Feb-Mar, 1968
1 103.00 309.00 975.00
2(Scarce) 49.00 147.00 440.00
3-5 34.00 103.00 275.00
6-10 24.00 73.00 195.00
11-20 18.00 53.00 140.00
21-30: 22-Last precode issue (2/55) 12.00 36.00 95.00
31-40 10.00 30.00 75.00
41-60 5.90 17.75 65.00
61-80 3.65 11.00 40.00
81-94: 94-(11/65)-The Brat Finks begin 2.80 8.40 28.00
95-Stanley & His Monster begins (origin & 1st app) 3.80 11.40 42.00
96-99,101-108 2.00 6.00 18.00
100 (10-11/66) 2.50 7.50 24.00
NOTE: *Many covers by **Mort Drucker.***

FOX AND THE HOUND, THE (Disney)(Movie)
Whitman Publishing Co.: Aug, 1981 - No. 3, Oct, 1981
11292(#1),2,3-Based on animated movie 2.40 6.00

FOXFIRE (See The Phoenix Resurrection)
Malibu Comics (Ultraverse): Feb, 1996 - No. 4, May, 1996 ($1.50)
1-4: Sludge, Ultraforce app. 4-Punisher app. 2.00

FOX GIANTS (Also see Giant Comics Edition)
Fox Features Syndicate: 1944 - 1950 (25¢, 132 - 196 pgs.)
Album of Crime nn(1949, 132p) 42.00 125.00 375.00
Album of Love nn(1949, 132p) 40.00 120.00 320.00
All Famous Crime Stories nn('49, 132p) 42.00 125.00 375.00
All Good Comics 1(1944, 132p)(R.W. Voigt)-The Bouncer, Purple Tigress, Rick

Take A Serious Look At A New World Of Comics.

For many years, Jay Parrino's The Mint has been a driving force in the world of coins, known as the home of the rarest, the finest, the best. Now we're shaking up the world of collectible comics.

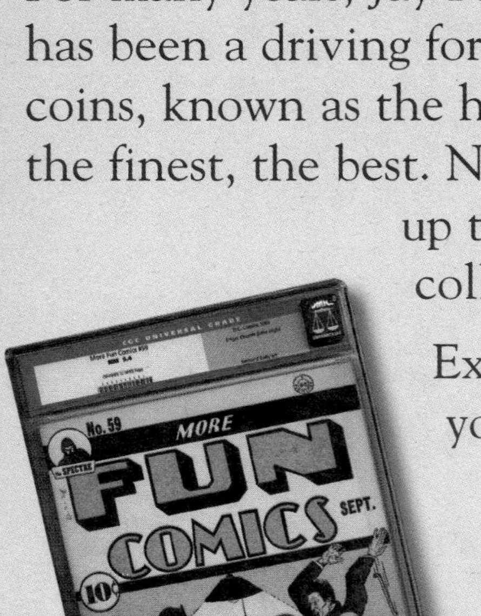

Explore possibilities you never dreamed of.

More Fun #59 CGC NM 9.4
$24,500

Included in these pages are a few items from our current inventory. Typical examples of the quality and rarity clients have come to expect from Jay Parrino's The Mint. Make collecting both FUN and rewarding.

Amazing Fantasy #15 CGC FN/VF 7.0
$11,500

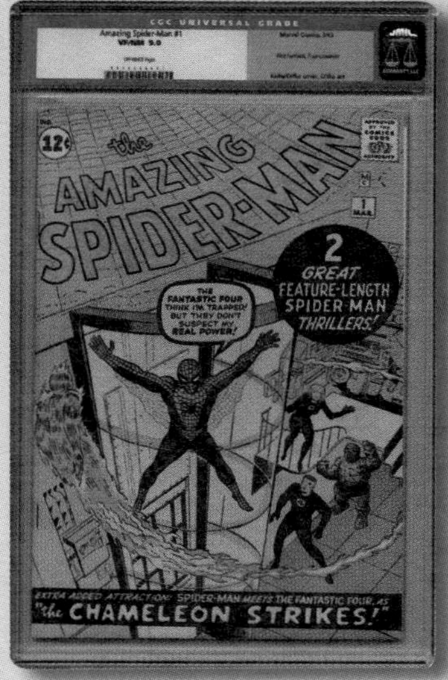

Amazing Spiderman #1 CGC VF/NM 9.0
$26,000

Batman #1 CGC VG+ 4.5
$27,500

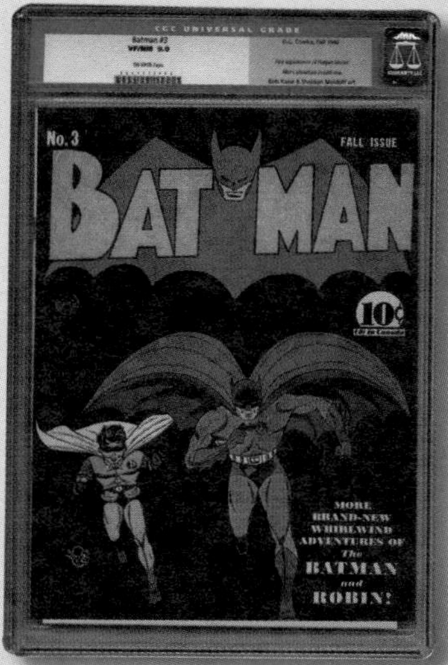

Batman #3 CGC VF/NM 9.0
$19,500

To buy any comics shown here call 1-800-280-4726
or to see our entire inventory visit www.jp-themint.com

Jay Parrino's The Mint, L.L.C.

Boy Commandos #3 CGC NM 9.4
$7,250

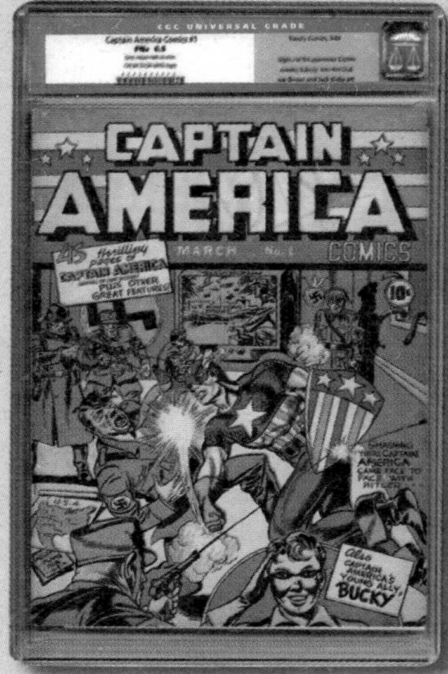

Captain America #1 CGC FN+ 6.5
$23,500

Crime Patrol #15 CGC NM+ 9.6
$7,950

Crypt of Terror #17 CGC NM+ 9.6
$10,500

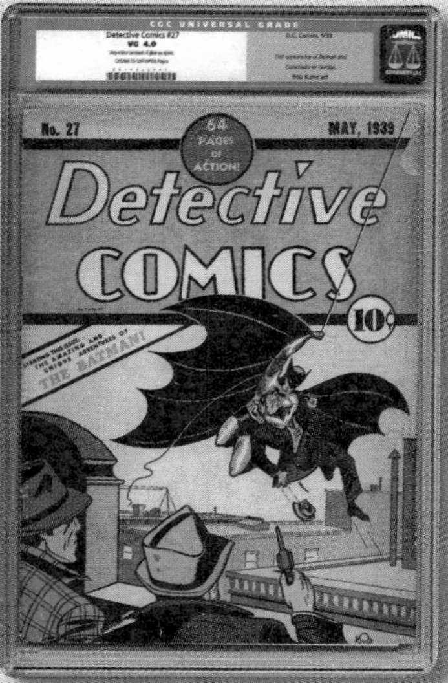

Detective #27 CGC VG 4.0
$82,500

Detective #37 CGC VF/NM 9.0
$16,500

Fantastic Four #1 CGC VF+ 8.5
$19,500

Flash #1 CGC FN-5.5
$27,500

To buy any comics shown here call 1-800-280-4726
or to see our entire inventory visit www.jp-themint.com

Jay Parrino's The Mint, L.L.C.

Funnies on Parade nn CGC FN/VF 7.0
$10,500

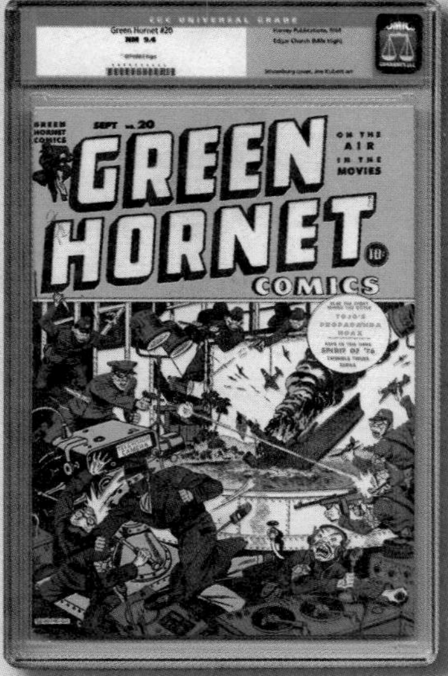

Green Hornet #20 CGC NM 9.4
$5,250

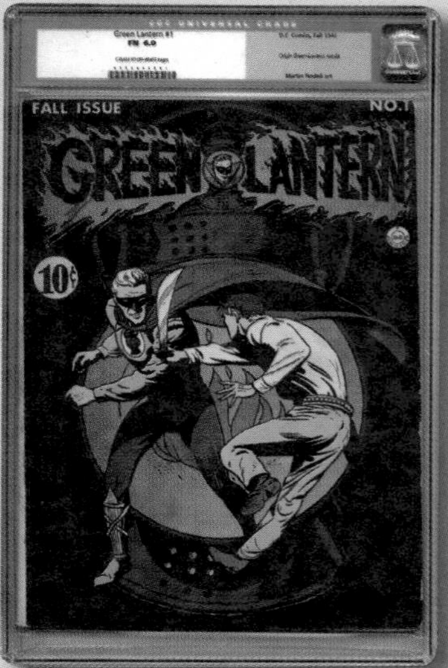

Green Lantern #1 CGC FN 6.0
$9,500

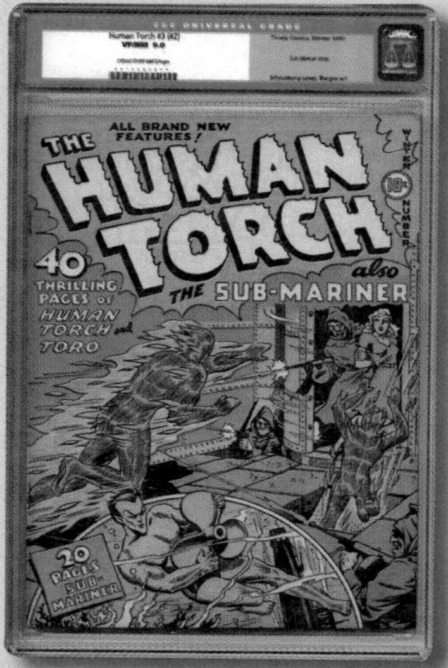

Human Torch #3(2) CGC VF/NM 9.0
$8,250

Ibis the Invincible #1 CGC NM+ 9.6
$12,000

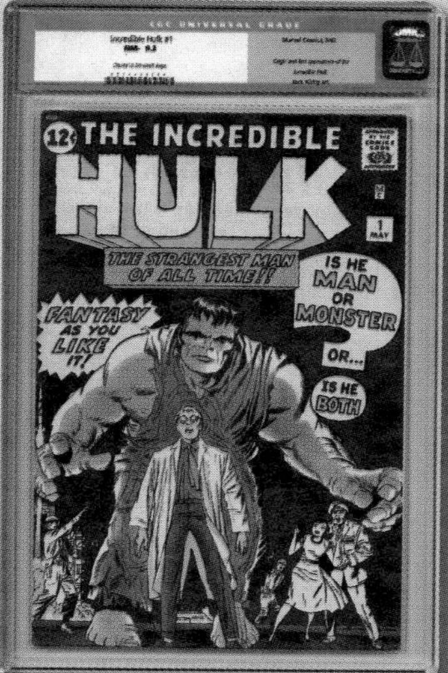

Incredible Hulk #1 CGC NM- 9.2
$24,500

Mad #1 CGC NM-9.2
$14,500

Marvel #1 CGC VG 4.0
$59,500

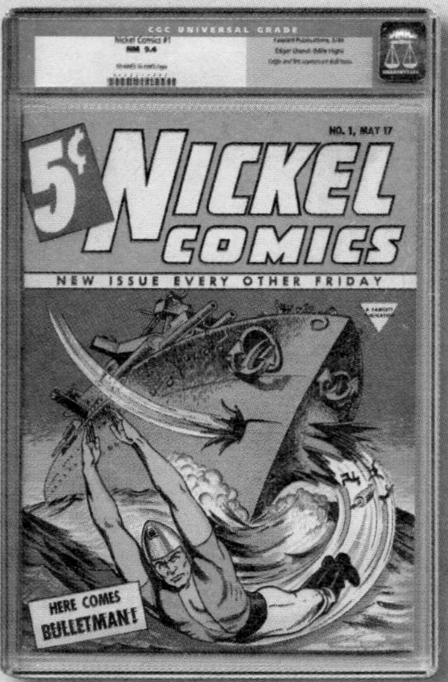

Nickel #1 CGC NM 9.4
$27,500

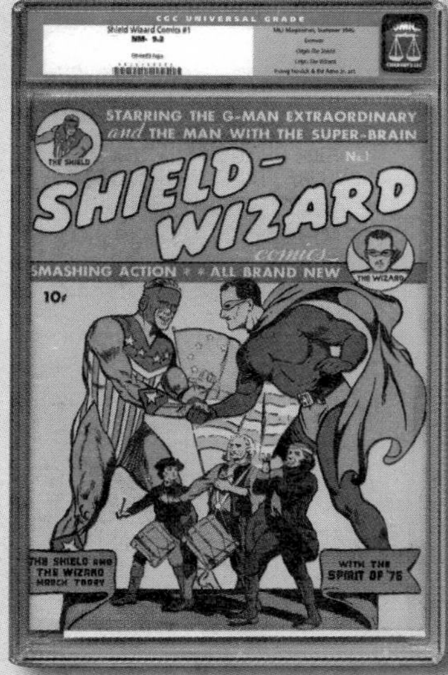

Shield Wizard #1 CGC NM- 9.2
$14,500

Showcase #4 CGC VF 8.0
$32,500

Showcase #9 CGC NM-9.2
$32,500

To buy any comics shown here call 1-800-280-4726
or to see our entire inventory visit www.jp-themint.com

Jay Parrino's The Mint, L.L.C.

Suspense #3 CGC FN/VF 7.0
$49,500

Terrific #5 CGC NM- 9.2
$19,500

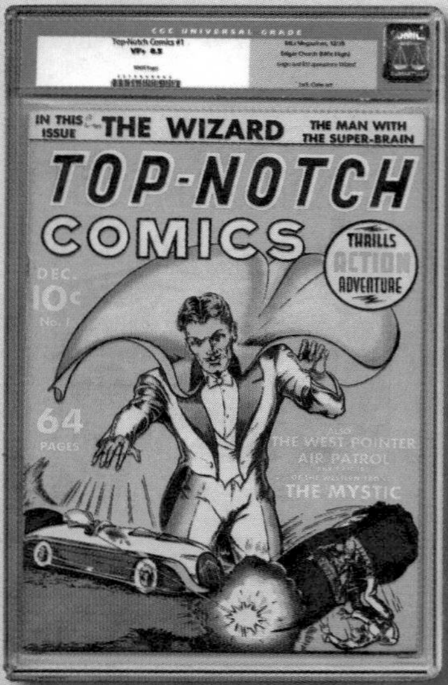

Top Notch #1 CGC VF+ 8.5
$26,500

Top Notch #9 CGC NM+ 9.6
$37,500

Fox Giant - Book of Love © FOX

Foxy Fagan Comics #6 © Dearfield

Frankenstein #13 © MAR

	GD2.0	FN6.0	NM9.4
Evans, Puppeteer, Green Mask; Infinity-c	39.00	118.00	315.00
All Great nn(1944, 132p)-Capt. Jack Terry, Rick Evans, Jaguar Man	39.00	118.00	315.00
All Great nn(Chicago Nite Life News)(1945, 132p)-Green Mask, Bouncer, Puppeteer, Rick Evans, Rocket Kelly	40.00	120.00	330.00
All-Great Confessions nn(1949, 132p)	38.00	113.00	300.00
All Great Crime Stories nn('49, 132p)	42.00	125.00	375.00
All Great Jungle Adventures nn('49, 132p)	47.00	140.00	420.00
All Real Confession Magazine 3 (3/49, 132p)	38.00	113.00	300.00
All Real Confession Magazine 4 (4/49, 132p)	38.00	113.00	300.00
All Your Comics 1(1944, 132p)-The Puppeteer, Red Robbins, & Merciless the Sorcerer	40.00	120.00	325.00
Almanac Of Crime nn(1948, 148p)-Phantom Lady	44.00	133.00	400.00
Almanac Of Crime 1(1950, 132p)	40.00	120.00	360.00
Book Of Love nn(1950, 132p)	35.00	105.00	280.00
Burning Romances 1(1949, 132p)	41.00	122.00	365.00
Crimes Incorporated nn(1950, 132p)	40.00	120.00	340.00
Daring Love Stories nn(1950, 132p)	36.00	108.00	290.00
Everybody's Comics 1(1944, 50¢, 196p)-The Green Mask, The Puppeteer, The Bouncer, Rocket Kelly, Rick Evans	42.00	125.00	375.00
Everybody's Comics 1(1946, 196p)-Green Lama, The Puppeteer	36.00	107.00	285.00
Everybody's Comics 1(1946, 196p)-Same as 1945 Ribtickler	28.00	83.00	220.00
Everybody's Comics nn(1947, 132p)-Jo-Jo, Purple Tigress, Cosmo Cat, Bronze Man	34.00	103.00	275.00
Exciting Romance Stories nn(1949, 132p)	35.00	105.00	280.00
Famous Love nn(1950, 132p)	35.00	105.00	280.00
Intimate Confessions nn(1950, 132p)	36.00	108.00	290.00
Journal Of Crime nn(1949, 132p)	42.00	125.00	375.00
Love Problems nn(1949, 132p)	38.00	113.00	300.00
Love Thrills nn(1950, 132p)	38.00	113.00	300.00
March of Crime nn('48, 132p)-Female w/rifle-c	40.00	120.00	325.00
March of Crime nn('49, 132p)-Cop w/pistol-c	40.00	120.00	325.00
March of Crime nn(1949, 132p)-Coffin & man w/machine-gun-c	40.00	120.00	325.00
Revealing Love Stories nn(1950, 132p)	36.00	108.00	290.00
Ribtickler nn(1945, 50¢, 196p)-Chicago Nite Life News; Marvel Mutt, Cosmo Cat, Flash Rabbit, The Nebbs app.	33.00	98.00	260.00
Romantic Thrills nn(1950, 132p)	35.00	105.00	280.00
Secret Love nn(1949, 132p)	35.00	105.00	280.00
Secret Love Stories nn(1949, 132p)	35.00	105.00	280.00
Strange Love nn(1950, 132p)-Photo-c	40.00	120.00	340.00
Sweetheart Scandals nn(1950, 132p)	35.00	105.00	280.00
Teen-Age Love nn(1950, 132p)	35.00	105.00	280.00
Throbbing Love nn(1950, 132p)-Photo-c; used in **POP**, pg. 107	40.00	120.00	330.00
Truth About Crime nn(1949, 132p)	42.00	125.00	375.00
Variety Comics 1(1946, 132p)-Blue Beetle, Jungle Jo	39.00	118.00	315.00
Variety Comics nn(1950, 132p)-Jungle Jo, My Secret Affair(w/Harrison/Wood-a), Crimes by Women & My Story	38.00	113.00	300.00
Western Roundup nn('50, 132p)-Hoot Gibson; Cody of the Pony Express app.	39.00	116.00	310.00

NOTE: *Each of the above usually contain four remaindered Fox books minus covers. Since these missing covers often had the first page of the first story, most Giants therefore are incomplete. Approximate values are listed. Books with appearances of Phantom Lady, Rulah, Jo-Jo, etc. could bring more.*

FOXHOLE (Becomes Never Again #8?)
Mainline/Charlton No. 5 on: 9-10/54 - No. 4, 3-4/55; No. 5, 7/55 - No. 7, 3/56

	GD2.0	FN6.0	NM9.4
1-Classic Kirby-c	42.00	125.00	375.00
2-Kirby-c/a(2); Kirby scripts based on his war time experiences	31.00	94.00	250.00
3-5-Kirby-c only	17.00	51.00	135.00
6-Kirby-c/a(2)	26.00	79.00	210.00
7	7.85	23.50	55.00
Super Reprints #10,15-17: 10-r/? 15,16-r/United States Marines #5,8. 17-r/Monty Hall #?	2.00	6.00	18.00
11,12,18-r/Foxhole #1,2,3; Kirby-c	2.50	7.50	24.00

NOTE: ***Kirby** a(r)-Super #11, 12. **Powell** a(r)-Super #15, 16. Stories by actual veterans.*

FOX KIDS FUNHOUSE (TV)
Acclaim Books: 1997 ($4.50, digest size)

1-The TIck 4.50

FOXY FAGAN COMICS (Funny Animal)
Dearfield Publishing Co.: Dec, 1946 - No. 7, Summer, 1948

	GD2.0	FN6.0	NM9.4
1-Foxy Fagan & Little Buck begin	12.00	36.00	95.00
2	7.00	21.00	48.00
3-7: 6-Rocket ship-c	5.70	17.00	40.00

FRACTURED FAIRY TALES (TV)
Gold Key: Oct, 1962 (Jay Ward)

	GD2.0	FN6.0	NM9.4
1 (10022-210)-From Bullwinkle TV show	11.00	33.00	130.00

FRAGGLE ROCK (TV)
Marvel Comics (Star Comics)/Marvel V2#1 on: Apr, 1985 - No. 8, Sept, 1986; V2#1, Apr, 1988 - No. 6, Sept, 1988

1-8 (75¢) 4.00
V2#1-6-($1.00): Reprints 1st series 2.00

FRANCIS, BROTHER OF THE UNIVERSE
Marvel Comics Group: 1980 (75¢, 52 pgs., one-shot)

nn-Buscema/Marie Severin-a; story of Francis Bernadone celebrating his 800th birthday in 1982 4.00

FRANCIS THE FAMOUS TALKING MULE (All based on movie)
Dell Publishing Co.: No. 335 (#1), June, 1951 - No. 1090, March, 1960

	GD2.0	FN6.0	NM9.4
Four Color 335 (#1)	7.50	22.50	90.00
Four Color 465	4.60	13.75	55.00
Four Color 501,547,579	4.10	12.30	45.00
Four Color 621,655,698,710,745	3.20	9.60	35.00
Four Color 810,863,906,953,991,1068,1090	3.00	9.00	30.00

FRANK
Nemesis Comics (Harvey): Apr (Mar inside), 1994 - No. 4, 1994 ($1.75/$2.50, limited series)

1-4-($2.50, direct sale): 1-Foil-c Edition 2.50
1-4-($1.75)-Newsstand Editions; Cowan-a in all 2.00

FRANK
Fantagraphics Books: Sept, 1996 ($2.95, B&W)

1-Woodring-c/a/scripts 3.00

FRANK BUCK (Formerly My True Love)
Fox Features Syndicate: No. 70, May, 1950 - No. 3, Sept, 1950

	GD2.0	FN6.0	NM9.4
70-Wood a(p)(3 stories)-Photo-c	33.00	98.00	260.00
71-Wood-a (9 pgs.); photo/painted-c	17.00	51.00	135.00
3: 3-Photo/painted-c	13.00	39.00	105.00

NOTE: *Based on "Bring 'Em Back Alive" TV show.*

FRANKENSTEIN (See Dracula, Movie Classics & Werewolf)
Dell Publishing Co.: Aug-Oct, 1964; No. 2, Sept, 1966 - No. 4, Mar, 1967

	GD2.0	FN6.0	NM9.4
1(12-283-410)(1964)	5.00	15.00	55.00
2-Intro. & origin super-hero character (9/66)	3.00	9.00	32.00
3,4	2.00	6.00	18.00

FRANKENSTEIN (The Monster of...; also see Monsters Unleashed #2, Power Record Comics, Psycho & Silver Surfer #7)
Marvel Comics Group: Jan, 1973 - No. 18, Sept, 1975

	GD2.0	FN6.0	NM9.4
1-Ploog-c/a begins, ends #6	3.65	11.00	40.00
2	2.50	7.50	25.00
3-5	2.00	6.00	18.00
6,7,10: 7-Dracula cameo	1.75	5.25	14.00
8,9-Dracula c/sty. 9-Death of Dracula	3.00	9.00	30.00
11-17	1.10	3.30	9.00
18-Wrightson-c(i)	1.50	4.50	12.00

NOTE: ***Adkins** c-17i. **Buscema** a-7-10p. **Ditko** a-12r. **G. Kane** c-15p. **Orlando** a-8r. **Ploog** a-1-3, 4p, 5p, 6; c-1-6. **Wrightson** c-18i.*

FRANKENSTEIN COMICS (Also See Prize Comics)
Prize Publ. (Crestwood/Feature): Sum, 1945 - V5#5(#33), Oct-Nov, 1954

1-Frankenstein begins by Dick Briefer (origin); Frank Sinatra parody

Frankenstein Comics #1 © PRIZE

Freckles and His Friends #11 © STD

Freedom Fighters #10 © DC

GD2.0 FN6.0 NM9.4

	GD2.0	FN6.0	NM9.4
	103.00	309.00	975.00
2	51.00	153.00	460.00
3-5	40.00	120.00	330.00
6-10: 7-S&K a(r)/Headline Comics. 8(7-8/47)-Superman satire	35.00	105.00	280.00
11-17(1-2/49)-11-Boris Karloff parody-c/story. 17-Last humor issue	30.00	90.00	240.00
18(3/52)-New origin, horror series begins	40.00	120.00	340.00
19,20(V3#4, 8-9/52)	26.00	79.00	210.00
21(V3#5), 22(V3#6), 23(V4#1) - #28(V4#6)	23.00	68.00	180.00
29(V5#1) - #33(V5#5)	23.00	68.00	180.00

NOTE: *Briefer c/a-all.* ***Meskin*** *a-21, 29.*

FRANKENSTEIN/DRACULA WAR, THE
Topps Comics: Feb, 1995 - No. 3, May, 1995 ($2.50, limited series)

1-3 — 2.50

FRANKENSTEIN, JR. (...& the Impossibles) (TV)
Gold Key: Jan, 1966 (Hanna-Barbera)

1-Super hero (scarce) — 10.00 30.00 120.00

FRANKENSTEIN: OR THE MODERN PROMETHEUS
Caliber Press: 1994 ($2.95, one-shot)

1 — 3.00

FRANK FRAZETTA FANTASY ILLUSTRATED (Magazine)
Quantum Cat Entertainment: Spring 1998 - Present ($5.95, quarterly)

1-Anthology; art by Corben, Horley, Jusko — 6.00
1-Linsner variant-c — 10.00
2-Battle Chasers by Madureira; Harris-a — 8.00
2-Madureira Battle Chasers variant-c — 12.00
3-8-Frazetta-c — 6.00
3-Tony Daniel variant-c — 15.00
5,6-Portacio variant-c, 7,8-Alex Nino variant-c — 10.00
8-Alex Ross Chicago Comicon variant-c — 10.00

FRANK FRAZETTA'S THUN'DA TALES
Fantagraphics Books: 1987 ($2.00, one-shot)

1-Frazetta-r — 3.00

FRANK FRAZETTA'S UNTAMED LOVE (Also see Untamed Love)
Fantagraphics Books: Nov, 1987 ($2.00, one-shot)

1-Frazetta-r from 1950's romance comics — 4.00

FRANKIE COMICS (...& Lana No. 13-15) (Formerly Movie Tunes; becomes Frankie Fuddle No. 16 on)
Marvel Comics (MgPC): No. 4, Wint, 1946-47 - No. 15, June, 1949

4-Mitzi, Margie, Daisy app. — 12.00 36.00 95.00
5-9 — 7.85 23.50 55.00
10-15: 13-Anti-Wertham editorial — 6.00 18.00 42.00

FRANKIE DOODLE (See Sparkler, both series)
United Features Syndicate: No. 7, 1939

Single Series 7 — 31.00 94.00 250.00

FRANKIE FUDDLE (Formerly Frankie & Lana)
Marvel Comics: No. 16, Aug, 1949 - No. 17, Nov, 1949

16,17 — 6.00 18.00 42.00

FRANK LUTHER'S SILLY PILLY COMICS (See Jingle Dingle...)
Children's Comics (Maltex Cereal): 1950 (10¢)

1-Characters from radio, records, & TV — 6.00 18.00 42.00

FRANK MERRIWELL AT YALE (Speed Demons No. 5 on?)
Charlton Comics: June, 1955 - No. 4, Jan, 1956 (Also see Shadow Comics)

1 — 5.50 16.50 38.00
2-4 — 5.00 15.00 30.00

FRANTIC (Magazine) (See Ratfink & Zany)
Pierce Publishing Co.: Oct, 1958 - V2#2, Apr, 1959 (Satire)

V1#1 — 9.30 28.00 65.00
2 — 7.15 21.50 50.00
V2#1,2: 1-Burgos-a, Severin-c/a; Powell-a? — 5.50 16.50 38.00

GD2.0 FN6.0 NM9.4

FREAK FORCE (Also see Savage Dragon)
Image Comics (Highbrow Ent.): Dec, 1993 - No. 18, July, 1995 ($1.95/$2.50)

1-18-Superpatriot & Mighty Man in all; Erik Larsen scripts in all. 4-Vanguard app. 8-Begin $2.50-c. 9-Cyberforce-c & app. 13-Variant-c — 2.50

FREAK FORCE (Also see Savage Dragon)
Image Comics: Apr, 1997 - No. 3, July, 1997 ($2.95)

1-3-Larsen-s — 3.00

FRECKLES AND HIS FRIENDS (See Crackajack Funnies, Famous Comics Cartoon Book, Honeybee Birdwhistle... & Red Ryder)

FRECKLES AND HIS FRIENDS
Standard Comics/Argo: No. 5, 11/47 - No. 12, 8/49; 11/55 - No. 4, 6/56

5-Reprints — 7.15 21.50 50.00
6-12-Reprints. 7-9-Airbrush-c (by Schomburg?). 11-Lingerie panels — 5.00 15.00 30.00

NOTE: *Some copies of No. 8 & 9 contain a printing oddity. The negatives were elongated in the engraving process, probably to conform to page dimensions on the filler pages. Those pages only look normal when viewed at a 45 degree angle.*

1(Argo,'55)-Reprints (NEA Service) — 5.00 15.00 32.00
2-4 — 4.00 12.00 24.00

FREDDY (Formerly My Little Margie's Boy Friends) (Also see Blue Bird)
Charlton Comics: V2#12, June, 1958 - No. 47, Feb, 1965

V2#12 — 3.00 9.00 30.00
13-15 — 2.30 7.00 20.00
16-47 — 1.75 5.25 14.00

FREDDY
Dell Publishing Co.: May-July, 1963 - No. 3, Oct-Dec, 1964

1 — 2.50 7.50 25.00
2,3 — 2.00 6.00 16.00

FREDDY KRUEGER'S A NIGHTMARE ON ELM STREET
Marvel Comics: Oct, 1989 - No. 2, Dec, 1989 ($2.25, B&W, movie adaptation)

1,2: Origin Freddy Krueger; Buckler/Alcala-a — 3.00

FREDDY'S DEAD: THE FINAL NIGHTMARE
Innovation Publishing: Oct, 1991 - No. 3, Dec 1991 ($2.50, color mini-series, adapts movie)

1-3: Dismukes (film poster artist) painted-c — 3.00

FRED HEMBECK DESTROYS THE MARVEL UNIVERSE
Marvel Comics: July, 1989 ($1.50, one-shot)

1-Punisher app.; Staton-i (5 pgs.) — 2.50

FRED HEMBECK SELLS THE MARVEL UNIVERSE
Marvel Comics: Oct, 1990 ($1.25, one-shot)

1-Punisher, Wolverine parodies; Hembeck/Austin-c — 2.50

FREEDOM AGENT (Also see John Steele)
Gold Key: Apr, 1963 (12¢)

1 (10054-304)-Painted-c — 3.20 9.60 35.00

FREEDOM FIGHTERS (See Justice League of America #107,108)
National Periodical Publ./DC Comics: Mar-Apr, 1976 - No. 15, July-Aug, 1978

1-Uncle Sam, The Ray, Black Condor, Doll Man, Human Bomb, & Phantom Lady begin (all former Quality characters) — 1.50 4.50 12.00
2-9: 4,5-Wonder Woman x-over. 7-1st app. Crusaders — 1.00 3.00 8.00
10-15: 10-Origin Doll Man; Cat-Man-c/story (4th app; 1st revival since Det. #325). 11-Origin The Ray. 12-Origin Firebrand. 13-Origin Black Condor. 14-Batgirl & Batwoman app. 15-Batgirl & Batwoman app.; origin Phantom Lady — 1.00 3.00 8.00

NOTE: ***Buckler*** *c-5-11p, 13p, 14p.*

FREE SPEECHES
Oni Press: Aug, 1998 ($2.95, one-shot)

1-Speeches against comic censorship; Frank Miller-c — 3.00

FREEX
Malibu Comics (Ultraverse): July, 1993 - No. 18, Mar, 1995 ($1.95)

1-3,5-14,16-18: 1-Polybagged w/trading card. 2-Some were polybagged w/card. 6-Nightman-c/story. 7-2 pg. origin Hardcase by Zeck. 17-Rune app.

The Friendly Ghost, Casper #3 © HARV

Frisky Fables V3 #6 © STAR

Frogman Comics #5 © HILL

	GD2.0	FN6.0	NM9.4
			2.00
1-Holographic-c edition		2.40	6.00
1-Ultra 5,000 limited silver ink-c			3.00
4-($2.50, 48 pgs.)-Rune flip-c/story by B. Smith (3 pgs.); 3 pg. Night Man preview			2.50
15 ($3.50)-w/Ultraverse Premiere #9 flip book; Alec Swan & Rafferty app.			3.50
Giant Size 1 (1994, $2.50)-Prime app.			2.50

NOTE: *Simonson c-1.*

FRENZY (Magazine) (Satire)
Picture Magazine: Apr, 1958 - No. 6, Mar, 1959

	GD2.0	FN6.0	NM9.4
1	9.30	28.00	65.00
2-6	6.00	18.00	42.00

FRIDAY FOSTER
Dell Publishing Co.: October, 1972

	GD2.0	FN6.0	NM9.4
1	2.80	8.40	28.00

FRIENDLY GHOST, CASPER, THE (Becomes Casper... #254 on)
Harvey Publications: Aug, 1958 - No. 224, Oct, 1982; No. 225, Oct, 1986 - No. 253, June, 1990

	GD2.0	FN6.0	NM9.4
1-Infinity-c	27.50	82.00	300.00
2	12.75	38.00	140.00
3-10: 6-X-Mas-c	6.35	19.00	70.00
11-20: 18-X-Mas-c	4.10	12.30	45.00
21-30	3.00	9.00	30.00
31-50	2.40	7.35	22.00
51-70,100: 54-X-Mas-c	2.00	6.00	18.00
71-99	2.00	6.00	16.00
101-131: 131-Last 12¢ issue	1.75	5.25	14.00
132-159	1.50	4.50	12.00
160-163: All 52 pg. Giants	2.00	6.00	18.00
164-199: 173,179,185-Cub Scout Specials	1.00	3.00	8.00
200	1.10	3.30	9.00
201-224		2.40	6.00
225-237: 230-X-mas-c. 232-Valentine's-c			5.00
238-253: 238-Begin $1.00-c. 238,244-Halloween-c. 243-Last new material			3.00

FRIENDS OF MAXX (Also see Maxx)
Image Comics (I Before E): Apr, 1996 ($2.95)

	GD2.0	FN6.0	NM9.4
1-Featuring Dude Japan; Sam Kieth-c/a/scripts			3.00

FRIGHT
Atlas/Seaboard Periodicals: June, 1975 (Aug on inside)

	GD2.0	FN6.0	NM9.4
1-Origin/1st app. The Son of Dracula; Frank Thorne-c/a			5.00

FRIGHT NIGHT
Now Comics: Oct, 1988 - No. 22, 1990 ($1.75)

	GD2.0	FN6.0	NM9.4
1-22: 1,2 Adapts movie. 8, 9-Evil Ed horror photo-c from movie			2.00

FRIGHT NIGHT II
Now Comics: 1989 ($3.95, 52 pgs.)

	GD2.0	FN6.0	NM9.4
1-Adapts movie sequel			4.00

FRISKY ANIMALS (Formerly Frisky Fables; Super Cat #56 on)
Star Publications: No. 44, Jan, 1951 - No. 55, Sept, 1953

	GD2.0	FN6.0	NM9.4
44-Super Cat; L.B. Cole	23.00	68.00	180.00
45-Classic L. B. Cole-c	33.00	99.00	265.00
46-51,53-55: Super Cat. 54-Super Cat-c begin	21.00	62.00	165.00
52-L. B. Cole-c/a, 3 1/2 pgs.; X-Mas-c	23.00	68.00	180.00

NOTE: *All have* ***L. B. Cole****-c. No. 47-No Super Cat.* ***Disbrow*** *a-49, 52.* ***Fago*** *a-51.*

FRISKY ANIMALS ON PARADE (Formerly Parade Comics; becomes Superspook)
Ajax-Farrell Publ. (Four Star Comic Corp.): Sept, 1957 - No. 3, Dec-Jan, 1957-1958

	GD2.0	FN6.0	NM9.4
1-L. B. Cole-c	19.00	58.00	155.00
2-No L. B. Cole-c	8.65	26.00	60.00
3-L. B. Cole-c	16.00	49.00	130.00

FRISKY FABLES (Frisky Animals No. 44 on)
Premium Group/Novelty Publ./Star Publ. V5#4 on: Spring, 1945 - No. 43, Oct, 1950

	GD2.0	FN6.0	NM9.4
V1#1-Funny animal; Al Fago-c/a #1-38	20.00	60.00	160.00
2,3(Fall & Winter, 1945)	10.00	30.00	75.00
V2#1(#4, 4/46) - 9,11,12(#15, 3/47): 4-Flag-c	7.85	23.50	55.00
10-Christmas-c	8.65	26.00	60.00
V3#1(#16, 4/47) - 12(#27, 3/48): 4-Flag-c. 7,9-Infinity-c. 10-X-Mas-c	6.40	19.25	45.00
V4#1(#28, 4/48) - 7(#34, 2-3/49)	6.40	19.25	45.00
V5#1(#35, 4-5/49) - 4(#38, 10-11/49)	6.40	19.25	45.00
39-43-L. B. Cole-c; 40-Xmas-c	22.00	66.00	175.00
Accepted Reprint No. 43 (nd); L.B. Cole-c	8.65	26.00	60.00

FRITZI RITZ (See Comics On Parade, Single Series #5, 1(reprint), Tip Top & United Comics)

FRITZI RITZ (United Comics No. 8-26)
United Features Synd./St. John No. 37?-55/Dell No. 56 on: Fall, 1948; No. 3, 1949 - No. 7, 1949; No. 27, 3-4/53 - No. 36, 9-10/54; No. 42, 1/55; No. 43, 6/56 - No. 55, 9-11/57; No. 56, 12-2/57-58 - No. 59, 9-11/58

	GD2.0	FN6.0	NM9.4
nn(1948)-Special Fall issue; by Ernie Bushmiller	14.00	43.00	115.00
3(#1)	8.65	26.00	60.00
4-7(1949): 6-Abbie & Slats app.	7.00	21.00	48.00
27-29(1953): 29-Five pg. Abbie & Slats; 1 pg. Mamie by Russell Patterson	5.00	15.00	35.00
30,32-59 (37-41 exist?): 36-1 pg. Mamie by Patterson	5.00	15.00	32.00
31-Peanuts by Schulz (1st app.?, 11-12/53)	5.00	15.00	35.00

NOTE: *Abbie & Slats in #6,7, 27-31. Li'l Abner in #33, 35, 36. Peanuts in #31, 43, 58, 59.*

FROGMAN COMICS
Hillman Periodicals: Jan-Feb, 1952 - No. 11, May, 1953

	GD2.0	FN6.0	NM9.4
1	12.50	37.50	100.00
2	7.85	23.50	55.00
3,4,6-11: 4-Meskin-a	6.00	18.00	42.00
5-Krigstein-a	7.15	21.50	50.00

FROGMEN, THE
Dell Publishing Co.: No. 1258, Feb-Apr, 1962 - No. 11, Nov-Jan, 1964-65 (Painted-c)

	GD2.0	FN6.0	NM9.4
Four Color 1258(#1)-Evans-a	6.70	20.00	80.00
2,3-Evans-a; part Frazetta inks in #2,3	5.00	15.00	60.00
4,6-11	3.00	9.00	30.00
5-Toth-a	3.65	11.00	40.00

FROM BEYOND THE UNKNOWN
National Periodical Publications: 10-11/69 - No. 25, 11-12/73

	GD2.0	FN6.0	NM9.4
1	4.10	12.30	45.00
2-6	2.30	7.00	20.00
7-11: (64 pgs.) 7-Intro Col. Glenn Merrit	2.50	7.50	25.00
12-17: (52 pgs.) 13-Wood-a(i)(r). 17-Pres. Nixon-c	2.30	7.00	20.00
18-25: Star Rovers-r begin #18,19. Space Museum in #23-25	1.75	5.25	14.00

NOTE: ***N. Adams*** *c-3, 6, 8, 9.* ***Anderson*** *c-2, 4, 5, 10, 11i, 15-17, 22; reprints-3, 4, 6-8, 10, 11, 13-16, 24, 25.* ***Infantino*** *r-1-5, 7-19, 23-25; c-11p.* ***Kaluta*** *c-18, 19.* ***Gil Kane*** *a-9r.* ***Kubert*** *c-1, 7, 12-14.* ***Toth*** *a-2r.* ***Wood*** *a-13i. Photo c-22.*

FROM DUSK TILL DAWN (Movie)
Big Entertainment: 1996 ($4.95, one-shot)

	GD2.0	FN6.0	NM9.4
nn-Adaptation of the film; Brereton-c			5.00
nn-($9.95)Deluxe Ed. w/ new material			10.00

FROM HERE TO INSANITY (Satire) (Formerly Eh! #1-7)
(See Frantic & Frenzy)
Charlton Comics: No. 8, Feb, 1955 - V3#1, 1956

	GD2.0	FN6.0	NM9.4
8	16.00	49.00	130.00
9	14.00	41.00	110.00
10-Ditko-c/a (3 pgs.)	23.00	68.00	180.00
11,12-All Kirby except 4 pgs.	31.00	94.00	250.00
V3#1(1956)-Ward-c/a(2) (signed McCartney); 5 pgs. Wolverton-a; 3 pgs. Ditko-a; magazine format (cover says "Crazy, Man, Crazy" and becomes Crazy, Man, Crazy with V2#2)	40.00	120.00	340.00

FROM THE PIT
Fantagor Press: 1994 ($4.95, one-shot, mature)

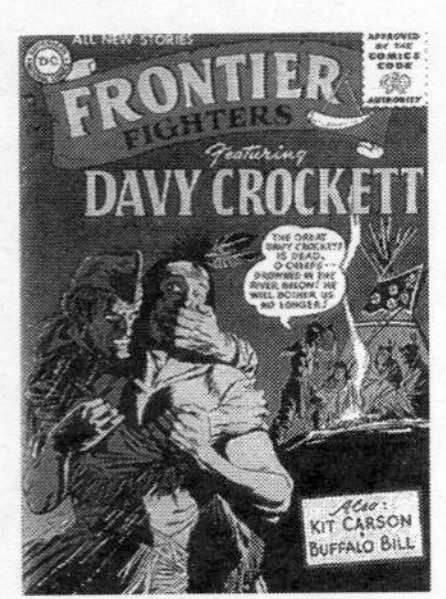

Frontier Fighters #4 © DC

F-Troop #7 © WB

Fun Comics #12 © STAR

GD2.0 FN6.0 NM9.4

1-R. Corben-a; HP Lovecraft back-up story 5.00

FRONTIER DOCTOR (TV)
Dell Publishing Co.: No. 877, Feb, 1958 (one-shot)

Four Color 877-Toth-a, Rex Allen photo-c 9.00 27.00 100.00

FRONTIER FIGHTERS
National Periodical Publications: Sept-Oct, 1955 - No. 8, Nov-Dec, 1956

1-Davy Crockett, Buffalo Bill (by Kubert), Kit Carson begin (Scarce) 58.00 174.00 550.00
2 40.00 120.00 360.00
3-8 40.00 120.00 320.00
NOTE: *Buffalo Bill by* ***Kubert*** *in all.*

FRONTIER ROMANCES
Avon Periodicals/I. W.: Nov-Dec, 1949 - No. 2, Feb-Mar, 1950 (Painted-c)

1-Used in **SOTI**, pg. 180(General reference) & illo. "Erotic spanking in a western comic book" 47.00 140.00 420.00
2 (Scarce)-Woodish-a by Stallman 38.00 113.00 300.00
I.W. Reprint #1-Reprints Avon's #1 3.65 11.00 40.00
I.W. Reprint #9-Reprints ? 2.50 7.50 25.00

FRONTIER SCOUT: DAN'L BOONE (Formerly Death Valley; The Masked Raider No. 14 on)
Charlton Comics: No. 10, Jan, 1956 - No. 13, Aug, 1956; V2#14, Mar, 1965

10 10.00 30.00 70.00
11-13(1956) 5.50 16.50 38.00
V2#14(3/65) 4.00 12.00 24.00

FRONTIER TRAIL (The Rider No. 1-5)
Ajax/Farrell Publ.: No. 6, May, 1958

6 5.00 15.00 32.00

FRONTIER WESTERN
Atlas Comics (PrPI): Feb, 1956 - No. 10, Aug, 1957

1 19.00 56.00 150.00
2,3,6-Williamson-a, 4 pgs. each 13.00 39.00 105.00
4,7,9,10: 10-Check-a 8.65 26.00 60.00
5-Crandall, Baker, Davis-a; Williamson text illos 12.00 36.00 95.00
8-Crandall, Morrow, & Wildey-a 8.65 26.00 60.00
NOTE: ***Baker*** *a-9.* ***Colan*** *a-2, 6.* ***Drucker*** *a-3, 4.* ***Heath*** *c-5.* ***Maneely*** *c/a-2, 7, 9.* ***Maurera*** *a-2.* ***Romita*** *a-7.* ***Severin*** *c-6, 8, 10.* ***Tuska*** *a-2.* ***Wildey*** *a-5, 8. Ringo Kid in No. 4.*

FRONTLINE COMBAT
E. C. Comics: July-Aug, 1951 - No. 15, Jan, 1954

1-Severin/Kurtzman-a 55.00 165.00 600.00
2 34.00 102.00 375.00
3 25.00 75.00 275.00
4-Used in **SOTI**, pg. 257; contains "Airburst" by Kurtzman which is his personal all-time favorite story 23.00 70.00 255.00
5 20.00 60.00 220.00
6-10 16.00 48.00 175.00
11-15 11.50 34.00 125.00
NOTE: ***Davis*** *a-in all; c-11, 12.* ***Evans*** *a-10-15.* ***Heath*** *a-1.* ***Kubert*** *a-14.* ***Kurtzman*** *a-1-5; c-1-9.* ***Severin*** *a-5-7, 9, 13, 15.* ***Severin/Elder*** *a-2-11; c-10.* ***Toth*** *a-8, 12.* ***Wood*** *a-1-4, 6-10, 12-15; c-13-15. Special issues: No. 7 (Iwo Jima), No. 9 (Civil War), No. 12 (Air Force).*
(Canadian reprints known; see Table of Contents.)

FRONTLINE COMBAT
Russ Cochran/Gemstone Publishing: Aug, 1995 - No. 14 ($2.00/$2.50)

1-14-E.C. reprints in all 2.50

FRONT PAGE COMIC BOOK
Front Page Comics (Harvey): 1945

1-Kubert-a; intro. & 1st app. Man in Black by Powell; Fuje-c 40.00 120.00 320.00

FROST AND FIRE (See DC Science Fiction Graphic Novel)

FROSTY THE SNOWMAN
Dell Publishing Co.: No. 359, Nov, 1951 - No. 1272, Dec-Feb?/1961-62

Four Color 359 (#1) 8.00 24.00 95.00
Four Color 435,514,601,661 4.10 12.30 45.00
Four Color 748,861,950,1065,1153,1272 3.65 11.00 40.00

GD2.0 FN6.0 NM9.4

FRUITMAN SPECIAL
Harvey Publications: Dec, 1969 (68 pgs.)

1-Funny super hero 2.80 8.40 28.00

F-TROOP (TV)
Dell Publishing Co.: Aug, 1966 - No. 7, Aug, 1967 (All have photo-c)

1 8.35 25.00 100.00
2-7 5.00 15.00 60.00

FUGITIVES FROM JUSTICE
St. John Publishing Co.: Feb, 1952 - No. 5, Oct, 1952

1 21.00 62.00 165.00
2-Matt Baker-r/Northwest Mounties #2; Vic Flint strip reprints begin 21.00 62.00 165.00
3-Reprints panel from Authentic Police Cases that was used in **SOTI** with changes; Tuska-a 20.00 60.00 160.00
4 10.00 30.00 70.00
5-Last Vic Flint-r; bondage-c 11.00 33.00 90.00

FUGITOID
Mirage Studios: 1985 (B&W, magazine size, one-shot)

1-Ties into Teenage Mutant Ninja Turtles #5 4.00

FULL COLOR COMICS
Fox Features Syndicate: 1946

nn 12.00 36.00 95.00

FULL METAL FICTION
London Night Studios: Mar, 1997 - Present ($3.95, B&W, mature)

1-8-Anthology: 1-Razor 4.00

FULL OF FUN
Red Top (Decker Publ.)(Farrell)/I. W. Enterprises: Aug, 1957 - No. 2, Nov, 1957; 1964

1(1957)-Funny animal; Dave Berg-a 6.40 19.25 45.00
2-Reprints Bingo, the Monkey Doodle Boy 4.65 14.00 28.00
8-I.W. Reprint('64) 1.75 5.25 14.00

FUN AT CHRISTMAS (See March of Comics No. 138)

FUN CLUB COMICS (See Interstate Theatres...)

FUN COMICS (Formerly Holiday Comics #1-8; Mighty Bear #13 on)
Star Publications: No. 9, Jan, 1953 - No. 12, Oct, 1953

9-(25¢ Giant)-L. B. Cole X-Mas-c; X-Mas issue 22.00 66.00 175.00
10-12-L. B. Cole-c. 12-Mighty Bear-c/story 19.00 56.00 150.00

FUNDAY FUNNIES (See Famous TV..., and Harvey Hits No. 35,40)

FUN-IN (TV)(Hanna-Barbera)
Gold Key: Feb, 1970 - No. 10, Jan, 1972; No. 11, 4/74 - No. 15, 12/74

1-Dastardly & Muttley in Their Flying Machines; Perils of Penelope Pitstop in #1-4; It's the Wolf in all 5.35 16.00 65.00
2-4,6-Cattanooga Cats in 2-4 3.00 9.00 32.00
5,7-Motormouse & Autocat, Dastardly & Muttley in both; It's the Wolf in #7 3.20 9.60 35.00
8,10-The Harlem Globetrotters, Dastardly & Muttley in #10 3.00 9.00 30.00
9-Where's Huddles?, Dastardly & Muttley, Motormouse & Autocat app. 3.20 9.60 35.00
11-Butch Cassidy 2.80 8.40 28.00
12-15: 12,15-Speed Buggy. 13-Hair Bear Bunch. 14-Inch High Private Eye 2.50 7.50 24.00

FUNKY PHANTOM, THE (TV)
Gold Key: Mar, 1972 - No. 13, Mar, 1975 (Hanna-Barbera)

1 4.55 13.65 50.00
2-5 2.50 7.50 25.00
6-13 2.00 6.00 18.00

FUNLAND
Ziff-Davis (Approved Comics): No date (1940s) (25¢)

nn-Contains games, puzzles, cut-outs, etc. 16.00 49.00 130.00

FUNLAND COMICS

The Funnies #2 © DELL

Funny Folks #10 © DC

Funny Pages V2 #12 © CEN

GD2.0 FN6.0 NM9.4

Croyden Publishers: 1945
1-Funny animal 15.00 45.00 120.00

FUNNIES, THE (New Funnies No. 65 on)
Dell Publishing Co.: Oct, 1936 - No. 64, May, 1942
1-Tailspin Tommy, Mutt & Jeff, Alley Oop (1st app?), Capt. Easy (1st app.), Don Dixon begin 350.00 1050.00 2800.00
2 (11/36)-Scribbly by Mayer begins (see Poplar #6 for 1st app.) 156.00 468.00 1250.00
3 113.00 338.00 900.00
4,5: 4(1/37)-Christmas-c 88.00 263.00 700.00
6-10 66.00 197.00 525.00
11-20: 16-Christmas-c 59.00 176.00 470.00
21-29: 25-Crime Busters by McWilliams(4pgs.) 45.00 135.00 360.00
30-John Carter of Mars (origin/1st app.) begins by Edgar Rice Burroughs; Warner Bros.' Bosko-c (4/39) 121.00 363.00 1150.00
31-44: 33-John Coleman Burroughs art begins on John Carter. 34-Last funny-c. 35-(9/39)-Mr. District Attorney begins; based on radio show 74.00 221.00 700.00
45-Origin/1st app. Phantasmo, the Master of the World (Dell's 1st super-hero, 7/40) & his sidekick Whizzer McGee 79.00 237.00 750.00
46-50: 46-The Black Knight begins, ends #62 50.00 150.00 450.00
51-56-Last ERB John Carter of Mars 44.00 133.00 400.00
57-Intro. & origin Captain Midnight (7/41) 263.00 790.00 2500.00
58-60: 58-Captain Midnight-c begin, end #63 87.00 261.00 825.00
61-Andy Panda begins by Walter Lantz 63.00 189.00 600.00
62,63: 63-Last Captain Midnight-c; bondage-c 63.00 189.00 600.00
64-Format change; Oswald the Rabbit, Felix the Cat, Li'l Eight Ball app.; origin & 1st app. Woody Woodpecker in Oswald; last Capt. Midnight; Oswald, Andy Panda, Li'l Eight Ball-c 111.00 332.00 1050.00
NOTE: ***Mayer** c-26, 48. **McWilliams** art in many issues on "Rex King of the Deep". Alley Oop c-17, 20. Captain Midnight c-57(i/2), 58-63. John Carter c-35-37, 40. Phantasmo c-45-56, 57(1/2), 58-61(part). Rex King c-38, 39, 42. Tailspin Tommy c-41.*

FUNNIES ANNUAL, THE
Avon Periodicals: 1959 ($1.00, approx. 7x10", B&W; tabloid-size)
1-(Rare)-Features the best newspaper comic strips of the year: Archie, Snuffy Smith, Beetle Bailey, Henry, Blondie, Steve Canyon, Buz Sawyer, The Little King, Hi & Lois, Popeye, & others. Also has a chronological history of the comics from 2000 B.C. to 1959. 42.00 125.00 375.00

FUNNY ANIMALS (See Fawcett's Funny Animals)
Charlton Comics: Sept, 1984 - No. 2, Nov, 1984
1,2-Atomic Mouse-r 4.00

FUNNYBONE (... The Laugh-Book of Comical Comics)
La Salle Publishing Co.: 1944 (25¢, 132 pgs.)
nn 28.00 83.00 220.00

FUNNY BOOK (...Magazine for Young Folks) (Hocus Pocus No. 9)
Parents' Magazine Press (Funny Book Publishing Corp.):
Dec, 1942 - No. 9, Aug-Sept, 1946 (Comics, stories, puzzles, games)
1-Funny animal; Alice In Wonderland app. 14.00 41.00 110.00
2-Gulliver in Giant-Land 8.65 26.00 60.00
3-9: 4-Advs. of Robin Hood. 9-Hocus-Pocus strip 6.00 18.00 42.00

FUNNY COMICS
Modern Store Publ.: 1955 (7¢, 5x7", 36 pgs.)
1-Funny animal 3.00 9.00 30.00

FUNNY COMIC TUNES (See Funny Tunes)

FUNNY FABLES
Decker Publications (Red Top Comics): Aug, 1957 - V2#2, Nov, 1957
V1#1 5.00 15.00 35.00
V1#2,V2#1,2: V1#2 (11/57)-Reissue of V1#1 4.00 11.00 22.00

FUNNY FILMS (Features funny animal characters from films)
American Comics Group(Michel Publ./Titan Publ.): Sept-Oct, 1949 - No. 29, May-June, 1954 (No. 1-4: 52 pgs.)
1-Puss An' Boots, Blunderbunny begin 19.00 56.00 150.00
2 10.00 30.00 75.00
3-10: 3-X-Mas-c 7.15 21.50 50.00
11-20 5.00 15.00 35.00
21-29 4.15 12.50 25.00

FUNNY FOLKS (Hollywood... on cover only No. 16-26; becomes Hollywood Funny Folks No. 27 on)
National Periodical Publications: April-May, 1946 - No. 26, June-July, 1950 (52 pgs., #16 on)
1-Nutsy Squirrel begins (1st app.) by Rube Grossman 40.00 120.00 330.00
2 19.00 56.00 150.00
3-5: 4-1st Nutsy Squirrel-c 14.00 41.00 110.00
6-10: 6,9-Nutsy Squirrel-c begin 10.00 30.00 80.00
11-26: 16-Begin 52 pg. issues (10-11/48) 10.00 30.00 70.00
NOTE: ***Sheldon Mayer** a-in some issues. **Post** a-18. Christmas c-12.*

FUNNY FROLICS
Timely/Marvel Comics (SPI): Summer, 1945 - No. 5, Dec, 1946
1-Sharpy Fox, Puffy Pig, Krazy Krow 22.00 66.00 175.00
2 12.00 36.00 95.00
3,4 10.00 30.00 70.00
5-Kurtzman-a 10.00 30.00 80.00

FUNNY FUNNIES
Nedor Publishing Co.: April, 1943 (68 pgs.)
1-Funny animals; Peter Porker app. 19.00 56.00 150.00

FUNNYMAN (Also see Cisco Kid Comics & Extra Comics)
Magazine Enterprises: Dec, 1947; No. 1, Jan, 1948 - No. 6, Aug, 1948
nn(12/47)-Prepublication B&W undistributed copy by Siegel & Shuster-(5-3/4x8"), 16 pgs.; Sold at auction in 1997 for $575.00
1-Siegel & Shuster-a in all; Dick Ayers 1st pro work (as assistant) on 1st few issues 44.00 133.00 400.00
2 28.00 84.00 225.00
3-6 23.00 69.00 185.00

FUNNY MOVIES (See 3-D Funny Movies)

FUNNY PAGES (Formerly The Comics Magazine)
Comics Magazine Co./Ultem Publ.(Chesler)/Centaur Publications:
No. 6, Nov, 1936 - No. 42, Oct, 1940
V1#6 (nn, nd)-The Clock begins (2 pgs., 1st app.), ends #11; The Clock is the 1st masked comic book hero 211.00 633.00 2000.00
7-11 84.00 253.00 800.00
V2#1-V2#3: V2#1 (9/37)(V2#2 on-c; V2#1 in indicia). V2#2 (10/37)(V2#3 on-c; V2#2 in indicia). V2#3(11/37)-5 58.00 174.00 550.00
6(1st Centaur, 3/38) 84.00 253.00 800.00
7-9 61.00 182.00 575.00
10(Scarce, 9/38)-1st app. of The Arrow by Gustavson (Blue costume) 295.00 885.00 2800.00
11,12 111.00 332.00 1050.00
V3#1-Bruce Wayne prototype in "Case of the Missing Heir," by Bob Kane, 3 months before app. Batman (See Det. Pic. Stories #5) 116.00 348.00 1100.00
2-6: 6,8-Last funny covers 103.00 308.00 975.00
7-1st Arrow-c (9/39) 211.00 633.00 2000.00
8,9: 9-Tarpe Mills jungle-c 105.00 316.00 1000.00
10-2nd Arrow-c 168.00 505.00 1600.00
V4#1(1/40, Arrow-c)-(Rare)-The Owl & The Phantom Rider app.; origin Mantoka, Maker of Magic by Jack Cole. Mad Ming begins, ends #42; Tarpe Mills-a 211.00 633.00 2000.00
35-Classic Arrow-c 211.00 633.00 2000.00
36-38-Mad Ming-c 103.00 308.00 975.00
39-41-Arrow-c 158.00 474.00 1500.00
42 (Scarce,10/40)-Last Arrow; Arrow-c 168.00 505.00 1600.00
NOTE: ***Biro** c-V2#9. **Burgos** c-V3#10. **Jack Cole** a-V2#3, 7, 8, 10, 11, V3#2, 6, 9, 10, V4#1, 37; c-V3#2, 4. **Eisner** a-V1#7, 8?, 10. **Ken Ernst** a-V1#7, 8. **Everett** a-V2#11 (illos). **Filchock** c-V2#10, V3#6. **Gill Fox** a-V2#11. **Sid Greene** a-39. **Guardineer** a-V2#2, 3, 5. **Gustavson** a-V2#5, 11, 12, V3#1-10, 35, 38-42; c-V3#7, 35, 39-42. **Bob Kane** a-V3#1. **McWilliams** a-V2#12, V3#1, 3-6. **Tarpe Mills** a-V3#8-10, V4#1; c-V3#9. **Ed Moore Jr.** a-V2#12. **Schwab** c-V3#1. **Bob Wood** a-V2#2, 3, 8, 11, V3#6, 9, 10; c-V2#6, 7. Arrow c-V3#7, 10, V4#1, 35, 40-42.*

FUNNY PICTURE STORIES (Comic Pages V3#4 on)
Comics Magazine Co./Centaur Publications: Nov, 1936 - V3#3, May, 1939

Funny Tunes #19 © MAR

Funtastic World of Hanna Barbera #2 © H-B

Futurama #1 © Bongo Entertainment

V1#1-The Clock begins (c-feature)(see Funny Pages for 1st app.) 305.00 915.00 3200.00
2 111.00 332.00 1050.00
3-7(6/37): 4-Eisner-a; X-Mas-c. 7-Racial humor-c 76.00 229.00 725.00
V2#1 (9/37; V1#10 on-c; V2#1 in indicia)-Jack Strand begins 53.00 159.00 475.00
2 (10/37; V1#11 on-c; V2#2 in indicia) 53.00 159.00 475.00
3-5,7-11(11/38): 4-Xmas-c 44.00 133.00 400.00
6-(1st Centaur, 3/38) 76.00 229.00 725.00
V3#1(1/39)-3 42.00 125.00 375.00
NOTE: ***Biro*** *c-V2#1, 8, 9, 11.* ***Guardineer*** *a-V1#11; c-V2#6, V3#5.* ***Bob Wood*** *c/a-V1#11, V2#2; c-V2#3, 5.*

FUNNY STUFF (Becomes The Dodo & the Frog No. 80)
All-American/National Periodical Publications No. 7 on: Summer, 1944 - No. 79, July-Aug, 1954 (#1-7 are quarterly)

1-The Three Mouseketeers (ends #28) & The "Terrific Whatzit" begin; Sheldon Mayer-a 89.00 268.00 850.00
2-Sheldon Mayer-a 42.00 125.00 375.00
3-5: 3-Flash parody. 5-All Mayer-a/scripts issue 30.00 90.00 240.00
6-10 10-(6/46) 20.00 60.00 160.00
11-17,19 15.00 45.00 120.00
18-The Dodo & the Frog (2/47, 1st app?) begin?; X-Mas-c 28.00 83.00 220.00
20-1st Dodo & the Frog-c (4/47) 18.00 53.00 140.00
21,23-30: 24-Infinity-c 10.00 30.00 80.00
22-Superman cameo 40.00 120.00 350.00
31-79: 70-1st Bo Bunny by Mayer & begins 9.30 28.00 65.00
NOTE: ***Mayer*** *a-1-8, 55, ,57, 58, 61, 62, 64, 65, 68, 70, 72, 74-79; c-2, 5, 6, 8.*

FUNNY STUFF STOCKING STUFFER
DC Comics: Mar, 1985 ($1.25, 52 pgs.)

1-Almost every DC funny animal featured 2.00

FUNNY 3-D
Harvey Publications: December, 1953 (25¢, came with 2 pair of glasses)

1-Shows cover in 3-D on inside 11.00 33.00 90.00

FUNNY TUNES (Animated Funny Comic Tunes No. 16-22; Funny Comic Tunes No. 23, on covers only; formerly Krazy Komics #15; Oscar No. 24 on)
U.S.A. Comics Magazine Corp. (Timely): No. 16, Summer, 1944 - No. 23, Fall, 1946

16-Silly Seal, Ziggy Pig, Krazy Krow begin 14.00 41.00 110.00
17 (Fall/44)-Becomes Gay Comics #18 on? 11.00 33.00 90.00
18-22: 21-Super Rabbit app. 9.30 28.00 65.00
23-Kurtzman-a 10.00 30.00 80.00

FUNNY TUNES (Becomes Space Comics #4 on)
Avon Periodicals: July, 1953 - No. 3, Dec-Jan, 1953-54

1-Space Mouse, Peter Rabbit, Merry Mouse, Spotty the Pup, Cicero the Cat begin; all continue in Space Comics 10.00 30.00 75.00
2,3 7.15 21.50 50.00

FUNNY WORLD
Marbak Press: 1947 - No. 3, 1948

1-The Berrys, The Toodles & other strip-r begin 7.85 23.50 55.00
2,3 6.00 18.00 42.00

FUNTASTIC WORLD OF HANNA-BARBERA, THE (TV)
Marvel Comics Group: Dec, 1977 - No. 3, June, 1978 ($1.25, oversized)

1-3: 1-The Flintstones Christmas Party(12/77). 2-Yogi Bear's Easter Parade(3/78). 3-Laff-a-lympics(6/78) 3.65 11.00 40.00

FUN TIME
Ace Periodicals: Spring, 1953; No. 2, Sum, 1953; No. 3(nn), Fall, 1953; No. 4, Wint, 1953-54

1-(25¢, 100 pgs.)-Funny animal 16.00 49.00 130.00
2-4 (All 25¢, 100 pgs.) 14.00 41.00 110.00

FUN WITH SANTA CLAUS (See March of Comics No. 11, 108, 325)

FURTHER ADVENTURES OF CYCLOPS AND PHOENIX (Also see Adventures of Cyclops and Phoenix, Uncanny X-Men & X-Men)
Marvel Comics: June, 1996 - No. 4, Sept, 1996 ($1.95, limited series)

1-4: Origin of Mr. Sinister; Peter Milligan scripts; John Paul Leon-c/a(p). 2-4-Apocalypse app. 3.00
Trade Paperback (1997, $14.99) r/1-4 15.00

FURTHER ADVENTURES OF INDIANA JONES, THE (Movie) (Also see Indiana Jones and the Last Crusade & Indiana Jones and the Temple of Doom)
Marvel Comics Group: Jan, 1983 - No. 34, Mar, 1986

1-34: 1-Byrne/Austin-a; Austin-c. 2-Byrne/Austin-c/a 2.00
NOTE: ***Austin*** *a-1i, 2i, 6i, 9i; c-1, 2i, 6i, 9i.* ***Byrne*** *a-1p, 2p; c-2p.* ***Chaykin*** *a-6p; c-6p, 8p-10p.* ***Ditko*** *a-21p, 25-28, 34.* ***Golden*** *c-24, 25.* ***Simonson*** *c-9. Painted c-14.*

FURTHER ADVENTURES OF NYOKA, THE JUNGLE GIRL, THE (See Nyoka)
AC Comics: 1988 - No. 5, 1989 ($1.95, color; $2.25/$2.50, B&W)

1-5 : 1,2-Bill Black-a plus reprints. 3-Photo-c. 4-Krigstein-r. 5-(B&W)-Reprints plus movie photos 2.50

FURY (Straight Arrow's Horse...) (See A-1 No. 119)

FURY (TV) (See March Of Comics #200)
Dell Publishing Co./Gold Key: No. 781, Mar, 1957 - Nov, 1962 (All photo-c)

Four Color 781 7.50 22.50 90.00
Four Color 885,975,1031,1080,1133,1172,1218,1296, 01292-208(#1-'62), 10020-211(11/62-G.K.) 5.85 17.50 70.00

FURY
Marvel Comics: May, 1994 ($2.95, one-shot)

1-Ironman, Red Skull, FF, Hatemonger, Logan, Scorpio app.; Origin Nick Fury 3.00

FURY/ AGENT 13
Marvel Comics: June, 1998 - No. 2, July, 1998 ($2.99, limited series)

1,2-Nick Fury returns 3.00

FURY OF FIRESTORM, THE (Becomes Firestorm The Nuclear Man on cover with #50, in indicia with #65) (Also see Firestorm)
DC Comics: June, 1982 - No. 64, Oct, 1987 (75¢ on)

1,41,42: 1-Intro The Black Bison; brief origin. 41,42-Crisis x-over 3.00
2-40,43-64: 4-JLA x-over. 17-1st app. Firehawk. 21-Death of Killer Frost. 22-Origin. 23-Intro. Byte. 24-(6/84)-1st app. Blue Devil & Bug (origin); origin Byte. 34-1st app./origin Killer Frost II. 39-Weasel's ID revealed. 48-Intro. Moonbow. 53-Origin/1st app. Silver Shade. 55,56-Legends x-over. 58-1st app./origin new Parasite 2.00
61-Test cover variant; Superman logo 3.20 9.60 35.00
Annual 1-4: 1(1983), 2(1984), 3(1985), 4(1986) 3.00
NOTE: ***Colan*** *a-19p, Annual 4p.* ***Giffen*** *a-Annual 4p.* ***Gil Kane*** *c-30.* ***Nino*** *a-37.* ***Tuska*** *a-(p)-17, 18, 32, 45.*

FURY OF SHIELD
Marvel Comics: Apr, 1995 - No. 4, July, 1995 ($2.50/$1.95, limited series)

1 ($2.50)-Foil-c 3.00
2-4: 4-Bagged w/ decoder 2.50

FUSION
Eclipse Comics: Jan, 1987 - No. 17, Oct, 1989 ($2.00, B&W, Baxter paper)

1-17: 11-The Weasel Patrol begins (1st app.?) 2.00

FUTURAMA (TV)
Bongo Comics: 2000 - Present ($2.50, bi-monthly)

1-Based on the FOX animated series; Groening/Morrison-c 2.50
1-San Diego Comic-Con Premiere Edition 4.00

FUTURE COMICS
David McKay Publications: June, 1940 - No. 4, Sept, 1940

1-(6/40, 64 pgs.)-Origin The Phantom (4 pgs.); The Lone Ranger (8 pgs.) & Saturn Against the Earth (4 pgs.) begin 253.00 758.00 2400.00
2 121.00 363.00 1150.00
3,4 97.00 292.00 925.00

FUTURE COP L.A.P.D. (Electronic Arts video game) (Also see Promotional Comics section)
DC Comics (WildStorm): Jan, 1999 ($4.95, magazine sized)

1-Stories & art by various 4.95

FUTURETECH
Mushroom Comics: Jan, 1996 ($2.50, limited series)

Gabby Hayes Western #6 © FAW

Galactus the Devourer #6 © MAR

Gambit V2 #2 © MAR

GD2.0 FN6.0 NM9.4

1-Flipbook w/SWARM 2.50

FUTURE WORLD COMICS
George W. Dougherty: Summer, 1946 - No. 2, Fall, 1946
1,2: H. C. Kiefer-c; preview of the World of Tomorrow 31.00 94.00 250.00

FUTURE WORLD COMIX (Warren Presents...)
Warren Publications: Sept, 1978
1-Corben, Morrow, Nino, Sutton-a; Todd-c 1.50 4.50 12.00

FUTURIANS, THE (See Marvel Graphic Novel #9)
Lodestone Publishing/Eternity Comics: Sept, 1985 - No. 3, 1985 ($1.50)
1-3: Indicia title "Dave Cockrum's..." 2.00
Graphic Novel 1 ($9.95, Eternity)-r/#1-3, plus never published #4 issue 10.00

G-8 (Listed at G-Eight)

GABBY (Formerly Ken Shannon) (Teen humor)
Quality Comics Group: No. 11, Jul, 1953; No. 2, Sep, 1953 - No. 9, Sep, 1954
11(#1)(7/53) 7.85 23.50 55.00
2 5.00 15.00 32.00
3-9 4.00 12.00 24.00

GABBY GOB (See Harvey Hits No. 85, 90, 94, 97, 100, 103, 106, 109)

GABBY HAYES ADVENTURE COMICS
Toby Press: Dec, 1953
1-Photo-c 15.00 45.00 120.00

GABBY HAYES WESTERN (Movie star) (See Monte Hale, Real Western Hero & Western Hero)
Fawcett Publications/Charlton Comics No. 51 on: Nov, 1948 - No. 50, Jan, 1953; No. 51, Dec, 1954 - No. 59, Jan, 1957
1-Gabby & his horse Corker begin; photo front/back-c begin
50.00 150.00 450.00
2 25.00 75.00 200.00
3-5 17.00 51.00 135.00
6-10: 9-Young Falcon begins 14.00 41.00 110.00
11-20: 19-Last photo back-c 11.00 33.00 90.00
21-49: 20,22,24,26,28,29-(52 pgs.) 9.30 28.00 65.00
50-(1/53)-Last Fawcett issue; last photo-c? 10.00 30.00 75.00
51-(12/54)-1st Charlton issue; photo-c 10.00 30.00 80.00
52-59(1955-57): 53,55-Photo-c. 58-Swayze-a 6.40 19.25 45.00

GAGS
United Features Synd./Triangle Publ. No. 9 on: July, 1937 - V3#10, Oct, 1944 (13-3/4x10-3/4")
1(7/37)-52 pgs.; 20 pgs. Grin & Bear It, Fellow Citizen
6.40 19.25 45.00
V1#9 (36 pgs.) (7/42) 4.65 14.00 28.00
V3#10 4.00 12.00 24.00

GALACTICA: THE NEW MILLENNIUM
Realm Press: Sept, 1999 - Present ($2.99)
1-Stories by Shooter, Braden, Kuhoric 3.00

GALACTIC GUARDIANS
Marvel Comics: July, 1994 - No. 4, Oct, 1994 ($1.50, limited series)
1-4 2.00

GALACTIC WAR COMIX (Warren Presents... on cover)
Warren Publications: December, 1978
nn-Wood, Williamson-r 1.50 4.50 12.00

GALACTUS THE DEVOURER
Marvel Comics: Sept, 1999 - No. 6, Mar, 2000 ($3.50/$2.50, limited series)
1-($3.50) L. Simonson-s/Muth & Sienkiewicz-a 3.50
2-5-($2.50) Buscema & Sienkiewicz-a 2.50
6-($3.50) Death of Galactus; Buscema & Sienkiewicz-a 3.50

GALLANT MEN, THE (TV)
Gold Key: Oct, 1963 (Photo-c)
1(1008-310)-Manning-a 2.50 7.50 25.00

GALLEGHER, BOY REPORTER (Disney, TV)
Gold Key: May, 1965
1(10149-505)-Photo-c 2.30 7.00 20.00

GAMBIT (See X-Men #266 & X-Men Annual #14)
Marvel Comics: Dec, 1993 - No. 4, Mar, 1994 ($2.00, limited series)
1-($2.50)-Lee Weeks-c/a in all; gold foil stamped-c. 5.00
1 (Gold) 1.85 5.50 15.00
2-4 3.00

GAMBIT
Marvel Comics: Sept, 1997 - No. 4, Dec, 1997 ($2.50, limited series)
1-4-Janson-a/ Mackie & Kavanagh-s 3.00

GAMBIT
Marvel Comics: Feb, 1999 - No. 25, Feb, 2001 ($2.99/$1.99)
1-($2.99) Five covers; Nicieza-a/Skroce-a 3.00
2-11,13-16-($1.99): 2-Two covers (Skroce & Adam Kubert) 2.00
12-($2.99) 3.00
17-24: 17-Begin $2.25-c. 21-Mystique-c/app. 2.25
25-($2.99) Leads into "Gambit & Bishop" 3.00
...1999 Annual ($3.50) Nicieza-s/McDaniel-a 3.50
...2000 Annual ($3.50) Nicieza-s/Derenick & Smith-a 3.50

GAMBIT AND BISHOP: SONS OF THE ATOM
Marvel Comics: Feb, 2001 - No. 6 ($2.25, bi-weekly limited series)
Alpha (2/01) Prelude to series; Nord-a 2.25
1-Jeanty-a/Williams-c 2.25

GAMBIT AND THE X-TERNALS
Marvel Comics: Mar, 1995 - No. 4, July, 1995 ($1.95, limited series)
1-4-Age of Apocalypse 2.00

GAMEBOY (Super Mario covers on all)
Valiant: 1990 - No. 5 ($1.95, coated-c)
1-5: 3,4-Layton-c. 4-Morrow-a. 5-Layton-c(i) 4.00

GAMERA
Dark Horse Comics: Aug, 1996 - No. 4, Nov, 1996 ($2.95, limited series)
1-4 3.00

GAMMARAUDERS
DC Comics: Jan, 1989 - No. 10, Dec, 1989 ($1.25/$1.50/$2.00)
1-10-Based on TSR game 2.00

GAMORRA SWIMSUIT SPECIAL
Image Comics (WildStorm Productions): June, 1996 ($2.50, one-shot)
1-Campbell wraparound-c; pinups 2.50

GANDY GOOSE (Movies/TV)(See All Surprise, Giant Comics Edition #5A &10, Paul Terry's Comics & Terry-Toons)
St. John Publ. Co./Pines No. 5,6: Mar, 1953 - No. 5, Nov, 1953; No. 5, Fall, 1956 - No. 6, Sum/58
1-All St. John issues are pre-code 10.00 30.00 70.00
2 5.00 15.00 32.00
3-5(1953)(St. John) 4.65 14.00 28.00
5,6(1956-58)(Pines)-CBS Televison Presents... 4.00 11.00 22.00

GANG BUSTERS (See Popular Comics #38)
David McKay/Dell Publishing Co.: 1938 - 1943
Feature Books 17(McKay)('38)-1st app. 50.00 150.00 600.00
Large Feature Comic 10('39)-(Scarce) 50.00 150.00 600.00
Large Feature Comic 17('41) 31.00 93.00 375.00
Four Color 7(1940) 35.00 105.00 420.00
Four Color 23,24('42-43) 27.00 80.00 320.00

GANG BUSTERS (Radio/TV)(Gangbusters #14 on)
National Periodical Publications: Dec-Jan, 1947-48 - No. 67, Dec-Jan, 1958-59 (No. 1-23: 52 pgs.)
1 84.00 253.00 800.00
2 40.00 120.00 350.00
3-5 30.00 90.00 240.00
6-10: 9-Dan Barry-a. 9,10-Photo-c 24.00 71.00 190.00
11-13-Photo-c 20.00 60.00 160.00

Gatecrasher #1 © Black Bull Ent.

Gay Comics #26 © MAR

Geisha #1 © Andi Watson

14,17-Frazetta-a, 8 pgs. each. 14-Photo-c 40.00 120.00 320.00
15,16,18-20,26: 26-Kirby-a 14.00 41.00 110.00
21-25,27-30 12.50 37.50 100.00
31-44: 44-Last Pre-code (2-3/55) 11.00 33.00 90.00
45-67 10.00 30.00 70.00
NOTE: ***Barry*** *a-6, 8, 10.* ***Drucker*** *a-51.* ***Moreira*** *a-48, 50, 59.* ***Roussos*** *a-8.*

GANGLAND
DC Comics (Vertigo): Jun, 1998 - No. 4, Sept, 1998 ($2.95, limited series)
1-4:Crime anthology by various. 2-Corben-a 3.00
TPB-(2000, $12.95) r/#1-4; Bradstreet-c 12.95

GANGSTERS AND GUN MOLLS
Avon Per./Realistic Comics: Sept, 1951 - No. 4, June, 1952 (Painted c-1-3)
1-Wood-a, 1 pg; c-/Avon paperback #292 47.00 142.00 425.00
2-Check-a, 8 pgs.; Kamen-a; Bonnie Parker story 40.00 120.00 325.00
3-Marijuana mentioned; used in **POP**, pg. 84,85 36.00 107.00 285.00
4-Syd Shores-c 28.00 84.00 225.00

GANGSTERS CAN'T WIN
D. S. Publishing Co.: Feb-Mar, 1948 - No. 9, June-July, 1949 (All 52 pgs?)
1-True crime stories 34.00 103.00 275.00
2 17.00 51.00 135.00
3,5,6 15.00 45.00 120.00
4-Acid in face story 19.00 56.00 150.00
7-9 11.00 33.00 90.00
NOTE: ***Ingles*** *a-5, 6.* ***McWilliams*** *a-5, 7.* ***Reinman*** *c-6.*

GANG WORLD
Standard Comics: No. 5, Nov, 1952 - No. 6, Jan, 1953
5-Bondage-c 19.00 56.00 150.00
6 14.00 43.00 115.00

GARGOYLE (See The Defenders #94)
Marvel Comics Group: June, 1985 - No. 4, Sept, 1985 (75¢, limited series)
1-Wrightson-c; character from Defenders 3.00
2-4 2.00

GARGOYLES (TV cartoon)
Marvel Comics: Feb, 1995 - No. 17, June, 1996 ($2.50)
1-17: Based on animated series 3.00

GARRISON'S GORILLAS (TV)
Dell Publishing Co.: Jan, 1968 - No. 4, Oct, 1968; No. 5, Oct, 1969 (Photo-c)
1 4.10 12.30 45.00
2-5: 5-Reprints #1 2.80 8.40 28.00

GARY GIANNI'S THE MONSTERMEN
Dark Horse Comics: Aug, 1999 ($2.95, one-shot)
1-Gianni-s/c/a; back-up Hellboy story by Mignola 3.00

GASM
Stories, Layouts & Press, Inc.: Nov, 1977 - nn(No. 4), Jun, 1978 (B&W/color)
1-Mark Wheatley-s/a; Gene Day-s/a; Workman-a 2.00 6.00 18.00
nn(#2, 2/78) Day-s/a; Wheatley-a; Workman-a 1.50 4.50 12.00
nn(#3, 4/78) Day-s/a; Wheatley-a; Corben-a 2.30 7.00 20.00
nn(#4, 6/78) Hempel-a; Howarth-a; Corben-a 2.40 7.35 22.00

GASOLINE ALLEY (Top Love Stories No. 3 on?)
Star Publications: Sept-Oct, 1950 - No. 2, Dec, 1950 (Newspaper-r)
1-Contains 1 pg. intro. history of the strip (The Life of Skeezix); reprints 15 scenes of highlights from 1921-1935, plus an adventure from 1935 and 1936 strips; a 2-pg. filler is included on the life of the creator Frank King, with photo of the cartoonist. 21.00 64.00 170.00
2-(1936-37 reprints)-L. B. Cole-c 25.00 75.00 200.00
(See Super Book No. 21)

GASP!
American Comics Group: Mar, 1967 - No. 4, Aug, 1967 (12¢)
1 3.20 9.60 35.00
2-4 2.30 7.00 20.00

GATECRASHER
Black Bull Entertainment: Mar, 2000 - No. 4, Jun, 2000 ($2.50, limited series)
1,2-Waid-s/Conner & Palmiotti-c/a; 1,2-variant-c by J.G. Jones 2.50
3,4: 3-Jusko var-c. 4-Linsner-c 2.50
... Ring of Fire TPB (11/00, $12.95) r/#1-4; Hughes-c; Ennis intro. 13.00

GATECRASHER (Regular series)
Black Bull Entertainment: Aug, 2000 - Present ($2.50)
1-5-Waid-s/Conner & Palmiotti-c/a; 1-3-Variant-c by Fabry. 4-Hildebrandts variant-c. 5-Art Adams var-c 2.50

GAY COMICS (Honeymoon No. 41)
Timely Comics/USA Comic Mag. Co. No. 18-24: Mar, 1944 (no month); No. 18, Fall, 1944 - No. 40, Oct, 1949
1-Wolverton's Powerhouse Pepper; Tessie the Typist begins; 1st app. Willie (one shot) 47.00 140.00 420.00
18-(Formerly Funny Tunes #17?)-Wolverton-a 28.00 83.00 220.00
19-29: Wolverton-a in all. 21,24-6 pg., 7 pg. Powerhouse Pepper; additional 2 pg. story in 24). 23-7 pg Wolverton story & 2 two pg stories(total of 11pgs.). 24,29-Kurtzman-a (24-"Hey Look"(2)) 22.00 66.00 175.00
30,33,36,37-Kurtzman's "Hey Look" 10.00 30.00 70.00
31-Kurtzman's "Hey Look" (1), Giggles 'N' Grins (1-1/2) 10.00 30.00 70.00
32,35,38-40: 35-Nellie The Nurse begins? 8.65 26.00 60.00
34-Three Kurtzman's "Hey Look" 10.00 30.00 75.00

GAY COMICS (Also see Smile, Tickle, & Whee Comics)
Modern Store Publ.: 1955 (7¢, 5x7-1/4", 52 pgs.)
1 3.00 9.00 30.00

GAY PURR-EE (See Movie Comics)

GAZILLION
Image Comics: Nov, 1998 ($2.50, one-shot)
1-Howard Shum-s/ Keron Grant-a 2.50

GEAR STATION, THE
Image Comics: Mar, 2000 - Present ($2.50)
1-Four covers by Ross, Turner, Pat Lee, Fraga 2.50
1-($6.95) DF Cover 6.95
2-5: 2-Two covers by Fraga and Art Adams 2.50

GEEK, THE (See Brother Power... & Vertigo Visions)

GEEKSVILLE (Also see 3 Geeks, The)
3 Finger Prints/ Image Comics: Aug, 1999 - Present ($2.75, B&W)
1-3-The 3 Geeks by Koslowski; Innocent Bystander by Sassaman 2.75
0-(3/00) First Image issue 2.75
(Vol. 2) 1-4-($2.95) 3-Mini-comic insert by the Geeks 2.95

G-8 AND HIS BATTLE ACES (Based on pulps)
Gold Key: Oct, 1966
1 (10184-610)-Painted-c 3.25 9.75 36.00

G-8 AND HIS BATTLE ACES
Blazing Comics: 1991 ($1.50, one-shot)
1-Glanzman-a; Truman-c 2.00
NOTE: *Flip book format with "The Spider's Web" #1 on other side w/****Glanzman****-a,* ***Truman****-c.*

GEISHA
Oni Press: Sept, 1998 - No. 4, Dec, 1998 ($2.95, limited series)
1-4-Andi Watson-s/a. 2-Adam Warren-c 3.00
...One Shot (5/00, $4.50) 4.50

GEM COMICS
Spotlight Publishers: Apr, 1945 (52 pgs)
1-Little Mohee, Steve Strong app.; Jungle bondage-c 40.00 120.00 350.00

GEMINAR
Image Comics: July, 2000 ($4.95, B&W)
1-(72-Page Special) Terry Collins-s/Al Bigley-a 4.95

GEMINI BLOOD
DC Comics (Helix): Sept, 1996 - No. 9, May, 1997 ($2.25, limited series)
1-9: 5-Simonson-c 2.25

Gen-Active #1 © WSP

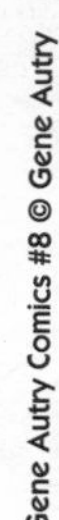
Gene Autry Comics #8 © Gene Autry

Generation X #40 © MAR

GD2.0 FN6.0 NM9.4

GEN ACTIVE
DC Comics (WildStorm): May, 2000 - Present ($3.95, 2 covers per issue)
1-4: 1-Covers by Campbell and Madureira; Gen 13 & DV8 app. 3.95

GENE AUTRY (See March of Comics No. 25, 28, 39, 54, 78, 90, 104, 120, 135, 150 & Western Roundup under Dell Giants)

GENE AUTRY COMICS (Movie, Radio star; singing cowboy)
Fawcett Publications: 1941 (On sale 12/31/41) - No. 10, 1943 (68 pgs.) (Dell takes over with No. 11)
1 (Rare)-Gene Autry & his horse Champion begin 730.00 2190.00 8400.00
2-(1942) 147.00 442.00 1400.00
3-5: 3-(11/1/42) 95.00 285.00 900.00
6-10 79.00 237.00 750.00

GENE AUTRY COMICS (...& Champion No. 102 on)
Dell Publishing Co.: No. 11, 1943 - No. 121, Jan-Mar, 1959 (TV - later issues)
11 (1943, 60 pgs.)-Continuation of Fawcett series; photo back-c 56.00 169.00 675.00
12 (2/44, 60 pgs.) 50.00 150.00 600.00
Four Color 47(1944, 60 pgs.) 42.00 125.00 500.00
Four Color 57(11/44),66('45)(52 pgs. each) 40.00 119.00 475.00
Four Color 75,83('45, 36 pgs. each) 30.00 90.00 360.00
Four Color 93,100('45-46, 36 pgs. each): 100-First Gene Autry photo-c 27.00 80.00 320.00
1(5-6/46, 52 pgs.) 42.00 125.00 500.00
2(7-8/46)-Photo-c begin, end #111 23.00 69.00 275.00
3-5: 4-Intro Flapjack Hobbs 17.00 50.00 200.00
6-10 14.00 43.00 170.00
11-20: 20-Panhandle Pete begins 12.00 35.00 140.00
21-29(36pgs.) 9.00 27.00 110.00
30-40(52pgs.) 7.50 22.50 90.00
41-56(52pgs.) 6.30 19.00 75.00
57-66(36pgs.): 58-X-mas-c 5.00 15.00 60.00
67-80(52pgs.) 4.60 13.75 55.00
81-90(52pgs.): 82-X-mas-c. 87-Blank inside-c 4.10 12.30 45.00
91-99(36pgs. No. 91-on). 94-X-mas-c 3.65 11.00 40.00
100 4.10 12.30 45.00
101-111-Last Gene Autry photo-c 3.20 9.60 35.00
112-121-All Champion painted-c, most by Savitt 3.00 9.00 30.00
NOTE: *Photo back covers 4-18, 20-45, 48-65.* ***Manning*** *a-118.* ***Jesse Marsh*** *art: 4-Color No. 66, 75, 93, 100, No. 1-25, 27-37, 39, 40.*

GENE AUTRY'S CHAMPION (TV)
Dell Publ. Co.: No. 287, 8/50; No. 319, 2/51; No. 3, 8-10/51 - No. 19, 8-10/55
Four Color 287(#1)('50, 52pgs.)-Photo-c 10.00 30.00 120.00
Four Color 319(#2, '51), 3: 2-Painted-c begin, most by Sam Savitt 4.55 13.65 50.00
4-19: 19-Last painted-c 3.65 11.00 40.00

GENE DOGS
Marvel Comics UK: Oct, 1993 - No. 4, Jan, 1994 ($1.75, limited series)
1-($2.75)-Polybagged w/4 trading cards 2.75
2-4: 2-Vs. Genetix 2.00

GENERAL DOUGLAS MACARTHUR
Fox Features Syndicate: 1951
nn-True life story 20.00 60.00 160.00

GENERIC COMIC, THE
Marvel Comics Group: Apr, 1984 (one-shot)
1 3.00

GENERATION HEX
DC Comics (Amalgam): June, 1997 ($1.95, one-shot)
1-Milligan-s/ Pollina & Morales-a 2.00

GENERATION NEXT
Marvel Comics: Mar, 1995 - No. 4, June, 1995 ($1.95, limited series)
1-4-Age of Apocalypse; Scott Lobdell scripts & Chris Bachalo-c/a 2.00

GENERATION X (See Gen 13/ Generation X)
Marvel Comics: Oct, 1994 - No. 75, May, 2001 ($1.50/$1.95/$1.99/$2.25)
Collectors Preview ($1.75), "Ashcan" Edition 2.00
-1(7/97) Flashback story 3.00
1/2 (San Diego giveaway) 1.50 4.50 12.00
1-($3.95)-Wraparound chromium-c; Scott Lobdell scripts & Chris Bachalo-a begins. 2.40 6.00
2-($1.95)-Deluxe edition, Bachalo-a 3.00
3,4-($1.95)-Deluxe Edition; Bachalo-a 3.00
2-4-Standard Edition; Bachalo-a 2.00
5-24, 26-28: 5-Returns from "Age of Apocalypse," begin $1.95-c. 6-Bachalo-a(p) ends, returns #17. 7-Roger Cruz-a(p). 10-Omega Red-c/app. 13,14-Bishop-app. 17-Stan Lee app. (Stan Lee scripts own dialogue); Bachalo/Buckingham-a; Onslaught update. 18-Toad cameo. 20-Franklin Richards app; Howard the Duck cameo. 21-Howard the Duck app. 22-Nightmare app. 2.00
25-($2.99)-Wraparound-c. Black Tom, Howard the Duck app. 3.00
29-37: 29-Begin $1.99-c, "Operation Zero Tolerance". 33-Hama-s 2.00
38-49: 38-Dodson-a begins. 40-Penance ID revealed. 49-Maggott app. 2.00
50,57-($2.99): 50-Crossover w/X-Man #50 3.00
51-56, 58-62: 59-Avengers & Spider-Man app. 2.00
63-72: 63-Ellis-s begin. 64-Begin $2.25-c. 69-71-Art Adams-c 2.25
'95 Special-($3.95) 4.00
'96 Special-($2.95)-Wraparound-c; Jeff Johnson-c/a 3.00
'97 Special-($2.99)-Wraparound-c; 3.00
'98 Annual-($3.50)-vs. Dracula 3.50
'99 Annual-($3.50)-Monet leaves 3.50
75¢ Ashcan Edition 5.00
...Holiday Special 1 (2/99, $3.50) Pollina-a 3.50
...Underground Special 1 (5/98, $2.50, B&W) Mahfood-a 2.50

GENERATION X/ GEN 13 (Also see Gen 13/ Generation X)
Marvel Comics: 1997 ($3.99, one-shot)
1-Robinson-s/Larroca-a(p) 4.00

GENE RODDENBERRY'S LOST UNIVERSE
Tekno Comix: Apr, 1995 - No. 7, Oct, 1995 ($1.95)
1-7: 1-3-w/ bound-in game piece & trading card. 4-w/bound-in trading card 2.25

GENE RODDENBERRY'S XANDER IN LOST UNIVERSE
Tekno Comix: No. 0, Nov, 1995; No. 1, Dec, 1995 - No. 8, July, 1996 ($2.25)
0,1-8: 1-5-Jae Lee-c. 4-Polybagged. 8-Pt. 5 of The Big Bang x-over 2.25

GENESIS (See DC related titles)
DC Comics: Oct, 1997 - No. 4, Oct, 1997 ($1.95, weekly limited series)
1-4: Byrne-s/Wagner-a(p) in all. 3.00

GENESIS: THE #1 COLLECTION (WildStorm Archives)
WildStorm Productions: 1998 ($9.99, TPB, B&W)
nn-Reprints #1 issues of WildStorm titles and pin-ups 10.00

GENETIX
Marvel Comics UK: Oct, 1993 - No. 6, Mar, 1994 ($1.75, limited series)
1-($2.75)-Polybagged w/4 cards; Dark Guard app. 2.75
2-6: 2-Intro Tektos. 4-Vs. Gene Dogs 2.00

GEN 12 (Also see Gen 13 and Team 7)
Image Comics (WildStorm Productions): Feb, 1998 - No. 5, June, 1998 ($2.50, limited series)
1-5: 1-Team 7 & Gen 13 app.; wraparound-c 3.00

GEN 13 (Also see Wild C.A.T.S. #1 & Deathmate Black #2)
Image Comics (WildStorm Productions): Feb, 1994 - No. 5, July 1994 ($1.95, limited series)
0 (8/95, $2.50)-Ch. 1 w/Jim Lee-p; Ch.4 w/Charest-p 3.00
1/2 1.25 3.75 10.00
1-($2.50)-Created by Jim Lee 2.00 6.00 16.00
1-2nd printing 2.50
1-"3-D" Edition (9/97, $4.95)-w/glasses 5.00
2-($2.50) 1.25 3.75 10.00
3-Pitt-c & story 2.40 6.00
4-Pitt-c & story; wraparound-c 5.00

Gen 13 #9 © WSP

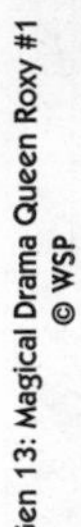
Gen 13: Magical Drama Queen Roxy #1 © WSP

Georgie Comics #4 © MAR

5 4.00
5-Alternate Portacio-c; see Deathblow #5 2.40 6.00
...Collected Edition ('94, $12.95)-r/#1-5 13.00
...Rave ($1.50, 3/95)-wraparound-c 2.00

NOTE: *Issues 1-4 contain coupons redeemable for the ashcan edition of Gen 13 #0. Price listed is for a complete book.*

GEN 13
Image Comics (WildStorm Productions): Mar, 1995 - No. 36, Dec, 1998; **DC Comics (WildStorm Prod.):** No. 37, Mar, 1999 - Present ($2.95/$2.50)

1-A (Charge)-Campbell/Gardner-c 4.00
1-B (Thumbs Up)-Campbell/Gardner-c 4.00
1-C-1-K,1-M: 1-C (Lil' GEN 13)-Art Adams-c. 1-D (Barbari-GEN)-Simon Bisley-c 1-E (Your Friendly Neighborhood Grunge)-John Cleary-c. 1-F (GEN 13 Goes Madison Ave.)-Michael Golden-c. 1-G (Lin-GEN-re)-Michael Lopez-c. 1-H (GEN-et Jackson)-Jason Pearson-c. 1-I (That's the way we became GEN 13)-Campbell/Gibson-c. 1-J (All Dolled Up)-Campbell/McWeeney-c. 1-K (Verti-GEN)-Joe Dunn-c. 1-L (Picto-Fiction). 1-M (Do it Yourself Cover) 2.40 6.00
1-"3-D" Edition (2/98, $4.95)-w/glasses 5.00
2 ($1.95, Newsstand)-WildStorm Rising Pt. 4; bound-in card 2.00
2-12: 2-($2.50, Direct Market)-WildStorm Rising Pt. 4, bound-in card. 6,7-Jim Lee-c/a(p). 9-Ramos-a. 10,11-Fire From Heaven Pt. 3. & Pt.9 3.00
11-($4.95)-Special European Tour Edition; chromium-c 12.00
13A,13B,13C-($1.30, 13 pgs.): 13A-Archie & Friends app. 13B-Bone-c/app.; Teenage Mutant Ninja Turtles, Madman, Spawn & Jim Lee app. 2.00
14-24: 20-Last Campbell-a 2.50
25-($3.50)-Two covers by Campbell and Charest 3.50
25-($3.50)-Voyager Pack w/Danger Girl preview 3.50
26-34: 26-Arcudi-s/Frank-a begins. 33-Flip book w/Planetary preview 34-Back-up story by Art Adams 2.50
35-49: 36,38,40-Two covers. 37-First DC issue. 41-Last Frank-a 2.50
50-($3.95) Two covers by Lee and Benes; art by various 3.95
51-61: 51-Moy-a; Fairchild loses her powers. 60-Warren-s/a 2.50
Annual 1 (1997, $2.95) Ellis-s/ Dillon-c/a. 3.00
Annual 1999 ($3.50, DC) Slipstream x-over w/ DV8 3.50
Annual 2000 ($3.50) Devil's Night x-over w/WildStorm titles; Bermejo-c 3.50
...: A Christmas Caper (1/00, $5.95, one-shot) McWeeney-s/a 5.95
... Archives (4/98, $12.99) B&W reprints of mini-series, #0,1/2,1-13ABC; includes cover gallery and sourcebook 13.00
...: Carny Folk (2/00, $3.50) Collect back-up stories 3.50
... European Vacation TPB ($6.95) r/#6,7 7.00
...: Going West (6/99, $2.50, one-shot) Pruett-s 2.50
...: Grunge Saves the World (5/99, $5.95, one-shot) Altieri-c/a 6.00
... I Love New York TPB ($9.95) r/part #25, 26-29; Frank-c 10.00
... Lost in Paradise TPB ($6.95) r/#3-5 7.00
.../ Maxx (12/95, $3.50, one-shot) Messner-Loebs-s, 1st Coker-c/a. 3.50
... Starting Over TPB ($14.95) r/#1-7 15.00
... #13 A,B&C Collected Edition ($6.95, TPB) r/#13A,B&C 7.00
... 3-D Special (1997, $4.95, one-shot) Art Adams-s/a(p) 5.00
...: The Unreal World (7/96, $2.95, one-shot) Humberto Ramos-c/a 3.00
... We'll Take Manhattan TPB ($14.95) r/#45-50; new Benes-c 15.00
...: Wired (4/99, $2.50, one-shot) Richard Bennett-c/a 2.50
...: 'Zine (12/96, $1.95, B&W, digest size) Campbell/Garner-c 2.00
Variant Collection-Four editions (all 13 variants w/Chromium variant-limited, signed) 16.50 49.00 180.00

GEN 13 BOOTLEG
Image Comics (WildStorm): Nov, 1996 - No. 20, Jul, 1998 ($2.50)

1-Alan Davis-a; alternate costumes-c 2.50
1-Team falling variant-c 3.00
2-7: 2-Alan Davis-a. 5,6-Terry Moore-s. 7-Robinson-s/Scott Hampton-a. 2.50
8-10-Adam Warren-s/a 4.00
11-20: 11,12-Lopresti-s/a & Simonson-s. 13-Wieringo-s/a. 14-Mariotte-s/Phillips-a. 15,16-Strnad-s/Shaw-a. 18-Altieri-s/a(p)/c, 18-Variant-c by Bruce Timm 2.50
Annual 1 (2/98, $2.95) Ellis-s/Dillon-c/a 3.00
... Grunge: The Movie (12/97, $9.95) r/#8-10, Warren-c 10.00
...Vol. 1 TPB (10/98, $11.95) r/#1-4 12.00

GEN 13/ GENERATION X (Also see Generation X / Gen 13)
Image Comics (WildStorm Publications): July, 1997 ($2.95, one-shot)

1-Choi-s/ Art Adams-p/Garner-i. Variant covers by Adams/Garner and Campbell/McWeeney 3.00
1-($4.95) 3-D Edition w/glasses; Campbell-c 5.00

GEN 13 INTERACTIVE
Image Comics (WildStorm): Oct, 1997 - No. 3, Dec, 1997 ($2.50, lim. series)

1-3-Internet voting used to determine storyline 2.50
... Plus! (7/98, $11.95) r/series & 3-D Special (in 2-D) 12.00

GEN 13 : MAGICAL DRAMA QUEEN ROXY
Image Comics (WildStorm): Oct, 1998 - No. 3, Dec, 1998 ($3.50, lim. series)

1-3-Adam Warren-s/c/a; manga style, 2-Variant-c by Hiroyuki Utatane 3.50
1-($6.95) Dynamic Forces Ed. w/Variant Warren-c 7.00

GEN 13 /MONKEYMAN & O'BRIEN
Image Comics (WildStorm): Jun, 1998 - No. 2, July, 1998 ($2.50, lim. series)

1,2-Art Adams-s/a(p); 1-Two covers 2.50
1-($4.95) Chromium-c, 1-($6.95) Dynamic Forces Ed. 6.00

GEN 13: ORDINARY HEROES
Image Comics (WildStorm Publications): Feb, 1996 - No. 2, July, 1996 ($2.50 limited series)

1,2-Adam Hughes-c/a/scripts 3.00

GENTLE BEN (TV)
Dell Publishing Co.: Feb, 1968 - No. 5, Oct, 1969 (All photo-c)

1 3.20 9.60 35.00
2-5: 5-Reprints #1 2.30 7.00 20.00

GEOMANCER (Also see Eternal Warrior: Fist & Steel)
Valiant: Nov, 1994 - No. 8, June, 1995 ($3.75/$2.25)

1 ($3.75)-Chromium wraparound-c; Eternal Warrior app. 3.75
2-8 2.25

GEORGE OF THE JUNGLE (TV)(See America's Best TV Comics)
Gold Key: Feb, 1969 - No. 2, Oct, 1969 (Jay Ward)

1 11.70 35.00 140.00
2 8.00 24.00 95.00

GEORGE PAL'S PUPPETOONS (Funny animal puppets)
Fawcett Publications: Dec, 1945 - No. 18, Dec, 1947; No. 19, 1950

1-Captain Marvel-c 40.00 120.00 350.00
2 22.00 66.00 175.00
3-10 13.00 39.00 105.00
11-19 11.00 33.00 90.00

GEORGIE COMICS (...& Judy Comics #20-35?; see All Teen & Teen Comics)
Timely Comics/GPI No. 1-34: Spr, 1945 - No. 39, Oct, 1952 (#1-3 are quarterly)

1-Dave Berg-a 23.00 69.00 185.00
2 11.00 33.00 90.00
3-5,7,8 10.00 30.00 70.00
6-Georgie visits Timely Comics 12.00 36.00 95.00
9,10-Kurtzman's "Hey Look" (1 & ?); Margie app. 10.00 30.00 75.00
11,12: 11-Margie, Millie app. 7.15 21.50 50.00
13-Kurtzman's "Hey Look", 3 pgs. 8.65 26.00 60.00
14-Wolverton-a(1 pg.); Kurtzman's "Hey Look" 10.00 30.00 70.00
15,16,18-20 6.00 18.00 42.00
17,29-Kurtzman's "Hey Look", 1 pg. 7.85 23.50 55.00
21-24,27,28,30-39: 21-Anti-Wertham editorial 5.50 16.50 38.00
25-Painted-c by classic pin-up artist Peter Driben 10.00 30.00 70.00
26-Logo design swipe from Archie Comics 6.00 18.00 42.00

GERALD McBOING-BOING AND THE NEARSIGHTED MR. MAGOO (TV) (Mr. Magoo No. 6 on)
Dell Publishing Co.: Aug-Oct, 1952 - No. 5, Aug-Oct, 1953

1 12.50 37.50 150.00
2-5 10.00 30.00 120.00

GERONIMO (See Fighting Indians of the Wild West!)
Avon Periodicals: 1950 - No. 4, Feb, 1952

1-Indian Fighter; Maneely-a; Texas Rangers-r/Cowpuncher #1; Fawcette-c 18.00 53.00 140.00

Get Smart #1 © Talent Assoc.

Ghost #2 © FH

Ghost #32 © DH

GD2.0 FN6.0 NM9.4

2-On the Warpath; Kit West app.; Kinstler-c/a 10.50 32.00 85.00
3-And His Apache Murderers; Kinstler-c/a(2); Kit West-r/Cowpuncher #6
15.00 32.00 85.00
4-Savage Raids of; Kinstler-c & inside front-c; Kinstlerish-a by McCann(3)
10.00 30.00 75.00

GERONIMO JONES
Charlton Comics: Sept, 1971 - No. 9, Jan, 1973
1 2.00 6.00 16.00
2-9 1.00 3.00 8.00
Modern Comics Reprint #7('78) 3.50

GETALONG GANG, THE (TV)
Marvel Comics (Star Comics): May, 1985 - No. 6, Mar, 1986
1-6: Saturday morning TV stars 2.00

GET LOST
Mikeross Publications/New Comics: Feb-Mar, 1954 - No. 3, June-July, 1954 (Satire)
1-Andru/Esposito-a in all? 30.00 90.00 240.00
2-Andru/Esposito-c; has 4 pg. E.C. parody featuring "The Sewer Keeper"
20.00 60.00 160.00
3-John Wayne 'Hondo' parody 16.00 49.00 130.00
1,2 (10,12/87-New Comics)-B&W r-original 2.00

GET SMART (TV)
Dell Publ. Co.: June, 1966 - No. 8, Sept, 1967 (All have Don Adams photo-c)
1 9.00 27.00 110.00
2,3-Ditko-a 6.30 19.00 75.00
4-8: 8-Reprints #1 (cover and insides) 5.00 15.00 60.00

GHOST (...Comics #9)
Fiction House Magazines: 1951(Winter) - No. 11, Summer, 1954
1-Most covers by Whitman 68.00 205.00 650.00
2-Ghost Gallery & Werewolf Hunter stories 38.00 113.00 300.00
3-9: 3,6,7,9-Bondage-c. 9-Abel, Discount-a 31.00 94.00 250.00
10,11-Dr. Drew by Grandenetti in each, reprinted from Rangers; 11-Evans-r/Rangers #39; Grandenetti-r/Rangers #49 28.00 84.00 225.00

GHOST (See Comic's Greatest World)
Dark Horse Comics: Apr, 1995 - No. 36, Apr, 1998 ($2.50/$2.95)
1-Adam Hughes-a 1.00 3.00 8.00
2,3-Hughes-a 4.00
4-24: 4-Barb Wire app. 5,6-Hughes-c. 12-Ghost/Hellboy preview. 15,21-X app. 18,19-Barb Wire app. 3.00
25-($3.50)-48 pgs. special 3.50
26-36: 26-Begin $2.95-c. 29-Flip book w/Timecop. 33-36-Jade Cathedral; Harris painted-c 3.00
Special 1 (7/94, $3.95, 48 pgs.) 1.00 2.80 7.00
Special 2 (6/98, $3.95) Barb Wire app. 4.00
...Black October (1/99, $14.95, trade paperback)-r/#6-9,26,27 15.00
...Nocturnes (1996, $9.95, trade paperback)-r/#1-3 & 5 10.00
...Stories (1995, $9.95, trade paperback)-r/Early Ghost app. 10.00

GHOST (Volume 2)
Dark Horse Comics: Sept, 1998 - No. 22, Aug, 2000 ($2.95)
1-22: 1-4-Ryan Benjamin-c/Zanier-a 3.00
Handbook (8/99, $2.95) guide to issues and characters 3.00
Special 3 (12/98, $3.95) 4.00

GHOST AND THE SHADOW
Dark Horse Comics: Dec, 1995 ($2.95, one-shot)
1-Moench scripts 3.00

GHOST/BATGIRL
Dark Horse Comics: Aug, 2000 - No. 4 ($2.95, limited series)
1,2-New Batgirl; Oracle & Bruce Wayne app.; Benjamin-c/a 3.00

GHOST/HELLBOY
Dark Horse Comics: May, 1996 - No. 2, June, 1996 ($2.50, limited series)
1,2: Mike Mignola-c/scripts & breakdowns; Scott Benefiel finished-a 3.00

GHOST BREAKERS (Also see Racket Squad in Action, Red Dragon & (CC) Sherlock Holmes Comics)
Street & Smith Publications: Sept, 1948 - No. 2, Dec, 1948 (52 pgs.)
1-Powell-c/a(3); Dr. Neff (magician) app. 40.00 120.00 350.00
2-Powell-c/a(2); Maneely-a 34.00 101.00 270.00

GHOSTBUSTERS (TV) (Also, see Real...and Slimer)
First Comics: Feb, 1987 - No. 6, Aug, 1987 ($1.25)
1-6: Based on new animated TV series 3.00

GHOSTBUSTERS II
Now Comics: Oct, 1989 - No. 3, Dec, 1989 ($1.95, mini-series)
1-3: Movie Adaptation 3.00

GHOST CASTLE (See Tales of...)

GHOSTDANCING
DC Comics (Vertigo): Mar, 1995 - No. 6, Sept, 1995 ($1.95, limited series)
1-6: Case-c/a 2.00

GHOST IN THE SHELL (Manga)
Dark Horse: Mar, 1995 - No. 8, Oct, 1995 ($3.95, B&W/color, lim. series)
1 2.50 7.50 25.00
2 2.80 8.40 28.00
3 1.85 5.50 15.00
4-8 1.25 3.75 10.00

GHOSTLY HAUNTS (Formerly Ghost Manor)
Charlton Comics: #20, 9/71 - #53, 12/76; #54, 9/77 - #55, 10/77; #56, 1/78 - #58, 4/78
20 2.30 7.00 20.00
21 1.50 4.50 12.00
22-25,27,31-34,36,37-Ditko-c/a. 27-Dr. Graves x-over. 32-New logo. 33-Back to old logo 1.85 5.50 15.00
26,29,30,35-Ditko-c 1.50 4.50 12.00
28,38-40-Ditko-a. 39-Origin & 1st app. Destiny Fox 1.50 4.50 12.00
41,42: 41-Sutton-c; Ditko-a. 42-Newton-c/a 1.85 5.50 15.00
43-46,48,50,52-Ditko-a 1.25 3.75 10.00
47,54,56-Ditko-c/a. 56-Ditko-a(r). 1.50 4.50 12.00
49,51,53,55,57 1.00 3.00 8.00
40,41(Modern Comics-r, 1977, 1978) 3.00

NOTE: ***Ditko*** *a-22-25, 27, 28, 31-34, 36-41, 43-48, 50, 52, 54, 56r; c-22-27, 29, 30, 33-37, 47, 54, 56.* ***Glanzman*** *a-20.* ***Howard*** *a-27, 30, 35, 40-43, 48, 54, 57.* ***Kim*** *a-38, 41, 57.* ***Larson*** *a-48, 50.* ***Newton*** *c/a-42.* ***Staton*** *a-32, 35; c-28, 46.* ***Sutton*** *c-33, 37, 39, 41.*

GHOSTLY TALES (Formerly Blue Beetle No. 50-54)
Charlton Comics: No. 55, 4-5/66 - No. 124, 12/76; No. 125, 9/77 - No. 169, 10/84
55-Intro. & origin Dr. Graves; Ditko-a 3.65 11.00 40.00
56-58,60,61,70,71-Ditko-a. 70-Dr. Graves ends. 71-Last 12¢ issue
2.40 7.35 22.00
59,62-66,68 2.00 6.00 18.00
67,69-Ditko-c/a 2.50 7.50 24.00
72,75,76,79-82,85-Ditko-a 1.75 5.25 14.00
73,77,78,83,84,86-90,92-95,97,99-Ditko-c/a 2.00 6.00 16.00
74,91,98,119,123,124 1.50 4.50 12.00
96-Ditko-c 1.75 5.25 14.00
100-Ditko-c; Sutton-a 1.75 5.25 14.00
101,103-105-Ditko-a 1.25 3.75 10.00
102,109,110,113: 102,109-Ditko-c/a. 110,113-Sutton-c; Ditko-a
1.50 4.50 12.00
106-Ditko & Sutton-a; Sutton-c 1.50 4.50 12.00
107-Ditko, Wood, Sutton-a 1.50 4.50 12.00
108,116,117,126-Ditko-a 1.25 3.75 10.00
111,112,114,115,127,130: 111-Ditko-c/a. 112,114-Ditko, Sutton-a. 114-Newton-a 115-Newton, Ditko-a. 127,130-Sutton-a 1.50 4.50 12.00
118,120-122,125-Ditko-c/a 1.75 5.25 14.00
119,128,129,134,135,142,145-151,153,154,156-160 2.40 6.00
131-133,163-Ditko-c/a 1.00 2.80 7.00
136-141,143,144,152,155-Ditko-a 2.40 6.00
161,162,164-169-Lower print run 1.00 2.80 7.00

NOTE: ***Aparo*** *a-65, 66, 68, 72, 141r, 142r; c-71, 72, 74-76, 81, 146r.* ***Ditko*** *a-55-58, 60, 61, 67, 69-73, 75-90, 92-95, 97, 99-118, 120-122, 125r, 126r, 131-133r, 136-141r, 143r, 144r, 152, 155, 161, 163; c-67, 69, 73, 77, 78, 83, 84, 86-90, 92-97, 99, 102, 109, 111, 118, 120-122, 125, 131-*

Ghost Manor #18 © CC

Ghost Rider #30 © MAR

Ghost Rider V2 #6 © MAR

133, 163. ***Glanzman*** *a-167.* ***Howard*** *a-95, 98, 99, 108, 117, 129; c-98, 107, 120, 121, 161.* ***Larson*** *a-117, 119.* ***Morisi*** *a-83, 84, 86.* ***Newton*** *a-114; c-115(painted).* ***Palais*** *a-61.* ***Staton*** *a-161; c-117.* ***Sutton*** *a-106, 107, 111-114, 127, 130; c-100, 106, 110, 113(painted).* ***Wood*** *a-107.*

GHOSTLY WEIRD STORIES (Formerly Blue Bolt Weird)
Star Publications: No. 120, Sept, 1953 - No. 124, Sept, 1954

120-Jo-Jo-r 40.00 120.00 320.00
121-124: 121-Jo-Jo-r. 122-The Mask-r/Capt. Flight #5; Rulah-r; has 1pg. story 'Death and the Devil Pills'-r/Western Outlaws #17. 123-Jo-Jo; Disbrow-a(2). 124-Torpedo Man 34.00 101.00 270.00
NOTE: ***Disbrow*** *a-120-124.* ***L. B. Cole*** *covers-all issues (#122 is a sci-fi cover).*

GHOST MANOR (Ghostly Haunts No. 20 on)
Charlton Comics: July, 1968 - No. 19, July, 1971

1 3.20 9.60 35.00
2-6: 6-Last 12¢ issue 2.30 7.00 20.00
7-12,17: 17-Morisi-a 2.00 6.00 16.00
13-16,18,19-Ditko-a; c-15,18,19 2.30 7.00 20.00

GHOST MANOR (2nd Series)
Charlton Comics: Oct, 1971-No. 32, Dec, 1976; No. 33, Sept, 1977-No. 77, 11/84

1 2.80 8.40 28.00
2,3,5-7,9-Ditko-c 1.75 5.25 14.00
4,10-Ditko-c/a 2.00 6.00 16.00
8-Wood, Ditko-a; Sutton-c 2.30 7.00 20.00
11,14-Ditko-c/a 1.75 5.25 14.00
12,17,27,30 1.25 3.75 10.00
13,15,16,19-21,23-26,29: 13-Ditko-a. 15,16-Ditko-c. 19-Newton, Sutton-a; nudity panels. 20-Ditko-a. 21-E-Man, Blue Beetle, Capt. Atom cameos; Ditko-a. 23-Sutton-a. 24-26,29-Ditko-a. 25-Sutton-a. 26-Early Zeck-a; Boyette-c 1.50 4.50 12.00
18-Newton's 1st pro art; Ditko-a; Sutton-c 2.00 6.00 16.00
22-Newton-c/a; Ditko-a 1.75 5.25 14.00
28,31,37,38-Ditko-c/a: 28-Nudity panels 1.75 5.25 14.00
32-36,39,41,45,48-50,53 1.00 3.00 8.00
40-Ditko-a; torture & drug use 1.10 3.30 9.00
42,43,46,47,51,52,60,62-Ditko-c/a 1.10 3.30 9.00
44,54,71-Ditko-a 1.00 2.80 7.00
55,56,58,59,61,63,65-70 5.00
57-Wood, Ditko, Howard-a 1.25 3.75 10.00
64-Ditko & Newton-a 1.00 2.80 7.00
71-77: 77-Aparo-r/Space Adventures V3#60 (Paul Mann) 2.40 6.00
19 (Modern Comics reprint, 1977) 3.00
NOTE: ***Ditko*** *a-4, 8, 10, 11(2), 13, 14, 18, 20-22, 24-26, 28, 29, 31, 37r, 38r, 40r, 42-44r, 46r, 47, 51r, 52r, 54r, 57, 60, 62(4), 64r, 71; c-2-7, 9-11, 14-16, 28, 31, 37, 38, 42, 43, 46, 47, 51, 52, 60, 62, 64.* ***Howard*** *a-4, 8, 12, 17, 19-21, 31, 41, 45, 57.* ***Newton*** *a-18-20, 22, 64; c-22.* ***Staton*** *a-13, 38, 44, 45.* ***Sutton*** *a-19, 23, 25, 45;c-8, 18.*

GHOST RIDER (See A-1 Comics, Best of the West, Black Phantom, Bobby Benson, Great Western, Red Mask & Tim Holt)
Magazine Enterprises: 1950 - No. 14, 1954
NOTE: *The character was inspired by Vaughn Monroe's "Ghost Riders in the Sky", and Disney's movie "The Headless Horseman".*

1(A-1 #27)-Origin Ghost Rider 71.00 213.00 675.00
2-5: 2(A-1 #29), 3(A-1 #31), 4(A-1 #34), 5(A-1 #37)-All Frazetta-c only 61.00 182.00 575.00
6,7: 6(A-1 #44)-Loco weed story, 7(A-1 #51) 28.00 83.00 220.00
8,9: 8(A-1 #57)-Drug use story, 9(A-1 #69) 24.00 71.00 190.00
10(A-1 #71)-Vs. Frankenstein 24.00 73.00 195.00
11-14: 11(A-1 #75). 12(A-1 #80)-Bondage-c; one-eyed Devil-c. 13(A-1 #84). 14(A-1 #112) 21.00 64.00 170.00
NOTE: ***Dick Ayers*** *art in all; c-1, 6-14.*

GHOST RIDER, THE (See Night Rider & Western Gunfighters)
Marvel Comics Group: Feb, 1967 - No. 7, Nov, 1967 (Western hero)(12¢)

1-Origin & 1st app. Ghost Rider; Kid Colt-reprints begin 6.35 19.00 70.00
2 3.45 10.35 38.00
3-7: 6-Last Kid Colt-r; All Ayers-c/a(p) 3.00 9.00 30.00

GHOST RIDER (See The Champions, Marvel Spotlight #5, Marvel Team-Up #15, 58, Marvel Treasury Edition #18, Marvel Two-In-One #8, The Original Ghost Rider & The Original Ghost Rider Rides Again)
Marvel Comics Group: Sept, 1973 - No. 81, June, 1983 (Super-hero)

1-Johnny Blaze, the Ghost Rider begins; 1st app. Daimon Hellstrom (Son of Satan) in cameo 6.35 19.00 70.00
2-1st full app. Daimon Hellstrom; gives glimpse of costume (1 panel); story continues in Marvel Spotlight #12 2.50 7.50 25.00
3-5: 3-Ghost Rider gets new cycle; Son of Satan app. 2.30 7.00 20.00
6-10: 10-Reprints origin/1st app. from Marvel Spotlight #5; Ploog-a 1.85 5.50 15.00
11-16 1.10 3.30 9.00
17,19-(Reg. 25¢ editions)(4,8/76) 1.10 3.30 9.00
17,19-(30¢-c variants, limited distribution) 1.75 5.25 14.00
18-(Reg. 25¢ edition)(6/76). Spider-Man-c & app. 1.25 3.75 10.00
18-(30¢-c variant, limited distribution) 1.85 5.50 15.00
20-Daredevil x-over; ties into D.D. #138; Byrne-a 1.85 5.50 15.00
21-30: 22-1st app. Enforcer. 29,30-Vs. Dr. Strange 2.40 6.00
31-34,36-49 5.00
35-Death Race classic; Starlin-c/a/sty 1.10 3.30 9.00
50-Double size 1.00 2.80 7.00
51-76,78-80: 80-Brief origin recap. 68,77-Origin retold 4.00
81-Death of Ghost Rider (Demon leaves Blaze) 1.10 3.30 9.00
NOTE: ***Anderson*** *c-64p.* ***Infantino*** *a(p)-43, 44, 51.* ***G. Kane*** *a-21p; c(p)-1, 2, 4, 5, 8, 9, 11-13, 19, 20, 24, 25.* ***Kirby*** *c-21-23.* ***Mooney*** *a-2-9p, 30i.* ***Nebres*** *c-26i.* ***Newton*** *a-23i.* ***Perez*** *c-26p.* ***Shores*** *a-2i. J.* ***Sparling*** *a-62p, 64p, 65p.* ***Starlin*** *a(p)-35.* ***Sutton*** *a-1p, 44i, 64i, 65i, 66, 67i.* ***Tuska*** *a-13p, 14p, 16p.*

GHOST RIDER (Volume 2) (Also see Doctor Strange/Ghost Rider Special, Marvel Comics Presents & Midnight Sons Unlimited)
Marvel Comics (Midnight Sons imprint #44 on): V2#1, May, 1990 - No. 93, Feb, 1998 ($1.50/$1.75/$1.95)

1-($1.95, 52 pgs.)-Origin/1st app. new Ghost Rider; Kingpin app. 2.40 6.00
1-2nd printing (not gold) 2.00
2-5: 3-Kingpin app. 5-Punisher app.; Jim Lee-c 3.00
5-Gold background 2nd printing 2.00
6-14,16-24,29,30,32-39: 6-Punisher app. 6,17-Spider-Man/Hobgoblin-c/story. 9-X-Factor app. 10-Reintro Johnny Blaze on the last pg. 11-Stroman-c/a(p). 12,13-Dr. Strange x-over cont'd in D.S. #28. 13-Painted-c. 14-Johnny Blaze vs. Ghost Rider; origin recap 1st Ghost Rider (Blaze). 18-Painted-c by Nelson. 29-Wolverine-c/story. 32-Dr. Strange x-over; Johnny Blaze app. 34-Williamson-a(i). 36-Daredevil app. 37-Archangel app. 2.00
15-Glow in the dark-c 3.00
25-27: 25-($2.75)-Contains pop-up scene insert. 26,27-X-Men x-over; Lee/Williams-c on both 2.75
28,31-($2.50, 52 pgs.)-Polybagged w/poster; part 1 & part 6 of Rise of the Midnight Sons storyline (see Ghost Rider/Blaze #1) 2.50
40-Outer-c is Darkhold envelope made of black parchment w/gold ink; Midnight Massacre; Demogoblin app. 2.50
41-48: 41-Lilith & Centurious app.; begin $1.75-c. 41-43-Neon ink-c. 43-Has free extra 16 pg. insert on Siege of Darkness. 44,45-Siege of Darkness parts 2 & 10. 44-Spot varnish-c. 46-Intro new Ghost Rider. 48-Spider-Man app. 2.00
49,51-60,62-74: 49-Begin $1.95-c; bound-in trading card sheet; Hulk app. 55-Werewolf by Night app. 65-Punisher app. 67,68-Gambit app. 68-Wolverine app. 73,74-Blaze, Vengeance app. 2.00
50,61: 50-($2.50, 52 pgs.)-Regular edition 2.50
50-($2.95, 52 pgs.)-Collectors Ed. die cut foil-c 3.00
75-92: 76-Vs. Vengeance. 77,78-Dr. Strange-app. 78-New costume 2.00
93-($2.99)-Saltares & Texeira-a 3.00
#(-1) Flashback (7/97) Saltares-a 2.00
Annual 1,2 ('93, '94, $2.95, 68 pgs.) 1-Bagged w/card 3.00
...And Cable 1 (9/92, $3.95, stiff-c, 68 pgs.)-Reprints Marvel Comics Presents #90-98 w/new Kieth-c 4.00
...:Crossroads (11/95, $3.95) Die cut cover; Nord-a 5.00
NOTE: ***Andy & Joe Kubert*** *c/a-28-31.* ***Quesada*** *c-21.* ***Williamson*** *a(i)-33-35; c-33i.*

GHOST RIDER/BALLISTIC
Marvel Comics: Feb, 1997 ($2.95, one-shot)

1-Devil's Reign pt. 3 3.00

GHOST RIDER/BLAZE: SPIRITS OF VENGEANCE (Also see Blaze)

Ghosts #79 © DC

Giant Comics Edition #11 © STJ

Giantkiller #4 © Dan Brereton

GD2.0 FN6.0 NM9.4

arvel Comics (Midnight Sons imprint #17 on): Aug, 1992 - No. 23, June, 994 ($1.75)

-($2.75, 52 pgs.)-Polybagged w/poster; part 2 of Rise of the Midnight Sons storyline; Adam Kubert-c/a begins 3.00
-11,14-21: 4-Art Adams & Joe Kubert-p. 5,6-Spirits of Venom parts 2 & 4 cont'd from Web of Spider-Man #95,96 w/Demogoblin. 14-17-Neon ink-c. 15-Intro Blaze's new costume & power. 17,18-Siege of Darkness parts 8 & 13. 17-Spot varnish-c 2.00
2-($2.95)-Glow-in-the-dark-c 3.00
3-($2.25)-Outer-c is Darkhold envelope made of black parchment w/gold ink; Midnight Massacre x-over 2.25
2,23: 22-Begin $1.95-c; bound-in trading card sheet 2.00
)TE: *Adam & Joe Kubert c-7, 8. Adam Kubert/Steacy c-6. J. Kubert a-13p(6 pgs.)*

HOST RIDER/CAPTAIN AMERICA: FEAR
arvel Comics: Oct, 1992 ($5.95, 52 pgs.)

-Wraparound gatefold-c; Williamson inks 2.40 6.00

HOST RIDER 2099
arvel Comics: May, 1994 - No. 25, May, 1996 ($1.50/$1.95)

($2.25)-Collector's Edition w/prismatic foil-c 3.00
($1.50)-Regular Edition; bound-in trading card sheet 2.00
-24: 7-Spider-Man 2099 app. 2.00
5 ($2.95) 3.00

HOST RIDER, WOLVERINE, PUNISHER: THE DARK DESIGN
arvel Comics: Dec, 1994 ($5.95, one-shot)

-Gatefold-c 2.40 6.00

HOST RIDER; WOLVERINE; PUNISHER: HEARTS OF DARKNESS
arvel Comics: Dec, 1991 ($4.95, one-shot, 52 pgs.)

-Double gatefold-c; John Romita, Jr.-c/a(p) 5.00

HOSTS (Ghost No. 1)
ational Periodical Publications/DC Comics: Sept-Oct, 1971 - No. 112, May, 982 (No. 1-5: 52 pgs.)

-Aparo-a 9.00 27.00 100.00
-Wood-a(i) 4.55 13.65 50.00
-5 3.20 9.60 35.00
-10 2.30 7.00 20.00
1-20 1.75 5.25 14.00
1-39 1.25 3.75 10.00
0-(68 pgs.) 2.00 6.00 18.00
1-60 1.00 2.80 7.00
1-96 5.00
7-99-The Spectre vs. Dr. 13 by Aparo. 97,98-Spectre-c by Aparo. 1.10 3.30 9.00
0-Infinity-c 5.00
1-112 4.00
)TE: *B. Baily a-77. Buckler c-99, 100. J. Craig a-108. Ditko a-77, 111. Giffen a-104p, 106p, 1p. Glanzman a-2. Golden a-88. Infantino a-8. Kaluta c-7, 93, 101. Kubert a-8; c-89, 105-8, 111. Mayer a-111. McWilliams a-99. Win Mortimer a-89, 91, 94. Nasser/Netzer a-97. wton a-92p, 94p. Nino a-35, 37, 57. Orlando a-74i; c-80. Redondo a-8, 13, 45. Sparling)-90, 93, 94. Spiegle a-103, 105. Tuska a-2i. Dr. 13, the Ghostbreaker back-ups in 95-99, 1.*

HOSTS SPECIAL (See DC Special Series No. 7)

HOST STORIES (See Amazing Ghost Stories)

HOST STORIES
ell Publ. Co.: Sept-Nov, 1962; No. 2, Apr-June, 1963 - No. 37, Oct, 1973

-295-211(#1)-Written by John Stanley 4.55 13.65 50.00
2.50 7.50 25.00
-10: Two No. 6's exist with different c/a(12-295-406 & 12-295-503) #12-295-503 is actually #9 with indicia to #6 2.30 7.00 20.00
1-21: 21-Last 12¢ issue 2.00 6.00 16.00
2-37 1.50 4.50 12.00
)TE: *#21-34, 36, 37 all reprint earlier issues.*

HOUL TALES (Magazine)
anley Publications: Nov, 1970 - No. 5, July, 1971 (52 pgs.) (B&W)

-Aragon pre-code reprints; Mr. Mystery as host; bondage-c 5.90 17.75 65.00
2,3: 2-(1/71)Reprint/Climax #1. 3-(3/71) 3.00 9.00 30.00
4-(5/71)Reprints story "The Way to a Man's Heart" used in **SOTI** 3.80 11.40 42.00
5-ACG reprints 2.50 7.50 25.00
NOTE: *No. 1-4 contain pre-code Aragon reprints.*

GIANT BOY BOOK OF COMICS (Also see Boy Comics)
Newsbook Publications (Gleason): 1945 (240 pgs., hard-c)

1-Crimebuster & Young Robin Hood; Biro-c 89.00 268.00 850.00

GIANT COMIC ALBUM
King Features Syndicate: 1972 (59¢, 11x14", 52 pgs., B&W, cardboard-c)

Newspaper reprints: Barney Google, Little Iodine, Katzenjammer Kids, Henry, Beetle Bailey, Blondie, & Snuffy Smith each... 3.00 9.00 30.00
Flash Gordon ('68-69 Dan Barry) 3.65 11.00 40.00
Mandrake the Magician ('59 Falk), Popeye 3.20 9.60 35.00

GIANT COMICS
Charlton Comics: Summer, 1957 - No. 3, Winter, 1957 (25¢, 100 pgs.)

1-Atomic Mouse, Hoppy app. 21.00 62.00 165.00
2,3: 2-Romance. 3-Christmas Book; Atomic Mouse, Atomic Rabbit, Li'l Genius, Li'l Tomboy & Atom the Cat stories 15.00 45.00 120.00
NOTE: *The above may be rebound comics; contents could vary.*

GIANT COMICS (See Wham-O Giant Comics)

GIANT COMICS EDITION (See Terry-Toons) (Also see Fox Giants)
St. John Publishing Co.: 1947 - No. 17, 1950 (25¢, 100-164 pgs.)

1-Mighty Mouse 43.00 127.00 475.00
2-Abbie & Slats 20.00 60.00 220.00
3-Terry-Toons Album; 100 pgs. 33.00 100.00 360.00
4-Crime comics; contains Red Seal No. 16, used & illo. in **SOTI** 50.00 150.00 550.00
5-Police Case Book (4/49, 132 pgs.)-Contents varies; contains remaindered St. John books - some volumes contain 5 copies rather than 4, with 160 pages; Matt Baker-c 48.00 143.00 525.00
5A-Terry-Toons Album (132 pgs.)-Mighty Mouse, Heckle & Jeckle, Gandy Goose & Dinky stories 30.00 90.00 325.00
6-Western Picture Stories; Baker-c/a(3); Tuska-a; The Sky Chief, Blue Monk, Ventrilo app., 132 pgs. 46.00 136.00 500.00
7-Contains a teen-age romance plus 3 Mopsy comics 27.00 80.00 295.00
8-The Adventures of Mighty Mouse (10/49) 30.00 90.00 325.00
9-Romance and Confession Stories; Kubert-a(4); Baker-a; photo-c (132 pgs.) 49.00 146.00 535.00
10-Terry-Toons Album (132 pgs.)-Mighty Mouse, Heckle & Jeckle, Gandy Goose stories 30.00 90.00 325.00
11-Western Picture Stories-Baker-c/a(4); The Sky Chief, Desperado, & Blue Monk app.; another version with Son of Sinbad by Kubert (132 pgs.) 44.00 131.00 480.00
12-Diary Secrets; Baker prostitute-c; 4 St. John romance comics; Baker-a 88.00 260.00 975.00
13-Romances; Baker, Kubert-a 43.00 128.00 470.00
14-Mighty Mouse Album (132 pgs.) 30.00 90.00 325.00
15-Romances (4 love comics)-Baker-c 50.00 150.00 550.00
16-Little Audrey; Abbott & Costello, Casper 31.00 91.00 335.00
17(nn)-Mighty Mouse Album (nn, no date, but did follow No. 16); 100 pgs. on cover but has 148 pgs. 30.00 90.00 325.00
NOTE: *The above books contain remaindered comics and contents could vary with each issue. No. 11, 12 have part photo magazine insides.*

GIANT COMICS EDITIONS
United Features Syndicate: 1940's (132 pgs.)

1-Abbie & Slats, Abbott & Costello, Jim Hardy, Ella Cinders, Iron Vic, Gordo, & Bill Bumlin 39.00 116.00 310.00
2-Jim Hardy, Ella Cinders, Elmo & Gordo 29.00 86.00 230.00
NOTE: *Above books contain rebound copies; contents can vary.*

GIANT GRAB BAG OF COMICS (See Archie All-Star Specials under Archie Comics)

GIANTKILLER
DC Comics: Aug, 1999 - No. 6, Jan, 2000 ($2.50, limited series)

1-6-Story and painted art by Dan Brereton 2.50

Giant Size Doc Savage #1 © MAR

Giant Size X-Men #1 © MAR

G.I. Combat #19 © QUA

...A to Z: A Field Guide to Big Monsters (8/99) 2.50

GIANTS (See Thrilling True Story of the Baseball...)

GIANT-SIZE...
Marvel Comics Group: May, 1974 - Dec, 1975 (35/50¢, 52/68 pgs.)
(Some titles quarterly) (Scarce in strict NM or better due to defective cutting, gluing and binding; warping, splitting and off-center pages are common)

Avengers 1(8/74)-New-a plus G.A. H. Torch-r; 1st modern app. The Whizzer; 1st & only modern app. Miss America; 2nd app. Invaders; Kang, Rama-Tut, Mantis app. 2.50 7.50 24.00
Avengers 2,3,5: 2(11/74)-Death of the Swordsman; origin of Rama-Tut. 3(2/75). 5(12/75)-Reprints Avengers Special #1 1.85 5.50 15.00
Avengers 4 (6/75)-Vision marries Scarlet Witch. 2.00 6.00 18.00
Captain America 1(12/75)-r/stories T.O.S. 59-63 by Kirby (#63 reprints origin) 2.40 7.35 22.00
Captain Marvel 1(12/75)-r/Capt. Marvel #17, 20, 21 by Gil Kane (p) 1.75 5.25 14.00
Chillers 1(6/74, 52 pgs)-Curse of Dracula; origin/1st app. Lilith, Dracula's daughter; Heath-r, Colan-c/a(p); becomes Giant-Size Dracula #2 on 3.00 9.00 30.00
Chillers 1(2/75, 50¢, 68 pgs.)-Alacala-a 2.00 6.00 18.00
Chillers 2(5/75)-All-r; Everett-r from Advs. into Weird Worlds 1.50 4.50 12.00
Chillers 3(8/75)-Wrightson-c(new)/a(r); Colan, Kirby, Smith-r 1.75 5.25 14.00
Conan 1(9/74)-B. Smith-r/#3; start adaptation of Howard's "Hour of the Dragon" (ends #4); 1st app. Belit; new-a begins 2.00 6.00 18.00
Conan 2(12/74)-B. Smith-r/#5; Sutton-a(i)(#1 also); Buscema-c 1.75 5.25 14.00
Conan 3-5: 3(4/75)-B. Smith-r/#6; Sutton-a(i). 4(6/75)-B. Smith-r/#7. 5(1975)-B. Smith-r/#14,15; Kirby-c 1.50 4.50 12.00
Creatures 1(5/74, 52 pgs.)-Werewolf app; 1st app. Tigra (formerly Cat); Crandall-r; becomes Giant-Size Werewolf w/#2 2.40 7.35 22.00
Daredevil 1(1975)-Reprints Daredevil Annual #1 1.85 5.50 15.00
Defenders 1(7/74)-Silver Surfer app.; Starlin-a; Ditko, Everett & Kirby reprints 2.50 7.50 24.00
Defenders 2(10/74, 68 pgs.)-New G. Kane-c/a(p); Son of Satan app.; Sub-Mariner-r by Everett; Ditko-r/Strange Tales #119 (Dr. Strange); Maneely-r. 1.75 5.25 14.00
Defenders 3-5: 3(1/75)-1st app. Korvac.; Newton, Starlin-a; Ditko, Everett-r. 4(4/75)-Ditko, Everett-r; G. Kane-c. 5-(7/75)-Guardians app. 1.50 4.50 12.00
Doc Savage 1(1975, 68 pgs.)-r/#1,2; Mooney-r 1.50 4.50 12.00
Doctor Strange 1(11/75)-Reprints stories from Strange Tales #164-168; Lawrence, Tuska-r 2.00 6.00 16.00
Dracula 2(9/74, 50¢)-Formerly Giant-Size Chillers 2.00 6.00 16.00
Dracula 3(12/74)-Fox-r/Uncanny Tales #6 1.75 5.25 14.00
Dracula 4(3/75)-Ditko-r(2) 1.75 5.25 14.00
Dracula 5(6/75)-1st Byrne art at Marvel 2.80 8.40 28.00
Fantastic Four 2-4: 2(8/74)-Formerly Giant-Size Super-Stars; Ditko-r. 3(11/74). 4(2/75)-1st Madrox; 2-4-All have Buscema-a 2.00 6.00 18.00
Fantastic Four 5,6: 5(5/75)-All-r; Kirby, G. Kane-r. 6(10/75)-All-r; Kirby-r 1.75 5.25 14.00
Hulk 1(1975) r/Hulk Special #1 2.40 7.35 22.00
Invaders 1(6/75, 50¢, 68 pgs.)-Origin; G.A. Sub-Mariner-r/Sub-Mariner #1; intro Master Man 2.30 7.00 20.00
Iron Man 1(1975)-Ditko reprint 2.00 6.00 18.00
Kid Colt 1-3: 1(1/75). 2(4/75). 3(7/75)-new Ayers-a 4.10 12.30 45.00
Man-Thing 1(8/74)-New Ploog-c/a (25 pgs.); Ditko-r/Amazing Adv. #11; Kirby-r/ Strange Tales Ann. #2 & T.O.S. #15; (#1-5 all have new Man-Thing stories, pre-hero-r & are 68 pgs.) 2.00 6.00 18.00
Man-Thing 2,3: 2(11/74)-Buscema-c/a(p); Kirby, Powell-r. 3(2/75)-Alcala-a; Ditko, Kirby, Sutton-r; Gil Kane-c 1.50 4.50 12.00
Man-Thing 4,5: 4(5/75)-Howard the Duck by Brunner-c/a; Ditko-r. 5(8/75)-Howard the Duck by Brunner (p); Dracaula cameo in Howard the Duck; Buscema-a(p); Sutton-a(i); G. Kane-c 2.00 6.00 18.00
Marvel Triple Action 1,2: 1(5/75). 2(7/75) 1.75 5.25 14.00
Master of Kung Fu 1(9/74)-Russell-a; Yellow Claw-r in #1-4; Gulacy-a in #1,2 2.30 7.00 20.00
Master of Kung Fu 2-4: 2-(12/74)-r/Yellow Claw #1. 3(3/75)-Gulacy-a; Kirby-a. 4(6/75)-Kirby-a 1.75 5.25 14.0
Power Man 1(1975) 1.75 5.25 14.0
Spider-Man 1(7/74)-Spider-Man /Human Torch-r by Kirby/Ditko; Byrne-r plus new-a (Dracula-c/story) 4.10 12.30 45.0
Spider-Man 2,3: 2(10/74)-Shang-Chi-c/app. 3(1/75)-Doc Savage-c/app.; Daredevil/Spider-Man-r w/Ditko-a 2.80 8.40 28.0
Spider-Man 4(4/75)-3rd Punisher app.; Byrne, Ditko-r 7.25 21.75 80.0
Spider-Man 5,6: 5(7/75)-Man-Thing/Lizard-c. 6(9/75) 2.30 7.00 20.0
Super-Heroes Featuring Spider-Man 1(6/74, 35¢, 52 pgs.)-Spider-Man vs. Man-Wolf; Morbius, the Living Vampire app.; Ditko-r; G. Kane-a(p); Spidey villains app. 5.00 15.00 55.0
Super-Stars 1(5/74, 35¢, 52 pgs.)-Fantastic Four; Thing vs. Hulk; Kirbyish-c/a by Buckler/Sinnott; F.F. villains profiled; becomes Giant-Size Fantastic Four #2 on 2.50 7.50 25.0
Super-Villain Team-Up 1(3/75, 68 pgs.)-Craig-r(i) (Also see Fantastic Four #6 for 1st super-villain team-up) 1.85 5.50 15.0
Super-Villain Team-Up 2(6/75, 68 pgs.)-Dr. Doom, Sub-Mariner app.; Spider-Man-r/Amazing Spider-Man #8 by Ditko; Sekowsky-a(p) 1.50 4.50 12.0
Thor 1(7/75) 1.85 5.50 15.0
Werewolf 2(10/74, 68 pgs.)-Formerly Giant-Size Creatures; Ditko-r; Frankenstein app. 1.75 5.25 14.0
Werewolf 3,5: 3(1/75, 68 pgs.). 5(7/75, 68 pgs.) 1.75 5.25 14.0
Werewolf 4(4/75, 68 pgs.)-Morbius the Living Vampire app. 2.00 8.00 18.0
X-Men 1(Summer, 1975, 50¢, 68 pgs.)-1st app. new X-Men; intro Nightcrawler, Storm, Colossus & Thunderbird; 2nd full app. Wolverine after Incredible Hulk #181 64.00 193.00 900.0
X-Men 2 (11/75)-N. Adams-r (51 pgs) 5.90 17.75 65.0

GIANT SPECTACULAR COMICS (See Archie All-Star Special under Archie Comics)

GIANT SUMMER FUN BOOK (See Terry-Toons...)

G. I. COMBAT
Quality Comics Group: Oct, 1952 - No. 43, Dec, 1956

	GD2.0	FN6.0	NM9.4
1-Crandall-c; Cuidera a-1-43i	63.00	189.00	600.0
2	31.00	94.00	250.0
3-5,10-Crandall-c/a	28.00	84.00	225.0
6-Crandall-a	25.00	75.00	200.0
7-9	21.00	64.00	170.0
11-20	16.00	48.00	125.0
21-31,33,35-43: 41-1st S.A. issue	13.00	39.00	105.0
32-Nuclear attack-c/story "Atomic Rocket Assault"	16.00	48.00	125.0
34-Crandall-a	14.00	41.00	110.0

G. I. COMBAT (See DC Special Series #22)
National Periodical Publ./DC Comics: No. 44, Jan, 1957 - No. 288, Mar, 1987

	GD2.0	FN6.0	NM9.4
44-Grey tone-c	45.00	135.00	585.0
45	26.50	79.00	290.0
46-50	20.50	61.00	225.0
51-Grey tone-c	19.50	58.00	215.0
52-54,59,60	17.00	51.00	185.0
55-minor Sgt. Rock prototype by Finger	18.00	54.00	200.0
56-Sgt. Rock prototype by Kanigher/Kubert	20.50	61.00	225.0
57,58-Pre-Sgt. Rock Easy Co. stories	19.50	58.00	215.0
61-65,69-74	12.50	37.00	135.0
66-Pre-Sgt. Rock Easy Co. story	18.00	54.00	200.0
67-1st Tank Killer	19.50	58.00	215.0
68-(1/59) Introduces "The Rock", Sgt. Rock prototype by Kanigher/Kubert; once considered his actual 1st app. (see Our Army at War #82,83)	40.00	120.00	475.0
75-80: 75-Greytone-c begin, end #109	13.50	40.00	150.0
81,82,84-86	9.50	28.50	105.0
83-1st Big Al, Little Al, & Charlie Cigar	12.75	38.00	140.0
87-1st Haunted Tank; series begins	45.00	135.00	585.0
88-2nd Haunted Tank	17.50	52.00	190.0
89-91: 90-Last 10¢ issue. 91-1st Haunted Tank-c	10.50	31.50	115.0
92-99	8.65	26.00	95.0

Giggle Comics #8 © ACG

G.I. Joe #16 © Z-D

G.I. Joe, A Real American Hero #21 © Hasbro

GD2.0 FN6.0 NM9.4

100,108: 108-1st Sgt. Rock x-over 9.50 28.50 105.00
101-107,109: 109-Grey tone-c 6.80 20.50 75.00
110-113,115-120: 113-Grey tone-c 5.00 15.00 55.00
114-Origin Haunted Tank 11.50 34.00 125.00
121-136: 121-1st app. Sgt. Rock's father. 136-Last 12¢ issue 3.20 9.60 35.00
137,139,140 3.00 9.00 30.00
138-Intro. The Losers (Capt. Storm, Gunner/Sarge, Johnny Cloud) in Haunted Tank (10-11/69) 7.65 23.00 85.00
141-143 2.00 6.00 18.00
144-148 (68pgs.) 2.50 7.50 25.00
149,151-154 (52 pgs.): 151-Capt. Storm story. 151,153-Medal of Honor series by Maurer 2.00 6.00 18.00
150- (52 pgs.) Ice Cream Soldier story (tells how he got his name); Death of Haunted Tank-c/s 2.50 7.50 25.00
155-167,169,170,200 1.10 3.30 9.00
168-Neal Adams-c 2.80 7.00 14.00
171-199 1.00 3.00 8.00
201,202 ($1.00 size) Neal Adams-c 2.40 6.00 12.00
203-210 ($1.00 size) 1.25 3.75 10.00
211-230 ($1.00 size) 1.00 2.80 7.00
231-259 ($1.00 size).232-Origin Kana the Ninja. 244-Death of Slim Stryker; 1st app. The Mercenaries. 246-(76 pgs., $1.50)-30th Anniversary issue. 257-Intro. Stuart's Raiders 2.40 6.00
260-281: 260-Begin $1.25, 52 pg. issues, end #281. 264-Intro Sgt. Bullet; origin Kana. 269-Intro. The Bravos of Vietnam. 274-Cameo of Monitor from Crisis on Infinite Earths x-over 4.00
282-288 (75¢): 282-New advs. begin 4.00

NOTE: ***N. Adams*** *c-168, 201, 202.* ***Check*** *a-168, 173.* ***Drucker*** *a-48, 61, 63, 66, 71, 72, 76, 134, 140, 141, 144, 147, 148, 153.* ***Evans*** *a-135, 138, 158, 164, 166, 201, 202, 204, 205, 215, 256.* ***Giffen*** *a-267.* ***Glanzman*** *a-most issues.* ***Kubert/Heath*** *a-most issues;* ***Kubert*** *covers most issues.* ***Morrow*** *a-159-161(2 pgs.).* ***Redondo*** *a-189, 240i, 243i.* ***Sekowsky*** *a-162p.* ***Severin*** *a-147, 152, 154.* ***Simonson*** *c-169.* ***Thorne*** *a-152, 156.* ***Wildey*** *a-153. Johnny Cloud app.-112, 115, 120. Mlle. Marie app.-123, 132, 200. Sgt. Rock app.-111-113, 115, 120, 125, 141, 146, 147, 149, 200. USS Stevens by* ***Glanzman****-145, 150-153, 157.* ***Grandenetti*** *c-44-48.*

GIDGET (TV)
Dell Publishing Co.: Apr, 1966 - No. 2, Dec, 1966

1-Sally Field photo-c 8.75 26.25 105.00
2 5.85 17.50 70.00

GIFT (See The Crusaders)

GIFT COMICS
Fawcett Publications: 1942 - No. 4, 1949 (50¢/25¢, 324 pgs./152 pgs.)

1-Captain Marvel, Bulletman, Golden Arrow, Ibis the Invincible, Mr. Scarlet, & Spy Smasher begin; not rebound, remaindered comics, printed at same time as originals; 50¢-c & 324 pgs. begin, end #3. 236.00 709.00 2600.00
2-Commando Yank, Phantom Eagle, others app. 155.00 465.00 1700.00
3 105.00 315.00 1150.00
4-(25¢, 152 pgs.)-The Marvel Family, Captain Marvel, etc.; each issue can vary in contents 64.00 191.00 700.00

GIFTS FROM SANTA (See March of Comics No. 137)

GIFTS OF THE NIGHT
DC Comics (Vertigo): Feb, 1999 - No. 4, May, 1999 ($2.95, limited series)

1-4-Bolton-c/a; Chadwick-s 3.00

GIGGLE COMICS (Spencer Spook No. 100) (Also see Ha Ha Comics)
Creston No.1-63/American Comics Group No. 64 on; Oct, 1943 - No. 99, Jan-Feb, 1955

1-Funny animal 31.00 94.00 250.00
2 15.00 45.00 120.00
3-5: Ken Hultgren-a begins? 11.00 33.00 90.00
6-10: 9-1st Superkatt (6/44) 10.00 30.00 70.00
11-20 7.15 21.50 50.00
21-40: 32-Patriotic-c. 37,61-X-Mas-c. 39-St. Valentine's Day-c 6.00 18.00 42.00
41-54,56-59,61-99: 95-Spencer Spook begins? 5.00 15.00 35.00
55,60-Milt Gross-a 6.40 19.25 45.00

G-I IN BATTLE (G-I No. 1 only)

GD2.0 FN6.0 NM9.4

Ajax-Farrell Publ./Four Star: Aug, 1952 - No. 9, July, 1953; Mar, 1957 - No. 6, May, 1958

1 10.00 30.00 75.00
2 5.50 16.50 38.00
3-9 5.00 15.00 32.00
Annual 1(1952, 25¢, 100 pgs.) 24.00 71.00 190.00
1(1957-Ajax) 6.40 19.25 45.00
2-6 4.65 14.00 28.00

G. I. JANE
Stanhall/Merit No. 11: May, 1953 - No. 11, Mar, 1955 (Misdated 3/54)

1-PX Pete begins; Bill Williams-c/a 12.00 36.00 95.00
2-7(5/54) 7.00 21.00 48.00
8-10(12/54, Stanhall) 5.55 16.50 38.00
11 (3/55, Merit) 5.00 15.00 32.00

G. I. JOE (Also see Advs. of..., Showcase #53, 54 & The Yardbirds)
Ziff-Davis Publ. Co. (Korean War): No. 10, 1950; No. 11, 4-5/51 - No. 51, 6/57(52pgs.: 10-14,6-17?)

10(#1, 1950)-Saunders painted-c begin 14.00 41.00 110.00
11-14(#2-5, 10/51): 11-New logo. 12-New logo 10.00 30.00 75.00
V2#6(12/51)-17-(11/52; Last 52 pgs.?) 10.00 30.00 70.00
18-(25¢, 100 pg. Giant, 12-1/52-53) 21.00 64.00 170.00
19-30: 20-22,24,28-31-The Yardbirds app. 7.85 23.50 55.00
31-47,49-51 7.15 21.50 50.00
48-Atom bomb story 7.85 23.50 55.00

NOTE: ***Powell*** *a-V2#7, 8, 11.* ***Norman Saunders*** *painted c-10-14, V2#6-14, 26, 30, 31, 35, 38, 39.* ***Tuska*** *a-7. Bondage c-29, 35, 38.*

G. I. JOE (America's Movable Fighting Man)
Custom Comics: 1967 (5-1/8x8-3/8", 36 pgs.)

nn-Schaffenberger-a; based on Hasbro toy 2.80 8.40 28.00

G.I. JOE
Dark Horse Comics: Dec, 1995 - No. 4, Apr, 1996 ($1.95, limited series)

1-4: Mike W. Barr scripts. 1,2-Miller-c. 3-Simonson-c 3.00

G.I. JOE
Dark Horse Comics: V2#1, June, 1996 - V2#4, Sept, 1996 ($2.50)

V2#1-4: Mike W. Barr scripts. 4-Painted-c 3.00

G. I. JOE AND THE TRANSFORMERS
Marvel Comics Group: Jan, 1987 - No. 4, Apr, 1987 (Limited series)

1-4 3.50

G. I. JOE, A REAL AMERICAN HERO (...Starring Snake-Eyes on-c #135 on)
Marvel Comics Group: June, 1982 - No. 155, Dec, 1994

1-Printed on Baxter paper; based on Hasbro toy 1.50 4.50 12.00
2-Printed on reg. paper 1.50 4.50 12.00
3-10 1.00 3.00 8.00
11-20: 11-Intro Airborne 1.00 2.80 7.00
21-1st Storm Shadow 1.00 3.00 8.00
22,26,27: 26,27-Origin Snake-Eyes parts 1 & 2 2.40 6.00
23-25,28-30,60: 60-Todd McFarlane-a 5.00
31-59,61-90: 33-New headquarters 3.00
91,92,94-99 4.00
93-Snake-Eyes' face first revealed 1.00 3.00 8.00
100,135-142: 139-142-New Transformers app. 5.00
101-134: 110-1st Ron Garney-a 4.00
143-149: 135-138-($1.75)-Bagged w/trading card. 144-Origin Snake-Eyes 5.00
150 1.25 3.75 10.00
151-154 1.10 3.30 9.00
155-Last issue 1.50 4.50 12.00
All 2nd printings 2.00
Special Treasury Edition (1982)-r/#1 2.00 6.00 16.00
Yearbook 1-4: (3/85-3/88)-r/#1; Golden-c. 2-Golden-c/a 3.00

NOTE: ***Garney*** *a(p)-110.* ***Golden*** *c-23, 29, 34, 36.* ***Heath*** *a-24.* ***Rogers*** *a(p)-75, 77-82, 84, 86; c-77.*

G. I. JOE COMICS MAGAZINE
Marvel Comics Group: Dec, 1986 - No. 13, 1988 ($1.50, digest-size)

1-13: G.I. Joe-r 1.00 2.80 7.00

Ginger #6 © AP

Girls' Life #1 © MAR

Girls' Romances #5 © DC

G.I. JOE EUROPEAN MISSIONS (Action Force in indicia)
Marvel Comics Ltd. (British): Jun, 1988 - No. 15, Dec, 1989 ($1.50/$1.75)

	GD2.0	FN6.0	NM9.4
1-15: Reprints Action Force			3.00

G. I. JOE ORDER OF BATTLE, THE
Marvel Comics Group: Dec, 1986 - No. 4, Mar, 1987 (limited series)

	GD2.0	FN6.0	NM9.4
1-4			2.50

G. I. JOE SPECIAL MISSIONS (Indicia title: Special Missions)
Marvel Comics Group: Oct, 1986 - No. 28, Dec, 1989 ($1.00)

	GD2.0	FN6.0	NM9.4
1-28			2.50

G. I. JUNIORS (See Harvey Hits No. 86,91,95,98,101,104,107,110,112,114,116,118,120,122)

GILGAMESH II
DC Comics: 1989 - No. 4, 1989 ($3.95, limited series, prestige format, mature)

	GD2.0	FN6.0	NM9.4
1-4: Starlin-c/a/scripts			4.00

GIL THORP
Dell Publishing Co.: May-July, 1963

	GD2.0	FN6.0	NM9.4
1-Caniffish-a	3.20	9.60	35.00

GINGER
Archie Publications: 1951 - No. 10, Summer, 1954

	GD2.0	FN6.0	NM9.4
1-Teenage humor	10.00	30.00	110.00
2-(1952)	5.90	17.75	65.00
3-6: 6-(Sum/53)	4.10	12.30	45.00
7-10-Katy Keene app.	6.35	19.00	70.00

GINGER FOX (Also see The World of Ginger Fox)
Comico: Sept, 1988 - No. 4, Dec, 1988 ($1.75, limited series)

	GD2.0	FN6.0	NM9.4
1-4: Part photo-c on all			2.00

G.I. R.A.M.B.O.T.
Wonder Color Comics/Pied Piper #2: Apr, 1987 - No. 2? ($1.95)

	GD2.0	FN6.0	NM9.4
1,2: 2-Exist?			2.00

GIRL
DC Comics (Vertigo Verite): Jul, 1996 - No. 3, 1996 ($2.50, lim. series, mature)

	GD2.0	FN6.0	NM9.4
1-3: Peter Milligan scripts; Fegredo-c/a			2.50

GIRL COMICS (Becomes Girl Confessions No. 13 on)
Marvel/Atlas Comics(CnPC): Oct, 1949 - No. 12, Jan, 1952 (#1-4: 52 pgs.)

	GD2.0	FN6.0	NM9.4
1-Photo-c	21.00	62.00	165.00
2-Kubert-a; photo-c	12.00	36.00	95.00
3-Everett-a; Liz Taylor photo-c	18.00	53.00	140.00
4-11: 4-Photo-c. 10-12-Sol Brodsky-c	10.00	30.00	70.00
12-Krigstein-a; Al Hartley-c	10.00	30.00	75.00

GIRL CONFESSIONS (Formerly Girl Comics)
Atlas Comics (CnPC/ZPC): No. 13, Mar, 1952 - No. 35, Aug, 1954

	GD2.0	FN6.0	NM9.4
13-Everett-a	11.00	33.00	90.00
14,15,19,20	7.85	23.50	55.00
16-18-Everett-a	9.30	28.00	65.00
21-35: Robinson-a	5.00	15.00	35.00

GIRL CRAZY
Dark Horse Comics: May, 1996 - No. 3, July, 1996 ($2.95, B&W, limited series)

	GD2.0	FN6.0	NM9.4
1-3: Gilbert Hernandez-a/scripts.			3.00

GIRL FROM U.N.C.L.E., THE (TV) (Also see The Man From...)
Gold Key: Jan, 1967 - No. 5, Oct, 1967

	GD2.0	FN6.0	NM9.4
1-McWilliams-a; Stephanie Powers photo front/back-c & pin-ups (no ads, 12¢)	8.35	25.00	100.00
2-5-Leonard Swift-Courier No. 5	5.85	17.50	70.00

GIRLS' FUN & FASHION MAGAZINE (Formerly Polly Pigtails)
Parents' Magazine Institute: V5#44, Jan, 1950 - V5#48, Sept., 1950

	GD2.0	FN6.0	NM9.4
V5#44	5.00	15.00	32.00
45-48	4.00	11.00	22.00

GIRLS IN LOVE
Fawcett Publications: May, 1950 - No. 2, July, 1950

	GD2.0	FN6.0	NM9.4
1,2-Photo-c	10.00	30.00	75.00

GIRLS IN LOVE (Formerly G. I. Sweethearts No. 45)
Quality Comics Group: No. 46, Sept, 1955 - No. 57, Dec, 1956

	GD2.0	FN6.0	NM9.4
46	7.15	21.50	50.00
47-53,55,56	5.00	15.00	32.00
54- 'Commie' story	5.50	16.50	38.00
57-Matt Baker-c/a	8.65	26.00	60.00

GIRLS IN WHITE (See Harvey Comics Hits No. 58)

GIRLS' LIFE (Patsy Walker's Own Magazine For Girls!)
Atlas Comics (BFP): Jan, 1954 - No. 6, Nov, 1954

	GD2.0	FN6.0	NM9.4
1	10.00	30.00	70.00
2-Al Hartley-c	6.00	18.00	42.00
3-6	5.00	15.00	32.00

GIRLS' LOVE STORIES
National Comics(Signal Publ. No. 9-65/Arleigh No. 83-117): Aug-Sept, 1949 - No. 180, Nov-Dec, 1973 (No. 1-13: 52 pgs.)

	GD2.0	FN6.0	NM9.4
1-Toth, Kinstler-a, 8 pgs. each; photo-c	53.00	158.00	475.00
2-Kinstler-a?	31.00	94.00	250.00
3-10: 1-9-Photo-c. 7-Infantino-c(p)	21.00	64.00	170.00
11-20	16.00	49.00	130.00
21-33: 21-Kinstler-a. 33-Last pre-code (1-2/55)	10.00	30.00	75.00
34-50	8.65	26.00	60.00
51-70	5.00	15.00	55.00
71-99: 83-Last 10¢ issue	3.20	9.60	35.00
100	3.80	11.40	42.00
101-146: 113-117-April O'Day app.	2.80	8.40	28.00
147-151- "Confessions" serial. 150-Wood-a	2.50	7.50	24.00
152-160,171-179	2.00	6.00	16.00
161-170 (52 pgs.)	3.00	9.00	30.00
180 Last issue	2.50	7.50	25.00

GIRLS' ROMANCES
National Periodical Publ.(Signal Publ. No. 7-79/Arleigh No. 84): Feb-Mar, 1950 - No. 160, Oct, 1971 (No. 1-11: 52 pgs.)

	GD2.0	FN6.0	NM9.4
1-Photo-c	53.00	158.00	475.00
2-Photo-c; Toth-a	30.00	90.00	240.00
3-10: 3-6-Photo-c	21.00	64.00	170.00
11,12,14-20	14.00	43.00	115.00
13-Toth-c	15.00	45.00	120.00
21-31: 31-Last pre-code (2-3/55)	10.00	30.00	70.00
32-50	5.00	15.00	55.00
51-99: 80-Last 10¢ issue	3.20	9.60	35.00
100	3.80	11.40	42.00
101-108,110-120	2.50	7.50	25.00
109-Beatles-c/story	11.50	34.00	125.00
121-133,135-140	2.30	7.00	20.00
134-Neal Adams-c (splash pg. is same as-c)	3.20	9.60	35.00
141-158	2.00	6.00	18.00
159,160-52 pgs.	3.00	9.00	30.00

GIRL WHO WOULD BE DEATH, THE
DC Comics (Vertigo): Dec, 1998 - No. 4, March, 1999 ($2.50, lim. series)

	GD2.0	FN6.0	NM9.4
1-4-Kiernan-s/Ormston-a			2.50

G. I. SWEETHEARTS (Formerly Diary Loves; Girls In Love #46 on)
Quality Comics Group: No. 32, June, 1953 - No. 45, May, 1955

	GD2.0	FN6.0	NM9.4
32	7.15	21.50	50.00
33-45: 44-Last pre-code (3/55)	5.00	15.00	32.00

G.I. TALES (Formerly Sgt. Barney Barker No. 1-3)
Atlas Comics (MCI): No. 4, Feb, 1957 - No. 6, July, 1957

	GD2.0	FN6.0	NM9.4
4-Severin-a(4)	7.85	23.50	55.00
5	5.50	16.50	38.00
6-Orlando, Powell, & Woodbridge-a	6.00	18.00	42.00

GIVE ME LIBERTY (Also see Dark Horse Presents Fifth Anniversary Special, Dark Horse Presents #100-4, Happy Birthday Martha Washington, Martha Washington Goes to War, Martha Washington Stranded In Space & San Diego Comicon Comics #2)
Dark Horse Comics: June, 1990 - No. 4, 1991 ($4.95, limited series, 52 pgs.)

Glamorous Romances #50 © ACE

Gloom Cookie #3 © Valentino & Naifeh

Glory V2 #0 © Awesome Ent.

GD2.0 FN6.0 NM9.4

1-4: 1st app. Martha Washington; Frank Miller scripts, Dave Gibbons-c/a in all. 5.00

G. I. WAR BRIDES
Superior Publishers Ltd.: Apr, 1954 - No. 8, June, 1955

	GD2.0	FN6.0	NM9.4
1	7.85	23.50	55.00
2	5.00	15.00	30.00
3-8: 4-Kamenesque-a; lingerie panels	4.30	13.00	26.00

G. I. WAR TALES
National Periodical Publications: Mar-Apr, 1973 - No. 4, Oct-Nov, 1973

	GD2.0	FN6.0	NM9.4
1-Reprints in all; dinosaur-c/s	2.30	7.00	20.00
2-N. Adams-a(r)	2.00	6.00	16.00
3,4: 4-Krigstein-a(r)	1.75	5.25	14.00

NOTE: ***Drucker** a-3r, 4r. **Heath** a-4r. **Kubert** a-2, 3; c-4r.*

GIZMO (Also see Domino Chance)
Chance Ent.: May-June, 1985 (B&W, one-shot)

1 4.00

GIZMO
Mirage Studios: 1986 - No. 6, July, 1987 ($1.50, B&W)

1-6 2.00

GLADSTONE COMIC ALBUM
Gladstone: 1987 - No. 28, 1990 ($5.95/$9.95, 8-1/2x11")(All Mickey Mouse albums are by Gottfredson)

1-10: 1-Uncle Scrooge; Barks-r; Beck-c. 2-Donald Duck; r/F.C. #108 by Barks. 3-Mickey Mouse-r by Gottfredson. 4-Uncle Scrooge; r/F.C. #456 by Barks w/ unedited story. 5-Donald Duck Advs.; r/F.C. #199. 6-Uncle Scrooge-r by Barks. 7-Donald Duck-r by Barks. 8-Mickey Mouse-r. 9-Bambi; r/F.C. #186? 10-Donald Duck Advs.; r/F.C. #275 1.25 3.75 10.00

11-20: 11-Uncle Scrooge; r/U.S. #4. 12-Donald And Daisy; r/F.C. #1055, WDC&S. 13-Donald Duck Advs.; r/F.C. #408. 14-Uncle Scrooge; Barks-r/ U.S #21. 15-Donald And Gladstone; Barks-r. 16-Donald Duck Advs.; r/F.C. #238. 17-Mickey Mouse strip-r (The World of Tomorrow, The Pirate Ghost Ship). 18-Donald Duck and the Junior Woodchucks; Barks-r. 19-Uncle Scrooge; r/U.S. #12; Rosa-c. 20-Uncle Scrooge; r/F.C. #386; Barks-c/a(r) 1.25 3.75 10.00

21-25: 21-Donald Duck Family; Barks-c/a(r). 22-Mickey Mouse strip-r. 23-Donald Duck; Barks-r/D.D. #26 w/unedited story. 24-Uncle Scrooge; Barks-r; Rosa-c. 25-D. Duck; Barks-c/a-r/F.C. #367 1.25 3.75 10.00

26-28: All have $9.95-c. 26-Mickey and Donald; Gottfredson-c/a(r). 27-Donald Duck; r/WDC&S by Barks; Barks painted-c. 28-Uncle Scrooge & Donald Duck; Rosa-c/a (4 stories) 1.25 3.75 10.00

Special 1-7: 1 ('89-'90, $9.95/13.95)-1-Donald Duck Finds Pirate Gold; r/F.C. #9 2 ('89, $8.95)-Uncle Scrooge and Donald Duck; Barks-r/Uncle Scrooge #5; Rosa-c. 3 ('89, $8.95)-Mickey Mouse strip-r. 4 ('89, $11.95)-Uncle Scrooge; Rosa-c/a-r/Son of the Sun from U.S. #219 plus Barks-r/U.S. 5 ('90, $11.95)-Donald Duck Advs.; Barks-r/F.C. #282 & 422 plus Barks painted-c. 6 ('90, $12.95)-Uncle Scrooge; Barks-c/a-r/Uncle Scrooge. 7 ('90, $13.95)-Mickey Mouse; Gottfredson strip-r 1.75 5.25 14.00

GLADSTONE COMIC ALBUM (2nd Series)(Also see The Original Dick Tracy)
Gladstone Publishing: 1990 ($5.95, 8-1/2 x 11," stiff-c, 52 pgs.)

	GD2.0	FN6.0	NM9.4
1,2-The Original Dick Tracy. 2-Origin of the 2-way wrist radio	2.40		6.00
3-D Tracy Meets the Mole-r by Gould ($6.95).	1.00	3.00	8.00

GLAMOROUS ROMANCES (Formerly Dotty)
Ace Magazines (A. A. Wyn): No. 41, July, 1949 - No. 90, Oct, 1956 (Photo-c 68-90)

	GD2.0	FN6.0	NM9.4
41-Dotty app.	7.85	23.50	55.00
42-72,74-80: 44-Begin 52 pg. issues. 45,50-61-Painted-c. 80-Last pre-code (2/55)	5.00	15.00	32.00
73-L.B. Cole-r/All Love #27	5.50	16.50	38.00
81-90	4.65	14.00	28.00

GLOBAL FORCE
Silverline Comics: 1987 - No. 2 ($1.95)

1,2 2.00

GLOOM COOKIE
SLG Publishing: June, 1999 - Present ($2.95, B&W)

1-6-Serena Valentino-s/Ted Naifeh-a 3.00

GLORY
Image Comics (Extreme Studios)/Maximum Press: Mar, 1995 - No. 22, Apr, 1997 ($2.50)

0-Deodato-c/a, 1-(3/95)-Deodato-a 2.50
1A-Variant-c 4.00
2-11,13-22: 4-Variant-c by Quesada & Palmiotti. 5-Bagged w/Youngblood gaming card. 7,8-Deodato-c/a(p). 8-Babewatch x-over. 9-Cruz-c; Extreme Destroyer Pt. 5; polybagged w/card. 10-Angela-c/app. 11-Deodato-c. 2.50
12-($3.50)-Photo-c 3.50
Trade Paperback (1995, $9.95)-r/#1-4 10.00

GLORY
Awesome Comics: Mar, 1999 ($2.50)

0-Liefeld-c; story and sketch pages 2.50

GLORY & FRIENDS BIKINI FEST
Image Comics (Extreme): Sept, 1995 - No. 2, Oct, 1995 ($2.50, limited series)

1,2: 1-Photo-c; centerfold photo; pin-ups 2.50

GLORY & FRIENDS CHRISTMAS SPECIAL
Image Comics (Extreme Studios): Dec, 1995 ($2.50, one-shot)

1-Deodato-c 2.50

GLORY & FRIENDS LINGIRIE SPECIAL
Image Comics (Extreme Studios): Sept, 1995 ($2.95, one-shot)

1-Pin-ups w/photos; photo-c; varant-c exists 3.00

GLORY/ANGELA: ANGELS IN HELL (See Angela/Glory: Rage of Angels)
Image Comics (Extreme Studios): Apr, 1996 ($2.50, one-shot)

1-Flip book w/Darkchylde #1 2.50

GLORY/AVENGELYNE
Image Comics (Extreme Studios): Oct, 1995 ($3.95, one-shot)

1-Chromium-c, 1-Regular-c 4.00

GLORY/CELESTINE: DARK ANGEL
Image Comics/Maximum Press (Extreme Studios): Sept, 1996 - No. 3, Nov, 1996 ($2.50, limited series)

1-3 2.50

GNOME MOBILE, THE (See Movie Comics)

GOBBLEDYGOOK
Mirage Studios: 1984 - No. 2, 1984 (B&W)(1st Mirage comics, published at same time)

1,2-(24 pgs.)-1st Teenage Mutant Ninja Turtles 19.00 57.00 210.00

GOBBLEDYGOOK
Mirage Studios: Dec, 1986 ($3.50, B&W, one-shot, 100 pgs.)

1-New 8 pg. TMNT story plus a Donatello/Michaelangelo 7 pg. story & a Gizmo story; Corben-i(r)/TMNT #7 5.00

GOBLIN, THE
Warren Publishing Co.: June, 1982 - No. 3, Dec, 1982 (Magazine, $2.25)

	GD2.0	FN6.0	NM9.4
1-The Gremlin app; Golden-a(p)	2.00	6.00	18.00
2,3: 2-1st Hobgoblin	1.50	4.50	12.00

GODDESS
DC Comics (Vertigo): June, 1995 - No. 8, Jan, 1996 ($2.95, limited series)

1-Garth Ennis scripts; Phil Winslade-c/a in all 5.00
2-8 4.00

GODFATHERS, THE (See The Crusaders)

GOD IS
Spire Christian Comics (Fleming H. Revell Co.): 1973, 1975 (35-49¢)

nn-By Al Hartley 1.00 2.80 7.00

GODS AND TULIPS
Westhampton House: Aug, 1999 ($3.00, B&W, one-shot for the CBLDF)

nn-Neil Gaiman speeches; Kaluta-c 3.00

GOD'S COUNTRY (Also see Marvel Comics Presents)

Godzilla #3 © Toho Co. Ltd

Golden Age Secret Files #1 © DC

Golden Arrow #4 © FAW

GD2.0 FN6.0 NM9.4

Marvel Comics: 1994 ($6.95)

nn-P. Craig Russell-a; Colossus story; r/Marvel Comics Presents #10-17 7.00

GODS FOR HIRE
Hot Comics: Dec, 1986 - No. 3 ($1.50)

1-3: Barry Crain-c/a(p) 2.00

GOD'S HEROES IN AMERICA
Catechetical Guild Educational Society: 1956 (nn) (25¢/35¢, 68 pgs.)

307 3.60 9.00 18.00

GOD'S SMUGGLER (Religious)
Spire Christian Comics/Fleming H. Revell Co.: 1972 (39¢/40¢)

1-Two variations exist 1.00 2.80 7.00

GODWHEEL
Malibu Comics (Ultraverse): No. 0, Jan, 1995 - No. 3, Feb, 1995 ($2.50, limited series)

0-3: 0-Flip-c. 1-1st app. of Primevil; Thor cameo (1 panel). 3-Perez-a in Chapter 3, Thor app. 2.50

GODZILLA (Movie)
Marvel Comics : August, 1977 - No. 24, July, 1979 (Based on movie series)

1-(Regular 30¢ edition)-Mooney-i 1.50 4.50 12.00
1-(35¢-c variant, limited distribution) 2.00 6.00 18.00
2-(Regular 30¢ edition)-Tuska-i. 1.00 3.00 8.00
2-(35¢-c variant, limited distribution) 1.50 4.50 12.00
3- Champions app.(w/o Ghost Rider) 1.25 3.75 10.00
4-10: 4,5-Sutton-a 1.00 2.80 7.00
11-23: 14-Shield app. 20-F.F. app. 21,22-Devil Dinosaur app. 2.40 6.00
24-Last issue 1.00 2.80 7.00

GODZILLA (Movie)
Dark Horse Comics: May, 1988 - No. 6, 1988 ($1.95, B&W, limited series) (Based on movie series)

1 5.00
2-6 3.00
...Collection (1990, $10.95)-r/1-6 with new-c 11.00
...Color Special 1 (Sum, 1992, $3.50, color, 44 pgs.)-Arthur Adams wrap-around-c/a & part scripts 4.00
...King Of The Monsters Special (8/87, $1.50)-Origin; Bissette-c/a 3.00
...Vs. Barkley nn (12/93, $2.95, color)-Dorman painted-c 3.00

GODZILLA (King of the Monsters) (Movie)
Dark Horse Comics: May, 1995 - No. 16, Sept, 1996 ($2.50) (Based on movies)

0-16: 0-r/Dark Horse Comics #10,11. 1-3-Kevin Maguire scripts. 3-8-Art Adams-c 4.00
...Vs. Hero Zero ($2.50) 2.50

GOG (VILLAINS) (See Kingdom Come)
DC Comics: Feb, 1998 ($1.95, one-shot)

1-Waid-s/Ordway-a(p)/Pearson-c 3.00

GO GIRL!
Image Comics: Aug, 2000 - Present ($3.50, B&W, quarterly)

1,2-Trina Robbins-s/Anne Timmons-a; pin-up gallery 3.50

GO-GO
Charlton Comics: June, 1966 - No. 9, Oct, 1967

1-Miss Bikini Luv begins w/Jim Aparo's 1st published work; Rolling Stones, Beatles, Elvis, Sonny & Cher, Bob Dylan, Sinatra, parody; Herman's Hermits pin-ups; D'Agostino-c/a in #1-8 6.35 19.00 70.00
2-Ringo Starr, David McCallum & Beatles photos on cover; Beatles story and photos 6.35 19.00 70.00
3,4: 3-Blooperman begins, ends #6; 1 pg. Batman & Robin satire; full pg. photo pin-ups Lovin' Spoonful & The Byrds 3.45 10.35 38.00
5-7,9: 5 (2/67)-Super Hero & TV satire by Jim Aparo & Grass Green begins. 6-8-Aparo-a. 6-Petula Clark photo-c. 7-Photo of Brian Wilson of Beach Boys on-c & Beach Boys photo inside f/b-c. 9-Aparo-c/a 3.45 10.35 38.00
8-Monkees photo on-c & photo inside f/b-c 4.55 13.65 50.00

GO-GO AND ANIMAL (See Tippy's Friends...)

GOING STEADY (Formerly Teen-Age Temptations)

GD2.0 FN6.0 NM9.4

St. John Publ. Co.: No. 10, Dec, 1954 - No. 13, June, 1955; No. 14, Oct, 1955

10(1954)-Matt Baker-c/a 20.00 60.00 160.00
11(2/55, last precode), 12(4/55)-Baker-c 11.00 33.00 90.00
13(6/55)-Baker-c/a 14.00 41.00 110.00
14(10/55)-Matt Baker-c/a, 25 pgs. 16.00 49.00 130.00

GOING STEADY (Formerly Personal Love)
Prize Publications/Headline: V3#3, Feb, 1960 - V3#6, Aug, 1960; V4#1, Sept-Oct, 1960

V3#3-6, V4#1 2.30 7.00 20.00

GOING STEADY WITH BETTY (Becomes Betty & Her Steady No. 2)
Avon Periodicals: Nov-Dec, 1949

1 14.00 41.00 110.00

GOLDEN AGE, THE
DC Comics (Elseworlds): 1993 - No. 4, 1994 ($4.95, limited series)

1-4: James Robinson scripts; Paul Smith-c/a; gold foil embossed-c 6.00
Trade Paperback (1995, $19.95) 20.00

GOLDEN AGE SECRET FILES
DC Comics: Feb, 2001 ($4.95, one-shot)

1-Origins and profiles of JSA members and other G.A. heroes; Lark-c 5.00

GOLDEN ARROW (See Fawcett Miniatures, Mighty Midget & Whiz Comics)

GOLDEN ARROW (...Western No. 6)
Fawcett Publications: Spring, 1942 - No. 6, Spring, 1947 (68 pgs.)

1-Golden Arrow begins 84.00 253.00 800.00
2-(1943) 42.00 125.00 375.00
3-5: 3-(Win/45-46). 4-(Spr/46). 5-(Fall/46) 34.00 101.00 270.00
6-Krigstein-a 36.00 108.00 290.00

GOLDEN COMICS DIGEST
Gold Key: May, 1969 - No. 48, Jan, 1976

NOTE: *Whitman editions exist of many titles and are generally valued the same.*

1-Tom & Jerry, Woody Woodpecker, Bugs Bunny 3.80 11.40 42.00
2-Hanna-Barbera TV Fun Favorites; Space Ghost, Flintstones, Atom Ant, Jetsons, Yogi Bear, Banana Splits, others app. 5.45 16.35 60.00
3-Tom & Jerry, Woody Woodpecker 2.30 7.00 20.00
4-Tarzan; Manning & Marsh-a 3.65 11.00 40.00
5,8-Tom & Jerry, W. Woodpecker, Bugs Bunny 2.00 6.00 18.00
6-Bugs Bunny 2.00 6.00 18.00
7-Hanna-Barbera TV Fun Favorites 3.65 11.00 40.00
9-Tarzan 3.65 11.00 40.00
10,12-17: 10-Bugs Bunny. 12-Tom & Jerry, Bugs Bunny, W. Woodpecker Journey to the Sun. 13-Tom & Jerry. 14-Bugs Bunny Fun Packed Funnies. 15-Tom & Jerry, Woody Woodpecker, Bugs Bunny. 16-Woody Woodpecker Cartoon Special. 17-Bugs Bunny 2.00 6.00 18.00
11-Hanna-Barbera TV Fun Favorites 3.65 11.00 40.00
18-Tom & Jerry; Barney Bear-r by Barks 2.30 7.00 20.00
19-Little Lulu 3.20 9.60 35.00
20-22: 20-Woody Woodpecker Falltime Funtime. 21-Bugs Bunny Showtime. 22-Tom & Jerry Winter Wingding 2.00 6.00 18.00
23-Little Lulu & Tubby Fun Fling 3.20 9.60 35.00
24-26,28: 24-Woody Woodpecker Fun Festival. 25-Tom & Jerry. 26-Bugs Bunny Halloween Hulla-Boo-Loo; Dr. Spektor article, also #25. 28-Tom & Jerry 2.00 6.00 16.00
27-Little Lulu & Tubby in Hawaii 3.00 9.00 30.00
29-Little Lulu & Tubby 3.00 9.00 30.00
30-Bugs Bunny Vacation Funnies 2.00 6.00 16.00
31-Turok, Son of Stone; r/4-Color #596,656; c-r/#9 3.20 9.60 35.00
32-Woody Woodpecker Summer Fun 2.00 6.00 16.00
33,36: 33-Little Lulu & Tubby Halloween Fun; Dr. Spektor app. 36-Little Lulu & Her Friends 3.20 9.60 35.00
34,35,37-39: 34-Bugs Bunny Winter Funnies. 35-Tom & Jerry Snowtime Funtime. 37-Woody Woodpecker County Fair. 39-Bugs Bunny Summer Fun 2.00 6.00 16.00
38-The Pink Panther 2.30 7.00 20.00
40,43: 40-Little Lulu & Tubby Trick or Treat; all by Stanley. 43-Little Lulu in Paris 3.20 9.60 35.00

Golden Comics Digest #4 © ERB

Golden Picture Classic #403 © WEST

Gon on Safari © Kodansha Ltd.

GD2.0 FN6.0 NM9.4

41,42,44,47: 41-Tom & Jerry Winter Carnival. 42-Bugs Bunny. 44-Woody Woodpecker Family Fun Festival. 47-Bugs Bunny 1.75 5.25 14.00
45-The Pink Panther 2.30 7.00 20.00
46-Little Lulu & Tubby 2.80 8.40 28.00
48-The Lone Ranger 2.30 7.00 20.00
NOTE: *#1-30, 164 pgs.; #31 on, 132 pgs..*

GOLDEN LAD
Spark/Fact & Fiction Publ.: July, 1945 - No. 5, June, 1946 (#4, 5: 52 pgs.)

1-Origin & 1st app. Golden Lad & Swift Arrow; Sandusky and the Senator begins 71.00 213.00 675.00
2-Mort Meskin-c/a 38.00 113.00 300.00
3,4-Mort Meskin-c/a 33.00 98.00 260.00
5-Origin/1st Golden Girl; Shaman & Flame app. 38.00 113.00 300.00
NOTE: *All have* ***Robinson,*** *and* ***Roussos*** *art plus* ***Meskin*** *covers and art.*

GOLDEN LEGACY
Fitzgerald Publishing Co.: 1966 - 1972 (Black History) (25¢)

1-Toussaint L'Ouverture (1966), 2-Harriet Tubman (1967), 3-Crispus Attucks & the Minutemen (1967), 4-Benjamin Banneker (1968), 5-Matthew Henson (1969), 6-Alexander Dumas & Family (1969), 7-Frederick Douglass, Part 1 (1969), 8-Frederick Douglass, Part 2 (1970), 9-Robert Smalls (1970), 10-J. Cinque & the Amistad Mutiny (1970), 11-Men in Action: White, Marshall J. Wilkins (1970), 12-Black Cowboys (1972), 13-The Life of Martin Luther King, Jr. (1972), 14-The Life of Alexander Pushkin (1971), 15-Ancient African Kingdoms (1972), 16-Black Inventors (1972)
each.... 1.50 4.50 12.00
1-10,12,13,15,16(1976)-Reprints 2.40 6.00

GOLDEN LOVE STORIES (Formerly Golden West Love)
Kirby Publishing Co.: No. 4, April, 1950

4-Powell-a; Glenn Ford/Janet Leigh photo-c 15.00 45.00 120.00

GOLDEN PICTURE CLASSIC, A
Western Printing Co. (Simon & Shuster): 1956-1957 (Text stories w/illustrations in color; 100 pgs. each)

CL-401: Treasure Island 9.30 28.00 65.00
CL-402,403: 402: Tom Sawyer. 403: Black Beauty 7.85 23.50 55.00
CL-404, 405: CL-404: Little Women. CL-405: Heidi 7.85 23.50 55.00
CL-406: Ben Hur 5.00 15.00 35.00
CL-407: Around the World in 80 Days 5.00 15.00 35.00
CL-408: Sherlock Holmes 6.40 19.25 45.00
CL-409: The Three Musketeers 5.00 15.00 35.00
CL-410: The Merry Advs. of Robin Hood 5.00 15.00 35.00
CL-411,412: 411: Hans Brinker. 412: The Count of Monte Cristo 6.40 19.25 45.00
(Both soft & hardcover editions are valued the same)
NOTE: *Recent research has uncovered new information. Apparently #s 1-6 were issued in 1956 and #7-12 in 1957. But they can be found in five different series listings: CL-1 to CL-12 (softbound); CL-401 to CL-412 (also softbound); CL-101 to CL-112 (hardbound); plus two new series discoveries: A Golden Reading Adventure, publ. by Golden Press; edited down to 60 pages and reduced in size to 6x9"; only #s discovered so far are #381 (CL-4), #382 (CL-6) & #387 (CL-3). They have no reorder list and some have covers different from GPC. There have also been found British hardbound editions of GPC with dust jackets. Copies of all five listed series vary from scarce to very rare. Some editions of some series have not yet been found at all.*

GOLDEN PICTURE STORY BOOK
Racine Press (Western): Dec, 1961 (50¢, Treasury size, 52 pgs.) (All are scarce)

ST-1-Huckleberry Hound (TV); Hokey Wolf, Pixie & Dixie, Quick Draw McGraw, Snooper and Blabber, Augie Doggie app. 20.00 60.00 220.00
ST-2-Yogi Bear (TV); Snagglepuss, Yakky Doodle, Quick Draw McGraw, Snooper and Blabber, Augie Doggie app. 20.00 60.00 220.00
ST-3-Babes in Toyland (Walt Disney's...)-Annette Funicello photo-c 24.00 71.00 260.00
ST-4-(...of Disney Ducks)-Walt Disney's Wonderful World of Ducks (Donald Duck, Uncle Scrooge, Donald's Nephews, Grandma Duck, Ludwig Von Drake, & Gyro Gearloose stories) 24.00 71.00 260.00

GOLDEN RECORD COMIC (See Amazing Spider-Man #1, Avengers #4, Fantastic Four #1, Journey Into Mystery #83)

GOLDEN STORY BOOKS
Western Printing Co. (Simon & Shuster): 1949 (Heavy covers, digest size, 128 pgs.) (Illustrated text in color)

7-Walt Disney's Mystery in Disneyville, a book-length adventure starring Donald and Nephews, Mickey and Nephews, and with Minnie, Daisy and Goofy. Art by Dick Moores & Manuel Gonzales (scarce) 28.00 84.00 225.00
10-Bugs Bunny's Treasure Hunt, a book-length adventure starring Bugs & Porky Pig, with Petunia Pig & Nephew, Cicero. Art by Tom McKimson (scarce) 19.00 56.00 150.00

GOLDEN WEST LOVE (Golden Love Stories No. 4)
Kirby Publishing Co.: Sept-Oct, 1949 - No. 3, Feb, 1950 (All 52 pgs.)

1-Powell-a in all; Roussos-a; painted-c 21.00 64.00 170.00
2,3: Photo-c 15.00 45.00 120.00

GOLDEN WEST RODEO TREASURY (See Dell Giants)

GOLDILOCKS (See March of Comics No. 1)

GOLD KEY CHAMPION
Gold Key: Mar, 1978 - No. 2, May, 1978 (50¢, 52pgs.)

1,2: 1-Space Family Robinson; half-r. 2-Mighty Samson; half-r 1.00 2.80 7.00

GOLD KEY SPOTLIGHT
Gold Key: May, 1976 - No. 11, Feb, 1978

1-Tom, Dick & Harriet 1.00 3.00 8.00
2-11: 2-Wacky Advs. of Cracky. 3-Wacky Witch. 4-Tom, Dick & Harriet. 5-Wacky Advs. of Cracky. 6-Dagar the Invincible; Santos-a; origin Demonomicon. 7-Wacky Witch & Greta Ghost 10-O. G. Whiz.11-Tom, Dick & Harriet. 8-The Occult Files of Dr. Spektor, Simbar, Lu-sai; Santos-a. 9-Tragg 2.40 6.00

GOLD MEDAL COMICS
Cambridge House: 1945 (25¢, one-shot, 132 pgs.)

nn-Captain Truth by Fugitani, Crime Detector, The Witch of Salem, Luckyman, others app. 28.00 83.00 220.00

GOMER PYLE (TV)
Gold Key: July, 1966 - No. 3, Jan, 1967

1-Photo front/back-c 7.00 21.00 85.00
2,3 5.00 15.00 60.00

GON
DC Comics (Paradox Press): July, 1996 - No. 4, Oct, 1996; No. 5, 1997 ($5.95, B&W, digest-size, limited series)

1-5: Misadventures of baby dinosaur; 1-Gon. 2-Gon Again. 3-Gon: Here Today, Gone Tomorrow. 4-Gon: Going, Going...Gon. 5-Gon Swimmin'. Tanaka-c/a/scripts in all 6.00

GON COLOR SPECTACULAR
DC Comics (Paradox Press): 1998 ($5.95, square-bound)

nn-Tanaka-c/a/scripts 6.00

GON ON SAFARI
DC Comics (Paradox Press): 2000 ($7.95, B&W, digest-size)

nn-Tanaka-c/a/scripts 8.00

GON UNDERGROUND
DC Comics (Paradox Press): 1999 ($7.95, B&W, digest-size)

nn-Tanaka-c/a/scripts 8.00

GON WILD
DC Comics (Paradox Press): 1997 ($9.95, B&W, digest-size)

nn-Tanaka-c/a/scripts in all. (Rep. Gon #3,4) 10.00

GOODBYE, MR. CHIPS (See Movie Comics)

GOOD GIRL ART QUARTERLY
AC Comics: Summer, 1990 - No. 15, Spring, 1994 (B&W/color, 52 pgs.)

1,3-15 ($3.50)-All have one new story (often FemForce) & rest reprints by Baker, Ward & other "good girl" artists 4.00
2 ($3.95) 4.00

GOOD GIRL COMICS (Formerly Good Girl Art Quarterly)
AC Comics: No. 16, Summer, 1994 - No. 18, 1995 (B&W)

16-18 4.00

GOOD GUYS, THE
Defiant: Nov, 1993 - No. 9, July, 1994 ($2.50/$3.25/$3.50)

1-($3.50, 52 pgs.)-Glory x-over from Plasm 3.50

Goofy Comics #9 © STD

Graphique Musique #1 © SLG

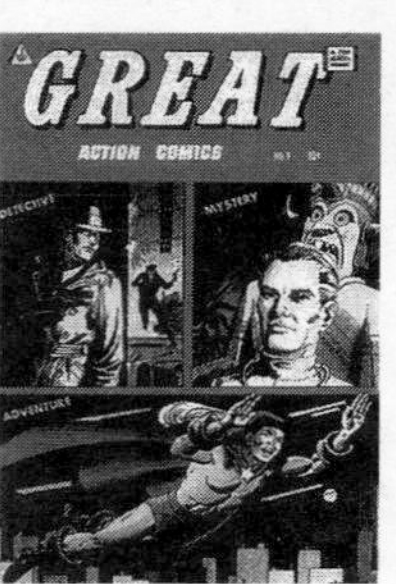

Great Action Comics #1 © I.W. Ent.

	GD2.0	FN6.0	NM9.4
2,3,5-9: 9-Pre-Schism issue			2.50
4-($3.25, 52 pgs.)			3.25

GOOFY (Disney)(See Dynabrite Comics, Mickey Mouse Magazine V4#7, Walt Disney Showcase #35 & Wheaties)
Dell Publishing Co.: No. 468, May, 1953 - Sept-Nov, 1962

	GD2.0	FN6.0	NM9.4
Four Color 468 (#1)	11.70	35.00	140.00
Four Color 562,627,658,702,747,802,857	6.70	20.00	80.00
Four Color 899,952,987,1053,1094,1149,1201	4.10	12.30	45.00
12-308-211(Dell, 9-11/62)	4.10	12.30	45.00

GOOFY ADVENTURES
Disney Comics: June, 1990 - No. 17, 1991 ($1.50)

	GD2.0	FN6.0	NM9.4
1-17: Most new stories. 2-Joshua Quagmire-a w/free poster. 7-WDC&S-r plus new-a. 9-Gottfredson-r. 14-Super Goof story. 15-All Super Goof issue. 17-Gene Colan-a(p)			2.00

GOOFY ADVENTURE STORY (See Goofy No. 857)

GOOFY COMICS (Companion to Happy Comics)(Not Disney)
Nedor Publ. Co. No. 1-14/Standard No. 14-48: June, 1943 - No. 48, 1953 (Animated Cartoons)

	GD2.0	FN6.0	NM9.4
1-Funny animal; Oriolo-c	28.00	83.00	220.00
2	14.00	41.00	110.00
3-10	11.00	33.00	90.00
11-19	9.30	28.00	65.00
20-35-Frazetta text illos in all	10.00	30.00	80.00
36-48	7.15	21.50	50.00

GOOFY SUCCESS STORY (See Goofy No. 702)

GOOSE (Humor magazine)
Cousins Publ. (Fawcett): Sept, 1976 - No. 3, 1976 (75¢, 52 pgs., B&W)

	GD2.0	FN6.0	NM9.4
1-Nudity in all	2.30	7.00	20.00
2,3: 2-(10/76) Fonz-c/s; Lone Ranger story. 3-Wonder Woman, King Kong, Six Million Dollar Man stories	1.75	5.25	14.00

GORDO (See Comics Revue No. 5 & Giant Comics Edition)

GORGO (Based on M.G.M. movie) (See Return of…)
Charlton Comics: May, 1961 - No. 23, Sept, 1965

	GD2.0	FN6.0	NM9.4
1-Ditko-a, 22 pgs.	23.00	68.00	250.00
2,3-Ditko-c/a	11.50	34.00	125.00
4-Ditko-c	6.80	20.50	75.00
5-11,13-16: 11,13-16-Ditko-a	6.35	19.00	70.00
12,17-23: 12-Reptisaurus x-over; Montes/Bache-a-No. 17-23. 20-Giordano-c	3.20	9.60	35.00
Gorgo's Revenge('62)-Becomes Return of…	4.55	13.65	50.00

GOSPEL BLIMP, THE
Spire Christian Comics (Fleming H. Revell Co.): 1973,1974 (35¢/39¢, 36 pgs.)

	GD2.0	FN6.0	NM9.4
nn	1.00	2.80	7.00

G.O.T.H.
Verotik: Dec, 1995 - No. 3, June, 1996 ($2.95, limited series, mature)

	GD2.0	FN6.0	NM9.4
1-3: Danzig scripts; Liam Sharpe-a.			3.00

GOTHAM BY GASLIGHT (A Tale of the Batman)(See Batman: Master of…)
DC Comics: 1989 ($3.95, one-shot, squarebound, 52 pgs.)

	GD2.0	FN6.0	NM9.4
nn-Mignola/Russell-a; intro by Robert Bloch			4.00

GOTHAM NIGHTS (See Batman: Gotham Nights II)
DC Comics: Mar, 1992 - No. 4, June, 1992 ($1.25, limited series)

	GD2.0	FN6.0	NM9.4
1-4: Featuring Batman			2.00

GOTHIC ROMANCES
Atlas/Seaboard Publ.: Dec, 1974 (75¢, B&W, magazine, 76 pgs.)

	GD2.0	FN6.0	NM9.4
1-Text w/ illos by N. Adams, Chaykin, Heath (2 pgs. ea.); painted cover (scarce)	6.35	19.00	70.00

GOTHIC TALES OF LOVE (Magazine)
Marvel Comics: Apr, 1975 - No. 2, Jun, 1975 (B&W, 76 pgs.)

	GD2.0	FN6.0	NM9.4
1,2-painted-c/a (scarce)	5.00	15.00	55.00

GOVERNOR & J. J., THE (TV)
Gold Key: Feb, 1970 - No. 3, Aug, 1970 (Photo-c)

	GD2.0	FN6.0	NM9.4
1	3.65	11.00	40.00
2,3	2.80	8.40	28.00

GRACKLE, THE
Acclaim Comics: Jan, 1997 - No. 4, Apr, 1997 ($2.95, B&W)

	GD2.0	FN6.0	NM9.4
1-4: Mike Baron scripts & Paul Gulacy-c/a. 1-4-Doublecross			3.00

GRAFIK MUSIK
Caliber Press: Nov, 1990 - No. 4, Aug, 1991 ($3.50/$2.50)

	GD2.0	FN6.0	NM9.4
1-($3.50, 48 pgs., color) Mike Allred-c/a/scripts-1st app. in color of Frank Einstein (Madman)			20.00
2-($2.50, 24 pgs., color)			10.00
3,4-($2.50, 24 pgs., B&W)			8.00

GRANDMA DUCK'S FARM FRIENDS(See Walt Disney's C&S 293 & Wheaties)
Dell Publishing Co.: No. 763, Jan, 1957 - No. 1279, Feb, 1962 (Disney)

	GD2.0	FN6.0	NM9.4
Four Color 763 (#1)	6.70	20.00	80.00
Four Color 873	4.60	13.75	55.00
Four Color 965,1279	4.10	12.30	45.00
Four Color 1010,1073,1161-Barks-a; 1073,1161-Barks c/a	12.50	37.50	150.00

GRAND PRIX (Formerly Hot Rod Racers)
Charlton Comics: No. 16, Sept, 1967 - No. 31, May, 1970

	GD2.0	FN6.0	NM9.4
16-Features Rick Roberts	3.00	9.00	30.00
17-20	2.50	7.50	24.00
21-31	2.00	6.00	18.00

GRAPHIQUE MUSIQUE
Slave Labor Graphics: Dec, 1989 - No. 3, May, 1990 ($2.95, 52 pgs.)

	GD2.0	FN6.0	NM9.4
1-Mike Allred-c/a/scripts	3.65	11.00	40.00
2,3	3.00	9.00	30.00

GRAVEDIGGERS
Acclaim Comics: Nov, 1996 - No. 4, Feb, 1997 ($2.95, B&W)

	GD2.0	FN6.0	NM9.4
1-4: Moretti scripts			3.00

GRAVESTONE
Malibu Comics: July, 1993 - No. 7, Feb, 1994 ($2.25)

	GD2.0	FN6.0	NM9.4
1-6: 3-Polybagged w/Skycap			2.25
7-($2.50)			2.50

GRAVE TALES
Hamilton Comics: Oct, 1991 - No. 3, Feb, 1992 ($3.95, B&W, mag., 52 pgs.)

	GD2.0	FN6.0	NM9.4
1-Staton-c/a	1.00	3.00	8.00
2,3: 2-Staton-a; Morrow-c		2.40	6.00

GRAY GHOST, THE
Dell Publishing Co.: No. 911, July, 1958; No. 1000, June-Aug, 1959

	GD2.0	FN6.0	NM9.4
Four Color 911 (#1), 1000-Photo-c each	8.35	25.00	100.00

GREASE MONKEY
Image Comics: Jan, 1998 - Present ($2.95, B&W)

	GD2.0	FN6.0	NM9.4
1,2-Tim Eldred-s/a			3.00

GREAT ACTION COMICS
I. W. Enterprises: 1958 (Reprints with new covers)

	GD2.0	FN6.0	NM9.4
1-Captain Truth reprinted from Gold Medal #1	2.50	7.50	25.00
8,9-Reprints Phantom Lady #15 & 23	8.65	26.00	95.00

GREAT AMERICAN COMICS PRESENTS - THE SECRET VOICE
Peter George 4-Star Publ./American Features Syndicate: 1945 (10¢)

	GD2.0	FN6.0	NM9.4
1-Anti-Nazi; "What Really Happened to Hitler"	31.00	94.00	250.00

GREAT AMERICAN WESTERN, THE
AC Comics: 1987 - No. 4, 1990? ($1.75/$2.95/$3.50, B&W with some color)

	GD2.0	FN6.0	NM9.4
1-4: 1-Western-r plus Bill Black-a. 2-Tribute to ME comics; Durango Kid photo-c 3-Tribute to Tom Mix plus Roy Rogers, Durango Kid; Billy the Kid-r by Severin; photo-c. 4- ($3.50, 52 pgs., 16 pgs. color)-Tribute to Lash LaRue; photo-c & interior photos; Fawcett-r			4.00
...Presents 1 (1991, $5.00) New Sunset Carson; film history			5.00

GREAT CAT FAMILY, THE (Disney-TV/Movie)

Greatest Team-Up Stories Ever Told SC © DC

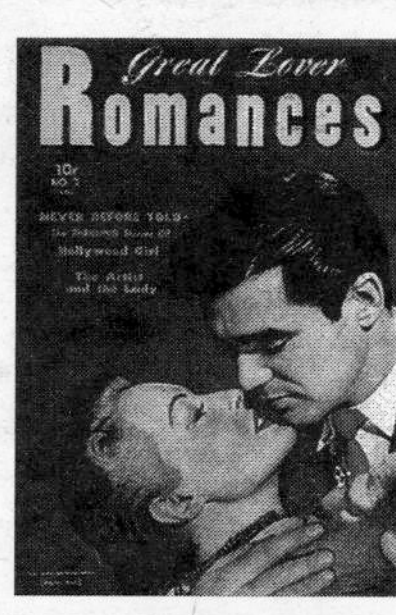

Great Lover Romances #2 © TOBY

Green Arrow #34 © DC

GD2.0 FN6.0 NM9.4

Dell Publishing Co.: No. 750, Nov, 1956 (one-shot)

Four Color 750-Pinocchio & Alice app. 5.85 17.50 70.00

GREAT COMICS
Great Comics Publications: Nov, 1941 - No. 3, Jan, 1942

1-Origin/1st app. The Great Zarro; Madame Strange & Guy Gorham, Wizard of Science & The Great Zarro begin 126.00 379.00 1200.00
2-Buck Johnson, Jungle Explorer app.; X-Mas-c 63.00 189.00 600.00
3-Futuro Takes Hitler to Hell-c/s; "The Lost City" movie story (starring William Boyd); continues in Choice Comics #3 211.00 633.00 2000.00

GREAT COMICS
Novack Publishing Co./Jubilee Comics/Barrel O' Fun: 1945

1-(Novack)-The Defenders, Capt. Power app.; L. B. Cole-c 40.00 120.00 350.00
1-(Jubilee)-Same cover; Boogey Man, Satanas, & The Sorcerer & His Apprentice 30.00 90.00 240.00
1-(Barrel O' Fun)-L. B. Cole-c; Barrel O' Fun overprinted in indicia; Li'l Cactus, Cuckoo Sheriff (humorous) 19.00 56.00 150.00

GREAT DOGPATCH MYSTERY (See Mammy Yokum & the...)

GREATEST BATMAN STORIES EVER TOLD, THE
DC Comics:

Hardcover ($24.95) 40.00
Softcover ($15.95) "Greatest DC Stories Vol. 2" on spine 17.00
Vol. 2 softcover (1992, $16.95)"Greatest DC Stories Vol. 7" on spine 17.00

GREATEST FLASH STORIES EVER TOLD, THE
DC Comics: 1991

nn-Hardcover ($29.95); Infantino-c 30.00
nn-Softcover ($14.95) 15.00

GREATEST GOLDEN AGE STORIES EVER TOLD, THE
DC Comics: 1990 ($24.95, hardcover)

nn-Ordway-c 45.00

GREATEST JOKER STORIES EVER TOLD, THE (See Batman)
DC Comics: 1983

Hardcover ($19.95)-Kyle Baker painted-c 35.00
Softcover ($14.95) 15.00
Stacked Deck...Expanded Edition (1992, $29.95)-Longmeadow Press Publ. 30.00

GREATEST 1950s STORIES EVER TOLD, THE
DC Comics: 1990

Hardcover ($29.95)-Kubert-c 45.00
Softcover ($14.95) "Greatest DC Stories Vol. 5" on spine 16.00

GREATEST TEAM-UP STORIES EVER TOLD, THE
DC Comics: 1989

Hardcover ($24.95)-DeVries and Infantino painted-c 45.00
Softcover ($14.95) "Greatest DC Stories Vol. 4" on spine; Adams-c 16.00

GREATEST SUPERMAN STORIES EVER TOLD, THE
DC Comics: 1987

Hardcover ($24.95) 40.00
Softcover ($15.95) 18.00

GREAT EXPLOITS
Decker Publ./Red Top: Oct, 1957

1-Krigstein-a(2) (re-issue on cover); reprints Daring Advs. #6 by Approved Comics 7.85 23.50 55.00

GREAT FOODINI, THE (See Foodini)

GREAT GAZOO, THE (The Flintstones)(TV)
Charlton Comics: Aug, 1973 - No. 20, Jan, 1977 (Hanna-Barbera)

1 3.00 9.00 30.00
2-10 2.00 6.00 16.00
11-20 1.25 3.75 10.00

GREAT GRAPE APE, THE (TV)(See TV Stars #1)
Charlton Comics: Sept, 1976 - No. 2, Nov, 1976 (Hanna-Barbera)

GD2.0 FN6.0 NM9.4

1 2.30 7.00 20.00
2 1.50 4.50 12.00

GREAT LOCOMOTIVE CHASE, THE (Disney)
Dell Publishing Co.: No. 712, Sept, 1956 (one-shot)

Four Color 712-Movie, photo-c 6.70 20.00 80.00

GREAT LOVER ROMANCES (Young Lover Romances #4,5)
Toby Press: 3/51; #2, 1951(nd); #3, 1952 (nd); #6, Oct?, 1952 - No. 22, May, 1955 (Photo-c #1-5, 10 ,13, 15, 17) (no #4, 5)

1-Jon Juan story-r/Jon Juan #1 by Schomburg; Dr. Anthony King app. 16.00 49.00 130.00
2-Jon Juan, Dr. Anthony King app. 9.30 28.00 65.00
3,7,9-14,16-22: 10-Rita Hayworth photo-c. 17-Rita Hayworth & Aldo Ray photo-c 5.50 16.50 38.00
6-Kurtzman-a (10/52) 9.30 28.00 65.00
8-Five pgs. of "Pin-Up Pete" by Sparling 10.00 30.00 70.00
15-Liz Taylor photo-c 10.00 30.00 80.00

GREAT RACE, THE (See Movie Classics)

GREAT SCOTT SHOE STORE (See Bulls-Eye)

GREAT WEST (Magazine)
M. F. Enterprises: 1969 (B&W, 52 pgs.)

V1#1 2.00 6.00 16.00

GREAT WESTERN
Magazine Enterprises: No. 8, Jan-Mar, 1954 - No. 11, Oct-Dec, 1954

8(A-1 93)-Trail Colt by Guardineer; Powell Red Hawk-r/Straight Arrow begins, ends #11; Durango Kid story 21.00 64.00 170.00
9(A-1 105), 11(A-1 127)-Ghost Rider, Durango Kid app. in each. 9-Red Mask-c, but no app. 12.50 37.50 100.00
10(A-1 113)-The Calico Kid by Guardineer-r/Tim Holt #8; Straight Arrow, Durango Kid app. 12.50 37.50 100.00
I.W. Reprint #1,2 9: 1,2-r/Straight Arrow #36,42. 9-r/Straight Arrow #? 2.50 7.50 24.00
I.W. Reprint #8-Origin Ghost Rider(r/Tim Holt #11); Tim Holt app.; Bolle-a 2.80 8.40 28.00

NOTE: ***Guardineer** c-8. **Powell** a(r)-8-11 (from Straight Arrow).*

GREEN ARROW (See Action #440, Adventure, Brave & the Bold, DC Super Stars #17, Detective #521, Flash #217, Green Lantern #76, Justice League of America #4, Leading Comics, More Fun #73 (1st app.), Showcase '95 #9 & World's Finest Comics)

GREEN ARROW
DC Comics: May, 1983 - No. 4, Aug, 1983 (limited series)

1-Origin; Speedy cameo; Mike W. Barr scripts, Trevor Von Eeden-c/a 5.00
2-4 4.00

GREEN ARROW
DC Comics: Feb, 1988 - No. 137, Oct, 1998 ($1.00-$2.50) (Painted-c #1-3)

1-Mike Grell scripts begin, ends #80 5.00
2-49,51-74,76-86: 27,28-Warlord app. 35-38-Co-stars Black Canary; Bill Wray-i. 40-Grell-a. 47-Begin $1.50-c. 63-No longer has mature readers on-c. 63-66-Shado app. 81-Aparo-a begins, ends #100; Nuklon app. 82-Intro & death of Rival. 83-Huntress-c/story. 84-Deathstroke cameo. 85-Deathstroke-c/app. 86-Catwoman-c/story w/Jim Balent layouts 2.00
50,75-($2.50, 52 pgs.): Anniversary issues. 75-Arsenal (Roy Harper) & Shado app. 2.50
0,87-96: 87-$1.95-c begins. 88-Guy Gardner, Martian Manhunter, & Wonder Woman-c/app.; Flash-c. 89-Anarky app. 90-(9/94)-Zero Hour tie-in. 0-(10/94)-1st app. Connor Hawke; Aparo-a(p). 91-(11/94). 93-1st app. Camorouge. 95-Hal Jordan cameo. 96-Intro new Force of July; Hal Jordan (Parallax) app; Oliver Queen learns that Connor Hawke is his son 2.00
97-99,102-109: 97-Begin $2.25-c; no Aparo-a. 97-99-Arsenal app. 102,103-Underworld Unleashed x-over. 104-GL(Kyle Rayner)-c/app. 105-Robin-c/app. 107-109-Thorn app. 109-Lois Lane cameo; Weeks-c. 2.50
100-($3.95)-Foil-c; Superman app. 5.00
101-Apparent death of Oliver Queen; Superman app. 1.50 4.50 12.00
110,111-124: 110,111-GL x-over. 110-Intro Hatchet. 114-Final Night. 115-117-Black Canary & Oracle app. 2.50
125-($3.50, 48 pgs)-GL x-over cont. in GL #92 3.50
126-137: 126-Begin $2.50-c. 130-GL & Flash x-over. 132,133-JLA app.

Green Goblin #4 © MAR

Green Hornet Comics #2 © HARV

Green Lama #3 © Spark Publ.

134,135-Brotherhood of the Fist pts. 1,5. 136-Hal Jordan-c/app.
137-Last issue; Superman app. 2.50
#1,000,000 (11/98) 853rd Century x-over 2.50
Annual 1-6 ('88-'94, 68 pgs.)-1-No Grell scripts. 2-No Grell scripts; recaps origin Green Arrow,Speedy, Black Canary & others. 3-Bill Wray-a. 4-50th anniversary issue. 5-Batman, Eclipso app. 6-Bloodlines; Hook app. 3.50
7-('95, $3.95)-Year One story 4.00

NOTE: *Aparo a-0, 81-85, 86 (partial),87p, 88p, 91-95, 96i, 98-100p, 109p; c-81,98-100p. **Austin** c-96i. **Balent** layouts-86. **Burchett** c-91-95. **Campanella** a-100-108i, 110-113i; c-99i, 101-108i,110-113i. **Denys Cowan** a-39p, 41-43p, 47p, 48p, 60p; c-41-43. **Damaggio** a(p)-97p, 100-108p, 110-112p; c-97-99p, 101-108p, 110-113p. **Mike Grell** c-1-4, 10p, 11, 39, 40, 44, 45, 47-80, Annual 4, 5. **Nasser/Netzer** a-89, 96. **Sienkiewicz** a-109i. **Springer** a-67, 68. **Weeks** c-109.*

GREEN ARROW: THE LONG BOW HUNTERS
DC Comics: Aug, 1987 - No. 3, Oct, 1987 ($2.95, limited series, mature)

1-Grell-c/a in all 4.00
1,2-2nd printings 2.50
2,3 3.00
Trade paperback (1989, $12.95)-r/#1-3 13.00

GREEN ARROW: THE WONDER YEAR
DC Comics: Feb, 1993 - No. 4, May, 1993 ($1.75, limited series)

1-4: Mike Grell-a(p)/scripts & Gray Morrow-a(i) 2.00

GREEN BERET, THE (See Tales of...)

GREEN CANDLES
DC Comics (Paradox Press): Sept, 1995 - No. 3, Dec, 1995 ($5.95, B&W, limited series, digest size)

1-3 2.40 6.00
Paperback ($9.95) 10.00

GREEN GIANT COMICS (Also see Colossus Comics)
Pelican Publ. (Funnies, Inc.): 1940 (No price on cover; distributed in New York City only)

	GD2.0	FN6.0	VF8.0	NM9.4
1-Dr. Nerod, Green Giant, Black Arrow, Mundoo & Master Mystic app.; origin Colossus (Rare)	957.00	2870.00	5980.00	11,000.00

NOTE: *The idea for this book came from George Kapitan. Printed by Moreau Publ. of Orange, N.J. as an experiment to see if they could profitably use the idle time of their 40-page Hoe color press. The experiment failed due to the difficulty of obtaining good quality color registration and Mr. Moreau believes the book never reached the stands. The book has no price or date which lends credence to this. Contains five pages reprinted from Motion Picture Funnies Weekly.*

GREEN GOBLIN
Marvel Comics: Oct, 1995 - No. 13, Oct, 1996 ($2.95/$1.95)

	GD2.0	FN6.0	NM9.4
1-($2.95)-Scott McDaniel-c/a begins, ends #7; foil-c			3.00
2-13: 2-Begin $1.95-c. 4-Hobgoblin-c/app; Thing app. 6-Daredevil-c/app. 8-Darrick Robertson-a; McDaniel-c. 10-Arcade app. 12,13-Onslaught x-over. 13-Green Goblin quits; Spider-Man app.			2.00

GREENHAVEN
Aircel Publishing: 1988 - No. 3, 1988 ($2.00, limited series, 28 pgs.)

1-3 2.00

GREEN HORNET, THE (TV)
Dell Publishing Co./Gold Key: Sept, 1953; Feb, 1967 - No. 3, Aug, 1967

Four Color 496-Painted-c.	23.00	70.00	280.00
1-All have Bruce Lee photo-c	20.00	60.00	240.00
2,3	14.00	42.00	170.00

GREEN HORNET, THE (Also see Kato of the... & Tales of the...)
Now Comics: Nov, 1989 - No. 14, Feb, 1991 ($1.75)
V2#1, Sept, 1991 - V2#39, Dec, 1994 ($1.95)

1 ($2.95, double-size)-Steranko painted-c; G.A. Green Hornet 2.40 6.00
1,2: 1-2nd printing ('90, $3.95)-New Butler-c 4.00
3-14: 5-Death of original ('30s) Green Hornet. 6-Dave Dorman painted-c. 11-Snyder-c 3.00
V2#1-11,13-21,24-26,28-30,32-37,39: 1-Butler painted-c. 9-Mayerik-c 2.50
12-($2.50)-Color Green Hornet button polybagged inside 3.00
22,23-($2.95)-Bagged w/color hologravure card 3.00
27-($2.95)-Newsstand ed. polybagged w/multi-dimensional card (1993 Anniversary Special on cover), 27-($2.95)-Direct Sale ed. polybagged w/multi-dimensional card; cover variations 3.00
31,38: 31-($2.50)-Polybagged w/trading card 2.50
1-($2.50)-Polybagged w/button (same as #12) 2.50
2,3-($1.95)-Same as #13 & 14 2.00
Annual 1 (12/92, $2.50), Annual 1994 (10/94, $2.95) 3.00

GREEN HORNET: DARK TOMORROW
Now Comics: Jun, 1993 - No. 3, Aug, 1993 ($2.50, limited series)

1-3: Future Green Hornet 2.50

GREEN HORNET: SOLITARY SENTINEL, THE
Now Comics: Dec, 1992 - No. 3, 1993 ($2.50, limited series)

1-3 2.50

GREEN HORNET COMICS (...Racket Buster #44) (Radio, movies)
Helnit Publ. Co.(Holyoke) No. 1-6/Family Comics(Harvey) No. 7-on:
Dec, 1940 - No. 47, Sept, 1949 (See All New #13,14)(Early issues: 68 pgs.)

1-1st app. Green Hornet & Kato; origin of Green Hornet on inside front-c; intro the Black Beauty (Green Hornet's car); painted-c	435.00	1305.00	5000.00
2-Early issues based on radio adventures	168.00	505.00	1600.00
3	132.00	395.00	1250.00
4-6: 6-(8/41)	103.00	308.00	975.00
7 (6/42)-Origin The Zebra & begins; Robin Hood, Spirit of '76, Blonde Bomber & Mighty Midgets begin; new logo	89.00	268.00	850.00
8,10	76.00	229.00	725.00
9-Kirby-c	95.00	285.00	900.00
11,12-Mr. Q in both	76.00	229.00	725.00
13-1st Nazi-c; shows Hitler poster on-c	84.00	253.00	800.00
14-19	58.00	174.00	550.00
20-Classic-c	63.00	189.00	600.00
21-23,25-30	47.00	142.00	425.00
24-Sci-Fi-c	50.00	150.00	450.00
31-The Man in Black Called Fate begins (11-12/45, early app.)	49.00	147.00	440.00
32-36	40.00	120.00	360.00
37,38: Shock Gibson app. by Powell. 37-S&K Kid Adonis reprinted from Stuntman #3. 38-Kid Adonis app.	40.00	120.00	360.00
39-Stuntman story by S&K	50.00	150.00	450.00
40-47: 42-47-Kerry Drake in all. 45-Boy Explorers on-c only. 46- "Case of the Marijuana Racket" cover/story; Kerry Drake app.	34.00	101.00	270.00

NOTE: ***Fuje** a-23, 24, 26. **Henkle** c-7-9. **Kubert** a-20, 30. **Powell** a-7-10, 12, 14, 16-21, 30, 31(2), 32(3), 33, 34(3), 35, 36, 37(2), 38. **Robinson** a-27. **Schomburg** c-15, 17-23. Kirbyish c-7, 15. Bondage c-8, 14, 18, 26, 36.*

GREEN JET COMICS, THE (See Comic Books, Series 1)

GREEN LAMA (Also see Comic Books, Series 1, Daring Adventures #17 & Prize Comics #7)
Spark Publications/Prize No. 7 on: Dec, 1944 - No. 8, Mar, 1946

1-Intro. Lt. Hercules & The Boy Champions; Mac Raboy-c/a #1-8	126.00	379.00	1200.00
2-Lt. Hercules borrows the Human Torch's powers for one panel	74.00	221.00	700.00
3-6,8: 4-Dick Tracy take-off in Lt. Hercules story by H. L. Gold (science fiction writer). 5-Lt. Hercules story; Little Orphan Annie, Smilin' Jack & Snuffy Smith take-off (5/45)	61.00	182.00	575.00
7-X-mas-c; Raboy craft tint-c/a	42.00	125.00	375.00

NOTE: ***Robinson** a-3-5, 8. Roussos a-8. Formerly a pulp hero who began in 1940.*

GREEN LANTERN (1st Series) (See All-American, All Flash Quarterly, All Star Comics, The Big All-American & Comic Cavalcade)
National Periodical Publications/All-American: Fall, 1941 - No. 38, May-June, 1949 (#1-18 are quarterly)

	GD2.0	FN6.0	VF8.0	NM9.4
1-Origin retold; classic Purcell-c	2500.00	7500.00	17,500.00	35,000.00

	GD2.0	FN6.0	NM9.4
2-1st book-length story	626.00	1878.00	7200.00
3-Classic German war-c by Mart Nodell	452.00	1357.00	5200.00
4-Green Lantern & Doiby Dickles join the Army	381.00	1143.00	4000.00
5	263.00	790.00	2500.00
6,8: 8-Hop Harrigan begins; classic-c	211.00	633.00	2000.00
7-Robot-c.	232.00	695.00	2200.00

Green Lantern #10 © DC

Green Lantern (2nd series) #123 © DC

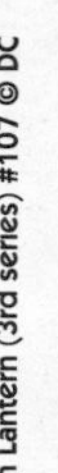
Green Lantern (3rd series) #107 © DC

GD2.0 FN6.0 NM9.4

9,10: 10-Origin/1st app. Vandal Savage 184.00 553.00 1750.00
11-17,19,20: 12-Origin/1st app. Gambler 129.00 387.00 1225.00
18-Christmas-c 142.00 426.00 1350.00
21-26,28-30: 30-Origin/1st app. Streak the Wonder Dog by Toth (2-3/48) 118.00 355.00 1125.00
27-Origin/1st app. Sky Pirate 121.00 363.00 1150.00
31-35: 35-Kubert-c. 35-38-New logo 99.00 297.00 940.00
36-38: 37-Sargon the Sorcerer app. 121.00 363.00 1150.00
NOTE: *Book-length stories #2-7.* ***Mayer/Moldoff*** *c-9.* ***Mayer/Purcell*** *c-8.* ***Purcell*** *c-1.* ***Mart Nodell*** *c-2, 3, 7.* ***Paul Reinman*** *c-11, 12, 15-22.* ***Toth*** *a-28, 30, 31, 34-38; c-28, 30, 34p, 36-38p. Cover to #8 says Fall while the indicia says Summer Issue. Streak the Wonder Dog c-30 (w/Green Lantern), 34, 36, 38.*

GREEN LANTERN (See Action Comics Weekly, Adventure Comics, Brave & the Bold, DC Special, DC Special Series, Flash, Guy Gardner, Guy Gardner Reborn, Justice League of America, Parallax: Emerald Night, Showcase, Showcase '93 #12 & Tales of The...Corps)

GREEN LANTERN (2nd Series)(Green Lantern Corps #206 on)
(See Showcase #22-24)
National Periodical Publ./DC Comics: 7-8/60 - No. 89, 4-5/72; No. 90, 8-9/76 - No. 205, 10/86

1-(7-8/60)-Origin retold; Gil Kane-c/a continues; 1st app. Guardians of the Universe 214.00 642.00 3400.00
2-1st Pieface 59.00 177.00 825.00
3-Contains readers poll 37.00 112.00 450.00
4,5: 5-Origin/1st app. Hector Hammond 31.00 93.00 350.00
6-Intro Tomar-Re the alien G.L. 29.00 88.00 325.00
7-Origin/1st app. Sinestro (7-8/61) 25.50 76.00 280.00
8-10: 8-1st 5700 A.D. story; grey tone-c. 9-1st Jordan Brothers; last 10¢ issue 23.00 68.00 250.00
11,12 15.50 46.50 170.00
13-Flash x-over 19.00 57.00 210.00
14-20: 14-Origin/1st app. Sonar. 16-Origin & 1st app. Star Sapphire. 20-Flash x-over 13.50 40.00 150.00
21-30: 21-Origin & 1st app. Dr. Polaris. 23-1st Tattooed Man. 24-Origin & 1st app. Shark. 29-JLA cameo; 1st Blackhand 12.00 36.00 130.00
31-39: 37-1st app. Evil Star (villain) 9.50 28.50 105.00
40-1st app. Crisis (10/65); 2nd solo G.A. Green Lantern in Silver Age (see Showcase #55); origin The Guardians; Doiby Dickles app. 42.00 126.00 550.00
41-44,46-50: 42-Zatanna x-over. 43-Flash x-over 7.65 23.00 85.00
45-2nd S.A. app. G.A. Green Lantern in title (6/66) 13.50 40.00 150.00
51,53-58 5.90 17.75 65.00
52-G.A. Green Lantern x-over 8.15 24.50 90.00
59-1st app. Guy Gardner (3/68) 20.00 60.00 220.00
60,62-69: 69-Wood inks; last 12¢ issue 4.10 12.30 45.00
61-G.A. Green Lantern x-over 5.45 16.35 60.00
70-75 3.00 9.00 30.00
76-(4/70)-Begin Green Lantern/Green Arrow series (by Neal Adams #76-89) ends #122 (see Flash #217 for 2nd series) 18.00 54.00 200.00
77 5.90 17.75 65.00
78-80 4.55 13.65 50.00
81-84: 82-Wrightson-i(1 pg.). 83-G.L. reveals i.d. to Carol Ferris. 84-N. Adams/ Wrightson-a(22 pgs.); last 15¢-c; partial photo-c 4.10 12.30 45.00
85,86-(52 pgs.)-Anti-drug issues. 86-G.A. Green Lantern-r; Toth-a 5.90 17.75 65.00
87-(52 pgs.): 2nd app. Guy Gardner (cameo); 1st app. John Stewart (12-1/71-72) (becomes 3rd Green Lantern in #182) 3.45 10.35 38.00
88-(2-3/72, 52 pgs.)-Unpubbed G.A. Green Lantern story; Green Lantern-r/ Showcase #23. N. Adams-c/a (1 pg.) 2.30 7.00 20.00
89-(4-5/72, 52 pgs.)-G.A. Green Lantern-r; Green Lantern & Green Arrow move to Flash #217 (2nd team-up series) 3.20 9.60 35.00
90 (8-9/76)-Begin 3rd Green Lantern/Green Arrow team-up series; Mike Grell-c/a begins, ends #111 1.75 5.25 14.00
91-99 1.00 2.80 7.00
100-(1/78, Giant)-1st app. Air Wave II 1.75 5.25 14.00
101-107,111,113-115,117-119: 107-1st Tales of the G.L. Corps story 2.40 6.00
108-110-(44 pgs)-G.A. Green Lantern back-ups in each. 111-Origin retold; G.A. Green Lantern app. 1.00 2.80 7.00
112-G.A. Green Lantern origin retold 1.50 4.50 12.00

GD2.0 FN6.0 NM9.4

116-1st app. Guy Gardner as a G.L. (5/79) 3.00 9.00 30.00
120-122,124-150: 22-Last Green Lantern/Green Arrow team-up. 130-132-Tales of the G.L. Corps. 132-Adam Strange series begins, ends147. 136,137-1st app. Citadel; Space Ranger app. 141-1st app. Omega Men (6/81). 142,143-Omega Men app.;Perez-c. 144-Omega Men cameo. 148-Tales of the G.L. Corps begins, ends #173. 150-Anniversary issue, 52 pgs.; no G.L. Corps 3.00
123-Green Lantern back to solo action; 2nd app. Guy Gardner as Green Lantern 4.00
151-180,183,184,186,187: 159-Origin Evil Star. 160,161-Omega Men app. 2.50
181,182,185,188: 181-Hal Jordan resigns as G.L. 182-John Stewart becomes new G.L.; origin recap of Hal Jordan as G.L. 185-Origin new G.L. (John Stewart).188-I.D. revealed; Alan Moore back-up scripts. 2.50
189-193,196-199,201-205: 191-Re-intro Star Sapphire (cameo). 192-Re-intro Star Sapphire (1st full app.). 194,198-Crisis x-over. 199-Hal Jordan returns as a member of G.L. Corps (3 G.L.s now). 201-Green Lantern Corps begins (is cover title, says premiere issue) 2.50
194-Hal Jordan/Guy Gardner battle; Guardians choose Guy Gardner to become new Green Lantern 4.00
195-Guy Gardner becomes Green Lantern; Crisis x-over 1.10 3.30 9.00
200-Double-size 4.00
Annual 1 (Listed as Tales Of The Green Lantern Corps Annual 1)
Annual 2,3 (See Green Lantern Corps Annual #2,3) 3.00
Special 1 (1988), 2 (1989)-(Both $1.50, 52 pgs.) 2.50
NOTE: ***N. Adams*** *a-76, 77-87p, 89; c-63, 76-89.* ***M. Anderson*** *a-137i.* ***Austin*** *a-93i, 94i, 171i.* ***Chaykin*** *c-196.* ***Greene*** *a-39-49i, 58-63i; c-54-58i.* ***Grell*** *a-90-106, 108-111; c-90-106, 108-112.* ***Heck*** *a-120-122p.* ***Infantino*** *a-137p, 145-147p, 151, 152p.* ***Gil Kane*** *a-1-49p, 50-57, 58-61p, 68-75p, 85p(r), 87p(r), 88p(r), 156, 177, 184p; c-1-52, 54-61p, 67-75, 123, 154, 156, 165-171, 177, 184.* ***Newton*** *a-148p, 149p, 181.* ***Perez*** *c-132p, 141-144.* ***Sekowsky*** *a-65p, 170p.* ***Simonson*** *c-200.* ***Sparling*** *a-63p.* ***Starlin*** *c-129, 133.* ***Staton*** *a-117p, 123-127p, 128, 129-131p, 132-139, 140p, 141-146, 147p, 148-150, 151-155p; c-107p, 117p, 135(i), 136p, 145p, 146, 147, 148-152p, 155p.* ***Toth*** *a-86r, 171p.* ***Tuska*** *a-166-168p, 170p.*

GREEN LANTERN (3rd Series)
DC Comics: June, 1990 - Present ($1.00/$1.25/$1.50/$1.75/$1.95/$1.99/$2.25)

1-Hal Jordan, John Stewart & Guy Gardner return; Batman app. 5.00
2-26: 9-12-Guy Gardner solo story. 13-(52 pgs.). 18-Guy Gardner solo story. 19-($1.75, 52 pgs.)-50th anniversary issue; Mart Nodell (original G.A. artist) part-p on G.A. Gr. Lantern; G. Kane-c. 25-($1.75, 52 pgs.)-Hal Jordan/Guy Gardner battle 4.00
27-45,47: 30,31-Gorilla Grodd-c/story(see Flash #69). 38,39-Adam Strange-c/ story. 42-Deathstroke-c/s. 47-Green Arrow x-over 3.00
46,48,49,50: 46-Superman app. cont'd in Superman #82. 48-Emerald Twilight part 1. 50-($2.95, 52 pgs.)-Glow-in-the-dark-c 2.40 6.00
0, 51-62: 51-1st app. New Green Lantern (Kyle Rayner) with new costume. 53-Superman-c/story. 55-(9/94)-Zero Hour. 0-(10/94). 56-(11/94) 4.00
63,64-Kyle Rayner vs. Hal Jordan. 4.00
65-80,82-92: 63-Begin $1.75-c. 65-New Titans app. 66,67-Flash app. 71-Batman & Robin app. 72-Shazam!-c/app. 73-Wonder Woman-c/app. 73-75-Adam Strange app. 76,77-Green Arrow x-over. 80-Final Night x-over. 87-JLA app. 91-Genesis x-over. 92-Green Arrow x-over. 3.00
81-(Regular Ed.)-Memorial for Hal Jordan (Parallax); most DC heroes app. 5.00
81-($3.95, Deluxe Edition)-Embossed prism-c 2.40 6.00
93-99: 93-Begin $1.95-c; Deadman app. 94-Superboy app. 95-Starlin-a(p). 98,99-Legion of Super-Heroes-c/app. 2.50
100-($2.95) Two covers (Jordan & Rayner); vs. Sinestro 5.00
101-106: 101-106-Hal Jordan-c/app. 103-JLA-c/app. 104-Green Arrow app. 105,106-Parallax app. 3.00
107-126: 107-Jade becomes a Green Lantern. 119-Hal Jordan/Spectre app. 125-JLA app. 2.00
127-134: 127-Begin $2.25-c. 129-Winick-s begin. 134-Guy Gardner app. 2.25
#1,000,000 (11/98) 853rd Century x-over 2.00
Annual 1-3: ('92-'94, 68 pgs.)-1-Eclipso app. 2 -Intro Nightblade. 3-Elseworlds story 3.50
Annual 4 (1995, $3.50)-Year One story 4.00
Annual 5,7,8 ('96, '98, '99, $2.95): 5-Legends of the Dead Earth. 7-Ghosts; Wrightson-c. 8-JLApe; Art Adams-c 3.00
Annual 6 (1997, $3.95)-Pulp Heroes story 5.00
Annual 9 (2000, $3.50) Planet DC 3.50
...80 Page Giant (12/98, $4.95) Stories by various 5.00

Green Lantern Secret Files #1 © DC

Green Mask #2 © FOX

Grendel #19 © Matt Wagner

...80 Page Giant 2 (6/99, $4.95) Team-ups 5.00
...80 Page Giant 3 (8/00, $5.95) Darkseid vs. the GL Corps 6.00
...3-D #1 (12/98, $3.95) Jeanty-a 4.00
...: A New Dawn TPB (1998, $9.95)-r/#50-55 10.00
...: Baptism of Fire TPB (1999, $12.95)-r/#59,66,67,70-75 13.00
...: Emerald Allies TPB (2000, $14.95)-r/GL/GA team-ups 15.00
...: Emerald Knights TPB (1998, $12.95)-r/Hal Jordan's return 13.00
...: Emerald Twilight nn (1994, $5.95)-r/#48-50 6.00
...: Ganthet's Tale nn (1992, $5.95, 68 pgs.)-Silver foil stamped logo; Larry Niven scripts; Byrne-c/a 6.00
.../Green Arrow Collection, Vol. 2-r/Gl #84-87,89 & Flash #217-219 & GL/GA #5-7 by O'Neil/Adams/Wrightson 13.00
...Plus 1 (12/1996, $2.95)-The Ray & Polaris-c/app. 3.00
...Secret Files 1,2- (7/98-6/99, $4.95)1- Origin stories & profiles. 2-Grell-c 5.00
.../Superman: Legend of the Green Flame (2000, $5.95) 1988 unpub. Neil Gaiman story of Hal Jordan with new art by various; Frank Miller-c 6.00
...The Road Back nn (1992, $8.95)-r/1-8 w/covers 9.00

NOTE: *Staton a(p)-9-12; c-9-12.*

GREEN LANTERN (See Tangent Comics/ Green Lantern)

GREEN LANTERN ANNUAL NO. 1, 1963
DC Comics: 1998 ($4.95, one-shot)

1-Reprints Golden Age & Silver Age stories in 1963-style 80 pg. Giant format; new Gil Kane sketch art 5.00

GREEN LANTERN: CIRCLE OF FIRE
DC Comics: Early Oct, 2000 - No. 2, Late Oct, 2000 (limited series)

1-($4.95) Intro. other Green Lanterns 4.95
2-($3.75) 3.75
Green Lantern (x-overs)- .../Adam Strange; .../Atom; .../Firestorm; ... /Green Lantern, Winick-s; .../Power Girl (all $2.50-c) 2.50

GREEN LANTERN CORPS, THE (Formerly Green Lantern; see Tales of...)
DC Comics: No. 206, Nov, 1986 - No. 224, May, 1988

206-223: 220,221-Millennium tie-ins 2.50
224-Double-size last issue 3.00
...Corps Annual 2,3- (12/86,8/87) 1-Formerly Tales of ...Annual #1; Alan Moore scripts. 3-Indicia says Green Lantern Annual #3; Moore scripts; Byrne-a 2.50

NOTE: ***Austin** a-Annual 3i. **Gil Kane** a-223, 224p; c-223, 224, Annual 2. **Russell** a-Annual 3i. **Staton** a-207-213p, 217p, 221p, 222p, Annual 3; c-207-213p, 217p, 221p, 222p. **Willingham** a-213p, 219p, 220p, 218p, 219p, Annual 2, 3p; c-218p, 219p.*

GREEN LANTERN CORPS QUARTERLY
DC Comics: Summer, 1992 - No. 8, Spring, 1994 ($2.50/$2.95, 68 pgs.)

1,7,8: 1-G.A. Green Lantern story; Staton-a(p). 7-Painted-c; Tim Vigil-a. 8-Lobo-c/s 3.50
2-6: 2-G.A. G.L.-c/story; Austin-c(i); Gulacy-a(p). 3-G.A. G.L. story. 4-Austin-i 3.00

GREEN LANTERN: EMERALD DAWN (Also see Emerald Dawn)
DC Comics: Dec, 1989 - No. 6, May, 1990 ($1.00, limited series)

1-Origin retold; Giffen plots in all 5.00
2-6 4.00

GREEN LANTERN: EMERALD DAWN II (Emerald Dawn II #1 & 2)
DC Comics: Apr, 1991 - No. 6, Sept, 1991 ($1.00, limited series)

1-6 2.00

GREEN LANTERN: FEAR ITSELF
DC Comics: 1999 (Graphic novel)

Hardcover ($24.95) Ron Marz-s/Brad Parker painted-a 25.00
Softcover ($14.95) 15.00

GREEN LANTERN/FLASH: FASTER FRIENDS (See Flash/Green Lantern...)
DC Comics: 1997 ($4.95, limited series)

1-Marz-s 5.00

GREEN LANTERN GALLERY
DC Comics: Dec, 1996 ($3.50, one-shot)

1-Wraparound-c; pin-ups by various 3.50

GREEN LANTERN/GREEN ARROW (Also see The Flash #217)
DC Comics: Oct, 1983 - No. 7, April, 1984 (52-60 pgs.)

1-7- r- Green Lantern #7689 4.0

NOTE: ***Neal Adams** r-1-7; c-1-4. **Wrightson** r-4, 5.*

GREEN LANTERN: MOSAIC (Also see Cosmic Odyssey #2)
DC Comics: June, 1992 - No. 18, Nov, 1993 ($1.25)

1-18: Featuring John Stewart. 1-Painted-c by Cully Hamner 2.0

GREEN LANTERN/SENTINEL: HEART OF DARKNESS
DC Comics: Mar, 1998 - No. 3, May, 1998 ($1.95, limited series)

1-3-Marz-s/Pelletier-a 3.0

GREEN LANTERN/SILVER SURFER: UNHOLY ALLIANCES
DC Comics: 1995 ($4.95, one-shot)(Prelude to DC Versus Marvel)

nn-Hal Jordan app. 5.0

GREEN LANTERN: THE NEW CORPS
DC Comics:1999 - No. 2, 1999 ($4.95, limited series)

1,2-Kyle recruits new GLs; Eaton-a 5.0

GREEN LANTERN VS. ALIENS
Dark Horse Comics: Sept, 2000 - No. 4 ($2.95, limited series)

1,2: 1-Hal Jordan and GL Corps vs. Aliens; Leonardi-p. 2-Kyle Rayner 3.0

GREEN MASK, THE (See Mystery Men)
Summer, 1940 - No. 9, 2/42; No. 10, 8/44 - No. 11, 11/44;
Fox Features Syndicate: V2#1, Spring, 1945 - No. 6, 10-11/46

	GD2.0	FN6.0	NM9.4
V1#1-Origin The Green Mask & Domino; reprints/Mystery Men #1-3,5-7; Lou Fine-c	362.00	1086.00	3800.0
2-Zanzibar The Magician by Tuska	132.00	395.00	1250.0
3-Powell-a; Marijuana story	84.00	253.00	800.0
4-Navy Jones begins, ends #6	68.00	205.00	650.0
5	55.00	165.00	500.0
6-The Nightbird begins, ends #9; bondage/torture-c	44.00	133.00	400.0
7-9: 9(2/42)-Becomes The Bouncer #10(nn) on? & Green Mask #10 on	40.00	120.00	320.0
10,11: 10-Origin One Round Hogan & Rocket Kelly	31.00	94.00	250.0
V2#1	24.00	71.00	190.0
2-6	20.00	60.00	160.0

GREEN PLANET, THE
Charlton Comics: 1962 (one-shot) (12¢)

nn-Giordano-c; sci-fi 6.35 19.00 70.0

GREEN TEAM (See Cancelled Comic Cavalcade & 1st Issue Special)

GREETINGS FROM SANTA (See March of Comics No. 48)

GRENDEL (Also see Primer #2, Mage and Comico Collection)
Comico: Mar, 1983 - No. 3, Feb, 1984 ($1.50, B&W)(#1 has indicia to Skrog #1)

1-Origin Hunter Rose 9.00 27.00 100.0
2,3: 2-Origin Argent 7.25 22.00 80.0

GRENDEL
Comico: Oct, 1986 - No. 40, Feb, 1991 ($1.50/$1.95/$2.50, mature)

1 2.40 6.0
1,2: 2nd printings 2.0
2-40: 4-Dave Stevens-c(i). 13-15-Ken Steacy-c. 16-Re-intro Mage (series begins, ends #19). 24-25, 27-28,30-31-Snyder-c/a; 26,29-Snyder-i 3.0
Devil by the Deed (Graphic Novel, 10/86, $5.95, 52 pgs.)-r/Grendel back-ups/ Mage 6-14; Alan Moore intro. 1.00 2.80 7.0
Devil's Legacy ($14.95, 1988, Graphic Novel) 1.85 5.50 15.0
Devil's Vagary (10/87, B&W & red)-No price; included in Comico Collection 1.50 4.50 12.0

GRENDEL (Title series): **Dark Horse Comics**

--BLACK, WHITE, AND RED, 11/98 - No. 4, 2/99 ($3.95, anthology)
1-Wagner-s in all. Art by Sale, Leon and others 5.0
2-4: 2-Mack, Chadwick-a. 3-Allred, Kristensen-a. 4-Pearson, Sprouse-a 4.0

--CLASSICS, 7/95 - 8/95 ($3.95,mature) 1,2-reprints; new Wagner-c 4.0

--CYCLE, 10/95 ($5.95) 1-nn-history of Grendel by M. Wagner & others 6.0

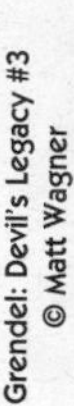
Grendel: Devil's Legacy #3 © Matt Wagner

Grifter V2 #4 © WSP

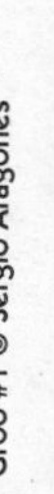
Groo #1 © Sergio Aragonés

--DEVIL BY THE DEED, 7/93 ($3.95, varnish-c) 1-nn-M. Wagner-c/a/scripts; r/Grendel back-ups from Mage #6-14 — 4.00
Reprint (12/97, $3.95) w/pin-ups by various — 4.00

--DEVIL CHILD, 6/99 - No. 2, 7/99 ($2.95, mature) 1,2-Sale & Kristiansen-a/ Diane Schutz-s — 3.00

--DEVIL QUEST, 11/95 ($4.95) 1-nn-Prequel to Batman/Grendel II; M. Wagner story & art; r/back-up story from Grendel Tales series. — 5.00

--DEVILS AND DEATHS, 10/94 - 11/94 ($2.95, mature) 1,2 — 3.00

: DEVIL'S LEGACY, 3/00 - No. 12 ($2.95, reprints 1986 series, recolored)
1-8-Wagner-s/c;Pander Bros.-a — 3.00

--TALES: DEVIL'S CHOICES, 3/95 - 6/95 ($2.95, mature) 1-4 — 3.00

--TALES: FOUR DEVILS, ONE HELL, 8/93 - 1/94 ($2.95, mature)
1-6-Wagner painted-c — 3.00
TPB (12/94, $17.95) r/#1-6 — 18.00

--TALES: HOMECOMING, 12/94 - 2/95 ($2.95, mature) 1-3 — 3.00

--TALES: THE DEVIL IN OUR MIDST, 5/94 - 9/95 ($2.95, mature) 1-5-Wagner painted-c. in all — 3.00

--TALES: THE DEVIL MAY CARE, 12/95 - No. 6, 5/96 ($2.95, mature)
1-6-Terry LaBan scripts. 5-Batman/Grendel II preview — 3.00

--TALES: THE DEVIL'S APPRENTICE, 9/97 - No. 3, 11/97 ($2.95, mature)
1-3 — 3.00

--TALES: THE DEVIL'S HAMMER, 2/94 - 4/94 ($2.95, mature) 1-3 — 3.00

GRENDEL: WAR CHILD
Dark Horse Comics: Aug, 1992 - No. 10, Jun, 1993 ($2.50, lim. series, mature)
1-9: 1-4-Bisley painted-c; Wagner-i & scripts in all — 2.50
10-($3.50, 52 pgs.) Wagner-c — 3.50
Limited Edition Hardcover ($99.95) — 100.00

GREYFRIARS BOBBY (Disney)(Movie)
Dell Publishing Co.: No. 1189, Nov, 1961 (one-shot)
Four Color 1189-Photo-c (scarce) — 6.70 — 20.00 — 80.00

GREYLORE
Sirius: 12/85 - No. 5, Sept, 1986 ($1.50/$1.75, high quality paper)
1-5: Bo Hampton-a in all — 2.00

GRIDIRON GIANTS
Ultimate Sports Ent.: 2000 - No. 3 ($3.95, cardstock covers)
1,2-NFL players Sanders, Marino, Plummer, T. Davis battle evil — 4.00

GRIFFIN, THE
DC Comics: 1991 - No. 6, 1992 ($4.95, limited series, 52 pgs.)
Book 1-6: Matt Wagner painted-c — 5.00

GRIFTER (Also see Team 7 & WildC.A.T.S)
Image Comics (WildStorm Prod.): May, 1995 - No. 10, Mar, 1996 ($1.95)
1 ($1.95, Newsstand)-WildStorm Rising Pt. 5 — 3.00
1-10:1 ($2.50, Direct)-WildStorm Rising Pt. 5, bound-in trading card — 3.00

GRIFTER
Image Comics (WildStorm Prod.): V2#1, July, 1996 - No. 14, Aug, 1997 ($2.50)
V2#1-14: Steven Grant scripts — 3.00

GRIFTER AND THE MASK
Dark Horse Comics: Sept, 1996 - No. 2, Oct, 1996 ($2.50, limited series) (1st Dark Horse Comics/Image x-over)
1,2: Steve Seagle scripts — 2.50

GRIFTER/BADROCK (Also see WildC.A.T.S & Youngblood)
Image Comics (Extreme Studios): Oct, 1995 - No.2, Nov, 1995 ($2.50, unfinished limited series)
1,2: 2-Flip book w/Badrock #2 — 2.50

GRIFTER: ONE SHOT
Image Comics (WildStorm Productions): Jan, 1995 ($4.95, one-shot)
1-Flip-c — 5.00

GRIFTER/SHI
Image Comics (WildStorm Productions): Apr, 1996 - No. 2, May, 1996 ($2.95, limited series)
1,2: 1-Jim Lee-c/a(p); Travis Charest-a(p). 2-Billy Tucci-c/a(p); Travis Charest-a(p) — 3.00

GRIM GHOST, THE
Atlas/Seaboard Publ.: Jan, 1975 - No. 3, July, 1975
1-3: Fleisher-s in all. 1-Origin. 2-Son of Satan; Colan-a. 3-Heath-c — 5.00

GRIMJACK (Also see Demon Knight & Starslayer)
First Comics: Aug, 1984 - No. 81, Apr, 1991 ($1.00/$1.95/$2.25)
1-John Ostrander scripts & Tim Truman-c/a begins. — 3.00
2-25: 20-Sutton-c/a begins. 22-Bolland-a. — 2.25
26-2nd color Teenage Mutant Ninja Turtles — 2.25
27-74,76-81 (Later issues $1.95, $2.25): 30-Dynamo Joe x-over; 31-Mandrake-c/a begins. 73,74-Kelley Jones-a — 2.25
75-($5.95, 52 pgs.)-Fold-out map; coated stock — 2.40 — 6.00
NOTE: ***Truman*** *c/a-1-17.*

GRIMJACK CASEFILES
First Comics: Nov, 1990 - No. 5, Mar, 1991 ($1.95, limited series)
1-5 Reprints 1st stories from Starslayer #10 on — 2.00

GRIMM'S GHOST STORIES (See Dan Curtis)
Gold Key/Whitman No. 55 on: Jan, 1972 - No. 60, June, 1982 (Painted-c #1-42,44,46-56)

	GD2.0	FN6.0	NM9.4
1	2.50	7.50	25.00
2-5,8: 5,8-Williamson-a	1.75	5.25	14.00
6,7,9,10	1.10	3.30	9.00
11-20	1.00	3.00	8.00
21-42,45-54: 32,34-Reprints. 45-Photo-c			6.00
43,44,55-60: 43,44-(52 pgs.). 43-Photo-c. 59-Williamson-a(r/#8)	1.00	3.00	8.00
Mini-Comic No. 1 (3-1/4x6-1/2", 1976)		2.40	6.00

NOTE: *Reprints-#32?, 34?, 39, 43, 44, 47?, 53; 56-60(1/3).* ***Bolle*** *a-8, 17, 22-25, 27, 29(2), 33, 35, 41, 43r, 45(2), 48(2), 50, 52.* ***Celardo*** *a-17, 26, 28p, 30, 31, 43(2), 45.* ***Lopez*** *a-24, 25.* ***McWilliams*** *a-33, 44r, 48, 54(2), 57, 58.* ***Win Mortimer*** *a-31, 33, 49, 51, 55, 56, 58(2), 59, 60.* ***Roussos*** *a-25, 30.* ***Sparling*** *a-23, 24, 28, 30, 31, 33, 43r, 44, 45, 51(2), 52, 56, 58, 59(2), 60.* ***Spiegle*** *a-44.*

GRIN (The American Funny Book) (Satire)
APAG House Pubs: Nov, 1972 - No. 3, April, 1973 (Magazine, 52 pgs.)
1-Parodies-Godfather, All in the Family — 2.50 — 7.50 — 23.00
2,3 — 1.85 — 5.50 — 15.00

GRIN & BEAR IT (See Gags)
Dell Publishing Co.: No. 28, 1941
Large Feature Comic 28 — 10.00 — 30.00 — 120.00

GRIPS (Extreme violence)
Silverwolf Comics: Sept, 1986 - No. 4, Dec, 1986 ($1.50, B&W, mature)
1-Tim Vigil-c/a in all — 5.00
2-4 — 4.00

GRIT GRADY (See Holyoke One-Shot No. 1)

GROO (Sergio Aragones'...)
Image Comics: Dec, 1994 - No. 12, Dec, 1995 ($1.95)
1-12: 2-Indicia reads #1, Jan, 1995; Aragones-c/a in all — 3.50

GROO (Sergio Aragones'...)
Dark Horse Comics: Jan, 1998 - No. 4, Apr, 1998 ($2.95)
1-4: Aragones-c/a in all — 4.00

GROO CHRONICLES, THE (Sergio Aragones)
Marvel Comics (Epic Comics): June, 1989 - No. 6, Feb, 1990 ($3.50)
Book 1-6: Reprints early Pacific issues — 3.50

GROO SPECIAL
Eclipse Comics: Oct, 1984 ($2.00, 52 pgs., Baxter paper)
1-Aragones-c/a — 1.75 — 5.25 — 14.00

GROO THE WANDERER (See Destroyer Duck #1 & Starslayer #5)
Pacific Comics: Dec, 1982 - No. 8, Apr, 1984
1-Aragones-c/a(p) in all; Aragones biog., photo — 2.25 — 6.75 — 18.00
2-8: 5-Deluxe paper (1.00-c) — 1.50 — 4.50 — 12.00

Grrl Scouts #4 © Jim Mahfood

The Gumps #2 © News Syndicate

Gunfire #4 © DC

GD2.0 FN6.0 NM9.4

GROO THE WANDERER (Sergio Aragones'...) (See Marvel Graphic Novel #32)
Marvel Comics (Epic Comics): March, 1985 - No. 120, Jan, 1995

1-Aragones-c/a in all 1.00 3.00 8.00
2-10 4.00
11-20,50-($1.50, double size) 3.00
21-49,51-99: 87-direct sale only, high quality paper 2.50
100-($2.95, 52 pgs.) 4.00
101-120 3.00
Groo Carnival, The (12/91, $8.95)-r/#9-12 9.00
Groo Garden, The (4/94, $10.95)-r/#25-28 11.00

GROOVY (Cartoon Comics - not CCA approved)
Marvel Comics Group: March, 1968 - No. 3, July, 1968

1-Monkees, Ringo Starr, Sonny & Cher, Mamas & Papas photos
7.25 21.75 80.00
2,3 5.00 15.00 55.00

GROSS POINT
DC Comics: Aug, 1997 - No. 14, Aug, 1998 ($2.50)

1-14: 1-Waid/Augustyn-s 2.50

GROUP LARUE, THE
Innovation Publishing: 1989 - No. 4, 1990 ($1.95, mini-series)

1-4-By Mike Baron 2.00

GRRL SCOUTS (Jim Mahfood's...)
Oni Press: Mar,1999 - No. 4, Dec, 1999 ($2.95, B&W, limited series)

1-4-Mahfood-s/c/a 3.00

GUADALCANAL DIARY (See American Library)

GUARDIANS OF JUSTICE & THE O-FORCE
Shadow Comics: 1990 (no date) ($1.50, 7-1/2 x10-1/4)

1-Super-hero group 2.00

GUARDIANS OF METROPOLIS
DC Comics: Nov, 1995 - Feb, 1995 ($1.50, limited series)

1-4: 1-Superman & Granny Goodness app. 2.00

GUARDIANS OF THE GALAXY (Also see The Defenders #26, Marvel Presents #3, Marvel Super-Heroes #18, Marvel Two-In-One #5)
Marvel Comics: June, 1990 - No. 62, July, 1995 ($1.00/$1.25)

1-Valentino-c/a(p) begin. 3.00
2-16: 2-Zeck-c(i). 5-McFarlane-c(i). 7-Intro Malevolence (Mephisto's daughter); Perez-c(i). 8-Intro Rancor (descendant of Wolverine) in cameo. 9-1st full app. Rancor; Rob Liefeld-c(i). 10-Jim Lee-c(i). 13,14-1st app. Spirit of Vengeance (futuristic Ghost Rider). 14-Spirit of Vengeance vs. The Guardians. 15-Starlin-c(i). 16-($1.50, 52 pgs.)-Starlin-c(i) 2.00
17-24,26-38,40-47: 17-20-31st century Punishers storyline. 20-Last $1.00-c. 21-Rancor app. 22-Reintro Starhawk. 24-Silver Surfer-c/story; Ron Lim-c. 26-Origin retold. 27-28-Infinity War x-over; 27-Inhumans app. 43-Intro Wooden (son of Thor) 2.00
25-($2.50)-Prism foil-c; Silver Surfer/Galactus-c/s 2.50
25-($2.50)-Without foil-c; newsstand edition 2.50
39-($2.95, 52 pgs.)-Embossed & holo-grafx foil-c; Dr. Doom vs. Rancor 3.00
48,49,51-62: 48-bound-in trading card sheet 2.00
50-($2.00, 52 pgs.)-Newsstand edition 2.00
50-($2.95, 52 pgs.)-Collectors ed. w/foil embossed-c 3.00
Annual 1-4: ('91-'94, 68 pgs.)-1-2 pg. origin. 2-Spirit of Vengeance-c/story. 3-Bagged w/card 3.00

GUERRILLA WAR (Formerly Jungle War Stories)
Dell Publishing Co.: No. 12, July-Sept, 1965 - No. 14, Mar, 1966

12-14 2.00 6.00 18.00

GUFF
Dark Horse Comics: Apr, 1998 ($1.95, B&W)

1-Flip book; Aragonés-c 2.00

GUILTY (See Justice Traps the Guilty)

GULLIVER'S TRAVELS (See Dell Jr. Treasury No. 3)
Dell Publishing Co.: Sept-Nov, 1965 - No. 3, May, 1966

1 4.60 13.75 55.00

GD2.0 FN6.0 NM9.4

2,3 3.45 10.35 38.00

GUMBY'S SUMMER FUN SPECIAL
Comico: July, 1987 ($2.50)

1-Art Adams-c/a; B. Burden scripts 3.00

GUMBY'S WINTER FUN SPECIAL
Comico: Dec, 1988 ($2.50, 44 pgs.)

1-Art Adams-c/a 3.00

GUMPS, THE (See Merry Christmas..., Popular & Super Comics)
Dell Publ. Co./Bridgeport Herald Corp.: No. 73, 1945; Mar-Apr, 1947 - No. 5, Nov-Dec, 1947

Four Color 73 (Dell)(1945) 11.70 35.00 140.00
1 (3-4/47) 15.00 45.00 120.00
2-5 10.00 30.00 75.00

GUNFIGHTER (Fat & Slat #1-4) (Becomes Haunt of Fear #15 on)
E. C. Comics (Fables Publ. Co.): No. 5, Sum, 1948 - No. 14, Mar-Apr, 1950

5,6-Moon Girl in each 53.00 158.00 475.00
7-14: 14-Bondage-c 40.00 120.00 325.00

NOTE: ***Craig & H. C. Kiefer*** *art in most issues.* ***Craig*** *c-5, 6, 13, 14.* ***Feldstein/Craig*** *a-10.* ***Feldstein*** *a-7-11.* ***Harrison/Wood*** *a-13, 14.* ***Ingels*** *a-5-14; c-7-12.*

GUNFIGHTERS, THE
Super Comics (Reprints): 1963 - 1964

10-12,15,16,18: 10,11-r/Billy the Kid #s? 12-r/The Rider #5(Swift Arrow). 15-r/Straight Arrow #42; Powell-r. 16-r/Billy the Kid #?(Toby). 18-r/The Rider #3; Severin-c 1.85 5.50 15.00

GUNFIGHTERS, THE (Formerly Kid Montana)
Charlton Comics: No. 51, 10/66 - No. 52, 10/67; No. 53, 6/79 - No. 85, 7/84

51,52 2.30 7.00 20.00
53,54,56:53,54-Williamson/Torres-r/Six Gun Heroes #47,49. 56-Williamson/Severin-c; Severin-r/Sheriff of Tombstone #1 1.00 3.00 8.00
55,57-80 5.00
81-84-Lower print run 2.40 6.00
85-S&K-r/1955 Bullseye 1.00 2.80 7.00

GUNFIRE (See Deathstroke Annual #2 & Showcase 94 #1,2)
DC Comics: May, 1994 - No. 13, June, 1995 ($1.75/$2.25)

1-5,0,6-13: 2-Ricochet-c/story. 5-(9/94). 0-(10/94). 6-(11/94) 2.25

GUN GLORY (Movie)
Dell Publishing Co.: No. 846, Oct, 1957 (one-shot)

Four Color 846-Toth-a, photo-c. 9.00 27.00 110.00

GUNHAWK, THE (Formerly Whip Wilson)(See Wild Western)
Marvel Comics/Atlas (MCI): No. 12, Nov, 1950 - No. 18, Dec, 1951
(Also see Two-Gun Western #5)

12 19.00 56.00 150.00
13-18: 13-Tuska-a. 16-Colan-a. 18-Maneely-c 13.00 39.00 105.00

GUNHAWKS (Gunhawk No. 7)
Marvel Comics Group: Oct, 1972 - No. 7, October, 1973

1,6: 1-Reno Jones, Kid Cassidy; Shores-c/a(p). 6-Kid Cassidy dies
2.00 6.00 16.00
2-5,7: 7-Reno Jones solo 1.50 4.50 12.00

GUNHED
Vix Comics: 1990 - No. 3, 1991? ($4.95, 7-1/8 x 9-1/8, 52 pgs., bi-monthly)

1-3: Japanese sci-fi based on 1991 movie 5.00

GUNMASTER (Becomes Judo Master #89 on)
Charlton Comics: 9/64 - No. 4, 1965; No. 84, 7/65 - No. 88, 3-4/66; No. 89, 10/67

V1#1 3.00 9.00 30.00
2,4, V5#84-86: 84-Formerly Six-Gun Heroes 2.30 7.00 20.00
V5#87-89 1.75 5.25 14.00

NOTE: *Vol. 5 was originally cancelled with #88 (3-4/66). #89 on, became Judo Master, then later in 1967, Charlton issued #89 as a Gunmaster one-shot.*

GUN RUNNER
Marvel Comics UK: Oct, 1993 - No. 6, Mar, 1994 ($1.75, limited series)

1-($2.75)-Polybagged w/4 trading cards; Spirits of Vengeance app.

Guns Against Gangsters #4 © NOVP

Gunsmoke #2 © WEST

Ha-Ha Comics #2 © ACG

GD2.0 FN6.0 NM9.4

2.75
2-6: 2-Ghost Rider & Blaze app. 2.00

GUNS AGAINST GANGSTERS (True-To-Life Romances #8 on)
Curtis Publications/Novelty Press: Sept-Oct, 1948 - No. 6, July-Aug, 1949; V2#1, Sept-Oct, 1949

1-Toni & Greg Gayle begins by Schomburg; L.B. Cole-c
38.00 113.00 300.00
2-L.B. Cole-c 28.00 84.00 225.00
3-6, V2#1: 6-Toni Gayle-c 24.00 71.00 190.00
NOTE: *L. B. Cole c-1-6, V2#1, 2; a-1, 2, 3(2), 4-6.*

GUNSLINGER
Dell Publishing Co.: No. 1220, Oct-Dec, 1961 (one-shot)

Four Color 1220-Photo-c 8.35 25.00 100.00

GUNSLINGER (Formerly Tex Dawson...)
Marvel Comics Group: No. 2, Apr, 1973 - No. 3, June, 1973

2,3 1.85 5.50 15.00

GUNSLINGERS
Marvel Comics: Feb, 2000 ($2.99)

1-Reprints stories of Two-Gun Kid, Rawhide Kid and Caleb Hammer 3.00

GUNSMITH CATS: (Title series), **Dark Horse Comics**
--BAD TRIP (Manga), 6/98 - No. 6, 11/98 ($2.95, B&W) 1-6 3.00
--BEAN BANDIT (Manga), 1/99 - No. 9 ($2.95, B&W, limited series) 1-9 3.00
--GOLDIE VS. MISTY (Manga), 11/97 - No. 7, 5/98 ($2.95, B&W) 1-7 3.00
--KIDNAPPED (Manga), 11/99 - No. 10, 8/00 ($2.95, B&W) 1-10 3.00
--MISTER V (Manga), 10/00 - No. 11 ($3.50, B&W) 1 3.50
--THE RETURN OF GRAY (Manga), 8/96 - No. 7, 2/97 ($2.95, B&W) 1-7 3.00
--SHADES OF GRAY (Manga), 5/97 - No. 5, 9/97 ($2.95, B&W) 1-5 3.00

GUNSMOKE (Blazing Stories of the West)
Western Comics (Youthful Magazines): Apr-May, 1949 - No. 16, Jan, 1952

1-Gunsmoke & Masked Marvel begin by Ingels; Ingels bondage-c
40.00 120.00 360.00
2-Ingels-c/a(2) 28.00 84.00 225.00
3-Ingels bondage-c/a 23.00 68.00 180.00
4-6: Ingels-c 18.00 53.00 140.00
7-10 10.00 30.00 80.00
11-16: 15,16-Western/horror stories 9.30 28.00 65.00
NOTE: ***Stallman** a-11, 14. **Wildey** a-15, 16.*

GUNSMOKE (TV)
Dell Publishing Co./Gold Key (All have James Arness photo-c): No. 679, Feb, 1956 - No. 27, Feb, 1969 - No. 6, Feb, 1970

Four Color 679(#1) 16.00 48.00 190.00
Four Color 720,769,797,844 (#2-5),6(11-1/57-58),7 7.50 22.50 90.00
8,9,11,12-Williamson-a in all, 4 pgs. each 8.00 24.00 95.00
10-Williamson/Crandall-a, 4 pgs. 8.00 24.00 95.00
13-27 6.30 19.00 75.00
1 (Gold Key) 4.60 13.75 55.00
2-6('69-70) 3.00 9.00 30.00

GUNSMOKE TRAIL
Ajax-Farrell Publ./Four Star Comic Corp.: June, 1957 - No. 4, Dec, 1957

1 10.00 30.00 75.00
2-4 6.00 18.00 42.00

GUNSMOKE WESTERN (Formerly Western Tales of Black Rider)
Atlas Comics No. 32-35(CPS/NPI); Marvel No. 36 on: No. 32, Dec, 1955 - No. 77, July, 1963

32-Baker & Drucker-a 16.00 49.00 130.00
33,35,36-Williamson-a in each: 5,6 & 4 pgs. plus Drucker-a #33. 33-Kinstler-a?
13.00 39.00 105.00
34-Baker-a, 4 pgs.; Kirby-c 11.00 33.00 90.00
37-Davis-a(2); Williamson text illo 10.00 30.00 80.00
38,39: 39-Williamson text illo (unsigned) 8.65 26.00 60.00
40-Williamson/Mayo-a (4 pgs.) 10.00 30.00 70.00
41,42,45,46,48,49,52-54,57,58,60: 49,52-Kid from Texas story. 57-1st Two Gun Kid by Severin. 60-Sam Hawk app. in Kid Colt 6.40 19.25 45.00
43,44-Torres-a 6.40 19.25 45.00
47,51,59,61: 47,51,59-Kirby-a. 61-Crandall-a 7.85 23.50 55.00
50-Kirby, Crandall-a 9.30 28.00 65.00
55,56-Matt Baker-a 8.65 26.00 60.00
62-67,69,71-73,77-Kirby-a. 72-Origin Kid Colt 4.10 12.30 45.00
68,70,74-76: 68-(10¢-c) 3.20 9.60 35.00
68-(10¢ cover price blacked out, 12¢ printed on) 6.35 19.00 70.00
NOTE: ***Colan** a-35-37, 39, 72, 76. **Davis** a-37, 52, 54, 55; c-50, 54. **Ditko** a-66; c-56p. **Drucker** a-32-34. **Heath** c-33. **Jack Keller** a-35, 40, 60, 72; c-72. **Kirby** a-47, 50, 51, 59, 62(3), 63-67, 69, 71, 73, 77; c-56(w/**Ditko**),57, 58, 60, 61(w/**Ayers**), 62, 63, 66, 68, 69, 71-77. **Robinson** a-35. **Severin** a-35, 59-61; c-34, 35, 39, 42, 43. **Tuska** a-34. **Wildey** a-10, 37, 42, 56, 57. Kid Colt in all. Two-Gun Kid in No. 57, 59, 60-63. Wyatt Earp in No. 45, 48, 49, 52, 54, 55, 58.*

GUNS OF FACT & FICTION (Also see A-1 Comics)
Magazine Enterprises: No. 13, 1948 (one-shot)

A-1 13-Used in **SOTI**, pg. 19; Ingels & J. Craig-a 29.00 86.00 230.00

GUNS OF THE DRAGON
DC Comics: Oct, 1998 - No. 4, Jan, 1999 ($2.50, limited series)

1-4-DCU in the 1920's; Enemy Ace & Bat Lash app. 2.50

GUY GARDNER (Guy Gardner: Warrior #17 on)(Also see Green Lantern #59)
DC Comics: Oct, 1992 - No. 44, July, 1996 ($1.25/$1.50/$1.75)

1-24,0,26-30: 1-Staton-c/a(p) begins. 6-Guy vs. Hal Jordan. 8-Vs. Lobo-c/story. 5-JLA x-over, begin $1.50-c. 18-Begin 4-part Emerald Fallout story; splash page x-over GL #50. 18-21-Vs. Hal Jordan. 24-(9/94)-Zero Hour. 0-(10/94) 2.50
25 (11/94, $2.50, 52 pgs.) 3.00
29 ($2.95)-Gatefold-c 3.50
29-Variant-c (Edward Hopper's Nighthawks) 2.50
31-44: 31-$1.75-c begins. 40-Gorilla Grodd-c/app. 44-Parallax-app. (1 pg.)
2.50
Annual 1 (1995, $3.50)-Year One story 4.00
Annual 2 (1996, $2.95)-Legends of the Dead Earth story 3.00

GUY GARDNER REBORN
DC Comics: 1992 - Book 3, 1992 ($4.95, limited series)

1-3: Staton-c/a(p). 1-Lobo-c/cameo. 2,3-Lobo-c/s 5.00

GYPSY COLT
Dell Publishing Co.: No. 568, June, 1954 (one-shot)

Four Color 568--Movie 4.10 12.30 45.00

GYRO GEARLOOSE (See Dynabrite Comics, Walt Disney's C&S #140 & Walt Disney Showcase #18)
Dell Publishing Co.: No. 1047, Nov-Jan/1959-60 - May-July, 1962 (Disney)

Four Color 1047 (No. 1)-All Barks-c/a 18.35 55.00 220.00
Four Color 1095,1184-All by Carl Barks 10.00 30.00 120.00
Four Color 1267-Barks c/a, 4 pgs. 7.00 21.00 85.00
01329-207 (#1, 5-7/62)-Barks-c only (intended as 4-Color 1329?)
5.00 15.00 60.00

HACKER FILES, THE
DC Comics: Aug, 1992 - No. 12, July, 1993 ($1.95)

1-12: 1-Sutton-a(p) begins; computer generated-c 2.00

HAGAR THE HORRIBLE (See Comics Reading Libraries)

HA HA COMICS (Teepee Tim No. 100 on; also see Giggle Comics)
Scope Mag.(Creston Publ.) No. 1-80/American Comics Group: Oct, 1943 - No. 99, Jan, 1955

1-Funny animal 31.00 94.00 250.00
2 15.00 45.00 120.00
3-5: Ken Hultgren-a begins? 11.00 33.00 90.00
6-10 10.00 30.00 70.00
11-20: 14-Infinity-c 7.15 21.50 50.00
21-40 6.00 18.00 42.00
41-94,96-99: 49-X-Mas-c 5.00 15.00 35.00
95-3-D effect-c 14.00 43.00 115.00

HAIR BEAR BUNCH, THE (TV) (See Fun-In No. 13)
Gold Key: Feb, 1972 - No. 9, Feb, 1974 (Hanna-Barbera)

Hammer of God: Butch #3 © DH

Hand of Fate #17 © ACE

Hangman Comics #6 © MLJ Mags.

1 3.20 9.60 35.00
2-9 2.30 7.00 20.00

HALLELUJAH TRAIL, THE (See Movie Classics)

HALL OF FAME FEATURING THE T.H.U.N.D.E.R. AGENTS
JC Productions(Archie Comics Group): May, 1983 - No. 3, Dec, 1983

1-3: Thunder Agents-r(Crandall, Kane, Tuska, Wood-a). 2-New Ditko-c 3.00

HALLOWEEN (Movie)
Chaos! Comics: Nov, 2000 ($2.95, one-shot)

1-Brewer-a; Michael Myers childhood at the Sanitarium 3.00

HALLOWEEN HORROR
Eclipse Comics: Oct, 1987 (Seduction of the Innocent #7)($1.75)

1-Pre-code horror-r 3.00

HALLOWEEN MEGAZINE
Marvel Comics: Dec, 1996 ($3.95, one-shot, 96 pgs.)

1-Reprints Tomb of Dracula 4.00

HALO, AN ANGEL'S STORY
Sirius Entertainment: Apr, 1996 - No. 4, Sept, 1996 ($2.95, limited series)

1-4: Knowles-c/a/scripts 3.00
TPB ($12.95) r/#1-4 13.00

HALO JONES (See The Ballad of...)

HAMMER, THE
Dark Horse Comics: Oct, 1997 - No. 4, Jan, 1998 ($2.95, limited series)

1-4-Kelley Jones-s/c/a, ...: Uncle Alex (8/98, $2.95) 3.00

HAMMER, THE: THE OUTSIDER
Dark Horse Comics: Feb, 1999 - No. 3, Apr, 1999 ($2.95, limited series)

1-3-Kelley Jones-s/c/a 3.00

HAMMERLOCKE
DC Comics: Sept, 1992 - No. 9, May, 1993 ($1.75, limited series)

1-($2.50, 52 pgs.)-Chris Sprouse-c/a in all 2.50
2-9 2.00

HAMMER OF GOD (Also see Nexus)
First Comics: Feb, 1990 - No. 4, May, 1990 ($1.95, limited series)

1-4 2.00

HAMMER OF GOD: BUTCH
Dark Horse Comics: May, 1994 - No. 4, Aug, 1994 ($2.50, limited series)

1-3 2.50

HAMMER OF GOD: PENTATHLON
Dark Horse Comics: Jan, 1994 ($2.50, one shot)

1-character from Nexus 2.50

HAMMER OF GOD: SWORD OF JUSTICE
First Comics: Feb 1991 - Mar 1991 ($4.95, lim. series, squarebound, 52 pgs.)

V2#1,2 5.00

HANDBOOK OF THE CONAN UNIVERSE, THE
Marvel Comics: June, 1985 ($1.25, one-shot)

1-Kaluta-c. 3.00

HAND OF FATE (Formerly Men Against Crime)
Ace Magazines: No. 8, Dec, 1951 - No. 25, Dec, 1954 (Weird/horror stories) (Two #25's)

8-Surrealistic text story 40.00 120.00 325.00
9,10,21-Necronomicon sty; drug belladonna used 23.00 69.00 185.00
11-18,20,22,23 19.00 56.00 150.00
19-Bondage, hypo needle scenes 20.00 60.00 160.00
24-Electric chair-c 30.00 90.00 240.00
25a(11/54), 25b(12/54)-Both have Cameron-a 15.00 45.00 120.00
NOTE: ***Cameron** a-9, 10, 19-25a, 25b; c-13. **Sekowsky** a-8, 9, 13, 14.*

HAND OF FATE
Eclipse Comics: Feb, 1988 - No. 3, Apr, 1988 ($1.75/$2.00, Baxter paper)

1-3; 3-B&W 2.00

HANDS OF THE DRAGON
Seaboard Periodicals (Atlas): June, 1975

1-Origin/1st app.; Craig-a(p)/Mooney inks 2.40 6.00

HANGMAN COMICS (Special Comics No. 1; Black Hood No. 9 on)
(Also see Flyman, Mighty Comics, Mighty Crusaders & Pep Comics)
MLJ Magazines: No. 2, Spring, 1942 - No. 8, Fall, 1943

2-The Hangman, Boy Buddies begin 190.00 570.00 1800.00
3-Beheading splash pg.; 1st Nazi war-c 121.00 363.00 1150.00
4-8: 5-1st Jap war-c. 8-2nd app. Super Duck (ties w/Jolly Jingles #11) 105.00 316.00 1000.00
NOTE: ***Fuje** a-7(3), 8(3); c-3. **Reinman** c/a-3. Bondage c-3. **Sahle** c-6.*

HANK
Pentagon Publishing Co.: 1946

nn-Coulton Waugh's newspaper reprint 7.15 21.50 50.00

HANNA-BARBERA (See Golden Comics Digest No. 2, 7, 11)

HANNA-BARBERA ALL-STARS
Archie Publications: Oct, 1995 - No. 6, Sept, 1996 ($1.50, bi-monthly)

1-6 3.00

HANNA-BARBERA BANDWAGON (TV)
Gold Key: Oct, 1962 - No. 3, Apr, 1963

1-Giant, 84 pgs. 1-Augie Doggie app.; 1st app. Lippy the Lion, Touché Turtle & Dum Dum, Wally Gator, Loopy de Loop, 11.70 35.00 140.00
2-Giant, 84 pgs.; Mr. & Mrs. J. Evil Scientist (1st app.) in Snagglepuss story; Yakky Doodle, Ruff and Reddy and others app. 8.75 26.25 105.00
3-Regular size; Mr. & Mrs. J. Evil Scientist app. (pre-#1), Snagglepuss, Wally Gator and others app. 6.30 19.00 75.00

HANNA-BARBERA GIANT SIZE
Harvey Comics: Oct, 1992 - No. 3 ($2.25, 68 pgs.)

V2#1-3:Flintstones, Yogi Bear, Magilla Gorilla, Huckleberry Hound, Quick Draw McGraw, Yakky Doodle & Chopper, Jetsons & others 3.50

HANNA-BARBERA HI-ADVENTURE HEROES (See Hi-Adventure...)

HANNA-BARBERA PARADE (TV)
Charlton Comics: Sept, 1971 - No. 10, Dec, 1972

1 7.25 21.75 80.00
2,4-10 3.65 11.00 40.00
3-(52 pgs.)- "Summer Picnic" 5.90 17.75 65.00
NOTE: *No. 4 (1/72) went on sale late in 1972 with the January 1973 issues.*

HANNA-BARBERA PRESENTS
Archie Publications: Nov, 1995 - No. 6 ($1.50, bi-monthly)

1-6: 2-Wacky Races. 4-Quick Draw McGraw & Magilla Gorilla. 5-A Pup Named Scooby-Doo 2.50

HANNA-BARBERA SPOTLIGHT (See Spotlight)

HANNA-BARBERA SUPER TV HEROES (TV)
Gold Key: Apr, 1968 - No. 7, Oct, 1969 (Hanna-Barbera)

1-The Birdman, The Herculoids(ends #6; not in #2), Moby Dick, Young Samson & Goliath(ends #2,4), and The Mighty Mightor begin; Spiegle-a in all 17.00 50.00 200.00
2-The Galaxy Trio app.; Shazzan begins; 12¢ & 15¢ versions exist 11.00 33.00 130.00
3,6,7-The Space Ghost app. 10.00 30.00 120.00
4,5 9.00 27.00 110.00

HANNA-BARBERA TV FUN FAVORITES (See Golden Comics Digest #2,7,11)

HANNA-BARBERA (TV STARS) (See TV Stars)

HANS BRINKER (Disney)
Dell Publishing Co.: No. 1273, Feb, 1962 (one-shot)

Four Color 1273-Movie, photo-c 5.85 17.50 70.00

HANS CHRISTIAN ANDERSEN
Ziff-Davis Publ. Co.: 1953 (100 pgs., Special Issue)

nn-Danny Kaye (movie)-Photo-c; fairy tales 16.00 49.00 130.00

HANSEL & GRETEL
Dell Publishing Co.: No. 590, Oct, 1954 (one-shot)

Hap Hazard Comics #9 © ACE

Harbinger #5 © VAL

Hardware #17 © Milestone Media

GD2.0 FN6.0 NM9.4

Four Color 590-Partial photo-c 5.85 17.50 70.00

HANSI, THE GIRL WHO LOVED THE SWASTIKA
Spire Christian Comics (Fleming H. Revell Co.): 1973, 1976 (39¢/49¢)

nn 2.30 7.00 20.00

HAP HAZARD COMICS (Real Love No. 25 on)
Ace Magazines (Readers' Research): Summer, 1944 - No. 24, Feb, 1949 (#1-6 are quarterly issues)

1 14.00 41.00 110.00
2 7.85 23.50 55.00
3-10 5.70 17.00 40.00
11-13,15-24 5.00 15.00 30.00
14-Feldstein-c (4/47) 8.65 26.00 60.00

HAP HOPPER (See Comics Revue No. 2)

HAPPIEST MILLIONAIRE, THE (See Movie Comics)

HAPPI TIM (See March of Comics No. 182)

HAPPY BIRTHDAY MARTHA WASHINGTON (Also see Give Me Liberty, Martha Washington Goes To War, & Martha Washington Stranded In Space)
Dark Horse Comics: Mar, 1995 ($2.95, one-shot)

1-Miller script; Gibbons-c/a 3.00

HAPPY COMICS (Happy Rabbit No. 41 on)
Nedor Publ./Standard Comics (Animated Cartoons): Aug, 1943 - No. 40, Dec, 1950 (Companion to Goofy Comics)

1-Funny animal 26.00 79.00 210.00
2 13.00 39.00 105.00
3-10 10.00 30.00 70.00
11-19 7.15 21.50 50.00
20-31,34-37-Frazetta text illos in all (2 in #34&35, 3 in #27,28,30). 27-Al Fago-a 10.00 30.00 70.00
32-Frazetta-a, 7 pgs. plus 2 text illos; Roussos-a 20.00 60.00 160.00
33-Frazetta-a(2), 6 pgs. each (Scarce) 28.00 83.00 220.00
38-40 5.00 15.00 35.00

HAPPYDALE: DEVILS IN THE DESERT
DC Comics (Vertigo): 1999 - No. 2, 1999 ($6.95, limited series)

1,2-Andrew Dabb-s/Seth Fisher-a 7.00

HAPPY DAYS (TV)(See Kite Fun Book)
Gold Key: Mar, 1979 - No. 6, Feb, 1980

1-Photo-c of TV cast 1.85 5.50 15.00
2-6 1.00 3.00 8.00

HAPPY HOLIDAY (See March of Comics No. 181)

HAPPY HOULIHANS (Saddle Justice No. 3 on; see Blackstone, The Magician Detective)
E. C. Comics: Fall, 1947 - No. 2, Winter, 1947-48

1-Origin Moon Girl (same date as Moon Girl #1) 44.00 133.00 400.00
2 28.00 83.00 220.00

HAPPY JACK
Red Top (Decker): Aug, 1957 - No. 2, Nov, 1957

V1#1,2 4.65 14.00 28.00

HAPPY JACK HOWARD
Red Top (Farrell)/Decker: 1957

nn-Reprints Handy Andy story from E. C. Dandy Comics #5, renamed "Happy Jack" 4.65 14.00 28.00

HAPPY RABBIT (Formerly Happy Comics)
Standard Comics (Animated Cartoons): No. 41, Feb, 1951 - No. 48, Apr, 1952

41-Funny animal 5.00 15.00 35.00
42-48 4.00 12.00 24.00

HARBINGER (Also see Unity)
Valiant: Jan, 1992 - No. 41, June, 1995 ($1.95/$2.50)

0-(Advance), 1-1st app. 5.00
2-4: 4-Low print run 4.00
5-24,26-41: 8,9-Unity x-overs. 8-Miller-c. 9-Simonson-c. 10-1st app. H.A.R.D Corps 10/92). 14-1st app. Stronghold18-Intro Screen. 19-1st app. Stunner. 22-Archer & Armstrong app. 24-Cover similar to #1. 26-Intro New Harbingers. 29-Bound-in trading card. 30-H.A.R.D. Corps app. 32-Eternal Warrior app. 33-Dr. Eclipse app. 2.50
25-($3.50, 52 pgs.)-Harada vs. Sting 3.50
...Files 1,2 (8/94,2/95 $2.50) 2.50
Trade paperback nn (11/92, $9.95)-Reprints #1-4 & comes polybagged with a copy of Harbinger #0 w/new-c. 10.00
NOTE: *Issues 1-6 have coupons with origin of Harada and are redeemable for Harbinger #0.*

HARD BOILED
Dark Horse Comics: Sept, 1990 - No. 3, 1992 ($4.95/$5.95, 8 1/2x11", lim. ser.)

1-3-Miller-s; Darrow-c/a; sexually explicit & violent 1.00 2.80 7.00
TPB (5/93, $15.95) 16.00
Big Damn Hard Boiled (12/97, $29.95, B&W) r/#1-3 30.00

HARDCASE (See Break Thru, Flood Relief & Ultraforce, 1st Series)
Malibu Comics (Ultraverse): June, 1993 - No. 26, Aug, 1995 ($1.95/$2.50)

1-Intro Hardcase; Dave Gibbons-c; has coupon for Ultraverse Premiere #0; Jim Callahan-a(p) begin, ends #3 3.00
1-With coupon missing 2.00
1-Platinum Edition 4.00
1-Holographic Cover Edition; 1st full-c holograph tied w/Prime 1 & Strangers 1 7.00
1-Ultra Limited silver foil-c 4.00
2,3-Callahan-a, 2-($2.50)-Newsstand edition bagged w/trading card 2.50
4,6-15, 17-19: 4-Strangers app. 7-Break-Thru x-over. 8-Solution app. 9-Vs. Turf. 12-Silver foil logo, wraparound-c. 17-Prime app. 2.00
5-($2.50, 48 pgs.)-Rune flip-c/story by B. Smith (3 pgs.) 2.50
16 ($3.50, 68 pgs.)-Rune pin-up 3.50
20-26: 23-Loki app. 2.50
NOTE: ***Perez** a-8(2); c-20i.*

HARDCORE STATION
DC Comics: July, 1998 - No. 6, Dec, 1998 ($2.50, limited series)

1-6-Starlin-s/a(p). 3-Green Lantern-c/app. 5,6-JLA-c/app. 3.00

H.A.R.D. CORPS, THE (See Harbinger #10)
Valiant: Dec, 1992 - No. 30, Feb, 1995 ($2.25) (Harbinger spin-off)

1-(Advance) 3.00
1-($2.50)-Gatefold-c by Jim Lee & Bob Layton 2.50
1-Gold variant 4.00
2-30: 5-Bloodshot-c/story cont'd from Bloodshot #3. 5-Variant edition; came w/Comic Defense System. 10-Turok app. 17-vs. Armorines. 18-Bound-in trad ing card. 20-Harbinger app. 2.25

HARDWARE
DC Comics (Milestone): Apr, 1993 - No. 50, Apr, 1997 ($1.50/$1.75/$2.50)

1-($2.95)-Collector's Edition polybagged w/poster & trading card (direct sale only) 3.00
1-Platinum Edition 4.00
1-15,17-19: 11-Shadow War x-over. 11,14-Simonson-c. 12-Buckler-a(p). 17-Worlds Collide Pt. 2. 18-Simonson-c; Worlds Collide Pt. 9. 15-1st Humberto Ramos DC work 2.50
16,50-($3.95, 52 pgs.)-16-Collector's Edition w/gatefold 2nd cover by Byrne; new armor; Icon app. 4.00
16,20-24,26-49: 16-($2.50, 52 pgs.)-Newsstand Ed. 49-Moebius-c 2.50
25-($2.95, 52 pgs.) 3.00

HARDY BOYS, THE (Disney
Dell Publ. Co.: No. 760, Dec, 1956 - No. 964, Jan, 1959 (Mickey Mouse Club)

Four Color 760 (#1)-Photo-c 10.50 31.00 125.00
Four Color 830(8/57), 887(1/58), 964-Photo-c 9.00 27.00 110.00

HARDY BOYS, THE (TV)
Gold Key: Apr, 1970 - No. 4, Jan, 1971

1 3.65 11.00 40.00
2-4 2.50 7.50 25.00

HARLAN ELLISON'S DREAM CORRIDOR
Dark Horse Comics: Mar, 1995 - No. 5, July, 1995 ($2.95, anthology)

1-5: Adaptation of Ellison stories. 1-4-Byrne-a. 3.00

Harley Quinn #1 © DC

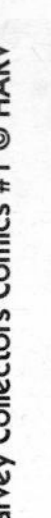

Harvey Collectors Comics #1 © HARV

Harvey Hits #10 © HARV

GD2.0 FN6.0 NM9.4

Special (1/95, $4.95) 5.00
Trade paperback-(1996, $18.95, 192 pgs)-r/#1-5 & Special #1 19.00

HARLAN ELLISON'S DREAM CORRIDOR QUARTERLY
Dark Horse Comics: V2#1, Aug, 1996 ($5.95, anthology, squarebound)

V2#1-Adaptations of Ellison's stories w/new material; Neal Adams-a 6.00

HARLEM GLOBETROTTERS (TV) (See Fun-In No. 8, 10)
Gold Key: Apr, 1972 - No. 12, Jan, 1975 (Hanna-Barbera)

1 3.00 9.00 30.00
2-5 2.00 6.00 18.00
6-12 1.75 5.25 14.00
NOTE: *#4, 8, and 12 contain 16 extra pages of advertising.*

HARLEY QUINN
DC Comics: Dec, 2000 - Present ($2.95/$2.25)

1-Joker and Poison Ivy app.; Terry & Rachel Dodson-a/c 3.00
2-4-($2.25). 2-Two-Face-c/app. 3-Slumber party 2.25

HAROLD TEEN (See Popular Comics, & Super Comics)
Dell Publishing Co.: No. 2, 1942 - No. 209, Jan, 1949

Four Color 2 27.00 80.00 320.00
Four Color 209 4.55 13.65 50.00

HARRIERS
Entity Comics: June, 1995 - No. 3, 1995 ($2.50)

1-Foil-c; polybagged w/PC game, 1-3 ($2.50) 3.00

HARROWERS, THE (See Clive Barker's...)

HARSH REALM (Inspired 1999 TV series)
Harris Comics: 1993- No. 6, 1994 ($2.95, limited series)

1-6: Painted-c. Hudnall-s/Paquette & Ridgway-a 3.50
TPB (2000, $14.95) r/series 14.95

HARVEY
Marvel Comics: Oct, 1970; No. 2, 12/70; No. 3, 6/72 - No. 6, 12/72

1 7.25 21.75 80.00
2-6 4.55 13.65 50.00

HARVEY COLLECTORS COMICS (Richie Rich Collectors Comics #10 on, cover title only)
Harvey Publ.: Sept, 1975 - No. 15, Jan, 1978; No. 16, Oct, 1979 (52 pgs.)

1-Reprints Richie Rich #1,2 1.75 5.25 14.00
2-10: 7-Splash pg. shows cover to Friendly Ghost Casper #1 1.00 3.00 8.00
11-16: 16-Sad Sack-r 2.40 6.00
NOTE: *All reprints: Casper-#2, 7, Richie Rich-#1, 3, 5, 6, 8-15, Sad Sack-#16. Wendy-#4. #6 titled 'Richie Rich...'on inside.*

HARVEY COMICS HITS (Formerly Joe Palooka #50)
Harvey Publications: No. 51, Oct, 1951 - No. 62, Apr, 1953

51-The Phantom 30.00 90.00 240.00
52-Steve Canyon's Air Power(Air Force sponsored) 12.00 36.00 95.00
53-Mandrake the Magician 22.00 66.00 175.00
54-Tim Tyler's Tales of Jungle Terror 12.00 36.00 95.00
55-Love Stories of Mary Worth 7.15 21.50 50.00
56-The Phantom; bondage-c 25.00 75.00 200.00
57-Rip Kirby Exposes the Kidnap Racket; entire book by Alex Raymond 15.00 45.00 120.00
58-Girls in White (nurses stories) 7.15 21.50 50.00
59-Tales of the Invisible featuring Scarlet O'Neil 10.50 32.00 85.00
60-Paramount Animated Comics #1 (9/52) (3rd app. Baby Huey); 2nd Harvey app. Baby Huey & Casper the Friendly Ghost (1st in Little Audrey #25 (8/52)); 1st app. Herman & Catnip (c/story) & Buzzy the Crow 40.00 120.00 325.00
61-Casper the Friendly Ghost #6 (3rd Harvey Casper, 10/52)-Casper-c 40.00 120.00 350.00
62-Paramount Animated Comics #2; Herman & Catnip, Baby Huey & Buzzy the Crow 14.00 41.00 110.00

HARVEY COMICS LIBRARY
Harvey Publications: Apr, 1952 - No. 2, 1952

1-Teen-Age Dope Slaves as exposed by Rex Morgan, M.D.; drug propaganda story; used in **SOTI,** pg. 27 95.00 285.00 900.00
2-Dick Tracy Presents Sparkle Plenty in "Blackmail Terror" 22.00 66.00 175.00

HARVEY COMICS SPOTLIGHT
Harvey Comics: Sept, 1987 - No. 4, Mar, 1988 (75¢/$1.00)

1-New material; begin 75¢, ends #3; Sand Sack 4.00
2-4: 2,4-All new material. 2-Baby Huey. 3-Little Dot; contains reprints w/5 pg. new story. 4-$1.00-c; Little Audrey 3.00
NOTE: No. 5 was advertised but not published.

HARVEY HITS
Harvey Publications: Sept, 1957 - No. 122, Nov, 1967

1-The Phantom 25.50 76.00 280.00
2-Rags Rabbit (10/57) 3.20 9.60 35.00
3-Richie Rich (11/57)-r/Little Dot; 1st book devoted to Richie Rich; see Little Dot for 1st app. 68.00 204.00 950.00
4-Little Dot's Uncles (12/57) 14.50 43.50 160.00
5-Stevie Mazie's Boy Friend (1/58) 2.50 7.50 25.00
6-The Phantom (2/58); Kirby-c; 2pg. Powell-a 18.00 54.00 200.00
7-Wendy the Good Little Witch (3/58, pre-dates Wendy #1; 1st book devoted to Wendy) 18.00 54.00 200.00
8-Sad Sack's Army Life; George Baker-c 5.90 17.75 65.00
9-Richie Rich's Golden Deeds; reprints (2nd book devoted to Richie Rich) 35.00 105.00 425.00
10-Little Lotta's Lunch Box 9.00 27.00 100.00
11-Little Audrey Summer Fun (7/58) 7.25 21.75 80.00
12-The Phantom; Kirby-c; 2pg. Powell-a (8/58) 14.50 43.50 160.00
13-Little Dot's Uncles (9/58); Richie Rich 1pg. 9.00 27.00 100.00
14-Herman & Katnip (10/58, TV/movies) 2.50 7.50 25.00
15-The Phantom (12/58)-1 pg. origin 14.50 43.50 160.00
16-Wendy the Good Little Witch (1/59); Casper app. 9.00 27.00 100.00
17-Sad Sack's Army Life (2/59) 4.55 13.65 50.00
18-Buzzy & the Crow 2.80 8.40 28.00
19-Little Audrey (4/59) 4.10 12.30 45.00
20-Casper & Spooky 5.90 17.75 65.00
21-Wendy the Witch 5.90 17.75 65.00
22-Sad Sack's Army Life 3.65 11.00 40.00
23-Wendy the Witch (8/59) 5.90 17.75 65.00
24-Little Dot's Uncles (9/59); Richie Rich 1pg. 7.25 21.75 80.00
25-Herman & Katnip (10/59) 2.30 7.00 20.00
26-The Phantom (11/59) 11.50 34.00 125.00
27-Wendy the Good Little Witch (12/59) 5.00 15.00 55.00
28-Sad Sack's Army Life (1/60) 2.50 7.50 25.00
29-Harvey-Toon (No.1)('60); Casper, Buzzy 3.65 11.00 40.00
30-Wendy the Witch (3/60) 5.90 17.75 65.00
31-Herman & Katnip (4/60) 2.30 7.00 20.00
32-Sad Sack's Army Life (5/60) 2.40 7.35 22.00
33-Wendy the Witch (6/60) 5.90 17.75 65.00
34-Harvey-Toon (7/60) 2.50 7.50 25.00
35-Funday Funnies (8/60) 2.30 7.00 20.00
36-The Phantom (1960) 10.00 30.00 110.00
37-Casper & Nightmare 4.10 12.30 45.00
38-Harvey-Toon 2.50 7.50 25.00
39-Sad Sack's Army Life (12/60) 2.40 7.35 22.00
40-Funday Funnies (1/61) 2.00 6.00 18.00
41-Herman & Katnip 2.30 7.00 20.00
42-Harvey-Toon (3/61) 2.40 7.35 22.00
43-Sad Sack's Army Life (4/61) 2.30 7.00 20.00
44-The Phantom (5/61) 9.50 28.50 105.00
45-Casper & Nightmare 3.20 9.60 35.00
46-Harvey-Toon (7/61) 2.30 7.00 20.00
47-Sad Sack's Army Life (8/61) 2.30 7.00 20.00
48-The Phantom (9/61) 9.50 28.50 105.00
49-Stumbo the Giant (1st app. in Hot Stuff) 8.65 26.00 95.00
50-Harvey-Toon (11/61) 2.00 6.00 18.00
51-Sad Sack's Army Life (12/61) 2.00 6.00 18.00
52-Casper & Nightmare 3.20 9.60 35.00
53-Harvey-Toons (2/62) 2.00 6.00 16.00
54-Stumbo the Giant 4.10 12.30 45.00

Hate #23 © Peter Bagge

Haunted Thrills #3 © AJAX

Haunt of Fear #17 © WMG

	GD2.0	FN6.0	NM9.4
55-Sad Sack's Army Life (4/62)	2.00	6.00	18.00
56-Casper & Nightmare	3.00	9.00	32.00
57-Stumbo the Giant	4.10	12.30	45.00
58-Sad Sack's Army Life	2.00	6.00	18.00
59-Casper & Nightmare (7/62)	3.00	9.00	32.00
60-Stumbo the Giant (9/62)	4.10	12.30	45.00
61-Sad Sack's Army Life	2.00	6.00	16.00
62-Casper & Nightmare	2.80	8.40	28.00
63-Stumbo the Giant	3.45	10.35	38.00
64-Sad Sack's Army Life (1/63)	2.00	6.00	16.00
65-Casper & Nightmare	2.80	8.40	28.00
66-Stumbo The Giant (3/63)	3.45	10.35	38.00
67-Sad Sack's Army Life (4/63)	2.00	6.00	16.00
68-Casper & Nightmare	2.80	8.40	28.00
69-Stumbo the Giant (6/63)	3.45	10.35	38.00
70-Sad Sack's Army Life (7/63)	2.00	6.00	16.00
71-Casper & Nightmare (8/63)	2.50	7.50	24.00
72-Stumbo the Giant	3.45	10.35	38.00
73-Little Sad Sack (10/63)	2.00	6.00	16.00
74-Sad Sack's Muttsy... (11/63)	2.00	6.00	16.00
75-Casper & Nightmare	2.40	7.35	22.00
76-Little Sad Sack	2.00	6.00	16.00
77-Sad Sack's Muttsy...	2.00	6.00	16.00
78-Stumbo the Giant (3/64); JFK caricature	3.45	10.35	38.00
79-87: 79-Little Sad Sack (4/64). 80-Sad Sack's Muttsy... (5/64). 81-Little Sad Sack. 82-Sad Sack's Muttsy... 83-Little Sad Sack(8/64). 84-Sad Sack's Muttsy... 85-Gabby Gob (#1)(10/64). 86-G. I. Juniors (#1)(11/64). 87-Sad Sack's Muttsy... (12/64)	2.00	6.00	16.00
88-Stumbo the Giant (1/65)	3.45	10.35	38.00
89-122: 89-Sad Sack's Muttsy... 90-Gabby Gob. 91-G. I. Juniors. 92-Sad Sack's Muttsy... (5/65). 93-Sadie Sack (6/65). 94-Gabby Gob. 95-G. I. Juniors (8/65). 96-Sad Sack's Muttsy... (9/65). 97-Gabby Gob (10/65). 98-G. I. Juniors (11/65). 99-Sad Sack's Muttsy... (12/65). 100-Gabby Gob(1/66). 101-G. I. Juniors (2/66). 102-Sad Sack's Muttsy... (3/66). 103-Gabby Gob. 104- G. I. Juniors. 105-Sad Sack's Muttsy... 106-Gabby Gob (7/66). 107-G. I. Juniors (8/66). 108-Sad Sack's Muttsy... 109-Gabby Gob. 110-G. I. Juniors (11/66). 111-Sad Sack's Muttsy... (12/66). 112-G. I. Juniors. 113-Sad Sack's Muttsy... 114-G. I. Juniors. 115-Sad Sack's Muttsy... 116-G. I. Juniors (5/67). 117-Sad Sack's Muttsy... 118-G. I. Juniors. 119-Sad Sack's Muttsy... (8/67). 120-G. I. Juniors (9/67). 121-Sad Sack's Muttsy... (10/67). 122-G. I. Juniors (11/67)	1.25	3.75	10.00

HARVEY HITS COMICS
Harvey Publications: Nov, 1986 - No. 6, Oct, 1987

	GD2.0	FN6.0	NM9.4
1-Little Lotta, Little Dot, Wendy & Baby Huey			5.00
2-6: 3-Xmas-c			3.00

HARVEY POP COMICS (Rock Happening) (Teen Humor)
Harvey Publications: Oct, 1968 - No. 2, Nov, 1969 (Both are 68 pg. Giants)

	GD2.0	FN6.0	NM9.4
1-The Cowsills	4.55	13.65	50.00
2-Bunny	4.10	12.30	45.00

HARVEY 3-D HITS (See Sad Sack)

HARVEY-TOON (...S) (See Harvey Hits No. 29, 34, 38, 42, 46, 50, 53)

HARVEY WISEGUYS (...Digest #? on)
Harvey Comics: Nov, 1987; #2, Nov, 1988; #3, Apr, 1989 - No. 4, Nov, 1989 (98 pgs., digest-size, $1.25/$1.75)

	GD2.0	FN6.0	NM9.4
1-Hot Stuff, Spooky, etc.		2.40	6.00
2-4: 2 (68 pgs.)			4.00

HATARI (See Movie Classics)

HATE
Fantagraphics Books: Spr, 1990 - No. 30, 1998 ($2.50/$2.95, B&W/color)

	GD2.0	FN6.0	NM9.4
1	1.85	5.50	15.00
2-3	1.00	3.00	8.00
4-10			5.00
11-20: 16- color begins			4.00
21-29			3.00
30-($3.95) Last issue			4.00
Buddy Go Home! (1997, $16.95) r/Buddy stories in color			17.00
Hate-Ball Special Edition ($3.95, giveaway)-reprints			4.00
Hate Jamboree (10/98, $4.50) old & new cartoons			4.50

HATHAWAYS, THE (TV)
Dell Publishing Co.: No. 1298, Feb-Apr, 1962 (one-shot)

	GD2.0	FN6.0	NM9.4
Four Color 1298-Photo-c	4.10	12.30	45.00

HAUNTED (See This Magazine Is Haunted)

HAUNTED (Baron Weirwulf's Haunted Library on-c #21 on)
Charlton Comics: 9/71 - No. 30, 11/76; No. 31, 9/77 - No. 75, 9/84

	GD2.0	FN6.0	NM9.4
1-All Ditko issue	2.80	8.40	28.00
2-7-Ditko-c/a	2.00	6.00	16.00
8,12,28-Ditko-a	1.50	4.50	12.00
9,19	1.25	3.75	10.00
10,20,15,18: 10,20-Sutton-a. 15,18-Sutton-c	1.50	4.50	12.00
11,13,14,16-Ditko-a	1.75	5.25	14.00
17-Sutton-c/a; Newton-a	1.75	5.25	14.00
21-Newton-c/a; Sutton-a; 1st Baron Weirwulf	2.00	6.00	18.00
22-Newton-c; Sutton-a	1.85	5.50	15.00
23,24-Sutton-c; Ditko-a	1.75	5.25	14.00
25-27,29,32,33	1.25	3.75	10.00
30,41,47,49-51,74-Ditko-c/a: 51-Reprints #1	1.75	5.25	14.00
31,35,37,38-Sutton-a	1.50	4.50	12.00
34,36,39,40,42,57,60-Ditko-a	1.50	4.50	12.00
43-46,48,52-56,58,59,61,62-73,75		2.40	6.00
59-Newton-a	1.00	3.00	8.00
64-Sutton-c	1.00	2.80	7.00

NOTE: ***Aparo** c-45. **Ditko** a-1-8, 11-16, 18, 23, 24, 28, 30, 34r, 36r, 39-42r, 47r, 49-51r, 57, 60, 74. c-1-7, 11, 13, 14, 16, 30, 41, 47, 49-51, 74. **Howard** a-6, 9, 18, 22, 25, 32. **Kim** a-9, 19. **Morisi** a-13. **Newton** a-17, 21, 59r; c-21, 22(painted). **Staton** a-11, 12, 18, 21, 22, 30, 33, 35, 38; c-18, 33. **Sutton** a-10, 17, 20-22, 31, 35, 37, 38; c-15, 17, 18, 23(painted), 24(painted), 64r. #49 reprints Tales of the Mysterious Traveler #4.*

HAUNTED LOVE
Charlton Comics: Apr, 1973 - No. 11, Sept, 1975

	GD2.0	FN6.0	NM9.4
1-Tom Sutton-a (16 pgs.)	4.10	12.30	45.00
2,3,6,7,10,11	2.30	7.00	20.00
4,5-Ditko-a	2.50	7.50	23.00
8,9-Newton-c	2.50	7.50	24.00
Modern Comics #1(1978)	1.50	4.50	12.00

NOTE: ***Howard** a-8i. **Kim** a-7-9. **Newton** c-8, 9. **Staton** a-1-6. **Sutton** a-1, 3-5, 10, 11.*

HAUNTED MAN, THE
Dark Horse Comics: Mar, 2000 - No. 3 ($2.95, limited series)

	GD2.0	FN6.0	NM9.4
1-Gerald Jones-s/Mark Badger-a			2.95

HAUNTED THRILLS (Tales of Horror and Terror)
Ajax/Farrell Publications: June, 1952 - No. 18, Nov-Dec, 1954

	GD2.0	FN6.0	NM9.4
1-r/Ellery Queen #1	42.00	125.00	375.00
2-L. B. Cole-a r-/Ellery Queen #1	33.00	98.00	260.00
3-5: 3-Drug use story	28.00	83.00	220.00
6-10,12: 7-Hitler story.	23.00	69.00	185.00
11-Nazi death camp story	24.00	73.00	195.00
13-18: 18-Lingerie panels. 14-Jesus Christ apps. in story by Webb. 15-Jo-Jo-r	19.00	58.00	155.00

NOTE: ***Kamenish** art in most issues. **Webb** a-12.*

HAUNT OF FEAR (Formerly Gunfighter)
E. C. Comics: No. 15, May-June, 1950 - No. 28, Nov-Dec, 1954

	GD2.0	FN6.0	NM9.4
15(#1, 1950)(Scarce)	255.00	765.00	2800.00
16-1st app. "The Witches Cauldron" & the Old Witch (by Kamen); begin series as hostess of HOF	109.00	327.00	1200.00
17-Origin of Crypt of Terror, Vault of Horror, & Haunt of Fear; used in **SOTI**, pg. 43; last pg. Ingels-a used by N.Y. Legis. Comm.; story "Monster Maker" based on Frankenstein. Old Witch by Feldstein	100.00	300.00	1100.00
4-Ingles becomes regular artist for Old Witch. 1st Vault Keeper & Crypt Keeper app. in HOF; begin series	66.00	198.00	725.00
5-Injury-to-eye panel, pg. 4 of Wood story	50.00	150.00	550.00
6-10: 6-Crypt Keeper by Feldstein begins. 8-Shrunken head cover. 9-Crypt Keeper by Davis begins. 10-Ingels biog.	38.00	113.00	415.00
11-13,15-18: 11-Kamen biog. 12-Feldstein biog. 16,18-Ray Bradbury adaptations. 18-Ray Bradbury biography	28.00	84.00	310.00

Haunt of Horror #4 © MAR

The Hawk #10 © Z-D

Hawkman #2 © DC

GD2.0 FN6.0 NM9.4

14-Origin Old Witch by Ingels 41.00 123.00 450.00
19-Used in **SOTI**, ill. "A comic book baseball game" & Senate investigation on juvenile delinq. bondage/decapitation-c 38.00 113.00 415.00
20-Feldstein-r/Vault of Horror #12 26.00 78.00 285.00
21-27: 23-Used in **SOTI**, pg. 241. 24-Used in Senate Investigative Report, pg.8. 26-Contains anti-censorship editorial, 'Are you a Red Dupe?' 27-Cannibalism story; Wertham cameo 19.00 57.00 210.00
28-Low distribution 21.00 63.00 230.00
NOTE: *(Canadian reprints known; see Table of Contents).* ***Craig*** *a-15-17, 5, 7, 10, 12, 13; c-15-17, 5-7.* ***Crandall*** *a-20, 21, 26, 27.* ***Davis*** *a-4-26, 28.* ***Evans*** *a-15-19, 22-25, 27.* ***Feldstein*** *a-15-17, 20; c-4, 8-10.* ***Ingels*** *a-16, 17, 4-28; c-11-28.* ***Kamen*** *a-16, 4, 6, 7, 9-11, 13-19, 21-28.* ***Krigstein*** *a-28.* ***Kurtzman*** *a-15(#1), 17(#3).* ***Orlando*** *a-9, 12.* ***Wood*** *a-15, 16, 4-6.*

HAUNT OF FEAR, THE
Gladstone Publishing: May, 1991 - No. 2, July, 1991 ($2.00, 68 pgs.)
1,2: 1-Ghastly Ingels-c(r); 2-Craig-c(r) 2.50

HAUNT OF FEAR
Russ Cochran/Gemstone Publ.: Sept, 1991 - No. 5, 1992 ($2.00, 68 pgs.); Nov, 1992 - Present ($1.50/$2.00/$2.50)
1-25: 1-Ingels-c(r). 1-3-r/HOF #15-17 with original-c. 4,5-r/HOF #4,5 with original-c 2.50
Annual 1-5: 1- r/#1-5. 2- r/#6-10. 3- r/#11-15. 4- r/#16-20. 5- r/#21-25 14.00
Annual 6-r/#26-28 8.95

HAUNT OF HORROR, THE (Digest)
Marvel Comics: Jun, 1973 - No. 2, Aug, 1973 (164 pgs.; text and art)
1-Morrow painted skull-c; stories by Ellison, Howard, and Leiber; Brunner-a 2.60 7.80 26.00
2-Kelly Freas painted bondage-c; stories by McCaffrey, Goulart,Leiber, Ellison; art by Simonson, Brunner, and Buscema 2.30 7.00 20.00

HAUNT OF HORROR, THE (Magazine)
Cadence Comics Publ. (Marvel): May, 1974 - No. 5, Jan, 1975 (75¢) (B&W)
1,2: 2-Origin & 1st app. Gabriel the Devil Hunter; Satana begins 1.50 4.50 12.00
3-5: 4-Neal Adams-a. 5-Evans-a(2) 1.85 5.50 15.00
NOTE: ***Alcala*** *a-2.* ***Colan*** *a-2p.* ***Heath*** *r-1.* ***Krigstein*** *r-3.* ***Reese*** *a-1.* ***Simonson*** *a-1.*

HAVE GUN, WILL TRAVEL (TV)
Dell Publishing Co.: No. 931, 8/58 - No. 14, 7-9/62 (All Richard Boone photo-c)
Four Color 931 (#1) 14.00 41.00 165.00
Four Color 983,1044 (#2,3) 8.75 26.25 105.00
4 (1-3/60) - 10 7.00 21.00 85.00
11-14 8.00 24.00 95.00

HAVOK & WOLVERINE - MELTDOWN (See Marvel Comics Presents #24)
Marvel Comics (Epic Comics): Mar, 1989 - No. 4, Oct, 1989 ($3.50, mini-series, squarebound, mature)
1-4: Violent content 4.00

HAWAIIAN EYE (TV)
Gold Key: July, 1963 (Troy Donahue, Connie Stevens photo-c)
1 (10073-307) 4.55 13.65 50.00

HAWAIIAN ILLUSTRATED LEGENDS SERIES
Hogarth Press: 1975 (B&W)(Cover printed w/blue, yellow, and green)
1-Kalelealuaka, the Mysterious Warrior 2/00

HAWK, THE (Also see Approved Comics #1, 7 & Tops In Adventure)
Ziff-Davis/St. John Publ. Co. No. 4 on: Wint/51 - No. 3, 11-12/52; No. 4, 1-2/53; No. 8, 9/54 - No. 12, 5/55 (Painted c-1-4)(#5-7 don't exist)
1-Anderson-a 20.00 60.00 160.00
2 (Sum, '52)-Kubert, Infantino-a 11.00 33.00 90.00
3-4,11: 11-Buckskin Belle & The Texan app. 10.00 30.00 70.00
8-10,12: 8(9/54)-Reprints #3 w/different-c by Baker. 9-Baker-c/a; Kubert-a(r)/#2. 10-Baker-c/a; r/one story from #2. 12-Baker-c/a; Buckskin Belle app. 12.00 36.00 95.00
3-D 1(11/53, 25¢)-Came w/glasses; Baker-c 34.00 101.00 270.00
NOTE: ***Baker*** *c-8-12.* ***Larsen*** *a-10.* ***Tuska*** *a-1, 9, 12. Painted c-1, 4, 7.*

HAWK AND THE DOVE, THE (See Showcase #75 & Teen Titans) (1st series)
National Periodical Publications: Aug-Sept, 1968 - No. 6, June-July, 1969

GD2.0 FN6.0 NM9.4

1-Ditko-c/a 6.80 20.50 75.00
2-6: 5-Teen Titans cameo 4.10 12.30 45.00
NOTE: ***Ditko*** *c/a-1, 2.* ***Gil Kane*** *a-3p, 4p, 5, 6p; c-3-6.*

HAWK AND DOVE (2nd Series)
DC Comics: Oct, 1988 - No. 5, Feb, 1989 ($1.00, limited series)
1-Rob Liefeld-c/a(p) in all 3.00
2-5 2.50
Trade paperback ('93, $9.95)-Reprints #1-5 10.00

HAWK AND DOVE
DC Comics: June, 1989 - No. 28, Oct, 1991 ($1.00)
1-28 2.00
Annual 1,2 ('90, '91; $2.00) 1-Liefeld pin-up. 2-Armageddon 2001 x-over 2.50

HAWK AND DOVE
DC Comics: Nov, 1997 - No.5, Mar, 1998 ($2.50, limited series)
1-5-Baron-s/Zachary & Giordano-a 3.50

HAWK AND WINDBLADE (See Elflord)
Warp Graphics: Aug, 1997 - No.2, Sept, 1997 ($2.95, limited series)
1,2-Blair-s/Chan-c/a 3.00

HAWKEYE (See The Avengers #16 & Tales Of Suspense #57)
Marvel Comics Group: Sept, 1983 - No. 4, Dec, 1983 (limited series)
1-4: Mark Gruenwald-a/scripts. 1-Origin Hawkeye. 3-Origin Mockingbird. 4-Hawkeye & Mockingbird elope 2.50

HAWKEYE
Marvel Comics: Jan, 1994 - No. 4, Apr, 1994 ($1.75, limited series)
1-4 2.00

HAWKEYE & THE LAST OF THE MOHICANS (TV)
Dell Publishing Co.: No. 884, Mar, 1958 (one-shot)
Four Color 884-Photo-c 6.70 20.00 80.00

HAWKEYE: EARTH'S MIGHTIEST MARKSMAN
Marvel Comics: Oct, 1998 ($2.99, one-shot)
1-Justice and Firestar app.; DeFalco-s 3.00

HAWKMAN (See Atom & Hawkman, The Brave & the Bold, DC Comics Presents, Detective, Flash Comics, Hawkworld, Justice League of America #31, Mystery in Space, Shadow War Of..., Showcase, & World's Finest #256)

HAWKMAN (1st Series) (Also see The Atom #7 & Brave & the Bold #34-36, 42-44, 51)
National Periodical Publications: Apr-May, 1964 - No. 27, Aug-Sept, 1968
1-(4-5/64)-Anderson-c/a begins, ends #21 50.00 150.00 650.00
2 20.50 61.00 225.00
3,5: 5-2nd app. Shadow Thief 12.00 36.00 130.00
4-Origin & 1st app. Zatanna (10-11/64) 16.50 49.00 180.00
6 11.00 33.00 120.00
7 9.50 28.50 105.00
8-10: 9-Atom cameo; Hawkman & Atom learn each other's I.D.; 3rd app. Shadow Thief 8.15 24.50 90.00
11-15 5.90 17.75 65.00
16-27: 18-Adam Strange x-over (cameo #19). 25-G.A. Hawkman-r by Moldoff. 26-Kirby-a(r). 27-Kubert-c 4.55 13.65 50.00

HAWKMAN (2nd Series)
DC Comics: Aug, 1986 - No. 17, Dec, 1987
1-17: 10-Byrne-c, Special #1 (1986, $1.25) 2.00
Trade paperback (1989, $19.95)-r/Brave and the Bold #34-36,42-44 by Kubert; Kubert-c 20.00

HAWKMAN (4th Series)(See both Hawkworld limited & ongoing series)
DC Comics: Sept, 1993 - No. 33, July, 1996 ($1.75/$1.95/$2.25)
1-($2.50)-Gold foil embossed-c; storyline cont'd from Hawkworld ongoing series; new costume & powers. 3.00
2-13,0,14-33: 2-Green Lantern x-over. 3-Airstryke app. 4,6-Won. Woman app. 13-(9/94)-Zero Hour. 0-(10/94). 14-(11/94). 15-Aquaman-c & app. 23-Wonder Woman app. 25-Kent Williams-c. 29,30-Chaykin-c. 32-Breyfogle-c 2.50
Annual 1 (1993, $2.50, 68 pgs.)-Bloodlines Earthplague 3.00
Annual 2 (1995, $3.95)-Year One story 4.00

Headline Comics #29 © PRIZE

Heart of Empire #6 © Bryan Talbot

Heart Throbs #2 © QUA

GD2.0 FN6.0 NM9.4

HAWKMOON: THE JEWEL IN THE SKULL
First Comics: May, 1986 - No. 4, Nov, 1986 ($1.75, limited series, Baxter paper)
1-4: Adapts novel by Michael Moorcock 2.50

HAWKMOON: THE MAD GOD'S AMULET
First Comics: Jan, 1987 - No. 4, July, 1987 ($1.75, limited series, Baxter paper)
1-4: Adapts novel by Michael Moorcock 2.50

HAWKMOON: THE RUNESTAFF
First Comics: Jun, 1988 -No. 4, Dec, 1988 ($1.75-$1.95, lim. series, Baxter paper)
1-4: ($1.75) Adapts novel by Michael Moorcock. 3,4 ($1.95) 2.50

HAWKMOON: THE SWORD OF DAWN
First Comics : Sept, 1987 - No. 4, Mar, 1988 ($1.75, lim. series, Baxter paper)
1-4: Dorman painted-c; adapts Moorcock novel 2.50

HAWKWORLD
DC Comics: 1989 - No. 3, 1989 ($3.95, prestige format, limited series)
Book 1-3: 1-Tim Truman story & art in all; Hawkman dons new costume; reintro Byth. 4.00
TPB (1991, $16.95) r/#1-3 17.00

HAWKWORLD (3rd Series)
DC Comics: June, 1990 - No. 32, Mar, 1993 ($1.50/$1.75)
1-Hawkman spin-off; story cont'd from limited series. 2.50
2-32: 15,16-War of the Gods x-over. 22-J'onn J'onzz app. 2.00
Annual 1-3 ('90-'92, $2.95, 68 pgs.), 2-2nd printing with silver ink-c 3.00
NOTE: ***Truman*** *a-30-32; c-27-32, Annual 1.*

HAYWIRE
DC Comics: Oct, 1988 - No. 13, Sept, 1989 ($1.25, mature)
1-13 2.00

HAZARD
Image Comics (WildStorm Prod.): June, 1996 - No. 7, Nov, 1996 ($1.75)
1-7: 1-Intro Hazard; Jeff Mariotte scripts begin; Jim Lee-c(p) 3.00

HEADBUSTERS
Antarctic Press: Oct, 1998 ($2.95, B&W)
1-Mallette-s 3.00

HEADHUNTERS
Image Comics: Apr, 1997 - No. 3, June, 1997 ($2.95, B&W)
1-3: Chris Marrinan-s/a 3.00

HEADLINE COMICS (...For the American Boy) (...Crime No. 32-39)
Prize Publ./American Boys' Comics: Feb, 1943 - No. 22, Nov-Dec, 1946; No. 23, 1947 - No. 77, Oct, 1956
1-Junior Rangers-c/stories begin; Yank & Doodle x-over in Junior Rangers (Junior Rangers are Uncle Sam's nephews) 47.00 142.00 425.00
2 24.00 71.00 190.00
3-Used in **POP**, pg. 84 19.00 56.00 150.00
4-7,9,10: 4,9,10-Hitler stories in each 16.00 49.00 130.00
8-Classic Hitler-c 44.00 133.00 400.00
11,12 13.00 39.00 105.00
13-15-Blue Streak in all 15.00 45.00 120.00
16-Origin & 1st app. Atomic Man (11-12/45) 26.00 79.00 210.00
17,18,20,21: 21-Atomic Man ends (9-10/46) 13.00 39.00 105.00
19-S&K-a 30.00 90.00 240.00
22-Last Junior Rangers; Kiefer-c 10.00 30.00 75.00
23,24: (All S&K-a). 23-Valentine's Day Massacre story; content changes to true crime. 24-Dope-crazy killer story 28.00 84.00 225.00
25-35-S&K-c/a. 25-Powell-a 26.00 79.00 210.00
36-S&K-a; photo-c begin 20.00 60.00 160.00
37-1 pg. S&K, Severin-a; rare Kirby photo-c app. 20.00 60.00 160.00
38,40-Meskin-a 7.85 23.50 55.00
39,41-43,46-50,52-55: 41-J. Edgar Hoover 26th Anniversary Issue with photo on-c. 43,49-Meskin-a 5.70 17.00 40.00
44-S&K-c; Severin/Elder, Meskin-a 12.00 36.00 95.00
45-Kirby-a 10.00 30.00 75.00
51-Kirby-c 6.40 19.25 45.00
56-S&K-a 12.00 36.00 95.00
57-77: 72-Meskin-c/a(i) 5.00 15.00 30.00
NOTE: ***Hollingsworth*** *a-30. Photo c-36-43.* ***H. C. Kiefer*** *c-12-16, 22. Atomic Man c-17-19.*

HEADMAN
Innovation Publishing: 1990 ($2.50, mature)
1-Sci/fi 2.50

HEAP, THE
Skywald Publications: Sept, 1971 (52 pgs.)
1-Kinstler-r/Strange Worlds #8 2.40 7.35 22.00

HEART AND SOUL
Mikeross Publications: April-May, 1954 - No. 2, June-July, 1954
1,2 6.40 19.25 45.00

HEARTBREAKERS (Also see Dark Horse Presents)
Dark Horse Comics: Apr, 1996 - No. 4, July, 1996 ($2.95, limited series)
1-4: 1-W/paper doll & pin-up. 2-Ross pin-up. 3-Evan Dorkin pin-ups. 4-Brereton-c; Matt Wagner pin-up 3.00
...Superdigest (7/98, $9.95, digest-size) new stories 10.00

HEARTLAND (See Hellblazer)
DC Comics (Vertigo): Mar, 1997 ($4.95, one-shot, mature)
1-Garth Ennis-s/Steve Dillon-c/a 5.00

HEART OF DARKNESS
Hardline Studios: 1994 ($2.95)
1-Brereton-c 3.00

HEART OF EMPIRE
Dark Horse Comics: Apr, 1999 - No. 9, Dec, 1999 ($2.95, limited series)
1-9-Bryan Talbot-s/a 3.00

HEART OF THE BEAST, THE
DC Comics (Vertigo): 1994 ($19.95, hardcover, mature)
1-Dean Motter scripts 20.00

HEARTS OF DARKNESS (See Ghost Rider; Wolverine; Punisher: Hearts of...)

HEART THROBS (Love Stories No. 147 on)
Quality Comics/National Periodical #47(4-5/57) on (Arleigh #48-101): 8/49 - No. 8, 10/50; No. 9, 3/52 - No. 146, Oct, 1972
1-Classic Ward-c, Gustavson-a, 9 pgs. 40.00 120.00 350.00
2-Ward-c/a (9 pgs); Gustavson-a 25.00 75.00 200.00
3-Gustavson-a 9.30 28.00 65.00
4,6,8-Ward-a, 8-9 pgs. 12.50 37.50 100.00
5,7 6.40 19.25 45.00
9-Robert Mitchum, Jane Russell photo-c 10.00 30.00 70.00
10,15-Ward-a 10.00 30.00 75.00
11-14,16-20: 12 (7/52) 5.00 15.00 35.00
21-Ward-c 9.30 28.00 65.00
22,23-Ward-a(p) 6.40 19.25 45.00
24-33: 33-Last pre-code (3/55) 5.00 15.00 30.00
34-39,41-46 (12/56; last Quality issue) 4.65 14.00 28.00
40-Ward-a; r-7 pgs./#21 6.00 18.00 42.00
47-(4-5/57; 1st DC issue) 23.00 68.00 250.00
48-60, 100 8.15 24.50 90.00
61-70 5.90 17.75 65.00
71-99: 74-Last 10 cent issue 4.35 13.00 48.00
101-The Beatles app. on-c 13.50 40.00 150.00
102-120: 102-123-(Serial)-Three Girls, Their Lives, Their Loves 2.50 7.50 25.00
121-132,143-146 2.30 7.00 20.00
133-142-(52 pgs.) 3.00 9.00 30.00
NOTE: ***Gustavson*** *a-8.* ***Tuska*** *a-128. Photo c-4, 5, 8-10, 15, 17.*

HEART THROBS - THE BEST OF DC ROMANCE COMICS (See Fireside Book Series)

HEART THROBS
DC Comics (Vertigo): Jan, 1999 - No. 4, Apr, 1999 ($2.95, lim. series)
1-4-Romance anthology. 1-Timm-c. 3-Corben-a 3.00

HEATHCLIFF (See Star Comics Magazine)
Marvel Comics (Star Comics)/Marvel Comics No. 23 on: Apr, 1985 - No. 56,

Hedy Devine Comics #27 © MAR

Hellblazer #143 © DC

Hellboy, Jr. #1 © DH

GD2.0 FN6.0 NM9.4

Feb, 1991 (#16-on, $1.00)

1-56: Post-a most issues. 43-X-Mas issue. 47-Batman parody (Catman vs. the Soaker), Annual 1 ('87) 3.00

HEATHCLIFF'S FUNHOUSE
Marvel Comics (Star Comics)/Marvel No. 6 on: May, 1987 - No. 10, 1988

1-10 3.00

HEAVY HITTERS
Marvel Comics (Epic Comics): 1993 ($3.75, 68 pgs.)

1-Bound w/trading card; Lawdog, Feud, Alien Legion, Trouble With Girls, & Spyke 3.75

HEAVY LIQUID
DC Comics (Vertigo): Oct, 1999 - No. 5, Feb, 2000 ($5.95, limited series)

1-5-Paul Pope-s/a; flip covers 6.00

HECKLE AND JECKLE (Paul Terry's...)(See Blue Ribbon, Giant Comics Edition #5A & 10, Paul Terry's, Terry-Toons Comics)
St. John Publ. Co. No. 1-24/Pines No. 25 on: No. 3, 2/52 - No. 24, 10/55; No. 25, Fall/56 - No. 34, 6/59

	GD2.0	FN6.0	NM9.4
3(#1)-Funny animal	25.00	75.00	200.00
4(6/52), 5	11.00	33.00	90.00
6-10(4/53)	7.85	23.50	55.00
11-20	6.00	18.00	42.00
21-34: 25-Begin CBS Television Presents on-c	5.00	15.00	30.00

HECKLE AND JECKLE (TV) (See New Terrytoons)
Gold Key/Dell Publ. Co.: 11/62 - No. 4, 8/63; 5/66; No. 2, 10/66; No. 3, 8/67

	GD2.0	FN6.0	NM9.4
1 (11/62; Gold Key)	5.85	17.50	70.00
2-4	3.00	9.00	32.00
1 (5/66; Dell)	3.65	11.00	40.00
2,3	2.80	8.40	28.00

(See March of Comics No. 379, 472, 484)

HECKLE AND JECKLE 3-D
Spotlight Comics: 1987 - No. 2?, 1987 ($2.50)

1,2 3.50

HECKLER, THE
DC Comics: Sept, 1992 - No. 6, Feb, 1993 ($1.25)

1-6-T&M Bierbaum-s/Keith Giffen-c/a 2.00

HECTIC PLANET
Slave Labor Graphics 1998 ($12.95/$14.95)

Book 1,2-r-Dorkin-s/a from Pirate Corp$ Vol. 1 & 2 15.00

HECTOR COMICS (The Keenest Teen in Town)
Key Publications: Nov, 1953 - No. 3, 1954

	GD2.0	FN6.0	NM9.4
1-Teen humor	4.65	14.00	28.00
2,3	3.20	8.00	16.00

HECTOR HEATHCOTE (TV)
Gold Key: Mar, 1964

	GD2.0	FN6.0	NM9.4
1 (10111-403)	6.70	20.00	80.00

HECTOR THE INSPECTOR (See Top Flight Comics)

HEDY DEVINE COMICS (Formerly All Winners #21? or Teen #22?(6/47); Hedy of Hollywood #36 on; also see Annie Oakley, Comedy & Venus)
Marvel Comics (RCM)/Atlas #50: No. 22, Aug, 1947 - No. 50, Sept, 1952

	GD2.0	FN6.0	NM9.4
22-1st app. Hedy Devine (also see Joker #32)	23.00	68.00	180.00
23,24,27-30: 23-Wolverton-a, 1 pg; Kurtzman's "Hey Look", 2 pgs. 24,27-30-"Hey Look" by Kurtzman, 1-3 pgs.	16.00	49.00	130.00
25-Classic "Hey Look" by Kurtzman, "Optical Illusion"	18.00	53.00	140.00
26- "Giggles 'n' Grins" by Kurtzman	10.00	30.00	80.00
31-34,36-50: 32-Anti-Wertham editorial	9.30	28.00	65.00
35-Four pgs. "Rusty" by Kurtzman	13.00	39.00	105.00

HEDY-MILLIE-TESSIE COMEDY (See Comedy Comics)

HEDY WOLFE (Also see Patsy & Hedy & Miss America Magazine V1#2)
Atlas Publishing Co. (Emgee): Aug, 1957

	GD2.0	FN6.0	NM9.4
1-Patsy Walker's rival; Al Hartley-c	10.00	30.00	80.00

HEE HAW (TV)
Charlton Press: July, 1970 - No. 7, Aug, 1971

	GD2.0	FN6.0	NM9.4
1	3.20	9.60	35.00
2-7	2.50	7.50	24.00

HEIDI (See Dell Jr. Treasury No. 6)

HELEN OF TROY (Movie)
Dell Publishing Co.: No. 684, Mar, 1956 (one-shot)

	GD2.0	FN6.0	NM9.4
Four Color 684-Buscema-a, photo-c	10.00	30.00	120.00

HELLBLAZER (John Constantine) (See Saga of Swamp Thing #37) (Also see Books of Magic limited series)
DC Comics (Vertigo #63 on): Jan, 1988 - Present ($1.25/$1.50/$1.95/$2.25)

	GD2.0	FN6.0	NM9.4
1-(44 pgs.)-John Constantine; McKean-c thru #21	1.75	5.25	14.00
2-5	1.10	3.30	9.00
6-8,10: 10-Swamp Thing cameo		2.40	6.00
9,19: 9-X-over w/Swamp Thing #76. 19-Sandman app.	1.00	2.80	7.00
11-18,20			5.00
21-26,28-30: 22-Williams-c. 24-Contains bound-in Shocker movie poster. 25,26-Grant Morrison scripts.			5.00
27-Neil Gaiman scripts; Dave McKean-a; low print run	1.25	3.75	10.00
31-39: 36-Preview of World Without End.			4.00
40-($2.25, 52 pgs.)-Dave McKean-a & colors; preview of Kid Eternity			4.00
41-Ennis scripts begin; ends #83			5.00
42-120: 44,45-Sutton-a(i). 50-($3.00, 52 pgs.). 52-Glenn Fabry painted-c begin. 62-Special Death insert by McKean. 63-Silver metallic ink on-c. 77-Totleben-c. 84-Sean Phillips-c/a begins; Delano story. 85-88-Eddie Campbell story. 75-($2.95, 52 pgs.). 89-Paul Jenkins scripts begin; 108-Adlard-a. 100,120 ($3.50,48 pgs.)			3.50
121-158: 129-Ennis-s, begin $2.50-c. 141-Bradstreet-a. 146-150-Corben-a			2.50
Annual 1 (1989, $2.95, 68 pgs.)-Bryan Talbot's 1st work in American comics		2.40	6.00
Special 1 (1993, $3.95, 68 pgs.)-Ennis story; w/pin-ups.		2.40	6.00
...Damnation's Flame (1999, $16.95, TPB) r/#72-77			17.00
...Dangerous Habits (1997, $14.95, TPB) r/#41-46			15.00
...Fear and Loathing (1997, $14.95, TPB) r/#62-67			18.00
...Fear and Loathing (2nd printing, $17.95)			18.00
...Hard Time (2001, $9.95, TPB) r/#146-150			10.00
...Original Sins (1993, $19.95, TPB) r/#1-9			20.00
...Tainted Love (1998, $16.95, TPB) r/#68-71, Vertigo Jam #1 and Hellblazer Special #1			17.00

NOTE: ***Alcala** a-8i, 9i, 18-22i. **Gaiman** scripts-27. **McKean** a-27,40; c-1-21. **Sutton** a-44i, 45i. **Talbot** a-Annual 1.*

HELLBLAZER SPECIAL: BAD BLOOD
DC Comics (Vertigo): Sept, 2000 - No. 4 ($2.95, mini-series)

1-4-Delano-s/Bond-a; Constantine in 2025 London 2.95

HELLBLAZER/THE BOOKS OF MAGIC
DC Comics (Vertigo): Dec, 1997 - No. 2, Jan, 1998 ($2.50, mini-series)

1,2-John Constantine and Tim Hunter 2.50

HELLBOY (Also see Dark Horse Presents, John Byrne's Next Men, San Diego Comic Con #2, Danger Unlimited #4, Gen13 #13B, Ghost/Hellboy, & Savage Dragon)

HELLBOY: ALMOST COLOSSUS
Dark Horse Comics (Legend): Jun, 1997 - No. 2, Jul, 1997 ($2.95, lim. series)

1,2-Mignola-s/a 3.00

HELLBOY: BOX FULL OF EVIL
Dark Horse Comics: Aug, 1999 - No. 2, Sept, 1999 ($2.95, lim. series)

1,2-Mignola-s/a; back-up story w/ Matt Smith-a 3.00

HELLBOY CHRISTMAS SPECIAL
Dark Horse Comics: Dec, 1997 ($3.95, one-shot)

nn-Christmas stories by Mignola, Gianni, Darrow, Purcell 4.00

HELLBOY, JR.
Dark Horse Comics: Oct, 1999 - No. 2, Nov, 1999 ($2.95, limited series)

1,2-Stories and art by various 3.00

HELLBOY, JR., HALLOWEEN SPECIAL

Hellcat #1 © MAR

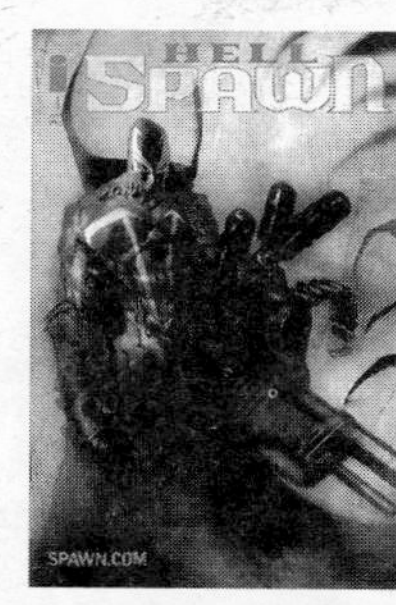

Hellspawn #1 © TMP

He-Man #1 © Z-D

GD2.0 FN6.0 NM9.4

Dark Horse Comics: Oct, 1997 ($3.95, one-shot)

nn-"Harvey" style renditions of Hellboy characters; Bill Wray, Mike Mignola & various-s/a; wraparound-c by Wray 4.00

HELLBOY: SEED OF DESTRUCTION
Dark Horse Comics (Legend): Mar, 1994 - No. 4, Jun, 1994 ($2.50, lim. series)

1-4-Mignola-c/a w/Byrne scripts; Monkeyman & O'Brien back-up story (origin) by Art Adams. 3.00
Trade paperback (1994, $17.95)-collects all four issues plus r/Hellboy's 1st app. in San Diego Comic Con #2 & pin-ups 18.00
Limited edition hardcover (1995, $99.95)-includes everything in trade paperback plus additional material. 100.00

HELLBOY: THE CHAINED COFFIN AND OTHERS
Dark Horse Comics (Legend): Aug, 1998 ($17.95, TPB)

nn-Mignola-c/a/s; reprints out-of-print one shots; pin-up gallery 18.00

HELLBOY: THE CORPSE AND THE IRON SHOES
Dark Horse Comics (Legend): Jan, 1996 ($2.95, one-shot)

nn-Mignola-c/a/scripts; reprints "The Corpse" serial from Capitol City's Advance Comics catalog w/new story 3.00

HELLBOY: THE WOLVES OF ST. AUGUST
Dark Horse Comics (Legend): 1995 ($4.95, squarebound, one-shot)

nn-Mignola--c/a/scripts; r/Dark Horse Presents #88-91 with additional story 5.00

HELLBOY: WAKE THE DEVIL (Sequel to Seed of Destruction)
Dark Horse Comics (Legend): Jun, 1996 - No. 5, Oct, 1996 ($2.95, lim. series)

1-5: Mignola-c/a & scripts; The Monstermen back-up story by Gary Gianni 3.00
TPB (1997, $17.95) r/#1-5 18.00

HELLCAT
Marvel Comics: Sept, 2000 - No. 3, Nov, 2000 ($2.99)

1-3-Englehart-s/Breyfogle-a; Hedy Wolfe app. 3.00

HELLCOP
Image Comics (Avalon Studios): Aug, 1998 - Present ($2.50)

1-4: 1-(Oct. on-c) Casey-s 2.50

HELL ETERNAL
DC Comics (Vertigo Verité): 1998 ($6.95, squarebound, one-shot)

1-Delano-s/Phillips-a 7.00

HELLHOLE
Image Comics: July, 1999 - No. 3, Oct, 1999 ($2.50)

1-3-Lobdell-s/Polina-a 2.50

HELLHOUNDS (...: Panzer Cops #3-6)
Dark Horse Comics: 1994 - No. 6, July, 1994 ($2.50, B&W, limited series)

1-6: 1-Hamner-c. 3-(4/94). 2-Joe Phillips-c 3.00

HELLHOUND, THE REDEMPTION QUEST
Marvel Comics (Epic Comics): Dec, 1993 - No. 4, Mar, 1994 ($2.25, limited series, coated stock)

1-4 2.25

HELLO, I'M JOHNNY CASH
Spire Christian Comics (Fleming H. Revell Co.): 1976 (39/49¢)

nn 2.40 6.00

HELL ON EARTH (See DC Science Fiction Graphic Novel)

HELLO PAL COMICS (Short Story Comics)
Harvey Publications: Jan, 1943 - No. 3, May, 1943 (Photo-c)

1-Rocketman & Rocketgirl begin; Yankee Doodle Jones app.; Mickey Rooney photo-c 63.00 189.00 600.00
2-Charlie McCarthy photo-c (scarce) 53.00 158.00 475.00
3-Bob Hope photo-c (scarce) 55.00 165.00 500.00

HELLRAISER/NIGHTBREED – JIHAD (Also see Clive Barker's...)
Epic Comics (Marvel Comics): 1991 - Book 2, 1991 ($4.50, 52 pgs.)

Book 1,2 4.50

HELL-RIDER (Magazine)
Skywald Publications: Aug, 1971 - No. 2, Oct, 1971 (B&W)

GD2.0 FN6.0 NM9.4

1-Origin & 1st app.; Butterfly & Wildbunch begins 4.10 12.30 45.00
2 3.00 9.00 32.00
NOTE: *#3 advertised in Psycho #5 but did not come out.* ***Buckler*** *a-1, 2.* ***Morrow*** *c-3.*

HELL'S ANGEL (Becomes Dark Angel #6 on)
Marvel Comics UK: July, 1992 - No. 5, Nov, 1993 ($1.75)

1-5: X-Men (Wolverine, Cyclops)-c/stories. 1-Origin. 3-Jim Lee cover swipe 2.00

HELLSHOCK
Image Comics: July, 1994 - No. 4, Nov, 1994 ($1.95, limited series)

1-4-Jae Lee-c/a & scripts. 4-variant-c. 2.00

HELLSHOCK
Image Comics: Jan, 1997 - No.2, Feb, 1997 ($2.95/$2.50, limited series)

1-($2.95)-Jae Lee-c/s/a, Villarrubia-painted-a 5.00
2-($2.50) 3.00

HELLSHOCK BOOK THREE: THE SCIENCE OF FAITH
Image Comics: Jan, 1998 ($2.50)

1-Jae Lee-c/s/a, Villarrubia-painted-a 2.50

HELLSPAWN
Image Comics: Aug, 2000 - Present ($2.50)

1-Bendis-s/Ashley Wood-c/a; Spawn and Clown app. 2.50
2-4 2.50

HELLSTORM: PRINCE OF LIES (See Ghost Rider #1 & Marvel Spotlight #12)
Marvel Comics: Apr, 1993 - No. 21, Dec, 1994 ($2.00)

1-($2.95)-Parchment-c w/red thermographic ink 3.00
2-21: 14-Bound-in trading card sheet. 18-P. Craig Russell-c 2.00

HE-MAN (See Masters Of The Universe)

HE-MAN (Also see Tops In Adventure)
Ziff-Davis Publ. Co. (Approved Comics): Fall, 1952

1-Kinstler painted-c; Powell-a 16.00 49.00 130.00

HE-MAN
Toby Press: May, 1954 - No. 2, July, 1954 (Painted-c by B. Safran)

1 15.00 45.00 120.00
2 12.50 37.50 100.00

HENNESSEY (TV)
Dell Publishing Co.: No. 1200, Aug-Oct, 1961 - No. 1280, Mar-May, 1962

Four Color 1200-Gil Kane-a, photo-c 6.70 20.00 80.00
Four Color 1280-Photo-c 5.85 17.50 70.00

HENRY (Also see Little Annie Rooney)
David McKay Publications: 1935 (52 pgs.) (Daily B&W strip reprints)(10"x10" cardboard-c)

1-By Carl Anderson 40.00 120.00 320.00

HENRY (See King Comics & Magic Comics)
Dell Publishing Co.: No. 122, Oct, 1946 - No. 65, Apr-June, 1961

Four Color 122-All new stories begin 13.00 40.00 160.00
Four Color 155 (7/47), 1 (1-3/48)-All new stories 8.00 24.00 95.00
2 4.10 12.30 45.00
3-10 3.45 10.35 38.00
11-20: 20-Infinity-c 2.50 7.50 24.00
21-30 2.30 7.00 20.00
31-40 1.85 5.50 15.00
41-65 1.50 4.50 12.00

HENRY (See Giant Comic Album and March of Comics No. 43, 58, 84, 101, 112, 129, 147, 162, 178, 189)

HENRY ALDRICH COMICS (TV)
Dell Publishing Co.: Aug-Sept, 1950 - No. 22, Sept-Nov, 1954

1-Part series written by John Stanley; Bill Williams-a 7.50 22.50 90.00
2 4.10 12.30 45.00
3-5 3.45 10.35 38.00
6-10 3.00 9.00 32.00
11-22 2.40 7.35 22.00

Hercules Unbound #3 © DC

Here's Howie Comics #9 © DC

Heroes For Hire #10 © MAR

HENRY BREWSTER
Country Wide (M.F. Ent.): Feb, 1966 - V2#7, Sept, 1967 (All 25¢ Giants)

1 2.50 7.50 24.00
2-6(12/66), V2#7-Powell-a in most 1.50 4.50 12.00

HEPCATS
Antarctic Press: Nov, 1996 - Present ($2.95, B&W)

0-12-Martin Wagner-c/s/a: 0-color 3.00
0-($9.95) CD Edition 10.00

HERBIE (See Forbidden Worlds & Unknown Worlds)
American Comics Group: April-May, 1964 - No. 23, Feb, 1967 (All 12¢)

1-Whitney-c/a in most issues 16.50 49.00 180.00
2-4 8.65 26.00 95.00
5-Beatles, Dean Martin, F. Sinatra app. 10.00 30.00 110.00
6,7,9,10 6.80 20.50 75.00
8-Origin & 1st app. The Fat Fury 8.15 24.50 90.00
11-23: 14-Nemesis & Magicman app. 17-r/2nd Herbie from Forbidden Worlds #94. 23-r/1st Herbie from F.W. #73 5.00 15.00 55.00

HERBIE
Dark Horse Comics: Oct, 1992 - No. 12, 1993 ($2.50, limited series)

1-Whitney-r plus new-c/a in all; Byrne-c/a & scripts.
2-6: 3-Bob Burden-c/a. 4-Art Adams-c 2.50

HERBIE GOES TO MONTE CARLO, HERBIE RIDES AGAIN (See Walt Disney Showcase No. 24, 41)

HERCULES (See Hit Comics #1-21, Journey Into Mystery Annual, Marvel Graphic Novel #37, Marvel Premiere #26 & The Mighty...)

HERCULES
Charlton Comics: Oct, 1967 - No. 13, Sept, 1969; Dec, 1968

1-Thane of Bagarth begins; Glanzman-a in all 3.00 9.00 30.00
2-13: 1-5,7-10-Aparo-a. 8-(12¢-c) 2.00 6.00 18.00
8-(Low distribution)(12/68, 35¢, B&W); magazine format; new Hercules story plus-r story/#1; Thane-r/#1-3 4.35 13.00 48.00
Modern Comics reprint 10('77), 11('78) 5.00

HERCULES (Prince of Power) (Also see The Champions)
Marvel Comics Group: V1#1, 9/82 - V1#4, 12/82; V2#1, 3/84 - V2#4, 6/84 (color, both limited series)

1-4, V2#1-4: Layton-c/a. 4-Death of Zeus. 3.00
NOTE: *Layton a-1, 2, 3p, 4p, V2#1-4; c-1-4, V2#1-4.*

HERCULES: HEART OF CHAOS
Marvel Comics: Aug, 1997 - No. 3, Oct, 1997 ($2.50, limited series)

1-3-DeFalco-s, Frenz-a 2.50

HERCULES: OFFICIAL COMICS MOVIE ADAPTION
Acclaim Books: 1997 ($4.50, digest size)

nn-Adaption of the Disney animated movie 4.50

HERCULES: THE LEGENDARY JOURNEYS (TV)
Topps Comics: June, 1996 - No. 5, Oct, 1996 ($2.95)

1-2: 1-Golden-c. 3.00
3-Xena-c/app. 1.00 2.80 7.00
3-Variant-c 1.85 5.50 15.00
4,5: Xena-c/app. 5.00

HERCULES UNBOUND
National Periodical Publications: Oct-Nov, 1975 - No. 12, Aug-Sept, 1977

1-Wood-i begins 1.00 3.00 8.00
2-12: 7-Adams ad. 10-Atomic Knights x-over 5.00
NOTE: ***Buckler** c-7p. **Layton** inks-No. 9, 10. **Simonson** a-7-10p, 11, 12; c- 8p, 9-12. **Wood** a-1-8i; c-7i, 8i.*

HERCULES (...Unchained #1121) (Movie)
Dell Publishing Co.: No. 1006, June-Aug, 1959 - No.1121, Aug, 1960

Four Color 1006-Buscema-a, photo-c 9.00 27.00 110.00
Four Color 1121-Crandall/Evans-a 9.00 27.00 110.00

HERE COMES SANTA (See March of Comics No. 30, 213, 340)

HERE COME THE BIG PEOPLE
Event Comics: Oct, 1997 ($2.95, one-shot)

1-Trace Beaulieu-s/Conner & Palmiotti-c/a; variant-c by Darrow 3.00

HERE'S HOWIE COMICS
National Periodical Publications: Jan-Feb, 1952 - No. 18, Nov-Dec, 1954

1 24.00 71.00 190.00
2 12.00 36.00 95.00
3-5: 5-Howie in the Army issues begin (9-10/52) 9.30 28.00 65.00
6-10 7.85 23.50 55.00
11-18 6.40 19.25 45.00

HERETIC, THE
Dark Horse Comics (Blanc Noir): Nov, 1996 - No. 4, Mar, 1997 ($2.95, limited series)

1-4:-w/back-up story 3.00

HERITAGE OF THE DESERT (See Zane Grey, 4-Color 236)

HERMAN & KATNIP (See Harvey Comics Hits #60 & 62, Harvey Hits #14,25,31,41 & Paramount Animated Comics #1)

HERMES VS. THE EYEBALL KID
Dark Horse Comics: Dec, 1994 - No. 3,Feb, 1995 ($2.95, B&W, limited series)

1-3: Eddie Campbell-c/a/scripts 3.00

HERO (Warrior of the Mystic Realms)
Marvel Comics: May, 1990 - No. 6, Oct, 1990 ($1.50, limited series)

1-6: 1-Portacio-i 2.00

HERO ALLIANCE, THE
Sirius Comics: Dec, 1985 - No. 2, Sept, 1986 (B&W)

1,2: 2-($1.50), Special Edition 1 (7/86, color) 2.00

HERO ALLIANCE
Wonder Color Comics: May, 1987 ($1.95)

1-Ron Lim-a 2.00

HERO ALLIANCE
Innovation Publishing: V2#1, Sept, 1989 - V2#17, Nov, 1991 ($1.95, 28 pgs.)

V2#1-17: 1,2-Ron Lim-a 2.00
Annual 1 (1990, $2.75, 36 pgs.)-Paul Smith-c/a 2.75
Special 1 (1992, $2.50, 32 pgs.)-Stuart Immonen-a (10 pgs.) 2.50

HERO ALLIANCE: END OF THE GOLDEN AGE
Innovation Publishing: July, 1989 - No. 3, Aug, 1989 ($1.75, bi-weekly limited series)

1-3: Bart Sears & Ron Lim-c/a; reprints & new-a 2.00

HEROES (Also see Shadow Cabinet & Static)
DC Comics (Milestone): May, 1996 - No. 6, Nov, 1996 ($2.50, limited series)

1-6: 1-Intro Heroes (Iota, Donner, Blitzen, Starlight, Payback & Static) 2.50

HEROES AGAINST HUNGER
DC Comics: 1986 ($1.50; one-shot for famine relief)

1-Superman, Batman app.; Neal Adams-c(p); includes many artists work; Jeff Jones assist (2 pg.) on B. Smith-a; Kirby-a 4.00

HEROES ALL CATHOLIC ACTION ILLUSTRATED
Heroes All Co.: 1943 - V6#5, Mar 10, 1948 (paper covers)

V1#1-(16 pgs., 8x11") 22.00 66.00 175.00
V1#2-(16 pgs., 8x11") 19.00 56.00 150.00
V2#1(1/44)-3(3/44)-(16 pgs., 8x11") 16.00 48.00 125.00
V3#1(1/45)-10(12/45)-(16 pgs., 8x11") 14.00 41.00 110.00
V4#1-35 (12/20/46)-(16 pgs.) 12.00 36.00 95.00
V5#1(1/10/47)-8(2/28/47)-(16 pgs.), V5#9(3/7/47)-20(11/25/47)-(32 pgs.), V6#1(1/10/48)-5(3/10/48)-(32 pgs.) 10.00 30.00 75.00

HEROES FOR HIRE
Marvel Comics: July, 1997 - No. 19, Jan, 1999 ($2.99/$1.99)

1-($2.99)-Wraparound cover 5.00
2-19: 2-Variant cover. 7-Thunderbolts app. 9-Punisher-c/app. 10,11 Deadpool-c/app. 18,19-Wolverine-c/app. 3.00
.../Quicksilver '98 Annual ($2.99) Siege of Wundagore pt.5 3.00

HEROES FOR HOPE STARRING THE X-MEN
Marvel Comics Group: Dec, 1985 ($1.50, one-shot, 52pgs., proceeds donated

Heroes Reborn: Doomsday #1 © MAR

Heroic Comics #17 © EAS

Hickory #6 © QUA

GD2.0 FN6.0 NM9.4

to famine relief)
1-Stephen King scripts; Byrne, Miller, Corben-a; Wrightson/J. Jones-a (3 pgs.); Art Adams-c; Starlin back-c 5.00

HEROES, INC. PRESENTS CANNON
Wally Wood/CPL/Gang Publ. No. 2: 1969 - No. 2, 1976 (Sold at Army PX's)
nn-Ditko, Wood-a; Wood-c; Reese-a(p) 1.75 5.25 14.00
2-Wood-c; Ditko, Byrne, Wood-a; 8-1/2x10-1/2"; B&W; $2.00 2.30 7.00 20.00
NOTE: *First issue not distributed by publisher; 1,800 copies were stored and 900 copies were stolen from warehouse. Many copies have surfaced in recent years.*

HEROES OF THE WILD FRONTIER (Formerly Baffling Mysteries)
Ace Periodicals: No. 27, Jan, 1956 - No. 2, Apr, 1956
27(#1),2-Davy Crockett, Daniel Boone, Buffalo Bill 5.00 15.00 30.00

HEROES REBORN (one-shots)
Marvel Comics: Jan, 2000 ($1.99)
...:Ashema; ...:Doom; ...:Doomsday; ...:Masters of Evil; ...:Rebel; ...:Remnants; ...:Young Allies 2.00

HEROES REBORN: THE RETURN
Marvel Comics: Dec, 1997 - No. 4 ($2.50, weekly mini-series)
1-4-Avengers, Fantastic Four, Iron Man & Captain America rejoin regular Marvel Universe; Peter David-s/Larocca-c/a 4.00
1-4-Variant-c for each 2.40 6.00
Wizard 1/2 1.10 3.30 9.00
Return of the Heroes TPB ('98, $14.95) r/#1-4 15.00

HERO FOR HIRE (Power Man No. 17 on; also see Cage)
Marvel Comics Group: June, 1972 - No. 16, Dec, 1973
1-Origin & 1st app. Luke Cage; Tuska-a(p) 4.55 13.65 50.00
2-Tuska-a(p) 2.30 7.00 20.00
3-5: 3-1st app. Mace. 4-1st app. Phil Fox of the Bugle 1.85 5.50 15.00
6-10: 8,9-Dr. Doom app. 9-F.F. app. 1.10 3.30 9.00
11-16: 14-Origin retold. 15-Everett Subby-r('53). 16-Origin Stilletto; death of Rackham 1.00 2.80 7.00

HERO HOTLINE (1st app. in Action Comics Weekly #637)
DC Comics: April, 1989 - No. 6, Sept, 1989 ($1.75, limited series)
1-6: Super-hero humor; Schaffenberger-i 2.00

HEROIC ADVENTURES (See Adventures)

HEROIC COMICS (Reg'lar Fellers...#1-15; New Heroic #41 on)
Eastern Color Printing Co./Famous Funnies(Funnies, Inc. No. 1): Aug, 1940 - No. 97, June, 1955
1-Hydroman (origin) by Bill Everett, The Purple Zombie (origin) & Mann of India by Tarpe Mills begins (all 1st apps.) 158.00 474.00 1500.00
2 71.00 213.00 675.00
3,4 49.00 147.00 440.00
5,6 40.00 120.00 350.00
7-Origin & 1st app. Man O'Metal (1 pg.) 43.00 130.00 390.00
8-10: 10-Lingerie panels 33.00 98.00 260.00
11,13: 13-Crandall/Fine-a 30.00 90.00 240.00
12-Music Master (origin/1st app.) begins by Everett, ends No. 31; last Purple Zombie & Mann of India 34.00 101.00 270.00
14,15-Hydroman x-over in Rainbow Boy. 14-Origin & 1st app. Rainbow Boy (super hero). 15-1st app. Downbeat 33.00 98.00 260.00
16-20: 16-New logo. 17-Rainbow Boy x-over in Hydroman. 19-Rainbow Boy x-over in Hydroman & vice versa 23.00 68.00 180.00
21-30:25-Rainbow Boy x-over in Hydroman. 28-Last Man O'Metal. 29-Last Hydroman 15.00 45.00 120.00
31,34,38 5.00 15.00 35.00
32,36,37-Toth-a (3-4 pgs. each) 7.15 21.50 50.00
33,35-Toth-a (8 & 9 pgs.) 7.85 23.50 55.00
39-42-Toth, Ingels-a 7.85 23.50 55.00
43,46,47,49-Toth-a (2-4 pgs.). 47-Ingels-a 6.40 19.25 45.00
44,45,50-Toth-a (6-9 pgs.) 7.15 21.50 50.00
48,53,54 5.00 15.00 32.00
51-Williamson-a 7.15 21.50 50.00
52-Williamson-a (3 pg. story) 5.50 16.50 38.00
55-Toth-c/a 6.40 19.25 45.00
56-60-Toth-c. 60-Everett-a 5.50 16.50 38.00
61-Everett-a 5.00 15.00 32.00
62,64-Everett-c/a 5.00 15.00 35.00
63-Everett-c 5.00 15.00 30.00
65-Williamson/Frazetta-a; Evans-a (2 pgs.) 9.30 28.00 65.00
66,75,94-Frazetta-a (2 pgs. each) 5.00 15.00 35.00
67,73-Frazetta-a (4 pgs. each) 6.40 19.25 45.00
68,74,76-80,84,85,88-93,95-97: 95-Last pre-code 4.65 14.00 28.00
69,72-Frazetta-a (6 & 8 pgs. each); 1st (?) app. Frazetta Red Cross ad 8.65 26.00 60.00
70,71,86,87-Frazetta, 3-4 pgs. each; 1 pg. ad by Frazetta in #70 5.00 15.00 35.00
81,82-Frazetta art (1 pg. each): 81-1st (?) app. Frazetta Boy Scout ad (tied w/ Buster Crabbe #9 5.00 15.00 30.00
83-Frazetta-a (1/2 pg.) 5.00 15.00 30.00
NOTE: ***Evans** a-64, 65. **Everett** a-(Hydroman-c/a-No. 1-9), 44, 60-64; c-1-9, 62-64. **Harvey Fuller** c-28-35. **Sid Greene** a-38-43, 46. **Guardineer** a-42(3), 43, 44, 45(2), 49(3), 50, 60, 61(2), 65, 67(2) 70-72. **Ingels** c-41. **Kiefer** a-46, 48; c-19-22, 24, 44, 46, 48, 51-53, 65, 67-69, 71-74, 76, 77, 79, 80, 82, 85, 86, 88, 89, 94, 95. **Mort Lawrence** a-45. **Tarpe Mills** a-2(2), 3(2), 10. **Ed Moore** a-49, 52-54, 56-63, 65-69, 72-74, 76, 77. **H.G. Peter** a-58-74, 76, 77, 87. **Paul Reinman** a-49. **Rico** a-31. Captain Tootsie by **Beck**-31, 32. Painted-c #16 on. Hydroman c-1-11. Music Master c-12, 13, 15. Rainbow Boy c-14.*

HERO ZERO (Also see Comics' Greatest World & Godzilla Versus Hero Zero)
Dark Horse Comics: Sept, 1994 ($2.50)
0 2.50

HEX (Replaces Jonah Hex)
DC Comics: Sept, 1985 - No. 18, Feb, 1987 (Story cont'd from Jonah Hex # 92)
1-Hex in post-atomic war world; origin 5.00
2-18: 6-Origin Stiletta. 11-13: All contain future Batman storyline. 13-Intro The Dogs of War (origin #15) 3.00
NOTE: ***Giffen** a(p)-15-18; c(p)-15,17,18. **Texeira** a-1, 2p, 3p, 5-7p, 9p, 11-14p; c(p)-1, 2, 4-7, 12.*

HEXBREAKER (See First Comics Graphic Novel #15)

HEY THERE, IT'S YOGI BEAR (See Movie Comics)

HI-ADVENTURE HEROES (TV)
Gold Key: May, 1969 - No. 2, Aug, 1969 (Hanna-Barbera)
1-Three Musketeers, Gulliver, Arabian Knights 4.55 13.65 50.00
2-Three Musketeers, Micro-Venture, Arabian Knights 3.65 11.00 40.00

HI AND LOIS
Dell Publishing Co.: No. 683, Mar, 1956 - No. 955, Nov, 1958
Four Color 683 (#1) 3.00 9.00 32.00
Four Color 774(3/57),955 2.40 7.35 22.00

HI AND LOIS
Charlton Comics: Nov, 1969 - No. 11, July, 1971
1 2.30 7.00 20.00
2-11 1.50 4.50 12.00

HICKORY (See All Humor Comics)
Quality Comics Group: Oct, 1949 - No. 6, Aug, 1950
1-Sahl-c/a in all; Feldstein?-a 16.00 48.00 125.00
2 9.30 28.00 65.00
3-6 8.65 26.00 60.00

HIDDEN CREW, THE (See The United States Air Force Presents:...)

HIDE-OUT (See Zane Grey, Four Color No. 346)

HIDING PLACE, THE
Spire Christian Comics (Fleming H. Revell Co.): 1973 (39¢/49¢)
nn 1.00 2.80 7.00

HIEROGLYPH
Dark Horse Comics: Nov, 1999 - No. 4, Feb, 2000 ($2.95, limited series)
1-4-Ricardo Delgado-s/a 3.00

HIGH ADVENTURE
Red Top(Decker) Comics (Farrell): Oct, 1957
1-Krigstein-r from Explorer Joe (re-issue on-c) 5.00 15.00 30.00

Hi-Jinx #3 © ACG

Hit Comics #7 © QUA

Hitman #50 © DC

HIGH ADVENTURE (TV)
Dell Publishing Co.: No. 949, Nov, 1958 - No. 1001, Aug-Oct, 1959 (Lowell Thomas)

Four Color 949 (#1)-Photo-c 5.00 15.00 60.00
Four Color 1001-Lowell Thomas'...(#2) 4.60 13.75 55.00

HIGH CHAPPARAL (TV)
Gold Key: Aug, 1968 (Photo-c)

1 (10226-808)-Tufts-a 4.55 13.65 50.00

HIGH SCHOOL CONFIDENTIAL DIARY (Confidential Diary #12 on)
Charlton Comics: June, 1960 - No. 11, Mar, 1962

1 3.65 11.00 40.00
2-11 2.50 7.50 24.00

HIGH VOLTAGE
Blackout Comics: 1996 ($2.95)

0-Mike Baron-s 3.00

HI-HO COMICS
Four Star Publications: nd (2/46?) - No. 3, 1946

1-Funny Animal; L. B. Cole-c 38.00 113.00 300.00
2,3: 2-L. B. Cole-c 21.00 62.00 165.00

HI-JINX (Teen-age Animal Funnies)
La Salle Publ. Co./B&I Publ. Co. (American Comics Group)/Creston: 1945; July-Aug, 1947 - No. 7, July-Aug, 1948

nn-(© 1945, 25 cents, 132 Pgs.)(La Salle) 22.00 66.00 175.00
1-Teen-age, funny animal 16.00 48.00 125.00
2,3 10.00 30.00 75.00
4-7-Milt Gross. 4-X-Mas-c 14.00 41.00 110.00

HI-LITE COMICS
E. R. Ross Publishing Co.: Fall, 1945

1-Miss Shady 19.00 56.00 150.00

HILLBILLY COMICS
Charlton Comics: Aug, 1955 - No. 4, July, 1956 (Satire)

1-By Art Gates 8.65 26.00 60.00
2-4 5.00 15.00 35.00

HILLY ROSE'S SPACE ADVENTURES
Astro Comics: May, 1995 - Present ($2.95, B&W)

1 1.10 3.30 9.00
2-5 5.00
6-9 3.00
Trade Paperback (1996, $12.95)-r/#1-5 13.00

HIP-IT-TY HOP (See March of Comics No. 15)

HI-SCHOOL ROMANCE (...Romances No. 41 on)
Harvey Publ./True Love(Home Comics): Oct, 1949 - No. 5, June, 1950; No. 6, Dec, 1950 - No. 73, Mar, 1958; No. 74, Sept, 1958 - No. 75, Nov, 1958

1-Photo-c 14.00 43.00 115.00
2-Photo-c 8.65 26.00 60.00
3-9: 3,5-Photo-c 6.00 18.00 42.00
10-Rape story 8.65 26.00 60.00
11-20 4.65 14.00 28.00
21-31 4.00 11.00 22.00
32- "Unholy passion" story 6.00 18.00 42.00
33-36: 36-Last pre-code (2/55) 4.00 10.00 20.00
37-75: 54-58,73-Kirby-c 3.00 7.50 15.00

NOTE: ***Powell*** *a-1-3, 5, 8, 12-16, 18, 21-23, 25-27, 30-34, 36, 37, 39, 45-48, 50-52, 57, 58, 60, 64, 65, 67, 69.*

HI-SCHOOL ROMANCE DATE BOOK
Harvey Publications: Nov, 1962 - No. 3, Mar, 1963 (25¢ Giants)

1-Powell, Baker-a 3.65 11.00 40.00
2,3 2.50 7.50 24.00

HIS NAME IS SAVAGE (Magazine format)
Adventure House Press: June, 1968 (35¢, 52 pgs.)

1-Gil Kane-a 3.65 11.00 40.00

HI-SPOT COMICS (Red Ryder No. 1 & No. 3 on)
Hawley Publications: No. 2, Nov, 1940

2-David Innes of Pellucidar; art by J. C. Burroughs; written by Edgar Rice Burroughs 116.00 348.00 1100.00

HISTORY OF THE DC UNIVERSE (Also see Crisis on Infinite Earths)
DC Comics: Sept, 1986 - No. 2, Nov, 1986 ($2.95, limited series)

1,2: 1-Perez-c/a 3.00
Limited Edition hardcover 4.10 12.30 45.00

HISTORY OF VIOLENCE, A
DC COMICS (Paradox Press) 1998?

nn-Paperback ($9.95) 10.00

HITCHHIKERS GUIDE TO THE GALAXY (See Life, the Universe and Everything & Restaraunt at the End of the Universe)
DC Comics: 1993 - No. 3, 1993 ($4.95, limited series)

1-3: Adaptation of Douglas Adams book 5.00
TPB (1997, $14.95) r/#1-3 15.00

HIT COMICS
Quality Comics Group: July, 1940 - No. 65, July, 1950

1-Origin/1st app. Neon, the Unknown & Hercules; intro. The Red Bee; Bob & Swab, Blaze Barton, the Strange Twins, X-5 Super Agent, Casey Jones & Jack & Jill (ends #7) begin 591.00 1775.00 6800.00
2-The Old Witch begins, ends #14 253.00 758.00 2400.00
3-Casey Jones ends; transvestism story "Jack & Jill" 232.00 695.00 2200.00
4-Super Agent (ends #17), & Betty Bates (ends #65) begin; X-5 ends 211.00 633.00 2000.00
5-Classic Lou Fine cover 505.00 1515.00 5800.00
6-10: 10-Old Witch by Crandall (4 pgs.); 1st work in comics (4/41) 184.00 553.00 1750.00
11-Classic cover 158.00 474.00 1500.00
12-17: 13-Blaze Barton ends. 17-Last Neon; Crandall Hercules in all; Last Lou Fine-c 113.00 340.00 1075.00
18-Origin & 1st app. Stormy Foster, the Great Defender (12/41); The Ghost of Flanders begins; Crandall-c 124.00 371.00 1175.00
19,20 100.00 300.00 950.00
21-24: 21-Last Hercules. 24-Last Red Bee & Strange Twins 95.00 285.00 900.00
25-Origin & 1st app. Kid Eternity and begins by Moldoff (12/42); 1st app. The Keeper (Kid Eternity's aide) 179.00 537.00 1700.00
26-Blackhawk x-over in Kid Eternity 100.00 300.00 950.00
27-29 50.00 150.00 450.00
30,31- "Bill the Magnificent" by Kurtzman, 11 pgs. in each 44.00 133.00 400.00
32-40: 32-Plastic Man x-over. 34-Last Stormy Foster 28.00 83.00 220.00
41-50 20.00 60.00 160.00
51-60-Last Kid Eternity 19.00 56.00 150.00
61-63-Crandall-c/a; 61-Jeb Rivers begins 20.00 60.00 160.00
64,65-Crandall-a 19.00 56.00 150.00

NOTE: ***Crandall*** *a-11-17(Hercules), 23, 24(Stormy Foster); c-18-20, 23, 24.* ***Fine*** *c-1-14, 16, 17(most).* ***Ward*** *c-33. Bondage c-7, 64. Hercules c-3, 10-17. Jeb Rivers c-61-65. Kid Eternity c-25-60 (w/Keeper-28-34, 36, 39-43, 45-55). Neon the Unknown c-2, 4, 8, 9. Red Bee c-1, 5-7. Stormy Foster c-18-24.*

HITLER'S ASTROLOGER (See Marvel Graphic Novel #35)

HITMAN (Also see Bloodbath #2, Batman Chronicles #4, Demon #43-45 & Demon Annual #2)
DC Comics: May, 1996 - No. 60, Apr, 2001 ($2.25/$2.50)

1-Garth Ennis-s & John McCrea-c/a begin; Batman app. 1.10 3.30 9.00
2-Joker-c;Two Face, Mad Hatter, Batman app. 2.40 6.00
3-5: 3-Batman-c/app.; Joker app. 4-1st app. Nightfist 4.00
6-20: 8-Final Night x-over. 10-GL cameo. 11-20: 11,12-GL-c/app. 15-20-"Ace of Killers". 16-18-Catwoman app. 17-19-Demon-app. 3.00
21-59: 34-Superman-c/app. 2.50
60-($3.95) Final issue 4.00
#1,000,000 (11/98) Hitman goes to the 853rd Century 2.50

Holiday Comics #2 © STAR

Hollywood Diary #3 © QUA

Holyoke One-Shot #7 © HOKE

GD2.0 FN6.0 NM9.4

Annual 1 (1997, $3.95) Pulp Heroes 4.00
.../Lobo: That Stupid Bastich (7/00, $3.95) Ennis-s/Mahnke-a 3.95
TPB-(1997, $9.95) r/#1-3, Demon Ann. #2, Batman Chronicles #4 10.00
Ace of Killers TPB ('00, $17.95) r/#15-22 18.00
Local Heroes TPB ('99, $17.95) r/#9-14 & Annual #1 18.00
10,000 Bullets TPB ('98, $9.95) r/#4-8 10.00

HI-YO SILVER (See Lone Ranger's Famous Horse... and also see The Lone Ranger and March of Comics No. 215)

HOBBIT, THE
Eclipse Comics: 1989 - No. 3, 1990 ($4.95, squarebound, 52 pgs.)

Book 1-3: Adapts novel; Wenzel-a 7.00
Book 1-Second printing 5.00
Graphic Novel (1990, Ballantine)-r/#1-3 20.00

HOCUS POCUS (Formerly Funny Book)
Parents' Magazine Press: No. 9, Aug-Sept, 1946

9 5.00 15.00 35.00

HOGAN'S HEROES (TV)
Dell Publishing Co.: June, 1966 - No. 8, Sept, 1967; No. 9, Oct, 1969

1: #1-7 photo-c 7.00 21.00 85.00
2,3-Ditko-a(p) 4.60 13.75 55.00
4-9: 9-Reprints #1 3.45 10.35 38.00

HOKUM & HEX (See Razorline)
Marvel Comics (Razorline): Sept, 1993 - No. 9, May, 1994 ($1.75/$1.95)

1-($2.50)-Foil embossed-c; by Clive Barker 2.50
2-9: 5-Hyperkind x-over 2.00

HOLIDAY COMICS
Fawcett Publications: 1942 (25¢, 196 pgs.)

1-Contains three Fawcett comics plus two page portrait of Captain Marvel; Capt. Marvel, Nyoka #1, & Whiz. Not rebound, remaindered comics; printed at the same time as originals 145.00 436.00 1600.00

HOLIDAY COMICS (Becomes Fun Comics #9-12)
Star Publications: Jan, 1951 - No. 8, Oct, 1952

1-Funny animal contents (Frisky Fables) in all; L. B. Cole X-Mas-c 35.00 105.00 280.00
2-Classic L. B. Cole-c 38.00 113.00 300.00
3-8: 5,8-X-Mas-c; all L.B. Cole-c 24.00 71.00 190.00
Accepted Reprint 4 (nd)-L.B. Cole-c 10.00 30.00 80.00

HOLIDAY DIGEST
Harvey Comics: 1988 ($1.25, digest-size)

1 2.40 6.00

HOLIDAY PARADE (Walt Disney's...)
W. D. Publications (Disney): Winter, 1990-91(no yr. given) - No. 2, Winter, 1990-91 ($2.95, 68 pgs.)

1-Reprints 1947 Firestone by Barks plus new-a 3.00
2-Barks-r plus other stories 3.00

HOLI-DAY SURPRISE (Formerly Summer Fun)
Charlton Comics: V2#55, Mar, 1967 (25¢ Giant)

V2#55 3.00 9.00 30.00

HOLLYWOOD COMICS
New Age Publishers: Winter, 1944 (52 pgs.)

1-Funny animal 18.00 53.00 140.00

HOLLYWOOD CONFESSIONS
St. John Publishing Co.: Oct, 1949 - No. 2, Dec, 1949

1-Kubert-c/a (entire book) 28.00 84.00 225.00
2-Kubert-c/a (entire book) (Scarce) 34.00 103.00 275.00

HOLLYWOOD DIARY
Quality Comics Group: Dec, 1949 - No. 5, July-Aug, 1950

1-No photo-c 19.00 56.00 150.00
2-Photo-c 12.00 36.00 95.00
3-5-Photo-c. 5-June Allyson/Peter Lawford photo-c 10.00 30.00 75.00

HOLLYWOOD FILM STORIES
Feature Publications/Prize: April, 1950 - No. 4, Oct, 1950 (All photo-c; "Fumetti" type movie comic)

1-June Allyson photo-c 19.00 56.00 150.00
2-4: 2-Lizabeth Scott photo-c. 3-Barbara Stanwick photo-c. 4-Betty Hutton photo-c 14.00 41.00 110.00

HOLLYWOOD FUNNY FOLKS (Formerly Funny Folks; Becomes Nutsy Squirrel #61 on)
National Periodical Publ.: No. 27, Aug-Sept, 1950 - No. 60, July-Aug, 1954

27 13.00 39.00 105.00
28-40 10.00 30.00 70.00
41-60 8.65 26.00 60.00

NOTE: ***Sheldon Mayer*** *a-27-35, 37-40, 43-46, 48-51, 53, 56, 57, 60.*

HOLLYWOOD LOVE DOCTOR (See Doctor Anthony King...)

HOLLYWOOD PICTORIAL (...Romances on cover)
St. John Publishing Co.: No. 3, Jan, 1950

3-Matt Baker-a; photo-c 23.00 69.00 185.00
(Becomes a movie magazine - Hollywood Pictorial Western with No. 4.)

HOLLYWOOD ROMANCES (Formerly Brides In Love; becomes For Lovers Only #60 on)
Charlton Comics: V2#46, 11/66; #47, 10/67; #48, 11/68;V3#49,11/69-V3#59, 6/71

V2#46-Rolling Stones-c/story 8.15 24.50 90.00
V2#47-V3#59: 56- "Born to Heart Break" begins 1.50 4.50 12.00

HOLLYWOOD SECRETS
Quality Comics Group: Nov, 1949 - No. 6, Sept, 1950

1-Ward-c/a (9 pgs.) 33.00 98.00 260.00
2-Crandall-a, Ward-c/a (9 pgs.) 22.00 66.00 175.00
3-6: All photo-c. 5-Lex Barker (Tarzan)-c 11.00 33.00 90.00
...of Romance, I.W. Reprint #9; r/#2 above w/Kinstler-c 2.00 6.00 16.00

HOLLYWOOD SUPERSTARS
Marvel Comics (Epic Comics): Nov, 1990 - No. 5, Apr, 1991 ($2.25)

1-($2.95, 52 pgs.)-Spiegle-c/a in all; Aragones-a, inside front-c plus 2-4 pgs. 3.00
2-5 ($2.25) 2.25

HOLO-MAN (See Power Record Comics)

HOLYOKE ONE-SHOT
Holyoke Publishing Co. (Tem Publ.): 1944 - No. 10, 1945 (All reprints)

1,2: 1-Grit Grady (on cover only), Miss Victory, Alias X (origin)-All reprints from Captain Fearless. 2-Rusty Dugan (Corporal); Capt. Fearless (origin), Mr. Miracle (origin) app. 13.00 39.00 105.00
3-Miss Victory; r/Crash #4; Cat Man (origin), Solar Legion by Kirby app.; Miss Victory on cover only (1945) 26.00 79.00 210.00
4,6,8: 4-Mr. Miracle; The Blue Streak app. 6-Capt. Fearless, Alias X, Capt. Stone (splash used as-c to #10); Diamond Jim & Rusty Dugan (splash from cover of #2). 8-Blue Streak, Strong Man (story matches cover to #7)-Crash reprints 11.00 33.00 90.00
5,7: 5-U.S. Border Patrol Comics (Sgt. Dick Carter of the...), Miss Victory (story matches cover to #3), Citizen Smith, & Mr. Miracle app. 7-Secret Agent Z-2, Strong Man, Blue Streak (story matches cover to #8); Reprints from Crash #2 13.00 39.00 105.00
9-Citizen Smith, The Blue Streak, Solar Legion by Kirby & Strongman, the Perfect Human app.; reprints from Crash #4 & 5; Citizen Smith on cover only-from story in #5 (1944-before #3) 18.00 53.00 140.00
10-Captain Stone; r/Crash; Solar Legion by S&K 18.00 53.00 140.00

HOMER COBB (See Adventures of...)

HOMER HOOPER
Atlas Comics: July, 1953 - No. 4, Dec, 1953

1-Teenage humor 9.30 28.00 65.00
2-4 6.00 18.00 42.00

HOMER, THE HAPPY GHOST (See Adventures of...)
Atlas(ACI/PPI/WPI)/Marvel: 3/55 - No. 22, 11/58; V2#1, 11/69 - V2#4, 5/70

V1#1-Dan DeCarlo-c/a begins, ends #22 16.00 48.00 125.00
2-1st code approved issue 9.30 28.00 65.00

Hooded Menace nn © AVON

Hopalong Cassidy #15 © FAW

Hoppy the Marvel Bunny #5 © FAW

GD2.0 FN6.0 NM9.4

3-10 7.15 21.50 50.00
11-22 6.00 18.00 42.00
V2#1 (11/69) 8.15 24.50 90.00
2-4 4.10 12.30 45.00

HOME RUN (Also see A-1 Comics)
Magazine Enterprises: No. 89, 1953 (one-shot)
A-1 89 (#3)-Powell-a; Stan Musial photo-c 12.00 36.00 95.00

HOMICIDE (Also see Dark Horse Presents)
Dark Horse Comics: Apr, 1990 ($1.95, B&W, one-shot)
1-Detective story 2.00

HOMICIDE: TEARS OF THE DEAD
Chaos! Comics: Apr, 1997 ($2.95, one-shot)
1-Brom-c, 1-Premium Ltd. Ed. w/wraparound-c 3.00

HONEYMOON (Formerly Gay Comics)
A Lover's Magazine(USA) (Marvel): No. 41, Jan, 1950
41-Photo-c; article by Betty Grable 10.00 30.00 70.00

HONEYMOONERS, THE (TV)
Lodestone: Oct, 1986 ($1.50)
1-Photo-c 4.00

HONEYMOONERS, THE (TV)
Triad Publications: Sept, 1987 - No. 13? ($2.00)
1-13 4.00

HONEYMOON ROMANCE
Artful Publications (Canadian): Apr, 1950 - No. 2, July, 1950 (25¢, digest size)
1,2-(Rare) 36.00 108.00 290.00

HONEY WEST (TV)
Gold Key: Sept, 1966 (Photo-c)
1 (10186-609) 10.00 30.00 120.00

HONG KONG PHOOEY (TV)
Charlton Comics: June, 1975 - No. 9, Nov, 1976 (Hanna-Barbera)
1 4.10 12.30 45.00
2 2.50 7.50 23.00
3-9 2.00 6.00 16.00

HONG ON THE RANGE
Image/Flypaper Press: Dec, 1997 - No. 3, Feb, 1998 ($2.50, lim. series)
1-3: Wu-s/Lafferty-a 2.50

HOODED HORSEMAN, THE (Formerly Blazing West)
American Comics Group (Michel Publ.): No. 21, 1-2/52 - No. 27, 1-2/54; No. 18, 12-1/54-55 - No. 22, 8-9/55
21(1-2/52)-Hooded Horseman, Injun Jones cont. 14.00 41.00 110.00
22 10.00 30.00 70.00
23,24,27(1-2/54) 7.85 23.50 55.00
25 (9-10/53)-Cowboy Sahib on cover only; Hooded Horseman i.d. revealed 8.65 26.00 60.00
26-Origin/1st app. Cowboy Sahib by L. Starr 10.00 30.00 80.00
18(12-1/54-55)(Formerly Out of the Night) 10.00 30.00 70.00
19,21,22: 19-Last precode (1-2/55) 7.15 21.50 50.00
20-Origin Johnny Injun 8.65 26.00 60.00
NOTE: *Whitney c/a-21('52), 20-22.*

HOODED MENACE, THE (Also see Daring Adventures)
Realistic/Avon Periodicals: 1951 (one-shot)
nn-Based on a band of hooded outlaws in the Pacific Northwest, 1900-1906; reprinted in Daring Advs. #15 47.00 140.00 420.00

HOODS UP
Fram Corp.: 1953 (15¢, distributed to service station owners, 16 pgs.)
1-(Very Rare; only 2 known); Eisner-c/a in all. 47.00 141.00 425.00
2-6-(Very Rare; only 1 known of #3, 4, 2 known of #2) 47.00 141.00 425.00
NOTE: *Convertible Connie gives tips for service stations, selling Fram oil filters.*

HOOK (Movie)
Marvel Comics: Early Feb, 1992 - No. 4, Late Mar, 1992 ($1.00, limited series)
1-4: Adapts movie; Vess-c; 1-Morrow-a(p) 2.00
nn (1991, $5.95, 84 pgs.)-Contains #1-4; Vess-c 2.40 6.00
1 (1991, $2.95, magazine, 84 pgs.)-Contains #1-4; Vess-c (same cover as nn issue) 3.00

HOOT GIBSON'S WESTERN ROUNDUP (See Western Roundup under Fox Giants)

HOOT GIBSON WESTERN (Formerly My Love Story)
Fox Features Syndicate: No. 5, May, 1950 - No. 3, Sept, 1950
5,6(#1,2): 5-Photo-c. 6-Photo/painted-c 28.00 83.00 220.00
3-Wood-a; painted-c 30.00 90.00 240.00

HOPALONG CASSIDY (Also see Bill Boyd Western, Master Comics, Real Western Hero, Six Gun Heroes & Western Hero; Bill Boyd starred as H. Cassidy in the movies; H. Cassidy in movies, radio & TV)
Fawcett Publications: Feb, 1943; No. 2, Summer, 1946 - No. 85, Nov, 1953
1 (1943, 68 pgs.)-H. Cassidy & his horse Topper begin (on sale 1/8/43)-Captain Marvel app. on-c 452.00 1357.00 5200.00
2-(Sum, '46) 76.00 229.00 725.00
3,4: 3-(Fall, '46, 52 pgs. begin) 40.00 120.00 340.00
5- "Mad Barber" story mentioned in **SOTI**, pgs. 308,309; photo-c 31.00 94.00 250.00
6-10: 8-Photo-c 26.00 79.00 210.00
11-19: 11,13-19-Photo-c 20.00 60.00 160.00
20-29 (52 pgs.)-Painted/photo-c 16.00 48.00 125.00
30,31,33,34,37-39,41 (52 pgs.)-Painted-c 11.00 33.00 90.00
32,40 (36pgs.)-Painted-c 10.00 30.00 75.00
35,42,43,45-47,49-51,53,54,56 (52 pgs.)-Photo-c 10.00 30.00 80.00
36,44,48 (36 pgs.)-Photo-c 10.00 30.00 70.00
52,55,57-70 (36 pgs.)-Photo-c 8.65 26.00 60.00
71-84-Photo-c 6.40 19.25 45.00
85-Last Fawcett issue; photo-c 8.65 26.00 60.00
NOTE: *Line-drawn c-1-4, 6, 7, 9, 10, 12.*
... & The 5 Men of Evil (AC Comics, 1991, $12.95) r/newspaper strips and Fawcett story "Signature of Death" 13.00

HOPALONG CASSIDY (TV)
National Periodical Publications: No. 86, Feb, 1954 - No. 135, May-June, 1959 (All-36 pgs.)
86-Gene Colan-a begins, ends #117; photo covers continue 40.00 120.00 325.00
87 22.00 66.00 175.00
88-91: 91-1 pg. Superboy-sty (6/54) 14.00 43.00 115.00
92-99 (98 has #93 on-c; last precode issue, 2/55). 95-Reversed photo-c to #52. 98-Reversed photo-c to #61. 99-Reversed photo-c to #60 12.50 37.50 100.00
100-Same cover as #50 14.00 41.00 110.00
101-108: 105-Same photo-c as #54. 107-Same photo-c as #51. 108-Last photo-c 6.80 20.50 75.00
109-130: 118-Gil Kane-a begins. 123-Kubert-a (2 pgs.). 124-Painted-c 5.90 17.75 65.00
131-135 6.35 19.00 70.00

HOPE SHIP
Dell Publishing Co.: June-Aug, 1963
1 2.00 6.00 18.00

HOPPY THE MARVEL BUNNY (See Fawcett's Funny Animals)
Fawcett Publications: Dec, 1945 - No. 15, Sept, 1947
1 29.00 86.00 230.00
2 14.00 41.00 110.00
3-15: 7-Xmas-c 12.00 36.00 95.00

HORACE & DOTTY DRIPPLE (Dotty Dripple No. 1-24)
Harvey Publications: No. 25, Aug, 1952 - No. 43, Oct, 1955
25-43 2.40 6.00 12.00

HORIZONTAL LIEUTENANT, THE (See Movie Classics)

HOROBI
Viz Premiere Comics: 1990 - No. 8, 1990 ($3.75, B&W, mature readers, 84 pgs.) V2#1, 1990 - No. 7, 1991 ($4.25, B&W, 68 pgs.)

Horrific #4 © Comic Media

Horse Feathers Comics #1 © LEV

Hot Rod Comics #4 © FAW

	GD2.0	FN6.0	NM9.4
1-8: Japanese manga, Part Two, #1-7			4.50

HORRIFIC (Terrific No. 14 on)
Artful/Comic Media/Harwell/Mystery: Sept, 1952 - No. 13, Sept, 1954

	GD2.0	FN6.0	NM9.4
1	42.00	125.00	375.00
2	25.00	75.00	200.00
3-Bullet in head-c	44.00	133.00	400.00
4,5,7,9,10: 4-Shrunken head-c. 7-Guillotine-c	21.00	62.00	165.00
6-Jack The Ripper story	22.00	66.00	175.00
8-Origin & 1st app. The Teller (E.C. parody)	25.00	75.00	200.00
11-13: 11-Swipe/Witches Tales #6,27; Devil-c	16.00	49.00	130.00

NOTE: *Don Heck a-8; c-3-13. **Hollingsworth** a-4. **Morisi** a-8. **Palais** a-5, 7-12.*

HORROR FROM THE TOMB (Mysterious Stories No. 2 on)
Premier Magazine Co.: Sept, 1954

	GD2.0	FN6.0	NM9.4
1-Woodbridge/Torres, Check-a; The Keeper of the Graveyard is host	40.00	120.00	340.00

HORRORIST, THE (Also see Hellblazer)
DC Comics (Vertigo): Dec, 1995 - No. 2, Jan, 1996 ($5.95, lim. series, mature)

	GD2.0	FN6.0	NM9.4
1,2: Jamie Delano scripts, David Lloyd-c/a; John Constantine (Hellblazer) app.		2.40	6.00

HORROR OF COLLIER COUNTY
Dark Horse Comics: Oct, 1999 - No. 5, Feb, 2000 ($2.95, B&W, limited series)

	GD2.0	FN6.0	NM9.4
1-5-Rich Tommaso-s/a			3.00

HORRORS, THE (Formerly Startling Terror Tales #10)
Star Publications: No. 11, Jan, 1953 - No. 15, Apr, 1954

	GD2.0	FN6.0	NM9.4
11-Horrors of War; Disbrow-a(2)	30.00	90.00	240.00
12-Horrors of War; color illo in **POP**	28.00	83.00	220.00
13-Horrors of Mystery; crime stories	26.00	77.00	205.00
14,15-Horrors of the Underworld; crime stories	28.00	83.00	220.00

NOTE: *All have **L. B. Cole** covers; a-12. **Hollingsworth** a-13. **Palais** a-13r.*

HORROR TALES (Magazine)
Eerie Publications: V1#7, 6/69 - V6#6, 12/74; V7#1, 2/75; V7#2, 5/76 - V8#5, 1977; V9#3, 8/78; (V1-V6: 52 pgs.; V7, V8#2: 112 pgs.; V8#4 on: 68 pgs.) (No V5#3, V8#1,3)

	GD2.0	FN6.0	NM9.4
V1#7	3.80	11.40	42.00
V1#8,9	2.80	8.40	28.00
V2#1-6('70), V3#1-6('71), V4#1-3,5-7('72)	2.50	7.50	24.00
V4#4-LSD story reprint/Weird V3#5	3.20	9.60	35.00
V5#1,2,4,5(6/73),5(10/73),6(12/73),V6#1-6('74),V7#1,2,4('76),V7#3('76)-Giant issue,V8#2,4,5('77)	2.50	7.50	24.00
V9#1-3(11/78, $1.50)	3.00	9.00	30.00

NOTE: *Bondage-c-V6#1, 3, V7#2.*

HORSE FEATHERS COMICS
Lev Gleason Publ.: Nov, 1945 - No. 4, July(Summer on-c), 1948 (52 pgs.)

	GD2.0	FN6.0	NM9.4
1-Wolverton's Scoop Scuttle, 2 pgs.	19.00	56.00	150.00
2	10.00	30.00	70.00
3,4: 3-(5/48)	7.15	21.50	50.00

HORSEMAN
Crusade Comics/Kevlar Studios: Mar, 1996 - No. 3, Nov, 1997 ($2.95)

	GD2.0	FN6.0	NM9.4
0-1st Kevlar Studios issue, 1-(3/96)-Crusade issue; Shi-c/app., 1-(11/96)-3-(11/97)-Kevlar Studios			3.00

HORSEMASTERS, THE (Disney)(TV, Movie)
Dell Publishing Co.: No. 1260, Dec-Feb, 1961/62

	GD2.0	FN6.0	NM9.4
Four Color 1260-Annette Funicello photo-c	11.70	35.00	140.00

HORSE SOLDIERS, THE
Dell Publishing Co.: No. 1048, Nov-Jan, 1959/60 (John Wayne movie)

	GD2.0	FN6.0	NM9.4
Four Color 1048-Painted-c, Sekowsky-a	13.00	40.00	160.00

HORSE WITHOUT A HEAD, THE (See Movie Comics)

HOT DOG
Magazine Enterprises: June-July, 1954 - No. 4, Dec-Jan, 1954-55

	GD2.0	FN6.0	NM9.4
1(A-1 #107)	7.15	21.50	50.00
2,3(A-1 #115),4(A-1 #136)	5.00	15.00	35.00

HOT DOG (See Jughead's Pal, Hotdog)

HOTEL DEPAREE - SUNDANCE (TV)
Dell Publishing Co.: No. 1126, Aug-Oct, 1960 (one-shot)

	GD2.0	FN6.0	NM9.4
Four Color 1126-Earl Holliman photo-c	5.85	17.50	70.00

HOT ROD AND SPEEDWAY COMICS
Hillman Periodicals: Feb-Mar, 1952 - No. 5, Apr-May, 1953

	GD2.0	FN6.0	NM9.4
1	26.00	79.00	210.00
2-Krigstein-a	19.00	56.00	150.00
3-5	10.00	30.00	80.00

HOT ROD COMICS (...Featuring Clint Curtis) (See XMas Comics)
Fawcett Publications: Nov, 1951 (no month given) - V2#7, Feb, 1953

	GD2.0	FN6.0	NM9.4
nn (V1#1)-Powell-c/a in all	31.00	94.00	250.00
2 (4/52)	18.00	53.00	140.00
3-6, V2#7	12.50	37.50	100.00

HOT ROD KING (Also see Speed Smith the Hot Rod King)
Ziff-Davis Publ. Co.: Fall, 1952

	GD2.0	FN6.0	NM9.4
1-Giacoia-a; Saunders painted-c	26.00	79.00	210.00

HOT ROD RACERS (Grand Prix No. 16 on)
Charlton Comics: Dec, 1964 - No. 15, July, 1967

	GD2.0	FN6.0	NM9.4
1	7.25	21.75	80.00
2-5	4.35	13.00	48.00
6-15	3.20	9.60	35.00

HOT RODS AND RACING CARS
Charlton Comics (Motor Mag. No. 1): Nov, 1951 - No. 120, June, 1973

	GD2.0	FN6.0	NM9.4
1-Speed Davis begins; Indianapolis 500 story	28.00	83.00	220.00
2	14.00	41.00	110.00
3-10	10.00	30.00	75.00
11-20	8.65	26.00	60.00
21-34,36-40	6.40	19.25	45.00
35 (6/58, 68 pgs.)	10.00	30.00	70.00
41-60	5.00	15.00	35.00
61-80	2.50	7.50	25.00
81-100	2.00	6.00	18.00
101-120	1.75	5.25	14.00

HOT SHOT CHARLIE
Hillman Periodicals: 1947 (Lee Elias)

	GD2.0	FN6.0	NM9.4
1	10.00	30.00	70.00

HOT SHOTS: AVENGERS
Marvel Comics: Oct, 1995 ($2.95, one-shot)

	GD2.0	FN6.0	NM9.4
nn-pin-ups			3.00

HOTSPUR
Eclipse Comics: Jun, 1987 - No. 3, Sep, 1987 ($1.75, lim. series, Baxter paper)

	GD2.0	FN6.0	NM9.4
1-3			2.00

HOT STUFF (See Stumbo Tinytown)
Harvey Comics: V2#1, Sept, 1991 - No. 12, June, 1994 ($1.00)

	GD2.0	FN6.0	NM9.4
V2#1-Stumbo back-up story			3.00
2-12 ($1.50)			2.00
...Big Book 1 (11/92), 2 (6/93) (Both $1.95, 52 pgs.)			3.00

HOT STUFF CREEPY CAVES
Harvey Publications: Nov, 1974 - No. 7, Nov, 1975

	GD2.0	FN6.0	NM9.4
1	3.00	9.00	30.00
2-7	2.00	6.00	16.00

HOT STUFF DIGEST
Harvey Comics: July, 1992 - No. 5, Nov, 1993 ($1.75, digest-size)

	GD2.0	FN6.0	NM9.4
V2#1-Hot Stuff, Stumbo, Richie Rich stories			3.50
2-5			2.00

HOT STUFF GIANT SIZE
Harvey Comics: Oct, 1992 - No. 3, Oct, 1993 ($2.25, 68 pgs.)

	GD2.0	FN6.0	NM9.4
V2#1-Hot Stuff & Stumbo stories			3.50
2,3			2.50

HOT STUFF SIZZLERS
Harvey Publications: July, 1960 - No. 59, Mar, 1974; V2#1, Aug, 1992

Hot Stuff, The Little Devil #1 © HARV

Hourman #1 © DC

House of Mystery #8 © DC

	GD2.0	FN6.0	NM9.4
1: 84 pgs. begin, ends #5; Hot Stuff, Stumbo begin	12.75	38.00	140.00
2-5	5.45	16.35	60.00
6-10: 6-68 pgs. begin, ends #45	3.45	10.35	38.00
11-20	3.00	9.00	30.00
21-45	2.30	7.00	20.00
46-52: 52 pgs. begin	1.85	5.50	15.00
53-59	1.25	3.75	10.00
V2#1-(8/92, $1.25)-Stumbo back-up			4.00

HOT STUFF, THE LITTLE DEVIL (Also see Devil Kids & Harvey Hits)
Harvey Publications (Illustrated Humor): 10/57 - No. 141, 7/77; No. 142, 2/78 - No. 164, 8/82; No. 165, 10/86 - No. 171, 11/87; No. 172, 11/88; No. 173, Sept, 1990 - No. 177, 1/91

	GD2.0	FN6.0	NM9.4
1	33.00	100.00	400.00
2-1st app. Stumbo the Giant (12/57)	18.00	53.00	195.00
3-5	12.75	38.00	140.00
6-10	7.65	23.00	85.00
11-20	5.90	17.75	65.00
21-40	3.45	10.35	38.00
41-60	2.50	7.50	24.00
61-80	2.00	6.00	18.00
81-105	1.75	5.25	14.00
106-112: All 52 pg. Giants	2.00	6.00	18.00
113-125	1.00	3.00	8.00
126-141		2.40	6.00
142-177: 172-177-($1.00)			4.00

HOT WHEELS (TV)
National Periodical Publications: Mar-Apr, 1970 - No. 6, Jan-Feb, 1971

	GD2.0	FN6.0	NM9.4
1	8.65	26.00	95.00
2,4,5	4.10	12.30	45.00
3-Neal Adams-c	4.55	13.65	50.00
6-Neal Adams-c/a	6.35	19.00	70.00

NOTE: ***Toth** a-1p, 2-5; c-1p, 5.*

HOURMAN (Justice Society member, see Adventure Comics #48)

HOURMAN (See JLA and DC One Million)
DC Comics: Apr, 1999 - No. 25, Apr, 2001 ($2.50)

	GD2.0	FN6.0	NM9.4
1-21: 1-JLA app.; McDaniel-c. 2-Tomorrow Woman-c/app. 6,7-Amazo app. 11-13-Justice Legion A app. 16-Silver Age flashback. 18,19-JSA-c/app. 22-Harris-c/a			2.50

HOUSE OF MYSTERY (See Brave and the Bold #93, Elvira's House of Mystery, Limited Collectors' Edition & Super DC Giant)

HOUSE OF MYSTERY, THE
National Periodical Publications/DC Comics: Dec-Jan, 1951-52 - No. 321, Oct, 1983 (No. 194-203: 52 pgs.)

	GD2.0	FN6.0	NM9.4
1-DC's first horror comic	211.00	633.00	2000.00
2	87.00	261.00	825.00
3	63.00	189.00	600.00
4,5	50.00	150.00	450.00
6-10	42.00	125.00	375.00
11-15	38.00	113.00	300.00
16(7/53)-25	28.00	84.00	225.00
26-35(2/55)-Last pre-code issue; 30-Woodish-a	22.00	66.00	175.00
36-50: 50-Text story of Orson Welles' War of the Worlds broadcast	13.50	40.00	150.00
51-60: 55-1st S.A. issue	11.00	33.00	120.00
61,63,65,66,70,72,76,85-Kirby-a	12.00	36.00	130.00
62,64,67-69,71,73-75,77-83,86-99	8.65	26.00	95.00
84-Prototype of Negative Man (Doom Patrol)	12.75	38.00	140.00
100 (7/60)	9.50	28.50	105.00
101-116: 109-Toth, Kubert-a. 116-Last 10¢ issue	8.15	24.50	90.00
117-130: 117-Swipes-c to HOS #20. 120-Toth-a	7.25	21.75	80.00
131-142	5.90	17.75	65.00
143-J'onn J'onzz, Manhunter begins (6/64), ends #173; story continues from Detective #326; intro. Idol-Head of Diabolu	22.00	65.00	240.00
144	10.00	30.00	110.00
145-155,157-159: 149-Toth-a. 155-The Human Hurricane app. (12/65), Red Tornado prototype. 158-Origin Diabolu Idol-Head	6.35	19.00	70.00
156-Robby Reed begins (origin/1st app.), ends #173	8.65	26.00	95.00
160-(7/66)-Robby Reed becomes Plastic Man in this issue only; 1st S.A. app. Plastic Man; intro Marco Xavier (Martian Manhunter) & Vulture Crime Organization; ends #173	11.50	34.00	125.00
161-173: 169-Origin/1st app. Gem Girl	4.55	13.65	50.00
174-Mystery format begins.	5.90	17.75	65.00
175-1st app. Cain (House of Mystery host)	4.10	12.30	45.00
176,177	3.65	11.00	40.00
178-Neal Adams-a (2/68)	4.55	13.65	50.00
179-N. Adams/Orlando, Wrightson-a (1st pro work, 3 pgs.)	7.25	21.75	80.00
180,181,183: Wrightson-a (3,10, & 3 pgs.). 180-Last 12¢ issue; Kane/Wood-a(2). 183-Wood-a	3.65	11.00	40.00
182,184: 182-Toth-a. 184-Kane/Wood, Toth-a	2.50	7.50	25.00
185-Williamson/Kaluta-a; Howard-a (3 pgs.)	3.00	9.00	30.00
186-N. Adams-c/a; Wrightson-a (10 pgs.)	3.20	9.60	35.00
187,190: Adams-c. 187-Toth-a. 190-Toth-a(r)	2.30	7.00	20.00
188-Wrightson-a (8 & 3pgs.); Adams-c	3.00	9.00	32.00
189,192,197: Adams-c on all. 189-Wood-a(i). 192-Last 15¢-c	2.30	7.00	20.00
191-Wrightson-a (8 & 3pgs.); Adams-c	3.00	9.00	30.00
193-Wrightson-c	2.40	7.35	22.00
194-Wrightson-c; 52 pgs begin, end #203; Toth,Kirby-a	2.80	8.40	28.00
195: Wrightson-c. Swamp creature story by Wrightson similar to Swamp Thing (10 pgs.)(10/71)	3.65	11.00	40.00
196,198	2.30	7.00	20.00
199-Adams-c; Wood-a(8pgs.); Kirby-a	2.50	7.50	25.00
200-(25¢, 52 pgs.)-One third-r (3/72)	2.80	8.40	28.00
201-203-(25¢, 52 pgs.)-One third-r	2.40	7.35	22.00
204-Wrightson-c/a, 9 pgs.	2.40	7.35	22.00
205,206,208,210,212,215,216,218	1.50	4.50	12.00
207-Wrightson c/a; Starlin, Redondo-a	2.30	7.00	20.00
209,211,213,214,217,219-Wrightson-c	2.00	6.00	16.00
220,222,223	1.25	3.75	10.00
221-Wrightson/Kaluta-a(8 pgs.)	2.30	7.00	20.00
224-229: 224-Wrightson-r from Spectre #9; Dillin/Adams-r from House of Secrets #82; begin 100 pg. issues; Phantom Stranger-r. 225,227-(100 pgs.): 225-Spectre app. 226-Wrightson/Redondo-a Phantom Stranger-r. 228-N. Adams inks; Wrightson-r. 229-Wrightson-a(r); Toth-r; last 100 pg. issue.	3.25	9.75	36.00
230,232-235,237-250	1.00	3.00	8.00
231-Classic Wrightson-c	3.20	8.00	16.00
236-Wrightson-c; Ditko-a(p); N. Adams-i	1.25	3.75	10.00
251-254-(84 pgs.)-Adams-c. 251-Wood-a	1.50	4.50	12.00
255,256-(84 pgs.)-Wrightson-c	1.50	4.50	12.00
257-259-(84 pgs.)	1.25	3.75	10.00
260-289,291-299: 282-(68 pgs.)-Has extra story "The Computers That Saved Metropolis" Radio Shack giveaway by Jim Starlin			5.00
290-1st "I, Vampire"	1.50	4.50	12.00
300,319,321: Death of "I, Vampire"	1.00	3.00	8.00
301-318,320: 301-318-"I, Vampire"	1.00	2.80	7.00
Welcome to the House of Mystery (7/98, $5.95) reprints stories with new framing story by Gaiman and Aragonés		2.40	6.00

NOTE: ***Neal Adams** a-236i; c-175-192, 197, 199, 251-254. **Alcala** a-209, 217, 219, 224, 227. **M. Anderson** a-212; c/a-37. **Aparo** a-209. **Aragones** a-185, 186, 194, 196, 200, 202, 229, 251. **Baily** a-279p. **Cameron** a-76, 79. **Colan** a-202r. **Craig** a-263, 275, 295, 300. **Dillin/Adams** r-224. **Ditko** a-236p, 247, 254, 258, 276; c-277. **Drucker** a-37. **Evans** c-218. **Fraden** a-251. **Giffen** a-284. **Giunta** a-199, 227r. **Golden** a-257, 259. **Heath** a-194r; c-203. **Howard** a-182, 185, 187, 196, 229r, 247i, 254, 279i. **Kaluta** a-195, 200, 250r; c-200-202, 210, 212, 233, 260, 261, 263, 265, 267, 268, 273, 276, 284, 287, 288, 293-295, 300, 302, 304, 305, 309-319, 321. **Bob Kane** a-84. **Gil Kane** a-196p, 253p, 300p. **Kirby** a-194r, 199r; c-65, 76, 78, 79, 85. **Kubert** c-282, 283, 285, 286, 289-292, 297-299, 301, 303, 306-308. **Maneely** a-68, 227r. **Mayer** a-317p. **Meskin** a-52-144 (most), 195r, 224r, 229r; c-63, 66, 124, 127. **Mooney** a-24, 159, 160. **Moreira** a-3, 4, 20-50, 58, 59, 62, 68, 77, 79, 90, 108, 113, 123, 201r, 228; c-4-28, 44, 47, 50, 54, 59, 62, 64, 68, 70, 73. **Morrow** a-192, 196, 255, 320i. **Mortimer** a-204(3 pgs.). **Nasser** a-276. **Newton** a-259, 272. **Nino** a-204, 212, 213, 220, 224, 225, 245, 250, 252-256, 283. **Orlando** a-175(2 pgs.), 178, 240i; c-240, 258p, 262, 264p, 270p, 271, 272, 274, 275, 278, 296i. **Redondo** a-194, 195, 197, 202, 203, 207, 211, 214, 217, 219, 226, 227, 229, 235, 241, 287(layout), 302p, 303i, 308; c-229. **Reese** a-195, 200, 205i. **Rogers** a-254, 274, 277. **Roussos** a-65, 84, 224i. **Sekowsky** a-282p. **Sparling** a-203. **Starlin** a-207(2 pgs.), 282p; c-281. **Leonard Starr** a-9. **Staton** a-300p. **Sutton***

House of Secrets #2 © DC

Howard the Duck #1 © MAR

Howdy Doody #7 © California National Prod.

GD2.0 FN6.0 NM9.4

a-189, 271, 290, 291, 293, 295, 297-299, 302, 303, 306-309, 310-313i, 314. ***Tuska*** *a-293p, 294p, 316p.* ***Wrightson*** *c-193-195, 204, 207, 209, 211, 213, 214, 217, 219, 221, 231, 236, 255, 256; r-224.*

HOUSE OF SECRETS (Combined with The Unexpected after #154)
National Periodical Publications/DC Comics: 11-12/56 - No. 80, 9-10/66; No. 81, 8-9/69 - No. 140, 2-3/76; No. 141, 8-9/76 - No. 154, 10-11/78

	GD2.0	FN6.0	NM9.4
1-Drucker-a; Moreira-c	107.00	321.00	1500.00
2-Moreira-a	41.00	123.00	525.00
3-Kirby-c/a	37.00	110.00	440.00
4-Kirby-a	29.00	88.00	325.00
5-7	19.00	57.00	210.00
8-Kirby-a	23.00	68.00	250.00
9-11: 11-Lou Cameron-a (unsigned)	17.00	51.00	185.00
12-Kirby-c/a; Lou Cameron-a	18.00	54.00	200.00
13-15: 14-Flying saucer-c	12.75	38.00	140.00
16-20	11.50	34.00	125.00
21,22,24-30	10.00	30.00	110.00
23-1st app. Mark Merlin & begin series (8/59)	11.50	34.00	125.00
31-50: 48-Toth-a. 50-Last 10¢ issue	8.65	26.00	90.00
51-60: 58-Origin Mark Merlin	7.25	21.75	80.00
61-First Eclipso (7-8/63) and begin series	17.00	51.00	185.00
62	8.15	24.50	90.00
63-65-Toth-a on Eclipso (see Brave and the Bold #64)	6.80	20.50	75.00
66-1st Eclipso-c (also #67,70,78,79); Toth-a	8.65	26.00	95.00
67,73: 67-Toth-a on Eclipso. 73-Mark Merlin becomes Prince Ra-Man (1st app.)	7.65	23.00	85.00
68-72,74-80: 76-Prince Ra-Man vs. Eclipso. 80-Eclipso, Prince Ra-Man end	6.80	20.50	75.00
81-Mystery format begins; 1st app. Abel (House Of Secrets host); (cameo in DC Special #4)	5.45	16.35	60.00
82-84: 82-Neal Adams-c(i)	3.00	9.00	30.00
85,90: 85-N. Adams-a(i). 90-Buckler (early work)/N. Adams-a(i)	3.25	9.75	36.00
86,88,89,91	2.50	7.50	25.00
87-Wrightson & Kaluta-a	3.65	11.00	40.00
92-1st app. Swamp Thing-c/story (8 pgs.)(6-7/71) by Berni Wrightson(p) w/JeffJones/Kaluta/Weiss ink assists; classic-c.	46.00	138.00	600.00
93,95,97,98-(52 pgs.)-Wrightson-c	2.50	7.50	25.00
94,96-Wrightson-c. 94-Wrightson-a(i);96-Wood-a	2.50	7.50	25.00
99-Wrightson splash pg.	2.30	7.00	20.00
100-Classic Wrightson-c	3.00	9.00	30.00
101,102,104,105,108-120	1.50	4.50	12.00
103,106,107-Wrightson-c	2.00	6.00	16.00
121-133	1.10	3.30	9.00
134-136,139-Wrightson-a	1.50	4.50	12.00
137,138,141-154	1.00	2.80	7.00
140-1st solo origin of the Patchworkman (see Swamp Thing #3)	2.30	7.00	20.00

NOTE: ***Neal Adams*** *c-81; 82, 84-88, 90, 91.* ***Alcala*** *a-104-107.* ***Anderson*** *a-91. Aparo a-93, 97, 105.* ***B. Bailey*** *a-107.* ***Cameron*** *a-13, 15.* ***Colan*** *a-63.* ***Ditko*** *a-139p, 148.* ***Elias*** *a-58.* ***Evans*** *a-118.* ***Finlay*** *a-7r(Real Fact?).* ***Glanzman*** *a-91.* ***Golden*** *a-151.* ***Heath*** *a-31.* ***Heck*** *a-85.* ***Kaluta*** *a-87, 98, 99; c-98, 99, 101, 102, 105, 149, 151, 154.* ***Bob Kane*** *a-18, 21.* ***G. Kane*** *a-85p.* ***Kirby*** *c-3, 11, 12.* ***Kubert*** *a-39.* ***Meskin*** *a-2-68 (most), 94r; c-55-60.* ***Moreira*** *a-7, 8, 51, 54, 102-104, 106, 108, 113, 116, 118, 121, 123, 127; c-1, 2, 4-10, 13-20.* ***Morrow*** *a-86, 89, 90; c-89, 146-148.* ***Nino*** *a-101, 103, 106, 109, 115, 117, 126, 128, 131, 147, 153.* ***Redondo*** *a-95, 99, 102, 104p, 113, 116, 134, 136, 139, 140.* ***Reese*** *a-85.* ***Severin*** *a-91.* ***Starlin*** *c-150.* ***Sutton*** *a-154.* ***Toth*** *a-63-67, 83, 93r, 94r, 96r-98r, 123.* ***Tuska*** *a-90, 104.* ***Wrightson*** *a-134; c-92-94, 96, 100, 103, 106, 107, 135, 136, 139.*

HOUSE OF SECRETS
DC Comics (Vertigo): Oct, 1996 - No. 25, Dec, 1998 ($2.50) (Creator-owned series)

	GD2.0	FN6.0	NM9.4
1-Steven Seagle-s/Kristiansen-c/a.			3.50
2-25: 5,7-Kristiansen-c/a. 6-Fegrado-a			3.00
TPB-(1997, $14.95) r/1-5			15.00

HOUSE OF TERROR (3-D)
St. John Publishing Co.: Oct, 1953 (25¢, came w/glasses)

	GD2.0	FN6.0	NM9.4
1-Kubert, Baker-a	33.00	99.00	265.00

HOUSE OF YANG, THE (See Yang)

Charlton Comics: July, 1975 - No. 6, June, 1976; 1978

	GD2.0	FN6.0	NM9.4
1-Sanho Kim-a in all	1.25	3.75	10.00
2-6		2.40	6.00
Modern Comics #1,2(1978)			3.00

HOUSE ON THE BORDERLAND
DC Comics (Vertigo): 2000 ($29.95, hardcover, one-shot)

	GD2.0	FN6.0	NM9.4
HC-Adaption of William Hope Hodgson book; Corben-a			30.00

HOUSE II: THE SECOND STORY
Marvel Comics: Oct, 1987 (One-shot)

	GD2.0	FN6.0	NM9.4
1-Adapts movie			2.00

HOWARD CHAYKIN'S AMERICAN FLAGG (See American Flagg!)
First Comics: V2#1, May, 1988 - V2#12, Apr, 1989 ($1.75/$1.95, Baxter paper)

	GD2.0	FN6.0	NM9.4
V2#1-9,11,12-Chaykin-c(p) in all			2.00
10-Elvis Presley photo-c			3.00

HOWARD THE DUCK (See Bizarre Adventures #34, Crazy Magazine, Fear, Man-Thing, Marvel Treasury Edition & Sensational She-Hulk #14-17)
Marvel Comics Group: Jan, 1976 - No. 31, May, 1979; No. 32, Jan, 1986; No. 33, Sept, 1986

	GD2.0	FN6.0	NM9.4
1-Brunner-c/a; Spider-Man x-over (low distr.)	1.85	5.50	15.00
2-Brunner-c/a (low distr.)		2.40	6.00
3,4-(Regular 25¢ edition). 3-Buscema-a(p), (7/76)			5.00
3,4-(30¢-c, limited distribution)	1.00	2.80	7.00
5			5.00
6-11: 8-Howard The Duck for president. 9-1st Sgt. Preston Dudley of RCMP. 10-Spider-Man-c/sty			4.00
12-1st app. Kiss (cameo, 3/77)	1.85	5.50	15.00
13-Kiss app. (1st full story, 6/77); Daimon Hellstrom app. plus cameo of Howard as Son of Satan	2.30	7.00	20.00
14-32: 14-Howard as Son of Satan-c/story; Son of Satan app. 16-Album issue; 3 pgs. comics. 22,23-Man-Thing-c/stories; Star Wars parody. 30,32-P. Smith-a			3.00
33-Last issue; low print run			4.00
Annual 1(1977, 52 pgs.)-Mayerik-a			5.00

NOTE: ***Austin*** *c-29i.* ***Bolland*** *c-33.* ***Brunner*** *a-1p, 2p; c-1, 2.* ***Buckler*** *c-3p.* ***Buscema*** *a-3p.* ***Colan*** *a(p)-4-15, 17-20, 24-27, 30, 31; c(p)-4-31, Annual 1p.* ***Leialoha*** *a-1-13i; c(i)-3-5, 8-11.* ***Mayerik*** *a-22, 23, 33.* ***Paul Smith*** *a-30p, 32. Man-Thing app. in #22, 23.*

HOWARD THE DUCK (Magazine)
Marvel Comics Group: Oct, 1979 - No. 9, Mar, 1981 (B&W, 68 pgs.)

	GD2.0	FN6.0	NM9.4
1-Art by Colan, Janson, Golden. Kidney Lady app.		2.40	6.00
2,3,5-9 (nudity in most): 2-Mayerick-c. 3-Xmas issue; Jack Davis-c; Duck World flashback. 5-Dracula app. 6-1st Street People back-up story. 7-Has poster by Byrne; Man-Thing-c/s(46 pgs.). 8-Batman parody w/Marshall Rogers-a; Dave Sim-a (1 pg.). 9-Marie Severin-a; John Pound painted-c			4.00
4-Beatles, John Lennon, Elvis, Kiss & Devo cameos; Hitler app.		2.40	6.00

NOTE: ***Buscema*** *a-4p.* ***Colan*** *a-1-5p, 7-9p.* ***Jack Davis*** *c-3.* ***Golden*** *a(p)-1, 5, 6(51pgs.).* ***Rogers*** *a-7, 8.* ***Simonson*** *a-7.*

HOWARD THE DUCK HOLIDAY SPECIAL
Marvel Comics: Feb, 1997 ($2.50, one-shot)

	GD2.0	FN6.0	NM9.4
1-Wraparound-c; Hama-s			2.50

HOWARD THE DUCK: THE MOVIE
Marvel Comics Group: Dec, 1986 - No. 3, Feb, 1987 (Limited series)

	GD2.0	FN6.0	NM9.4
1-3: Movie adaptation; r/Marvel Super Special			2.00

HOW BOYS AND GIRLS CAN HELP WIN THE WAR
The Parents' Magazine Institute: 1942 (10¢, one-shot)

	GD2.0	FN6.0	NM9.4
1-All proceeds used to buy war bonds	25.00	75.00	200.00

HOWDY DOODY (TV)(See Jackpot of Fun-- & Poll Parrot)
Dell Publishing Co.: 1/50 - No. 38, 7-9/56; No. 761, 1/57; No. 811, 7/57

	GD2.0	FN6.0	NM9.4
1-(Scarce)-Photo-c; 1st TV comic	83.00	250.00	1000.00
2-Photo-c	35.00	106.00	425.00
3-5: All photo-c	20.00	60.00	240.00
6-Used in **SOTI**, pg. 309; painted-c begin	17.00	50.00	200.00
7-10	13.00	40.00	160.00
11-20: 13-X-Mas-c	11.00	33.00	130.00
21-38, Four Color 761,811	9.00	27.00	110.00

Hulk #1 © MAR

Human Fly #10 © Human Fly Spectacles Ltd.

Human Target #1 © DC

HOW IT BEGAN
United Features Syndicate: No. 15, 1939 (one-shot)

Single Series 15 33.00 98.00 260.00

HOW SANTA GOT HIS RED SUIT (See March of Comics No. 2)

HOW THE WEST WAS WON (See Movie Comics)

HOW TO DRAW FOR THE COMICS
Street and Smith: No date (1942?) (10¢, 64 pgs., B&W & color, no ads)

nn-Art by Robert Winsor McCay (recreating his father's art), George Marcoux (Supersnipe artist), Vernon Greene (The Shadow artist), Jack Binder (with biog.), Thorton Fisher, Jon Small, & Jack Farr; has biographies of each artist 28.00 83.00 220.00

H. P. LOVECRAFT'S CTHULHU
Millennium Publications: Dec, 1991 - No. 3, May, 1992 ($2.50, limited series)

1-3: 1-Contains trading cards on thin stock 3.00

H. R. PUFNSTUF (TV) (See March of Comics #360)
Gold Key: Oct, 1970 - No. 8, July, 1972

1-Photo-c (all have photo-c?) 19.00 57.00 225.00
2-8 9.00 27.00 110.00

HUBERT AT CAMP MOONBEAM
Dell Publishing Co.: No. 251, Oct, 1949 (one shot)

Four Color 251 4.10 12.30 45.00

HUCK & YOGI JAMBOREE (TV)
Dell Publishing Co.: Mar, 1961 ($1.00, 6-1/4x9", 116 pgs., cardboard-c, high quality paper) (B&W original material)

nn (scarce) 9.00 27.00 110.00

HUCK & YOGI WINTER SPORTS (TV)
Dell Publishing Co.: No. 1310, Mar, 1962 (Hanna-Barbara) (one-shot)

Four Color 1310 8.75 26.25 105.00

HUCK FINN (See The New Adventures of... & Power Record Comics)

HUCKLEBERRY FINN (Movie)
Dell Publishing Co.: No. 1114, July, 1960

Four Color 1114-Photo-c 4.60 13.75 55.00

HUCKLEBERRY HOUND (See Dell Giant #31,44, Golden Picture Story Book, Kite Fun Book, March of Comics #199, 214, 235, Spotlight #1 & Whitman Comic Books)

HUCKLEBERRY HOUND (TV)
Dell/Gold Key No. 18 (10/62) on: No. 990, 5-7/59 - No. 43, 10/70 (Hanna-Barbera)

Four Color 990(#1)-1st app. Huckleberry Hound, Yogi Bear, & Pixie & Dixie & Mr. Jinks 11.70 35.00 140.00
Four Color 1050,1054 (12/59) 8.00 24.00 95.00
3(1-2/60) - 7 (9-10/60), Four Color 1141 (10/60) 7.50 22.50 90.00
8-10 5.35 16.00 65.00
11,13-17 (6-8/62) 4.10 12.30 45.00
12-1st Hokey Wolf & Ding-a-Ling 4.60 13.75 55.00
18,19 (84pgs.; 18-20 titled ...Chuckleberry Tales) 7.50 22.50 90.00
20-Titled Chuckleberry Tales 3.65 11.00 40.00
21-30: 28-30-Reprints 3.20 9.60 35.00
31-43: 31,32,35,37-43-Reprints 2.50 7.50 25.00

HUCKLEBERRY HOUND (TV)
Charlton Comics: Nov, 1970 - No. 8, Jan, 1972 (Hanna-Barbera)

1 4.10 12.30 45.00
2-8 2.50 7.50 25.00

HUEY, DEWEY, & LOUIE (See Donald Duck, 1938 for 1st app. Also see Mickey Mouse Magazine V4#2, V5#7 & Walt Disney's Junior Woodchucks Limited Series)

HUEY, DEWEY, & LOUIE BACK TO SCHOOL (See Dell Giant #22, 35, 49 & Dell Giants)

HUEY, DEWEY, AND LOUIE JUNIOR WOODCHUCKS (Disney)
Gold Key No. 1-61/Whitman No. 62 on: Aug, 1966 - No. 81, 1984 (See Walt Disney's Comics & Stories #125)

1 4.60 13.75 55.00
2,3(12/68) 3.00 9.00 32.00
4,5(4/70)-r/two WDC&S D.Duck stories by Barks 3.00 9.00 30.00
6-17 2.80 8.40 28.00
18,27-30 2.00 6.00 18.00
19-23,25-New storyboarded scripts by Barks, 13-25 pgs. per issue 2.80 8.40 28.00
24,26: 26-r/Barks Donald Duck WDC&S stories 2.00 6.00 18.00
31-57,60,61: 35,41-r/Barks J.W. scripts 1.10 3.30 9.00
58,59: 58-r/Barks Donald Duck WDC&S stories 1.25 3.75 10.00
62-64 (Whitman) 1.25 3.75 10.00
65-(9/80), 66 (Pre-pack? scarce) 2.00 6.00 18.00
67 (1/81),68 1.75 5.25 14.00
69-74 1.50 4.50 12.00
75-81 (all #90183; pre-pack?; nd, nd code; scarce) 1.75 5.25 14.00

HUGGA BUNCH (TV)
Marvel Comics (Star Comics): Oct, 1986 - No. 6, Aug, 1987

1-6 3.00

HULK (Magazine)(Formerly The Rampaging Hulk)(Also see The Incredible Hulk)
Marvel Comics: No. 10, Aug., 1978 - No. 27, June, 1981 ($1.50)

10-18: 10-Bill Bixby interview. 11-Moon Knight begins. 12-15,17,18-Moon Knight stories. 12-Lou Ferrigno interview. 1.00 3.00 8.00
19-27: 20-Moon Knight story. 23-Last full color issue; Banner is attacked. 24-Part color, Lou Ferrigno interview. 25-Part color. 26,27-are B&W 5.00

NOTE: #10-20 have fragile spines which split easily. ***Alcala*** *a(i)-15, 17-20, 22, 24-27.* ***Buscema*** *a-23; c-26.* ***Chaykin*** *a-21-25.* ***Colan*** *a(p)-11, 19, 24-27.* ***Jusko*** *painted c-12.* ***Nebres*** *a-16.* ***Severin*** *a-19i. Moon Knight by* ***Sienkiewicz*** *in 13-15, 17, 18, 20.* ***Simonson*** *a-27; c-23. Domini Fortune appears in #21-24.*

HULK (Becomes Incredible Hulk Vol. 2 with issue #12)
Marvel Comics: Apr, 1999 - No. 11, Feb, 2000 ($2.99/$1.99)

1-($2.99) Byrne-s/Garney-a 4.00
1-Variant-c 10.00
1-Gold foil variant 10.00
2-11-($1.99): 2-Two covers. 5-Art by Jurgens, Buscema & Texeira. 7-Avengers app. 11-She-Hulk app. 2.00
1999 Annual ($3.50) Chapter One story; Byrne-s/Weeks-a 3.50
Hulk Vs. The Thing (12/99, $3.99, TPB) reprints their notable battles 4.00

HULK: FUTURE IMPERFECT
Marvel Comics: Jan, 1993 - No. 2, Dec, 1992 (In error) ($5.95, 52 pgs., square-bound, limited series)

1,2: Embossed-c; Peter David story & George Perez-c/a. 1-1st app. Maestro. 1.00 3.00 8.00

HULK/ PITT
Marvel Comics: 1997 ($5.99, one-shot)

1-David-s/Keown-c/a 2.00 6.00

HULK SMASH
Marvel Comics: Mar, 2001 - No. 2, Apr, 2001 ($2.99, limited series)

1,2-Ennis-s/McCrea & Janson-a/Nowlan painted-c 3.00

HULK 2099
Marvel Comics: Dec, 1994 - No. 10, Sept, 1995 ($1.50/$1.95)

1-($2.50)-Green foil-c 2.50
2-10: 2-A. Kubert-c 2.00

HUMAN FLY
I.W. Enterprises/Super: 1963 - 1964 (Reprints)

I.W. Reprint #1-Reprints Blue Beetle #44('46) 2.00 6.00 18.00
Super Reprint #10-R/Blue Beetle #46('47) 2.00 6.00 18.00

HUMAN FLY, THE
Marvel Comics Group: Sept, 1977 - No. 19, Mar, 1979

1,2,9,19: 1-Origin; Spider-Man x-over. 2-Ghost Rider app. 9-Daredevil x-over; Byrne-c(p). 19-Last issue 2.40 6.00
3-8,10-18 3.00

NOTE: ***Austin*** *c-4i, 9i.* ***Elias*** *a-1, 3p, 4p, 7p, 10-12p, 15p, 18p, 19p.* ***Layton*** *c-19.*

HUMAN TARGET
DC Comics (Vertigo): Apr, 1999 - No. 4, July, 1999 ($2.95, limited series)

1-4-Milligan-s/Bradstreet-c/Biuković-a 3.00

Human Torch #12 © MAR

Humdinger #1 © NOVP

Hurricane Comics #1 © Cambridge House

TPB (2000, $12.95) new Bradstreet-c 12.95

HUMAN TARGET SPECIAL (TV)
DC Comics: Nov, 1991 ($2.00, 52 pgs., one-shot)

1 2.00

HUMAN TORCH, THE (Red Raven #1)(See All-Select, All Winners, Marvel Mystery, Men's Adventures, Mystic Comics (2nd series), Sub-Mariner, USA & Young Men)
Timely/Marvel Comics (TP 2,3/TCI 4-9/SePI 10/SnPC 11-25/CnPC 26-35/Atlas Comics (CPC 36-38)): No. 2, Fall, 1940 - No. 15, Spring, 1944; No. 16, Fall, 1944 - No. 35, Mar, 1949 (Becomes Love Tales #36 on); No. 36, April, 1954 - No. 38, Aug, 1954

GD2.0 FN6.0 VF8.0 NM9.4
2(#1)-Intro & Origin Toro; The Falcon, The Fiery Mask, Mantor the Magician, & Microman only app.; Human Torch by Burgos, Sub-Mariner by Everett begin (origin of each in text) 2240.00 6720.00 14,560.00 28,000.00
GD2.0 FN6.0 NM9.4
3(#2)-40 pg. H.T. story; H.T. & S.M. battle over who is best artist in text-Everett or Burgos 461.00 1383.00 5300.00
4(#3)-Origin The Patriot in text; last Everett Sub-Mariner; Sid Greene-a 381.00 1143.00 4000.00
5(#4)-The Patriot app; Angel x-over in Sub-Mariner (Summer, 1941); 1st Nazi war-c this title 300.00 900.00 3000.00
5-Human Torch battles Sub-Mariner (Fall, '41); 60 pg. story 435.00 1305.00 5000.00
6,9 200.00 600.00 1900.00
7-1st Japanese war-c 211.00 633.00 2000.00
8-Human Torch battles Sub-Mariner; 52 pg. story; Wolverton-a, 1 pg. 305.00 915.00 3200.00
10-Human Torch battles Sub-Mariner, 45 pg. story; Wolverton-a, 1 pg. 274.00 821.00 2600.00
11,13-15: 14-1st Atlas Globe logo (Winter, 1943-44; see All Winners #11 also) 163.00 490.00 1550.00
12-Classic-c 284.00 853.00 2700.00
16-20: 20-Last War issue 116.00 348.00 1100.00
21,22,24-30: 105.00 316.00 1000.00
23 (Sum/46)-Becomes Junior Miss 24? Classic Schomburg Robot-c 121.00 363.00 1150.00
31,32: 31-Namora x-over in Sub-Mariner (also #30); last Toro. 32-Sungirl, Namora app.; Sungirl-c 89.00 268.00 850.00
33-Capt. America x-over 92.00 276.00 875.00
34-Sungirl solo 82.00 245.00 775.00
35-Captain America & Sungirl app. (1949) 89.00 268.00 850.00
36-38(1954)-Sub-Mariner in all 84.00 253.00 800.00

NOTE: *Ayers Human Torch in 36(3). **Brodsky** c-25, 31-33?, 37, 38. **Burgos** c-36. **Everett** a-1-3, 27, 28, 30, 37, 38. **Powell** a-36(Sub-Mariner). **Schomburg** c-1-3, 5-8, 10-23. **Sekowsky** c-28, 34?, 35? **Shores** c-24, 26, 27, 29, 30. **Mickey Spillane** text 4-6. Bondage c-2, 12, 19.*

HUMAN TORCH, THE (Also see Avengers West Coast, Fantastic Four, The Invaders, Saga of the Original... & Strange Tales #101)
Marvel Comics Group: Sept, 1974 - No. 8, Nov, 1975

1: 1-8-r/stories from Strange Tales #101-108 1.85 5.50 15.00
2-8: 1st H.T. title since G.A. 7-vs. Sub-Mariner 1.10 3.30 9.00

NOTE: *Golden Age & Silver Age Human Torch-r #1-8. **Ayers** r-6, 7. **Kirby/Ayers** r-1-5, 8.*

HUMBUG (Satire by Harvey Kurtzman)
Humbug Publications: Aug, 1957 - No. 9, May, 1958; No. 10, June, 1958; No. 11, Oct, 1958

1-Wood-a (intro pgs. only) 28.00 83.00 220.00
2 13.00 39.00 105.00
3-9: 8-Elvis in Jailbreak Rock 11.00 33.00 90.00
10,11-Magazine format. 10-Photo-c 15.00 45.00 120.00
Bound Volume(#1-9)(extremely rare) 63.00 189.00 600.00

NOTE: ***Davis** a-1-11. **Elder** a-2-4, 6-9, 11. **Heath** a-2, 4-8, 10. **Jaffee** a-2, 4-9. **Kurtzman** a-11.*

HUMDINGER (Becomes White Rider and Super Horse #3 on?)
Novelty Press/Premium Group: May-June, 1946 - V2#2, July-Aug, 1947

1-Jerkwater Line, Mickey Starlight by Don Rico, Dink begin 35.00 105.00 280.00
2 15.00 45.00 120.00
3-6, V2#1,2 10.00 30.00 80.00

HUMONGOUS MAN
Alternative Press (Ikon Press): Sept, 1997 -Present ($2.25, B&W)

1-3-Stepp & Harrison-c/s/a. 2.25

HUMOR (See All Humor Comics)

HUMPHREY COMICS (Joe Palooka Presents...; also see Joe Palooka)
Harvey Publications: Oct, 1948 - No. 22, Apr, 1952

1-Joe Palooka's pal (r); (52 pgs.)-Powell-a 12.00 36.00 95.00
2,3: Powell-a 6.40 19.25 45.00
4-Boy Heroes app.; Powell-a 7.15 21.50 50.00
5-8,10: 5,6-Powell-a. 7-Little Dot app. 5.00 15.00 32.00
9-Origin Humphrey 6.40 19.25 45.00
11-22 4.65 14.00 28.00

HUNCHBACK OF NOTRE DAME, THE
Dell Publishing Co.: No. 854, Oct, 1957 (one shot)

Four Color 854-Movie, photo-c 12.50 37.50 150.00

HUNK
Charlton Comics: Aug, 1961 - No. 11, 1963

1 3.20 9.60 35.00
2-11 2.00 6.00 18.00

HUNTED (Formerly My Love Memoirs)
Fox Features Syndicate: No. 13, July, 1950 - No. 2, Sept, 1950

13(#1)-Used in **SOTI**, pg. 42 & illo. "Treating police contemptuously" (lower left); Hollingsworth bondage-c 35.00 105.00 280.00
2 15.00 43.00 120.00

HUNTER'S HEART
DC Comics: June, 1995 - No. 3, Aug, 1995 ($5.95, B&W, limited series)

1-3 2.40 6.00

HUNTRESS, THE (See All-Star Comics #69, Batman Family, Brave & the Bold #62, DC Super Stars #17, Detective #652, Infinity, Inc. #1, Sensation Comics #68 & Wonder Woman #271)
DC Comics: Apr, 1989 - No. 19, Oct, 1990 ($1.00, mature)

1-16: Staton-c/a(p) in all 2.00
17-19-Batman-c/stories 2.50

HUNTRESS, THE
DC Comics: June, 1994 - No. 4, Sept, 1994 ($1.50, limited series)

1-4-Netzer-c/a: 2-Batman app. 2.00

HURRICANE COMICS
Cambridge House: 1945 (52 pgs.)

1-(Humor, funny animal) 23.00 68.00 180.00

HYBRIDS
Continunity Comics: Jan, 1994 ($2.50, one-shot)

1-Neal Adams-c(p) & part-a(i); embossed-c. 2.50

HYBRIDS DEATHWATCH 2000
Continuity Comics: Apr, 1993 - No. 3, Aug, 1993 ($2.50)

0-(Giveaway)-Foil-c; Neal Adams-c(i) & plots (also #1,2) 2.50
1-3: 1-Polybagged w/card; die-cut-c. 2-Thermal-c. 3-Polybagged w/card; indestructible-c; Adams plot 2.50

HYBRIDS ORIGIN
Continuity Comics: 1993 - No. 5, Jan, 1994 ($2.50)

1-5: 2,3-Neal Adams-c. 4,5-Valeria the She-Bat app. Adams-c(i) 2.50

HYDE-25
Harris Publications: Apr, 1995 ($2.95, one-shot)

0-coupon for poster; r/Vampirella's 1st app. 3.00

HYDROMAN (See Heroic Comics)

HYPERKIND (See Razorline)
Marvel Comics: Sept, 1993 - No. 9, May, 1994 ($1.75/$1.95)

1-($2.50)-Foil embossed-c; by Clive Barker 2.50
2-9 2.00

HYPERKIND UNLEASED

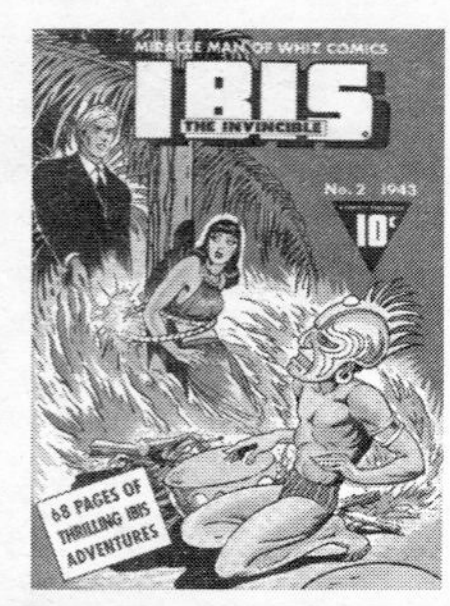

Ibis, The Invincible #2 © FAW

Icon #13 © Milestone Media

I Die at Midnight © Kyle Baker

GD2.0 FN6.0 NM9.4

Marvel Comics: Aug, 1994 ($2.95, 52 pgs., one-shot)

1 3.00

HYPER MYSTERY COMICS
Hyper Publications: May, 1940 - No. 2, June, 1940 (68 pgs.)

1-Hyper, the Phenomenal begins; Calkins-a 200.00 600.00 1900.00
2 105.00 316.00 1000.00

HYPERSONIC
Dark Horse Comics: Nov, 1997 - No. 4, Feb, 1998 ($2.95, limited series)

1-4: Abnett & White/Erskine-a 3.00

I AIM AT THE STARS (Movie)
Dell Publishing Co.: No. 1148, Nov-Jan/1960-61 (one-shot)

Four Color 1148-The Werner Von Braun Sty-photo-c 6.70 20.00 80.00

I AM COYOTE (See Eclipse Graphic Album Series & Eclipse Magazine #2)

I AM LEGEND
Eclipse Books: 1991 - No. 4, 1991 ($5.95, B&W, squarebound, 68 pgs.)

1-4: Based on 1954 novel 2.40 6.00

IBIS, THE INVINCIBLE (See Fawcett Miniatures, Mighty Midget & Whiz)
Fawcett Publications: 1942 (Fall?); #2, Mar.,1943; #3, Wint, 1945 - #5, Fall, 1946; #6, Spring, 1948

1-Origin Ibis; Raboy-c; on sale 1/2/43 179.00 537.00 1700.00
2-Bondage-c (on sale 2/5/43) 89.00 268.00 850.00
3-Wolverton-a #3-6 (4 pgs. each) 71.00 213.00 675.00
4-6: 5-Bondage-c 50.00 150.00 450.00
NOTE: ***Mac Raboy*** *c(p)-3-5.* ***Shaffenberger*** *c-6.*

I–BOTS (See Isaac Asimov's I-BOTS)

ICE AGE ON THE WORLD OF MAGIC: THE GATHERING (See Magic The Gathering)

ICE KING OF OZ, THE (See First Comics Graphic Novel #13)

ICEMAN (Also see The Champions & X-Men #94)
Marvel Comics Group: Dec, 1984 - No. 4, June, 1985 (Limited series)

1,2,4: Zeck covers on all 2.00
3-The Defenders, Champions (Ghost Rider) & the original X-Men x-over 3.00

ICON
DC Comics (Milestone): May, 1993 - No. 42, Feb, 1997($1.50/$1.75/$2.50)

1-($2.95)-Collector's Edition polybagged w/poster & trading card (direct sale only) 3.00
1-24,30-42: 9-Simonson-c. 15,16-Worlds Collide Pt. 4 & 11. 15-Superboy app. 16-Superman-c/story. 40-Vs. Blood Syndicate 2.50
25-($2.95, 52 pgs.) 3.00

IDAHO
Dell Publishing Co.: June-Aug, 1963 - No. 8, July-Sept, 1965

1 2.30 7.00 20.00
2-8: 5-7-Painted-c 1.50 4.50 12.00

IDEAL (... a Classical Comic) (2nd Series) (Love Romances No. 6 on)
Timely Comics: July, 1948 - No. 5, March, 1949 (Feature length stories)

1-Antony & Cleopatra 35.00 105.00 280.00
2-The Corpses of Dr. Sacotti 30.00 90.00 240.00
3-Joan of Arc; used in **SOTI**, pg. 308 'Boer War' 28.00 83.00 220.00
4-Richard the Lion-hearted; titled "...the World's Greatest Comics"; The Witness app. 40.00 120.00 360.00
5-Ideal Love & Romance; change to love; photo-c 18.00 53.00 140.00

IDEAL COMICS (1st Series) (Willie Comics No. 5 on)
Timely Comics (MgPC): Fall, 1944 - No. 4, Spring, 1946

1-Funny animal; Super Rabbit in all 22.00 66.00 175.00
2 12.50 37.50 100.00
3,4 12.00 36.00 95.00

IDEAL LOVE & ROMANCE (See Ideal, A Classical Comic)

IDEAL ROMANCE (Formerly Tender Romance)
Key Publ.: No. 3, April, 1954 - No. 8, Feb, 1955 (Diary Confessions No. 9 on)

3-Bernard Baily-c 8.65 26.00 60.00

GD2.0 FN6.0 NM9.4

4-8: 4,5-B. Baily-c 5.00 15.00 35.00

IDEALS (Secret Stories)
Ideals Publ., USA: 1981 (68 pgs, graphic novels, 7x10", stiff-c)

Captain America - Star Spangled Super Hero 2.50 7.50 25.00
Fantastic Four - Cosmic Quartet 2.50 7.50 25.00
Incredible Hulk - Gamma Powered Goliath 3.00 9.00 30.00
Spider-Man - World Famous Wall Crawler 3.60 10.80 36.00

I DIE AT MIDNIGHT (Vertigo V2K)
DC Comics (Vertigo): 2000 ($6.95, prestige format, one-shot)

1-Kyle Baker-s/a 6.95

IDOL
Marvel Comics (Epic Comics): 1992 - No. 3, 1992 ($2.95, mini-series, 52 pgs.)

Book 1-3 3.00

I DREAM OF JEANNIE (TV)
Dell Publishing Co.: Apr, 1965 - No. 2, Dec, 1966 (Photo-c)

1-Barbara Eden photo-c, each 15.00 45.00 180.00
2 11.30 34.00 135.00

I FEEL SICK
Slave Labor Graphics: Aug, 1999 - No. 2, May, 2000 ($3.95, limited series)

1,2-Jhonen Vasquez-s/a 4.00

ILLUMINATOR
Marvel Comics/Nelson Publ.: 1993 - No. 4, 1993 ($4.99/$2.95, 52 pgs.)

1,2-($4.99) Religious themed 5.00
3,4 3.00

ILLUSTRATED GAGS
United Features Syndicate: No. 16, 1940

Single Series 16 16.00 49.00 130.00

ILLUSTRATED LIBRARY OF..., AN (See Classics Illustrated Giants)

ILLUSTRATED STORIES OF THE OPERAS
Baily (Bernard) Publ. Co.: 1943 (16 pgs.; B&W) (25 cents) (cover-B&W & red)

nn-(Rare)(4 diff. issues)-Faust (part-r in Cisco Kid #1), nn-Aida, nn-Carmen; Baily-a, nn-Rigoleito 55.00 165.00 500.00

ILLUSTRATED STORY OF ROBIN HOOD & HIS MERRY MEN, THE (See Classics Giveaways, 12/44)

ILLUSTRATED TARZAN BOOK, THE (See Tarzan Book)

I LOVED (Formerly Rulah; Colossal Features Magazine No. 33 on)
Fox Features Syndicate: No. 28, July, 1949 - No. 32, Mar, 1950

28 10.00 30.00 70.00
29-32 7.00 21.00 48.00

I LOVE LUCY
Eternity Comics : 6/90 - No. 6, 1990;V2#1, 11/90 - No. 6, 1991 ($2.95, B&W, mini-series)

1-6: Reprints 1950s comic strip; photo-c 3.50
Book II #1-6: Reprints comic strip; photo-c 3.50
...In Full Color 1 (1991, $5.95, 52 pgs.)-Reprints I Love Lucy Comics #4,5,8,16; photo-c with embossed logo (2 versions exist, one with pgs. 18 & 19 reversed the other corrected) 2.40 6.00
...In 3-D 1 (1991, $3.95, w/glasses)-Reprints I Love Lucy Comics; photo-c sealed in plastic bag 5.00

I LOVE LUCY COMICS (TV) (Also see The Lucy Show)
Dell Publishing Co.: No. 535, Feb, 1954 - No. 35, Apr-June, 1962 (All have Lucille Ball photo-c)

Four Color 535(#1) 50.00 150.00 600.00
Four Color 559(#2, 5/54) 30.00 90.00 360.00
3 (8-10/54) - 5 18.35 55.00 220.00
6-10 14.00 42.00 170.00
11-20 10.50 31.00 125.00
21-35 8.00 24.00 95.00

I LOVE YOU
Fawcett Publications: June, 1950 (one-shot)

Impact #4 © WMG

Impulse #56 © DC

The Incredible Hulk #3 © MAR

GD2.0 FN6.0 NM9.4

1-Photo-c 14.00 41.00 110.00

LOVE YOU (Formerly In Love)
:harlton Comics: No. 7, 9/55 - No. 121, 12/76; No. 122, 3/79 - No. 130, 5/80

7-Kirby-c; Powell-a 8.15 24.50 90.00
8-10 3.20 9.60 35.00
1-16,18-20 2.80 8.40 28.00
7-(68 pg. Giant) 5.90 17.75 65.00
21-50: 26-No Torres-a 2.50 7.50 25.00
51-59 2.00 6.00 16.00
60-(1/66)-Elvis Presley line drawn c/story 13.50 40.00 150.00
61-85 1.50 4.50 12.00
86-110 1.00 3.00 8.00
11-130 5.00

LUSIPHER (Becomes Poison Elves, 1st series #8 on)
ulehide Graphics: 1991 - No. 7, 1992 (B&W, magazine size)

1-Drew Hayes-c/a/scripts 5.45 16.35 60.00
2,4,5 3.00 9.00 30.00
3-Low print run 6.80 20.50 75.00
6,7 2.00 6.00 18.00
'oison Elves: Requiem For An Elf (Sirius Ent., 6/96, $14.95, trade paperback)-
Reprints I, Lusiphur #1,2 as text, and 3-6 12.00

M A COP
lagazine Enterprises: 1954 - No. 3, 1954?

1(A-1 #111)-Powell-c/a in all 15.00 45.00 120.00
2(A-1 #126), 3(A-1 #128) 9.30 28.00 65.00

MAGE GRAPHIC NOVEL
nage Int.: 1984 ($6.95)(Advertised as Pacific Comics Graphic Novel #1)

1-The Seven Samuroid; Brunner-c/a 7.00

MAGES OF A DISTANT SOIL
nage Comics: Feb, 1997 ($2.95, B&W, one-shot)

1-Sketches by various 3.00

MAGES OF SHADOWHAWK (Also see Shadowhawk)
nage Comics: Sept, 1993 - No. 3, 1994 ($1.95, limited series)

1-3: Keith Giffen-c/a; Trencher app. 2.00

MAGE ZERO
nage Comics: 1993 (Received through mail w/coupons from Image books)

0-Savage Dragon, StormWatch, Shadowhawk, Strykeforce; 1st app. Troll; 1st app. McFarlane's Freak, Blotch, Sweat and Bludd 5.00

M DICKENS - HE'S FENSTER (TV)
ell Publishing Co.: May-July, 1963 - No. 2, Aug-Oct, 1963 (Photo-c)

1 4.60 13.75 55.00
2 4.55 13.65 50.00

MET A HANDSOME COWBOY
ell Publishing Co.: No. 324, Mar, 1951

'our Color 324 8.35 25.00 100.00

MMORTAL DOCTOR FATE, THE
C Comics: Jan, 1985 - No. 3, Mar, 1985 ($1.25, limited series)

1-3: 1-Simonson-c/a. 2-Giffen-c/a(p) 3.00

MMORTALIS (See Mortigan Goth: Immortalis)

MMORTAL II
nage Comics: Apr, 1997 - No. 5, Feb, 1998 ($2.50, B&W&Grey, lim. series)

1-5: 1-B&W w/ color pull-out poster 2.50

MPACT
:. C. Comics: Mar-Apr, 1955 - No. 5, Nov-Dec, 1955

1-Not code approved 14.00 41.00 150.00
2 9.00 27.00 100.00
3-5: 4-Crandall-a 7.00 22.00 80.00
IOTE: ***Crandall*** *a-1-4.* ***Davis*** *a-2-4; c-1-5.* ***Evans*** *a-1, 4, 5.* ***Ingels*** *a-in all.* ***Kamen*** *a-3.* ***:rigstein*** *a-1, 5.* ***Orlando*** *a-2, 5.*

MPACT
;emstone Publishing: Apr, 1999 - No. 5, Aug, 1999 ($2.50)

GD2.0 FN6.0 NM9.4

1-5-Reprints E.C. series 2.50

IMPACT CHRISTMAS SPECIAL
DC Comics (Impact Comics): 1991 ($2.50, 68 pgs.)

1-Gift of the Magi by Infantino/Rogers; The Black Hood, The Fly, The Jaguar, & The Shield stories 2.50

IMPOSSIBLE MAN SUMMER VACATION SPECTACULAR, THE
Marvel Comics: Aug, 1990; No. 2, Sept, 1991 ($2.00, 68 pgs.) (See Fantastic Four#11)

1-Spider Man, Quasar, Dr. Strange, She-Hulk, Punisher & Dr. Doom stories; Barry Crain, Guice-a; Art Adams-c(i) 2.00
2-Ka Zar & Thor app.; Cable Wolverine-c app. 2.00

IMPERIAL GUARD
Marvel Comics: Jan, 1997 - No. 3, Mar, 1997 ($1.95, limited series)

1-3: Augustyn-s in all; 1-Wraparound-c 2.00

IMPULSE (See Flash #92, 2nd Series for 1st app.) (Also see Young Justice)
DC Comics: Apr, 1995 - Present ($1.50/$1.75/$1.95/$2.25/$2.50)

1-Mark Waid scripts & Humberto Ramos-c/a(p) begin; brief retelling of origin 2.40 6.00
2-12: 9-XS from Legion (Impulse's cousin) comes to the 20th Century, returns to the 30th Century in #12. 10-Dead Heat Pt. 3 (cont'd in Flash #110). 11-Dead Heat Pt. 4 (cont'd in Flash #111); Johnny Quick dies. 3.00
13-25: 14-Trickster app. 17-Zatanna-c/app. 21-Legion-c/app. 22-Jesse Quick-c/app. 24-Origin; Flash app. 25-Last Ramos-a. 2.50
26-55: 26-Rousseau-a begins. 28-1st new Arrowette (see World's Finest #113). 30-Genesis x-over.41-Arrowette-c/app. 47-Superman-c/app. 50-Batman & Joker-c/app. Van Sciver-a begins. 52,53-Simonson art pages 2.50
56-62: 56-Young Justice app. 2.25
63-70: 63-Begin $2.50-c. 66-JLA,JSA-c/app. 68,69-Adam Strange, GL app. 2.50
#1,000,000 (11/98) John Fox app. 2.25
Annual 1 (1996, $2.95)-Legends of the Dead Earth; Parobeck-a 4.00
Annual 2 (1997, $3.95)-Pulp Heroes stories; Orbik painted-c 4.00
.../Atom Double-Shot 1(2/98, $1.95) Jurgens-s/Mhan-a 3.00
...: Bart Saves the Universe (4/99, $5.95) JSA app. 6.00
...Plus(9/97, $2.95) w/Gross Out (Scare Tactics)-c/app. 3.00
...Reckless Youth (1997, $14.95, TPB) r/Flash #92-94, Impulse #1-6 15.00

INCAL, THE
Marvel Comics (Epic): Nov, 1988 - No. 3, Jan, 1989 ($10.95/$12.95, mature)

1-3: Moebius-c/a in all; sexual content 14.00

INCOMPLETE DEATH'S HEAD (Also see Death's Head)
Marvel Comics UK: Jan, 1993 - No. 12, Dec, 1993 ($1.75, limited series)

1-($2.95, 56 pgs.)-Die-cut cover 3.00
2-11: 2-Re-intro original Death's Head. 3-Original Death's Head vs. Dragon's Claws 2.00
12-($2.50, 52 pgs.)-She Hulk app. 2.50

INCREDIBLE HULK, THE (See Aurora, The Avengers #1, The Defenders #1, Giant-Size..., Hulk, Marvel Collectors Item Classics, Marvel Comics Presents #26, Marvel Fanfare, Marvel Treasury Edition, Power Record Comics, Rampaging Hulk, She-Hulk & 2099 Unlimited)

INCREDIBLE HULK, THE
Marvel Comics: May, 1962 - No. 6, Mar, 1963; No. 102, Apr, 1968 - No. 474, Mar, 1999

GD2.0 FN6.0 VF8.0 NM9.4
1-Origin & 1st app. (skin is grey colored); Kirby pencils begin, end #5 600.00 1800.00 6000.00 15,000.00

GD2.0 FN6.0 NM9.4
2-1st green skinned Hulk; Kirby/Ditko-a 180.00 540.00 2700.00
3-Origin retold; 1st app. Ringmaster & Hercules (9/62) 118.00 354.00 1650.00
4,5: 4-Brief origin retold 111.00 332.00 1550.00
6-(3/63) Intro. Teen Brigade; all Ditko-a 154.00 462.00 2300.00
102-(4/68) (Formerly Tales to Astonish)-Origin retold; story continued from Tales to Astonish #101 20.50 61.00 225.00
103 8.15 24.50 90.00
104-Rhino app. 8.15 24.50 90.00
105-108: 105-1st Missing Link. 107-Mandarin app.(9/68). 108-Mandarin & Nick Fury app. (10/68). 5.90 17.75 65.00

The Incredible Hulk #181 © MAR

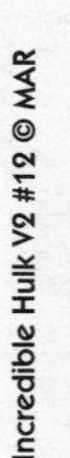
The Incredible Hulk #461 © MAR

The Incredible Hulk V2 #12 © MAR

GD2.0 FN6.0 NM9.4

109,110: 109-Ka-Zar app. 4.10 12.30 45.00
111-117: 117-Last 12¢ issue 3.20 9.60 35.00
118-Hulk vs. Sub-Mariner 3.45 10.35 38.00
119-121,123-125 2.50 7.50 25.00
122-Hulk battles Thing (12/69) 4.55 13.65 50.00
126-1st Barbara Norriss (Valkyrie) 2.80 8.40 28.00
127-139: 131-Hulk vs. Iron Man; 1st Jim Wilson, Hulk's new sidekick. 136-1st Xeron, The Star-Slayer 2.00 6.00 16.00
140-Written by Harlan Ellison; 1st Jarella, Hulk's love 2.30 7.00 20.00
141-1st app. Doc Samson (7/71) 3.20 9.60 35.00
142-144: 144-Last 15¢ issue 1.50 4.50 12.00
145-(52 pgs.)-Origin retold 2.00 6.00 18.00
146-160: 149-1st app. The Inheritor. 155-1st app. Shaper. 158-Warlock cameo(12/72) 1.10 3.30 9.00
161-The Mimic dies; Beast app. 1.85 5.50 15.00
162-1st app. The Wendigo (4/73); Beast app. 2.00 6.00 16.00
163-171,173-176: 163-1st app. The Gremlin. 164-1st Capt. Omen & Colonel John D. Armbruster. 166-1st Zzzax. 168-1st The Harpy; nudity panels of Betty Brant. 169-1st app. Bi-Beast.176-Warlock cameo (2 panels only); same date as Strange Tales #178 (6/74) 1.00 3.00 8.00
172-X-Men cameo; origin Juggernaut retold 2.30 7.00 20.00
177-1st actual death of Warlock (last panel only) 1.50 4.50 12.00
178-Rebirth of Warlock 1.75 5.25 14.00
179-No Warlock 1.00 2.80 7.00
180-(10/74)-1st app. Wolverine (cameo last pg.) 8.15 24.50 90.00
181-(11/74)-1st full Wolverine story; Trimpe-a 64.00 193.00 900.00
182-Wolverine cameo; see Giant-Size X-Men #1 for next app.; 1st Crackajack Jackson 7.25 21.75 80.00
183-199: 185-Death of Col. Armbruster 1.00 2.80 7.00
198,199, 201-203-(30¢-c variants, lim. distribution) 1.10 3.30 9.00
200-(25¢-c) Silver Surfer app.; anniversary issue 2.50 7.50 24.00
200-(30¢-c variant, limited distribution)(6/76) 3.25 9.75 36.00
201-220: 201-Conan swipe-c/sty. 212-1st app. The Constrictor 5.00
221-249: 227-Original Avengers app. 232-Capt. America x-over from C.A. #230. 233-Marvel Man app. 234-(4/79)-1st app. Quasar (formerly Marvel Man & changes name to Quasar). 243-Cage app. 4.00
250-Giant size; Silver Surfer app. 1.10 3.30 9.00
251-277,280-299: 271-Rocket Raccoon app. 272-Sasquatch & Wendigo app.; Wolverine & Alpha Flight cameo in flashback. 282-284-She-Hulk app. 293-F.F. app. 3.50
278,279-Most Marvel characters app. (Wolverine in both). 279-X-Men & Alpha Flight cameos 5.00
300-(11/84, 52 pgs.)-Spider-Man app in new black costume on-c & 2 pg. cameo 2.40 6.00
301-313: 312-Origin Hulk retold 3.00
314-Byrne-c/a begins, ends #319 4.00
315-319: 319-Bruce Banner & Betty Talbot wed 3.00
320-323,325,327-329 3.00
324-1st app. Grey Hulk since #1 (c-swipe of #1) 1.25 3.75 10.00
326-Grey vs. Green Hulk 4.00
330,331: 330-1st McFarlane ish (4/87); Thunderbolt Ross dies. 331-Grey Hulk series begins 1.85 5.50 15.00
332-334,336-339: 336,337-X-Factor app. 1.10 3.30 9.00
335-No McFarlane-a 4.00
340-Hulk battles Wolverine by McFarlane 2.40 7.35 22.00
341-346: 345-($1.50, 52 pgs.). 346-Last McFarlane issue 5.00
347-349,351-358,360-366: 347-1st app. Marlo 2.50
350-Hulk/Thing battle 5.00
359-Wolverine app. (illusion only) 2.50
367,372,377: 367-1st Dale Keown-a on Hulk (3/90). 372-Green Hulk app.;Keown-c/a. 377-1st all new Hulk; fluorescent-c; Keown-c/a 1.00 2.80 7.00
368-371,373-376: 368-Sam Kieth-c/a, 1st app. Pantheon. 369,370-Dale Keown-c/a. 370,371-Original Defenders app. 371,373-376: Keown-c/a. 376-Green vs. Grey Hulk 4.00
377-Fluorescent green logo 2nd printing 3.00
378,380,389: No Keown-a. 380-Doc Samson app. 2.50
379,381-388,390-393-Keown-a. 385-Infinity Gauntlet x-over. 389-Last $1.00-c. 392-X-Factor app. 393-($2.50, 72 pgs.)-30th anniversary issue; green foil stamped-c; swipes-c to #1; has pin-ups of classic battles; Keown-c/a 4.0
393-2nd printing 2.5
394-399: 394-No Keown-c/a; intro Trauma. 395,396-Punisher-c/stories; Keown-c/a. 397-Begin "Ghost of the Past" 4-part sty; Keown c/a. 398-Last Keown-c/ 2.0
400-($2.50, 68 pgs.)-Holo-grafx foil-c & r/TTA #63 3.0
400-416: 400-2nd print-Diff. color foil-c. 402-Return of Doc Samson 2.0
417-424: 417-Begin $1.50-c; Rick Jones' bachelor party; Hulk returns from "Future Imperfect"; bound-in trading card sheet. 418-(Regular edition)-Rick Jones marries Marlo; includes cameo apps of various Marvel characters as well as DC's Death & Peter David. 420-Death of Jim Wilson 2.0
418-($2.50)-Collector's Edition w/gatefold die-cut-c 2.5
425 ($2.25, 52 pgs.) 2.2
425 ($3.50, 52 pgs.)-Holographic-c 3.5
426-434, 436-442: 426-Begin $1.95-c. 427, 428-Man-Thing app. 431,432-Abomination app. 434-Funeral for Nick Fury. 436-Ghosts of the Future begin ends #440. 439-Hulk becomes Maestro, Avengers app. 440-Thor-c/app. 441,442-She-Hulk-c/app. 442-Molecule Man app. 2.0
435 ($2.50)-Rhino-app; excerpt from "What Savage Beast" 2.5
443,446-448: 443-Begin $1.50-c; re-app. of Hulk. 446-w/card insert. 447-Begin Deodato-c/a(p) 2.0
444,445: 444-Cable-c/app.; "Onslaught". 445-"Onslaught" 4.0
447-Variant cover 4.0
449-1st app. Thunderbolts 6.0
450-($2.95)-Thunderbolts app.; 2 stories; Heroes Reborn-c/app. 5.0
451-473: 455-X-Men-c/app. 460-Bruce Banner returns. 464-Silver Surfer-c/app. 466,467: Betty dies. 467-Last Peter David-s/Kubert-a. 468-Casey-s/Pulido-a begin 2.0
474-($2.99) Last issue; Abomination app. 4.0
#(-1) Flashback (7/97) Kubert-a 2.5
Special 1 (10/68, 25¢, 68 pg.)-New 51 pg. story, Hulk battles The Inhumans (early app.); Steranko-c. 8.15 24.50 90.0
Special 2 (10/69, 25¢, 68 pg.)-Origin retold 4.55 13.65 50.0
Special 3,4: 3-(1/71, 25¢, 68 pg.). 4-(1/72, 52pgs.) 2.00 6.00 16.0
Annual 5 (1976) 1.10 3.30 9.0
Annual 6-8 ('77-79)-7-Byrne/Layton-c/a; Iceman & Angel app. in book-length story. 8-Book-length Sasquatch-c/sty 2.40 6.0
Annual 9,12-17: 9('80). 12 ('83). 13('84). 14('85). 15('86). 16('90, $2.00, 68 pgs.)-She-Hulk app. 17(1991, $2.00)-Origin retold 3.0
Annual 10,11: 10 ('81). 11('82)-Doc Samson back-up by Miller(p)(5 pgs.); Spider-Man & Avengers app. Buckler-a(p) 3.5
Annual 18-20 ('92-'94 68 pgs.)-18-Return of the Defenders, Pt. I; no Keown-c/a 19-Bagged w/card 3.0
...'97 ($2.99) Pollina-c 3.0
...And Wolverine 1 (10/86, $2.50)-r/1st app. #180-181 1.25 3.75 10.0
...: Beauty and the Behemoth ('98, $19.95, TPB) r/Bruce & Betty stories 20.0
...Ground Zero ('95, $12.95) r/#340-346 13.0
...Hercules Unleashed (10/96, $2.50) David-s/Deodato-c/a 2.5
.../Sub-Mariner '98 Annual ($2.99) 3.0
...Versus Quasimodo 1 (3/83, one-shot)-Based on Saturday morning cartoon 4.0
...Vs. Superman 1 (7/99, $5.95, one-shot)-painted-c by Rude 6.0
...Versus Venom 1 (4/94, $2.50, one-shot)-Embossed-c; red foil logo 2.7

(Also see titles listed under **Hulk**)

NOTE: ***Adkins*** *a-111-116i.* ***Austin*** *a(i)-350, 351, 353, 354; c-302i, 350i.* ***Ayers*** *a-3-5i.* ***Buckler*** *a Annual 5; c-252.* ***John Buscema*** *c-202p.* ***Byrne*** *a-314-319p; c-314-316, 318, 319, 359, Annual 14i.* ***Colan*** *c-363.* ***Ditko*** *a-2i, 6, 249, Annual 2r(5), 3r, 9p; c-2i, 6, 235, 249.* ***Everett*** *c-133i.* ***Golden*** *c-248, 251.* ***Kane*** *c(p)-193, 194, 196, 198.* ***Dale Keown*** *a(p)-367, 369-377, 379, 381-388, 390-393, 395-398; c-369-377p, 381, 382p, 384, 385, 386, 387p, 388, 390p, 391-393, 395p, 396, 397p, 398.* ***Kirby*** *a-1-5p, Special 2, 3p, Annual 5p; c-1-5, Annual 5.* ***McFarlane*** *a-330-334p 336-339p, 340-343, 344-346p; c-330p, 340p, 341-343, 344p, 345, 346p.* ***Mignola*** *c-302, 305, 313.* ***Miller*** *c-258p, 261, 264, 268.* ***Mooney*** *a-230p, 287i, 288i.* ***Powell*** *a-Special 3r(2).* ***Romita*** *a Annual 17p.* ***Severin*** *a(i)-108-110, 131-133, 141-151, 153-155; c(i)-109, 110, 132, 142, 144-155* ***Simonson*** *c-283, 364-367.* ***Starlin*** *a-222p; c-217.* ***Staton*** *a(i)-187-189, 191-209.* ***Tuska*** *a-102i, 105i, 106i, 218p.* ***Williamson*** *a-310i; c-310i, 311i.* ***Wrightson*** *c-197.*

INCREDIBLE HULK (Vol. 2) (Formerly Hulk #1-11)
Marvel Comics: No. 12, Mar, 2000 - Present ($2.99, $1.99)

12-Jenkins-s/Garney & McKone-a 3.0
13,14-($1.99) Garney & Buscema-a 2.0
15-23: 15-Begin $2.25-c. 21-Maximum Security x-over 2.2

Incredible Science Fiction #33 © WMG

Indian Chief #4 © Western Printing

Inferior Five #6 © DC

GD2.0 FN6.0 NM9.4

..nnual 2000 ($3.50) Texeira-a/Jenkins-s; Avengers app. 3.50

..NCREDIBLE MR. LIMPET, THE (See Movie Classics)

..NCREDIBLE SCIENCE FICTION (Formerly Weird Science-Fantasy)
.. C. Comics: No. 30, July-Aug, 1955 - No. 33, Jan-Feb, 1956

..0,33: 33-Story-r/Weird Fantasy #18 34.00 102.00 375.00
..1-Williamson/Krenkel-a, Wood-a(2) 35.00 105.00 385.00
..2-Williamson/Krenkel-a 35.00 105.00 385.00
..OTE: ***Davis** a-30, 32, 33; c-30-32. **Krigstein** a-in all. **Orlando** a-30, 32, 33("Judgement Day" ..eprint). **Wood** a-30, 31, 33; c-33.*

..NCREDIBLE SCIENCE FICTION (Formerly Weird Science-Fantasy)
..uss Cochran/Gemstone Publ.: No. 8, Aug, 1994 - No. 11, May, 1995 ($2.00)

..8-11: Reprints #30-33 of E.C. series 2.50

..NDEPENDENCE DAY (Movie)
..larvel Comics: No. 0, June, 1996 - No. 2, Aug, 1996 ($1.95, limited series)

..0-Special Edition; photo-c 5.00
..0-2 2.00

..NDEPENDENT VOICES
..eregrine Entertainment: Sept, 1998 ($1.95, B&W)

..1-Sampler of Indy titles for CBLDF 2.00

..NDIANA JONES (Title series), **Dark Horse Comics**
..AND THE ARMS OF GOLD, 2/94 - 5/94 ($2.50) 1-4 2.50
..AND THE FATE OF ATLANTIS, 3/91 - 9/91 ($2.50) 1-4-Dorman painted-c on all; contain trading cards (#1 has a 2nd printing, 10/91) 2.50
..AND THE GOLDEN FLEECE, 6/94 - 7/94 ($2.50) 1,2 2.50
..AND THE IRON PHOENIX, 12/94 - 3/95 ($2.50) 1-4 2.50

..NDIANA JONES AND THE LAST CRUSADE
..larvel Comics: 1989 - No. 4, 1989 ($1.00, limited series, movie adaptation)

..1-4: Williamson-i assist 2.50
..1-(1989, $2.95, B&W mag., 80 pgs.) 4.00

..AND THE SHRINE OF THE SEA DEVIL: Dark Horse, 9/94 ($2.50, one shot)
..1-Gary Gianni-a 2.50
..AND THE SPEAR OF DESTINY: Dark Horse, 4/95 - 8/95 ($2.50) 1-4 2.50
..THUNDER IN THE ORIENT: Dark Horse, 9/93 - '94 ($2.50)
..1-6: Dan Barry story & art in all; 1-Dorman painted-c 2.50

..NDIANA JONES AND THE TEMPLE OF DOOM
..larvel Comics Group: Sept, 1984 - No. 3, Nov, 1984 (Movie adaptation)

..1-3-r/Marvel Super Special; Guice-a 2.50

..NDIAN BRAVES (Baffling Mysteries No. 5 on)
..ce Magazines: March, 1951 - No. 4, Sept, 1951

..1-Green Arrowhead begins, ends #3 11.00 33.00 90.00
..2 6.40 19.25 45.00
..3,4 5.00 15.00 35.00
..W. Reprint #1 (nd)-r/Indian Braves #4 1.75 5.25 14.00

..NDIAN CHIEF (White Eagle...) (Formerly The Chief, Four Color 290)
..ell Publ. Co.: No. 3, July-Sept, 1951 - No. 33, Jan-Mar, 1959 (All painted-c)

..3 3.65 11.00 40.00
..4-11: 6-White Eagle app. 3.00 9.00 32.00
..12-1st White Eagle(10-12/53)-Not same as earlier character 3.65 11.00 40.00
..13-29 2.50 7.50 24.00
..30-33-Buscema-a 2.50 7.50 25.00

..NDIAN CHIEF (See March of Comics No. 94, 110, 127, 140, 159, 170, 187)

..NDIAN FIGHTER, THE (Movie)
..ell Publishing Co.: No. 687, May, 1956 (one-shot)

..our Color 687-Kirk Douglas photo-c 7.50 22.50 90.00

..NDIAN FIGHTER
..outhful Magazines: May, 1950 - No. 11, Jan, 1952

..1 12.00 36.00 95.00
..2-Wildey-a/c(bondage) 8.65 26.00 60.00
..3-11: 3,4-Wildey-a 5.75 17.00 40.00

GD2.0 FN6.0 NM9.4

*NOTE: **Walter Johnson** c-1, 3, 4, 6. **Palais** a-10. **Stallman** a-7. **Wildey** a-2-4; c-2, 5.*

INDIAN LEGENDS OF THE NIAGARA (See American Graphics)

INDIANS
Fiction House Magazines (Wings Publ. Co.): Spring, 1950 - No. 17, Spring, 1953 (1-8: 52 pgs.)

1-Manzar The White Indian, Long Bow & Orphan of the Storm begin 28.00 83.00 220.00
2-Starlight begins 14.00 41.00 110.00
3-5: 5-17-Most-c by Whitman 12.00 36.00 95.00
6-10 10.00 30.00 75.00
11-17 9.30 28.00 65.00

INDIANS OF THE WILD WEST
I. W. Enterprises: Circa 1958? (no date) (Reprints)

9-Kinstler-c; Whitman-a; r/Indians #? 2.00 6.00 16.00

INDIANS ON THE WARPATH
St. John Publishing Co.: No date (Late 40s, early 50s) (132 pgs.)

nn-Matt Baker-c; contains St. John comics rebound. Many combinations possible 33.00 98.00 260.00

INDIAN TRIBES (See Famous Indian Tribes)

INDIAN WARRIORS (Formerly White Rider and Super Horse; becomes Western Crime Cases #9)
Star Publications: No. 7, June, 1951 - No. 8, Sept, 1951

7-White Rider & Superhorse continue; "Last of the Mohicans" serial begins; L.B. Cole-c 18.00 53.00 140.00
8-L. B. Cole-c 16.00 49.00 130.00
3-D 1(12/53, 25¢)-Came w/glasses; L. B. Cole-c 40.00 120.00 330.00
Accepted Reprint(nn)(inside cover shows White Rider & Superhorse #11)-r/cover to #7; origin White Rider &...;. L. B. Cole-c 6.40 19.25 45.00
Accepted Reprint #8 (nd); L.B. Cole-c (r-cover to #8) 6.40 19.25 45.00

INDOORS-OUTDOORS (See Wisco)

INDOOR SPORTS
National Specials Co.: nd (6x9", 64 pgs., B&W-r, hard-c)

nn-By Tad 5.00 15.00 35.00

INDUSTRIAL GOTHIC
DC Comics (Vertigo): Dec, 1995 - No. 5, Apr, 1996 ($2.50, limited series)

1-5: Ted McKeever-c/a/scripts 2.50

INFERIOR FIVE, THE (Inferior 5 #11, 12) (See Showcase #62, 63, 65)
National Periodical Publications (#1-10: 12¢): 3-4/67 - No. 10, 9-10/68; No. 11, 8-9/72 - No. 12, 10-11/72

1-(3-4/67)-Sekowsky-a(p); 4th app. 4.10 12.30 45.00
2-5: 2-Plastic Man, F.F. app. 4-Thor app. 2.50 7.50 25.00
6-9: 6-Stars DC staff 2.00 6.00 18.00
10-Superman x-over; F.F., Spider-Man & Sub-Mariner app. 2.50 7.50 24.00
11,12: Orlando-c/a; both r/Showcase #62,63 2.00 6.00 18.00

INFERNO
Caliber Comics: 1995 - No. 5 ($2.95, B&W)

1-5 3.00

INFERNO (See Legion of Super-Heroes)
DC Comics: Oct, 1997 - No. 4, Feb, 1998 ($2.50, limited series)

1-Immonen-s/c/a in all 4.00
2-4 3.00

INFINITY CRUSADE
Marvel Comics: June, 1993 - No. 6, Nov, 1993 ($2.50, limited series, 52 pgs.)

1-6: By Jim Starlin & Ron Lim 2.50

INFINITY GAUNTLET (The... #2 on; see Infinity Crusade, The Infinity War & Warlock & the Infinity Watch)
Marvel Comics: July, 1991 - No. 6, Dec, 1991 ($2.50, limited series)

1-6:Thanos-c/stories in all; Starlin scripts in all; 5,6-Ron Lim-c/a 2.50
TPB (4/99, $24.95) r/#1-6 24.95
*NOTE: **Lim** a-3p(part), 5p, 6p; c-5i, 6i. **Perez** a-1-3p, 4p(part); c-1(painted), 2-4, 5i, 6i.*

Infinity, Inc. #42 © DC

Inhumans V2 #12 © MAR

Interface #2 © James D. Hudnall

INFINITY, INC. (See All-Star Squadron #25)
DC Comics: Mar, 1984 - No. 53, Aug, 1988 ($1.25, Baxter paper, 36 pgs.)
1-Brainwave, Jr., Fury, The Huntress, Jade, Northwind, Nuklon, Obsidian, Power Girl, Silver Scarab & Star Spangled Kid begin 4.00
2-13,38-49,51-53: 2-Dr. Midnite, G.A. Flash, W. Woman, Dr. Fate, Hourman, Green Lantern, Wildcat app. 5-Nudity panels. 46,47-Millennium tie-ins 3.00
14-Todd McFarlane-a (5/85, 2nd full story) 1.10 3.30 9.00
15-37-McFarlane-a (20,23,24: 5 pgs. only; 33: 2 pgs.); 18-24-Crisis x-over. 21-Intro new Hourman & Dr. Midnight. 26-New Wildcat app. 31-Star Spangled Kid becomes Skyman. 32-Green Fury becomes Green Flame. 33-Origin Obsidian. 35-1st modern app. G.A. Fury 4.00
50 ($2.50, 52 pgs.) 3.00
Annual 1,2: 1(12/85)-Crisis x-over. 2('88, $2.00), Special 1 ('87, $1.50) 3.00
NOTE: **Kubert** r-4. **McFarlane** a-14-37p, Annual 1p; c(p)-14-19, 22, 25, 26, 31-33, 37, Annual 1. **Newton** a-12p, 13p(last work 4/85). **Tuska** a-11p. JSA app. 3-10.

INFINITY WAR, THE (Also see Infinity Gauntlet & Warlock and the Infinity...)
Marvel Comics: June, 1992 - No. 6, Nov, 1992 ($2.50, mini-series)
1-Starlin scripts, Lim-c/a(p), Thanos app. in all 2.50
2-6: All have wraparound gatefold covers 2.50

INFORMER, THE
Feature Television Productions: April, 1954 - No. 5, Dec, 1954
1-Sekowsky-a begins 10.50 32.00 85.00
2 7.85 23.50 55.00
3-5 7.00 21.00 48.00

IN HIS STEPS
Spire Christian Comics (Fleming H. Revell Co.): 1973, 1977 (39/49¢)
nn 1.00 2.80 7.00

INHUMANOIDS, THE (TV)
Marvel Comics (Star Comics): Jan, 1987 - No. 4, July 1987
1-4: Based on Hasbro toys 3.00

INHUMANS, THE (See Amazing Adventures, Fantastic Four #54 & Special #5, Incredible Hulk Special #1, Marvel Graphic Novel & Thor #146)
Marvel Comics Group: Oct, 1975 - No. 12, Aug, 1977
1: #1-4,6 are 25¢ issues 1.50 4.50 12.00
2-12: 9-Reprints Amazing Adventures #1,2('70). 12-Hulk app. 2.40 6.00
4,6-(30¢-c variants, limited distribution)(4,8/76) 1.10 3.30 9.00
Special 1(4/90, $1.50, 52 pgs.)-F.F. cameo 3.00
NOTE: **Buckler** c-2-4p, 5. **Gil Kane** a-5-7p; c-1p, 7p, 8p. **Kirby** a-9r. **Mooney** a-11i. **Perez** a-1-4p, 8p.

INHUMANS (Marvel Knights)
Marvel Comics: Nov, 1998 - No. 12, Oct, 1999 ($2.99, limited series)
1-Jae Lee-c/a; Paul Jenkins-s 10.00
1-($6.95) DF Edition; Jae Lee variant-c 7.00
2-Two covers by Lee and Darrow 4.00
3-12 3.00
TPB (10/00, $24.95) r/#1-12 24.95

INHUMANS (Volume 3)
Marvel Comics: Jun, 2000 - No. 4, Oct, 2000 ($2.99, limited series)
1-4-Ladronn-c/Pacheco & Marin-s. 1-3-Ladronn-a. 4-Lucas-a 3.00

INHUMANS: THE GREAT REFUGE
Marvel Comics: May, 1995 ($2.95, one-shot)
1 3.00

INKY & DINKY (See Felix's Nephews...)

IN LOVE (...Magazine on-c; I Love You No. 7 on)
Mainline/Charlton No. 5 (5/55)-on: Aug-Sept, 1954 - No. 6, July, 1955 ('Adult Reading' on-c)
1-Simon & Kirby-a; book-length novel in all issues 38.00 113.00 300.00
2,3-S&K-a. 3-Last pre-code (12-1/54-55) 22.00 66.00 175.00
4-S&K-a.(Rare) 22.00 66.00 175.00
5-S&K-c only 10.00 30.00 70.00
6-No S&K-a 6.40 19.25 45.00

INNOVATION SPECTACULAR
Innovation Publishing: 1991 - No. 2, 1991 ($2.95, squarebound, 100 pgs.)
1,2: Contains rebound comics w/o covers 3.0

INNOVATION SUMMER FUN SPECIAL
Innovation Publishing: 1991 ($3.50, B&W/color, squarebound)
1-Contains rebound comics (Power Factory) 3.5

INSANE
Dark Horse Comics: Feb, 1988 - No. 2 ($1.75, B&W)
1,2: 1-X-Men, Godzilla parodies. 2-Concrete 2.0

INSANE CLOWN POSSE
Chaos Comics: June, 1999 - No. 3, Nov, 1999 ($2.95)
1-3-McCann-s 4.0
TPB ('00, $8.95) r/#1-3 8.9

INSANE CLOWN POSSE: THE PENDULUM
Chaos Comics: Jan, 2000 - No. 12 ($2.95)
1-6-($5.95) polybagged w/CD 5.9

IN SEARCH OF THE CASTAWAYS (See Movie Comics)

INSIDE CRIME (Formerly My Intimate Affair)
Fox Features Syndicate (Hero Books): No. 3, July, 1950 - No. 2, Sept, 1950
3-Wood-a (10 pgs.); L. B. Cole-c 28.00 84.00 225.0
2-Used in **SOTI**, pg. 182,183; r/Spook #24 22.00 66.00 175.0
nn(no publ. listed, nd) 9.30 28.00 65.0

INSPECTOR, THE (TV) (Also see The Pink Panther)
Gold Key: July, 1974 - No. 19, Feb, 1978
1 2.50 7.50 25.0
2-5 1.85 5.50 15.0
6-9 1.50 4.50 12.0
10-19: 11-Reprints 1.00 2.80 7.0

INSPECTOR GILL OF THE FISH POLICE (See Fish Police)

INSPECTOR WADE
David McKay Publications: No. 13, May, 1938
Feature Books 13 19.00 57.00 225.0

INSTANT PIANO
Dark Horse Comics: Aug, 1994 - No. 4, Feb, 1995 ($3.95, B&W, bimonthly, mature)
1-4 4.0

INTERFACE
Marvel Comics (Epic Comics): Dec, 1989 - No. 8, Dec, 1990 ($1.95, mature, coated paper)
1-8: Cont. from 1st ESPers series; painted-c/a 2.2
Espers: Interface TPB ('98, $16.95) r/#1-6 17.0

INTERNATIONAL COMICS (...Crime Patrol No. 6)
E. C. Comics: Spring, 1947 - No. 5, Nov-Dec, 1947
1-Schaffenberger-a begins, ends #4 55.00 165.00 520.0
2 41.00 123.00 370.0
3-5 39.00 116.00 310.0

INTERNATIONAL CRIME PATROL (Formerly International Comics #1-5; becomes Crime Patrol No. 7 on)
E. C. Comics: No. 6, Spring, 1948
6-Moon Girl app. 55.00 165.00 525.0

IN THE DAYS OF THE MOB (Magazine)
Hampshire Dist. Ltd. (National): Fall, 1971 (B&W)
1-Kirby-a; John Dillinger wanted poster inside 7.65 23.00 85.0

IN THE PRESENCE OF MINE ENEMIES
Spire Christian Comics/Fleming H. Revell Co.: 1973 (35/49¢)
nn 1.00 2.80 7.0

INTIMATE
Charlton Comics: Dec, 1957 - No. 3, May, 1958
1 4.65 14.00 28.0
2,3 4.00 10.00 20.0

INTIMATE CONFESSIONS (See Fox Giants)

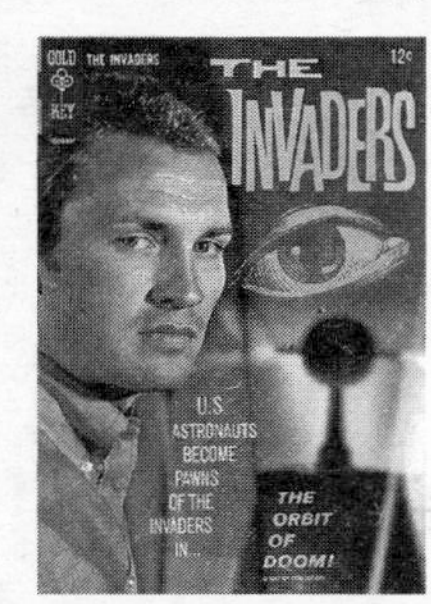

The Invaders (TV) #2 © QM Productions

The Invaders #19 © MAR

The Invisibles #16 © Grant Morrison

GD2.0 FN6.0 NM9.4

TIMATE CONFESSIONS
ealistic Comics: July-Aug, 1951 - No. 7, Aug, 1952; No. 8, Mar, 1953 (All inted-c)

	GD2.0	FN6.0	NM9.4
-Kinstler-c/a; c/Avon paperback #222	74.00	221.00	700.00
	20.00	60.00	160.00
-c/Avon paperback #250; Kinstler-c/a	23.00	68.00	180.00
-6,8: 4-c/Avon paperback #304; Kinstler-c. 6-c/Avon paperback #120. 8-c/Avon paperback #375; Kinstler-a	20.00	60.00	160.00
-Spanking panel	20.00	60.00	160.00

TIMATE CONFESSIONS
W. Enterprises/Super Comics: 1964

V. Reprint #9,10, Super Reprint #10,12,18	2.00	6.00	16.00

TIMATE LOVE
andard Comics: No. 5, 1950 - No. 28, Aug, 1954

-8: 6-8-Severin/Elder-a	7.85	23.50	55.00
	4.65	14.00	28.00
)-Jane Russell, Robert Mitchum photo-c	9.30	28.00	65.00
1-18,20,23,25,27,28	4.00	11.00	22.00
),21,22,24,26-Toth-a	5.50	16.50	38.00

*TE: **Celardo** a-8, 10. **Colletta** a-23. **Moreira** a-13(2). Photo-c-6, 7, 10, 12, 14, 15, 18-20, 24, 27.*

TIMATE SECRETS OF ROMANCE
ar Publications: Sept, 1953 - No. 2, Apr, 1954

,2-L. B. Cole-c	19.00	56.00	150.00

TRIGUE
uality Comics Group: Jan, 1955

-Horror; Jack Cole reprint/Web of Evil	31.00	94.00	250.00

TRIGUE
age Comics: Aug, 1999 - Present ($2.50/$2.95)

,2: 1-Two covers (Andrews, Wieringo); Shum-s/Andrews-a	2.50
-($2.95)	2.95

TRUDER
R, Inc.: 1990 - No. 10, 1991 ($2.95, 44 pgs.)

-10	3.00

VADERS, THE (TV)
old Key: Oct, 1967 - No. 4, Oct, 1968 (All have photo-c)

-Spiegle-a in all	10.00	30.00	120.00
-4	6.70	20.00	80.00

VADERS, THE (Also see The Avengers #71 & Giant-Size Invaders)
arvel Comics Group: August, 1975 - No. 40, May, 1979; No. 41, Sept, 1979

-Captain America & Bucky, Human Torch & Toro, & Sub-Mariner begin; cont'd. from Giant Size Invaders #1; #1-7 are 25¢ issues	2.80	8.40	28.00
-5: 2-1st app. Brain-Drain. 3-Battle issue; Cap vs. Namor vs. Torch; intro U-Man	1.50	4.50	12.00
-10: 6,7-(Regular 25¢ edition). 6-(7/76) Liberty Legion app. 7-Intro Baron Blood & intro/1st app. Union Jack; Human Torch origin retold. 8-Union Jack-c/story. 9-Origin Baron Blood. 10-G.A. Capt. America-r/C.A #22	1.25	3.75	10.00
,7-(30¢-c variant, limited distribution)	1.85	5.50	15.00
-19: 11-Origin Spitfire; intro The Blue Bullet. 14-1st app. The Crusaders. 16-Re-intro The Destroyer. 17-Intro Warrior Woman. 18-Re-intro The Destroyer w/new origin. 19-Hitler-c/story		2.40	6.00
)-Reprints origin/1st app. Sub-Mariner from Motion Picture Funnies Weekly with color added & brief write-up about MPFW; 1st app. new Union Jack II	1.25	3.75	10.00
-(Regular 30¢ edition)-r/Marvel Mystery #10 (battle issue)			5.00
-(35¢-c variant, limited distribution)	1.00	3.00	8.00
2-30,34-40: 22-New origin Toro. 24-r/Marvel Mystery #17 (team-up issue; all-r). 25-All new-a begins. 28-Intro new Human Top & Golden Girl. 29-Intro Teutonic Knight. 34-Mighty Destroyer joins. 35-The Whizzer app.			5.00
-33: 31-Frankenstein-c/sty. 32,33-Thor app.	1.00	2.80	7.00
-Double size last issue	1.10	3.30	9.00
nual 1 (9/77)-Schomburg, Rico stories (new); Schomburg-c/a (1st for Marvel in 30 years); Avengers app.; re-intro The Shark & The Hyena	1.85	5.50	15.00

*NOTE: **Buckler** a-5. **Everett** r-20('39), 21(1940), 24, Annual 1. **Gil Kane** c(p)-13, 17, 18, 20-27. **Kirby** c(p)-3-12, 14-16, 32, 33. **Mooney** a-5i, 16, 22. **Robbins** a-1-4, 6-9, 10(3 pg.), 11-15, 17-21, 23, 25-28; c-28.*

INVADERS (See Namor, the Sub-Mariner #12)
Marvel Comics Group: May, 1993 - No. 4, Aug, 1993 ($1.75, limited series)

1-4	2.00

INVADERS FROM HOME
DC Comics (Piranha Press): 1990 - No. 6, 1990 ($2.50, mature)

1-6	2.50

INVASION
DC Comics: Holiday, 1988-'89 - No. 3, Jan, 1989 ($2.95, lim. series, 84 pgs.)

1-3:1-McFarlane/Russell-a. 2-McFarlane/Russell & Giffen/Gordon-a	3.00

INVINCIBLE FOUR OF KUNG FU & NINJA
Leung Publications: April, 1988 - No. 6, 1989 ($2.00)

1-($2.75)	2.75
2-6: 2-Begin $2.00-c	2.00

INVISIBLE BOY (See Approved Comics)

INVISIBLE MAN, THE (See Superior Stories #1 & Supernatural Thrillers #2)

INVISIBLE PEOPLE
Kitchen Sink Press: 1992 (B&W, lim. series)

Book One: Sanctum; Book Two: "The Power": Will Eisner-s/a in all	2.00
Book Three: "Mortal Combat"	4.00
Hardcover ($34.95)	34.95
TPB (DC Comics, 9/00, $12.95) reprints series	13.00

INVISIBLES, THE (1st Series)
DC Comics (Vertigo): Sept, 1994 - No. 25, Oct, 1996 ($1.95/$2.50, mature)

1-($2.95, 52 pgs.)-Intro King Mob, Ragged Robin, Boy, Lord Fanny & Dane (Jack Frost); Grant Morrison scripts in all	6.00
2-8: 4-Includes bound-in trading cards. 5-1st app. Orlando; brown paper-c	4.00
9-25: 10-Intro Jim Crow. 13-15-Origin Lord Fanny. 19-Origin King Mob; polybagged. 20-Origin Boy. 21-Mister Six revealed. 25-Intro Division X	2.50
Say You Want A Revolution (1996, $17.50, TPB)-r/#1-8	18.00

*NOTE: **Buckingham** a-25p. **Rian Hughes** c-1, 5. **Phil Jimenez** a-17p-19p. **Paul Johnson** a-16, 21. **Sean Phillips** c-2-4, 6-25. **Weston** a-10p. **Yeowell** a-1p-4p, 22p-24p.*

INVISIBLES, THE (2nd Series)
DC Comics (Vertigo): V2#1, Feb, 1997 - No. 22, Feb, 1999 ($2.50, mature)

1-Intro Jolly Roger; Grant Morrison scripts, Phil Jimenez-a, & Brian Bolland-c begins	4.00
2-22: 9,14-Weston-a	2.50
Bloody Hell in America TPB ('98, $12.95) r/#1-4	13.00
Counting to None TPB ('99, $19.95) r/#5-13	20.00
Kissing Mr. Quimper TPB ('00, $19.95) r/#14-22	20.00

INVISIBLES, THE (3rd Series) (Issue #'s go in reverse from #12 to #1)
DC Comics (Vertigo): V3#12, Apr, 1999 - No. 1, June, 2000 ($2.95, mature)

1-12-Bolland-c; Morrison-s on all. 1-Quitely-a. 2-4-Art by various. 5-8-Phillips-a. 9-12-Phillip Bond-a.	3.00

INVISIBLE SCARLET O'NEIL (Also see Famous Funnies #81 & Harvey Comics Hits #59)
Famous Funnies (Harvey): Dec, 1950 - No. 3, Apr, 1951
(2-3 pgs. of Powell-a in each issue.)

1	14.00	41.00	110.00
2,3	10.00	30.00	80.00

IRON CORPORAL, THE (See Army War Heroes #22)
Charlton Comics: No. 23, Oct, 1985 - No. 25, Feb, 1986

23-25: Glanzman-a(r)	4.00

IRON FIST (See Deadly Hands of Kung Fu, Marvel Premiere & Power Man)
Marvel Comics: Nov, 1975 - No. 15, Sept, 1977

1-Iron Fist battles Iron Man (#1-6: 25¢)	3.20	9.60	35.00
2	2.50	7.50	23.00
3-10: 4-6-(Regular 25¢ edition)(4-6/76). 8-Origin retold			

Iron Fist #2 © MAR

Iron Man #110 © MAR

Iron Man #308 © MAR

	GD2.0	FN6.0	NM9.4
	2.00	6.00	16.00
4-6-(30¢-c variant, limited distribution)	2.50	7.50	24.00
11-13: 12-Capt. America app.	1.25	3.75	10.00
14-1st app. Sabretooth (8/77)(see Power Man)	10.00	30.00	110.00
14-(35¢-c variant, limited distribution)	18.00	54.00	200.00
15-(Regular 30¢ ed.) X-Men app., Byrne-a	4.10	12.30	45.00
15-(35¢-c variant, limited distribution)	5.90	17.75	65.00

NOTE: ***Adkins** a-8p, 10i, 13i; c-8i. **Byrne** a-1-15p; c-8p, 15p. **G. Kane** c-4-6p. **McWilliams** a-1i.*

IRON FIST
Marvel Comics: Sept, 1996 - No. 2, Oct, 1996 ($1.50, limited series)

1,2 — 3.00

IRON FIST
Marvel Comics: Jul, 1998 - No. 3, Sept, 1998 ($2.50, limited series)

1-3: Jurgens-s/Guice-a — 2.50

IRON FIST: WOLVERINE
Marvel Comics: Nov, 2000 - No. 4, Feb, 2001 ($2.99, limited series)

1-4-Igle-c/a; Kingpin app. 2-Iron Man app. 3,4-Capt. America app. — 3.00

IRONHAND OF ALMURIC (Robert E. Howard's...)
Dark Horse Comics: Aug, 1991 - No. 4, 1991 ($2.00, B&W, mini-series)

1-4: 1-Conrad painted-c — 2.00

IRON HORSE (TV)
Dell Publishing Co.: March, 1967 - No. 2, June, 1967

1,2-Dale Robertson photo covers on both — 2.00 6.00 18.00

IRONJAW (Also see The Barbarians)
Atlas/Seaboard Publ.: Jan, 1975 - No. 4, July, 1975

1,2-Neal Adams-c. 1-1st app. Iron Jaw; Sekowsky-a(p); Fleisher-s — 5.00
3,4-Marcos. 4-Origin — 4.00

IRON LANTERN
Marvel Comics (Amalgam): June, 1997 ($1.95, one-shot)

1-Kurt Busiek-s/Paul Smith & Al Williamson-a — 2.00

IRON MAN (Also see The Avengers #1, Giant-Size..., Marvel Collectors Item Classics, Marvel Double Feature, Marvel Fanfare & Tales of Suspense #39)
Marvel Comics: May, 1968 - No. 332, Sept, 1996

	GD2.0	FN6.0	NM9.4
1-Origin; Colan-c/a(p); story continued from Iron Man & Sub-Mariner #1	40.00	120.00	475.00
2	13.50	40.00	150.00
3	6.80	20.50	75.00
4,5	5.45	16.35	60.00
6-10: 9-Iron Man battles green Hulk-like android	4.55	13.65	50.00
11-15: 15-Last 12¢ issue	3.20	9.60	35.00
16-20	2.50	7.50	25.00
21-24,26-30: 22-Death of Janice Cord. 27-Intro Fire Brand	2.00	6.00	18.00
25-Iron Man battles Sub-Mariner	2.40	7.35	22.00
31-42: 33-1st app. Spymaster. 35-Nick Fury & Daredevil x-over. 42-Last 15¢ issue	2.00	6.00	16.00
43-Intro The Guardsman; 25¢ giant (52 pgs.)	2.30	7.00	20.00
44-46,48-50: 43-Giant-Man back-up by Ayers. 44-Ant-Man by Tuska. 46-The Guardsman dies. 50-Princess Python app.	1.75	5.25	14.00
47-Origin retold; Barry Smith-a(p)	2.00	6.00	18.00
51-53: 53-Starlin part pencils	1.25	3.75	10.00
54-Iron Man battles Sub-Mariner; 1st app. Moondragon (1/73) as Madame MacEvil; Everett part-c	2.40	7.35	22.00
55-1st app. Thanos (cameo), Drax the Destroyer, Mentor, Starfox & Kronos (2/73); Starlin-c/a	8.15	24.50	90.00
56-Starlin-a	2.00	6.00	18.00
57-65,67-70: 59-Firebrand returns. 65-Origin Dr. Spectrum. 67-Last 20¢ issue. 68-Sunfire & Unicorn app.; origin retold; Starlin-c	1.25	3.75	10.00
66-Iron Man vs. Thor.	1.50	4.50	12.00
71-84: 72-Cameo portraits of N. Adams. 73-Rename Stark Industries to Stark International; Brunner. 76-r/#9.	1.00	3.00	8.00
85-88-(Regular 25¢ editions): 86-1st app. Blizzard. 87-Origin Blizzard. 88-Thanos app.	1.00	2.80	7.00
85-88-(30¢-c variants, limited distribution)(4-8/76)	1.25	3.75	10.00

	GD2.0	FN6.0	NM9.4
89-99: 89-Daredevil app.; last 25¢ issue. 96-1st app. new Guardsman	1.00	2.80	7.0
100-(7/77)-Starlin-c	1.85	5.50	15.0
101-117: 101-Intro DreadKnight. 109-1st app. new Crimson Dynamo; 1st app. Vanguard. 110-Origin Jack of Hearts retold; death of Count Nefaria. 114-Avengers app.		2.40	6.0
102-(35¢-c variant, limited dist.)(9/77)	1.10	3.30	9.0
118-Byrne-a(p); 1st app. Jim Rhodes	1.00	3.00	8.0
119-127: 120,121-Sub-Mariner x-over. 122-Origin. 123-128-Tony Stark treated for alcohol problem. 125-Ant-Man app.		2.40	6.0
128-Classic Tony Stark alcoholism cover	1.00	3.00	8.0
129,130,133-149			4.0
131,132-Hulk x-over			5.0
150-Double size			5.0
151-168: 152-New armor. 161-Moon Knight app. 167-Tony Stark alcohol problem resurfaces			3.0
169-New Iron Man (Jim Rhodes replaces Tony Stark)			5.0
170,171			4.0
172-199: 172-Captain America x-over. 186-Intro Vibro. 190-Scarlet Witch app. 191-198-Tony Stark returns as original Iron Man. 192-Both Iron Men battle			3.0
200-(11/85, $1.25, 52 pgs.)-Tony Stark returns as new Iron Man (red & white armor) thru #230			4.0
201-213,215-224: 213-Intro new Dominic Fortune			2.5
214,225,228,231,234,247: 214-Spider-Woman app. in new black costume (1/87 225-Double size ($1.25). 228-vs. Capt. America. 231-Intro new Iron Man. 234-Spider-Man x-over. 247-Hulk x-over			3.0
226,227,229,230,232,233,235-243,245,246,248,249: 233-Ant-Man app. 243-Tony Stark loses use of legs			2.5
244-($1.50, 52 pgs.)-New Armor makes him walk			3.0
250-($1.50, 52 pgs.)-Dr. Doom-c/story			3.0
251-274,276-281,283,285-287,289,291-299: 258-277-Byrne scripts. 271-Fin Fang Foom app. 276-Black Widow-c/story; last $1.00-c. 281-1st app. ;War Machine (cameo). 283-2nd full app. War Machine			2.0
275-($1.50, 52 pgs.)			3.0
282-1st full app. War Machine (7/92)			4.0
284-Death of Iron Man (Tony Stark)			4.0
288-($2.50, 52pg.)-Silver foil stamped-c; Iron Man's 350th app. in comics			3.0
290-($2.95, 52pg.)-Gold foil stamped-c; 30th ann.			3.0
300-($3.95, 68 pgs.)-Collector's Edition w/embossed foil-c; anniversary issue; War Machine-c/story			4.0
300-($2.50, 68 pgs.)-Newsstand Edition			2.5
301-303: 302-Venom-c/story (cameo #301)			2.0
304-316,318-324,326-331: 304-Begin $1.50-c; bound-in trading card sheet; Thunderstrike-c/story. 310-Orange logo. 312-w/bound-in Power Ranger Card. 319-Prologue to "The Crossing." 326-New Tony Stark; Pratt-c. 330-War Machine & Stockpile app; return of Morgan Stark			2.0
310,325: 310 ($2.95)-Polybagged w/ 16 pg. Marvel Action Hour preview & acetate print; white logo. 325-($2.95)-Wraparound-c			3.0
317 ($2.50)-Flip book			2.5
332-Onslaught x-over			3.0
Special 1 (8/70)-Sub-Mariner x-over; Everett-c	3.00	9.00	30.0
Special 2 (11/71, 52 pgs.)-r/TOS #81,82,91 (all-r)	1.85	5.50	15.0
Annual 3 (1976)-Man-Thing app.	1.00	2.80	7.0
King Size 4 (8/77)-The Champions (w/Ghost Rider) app.; Newton-a(i)			5.0
Annual 5 ('82) New-a			4.0
Annual 6-15: ('83-'94) 6-New Iron Man (J. Rhodes) app. 8-X-Factor app. 10-Atlantis Attacks x-over; P. Smith-a; Layton/Guice-a; Sub-Mariner app. 11-(1990)-Origin of Mrs. Arbogast by Ditko (p&i). 12-1 pg. origin recap; Ant-Man back-up story. 13-Darkhawk & Avengers West Coast app.; Colan/Williamson-a. 14-Bagged w/card			3.0
Manual 1 (1993, $1.75)-Operations handbook			2.0
Graphic Novel: Crash (1988, $12.95, Adults, 72 pgs)-Computer generated art & color; violence & nudity			13.0
...Collector's Preview 1(11/94, $1.95)-wraparound-c; text & illos-no comics			2.0
...Vs. Dr. Doom (12/94, $12.95)-r/#149-150, 249,250. Julie Bell-c			13.0

NOTE: ***Austin** c-105i, 109-111i, 151i. **Byrne** a-118p; c-109p, 197, 253. **Colan** a-1p, 253, Speci 1p(3); c-1p. **Craig** a-1i, 2-4, 5-13i, 14, 15-19i, 24p, 25p, 26-28i; c-2-4. **Ditko** a-160p. **Everett** c-2 **Guice** a-233-241p. **G. Kane** c(p)-52-54, 63, 67, 72-75, 77-79, 88, 98. **Kirby** a-Special 1p; c-13, 80p, 90, 92-95. **Mooney** a-40i, 43i, 47i. **Perez** c-103p. **Simonson** c-Annual 8. **B. Smith** a-232p,*

Iron Man V3 #2 © MAR

I Spy #2 © GK

It Really Happened #3 © STD

3i; c-232. **P. Smith** a-159p, 245p, Annual 10p; c-159. **Starlin** a-53p(part), 55p, 56p; c-55p, 160, 3. **Tuska** a-5-13p, 15-23p, 24i, 32p, 38-46p, 48-54p, 57-61p, 63-69p, 70-72p, 78p, 86-92p, 95-5p, Annual 4p. **Wood** a-Special 1i.

ON MAN (The Invincible...) (Volume Two)
rvel Comics: Nov, 1996 - No. 13, Nov, 1997 ($2.95/$1.95/$1.99)
roduced by WildStorm Productions)

	GD2.0	FN6.0	NM9.4
#1-3-Heroes Reborn begins; Scott Lobdell scripts & Whilce Portacio-c/a begin; new origin Iron Man & Hulk. 2-Hulk app. 3-Fantastic Four app.			4.00
-Variant-c			5.00
-11: 4-Two covers. 6-Fantastic Four app.; Industrial Revolution; Hulk app. 7-Return of Rebel. 11-($1.99) Dr. Doom-c/app.			3.00
-($2.99) "Heroes Reunited"-pt. 3; Hulk-c/app.			3.50
-($1.99) "World War 3"-pt. 3, x-over w/Image			3.00

ON MAN (The Invincible...) (Volume Three)
rvel Comics: Feb, 1998 - Present ($2.99/$1.99/$2.25)

	GD2.0	FN6.0	NM9.4
#1-($2.99)-Follows Heroes Return; Busiek scripts & Chen-c/a begin; Deathsquad app.			5.00
-Alternate Ed.	1.00	3.00	8.00
-12: 2-Two covers. 6-Black Widow-c/app. 7-Warbird-c/app. 8-Black Widow app. 9-Mandarin returns			3.00
-($2.99) battles the Controller			3.50
-24, 26-28: 14-Fantastic Four-c/app.			2.50
-($2.99) Iron Man and Warbird battle Ultimo; Avengers app.			3.00
-37: 29-Begin $2.25-c. 35-Maximum Security x-over; FF-c/app.			2.25
Captain America '98 Annual ($3.50) vs. Modok			3.50
99 Annual ($3.50)			3.50
00 Annual ($3.50)			3.50

ON MAN & SUB-MARINER
rvel Comics Group: Apr, 1968 (12¢, one-shot) (Pre-dates Iron Man #1 & b-Mariner #1)

	GD2.0	FN6.0	NM9.4
-Iron Man story by Colan/Craig continued from Tales of Suspense #99 & continued in Iron Man #1; Sub-Mariner story by Colan continued from Tales to Astonish #101 & continued in Sub-Mariner #1; Colan/Everett-c	13.50	40.00	150.00

ON MAN: BAD BLOOD
rvel Comics: Sept, 2000 - No. 4, Dec, 2000 ($2.99, limited series)

	GD2.0	FN6.0	NM9.4
-4-Micheline-s/Layton-a			3.00

ON MAN: THE IRON AGE
rvel Comics: Aug, 1998 - No. 2, Sept, 1998 ($5.99, limited series)

	GD2.0	FN6.0	NM9.4
,2-Busiek-s; flashback story from gold armor days		2.40	6.00

ON MAN: THE LEGEND
rvel Comics: Sept, 1996 ($3.95, one-shot)

	GD2.0	FN6.0	NM9.4
-Tribute issue			4.50

ON MAN 2020 (Also see Machine Man limited series)
rvel Comics: June, 1994 ($5.95, one-shot)

	GD2.0	FN6.0	NM9.4
		2.40	6.00

ON MAN/X-O MANOWAR: HEAVY METAL (See X-O Manowar/Iron Man: Heavy Metal)
rvel Comics: Sept, 1996 ($2.50, one-shot) (1st Marvel/Valiant x-over)

	GD2.0	FN6.0	NM9.4
-Pt. II of Iron Man/X-O Manowar x-over; Fabian Nicieza scripts; 1st app. Rand Banion			2.50

ON MARSHALL
deman Comics: July, 1990 - No. 32, Feb, 1993 ($1.75, plastic coated-c)

	GD2.0	FN6.0	NM9.4
-32: Kung Fu stories. 1-Poster centerfold			2.00

ON VIC (See Comics Revue No. 3 & Giant Comics Editions)
ited Features Syndicate/St. John Publ. Co.: 1940

	GD2.0	FN6.0	NM9.4
ngle Series 22	33.00	98.00	260.00

ON WINGS
age Comics: Apr, 2000 - Present ($2.50)

	GD2.0	FN6.0	NM9.4
,2: 1-Two covers			2.50

ONWOLF
: Comics: 1986 ($2.00, one shot)

	GD2.0	FN6.0	NM9.4
1-r/Weird Worlds 8-10; Chaykin story & art			2.00

IRONWOLF: FIRES OF THE REVOLUTION (See Weird Worlds #8-10)
DC Comics: 1992 ($29.95, hardcover)

	GD2.0	FN6.0	NM9.4
nn-Chaykin/Moore story, Mignola-a w/Russell inks.			30.00

ISAAC ASIMOV'S I-BOTS
Tekno Comix: Dec, 1995 - No. 7, May, 1996 ($1.95)

	GD2.0	FN6.0	NM9.4
1-7: 1-6-Perez-c/a. 2-Chaykin variant-c exists. 3-Polybagged. 7-Lady Justice-c/app.			2.25

ISAAC ASIMOV'S I-BOTS
BIG Entertainment: V2#1, June, 1996 - Present ($2.25)

	GD2.0	FN6.0	NM9.4
V2#1-9: 1-Lady Justice-c/app. 6-Gil Kane-c			2.25

ISIS (TV) (Also see Shazam)
National Per.l Publ./DC Comics: Oct-Nov, 1976 - No. 8, Dec-Jan, 1977-78

	GD2.0	FN6.0	NM9.4
1-Wood inks	1.25	3.75	10.00
2-8: 5-Isis new look. 7-Origin		2.40	6.00

ISLAND AT THE TOP OF THE WORLD (See Walt Disney Showcase #27)

ISLAND OF DR. MOREAU, THE (Movie)
Marvel Comics Group: Oct, 1977 (52 pgs.)

	GD2.0	FN6.0	NM9.4
1-Gil Kane-c			5.00

I SPY (TV)
Gold Key: Aug, 1966 - No. 6, Sept, 1968 (All have photo-c)

	GD2.0	FN6.0	NM9.4
1-Bill Cosby, Robert Culp photo covers	23.00	68.00	270.00
2-6: 3,4-McWilliams-a	13.00	40.00	160.00

IT! (See Astonishing Tales No. 21-24 & Supernatural Thrillers No. 1)

ITCHY & SCRATCHY COMICS (The Simpsons TV show)
Bongo Comics: 1993 - No. 3, 1993 ($1.95)

	GD2.0	FN6.0	NM9.4
1-3: 1-Bound-in jumbo poster. 3-w/decoder screen trading card			3.00
Holiday Special ('94, $1.95)			3.00

IT REALLY HAPPENED
William H. Wise No. 1,2/Standard (Visual Editions): 1944 - No. 11, Oct, 1947

	GD2.0	FN6.0	NM9.4
1-Kit Carson & Ben Franklin stories	19.00	56.00	150.00
2	10.00	30.00	80.00
3,4,6,9,11: 6-Joan of Arc story. 9-Captain Kidd & Frank Buck stories	9.30	28.00	65.00
5-Lou Gehrig & Lewis Carroll stories	15.00	45.00	120.00
7-Teddy Roosevelt story	10.00	30.00	70.00
8-Story of Roy Rogers	16.00	49.00	130.00
10-Honus Wagner & Mark Twain stories	12.00	36.00	95.00

NOTE: **Guardineer** a-7(2), 8(2), 11. **Schomburg** c-1-7, 9-11.

IT RHYMES WITH LUST (Also see Bold Stories & Candid Tales)
St. John Publishing Co.: 1950 (Digest size, 128 pgs.)

	GD2.0	FN6.0	NM9.4
nn (Rare)-Matt Baker & Ray Osrin-a	58.00	174.00	550.00

IT'S ABOUT TIME (TV)
Gold Key: Jan, 1967

	GD2.0	FN6.0	NM9.4
1 (10195-701)-Photo-c	3.80	11.40	42.00

IT'S A DUCK'S LIFE
Marvel Comics/Atlas(MMC): Feb, 1950 - No. 11, Feb, 1952

	GD2.0	FN6.0	NM9.4
1-Buck Duck, Super Rabbit begin	14.00	41.00	110.00
2	7.85	23.50	55.00
3-11	6.40	19.25	45.00

IT'S GAMETIME
National Periodical Publications: Sept-Oct, 1955 - No. 4, Mar-Apr, 1956

	GD2.0	FN6.0	NM9.4
1-(Scarce)-Infinity-c; Davy Crockett app. in puzzle	74.00	221.00	700.00
2,3 (Scarce): 2-Dodo & The Frog	58.00	174.00	550.00
4 (Rare)	61.00	182.00	575.00

IT'S LOVE, LOVE, LOVE
St. John Publishing Co.: Nov, 1957 - No. 2, Jan, 1958 (10¢)

	GD2.0	FN6.0	NM9.4
1,2	5.00	15.00	32.00

IVANHOE (See Fawcett Movie Comics No. 20)

Jackie Gleason and the Honeymooners #8 © DC

Jack Kirby's Fourth World #13 © DC

Jackpot Comics #1 © MLJ

GD2.0 FN6.0 NM9.4 — GD2.0 FN6.0 NM9

IVANHOE
Dell Publishing Co.: July-Sept, 1963

1 (12-373-309) 3.00 9.00 32.00

IWO JIMA (See Spectacular Features Magazine)

JACE PEARSON OF THE TEXAS RANGERS (Radio/TV)(4-Color #396 is titled Tales of the Texas Rangers; ...'s Tales of ... #11-on)(See Western Roundup under Dell Giants)
Dell Publishing Co.: No. 396, 5/52 - No. 1021, 8-10/59 (No #10) (All-Photo-c)

Four Color 396 (#1) 10.50 31.00 125.00
2(5-7/53) - 9(2-4/55) 5.85 17.50 70.00
Four Color 648(#10, 9/55) 4.60 13.75 55.00
11(11-2/55-56) - 14,17-20(6-8/58) 4.55 13.65 50.00
15,16-Toth-a 4.60 13.75 55.00
Four Color 961, 1021: 961--Spiegle-a 4.55 13.65 50.00

NOTE: *Joel McCrea photo c-1-9, F.C. 648 (starred on radio show only); Willard Parker photo c-11-on (starred on TV series).*

JACK ARMSTRONG (Radio)(See True Comics)
Parents' Institute: Nov, 1947 - No. 9, Sept, 1948; No. 10, Mar, 1949 - No. 13, Sept, 1949

1-(Scarce) (odd size) Cast intro. inside front-c 42.00 125.00 375.00
2 20.00 60.00 160.00
3-5 14.00 41.00 110.00
6-13: 7-Vic Hardy's Crime Lab begins? 11.00 33.00 90.00

JACK HUNTER
Blackthorne Publishing: July, 1987 - No. 3 ($1.25)

1-3 2.00

JACKIE CHAN'S SPARTAN X
Topps Comics: May, 1997 - No. 3 ($2.95, limited series)

1-3-Michael Golden-s/a; variant photo-c 3.00

JACKIE CHAN'S SPARTAN X: HELL BENT HERO FOR HIRE
Image Comics (Little Eva Ink): Mar, 1998 - No. 3 ($2.95, B&W)

1-3-Michael Golden-s/a: 1-variant photo-c 3.00

JACKIE GLEASON (TV) (Also see The Honeymooners)
St. John Publishing Co.: Sept, 1955 - No. 4, Dec, 1955?

1(1955)(TV)-Photo-c 58.00 174.00 550.00
2-4 40.00 120.00 350.00

JACKIE GLEASON AND THE HONEYMOONERS (TV)
National Periodical Publications: June-July, 1956 - No. 12, Apr-May, 1958

1-1st app. Ralph Kramden 84.00 253.00 800.00
2 53.00 160.00 480.00
3-11 40.00 120.00 360.00
12 (Scarce) 58.00 174.00 550.00

JACKIE JOKERS (Became Richie Rich &...)
Harvey Publications: March, 1973 - No. 4, Sept, 1973 (#5 was advertised, but not published)

1-1st app. 2.50 7.50 23.00
2-4: 2-President Nixon app. 1.50 4.50 12.00

JACKIE ROBINSON (Famous Plays of...) (Also see Negro Heroes #2 & Picture News #4)
Fawcett Publications: May, 1950 - No. 6, 1952 (Baseball hero) (All photo-c)

nn 89.00 268.00 850.00
2 54.00 163.00 490.00
3-6 44.00 133.00 400.00

JACK IN THE BOX (Formerly Yellowjacket Comics #1-10; becomes Cowboy Western Comics #17 on)
Frank Comunale/Charlton Comics No. 11 on: Feb, 1946; No. 11, Oct, 1946 - No. 16, Nov-Dec, 1947

1-Stitches, Marty Mouse & Nutsy McKrow 13.00 39.00 105.00
11-Yellowjacket (early Charlton comic) 19.00 56.00 150.00
12,14,15 8.65 26.00 60.00
13-Wolverton-a 20.00 60.00 160.00
16-12 pg. adapt. of Silas Marner; Kiefer-a 10.00 30.00 80.00

JACK KIRBY'S FOURTH WORLD (See New Gods, 3rd Series)
DC Comics: Mar, 1997 - No. 20, Oct, 1998 ($1.95/$2.25)

1-20: 1-Byrne-a/scripts & Simonson-c begin; story cont'd from New Gods, 3rc Series #15; retells "The Pact" (New Gods, 1st Series #7); 1st DC app. Thor (cameo). 2-Thor vs. Big Barda; "Apokolips Then" back-up begins; Kirby-c/swipe (Thor #126) 8-Genesis x-over. 10-Simonson-s/a 13-Simonson back-up story. 20-Superman-c/app. 2.

JACK KIRBY'S SECRET CITY SAGA
Topps Comics (Kirbyverse): No. 0, Apr, 1993; No. 1, May, 1993 - No. 4, Aug 1993 ($2.95, limited series)

0-(No cover price, 20 pgs.)-Simonson-c/a 3.
1-4-Bagged w/3 trading cards; Ditko-c/a: 1-Ditko/Art Adams-c. 2-Ditko/Byrne-has coupon for Pres. Clinton holo-foil trading card. 3-Dorman poster; has coupon for Gore holo-foil trading card. 4-Ditko/Perez-c 3.

NOTE: *Issues #1-4 contain coupons redeemable for Kirbychrome version of #1*

JACK KIRBY'S SILVER STAR (Also see Silver Star)
Topps Comics (Kirbyverse): Oct, 1993 ($2.95)(Intended as a 4-issue limited series)

1-Silver ink-c; Austin-c/a(i); polybagged w/3 cards 3.

JACK KIRBY'S TEENAGENTS (See Satan's Six)
Topps Comics (Kirbyverse): Aug, 1993 - No. 3, Oct, 1993 ($2.95)(Intended a a 4-issue limited series)

1-3: Bagged with/3 trading cards; 1-3-Austin-c(i): 3-Liberty Project app. 3.

JACK OF HEARTS (Also see The Deadly Hands of Kung Fu #22 & Marvel Premiere #44)
Marvel Comics Group: Jan, 1984 - No. 4, Apr, 1984 (60¢, limited series)

1-4 2.

JACKPOT COMICS (Jolly Jingles #10 on)
MLJ Magazines: Spring, 1941 - No. 9, Spring, 1943

1-The Black Hood, Mr. Justice, Steel Sterling & Sgt. Boyle begin; Biro-c 295.00 885.00 2800.
2-S. Cooper-c 132.00 395.00 1250.
3-Hubbell-c 97.00 292.00 925.
4-Archie begins (Win/41; on sale 12/41)-(also see Pep Comics #22); 1st app. Mrs. Grundy, the principal; Novick-c 343.00 1030.00 3600.
5-Hitler, Tojo, Mussolini-c by Montana; 1st definitive Mr. Weatherbee; 1st app Reggie in 1 panel cameo 147.00 442.00 1400.
6-9: 6,7-Bondage-c by Novick. 8,9-Sahle-c 103.00 309.00 975.

JACK Q FROST (See Unearthly Spectaculars)

JACK THE GIANT KILLER (See Movie Classics)

JACK THE GIANT KILLER (New Adventures of...)
Bimfort & Co.: Aug-Sept, 1953

V1#1-H. C. Kiefer-c/a 23.00 68.00 180.

JACKY'S DIARY
Dell Publishing Co.: No. 1091, Apr-June, 1960 (one-shot)

Four Color 1091 4.10 12.30 45.

JADEMAN COLLECTION
Jademan Comics: Dec, 1989 - No. 3, 1990 ($2.50, plastic coated-c, 68 pgs.)

1-3: 1-Wraparound-c w/fold-out poster 2.

JADEMAN KUNG FU SPECIAL
Jademan Comics: 1988 ($1.50, 64 pgs.)

1 2.

JADE WARRIORS (Mike Deodato's...)
Image Comics (Glass House Graphics): Nov, 1999 - Present ($2.50)

1-3-Deodato-a 2.
1-Variant-c 2.

JAGUAR, THE (Also see The Adventures of...)
Impact Comics (DC): Aug, 1991 - No. 14, Oct, 1992 ($1.00)

1-14: 4-The Black Hood x-over. 7-Sienkiewicz-c. 9-Contains Crusaders trading card 2.
Annual 1 (1992, $2.50, 68 pgs.)-With trading card 2.

Jaguar God #3 © Verotik

Jay & Silent Bob #1 © View Askew

Jenny Sparks: The Secret History of the Authority #2 © WSP

GD2.0 FN6.0 NM9.4

ꞁUAR GOD
otik: Mar, 1995 - No. 7, June, 1997 ($2.95, mature)
2/96, $3.50)-Embossed Frazetta-c; Bisley-a; w/pin-ups. 2.40 6.00
-razetta-c. 2.40 6.00
: 2-Frazetta-c. 3-Bisley-c. 4-Emond-c. 7-($2.95)-Frazetta-c 5.00

E THRASH
el Publishing: 1988 - No. 3, 1988 ($2.00)
3 2.00

, THE (...Urban Adventure)
e Labor Nos. 1-5/Dark Horse Comics Nos. 6-8/Caliber Comics No. 9 on:
, 1989 - No. 14, 1997 ($1.95/$2.50/$2.95, B&W)
4: Bernie Mireault-c/a/scripts. 6-1st Dark Horse issue. 9-1st Caliber issue 3.00

BOREE
nd Publishing Co.: Feb, 1946(no mo. given) - No. 3, Apr, 1946
-unny animal 25.00 75.00 200.00
3 15.00 45.00 120.00

ES BOND 007: A SILENT ARMAGEDDON
k Horse Comics/Acme Press: Mar, 1993 - Apr 1993 (limited series)
2 3.50

ES BOND 007: GOLDENEYE (Movie)
ps Comics: Jan, 1996 ($2.95, unfinished limited series of 3)
Movie adaptation; Stelfreeze-c 3.00

ES BOND 007: SERPENT'S TOOTH
k Horse Comics/Acme Press: July 1992 - Aug 1992 ($4.95, limited series)
-Paul Gulacy-c/a 5.00

ES BOND 007: SHATTERED HELIX
k Horse Comics: Jun 1994 - July 1994 ($2.50, limited series)
2 3.00

ES BOND 007: THE QUASIMODO GAMBIT
k Horse Comics: Jan 1995 - May 1995 ($3.95, limited series)
3 4.50

ES BOND FOR YOUR EYES ONLY
vel Comics Group: Oct, 1981 - No. 2, Nov, 1981
-Movie adapt.; r/Marvel Super Special #19 3.00

ES BOND JR. (TV)
vel Comics: Jan, 1992 - No. 12, Dec, 1992 (#1: $1.00, #2-on: $1.25)
2: Based on animated TV show 2.00

ES BOND: LICENCE TO KILL (See Licence To Kill)

ES BOND: PERMISSION TO DIE
pse Comics/ACME Press: 1989 - No. 3, 1991 ($3.95, limited series, square-nd, 52 pgs.)
: Mike Grell-c/a/scripts in all. 3-($4.95) 5.00

, THE: SUPER COOL COLOR INJECTED TURBO ADVENTURE #1 M HELL!
nico: May, 1988 ($2.50, 44 pgs., one-shot)
2.50

E ARDEN (See Feature Funnies & Pageant of Comics)
John (United Features Syndicate): Mar, 1948 - No. 2, June, 1948
Newspaper reprints 15.00 45.00 120.00
11.00 33.00 90.00

N OF THE JUNGLE (Jungle Tales No. 1-7)
s Comics (CSI): No. 8, Nov, 1955 - No. 17, June, 1957
#1) 33.00 98.00 260.00
1-15 19.00 56.00 150.00
Williamson/Colletta-c 19.00 58.00 155.00
17-Williamson/Mayo-a(3), 5 pgs. each 20.00 60.00 160.00
E: ***Everett** c-15-17. **Heck** a-8, 15, 17. **Maneely** c-11. **Shores** a-8.*

OF FOOLS
Penny Dreadful Press: 1994 ($5.95, B&W)
1-Jason Lutes-c/a/scripts 6.00

JAR OF FOOLS
Black Eye Productions: 1994 - No. 2, 1994 ($6.95, B&W)
1,2: 1-Reprints of earlier ed. Jason Lutes-c/a/scripts 7.00

JASON & THE ARGONAUTS (See Movie Classics)

JASON GOES TO HELL: THE FINAL FRIDAY (Movie)
Topps Comics: July, 1993 - No. 3, Sept, 1993 ($2.95, limited series)
1-3: Adaptation of film. 1-Glow-in-the-dark-c 3.00

JASON'S QUEST (See Showcase #88-90)

JASON VS. LEATHERFACE
Topps Comics: Oct, 1995 - No. 3, Jan, 1996 ($2.95, limited series)
1-3: Collins scripts; Bisley-c 3.00

JAWS 2 (See Marvel Comics Super Special, A)

JAY & SILENT BOB (See Clerks & Oni Double Feature)
Oni Press: July, 1998 - No. 4, Oct, 1999 ($2.95, B&W, limited series)
1-Kevin Smith-s/Fegredo-a; photo-c & Quesada/Palmiotti-c 8.00
1-San Diego Comic Con variant covers (2 different covers, came packaged with action figures) 10.00
1-2nd & 3rd printings, 2-4: 2-Allred-c. 3-Flip-c by Jaime Hernandez 3.00
Chasing Dogma TPB (1999, $11.95) r/#1-4; Alanis Morissette intro. 12.00
Chasing Dogma HC (1999, $69.95, S&N) r/#1-4 in color; Morissette intro. 70.00

JCP FEATURES
J.C. Productions (Archie): Feb, 1982-c; Dec, 1981-indicia ($2.00, one-shot, B&W magazine)
1-T.H.U.N.D.E.R. Agents; Black Hood by Morrow & Neal Adams; Texeira-a; 2 pgs. S&K-a from Fly #1 1.00 3.00 8.00

JEANIE COMICS (Formerly All Surprise; Cowgirl Romances #28)
Marvel Comics/Atlas(CPC): No. 13, April, 1947 - No. 27, Oct, 1949
13-Mitzi, Willie begin 16.00 49.00 130.00
14,15 12.00 36.00 95.00
16-Used in Love and Death by Legman; Kurtzman's "Hey Look" 14.00 43.00 115.00
17-19,22-Kurtzman's "Hey Look", (1-3 pgs. each) 10.00 30.00 80.00
20,21,23-27 9.30 28.00 65.00

JEEP COMICS (Also see G.I. Comics and Overseas Comics)
R. B. Leffingwell & Co.: Winter, 1944 - No. 3, Mar-Apr, 1948
1-Capt. Power, Criss Cross & Jeep & Peep (costumed) begin 50.00 150.00 450.00
2 34.00 101.00 270.00
3-L. B. Cole dinosaur-c 44.00 133.00 400.00

JEFF JORDAN, U.S. AGENT
D. S. Publishing Co.: Dec, 1947 - Jan, 1948
1 14.00 41.00 110.00

JEMM, SON OF SATURN
DC Comics: Sept, 1984 - No. 12, Aug, 1985 (Maxi-series, mando paper)
1-12: 3-Origin 2.00
NOTE: ***Colan** a-1-12p; c-1-5, 7-12p.*

JENNY FINN
Oni Press: June, 1999 - No. 2, Sept, 1999 ($2.95, B&W, unfinished lim. series)
1,2-Mignola & Nixey-s/Nixey-a/Mignola-c 3.00

JENNY SPARKS: THE SECRET HISTORY OF THE AUTHORITY
DC Comics (WildStorm): Aug, 2000 - No. 5, Mar, 2001 ($2.50, limited series)
1-Millar-s/McCrea & Hodgkins-a/Hitch & Neary-c 3.00
1-Variant-c by McCrea 5.00
2-5: 2-Apollo & Midnighter. 3-Jack Hawksmoor. 4-Shen. 5-Engineer 2.50

JERRY DRUMMER (Formerly Soldier & Marine V2#9)
Charlton Comics: V2#10, Apr, 1957 - V3#12, Oct, 1957
V2#10, V3#11,12: 11-Whitman-c/a 5.00 15.00 35.00

JERRY IGER'S... (All titles, Blackthorne/First)(Value: cover or less)

Jesse James #6 © AVON

Jet #1 © WSP

Jetta of the 21st Century #6 © STD

JERRY LEWIS (See The Adventures of...)

JESSE JAMES (The True Story Of..., also seeThe Legend of...)
Dell Publishing Co.: No. 757, Dec, 1956 (one shot)

Four Color 757-Movie, photo-c 9.00 27.00 110.00

JESSE JAMES (See Badmen of the West & Blazing Sixguns)
Avon Periodicals: 8/50 - No. 9, 11/52; No. 15, 10/53 - No. 29, 8-9/56

1-Kubert Alabam-r/Cowpuncher #1 16.00 49.00 130.00
2-Kubert-a(3) 13.00 39.00 105.00
3-Kubert Alabam-r/Cowpuncher #2 12.00 36.00 95.00
4,9-No Kubert 5.70 17.00 40.00
5,6-Kubert Jesse James-a(3); 5-Wood-a(1pg.) 12.00 36.00 95.00
7-Kubert Jesse James-a(2) 10.00 30.00 75.00
8-Kinstler-a(3) 7.15 21.50 50.00
15-Kinstler-r/#3 5.00 15.00 35.00
16-Kinstler-r/#3 & story-r/Butch Cassidy #1 5.50 16.50 38.00
17-19,21: 17-Jesse James-r/#4; Kinstler-c idea from Kubert splash in #6. 18-Kubert Jesse James-r/#5. 19-Kubert Jesse James-r/#6. 21-Two Jesse James-r/#4, Kinstler-r/#4 5.00 15.00 32.00
20-Williamson/Frazetta-a; r/Chief Vic. Apache Massacre; Kubert Jesse James-r/#6; Kit West story by Larsen 12.50 37.50 100.00
22-29: 22,23-No Kubert. 24-New McCarty strip by Kinstler; Kinstler-r. 25-New McCarty Jesse James strip by Kinstler; Jesse James-r/#7,9. 26,27-New McCarty Jesse James strip plus a Kinstler/McCann Jesse James-r. 28-Reprints most of Red Mountain, Featuring Quantrells Raiders 5.00 15.00 32.00
Annual nn (1952; 25¢, 100 pgs.)- "...Brings Six-Gun Justice to the West"- 3 earlier issues rebound; Kubert, Kinstler-a(3) 28.00 84.00 225.00

NOTE: *Mostly reprints #10 on.* ***Fawcette*** *c-1, 2.* ***Kida*** *a-5.* ***Kinstler*** *a-3, 4, 7-9, 15r, 16r(2), 21-27; c-3, 4, 9, 17-27. Painted c-5-8. 22 has 2 stories r/Sheriff Bob Dixon's Chuck Wagon #1 with name changed to Sheriff Bob Trent.*

JESSE JAMES
Realistic Publications: July, 1953

nn-Reprints Avon's #1; same-c, colors different 10.00 30.00 70.00

JEST (Formerly Snap; becomes Kayo #12)
Harry 'A' Chesler: No. 10, 1944; No. 11, 1944

10-Johnny Rebel & Yankee Boy app. in text 16.00 48.00 125.00
11-Little Nemo in Adventure Land 16.00 48.00 125.00

JESTER
Harry 'A' Chesler: No. 10, 1945

10 14.00 41.00 110.00

JESUS
Spire Christian Comics (Fleming H. Revell Co.): 1979 (49¢)

nn 2.40 6.00

JET (See Jet Powers)

JET (Crimson from Wildcore & Backlash)
DC Comics (WildStorm): Nov, 2000 - No. 4, Feb, 2001 ($2.50, limited series)

1-4-Nguyen-a/Abnett & Lanning-s 2.50

JET ACES
Fiction House Magazines: 1952 - No. 4, 1953

1 12.50 37.50 100.00
2-4 8.65 26.00 60.00

JET DREAM (...and Her Stunt-Girl Counterspies)(See The Man from Uncle #7)
Gold Key: June, 1968 (12¢)

1-Painted-c 3.20 9.60 35.00

JET FIGHTERS (Korean War)
Standard Magazines: No. 5, Nov, 1952 - No. 7, Mar, 1953

5,7-Toth-a. 5-Toth-c 11.00 33.00 90.00
6-Celardo-a 5.00 15.00 35.00

JET POWER
I.W. Enterprises: 1963

I.W. Reprint 1,2-r/Jet Powers #1,2 3.00 9.00 30.00

JET POWERS (American Air Forces No. 5 on)
Magazine Enterprises: 1950 - No. 4, 1951

1(A-1 #30)-Powell-c/a begins 33.00 98.00 260
2(A-1 #32) 23.00 69.00 185
3(A-1 #35)-Williamson/Evans-a 39.00 116.00 310
4(A-1 #38)-Williamson/Wood-a; "The Rain of Sleep" drug story 39.00 116.00 310

JET PUP (See 3-D Features)

JETSONS, THE (TV) (See March of Comics #276, 330, 348 & Spotlight #3)
Gold Key: Jan, 1963 - No. 36, Oct, 1970 (Hanna-Barbera)

1-1st comic book app. 23.00 68.00 270
2 11.00 33.00 130
3-10 8.35 25.00 100
11-20 5.85 17.50 70
21-36: 23-36-Reprints 4.60 13.75 55

JETSONS, THE (TV) (Also see Golden Comics Digest)
Charlton Comics: Nov, 1970 - No. 20, Dec, 1973 (Hanna-Barbera)

1 7.25 21.75 80
2 3.65 11.00 40
3-10 3.00 9.00 30
11-20 2.30 7.00 20

JETSONS, THE (TV)
Harvey Comics: V2#1, Sept, 1992 - No. 5, Nov, 1993 ($1.25/$1.50) (Hanna-Barbera)

V2#1-5 3
...Big Book V2#1,2,3 ($1.95, 52 pgs.): 1-(11/92). 2-(4/93). 3-(7/93) 3
...Giant Size 1,2,3 ($2.25, 68 pgs): 1-(10/92). 2-(4/93). 3-(10/93) 3

JETSONS, THE (TV)
Archie Comics: Sept, 1995 - No. 17, Aug, 1996 ($1.50)

1-17 2

JETTA OF THE 21ST CENTURY
Standard Comics: No. 5, Dec, 1952 - No. 7, Apr, 1953 (Teen-age Archie typ

5 22.00 66.00 175
6,7: 6-Robot-c 12.50 37.50 100

JEZEBEL JADE (Hanna-Barbera)
Comico: Oct, 1988 - No. 3, Dec, 1988 ($2.00, mini-series)

1-3: Johnny Quest spin-off 3

JIGGS & MAGGIE
Dell Publishing Co.: No. 18, 1941 (one shot)

Four Color 18 (#1)-(1936-38-r) 38.00 115.00 460

JIGGS & MAGGIE
Standard Comics/Harvey Publications No. 22 on: No. 11, 1949(June) - No 21, 2/53; No. 22, 4/53 - No. 27, 2-3/54

11 10.50 32.00 85
12-15,17-21 6.40 19.25 45
16-Wood text illos. 7.85 23.50 55
22-24-Little Dot app. 5.50 16.50 38
25,27 5.00 15.00 35
26-Four pgs. partially in 3-D 13.00 39.00 105

NOTE: *Sunday page reprints by McManus loosely blended into story continuity. Based on Bringing Up Father strip. Advertised on covers as "All New."*

JIGSAW (Big Hero Adventures)
Harvey Publ. (Funday Funnies): Sept, 1966 - No. 2, Dec, 1966 (36 pgs.)

1-Origin & 1st app.; Crandall-a (5 pgs.) 2.30 7.00 20
2-Man From S.R.A.M. 1.75 5.25 14

JIGSAW OF DOOM (See Complete Mystery No. 2)

JIM BOWIE (Formerly Danger?; Black Jack No. 20 on)
Charlton Comics: No. 16, 1955? - No. 19, Apr, 1957

16 7.00 21.00 48
17-19 5.00 15.00 32

JIM BOWIE (TV, see Western Tales)
Dell Publishing Co.: No. 893, Mar, 1958 - No. 993, May-July, 1959

Jimmy Wakely #13 © DC

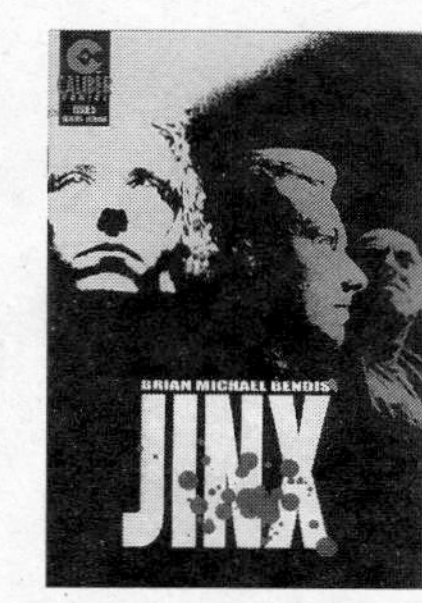

Jinx #5 © Brian Michael Bendis

JLA #15 © DC

GD2.0 FN6.0 NM9.4

Four Color 893 (#1), 993-Photo-c 4.60 13.75 55.00

JIM DANDY
Dandy Magazine (Lev Gleason): May, 1956 - No. 3, Sept, 1956 (Charles Biro)

1-Biro-c 7.15 21.50 50.00
2,3 5.00 15.00 30.00

JIM HARDY (See Giant Comics Eds., Sparkler & Treasury of Comics #2 & 5)
United Features Syndicate/Spotlight Publ.: 1939; 1942; 1947 - No. 2, 1947

Single Series 6 ('39) 40.00 120.00 350.00
Single Series 27('42) 35.00 105.00 280.00
1('47)-Spotlight Publ. 14.00 41.00 110.00
2 8.65 26.00 60.00

JIM HARDY
Spotlight/United Features Synd.: 1944 (25¢, 132 pgs.) (Tip Top, Sparkler-r)

nn-Origin Mirror Man; Triple Terror app. 40.00 120.00 350.00

JIMINY CRICKET (Disney,, see Mickey Mouse Mag. V5#3 & Walt Disney Showcase #37)
Dell Publishing Co.: No. 701, May, 1956 - No. 989, May-July, 1959

Four Color 701 8.35 25.00 100.00
Four Color 795, 897, 989 5.85 17.50 70.00

JIMMY CORRIGAN (See Acme Novelty Library)

JIMMY DURANTE (Also see A-1 Comics)
Magazine Enterprises: No. 18, 1949 - No. 20, 1949

A-1 18,20-Photo-c 42.00 125.00 375.00

JIMMY OLSEN (See Superman's Pal...)

JIMMY WAKELY (Cowboy movie star)
National Per. Publ.: Sept-Oct, 1949 - No. 18, July-Aug, 1952 (1-13: 52pgs.)

1-Photo-c, 52 pgs. begin; Alex Toth-a; Kit Colby Girl Sheriff begins
111.00 332.00 1050.00
2-Toth-a 47.00 140.00 420.00
3,4,6,7-Frazetta-a in all, 3 pgs. each; Toth-a in all. 7-Last photo-c. 4-Kurtzman "Pot-Shot Pete", 1 pg; Toth-a 47.00 142.00 425.00
5,8-15,18-Toth-a; 12,14-Kubert-a (3 & 2 pgs.) 40.00 120.00 320.00
16,17 33.00 98.00 260.00

NOTE: *Gil Kane c-10-19p.*

JIM RAY'S AVIATION SKETCH BOOK
Vital Publishers: Mar-Apr, 1946 - No. 2, May-June, 1946

1-Picture stories about planes and pilots 38.00 113.00 300.00
2 26.00 79.00 210.00

JIM SOLAR (See Wisco/Klarer)

JINGLE BELLE
Oni Press: Nov, 1999 - No. 2, Dec, 1999 ($2.95, B&W, limited series)

1,2-Paul Dini-s. 2-Alex Ross flip-c 3.00
Paul Dini's Jingle Belle's All-Star Holiday Hullabaloo (11/00, $4.95) stories by various incl. Dini, Aragonés, Jeff Smith, Bill Morrison; Frank Cho-c 5.00
TPB (10/00, $8.95) r/#1&2, and app. from Oni Double Feature #13 9.00

JINGLE BELLS (See March of Comics No. 65)

JINGLE DINGLE CHRISTMAS STOCKING COMICS (See Foodini #2)
Stanhall Publications: V2#1, 1951 (no date listed) (25¢, 100 pgs.; giant-size) (Publ. annually)

V2#1-Foodini & Pinhead, Silly Pilly plus games & puzzles
17.00 51.00 135.00

JINGLE JANGLE COMICS (Also see Puzzle Fun Comics)
Eastern Color Printing Co.: Feb, 1942 - No. 42, Dec, 1949

1-Pie-Face Prince of Old Pretzleburg, Jingle Jangle Tales by George Carlson, Hortense, & Benny Bear begin 40.00 120.00 350.00
2-4: 2,3-No Pie-Face Prince. 4-Pie-Face Prince-c 20.00 60.00 160.00
5 18.00 53.00 140.00
6-10: 8-No Pie-Face Prince 14.00 43.00 115.00
11-15 11.00 33.00 90.00
16-30: 17,18-No Pie-Face Prince. 30-XMas-c 10.00 30.00 70.00
31-42: 36,42-Xmas-c 8.65 26.00 60.00

NOTE: *George Carlson a-(2) in all except No. 2, 3, 8; c-1-6. Carlson 1 pg. puzzles in 9, 10, 12-15, 18, 20. Carlson illustrated a series of Uncle Wiggily books in 1930's.*

JING PALS
Victory Publishing Corp.: Feb, 1946 - No. 4, Aug?, 1946 (Funny animal)

1-Wishing Willie, Puggy Panda & Johnny Rabbit begin
14.00 41.00 110.00
2-4 7.85 23.50 55.00

JINKS, PIXIE, AND DIXIE (See Kite Fun Book & Whitman Comic Books)

JINN
Image Comics (Avalon Studios): Mar, 2000 - No. 3, Oct, 2000 ($2.50)

1-3-Rearte-c/a 3.00

JINX
Caliber Press: 1996 - No. 7, 1996 ($2.95, B&W, 32 pgs.)

1-7: Brian Michael Bendis-c/a/scripts. 2-Photo-c 3.00

JINX (Volume 2)
Image Comics: 1997 - No. 5, 1998 ($2.95, B&W, bi-monthly)

1-4: Brian Michael Bendis-c/a/scripts. 3.00
5-($3.95) Brereton-c 4.00
...Buried Treasures ('98, $3.95) short stories, ...Confessions ('98, $3.95) short stories, ...Pop Culture Hoo-Hah ('98, $3.95) humor shorts 4.00
TPB (1997, $10.95) r/Vol 1,#1-4 11.00

JINX: TORSO
Image Comics: 1998 - No. 6, 1999 ($3.95/$4.95, B&W)

1-6-Brian Michael Bendis & Marc Andreyko-s/Bendis-a. 3-6-($4.95) 5.00

JLA (See Justice League of America)
DC Comics: Jan, 1997 - Present ($1.95/$1.99/$2.25)

1-Morrison-s/Porter & Dell-a. The Hyperclan app. 1.85 5.50 15.00
2 1.25 3.75 10.00
3,4 1.00 3.00 8.00
5-Membership drive; Tomorrow Woman app. 2.40 6.00
6-9: 8-Green Arrow joins. 2.40 6.00
10-21: 10-Rock of Ages begins. 11-Joker and Luthor-c/app. 15-($2.95) Rock of Ages concludes. 16-New members join; Prometheus app. 17,20-Jorgensen-a. 18-21-Waid-s. 20,21-Adam Strange c/app. 5.00
22-40: 22-Begin $1.99-c; Sandman (Daniel) app. 27-Amazo app. 28-31-JSA app. 35-Hal Jordan/Spectre app. 36-40-World War 3 2.50
41-($2.99) Conclusion of World War 3; last Morrison-s 3.00
42-46: 43-Waid-s; Ra's al Ghul app. 44-Begin $2.25-c. 46-Batman leaves 2.25
47-49: 47-Hitch & Neary-a begins; JLA battles Queen of Fables 2.25
#1,000,000 (11/98)853rd Century x-over 2.00
Annual 1 (1997, $3.95) Pulp Heroes; Augustyn-s/Olivetti & Ha-a 4.00
Annual 2 (1998, $2.95) Ghosts; Wrightson-c 4.00
Annual 3 (1999, $2.95) JLApe; Art Adams-c 3.00
...80-Page Giant 1 (7/98, $4.95) stories & art by various 5.00
...80-Page Giant 2 (11/99, $4.95) Green Arrow & Hawkman app. Hitch-c 5.00
...80-Page Giant 3 (10/00, $5.95) Pariah & Harbinger; intro. Moon Maiden 6.00
...Foreign Bodies (1999, $5.95) Kobra app.; Semeiks-a 6.00
...Gallery (1997, $2.95) pin-ups by various; Quitely-c 3.00
...In Crisis Secret Files 1 (11/98, $4.95) recap of JLA in DC x-overs 5.00
...Primeval (1999, $5.95) Abnett & Lanning-s/Olivetti-a 6.00
...: Seven Caskets (2000, $5.95) Brereton-s/painted-c/a 6.00
...Showcase 80-Page Giant (2/00, $4.95) Hitch-c 5.00
...Superpower (1999, $5.95) Arcudi-s/Eaton-a; Mark Antaeus joins 6.00
...Vs. Predator (DC/Dark Horse, 2000, $5.95) Nolan-c/a 6.00
American Dreams (1998, $7.95, TPB) r/#5-9 8.00
Justice For All (1999, $14.95, TPB) r/#24-33 15.00
New World Order (1997, $5.95, TPB) r/#1-4 6.00
Rock of Ages (1998, $9.95, TPB) r/#10-15 10.00
Strength in Numbers (1998, $12.95, TPB) r/#16-23, Secret Files #2 and Prometheus #1 13.00
World War III (2000, $12.95, TPB) r/#34-41 13.00

JLA: ACT OF GOD
DC Comics: 2000 - No. 3, 2001 ($4.95, limited series)

1-3-Elseworlds; metahumans lose their powers; Moench-s/Dave Ross-a 5.00

JLA: A League of One © DC

JLA/ Titans #1 © DC

Joe Palooka #8 © HARV

JLA: A LEAGUE OF ONE
DC Comics: 2000 (Graphic novel)

Hardcover ($24.95) Christopher Moeller-s/painted-a 25.00

JLA: CREATED EQUAL
DC Comics: 2000 - No. 2, 2000 ($5.95, limited series, prestige format)

1,2-Nicieza-s/Maguire-a; Elseworlds-Superman as the last man on Earth 5.95

JLA: EARTH 2
DC Comics: 2000 (Graphic novel)

Hardcover ($24.95) Morrison-s/Quitely-a; Crime Syndicate app. 25.00
Softcover ($14.95) 15.00

JLA: HEAVEN'S LADDER
DC Comics: 2000 ($9.95, Treasury-size one-shot)

nn-Bryan Hitch & Paul Neary-c/a; Mark Waid-s 10.00

JLA PARADISE LOST
DC Comics: Jan, 1998 - No. 3, Mar, 1998 ($1.95, limited series)

1-3-Millar-s/Olivetti-a 2.00

JLA SECRET FILES
DC Comics: Sept, 1997 - Present ($4.95)

1-Standard Ed. w/origin-s & pin-ups 5.00
1-Collector's Ed. w/origin-s & pin-ups; cardstock-c 2.40 6.00
2,3: 2-(8/98) origin-s of JLA #16's newer members. 3-(12/00) 5.00

JLA: SECRET SOCIETY OF SUPER-HEROES
DC Comics: 2000 - No. 2, 2000 ($5.95, limited series, prestige format)

1,2-Elseworlds JLA; Chaykin and Tischman-s/McKone-a 5.95

JLA: THE NAIL (Elseworlds)
DC Comics: Aug, 1998 - No. 3, Oct, 1998 ($4.95, prestige format)

1-3-JLA in a world without Superman; Alan Davis-s/a(p) 5.00
TPB ('98, $12.95) r/series w/new Davis-c 13.00

JLA / TITANS
DC Comics: Dec, 1998 - No. 3, Feb, 1999 ($2.95, limited series)

1-3-Grayson-s; P. Jimenez-c/a 3.00
...:The Technis Imperative ('99, $12.95, TPB) r/#1-3; Titans Secret Files 12.95

JLA: TOMORROW WOMAN (Girlfrenzy)
DC Comics: June, 1998 ($1.95, one-shot)

1-Peyer-s; story takes place during JLA #5 2.50

JLA/ WILDC.A.T.S
DC Comics: 1997 ($5.95, one-shot, prestige format)

1-Morrison-s/Semeiks & Conrad-a 2.40 6.00

JLA/WITCHBLADE
DC Comics/Top Cow: 2000 ($5.95, prestige format, one-shot)

1-Pararillo-c/a 6.00

JLA/ WORLD WITHOUT GROWN-UPS (See Young Justice)
DC Comics: Aug, 1998 - No. 2, Sept, 1998 ($4.95, prestige format)

1,2-JLA, Robin, Impulse & Superboy app.; Ramos & McKone-a 6.00
TPB ('98, $9.95) r/series & Young Justice: The Secret #1 10.00

JLA: YEAR ONE
DC Comics: Jan, 1998 - No. 12, Dec, 1998 ($2.95/$1.95, limited series)

1-($2.95)-Waid & Augustyn-s/Kitson-a 4.00
1-Platinum Edition 12.00
2-8-($1.95): 5-Doom Patrol-c/app. 7-Superman app. 4.00
9-12 3.00
TPB ('99, $19.95) r/#1-12; Busiek intro. 20.00

JLX
DC Comics (Amalgam): Apr, 1996 ($1.95, one-shot)

1-Mark Waid scripts 2.00

JLX UNLEASHED
DC Comics (Amalgam): June, 1997 ($1.95, one-shot)

1-Priest-s/ Oscar Jimenez & Rodriquez/a 2.00

JOAN OF ARC (Also see A-1 Comics & Ideal a Classical Comic)
Magazine Enterprises: No. 21, 1949 (one shot)

A-1 21-Movie adaptation; Ingrid Bergman photo-covers & interior photos; Whitney-a 28.00 83.00 220.00

JOE COLLEGE
Hillman Periodicals: Fall, 1949 - No. 2, Wint, 1950 (Teen-age humor, 52 pgs.)

1,2: Powell-a; 1-Briefer-a 10.00 30.00 75.00

JOE JINKS
United Features Syndicate: No. 12, 1939

Single Series 12 30.00 90.00 240.00

JOE LOUIS (See Fight Comics #2, Picture News #6 & True Comics #5)
Fawcett Publications: Sept, 1950 - No. 2, Nov, 1950 (Photo-c) (Boxing champ) (See Dick Cole #10)

1-Photo-c; life story 55.00 165.00 500.00
2-Photo-c 40.00 120.00 320.00

JOE PALOOKA (1st Series)(Also see Big Shot Comics, Columbia Comics & Feature Funnies)
Columbia Comic Corp. (Publication Enterprises): 1942 - No. 4, 1944

1-1st to portray American president; gov't permission required 79.00 237.00 750.00
2 (1943)-Hitler-c 50.00 150.00 450.00
3,4: 3-Nazi Sub-c 33.00 98.00 260.00

JOE PALOOKA (2nd Series) (Battle Adv. #68-74; ...Advs. #75, 77-81, 83-85, 87; Champ of the Comics #76, 82, 86, 89-93) (See All-New)
Harvey Publications: Nov, 1945 - No. 118, Mar, 1961

1 44.00 133.00 400.00
2 23.00 68.00 180.00
3,4,6,7-1st Flyin' Fool, ends #25 14.00 41.00 110.00
5-Boy Explorers by S&K (7-8/46) 20.00 60.00 160.00
8-10 10.50 32.00 85.00
11-14,16,18-20: 14-Black Cat text-s(2). 18-Powell-a.; Little Max app. 19-Freedom Train-c 10.00 30.00 70.00
15-Origin & 1st app. Humphrey (12/47); Super-heroine Atoma app. by Powell 14.00 41.00 110.00
17-Humphrey vs. Palooka-c/s; 1st app. Little Max 14.00 41.00 110.00
21-26,29,30: 22-Powell-a. 30-Nude female painting 7.85 23.50 55.00
27-Little Max app.; Howie Morenz-s 8.65 26.00 60.00
28-Babe Ruth 4 pg. sty. 8.65 26.00 60.00
31,39,51: 31-Dizzy Dean 4 pg. sty. 39-(12/49) Humphrey & Little Max begin; Sonny Baugh football-s; Sherlock Max-s. 51-Babe Ruth 2 pg. sty; Jake Lamotta 1/2 pg. sty 6.40 19.25 45.00
32-38,40-50,52-61: 35-Little Max-c/story(4 pgs.); Joe Louis 1 pg. sty. 36-Humphrey story. 41-Bing Crosby photo on-c. 44-Palooka marries Ann Howe. 50-(11/51)-Becomes Harvey Comics Hits #51 5.70 17.00 40.00
62-S&K Boy Explorers-r 7.00 21.00 48.00
63-65,73-80,100: 79-Story of 1st meeting with Ann 5.00 15.00 35.00
66,67-'Commie' torture story "Drug-Diet Horror" 7.15 21.50 50.00
68,70-72: 68,70-Joe vs. "Gooks"-c. 71-Bloody bayonets-c. 72-Tank-c 6.40 19.25 45.00
69-1st "Battle Adventures" issue; torture & bondage 7.15 21.50 50.00
81-99,101-115: 104,107-Humphrey & Little Max-s 5.00 15.00 30.00
116-S&K Boy Explorers-r (Giant, '60) 7.00 21.00 48.00
117-(84 pg. Giant) r/Commie issues #66,67; Powell-a 7.15 21.50 50.00
118-(84 pg. Giant) Jack Dempsey 2 pg. sty, Powell-a 6.40 19.25 45.00
...**Visits the Lost City** nn (1945)(One Shot)(50¢)-164 page continuous story strip reprint. Has biography & photo of Ham Fisher; possibly the single longest comic book story published in that era (159 pgs.?) 150.00 450.00 1650.00

NOTE: ***Nostrand/Powell** a-73. **Powell** a-7, 8, 10, 12, 14, 17, 19, 26-45, 47-53, 70, 73 at least. Black Cat text stories #8, 12, 13, 19.*

JOE PSYCHO & MOO FROG
Goblin Studios: 1996 - No. 5, 1997 ($2.50, B&W)

1-5: 4-Two covers 2.50
...Full Color Extravagarbonzo ($2.95, color) 3.00

JOE YANK (Korean War)

John Byrne's Next Men #10 © John Byrne

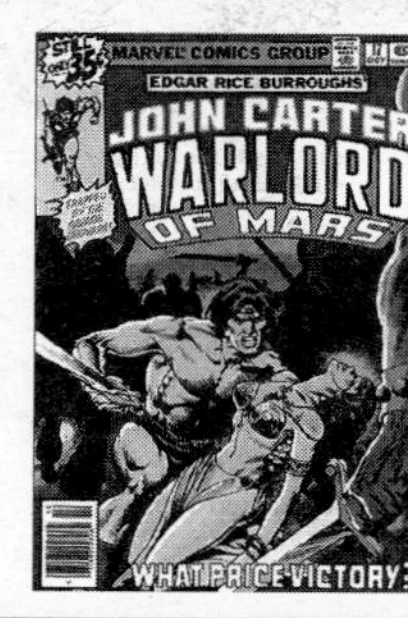

John Carter, Warlord of Mars #17 © ERB

Johnny Hazard #8 © STD

GD2.0 FN6.0 NM9.4

Standard Comics (Visual Editions): No. 5, Mar, 1952 - No. 16, 1954
5-Toth, Celardo, Tuska-a 7.15 21.50 50.00
6-Toth, Severin/Elder-a 8.65 26.00 60.00
7 5.00 15.00 30.00
8-Toth-c 6.40 19.25 45.00
9-16: 9-Andru-c. 12-Andru-a 4.65 14.00 28.00

JOHN BOLTON'S HALLS OF HORROR
Eclipse Comics: June, 1985 - No. 2, June, 1985 ($1.75, limited series)
1,2-British-r; Bolton-c/a 3.00

JOHN BOLTON'S STRANGE WINK
Dark Horse Comics: Mar, 1998 - No. 3, May, 1998 ($2.95, B&W, limited series)
1-3-Anthology; Bolton-s/c/a 3.00

JOHN BYRNE'S NEXT MEN (See Dark Horse Presents #54)
Dark Horse Comics (Legend imprint #19 on): Jan, 1992 - No. 30, Dec, 1994 ($2.50, mature)
1-Silver foil embossed-c; Byrne-c/a/scripts in all 4.00
1-4: 1-2nd printing with gold ink logo 2.50
0-(2/92)-r/chapters 1-4 from DHP w/new Byrne-c 2.50
5-20,22-30: 7-10-MA #1-4 mini-series on flip side. 16-Origin of Mark IV. 17-Miller-c. 19-22-Faith storyline. 23-26-Power storyline. 27-30-Lies storyline Pt. 1-4. 2.50
21-1st Hellboy 5.00
...Parallel, Book 2 ($16.95)-TPB; r/#7-12 17.00
...Fame, Book 3($16.95)-TPB r/#13-18 17.00
...Faith, Book 4($14.95)-TPB r/#19-22 15.00
NOTE: *Issues 1 through 6 contain certificates redeemable for an exclusive Next Men trading card set by Byrne. Prices are for complete books.* ***Cody*** *painted c-23-26.* ***Mignola*** *a-21(part); c-21.*

JOHN BYRNE'S 2112
Dark Horse Comics (Legend): Oct, 1994 ($9.95, TPB)
1-Byrne-c/a/s 10.00

JOHN CARTER OF MARS (See The Funnies & Tarzan #207)
Dell Publishing Co.: No. 375, Mar-May, 1952 - No. 488, Aug-Oct, 1953 (Edgar Rice Burroughs)
Four Color 375 (#1)-Origin; Jesse Marsh-a 24.00 73.00 290.00
Four Color 437, 488-Painted-c 15.00 45.00 180.00

JOHN CARTER OF MARS
Gold Key: Apr, 1964 - No. 3, Oct, 1964
1(10104-404)-r/4-Color #375; Jesse Marsh-a 5.00 15.00 60.00
2(407), 3(410)-r/4-Color #437 & 488; Marsh-a 3.65 11.00 40.00

JOHN CARTER OF MARS
House of Greystroke: 1970 (10-1/2x16-1/2", 72 pgs., B&W, paper-c)
1941-42 Sunday strip-r; John Coleman Burroughs-a 3.00 9.00 30.00

JOHN CARTER, WARLORD OF MARS (Also see Weird Worlds)
Marvel Comics: June, 1977 - No. 28, Oct, 1979
1,18: 18-Frank Miller-a(p)(1st publ. Marvel work) 5.00
2-17,19-28: 1-Origin. 11-Origin Dejah Thoris 3.00
Annuals 1-3: 1(1977). 2(1978). 3(1979)-All 52 pgs. with new book-length stories 3.00
NOTE: ***Austin*** *c-24i.* ***Gil Kane*** *a-1-10p; c-1p, 2p, 3, 4-9p, 10, 15p, Annual 1p.* ***Layton*** *a-17i.* ***Miller*** *c-25, 26p.* ***Nebres*** *a-2-4i, 8-16i; c(i)-6-9, 11-22, 25, Annual 1.* ***Perez*** *c-24p.* ***Simonson*** *a-15p.* ***Sutton*** *a-7i.*

JOHN F. KENNEDY, CHAMPION OF FREEDOM
Worden & Childs: 1964 (no month) (25¢)
nn-Photo-c 5.00 15.00 55.00

JOHN F. KENNEDY LIFE STORY
Dell Publishing Co.: Aug-Oct, 1964; Nov, 1965; June, 1966 (12¢)
12-378-410-Photo-c 3.65 11.00 40.00
12-378-511 (reprint, 11/65) 2.50 7.50 25.00
12-378-606 (reprint, 6/66) 2.50 7.50 23.00

JOHN FORCE (See Magic Agent)

JOHN HIX SCRAP BOOK, THE
Eastern Color Printing Co. (McNaught Synd.): Late 1930's (no date) (10¢, 68 pgs., regular size)
1-Strange As It Seems (resembles Single Series books) 38.00 113.00 300.00
2-Strange As It Seems 26.00 79.00 210.00

JOHN JAKES' MULLKON EMPIRE
Tekno Comix: Sept, 1995 - No. 6, Feb, 1996 ($1.95)
1-6 2.00

JOHN LAW DETECTIVE (See Smash Comics #3)
Eclipse Comics: April, 1983 ($1.50, Baxter paper)
1-Three Eisner stories originally drawn in 1948 for the never published John Law #1; original cover pencilled in 1948 & inked in 1982 by Eisner 3.00

JOHNNY APPLESEED (See Story Hour Series)

JOHNNY CASH (See Hello, I'm...)

JOHNNY DANGER (See Movie Comics, 1946)
Toby Press: 1950 (Based on movie serial)
1-Photo-c; Sparling-a 17.00 51.00 135.00

JOHNNY DANGER PRIVATE DETECTIVE
Toby Press: Aug, 1954 (Reprinted in Danger #11 by Super)
1-Photo-c; Opium den story 13.00 39.00 105.00

JOHNNY DYNAMITE (Formerly Dynamite #1-9; Foreign Intrigues #14 on)
Charlton Comics: No. 10, June, 1955 - No. 12, Oct, 1955
10-12 8.65 26.00 60.00

JOHNNY DYNAMITE
Dark Horse Comics: Sept, 1994 - Dec, 1994 ($2.95, B&W & red, limited series)
1-4: Max Allan Collins scripts in all. 3.00

JOHNNY HAZARD
Best Books (Standard Comics) (King Features): No. 5, Aug, 1948 - No. 8, May, 1949; No. 35, date?
5-Strip reprints by Frank Robbins (c/a) 18.00 53.00 140.00
6,8-Strip reprints by Frank Robbins 15.00 45.00 120.00
7,35: 7-New art, not Robbins 10.00 30.00 80.00

JOHNNY JASON (...Teen Reporter)
Dell Publishing Co.: Feb-Apr, 1962 - No. 2, June-Aug, 1962
Four Color 1302, 2(01380-208) 3.20 9.60 35.00

JOHNNY LAW, SKY RANGER
Good Comics (Lev Gleason): Apr, 1955 - No. 3, Aug, 1955; No. 4, Nov, 1955
1-Edmond Good-c/a 10.00 30.00 70.00
2-4 5.70 17.00 40.00

JOHNNY MACK BROWN (TV western star; see Western Roundup under Dell Giants)
Dell Publishing Co.: No. 269, Mar, 1950 - No. 963, Feb, 1959 (All Photo-c)
Four Color 269(#1)(3/50, 52pgs.)-Johnny Mack Brown & his horse Rebel begin; photo front/back-c begin; Marsh-a in #1-9 23.00 69.00 275.00
2(10-12/50, 52pgs.) 11.30 34.00 135.00
3(1-3/51, 52pgs.) 8.75 26.25 105.00
4-10 (9-11/52)(36pgs.), Four Color 455,493,541,584,618,645,685,722,776, 834,963 5.85 17.50 70.00
Four Color 922-Manning-a 6.30 19.00 75.00

JOHNNY NEMO
Eclipse Comics: Sept, 1985 - No. 3, Feb, 1986 (Mini-series)
1-3 2.00

JOHNNY PERIL (See Comic Cavalcade #15, Danger Trail #5, Sensation Comics #107 & Sensation Mystery)

JOHNNY RINGO (TV)
Dell Publishing Co.: No. 1142, Nov-Jan, 1960/61 (one shot)
Four Color 1142-Photo-c 6.70 20.00 80.00

JOHNNY STARBOARD (See Wisco)

JOHNNY THE HOMICIDAL MANIAC
Slave Labor Graphics: Aug, 1995 - No. 7, Jan, 1997 ($2.95, B&W, lim. series)

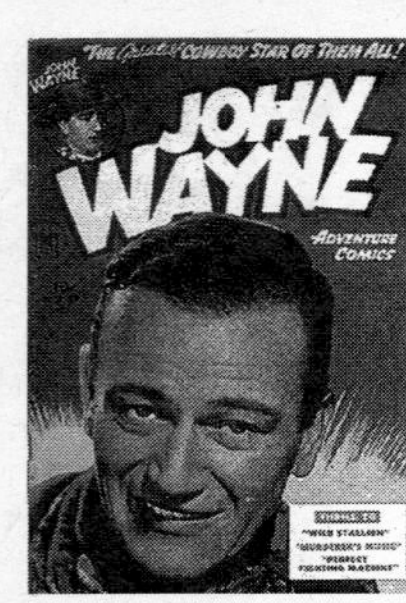

John Wayne Adventure Comics #17 © TOBY

Jo-Jo Comics #14 © FOX

Jonah Hex #19 © DC

GD2.0 FN6.0 NM9.4

1-Jhonen Vasquez-c/s/a 1.85 5.50 15.00
1-Signed & numbered edition 2.50 7.50 20.00
2,3: 2-(11/95). 3-(2/96) 1.00 3.00 8.00
4-7: 4-(5-96). 5-(8/96) 4.00
Hardcover-($29.95) r/#1-7 30.00
TPB-($19.95) 20.00

JOHNNY THUNDER
National Periodical Publications: Feb-Mar, 1973 - No. 3, July-Aug, 1973

1-Johnny Thunder & Nighthawk-r. in all 1.75 5.25 14.00
2,3: 2-Trigger Twins app. 1.10 3.30 9.00
NOTE: *All contain 1950s DC reprints from All-American Western.* ***Drucker*** *r-2, 3.* ***G. Kane*** *r-2, 3.* ***Moriera*** *r-1.* ***Toth*** *r-1, 3; c-1r, 3r. Also see All-American, All-Star Western, Flash Comics, Western Comics, World's Best & World's Finest.*

JOHN PAUL JONES
Dell Publishing Co.: No. 1007, July-Sept, 1959 (one-shot)

Four Color 1007-Movie, Robert Stack photo-c 4.60 13.75 55.00

JOHN STEED & EMMA PEEL (See The Avengers, Gold Key series)

JOHN STEELE SECRET AGENT (Also see Freedom Agent)
Gold Key: Dec, 1964

1-Freedom Agent 8.00 24.00 95.00

JOHN WAYNE ADVENTURE COMICS (Movie star; See Big Tex, Oxydol-Dreft, Tim McCoy, & With The Marines...#1)
Toby Press: Winter, 1949-50 - No. 31, May, 1955 (Photo-c: 1-12,17,25-on)

1 (36pgs.)-Photo-c begin (1st time in comics on-c) 153.00 458.00 1450.00
2-4: 2 (4/50, 36pgs.)-Williamson/Frazetta-a(2) 6 & 2 pgs. (one story-r/Billy the Kid #1); photo back-c. 3 (36pgs.)-Williamson/Frazetta-a(2), 16 pgs. total; photo back-c. 4 (52pgs.)-Williamson/Frazetta-a(2), 16 pgs. total 63.00 189.00 600.00
5 (52pgs.)-Kurtzman-a-(Alfred "L" Newman in Potshot Pete) 47.00 140.00 420.00
6 (52pgs.)-Williamson/Frazetta-a (10 pgs.); Kurtzman-a "Pot-Shot Pete", (5 pgs.); & "Genius Jones", (1 pg.) 58.00 174.00 550.00
7 (52pgs.)-Williamson/Frazetta-a (10 pgs.) 47.00 140.00 420.00
8 (36pgs.)-Williamson/Frazetta-a(2) (12 & 9 pgs.) 58.00 174.00 550.00
9-11: Photo western-c 37.00 111.00 295.00
12,14-Photo war-c. 12-Kurtzman-a(2 pg.) "Genius" 37.00 111.00 295.00
13,15: 13,15-Line-drawn-c begin, end #24 33.00 98.00 260.00
16-Williamson/Frazetta-r/Billy the Kid #1 36.00 107.00 285.00
17-Photo-c 36.00 107.00 285.00
18-Williamson/Frazetta-a (r/#4 & 8, 19 pgs.) 40.00 120.00 320.00
19-24: 23-Evans-a? 30.00 90.00 240.00
25-Photo-c resume; end #31; Williamson/Frazetta-r/Billy the Kid #3 39.00 116.00 310.00
26-28,30-Photo-c 34.00 101.00 270.00
29,31-Williamson/Frazetta-a in each (r/#4, 2) 38.00 113.00 300.00
NOTE: *Williamsonish art in later issues by* ***Gerald McCann.***

JO-JO COMICS (...Congo King #7-29; My Desire #30 on)
(Also see Fantastic Fears and Jungle Jo)
Fox Feature Syndicate: 1945 - No. 29, July, 1949 (Two No.7's; no #13)

nn(1945)-Funny animal, humor 16.00 49.00 130.00
2(Sum,'46)-6(4-5/47): Funny animal. 2-Ten pg. Electro story (Fall/46) 9.30 28.00 65.00
7(7/47)-Jo-Jo, Congo King begins (1st app.); Bronze Man & Purple Tigress app. 87.00 261.00 825.00
7(#8) (9/47) 63.00 189.00 600.00
8-10(#9-11): 8-Tanee begins 53.00 159.00 475.00
11,12(#12,13),14,16: 11,16-Kamen bondage-c 47.00 140.00 420.00
15,17: 15-Cited by Dr. Wertham in 5/47 Saturday Review of Literature. 17-Kamen bondage-c 49.00 147.00 440.00
18-20 47.00 140.00 420.00
21-29: 21-Hollingsworth-a(4 pgs.; 23-1 pg.) 40.00 120.00 340.00
NOTE: *Many bondage-c/a by* ***Baker/Kamen/Feldstein/Good.*** *No. 7's have Princesses Gwenna, Geesa, Yolda, & Safra before settling down on Tanee.*

JOKEBOOK COMICS DIGEST ANNUAL (...Magazine No. 5 on)
Archie Publications: Oct, 1977 - No. 13, Oct, 1983 (Digest Size)

1(10/77)-Reprints; Neal Adams-a 1.85 5.50 15.00
2(4/78)-5 1.25 3.75 10.00
6-11 1.00 3.00 8.00

JOKER, THE (See Batman #1, Batman: The Killing Joke, Brave & the Bold, Detective, Greatest Joker Stories & Justice League Annual #2)
National Periodical Publications: May, 1975 - No. 9, Sept-Oct, 1976

1-Two-Face app. 3.00 9.00 30.00
2,3: 3-The Creeper app. 1.85 5.50 15.00
4-9: 4-Green Arrow-c/sty. 6-Sherlock Holmes-c/sty. 7-Lex Luthor-c/story. 8-Scarecrow-c/story. 9-Catwoman-c/story 1.50 4.50 12.00

JOKER, THE (See Tangent Comics/ The Joker)

JOKER COMICS (Adventures Into Terror No. 43 on)
Timely/Marvel Comics No. 36 on (TCI/CDS): Apr, 1942 - No. 42, Aug, 1950

1-(Rare)-Powerhouse Pepper (1st app.) begins by Wolverton; Stuporman app. from Daring Comics 232.00 695.00 2200.00
2-Wolverton-a; 1st app. Tessie the Typist & begin series 84.00 253.00 800.00
3-5-Wolverton-a 53.00 160.00 480.00
6-10-Wolverton-a. 6-Tessie-c begin 40.00 120.00 325.00
11-20-Wolverton-a 33.00 98.00 260.00
21,22,24-27,29,30-Wolverton cont'd. & Kurtzman's "Hey Look" in #23-27 28.00 83.00 220.00
23-1st "Hey Look" by Kurtzman; Wolverton-a 30.00 90.00 240.00
28,32,34,37-41: 28-Millie the Model begins. 32-Hedy begins. 41-Nellie the Nurse app. 9.30 28.00 65.00
31-Last Powerhouse Pepper; not in #28 20.00 60.00 160.00
33,35,36-Kurtzman's "Hey Look" 10.00 30.00 80.00
42-Only app. 'Patty Pinup,' clone of Millie the Model 10.00 30.00 70.00

JOKER: DEVIL'S ADVOCATE
DC Comics: 1996 ($24.95/$12.95, one-shot)

nn-(Hardcover)-Dixon scripts/Nolan & Hanna-a 25.00
nn-(Softcover) 13.00

JOKER / MASK
Dark Horse Comics: May, 2000 - No. 4, Aug, 2000 ($2.95, limited series)

1-4-Batman, Harley Quinn, Poison Ivy app. 3.00

JOLLY CHRISTMAS, A (See March of Comics No. 269)

JOLLY COMICS: Four Star Publishing Co.: 1947 (Advertised, not published)

JOLLY JINGLES (Formerly Jackpot Comics)
MLJ Magazines: No. 10, Sum, 1943 - No. 16, Wint, 1944/45

10-Super Duck begins (origin & 1st app.); Woody The Woodpecker begins (not same as Lantz character) 38.00 113.00 300.00
11 (Fall, '43)-2nd Super Duck(see Hangman #8) 19.00 56.00 150.00
12-Hitler-c 22.00 66.00 175.00
13-16: 13-Sahle-c. 15-Vigoda-c 12.00 36.00 95.00

JONAH HEX (See All-Star Western, Hex and Weird Western Tales)
National Periodical Pub./DC Comics: Mar-Apr, 1977 - No. 92, Aug, 1985

1 6.80 20.50 75.00
2 3.00 9.00 30.00
3,4,9: 9-Wrightson-c. 2.50 7.50 25.00
5,6,10: 5-Rep 1st app. from All-Star Western #10 2.30 7.00 20.00
7,8-Explains Hex's face disfigurement (origin) 3.00 9.00 30.00
11-20: 12-Starlin-c 1.50 4.50 12.00
21-50: 31,32-Origin retold 1.00 2.80 7.00
51-91: 89-Mark Texeira-a. 92-Story contd in Hex #1 5.00
92 1.85 5.50 15.00
NOTE: ***Ayers*** *a(p)-35-37, 40, 41, 44-53, 56, 58-82.* ***Buckler*** *a-11; c-11, 13-16.* ***Kubert*** *c-43-46.* ***Morrow*** *a-90-92; c-10.* ***Spiegle(Tothish)*** *a-34, 38, 40, 49, 52.* ***Texeira*** *a-89p. Batlash back-ups in 49, 52. El Diablo back-ups in 48, 56-60, 73-75. Scalphunter back-ups in 40, 41, 45-47.*

JONAH HEX AND OTHER WESTERN TALES (Blue Ribbon Digest)
DC Comics: Sept-Oct, 1979 - No. 3, Jan-Feb, 1980 (100 pgs.)

1-3: 1-Origin Scalphunter-r, Ayers/Evans, Neal Adams-a.; painted-c. 2-Weird Western Tales-r; Neal Adams, Toth, Aragones-a. 3-Outlaw-r, Scalphunter-r; Gil Kane, Wildey-a 1.25 3.75 10.00

JONAH HEX: RIDERS OF THE WORM AND SUCH
DC Comics (Vertigo): Mar, 1995 - No. 5, July, 1995 ($2.95, limited series)

Jonny Quest #5 © H-B

Journey Into Fear #3 © SUPR

Journey Into Mystery #5 © MAR

	GD2.0	FN6.0	NM9.4
1-5-Lansdale story, Truman -a			4.00

JONAH HEX: SHADOWS WEST
DC Comics (Vertigo): Feb, 1999 - No. 3, Apr, 1999 ($2.95, limited series)

	GD2.0	FN6.0	NM9.4
1-3-Lansdale-s/Truman -a			4.00

JONAH HEX SPECTACULAR (See DC Special Series No. 16)

JONAH HEX: TWO-GUN MOJO
DC Comics (Vertigo): Aug, 1993 - No. 5, Dec, 1993 ($2.95, limited series)

	GD2.0	FN6.0	NM9.4
1-Lansdale scripts in all;Truman/Glanzman-a in all w/Truman-c		2.40	6.00
1-Platinum edition with no price on cover			20.00
2-5			4.00
TPB-(1994, $12.95) r/#1-5			13.00

JONESY (Formerly Crack Western)
Comic Favorite/Quality Comics Group: No. 85, Aug, 1953; No. 2, Oct, 1953 - No. 8, Oct, 1954

	GD2.0	FN6.0	NM9.4
85(#1)-Teen-age humor	6.40	19.25	45.00
2	4.65	14.00	28.00
3-8	4.00	11.00	22.00

JON JUAN (Also see Great Lover Romances)
Toby Press: Spring, 1950

	GD2.0	FN6.0	NM9.4
1-All Schomburg-a (signed Al Reid on-c); written by Siegel; used in **SOTI**, pg. 38 (Scarce)	58.00	174.00	550.00

JONNI THUNDER (...A.K.A. Thunderbolt)
DC Comics: Feb, 1985 - No. 4, Aug, 1985 (75¢, limited series)

	GD2.0	FN6.0	NM9.4
1-4: 1-Origin & 1st app.			2.00

JONNY DEMON
Dark Horse Comics: May, 1994 - No. 3, July, 1994 ($2.50, limited series)

	GD2.0	FN6.0	NM9.4
1-3			2.50

JONNY DOUBLE
DC Comics (Vertigo): Sept, 1998 - No. 4, Dec, 1998 ($2.95, limited series)

	GD2.0	FN6.0	NM9.4
1-4-Azzarello-s			3.00

JONNY QUEST (TV)
Gold Key: Dec, 1964 (Hanna-Barbera)

	GD2.0	FN6.0	NM9.4
1 (10139-412)	33.00	100.00	400.00

JONNY QUEST (TV)
Comico: June 1986 - No. 31, Dec, 1988 ($1.50/$1.75)(Hanna-Barbera)

	GD2.0	FN6.0	NM9.4
1			4.00
2,3,5: 3,5-Dave Stevens-c			4.00
4,6-31: 30-Adapts TV episode			3.00
Special 1(9/88, $1.75), 2(10/88, $1.75)			4.00

NOTE: ***M. Anderson** a-9. **Mooney** a-Special 1. **Pini** a-2. **Quagmire** a-31p. **Rude** a-1; c-2i. **Sienkiewicz** c-11. **Spiegle** a-7, 12, 21; c-21 **Staton** a-2i, 11p. **Steacy** c-8. **Stevens** a-4i; c-3,5. **Wildey** a-1, c-1, 7, 12. **Williamson** a-4i; c-4i.*

JONNY QUEST CLASSICS (TV)
Comico: May, 1987 - No. 3, July, 1987 ($2.00) (Hanna-Barbera)

	GD2.0	FN6.0	NM9.4
1-3: Wildey-c/a; 3-Based on TV episode			3.00

JON SABLE, FREELANCE (Also see Mike Grell's Sable & Sable)
First Comics: 6/83 - No. 56, 2/88 (#1-17, $1; #18-33, $1.25, #34-on, $1.75)

	GD2.0	FN6.0	NM9.4
1-Mike Grell-c/a/scripts			3.00
2-56: 3-5-Origin, parts 1-3. 6-Origin, part 4. 11-1st app. of Maggie the Cat. 14-Mando paper begins. 16-Maggie the Cat. app. 25-30-Shatter app. 34-Deluxe format begins ($1.75)			2.00

NOTE: ***Aragones** a-33; c-33(part). **Grell** a-1-43;c-1-52, 53p, 54-56.*

JOSEPH & HIS BRETHREN (See The Living Bible)

JOSIE (She's... #1-16) (...& the Pussycats #45 on) (See Archie Giant Series Magazine #528, 540, 551, 562, 571, 584, 597, 610, 622)
Archie Publications/Radio Comics: Feb, 1963; No. 2, Aug, 1963 - No. 106, Oct, 1982

	GD2.0	FN6.0	NM9.4
1	16.50	49.00	180.00
2	8.15	24.50	90.00
3-5	5.45	16.35	60.00
6-10	3.65	11.00	40.00
11-20	3.00	9.00	30.00
21, 23-30	2.40	7.35	22.00
22 (9/66)-Mighty Man & Mighty (Josie Girl) app.	3.20	9.60	35.00
31-44	2.00	6.00	18.00
45 (12/69)-Josie and the Pussycats begins (Hanna Barbera TV cartoon); 1st app. of the Pussycats	7.25	21.75	80.00
46-2nd app./1st cover Pussycats	4.55	13.65	50.00
47-3rd app. of the Pussycats	3.00	9.00	32.00
48,49-Pussycats band-c/s	3.65	11.00	40.00
50-J&P-c; go to Hollywood, meet Hanna & Barbera	4.55	13.65	50.00
51-54	2.50	7.50	25.00
55-74 (2/74)(52pg. issues)	2.30	7.00	20.00
75-90(8/76)	1.50	4.50	12.00
91-99	1.75	5.25	14.00
100 (10/79)	2.00	6.00	18.00
101-106	2.00	6.00	16.00

JOSIE & THE PUSSYCATS (TV)
Archie Comics: 1993 - No. 2, 1994 ($2.00, 52 pgs.)(Published annually)

	GD2.0	FN6.0	NM9.4
1,2-Bound-in pull-out poster in each. 2-(Spr/94)			4.00

JOURNAL OF CRIME (See Fox Giants)

JOURNEY
Aardvark-Vanaheim #1-14/Fantagraphics Books #15-on: 1983 - No. 14, 9/84; No. 15, 4/85 - No. 27, 7/86 (B&W)

	GD2.0	FN6.0	NM9.4
1			3.00
2-27: 20-Sam Kieth-a			2.00

JOURNEY INTO FEAR
Superior-Dynamic Publications: May, 1951 - No. 21, Sept, 1954

	GD2.0	FN6.0	NM9.4
1-Baker-r(2)	61.00	182.00	575.00
2	41.00	123.00	370.00
3,4	39.00	116.00	310.00
5-10,15: 15-Used in **SOTI**, pg. 389	26.00	77.00	205.00
11-14,16-21	24.00	71.00	190.00

NOTE: *Kamenish 'headlight'-a most issues. **Robinson** a-10.*

JOURNEY INTO MYSTERY (1st Series) (Thor Nos. 126-502)
Atlas(CPS No. 1-48/AMI No. 49-68/Marvel No. 69 (6/61) on): 6/52 - No. 48, 8/57; No. 49, 11/58 - No. 125, 2/66; 503, 11/96 - No. 521, June, 1998

	GD2.0	FN6.0	NM9.4
1-Weird/horror stories begin	300.00	900.00	3100.00
2	100.00	300.00	950.00
3,4	76.00	229.00	725.00
5-11	53.00	158.00	475.00
12-20,22: 15-Atomic explosion panel. 22-Davisesque-a; last pre-code issue (2/55)	41.00	123.00	370.00
21-Kubert-a; Tothish-a by Andru	42.00	125.00	375.00
23-32,35-38,40: 24-Torres?-a. 38-Ditko-a	29.00	87.00	235.00
33-Williamson-a; Ditko-a (his 1st for Atlas?)	33.00	98.00	260.00
34,39: 34-Krigstein-a. 39-1st S.A. issue; Wood-a	30.00	90.00	240.00
41-Crandall-a; Frazettaesque-a by Morrow	19.00	57.00	210.00
42,46,48: 42,48-Torres-a. 46-Torres & Krigstein-a	19.00	57.00	210.00
43,44-Williamson/Mayo-a in both	20.00	60.00	220.00
45,47,50,52-54: 50-Davis-a. 54-Williamson-a	18.00	53.00	195.00
49-Matt Fox, Check-a	19.00	57.00	210.00
51-Kirby/Wood-a	21.00	63.00	230.00
55-61,63-65,67-69,71,72,74,75: 74-Contents change to Fantasy. 75-Last 10¢ issue	18.00	54.00	200.00
62-Prototype ish. (The Hulk); 1st app. Xemnu (Titan) called "The Hulk"	27.50	82.00	300.00
66-Prototype ish. (The Hulk)-Return of Xemnu "The Hulk"	24.50	74.00	270.00
70-Prototype ish. (The Sandman)(7/61); similar to Spidey villain	23.50	71.00	260.00
73-Story titled "The Spider" where a spider is exposed to radiation & gets powers of a human and shoots webbing; a reverse prototype of Spider-Man's origin	35.00	105.00	415.00
76,77,80-82: 80-Anti-communist propaganda story	14.50	43.50	160.00
76-(10¢ cover price blacked out, 12¢ printed on)	31.00	93.00	350.00
78-The Sorceror (Dr. Strange prototype) app. (3/62)			

Journey Into Mystery #87 © MAR

Journey Into Unknown Worlds #20 © MAR

JSA: The Liberty File #1 © DC

GD2.0 FN6.0 NM9.4

23.50 71.00 260.00
79-Prototype issue. (Mr. Hyde) 20.50 61.00 225.00
GD2.0 FN6.0 VF8.0 NM9.4
83-Origin & 1st app. The Mighty Thor by Kirby (8/62) and begin series; Thor-c also begin 325.00 975.00 2600.00 5500.00
GD2.0 FN6.0 NM9.4
83-Reprint from the Golden Record Comic Set 11.00 33.00 120.00
with the record (1966) 16.50 49.00 180.00
84-2nd app. Thor 86.00 251.00 1200.00
85-1st app. Loki & Heimdall; Odin cameo (1 panel) 54.00 161.00 750.00
86-1st full app. Odin 41.00 123.00 500.00
87-89: 89-Origin Thor retold 31.00 93.00 350.00
90-No Kirby-a 20.00 60.00 220.00
91,92,94,96-Sinnott-a 16.00 48.00 175.00
93,97-Kirby-a; Tales of Asgard series begins #97 (origin which concludes in #99) 97-Origin/1st app. Lava Man 18.00 54.00 200.00
95-Sinnott-a (scarce in VF/NM) 17.00 51.00 185.00
98-100-Kirby/Heck-a. 98-Origin/1st app. The Human Cobra. 99-1st app. Surtur & Mr. Hyde 13.50 40.00 150.00
101,108: 101-(2/64)-2nd Avengers x-over (w/o Capt. America); see Tales Of Suspense #49 for 1st x-over. 108-(9/64)-Early Dr. Strange & Avengers x-over; ten extra pgs. Kirby-a 9.50 28.50 105.00
102-107,110: 102-Intro Sif. 103-1st app. Enchantress. 105-109-Ten extra pgs. Kirby-a in each. 107-1st app. Grey Gargoyle 8.65 26.00 95.00
109-Magneto-c & app. (1st x-over, 10/64) 12.50 37.00 135.00
111,113,114,116-123,125: 113-Origin Loki. 114-Origin/1st app. Absorbing Man. 118-1st app. Destroyer. 119-Intro Hogun, Fandrall, Volstagg
7.65 23.00 85.00
112-Thor Vs. Hulk (1/65). 112-Origin Loki 22.00 65.00 240.00
115-Origin Loki 10.00 30.00 110.00
124-Hercules-c/story 8.65 26.00 95.00
503-521: 503-(11/96, $1.50)-The Lost Gods begin; Tom DeFalco scripts & Deodato Studios-c/a. 505-Spider-Man-c/app. 509-Loki-c/app. 514-516-Shang-Chi 2.00
#(-1) Flashback (7/97) Tales of Asgard Donald Blake app. 2.00
Annual 1(1965, 25¢, 72 pgs.)-New Thor vs. Hercules(1st app.)-c/story (see Incredible Hulk #3); Kirby-c/a; r/#85,93,95,97 18.00 54.00 200.00

NOTE: ***Ayers*** *a-14, 39, 64i, 71i, 74i, 80i.* ***Bailey*** *a-43.* ***Briefer*** *a-5, 12.* ***Cameron*** *a-35.* ***Check*** *a-17.* ***Colan*** *a-23, 81; c-14.* ***Ditko*** *a-33, 38, 50-96; c-58, 67, 71, 88i.* ***Kirby/Ditko*** *a-50-83.* ***Everett*** *a-20, 48; c-4-7, 9, 36, 37, 39-42, 44, 45, 47.* ***Forte*** *a-19, 35, 40, 53.* ***Heath*** *a-4-6, 11, 14; c-1, 8, 11, 15, 51.* ***Heck*** *a-53, 73.* ***Kirby*** *a(p)-51, 52, 56, 57, 60, 62, 64, 66, 69, 71-74, 76, 79, 80-89, 93, 97, 98, 100(w/****Heck****), 101-125; c-50-57, 59-66, 68-70, 72-82, 88(w/****Ditko****), 83 & 84(w/****Sinnott****), 85-96(w/****Ayers****), 97-125p.* ***Leiber/Fox*** *a-93, 98-102.* ***Maneely*** *c-20-22.* ***Morisi*** *a-42.* ***Morrow*** *a-41, 42.* ***Orlando*** *a-30, 45, 57.* ***Mac Pakula*** *(Tothish) a-9, 35, 41.* ***Powell*** *a-20, 27, 34.* ***Reinman*** *a-39, 87, 92, 96i.* ***Robinson*** *a-9.* ***Roussos*** *a-39.* ***Robert Sale*** *a-14.* ***Severin*** *a-27; c-30.* ***Sinnott*** *a-41; c-50.* ***Tuska*** *a-11.* ***Wildey*** *a-16.*

JOURNEY INTO MYSTERY (2nd Series)
Marvel Comics: Oct, 1972 - No. 19, Oct, 1975

1-Robert Howard adaptation; Starlin/Ploog-a 2.30 7.00 20.00
2-5: 2,3,5-Bloch adapt. 4-H. P. Lovecraft adapt. 1.75 5.25 14.00
6-19: Reprints 1.25 3.75 10.00

NOTE: ***N. Adams*** *a-2i.* ***Ditko*** *r-7, 10, 12, 14, 15, 19; c-10.* ***Everett*** *r-9, 14.* ***G. Kane*** *a-1p, 2p; c-1-3p.* ***Kirby*** *r-7, 13, 15, 18, 19; c-7.* ***Mort Lawrence*** *r-2.* ***Maneely*** *r-3.* ***Orlando*** *r-16.* ***Reese*** *a-1, 2i.* ***Starlin*** *a-1p, 3p.* ***Torres*** *r-16.* ***Wildey*** *r-9, 14.*

JOURNEY INTO UNKNOWN WORLDS (Formerly Teen)
Atlas Comics (WFP): No. 36, 9/50 - No. 38, 2/51; No. 4, 4/51 - No. 59, 8/57

36(#1)-Science fiction/weird; "End Of The Earth" c/story
221.00 663.00 2100.00
37(#2)-Science fiction; "When Worlds Collide" c/story; Everett-c/a; Hitler story
98.00 295.00 935.00
38(#3)-Science fiction 82.00 245.00 775.00
4-6,8,10-Science fiction/weird 53.00 158.00 475.00
7-Wolverton-a "Planet of Terror", 6 pgs; electric chair c-inset/story
87.00 261.00 825.00
9-Giant eyeball story 63.00 189.00 600.00
11,12-Krigstein-a 40.00 120.00 360.00
13,16,17,20 34.00 101.00 270.00
14-Wolverton-a "One of Our Graveyards Is Missing", 4 pgs; Tuska-a
66.00 197.00 625.00
15-Wolverton-a "They Crawl by Night", 5 pgs.; 2 pg. Maneely s/f story
66.00 197.00 625.00
18,19-Matt Fox-a 39.00 116.00 310.00
21-33: 21-Decapitation-c. 24-Sci/fic story. 26-Atom bomb panel. 27-Sid Check-a. 33-Last pre-code (2/55) 26.00 79.00 210.00
34-Kubert, Torres-a 20.00 60.00 160.00
35-Torres-a 18.00 53.00 140.00
36-45,48,50,53,55,59: 43-Krigstein-a. 44-Davis-a. 45,55,59-Williamson-a in all; with Mayo #55,59. 55-Crandall-a. 48,53-Crandall-a (4 pgs. #48). 48-Check-a. 50-Davis, Crandall-a 17.00 51.00 135.00
46,47,49,52,54,56-58: 54-Torres-a 15.00 45.00 120.00
51-Ditko, Wood-a 19.00 56.00 150.00

NOTE: ***Ayers*** *a-24, 43,* ***Berg*** *a-38(#3), 43.* ***Lou Cameron*** *a-33.* ***Colan*** *a-37(#2), 6, 17, 19, 20, 23, 39.* ***Ditko*** *a-45, 51.* ***Drucker*** *a-35, 58.* ***Everett*** *a-37(#2), 11, 14, 41, 55, 56; c-37(#2), 11, 13, 14, 17, 22, 47, 48, 50, 53-55, 59.* ***Forte*** *a-49.* ***Fox*** *a-21i.* ***Heath*** *a-36(#1), 4, 6-8, 17, 20, 22, 36i; c-18.* ***Keller*** *a-15.* ***Mort Lawrence*** *a-38, 39.* ***Maneely*** *a-7, 8, 15, 16, 22, 49, 58; c-19, 25, 52.* ***Morrow*** *a-48.* ***Orlando*** *a-44, 57.* ***Pakula*** *a-36.* ***Powell*** *a-42, 53, 54.* ***Reinman*** *a-8.* ***Rico*** *a-21.* ***Robert Sale*** *a-24, 49.* ***Sekowsky*** *a-4, 5, 9.* ***Severin*** *a-38, 51; c-38, 48i, 56.* ***Sinnott*** *a-9, 21, 24.* ***Tuska*** *a-38(#3), 14.* ***Wildey*** *a-25, 43, 44.*

JOURNEYMAN
Image Comics: Aug, 1999 - No. 3, Oct, 1999 ($2.95, B&W, limited series)

1-3-Brandon McKinney-s/a 3.00

JOURNEY TO THE CENTER OF THE EARTH (Movie)
Dell Publishing Co.: No. 1060, Nov-Jan, 1959/60 (one-shot)

Four Color 1060-Pat Boone & James Mason photo-c 11.30 34.00 135.00

JSA (Justice Society of America) (Also see All Star Comics)
DC Comics: Aug, 1999 - Present ($2.50)

1-Robinson and Goyer-s; funeral of Wesley Dodds 2.50
2-20: 4-Return of Dr. Fate. 6-Black Adam-c/app. 11,12-Kobra. 16-20-JSA vs. Johnny Sorrow. 19,20-Spectre app. 2.50
Annual 1 (10/00, $3.50) Planet DC; intro. Nemesis 3.50
... Secret Files 1 (8/99, $4.95) Origin stories and pin-ups; death of Wesley Dodds (G.A. Sandman); intro new Hawkgirl 5.00
Justice Be Done TPB (2000, $14.95) r/Secret Files & #1-5 14.95

JSA: THE LIBERTY FILE (Elseworlds)
DC Comics: Feb, 2000 - No. 2, Mar, 2000 ($6.95, limited series)

1,2-Batman, Dr. Mid-Nite and Hourman vs. WW2 Joker 6.95

J2 (Also see A-Next and Juggernaut)
Marvel Comics: Oct, 1998 - No. 12, Sept, 1999 ($1.99)

1-Juggernaut's son; Lim-a 2.00
2-12: 2-Two covers; X-People app. 3-J2 battles the Hulk 2.00

JUDE, THE FORGOTTEN SAINT
Catechetical Guild Education Soc.: 1954 (16 pgs.; 8x11"; full color; paper-c)

nn 3.20 8.00 16.00

J.U.D.G.E.: THE SECRET RAGE
Image Comics: Mar, 2000 - Present ($2.95)

1-3-Greg Horn-s/c/a 2.95

JUDGE COLT
Gold Key: Oct, 1969 - No. 4, Sept, 1970

1 2.00 6.00 18.00
2-4 1.25 3.75 10.00

JUDGE DREDD (...Classics #62 on; also see Batman - Judge Dredd, The Law of Dredd & 2000 A.D. Monthly)
Eagle Comics/IPC Magazines Ltd./Quality Comics #34-35, V2#1-37/ Fleetway #38 on: Nov, 1983 - No. 35, 1986; V2#1, Oct, 1986 - No. 77, 1993

1-Bolland-c/a 2.40 6.00
2-35 2.50
V2#1-77: 1-('86)-New look begins. 20-Begin $1.50-c. 21/22, 23/24-Two issue numbers in one. 28-1st app. Megaman (super-hero). 39-Begin $1.75-c. 51-Begin $1.95-c. 53-Bolland-a. 57-Reprints 1st published Judge Dredd story 2.50
Special 1 2.50

NOTE: ***Bolland*** *a-1-6, 8, 10; c-1-10, 15.* ***Guice*** *c-V2#23/24, 26, 27.*

JUDGE DREDD (3rd Series)
DC Comics: Aug, 1994 - No. 18, Jan, 1996 ($1.95)

Judge Dredd #2 © DC

Jughead #325 © AP

Jughead's Baby Tales #1 © AP

GD2.0 FN6.0 NM9.4

- 1-18: 12-Begin $2.25-c — 2.50
- nn ($5.95)-Movie adaptation, Sienkiewicz-c — 2.40 6.00

JUDGE DREDD'S CRIME FILE
Eagle Comics: Aug, 1989 - No. 6, Feb, 1986 ($1.25, limited series)

- 1-6: 1-Byrne-a — 2.50

JUDGE DREDD: LEGENDS OF THE LAW
DC Comics: Dec, 1994 - No. 13, Dec, 1995 ($1.95)

- 1-13: 1-5-Dorman-c — 2.50

JUDGE DREDD: THE EARLY CASES
Eagle Comics: Feb, 1986 - No. 6, Jul, 1986 ($1.25, Mega-series, Mando paper)

- 1-6: 2000 A.D.-r — 2.50

JUDGE DREDD: THE JUDGE CHILD QUEST (Judge Child in indicia)
Eagle Comics: Aug, 1984 - No. 5, Oct, 1984 ($1.25, Lim. series, Baxter paper)

- 1-5: 2000A.D.-r; Bolland-c/a — 2.50

JUDGE DREDD: THE MEGAZINE
Fleetway/Quality: 1991 - Present ($4.95, stiff-c, squarebound, 52 pgs.)

- 1-3 — 5.00

JUDGE PARKER
Argo: Feb, 1956 - No. 2, 1956

- 1-Newspaper strip reprints — 5.70 17.00 40.00
- 2 — 4.30 13.00 26.00

JUDGMENT DAY
Awesome Entertainment: June, 1997 - No. 3, Oct, 1997 ($2.50, limited series)

- 1-3: 1 Alpha-Moore-s/Liefeld-c/a(p) flashback art by various in all. 2 Omega. 3 Final Judgment, — 2.50
- 1-3-Variant cover by Dave Gibbons — 2.50
- ...Aftermath-($3.50) Moore-s/Kane-a; Youngblood, Glory, New Men, Maximage Allies and Spacehunter short stories — 3.50
- ...Aftermath-Variant cover by Dave Gibbons — 3.50

JUDGMENT PAWNS
Antarctic Press: Feb, 1997 ($2.95, one-shot)

- 1 — 3.00

JUDO JOE
Jay-Jay Corp.: Aug, 1953 - No. 3, Dec, 1953 (Judo lessons in each issue)

- 1-Drug ring story — 8.65 26.00 60.00
- 2,3: 3-Hypo needle story — 6.00 18.00 42.00

JUDOMASTER (Gun Master #84-89) (Also see Crisis on Infinite Earths, Sarge Steel #6 & Special War Series)
Charlton Comics: No. 89, May-June, 1966 - No. 98, Dec, 1967 (Two No. 89's)

- 89-3rd app. Judomaster — 3.45 10.35 38.00
- 90,92-98: 93-Intro. Tiger — 3.00 9.00 30.00
- 91-Sarge Steel begins — 3.00 9.00 32.00
- 93,94,96,98 (Modern Comics reprint, 1977) — 4.00

NOTE: ***Morisi*** *Thunderbolt #90. #91 has 1 pg. biography on writer/artist Frank McLaughlin.*

JUDY CANOVA (Formerly My Experience) (Stage, screen, radio)
Fox Features Syndicate: No. 23, May, 1950 - No. 3, Sept, 1950

- 23(#1)-Wood-c,a(p)? — 21.00 64.00 170.00
- 24-Wood-a(p) — 21.00 64.00 170.00
- 3-Wood-c; Wood/Orlando-a — 23.00 69.00 185.00

JUDY GARLAND (See Famous Stars)

JUDY JOINS THE WAVES
Toby Press: 1951 (For U.S. Navy)

- nn — 5.70 17.00 40.00

JUGGERNAUT (See X-Men)
Marvel Comics: Apr, 1997, Nov, 1999 ($2.99, one-shots)

- 1-(4/97) Kelly-s/ Rouleau-a — 3.00
- 1-(11/99) Casey-s; Eighth Day x-over; Thor, Iron Man, Spidey app. — 3.00

JUGHEAD (Formerly Archie's Pal...)
Archie Publications: No. 127, Dec, 1965 - No. 352, June, 1987

- 127-130 — 2.50 7.50 24.00
- 131,133,135-160(9/68) — 2.30 7.00 20.00
- 132,134: 132-Shield-c; The Fly & Black Hood app.; Shield cameo. 134-Shield-c — 2.80 8.40 28.00
- 161-180 — 1.85 5.50 15.00
- 181-199 — 1.50 4.50 12.00
- 200(1/'72) — 1.75 5.25 14.00
- 201-240(5/75) — 1.00 3.00 8.00
- 241-270(11/77) — 2.40 6.00
- 271-299 — 5.00
- 300(5/80)-Anniversary issue; infinity-c — 2.40 6.00
- 301-320(1/82) — 4.00
- 321-324,326-352 — 3.00
- 325-(10/82) Cheryl Blossom app. (not on cover); same month as intro. (cover & story) in Archie's Girls, Betty & Veronica #320; Jason Blossom app.; DeCarlo-a — 2.30 7.00 20.00

JUGHEAD (2nd Series)(Becomes Archie's Pal Jughead Comics #46 on)
Archie Enterprises: Aug, 1987 - No. 45, May, 1993 (.75/$1.00/$1.25)

- 1 — 5.00
- 2-10 — 3.00
- 11-45: 4-X-Mas issue. 17-Colan-c/a — 2.00

JUGHEAD AS CAPTAIN HERO (See Archie as Purehear the Powerful, Archie Giant Series Magazine #142 & Life With Archie)
Archie Publications: Oct, 1966 - No. 7, Nov, 1967

- 1-Super hero parody — 5.45 16.35 60.00
- 2 — 3.65 11.00 40.00
- 3-7 — 2.80 8.40 28.00

JUGHEAD JONES COMICS DIGEST, THE (...Magazine No. 10-64; Jughead Jones Digest Magazine #65)
Archie Publ.: June, 1977 - No. 100, May, 1996 ($1.35/$1.50/$1.75, digest-size, 128 pgs.)

- 1-Neal Adams-a; Capt. Hero-r — 2.60 7.80 26.00
- 2(9/77)-Neal Adams-a — 2.30 7.00 20.00
- 3-6,8-10 — 1.75 5.25 14.00
- 7-Origin Jaguar-r; N. Adams-a. — 2.00 6.00 18.00
- 11-20: 13-r/1957 Jughead's Folly — 1.25 3.75 10.00
- 21-50 — 1.00 2.80 7.00
- 51-70 — 5.00
- 71-100 — 3.00

JUGHEAD'S BABY TALES
Archie Comics: Spring, 1994 - No. 2, Wint. 1994 ($2.00, 52 pgs.)

- 1,2: 1-Bound-in pull-out poster — 3.00

JUGHEAD'S DINER
Archie Comics: Apr, 1990 - No. 7, Apr, 1991 ($1.00)

- 1 — 3.00
- 2-7 — 2.00

JUGHEAD'S DOUBLE DIGEST (...Magazine #5)
Archie Comics: Oct, 1989 - Present ($2.25/$2.50/$2.75/$2.79/$2.95/$2.99)

- 1 — 1.25 3.75 10.00
- 2-10: 2,5-Capt. Hero stories — 1.00 2.80 7.00
- 11-25 — 4.00
- 26-74: 58-Begin $2.99-c. 66-Begin $3.19-c — 3.20

JUGHEAD'S EAT-OUT COMIC BOOK MAGAZINE (See Archie Giant Series Magazine No. 170)

JUGHEAD'S FANTASY
Archie Publications: Aug, 1960 - No. 3, Dec, 1960

- 1 — 17.50 52.00 190.00
- 2 — 11.50 34.00 125.00
- 3 — 10.00 30.00 110.00

JUGHEAD'S FOLLY
Archie Publications (Close-Up): 1957 (36 pgs.)(one-shot)

- 1-Jughead a la Elvis (Rare) (1st reference to Elvis in comics?) — 50.00 150.00 450.00

JUGHEAD'S JOKES

Jughead's Jokes #5 © AP

Jumbo Comics #27 © FH

Jungle Action #2 © ATLAS

Archie Publications: Aug, 1967 - No. 78, Sept, 1982
(No. 1-8, 38 on: reg. size; No. 9-23: 68 pgs.; No. 24-37: 52 pgs.)

	GD2.0	FN6.0	NM9.4
1	6.35	19.00	70.00
2	3.20	9.60	35.00
3-8	2.50	7.50	25.00
9,10 (68 pgs.)	2.80	8.40	28.00
11-23(4/71) (68 pgs.)	2.30	7.00	20.00
24-37(1/74) (52 pgs.)	2.00	6.00	16.00
38-50(9/76)	1.00	3.00	8.00
51-78			4.00

JUGHEAD'S PAL HOT DOG (See Laugh #14 for 1st app.)
Archie Comics: Jan, 1990 - No. 5, Oct, 1990 ($1.00)

	GD2.0	FN6.0	NM9.4
1			3.00
2-5			2.00

JUGHEAD'S SOUL FOOD
Spire Christian Comics (Fleming H. Revell Co.): 1979 (49 cents)

	GD2.0	FN6.0	NM9.4
nn	1.25	3.75	10.00

JUGHEAD'S TIME POLICE
Archie Comics: July, 1990 - No. 6, May, 1991 ($1.00, bi-monthly)

	GD2.0	FN6.0	NM9.4
1			3.00
2-6: Colan a-3-6p; c-3-6			2.00

JUGHEAD WITH ARCHIE DIGEST (...Plus Betty & Veronica & Reggie Too No. 1,2; ...Magazine #33-?, 101-on; ...Comics Digest Mag.)
Archie Pub.: Mar, 1974 - Present ($1.00/$1.25/$1.35/$1.50/$1.75/$1.95/$1.99)

	GD2.0	FN6.0	NM9.4
1	4.55	13.65	50.00
2	3.00	9.00	30.00
3-10	2.30	7.00	20.00
11-13,15-17,19,20: Capt. Hero-r in #14-16; Capt. Pureheart #17,19	1.75	5.25	14.00
14,18,21,22-Pureheart the Powerful in #18,21,22	1.75	5.25	14.00
23-30: 29-The Shield-r. 30-The Fly-r	1.25	3.75	10.00
31-50,100	1.00	3.00	8.00
51-99	1.00	2.80	7.00
101-121			4.00
122-163: 156-Begin $2.19-c			2.20

JUKE BOX COMICS
Famous Funnies: Mar, 1948 - No. 6, Jan, 1949

	GD2.0	FN6.0	NM9.4
1-Toth-c/a; Hollingsworth-a	40.00	120.00	350.00
2-Transvestism story	26.00	79.00	210.00
3-6: 3-Peggy Lee story. 4-Jimmy Durante line drawn-c. 6-Features Desi Arnaz plus Arnaz line drawn-c	20.00	60.00	160.00

JUMBO COMICS (Created by S.M. Iger)
Fiction House Magazines (Real Adv. Publ. Co.): Sept, 1938 - No. 167, Mar, 1953 (No. 1-3: 68 pgs.; No. 4-8: 52 pgs.)(No. 1-8 oversized-10-1/2x14-1/2"; black & white)

	GD2.0	FN6.0	VF8.0
1-(Rare)-Sheena Queen of the Jungle(1st app.) by Meskin, Hawks of the Seas (The Hawk #10 on; see Feature Funnies #3) by Eisner, The Hunchback by Dick Briefer (ends #8), Wilton of the West (ends #24), Inspector Dayton (ends #67) & ZX-5 (ends #140) begin; 1st comic art by Jack Kirby (Count of Monte Cristo & Wilton of the West); Mickey Mouse appears (1 panel) with brief biography of Walt Disney; 1st app. Peter Pupp by Bob Kane. Note: Sheena was created by Iger for publication in England as a newspaper strip. The early issues of Jumbo contain Sheena strip-r; multiple panel-c 1,2,7	1900.00	5700.00	19,000.00
2-(Rare)-Origin Sheena. Diary of Dr. Hayward by Kirby (also #3) plus 2 other stories; contains strip from Universal Film featuring Edgar Bergen & Charlie McCarthy plus-c (preview of film)	620.00	1860.00	6200.00
3-Last Kirby issue	420.00	1260.00	4200.00
4-(Scarce)-Origin The Hawk by Eisner; Wilton of the West by Fine (ends #14)(1st comic work); Count of Monte Cristo by Fine (ends #15); The Diary of Dr. Hayward by Fine (cont'd #8,9)	390.00	1170.00	3900.00
5-Christmas-c	340.00	1020.00	3400.00
6-8-Last B&W issue. #8 was a 1939 N. Y. World's Fair Special Edition; Frank Buck's Jungleland story	300.00	900.00	3000.00
9-Stuart Taylor begins by Fine (ends #140); Fine-c; 1st color issue (8-9/39)-1st Sheena (jungle) cover; 8-1/4x10-1/4" (oversized in width only)	270.00	810.00	2700.00

	GD2.0	FN6.0	NM9.4
10-Regular size 68 pg. issues begin; Sheena dons new costume w/ origin costume; Stuart Taylor sci/fi-c; classic Lou Fine-c.	179.00	537.00	1700.00
11-13: 12-The Hawk-c by Eisner. 13-Eisner-c	121.00	363.00	1150.00
14-Intro. Lightning (super-hero) on-c only	126.00	379.00	1200.00
15,17-20: 15-1st Lightning story and begins, ends #41. 17-Lightning part-c	76.00	229.00	725.00
16-Lightning-c	95.00	285.00	900.00
21-30: 22-1st Tom, Dick & Harry; origin The Hawk retold. 25-Midnight the Black Stallion begins, ends #65	61.00	182.00	575.00
31-40: 31-(9/41)-1st app. Mars God of War in Stuart Taylor story (see Planet Comics #15. 35-Shows V2#11 (correct number does not appear)	50.00	150.00	450.00
41-50: 42-Ghost Gallery begins, ends #167	40.00	120.00	350.00
51-60: 52-Last Tom, Dick & Harry	35.00	105.00	280.00
61-70: 68-Sky Girl begins, ends #130; not in #79	26.00	79.00	210.00
71-93,95-99: 89-ZX5 becomes a private eye.	20.00	60.00	160.00
94-Used in Love and Death by Legman	22.00	66.00	175.00
100	22.00	66.00	175.00
101-140,150-158: 155-Used in **POP**, pg. 98	16.00	49.00	130.00
141-149-Two Sheena stories. 141-Long Bow, Indian Boy begins, ends #160	16.00	49.00	130.00
159-163: Space Scouts serial in all. 160-Last jungle-c (6/52). 161-Ghost Gallery covers begin, end #167. 163-Suicide Smith app.	15.00	45.00	120.00
164-The Star Pirate begins, ends #165	15.00	45.00	120.00
165-167: 165,167-Space Rangers app.	15.00	45.00	120.00

NOTE: *Bondage covers, negligee panels, torture, etc. are common in this series. Hawks of the Seas, Inspector Dayton, Spies in Action, Sports Shorts, & Uncle Otto by Eisner, #1-7. Hawk by* ***Eisner****-#10-15.* ***Eisner*** *c-1-8, 12-14. 1pg. Patsy pin-ups in 92-97, 99-101. Sheena by* ***Meskin****-#1, 4; by* ***Powell****-#2, 3, 5-28;* ***Powell*** *c-14, 16, 17, 19.* ***Powell/Eisner*** *c-15. Sky Girl by* ***Matt Baker****-#69-78, 80-130. ZX-5 & Ghost Gallery by* ***Kamen****-#90-130.* ***Bailey*** *a-3-8.* ***Briefer*** *a-1-8, 10.* ***Fine*** *a-14; c-9-11.* ***Kamen*** *a-101, 105, 123, 132; c-105, 121-145.* ***Bob Kane*** *a-1-8.* ***Whitman*** *c-146-167(most). Jungle c-9, 13, 15, 17 on.*

JUNGLE ACTION
Atlas Comics (IPC): Oct, 1954 - No. 6, Aug, 1955

	GD2.0	FN6.0	NM9.4
1-Leopard Girl begins by Al Hartley (#1,3); Jungle Boy by Forte; Maneely-a in all	38.00	113.00	300.00
2-(3-D effect cover)	38.00	113.00	300.00
3-6: 3-Last precode (2/55)	24.00	71.00	190.00

NOTE: ***Maneely*** *c-1, 2, 5, 6.* ***Romita*** *a-3, 6.* ***Shores*** *a-3, 6; c-3, 4?.*

JUNGLE ACTION (...& Black Panther #18-21?)
Marvel Comics Group: Oct, 1972 - No. 24, Nov, 1976

	GD2.0	FN6.0	NM9.4
1-Lorna, Jann-r (All reprints in 1-4)	2.00	6.00	18.00
2-4	1.25	3.75	10.00
5-Black Panther begins (r/Avengers #62)	2.00	6.00	18.00
6,8: 6-New stories begin. 8-Origin Black Panther	1.75	5.25	14.00
7,9,10: 9-Contains pull-out centerfold ad by Mark Jewelers	1.25	3.75	10.00
11-20,23,24: 19-23-KKK x-over. 23-r/#22. 24-1st Wind Eagle; sty contd in Marvel Premiere #51-#53		2.40	6.00
21,22-(Regular 25¢ edition)(5,7/76)		2.40	6.00
21,22-(30¢-c variant, limited distribution)	1.10	3.30	9.00

NOTE: ***Buckler*** *a-6-9p, 22; c-8p, 12p.* ***Buscema*** *a-5p; c-22.* ***Byrne*** *c-23.* ***Gil Kane*** *a-8p; c-2, 4, 10p, 11p, 13-17, 19, 24.* ***Kirby*** *c-18.* ***Maneely*** *r-1.* ***Russell*** *a-13i.* ***Starlin*** *c-3p.*

JUNGLE ADVENTURES
Super Comics: 1963 - 1964 (Reprints)

	GD2.0	FN6.0	NM9.4
10,12,15,17,18: 10-r/Terrors of the Jungle #4 & #10(Rulah). 12-r/Zoot #14 (Rulah).15-r/Kaanga from Jungle #152 & Tiger Girl . 17-All Jo-Jo-r. 18-Reprints/White Princess of the Jungle #1; no Kinstler-a; origin of both White Princess & Cap'n Courage	3.20	9.60	35.00

JUNGLE ADVENTURES
Skywald Comics: Mar, 1971 - No. 3, June, 1971 (25¢, 52 pgs.)

	GD2.0	FN6.0	NM9.4
1-Zangar origin; reprints of Jo-Jo, Blue Gorilla(origin)/White Princess #3, Kinstler-r/White Princess #2	2.30	7.00	20.00
2,3: 2-Zangar, Sheena-r/Sheena #17 & Jumbo #162, Jo-Jo, origin Slave Girl-r.			

Jungle Comics #26 © FH

Jungle Comics #158 © FH

Jungle Jim #13 © STD

GD2.0 FN6.0 NM9.4

3-Zangar, Jo-Jo, White Princess, Rulah-r 1.75 5.25 14.00

JUNGLE BOOK (See King Louie and Mowgli, Movie Comics, Mowgli..., Walt Disney Showcase #45 & Walt Disney's The Jungle Book)

JUNGLE CAT (Disney)
Dell Publishing Co.: No. 1136, Sept-Nov, 1960 (one shot)

Four Color 1136-Movie, photo-c 5.85 17.50 70.00

JUNGLE COMICS
Fiction House Magazines: 1/40 - No. 157, 3/53; No. 158, Spr, 1953 - No. 163, Summer, 1954

1-Origin The White Panther, Kaanga, Lord of the Jungle, Tabu, Wizard of the Jungle; Wambi, the Jungle Boy, Camilla & Capt. Terry Thunder begin (all 1st app.). Lou Fine-c 429.00 1286.00 4500.00
2-Fantomah, Mystery Woman of the Jungle begins, ends #51; The Red Panther begins, ends #26 158.00 474.00 1500.00
3,4 132.00 395.00 1250.00
5-Classic Eisner-c 142.00 426.00 1350.00
6-10: 7,8-Powell-c 74.00 221.00 700.00
11-20: 13-Tuska-c 53.00 158.00 475.00
21-30: 25-Shows V2#1 (correct number does not appear). #27-New origin Fantomah, Daughter of the Pharoahs; Camilla dons new costume 42.00 125.00 375.00
31-40 34.00 101.00 270.00
41,43-50 30.00 90.00 240.00
42-Kaanga by Crandall, 12 pgs. 33.00 98.00 260.00
51-60 26.00 79.00 210.00
61-70: 67-Cover swipes Crandall splash pg. in #42 22.00 66.00 175.00
71-80: 79-New origin Tabu 20.00 60.00 160.00
81-97,99,101-110 18.00 53.00 140.00
98-Used in **SOTI**, pg. 185 & illo "In ordinary comic books, there are pictures within pictures for children who know how to look;" used by N.Y. Legis. Comm. 31.00 94.00 250.00
100 22.00 66.00 175.00
111-163: 104-In Camilla story villain is Dr. Wertham. 118-Clyde Beatty app. 135-Desert Panther begins in Terry Thunder (origin), not in #137; ends (dies) #138. 139-Last 52 pg. issue. 141-Last Tabu. 143,145-Used in **POP**, pg. 99. 151-Last Camilla & Terry Thunder. 152-Tiger Girl begins. 158-Last Wambi; Sheena app. 16.00 49.00 130.00
I.W. Reprint #1,9: 1-r/? 9-r/#151 3.00 9.00 30.00

NOTE: *Bondage covers, negligee panels, torture, etc. are common to this series. Camilla by* ***Fran Hopper****-#70-92; by* ***Baker****-#69, 100-113, 115, 116; by* ***Lubbers****-#97-99 by* ***Tuska****-#63, 65. Kaanga by* ***John Celardo****-#80-113; by* ***Larsen****-#71, 75-79; by* ***Moreira****-#58, 60, 61, 63-70, 72-74; by* ***Tuska****-#37, 62; by* ***Whitman****-#114-163. Tabu by* ***Larsen****-#59-75, 82-92; by* ***Whitman****-#93-115. Terry Thunder by* ***Hopper****-#71, 72; by* ***Celardo****-#78, 79; by* ***Lubbers****-#80-85. Tiger Girl-r by* ***Baker****-#152, 153, 155-157, 159. Wambi by* ***Baker****-#62-67, 74.* ***Astarita*** *c-45, 46.* ***Celardo*** *a-78; c-98-113.* ***Crandall*** *c-67 from splash pg.* ***Eisner*** *c-2, 5, 6.* ***Fine*** *c-1.* ***Larsen*** *a-65, 66, 71, 72, 74, 75, 79, 83, 84, 87-90.* ***Moriera*** *c-43, 44.* ***Morisi*** *a-51.* ***Powell*** *c-7, 8.* ***Sultan*** *c-3, 4.* ***Tuska*** *c-13.* ***Whitman*** *c-132-163(most).* ***Zolnerowich*** *c-11, 12, 18-41.*

JUNGLE COMICS
Blackthorne Publishing: May, 1988 - No. 4 ($2.00, B&W/color)

1-Dave Stevens-c; B. Jones scripts in all. 3.00
2-4: 2-B&W-a begins 2.00

JUNGLE GIRL (See Lorna, the...)

JUNGLE GIRL (Nyoka, Jungle Girl No. 2 on)
Fawcett Publications: Fall, 1942 (one-shot)(No month listed)

1-Bondage-c; photo of Kay Aldridge who played Nyoka in movie serial app. on-c. Adaptation of the classic Republic movie serial Perils of Nyoka. 1st comic to devote entire contents to a movie serial adaptation 126.00 379.00 1200.00

JUNGLE GIRLS
AC Comics: 1989 - No. 16, 1993 (B&W)

1-16: 1-4,10,13-16-New story & "good girl" reprints. 5-9,11,12-All g.g. reprints (Baker, Powell, Lubbers, others) 3.00

JUNGLE JIM (Also see Ace Comics)
Standard Comics (Best Books): No. 11, Jan, 1949 - No. 20, Apr, 1951

11 10.00 30.00 70.00
12-20 5.70 17.00 40.00

GD2.0 FN6.0 NM9.4

JUNGLE JIM
Dell Publishing Co.: No. 490, 8/53 - No. 1020, 8-10/59 (Painted-c)

Four Color 490(#1) 5.85 17.50 70.00
Four Color 565(#2, 6/54) 3.20 9.60 35.00
3(10-12/54)-5 3.00 9.00 32.00
6-19(1-3/59), Four Color 1020(#20) 3.00 9.00 30.00

JUNGLE JIM
King Features Syndicate: No. 5, Dec, 1967

5-Reprints Dell #5; Wood-c 1.75 5.25 14.00

JUNGLE JIM (Continued from Dell series)
Charlton Comics: No. 22, Feb, 1969 - No. 28, Feb, 1970 (#21 was an overseas edition only)

22-Dan Flagg begins; Ditko/Wood-a 3.00 9.00 30.00
23-26: 23-Last Dan Flagg; Howard-c. 24-Jungle People begin 2.30 7.00 20.00
27,28: 27-Ditko/Howard-a. 28-Ditko-a 2.50 7.50 25.00

NOTE: *Ditko cover of #22 reprints story panels*

JUNGLE JO
Fox Feature Syndicate (Hero Books): Mar, 1950 - No. 3, Sept, 1950

nn-Jo-Jo blanked out, leaving Congo King; came out after Jo-Jo #29 (intended as Jo-Jo #30?) 42.00 125.00 375.00
1-Tangi begins; part Wood-a 45.00 135.00 405.00
2,3 36.00 107.00 285.00

JUNGLE LIL (Dorothy Lamour #2 on; also see Feature Stories Magazine)
Fox Feature Syndicate (Hero Books): April, 1950

1 39.00 116.00 310.00

JUNGLE TALES (Jann of the Jungle No. 8 on)
Atlas Comics (CSI): Sept, 1954 - No. 7, Sept, 1955

1-Jann of the Jungle 38.00 113.00 300.00
2-7: 3-Last precode (1/55) 26.00 79.00 210.00

NOTE: ***Heath*** *c-5.* ***Heck*** *a-6, 7.* ***Maneely*** *a-2; c-1, 3.* ***Shores*** *a-5-7; c-4, 6.* ***Tuska*** *a-2.*

JUNGLE TALES OF CAVEWOMAN
Basement Comics: 1998 ($2.95, B&W)

1-Budd Root-s/a 3.00

JUNGLE TALES OF TARZAN
Charlton Comics: Dec, 1964 - No. 4, July, 1965

1 4.55 13.65 50.00
2-4 3.20 9.60 35.00

NOTE: ***Giordano*** *c-3p.* ***Glanzman*** *a-1-3.* ***Montes/Bache*** *a-4.*

JUNGLE TERROR (See Harvey Comics Hits No. 54)

JUNGLE THRILLS (Formerly Sports Thrills; Terrors of the Jungle #17 on)
Star Publications: No. 16, Feb, 1952; Dec, 1953; No. 7, 1954

16-Phantom Lady & Rulah story-reprint/All Top No. 15; used in **POP**, pg. 98,99; L. B. Cole-c 50.00 150.00 450.00
3-D 1(12/53, 25¢)-Came w/glasses; Jungle Lil & Jungle Jo appear; L. B. Cole-c 52.00 156.00 470.00
7-Titled 'Picture Scope Jungle Adventures;' (1954, 36 pgs, 15¢)-3-D effect c/stories; story & coloring book; Disbrow-a/script; L.B. Cole-c 48.00 144.00 435.00

JUNGLE TWINS, THE (Tono & Kono)
Gold Key/Whitman No. 18: Apr, 1972 - No. 17, Nov, 1975; No. 18, May, 1982

1 2.00 6.00 16.00
2-5 1.10 3.30 9.00
6-18: 18-Reprints 2.40 6.00

NOTE: *UFO c/story No. 13. Painted-c No. 1-17.* ***Spiegle*** *c-18.*

JUNGLE WAR STORIES (Guerrilla War No. 12 on)
Dell Publishing Co.: July-Sept, 1962 - No. 11, Apr-June, 1965 (Painted-c)

01-384-209 (#1) 3.00 9.00 30.00
2-11 2.30 7.00 20.00

JUNIE PROM (Also see Dexter Comics)
Dearfield Publishing Co.: Winter, 1947-48 - No. 7, Aug, 1949

Junior Comics #11 © FOX

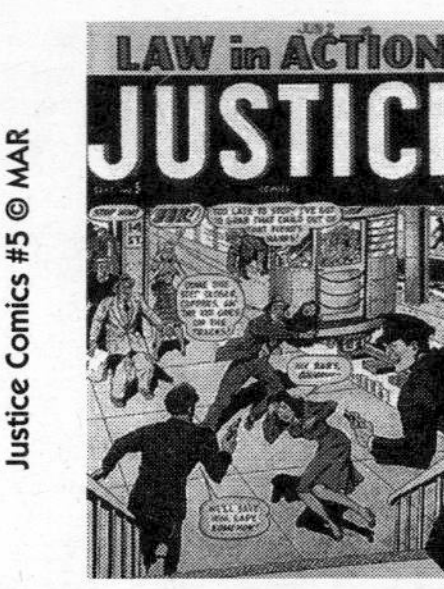

Justice Comics #5 © MAR

Justice League America #45 © DC

	GD2.0	FN6.0	NM9.4
1-Teen-age	12.00	36.00	95.00
2	7.15	21.50	50.00
3-7	5.00	15.00	35.00

JUNIOR
Fantagraphics Books: June, 2000 - No. 5 ($2.95, B&W)

1-4-Peter Bagge-s/a 2.95

JUNIOR CARROT PATROL (Jr. Carrot Patrol #2)
Dark Horse Comics: May, 1989; No. 2, Nov, 1990 ($2.00, B&W)

1,2-Flaming Carrot spin-off. 1-Bob Burden-c(i) 2.00

JUNIOR COMICS (Formerly Li'l Pan; becomes Western Outlaws with #17)
Fox Feature Syndicate: No. 9, Sept, 1947 - No. 16, July, 1948

	GD2.0	FN6.0	NM9.4
9-Feldstein-c/a; headlights-c	77.00	232.00	735.00
10-16-Feldstein-c/a; headlights-c on all	68.00	205.00	650.00

JUNIOR FUNNIES (Formerly Tiny Tot Funnies No. 9)
Harvey Publ. (King Features Synd.): No. 10, Aug, 1951 - No. 13, Feb, 1952

	GD2.0	FN6.0	NM9.4
10-Partial reprints in all; Blondie, Dagwood, Daisy, Henry, Popeye, Felix, Katzenjammer Kids	4.30	13.00	26.00
11-13	4.00	11.00	22.00

JUNIOR HOPP COMICS
Stanmor Publ.: Feb, 1952 - No. 3, July, 1952

	GD2.0	FN6.0	NM9.4
1-Teenage humor	9.30	28.00	65.00
2,3: 3-Dave Berg-a	5.00	15.00	35.00

JUNIOR MEDICS OF AMERICA, THE
E. R. Squire & Sons: No. 1359, 1957 (15¢)

	GD2.0	FN6.0	NM9.4
1359	3.60	9.00	18.00

JUNIOR MISS
Timely/Marvel (CnPC): Wint, 1944; No. 24, Apr, 1947 - No. 39, Aug, 1950

	GD2.0	FN6.0	NM9.4
1-Frank Sinatra & June Allyson life story	26.00	79.00	210.00
24-Formerly The Human Torch #23?	12.00	36.00	95.00
25-38: 29,31,34-Cindy-c/stories (others?)	7.15	21.50	50.00
39-Kurtzman-a	9.30	28.00	65.00

NOTE: *Painted-c 35-37. 35, 37-all romance. 36, 38-mostly teen humor.*

JUNIOR PARTNERS (Formerly Oral Roberts' True Stories)
Oral Roberts Evangelistic Assn.: No. 120, Aug, 1959 - V3#12, Dec, 1961

	GD2.0	FN6.0	NM9.4
120(#1)	3.20	9.60	35.00
2(9/59)	2.50	7.50	25.00
3-12(7/60)	2.00	6.00	16.00
V2#1(8/60)-5(12/60)	1.50	4.50	12.00
V3#1(1/61)-12	1.10	3.30	9.00

JUNIOR TREASURY (See Dell Junior...)

JUNIOR WOODCHUCKS GUIDE (Walt Disney's...)
Danbury Press: 1973 (8-3/4"x5-3/4", 214 pgs., hardcover)

	GD2.0	FN6.0	NM9.4
nn-Illustrated text based on the long-standing J.W. Guide used by Donald Duck's nephews Huey, Dewey & Louie by Carl Barks. The guidebook was a popular plot devise to enable the nephews to solve problems facing their uncle or Scrooge McDuck (scarce)	4.10	12.30	45.00

JUNIOR WOODCHUCKS LIMITED SERIES (Walt Disney's...)
W. D. Publications (Disney): July, 1991 - No. 4, Oct, 1991 ($1.50, limited series; new & reprint-a)

1-4: 1-The Beagle Boys app.; Barks-r 2.00

JUNIOR WOODCHUCKS (See Huey, Dewey & Louie...)

JUNK CULTURE
DC Comics (Vertigo): July, 1997 - No. 2, Aug, 1997 ($2.50, limited series)

1,2: Ted McKeever-s/a in all 2.50

JURASSIC PARK
Topps Comics: 6/93 - No. 4, 8/93; #5, 10/94 - #10, 2/95

	GD2.0	FN6.0	NM9.4
1-($2.50)-Newsstand Edition; Kane/Perez-a in all; 1-4: movie adaptation			2.50
1-($2.95)-Collector's Ed.; polybagged w/3 cards			4.00
1-Amberchrome Edition w/no price or ads	1.00	2.80	7.00
2-4-($2.50)-Newsstand Edition			2.50
2,3-($2.95)-Collector's Ed.; polybagged w/3 cards			3.00
4-10: 4-($2.95)-Collector's Ed.; polybagged w/1 of 4 different action hologram trading card; Gil Kane/Perez-a. 5-becomes Advs. of			3.00
Annual 1 ($3.95, 5/95)			4.00
Trade paperback (1993, $9.95)-r/#1-4; bagged w/#0			10.00

JURASSIC PARK: RAPTOR
Topps Comics: Nov, 1993 - No. 2, Dec, 1993 ($2.95, limited series)

1,2: 1-Bagged w/3 trading cards & Zorro #0; Golden c-1,2 3.00

JURASSIC PARK: RAPTORS ATTACK
Topps Comics: Mar, 1994 - No. 4, June, 1994 ($2.50, limited series)

1-4-Michael Golden-c/frontispiece 2.50

JURASSIC PARK: RAPTORS HIJACK
Topps Comics: July, 1994 - No. 4, Oct, 1994 ($2.50, limited series)

1-4: Michael Golden-c/front piece 2.50

JUSTICE
Marvel Comics Group (New Universe): Nov, 1986 - No. 32, June, 1989

	GD2.0	FN6.0	NM9.4
1-25			2.00
26-32-$1.50-c (low print run)			3.00

JUSTICE COMICS (Formerly Wacky Duck; Tales of Justice #53 on)
Marvel/Atlas Comics (NPP 7-9,4-19/CnPC 20-23/MjMC 24-38/Male 39-52: No. 7, Fall/47 - No. 9, 6/48; No. 4, 8/48 - No. 52, 3/55

	GD2.0	FN6.0	NM9.4
7(#1, 1947)	28.00	83.00	220.00
8(#2)-Kurtzman-a "Giggles 'n' Grins" (3)	19.00	56.00	150.00
9(#3, 6/48)	17.00	51.00	135.00
4	15.00	45.00	120.00
5(9/48)-9: 8-Anti-Wertham editorial	13.00	39.00	105.00
10-15-Photo-c	10.00	30.00	80.00
16-30	9.30	28.00	65.00
31-40,42-52: 35-Gene Colan-a. 48-Last precode; Pakula & Tuska-a.	8.65	26.00	60.00
41-Electrocution-c	16.00	48.00	125.00

NOTE: ***Heath** a-24. **Maneely** c-44, 52. **Pakula** a-43, 45, 48. **Louis Ravielli** a-39. **Robinson** a-22, 25, 41. **Shores** c-7(#1), 8(#2)? **Tuska** a-48. **Wildey** a-52.*

JUSTICE: FOUR BALANCE
Marvel Comics: Sept, 1994 - No. 4, Dec, 1994 ($1.75, limited series)

1-4: 1-Thing & Firestar app. 2.00

JUSTICE, INC. (The Avenger) (Pulp)
National Periodical Publications: May-June, 1975 - No. 4, Nov-Dec, 1975

	GD2.0	FN6.0	NM9.4
1-McWilliams-a, Kubert-c; origin	1.25	3.75	10.00
2-4: 2-4-Kirby-a(p), c-2,3p. 4-Kubert-c	1.00	2.80	7.00

NOTE: *Adapted from Kenneth Robeson novel, creator of Doc Savage.*

JUSTICE, INC. (Pulp)
DC Comics: 1989 - No. 2, 1989 ($3.95, 52 pgs., squarebound, mature)

1,2: Re-intro The Avenger; Andrew Helfer scripts & Kyle Baker-c/a 4.00

JUSTICE LEAGUE (...International #7-25; ...America #26 on)
DC Comics: May, 1987 - No. 113, Aug, 1996 (Also see Legends #6)

	GD2.0	FN6.0	NM9.4
1-Batman, Green Lantern (Guy Gardner), Blue Beetle, Mr. Miracle, Capt. Marvel & Martian Manhunter begin		2.40	6.00
2,3: 3-Regular-c (white background)			4.00
3-Limited-c (yellow background, Superman logo)	3.65	11.00	40.00
4-10: 4-Booster Gold joins. 5-Origin Gray Man; Batman vs. Guy Gardner; Creeper app. 7-($1.25, 52 pgs.)-Capt. Marvel & Dr. Fate resign; Capt. Atom & Rocket Red join. 9,10-Millennium x-over			3.00
11-17,22,23,25-49,51-68,72-82: 16-Bruce Wayne-c/story. 31,32-J. L. Europe x-over. 58-Lobo app. 61-New team begins; swipes-c to J.L. of A. #1('60). 70-Newsstand version w/o outer-c. 71-Direct sales version w/black outer-c. 71-Newsstand version w/o outer-c.80-Intro new Booster Gold. 82,83-Guy Gardner-c/stories			2.00
18-21,24,50: 18-21-Lobo app. 24-($1.50)-1st app. Justice League Europe. 50-($1.75, 52 pgs.)			3.00
69-Doomsday tie-in; takes place between Superman: The Man of Steel #18 & Superman #74			5.00
69,70-2nd printings			2.00
70-Funeral for a Friend part 1; red 3/4 outer-c			4.00

83-99,101-113: 92-(9/94)-Zero Hour x-over; Triumph app. 113-Green Lantern,

Justice League Europe #14 © DC

Justice League of America #9 © DC

Justice League of America #124 © DC

GD2.0 FN6.0 NM9.4

Flash & Hawkman app. 2.00
100 ($3.95)-Foil-c; 52 pgs. 4.00
100 ($2.95)-Newstand 3.00
#0-(10/94) Zero Hour (publ between #92 & #93); new team begins (Hawkman, Wonder Woman, Flash, Metamorpho, Nuklon, Crimson Fox, Obsidian & Fire) 2.00
Annual 1-8,10 ('87-'94, '96, 68 pgs.): 2-Joker-c/story; Batman cameo. 5-Armageddon 2001 x-over; Silver ink 2nd print. 7-Bloodlines x-over. 8-Elseworlds story. 10-Legends of the Dead Earth 3.00
Annual 9 (1995, $3.50)-Year One story 3.50
Special 1,2 ('90,'91, 52 pgs.): 1-Giffen plots. 2-Staton-a(p) 3.00
Spectacular 1 (1992, $1.50, 52 pgs.)-Intro new JLI & JLE teams; ties into JLI #61 & JLE #37; two interlocking covers by Jurgens 3.00
A New Beginning Trade Paperback (1989, $12.95)-r/#1-7 13.00
*NOTE: **Anderson** c-61i. **Austin** a-1i, 60i; c-1i. **Giffen** a-13; c-21p. **Guice** a-62i. **Maguire** a-1-12, 16-19, 22, 23. **Russell** a-Annual 1i; c-54i. **Willingham** a-30p, Annual 2.*

JUSTICE LEAGUE: A MIDSUMMER'S NIGHTMARE
DC Comics: Sept, 1996 - No. 3, Nov, 1996 ($2.95, limited series, 38 pgs.)
1-3: Re-establishes Superman, Batman, Green Lantern, The Martian Manhunter, Flash, Aquaman & Wonder Woman as the Justice League; Mark Waid & Fabian Nicieza co-scripts; Jeff Johnson & Darick Robertson-a(p); Kevin Maguire-c. 5.00
TPB-(1997, $8.95) r/1-3 9.00

JUSTICE LEAGUE EUROPE (Justice League International #51 on)
DC Comics: Apr, 1989 - No. 68, Sept., 1994 (75¢/ $1.00/$1.25/$1.50)
1-Giffen plots in all, breakdowns in #1-8,13-30; Justice League #1-c/swipe 3.00
2-10: 7-9-Batman app. 7,8-JLA x-over. 8,9-Superman app. 2.50
11-49: 12-Metal Men app. 20-22-Rogers-c/a(p). 33,34-Lobo vs. Despero. 37-New team begins; swipes-c to JLA #9; see JLA Spectacular 2.00
50-($2.50, 68 pgs.)-Battles Sonar 2.50
51-68: 68-Zero Hour x-over; Triumph joins Justice League Task Force (See JLTF #17) 2.00
Annual 1-5 ('90-'94, 68 pgs.)-1-Return of the Global Guardians; Giffen plots/ breakdowns. 2-Armageddon 2001; Giffen-a(p); Rogers-a(p); Golden-a(i) 3-Eclipso app. 4-Intro Lionheart. 5-Elseworlds story 3.00
*NOTE: **Phil Jimenez** a-68p. **Rogers** c/a-20-22. **Sears** a-1-12, 14-19, 23-29; c-1-10, 12, 14-19, 23-29.*

JUSTICE LEAGUE INTERNATIONAL (See Justice League Europe)

JUSTICE LEAGUE OF AMERICA (See Brave & the Bold #28-30, Mystery In Space #75 & Official... Index)
National Periodical Publ./DC Comics: Oct-Nov, 1960 - No. 261, Apr, 1987 (#91-99,139-157: 52 pgs.)

	GD2.0	FN6.0	VF8.0	NM9.4
1-(10-11/60)-Origin & 1st app. Despero; Aquaman, Batman, Flash, Green Lantern, J'onn J'onzz, Superman & Wonder Woman continue from Brave and the Bold	263.00	790.00	2100.00	4200.00

	GD2.0	FN6.0	NM9.4
2	61.00	182.00	850.00
3-Origin/1st app. Kanjar Ro (see Mystery in Space #75)(scarce in high grade due to black-c)	52.00	156.00	675.00
4-Green Arrow joins JLA	37.00	112.00	450.00
5-Origin & 1st app. Dr. Destiny	31.00	93.00	350.00
6-8,10: 6-Origin & 1st app. Prof. Amos Fortune. 7-(10-11/61)-Last 10¢ issue. 10-(3/62)-Origin & 1st app. Felix Faust; 1st app. Lord of Time.	27.50	82.00	300.00
9-(2/62)-Origin JLA (1st origin)	40.00	119.00	475.00
11-15: 12-(6/62)-Origin & 1st app. Dr. Light. 13-(8/62)-Speedy app. 14-(9/62)-Atom joins JLA.	19.00	57.00	210.00
16-20: 17-Adam Strange flashback	16.50	49.00	180.00
21-(8/63)-"Crisis on Earth-One"; re-intro. of JSA in this title (see Flash #129) (1st S.A. app. Hourman & Dr. Fate)	31.00	93.00	350.00
22- "Crisis on Earth-Two"; JSA x-over (story continued from #21)	27.50	82.00	300.00
23-28: 24-Adam Strange app. 27-Robin app.	11.50	34.00	125.00
29-JSA x-over; 1st S.A. app. Starman; "Crisis on Earth-Three"	15.00	45.00	165.00
30-JSA x-over	13.50	40.00	150.00
31-Hawkman joins JLA, Hawkgirl cameo (11/64)	11.00	33.00	120.00
32,34: 32-Intro & Origin Brain Storm. 34-Joker-c/sty	7.65	23.00	85.00
33,35,36,40,41: 40-3rd S.A. Penguin app. 41-Intro & origin The Key	6.80	20.50	75.00
37-39: 37,38-JSA x-over. 37-1st S.A. app. Mr. Terrific; Batman cameo. 38-"Crisis on Earth-A". 39-Giant G-16; r/B&B #28,30 & JLA #5	10.00	30.00	110.00
42-45: 42-Metamorpho app. 43-Intro. Royal Flush Gang	5.45	16.35	60.00
46-JSA x-over; 1st S.A. app. Sandman; 3rd S.A. app. of G.A. Spectre (8/66)	11.00	33.00	120.00
47-JSA x-over; 4th S.A. app of G.A. Spectre.	7.25	21.75	80.00
48-Giant G-29; r/JLA #2,3 & B&B #29	6.80	20.50	75.00
49-54,57,59,60	5.00	15.00	55.00
55-Intro. Earth 2 Robin (1st G.A. Robin in S.A.)	6.80	20.50	75.00
56-JLA vs. JSA (1st G.A. Wonder Woman in S.A.)	5.90	17.75	65.00
58-Giant G-41; r/JLA #6,8,1	5.90	17.75	65.00
61-63,66,68-72: 69-Wonder Woman quits. 71-Manhunter leaves. 72-Last 12¢ issue	3.65	11.00	40.00
64,65-JSA story. 64-(8/68)-Origin/1st app. S.A. Red Tornado	4.10	12.30	45.00
67-Giant G-53; r/JLA #4,14,31	5.45	16.35	60.00
73-1st S.A. app. of G.A. Superman; 1st app. of S. A. Black Canary	4.10	12.30	45.00
74-Black Canary joins; 1st meeting of G.A. & S.A. Superman.	3.65	11.00	40.00
75-2nd app. Green Arrow in new costume (see Brave & the Bold #85)	3.20	9.60	35.00
76-Giant G-65	4.10	12.30	45.00
77-80: 78-Re-intro Vigilante (1st S.A. app?)	2.50	7.50	25.00
81-84,86-90: 82-1st S.A. app. of G.A. Batman (cameo). 83-Death of Spectre. 90-Last 15¢ issue	2.50	7.50	23.00
85,93-(Giant G-77,G-89; 68 pgs.)	3.20	9.60	35.00
91,92: 91-1st meeting of the G.A. & S.A. Robin; begin 25¢, 52 pgs. issues, ends #99. 92-S.A. Robin tries on costume that is similar to that of G.A. Robin in All Star Comics #58.	2.80	8.40	28.00
94-Reprints 1st Sandman story (Adv. #40) & origin/1st app. Starman (Adv. #61); Deadman x-over; N. Adams-a (4 pgs.)	7.25	21.75	80.00
95,96: 95-Origin Dr. Fate & Dr. Midnight -r/ More Fun #67, All-American #25). 96-Origin Hourman (Adv. #48); Wildcat-r	3.00	9.00	30.00
97-99: 97-Origin JLA retold; Sargon, Starman-r. 98-G.A. Sargon, Starman-r. 99-G.A. Sandman, Atom-r; last 52 pg. issue	2.50	7.50	25.00
100-(8/72)-1st meeting of G.A. & S.A. W. Woman	3.20	9.60	35.00
101,102: JSA x-overs. 102-Red Tornado dies	2.40	7.35	22.00
103-106,109: 103-Phantom Stranger joins. 105-Elongated Man joins. 106-New Red Tornado joins. 109-Hawkman resigns	1.85	5.50	15.00
107,108-G.A. Uncle Sam, Black Condor, The Ray, Dollman, Phantom Lady & The Human Bomb (JSA) x-over, 1st S.A. app.	2.00	6.00	18.00
110-116: All 100 pgs. 111-JLA vs. Injustice Gang; Shining Knight, Green Arrow-r. 112-Amazo app; Crimson Avenger, Vigilante-r; origin Starman-r/Adv. #81. 115-Martian Manhunter app.	2.80	8.40	28.00
117-122,125-134: 117-Hawkman rejoins. 120,121-Adam Strange app. 125,126-Two-Face-c/story. 128-Wonder Woman rejoins. 129-Destruction of Red Tornado	1.25	3.75	10.00
123-(10/75),124: JLA/JSA x-over. DC editor Julie Schwartz & JLA writers Cary Bates & Elliot S! Maggin appear in story as themselves. 1st named app. Earth-Prime (3rd app. after Flash; 1st Series #179 & 228)	1.50	4.50	12.00
135-136: 135-137-G.A. Bulletman, Bulletgirl, Spy Smasher, Mr. Scarlet, Pinky & Ibis x-over, 1st S.A. appearances	1.50	4.50	12.00
137-Superman battles G.A. Capt. Marvel	1.85	5.50	15.00
138,139-157: 138-Adam Strange app. w/c by Neal Adams; 1st app. Green Lantern of the 73rd Century. 139-157-(52 pgs.): 139-Adam Strange app. 144-Origin retold; origin J'onn J'onzz. 145-Red Tornado resurrected. 147,148-Legion x-over	1.10	3.30	9.00
158-160-(44 pgs.)	1.00	2.80	7.00
161-182: 161-Zatanna joins & new costume. 171-Mr. Terrific murdered. 178-Cover similar to #1; J'onn J'onzz app. 179-Firestorm joins. 181-Green Arrow leaves JLA			5.00
183-185-JSA/New Gods/Darkseid/Mr.Miracle x-over		2.40	6.00

Justice League of America #207 © DC

Justice Society of America #3 © DC

Justice Traps the Guilty #10 © PRIZE

186-199: 192,193-Real origin Red Tornado. 193-1st app. All-Star Squadron as free 16 pg. insert 3.00
200 ($1.50, Anniversary issue, 76pgs.)-JLA origin retold; Green Arrow rejoins; Bolland, Broderick, Aparo, Giordano, Gil Kane, Infantino, Kubert-a; Perez-c/a. 4.00
201-206,209-243,246-259: 203-Intro/origin new Royal Flush Gang. 219,220-True origin Black Canary. 228-Re-intro Martian Manhunter. 228-230-War of the Worlds storyline; JLA Satellite destroyed by Martians. 233-Story cont'd from Annual #2. 243-Aquaman leaves. 250-Batman rejoins. 253-Origin Despero. 258-Death of Vibe. 258-261-Legends x-over 2.50
207,208-JSA, JLA, & All-Star Squadron team-up 3.00
244,245-Crisis x-over 3.00
260-Death of Steel 4.00
261-Last issue 2.40 6.00
Annual 1-3 ('83-'85), 2-Intro new J.L.A. (Aquaman, Martian Manhunter, Steel, Gypsy,Vixen, Vibe, Elongated Man, & Zatanna). 3-Crisis x-over 3.00

NOTE: ***Neal Adams** c-63, 66, 67, 70, 74, 79, 81, 82, 86-89, 91, 92, 94, 96-98, 138, 139. **M. Anderson** c-1-4, 6, 7, 10, 12-14. **Aparo** a-200. **Austin** a-200i. **Baily** a-96r. **Bolland** a-200. **Buckler** c-158, 163, 164. **Burnley** r-94, 98, 99. **Greene** a-46-61i, 64-73i, 110i(r). **Grell** c-117, 122. **Kaluta** c-154p. **Gil Kane** a-200. **Krigstein** a-96(r/Sensation #84). **Kubert** a-200; c-72, 73. **Nino** a-228i, 230i. **Orlando** c-151i. **Perez** a-184-186p, 192-197p, 200p; c-184p, 186, 192-195, 196p, 197p, 199, 200, 201p, 202, 203-205p, 207-209, 212-215, 217, 219, 220. **Reinman** r-97. **Roussos** a-62i. **Sekowsky** a-37, 38, 44-63p, 110-112p(r); c-46-48p, 51p. **Sekowsky/Anderson** c-5, 8, 9, 11, 15. **B. Smith** c-185i. **Starlin** c-178-180, 183, 185p. **Staton** a-244p; c-157p, 244p. **Toth** r-110. **Tuska** a-153, 228p, 241-243p. JSA x-overs-21, 22, 29, 30, 37, 38, 46, 47, 55, 56, 64, 65, 73, 74, 82, 83, 91, 92, 100, 101, 102, 107, 108, 110, 113, 115, 123, 124, 135-137, 147, 148, 159, 160, 171, 172, 183-185, 195-197, 207-209, 219, 220, 231, 232, 244.*

JUSTICE LEAGUE OF AMERICA SUPER SPECTACULAR
DC Comics: 1999 ($5.95, mimics format of DC 100 Page Super Spectaculars)
1-Reprints Silver Age JLA and Golden Age JSA 6.00

JUSTICE LEAGUE QUARTERLY (...International Quarterly #6 on)
DC Comics: Winter, 1990-91 - No. 17, Winter, 1994 ($2.95/$3.50, 84 pgs.)
1-12,14-17: 1-Intro The Conglomerate (Booster Gold, Praxis, Gypsy, Vapor, Echo, Maxi-Man, & Reverb); Justice League #1-c/swipe. 1,2-Giffen plots/ breakdowns. 3-Giffen plot; 72 pg. story. 4-Rogers/Russell-a in back-up. 5,6-Waid scripts. 8,17-Global Guardians app. 12-Waid script 3.50
13-Linsner-c 5.00
NOTE: ***Phil Jimenez** a-17p. **Sprouse** a-1p.*

JUSTICE LEAGUE TASK FORCE
DC Comics: June, 1993 - No. 37, Aug, 1996 ($1.25/$1.50/$1.75)
1-16,0,17-37: Aquaman, Nightwing, Flash, J'onn J'onzz, & Gypsy form team. 5,6-Knight-quest tie-ins (new Batman cameo #5, 1 pg.). 15-Triumph cameo. 16-(9/94)-Zero Hour x-over;Triumph app. 0-(10/94). 17-(11/94)-Triumph becomes part of Justice League Task Force (See JLE #68). 26-Impulse app. 35-Warlord app. 37-Triumph quits team 2.00

JUSTICE MACHINE, THE
Noble Comics: June, 1981 - No. 5, Nov, 1983 ($2.00, nos. 1-3 are mag. size)

	GD2.0	FN6.0	NM9.4
1-Byrne-c(p)	2.50	7.50	23.00
2-Austin-c(i)	1.75	5.25	14.00
3	1.10	3.30	9.00
4,5, Annual 1 (1/84, 68 pgs.)(published by Texas Comics); 1st app. The Elementals; Golden-c(p)			5.00

JUSTICE MACHINE (Also see The New Justice Machine)
Comico/Innovation Publishing: Jan, 1987 - No. 29, May 1989 ($1.50/$1.75)
1-29 2.25
Annual 1(6/89, $2.50, 36 pgs.)-Last Comico ish. 3.00
Summer Spectacular 1 ('89, $2.75)-Innovation Publ.; Byrne/Gustovich cover 3.00

JUSTICE MACHINE, THE
Innovation Publishing: 1990 - No. 4, 1990 ($1.95/$2.25, deluxe format, mature)
1-4: Gustovich-c/a in all 2.25

JUSTICE MACHINE FEATURING THE ELEMENTALS
Comico: May, 1986 - No. 4, Aug, 1986 ($1.50, limited series)
1-4 2.25

JUSTICE RIDERS
DC Comics: 1997 ($5.95, one-shot, prestige format)
1-Elseworlds; Dixon-s/Williams & Gray-a 2.40 6.00

JUSTICE SOCIETY OF AMERICA (See Adventure #461 & All-Star #3)
DC Comics: April, 1991 - No. 8, Nov, 1991 ($1.00, limited series)
1-8: 1-Flash. 2-Black Canary. 3-Green Lantern. 4-Hawkman. 5-Flash/ Hawkman. 6-Green Lantern/Black Canary. 7-JSA 2.00

JUSTICE SOCIETY OF AMERICA (Also see Last Days of the... Special)
DC Comics: Aug, 1992 - No. 10, May, 1993 ($1.25)
1-10 2.00

JUSTICE SOCIETY OF AMERICA 100-PAGE SUPER SPECTACULAR
DC Comics: 2000 ($6.95, mimics format of DC 100 Page Super Spectaculars)
1-"1975 Issue" reprints Flash team-up and Golden Age JSA 7.00

JUSTICE TRAPS THE GUILTY (Fargo Kid V11#3 on)
Prize/Headline Publications: Oct-Nov, 1947 - V11#2(#92), Apr-May, 1958 (Tru FBI Cases)

	GD2.0	FN6.0	NM9.4
V2#1-S&K-c/a; electrocution-c	55.00	165.00	500.00
2-S&K-c/a	35.00	105.00	280.00
3-5-S&K-c/a	33.00	98.00	260.00
6-S&K-c/a; Feldstein-a	34.00	101.00	270.00
7,9-S&K-c/a. 7-9-V2#1-3 in indicia; #7-9 on-c	28.00	84.00	225.00
8,10-Krigstein-a; S&K-c. 10-S&K-a	28.00	84.00	225.00
11,18,19-S&K-c	12.50	37.50	100.00
12,14-17,20-No S&K. 14-Severin/Elder-a (8pg.)	7.15	21.50	50.00
13-Used in **SOTI**, pg. 110-111	9.30	28.00	65.00
21,30-S&K-c/a	11.00	33.00	90.00
22,23,27-S&K-c	9.30	28.00	65.00
24-26,29,31-50: 32-Meskin story	5.70	17.00	40.00
28-Kirby-c	7.15	21.50	50.00
51-55,57,59-70	5.00	15.00	35.00
56-Ben Oda, Joe Simon, Joe Genola, Mort Meskin & Jack Kirby app. in police line-up on classic-c	10.00	30.00	70.00
58-Illo. in **SOTI**, "Treating police contemptuously" (top left); text on heroin	26.00	79.00	210.00
71-92: 76-Orlando-a	5.00	15.00	30.00

NOTE: ***Bailey** a-12, 13. **Elder** a-8. **Kirby** a-19p. **Meskin** a-22, 27, 63, 64; c-45, 46. **Robinson/Meskin** a-5, 19. **Severin** a-8, 11p. Photo c-12, 15-17.*

JUST MARRIED
Charlton Comics: January, 1958 - No. 114, Dec, 1976

	GD2.0	FN6.0	NM9.4
1	5.90	17.75	65.00
2	3.20	9.60	35.00
3-10	2.50	7.50	25.00
11-30	2.00	6.00	18.00
31-50	1.75	5.25	14.00
51-70	1.25	3.75	10.00
71-90	1.00	2.80	7.00
91-114		2.40	6.00

JUSTY
Viz Comics: Dec 6, 1988 - No. 9, 1989 ($1.75, B&W, bi-weekly mini-series)
1-9: Japanese manga 1.75

KA'A'NGA COMICS (...Jungle King)(See Jungle Comics)
Fiction House Magazines (Glen-Kel Publ. Co.): Spring, 1949 - No. 20, Summer, 1954

	GD2.0	FN6.0	NM9.4
1-Ka'a'nga, Lord of the Jungle begins	51.00	153.00	460.00
2 (Winter, '49-'50)	29.00	86.00	230.00
3,4	21.00	62.00	165.00
5-Camilla app.	16.00	48.00	125.00
6-10: 7-Tuska-a. 9-Tabu, Wizard of the Jungle app. 10-Used in **POP**, pg. 99	14.00	41.00	110.00
11-15: 15-Camilla-r by Baker/Jungle #106	11.00	33.00	90.00
16-Sheena app.	12.00	36.00	95.00
17-20	10.00	30.00	80.00
I.W. Reprint #1,8: 1-r/#18; Kinstler-c. 8-r/#10	2.50	7.50	23.00

NOTE: ***Celardo** c-1. **Whitman** c-8-20(most).*

KABOOM
Awesome Entertainment: Sept, 1997 - No. 3, Nov, 1997 ($2.50)

Kabuki Agents #4 © David Mack

Kamandi, The Last Boy on Earth #12 © DC

Katy Keene #4 © AP

GD2.0 FN6.0 NM9.4

1-3: 1-Matsuda-a/Loeb-s; 4 covers exist (Matsuda, Sale, Pollina and McGuinness), 1-Dynamic Forces Edition, 2-Regular, 2-Alicia Watcher variant-c, 2-Gold logo variant -c, 3-Two covers by Liefeld & Matsuda, 3-Dynamic Forces Ed., Prelude ED. 2.50
Prelude Gold Edition 4.00

KABOOM (2nd series)
Awesome Entertainment: July, 1999 - No. 3, Dec, 1999 ($2.50)
1-3: 1-Grant-a(p); at least 4 variant covers 2.50

KABUKI
Caliber: Nov, 1994 ($3.50, B&W, one-shot)
nn-(Fear The Reaper) 1st app.; David Mack-c/a/scripts 1.00 3.00 8.00
Color Special (1/96, $2.95)-Mack-c/a/scripts; pin-ups by Tucci, Harris & Quesada 4.00
Gallery (8/95, $2.95)- pinups from Mack, Bradstreet, Paul Pope & others 3.00

KABUKI
Image Comics: Oct, 1997 - Present ($2.95, color)
1-David Mack-c/s/a 4.00
1-($10.00)-Dynamic Forces Edition 10.00
2-9 3.00
...Classics (2/99, $3.95) Reprints Fear the Reaper 4.00
...Classics 2 (3/99, $3.95) Reprints Dance of Dance 4.00
...Classics 3-5 (3-6/99, $4.95) Reprints Circle of Blood-Acts 1-3 5.00
...Classics 6-12 (7/99-3/00, $3.25) Various reprints 3.25
...Images (6/98, $4.95) r/#1 with new pin-ups 5.00
...Images 2 (1/99, $4.95) r/#1 with new pin-ups 5.00
...Reflections 1-3 (7/98, 12/98, 1/00; $4.95) new story plus art techniques 5.00

KABUKI AGENTS (SCARAB)
Image Comics: Aug, 1999 - Present ($2.95, B&W)
1-6-David Mack-s/Rick Mays-a 3.00

KABUKI: CIRCLE OF BLOOD
Caliber Press: Jan, 1995 - No. 6, Nov, 1995 ($2.95, B&W)
1-David Mack story/a in all 5.00
2-6: 3-#1on inside indicia. 3.00
6-Variant-c 3.00
TPB ($16.95) r/#1-6, intro. by Steranko 17.00
TPB (1997, $17.95) Image Edition-r/#1-6, intro. by Steranko 18.00
TPB ($24.95) Deluxe Edition 25.00

KABUKI: DANCE OF DEATH
London Night Studios: Jan, 1995 ($3.00, B&W, one-shot)
1-David Mack-c/a/scripts 1.00 3.00 8.00

KABUKI: DREAMS
Image Comics: Jan, 1998 ($4.95, TPB)
nn-Reprints Color Special & Dreams of the Dead 5.00

KABUKI: DREAMS OF THE DEAD
Caliber: July, 1996 ($2.95, one-shot)
nn-David Mack-c/a/scripts 3.00

KABUKI FAN EDITION
Gemstone Publ./Caliber: Feb, 1997 (mail-in offer, one-shot)
nn-David Mack-c/a/scripts 4.00

KABUKI: MASKS OF THE NOH
Caliber: May, 1996 - No. 4, Feb, 1997 ($2.95, limited series)
1-4: 1-Three-c (1A-Quesada, 1B-Buzz, &1C-Mack). 3-Terry Moore pin-up 3.00
TPB-(4/98, $10.95) r/#1-4; intro by Terry Moore 11.00

KABUKI: SKIN DEEP
Caliber Comics: Oct, 1996 - No. 3, May, 1997 ($2.95)
1-3:David Mack-c/a/scripts. 2-Two-c (1-Mack, 1-Ross) 3.00
TPB-(5/98, $9.95) r/#1-3; intro by Alex Ross 10.00

KAMANDI: AT EARTH'S END
DC Comics: June, 1993 - No. 6, Nov, 1993 ($1.75, limited series)
1-6: Elseworlds storyline 2.50

GD2.0 FN6.0 NM9.4

KAMANDI, THE LAST BOY ON EARTH (Also see Alarming Tales #1, Brave and the Bold #120 & 157 & Cancelled Comic Cavalcade)
National Periodical Publ./DC Comics: Oct-Nov, 1972 - 59, Sept-Oct, 1978
1-Origin & 1st app. Kamandi 4.10 12.30 45.00
2 2.40 7.35 22.00
3-5: 4-Intro. Prince Tuftan of the Tigers 1.85 5.50 15.00
6-10 1.50 4.50 12.00
11-20 1.25 3.75 10.00
21-28,30,31,33-40: 24-Last 20¢ issue. 31-Intro Pyra. 1.00 3.00 8.00
29,32: 29-Superman x-over. 32-(68 pgs.)-r/origin from #1 plus one new story; 4 pg. biog. of Jack Kirby with B&W photos 1.50 4.50 12.00
41-57 5.00
58-(44 pgs.)-Karate Kid x-over from LSH 1.10 3.30 9.00
59-(44 pgs.)-Cont'd in B&B #157; The Return of Omac back-up by Starlin-c/a(p) 1.10 3.30 9.00
NOTE: *Ayers a(p)-48-59 (most).* ***Giffen*** *a-44p, 45p.* ***Kirby*** *a-1-40p; c-1-33.* ***Kubert*** *c-34-41.* ***Nasser*** *a-45p, 46p.* ***Starlin*** *a-59p; c-57, 59p.*

KAMUI (Legend Of...#2 on)
Eclipse Comics/Viz Comics: May 12, 1987 - No. 37, Nov. 15, 1988 ($1.50, B&W, bi-weekly)
1-37: 1-3 have 2nd printings 2.00

KAOS MOON (Also see Negative Burn #34)
Caliber Comics: 1996 - No. 4, 1997 ($2.95, B&W)
1-4-David Boller-s/a 3.00
3,4-Limited Alternate-c 4.00
3,4-Gold Alternate-c, Full Circle TPB ($5.95) r/#1,2 2.40 6.00

KARATE KID (See Action, Adventure, Legion of Super-Heroes, & Superboy)
National Periodical Publications/DC Comics: Mar-Apr, 1976 - No. 15, July-Aug, 1978 (Legion of Super-Heroes spin-off)
1,15: 1-Meets Iris Jacobs; Estrada/Staton-a. 15-Continued into Kamandi #58 1.25 3.75 10.00
2-14: 2-Major Disaster app. 14-Robin x-over 2.40 6.00
NOTE: ***Grell*** *c-1-4, 5p, 6p, 7, 8.* ***Staton*** *a-1-9i. Legion x-over-No. 1, 2, 4, 6, 10, 12, 13. Princess Projectra x-over-#8, 9.*

KATHY
Standard Comics: Sept, 1949 - No. 17, Sept, 1955
1-Teen-age 10.00 30.00 70.00
2-Schomburg-c 6.40 19.25 45.00
3-5 4.65 14.00 28.00
6-17: 17-Code approved 4.00 10.00 20.00

KATHY (The Teenage Tornado)
Atlas Comics/Marvel (ZPC): Oct, 1959 - No. 27, Feb, 1964
1-Teen-age 5.90 17.75 65.00
2 3.00 9.00 32.00
3-15 2.30 7.00 20.00
16-27 1.50 4.50 12.00

KAT KARSON
I. W. Enterprises: No date (Reprint)
1-Funny animals 1.75 5.25 14.00

KATO OF THE GREEN HORNET (Also see The Green Hornet)
Now Comics: Nov, 1991 - No. 4, Feb, 1992 ($2.50, mini-series)
1-4: Brent Anderson-c/a 2.50

KATO OF THE GREEN HORNET II (Also see The Green Hornet)
Now Comics: Nov, 1992 - No. 2, Dec, 1993 ($2.50, mini-series)
1,2-Baron-s/Mayerik & Sherman-a 2.50

KATY KEENE (Also see Kasco Komics, Laugh, Pep, Suzie, & Wilbur)
Archie Publ./Close-Up/Radio Comics: 1949 - No. 4, 1951; No. 5, 3/52 - No. 62, Oct, 1961 (50-53-Adventures of...on-c)
1-Bill Woggon-c/a begins; swipes-c to Mopsy #1 95.00 285.00 900.00
2-(1950) 47.00 141.00 425.00
3-5: 3-(1951). 4-(1951) 40.00 120.00 320.00
6-10 33.00 99.00 265.00
11,13-21: 21-Last pre-code issue (3/55) 28.00 84.00 225.00
12-(Scarce) 33.00 98.00 260.00

Katzenjammer Kids #6 © KING

Ka-Zar #5 © MAR

Keen Detective Funnies V2 #6 © CEN

22-40 20.00 60.00 160.00
41-62: 54-Wedding Album plus wedding pin-up. 62-Robot-c
16.00 49.00 130.00
Annual 1('54, 25¢)-All new stories; last pre-code 44.00 133.00 400.00
Annual 2-6('55-59, 25¢)-All new stories 28.00 84.00 225.00
3-D 1(1953, 25¢, large size)-Came w/glasses 40.00 120.00 325.00
Charm 1(9/58)-Woggon-c/a; new stories, and cut-outs
28.00 83.00 220.00
Glamour 1(1957)-Puzzles, games, cut-outs 28.00 83.00 220.00
Spectacular 1('56) 28.00 83.00 220.00
NOTE: *Debby's Diary in #45, 47-49, 52, 57.*

KATY KEENE COMICS DIGEST MAGAZINE
Close-Up, Inc. (Archie Ent.): 1987 - No. 10, July, 1990 ($1.25/$1.35/$1.50, digest size)
1 1.10 3.30 9.00
2-10 2.40 6.00

KATY KEENE FASHION BOOK MAGAZINE
Radio Comics/Archie Publications: 1955 - No. 13, Sum, '56 - N. 23, Wint, '58-59 (nn 3-10)
1-Bill Woggon-c/a 44.00 133.00 400.00
2 28.00 84.00 225.00
11-18: 18-Photo Bill Woggon 20.00 60.00 160.00
19-23 16.00 49.00 130.00

KATY KEENE HOLIDAY FUN (See Archie Giant Series Magazine No. 7, 12)

KATY KEENE PINUP PARADE
Radio Comics/Archie Publications: 1955 - No. 15, Summer, 1961 (25¢) (Cut-out & missing pages are common)
1-Cut-outs in all?; last pre-code issue 44.00 133.00 400.00
2-(1956) 26.00 79.00 210.00
3-5: 3-(1957) 23.00 68.00 180.00
6-10,12-14: 8-Mad parody. 10-Bill Woggon photo 19.00 56.00 150.00
11-Story of how comics get CCA approved, narrated by Katy
25.00 75.00 200.00
15(Rare)-Photo artist & family 40.00 120.00 360.00

KATY KEENE SPECIAL (Katy Keene #7 on; see Laugh Comics Digest)
Archie Ent.: Sept, 1983 - No. 33, 1990 (Later issues published quarterly)
1-10: 1-Woggon-r; new Woggon-c. 3-Woggon-r 4.00
11-25 2.40 6.00
26-32-(Low print run) 1.00 3.00 8.00
33 1.25 3.75 10.00

KATZENJAMMER KIDS, THE (See Captain & the Kids & Giant Comic Album)
David McKay Publ./Standard No. 12-21(Spring/'50 - 53)/Harvey No. 22, 4/53 on: 1945-1946; Summer, 1947 - No. 27, Feb-Mar, 1954
Feature Books 30 19.00 56.00 150.00
Feature Books 32,35('45),41,44('46) 16.00 49.00 130.00
Feature Book 37-Has photos & biography of Harold Knerr
18.00 53.00 140.00
1(1947)-All new stories begin 18.00 53.00 140.00
2 10.00 30.00 70.00
3-11 6.40 19.25 45.00
12-14(Standard) 5.00 15.00 32.00
15-21(Standard) 4.65 14.00 28.00
22-25,27(Harvey): 22-24-Henry app. 5.00 15.00 32.00
26-Half in 3-D 19.00 56.00 150.00

KAYO (Formerly Bullseye & Jest; becomes Carnival Comics)
Harry 'A' Chesler: No. 12, Mar, 1945
12-Green Knight, Capt. Glory, Little Nemo (not by McCay)
16.00 48.00 125.00

KA-ZAR (Also see Marvel Comics #1, Savage Tales #6 & X-Men #10)
Marvel Comics Group: Aug, 1970 - No. 3, Mar, 1971 (Giant-Size, 68 pgs.)
1-Reprints earlier Ka-Zar stories; Avengers x-over in Hercules; Daredevil, X-Men app.; hidden profanity-c 2.60 7.80 26.00
2,3-Daredevil-r. 2-r/Daredevil #13 w/Kirby layouts; Ka-Zar origin, Angel-r from X-Men by Tuska. 3-Romita & Heck-a (no Kirby) 2.30 7.00 20.00
NOTE: ***Buscema** r-2. **Colan** a-1p(r). **Kirby** c/a-1, 2. #1-Reprints X-Men #10 & Daredevil #24*

KA-ZAR
Marvel Comics Group: Jan, 1974 - No. 20, Feb, 1977 (Regular Size)
1 1.75 5.25 14.00
2,3-new X-Men Angel; w/death of parents (see Marvel Tales #30)
1.10 3.30 9.00
4-10 1.00 2.80 7.00
11-14,16,18-20 5.00
15,17-(Regular 25¢ edition)(8/76) 5.00
15,17-(30¢-c, limited distribution) 2.40 6.00
NOTE: ***Alcala** a-6i, 8i. **Brunner** c-4. **J. Buscema** a-6-10p; c-1, 5, 7. **Heath** a-12. **G. Kane** c(p)-3, 5, 8-11, 15, 20. **Kirby** c-12p. **Reinman** a-1p.*

KA-ZAR (Volume 2)
Marvel Comics: May, 1997 - No. 20, Dec, 1998 ($1.95/$1.99)
1-Waid-s/Andy Kubert-c/a. thru #4 3.00
1-2nd printing; new cover 2.00
2,4: 2-Two-c 2.00
3-Alpha Flight #1 preview 3.00
5-13,15-20: 8-Includes Spider-Man Cybercomic CD-ROM. 9-11-Thanos app. 15-Priest-s/Martinez & Rodriguez-a begin; Punisher app. 2.00
14-($2.99) Last Waid/Kubert issue; flip book with 2nd story previewing new creative team of Priest-s/Martinez & Rodriguez-a 3.00
'97 Annual ($2.99)-Wraparound-c 3.00

KA-ZAR OF THE SAVAGE LAND
Marvel Comics: Feb, 1997 ($2.50, one-shot)
1-Wraparound-c 2.50

KA-ZAR: SIBLING RIVALRY
Marvel Comics: July, 1997 ($1.95, one-shot)
(# -1) Flashback story w/Alpha Flight #1 preview 2.00

KA-ZAR THE SAVAGE (See Marvel Fanfare)
Marvel Comics Group: Apr, 1981 - No. 34, Oct, 1984 (Regular size) (Mando paper #10 on)
1 3.00
2-20,24,27,28,30-34: 11-Origin Zabu. 12-One of two versions with panel missing on pg. 10. 20-Kraven the Hunter-c/story (also apps. in #21) 2.00
12-Version with panel on pg. 10 (1600 printed) 5.00
21-23, 25,26-Spider-Man app. 26-Photo-c. 3.00
29-Double size; Ka-Zar & Shanna wed 3.00
NOTE: ***B. Anderson** a-1-15p, 18, 19; c-1-17, 18p, 20(back). **G. Kane** a(back-up)-11, 12, 14.*

KEEN DETECTIVE FUNNIES (Formerly Detective Picture Stories?)
Centaur Publications: No. 8, July, 1938 - No. 24, Sept, 1940
V1#8-The Clock continues-r/Funny Picture Stories #1; Roy Crane-a (1st?)
211.00 633.00 2000.00
9-Tex Martin by Eisner; The Gang Buster app. 82.00 245.00 775.00
10,11: 11-Dean Denton story (begins?) 74.00 221.00 700.00
V2#1,2-The Eye Sees by Frank Thomas begins; ends #23(Not in V2#3&5).
2-Jack Cole-a 68.00 205.00 650.00
3-6: 3-TNT Todd begins. 4-Gabby Flynn begins. 5,6-Dean Denton story
63.00 189.00 600.00
7-The Masked Marvel by Ben Thompson begins (7/39, 1st app.)(scarce)
232.00 695.00 2200.00
8-Nudist ranch panel w/four girls 82.00 245.00 775.00
9-11 71.00 213.00 675.00
12(12/39)-Origin The Eye Sees by Frank Thomas; death of Masked Marvel's sidekick ZL 90.00 269.00 850.00
V3#1,2 68.00 205.00 650.00
18,19,21,22: 18-Bondage/torture-c 68.00 205.00 650.00
20-Classic Eye Sees-c by Thomas 95.00 285.00 900.00
23-Air Man begins (intro); Air Man-c 90.00 269.00 850.00
24-(scarce) Air Man-c 95.00 285.00 900.00
NOTE: ***Burgos** a-V2#2. **Jack Cole** a-V2#2. **Eisner** a-10, V2#6r. **Ken Ernst** a-V2#4-7, 9, 10, 19, 21; c-V2#4. **Everett** a-V2#6, 7, 9, 11, 12, 20. **Guardineer** a-V2#5, 66. **Gustavson** a-V2#4-6. **Simon** c-V3#1. **Thompson** c-V2#7, 9, 10, 22.*

KEEN KOMICS
Centaur Publications: V2#1, May, 1939 - V2#3, Nov, 1939
V2#1(Large size)-Dan Hastings (s/f), The Big Top, Bob Phantom the Magician, The Mad Goddess app. 95.00 285.00 900.00

Keif Llama nn © Matt Howarth

Kerry Drake Detective Cases #5 © HARV

Kid Colt Outlaw #3 © MAR

GD2.0 FN6.0 NM9.4 | GD2.0 FN6.0 NM9.4

V2#2(Reg. size)-The Forbidden Idol of Machu Picchu; Cut Carson by Burgos begins 61.00 182.00 575.00
V2#3-Saddle Sniffl by Jack Cole, Circus Pays, Kings Revenge app. 61.00 182.00 575.00
NOTE: *Binder a-V2#2. Burgos a-V2#2, 3. Ken Ernst a-V2#3. Gustavson a-V2#2. Jack Cole a-V2#3.*

KEEN TEENS (Girls magazine)
Life's Romances Publ./Leader/Magazine Ent.: 1945 - No. 6, Aug-Sept, 1947
nn (#1)-14 pgs. Claire Voyant (cont'd. in other nn issue) movie photos, Dotty Dripple, Gertie O'Grady & Sissy; Van Johnson, Frank Sinatra photo-c 30.00 90.00 240.00
nn (#2, 1946)-16 pgs. Claire Voyant & 16 pgs. movie photos 26.00 79.00 210.00
3-6: 4-Glenn Ford photo-c. 5-Perry Como-c 10.00 30.00 75.00

KEIF LLAMA
Oni Press: Mar, 1999 ($2.95, B&W, one-shot)
1-Matt Howarth-s/a 3.00

KELLYS, THE (Formerly Rusty Comics; Spy Cases No. 26 on)
Marvel Comics (HPC): No. 23, Jan, 1950 - No. 25, June, 1950 (52 pgs.)
23-Teenage 11.00 33.00 90.00
24,25: 24-Margie app. 7.85 23.50 55.00

KELVIN MACE
Vortex Publications: 1986 - No. 2, 1986 ($2.00, B&W)
1,2: 1-(B&W). 1-2nd print (1/87, $1.75). 2-(Color) 2.00

KEN MAYNARD WESTERN (Movie star)(See Wow Comics, 1936)
Fawcett Publ.: Sept, 1950 - No. 8, Feb, 1952 (All 36 pgs; photo front/back-c)
1-Ken Maynard & his horse Tarzan begin 58.00 174.00 550.00
2 38.00 113.00 300.00
3-8: 6-Atomic bomb explosion panel 29.00 86.00 230.00

KEN SHANNON (Becomes Gabby #11 on) (Also see Police Comics #103)
Quality Comics Group: Oct, 1951 - No. 10, Apr, 1953 (A private eye)
1-Crandall-a 37.00 111.00 295.00
2-Crandall c/a(2) 30.00 90.00 240.00
3-5-Crandall-a. 3-Horror-c 21.00 64.00 170.00
6-Crandall-c/a; "The Weird Vampire Mob"-c/s 24.00 71.00 190.00
7,10: 7-Crandall-a. 10-Crandall-c 17.00 51.00 135.00
8,9: 8-Opium den drug use story 16.00 49.00 130.00
NOTE: *Crandall/Cuidera c-1-10. Jack Cole a-1-9. #1-15 published after title change to Gabby.*

KEN STUART
Publication Enterprises: Jan, 1949 (Sea Adventures)
1-Frank Borth-c/a 10.00 30.00 70.00

KENT BLAKE OF THE SECRET SERVICE (Spy)
Marvel/Atlas Comics(20CC): May, 1951 - No. 14, July, 1953
1-Injury to eye, bondage, torture; Brodsky-c 20.00 60.00 160.00
2-Drug use w/hypo scenes; Brodsky-c 14.00 41.00 110.00
3-14: 8-R.Q. Sale-a (2 pgs.) 8.65 26.00 60.00
NOTE: *Heath c-5, 7, 8. Infantino c-12. Maneely c-3. Sinnott a-2(3). Tuska a-8(3pg.).*

KENTS, THE
DC Comics: Aug, 1997 - No. 12, July, 1998 ($2.50, limited series)
1-12-Ostrander-s/art by Truman and Bair (#1-8), Mandrake (#9-12) 3.00
TPB ($19.95) r/#1-12 19.95

KERRY DRAKE (Also see A-1 Comics)
Argo: Jan, 1956 - No. 2, March, 1956
1,2-Newspaper-r 7.85 23.50 55.00

KERRY DRAKE DETECTIVE CASES (...Racket Buster No. 32,33)
(Also see Chamber of Clues & Green Hornet Comics #42-47)
Life's Romances/Com/Magazine Ent. No.1-5/Harvey No.6 on: 1944 - No. 5, 1944; No. 6, Jan, 1948 - No. 33, Aug, 1952
nn(1944)(A-1 Comics)(slightly over-size) 28.00 84.00 225.00
2 18.00 53.00 140.00
3-5(1944) 15.00 45.00 120.00
6,8(1948): Lady Crime by Powell. 8-Bondage-c 10.00 30.00 75.00
7-Kubert-a; biog of Andriola (artist) 11.00 33.00 90.00
9,10-Two-part marijuana story; Kerry smokes marijuana in #10 15.00 45.00 120.00
11-15 9.30 28.00 65.00
16-33 7.15 21.50 50.00
NOTE: *Andiola c-6-9. Berg a-5. Powell a-10-23, 28, 29.*

KEWPIES
Will Eisner Publications: Spring, 1949
1-Feiffer-a; Kewpie Doll ad on back cover 44.00 133.00 400.00

KEY COMICS
Consolidated Magazines: Jan, 1944 - No. 5, Aug, 1946
1-The Key, Will-O-The-Wisp begin 40.00 120.00 350.00
2 (3/44) 22.00 66.00 175.00
3,4: 4-(5/46)-Origin John Quincy The Atom (begins); Walter Johnson c-3-5 19.00 56.00 150.00
5-4pg. Faust Opera adaptation; Kiefer-a; back-c advertises "Masterpieces Illustrated" by Lloyd Jacquet after he left Classic Comics (no copies of Masterpieces Illustrated known) 24.00 71.00 190.00

KEY RING COMICS
Dell Publishing Co.: 1941 (16 pgs.; two colors) (sold 5 for 10¢)
1-Sky Hawk, 1-Viking Carter, 1-Features Sleepy Samson, 1-Origin Greg Gilday-r/War Comics #2 5.70 17.00 40.00
1-Radior (Super hero) 7.15 21.50 50.00
NOTE: *Each book has two holes in spine to put in binder.*

KICKERS, INC.
Marvel Comics Group: Nov, 1986 - No. 12, Oct, 1987
1-12 2.00

KID CARROTS
St. John Publishing Co.: September, 1953
1-Funny animal 6.40 19.25 45.00

KID COLT OUTLAW (Kid Colt #1-4; ...Outlaw #5-on)(Also see All Western Winners, Best Western, Black Rider, Giant-Size..., Two-Gun Kid, Two-Gun Western, Western Winners, Wild Western, Wisco)
Marvel Comics(LCC) 1-16; Atlas(LMC) 17-102; Marvel 103-on: 8/48 - No. 139, 3/68; No. 140, 11/69 - No. 229, 4/79
1-Kid Colt & his horse Steel begin. 95.00 285.00 900.00
2 47.00 142.00 425.00
3-5: 4-Anti-Wertham editorial; Tex Taylor app. 5-Blaze Carson app. 40.00 120.00 350.00
6-8: 6-Tex Taylor app; 7-Nimo the Lion begins, ends #10 28.00 83.00 220.00
9,10 (52 pgs.) 28.00 83.00 220.00
11-Origin 31.00 94.00 250.00
12-20 20.00 60.00 160.00
21-32 16.00 49.00 130.00
33-45: Black Rider in all 12.00 36.00 95.00
46,47,49,50 10.00 30.00 75.00
48-Kubert-a 10.00 30.00 80.00
51-53,55,56 8.65 26.00 60.00
54-Williamson/Maneely-c 10.00 30.00 70.00
57-60,66: 4-pg. Williamson-a in all 6.80 20.50 75.00
61-63,67-78,80-86: 70-Severin-c. 73-Maneely-c. 86-Kirby-a(r). 4.10 12.30 45.00
64,65-Crandall-a 4.55 13.65 50.00
79,87: 79-Origin retold. 87-Davis-a(r) 4.55 13.65 50.00
88,89-Williamson-a in both (4 pgs.). 89-Redrawn Matt Slade #2 5.45 16.35 60.00
90-99,101-106,108,109: 91-Kirby/Ayers-c. 95-Kirby/Ayers-c/story. 101-Last 10¢ issue 3.20 9.60 35.00
100 3.80 11.40 42.00
107-Only Kirby sci-fi cover of title; Kirby -a. 3.65 11.00 40.00
110-(5/63)-1st app. Iron Mask (Iron Man type villain) 3.65 11.00 40.00
111-120: 114-(1/64)-2nd app. Iron Mask 3.00 9.00 30.00
121-129,133-139: 121-Rawhide Kid x-over. 125-Two-Gun Kid x-over 139-Last 12¢ issue 2.30 7.00 20.00
130-132 (68 pgs.)-one new story each. 130-Origin 3.00 9.00 30.00
140-155: 140-Reprints begin (later issues all-r). 155-Last 15¢ issue

Kid Cowboy #4 © Z-D

Kid Eternity #7 © QUA

Kid Movie Komics #11 © MAR

GD2.0 FN6.0 NM9.4

1.75 5.25 14.00
156-Giant; reprints (52 pgs.) 2.30 7.00 20.00
157-180,200: 170-Origin retold. 1.50 4.50 12.00
181-199 1.25 3.75 10.00
201-229: 229-Rawhide Kid-r 1.00 3.00 8.00
...Album (no date; 1950's; Atlas Comics)-132 pgs.; random binding, cardboard cover, B&W stories; contents can vary (Rare) 76.00 228.00 725.00

NOTE: ***Ayers*** *a-many.* ***Colan*** *a-52, 53; c(p)-223, 228, 229.* ***Crandall*** *a-140r, 167r.* ***Everett*** *a-90, 137i, 225i(r).* ***Heath*** *a-8(2); c-34, 35, 39, 44, 46, 48, 49, 57, 64.* ***Heck*** *a-135, 139.* ***Jack Keller*** *a-25(2), 26-68(3-4), 78, 94p, 98, 99, 108, 110, 130, 132, 140-150r.* ***Kirby*** *a-86r, 93, 96, 107, 119, 176(part); c-87, 92-95, 97, 99-112, 114-117, 121-123, 197r; w/****Ditko*** *c-89.* ***Maneely*** *a-12, 68, 81; c-17, 19, 40-43, 47, 52, 53, 62, 65, 68, 78, 81, 142r, 150r.* ***Morrow*** *a-173r, 216r.* ***Rico*** *a-13, 18.* ***Severin*** *c-58, 59, 143, 148, 149i.* ***Shores*** *a-39, 41-43, 143r; c-1-10(most), 24.* ***Sutton*** *a-136, 137p, 225p(r).* ***Wildey*** *a-47, 54, 82, 144r.* ***Williamson*** *r-147, 170, 172, 216.* ***Woodbridge*** *a-64, 81. Black Rider in #33-45, 74, 86. Iron Mask in #110, 114, 121, 127. Sam Hawk in #84, 101, 111, 121, 146, 174, 181, 188.*

KID COWBOY (Also see Approved Comics #4 & Boy Cowboy)
Ziff-Davis Publ./St. John (Approved Comics) #11,14: 1950 - No. 11, Wint, '52-'53; No. 14, June, 1954 (No #12,13)
(Painted covers #1-10, 14)

1-Lucy Belle & Red Feather begin 15.00 45.00 120.00
2-Maneely-c 10.00 30.00 70.00
3-11,14: (#3, spr. '51). 5-Berg-a. 14-Code approved 8.65 26.00 60.00

KID DEATH & FLUFFY HALLOWEEN SPECIAL
Event Comics: Oct, 1997 ($2.95, B&W, one-shot)

1-Variant-c by Cebollero & Quesada/Palmiotti 3.00

KID DEATH & FLUFFY SPRING BREAK SPECIAL
Event Comics: July, 1996 ($2.50, B&W, one-shot)

1-Quesada & Palmiotti-c/scripts 2.50

KIDDIE KAPERS
Kiddie Kapers Co., 1945/Decker Publ. (Red Top-Farrell): 1945?(nd); Oct, 1957; 1963 - 1964

1(nd, 1945-46?, 36 pgs.)-Infinity-c; funny animal 8.65 26.00 60.00
1(10/57)(Decker)-Little Bit-r from Kiddie Karnival 4.65 14.00 28.00
Super Reprint #7, 10('63), 12, 14('63), 15,17('64), 18('64): 10, 14-r/Animal Adventures #1. 15-Animal Adventures #? 17-Cowboys 'N' Injuns #? 1.50 4.50 12.00

KIDDIE KARNIVAL
Ziff-Davis Publ. Co. (Approved Comics): 1952 (25¢, 100 pgs.) (One Shot)

nn-Rebound Little Bit #1,2; painted-c 36.00 108.00 290.00

KID ETERNITY (Becomes Buccaneers) (See Hit Comics)
Quality Comics Group: Spring, 1946 - No. 18, Nov, 1949

1 84.00 253.00 800.00
2 40.00 120.00 340.00
3-Mac Raboy-a 40.00 120.00 350.00
4-10 24.00 71.00 190.00
11-18 19.00 56.00 150.00

KID ETERNITY
DC Comics: 1991 - No. 3, Nov, 1991 ($4.95, limited series)

1-3: Grant Morrison scripts 6.00

KID ETERNITY
DC Comics (Vertigo): May, 1993 - No. 16, Sept, 1994 ($1.95, mature)

1-16: 1-Gold ink-c. 6-Photo-c. All Sean Phillips-c/a except #15 (Phillips-c/i only) 2.00

KID FROM DODGE CITY, THE
Atlas Comics (MMC): July, 1957 - No. 2, Sept, 1957

1-Don Heck-c 10.00 30.00 70.00
2-Everett-c 6.00 18.00 42.00

KID FROM TEXAS, THE (A Texas Ranger)
Atlas Comics (CSI): June, 1957 - No. 2, Aug, 1957

1-Powell-a; Severin-c 10.00 30.00 75.00
2 6.00 18.00 42.00

KID KOKO
I. W. Enterprises: 1958

Reprint #1,2-(r/M.E.'s Koko & Kola #4, 1947) 1.50 4.50 12.00

KID KOMICS (Kid Movie Komics No. 11)
Timely Comics (USA 1,2/FCI 3-10): Feb, 1943 - No. 10, Spring, 1946

1-Origin Captain Wonder & sidekick Tim Mullrooney, & Subbie; intro the Sea-Going Lad, Pinto Pete, & Trixie Trouble; Knuckles & Whitewash Jones (from Young Allies) app.; Wolverton-a (7 pgs.) 381.00 1143.00 4000.00
2-The Young Allies, Red Hawk, & Tommy Tyme begin; last Captain Wonder & Subbie 168.00 505.00 1600.00
3-The Vision, Daredevils & Red Hawk app. 129.00 387.00 1225.00
4-The Destroyer begins; Sub-Mariner app.; Red Hawk & Tommy Tyme end 111.00 332.00 1050.00
5,6: 5-Tommy Tyme begins, ends #10 84.00 253.00 800.00
7-10: 7,10-The Whizzer app. Destroyer not in #7,8. 10-Last Destroyer, Young Allies & Whizzer 77.00 232.00 735.00

NOTE: ***Brodsky*** *c-5.* ***Schomburg*** *c-2-4, 6-10.* ***Shores*** *c-1. Captain Wonder c-1, 2. The Young Allies c-3-10.*

KID MONTANA (Formerly Davy Crockett Frontier Fighter; The Gunfighters No. 51 on)
Charlton Comics: V2#9, Nov, 1957 - No. 50, Mar, 1965

V2#9 4.10 12.30 45.00
10 3.20 9.60 35.00
11,12,14-20 2.50 7.50 24.00
13-Williamson-a 3.20 9.60 35.00
21-35 2.00 6.00 16.00
36-50 1.50 4.50 12.00

NOTE: *Title change to Montana Kid on cover only #44 & 45; remained Kid Montana on inside.*

KID MOVIE KOMICS (Formerly Kid Komics; Rusty Comics #12 on)
Timely Comics: No. 11, Summer, 1946

11-Silly Seal & Ziggy Pig; 2 pgs. Kurtzman "Hey Look" plus 6 pg. "Pigtales" story 26.00 79.00 210.00

KIDNAPPED (Robert Louis Stevenson's...also see Movie Comics)(Disney)
Dell Publishing Co.: No. 1101, May, 1960

Four Color 1101-Movie, photo-c 5.85 17.50 70.00

KIDNAP RACKET (See Harvey Comics Hits No. 57)

KID SLADE GUNFIGHTER (Formerly Matt Slade...)
Atlas Comics (SPI): No. 5, Jan, 1957 - No. 8, July, 1957

5-Maneely, Roth, Severin-a in all; Maneely-c 12.00 36.00 95.00
6,8-Severin-c 7.15 21.50 50.00
7-Williamson/Mayo-a, 4 pgs. 10.00 30.00 75.00

KID SUPREME (See Supreme)
Image Comics (Extreme Studios): Mar, 1996 - No. 3, July, 1996 ($2.50)

1-3: Fraga-a/scripts. 3-Glory-c/app. 2.50

KID TERRIFIC
Image Comics: Nov, 1998 ($2.95, B&W)

1-Snyder & Diliberto-s/a 3.00

KID ZOO COMICS
Street & Smith Publications: July, 1948 (52 pgs.)

1-Funny Animal 26.00 79.00 210.00

KILLER (...Tales By Timothy Truman)
Eclipse Comics: March, 1985 ($1.75, one-shot, Baxter paper)

1-Timothy Truman-c/a 2.00

KILLER INSTINCT (Video game)
Acclaim Comics: June, 1996 - No. 6 ($2.50, limited series)

1-6: 1-Bart Sears-a(p). 4-Special #1. 5-Special #2. 6-Special #3 3.00

KILLERS, THE
Magazine Enterprises: 1947 - No. 2, 1948 (No month)

1-Mr. Zin, the Hatchet Killer; mentioned in **SOTI**, pgs. 179,180; used by N.Y. Legis. Comm.; L. B. Cole-c 100.00 300.00 950.00
2-(Scarce)-Hashish smoking story; "Dying, Dying, Dead" drug story; Whitney, Ingels-a; Whitney hanging-c 84.00 253.00 800.00

KILLING JOKE, THE (See Batman: The Killing Joke under Batman one-shots)

Kin #4 © Gary Frank

King Comics #26 © DMP

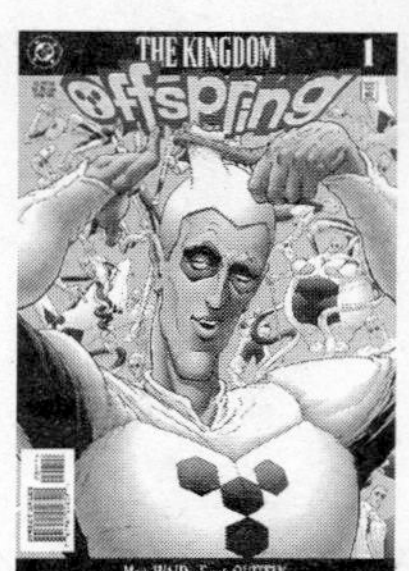

The Kingdom: Offspring #1 © DC

GD2.0 FN6.0 NM9.4

KILLPOWER: THE EARLY YEARS
Marvel Comics UK: Sept, 1993 - No. 4, Dec, 1993 ($1.75, mini-series)
1-($2.95)-Foil embossed-c 3.00
2-4: 2-Genetix app. 3-Punisher app. 2.00

KILLRAVEN (See Amazing Adventures #18 (5/73))
Marvel Comics: Feb, 2001 ($2.99, one-shot)
1-Linsner-s/a/c 3.00

KILLRAZOR
Image Comics (Top Cow Productions): Aug, 1995 ($2.50, one-shot)
1 2.50

KILL YOUR BOYFRIEND
DC Comics (Vertigo): June, 1995 ($4.95, one-shot)
1-Grant Morrison story 2.40 6.00
1($5.95, 1998) 2nd printing 6.00

KILROY (Volume 2)
Caliber Press: 1998 ($2.95, B&W)
1-Pruett-s 3.00

KILROY IS HERE
Caliber Press: 1995 ($2.95, B&W)
1-10 3.00

KILROYS, THE
B&I Publ. Co. No. 1-19/American Comics Group: June-July, 1947 - No. 54, June-July, 1955

	GD2.0	FN6.0	NM9.4
1	22.00	66.00	175.00
2	11.00	33.00	90.00
3-5: 5-Gross-a	9.30	28.00	65.00
6-10: 8-Milt Gross's Moronica	7.00	21.00	48.00
11-20: 14-Gross-a	6.00	18.00	42.00
21-30	5.00	15.00	30.00
31-47,50-54	4.65	14.00	28.00
48,49-(3-D effect-c/stories)	17.00	51.00	135.00

KILROY: THE SHORT STORIES
Caliber Press: 1995 ($2.95, B&W)
1 3.00

KIN
Image Comics (Top Cow): Mar, 2000 - Present ($2.95)
1-5-Gary Frank-s/c/a 3.00
1-($6.95) DF Alternate footprint cover 6.95
6-($3.95) 3.95

KINDRED, THE
Image Comics (WildStorm Productions): Mar, 1994 - No. 4, July, 1995 ($1.95, limited series)
1-($2.50)-Grifter & Backlash app. in all; bound-in trading card 2.50
2-4 2.50
2,3: 2-Variant-c. 3-Alternate-c by Portacio, see Deathblow #5 4.00
Trade paperback (2/95, $9.95) 10.00
NOTE: ***Booth*** *c/a-1-4. The first four issues contain coupons redeemable for a Jim Lee Grifter/Backlash print.*

KING ARTHUR AND THE KNIGHTS OF JUSTICE
Marvel Comics UK: Dec, 1993 - No. 3, Feb, 1994 ($1.25, limited series)
1-3: TV adaptation 2.00

KING CLASSICS
King Features : 1977 (36 pgs., cardboard-c)
(Printed in Spain for U.S. distr.)
1-Connecticut Yankee, 2-Last of the Mohicans, 3-Moby Dick, 4-Robin Hood, 5-Swiss Family Robinson, 6-Robinson Crusoe, 7-Treasure Island, 8-20,000 Leagues, 9-Christmas Carol, 10-Huck Finn, 11-Around the World in 80 Days, 12-Davy Crockett, 13-Don Quixote, 14-Gold Bug, 15-Ivanhoe, 16-Three Musketeers, 17-Baron Munchausen, 18-Alice in Wonderland, 19-Black Arrow, 20-Five Weeks in a Balloon, 21-Great Expectations, 22-Gulliver's Travels, 23-Prince & Pauper, 24-Lawrence of Arabia (Originals, 1977-78)

	GD2.0	FN6.0	NM9.4
each....	1.50	4.50	12.00
Reprints (1979; HRN-24)	1.00	3.00	8.00

NOTE: *The first eight issues were not numbered. Issues No. 25-32 were advertised but not published. The 1977 originals have HRN 32a; the 1978 originals have HRN 32b.*

KING COLT (See Luke Short's Western Stories)

KING COMICS (Strip reprints)
David McKay Publications/Standard #156-on: 4/36 - No. 155, 11-12/49; No. 156, Spr/50 - No. 159, 2/52 (Winter on-c)

	GD2.0	FN6.0	VF8.0
1-1st app. Flash Gordon by Alex Raymond; Brick Bradford (1st app.), Popeye, Henry (1st app.) & Mandrake the Magician (1st app.) begin; Popeye-c begin	1200.00	3600.00	8400.00
	GD2.0	**FN6.0**	**NM9.4**
2	338.00	1013.00	2700.00
3	225.00	675.00	1800.00
4	175.00	525.00	1400.00
5	125.00	375.00	1000.00
6-10: 9-X-Mas-c	88.00	263.00	700.00
11-20	69.00	206.00	550.00
21-30: 21-X-Mas-c	50.00	150.00	400.00
31-40: 33-Last Segar Popeye	40.00	120.00	320.00
41-50: 46-Text illos by Marge Buell contain characters similar to Lulu, Alvin & Tubby. 50-The Lone Ranger begins	33.00	98.00	260.00
51-60: 52-Barney Baxter begins?	22.00	66.00	175.00
61-The Phantom begins	22.00	66.00	175.00
62-80: 76-Flag-c. 79-Blondie begins	17.00	51.00	135.00
81-99	13.00	39.00	105.00
100	16.00	48.00	125.00
101-114: 114-Last Raymond issue (1 pg.); Flash Gordon by Austin Briggs begins, ends #155	12.00	36.00	95.00
115-145: 117-Phantom origin retold	10.00	30.00	70.00
146,147-Prince Valiant in both	7.85	23.50	55.00
148-155: 155-Flash Gordon ends (11-12/49)	7.85	23.50	55.00
156-159: 156-New logo begins (Standard)	7.15	21.50	50.00

NOTE: *Marge Buell text illos in No. 24-46 at least.*

KING CONAN (Conan The King No. 20 on)
Marvel Comics Group: Mar, 1980 - No. 19, Nov, 1983 (52 pgs.)
1 5.00
2-19: 4-Death of Thoth Amon. 7-1st Paul Smith-a, 1 pg. pin-up (9/81) 3.00
NOTE: ***J. Buscema*** *a-1-9p, 17p; c(p)-1-5, 7-9, 14, 17.* ***Kaluta*** *c-19.* ***Nebres*** *a-17i, 18, 19i.* ***Severin*** *c-18.* ***Simonson*** *c-6.*

KINGDOM, THE
DC Comics: Feb, 1999 - No. 2, Feb, 1999 ($2.95, limited series)
1,2-Waid-s; sequel to Kingdom Come; introduces Hypertime 4.00
...: Kid Flash 1 (2/99, $1.99) Waid-s/Pararillo-a, ...: Nightstar 1 (2/99, $1.99) Waid-s/Haley-a, ...: Offspring 1 (2/99, $1.99) Waid-s/Quitely-a, ...: Planet Krypton 1 (2/99, $1.99) Waid-s/Kitson-a, ...: Son of the Bat 1 (2/99, $1.99) Waid-s/Apthorp-a 2.00

KINGDOM COME
DC Comics: 1996 - No. 4, 1996 ($4.95, painted limited series)

	GD2.0	FN6.0	NM9.4
1- Mark Waid scripts & Alex Ross-painted c/a in all; tells the last days of the DC Universe; 1st app. Magog	1.25	3.75	10.00
2-Superman forms new Justice League	1.25	3.75	10.00
3-Return of Capt. Marvel	1.00	3.00	8.00
4-Final battle of Superman and Capt. Marvel	1.00	3.00	8.00

Deluxe Slipcase Edition-($89.95) w/Revelations companion book, 12 new story pages, foil stamped covers, signed and numbered 160.00
Hardcover Edition-($29.95)-Includes 12 new story pages and artwork from Revelations, new cover artwork with gold foil inlay 35.00
Hardcover 2nd printing 30.00
Softcover Ed.-($14.95)-Includes 12 new story pgs. & artwork from Revelations, new c-artwork 15.00

KING KONG (See Movie Comics)

KING LEONARDO & HIS SHORT SUBJECTS (TV)
Dell Publishing Co./Gold Key: Nov-Jan, 1961-62 - No. 4, Sept, 1963

	GD2.0	FN6.0	NM9.4
Four Color 1242,1278	13.00	40.00	160.00
01390-207(5-7/62)(Dell)	10.00	30.00	120.00
1 (10/62)	11.00	33.00	130.00
2-4	8.75	26.25	105.00

KISS Psycho Circus #30 © KISS Catalog

Kit Carson nn © AVON

Knightmare #4 © Rob Liefeld

GD2.0 FN6.0 NM9.4

KING LOUIE & MOWGLI (See Jungle Book under Movie Comics)
Gold Key: May, 1968 (Disney)
1 (#10223-805)-Characters from Jungle Book 2.50 7.50 25.00

KING OF DIAMONDS (TV)
Dell Publishing Co.: July-Sept, 1962
01-391-209-Photo-c 3.45 10.35 38.00

KING OF KINGS (Movie)
Dell Publishing Co.: No. 1236, Oct-Nov, 1961
Four Color 1236-Photo-c 7.50 22.50 90.00

KING OF THE BAD MEN OF DEADWOOD
Avon Periodicals: 1950 (See Wild Bill Hickok #16)
nn-Kinstler-c; Kamen/Feldstein-r/Cowpuncher #2 15.00 45.00 125.00

KING OF THE ROYAL MOUNTED (See Famous Feature Stories, King Comics, Red Ryder #3 & Super Book #2, 6)

KING OF THE ROYAL MOUNTED (Zane Grey's...)
David McKay/Dell Publishing Co.: No. 1, May, 1937; No. 9, 1940; No. 207, Dec, 1948 - No. 935, Sept-Nov, 1958
Feature Books 1 (5/37)(McKay) 71.00 213.00 850.00
Large Feature Comic 9 (1940) 38.00 113.00 450.00
Four Color 207(#1, 12/48) 14.00 42.00 170.00
Four Color 265,283 7.50 22.50 90.00
Four Color 310,340 5.85 17.50 70.00
Four Color 363,384, 8(6-8/52)-10 5.00 15.00 60.00
11-20 4.55 13.65 50.00
21-28(3-5/58), Four Color 935(9-11/58) 3.45 10.35 38.00
NOTE: *4-Color No. 207, 265, 283, 310, 340, 363, 384 are all newspaper reprints with* ***Jim Gary*** *art. No. 8 on are all Dell originals. Painted c-No. 9-on.*

KINGPIN
Marvel Comics: Nov, 1997 ($5.99, squarebound, one-shot)
nn-Spider-Man & Daredevil vs. Kingpin; Stan Lee-s/ John Romita Sr.-a 2.40 6.00

KING RICHARD & THE CRUSADERS
Dell Publishing Co.: No. 588, Oct, 1954
Four Color 588-Movie, Matt Baker-a, photo-c 10.00 30.00 120.00

KINGS OF THE NIGHT
Dark Horse Comics: 1990 - No. 2, 1990 ($2.25, limited series)
1,2-Robert E. Howard adaptation; Bolton-c 2.25

KING SOLOMON'S MINES (Movie)
Avon Periodicals: 1951
nn (#1 on 1st page) 40.00 120.00 320.00

KING TIGER & MOTORHEAD
Dark Horse Comics: Aug, 1996 - No. 2, Sept, 1996 ($2.95, limited series)
1,2: Chichester scripts 3.00

KIPLING, RUDYARD (See Mowgli, The Jungle Book)

KISS (See Crazy Magazine, Howard the Duck #12, 13, Marvel Comics Super Special #1, 5, Rock Fantasy Comics #10 & Rock N' Roll Comics #9)

KISS: THE PSYCHO CIRCUS
Image Comics: Aug, 1997 - Present ($1.95/$2.25/$2.50)
1-Holguin-s/Medina-a(p) 1.50 4.50 12.00
1-2nd & 3rd printings 2.50
2 1.00 2.80 7.00
3,4: 4-Photo-c 5.00
5-8: 5-Begin $2.25-c 4.00
9-29 2.50
30,31: 30-Begin $2.50-c 2.50
Book 1 TPB ('98, $12.95) r/#1-6 13.00
Book 2 Destroyer TPB (8/99, $9.95) r/#10-13 10.00
Book 3 Whispered Scream TPB ('00, $9.95) r/#7-9,18 10.00
...Magazine 1 ($6.95) r/#1-3 plus interviews 7.00
...Magazine 2-5 ($4.95) 2-r/#4,5 plus interviews. 3-r/#6,7. 4-r/#8,9 5.00
Wizard Edition ('98, supplement) Bios, tour preview and interviews 2.00

GD2.0 FN6.0 NM9.4

KISSYFUR (TV)
DC Comics: 1989 (Sept.) ($2.00, 52 pgs., one-shot)
1-Based on Saturday morning cartoon 3.00

KIT CARSON (Formerly All True Detective Cases No. 4; Fighting Davy Crockett No. 9; see Blazing Sixguns & Frontier Fighters)
Avon Periodicals: 1950; No. 2, 8/51 - No. 3, 12/51; No. 5, 11-12/54 - No. 8, 9/55 (No #4)
nn(#1) (1950)- "...Indian Scout" ; r-Cowboys 'N' Injuns #? 13.00 39.00 105.00
2(8/51) 9.30 28.00 65.00
3(12/51)- "...Fights the Comanche Raiders" 7.85 23.50 55.00
5-6,8(11-12/54-9/55): 5-Formerly All True Detective Cases (last pre-code); titled "...and the Trail of Doom" 7.15 21.50 50.00
7-McCann-a? 7.85 23.50 55.00
I.W. Reprint #10('63)-r/Kit Carson #1; Severin-c 2.00 6.00 16.00
NOTE: ***Kinstler*** *c-1-3, 5-8.*

KIT CARSON & THE BLACKFEET WARRIORS
Realistic: 1953
nn-Reprint; Kinstler-c 9.30 28.00 65.00

KIT KARTER
Dell Publishing Co.: May-July, 1962
1 2.80 8.40 28.00

KITTY
St. John Publishing Co.: Oct, 1948
1-Teenage; Lily Renee-c/a 7.00 21.00 48.00

KITTY PRYDE, AGENT OF S.H.I.E.L.D. (Also see Excalibur)
Marvel Comics: Dec, 1997 - No. 3, Feb, 1998 ($2.50, limited series)
1-3-Hama-s 2.50

KITTY PRYDE AND WOLVERINE (Also see Uncanny X-Men & X-Men)
Marvel Comics Group: Nov, 1984 - No. 6, Apr, 1985 (Limited series)
1-6: Characters from X-Men 4.00

KLARER GIVEAWAYS (See Wisco)

KNIGHTHAWK
Acclaim Comics (Windjammer): Sept, 1995 - No. 6, Nov, 1995 ($2.50, lim. series)
1-6: 6-origin 2.50

KNIGHTMARE
Antarctic Press: July, 1994 - May, 1995 ($2.75, B&W, mature readers)
1-6 2.75

KNIGHTMARE
Image Comics (Extreme Studios): Feb, 1995 - No. 5, June, 1995 ($2.50)
0 ($3.50) 3.50
1-5: 4-Quesada & Palmiotti variant-c, 5-Flip book w/Warcry 2.50

KNIGHTS OF PENDRAGON, THE (Also see Pendragon)
Marvel Comics Ltd.: July, 1990 - No. 18, Dec, 1991 ($1.95)
1-18: 1-Capt. Britain app. 2,8-Free poster inside. 9,10-Bolton-c. 11,18-Iron Man app. 2.00

KNIGHTS OF THE ROUND TABLE
Dell Publishing Co.: No. 540, Mar, 1954
Four Color 540-Movie, photo-c 6.70 20.00 80.00

KNIGHTS OF THE ROUND TABLE
Pines Comics: No. 10, April, 1957
10 4.65 14.00 28.00

KNIGHTS OF THE ROUND TABLE
Dell Publishing Co.: Nov-Jan, 1963-64
1 (12-397-401)-Painted-c 3.00 9.00 32.00

KNIGHTSTRIKE (Also see Operation: Knightstrike)
Image Comics (Extreme Studios): Jan, 1996 ($2.50)
1-Rob Liefeld & Eric Stephenson story; Extreme Destroyer Part 6. 2.50

KNIGHT WATCHMAN (See Big Bang Comics & Dr. Weird)

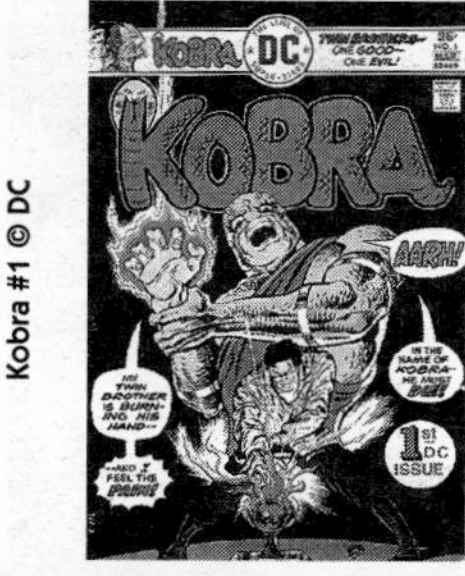

Kobra #1 © DC

Komic Kartoons #1 © MAR

Korak, Son of Tarzan #50 © ERB

GD2.0 FN6.0 NM9.4

Image Comics: June, 1998 - No. 4, Oct, 1998 ($2.95/$3.50, B&W, lim. series)
1-3-Ben Torres-c/a in all 3.00
4-($3.50) 3.50

KNIGHT WATCHMAN: GRAVEYARD SHIFT
Caliber Press: 1994 ($2.95, B&W)
1,2-Ben Torres-a 3.00

KNOCK KNOCK (...Who's There?)
Whitman Publ./Gerona Publications: No. 801, 1936 (52 pgs.) (8x9", B&W)
801-Joke book; Bob Dunn-a 7.15 21.50 50.00

KNOCKOUT ADVENTURES
Fiction House Magazines: Winter, 1953-54
1-Reprints Fight Comics #53 w/Rip Carson-c/s 13.00 39.00 105.00

KNUCKLES (Spin-off of Sonic the Hedgehog)
Archie Publications: Apr, 1997 - Present ($1.50/$1.75/$1.79)
1-29 2.00

KNUCKLES' CHAOTIX
Archie Publications: Jan, 1996 ($2.00, annual)
1 2.00

KOBALT
DC Comics (Milestone): June, 1994 - No. 16, Sept, 1995 ($1.75/$2.50)
1-16: 1-Byrne-c. 4-Intro Page. 16-Kent Williams-c 2.50

KOBRA (See DC Special Series No. 1)
National Periodical Publications: Feb-Mar, 1976 - No. 7, Mar-Apr, 1977
1-1st app.; Kirby-a redrawn by Marcos; only 25¢-c 1.00 3.00 8.00
2-7: (All 30¢ issues) 3-Giffen-a 5.00
NOTE: ***Austin** a-3i. **Buckler** a-5p; c-5p. **Kubert** c-4. **Nasser** a-6p, 7; c-7.*

KOKEY KOALA (...and the Magic Button)
Toby Press: May, 1952
1 10.00 30.00 80.00

KOKO AND KOLA (Also see A-1 Comics #16 & Tick Tock Tales)
Com/Magazine Enterprises: Fall, 1946 - No. 5, May, 1947; No. 6, 1950
1-Funny animal 10.00 30.00 80.00
2-X-Mas-c 6.40 19.25 45.00
3-6: 6(A-1 28) 5.00 15.00 35.00

KO KOMICS
Gerona Publications: Oct, 1945
1-The Duke of Darkness & The Menace (hero) 66.00 197.00 625.00

KOMIC KARTOONS
Timely Comics (EPC): Fall, 1945 - No. 2, Winter, 1945
1,2-Andy Wolf, Bertie Mouse 19.00 56.00 150.00

KOMIK PAGES (Formerly Snap; becomes Bullseye #11)
Harry 'A' Chesler, Jr. (Our Army, Inc.): Apr, 1945 (All reprints)
10(#1 on inside)-Land O' Nod by Rick Yager (2 pgs.), Animal Crackers, Foxy GrandPa, Tom, Dick & Mary, Cheerio Minstrels, Red Starr plus other 1-2 pg. strips; Cole-a 23.00 69.00 185.00

KONA (...Monarch of Monster Isle)
Dell Publishing Co.: Feb-Apr, 1962 - No. 21, Jan-Mar, 1967 (Painted-c)
Four Color 1256 (#1) 6.80 20.50 75.00
2-10: 4-Anak begins 3.20 9.60 35.00
11-21 2.50 7.50 25.00
NOTE: ***Glanzman** a-all issues.*

KONGA (Fantastic Giants No. 24) (See Return of...)
Charlton Comics: 1960; No. 2, Aug, 1961 - No. 23, Nov, 1965
1(1960)-Based on movie; Giordano-c 23.50 71.00 260.00
2-5: 2-Giordano-c; no Ditko-a 10.00 30.00 110.00
6-15 7.65 23.00 85.00
16-23 4.55 13.65 50.00
NOTE: ***Ditko** a-1, 3-15; c-4, 6-9. **Glanzman** a-12. **Montes** & **Bache** a-16-23.*

KONGA'S REVENGE (Formerly Return of...)
Charlton Comics: No. 2, Summer, 1963 - No. 3, Fall, 1964; Dec, 1968
2,3: 2-Ditko-c/a 5.45 16.35 60.00
1(12/68)-Reprints Konga's Revenge #3 2.80 8.40 28.00

KONG THE UNTAMED
National Periodical Publications: June-July, 1975 - V2#5, Feb-Mar, 1976
1-1st app. Kong; Wrightson-c; Alcala-a 1.00 2.80 7.00
2-5: 2-Wrightson-c. 2,3-Alcala-a 5.00

KOOKIE
Dell Publishing Co.: Feb-Apr, 1962 - No. 2, May-July, 1962 (15 cents)
1-Written by John Stanley; Bill Williams-a 8.00 24.00 95.00
2 7.00 21.00 85.00

KOOSH KINS
Archie Comics: Oct, 1991 - No. 3, Feb, 1992 ($1.00, bi-monthly, limited series)
1-3 2.00
NOTE: *No. 4 was planned, but cancelled.*

KORAK, SON OF TARZAN (Edgar Rice Burroughs)(See Tarzan #139)
Gold Key: Jan, 1964 - No. 45, Jan, 1972 (Painted-c No. 1-?)
1-Russ Manning-a 5.85 17.50 70.00
2-11-Russ Manning-a 3.20 9.60 35.00
12-23: 12,13-Warren Tufts-a. 14-Jon of the Kalahari ends. 15-Mabu, Jungle Boy begins. 21-Manning-a. 23-Last 12¢ issue 2.50 7.50 25.00
24-30 2.00 6.00 18.00
31-45 1.50 4.50 12.00

KORAK, SON OF TARZAN (Tarzan Family #60 on; see Tarzan #230)
National Periodical Publications: V9#46, May-June, 1972 - V12#56, Feb-Mar, 1974; No. 57, May-June, 1975 - No. 59, Sept-Oct, 1975 (Edgar Rice Burroughs)
46-(52 pgs.)-Carson of Venus begins (origin), ends #56; Pellucidar feature; Weiss-a 1.75 5.25 14.00
47-59: 49-Origin Korak retold 2.40 6.00
NOTE: *All have covers by **Joe Kubert. Manning** strip reprints-No. 57-59. **Murphy Anderson** a-52. **Michael Kaluta** a-46-56. **Frank Thorne** a-46-51.*

KORG: 70,000 B. C. (TV)
Charlton Publications: May, 1975 - No. 9, Nov, 1976 (Hanna-Barbera)
1,2: 1-Boyette-c/a. 2-Painted-c; Byrne text illos 1.75 5.25 14.00
3-9 1.10 3.30 9.00

KORNER KID COMICS: Four Star Publications: 1947 (Advertised, not pub.)

KOSMIC KAT ACTIVITY BOOK (See Deity)
Image Comics: Aug, 1999 ($2.95, one-shot)
1-Stories and games by various 3.00

KRAZY KAT
Holt: 1946 (Hardcover)
Reprints daily & Sunday strips by Herriman 58.00 174.00 550.00
dust jacket only 44.00 133.00 400.00

KRAZY KAT (See Ace Comics & March of Comics No. 72, 87)

KRAZY KAT COMICS (...& Ignatz the Mouse early issues)
Dell Publ. Co./Gold Key: May-June, 1951 - F.C. #696, Apr, 1956; Jan, 1964 (None by Herriman)
1(1951) 6.70 20.00 80.00
2-5 (#5, 8-10/52) 4.10 12.30 45.00
Four Color 454,504 3.65 11.00 40.00
Four Color 548,619,696 (4/56) 3.20 9.60 35.00
1(10098-401)(1/64-Gold Key)(TV) 3.20 9.60 35.00

KRAZY KOMICS (1st Series) (Cindy Comics No. 27 on)
Timely Comics (USA No. 1-21/JPC No. 22-26): July, 1942 - No. 26, Spr, 1947 (Also see Ziggy Pig)
1-Toughy Tomcat, Ziggy Pig (by Jaffee) & Silly Seal begin 55.00 165.00 500.00
2 26.00 79.00 210.00
3-8,10 19.00 56.00 150.00
9-Hitler parody 20.00 60.00 160.00
11,13,14 12.50 37.50 100.00
12-Timely's entire art staff drew themselves into a Creeper story

Krypton Chronicles #1 © DC

Kull the Destroyer #15 © MAR

Kurt Busiek's Astro City #2 © Juke Box Productions

25.00 75.00 200.00
15-(8-9/44)-Becomes Funny Tunes #16; has "Super Soldier" by Pfc. Stan Lee 12.50 37.50 100.00
16-24,26: 16-(10-11/44). 26-Super Rabbit-c/story 10.00 30.00 80.00
25-Wacky Duck-c/story & begin; Kurtzman-a (6pgs.) 12.50 37.50 100.00

KRAZY KOMICS (2nd Series)
Timely/Marvel Comics: Aug, 1948 - No. 2, Nov, 1948

1-Wolverton (10 pgs.) & Kurtzman (8 pgs.)-a; Eustice Hayseed begins (Li'l Abner swipe) 40.00 120.00 350.00
2-Wolverton-a (10 pgs.); Powerhouse Pepper cameo 31.00 94.00 250.00

KRAZY KROW (Also see Dopey Duck, Film Funnies, Funny Frolics & Movie Tunes)
Marvel Comics (ZPC): Summer, 1945 - No. 3, Wint, 1945/46

1 19.00 56.00 150.00
2,3 12.00 36.00 95.00
I.W. Reprint #1('57), 2('58), 7 2.00 6.00 18.00

KRAZYLIFE (Becomes Nutty Life #2)
Fox Feature Syndicate: 1945 (no month)

1-Funny animal 16.00 48.00 125.00

KREE/SKRULL WAR STARRING THE AVENGERS, THE
Marvel Comics: Sept, 1983 - No. 2, Oct, 1983 ($2.50, 68 pgs., Baxter paper)

1,2 3.00
NOTE: *Neal Adams p-1r, 2.* ***Buscema*** *a-1r, 2r.* ***Simonson*** *a-1p; c-1p.*

KROFFT SUPERSHOW (TV)
Gold Key: Apr, 1978 - No. 6, Jan, 1979

1-Photo-c 2.00 6.00 18.00
2-6: 6-Photo-c 1.50 4.50 12.00

KRULL
Marvel Comics Group: Nov, 1983 - No. 2, Dec, 1983

1,2-Adaptation of film; r/Marvel Super Special. 1-Photo-c from movie 2.00

KRUSTY COMICS (TV)(See Simpsons Comics)
Bongo Comics: 1995 - No. 3, 1995 ($2.25, limited series)

1-3 2.50

KRYPTON CHRONICLES
DC Comics: Sept, 1981 - No. 3, Nov, 1981

1-3: 1-Buckler-c(p) 3.00

KULL AND THE BARBARIANS
Marvel Comics: May, 1975 - No. 3, Sept, 1975 ($1.00, B&W, magazine)

1-(84 pgs.) Andru/Wood-r/Kull #1; 2 pgs. Neal Adams; Gil Kane(p), Marie & John Severin-a(r); Krenkel text illo. 1.50 4.50 12.00
2,3: 2-(84 pgs.) Red Sonja by Chaykin begins; Solomon Kane by Weiss/Adams; Gil Kane-a; Solomon Kane pin-up by Wrightson. 3-(76 pgs.) Origin Red Sonja by Chaykin; Adams-a; Solomon Kane app. 1.00 3.00 8.00

KULL THE CONQUEROR (...the Destroyer #11 on; see Conan #1, Creatures on the Loose #10, Marvel Preview, Monsters on the Prowl)
Marvel Comics Group: June, 1971 - No. 2, Sept, 1971; No. 3, July, 1972 - No. 15, Aug, 1974; No. 16, Aug, 1976 - No. 29, Oct, 1978

1-Andru/Wood-a; 2nd app. & origin Kull; 15¢ issue 3.00 9.00 30.00
2-5: 2-3rd Kull app. Last 15¢ iss. 3-13: 20¢ issues 1.50 4.50 12.00
6-10 1.00 3.00 8.00
11-15: 11-15-Ploog-a. 14,15: 25¢ issues 2.40 6.00
16-(Regular 25¢ edition)(8/76) 2.40 6.00
16-(30¢-c variant, limited distribution) 1.10 3.30 9.00
17-29 5.00
NOTE: *No. 1, 2, 7-9, 11 are based on Robert E. Howard stories.* ***Alcala*** *a-17p, 18-20i; c-24.* ***Ditko*** *a-12r, 15r.* ***Gil Kane*** *c-15p, 21.* ***Nebres*** *a-22i-27i; c-25i, 27i.* ***Ploog*** *c-11, 12p, 13.* ***Severin*** *a-2-9i; c-2-10i, 19.* ***Starlin*** *c-14.*

KULL THE CONQUEROR
Marvel Comics Group: Dec, 1982 - No. 2, Mar, 1983 (52 pgs., Baxter paper)

1,2: 1-Buscema-a(p) 4.00

KULL THE CONQUEROR (No. 9,10 titled "Kull")
Marvel Comics Group: 5/83 - No. 10, 6/85 (52 pgs., Baxter paper)

V3#1-10: Buscema-a in #1-3,5-10 3.00
NOTE: Bolton a-4. Golden painted c-3-8. Guice a-4p. Sienkiewicz a-4; c-2.

KUNG FU (See Deadly Hands of..., & Master of...)

KUNG FU FIGHTER (See Richard Dragon...)

KURT BUSIEK'S ASTRO CITY (Limited series)
Image Comics (Juke Box Productions): Aug, 1995 - No. 6, Jan, 1996 ($2.25)

1-Kurt Busiek scripts, Brent Anderson-a & Alex Ross front & back-c begins; 1st app. Samaritan & Honor Guard (Cleopatra, MHP, Beautie, The Black Rapier, Quarrel & N-Forcer) 1.50 4.50 12.00
2-6: 2-1st app. The Silver Agent, The Old Soldier, & the "original" Honor Guard (Max O'Millions, Starwoman, the "original" Cleopatra, the "original" N-Forcer, the Bouncing Beatnik, Leopardman & Kitkat). 3-1st app. Jack-in-the-Box & The Deacon. 4-1st app. Winged Victory (cameo), The Hanged Man & The First Family. 5-1st app. Crackerjack, The Astro City Irregulars, Nightingale & Sunbird. 6-Origin Samaritan; 1st full app Winged Victory 1.25 3.75 10.00
Life In The Big City-(8/96, $19.95, trade paperback)-r/Image Comics limited series w/sketchbook & cover gallery; Ross-c 20.00
Life In The Big City-(8/96, $49.95, hardcover, 1000 print run)-r/Image Comics limited series w/sketchbook & cover gallery; Ross-c 50.00

KURT BUSIEK'S ASTRO CITY (1st Homage Comics series)
Image Comics (Homage Comics): V2#1, Sept, 1996 - No. 15, Dec, 1998;
DC Comics (Homage Comics): No. 16, Mar, 1999 - Present ($2.50)

1/2-(10/96)-The Hanged Man story; 1st app. The All-American & Slugger, The Lamplighter, The Time-Keeper & Eterneon 1.25 3.75 10.00
1/2-(1/98) 2nd printing w/new cover 2.50
1- Kurt Busiek scripts, Alex Ross-c, Brent Anderson-p & Will Blyberg-i begin; intro The Gentleman, Thunderhead & Helia. 1.00 3.00 8.00
1-(12/97, $4.95) "3-D Edition" w/glasses 5.00
2-Origin The First Family; Astra story 1.00 2.80 7.00
3-5: 4-1st app. The Crossbreed, Ironhorse, Glue Gun & The Confessor (cameo) 2.40 6.00
6-10 5.00
11-22: 14-20-Steeljack story arc. 16-(3/99) First DC issue 2.50
TPB-($19.95) Ross-c, r/#4-9, #1/2 w/sketchbook 20.00
Family Album TPB ($19.95) r/#1-3,10-13 20.00
The Tarnished Angel HC ($29.95) r/#14-20; new Ross dust jacket; sketch pages by Anderson & Ross; cover gallery with reference photos 30.00

LABMAN
Image Comics: Nov, 1996 ($3.50, one-shot)

1-Allred-c 4.00

LABYRINTH
Marvel Comics Group: Nov, 1986 - No. 3, Jan, 1987 (Limited series)

1-3: David Bowie movie adaptation; r/Marvel Super Special #40 3.00

LA COSA NOSTROID (See Scud: The Disposible Assassin)
Fireman Press: Mar, 1996 - Present ($2.95, B&W)

1-9-Dan Harmon-s/Rob Schrab-c/a 3.00

LAD: A DOG (Movie)
Dell Publishing Co.: 1961 - No. 2, July-Sept, 1962

Four Color 1303 3.65 11.00 40.00
2 3.20 9.60 35.00

LADY AND THE TRAMP (Disney, See Dell Giants & Movie Comics)
Dell Publishing Co.: No. 629, May, 1955 - No. 634, June, 1955

Four Color 629 (#1)-..with Jock 6.70 20.00 80.00
Four Color 634-...Album 4.55 13.65 50.00

LADY COP (See 1st Issue Special)

LADY DEATH (See Evil Ernie)
Chaos! Comics: Jan, 1994 - No. 3, Mar, 1994 ($2.75, limited series)

1/2-S. Hughes-c/a in all, 1/2 Velvet 1.00 3.00 8.00
1/2 Gold 1.50 4.50 12.00

Lady Death #13 © Chaos!

Lady Pendragon V2 #1 © Matt Hawkins

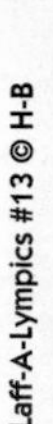

Laff-A-Lympics #13 © H-B

	GD2.0	FN6.0	NM9.4
1/2 Signed Limited Edition	1.75	5.25	14.00
1-($3.50)-Chromium-c	2.30	7.00	20.00
1-Commemorative	2.00	6.00	18.00
1-(9/96, $2.95) "Encore Presentation"; r/#1			3.00
2	1.25	3.75	10.00
3		2.40	6.00
...And The Women of Chaos! Gallery #1 (11/96, $2.25) pin-ups by various			2.25
...By Steven Hughes (6/00, $2.95) Tribute issue to Steven Hughes			3.00
...By Steven Hughes Deluxe Edition(6/00, $15.95)			16.00
...Death Becomes Her #0 (11/97, $2.95) Hughes-c/a			3.00
...FAN Edition: All Hallow's Eve #1 (1/97, mail-in)			5.00
...In Lingerie #1 (8/95, $2.95) pin-ups, wraparound-c			3.00
...In Lingerie #1-Leather Edition (10,000)	1.75	5.25	14.00
...In Lingerie #1-Micro Premium Edition; Lady Demon-c (2,000)	3.65	11.00	40.00
...Swimsuit Special #1-($2.50)-Wraparound-c			3.00
...Swimsuit Special #1-Red velvet-c	2.00	6.00	16.00
...: The Reckoning (7/94, $6.95)-r/#1-3			7.00
...: The Reckoning (8/95, $12.95)- new printing including Lady Death 1/2 & Swimsuit Special #1			13.00
.../Vampirella (3/99, $3.50) Hughes-c/a			3.50
.../Vampirella 2 (3/00, $3.50) Deodato-c/a			3.50
... Vs. Purgatori (12/99, $3.50) Deodato-a			3.50
... Vs. Vampirella Preview (2/00, $1.00) Deodato-a/c			1.00

LADY DEATH (Ongoing series)
Chaos! Comics: Feb, 1998 - No. 16, May, 1999 ($2.95)

1-16: 1-4: Pulido-s/Hughes-c/a. 5-8,13-16-Deodato-a. 9-11-Hughes-a			3.00
...Retribution (8/98, $2.95) Jadsen-a			3.00
...Retribution Premium Ed.			8.00

LADY DEATH: DARK MILLENNIUM
Chaos! Comics: Feb, 2000 - No. 3, Apr, 2000 ($2.95, limited series)

Preview (6/00, $5.00)			5.00
1-3-Ivan Reis-a			3.00

LADY DEATH: JUDGEMENT WAR
Chaos! Comics: Nov, 1999 - No. 3, Jan, 2000 ($2.95, limited series)

Prelude (10/99) two covers			3.00
1-3-Ivan Reis-a			3.00

LADY DEATH: THE CRUCIBLE
Chaos! Comics: Nov, 1996 - No. 6, Oct, 1997 ($3.50/$2.95, limited series)

1/2			4.00
1/2 Cloth Edition	1.00	3.00	8.00
1-Wraparound silver foil embossed-c			4.00
1-($19.95)-Leather Edition			20.00
2-6-($2.95)			3.00

LADY DEATH: THE ODYSSEY
Chaos! Comics: Apr, 1996 - No. 4, Aug, 1996 ($3.50/$2.95)

1-($1.50)-Sneak Peek Preview			2.00
1-($1.50)-Sneak Peek Preview Micro Premium Edition (2500 print run)	1.50	4.50	12.00
1-($3.50)-Embossed, wraparound goil foil-c			5.00
1-Black Onyx Edition (200 print run)	7.25	21.75	80.00
1-($19.95)-Premium Edition (10,000 print run)			18.00
2-4-($2.95)			3.00

LADY DEATH: THE RAPTURE
Chaos! Comics: Jun, 1999 - No. 4, Sept, 1999 ($2.95, limited series)

1-4-Ivan Reis-c/a; Pulido-s			3.00

LADY DEATH: TRIBULATION
Chaos! Comics: Dec, 2000 - No. 4 ($2.95, limited series)

1,2-Ivan Reis-a; Kaminski-s			3.00

LADY DEATH II: BETWEEN HEAVEN & HELL
Chaos! Comics: Mar, 1995 - No. 4, July, 1995 ($3.50, limited series)

1-Chromium wraparound-c; Evil Ernie cameo			5.00
1-Commemorative (4,000), 1-Black Velvet-c	2.00	6.00	18.00
1-Gold	1.25	3.75	10.00

	GD2.0	FN6.0	NM9.4
1-"Refractor" edition (5,000)	2.30	7.00	20.00
2-4			3.50
4-Lady Demon variant-c	1.10	3.30	9.00
Trade paperback-($12.95)-r/#1-4			13.00

LADY DEMON
Chaos! Comics: Mar, 2000 - No. 3, May, 2000 ($2.95, limited series)

1-3-Kaminski-s/Brewer-a			2.95
1-Premium Edition			10.00

LADY FOR A NIGHT (See Cinema Comics Herald)

LADY JUSTICE (See Neil Gaiman's...)

LADY LUCK (Formerly Smash #1-85) (Also see Spirit Sections #1)
Quality Comics Group: No. 86, Dec, 1949 - No. 90, Aug, 1950

86(#1)	84.00	253.00	800.00
87-90	63.00	189.00	600.00

LADY PENDRAGON
Maximum Press: Mar, 1996 ($2.50)

1-Matt Hawkins script			2.50

LADY PENDRAGON
Image Comics: Nov, 1998 - No. 3, Jan, 1999 ($2.50, mini-series)

Preview (6/98) Flip book w/ Deity preview			3.00
1-3: 1-Matt Hawkins-s/Stinsman-a			3.00
1-($6.95) DF Ed. with variant-c by Jusko			7.00
2-($4.95)Variant edition			5.00
0-(3/99) Origin; flip book			2.50

LADY PENDRAGON (Volume 3)
Image Comics: Apr, 1999 - No. 9, Mar, 2000 ($2.50, mini-series)

1,2,4-6,8-10: 1-Matt Hawkins-s/Stinsman-a. 2-Peterson-c			2.50
3-Flip book w/Alley Cat preview (1st app.)			3.00
7-($3.95) Flip book; Stinsman-a/Cleavenger painted-a			3.95
Gallery Edition (10/99, $2.95) pin-ups			3.00
...Merlin (1/00, $2.95) Stinsman-a			3.00

LADY PENDRAGON/ MORE THAN MORTAL
Image Comics: May, 1999 ($2.50, one-shot)

Preview (2/99) Diamond Dateline suppl.			2.00
1-Scott-s/Norton-a; 2 covers by Norton & Finch			2.50

LADY RAWHIDE
Topps Comics: July, 1995 - No. 5, Mar, 1996 ($2.95, bi-monthly, limited series)

1-5: Don McGregor scripts & Mayhew-a. in all. 2-Stelfreeze-c. 3-Hughes-c. 4-Golden-c. 5-Julie Bell-c.			3.00
It Can't Happen Here TPB (8/99, $16.95) r/#1-5			17.00
Mini Comic 1 (7/95) Maroto-a; Zorro app.			1.00
Special Edition 1 (6/95, $3.95)-Reprints			4.00

LADY RAWHIDE (Volume 2)
Topps Comics: Oct, 1996 -No. 5, June, 1997 ($2.95, limited series)

1-5: 1-Julie Bell-c.			3.00

LADY RAWHIDE OTHER PEOPLE'S BLOOD (ZORRO'S ...)
Image Comics: Mar, 1999 - No. 5, July, 1999 ($2.95, B&W)

1-5-Reprints Lady Rawhide series in B&W			3.00

LADY SUPREME (See Asylum)(Also see Supreme & Kid Supreme)
Image Comics (Extreme): May, 1996 - No. 2, June, 1996 ($2.50, limited series)

1,2-Terry Moore -s: 1-Terry Moore-c. 2-Flip book w/Newmen preview			2.50

LAFF-A-LYMPICS (TV)(See The Funtastic World of Hanna-Barbera)
Marvel Comics: Mar, 1978 - No. 13, Mar, 1979 (Newsstand sales only)

1-Yogi Bear, Scooby Doo, Pixie & Dixie, etc.	2.00	6.00	18.00
2-8	1.75	5.25	14.00
9-13: 11-Jetsons x-over; 1 pg. illustrated bio of Mighty Mightor, Herculoids, Shazzan, Galaxy Trio & Space Ghost	2.00	6.00	18.00

LAFFY-DAFFY COMICS
Rural Home Publ. Co.: Feb, 1945 - No. 2, Mar, 1945

1,2-Funny animal	9.30	28.00	65.00

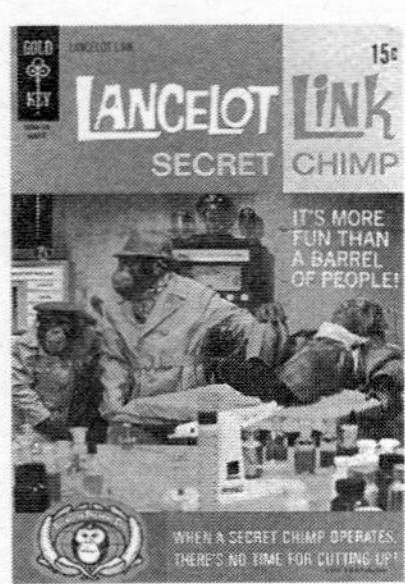

Lancelot Link, Secret Chimp #2 © GK

Land of the Lost Comics #8 © WMG

Large Feature Comic #20 © WDC

LANA (Little Lana No. 8 on)
Marvel Comics (MjMC): Aug, 1948 - No. 7, Aug, 1949 (Also see Annie Oakley)

	GD2.0	FN6.0	NM9.4
1-Rusty, Millie begin	18.00	53.00	140.00
2-Kurtzman's "Hey Look" (1); last Rusty	11.00	33.00	90.00
3-7: 3-Nellie begins	8.65	26.00	60.00

LANCELOT & GUINEVERE (See Movie Classics)

LANCELOT LINK, SECRET CHIMP (TV)
Gold Key: Apr, 1971 - No. 8, Feb, 1973

	GD2.0	FN6.0	NM9.4
1-Photo-c	4.55	13.65	50.00
2-8: 2-Photo-c	2.80	8.40	28.00

LANCELOT STRONG (See The Shield)

LANCE O'CASEY (See Mighty Midget & Whiz Comics)
Fawcett Publications: Spring, 1946 - No. 3, Fall, 1946; No. 4, Summer, 1948

	GD2.0	FN6.0	NM9.4
1-Captain Marvel app. on-c	35.00	105.00	280.00
2	22.00	66.00	175.00
3,4	16.00	49.00	130.00

NOTE: *The cover for the 1st issue was done in 1942 but was not published until 1946. The cover shows 68 pages but actually has only 36 pages.*

LANCER (TV)(Western)
Gold Key: Feb, 1969 - No. 3, Sept, 1969 (All photo-c)

	GD2.0	FN6.0	NM9.4
1	3.20	9.60	35.00
2,3	2.50	7.50	25.00

LAND OF NOD, THE
Dark Horse Comics: July, 1997 - Present ($2.95, B&W)

1-3-Jetcat; Jay Stephens-s/a 3.00

LAND OF OZ
Arrow Comics: 1998 - Present ($2.95, B&W)

1-9-Bishop-s/Bryan-s/a 3.00

LAND OF THE GIANTS (TV)
Gold Key: Nov, 1968 - No. 5, Sept, 1969 (All have photo-c)

	GD2.0	FN6.0	NM9.4
1	5.00	15.00	60.00
2-5	3.20	9.60	35.00

LAND OF THE LOST COMICS (Radio)
E. C. Comics: July-Aug, 1946 - No. 9, Spring, 1948

	GD2.0	FN6.0	NM9.4
1	34.00	101.00	270.00
2	23.00	68.00	180.00
3-9	19.00	56.00	150.00

LAND UNKNOWN, THE (Movie)
Dell Publishing Co.: No. 845, Sept, 1957

	GD2.0	FN6.0	NM9.4
Four Color 845-Alex Toth-a	11.70	35.00	140.00

LA PACIFICA
DC Comics (Paradox Press): 1994/1995 ($4.95, B&W, limited series, digest size, mature readers)

1-3 5.00

LARAMIE (TV)
Dell Publishing Co.: Aug, 1960 - July, 1962 (All photo-c)

	GD2.0	FN6.0	NM9.4
Four Color 1125-Gil Kane/Heath-a	9.00	27.00	110.00
Four Color 1223,1284, 01-418-207 (7/62)	5.85	17.50	70.00

LAREDO (TV)
Gold Key: June, 1966

	GD2.0	FN6.0	NM9.4
1 (10179-606)-Photo-c	3.20	9.60	35.00

LARGE FEATURE COMIC (Formerly called Black & White in previous guides)
Dell Publishing Co.: 1939 - No. 13, 1943

Note: See individual alphabetical listings for prices

1 (Series I)-Dick Tracy Meets the Blank
2-Terry and the Pirates (#1)
3-Heigh-Yo Silver! The Lone Ranger (text & ill.)(76 pgs.); also exists as a Whitman #710; based on radio
4-Dick Tracy Gets His Man
5-Tarzan of the Apes (#1) by Harold Foster (origin); reprints 1st Tarzan dailies from 1929
6-Terry & the Pirates & The Dragon Lady; reprints dailies from 1936
7-(Scarce, 52 pgs.)-Hi-Yo Silver the Lone Ranger to the Rescue; also exists as a Whitman #715, based on radio program
8-Dick Tracy the Racket Buster
9-King of the Royal Mounted (Zane Grey's...)
10-(Scarce)-Gang Busters (No. appears on inside front cover); first slick cover (based on radio program)
11-Dick Tracy Foils the Mad Doc Hump
12-Smilin' Jack; no number on-c
13-Dick Tracy and Scottie of Scotland Yard
14-Smilin' Jack Helps G-Men Solve a Case!
15-Dick Tracy and the Kidnapped Princes
16-Donald Duck; 1st app. Daisy Duck on back cover (6/41-Disney)
17-Gang Busters (1941)
18-Phantasmo (see The Funnies #45)
19-Dumbo Comic Paint Book (Disney); partial-r from 4-Color #17
20-Donald Duck Comic Paint Book (rarer than #16) (Disney)
21,22: 21-Private Buck. 22-Nuts & Jolts
23-The Nebbs
24-Popeye in "Thimble Theatre" by Segar
25-Smilin' Jack-1st issue to show title on-c
26-Smitty
27-Terry and the Pirates; Caniff-c/a
28-Grin and Bear It
29-Moon Mullins
30-Tillie the Toiler
1 (Series II)-Peter Rabbit by Harrison Cady; arrival date-3/27/42
2-Winnie Winkle (#1)
3-Dick Tracy
4-Tiny Tim (#1)
5-Toots and Casper
6-Terry and the Pirates; Caniff-a
7-Pluto Saves the Ship (#1) (Disney)-Written by Carl Barks, Jack Hannah, & Nick George (Barks' 1st comic book work)
8-Bugs Bunny (#1)('42)
9-Bringing Up Father
10-Popeye (Thimble Theatre)
11-Barney Google and Snuffy Smith
12-Private Buck
13-(nn)-1001 Hours Of Fun; puzzles & games; by A. W. Nugent. This book was bound as #13 with Large Feature Comics in publisher's files

NOTE: *The Black & White Feature Books are oversized 8-1/2x11-3/8" comics with color covers and black and white interiors. The first nine issues all have rough, heavy stock covers and, except for #7, all have 76 pages, including covers. #7 and #10-on all have 52 pages. Beginning with #10 the covers are slick and thin and, because of their size, are difficult to handle without damaging. For this reason, they are seldom found in fine to mint condition. The paper stock, unlike Wow #1 and Capt. Marvel #1, is itself not unstable ...just thin.*

LARRY DOBY, BASEBALL HERO
Fawcett Publications: 1950 (Cleveland Indians)

	GD2.0	FN6.0	NM9.4
nn-Bill Ward-a; photo-c	74.00	221.00	700.00

LARRY HARMON'S LAUREL AND HARDY (...Comics)
National Periodical Publ.: July-Aug, 1972 (Digest advertised, not published)

	GD2.0	FN6.0	NM9.4
1	6.80	20.50	75.00

LARS OF MARS
Ziff-Davis Publishing Co.: No. 10, Apr-May, 1951 - No. 11, July-Aug, 1951 (Painted-c) (Created by Jerry Siegel, editor)

	GD2.0	FN6.0	NM9.4
10-Origin; Anderson-a(3) in each; classic robot-c	79.00	237.00	750.00
11-Gene Colan-a; classic-c	63.00	189.00	600.00

LARS OF MARS 3-D
Eclipse Comics: Apr, 1987 ($2.50)

1-r/Lars of Mars #10,11 in 3-D plus new story 3.00
2-D limited edition (B&W, 100 copies) 5.00

LASER ERASER & PRESSBUTTON (See Axel Pressbutton & Miracle Man 9)
Eclipse Comics: Nov, 1985 - No. 6, 1987 (95¢/$2.50, limited series)

1-6: 5,6-(95¢) 2.00
...In 3-D 1 (8/86, $2.50) 2.50
2-D 1 (B&W, limited to 100 copies signed & numbered) 4.00

LASH LARUE WESTERN (Movie star; king of the bullwhip)(See Fawcett Movie Comic, Motion Picture Comics & Six-Gun Heroes)
Fawcett Publications: Sum, 1949 - No. 46, Jan, 1954 (36pgs., 1-7,9,13,16-on)

	GD2.0	FN6.0	NM9.4
1-Lash & his horse Black Diamond begin; photo front/back-c begin	105.00	316.00	1000.00
2(11/49)	44.00	133.00	400.00
3-5	40.00	120.00	325.00

Lash Larue Western #9 © FAW

Lassie #4 © MGM

Laugh Comics #43 © AP

GD2.0 FN6.0 NM9.4

6,7,9: 6-Last photo back-c; intro. Frontier Phantom (Lash's twin brother) 33.00 98.00 260.00
8,10 (52pgs.) 34.00 101.00 270.00
11,12,14,15 (52pgs.) 23.00 68.00 180.00
13,16-20 (36pgs.) 20.00 60.00 160.00
21-30: 21-The Frontier Phantom app. 17.00 51.00 135.00
31-45 14.00 43.00 115.00
46-Last Fawcett issue & photo-c 15.00 45.00 120.00

LASH LARUE WESTERN (Continues from Fawcett series)
Charlton Comics: No. 47, Mar-Apr, 1954 - No. 84, June, 1961
47-Photo-c 19.00 56.00 150.00
48 14.00 41.00 110.00
49-60, 67,68-(68 pgs.). 68-Check-a 10.00 30.00 80.00
61-66,69,70: 52-r/#8; 53-r/#22 10.00 30.00 75.00
71-83 7.15 21.50 50.00
84-Last issue 9.30 28.00 65.00

LASH LARUE WESTERN
AC Comics: 1990 ($3.50, 44 pgs) (24 pgs. of color, 16 pgs. of B&W)
1-Photo covers; r/Lash #6; r/old movie posters 3.50
Annual 1 (1990, $2.95, B&W, 44 pgs.)-Photo covers 3.00

LASSIE (TV)(M-G-M's... #1-36; see Kite Fun Book)
Dell Publ. Co./Gold Key No. 59 (10/62) on: June, 1950 - No. 70, July, 1969
1 (52 pgs.)-Photo-c; inside lists One Shot #282 in error 13.00 40.00 160.00
2-Painted-c begin 5.85 17.50 70.00
3-10 4.10 12.30 45.00
11-19: 12-Rocky Langford (Lassie's master) marries Gerry Lawrence. 15-1st app. Timbu 3.20 9.60 35.00
20-22-Matt Baker-a 3.65 11.00 40.00
23-38,40: 33-Robinson-a. 3.00 9.00 32.00
39-1st app. Timmy as Lassie picks up her TV family 4.55 13.65 50.00
41-50 3.00 9.00 30.00
51-58 2.80 8.40 28.00
59 (10/62)-1st Gold Key 3.65 11.00 40.00
60-70: 63-Last Timmy (10/63). 64-r/#19. 65-Forest Ranger Corey Stuart begins, ends #69. 70-Forest Rangers Bob Ericson & Scott Turner app. (Lassie's new masters) 2.80 8.40 28.00
11193(1978, $1.95, 224 pgs., Golden Press)-Baker-r (92 pgs.) 3.00 9.00 30.00
NOTE: *Photo c-57, 63. (See March of Comics #210, 217, 230, 254, 266, 278, 296, 308, 324, 334, 346, 358, 370, 381, 394, 411, 432)*

LAST AMERICAN, THE
Marvel Comics (Epic): Dec, 1990 - No. 4, March, 1991 ($2.25, mini-series)
1-4: Alan Grant scripts 2.25

LAST AVENGERS STORY, THE (Last Avengers #1)
Marvel Comics: Nov, 1995 - No. 2, Dec, 1995 ($5.95, painted, limited series) (Alterniverse)
1,2: Peter David story; acetate-c in all. 1-New team (Hank Pym, Wasp, Human Torch, Cannonball, She-Hulk, Hotshot, Bombshell, Tommy Maximoff, Hawkeye, & Mockingbird) forms to battle Ultron 59, Kang the Conqueror, The Grim Reaper & Oddball 2.40 6.00

LAST DAYS OF THE JUSTICE SOCIETY SPECIAL
DC Comics: 1986 ($2.50, one-shot, 68 pgs.)
1-62 pg. JSA story plus unpubbed G.A. pg. 2.40 6.00

LAST GENERATION, THE
Black Tie Studios: 1986 - No. 5, 1989 ($1.95, B&W, high quality paper)
1-5 2.00
Book 1 (1989, $6.95)-By Caliber Press 7.00

LAST HUNT, THE
Dell Publishing Co.: No. 678, Feb, 1956
Four Color 678-Movie, photo-c 7.50 22.50 90.00

LAST KISS
ACME Press (Eclipse): 1988 ($3.95, B&W, squarebound, 52 pgs.)
1-One story adapts E.A. Poe's The Black Cat 4.00

GD2.0 FN6.0 NM9.4

LAST OF THE COMANCHES (Movie) (See Wild Bill Hickok #28)
Avon Periodicals: 1953
nn-Kinstler-c/a, 21pgs.; Ravielli-a 15.00 45.00 120.00

LAST OF THE ERIES, THE (See American Graphics)

LAST OF THE FAST GUNS, THE
Dell Publishing Co.: No. 925, Aug, 1958
Four Color 925-Movie, photo-c 6.70 20.00 80.00

LAST OF THE MOHICANS (See King Classics & White Rider and...)

LAST OF THE VIKING HEROES, THE (Also see Silver Star #1)
Genesis West Comics: Mar, 1987 - No. 12 ($1.50/$1.95)
1-4,5A,5B,6-12: 4-Intro The Phantom Force, 1-Signed edition ($1.50), 5A-Kirby/Stevens-c. 5B,6 ($1.95). 7-Art Adams-c. 8-Kirby back-c. 4.00
Summer Special 1-3: 1-(1988)-Frazetta-c & illos. 2 (1990, $2.50)-A TMNT app. 3 (1991, $2.50)-Teenage Mutant Ninja Turtles 4.00
Summer Special 1-Signed edition (sold for $1.95) 4.00
NOTE: ***Art Adams** c-7. **Byrne** c-3. **Kirby** c-1p, 5p. **Perez** c-2i. **Stevens** c-5Ai.*

LAST ONE, THE
DC Comics (Vertigo): July, 1993 - No. 6, Dec, 1993 ($2.50, lim. series, mature)
1-6 2.50

LAST STARFIGHTER, THE
Marvel Comics Group: Oct, 1984 - No. 3, Dec, 1984 (75¢, movie adaptation)
1-3: r/Marvel Super Special; Guice-c 2.00

LAST TEMPTATION, THE
Marvel Comics: 1994 - No. 3, 1994 ($4.95, limited series)
1-3-Alice Cooper story; Neil Gaiman scripts; McKean-c; Zulli-a: 1-Two covers. 5.00

LAST TRAIN FROM GUN HILL
Dell Publishing Co.: No. 1012, July, 1959
Four Color 1012-Movie, photo-c 8.35 25.00 100.00

LATEST ADVENTURES OF FOXY GRANDPA (See Foxy Grandpa)

LATEST COMICS (Super Duper No. 3?)
Spotlight Publ./Palace Promotions (Jubilee): Mar, 1945 - No. 2, 1945?
1-Super Duper 16.00 48.00 125.00
2-Bee-29 (nd); Jubilee in indicia blacked out 12.00 36.00 95.00

LAUGH
Archie Enterprises: June, 1987 - No. 29, Aug, 1991 (75¢/$1.00)
V2#1 5.00
2-10,14,24: 5-X-Mas issue. 14-1st app. Hot Dog. 24-Re-intro Super Duck 4.00
11-13,15-23,25-29: 19-X-Mas issue 2.50

LAUGH COMICS (Teenage) (Formerly Black Hood #9-19) (Laugh #226 on)
Archie Publications (Close-Up): No. 20, Fall, 1946 - No. 400, Apr, 1987
20-Archie begins; Katy Keene & Taffy begin by Woggon; Suzie & Wilbur also begin; Archie covers begin 61.00 182.00 575.00
21-23,25 34.00 101.00 270.00
24- "Pipsy" by Kirby (6 pgs.) 35.00 105.00 280.00
26-30 18.00 53.00 140.00
31-40 13.00 39.00 105.00
41-60: 41,54-Debbi by Woggon 10.00 30.00 70.00
61-80: 67-Debbi by Woggon 7.15 21.50 50.00
81-99 3.65 11.00 40.00
100 4.10 12.30 45.00
101-126: 125-Debbi app. 3.00 9.00 30.00
127-144: Super-hero app. in all (see note) 3.20 9.60 35.00
145-156,158-160 2.50 7.50 25.00
157-Josie app.(4/64) 3.00 9.00 32.00
161-165,167-180, 200 (12/67) 2.30 7.00 20.00
166-Beatles-c (1/65) 3.65 11.00 40.00
181-199 2.00 6.00 16.00
201-240(3/71) 1.50 4.50 12.00
241-280(7/74) 1.10 3.30 9.00
281-299 1.00 2.80 7.00

Laugh Comics Digest #133 © AP

The L.A.W. #6 © DC

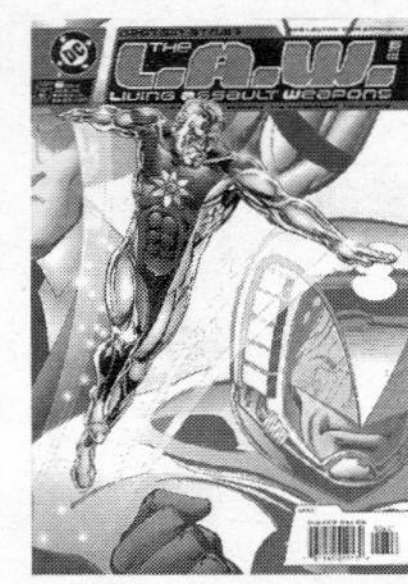

Leading Comics #4 © DC

300(3/76) 1.00 3.00 8.00
301-340 (7/79) 5.00
341-370 (1/82) 4.00
371-380,385-399 3.00
381-384,400: 381-384-Katy Keene app.; by Woggon-381,382 4.00
NOTE: *The Fly app. in 128, 129, 132, 134, 138, 139. Flygirl app. in 136, 137, 143. Flyman app. in 137. The Jaguar app. in 127, 130, 131, 133, 135, 140-142, 144. Josie app. in 145, 160, 164. Katy Keene app. in 20-125, 129, 130, 133. Many issues contain paper dolls.* ***Al Fagaly*** *c-20-29.* ***Montana*** *c-33, 36, 37, 42.* ***BillVigoda*** *c-30, 50.*

LAUGH COMICS DIGEST (...Magazine #23-89; Laugh Digest Mag. #90 on)
Archie Publ. (Close-Up No. 1, 3 on): 8/74; No. 2, 9/75; No. 3, 3/76 - Present (Digest-size)

1-Neal Adams-a 3.65 11.00 40.00
2,7,8,19-Neal Adams-a 2.50 7.50 24.00
3-6,9,10 2.00 6.00 16.00
11-18,20 1.75 5.25 14.00
21-40 1.25 3.75 10.00
41-80 1.00 2.80 7.00
81-99 5.00
100 5.50
101-138 2.50
139-163: 139-Begin $1.95-c. 148-Begin $1.99-c. 156-Begin $2.19-c 2.20
NOTE: *Katy Keene in 23, 25, 27, 32-38, 40, 45-48, 50. The Fly-r in 19, 20. The Jaguar-r in 25, 27. Mr. Justice-r in 21. The Web-r in 23.*

LAUGH COMIX (Formerly Top Notch Laugh; Suzie Comics No. 49 on)
MLJ Magazines: No. 46, Summer, 1944 - No. 48, Winter, 1944-45

46-Wilbur & Suzie in all; Harry Sahle-c 22.00 66.00 175.00
47,48: 47-Sahle-c. 48-Bill Vigoda-c 15.00 45.00 120.00

LAUGH-IN MAGAZINE (TV)(Magazine)
Laufer Publ. Co.: Oct, 1968 - No. 12, Oct, 1969 (50¢) (Satire)

V1#1 4.10 12.30 45.00
2-12 3.00 9.00 32.00

LAUREL & HARDY (See Larry Harmon's... & March of Comics No. 302, 314)

LAUREL AND HARDY (...Comics)
St. John Publ. Co.: 3/49 - No. 3, 9/49; No. 26, 11/55 - No. 28, 3/56 (No #4-25)

1 68.00 205.00 650.00
2 40.00 120.00 350.00
3 30.00 90.00 240.00
26-28 (Reprints) 16.00 49.00 130.00

LAUREL AND HARDY (TV)
Dell Publishing Co.: Oct, 1962 - No. 4, Sept-Nov, 1963

12-423-210 (8-10/62) 5.00 15.00 60.00
2-4 (Dell) 3.65 11.00 40.00

LAUREL AND HARDY (Larry Harmon's...)
Gold Key: Jan, 1967 - No. 2, Oct, 1967

1-Photo back-c 4.55 13.65 50.00
2 3.65 11.00 40.00

LAURAL AND HARDY DIGEST: DC Comics. 1972 (Advertised, not published)

L.A.W., THE (LIVING ASSAULT WEAPONS)
DC Comics: Sept, 1999 - No. 6, Feb, 2000 ($2.50, limited series)

1-6-Blue Beetle, Question, Judomaster, Capt. Atom app.; Giordano-a 5-JLA app. 2.50

LAW AGAINST CRIME (Law-Crime on cover)
Essenkay Publishing Co.: April, 1948 - No. 3, Aug, 1948 (Real Stories from Police Files)

1-(#1-3 are half funny animal, half crime stories)-L. B. Cole-c/a in all; electrocution-c 70.00 210.00 665.00
2-L. B. Cole-c/a 53.00 160.00 480.00
3-Used in **SOTI**, pg. 180,181 & illo "The wish to hurt or kill couples in lovers' lanes;" reprinted in All-Famous Crime #9 66.00 197.00 625.00

LAW AND ORDER
Maximum Press: Sept, 1995 - No. 2, 1995 ($2.50, unfinished limited series)

1,2 2.50

LAWBREAKERS (...Suspense Stories No. 10 on)
Law and Order Magazines (Charlton): Mar, 1951 - No. 9, Oct-Nov, 1952

1 34.00 103.00 275.00
2 19.00 56.00 150.00
3,5,6,8,9 14.00 41.00 110.00
4- "White Death" junkie story 18.00 53.00 140.00
7- "The Deadly Dopesters" drug story 18.00 53.00 140.00

LAWBREAKERS ALWAYS LOSE!
Marvel Comics (CBS): Spring, 1948 - No. 10, Oct, 1949

1-2pg. Kurtzman-a, "Giggles 'n' Grins" 34.00 103.00 275.00
2 18.00 53.00 140.00
3-5: 4-Vampire story 13.00 39.00 105.00
6(2/49)-Has editorial defense against charges of Dr. Wertham 14.00 41.00 110.00
7-Used in **SOTI**, illo "Comic-book philosophy" 30.00 90.00 240.00
8-10: 9,10-Photo-c 12.00 36.00 95.00
NOTE: ***Brodsky*** *c-4, 5.* ***Shores*** *c-1-3, 6-8.*

LAWBREAKERS SUSPENSE STORIES (Formerly Lawbreakers; Strange Suspense Stories No. 16 on)
Capitol Stories/Charlton Comics: No. 10, Jan, 1953 - No. 15, Nov, 1953

10 35.00 105.00 280.00
11 (3/53)-Severed tongues-c/story & woman negligee scene 89.00 268.00 850.00
12-14: 13-Giordano-c begin, end #15 20.00 60.00 160.00
15-Acid-in-face-c/story; hands dissolved in acid sty 47.00 142.00 425.00

LAW-CRIME (See Law Against Crime)

LAWDOG
Marvel Comics (Epic Comics): May, 1993 - No. 10, Feb, 1993

1-10 2.00

LAWDOG/GRIMROD: TERROR AT THE CROSSROADS
Marvel Comics (Epic Comics): Sept, 1993 ($3.50)

1 3.50

LAWMAN (TV)
Dell Publishing Co.: No. 970, Feb, 1959 - No. 11, Apr-June, 1962 (All photo-c)

Four Color 970(#1) 12.50 37.50 150.00
Four Color 1035('60), 3(2-4/60)-Toth-a 6.70 20.00 80.00
4-11 4.60 13.75 55.00

LAW OF DREDD, THE (Also see Judge Dredd)
Quality Comics/Fleetway #8 on: 1989 - No. 33, 1992 ($1.50/$1.75)

1-33: Bolland a-1-6,8,10-12,14(2 pg),15,19 2.00

LAWRENCE (See Movie Classics)

LAZARUS CHURCHYARD
Tundra Publishing: June, 1992 - No. 3, 1992 ($3.95, 44 pgs., coated stock)

1-3 4.00

LAZARUS FIVE
DC Comics: July, 2000 - No. 5 ($2.50, limited series)

1-5-Harris-c/Abell-a(p) 2.50

LEADING COMICS (...Screen Comics No. 42 on)
National Periodical Publications: Winter, 1941-42 - No. 41, Feb-Mar, 1950

1-Origin The Seven Soldiers of Victory; Crimson Avenger, Green Arrow & Speedy, Shining Knight, The Vigilante, Star Spangled Kid & Stripesy begin; The Dummy (Vigilante villain) 1st app. 400.00 1200.00 4200.00
2-Meskin-a; Fred Ray-c 158.00 474.00 1500.00
3 126.00 379.00 1200.00
4,5 90.00 270.00 850.00
6-10 79.00 237.00 750.00
11,12,14(Spring, 1945) 55.00 165.00 500.00
13-Robot-c 79.00 237.00 750.00
15-(Sum,'45)-Contents change to funny animal 28.00 83.00 220.00
16-22,24-30: 16-Nero Fox-c begin, end #22 12.00 36.00 95.00
23-1st app. Peter Porkchops by Otto Feur & begins 28.00 83.00 220.00
31,32,34-41: 34-41-Leading Screen... on-c only 10.00 30.00 75.00

Leave It To Binky #1 © DC

Leave It To Chance #12 © James Robinson & Paul Smith

Legend of the Hawkman #1 © DC

GD2.0 FN6.0 NM9.4

33-(Scarce) 20.00 60.00 160.00
NOTE: ***Rube Grossman**-a(Peter Porkchops)-most #15-on; c-15-41. **Post** a-23-37, 39, 41.*

LEADING SCREEN COMICS (Formerly Leading Comics)
National Periodical Publ.: No. 42, Apr-May, 1950 - No. 77, Aug-Sept, 1955

42-Peter Porkchops-c/stories continue 10.00 30.00 75.00
43-77 9.30 28.00 65.00
NOTE: ***Grossman** a-most. **Mayer** a-45-48, 50, 54-57, 60, 62-74, 75(3), 76, 77.*

LEAGUE OF CHAMPIONS, THE (Also see The Champions)
Hero Graphics: Dec, 1990 - No. 12, 1992 ($2.95, 52 pgs.)

1-12: 1-Flare app. 2-Origin Malice 3.00

LEAGUE OF EXTRAORDINARY GENTLEMEN, THE
America's Best Comics: Mar, 1999 - No. 6, Sept, 2000 ($2.95, limited series)

1-Alan Moore-s/Kevin O'Neill-a 1.00 3.00 8.00
1-DF Edition ($10.00) O'Neill-c 10.00
2,3 4.00
4-6 3.00
... Compendium 1,2: 1-r/#1,2. 2-r/#3,4 5.95

LEAGUE OF JUSTICE
DC Comics (Elseworlds): 1996 - No. 2, 1996 ($5.95, 48 pgs., squarebound)

1,2: Magic-based alternate DC Universe story; Giordano-i 2.40 6.00

LEATHERFACE
Arpad Publishing: May (April on-c), 1991 - No. 4, May, 1992 ($2.75, painted-c)

1-4-Based on Texas Chainsaw movie; Dorman-c 3.00

LEATHERNECK THE MARINE (See Mighty Midget Comics)

LEAVE IT TO BEAVER (TV)
Dell Publishing Co.: No. 912, June, 1958; May-July, 1962 (All photo-c)

Four Color 912 17.50 52.50 210.00
Four Color 999,1103,1191,1285, 01-428-207 15.00 45.00 175.00

LEAVE IT TO BINKY (Binky No. 72 on) (Super DC Giant) (No. 1-22: 52 pgs.)
National Periodical Publications: 2-3/48 - #60, 10/58; #61, 6-7/68 - #71, 2-3/70 (Teen-age humor)

1-Lucy wears Superman costume 35.00 105.00 280.00
2 18.00 53.00 140.00
3,4 10.00 30.00 75.00
5-Superman cameo 17.00 51.00 135.00
6-10 9.35 28.00 65.00
11-14,16-22: Last 52 pg. issue 7.85 23.50 55.00
15-Scribbly story by Mayer 10.00 30.00 75.00
23-28,30-45: 45-Last pre-code (2/55) 5.00 15.00 35.00
29-Used in **POP**, pg. 78 5.50 16.50 38.00
46-60: 60-(10/58) 2.80 8.40 28.00
61 (6-7/68) 4.10 12.30 45.00
62-69: 67-Last 12¢ issue 2.50 7.50 25.00
70-7pg. app. Bus Driver who looks like Ralph from Honeymooners
3.20 9.60 35.00
71-Last issue 3.00 9.00 30.00
NOTE: ***Aragones**-a-61, 62, 67. **Drucker** a-28. **Mayer** a-1, 2, 15. Created by **Mayer**.*

LEAVE IT TO CHANCE
Image Comics (Homage Comics): Sept, 1996 - No. 11, Sept, 1998;
DC Comics (Homage Comics): No. 12, Jun, 1999 - Present ($2.50/$2.95)

1-3: 1-Intro Chance Falconer & St. George; James Robinson scripts & Paul Smith-c/a begins 5.00
4-12 3.00
Shaman's Rain TPB (1997, $9.95) r/#1-4 10.00
Trick or Threat TPB (1997, $12.95) r/#5-8 13.00

LEE HUNTER, INDIAN FIGHTER
Dell Publishing Co.: No. 779, Mar, 1957; No. 904, May, 1958

Four Color 779 (#1) 4.10 12.30 45.00
Four Color 904 3.20 9.60 35.00

LEFT-HANDED GUN, THE (Movie)
Dell Publishing Co.: No. 913, July, 1958

Four Color 913-Paul Newman photo-c 10.00 30.00 120.00

GD2.0 FN6.0 NM9.4

LEGACY
Majestic Entertainment: Oct, 1993 - No. 2, Nov, 1993; No. 0, 1994 ($2.25)

1-2,0: 1-Glow-in-the-dark-c. 0-Platinum 2.25

LEGACY OF KAIN: SOUL REAVER
Top Cow Productions: Oct, 1999 (Diamond Dateline supplement)

1-Based on the Eidos video game; Benitez-c 2.00

LEGEND OF CUSTER, THE (TV)
Dell Publishing Co.: Jan, 1968

1-Wayne Maunder photo-c 2.60 7.80 26.00

LEGEND OF JESSE JAMES, THE (TV)
Gold Key: Feb, 1966

10172-602-Photo-c 2.60 7.80 26.00

LEGEND OF KAMUI, THE (See Kamui)

LEGEND OF LOBO, THE (See Movie Comics)

LEGEND OF MOTHER SARAH (Manga)
Dark Horse Comics: Apr, 1995 - No. 8, Nov, 1995 ($2.50, limited series)

1-8: Katsuhiro Otomo scripts 4.00

LEGEND OF MOTHER SARAH: CITY OF THE ANGELS (Manga)
Dark Horse Comics: Oct, 1996 - Present ($3.95, B&W, limited series)

1(10/96), 2(12/97),3-9: Otomo scripts 4.00

LEGEND OF MOTHER SARAH: CITY OF THE CHILDREN (Manga)
Dark Horse Comics: Jan, 1996 - No. 7, July, 1996 ($3.95, B&W, limited series)

1-7: Otomo scripts 4.00

LEGEND OF SUPREME
Image Comics (Extreme): Dec, 1994 - No. 3, Feb, 1995 ($2.50, limited series)

1-3 2.50

LEGEND OF THE ELFLORD
DavDez Arts: July, 1998 ($2.95)

1-Barry Blair & Colin Chin-s/a 3.00

LEGEND OF THE HAWKMAN
DC Comics: 2000 - No. 3, 2000 ($4.95, limited series)

1-3-Raab-s/Lark-c/a 4.95

LEGEND OF THE SHIELD, THE
DC Comics (Impact Comics): July, 1991 - No. 16, Oct, 1992 ($1.00)

1-16: 6,7-The Fly x-over. 12-Contains trading card 2.00
Annual 1 (1992, $2.50, 68 pgs.)-Snyder-a; w/trading card 2.50

LEGEND OF WONDER WOMAN, THE
DC Comics: May, 1986 - No. 4, Aug, 1986 (75¢, limited series)

1-4 3.00

LEGEND OF YOUNG DICK TURPIN, THE (Disney)(TV)
Gold Key: May, 1966

1 (10176-605)-Photo/painted-c 2.60 7.80 26.00

LEGEND OF ZELDA, THE (Link: The Legend... in indicia)
Valiant Comics: 1990 - No. 4, 1990 ($1.95, coated stiff-c)
V2#1, 1990 - No. 5, 1990 ($1.50)

1-4: 4-Layton-c(i) 3.00
V2#1-5 3.00

LEGENDS
DC Comics: Nov, 1986 - No. 6, Apr, 1987 (75¢, limited series)

1-6: 1-Byrne-c/a(p) in all; 1st app. new Capt. Marvel. 3-1st app. new Suicide Squad; death of Blockbuster. 6-1st app. new Justice League 3.00

LEGENDS OF DANIEL BOONE, THE (...Frontier Scout)
National Periodical Publications: Oct-Nov, 1955 - No. 8, Dec-Jan, 1956-57

1 (Scarce)-Nick Cardy c-1-8 61.00 182.00 575.00
2 (Scarce) 43.00 130.00 390.00
3-8 (Scarce) 40.00 120.00 350.00

LEGENDS OF KID DEATH AND FLUFFY
Event Comics: Feb, 1997 ($2.95, B&W, one-shot)

Legends of the DC Universe #29 © DC

Legion Lost #1 © DC

Legionnaires #54 © DC

1-Five covers 3.00

LEGENDS OF NASCAR, THE
Vortex Comics: Nov, 1990 - No. 14, 1992? (#1 3rd printing (1/91) says 2nd printing inside)

1-Bill Elliott biog.; Trimpe-a ($1.50) 5.00
1-2nd printing (11/90, $2.00) 2.00
1-3rd print; contains Maxx racecards ($3.00) 3.00
2-14: 2-Richard Petty. 3-Ken Schrader (7/91). 4-Bobby Allison; Spiegle-a(p); Adkins part-i. 5-Sterling Marlin. 6-Bill Elliott. 7-Junior Johnson; Spiegle-c/a. 8-Benny Parsons; Heck-a 3.00
1-13-Hologram cover versions. 2-Hologram shows Bill Elliott's car by mistake (all are numbered & limited) 5.00
2-Hologram corrected version 5.00
Christmas Special ($5.95) 2.40 6.00

LEGENDS OF THE DARK CLAW
DC Comics (Amalgam): Apr, 1996 ($1.95)

1-Jim Balent-c/a 3.00

LEGENDS OF THE DARK KNIGHT (See Batman: ...)

LEGENDS OF THE DC UNIVERSE
DC Comics: Feb, 1998 - No. 41, June, 2001 ($1.95/$1.99/$2.50)

1-13,15-21: 1-3-Superman; Robinson-s/Semeiks-a/Orbik-painted-c. 4,5-Wonder Woman; Deodato-a/Rude painted-c. 8-GL/GA, O'Neil-s. 10,11-Batgirl; Dodson-a. 12,13-Justice League. 15-17-Flash. 18-Kid Flash; Guice-a. 19-Impulse; prelude to JLApe Annuals. 20,21-Abin Sur 3.00
14-($3.95) Jimmy Olsen; Kirby-esque-c by Rude 4.00
22-27,30: 22,23-Superman; Rude-c/Ladronn-a. 26,27-Aquaman/Joker 2.00
28,29: Green Lantern & the Atom; Gil Kane-a; covers by Kane and Ross 2.00
31,32: 32-Begin $2.50-c; Wonder Woman; Texeira-c 2.50
33-36-Hal Jordan as The Spectre; DeMatteis-s/Zulli-a; Hale painted-c 2.50
37-41: 37,38-Kyle Rayner. 39-Superman. 40,41-Atom; Harris-c 2.50
... Crisis on Infinite Earths 1 (2/99, $4.95) Untold story during and after Crisis on I.E. #4; Wolfman-s/Ryan-a/Orbik-c 5.00
... 80 Page Giant 1 (9/98, $4.95) Stories and art by various incl. Ditko, Perez, Gibbons, Mumy; Joe Kubert-c 5.00
... 80 Page Giant 2 (1/00, $4.95) Stories and art by various incl. Challengers by Art Adams; Sean Phillips-c 5.00
... 3-D Gallery (12/98, $2.95) Pin-ups w/glasses 3.00

LEGENDS OF THE LEGION (See Legion of Super-Heroes)
DC Comics: Feb, 1998 - No. 4, May, 1998 ($2.25, limited series)

1-4:1-Origin-s of Ultra Boy. 2-Spark. 3-Umbra. 4-Star Boy 3.00

LEGENDS OF THE STARGRAZERS (See Vanguard Illustrated #2)
Innovation Publishing: Aug, 1989 - No. 6, 1990 ($1.95, limited series, mature)

1-6: 1-Redondo part inks 2.00

LEGENDS OF THE WORLD'S FINEST (See World's Finest)
DC Comics: 1994 - No. 3, 1994 ($4.95, squarebound, limited series)

1-3: Simonson scripts; Brereton-c/a; embossed foil logos 2.40 6.00
TPB-(1995, $14.95) r/#1-3 15.00

L.E.G.I.O.N. (The # to right of title represents year of print)(Also see Lobo & R.E.B.E.L.S.)
DC Comics: Feb, 1989 - No. 70, Sept, 1994 ($1.50/$1.75)

1-Giffen plots/breakdowns in #1-12,28 5.00
2-22,24-47: 3-Lobo app. #3 on. 4-1st Lobo-c this title. 5-Lobo joins L.E.G.I.O.N. 13-Lar Gand app. 16-Lar Gand joins L.E.G.I.O.N., leaves #19. 31-Capt. Marvel app. 35-L.E.G.I.O.N. '92 begins 3.00
23,70-($2.50, 52 pgs.)-L.E.G.I.O.N. '91 begins. 70-Zero Hour 4.00
48,49,51-69: 48-Begin $1.75-c. 63-L.E.G.I.O.N. '94 begins; Superman x-over 3.00
50-($3.50, 68 pgs.) 4.00
Annual 1-5 ('90-94, 68 pgs.): 1-Lobo, Superman app. 2-Alan Grant scripts. 5-Elseworlds story; Lobo app. 4.00
NOTE: ***Alan Grant*** *scripts in #1-39, 51, Annual 1, 2.*

LEGION LOST (Continued from Legion of Super-Heroes [4th series] #125)
DC Comics: May, 2000 - No. 12, Apr, 2001 ($2.50, limited series)

1-12-Abnett & Lanning-s/ Coipel & Lanning-c/a. 4,9-Alixe-a 2.50

GD2.0 FN6.0 NM9.4

LEGIONNAIRES (See Legion of Super-Heroes #40, 41 & Showcase 95 #6)
DC Comics: Apr, 1992 - No. 81, Mar, 2000 ($1.25/$1.50/$2.25)

0-(10/94)-Zero Hour restart of Legion; released between #18 & #19 2.50
1-49,51-77: 1-(4/92)-Chris Sprouse-c/a; polybagged w/SkyBox trading card. 11-Kid Quantum joins. 18-(9/94)-Zero Hour. 19(11/94). 37-Valor (Lar Gand) becomes M'onel (5/96). 43-Legion tryouts; reintro Princess Projectra, Shadow Lass & others. 47-Forms one cover image with LSH #91. 60-Karate Kid & Kid Quantum join. 61-Silver Age & 70's Legion app. 76-Return of Wildfire. 79,80-Coipel-c/a; Legion vs. the Blight 2.50
50-($3.95) Pullout poster by Davis/Farmer 4.00
#1,000,000 (11/98) Sean Phillips-a 2.50
Annual 1,3 ('94,'96 $2.95)-1-Elseworlds-s. 3-Legends of the Dead Earth-s 3.00
Annual 2 (1995, $3.95)-Year One-s 4.50

LEGIONNAIRES THREE
DC Comics: Jan, 1986 - No. 4, May, 1986 (75¢, limited series)

1-4 3.00

LEGION OF MONSTERS (Also see Marvel Premiere #28 & Marvel Preview #8)
Marvel Comics Group: Sept, 1975 ($1.00, B&W, magazine, 76 pgs.)

1-Origin & 1st app. Legion of Monsters; Neal Adams-c; Morrow-a; origin & only app. The Manphibian; Frankenstein by Mayerik; Bram Stoker's Dracula adaptation; Reese-a; painted-c (#2 was advertised with Morbius & Satana, but was never published) 2.50 7.50 24.00

LEGION OF NIGHT, THE
Marvel Comics: Oct, 1991 - No. 2, Oct, 1991 ($4.95, 52 pgs.)

1,2-Whilce Portacio-c/a(p) 5.00

LEGION OF SUBSTITUTE HEROES SPECIAL (See Adventure Comics #306)
DC Comics: July, 1985 ($1.25, one-shot, 52 pgs.)

1-Giffen-c/a(p) 3.00

LEGION OF SUPER-HEROES (See Action, Adventure, All New Collectors Edition, Legionnaires, Legends of the Legion, Limited Collectors Edition, Secrets of the..., Superboy & Superman)
National Periodical Publications: Feb, 1973 - No. 4, July-Aug, 1973

1-Legion & Tommy Tomorrow reprints begin 2.40 7.35 22.00
2-4: 2-Forte-r. 3-r/Adv. #340. Action #240. 4-r/Adv. #341, Action #233; Mooney-r 1.50 4.50 12.00

LEGION OF SUPER-HEROES, THE (Formerly Superboy and...; Tales of The Legion No. 314 on)
DC Comics: No. 259, Jan, 1980 - No. 313, July, 1984

259(#1)-Superboy leaves Legion 1.00 3.00 8.00
260-270,285-290,294: 265-Contains 28 pg. insert "Superman & the TRS-80 computer"; origin Tyroc; Tyroc leaves Legion. 290-294-Great Darkness saga. 294-Double size (52 pgs.) 5.00
271-284,291-293: 272-Blok joins; origin; 20 pg. insert-Dial 'H' For Hero. 277-Intro Reflecto. 280-Superboy re-joins Legion. 282-Origin Reflecto. 283-Origin Wildfire 4.00
295-299,301-313: 297-Origin retold. 298-Free 16pg. Amethyst preview. 306-Brief origin Star Boy 2.50
300-(68 pgs., Mando paper)-Anniversary issue; has c/a by almost everyone at DC 4.00
Annual 1-3(82-84, 52 pgs.)-1-Giffen-c/a; 1st app./origin new Invisible Kid who joins Legion. 2-Karate Kid & Princess Projectra wed & resign 3.00
...The Great Darkness Saga (1989, $17.95, 196 pgs.)-r/LSH #287,290-294 & Annual #3; Giffen-c/a 1.80 5.40 18.00
NOTE: ***Aparo*** *c-282, 283, 300(part).* ***Austin*** *c-268i.* ***Buckler*** *c-273p, 274p, 276p.* ***Colan*** *a-311p.* ***Ditko*** *a(p)-267, 268, 272, 274, 276, 281.* ***Giffen*** *a-285-313p, Annual 1p; c-287p, 288p, 289, 290p, 291p, 292, 293, 294-299p, 300, 301-313p, Annual 1p, 2p.* ***Perez*** *c-268p, 277-280, 281p.* ***Starlin*** *a-265.* ***Staton*** *a-259p, 260p, 280.* ***Tuska*** *a-308p.*

LEGION OF SUPER-HEROES (3rd Series) (Reprinted in Tales of the Legion)
DC Comics: Aug, 1984 - No. 63, Aug, 1989 ($1.25/$1.75, deluxe format)

1-Silver ink logo 5.00
2-36,39-44,46-49,51-62: 4-Death of Karate Kid. 5-Death of Nemesis Kid. 12-Cosmic Boy, Lightning Lad, & Saturn Girl resign. 14-Intro new members: Tellus, Sensor Girl, Quislet. 15-17-Crisis tie-ins. 18-Crisis x-over. 25-Sensor Girl i.d. revealed as Princess Projectra. 35-Saturn Girl rejoins. 42,43-Millennium tie-ins. 44-Origin Quislet 3.00

Legion of Super-Heroes #105 © DC

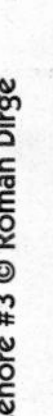
Legion Science Police #1 © DC

Lenore #3 © Roman Dirge

GD2.0 FN6.0 NM9.4

7,38-Death of Superboy 1.75 5.25 14.00
5,50: 45 ($2.95, 68 pgs.)-Anniversary ish. 50-Double size ($2.50-c) 4.00
3-Final issue 4.00
nnual 1-4 (10/85-'88, 52 pgs.)-1-Crisis tie-in 3.00
)TE: *Byrne c-36p.* *Giffen a(p)-1, 2, 50-55, 57-63, Annual 1p, 2; c-1-5p, 54p, Annual 1.* *'lando a-6p.* *Steacy c-45-50, Annual 3.*

EGION OF SUPER-HEROES (4th Series)
C Comics: Nov, 1989 - No. 125, Mar, 2000 ($1.75/$1.95/$2.25)

)-(10/94)-Zero Hour restart of Legion; released between #61 & #62 2.50
-Giffen-c/a(p)/scripts begin (4 pg.-a only #18) 4.00
2-20,26-49,51-53,55-58: 4-Mon-El (Lar Gand) destroys Time Trapper, changes reality. 5-Alt. reality story where Mordru rules all; Ferro Lad app. 6-1st app. of Laurel Gand (Lar Gand's cousin). 8-Origin. 13-Free poster by Giffen showing new costumes. 15-(2/91)-1st reference of Lar Gand as Valor. 26-New map of headquarters. 34-Six pg. preview of Timber Wolf mini-series. 40-Minor Legionnaires app. 41-(3/93)-SW6 Legion renamed Legionnaires w/new costumes and some new code-names 3.00
1-25: 21-24-Lobo & Darkseid storyline. 24-Cameo SW6 younger Legion duplicates. 25-SW6 Legion full intro. 3.50
0-($3.50, 68 pgs.) 4.00
4-($2.95)-Die-cut & foil stamped-c 4.00
9-99: 61-(9/94)-Zero Hour. 62-(11/94). 75-XS travels back to the 20th Century (cont'd in Impulse #9). 77-Origin of Brainiac 5. 81-Reintro Sun Boy. 85-Half of the Legion sent to the 20th century, Superman-c/app. 86-Final Night. 87-Deadman-c/app. 88-Impulse-c/app. Adventure Comics #247 cover swipe. 91-Forms one cover image with Legionnaires #47. 96-Wedding of Ultra Boy and Apparition. 99-Robin, Impulse, Superboy app. 2.50
)0-($5.95, 96 pgs.)-Legionnaires return to the 30th Century; gatefold-c; 5 stories-art by Simonson, Davis and others 1.00 2.80 7.00
)1-125: 101-Armstrong-a(p) begins. 105-Legion past & present vs. Time Trapper. 109-Moder-a. 110-Thunder joins. 114,115-Bizarro Legion. 120,121-Fatal Five. 122,123-Coipel-c/a. 125-Leads into "Legion Lost" maxi-series 2.50
,000,000 (11/98) Giffen-a 2.50
nnual 1-5 (1990-1994, $3.50, 68 pgs.): 4-Bloodlines. 5-Elseworlds story 3.50
nnual 6 (1995,$3.95)-Year One story 4.00
nnual 7 (1996, $3.50, 48 pgs.)-Legends of the Dead Earth story; intro 75th Century Legion of Super-Heroes; Wildfire app. 3.50
egion: Secret Files 1 (1/98, $4.95) Retold origin & pin-ups 5.00
egion: Secret Files 2 (6/99, $4.95) Story and profile pages 5.00
he Beginning of Tomorrow TPB ('99, $17.95) r/post-Zero Hour reboot 18.00
)TE: *Giffen a-1-24; breakdowns-26-32, 34-36; c-1-7, 8(part), 9-24.* *Brandon Peterson a(p)-(1st for DC), 16, 18, Annual 2(54 pgs.); c-Annual 2p.* *Swan/Anderson c-8(part).*

EGION: SCIENCE POLICE (See Legion of Super-Heroes)
C Comics: Aug, 1998 - No. 4, Nov, 1998 ($2.25, limited series)

-4-Ryan-a 2.50

EMONADE KID, THE (See Bobby Benson's B-Bar-B Riders)
C Comics: 1990 ($2.50, 28 pgs.)

-Powell-c(r); Red Hawk-r by Powell; Lemonade Kid-r/Bobby Benson by Powell (2 stories) 2.50

ENNON SISTERS LIFE STORY, THE
ell Publishing Co.: No. 951, Nov, 1958 - No. 1014, Aug, 1959

our Color 951 (#1)-Toth-a, 32pgs, photo-c 14.00 42.00 170.00
our Color 1014-Toth-a, photo-c 13.00 40.00 160.00

ENORE
ave Labor Graphics: Feb, 1998 - Present ($2.95, B&W)

-8: 1-Roman Dirge-s/a, 1,2-2nd printing 3.00
.: Noogies TPB ($11.95) r/#1-4 12.00
.: Wedgies TPB (2000, $13.95) r/#5-8 14.00

EONARD NIMOY'S PRIMORTALS
ekno Comix: Mar, 1995 - No. 15, May, 1996 ($1.95)

-15: Concept by Leonard Nimoy & Isaac Asimov 1-3-w/bound-in game piece & trading card. 4-w/Teknophage Steel Edition coupon. 13,14-Art Adams-c. 15-Simonson-c 2.25

EONARD NIMOY'S PRIMORTALS
G Entertainment: V2#0, June, 1996 - No. 8, Feb, 1997 ($2.25)

GD2.0 FN6.0 NM9.4

V2#0-8: 0-Includes Pt. 9 of "The Big Bang" x-over. 0,1-Simonson-c. 3-Kelley Jones-c 2.25

LEONARD NIMOY'S PRIMORTALS ORIGINS
Tekno Comix: Nov, 1995 - No. 2, Dec, 1995 ($2.95, limited series)

1,2: Nimoy scripts; Art Adams-c; polybagged 3.00

LEONARDO (Also see Teenage Mutant Ninja Turtles)
Mirage Studios: Dec, 1986 ($1.50, B&W, one-shot)

1 4.00

LEO THE LION
I. W. Enterprises: No date(1960s) (10¢)

1-Reprint 1.75 5.25 14.00

LEROY (Teen-age)
Standard Comics: Nov, 1949 - No. 6, Nov, 1950

1 7.15 21.50 50.00
2-Frazetta text illo. 5.00 15.00 35.00
3-6: 3-Lubbers-a 4.65 14.00 28.00

LETHAL (Also see Brigade)
Image Comics (Extreme Studios): Feb, 1996 ($2.50, unfinished limited series)

1-Marat Mychaels-c/a. 2.50

LETHAL FOES OF SPIDER-MAN (Sequel to Deadly Foes of Spider-Man)
Marvel Comics: Sept, 1993 - No. 4, Dec, 1993 ($1.75, limited series)

1-4 2.00

LETHAL STRYKE
London Night Studios: June, 1995 - No. 3, 1995 ($3.00)

0-(8/95, $5.95)-Collector's ed. 2.40 6.00
1/2, 1-3: 1-polybagged w/card 3.00
Annual 1-(1996, $3.00) 3.00
Annual 1-Platinum Edition 10.00
Trade paperback-(1996, $12.95)-r/#(1/2)-3 13.00

LETHAL STRYKE/DOUBLE IMPACT: LETHAL IMPACT
London Night Studios: May, 1996 ($3.00, one-shot)

1-Hartsoe/Lyon-a(p) 3.00
1-Natural Born Killers Edition 5.00

LETHARGIC LAD
Crusade Ent.: June, 1996 - No. 3, Sept, 1996 ($2.95, B&W, limited series)

1,2 3.00
3-Alex Ross-c/swipe (Kingdom Come) 4.00

LETHARGIC LAD ADVENTURES
Crusade Ent./Destination Ent.#3 on: Oct, 1997 - Present ($2.95, B&W)

1-12-Hyland-s/a. 9-Alex Ross sketch page & back-c 3.00

LET'S PRETEND (CBS radio)
D. S. Publishing Co.: May-June, 1950 - No. 3, Sept-Oct, 1950

1 16.00 48.00 125.00
2,3 12.00 36.00 95.00

LET'S READ THE NEWSPAPER
Charlton Press: 1974

nn-Features Quincy by Ted Sheares 1.00 3.00 8.00

LET'S TAKE A TRIP (TV) (CBS Television Presents)
Pines Comics: Spring, 1958

1-Marv Levy-c/a 4.65 14.00 28.00

LETTERS TO SANTA (See March of Comics No. 228)

LEX LUTHOR: THE UNAUTHORIZED BIOGRAPHY
DC Comics: 1989 ($3.95, 52 pgs., one-shot, squarebound)

1-Painted-c; Clark Kent app. 4.00

LIBERTY COMICS (Miss Liberty No. 1)
Green Publishing Co.: No. 5, May, '46 - No. 15, July, 1946 (MLJ & other-r)

5 (5/46)-The Prankster app; Starr-a 19.00 56.00 150.00
10-Hangman & Boy Buddies app.; Suzie & Wilbur begin; reprints Hangman story from Hangman #8 20.00 60.00 160.00

Liberty Meadows #9 © Creators Syndicate

Life of Captain Marvel #3 © MAR

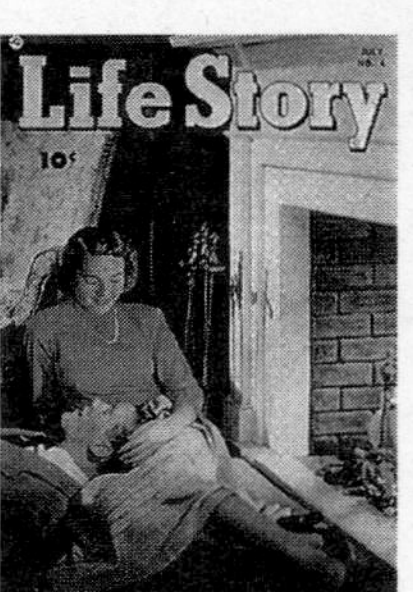

Life Story #4 © FAW

GD2.0 FN6.0 NM9.4

11(V2#2, 1/46)-Wilbur in women's clothes 16.00 49.00 130.00
12-Black Hood & Suzie app.; Skull-c 19.00 56.00 150.00
14,15-Patty of Airliner; Starr-a in both 11.00 33.00 90.00

LIBERTY GUARDS
Chicago Mail Order: No date (1946?)
nn-Reprints Man of War #1 with cover of Liberty Scouts #1; Gustavson-c 36.00 108.00 290.00

LIBERTY MEADOWS
Insight Studios Group: 1999 - Present ($2.95, B&W)
1-Frank Cho-s/a; reprints newspaper strips 2.40 6.00
2,3 4.00
4-16 2.95

LIBERTY PROJECT, THE
Eclipse Comics: June, 1987 - No. 8, May, 1988 ($1.75, color, Baxter paper)
1-8: 6-Valkyrie app. 2.00

LIBERTY SCOUTS (See Liberty Guards & Man of War)
Centaur Publications: No. 2, June, 1941 - No. 3, Aug, 1941
2(#1)-Origin The Fire-Man, Man of War; Vapo-Man & Liberty Scouts begin; intro Liberty Scouts; Gustavson-c/a in both 126.00 379.00 1200.00
3(#2)-Origin & 1st app. The Sentinel 92.00 276.00 875.00

LICENCE TO KILL (James Bond 007) (Movie)
Eclipse Comics: 1989 ($7.95, slick paper, 52 pgs.)
nn-Movie adaptation; Timothy Dalton photo-c 1.00 3.00 8.00
Limited Hardcover ($24.95) 25.00

LIDSVILLE (TV)
Gold Key: Oct, 1972 - No. 5, Oct, 1973
1-Photo-c 4.10 12.30 45.00
2-5 2.80 8.40 28.00

LIEUTENANT, THE (TV)
Dell Publishing Co.: April-June, 1964
1-Photo-c 2.60 7.80 26.00

LIEUTENANT BLUEBERRY (Also see Blueberry)
Marvel Comics (Epic Comics): 1991 - No. 3, 1991 (Graphic novel)
1,2 ($8.95)-Moebius-a in all 9.00
3 ($14.95) 15.00

LT. ROBIN CRUSOE, U.S.N. (See Movie Comics & Walt Disney Showcase #26)

LIFE OF CAPTAIN MARVEL, THE
Marvel Comics Group: Aug, 1985 - No. 5, Dec, 1985 ($2.00, Baxter paper)
1-5: 1-All reprint Starlin issues of Iron Man #55, Capt. Marvel #25-34 plus Marvel Feature #12 (all with Thanos). 4-New Thanos back-c by Starlin 3.00

LIFE OF CHRIST, THE
Catechetical Guild Educational Society: No. 301, 1949 (35¢, 100 pgs.)
301-Reprints from Topix(1949)-V5#11,12 8.65 26.00 60.00

LIFE OF CHRIST: THE CHRISTMAS STORY, THE
Marvel Comics/Nelson: Feb, 1993 ($2.99, slick stock)
nn 4.00

LIFE OF CHRIST: THE EASTER STORY, THE
Marvel Comics/Nelson: 1993 ($2.99, slick stock)
nn 3.00

LIFE OF CHRIST VISUALIZED
Standard Publishers: 1942 - No. 3, 1943
1-3: All came in cardboard case 6.40 19.25 45.00
With case..... 10.00 30.00 75.00

LIFE OF CHRIST VISUALIZED
The Standard Publ. Co.: 1946? (48 pgs. in color)
nn 4.00 12.00 24.00

LIFE OF ESTHER VISUALIZED
The Standard Publ. Co.: No. 2062, 1947 (48 pgs. in color)
2062 4.00 12.00 24.00

GD2.0 FN6.0 NM9

LIFE OF JOSEPH VISUALIZED
The Standard Publ. Co.: No. 1054, 1946 (48 pgs. in color)
1054 4.00 12.00 24.0

LIFE OF PAUL (See The Living Bible)

LIFE OF POPE JOHN PAUL II, THE
Marvel Comics Group: Jan, 1983 ($1.50/$1.75)
1 5.0

LIFE OF RILEY, THE (TV)
Dell Publishing Co.: No. 917, July, 1958
Four Color 917-Photo-c 11.30 34.00 135.0

LIFE ON ANOTHER PLANET
Kitchen Sink Press: 1978 (B&W, graphic novel, magazine size)
nn-Will Eisner-s/a 13.0
Reprint (DC Comics, 5/00, $12.95) 13.0

LIFE'S LIKE THAT
Croyden Publ. Co.: 1945 (25¢, B&W, 68 pgs.)
nn-Newspaper Sunday strip-r by Neher 6.00 18.00 42.0

LIFE STORIES OF AMERICAN PRESIDENTS (See Dell Giants)

LIFE STORY
Fawcett Publications: Apr, 1949 - V8#46, Jan, 1953; V8#47, Apr, 1953 (All have photo-c?)
V1#1 12.50 37.50 100.0
2 6.40 19.25 45.0
3-6, V2#7-12 5.00 15.00 35.0
V3#13-Wood-a 13.00 39.00 105.0
V3#14-18, V4#19-24, V5#25-30, V6#31-35 5.00 15.00 30.0
V6#36- "I sold drugs" on-c 5.75 17.00 40.0
V7#37,40-42, V8#44,45 4.15 12.50 25.0
V7#38, V8#43-Evans-a 5.00 15.00 35.0
V7#39-Drug Smuggling & Junkie story 5.00 15.00 35.0
V8#46,47 (Scarce) 5.00 15.00 35.0
NOTE: ***Powell** a-13, 23, 24, 26, 28, 30, 32, 39. **Marcus Swayze** a-1-3, 10-12, 15, 16, 20, 21, 2 25, 31, 35, 37, 40, 44, 46.*

LIFE, THE UNIVERSE AND EVERYTHING (See Hitchhikers Guide to the Galaxy & Restaurant at the End of the Universe)
DC Comics: 1996 - No. 3, 1996 ($6.95, squarebound, limited series)
1-3: Adaptation of novel by Douglas Adams. .85 2.60 7.0

LIFE WITH ARCHIE
Archie Publications: Sept, 1958 - No. 285, July, 1991
1 27.50 82.00 300.0
2-(9/59) 13.50 40.00 150.0
3-5: 3-(7/60) 9.00 27.00 100.0
6-10 6.35 19.00 70.0
11-20 4.55 13.65 50.0
21(7/63)-30 3.20 9.60 35.0
31-41 2.80 8.40 28.0
42-Pureheart begins (1st app.-c/s, 10/65) 5.90 17.75 65.0
43,44 3.20 9.60 35.0
45(1/66) 1st Man From R.I.V.E.R.D.A.L.E. 4.55 13.65 50.0
46-Origin Pureheart 3.20 9.60 35.0
47-49 3.00 9.00 30.0
50-United Three begin: Pureheart (Archie), Superteen (Betty), Captain Hero (Jughead) 3.20 9.60 35.0
51-59: 59-Pureheart ends 2.80 8.40 28.0
60-Archie band begins, ends #66 3.20 9.60 35.0
61-66: 61-Man From R.I.V.E.R.D.A.L.E.-c/s 2.50 7.50 25.0
67-80 2.00 6.00 16.0
81-99 1.75 5.25 14.0
100 (8/70), 113-Sabrina & Salem app. 2.40 7.35 22.0
101-112, 114-130(2/73), 139(11/73)-Archie Band c/s 1.25 3.75 10.0
131,134-138,140-146,148-161,164-170(6/76) 1.00 3.00 8.0
132,133,147,163-all horror-c/s 1.50 4.50 12.0
162-UFO c/s 1.50 4.50 12.0
171,173-175,177-184,186,189,191-194,196 2.40 6.0

Life With Archie #34 © AP

Limited Collectors' Edition C-48 © DC

Linda #1 © AJAX

GD2.0 FN6.0 NM9.4 | GD2.0 FN6.0 NM9.4

'2,185,197 : 172-(9/77)-Bi-Cent. spec. ish, 185-2nd 24th cent.-c/s, 197-Time machine/SF-c/s 1.00 2.80 7.00
6(12/76)-1st app. Capt. Archie of Starship Rivda, in 24th century c/s; 1st app. Stella the Robot 1.50 4.50 12.00
7,188,195,198,199-all horror-c/s 1.00 2.80 7.00
0-1st Dr. Doom-c/s 1.00 2.80 7.00
0 (12/78) Maltese Pigeon-s 1.00 3.00 8.00
1-203,205-237,239,240(1/84): 208-Reintro Veronica. 4.00
4-Flying saucer-c/s 2.40 6.00
8-(9/83)-25th anniversary issue; Ol' Betsy (jalopy) replaced 5.00
1-278,280-284: 250-Comic book convention-s 3.00
'9,285: 279-Intro Mustang Sally ($1.00, 7/90) 4.00
)TE: *Gene Colan a-272-279, 285, 286.*

FE WITH MILLIE (Formerly A Date With Millie) (Modeling With Millie #21 on)
las/Marvel Comics Group: No. 8, Dec, 1960 - No. 20, Dec, 1962

-Teenage 6.80 20.50 75.00
-11 4.35 13.00 48.00
2-20 3.45 10.35 38.00

FE WITH SNARKY PARKER (TV)
x Feature Syndicate: Aug, 1950

-Early TV comic; photo-c from TV puppet show 26.00 79.00 210.00

GHT AND DARKNESS WAR, THE
arvel Comics (Epic Comics): Oct, 1988 - No. 6, Dec, 1989 ($1.95, lim. series)

-6 2.00

GHT FANTASTIC, THE (Terry Pratchett's)
novation Publishing: June, 1992 - No. 4, Sept, 1992 ($2.50, mini-series)

-4: Adapts 2nd novel in Discworld series 2.50

GHT IN THE FOREST (Disney)
ell Publishing Co.: No. 891, Mar, 1958

our Color 891-Movie, Fess Parker photo-c 7.50 22.50 90.00

GHTNING COMICS (Formerly Sure-Fire No. 1-3)
ce Magazines: No. 4, Dec, 1940 - No. 13(V3#1), June, 1942

-Characters continue from Sure-Fire 99.00 297.00 940.00
,6: 6-Dr. Nemesis begins 66.00 197.00 625.00
2#1-6: 2- "Flash Lightning" becomes "Lash..." 53.00 158.00 475.00
3#1-Intro. Lightning Girl & The Sword 53.00 158.00 475.00
)TE: ***Anderson** a-V2#6. **Mooney** c-V1#5, 6, V2#1-6, V3#1. Bondage c-V2#6. Lightning-c on*

GHTNING COMICS PRESENTS
ghtning Comics: May, 1994 ($3.50)

-Red foil-c distr. by Diamond Distr., 1-Black/yellow/blue-c distrib. by Capital Distr., 1-Red/yellow-c distributed by H. World, 1-Platinum 3.50

'L ... (See Little ...)

LI
nage Comics: No. 0, 1999 ($4.95, B&W, limited series)

-Bendis & Yanover-s 5.00

LLITH (See Warrior Nun...)
ntarctic Press: Sept, 1996 - No. 3, Feb, 1997 ($2.95, limited series)

-3: 1-Variant-c 3.00

MITED COLLECTORS' EDITION (See Famous First Edition, Marvel Treasury '8, Rudolph The Red-Nosed Reindeer, & Superman Vs. The Amazing Spider-an; becomes All-New Collectors' Edition)
ational Periodical Publications/DC Comics:
21-34,51-59: 84 pgs.; #35-41: 68 pgs.; #42-50: 60 pgs.)
21, Summer, 1973 - No. C-59, 1978 ($1.00) (10x13-1/2")

udolph...C-20 (implied), 12/72)-See Rudolph The Red-Nosed Reindeer
21: Shazam (TV); r/Captain Marvel Jr. #11 by Raboy; C.C. Beck-c, biog. & photo 3.00 9.00 30.00
22: Tarzan; complete origin reprinted from #207-210; all Kubert-c/a; Joe Kubert biography & photo inside 2.50 7.50 24.00
23: House of Mystery; Wrightson, N. Adams/Orlando, G. Kane/Wood, Toth, Aragones, Sparling reprints 3.20 9.60 35.00
24: Rudolph The Red-Nosed Reindeer 7.25 21.75 80.00
C-25: Batman; Neal Adams-c/a(r); G.A. Joker-r; Batman/Enemy Ace-r; has photos from TV show 3.80 11.40 42.00
C-26: See Famous First Edition C-26 (same contents)
C-27,C-29,C-31: C-27: Shazam (TV); G.A. Capt. Marvel & Mary Marvel-r; Beck-r. C-29: Tarzan; reprints "Return of Tarzan" from #219-223 by Kubert; Kubert-c. C-31: Superman; origin-r; N. Adams-a; photos of George Reeves from 1950s TV show on inside b/c; Burnley, Boring-r 2.40 7.35 22.00
C-32: Ghosts (new-a) 3.20 9.60 35.00
C-33: Rudolph The Red-Nosed Reindeer(new-a) 6.35 19.00 70.00
C-34: Christmas with the Super-Heroes; unpublished Angel & Ape story by Oksner & Wood; Batman & Teen Titans-r 2.40 7.35 22.00
C-35: Shazam (TV); photo cover features TV's Captain Marvel, Jackson Bostwick; Beck-r; TV photos inside b/c 2.30 7.00 20.00
C-36: The Bible; all new adaptation beginning with Genesis by Kubert, Redondo & Mayer; Kubert-c 2.30 7.00 20.00
C-37: Batman; r-1946 Sundays; inside b/c photos of Batman TV show villains (all villain issue; r/G.A. Joker, Catwoman, Penguin, Two-Face, & Scarecrow stories plus 1946 Sundays-r) 2.50 7.50 25.00
C-38: Superman; 1 pg. N. Adams; part photo-c; photos from TV show on inside back-c 2.30 7.00 20.00
C-39: Secret Origins of Super-Villains; N. Adams-i(r); collection reprints 1950's Joker origin, Luthor origin from Adv. Comics #271, Capt. Cold origin from Showcase #8 among others; G.A. Batman-r; Beck-r. 2.30 7.00 20.00
C-40: Dick Tracy by Gould featuring Flattop; newspaper-r from 12/21/43 - 5/17/44; biog. of Chester Gould 2.30 7.00 20.00
C-41: Super Friends (TV); JLA-r(1965); Toth-c/a 2.40 7.35 22.00
C-42: Rudolph 4.55 13.65 50.00
C-43-C-47: C-43: Christmas with the Super-Heroes; Wrightson, S&K, Neal Adams-a. C-44: Batman; N. Adams-p(r) & G.A.-r; painted-c. C-45: More Secret Origins of Super-Villains; Flash-r/#105; G.A. Wonder Woman & Batman/Catwoman-r. C-46: Justice League of America(1963-r); 3 pgs. Toth-a C-47: Superman Salutes the Bicentennial (Tomahawk interior); 2 pgs. new-a 2.00 6.00 18.00
C-48,C-49: C-48: Superman Vs. The Flash (Superman/Flash race); swipes-c to Superman #199; r/Superman #199 & Flash #175; 6 pgs. Neal Adams-a. C-49 C-49: Superboy & the Legion of Super-Heroes 2.40 7.00 22.00
C-50: Rudolph The Red-Nosed Reindeer 4.55 13.65 50.00
C-51: Batman; Neal Adams-c/a 2.50 7.50 24.00
C-52,C-57: C-52: The Best of DC; Neal Adams-c/a; Toth, Kubert-a. C-57: Welcome Back, Kotter-r(TV)(5/78) 2.40 7.35 22.00
C-59: Batman's Strangest Cases; N. Adams-r; Wrightson-r/Swamp Thing #7; N. Adams/Wrightson-c 2.30 7.00 20.00
NOTE: *All-r with exception of some special features and covers.* ***Aparo** a-52r; c-37. **Grell** c-49. **Infantino** a-25, 39, 44, 45, 52. **Bob Kane** r-25. **Robinson** r-25, 44. **Sprang** r-44. Issues #21-31, 35-39, 45, 48 have back cover cut-outs.*

LINDA (Everybody Loves...) (Phantom Lady No. 5 on)
Ajax-Farrell Publ. Co.: Apr-May, 1954 - No. 4, Oct-Nov, 1954

1-Kamenish-a 15.00 45.00 120.00
2-Lingerie panel 12.00 36.00 95.00
3,4 10.00 30.00 70.00

LINDA CARTER, STUDENT NURSE
Atlas Comics (AMI): Sept, 1961 - No. 9, Jan, 1963

1-Al Hartley-c 4.10 12.30 45.00
2-9 3.00 9.00 32.00

LINDA LARK
Dell Publishing Co.: Oct-Dec, 1961 - No. 8, Aug-Oct, 1963

1 2.50 7.50 25.00
2-8 1.85 5.50 15.00

LINUS, THE LIONHEARTED (TV)
Gold Key: Sept, 1965

1 (10155-509) 8.00 24.00 95.00

LION, THE (See Movie Comics)

LIONHEART
Awesome Comics: Sept, 1999 - Present ($2.99/$2.50)

1-Ian Churchill-story/a, Jeph Loeb-s; Coven app. 3.00

Li'l Abner #73 © TOBY

Little Archie #38 © AP

Little Audrey #10 © HARV

GD2.0 FN6.0 NM9.4

2-Flip book w/Coven #4 2.50

LION OF SPARTA (See Movie Classics)

LIPPY THE LION AND HARDY HAR HAR (TV)
Gold Key: Mar, 1963 (12¢) (See Hanna-Barbera Band Wagon #1)

1 (10049-303) 9.00 27.00 110.00

LISA COMICS (TV)(See Simpsons Comics)
Bongo Comics: 1995 ($2.25)

1-Lisa in Wonderland 2.25

LI'L ABNER (See Comics on Parade, Sparkle, Sparkler Comics, Tip Top Comics & Tip Topper)
United Features Syndicate: 1939 - 1940

Single Series 4 ('39) 71.00 213.00 675.00
Single Series 18 ('40) (#18 on inside, #2 on-c) 58.00 174.00 550.00

LI'L ABNER (Al Capp's; continued from Comics on Parade #58)
Harvey Publ. No. 61-69 (2/49)/Toby Press No. 70 on: No. 61, Dec, 1947 - No. 97, Jan, 1955 (See Oxydol-Dreft)

61(#1)-Wolverton & Powell-a 34.00 101.00 270.00
62-65: 63-The Wolf Girl app. 65-Powell-a 20.00 60.00 160.00
66,67,69,70 18.00 53.00 140.00
68-Full length Fearless Fosdick-c/story 19.00 56.00 150.00
71-74,76,80 14.00 41.00 110.00
75,77-79,86,91-All with Kurtzman art; 91-r/#77 18.00 53.00 140.00
81-85,87-90,92-94,96,97 12.50 37.50 100.00
95-Full length Fearless Fosdick story 15.00 45.00 120.00

LI'L ABNER
Toby Press: 1951

1 18.00 53.00 140.00

LI'L ABNER'S DOGPATCH (See Al Capp's...)

LITTLE AL OF THE F.B.I.
Ziff-Davis Publications: No. 10, 1950 (no month) - No. 11, Apr-May, 1951 (Saunders painted-c)

10(1950) 16.00 48.00 125.00
11(1951) 12.50 37.50 100.00

LITTLE AL OF THE SECRET SERVICE
Ziff-Davis Publications: No. 10, 7-8/51; No, 2, 9-10/51; No. 3, Winter, 1951 (Saunders painted-c)

10(#1)-Spanking panels (2) 16.00 49.00 130.00
2,3 12.50 37.50 100.00

LITTLE AMBROSE
Archie Publications: September, 1958

1-Bob Bolling-c 14.00 43.00 115.00

LITTLE ANGEL
Standard (Visual Editions)/Pines: No. 5, Sept, 1954; No. 6, Sept, 1955 - No. 16, Sept, 1959

5-Last pre-code issue 6.40 19.25 45.00
6-16 4.65 14.00 28.00

LITTLE ANNIE ROONEY (Also see Henry)
David McKay Publ.: 1935 (25¢, B&W dailies, 48 pgs.)(10"x10", cardboard-c)

Book 1-Daily strip-r by Darrell McClure 38.00 113.00 300.00

LITTLE ANNIE ROONEY (See King Comics & Treasury of Comics)
David McKay/St. John/Standard: 1938; Aug, 1948 - No. 3, Oct, 1948

Feature Books 11 (McKay, 1938) 38.00 113.00 300.00
1 (St. John) 14.00 41.00 110.00
2,3 8.65 26.00 60.00

LITTLE ARCHIE (The Adventures of... #13-on) (See Archie Giant Series Mag. #527, 534, 538, 545, 549, 556, 560, 566, 570, 583, 594, 596, 607, 609, 619)
Archie Publications: 1956 - No. 180, Feb, 1983 (Giants No. 3-84)

1-(Scarce) 52.00 156.00 700.00
2 (1957) 24.50 74.00 270.00
3-5: 3-(1958)-Bob Bolling-c & giant issues begin 13.50 40.00 150.00
6-10 10.00 30.00 110.00
11-22 (84 pgs.) 6.35 19.00 70.
23-39 (68 pgs.) 4.10 12.30 45.
40 (Fall/66)-Intro. Little Pureheart-c/s (68 pgs.) 5.00 15.00 55.
41,44-Little Pureheart (68 pgs.) 3.65 11.00 40.
42-Intro The Little Archies Band, ends #66 (68 pgs.) 4.55 13.65 50.
43-1st Boy From R.I.V.E.R.D.A.L.E. (68 pgs.) 4.10 12.30 45.
45-58 (68pgs.) 2.80 8.40 28.
59 (68pgs.)-Little Sabrina begins 6.80 20.50 75.
60-66 (68 pgs.) 3.00 9.00 30.
67(9/71)-84: 84-Last 52pg. Giant-Size (2/74) 2.00 6.00 16.
85-99 1.25 3.75 10.
100 1.50 4.50 12.
101-112,114-116,118-129 1.00 2.80 7.
113,117,130: 113-Halloween Special issue(12/76). 117-Donny Osmond-c cam
130-UFO cover (5/78) 1.25 3.75 10.
131-150(1/80), 180(Last issue, 2/83) 2.40 6.
151-179 4.
...In Animal Land 1 (1957) 12.50 37.50 135.
...In Animal Land 17 (Winter, 1957-58)-19 (Summer,1958)-Formerly Li'l Jinx
6.80 20.50 75.

NOTE: *Little Archie Band app. 42-66. Little Sabrina in 59-78,80-180*

LITTLE ARCHIE CHRISTMAS SPECIAL (See Archie Giant Series #581)

LITTLE ARCHIE COMICS DIGEST ANNUAL (...Magazine #5 on)
Archie Publications: 10/77 - No. 48, 5/91 (Digest-size, 128 pgs., later issues $1.35-$1.50)

1(10/77)-Reprints 2.30 7.00 20.
2(4/78,3(11/78)-Neal Adams-a. 3-The Fly-r by S&K 2.00 6.00 18.
4(4/79) - 10 1.75 5.25 14.
11-20 1.25 3.75 10.
21-30: 28-Christmas-c 1.00 2.80 7.
31-48: 40,46-Christmas-c 5.

NOTE: *Little Archie, Little Jinx, Little Jughead & Little Sabrina in most issues.*

LITTLE ARCHIE DIGEST MAGAZINE
Archie Comics: July, 1991 - No. 25 ($1.50/$1.79/$1.89, digest size, bi-annual)

V2#1 5.
2-10 3.
11-25 2.

LITTLE ARCHIE MYSTERY
Archie Publications: Aug, 1963 - No. 2, Oct, 1963 (12¢ issues)

1 11.00 33.00 120.
2 5.90 17.75 65.

LITTLE ASPIRIN (See Little Lenny & Wisco)
Marvel Comics (CnPC): July, 1949 - No. 3, Dec, 1949 (52 pgs.)

1-Oscar app.; Kurtzman-a (4 pgs.) 16.00 48.00 125.
2-Kurtzman-a (4 pgs.) 10.00 30.00 70.
3-No Kurtzman-a 5.70 17.00 40.

LITTLE AUDREY (Also see Playful...)
St. John Publ.: Apr, 1948 - No. 24, May, 1952

1-1st app. Little Audrey 40.00 120.00 350.
2 22.00 66.00 175.
3-5 14.00 41.00 110.
6-10 10.00 30.00 75.
11-20: 16-X-Mas-c 7.85 23.50 55.
21-24 6.00 18.00 42.

LITTLE AUDREY (See Harvey Hits #11, 19)
Harvey Publications: No. 25, Aug, 1952 - No. 53, April, 1957

25-(Paramount Pictures Famous Star... on-c); 1st Harvey Casper and Baby Huey (1 month earlier than Harvey Comic Hits #60(9/52))
11.50 34.00 125.
26-30: 26-28-Casper app. 5.90 17.75 65.
31-40: 32-35-Casper app. 4.55 13.65 50.
41-53 3.00 9.00 32.
...Clubhouse 1 (9/61, 68 pg. Giant)-New stories & reprints
7.65 23.00 85.

LITTLE AUDREY

Little Dot #4 © HARV

Little Eva #4 © STJ

Little Giant Detective Funnies #1 © DC

GD2.0 FN6.0 NM9.4 GD2.0 FN6.0 NM9.4

rvey Comics: Aug, 1992 - No. 8, July, 1993 ($1.25/$1.50)
#1 3.00
2-8 2.00

TLE AUDREY (...Yearbook)
John Publishing Co.: 1950 (50¢, 260 pgs.)
ıtains 8 complete 1949 comics rebound; Casper, Alice in Wonderland, Little Audrey,
ott & Costello, Pinocchio, Moon Mullins, Three Stooges (from Jubilee), Little Annie
ıney app. (Rare) 61.00 184.00 675.00
(Also see All Good & Treasury of Comics)
TE: *This book contains remaindered St. John comics; many variations possible.*

TLE AUDREY & MELVIN (Audrey & Melvin No. 62)
rvey Publications: May, 1962 - No. 61, Dec, 1973
8.15 24.50 90.00
5 4.10 12.30 45.00
10 3.20 9.60 35.00
-20 2.40 7.35 22.00
-40: 22-Richie Rich app. 2.00 6.00 16.00
-50,55-61 1.50 4.50 12.00
-54: All 52 pg. Giants 2.00 6.00 16.00

TLE AUDREY TV FUNTIME
rvey Publ.: Sept, 1962 - No. 33, Oct, 1971 (#1-31: 68 pgs.; #32,33: 52 pgs.)
Richie Rich app. 7.65 23.00 85.00
3: Richie Rich app. 5.00 15.00 55.00
5: 5-25¢ & 35¢ issues exist 4.10 12.30 45.00
10 2.80 8.40 28.00
-20 2.00 6.00 18.00
-33 1.75 5.25 14.00

TLE BAD WOLF (Disney; seeWalt Disney's C&S #52, Walt Disney
owcase #21 & Wheaties)
ll Publishing Co.: No. 403, June, 1952 - No. 564, June, 1954
ır Color 403 (#1) 6.70 20.00 80.00
ır Color 473 (6/53), 564 4.10 12.30 45.00

TLE BEAVER
ll Publishing Co.: No. 211, Jan, 1949 - No. 870, Jan, 1958 (All painted-c)
ır Color 211('49)-All Harman-a 7.50 22.50 90.00
ır Color 267,294,332(5/51) 4.10 12.30 45.00
10-12/51)-8(1-3/53) 3.65 11.00 40.00
ır Color 483(8-10/53),529 3.20 9.60 35.00
ır Color 612,660,695,744,817,870 3.20 9.60 35.00

TLE BIT
bilee/St. John Publishing Co.: Mar, 1949 - No. 2, June, 1949
2 6.40 19.25 45.00

TLE DOT (See Humphrey, Li'l Max, Sad Sack, and Tastee-Freez Comics)
rvey Publications: Sept, 1953 - No. 164, Apr, 1976
Intro./1st app. Richie Rich & Little Lotta 100.00 300.00 1100.00
1st app. Freckles & Pee Wee (Richie Rich's poor friends)
39.00 116.00 425.00
25.00 76.00 280.00
18.00 55.00 200.00
Origin dots on Little Dot's dress 25.00 76.00 280.00
Richie Rich, Little Lotta, & Little Dot all on cover; 1st Richie Rich cover
featured 25.00 76.00 280.00
10: 9-Last pre-code issue (1/55) 13.70 40.00 150.00
20 9.00 27.00 100.00
40 4.50 13.50 50.00
60 2.70 8.00 30.00
80 2.00 6.00 22.00
-100 1.80 5.40 18.00
-141 1.20 3.60 12.00
2-145: All 52 pg. Giants 1.80 5.40 18.00
5-164 1.00 3.00 8.00
TE: *Richie Rich & Little Lotta in all.*

TLE DOT
rvey Comics: Sept, 1992 - No. 7, June, 1994 ($1.25/$1.50)
V2#1-Little Dot, Little Lotta, Richie Rich in all 3.00
2-7 ($1.50) 2.00

LITTLE DOT DOTLAND (Dot Dotland No. 62, 63)
Harvey Publications: July, 1962 - No. 61, Dec, 1973
1-Richie Rich begins 10.00 30.00 110.00
2,3 4.55 13.65 50.00
4,5 4.10 12.30 45.00
6-10 3.00 9.00 30.00
11-20 2.40 7.20 24.00
21-30 1.60 4.80 16.00
31-50 1.40 4.20 14.00
51-54: All 52 pg. Giants 1.80 5.40 18.00
55-61 1.00 3.00 10.00

LITTLE DOT'S UNCLES & AUNTS (See Harvey Hits No. 4, 13, 24)
Harvey Enterprises: Oct, 1961; No. 2, Aug, 1962 - No. 52, Apr, 1974
1-Richie Rich begins; 68 pgs. begin 11.50 34.00 125.00
2,3 6.35 19.00 70.00
4,5 4.10 12.30 45.00
6-10 3.20 9.60 35.00
11-20 2.80 8.40 28.00
21-37: Last 68 pg. issue 2.00 6.00 20.00
38-52: All 52 pg. Giants 1.80 5.40 18.00

LITTLE DRACULA
Harvey Comics: Jan, 1992 - No. 3, May, 1992 ($1.25, quarterly, mini-series)
1-3 2.00

LITTLE EVA
St. John Publishing Co.: May, 1952 - No. 31, Nov, 1956
1 15.00 45.00 120.00
2 8.65 26.00 60.00
3-5 5.70 17.00 40.00
6-10 5.00 15.00 32.00
11-31 4.65 14.00 28.00
3-D 1,2(10/53, 11/53, 25¢)-Both came w/glasses. 1-Infinity-c
22.00 66.00 175.00
I.W. Reprint #1-3,6-8: 1-r/Little Eva #28. 2-r/Little Eva #29. 3-r/Little Eva #24
1.50 4.50 12.00
Super Reprint #10,12('63),14,16,18('64): 18-r/Little Eva #25.
1.50 4.50 12.00

LI'L GENIUS (Formerly Super Brat; Summer Fun No. 54) (See Blue Bird & Giant Comics #3)
Charlton Comics: 1954 - No. 52, 1/65; No. 53, 10/65; No. 54, 10/85 - No. 55, 1/86
5(#1?) 10.00 30.00 75.00
6-10 5.50 16.50 38.00
11-15,19,20 5.00 15.00 30.00
16,17-(68 pgs.) 6.40 19.25 45.00
18-(100 pgs., 10/58) 10.00 30.00 70.00
21-35 2.50 7.50 23.00
36-53 1.85 5.50 15.00
54,55 (Low print) 5.00

LI'L GHOST
St. John Publ. Co./Fago No. 1 on: 2/58; No. 2,1/59 - No. 3, Mar, 1959
1(St. John) 8.65 26.00 60.00
2,3 4.65 14.00 28.00

LITTLE GIANT COMICS
Centaur Publications: 7/38 - No. 3, 10/38; No. 4, 2/39 (132 pgs.) (6-3/4x4-1/2")
1-B&W with color-c; stories, puzzles, magic 63.00 189.00 600.00
2,3-B&W with color-c 55.00 165.00 525.00
4 (6-5/8x9-3/8")(68 pgs., B&W inside) 55.00 165.00 525.00
NOTE: ***Filchock** c-2, 4. **Gustavson** a-1. **Pinajian** a-4. **Bob Wood** a-1.*

LITTLE GIANT DETECTIVE FUNNIES
Centaur Publ.: Oct, 1938; No. 4, Jan, 1939 (6-3/4x4-1/2", 132 pgs., B&W)
1-B&W with color-c 74.00 221.00 700.00
4(1/39, B&W; color-c; 68 pgs., 6-1/2x9-1/2")-Eisner-r
55.00 165.00 525.00

Little Giant Movie Funnies #2 © CEN

Little Lizzie #1 © MAR

Little Lotta #4 © HARV

GD2.0 FN6.0 NM9.4

LITTLE GIANT MOVIE FUNNIES
Centaur Publ.: Aug, 1938 - No. 2, Oct, 1938 (6-3/4x4-1/2", 132 pgs., B&W)

	GD2.0	FN6.0	NM9.4
1-Ed Wheelan's "Minute Movies" reprints	74.00	221.00	700.00
2-Ed Wheelan's "Minute Movies" reprints	55.00	165.00	525.00

LITTLE GROUCHO (...the Red-Headed Tornado; ...Grouchy No. 2)
Reston Publ. Co.: No. 16; Feb-Mar, 1955 - No. 2, June-July, 1955
(See Tippy Terry)

	GD2.0	FN6.0	NM9.4
16, 1 (2-3/55)	7.85	23.50	55.00
2(6-7/55)	5.00	15.00	35.00

LITTLE HIAWATHA (Disney; see Walt Disney's C&S #143)
Dell Publishing Co.: No. 439, Dec, 1952 - No. 988, May-July, 1959

	GD2.0	FN6.0	NM9.4
Four Color 439 (#1)	5.00	15.00	60.00
Four Color 787 (4/57), 901 (5/58), 988	4.10	12.30	45.00

LITTLE IKE
St. John Publishing Co.: April, 1953 - No. 4, Oct, 1953

	GD2.0	FN6.0	NM9.4
1	9.30	28.00	65.00
2	5.00	15.00	35.00
3,4	4.65	14.00	28.00

LITTLE IODINE (See Giant Comic Album)
Dell Publ. Co.: No. 224, 4/49 - No. 257, 1949: 3-5/50 - No. 56, 4-6/62 (1-4-52pgs.)

	GD2.0	FN6.0	NM9.4
Four Color 224-By Jimmy Hatlo	9.00	27.00	110.00
Four Color 257	6.70	20.00	80.00
1(3-5/50)	8.35	25.00	100.00
2-5	3.65	11.00	40.00
6-10	3.00	9.00	30.00
11-20	2.30	7.00	20.00
21-30: 27-Xmas-c	2.00	6.00	18.00
31-40	1.85	5.50	15.00
41-56	1.50	4.50	12.00

LITTLE JACK FROST
Avon Periodicals: 1951

	GD2.0	FN6.0	NM9.4
1	9.30	28.00	65.00

LI'L JINX (Little Archie in Animal Land #17) (Also see Pep Comics #62)
Archie Publications: No. 11, Nov, 1956 - No. 16, Sept, 1957

	GD2.0	FN6.0	NM9.4
11-By Joe Edwards	12.00	36.00	95.00
12(1/57)-16	9.30	28.00	65.00

LI'L JINX (See Archie Giant Series Magazine No. 223)

LI'L JINX CHRISTMAS BAG (See Archie Giant Series Mag. No. 195, 206, 219)

LI'L JINX GIANT LAUGH-OUT (See Archie Giant Series Mag. No. 176, 185)
Archie Publications: No. 33, Sept, 1971 - No. 43, Nov, 1973 (52 pgs.)

	GD2.0	FN6.0	NM9.4
33-43 (52 pgs.)	2.00	6.00	16.00

LITTLE JOE (See Popular Comics & Super Comics)
Dell Publishing Co.: No. 1, 1942

	GD2.0	FN6.0	NM9.4
Four Color 1	50.00	150.00	600.00

LITTLE JOE
St. John Publishing Co.: Apr, 1953

	GD2.0	FN6.0	NM9.4
1	4.15	12.50	25.00

LI'L KIDS (Also see Li'l Pals)
Marvel Comics Group: 8/70 - No. 2, 10/70; No. 3, 11/71 - No. 12, 6/73

	GD2.0	FN6.0	NM9.4
1	5.00	15.00	55.00
2-9	3.00	9.00	30.00
10-12-Calvin app.	3.20	9.60	35.00

LITTLE KING
Dell Publishing Co.: No. 494, Aug, 1953 - No. 677, Feb, 1956

	GD2.0	FN6.0	NM9.4
Four Color 494 (#1)	9.00	27.00	110.00
Four Color 597, 677	4.60	13.75	55.00

LITTLE LANA (Formerly Lana)
Marvel Comics (MjMC): No. 8, Nov, 1949; No. 9, Mar, 1950

	GD2.0	FN6.0	NM9.4
8,9	7.85	23.50	55.00

LITTLE LENNY
Marvel Comics (CDS): June, 1949 - No. 3, Nov, 1949

	GD2.0	FN6.0	NM
1-Little Aspirin app.	10.50	32.00	85.
2,3	6.40	19.25	45.

LITTLE LIZZIE
Marvel Comics (PrPl)/Atlas (OMC): 6/49 - No. 5, 4/50; 9/53 - No. 3, Jan, 195

	GD2.0	FN6.0	NM
1	12.00	36.00	95.
2-5	7.85	23.50	55.
1 (9/53, 2nd series by Atlas)-Howie Post-c	8.65	26.00	60.
2,3	6.00	18.00	42.

LITTLE LOTTA (See Harvey Hits No. 10)
Harvey Publications: 11/55 - No. 110, 11/73; No. 111, 9/74 - No. 120, 5/76
V2#1, Oct, 1992 - No. 4, July, 1993 ($1.25)

	GD2.0	FN6.0	NM
1-Richie Rich (r) & Little Dot begin	31.00	93.00	350.
2,3	13.50	40.00	150.
4,5	8.15	24.50	90.
6-10	6.80	20.50	75.
11-20	4.10	12.30	45.
21-40	3.00	9.00	30.
41-60	2.50	7.50	25.
61-80: 62-1st app. Nurse Jenny	2.00	6.00	20.
81-99	1.40	4.20	14.
100-103: All 52 pg. Giants	1.80	5.40	18.
104-120	1.00	3.00	9.
V2#1-4 (1992-93)			2.

NOTE: *No. 121 was advertised, but never released.*

LITTLE LOTTA FOODLAND
Harvey Publications: 9/63 - No. 14, 10/67; No. 15, 10/68 - No. 29, Oct, 1972

	GD2.0	FN6.0	NM
1-Little Lotta, Little Dot, Richie Rich, 68 pgs. begin	11.50	34.00	125.
2,3	7.25	21.75	80.
4,5	5.00	15.00	55.
6-10	3.60	11.00	40.
11-20	2.80	8.40	28.
21-26: 26-Last 68 pg. issue	2.20	6.60	22.
27,28: Both 52 pgs.	2.00	6.00	20.
29-(36 pgs.)	1.20	3.60	12.

LITTLE LULU (Formerly Marge's Little Lulu)
Gold Key 207-257/Whitman 258 on: No. 207, Sept, 1972 - No. 268, April, 19

	GD2.0	FN6.0	NM
207,209,220-Stanley-r. 207-1st app. Henrietta	1.50	4.50	12.
208,210-219: 208-1st app. Snobbly, Wilbur's butler	1.10	3.30	9.
221-240,242-249, 250(r/#166), 251-254(r/#206)		2.40	6.
241,263-Stanley-r	1.00	2.80	7.
255-257(Gold Key): 256-r/#212			5.
258,259,262,264,265 (Whitman)	1.00	3.00	8.
260,261	1.25	3.75	10.
266-268 (All #90028 on-c; no date, no date code; 3-pack?): 268-Stanley-r	1.75	5.25	14.

LITTLE MARY MIXUP (See Comics On Parade)
United Features Syndicate: No. 10, 1939, - No. 26, 1940

	GD2.0	FN6.0	NM
Single Series 10, 26	35.00	105.00	280.

LITTLE MAX COMICS (Joe Palooka's Pal; see Joe Palooka)
Harvey Publications: Oct, 1949 - No. 73, Nov, 1961

	GD2.0	FN6.0	NM
1-Infinity-c; Little Dot begins; Joe Palooka on-c	19.00	56.00	150.
2-Little Dot app.; Joe Palooka on-c	10.00	30.00	75.
3-Little Dot app.; Joe Palooka on-c	7.85	23.50	55.
4-10: 5-Little Dot app., 1pg.	5.00	15.00	35.
11-20	5.00	15.00	30.
21-40: 23-Little Dot app. 38-r/#20	4.65	14.00	28.
41-73: 63-65,67-73-Include new five pg. Richie Rich stories. 70-73-Little Lotta app.	2.30	7.00	20.

LI'L MENACE
Fago Magazine Co.: Dec, 1958 - No. 3, May, 1959

	GD2.0	FN6.0	NM
1-Peter Rabbit app.	7.15	21.50	50.
2-Peter Rabbit (Vincent Fago's)	5.70	17.00	40.
3	5.00	15.00	32.

Little Miss Muffet #11 © STD

Li'l Pan #2 © FOX

Little Roquefort #10 © Pines

LITTLE MERMAID, THE (Walt Disney's...; also see Disney's...)
W. D. Publications (Disney): 1990 (no date given)($5.95, no ads, 52 pgs.)

	GD2.0	FN6.0	NM9.4
nn-Adapts animated movie	1.00	2.80	7.00
nn-Comic version ($2.50)			3.00

LITTLE MERMAID, THE
Disney Comics: 1992 - No. 4, 1992 ($1.50, mini-series)

	GD2.0	FN6.0	NM9.4
1-4: Based on movie			3.00
1-4: 2nd printings sold at Wal-Mart w/different-c			2.00

LITTLE MISS MUFFET
Best Books (Standard Comics)/King Features Synd.: No. 11, Dec, 1948 - No. 13, March, 1949

	GD2.0	FN6.0	NM9.4
11-Strip reprints; Fanny Cory-c/a	7.85	23.50	55.00
12,13-Strip reprints; Fanny Cory-c/a	5.00	15.00	35.00

LITTLE MISS SUNBEAM COMICS
Magazine Enterprises/Quality Bakers of America: June-July, 1950 - No. 4, Dec-Jan, 1950-51

	GD2.0	FN6.0	NM9.4
1	16.00	48.00	125.00
2-4	9.30	28.00	65.00
...Advs. In Space ('55)	5.70	17.00	40.00

LITTLE MONSTERS, THE (See March of Comics #423, Three Stooges #17)
Gold Key: Nov, 1964 - No. 44, Feb, 1978

	GD2.0	FN6.0	NM9.4
1	5.00	15.00	60.00
2	3.00	9.00	30.00
3-10	2.50	7.50	24.00
11-20	2.00	6.00	18.00
21-30	1.75	5.25	14.00
31-44: 20,34-39,43-Reprints	1.00	3.00	8.00

LITTLE MONSTERS (Movie)
Now Comics: 1989 - No. 6, June, 1990 ($1.75)

	GD2.0	FN6.0	NM9.4
1-6: Photo-c from movie			2.00

LITTLE NEMO (See Cocomalt, Future Comics, Help, Jest, Kayo, Punch, Red Seal, & Superworld; most by Winsor McCay Jr., son of famous artist) (Other McCay books: see Little Sammy Sneeze & Dreams of the Rarebit Fiend)

LITTLE NEMO (...in Slumberland)
McCay Features/Nostalgia Press('69): 1945 (11x7-1/4", 28 pgs., B&W)

	GD2.0	FN6.0	NM9.4
1905 & 1911 reprints by Winsor McCay	10.00	30.00	75.00
1969-70 (Exact reprint)	1.50	4.50	12.00

LITTLE ORPHAN ANNIE (See Annie, Famous Feature Stories, Marvel Super Special, Merry Christmas..., Popular Comics, Super Book #7, 11, 23 & Super Comics)

LITTLE ORPHAN ANNIE
David McKay Publ./Dell Publishing Co.: No. 7, 1937 - No. 3, Sept-Nov, 1948; No. 206, Dec, 1948

	GD2.0	FN6.0	NM9.4
Feature Books(McKay) 7-(1937) (Rare)	81.00	244.00	975.00
Four Color 12(1941)	48.00	144.00	575.00
Four Color 18(1943)-Flag-c	38.00	113.00	450.00
Four Color 52(1944)	29.00	87.00	350.00
Four Color 76(1945)	24.00	72.00	290.00
Four Color 107(1946)	21.00	63.00	250.00
Four Color 152(1947)	13.00	40.00	160.00
1(3-5/48)-r/strips from 5/7/44 to 7/30/44	13.00	40.00	160.00
2-r/strips from 7/21/40 to 9/9/40	9.00	27.00	110.00
3-r/strips from 9/10/40 to 11/9/40	9.00	27.00	110.00
Four Color 206(12/48)	7.00	20.00	85.00

LI'L PALS (Also see Li'l Kids)
Marvel Comics Group: Sept, 1972 - No. 5, May, 1973

	GD2.0	FN6.0	NM9.4
1	4.55	13.65	50.00
2-5	3.00	9.00	30.00

LI'L PAN (Formerly Rocket Kelly; becomes Junior Comics with #9)
Fox Features Syndicate: No. 6, Dec-Jan, 1946-47 - No. 8, Apr-May, 1947
Also see Wotalife Comics)

	GD2.0	FN6.0	NM9.4
6	9.30	28.00	65.00
7,8: 7-Atomic bomb story; robot-c	6.40	19.25	45.00

LITTLE PEOPLE
Dell Publishing Co.: No. 485, Aug-Oct, 1953 - No. 1062, Dec, 1959
(Walt Scott's)

	GD2.0	FN6.0	NM9.4
Four Color 485 (#1)	5.85	17.50	70.00
Four Color 573(7/54), 633(6/55)	3.65	11.00	40.00
Four Color 692(3/56),753(11/56),809(7/57),868(12/57),908(5/58), 959(12/58), 1062	3.65	11.00	40.00
Four Color 1024-Darby O'Gill &...-Movie, Toth-a, photo-c	9.00	27.00	110.00

LITTLE RASCALS
Dell Publishing Co.: No. 674, Jan, 1956 - No. 1297, Mar-May, 1962

	GD2.0	FN6.0	NM9.4
Four Color 674 (#1)	6.70	20.00	80.00
Four Color 778(3/57),825(8/57)	4.35	13.00	48.00
Four Color 883(3/58),936(9/58),974(3/59),1030(9/59),1079(2-4/60),1137 (9-11/60)	4.35	13.00	48.00
Four Color 1174(3-5/61),1224(10-12/61),1297	3.45	10.35	38.00

LI'L RASCAL TWINS (Formerly Nature Boy)
Charlton Comics: No. 6, 1957 - No. 18, Jan, 1960

	GD2.0	FN6.0	NM9.4
6-Li'l Genius & Tomboy in all	5.00	15.00	35.00
7-18: 7-Timmy the Timid Ghost app.	4.00	11.00	22.00

LITTLE RED HOT: (CHANE OF FOOLS)
Image Comics: Feb, 1999 - No. 3, Apr, 1999 ($2.95/$3.50, B&W, limited series)

	GD2.0	FN6.0	NM9.4
1-3-Dawn Brown-s/a. 2,3-($3.50-c)			3.50

LITTLE ROQUEFORT COMICS (See Paul Terry's Comics #105)
St. John Publishing Co.(all pre-code)/Pines No. 10: June, 1952 - No. 9, Oct, 1953; No. 10, Summer, 1958

	GD2.0	FN6.0	NM9.4
1-By Paul Terry	10.00	30.00	70.00
2	5.00	15.00	32.00
3-10: 10-CBS Television Presents on-c	4.30	13.00	26.00

LITTLE SAD SACK (See Harvey Hits No. 73, 76, 79, 81, 83)
Harvey Publications: Oct, 1964 - No. 19, Nov, 1967

	GD2.0	FN6.0	NM9.4
1-Richie Rich app. on cover only	4.10	12.30	45.00
2-10	2.50	7.50	25.00
11-19	2.30	7.00	20.00

LITTLE SCOUTS
Dell Publishing Co.: No. 321, Mar, 1951 - No. 587, Oct, 1954

	GD2.0	FN6.0	NM9.4
Four Color #321 (#1, 3/51)	3.20	9.60	35.00
2(10-12/51) - 6(10-12/52)	2.30	7.00	20.00
Four Color #462,506,550,587	2.30	7.00	20.00

LITTLE SHOP OF HORRORS SPECIAL (Movie)
DC Comics: Feb, 1987 ($2.00, 68 pgs.)

	GD2.0	FN6.0	NM9.4
1-Colan-c/a			3.00

LITTLE SPUNKY
I. W. Enterprises: No date (1963?) (10¢)

	GD2.0	FN6.0	NM9.4
1-r/Frisky Fables #1	1.50	4.50	12.00

LITTLE STOOGES, THE (The Three Stooges' Sons)
Gold Key: Sept, 1972 - No. 7, Mar, 1974

	GD2.0	FN6.0	NM9.4
1-Norman Maurer cover/stories in all	2.80	8.40	28.00
2-7	2.00	6.00	16.00

LITTLEST OUTLAW (Disney)
Dell Publishing Co.: No. 609, Jan, 1955

	GD2.0	FN6.0	NM9.4
Four Color 609-Movie, photo-c	5.85	17.50	70.00

LITTLEST SNOWMAN, THE
Dell Publishing Co.: No. 755, 12/56; No. 864, 12/57; 12-2/1963-64

	GD2.0	FN6.0	NM9.4
Four Color #755,864, 1(1964)	4.10	12.30	45.00

LI'L TOMBOY (Formerly Fawcett's Funny Animals; see Giant Comics #3)
Charlton Comics: V14#92, Oct, 1956; No. 93, Mar, 1957 - No. 107, Feb, 1960

	GD2.0	FN6.0	NM9.4
V14#92	5.00	15.00	30.00
93-107: 97-Atomic Bunny app.	4.00	12.00	24.00

LI'L WILLIE COMICS (Formerly & becomes Willie Comics #22 on)
Marvel Comics (MgPC): No. 20, July, 1949 - No. 21, Sept, 1949

Lobo #24 © DC

Logan's Run #5 © MAR

Lonely Heart #9 © AJAX

GD2.0 FN6.0 NM9.4

20,21: 20-Little Aspirin app. 7.85 23.50 55.00

LITTLE WOMEN (See Power Record Comics)

LIVE IT UP
Spire Christian Comics (Fleming H. Revell Co.): 1973, 1976 (39-49 cents)

nn 1.00 2.80 7.00

LIVING BIBLE, THE
Living Bible Corp.: Fall, 1945 - No. 3, Spring, 1946

1-The Life of Paul; all have L. B. Cole-c 40.00 120.00 325.00
2-Joseph & His Brethren; Jonah & the Whale 29.00 87.00 235.00
3-Chaplains At War (classic-c) 40.00 120.00 340.00

LOBO
Dell Publishing Co.: Dec, 1965; No. 2, Oct, 1966

1-1st black character to have his own title 2.50 7.50 20.00
2 2.25 6.75 18.00

LOBO (Also see Action #650, Adventures of Superman, Demon (2nd series), Justice League, L.E.G.I.O.N., Mister Miracle, Omega Men #3 & Superman #41)
DC Comics: Nov, 1990 - No. 4, Feb, 1991 ($1.50, color, limited series)

1-(99¢)-Giffen plots/Breakdowns in all 4.00
1-2nd printing 2.50
2-4: 2-Legion '89 spin-off. 1-4 have Bisley painted covers & art 2.50
...: Blazing Chain of Love 1 (9/92, $1.50)-Denys Cowan-c/a; Alan Grant scripts, ...Convention Special 1 (1993, $1.75), ...Paramilitary Christmas Special 1 (1991, $2.39, 52 pgs.)-Bisley-c/a, ...: Portrait of a Victim 1 (1993, $1.75) 2.50

LOBO (Also see Showcase '95 #9)
DC Comics: Dec, 1993 - No. 64, Jul, 1999 ($1.75/$1.95/$2.25/$2.50, mature)

1 ($2.95)-Foil enhanced-c; Alan Grant scripts begin 3.00
2-9,0,10-64: 2-7-Alan Grant scripts. 9-(9/94). 0-(10/94)-Origin retold. 50-Lobo vs. the DCU. 58-Giffen-a 2.50
#1,000,000 (11/98) 853rd Century x-over 2.50
Annual 1 (1993, $3.50, 68 pgs.)-Bloodlines x-over 3.50
Annual 2 (1994, $3.50)-21 artists (20 listed on-c); Alan Grant script; Elseworlds story 3.50
Annual 3 (1995, $3.95)-Year One story 4.00
...Big Babe Spring Break Special (Spr, '95, $1.95)-Balent-a 2.50
...Bounty Hunting for Fun and Profit ('95)-Bisley-c 5.00
... Chained (5/97, $2.50)-Alan Grant story 2.50
.../Deadman: The Brave And The Bald (2/95, $3.50) 3.50
.../Demon: Helloween (12/96, $2.25)-Giarrano-a 2.50
...Fragtastic Voyage 1 ('97, $5.95)-Mejia painted-c/a 6.00
...Gallery (9/95, $3.50)-pin-ups. 3.50
...In the Chair 1 (8/94, $1.95, 36 pgs.), ...I Quit-(12/95, $2.25) 2.50
.../Judge Dredd ('95, $4.95). 5.00
...Lobocop 1 (2/94, $1.95)-Alan Grant scripts; painted-c 2.50

LOBO: (Title Series), DC Comics

--A CONTRACT ON GAWD, 4/94 - 7/94 (mature) 1-4: Alan Grant scripts. 3-Groo cameo 2.50

--DEATH AND TAXES, 10/96 - No. 4, 1/97, 1-4-Giffen/Grant scripts 2.50

--GOES TO HOLLYWOOD, 8/96 ($2.25), 1-Grant scripts 2.50

--INFANTICIDE, 10/92 - 1/93 ($1.50, mature), 1-4-Giffen-c/a; Grant scripts 2.50

--/ MASK, 2/97 - No. 2, 3/97 ($5.95), 1,2 6.00

--'S BACK, 5/92 - No. 4, 11/92 ($1.50, mature), 1-4: 1-Has 3 outer covers. Bisley painted-c 1,2; a-1-3. 3-Sam Kieth-c; all have Giffen plots/breakdown & Grant scripts 2.50
Trade paperback (1993, $9.95)-r/1-4 10.00

--THE DUCK, 6/97 ($1.95), 1-A. Grant-s/V. Semeiks & R. Kryssing-a 2.00

--UNAMERICAN GLADIATORS, 6/93 - 9/93 ($1.75, mature), 1-4-Mignola-c; Grant/Wagner scripts 2.50

LOCKE!
Blackthorne Publishing: 1987 - No. 3, ($1.25, limited series)

1-3 2.00

LOCO (Magazine) (Satire)
Satire Publications: Aug, 1958 - V1#3, Jan, 1959

V1#1-Chic Stone-a 7.85 23.50 55.00
V1#2,3-Severin-a, 2 pgs. Davis; 3-Heath-a 6.00 18.00 42.00

LOGAN: PATH OF THE WARLORD
Marvel Comics: Feb, 1996 ($5.95, one-shot)

1-John Paul Leon-a 6.00

LOGAN: SHADOW SOCIETY
Marvel Comics: 1996 ($5.95, one-shot)

1 6.00

LOGAN'S RUN
Marvel Comics Group: Jan, 1977 - No. 7, July, 1977

1: 1-5-Based on novel & movie 2.40 6.00
2-5,7: 6,7-New stories adapted from novel 5.00
6-1st Thanos (also see Iron Man #55) solo story (back-up) by Zeck (6/77) 1.50 4.50 12.00

NOTE: ***Austin*** *a-6i.* ***Gulacy*** *c-6.* ***Kane*** *c-7p.* ***Perez*** *a-1-5p; c-1-5p.* ***Sutton*** *a-6p, 7p.*

LOIS & CLARK, THE NEW ADVENTURES OF SUPERMAN
DC Comics: 1994 ($9.95, one-shot)

1-r/Man of Steel #2, Superman Annual 1, Superman #9 & 11, Action #600 & 655, Adventures of Superman #445, 462 & 466 1.25 3.75 10.00

LOIS LANE (Also see Daring New Adventures of Supergirl, Showcase #9,10 & Superman's Girlfriend...)
DC Comics: Aug, 1986 - No. 2, Sept, 1986 ($1.50, 52 pgs.)

1,2-Morrow-c/a in each 4.00

LOLLY AND PEPPER
Dell Publishing Co.: No. 832, Sept, 1957 - July, 1962

Four Color 832(#1) 3.20 9.60 35.00
Four Color 940,978,1086,1206 2.50 7.50 25.00
01-459-207 (7/62) 2.40 7.35 22.00

LOMAX (See Police Action)

LONDON'S DARK
Escape/Titan: 1989 ($8.95, B&W, graphic novel)

nn-James Robinson script; Paul Johnson-c/a .90 2.70 9.00

LONE EAGLE (The Flame No. 5 on)
Ajax/Farrell Publications: Apr-May, 1954 - No. 4, Oct-Nov, 1954

1 12.00 36.00 95.00
2-4: 3-Bondage-c 8.65 26.00 60.00

LONELY HEART (Formerly Dear Lonely Hearts; Dear Heart #15 on)
Ajax/Farrell Publ. (Excellent Publ.): No. 9, Mar, 1955 - No. 14, Feb, 1956

9-Kamenesque-a; (Last precode) 9.30 28.00 65.00
10-14 5.50 16.50 38.00

LONE RANGER, THE (See Ace Comics, Aurora, Dell Giants, Future Comics, Golden Comics Digest #48, King Comics, Magic Comics & March of Comics #165, 174, 193, 208, 225, 238, 310, 322, 338, 350)

LONE RANGER, THE
Dell Publishing Co.: No. 3, 1939 - No. 167, Feb, 1947

Large Feature Comic 3(1939)-Heigh-Yo Silver; text with illus. by Robert Weisman; also exists as a Whitman #710 114.00 341.00 1250.00
Large Feature Comic 7(1939)-Illustr. by Henry Vallely; Hi-Yo Silver the Lone Ranger to the Rescue; also exists as a Whitman #715 109.00 327.00 1200.00
Feature Book 21(1940), 24(1941) 73.00 218.00 800.00
Four Color 82(1945) 42.00 125.00 500.00
Four Color 98(1945),118(1946) 31.00 94.00 375.00
Four Color 125(1946),136(1947) 21.00 63.00 250.00
Four Color 151,167(1947) 17.50 52.50 210.00

LONE RANGER, THE (Movie, radio & TV; Clayton Moore starred as Lone Ranger in the movies; No. 1-37: strip reprints)(See Dell Giants)
Dell Publishing Co.: Jan-Feb, 1948 - No. 145, May-July, 1962

1 (36 pgs.)-The Lone Ranger, his horse Silver, companion Tonto & his horse Scout begin 63.00 188.00 750.00

Lone Ranger #6 © Lone Ranger Inc.

Lone Rider #8 © Farrell

Lone Wolf and Cub #7 © Kazuo Koike

GD2.0 FN6.0 NM9.4

2 (52 pgs. begin, end #41) 28.00 85.00 340.00
3-5 21.00 63.00 250.00
6,7,9,10 17.50 52.50 210.00
8-Origin retold; Indian back-c begin, end #35 21.00 63.00 250.00
11-20: 11- "Young Hawk" Indian boy serial begins, ends #145
11.30 34.00 135.00
21,22,24-31: 51-Reprint. 31-1st Mask logo 9.00 27.00 110.00
23-Origin retold 11.70 35.00 140.00
32-37: 32-Painted-c begin. 36-Animal photo back-c begin, end #49. 37-Last newspaper-r issue; new outfit 7.50 22.50 90.00
38-41 (All 52 pgs.) 38-Paul S. Newman-s (wrote most of the stories #38-on)
6.70 20.00 80.00
42-50 (36 pgs.) 5.35 16.00 65.00
51-74 (52 pgs.): 56-One pg. origin story of Lone Ranger & Tonto. 71-Blank inside-c 5.35 16.00 65.00
75,77-99: 79-X-mas-c 4.60 13.75 55.00
76-Classic flag-c 5.35 16.00 65.00
100 6.30 19.00 75.00
101-111: Last painted-c 4.60 13.75 55.00
112-Clayton Moore photo-c begin, end #145 17.00 50.00 200.00
113-117 9.00 27.00 110.00
118-Origin Lone Ranger, Tonto, & Silver retold; Special anniversary issue
22.50 68.00 270.00
119-140: 139-Fran Striker-s 8.00 24.00 95.00
141-145 8.75 26.25 105.00

NOTE: ***Hank Hartman*** *painted c(signed)-65, 66, 70, 75, 82; unsigned-64?, 67-69?, 71, 72, 73?, 74?, 76-78, 80, 81, 83-91, 92?, 93-111.* ***Ernest Nordli*** *painted c(signed)-42, 50, 52, 53, 56, 59, 60; unsigned-39-41, 44-49, 51, 54, 55, 57, 58, 61-63?*

LONE RANGER, THE
Gold Key (Reprints in #13-20): 9/64 - No. 16, 12/69; No. 17, 11/72; No. 18, 9/74 - No. 28, 3/77

1-Retells origin 5.00 15.00 60.00
2 3.00 9.00 30.00
3-10: Small Bear-r in #6-12. 10-Last 12¢ issue 2.50 7.50 25.00
11-17 2.00 6.00 18.00
18-28 1.25 3.75 10.00
Golden West 1(30029-610, 10/66)-Giant; r/most Golden West #3 including Clayton Moore photo front/back-c 6.30 19.00 75.00

LONE RANGER AND TONTO, THE
Topps Comics: Aug, 1994 - No. 4, Nov, 1994 ($2.50, limited series)

1-4: 3-Origin of Lone Ranger; Tonto leaves; Lansdale story, Truman-c/a in all.
2.50
1-4: Silver logo. 1-Signed by Lansdale and Truman 2.40 6.00
Trade paperback (1/95, $9.95) 10.00

LONE RANGER'S COMPANION TONTO, THE (TV)
Dell Publishing Co.: No. 312, Jan, 1951 - No. 33, Nov-Jan/58-59 (All painted-c)

Four Color 312(#1, 1/51) 9.00 27.00 110.00
2(8-10/51),3: (#2 titled "Tonto") 4.60 13.75 55.00
4-10 4.55 13.65 50.00
11-20 3.45 10.35 38.00
21-33 2.80 8.40 28.00

NOTE: ***Ernest Nordli*** *painted c(signed)-2, 7; unsigned-3-6, 8-11, 12?, 13, 14, 18?, 22-24? See Aurora Comic Booklets.*

LONE RANGER'S FAMOUS HORSE HI-YO SILVER, THE (TV)
Dell Publishing Co.: No. 369, Jan, 1952 - No. 36, Oct-Dec, 1960 (All painted-c, most by Sam Savitt)

Four Color 369(#1)-Silver's origin as told by The Lone Ranger
8.35 25.00 100.00
Four Color 392(#2, 4/52) 4.55 13.65 50.00
3(7-9/52)-10(4-6/52) 3.80 11.40 42.00
11-36 3.00 9.00 32.00

LONE RIDER (Also see The Rider)
Superior Comics(Farrell Publ.): Apr, 1951 - No. 26, Jul, 1955 (#3-on: 36 pgs.)

1 (52 pgs.)-The Lone Rider & his horse Lightnin' begin; Kamenish-a begins
20.00 60.00 160.00
2 (52 pgs.)-The Golden Arrow begins (origin) 10.00 30.00 80.00
3-6: 6-Last Golden Arrow 10.00 30.00 70.00

GD2.0 FN6.0 NM9.4

7-Golden Arrow becomes Swift Arrow; origin of his shield
10.00 30.00 80.00
8-Origin Swift Arrow 12.00 36.00 95.00
9,10 8.65 26.00 60.00
11-14 6.40 19.25 45.00
15-Golden Arrow origin-r from #2, changing name to Swift Arrow
8.65 26.00 60.00
16-20,22-26: 23-Apache Kid app. 6.40 19.25 45.00
21-3-D effect-c 13.00 39.00 105.00

LONE WOLF AND CUB
First Comics: May, 1987 - No. 45, Apr, 1991 ($1.95-$3.25, B&W, deluxe size)

1-12: Frank Miller-c & intro. 6-72 pgs. origin issue 4.00
1-2nd print, 3rd print, 2-2nd print 3.25
13-38,40,42-45: 40,42-Ploog-c 3.25
39-($5.95, 120 pgs.)-Ploog-c 6.00
41-($3.95, 84 pgs.)-Ploog-c 4.00
Deluxe Edition ($19.95, B&W) 20.00

NOTE: ***Sienkiewicz*** *c-13-24.* ***Matt Wagner*** *c-25-30.*

LONG BOW (...Indian Boy)(See Indians & Jumbo Comics #141)
Fiction House Mag. (Real Adventures Publ.): 1951 - No. 9, Wint, 1952/53

1-Most covers by Maurice Whitman 15.00 45.00 120.00
2 10.00 30.00 75.00
3-9 8.65 26.00 60.00

LONG HOT SUMMER, THE
DC Comics (Milestone): Jul, 1995 - No. 3, Sept, 1995 ($2.95/$2.50, lim. series)

1-3: 1-($2.95-c). 2,3-($2.50-c) 2.50

LONG JOHN SILVER & THE PIRATES (Formerly Terry & the Pirates)
Charlton Comics: No. 30, Aug, 1956 - No. 32, March, 1957 (TV)

30-32: Whitman-c 9.30 28.00 65.00

LONGSHOT (Also see X-Men, 2nd Series #10)
Marvel Comics: Sept, 1985 - No. 6, Feb, 1986 (60¢, limited series)

1-6: 1-Art Adams/Whilce Portacio-c/a in all. 4-Spider-Man app. 6-Double size
2.40 6.00
Trade Paperback (1989, $16.95)-r/#1-6 17.00

LONGSHOT
Marvel Comics: Feb, 1998 ($3.99, one-shot)

1-DeMatteis-s/Zulli-a 4.00

LOONEY TUNES (2nd Series) (TV)
Gold Key/Whitman: April, 1975 - No. 47, July, 1984

1 -Reprints 2.80 8.40 28.00
2-10: 2,4-reprints 1.85 5.50 15.00
11-20: 16-reprints 1.25 3.75 10.00
21-30 1.00 2.80 7.00
31,32,36-42 5.00
33-35('80) (Whitman, scarce) 1.75 5.25 14.00
43,44 (low distribution) 1.00 3.00 8.00
45-47 (All #90296 on-c; nd, nd code, pre-pack?) 1.50 4.50 12.00

LOONEY TUNES (3rd Series) (TV)
DC Comics: Apr, 1994 - Present ($1.50/$1.75/$1.95/$1.99)

1-75: 1-Marvin Martian-c/sty; Bugs Bunny, Roadrunner, Daffy begin. 23-34-($1.75-c). 35-43-($1.95-c). 44-Begin $1.99-c 2.00

LOONEY TUNES AND MERRIE MELODIES COMICS ("Looney Tunes" #166 (8/55) on)(Also see Porky's Duck Hunt)
Dell Publishing Co.: 1941 - No. 246, July-Sept, 1962

GD2.0 FN6.0 VF8.0 NM9.4

1-Porky Pig, Bugs Bunny, Daffy Duck, Elmer Fudd, Mary Jane & Sniffles, Pat Patsy and Pete begin (1st comic book app. of each). Bugs Bunny story by Win Smith (early Mickey Mouse artist)
1000.00 3000.00 6250.00 12,000.00

GD2.0 FN6.0 NM9.4

2 (11/41) 145.00 435.00 1740.00
3-Kandi the Cave Kid begins by Walt Kelly; also in #4-6,8,11,15
123.00 369.00 1475.00
4-Kelly-a 123.00 369.00 1475.00

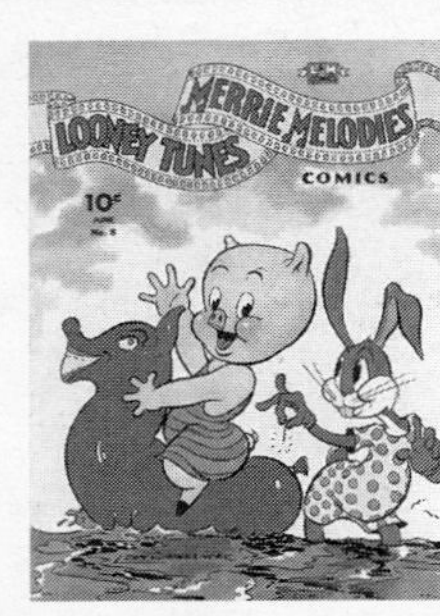

Looney Tunes & Merrie Melodies #8 © WB

Lorna the Jungle Girl #9 © MAR

The Lost Ones #1 © Ken Panders

	GD2.0	FN6.0	NM9.4
5-Bugs Bunny The Super-Duper Rabbit story (1st funny animal super hero, 3/42; also see Coo Coo); Kelly-a	93.00	280.00	1115.00
6,8-Kelly-a	69.00	206.00	825.00
7,9,10: 9-Painted-c. 10-Flag-c	52.00	156.00	625.00
11,15-Kelly-a; 15-X-Mas-c	52.00	156.00	625.00
12-14,16-19	37.00	111.00	445.00
20-25: Pat, Patsy & Pete by Walt Kelly in all	32.00	96.00	385.00
26-30	23.00	69.00	275.00
31-40: 33-War bond-c. 39-X-Mas-c	19.00	56.00	225.00
41-50	14.00	43.00	165.00
51-60	10.00	30.00	120.00
61-80	6.70	20.00	80.00
81-99: 87-X-Mas-c	5.00	15.00	60.00
100	5.85	17.50	70.00
101-120	4.10	12.30	45.00
121-150	3.20	9.60	35.00
151-200: 159-X-Mas-c	2.80	8.40	28.00
201-240	2.40	7.35	22.00
241-246	2.50	7.50	24.00

LOONY SPORTS (Magazine)
3-Strikes Publishing Co.: Spring, 1975 (68 pgs.)

	GD2.0	FN6.0	NM9.4
1-Sports satire	1.25	3.75	10.00

LOOSE CANNON (Also see Action Comics Annual #5 & Showcase '94 #5)
DC Comics: June, 1995 - No. 4, Sept, 1995 ($1.75, limited series)

1-4: Adam Pollina-a. 1-Superman app. 2.50

LOOY DOT DOPE
United Features Syndicate: No. 13, 1939

	GD2.0	FN6.0	NM9.4
Single Series 13	30.00	90.00	240.00

LORD JIM (See Movie Comics)

LORD PUMPKIN
Malibu Comics (Ultraverse): Oct, 1994 ($2.50, one-shot)

0-Two covers 2.50

LORD PUMPKIN/NECROMANTRA
Malibu Comics (Ultraverse): Apr, 1995 - No. 4, July, 1995 ($2.95, limited series, flip book)

1-4 3.00

LORDS OF MISRULE
Dark Horse Comics: Jan, 1997 - No. 6, Jun, 1997 ($2.95, B&W, limited series)

1-6: 1-Wraparound-c 3.00

LORDS OF THE ULTRA-REALM
DC Comics: June, 1986 - No. 6, Nov, 1986 (Mini-series)

1-6, Special 1(12/87, $2.25) 2.25

LORNA THE JUNGLE GIRL (...Jungle Queen #1-5)
Atlas Comics (NPI 1/OMC 2-11/NPI 12-26): July, 1953 - No. 26, Aug, 1957

	GD2.0	FN6.0	NM9.4
1-Origin & 1st app.	38.00	113.00	300.00
2-Intro. & 1st app. Greg Knight	19.00	56.00	150.00
3-5	16.00	48.00	125.00
6-11: 11-Last pre-code (1/55)	13.00	39.00	105.00
12-17,19-26: 14-Colletta & Maneely-c	10.00	30.00	80.00
18-Williamson/Colletta-c	11.00	33.00	90.00

NOTE: ***Brodsky*** *c-1-3, 5, 9.* ***Everett*** *c-21, 23-26.* ***Heath*** *c-6, 7.* ***Maneely*** *c-12, 15.* ***Romita*** *a-20, 22, 24, 26.* ***Shores*** *a-14-16, 24, 26; c-11, 13, 16.* ***Tuska*** *a-6.*

LOSERS SPECIAL (See Our Fighting Forces #123)(Also see G.I. Combat & Our Fighting Forces)
DC Comics: Sept, 1985 ($1.25, one-shot)

1-Capt. Storm, Gunner & Sarge; Crisis x-over 4.00

LOST, THE
Chaos! Comics: Dec, 1997 - No. 3 ($2.95, B&W, unfinished limited series)

1-3-Andreyko-script: 1-Russell back-c 3.00

LOST CONTINENT
Eclipse Int'l: Sept, 1990 - No. 6, 1991 ($3.50, B&W, squarebound, 60 pgs.)

1-6: Japanese story translated to English 3.50

LOST HEROES
Davdez Arts: Mar, 1998 - No. 4 ($2.95)

0-4-Rob Prior-s/painted-a 3.00

LOST IN SPACE (Movie)
Dark Horse Comics: Apr, 1998 - No. 3, July, 1998 ($2.95, limited series)

1-3-Continuation of 1998 movie; Erskine-c 3.00

LOST IN SPACE (TV)(Also see Space Family Robinson)
Innovation Publishing: Aug, 1991 - No. 12, Jan, 1993 ($2.50, limited series)

1-12: Bill Mumy (Will Robinson) scripts in #1-9. 9-Perez-c 2.50
1,2-Special Ed.; r/#1,2 plus new art & new-c 2.50
Annual 1,2 (1991, 1992, $2.95, 52 pgs.) 3.00
...: Project Robinson (11/93, $2.50) 1st & only part of intended series 2.50

LOST IN SPACE: VOYAGE TO THE BOTTOM OF THE SOUL
Innovation Publishing: No. 13, Aug, 1993 - No. 18, 1994 ($2.50, limited series)

13(V1#1, $2.95)-Embossed silver logo edition; Bill Mumy scripts begin; painted-c 3.00
13(V1#1, $4.95)-Embossed gold logo edition bagged w/poster 5.00
14-18: Painted-c 2.50

NOTE: *Originally intended to be a 12 issue limited series.*

LOST ONES, THE
Image Comics: Mar, 2000 ($2.95)

1-Ken Penders-s/a 2.95

LOST PLANET
Eclipse Comics: 5/87 - No. 5, 2/88; No. 6, 3/89 (Mini-series, Baxter paper)

1-6-Bo Hampton-c/a in all 2.00

LOST WAGON TRAIN, THE (See Zane Grey Four Color 583)

LOST WORLD, THE
Dell Publishing Co.: No. 1145, Nov-Jan, 1960-61

	GD2.0	FN6.0	NM9.4
Four Color 1145-Movie, Gil Kane-a, photo-c; 1pg. Conan Doyle biography by Torres	10.00	30.00	120.00

LOST WORLD, THE (See Jurassic Park)
Topps Comics: May, 1997 - No. 4, Aug, 1997 ($2.95, limited series)

1-4-Movie adaption 3.00

LOST WORLDS (Weird Tales of the Past and Future)
Standard Comics: No. 5, Oct, 1952 - No. 6, Dec, 1952

	GD2.0	FN6.0	NM9.4
5- "Alice in Terrorland" by Alex Toth; J. Katz-a	42.00	125.00	375.00
6-Toth-a	36.00	108.00	290.00

LOTS 'O' FUN COMICS
Robert Allen Co.: 1940's? (5¢, heavy stock, blue covers)

nn-Contents can vary; Felix, Planet Comics known; contents would determine value. Similar to Up-To-Date Comics. Remainders - re-packaged.

LOU GEHRIG (See The Pride of the Yankees)

LOVE ADVENTURES (Actual Confessions #13)
Marvel (IPS)/Atlas Comics (MPI): Oct, 1949; No. 2, Jan, 1950; No. 3, Feb, 1951 - No. 12, Aug, 1952

	GD2.0	FN6.0	NM9.4
1-Photo-c	15.00	45.00	120.00
2-Powell-a; Tyrone Power, Gene Tierney photo-c	14.00	41.00	110.00
3-8,10-12: 8-Robinson-a	7.85	23.50	55.00
9-Everett-a	8.65	26.00	60.00

LOVE AND MARRIAGE
Superior Comics Ltd. (Canada): Mar, 1952 - No. 16, Sept, 1954

	GD2.0	FN6.0	NM9.4
1	12.00	36.00	95.00
2	7.00	21.00	48.00
3-10	5.00	15.00	35.00
11-16	5.00	15.00	30.00
I.W. Reprint #1,2,8,11,14: 8-r/Love and Marriage #3. 11-r/Love and Marriage #11.	1.75	5.25	14.00
Super Reprint #10('63),15,17('64):15-Love and Marriage #?	1.75	5.25	14.00

NOTE: *All issues have* ***Kamenish*** *art.*

LOVE AND ROCKETS

Love Classics #2 © MAR

Love Diary #2 © QUA

Love Lessons #1 © HARV

GD2.0 FN6.0 NM9.4

Fantagraphics Books: July, 1982 - No. 50, May, 1996 ($2.95/$2.50/$4.95, B&W, mature)

	GD2.0	FN6.0	NM9.4
1-B&W-c (6/82, $2.95; small size, publ. by Hernandez Bros.)(800 printed)	2.30	7.00	20.00
1 (Fall, '82; color-c)	2.00	6.00	18.00
1-2nd & 3rd printing, 2-11,29-31: 2nd printings			3.00
2		2.40	6.00
3-10			4.00
11-49: 30 ($2.95, 52 pgs.)			3.00
50-($4.95)			5.00

LOVE AND ROMANCE
Charlton Comics: Sept, 1971 - No. 24, Sept, 1975

	GD2.0	FN6.0	NM9.4
1	2.50	7.50	24.00
2-10	1.75	5.25	14.00
11-24	1.10	3.30	9.00

LOVE AT FIRST SIGHT
Ace Magazines (RAR Publ. Co./Periodical House): Oct, 1949 - No. 43, Nov, 1956 (Photo-c: 21-42)

	GD2.0	FN6.0	NM9.4
1-Painted-c	12.50	37.50	100.00
2-Painted-c	7.15	21.50	50.00
3-10: 4-Painted-c	5.00	15.00	35.00
11-20	5.00	15.00	30.00
21-33: 33-Last pre-code	4.15	12.50	25.00
34-43	4.00	10.00	20.00

LOVE BUG, THE (See Movie Comics)

LOVE CLASSICS
A Lover's Magazine/Marvel: Nov, 1949 - No. 2, Feb, 1950 (Photo-c, 52 pgs.)

	GD2.0	FN6.0	NM9.4
1,2: 2-Virginia Mayo photo-c; 30 pg. story "I Was a Small Town Flirt"	12.50	37.50	100.00

LOVE CONFESSIONS
Quality Comics: Oct, 1949 - No. 54, Dec, 1956 (Photo-c: 3,4,6,7,9,11-18,21)

	GD2.0	FN6.0	NM9.4
1-Ward-c/a, 9 pgs; Gustavson-a	29.00	86.00	230.00
2-Gustavson-a; Ward-c	12.50	37.50	100.00
3	7.85	23.50	55.00
4-Crandall-a	10.00	30.00	70.00
5-Ward-a, 7 pgs.	11.00	33.00	90.00
6,7,9,11-13,15,16,18: 7-Van Johnson photo-c. 8-Robert Mitchum & Jane Russell photo-c	5.50	16.50	38.00
8,10-Ward-a(2 stories in #10)	11.00	33.00	90.00
14,17,19,22-Ward-a; 17-Faith Domerque photo-c	10.00	30.00	75.00
20-Ward-a(2)	11.00	33.00	90.00
21,23-28,30-38,40-42: Last precode, 4/55	4.15	12.50	25.00
29-Ward-a	10.00	30.00	70.00
39-Matt Baker-a	6.40	19.25	45.00
43,44,46-48,50-54: 47-Ward-c?	4.00	11.00	22.00
45-Ward-a	5.70	17.00	40.00
49-Baker-c/a	7.85	23.50	55.00

LOVE DIARY
Our Publishing Co./Toytown/Patches: July, 1949 - No. 48, Oct, 1955 (Photo-c: 1-24,27-29) (52 pgs. #1-11?)

	GD2.0	FN6.0	NM9.4
1-Krigstein-a	16.00	49.00	130.00
2,3-Krigstein & Mort Leav-a in each	10.00	30.00	80.00
4-8	5.50	16.50	38.00
9,10-Everett-a	6.00	18.00	42.00
11-20: 16- Mort Leav-a, 3 pg. Baker-sty. Leav-a	5.00	15.00	32.00
21-30,32-48: 45-Leav-a. 47-Last precode(12/54)	4.65	14.00	28.00
31-John Buscema headlights-c	5.00	15.00	35.00

LOVE DIARY (Diary Loves #2 on; title change due to previously published title)
Quality Comics Group: Sept, 1949

	GD2.0	FN6.0	NM9.4
1-Ward-c/a, 9 pgs.	30.00	90.00	240.00

LOVE DIARY
Charlton Comics: July, 1958 - No. 102, Dec, 1976

	GD2.0	FN6.0	NM9.4
1	8.65	26.00	60.00
2	5.50	16.50	38.00
3-5,7-10: 10-Photo-c	4.65	14.00	28.00
6-Torres-a	5.50	16.50	38.00
11-20: 20-Photo-c	2.30	7.00	20.00
21-40	2.00	6.00	16.00
41-60	1.50	4.50	12.00
61-80,100-102	1.10	3.30	9.00
81-99	1.00	2.80	7.00

LOVE DOCTOR (See Dr. Anthony King...)

LOVE DRAMAS (True Secrets No. 3 on?)
Marvel Comics (IPS): Oct, 1949 - No. 2, Jan, 1950

	GD2.0	FN6.0	NM9.4
1-Jack Kamen-a; photo-c	16.00	49.00	130.00
2	12.00	36.00	95.00

LOVE EXPERIENCES (Challenge of the Unknown No. 6)
Ace Periodicals (A.A. Wyn/Periodical House): Oct, 1949 - No. 5, June, 1950; No. 6, Apr, 1951 - No. 38, June, 1956

	GD2.0	FN6.0	NM9.4
1-Painted-c	11.00	33.00	90.00
2	5.70	17.00	40.00
3-5: 5-Painted-c	5.00	15.00	30.00
6-10	4.15	12.50	25.00
11-30: 30-Last pre-code (2/55)	4.00	10.00	20.00
31-38: 38-Indicia date-6/56; c-date-8/56	3.60	9.00	18.00

NOTE: ***Anne Brewster** a-15. Photo c-4, 15-35, 38.*

LOVE JOURNAL
Our Publishing Co.: No. 10, Oct, 1951 - No. 25, July, 1954

	GD2.0	FN6.0	NM9.4
10	10.00	30.00	75.00
11-25: 19-Mort Leav-a	5.50	16.50	38.00

LOVELAND
Mutual Mag./Eye Publ. (Marvel): Nov, 1949 - No. 2, Feb, 1950 (52 pgs.)

	GD2.0	FN6.0	NM9.4
1,2-Photo-c	10.00	30.00	70.00

LOVE LESSONS
Harvey Comics/Key Publ. No. 5: Oct, 1949 - No. 5, June, 1950

	GD2.0	FN6.0	NM9.4
1-Metallic silver-c printed over the cancelled covers of Love Letters #1; indicia title is "Love Letters"	12.50	37.50	100.00
2-Powell-a; photo-c	6.40	19.25	45.00
3-5: 3-Photo-c	5.00	15.00	35.00

LOVE LETTERS (10/49, Harvey; advertised but never published; covers were printed before cancellation and were used as the cover to Love Lessons #1)

LOVE LETTERS (Love Secrets No. 32 on)
Quality Comics: 11/49 - #6, 9/50; #7, 3/51 - #31, 6/53; #32, 2/54 - #51, 12/56

	GD2.0	FN6.0	NM9.4
1-Ward-c, Gustavson-a	23.00	69.00	185.00
2-Ward-c, Gustavson-a	19.00	56.00	150.00
3-Gustavson-a	12.50	37.50	100.00
4-Ward-a, 9 pgs.	18.00	53.00	140.00
5-8,10	5.70	17.00	40.00
9-One pg. Ward "Be Popular with the Opposite Sex"; Robert Mitchum photo-c	7.85	23.50	55.00
11-Ward-r/Broadway Romances #2 & retitled	7.85	23.50	55.00
12-15,18-20	5.00	15.00	35.00
16,17-Ward-a; 16-Anthony Quinn photo-c. 17-Jane Russell photo-c	10.00	30.00	80.00
21-29	5.00	15.00	30.00
30,31(6/53)-Ward-a	7.00	21.00	48.00
32(2/54)-39: 38-Crandall-a. 39-Last precode (4/55)	4.15	12.50	25.00
40-48	4.00	10.00	20.00
49,50-Baker-a	7.85	23.50	55.00
51-Baker-c	6.00	18.00	42.00

NOTE: *Photo-c on most 3-28.*

LOVE LIFE
P. L. Publishing Co.: Nov, 1951

	GD2.0	FN6.0	NM9.4
1	9.30	28.00	65.00

LOVELORN (Confessions of the Lovelorn #52 on)
American Comics Group (Michel Publ./Regis Publ.): Aug-Sept, 1949 - No. 51, July, 1954 (No. 1-26: 52 pgs.)

	GD2.0	FN6.0	NM9.4
1	14.00	41.00	110.00

Lovelorn #49 © ACG

Lovers' Lane #1 © LEV

Lucifer #4 © DC

	GD2.0	FN6.0	NM9.4
2	8.65	26.00	60.00
3-10	5.70	17.00	40.00
11-20,22-48: 18-Drucker-a(2 pgs.). 46-Lazarus-a	5.00	15.00	32.00
21-Prostitution story	6.40	19.25	45.00
49-51-Has 3-D effect-c/stories	15.00	45.00	120.00

LOVE MEMORIES
Fawcett Publications: 1949 (no month) - No. 4, July, 1950 (All photo-c)

	GD2.0	FN6.0	NM9.4
1	12.50	37.50	100.00
2-4: 2-(Win/49-50)	7.85	23.50	55.00

LOVE MYSTERY
Fawcett Publications: June, 1950 - No. 3, Oct, 1950 (All photo-c)

	GD2.0	FN6.0	NM9.4
1-George Evans-a	20.00	60.00	160.00
2,3-Evans-a. 3-Powell-a	16.00	49.00	130.00

LOVE PROBLEMS (See Fox Giants)

LOVE PROBLEMS AND ADVICE ILLUSTRATED (see True Love...)

LOVE ROMANCES (Formerly Ideal #5)
Timely/Marvel/Atlas(TCI No. 7-71/Male No. 72-106): No. 6, May, 1949 - No. 106, July, 1963

	GD2.0	FN6.0	NM9.4
6-Photo-c	12.50	37.50	100.00
7-Photo-c; Kamen-a	8.65	26.00	60.00
8-Kubert-a; photo-c	8.65	26.00	60.00
9-20: 9-12-Photo-c	6.40	19.25	45.00
21,24-Krigstein-a	7.85	23.50	55.00
22,23,25-35,37,39,40	5.70	17.00	40.00
36,38-Krigstein-a	7.00	21.00	48.00
41-44,46,47: Last precode (2/55)	5.00	15.00	35.00
45,57-Matt Baker-a	7.85	23.50	55.00
48,50-52,54-56,58-74	3.00	9.00	30.00
49,53-Toth-a, 6 & ? pgs.	4.10	12.30	45.00
75,77,82-Matt Baker-a	4.35	13.00	48.00
76,78-81,86,88-90,92-95: 80-Heath-c. 95-Last 10¢-c?	2.80	8.40	28.00
83,84,87,91-Kirby-c. 83-Severin-a	4.10	12.30	45.00
85,96,97,99-106-Kirby-c/a	5.90	17.75	65.00
98-Kirby-c/a	6.80	20.50	75.00

NOTE: ***Anne Brewster** a-67, 72. **Colletta** a-37, 40, 42, 44, 67(2); c-42, 44, 49, 54, 80. **Everett** c-70. **Heath** a-87. **Kirby** c-80, 85, 88. **Robinson** a-29.*

LOVERS (Formerly Blonde Phantom)
Marvel Comics No. 23,24/Atlas No. 25 on (ANC): No. 23, May, 1949 - No. 86, Aug?, 1957

	GD2.0	FN6.0	NM9.4
23-Photo-c begin, end #28	12.50	37.50	100.00
24-Tothish plus Robinson-a	7.15	21.50	50.00
25,30-Kubert-a; 7, 10 pgs.	7.85	23.50	55.00
26-29,31-36,39,40	5.50	16.50	38.00
37,38-Krigstein-a	7.85	23.50	55.00
41-Everett-a(2)	7.15	21.50	50.00
42,44-65: 65-Last pre-code (1/55)	5.00	15.00	35.00
43-Frazetta 1 pg. ad	5.50	16.50	38.00
66,68-86	5.00	15.00	30.00
67-Toth-a	5.50	16.50	38.00

NOTE: ***Anne Brewster** a-86. **Colletta** a-54, 59, 62, 64, 65, 69, 85; c-61, 64, 65, 75. **Heath** a-61. **Maneely** a-57. **Powell** a-27, 30. **Robinson** a-54, 56.*

LOVERS' LANE
Lev Gleason Publications: Oct, 1949 - No. 41, June, 1954 (No. 1-18: 52 pgs.)

	GD2.0	FN6.0	NM9.4
1-Biro-c	10.00	30.00	75.00
2-Biro-c	5.50	16.50	38.00
3-20: 3,4-Painted-c. 20-Frazetta 1 pg. ad	5.00	15.00	30.00
21-38,40,41	4.00	11.00	22.00
39-Story narrated by Frank Sinatra	5.70	17.00	40.00

NOTE: ***Briefer** a-6, 21. **Fuje** a-4, 16; c-many. **Guardineer** a-1. **Kinstler** c-41. **Tuska** a-6. Painted c-3-18. Photo c-19-22, 26-28.*

LOVE SCANDALS
Quality Comics: Feb, 1950 - No. 5, Oct, 1950 (Photo-c #2-5) (All 52 pgs.)

	GD2.0	FN6.0	NM9.4
1-Ward-c/a, 9 pgs.	25.00	75.00	200.00
2,3: 2-Gustavson-a	10.00	30.00	70.00
4-Ward-a, 18 pgs; Gil Fox-a	20.00	60.00	160.00
5-C. Cuidera-a; tomboy story "I Hated Being a Woman"	10.00	30.00	70.00

LOVE SECRETS
Marvel Comics(IPC): Oct, 1949 - No. 2, Jan, 1950 (52 pgs., photo-c)

	GD2.0	FN6.0	NM9.4
1	12.50	37.50	100.00
2	8.65	26.00	60.00

LOVE SECRETS (Formerly Love Letters #31)
Quality Comics Group: No. 32, Aug, 1953 - No. 56, Dec, 1956

	GD2.0	FN6.0	NM9.4
32	9.30	28.00	65.00
33,35-39	5.00	15.00	32.00
34-Ward-a	9.30	28.00	65.00
40-Matt Baker-c	7.00	21.00	48.00
41-43: 43-Last precode (3/55)	5.00	15.00	30.00
44,47-50,53,54	4.00	12.00	24.00
45,46-Ward-a. 46-Baker-a	7.85	23.50	55.00
51,52-Ward(r). 52-r/Love Confessions #17	5.00	15.00	35.00
55,56: 55-Baker-a. 56-Baker-c	6.00	18.00	42.00

LOVE STORIES (See Top Love Stories)

LOVE STORIES (Formerly Heart Throbs)
National Periodical Publ.: No. 147, Nov, 1972 - No. 152, Oct-Nov, 1973

	GD2.0	FN6.0	NM9.4
147-152	2.00	6.00	16.00

LOVE STORIES OF MARY WORTH (See Harvey Comics Hits #55 & Mary Worth)
Harvey Publications: Sept, 1949 - No. 5, May, 1950

	GD2.0	FN6.0	NM9.4
1-1940's newspaper reprints-#1-4	7.15	21.50	50.00
2-5: 3-Kamen/Baker-a?	5.00	15.00	35.00

LOVE SUCKS
Ace Comics: 1995; Oct, 1996 - Present ($2.95, B&W)

	GD2.0	FN6.0	NM9.4
1-5: 1-(1995) Hynes-s/Juch-a, 1-(10/96) Santiago-s/Juch-a			3.00

LOVE TALES (Formerly The Human Torch #35)
Marvel/Atlas Comics (ZPC No. 36-50/MMC No. 67-75): No. 36, 5/49 - No. 58, 8/52; No. 59, date? - No. 75, Sept, 1957

	GD2.0	FN6.0	NM9.4
36-Photo-c	12.50	37.50	100.00
37	7.85	23.50	55.00
38-44,46-50: 39-41-Photo-c	5.70	17.00	40.00
45,51,52,69: 45-Powell-a. 51,69-Everett-a. 52-Krigstein-a	6.40	19.25	45.00
53-60: 60-Last pre-code (2/55)	5.00	15.00	30.00
61-68,70-75: 75-Brewster, Cameron, Colletta-a	4.15	12.50	25.00

LOVE THRILLS (See Fox Giants)

LOVE TRAILS (Western romance)
A Lover's Magazine (CDS)(Marvel): Dec, 1949 - No. 2, Mar, 1950 (52 pgs.)

	GD2.0	FN6.0	NM9.4
1,2: 1-Photo-c	12.50	37.50	100.00

LOWELL THOMAS' HIGH ADVENTURE (See High Adventure)

LT. (See Lieutenant)

LUBA
Fantographics Books: Feb, 1998 - Present ($2.95/$3.50, B&W, mature)

	GD2.0	FN6.0	NM9.4
1-4-Gilbert Hernandez-s/a			3.00
5-($3.50)			3.50

LUBA'S COMICS AND STORIES
Fantographics Books: Mar, 2000 - Present ($2.95/$3.50, B&W, mature)

	GD2.0	FN6.0	NM9.4
1-Gilbert Hernandez-s/a			3.00
2-($3.50)			3.50

LUCIFER (See The Sandman #4)
DC Comics (Vertigo): Jun, 2000 - Present ($2.50)

	GD2.0	FN6.0	NM9.4
1-11: 1-3-Carey-s/Weston-a/Fegredo-c. 5-8-Gross-a			2.50
Preview-16 pg. flip book w/Swamp Thing Preview			1.00

LUCIFER'S HAMMER (Larry Niven & Jerry Pournelle's...)
Innovation Publishing: Nov, 1993 - No. 6, 1994 ($2.50, painted, limited series)

	GD2.0	FN6.0	NM9.4
1-6: Adaptatin of novel, painted-c & art			2.50

LUCKY COMICS

Lucy, The Real Gone Gal #3 © STJ

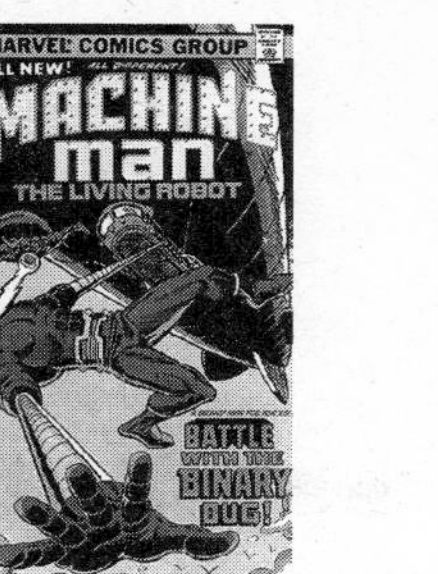

Machine Man #11 © MAR

Machine Man 2020 #1 © MAR

GD2.0 FN6.0 NM9.4

onsolidated Magazines: Jan, 1944; No. 2, Sum, 1945 - No. 5, Sum, 1946
1-Lucky Starr & Bobbie begin 20.00 60.00 160.00
2-5: 5-Devil-c by Walter Johnson 11.00 33.00 90.00

UCKY DUCK
tandard Comics (Literary Ent.): No. 5, Jan, 1953 - No. 8, Sept, 1953
5-Funny animal; Irving Spector-a 10.00 30.00 80.00
6-8-Irving Spector-a 9.30 28.00 65.00
OTE: *Harvey Kurtzman tried to hire Spector for Mad #1.*

UCKY "7" COMICS
oward Publishers Ltd.: 1944 (No date listed)
1-Pioneer, Sir Gallagher, Dick Royce, Congo Raider, Punch Powers; bondage-c 38.00 113.00 300.00

UCKY STAR (Western)
ation Wide Publ. Co.: 1950 - No. 7, 1951; No. 8, 1953 - No. 14, 1955 (5x7-¼"; full color, 5¢)
n (#1)-(5¢, 52 pgs.)-Davis-a 14.00 41.00 110.00
2,3-(5¢, 52 pgs.)-Davis-a 10.00 30.00 70.00
4-7-(5¢, 52 pgs.)-Davis-a 8.65 26.00 60.00
8-14-(36 pgs.)(Exist?) 6.40 19.25 45.00
iven away with Lucky Star Western Wear by the Juvenile Mfg. Co. 4.65 14.00 28.00

UCY SHOW, THE (TV) (Also see I Love Lucy)
old Key: June, 1963 - No. 5, June, 1964 (Photo-c: 1,2)
1 12.50 37.50 150.00
2 6.70 20.00 80.00
3-5: Photo back c-1,2,4,5 5.85 17.50 70.00

UCY, THE REAL GONE GAL (Meet Miss Pepper #5 on)
t. John Publishing Co.: June, 1953 - No. 4, Dec, 1953
1-Negligee panels 11.00 33.00 90.00
2 7.15 21.50 50.00
3,4: 3-Drucker-a 5.70 17.00 40.00

UDWIG BEMELMAN'S MADELEINE & GENEVIEVE
ell Publishing Co.: No. 796, May, 1957
our Color 796 3.20 9.60 35.00

UDWIG VON DRAKE (TV)(Disney)(See Walt Disney's C&S #256)
ell Publishing Co.: Nov-Dec, 1961 - No. 4, June-Aug, 1962
1 6.30 19.00 75.00
2-4 4.55 13.65 50.00

UFTWAFFE: 1946 (Volume 1)
ntarctic Press: July, 1996 - No. 4, Jan, 1997 ($2.95, B&W, limited series)
1-4-Ben Dunn & Ted Nomura-s/a, ...Special Ed. 3.00

UFTWAFFE: 1946 (Volume 2)
ntarctic Press: Mar, 1997 - No. 18 ($2.95/$2.99, B&W, limited series)
1-18: 8-Reviews Tigers of Terra series 3.00
nnual 1 (4/98, $2.95)-Reprints early Nomura pages 3.00
Color Special (4/98) 3.00
Technical Manual 1,2 (2/98, 4/99) 4.00

UGER
clipse Comics: Oct, 1986 - No. 3, Feb, 1987 ($1.75, miniseries, Baxter paper)
1-3: Bruce Jones scripts; Yeates-c/a 2.00

UKE CAGE (See Cage & Hero for Hire)

UKE SHORT'S WESTERN STORIES
ell Publishing Co.: No. 580, Aug, 1954 - No. 927, Aug, 1958
our Color 580(8/54), 651(9/55)-Kinstler-a 3.20 9.60 35.00
our Color 739,771,807,848,875,927 3.20 9.60 35.00

UNATIC FRINGE, THE
novation Publishing: July, 1989 - No. 2, 1989 ($1.75, deluxe format)
1,2 2.00

UNATICKLE (Magazine) (Satire)
hitstone Publ.: Feb, 1956 - No. 2, Apr, 1956
1,2-Kubert-a (scarce) 5.00 15.00 30.00

LUNATIK
Marvel Comics: Dec, 1995 - No. 3, Feb, 1996 ($1.95, limited series)
1-3 2.00

LUST FOR LIFE
Slave Labor Graphics: Feb, 1997 - No. 4, Jan, 1998 ($2.95, B&W)
1-4: 1-Jeff Levin-s/a 3.00

LYCANTHROPE LEO
Viz Communications: 1994 - No. 7($2.95, B&W, limited series, 44 pgs.)
1-7 3.00

LYNCH (See Gen [13])
Image Comics (WildStorm Productions): May, 1997 ($2.50, one-shot)
1-Helmut-c/app. 2.50

LYNCH MOB
Chaos! Comics: June, 1994 - No. 4, Sept, 1994 ($2.50, limited series)
1-4 2.50
1-Special edition full foil-c 5.00

LYNDON B. JOHNSON
Dell Publishing Co.: Mar, 1965
12-445-503-Photo-c 2.50 7.50 23.00

M
Eclipse Books: 1990 - No. 4, 1991 ($4.95, painted, 52 pgs.)
1-Adapts movie; contains flexi-disc ($5.95) 6.00
2-4 5.00

MACHINE, THE
Dark Horse Comics: Nov, 1994 - Feb, 1995 ($2.50, color)
1-4 2.50

MACHINE MAN (Also see 2001, A Space Odyssey)
Marvel Comics Group: Apr, 1978 - No. 9, Dec, 1978; No. 10, Aug, 1979 - No. 19, Feb, 1981
1-Jack Kirby-c/a/scripts begin; end #9 1.25 3.75 10.00
2-9-Kirby-c/a/s. 9-(12/78) 2.40 6.00
10-17: 10-(8/79) Marv Wolfman scripts & Ditko-a begins 4.00
18-Wendigo, Alpha Flight-ties into X-Men #140 1.85 5.50 15.00
19-Intro/1st app. Jack O'Lantern (Macendale), later becomes 2nd Hobgoblin 1.50 4.50 12.00
NOTE: ***Austin*** *c-7i, 19i.* ***Buckler*** *c-17p, 18p.* ***Byrne*** *c-14p.* ***Ditko*** *a-10-19; c-10-13, 14i, 15, 16.* ***Kirby*** *a-1-9p; c-1-5, 7-9p.* ***Layton*** *c-7i.* ***Miller*** *c-19p.* ***Simonson*** *c-6.*

MACHINE MAN (Also see X-51)
Marvel Comics Group: Oct, 1984 - No. 4, Jan, 1985 (Limited-series)
1-4-Barry Smith-c/a(i) & colors in all 4.00
TPB (1988, $6.95) r/ #1-4; Barry Smith-c 7.00
.../Bastion '98 Annual ($2.99) wraparound-c 3.00

MACHINE MAN 2020
Marvel Comics: Aug, 1994 - Nov, 1994 ($2.00, 52 pgs., limited series)
1-4: Reprints Machine Man limited series; Barry Windsor-Smith-c/i(r) 2.00

MACK BOLAN: THE EXECUTIONER (Don Pendleton's...)
Innovation Publishing: July, 1993 ($2.50)
1-3-($2.50) 2.50
1-($3.95)-Indestructible Cover Edition 4.00
1-($2.95)-Collector's Gold Edition; foil stamped 3.00
1-($3.50)-Double Cover Edition; red foil outer-c 3.50

MACKENZIE'S RAIDERS (Movie, TV)
Dell Publishing Co.: No. 1093, Apr-June, 1960
Four Color 1093-Richard Carlson photo-c from TV show 5.85 17.50 70.00

MACROSS (Becomes Robotech: The Macross Saga #2 on)
Comico: Dec, 1984 ($1.50)(Low print run)
1-Early manga app. 2.30 7.00 20.00

MACROSS II

Mad #3 © E.C. Publications

Mad #193 © E.C. Publications

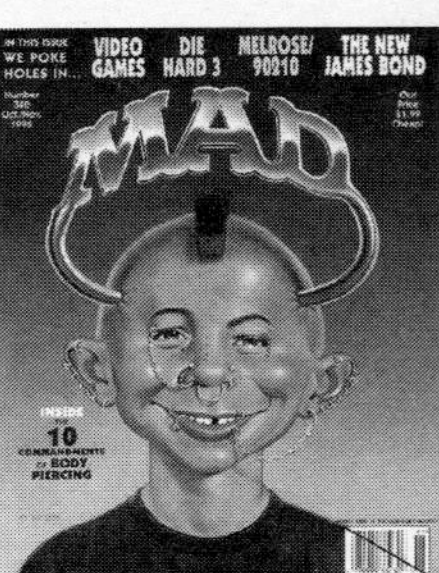

Mad #340 © E.C. Publications

Viz Select Comics: 1992 - No. 10, 1993 ($2.75, B&W, limited series)

1-10: Based on video series 2.75

MAD (Tales Calculated to Drive You...)
E. C. Comics (Educational Comics): Oct-Nov, 1952 - Present (No. 24 on are magazine format) (Kurtzman editor No. 1-28, Feldstein No. 29 - No. ?)

1-Wood, Davis, Elder start as regulars 520.00 1560.00 6500.00
2-Dick Tracy cameo 136.00 409.00 1500.00
3,4: 3-Stan Lee mentioned. 4-Reefer mention story "Flob Was a Slob" by Davis; Superman parody 82.00 245.00 900.00
5-Low distr.; W.M. Gaines biog. 145.00 436.00 1600.00
6-11: 6-Popeye cameo. 7,8- "Hey Look" reprints by Kurtzman. 11-Wolverton-a; Davis story was-r/Crime Suspenstories #12 w/new Kurtzman dialogue 59.00 177.00 650.00
12-15: 15,18-Pot Shot Pete-r by Kurtzman 48.00 143.00 525.00
16-23(5/55): 18-Alice in Wonderland by Jack Davis. 21-1st app. Alfred E. Neuman on-c in fake ad. 22-All by Elder plus photo-montages by Kurtzman. 23-Special cancel announcement 38.00 115.00 420.00
24(7/55)-1st magazine issue (25¢); Kurtzman logo & border on-c; 1st "What? Me Worry?" on-c; 2nd printing exists 90.00 270.00 900.00
25-Jaffee starts as regular writer 40.00 120.00 400.00
26,27: 27-Jaffee starts as story artist; new logo 36.00 107.00 320.00
28-Last issue edited by Kurtzman; (three cover variations exist with different wording on contents banner on lower right of cover; value of each the same) 31.00 93.00 280.00
29-Kamen-a; Don Martin starts as regular; Feldstein editing begins 31.00 93.00 280.00
30-1st A. E. Neuman cover by Mingo; last Elder-a; Bob Clarke starts as regular; Disneyland & Elvis Presley spoof 45.00 135.00 450.00
31-Freas starts as regular; last Davis-a until #99 27.00 80.00 240.00
32,33: 32-Orlando, Drucker, Woodbridge start as regulars; Wood back-c. 33-Orlando back-c 24.00 73.00 220.00
34-Berg starts as regular 20.00 60.00 180.00
35-Mingo wraparound-c; Crandall-a 20.00 60.00 180.00
36-40 (7/58) 14.00 43.00 130.00
41-50: 42-Danny Kaye-s. 44-Xmas-c. 47-49-Sid Caesar-s. 48-Uncle Sam-c. 50 (10/59)-Peter Gunn-s 11.00 33.00 100.00
51-59: 52-Xmas-c; 77 Sunset Strip. 53-Rifleman-s. 55-Sid Caesar-s. 59-Strips of Superman, Flash Gordon, Donald Duck & others. 59-Halloween/Headless Horseman-c 10.00 30.00 90.00
60 (1/61)-JFK/Nixon flip-c; 1st Spy vs. Spy by Prohias, who starts as regular 12.00 35.00 105.00
61-70: 64-Rickard starts as regular. 65-JFK-s. 66-JFK-c. 68-Xmas-c by Martin. 70-Route 66-s 7.00 20.00 60.00
71-75,77-80 (7/63): 72-10th Anniv. special; 1/3 pg. strips of Superman, Tarzan & others. 73-Bonanza-s. 74-Dr. Kildare-s 4.10 12.30 45.00
76-Aragonés starts as regular 5.00 15.00 55.00
81-85: 81-Superman strip. 82-Castro-c. 85-Lincoln-c 3.65 11.00 40.00
86-1st Fold-in; commonly creased back covers makes these and later issues scarcer in NM 4.10 12.30 45.00
87,88 3.80 11.40 42.00
89,90: 89-One strip by Walt Kelly; Frankenstein-c; Fugitive-s. 90-Ringo back-c by Frazetta; Beatles app. 4.10 12.30 45.00
91,94,96,100: 91-Jaffee starts as story artist. 94-King Kong-c. 96-Man From U.N.C.L.E. 100-(1/66)-Anniversary issue 3.65 11.00 40.00
92,93,95,97-99: 99-Davis-a resumes 3.25 9.75 36.00
101,104,106,108,114,115,119,121: 101-Infinity-c; Voyage to the Bottom of the Sea-s. 104-Lost in Space-s. 106-Tarzan back-c by Frazetta; 2 pg. Batman by Aragonés. 108-Hogan's Heroes by Davis. 114-Rat Patrol-s. 115-Star Trek. 119-Invaders (TV). 121-Beatles-c; Ringo pin-up; flip-c of Sik-Teen; Flying Nun-s 3.00 9.00 30.00
102,103,107,109-113,116-118,120(7/68): 118-Beatles cameo 2.70 8.00 27.00
105-Batman-c/s, TV show parody (9/66) 3.45 10.35 38.00
122,124,126,128,129,131-134,136,137,139,140: 122-Ronald Reagan photo inside; Drucker & Mingo-c. 126-Family Affair-s. 128-Last Orlando. 131-Reagan photo back-c. 132-Xmas-c. 133-John Wayne/True Grit. 136-Room 222 2.00 6.00 18.00
123-Three different covers 2.30 7.00 20.00
125,127,130,135,138: 125-2001 Space Odyssey; Hitler back-c. 127-Mod Squad-c/s. 130-Land of the Giants-s; Torres begins as reg. 135-Easy Rider-c by Davis. 138-Snoopy-c; MASH-s 2.50 7.50 24.00
141-149,151-156,158-170: 141-Hawaii Five-0. 147-All in the Family-s. 153-Dirty Harry-s. 155-Godfather-c/s. 156-Columbo-s. 159-Clockwork Orange-c/s. 161-Tarzan-s. 164-Kung Fu (TV)-s. 165-James Bond-s; Dean Martin-c. 169-Drucker-c; McCloud-s. 170-Exorcist-s 2.00 6.00 16.00
150-(4/72) Partridge Family-s 2.00 6.00 18.00
157-(4/72) Planet of the Apes-c/s 2.40 7.35 22.00
171-185,187,189-192,194,195,198,199: 172-Six Million Dollar Man-s; Hitler back-c. 178-Godfather II-c/s. 180-Jaws-c/s (1/76). 182-Bob Jones starts as regular. 185-Starsky & Hutch-s. 187-Fonz/Happy Days-c/s; Harry North starts as regular. 189-Travolta/Kotter-c/s. 190-John Wayne-c/s. 192-King Kong-c/s. 194-Rocky-c/s; Laverne & Shirley-s. 199-James Bond-s. 1.75 5.25 14.00
186,188,197,200: 186-Star Trek-c/s. 188-Six Million Dollar Man/ Bionic Woman. 197-Spock-s; Star Wars-s. 200-Close Encounters 2.00 6.00 18.00
193,196: 193-Farrah/Charlie's Angels-c/s. 196-Star Wars-c/s 2.30 7.00 20.00
201,203,205,220: 201-Sat. Night Fever-c/s. 203-Star Wars. 205-Travolta/Grease 220-Yoda-c, Empire Strikes Back-s 1.75 5.25 14.00
202,204,206,207,209-219,221-227,229,230: 204-Hulk TV show. 206-Tarzan. 208-Superman movie. 209-Mork & Mindy. 210-Lord of the Rings. 212-Spider Man-s; Alien (movie)-s. 213-James Bond, Dracula, Rocky II-s 216-Star Trek. 219-Martin-c. 221-Shining-s. 223-Dallas-c/s. 225-Popeye. 226-Superman II. 229-James Bond. 230-Star Wars 1.00 3.00 8.00
208,228: 208-Superman movie-c/s; Battlestar Galactica-s. 228-Raiders of the Lost Ark-c/s 1.50 4.50 12.00
231-235,237-241,243-249,251-260: 233-Pac-Man-c. 234-MASH-c/s. 235-Flip-c with Rocky III & Conan; Boris-a. 239-Mickey Mouse-c. 241-Knight Rider-s. 243-Superman III. 245- Last Rickard-a. 247-Seven Dwarfs-c. 253-Supergirl movie-s; Prince/Purple Rain-s. 254-Rock stars-s. 255-Reagan-c; Cosby-s. 256-Last issue edited by Feldstein; Dynasty, Bev. Hills Cop. 259-Rambo. 260-Back to the Future-c/s; Honeymooners-s 1.00 2.80 7.00
236,242,250: 236-E.T.-c/s;Star Trek II-s. 242-Star Wars/A-Team-c/s. 250-Temple of Doom-c/s; Tarzan-s 1.00 3.00 8.00
261-267,269-276,278-288,290-297: 261-Miami Vice. 262-Rocky IV-c/s, Leave It To Beaver-s. 263-Young Sherlock Holmes-s. 264-Hulk Hogan-c; Rambo-s. 267-Top Gun. 271-Star Trek IV-c/s. 272-ALF-c; Get Smart-s. 273-Pee Wee Herman-c/s. 274-Last Martin-a. 281-California Raisins-c. 282-Star Trek:TNG-s; ALF-s. 283-Rambo III-c/s. 284-Roger Rabbit-c/s. 285-Hulk Hogan-c. 287-3 pgs. Eisner-a. 291-TMNT-c; Indiana Jones-s. 292-Super Mario Bros.-c; Married with Children-s. 295-Back to the Future II. 297-Mike Tyson-c 5.00
268,277,289,298-300: 268-Aliens-c/s. 277-Michael Jackson-c/s; Robocop-s. 289-Batman movie parody. 298-Gremlins II-c/s; Robocop II. Batman-s. 299-Simpsons-c/story; Total Recall-s. 300(1/91) Casablanca-s, Dick Tracy-s, Wizard of Oz-s, Gone With The Wind-s 1.00 2.80 7.00
300-303 (1/91-6/91)-Special Hussein Asylum Editions; only distributed to the troops in the Middle East (see Mad Super Spec.) 1.00 3.00 8.00
301-310,312,313,315-320,322,324,326-334,337-349: 303-Home Alone-c/s. 305-Simpsons-s. 306-TMNT II movie. 308-Terminator II. 315-Tribute to William Gaines. 316-Photo-c. 319-Dracula-c/s. 320-Disney's Aladdin-s. 322-Batman Animated series. 327-Seinfeld-s; X-Men-s. 331-Flintstones-c/s. 332-O.J. Simpson-c/s; Simpsons app. in Lion King. 334-Frankenstein-c/s. 338-Judge Dredd-c by Frazetta. 341-Pocahontas-s. 345-Beatles app. (1 pg.) 347-Broken Arrow & Mission Impossible 3.00
311,314,321,323,325,335,336,350,354,358: 311-Addams Family-c/story, Home Improvement-s. 314-Batman Returns-c/story. 321-Star Trek DS9-c/s. 323-Jurassic Park-c/s. 325,336-Beavis & Butthead-c/s. 335-X-Files-s; Pulp Fiction-s; Interview with the Vampire-s. 336-Lois & Clark-s. 350-Polybagged w/CD Rom. 354-Star Wars; Beavis & Butthead-s. 358-X-Files 4.00
351-353,355-357,359-388 2.50

NOTE: ***Aragones*** *c-210, 293.* ***Davis*** *c-2, 27, 135, 139, 173, 178, 212, 213, 219, 246, 260, 296, 308.* ***Drucker*** *c-122, 169, 176, 225, 234, 264, 266, 274, 280, 285, 297, 299, 303, 314, 315, 321.* ***Elder*** *c-5, 259, 261, 268.* ***Elder/Kurtzman*** *a-258-274.* ***Jules Feiffer*** *a(r)-42.* ***Freas*** *c-39-59, 62-67, 69-70, 72, 74.* ***Heath*** *a-14, 27.* ***Jaffee*** *c-199, 217, 224, 258.* ***Kamen*** *a-29.* ***Krigstein*** *a-12, 17, 24, 26.* ***Kurtzman*** *c-1, 3, 4, 6-10, 13, 16, 18.* ***Martin*** *c-68, 165, 229.* ***Mingo*** *c-30-37, 61, 71, 75-80, 82-114, 117-124, 126, 129, 131, 133, 134, 136, 140, 143-148, 150-162, 164, 166-168, 171, 172, 174, 175, 177, 179, 181, 183, 185, 198, 206, 209, 211, 214, 218, 221, 222, 300.* ***John Severin*** *a-1-6, 9, 10.* ***Wolverton*** *c-11; a-11, 17, 29, 31, 36, 40, 82, 137.* ***Wood*** *a-24-45, 59; c-2*

Mad-Dog #4 © Paramount

Mad Hatter #1 © O.W. Comics

Madman #1 © Mike Allred

*28, 29. **Woodbridge** a-43. Issues 1-23 are 36 pgs.; 24-28 are 58 pgs.; 29 on are 52 pgs.*

MAD (See Mad Follies, ...Special, More Trash from..., and The Worst from...)

MAD ABOUT MILLIE (Also see Millie the Model)
Marvel Comics Group: April, 1969 - No. 16, Nov, 1970

	GD2.0	FN6.0	NM9.4
1-Giant issue	6.35	19.00	70.00
2,3 (Giants)	3.80	11.40	42.00
4-10	2.50	7.50	25.00
11-16: 16-r	2.30	7.00	20.00
Annual 1(11/71, 52 pgs.)	2.50	7.50	25.00

MADAME XANADU
DC Comics: July, 1981 ($1.00, no ads, 36 pgs.)

1-Marshall Rogers-a(25 pgs.); Kaluta-c/a(2pgs.); pin-up 4.00

MADBALLS
Star Comics/Marvel Comics #9 on: Sept, 1986 - No. 3, Nov, 1986; No. 4, June, 1987 - No. 10, June, 1988

1-10: Based on toys. 9-Post-a 3.50

MAD DISCO
E.C. Comics: 1980 (one-shot, 36 pgs.)

1-Includes 30 minute flexi-disc of Mad disco music 2.00 6.00 18.00

MAD-DOG
Marvel Comics: May, 1993 - No. 6, Oct, 1993 ($1.25)

1-6-Flip book w/2nd story "created" by Bob Newhart's character from his TV show "Bob" set at a comic book company; actual s/a-Ty Templeton 1.50

MAD DOGS
Eclipse Comics: Feb, 1992 - No. 3, July, 1992 ($2.50, B&W, limited series)

1-3 2.50

MAD 84 (Mad Extra)
E.C. Comics: 1984 (84 pgs.)

1 1.00 2.80 7.00

MAD FOLLIES (Special)
E. C. Comics: 1963 - No. 7, 1969

	GD2.0	FN6.0	NM9.4
nn(1963)-Paperback book covers	23.00	70.00	280.00
2(1964)-Calendar	17.50	53.00	210.00
3(1965)-Mischief Stickers	13.00	40.00	160.00
4(1966)-Mobile; Frazetta-r/back-c Mad #90	10.00	30.00	120.00
5,6: 5(1967)-Stencils. 6(1968)-Mischief Stickers	7.00	21.00	85.00
7(1969)-Nasty Cards	7.00	21.00	85.00

If bonus is missing, issue is half price)
NOTE: ***Clarke** c-4. **Frazetta** r-4, 6 (1 pg. ea.). **Mingo** c-1-3. **Orlando** a-5.*

MAD HATTER, THE (Costumed Hero)
O. W. Comics Corp.: Jan-Feb, 1946; No. 2, Sept-Oct, 1946

	GD2.0	FN6.0	NM9.4
1-Freddy the Firefly begins; Giunta-c/a	84.00	253.00	800.00
2-Has ad for E.C.'s Animal Fables #1	40.00	120.00	360.00

MADHOUSE
Ajax/Farrell Publ. (Excellent Publ./4-Star): 3-4/54 - No. 4, 9-10/54; 6/57 - No. 4, Dec?, 1957

	GD2.0	FN6.0	NM9.4
1(1954)	30.00	90.00	240.00
2,3	16.00	49.00	130.00
4-Surrealistic-c	25.00	75.00	200.00
1(1957, 2nd series)	12.50	37.50	100.00
2-4 (#4 exist?)	9.30	28.00	65.00

MAD HOUSE (Formerly Madhouse Glads; ...Comics #104? on)
Red Circle Productions/Archie Publications: No. 95, 9/74 - No. 97, 1/75; No. 98, 8/75 - No. 130, 10/82

	GD2.0	FN6.0	NM9.4
95,96-Horror stories through #97; Morrow-c	1.50	4.50	12.00
97-Intro. Henry Hobson; Morrow-a/c, Thorne-a	1.10	3.30	9.00
98,99,101-120-Satire/humor stories. 110-Sabrina app.,1pg.	1.00	2.80	7.00
100	1.00	3.00	8.00
121-130	1.00	3.00	8.00
Annual 8(1970-71)-Formerly Madhouse Ma-ad Annual; Sabrina app. (6 pgs.)	3.00	9.00	30.00
Annual 9- 12(1974-75): 11-Wood-a(r)	2.00	6.00	16.00
...Comics Digest 1('75-76)	1.85	5.50	15.00
2-8(8/82)(...Mag. #5 on)-Sabrina in many	1.50	4.50	12.00

NOTE: ***B. Jones** a-96. **McWilliams** a-97. **Wildey** a-95, 96. See Archie Comics Digest #1, 13.*

MADHOUSE GLADS (Formerly ...Ma-ad; Madhouse #95 on)
Archie Publ.: No. 73, May, 1970 - No. 94, Aug, 1974 (No. 78-92: 52 pgs.)

	GD2.0	FN6.0	NM9.4
73-77,93,94: 74-1 pg. Sabrina	1.50	4.50	12.00
78-92 (52 pgs.)	1.85	5.50	15.00

MADHOUSE MA-AD (...Jokes #67-70; ...Freak-Out #71-74) (Formerly Archie's Madhouse) (Becomes Madhouse Glads #73 on)
Archie Publications: No. 67, April, 1969 - No. 72, Jan, 1970

	GD2.0	FN6.0	NM9.4
67-71: 70-1 pg. Sabrina	1.75	5.25	14.00
72-6 pgs. Sabrina	2.30	7.00	20.00
...Annual 7(1969-70)-Formerly Archie's Madhouse Annual; becomes Madhouse Annual; 6 pgs. Sabrina	3.00	9.00	30.00

MADMAN (See Creatures of the Id #1)
Tundra Publishing: Mar, 1992 - No. 3, 1992 ($3.95, duotone, high quality, limited series, 52 pgs.)

	GD2.0	FN6.0	NM9.4
1-Mike Allred-c/a in all	1.50	4.50	12.00
1-2nd printing			4.00
2,3		2.40	6.00

MADMAN ADVENTURES
Tundra Publishing: 1992 - No. 3, 1993 ($2.95, limited series)

	GD2.0	FN6.0	NM9.4
1-Mike Allred-c/a in all	1.10	3.30	9.00
2,3			5.00

MADMAN COMICS
Dark Horse Comics (Legend No. 2 on): Apr, 1994 - Present ($2.95, bi-monthly)

	GD2.0	FN6.0	NM9.4
1-Allred-c/a; F. Miller back-c.	1.00	3.00	8.00
2-3: 3-Alex Toth back-c.			5.00
4-11: 4-Dave Stevens back-c. 6,7-Miller/Darrow's Big Guy app. 6-Bruce Timm back-c. 7-Darrow back-c. 8-Origin?; Bagge back-c. 10-Allred/Ross-c; Ross back-c. 11-Frazetta back-c			4.00
12-16: 12-(4/99)			3.00
17-19: 17-The G-Men From Hell #1 on cover; Brereton back-c. 18-(#2)			2.95
... Boogaloo TPB (6/99, $8.95) r/Nexus Meets Madman & Madman/The Jam			8.95
Ltd. Ed. Slipcover (1997, $99.95, signed and numbered) w/Vol.1 & Vol. 2. Vol.1- reprints #1-5; Vol. 2- reprints #6-10			100.00
The Complete Madman Comics: Volume 2 (11/96, $17.95, TPB) r/#6-10 plus new material			18.00
Yearbook '95 (1996, $17.95, TPB)-r/#1-5, intro by Teller			18.00

MADMAN / THE JAM
Dark Horse Comics: Jul, 1998 - No. 2, Aug, 1998 ($2.95, mini-series)

1,2-Allred & Mireault-s/a 3.00

MAD MONSTER PARTY (See Movie Classics)

MADNESS IN MURDERWORLD
Marvel Comics: 1989 (Came with computer game from Paragon Software)

V1#1-Starring The X-Men 2.00

MADRAVEN HALLOWEEN SPECIAL
Hamilton Comics: Oct, 1995 ($2.95, one-shot)

nn-Morrow-a 3.00

MAD SPECIAL (...Super Special)
E. C. Publications, Inc.: Fall, 1970 - Present (84 - 116 pgs.)
(If bonus is missing, issue is one third price)

	GD2.0	FN6.0	NM9.4
Fall 1970(#1)-Bonus-Voodoo Doll; contains 17 pgs. new material	7.50	22.50	90.00
Spring 1971(#2)-Wall Nuts; 17 pgs. new material	4.55	13.65	50.00
3-Protest Stickers	4.55	13.65	50.00
4-8: 4-Mini Posters. 5-Mad Flag. 6-Mad Mischief Stickers. 7-Presidential candidate posters, Wild Shocking Message posters. 8-TV Guise	3.80	11.40	42.00
9(1972)-Contains Nostalgic Mad #1 (28 pgs.)	3.00	9.00	32.00

10-13: 10-Nonsense Stickers (Don Martin). 13-Sickie Stickers; 3 pgs. Wolverton-r/Mad #137. 11-Contains 33-1/3 RPM record . 12-Contains

The Magdalena #1 © Top Cow

Mage (The Hero Defined) #5 © Matt Wagner

Magic Comics #40 © DMP

Nostalgic Mad #2 (36 pgs.); Davis, Wolverton-a 2.80 8.40 28.00
14,16-21,24: 4-Vital Message posters & Art Depreciation paintings. 16-Mad-hesive Stickers. 17-Don Martin posters. 20-Martin Stickers. 18-Contains Nostalgic Mad #4 (36 pgs.). 21,24-Contains Nostalgic Mad #5 (28 pgs.) & #6 (28 pgs.) 2.00 6.00 18.00
15-Contains Nostalgic Mad #3 (28 pgs.) 2.30 7.00 20.00
22,23,25,27-29,30: 22-Diplomas. 23-Martin Stickers. 25-Martin Posters.27-Mad Shock-Sticks. 28-Contains Nostalgic Mad #7 (36 pgs.). 29-Mad Collectable-Correctables Posters. 30-The Movies 1.50 4.50 12.00
26-Has 33-1/3 RPM record 1.85 5.50 15.00
31-50: 32-Contains Nostalgic Mad #8. 36-Has 96 pgs. of comic book & comic strip spoofs: titles "The Comics" on-c 1.50 4.50 12.00
51-70 1.10 3.30 9.00
71-88,90-100: 71-Batman parodies-r by Wood, Drucker. 72-Wolverton-c r-from 1st panel in Mad #11; Wolverton-s r/new dialogue. 83-All Star Trek spoof issue 1.00 2.80 7.00
76-(Fall, 1991)-Special Hussein Asylum Edition; distributed only to the troops in the Middle East (see Mad #300-303) 1.00 2.80 7.00
89-($3.95)-Polybagged w/1st of 3 Spy vs. Spy hologram trading cards (direct sale only issue)(other cards came w/card set) 1.00 2.80 7.00
101-135: 117-Sci-Fi parodies-r. 4.00
NOTE: *#28-30 have no number on cover.* ***Freas*** *c-76.* ***Mingo*** *c-9, 11, 15, 19, 23.*

MAGDALENA, THE (See The Darkness)
Image Comics (Top Cow): Apr, 2000 - No. 3 ($2.50)

Preview Special ('00, $4.95) Flip book w/Blood Legacy preview 4.95
1-Benitez-c/a; variant covers by Silvestri & Turner 2.50
2-Two covers 2.50

MAGE (The Hero Discovered...; also see Grendel #16)
Comico: Feb, 1984 (no month) - No. 15, Dec, 1986 ($1.50, Mando paper)

1-Comico's 1st color comic 1.75 5.25 14.00
2-5: 3-Intro Edsel 2.40 6.00
6-Grendel begins (1st in color) 2.50 7.50 25.00
7-1st new Grendel story 1.50 4.50 12.00
8-14: 13-Grendel dies. 14-Grendel story ends 2.40 6.00
15-($2.95) Double size w/pullout poster 1.00 3.00 8.00
TPB Volume 1-4 ($5.95) 1- r/#1,2. 2- r/#3,4. 3- r/#5,6. 4- r/#7,8 6.00
TPB Volume 5,6 ($6.95) 5- r/#9,10. 6- r/#11,12 7.00

MAGE (The Hero Defined)
Image Comics: July, 1997 - No. 15, Oct, 1999 ($2.50)

0-(7/97, $5.00) American Ent. Ed. 5.00
1-14:Matt Wagner-c/s/a in all. 13-Three covers 2.50
1-"3-D Edition" (2/98, $4.95) w/glasses 5.00
15-($5.95) Acetate cover 5.95
Volume 1,2 TPB ('98,'99, $9.95) 1- r/#1-4. 2-r/#5-8 10.00
Volume 3 TPB ('00, $12.95) r/#9-12 13.00

MAGGIE AND HOPEY COLOR SPECIAL (See Love and Rockets)
Fantagraphics Books: May, 1997 ($3.50, one-shot)

1 3.50

MAGGIE THE CAT (Also see Jon Sable, Freelance #11 & Shaman's Tears #12)
Image Comics (Creative Fire Studio): Jan, 1996 - No. 2, Feb, 1996 ($2.50, unfinished limited series)

1,2: Mike Grell-c/a/scripts 2.50

MAGICA DE SPELL (See Walt Disney Showcase #30)

MAGIC AGENT (See Forbidden Worlds & Unknown Worlds)
American Comics Group: Jan-Feb, 1962 - No. 3, May-June, 1962

1-Origin & 1st app. John Force 3.20 9.60 35.00
2,3 2.50 7.50 25.00

MAGICAL POKÉMON JOURNEY
Viz Comics: 2000 - Present ($4.95, B&W, magazine-size)

1-4 5.00
Part 2: 1-3 5.00
Part 3: 1,2: 1-Includes color poster 5.00

MAGIC COMICS
David McKay Publications: Aug, 1939 - No. 123, Nov-Dec, 1949

1-Mandrake the Magician, Henry, Popeye , Blondie, Barney Baxter, Secret Agent X-9 (not by Raymond), Bunky by Billy DeBeck & Thornton Burgess text stories illustrated by Harrison Cady begin; Henry covers begin 325.00 975.00 2600.00
2 112.00 337.00 900.00
3 88.00 263.00 700.00
4 69.00 206.00 550.00
5 53.00 158.00 420.00
6-10: 8-11,21-Mandrake/Henry-c 43.00 128.00 340.00
11-16,18,20: 12-Mandrake-c begin. 41.00 124.00 290.00
17-The Lone Ranger begins 40.00 120.00 320.00
19-Robot-c 44.00 131.00 350.00
21-30: 25-Only Blondie-c. 26-Dagwood-c begin 24.00 71.00 190.00
31-40: 36-Flag-c 17.50 53.00 140.00
41-50 14.00 42.00 110.00
51-60 12.00 36.00 95.00
61-70 9.30 28.00 75.00
71-99, 107,108-Flash Gordon app; not by Raymond 7.50 22.50 60.00
100 9.00 26.00 70.00
101-106,109-123: 123-Last Dagwood-c 6.30 19.00 50.00

MAGIC FLUTE, THE (See Night Music #9-11)

MAGIC SWORD, THE (See Movie Classics)

MAGIC THE GATHERING (Title Series), **Acclaim Comics (Armada)**

...ANTIQUITIES WAR,11/95 - 2/96 ($2.50), 1-4-Paul Smith-a(p) 2.50
...ARABIAN NIGHTS, 12/95 - 1/96 ($2.50), 1,2 2.50
...COLLECTION ,'95 ($4.95), 1,2-polybagged 5.00
...CONVOCATIONS, '95 ($2.50), 1-nn-pin-ups 2.50
...ELDER DRAGONS ,'95 ($2.50), 1,2-Doug Wheatley-a 2.50
...FALLEN ANGEL ,'95 ($5.95), nn 6.00
...FALLEN EMPIRES ,9/95 - 10/95 ($2.75), 1,2 2.75
...Collection ($4.95)-polybagged 5.00
...HOMELANDS ,'95 ($5.95), nn-polybagged w/card; Hildebrandts-c 6.00
... ICE AGE (On The World of...) ,7/5 -11/95 ($2.50), 1-4: 1,2-bound-in Magic Card. 3,4-bound-in insert 2.50
...LEGEND OF JEDIT OJANEN, '96 ($2.50), 1,2 2.50
...NIGHTMARE, '95 ($2.50, one shot), 1 2.50
...THE SHADOW MAGE, 7/95 - 10/95 ($2.50), 1-4--polybagged w/Magic The Gathering card 2.50
...Collection 1,2 (1995, $4.95)-Trade paperback; polybagged 5.00
...SHANDALAR ,'96 ($2.50), 1,2 2.50
...WAYFARER ,11/95 - 2/96 ($2.50), 1-5 2.50

MAGIC: THE GATHERING: GERRARD'S QUEST
Dark Horse Comics: Mar, 1998 - No. 4, June, 1998 ($2.95, limited series)

1-4: Grell-s/Mhan-a 3.00

MAGIK (Illyana and Storm Limited Series)
Marvel Comics Group: Dec, 1983 - No. 4, Mar, 1984 (60¢, limited series)

1-4: 1-Characters from X-Men; Inferno begins; X-Men cameo (Buscema pencils in #1,2; c-1p. 2-4: 2-Nightcrawler app. & X-Men cameo 2.50

MAGIK (See Black Sun mini-series)
Marvel Comics: Dec, 2000 - No. 4, Mar, 2001 ($2.99, limited series)

1-4-Liam Sharp-a/Abnett & Lanning-s; Nightcrawler app. 3.00

MAGILLA GORILLA (TV) (See Kite Fun Book)
Gold Key: May, 1964 - No. 10, Dec, 1968 (Hanna-Barbera)

1-1st comic app. 9.00 27.00 110.00
2-4: 3-Vs. Yogi Bear for President. 4-1st Punkin Puss & Mushmouse, Ricochet Rabbit & Droop-a-Long 5.85 17.50 70.00
5-10: 10-Reprints 5.00 15.00 60.00

MAGILLA GORILLA (TV)(See Spotlight #4)
Charlton Comics: Nov, 1970 - No. 5, July, 1971 (Hanna-Barbera)

1 4.10 12.30 45.00

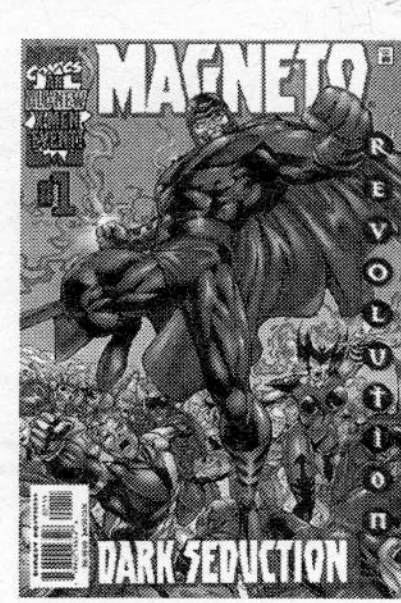

Magneto Dark Seduction #1 © MAR

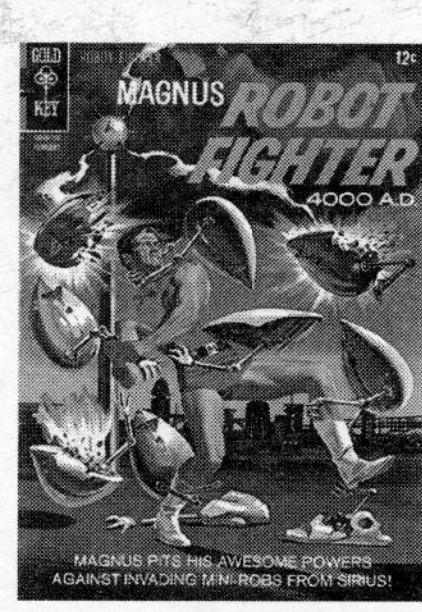

Magnus Robot Fighter #17 © GK

Major Victory Comics #2 © CHES

GD2.0 FN6.0 NM9.4

2-5 2.80 8.40 28.00

AGNETIC MEN FEATURING MAGNETO
arvel Comics (Amalgam): June, 1997 ($1.95, one-shot)
1-Tom Peyer-s/Barry Kitson & Dan Panosian-a 2.00

AGNETO (See X-Men #1)
arvel Comics: nd (Sept, 1993) (Giveaway) (one-shot)
)-Embossed foil-c by Sienkiewicz; r/Classic X-Men #19 & 12 by Bolton 5.00

AGNETO
arvel Comics: Nov, 1996 - No. 4, Feb, 1997 ($1.95, limited series)
1-4: Peter Milligan scripts & Kelley Jones-a(p) 2.00

AGNETO AND THE MAGNETIC MEN
arvel Comics (Amalgam): Apr, 1996 ($1.95, one-shot)
1-Jeff Matsuda-a(p) 2.00

AGNETO ASCENDANT
arvel Comics: May, 1999 ($3.99, squarebound one-shot)
1-Reprints early Magneto appearances 4.00

AGNETO: DARK SEDUCTION
arvel Comics: Jun, 2000 - No. 4, Sept, 2000 ($2.99, limited series)
1-4: Nicieza-s/Cruz-a. 3,4-Avengers-c/app. 3.00

AGNETO REX
arvel Comics: Apr, 1999 - No. 3, July, 1999 ($2.50, limited series)
1-3-Rogue, Quicksilver app.; Peterson-a(p) 2.50

AGNUS, ROBOT FIGHTER (...4000 A.D.)(See Doctor Solar)
old Key: Feb, 1963 - No. 46, Jan, 1977 (All painted covers except #5,31)

	GD2.0	FN6.0	NM9.4
1-Origin & 1st app. Magnus; Aliens (1st app.) series begins	23.00	68.00	250.00
2,3	10.00	30.00	110.00
4-10: 10-Simonson fan club illo (5/65, 1st-a?)	5.90	17.75	65.00
1-20	3.65	11.00	40.00
1,24-28: 28-Aliens ends	2.80	8.40	28.00
2,23: 22-Origin-r/#1; last 12¢ issue	3.00	9.00	30.00
9-46-Mostly reprints	1.50	4.50	12.00

)TE: *Manning a-1-22, 28-43(r).* ***Spiegle** a-23, 44r.*

AGNUS ROBOT FIGHTER (Also see Vintage Magnus)
aliant/Acclaim Comics: May, 1991 - No. 64, Feb, 1996
1.75/$1.95/$2.25/$2.50)

	GD2.0	FN6.0	NM9.4
-Nichols/Layton-c/a; 1-8 have trading cards		2.40	6.00
2-8: 4-Rai cameo. 5-Origin & 1st full app. Rai (10/91); 5-8 are in flip book format and back-c & half of book are Rai #1-4 mini-series. 6-1st Solar x-over. 7-Magnus vs. Rai-c/story; 1st X-O Armor			4.00
)-Origin issue; Layton-a; ordered through mail w/coupons from 1st 8 issues plus 50¢; B. Smith trading card		2.40	6.00
)-Sold thru comic shops without trading card			3.00
)-11			3.00
2-(3.25, 44 pgs.)-Turok-c/story (1st app. in Valiant universe, 5/92); has 8 pg. Magnus story insert	1.00	3.00	8.00
3-24,26-48, 50-63: 14-1st app. Isak. 15,16-Unity x-overs. 15-Miller-c. 16-Birth of Magnus. 24-Story cont'd in Rai & the Future Force #9. 33-Timewalker app.36-Bound-in trading cards. 37-Rai & Starwatchers app. 44-Bound-in sneak peek card. 21-New direction & new logo; Reese inks. 21-Gold ink vari ant			2.50
5-($2.95)-Embossed silver foil-c; new costume			3.00
9, 64 ($2.50): 64-Magnus dies?			3.00
Invasion (1994, $9.95)-r/Rai #1-4 & Magnus #5-8			10.00
earbook (1994, $3.95, 52 pgs.)			4.00

)TE: ***Ditko/Reese** a-18. **Layton** a(i)-5; c-6-9i, 25; back(i)-5-8. **Reese** a(i)-22, 25, 28; c(i)-22, 24, . **Simonson** c-16. Prices for issues 1-8 are for trading cards and coupons intact.*

AGNUS ROBOT FIGHTER
cclaim Comics (Valiant Heroes): V2#1, May, 1997 - No. 18, Jun, 1998 ($2.50)
-18: 1-Reintro Magnus; Donavon Wylie (X-O Manowar) cameo; Tom Peyer scripts & Mike McKone-c/a begin; painted variant-c exists 2.50

AGNUS ROBOT FIGHTER 4000 A.D.
aliant: 1990 - No. 2?, 1991 ($7.95, high quality paper, card stock-c, 96 pgs.)
1,2: Russ Manning-r in all. 1-Origin 8.00

MAGNUS ROBOT FIGHTER/NEXUS
Valiant/Dark Horse Comics: Dec, 1993 - No. 2, Apr, 1994 ($2.95, lim. series)
1,2: Steve Rude painted-c & pencils in all 3.00

MAID OF THE MIST (See American Graphics)

MAI, THE PSYCHIC GIRL
Eclipse Comics: May, 1987 - No. 28, July, 1989 ($1.50, B&W, bi-weekly, 44pgs.)
1-28, 1,2-2nd print 2.00

MAJOR BUMMER
DC Comics: Aug, 1997 - No. 15, Oct, 1998 ($2.50)
1-15: 1-Origin and 1st app. Major Bummer 2.50

MAJOR HOOPLE COMICS (See Crackajack Funnies)
Nedor Publications: nd (Jan, 1943)
1-Mary Worth, Phantom Soldier app. by Moldoff 40.00 120.00 350.00

MAJOR VICTORY COMICS (Also see Dynamic Comics)
H. Clay Glover/Service Publ./Harry 'A' Chesler: 1944 - No. 3, Summer, 1945

	GD2.0	FN6.0	NM9.4
1-Origin Major Victory (patriotic hero) by C. Sultan (reprint from Dynamic #1); 1st app. Spider Woman	61.00	182.00	575.00
2-Dynamic Boy app.	40.00	120.00	350.00
3-Rocket Boy app.	38.00	113.00	300.00

MALIBU ASHCAN: RAFFERTY (See Firearm #12)
Malibu Comics (Ultraverse): Nov, 1994 (99¢, B&W w/color-c; one-shot)
1-Previews "The Rafferty Saga" storyline in Firearm; Chaykin-c 2.00

MALTESE FALCON
David McKay Publications: No. 48, 1946
Feature Books 48-by Dashiell Hammett 74.00 221.00 700.00

MALU IN THE LAND OF ADVENTURE
I. W. Enterprises: 1964 (See White Princess of Jungle #2)
1-r/Avon's Slave Girl Comics #1; Severin-c 5.00 15.00 55.00

MAMMOTH COMICS
Whitman Publishing Co.(K. K. Publ.): 1938 (84 pgs.) (B&W, 8-1/2x11-1/2")
1-Alley Oop, Terry & the Pirates, Dick Tracy, Little Orphan Annie, Wash Tubbs, Moon Mullins, Smilin' Jack, Tailspin Tommy, Don Winslow, Dan Dunn, Smokey Stover & other reprints 190.00 570.00 1800.00

MAN AGAINST TIME
Image Comics (Motown Machineworks): May, 1996 - No. 4, Aug, 1996 ($2.25, limited series)
1-4: 1-Simonson-c. 2,3-Leon-c. 4-Barreto & Leon-c 2.25

MAN-BAT (See Batman Family, Brave & the Bold, & Detective #400)
National Periodical Publications/DC Comics: Dec-Jan, 1975-76 - No. 2, Feb-Mar, 1976; Dec, 1984

	GD2.0	FN6.0	NM9.4
1-Ditko-a(p); Aparo-c; Batman app.; 1st app. She-Bat?	1.85	5.50	15.00
2-Aparo-c	1.25	3.75	10.00
1 (12/84)-N. Adams-r(3)/Det.(Vs. Batman on-c)			4.00

MAN-BAT
DC Comics: Feb, 1996 - No. 3, Apr, 1996 ($2.25, limited series)
1-3: Dixon scripts in all. 2-Killer Croc-c/app. 2.25

MAN CALLED A-X, THE
Malibu Comics (Bravura): Nov, 1994 - No. 4, Jun, 1995 ($2.95, limited series)
0-4: Marv Wolfman scripts & Shawn McManus-c/a. 0-(2/95). 1-"1A" on cover 3.00

MAN CALLED A-X, THE
DC Comics: Oct, 1997 - No. 8, May, 1998 ($2.50)
1-8: Marv Wolfman scripts & Shawn McManus-c/a. 2.50

MAN COMICS
Marvel/Atlas Comics (NPI): Dec, 1949 - No. 28, Sept, 1953 (#1-6: 52 pgs.)

	GD2.0	FN6.0	NM9.4
1-Tuska-a	22.00	66.00	175.00
2-Tuska-a	12.50	37.50	100.00

Man Comics #16 © DC

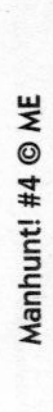
Manhunt! #4 © ME

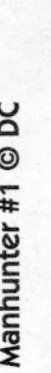
Manhunter #1 © DC

3-6 10.00 30.00 75.00
7,8 10.00 30.00 70.00
9-13,15: 9-Format changes to war 6.40 19.25 45.00
14-Henkel (3 pgs.); Pakula-a 7.85 23.50 55.00
16-21,23-28: 28-Crime issue (Bob Brant) 5.50 16.50 38.00
22-Krigstein-a, 5 pgs. 7.85 23.50 55.00

NOTE: ***Berg*** *a-14, 15, 19.* ***Colan*** *a-9, 21.* ***Everett*** *a-8, 22; c-22, 25.* ***Heath*** *a-11, 17, 21. Kubertish a-by* ***Bob Brown****-3.* ***Maneely*** *a-11; c-10, 11.* ***Reinman*** *a-11.* ***Robinson*** *a-7, 10, 14.* ***Robert Sale*** *a-9, 11.* ***Sinnott*** *a-22, 23.* ***Tuska*** *a-14, 23.*

MANDRAKE THE MAGICIAN (See Defenders Of The Earth, 123, 46, 52, 55, Giant Comic Album, King Comics, Magic Comics, The Phantom #21, Tiny Tot Funnies & Wow Comics, '36)

MANDRAKE THE MAGICIAN (See Harvey Comics Hits #53)
David McKay Publ./Dell/King Comics (All 12¢): 1938 - 1948; Sept, 1966 - No. 10, Nov, 1967 (Also see Four Color #752)

Feature Books 18,19,25 (1938) 50.00 150.00 550.00
Feature Books 46 41.00 124.00 350.00
Feature Books 52,55 35.00 105.00 280.00
Four Color 752 (11/56) 10.00 30.00 120.00
1-Begin S.O.S. Phantom, ends #3 4.10 12.30 45.00
2-7,9: 4-Girl Phantom app. 5-Flying Saucer-c/story. 5,6-Brick Bradford app. 7-Origin Lothar. 9-Brick Bradford app. 2.50 7.50 25.00
8-Jeff Jones-a (4 pgs.) 3.00 9.00 32.00
10-Rip Kirby app.; Raymond-a (14 pgs.) 3.20 9.60 35.00

MANDRAKE THE MAGICIAN
Marvel Comics: Apr, 1995 - No. 2, May, 1995 ($2.95, unfinished limited series)

1,2: Mike Barr scripts 3.00

MAN-EATING COW (See Tick #7,8)
New England Comics: July, 1992 - No. 10, 1994? ($2.75, B&W, limited series)

1-10 3.00
Man-Eating Cow Bonanza (6/96, $4.95, 128 pgs.)-r/#1-4. 5.00

MAN FROM ATLANTIS (TV)
Marvel Comics: Feb, 1978 - No. 7, Aug, 1978

1-(84 pgs.)-Sutton-a(p), Buscema-c; origin & cast photos 2.40 6.00
2-7 3.50

MAN FROM PLANET X, THE
Planet X Productions: 1987 (no price;probably unlicensed)

1-Reprints Fawcett Movie Comic 2.00

MAN FROM U.N.C.L.E., THE (TV) (Also see The Girl From Uncle)
Gold Key: Feb, 1965 - No. 22, Apr, 1969 (All photo-c)

1 15.00 45.00 180.00
2-Photo back c-2-8 8.00 24.00 95.00
3-10: 7-Jet Dream begins (1st app., also see Jet Dream) (all new stories) 5.35 16.00 65.00
11-22: 19-Last 12¢ issue. 21,22-Reprint #10 & 7 4.60 13.75 55.00

MAN FROM U.N.C.L.E., THE (TV)
Entertainment Publishing: 1987 - No. 11 ($1.50/$1.75, B&W)

1-7 ($1.50), 8-11 ($1.75) 3.00

MAN FROM WELLS FARGO (TV)
Dell Publishing Co.: No. 1287, Feb-Apr, 1962 - May-July, 1962 (Photo-c)

Four Color 1287, #01-495-207 5.00 15.00 60.00

MANGA SHI (See Tomoe)
Crusade Entertainment: Aug, 1996 ($2.95)

1-Printed backwards (manga-style) 3.00

MANGA SHI 2000
Crusade Entertainment: Feb, 1997 - No. 3, June, 1997 ($2.95, mini-series)

1-3: 1-Two covers 3.00

MANGA ZEN (Also see Zen Intergalactic Ninja)
Zen Comics (Fusion Studios): 1996 - No. 3, 1996 ($2.50, B&W)

1-3 2.50

MANGAZINE
Antarctic Press: Aug, 1985 - No. 4, Sept, 1986 (B&W)

1-Soft paper-c 1.50 4.50 12.00

GD2.0 FN6.0 NM9.4

2-4 1.00 3.00 8.00

MANGLE TANGLE TALES
Innovation Publishing: 1990 ($2.95, deluxe format)

1-Intro by Harlan Ellison 3.00

MANHUNT! (Becomes Red Fox #15 on)
Magazine Enterprises: 10/47 - No. 11, 8/48; #13,14, 1953 (no #12)

1-Red Fox by L. B. Cole, Undercover Girl by Whitney, Space Ace begin (1st app.); negligee panels 47.00 140.00 420.00
2-Electrocution-c 39.00 116.00 310.00
3-6 33.00 98.00 260.00
7-10: 7-Space Ace ends. 8-Trail Colt begins (intro/1st app., 5/48) by Guardineer; Trail Colt-c. 10-G. Ingels-a 29.00 86.00 230.00
11(8/48)-Frazetta-a, 7 pgs.; The Duke, Scotland Yard begin 40.00 120.00 340.00
13(A-1 #63)-Frazetta, r-/Trail Colt #1, 7 pgs. 39.00 116.00 310.00
14(A-1 #77)-Bondage/hypo-c; last L. B. Cole Red Fox; Ingels-a 32.00 96.00 255.00

NOTE: ***Guardineer*** *a-1-5; c-8.* ***Whitney*** *a-2-14; c-1-6, 10. Red Fox by* ***L. B. Cole****-#1-14. #15 wa advertised but came out as Red Fox #15. Bondage c-6.*

MANHUNTER (See Adventure #58, 73, Brave & the Bold, Detective Comics, 1st Issue Special, House of Mystery #143 and Justice League of America)
DC Comics: 1984 ($2.50, 76 pgs; high quality paper)

1-Simonson-c/a(r)/Detective; Batman app. 3.00

MANHUNTER
DC Comics: July, 1988 - No. 24, Apr, 1990 ($1.00)

1-24: 8,9-Flash app. 9-Invasion. 17-Batman-c/sty 2.25

MANHUNTER
DC Comics: No. 0, Nov, 1994 - No. 12, Nov, 1995 ($1.95/$2.25)

0-12 2.25

MANHUNTER: THE SPECIAL EDITION
DC Comics: 1999 ($9.95)

TPB-Reprints Detective Comics stories by Goodwin and Simonson 10.00

MAN IN BLACK (See Thrill-O-Rama) (Also see All New Comics, Front Page, Green Hornet #31, Strange Story & Tally-Ho Comics)
Harvey Publications: Sept, 1957 - No. 4, Mar, 1958

1-Bob Powell-c/a 16.00 49.00 130.00
2-4: Powell-c/a 12.50 37.50 100.00

MAN IN BLACK
Lorne-Harvey Publications (Recollections): 1990 - No. 2, July, 1991 (B&W)

1,2 2.00

MAN IN FLIGHT (Disney, TV)
Dell Publishing Co.: No. 836, Sept, 1957

Four Color 836 6.70 20.00 80.00

MAN IN SPACE (Disney, TV, see Dell Giant #27)
Dell Publishing Co.: No. 716, Aug, 1956 - No. 954, Nov, 1958

Four Color 716-A science feat. from Tomorrowland 8.35 25.00 100.00
Four Color 954-Satellites 6.70 20.00 80.00

MANKIND (WWF Wrestling)
Chaos Comics: Sept, 1999 ($2.95, one-shot)

1-Regular and photo-c 3.00
1-Premium Edition ($10.00) Dwayne Turner & Danny Miki-c 10.00

MANN AND SUPERMAN
DC Comics: 2000 ($5.95, prestige format, one-shot)

nn-Michael T. Gilbert-s/a 5.95

MAN OF STEEL, THE (Also see Superman: The Man of Steel)
DC Comics: 1986 (June release) - No. 6, 1986 (75¢, limited series)

1-6: 1-Silver logo; Byrne-c/a/scripts in all; origin, 1-Alternate-c for newsstand sales,1-Distr. to toy stores by So Much Fun, 2-6: 2-Intro. Lois Lane, Jimmy Olsen. 3-Intro/origin Magpie; Batman-c/story. 4-Intro. new Lex Luthor 3.00
1-6-Silver Editions (1993, $1.95)-r/1-6 3.00
...The Complete Saga nn-Contains #1-6, given away in contest 3.00

Man-Thing #9 © MAR

Mantra #16 © MAL

Many Loves of Dobie Gillis #20 © DC

GD2.0 FN6.0 NM9.4

imited Edition, softcover 4.55 13.65 50.00
IOTE: Issues 1-6 were released between Action #583 (9/86) & Action #584 (1/87) plus Superman #423 (9/86) & Advs. of Superman #424 (1/87).

IAN OF THE ATOM (See Solar, Man of the Atom Vol. 2)

IAN OF WAR (See Liberty Guards & Liberty Scouts)
entaur Publications: Nov, 1941 - No. 2, Jan, 1942
1-The Fire-Man, Man of War, The Sentinel, Liberty Guards, & Vapo-Man begin; Gustavson-c/a; Flag-c 158.00 474.00 1500.00
2-Intro The Ferret; Gustavson-c/a 121.00 363.00 1150.00

IAN OF WAR
clipse Comics: Aug, 1987 - No. 3, Feb, 1988 ($1.75, Baxter paper)
1-3: Bruce Jones scripts 2.00

IAN OF WAR (See The Protectors)
Ialibu Comics: 1993 - No, 8, Feb, 1994 ($1.95/$2.50/$2.25)
1-5 ($1.95)-Newsstand Editions w/different-c 2.00
1-8-1-5-Collector's Edi. w/poste.r. 6-8 ($2.25): 6-Polybagged w/Skycap. 8-Vs. Rocket Rangers 2.50

IAN O' MARS
iction House Magazines: 1953; 1964
1-Space Rangers; Whitman-c 40.00 120.00 350.00
W. Reprint #1-r/Man O'Mars #1 & Star Pirate; Murphy Anderson-a 5.00 15.00 55.00

IANTECH ROBOT WARRIORS
rchie Enterprises, Inc.: Sept, 1984 - No. 4, Apr, 1985 (75¢)
1-4: Ayers-c/a(p). 1-Buckler-c(i) 3.00

IAN-THING (See Fear, Giant-Size..., Marvel Comics Presents, Marvel Fanfare, Ionsters Unleashed, Power Record Comics & Savage Tales)
Iarvel Comics Group: Jan, 1974 - No. 22, Oct, 1975; V2#1, Nov, 1979 - 2#11, July, 1981
1-Howard the Duck(2nd app.) cont'd/Fear #19 3.00 9.00 30.00
2 1.75 5.25 14.00
3-1st app. original Foolkiller 1.25 3.75 10.00
4-Origin Foolkiller; last app. 1st Foolkiller 1.00 3.00 8.00
5-11-Ploog-a. 11-Foolkiller cameo (flashback) 1.00 2.80 7.00
12-22: 19-1st app. Scavenger. 20-Spidey cameo. 21-Origin Scavenger, Man-Thing. 22-Howard the Duck cameo 2.40 6.00
/2#1(1979) 2.40 6.00
/2#2-11: 4-Dr. Strange-c/app. 11-Mayerik-a 4.00
*IOTE: **Alcala** a-14. **Brunner** c-1. J. **Buscema** a-12p, 13p, 16p. **Gil Kane** c-4p, 10p, 12-20p, 21. **Iooney** a-17, 18, 19p, 20-22, V2#1-3p. **Ploog** Man-Thing-5p, 6p, 7, 8, 9-11p; c-5, 6, 8, 9, 11. **utton** a-13i. No. 19 says #10 in indicia.*

IAN-THING (Volume Three, continues in Strange Tales #1 (9/98))
Iarvel Comics: Dec, 1997 - No. 8, July, 1998 ($2.99)
1-8-DeMatteis-s/Sharp-a. 2-Two covers. 6-Howard the Duck-c/app. 3.00

IANTRA
Ialibu Comics (Ultraverse): July, 1993 - No. 24, Aug, 1995 ($1.95/$2.50)
1-Polybagged w/trading card & coupon 2.50
1-Newsstand edition w/o trading card or coupon 2.00
1-Full cover holographic edition 1.25 3.75 10.00
1-Ultra-limited silver foil-c 5.00
2-9,11-24: 3-Intro Warstrike & Kismet. 6-Break-Thru x-over. 2-($2.50-Newsstand edition bagged w/card. 4-($2.50, 48 pgs.)-Rune flip-c/story by B. Smith (3 pgs.). 7-Prime app.; origin Prototype by Jurgens/Austin (2 pgs.). 11-New costume. 17-Intro NecroMantra & Pinnacle; prelude to Godwheel 2.50
10-($3.50, 68 pgs.)-Flip-c w/Ultraverse Premiere #2 3.50
iant Size 1 (7/94, $2.50, 44 pgs.) 2.50
..Spear of Destiny 1,2 (4/95, $2.50, 36pgs.) 2.50

IANTRA (2nd Series) (Also See Black September)
Ialibu Comics (Ultraverse): Infinity, Sept, 1995 - No. 7, Apr, 1996 ($1.50)
nfinity (9/95, $1.50)-Black September x-over, Intro new Mantra. 2.00
1-7: 1-(10/95). 5-Return of Eden (original Mantra). 6,7-Rush app. 2.00

IAN WITH THE X-RAY EYES, THE (See X,... under Movie Comics)

IANY GHOSTS OF DR. GRAVES, THE (Doctor Graves #73 on)
Charlton Comics: 5/67 - No. 60, 12/76; No. 61, 9/77 - No. 62, 10/77; No. 63, 2/78 - No. 65, 4/78; No. 66, 6/81 - No. 72, 5/82
1-Ditko-a; Palais-a; early issues 12¢-c 3.65 11.00 40.00
2-6,8,10 2.00 6.00 18.00
7,9-Ditko-a 2.30 7.00 20.00
11-13,16-18-Ditko-c/a 1.50 4.50 12.00
14,19,23,25 1.00 3.00 8.00
15,20,21-Ditko-a 1.25 3.75 10.00
22,24,26,27,29-35,38,40-Ditko-c/a 1.10 3.30 9.00
28-Ditko-c 1.00 3.00 8.00
36,46,56,57,59,66-69,71 1.00 2.80 7.00
37,41,43,51,54,60,61,70,72-Ditko-a 1.00 3.00 8.00
39,58-Ditko-c. 39-Sutton-a. 58-Ditko-a 1.10 3.30 9.00
42,44,53-Sutton-c; Ditko-a. 42-Sutton-a 1.00 2.80 7.00
45-1st Newton comic work (8 pgs.); new logo; Sutton-c 1.50 4.50 12.00
47-Newton, Sutton, Ditko-a 1.00 2.80 7.00
48-Ditko, Sutton-a 1.00 2.80 7.00
49-Newton-c/a; Sutton-a. 1.00 3.00 8.00
50-Sutton-a 2.40 6.00
52-Newton-c; Ditko-a 1.00 3.00 8.00
55-Ditko-c; Sutton-a 1.00 2.80 7.00
62-65-Ditko-c/a. 65-Sutton-a 1.00 2.80 7.00
Modern Comics Reprint 12,25 (1978) 4.00
*NOTE: **Aparo** a-4, 5, 7, 8, 66r, 69r; c-8, 14, 19, 66r, 67r. **Byrne** c-54. **Ditko** a-1, 7, 9, 11-13, 15-18, 20-22, 24, 26, 27, 29, 30-35, 37, 38, 40-44, 47, 48, 51-54, 58, 60r-65r, 70, 72; c-11-13, 16-18, 22, 24, 26-35, 38, 40, 55, 58, 62-65. **Howard** a-38, 39, 45i, 65; c-48. **Kim** a-36, 46, 52. **Larson** a-58. **Morisi** a-13, 14, 23, 26. **Newton** a-45, 47p, 49p; c-49, 52. **Staton** a-36, 37, 41, 43. **Sutton** a-39, 42, 47-50, 55, 65; c-42, 44, 45; painted c-53. **Zeck** a-56, 59.*

MANY LOVES OF DOBIE GILLIS (TV)
National Periodical Publications: May-June, 1960 - No. 26, Oct, 1964
1-Most covers by Bob Oskner 23.50 71.00 260.00
2-5 12.75 38.00 140.00
6-10: 10-Last 10¢-c 8.65 26.00 95.00
11-26: 20-Drucker-a. 24-(3-4/64). 25-(9/64) 7.65 23.00 85.00

MARAUDER'S MOON (See Luke Short, Four Color #848)

MARCH OF COMICS (See Promotional Comics section)

MARCH OF CRIME (Formerly My Love Affair #1-6) (See Fox Giants)
Fox Features Synd.: No. 7, July, 1950 - No. 2, Sept, 1950; No. 3, Sept, 1951
7(#1)(7/50)-True crime stories; Wood-a 40.00 120.00 320.00
2(9/50)-Wood-a (exceptional) 38.00 113.00 300.00
3(9/51) 18.00 53.00 140.00

MARCO POLO
Charlton Comics Group: 1962 (Movie classic)
nn (Scarce)-Glanzman-c/a (25 pgs.) 11.00 33.00 120.00

MARC SPECTOR: MOON KNIGHT (Also see Moon Knight)
Marvel Comics: June, 1989 - No. 60, Mar, 1994 ($1.50/$1.75, direct sales)
1-24,26-49,51-54,58,59: 4-Intro new Midnight. 8,9-Punisher app. 15-Silver Sable app. 19-21-Spider-Man & Punisher app. 25-(52 pgs.)-Ghost Rider app. 32,33-Hobgoblin II (Macendale) & Spider-Man (in black costume) app. 35-38-Punisher story. 42-44-Infinity War x-over. 46-Demogoblin app. 51,53-Gambit app. 55-New look. 57-Spider-Man-c/story. 60-Moon Knight dies 2.50
50-(56 pgs.)-Special die-cut-c 3.00
55-57,60-Platt a 3.50
...: Divided We Fall ($4.95, 52 pgs.) 5.00
Special 1 (1992, $2.50) 2.50
NOTE: Cowan c(p) 20-23. Guice c-20. Heath c/a-4. Platt -a 55-57,60; c-55-60.

MARGARET O'BRIEN (See The Adventures of...)

MARGE'S LITTLE LULU (Continues as Little Lulu from #207 on)
Dell Publishing Co./Gold Key #165-206: No. 74, 6/45 - No. 164, 7-9/62; No. 165, 10/62 - No. 206, 8/72
Marjorie Henderson Buell, born in Philadelphia, Pa., in 1904, created Little Lulu, a cartoon character that appeared weekly in the Saturday Evening Post from Feb. 23, 1935 through Dec. 30, 1944. She was not responsible for any of the comic books. **John Stanley** did pencils only on all Little Lulu comics through at least #135 (1959). He did pencils and inks on Four Color #74 & 97. **Irving Tripp** began inking stories from #1 on, and remained the comic's illustrator throughout its

Marge's Little Lulu #55 © Marjorie Buell

Margie Comics #36 © MAR

The Mark #4 © DH

entire run. **Stanley** did storyboards (layouts), pencils, and scripts in all cases and inking only on covers. His word balloons were written in cursive. **Tripp** and occasionally other artists at Western Publ. in Poughkeepsie, N.Y. blew up the pencilled pages, inked the blowups, and lettered them. **Arnold Drake** did storyboards, pencils and scripts starting with #197 (1970) on, amidst reprinted issues. **Buell** sold her rights exclusively to Western Publ. in Dec., 1971. The earlier issues had to be approved by **Buell** prior to publication.

Four Color 74('45)-Intro Lulu, Tubby & Alvin 104.00 313.00 1250.00
Four Color 97(2/46) 48.00 144.00 575.00
(Above two books are all John Stanley - cover, pencils, and inks.)
Four Color 110('46)-1st Alvin Story Telling Time; 1st app. Willy; variant cover may exist 33.00 100.00 400.00
Four Color 115-1st app. Boys' Clubhouse 33.00 100.00 400.00
Four Color 120, 131: 120-1st app. Eddie 29.00 88.00 350.00
Four Color 139('47),146,158 27.00 81.00 325.00
Four Color 165 (10/47)-Smokes doll hair & has wild hallucinations. 1st Tubby detective story 27.00 81.00 325.00
1(1-2/48)-Lulu's Diary feature begins 58.00 175.00 700.00
2-1st app. Gloria; 1st Tubby story in a L.L. comic; 1st app. Miss Feeny 28.00 85.00 340.00
3-5 26.00 78.00 310.00
6-10: 7-1st app. Annie; Xmas-c 20.00 60.00 240.00
11-20: 18-X-Mas-c. 19-1st app. Wilbur. 20-1st app. Mr. McNabbem 17.00 50.00 200.00
21-30: 26-r/F.C. 110. 30-Xmas-c 13.00 40.00 160.00
31-38,40: 35-1st Mumday story 11.70 35.00 140.00
39-Intro. Witch Hazel in "That Awful Witch Hazel" 12.50 37.50 150.00
41-60: 42-Xmas-c. 45-2nd Witch Hazel app. 49-Gives Stanley & others credit 11.00 33.00 130.00
61-80: 63-1st app. Chubby (Tubby's cousin). 68-1st app. Prof. Cleff. 78-Xmas-c. 80-Intro. Little Itch (2/55) 7.50 22.50 90.00
81-99: 90-Xmas-c 5.85 17.50 70.00
100 6.30 19.00 75.00
101-130: 123-1st app. Fifi 5.00 15.00 60.00
131-164: 135-Last Stanley-p 4.55 13.65 50.00
165-Giant; ...in Paris ('62) 11.30 34.00 135.00
166-Giant; ...Christmas Diary (1962 - '63) 11.30 34.00 135.00
167-169 3.80 11.40 42.00
170,172,175,176,178-196,198-200-Stanley-r. 182-1st app. Little Scarecrow Boy 2.30 7.00 20.00
171,173,174,177,197 1.85 5.50 15.00
201,203,206-Last issue to carry Marge's name 1.50 4.50 12.00
202,204,205-Stanley-r 1.85 5.50 15.00
...& Tubby in Japan (12¢)(5-7/62) 01476-207 6.30 19.00 75.00
...Summer Camp 1(8/67-G.K.-Giant) '57-58-r 4.55 13.65 50.00
...Trick 'N' Treat 1(12¢)(12/62-Gold Key) 5.00 15.00 60.00
NOTE: *See Dell Giant Comics #23, 29, 36, 42, 50, & Dell Giants for annuals. All Giants not by Stanley from L.L. on Vacation (7/54) on. Irving Tripp a-#1-on. Christmas c-7, 18, 30, 42, 78, 90, 126, 166, 250. Summer Camp issues #173, 177, 181, 189, 197, 201, 206.*

MARGE'S LITTLE LULU (See Golden Comics Digest #19, 23, 27, 29, 33, 36, 40, 43, 46, & March of Comics #251, 267, 275, 293, 307, 323, 335, 349, 355, 369, 385, 406, 417, 427, 439, 456, 468, 475, 488)

MARGE'S TUBBY (Little Lulu)(See Dell Giants)
Dell Publishing Co./Gold Key: No. 381, Aug, 1952 - No. 49, Dec-Feb, 1961-62

Four Color 381(#1)-Stanley script; Irving Tripp-a 20.00 60.00 240.00
Four Color 430,444-Stanley-a 11.30 34.00 135.00
Four Color 461 (4/53)-1st Tubby & Men From Mars story; Stanley-a 10.00 30.00 120.00
5 (7-9/53)-Stanley-a 8.00 24.00 95.00
6-10 6.30 19.00 75.00
11-20 4.55 13.65 50.00
21-30 3.20 9.60 35.00
31-49 3.00 9.00 32.00
...& the Little Men From Mars No. 30020-410(10/64-G.K.)-25¢, 68 pgs. 7.00 21.00 85.00
NOTE: ***John Stanley** did all storyboards & scripts through at least #35 (1959). **Lloyd White** did all art except F.C. 381, 430, 444, 461 & #5.*

MARGIE (See My Little...)

MARGIE (TV)
Dell Publ. Co.: No. 1307, Mar-May, 1962 - No. 2, July-Sept, 1962 (Photo-c)

Four Color 1307(#1) 5.00 15.00 60.00
2 4.10 12.30 45.00

MARGIE COMICS (Formerly Comedy Comics; Reno Browne #50 on)
(Also see Cindy Comics & Teen Comics)
Marvel Comics (ACI): No. 35, Winter, 1946-47 - No. 49, Dec, 1949

35 14.00 41.00 110.00
36-38,42,45,47-49 8.65 26.00 60.00
39,41,43(2),44,46-Kurtzman's "Hey Look" 10.00 30.00 75.00
40-Three "Hey Looks", three "Giggles 'n' Grins" by Kurtzman 11.00 33.00 90.00

MARINES (See Tell It to the...)

MARINES ATTACK
Charlton Comics: Aug, 1964 - No. 9, Feb-Mar, 1966

1-Glanzman-a begins 3.00 9.00 30.00
2-9 2.00 6.00 18.00

MARINES AT WAR (Formerly Tales of the Marines #4)
Atlas Comics (OPI): No. 5, Apr, 1957 - No. 7, Aug, 1957

5-7 7.15 21.50 50.00
NOTE: ***Colan** a-5. **Drucker** a-5. **Everett** a-5. **Maneely** a-5. **Orlando** a-7. **Severin** c-5.*

MARINES IN ACTION
Atlas News Co.: June, 1955 - No. 14, Sept, 1957

1-Rock Murdock, Boot Camp Brady begin 10.00 30.00 75.00
2-14 7.15 21.50 50.00
NOTE: ***Berg** a-2, 8, 9, 11, 14. **Heath** c-2, 9. **Maneely** c-1. **Severin** a-4; c-7-11, 14.*

MARINES IN BATTLE
Atlas Comics (ACI No. 1-12/WPI No. 13-25): Aug, 1954 - No. 25, Sept, 1958

1-Heath-c; Iron Mike McGraw by Heath; history of U.S. Marine Corps. begins 19.00 56.00 150.00
2-Heath-c 10.00 30.00 75.00
3-6,8-10: 4-Last precode (2/55) 7.85 23.50 55.00
7-Kubert/Moskowitz-a (6 pgs.) 8.65 26.00 60.00
11-16,18-21,24 7.15 21.50 50.00
17-Williamson-a (3 pgs.) 10.00 30.00 70.00
22,25-Torres-a 7.85 23.50 55.00
23-Crandall-a; Mark Murdock app. 8.65 26.00 60.00
NOTE: ***Berg** a-22. **G. Colan** a-22, 23. **Drucker** a-6. **Everett** a-4, 15; c-21. **Heath** c-1, 2, 4. **Maneely** c-23, 24. **Orlando** a-14. **Pakula** a-6, 23. **Powell** a-16. **Severin** a-22; c-12. **Sinnott** a-23. **Tuska** a-15.*

MARINE WAR HEROES (Charlton Premiere #19 on)
Charlton Comics: Jan, 1964 - No. 18, Mar, 1967

1-Montes/Bache-c/a 3.00 9.00 30.00
2-18: 14,18-Montes/Bache-a 2.00 6.00 18.00

MARK, THE (Also see Mayhem)
Dark Horse Comics: Dec, 1993 - No. 4, Mar, 1994 ($2.50, limited series)

1-4 2.50

MARK HAZZARD: MERC
Marvel Comics Group: Nov, 1986 - No. 12, Oct, 1987 (75¢)

1-12: Morrow-a, Annual 1 (11/87, $1.25) 2.00

MARK OF ZORRO (See Zorro, Four Color #228)

MARK 1 COMICS (Also see Shaloman)
Mark 1 Comics: Apr, 1988 - No. 3, Mar, 1989 ($1.50)

1-3: Early Shaloman app. 2-Origin 2.00

MARKSMAN, THE (Also see Champions)
Hero Comics: Jan, 1988 - No. 5, 1988 ($1.95)

1-5: 1-Rose begins. 1-3-Origin The Marksman 2.00
Annual 1 ('88, $2.75, 52pgs)-Champions app. 2.75

MARK TRAIL
Standard Magazines (Hall Syndicate)/Fawcett Publ. No. 5: Oct, 1955; No. 5, Summer, 1959

1(1955)-Sunday strip-r 6.00 18.00 42.00
5(1959) 4.15 12.50 25.00
...Adventure Book of Nature 1 (Summer, 1958, 25¢, Pines)-100 pg. Giant;

Marmaduke Mouse #6 © QUA

Martha Washington Goes To War #5 © Frank Miller & Dave Gibbons

Martian Manhunter #9 © DC

GD2.0 FN6.0 NM9.4

Special Camp Issue; contains 78 Sunday strip-r 10.00 30.00 70.00

MARMADUKE MONK
I. W. Enterprises/Super Comics: No date; 1963 (10¢)

I.W. Reprint 1 (nd) 1.50 4.50 12.00
Super Reprint 14 (1963)-r/Monkeyshines Comics #? 1.50 4.50 12.00

MARMADUKE MOUSE
Quality Comics Group (Arnold Publ.): Spring, 1946 - No. 65, Dec, 1956 (Early issues: 52 pgs.)

1-Funny animal 16.00 49.00 130.00
2 9.30 28.00 65.00
3-10 7.00 21.00 48.00
11-30 5.00 15.00 35.00
31-65: Later issues are 36 pgs. 4.65 14.00 28.00
Super Reprint #14(1963) 1.75 5.25 14.00

MARQUIS, THE: DANSE MACABRE
Oni Press: May, 2000 - No. 5 ($2.95, B&W, limited series)

1-3-Guy Davis-s/a. 1-Wagner-c. 2-Mignola-c. 3-Vess-c 3.00

MARRIAGE OF HERCULES AND XENA, THE
Topps Comics: July, 1998 ($2.95, one-shot)

1-Photo-c; Lopresti-a; Alex Ross pin-up, 1-Alex Ross painted-c 3.00
1-Gold foil logo-c 5.00

MARRIED ... WITH CHILDREN (TV)(Based on Fox TV show)
Now Comics: June, 1990 - No. 7, Feb, 1991(12/90 inside) ($1.75)
V2#1, Sept, 1991 - No. 12, 1992 ($1.95)

1-7: 2-Photo-c, 1,2-2nd printing, V2#1-12: 1,4,5,9-Photo-c 2.00
...Buck's Tale (6/94, $1.95) 2.00
...1994 Annual nn (2/94, $2.50, 52 pgs.)-Flip book format 2.50
Special 1 (7/92, $1.95)-Kelly Bundy photo-c/poster 2.00

MARRIED ... WITH CHILDREN: KELLY BUNDY
Now Comics: Aug, 1992 - No. 3, Oct, 1992 ($1.95, limited series)

1-3: Kelly Bundy photo-c & poster in each 2.00

MARRIED ... WITH CHILDREN: QUANTUM QUARTET
Now Comics: Oct, 1993 - No. 4, 1994, ($1.95, limited series)

1-4: Fantastic Four parody 2.00

MARRIED ... WITH CHILDREN: 2099
Now Comics: June, 1993 - No. 3, Aug, 1993 ($1.95, limited series)

1-3 2.00

MARS
First Comics: Jan, 1984 - No. 12, Jan, 1985 ($1.00, Mando paper)

nn: 1-12: Marc Hempel & Mark Wheatley story & art. 2-The Black Flame begins. 10-Dynamo Joe begins 2.00

MARS & BEYOND (Disney, TV)
Dell Publishing Co.: No. 866, Dec, 1957

Four Color 866-A Science feat. from Tomorrowland 8.35 25.00 100.00

MARS ATTACKS
Topps Comics: May, 1994 - No. 5, Sept, 1994 ($2.95, limited series)

1-5-Giffen story; flip books 4.00
Special Edition 1.50 4.50 12.00
Trade paperback (12/94, $12.95)-r/limited series plus new 8 pg. story 13.00

MARS ATTACKS
Topps Comics: V2#1, 8/95 - V2#3, 10/95; V2#4, 1/96 - No. 7, 5/96($2.95, bi-monthly #6 on)

V2#1-7: 1-Counterstrike storyline begins. 4-(1/96). 5-(1/96). 5,7-Brereton-c. 6-(3/96)-Simonson-c. 7-Story leads into Baseball Special #1 3.00
Baseball Special 1 (6/96, $2.95)-Bisley-c. 3.00

MARS ATTACKS HIGH SCHOOL
Topps Comics: May, 1997 - No. 2, Sept, 1997 ($2.95, B&W, limited series)

1,2-Stelfreeze-c 3.00

MARS ATTACKS IMAGE
Topps Comics: Dec, 1996 - No. 4, Mar, 1997 ($2.50, limited series)

1-4-Giffen-s/Smith/Sienkiewicz-a 3.00

MARS ATTACKS THE SAVAGE DRAGON
Topps Comics: Dec, 1996 - No. 4, Mar, 1997 ($2.95, limited series)

1-4: 1-w/bound-in card 3.00

MARSHAL BLUEBERRY (See Blueberry)
Marvel Comics (Epic Comics): 1991 (14.95, graphic novel)

1-Moebius-a 15.00

MARSHAL LAW (Also see Crime And Punishment: Marshall Law...)
Marvel Comics (Epic Comics): Oct, 1987 - No. 6, May, 1989 ($1.95, mature)

1-6 2.00

M.A.R.S. PATROL TOTAL WAR (Formerly Total War #1,2)
Gold Key: No. 3, Sept, 1966 - No. 10, Aug, 1969 (All-Painted-c except #7)

3-Wood-a; aliens invade USA 5.00 15.00 60.00
4-10 3.00 9.00 30.00

MARTHA WASHINGTON (Also see Dark Horse Presents Fifth Anniversary Special, Dark Horse Presents #100-4, Give Me Liberty, Happy Birthday Martha Washington & San Diego Comicon Comics #2)

MARTHA WASHINGTON GOES TO WAR
Dark Horse Comics (Legend): May, 1994 - No. 5, Sep, 1994 ($2.95, lim. series)

1-5-Miller scripts; Gibbons-c/a 3.00
TPB ($17.95) r/#1-5 18.00

MARTHA WASHINGTON SAVES THE WORLD
Dark Horse Comics: Dec, 1997 - No. 3, Feb, 1998 ($2.95/$3.95, lim. series)

1,2-Miller scripts; Gibbons-c/a in all 3.00
3-($3.95) 4.00

MARTHA WASHINGTON STRANDED IN SPACE
Dark Horse Comics (Legend): Nov, 1995 ($2.95, one-shot)

nn-Miller-s/Gibbons-a; Big Guy app. 3.00

MARTHA WAYNE (See The Story of...)

MARTIAN MANHUNTER (See Detective Comics & Showcase '95 #9)
DC Comics: May, 1988 - No. 4, Aug,. 1988 ($1.25, limited series)

1-4: 1,4-Batman app. 2-Batman cameo 2.00
Special 1-(1996, $3.50) 3.50

MARTIAN MANHUNTER (See JLA)
DC Comics: No. 0, Oct, 1998 - Present ($1.99)

0-(10/98) Origin retold; Ostrander-s/Mandrake-c/a 3.00
1-29: 1-(12/98). 6-9-JLA app. 18,19-JSA app. 24-Mahnke-a 2.50
#1,000,000 (11/98) 853rd Century x-over 2.50
Annual 1,2 (1998,1999; $2.95) 1-Ghosts; Wrightson-c. 2-JLApe 3.00

MARTIAN MANHUNTER: AMERICAN SECRETS
DC Comics: 1992 - Book Three, 1992 ($4.95, limited series, prestige format)

1-3: Barreto-a 5.00

MARTIN KANE (William Gargan as... Private Eye)(Stage/Screen/Radio/TV)
Fox Features Syndicate (Hero Books): No. 4, June, 1950 - No. 2, Aug, 1950 (Formerly My Secret Affair)

4(#1)-True crime stories; Wood-c/a(2); used in **SOTI**, pg. 160; photo back-c 30.00 90.00 240.00
2-Wood/Orlando story, 5 pgs; Wood-a(2) 23.00 69.00 185.00

MARTIN MYSTERY
Dark Horse (Bonelli Comics): Mar, 1999 - No. 6, Aug, 1999 ($4.95, B&W, digest size)

1-6-Reprints Italian series in English; Gibbons-c on #1-3 5.00

MARTY MOUSE
I. W. Enterprises: No date (1958?) (10¢)

1-Reprint 1.50 4.50 12.00

MARVEL ACTION HOUR FEATURING IRON MAN (TV cartoon)
Marvel Comics: Nov, 1994 - No. 8, June, 1995 ($1.50/$2.95)

1-8: Based on cartoon series 2.00
1 ($2.95)-Polybagged w/16 pg Marvel Action Hour Preview & acetate print 3.00

Marvel Boy #1 © MAR

Marvel Chillers #3 © MAR

Marvel Comics Presents #39 © MAR

MARVEL ACTION HOUR FEATURING THE FANTASTIC FOUR (TV cartoon)
Marvel Comics: Nov, 1994 - No. 8, June, 1995 ($1.50/$2.95)

1-8: Based on cartoon series 2.00
1-($2.95)-Polybagged w/ 16 pg. Marvel Action Hour Preview & acetate print 3.00

MARVEL ACTION UNIVERSE (TV cartoon)
Marvel Comics: Jan, 1989 ($1.00, one-shot)

1-r/Spider-Man And His Amazing Friends 2.00

MARVEL ADVENTURES
Marvel Comics: Apr, 1997 - No. 18, Sept, 1998 ($1.50)

1-18-"Animated style": 1,4,7-Hulk-c/app. 2,11-Spider-Man. 3,8,15-X-Men. 5-Spider-Man & X-Men. 6-Spider-Man & Human Torch. 9,12-Fantastic Four. 10,16-Silver Surfer. 13-Spider-Man & Silver Surfer. 14-Hulk & Dr. Strange 18-Capt. America 2.00

MARVEL ADVENTURES STARRING DAREDEVIL (...Adventure #3 on)
Marvel Comics Group: Dec, 1975 - No. 6, Oct, 1976

1 1.25 3.75 10.00
2-6-r/Daredevil #22-27 by Colan. 3-5-(25¢-c) 2.40 6.00
3-5-(30¢-c variants, limited distribution)(4,6,8/76) 1.10 3.30 9.00

MARVEL AND DC PRESENT FEATURING THE UNCANNY X-MEN AND THE NEW TEEN TITANS
Marvel Comics/DC Comics: 1982 ($2.00, 68 pgs., one-shot, Baxter paper)

1-3rd app. Deathstroke the Terminator; Darkseid app.; Simonson/Austin-c/a 1.85 5.50 15.00

MARVEL BOY (Astonishing #3 on; see Marvel Super Action #4)
Marvel Comics (MPC): Dec, 1950 - No. 2, Feb, 1951

1-Origin Marvel Boy by Russ Heath 103.00 308.00 975.00
2-Everett-a 74.00 221.00 700.00

MARVEL BOY (Marvel Knights)
Marvel Comics: Aug, 2000 - No. 6, Mar, 2001 ($2.99, limited series)

1-Intro. Marvel Boy; Morrison-s/J.G. Jones-c/a 3.50
1-DF Variant-c 5.00
2-6 3.00

MARVEL CHILLERS (Also see Giant-Size Chillers)
Marvel Comics Group: Oct, 1975 - No. 7, Oct, 1976 (All 25¢ issues)

1-Intro. Modred the Mystic, ends #2; Kane-c(p) 1.25 3.75 10.00
2,4,5,7: 4-Kraven app. 5,6-Red Wolf app. 7-Kirby-c; Tuska-p 2.40 6.00
3-Tigra, the Were-Woman begins (origin), ends #7 (see Giant-Size Creatures #1). Chaykin/Wrightson-c. 1.85 5.50 15.00
4-6-(30¢-c variants, limited distribution)(4-8/76) 1.10 3.30 9.00
6-Byrne-a(p); Buckler-c(p) 1.00 3.00 8.00

NOTE: ***Bolle** a-1. **Buckler** c-2. **Kirby** c-7.*

MARVEL CLASSICS COMICS SERIES FEATURING... (Also see Pendulum Illustrated Classics)
Marvel Comics Group: 1976 - No. 36, Dec, 1978 (52 pgs., no ads)

1-Dr. Jekyll and Mr. Hyde 2.00 6.00 16.00
2-10,28: 28-1st Golden-c/a; Pit and the Pendulum 1.50 4.50 12.00
11-27,29-36 1.10 3.30 9.00

NOTE: ***Adkins** c-1i, 4i, 12i. **Alcala** a-34i; c-34. **Bolle** a-35. **Buscema** c-17p, 19p, 26p. **Golden** c/a-28. **Gil Kane** c-1-16p, 21p, 22p, 24p, 32p. **Nebres** a-5; c-24i. **Nino** a-2, 8, 12. **Redondo** a-1, 9. No. 1-12 were reprinted from Pendulum Illustrated Classics.*

MARVEL COLLECTIBLE CLASSICS: AVENGERS
Marvel Comics: 1998 ($10.00, reprints with chromium wraparound-c)

1-Reprints Avengers Vol.3, #1; Perez-c 10.00

MARVEL COLLECTIBLE CLASSICS: SPIDER-MAN
Marvel Comics: 1998 ($10.00, reprints with chromium wraparound-c)

1-Reprints Amazing Spider-Man #300; McFarlane-c 10.00
2-Reprints Spider-Man #1; McFarlane-c 10.00

MARVEL COLLECTIBLE CLASSICS: X-MEN
Marvel Comics: 1998 ($10.00, reprints with chromium wraparound-c)

1-6: 1-Reprints (Uncanny) X-Men #1 & 2; Adam Kubert-c. 2-Reprints Uncanny X-Men #141 & 142; Byrne-c. 3-Reprints (Uncanny) X-Men #137; Larroca-c. 4-Reprints X-Men #25; Andy Kubert-c. 5-Reprints Giant Size X-Men #1; Gary Frank-c. 6-Reprints X-Men V2#1; Ramos-c 10.00

MARVEL COLLECTOR'S EDITION
Marvel Comics: 1992 (Ordered thru mail with Charleston Chew candy wrapper)

1-Flip-book format; Spider-Man, Silver Surfer, Wolverine (by Sam Kieth), & Ghost Rider stories; Wolverine back-c by Kieth 3.00

MARVEL COLLECTORS' ITEM CLASSICS (Marvel's Greatest #23 on)
Marvel Comics Group(ATF): Feb, 1965 - No. 22, Aug, 1969 (25¢, 68 pgs.)

1-Fantastic Four, Spider-Man, Thor, Hulk, Iron Man-r begin 8.15 24.50 90.00
2 (4/66) 4.10 12.30 45.00
3,4 3.20 9.60 35.00
5-10 2.80 8.40 28.00
11-22: 22-r/The Man in the Ant Hill/TTA #27 2.30 7.00 20.00

NOTE: *All reprints; **Ditko, Kirby** art in all.*

MARVEL COMICS (Marvel Mystery Comics #2 on)
Timely Comics (Funnies, Inc.): Oct, Nov, 1939

NOTE: The first issue was originally dated October 1939. Most copies have a black circle stamped over the date (on cover and inside) with "November" printed over it. However, some copies do not have the November overprint and could have a higher value. Most No. 1's have printing defects, i.e., tilted pages which caused trimming into the panels usually on right side and bottom. Covers exist with and without gloss finish.

GD2.0 FN6.0 VF8.0 NM9.4

1-Origin Sub-Mariner by Bill Everett(1st newsstand app.); 1st 8 pgs. were produced for Motion Picture Funnies Weekly #1 which was probably not distributed outside of advance copies; intro Human Torch by Carl Burgos, Kazar the Great (1st Tarzan clone), & Jungle Terror(only app.); intro. The Angel by Gustavson, The Masked Raider & his horse Lightning (ends #12); cover by sci/fi pulp illustrator Frank R. Paul 14,000.00 42,000.00 91,000.00 175,000.00

MARVEL COMICS PRESENTS
Marvel Comics (Midnight Sons imprint #143 on): Early Sept, 1988 - No. 175, Feb, 1995 ($1.25/$1.50/$1.75, bi-weekly)

GD2.0 FN6.0 NM9.4

1-Wolverine by Buscema in #1-10 2.40 6.00
2-5 4.00
6-10: 6-Sub-Mariner app. 10-Colossus begins 3.00
11-47,51-71: 17-Cyclops begins. 19-1st app. Damage Control. 24-Havok begins. 25-Origin/1st app. Nth Man. 26-Hulk begins by Rogers. 29-Quasar app. 31-Excalibur begins by Austin (i). 32-McFarlane-a(p). 37-Devil-Slayer app. 33-Capt. America; Jim Lee-a. 38-Wolverine begins by Buscema; Hulk app. 39-Spider-Man app. 46-Liefeld Wolverine-c. 51-53-Wolverine by Rob Liefeld. 54-61-Wolverine/Hulk story: 54-Werewolf by Night begins; The Shroud by Ditko. 58-Iron Man by Ditko. 59-Punisher. 62-Deathlok & Wolverine stories 63-Wolverine. 64-71-Wolverine/Ghost Rider 8-part story. 70-Liefeld Ghost Rider/Wolverine-c 2.50
48-50-Wolverine & Spider-Man team-up by Erik Larsen-c/a. 48-Wasp app. 49, 50-Savage Dragon prototype app. by Larsen. 50-Silver Surfer. 50-53-Comet Man; Bill Mumy scripts 4.00
72-Begin13-part Weapon-X story (Wolverine origin) by B. Windsor-Smith (prologue) 5.00
73-Weapon-X part 1; Black Knight, Sub-Mariner 4.00
74-84: 74-Weapon-X part 2; Black Knight, Sub-Mariner. 76-Death's Head story. 77-Mr. Fantastic story. 78-Iron Man by Steacy. 80,81-Capt. America by Ditko/Austin. 81-Daredevil by Rogers/Williamson. 82-Power Man. 83-Human Torch by Ditko(a&scripts); $1.00-c direct, $1.25 newsstand. 84-Last Weapon-X(24 pg. conclusion) 3.00
85-Begin 8-part Wolverine story by Sam Kieth (c/a); 1st Kieth-a on Wolverine; begin 8-part Beast story by Jae Lee(p) with Liefeld part pencils #85,86; 1st Jae Lee-a (assisted w/Liefeld, 1991) 4.00
86-90: 86-89-Wolverine, Beast stories continue. 90-Begin 8-part Ghost Rider & Cable story, ends #97; begin flip book format w/two-c 3.00
91-175: 93-Begin 6-part Wolverine story, ends #98. 98-Begin 2-part Ghost Rider story. 99-Spider-Man story. 101-Begin 6-part Ghost Rider/Dr. Strange story & begin 8-part Wolverine/Nightcrawler story by Colan/Williamson; Punisher story. 107-Begin 6-part Ghost Rider/Werewolf by Night story. 112-Demogoblin story by Colan/Williamson; Pip the Troll story w/Starlin scripts & Gamora cameo. 113-Begin 6-part Giant-Man & begin 6-part Ghost Rider/Iron Fist sto

Marvel Double Feature #4 © MAR

Marvel Family #3 © FAW

Marvel Fanfare #48 © MAR

ries. 100-Full-length Ghost Rider/Wolverine story by Sam Keith w/Tim Vigil assists; anniversary issue, non flip-book. 108-Begin 4 part Thanos story; Starlin scripts. 109-Begin 8 part Wolverine/Typhoid Mary story. 111-Iron Fist. 117-Preview of Ravage 2099 (1st app.); begin 6 part Wolverine/Venom story w/Kieth-a. 118-Preview of Doom 2099 (1st app.). 119-Begin Ghost Rider/ Cloak & Dagger story by Colan. 120,136,138-Spider-Man. 123-Begin 8-part Ghost Rider/Typhoid Mary story; begin 4-part She Hulk story; begin 8-part Wolverine/Lynx story. 125-Begin 6-part Iron Fist story. 129-Jae Lee back-c. 130-Begin 6-part Ghost Rider/ Cage story. 131-Begin 6-part Ghost Rider/ Cage story. 132-Begin 5-part Wolverine story. 133-136-Iron Fist vs. Sabretooth. 136-Daredevil. 137-Begin 6-part Wolverine story & 6-part Ghost Rider story. 147-Begin 2-part Vengeance-c/story w/new Ghost Rider. 149-Vengeance-c/story w/new Ghost Rider. 150-Silver ink-c; begin 2-part Bloody Mary story w/Typhoid Mary,Wolverine, Daredevil, new Ghost Rider; intro Steel Raven. 152-Begin 4-part Wolverine, 4-part War Machine, 4-part Vengeance, 3-part Moon Knight stories; same date as War Machine #1. 143-146: Siege of Darkness parts 3,6,11,14; all have spot-varnished-c. 143-Ghost Rider/ Scarlet Witch; intro new Werewolf. 144-Begin 2-part Morbius story. 145-Begin 2-part Nightstalkers story. 153-155-Bound-in Spider-Man trading card sheet 2.00

...Colossus: God's Country (1994, $6.95) r/#10-17 1.00 2.80 7.00

NOTE: ***Austin*** *a-31-37i; c(i)-48, 50, 99, 122.* ***Buscema*** *a-1-10, 38-47; c-6.* ***Byrne*** *a-79; c-71.* ***Colan*** *a(p)-36, 37.* ***Colan/Williamson*** *a-101-108.* ***Ditko*** *a-7p, 10, 56p, 58, 80, 81, 83.* ***Guice*** *a-62.* ***Sam Kieth*** *a-85-92, 117-122; c-85-98, 99p, 100-108, 117, 118, 120-122; back c-109-113, 117.* ***Jae Lee*** *c-129(back).* ***Liefeld*** *a-51, 52, 53p(2), 85p; c-46, 70.* ***McFarlane*** *c-32.* ***Mooney*** *a-73.* ***Rogers*** *a-26, 38, 46i, 81p.* ***Russell*** *a-10-14,16,17i; c-4,19, 30,31i.* ***Saltares*** *a-8p(early), 38-45p.* ***Simonson*** *c-1.* ***B. Smith*** *a-72-84; c-72-84.* ***P. Smith*** *c-34.* ***Sparling*** *a-33.* ***Starlin*** *a-89i.* ***Staton*** *a-74.* ***Steacy*** *a-78.* ***Sutton*** *a-101-105.* ***Williamson*** *c-62i. Two Gun Kid by* ***Gil Kane*** *in #116, 122.*

MARVEL COMICS SUPER SPECIAL, A (Marvel Super Special #5 on)
Marvel Comics: Sept, 1977 - No. 41(?), Nov, 1986 (nn 7) ($1.50, magazine)

1-Kiss, 40 pgs. comics plus photos & features; Simonson-a(p); also see Howard the Duck #12; ink contains real KISS blood; Dr. Doom, Spider-Man, Avengers, Fantastic Four, Mephisto app. 11.00 33.00 120.00
2-Conan (1978) 1.75 5.25 14.00
3-Close Encounters of the Third Kind (1978); Simonson-a 1.25 3.75 10.00
4-The Beatles Story (1978)-Perez/Janson-a; has photos & articles 3.20 9.60 35.00
5-Kiss (1978)-Includes poster 11.00 33.00 120.00
6-Jaws II (1978) 1.25 3.75 10.00
7-Sgt. Pepper; Beatles movie adaptation; withdrawn from U.S. distribution
8-Battlestar Galactica; tabloid size ($1.50, 1978); adapts TV show 2.00 6.00 18.00
8-Modern-r of tabloid size; scarce 3.00 9.00 32.00
8-Battlestar Galactica; publ. in regular magazine format; low distribution ($1.50, 8-1/2x11") 2.00 6.00 18.00
9-Conan 1.25 3.75 10.00
10-Star-Lord 1.00 3.00 8.00
11-13-Weirdworld begins #11; 25 copy special press run of each with gold seal and signed by artists (Proof quality), Spring-June, 1979 8.15 24.50 90.00
11-15: 11-13-Weirdworld (regular issues): 11-Fold-out centerfold. 14-Miller-c(p); adapts movie "Meteor." 15-Star Trek with photos & pin-ups ($1.50-c) 2.40 6.00
15-With $2.00 price (scarce); the price was changed at tail end of a 200,000 press run 1.00 3.00 8.00
16-Empire Strikes Back adaption; Williamson-a 1.00 3.00 8.00
17-20 (Movie adaptations):17-Xanadu. 18-Raiders of the Lost Ark. 19-For Your Eyes Only (James Bond). 20-Dragonslayer 5.00
21-26,28-30 (Movie adaptations): 21-Conan. 22-Blade Runner; Williamson-a; Steranko-c. 23-Annie. 24-The Dark Crystal. 25-Rock and Rule-w/photos; artwork is from movie. 26-Octopussy (James Bond). 28-Krull; photo-c. 29-Tarzan of the Apes (Greystoke movie). 30-Indiana Jones and the Temple of Doom 2.40 6.00
27,31-41: 27-Return of the Jedi. 31-The Last Star Fighter. 32-The Muppets Take Manhattan. 33-Buckaroo Banzai. 34-Sheena. 35-Conan The Destroyer. 36-Dune. 37-2010. 38-Red Sonja. 39-Santa Claus:The Movie. 40-Labyrinth. 41-Howard The Duck 1.00 2.80 7.00

NOTE: ***J. Buscema*** *a-1, 2, 9, 11-13, 18p, 21, 35, 40; c-11(part), 12.* ***Chaykin*** *a-9, 19p; c-18, 19.* ***Colan*** *a(p)-6, 10, 14.* ***Morrow*** *a-34; c-1i, 34.* ***Nebres*** *a-11.* ***Spiegle*** *a-29.* ***Stevens*** *a-27.* ***Williamson*** *a-27. #22-28 contain photos from movies.*

MARVEL DOUBLE FEATURE
Marvel Comics Group: Dec, 1973 - No. 21, Mar, 1977

1-Capt. America, Iron Man-r/T.O.S. begin 1.50 4.50 12.00
2-10: 3-Last 20¢ issue 1.00 2.80 7.00
11-17,20,21:17-Story-r/Iron Man & Sub-Mariner #1; last 25¢ issue 5.00
15-17-(30¢-c variants, limited distribution)(4,6,8/76) 2.40 6.00
18,19-Colan/Craig-r from Iron Man #1 in both 2.40 6.00

NOTE: ***Colan*** *r-1-19p.* ***Craig*** *r-17-19i.* ***G. Kane*** *r-15p; c-15p.* ***Kirby*** *r-1-16p, 20, 21; c-17-20.*

MARVEL FAMILY (Also see Captain Marvel Adventures No. 18)
Fawcett Publications: Dec, 1945 - No. 89, Jan, 1954

1-Origin Captain Marvel, Captain Marvel Jr., Mary Marvel, & Uncle Marvel retold; origin/1st app. Black Adam 158.00 474.00 1500.00
2-The 3 Lt. Marvels & Uncle Marvel app. 74.00 221.00 700.00
3 53.00 158.00 475.00
4,5 42.00 125.00 375.00
6-10: 7-Shazam app. 38.00 113.00 300.00
11-20 28.00 84.00 225.00
21-30 23.00 68.00 180.00
31-40 20.00 60.00 160.00
41-46,48-50 15.00 45.00 120.00
47-Flying Saucer-c/story (5/50) 21.00 62.00 165.00
51-76,79,80,82-89: 79-Horror satire-c 14.00 41.00 110.00
77-Communist Threat-c 23.00 68.00 180.00
78,81-Used in **POP**, pg. 92,93. 15.00 45.00 120.00

MARVEL FANFARE (1st Series)
Marvel Comics Group: March, 1982 - No. 60, Jan, 1992 ($1.25/$2.25, slick paper, direct sales)

1-Spider-Man/Angel team-up; 1st Paul Smith-a (1st full story; see King Conan #7); Daredevil app. 2.40 6.00
2-Spider-Man, Ka-Zar, The Angel. F.F. origin retold 5.00
3,4-X-Men & Ka-Zar. 4-Deathlok, Spidey app. 4.00
5-14,16-23,25-32,34-44,46-50: 5-Dr. Strange, Capt. America. 6-Spider-Man, Scarlet Witch. 7-Incredible Hulk; D.D. back-up(also 15). 8-Dr. Strange; Wolf Boy begins. 9-Man-Thing. 10-13-Black Widow. 14-The Vision. 16,17-Skywolf. 16-Sub-Mariner back-up. 17-Hulk back-up. 18-Capt. America by Miller. 19-Cloak and Dagger. 20-Thing/Dr. Strange. 21-Thing/Dr. Strange /Hulk. 22,23-Iron Man vs. Dr. Octopus. 25,26-Weirdworld. 27-Daredevil/Spider-Man. 28-Alpha Flight. 29-Hulk. 30-Moon Knight. 31,32-Captain America. 34-37-Warriors Three. 38-Moon Knight/Dazzler. 39-Moon Knight/Hawkeye. 40-Angel/Rogue & Storm. 41-Dr. Strange. 42-Spider-Man. 43-Sub-Mariner/ Human Torch. 44-Iron Man vs. Dr. Doom by Ken Steacy. 46-Fantastic Four. 47-Hulk. 48-She-Hulk/Vision. 49-Dr. Strange/Nick Fury. 50-X-Factor 2.50
15,24,33,45: 15-The Thing by Barry Smith, c/a. 24-Weirdworld; Wolverine back-up. 33-X-Men, Wolverine app.; Punisher pin-up. 45-All pin-up issue by Steacy, Art Adams & others 4.00
51-($2.95, 52 pgs.)-Silver Surfer; Fantastic Four & Capt. Marvel app.; 51,52-Colan/Williamson back-up (Dr. Strange) 3.00
52,53,56-60: 52,53-Black Knight; 53-Iron Man back up. 56-59-Shanna the She-Devil. 58-Vision & Scarlet Witch back-up. 60-Black Panther/Rogue/Daredevil stories 2.50
54,55-Wolverine back-ups. 54-Black Knight. 55-Power Pack 4.00

NOTE: ***Art Adams*** *c-13.* ***Austin*** *a-1i, 4i, 33i, 38i; c-8i, 33i.* ***Buscema*** *a-51p.* ***Byrne*** *a-1p, 29, 48; c-29.* ***Chiodo*** *painted c-56-59.* ***Colan*** *a-51p.* ***Cowan/Simonson*** *c/a-60.* ***Golden*** *a-1, 2, 4p, 47; c-1, 2, 47.* ***Infantino*** *c/a(p)-8.* ***Gil Kane*** *a-8-11p.* ***Miller*** *a-18; c-1(Back-c), 18.* ***Perez*** *a-10, 11p, 12, 13p; c-10-13p.* ***Rogers*** *a-5p; c-5p.* ***Russell*** *a-5i, 6i, 8-11i, 43i; c-5i, 6.* ***Paul Smith*** *a-1p, 4p, 32, 60; c-4p. Staton c/a-50(p).* ***Williamson*** *a-30i, 51i.*

MARVEL FANFARE (2nd Series)
Marvel Comics: Sept, 1996 - No. 6, Feb, 1997 (99¢)

1-6: 1-Capt. America & The Falcon-c/story; Deathlok app. 2-Wolverine & Hulk-c/app. 3-Ghost Rider & Spider-Man-c/app. 5-Longshot-c/app. 6-Sabretooth, Power Man, & Iron Fist-c/app 2.00

MARVEL FEATURE (See Marvel Two-In-One)
Marvel Comics Group: Dec, 1971 - No. 12, Nov, 1973 (1,2: 25¢, 52 pg. giants) (#1-3: quarterly)

1-Origin/1st app. The Defenders (Sub-Mariner, Hulk & Dr. Strange); see

Marvel Feature (2nd series) #3 © MAR

Marvel Graphic Novel - Black Widow The Coldest War © MAR

Marvel Knights #2 © MAR

GD2.0 FN6.0 NM9.4

Sub-Mariner #34,35 for prequel; Dr. Strange solo story (predates D.S. #1) plus 1950s Sub-Mariner-r; Neal Adams-c 12.75 38.00 140.00
2-2nd app. Defenders; 1950s Sub-Mariner-r 5.90 17.75 65.00
3-Defenders ends 4.10 12.30 45.00
4-Re-intro Antman (1st app. since 1960s), begin series; brief origin; Spider-Man app. 2.40 7.35 22.00
5-7,9,10: 6-Wasp app. & begins team-ups. 9-Iron Man app. 10-Last Antman 1.25 3.75 10.00
8-Origin Antman & Wasp-r/TTA #44; Kirby-a 1.75 5.25 14.00
11-Thing vs. Hulk; 1st Thing solo book (9/73); origin Fantastic Four retold 3.65 11.00 40.00
12-Thing/Iron Man; early Thanos app.; occurs after Capt. Marvel #33; Starlin-a(p) 2.00 6.00 18.00
NOTE: ***Bolle** a-9i. **Everett** a-1i, 3i. **Hartley** r-10. **Kane** c-3p, 7p. **Russell** a-7-10p. **Starlin** a-8, 11, 12; c-8.*

MARVEL FEATURE (Also see Red Sonja)
Marvel Comics: Nov, 1975 - No. 7, Nov, 1976 (Story cont'd in Conan #68)

1,7: 1-Red Sonja begins (pre-dates Red Sonja #1); adapts Howard short story; Adams-r/Savage Sword of Conan #1. 7-Battles Conan 2.40 6.00
2-6: Thorne-c/a in #2-7. 4,5-(Regular 25¢ edition)(5,7/76) 4.00
4,5-(30¢-c variant, limited distribution) 2.40 6.00

MARVEL FRONTIER COMICS UNLIMITED
Marvel Frontier Comics: Jan, 1994 ($2.95, 68 pgs.)

1-Dances with Demons, Immortalis, Children of the Voyager, Evil Eye, The Fallen stories 3.00

MARVEL FUMETTI BOOK
Marvel Comics Group: Apr, 1984 ($1.00, one-shot)

1-All photos; Stan Lee photo-c; Art Adams touch-ups 4.00

MARVEL FUN & GAMES
Marvel Comics Group: 1979/80 (color comic for kids)

1,11: 1-Games, puzzles, etc. 11-X-Men-c 1.00 3.00 8.00
2-10,12,13: (beware marked pages) 2.40 6.00

MARVEL GRAPHIC NOVEL
Marvel Comics Group (Epic Comics): 1982 - No. 38, 1990? ($5.95/$6.95)

1-Death of Captain Marvel (2nd Marvel graphic novel); Capt. Marvel battles Thanos by Jim Starlin (c/a/scripts) 2.00 6.00 18.00
1 (2nd & 3rd printings) 1.00 3.00 8.00
2-Elric: The Dreaming City 1.50 4.50 12.00
3-Dreadstar; Starlin-c/a, 52 pgs. 1.50 4.50 12.00
4-Origin/1st app. The New Mutants (1982) 1.75 5.25 14.00
4,5-2nd printings 1.00 2.80 7.00
5-X-Men; book-length story (1982) 2.00 6.00 18.00
6-17,20,21,23-25,29-31: 6-The Star Slammers. 7-Killraven. 8-Super Boxers; Byrne scripts. 9-The Futurians. 10-Heartburst. 11-Void Indigo. 12-Dazzler. 13-Starstruck. 14-The Swords Of The Swashbucklers. 15-The Raven Banner (a Tale of Asgard). 16-The Aladdin Effect (Storm, Tigra, Wasp, She-Hulk). 17-Revenge Of The Living Monolith (Spider-Man, Avengers, FF app.). 20-Greenberg the Vampire. 21-Marada the She-Wolf. 23-Dr. Strange. 24-Love and War (Daredevil); Miller scripts. 25-Alien Legion. 29-The Big Chance (Thing vs. Hulk). 30-A Sailor's Story. 31-Wolfpack 1.10 3.30 9.00
18,19,26-28: 18-She Hulk. 19-Witch Queen of Acheron (Conan). 26-Dracula. 27-Avengers (Emperor Doom). 28-Conan the Reaver 1.50 4.50 12.00
22-Amaz. Spider-Man in Hooky by Wrightson 1.75 5.25 14.00
32-Death of Groo 1.75 5.25 14.00
32-2nd printing ($5.95) 1.00 3.00 8.00
33,34,36,37: 33-Thor. 34-Predator & Prey (Cloak & Dagger). 36-Willow (movie adapt.). 37-Hercules 1.10 3.30 9.00
35-Hitler's Astrologer (The Shadow, $12.95, HC) 2.00 6.00 16.00
35-Soft-c reprint (1990, $10.95) 1.50 4.50 12.00
38-Silver Surfer (Judgement Day)($14.95, HC) 2.00 6.00 16.00
38-Soft-c reprint (1990, $10.95) 1.50 4.50 12.00
nn-Abslom Daak: Dalak Killer (1990, $8.95) Dr. Who 1.25 3.75 10.00
nn-Arena by Bruce Jones (1989, $5.95) Dinosaurs 1.00 3.00 8.00
nn- A-Team Storybook Comics Illustrated (1983) r/ A-Team mini-series #1-3 1.25 3.75 10.00
nn-Ax (1988, $5.95) Ernie Colan-s/a 1.25 3.75 10.00
nn-Black Widow Coldest War (4/90, $9.95) 1.50 4.50 12.00
nn-Chronicles of Genghis Grimtoad (1990, $8.95)-Alan Grant-s 1.25 3.75 10.00
nn-Conan the Barbarian in the Horn of Azoth (1990, $8.95) 1.50 4.50 12.00
nn-Conan of Isles ($8.95) 1.50 4.50 12.00
nn-Conan Ravagers of Time (1992, $9.95) Kull & Red Sonja app. 1.50 4.50 12.00
nn-Conan -The Skull of Set 1.50 4.50 12.00
nn-Doctor Strange and Doctor Doom Triumph and Torment (1989, $17.95, HC) 2.50 7.50 22.00
nn-Dreamwalker (1989, $6.95)-Morrow-a 1.10 3.30 9.00
nn-Excalibur Weird War III (1990, $9.95) 1.50 4.50 12.00
nn-G.I. Joe - The Trojan Gambit (1983, 68 pgs.) 1.25 3.75 10.00
nn-Harvey Kurtzman Strange Adventures (Epic, $19.95, HC) Aragonés, Crumb 2.50 7.50 25.00
nn-Hearts and Minds (1990, $8.95) Heath-a 1.25 3.75 10.00
nn-Inhumans (1988, $7.95)-Williamson-i 1.10 3.30 9.00
nn-Jhereg (Epic, 1990, $8.95) 1.25 3.75 10.00
nn-Kazar-Guns of the Savage Land (7/90, $8.95) 1.25 3.75 10.00
nn-Kull-The Vale of Shadow ('89, $6.95) 1.25 3.75 10.00
nn-Last of the Dragons (1988, $6.95) Austin-a(i) 1.00 2.80 7.00
nn-Nightraven: House of Cards (1991, $14.95) 1.85 5.50 15.00
nn-Nightraven: The Collected Stories (1990, $9.95) Bolton-r/British Hulk mag.; David Lloyd-c/a 1.50 4.50 12.00
nn-Original Adventures of Cholly and Flytrap (Epic, 1991, $9.95) Suydam-s/c/a 1.85 5.50 15.00
nn-Rick Mason Agent (1989, $9.95) 1.25 3.75 10.00
nn-Roger Rabbit In The Resurrection Of Doom (1989, $8.95) 1.25 3.75 10.00
nn-A Sailor's Story Book II: Winds, Dreams and Dragons ('86, $6.95, softcover) Glansman-s/c/a 1.25 3.75 10.00
nn-Squadron Supreme: Death of a Universe (1989, $9.95) Gruenwald-s; Ryan & Williamson-a 1.25 3.75 10.00
nn-Who Framed Roger Rabbit (1989, $6.95) 1.25 3.75 10.00
NOTE: ***Aragones** a-27, 32. **Buscema** a-38. **Byrne** c/a-18. **Heath** a-35i. **Kaluta** a-13, 35p; c-13. **Miller** a-24p. **Simonson** a-6; c-6. **Starlin** c/a-1,3. **Williamson** a-34. **Wrightson** c-29i.*

MARVEL-HEROES & LEGENDS
Marvel Comics: Oct, 1996; 1997 ($2.95)

nn-Wraparound-c, ...1997 ($2.99) -Original Avengers story 3.00

MARVEL HOLIDAY SPECIAL
Marvel Comics: No. 1, 1991 ($2.25, 84 pgs.) - 1996

1-X-Men, Fantastic Four, Punisher, Thor, Capt. America, Ghost Rider, Capt. Ultra, Spidey stories; Art Adams-c/a 3.00
nn (1/93)-Wolverine, Thanos (by Starlin/Lim/Austin) 3.00
nn (1994)-Capt. America, X-Men, Silver Surfer 3.00
...1996-Spider-Man by Waid & Olliffe; X-Men, Silver Surfer 3.00
NOTE: ***Art Adams** c-'93. **Golden** a-'93. **Perez** c-'94.*

MARVEL ILLUSTRATED: SWIMSUIT ISSUE (See Marvel Swimsuit Spec.)
Marvel Comics: 1991 ($3.95, magazine, 52 pgs.)

V1#1-Parody of Sports Illustrated swimsuit issue; Mary Jane Parker centerfold pin-up by Jusko; 2nd print exists 1.00 2.80 7.00

MARVEL KNIGHTS (See Black Panther, Daredevil, Inhumans, & Punisher)
Marvel Comics: 1998 (Previews for upcoming series)

Sketchbook-Wizard suppl.; Quesada & Palmiotti-c 3.00
Tourbook-($2.99) Interviews and art previews 3.00

MARVEL KNIGHTS
Marvel Comics: July, 2000 - Present ($2.99)

1-Daredevil, Punisher, Black Widow, Shang-Chi, Dagger app. 3.00
2-8: 2-Two covers by Barreto & Quesada 3.00
.../Marvel Boy Genesis Edition (6/00) Sketchbook preview 1.00

MARVEL MASTERPIECES COLLECTION, THE
Marvel Comics: May, 1993 - No. 4, Aug, 1993 ($2.95, coated paper, lim. series)

1-4-Reprints Marvel Masterpieces trading cards w/ new Jusko paintings in

Marvel Milestone Edition - Captain America Comics #1 © MAR

Marvel Mystery Comics #2 © MAR

Marvel Mystery Comics #73 © MAR

in each; Jusko painted-c/a 3.00

MARVEL MASTERPIECES 2 COLLECTION, THE
Marvel Comics: July, 1994 - No. 3, Sept, 1994 ($2.95, limited series)

1-3: 1-Kaluta-c; r/trading cards; new Steranko centerfold 3.00

MARVEL MILESTONE EDITION
Marvel Comics: 1991 - Present ($2.95, coated stock)(r/originals with original ads w/silver ink-c)

...: X-Men #1-Reprints X-Men #1 (1991) 3.00
...: Giant Size X-Men #1-(1991, $3.95, 68 pgs.) 4.00
...: Fantastic Four #1 (11/91), ...: Incredible Hulk #1 (3/92, says 3/91 by error), ...: Amazing Fantasy #15 (3/92), ...: Fantastic Four #5 (11/92), ...: Amazing Spider-Man #129 (11/92), ...: Iron Man #55 (11/92), ...: Iron Fist #14 (11/92) ...: Amazing Spider-Man #1 (1/93), ...: Amazing Spider-Man #1 (1/93) variation- no price on-c, ...: Tales of Suspense #39 (3/93), ...: Avengers #1 (9/93) ...: X-Men #9 (10/93), ...: Avengers #16 (10/93), ...:Amazing Spider-Man #149 (11/94, $2.95), ...:X-Men #28 (11/94, $2.95) 3.00
...:Captain America #1 (3/95, $3.95) 4.00
...:Amazing Spider-Man #3 (3/95, $2.95), ...:Avengers #4 (3/95, $2.95), ...:Strange Tales-r/Dr. Strange stories from #110, 111, 114, & 115 3.00
....:Hulk #181 (8/99, $2.99) 3.00

MARVEL MINI-BOOKS (See Promotional Comics section)

MARVEL MOVIE PREMIERE (Magazine)
Marvel Comics Group: Sept, 1975 (B&W, one-shot)

1-Burroughs' "The Land That Time Forgot" adapt. 1.25 3.75 10.00

MARVEL MOVIE SHOWCASE FEATURING STAR WARS
Marvel Comics Group: Nov, 1982 - No. 2, Dec, 1982 ($1.25, 68 pgs.)

1,2-Star Wars movie adaptation; reprints Star Wars #1-6 by Chaykin; 1-Reprints-c to Star Wars #1. 2-Stevens-r 4.00

MARVEL MOVIE SPOTLIGHT FEATURING RAIDERS OF THE LOST ARK
Marvel Comics Group: Nov, 1982 ($1.25, 68 pgs.)

1-Edited-r/Raiders of the Lost Ark #1-3; Buscema-c/a(p); movie adapt. 3.00

MARVEL MYSTERY COMICS (Formerly Marvel Comics) (Becomes Marvel Tales No. 93 on)
Timely /Marvel Comics (TP #2-17/TCI #18-54/MCI #55-92): No. 2, Dec, 1939 - No. 92, June, 1949

GD2.0 FN6.0 VF8.0 NM9.4
2-(Rare)-American Ace begins, ends #3; Human Torch (blue costume) by Burgos, Sub-Mariner by Everett continue; 2 pg. origin recap of Human Torch 2000.00 6000.00 13,000.00 25,000.00

GD2.0 FN6.0 NM9.4
3-New logo from Marvel pulp begins; 1st app. of television in comics? in Human Torch story (1/40) 1000.00 3000.00 11,500.00
4-Intro. Electro, the Marvel of the Age (ends #19), The Ferret, Mystery Detective (ends #9); 1st Sub-Mariner-c by Schomburg; 1st Nazi war-c on a comic book & 1st German flag (Swastika) on-c of a comic (2/40) 1000.00 3000.00 9000.00

GD2.0 FN6.0 VF8.0 NM9.4
5 Classic Schomburg-c (Scarce) 1560.00 4680.00 10,140.00 19,500.00

GD2.0 FN6.0 NM9.4
6,7: 6-Gustavson Angel story 539.00 1617.00 6200.00
8-1st Human Torch & Sub-Mariner battle(6/40) 826.00 2478.00 9500.00

GD2.0 FN6.0 VF8.0 NM9.4
9-(Scarce)-Human Torch & Sub-Mariner battle (cover/story); classic-c 1840.00 5520.00 11960.00 23,000.00

GD2.0 FN6.0 NM9.4
10-Human Torch & Sub-Mariner battle, conclusion; Terry Vance, the Schoolboy Sleuth begins, ends #57 565.00 1695.00 6500.00
11 305.00 915.00 3200.00
12-Classic Kirby-c 362.00 1086.00 3800.00
13-Intro. & 1st app. The Vision by S&K (11/40); Sub-Mariner dons new costume, ends #15 420.00 1260.00 4800.00
14-16: 14-Shows-c to Human Torch #1 on-c (12/40). 15-S&K Vision, Gustavson Angel story 232.00 695.00 2200.00
17-Human Torch/Sub-Mariner team-up by Burgos/Everett; pin-up on back-c; shows-c to Human Torch #2 on-c 263.00 790.00 2500.00
18 211.00 633.00 2000.00
19,20: 19-Origin Toro in text; shows-c to Sub-Mariner #1 on-c. 20-Origin The Angel in text 221.00 663.00 2100.00
21-The Patriot begins, (intro. in Human Torch #4 (#3)); not in #46-48; pin-up on back-c (7/41) 211.00 633.00 2000.00
22-25: 23-Last Gustavson Angel; origin The Vision in text. 24-Injury-to-eye story 184.00 553.00 1750.00
26-30: 27-Ka-Zar ends; last S&K Vision who battles Satan. 28-Jimmy Jupiter in the Land of Nowhere begins, ends #48; Sub-Mariner vs. The Flying Dutchman. 30-1st Japanese war-c 168.00 505.00 1600.00
31-33,35,36,38,39: 31-Sub-Mariner by Everett ends, resumes #84. 32-1st app. The Boboes 153.00 458.00 1450.00
34-Everett, Burgos, Martin Goodman, Funnies, Inc. office appear in story & battles Hitler; last Burgos Human Torch 168.00 505.00 1600.00
37-Classic Hitler-c 168.00 505.00 1600.00
40-Classic Zeppelin-c 158.00 474.00 1500.00
41-43,45,47,48: 48-Last Vision; flag-c 126.00 379.00 1200.00
44-Classic Super Plane-c 137.00 411.00 1300.00
46-Classic Hitler-c 137.00 411.00 1300.00
49-Origin Miss America 168.00 505.00 1600.00
50-Mary becomes Miss Patriot (origin) 132.00 395.00 1250.00
51-60: 53-Bondage-c. 60-Last Japanese war-c 118.00 355.00 1125.00
61,62,64-Last German war-c 111.00 332.00 1050.00
63-Classic Hitler War-c; The Villainess Cat-Woman only app. 126.00 379.00 1200.00
65,66-Last Japanese War-c 111.00 332.00 1050.00
67-78: 74-Last Patriot. 75-Young Allies begin. 76-Ten Chapter Miss America serial begins, ends #85 100.00 300.00 950.00
79-New cover format; Super Villains begin on cover; last Angel 103.00 308.00 975.00
80-1st app. Capt. America in Marvel Comics 126.00 379.00 1200.00
81-Captain America app. 100.00 300.00 950.00
82-Origin & 1st app. Namora (5/47); 1st Sub-Mariner/Namora team-up; Captain America app. 253.00 758.00 2400.00
83,85: 83-Last Young Allies. 85-Last Miss America; Blonde Phantom app. 89.00 268.00 850.00
84-Blonde Phantom begins (on-c of #84,88,89); Sub-Mariner by Everett begins; Captain America app. 126.00 379.00 1200.00
86-Blonde Phantom i.d. revealed; Captain America app.; last Bucky app. 100.00 300.00 950.00
87-1st Capt. America/Golden Girl team-up 105.00 316.00 1000.00
88-Golden Girl, Namora, & Sun Girl (1st in Marvel Comics) x-over; Captain America, Blonde Phantom app.; last Toro 100.00 300.00 950.00
89-1st Human Torch/Sun Girl team-up; 1st Captain America solo; Blonde Phantom app. 100.00 300.00 950.00
90,91: 90-Blonde Phantom un-masked; Captain America app. 91-Capt. America app.; Blonde Phantom & Sub-Mariner end; early Venus app. (4/49) (scarce) 116.00 348.00 1100.00
92-Feature story on the birth of the Human Torch and the death of Professor Horton (his creator); 1st app. The Witness in Marvel Comics; Captain America app. (scarce) 274.00 821.00 2600.00
132 Pg. issue, B&W, 25¢ (1943-44)-printed in N. Y.; square binding, blank inside covers; has Marvel No. 33-c in color; contains Capt. America #18 & Marvel Mystery Comics #33; same contents as Captain America Annual

GD2.0 FN6.0 VF8.0
(Less than 5 copies known to exist) 3000.00 9000.00 18,000.00

NOTE: ***Brodsky*** *c-49, 72, 86, 88-92.* ***Crandall*** *a-26i.* ***Everett*** *c-7-9, 27, 84.* ***Gabrielle*** *c-30-32.* ***Schomburg*** *c-3-11, 13-29, 33-36, 39-48, 50-59, 63-69, 74, 76, 132 pg. issue.* ***Shores*** *c-37, 38, 75p, 77, 78p, 79p, 80, 81p, 82-84, 85p, 87p.* ***Sekowsky*** *c-73. Bondage covers-3, 4, 7, 12, 28, 29, 49, 50, 52, 56, 57, 58, 59, 65. Angel c-2, 3, 8, 12. Remember Pearl Harbor issues-#30-32.*

MARVEL MYSTERY COMICS
Marvel Comics: Dec, 1999 ($3.95, reprints)

GD2.0 FN6.0 NM9.4
1-Reprints original 1940s stories; Schomburg-c from #74 4.00

MARVEL NO-PRIZE BOOK, THE (The Official... on-c)
Marvel Comics Group: Jan, 1983 (one-shot, direct sales only)

1-Golden-c; Kirby-a 3.00

MARVEL PREMIERE
Marvel Comics Group: April, 1972 - No. 61, Aug, 1981 (A tryout book for new

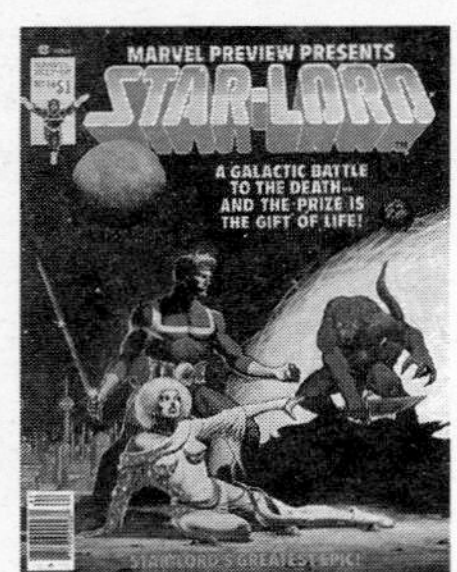

Marvel Preview #14 © MAR

Marvels Comics X-Men #1 © MAR

Marvel Selects Fantastic Four #1 © MAR

GD2.0 FN6.0 NM9.4

characters)

1-Origin Warlock (pre-#1) by Gil Kane/Adkins; origin Counter-Earth; Hulk & Thor cameo (#1-14 are 20¢-c) 4.10 12.30 45.00
2-Warlock ends; Kirby Yellow Claw-r 2.40 7.35 22.00
3-Dr. Strange series begins (pre #1, 7/72), B. Smith-c/a(p) 3.20 9.60 35.00
4-Smith/Brunner-a 2.00 6.00 16.00
5-9: 8-Starlin-c/a(p) 1.25 3.75 10.00
10-Death of the Ancient One 1.75 5.25 14.00
11-14: 11-Dr. Strange origin-r by Ditko. 14-Last Dr. Strange (3/74), gets own title 3 months later 1.00 2.80 7.00
15-Origin/1st app. Iron Fist (5/74), ends #25 5.45 16.35 60.00
16,25: 16-2nd app. Iron Fist; origin cont'd from #15; Hama's 1st Marvel-a. 25-1st Byrne Iron Fist (moves to own title next) 2.40 7.35 22.00
17-24: Iron Fist in all 1.75 5.25 14.00
26-Hercules. 2.40 6.00
27-Satana 1.00 3.00 8.00
28-Legion of Monsters (Ghost Rider, Man-Thing, Morbius, Werewolf) 1.85 5.50 15.00
29-46,49: 29,30-The Liberty Legion. 29-1st modern app. Patriot. 31-1st app. Woodgod; last 25¢ issue. 32-1st app. Monark Starstalker. 33,34-1st color app. Solomon Kane (Robert E. Howard adaptation "Red Shadows".) 35-Origin/1st app. 3-D Man. 36,37-3-D Man. 38-1st Weirdworld. 39,40-Torpedo. 41-1st Seeker 3000! 42-Tigra. 43-Paladin. 44-Jack of Hearts (1st solo book, 10/78). 45,46-Man-Wolf. 49-The Falcon (1st solo book, 8/79) 3.50
29-31-(30¢-c variants, limited distribution)(4-8/76) 4.00
47,48-Byrne-a: 47-Origin/1st app. new Ant-Man. 48-Ant-Man 5.00
50-1st app. Alice Cooper; co-plotted by Alice 1.75 5.25 14.00
51-56,58-61: 51-53-Black Panther. 54-1st Caleb Hammer. 55-Wonder Man. 56-1st color app. Dominic Fortune. 58-60-Dr. Who. 61-Star Lord 2.50
57-Dr. Who (2nd U.S. app.-see Movie Classics) 5.00

NOTE: ***N. Adams*** *(Crusty Bunkers) part inks-10, 12, 13.* ***Austin*** *a-50i, 56i; c-46i, 50i, 56i, 58.* ***Brunner*** *a-4i, 6p, 9-14p; c-9-14.* ***Byrne*** *a-47p, 48p.* ***Chaykin*** *a-32-34; c-32, 33, 56.* ***Giffen*** *a-31p, 44p; c-44.* ***Gil Kane*** *a(p)-1, 2, 15; c(p)-1, 2, 15, 16, 22-24, 27, 36, 37.* ***Kirby*** *c-26, 29-31, 35.* ***Layton*** *a-47i, 48i; c-47.* ***McWilliams*** *a-25i.* ***Miller*** *c-49p, 53p, 58p.* ***Nebres*** *a-44i; c-38i.* ***Nino*** *a-38i.* ***Perez*** *c/a-38p, 45p, 46p.* ***Ploog*** *a-38; c-5-7.* ***Russell*** *a-7p.* ***Simonson*** *a-60(2pgs.); c-57.* ***Starlin*** *a-8p; c-8.* ***Sutton*** *a-41, 43, 50p, 61; c-50p, 61. #57-60 publ'd w/two different prices on-c.*

MARVEL PRESENTS
Marvel Comics: October, 1975 - No. 12, Aug, 1977 (#1-6 are 25¢ issues)

1-Origin & 1st app. Bloodstone 1.10 3.30 9.00
2-Origin Bloodstone continued; Kirby-c 2.40 6.00
3-Guardians of the Galaxy (1st solo book, 2/76) begins, ends #12 1.25 3.75 10.00
4-7,9-12: 9,10-Origin Starhawk 2.40 6.00
4-6-(30¢-c variants, limited distribution)(4-8/76) 1.10 3.30 9.00
8-r/story from Silver Surfer #2 plus 4 pgs. new-a 2.40 6.00

NOTE: ***Austin*** *a-6i.* ***Buscema*** *r-8p.* ***Chaykin*** *a-5p.* ***Kane*** *c-1p.* ***Starlin*** *layouts-10.*

MARVEL PREVIEW (Magazine) (Bizarre Adventures #25 on)
Marvel Comics: Feb (no month), 1975 - No. 24, Winter, 1980 (B&W) ($1.00)

1-Man-Gods From Beyond the Stars; Crusty Bunkers (Neal Adams)-a(i) & cover; Nino-a 1.25 3.75 10.00
2-1st origin The Punisher (see Amaz. Spider-Man #129 & Classic Punisher); 1st app. Dominic Fortune; Morrow-c 6.35 19.00 70.00
3,8,10: 3-Blade the Vampire Slayer. 8-Legion of Monsters; Morbius app. 10-Thor the Mighty; Starlin frontispiece 1.50 4.50 12.00
4,5: 4-Star-Lord & Sword in the Star (origins & 1st app.). 5,6-Sherlock Holmes. 1.10 3.30 9.00
6,9: 6-Sherlock Holmes; N. Adams frontispiece. 9-Man-God; origin Star Hawk, ends #20 2.40 6.00
7-Satana, Sword in the Star app. 1.00 3.00 8.00
11,16,19: 11-Star-Lord; Byrne-a; Starlin frontispiece. 16-Masters of Terror. 19-Kull 5.00
12-15,17,18,20-24: 12-Haunt of Horror. 14,15-Star-Lord. 14-Starlin painted-c. 16-Masters of Terror. 17-Blackmark by G. Kane (see SSOC #1-3). 18-Star-Lord. 20-Bizarre Advs. 21-Moon Knight (Spr/80)-Predates Moon Knight #1; The Shroud by Ditko. 22-King Arthur. 23-Bizarre Advs.; Miller-a. 24-Debut Paradox 4.00

NOTE: ***N. Adams*** *(C. Bunkers) r-20i.* ***Buscema*** *a-22, 23.* ***Byrne*** *a-11.* ***Chaykin*** *a-20r; c-20 (new).* ***Colan*** *a-8, 16p(3), 18p, 23p; c-16p.* ***Elias*** *a-18.* ***Giffen*** *a-7.* ***Infantino*** *a-14p.* ***Kaluta*** *a-12; c-15.* ***Miller*** *a-23.* ***Morrow*** *a-8i; c-2-4.* ***Perez*** *a-20p.* ***Ploog*** *a-8.* ***Starlin*** *c-13, 14. Nudity in some issues*

MARVEL RIOT
Marvel Comics: Dec, 1995 ($1.95, one-shot)

1-"Age of Apocalypse" spoof; Lobdell script 2.00

MARVELS
Marvel Comics: Jan, 1994 - No. 4, Apr, 1994 ($5.95, painted lim. series)
No. 1 (2nd Printing), Apr, 1996 - No. 4 (2nd Printing), July, 1996 ($2.95)

1-4: Kurt Busiek scripts & Alex Ross painted-c/a in all; double-c w/acetate overlay 1.00 3.00 8.00
Marvel Classic Collectors Pack ($11.90)-Issues #1 & 2 boxed (1st printings). 2.00 6.00 16.00
0-(8/94, $2.95)-no acetate overlay. 4.00
1-4-(2nd printing): r/original limited series w/o acetate overlay 3.00
Hardcover (1994, $59.95)-r/#0-4; w/intros by Stan Lee, John Romita, Sr., Kurt Busiek & Scott McCloud. 60.00
Trade paperback ($19.95) 20.00

MARVEL SAGA, THE
Marvel Comics Group: Dec, 1985 - No. 25, Dec, 1987

1-25 2.00

NOTE: ***Williamson*** *a(i)-9, 10; c(i)-7, 10-12, 14, 16.*

MARVELS COMICS: ... (Marvel-type Comics read in the Marvel Universe)
Marvel Comics: Jul, 2000 ($2.25, one-shots)

...Captain America #1 -Frenz & Sinnott-a; ...Daredevil #1 -Isabella-s/Newell-a; ...Fantastic Four #1 -Kesel-s/Paul Smith-a; Spider-Man #1 -Oliff-a; ...Thor #1 -Templeton-s/Aucoin-a 2.25
...X-Men #1 -Millar-s/ Sean Phillips & Duncan Fegredo-a 2.25
The History of Marvels Comics (no cover price)-Faux history; previews titles 2.00

MARVEL SELECTS:
Marvel Comics: Jan, 2000 - Present ($2.75/$2.99, reprints)

...Fantastic Four 1-6: Reprints F.F. #107-112; new Davis-c 2.75
...Spider-Man 1,2,4-6: Reprints AS-M #100,101,103,104,93; Wieringo-c 2.75
...Spider-Man 3 ($2.99): Reprints AS-M #102; new Wieringo-c 2.99

MARVEL'S GREATEST COMICS (Marvel Collectors' Item Classics #1-22)
Marvel Comics Group: No. 23, Oct, 1969 - No. 96, Jan, 1981

23-34 (Giants). Begin Fantastic Four-r/#30s?-116 2.00 6.00 18.00
35-37-Silver Surfer-r/Fantastic Four #48-50 1.10 3.30 9.00
38-50: 42-Silver Surfer-r/F.F.(others?) 2.40 6.00
51-70: 63,64-(25¢ editions) 3.00
63,64-(30¢-c variants, limited distribution)(5,7/76) 4.00
71-96 2.50

NOTE: *Dr. Strange, Fantastic Four, Iron Man, Watcher-#23, 24. Capt. America, Dr. Strange, Iron Man, Fantastic Four-#25-28. Fantastic Four-#38-96.* ***Buscema*** *r-85-92; c-87-92r.* ***Ditko*** *r-23-28.* ***Kirby*** *r-23-82; c-75, 77p, 80p. #81 reprints Fantastic Four #100.*

MARVEL'S GREATEST SUPERHERO BATTLES (See Fireside Book Series)

MARVEL: SHADOWS AND LIGHT
Marvel Comics: Feb, 1997 ($2.95, B&W, one-shot)

1-Tony Daniel-c 3.00

MARVELS OF SCIENCE
Charlton Comics: March, 1946 - No. 4, June, 1946

1-A-Bomb story 22.00 66.00 175.00
2-4 13.00 39.00 105.00

MARVEL SPECIAL EDITION FEATURING... (Also see Special Collectors' Ed.)
Marvel Comics Group: 1975 - 1978 (84 pgs.) (Oversized)

1-The Spectacular Spider-Man ($1.50); r/Amazing Spider-Man #6,35, Annual 1; Ditko-a(r) 2.30 7.00 20.00
1,2-Star Wars ('77,'78; r/Star Wars #1-3 & #4-6 1.75 5.25 14.00
3-Star Wars ('78, $2.50, 116pgs.); r/S. Wars #1-6 2.00 6.00 16.00
3-Close Encounters of the Third Kind (1978, $1.50, 56 pgs.)-Movie adaptation; Simonson-a(p) 1.75 5.25 14.00
V2#2(Spring, 1980, $2.00, oversized)- "Star Wars: The Empire Strikes Back"; r/Marvel Comics Super Special #16 2.50 7.50 24.00

NOTE: ***Chaykin*** *c/a(r)-1(1977), 2, 3.* ***Stevens*** *a(r)-2i, 3i.* ***Williamson*** *a(r)-V2#2.*

MARVEL SPECTACULAR

Marvel Spotlight V2 #1 © MAR

Marvel Super-Heroes #86 © MAR

Marvel Super-Heroes Megazine #4 © MAR

Marvel Comics Group: Aug, 1973 - No. 19, Nov, 1975

1-Thor-r from mid-sixties begin by Kirby 1.10 3.30 9.00
2-19 4.00

MARVELS: PORTRAITS
Marvel Comics: Mar, 1995 - No. 4, June, 1995 ($2.95, limited series)

1-4:Different artists renditions of Marvel characters 3.00

MARVEL SPOTLIGHT (...& Son of Satan #19, 20, 23, 24)
Marvel Comics Group: Nov, 1971 - No. 33, Apr, 1977; V2#1, July, 1979 - V2#11, Mar, 1981 (A try-out book for new characters)

1-Origin Red Wolf (western hero)(1st solo book, pre-#1); Wood inks, Neal Adams-c; only 15¢ issue 3.00 9.00 30.00
2-(25¢, 52 pgs.)-Venus-r by Everett; origin/1st app. Werewolf By Night (begins) by Ploog; N. Adams-c 13.50 40.00 150.00
3,4: 4-Werewolf By Night ends (6/72); gets own title 9/72 4.10 12.30 45.00
5-Origin/1st app. Ghost Rider (8/72) & begins 9.00 27.00 100.00
6-8: 6-Origin G.R. retold. 8-Last Ploog issue 3.45 10.35 38.00
9-11-Last Ghost Rider (gets own title next mo.) 2.80 8.40 28.00
12-Origin & 2nd full app. The Son of Satan (10/73); story cont'd from Ghost Rider #2 & into #3; series begins, ends #24 2.80 8.40 28.00
13-24: 13-Partial origin Son of Satan. 14-Last 20¢ issue. 22-Ghost Rider-c & cameo (5 panels). 24-Last Son of Satan (10/75); gets own title 12/75 1.00 3.00 8.00
25,27,30,31: 27-(Regular 25¢-c), Sub-Mariner app. 30-The Warriors Three. 31-Nick Fury 5.00
26-Scarecrow 1.10 3.30 9.00
27-(30¢-c variant, limited distribution) 1.00 3.00 8.00
28-(Regular 25¢-c) 1st solo Moon Knight app. 2.50 7.50 25.00
28-(30¢-c variant, limited distribution) 3.20 9.60 35.00
29,32: 29-(Regular 25¢-c) (8/76) Moon Knight app.; last 25¢ issue. 32-1st app./partial origin Spider-Woman (2/77); Nick Fury app. 2.30 7.00 20.00
29-(30¢-c variant, limited distribution) 3.00 9.00 30.00
33-Deathlok; 1st app. Devil-Slayer 1.00 2.80 7.00
V2#1-7,9-11: 1-4-Capt. Marvel. 5-Dragon Lord. 6,7-StarLord; origin #6. 9-11-Capt. Universe (see Micronauts #8) 2.00
1-Variant copy missing issue #1 on cover 1.25 3.75 10.00
8-Capt. Marvel; Miller-c/a(p) 4.00

NOTE: ***Austin*** *c-V2#2i, 8.* ***J. Buscema*** *c/a-30p.* ***Chaykin*** *a-31; c-26, 31.* ***Colan*** *a-18p, 19p.* ***Ditko*** *a-V2#4, 5, 9-11; c-V2#4, 9-11.* ***Kane*** *c-21p, 32p.* ***Kirby*** *c-29p.* ***McWilliams*** *a-20i.* ***Miller*** *a-V2#8p; c(p)-V2#2, 5, 7, 8.* ***Mooney*** *a-8i, 10i, 14p, 15, 16p, 17p, 24p, 27, 32i.* ***Nasser*** *a-33p.* ***Ploog*** *a-2-5, 6-8p; c-3-9.* ***Romita*** *c-13.* ***Sutton*** *a-9-11p, V2#6, 7. #29-25¢ & 30¢ issues exist.*

MARVEL SUPER ACTION (Magazine)
Marvel Comics Group: Jan, 1976 (B&W, 76 pgs.)

1-Origin/2nd app. Dominic Fortune(see Marvel Preview); early Punisher app.; Weird World & The Huntress; Evans, Ploog-a 4.10 12.30 45.00

MARVEL SUPER ACTION
Marvel Comics Group: May, 1977 - No. 37, Nov, 1981

1-Reprints Capt. America #100 by Kirby 1.10 3.30 9.00
2-13: 2,3,5-13 r/Capt. America #101,102,103-111. 11-Origin-r. 12,13-Classic Steranko-c/a(r). 4-Marvel Boy-r(origin)/M. Boy #1 5.00
14-20: r/Avengers #55,56, Annual 2, others 3.00
21-37: 30-r/Hulk #6 from U.K. 2.00

NOTE: ***Buscema*** *a(r)-14p, 15p; c-18-20, 22, 35r-37.* ***Everett*** *a-4.* ***Heath*** *a-4r.* ***Kirby*** *r-1-3, 5-11.* ***B. Smith*** *a-27r, 28r.* ***Steranko*** *a(r)-12p, 13p; c-12r, 13r.*

MARVEL SUPER HERO CONTEST OF CHAMPIONS
Marvel Comics Group: June, 1982 - No. 3, Aug, 1982 (Limited series)

1-3: Features nearly all Marvel characters currently appearing in their comics; 1st Marvel limited series 5.00

MARVEL SUPER HEROES
Marvel Comics Group: October, 1966 (25¢, 68 pgs.) (1st Marvel one-shot)

1-r/origin Daredevil from D.D. #1; r/Avengers #2; G.A. Sub-Mariner-r/Marvel Mystery #8 (Human Torch app.). Kirby-a 8.15 24.50 90.00

MARVEL SUPER-HEROES (Formerly Fantasy Masterpieces #1-11) (Also see Giant-Size Super Heroes) (#12-20: 25¢, 68 pgs.)
Marvel Comics: No. 12, 12/67 - No. 31, 11/71; No. 32, 9/72 - No. 105, 1/82

12-Origin & 1st app. Capt. Marvel of the Kree; G.A. Human Torch, Destroyer, Capt. America, Black Knight, Sub-Mariner-r (#12-20 all contain new stories and reprints) 10.00 30.00 110.00
13-2nd app. Capt. Marvel; G.A. Black Knight, Torch, Vision, Capt. America, Sub-Mariner-r 4.55 13.65 50.00
14-Amazing Spider-Man (5/68, new-a by Andru/Everett); G.A. Sub-Mariner, Torch, Mercury (1st Kirby-a at Marvel), Black Knight, Capt. America reprints 7.25 21.75 80.00
15-17: 15-Black Bolt cameo in Medusa (new-a); Black Knight, Sub-Mariner, Black Marvel, Capt. America-r. 16-Origin & 1st app. S. A. Phantom Eagle; G.A. Torch, Capt. America, Black Knight, Patriot, Sub-Mariner-r. 17-Origin Black Knight (new-a); G.A. Torch, Sub-Mariner-r; reprint from All- Winners Squad #21 (cover & story) 3.00 9.00 30.00
18-Origin/1st app. Guardians of the Galaxy (1/69); G.A. Sub-Mariner, All-Winners Squad-r 3.65 11.00 40.00
19-Ka-Zar (new-a); G.A. Torch, Marvel Boy, Black Knight, Sub-Mariner reprints; Smith-c(p); Tuska-a(r) 2.00 6.00 18.00
20-Doctor Doom (5/69); r/Young Men #24 w/-c 2.50 7.50 25.00
21-31: All-r issues. 21-X-Men, Daredevil, Iron Man-r begin, end #31. 31-Last Giant issue 1.50 4.50 12.00
32-50: 32-Hulk/Sub-Mariner-r begin from TTA. 5.00
51-105: 56-r/origin Hulk/Inc. Hulk #102; Hulk-r begin 3.00
57,58-(30¢-c variants, limited distribution)(5,7/76) 4.00

NOTE: ***Austin*** *a-104.* ***Colan*** *a(p)-12, 13, 15, 18; c-12, 13, 15, 18.* ***Everett*** *a-14i(new); r-14, 15i, 18, 19, 33; c-85(r). New* ***Kirby*** *c-22, 27, 54.* ***Maneely*** *r-14, 15, 19.* ***Severin*** *r-83-85i, 100-102; c-100-102r.* ***Starlin*** *c-47.* ***Tuska*** *a-19p. Black Knight-r by* ***Maneely*** *in 12-16, 19. Sub-Mariner-r by* ***Everett*** *in 12-20.*

MARVEL SUPER-HEROES
Marvel Comics: May, 1990 - V2#15, Oct, 1993 ($2.95/$2.50, quart., 68-84 pgs.)

1-Moon Knight, Hercules, Black Panther, Magik, Brother Voodoo, Speedball (by Ditko) & Hellcat; Hembeck-a 3.00
2,4,5,V2#3,6-15: 2-Summer Special(7/90); Rogue, Speedball (by Ditko), Iron Man, Falcon,Tigra & Daredevil. 4-Spider-Man/Nick Fury, Daredevil,Speedball, Wonder Man, Spitfire & Black Knight; Byrne-c. 5-Thor, Dr. Strange, Thing & She-Hulk; Speedball by Ditko(p). V2#3-Retells origin Capt. America w/new facts; Blue Shield, Capt. Marvel,Speedball, Wasp; Hulk by Ditko/Rogers V2#6-9: 6-8-$2.25-c. 6,7-X-Men, Cloak & Dagger, The Shroud (by Ditko) & Marvel Boy in each. 8-X-Men, Namor & Iron Man (by Ditko); Larsen-c. 9-W.C Avengers, Iron Man app.; Kieth-c(p). V2#10-Ms. Marvel/Sabretooth-c/story (intended for Ms. Marvel #24; shows-c to #24); Namor, Vision, Scarlet Witch stories. V2#11,12 :11-Original Ghost Rider-c/story; Giant-Man, Ms. Marvel stories. 12-Dr. Strange, Falcon, Iron Man. V2#13-15 ($2.75, 84 pgs.): 13-All Iron Man 30th anniversary. 15-Iron Man/Thor/Volstagg/Dr. Druid 2.75

MARVEL SUPER-HEROES MEGAZINE
Marvel Comics: Oct, 1994 - No. 6, Mar, 1995 ($2.95, 100 pgs.)

1-6: 1-r/FF #232, DD #159, Iron Man #115, Incred. Hulk #314 3.00

MARVEL SUPER-HEROES SECRET WARS (See Secret Wars II)
Marvel Comics Group: May, 1984 - No. 12, Apr, 1985 (limited series)

1 2.40 6.00
1-3-(2nd printings, sold in multi-packs) 2.00
2-6,9-11: 6-The Wasp dies 5.00
7,12: 7-Intro. new Spider-Woman. 12-($1.00, 52 pgs.) 2.40 6.00
8-Spider-Man's new black costume explained as alien costume (1st app. Venom as alien costume) 2.50 7.50 24.00

NOTE: ***Zeck*** *a-1-12; c-1,3,8-12.*

MARVEL SUPER SPECIAL, A (See Marvel Comics Super...)

MARVEL SWIMSUIT SPECIAL (Also see Marvel Illustrated...)
Marvel Comics: 1992 - No. 4, 1995 ($3.95/$4.50, magazine, 52 pgs.)

1-4-Silvestri-c; pin-ups by diff. artists. 2-Jusko-c. 3-Hughes-c 2.40 6.00

MARVEL TAILS STARRING PETER PORKER THE SPECTACULAR SPIDER-HAM (Also see Peter Porker...)
Marvel Comics Group: Nov, 1983 (one-shot)

1-Peter Porker, the Spectacular Spider-Ham, Captain Americat, Goose Rider, Hulk Bunny app. 3.00

MARVEL TALES (Formerly Marvel Mystery Comics #1-92)
Marvel/Atlas Comics (MCI): No. 93, Aug, 1949 - No. 159, Aug, 1957

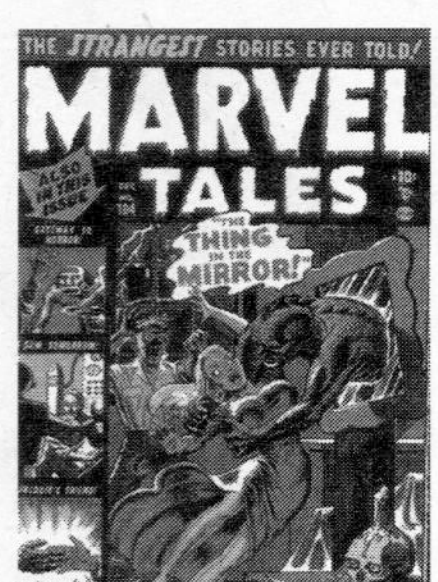

Marvel Tales #104 © MAR

Marvel Tales #290 © MAR

Marvel Team-Up #41 © MAR

GD2.0 FN6.0 NM9.4

	GD2.0	FN6.0	NM9.4
93-Horror/weird stories begin	137.00	411.00	1300.00
94-Everett-a	93.00	280.00	885.00
95,96,99,101,103,105: 95-New logo	62.00	186.00	590.00
97-Sun Girl, 2 pgs; Kirbyish-a; one story used in N.Y. State Legislative document	75.00	221.00	700.00
98,100: 98-Krigstein-a	65.00	196.00	620.00
102-Wolverton-a "The End of the World", (6 pgs.)	90.00	270.00	855.00
104-Wolverton-a "Gateway to Horror", (6 pgs.)	87.00	261.00	825.00
106,107-Krigstein-a. 106-Decapitation story	53.00	158.00	475.00
108-120: 118-Hypo-c/panels in End of World story. 120-Jack Katz-a	40.00	120.00	340.00
121,123-131: 128-Flying Saucer-c. 131-Last precode (2/55)	33.00	98.00	260.00
122-Kubert-a	33.00	99.00	265.00
132,133,135-141,143,145	21.00	62.00	165.00
134-Krigstein, Kubert-a; flying saucer-c	23.00	68.00	180.00
142-Krigstein-a	21.00	64.00	170.00
144-Williamson/Krenkel-a, 3 pgs.	21.00	64.00	170.00
146,148-151,154-156,158: 150-1st S.A. issue. 156-Torres-a	16.00	48.00	125.00
147,152: 147-Ditko-a. 152-Wood, Morrow-a	19.00	56.00	150.00
153-Everett End of World c/story	21.00	64.00	170.00
157,159-Krigstein-a	17.00	51.00	135.00

NOTE: ***Andru** a-103. **Briefer** a-118. **Check** a-147. **Colan** a-105, 107, 118, 120, 121, 127, 131. **Drucker** a-127, 135, 141, 146, 150. **Everett** a-98, 104, 106(2), 108(2), 131, 148, 151, 153, 155; c-107, 109, 111, 112, 114, 117, 127, 143, 147-151, 153, 155, 156. **Forte** a-119, 125, 130. **Heath** a-110, 113, 118, 119; c-104-106, 110, 130. **Gil Kane** a-117. **Lawrence** a-130. **Maneely** a-111, 126, 129; c-108, 116, 120, 129, 152. **Mooney** a-114. **Morisi** a-153. **Morrow** a-150, 152, 156. **Orlando** a-149, 151, 157. **Pakula** a-119, 121, 135, 144, 150, 152, 156. **Powell** a-136, 137, 150, 154. **Ravielli** a-117. **Rico** a-97, 99. **Romita** a-108. **Sekowsky** a-96-98. **Shores** a-110; c-96. **Sinnott** a-105, 116. **Tuska** a-114. **Whitney** a-107. **Wildey** a-126, 138.*

MARVEL TALES (…Annual #1,2; …Starring Spider-Man #123 on)
Marvel Comics Group (NPP earlier issues): 1964 - No. 291, Nov, 1994 (No. 1-32: 72 pgs.)

	GD2.0	FN6.0	NM9.4
1-Reprints origins of Spider-Man/Amazing Fantasy #15, Hulk/Inc. Hulk#1, Ant-Man/T.T.A. #35, Giant Man/T.T.A. #49, Iron Man/T.O.S. #39,48, Thor/J.I.M. #83 & r/Sgt. Fury #1	29.00	87.00	320.00
2 ('65)-r/X-Men #1(origin), Avengers #1(origin), origin Dr. Strange-r/Strange Tales #115 & origin Hulk(Hulk #3)	9.50	28.50	105.00
3 (7/66)-Spider-Man, Strange Tales (H. Torch), Journey into Mystery (Thor), Tales to Astonish (Ant-Man)-r begin (r/Strange Tales #101)	4.10	12.30	45.00
4,5	3.00	9.00	32.00
6-8,10: 10-Reprints 1st Kraven/Amaz. S-M #15	2.30	7.00	20.00
9-r/Amazing Spider-Man #14 w/cover	2.50	7.50	25.00
11-33: 11-Spider-Man battles Daredevil-r/Amaz. Spider-Man #16. 13-Origin Marvel Boy-r/M. Boy #1. 22-Green Goblin-c/story-r/Amaz. Spider-Man #27. 30-New Angel story (x-over w/Ka-Zar #2,3). 32-Last 72 pg. iss. 33-(52 pgs.) Kraven-r	2.00	6.00	18.00
34-50: 34-Begin regular size issues		2.40	6.00
51-65			4.00
66-70-(Regular 25¢ editions)(4-8/76)			4.00
66-70-(30¢-c variants, limited distribution)		2.40	6.00
71-105: 75-Origin Spider-Man-r. 77-79-Drug issues-r/Amaz. Spider-Man #96-98. 98-Death of Gwen Stacy-r/Amaz. Spider-Man #121 (Green Goblin). 99-Death Green Goblin-r/Amaz. Spider-Man #122. 100-(52 pgs.)-New Hawkeye/Two Gun Kid story. 101-105-All Spider-Man-r			3.00
106-r/1st Punisher-Amazing Spider-Man #129			4.00
107-136: 107-133-All Spider-Man-r. 111,112-r/Spider-Man #134,135 (Punisher). 113,114-r/Spider-Man #136,137(Green Goblin). 126-128-r/clone story from Amazing Spider-Man #149-151. 134-136-Dr. Strange-r begin; SpM stories continue. 134-Dr. Strange-r/Strange Tales #110			3.00
137-Origin-r Dr. Strange; shows original unprinted-c & origin Spider-Man/Amazing Fantasy #15			5.00
137-Nabisco giveaway		2.40	6.00
138-Reprints all Amazing Spider-Man #1; begin reprints of Spider-Man with covers similar to originals			4.00
139-144: r/Amazing Spider-Man #2-7			3.00
145-200: Spider-Man-r continue w/#8 on. 149-Contains skin "Tattooz" decals. 150-($1.00, 52pgs.)-r/Spider-Man Annual 1(Kraven app.). 153-r/1st Kraven/Spider-Man #15. 155-r/2nd Green Goblin/Spider-Man #17. 161,164,165-Gr. Goblin-c/stories-r/Spider-Man #23,26,27. 178,179-Green Goblin-c/story-r/Spider-Man #39,40. 187,189-Kraven-r. 191-($1.50, 68 pgs.)-r/Spider-Man #96-98. 193-Byrne-r/Marvel Team-Up begin w/scripts. 192-($1.25, 52 pgs.)-r/Spider-Man #121,122. 200-Double size ($1.25)-Miller-c & r/Annual #14			2.50
201-257: 208-Last Byrne-r. 210,211-r/Spidey #134,135. 212,213-r/Giant-Size Spidey #4. 213-r/1st solo Silver Surfer story/F.F. Annual #5. 214,215-r/Spidey #161,162. 222-Reprints origin Punisher/Spectacular Spider-Man #83; last Punisher reprint. 209-Reprints 1st app. The Punisher/Amazing Spider-Man #129; Punisher reprints begin, end #222. 223-McFarlane-c begins, end #239. 233-Spider-Man/X-Men team-ups begin; r/X-Men #35. 234-r/Marvel Team-Up #4. 235,236-r/M. Team-Up Annual #1. 237,238-r/M. Team-Up #150. 239,240-r/M. Team-Up #38,90(Beast). 242-r/M.Team-Up #89. 243-r/M. Team-Up #117(Wolverine). 250-($1.50, 52pgs.)-r/1st Karma/M. Team-Up #100. 251-r/Spider-Man #100 (Green Goblin-c/story). 252-r/1st app. Morbius/Amaz. Spider-Man #101. 253-($1.50, 52 pgs.)-r/Amaz. S-M #102254-r/M. Team-Up #15(Ghost Rider); new painted-c. 255,256-Spider-Man & Ghost Rider-r/Marvel Team-Up #58,91. 257-Hobgoblin-r begin(r/Amazing Spider-Man #238).			2.00
258-291: 258-261-r/A. Spider-Man #239,249-251(Hobgoblin). 262,263-r/Marv. Team-Up #53,54. 262-New X-Men vs. Sunstroke story. 263-New Woodgod origin story. 264,265-r/A. Spider-Man Annual 5. 266-273-Reprints alien costume stories/A. S-M 252-259. 277-r/1st Silver Sable/A. S-M 265. 283-r/A. S-M 275 (Hobgoblin). 284-r/A. S-M 276 (Hobgoblin)			2.00
285-variant w/Wonder-Con logo on c-no price-giveaway			2.00
286-($2.95)-p/bagged w/16 page insert & animation print			3.00

NOTE: *All contain reprints; some have new art. #89-97-r/Amazing Spider-Man #110-118; #98-136-r/#121-159; #137-150-r/Amazing Fantasy #15, #1-12 & Annual 1; #151-167-r/#13-28 & Annual 2; #168-186-r/#29-46. **Austin** a-100i; c-272i, 273i. **Byrne** a(r)-193-198p, 201-208p. **Ditko** a-1-30, 83, 100, 137-155. **G. Kane** a-71, 81, 98-101p, 249r; c-125-127p, 130p, 137-155. **Sam Kieth** c-255, 262, 263. **Ron Lim** c-266p-281p, 283p-285p. **McFarlane** c-223-239. **Mooney** a-63, 95-97i, 103(i). **Nasser** a-100p. **Nebres** a-242i. **Perez** c-259-261. **Rogers** c-240, 241, 243-252.*

MARVEL TEAM-UP (See Marvel Treasury Edition #18 & Official Marvel Index To…) (Replaced by Web of Spider-Man)
Marvel Comics Group: March, 1972 - No. 150, Feb, 1985
NOTE: *Spider-Man team-ups in all but Nos. 18, 23, 26, 29, 32, 35, 97, 104, 105, 137.*

	GD2.0	FN6.0	NM9.4
1-Human Torch	12.00	36.00	130.00
2-Human Torch	3.45	10.35	38.00
3-Spider-Man/Human Torch vs. Morbius (part 1); 3rd app. of Morbius (7/72)	3.80	11.40	42.00
4-Spider-Man/X-Men vs. Morbius (part 2 of story); 4th app. of Morbius	4.35	13.00	48.00
5-10: 5-Vision. 6-Thing. 7-Thor. 8-The Cat (4/73, came out between The Cat #3 & 4). 9-Iron Man. 10-H-T	2.00	6.00	18.00
11,13,14,16-20: 11-Inhumans. 13-Capt. America. 14-Sub-Mariner. 16-Capt. Marvel. 17-Mr. Fantastic. 18-H-T/Hulk. 19-Ka-Zar. 20-Black Panther; last 20¢ issue	1.50	4.50	12.00
12-Werewolf (8/73, 1 month before Werewolf #1).	2.50	7.50	23.00
15-1st Spider-Man/Ghost Rider team-up (11/73)	2.50	7.50	20.00
21-30: 21-Dr. Strange. 22-Hawkeye. 23-H-T/Iceman (X-Men cameo). 24-Brother Voodoo. 25-Daredevil. 26-H-T/Thor. 27-Hulk. 28-Hercules. 29-H-T/Iron Man. 30-Falcon	1.00	2.80	7.00
31-45,47-50: 31-Iron Fist. 32-H-T/Son of Satan. 33-Nighthawk. 34-Valkyrie. 35-H-T/Dr. Strange. 36-Frankenstein. 37-Man-Wolf. 38-Beast. 39-H-T. 40-Sons of the Tiger/H-T. 41-Scarlet Witch. 42-The Vision. 43-Dr. Doom; retells origin. 44-Moondragon. 45-Killraven. 47-Thing. 48-Iron Man; last 25¢ issue. 49-Dr. Strange; Iron Man app. 50-Iron Man; Dr. Strange app.			5.00
44-48-(30¢-c variants, limited distribution)(4-8/76)	1.00	3.00	8.00
46-Spider-Man/Deathlok team-up		2.40	6.00
51,52,56,57: 51-Iron Man; Dr. Strange app. 52-Capt. America. 56-Daredevil. 57-Black Widow			4.00
53-Hulk; Woodgod & X-Men app., 1st Byrne-a on X-Men (1/77)	2.50	7.50	25.00
54,55,58-60: 54,59,60: 54-Hulk; Woodgod app. 59-Yellowjacket/The Wasp. 60-The Wasp (Byrne-a in all). 55-Warlock-c/story; Byrne-a. 58-Ghost Rider		2.40	6.00

61-70: All Byrne-a; 61-H-T. 62-Ms. Marvel; last 30¢ issue. 63-Iron Fist. 64-Daughters of the Dragon. 65-Capt. Britain (1st U.S. app.). 66-Capt. Britain;

Marvel Team-Up #100 © MAR

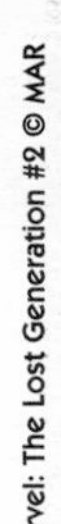
Marvel: The Lost Generation #2 © MAR

Marvel Two-In-One #47 © MAR

1st app. Arcade. 67-Tigra; Kraven the Hunter app. 68-Man-Thing. 69-Havok (from X-Men). 70-Thor 5.00
71-74,76-78,80: 71-Falcon. 72-Iron Man. 73-Daredevil. 74-Not Ready for Prime Time Players (Belushi). 76-Dr. Strange. 77-Ms. Marvel. 78-Wonder Man. 80-Dr. Strange/Clea; last 35¢ issue 3.00
75,79,81: Byrne-a(p). 75-Power Man; Cage app. 79-Mary Jane Watson as Red Sonja; Clark Kent cameo (1 panel, 3/79). 81-Death of Satana 4.00
82-99: 82-Black Widow. 83-Nick Fury. 84-Shang-Chi. 86-Guardians of the Galaxy. 89-Nightcrawler (from X-Men). 91-Ghost Rider. 92-Hawkeye. 93-Werewolf by Night. 94-Spider-Man vs. The Shroud. 95-Mockingbird (intro.); Nick Fury app. 96-Howard the Duck; last 40¢ issue. 97-Spider-Woman/ Hulk. 98-Black Widow. 99-Machine Man. 85-Shang-Chi/Black Widow/Nick Fury. 87-Black Panther. 88-Invisible Girl. 90-Beast 2.50
100-(Double-size)-Fantastic Four/Storm/Black Panther; origin/1st app. Karma, one of the New Mutants; origin Storm; X-Men x-over; Miller-c/a(p); Byrne-a (on X-Men app. only) 5.00
101-116: 101-Nighthawk(Ditko-a). 102-Doc Samson. 103-Ant-Man. 104-Hulk/Ka-Zar. 105-Hulk/Powerman/Iron Fist. 106-Capt. America. 107-She-Hulk. 108-Paladin; Dazzler cameo. 109-Dazzler; Paladin app. 110-Iron Man. 111-Devil-Slayer. 112-King Kull; last 50¢ issue. 113-Quasar. 114-Falcon. 115-Thor. 116-Valkyrie 2.50
117-Wolverine-c/story 1.25 3.75 10.00
118-140,142-149: 118-Professor X; Wolverine app. (4 pgs.); X-Men cameo. 119-Gargoyle. 120-Dominic Fortune. 121-Human Torch. 122-Man-Thing. 123-Daredevil. 124-The Beast. 125-Tigra. 126-Hulk & Powerman/Son of Satan. 127-The Watcher. 128-Capt. America; Spider-Man/Capt. America photo-c. 129-The Vision. 130-Scarlet Witch. 131-Frogman. 132-Mr. Fantastic. 133-Fantastic Four. 134-Jack of Hearts. 135-Kitty Pryde; X-Men cameo. 136-Wonder Man. 137-Aunt May/Franklin Richards. 138-Sandman. 139-Nick Fury. 140-Black Widow. 142-Capt. Marvel. 143-Starfox. 144-Moon Knight. 145-Iron Man. 146-Nomad. 147-Human Torch; SpM back to old costume. 148-Thor. 149-Cannonball 2.50
141-Daredevil; SpM/Black Widow app. (Spidey in new black costume; ties w/ Amaz. S-M #252 for 1st black costume) 3.00
150-X-Men ($1.00, double-size); B. Smith-c 4.00
Annual 1 (1976)-Spider-Man/X-Men (early app.) 2.30 7.00 20.00
Annual 2 (1979)-Spider-Man/Hulk 1.00 2.80 7.00
Annuals 3,4: 3 (1980)-Hulk/Power Man/Machine Man/Iron Fist; Miller-c(p). 4 (1981)-SpM/Daredevil/Moon Knight/Power Man/Iron Fist; brief origins of each; Miller-c; Miller scripts on Daredevil 5.00
Annuals 5-7: 5 (1982)-SpM/The Thing/Scarlet Witch/Dr. Strange/Quasar. 6 (1983)-SpM/New Mutants (early app.), Cloak & Dagger. 7(1984)-Alpha Flight; Byrne-c(i) 3.00

NOTE: ***Art Adams*** *c-141p.* ***Austin*** *a-79i; c-76i, 79i, 96i, 101i, 112i, 130i.* ***Bolle*** *a-9i.* ***Byrne*** *a(p)-53-55, 59-70, 75, 79, 100; c-68p, 70p, 72p, 75, 76p, 79p, 129i, 133i.* ***Colan*** *a-87p.* ***Ditko*** *a-101.* ***Kane*** *a(p)-4-6, 13, 14, 16-19, 23; c(p)-4, 13, 14, 17-19, 23, 25, 26, 32-35, 37, 41, 44, 45, 47, 53, 54.* ***Miller*** *a-100p; c-95p, 99p, 100p, 102p, 106.* ***Mooney*** *a-2i, 7i, 8, 10p, 11p, 16i, 24-31p, 72, 93i, Annual 5i.* ***Nasser*** *a-89p; c-101p.* ***Simonson*** *c-99i, 148.* ***Paul Smith*** *c-131, 132.* ***Starlin*** *c-27.* ***Sutton*** *a-93p. "H-T" means Human Torch; "SpM" means Spider-Man; "S-M" means Sub-Mariner.*

MARVEL TEAM-UP (2nd Series)
Marvel Comics: Sept, 1997 - No. 11, July, 1998 ($1.99)

1-11: 1-Spider-Man team-ups begin, Generation x-app. 2-Hercules-c/app.; two covers. 3-Sandman. 4-Man-Thing. 7-Blade. 8-Namor team-ups begin, Dr. Strange app. 9-Capt. America. 10-Thing. 11-Iron Man 2.00

MARVEL: THE LOST GENERATION
Marvel Comics: No. 12, Mar, 2000 - No. 1, Feb, 2001 ($2.99, issue #s go in reverse)

1-12-Stern-s/Byrne-s/a; untold story of The First Line. 5-Thor app. 3.00

MARVEL TREASURY EDITION
Marvel Comics Group/Whitman #17,18: 1974; #2, Dec, 1974 - #28, 1981 ($1.50/$2.50, 100 pgs., oversized, new-a &-r)(Also see Amazing Spider-Man, The, Marvel Spec. Ed. Feat.--, Savage Fists of Kung Fu, Superman Vs., & 2001, A Space Odyssey)

1-Spectacular Spider-Man; story-r/Marvel Super-Heroes #14; Romita-c/a(r); G. Kane, Ditko-r; Green Goblin/Hulk-r 4.10 12.30 45.00
1-1,000 numbered copies signed by Stan Lee & John Romita on front-c & sold thru mail for $5.00; these were the1st 1,000 copies off the press 11.00 33.00 120.00
2-10: 2-Fantastic Four-r/F.F. 6,11,48-50(Silver Surfer). 3-The Mighty Thor-r/Thor #125-130. 4-Conan the Barbarian; Barry Smith-c/a(r)/Conan #11. 5-The Hulk (origin-r/Hulk #3). 6-Dr. Strange. 7-Mighty Avengers. 8-Giant Superhero Holiday Grab-Bag; Spider-Man, Hulk, Nick Fury. 9-Giant; Super-hero Team-up. 10-Thor; r/Thor #154-157 2.00 6.00 18.00
11-25,27: 11-Fantastic Four. 12-Howard the Duck (r/#H. the Duck #1 & G.S. Man-Thing #4,5) plus new Defenders story. 13-Giant Super-Hero Holiday Grab-Bag. 14-The Sensational Spider-Man; r/1st Morbius from Amazing S-M #101,102 plus #100 & r/Not Brand Echh #6. 15-Conan; B. Smith, Neal Adams-i; r/Conan #24. 16-The Defenders (origin) & Valkyrie; r/Defenders #1,4,13,14. 17-The Hulk. 18-The Astonishing Spider-Man; r/Spider-Man's 1st team-ups with Iron Fist, The X-Men, Ghost Rider & Werewolf by Night; inside back-c has photos from 1978 Spider-Man TV show. 19-Conan the Barbarian. 20-Hulk. 21-Fantastic Four. 22-Spider-Man. 23-Conan. 24-Rampaging Hulk. 25-Spider-Man vs. The Hulk. 27-Spider-Man 1.75 5.25 14.00
26-The Hulk; 6 pg. new Wolverine/Hercules-s 2.00 6.00 18.00
28-Spider-Man/Superman; (origin of each) 3.00 9.00 30.00

NOTE: *Reprints-2, 3, 5, 7-9, 13, 14, 16, 17.* ***Neal Adams*** *a(i)-6, 15.* ***Brunner*** *a-6, 12; c-6.* ***Buscema*** *a-15, 19, 28; c-28.* ***Colan*** *a-6r; c-12p.* ***Ditko*** *a-1, 6.* ***Gil Kane*** *c-16p.* ***Kirby*** *a-1-3, 5, 7, 9-11; c-7.* ***Perez*** *a-26.* ***Romita*** *c-1, 5.* ***B. Smith*** *a-4, 15, 19; c-4, 19.*

MARVEL TREASURY OF OZ FEATURING THE MARVELOUS LAND OF OZ
Marvel Comics Group: 1975 ($1.50, oversized) (See MGM's Marvelous...)

1-Buscema-a; Romita-c 2.00 6.00 18.00

MARVEL TREASURY SPECIAL (Also see 2001: A Space Odyssey)
Marvel Comics Group: 1974; 1976 ($1.50, oversized, 84 pgs.)

Vol. 1-Spider-Man, Torch, Sub-Mariner, Avengers "Giant Superhero Holiday Grab-Bag"; Wood, Colan/Everett, plus 2 Kirby-r; reprints Hulk vs. Thing from Fantastic Four #25,26 2.00 6.00 18.00
Vol. 1-... Featuring Captain America's Bicentennial Battles (6/76)-Kirby-a; B. Smith inks, 11 pgs. 2.50 7.50 23.00

MARVEL TRIPLE ACTION (See Giant-Size...)
Marvel Comics Group: Feb, 1972 - No. 24, Mar, 1975; No. 25, Aug, 1975 - No. 47, Apr, 1979

1-(25¢ giant, 52 pgs.)-Dr. Doom, Silver Surfer, The Thing begin, end #4 ('66 reprints from Fantastic Four) 2.30 7.00 20.00
2-5 1.10 3.30 9.00
6-10 2.40 6.00
11-47: 45-r/X-Men #45. 46-r/Avengers #53(X-Men) 3.00
29,30-(30¢-c variants, limited distribution)(5,7/76) 5.00

NOTE: *#5-44, 46, 47 reprint Avengers #11 thru ?. #40-r/Avengers #48(1st Black Knight).* ***Buscema*** *a(r)-35p, 36p, 38p, 39p, 41, 42, 43p, 44p, 46p, 47p.* ***Ditko*** *a-2r; c-47.* ***Kirby*** *a(r)-1-4p; c-1-4, 9-19, 22, 24, 29.* ***Starlin*** *c-7.* ***Tuska*** *a(r)-40p, 43i, 46i, 47i. #2 through #17 are 20¢-c.*

MARVEL TWO-IN-ONE (...Featuring ... #82 on; also see The Thing)
Marvel Comics Group: January, 1974 - No. 100, June, 1983

1-Thing team-ups begin; Man-Thing 4.50 13.65 50.00
2-6: 2-Sub-Mariner; last 20¢ issue. 3-Daredevil. 4-Capt. America. 5-Guardians of the Galaxy (9/74, 2nd app.?). 6-Dr. Strange (11/74) 1.75 5.25 14.00
7,9,10 1.10 3.30 9.00
8-Early Ghost Rider app. (3/75) 1.50 4.50 12.00
11-14,18-20: 13-Power Man. 14-Son of Satan (early app.). 18-Last 25¢ issue 2.40 6.00
15-17-(Regular 25¢ editions)(5-7/76) 17-Spider-Man. 2.40 6.00
15-17-(30¢-c variants, limited distribution) 1.10 3.30 9.00
21-27,29,31-40: 27-Deathlok. 9-Master of Kung Fu; Spider-Woman cameo. 31-33-Spider-Woman. 39-Vision 4.00
28-(Regular 30¢ edition)(6/77) 4.00
28-(35¢-c variant, limited distribution) 2.40 6.00
30-2nd full app. Spider-Woman (see Marvel Spotlight #32 for 1st app.) 1.00 2.80 7.00
41,42,44,45,47-49: 42-Capt. America. 45-Capt. Marvel 3.00
43,50,53,55-Byrne-a(p). 53-Quasar(7/79, 2nd app.) 5.00
46-Thing battles Hulk-c/story 1.00 2.80 7.00
51-The Beast, Nick Fury, Ms. Marvel; Miller-p 5.00
52-Moon Knight app. 3.00
54-Death of Deathlok: Byrne-a 1.00 3.00 8.00

Marvel Universe #2 © MAR

Mary Marvel Comics #3 © FAW

The Mask World Tour #2 © DH

GD2.0 FN6.0 NM9.4

56-60,64-74,76-79,81,82: 60-Intro. Impossible Woman. 68-Angel. 69-Guardians of the Galaxy. 71-1st app. Maelstrom. 76-Iceman 2.50
61-63: 61-Starhawk (from Guardians); "The Coming of Her" storyline begins, ends #63; cover similar to F.F. #67 (Him-c). 62-Moondragon; Thanos & Warlock cameo in flashback; Starhawk app. 63-Warlock revived shortly; Starhawk & Moondragon app. 3.50
75-Avengers (52 pgs.) 3.50
80,90,100: 80-Ghost Rider. 90-Spider-Man. 100-Double size, Byrne-s 4.00
83-89,91-99: 83-Sasquatch. 84-Alpha Flight app. 93-Jocasta dies. 96-X-Men-c & cameo 3.00
Annual 1 (1976, 52 pgs.)-Thing/Liberty Legion; Kirby-c 2.40 6.00
Annual 2(1977, 52 pgs.)-Thing/Spider-Man; 2nd death of Thanos; end of Thanos saga; Warlock app.; Starlin-c/a 2.30 7.00 20.00
Annual 3,4 (1978-79, 52 pgs.): 3-Nova. 4-Black Bolt 3.00
Annual 5-7 (1980-82, 52 pgs.): 5-Hulk. 6-1st app. American Eagle. 7-The Thing/Champion; Sasquatch, Colossus app.; X-Men cameo (1 pg.) 3.00

NOTE: ***Austin*** *c(i)-42, 54, 56, 58, 61, 63, 66.* ***John Buscema*** *a-30p, 45; c-30p.* ***Byrne*** *(p)-43, 50, 53-55; c-43, 53p, 56p, 98i, 99i.* ***Gil Kane*** *a-1p, 2p; c(p)-1-3, 9, 11, 14, 28.* ***Kirby*** *c-10, 12, 19p, 20, 25, 27.* ***Mooney*** *a-18i, 38i, 90i.* ***Nasser*** *a-70p.* ***Perez*** *a(p)-56-58, 60, 64, 65; c(p)-32, 33, 42, 50-52, 54, 55, 57, 58, 61-66, 70.* ***Roussos*** *a-Annual 1i.* ***Simonson*** *c-43i, 97p, Annual 6i.* ***Starlin*** *c-6, Annual 1.* ***Tuska*** *a-6p.*

MARVEL UNIVERSE (See Official Handbook Of The...)

MARVEL UNIVERSE
Marvel Comics: June, 1998 - No. 7, Dec, 1998 ($2.99/$1.99)
1-($2.99)-Invaders stories from WW2; Stern-s 3.00
2-7-($1.99): 2-Two covers. 4-7-Monster Hunters; Manley-a/Stern-s 2.00

MARVEL VALENTINE SPECIAL
Marvel Comics: Mar, 1997 ($2.99, one-shot)
1-Valentine stories w/Spider-Man, Daredevil, Cyclops, Phoenix 3.00

MARVEL VERSUS DC (See DC Versus Marvel) (Also see Amazon, Assassins, Bruce Wayne: Agent of S.H.I.E.L.D., Bullets & Bracelets, Doctor Strangefate, JLX, Legend of the Dark Claw, Magneto & The Magnetic Men, Speed Demon, Spider-Boy, Super Soldier, & X-Patrol)
Marvel Comics: No. 2, 1996 - No. 3, 1996 ($3.95, limited series)
2,3: 2-Peter David script. 3-Ron Marz script; Dan Jurgens-a(p). 1st app. of Super Soldier, Spider-Boy, Dr. Doomsday, Doctor Strangefate, The Dark Claw, Nightcreeper, Amazon, Wraith & others. Storyline continues in Amalgam books. 4.00

MARVEL X-MEN COLLECTION, THE
Marvel Comics: Jan, 1994 - No. 3, Mar, 1994 ($2.95, limited series)
1-3-r/X-Men trading cards by Jim Lee 3.00

MARVEL - YEAR IN REVIEW (Magazine)
Marvel Comics: 1989 - No. 3, 1991 (52 pgs.)
1-3: 1-Spider-Man-c by McFarlane. 2-Capt. America-c. 3-X-Men/Wolverine-c 5.00

MARVIN MOUSE
Atlas Comics (BPC): September, 1957
1-Everett-c/a; Maneely-a 12.00 36.00 95.00

MARY JANE & SNIFFLES (See Looney Tunes)
Dell Publishing Co.: No. 402, June, 1952 - No. 474, June, 1953
Four Color 402 (#1) 7.50 22.50 90.00
Four Color 474 6.70 20.00 80.00

MARY MARVEL COMICS (Monte Hale #29 on) (Also see Captain Marvel #18, Marvel Family, Shazam, & Wow Comics)
Fawcett Publications: Dec, 1945 - No. 28, Sept, 1948
1-Captain Marvel introduces Mary on-c; intro/origin Georgia Sivana 190.00 570.00 1800.00
2 74.00 221.00 700.00
3,4: 3-New logo 50.00 150.00 450.00
5-8: 8-Bulletgirl x-over in Mary Marvel; X-Mas-c 40.00 120.00 320.00
9,10 35.00 105.00 280.00
11-20 23.00 68.00 180.00
21-28: 28-Western-c 20.00 60.00 160.00

MARY POPPINS (See Movie Comics & Walt Disney Showcase No. 17)

MARY SHELLEY'S FRANKENSTEIN
Topps Comics: Oct, 1994 - Jan, 1995 ($2.95, limited series)
1-4-polybagged w/3 trading cards 3.00
1-4 ($2.50)-Newstand ed. 2.50

MARY WORTH (See Harvey Comics Hits #55 & Love Stories of...)
Argo: March, 1956 (Also see Romantic Picture Novelettes)
1 7.15 21.50 50.00

MASK (TV)
DC Comics: Dec, 1985 - No. 4, Mar, 1986; Feb, 1987 - No. 9, Oct, 1987
1-4; 1-9 (2nd series)-Sat. morning TV show. 2.00

MASK, THE (Also see Mayhem)
Dark Horse Comics: Aug, 1991 - No. 4, Oct, 1991; No. 0, Dec, 1991 ($2.50, 36 pgs., limited series)
1-4: 1-1st app. Lt. Kellaway as The Mask (see Dark Horse Presents #10 for 1st app.) 5.00
0-(12/91, B&W, 56 pgs.)-r/Mayhem #1-4 4.00

...: HUNT FOR GREEN OCTOBER July, 1995 - Oct, 1995 ($2.50, lim. series)
1-4-Evan Dorkin scripts 2.50

.../ MARSHALL LAW Feb, 1998 - No. 2, Mar, 1998 ($2.95, lim. series)
1,2-Mills-s/O'Neill-a 3.00

...: OFFICIAL MOVIE ADAPTATION July, 1994 - Aug, 1994 ($2.50, lim. series)
1,2 2.50

... RETURNS Oct, 1992 - No. 4, Mar, 1993 ($2.50, limited series)
1-4 4.00

... SOUTHERN DISCOMFORT Mar, 1996 - No. 4, July, 1996 ($2.50, lim. series)
1-4 2.50

... STRIKES BACK Feb, 1995 - No. 5, Jun, 1995 ($2.50, limited series)
1-5 2.50

... SUMMER VACATION July, 1995 ($10.95, one shot, hard-c)
1-nn-Rick Geary-c/a 11.00

... TOYS IN THE ATTIC Aug, 1998 - No. 4, Nov, 1998 ($2.95, limited series)
1-4-Fingerman-s 3.00

... VIRTUAL SURREALITY July, 1997 ($2.95, one shot)
nn-Mignola, Aragonés, and others-s/a 3.00

... WORLD TOUR Dec, 1995 - No. 4, Mar, 1996 ($2.50, limited series)
1-4: 3-X & Ghost-c/app. 2.50

MASK COMICS
Rural Home Publ.: Feb-Mar, 1945 - No. 2, Apr-May, 1945; No. 2, Fall, 1945
1-Classic L. B. Cole Satan-c/a; Palais-a 263.00 790.00 2500.00
2-(Scarce)-Classic L. B. Cole Satan-c; Black Rider, The Boy Magician, & The Collector app. 168.00 505.00 1600.00
2-(Fall, 1945)-No publ.-same as regular #2; L. B. Cole-c 132.00 395.00 1250.00

MASKED BANDIT, THE
Avon Periodicals: 1952
nn-Kinstler-a 16.00 48.00 125.00

MASKED MAN, THE
Eclipse Comics: 12/84 - #10, 4/86; #11, 10/87; #12, 4/88 ($1.75/$2.00, color/B&W #9 on, Baxter paper)
1-12: 1-Origin retold. 3-Origin Aphid-Man; begin $2.00-c 2.00

MASKED MARVEL (See Keen Detective Funnies)
Centaur Publications: Sept, 1940 - No. 3, Dec, 1940
1-The Masked Marvel begins 163.00 490.00 1550.00
2,3: 2-Gustavson, Tarpe Mills-a 111.00 332.00 1050.00

MASKED RAIDER, THE (Billy The Kid #9 on; Frontier Scout, Daniel Boone #10-13) (Also see Blue Bird)
Charlton Comics: June, 1955 - No. 8, July, 1957; No. 14, Aug, 1958 - No. 30, June, 1961
1-Masked Raider & Talon the Golden Eagle begin; painted-c 11.00 33.00 90.00

Masked Ranger #2 © Premiere Mags.

Master Comics #26 © FAW

Master of Kung-Fu #111 © MAR

GD2.0 FN6.0 NM9.4

2 7.15 21.50 50.00
3-8,15: 8-Billy The Kid app. 15-Williamson-a, 7 pgs. 5.00 15.00 35.00
14,16-30: 22-Rocky Lane app. 4.65 14.00 28.00

MASKED RANGER
Premier Magazines: Apr, 1954 - No. 9, Aug, 1955

1-The Masked Ranger, his horse Streak, & The Crimson Avenger (origin) begin, end #9; Woodbridge/Frazetta-a 40.00 120.00 350.00
2,3 12.50 37.50 100.00
4-8-All Woodbridge-a. 5-Jesse James by Woodbridge. 6-Billy The Kid by Woodbridge. 7-Wild Bill Hickok by Woodbridge. 8-Jim Bowie's Life Story 14.00 41.00 110.00
9-Torres-a; Wyatt Earp by Woodbridge; Says Death of Masked Ranger on-c 15.00 45.00 120.00

NOTE: *Check a-1. **Woodbridge** c/a-1, 4-9.*

MASK OF DR. FU MANCHU, THE (See Dr. Fu Manchu)
Avon Periodicals: 1951

1-Sax Rohmer adapt.; Wood-c/a (26 pgs.); Hollingsworth-a 89.00 268.00 850.00

MASK OF ZORRO, THE
Image Comics: Aug, 1998 - No. 4, Dec, 1998 ($2.95, limited series)

1-4-Movie adapt. Photo variant-c 3.00

MASQUE OF THE RED DEATH (See Movie Classics)

MASTER COMICS (Combined with Slam Bang Comics #7 on)
Fawcett Publications: Mar, 1940 - No. 133, Apr, 1953 (No. 1-6: oversized issues) (#1-3: 15¢, 52 pgs.; #4-6: 10¢, 36 pgs.; #7-Begin 68 pg. issues)

1-Origin & 1st app. Master Man; The Devil's Dagger, El Carim, Master of Magic, Rick O'Say, Morton Murch, White Rajah, Shipwreck Roberts, Frontier Marshal, Streak Sloan, Mr. Clue begin (all features end #6) 713.00 2140.00 8200.00
2 211.00 633.00 2000.00
3-6: 6-Last Master Man 163.00 490.00 1550.00

NOTE: *#1-6 rarely found in near mint to mint condition due to large-size format.*

7-(10/40)-Bulletman, Zoro, the Mystery Man (ends #22), Lee Granger, Jungle King, & Buck Jones begin; only app. The War Bird & Mark Swift & the Time Retarder; Zoro, Lee Granger, Jungle King & Mark Swift all continue from Slam Bang; Bulletman moves from Nickel 284.00 853.00 2700.00
8-The Red Gaucho (ends #13), Captain Venture (ends #22) & The Planet Princess begin 147.00 442.00 1400.00
9,10: 10-Lee Granger ends 116.00 348.00 1100.00
11-Origin & 1st app. Minute-Man (2/41) 253.00 758.00 2400.00
12 126.00 379.00 1200.00
13-Origin & 1st app. Bulletgirl; Hitler-c 195.00 584.00 1850.00
14-16: 14-Companions Three begins, ends #31 105.00 316.00 1000.00
17-20: 17-Raboy-a on Bulletman begins. 20-Captain Marvel cameo app. in Bulletman 97.00 292.00 925.00
21-(12/41; Scarce)-Captain Marvel & Bulletman team up against Capt. Nazi; origin & 1st app. Capt. Marvel Jr's most famous nemesis Captain Nazi who will cause creation of Capt. Marvel Jr. in Whiz #25. Part I of trilogy origin of Capt. Marvel Jr.; 1st Mac Raboy-c for Fawcett; Capt. Nazi-c 478.00 1435.00 5500.00
22-(1/42)-Captain Marvel Jr. moves over from Whiz #25 & teams up with Bulletman against Captain Nazi; part III of trilogy origin of Capt. Marvel Jr. & his 1st cover and adventure 435.00 1305.00 5000.00
23-Capt. Marvel Jr. c/stories begin (1st solo story); fights Capt. Nazi by himself. 284.00 853.00 2700.00
24,25 95.00 285.00 900.00
26-28,30-Captain Marvel Jr. vs. Capt. Nazi. 30-Flag-c 84.00 253.00 800.00
29-Hitler & Hirohito-c 103.00 308.00 975.00
31-33,35: 32-Last El Carim & Buck Jones; intro Balbo, the Boy Magician in El Carim story; classic Eagle-c by Raboy. 33-Balbo, the Boy Magician (ends #47), Hopalong Cassidy (ends #49) begins 63.00 189.00 600.00
34-Capt. Marvel Jr. vs. Capt. Nazi-c/story 71.00 213.00 675.00
36-40: 40-Flag-c 58.00 174.00 550.00
41-(8/43)-Bulletman, Capt. Marvel Jr. & Bulletgirl x-over in Minute-Man; only app.Crime Crusaders Club (Capt. Marvel Jr., Minute-Man, Bulletman & Bulletgirl) 63.00 189.00 600.00

GD2.0 FN6.0 NM9.4

42-47,49: 47-Hitler becomes Corpl. Hitler Jr. 49-Last Minute-Man 40.00 120.00 350.00
48-Intro. Bulletboy; Capt. Marvel cameo in Minute-Man 44.00 133.00 400.00
50-Intro Radar & Nyoka the Jungle Girl & begin series (5/44); Radar also intro in Captain Marvel #35 (same date); Capt. Marvel x-over in Radar; origin Radar; Capt. Marvel & Capt. Marvel, Jr. introduce Radar on-c 40.00 120.00 360.00
51-58 22.00 66.00 175.00
59-62: Nyoka serial "Terrible Tiara" in all; 61-Capt. Marvel Jr. 1st meets Uncle Marvel 25.00 75.00 200.00
63-80 18.00 53.00 140.00
81,83-87,89-91,95-99: 88-Hopalong Cassidy begins (ends #94). 95-Tom Mix begins (ends #133) 15.00 45.00 120.00
82,88,92-94-Krigstein-a 16.00 49.00 130.00
100 16.00 48.00 125.00
101-106-Last Bulletman 14.00 41.00 110.00
107-131 12.50 37.50 100.00
132-B&W and color illos in **POP** 13.00 39.00 105.00
133-Bill Battle app. 19.00 56.00 150.00

NOTE: ***Mac Raboy** a-15-39, 40(part), 42, 58. c-21-49, 51, 52, 54, 56, 58, 68(part), 69(part). Bulletman c-7-11, 13(half), 15, 18(part), 19, 20, 21(w/Capt. Marvel & Capt. Nazi), 22(w/Capt. Marvel, Jr.). Capt. Marvel, Jr. c-23-133. Master Man c-1-6. Minute Man c-12, 13(half), 14, 16, 17, 18(part).*

MASTER DARQUE
Acclaim Comics (Valiant): Feb, 1998 ($3.95)

1-Manco-a/Christina Z.-s 4.00

MASTER DETECTIVE
Super Comics: 1964 (Reprints)

17-r/Criminals on the Loose V4 #2; r/Young King Cole #?; McWilliams-r 1.50 4.50 12.00

MASTER OF KUNG FU (Formerly Special Marvel Edition; see Deadly Hands of Kung Fu & Giant-Size...)
Marvel Comics Group: No. 17, April, 1974 - No. 125, June, 1983

17-Starlin-a; intro Black Jack Tarr; 3rd Shang-Chi (ties w/Deadly Hands #1) 2.30 7.00 20.00
18-20: 19-Man-Thing-c/story 1.50 4.50 12.00
21-23,25-30 1.00 2.80 7.00
24-Starlin, Simonson-a 1.10 3.30 9.00
31-50: 33-1st Leiko Wu. 43-Last 25¢ issue 4.00
40-42-(30¢-c variants, limited distribution)(5-7/76) 2.40 6.00
51-99 3.50
100118,125-Double size 4.00
101-117,119-124 3.00
Annual 1(4/76)-Iron Fist app. 1.50 4.50 12.00

NOTE: ***Austin** c-63i, 74i. **Buscema** c-44p. **Gulacy** a(p)-18-20, 22, 25, 29-31, 33-35, 38, 39, 40(p&i), 42-50, 53r(#20); c-51, 55, 64, 67. **Gil Kane** c(p)-20, 38, 39, 42, 45, 59, 63. **Nebres** c-73i. **Starlin** a-17p, 24; c-54. **Sutton** a-42i. #53 reprints #20.*

MASTER OF KUNG-FU: BLEEDING BLACK
Marvel Comics: Feb, 1991 ($2.95, 84 pgs., one-shot)

1-The Return of Shang-Chi 3.00

MASTER OF THE WORLD
Dell Publishing Co.: No. 1157, July, 1961

Four Color 1157-Movie 4.60 13.75 55.00

MASTERS OF TERROR (Magazine)
Marvel Comics Group: July, 1975 - No. 2, Sept, 1975 (B&W) (All reprints)

1-Brunner, Barry Smith-a; Morrow/Steranko-c; Starlin-a(p); Gil Kane-a 1.75 5.25 14.00
2-Reese, Kane, Mayerik-a; Adkins/Steranko-c 1.50 4.50 12.00

MASTERS OF THE UNIVERSE (See DC Comics Presents #47 for 1st app.)
DC Comics: Dec, 1982 - No. 3, Feb, 1983 (Mini-series)

1-3: 2-Origin He-Man & Ceril 3.00

NOTE: ***Alcala** a-1i,, 2i. **Tuska** a-1-3p; c-1-3p. #2 has 75 & 95 cent cover price.*

MASTERS OF THE UNIVERSE (Comic Album)
Western Publishing Co.: 1984 (8-1/2x11", $2.95, 64 pgs.)

Maverick #7 © MAR

Maximum Security #1 © MAR

MD #1 © WMG

11362-Based on Mattel toy & cartoon 1.25 3.75 10.00

MASTERS OF THE UNIVERSE
Star Comics/Marvel #7 on: May 1986 - No. 13, May, 1988 (75¢/$1.00)

1-11: 8-Begin $1.00-c 4.00
12-Death of He-Man (1st Marvel app.) 5.00
13-Return of He-Man & death of Skeletor 5.00
The Motion Picture (11/87, $2.00)-Tuska-p 3.00

MASTERWORKS SERIES OF GREAT COMIC BOOK ARTISTS, THE
Sea Gate Dist./DC Comics: May, 1983 - No. 3, Dec, 1983 (Baxter paper)

1-3: 1,2-Shining Knight by Frazetta r-/Adventure. 2-Tomahawk by Frazetta-r. 3-Wrightson-c/a(r) 4.00

MATT SLADE GUNFIGHTER (Kid Slade Gunfighter #5 on; See Western Gunfighters)
Atlas Comics (SPI): May, 1956 - No. 4, Nov, 1956

1-Intro Matt & horse Eagle; Williamson/Torres-a 20.00 60.00 160.00
2-Williamson-a 12.00 36.00 95.00
3,4 10.00 30.00 60.00
NOTE: ***Maneely*** *a-1, 3, 4; c-1, 2, 4.* ***Roth*** *a-2-4.* ***Severin*** *a-1, 3, 4.* ***Maneely*** *c/a-1. Issue #s stamped on cover after printing.*

MAUS: A SURVIVOR'S TALE (First graphic novel to win a Pulitzer Prize)
Pantheon Books: 1986, 1991 (B&W)

Vol. 1-(...: My Father Bleeds History)(1986) Art Spiegelman-s/a; recounts stories of Spiegelman's father in 1930s-40s Nazi-occupied Poland; collects first six stories serialized in Raw Magazine from 1980-1985 20.00
Vol. 2-(...: And Here My Troubles Began)(1991) 20.00
Complete Maus Survivor's Tale -HC Vols. 1& 2 w/slipcase 35.00
Hardcover Vol. 1 (1991) 24.00
Hardcover Vol. 2 (1991) 24.00
TPB (1992, $14.00) Vols. 1& 2 14.00

MAVERICK (TV)
Dell Publishing Co.: No. 892, 4/58 - No. 19, 4-6/62 (All have photo-c)

Four Color 892 (#1)-James Garner photo-c begin 25.00 75.00 300.00
Four Color 930,945,962,980,1005 (6-8/59): 945-James Garner/Jack Kelly photo-c begin 10.00 30.00 120.00
7 (10-12/59) - 14: Last Garner/Kelly-c 8.00 24.00 95.00
15-18: Jack Kelly/Roger Moore photo-c 6.70 20.00 80.00
19-Jack Kelly photo-c 6.70 20.00 80.00

MAVERICK (See X-Men)
Marvel Comics: Jan, 1997 ($2.95, one-shot)

1-Hama-s 3.00

MAVERICK (See X-Men)
Marvel Comics: Sept, 1997 - No. 12, Aug, 1998 ($2.99/$1.99)

1,12: 1-($2.99)-Wraparound-c. 12-($2.99) Battles Omega Red 4.00
2-11: 2-Two covers. 4-Wolverine app. 6,7-Sabretooth app. 3.00

MAVERICK MARSHAL
Charlton Comics: Nov, 1958 - No. 7, May, 1960

1 5.50 16.50 38.00
2-7 4.30 13.00 26.00

MAVERICKS
Daggar Comics Group: Jan, 1994 - No. 5, 1994 (#1-$2.75, #2-5-$2.50)

1-5: 1-Bronze. 1-Gold. 1-Silver 2.75

MAX BRAND (See Silvertip)

MAXIMAGE
Image Comics (Extreme Studios): Dec, 1995 - No. 7, June 1996 ($2.50)

1-7: 1-Liefeld-c. 2-Extreme Destroyer Pt. 2; polybagged w/card. 4-Angela & Glory-c/app. 2.50

MAXIMUM SECURITY (Crossover)
Marvel Comics: Oct, 2000 - No. 3, Jan, 2001 ($2.99)

1-3-Busiek-s/Ordway-a; Ronan the Accuser, Avengers app. 3.00
...Dangerous Planet 1: Busiek-s/Ordway-a; Ego, the Living Planet 3.00
Thor vs. Ego (11/00, $2.99) Reprints Thor #133,160,161; Kirby-a 3.00

MAXX (Also see Darker Image, Primer #5, & Friends of Maxx)
Image Comics (I Before E): Mar, 1993 - Present ($1.95)

1/2 1.25 3.75 10.00
1/2 (Gold) 20.00
1-Sam Kieth-c/a/scripts 4.00
1-Glow-in-the-dark variant 1.50 4.50 12.00
1-"3-D Edition" (1/98, $4.95) plus new back-up story 5.00
2-12: 6-Savage Dragon cameo(1 pg.). 7,8-Pitt-c & story 2.50
13-16 2.50
17-35: 21-Alan Moore-s 2.00

MAYA (See Movie Classics)
Gold Key: Mar, 1968

1 (10218-803)(TV) 2.50 7.50 23.00

MAYHEM
Dark Horse Comics: May, 1989 - No. 4, Sept, 1989 ($2.50, B&W, 52 pgs.)

1- Four part Stanley Ipkiss/Mask story begins; Mask-c 1.25 3.75 10.00
2-4: 2-Mask 1/2 back-c. 4-Mask-c 1.10 3.30 9.00

MAZE AGENCY, THE
Comico/Innovation Publ. #8 on: Dec, 1988 - No. 20, 1991 ($1.95-$2.50, color)

1-20: 9-Ellery Queen app. 7 ($2.50)-Last Comico issue 2.50
Annual 1 (1990, $2.75)-Ploog-c; Spirit tribute ish 2.75
Special 1 (1989, $2.75)-Staton-p (Innovation) 2.75

MAZE AGENCY, THE (Vol. 2)
Caliber Comics: July, 1997 - Present ($2.95, B&W)

1-3: 1-Barr-s/Gonzales-a(p). 3-Hughes-c 3.00

MAZIE (...& Her Friends) (See Flat-Top, Mortie, Stevie & Tastee-Freez)
Mazie Comics(Magazine Publ.)/Harvey Publ. No. 13-on: 1953 - #12, 1954; #13, 12/54 - #22, 9/56; #23, 9/57 - #28, 8/58

1-(Teen-age)-Stevie's girlfriend 7.85 23.50 55.00
2 4.65 14.00 28.00
3-10 4.00 11.00 22.00
11-28 3.00 7.50 15.00

MAZIE
Nation Wide Publishers: 1950 - No. 7, 1951 (5¢) (5x7-1/4"-miniature)(52 pgs.)

1-Teen-age 15.00 45.00 120.00
2-7 8.65 26.00 60.00

MAZINGER (See First Comics Graphic Novel #17)

'MAZING MAN
DC Comics: Jan, 1986 - No. 12, Dec, 1986

1-11: 7,8-Hembeck-a 2.00
12-Dark Knight part-c by Miller 3.00
Special 1 ('87), 2 (4/88), 3 ('90)-All $2.00, 52pgs. 2.00

McHALE'S NAVY (TV) (See Movie Classics)
Dell Publ. Co.: May-July, 1963 - No. 3, Nov-Jan, 1963-64 (All have photo-c)

1 5.00 15.00 60.00
2,3 4.55 13.65 50.00

McKEEVER & THE COLONEL (TV)
Dell Publishing Co.: Feb-Apr, 1963 - No. 3, Aug-Oct, 1963

1-Photo-c 5.00 15.00 60.00
2,3 3.80 11.50 45.00

McLINTOCK (See Movie Comics)

MD
E. C. Comics: Apr-May, 1955 - No. 5, Dec-Jan, 1955-56

1-Not approved by code; Craig-c 11.00 33.00 120.00
2-5 8.00 24.00 90.00
NOTE: ***Crandall, Evans, Ingels, Orlando*** *art in all issues;* ***Craig*** *c-1-5.*

MD
Russ Cochran/Gemstone Publishing: Sept, 1999 - No. 5, Jan, 2000 ($2.50)

1-5-Reprints original EC series 2.50
Annual 1 (1999, $13.50) r/#1-5 13.50

M.D. GEIST
CPM Comics: 1995 - No. 3, 1995 (Limited series)

Measles #4 © Fantagraphics Books

Meet Miss Pepper #5 © STJ

Megaton #8 © Gary S. Carlson

GD2.0 FN6.0 NM9.4

1-3 3.00

.D. GEIST DATA ALBUM
'PM Comics: June, 1996 ($9.95, trade paperback)

1 10.00

.D. GEIST: GROUND ZERO
:PM Comics: Mar, 1996 - No. 3, May, 1996 ($2.95, limited series)

1-3 3.00

IEASLES
antagraphics Books: Christmas 1998 - Present ($2.95, B&W, quarterly)

1-7-Anthology: 1-Venus-s by Hernandez 3.00

IEAT CAKE
:onographix: 1992 (B&W)

1 2.00

IEAT CAKE
antagraphics Books: No. 1, Oct, 1993 - Present (B&W)

0-8: 3-Sal Buscema-a. 0-(1996)-r/Meat Cake #1 from Iconographix. 2.50
9-($3.95) Alan Moore-s 4.00

IECHA (Also see Mayhem)
ark Horse Comics: June, 1987 - No. 6, 1988 ($1.50/$1.95, color/B&W)

1-6: 1,2 ($1.95, color), 3,4-($1.75, B&W), 5,6-($1.50, B&W) 2.00

IECHANIC, THE
nage Comics: 1998 ($5.95, one-shot, squarebound)

1-Chiodo-painted art; Peterson-s 2.40 6.00
1-($10.00) DF Alternate Cover Ed. 10.00

IECHA SPECIAL
ark Horse Comics: May, 1995 ($2.95, one-shot)

1 3.00

IEDAL FOR BOWZER, A
merican Visuals: 1966 (8 pgs.)

n-Eisner-c/script 25.00 65.00 240.00

IEDAL OF HONOR COMICS
. S. Curtis: Spring, 1946

1-War stories 11.00 33.00 90.00

IEDAL OF HONOR SPECIAL
ark Horse Comics: 1994 ($2.50, one-shot)

1-Kubert-c/a (first story) 2.50

IEDIA STARR
nnovation Publ.: July, 1989 - No. 3, Sept, 1989 ($1.95, mini-series, 28pgs.)

1-3: Deluxe format 2.00

IEDIEVAL SPAWN/WITCHBLADE
nage Comics (Top Cow Productions): May, 1996 - No. 3, June, 1996 ($2.95, mited series)

1-3-Garth Ennis scripts in all 2.40 6.00
1-Platinum foil-c (500 copies from Pittsburgh Con) 35.00
1-Gold 10.00
1-ETM Exclusive Edition; gold foil logo 7.00
'PB ($9.95) r/#1-3 10.00

IEET ANGEL (Formerly Angel & the Ape)
lational Periodical Publications: No. 7, Nov-Dec, 1969

7-Wood-a(i) 2.30 7.00 20.00

IEET CORLISS ARCHER (Radio/Movie)(My Life #4 on)
ox Features Syndicate: Mar, 1948 - No. 3, July, 1948

1-(Teen-age)-Feldstein-c/a; headlight-c 95.00 285.00 900.00
2-Feldstein-c only 55.00 165.00 500.00
3-Part Feldstein-c only 50.00 150.00 450.00
IOTE: *No. 1-3 used in Seduction of the Innocent, pg. 39.*

IEET HERCULES (See Three Stooges)

IEET MERTON
'oby Press: Dec, 1953 - No. 4, June, 1954

GD2.0 FN6.0 NM9.4

1-(Teen-age)-Dave Berg-c/a 8.65 26.00 60.00
2-Dave Berg-c/a 5.00 15.00 32.00
3,4-Dave Berg-c/a 5.00 15.00 30.00
I.W. Reprint #9, Super Reprint #11('63), 18 1.50 4.50 12.00

MEET MISS BLISS (Becomes Stories Of Romance #5 on)
Atlas Comics (LMC): May, 1955 - No. 4, Nov, 1955

1-Al Hartley-c/a 12.50 37.50 100.00
2-4 8.65 26.00 60.00

MEET MISS PEPPER (Formerly Lucy, The Real Gone Gal)
St. John Publishing Co.: No. 5, April, 1954 - No. 6, June, 1954

5-Kubert/Maurer-a 20.00 60.00 160.00
6-Kubert/Maurer-a; Kubert-c 16.00 49.00 130.00

MEGA DRAGON & TIGER
Image Comics: Mar, 1999 - No. 5 ($2.95)

1-5-Tony Wong-s/a 3.00

MEGAHURTZ
Image Comics: Aug, 1997 - No. 3, Oct, 1997 ($2.95, B&W)

1-3-St. Pierre-s 3.00

MEGALITH (Megalith Deathwatch 2000 #1,2 of second series)
Continuity: 1989 - No. 9, Mar, 1992; No, 0, Apr, 1993 - No. 7, Jan, 1994

1-9-($2.00-c) 1-Adams & Texiera-c/Texiera & Nebres-a 2.00
2nd series: 0-(4/93)-Foil-c; no c-price, giveaway; Adams plot 3.00
1-7: 1-3-Bagged w/card: 1-Gatefold-c by Nebres; Adams plot. 2-Fold-out-c; Adamsplot. 3-Indestructible-c. 4-7-Embossed-c: 4-Adams/Nebres-c; Adams part-i. 5-Sienkiewicz-i. 6-Adams part-i. 7-Adams-c(p); Adams plot 3.00

MEGATON (A super hero)
Megaton Publ.: Nov, 1983; No. 2, Oct, 1985 - No. 8, Aug, 1987 (B&W)

1-($2.00, 68 pgs.)-Erik Larsen's 1st pro work; Vanguard by Larsen begins (1st app.), ends #4; 1st app. Megaton, Berzerker, & Ethrian; Guice-c/a(p); Gustovich-a(p) in #1,2 1.00 3.00 8.00
2-($2.00, 68 pgs.)-The Dragon cameo (1 pg.) by Larsen (later The Savage Dragon in Image Comics); Guice-c/a(p) 5.00
3-(44 pgs.)-1st full app. Savage Dragon-c/story by Larsen; 1st comic book work by Angel Medina (pin-up) 1.50 4.50 12.00
4-(52 pgs.)-2nd full app. Savage Dragon by Larsen; 4,5-Wildman by Grass Green 1.00 2.80 7.00
5-1st Liefeld published-a (inside f/c, 6/86) 4.00
6,7: 6-Larsen-c 3.00
8-1st Liefeld story-a (7 pg. super hero story) plus 1 pg. Youngblood ad 5.00
...Explosion (6/87, 16 pg. color giveaway)-1st app. Youngblood by Rob Liefeld (2 pg. spread); shows Megaton heroes 1.85 5.50 15.00
...Holiday Special 1 (1994, $2.95, color, 40 pgs., publ. by Entity Comics)-Gold foil logo; bagged w/Kelley Jones card; Vanguard, Megaton plus shows unpublished-c to 1987 Youngblood #1 by Liefeld/Ordway 3.00
NOTE: *Copies of Megaton Explosion were also released in early 1992 all signed by Rob Liefeld and were made available to retailers.*

MEGATON MAN (See Don Simpson's Bizarre Heroes)
Kitchen Sink Enterprises: Nov, 1984 - No. 10, 1986

1-10, 1-2nd printing (1989) 2.00
...Meets The Uncategorizable X-Thems 1 (4/89, $2.00) 2.00

MEGATON MAN: BOMB SHELL
Image Comics: Jul, 1999 - No. 2 ($2.95, B&W, mini-series)

1-Reprints stories from Megaton Man internet site 3.00

MEGATON MAN: HARD COPY
Image Comics: Feb, 1999 - No. 2, Apr, 1999 ($2.95, B&W, mini-series)

1,2-Reprints stories from Megaton Man internet site 3.00

MEGATON MAN VS. FORBIDDEN FRANKENSTEIN
Fiasco Comics: Apr, 1996 ($2.95, B&W, one-shot)

1-Intro The Tomb Team (Forbidden Frankenstein, Drekula, Bride of the Monster, & Moon Wolf). 3.00

MEL ALLEN SPORTS COMICS (The Voice of the Yankees)
Standard Comics: No. 5, Nov, 1949; No. 6, June, 1950

Menace #1 © Awesome Ent.

Men in Action #5 © MAR

Meridian #1 © CRO

GD2.0 FN6.0 NM9.4

5(#1 on inside)-Tuska-a 23.00 68.00 180.00
6(#2)-Lou Gehrig story 15.00 45.00 120.00

MELTING POT
Kitchen Sink Press: Dec, 1993 - No. 4, Sept, 1994 ($2.95)

1-4: Bisley-painted-c 3.00

MELVIN MONSTER
Dell Publishing Co.: Apr-June, 1965 - No. 10, Oct, 1969

1-By John Stanley 10.00 30.00 120.00
2-10-All by Stanley. #10-r/#1 7.00 21.00 85.00

MELVIN THE MONSTER (See Peter, the Little Pest & Dexter The Demon #7)
Atlas Comics (HPC): July, 1956 - No. 6, July, 1957

1-Maneely-c/a 12.50 37.50 100.00
2-6: 4-Maneely-c/a 9.30 28.00 65.00

MENACE
Atlas Comics (HPC): Mar, 1953 - No. 11, May, 1954

1-Horror & sci/fi stories begin; Everett-c/a 63.00 189.00 600.00
2-Post-atom bomb disaster by Everett; anti-Communist propaganda/torture scenes; Sinnott sci/fi story "Rocket to the Moon" 44.00 133.00 400.00
3,4,6-Everett-a. 4-Sci/fi story "Escape to the Moon". 6-Romita sci/fi story "Science Fiction" 38.00 113.00 300.00
5-Origin & 1st app. The Zombie by Everett (reprinted in Tales of the Zombie #1)(7/53); 5-Sci/fi story "Rocket Ship" 53.00 158.00 475.00
7,8,10,11: 7-Frankenstein story. 8-End of world story; Heath 3-D art(3 pgs.). 10-H-Bomb panels 28.00 84.00 225.00
9-Everett-a r-in Vampire Tales #1 33.00 98.00 260.00
NOTE: ***Brodsky*** *c-7, 8, 11.* ***Colan*** *a-6; c-9.* ***Everett*** *a-1-6, 9; c-1-6.* ***Heath*** *a-1-8; c-10.* ***Katz*** *a-11.* ***Maneely*** *a-3, 5, 7-9.* ***Powell*** *a-11.* ***Romita*** *a-3, 6, 8, 11.* ***Shelly*** *a-10.* ***Shores*** *a-7.* ***Sinnott*** *a-2, 7.* ***Tuska*** *a-1, 2, 5.*

MENACE
Awesome-Hyperwerks: Nov, 1998 ($2.50)

1-Jada Pinkett Smith-s/Fraga-a 2.50

MEN AGAINST CRIME (Formerly Mr. Risk; Hand of Fate #8 on)
Ace Magazines: No. 3, Feb, 1951 - No. 7, Oct, 1951

3-Mr. Risk app. 10.00 30.00 80.00
4-7: 4-Colan-a; entire book-r as Trapped! #4. 5-Meskin-a 7.15 21.50 50.00

MEN, GUNS, & CATTLE (See Classics Illustrated Special Issue)

MEN IN ACTION (Battle Brady #10 on)
Atlas Comics (IPS): April, 1952 - No. 9, Dec, 1952 (War stories)

1-Berg, Reinman-a 16.00 48.00 125.00
2 10.00 30.00 70.00
3-6,8,9: 3-Heath-c/a 7.85 23.50 55.00
7-Krigstein-a; Heath-c 10.00 30.00 75.00
NOTE: ***Brodsky*** *c-1, 4-6.* ***Maneely*** *c-5.* ***Pakula*** *a-1, 6.* ***Robinson*** *c-8.* ***Shores*** *c-9.*

MEN IN ACTION
Ajax/Farrell Publications: April, 1957 - No. 6, 1958

1 8.65 26.00 60.00
2 5.00 15.00 35.00
3-6 4.65 14.00 28.00

MEN IN BLACK, THE (1st series)
Aircel Comics (Malibu): Jan, 1990 - No. 3 Mar, 1990 ($2.25, B&W, lim. series)

1-Cunningham-s/a in all 3.20 9.60 35.00
2,3 2.00 6.00 18.00
Graphic Novel (Jan, 1991) r/#1-3 2.30 7.00 20.00

MEN IN BLACK (2nd series)
Aircel Comics (Malibu): May, 1991 - No. 3, Jul, 1991 ($2.50, B&W, lim. series)

1-Cunningham-s/a in all 2.00 6.00 16.00
2,3 1.00 3.00 8.00

MEN IN BLACK: FAR CRY
Marvel Comics: Aug, 1997 ($3.99, color, one-shot)

1-Cunningham-s 4.00

MEN IN BLACK: RETRIBUTION

GD2.0 FN6.0 NM9.4

Marvel Comics: Dec, 1997 ($3.99, color, one-shot)

1-Cunningham-s; continuation of the movie 4.00

MEN IN BLACK: THE MOVIE
Marvel Comics: Oct, 1997 ($3.99, one-shot, movie adaption)

1-Cunningham-s 4.00

MEN INTO SPACE
Dell Publishing Co.: No. 1083, Feb-Apr, 1960

Four Color 1083-Anderson-a, photo-c 4.60 13.75 55.00

MEN OF BATTLE (Also see New Men of Battle)
Catechetical Guild: V1#5, March, 1943 (Hardcover)

V1#5-Topix reprints 4.65 14.00 28.00

MEN OF WAR
DC Comics, Inc.: August, 1977 - No. 26, March, 1980 (#9,10: 44 pgs.)

1-Enemy Ace, Gravedigger (origin #1,2) begin 1.10 3.30 9.00
2-4,8-10,12-14,19,20: All Enemy Ace stories. 4-1st Dateline Frontline. 9-Unknown Soldier app. 2.40 6.00
5-7,11,15-18,21-25: 17-1st app. Rosa 5.00
26-Sgt. Rock & Easy Co.-c/s 1.10 3.30 9.00
NOTE: ***Chaykin*** *a-9, 10, 12-14, 19, 20.* ***Evans*** *c-25.* ***Kubert*** *c-2-23, 24p, 26.*

MEN'S ADVENTURES (Formerly True Adventures)
Marvel/Atlas Comics (CCC): No. 4, Aug, 1950 - No. 28, July, 1954

4(#1)(52 pgs.) 32.00 96.00 255.00
5-Flying Saucer story 20.00 60.00 160.00
6-8: 7-Buried alive story. 8-Sci/fic story 18.00 53.00 140.00
9-20: All war format 11.00 33.00 90.00
21,22,24,26: All horror format 19.00 56.00 150.00
23-Crandall-a; Fox-a(i); horror format 19.00 58.00 135.00
25-Shrunken head-c 31.00 94.00 250.00
27,28-Human Torch & Toro-c/stories; Captain America & Sub-Mariner stories in each (also see Young Men #24-28) 97.00 292.00 925.00
NOTE: ***Ayers*** *a-27(H. Torch).* ***Berg*** *a-15, 16.* ***Brodsky*** *c-4-9, 11, 12, 16-18, 24.* ***Burgos*** *c-27, 28(Human Torch).* ***Colan*** *a-14, 19.* ***Everett*** *a-10, 14, 22, 25, 28; c-14, 21-23.* ***Heath*** *a-8, 11, 24; c-13, 20, 26.* ***Lawrence*** *a-23; 27(Captain America).* ***Maneely*** *a-24; c-10, 15.* ***Mac Pakula*** *a-15, 25.* ***Post*** *a-23.* ***Powell*** *a-27(Sub-Mariner).* ***Reinman*** *a-11, 12.* ***Robinson*** *c-19.* ***Romita*** *a-22.* ***Shores*** *c-25.* ***Sinnott*** *a-21.* ***Tuska*** *a-24. Adventure-#4-8; War-#9-20; Weird/Horror-#21-26.*

MENZ INSANA
DC Comics (Vertigo): 1997 ($7.95, one-shot)

nn-Fowler-s/Bolton painted art 1.00 3.00 8.00

MEPHISTO VS... (See Silver Surfer #3)
Marvel Comics Group: Apr, 1987 - No. 4, July, 1987 ($1.50, mini-series)

1-4: 1-Fantastic Four; Austin-i. 2-X-Factor. 3-X-Men. 4-Avengers 3.00

MERC (See Mark Hazzard: Merc)

MERCHANTS OF DEATH
Acme Press (Eclipse): Jul, 1988 - No. 4, Nov, 1988 ($3.50, B&W/16 pgs. color, 44pg. mag.)

1-4: 4-Toth-c 3.50

MERCY
DC Comics (Vertigo): 1993 ($5.95, 68 pgs., mature)

nn 2.40 6.00

MERIDIAN
CrossGeneration Comics: Jul, 2000 - Present ($2.95)

1-8: Barbara Kesel-s 3.00

MERLIN JONES AS THE MONKEY'S UNCLE (See Movie Comics and The Misadventures of... under Movie Comics)

MERRILL'S MARAUDERS (See Movie Classics)

MERRY CHRISTMAS (See A Christmas Adventure, Donald Duck..., Dell Giant #39, & March of Comics #153)

MERRY COMICS
Carlton Publishing Co.: Dec, 1945 (No cover price)

nn-Boogeyman app. 20.00 60.00 160.00

MERRY COMICS: Four Star Publications: 1947 (Advertised, not published)

Merv Pumpkinhead, Agent of D.R.E.A.M. #1 © DC

Meta-4 #3 © FC

Mickey Finn #4 © McNaught Syndicate

GD2.0 FN6.0 NM9.4

ERRY-GO-ROUND COMICS
aSalle Publ. Co./Croyden Publ./Rotary Litho.: 1944 (25¢, 132 pgs.); 1946; 9-
)/47 - No. 2, 1948

	GD2.0	FN6.0	NM9.4
ı(1944)(LaSalle)-Funny animal; 29 new features	18.00	53.00	140.00
:1 (Publisher?)	7.15	21.50	50.00
1(1946)(Croyden)-Al Fago-c; funny animal	10.00	30.00	70.00
1#1,2(1947-48; 52 pgs.)(Rotary Litho. Co. Ltd., Canada); Ken Hultgren-a	7.15	21.50	50.00

ERRY MAILMAN (See Fawcett's Funny Animals #87-89)

ERRY MOUSE (Also see Funny Tunes & Space Comics)
von Periodicals: June, 1953 - No. 4, Jan-Feb, 1954

	GD2.0	FN6.0	NM9.4
1-1st app.; funny animal; Frank Carin-c/a	9.30	28.00	65.00
2-4	5.50	16.50	38.00

ERV PUMPKINHEAD, AGENT OF D.R.E.A.M. (See The Sandman)
C Comics (Vertigo): 2000 ($5.95, one-shot)

1-Buckingham-a(p); Nowlan painted-c 6.00

ESSENGER, THE
nage Comics: July, 2000 ($5.95, one-shot)

1-Ordway-s/c/a 6.00

ETA-4
irst Comics: Feb, 1991 - No. 4, 1991 ($2.25)

1-($3.95, 52pgs.) 4.00
2-4 2.25

ETAL MEN (See Brave & the Bold, DC Comics Presents, and
howcase #37-40)
ational Periodical Publications/DC Comics: 4-5/63 - No. 41, 12-1/69-70; No.
2, 2-3/73 - No. 44, 7-8/73; No. 45, 4-5/76 - No. 56, 2-3/78

	GD2.0	FN6.0	NM9.4
1-(4-5/63)-5th app. Metal Men	50.00	150.00	650.00
2	18.00	54.00	200.00
3-5	11.00	33.00	120.00
6-10	6.80	20.50	75.00
1 1-20: 12-Beatles cameo (12/65)	5.45	16.35	60.00
21-26,28-30: 21-Batman, Robin & Flash x-over	3.65	11.00	40.00
27-Origin Metal Men retold	5.45	16.35	60.00
31-41(1968-70): 38-Last 12¢ issue. 41-Last 15¢	2.50	7.50	25.00
42-44(1973)-Reprints	1.50	4.50	12.00
45('76)-49-Simonson-a in all: 48,49-Re-intro Eclipso	1.00	2.80	7.00
50-56: 50-Part-r. 54,55-Green Lantern x-over	1.00	2.80	7.00

OTE: ***Andru/Esposito** c-1-30. **Aparo** c-53-56. **Giordano** c-45, 46. **Kane/Esposito** a-30, 31; c-1. **Simonson** a-45-49; c-47-52. **Staton** a-50-56.*

ETAL MEN
C Comics: Oct, 1993 - No. 4, Jan, 1994 ($1.25, mini-series)

1-($2.50)-Multi-colored foil-c 3.00
2-4: 2-Origin 2.00

ETAL MEN (See Tangent Comics/ Metal Men)

ETAMORPHO (See Action Comics #413, Brave & the Bold #57,58, 1st Issue
pecial,& World's Finest #217)
ational Periodical Publications: July-Aug, 1965 - No. 17, Mar-Apr, 1968
All 12¢ issues)

	GD2.0	FN6.0	NM9.4
1-(7-8/65)-3rd app. Metamorpho	11.50	34.00	125.00
2,3	5.45	16.35	60.00
4-6,10:10-Origin & 1st app. Element Girl (1-2/67)	3.80	11.40	42.00
7-9	3.20	9.60	35.00
11-17: 17-Sparling-c/a	2.50	7.50	25.00

OTE: ***Ramona Fradon** a-B&B 57, 58, 1-4. **Orlando** a-5, 6; c-5-9, 11. **Trapani** a(p)-7-16; i-16.*

ETAMORPHO
C Comics: Aug, 1993 - No. 4, Nov, 1993 ($1.50, mini-series)

1-4 2.00

ETAPHYSIQUE
Malibu Comics (Bravura): Apr, 1995 - No. 6, Oct, 1995 ($2.95, limited series)

1-6: Norm Breyfogle-c/a/scripts 3.00

ETEOR COMICS
L. L. Baird (Croyden): Nov, 1945

	GD2.0	FN6.0	NM9.4
1-Captain Wizard, Impossible Man, Race Wilkins app.; origin Baldy Bean, Capt. Wizard's sidekick; bare-breasted mermaids story	40.00	120.00	350.00

METEOR MAN
Marvel Comics: Aug, 1993 - No. 6, Jan, 1994 ($1.25, limited series)

1-6: 1-Polybagged w/button & rap newspaper. 4-Night Thrasher-c/story. 6-Terry Austin-c(i) 2.00

METROPOL (See Ted McKeever's...)

METROPOL A.D. (See Ted McKeever's...)

METROPOLIS S.C.U. (Also see Showcase '96 #1)
DC Comics: Nov, 1995 - No. 4, Feb, 1996 ($1.50, limited series)

1-4:1-Superman-c & app. 2.00

MEZZ: GALACTIC TOUR 2494 (Also See Nexus)
Dark Horse Comics: May, 1994 ($2.50, one-shot)

1 2.50

MGM'S MARVELOUS WIZARD OF OZ (See Marvel Treasury of Oz)
Marvel Comics Group/National Periodical Publications: 1975 ($1.50, 84 pgs.; oversize)

	GD2.0	FN6.0	NM9.4
1-Adaptation of MGM's movie; J. Buscema-a	2.00	6.00	18.00

M.G.M'S MOUSE MUSKETEERS (Formerly M.G.M.'s The Two Mouseketeers)
Dell Publishing Co.: No. 670, Jan, 1956 - No. 1290, Mar-May, 1962

	GD2.0	FN6.0	NM9.4
Four Color 670 (#4)	3.65	11.00	40.00
Four Color 711,728,764	2.50	7.50	25.00
8 (4-6/57) - 21 (3-5/60)	2.40	7.35	22.00
Four Color 1135,1175,1290	2.50	7.50	25.00

M.G.M.'S SPIKE AND TYKE (also see Tom & Jerry #79)
Dell Publishing Co.: No. 499, Sept, 1953 - No. 1266, Dec-Feb, 1961-62

	GD2.0	FN6.0	NM9.4
Four Color 499 (#1)	3.65	11.00	40.00
Four Color 577,638	2.50	7.50	25.00
4(12-2/55-56)-10	2.40	7.35	22.00
11-24(12-2/60-61)	2.00	6.00	18.00
Four Color 1266	2.40	7.35	22.00

M.G.M.'S THE TWO MOUSKETEERS
Dell Publishing Co.: No. 475, June, 1953 - No. 642, July, 1955

	GD2.0	FN6.0	NM9.4
Four Color 475 (#1)	6.70	20.00	80.00
Four Color 603 (11/54), 642	4.10	12.30	45.00

MICHAELANGELO CHRISTMAS SPECIAL (See Teenage Mutant Ninja Turtles Christmas Special)

MICHAELANGELO, TEENAGE MUTANT NINJA TURTLE
Mirage Studios: 1986 (One shot) ($1.50, B&W)

1 4.00
1-2nd printing ('89, $1.75)-Reprint plus new-a 2.00

MICHAEL MOORCOCK'S MULTIVERSE
DC Comics (Helix): Nov, 1997 - No. 12, Oct, 1998 ($2.50, limited series)

1-12: Simonson, Reeve & Ridgway-a 2.50
TPB (1999, $19.95) r/#1-12 20.00

MICKEY AND DONALD (See Walt Disney's...)

MICKEY AND DONALD IN VACATIONLAND (See Dell Giant No. 47)

MICKEY & THE BEANSTALK (See Story Hour Series)

MICKEY & THE SLEUTH (See Walt Disney Showcase #38, 39, 42)

MICKEY FINN (Also see Big Shot Comics #74 & Feature Funnies)
Eastern Color 1-4/McNaught Synd. #5 on (Columbia)/Headline V3#2: Nov?, 1942 - V3#2, May, 1952

	GD2.0	FN6.0	NM9.4
1	30.00	90.00	240.00
2	15.00	45.00	120.00
3-Charlie Chan story	10.00	30.00	80.00
4	8.65	26.00	60.00
5-10	6.40	19.25	45.00
11-15(1949): 12-Sparky Watts app.	5.00	15.00	32.00

Mickey Mouse Four Color #116 © WDC

Mickey Mouse #253 © WDC

Mickey Mouse Magazine V2 #3 © WDC

V3#1,2(1952) 4.30 13.00 26.00

MICKEY MALONE
Hale Nass Corp.: 1936 (Color, punchout-c) (B&W-a on back)

GD2.0 FN6.0 VF8.0

nn-1pg. of comics 140.00 280.00 560.00

MICKEY MANTLE (See Baseball's Greatest Heroes #1)

MICKEY MOUSE (See Adventures of Mickey Mouse, The Best of Walt Disney Comics, Cheerios giveaways, Donald and ..., Dynabrite Comics, 40 Big Pages..., Gladstone Comic Album, Merry Christmas From..., Walt Disney's Mickey and Donald, Walt Disney's Comics & Stories, Walt Disney's..., & Wheaties)

MICKEY MOUSE (...Secret Agent #107-109; Walt Disney's... #148-205?) (See Dell Giants for annuals) (#204 exists from both G.K. & Whitman)
Dell Publ. Co./Gold Key #85-204/Whitman #204-218/Gladstone #219 on: #16, 1941 - #84, 7-9/62; #85, 11/62 - #218, 8/82; #219, 10/86 - #256, 4/90

GD2.0 FN6.0 VF8.0

Four Color 16(1941)-1st Mickey Mouse comic book; "...vs. the Phantom Blot" by Gottfredson 1000.00 3000.00 11,000.00

GD2.0 FN6.0 NM9.4

Four Color 27(1943)- "7 Colored Terror" 83.00 250.00 1000.00
Four Color 79(1945)-By Carl Barks (1 story) 104.00 313.00 1250.00
Four Color 116(1946) 23.00 69.00 275.00
Four Color 141,157(1947) 20.00 60.00 240.00
Four Color 170,181,194('48) 17.00 50.00 200.00
Four Color 214('49),231,248,261 13.00 40.00 160.00
Four Color 268-Reprints/WDC&S #22-24 by Gottfredson ("Surprise Visitor") 12.50 37.50 150.00
Four Color 279,286,296 9.00 27.00 110.00
Four Color 304,313(#1),325(#2),334 7.50 22.50 90.00
Four Color 343,352,362,371,387 5.85 17.50 70.00
Four Color 401,411,427(10-11/52) 4.10 12.30 45.00
Four Color 819-Mickey Mouse in Magicland 3.65 11.00 40.00
Four Color 1057,1151,1246(1959-61)-Album 3.45 10.35 38.00
28(12-1/52-53)-32,34 3.20 9.60 35.00
33-(Exists with 2 dates, 10-11/53 & 12-1/54) 3.20 9.60 35.00
35-50 3.00 9.00 30.00
51-73,75-80 2.30 7.00 20.00
74-Story swipe "The Rare Stamp Search" from 4-Color #422- "The Gilded Man" 2.50 7.50 24.00
81-105: 93,95-titled "Mickey Mouse Club Album". 100-105: Reprint 4-Color #427,194,279,170,343,214 in that order 2.40 7.35 22.00
106-120 2.00 6.00 16.00
121-130 1.75 5.25 14.00
131-146 1.50 4.50 12.00
147,148: 147-Reprints "The Phantom Fires" from WDC&S #200-202.148-Reprints "The Mystery of Lonely Valley" from WDC&S #208-210 1.50 4.50 12.00
149-158 1.00 2.80 7.00
159-Reprints "The Sunken City" from WDC&S #205-207 1.10 3.30 9.00
160-178,180-203: 162-170-r. 200-r/Four Color #371 2.40 6.00
179-(52 pgs.) 1.00 2.80 7.00
204-(Whitman or G.K.), 205,206 1.10 3.30 9.00
207(8/80), 209(pre-pack?) 2.00 6.00 16.00
208-(8-12/80)-Only distr. in Whitman 3-pack 4.10 12.30 45.00
210(2/81),211-214 1.00 3.00 8.00
215-218 1.25 3.75 10.00
219-1st Gladstone issue; The Seven Ghosts serial-r begins by Gottfredson 2.00 6.00 16.00
220,221 1.00 3.00 8.00
222-225: 222-Editor-in Grief strip-r 4.00
226-230 4.00
231-243,246-254: 240-r/March of Comics #27. 245-r/F.C. #279. 250-r/F.C. #248 3.00
244 (1/89, $2.95, 100 pgs.)-Squarebound 60th anniversary issue; gives history of Mickey 4.00
245, 256: 245-r/F.C. #279. 256-$1.95, 68 pgs. 4.00
255 ($1.95, 68 pgs.) 3.00
NOTE: *Reprints #195-197, 198(2/3), 199(1/3), 200-208, 211(1/2), 212, 213, 215(1/3), 216-on. Gottfredson Mickey Mouse serials in #219-239, 241-244, 246-249, 251-253, 255.*
Album 01-518-210(Dell), 1(10082-309)(9/63-Gold Key) 2.30 7.00 20.00
...Club 1(1/64-Gold Key)(TV) 3.00 9.00 30.00
Mini Comic 1(1976)(3-1/4x6-1/2")-Reprints 158 1.00 2.80 7.00
New Mickey Mouse Club Fun Book 11190 (Golden Press, 1977, $1.95, 224 pgs.) 2.40 7.35 22.00
Surprise Party 1(30037-901, G.K.)(1/69)-40th Anniversary (see Walt Disney Showcase #47) 2.80 8.40 28.00
Surprise Party 1(1979)-r/1969 issue 5.00

MICKEY MOUSE ADVENTURES
Disney Comics: June, 1990 - No. 18, Nov, 1991 ($1.50)
1,8,9: 1-Bradbury, Murry-r/M.M. #45,73 plus new-a. 8-Byrne-c. 9-Fantasia 50th ann. issue w/new adapt. of movie 3.00
2-7,10-18: 2-Begin all new stories. 10-r/F.C. #214 2.50

MICKEY MOUSE CLUB MAGAZINE (See Walt Disney...)

MICKEY MOUSE COMICS DIGEST
Gladstone: 1986 - No. 5, 1987 (96 pgs.)
1 ($1.25-c) 1.00 3.00 8.00
2-5: 3-5 ($1.50-c) 5.00

MICKEY MOUSE IN COLOR
Another Rainbow/Pantheon: 1988 (Deluxe, 13"x17", hard-c, $250.00) (Trade, 9-7/8"x11-1/2", hard-c, $39.95)
Deluxe limited edition of 3,000 copies signed by Floyd Gottfredson and Carl Barks, designated as the "Official Mickey Mouse 60th Anniversary" book. Mickey Sunday and daily reprints, plus Barks "Riddle of the Red Hat" from Four Color #79. Comes with 45 r.p.m. record interview with Gottfredson and Barks. 240 pgs. 23.00 68.00 250.00
Deluxe, limited to 100 copies, as above, but with a unique colored pencil original drawing of Mickey Mouse by Carl Barks. Add value of art to book price. 750.00
Pantheon trade edition, edited down & without Barks, 192 pgs. 3.65 11.00 40.00

MICKEY MOUSE MAGAZINE (Becomes Walt Disney's Comics & Stories)
K. K. Publ./Western Publishing Co.: Summer, 1935 (June-Aug, indicia) - V5#12, Sept, 1940; V1#1-5, V3#11,12, V4#1-3 are 44 pgs; V2#3-100 pgs; V5#12-68 pgs; rest are 36 pgs.(No V3#1, V4#6)

GD2.0 FN6.0 VF8.0 NM9.4

V1#1 (Large size, 13-1/4x10-1/4"; 25¢)-Contains puzzles, games, cels, stories & comics of Disney characters. Promotional magazine for Disney cartoon movies and paraphernalia 1120.00 3360.00 7280.00 14000.00

Note: *Some copies were autographed by the editors & given away with all early one year subscriptions.*

GD2.0 FN6.0 VF8.0

2 (Size change, 11-1/2x8-1/2"; 10/35; 10¢)-High quality paper begins; Messmer-a 150.00 450.00 1200.00
3,4: 3-Messmer-a 78.00 234.00 625.00
5-1st Donald Duck solo-c; 2nd cover app. ever; last 44 pg. & high quality paper issue 88.00 263.00 700.00
6-9: 6-36 pg. issues begin; Donald becomes editor. 8-2nd Donald solo-c. 9-1st Mickey/Minnie-c 72.00 216.00 575.00
10-12, V2#1,2: 11-1st Pluto/Mickey-c; Donald fires himself and appoints Mickey as editor 66.00 197.00 525.00
V2#3-Special 100 pg. Christmas issue (25¢); Messmer-a; Donald becomes editor of Wise Quacks 300.00 900.00 2400.00
4-Mickey Mouse Comics & Roy Ranger (adventure strip) begin; both end V2#9; Messmer-a 56.00 169.00 450.00

GD2.0 FN6.0 NM9.4

5-9: 5-Ted True (adventure strip, ends V2#9) & Silly Symphony Comics (ends V3#3) begin. 6-1st solo Minnie-c. 6-9-Mickey Mouse Movies cut-out in each 44.00 132.00 375.00
10-1st full color issue; Mickey Mouse (by Gottfredson; ends V3#12) & Silly Symphony (ends V3#3) full color Sunday-r, Peter The Farm Detective (ends V5#8) & Ole Of The North (ends V3#3) begins 68.00 205.00 650.00
11-13: 12-Hiawatha-c & feature story 43.00 130.00 390.00
V3#2-Big Bad Wolf Halloween-c 53.00 160.00 480.00

Mickey Mouse Magazine (Russian Version) © WDC

Midget Comics #2 © STJ

Midnight Nation #1 © J. Michael Straczynski & Top Cow

GD2.0 FN6.0 NM9.4

3 (12/37)-1st app. Snow White & The Seven Dwarfs (before release of movie)(possibly 1st in print); Mickey X-Mas-c 92.00 276.00 875.00
4 (1/38)-Snow White & The Seven Dwarfs serial begins (on stands before release of movie); Ducky Symphony (ends V3#11) begins 74.00 221.00 700.00
5-1st Snow White & Seven Dwarfs-c (St. Valentine's Day) 95.00 285.00 900.00
6-Snow White serial ends; Lonesome Ghosts app. (2 pp.) 51.00 153.00 460.00
7-Seven Dwarfs Easter-c 49.00 145.00 440.00
8-10: 9-Dopey-c. 10-1st solo Goofy-c 40.00 120.00 350.00
11,12 (44 pgs; 8 more pgs. color added). 11-Mickey the Sheriff serial (ends V4#3) & Donald Duck strip-r (ends V3#12) begin. Color feature on Snow White's Forest Friends 43.00 130.00 390.00
4#1 (10/38; 44 pgs.)-Brave Little Tailor-c/feature story, nominated for Academy Award; Bobby & Chip by Otto Messmer (ends V4#2) & The Practical Pig (ends V4#2) begin 43.00 130.00 390.00
2 (44 pgs.)-1st Huey, Dewey & Louie-c 44.00 132.00 400.00
3 (12/38, 44 pgs.)-Ferdinand The Bull-c/feature story, Academy Award winner; Mickey Mouse & The Whalers serial begins, ends V4#12 43.00 130.00 390.00
4-Spotty, Mother Pluto strip-r begin, end V4#8 40.00 120.00 350.00
5-St. Valentine's day-c. 1st Pluto solo-c 47.00 141.00 420.00
7 (3/39)-The Ugly Duckling-c/feature story, Academy Award winner 43.00 130.00 390.00
7 (4/39)-Goofy & Wilbur The Grasshopper classic-c/feature story from 1st Goofy solo cartoon movie; Timid Elmer begins, ends V5#5 43.00 130.00 390.00
8-Big Bad Wolf-c from Practical Pig movie poster; Practical Pig feature story 43.00 130.00 390.00
9-Donald Duck & Mickey Mouse Sunday-r begin; The Pointer feature story, nominated for Academy Award 43.00 130.00 390.00
10-Classic July 4th drum & fife-c; last Donald Sunday-r 55.00 165.00 500.00
11-1st slick-c; last over-sized issue 40.00 120.00 350.00
12 (9/39; format change, 10-1/4x8-1/4")-1st full color, cover to cover issue; Donald's Penguin-c/feature story 49.00 147.00 440.00
'5#1-Black Pete-c; Officer Duck-c/feature story; Autograph Hound feature story; Robinson Crusoe serial begins 48.00 145.00 430.00
2-Goofy-c; 1st app. Pinocchio (cameo) 64.00 195.00 605.00
3 (12/39)-Pinocchio Christmas-c (Before movie release). 1st app. Jiminy Cricket; Pinocchio serial begins 72.00 215.00 685.00
4,5: 5-Jiminy Cricket-c; Pinocchio serial ends; Donald's Dog Laundry feature story 48.00 145.00 430.00
6,7: 6-Tugboat Mickey feature story; Rip Van Winkle feature begins, ends V5#8. 7-2nd Huey, Dewey & Louie-c 47.00 140.00 420.00
8-Last magazine size issue; 2nd solo Pluto-c; Figaro & Cleo feature story 48.00 144.00 430.00
9-11: 9 (6/40; change to comic book size)-Jiminy Cricket feature story; Donald-c & Sunday-r begin. 10-Special Independence Day issue. 11-Hawaiian Holiday & Mickey's Trailer feature stories; last 36 pg. issue 52.00 155.00 470.00
12 (Format change)-The transition issue (68 pgs.) becoming a comic book. With only a title change to follow, becomes Walt Disney's Comics & Stories #1 with the next issue 420.00 1260.00 4400.00

OTE: *Otto Messmer-a is in many issues of the first two-three years. The following story titles nd issues have gags created by* ***Carl Barks:*** *V4#3(12/38)-'Donald's Better Self' & 'Donald's Golf ame;' V4#4(1/39)-'Donald's Lucky Day;' V4#7(3/39)-'Hockey Champ;' V4#7(4/39)-'Donald's ousin Gus;' V4#9(6/39)-'Sea Scouts;' V4#12(9/39)-'Donald's Penguin;' V5#9 (6/40)-'Donald's acation;' V5#10(7/40)-'Bone Trouble;' V5#12(9/40)-'Window Cleaners.'*

IICKEY MOUSE MAGAZINE (Russian Version)
Iay 16, 1991 (1st Russian printing of a modern comic book)

1-Bagged w/gold label commemoration in English 10.00

IICKEY MOUSE MARCH OF COMICS (See March of Comics #8,27,45,60,74)

IICKEY MOUSE'S SUMMER VACATION (See Story Hour Series)

IICKEY MOUSE SUMMER FUN (See Dell Giants)

IICKEY SPILLANE'S MIKE DANGER
'ekno Comix: Sept, 1995 - No. 11, May, 1996 ($1.95)

GD2.0 FN6.0 NM9.4

1-11: 1-Frank Miller-c. 7-polybagged; Simonson-c. 8,9-Simonson-c 2.00

MICKEY SPILLANE'S MIKE DANGER
Big Entertainment: V2#1, June, 1996 - No. 10, Apr, 1997 ($2.25)

V2#1-10: Max Allan Collins scripts 2.25

MICROBOTS, THE
Gold Key: Dec, 1971 (one-shot)

1 (10271-112) 2.00 6.00 18.00

MICRONAUTS (Toys)
Marvel Comics Group: Jan, 1979 - No. 59, Aug, 1984 (Mando paper #53 on)

1-Intro/1st app. Baron Karza 3.00
2-10,35,37,57: 7-Man-Thing app. 8-1st app. Capt. Universe (8/79). 9-1st app. Cilicia. 35-Double size; origin Microverse; intro Death Squad; Dr. Strange app. 37-Nightcrawler app.; X-Men cameo (2 pgs.). 57-(52 pgs.) 2.50
11-34,36,38-56,58,59: 13-1st app. Jasmine. 15-Death of Microtron. 15-17-Fantastic Four app. 17-Death of Jasmine. 20-Ant-Man app. 21-Microverse series begins. 25-Origin Baron Karza. 25-29-Nick Fury app. 27-Death of Biotron. 34-Dr. Strange app. 38-First direct sale. 40-Fantastic Four app. 59-Golden painted-c 2.00
nn-Reprints #1-3; blank UPC; diamond on top 2.00
Annual 1,2 (12/79,10/80)-Ditko-c/a 2.50

NOTE: *#38-on distributed only through comic shops.* ***N. Adams*** *c-7i.* ***Chaykin*** *a-13-18p.* ***Ditko*** *a-39p.* ***Giffen*** *a-36p, 37p(part).* ***Golden*** *a-1-12p; c-2-7p, 8-23, 24p, 38, 39, 59.* ***Guice*** *a-48-58p; c-49-58.* ***Gil Kane*** *a-38, 40-45p; c-40-45.* ***Layton*** *c-33-37.* ***Miller*** *c-31.*

MICRONAUTS (Toys)
Marvel Comics Group: Oct, 1984 - No. 20, May, 1986

V2#1-20 2.00

NOTE: ***Kelley Jones*** *a-1; c-1, 6.* ***Guice*** *a-4p; c-2p.*

MICRONAUTS SPECIAL EDITION
Marvel Comics Group: Dec, 1983 - No. 5, Apr, 1984 ($2.00, limited series, Baxter paper)

1-5: r-/original series 1-12; Guice-c(p)-all 3.00

MIDGET COMICS (Fighting Indian Stories)
St. John Publishng Co.: Feb, 1950 - No. 2, Apr, 1950 (5-3/8x7-3/8", 68 pgs.)

1-Fighting Indian Stories; Matt Baker-c 19.00 56.00 150.00
2-Tex West, Cowboy Marshal (also in #1) 10.00 30.00 70.00

MIDNIGHT (See Smash Comics #18)

MIDNIGHT
Ajax/Farrell Publ. (Four Star Comic Corp.): Apr, 1957 - No. 6, June, 1958

1-Reprints from Voodoo & Strange Fantasy with some changes 14.00 41.00 110.00
2-6 8.65 26.00 60.00

MIDNIGHT EYE
Viz Premiere Comics: 1991 - No. 6, 1992 ($4.95, 44 pgs., mature)

1-6: Japanese stories translated into English 5.00

MIDNIGHT MEN
Marvel Comics (Epic Comics/Heavy Hitters): June, 1993 - No. 4, Sept, 1993 ($2.50/$1.95, limited series)

1-($2.50)-Embossed-c; Chaykin-c/a & scripts in all. 2.50
2-4 2.00

MIDNIGHT MYSTERY
American Comics Group: Jan-Feb, 1961 - No. 7, Oct, 1961

1-Sci/Fi story 8.65 26.00 95.00
2-7: 7-Gustavson-a 4.35 13.00 48.00

NOTE: ***Reinman*** *a-1, 3.* ***Whitney*** *a-1, 4-6; c-1-3, 5, 7.*

MIDNIGHT NATION
Image Comics (Top Cow): Oct, 2000 - Present ($2.50)

1-Straczynski-s/Frank-a; 2 covers 2.50
2-4 2.50

MIDNIGHT SONS UNLIMITED
Marvel Comics (Midnight Sons imprint #4 on): Apr, 1993 - No. 9, May, 1995 ($3.95, 68 pgs.)

1-9: Blaze, Darkhold (by Quesada #1), Ghost Rider, Morbius & Nightstalkers

Midnight Tales #12 © DC

Mighty Crusaders #10 © AP

Mighty Marvel Western #17 © MAR

in all. 1-Painted-c. 3-Spider-Man app. 4-Siege of Darkness part 17; new Dr. Strange & new Ghost Rider app.; spot varnish-c — 4.00

NOTE: ***Sears** a-2.*

MIDNIGHT TALES
Charlton Press: Dec, 1972 - No. 18, May, 1976

	GD2.0	FN6.0	NM9.4
V1#1	2.30	7.00	20.00
2-10	1.50	4.50	12.00
11-18: 11-14-Newton-a(p)	1.10	3.30	9.00
12,17(Modern Comics reprint, 1977)			4.00

NOTE: ***Adkins** a-12i, 13i. **Ditko** a-12. **Howard** (Wood imitator) a-1-15, 17, 18; c-1-18. **Don Newton** a-11-14p. **Staton** a-1, 3-11, 13. **Sutton** a-3-10.*

MIGHTY ATOM, THE (...& the Pixies #6) (Formerly The Pixies #1-5)
Magazine Enterprises: No. 6, 1949; Nov, 1957 - No. 6, Aug-Sept, 1958

6(1949-M.E.)-no month (1st Series)	5.70	17.00	40.00
1-6(2nd Series)-Pixies-r	4.00	11.00	22.00
I.W. Reprint #1(nd)	1.25	3.75	10.00

MIGHTY BEAR (Formerly Fun Comics; becomes Unsane #15)
Star Publ. No. 13,14/Ajax-Farrell (Four Star): No. 13, Jan, 1954 - No. 14, Mar, 1954; 9/57 - No. 3, 2/58

13,14-L. B. Cole-c	18.00	53.00	140.00
1-3('57-58)Four Star; becomes Mighty Ghost #4	5.00	15.00	35.00

MIGHTY COMICS (...Presents) (Formerly Flyman)
Radio Comics (Archie): No. 40, Nov, 1966 - No. 50, Oct, 1967 (All 12¢ issues)

40-Web	3.00	9.00	30.00
41-50: 41-Shield, Black Hood. 42-Black Hood. 43-Shield, Web & Black Hood. 44-Black Hood, Steel Sterling & The Shield. 45-Shield & Hangman; origin Web retold. 46-Steel Sterling, Web & Black Hood. 47-Black Hood & Mr. Justice. 48-Shield & Hangman; Wizard x-over in Shield. 49-Steel Sterling & Fox; Black Hood x-over in Steel Sterling. 50-Black Hood & Web; Inferno x-over in Web	2.50	7.50	25.00

NOTE: ***Paul Reinman** a-40-50.*

MIGHTY CRUSADERS, THE (Also see Adventures of the Fly, The Crusaders & Fly Man)
Mighty Comics Group (Radio Comics): Nov, 1965 - No. 7, Oct, 1966 (All 12¢)

1-Origin The Shield	5.00	15.00	55.00
2-Origin Comet	3.00	9.00	30.00
3,5-7: 3-Origin Fly-Man. 5-Intro. Ultra-Men (Fox, Web, Capt. Flag) & Terrific Three (Jaguar, Mr. Justice, Steel Sterling). 7-Steel Sterling feature; origin Fly-Girl	2.50	7.50	25.00
4-1st S.A. app. Fireball, Inferno & Fox; Firefly, Web, Bob Phantom, Blackjack, Hangman, Zambini, Kardak, Steel Sterling, Mr. Justice, Wizard, Capt. Flag, Jaguar x-over	2.80	8.40	28.00

NOTE: ***Reinman** a-6.*

MIGHTY CRUSADERS, THE (All New Advs. of...#2)
Red Circle Prod./Archie Ent. No. 6 on: Mar, 1983 - No. 13, Sept, 1985 ($1.00, 36 pgs, Mando paper)

1-Origin Black Hood, The Fly, Fly Girl, The Shield, The Wizard, The Jaguar, Pvt. Strong & The Web.			4.00
2-13: 2-Mister Midnight begins. 4-Darkling replaces Shield. 5-Origin Jaguar, Shield begins. 7-Untold origin Jaguar. 10-Veitch-a			3.00

NOTE: ***Buckler** a-1-3, 4i, 5p, 7p, 8i, 9i; c-1-10p.*

MIGHTY GHOST (Formerly Mighty Bear #1-3)
Ajax/Farrell Publ.: No. 4, June, 1958

4	4.65	14.00	28.00

MIGHTY HERCULES, THE (TV)
Gold Key: July, 1963 - No. 2, Nov, 1963

1 (10072-307), 2 (10072-311)	14.00	41.00	165.00

MIGHTY HEROES, THE (TV) (Funny)
Dell Publishing Co.: Mar, 1967 - No. 4, July, 1967

1-Also has a 1957 Heckle & Jeckle-r	14.00	41.00	165.00
2-4: 4-Has two 1958 Mighty Mouse-r	9.50	29.00	115.00

MIGHTY HEROES
Spotlight Comics: 1987 (B&W, one-shot)

1-Heckle & Jeckle backup			3.0

MIGHTY HEROES
Marvel Comics: Jan, 1998 ($2.99, one-shot)

1-Origin of the Mighty Heroes			3.0

MIGHTY MARVEL TEAM-UP THRILLERS
Marvel Comics: 1983 ($5.95, trade paperback)

1-Reprints team-up stories			20.0

MIGHTY MARVEL WESTERN, THE
Marvel Comics Group (LMC earlier issues): Oct, 1968 - No. 46, Sept, 1976 (#1-14: 68 pgs.; #15,16: 52 pgs.)

1-Begin Kid Colt, Rawhide Kid, Two-Gun Kid-r	4.10	12.30	45.0
2-16: (2-14-68 pgs./ 15,16-52 pgs.)	2.80	8.40	28.0
17-20	1.75	5.25	14.0
21-30,32,37: 24-Kid Colt-r end. 25-Matt Slade-r begin. 32-Origin-r/Rawhide Kid #23; Williamson-r/Kid Slade #7. 37-Williamson, Kirby-r/Two-Gun Kid 51	1.50	4.50	12.0
31,33-36,38-46: 31-Baker-r.	1.25	3.75	10.0
44-46-(30¢-c variants, limited distribution)(4-8/76)	1.85	5.50	15.0

NOTE: ***Jack Davis** a(r)-21-24. **Keller** r-1-13, 22. **Kirby** a(r)-1-3, 6, 9, 12-14, 16, 25-29, 32-38, 4 41, 43-46; c-29. **Maneely** a(r)-22. **Severin** c-3i, 9. No Matt Slade-#43.*

MIGHTY MIDGET COMICS, THE (Miniature)
Samuel E. Lowe & Co.: No date; circa 1942-1943 (Sold 2 for 5¢, B&W and red 36 pgs, approx. 5x4")

Bulletman #11(1943)-r/cover/Bulletman #3	21.00	64.00	170.0
Captain Marvel Adventures #11	21.00	64.00	170.0
Captain Marvel #11 (Same as above except for full color ad on back cover; this issue was glued to cover of Captain Marvel #20 and is not found in fine-mint condition)	275.00	825.00	–
Captain Marvel Jr. #11 (Same-c as Master #27	21.00	64.00	170.0
Captain Marvel Jr. #11 (Same as above except for full color ad on back-c; this issue was glued to cover of Captain Marvel #21 and is not found in fine-mint condition)	275.00	825.00	–
Golden Arrow #11	19.00	56.00	150.0
Golden Arrow #11 (Same as above except for full color ad on back-c; this issue was glued to cover of Captain Marvel #21 and is not found in fine-mint condition)	225.00	675.00	–
Ibis the Invincible #11(1942)-Origin; reprints cover to Ibis #1 (Predates Fawcett's Ibis the Invincible #1).	21.00	64.00	170.0
Spy Smasher #11(1942)	21.00	64.00	170.0

NOTE: *The above books came in a box called "box full of books" and was distributed with oth Samuel Lowe puzzles, paper dolls, coloring books, etc. They are not titled Mighty Midget Comic All have a war bond seal on back cover which is otherwise blank. These books came in a "Migh Midget" flat cardboard counter display rack.*

Balbo, the Boy Magician #12 (1943)-1st book devoted entirely to character.	10.00	30.00	70.0
Bulletman #12	15.00	45.00	120.0
Commando Yank #12 (1943)-Only comic devoted entirely to character.	10.50	32.00	85.0
Dr. Voltz the Human Generator (1943)-Only comic devoted entirely to character.	10.00	30.00	70.0
Lance O'Casey #12 (1943)-1st comic devoted entirely to character (Predates Fawcett's Lance O'Casey #1).	10.00	30.00	70.0
Leatherneck the Marine (1943)-Only comic devoted entirely to character.	10.00	30.00	70.0
Minute Man #12	15.00	45.00	120.0
Mister "Q" (1943)-Only comic devoted entirely to character.	10.00	30.00	70.0
Mr. Scarlet and Pinky #12 (1943)-Only comic devoted entirely to character.	12.00	36.00	95.0
Pat Wilton and His Flying Fortress (1943)-1st comic devoted entirely to character.	10.00	30.00	70.0
The Phantom Eagle #12 (1943)-Only comic devoted entirely to character.	10.00	30.00	75.0
State Trooper Stops Crime (1943)-Only comic devoted entirely to character.	10.00	30.00	70.0
Tornado Tom (1943)-Origin, r/from Cyclone #1-3; only comic devoted entirely to character.	10.00	30.00	70.0

Mighty Mouse #3 © Terry Toons

Mike Barrett, Man Against Crime #1 © FAW

Military Comics #4 © QUA

MIGHTY MORPHIN' POWER RANGERS: THE MOVIE (Also see Saban's Mighty Morphin' Power Rangers)
Marvel Comics: Sept, 1995 ($3.95, one-shot)

	GD2.0	FN6.0	NM9.4
nn-adaptation of movie			4.00

MIGHTY MOUSE (See Adventures of..., Dell Giant #43, Giant Comics Edition, March of Comics #205, 237, 247, 257, 447, 459, 471, 483, Oxydol-Dreft, Paul Terry's, & Terry-Toons Comics)

MIGHTY MOUSE (1st Series)
Timely/Marvel Comics (20th Century Fox): Fall, 1946 - No. 4, Summer, 1947

	GD2.0	FN6.0	NM9.4
1	121.00	363.00	1150.00
2	55.00	165.00	500.00
3,4	40.00	120.00	350.00

MIGHTY MOUSE (2nd Series) (Paul Terry's... #62-71)
St. John Publishing Co./Pines No. 68 (3/56) on (TV issues #72 on): Aug, 1947 - No. 67, 11/55; No. 68, 3/56 - No. 83, 6/59

	GD2.0	FN6.0	NM9.4
5(#1)	38.00	113.00	300.00
6-10	19.00	56.00	150.00
11-19	12.00	36.00	95.00
20 (11/50) - 25-(52 pg. editions)	10.00	30.00	70.00
20-25-(36 pg. editions)	8.65	26.00	60.00
26-37: 35-Flying saucer-c	7.00	21.00	48.00
38-45-(100 pgs.)	18.00	53.00	140.00
46-83: 62-64,67-Painted-c. 82-Infinity-c	6.40	19.25	45.00
Album nn (nd, 1952/53?, St. John)(100 pgs.)(Rebound issues w/new cover)	22.00	66.00	175.00
Album 1(10/52, 25¢, 100 pgs., St. John)-Gandy Goose app.	28.00	84.00	225.00
Album 2,3(11/52 & 12/52, St. John) (100 pgs.)	22.00	66.00	175.00
Fun Club Magazine 1(Fall, 1957-Pines, 25¢, 100 pgs.) (CBS TV)-Tom Terrific, Heckle & Jeckle, Dinky Duck, Gandy Goose	15.00	45.00	120.00
Fun Club Magazine 2-6(Winter, 1958-Pines)	10.00	30.00	75.00
3-D 1-(1st printing-9/53, 25¢)(St. John)-Came w/glasses; stiff covers; says World's First! on-c; 1st 3-D comic	29.00	86.00	230.00
3-D 1-(2nd printing-10/53, 25¢)-Came w/glasses; slick, glossy covers, slightly smaller	26.00	79.00	210.00
3-D 2,3(11/53, 12/53, 25¢)-(St. John)-With glasses	25.00	75.00	200.00

MIGHTY MOUSE (TV)(3rd Series)(Formerly Adventures of Mighty Mouse)
Gold Key/Dell Publ. Co. No. 166-on: No. 161, Oct, 1964 - No. 172, Oct, 1968

	GD2.0	FN6.0	NM9.4
161(10/64)-165(9/65)-(Becomes Adventures of... No. 166 on)	4.10	12.30	45.00
166(3/66), 167(6/66)-172	3.00	9.00	32.00

MIGHTY MOUSE (TV)
Spotlight Comics: 1987 - No. 2, 1987 ($1.50, color)

	GD2.0	FN6.0	NM9.4
1,2-New stories			3.00
...And Friends Holiday Special (11/87, $1.75)			3.00

MIGHTY MOUSE (TV)
Marvel Comics: Oct, 1990 - No. 10, July, 1991 ($1.00)(Based on Sat. cartoon)

	GD2.0	FN6.0	NM9.4
1-10: 1-Dark Knight-c parody. 2-10: 3-Intro Bat-Bat; Byrne-c. 4,5-Crisis-c/story parodies w/Perez-c. 6-Spider-Man-c parody. 7-Origin Bat-Bat			2.00

MIGHTY MOUSE ADVENTURE MAGAZINE
Spotlight Comics: 1987 ($2.00, B&W, 52 pgs., magazine size, one-shot)

	GD2.0	FN6.0	NM9.4
1-Deputy Dawg, Heckle & Jeckle backup stories			4.00

MIGHTY MOUSE ADVENTURES (Adventures of... #2 on)
St. John Publishing Co.: November, 1951

	GD2.0	FN6.0	NM9.4
1	33.00	99.00	265.00

MIGHTY MOUSE ADVENTURE STORIES (Paul Terry's... on-c only)
St. John Publishing Co.: 1953 (50¢, 384 pgs.)

	GD2.0	FN6.0	NM9.4
nn-Rebound issues	42.00	125.00	375.00

MIGHTY MUTANIMALS (See Teenage Mutant Ninja Turtles Adventures #19)
May, 1991 - No. 3, July, 1991 ($1.00, limited series)
Archie Comics: Apr, 1992 - Present ($1.25)

	GD2.0	FN6.0	NM9.4
1-3: 1-Story cont'd from TMNT Advs. #19.			2.00
1-8 (1992): 7-1st app. Merdude			2.00

MIGHTY SAMSON (Also see Gold Key Champion)
Gold Key: 7/64 - #20, 11/69; #21, 8/72; #22, 12/73 - #31, 3/76; #32, 8/82 (Painted c-1-31)

	GD2.0	FN6.0	NM9.4
1-Origin/1st app.; Thorne-a begins	7.50	22.50	90.00
2-5	4.10	12.30	45.00
6-10: 7-Tom Morrow begins, ends #20	2.80	8.40	28.00
11-20	2.30	7.00	20.00
21-31: 21,22-r	1.75	5.25	14.00
32-r	1.00	3.00	8.00

MIGHTY THOR (See Thor)

MIKE BARNETT, MAN AGAINST CRIME (TV)
Fawcett Publications: Dec, 1951 - No. 6, Oct, 1952

	GD2.0	FN6.0	NM9.4
1	19.00	56.00	150.00
2	11.00	33.00	90.00
3,4,6	10.00	30.00	75.00
5- "Market for Morphine" cover/story	12.00	36.00	95.00

MIKE DANGER (See Mickey Spillane's...)

MIKE DEODATO'S...
Caliber Comics: 1996, ($2.95, B&W)

	GD2.0	FN6.0	NM9.4
...FALLOUT 3000 #1, **...JONAS** (mag. size) #1,**...PRIME CUTS** (mag. size) #1, **...PROTHEUS** #1,2, **...RAMTHAR** #1,**...RAZOR NIGHTS** #1			3.00

MIKE GRELL'S SABLE (Also see Jon Sable & Sable)
First Comics: Mar, 1990 - No. 10, Dec, 1990 ($1.75)

	GD2.0	FN6.0	NM9.4
1-10: r/Jon Sable Freelance #1-10 by Grell			2.00

MIKE MIST MINUTE MIST-ERIES (See Ms. Tree/Mike Mist in 3-D)
Eclipse Comics: April, 1981 ($1.25, B&W, one-shot)

	GD2.0	FN6.0	NM9.4
1			2.00

MIKE SHAYNE PRIVATE EYE
Dell Publishing Co.: Nov-Jan, 1962 - No. 3, Sept-Nov, 1962

	GD2.0	FN6.0	NM9.4
1	3.00	9.00	30.00
2,3	2.30	7.00	20.00

MILITARY COMICS (Becomes Modern Comics #44 on)
Quality Comics Group: Aug, 1941 - No. 43, Oct, 1945

	GD2.0	FN6.0	VF8.0	NM9.4
1-Origin/1st app. Blackhawk by C. Cuidera (Eisner scripts); Miss America, The Death Patrol by Jack Cole (also #2-7,27-30), & The Blue Tracer by Guardineer; X of the Underground, The Yankee Eagle, Q-Boat & Shot & Shell, Archie Atkins, Loops & Banks by Bud Ernest (Bob Powell)(ends #13) begin	825.00	2475.00	5150.00	9500.00

	GD2.0	FN6.0	NM9.4
2-Secret War News begins (by McWilliams #2-16); Cole-a; new uniform with yellow circle & hawk's head for Blackhawk	253.00	758.00	2400.00
3-Origin/1st app. Chop Chop	216.00	647.00	2050.00
4	174.00	521.00	1650.00
5-The Sniper begins; Miss America in costume #4-7	147.00	442.00	1400.00
6-9: 8-X of the Underground begins (ends #13). 9-The Phantom Clipper begins (ends #16)	108.00	324.00	1025.00
10-Classic Eisner-c	111.00	332.00	1050.00
11-Flag-c	86.00	258.00	815.00
12-Blackhawk by Crandall begins, ends #22	111.00	332.00	1050.00
13-15: 14-Private Dogtag begins (ends #83)	83.00	250.00	790.00
16-20: 16-Blue Tracer ends. 17-P.T. Boat begins	72.00	216.00	685.00
21-31: 22-Last Crandall Blackhawk. 23-Shrunken head-c. 27-Death Patrol revived	62.00	186.00	590.00
32-43	55.00	165.00	500.00

NOTE: ***Berg*** *a-6.* ***Al Bryant*** *c-31-34, 38, 40-43.* ***J. Cole*** *a-1-3, 27-32.* ***Crandall*** *a-12-22; c-13-20.* ***Cuidera*** *c-2-9.* ***Eisner*** *c-1, 2(part), 9, 10.* ***Kotsky*** *c-21-29, 35, 37, 39.* ***McWilliams*** *a-2-16.* ***Powell*** *a-1-13.* ***Ward*** *Blackhawk-30, 31(15 pgs. each); c-30.*

MILK AND CHEESE (Also see Cerebus Bi-Weekly #20)
Slave Labor: 1991 - Present ($2.50, B&W)

	GD2.0	FN6.0	NM9.4
1-Evan Dorkin story & art in all.	4.55	13.65	50.00
1-2nd-6th printings			4.00
2-"Other #1"	3.00	9.00	30.00

Millennium Edition - Action Comics #1 © DC

Minute Man #2 © FAW

Minor Miracles nn © Will Eisner

GD2.0 FN6.0 NM9.4

2-reprint 3.00
3-"Third #1" 2.30 7.00 20.00
4-"Fourth #1", 5-"First Second Issue" 1.25 3.75 10.00
6,7: 6-"#666" 5.00
NOTE: *Multiple printings of all issues exist and are worth cover price unless listed here.*

MILLENNIUM
DC Comics: Jan, 1988 - No. 8, Feb, 1988 (Weekly limited series)
1-Staton c/a(p) begins 3.00
2-8 2.00

MILLENNIUM EDITION:... (Reprints of classic DC issues)
DC Comics: Feb, 2000 - Feb, 2001 (gold foil cover stamps)
Action Comics #1, Adventure Comics #61, All Star Comics #3, All Star Comics #8, Batman #1, Detective Comics #1, Detective Comics #27, Detective Comics #38, Flash Comics #1, Military Comics #1, More Fun Comics #73, Police Comics #1, Sensation Comics #1, Superman #1, Whiz Comics #2, Wonder Woman #1 -($3.95-c) 3.95
Action Comics #252, Adventure Comics #247, Brave and the Bold #28, Brave and the Bold #85, Crisis on Infinte Earths #1, Detective #225, Detective #327, Detective #359, Detective #395, Flash #123, Gen13 #1, Green Lantern #76, House of Mystery #1, House of Secrets #92, JLA #1, Justice League #1, Mad #1, Man of Steel #1, Mysterious Suspense #1, New Gods, #1, New Teen Titans #1, Our Army at War #81, Plop! #1, Saga of the Swamp Thing #21, Shadow #1, Showcase #4, Showcase #9, Showcase #22, Superman #233, Superman (2nd) #75, Superman's Pal Jimmy Olsen #1, Watchmen #1, WildC.A.T.s #1, Wonder Woman (2nd) #1, World's Finest #71 -($2.50-c) 2.50
All-Star Western #10, Hellblazer #1, More Fun Comics #101, Preacher #1, Sandman #1, Spirit #1, Superboy #1, Superman #76, Young Romance #1 -($2.95-c) 2.95
Batman: The Dark Knight Returns #1, Kingdom Come #1 -($5.95-c) 5.95
All Star Comics #3, Batman #1, Justice League #1: Chromium cover 10.00
Crisis on Infinite Earths #1 Chromium cover 20.00

MILLENNIUM FEVER
DC Comics (Vertigo): Oct, 1995 - No.4, Jan, 1996 ($2.50, limited series)
1-4: Duncan Fegredo-c/a 2.50

MILLENNIUM INDEX
Independent Comics Group: Mar, 1988 - No. 2, Mar, 1988 ($2.00)
1,2 2.00

MILLIE, THE LOVABLE MONSTER
Dell Publishing Co.: Sept-Nov, 1962 - No. 6, Jan, 1973
12-523-211 4.10 12.30 45.00
2(8-10/63)-Bill Woggon c/a 3.45 10.35 38.00
3(8-10/64) 3.00 9.00 32.00
4(7/72), 5(10/72), 6(1/73) 2.00 6.00 16.00
NOTE: ***Woggon** a-3-6; c-3-6. 4 reprints 1; 5 reprints 2; 6 reprints 3.*

MILLIE THE MODEL (See Comedy Comics, A Date With..., Joker Comics #28, Life With..., Mad About..., Marvel Mini-Books, Misty & Modeling With...)
Marvel/Atlas/Marvel Comics(CnPC #1)(SPI/Male/VPI): 1945 - No. 207, Dec, 1973
1-Origin 79.00 237.00 750.00
2 (10/46)-Millie becomes The Blonde Phantom to sell Blonde Phantom perfume; a pre-Blonde Phantom app. (see All-Select #11, Fall, 1946) 40.00 120.00 350.00
3-8,10: 4-7-Willie app. 7-Willie smokes extra strong tobacco. 8,10-Kurtzman's "Hey Look". 8-Willie & Rusty app. 28.00 83.00 220.00
9-Powerhouse Pepper by Wolverton, 4 pgs. 31.00 94.00 250.00
11-Kurtzman-a, "Giggles 'n' Grins" 19.00 56.00 150.00
12,15,17-20: 12-Rusty & Hedy Devine app. 12.50 37.50 100.00
13,14,16-Kurtzman's "Hey Look". 13-Hedy Devine app. 14.00 41.00 110.00
21-30 10.00 30.00 70.00
31-60 4.55 13.65 50.00
61-99 3.20 9.60 35.00
100 3.80 11.40 42.00
101-130: 107-Jack Kirby app. in story 3.00 9.00 32.00
131-153: 141-Groovy Gears-c/s 2.50 7.50 25.00
154-New Millie begins (10/67) 3.20 9.60 35.00
155-190 2.50 7.50 23.00
191,193-199,201-206 2.30 7.00 20.00
192-(52 pgs.) 2.80 8.40 28.00
200,207(Last issue) 2.80 8.40 28.00
(Beware: cut-up pages are common in all Annuals)
Annual 1(1962)-Early Marvel annual (2nd?) 18.00 54.00 200.00
Annual 2(1963) 12.75 38.00 140.00
Annual 3-5 (1964-1966) 7.25 21.75 80.00
Annual 6-10(1967-11/71) 5.90 17.75 65.00
Queen-Size 11(9/74), 12(1975) 4.55 13.65 50.00
NOTE: ***Dan DeCarlo** a-18-93.*

MILLION DOLLAR DIGEST (Richie Rich... #23 on; also see Richie Rich...)
Harvey Publications: 11/86 - No. 7, 11/87; No. 8, 4/88 - No. 34, Nov, 1994 ($1.25/$1.75, digest size)
1 5.00
2-8: 8-(68 pgs.) 4.00
9-34: 9-Begin $1.75-c. 14-May not exist 2.00

MILT GROSS FUNNIES (Also see Picture News #1)
Milt Gross, Inc. (ACG?): Aug, 1947 - No. 2, Sept, 1947
1 16.00 48.00 125.00
2 12.00 36.00 95.00

MILTON THE MONSTER & FEARLESS FLY (TV)
Gold Key: May, 1966
1 (10175-605) 10.00 30.00 120.00

MINIMUM WAGE
Fantagraphics Books: V1#1, July, 1995 ($9.95, B&W, graphic novel, mature) V2#1, 1995 - Present ($2.95, B&W, mature)
V1#1-Bob Fingerman story & art 1.25 3.75 10.00
V2#1-9($2.95): Bob Fingerman story & art. 2-Kevin Nowlan back-c. 4-w/pin-ups. 5-Mignola back-c 3.00
Book Two TPB ('97, $12.95) r/V2#1-5 13.00

MINOR MIRACLES
DC Comics: 2000 ($12.95, B&W, squarebound)
nn-Will Eisner-s/a 12.95

MINUTE MAN (See Master Comics & Mighty Midget Comics)
Fawcett Publications: Summer, 1941 - No. 3, Spring, 1942 (68 pgs.)
1 168.00 505.00 1600.00
2,3 105.00 316.00 1000.00

MINX, THE
DC Comics (Vertigo): Oct, 1998 - No. 8, May, 1999 ($2.50, limited series)
1-8-Milligan-s/Phillips-c/a 3.00

MIRACLE COMICS
Hillman Periodicals: Feb, 1940 - No. 4, Mar, 1941
1-Sky Wizard Master of Space, Dash Dixon, Man of Might, Pinkie Parker, Dusty Doyle, The Kid Cop, K-7, Secret Agent, The Scorpion, & Blandu, Jungle Queen begin; Masked Angel only app. (all 1st app.) 179.00 537.00 1700.00
2 89.00 268.00 850.00
3,4: 3-Bill Colt, the Ghost Rider begins. 4-The Veiled Prophet & Bullet Bob (by Burnley) app. 76.00 229.00 725.00

MIRACLEMAN
Eclipse Comics: Aug, 1985 - No. 15, Nov, 1988; No. 16, Dec, 1989 - No. 24, 1994
1-r/British Marvelman series; Alan Moore scripts in #1-16 5.00
1-Gold & Silver editions 2.40 6.00
2-12: 8-Airboy preview. 9,10-Origin Miracleman. 9-Shows graphic scenes of childbirth. 10-Snyder-c 4.00
13,14 1.00 3.00 8.00
15-($1.75-c, scarce) end of Kid Miracleman 2.30 7.00 20.00
16-Last Alan Moore-s; 1st $1.95-c (low print) 1.25 3.75 10.00
17,18-($1.95): 17-"The Golden Age" begins, ends #22. Dave McKean-c begins, end #22; Neil Gaiman scripts in #17-24 4.00
19-24-($2.50); 23-"The Silver Age" begins. 23,24-B. Smith-c. 4.00
3-D 1 (12/85) 4.00

Miracleman Family #1 © ECL

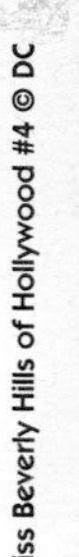
Miss Beverly Hills of Hollywood #4 © DC

Miss Fury Comics #7 © TCI

Book One: A Dream of Flying (1988, $10.95, TPB) r/#1-5 22.00
Book Two: The Red King Syndrome (1990, $14.95, TPB) r/#6-10 22.00
Book Three: Olympus (1990, $12.95, TPB) r/#11-16 45.00
Book Four: The Golden Age (1992, $14.95, TPB) r/#17-22 22.00
Book Four: The Golden Age (1993, $12.99, TPB) new McKean-c 15.00
NOTE: ***Chaykin*** *c-3.* ***Gulacy*** *c-7.* ***McKean*** *c-17-22.* ***B. Smith*** *c-23, 24.* ***Starlin*** *c-4.* ***Totleben*** *a-11-13; c-9, 11-13.* ***Truman*** *c-6.*

MIRACLEMAN: APOCRYPHA
Eclipse Comics: Nov, 1991 - No. 3, Feb, 1992 ($2.50, limited series)
1-3: 1-Stories by Neil Gaiman, Mark Buckingham, Alex Ross & others. 3-Stories by James Robinson, Kelley Jones, Matt Wagner, Neil Gaiman, Mark Buckingham & others 2.50
TPB (12/92, $15.95) r/#1-3; Buckingham-c 20.00

MIRACLEMAN FAMILY
Eclipse Comics: May, 1988 - No. 2, Sept, 1988 ($1.95, lim. series, Baxter paper)
1,2: 2-Gulacy-c 2.00

MIRACLE OF THE WHITE STALLIONS, THE (See Movie Comics)

MIRACLE SQUAD, THE
Upshot Graphics (Fantagraphics Books): Aug, 1986 - No. 4, 1987 ($2.00)
1-4 2.00

MIRACLE SQUAD: BLOOD AND DUST, THE
Apple Comics: Jan, 1989 - No. 4, July, 1989 ($1.95, B&W, limited series)
1-4 2.00

MIRRORWORLD: RAIN
NetCo Partners (Big Ent.): Feb, 1997 - No. 0, Apr, 1997 ($3.25, limited series)
0,1-Tad Williams-s 3.25

MISADVENTURES OF MERLIN JONES, THE (See Movie Comics & Merlin Jones as the Monkey's Uncle under Movie Comics)

MISS AMERICA COMICS (Miss America Magazine #2 on; also see Blonde Phantom & Marvel Mystery Comics)
Marvel Comics (20CC): 1944 (one-shot)
1-2 pgs. pin-ups 153.00 458.00 1450.00

MISS AMERICA MAGAZINE (Formerly Miss America; Miss America #51 on)
Miss America Publ. Corp./Marvel/Atlas (MAP): V1#2, Nov, 1944 - No. 93, Nov, 1958
V1#2-Photo-c of teenage girl in Miss America costume; Miss America, Patsy Walker (intro.) comic stories plus movie reviews & stories; intro. Buzz Baxter & Hedy Wolfe; 1 pg. origin Miss America 125.00 375.00 1190.00
3-5-Miss America & Patsy Walker stories 47.00 140.00 420.00
6-Patsy Walker only 12.50 37.50 100.00
V2#1(4/45)-6(9/45)-Patsy Walker continues 8.65 26.00 60.00
V3#1(10/45)-6(4/46) 7.15 21.50 50.00
V4#1(5/46),2,5(9/46) 6.40 19.25 45.00
V4#3(7/46)-Liz Taylor photo-c 12.50 37.50 100.00
V4#4 (8/46; 68 pgs.), V4#6 (10/46; 92 pgs.) 5.70 17.00 40.00
V5#1(11/46)-6(4/47), V6#1(5/47)-3(7/47) 5.70 17.00 40.00
V7#1(8/47)-14,16-23(#56, 6/49) 5.00 15.00 35.00
V7#15-All comics 6.40 19.25 45.00
V7#24(#57, 7/49)-Kamen-a (becomes Best Western #58 on?) 5.70 17.00 40.00
V7#25(8/49), 27-44(3/52), VII,nn(5/52) 5.00 15.00 32.00
V7#26(9/49)-All comics 5.70 17.00 40.00
V1,nn(7/52)-V1,nn(1/53)(#46-49), V7#50(Spring '53), V1#51-V7?#54(7/53), 55-93 5.00 15.00 32.00
NOTE: *Photo-c #1, 4, V2#1, 4, 5, V3#5, V4#3, 4, 6, V7#15, 16, 24, 26, 34, 37, 38. Painted c-3.* ***Powell*** *a-V7#31.*

MISS BEVERLY HILLS OF HOLLYWOOD (See Adventures of Bob Hope)
National Periodical Publ.: Mar-Apr, 1949 - No. 9, July-Aug, 1950 (52 pgs.)
1 (Meets Alan Ladd) 58.00 174.00 550.00
2-William Holden photo on-c 42.00 125.00 375.00
3-5: 2-9-Part photo-c. 5-Bob Hope photo on-c 40.00 120.00 325.00
6,7,9: 6-Lucille Ball photo on-c 35.00 105.00 280.00
8-Reagan photo on-c 40.00 120.00 350.00

NOTE: *Beverly meets Alan Ladd in #1, Eve Arden #2, Betty Hutton #4, Bob Hope #5.*

MISS CAIRO JONES
Croyden Publishers: 1945
1-Bob Oksner daily newspaper-r (1st strip story); lingerie panels 20.00 60.00 160.00

MISS FURY COMICS (Newspaper strip reprints)
Timely Comics (NPI 1/CmPI 2/MPC 3-8): Winter, 1942-43 - No. 8, Winter, 1946 (Published quarterly)
1-Origin Miss Fury by Tarpe' Mills (68 pgs.) in costume w/pin-ups 333.00 1000.00 3500.00
2-(60 pgs.)-In costume w/pin-ups 168.00 505.00 1600.00
3-(60 pgs.)-In costume w/pin-ups; Hitler-c 137.00 411.00 1300.00
4-(52 pgs.)-In costume, 2 pgs. w/pin-ups 105.00 316.00 1000.00
5-(52 pgs.)-In costume w/pin-ups 89.00 268.00 850.00
6-(52 pgs.)-Not in costume in inside stories, w/pin-ups 84.00 253.00 800.00
7,8-(36 pgs.)-In costume 1 pg. each; no pin-ups 77.00 232.00 735.00
NOTE: ***Schomburg*** *c-1, 5, 6.*

MISS FURY
Adventure Comics: 1991 - No. 4, 1991 ($2.50, limited series)
1-4: 1-Origin; granddaughter of original Miss Fury 2.50
1-Limited ed. ($4.95) 5.00

MISSION IMPOSSIBLE (TV)
Dell Publ. Co.: May, 1967 - No. 4, Oct, 1968; No. 5, Oct, 1969 (All have photo-c)
1 8.35 25.00 100.00
2-5: 5-Reprints #1 5.35 16.00 65.00

MISSION IMPOSSIBLE (Movie)
Marvel Comics (Paramount Comics): May, 1996 ($2.95, one-shot) (1st Paramount Comics book)
1-Liefeld-c & back-up story 3.00

MISS LIBERTY (Becomes Liberty Comics)
Burten Publishing Co.: 1945 (MLJ reprints)
1-The Shield & Dusty, The Wizard, & Roy, the Super Boy app.; r/Shield-Wizard #13 29.00 86.00 230.00

MISS MELODY LANE OF BROADWAY (See The Adventures of Bob Hope)
National Periodical Publ.: Feb-Mar, 1950 - No. 3, June-July, 1950 (52 pgs.)
1-Movie stars photos app. on all-c. 58.00 174.00 550.00
2,3: 3-Ed Sullivan photo on-c. 40.00 120.00 350.00

MISS PEACH
Dell Publishing Co.: Oct-Dec, 1963; 1969
1-Jack Mendelsohn-a/script 7.25 21.75 80.00
...Tells You How to Grow (1969; 25¢)-Mel Lazarus-a; also given away (36 pgs.) 4.10 12.30 45.00

MISS PEPPER (See Meet Miss Pepper)

MISS SUNBEAM (See Little Miss...)

MISS VICTORY (See Captain Fearless #1,2, Holyoke One-Shot #3, Veri Best Sure Fire & Veri Best Sure Shot Comics)

MISTER AMERICA
Endeavor Comics: Apr, 1994 - No. 2, May, 1994 ($2.95, limited series)
1,2 3.00

MR. & MRS. BEANS
United Features Syndicate: No. 11, 1939
Single Series 11 35.00 105.00 280.00

MR. & MRS. J. EVIL SCIENTIST (TV)(See The Flintstones & Hanna-Barbera Band Wagon #3)
Gold Key: Nov, 1963 - No. 4, Sept, 1966 (Hanna-Barbera, all 12¢)
1 7.50 22.50 90.00
2-4 4.60 13.75 55.00

MR. ANTHONY'S LOVE CLINIC (Based on radio show)
Hillman Periodicals: Nov, 1949 - No. 5, Apr-May, 1950 (52 pgs.)
1-Photo-c 12.50 37.50 100.00

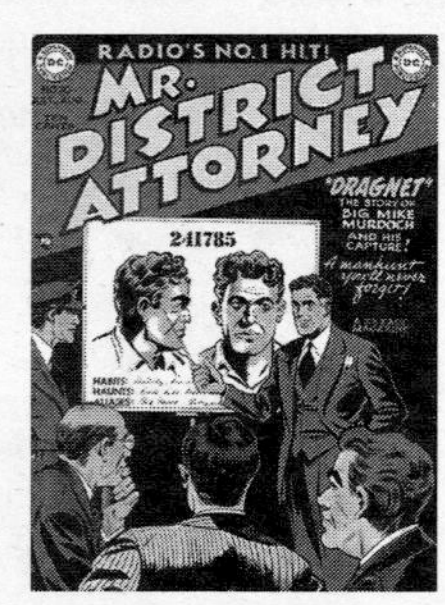

Mr. District Attorney #10 © DC

Mister Miracle #24 © DC

Mister Mystery #8 © Media Pub.

	GD2.0	FN6.0	NM9.4
2	8.65	26.00	60.00
3-5: 5-Photo-c	7.15	21.50	50.00

MISTER BLANK
Amaze Ink: No. 0, Jan, 1996 - No. 14, May, 2000 ($1.75/$2.95, B&W)

0-($1.75, 16 pgs.) Origin of Mr. Blank 2.00
1-14-($2.95) Chris Hicks-s/a 3.00

MR. DISTRICT ATTORNEY (Radio/TV)
National Per. Publ.: Jan-Feb, 1948 - No. 67, Jan-Feb, 1959 (1-23: 52 pgs.)

	GD2.0	FN6.0	NM9.4
1-Howard Purcell c-5-23 (most)	100.00	300.00	950.00
2	44.00	133.00	400.00
3-5	35.00	105.00	280.00
6-10	28.00	83.00	220.00
11-20	21.00	64.00	170.00
21-43: 43-Last pre-code (1-2/55)	14.00	41.00	110.00
44-67	11.00	33.00	90.00

MR. DISTRICT ATTORNEY (SeeThe Funnies #35)
Dell Publishing Co.: No. 13, 1942

	GD2.0	FN6.0	NM9.4
Four Color 13-See The Funnies #35 for 1st app.	29.00	87.00	350.00

MISTER E (Also see Books of Magic limited series)
DC Comics: Jun, 1991- No. 4, Sept, 1991($1.75, limited series)

1-4-Snyder III-c/a; follow-up to Books of Magic limited series 3.00

MISTER ED, THE TALKING HORSE (TV)
Dell Publishing Co./Gold Key: Mar-May, 1962 - No. 6, Feb, 1964 (All photo-c; photo back-c: 1-6)

	GD2.0	FN6.0	NM9.4
Four Color 1295	12.50	37.50	150.00
1(11/62) (Gold Key)-Photo-c	9.00	27.00	110.00
2-6: Photo-c	5.00	15.00	60.00

(See March of Comics #244, 260, 282, 290)

MR. HERO, THE NEWMATIC MAN (See Neil Gaiman's...)

MR. MAGOO (TV) (The Nearsighted..., ...& Gerald McBoing Boing 1954 issues; formerly Gerald McBoing-Boing And ...)
Dell Publishing Co.: No. 6, Nov-Jan, 1953-54; 5/54 - 3-5/62; 9-11/63 - 3-5/65

	GD2.0	FN6.0	NM9.4
6	11.00	33.00	120.00
Four Color 561(5/54),602(11/54)	11.00	33.00	120.00
Four Color 1235(#1, 12-2/62),1305(#2, 3-5/62)	9.00	27.00	100.00
3(9-11/63) - 5	8.00	23.00	85.00
Four Color 1235(12-536-505)(3-5/65)-2nd Printing	5.50	16.50	60.00

MR. MAJESTIC (See WildC.A.T.S.)
DC Comics (WildStorm): Sept, 1999 - No. 9, May, 2000 ($2.50)

1-9: 1-McGuinness-a/Casey & Holguin-s. 2-Two covers 2.50

MISTER MIRACLE (1st series) (See Cancelled Comic Cavalcade)
National Periodical Publications/DC Comics: 3-4/71 - V4#18, 2-3/74; V5#19, 9/77 - V6#25, 8-9/78; 1987 (Fourth World)

	GD2.0	FN6.0	NM9.4
1-1st app. Mr. Miracle (#1-3 are 15¢)	4.55	13.65	50.00
2,3: 3-Last 15¢ issue	2.50	7.50	25.00
4-8: 4-Boy Commandos-r begin; all 52 pgs.	3.00	9.00	30.00
9-18: 9-Origin Mr. Miracle; Darkseid cameo. 15-Intro/1st app. Shilo Norman. 18-Barda & Scott Free wed; New Gods app. & Darkseid cameo; Last Kirby issue.	1.85	5.50	15.00
19-25 (1977-78)	1.00	2.80	7.00
Special 1(1987, $1.25, 52 pgs.)			3.00
Jack Kirby's Mister Miracle TPB ('98, $12.95) B&W&Grey-toned reprint of #1-10; David Copperfield intro.			13.00

NOTE: ***Austin** a-19i. **Ditko** a-6r. **Golden** a-23-25p; c-25p. **Heath** a-24i, 25i; c-25i. **Kirby** a(p)/c-1-18. **Nasser** a-19i. **Rogers** a-19-22p; c-19, 20p, 21p, 22-24. 4-8 contain **Simon & Kirby** Boy Commandos reprints from Detective 82,76, Boy Commandos 1, 3 & Detective 64 in that order.*

MISTER MIRACLE (2nd Series) (See Justice League)
DC Comics: Jan, 1989 - No. 28, June, 1991 ($1.00/$1.25)

1-28: 13,14-Lobo app. 22-1st new Mr. Miracle w/new costume 2.00

MISTER MIRACLE (3rd Series)
DC Comics: Apr, 1996 - No. 7, Oct, 1996 ($1.95)

1-7: 2-Vs. JLA. 6-Simonson-c 2.00

MR. MIRACLE (See Capt. Fearless #1 & Holyoke One-Shot #4)

MR. MONSTER (1st Series)(Doc Stearn... #7 on; See Airboy-Mr. Monster Special, Dark Horse Presents, Super Duper Comics & Vanguard Illustrated #7)
Eclipse Comics: Jan, 1985 - No. 10, June, 1987 ($1.75, Baxter paper)

1-1st story-r from Vanguard Ill. #7(1st app.) 4.00
2-10: 2-Dave Stevens-c. 3-Alan Moore scripts; Wolverton-r/Weird Mysteries #5. 6-Ditko-r/Fantastic Fears #5 plus new Giffen-a 10 6-D issue 3.00

MR. MONSTER
Dark Horse Comics: Feb, 1988 - No. 8, July, 1991 ($1.75, B&W)

1-7 2.00
8-($4.95, 60 pgs.)-Origins conclusion 5.00

MR. MONSTER ATTACKS! (Doc Stearn...)
Tundra Publ.: Aug, 1992 - No. 3, Oct, 1992 ($3.95, limited series, 32 pgs.)

1-3: Michael T. Gilbert-a/scripts; Gilbert/Dorman painted-c 4.00

MR. MONSTER PRESENTS (CRACK-A-BOOM!)
Caliber Comics: 1997 - No. 3, 1997 ($2.95, B&W&Red, limited series)

1-3: Michael T. Gilbert-a/scripts: 1-Wraparound-c 3.00

MR. MONSTER'S GAL FRIDAY...KELLY!
Image Comics: Jan, 2000 - Present ($3.50, B&W)

1-3- Michael T. Gilbert-c; story & art by various. 3-Alan Moore-s 3.50

MR. MONSTER'S SUPER-DUPER SPECIAL
Eclipse Comics: May, 1986 - No. 8, July, 1987

	GD2.0	FN6.0	NM9.4
1-(5/86)...3-D High Octane Horror #1			4.00
1-(5/86)...2-D version, 100 copies	1.75	5.25	14.00
2-(8/86)...High Octane Horror #1, 3-(9/86)...True Crime #1, 4-(11/86)...True Crime #2, 5-(1/87)...Hi-Voltage Super Science #1, 6-(3/87)...High Shock Schlock #1, 7-(5/87)...High Shock Schlock #2, 8-(7/87)...Weird Tales Of The Future #1			4.00

NOTE: ***Jack Cole** r-3, 4. **Evans** a-2r. **Kubert** a-1r. **Powell** a-5r. **Wolverton** a-2r, 7r, 8r.*

MR. MONSTER VS. GORZILLA
Image Comics: July, 1998 ($2.95, one-shot)

1- Michael T. Gilbert-a 3.00

MR. MUSCLES (Formerly Blue Beetle #18-21)
Charlton Comics: No. 22, Mar, 1956; No. 23, Aug, 1956

	GD2.0	FN6.0	NM9.4
22,23	7.15	21.50	50.00

MR. MXYZPTLK (VILLAINS)
DC Comics: Feb, 1998 ($1.95, one-shot)

1-Grant-s/Morgan-a/Pearson-c 2.00

MISTER MYSTERY (Tales of Horror and Suspense)
Mr. Publ. (Media Publ.) No. 1-3/SPM Publ./Stanmore (Aragon): Sept, 1951 - No. 19, Oct, 1954

	GD2.0	FN6.0	NM9.4
1-Kurtzmanesque horror story	84.00	253.00	800.00
2,3-Kurtzmanesque story. 3-Anti-Wertham edit.	55.00	165.00	525.00
4,6: Bondage-c; 6-Torture	55.00	165.00	525.00
5,8,10	53.00	158.00	475.00
7- "The Brain Bats of Venus" by Wolverton; partially re-used in Weird Tales of the Future #7	116.00	348.00	1100.00
9-Nostrand-a	53.00	158.00	475.00
11-Wolverton "Robot Woman" story/Weird Mysteries #2, cut up, rewritten & partially redrawn	79.00	239.00	750.00
12-Classic injury to eye-c	116.00	348.00	1100.00
13-17,19: 15- "Living Dead" junkie story. 17-Severed heads-c. 19-Reprints	40.00	120.00	325.00
18- "Robot Woman" by Wolverton reprinted from Weird Mysteries #2; decapitation, bondage-c	58.00	174.00	550.00

NOTE: ***Andru** a-1, 2p, 3p. **Andru/Esposito** c-1-3. **Baily** c-10-18(most). **Mortellaro** c-5-7. Bondage c-7. Some issues have graphic dismemberment scenes.*

MR. PUNCH
DC Comics (Vertigo): 1994 ($24.95, one-shot)

nn (Hard-c)-Gaiman scripts; McKean-c/a 40.00
nn (Soft-c) 15.00

MISTER Q (See Mighty Midget Comics & Our Flag Comics #5)

Mr. T and the T-Force #4 © Now Comics

Modern Comics #59 © QUA

Modern Love #2 © WMG

GD2.0 FN6.0 NM9.4

MR. RISK (Formerly All Romances; Men Against Crime #3 on)(Also see Our Flag Comics & Super-Mystery Comics)
Ace Magazines: No. 7, Oct, 1950 - No. 2, Dec, 1950

7,2 8.65 26.00 60.00

MR. SCARLET & PINKY (See Mighty Midget Comics)

MR. T AND THE T-FORCE
Now Comics: June, 1993 - No. 10, May, 1994 ($1.95, color)

1-10-Newsstand editions: 1-7-polybagged with photo trading card in each. 1,2-Neal Adams-c/a(p). 3-Dave Dorman painted-c 2.00
1-10-Direct Sale editions polybagged w/line drawn trading cards. 1-Contains gold foil trading card by Neal Adams 2.00

MISTER UNIVERSE (Professional wrestler)
Mr. Publications Media Publ. (Stanmor, Aragon): July, 1951; No. 2, Oct, 1951 - No. 5, April, 1952

1 21.00 64.00 170.00
2- "Jungle That Time Forgot", (24 pg. story); Andru/Esposito-c 13.00 39.00 105.00
3-Marijuana story 13.00 39.00 105.00
4,5- "Goes to War" cover/stories 10.00 30.00 75.00

MISTER X (See Vortex)
Mr. Publications/Vortex Comics/Caliber V3#1 on: 6/84 - No. 14, 8/88 ($1.50/$2.25, direct sales, coated paper);V2#1, Apr, 1989 - V2#12, Mar, 1990 ($2.00/$2.50, B&W, newsprint) V3#1, 1996 - Present ($2.95, B&W)

1-10,12-14 4.00
11-Dave McKean story & art (6 pgs.) 5.00
V2 #1-12: 1-11 (Second Coming, B&W): 1-Four diff.-c. 10-Photo-c 3.00
V3 #1-4 3.00
Return of... ($11.95, graphic novel)-r/V1#1-4 12.00
Return of... ($34.95, hardcover limited edition)-r/1-4 35.00
Special (no date, 1990?) 3.00

MISTY
Marvel Comics (Star Comics): Dec, 1985 - No. 6, May, 1986 (Limited series)

1-6: Millie The Model's niece 3.00

MITZI COMICS (Becomes Mitzi's Boy Friend #2-7)(See All Teen)
Timely Comics: Spring, 1948 (one-shot)

1-Kurtzman's "Hey Look" plus 3 pgs. "Giggles 'n' Grins" 22.00 66.00 175.00

MITZI'S BOY FRIEND (Formerly Mitzi Comics; becomes Mitzi's Romances)
Marvel Comics (TCI): No. 2, June, 1948 - No. 7, April, 1949

2 10.00 30.00 80.00
3-7 8.65 26.00 60.00

MITZI'S ROMANCES (Formerly Mitzi's Boy Friend)
Timely/Marvel Comics (TCI): No. 8, June, 1949 - No. 10, Dec, 1949

8-Becomes True Life Tales #8 (10/49) on? 10.00 30.00 80.00
9,10: 10-Painted-c 8.65 26.00 60.00

MOBFIRE
DC Comics (Vertigo): Dec, 1994 - No. 6, May, 1995 ($2.50, limited series)

1-6 2.50

MOBY DICK (See Feature Presentations #6, and King Classics)
Dell Publishing Co.: No. 717, Aug, 1956

Four Color 717-Movie, Gregory Peck photo-c 8.35 25.00 100.00

MOBY DUCK (See Donald Duck #112 & Walt Disney Showcase #2,11)
Gold Key (Disney): Oct, 1967 - No. 11, Oct, 1970; No. 12, Jan, 1974 - No. 30, Feb, 1978

1 2.50 7.50 25.00
2-5 1.75 5.25 14.00
6-11 1.25 3.75 10.00
12-30: 21,30-r 2.40 6.00

MODEL FUN (With Bobby Benson)
Harle Publications: No. 3, Winter, 1954-55 - No. 5, July, 1955

3-Bobby Benson 6.40 19.25 45.00
4,5-Bobby Benson 4.65 14.00 28.00

MODELING WITH MILLIE (Formerly Life With Millie)
Atlas/Marvel Comics (Male Publ.): No. 21, Feb, 1963 - No. 54, June, 1967

21 7.65 23.00 85.00
22-30 4.35 13.00 48.00
31-54 3.20 9.60 35.00

MODERN COMICS (Formerly Military Comics #1-43)
Quality Comics Group: No. 44, Nov, 1945 - No. 102, Oct, 1950

44-Blackhawk continues 55.00 165.00 500.00
45-52: 49-1st app. Fear, Lady Adventuress 40.00 120.00 350.00
53-Torchy by Ward begins (9/46) 42.00 125.00 375.00
54-60: 55-J. Cole-a 35.00 105.00 280.00
61-77,79,80: 73-J. Cole-a 33.00 98.00 260.00
78-1st app. Madame Butterfly 35.00 105.00 280.00
81-99,101: 82,83-One pg. J. Cole-a. 83-The Spirit app.; last 52 pg. issue? 99-Blackhawks on the moon-c/story 33.00 98.00 260.00
100 33.00 98.00 260.00
102-(Scarce)-J. Cole-a; Spirit by Eisner app. 38.00 113.00 300.00

NOTE: ***Al Bryant** c-44-51, 54, 55, 66, 69. **Jack Cole** a-55, 73. **Crandall** Blackhawk-#46, 47, 50, 51, 54, 56, 58-60, 64, 67-70, 73, 74, 76-78, 80-83; c-60-65, 67, 68, 70-95. **Crandall/Cuidera** c-56-59, 96-102. **Gustavson** a-47. **Ward** Blackhawk-#52, 53, 55 (15 pgs. each). Torchy in #53-102; by **Ward** only in #53-89(9/49); by **Gil Fox** #93, 102.*

MODERN LOVE
E. C. Comics: June-July, 1949 - No. 8, Aug-Sept, 1950

1 55.00 165.00 500.00
2-Craig/Feldstein-c 40.00 120.00 350.00
3-Spanking panel 38.00 113.00 300.00
4-6 (Scarce): 4-Bra/panties panels 49.00 147.00 440.00
7,8 38.00 113.00 300.00

NOTE: ***Craig** a-3. **Feldstein** a-in most issues; c-1, 2i, 3-8. **Harrison** a-4. **Iger** a-6-8. **Ingels** a-1, 2, 4-7. **Palais** a-5. **Wood** a-7. **Wood/Harrison** a-5-7. (Canadian reprints known; see Table of Contents.)*

MOD LOVE
Western Publishing Co.: 1967 (50¢, 36 pgs.)

1 3.25 9.75 36.00

MODNIKS, THE
Gold Key: Aug, 1967 - No. 2, Aug, 1970

10206-708(#1) 2.80 8.40 28.00
2 2.00 6.00 18.00

MOD SQUAD (TV)
Dell Publishing Co.: Jan, 1969 - No. 3, Oct, 1969 - No. 8, April, 1971

1-Photo-c 5.00 15.00 60.00
2-4: 2-4-Photo-c 3.20 9.60 35.00
5-8: 8-Photo-c; Reprints #2 3.00 9.00 30.00

MOD WHEELS
Gold Key: Mar, 1971 - No. 19, Jan, 1976

1 3.00 9.00 30.00
2-9 2.00 6.00 18.00
10-19: 11,15-Extra 16 pgs. ads 1.75 5.25 14.00

MOE & SHMOE COMICS
O. S. Publ. Co.: Spring, 1948 - No. 2, Summer, 1948

1 8.65 26.00 60.00
2 5.70 17.00 40.00

MOEBIUS (Graphic novel)
Marvel Comics (Epic Comics): Oct, 1987 - No. 6, 1988; No. 7, 1990; No. 8, 1991 ($9.95, 8x11", mature)

1,2,4-6,8: (#2, 2nd printing, $9.95) 10.00
3,7,0: 3-(1st & 2nd printings, $12.95). 0 (1990, $12.95) 13.00
Moebius I-Signed & numbered hard-c ($45.95, Graphitti Designs, 1,500 copies printed)-r/#1-3 46.00

MOEBIUS COMICS
Caliber: May, 1996 - No. 6 ($2.95, B&W)

1-6: Moebius-c/a. 1-William Stout-a 3.00

Monkees #1 © Raybert Prod.

Monster Crime Comics #1 © HILL

Monster Fighters Inc. #1 © J. Torres

MOEBIUS: THE MAN FROM CIGURI
Dark Horse Comics: 1996 ($7.95, digest-size)
nn-Moebius-c/a 8.00

MOLLY MANTON'S ROMANCES (Romantic Affairs #3)
Marvel Comics (SePI): Sept, 1949 - No. 2, Dec, 1949 (52 pgs.)
1-Photo-c (becomes Blaze the Wonder Collie #2 (10/49) on? & Molly Manton's Romances #2 12.50 37.50 100.00
2-Titled "Romances of…"; photo-c 10.00 30.00 70.00

MOLLY O'DAY (Super Sleuth)
Avon Periodicals: February, 1945 (1st Avon comic)
1-Molly O'Day, The Enchanted Dagger by Tuska (r/Yankee #1), Capt'n Courage, Corporal Grant app. 50.00 150.00 450.00

MONA
Kitchen Sink Press: 1999 ($4.95, B&W, one-shot)
1-Cartoons by Kurtzman and various; Hernandez-c 5.00

MONKEES, THE (TV)(Also see Circus Boy, Groovy, Not Brand Echh #3, Teen-Age Talk, Teen Beam & Teen Beat)
Dell Publishing Co.: March, 1967 - No. 17, Oct, 1969 (#1-4,6,7,9,10,12,15,16 have photo-c)
1-Photo-c 9.00 27.00 110.00
2-6,7,9,10,12,15,16: All photo-c 5.35 16.00 65.00
8,11,13,14,17-No photo-c: 17-Reprints #1 4.10 12.30 45.00

MONKEY AND THE BEAR, THE
Atlas Comics (ZPC): Sept, 1953 - No. 3, Jan, 1954
1-Howie Post-c/a in all; funny animal 8.65 26.00 60.00
2,3 5.00 15.00 35.00

MONKEYMAN AND O'BRIEN (Also see Dark Horse Presents #80, 100-5, Gen13/…, Hellboy: Seed of Destruction, & San Diego Comic Con #2)
Dark Horse Comics (Legend): Jul, 1996 - No. 3, Sept, 1996 ($2.95, lim. series)
1-3: New stories; Art Adams-c/a/scripts 3.50
nn-(2/96, $2.95)-r/back-up stories from Hellboy: Seed of Destruction; Adams-c/a/scripts 3.50

MONKEYSHINES COMICS
Ace Periodicals/Publishers Specialists/Current Books/Unity Publ.: Summer, 1944 - No. 27, July, 1949
1-Funny animal 10.50 32.00 85.00
2-(Aut/44) 6.40 19.25 45.00
3-10: 3-(Win/44) 5.00 15.00 35.00
11-17,19-27: 23,24-Fago-c/a 5.00 15.00 30.00
18-Frazetta-a 6.40 19.25 45.00

MONKEY'S UNCLE, THE (See Merlin Jones As… under Movie Comics)

MONROES, THE (TV)
Dell Publishing Co.: Apr, 1967
1-Photo-c 2.50 7.50 25.00

MONSTER
Fiction House Magazines: 1953 - No. 2, 1953
1-Dr. Drew by Grandenetti; reprint from Rangers Comics #48; Whitman-c
50.00 150.00 450.00
2-Whitman-c 40.00 120.00 325.00

MONSTER CRIME COMICS (Also see Crime Must Stop)
Hillman Periodicals: Oct, 1952 (15¢, 52 pgs.)
1 (Scarce) 99.00 300.00 940.00

MONSTER FIGHTERS INC.
Image Comics (Bright Anvil Studios): Apr, 1999; Dec, 1999 ($3.50/$3.95)
1-Torres-s/Lubera & Yeung-a 3.50
…: The Black Book 1 (9/00, $3.50) Manapul-a 3.50
…The Ghosts of Christmas 1 (12/99, $3.95) 3.95

MONSTER HOWLS (Magazine)
Humor-Vision: December, 1966 (Satire) (35¢, 68 pgs.)
1 4.55 13.65 50.00

MONSTER HUNTERS
Charlton Comics: Aug, 1975 - No. 9, Jan, 1977; No. 10, Oct, 1977 - No. 18, Feb, 1979
1-Howard-a; Newton-c. 2.40 7.35 22.00
2-Sutton-c/a; Ditko-a 2.00 6.00 16.00
3,5,7 1.25 3.75 10.00
4,6,8,10: 4-Sutton-c/a. 6,8,10-Ditko-a 1.50 4.50 12.00
9,11,12 1.00 3.00 8.00
13,15,18-Ditko-c/a. 18-Sutton-a 1.10 3.30 9.00
14-Special all-Ditko issue 2.00 6.00 18.00
16,17-Sutton-a 1.00 2.80 7.00
1,2 (Modern Comics reprints, 1977) 4.00
NOTE: *Ditko a-2, 6, 8, 10, 13-15r, 18r; c-13-15, 18.* ***Howard*** *a-1, 3, 17; r-13.* ***Morisi*** *a-1.* ***Staton*** *a-1, 13.* ***Sutton*** *a-2, 4; c-2, 4; r-16-18.* ***Zeck*** *a-4-9. Reprints in #12-18.*

MONSTER MADNESS (Magazine)
Marvel Comics: 1972 - #3, 1973 (60¢, B&W)
1-3: Stories by "Sinister" Stan Lee 2.60 7.80 26.00

MONSTER MAN
Image Comics (Action Planet): Sept, 1997 ($2.95, B&W)
1-Mike Manley-c/s/a 3.00

MONSTER MASTERWORKS
Marvel Comics: 1989 ($12.95, TPB)
nn-Reprints 1960's monster stories; art by Kirby, Ditko, Ayers, Everett 13.00

MONSTER MATINEE
Chaos! Comics: Oct, 1997 - No. 3, Oct, 1997 ($2.50, limited series)
1-3: pin-ups 2.50

MONSTER MENACE
Marvel Comics: Dec, 1993 - No. 4, Mar, 1994 ($1.25, limited series)
1-4: Pre-code Atlas horror reprints. 3.00
NOTE: ***Ditko****-r &* ***Kirby****-r in all.*

MONSTER OF FRANKENSTEIN (See Frankenstein)

MONSTERS ON THE PROWL (Chamber of Darkness #1-8)
Marvel Comics Group (No. 13,14: 52 pgs.): No. 9, 2/71 - No. 27, 11/73; No. 28, 6/74 - No. 30, 10/74
9-Barry Smith inks 2.50 7.50 25.00
10-12,15: 12-Last 15¢ issue 1.75 5.25 14.00
13,14-(52 pgs.) 2.30 7.00 20.00
16-(4/72)-King Kull 4th app.; Severin-c 1.85 5.50 15.00
17-30 1.50 4.50 12.00
NOTE: ***Ditko*** *r-9, 14, 16.* ***Kirby*** *r-10-17, 21, 23, 25, 27, 28, 30; c-9, 25.* ***Kirby/Ditko*** *r-14, 17-20, 22, 24, 26, 29.* ***Marie/John Severin*** *a-16(Kull). 9-13, 15 contain one new story. Woodish art by* ***Reese****-11. King Kull created by Robert E. Howard.*

MONSTERS TO LAUGH WITH (Magazine) (Becomes Monsters Unlimited #4)
Marvel Comics Group: 1964 - No. 3, 1965 (B&W)
1-Humor by Stan Lee 5.90 17.75 65.00
2,3 3.20 9.60 35.00

MONSTERS UNLEASHED (Magazine)
Marvel Comics Group: July, 1973 - No. 11, Apr, 1975; Summer, 1975 (B&W)
1-Soloman Kane sty; Werewolf app. 3.00 9.00 30.00
2-4: 2-The Frankenstein Monster begins, ends #10. 3-Neal Adams-c/a; The Man-Thing begins (origin-r); Son of Satan preview. 4-Werewolf app.
2.60 7.80 26.00
5-7: Werewolf in all. 5-Man-Thing. 7-Williamson-a(r) 2.00 6.00 16.00
8-11: 8-Man-Thing; N. Adams-r. 9-Man-Thing; Wendigo app. 10-Origin Tigra
2.30 7.00 20.00
Annual 1 (Summer,1975, 92 pgs.)-Kane-a 2.00 6.00 18.00
NOTE: ***Boris*** *c-2, 6.* ***Brunner*** *a-2; c-11.* ***J. Buscema*** *a-2p, 4p, 5p.* ***Colan*** *a-1, 4r.* ***Davis*** *a-3r.* ***Everett*** *a-2r.* ***G. Kane*** *a-3.* ***Krigstein*** *r-4.* ***Morrow*** *a-3; c-1.* ***Perez*** *a-8.* ***Ploog*** *a-6.* ***Reese*** *a-1, 2.* ***Tuska*** *a-3p.* ***Wildey*** *a-1r.*

MONSTERS UNLIMITED (Magazine) (Formerly Monsters To Laugh With)
Marvel Comics Group: No. 4, 1965 - No. 7, 1966 (B&W)
4-7 3.00 9.00 32.00

MONTANA KID, THE (See Kid Montana)

MONTE HALE WESTERN (Movie star; Formerly Mary Marvel #1-28; also

Monte Hale Western #30 © FAW

Moon Girl #5 © WMG

Moon Knight V3 #4 © MAR

see Fawcett Movie Comic, Motion Picture Comics, Picture News #8, Real Western Hero, Six-Gun Heroes, Western Hero & XMas Comics)
Fawcett Publ./Charlton No. 83 on: No. 29, Oct, 1948 - No. 88, Jan, 1956

	GD2.0	FN6.0	NM9.4
29-(#1, 52 pgs.)-Photo-c begin, end #82; Monte Hale & his horse Pardner begin	50.00	150.00	450.00
30-(52 pgs.)-Big Bow and Little Arrow begin, end #34; Captain Tootsie by Beck	26.00	79.00	210.00
31-36,38-40-(52 pgs.): 34-Gabby Hayes begins, ends #80. 39-Captain Tootsie by Beck	19.00	56.00	150.00
37,41,45,49-(36 pgs.)	13.00	39.00	105.00
42-44,46-48,50-(52 pgs.): 47-Big Bow & Little Arrow app.	14.00	41.00	110.00
51,52,54-56,58,59-(52 pgs.)	11.00	33.00	90.00
53,57-(36 pgs.): 53-Slim Pickens app.	10.00	30.00	70.00
60-81: 36 pgs. #60-on. 80-Gabby Hayes ends	10.00	30.00	70.00
82-Last Fawcett issue (6/53)	11.00	33.00	90.00
83-1st Charlton issue (2/55); B&W photo back-c begin. Gabby Hayes returns, ends #86	12.50	37.50	100.00
84 (4/55)	10.00	30.00	75.00
85-86	10.00	30.00	70.00
87,88: 87-Wolverton-r, 1/2 pg. 88-Last issue	10.00	30.00	75.00

NOTE: ***Gil Kane** a-33?, 34? Rocky Lane -1 pg. (Carnation ad)-38, 40, 41, 43, 44, 46, 55.*

MONTY HALL OF THE U.S. MARINES (See With the Marines...)
Toby Press: Aug, 1951 - No. 11, Apr, 1953

	GD2.0	FN6.0	NM9.4
1	10.00	30.00	80.00
2	6.40	19.25	45.00
3-5	5.70	17.00	40.00
6-11	5.00	15.00	35.00

NOTE: *Full page pin-ups (Pin-Up Pete) by **Jack Sparling** in #1-9.*

MOON, A GIRL...ROMANCE, A (Becomes Weird Fantasy #13 on; formerly Moon Girl #1-8)
E. C. Comics: No. 9, Sept-Oct, 1949 - No. 12, Mar-Apr, 1950

	GD2.0	FN6.0	NM9.4
9-Moon Girl cameo; spanking panel	68.00	205.00	650.00
10,11	55.00	165.00	500.00
12-(Scarce)	69.00	208.00	660.00

NOTE: ***Feldstein, Ingels** art in all. **Feldstein** c-9-12. **Wood/Harrison** a-10-12. Canadian reprints known; see Table of Contents.*

MOON GIRL AND THE PRINCE (#1) (Moon Girl #2-6; Moon Girl Fights Crime #7, 8; becomes A Moon, A Girl, Romance #9 on)(Also see Animal Fables #7 and Happy Houlihans)
E. C. Comics: Fall, 1947 - No. 8, Summer, 1949

	GD2.0	FN6.0	NM9.4
1-Origin Moon Girl (see Happy Houlihans #1)	89.00	268.00	850.00
2	50.00	150.00	450.00
3,4: 4-Moon Girl vs. a vampire	44.00	133.00	400.00
5-E.C.'s 1st horror story, "Zombie Terror"	95.00	285.00	900.00
6-8 (Scarce): 7-Origin Star (Moongirl's sidekick)	50.00	150.00	450.00

NOTE: ***Craig** a-2, 5. **Moldoff** a-1-8; c-2-6. **Wheelan's** Fat and Slat app. in #3, 4, 6. #2 & #3 are 52 pgs., #4 on, 36 pgs. Canadian reprints known; (see Table of Contents.)*

MOON KNIGHT (Also see The Hulk, Marc Spector..., Marvel Preview #21, Marvel Spotlight & Werewolf by Night #32)
Marvel Comics Group: Nov, 1980 - No. 38, Jul, 1984 (Mando paper #33 on)

	NM9.4
1-Origin resumed in #4	4.00
2-15,25,35: 4-Intro Midnight Man. 25-Double size. 35-($1.00, 52 pgs.)-X-men app.; F.F. cameo	2.50
16-24,26-34,36-38: 16-The Thing app.	2.00

NOTE: ***Austin** c-27i, 31i. **Cowan** a-16; c-16, 17. **Kaluta** c-36-38; back c-35. **Miller** c-9, 12p, 13p, 15p, 27p. **Ploog** back c-35. **Sienkiewicz** a-1-15, 17-20, 22-26, 28-30, 33i, 36(4), 37; c-1-5, 7, 8, 10, 11, 14-16, 18-26, 28-30, 31p, 33, 34.*

MOON KNIGHT
Marvel Comics Group: June, 1985 - V2#6, Dec, 1985

V2#1-6: 1-Double size; new costume. 6-Sienkiewicz painted-c. 2.00

MOON KNIGHT
Marvel Comics: Jan, 1998 - No. 4, Apr, 1998 ($2.50, limited series)

1-4-Moench-s/Edwards-c/a 2.50

MOON KNIGHT (Volume 3)
Marvel Comics: Jan, 1999 - No. 4, Feb, 1999 ($2.99, limited series)

1-4-Moench-s/Texeira-a(p) 3.00

MOON KNIGHT: DIVIDED WE FALL
Marvel Comics: 1992 ($4.95, 52 pgs.)

nn-Denys Cowan-c/a(p) 5.00

MOON KNIGHT SPECIAL
Marvel Comics: Oct, 1992 ($2.50, 52 pgs.)

1-Shang Chi, Master of Kung Fu-c/story 2.50

MOON KNIGHT SPECIAL EDITION
Marvel Comics Group: Nov, 1983 - No. 3, Jan, 1984 ($2.00, limited series, Baxter paper)

1-3: Reprints from Hulk mag. by Sienkiewicz 3.00

MOON MULLINS (See Popular Comics, Super Book #3 & Super Comics)
Dell Publishing Co.: 1941 - 1945

	GD2.0	FN6.0	NM9.4
Four Color 14(1941)	35.00	105.00	420.00
Large Feature Comic 29(1941)	25.00	75.00	300.00
Four Color 31(1943)	18.35	55.00	220.00
Four Color 81(1945)	10.00	30.00	120.00

MOON MULLINS
Michel Publ. (American Comics Group)#1-6/St. John #7,8: Dec-Jan, 1947-48 - No. 8, 1949 (52 pgs)

	GD2.0	FN6.0	NM9.4
1-Alternating Sunday & daily strip-r	20.00	60.00	160.00
2	10.00	30.00	80.00
3-8: 7,8-St. John Publ. 8-...Featuring Kayo on-c	9.30	28.00	65.00

NOTE: ***Milt Gross** a-2-6, 8. **Frank Willard** r-all.*

MOON PILOT
Dell Publishing Co.: No. 1313, Mar-May, 1962

	GD2.0	FN6.0	NM9.4
Four Color 1313-Movie, photo-c	6.70	20.00	80.00

MOONSHADOW (Also see Farewell, Moonshadow)
Marvel Comics (Epic Comics): 5/85 - #12, 2/87 ($1.50/$1.75, mature) (1st fully painted comic book)

	GD2.0	FN6.0	NM9.4
1-Origin; J. M. DeMatteis scripts & Jon J. Muth painted-c/a.		2.40	6.00
2-12: 11-Origin			4.00
Trade paperback (1987?)-r/#1-12			14.00
Signed & numbered hard-c ($39.95, 1,200 copies)-r/#1-12	5.45	16.35	60.00

MOONSHADOW
DC Comics (Vertigo): Oct, 1994 - No. 12, Aug, 1995 ($2.25/$2.95)

	NM9.4
1-11: Reprints Epic series.	2.50
12 ($2.95)-w/expanded ending	3.00
The Complete Moonshadow TPB ('98, $39.95) r/#1-12 and Farewell Moonshadow; new Muth painted-c	40.00

MOON-SPINNERS, THE (See Movie Comics)

MOPSY (See Pageant of Comics & TV Teens)
St. John Publ. Co.: Feb, 1948 - No. 19, Sept, 1953

	GD2.0	FN6.0	NM9.4
1-Part-r; reprints "Some Punkins" by Neher	18.00	53.00	140.00
2	10.00	30.00	75.00
3-10(1953): 8-Lingerie panels	8.65	26.00	60.00
11-19: 19-Lingerie-c	7.15	21.50	50.00

NOTE: *#1, 3-6, 13, 18, 19 have paper dolls.*

MORBID ANGEL
London Night Studios: Oct, 1995 ($3.00, B&W)

1-Hartsoe-c 3.00

MORBID ANGEL
London Night Studios: July, 1996 - No. 3, Jan, 1997 ($3.00, limited series)

	NM9.4
1/2-($9.95)-Angel Tear Edition; foil logo	10.00
1-3, 1-Penance-c, ...-To Hell and Back-(10/96, $3.00, B&W)	3.00

MORBIUS REVISITED
Marvel Comic: Aug, 1993 - No. 5, Dec, 1993 ($1.95, mini-series)

1-5-Reprints Fear #27-31 2.00

MORBIUS: THE LIVING VAMPIRE (Also see Amazing Spider-Man #101, 102, Fear #20, Marvel Team-Up #3, 4, Midnight Sons Unl. & Vampire Tales)

Morbius: The Living Vampire #25 © MAR

More Fun Comics #48 © DC

More Than Mortal #5 © Sharon Scott

GD2.0 FN6.0 NM9.4

Marvel Comics (Midnight Sons imprint #16 on): Sept, 1992 - No. 32, Apr, 1995 ($1.75/$1.95)

1-($2.75, 52 pgs.)-Polybagged w/poster; Ghost Rider & Johnny Blaze x-over (part 3 of Rise of the Midnight Sons) 3.00
2-11,13-24,26-32: 3,4-Vs. Spider-Man-c/s.15-Ghost Rider app. 16-Spot varnish-c. 16,17-Siege of Darkness,parts 5 &13. 18-Deathlok app. 21-Bound-in Spider-Man trading card sheet; S-M app. 2.00
12-($2.25)-Outer-c is a Darkhold envelope made of black parchment w/gold ink; Midnight Massacre x-over 2.50
25-($2.50, 52 pgs.)-Gold foil logo 2.50

MORE FUN COMICS (Formerly New Fun Comics #1-6)
National Periodical Publications: No. 7, Jan, 1936 - No. 127, Nov-Dec, 1947 (No. 7,9-11: paper-c) **GD2.0 FN6.0 VF8.0**

7(1/36)-Oversized, paper-c; 1 pg. Kelly-a 769.00 2310.00 5000.00
8(2/36)-Oversized (10x12"), paper-c; 1 pg. Kelly-a; Sullivan-c 769.00 2310.00 5000.00
9(3-4/36)(Very rare, 1st standard-sized comic book with original material)-Last multiple panel-c 923.00 2770.00 6000.00
10,11(7/36): 10-Last Henri Duval by Siegel & Shuster. 11-1st "Calling All Cars" by Siegel & Shuster; new classic logo begins 538.00 1615.00 3500.00
12(8/36)-Slick-c begin 415.00 1245.00 2700.00
V2#1(9/36, #13) 385.00 1154.00 2500.00
2(10/36, #14)-Dr. Occult in costume (1st in color)(Superman proto-type; 1st DC appearance) continues from The Comics Magazine, ends #17 1846.00 5539.00 12,000.00
V2#3(11/36, #15), 16(V2#4), 17(V2#5): 16-Cover numbering begins; Xmas-c; last Superman tryout issue 738.00 2215.00 4800.00
18-20(V2#8, 5/37) 292.00 877.00 1900.00
GD2.0 FN6.0 NM9.4
21(V2#9)-24(V2#12, 9/37) 275.00 825.00 2200.00
25(V3#1, 10/37)-27(V3#3, 12/37): 27-Xmas-c 275.00 825.00 2200.00
28-30: 30-1st non-funny cover 250.00 750.00 2000.00
31-Has ad for Action #1 263.00 788.00 2100.00
32-35: 32-Last Dr. Occult 250.00 750.00 2000.00
36-40: 36-(10/38)-The Masked Ranger & sidekick Pedro begins; Ginger Snap by Bob Kane (2 pgs.; 1st-a?). 39-Xmas-c 250.00 750.00 2000.00
41-50: 41-Last Masked Ranger 200.00 600.00 1600.00
51-The Spectre app. (in costume) in one panel ad at end of Buccaneer story 725.00 2175.00 5500.00
GD2.0 FN6.0 VF8.0 NM9.4
52-(2/40)-Origin/1st app. The Spectre (in costume splash panel only), part 1 by Bernard Baily (parts 1 & 2 written by Jerry Siegel; Spectre's costume changes color from purple & blue to green & grey; last Wing Brady; Spectre-c 4960.00 14,880.00 32,240.00 62,000.00
53-Origin The Spectre (in costume at end of story), part 2; Capt. Desmo begins;Spectre-c 2358.00 7075.00 16,500.00 33,000.00
54-The Spectre in costume; last King Carter; classic-Spectre-c 957.00 2870.00 5980.00 11,000.00
55-(Scarce, 5/40)-Dr. Fate begins (Intro & 1st app.); last Bulldog Martin; Spectre-c 1120.00 3360.00 7280.00 14,000.00
GD2.0 FN6.0 NM9.4
56-1st Dr. Fate-c (classic), origin continues. Congo Bill begins (6/40), 1st app.; 478.00 1435.00 5500.00
57-60-All Spectre-c 333.00 1000.00 3500.00
61,65: 61-Classic Dr. Fate-c. 65-Classic Spectre-c 305.00 915.00 3200.00
62-64,66: 63-Last St. Bob Neal. 64-Lance Larkin begins; all Spectre-c 290.00 870.00 2750.00
GD2.0 FN6.0 VF8.0 NM9.4
67-(5/41)-Origin (1st) Dr. Fate; last Congo Bill & Biff Bronson (C.B. cont. in Action Comics #37, 6/41)-Spectre-c 609.00 1826.00 3654.00 7000.00
GD2.0 FN6.0 NM9.4
68-70: 68-Clip Carson begins. 70-Last Lance Larkin; all Dr. Fate-c 226.00 679.00 2150.00
GD2.0 FN6.0 VF8.0 NM9.4
71-Origin & 1st app. Johnny Quick by Mort Weisinger (9/41); classic sci/fi Dr. Fate-c 496.00 1487.00 2976.00 5700.00
GD2.0 FN6.0 NM9.4
72-Dr. Fate's new helmet; last Sgt. Carey, Sgt. O'Malley & Captain Desmo; German submarine-c (only German war-c) 221.00 663.00 2100.00
GD2.0 FN6.0 VF8.0 NM9.4
73-Origin & 1st app. Aquaman (11/41) by Paul Norris; intro. Green Arrow & Speedy; Dr. Fate-c 1000.00 3000.00 6500.00 12,500.00
GD2.0 FN6.0 NM9.4
74-2nd Aquaman; 1st Percival Popp, Supercop; Dr. Fate-c 253.00 758.00 2400.00
75,76: 75-New origin Spectre; Nazi spy ring cover w/Hitler's photo. 76-Last Dr. Fate-c; Johnny Quick (by Meskin #76-97) begins, ends #107; Last Clip Carson 226.00 679.00 2150.00
77-80: 77-Green Arrow-c begin 216.00 647.00 2050.00
81-83,85,88,90: 81-Last large logo. 82-1st small logo. 126.00 379.00 1200.00
84-Green Arrow Japanese war-c 132.00 395.00 1250.00
86,87-Johnny Quick-c. 87-Last Radio Squad 126.00 379.00 1200.00
89-Origin Green Arrow & Speedy Team-up 137.00 411.00 1300.00
91-97,99: 91-1st bi-monthly issue. 93-Dover & Clover begin (1st app., 9-10/43). 97-Kubert-a 79.00 237.00 750.00
98-Last Dr. Fate (scarce) 95.00 285.00 900.00
100 (11-12/44)-Johnny Quick-c 116.00 348.00 1100.00
GD2.0 FN6.0 VF8.0 NM9.4
101-Origin & 1st app. Superboy (1-2/45)(not by Siegel & Shuster); last Spectre issue; Green Arrow-c 739.00 2217.00 4435.00 8500.00
GD2.0 FN6.0 NM9.4
102-2nd Superboy app; 1st Dover & Clover-c 126.00 379.00 1200.00
103-3rd Superboy app; last Green Arrow-c 95.00 285.00 900.00
104-1st Superboy-c w/Dover & Clover 84.00 253.00 800.00
105,106-Superboy-c 79.00 237.00 750.00
107-Last Johnny Quick & Superboy 79.00 237.00 750.00
108-120: 108-Genius Jones begins; 1st c-app. (3-4/46; cont'd from Adventure Comics #102) 22.00 66.00 175.00
121-124,126: 121-123,126-Post funny animal(Jimminy & the Magic Book)-c 19.00 56.00 150.00
125-Superman c-app.w/Jimminy 74.00 221.00 700.00
127-(Scarce)-Post-c/a 34.00 103.00 275.00

NOTE: *All issues are scarce to rare. Cover features: The Spectre-#52-55, 57-60, 62-67. Dr. Fate-#56, 61, 68-76. The Green Arrow & Speedy-#77-85, 88-97, 99, 101 (w/Dover & Clover-#98, 103). Johnny Quick-#86, 87, 100. Dover & Clover-#102, (104, 106 w/Superboy), 107, 108(w/Genius Jones), 110, 112, 114, 117, 119. Genius Jones-#109, 111, 113, 115, 118, 120.* ***Baily*** *a-45, 52-on; c-52-55, 57-60, 62-67.* ***Al Capp*** *a-45(signed Koppy).* ***Ellsworth*** *c-7.* ***Creig Flessel*** *c-30, 31, 35-48(most).* ***Guardineer*** *c-47, 49, 50.* ***Kiefer*** *a-20.* ***Meskin*** *c-86, 87, 100?* ***Moldoff*** *c-51.* ***George Papp*** *c-77-85.* ***Post*** *c-121-127.* ***Vincent Sullivan*** *c-8-28, 32-34.*

MORE SEYMOUR (See Seymour My Son)
Archie Publications: Oct, 1963

1 2.30 7.00 20.00

MORE THAN MORTAL (Also see Lady Pendragon/...)
Liar Comics: June, 1997 - No. 4, Apr, 1998 ($2.95, limited series)
Image Comics: No. 5, Dec, 1999 - Present ($2.95)

1-Blue forest background-c, 1-Variant-c 4.00
1-White-c 2.40 6.00
1-2nd printing; purple sky cover 3.00
2-4: 3-Silvestri-c, 4-Two-c, one by Randy Queen 3.00
5,6: 5-1st Image Comics issue 3.00

MORE THAN MORTAL: OTHERWORLDS
Image Comics: July, 1999 - No. 4, Dec, 1999 ($2.95, limited series)

1-4-Firchow-a. 1-Two covers 3.00

MORE THAN MORTAL SAGAS
Liar Comics: Jun, 1998 - No. 3, Dec, 1998 ($2.95, limited series)

1,2-Painted art by Romano. 2-Two-c, one by Firchow 3.00
1-Variant-c by Linsner 5.00

MORE THAN MORTAL TRUTHS AND LEGENDS
Liar Comics: Aug, 1998 - No. 6, Apr, 1999 ($2.95)

1-6-Firchow-a(p) 3.00
1-Variant-c by Dan Norton 4.50

MORE TRASH FROM MAD (Annual)
E. C. Comics: 1958 - No. 12, 1969

Mostly Wanted #4 © DC

Motion Picture Comics #102 © FAW

Movie Classics - Dr. Who & the Daleks © BBC

GD2.0 FN6.0 NM9.4

(Note: Bonus missing = one third price)
nn(1958)-8 pgs. color Mad reprint from #20 19.00 57.00 210.00
2(1959)-Market Product Labels 13.50 40.00 150.00
3(1960)-Text book covers 12.50 37.00 135.00
4(1961)-Sing Along with Mad booklet 12.50 37.00 135.00
5(1962)-Window Stickers; r/from Mad #39 8.15 24.50 90.00
6(1963)-TV Guise booklet 9.00 27.00 100.00
7(1964)-Alfred E. Neuman commemorative stamps 6.80 20.50 75.00
8(1965)-Life size poster-Alfred E. Neuman 4.55 13.65 50.00
9-12: 9,10(1966-67)-Mischief Sticker. 11(1968)-Campaign poster & bumper sticker. 12(1969)-Pocket medals 4.10 12.30 45.00
NOTE: ***Kelly Freas** c-1, 2, 4. **Mingo** c-3, 5-9, 12.*

MORGAN THE PIRATE (Movie)
Dell Publishing Co.: No. 1227, Sept-Nov, 1961
Four Color 1227-Photo-c 7.50 22.50 90.00

MORLOCK 2001
Atlas/Seaboard Publ.: Feb, 1975 - No. 3, July, 1975
1,2: 1-(Super-hero)-Origin & 1st app.; Milgrom-c 5.00
3-Ditko/Wrightson-a; origin The Midnight Man & The Mystery Men 2.40 6.00

MORNINGSTAR SPECIAL
Comico: Apr, 1990 ($2.50)
1-From the Elementals; Willingham-c/a/scripts 3.00

MORRIGAN
Dimension X: Aug, 1993 ($2.75, B&W)
1-Foil stamped-c 3.00

MORRIGAN
Sirius Entertainment: 1997 ($2.95, limited series)
1-Tenuta-c/a 3.00

MORTAL KOMBAT
Malibu Comics: July, 1994 - No. 6, Dec, 1994 ($2.95)
1-6: 1-Two diff. covers exist 3.00
1-Limited edition gold foil embossed-c 4.00
0 (12/94), Special Edition 1 (11/94) 3.00
Tournament Edition I12/94, $3.95), II('95)($3.95) 4.00
...: **BARAKA** ,June, 1995 ($2.95, one-shot) #1; ...**BATTLEWAVE** ,2/95 - No. 6, 7/95 , #1-6; ...**GORO, PRINCE OF PAIN** ,9/94 - No. 3, 11/94, #1-3; ... **KITANA AND MILEENA** ,8/95 , #1; ...**KUNG LAO** ,7/95 , #1; ... **RAYDON & KANO** ,3/95 - No. 3, 5/95, #1-3: ...(all $2.95) 3.00
U.S. SPECIAL FORCES ,1/95 - No. 2, ($3.50), #1,2 3.50

MORTIE (Mazie's Friend; also see Flat-Top)
Magazine Publishers: Dec, 1952 - No. 4, June, 1953?
1 7.85 23.50 55.00
2-4 5.00 15.00 30.00

MORTIGAN GOTH: IMMORTALIS (See Marvel Frontier Comics Unlimited)
Marvel Comics: Sept, 1993 - No. 4, Mar, 1994 ($1.95, mini-series)
1-($2.95)-Foil-c 3.00
2-4 2.00

MORT THE DEAD TEENAGER
Marvel Comics: Nov, 1993 - No. 4, Mar, 1994 ($1.75, mini-series)
1-4 2.00

MORTY MEEKLE
Dell Publishing Co.: No. 793, May, 1957
Four Color 793 2.50 7.50 25.00

MOSES & THE TEN COMMANDMENTS (See Dell Giants)

MOSTLY WANTED
DC Comics (WildStorm): Jul, 2000 - No. 4, Nov, 2000 ($2.50, limited series)
1-4-Lobdell-s/Flores-a 2.50

MOTHER GOOSE AND NURSERY RHYME COMICS (See Christmas With Mother Goose)
Dell Publishing Co.: No. 41, 1944 - No. 862, Nov, 1957
Four Color 41-Walt Kelly-c/a 22.00 65.00 260.00
Four Color 59, 68-Kelly c/a 19.00 57.00 225.00
Four Color 862-The Truth About..., Movie (Disney) 6.70 20.00 80.00

MOTHER TERESA OF CALCUTTA
Marvel Comics Group: 1984
1-(52 pgs.) No ads 4.00

MOTION PICTURE COMICS (See Fawcett Movie Comics)
Fawcett Publications: No. 101, 1950 - No. 114, Jan, 1953 (All-photo-c)
101- "Vanishing Westerner"; Monte Hale (1950) 30.00 90.00 240.00
102- "Code of the Silver Sage"; Rocky Lane (1/51) 28.00 84.00 225.00
103- "Covered Wagon Raid"; Rocky Lane (3/51) 28.00 84.00 225.00
104- "Vigilante Hideout"; Rocky Lane (5/51)-Book length Powell-a 28.00 84.00 225.00
105- "Red Badge of Courage"; Audie Murphy; Bob Powell-a (7/51) 34.00 101.00 270.00
106- "The Texas Rangers"; George Montgomery (9/51) 29.00 86.00 230.00
107- "Frisco Tornado"; Rocky Lane (11/51) 25.00 75.00 200.00
108- "Mask of the Avenger"; John Derek 19.00 56.00 150.00
109- "Rough Rider of Durango"; Rocky Lane 26.00 79.00 210.00
110- "When Worlds Collide"; George Evans-a (5/52); Williamson & Evans drew themselves in story; (also see Famous Funnies No. 72-88) 95.00 285.00 900.00
111- "The Vanishing Outpost"; Lash LaRue 31.00 94.00 250.00
112- "Brave Warrior"; Jon Hall & Jay Silverheels 18.00 53.00 140.00
113- "Walk East on Beacon"; George Murphy; Schaffenberger-a 12.50 37.50 100.00
114- "Cripple Creek"; George Montgomery (1/53) 14.00 41.00 110.00

MOTION PICTURE FUNNIES WEEKLY (See Promotional Comics section)

MOTORHEAD (See Comic's Greatest World)
Dark Horse Comics: Aug, 1995 - No. 6, Jan, 1996 ($2.50)
1-6: Bisley-c on all. 1-Predator app. 2.50
Special 1 (3/94, $3.95, 52pgs.)-Jae Lee-c; Barb Wire, The Machine & Wolf Gang app. 4.00

MOTORMOUTH (... & Killpower #7? on)
Marvel Comics UK: June, 1992 - No. 12, May, 1993 ($1.75)
1-13: 1,2-Nick Fury app. 3-Punisher-c/story. 5,6-Nick Fury & Punisher app. 6-Cable cameo. 7-9-Cable app. 2.00

MOUNTAIN MEN (See Ben Bowie)

MOUSE MUSKETEERS (See M.G.M.'s...)

MOUSE ON THE MOON, THE (See Movie Classics)

MOVIE CLASSICS
Dell Publishing Co.: Apr, 1956; May-Jul, 1962 - Dec, 1969
(Before 1963, most movie adaptations were part of the 4-Color series)
(Disney movie adaptations after 1970 are in Walt Disney Showcase)
Around the World Under the Sea 12-030-612 (12/66) 3.00 9.00 30.00
Bambi 3(4/56)-Disney; r/4-Color #186 3.45 10.35 38.00
Battle of the Bulge 12-056-606 (6/66) 3.00 9.00 32.00
Beach Blanket Bingo 12-058-509 5.85 17.50 70.00
Bon Voyage 01-068-212 (12/62)-Disney; photo-c 3.20 9.60 35.00
Castilian, The 12-110-401 3.00 9.00 30.00
Cat, The 12-109-612 (12/66) 2.80 8.40 28.00
Cheyenne Autumn 12-112-506 (4-6/65) 5.00 15.00 55.00
Circus World, Samuel Bronston's 12-115-411; John Wayne app.; John Wayne photo-c 9.00 27.00 110.00
Countdown 12-150-710 (10/67)-James Caan photo-c 3.00 9.00 32.00
Creature, The 1 (12-142-302) (12-2/62-63) 5.85 17.50 70.00
Creature, The 12-142-410 (10/64) 4.10 12.30 45.00
David Ladd's Life Story 12-173-212 (10-12/62)-Photo-c 6.70 20.00 80.00
Die, Monster, Die 12-175-603 (3/66)-Photo-c 4.10 12.30 45.00
Dirty Dozen 12-180-710 (10/67) 3.80 11.40 42.00
Dr. Who & the Daleks 12-190-612 (12/66)-Peter Cushing photo-c; 1st U.S. app. of Dr. Who 9.50 28.00 115.00
Dracula 12-231-212 (10-12/62) 5.00 15.00 60.00
El Dorado 12-240-710 (10/67)-John Wayne; photo-c 11.70 35.00 140.00

Movie Classics - El Dorado © DELL

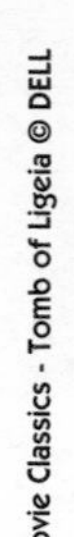
Movie Classics - Tomb of Ligeia © DELL

Movie Comics #4 © DC

GD2.0 FN6.0 NM9.4

Ensign Pulver 12-257-410 (8-10/64) 2.80 8.40 28.00
Frankenstein 12-283-305 (3-5/63) 5.00 15.00 60.00
Great Race, The 12-299-603 (3/66)-Natallie Wood, Tony Curtis photo-c
3.80 11.40 42.00
Hallelujah Trail, The 12-307-602 (2/66) (Shows 1/66 inside); Burt Lancaster, Lee Remick photo-c 4.10 12.30 45.00
Hatari 12-340-301 (1/63)-John Wayne 7.00 21.00 85.00
Horizontal Lieutenant, The 01-348-210 (10/62) 2.80 8.40 28.00
Incredible Mr. Limpet, The 12-370-408; Don Knotts photo-c
3.20 9.60 35.00
Jack the Giant Killer 12-374-301 (1/63) 7.50 22.50 90.00
Jason & the Argonauts 12-376-310 (8-10/63)-Photo-c
9.00 27.00 100.00
Lancelot & Guinevere 12-416-310 (10/63) 4.55 13.65 50.00
Lawrence 12-426-308 (8/63)-Story of Lawrence of Arabia; movie ad on back-c; not exactly like movie 4.55 13.65 50.00
Lion of Sparta 12-439-301 (1/63) 3.20 9.60 35.00
Mad Monster Party 12-460-801 (9/67)-Based on Kurtzman's screenplay
5.00 15.00 60.00
Magic Sword, The 01-496-209 (9/62) 5.00 15.00 55.00
Masque of the Red Death 12-490-410 (8-10/64)-Vincent Price photo-c
5.00 15.00 55.00
Maya 12-495-612 (12/66)-Clint Walker & Jay North part photo-c
3.65 11.00 40.00
McHale's Navy 12-500-412 (10-12/64) 3.65 11.00 40.00
Merrill's Marauders 12-510-301 (1/63)-Photo-c 2.80 8.40 28.00
Mouse on the Moon, The 12-530-312 (10/12/63)-Photo-c
3.20 9.60 35.00
Mummy, The 12-537-211 (9-11/62) 2 versions with different back-c
5.85 17.50 70.00
Music Man, The 12-538-301 (1/63) 2.80 8.40 28.00
Naked Prey, The 12-545-612 (12/66)-Photo-c 5.00 15.00 55.00
Night of the Grizzly, The 12-558-612 (12/66)-Photo-c 3.00 9.00 35.00
None But the Brave 12-565-506 (4-6/65) 5.00 15.00 55.00
Operation Bikini 12-597-310 (10/63)-Photo-c 3.00 9.00 30.00
Operation Crossbow 12-590-512 (10-12/65) 3.00 9.00 30.00
Prince & the Pauper, The 01-654-207 (5-7/62)-Disney
3.20 9.60 35.00
Raven, The 12-680-309 (9/63)-Vincent Price photo-c 5.00 15.00 55.00
Ring of Bright Water 01-701-910 (10/69) (inside shows #12-701-909)
3.00 9.00 35.00
Runaway, The 12-707-412 (10-12/64) 2.80 8.40 28.00
Santa Claus Conquers the Martians #? (1964)-Photo-c
7.50 22.50 90.00
Santa Claus Conquers the Martians 12-725-603 (3/66, 12¢)-Reprints 1964 issue; photo-c 6.30 19.00 75.00
Another version given away with a Golden Record, SLP 170, nn, no price (3/66)-Complete with record 13.00 40.00 160.00
Six Black Horses 12-750-301 (1/63)-Photo-c 3.00 9.00 30.00
Ski Party 12-743-511 (9-11/65)-Frankie Avalon photo-c
4.10 12.30 45.00
Smoky 12-746-702 (2/67) 2.80 8.40 28.00
Sons of Katie Elder 12-748-511 (9-11/65); John Wayne app.; photo-c
12.00 36.00 145.00
Tales of Terror 12-793-302 (2/63)-Evans-a 4.10 12.30 45.00
Three Stooges Meet Hercules 01-828-208 (8/62)-Photo-c
7.50 22.50 90.00
Tomb of Ligeia 12-830-506 (4-6/65) 4.10 12.30 45.00
Treasure Island 01-845-211 (7-9/62)-Disney; r/4-Color #624
3.00 9.00 30.00
Twice Told Tales (Nathaniel Hawthorne) 12-840-401 (11-1/63-64); Vincent Price photo-c 4.10 12.30 45.00
Two on a Guillotine 12-850-506 (4-6/65) 3.20 9.60 35.00
Valley of Gwangi 01-880-912 (12/69) 8.00 24.00 95.00
War Gods of the Deep 12-900-509 (7-9/65) 3.00 9.00 30.00
War Wagon, The 12-533-709 (9/67); John Wayne app.
7.50 22.50 90.00
Who's Minding the Mint? 12-924-708 (8/67) 2.80 8.40 28.00
Wolfman, The 12-922-308 (6-8/63) 5.00 15.00 60.00

GD2.0 FN6.0 NM9.4

Wolfman, The 1(12-922-410)(8-10/64)-2nd printing; r/#12-922-308
3.20 9.60 35.00
Zulu 12-950-410 (8-10/64)-Photo-c 7.00 21.00 85.00

MOVIE COMICS (See Cinema Comics Herald & Fawcett Movie Comics)

MOVIE COMICS
National Periodical Publications/Picture Comics: April, 1939 - No. 6, Sept-Oct, 1939 (Most all photo-c)

1- "Gunga Din", "Son of Frankenstein", "The Great Man Votes", "Fisherman's Wharf", & "Scouts to the Rescue" part 1; Wheelan "Minute Movies" begin
314.00 943.00 3300.00
2- "Stagecoach", "The Saint Strikes Back", "King of the Turf","Scouts to the Rescue" part 2, "Arizona Legion", Andy Devine photo-c
221.00 663.00 2100.00
3- "East Side of Heaven", "Mystery in the White Room", "Four Feathers", "Mexican Rose" with Gene Autry, "Spirit of Culver", "Many Secrets", "The Mikado" (1st Gene Autry photo cover) 158.00 474.00 1500.00
4- "Captain Fury", Gene Autry in "Blue Montana Skies", "Streets of N.Y." with Jackie Cooper, "Oregon Trail" part 1 with Johnny Mack Brown, "Big Town Czar" with Barton MacLane, & "Star Reporter" with Warren Hull
126.00 379.00 1200.00
5- "The Man in the Iron Mask", "Five Came Back", "Wolf Call", "The Girl & the Gambler", "The House of Fear", "The Family Next Door", "Oregon Trail" part 2 147.00 442.00 1400.00
6- "The Phantom Creeps", "Chumps at Oxford", & "The Oregon Trail" part 3; 2nd Robot-c 190.00 570.00 1800.00

NOTE: *Above books contain many original movie stills with dialogue from movie scripts. All issues are scarce.*

MOVIE COMICS
Fiction House Magazines: Dec, 1946 - No. 4, 1947

1-Big Town (by Lubbers), Johnny Danger begin; Celardo-a; Mitzi of the Movies by Fran Hopper 53.00 158.00 475.00
2-(2/47)- "White Tie & Tails" with William Bendix; Mitzi of the Movies begins by Matt Baker, ends #4 40.00 120.00 360.00
3-(6/47)-Andy Hardy starring Mickey Rooney 40.00 120.00 360.00
4-Mitzi In Hollywood by Matt Baker; Merton of the Movies with Red Skelton; Yvonne DeCarlo & George Brent in "Slave Girl" 47.00 141.00 425.00

MOVIE COMICS
Gold Key/Whitman: Oct, 1962 - 1984

Alice in Wonderland 10144-503 (3/65)-Disney; partial reprint of 4-Color #331
3.45 10.35 38.00
Aristocats, The 1 (30045-103)(3/71)-Disney; with pull-out poster (25¢) (No poster = half price) 6.70 20.00 80.00
Bambi 1 (10087-309)(9/63)-Disney; r/4-C #186 3.65 11.00 40.00
Bambi 2 (10087-607)(7/66)-Disney; r/4-C #186 3.00 9.00 30.00
Beneath the Planet of the Apes 30044-012 (12/70)-with pull-out poster; photo-c (No poster = half price) 8.00 24.00 95.00
Big Red 10026-211 (11/62)-Disney; photo-c 3.00 9.00 30.00
Big Red 10026-503 (3/65)-Disney; reprints 10026-211; photo-c
2.50 7.50 25.00
Blackbeard's Ghost 10222-806 (6/68)-Disney 2.80 8.40 28.00
Bullwhip Griffin 10181-706 (6/67)-Disney; Manning-a; photo-c
3.20 9.60 35.00
Captain Sindbad 10077-309 (9/63)-Manning-a; photo-c
5.00 15.00 60.00
Chitty Chitty Bang Bang 1 (30038-902)(2/69)-with pull-out poster; Disney; photo-c (No poster = half price) 6.00 18.00 72.00
Cinderella 10152-508 (8/65)-Disney; r/4-C #786 3.20 9.60 35.00
Darby O'Gill & the Little People 10251-001(1/70)-Disney; reprints 4-Color #1024 (Toth-a); photo-c 4.55 13.65 50.00
Dumbo 1 (10090-310)(10/63)-Disney; r/4-C #668 3.20 9.60 35.00
Emil & the Detectives 10120-502 (2/65)-Disney; photo-c
3.00 9.00 30.00
Escapade in Florence 1 (10043-301)(1/63)-Disney; starring Annette Funicello
7.50 22.50 90.00
Fall of the Roman Empire 10118-407 (7/64); Sophia Loren photo-c
3.20 9.60 35.00
Fantastic Voyage 10178-702 (2/67)-Wood/Adkins-a; photo-c

Movie Comics - PT 109 © GK

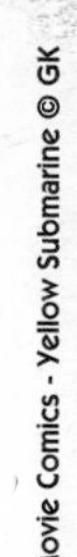
Movie Comics - Yellow Submarine © GK

Movie Love #5 © FF

GD2.0 FN6.0 NM9.4

5.00 15.00 55.00
55 Days at Peking 10081-309 (9/63)-Photo-c 3.00 9.00 30.00
Fighting Prince of Donegal, The 10193-701 (1/67)-Disney 2.80 8.40 28.00
First Men in the Moon 10132-503 (3/65)-Fred Fredericks-a; photo-c 3.00 9.00 32.00
Gay Purr-ee 30017-301(1/63, 84 pgs.) 4.55 13.65 50.00
Gnome Mobile, The 10207-710 (10/67)-Disney 3.20 9.60 35.00
Goodbye, Mr. Chips 10246-006 (6/70)-Peter O'Toole photo-c 3.00 9.00 30.00
Happiest Millionaire, The 10221-804 (4/68)-Disney 3.20 9.60 35.00
Hey There, It's Yogi Bear 10122-409 (9/64)-Hanna-Barbera 5.85 17.50 70.00
Horse Without a Head, The 10109-401 (1/64)-Disney 2.80 8.40 28.00
How the West Was Won 10074-307 (7/63)-Tufts-a 3.20 9.60 35.00
In Search of the Castaways 10048-303 (3/63)-Disney; Hayley Mills photo-c 6.00 18.00 72.00
Jungle Book, The 1 (6022-801)(1/68-Whitman)-Disney; large size (10x13-1/2"); 59¢ 5.85 17.50 70.00
Jungle Book, The 1 (30033-803)(3/68, 68 pgs.)-Disney; same contents as Whitman #1 3.65 11.00 40.00
Jungle Book, The 1 (6/78, $1.00 tabloid) 2.30 7.00 20.00
Jungle Book (1984)-r/Giant 2.40 6.00
Kidnapped 10080-306 (6/63)-Disney; reprints 4-Color #1101; photo-c 3.00 9.00 30.00
King Kong 30036-809(9/68-68 pgs.)-painted-c 3.20 9.60 35.00
King Kong nn-Whitman Treasury($1.00, 68 pgs.,1968), same cover as Gold Key issue 4.55 13.65 50.00
King Kong 11299(#1-786, 10x13-1/4", 68 pgs., $1.00, 1978) 2.40 7.35 22.00
Lady and the Tramp 10042-301 (1/63)-Disney; r/4-Color #629 3.20 9.60 35.00
Lady and the Tramp 1 (1967-Giant; 25¢)-Disney; reprints part of Dell #1 5.00 15.00 60.00
Lady and the Tramp 2 (10042-203)(3/72)-Disney; r/4-Color #629 2.40 7.35 22.00
Legend of Lobo, The 1 (10059-303)(3/63)-Disney; photo-c 2.50 7.50 24.00
Lt. Robin Crusoe, U.S.N. 10191-610 (10/66)-Disney; Dick Van Dyke photo-c 2.50 7.50 24.00
Lion, The 10035-301 (1/63)-Photo-c 2.40 7.35 22.00
Lord Jim 10156-509 (9/65)-Photo-c 2.50 7.50 24.00
Love Bug, The 10237-906 (6/69)-Disney; Buddy Hackett photo-c 2.80 8.40 28.00
Mary Poppins 10136-501 (1/65)-Disney; photo-c 3.80 11.40 42.00
Mary Poppins 30023-501 (1/65-68 pgs.)-Disney; photo-c 6.00 18.00 72.00
McLintock 10110-403 (3/64); John Wayne app.; John Wayne & Maureen O'Hara photo-c 11.00 33.00 130.00
Merlin Jones as the Monkey's Uncle 10115-510 (10/65)-Disney; Annette Funicello front/back photo-c 4.55 13.65 50.00
Miracle of the White Stallions, The 10065-306 (6/63)-Disney 2.80 8.40 28.00
Misadventures of Merlin Jones, The 10115-405 (5/64)-Disney; Annette Funicello photo front/back-c 4.55 13.65 50.00
Moon-Spinners, The 10124-410 (10/64)-Disney; Haley Mills photo-c 6.00 18.00 72.00
Mutiny on the Bounty 1 (10040-302)(2/63)-Marlon Brando photo-c 3.00 9.00 30.00
Nikki, Wild Dog of the North 10141-412 (12/64)-Disney; reprints 4-Color #1226 2.50 7.50 24.00
Old Yeller 10168-601 (1/66)-Disney; reprints 4-Color #869; photo-c 2.50 7.50 25.00
One Hundred & One Dalmations 1 (10247-002) (2/70)-Disney; reprints Four Color #1183 2.80 8.40 28.00
Peter Pan 1 (10086-309)(9/63)-Disney; reprints Four Color #442 3.20 9.60 35.00
Peter Pan 2 (10086-909)(9/69)-Disney; reprints Four Color #442 2.50 7.50 24.00
Peter Pan 1 ('83)-r/4-Color #442 3.00
P.T. 109 10123-409 (9/64)-John F. Kennedy 3.65 11.00 40.00
Rio Conchos 10143-503(3/65) 3.20 9.60 35.00
Robin Hood 10163-506 (6/65)-Disney; reprints Four Color #413 2.80 8.40 28.00
Shaggy Dog & the Absent-Minded Professor 30032-708 (8/67-Giant, 68 pgs.) Disney; reprints 4-Color #985,1199 5.00 15.00 55.00
Sleeping Beauty 1 (30042-009)(9/70)-Disney; reprints Four Color #973; with pull-out poster (No poster = half price) 5.85 17.50 70.00
Snow White & the Seven Dwarfs 1 (10091-310)(10/63)-Disney; reprints Four Color #382 3.00 9.00 30.00
Snow White & the Seven Dwarfs 10091-709 (9/67)-Disney; reprints Four Color #382 2.50 7.50 24.00
Snow White & the Seven Dwarfs 90091-204 (2/84)-Reprints Four Color #382 3.00
Son of Flubber 1 (10057-304)(4/63)-Disney; sequel to "The Absent-Minded Professor" 3.00 9.00 30.00
Summer Magic 10076-309 (9/63)-Disney; Hayley Mills photo-c; Manning-a 6.00 18.00 72.00
Swiss Family Robinson 10236-904 (4/69)-Disney; reprints Four Color #1156; photo-c 2.80 8.40 28.00
Sword in the Stone, The 30019-402 (2/64-Giant, 68 pgs.)-Disney (see March of Comics #258 & Wart and the Wizard 5.85 17.50 70.00
That Darn Cat 10171-602 (2/66)-Disney; Hayley Mills photo-c 5.85 17.50 70.00
Those Magnificent Men in Their Flying Machines 10162-510 (10/65); photo-c 3.00 9.00 30.00
Three Stooges in Orbit 30016-211 (11/62-Giant, 32 pgs.)-All photos from movie; stiff-photo-c 9.00 27.00 110.00
Tiger Walks, A 10117-406 (6/64)-Disney; Torres?, Tufts-a; photo-c 3.65 11.00 40.00
Toby Tyler 10142-502 (2/65)-Disney; reprints Four Color #1092; photo-c 2.80 8.40 28.00
Treasure Island 1 (10200-703)(3/67)-Disney; reprints Four Color #624; photo-c 2.50 7.50 25.00
20,000 Leagues Under the Sea 1 (10095-312)(12/63)-Disney; reprints Four Color #614 2.80 8.40 28.00
Wonderful Adventures of Pinocchio, The 1 (10089-310)(10/63)-Disney; reprints Four Color #545 (see Wonderful Advs. of...) 3.20 9.60 35.00
Wonderful Adventures of Pinocchio, The 10089-109 (9/71)-Disney; reprints Four Color #545 2.50 7.50 25.00
Wonderful World of the Brothers Grimm 1 (10008-210)(10/62) 3.80 11.40 42.00
X, the Man with the X-Ray Eyes 10083-309 (9/63)-Ray Milland photo on-c 6.30 19.00 75.00
Yellow Submarine 35000-902 (2/69-Giant, 68 pgs.)-With pull-out poster; The Beatles cartoon movie; Paul S. Newman-s 22.00 66.00 265.00
Without poster 7.50 22.50 90.00

MOVIE LOVE (Also see Personal Love)
Famous Funnies: Feb, 1950 - No. 22, Aug, 1953 (All photo-c)

1-Dick Powell, Evelyn Keyes, & Mickey Rooney photo-c 14.00 41.00 110.00
2-Myrna Loy photo-c 7.85 23.50 55.00
3-7,9: 6-Ricardo Montalban photo-c. 9-Gene Tierney, John Lund, Glenn Ford, & Rhonda Fleming photo-c. 6.40 19.25 45.00
8-Williamson/Frazetta-a, 6 pgs. 40.00 120.00 320.00
10-Frazetta-a, 6 pgs. 40.00 120.00 340.00
11,14-16: 14-Janet Leigh photo-c 5.70 17.00 40.00
12-Dean Martin & Jerry Lewis photo-c (12/51, pre-dates Advs. of Dean Martin & Jerry Lewis comic) 10.00 30.00 75.00
13-Ronald Reagan photo-c with 1 pg. biog. 20.00 60.00 160.00
17-Leslie Caron & Ralph Meeker photo-c; 1 pg. Frazetta ad 5.70 17.00 40.00
18-22: 19-John Derek photo-c. 20-Donald O'Connor & Debbie Reynolds photo-c. 21-Paul Henreid & Patricia Medina photo-c. 22-John Payne & Coleen Gray photo-c 5.00 15.00 35.00

NOTE: *Each issue has a full-length movie adaptation with photo covers.*

MOVIE THRILLERS (Movie)

M. Rex #1 © Joe Kelly & Duncan Rouleau

Ms. Marvel #10 © MAR

Murder Incorporated #6 © FOX

Magazine Enterprises: 1949
1-Adaptation of "Rope of Sand" w/Burt Lancaster; Burt Lancaster photo-c 30.00 90.00 240.00

MOVIE TOWN ANIMAL ANTICS (Formerly Animal Antics; becomes Raccoon Kids #52 on)
National Periodical Publ.: No. 24, Jan-Feb, 1950 - No. 51, July-Aug, 1954
24-Raccoon Kids continue 11.00 33.00 90.00
25-51 10.00 30.00 75.00
NOTE: ***Sheldon Mayer** a-28-33, 35, 37-41, 43, 44, 47, 49-51.*

MOVIE TUNES COMICS (Formerly Animated...; Frankie No. 4 on)
Marvel Comics (MgPC): No. 3, Fall, 1946
3-Super Rabbit, Krazy Krow, Silly Seal & Ziggy Pig 12.00 36.00 95.00

MOWGLI JUNGLE BOOK (Rudyard Kipling's...)
Dell Publ. Co.: No. 487, Aug-Oct, 1953 - No. 620, Apr, 1955
Four Color 487 (#1) 5.00 15.00 60.00
Four Color 582 (8/54), 620 4.10 12.30 45.00

MR. (See Mister)

M. REX
Image Comics: July, 1999 - Present ($2.95)
Preview ($5.00) B&W pages and sketchbook; Rouleau-a 5.00
1,2-($2.95) 1-Joe Kelly-s/Rouleau-a/Anacleto-c. 2-Rouleau-c 2.95

MS. CYANIDE & ICE
Blackout Comics: June, 1995 - No. 1, 1995 ($2.95, B&W)
0,1 3.00

MS. FORTUNE
Image Comics: Jan, 1998 ($2.95, B&W, one-shot)
1-Chris Marrinan-s/a 3.00

MS. MARVEL (Also see The Avengers #183)
Marvel Comics Group: Jan, 1977 - No. 23, Apr, 1979
1-1st app. Ms. Marvel; Scorpion app. in #1,2 1.00 3.00 8.00
2-10: 2-Origin. 5-Vision app. 6-(Reg. 30¢-c). 10-Last 30¢ issue 4.00
6-(35¢-c variant, limited dist.)(6/77) 2.40 6.00
11-15,19-23: 19-Capt. Marvel app. 20-New costume. 23-Vance Astro (leader of the Guardians) app. 3.00
16,17-Mystique cameo 1.00 3.00 8.00
18-1st full Mystique; Avengers x-over 1.50 4.50 12.00
NOTE: ***Austin** c-14i, 16i, 17i, 22i. **Buscema** a-1-3p; c(p)-2, 4, 6, 7, 15. **Infantino** a-14p, 19p. **Gil Kane** c-8. **Mooney** a-4-8p, 13p, 15-18p. **Starlin** c-12.*

MS. MYSTIC
Pacific Comics: Oct, 1982 - No. 2, Feb, 1984 ($1.00/$1.50)
1,2: Neal Adams-c/a/script. 1-Origin; intro Erth, Ayre, Fyre & Watr 4.00

MS. MYSTIC
Continuity Comics: 1988 - No. 9, May, 1992 ($2.00)
1-9: 1,2-Reprint Pacific Comics issues 3.00

MS. MYSTIC
Continunity Comics: V2#1, Oct, 1993 - V2#4, Jan, 1994 ($2.50)
V2#1-4: 1-Adams-c(i)/part-i. 2-4-Embossed-c. 2-Nebres part-i. 3-Adams-c(i)/plot. 4-Adams-c(p)/plot 2.50

MS. MYSTIC DEATHWATCH 2000 (Ms. Mystic #3)
Continuity: May, 1993 - No. 3, Aug, 1993 ($2.50)
1-3-Bagged w/card; Adams plots 2.50

MS. TREE QUARTERLY / SPECIAL
DC Comics: Summer, 1990 -No. 10, 1992 ($3.95/$3.50, 84 pgs, mature)
1-10: 1-Midnight story; Batman text story, Grell-a. 2,3-Midnight stories; The Butcher text stories 4.00
NOTE: ***Cowan** c-2. **Grell** c-1, 6. **Infantino** a-8.*

MS. TREE'S THRILLING DETECTIVE ADVS (Ms. Tree #4 on; also see The Best of Ms. Tree)(Baxter paper #4-9)
Eclipse Comics/Aardvark-Vanaheim 10-18/Renegade Press 19 on: 2/83 - #9, 7/84; #10, 8/84 - #18, 5/85; #19, 6/85 - #50, 6/89
1 3.00
2-49: 2-Schythe begins. 9-Last Eclipse & last color issue. 10,11-2-tone 2.00
50-Contains flexi-disc ($3.95, 52pgs.) 4.00
Summer Special 1 (8/86) 3.00
1950s 3-D Crime (7/87, no glasses)-Johnny Dynamite in 3-D 3.00
Mike Mist in 3-D (8/85)-With glasses 3.00
NOTE; ***Miller** pin-up 1-4. Johnny Dynamite-r begin #36 by **Morisi**.*

MS. VICTORY SPECIAL(Also see Capt. Paragon & Femforce)
Americomics: Jan, 1985 (nd)
1 2.00

MUGGSY MOUSE (Also see Tick Tock Tales)
Magazine Enterprises: 1951 - No. 3, 1951; No. 4, 1954 - No. 5, 1954; 1963
1(A-1 #33) 6.40 19.25 45.00
2(A-1 #36)-Racist-c 8.65 26.00 60.00
3(A-1 #39), 4(A-1 #95), 5(A-1 #99) 4.15 12.50 25.00
Super Reprint #14(1963), I.W. Reprint #1,2 (nd) 1.25 3.75 10.00

MUGGY-DOO, BOY CAT
Stanhall Publ.: July, 1953 - No. 4, Jan, 1954
1-Funny animal; Irving Spector-a 7.15 21.50 50.00
2-4 5.00 15.00 32.00
Super Reprint #12('63), 16('64) 1.25 3.75 10.00

MUKTUK WOLFSBREATH: HARD-BOILED SHAMAN
DC Comics (Vertigo): Aug, 1998 - No. 3, Oct, 1998 ($2.50)
1-3-Terry LaBan-s/Steve Parkhouse-a 2.50

MULLKON EMPIRE (See John Jake's...)

MUMMY, THE (See Universal Presents... under Dell Giants & Movie Classics)

MUNDEN'S BAR ANNUAL
First Comics: Apr, 1988; 1989 ($2.95/$5.95)
1-($2.95)-r/from Grimjack; Fish Police story; Ordway-c 3.00
2-($5.95)-Teenage Mutant Ninja Turtles app. 2.40 6.00

MUNSTERS, THE (TV)
Gold Key: Jan, 1965 - No. 16, Jan, 1968 (All photo-c)
1 (10134-501) 19.00 57.00 225.00
2 9.00 27.00 110.00
3-5 7.00 21.00 85.00
6-16 6.30 19.00 75.00

MUNSTERS, THE (TV)
TV Comics!: Aug, 1997 - No. 4 ($2.95, B&W)
1-4-All have photo-c 3.00
1,4-($7.95)-Variant-c 8.00
2-Variant-c w/Beverly Owens as Marilyn 3.00
Special Comic Con Ed. (7/97, $9.95) 10.00

MUPPET BABIES, THE (TV)(See Star Comics Magazine)
Marvel Comics (Star Comics)/Marvel #18 on: Aug, 1985 - No. 26, July, 1989 (Children's book)
1-26 3.00

MUPPETS TAKE MANHATTAN, THE
Marvel Comics (Star Comics): Nov, 1984 - No. 3, Jan, 1985
1-3-Movie adapt. r-/Marvel Super Special 3.00

MURCIELAGA, SHE-BAT
Heroic Publishing: Jan, 1993 - No. 2, 1993 (B&W)
1-($1.50, 28 pgs.) 2.00
2-($2.95, 36 pgs.)-Coated-c 3.00

MURDER CAN BE FUN
Slave Labor Graphics: Feb, 1996 - Present ($2.95, B&W)
1-12: 1-Dorkin-c. 2-Vasquez-c. 3.00

MURDER INCORPORATED (My Private Life #16 on)
Fox Feature Syndicate: 1/48 - No. 15, 12/49; (2 No.9's); 6/50 - No. 3, 8/51
1 (1st Series); 1,2 have 'For Adults Only' on-c 50.00 150.00 450.00
2-Electrocution story 40.00 120.00 350.00
3-7,9(4/49),10(5/49),11-15 23.00 68.00 180.00
8-Used in **SOTI**, pg. 160 25.00 75.00 200.00

Mutant X #2 © MAR

Mutiny #1 © Aragon Mags.

My Favorite Martian #7 © Jack Chertok TV

GD2.0 FN6.0 NM9.4

9(3/49)-Possible use in **SOTI**, pg. 145; r/Blue Beetle #56('48) 23.00 68.00 180.00
5(#1, 6/50)(2nd Series)-Formerly My Desire #4; bondage-c. 18.00 53.00 140.00
2(8/50)-Morisi-a 15.00 45.00 120.00
3(8/51)-Used in **POP**, pg. 81; Rico-a; lingerie-c/panels 17.00 51.00 135.00

MURDER ME DEAD
El Capitán Books: July, 2000 - Present ($2.95, B&W)
1-David Lapham-s/a 2.95

MURDEROUS GANGSTERS
Avon Per./Realistic No. 3 on: Jul, 1951; No. 2, Dec, 1951 - No. 4, Jun, 1952
1-Pretty Boy Floyd, Leggs Diamond; 1 pg. Wood-a 42.00 125.00 375.00
2-Baby-Face Nelson; 1 pg. Wood-a; painted-c 29.00 87.00 230.00
3-Painted-c 23.00 69.00 180.00
4- "Murder by Needle" drug story; Mort Lawrence-a; Kinstler-c 29.00 87.00 230.00

MURDER TALES (Magazine)
World Famous Publications: V1#10, Nov, 1970 - V1#11, Jan, 1971 (52 pgs.)
V1#10-One pg. Frazetta ad 3.20 9.60 35.00
11-Guardineer-r; bondage-c 2.60 7.80 26.00

MUSHMOUSE AND PUNKIN PUSS (TV)
Gold Key: September, 1965 (Hanna-Barbera)
1 (10153-509) 9.00 27.00 110.00

MUSIC MAN, THE (See Movie Classics)

MUTANT CHRONICLES (Video game)
Acclaim Comics (Armada): May, 1996 - No. 4, Aug, 1996 ($2.95, lim. series)
1-4: Simon Bisley-c on all, Sourcebook (#5) 3.00

MUTANT MISADVENTURES OF CLOAK AND DAGGER, THE (Becomes Cloak and Dagger #14 on)
Marvel Comics: Oct, 1988 - No. 19, Aug, 1991 ($1.25/$1.50)
1-8,10-15: 1-X-Factor app. 10-Painted-c. 12-Dr. Doom app. 14-Begin new direction 2.00
9,16-19: 9-(52 pgs.) The Avengers x-over; painted-c. 16-18-Spider-Man x-over. 18-Infinity Gauntlet x-over; Thanos cameo; Ghost Rider app. 19-(52 pgs.) Origin Cloak & Dagger 2.50
NOTE: ***Austin** a-12i; c(i)-4, 12, 13; scripts-all. **Russell** a-2i. **Williamson** a-14i-16i; c-15i.*

MUTANTS & MISFITS
Silverline Comics (Solson): 1987 - No. 3, 1987 ($1.95)
1-3 2.00

MUTANTS VS. ULTRAS
Malibu Comics (Ultraverse): Nov, 1995 ($6.95, one-shot)
1-r/Exiles vs. X-Men, Night Man vs. Wolverine, Prime vs. Hulk 7.00

MUTANT X (See X-Factor)
Marvel Comics: Nov, 1998 - No. 32, June, 2001 ($2.99/$1.99/$2.25)
1-($2.99) Alex Summers with alternate world's X-Men 3.00
2-11,13-19-($1.99): 2-Two covers. 5-Man-Spider-c/app. 2.00
12,25-($2.99): 12-Pin-up gallery by Kaluta, Romita, Byrne 3.00
20-24,26-29: 20-Begin $2.25-c. 28,29-Logan-c/app. 2.25
Annual '99, '00 (5/99,'00, $3.50) '00-Doran-a(p) 3.50

MUTATIS
Marvel Comics (Epic Comics): 1992 - No. 3, 1992 ($2.25, mini-series)
1-3: Painted-c 2.25

MUTINY (Stormy Tales of the Seven Seas)
Aragon Magazines: Oct, 1954 - No. 3, Feb, 1955
1 16.00 49.00 130.00
2,3: 2-Capt. Mutiny. 3-Bondage-c 12.50 37.50 100.00

MUTINY ON THE BOUNTY (See Classics Illustrated #100 & Movie Comics)

MUTT AND JEFF (See All-American, All-Flash #18, Cicero's Cat, Comic Cavalcade, Famous Feature Stories, The Funnies, Popular & Xmas Comics)
All American/National 1-103(6/58)/Dell 104(10/58)-115 (10-12/59)/

GD2.0 FN6.0 NM9.4

Harvey 116(2/60)-148: Summer, 1939 (nd) - No. 148, Nov, 1965
1(nn)-Lost Wheels 125.00 375.00 1250.00
2(nn)-Charging Bull (Summer, 1940, nd; on sale 6/20/40) 66.00 200.00 660.00
3(nn)-Bucking Broncos (Summer, 1941, nd) 47.00 141.00 470.00
4(Winter, '41), 5(Summer, '42) 42.00 126.00 420.00
6-10 20.00 60.00 200.00
11-20: 20-X-Mas-c 13.00 39.00 130.00
21-30 9.00 27.00 90.00
31-50: 32-X-Mas-c 7.00 21.00 65.00
51-75-Last Fisher issue. 53-Last 52 pgs. 6.00 18.00 50.00
76-99,101-103: 76-Last pre-code issue(1/55) 3.20 9.60 35.00
100 3.80 11.40 42.00
104-148: 116-131-Richie Rich app. 2.50 7.50 24.00
...Jokes 1-3(8/60-61, Harvey)-84 pgs.; Richie Rich in all; Little Dot in #2,3 Lotta in #2 3.00 9.00 32.00
...New Jokes 1-4(10/63-11/65, Harvey)-68 pgs.; Richie Rich in #1-3; Stumbo in #1 2.40 7.35 22.00
NOTE: *Most all issues by **Al Smith**. Issues from 1963 on have **Fisher** reprints. Clarification: early issues signed by Fisher are mostly drawn by Smith.*

MY BROTHERS' KEEPER
Spire Christian Comics (Fleming H. Revell Co.): 1973 (35/49¢, 36 pgs.)
nn 2.40 6.00

MY CONFESSIONS (My Confession #7&8; formerly Western True Crime; A Spectacular Feature Magazine #11)
Fox Feature Syndicate: No. 7, Aug, 1949 - No. 10, Jan-Feb, 1950
7-Wood-a (10 pgs.) 22.00 66.00 175.00
8,9: 8-Harrison/Wood-a (19 pgs.). 9-Wood-a 20.00 60.00 160.00
10 10.00 30.00 70.00

MY DATE COMICS (Teen-age)
Hillman Periodicals: July, 1947 - V1#4, Jan, 1948 (2nd Romance comic; see Young Romance)
1-S&K-c/a 36.00 108.00 290.00
2-4-S&K-c/a; Dan Barry-a 25.00 75.00 200.00

MY DESIRE (Formerly Jo-Jo Comics; becomes Murder, Inc. #5 on)
Fox Feature Syndicate: No. 30, Aug, 1949 - No. 4, April, 1950
30(#1) 15.00 45.00 120.00
31 (#2, 10/49),3(2/50),4 10.00 30.00 80.00
31 (Canadian edition) 6.40 19.25 45.00
32(12/49)-Wood-a 20.00 60.00 160.00

MY DIARY (Becomes My Friend Irma #3 on?)
Marvel Comics (A Lovers Mag.): Dec, 1949 - No. 2, Mar, 1950
1,2-Photo-c 14.00 41.00 110.00

MY EXPERIENCE (Formerly All Top; becomes Judy Canova #23 on)
Fox Feature Syndicate: No. 19, Sept, 1949 - No. 22, Mar, 1950
19,21: 19-Wood-a. 21-Wood-a(2) 25.00 75.00 200.00
20 10.00 30.00 80.00
22-Wood-a (9 pgs.) 20.00 60.00 160.00

MY FAVORITE MARTIAN (TV)
Gold Key: 1/64; No.2, 7/64 - No. 9, 10/66 (No. 1,3-9 have photo-c)
1-Russ Manning-a 12.50 37.50 150.00
2 6.30 19.00 75.00
3-9 5.35 16.00 65.00

MY FRIEND IRMA (Radio/TV) (Formerly My Diary? and/or Western Life Romances?)
Marvel/Atlas Comics (BFP): No. 3, June, 1950 - No. 47, Dec, 1954; No. 48, Feb, 1955
3-Dan DeCarlo-a in all; 52 pgs. begin, end ? 14.00 41.00 110.00
4-Kurtzman-a (10 pgs.) 18.00 54.00 145.00
5- "Egghead Doodle" by Kurtzman (4 pgs.) 13.00 39.00 105.00
6,8-10: 9-paper dolls, 1 pg; Millie app. (5 pgs.) 10.00 30.00 70.00
7-One pg. Kurtzman-a 10.00 30.00 70.00
11-23: 23-One pg. Frazetta-a 5.70 17.00 40.00
24-48: 41,48-Stan Lee & Dan DeCarlo app. 5.00 15.00 32.00

My Life #9 © FOX

My Little Margie #5 © CC

My Love Story #2 © MAR

MY GIRL PEARL
Atlas Comics: 4/55 - #4, 10/55; #5, 7/57 - #6, 9/57; #7, 8/60 - #11, ?/61

	GD2.0	FN6.0	NM9.4
1-Dan DeCarlo-c/a in #1-6	13.00	39.00	105.00
2	7.15	21.50	50.00
3-6	5.00	15.00	35.00
7-11	2.50	7.50	25.00

MY GREATEST ADVENTURE (Doom Patrol #86 on)
National Periodical Publications: Jan-Feb, 1955 - No. 85, Feb, 1964

	GD2.0	FN6.0	NM9.4
1-Before CCA	125.00	375.00	1500.00
2	50.00	150.00	650.00
3-5	35.00	105.00	420.00
6-10: 6-Science fiction format begins	31.00	93.00	360.00
11-14: 12-1st S.A. issue	23.00	68.00	250.00
15-17: Kirby-a in all	25.00	75.00	275.00
18-Kirby-c/a	27.50	82.00	300.00
19,22-25	19.00	57.00	210.00
20,21,28-Kirby-a	23.00	68.00	250.00
26,27,29,30	13.50	40.00	150.00
31-40	11.50	34.00	125.00
41,42,44-57,59	8.65	26.00	95.00
43-Kirby-c/a	10.00	30.00	110.00
58,60,61-Toth-a; Last 10¢ issue	8.65	26.00	95.00
62-76,78,79: 79-Promotes "Legion of the Strange" for next issue; renamed Doom Patrol for #80	5.90	17.75	65.00
77-Toth-a; Robotman prototype	6.35	19.00	70.00
80-(6/63)-Intro/origin Doom Patrol and begin series; origin & 1st app. Negative Man, Elasti-Girl & S.A. Robotman	41.00	123.00	500.00
81,85-Toth-a	16.50	49.00	180.00
82-84	15.00	45.00	165.00

NOTE: ***Anderson** a-42. **Cameron** a-24. **Colan** a-77. **Meskin** a-25, 26, 32, 39, 45, 50, 56, 57, 61, 64, 70, 73, 74, 76, 79; c-76. **Moreira** a-11, 12, 15, 17, 20, 23, 25, 27, 37, 40-43, 46, 48, 55-57, 59, 60, 62-65, 67, 69, 70; c-1-4, 7-10. **Roussos** c/a-71-73. **Wildey** a-32.*

MY GREAT LOVE (Becomes Will Rogers Western #5)
Fox Feature Syndicate: Oct, 1949 - No. 4, Apr, 1950

	GD2.0	FN6.0	NM9.4
1	14.00	41.00	110.00
2-4	8.65	26.00	60.00

MY INTIMATE AFFAIR (Inside Crime #3)
Fox Feature Syndicate: Mar, 1950 - No. 2, May, 1950

	GD2.0	FN6.0	NM9.4
1	14.00	41.00	110.00
2	8.65	26.00	60.00

MY LIFE (Formerly Meet Corliss Archer)
Fox Feature Syndicate: No. 4, Sept, 1948 - No. 15, July, 1950

	GD2.0	FN6.0	NM9.4
4-Used in **SOTI**, pg. 39; Kamen/Feldstein-a	40.00	120.00	330.00
5-Kamen-a	22.00	66.00	175.00
6-Kamen/Feldstein-a	23.00	68.00	180.00
7-Wood-a; wash cover	20.00	60.00	160.00
8,9,11-15	9.30	28.00	65.00
10-Wood-a	18.00	54.00	145.00

MY LITTLE MARGIE (TV)
Charlton Comics: July, 1954 - No. 54, Nov, 1964

	GD2.0	FN6.0	NM9.4
1-Photo front/back-c	34.00	101.00	270.00
2-Photo front/back-c	16.00	48.00	125.00
3-7,10	10.00	30.00	70.00
8,9-Infinity-c	10.00	30.00	75.00
11-14: Part-photo-c (#13, 8/56)	8.65	26.00	60.00
15-19	4.55	13.65	50.00
20-(25¢, 100 pg. issue)	9.00	27.00	100.00
21-39-Last 10¢ issue?	3.65	11.00	40.00
40-53	3.20	9.60	35.00
54-Beatles on cover; lead story spoofs the Beatle haircut craze of the 1960's (scarce)	16.00	48.00	175.00

NOTE: *Doll cut-outs in 32, 33, 40, 45, 50.*

MY LITTLE MARGIE'S BOY FRIENDS (TV) (Freddy V2#12 on)
Charlton Comics: Aug, 1955 - No. 11, Apr?, 1958

	GD2.0	FN6.0	NM9.4
1-Has several Archie swipes	14.00	41.00	110.00
2	8.65	26.00	60.00
3-11	6.40	19.25	45.00

MY LITTLE MARGIE'S FASHIONS (TV)
Charlton Comics: Feb, 1959 - No. 5, Nov, 1959

	GD2.0	FN6.0	NM9.4
1	12.50	37.50	100.00
2-5	7.15	21.50	50.00

MY LOVE (Becomes Two Gun Western #5 (11/50) on?)
Marvel Comics (CLDS): July, 1949 - No. 4, Apr, 1950 (All photo-c)

	GD2.0	FN6.0	NM9.4
1	12.50	37.50	100.00
2,3	8.65	26.00	60.00
4-Bettie Page photo-c (see Cupid #2)	31.00	94.00	250.00

MY LOVE
Marvel Comics Group: Sept, 1969 - No. 39, Mar, 1976

	GD2.0	FN6.0	NM9.4
1	4.10	12.30	45.00
2-9: 4-6-Colan-a	2.40	7.35	22.00
10-Williamson-r/My Own Romance #71; Kirby-a	2.50	7.50	25.00
11-13,15-19	2.00	6.00	18.00
14-(52 pgs.)-Woodstock-c/sty; Morrow-c/a; Kirby/Colletta-r	3.00	9.00	32.00
20-Starlin-a	2.30	7.00	20.00
21,22,24-27,29-38: 38-Reprints	1.75	5.25	14.00
23-Steranko-r/Our Love Story #5	2.30	7.00	20.00
28-Kirby-a	2.00	6.00	16.00
39-Last issue; reprints	2.00	6.00	18.00
Special 1 (12/71)(52 pgs.)	3.20	9.60	35.00

NOTE: ***John Buscema** a-1-7, 10, 18-21, 22r(2), 24r, 25r, 29r, 34r, 36r, 37r, Spec. (r)(4); c-13, 15, 25, 27, Spec. **Colan** a-4, 5, 6, 8, 9, 16, 17, 20, 21, 22, 24r, 27r, 30r, 35r, 39r. **Colan/Everett** a-13, 15, 16, 27(r/#13). **Kirby** a-(r)-10, 14, 26, 28. **Romita** a-1-3, 19, 20, 25, 34, 38; c-1-3, 15.*

MY LOVE AFFAIR (March of Crime #7 on)
Fox Feature Syndicate: July, 1949 - No. 6, May, 1950

	GD2.0	FN6.0	NM9.4
1	14.00	43.00	110.00
2	8.65	26.00	60.00
3-6-Wood-a. 5-(3/50)-Becomes Love Stories #6	18.00	54.00	145.00

MY LOVE LIFE (Formerly Zegra)
Fox Feature Synd.: No. 6, June, 1949 - No. 13, Aug, 1950; No. 13, Sept, 1951

	GD2.0	FN6.0	NM9.4
6-Kamenish-a	15.00	45.00	120.00
7-13	8.65	26.00	60.00
13 (9/51)(Formerly My Story #12)	7.85	23.50	55.00

MY LOVE MEMOIRS (Formerly Women Outlaws; Hunted #13 on)
Fox Feature Syndicate: No. 9, Nov, 1949 - No. 12, May, 1950

	GD2.0	FN6.0	NM9.4
9,11,12-Wood-a	17.00	51.00	135.00
10	8.65	26.00	60.00

MY LOVE SECRET (Formerly Phantom Lady; Animal Crackers #31)
Fox Feature Syndicate/M. S. Distr.: No. 24, June, 1949 - No. 30, June, 1950; No. 53, 1954

	GD2.0	FN6.0	NM9.4
24-Kamen/Feldstein-a	17.00	51.00	135.00
25-Possible caricature of Wood on-c?	10.00	30.00	70.00
26,28-Wood-a	17.00	51.00	135.00
27,29,30: 30-Photo-c	8.65	26.00	60.00
53-(Reprint, M.S. Distr.) 1954? nd given; formerly Western Thrillers; becomes Crimes by Women #54; photo-c	5.00	15.00	35.00

MY LOVE STORY (Hoot Gibson Western #5 on)
Fox Feature Syndicate: Sept, 1949 - No. 4, Mar, 1950

	GD2.0	FN6.0	NM9.4
1	14.00	41.00	110.00
2	8.65	26.00	60.00
3,4-Wood-a	18.00	54.00	145.00

MY LOVE STORY
Atlas Comics (GPS): April, 1956 - No. 9, Aug, 1957

	GD2.0	FN6.0	NM9.4
1	10.00	30.00	80.00
2	5.75	17.00	40.00
3,7: Matt Baker-a. 7-Toth-a	8.65	26.00	60.00
4-6,8,9	5.00	15.00	35.00

NOTE: ***Brewster** a-3. **Colletta** a-1(2), 3, 4(2), 5; c-3.*

MY NAME IS CHAOS
DC Comics: 1992 - No. 4, 1992 ($4.95, limited series, 52 pgs.)

My Name is Holocaust #3 © Milestone Media

My Secret #2 © SUPR

Mysteries (Weird & Strange) #4 © SUPR

	GD2.0	FN6.0	NM9.4
Book 1-4: Tom Veitch scripts; painted-c			5.00

MY NAME IS HOLOCAUST
DC Comics: May, 1995 - No. 5, Sept, 1995 ($2.50, limited series)

1-5			2.50

MY ONLY LOVE
Charlton Comics: July, 1975 - No. 9, Nov, 1976

1	2.00	6.00	18.00
2,4-9	1.50	4.50	12.00
3-Toth-a	1.85	5.50	15.00

MY OWN ROMANCE (Formerly My Romance; Teen-Age Romance #77 on)
Marvel/Atlas (MjPC/RCM No. 4-59/ZPC No. 60-76): No. 4, Mar, 1949 - No. 76, July, 1960

4-Photo-c	14.00	41.00	110.00
5-10: 5,6,8-10-Photo-c	7.15	21.50	50.00
11-20: 14-Powell-a	6.40	19.25	45.00
21-42,55: 42-Last precode (2/55). 55-Toth-a	5.70	17.00	40.00
43-54,56-60	3.00	9.00	30.00
61-70,72,73,75,76	2.50	7.50	25.00
71-Williamson-a	3.65	11.00	40.00
74-Kirby-a	3.20	9.60	35.00

NOTE: ***Brewster** a-59. **Colletta** a-45(2), 48, 50, 55, 57(2), 59; c-58i, 59, 61. **Everett** a-25; c-58p. **Kirby** c-71, 75, 76. **Morisi** a-18. **Orlando** a-61. **Romita** a-36. **Tuska** a-10.*

MY PAL DIZZY (See Comic Books, Series I)

MY PAST (...Confessions) (Formerly Western Thrillers)
Fox Feature Syndicate: No. 7, Aug, 1949 - No. 11, Apr, 1950 (Crimes Inc. #12)

7	14.00	41.00	110.00
8-10	8.65	26.00	60.00
11-Wood-a	17.00	51.00	135.00

MY PERSONAL PROBLEM
Ajax/Farrell/Steinway Comic: 11/55; No. 2, 2/56; No. 3, 9/56 - No. 4, 11/56; 10/57 - No. 3, 5/58

1	8.65	26.00	60.00
2-4	5.70	17.00	40.00
1-3('57-'58)-Steinway	5.00	15.00	32.00

MY PRIVATE LIFE (Formerly Murder, Inc.; becomes Pedro #18)
Fox Feature Syndicate: No. 16, Feb, 1950 - No. 17, April, 1950

16,17	12.00	36.00	95.00

MYRA NORTH (See The Comics, Crackajack Funnies & Red Ryder)
Dell Publishing Co.: No. 3, Jan, 1940

Four Color 3	75.00	225.00	900.00

MY REAL LOVE
Standard Comics: No. 5, June, 1952 (Photo-c)

5-Toth-a, 3 pgs.; Tuska, Cardy, Vern Greene-a	12.50	37.50	100.00

MY ROMANCE (Becomes My Own Romance #4 on)
Marvel Comics (RCM): Sept, 1948 - No. 3, Jan, 1949

1	14.00	41.00	110.00
2,3: 2-Anti-Wertham editorial (11/48)	8.65	26.00	60.00

MY ROMANTIC ADVENTURES (Formerly Romantic Adventures)
American Comics Group: No. 68, 8/56 - No. 115, 12/60; No. 116, 7/61 - No. 138, 3/64

68	8.65	26.00	60.00
69-85	5.00	15.00	30.00
86-Three pg. Williamson-a (2/58)	7.00	21.00	48.00
87-100	2.40	7.35	22.00
101-138	1.85	5.50	15.00

NOTE: ***Whitney** art in most issues.*

MY SECRET (Becomes Our Secret #4 on)
Superior Comics, Ltd.: Aug, 1949 - No. 3, Oct, 1949

1	12.50	37.50	100.00
2,3	8.65	26.00	60.00

MY SECRET AFFAIR (Becomes Martin Kane #4)
Hero Book (Fox Feature Syndicate): Dec, 1949 - No. 3, April, 1950

	GD2.0	FN6.0	NM9.4
1-Harrison/Wood-a (10 pgs.)	20.00	60.00	160.00
2-Wood-a	16.00	48.00	125.00
3-Wood-a	17.00	51.00	135.00

MY SECRET CONFESSION
Sterling Comics: September, 1955

1-Sekowsky-a	8.65	26.00	60.00

MY SECRET LIFE (Formerly Western Outlaws; Romeo Tubbs #26 on)
Fox Feature Syndicate: No. 22, July, 1949 - No. 27, July, 1950; No. 27, 9/51

22	10.00	30.00	80.00
23,26-Wood-a, 6 pgs.	17.00	51.00	135.00
24,25,27	8.65	26.00	60.00
27 (9/51)	7.85	23.50	55.00

NOTE: *The title was changed to Romeo Tubbs after #25 even though #26 & 27 did come out.*

MY SECRET LIFE (Formerly Young Lovers; Sue & Sally Smith #48)
Charlton Comics: No. 19, Aug, 1957 - No. 47, Sept, 1962

19	3.00	9.00	32.00
20-35	2.00	6.00	18.00
36-47: 44-Last 10¢ issue	1.75	5.25	14.00

MY SECRET MARRIAGE
Superior Comics, Ltd.: May, 1953 - No. 24, July, 1956

1	10.50	32.00	85.00
2	6.40	19.25	45.00
3-24	5.00	15.00	32.00
I.W. Reprint #9	1.50	4.50	12.00

NOTE: *Many issues contain **Kamenish** art.*

MY SECRET ROMANCE (Becomes A Star Presentation #3)
Hero Book (Fox Feature Syndicate): Jan, 1950 - No. 2, March, 1950

1	13.00	39.00	105.00
2-Wood-a	17.00	51.00	135.00

MY SECRET STORY (Formerly Captain Kidd #25; Sabu #30 on)
Fox Feature Syndicate: No. 26, Oct, 1949 - No. 29, April, 1950

26	14.00	41.00	110.00
27-29	8.65	26.00	60.00

MYS-TECH WARS
Marvel Comics UK: Mar, 1993 - No. 4, June, 1993 ($1.75, mini-series)

1-4: 1-Gatefold-c			2.00

MYSTERIES (...Weird & Strange)
Superior/Dynamic Publ. (Randall Publ. Ltd.): May, 1953 - No. 11, Jan, 1955

1-All horror stories	40.00	120.00	325.00
2-A-Bomb blast story	24.00	73.00	195.00
3-11: 10-Kamenish-c/a reprinted from Strange Mysteries #2; cover is from a panel in Strange Mysteries #2	21.00	64.00	170.00

MYSTERIES IN SPACE (See Fireside Book Series)

MYSTERIES OF SCOTLAND YARD (Also see A-1 Comics)
Magazine Enterprises: No. 121, 1954 (one shot)

A-1 121-Reprinted from Manhunt (5 stories)	16.00	49.00	130.00

MYSTERIES OF UNEXPLORED WORLDS (See Blue Bird) (Becomes Son of Vulcan V2#49 on)
Charlton Comics: Aug, 1956; No. 2, Jan, 1957 - No. 48, Sept, 1965

1	36.00	108.00	285.00
2-No Ditko	14.00	41.00	110.00
3,4,8,9 Ditko-a. 3-Diko c/a (4). 4-Ditko c/a (2).	28.00	83.00	220.00
5,6,10,11: 5,6-Ditko-c/a (all). 10-Ditko-c/a(4). 11-Ditko-c/a(3); signed J. Kotdi	30.00	90.00	240.00
7-(2/58, 68 pgs.) 4 stories w/Ditko-a	33.00	98.00	260.00
12,19,21-24,26-Ditko-a. 12-Ditko sty (3); Baker story "The Charm Bracelet."	21.00	62.00	165.00
13-18,20,	6.40	19.25	45.00
25,27-30	3.00	9.00	30.00
31-45	2.50	7.50	25.00
46(5/65)-Son of Vulcan begins (origin/1st app.)	3.65	11.00	40.00
47,48	2.50	7.50	25.00

NOTE: ***Ditko** c-3-6, 10, 11, 19, 21-24. Covers to #19, 21-24 reprint story panels.*

Mysterious Adventures #12 © Story Comics

Mystery Comics #4 © WHW

Mystery in Space #1 © DC

MYSTERIOUS ADVENTURES
Story Comics: Mar, 1951 - No. 24, Mar, 1955; No. 25, Aug, 1955

	GD2.0	FN6.0	NM9.4
1-All horror stories	55.00	165.00	500.00
2	31.00	94.00	250.00
3,4,6,10	28.00	84.00	225.00
5-Bondage-c	31.00	94.00	250.00
7-Daggar in eye panel	40.00	120.00	325.00
8-Eyeball story	43.00	130.00	390.00
9-Extreme violence	35.00	105.00	280.00
11(12/52)-Used in **SOTI**, pg. 84	35.00	105.00	280.00
12,14: 14-E.C. Old Witch swipe	29.00	87.00	235.00
13-Classic skull-c	33.00	99.00	260.00
15-21: 18-Used in Senate Investigative report, pgs. 5,6; E.C. swipe/TFTC #35; The Coffin-Keeper & Corpse (hosts). 20-Used by Wertham in the Senate hearings. 21-Bondage/beheading-c	38.00	113.00	300.00
22- "Cinderella" parody	30.00	90.00	240.00
23-Disbrow-a (6 pgs.); E.C. swipe "The Mystery Keeper's Tale" (host) and "Mother Ghoul's Nursery Tale"	30.00	90.00	240.00
24,25	23.00	68.00	180.00

NOTE: ***Tothish** art by **Ross Andru**-#22, 23. **Bache** a-8. **Cameron** a-5-7. **Harrison** a-12. **Hollingsworth** a-3-8, 12. **Schaffenberger** a-24, 25. **Wildey** a-15, 17.*

MYSTERIOUS ISLAND
Dell Publishing Co.: No. 1213, July-Sept, 1961

Four Color 1213-Movie, photo-c	8.35	25.00	100.00

MYSTERIOUS ISLE
Dell Publishing Co.: Nov-Jan, 1963/64 (Jules Verne)

1	2.50	7.50	25.00

MYSTERIOUS RIDER, THE (See Zane Grey, 4-Color 301)

MYSTERIOUS STORIES (Formerly Horror From the Tomb #1)
Premier Magazines: No. 2, Dec-Jan, 1954-1955 - No. 7, Dec, 1955

2-Woodbridge-c; last pre-code issue	42.00	126.00	375.00
3-Woodbridge-c/a	29.00	87.00	235.00
4-7: 5-Cinderella parody. 6-Woodbridge-c	27.00	81.00	215.00

NOTE: ***Hollingsworth** a-2, 4.*

MYSTERIOUS SUSPENSE
Charlton Comics: Oct, 1968 (12¢)

1-Return of the Question by Ditko (c/a)	5.90	17.75	65.00

MYSTERIOUS TRAVELER (See Tales of the...)

MYSTERIOUS TRAVELER COMICS (Radio)
Trans-World Publications: Nov, 1948

1-Powell-c/a(2); Poe adaptation, "Tell Tale Heart"	55.00	165.00	525.00

MYSTERY COMICS
William H. Wise & Co.: 1944 - No. 4, 1944 (No months given)

1-The Magnet, The Silver Knight, Brad Spencer, Wonderman, Dick Devins, King of Futuria, & Zudo the Jungle Boy begin (all 1st app.); Schomburg-c on all	105.00	316.00	1000.00
2-Bondage-c	68.00	205.00	650.00
3,4: 3-Lance Lewis, Space Detective begins (1st app.); Robot-c. 4(V2#1 inside)	61.00	182.00	575.00

MYSTERY COMICS DIGEST
Gold Key/Whitman?: Mar, 1972 - No. 26, Oct, 1975

1-Ripley's Believe It or Not; reprint of Ripley's #1 origin Ra-Ka-Tep the Mummy; Wood-a	3.65	11.00	40.00
2-9: 2-Boris Karloff Tales of Mystery; Wood-a; 1st app. Werewolf Count Wulfstein 3-Twilight Zone (TV); Crandall, Toth & George Evans-a; 1st app. Tragg & Simbar the Lion Lord; (2) Crandall/Frazetta-r/Twilight Zone #1 4-Ripley's Believe It or Not; 1st app. Baron Tibor, the Vampire. 5-Boris Karloff Tales of Mystery; 1st app. Dr. Spektor. 6-Twilight Zone (TV); 1st app. U.S. Marshal Reid & Sir Duane; Evans-r. 7-Ripley's Believe It or Not; origin The Lurker in the Swamp; 1st app. Duroc. 8-Boris Karloff Tales of Mystery; McWilliams-r; Orlando-r. 9-Twilight Zone (TV); Williamson, Crandall, McWilliams-a; 2nd Tragg app.;Torres, Evans, Heck/Tuska-r	2.80	8.40	28.00
10-26: 10,13-Ripley's Believe It or Not: 13-Orlando-r. 11,14-Boris Karloff Tales of Mystery. 14-1st app. Xorkon. 12,15-Twilight Zone (TV). 16,19,22,25-Ripley's Believe It or Not. 17-Boris Karloff Tales of Mystery; Williamson-r; Orlando-r. 18,21,24-Twilight Zone (TV). 20,23,26-Boris Karloff Tales of Mystery	2.30	7.00	20.00

NOTE: *Dr. Spektor app.-#5, 10-12, 21. Durak app.-#15. Duroc app.-#14 (later called Durak). King George 1st app.-#8.*

MYSTERY IN SPACE (Also see Fireside Book Series and Pulp Fiction Library)
National Periodical Publ.: 4-5/51 - No. 110, 9/66; No. 111, 9/80 - No. 117, 3/81 (#1-3: 52 pgs.)

1-Frazetta-a, 8 pgs.; Knights of the Galaxy begins, ends #8	214.00	642.00	3200.00
2	86.00	257.00	1200.00
3	70.00	210.00	975.00
4,5	55.00	166.00	775.00
6-10: 7-Toth-a	48.00	144.00	625.00
11-15: 13-Toth-a	37.00	110.00	440.00
16-18,20-25: Interplanetary Insurance feature by Infantino in all. 21-1st app. Space Cabbie. 24-Last pre-code issue	32.00	97.00	390.00
19-Virgil Finlay-a	35.00	105.00	420.00
26-40: 26-Space Cabbie feature begins. 34-1st S.A. issue	29.00	88.00	325.00
41-52: 47-Space Cabbie feature ends	22.00	65.00	240.00
53-Adam Strange begins (8/59, 10pg. sty); robot-c	143.00	429.00	2000.00
54	40.00	120.00	475.00
55-Grey tone-c	31.00	93.00	350.00
56-60: 59-Kane/Anderson-a	22.00	65.00	240.00
61-71: 61-1st app. Adam Strange foe Ulthoon. 62-1st app. A.S. foe Mortan. 63-Origin Vandor. 66-Star Rovers begin (1st app.). 68-1st app. Dust Devils (6/61). 69-1st Mailbag. 70-2nd app. Dust Devils. 71-Last 10¢ issue	16.50	49.00	180.00
72-74,76-80	11.50	34.00	125.00
75-JLA x-over in Adam Strange (5/62)(sequel to JLA #3)	25.00	75.00	275.00
81-86	8.15	24.50	90.00
87-(11/63)-Adam Strange/Hawkman double feat begins; 3rd Hawkman tryout series	19.00	57.00	210.00
88-Adam Strange & Hawkman stories	17.00	51.00	185.00
89-Adam Strange & Hawkman stories	16.00	48.00	175.00
90-Adam Strange & Hawkman team-up for 1st time (3/64); Hawkman moves to own title next month	18.00	53.00	195.00
91-103: 91-End Infantino art on Adam Strange; double-length Adam Strange story. 92-Space Ranger begins (6/64), ends #103. 92-94,96,98-Space Ranger-c. 94,98-Adam Strange/Space Ranger team-up. 102-Adam Strange ends (no Space Ranger). 103-Origin Ultra, the Multi-Alien; last Space Ranger	4.10	12.30	45.00
104-110: 110-(9/66)-Last 12¢ issue	2.80	8.40	28.00
V17#111(9/80)-117: 117-Newton-a(3 pgs.)		2.40	6.00

NOTE: ***Anderson** a-2, 4, 8-10, 12-17, 19, 45-48, 51, 57, 59i, 61-64, 70, 76, 87-91; c-9, 10, 15-25, 87, 89, 105-108, 110. **Aparo** a-111. **Austin** a-112i. **Bolland** a-115. **Craig** a-114, 116. **Ditko** a-111, 114-116. **Drucker** a-13, 14. **Elias** a-98, 102, 103. **Golden** a-113p. **Sid Greene** a-78, 91. **Infantino** a-1-8, 11, 14-25, 27-46, 48, 49, 51, 53-91, 103, 117; c-60-86, 88, 90, 91, 105, 107. **Gil Kane** a-14p, 15p, 18p, 19p, 26p, 29-59p(most), 100-102; c-52, 101. **Kubert** a-113; c-111-115. **Moriera** c-27, 28. **Rogers** a-111. **Sekowsky** a-52. **Simon** & **Kirby** a-4(2 pgs.). **Spiegle** a-111, 114. **Starlin** c-116. **Sutton** a-112. **Tuska** a-115p, 117p.*

MYSTERY MEN COMICS
Fox Features Syndicate: Aug, 1939 - No. 31, Feb, 1942

1-Intro. & 1st app. The Blue Beetle, The Green Mask, Rex Dexter of Mars by Briefer, Zanzibar by Tuska, Lt. Drake, D-13-Secret Agent by Powell, Chen Chang, Wing Turner, & Captain Denny Scott	957.00	2870.00	11,000.00
2-Robot & sci/fi-c (2nd Robot-c w/Movie #6)	305.00	915.00	3200.00
3 (10/39)-Classic Lou Fine-c	381.00	1143.00	4000.00
4,5: 4-Capt. Savage begins (11/39)	242.00	726.00	2300.00
6-Tuska-c	200.00	600.00	1900.00
7-1st Blue Beetle-c app.	242.00	726.00	2300.00
8-Lou Fine-c	216.00	647.00	2050.00
9-The Moth begins; Lou Fine-c	111.00	332.00	1050.00
10-12: All Joe Simon-c. 10-Wing Turner by Kirby; Simon-c. 11-Intro. Domino	95.00	285.00	900.00
13-Intro. Lynx & sidekick Blackie (8/40)	63.00	189.00	600.00

Mystery Men Movie Adaption #1 © Universal Studios

Mystery Tales #9 © MAR

Mystical Tales #4 © MAR

	GD2.0	FN6.0	NM9.4
14-18	61.00	182.00	575.00
19-Intro. & 1st app. Miss X (ends #21)	63.00	189.00	600.00
20-31: 26-The Wraith begins	57.00	171.00	540.00

NOTE: ***Briefer** a-1-15, 20, 24; c-9. **Cuidera** a-22. **Lou Fine** c-1-5,8,9. **Powell** a-1-15, 24. **Simon** c-10-12. **Tuska** a-1-16, 22, 24, 27; c-6. Bondage-c 1, 3, 7, 8, 25, 27-29, 31. Blue Beetle c-7, 8, 10-31. D-13 Secret Agent c-6. Green Mask c-1, 3-5. Rex Dexter of Mars c-2, 9.*

MYSTERY MEN MOVIE ADAPTION
Dark Horse Comics: July, 1999 - No. 2, Aug, 1999 ($2.95, mini-series)

	GD2.0	FN6.0	NM9.4
1,2-Fingerman-s; photo-c			3.00

MYSTERY PLAY, THE
DC Comics (Vertigo): 1994 ($19.95, one-shot)

	GD2.0	FN6.0	NM9.4
nn-Hardcover-Morrison-s/Muth-painted art			25.00
Softcover ($9.95)-New Muth cover			10.00

MYSTERY TALES
Atlas Comics (20CC): Mar, 1952 - No. 54, Aug, 1957

	GD2.0	FN6.0	NM9.4
1-Horror/weird stories in all	83.00	250.00	785.00
2-Krigstein-a	44.00	133.00	400.00
3-10: 6-A-Bomb panel. 10-Story similar to "The Assassin" from Shock SuspenStories	39.00	116.00	310.00
11,13-21: 14-Maneely s/f story. 20-Electric chair issue. 21-Matt Fox-a; decapitation story	29.00	87.00	230.00
12,22: 12-Matt Fox-a. 22-Forte/Matt Fox-c; a(i)	31.00	94.00	250.00
23-26 (2/55)-Last precode issue	23.00	68.00	180.00
27,29-35,37,38,41-43,48,49: 43-Morisi story contains Frazetta art swipes from Untamed Love	18.00	54.00	140.00
28,36,39,40,45: 28-Jack Katz-a. 36,39-Krigstein-a. 40,45-Ditko-a (#45 is 3 pgs. only)	19.00	57.00	150.00
44,51-Williamson/Krenkel-a	20.00	60.00	160.00
46-Williamson/Krenkel-a; Crandall text illos	20.00	60.00	160.00
47-Crandall, Ditko, Powell-a	20.00	60.00	160.00
50,52,53: 50-Torres, Morrow-a	18.00	53.00	140.00
54-Crandall, Check-a	19.00	56.00	150.00

NOTE: ***Ayers** a-18, 49, 52. **Berg** a-17, 51. **Colan** a-1, 3, 18, 35, 43. **Colletta** a-18. **Drucker** a-41. **Everett** a-2, 29, 33, 35, 41; c-8-11, 14, 38, 39, 41, 43, 44, 46, 48-51, 53. **Fass** a-16. **Forte** a-21, 22, 45, 46. **Matt Fox** a-12?, 21, 22; c-22. **Heath** a-3; c-3, 15, 17, 26. **Heck** a-25. **Kinstler** a-15. **Mort Lawrence** a-26, 32, 34. **Maneely** a-1, 9, 14, 22; c-12, 23, 24, 27. **Mooney** a-3, 40. **Morisi** a-43, 49, 52. **Morrow** a-50. **Orlando** a-51. **Pakula** a-16. **Powell** a-21, 29, 37, 38, 47. **Reinman** a-1, 14, 17. **Robinson** a-7p, 42. **Romita** a-37. **Roussos** a-4, 44. **R.Q. Sale** a-45, 46, 49. **Severin** c-52. **Shores** a-17, 45. **Tuska** a-10, 12, 14. **Whitney** a-2. **Wildey** a-37.*

MYSTERY TALES
Super Comics: 1964

	GD2.0	FN6.0	NM9.4
Super Reprint #16,17('64): 16-r/Tales of Horror #2. 17-r/Eerie #14(Avon), 18-Kubert-r/Strange Terrors #4	2.24	7.35	22.00

MYSTIC (3rd Series)
Marvel/Atlas Comics (CLDS 1/CSI 2-21/OMC 22-35/CSI 35-61): March, 1951 - No. 61, Aug, 1957

	GD2.0	FN6.0	NM9.4
1-Atom bomb panels; horror/weird stories in all	87.00	261.00	825.00
2	50.00	150.00	450.00
3-Eyes torn out	42.00	125.00	375.00
4- "The Devil Birds" by Wolverton (6 pgs.)	75.00	225.00	715.00
5,7-10	33.00	98.00	260.00
6- "The Eye of Doom" by Wolverton (7 pgs.)	75.00	225.00	715.00
11-20: 16-Bondage/torture c/story	28.00	84.00	225.00
21-25,27-36-Last precode (3/55). 25-E.C. swipe	23.00	68.00	180.00
26-Atomic War, severed head stories	25.00	75.00	200.00
37-51,53-56,61	19.00	56.00	150.00
52-Wood-a; Crandall-a?	21.00	62.00	165.00
57-Story "Trapped in the Ant-Hill" (1957) is very similar to "The Man in the Ant Hill" in TTA #27	21.00	64.00	170.00
58,59-Krigstein-a	19.00	56.00	150.00
60-Williamson/Mayo-a (4 pgs.)	19.00	56.00	150.00

NOTE: ***Andru** a-23, 25. **Ayers** a-35, 53; c-8. **Berg** a-49. **Cameron** a-49, 51. **Check** a-31, 60. **Colan** a-3, 7, 12, 21, 37, 60. **Colletta** a-29. **Drucker** a-46, 52, 56. **Everett** a-8, 9, 17, 40, 44, 57; c-13, 18, 21, 42, 47, 49, 51-55, 57-59, 61. **Forte** a-35, 52, 58. **Fox** a-24i. **Al Hartley** a-35. **Heath** a-10; c-10, 20, 22, 23, 25, 30. **Infantino** a-12. **Kane** a-8, 24p. **Jack Katz** a-31, 33. **Mort Law.rence** a-19, 37. **Maneely** a-22, 24, 58; c-7, 15, 28, 29, 31. **Moldoff** a-29. **Morisi** a-48, 49, 52. **Morrow** a-51. **Orlando** a-57, 61. **Pakula** a-52, 57, 59. **Powell** a-52, 54-56. **Robinson** a-5. **Romita** a-11, 15. **R.Q. Sale** a-35, 53, 58. **Sekowsky** a-1, 2, 4, 5. **Severin** c-56, 60. **Tuska** a-15. **Whitney** a-33. **Wildey** a-28, 30. **Ed Win** a-17, 20. Canadian reprints known-title 'Startling.'*

MYSTIC (Also see CrossGen Chronicles)
CrossGeneration Comics: Jul, 2000 - Present ($2.95)

	GD2.0	FN6.0	NM9.4
1-8: Marz-s/Peterson & Dell-a			3.00

MYSTICAL TALES
Atlas Comics (CCC 1/EPI 2-8): June, 1956 - No. 8, Aug, 1957

	GD2.0	FN6.0	NM9.4
1-Everett-c/a	47.00	140.00	420.00
2-4: 2-Berg-a. 3,4-Crandall-a.	26.00	79.00	210.00
5-Williamson-a (4 pgs.)	28.00	83.00	220.00
6-Torres, Krigstein-a	24.00	73.00	195.00
7-Bolle, Forte, Torres, Orlando-a	24.00	73.00	195.00
8-Krigstein, Check-a	24.00	73.00	195.00

NOTE: ***Everett** a-1; c-1-4, 6, 7. **Orlando** a-1, 2, 7. **Pakula** a-3. **Powell** a-1, 4.*

MYSTIC COMICS (1st Series)
Timely Comics (TPI 1-5/TCI 8-10): March, 1940 - No. 10, Aug, 1942

	GD2.0	FN6.0	VF8.0	NM9.4
1-Origin The Blue Blaze, The Dynamic Man, & Flexo the Rubber Robot; Zephyr Jones, 3X's & Deep Sea Demon app.; The Magician begins (all 1st app.); c-from Spider pulp V18#1, 6/39	1200.00	3600.00	7800.00	15,000.00

	GD2.0	FN6.0	NM9.4
2-The Invisible Man & Master Mind Excello begin; Space Rangers, Zara of the Jungle, Taxi Taylor app.	381.00	1143.00	4000.00
3-Origin Hercules, who last appears in #4	300.00	900.00	3000.00
4-Origin The Thin Man & The Black Widow; Merzak the Mystic app.; last Flexo, Dynamic Man, Invisible Man & Blue Blaze (some issues have date sticker on cover; others have July w/August overprint in silver color); Roosevelt assassination-c	314.00	943.00	3300.00
5-(3/41)-Origin The Black Marvel, The Blazing Skull, The Sub-Earth Man, Super Slave & The Terror; The Moon Man & Black Widow app.; 5-German war-c begin, end #10	300.00	900.00	3000.00
6-(10/41)-Origin The Challenger & The Destroyer (1st app.?; also see All-Winners #2, Fall, 1941)	333.00	1000.00	3500.00
7-The Witness begins (12/41, origin & 1st app.); origin Davey & the Demon; last Black Widow; Hitler opens his trunk of terror-c by Simon & Kirby (classic-c)	352.00	1057.00	3700.00
8,10: 10-Father Time, World of Wonder, & Red Skeleton app.; last Challenger & Terror	200.00	600.00	1900.00
9-Gary Gaunt app.; last Black Marvel, Mystic & Blazing Skull; Hitler-c	211.00	633.00	2000.00

NOTE: ***Gabrielle** c-8-10. **Kirby/Schomburg** c-6. **Rico** a-9(2). **Schomburg** a-1-4; c-1-5. **Sekowsky** a-9. **Sekowsky/Klein** a-8(Challenger). Bondage c-1, 2, 9.*

MYSTIC COMICS (2nd Series)
Timely Comics (ANC): Oct, 1944 - No. 3, Win, 1944-45; No. 4, Mar, 1945

	GD2.0	FN6.0	NM9.4
1-The Angel, The Destroyer, The Human Torch, Terry Vance the Schoolboy Sleuth, & Tommy Tyme begin	221.00	663.00	2100.00
2-(Fall/44)-Last Human Torch & Terry Vance; bondage/hypo-c	116.00	348.00	1100.00
3-Last Angel (two stories) & Tommy Tyme	111.00	332.00	1050.00
4-The Young Allies-c & app.; Schomburg-c	103.00	308.00	975.00

MYSTIC EDGE (Manga)
Antarctic Press: Oct, 1998 ($2.95, one-shot)

	GD2.0	FN6.0	NM9.4
1-Ryan Kinnaird-s/a/c			3.00

MYSTIQUE & SABRETOOTH (Sabretooth and Mystique on-c)
Marvel Comics: Dec, 1996 - No. 4, Mar, 1997 ($1.95, limited series)

	GD2.0	FN6.0	NM9.4
1-4: Characters from X-Men			3.00

MY STORY (...True Romances in Pictures #5,6; becomes My Love Life #13) (Formerly Zago)
Hero Books (Fox Features Syndicate): No. 5, May, 1949 - No. 12, Aug, 1950

	GD2.0	FN6.0	NM9.4
5-Kamen/Feldstein-a	19.00	56.00	150.00
6-8,11,12: 12-Photo-c	10.00	30.00	70.00
9,10-Wood-a	18.00	53.00	140.00

MYTHOGRAPHY
Bardic Press: Sept, 1996 - Present ($3.95/$4.25, B&W, anthology)

	GD2.0	FN6.0	NM9.4
1-3: 1-Drew Hayes-s/a			5.00
4-8			4.25

MYTHOS: THE FINAL TOUR

Namora #3 © MAR

Nathaniel Dusk #2 © DC

National Comics #14 © QUA

DC Comics/Vertigo: Dec, 1996 - No. 3, Feb, 1997 ($5.95, limited series)

1-3: 1-Ney Rieber-s/Amaro-a. 2-Snejbjerg-a; Constantine-app. 3-Kristiansen-a; Black Orchid-app. 6.00

MY TRUE LOVE (Formerly Western Killers #64; Frank Buck #70 on)
Fox Features Syndicate: No. 65, July, 1949 - No. 69, March, 1950

65 14.00 41.00 110.00
66,68,69: 69-Morisi-a 9.30 28.00 65.00
67-Wood-a 18.00 53.00 140.00

NAKED PREY, THE (See Movie Classics)

'NAM, THE (See Savage Tales #1, 2nd series & Punisher Invades...)
Marvel Comics Group: Dec, 1986 - No. 84, Sept, 1993

1-Golden a(p)/c begins, ends #13 3.00
1 (2nd printing) 2.00
2-74,76-84: 7-Golden-a (2 pgs.). 32-Death R. Kennedy. 52,53-Frank Castle (The Punisher) app. 52,53-Gold 2nd printings. 58-Silver logo. 65-Heath-c/a. 67-69-Punisher 3 part story. 70-Lomax scripts begin 2.00
75-($2.25, 52 pgs.) 2.25
Trade Paperback 1,2: 1-r/#1-4. 2-r/#5-8 4.50
TPB ('99, $14.95) r/#1-4; recolored 15.00

'NAM MAGAZINE, THE
Marvel Comics: Aug, 1988 - No. 10, May, 1989 ($2.00, B&W, 52pgs.)

1-10: Each issue reprints 2 of the comic 2.00

NAMELESS, THE
Image Comics: May, 1997 - No. 5, Sept, 1997 ($2.95, B&W)

1-5: Pruett/Hester-s/a 3.00

NAMES OF MAGIC, THE (Also see Books of Magic)
DC Comics (Vertigo): Feb, 2001 - No. 5, June, 2001 ($2.50, limited series)

1-5: Bolton painted-c on all; Case-a 2.50

NAMORA (See Marvel Mystery Comics #82 & Sub-Mariner Comics)
Marvel Comics (PrPl): Fall, 1948 - No. 3, Dec, 1948

1-Sub-Mariner x-over in Namora; Namora by Everett(2), Sub-Mariner by Rico (10 pgs.) 232.00 695.00 2200.00
2-The Blonde Phantom & Sub-Mariner story; Everett-a 121.00 363.00 1150.00
3-(Scarce)-Sub-Mariner app.; Everett-a 132.00 395.00 1250.00

NAMOR, THE SUB-MARINER (See Prince Namor & Sub-Mariner)
Marvel Comics: Apr, 1990 - No. 62, May, 1995 ($1.00/$1.25/$1.50)

1-Byrne-c/a/scripts in 1-25 (scripts only #26-32) 4.00
2-5: 5-Iron Man app. 3.00
6-11,13-23,25,27-49,51-62: 16-Re-intro Iron Fist (8-cameo only). 18-Punisher cameo (1 panel); 21-23,25-Wolverine cameos. 22,23-Iron Fist app. 28-Iron Fist-c/story. 31-Dr. Doom-c/story. 33,34-Iron Fist cameo. 35-New Tiger Shark-c/story. 37-Aqua holografx foil-c. 48-The Thing app. 2.00
12,24: 12-(52pgs.)-Re-intro. The Invaders. 24-Namor vs. Wolverine 2.50
26-Namor w/new costume; 1st Jae Lee-c/a this title (5/92) & begins 3.00
50-($1.75, 52 pgs.)-Newsstand edition; w/bound-in S-M trading card sheet (both versions) 2.00
50-($2.95, 52 pgs.)-Collector edition w/foil-c 3.00
Annual 1-4 ('91-94, 68 pgs.): 1-3 pg. origin recap. 2-Return/Defenders. 3-Bagged w/card. 4-Painted-c 3.00

NOTE: *Jae Lee a-26-30p, 31-37, 38p, 39, 40; c-26-40.*

NANCY AND SLUGGO (See Comics On Parade & Sparkle Comics)
United Features Syndicate: No. 16, 1949 - No. 23, 1954

16(#1) 8.65 26.00 60.00
17-23 5.00 15.00 35.00

NANCY & SLUGGO (Nancy #146-173; formerly Sparkler Comics)
St. John/Dell #146-187/Gold Key #188 on: No. 121, Apr, 1955-No. 192, Oct, 1963

121(4/55)(St. John) 6.40 19.25 45.00
122-145(7/57)(St. John) 5.00 15.00 32.00
146(9/57)-Peanuts begins, ends #192 (Dell) 4.10 12.30 45.00
147-161 (Dell) 3.20 9.60 35.00
162-165,177-180-John Stanley-a 6.70 20.00 80.00
166-176-Oona & Her Haunted House series; Stanley-a 7.50 22.50 90.00
181-187(3-5/62)(Dell) 3.20 9.60 35.00
188(10/62)-192 (Gold Key) 3.65 11.00 40.00
Four Color 1034(9-11/59)-Summer Camp 3.65 11.00 40.00
(See Dell Giant #34, 45 & Dell Giants)

NANNY AND THE PROFESSOR (TV)
Dell Publishing Co.: Aug, 1970 - No. 2, Oct, 1970 (Photo-c)

1-(01-546-008) 3.65 11.00 40.00
2 3.20 9.60 35.00

NAPOLEON
Dell Publishing Co.: No. 526, Dec, 1953

Four Color 526 2.50 7.50 25.00

NAPOLEON & SAMANTHA (See Walt Disney Showcase No. 10)

NAPOLEON & UNCLE ELBY (See Clifford McBride's...)
Eastern Color Printing Co.: July, 1942 (68 pgs.) (One Shot)

1 42.00 125.00 375.00
1945-American Book-Strafford Press (128 pgs.) (8x10-1/2"; B&W reprints; hardcover) 14.00 41.00 110.00

NARRATIVE ILLUSTRATION, THE STORY OF THE COMICS
M.C. Gaines: Summer, 1942 (32 pgs., 7-1/4"x10", B&W w/color inserts)

nn-16pgs. text with illustrations of ancient art, strips and comic covers; 4 pg. WWII War Bond promo, "The Minute Man Answers the Call" color comic drawn by Shelly and a special 8-page color comic insert of "The Story of Saul" from Picture Stories from the Bible #1 or soon to appear in PS #1. Insert has special title page indicating it was No. 10 of a Sunday newspaper supplement insert series that had already run in a New England "Sunday Herald." (very rare; only two known copies.) Estimated value... 1200.00

NASH (WCW Wrestling)
Image Comics: July, 1999 - No. 2, July, 1999 ($2.95)

1,2-Regular and photo-c 3.00
1-($6.95) Photo-split-cover Edition 7.00

NATHANIEL DUSK
DC Comics: Feb, 1984 - No. 4, May, 1984 ($1.25, mini-series, direct sales, Baxter paper)

1-4: 1-Intro/origin; Gene Colan-c/a in all 2.00

NATHANIEL DUSK II
DC Comics: Oct, 1985 - No. 4, Jan, 1986 ($2.00, mini-series, Baxter paper)

1-4: Gene Colan-c/a in all 2.00

NATHAN NEVER
Dark Horse (Bonelli Comics): Mar, 1999 - No. 6, Aug, 1999 ($4.95, B&W, digest size)

1-6-Reprints Italian series in English. 1-4-Art Adams-c 5.00

NATIONAL COMICS
Quality Comics Group: July, 1940 - No. 75, Nov, 1949

1-Uncle Sam begins (1st app.); origin sidekick Buddy by Eisner; origin Wonder Boy & Kid Dixon; Merlin the Magician (ends #45); Cyclone, Kid Patrol, Sally O'Neil Policewoman, Pen Miller (by Klaus Nordling; ends #22), Prop Powers (ends #26), & Paul Bunyan (ends #22) begin 496.00 1487.00 5700.00
2 232.00 695.00 2200.00
3-Last Eisner Uncle Sam 158.00 474.00 1500.00
4-Last Cyclone 126.00 379.00 1200.00
5-(11/40)-Quicksilver begins (1st app.; 3rd w/lightning speed?; re-intro'd by DC in 1993 as Max Mercury in Flash #76, 2nd series); origin Uncle Sam; bondage-c 147.00 442.00 1400.00
6,8-11: 8-Jack & Jill begins (ends #22). 9-Flag-c 126.00 379.00 1200.00
7-Classic Lou Fine-c 211.00 633.00 2000.00
12 95.00 285.00 900.00
13-16-Lou Fine-a 84.00 253.00 800.00
17,19-22: 22-Last Pen Miller (moves to Crack #23) 63.00 189.00 600.00
18-(12/41)-Shows orientals attacking Pearl Harbor; on stands one month before actual event 116.00 348.00 1100.00
23-The Unknown & Destroyer 171 begin 66.00 197.00 625.00

Navy Action #2 © MAR

Negative Burn #31 © Caliber

Neil Gaiman's Lady Justice #4 © Big Ent.

GD2.0 FN6.0 NM9.4

24-Japanese War-c 66.00 197.00 625.00
25-30: 26-Wonder Boy ends. 27- G-2 the Unknown begins (ends #46). 29-Origin The Unknown 47.00 142.00 425.00
31-33: 33-Chic Carter begins (ends #47) 42.00 125.00 375.00
34-38,40: 35-Last Kid Patrol 38.00 113.00 300.00
39-Hitler-c 42.00 125.00 375.00
41-50: 42-The Barker begins (1st app?, 5/44); The Barker covers begin. 48-Origin The Whistler 23.00 68.00 180.00
51-Sally O'Neil by Ward, 8 pgs. (12/45) 28.00 84.00 225.00
52-60 19.00 56.00 150.00
61-67: 67-Format change; Quicksilver app. 14.00 41.00 110.00
68-75: The Barker ends 10.50 32.00 85.00
NOTE: ***Cole** Quicksilver-13; Barker-43; c-43, 46, 47, 49-51. **Crandall** Uncle Sam-11-13 (with **Fine**), 25, 26; c-24-26, 30-33, 43. **Crandall** Paul Bunyan-10-13. **Fine** Uncle Sam-13 (w/**Crandall**), 17, 18; c-1-14, 16, 18, 21. **Gill Fox** c-69-74. **Guardineer** Quicksilver-27, 35. **Gustavson** Quicksilver-14-26. **McWilliams** a-23-28, 55, 57. Uncle Sam c-1-41. Barker c-42-75.*

NATIONAL COMICS (Also see All Star Comics 1999 crossover titles)
DC Comics: May, 1999 ($1.99, one-shot)
1-Golden Age Flash and Mr. Terrific; Waid-s/Lopresti-a 2.00

NATIONAL CRUMB, THE (Magazine-Size)
Mayfair Publications: August, 1975 (52 pgs., B&W) (Satire)
1-Grandenetti-c/a, Ayers-a 1.75 5.25 14.00

NATIONAL VELVET (TV)
Dell Publishing Co./Gold Key: May-July, 1961 - No. 2, Mar, 1963 (All photo-c)
Four Color 1195 (#1) 5.85 17.50 70.00
Four Color 1312, 01-556-207, 12-556-210 (Dell) 3.20 9.60 35.00
1,2: 1(12/62) (Gold Key). 2(3/63) 3.45 10.35 38.00

NATION OF SNITCHES
Piranha Press (DC): 1990 ($4.95, color, 52 pgs.)
nn 5.00

NATURE BOY (Formerly Danny Blaze; Li'l Rascal Twins #6 on)
Charlton Comics: No. 3, March, 1956 - No. 5, Feb, 1957
3-Origin; Blue Beetle story; Buscema-c/a 23.00 68.00 180.00
4,5 16.00 49.00 130.00
NOTE: ***John Buscema** a-3, 4p, 5; c-3. **Powell** a-4.*

NATURE OF THINGS (Disney, TV/Movie)
Dell Publishing Co.: No. 727, Sept, 1956 - No. 842, Sept, 1957
Four Color 727 (#1), 842-Jesse Marsh-a 4.60 13.75 55.00

NAUSICAA OF THE VALLEY OF WIND
Viz Comics: 1988 - No. 7, 1989; 1989 - No. 4, 1990 ($2.50, B&W, 68pgs.)
Book 1-7: 1-Contains Moebius poster 3.25
Part II, Book 1-4 ($2.95) 3.25

NAVY ACTION (Sailor Sweeney #12-14)
Atlas Comics (CDS): Aug, 1954 - No. 11, Apr, 1956; No. 15, 1/57 - No. 18, 8/57
1-Powell-a 18.00 53.00 140.00
2-Lawrence-a 10.00 30.00 70.00
3-11: 4-Last precode (2/55) 7.15 21.50 50.00
15-18 6.40 19.25 45.00
NOTE: ***Berg** a-7, 9. **Colan** a-8. **Drucker** a-7, 17. **Everett** a-3, 7, 16; c-16, 17. **Heath** c-1, 2, 6. **Maneely** a-7, 8, 18; c-9, 11. **Pakula** a-2, 3, 9. **Reinman** a-17.*

NAVY COMBAT
Atlas Comics (MPI): June, 1955 - No. 20, Oct, 1958
1-Torpedo Taylor begins by Don Heck 18.00 53.00 140.00
2 10.00 30.00 70.00
3-10 7.15 21.50 50.00
11,13,15,16,18-20 6.40 19.25 45.00
12-Crandall-a 10.00 30.00 70.00
14-Torres-a 7.15 21.50 50.00
17-Williamson-a, 4 pgs.; Torres-a 7.85 23.50 55.00
NOTE: ***Berg** a-10, 11. **Colan** a-11. **Drucker** a-7. **Everett** a-3, 20; c-8 & 9 w/**Tuska**, 10, 13-16. **Heck** a-11(2). **Maneely** c-1, 6, 11, 17. **Morisi** a-8. **Pakula** a-7. **Powell** a-20.*

NAVY HEROES
Almanac Publishing Co.: 1945
1-Heavy in propaganda 11.00 33.00 90.00

GD2.0 FN6.0 NM9.4

NAVY PATROL
Key Publications: May, 1955 - No. 4, Nov, 1955
1 6.40 19.25 45.00
2-4 4.65 14.00 28.00

NAVY TALES
Atlas Comics (CDS): Jan, 1957 - No. 4, July, 1957
1-Everett-c; Berg, Powell-a 15.00 45.00 120.00
2-Williamson/Mayo-a(5 pgs); Crandall-a 12.50 37.50 100.00
3,4-Reinman-a; Severin-c. 4-Crandall-a 11.00 33.00 90.00
NOTE: ***Colan** a-4. **Maneely** c-2. **Sinnott** a-4.*

NAVY TASK FORCE
Stanmor Publications/Aragon Mag. No. 4-8: Feb, 1954 - No. 8, April, 1956
1 7.85 23.50 55.00
2 4.65 14.00 28.00
3-8: #8-r/Navy Patrol #1 4.00 12.00 24.00

NAVY WAR HEROES
Charlton Comics: Jan, 1964 - No. 7, Mar-Apr, 1965
1 3.00 9.00 30.00
2-7 2.00 6.00 18.00

NAZA (Stone Age Warrior)
Dell Publishing Co.: Nov-Jan, 1963-64 - No. 9, March, 1966
12-555-401 (#1)-Painted-c 3.65 11.00 40.00
2-9: 2-4-Painted-c 2.80 8.40 28.00

NAZZ, THE
DC Comics: 1990 - No. 4, 1991 ($4.95, 52 pgs., mature)
1-4 5.00

NEBBS, THE (Also see Crackajack Funnies)
Dell Publishing Co./Croydon Publishing Co.: 1941; 1945
Large Feature Comic 23(1941) 14.00 42.00 170.00
1(1945, 36 pgs.)-Reprints 11.00 33.00 90.00

NECROMANCER: THE GRAPHIC NOVEL
Marvel Comics (Epic Comics): 1989 ($8.95)
nn 9.00

NEGATIVE BURN
Caliber : 1993 - No. 50, 1997 ($2.95, B&W, anthology)
1,2,4-12,14-47: Anthology by various including Bolland, Burden, Doran, Gaiman, Moebius, Moore, & Pope 4.00
3,13: 3-Bone story. 13-Strangers in Paradise story 1.50 4.50 12.00
48,49-($4.95) 5.00
50-($6.95, 96 pgs.)-Gaiman, Robinson, Bolland 7.00

NEGRO (See All-Negro)

NEGRO HEROES (Calling All Girls, Real Heroes, & True Comics reprints)
Parents' Magazine Institute: Spring, 1947 - No. 2, Summer, 1948
1 84.00 253.00 800.00
2-Jackie Robinson-c/story 89.00 268.00 850.00

NEGRO ROMANCE (Negro Romances #4)
Fawcett Publications: June, 1950 - No. 3, Oct, 1950 (All photo-c)
1-Evans-a 111.00 332.00 1050.00
2,3 84.00 253.00 800.00

NEGRO ROMANCES (Formerly Negro Romance; Romantic Secrets #5 on)
Charlton Comics: No. 4, May, 1955
4-Reprints Fawcett #2 68.00 205.00 650.00

NEIL GAIMAN AND CHARLES VESS' STARDUST
DC Comics (Vertigo): 1997 - No. 4, 1998 ($5.95/$6.95, square-bound, lim. series)
1-4: Gaiman text with Vess paintings in all 7.00
Hardcover (1998, $29.95) r/series with new sketches 35.00
Softcover (1999, $19.95) oversized; new Vess-c 20.00

NEIL GAIMAN'S LADY JUSTICE
Tekno Comix: Sept, 1995 - No. 11, May, 1996 ($1.95/$2.25)
1-11: 1-Sienkiewicz-c; pin-ups. 1-5-Brereton-c. 7-polybagged. 11-Includes The

Neon Cyber #1 © Dreamwave Prod.

Nevada #1 © Steve Gerber

New Adventure Comics #19 © DC

Big Bang Pt. 7 2.25

NEIL GAIMAN'S LADY JUSTICE
BIG Entertainment: V2#1, June, 1996 - No. 9, Feb, 1997 ($2.25)

V2#1-9: Dan Brereton-c on all. 6-8-Dan Brereton script 2.25

NEIL GAIMAN'S MIDNIGHT DAYS
DC Comics (Vertigo): 1999 ($17.95, trade paperback)

nn-Reprints Gaiman's short stories; new Swamp Thing w/ Bissette-a 17.95

NEIL GAIMAN'S MR. HERO-THE NEWMATIC MAN
Tekno Comix: Mar, 1995 - No. 17, May, 1996 ($1.95/$2.25)

1-17: 1-Intro Mr. Hero & Teknophage; bound-in game piece and trading card 4-w/Steel edition Neil Gaiman's Teknophage #1 coupon. 13-polybagged. 2.25

NEIL GAIMAN'S MR. HERO-THE NEWMATIC MAN
BIG Entertainment: V2#1, June, 1996 ($2.25)

V2#1-Teknophage destroys Mr. Hero; includes The Big Bang Pt. 10 2.25

NEIL GAIMAN'S PHAGE-SHADOWDEATH
BIG Entertainment: June, 1996 - No. 6, Nov, 1996 ($2.25, limited series)

1-6: Bryan Talbot-c & scripts in all. 1-1st app. Orlando Holmes 2.25

NEIL GAIMAN'S TEKNOPHAGE
Tekno Comix: Aug, 1995 - No. 10, Mar, 1996 ($1.95/$2.25)

1-6-Rick Veitch scripts & Bryan Talbot-c/a. 2.25
1-Steel Edition 4.00
7-10: Paul Jenkins scripts in all. 8-polybagged 2.25

NEIL GAIMAN'S WHEEL OF WORLDS
Tekno Comix: Apr, 1995 - No. 1, May, 1996 ($2.95/$3.25)

0-1st app. Lady Justice; 48 pgs.; bound-in poster 3.25
0-Regular edition 2.00
1 ($3.25, 5/96)-Bruce Jones scripts; Lady Justice & Teknophage app.; computer-generated photo-c. 3.25

NEIL THE HORSE (See Charlton Bullseye #2)
Aardvark-Vanaheim #1-10/Renegade Press #11 on: 2/83 - No. 10, 12/84; No. 11, 4/85 - #15, 1985 (B&W)

1($1.40) 4.00
1-2nd print 2.00
2-13: 13-Double size; 11,13-w/paperdolls 2.00
14,15: Double size ($3.00). 15 is a flip book(2-c) 3.00

NELLIE THE NURSE (Also see Gay Comics & Joker Comics)
Marvel/Atlas Comics (SPI/LMC): 1945 - No. 36, Oct, 1952; 1957

	GD2.0	FN6.0	NM9.4
1-(1945)	40.00	120.00	320.00
2-(Spring/46)	19.00	56.00	150.00
3,4: 3-New logo (9/46)	14.00	41.00	110.00
5-Kurtzman's "Hey Look" (3); Georgie app.	16.00	49.00	130.00
6-8,10: 7,8-Georgie app. 10-Millie app.	12.50	37.50	100.00
9-Wolverton-a (1 pg.); Mille the Model app.	13.00	39.00	105.00
11,14-16,18-Kurtzman's "Hey Look"	14.00	41.00	110.00
12- "Giggles 'n' Grins" by Kurtzman	12.50	37.50	100.00
13,17,19,20: 17-Annie Oakley app.	10.00	30.00	70.00
21-27,29,30	8.65	26.00	60.00
28-Mr. Nexdoor-r (3 pgs.) by Kurtzman/Rusty #22	8.65	26.00	60.00
31-36: 36-Post-c	7.15	21.50	50.00
1('57)-Leading Mag. (Atlas)-Everett-a, 20 pgs	8.65	26.00	60.00

NELLIE THE NURSE
Dell Publishing Co.: No. 1304, Mar-May, 1962

Four Color 1304-Stanley-a 6.70 20.00 80.00

NEMESIS THE WARLOCK (Also see Spellbinders)
Eagle Comics: Sept, 1984 - No. 7, Mar, 1985 (limited series, Baxter paper)

1-7: 2000 A.D. reprints 2.00

NEMESIS THE WARLOCK
Quality Comics/Fleetway Quality #2 on: 1989 - No. 19, 1991 ($1.95, B&W)

1-19 2.00

NEON CYBER
Image Comics (Dreamwave Prod.): Jul, 1999 - No. 8, Jun, 2000 ($2.50)

1-8-Adrian Tsang-s 2.50

NEUTRO
Dell Publishing Co.: Jan, 1967

1-Jack Sparling-c/a (super hero); UFO-s 3.20 9.60 35.00

NEVADA (See Zane Grey's Four Color 412, 996 & Zane Grey's Stories of the West #1)

NEVADA (Also see Vertigo Winter's Edge #1)
DC Comics (Vertigo): May, 1998 - No. 6, Oct, 1998 ($2.50, limited series)

1-6-Gerber-s/Winslade-c/a 2.50
TPB-(1999, $14.95) r/#1-6 & Vertigo Winter's Edge preview 15.00

NEVER AGAIN (War stories; becomes Soldier & Marine V2#9)
Charlton Comics: Aug, 1955; No. 8, July, 1956 (No #2-7)

1 8.65 26.00 60.00
8-(Formerly Foxhole?) 5.00 15.00 32.00

NEVERMEN, THE (See Dark Horse Presents #148-150)
Dark Horse Comics: May, 2000 - Present ($2.95)

1-3-Phil Amara-s/Guy Davis-a 2.95

NEW ADVENTURE COMICS (Formerly New Comics; becomes Adventure Comics #32 on; V1#12 indicia says NEW COMICS #12)
National Periodical Publications: V1#12, Jan, 1937 - No. 31, Oct, 1938

	GD2.0	FN6.0	VF8.0	NM9.4
V1#12-Federal Men by Siegel & Shuster continues; Jor-L mentioned; Whitney Ellsworth-c begin, end #14	508.00	1523.00	3300.00	–
V2#1(2/37, #13)-(Rare)	477.00	1431.00	3100.00	–
V2#2 (#14)	415.00	1246.00	2700.00	–

	GD2.0	FN6.0	NM9.4
15(V2#3)-20(V2#8): 15-1st Adventure logo; Creig Flessel-c begin, end #31. 16-1st non-funny cover. 17-Nadir, Master of Magic begins, ends #30	356.00	1069.00	2850.00
21(V2#9),22(V2#10, 2/37): 22-X-Mas-c	325.00	975.00	2600.00
23-31	275.00	825.00	2200.00

NEW ADVENTURES OF ABRAHAM LINCOLN, THE
Image Comics (Homage): 1998 ($19.95, one-shot)

1-Scott McCloud-s/computer art 20.00

NEW ADVENTURES OF CHARLIE CHAN, THE (TV)
National Periodical Publications: May-June, 1958 - No. 6, Mar-Apr, 1959

	GD2.0	FN6.0	NM9.4
1 (Scarce)-Gil Kane/Sid Greene-a in all	66.00	197.00	625.00
2 (Scarce)	44.00	133.00	400.00
3-6 (Scarce)-Greene/Giella-a	40.00	120.00	340.00

NEW ADVENTURES OF HUCK FINN, THE (TV)
Gold Key: December, 1968 (Hanna-Barbera)

1- "The Curse of Thut"; part photo-c 3.45 10.35 38.00

NEW ADVENTURES OF PINOCCHIO (TV)
Dell Publishing Co.: Oct-Dec, 1962 - No. 3, Sept-Nov, 1963

12-562-212(#1) 8.75 26.25 105.00
2,3 6.30 19.00 75.00

NEW ADVENTURES OF ROBIN HOOD (See Robin Hood)

NEW ADVENTURES OF SHERLOCK HOLMES (Also see Sherlock Holmes)
Dell Publishing Co.: No. 1169, Mar-May, 1961 - No. 1245, Nov-Jan, 1961/62

Four Color 1169(#1) 16.00 48.00 190.00
Four Color 1245 15.00 45.00 175.00

NEW ADVENTURES OF SPEED RACER
Now Comics: Dec, 1993 - No. 7, 1994? ($1.95)

1-7 2.00
0-(Premiere)-3-D cover 3.00

NEW ADVENTURES OF SUPERBOY, THE (Also see Superboy)
DC Comics: Jan, 1980 - No. 54, June, 1984

1,7,50: 7-Has extra story "The Computers That Saved Metropolis" by Starlin (Radio Shack giveaway w/indicia). 50-Legion app. 3.00
2-6,8-49,51-54: 11-Superboy gets new power. 14-Lex Luthor app. 15-Superboy

New Eternals: Apocalypse Now #1 © MAR

New Fun Comics #2 © DC

The New Gods #10 © DC

gets new parents. 28-Dial "H" For Hero begins, ends #49.
45-47-1st app. Sunburst. 48-Begin 75¢-c. 2.00

NOTE: *Buckler a-9p; c-36p.* ***Giffen*** *a-50; c-50. 40i.* ***Gil Kane*** *c-32p, 33p, 35, 39, 41-49.* ***Miller*** *c-51.* ***Starlin*** *a-7. Krypto back-ups in 17, 22. Superbaby in 11, 14, 19, 24.*

NEW ADVENTURES OF THE PHANTOM BLOT, THE (See The Phantom Blot)

NEW AMERICA
Eclipse Comics: Nov, 1987 - No. 4, Feb, 1988 ($1.75, Baxter paper)
1-4: Scout limited series 2.00

NEW ARCHIES, THE (TV)
Archie Comic Publications: Oct, 1987 - No. 22, May, 1990 (75¢)
1 4.00
2-10: 3-Xmas issue 3.00
11-22: 17-22 (95¢-$1.00): 21-Xmas issue 2.00

NEW ARCHIES DIGEST (TV)(...Comics Digest Magazine #4?-10; ...Digest Magazine #11 on)
Archie Comics: May, 1988 - No. 14, July, 1991 ($1.35/$1.50, quarterly)
1 2.40 6.00
2-14: 6-Begin $1.50-c 3.50

NEW BOOK OF COMICS (Also see Big Book Of Fun)
National Periodical Publ.: 1937; No. 2, Spring, 1938 (100 pgs. each) (Reprints)
GD2.0 FN6.0 VF8.0 NM9.4
1(Rare)-1st regular size comic annual; 2nd DC annual; contains r/New Comics #1-4 & More Fun #9; r/Federal Men (8 pgs.), Henri Duval (1 pg.), & Dr. Occult in costume (1 pg.) by Siegel & Shuster; Moldoff, Sheldon Mayer (15 pgs.)-a 2000.00 6000.00 13,000.00 –
2-Contains-r/More Fun #15 & 16; r/Dr. Occult in costume (a Superman prototype), & Calling All Cars (4 pgs.) by Siegel & Shuster
1000.00 3000.00 6500.00 –

NEW COMICS (New Adventure #12 on)
National Periodical Publ.: 12/35 - No. 11, 12/36 (No. 1-6: paper cover) (No. 1-5: 84 pgs.)
V1#1-Billy the Kid, Sagebrush 'n' Cactus, Jibby Jones, Needles, The Vikings, Sir Loin of Beef, Now-When I Was a Boy, & other 1-2 pg. strips; 2 pgs. Kelly art(1st)-(Gulliver's Travels); Sheldon Mayer-a(1st)(2 2pg. strips); Vincent Sullivan-c(1st) 2850.00 8550.00 18,500.00 –
2-1st app. Federal Men by Siegel & Shuster & begins (also see The Comics Magazine #2); Mayer, Kelly-a (Rare)(1/36)
1000.00 3000.00 6500.00 –
3-6: 3,4-Sheldon Mayer-a which continues in The Comics Magazine #1. 3-Vincent Sullivan-c. 4-Dickens' "A Tale of Two Cities" adaptation begins. 5-Junior Federal Men Club; Kiefer-a. 6- "She" adaptation begins
575.00 1725.00 3800.00 –
7-11: 11-Christmas-c 475.00 1425.00 3100.00 –

NOTE: *#1-6 rarely occur in mint condition.* ***Whitney Ellsworth*** *c-4-11.*

NEW DEFENDERS (See Defenders)

NEW DNAGENTS, THE (Formerly DNAgents)
Eclipse Comics: V2#1, Oct, 1985 - V2#17, Mar, 1987 (Whole #s 25-40; Mando paper)
GD2.0 FN6.0 NM9.4
V2#1-17: 1-Origin recap. 7-Begin 95 cent-c. 9,10-Airboy preview 2.00
3-D 1 (1/86, $2.25) 2.25
2-D 1 (1/86)-Limited ed. (100 copies) 4.00

NEW ETERNALS: APOCALYPSE NOW (Also see Eternals, The)
Marvel Comics: Feb, 2000 ($3.99, one-shot)
1-Bennett & Hanna-a; Ladronn-c 4.00

NEWFORCE (Also see Newmen)
Image Comics (Extreme Studios): Jan, 1996-No. 4, Apr, 1996 ($2.50, lim. series)
1-4: 1-"Extreme Destroyer" Pt. 8; polybagged w/gaming card. 4-Newforce disbands. 2.50

NEW FUN COMICS (More Fun #7 on; see Big Book of Fun Comics)
National Periodical Publications: Feb, 1935 - No. 6, Oct, 1935 (10x15", No. 1-4,: slick-c) (No. 1-5: 36 pgs; 40 pgs. No. 6)
GD2.0 FN6.0 VF8.0 NM9.4
V1#1 (1st DC comic); 1st app. Oswald The Rabbit; Jack Woods (cowboy) begins 6500.00 19,500.00 42,000.00 –
2(3/35)-(Very Rare) 2750.00 8250.00 18,000.00 –
3-5(8/35): 3-Don Drake on the Planet Soro-c/story (sci/fi, 4/35). 5-Soft-c
1400.00 4200.00 9,000.00 –
6(10/35)-1st Dr. Occult by Siegel & Shuster (Leger & Reuths); last "New Fun" title. "New Comics" #1 begins in Dec. which is reason for title change to More Fun; Henri Duval (ends #10) by Siegel & Shuster begins; paper-c 3100.00 9300.00 20,000.00 –

NEW FUNNIES (The Funnies #1-64; Walter Lantz...#109 on; New TV... #259, 260, 272, 273; TV Funnies #261-271)
Dell Publishing Co.: No. 65, July, 1942 - No. 288, Mar-Apr, 1962
GD2.0 FN6.0 NM9.4
65(#1)-Andy Panda in a world of real people, Raggedy Ann & Andy, Oswald the Rabbit (with Woody Woodpecker x-overs), Li'l Eight Ball & Peter Rabbit begin 67.00 200.00 800.00
66-70: 66-Felix the Cat begins. 67-Billy & Bonnie Bee by Frank Thomas begins. 69-Kelly-a (2 pgs.); The Brownies begin (not by Kelly)
30.00 90.00 360.00
71-75: 72-Kelly illos. 75-Brownies by Kelly? 19.00 57.00 225.00
76-Andy Panda (Carl Barks & Pabian-a); Woody Woodpecker x-over in Oswald ends 92.00 275.00 1100.00
77,78: 77-Kelly-c. 78-Andy Panda in a world with real people ends
19.00 57.00 225.00
79-81 13.00 40.00 160.00
82-Brownies by Kelly begins; Homer Pigeon begins 14.00 42.00 170.00
83-85-Brownies by Kelly in ea. 83-X-mas-c. 85-Woody Woodpecker, 1 pg. strip begins 14.00 42.00 170.00
86-90: 87-Woody Woodpecker stories begin 10.00 30.00 120.00
91-99 6.70 20.00 80.00
100 (6/45) 7.00 21.00 85.00
101-120: 119-X-Mas-c 4.60 13.75 55.00
121-150: 131,143-X-Mas-c 4.10 12.30 45.00
151-200: 155-X-Mas-c. 168-X-Mas-c. 182-Origin & 1st app. Knothead & Splinter. 191-X-Mas-c 3.20 9.60 35.00
201-240 2.50 7.50 25.00
241-288: 270,271-Walter Lantz c-app. 281-1st story swipes/WDC&S #100
2.30 7.00 20.00

NOTE: *Early issues written by* ***John Stanley.***

NEW GODS, THE (1st Series)(New Gods #12 on)(See Adventure #459, DC Graphic Novel #4, 1st Issue Special #13 & Super-Team Family)
National Periodical Publications/DC Comics: 2-3/71 - V2#11, 10-11/72; V3#12, 7/77 - V3#19, 7-8/78 (Fourth World)
1-Intro/1st app. Orion; 4th app. Darkseid (cameo; 3 weeks after Forever People #1) (#1-3 are 15¢ issues) 7.25 21.75 80.00
2-Darkseid-c/story (2nd full app., 4-5/71) 3.65 11.00 40.00
3-1st app. Black Racer; last 15¢ issue 2.50 7.50 25.00
4-9: (25¢, 52 pg. giants): 4-Darkseid cameo; origin Manhunter-r. 5,7,8-Young Gods feature. 7-Darkseid app. (2-3/72); origin Orion; 1st origin of all New Gods as a group. 9-1st app. Forager 2.80 8.40 28.00
10,11: 11-Last Kirby issue. 1.85 5.50 15.00
12-19: Darkseid storyline w/minor apps. 12-New costume Orion (see 1st Issue Special #13 for 1st new costume). 19-Story continued in Adventure Comics #459,460 1.00 2.80 7.00
Jack Kirby's New Gods TPB ('98, $11.95, B&W&Grey) r/#1-11 plus cover gallery of original series and "84 reprints 12.00

NOTE: *#4-9(25¢, 52 pgs.) contain Manhunter-r by* ***Simon*** *&* ***Kirby*** *from Adventure #73, 74, 75, 76, 77, 78 with covers in that order.* ***Adkins*** *i-12-14, 17-19.* ***Buckler*** *a(p)-15.* ***Kirby*** *c/a-1-11p.* ***Newton*** *a(p)-12-14, 16-19.* ***Starlin*** *c-17.* ***Staton*** *c-19p.*

NEW GODS (Also see DC Graphic Novel #4)
DC Comics: June, 1984 - No. 6, Nov, 1984 ($2.00, Baxter paper)
1-5: New Kirby-c; r/New Gods #1-10. 3.00
6-Reprints New Gods #11 w/48 pgs of new Kirby story & art; leads into DC Graphic Novel #4 1.00 3.00 8.00

NEW GODS (2nd Series)
DC Comics: Feb, 1989 - No. 28, Aug, 1991 ($1.50)
1-28 2.00

NEW GODS (3rd Series) (Becomes Jack Kirby's Fourth World) (Also see Showcase '94 #1 & Showcase '95 #7)

New Mutants #7 © MAR

New Romances #5 © STD

New Teen Titans #9 © DC

GD2.0 FN6.0 NM9.4

DC Comics: Oct, 1995 - No. 15, Feb, 1997 ($1.95)

1-11,13-15: 9-Giffen-a(p). 10,11-Superman app. 13-Takion, Mr. Miracle & Big Barda app. 13-15-Byrne-a(p)/scripts & Simonson-c. 15-Apokolips merged w/ New Genesis; story cont'd in Jack Kirby's Fourth World 2.50
12-(11/96, 99¢)-Byrne-a(p)/scripts & Simonson-c begin; Takion cameo; indicia reads October 1996 2.00
...Secret Files 1 (9/98, $4.95) Origin-s 5.00

NEW GUARDIANS, THE
DC Comics: Sept, 1988 - No. 12, Sept, 1989 ($1.25)

1-($2.00, 52pgs)-Staton-c/a in #1-9 3.00
2-12 2.00

NEW HEROIC (See Heroic)

NEW JUSTICE MACHINE, THE (Also see The Justice Machine)
Innovation Publishing: 1989 - No. 3, 1989 ($1.95, limited series)

1-3 2.00

NEW KIDS ON THE BLOCK, THE (Also see Richie Rich and...)
Harvey Comics: Dec, 1990 -1991 ($1.25)

1-5 2.00
...**Backstage Pass** 1(12/90) - 5 **Chillin'** 1(12/90) - 5: 1-Photo-c...**Comics Tour** '90/91 1 (12/90) - 5 **Hanging Tough** 1 (2/91) - 3 **Live** 1 (2/91) - 3 **Magic Summer Tour** 1 (Fall/90, one-shot) **Step By Step** 1 (Fall/90, one-shot) **Valentine Girl** 1 (Fall/90, one-shot)-Photo-c 2.00

NEW LOVE (See Love & Rockets)
Fantagraphics Books: Aug, 1996 - No. 6, Dec, 1997 ($2.95, B&W, lim. series)

1-6: Gilbert Hernandez-s/a 3.00

NEWMAN
Image Comics (Extreme Studios): Jan, 1996 - No. 4, Apr, 1996 ($2.50, lim. series)

1-4: 1-Extreme Destroyer Pt. 3; polybagged w/card. 4-Shadowhunt tie-in; Eddie Collins becomes new Shadowhawk 2.50

NEWMEN (becomes The Adventures Of The...#22)
Image Comics (Extreme Studios): Apr, 1994 - No. 20, Nov, 1995; No. 21, Nov, 1996 ($1.95/$2.50)

1-21: 1-5: Matsuda-c/a. 1-Liefeld/Matsuda plot. 10-Polybagged w/trading card. 11-Polybagged. 20-Has a variant-c; Babewatch! x-over. 21-(11/96)-Series relaunch; ChrisSprouse-a begins; pin-up. 16-Has a variant-c by Quesada & Palmiotti 2.50
TPB-(1996, $12.95) r/#1-4 w/pin-ups 13.00

NEW MEN OF BATTLE, THE
Catechetical Guild: 1949 (nn) (Carboard-c)

nn(V8#1-3,5,6)-192 pgs.; contains 5 issues of Topix rebound 7.15 21.50 50.00
nn(V8#7-V8#11)-160 pgs.; contains 5 iss. of Topix 7.15 21.50 50.00

NEW MUTANTS, THE (See Marvel Graphic Novel #4 for 1st app.)(Also see X-Force & Uncanny X-Men #167)
Marvel Comics Group: Mar, 1983 - No. 100, Apr, 1991

1 5.00
2-10: 3,4-Ties into X-Men #167. 10-1st app. Magma 3.00
11-17,19,20: 13-Kitty Pryde app. 16-1st app. Warpath (w/out costume); see X-Men #193 2.50
18,21: 18-Intro. new Warlock. 21-Double size; origin new Warlock; newsstand version has cover price written in by Sienkiewicz 3.00
22-24,27-30: 23-25-Cloak & Dagger app. 2.50
25,26: 25-Legion app. (cameo). 26-1st full Legion app. 4.00
31-58: 35-Magneto intro'd as new headmaster. 43-Portacio-i. 50-Double size. 58-Contains pull-out mutant registration form 2.00
59-61: Fall of The Mutants series. 60(52 pgs.) 3.00
62-85: 68-Intro Spyder. 63-X-Men & Wolverine clones app. 73-(52 pgs.). 76-X-Factor & X-Terminator app. 85-Liefeld-c begin 2.00
86-Rob Liefeld-a begins; McFarlane-c(i) swiped from Ditko splash pg.; Cable cameo (last page teaser) 2.40 6.00
87-1st full app. Cable (3/90) 1.85 5.50 15.00
87-2nd printing; gold metallic ink-c ($1.00) 2.00
88-2nd app. Cable 1.00 2.80 7.00
92-No Liefeld-a; Liefeld-c 4.00
89,90,91,93-100: 89-3rd app. Cable. 90-New costumes. 90,91-Sabretooth app. 93,94-Cable vs. Wolverine. 95-97-X-Tinction Agenda x-over. 95-Death of new Warlock. 97-Wolverine & Cable-c, but no app. 98-1st app. Deadpool, Gideon & Domino (2/91);2nd Shatterstar (cameo). 99-1st app. of Feral (of X-Force); Byrne-c/swipe (X-Men, 1st Series #138). 100-(52 pgs.)-1st app. X-Force (cameo) 5.00
95,100-Gold 2nd printing. 100-Silver ink 3rd printing 2.00
Annual 1 (1984) 4.00
Annual 2 (1986, $1.25)-1st Psylocke 1.00 3.00 8.00
Annual 3,4,6,7 ('87, '88,'90,'91, 68 pgs.): 4-Evolutionary War x-over. 6-1st new costumes by Liefeld (3 pgs.); 1st app. (cameo) Shatterstar (of X-Force). 7-Liefeld pin-up only; X-Terminators back-up story; 2nd app. X-Force (contin ued in New Warriors Annual #1) 3.00
Annual 5 (1989, $2.00, 68 pgs.)-Atlantis Attacks; 1st Liefeld-a on New Mutants 4.00
Special 1-Special Edition ('85, 68 pgs.)-Ties in w/X-Men Alpha Flight limited series; cont'd in X-Men Annual #9; Art Adams/Austin-a 5.00
Summer Special 1(Sum/90, $2.95, 84 pgs.) 3.00

NOTE: ***Art Adams** c-38, 39. **Austin** c-57i. **Byrne** c/a-75p. **Liefeld** a-86-91p, 93-96p, 98-100, Annual 5p, 6(3 pgs.); c-85-91p, 92, 93p, 94, 95, 96p, 97-100, Annual 5, 6p. **McFarlane** c-85-89i, 93i. **Portacio** a(i)-43. **Russell** a-48i. **Sienkiewicz** a-18-31, 35-38i; c-17-31, 35i, 37i, Annual 1. **Simonson** c-11p. **B. Smith** c-36, 40-48. **Williamson** a(i)-69, 71-73, 78-80, 82, 83; c(i)-69, 72, 73, 78i.*

NEW MUTANTS, THE: TRUTH OR DEATH
Marvel Comics: Nov, 1997 - No. 3, Jan, 1998 ($2.50, limited series)

1-3-Raab-s/Chang-a(p) 2.50

NEW ORDER, THE
CFD Publishing: Nov, 1994 ($2.95)

1 3.00

NEW PEOPLE, THE (TV)
Dell Publishing Co.: Jan, 1970 - No. 2, May, 1970

1 2.40 7.35 22.00
2 2.00 6.00 18.00

NEW ROMANCES
Standard Comics: No. 5, May, 1951 - No. 21, May, 1954

5-Photo-c 11.00 33.00 90.00
6-9: 6-Barbara Bel Geddes, Richard Basehart "Fourteen Hours" photo-c. 7-Ray Milland & Joan Fontaine photo-c. 9-Photo-c from '50s movie 6.40 19.25 45.00
10,14,16,17-Toth-a 7.85 23.50 55.00
11-Toth-a; Liz Taylor, Montgomery Cliff photo-c 15.00 45.00 120.00
12,13,15,18-21 5.00 15.00 35.00

NOTE: ***Celardo** a-9. **Moreira** a-6. **Tuska** a-7, 20. Photo c-5-16.*

NEW SHADOWHAWK, THE (Also see Shadowhawk & Shadowhunt)
Image Comics (Shadowline Ink): June, 1995 - No. 7, Mar, 1996 ($2.50)

1-7: Kurt Busiek scripts in all 3.00

NEW STATESMEN, THE
Fleetway Publications (Quality Comics): 1989 - No. 5, 1990 ($3.95, limited series, mature readers, 52pgs.)

1-5: Futuristic; squarebound; 3-Photo-c 4.00

NEWSTRALIA
Innovation Publ.: July, 1989 - No. 5, 1989 ($1.75, color)(#2 on, $2.25, B&W)

1-5: 1,2: Timothy Truman-c/a; Gustovich-i 2.25

NEW TALENT SHOWCASE (Talent Showcase #16 on)
DC Comics: Jan, 1984 - No. 19, Oct, 1985 (Direct sales only)

1-19: Features new strips & artists. 18-Williamson-c(i) 2.00

NEW TEEN TITANS, THE (See DC Comics Presents 26, Marvel and DC Present & Teen Titans; Tales of the Teen Titans #41 on)
DC Comics: Nov, 1980 - No. 40, Mar, 1984

1-Robin, Kid Flash, Wonder Girl, The Changeling (1st app.), Starfire, The Raven, Cyborg begin; partial origin 1.10 3.30 9.00
2-1st app. Deathstroke the Terminator 1.00 2.80 7.00
3-10: 3-Origin Starfire; Intro The Fearsome Five. 4-Origin continues; J.L.A. app.

New Titans #72 © DC

New Warriors V2 #9 © MAR

New York World's Fair 1939 © DC

GD2.0 FN6.0 NM9.4 GD2.0 FN6.0 NM9.4

6-Origin Raven. 7-Cyborg origin. 8-Origin Kid Flash retold. 9-Minor cameo Deathstroke on last pg. 10-2nd app. Deathstroke the Terminator (see Marvel & DC Present for 3rd app.); origin Changeling retold 5.00

11-40: 13-Return of Madame Rouge & Capt. Zahl; Robotman revived. 14-Return of Mento; origin Doom Patrol. 15-Death of Madame Rouge & Capt. Zahl; intro. new Brotherhood of Evil. 16-1st app. Captain Carrot (free 16 pg. preview). 18-Return of Starfire. 19-Hawkman teams-up. 21-Intro Night Force in free 16 pg. insert; intro Brother Blood. 23-1st app. Vigilante (not in costume), & Blackfire. 24-Omega Men app. 25-Omega Men cameo; free 16 pg. preview Masters of the Universe. 26-1st app. Terra. 27-Free 16 pg. preview Atari Force. 29-The New Brotherhood of Evil & Speedy app. 30-Terra joins the Titans. 37-Batman & The Outsiders x-over. 38-Origin Wonder Girl. 34-4th app. Deathstroke the Terminator. 39-Last Dick Grayson as Robin; Kid Flash quits 3.00

Annual 1(11/82)-Omega Men app. 3.50

Annual V2#2(9/83)-1st app. Vigilante in costume 3.50

Annual 3 (See Tales of the Teen Titans Annual #3)

NOTE: ***Perez*** *a-1-4p, 6-34p, 37-40p, Annual 1p, 2p; c-1-12, 13-17p, 18-21, 22p, 23p, 24-37, 38, 39(painted), 40, Annual 1, 2.*

NEW TEEN TITANS, THE (Becomes The New Titans #50 on)
DC Comics: Aug, 1984 - No. 49, Nov, 1988 ($1.25/$1.75; deluxe format)

1-New storyline; Perez-c/a begins 5.00
2,3: 2-Re-intro Lilith 4.00
4-10: 5-Death of Trigon. 7-9-Origin Lilith. 8-Intro Kole. 10-Kole joins 3.00
11-49: 13,14-Crisis x-over. 20-Robin (Jason Todd) joins; original Teen Titans return. 38-Infinity, Inc. x-over. 47-Origin of all Titans; Titans (East & West) pin-up by George Perez. 2.25
Annual 1-4 (9/85-'88): 1-Intro. Vanguard. 2-Byrne c/a(p); origin Brother Blood; intro new Dr. Light. 3-Intro. Danny Chase. 4-Perez-c 2.50

NOTE: ***Buckler*** *c-10.* ***Kelley Jones*** *a-47, Annual 4.* ***Erik Larsen*** *a-33.* ***Orlando*** *c-33p.* ***Perez*** *a-1-5; c-1-7, 19-23, 43.* ***Steacy*** *c-47.*

NEW TERRYTOONS (TV)
Dell Publishing Co./Gold Key: 6-8/60 - No. 8, 3-5/62; 10/62 - No. 54, 1/79

1(1960-Dell)-Deputy Dawg, Dinky Duck & Hashimoto-San begin (1st app. of each)	4.60	13.75	55.00
2-8(1962)	3.00	9.00	30.00
1(30010-210)(10/62-Gold Key, 84 pgs.)-Heckle & Jeckle begins	6.70	20.00	80.00
2(30010-301)-84 pgs.	5.85	17.50	70.00
3-5	2.50	7.50	25.00
6-10	2.30	7.00	20.00
11-20	1.85	5.50	15.00
21-30	1.25	3.75	10.00
31-43	1.00	2.80	7.00
44-54: Mighty Mouse-c/s in all	1.00	3.00	8.00

NOTE: *Reprints: #4-12, 38, 40, 47. (See March of Comics #379, 393, 412, 435)*

NEW TESTAMENT STORIES VISUALIZED
Standard Publishing Co.: 1946 - 1947

'New Testament Heroes–Acts of Apostles Visualized, Book I"
'New Testament Heroes–Acts of Apostles Visualized, Book II"
'Parables Jesus Told" Set.... 15.00 45.00 120.00

NOTE: *All three are contained in a cardboard case, illustrated on front and info about the set.*

NEW TITANS, THE (Formerly The New Teen Titans)
DC Comics: No. 50, Dec, 1988 - No. 130, Feb, 1996 ($1.75/$2.25)

50-Perez-c/a begins; new origin Wonder Girl 5.00
51-59: 50-55-Painted-c. 55-Nightwing (Dick Grayson) forces Danny Chase to resign; Batman app. in flashback, Wonder Girl becomes Troia 3.00
60,61: 60-A Lonely Place of Dying Part 2 continues from Batman #440; new Robin tie-in; Timothy Drake app. 61-A Lonely Place of Dying Part 4 3.00
62-99,101-124,126-130: 62-65: Deathstroke the Terminator app. 65-Tim Drake (Robin) app. 70-1st Deathstroke solo cover/sty. 71-(44 pgs.)-10th anniversary issue; Deathstroke cameo. 72-79-Deathstroke in all: 74-Intro. Pantha. 79-Terra brought back to life;1 panel cameo Team Titans (1st app.). Deathstroke in #80-84,86. 80-2nd full app. Team Titans. 83,84-Deathstroke kills his son, Jericho. 85-Team Titans app. 86-Deathstroke vs. Nightwing-c/story; last Deathstroke app. 87-New costume Nightwing. 90-92-Parts 2,5,8 Total Chaos (Team Titans). 115-(11/94) 2.50
100-($3.50, 52 pgs.)-Holo-grafx foil-c 3.50
125 (3.50)-wraparound-c 3.50
#0-(10/94) Zero Hour, released between #114 & 115 2.50
Annual 5-10 ('89-'94, 68 pgs.. 7-Armaggedon 2001 x-over; 1st full app. Teen (Team) Titans (new group). 8-Deathstroke app.; Eclipso app. (minor). 10-Elseworlds story 3.50
Annual 11 (1995, $3.95)-Year One story 4.00

NOTE: ***Perez*** *a-50-55p, 57,60p, 58,59,61(layouts); c-50-61, 62-67i, Annual 5i; co-plots-66.*

NEW TV FUNNIES (See New Funnies)

NEW TWO-FISTED TALES, THE
Dark Horse Comics/Byron Preiss: 1993 ($4.95, limited series, 52 pgs.)

1-Kurtzman-r & new-a 5.00

NOTE: ***Eisner*** *c-1i.* ***Kurtzman*** *c-1p, 2.*

NEW WARRIORS, THE (See Thor #411,412)
Marvel Comics: July, 1990 - No. 75, 1996 ($1.00/$1.25/$1.50)

1-Williamson-i; Bagley-c/a(p) in 1-13, Annual 1 5.00
1-Gold 2nd printing (7/91) 2.00
2-5: 1,3-Guice-c(i). 2-Williamson-c/a(i). 3.00
6-24,26-49,51-75: 7-Punisher cameo (last pg.). 8,9-Punisher app. 14-Darkhawk & Namor x-over. 17-Fantastic Four & Silver Surfer x-over. 19-Gideon (of X-Force) app. 28-Intro Turbo & Cardinal. 31-Cannonball & Warpath app. 42-Nova vs. Firelord. 46-Photo-c. 47-Bound-in S-M trading card sheet. 52-12 pg. ad insert. 62-Scarlet Spider-c/app. 70-Spider-Man-c/app. 72-Avengers-c/app. 2.00
25-($2.50, 52 pgs.)-Die-cut cover 2.50
40,60: 40-($2.25)-Gold foil collector's edition 2.50
50-($2.95, 52 pgs.)-Glow in the dark-c 3.00
Annual 1-4('91-'94,68 pgs.)-1-Origins all members; 3rd app. X-Force (cont'd from New Mutants Ann. #7 & cont'd in X-Men Ann. #15); x-over before X-Force #1. 3-Bagged w/card 3.00

NEW WARRIORS, THE
Marvel Comics: Oct, 1999 - No. 10, July, 2000 ($2.99/$2.50)

0-Wizard supplement; short story and preview sketchbook 1.00
1-($2.99) 3.00
2-10: 2-Two covers. 5-Generation X app. 9-Iron Man-c 2.50

NEW WAVE, THE
Eclipse Comics: 6/10/86 - No. 13, 3/87 (#1-8: bi-weekly, 20pgs; #9-13: monthly)

1-13:1-Origin, concludes #5. 6-Origin Megabyte. 8,9-The Heap returns. 13-Snyder-c 2.00
Versus the Volunteers 3-D #1,2(4/87): 1-Snyder-c 2.50

NEW WORLD (See Comic Books, series I)

NEW WORLDS
Caliber: 1996 - No. 6 ($2.95, 80 pgs., B&W, anthology)

1-6: 1-Mister X & other stories 3.00

NEW YORK GIANTS (See Thrilling True Story of the Baseball Giants)

NEW YORK STATE JOINT LEGISLATIVE COMMITTEE TO STUDY THE PUBLICATION OF COMICS, THE
N.Y. State Legislative Document: 1951, 1955

This document was referenced by Wertham for **Seduction of the Innocent.** Contains numerous repros from comics showing violence, sadism, torture, and sex.
1955 version (196p, No. 37, 2/23/55)-Sold for $180 in 1986.

NEW YORK, THE BIG CITY
Kitchen Sink Press: 1986 ($10.95, B&W)
DC Comics: July, 2000 ($12.95, B&W)

nn-Will Eisner-s/a 13.00

NEW YORK WORLD'S FAIR (Also see Big Book of Fun & New Book of Fun)
National Periodical Publ.: 1939, 1940 (100 pgs.; cardboard covers)
(DC's 4th & 5th annuals)

	GD2.0	FN6.0	VF8.0	NM9.4
1939-Scoop Scanlon, Superman (blond haired Superman on-c), Sandman, Zatara, Slam Bradley, Ginger Snap by Bob Kane begin; 1st published app. The Sandman (see Adventure #40 for his 1st drawn story); Vincent Sullivan-c; cover background by Guardineer	2080.00	6240.00	13,520.00	26,000.00

1940-Batman, Hourman, Johnny Thunderbolt, Red, White & Blue & Hanko (by Creig Flessel) app.; Superman, Batman & Robin-c (1st time they all

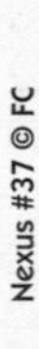
Nexus #37 © FC

Nickel Comics #5 © FAW

Nick Fury V2 #9 © MAR

appear together); early Robin app.; 1st Burnley-c/a (per Burnley) 1120.00 3360.00 7280.00 14,000.00

NOTE: *The 1939 edition was published 4/29/39 and released 4/30/39, the day the fair opened, at 25¢, and was first sold only at the fair. Since all other comics were 10¢, it didn't sell. Remaining copies were advertised beginning in the August issues of most DC comics for 25¢, but soon the price was dropped to 15¢. Everyone that sent a quarter through the mail for it received a free Superman #1 or a #2 to make up the dime difference. 15¢ stickers were placed over the 25¢ price. Four variations on the 15¢ stickers are known. The 1940 edition was published 5/11/40 and was priced at 15¢. It was a precursor to World's Best #1.*

NEW YORK: YEAR ZERO
Eclipse Comics: July, 1988 - No. 4, Oct, 1988 ($2.00, B&W, limited series)
1-4 2.00

NEXT MAN
Comico: Mar, 1985 - No. 5, Oct, 1985 ($1.50, color, Baxter paper)
1-5 2.00

NEXT MEN (See John Byrne's...)

NEXT NEXUS, THE
First Comics: Jan, 1989 - No. 4, April, 1989 ($1.95, limited series, Baxter paper)
1-4: Mike Baron scripts & Steve Rude-c/a. 2.00
TPB (10/89, $9.95) r/series 10.00

NEXUS (See First Comics Graphic Novel #4, 19 & The Next Nexus)
Capital Comics/First Comics No. 7 on: June, 1981 - No. 6, Mar, 1984; No. 7, Apr, 1985 - No. 80?, May, 1991
(Direct sales only, 36 pgs.; V2#1('83)-printed on Baxter paper
1-B&W version; mag. size; w/double size poster 2.00 6.00 18.00
1-B&W 1981 limited edition; 500 copies printed and signed; same as above except this version has a 2-pg. poster & a pencil sketch on paperboard by Rude 2.50 7.50 25.00
2-B&W, magazine size 1.75 5.25 14.00
3-B&W, magazine size; contains 33-1/3 rpm record ($2.95 price) 1.10 3.30 9.00
V2#1-Color version 4.00
2-49,51-80: 2-Nexus' origin begins. 67-Snyder-c/a 2.25
50-($3.50, 52 pgs.) 3.50

NOTE: ***Bissette** c-V2#29. **Giffen** c/a-V2#23. **Gulacy** c-1 (B&W), 2(B&W). **Mignola** c/a-V2#28. **Rude** c-3(B&W), V2#1-22, 24-27, 33-36, 39-42, 45-48, 50, 58-60, 75; a-1-3, V2#1-7, 8-16p, 18-22p, 24-27p, 33-36p, 39-42p, 45-48p, 50, 58, 59p, 60. **Paul Smith** a-V2#37, 38, 43, 44, 51-55p; c-V2#37, 38, 43, 44, 51-55.*

NEXUS: ALIEN JUSTICE
Dark Horse Comics: Dec, 1992 - No. 3, Feb, 1993 ($3.95, limited series)
1-3: Mike Baron scripts & Steve Rude-c/a 4.00

NEXUS: EXECUTIONER'S SONG
Dark Horse Comics: June, 1996 - No. 4, Sept, 1996 ($2.95, limited series)
1-4: Mike Baron scripts & Steve Rude-c/a 3.00

NEXUS FILES
First Comics: 1989 ($4.50, color/16pgs. B&W, one-shot, squarebound, 52pgs.)
1-New Rude-a; info on Nexus 4.50

NEXUS: GOD CON
Dark Horse Comics: Apr, 1997 - No. 2, May, 1997 ($2.95, limited series)
1,2-Baron-s/Rude-c/a 3.00

NEXUS LEGENDS
First Comics: May, 1989 - No. 23, Mar, 1991 ($1.50, Baxter paper)\
1-23: R/1-3(Capital) & early First Comics issues w/new Rude covers #1-6,9,10 2.00

NEXUS MEETS MADMAN (...Special)
Dark Horse Comics: May, 1996 ($2.95, one-shot)
nn-Mike Baron & Mike Allred scripts, Steve Rude-c/a. 3.00

NEXUS: NIGHTMARE IN BLUE
Dark Horse Comics: July, 1997 - No. 4, Oct, 1997 ($2.95, limited series)
1-4: 1,2,4-Adam Hughes-c 3.00

NEXUS: THE LIBERATOR
Dark Horse Comics: Aug, 1992 - No. 4, Nov, 1992 ($2.95, limited series)
1-4 3.00

NEXUS: THE ORIGIN
Dark Horse Comics: July, 1996 ($3.95, one-shot)
nn-Mike Baron- scripts, Steve Rude-c/a. 4.00

NEXUS: THE WAGES OF SIN
Dark Horse Comics: Mar, 1995 - No. 4, June, 1995 ($2.95, limited series)
1-4 3.00

NICKEL COMICS
Dell Publishing Co.: 1938 (Pocket size - 7-1/2x5-1/2")(132 pgs.)
1- "Bobby & Chip" by Otto Messmer, Felix the Cat artist. Contains some English reprints 68.00 205.00 650.00

NICKEL COMICS
Fawcett Publications: May, 1940 - No. 8, Aug, 1940 (36 pgs.; Bi-Weekly; 5¢)
1-Origin/1st app. Bulletman 381.00 1143.00 4000.00
2 126.00 379.00 1200.00
3 95.00 285.00 900.00
4-The Red Gaucho begins 79.00 237.00 750.00
5-7 74.00 221.00 700.00
8-World's Fair-c; Bulletman moved to Master Comics #7 in October (scarce) 79.00 237.00 750.00

NOTE: ***Beck** c-5-8. **Jack Binder** c-1-4. Bondage c-5. Bulletman c-1-8.*

NICK FURY, AGENT OF SHIELD (See Fury, Marvel Spotlight #31 & Shield)
Marvel Comics Group: 6/68 - No. 15, 11/69; No. 16, 11/70 - No. 18, 3/71
1 10.00 30.00 110.00
2-4: 4-Origin retold 4.55 13.65 50.00
5-Classic-c 5.00 15.00 55.00
6,7: 7-Salvador Dali painting swipe 3.20 9.60 35.00
8-11,13: 9-Hate Monger begins, ends #11. 10-Smith layouts/pencil. 11-Smith-c. 13-1st app. Super-Patriot; last 12¢ issue 2.30 7.00 20.00
12-Smith-c/a 2.50 7.50 25.00
14-Begin 15¢ issues 2.00 6.00 18.00
15-1st app. & death of Bullseye-c/story(11/69); Nick Fury shot & killed; last 15¢ issue 5.00 15.00 55.00
16-18-(25¢, 52 pgs.)-r/Str. Tales #135-143 2.00 6.00 18.00
TPB (May 2000, $19.95) r/ Strange Tales #150-168 20.00
...: Who is Scorpio? TPB (11/00, $12.95) r/#1-3,5; Steranko-c 13.00

NOTE: ***Adkins** a-3i. **Craig** a-10i. **Sid Greene** a-12i. **Kirby** a-16-18r. **Springer** a-4, 6, 7, 8p, 9, 10p, 11; c-8, 9. **Steranko** a(p)-1-3, 5; c-1-7.*

NICK FURY AGENT OF SHIELD (Also see Strange Tales #135)
Marvel Comics: Dec, 1983 - No. 2, Jan, 1984 (2.00, 52 pgs., Baxter paper)
1,2-r/Nick Fury #1-4; new Steranko-c 3.00

NICK FURY, AGENT OF S.H.I.E.L.D.
Marvel Comics: Sept, 1989 - No. 47, May, 1993 ($1.50/$1.75)
V2#1-26,30-47: 10-Capt. America app. 13-Return of The Yellow Claw. 15-Fantastic Four app. 30,31-Deathlok app. 36-Cage app. 37-Woodgod c/story. 38-41-Flashes back to pre-Shield days after WWII. 44-Capt. America-c/s. 45-Viper-c/s. 46-Gideon x-over 2.00
27-29-Wolverine-c/stories 2.50

NOTE: ***Alan Grant** scripts-11. **Guice** a(p)-20-23, 25, 26; c-20-28.*

NICK FURY VS. S.H.I.E.L.D.
Marvel Comics: June, 1988 - No. 6, Nov, 1988 ($3.50, 52 pgs, deluxe format)
1,2: 1-Steranko-c. 2-(Low print run) Sienkiewicz-c 5.00
3-6 4.00

NICK HALIDAY (Thrill of the Sea)
Argo: May, 1956
1-Daily & Sunday strip-r by Petree 7.85 23.50 55.00

NIGHT AND THE ENEMY (Graphic Novel)
Comico: 1988 (8-1/2x11") ($11.95, color, 80 pgs.)
1-Harlan Ellison scripts/Ken Steacy-c/a; r/Epic Illustrated & new-a (1st and 2nd printings) 12.00
1-Limited edition ($39.95) 40.00

NIGHT BEFORE CHRISTMAS, THE (See March of Comics No. 152)

NIGHT BEFORE CHRISTMASK, THE
Dark Horse Comics: Nov, 1994 ($9.95, one-shot)

Night Force (1st series) #5 © DC

Nightmare #2 © Z-D

Nightmare Theater #1 © Chaos!

GD2.0 FN6.0 NM9.4

nn-Hardcover book; Rick Geary -c/a 10.00

NIGHTBREED (See Clive Barker's Nightbreed)

NIGHTCRAWLER
Marvel Comics Group: Nov, 1985 - No. 4, Feb, 1986 (Mini-series from X-Men)

1-4: 1-Cockrum-c/a 3.00

NIGHTFALL: THE BLACK CHRONICLES
DC Comics (Homage): Dec, 1999 - No. 3, Feb, 2000 ($2.95, limited series)

1-3-Coker-a/Gilmore-s 3.00

NIGHT FORCE, THE (See New Teen Titans #21)
DC Comics: Aug, 1982 - No. 14, Sept, 1983 (60¢)

1 4.00
2-14: 13-Origin Baron Winter. 14-Nudity panels 3.00
NOTE: ***Colan** c/a-1-14p.* ***Giordano** c-1i, 2i, 4i, 5i, 7i, 12i.*

NIGHT FORCE
DC Comics: Dec, 1996 - No. 12, Nov, 1997 ($2.25)

1-12: 1-3-Wolfman-s/Anderson-a(p). 8-"Convergence" part 2 2.25

NIGHT GLIDER
Topps Comics (Kirbyverse): April, 1993 ($2.95, one-shot)

1-Kirby c-1, Heck-a; polybagged w/Kirbychrome trading card 3.00

NIGHTHAWK
Marvel Comics: Sept, 1998 - No. 3, Nov, 1998 ($2.99, mini-series)

1-3-Krueger-s; Daredevil app. 3.00

NIGHTINGALE, THE
Henry H. Stansbury Once-Upon-A-Time Press, Inc.: 1948 (10¢, 7-1/4x10-1/4", 14 pgs., 1/2 B&W)

(Very Rare)-Low distribution; distributed to Westchester County & Bronx, N.Y. only; used in **Seduction of the Innocent**, pg. 312,313 as the 1st and only "good" comic book ever published. Ill. by Dong Kingman; 1,500 words of text, printed on high quality paper & no word balloons. Copyright registered 10/22/48, distributed week of 12/5/48. (By Hans Christian Andersen)
Estimated value........ $200

NIGHT MAN, THE (See Sludge #1)
Malibu Comics (Ultraverse): Oct, 1993 - No. 23, Aug, 1995 ($1.95/$2.50)

1-($2.50, 48 pgs.)-Rune flip-c/story by B. Smith (3 pgs.) 2.50
1-Ultra-Limited silver foil-c 2.40 6.00
2-15, 17: 3-Break-Thru x-over; Freex app. 4-Origin Firearm (2 pgs.) by Chaykin. 6-TNTNT app. 8-1st app. Teknight 2.50
16 ($3.50)-flip book (Ultraverse Premiere #11) 3.50
...:The Pilgrim Conundrum Saga (1/95, $3.95, 68 pgs.)-Strangers app. 4.00
18-23: 22-Loki-c/a 2.50
Infinity ($1.50) 2.50
...Vs. Wolverine #0-Kelley Jones-c; mail in offer 1.25 3.75 10.00
*NOTE: **Zeck** a-16.*

NIGHT MAN, THE
Malibu Comics (Ultraverse): Sept, 1995 - No.4, Dec, 1995 ($1.50, lim. series)

1-4: Post Black September storyline 2.00

NIGHT MAN, THE /GAMBIT
Malibu Comics (Ultraverse): Mar, 1996 - No. 3, May, 1996 ($1.95, lim. series)

0-Limited Premium Edition 4.00
1-3: David Quinn scripts in all. 3-Rhiannon discovered to be The Night Man's mother 2.00

NIGHTMARE
Ziff-Davis (Approved Comics)/St. John No. 3: Summer, 1952 - No. 3, Winter, 1952, 53 (Painted-c)

1-1 pg. Kinstler-a; Tuska-a(2) 55.00 165.00 500.00
2-Kinstler-a-Poe's "Pit & the Pendulum" 40.00 120.00 340.00
3-Kinstler-a 34.00 101.00 270.00

NIGHTMARE (Weird Horrors #1-9) (Amazing Ghost Stories #14 on)
St. John Publishing Co.: No. 10, Dec, 1953 - No. 13, Aug, 1954

10-Reprints Ziff-Davis Weird Thrillers #2 w/new Kubert-c plus 2 pgs. Kinstler-a; Anderson, Colan & Toth-a 53.00 158.00 475.00
11-Krigstein-a; painted-c; Poe adapt., "Hop Frog" 40.00 120.00 340.00
12-Kubert bondage-c; adaptation of Poe's "The Black Cat"; Cannibalism story 38.00 113.00 300.00
13-Reprints Z-D Weird Thrillers #3 with new cover; Powell-a(2), Tuska-a; Baker-c 28.00 84.00 225.00

NIGHTMARE (Magazine)
Skywald Publishing Corp.: Dec, 1970 - No. 23, Feb, 1975 (B&W, 68 pgs.)

1-Everett-a 5.45 16.35 60.00
2-6,8,9: 4-Decapitation story. 6-Kaluta-a; Jeff Jones photo & interview. 8-Features E. C. movie "Tales From the Crypt"; reprints some E.C. comics panels. 9-Wrightson-a 3.00 9.00 32.00
7,10 2.50 7.50 25.00
11-19: 12-Excessive gore, severed heads 2.40 7.35 22.00
20-Byrne's 1st artwork (8/74); severed head-c 3.20 9.60 35.00
21-23: 21-(1974 Summer Special)-Kaluta-a. 22-Tomb of Horror issue. 23-(1975 Winter Special) 2.80 8.40 28.00
Annual 1(1972)-B. Jones-a 3.00 9.00 32.00
Winter Special 1(1973) 2.50 7.50 25.00
Yearbook nn(1974)-B. Jones, Reese, Wildey-a 2.50 7.50 25.00
*NOTE: **Adkins** a-5. **Boris** c-2, 3, 5 (#4 is not by Boris). **Buckler** a-3, 15. **Byrne** a-20p. **Everett** a-4, 5, 12. **Jeff Jones** a-6, 21r(Psycho #6); c-6. **Katz** a-5. **Reese** a-4, 5. **Wildey** a-4, 5, 6, 21, '74 Yearbook.*

NIGHTMARE (Alex Nino's)
Innovation Publishing: 1989 ($1.95)

1-Alex Nino-a 2.00

NIGHTMARE
Marvel Comics: Dec, 1994 - No. 4, Mar, 1995 ($1.95, limited series)

1-4 2.00

NIGHTMARE & CASPER (See Harvey Hits #71) (Casper & Nightmare #6 on) (See Casper The Friendly Ghost #19)
Harvey Publications: Aug, 1963 - No. 5, Aug, 1964 (25¢)

1-All reprints? 6.35 19.00 70.00
2-5: All reprints? 3.65 11.00 40.00

NIGHTMARE ON ELM STREET, A (See Freddy Krueger's...)

NIGHTMARES (See Do You Believe in Nightmares)

NIGHTMARES
Eclipse Comics: May, 1985 - No. 2, May, 1985 ($1.75, Baxter paper)

1,2 3.00

NIGHTMARE THEATER
Chaos! Comics: Nov, 1997 - No. 4, Nov, 1997 ($2.50, mini-series)

1-4-Horror stories by various; Wrightson-a 2.50

NIGHTMARK: BLOOD & HONOR
Alpha Productions: 1994 - No. 3, 1994 ($2.50, B&W, mini-series)

1,2 2.50

NIGHTMARK MYSTERY SPECIAL
Alpha Productions: Jan, 1994 ($2.50, B&W)

1 2.50

NIGHTMASK
Marvel Comics Group: Nov, 1986 - No. 12, Oct, 1987

1-12 2.00

NIGHT MASTER
Silverwolf: Feb, 1987 ($1.50, B&W)

1-Tim Vigil-c/a 3.00

NIGHT MUSIC (See Eclipse Graphic Album Series, The Magic Flute)
Eclipse Comics: Dec, 1984 - No. 11, 1990 ($1.75/$3.95/$4.95, Baxter paper)

1-7: 3-Russell's Jungle Book adapt. 4,5-Pelleas And Melisande (double titled) 6-Salome' (double titled). 7-Red Dog #1 2.00
8-($3.95) Ariane and Bluebeard 4.00
9-11-($4.95) The Magic Flute; Russell adapt. 5.00

NIGHT NURSE
Marvel Comics Group: Nov, 1972 - No. 4, May, 1973

1 10.00 30.00 110.00
2-4 6.80 20.50 75.00

Night of Mystery nn © AVON

Night Thrasher #14 © MAR

Nightwing #41 © DC

GD2.0 FN6.0 NM9.4

NIGHT OF MYSTERY
Avon Periodicals: 1953 (no month) (one-shot)
nn-1 pg. Kinstler-a, Hollingsworth-c 42.00 125.00 375.00

NIGHT OF THE GRIZZLY, THE (See Movie Classics)

NIGHTRAVEN (See Marvel Graphic Novel)

NIGHT RIDER (Western)
Marvel Comics Group: Oct, 1974 - No. 6, Aug, 1975
1: 1-6 reprint Ghost Rider #1-6 (#1-origin) 1.85 5.50 15.00
2-6 1.25 3.75 10.00

NIGHT'S CHILDREN: THE VAMPIRE
Millenium: July, 1995 - No. 2, Aug, 1995 ($2.95, B&W)
1,2: Wendy Snow-Lang story & art 3.00

NIGHTSHADE
No Mercy Comics: Aug, 1997 ($2.50)
1-Mark Williams-s/a 2.50

NIGHTS INTO DREAMS (Based on video game)
Archie Comics: Feb, 1998 -No. 6, Oct, 1998 ($1.75, limited series)
1-6 2.00

NIGHTSTALKERS (Also see Midnight Sons Unlimited)
Marvel Comics (Midnight Sons #14 on): Nov, 1992 - No. 18, Apr, 1994 ($1.75)
1-($2.75, 52 pgs.)-Polybagged w/poster; part 5 of Rise of the Midnight Sons storyline; Garney/Palmer-c/a begins; Hannibal King, Blade & Frank Drake begin (see Tomb of Dracula for & Dr. Strange) 2.75
2-9,11-18: 5-Punisher app. 7-Ghost Rider app. 8,9-Morbius app. 14-Spot varnish-c. 14,15-Siege of Darkness Pts 1 & 9 2.00
10-($2.25)-Outer-c is a Darkhold envelope made of black parchment w/gold ink; Midnight Massacre part 1 2.25

NIGHT TERRORS,THE
Chanting Monks Studios: 2000 ($2.75, B&W)
1-Bernie Wrightson-c; short stories, one by Wrightson-s/a 2.75

NIGHT THRASHER (Also see The New Warriors)
Marvel Comics: Aug, 1993 - No. 21, Apr, 1995 ($1.75/$1.95)
1-($2.95, 52 pgs.)-Red holo-grafx foil-c; origin 3.00
2-21: 2-Intro Tantrum. 3-Gideon (of X-Force) app. 10-Bound-in trading card sheet; Iron Man app. 15-Hulk app. 2.00

NIGHT THRASHER: FOUR CONTROL
Marvel Comics: Oct, 1992 - No. 4, Jan, 1993 ($2.00, limited series)
1-4: 2-Intro Tantrum. 3-Gideon (of X-Force) app. 2.00

NIGHT TRIBES
DC Comics (WildStorm): July, 1999 ($4.95, one-shot)
1-Golden & Sniegoski-s/Chin-a 5.00

NIGHTVEIL (Also see Femforce)
Americomics/AC Comics: Nov, 1984 - No. 7, 1987 ($1.75)
1-7 2.00
...'s Cauldron Of Horror 1 (1989, B&W)-Kubert, Powell, Wood-r plus new Nightveil story 3.00
...'s Cauldron Of Horror 2 (1990, $2.95, B&W, 44pgs)-Pre-code horror-r by Kubert & Powell 3.00
...'s Cauldron Of Horror 3 (1991) 3.00
Special 1 ('88, $1.95)-Kaluta-c 2.00
One Shot ('96, $5.95)-Flip book w/ Colt 6.00

NIGHTWATCH
Marvel Comics: Apr, 1994 - No. 12, Mar, 1995 ($1.50)
1-($2.95)-Collectors edition; foil-c; Ron Lim-c/a begins; Spider-Man app. 3.00
1-12-Regular edition. 2-Bound-in S-M trading card sheet; 5,6-Venom-c & app. 7,11-Cardiac app. 2.00

NIGHTWING (Also see New Teen Titans, New Titans, Showcase '93 #11,12, Tales of the New Teen Titans & Teen Titans Spotlight)
DC Comics: Sept, 1995 - No. 4, Dec, 1995 ($2.25, limited series)
1-Dennis O'Neil story/Greg Land-a in all 5.00
2-4 4.00
...: Alfred's Return (7/95, $3.50) Giordano-a 4.00
...Ties That Bind (1997, $12.95, TPB) r/mini-series & Alfred's Return 13.00

NIGHTWING
DC Comics: Oct, 1996 - Present ($1.95/$1.99/$2.25)
1-Chuck Dixon scripts & Scott McDaniel-c/a 1.50 4.50 12.00
2,3 1.00 2.80 7.00
4-10: 6-Robin-c/app. 5.00
11-20: 13-15-Batman app. 19,20-Cataclysm pts. 2,11 3.00
21-49,51-53: 23-Green Arrow app. 26-29-Huntress-c/app. 30-Superman-c/app. 35-39-No Man's Land. 41-Land/Geraci-a begins. 46-Begin $2.25-c. 47-Texiera-c. 52-Catwoman-c/app. 2.25
50-($3.50) Nightwing battles Torque 3.50
#1,000,000 (11/98) teams with future Batman 2.00
Annual 1(1997, $3.95) Pulp Heroes 4.00
...Eighty Page Giant 1 (12/00, $5.95) Intro. of Hella; Dixon-s/Haley-c 6.00
...: A Knight in Blüdhaven (1998, $14.95, TPB) r/#1-8 15.00
...: Love and Bullets (2000, $17.95, TPB) r/#1/2, 19,21,22,24-29 18.00
...: Rough Justice (1999, $17.95, TPB) r/#9-18 18.00
Secret Files 1 (10/99, $4.95) Origin-s and pin-ups 5.00
Wizard 1/2 (Mail offer) 5.00

NIGHTWING (See Tangent Comics/ Nightwing)

NIGHTWING AND HUNTRESS
DC Comics: May, 1998 - No. 4, Aug, 1998 ($1.95, limited series)
1-4-Grayson-s/Land & Sienkiewicz-a 2.50

NIGHTWINGS (See DC Science Fiction Graphic Novel)

NIKKI, WILD DOG OF THE NORTH (Disney, see Movie Comics)
Dell Publishing Co.: No. 1226, Sept, 1961
Four Color 1226-Movie, photo-c 4.60 13.75 55.00

NINE RINGS OF WU-TANG
Image Comics: July, 1999 - Present ($2.95)
Preview (7/99, $5.00, B&W) 5.00
1-5: 1-(11/99, $2.95) Clayton Henry-a 2.95
Tower Records Variant-c 5.00
Wizard #0 Prelude 1.00

1963
Image Comics (Shadowline Ink): Apr, 1993 - No. 6, Oct, 1993 ($1.95, lim. series)
1-6: Alan Moore scripts; Veitch, Bissette & Gibbons-a(p) 2.00
1-Gold 3.00
NOTE: ***Bissette*** *a-2-4;* ***Gibbons*** *a-1i, 2i, 6i; c-2.*

1984 (Magazine) (1994 #11 on)
Warren Publishing Co.: June, 1978 - No. 10, Jan, 1980 ($1.50)
1-Nino-a in all 2.00 6.00 18.00
2-10 1.50 4.50 12.00
NOTE: ***Alacla*** *a-1-3, 5i.* ***Corben*** *a-1-8; c-1, 2.* ***Thorne*** *a-7-10.* ***Wood*** *a-1, 2, 5i.*

1994 (Formerly 1984) (Magazine)
Warren Publishing Co.: No. 11, Feb, 1980 - No. 29, Feb, 1983
11-29: 27-The Warhawks return 1.00 3.00 8.00
NOTE: ***Corben*** *c-26.* ***Nino*** *a-11-19, 20(2), 21, 25, 26, 28; c-21.* ***Redondo*** *c-20.* ***Thorne*** *a-11-14, 17-21, 25, 26, 28, 29.*

NINE VOLT
Image Comics (Top Cow Productions): July, 1997 - No. 4, Oct, 1997 ($2.50)
1-4 2.50

NINJA HIGH SCHOOL (1st series)
Antarctic Press: 1986 - No. 3, Aug, 1987 (B&W)
1-Ben Dunn-s/c/a; early Manga series 1.85 5.50 15.00
2,3 1.25 3.75 10.00

NINJAK (See Bloodshot #6, 7 & Deathmate)
Valiant/Acclaim Comics (Valiant) No. 16 on: Feb, 1994 - No. 26, Nov. 1995 ($2.25/$2.50)
1 ($3.50)-Chromium-c; Quesada-c/a(p) in #1-3 3.50
1-Gold 5.00
2-13: 3-Batman, Spawn & Random (from X-Factor) app. as costumes at party

Nocturnals Troll Bridge nn © Dan Brereton

Northwest Mounties #3 © STJ

Nova #19 © MAR

GD2.0 FN6.0 NM9.4

(cameo). 4-w/bound-in trading card. 5,6-X-O app. 2.50
0,00,14-26: 14-(4/95)-Begin $2.50-c. 0-(6/95, $2.50). 00-(6/95, $2.50) 2.50
Yearbook 1 (1994, $3.95) 4.00

NINJAK
Acclaim Comics (Valiant Heroes): V2#1, Mar, 1997 -No. 12, Feb, 1998 ($2.50)
V2#1-12: 1-Intro new Ninjak; 1st app. Brutakon; Kurt Busiek scripts begin; painted variant-c exists. 2-1st app. Karnivor & Zeer. 3-1st app. Gigantik, Shurikai, & Nixie. 4-Origin; 1st app. Yasuiti Motomiya; intro The Dark Dozen; Colin King (original Ninjak) cameo. 9-Copycat-c 2.50

NINTENDO COMICS SYSTEM (Also see Adv. of Super Mario Brothers)
Valiant Comics: Feb, 1990 - No. 9, Oct, 1991 ($4.95, card stock-c, 68pgs.)
1-9: 1-Featuring Game Boy, Super Mario, Clappwall. 3-Layton-c. 5-8-Super Mario Bros. 9-Dr. Mario 1st app. 5.00

N.I.O.
Acclaim Comics: Nov, 1998 - No. 4, Feb, 1999 ($2.50, limited series)
1-4-Bury-s 2.50

NOAH'S ARK
Spire Christian Comics/Fleming H. Revell Co.: 1973 (35/49¢)
nn-By Al Hartley 2.40 6.00

NOBODY (Amado, Cho & Adlard's...)
Oni Press: Nov, 1998 - No. 4, Feb, 1999 ($2.95. B&W, mini-series)
1-4 3.00

NOCTURNALS, THE
Malibu Comics (Bravura): Jan, 1995 - No. 6, Aug, 1995 ($2.95, limited series)
1-6: Dan Brereton painted-c/a & scripts 3.00
1-Glow-in-the-Dark premium edition 5.00
Black Planet TPB ('98, $19.95, Oni Press) r/#1-6 20.00

NOCTURNALS: TROLL BRIDGE
Oni Press: Oct, 2000 ($4.95, B&W & orange, one-shot)
nn-Brereton-s/painted-c; art by Brereton, Chin, Art Adams, Sakai, Timm, Warren, Thompson, Purcell, Stephens and others 5.00

NOCTURNALS, THE :WITCHING HOUR
Dark Horse Comics: May 1998 ($4.95, one-shot)
1-Brereton-s/painted-a; reprints DHP stories + 8 new pgs. 5.00

NOCTURNE
Marvel Comics: June, 1995 - No. 4, Sept. 1995 ($1.50, limited series)
1-4 2.00

NO ESCAPE (Movie)
Marvel Comics: June, 1994 - No. 3, Aug, 1994 ($1.50)
1-3: Based on movie 2.00

NOMAD (See Captain America #180)
Marvel Comics: Nov, 1990 - No. 4, Feb, 1991 ($1.50, limited series)
1-4: 1,4-Captain America app. 2.00

NOMAD
Marvel Comics: V2#1, May, 1992 - No. 25, May, 1994 ($1.75)
V2#1-25: 1-Has gatefold-c w/map/wanted poster. 4-Deadpool x-over. 5-Punisher vs. Nomad-c/story. 6-Punisher & Daredevil-c/story cont'd in Punisher War Journal #48. 7-Gambit-c/story. 10-Red Wolf app. 21-Man-Thing-c/story. 25-Bound-in trading card sheet 2.00

NOMAN (See Thunder Agents)
Tower Comics: Nov, 1966 - No. 2, March, 1967 (25¢, 68 pgs.)
1-Wood/Williamson-c; Lightning begins; Dynamo cameo; Kane-a(p) & Whitney-a 7.25 21.75 80.00
2-Wood-c only; Dynamo x-over; Whitney-a 4.55 13.65 50.00

NONE BUT THE BRAVE (See Movie Classics)

NOODNIK COMICS (See Pinky the Egghead)
Comic Media/Mystery/Biltmore: Dec, 1953; No. 2, Feb, 1954 - No. 5, Aug, 1954
3-D(1953, 25¢; Comic Media)(#1)-Came w/glasses 33.00 99.00 265.00
2-5 6.40 19.25 45.00

GD2.0 FN6.0 NM9.4

NORMALMAN (See Cerebus the Aardvark #55, 56)
Aardvark-Vanaheim/Renegade Press #6 on: Jan, 1984 - No. 12, Dec, 1985 ($1.70/$2.00)
1-12: 1-Jim Valentino-c/a in all. 6-12 ($2.00, B&W): 10-Cerebus cameo; Sim-a (2 pgs.) 2.25
...3-D 1 (Annual, 1986, $2.25) 2.25

NORMALMAN-MEGATON MAN SPECIAL
Image Comics: Aug, 1994 ($2.50, color)
1 2.50

NORTH AVENUE IRREGULARS (See Walt Disney Showcase #49)

NORTHSTAR
Marvel Comics: Apr, 1994 - No. 4, July, 1994 ($1.75, mini-series)
1-4: Character from Alpha Flight 2.00

NORTH TO ALASKA
Dell Publishing Co.: No. 1155, Dec, 1960
Four Color 1155-Movie, John Wayne photo-c 16.00 48.00 190.00

NORTHWEST MOUNTIES (Also see Approved Comics #12)
Jubilee Publications/St. John: Oct, 1948 - No. 4, July, 1949
1-Rose of the Yukon by Matt Baker; Walter Johnson-a; Lubbers-c 47.00 142.00 425.00
2-Baker-a; Lubbers-c. Ventrilo app. 40.00 120.00 320.00
3-Bondage-c, Baker-a; Sky Chief, K-9 app. 40.00 120.00 340.00
4-Baker-c/a(2 pgs.); Blue Monk & The Desperado app. 40.00 120.00 340.00

NO SLEEP 'TIL DAWN
Dell Publishing Co.: No. 831, Aug, 1957
Four Color 831-Movie, Karl Malden photo-c 5.85 17.50 70.00

NOSTALGIA ILLUSTRATED
Marvel Comics: Nov, 1974 - V2#8, Aug, 1975 (B&W, 76 pgs.)
V1#1 2.80 8.40 28.00
V1#2, V2#1-8 1.85 5.50 15.00

NOT BRAND ECHH (Brand Echh #1-4; See Crazy, 1973)
Marvel Comics Group (LMC): Aug, 1967 - No. 13, May, 1969 (1st Marvel parody book)
1: 1-8 are 12¢ issues 4.10 12.30 45.00
2-8: 3-Origin Thor, Hulk & Capt. America; Monkees, Alfred E. Neuman cameo. 4-X-Men app. 5-Origin/intro. Forbush Man. 7-Origin Fantastical-4 & Stupor-man. Beatles cameo; X-Men satire; last 12¢-c 2.50 7.50 25.00
9-13 (25¢, 68 pgs., all Giants) 9-Beatles cameo. 10-All-r; The Old Witch, Crypt Keeper & Vault Keeper cameos. 12,13-Beatles cameo 3.20 9.60 35.00
NOTE: ***Colan** a(p)-4, 5, 8, 9, 13. **Everett** a-1i. **Kirby** a(p)-1, 3, 5-7, 10r; c-1p. **J. Severin** a-1; c-3, 6-8, 11. **M. Severin** a-1-13; c-2, 9, 10, 12, 13. **Sutton** a-3, 4, 5i, 6i, 8, 9, 10r, 11-13; c-5. Archie satire in #9. Avengers satire in #8, 12.*

NOTHING CAN STOP THE JUGGERNAUT
Marvel Comics: 1989 ($3.95)
1-r/Amazing Spider-Man #229 & 230 4.00

NO TIME FOR SERGEANTS (TV)
Dell Publ. Co.: No. 914, July, 1958; Feb-Apr, 1965 - No. 3, Aug-Oct, 1965
Four Color 914 (Movie)-Toth-a; Andy Griffith photo-c 9.00 27.00 110.00
1(2-4/65) (TV): Photo-c 4.60 13.75 55.00
2,3 (TV): Photo-c 4.10 12.30 45.00

NOVA (The Man Called... No. 22-25)(See New Warriors)
Marvel Comics Group: Sept, 1976 - No. 25, May, 1979
1-Origin/1st app. Nova 1.50 4.50 12.00
2-4,12: 4-Thor x-over. 12-Spider-Man x-over 2.40 6.00
5-11 5.00
13-(Regular 30¢ edition)(9/77) Intro Crime-Buster. 4.00
13-(35¢-c variant, limited distribution) 2.40 6.00
14-24: 18-Yellow Claw app. 19-Wally West (Kid Flash) cameo 4.00
25-Last issue 5.00
NOTE: ***Austin** c-21i, 23i. **John Buscema** a(p)-1-3, 8, 21; c-1p, 2, 15. **Infantino** a(p)-15-20, 22-25; c-17-20, 21p, 23p, 24p. **Kirby** c-4p, 5, 7. **Nebres** c-25i. **Simonson** a-23i.*

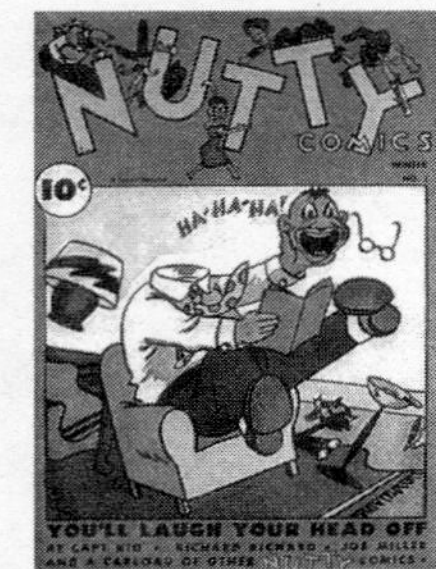

Nutty Comics #1 © FAW

Nyoka, the Jungle Girl #66 © FAW

Oaky Doaks #1 © EAS

NOVA
Marvel Comics: Jan, 1994 - June, 1995 ($1.75/$1.95)
(Started as 4-part mini-series)

1-($2.95, 52 pgs.)-Collector's Edition w/gold foil-c; new Nova costume 3.00
1-($2.25, 52 pgs.)-Newsstand Edition w/o foil-c 2.25
2-18: 3-Spider-Man-c/story. 5-Stan Lee app. 5-Bound-in card sheet. 13-Firestar & Night Thrasher app.14-Darkhawk 2.00

NOVA
Marvel Comics: May, 1999 - No. 7, Nov, 1999 ($2.99/$1.99)

1-($2.99) Larsen-s/Bennett-a; wraparound-c by Larsen 3.00
2-7-($1.99): 2-Two covers; Capt. America app. 5-Spider-Man. 7-Venom 2.00

NOW AGE ILLUSTRATED (See Pendulum Illustrated Classics)

NOW AGE BOOKS ILLUSTRATED (See Pendulum Illustrated Classics)

NTH MAN THE ULTIMATE NINJA (See Marvel Comics Presents 25)
Marvel Comics: Aug, 1989 - No. 16, Sept, 1990 ($1.00)

1-16-Ninja mercenary. 8-Dale Keown's 1st Marvel work (1/90, pencils) 2.00

NUCLEUS (Also see Cerebus)
Heiro-Graphic Publications: May, 1979 ($1.50, B&W, adult fanzine)

1-Contains "Demonhorn" by Dave Sim; early app. of Cerebus The Aardvark (4 pg. story) 3.45 10.35 38.00

NUKLA
Dell Publishing Co.: Oct-Dec, 1965 - No. 4, Sept, 1966

	GD2.0	FN6.0	NM9.4
1-Origin & 1st app. Nukla (super hero)	3.65	11.00	40.00
2,3	2.50	7.50	25.00
4-Ditko-a, c(p)	3.20	9.60	35.00

NURSE BETSY CRANE (Formerly Teen Secret Diary)
Charlton Comics: V2#12, Aug, 1961 - V2#27, Mar, 1964 (See Soap Opera Romances)

V2#12-27 2.00 6.00 18.00

NURSE HELEN GRANT (See The Romances of...)

NURSE LINDA LARK (See Linda Lark)

NURSERY RHYMES
Ziff-Davis Publ. Co. (Approved Comics): No. 10, July-Aug, 1951 - No. 2, Winter, 1951 (Painted-c)

10 (#1), 2: 10-Howie Post-a 15.00 45.00 120.00

NURSES, THE (TV)
Gold Key: April, 1963 - No. 3, Oct, 1963 (Photo-c: #1,2)

	GD2.0	FN6.0	NM9.4
1	3.20	9.60	35.00
2,3	2.50	7.50	24.00

NUTS! (Satire)
Premiere Comics Group: March, 1954 - No. 5, Nov, 1954

	GD2.0	FN6.0	NM9.4
1-Hollingsworth-a	30.00	90.00	240.00
2,4,5: 5-Capt. Marvel parody	20.00	60.00	160.00
3-Drug "reefers" mentioned	20.00	60.00	160.00

NUTS (Magazine) (Satire)
Health Knowledge: Feb, 1958 - No. 2, April, 1958

	GD2.0	FN6.0	NM9.4
1	8.65	26.00	60.00
2	6.00	18.00	42.00

NUTS & JOLTS
Dell Publishing Co.: No. 22, 1941

Large Feature Comic 22 10.00 30.00 120.00

NUTSY SQUIRREL (Formerly Hollywood Funny Folks)(See Comic Cavalcade)
National Periodical Publications: #61, 9-10/54 - #69, 1-2/56; #70, 8-9/56 - #71, 10-11/56; #72, 11/57

	GD2.0	FN6.0	NM9.4
61-Mayer-a; Grossman-a in all	13.00	39.00	105.00
62-72: Mayer a-62,65,67-72	10.00	30.00	70.00

NUTTY COMICS
Fawcett Publications: Winter, 1946 (Funny animal)

1-Capt. Kidd story; 1 pg. Wolverton-a 12.50 37.50 100.00

NUTTY COMICS
Home Comics (Harvey Publications): 1945; No. 4, May-June, 1946 - No. 8, June-July, 1947 (No #2,3)

	GD2.0	FN6.0	NM9.4
nn-Helpful Hank, Bozo Bear & others (funny animal)	7.85	23.50	55.00
4	5.00	15.00	35.00
5-8: 5-Rags Rabbit begins(1st app.); infinity-c	4.65	14.00	28.00

NUTTY LIFE (Formerly Krazy Life #1; becomes Wotalife Comics #3 on)
Fox Features Syndicate: No. 2, Summer, 1946

2 10.00 30.00 75.00

NYOKA, THE JUNGLE GIRL (Formerly Jungle Girl; see The Further Adventures of..., Master Comics #50 & XMas Comics)
Fawcett Publications: No. 2, Winter, 1945 - No. 77, June, 1953 (Movie serial)

	GD2.0	FN6.0	NM9.4
2	55.00	165.00	500.00
3	33.00	98.00	260.00
4,5	28.00	84.00	225.00
6-11,13,14,16-18-Krigstein-a: 17-Sam Spade ad by Lou Fine	20.00	60.00	160.00
12,15,19,20	18.00	53.00	140.00
21-30: 25-Clayton Moore photo-c?	12.00	36.00	95.00
31-40	10.00	30.00	75.00
41-50	8.65	26.00	60.00
51-60	6.40	19.25	45.00
61-77	5.70	17.00	40.00

NOTE: *Photo-c from movies 25, 30-70, 72, 75-77. Bondage c-4, 5, 7, 8, 14, 24.*

NYOKA, THE JUNGLE GIRL (Formerly Zoo Funnies; Space Adventures #23 on)
Charlton Comics: No. 14, Nov, 1955 - No. 22, Nov, 1957

	GD2.0	FN6.0	NM9.4
14	10.00	30.00	80.00
15-22	8.65	26.00	60.00

OAKLAND PRESS FUNNYBOOK, THE
The Oakland Press: 9/17/78 - 4/13/80 (16 pgs.) (Weekly)
Full color in comic book form; changes to tabloid size 4/20/80-on

Contains Tarzan by Manning, Marmaduke, Bugs Bunny, etc. (low distribution); 9/23/79 - 4/13/80 contain Buck Rogers by Gray Morrow & Jim Lawrence 2.00

OAKY DOAKS (See Famous Funnies #190)
Eastern Color Printing Co.: July, 1942 (One Shot)

1 35.00 105.00 280.00

OBIE
Store Comics: 1953 (6¢)

1 4.15 12.50 25.00

OBJECTIVE FIVE
Image Comics: July, 2000 - Present ($2.95)

1-5-Lizalde-a 3.00

OBLIVION
Comico: Aug, 1995 - No. 3, May, 1996 ($2.50)

1-3: 1-Art Adams-c. 2-(1/96)-Bagged w/gaming card. 3-(5/96)-Darrow-c 2.50

OBNOXIO THE CLOWN (Character from Crazy Magazine)
Marvel Comics Group: April, 1983 (one-shot)

1-Vs. the X-Men 3.00

OCCULT FILES OF DR. SPEKTOR, THE
Gold Key/Whitman No. 25: Apr, 1973 - No. 24, Feb, 1977; No. 25, May, 1982 (Painted-c #1-24)

	GD2.0	FN6.0	NM9.4
1-1st app. Lakota; Baron Tibor begins	3.00	9.00	32.00
2-5: 3-Mummy-c/s. 5-Jekyll & Hyde-c/s	1.75	5.25	14.00
6-10: 6,9-Frankenstein. 8,9-Dracula c/s. 9.-Jekyll & Hyde c/s. 9,10-Mummy-c/s	1.25	3.75	10.00
11-13,15-17,19-22,24,25: 11-1st app. Spektor as Werewolf. 11-13-Werewolf-c/s 12,16-Frankenstein c/s. 17-Zombie/Voodoo-c. 19-Sea monster-c/s. 20-mummy-s. 21-Swamp monster c/s. 24-Dragon c/s.25-R/ #1 with line drawn-c	3.00	8.00	
14-Dr. Solar app.	1.85	5.50	15.00

Official Handbook of the Marvel Universe V1 #3 © MAR

Official True Crime Cases #25 © MAR

Oh My Goddess Part 9 #4 © Kosuke Fujishima

GD2.0 FN6.0 NM9.4

18,23-Dr. Solar cameo 1.25 3.70 10.00
22-Return of the Owl c/s 1.50 4.50 12.00
9(Modern Comics reprint, 1977)(exist?) 5.00
OTE: *Also see Dan Curtis, Golden Comics Digest 33, Gold Key Spotlight, Mystery Comics igest 5, & Spine Tingling Tales.*

DELL'S ADVENTURES IN 3-D (See Adventures in 3-D)

FFCASTES
larvel Comics (Epic Comics/Heavy Hitters): July, 1993 - No. 3, Sept, 1993 $1.95, limited series)
1-3: Mike Vosburg-c/a/scripts in all 2.00

FFICIAL CRISIS ON INFINITE EARTHS INDEX, THE
ndependent Comics Group (Eclipse): Mar, 1986 ($1.75)
1 5.00

FFICIAL CRISIS ON INFINITE EARTHS CROSSOVER INDEX, THE
ndependent Comics Group (Eclipse): July, 1986 ($1.75)
1-Perez-c. 5.00

FFICIAL DOOM PATROL INDEX, THE
ndependent Comics Group (Eclipse): Feb, 1986 - No. 2, Mar, 1986 ($1.50, mited series)
1,2: Byrne-c. 4.00

FFICIAL HANDBOOK OF THE CONAN UNIVERSE (See Handbook of...)

FFICIAL HANDBOOK OF THE MARVEL UNIVERSE, THE
larvel Comics Group: Jan, 1983 - No. 15, May, 1984 (Limited series)
1-Lists Marvel heroes & villains (letter A) 5.00
2-15: 2 (B-C, 3-(C-D). 4-(D-G). 5-(H-J), 6-(K-L). 7-(M). 8-(N-P); Punisher-c. 9-(Q-S), 10-(S). 11-(S-U). 12-(V-Z); Wolverine-c. 13,14-Book of the Dead. 15-Weaponry catalogue 4.00
OTE: ***Bolland** a-8. **Byrne** c/a(p)-1-14; c-15p. **Grell** a-6, 9. **Kirby** a-1, 3. **Layton** a-2, 5, 7. **lignola** a-3, 4, 5, 6, 8, 12. **Miller** a-4-6, 8, 10. **Nebres** a-3, 4, 8. **Redondo** a-3, 4, 8, 13, 14. **imonson** a-1, 4, 6-13. **Paul Smith** a-1-12. **Starlin** a-5, 7, 8, 10, 13, 14. **Steranko** a-8p. **Zeck**-2-4.*

FFICIAL HANDBOOK OF THE MARVEL UNIVERSE, THE
larvel Comics Group: Dec, 1985 - No. 20, Feb, 1988 ($1.50, maxi-series)
'2#1-Byrne-c 4.00
2-20: 2,3-Byrne-c 3.00
Trade paperback Vol. 1-10 ($6.95) 1.00 3.00 8.00
OTE: ***Art Adams** a-7, 8, 11, 12, 14. **Bolland** a-8, 10, 13. **Buckler** a-1, 3, 5, 10. **Buscema** a-1, , 8, 9, 10, 13, 14. **Byrne** a-1-14; c-1-11. **Ditko** a-1, 2, 4, 6, 7, 11, 13. a-7, 11. **Mignola** a-2, 4, 9, 1, 13. **Miller** a-2, 4, 12. **Simonson** a-1, 2, 4-13, 15. **Paul Smith** a-1-5, 7-12, 14. **Starlin** a-6, 8, , 12, 16. **Zeck** a-1-4, 6, 7, 9-14, 16.*

FFICIAL HANDBOOK OF THE MARVEL UNIVERSE, THE
larvel Comics: July, 1989 - No. 8, Mid-Dec, 1990 ($1.50, lim. series, 52 pgs.)
'3#1-8: 1-McFarlane-a (2 pgs.) 3.00

FFICIAL HAWKMAN INDEX, THE
ndependent Comics Group: Nov, 1986 - No. 2, Dec, 1986 ($2.00)
1,2 4.00

FFICIAL JUSTICE LEAGUE OF AMERICA INDEX, THE
ndependent Comics Group (Eclipse): April, 1986 - No. 8, Mar, 1987 ($2.00, axter paper)
1-8: 1,2-Perez-c. 2.40 6.00

FFICIAL LEGION OF SUPER-HEROES INDEX, THE
ndependent Comics Group (Eclipse): Dec, 1986 - No. 5, 1987 ($2.00, limited eries)(No Official in Title #2 on)
1-5: 4-Mooney-c 2.40 6.00

FFICIAL MARVEL INDEX TO MARVEL TEAM-UP
larvel Comics Group: Jan, 1986 - No. 6, 1987 ($1.25, limited series)
1-6 4.00

FFICIAL MARVEL INDEX TO THE AMAZING SPIDER-MAN
larvel Comics Group: Apr, 1985 - No. 9, Dec, 1985 ($1.25, limited series)
1 ($1.00)-Byrne-c. 4.00
2-9: 5,6,8,9-Punisher-c. 3.00

FFICIAL MARVEL INDEX TO THE AVENGERS, THE
Marvel Comics: Jun, 1987 - No. 7, Aug, 1988 ($2.95, limited series)
1-7 5.00

OFFICIAL MARVEL INDEX TO THE AVENGERS, THE
Marvel Comics: V2#1, Oct, 1994 - V2#6, 1995 ($1.95, limited series)
V2#1-#6 3.00

OFFICIAL MARVEL INDEX TO THE FANTASTIC FOUR
Marvel Comics Group: Dec, 1985 - No. 12, Jan, 1987 ($1.25, limited series)
1-12: 1-Byrne-c. 1,2-Kirby back-c (unpub. art) 3.00

OFFICIAL MARVEL INDEX TO THE X-MEN, THE
Marvel Comics: May, 1987 - No. 7, July, 1988 ($2.95, limited series)
1-7 5.00

OFFICIAL MARVEL INDEX TO THE X-MEN, THE
Marvel Comics: V2#1, Apr, 1994 - V2#5, 1994 ($1.95, limited series)
V2#1-5: 1-Covers X-Men #1-51. 2-Covers #52-122,Special #1,2,Giant-Size #1,2. 3-Byrne-c; covers #123-177, Annuals 3-7, Spec. Ed. #1. 4-Covers Uncanny X-Men #178-234, Annuals 8-12. 5-Covers #235-287, Annuals 13-15 3.00

OFFICIAL SOUPY SALES COMIC (See Soupy Sales)

OFFICIAL TEEN TITANS INDEX, THE
Indep. Comics Group (Eclipse): Aug, 1985 - No. 5, 1986 ($1.50, lim. series)
1-5 4.00

OFFICIAL TRUE CRIME CASES (Formerly Sub-Mariner #23; All-True Crime Cases #26 on)
Marvel Comics (OCI): No. 24, Fall, 1947 - No. 25, Winter, 1947-48
24(#1)-Burgos-a; Syd Shores-c 22.00 66.00 175.00
25-Syd Shores-c; Kurtzman's "Hey Look" 18.00 53.00 140.00

OF SUCH IS THE KINGDOM
George A. Pflaum: 1955 (15¢, 36 pgs.)
nn-Reprints from 1951 Treasure Chest 3.60 9.00 18.00

O.G. WHIZ (See Gold Key Spotlight #10)
Gold Key: 2/71 - No. 6, 5/72; No. 7, 5/78 - No. 11, 1/79 (No. 7: 52 pgs.)
1,2-John Stanley scripts 5.00 15.00 60.00
3-6(1972) 3.00 9.00 30.00
7-11(1978-79)-Part-r: 9-Tubby issue 1.75 5.25 14.00

OH, BROTHER! (Teen Comedy)
Stanhall Publ.: Jan, 1953 - No. 5, Oct, 1953
1-By Bill Williams 6.40 19.25 45.00
2-5 4.65 14.00 28.00

OH MY GODDESS! (Manga)
Dark Horse Comics: Aug, 1994 - No. 6, Jan, 1995 ($2.50, B&W, limited series)
1-6 3.00
... PART II 2/95 - No. 9, 9/95 ($2.50, B&W, lim.series) #1-9 3.00
... PART III 11/95 - No. 11, 9/96 ($2.95, B&W, lim. series) #1-11 3.00
... PART IV 12/96 - No. 8, 7/97 ($2.95, B&W, lim. series) #1-8 3.00
... PART V 9/97 - Np. 12, 8/98 ($2.95, B&W, lim. series)
1,2,5,8: 5-Ninja Master pt. 1 3.00
3,4,6,7,10-12-($3.95, 48 pgs.) 10-Fallen Angel. 11-Play The Game 4.00
9-($3.50) "It's Lonely At The Top" 3.50
... PART VI 10/98 - No. 5, 3/99 ($3.50/$2.95, B&W, lim. series)
1-($3.50) 3.50
2-6-($2.95)-6-Super Urd one-shot 3.00
... PART VII 5/99 - No. 8, 12/99 ($2.95, B&W, lim. series) #1-3 3.00
4-8-($3.50) 3.50
... PART VIII 1/00 - No. 6, 6/00 ($3.50, B&W, lim. series) #1-3,5,7 3.50
4-($2.95) "Hail To The Chief" begins 2.95
... PART IX 7/00 - No. 7, ($3.50/$2.99) #1-4: 3-Queen Sayoko 3.50
5-($2.99) 3.00

OH MY GOTH
Sirius Entertainment (Dog Star Press): 1998 - No. 4, 1999 ($2.95, B&W)
1-4-Voltaire-s/a 3.00
... Humans Suck! (2000 - No. 3) 1,2-Voltaire-s/a 2.95

OH SUSANNA (TV)

O.K. Comics #2 © UFS

The Omen #2 © Chaos!

100 Bullets #11 © Brian Azzarello & DC

GD2.0 FN6.0 NM9.4

Dell Publishing Co.: No. 1105, June-Aug, 1960 (Gale Storm)

Four Color 1105-Toth-a, photo-c 12.50 37.50 150.00

OINK: BLOOD AND CIRCUS
Kitchen Sink: 1998 - No. 4, July, 1998 ($4.95, limited series)

1-4-John Mueller-s/a 5.00

OKAY COMICS
United Features Syndicate: July, 1940

1-Captain & the Kids & Hawkshaw the Detective reprints
42.00 125.00 375.00

O.K. COMICS
United Features Syndicate/Hit Publications: July, 1940 - No. 2, Oct, 1940

1-Little Giant (w/super powers), Phantom Knight, Sunset Smith, & The Teller Twins begin 76.00 229.00 725.00
2 (Rare)-Origin Mister Mist by Chas. Quinlan 79.00 237.00 750.00

OKLAHOMA KID
Ajax/Farrell Publ.: June, 1957 - No. 4, 1958

1 10.00 30.00 80.00
2-4 6.40 19.25 45.00

OKLAHOMAN, THE
Dell Publishing Co.: No. 820, July, 1957

Four Color 820-Movie, photo-c 9.00 27.00 110.00

OKTANE
Dark Horse Comics: Aug, 1995 - Nov, 1995($2.50, color, limited series)

1-4-Gene Ha-a 2.50

OLD IRONSIDES (Disney)
Dell Publishing Co.: No. 874, Jan, 1958

Four Color 874-Movie w/Johnny Tremain 5.85 17.50 70.00

OLD YELLER (Disney, see Movie Comics, and Walt Disney Showcase #25)
Dell Publishing Co.: No. 869, Jan, 1958

Four Color 869-Movie, photo-c 4.60 13.75 55.00

OMAC (One Man Army; ...Corps. #4 on; also see Kamandi #59 & Warlord) (See Cancelled Comic Cavalcade)
National Periodical Publications: Sept-Oct, 1974 - No. 8, Nov-Dec, 1975

1-Origin 2.00 6.00 18.00
2-8: 8-2 pg. Neal Adams ad 1.00 3.00 9.00
NOTE: ***Kirby*** *a-1-8p; c-1-7p.* ***Kubert*** *c-8.*

OMAC: ONE MAN ARMY CORPS
DC Comics: 1991 - No. 4, 1991 ($3.95, B&W, mini-series, mature, 52 pgs.)

Book One - Four: John Byrne-c/a & scripts 4.00

O'MALLEY AND THE ALLEY CATS
Gold Key: April, 1971 - No. 9, Jan, 1974 (Disney)

1 2.30 7.00 20.00
2-9 1.50 4.50 12.00

OMEGA ELITE
Blackthorne Publishing: 1987 ($1.25)

1-Starlin-c 3.00

OMEGA MEN, THE (See Green Lantern #141)
DC Comics: Dec, 1982 - No. 38, May, 1986 ($1.00/$1.50; Baxter paper)

1,20: 20-2nd full Lobo story 3.00
2,4-9,11-19,21-25,28-30,32,33,36,38: 2-Origin Broot. 5,9-2nd & 3rd app. Lobo (cameo, 2 pgs. each). 7-Origin The Citadel. 19-Lobo cameo. 30-Intro new Primus 2.00
3-1st app. Lobo (5 pgs.)(6/83); Lobo-c 1.00 2.80 7.00
10-1st full Lobo story 5.00
26,27,31,34,35: 26,27-Alan Moore scripts. 31-Crisis x-over. 34,35-Teen Titans x-over 3.00
37-1st solo Lobo story (8 pg. back-up by Giffen) 4.00
Annual 1(11/84, 52 pgs.), 2(11/85) 3.00
NOTE: ***Giffen*** *c/a-1-6p.* ***Morrow*** *a-24r.* ***Nino*** *c/a-16, 21; a-Annual 1i.*

OMEGA THE UNKNOWN
Marvel Comics Group: March, 1976 - No. 10, Oct, 1977

1-1st app. Omega 1.00 3.00 8.00
2,3-(Regular 25¢ editions). 2-Hulk-c/story. 3-Electro-c/story. 5.00
2,3-(30¢-c variants, limited distribution) 1.00 3.00 8.00
4-10: 8-1st app. 2nd Foolkiller (Greg Salinger), 1 panel only (cameo). 9-Regular 30¢ edition)(7/77)-1st full app. 2nd Foolkiller 5.00
9-(35¢-c variant, limited distribution) 1.00 3.00 8.00
NOTE: ***Kane*** *c(p)-3, 5, 8, 9.* ***Mooney*** *a-1-3, 4p, 5, 6p, 7, 8i, 9, 10.*

OMEN
Northstar Publishing: 1989 - No. 3, 1989 ($2.00, B&W, mature)

1-Tim Vigil-c/a in all 1.00 2.80 7.00
1, (2nd printing) 3.00
2,3 5.00

OMEN, THE
Chaos! Comics: May, 1998 - No. 5, Sept, 1998 ($2.95, limited series)

1-5: 1-Six covers, ...: Vexed (10/98, $2.95) Chaos! characters appear 3.00

OMNI MEN
Blackthorne Publishing: 1987 - No. 3, 1987 ($1.25)

1-3 2.00

ONE, THE
Marvel Comics (Epic Comics): July, 1985 - No. 6, Feb, 1986 (Limited series, mature)

1-6: Post nuclear holocaust super-hero. 2-Intro The Other 2.00

ONE-ARM SWORDSMAN, THE
Victory Prod./Lueng's Publ. #4 on: 1987 - No. 12, 1990 ($2.75/$1.80, 52pgs.)

1-3 ($2.75) 2.75
4-12: 4-6-$1.80-c. 7-12-$2.00-c 2.00

ONE HUNDRED AND ONE DALMATIANS (Disney, see Cartoon Tales, Movie Comics, and Walt Disney Showcase #9, 51)
Dell Publishing Co.: No. 1183, Mar, 1961

Four Color 1183-Movie 10.00 30.00 120.00

101 DALMATIONS (Movie)
Disney Comics: 1991 (52 pgs., graphic novel)

nn-($4.95, direct sales)-r/movie adaptation & more 5.00
1-($2.95, newsstand edition) 3.00

101 WAYS TO END THE CLONE SAGA (See Spider-Man)
Marvel Comics: Jan, 1997 ($2.50, one-shot)

1 2.50

100 BULLETS
DC Comics (Vertigo): Aug, 1999 - Present ($2.50)

1-Azzarello-s/Risso-a/Dave Johnson-c 4.00
2-5 3.00
6-20 2.50
First Shot, Last Call TPB (2000, $9.95) r/#1-5, Vertigo Winter's Edge #3 9.95

100 PAGES OF COMICS
Dell Publishing Co.: 1937 (Stiff covers, square binding)

101(Found on back cover)-Alley Oop, Wash Tubbs, Capt. Easy, Og Son of Fire, Apple Mary, Tom Mix, Dan Dunn, Tailspin Tommy, Doctor Doom
158.00 474.00 1500.00

100 PAGE SUPER SPECTACULAR (See DC 100 Page...)

100% TRUE?
DC Comics (Paradox Press): Summer 1996 - No. 2 ($4.95, B&W)

1,2-Reprints stories from various Paradox Press books. 5.00

$1,000,000 DUCK (See Walt Disney Showcase #5)

ONE MILLION YEARS AGO (Tor #2 on)
St. John Publishing Co.: Sept, 1953

1-Origin & 1st app. Tor; Kubert-c/a; Kubert photo inside front cover
20.00 60.00 160.00

ONE SHOT (See Four Color...)

1001 HOURS OF FUN

Oni Double Feature #13 © Oni Press

Operation Peril #11 © ACG

Original Dick Tracy #2 © Tribune Media Services

GD2.0 FN6.0 NM9.4

ell Publishing Co.: No. 13, 1943
rge Feature Comic 13 (nn)-Puzzles & games; by A.W. Nugent. This book was bound as #13 w/Large Feature Comics in publisher's files 27.00 81.00 190.00

NE TRICK RIP OFF, THE (See Dark Horse Presents)

NI DOUBLE FEATURE (See Clerks: The Comic Book and Jay & Silent Bob)
ni Press: Jan, 1998 - No. 13, Sept, 1999 ($2.95, B&W)
-Jay & Silent Bob; Kevin Smith-s/Matt Wagner-a 1.25 3.75 10.00
-2nd printing 3.00
-11,13: 2,3-Paul Pope-s/a. 3,4-Nixey-s/a. 4,5-Sienkewicz-s/a. 6,7-Gaiman-s. 9-Bagge-c. 13-All Paul Dini-s; Jingle Belle 3.00
2-Jay & Silent Bob as Bluntman & Chronic; Smith-s/Allred-a 5.00

NIGAMI (See Warrior Nun Areala: Black & White)
ntarctic Press: Apr, 1998 - No. 3, July, 1998 ($2.95, B&W, limited series)
-3-Michel Lacombe-s/a 3.00

NSLAUGHT: EPILOGUE
arvel Comics: Feb, 1997 ($2.95, one-shot)
-Hama-s/Green-a; Xavier-c; Bastion-app. 3.00

NSLAUGHT: MARVEL
arvel Comics: Oct, 1996 ($3.95, one-shot)
-Conclusion to Onslaught x-over; wraparound-c 1.00 2.80 7.00

NSLAUGHT: X-MEN
arvel Comics: Aug, 1996 ($3.95, one-shot)
-Mark Waid & Scott Lobdell script; Fantastic Four & Avengers app.; Xavier as Onslaught 5.00
-Variant-c 1.50 4.50 12.00

N STAGE
ell Publishing Co.: No. 1336, Apr-June, 1962
ur Color 1336-Not by Leonard Starr 4.10 12.30 45.00

N THE DOUBLE (Movie)
ell Publishing Co.: No. 1232, Sept-Nov, 1961
ur Color 1232 4.10 12.30 45.00

N THE ROAD WITH ANDRAE CROUCH
ire Christian Comics (Fleming H. Revell): 1973, 1977 (39¢)
2.40 6.00

N THE SPOT (Pretty Boy Floyd…)
wcett Publications: Fall, 1948
-Pretty Boy Floyd photo on-c; bondage-c 34.00 101.00 270.00

NYX OVERLORD
arvel Comics (Epic): Oct, 1992 - No. 4, Jan, 1993 ($2.75, mini-series)
-4: Moebius scripts 2.75

PEN SPACE
arvel Comics: Mid-Dec, 1989 - No. 4, Aug, 1990 ($4.95, bi-monthly, 68 pgs.)
-4: 1-Bill Wray-a; Freas-c 5.00
-(1999) Wizard supplement; unpubl. early Alex Ross-a; new Ross-c 2.00

PERATION BIKINI (See Movie Classics)

PERATION BUCHAREST (See The Crusaders)

PERATION CROSSBOW (See Movie Classics)

PERATION: KNIGHTSTRIKE (See Knightstrike)
age Comics (Extreme Studios): May, 1995 - No.3, July, 1995 ($2.50)
-3 2.50

PERATION PERIL
nerican Comics Group (Michel Publ.): Oct-Nov, 1950 - No. 16, Apr-May, 53 (#1-5: 52 pgs.)
-Time Travelers, Danny Danger (by Leonard Starr) & Typhoon Tyler (by Ogden Whitney) begin 38.00 113.00 300.00
-War-c 23.00 68.00 180.00
-War-c; horror story 20.00 60.00 160.00
,5-Sci/fi-c/story 22.00 66.00 175.00
6-10: 6,8,9,10-Sci/fi-c. 6-Dinosaur-c. 7-Sabretooth-c 19.00 56.00 150.00
11,12-War-c; last Time Travelers 12.50 37.50 100.00
13-16: All war format 9.30 28.00 65.00
NOTE: *Starr a-2, 5. Whitney a-1, 2, 5-10, 12; c-1, 3, 5, 8, 9.*

OPERATION: STORMBREAKER
Acclaim Comics (Valiant Heroes): Aug, 1997 ($3.95, one-shot)
1-Waid/Augustyn-s, Braithwaite-a 4.00

OPTIC NERVE
Drawn and Quarterly: Apr, 1995 - Present ($2.95, bi-annual)
1-7: Adrian Tomine-c/a/scripts in all 3.00
32 Stories-($9.95, trade paperback)-r/Optic Nerve mini-comics 10.00
32 Stories-($29.95, hardcover)-r/Optic Nerve mini-comics; signed & numbered 30.00

ORAL ROBERTS' TRUE STORIES (Junior Partners #120 on)
TelePix Publ. (Oral Roberts' Evangelistic Assoc./Healing Waters): 1956 (no month) - No. 119, 7/59 (15¢)(No. 102: 25¢)
V1#1(1956)-(Not code approved)- "The Miracle Touch" 20.00 60.00 160.00
102-(Only issue approved by code, 10/56) "Now I See" 12.00 36.00 95.00
103-119: 115-(114 on inside) 8.65 26.00 60.00
NOTE: *Also see Happiness & Healing For You.*

ORANGE BIRD, THE
Walt Disney Educational Media Co.: No date (1980) (36 pgs.; in color; slick cover)
nn-Included with educational kit on foods, …in Nutrition Adventures nn (1980) …and the Nutrition Know-How Revue nn (1983) 3.00

ORB (Magazine)
Orb Publishing: 1974 - No. 6, Mar/Apr 1976 (B&W/color)
1-1st app. Northern Light & Kadaver, both series begin 2.50 7.50 24.00
2,3 (72 pgs.) 2.00 6.00 16.00
4-6 (60 pgs.): 4,5-origin Northern Light 1.50 4.50 12.00
NOTE: *Allison a-1-3. Gene Day a-1-6. P. Hsu a-4-6. Steacy s/a-3,4.*

ORBIT
Eclipse Books: 1990 - No. 3, 1990 ($4.95, 52 pgs., squarebound)
1-3: Reprints from Isaac Asimov's Science Fiction Magazine; 1-Dave Stevens-c, Bolton-a. 3-Bolton-c/a, Yeates-a 5.00

ORIENTAL HEROES
Jademan Comics: Aug, 1988 - No. 55, Feb, 1993 ($1.50/$1.95, 68pgs.)
1-55 2.00

ORIGINAL ASTRO BOY, THE
Now Comics: Sept, 1987 - No. 20, Jun, 1989 ($1.50/$1.75)
1-20-All have Ken Steacy painted-c/a 3.00

ORIGINAL BLACK CAT, THE
Recollections: Oct. 6, 1988 - No. 9, 1992 ($2.00, limited series)
1-9: Elias-r; 1-Bondage-c. 2-Murphy Anderson-c 3.00

ORIGINAL DICK TRACY, THE
Gladstone Publishing: Sept, 1990 - No. 5, 1991 ($1.95, bi-monthly, 68pgs.)
1-5: 1-Vs. Pruneface. 2-& the Evil influence; begin $2.00-c 2.00
NOTE: *#1 reprints strips 7/16/43 - 9/30/43. #2 reprints strips 12/1/46 - 2/2/47. #3 reprints 8/31/46 - 11/14/46. #4 reprints 9/17/45 - 12/23/45. #5 reprints 6/10/46 - 8/28/46.*

ORIGINAL DOCTOR SOLAR, MAN OF THE ATOM, THE
Valiant: Apr, 1995 ($2.95, one-shot)
1-Reprints Doctor Solar, Man of the Atom #1,5; Bob Fugitani-r; Paul Smith-c; afterword by Seaborn Adamson 3.00

ORIGINAL E-MAN AND MICHAEL MAUSER, THE
First Comics: Oct, 1985 - No. 7, April, 1986 ($1.75, Baxter paper)
1-7: 1-Has r-/Charlton's E-Man, Vengeance Squad. 2-Shows #4 in indicia by mistake. 7 ($2.00, 44pgs.)-Staton-a 2.00

ORIGINAL GHOST RIDER, THE
Marvel Comics: July, 1992 - No. 20, Feb, 1994 ($1.75)

Orion #1 © DC

Oscar Comics #6 © MAR

Our Army at War #2 © DC

GD2.0 FN6.0 NM9.4

1-20: 1-7-r/Marvel Spotlight #5-11 by Ploog w/new-c. 3-New Phantom Rider (former Night Rider) back-ups begin by Ayers. 4-Quesada-c(p). 8-Ploog-c. 8,9-r/Ghost Rider #1,2. 10-r/Marvel Spotlight #12. 11-18,20-r/Ghost Rider #3-12. 19-r/Marvel Two-in-One #8 — 2.00

ORIGINAL GHOST RIDER RIDES AGAIN, THE
Marvel Comics: July, 1991 - No. 7, Jan, 1992, ($1.50, limited series, 52 pgs.)

1-7: 1-R/Ghost Rider #68(origin),69 w/covers. 2-7: R/ G.R. #70-81 w/covers — 2.00

ORIGINAL MAGNUS ROBOT FIGHTER, THE
Valiant: Apr, 1995 ($2.95, one-shot)

1-Reprints Magnus, Robot Fighter 4000 #2; Russ Manning-r; Rick Leonardi-c; afterword by Seaborn Adamson — 3.00

ORIGINAL NEXUS GRAPHIC NOVEL (See First Comics Graphic Novel #19)

ORIGINAL SHIELD, THE
Archie Enterprises, Inc.: Apr, 1984 - No. 4, Oct, 1984

1-4: 1,2-Origin Shield; Ayers p-1-4, Nebres c-1,2 — 4.00

ORIGINAL SWAMP THING SAGA, THE (See DC Special Series #2, 14, 17, 20)

ORIGINAL TUROK, SON OF STONE, THE
Valiant: Apr, 1995 - No. 2, May, 1995 ($2.95, limited series)

1,2: 1-Reprints Turok, Son of Stone #24,25,42; Alberto Gioletti-r; Rags Morales-c; afterword by Seaborn Adamson. 2-Reprints Turok, Son of Stone #24,33; Gioletti-r; Mike McKone-c — 3.00

ORIGIN OF GALACTUS (See Fantastic Four #48-50)
Marvel Comics: Feb, 1996 ($2.50, one-shot)

1-Lee & Kirby reprints w/pin-ups — 2.50

ORIGIN OF THE DEFIANT UNIVERSE, THE
Defiant Comics: Feb, 1994 ($1.50, 20 pgs., one-shot)

1-David Lapham, Adam Pollina & Alan Weiss-a; Weiss-c — 5.00

NOTE: *The comic was originally published as Defiant Genesis and was distributed at the 1994 Philadelphia ComicCon.*

ORIGINS OF MARVEL COMICS (See Fireside Book Series)

ORION (Manga)
Dark Horse Comics: Sept, 1992 - No. 6, July, 1993 ($2.95/$3.95, B&W, bimonthly, limited series)

1-6:1,2,6-Squarebound): 1-Masamune Shirow-c/a/s in all — 4.00

ORION (See New Gods)
DC Comics: June, 2000 - Present ($2.50)

1-10-Simonson-s/a. 3-Back-up story w/Miller-a. 4-Gibbons-a back-up. 7-Chaykin back-up. 8-Loeb/Liefeld back-up — 2.50

OSBORNE JOURNALS (See Spider-Man titles)
Marvel Comics: Feb, 1997 ($2.95, one-shot)

1-Hotz-c/a — 3.00

OSCAR COMICS (Formerly Funny Tunes; Awful...#11 & 12) (Also see Cindy Comics)
Marvel Comics: No. 24, Spring, 1947 - No. 10, Apr, 1949; No. 13, Oct, 1949

	GD2.0	FN6.0	NM9.4
24(#1, Spring, 1947)	16.00	48.00	125.00
25(#2, Sum, 1947)-Wolverton-a plus Kurtzman's "Hey Look"	18.00	53.00	140.00
26(#3)-Same as regular #3 except #26 was printed over in black ink with #3 appearing on-c below the over print	10.00	30.00	80.00
3-9,13: 8-Margie app.	10.00	30.00	80.00
10-Kurtzman's "Hey Look"	12.00	36.00	95.00

OSWALD THE RABBIT (Also see New Fun Comics #1)
Dell Publishing Co.: No. 21, 1943 - No. 1268, 12-2/61-62 (Walter Lantz)

	GD2.0	FN6.0	NM9.4
Four Color 21(1943)	50.00	150.00	600.00
Four Color 39(1943)	35.00	105.00	420.00
Four Color 67(1944)	17.50	52.50	210.00
Four Color 102(1946)-Kelly-a, 1 pg.	15.00	45.00	180.00
Four Color 143,183	9.00	27.00	110.00
Four Color 225,273	5.00	15.00	60.00
Four Color 315,388	4.60	13.75	55.00
Four Color 458,507,549,593	3.20	9.60	35.00
Four Color 623,697,792,894,979,1268	3.00	9.00	30.00

OSWALD THE RABBIT (See The Funnies, March of Comics #7, 38, 53, 67, 81, 95, 111, 126, 141, 156, 171, 186, New Funnies & Super Book #8, 20)

OTHERS, THE
Image Comics (Shadowline Ink): 1995 - No. 3, 1995 ($2.50)

0 ($1.00)-16 pg. preview — 2.00
1-3 — 2.50

OTIS GOES TO HOLLYWOOD
Dark Horse Comics: Apr, 1997 - No.2, May, 1997 ($2.95, B&W, mini-series)

1,2-Fingerman-c/s/a — 3.00

OUR ARMY AT WAR (Becomes Sgt. Rock #302 on; also see Army At War)
National Periodical Publications: Aug, 1952 - No. 301, Feb, 1977

	GD2.0	FN6.0	NM9.4
1	129.00	386.00	1800.00
2	57.00	171.00	800.00
3,4: 4-Krigstein-a	46.00	138.00	600.00
5-7	40.00	120.00	480.00
8-11,14-Krigstein-a	37.00	112.00	450.00
12,15-20	31.00	93.00	350.00
13-Krigstein-c/a; flag-c	38.00	115.00	460.00
21-31: Last precode (2/55)	22.00	65.00	240.00
32-40	18.00	53.00	195.00
41-60: 51-1st S.A. issue	15.00	45.00	165.00
61-70: 67-Minor Sgt. Rock prototype	12.75	38.00	140.00
71-80	11.00	33.00	120.00
81- (4/59)-Sgt. Rocky of Easy Co. app. by Andru & Esposito-a/ Haney-s; (the last Sgt. Rock prototype)	180.00	540.00	2700.00
82-1st Sgt. Rock app., in name only, in Easy Co. story (6 panels) by Kanigher & Drucker	46.00	138.00	600.00
83-(6/59)-1st true Sgt. Rock app. in "The Rock and the Wall" by Kubert & Kanigher; (most similar to prototype in G.I. Combat #68)	129.00	386.00	1800.00
84-Kubert-c	25.50	76.00	280.00
85-Origin & 1st app. Ice Cream Soldier	34.00	102.00	405.00
86,87-Early Sgt. Rock; Kubert-a	24.50	74.00	270.00
88-1st Sgt. Rock-c; Kubert-c/a	28.00	85.00	310.00
89	23.00	68.00	250.00
90-Kubert-c/a; How Rock got his stripes	30.00	90.00	330.00
91-All-Sgt. Rock issue; Grandenetti-c/Kubert-a	52.00	156.00	675.00
92,94,96-99: 97-Regular Kubert-c begin	15.50	46.50	170.00
93-1st Zack Nolan	16.00	48.00	175.00
95,100: 95-1st app. Bulldozer	16.50	49.00	180.00
101,105,108,113,115: 101-1st app. Buster. 105-1st app. Junior. 113-1st app. Wildman & Jackie Johnson. 115-Rock revealed as orphan; 1st x-over Mlle. Marie. 1st Sgt. Rock's battle family	11.50	34.00	125.00
102-104,106,107,109,110,114,116-120: 104-Nurse Jane-c/s. 109-Pre Easy Co. Sgt. Rock-s. 118-Sunny injured	10.00	30.00	110.00
111-1st app. Wee Willie & Sunny	11.50	34.00	125.00
112-Classic Easy Co. roster-c	12.75	38.00	140.00
121-125,130-133,135-139,141-150: 138-1st Sparrow. 141-1st Shaker. 147,148-Rock becomes a General	6.35	19.00	70.00
126,129,134: 126-1st app. Canary; grey tone-c	7.25	21.75	80.00
127-2nd all-Sgt. Rock issue; 1st app. Little Sure	8.15	24.50	90.00
128-Training & origin Sgt. Rock; 1st Sgt. Krupp	23.00	68.00	250.00
140-3rd all-Sgt. Rock issue	6.80	20.50	75.00
151-Intro. Enemy Ace by Kubert (2/65)	34.00	102.00	405.00
152-4th all-Sgt. Rock issue	6.80	20.50	75.00
153-2nd app. Enemy Ace (4/65)	15.50	46.50	170.00
154,156,157,159-161,165-167: 157-2 pg. pin-up: 159-1st Nurse Wendy Winston-c/s. 165-2nd Iron Major	5.45	16.35	60.00
155-3rd app. Enemy Ace (6/65)(see Showcase)	11.00	33.00	120.00
158-Origin & 1st app. Iron Major(9/65), formerly Iron Captain	6.35	19.00	70.00
162,163-Viking Prince x-over in Sgt. Rock	5.90	17.75	65.00
164-Giant G-19	11.50	34.00	125.00
168-1st Unknown Soldier app.; referenced in Star-Spangled War Stories #157; (Sgt. Rock x-over) (6/66)	11.00	33.00	120.00

Our Fighting Forces #5 © DC

Our Flag Comics #1 © ACE

Our Love #1 © MAR

	GD2.0	FN6.0	NM9.4
169,170	5.00	15.00	55.00
171-176,178-181: 171-1st Mad Emperor	4.10	12.30	45.00
177-(80 pg. Giant G-32)	6.80	20.50	75.00
182,183,186-Neal Adams-a. 186-Origin retold	5.00	15.00	55.00
184,185,187,188,193-195,197-199: 184-Wee Willie dies	3.65	11.00	40.00
189,191,192,196: 189-Intro. The Teen-age Underground Fighters of Unit 3. 196-Hitler cameo	3.65	11.00	40.00
190-(80 pg. Giant G-44)	5.45	16.35	60.00
200-12 pg. Rock story told in verse; Evans-a	4.10	12.30	45.00
201,202,204-207: 201-Krigstein-r/#14. 204,205-All reprints; no Sgt. Rock. 207-Last 12¢ cover	2.50	7.50	25.00
203-(80 pg. Giant G-56)-All-r, Sgt. Rock story	5.00	15.00	55.00
208-215	2.30	7.00	20.00
216,229-(80 pg. Giants G-68, G-80): 216-Has G-58 on-c by mistake	4.55	13.65	50.00
217-219: 218-1st U.S.S. Stevens	2.00	6.00	18.00
220-Classic dinosaur/Sgt. Rock-c/s	2.50	7.50	25.00
221-228,230-234: 231-Intro/death Rock's brother. 234-Last 15¢ issue	2.00	6.00	16.00
235-239,241: 52 pg. Giants	2.40	7.35	22.00
240-Neal Adams-a; 52 pg. Giant	3.00	9.00	30.00
242-Also listed as **DC 100 Page Super Spectacular #9**; see for price			-
243-246: 244-(52 pgs.) no Adams-a	2.30	7.00	20.00
247-250,254-268,270: 247-Joan of Arc	1.75	5.25	14.00
251-253-Return of Iron Major	1.75	5.25	14.00
269,275-(100 pgs.)	3.20	9.60	35.00
271-274,276-279: 273-Crucifixion-c	1.50	4.50	12.00
280-(68 pgs.)-200th app. Sgt. Rock; reprints Our Army at War #81,83	2.50	7.50	25.00
281-299,301: 295-Bicentennial cover	1.25	3.75	10.00
300-Sgt. Rock-s by Kubert (2/77)	1.50	4.50	12.00

NOTE ***Alcala*** *a-251.* ***Drucker*** *a-27, 67, 68, 79, 82, 83, 96, 164, 177, 203, 212, 243r, 244, 269r, 275r, 280r.* ***Evans*** *a-165-175, 200, 266, 269, 270, 274, 276, 278, 280.* ***Glanzman*** *a-218, 220, 222, 223, 225, 227, 230-232, 238-241, 244, 247, 248, 256-259, 261, 265-267, 271, 282, 283, 298.* ***Grandenetti*** *c-91.* ***Grell*** *a-287.* ***Heath*** *a-50, 164, & most 176-281.* ***Kubert*** *a-38, 59, 67, 68 & most issues from 83-165, 233, 236, 267, 275, 300; c-84, 280.* ***Maurer*** *a-233, 237, 239, 240, 45, 280, 284, 288, 290, 291, 295.* ***Severin*** *a-236, 252, 265, 267, 269r, 272.* ***Toth*** *a-235, 241, 254.* ***Wildey*** *a-283-285, 287p.* ***Wood*** *a-249.*

OUR FIGHTING FORCES
National Per. Publ./DC Comics: Oct-Nov, 1954 - No. 181, Sept-Oct, 1978

	GD2.0	FN6.0	NM9.4
1-Grandenetti-c/a	80.00	240.00	1120.00
2	37.00	112.00	450.00
3-Kubert-c; last precode issue (3/55)	32.00	96.00	390.00
4,5	26.50	79.00	290.00
6-9: 7-1st S.A. issue	23.00	68.00	250.00
10-Wood-a	23.50	71.00	260.00
11-19	18.00	54.00	200.00
20-Grey tone-c (4/57)	20.50	61.00	225.00
21-30	12.75	38.00	140.00
31-40	12.00	36.00	130.00
41-Unknown Soldier tryout	14.50	43.50	160.00
42-44	10.00	30.00	110.00
45-Gunner & Sarge begins, end #94	34.00	102.00	405.00
46	14.50	43.50	160.00
47	10.00	30.00	110.00
48,50	8.15	24.50	90.00
49-1st Pooch	11.50	34.00	125.00
51-64: 51-Grey tone-c. 64-Last 10¢ issue	7.25	21.75	80.00
65-70	5.00	15.00	55.00
71-80: 71-Grey tone-c	3.65	11.00	40.00
81-90	3.20	9.60	35.00
91-98: 95-Devil-Dog begins, ends #98.	2.50	7.50	25.00
99-Capt. Hunter begins, ends #106	3.00	9.00	30.00
100	2.80	8.40	28.00
101-105,107-120: 116-Mlle. Marie app. 120-Last 12¢ issue	2.30	7.00	20.00
106-Hunters Hellcats begin	2.40	7.35	22.00
121,122: 121-Intro. Heller	2.30	7.00	20.00
123-Losers (Capt. Storm, Gunner & Sarge, Johnny Cloud) begin	4.10	12.30	45.00
124-132: 132-Last 15¢ issue	2.00	6.00	16.00
133-137 (Giants). 134-Toth-a	2.30	7.00	20.00
138-150: 146-Toth-a	1.50	4.50	12.00
151-162-Kirby a(p)	2.00	6.00	16.00
163-180	1.10	3.30	9.00
181-Last issue	1.50	4.50	12.00

NOTE: ***N. Adams*** *c-147.* ***Drucker*** *a-28, 37, 39, 42-44, 49, 53, 133r.* ***Evans*** *a-149, 164-174, 177-181.* ***Glanzman*** *a-125-128, 132, 134, 138-141, 143, 144.* ***Heath*** *a-2, 16, 18, 28, 41, 44, 49, 114, 135-138r; c-51.* ***Kirby*** *a-151-162p; c-152-159.* ***Kubert*** *c/a in many issues.* ***Maurer*** *a-135.* ***Redondo*** *a-166.* ***Severin*** *a-123-130, 131i, 132-150.*

OUR FIGHTING MEN IN ACTION (See Men In Action)

OUR FLAG COMICS
Ace Magazines: Aug, 1941 - No. 5, April, 1942

	GD2.0	FN6.0	NM9.4
1-Captain Victory, The Unknown Soldier (intro.) & The Three Cheers begin	263.00	790.00	2500.00
2-Origin The Flag (patriotic hero); 1st app?	116.00	348.00	1100.00
3-5: 5-Intro & 1st app. Mr. Risk	89.00	268.00	850.00

NOTE: ***Anderson*** *a-1, 4.* ***Mooney*** *a-1, 2; c-2.*

OUR GANG COMICS (With Tom & Jerry #39-59; becomes Tom & Jerry #60 on; based on film characters)
Dell Publishing Co.: Sept-Oct, 1942 - No. 59, June, 1949

	GD2.0	FN6.0	NM9.4
1-Our Gang & Barney Bear by Kelly, Tom & Jerry, Pete Smith, Flip & Dip, The Milky Way begin (all 1st app.)	83.00	250.00	1000.00
2-Benny Burro begins (#2 by Kelly)	42.00	125.00	500.00
3-5	28.00	83.00	330.00
6-Bumbazine & Albert only app. by Kelly	42.00	125.00	500.00
7-No Kelly story	22.00	65.00	260.00
8-Benny Burro begins by Barks	54.00	163.00	650.00
9-Barks-a(2): Benny Burro & Happy Hound; no Kelly story	48.00	144.00	575.00
10-Benny Burro by Barks	34.00	103.00	410.00
11-1st Barney Bear & Benny Burro by Barks (5-6/44); Happy Hound by Barks	48.00	144.00	575.00
12-20	22.00	65.00	260.00
21-30: 30-X-Mas-c	14.00	42.00	170.00
31-36-Last Barks issue	10.50	31.00	125.00
37-40	6.30	19.00	75.00
41-50	4.60	13.75	55.00
51-57	4.10	12.30	45.00
58,59-No Kelly art or Our Gang stories	3.65	11.00	40.00

NOTE: ***Barks*** *art in part only.* ***Barks*** *did not write Barney Bear stories #30-34. (See March of Comics #3, 26). Early issues have photo back-c.*

OUR LADY OF FATIMA
Catechetical Guild Educational Society: 3/11/55 (15¢) (36 pgs.)

	GD2.0	FN6.0	NM9.4
395	4.65	14.00	28.00

OUR LOVE (True Secrets #3 on? or Romantic Affairs #3 on?)
Marvel Comics (SPC): Sept, 1949 - No. 2, Jan, 1950

	GD2.0	FN6.0	NM9.4
1-Photo-c	12.50	37.50	100.00
2-Photo-c	8.65	26.00	60.00

OUR LOVE STORY
Marvel Comics Group: Oct, 1969 - No. 38, Feb, 1976

	GD2.0	FN6.0	NM9.4
1	4.10	12.30	45.00
2-4,6-8,10,11	2.30	7.00	20.00
5-Steranko-a	6.35	19.00	70.00
9,12-Kirby-a	2.50	7.50	25.00
13-(10/71, 52 pgs.)	3.20	9.60	35.00
14-New story by Gary Fredrich & Tarpe' Mills	2.50	7.50	23.00
15-20,27:27-Colan/Everett-a(r?); Kirby/Colletta-r	2.00	6.00	16.00
21-26,28-37:	1.50	4.50	12.00
38-Last issue	2.00	6.00	18.00

NOTE: ***J. Buscema*** *a-1-3, 5-7, 9, 13r, 16r, 19r(2), 21r, 22r(2), 23r, 34r, 35r; c-11, 13, 16, 22, 23, 24, 27, 35.* ***Colan*** *a-3-6, 21r(#6), 22r, 23r(#3), 24r(#4), 27; c-19.* ***Katz*** *a-17.* ***Maneely*** *a-13r.* ***Romita*** *a-13r; c-1, 2, 4-6.* ***Weiss*** *a-16, 17, 29r(#17).*

OUR MISS BROOKS
Dell Publishing Co.: No. 751, Nov, 1956

	GD2.0	FN6.0	NM9.4
Four Color 751-Photo-c	7.50	22.50	90.00

Outer Space #23 © CC

Outlaw Nation #1 © Delano & Sudzuka

Out of the Shadows #9 © STD

GD2.0 FN6.0 NM9.4 GD2.0 FN6.0 NM9.4

OUR SECRET (Exciting Love Stories)(Formerly My Secret)
Superior Comics Ltd.: No. 4, Nov, 1949 - No. 8, Jun, 1950

4-Kamen-a; spanking scene 18.00 53.00 140.00
5,6,8 10.00 30.00 70.00
7-Contains 9 pg. story intended for unpublished Ellery Queen #5; lingerie panels 10.00 30.00 80.00

OUTBREED 999
Blackout Comics: May, 1994 - No. 6, 1994 ($2.95)

1-6: 4-1st app. of Extreme Violet in 7 pg. backup story 3.00

OUTCAST, THE
Valiant: Dec, 1995 ($2.50, one-shot)

1-Breyfogle-a. 2.50

OUTCASTS
DC Comics: Oct, 1987 - No. 12, Sept, 1988 ($1.75, limited series)

1-12: John Wagner & Alan Grant scripts in all 2.00

OUTER LIMITS, THE (TV)
Dell Publishing Co.: Jan-Mar, 1964 - No. 18, Oct, 1969 (Most painted-c)

1 11.00 33.00 130.00
2-5 6.00 18.00 72.00
6-10 5.00 15.00 60.00
11-18: 17-Reprints #1. 18-r/#2 3.65 11.00 40.00

OUTER SPACE (Formerly This Magazine Is Haunted, 2nd Series)
Charlton Comics: No. 17, May, 1958 - No. 25, Dec, 1959; Nov, 1968

17-Williamson/Wood style art; not by them (Sid Check?) 14.00 41.00 110.00
18-20-Ditko-a 22.00 66.00 175.00
21-25: 21-Ditko-c 12.50 37.50 100.00
V2#1(11/68)-Ditko-a, Boyette-c 4.55 13.65 50.00

OUTER SPACE BABES, THE
Silhouette Studios: Feb, 1994 ($2.95)

V3#1 3.00

OUT FOR BLOOD
Dark Horse: Sept, 1999 - No. 4, Dec, 1999 ($2.95, B&W, limited series)

1-4-Kelley Jones-c; Erskine-a 2.95

OUTLANDERS (Manga)
Dark Horse Comics: Dec, 1988 - No. 33, Sep,1991 ($2.00-$2.50, B&W, 44pgs.)

1-33: Japanese Sci-fi manga 2.50

OUTLAW (See Return of the...)

OUTLAW FIGHTERS
Atlas Comics (IPC): Aug, 1954 - No. 5, Apr, 1955

1-Tuska-a 12.50 37.50 100.00
2-5: 5-Heath-c/a, 7 pgs. 8.65 26.00 60.00
NOTE: ***Heath** c/a-5. **Maneely** c-2. **Pakula** a-2. **Reinman** a-2. **Tuska** a-1, 2.*

OUTLAW KID, THE (1st Series; see Wild Western)
Atlas Comics (CCC No. 1-11/EPI No. 12-29): Sept, 1954 - No. 19, Sept, 1957

1-Origin; The Outlaw Kid & his horse Thunder begin; Black Rider app. 27.00 81.00 215.00
2-Black Rider app. 12.50 37.50 100.00
3-7,9: 3-Wildey-a(3) 11.00 33.00 90.00
8-Williamson/Woodbridge-a, 4 pgs. 12.00 36.00 95.00
10-Williamson-a 11.00 33.00 90.00
11-17,19: 13-Baker text illo. 15-Williamson text illo (unsigned) 8.65 26.00 60.00
18-Williamson/Mayo-a 10.00 30.00 70.00
NOTE: ***Berg** a-4, 7, 13. **Maneely** c-1-3, 5-8, 11-13, 15, 16, 18. **Pakula** a-3. **Severin** c-10, 17, 19. **Shores** a-1. **Wildey** a-1(3), 2-8, 10, 11, 12(4), 13(4), 15-19(4 each); c-4.*

OUTLAW KID, THE (2nd Series)
Marvel Comics Group: Aug, 1970 - No. 30, Oct, 1975

1-Reprints; 1-Orlando-r, Wildey-r(3) 2.50 7.50 25.00
2,3,9: 2-Reps. 3,9-Williamson-a(r) 2.00 6.00 16.00
4-7: 7-Last 15¢ issue 1.75 5.25 14.00
8-Double size (52 pgs.); Crandall-r 2.30 7.00 20.00
10-Origin 2.50 7.50 25.00
11-20: new-a in #10-16 1.75 5.25 14.00
21-30: 27-Origin-r/#10 1.10 3.30 9.00
NOTE: ***Ayers** a-10, 27r. **Berg** a-7, 25r. **Everett** a-2(2 pgs.). **Gil Kane** c-10, 11, 15, 27r, 28. **Roussos** a-10i, 27i(r). **Severin** c-1, 9, 20, 25. **Wildey** r-1-4, 6-9, 19-22, 25, 26. **Williamson** a-28r. **Woodbridge/Williamson** a-9r.*

OUTLAW NATION
DC Comics (Vertigo): Nov, 2000 - Present ($2.50)

1-5-Fabry panited-c/Delano-s/Sudzuka-a 2.50

OUTLAWS
D. S. Publishing Co.: Feb-Mar, 1948 - No. 9, June-July, 1949

1-Violent & suggestive stories 34.00 101.00 270.00
2-Ingels-a; Baker-a 34.00 101.00 270.00
3,5,6: 3-Not Frazetta. 5-Sky Sheriff by Good app. 6-McWilliams-a 15.00 45.00 120.00
4-Orlando-a 17.00 51.00 135.00
7,8-Ingels-a in each 25.00 75.00 200.00
9-(Scarce)-Frazetta-a (7 pgs.) 47.00 142.00 425.00
NOTE: *Another #3 was printed in Canada with **Frazetta** art "Prairie Jinx," 7 pgs.*

OUTLAWS, THE (Formerly Western Crime Cases)
Star Publishing Co.: No. 10, May, 1952 - No. 13, Sep, 1953; No. 14, Apr, 1954

10-L. B. Cole-c 21.00 62.00 165.00
11-14-L. B. Cole-c. 14-Reprints Western Thrillers #4 (Fox) w/new L.B. Cole-c; Kamen, Feldstein-r 16.00 48.00 125.00

OUTLAWS
DC Comics: Sept, 1991 - No. 8, Apr, 1992 ($1.95, limited series)

1-8: Post-apocalyptic Robin Hood. 2.00

OUTLAWS OF THE WEST (Formerly Cody of the Pony Express #10)
Charlton Comics: No. 11, 7/57 - No. 81, 5/70; No. 82, 7/79 - No. 88, 4/80

11 7.85 23.50 55.00
12,13,15-17,19,20 5.00 15.00 30.00
14-(68 pgs., 2/58) 8.65 26.00 60.00
18-Ditko-a 10.00 30.00 70.00
21-30 2.50 7.50 23.00
31-50: 34-Gunmaster app. 2.00 6.00 18.00
51-63,65,67-70: 54-Kid Montana app. 1.75 5.25 14.00
64,66: 64-Captain Doom begins (1st app.). 68-Kid Montana series begins 2.00 6.00 18.00
71-79: 73-Origin & 1st app. The Sharp Shooter, last app. #74. 75-Last Capt. Doom 1.50 4.50 12.00
80,81-Ditko-a 2.00 6.00 18.00
82-88 4.00
64,79(Modern Comics-r, 1977, '78) 3.00

OUTLAWS OF THE WILD WEST
Avon Periodicals: 1952 (25¢, 132 pgs.) (4 rebound comics)

1-Wood back-c; Kubert-a (3 Jesse James-r) 33.00 98.00 260.00

OUTLAW TRAIL (See Zane Grey 4-Color 511)

OUT OF SANTA'S BAG (See March of Comics #10)

OUT OF THE NIGHT (The Hooded Horseman #18 on)
Amer. Comics Group (Creston/Scope): Feb-Mar, 1952 - No. 17, Oct-Nov, 1954

1-Williamson/LeDoux-a (9 pgs.) 61.00 182.00 575.00
2-Williamson-a (5 pgs.) 47.00 140.00 420.00
3,5-10: 9-Sci/Fic story 27.00 81.00 215.00
4-Williamson-a (7 pgs.) 40.00 120.00 350.00
11-17: 13-Nostrand-a? 17-E.C. Wood swipe 21.00 62.00 165.00
NOTE: ***Landau** a-14, 16, 17. **Shelly** a-12.*

OUT OF THE SHADOWS
Standard Comics/Visual Editions: No. 5, July, 1952 - No. 14, Aug, 1954

5-Toth-p; Moreira, Tuska-a; Roussos-c 54.00 162.00 485.00
6-Toth/Celardo-a; Katz-a(2) 40.00 120.00 325.00
7,9: 7-Jack Katz-c/a(2). 9-Crandall-a(2) 29.00 87.00 235.00
8-Katz shrunken head-c 44.00 133.00 400.00
10-Spider-c; Sekowsky-a 26.00 79.00 210.00
11-Toth-a, 2 pgs.; Katz-a; Andru-c 29.00 87.00 235.00

Out of This World #1 © AVON

Outsiders #9 © DC

Ozzie and Harriet #1 © DC

GD2.0 FN6.0 NM9.4

12-Toth/Peppe-a(2); Katz-a 39.00 118.00 315.00
13-Cannabalism story; Sekowsky-a; Roussos-c 33.00 98.00 260.00
14-Toth-a 29.00 87.00 235.00

OUT OF THE VORTEX (Comics' Greatest World:... #1-4)
Dark Horse Comics: Oct., 1993 - No. 12, Oct, 1994 ($2.00, limited series)

1-11: 1-Foil logo. 4-Dorman-c(p). 6-Hero Zero x-over 2.00
12 ($2.50) 2.50
NOTE: ***Art Adams*** *c-7.* ***Golden*** *c-8.* ***Mignola*** *c-2.* ***Simonson*** *c-3.* ***Zeck*** *c-10.*

OUT OF THIS WORLD
Charlton Comics: Aug, 1956 - No. 16, Dec, 1959

1 24.00 71.00 190.00
2 12.00 36.00 95.00
3-6-Ditko-c/a (3) each 30.00 90.00 240.00
7-(2/58, 15¢, 68 pgs.)-Ditko-c/a(4) 31.00 94.00 250.00
8-(5/58, 15¢, 68 pgs.)-Ditko-a(2) 26.00 77.00 205.00
9,10,12,16-Ditko-a 21.00 62.00 165.00
11-Ditko c/a (3) 24.00 71.00 190.00
13-15 9.30 28.00 65.00
NOTE: ***Ditko*** *c-3-12, 16.* ***Reinman*** *a-10.*

OUT OF THIS WORLD
Avon Periodicals: June, 1950; Aug, 1950 (25¢ pulp)

1-Kubert-a(2) (one reprinted/Eerie #1, 1947) plus Crom the Barbarian by Gardner Fox & John Giunta (origin); Fawcette-c 63.00 189.00 600.00
1-(8/50) Reprint; no month on cover 44.00 133.00 400.00

OUT OF THIS WORLD ADVENTURES
Avon Periodicals: July, 1950 - No. 2, Dec, 1950 (25¢ pulp)

1-Kubert-a 63.00 189.00 600.00
2-Kubert-a plus The Spider God of Akka by Gardner Fox & John Giunta. pulp magazine w/comic insert 44.00 133.00 400.00
NOTE: *Out of This World Adventures is a sci-fi pulp magazine w/32 pgs. of color comics.*

OUT OUR WAY WITH WORRY WART
Dell Publishing Co.: No. 680, Feb, 1956

Four Color 680 2.50 7.50 25.00

OUTPOSTS
Blackthorne Publishing: June, 1987 - No. 4, 1987 ($1.25)

1-4: 1-Kaluta-c(p) 2.00

OUTSIDERS, THE
DC Comics: Nov, 1985 - No. 28, Feb, 1988

1 3.00
2-28: 18-26-Batman returns. 21-Intro. Strike Force Kobra; 1st app. Clayface IV 22-E.C. parody; Orlando-a. 21- 25-Atomic Knight app. 27,28-Millennium tie-ins. 2.25
Annual 1 (12/86, $2.50), Special 1 (7/87, $1.50) 2.50
NOTE: ***Aparo*** *a-1-7, 9-14, 17-22, 25, 26; c-1-7, 9-14, 17, 19-26.* ***Byrne*** *a-11.* ***Bolland*** *a-6, 18; c-16.* ***Ditko*** *a-13p.* ***Erik Larsen*** *a-24, 27 28; c-27, 28.* ***Morrow*** *a-12.*

OUTSIDERS
DC Comics: Nov, 1993 - No. 24, Nov, 1995 ($1.75/$1.95/$2.25)

1-11,0,12-24: 1-Alpha; Travis Charest-c. 1-Omega; Travis Charest-c. 5-Atomic Knight app. 8-New Batman-c/story. 11-(9/94)-Zero Hour. 0-(10/94).12-(11/94). 21-Darkseid cameo. 22-New Gods app. 2.25

OVERKILL: WITCHBLADE/ ALIENS/ DARKNESS/ PREDATOR
Image Comics/Dark Horse Comics: Dec, 2000 ($5.95)

1-Jenkins-s/Benitez-a 5.95

OVER THE EDGE
Marvel Comics: Nov, 1995 - No. 10, Aug, 1996 (99¢)

1-10: 1,6,10-Daredevil-c/story. 2,7-Dr. Strange-c/story. 3-Hulk-c/story. 4,9-Ghost Rider-c/story. 5-Punisher-c/story. 8-Elektra-c/story 2.00

OWL, THE (See Crackajack Funnies #25, Popular Comics #72 and Occult Files of Dr. Spektor #22)
Gold Key: April, 1967; No. 2, April, 1968

1-Written by Jerry Siegel; '40s super hero 4.60 13.75 55.00
2 4.10 12.30 45.00

OZ (See First Comics Graphic Novel, Marvel Treaury Of Oz & MGM's Marvelous...)

OZ
Caliber Press: 1994 - 1997 ($2.95, B&W)

0-20: 0-Released between #10 & #11 3.00
1 ($5.95)-Limited Edition; double-c 6.00
...Specials: Freedom Fighters. Lion. Scarecrow. Tin Man 3.00

OZARK IKE
Dell Publishing Co./Standard Comics B11 on: Feb, 1948; Nov, 1948 - No. 24, Dec, 1951; No. 25, Sept, 1952

Four Color 180(1948-Dell) 10.00 30.00 120.00
B11, B12, 13-15 8.65 26.00 60.00
16-25 6.40 19.25 45.00

OZ: DAEMONSTORM
Caliber Press: 1997 ($3.95, B&W, one-shot)

1 4.00

OZ: ROMANCE IN RAGS
Caliber Press: 1996 ($2.95, B&W, limited series)

1-3, ..Special 3.00

OZ SQUAD
Brave New Worlds/Patchwork Press: 1992 - No. 4, 1994 ($2.50/$2.75, B&W)

1-4-Patchwork Press 2.75

OZ SQUAD
Patchwork Press: Dec, 1995 - No. 10, 1996 ($2.95, B&W)

1 ($3.95)-10 3.00

OZ: STRAW AND SORCERY
Caliber Press: 1997 ($2.95, B&W, limited series)

1-3 3.00

OZ-WONDERLAND WARS, THE
DC Comics: Jan, 1986 - No. 3, March, 1986 (Mini-series)

1-3-Capt Carrot app.; funny animals 4.00

OZZIE & BABS (TV Teens #14 on)
Fawcett Publications: Dec, 1947 - No. 13, Fall, 1949

1-Teen-age 8.65 26.00 60.00
2 5.00 15.00 30.00
3-13 4.00 12.00 24.00

OZZIE AND HARRIET (The Adventures of... on cover) (Radio)
National Periodical Publications: Oct-Nov, 1949 - No. 5, June-July, 1950

1-Photo-c 92.00 276.00 875.00
2 47.00 140.00 420.00
3-5 40.00 120.00 340.00

OZZY OSBOURNE (Todd McFarland Presents)
Image Comics (Todd McFarlane Prod.): June, 1999 ($4.95, magazine-sized)

1-Bio, interview and comic story; Ormston painted-a; Ashley Wood-c 5.00

PACIFIC COMICS GRAPHIC NOVEL (See Image Graphic Novel)

PACIFIC PRESENTS (Also see Starslayer #2, 3)
Pacific Comics: Oct, 1982 - No. 2, Apr, 1983; No. 3, Mar, 1984 - No. 4, Jun, 1984

1-Chapter 3 of The Rocketeer; Stevens-c/a; Bettie Page model 1.00 2.80 7.00
2-Chapter 4 of The Rocketeer (4th app.); nudity; Stevens-c/a 1.00 2.80 7.00
3,4: 3-1st app. Vanity 3.00
NOTE: ***Conrad*** *a-3, 4; c-3.* ***Ditko*** *a-1-3; c-1(1/2).* ***Dave Stevens*** *a-1, 2; c-1(1/2), 2.*

PACT, THE
Image Comics: Feb, 1994 - No. 3, June, 1994 ($1.95, limited series)

1-3: Valentino co-scripts & layouts 2.00

PAGEANT OF COMICS (See Jane Arden & Mopsy)
Archer St. John: Sept, 1947 - No. 2, Oct, 1947

1,2: 1-Mopsy strip-r. 2-Jane Arden strip-r 9.30 28.00 65.00

PAINKILLER JANE
Event Comics: June, 1997 - Present ($3.95/$2.95)

Pancho Villa nn © AVON

Panic #4 © WMG

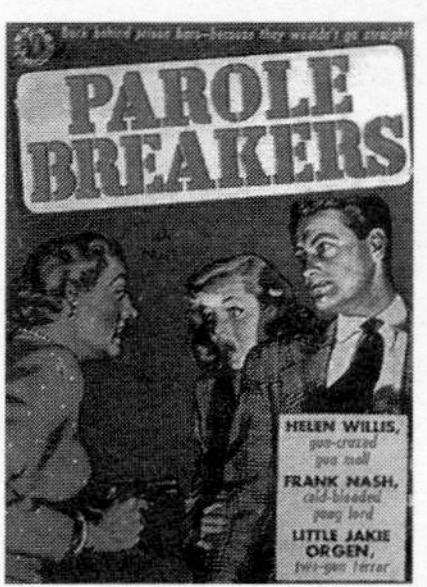

Parole Breakers #1 © AVON

GD2.0 FN6.0 NM9.4

GD2.0 FN6.0 NM9.4

1-Augustyn/Waid-s/Leonardi/Palmiotti-a, variant-c 4.00
2-5: Two covers (Quesada, Leonardi) 3.00
0-(1/99, $3.95) Retells origin; two covers 4.00

PAINKILLER JANE / DARKCHYLDE
Event Comics: Oct, 1998 ($2.95, one-shot)

Preview-($6.95) DF Edition, 1-($6.95) DF Edition 7.00
1-Three covers; J.G. Jones-a 3.00

PAINKILLER JANE / HELLBOY
Event Comics: Aug, 1998 ($2.95, one-shot)

1-Leonardi & Palmiotti-a 3.00

PAINKILLER JANE VS. THE DARKNESS
Event Comics: Apr, 1997 ($2.95, one-shot)

1-Ennis-s; four variant-c (Conner, Hildebrandts, Quesada, Silvestri) 3.50

PAKKINS' LAND
Caliber Comics (Tapestry): Oct, 1996 - No. 6, July, 1997 ($2.95, B&W)

1-Gary and Rhoda Shipman-s/a 2.40 6.00
2,3 4.00
1-3-2nd printing 3.00
4-6 3.00
0-(6/97, $1.95) 3.00

PAKKINS' LAND: FORGOTTEN DREAMS
Caliber Comics/Image Comics #4: Apr, 1998 - No. 4, Mar, 2000 ($2.95, B&W)

1-4-Gary and Rhoda Shipman-s/a 3.00

PAKKINS' LAND: QUEST FOR KINGS
Caliber Comics: Aug, 1997 - No. 6, Mar, 1998 ($2.95, B&W)

1-6: 1-Gary and Rhoda Shipman-s/a; Jeff Smith var-c 3.00

PANCHO VILLA
Avon Periodicals: 1950

nn-Kinstler-c 24.00 71.00 190.00

PANDEMONIUM
Chaos! Comics: Sept, 1998 ($2.95, one-shot)

1-Al Rio-c 3.00

PANHANDLE PETE AND JENNIFER (TV) (See Gene Autry #20)
J. Charles Laue Publishing Co.: July, 1951 - No. 3, Nov, 1951

1 10.00 30.00 70.00
2,3 7.00 21.00 48.00

PANIC (Companion to Mad)
E. C. Comics (Tiny Tot Comics): Feb-Mar, 1954 - No. 12, Dec-Jan, 1955-56

1-Used in Senate Investigation hearings; Elder draws entire E. C. staff; Santa Claus & Mickey Spillane parody 24.00 71.00 260.00
2 11.00 33.00 120.00
3,4: 3-Senate Subcommittee parody; Davis draws Gaines, Feldstein & Kelly, 1 pg.; Old King Cole smokes marijuana. 4-Infinity-c; John Wayne parody 10.00 30.00 110.00
5-11: 8-Last pre-code issue (5/55). 9-Superman, Smilin' Jack & Dick Tracy app. on-c; has photo of Walter Winchell on-c. 11-Wheedies cereal box-c 9.00 26.00 95.00
12 (Low distribution; thousands were destroyed) 11.00 33.00 120.00

NOTE: ***Davis** a-1-12; c-12. **Elder** a-1-12. **Feldstein** c-1-3, 5. **Kamen** a-1. **Orlando** a-1-9. **Wolverton** c-4, panel-3. **Wood** a-2-9, 11, 12.*

PANIC (Magazine) (Satire)
Panic Publ.: July, 1958 - No. 6, July, 1959; V2#10, Dec, 1965 - V2#12, 1966

1 10.00 30.00 80.00
2-6 6.40 19.25 45.00
V2#10-12: Reprints earlier issues 3.00 9.00 30.00

NOTE: ***Davis** a-3(2 pgs.), 4, 5, 10; c-10. **Elder** a-5. **Powell** a-V2#10, 11. **Torres** a-1-5. **Tuska** a-V2#11.*

PANIC
Gemstone Publishing: March, 1997 - Present ($2.50, quarterly)

1-11: E.C. reprints 2.50

PANTHA (See Vampirella-The New Monthly #16,17)

PANTHA: HAUNTED PASSION (Also see Vampirella Monthly #0)
Harris Comics: May, 1997 ($2.95, B&W, one-shot)

1-r/Vampirella #30,31 3.00

PARADAX (Also see Strange Days)
Eclipse Comics: 1986 (one-shot)

1 2.00

PARADAX
Vortex Comics: April, 1987 - No. 2, Aug, 1987 ($1.75, mature)

1,2-Nudity, adult language 2.00

PARADE (See Hanna-Barbera...)

PARADE COMICS (Frisky Animals on Parade #2 on)
Ajax/Farrell Publ. (World Famous Publ.): Sept, 1957

1 6.40 19.25 45.00

NOTE: *Cover title: Frisky Animals on Parade.*

PARADE OF PLEASURE
Derric Verschoyle Ltd., London, England: 1954 (192 pgs.) (Hardback book)

By Geoffrey Wagner. Contains section devoted to the censorship of American comic books with illustrations in color and black and white. (Also see **Seduction of the Innocent**). Distributed in USA by Library Publishers, N. Y. 40.00 120.00 325.00
with dust jacket.... 76.00 229.00 725.00

PARADOX
Dark Visions Publ: June, 1994 - No. 2, Aug, 1994 ($2.95, B&W, mature)

1,2: 1-Linsner-c. 2-Boris-c. 3.00

PARALLAX: EMERALD NIGHT (See Final Night)
DC Comics: Nov, 1996 ($2.95, one-shot, 48 pgs.)

1-Final Night tie-in; Green Lantern (Kyle Rayner) app. 4.00

PARAMOUNT ANIMATED COMICS (See Harvey Comics Hits #60, 62)
Harvey Publications: No. 3, Feb, 1953 - No. 22, July, 1956

3-Baby Huey, Herman & Katnip, Buzzy the Crow begin 21.00 62.00 165.00
4-6 10.00 30.00 75.00
7-Baby Huey becomes permanent cover feature; cover title becomes Baby Huey with #9 20.00 60.00 160.00
8-10: 9-Infinity-c 9.30 28.00 65.00
11-22 7.15 21.50 50.00

PARENT TRAP, THE (Disney)
Dell Publishing Co.: No. 1210, Oct-Dec, 1961

Four Color 1210-Movie, Haley Mills photo-c 9.00 27.00 110.00

PARODY
Armour Publishing: Mar, 1977 - No. 3, Aug, 1977 (B&W humor magazine)

1 2.00 6.00 18.00
2,3: 2-King Kong, Happy Days. 3-Charlie's Angels, Rocky 1.75 5.25 14.00

PAROLE BREAKERS
Avon Periodicals/Realistic #2 on: Dec, 1951 - No. 3, July, 1952

1(#2 on inside)-r-c/Avon paperback #283 (painted) 42.00 125.00 375.00
2-Kubert-a; r-c/Avon paperback #114 (photo-c) 32.00 96.00 255.00
3-Kinstler-c 29.00 86.00 230.00

PARTRIDGE FAMILY, THE (TV)(Also see David Cassidy)
Charlton Comics: Mar, 1971 - No. 21, Dec, 1973

1 5.45 16.35 60.00
2-4,6-10 2.80 8.40 28.00
5-Partridge Family Summer Special (52 pgs.); The Shadow, Lone Ranger, Charlie McCarthy, Flash Gordon, Hopalong Cassidy, Gene Autry & others app. 6.80 20.50 75.00
11-21 2.40 7.35 22.00

PARTS UNKNOWN
Eclipse Comics/FX: July, 1992 - No. 4, Oct, 1992 ($2.50, B&W, mature)

1-4: All contain FX gaming cards 2.50

Patches #1 © RH

The Patriots #2 © WSP

Patsy and Hedy #64 © MAR

GD2.0 FN6.0 NM9.4

PARTS UNKNOWN
Image Comics: May, 2000 - Present ($2.95, B&W)
...: Killing Attractions 1 (5/00) Beau Smith-s/Brad Gorby-a 2.95
...: Hostile Takeover 1-4 (6-9/00) 2.95

PASSION, THE
Catechetical Guild: No. 394, 1955
394 4.30 13.00 26.00

PASSOVER (See Avengelyne)
Maximum Press: Dec, 1996 ($2.99, one-shot)
1 3.00

PAT BOONE (TV)(Also see Superman's Girlfriend Lois Lane #9)
National Per. Publ.: Sept-Oct, 1959 - No. 5, May-Jun, 1960 (All have photo-c)
1 44.00 133.00 400.00
2-5: 3-Fabian, Connie Francis & Paul Anka photos on-c. 4-Previews "Journey To The Center Of The Earth". 4-Johnny Mathis & Bobby Darin photos on-c. 5-Dick Clark & Frankie Avalon photos on-c 38.00 113.00 300.00

PATCHES
Rural Home/Patches Publ. (Orbit): Mar-Apr, 1945 - No. 11, Nov, 1947
1-L. B. Cole-c 40.00 120.00 325.00
2 14.00 41.00 110.00
3,4,6,8-11: 6-Henry Aldrich story. 8-Smiley Burnette-c/s (6/47); pre-dates Smiley Burnette #1. 9-Mr. District Attorney story (radio). Leav/Keigstein-a (16 pgs.). 9-11-Leav-c. 10-Jack Carson (radio) c/story; Leav-c. 11-Red Skelton story 12.50 37.50 100.00
5-Danny Kaye-c/story; L.B. Cole-c. 20.00 60.00 160.00
7-Hopalong Cassidy-c/story 16.00 48.00 125.00

PATHWAYS TO FANTASY
Pacific Comics: July, 1984
1-Barry Smith-c/a; Jeff Jones-a (4 pgs.) 4.00

PATORUZU (See Adventures of...)

PATRIOTS, THE
DC Comics (WildStorm): Jan, 2000 - No. 10, Oct, 2000 ($2.50)
1-10-Choi and Peterson-s/Ryan-a 2.50

PATSY & HEDY (Teenage)(Also see Hedy Wolfe)
Atlas Comics/Marvel (GPI/Male): Feb, 1952 - No. 110, Feb, 1967
1-Patsy Walker & Hedy Wolfe; Al Jaffee-c 21.00 64.00 170.00
2 11.00 33.00 90.00
3-10: 3,8-Al Jaffee-c 9.30 28.00 65.00
11-20 7.15 21.50 50.00
21-40 5.70 17.00 40.00
41-60 3.00 9.00 30.00
61-80,100: 88-Lingerie panel 2.40 7.35 22.00
81-87,89-99,101-110 2.00 6.00 18.00
Annual 1(1963)-Early Marvel annual 8.65 26.00 95.00

PATSY & HER PALS (Teenage)
Atlas Comics (PPI): May, 1953 - No. 29, Aug, 1957
1-Patsy Walker 18.00 53.00 140.00
2 10.00 30.00 70.00
3-10 8.65 26.00 60.00
11-29: 24-Everett-c 6.00 18.00 42.00

PATSY WALKER (See All Teen, A Date With Patsy, Girls' Life, Miss America Magazine, Patsy & Hedy, Patsy & Her Pals & Teen Comics)
Marvel/Atlas Comics (BPC): 1945 (no month) - No. 124, Dec, 1965
1-Teenage 47.00 140.00 420.00
2 24.00 71.00 190.00
3,4,6-10 19.00 56.00 150.00
5-Injury-to-eye-c; spanking panel 22.00 66.00 175.00
11,12,15,16,18 12.00 36.00 95.00
13,14,17,19-22-Kurtzman's "Hey Look" 12.50 37.50 100.00
23,24 10.00 30.00 70.00
25-Rusty by Kurtzman; painted-c 12.50 37.50 100.00
26-29,31: 26-31: 52 pgs. 8.65 26.00 60.00
30(52 pgs.)-Egghead Doodle by Kurtzman (1 pg.) 9.30 28.00 65.00
32-57: Last precode (3/55) 6.40 19.25 45.00
58-80,100 3.00 9.00 30.00
81-99: 92,98-Millie x-over 2.30 7.00 20.00
101-124 2.00 6.00 18.00
Fashion Parade 1(1966, 68 pgs.) (Beware cut-out & marked pages) 6.80 20.50 75.00

NOTE: *Painted c-25-28. Anti-Wertham editorial in #21. Georgie app. in #8, 11. Millie app. in #10, 92, 98. Mitzi app. in #11. Rusty app. in #12, 25. Willie app. in #12.* ***Al Jaffee*** *c-57, 58.*

PAT THE BRAT (Adventures of Pipsqueak #34 on)
Archie Publications (Radio): June, 1953; Summer, 1955 - No. 4, 5/56; No. 15, 7/56 - No. 33, 7/59
nn(6/53) 12.50 37.50 100.00
1(Summer, 1955) 10.00 30.00 70.00
2-4-(5/56) (#5-14 not published) 5.70 17.00 40.00
15-(7/56)-33 3.00 9.00 30.00

PAT THE BRAT COMICS DIGEST MAGAZINE
Archie Publications: October, 1980
1-Li'l Jinx & Super Duck app. 1.75 5.25 14.00

PATTY CAKE
Permanent Press: Mar, 1995 - No. 9, Jul, 1996 ($2.95, B&W)
1-9: Scott Roberts-s/a 3.00

PATTY CAKE
Caliber Press (Tapestry): Oct, 1996 - No. 3, Apr, 1997 ($2.95, B&W)
1-3: Scott Roberts-s/a, ...Christmas (12/96) 3.00

PATTY CAKE & FRIENDS
Slave Labor Graphics: Nov, 1997 - Present ($2.95, B&W)
Here There Be Monsters (10/97), 1-14: Scott Roberts-s/a 3.00
Volume 2 #1 (11/00, $4.95) 4.95

PATTY POWERS (Formerly Della Vision #3)
Atlas Comics: No. 4, Oct, 1955 - No. 7, Oct, 1956
4 9.30 28.00 65.00
5-7 5.00 15.00 32.00

PAT WILTON (See Mighty Midget Comics)

PAUL
Spire Christian Comics (Fleming H. Revell Co.): 1978 (49¢)
nn 1.00 3.00 8.00

PAULINE PERIL (See The Close Shaves of...)

PAUL REVERE'S RIDE (TV, Disney, see Walt Disney Showcase #34)
Dell Publishing Co.: No. 822, July, 1957
Four Color 822-w/Johnny Tremain, Toth-a 9.00 27.00 110.00

PAUL TERRY (See Heckle and Jeckle)

PAUL TERRY'S ADVENTURES OF MIGHTY MOUSE (See Adventures of...)

PAUL TERRY'S COMICS (Formerly Terry-Toons Comics; becomes Adventures of Mighty Mouse No. 126 on)
St. John Publishing Co.: No. 85, Mar, 1951 - No. 125, May, 1955
85,86-Same as Terry-Toons #85, & 86 with only a title change; published at same time?; Mighty Mouse, Heckle & Jeckle & Gandy Goose continue from Terry-Toons 10.00 30.00 80.00
87-99 7.15 21.50 50.00
100 8.65 26.00 60.00
101-104,107-125: 121,122,125-Painted-c 7.00 21.00 48.00
105,106-Giant Comics Edition (25¢, 100 pgs.) (9/53 & ?). 105-Little Roquefort-c/story 18.00 53.00 140.00

PAUL TERRY'S MIGHTY MOUSE (See Mighty Mouse)

PAUL TERRY'S MIGHTY MOUSE ADVENTURE STORIES (See Mighty Mouse Adventure Stories)

PAUL THE SAMURAI (See The Tick #4)
New England Comics: July, 1992 - No. 6, July, 1993 ($2.75, B&W)
1-6 2.75

PAWNEE BILL
Story Comics (Youthful Magazines?): Feb, 1951 - No. 3, July, 1951

Pay-Off #5 © DS

Peanuts Four Color #878 © UFS

Penny Century #3 © Jaime Hernandez

	GD2.0	FN6.0	NM9.4
1-Bat Masterson, Wyatt Earp app.	12.00	36.00	95.00
2,3: 3-Origin Golden Warrior; Cameron-a	7.85	23.50	55.00

PAY-OFF (This Is the..., ...Crime, ...Detective Stories)
D. S. Publishing Co.: July-Aug, 1948 - No. 5, Mar-Apr, 1949 (52 pgs.)

	GD2.0	FN6.0	NM9.4
1-True Crime Cases #1,2	25.00	75.00	200.00
2	15.00	45.00	120.00
3-5-Thrilling Detective Stories	13.00	39.00	105.00

PEACEMAKER, THE (Also see Fightin' Five)
Charlton Comics: V3#1, Mar, 1967 - No. 5, Nov, 1967 (All 12¢ cover price)

	GD2.0	FN6.0	NM9.4
1-Fightin' Five begins	4.10	12.30	45.00
2,3,5	2.50	7.50	25.00
4-Origin The Peacemaker	3.20	9.60	35.00
1,2(Modern Comics reprint, 1978)			3.00

PEACEMAKER (Also see Crisis On Infinite Earths & Showcase '93 #7,9,10)
DC Comics: Jan, 1988 - No. 4, Apr, 1988 ($1.25, limited series)

	GD2.0	FN6.0	NM9.4
1-4			2.00

PEANUTS (Charlie Brown) (See Fritzi Ritz, Nancy & Sluggo, Tip Top, Tip Topper & United Comics)
Dell Publishing Co./Gold Key: 1953-54; No. 878, 2/58 - No. 13, 5-7/62; 5/63 - No. 4, 2/64

	GD2.0	FN6.0	NM9.4
1(1953-54)-Reprints United Features' Strange As It Seems, Willie, Ferdnand	11.70	35.00	140.00
Four Color 878(#1) Schulz-s/a, with assistance from Dale Hale and Jim Sasseville thru #4	14.00	42.00	170.00
Four Color 969,1015('59)	10.00	30.00	120.00
4(2-4/60) Schulz-s/a; one story by Anthony Pocrnich, Schulz's assistant cartoonist	8.00	24.00	95.00
5-13-Schulz-c only; s/a by Pocrnich	5.85	17.50	70.00
1(Gold Key, 5/63)	11.00	33.00	130.00
2-4	6.70	20.00	80.00

PEBBLES & BAMM BAMM (TV) (See Cave Kids #7, 12)
Charlton Comics: Jan, 1972 - No. 36, Dec, 1976 (Hanna-Barbera)

	GD2.0	FN6.0	NM9.4
1-From the Flintstones; "Teen Age..." on cover	4.55	13.65	50.00
2-10	2.50	7.50	24.00
11-20	2.00	6.00	18.00
21-36	1.75	5.25	14.00

PEBBLES & BAMM BAMM (TV)
Harvey Comics: Nov, 1993 - No. 3, Mar, 1994 ($1.50) (Hanna-Barbera)

	GD2.0	FN6.0	NM9.4
V2#1-3			3.00
...Giant Size 1 (10/93, $2.25, 68 pgs.)("Summer Special" on-c)			4.00

PEBBLES FLINTSTONE (TV) (See The Flintstones #11)
Gold Key: Sept, 1963 (Hanna-Barbera)

	GD2.0	FN6.0	NM9.4
1 (10088-309)-Early Pebbles app.	9.00	27.00	110.00

PEDRO (Formerly My Private Life #17; also see Romeo Tubbs)
Fox Features Syndicate: No. 18, June, 1950 - No. 2, Aug, 1950?

	GD2.0	FN6.0	NM9.4
18(#1)-Wood-c/a(p)	22.00	66.00	175.00
2-Wood-a?	16.00	49.00	130.00

PEE-WEE PIXIES (See The Pixies)

PELLEAS AND MELISANDE (See Night Music #4, 5)

PENALTY (See Crime Must Pay the...)

PENDRAGON (Knights of... #5 on; also see Knights of...)
Marvel Comics UK, Ltd.: July, 1992 - No. 15, Sept, 1993 ($1.75)

	GD2.0	FN6.0	NM9.4
1-15: 1-4-Iron Man app. 6-8-Spider-Man app.			2.00

PENDULUM ILLUSTRATED BIOGRAPHIES
Pendulum Press: 1979 (B&W)

19-355x-George Washington/Thomas Jefferson, 19-3495-Charles Lindbergh/Amelia Earhart, 19-3509-Harry Houdini/Walt Disney, 19-3517-Davy Crockett/Daniel Boone-Redondo-a, 19-3525-Elvis Presley/Beatles, 19-3533-Benjamin Franklin/Martin Luther King Jr, 19-3541-Abraham Lincoln/Franklin D. Roosevelt, 19-3568-Marie Curie/Albert Einstein-Redondo-a, 19-3576-Thomas Edison/Alexander Graham Bell-Redondo-a, 19-3584-Vince Lombardi/Pele, 19-3592-Babe Ruth/Jackie Robinson, 19-3606-Jim Thorpe/Althea Gibson

	GD2.0	FN6.0	NM9.4
Softback			3.00
Hardback			5.00

NOTE: *Above books still available from publisher.*

PENDULUM ILLUSTRATED CLASSICS (Now Age Illustrated)
Pendulum Press: 1973 - 1978 (75¢, 62pp, B&W, 5-3/8x8")
(Also see Marvel Classics)

64-100x(1973)-Dracula-Redondo art, 64-131x-The Invisible Man-Nino art, 64-0968-Dr. Jekyll and Mr. Hyde-Redondo art, 64-1005-Black Beauty, 64-1010-Call of the Wild, 64-1020-Frankenstein, 64-1025-Huckleburry Finn, 64-1030-Moby Dick-Nino-a, 64-1040-Red Badge of Courage, 64-1045-The Time Machine-Nino-a, 64-1050-Tom Sawyer, 64-1055-Twenty Thousand Leagues Under the Sea, 64-1069-Treasure Island, 64-1328(1974)-Kidnapped, 64-1336-Three Musketeers-Nino art, 64-1344-A Tale of Two Cities, 64-1352-Journey to the Center of the Earth, 64-1360-The War of the Worlds-Nino-a, 64-1379-The Greatest Advs. of Sherlock Holmes-Redondo art, 64-1387-Mysterious Island, 64-1395-Hunchback of Notre Dame, 64-1409-Helen Keller-story of my life, 64-1417-Scarlet Letter, 64-1425-Gulliver's Travels, 64-2618(1977)-Around the World in Eighty Days, 64-2626-Captains Courageous, 64-2634-Connecticut Yankee, 64-2642-The Hound of the Baskervilles, 64-2650-The House of Seven Gables, 64-2669-Jane Eyre, 64-2677-The Last of the Mohicans, 64-2685-The Best of O'Henry, 64-2693-The Best of Poe-Redondo-a, 64-2707-Two Years Before the Mast, 64-2715-White Fang, 64-2723-Wuthering Heights, 64-3126(1978)-Ben Hur-Redondo art, 64-3134-A Christmas Carol, 64-3142-The Food of the Gods, 64-3150-Ivanhoe, 64-3169-The Man in the Iron Mask, 64-3177-The Prince and the Pauper, 64-3185-The Prisoner of Zenda, 64-3193-The Return of the Native, 64-3207-Robinson Crusoe, 64-3215-The Scarlet Pimpernel, 64-3223-The Sea Wolf, 64-3231-The Swiss Family Robinson, 64-3851-Billy Budd, 64-386x-Crime and Punishment, 64-3878-Don Quixote, 64-3886-Great Expectations, 64-3894-Heidi, 64-3908-The Iliad, 64-3916-Lord Jim, 64-3924-The Mutiny on Board H.M.S. Bounty, 64-3932-The Odyssey, 64-3940-Oliver Twist, 64-3959-Pride and Prejudice, 64-3967-The Turn of the Screw

	GD2.0	FN6.0	NM9.4
Softback			3.00
Hardback			5.00

NOTE: *All of the above books can be ordered from the publisher; some were reprinted as Marvel Classic Comics #1-12. In 1972 there was another brief series of 12 titles which contained Classics Ill. artwork. They were entitled **Now Age Books** Illustrated, but can be easily distinguished from later series by the small Classics Illustrated logo at the top of the front cover. The format is the same as the later series. The 48 pg. C.I. art was stretched out to make 62 pgs. After Twin Circle Publ. terminated the Classics Ill. series in 1971, they made a one year contract with Pendulum Press to print these twelve titles of C.I. art. Pendulum was unhappy with the contract, and at the end of 1972 began their own art series, utilizing the talents of the Filipino artist group. One detail which makes this rather confusing is that when they redid the art in 1973, they gave it the same identifying no. as the 1972 series. All 12 of the 1972 C.I. editions have new covers, taken from internal art panels. In spite of their recent age, all of the 1972 C.I. series are very rare. Mint copies would fetch at least $50. Here is a list of the 1972 series, with C.I. title no. counterpart:*

64-1005 (CI#60-A2) 64-1010 (CI#91) 64-1015 (CI-Jr #503) 64-1020 (CI#26)
64-1025 (CI#19-A2) 64-1030 (CI#5-A2) 64-1035 (CI#169) 64-1040 (CI#98)
64-1045 (CI#133) 64-1050 (CI#50-A2) 64-1055 (CI#47) 64-1060 (CI-Jr#535)

PENDULUM ILLUSTRATED ORIGINALS
Pendulum Press: 1979 (In color)

	GD2.0	FN6.0	NM9.4
94-4254-Solarman: The Beginning (See Solarman)			4.00

PENDULUM'S ILLUSTRATED STORIES
Pendulum Press: 1990 - No. 72, 1990? (No cover price ($4.95), squarebound, 68 pgs.)

	GD2.0	FN6.0	NM9.4
1-72: Reprints Pendulum Ill. Classics series			5.00

PENNY
Avon Comics: 1947 - No. 6, Sept-Oct, 1949 (Newspaper reprints)

	GD2.0	FN6.0	NM9.4
1-Photo & biography of creator	11.00	33.00	90.00
2-5	7.85	23.50	55.00
6-Perry Como photo on-c	8.65	26.00	60.00

PENNY CENTURY (See Love and Rockets)
Fantagraphics Books: Dec, 1997 - Present ($2.95, B&W, mini-series)

	GD2.0	FN6.0	NM9.4
1-7-Jaime Hernandez-s/a			3.00

PENTHOUSE COMIX
General Media Int.: 1994 - No. 33, July, 1998 ($4.95, bimonthly, magazine & comic sized, mature)

	GD2.0	FN6.0	NM9.4
1	1.10	3.30	9.00
2-5		2.40	6.00
6-33: 15-Corben-c. 16-Dorman-c. 17-Manara-c. 20-Chiodo-c. 21,23-Boris-c 24-Scott Hampton-c. 26-33-Comic-sized			5.00

PENTHOUSE MAX
General Media International: July, 1996 - No. 3 ($4.95, magazine, mature)

	GD2.0	FN6.0	NM9.4
1-3: 1-Giffen, Sears, Maguire-a. 2-Political satire. 3-Mr. Monster-c/app.; Dorman-c			5.00

Pep Comics #31 © AP

The Perfect Crime #9 © Cross Publ.

Personal Love #1 © FF

PENTHOUSE MEN'S ADVENTURE COMIX
General Media International: 1995 - No. 7, 1996 ($4.95, magazine, mature)
1-7 (Magazine Size): 1-Boris-c, 1-5 (Comic Size): 1-Boris-c 5.00

PEP COMICS (See Archie Giant Series #576, 589, 601, 614, 624)
MLJ Magazines/Archie Publications No. 56 (3/46) on: Jan, 1940 - No. 411, Mar, 1987

	GD2.0	FN6.0	VF8.0	NM9.4
1-Intro. The Shield (1st patriotic hero) by Irving Novick; origin & 1st app. The Comet by Jack Cole, The Queen of Diamonds & Kayo Ward; The Rocket, The Press Guardian (The Falcon #1 only), Sergeant Boyle, Fu Chang, & Bentley of of Scotland Yard; Robot-c; Shield-c begin	783.00	2350.00	4900.00	9000.00

	GD2.0	FN6.0	NM9.4
2-Origin The Rocket	221.00	663.00	2100.00
3	158.00	474.00	1500.00
4-Wizard cameo	132.00	395.00	1250.00
5-Wizard cameo in Shield story	132.00	395.00	1250.00
6-10: 8-Last Cole Comet; no Cole-a in #6,7	100.00	300.00	950.00
11-Dusty, Shield's sidekick begins (1st app.); last Press Guardian, Fu Chang	105.00	316.00	1000.00
12-Origin & 1st app. Fireball (2/41); last Rocket & Queen of Diamonds; Danny in Wonderland begins	126.00	379.00	1200.00
13-15	82.00	245.00	775.00
16-Origin Madam Satan; blood drainage-c	132.00	395.00	1250.00
17-Origin/1st app. The Hangman (7/41); death of The Comet; Comet is revealed as Hangman's brother	314.00	943.00	3300.00
18-21: 20-Last Fireball. 21-Last Madam Satan	82.00	245.00	775.00

	GD2.0	FN6.0	VF8.0	NM9.4
22-Intro. & 1st app. Archie, Betty, & Jughead(12/41); (also see Jackpot)	1120.00	3360.00	7280.00	14,000.00

	GD2.0	FN6.0	NM9.4
23	147.00	442.00	1400.00
24,25: 24-Coach Kleets app. (unnamed until Archie #94); bondage/torture-c. 25-1st app. Archie's jalopy; 1st skinny Mr. Weatherbee prototype	111.00	332.00	1050.00
26-1st app. Veronica Lodge (4/42)	158.00	474.00	1500.00
27-30: 29-Origin Shield retold; 30-Capt. Commando begins; bondage/torture-c; 1st Miss Grundy (definitive version); see Jackpot #4	89.00	268.00	850.00
31-35: 31-MLJ offices & artists are visited in Sgt. Boyle story; 1st app. Mr. Lodge. 32-Shield dons new costume. 34-Bondage/Hypo-c. 33-Pre-Moose tryout (see Jughead #1)	71.00	213.00	675.00
36-1st Archie-c (2/43) w/Shield & Hangman	168.00	505.00	1600.00
37-40	55.00	165.00	500.00
41-50: 41-Archie-c begin. 47-Last Hangman issue; infinity-c. 48-Black Hood begins (5/44); ends #51,59,60	40.00	120.00	325.00
51-60: 52-Suzie begins. 56-Last Capt. Commando. 59-Black Hood not in costume; spanking & lingerie panels; Archie dresses as his aunt; Suzie ends. 60-Katy Keene begins(3/47), ends #154	26.00	79.00	210.00
61-65-Last Shield. 62-1st app. Li'l Jinx (7/47)	22.00	66.00	175.00
66-80: 66-G-Man Club becomes Archie Club (2/48); Nevada Jones by Bill Woggon. 78-1st app. Dilton	13.00	39.00	105.00
81-99	10.00	30.00	80.00
100	12.50	37.50	100.00
101-130	6.40	19.25	45.00
131(2/59)-149(9/61)	3.00	9.00	30.00
150-160-Super-heroes app. in each (see note). 150 (10/61?)-2nd or 3rd app. The Jaguar? 152-157-Sci/Fi-c. 157-Li'l Jinx story	3.65	11.00	40.00
161(3/63)-167,169-180	2.30	7.00	20.00
168.200: 168-.(1/64)-Jaguar app. 200 (12/66)	2.50	7.50	25.00
181(5/65)-199: 192-UFO-c. 198-Giantman-c(only)	2.00	6.00	18.00
201-217,219-226,228-240(4/70)	1.75	5.25	14.00
218,227-Archies Band-c only	2.00	6.00	16.00
241-270(10/72)	1.50	4.50	12.00
271-299: 298-Josie and the Pussycats-c	1.10	3.30	9.00
300(4/75)	1.50	4.50	12.00
301-340(8/78)			5.00
341-382			4.00
383(4/82),393(3/84): 383-Marvelous Maureen begins (Sci/fi). 393-Thunder-bunny begins			5.00
384-392,394-399,401-410			3.00
400(5/85),411: 400-Story featuring Archie staff (DeCarlo-a)			5.00

NOTE: ***Biro** a-2, 4, 5. **Jack Cole** a-1-5, 8. **Al Fagaly** c-55-72. **Fuje** a-39, 45, 47; c-34. **Meskin** a-2, 4, 5, 11(2). **Montana** c-30, 32, 33, 36, 73-87(most). **Novick** c-1-28, 29(w/**Schomburg**), 31i. **Harry Sahle** c-35, 39-50. **Schomburg** c-38. **Bob Wood** a-2, 4-6, 11. The Fly app. in 151, 154, 160. Flygirl app. in 153, 155, 156, 158. Jaguar app. in 150, 152, 157, 159, 168. Katy Keene by **Bill Woggon** in many later issues. Bondage c-7, 12, 13, 15, 18, 21, 31, 32. Cover features: Shield #1-16; Shield/Hangman #17-27, 29-41; Hangman #28. Archie #36, 41-on.*

PEPE
Dell Publishing Co.: No. 1194, Apr, 1961

Four Color 1194-Movie, photo-c	2.40	7.35	22.00

PERFECT CRIME, THE
Cross Publications: Oct, 1949 - No. 33, May, 1953 (#2-12, 52 pgs.)

1-Powell-a(2)	31.00	94.00	250.00
2 (4/50)	18.00	53.00	140.00
3-10: 7-Steve Duncan begins, ends #30. 10-Flag-c	15.00	45.00	120.00
11-Used in **SOTI**, pg. 159	17.00	51.00	135.00
12-14	14.00	43.00	115.00
15- "The Most Terrible Menace" 2 pg. drug editorial	15.00	45.00	120.00
16,17,19-25,27-29,31-33	10.00	30.00	80.00
18-Drug cover, heroin drug propaganda story, plus 2 pg. anti-drug editorial	22.00	66.00	175.00
26-Drug-c with hypodermic; drug propaganda story	24.00	72.00	190.00
30-Strangulation cover	24.00	72.00	190.00

NOTE: ***Powell** a-No. 1, 2, 4. **Wildey** a-1, 5. Bondage c-11.*

PERFECT LOVE
Ziff-Davis(Approved Comics)/St. John No. 9 on: #10, 8-9/51 (cover date; 5-6/51 indicia date); #2, 10-11/51 - #10, 12/53

10(#1)(8-9/51)-Painted-c	19.00	56.00	150.00
2(10-11/51)	12.50	37.50	100.00
3,5-7: 3-Painted-c. 5-Photo-c	10.00	30.00	70.00
4,8 (Fall, 1952)-Kinstler-a; last Z-D issue	10.00	30.00	75.00
9,10 (10/53, 12/53, St. John): 9-Painted-c. 10-Photo-c	9.30	28.00	65.00

PERG (Also see Hellina)
Lightning Comics: Oct, 1993 - No. 8, May, 1994 ($2.95)

1-($3.50)-Flip-c is glow-in-the-dark by Saltares			3.50
1-4: Platinum Editions			3.00
2-8: 4-Origin Perg. 7-Blue & Pink cover versions			3.00

PERRI (Disney)
Dell Publishing Co.: No. 847, Jan, 1958

Four Color 847-Movie, w/2 diff-c publ.	4.60	13.75	55.00

PERRY MASON
David McKay Publications: No. 49, 1946 - No. 50, 1946

Feature Books 49, 59-Based on Gardner novels	28.00	84.00	225.00

PERRY MASON MYSTERY MAGAZINE (TV)
Dell Publishing Co.: June-Aug, 1964 - No. 2, Oct-Dec, 1964

1	3.00	9.00	40.00
2-Raymond Burr photo-c	3.00	9.00	35.00

PERSONAL LOVE (Also see Movie Love)
Famous Funnies: Jan, 1950 - No. 33, June, 1955

1-Photo-c	17.00	51.00	135.00
2-Kathryn Grayson & Mario Lanza photo-c	10.00	30.00	70.00
3-7,10: 7-Robert Walker & Joanne Dru photo-c. 10-Loretta Young & Joseph Cotton photo-c	7.85	23.50	55.00
8,9: 8-Esther Williams & Howard Keel photo-c. 9-Debra Paget & Louis Jourdan photo-c	8.65	26.00	60.00
11-Toth-a; Glenn Ford & Gene Tierney photo-c	10.00	30.00	80.00
12,16,17-One pg. Frazetta each. 17-Rock Hudson & Yvonne DeCarlo photo-c	7.85	23.50	55.00

13-15,18-23: 12-Jane Greer & William Lundigan photo-c. 14-Kirk Douglas photo-c. 15-Dale Robertson & Joanne Dru photo-c. 18-Gregory Peck & Susan Hayworth photo-c. 19-Anthony Quinn & Suzan Ball photo-c. 20-Robert Wagner & Kathleen Crowley photo-c. 21-Roberta Peters & Byron Palmer

Peter Panda #10 © DC

Peter Parker: Spider-Man #10 © MAR

Petticoat Junction #2 © Way Films

photo-c. 22-Dale Robertson photo-c. 23-Rhonda Fleming-c 6.40 19.25 45.00
24,27,28-Frazetta-a in each (8,8&6 pgs.). 27-Rhonda Fleming & Fernando Lamas photo-c. 28,30-Mitzi Gaynor photo-c 40.00 120.00 320.00
25-Frazetta-a (tribute to Betty Page, 7 pg. story); Tyrone Power/Terry Moore photo-c from "King of the Khyber Rifles" 40.00 120.00 360.00
26,29,30,33: 26-Constance Smith & Byron Palmer photo-c. 29-Charlton Heston & Nicol Morey photo-c. 30-Johnny Ray & Mitzi Gaynor photo-c. 33-Dana Andrews & Piper Laurie photo-c 6.40 19.25 45.00
31-Marlon Brando & Jean Simmons photo-c; last pre-code (2/55) 10.00 30.00 70.00
32-Classic Frazetta-a (8 pgs.); Kirk Douglas & Bella Darvi photo-c 50.00 150.00 450.00
NOTE: *All have photo-c. Many feature movie stars.* ***Everett*** *a-5, 9, 10, 24.*

PERSONAL LOVE (Going Steady V3#3 on)
Prize Publ. (Headline): V1#1, Sept, 1957 - V3#2, Nov-Dec, 1959

V1#1 8.65 26.00 60.00
2 5.00 15.00 32.00
3-6(7-8/58) 5.00 15.00 30.00
V2#1(9-10/58)-V2#6(7-8/59) 4.30 13.00 26.00
V3#1-Wood?/Orlando-a 5.00 15.00 35.00
2 4.00 12.00 24.00

PETER CANNON - THUNDERBOLT (See Crisis on Infinite Earths)(Also see Thunderbolt)
DC Comics: Sept, 1992 - No. 12, Aug, 1993 ($1.25)

1-12 2.00

PETER COTTONTAIL
Key Publications: Jan, 1954; Feb, 1954 - No. 2, Mar, 1954 (Says 3/53 in error)

1(1/54)-Not 3-D 8.65 26.00 60.00
1(2/54)-(3-D, 25¢)-Came w/glasses; written by Bruce Hamilton 22.00 66.00 175.00
2-Reprints 3-D #1 but not in 3-D 5.70 17.00 40.00

PETER GUNN (TV)
Dell Publishing Co.: No. 1087, Apr-June, 1960

Four Color 1087-Photo-c 9.00 27.00 110.00

PETER PAN (Disney) (See Hook, Movie Classics & Comics, New Adventures of… & Walt Disney Showcase #36)
Dell Publishing Co.: No. 442, Dec, 1952 - No. 926, Aug, 1958

Four Color 442 (#1)-Movie 9.00 27.00 110.00
Four Color 926-Reprint of 442 4.10 12.30 45.00

PETER PAN
Disney Comics: 1991 ($5.95, graphic novel, 68 pgs.)(Celebrates video release)

nn-r/Peter Pan Treasure Chest from 1953 7.00

PETER PANDA
National Periodical Publications: Aug-Sept, 1953 - No. 31, Aug-Sept, 1958

1-Grossman-c/a in all 40.00 120.00 350.00
2 22.00 66.00 175.00
3-10: 9-Robot-c 18.00 53.00 140.00
11-31 10.50 32.00 85.00

PETER PAN TREASURE CHEST (See Dell Giants)

PETER PARKER (See The Spectacular Spider-Man)

PETER PARKER: SPIDER-MAN
Marvel Comics: Jan, 1999 - Present ($2.99/$1.99/$2.25)

1-Mackie-s/Romita Jr.-a; wraparound-c 3.00
1-($6.95) DF Edition w/variant cover by the Romitas 7.00
2-11,13-17-($1.99): 2-Two covers; Thor app. 3-Iceman-c/app. 4-Marrow-c/app. 5-Spider-Woman app. 7,8-Blade app. 9,10-Venom app. 11-Iron Man & Thor-c/app. 2.00
12-($2.99) Sinister Six and Venom app. 3.00
18-24: 18-Begin $2.25-c. 20-Jenkins-s/Buckingham-a start. 23-Intro Typeface. 24-Maximum Security x-over 2.25
25-($2.99) Two covers; Spider-Man & Green Goblin 3.00
...'99 Annual (8/99, $3.50) Man-Thing app. 3.50
...'00 Annual ($3.50) Bounty app.; Joe Bennett-a; Black Cat back-up story 3.50

PETER PAT
United Features Syndicate: No. 8, 1939

Single Series 8 34.00 101.00 270.00

PETER PAUL'S 4 IN 1 JUMBO COMIC BOOK
Capitol Stories (Charlton): No date (1953)

1-Contains 4 comics bound; Space Adventures, Space Western, Crime & Justice, Racket Squad in Action 40.00 120.00 340.00

PETER PIG
Standard Comics: No. 5, May, 1953 - No. 6, Aug, 1953

5,6 5.70 17.00 40.00

PETER PORKCHOPS (See Leading Comics #23)
National Periodical Publications: 11-12/49 - No. 61, 9-11/59; No. 62, 10-12/60 (1-11: 52 pgs.)

1 34.00 101.00 270.00
2 16.00 49.00 130.00
3-10: 6- "Peter Rockets to Mars!" c/story 12.00 36.00 95.00
11-30 10.00 30.00 70.00
31-62 8.65 26.00 60.00
NOTE: ***Otto Feur*** *a-all.* ***Sheldon Mayer*** *a-30-38, 40-44, 46-52, 61.*

PETER PORKER, THE SPECTACULAR SPIDER-HAM
Star Comics (Marvel): May, 1985 - No. 17, Sept, 1987 (Also see Marvel Tails)

1-Michael Golden-c 4.00
2-17: 12-Origin/1st app. Bizarro Phil. 13-Halloween issue 3.00
NOTE: *Back-up features: 2-X-Bugs. 3-Iron Mouse. 4-Croctor Strange. 5-Thrr, Dog of Thunder.*

PETER POTAMUS (TV)
Gold Key: Jan, 1965 (Hanna-Barbera)

1-1st app. Peter Potamus & So-So, Breezly & Sneezly 9.00 27.00 110.00

PETER RABBIT (See New Funnies #65 & Space Comics)
Dell Publishing Co.: No. 1, 1942

Large Feature Comic 1 42.00 125.00 500.00

PETER RABBIT (Adventures of…; New Advs. of… #9 on)(Also see Funny Tunes & Space Comics)
Avon Periodicals: 1947 - No. 34, Aug-Sept, 1956

1(1947)-Reprints 1943-44 Sunday strips; contains a biography & drawing of Cady 35.00 105.00 280.00
2 (4/48) 25.00 75.00 200.00
3 ('48) - 6(7/49)-Last Cady issue 22.00 66.00 175.00
7-10(1950-8/51): 9-New logo 8.65 26.00 60.00
11(11/51)-34('56)-Avon's character 5.70 17.00 40.00
...Easter Parade (1952, 25¢, 132 pgs.) 18.00 53.00 140.00
...Jumbo Book (1954-Giant Size, 25¢)-Jesse James by Kinstler (6 pgs.); space ship-c 23.00 68.00 180.00

PETER RABBIT 3-D
Eternity Comics: April, 1990 ($2.95, with glasses; sealed in plastic bag)

1-By Harrison Cady (reprints) 3.00

PETER, THE LITTLE PEST (#4 titled Petey)
Marvel Comics Group: Nov, 1969 - No. 4, May, 1970

1 5.00 15.00 55.00
2-4-r-Dexter the Demon & Melvin the Monster 3.45 10.35 38.00

PETE'S DRAGON (See Walt Disney Showcase #43)

PETE THE PANIC
Stanmor Publications: November, 1955

nn-Code approved 4.30 13.00 26.00

PETEY (See Peter, the Little Pest)

PETTICOAT JUNCTION (TV, inspired Green Acres)
Dell Publ. Co.: Oct-Dec, 1964 - No. 5, Oct-Dec, 1965 (#1-3, 5 have photo-c)

1 5.85 17.50 70.00
2-5 4.55 13.65 50.00

PETUNIA (Also see Looney Tunes and Porky Pig)

The Phantom #6 © GK

Phantom Lady #23 © FOX

Phantom Stranger #5 © DC

GD2.0 FN6.0 NM9.4

Dell Publishing Co.: No. 463, Apr, 1953
Four Color 463 3.65 11.00 40.00

PHAGE (See Neil Gaiman's Teknophage & Neil Gaiman's Phage-Shadowdeath)

PHANTACEA
McPherson Publishing Co.: Sept, 1977 - No. 6, Summer, 1980 (B&W)
1-Early Dave Sim-a (32 pgs.) 3.00 9.00 30.00
2-Dave Sim-a(10 pgs.) 2.00 6.00 16.00
3,5: 3-Flip-c w/Damnation Bridge 1.10 3.30 9.00
4,6: 4-Gene Day-a 1.10 3.30 9.00

PHANTASMO (See The Funnies #45)
Dell Publishing Co.: No. 18, 1941
Large Feature Comic 18 27.00 81.00 325.00

PHANTOM, THE
David McKay Publishing Co.: 1939 - 1949
Feature Books 20 71.00 213.00 850.00
Feature Books 22 54.00 163.00 650.00
Feature Books 39 50.00 150.00 450.00
Feature Books 53,56,57 40.00 120.00 350.00

PHANTOM, THE (See Ace Comics, Defenders Of The Earth, Eat Right to Work and Win, Future Comics, Harvey Comics Hits #51,56, Harvey Hits #1, 6, 12, 15, 26, 36, 44, 48, & King Comics)

PHANTOM, THE (nn (#29)-Published overseas only) (Also see Comics Reading Library)
Gold Key(#1-17)/King(#18-28)/Charlton(#30 on): Nov, 1962 - No. 17, Jul, 1966; No. 18, Sept, 1966 - No. 28, Dec, 1967; No. 30, Feb, 1969 - No. 74, Jan, 1977
1-Manning-a; origin revealed on inside-c. & back-c 15.00 45.00 175.00
2-King, Queen & Jack begins, ends #11 7.50 22.50 90.00
3-5 6.30 19.00 75.00
6-10 5.85 17.50 70.00
11-17: 12-Track Hunter begins 4.60 13.75 55.00
18-Flash Gordon begins; Wood-a 4.10 12.30 45.00
19-24: 20-Flash Gordon ends (both by Gil Kane). 21-Mandrake begins. 20,24-Girl Phantom app. 3.65 11.00 40.00
25-28: 25-Jeff Jones-a(4 pgs.); 1 pg. Williamson ad. 26-Brick Bradford app. 28(nn)-Brick Bradford app. 3.20 9.60 35.00
30-33: 33-Last 12¢ issue 2.50 7.50 24.00
34-40: 36,39-Ditko-a 2.30 7.00 20.00
41-66: 46-Intro. The Piranha. 62-Bolle-c 2.00 6.00 18.00
67-Origin retold; Newton-c/a 2.30 7.00 20.00
68-73-Newton-c/a 1.75 5.25 14.00
74-Classic flag-c by Newton; Newton-a; 2.30 7.00 20.00
NOTE: ***Aparo** a-31-34, 36-38; c-31-38, 60, 61. Painted c-1-17.*

PHANTOM, THE
DC Comics: May, 1988 - No. 4, Aug, 1988 ($1.25, mini-series)
1-4: Orlando-c/a in all 3.00

PHANTOM, THE
DC Comics: Mar, 1989 - No. 13, Mar, 1990 ($1.50)
1-13: 1-Brief origin 3.00

PHANTOM, THE
Wolf Publishing: 1992 - No. 8, 1993 ($2.25)
1-8 2.25

PHANTOM BLOT, THE (#1 titled New Adventures of...)
Gold Key: Oct, 1964 - No. 7, Nov, 1966 (Disney)
1 (Meets The Beagle Boys) 5.00 15.00 55.00
2-1st Super Goof 4.55 13.65 50.00
3-7 3.00 9.00 30.00

PHANTOM EAGLE (See Mighty Midget, Marvel Super Heroes #16 & Wow #6)

PHANTOM FORCE
Image Comics/Genesis West #0, 3-7: 12/93 - #2, 1994; #0, 3/94; #3, 5/94 - #8, 10/94 ($2.50/$3.50, limited series)
0 (3/94, $2.50)-Kirby/Jim Lee-c; Kirby-p pgs. 1,5,24-29. 3.00
1 (12/93, $2.50)-Polybagged w/trading card; Kirby Liefeld-c; Kirby plots/pencils w/inks by Liefeld, McFarlane, Jim Lee, Silvestri, Larsen, Williams, Ordway & Miki. 3.00
2 ($3.50)-Kirby-a(p); Kirby/Larson-c 3.50
3-8: 3-(5/94, $2.50)-Kirby/McFarlane-c 4-(5/94)-Kirby-c(p). 5-(6/94) 3.00

PHANTOM GUARD
Image Comics (WildStorm Productions): Oct, 1997 - No. 6, Mar, 1998 ($2.50)
1-6: 1-Two covers 3.00
1-($3.50)-Voyager Pack w/Wildcore preview 3.50

PHANTOM LADY (1st Series) (My Love Secret #24 on) (Also see All Top, Daring Adventures, Freedom Fighters, Jungle Thrills, & Wonder Boy)
Fox Features Syndicate: No. 13, Aug, 1947 - No. 23 Apr, 1949
13(#1)-Phantom Lady by Matt Baker begins (1st app.); The Blue Beetle story 381.00 1143.00 4000.00
14-16: 14(#2)-Not Baker-c. 15-P.L. injected with experimental drug. 16-Negligee-c, panels; true crime stories begin 237.00 711.00 2250.00
17-Classic bondage cover; used in **SOTI**, illo "Sexual stimulation by combining 'headlights' with the sadist's dream of tying up a woman" 504.00 1513.00 5800.00
18,19 168.00 505.00 1600.00
20-22 132.00 395.00 1250.00
23-Bondage-c 147.00 442.00 1400.00
NOTE: ***Matt Baker** a-in all; c-13, 15-21. **Kamen** a-22, 23.*

PHANTOM LADY (2nd Series) (See Terrific Comics) (Formerly Linda)
Ajax/Farrell Publ.: V1#5, Dec-Jan, 1954/1955 - No. 4, June, 1955
V1#5(#1)-By Matt Baker 111.00 332.00 1050.00
V1#2-Last pre-code 84.00 252.00 800.00
3,4-Red Rocket. 3-Heroin story 68.00 204.00 650.00

PHANTOM LADY
Verotik Publications: 1994 ($9.95)
1-Reprints G. A. stories from Phantom Lady and All Top Comics; Adam Hughes-c 10.00

PHANTOM PLANET, THE
Dell Publishing Co.: No. 1234, 1961
Four Color 1234-Movie 6.70 20.00 80.00

PHANTOM STRANGER, THE (1st Series)(See Saga of Swamp Thing)
National Periodical Publications: Aug-Sept, 1952 - No. 6, June-July, 1953
1(Scarce)-1st app. 190.00 570.00 1800.00
2 (Scarce) 105.00 316.00 1000.00
3-6 (Scarce) 92.00 276.00 875.00

PHANTOM STRANGER, THE (2nd Series) (See Showcase #80)
National Periodical Publications: May-June, 1969 - No. 41, Feb-Mar, 1976
1-2nd S.A. app. P. Stranger; only 12¢ issue 9.00 27.00 100.00
2,3 3.65 11.00 40.00
4-1st new look Phantom Stranger; N. Adams-a 4.10 12.30 45.00
5-7 3.00 9.00 30.00
8-14: 14-Last 15¢ issue 2.50 7.50 23.00
15-19: All 25¢ giants (52 pgs.) 2.50 7.50 25.00
20-Dark Circle begins, ends #24. 2.00 6.00 18.00
21,22 1.50 4.50 12.00
23-Spawn of Frankenstein begins by Kaluta 2.50 7.50 25.00
24,25,27-30-Last Spawn of Frankenstein 2.00 6.00 18.00
26- Book-length story featuring Phantom Stranger, Dr.13 & Spawn of Frankenstein 2.30 7.00 20.00
31-The Black Orchid begins (6-7/74). 2.50 7.50 23.00
32,34-38: 34-Last 20¢ issue (#35 on are 25¢) 1.50 4.50 12.00
33,39-41: 33-Deadman-c/story. 39-41-Deadman ap. 1.85 5.50 15.00
NOTE: ***N. Adams** a-4; c-3-19. **Anderson** a-4, 5i. **Aparo** a-7-17, 19-26; c-20-24, 33-41. **B. Bailey** a-27-30. **DeZuniga** a-12-16, 18, 19, 21, 22, 31, 34. **Grell** a-33. **Kaluta** a-23-25; c-26. **Meskin** r-15, 16, 18, 19. **Redondo** a-32, 35, 36. **Sparling** a-20. **Starr** a-17r. **Toth** a-15r. Black Orchid by **Carrilo**-38-41. Dr. 13 solo in-13, 18, 19, 20, 21, 34. Frankenstein by **Kaluta**-23-25; by **Baily**-27-30. No Black Orchid-33, 34, 37.*

PHANTOM STRANGER (See Justice League of America #103)
DC Comics: Oct, 1987 - No. 4, Jan, 1988 (75¢, limited series)
1-4-Mignola/Russell-c/a & Eclipso app. in all. 3,4-Eclipso-c 3.00

PHANTOM STRANGER (See Vertigo Visions-The Phantom Stranger)

Phantom Witch Doctor #1 © AVON

Pictorial Romances #9 © STJ

Picture Stories From American History #2 © WMG

GD2.0 FN6.0 NM9.4

PHANTOM: THE GHOST WHO WALKS
Marvel Comics: Feb, 1995 - No. 3, Apr, 1995 ($2.95, limited series)

1-3 3.00

PHANTOM 2040 (TV cartoon)
Marvel Comics: May, 1995 - No. 4, Aug, 1995 ($1.50)

1-4-Based on animated series 2.00

PHANTOM WITCH DOCTOR (Also see Durango Kid #8 & Eerie #8)
Avon Periodicals: 1952

1-Kinstler-c/a (7 pgs.) 44.00 133.00 400.00

PHANTOM ZONE, THE (See Adventure #283 & Superboy #100, 104)
DC Comics: January, 1982 - No. 4, April, 1982

1-4-Superman app. in all. 2-4: Batman, Green Lantern app. 3.00
NOTE: *Colan a-1-4p; c-1-4p.* ***Giordano*** *c-1-4i.*

PHAZE
Eclipse Comics: Apr, 1988 - No. 2, Oct, 1988 ($2.25)

1,2: 1-Sienkiewicz-c. 2-Gulacy painted-c 2.25

PHIL RIZZUTO (Baseball Hero)(See Sport Thrills, Accepted reprint)
Fawcett Publications: 1951 (New York Yankees)

nn-Photo-c 68.00 205.00 650.00

PHOENIX
Atlas/Seaboard Publ.: Jan, 1975 - No. 4, Oct, 1975

1-Origin; Rovin-s/Amendola-a 6.00
2-4: 3-Origin & only app. The Dark Avenger. 4-New origin/costume The Protector (formerly Phoenix) 5.00
NOTE: ***Infantino*** *appears in #1, 2.* ***Austin*** *a-3i.* ***Thorne*** *c-3.*

PHOENIX (...The Untold Story)
Marvel Comics Group: April, 1984 ($2.00, one-shot)

1-Byrne/Austin-r/X-Men #137 with original unpublished ending 1.25 3.75 10.00

PHOENIX RESURRECTION, THE
Malibu Comics (Ultraverse): 1995 - 1996 ($3.95)

Genesis #1 (12/95)-X-Men app; wraparound-c, Revelations #1 (12/95)-X-Men app; wraparound-c, Aftermath #1 (1/96)-X-Men app. 4.00
0-($1.95)-r/series 2.00
0-American Entertainment Ed. 4.00

PICNIC PARTY (See Dell Giants)

PICTORIAL CONFESSIONS (Pictorial Romances #4 on)
St. John Publishing Co.: Sept, 1949 - No. 3, Dec, 1949

1-Baker-c/a(3) 30.00 90.00 240.00
2-Baker-a; photo-c 19.00 56.00 150.00
3-Kubert, Baker-a; part Kubert-c 21.00 62.00 165.00

PICTORIAL LOVE STORIES (Formerly Tim McCoy)
Charlton Comics: No. 22, Oct, 1949 - No. 26, July, 1950 (all photo-c)

22-26: All have "Me-Dan Cupid". 25-Fred Astaire-c 20.00 60.00 160.00

PICTORIAL LOVE STORIES
St. John Publishing Co.: October, 1952

1-Baker-c 28.00 83.00 220.00

PICTORIAL ROMANCES (Formerly Pictorial Confessions)
St. John Publ. Co.: No. 4, Jan, 1950; No. 5, Jan, 1951 - No. 24, Mar, 1954

4-Baker-a; photo-c 29.00 87.00 235.00
5,10-All Matt Baker issues. 5-Reprints all stories from #4 w/new Baker-c 22.00 66.00 175.00
6-9,12,13,15,16-Baker-c, 2-3 stories 16.00 49.00 130.00
11-Baker-c/a(3); Kubert-r/Hollywood Confessions #1 18.00 53.00 140.00
14,21-24: Baker-c/a each. 21,24-Each has signed story by Estrada 14.00 43.00 115.00
17-20(7/53, 25¢, 100 pgs.): Baker-c/a; each has two signed stories by Estrada 29.00 87.00 235.00
NOTE: ***Matt Baker*** *art in most issues.* ***Estrada*** *a-17-20(2), 21, 24.*

PICTURE NEWS
Lafayette Street Corp.: Jan, 1946 - No. 10, Jan-Feb, 1947

1-Milt Gross begins, ends No. 6; 4 pg. Kirby-a; A-Bomb-c/story 40.00 120.00 340.00
2-Atomic explosion panels; Frank Sinatra/Perry Como story 21.00 64.00 170.00
3-Atomic explosion panels; Frank Sinatra, June Allyson, Benny Goodman stories 18.00 53.00 140.00
4-Atomic explosion panels; "Caesar and Cleopatra" movie adapt. w/Claude Raines & Vivian Leigh; Jackie Robinson story 20.00 60.00 160.00
5-7: 5-Hank Greenberg story. 6-Joe Louis-c/story 14.00 41.00 110.00
8,10: 8-Monte Hale story (9-10/46; 1st?). 10-Dick Quick; A-Bomb story; Krigstein, Gross-a 15.00 45.00 120.00
9-A-Bomb story; "Crooked Mile" movie adaptation; Joe DiMaggio story. 18.00 53.00 140.00

PICTURE PARADE (Picture Progress #5 on)
Gilberton Company (Also see A Christmas Adventure): Sept, 1953 - V1#4, Dec, 1953 (28 pgs.)

V1#1-Andy's Atomic Adventures; A-bomb blast-c; (Teachers version distributed to schools exists) 19.00 56.00 150.00
2-Around the World with the United Nations 11.00 33.00 90.00
3-Adventures of the Lost One(The American Indian), 4-A Christmas Adventure (r-under same title in 1969) 11.00 33.00 90.00

PICTURE PROGRESS (Formerly Picture Parade)
Gilberton Corp.: V1#5, Jan, 1954 - V3#2, Oct, 1955 (28-36 pgs.)

V1#5-9,V2#1-9: 5-News in Review 1953. 6-The Birth of America. 7-The Four Seasons. 8-Paul Revere's Ride. 9-The Hawaiian Islands(5/54). V2#1-The Story of Flight(9/54). 2-Vote for Crazy River (The Meaning of Elections). 3-Louis Pasteur. 4-The Star Spangled Banner. 5-News in Review 1954. 6-Alaska: The Great Land. 7-Life in the Circus. 8-The Time of the Cave Man. 9-Summer Fun(5/55) 6.40 19.25 45.00
V3#1,2: 1-The Man Who Discovered America. 2-The Lewis & Clark Expedition 6.40 19.25 45.00

PICTURE SCOPE JUNGLE ADVENTURES (See Jungle Thrills)

PICTURE STORIES FROM AMERICAN HISTORY
National/All-American/E. C. Comics: 1945 - No. 4, Sum, 1947 (#1,2: 10¢, 56 pgs.; #3,4: 15¢, 52 pgs.)

1 30.00 90.00 240.00
2-4 24.00 73.00 195.00

PICTURE STORIES FROM SCIENCE
E.C. Comics: Spring, 1947 - No. 2, Fall, 1947

1-(15¢) 30.00 90.00 240.00
2-(10¢) 26.00 79.00 210.00

PICTURE STORIES FROM THE BIBLE (See Narrative Illustration, the Story of the Comics by M.C. Gaines)
National/All-American/E.C. Comics: 1942 - No. 4, Fall, 1943; 1944-46

1-4('42-Fall, '43)-Old Testament (DC) 24.00 71.00 190.00
Complete Old Testament Edition, (12/43-DC, 50¢, 232 pgs.);-1st printing; contains #1-4; 2nd - 8th (1/47) printings exist; later printings by E.C. 28.00 84.00 225.00
Complete Old Testament Edition (1945-publ. by Bible Pictures Ltd.)-232 pgs., hardbound, in color with dust jacket 28.00 84.00 225.00
NOTE: *Both Old and New Testaments published in England by Bible Pictures Ltd. in hardback, 1943, in color, 376 pgs. (2 vols.: O.T. 232 pgs. & N.T. 144 pgs.), and were also published by Scarf Press in 1979 (Old Test., $9.95) and in 1980 (New Test., $7.95)*

1-3(New Test.; 1944-46, DC)-52 pgs. ea. 18.00 53.00 140.00
The Complete Life of Christ Edition (1945, 25¢, 96 pgs.)-Contains #1&2 of the New Testament Edition 24.00 71.00 190.00
1,2(Old Testament-r in comic book form)(E.C., 1946; 52 pgs.) 18.00 53.00 140.00
1(DC),2(AA),3(EC)(New Testament-r in comic book form)(E.C., 1946; 52 pgs.) 18.00 53.00 140.00
Complete New Testament Edition (1946-E.C., 50¢, 144 pgs.)-Contains #1-3 24.00 71.00 190.00
NOTE: *Another British series entitled* ***The Bible Illustrated*** *from 1947 has recently been discov ered, with the same internal artwork. This eight edition series (5-OT, 3-NT) is of particular intere to Classics Ill. collectors because it exactly copied the C.I. logo format. The British publisher wa*

Pinhead & Foodini #2 © FAW

Pinky and the Brain #2 © WB

Pin-Up Pete #1 © Minoan Mags.

Thorpe & Porter, who in 1951 began publishing the British Classics Ill. series. All editions of The Bible Ill. have new British painted covers. While this market is still new, and not all editions have as yet been found, current market value is about the same as the first U.S. editions of Picture Stories From The Bible.

PICTURE STORIES FROM WORLD HISTORY
E.C. Comics: Spring, 1947 - No. 2, Summer, 1947 (52, 48 pgs.)

	GD2.0	FN6.0	NM9.4
1-(15¢)	30.00	90.00	240.00
2-(10¢)	26.00	79.00	210.00

PINHEAD
Marvel Comics (Epic Comics): Dec, 1993 - No. 6, May, 1994 ($2.50)

	GD2.0	FN6.0	NM9.4
1-($2.95)-Embossed foil-c by Kelley Jones; Intro Pinhead & Disciples (Snakeoil, Hangman, Fan Dancer & Dixie)			3.00
2-6			2.50

PINHEAD & FOODINI (TV)(Also see Foodini & Jingle Dingle Christmas...)
Fawcett Publications: July, 1951 - No. 4, Jan, 1952 (Early TV comic)

	GD2.0	FN6.0	NM9.4
1-(52 pgs.)-Photo-c; based on TV puppet show	33.00	98.00	260.00
2,3-Photo-c	16.00	48.00	125.00
4	12.50	37.50	100.00

PINHEAD VS. MARSHALL LAW (Law in Hell)
Marvel Comics (Epic): Nov, 1993 - No. 2, Dec, 1993 ($2.95, lim. series)

	GD2.0	FN6.0	NM9.4
1,2: 1-Embossed red foil-c. 2-Embossed silver foil-c			3.00

PINK DUST
Kitchen Sink Press: 1998 ($3.50, B&W, mature)

	GD2.0	FN6.0	NM9.4
1-J. O'Barr-s/a			3.50

PINK PANTHER, THE (TV)(See The Inspector & Kite Fun Book)
Gold Key #1-70/Whitman #71-87: April, 1971 - No. 87, 1984

	GD2.0	FN6.0	NM9.4
1-The Inspector begins	4.10	12.30	45.00
2-5	2.30	7.00	20.00
6-10	1.85	5.50	15.00
11-30: Warren Tufts-a #16-on	1.50	4.50	12.00
31-60	1.10	3.30	9.00
61-70		2.40	6.00
71-74,81-83	1.00	3.00	8.00
75(8/80),76-80(pre-pack?)	1.75	5.25	14.00
84-87(All #90266 on-c, no date or date code)	1.50	4.50	12.00
Mini-comic No. 1(1976)(3-1/4x6-1/2")	1.10	3.30	9.00

NOTE: *Pink Panther began as a movie cartoon. (See Golden Comics Digest #38, 45 and March of Comics #376, 384, 390, 409, 418, 429, 441, 449, 461, 473, 486); #37, 72, 80-85 contain reprints.*

PINK PANTHER SUPER SPECIAL (TV)
Harvey Comics: Oct, 1993 ($2.25, 68 pgs.)

	GD2.0	FN6.0	NM9.4
V2#1-The Inspector & Wendy Witch stories also			3.00

PINK PANTHER, THE
Harvey Comics: Nov, 1993 - No. 9, July, 1994 ($1.50)

	GD2.0	FN6.0	NM9.4
V2#1-9			2.00

PINKY & THE BRAIN (See Animaniacs)
DC Comics: July, 1996 - No. 27, Nov, 1998 ($1.75/$1.95/$1.99)

	GD2.0	FN6.0	NM9.4
1-27, ...Christmas Special (1/96, $1.50)			2.50

PINKY LEE (See Adventures of...)

PINKY THE EGGHEAD
I.W./Super Comics: 1963 (Reprints from Noodnik)

	GD2.0	FN6.0	NM9.4
I.W. Reprint #1,2(nd)	1.50	4.50	12.00
Super Reprint #14-r/Noodnik Comics #4	1.50	4.50	12.00

PINOCCHIO (See 4-Color #92, 252, 545, 1203, Mickey Mouse Mag. V5#3, Movie Comics under Wonderful Advs. of..., New Advs. of..., Thrilling Comics #2, Walt Disney Showcase, Walt Disney's..., Wonderful Advs. of..., & World's Greatest Stories #2)
Dell Publishing Co.: No. 92, 1945 - No. 1203, Mar, 1962 (Disney)

	GD2.0	FN6.0	NM9.4
Four Color 92-The Wonderful Adventures of...; 16 pg. Donald Duck story ; entire book by Kelly	58.00	175.00	700.00
Four Color 252 (10/49)-Origin, not by Kelly	10.00	30.00	120.00
Four Color 545 (3/54)-The Wonderful Advs. of...; part-r of 4-Color #92; Disney-movie	6.70	20.00	80.00
Four Color 1203 (3/62)	4.60	13.75	55.00

PINOCCHIO AND THE EMPEROR OF THE NIGHT
Marvel Comics: Mar, 1988 ($1.25, 52 pgs.)

	GD2.0	FN6.0	NM9.4
1-Adapts film			3.00

PINOCCHIO LEARNS ABOUT KITES (See Kite Fun Book)

PIN-UP PETE (Also see Great Lover Romances & Monty Hall...)
Toby Press: 1952

	GD2.0	FN6.0	NM9.4
1-Jack Sparling pin-ups	19.00	56.00	150.00

PIONEER MARSHAL (See Fawcett Movie Comics)

PIONEER PICTURE STORIES
Street & Smith Publications: Dec, 1941 - No. 9, Dec, 1943

	GD2.0	FN6.0	NM9.4
1-The Legless Air Ace begins	30.00	90.00	240.00
2 -True life story of Errol Flynn	15.00	45.00	120.00
3-9	12.50	37.50	100.00

PIONEER WEST ROMANCES (Firehair #1,2,7-11)
Fiction House Magazines: No. 3, Spring, 1950 - No. 6, Winter, 1950-51

	GD2.0	FN6.0	NM9.4
3-(52 pgs.)-Firehair continues	20.00	60.00	160.00
4-6	20.00	60.00	160.00

PIPSQUEAK (See The Adventures of...)

PIRACY
E. C. Comics: Oct-Nov, 1954 - No. 7, Oct-Nov, 1955

	GD2.0	FN6.0	NM9.4
1-Williamson/Torres-a	23.00	68.00	250.00
2-Williamson/Torres-a	14.00	41.00	150.00
3-7: 5-7-Comics Code symbol on cover	11.35	34.00	125.00

NOTE: ***Crandall** a-in all; c-2-4. **Davis** a-1, 2, 6. **Evans** a-3-7; c-7. **Ingels** a-3-7. **Krigstein** a-3-5, 7; c-5, 6. **Wood** a-1, 2; c-1.*

PIRACY
Gemstone Publishing: March, 1998 - No. 7, Sept, 1998 ($2.50)

	GD2.0	FN6.0	NM9.4
1-7: E.C. reprints			2.50
Annual 1 ($10.95) Collects #1-4			11.00
Annual 2 ($7.95) Collects #5-7			8.00

PIRANA (See The Phantom #46 & Thrill-O-Rama #2, 3)

PIRATE CORP$, THE (See Hectic Planet)
Eternity Comics/Slave Labor Graphics: 1987 - No. 4, 1988 ($1.95)

	GD2.0	FN6.0	NM9.4
1-4: 1,2-Color. 3,4-B&W			2.00
Special 1 ('89, B&W)-Slave Labor Publ.			2.00

PIRATE CORP$, THE (Volume 2)
Slave Labor Graphics: 1989 - No. 4, 1992 ($1.95)

	GD2.0	FN6.0	NM9.4
1-4-Dorkin-s/a			2.00

PIRATE OF THE GULF, THE (See Superior Stories #2)

PIRATES COMICS
Hillman Periodicals: Feb-Mar, 1950 - No. 4, Aug-Sept, 1950 (All 52 pgs.)

	GD2.0	FN6.0	NM9.4
1	25.00	75.00	200.00
2-Dave Berg-a	18.00	53.00	140.00
3,4-Berg-a	16.00	49.00	130.00

PIRATES OF DARK WATER, THE (Hanna Barbera)
Marvel Comics: Nov, 1991 - No. 9, Aug, 1992 ($1.95)

	GD2.0	FN6.0	NM9.4
1-9: 9-Vess-c			2.00

P.I.'S: MICHAEL MAUSER AND MS. TREE, THE
First Comics: Jan, 1985 - No. 3, May, 1985 ($1.25, limited series)

	GD2.0	FN6.0	NM9.4
1-3: Staton-c/a(p)			2.00

PITT, THE (Also see The Draft & The War)
Marvel Comics: Mar, 1988 ($3.25, 52 pgs., one-shot)

	GD2.0	FN6.0	NM9.4
1-Ties into Starbrand, D.P.7			3.50

PITT (See Youngblood #4 & Gen 13 #3,#4)
Image Comics #1-9/Full Bleed #1/2,10-on: Jan, 1993 - Present ($1.95, intended as a four part limited series)

	GD2.0	FN6.0	NM9.4
1/2-(12/95)-1st Full Bleed issue			4.00
1-Dale Keown-c/a. 1-1st app. The Pitt			4.00

Pixie Puzzle Rocket to Adventureland #1 © AVON

Planetary #1 © WSP

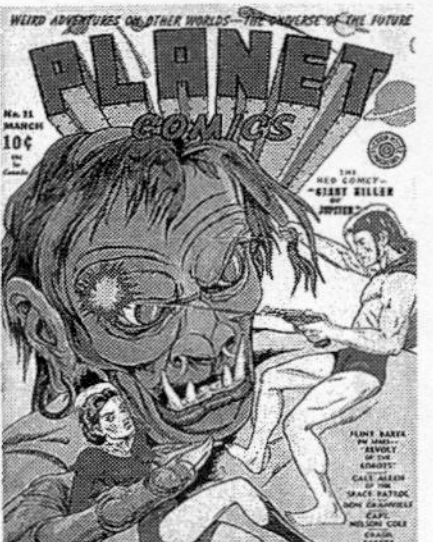

Planet Comics #11 © FH

2-13: All Dale Keown-c/a. 3 (Low distribution). 10 (1/96)-Indicia reads "January 1995" 3.00
14-20: 14-Begin $2.50-c, pullout poster 2.50
TPB-(1997, $9.95) r/#1/2, 1-4 10.00
TPB 2-(1999, $11.95) r/#5-9 12.00

PITT CREW
Full Bleed Studios: Aug, 1998 - Present ($2.50)
1-5: 1-Richard Pace-s/Ken Lashley-a. 2-4-Scott Lee-a 2.50

PITT IN THE BLOOD
Full Bleed Studios: Aug, 1996 ($2.50, one-shot)
nn-Richard Pace-a/script 2.50

PIXIE & DIXIE & MR. JINKS (TV)(See Jinks, Pixie, and Dixie & Whitman Comic Books)
Dell Publishing Co./Gold Key: July-Sept, 1960 - Feb, 1963 (Hanna-Barbera)
Four Color 1112 7.00 21.00 85.00
Four Color 1196,1264, 01-631-207 (Dell, 7/62) 5.00 15.00 60.00
1(2/63-Gold Key) 5.85 17.50 70.00

PIXIE PUZZLE ROCKET TO ADVENTURELAND
Avon Periodicals: Nov, 1952
1 12.50 37.50 100.00

PIXIES, THE (Advs. of...)(The Mighty Atom and ...#6 on)(See A-1 Comics #16)
Magazine Enterprises: Winter, 1946 - No. 4, Fall?, 1947; No. 5, 1948
1-Mighty Atom 8.65 26.00 60.00
2-5-Mighty Atom 5.00 15.00 30.00
I.W. Reprint #1(1958), 8-(Pee-Wee Pixies), 10-I.W. on cover, Super on inside 1.50 4.50 12.00

PIZZAZZ
Marvel Comics: Oct, 1977 - No. 16, Jan, 1979 (slick-color kids mag. w/puzzles, games, comics)
1-Star Wars photo-c/article; origin Tarzan; KISS photos/article; Iron-On bonus; 2 pg. pin-up calendars thru #8 2.50 7.50 24.00
2-Spider-Man-c; Beatles pin-up calendar 1.75 5.25 14.00
3-8: 3-Close Encounters-s; Bradbury-s. 4-Alice Cooper, Travolta; Charlie's Angels/Fonz/Hulk/Spider-Man-c. 5-Star Trek quiz. 6-Asimov-s. 7-James Bond; Spock/Darth Vader-c. 8-TV Spider-Man photo-c/article 1.75 5.25 14.00
9-14: 9-Shaun Cassidy-c. 10-Sgt. Pepper-c/s. 12-Battlestar Galactica-s; Spider-Man app. 13-TV Hulk-c/s. 14-Meatloaf-c/s 1.25 3.75 10.00
15,16: 15-Battlestar Galactica-s. 16-Movie Superman photo-c/s, Hulk. 1.50 4.50 12.00

NOTE: ***Star Wars*** *comics in all (1-6:Chaykin-a, 7-9: DeZuniga-a, 10-13:Simonson/Janson-a. 14-16:Cockrum-a).* ***Tarzan*** *comics, 1pg.-#1-8. 1pg. "Hey Look" by Kurtzman #12-16.*

PLANETARY (See Preview in flip book Gen13 #33)
DC Comics (WildStorm Prod.): Apr, 1999 - Present ($2.50)
1,2-Ellis-s/Cassaday-a/c 4.00
3-13: 12-Fourth Man revealed 2.50
...: All Over the World and Other Stories (2000, $14.95) r/#1-6 & Preview 14.95
.../The Authority: Ruling the World (8/00, $5.95) Ellis-s/Phil Jimenez-a 5.95

PLANET COMICS
Fiction House Magazines: 1/40 - No. 62, 9/49; No. 63, Wint, 1949-50; No. 64, Spring, 1950; No. 65, 1951(nd); No. 66-68, 1952(nd); No. 69, Wint, 1952-53; No. 70-72, 1953(nd); No. 73, Winter, 1953-54

	GD2.0	FN6.0	VF8.0	NM9.4
1-Origin Auro, Lord of Jupiter by Briefer (ends #61); Flint Baker & The Red Comet begin; Eisner/Fine-c	1000.00	3000.00	6250.00	11,500.00

	GD2.0	FN6.0	NM9.4
2-Lou Fine-c (Scarce)	410.00	1230.00	4300.00
3-Eisner-c	295.00	885.00	2800.00
4-Gale Allen and the Girl Squadron begins	253.00	758.00	2400.00
5,6-(Scarce): 5-Eisner/Fine-c	242.00	726.00	2300.00
7-12: 8-Robot-c. 12-The Star Pirate begins	200.00	600.00	1900.00
13,14: 13-Reff Ryan begins	147.00	442.00	1400.00
15-(Scarce)-Mars, God of War begins (11/41); see Jumbo Comics #31 for 1st app.	295.00	885.00	2800.00
16-20,22	132.00	395.00	1250.00
21-The Lost World & Hunt Bowman begin	137.00	412.00	1300.00
23-26: 26-Space Rangers begin (9/43), end #71	126.00	379.00	1200.00
27-30	101.00	303.00	960.00
31-35: 33-Origin Star Pirates Wonder Boots, reprinted in #52. 35-Mysta of the Moon begins, ends #62	84.00	253.00	800.00
36-45: 38-1st Mysta of the Moon-c. 41-New origin of "Auro, Lord of Jupiter". 42-Last Gale Allen. 43-Futura begins	76.00	229.00	725.00
46-60: 48-Robot-c. 53-Used in **SOTI**, pg. 32	61.00	182.00	575.00
61-68,70: 64,70-Robot-c. 65-70-All partial-r of earlier issues. 70-r/stories from #41	47.00	140.00	420.00
69-Used in **POP**, pgs. 101,102	47.00	140.00	420.00
71-73-No series stories. 71-Space Rangers strip	38.00	113.00	300.00
I.W. Reprint 1,8,9: 1(nd)-r/#70; cover-r from Attack on Planet Mars. 8 (r/#72), 9-r/#73	7.25	21.75	80.00

NOTE: ***Anderson*** *a-33-38, 40-51 (Star Pirate).* ***Matt Baker*** *a-53-59 (Mysta of the Moon).* ***Celardo*** *c-12.* ***Bill Discount*** *a-71 (Space Rangers).* ***Elias*** *c-70.* ***Evans*** *a-46-49 (Auro, Lord of Jupiter), 50-64 (Lost World).* ***Fine*** *c-2, 5.* ***Hopper*** *a-31, 35 (Gale Allen), 41, 42, 48, 49 (Mysta of the Moon).* ***Ingels*** *a-24-31 (Lost World), 56-61 (Auro, Lord of Jupiter).* ***Lubbers*** *a-44-47 (Space Rangers); c-40, 41.* ***Moriera*** *a-43, 44 (Mysta of the Moon.* ***Renee*** *a-40-49 (Lost World); c-33, 35, 39.* ***Tuska*** *a-30 (Star Pirate).* ***M. Whitman*** *a-50-52 (Mysta of the Moon), 53-58 (Star Pirate); c-71-73.* ***Starr*** *a-59.* ***Zolnerwich*** *c-10. 13-25. Bondage c-53.*

PLANET COMICS
Pacific Comics: 1984 ($5.95)
1-Reprints Planet Comics #1(1940) 6.00

PLANET COMICS
Blackthorne Publishing: Apr, 1988 - No. 3 ($2.00, color/B&W #3)
1-3: New stories. 1-Dave Stevens-c 3.00

PLANET OF THE APES (Magazine) (Also see Adventures on the... & Power Record Comics)
Marvel Comics Group: Aug, 1974 - No. 29, Feb, 1977 (B&W) (Based on movies)
1-Ploog-a 2.80 8.40 28.00
2-Ploog-a 2.00 6.00 16.00
3-10 1.50 4.50 12.00
11-20 (uncommon) 1.85 5.50 15.00
21-28 (low distribution) 2.00 6.00 18.00
29 (scarce) 3.20 9.60 35.00

NOTE: ***Alcala*** *a-7-11, 17-22, 24.* ***Ploog*** *a-1-4, 6, 8, 11, 13, 14, 19.* ***Sutton*** *a-11, 12, 15, 17, 19, 20, 23, 24, 29.* ***Tuska*** *a-1-6.*

PLANET OF THE APES
Adventure Comics: Apr, 1990 - No. 24, 1992 ($2.50, B&W)
1-New movie tie-in; comes w/outer-c (3 colors) 4.00
1-Limited serial numbered edition ($5.00) 5.00
1-2nd printing (no outer-c, $2.50) 2.50
2-24 3.00
Annual 1 ($3.50) 4.00
...Urchak's Folly 1-4 ($2.50, mini-series) 3.00

PLANET OF VAMPIRES
Seaboard Publications (Atlas): Feb, 1975 - No. 3, July, 1975
1-Neal Adams-c(i); 1st Broderick c/a(p); Hama-s 2.40 6.00
2,3: 2-Neal Adams-c. 3-Heath-c/a 5.00

PLANET TERRY
Marvel Comics (Star Comics)/Marvel: April, 1985 - No. 12, March, 1986 (Children's comic)
1-12 3.00

PLASM (See Warriors of Plasm)
Defiant Comics: June, 1993
0-Came bound into Diamond Previews V3#6 (6/93); price is for complete Previews with comic still attached 3.00
0-Comic only removed from Previews 2.00

PLASMER
Marvel Comics UK: Nov, 1993 - No. 4, Feb, 1994 ($1.95, limited series)
1-($2.50)-Polybagged w/4 trading cards 2.50
2-4: Capt. America & Silver Surfer app. 2.00

PLASTIC FORKS

Plastic Man #28 © QUA

Pocket Comics #4 © HARV

Poison Elves #50 © Drew Hayes

GD2.0 FN6.0 NM9.4

Marvel Comis (Epic Comics): 1990 - No. 5, 1990 ($4.95, 68 pgs., limited series, mature)
Book 1-5: Squarebound 5.00

PLASTIC MAN (Also see Police Comics & Smash Comics #17)
Vital Publ. No. 1,2/Quality Comics No. 3 on: Sum, 1943 - No. 64, Nov, 1956
nn(#1)- "In The Game of Death"; Skull-c; Jack Cole-c/a begins; ends-#64? 381.00 1143.00 4000.00
nn(#2, 2/44)- "The Gay Nineties Nightmare" 168.00 505.00 1600.00
3 (Spr, '46) 105.00 316.00 1000.00
4 (Sum, '46) 84.00 253.00 800.00
5 (Aut, '46) 71.00 213.00 675.00
6-10 58.00 174.00 550.00
11-20 53.00 158.00 475.00
21-30: 26-Last non-r issue? 42.00 127.00 380.00
31-40: 40-Used in POP, pg. 91 36.00 108.00 290.00
41-64: 53-Last precode issue. 54-Robot-c 30.00 90.00 240.00
Super Reprint 11,16,18: 11('63)-r/#16. 16-r/#18 & #21; Cole-a. 18('64)-Spirit-r by Eisner from Police #95 4.35 13.00 48.00
NOTE: ***Cole** r-44, 49, 56, 58, 59 at least. **Cuidera** c-32-64i.*

PLASTIC MAN (See DC Special #15 & House of Mystery #160)
National Periodical Publications/DC Comics: 11-12/66 - No. 10, 5-6/68; V4#11, 2-3/76 - No. 20, 10-11/77
1-Real 1st app. Silver Age Plastic Man (House of Mystery #160 is actually tryout); Gil Kane-c/a; 12¢ issues begin 7.25 21.75 80.00
2-5: 4-Infantino-c; Mortimer-a 3.20 9.60 35.00
6-10('68): 7-G.A. Plastic Man & Woozy Winks (1st S.A. app.) app.; origin retold. 10-Sparling-a; last 12¢ issue 2.50 7.50 25.00
V4#11('76)-20: 11-20-Fradon-p. 17-Origin retold 1.00 2.80 7.00

PLASTIC MAN
DC Comics: Nov, 1988 - No. 4, Feb, 1989 ($1.00, mini-series)
1-4: 1-Origin; Woozy Winks app. 2.00

PLASTRON CAFE
Mirage Studios: Dec, 1992 - No. 4, July, 1993 ($2.25, B&W)
1-4: 1-Teenage Mutant Ninja Turtles app.; Kelly Freas-c. 2-Hildebrandt painted-c. 4-Spaced & Alien Fire stories 2.25

PLAYFUL LITTLE AUDREY (TV)(Also see Little Audrey #25)
Harvey Publications: 6/57 - No. 110, 11/73; No. 111, 8/74 - No. 121, 4/76
1 22.00 65.00 240.00
2 11.00 33.00 120.00
3-5 7.65 23.00 85.00
6-10 5.00 15.00 55.00
11-20 3.45 10.35 38.00
21-40 2.50 7.50 25.00
41-60 2.30 7.00 20.00
61-84: 84-Last 12¢ issue 2.00 6.00 16.00
85-99 1.50 4.50 12.00
100-52 pg. Giant 2.30 7.00 20.00
101-103: 52 pg. Giants 2.00 6.00 18.00
104-121 1.00 3.00 8.00
...In 3-D (Spring, 1988, $2.25, Blackthorne #66) 4.00

PLOP! (Also see The Best of DC #60)
National Periodical Publications: Sept-Oct, 1973 - No. 24, Nov-Dec, 1976
1-Sergio Aragonés-a begins; Wrightson-a 2.50 7.50 25.00
2-4,6-20 1.50 4.50 12.00
5-Wrightson-a 1.75 5.25 14.00
21-24 (52 pgs.). 23-No Aragonés-a 2.00 6.00 16.00
NOTE: ***Alcala** a-1-3. **Anderson** a-5. **Aragonés** a-1-22, 24. **Ditko** a-16p. **Evans** a-1. **Mayer** a-1. **Orlando** a-21, 22; c-21. **Sekowsky** a-5, 6p. **Toth** a-11. **Wolverton** r-4, 22-24(1 pg.ea.); c-1-12, 14, 17, 18. **Wood** a-14, 16i, 18-24; c-13, 15, 16, 19.*

PLUTO (See Cheerios Premiums, Four Color #537, Mickey Mouse Magazine, Walt Disney Showcase #4, 7, 13, 20, 23, 33 & Wheaties)
Dell Publ. Co.: No. 7, 1942; No. 429, 10/52 - No. 1248, 11-1/61-62 (Disney)
Large Feature Comic 7(1942)-Written by Carl Barks, Jack Hannah, & Nick George (Barks' 1st comic book work) 117.00 350.00 1400.00
Four Color 429 (#1) 8.35 25.00 100.00

GD2.0 FN6.0 NM9.4

Four Color 509 5.00 15.00 60.00
Four Color 595,654,736,853 3.20 9.60 35.00
Four Color 941,1039,1143,1248 3.20 9.60 35.00

POCKET COMICS (Also see Double Up)
Harvey Publications: Aug, 1941 - No. 4, Jan, 1942 (Pocket size; 100 pgs.) (1st Harvey comic)
1-Origin & 1st app. The Black Cat, Cadet Blakey the Spirit of '76, The Red Blazer, The Phantom, Sphinx, & The Zebra; Phantom Ranger, British Agent #99, Spin Hawkins, Satan, Lord of Evil begin (1st app. of each); Simon-c/a in #1-3 95.00 285.00 900.00
2 (9/41)-Black Cat on-c #2-4 63.00 189.00 600.00
3,4 50.00 150.00 450.00

POE
Cheese Comics: Sept, 1996 - No. 6, Apr, 1997 ($2.00, B&W)
1-6-Jason Asala-s/a 2.50

POE
Sirius Entertainment (Dogstar Press): Oct, 1997 - Present ($2.50/$2.95, B&W)
1-19-Jason Asala-s/a 2.50
20-24 ($2.95) 2.95
... Color Special (12/98, $2.95) Linsner-c 3.00

POGO PARADE (See Dell Giants)

POGO POSSUM (Also see Animal Comics & Special Delivery)
Dell Publishing Co.: No. 105, 4/46 - No. 148, 5/47; 10-12/49 - No. 16, 4-6/54
Four Color 105(1946)-Kelly-c/a 71.00 213.00 850.00
Four Color 148-Kelly-c/a 58.00 175.00 700.00
1-(10-12/49)-Kelly-c/a in all 48.00 143.00 575.00
2 38.00 115.00 460.00
3-5 27.00 80.00 320.00
6-10: 10-Infinity-c 23.00 68.00 270.00
11-16: 11-X-Mas-c 17.50 52.50 210.00
NOTE: *#1-4, 9-13: 52 pgs.; #5-8, 14-16: 36 pgs.*

POINT BLANK
Acme Press (Eclipse): May, 1989 - No. 2, 1989 ($2.95, B&W, magazine)
1,2-European-r 3.00

POISON ELVES (Formerly I, Lusiphur)
Mulehide Graphics: No. 8, 1993- No. 20, 1995 (B&W, magazine/comic size, mature readers)
8-Drew Hayes-c/a/scripts. 1.50 4.50 12.00
9-11: 11-1st comic size issue 1.50 4.50 12.00
12,14,16 1.00 3.00 8.00
13,15-scarce 1.85 5.50 15.00
15-2nd print 4.00
17-20 1.00 3.00 8.00
...Desert of the Third Sin-(1997, $14.95, TPB)-r/#13-18 15.00
...Patrons-($4.95, TPB)-r/#19,20 5.00
...Traumatic Dogs-(1996, $14.95,TPB)-Reprints I, Lusiphur #7, Poison Elves #8-12 15.00

POISON ELVES (See I, Lusiphur)
Sirius Entertainment: June, 1995 - Present ($2.50, B&W, mature readers)
1-Linsner-c; Drew Hayes-a/scripts in all. 5.00
1-2nd print 2.50
2-25: 12-Purple Marauder-c/app. 3.00
26-45, 47-49 2.50
46,50-62: 61-Fillbäch Brothers-s/a 2.95
... Color Special #1 (12/98, $2.95) 5.00
... FAN Edition #1 mail-in offer; Drew Hayes-c/s/a 1.00 3.00 8.00
...Sanctuary-(1999, $14.95, TPB)-r/#1-12 15.00

POKÉMON (TV) (Also see Magical Pokémon Journey)
Viz Comics: Nov, 1998 - Present ($3.25/$3.50, B&W)
...Part 1: The Electric Tale of Pikachu
1-Toshiro Ono-s/a 1.25 3.75 10.00
1-4 (2nd through current printings) 3.00
2 2.40 6.00
3,4 3.00

Pokémon Part 2 #3 © Nintendo

Police Comics #13 © QUA

Polly Pigtails #3 © PMI

GD2.0 FN6.0 NM9.4

TPB ($12.95) 13.00
...Part 2: Pikachu Strikes Back
1 3.00
2-4 4.00
TPB 13.00
...Part 3: Electric Pikachu Boogaloo
1 3.50
2-4 ($2.95-c) 3.00
TPB 13.00
...Part 4: Surf's Up Pikachu
1,3,4 3.50
2 ($2.95-c) 3.00
TPB 13.00
NOTE: Multiple printings exist for most issues

POKÉMON ADVENTURES
Viz Comics: Sept, 1999 - No. 4 ($5.95, B&W, magazine-size)
1-4-Includes stickers bound in 6.00

POKÉMON ADVENTURES
Viz Comics: 2000 - Present ($2.95, B&W)
Part 2 (2/00-7/00) 1-6-Includes stickers bound in 3.00
Part 3 (8/00-2/01) 1-7 3.00

POKÉMON: THE FIRST MOVIE
Viz Comics: 1999 ($3.95)
Mewtwo Strikes Back 1-4 4.00
Pikachu's Vacation 4.00

POKÉMON: THE MOVIE 2000
Viz Comics: 2000 ($3.95)
1-Official movie adaption 4.00
Pikachu's Rescue Adventure 4.00
...:The Power of One (mini-series) 1-3 3.95

POLICE ACADEMY (TV)
Marvel Comics: Nov, 1989 - No. 6, Feb, 1990 ($1.00)
1-6: Based on TV cartoon; Post-c/a(p) in all 2.00

POLICE ACTION
Atlas News Co.: Jan, 1954 - No. 7, Nov, 1954
1-Violent-a by Robert Q. Sale 20.00 60.00 160.00
2 10.00 30.00 80.00
3-7: 7-Powell-a 10.00 30.00 70.00
NOTE: ***Ayers** a-4, 5. **Colan** a-1. **Forte** a-1, 2. **Mort Lawrence** a-5. **Maneely** a-3; c-1, 5. **Reinman** a-6, 7.*

POLICE ACTION
Atlas/Seaboard Publ.: Feb, 1975 - No. 3, June, 1975
1-3: 1-Lomax, N.Y.P.D., Luke Malone begin; McWilliams-a. 2-Origin Luke Malone, Manhunter; Ploog-a 5.00
NOTE: ***Ploog** art in all. **Sekowsky/McWilliams** a-1-3. **Thorne** c-3.*

POLICE AGAINST CRIME
Premiere Magazines: April, 1954 - No. 9, Aug, 1955
1-Disbrow-a; extreme violence (man's face slashed with knife); Hollingsworth-a 24.00 71.00 190.00
2-Hollingsworth-a 12.50 37.50 100.00
3-9 10.00 30.00 80.00

POLICE BADGE #479 (Formerly Spy Thrillers #1-4)
Atlas Comics (PrPl): No. 5, Sept, 1955
5-Maneely-c/a (6 pgs.) 10.00 30.00 80.00

POLICE CASE BOOK (See Giant Comics Editions)

POLICE CASES (See Authentic... & Record Book of...)

POLICE COMICS
Quality Comics Group (Comic Magazines): Aug, 1941 - No. 127, Oct, 1953
1-Origin/1st app. Plastic Man by Jack Cole (r-in DC Special #15), The Human Bomb by Gustavson, & No. 711; intro. Chic Carter by Eisner, The Firebrand by Reed Crandall, The Mouthpiece by Guardineer, Phantom Lady, & The Sword; Firebrand-c 1-4 697.00 2090.00 8000.00
2-Plastic Man smuggles opium 305.00 915.00 3200.00

GD2.0 FN6.0 NM9.4

3 211.00 633.00 2000.00
4 190.00 570.00 1800.00
5-Plastic Man-c begin; Plastic Man forced to smoke marijuana; Plastic Man covers begin, end #102 179.00 537.00 1700.00
6,7 158.00 474.00 1500.00
8-Manhunter begins (origin/1st app.) (3/42) 184.00 553.00 1750.00
9,10 126.00 379.00 1200.00
11-The Spirit strip reprints begin by Eisner (origin-strip #1); 1st comic book app. The Spirit & 1st cover app. (9/42) 211.00 633.00 2000.00
12-Intro. Ebony 132.00 395.00 1250.00
13-Intro. Woozy Winks; last Firebrand 126.00 379.00 1200.00
14-19: 15-Last No. 711; Destiny begins 92.00 276.00 875.00
20-The Raven x-over in Phantom Lady; features Jack Cole himself 92.00 276.00 875.00
21,22: 21-Raven & Spider Widow x-over in Phantom Lady (cameo in #22) 76.00 229.00 725.00
23-30: 23-Last Phantom Lady. 24-26-Flatfoot Burns by Kurtzman in all 71.00 213.00 675.00
31-41: 37-1st app. Candy by Sahle & begins (12/44). 41-Last Spirit-r by Eisner 50.00 150.00 450.00
42,43-Spirit-r by Eisner/Fine 40.00 120.00 360.00
44-Fine Spirit-r begin, end #88,90,92 40.00 120.00 325.00
45-50: 50-(#50 on-c, #49 on inside, 1/46) 39.00 116.00 310.00
51-60: 58-Last Human Bomb 34.00 101.00 270.00
61-88,90,92: 63-(Some issues have #65 printed on cover, but #63 on inside) Kurtzman-a, 6 pgs. 90,92-Spirit by Fine 25.00 75.00 200.00
89,91,93-No Spirit stories 22.00 66.00 175.00
94-99,101,102: Spirit by Eisner in all; 101-Last Manhunter. 102-Last Spirit & Plastic Man by Jack Cole 33.00 99.00 265.00
100 40.00 120.00 320.00
103-Content change to crime; Ken Shannon & T-Man begin (1st app. of each, 12/50) 26.00 79.00 210.00
104-112,114-127: Crandall-a most issues (not in 104,105,122,125-127). 109-Atomic bomb story. 112-Crandall-a 19.00 56.00 150.00
113-Crandall-c/a(2), 9 pgs. each 20.00 60.00 160.00
NOTE: *Most Spirit stories signed by Eisner are not by him; all are reprints. **Cole** c-17, 19-21, 24-26, 28-31, 36-38, 40-42, 45-48, 65-68, 69, 73, 75. **Crandall** Firebrand-1-8. Spirit by **Eisner** 1-41, 94-102; by **Eisner/Fine**-42, 43; by **Fine**-44-88, 90, 92. 103, 109. **Al Bryant** c-33, 34. **Cole** c-17-32, 35-102(most). **Crandall** c-13, 14. **Crandall/Cuidera** c-105-127. **Eisner** c-4i. **Gill Fox** c-1-3, 4p, 5-12, 15. Bondage c-103, 109, 125.*

POLICE LINE-UP
Avon Periodicals/Realistic Comics #3,4: Aug, 1951 - No. 4, July, 1952 (Painted-c #1-3)
1-Wood-a, 1 pg. plus part-c; spanking panel-r/Saint #5 40.00 120.00 320.00
2-Classic story "The Religious Murder Cult", drugs, perversion; r/Saint #5; c-r/Avon paperback #329 28.00 83.00 220.00
3,4: 3-Kubert-a(r?)/part-c; Kinstler-a (inside-c only) 21.00 62.00 165.00

POLICE TRAP (Public Defender In Action #7 on)
Mainline #1-4/Charlton #5,6: 8-9/54 - No. 4, 2-3/55; No. 5, 7/55 - No. 6, 9/55
1-S&K covers-all issues; Meskin-a; Kirby scripts 30.00 90.00 240.00
2-4 18.00 53.00 140.00
5,6-S&K-c/a 24.00 71.00 190.00

POLICE TRAP
Super Comics: No. 11, 1963; No. 16-18, 1964
Reprint #11,16-18: 11-r/Police Trap #3. 16-r/Justice Traps the Guilty #? 17-r/Inside Crime #3 & r/Justice Traps The Guilty #83; 18-r/Inside Crime #3 1.75 5.25 14.00

POLLY & HER PALS (See Comic Monthly #1)

POLLYANNA (Disney)
Dell Publishing Co.: No. 1129, Aug-Oct, 1960
Four Color 1129-Movie, Haley Mills photo-c 7.50 22.50 90.00

POLLY PIGTAILS (Girls' Fun & Fashion Magazine #44 on)
Parents' Magazine Institute/Polly Pigtails: Jan, 1946 - V4#43, Oct-Nov, 1949
1-Infinity-c; photo-c 10.50 32.00 85.00
2-Photo-c 6.00 18.00 42.00

Popeye #8 © KING

Popular Comics #57 © DELL

Popular Romance #10 © STD

	GD2.0	FN6.0	NM9.4
3-5: 3,4-Photo-c	5.00	15.00	32.00
6-10: 7-Photo-c	4.65	14.00	28.00
11-30: 22-Photo-c	4.00	10.00	20.00
31-43	3.60	9.00	18.00

PONY EXPRESS (See Tales of the...)

PONYTAIL
Dell Publishing Co./Charlton No. 13 on: 7-9/62 - No. 12, 10-12/65; No. 13, 11/69 - No. 20, 1/71

	GD2.0	FN6.0	NM9.4
12-641-209(#1)	3.00	9.00	32.00
2-12	2.30	7.00	20.00
13-20	1.75	5.25	14.00

POP COMICS
Modern Store Publ.: 1955 (36 pgs.; 5x7"; in color) (7¢)

	GD2.0	FN6.0	NM9.4
1-Funny animal	5.00	15.00	30.00

POPEYE (See Comic Album #7, 11, 15, Comics Reading Libraries, Eat Right to Work and Win, Giant Comic Album, King Comics, Kite Fun Book, Magic Comics, March of Comics #37, 52, 66, 80, 96, 117, 134, 148, 157, 169, 194, 246, 264, 274, 294, 453, 465, 477 & Wow Comics, 1st series)

POPEYE
David McKay Publications: 1937 - 1939 (All by Segar)

	GD2.0	FN6.0	NM9.4
Feature Books nn (100 pgs.) (Very Rare)	600.00	1800.00	6600.00
Feature Books 2 (52 pgs.)	67.00	200.00	800.00
Feature Books 3 (100 pgs.)-r/nn issue with a new-c	65.00	195.00	775.00
Feature Books 5,10 (76 pgs.)	56.00	169.00	675.00
Feature Books 14 (76 pgs.) (Scarce)	65.00	195.00	775.00

POPEYE (Strip reprints through 4-Color #70)
Dell #1-65/Gold Key #66-80/King #81-92/Charlton #94-138/Gold Key #139-155/Whitman #156 on: 1941 - 1947; #1, 2-4/48 - #65, 7-9/62; #66, 10/62 - #80, 5/66; #81, 8/66 - #92, 12/67; #94, 2/69 - #138, 1/77; #139, 5/78 - #171, 7/84 (no #93,160,161)

	GD2.0	FN6.0	NM9.4
Large Feature Comic 24('41)-Half by Segar	54.00	163.00	650.00
Four Color 25('41)-by Segar	69.00	206.00	825.00
Large Feature Comic 10('43)	44.00	131.00	525.00
Four Color 17('43),26('43)-by Segar	50.00	150.00	600.00
Four Color 43('44)	31.00	93.00	375.00
Four Color 70('45)-Title: ...& Wimpy	25.00	75.00	300.00
Four Color 113('46-original strips begin),127,145('47),168	12.50	37.50	150.00
1(2-4/48)(Dell)-All new stories continue	27.00	81.00	325.00
2	13.00	40.00	160.00
3-10: 5-Popeye on moon w/rocket-c	11.30	34.00	135.00
11-20	9.00	27.00	110.00
21-40,46: 46-Origin Swee' Pee	7.50	22.50	90.00
41-45,47-50	5.85	17.50	70.00
51-60	5.00	15.00	60.00
61-65 (Last Dell issue)	4.55	13.65	50.00
66,67-Both 84 pgs. (Gold Key)	5.85	17.50	70.00
68-80	3.00	9.00	30.00
81-92,94-97 (no #93): 97-Last 12¢ issue	2.40	7.35	22.00
98,99,101-130	1.85	5.50	15.00
100	2.50	7.50	25.00
131-155: 144-50th Anniversary issue	1.00	2.80	7.00
156,157,162-167(Whitman) (no #160,161,168)	1.25	3.75	10.00
158(9/80),159(11/80)-pre-pack?	2.00	6.00	18.00
169-171: 169(#168 on-c). All #90069 on-c; pre-pack?	1.75	5.25	14.00

NOTE: *Reprints-#145, 147, 149, 151, 153, 155, 157, 163-68(1/3), 170.*

POPEYE
Harvey Comics: Nov, 1993 - No. 7, Aug, 1994 ($1.50)

	NM9.4
V2#1-7	3.00
...Summer Special V2#1-(10/93, $2.25, 68 pgs.)-Sagendorf-r & others	4.00

POPEYE SPECIAL
Ocean Comics: Summer, 1987 - No. 2, Sept, 1988 ($1.75/$2.00)

	NM9.4
1,2: 1-Origin	3.00

POPPLES (TV, movie)
Star Comics (Marvel): Dec, 1986 - No. 5, Aug, 1987

	NM9.4
1-5-Based on toys	3.00

POPPO OF THE POPCORN THEATRE
Fuller Publishing Co. (Publishers Weekly): 10/29/55 - No. 13, 1956 (weekly)

	GD2.0	FN6.0	NM9.4
1	8.65	26.00	60.00
2-5	5.70	17.00	40.00
6-13	5.00	15.00	30.00

NOTE: *By **Charles Biro**. 10¢ cover, given away by supermarkets such as IGA.*

POP-POP COMICS
R. B. Leffingwell Co.: No date (Circa 1945) (52 pgs.)

	GD2.0	FN6.0	NM9.4
1-Funny animal	10.50	32.00	85.00

POPULAR COMICS
Dell Publishing Co.: Feb, 1936 - No. 145, July-Sept, 1948

	GD2.0	FN6.0	VF8.0
1-Dick Tracy (1st comic book app.), Little Orphan Annie, Terry & the Pirates, Gasoline Alley, Don Winslow (1st app.), Harold Teen, Little Joe, Skippy, Moon Mullins, Mutt & Jeff, Tailspin Tommy, Smitty, Smokey Stover, Winnie Winkle & The Gumps begin (all strip-r)	615.00	1846.00	4000.00
2	215.00	646.00	1400.00
3	162.00	485.00	1050.00
4-6(7/36): 5-Tom Mix begins. 6-1st app. Scribbly	131.00	392.00	850.00
7-10: 8,9-Scribbly & Reglar Fellers app.	100.00	300.00	650.00

	GD2.0	FN6.0	NM9.4
11-20: 12-X-Mas-c	78.00	234.00	625.00
21-27: 27-Last Terry & the Pirates, Little Orphan Annie, & Dick Tracy	56.00	169.00	450.00
28-37: 28-Gene Autry app. 31,32-Tim McCoy app. 35-Christmas-c; Tex Ritter app.	47.00	141.00	375.00
38-43: Tarzan in text only. 38-(4/39)-Gang Busters (Radio, 2nd app.) & Zane Grey's Tex Thorne begins? 43-The Masked Pilot app.; 1st non-funny-c?	45.00	135.00	360.00
44,45: 45-Hurricane Kid-c	31.00	94.00	250.00
46-Origin/1st app. Martan, the Marvel Man(12/39)	41.00	122.00	325.00
47-50	30.00	90.00	240.00
51-Origin The Voice (The Invisible Detective) strip begins (5/40)	31.00	94.00	250.00
52-59: 52-Robot-c. 55-End of World story	24.00	73.00	195.00
60-Origin/1st app. Professor Supermind and Son (2/41)	25.00	75.00	200.00
61-71: 63-Smilin' Jack begins	20.00	60.00	160.00
72-The Owl & Terry & the Pirates begin (2/42); Smokey Stover reprints begin	40.00	120.00	320.00
73-75	26.00	77.00	210.00
76-78-Capt. Midnight in all (see The Funnies #57)	38.00	113.00	300.00
79-85-Last Owl	23.00	69.00	185.00
86-99: 98-Felix the Cat, Smokey Stover-r begin	17.50	53.00	140.00
100	19.00	56.00	150.00
101-130	10.50	32.00	85.00
131-145: 142-Last Terry & the Pirates	10.00	30.00	80.00

NOTE: *Martan, the Marvel Man c-47-49, 52, 57-59. Professor Supermind c-60-63, 64(1/2), 65, 66. The Voice c-53.*

POPULAR FAIRY TALES (See March of Comics #6, 18)

POPULAR ROMANCE
Better-Standard Publications: No. 5, Dec, 1949 - No. 29, July, 1954

	GD2.0	FN6.0	NM9.4
5	10.00	30.00	75.00
6-9: 7-Palais-a; lingerie panels	6.40	19.25	45.00
10-Wood-a (2 pgs.)	8.65	26.00	60.00
11,12,14-16,18-21,28,29	5.00	15.00	35.00
13,17-Severin/Elder-a (3&8 pgs.)	6.40	19.25	45.00
22-27-Toth-a	8.65	26.00	60.00

NOTE: *All have photo-c. **Tuska** art in most issues.*

POPULAR TEEN-AGERS (Secrets of Love) (School Day Romances #1-4)
Star Publications: No. 5, Sept, 1950 - No. 23, Nov, 1954

	GD2.0	FN6.0	NM9.4
5-Toni Gay, Midge Martin & Eve Adams continue from School Day Romances; Ginger Bunn (formerly Ginger Snapp & becomes Honey Bunn #6 on) begins; all features end #8	34.00	101.00	270.00

6-8 (7/51)-Honey Bunn begins; all have L. B. Cole-c; 6-Negligee panels

Popular Teen-Agers #16 © STAR

Porky Pig Four Color #303 © WB

Powerhouse Pepper #1 © MAR

	GD2.0	FN6.0	NM9.4
	31.00	94.00	250.00
9-(…Romances; 1st romance issue, 10/51)	20.00	60.00	160.00
10-(…Secrets of Love thru #23)	19.00	56.00	150.00
11,16,18,19,22,23	15.00	45.00	120.00
12,13,17,20,21-Disbrow-a	17.00	51.00	135.00
14-Harrison/Wood-a; 2 spanking scenes	22.00	66.00	175.00
15-Wood?, Disbrow-a	18.00	54.00	145.00
Accepted Reprint 5,6 (nd); L.B. Cole-c	8.65	26.00	60.00

NOTE: *All have* ***L. B. Cole*** *covers.*

PORKY PIG (See Bugs Bunny &…, Kite Fun Book, Looney Tunes, March of Comics #42, 57, 71, 89, 99, 113, 130, 143, 164, 175, 192, 209, 218, 367, and Super Book #6, 18, 30)

PORKY PIG (…& Bugs Bunny #40-69)
Dell Publishing Co./Gold Key No. 1-93/Whitman No. 94 on: No. 16, 1942 - No. 81, Mar-Apr, 1962; Jan, 1965 - No. 109, July, 1984

	GD2.0	FN6.0	NM9.4
Four Color 16(#1, 1942)	83.00	250.00	1000.00
Four Color 48(1944)-Carl Barks-a	96.00	288.00	1150.00
Four Color 78(1945)	23.00	68.00	280.00
Four Color 112(7/46)	14.00	42.00	170.00
Four Color 156,182,191('49)	10.00	30.00	120.00
Four Color 226,241('49),260,271,277,284,295	7.50	22.50	90.00
Four Color 303,311,322,330: 322-Sci/fi-c/story	5.00	15.00	60.00
Four Color 342,351,360,370,385,399,410,426	4.10	12.30	45.00
25 (11-12/52)-30	3.20	9.60	35.00
31-40	2.30	7.00	20.00
41-60	2.00	6.00	18.00
61-81(3-4/62)	2.00	6.00	16.00
1(1/65-Gold Key)(2nd Series)	4.10	12.30	45.00
2,4,5-r/4-Color 226,284 & 271 in that order	2.50	7.50	25.00
3,6-10: 3-r/Four Color #342	2.00	6.00	18.00
11-30	1.75	5.25	14.00
31-54	1.25	3.75	10.00
55-70	1.00	3.00	8.00
71-93(Gold Key)		2.40	6.00
94-96	1.00	2.80	7.00
97(9/80),98,99-pre-pack?	1.75	5.25	14.00
100	1.10	3.30	9.00
101-105	1.00	2.80	7.00
106-109 (All #90140 on-c, no date or date code)	1.50	4.50	12.00

NOTE: *Reprints-#1-8, 9-35(2/3); 36-46, 58, 67, 69-74, 76, 78, 102-109(1/3-1/2).*

PORKY PIG'S DUCK HUNT
Saalfield Publishing Co.: 1938 (12pgs.)(large size)(heavy linen-like paper)

	GD2.0	FN6.0	NM9.4
2178-1st app. Porky Pig & Daffy Duck by Leon Schlesinger. Illustrated text story book written in verse.1st book ever devoted to these characters. (see Looney Tunes #1 for their 1st comic book app.)	68.00	205.00	650.00

PORTIA PRINZ OF THE GLAMAZONS
Eclipse Comics: Dec, 1986 - No. 6, Oct, 1987 ($2.00, B&W, Baxter paper)

1-6 — 2.00

POST GAZETTE (See Meet the New…)

POWDER RIVER RUSTLERS (See Fawcett Movie Comics)

POWER & GLORY (See American Flagg! & Howard Chaykin's American Flagg!
Malibu Comics (Bravura): Feb, 1994 - No. 4, May, 1994 ($2.50, limited series, mature)

	NM9.4
1A, 1B-By Howard Chaykin; w/Bravura stamp	2.50
1-Newsstand ed. (polybagged w/children's warning on bag), Gold ed., Silver-foil ed., Blue-foil ed.(print run of 10,000), Serigraph ed. (print run of 3,000)($2.95)-Howard Chaykin-c/a begin	3.00
2-4-Contains Bravura stamp	2.50
Holiday Special (Win '94, $2.95)	3.00

POWER COMICS
Holyoke Publ. Co./Narrative Publ.: 1944 - No. 4, 1945

	GD2.0	FN6.0	NM9.4
1-L. B. Cole-c	147.00	442.00	1400.00
2-Hitler, Hirohito-c (scarce)	147.00	442.00	1400.00
3-Classic L.B. Cole-c; Dr. Mephisto begins?	168.00	505.00	1600.00
4-L.B. Cole-c; Miss Espionage app. #3,4; Leav-a	147.00	442.00	1400.00

POWER COMICS
Power Comics Co.: 1977 - No. 5, Dec, 1977 (B&W)

	GD2.0	FN6.0	NM9.4
1- "A Boy And His Aardvark" by Dave Sim; first Dave Sim aardvark (not Cerebus)	1.85	5.50	15.00
1-Reprint (3/77, black-c)		2.40	6.00
2-Cobalt Blue by Gustovich	1.00	3.00	8.00
3-5: 3-Nightwitch. 4-Northern Light. 5-Bluebird	1.00	3.00	8.00

POWER COMICS
Eclipse Comics (Acme Press): Mar, 1988 - No. 4, Sept, 1988 ($2.00, B&W, mini-series)

1-4: Bolland, Gibbons-r in all — 2.00

POWER FACTOR
Wonder Color Comics #1/Pied Piper #2: May, 1987 - No. 2, 1987 ($1.95)

1,2: Super team. 2-Infantino-c — 2.00

POWER FACTOR
Innovation Publishing: Oct, 1990 - No. 3, 1991 ($1.95/$2.25)

1-3: 1-R-/1st story + new-a, 2-r/2nd story + new-a. 3-Infantino-a — 2.25

POWER GIRL (See All-Star #58, Infinity, Inc., Showcase #97-99)
DC Comics: June, 1988 - No. 4, Sept, 1988 ($1.00, color, limited series)

1-4 — 3.00

POWERHOUSE PEPPER COMICS (See Gay Comics, Joker Comics & Tessie the Typist)
Marvel Comics (20CC): No. 1, 1943; No. 2, May, 1948 - No. 5, Nov, 1948

	GD2.0	FN6.0	NM9.4
1-(60 pgs.)-Wolverton-a in all; c-2,3	158.00	474.00	1500.00
2	82.00	245.00	775.00
3,4	76.00	229.00	725.00
5-(Scarce)	90.00	268.00	850.00

POWER LINE
Marvel Comics (Epic Comics): May, 1988 - No. 8, Sept, 1989 ($1.25/$1.50)

1-8: 2-Williamson-i. 3- Dr. Zero app. 4-7-Morrow-a. 8-Williamson-i — 2.00

POWER LORDS
DC Comics: Dec, 1983 - No. 3, Feb, 1984 (Limited series, Mando paper)

1-3: Based on Revell toys — 2.00

POWER MAN (Formerly Hero for Hire; …& Iron Fist #50 on; see Cage & Giant-Size…)
Marvel Comics Group: No. 17, Feb, 1974 - No. 125, Sept, 1986

	GD2.0	FN6.0	NM9.4
17-Luke Cage continues; Iron Man app.	1.25	3.75	10.00
18-20: 18-Last 20¢ issue		2.40	6.00
21-30			5.00
30-(30¢-c variant, limited distribution)(4/76)	1.00	2.80	7.00
31-(30¢-c variant, limited distribution)(5/76)		2.40	6.00
31-46: 31-Part Neal Adams-i. 34-Last 25¢ issue. 36-r/Hero For Hire #12. 41-1st app. Thunderbolt. 45-Starlin-c.			4.00
32-34-(30¢-c variants, limited distribution)(6-8/76)		2.40	6.00
47-Barry Smith-a		2.40	6.00
48-50-Byrne-a(p); 48-Power Man/Iron Fist 1st meet. 50-Iron Fist joins Cage	1.25	3.75	10.00
51-56,58-65,67-77: 58-Intro El Aguila. 75-Double size. 77-Daredevil app.			3.00
57-New X-Men app. (6/79)	1.85	5.50	15.00
66-2nd app. Sabretooth (see Iron Fist #14)	2.30	7.00	20.00
78,84: 78-3rd app. Sabretooth (cameo under cloak). 84-4th app. Sabretooth	1.25	3.75	10.00
79-83,85-125: 87-Moon Knight app. 90-Unus app. 100-Double size; origin K'un L'un. 109-The Reaper app. 125-Double size; death of Iron Fist			2.00
Annual 1(1976)-Punisher cameo in flashback	1.25	3.75	10.00

NOTE: ***Austin*** *c-102i.* ***Byrne*** *a-48-50; c-102, 104, 106, 107, 112-116.* ***Kane*** *c(p)-24, 25, 28, 48.* ***Miller*** *a-68, 76(2 pgs.); c-66-68, 70-74, 80i.* ***Mooney*** *a-38i, 53i, 55i.* ***Nebres*** *a-76p.* ***Nino*** *a-42i, 43i.* ***Perez*** *a-27.* ***B. Smith*** *a-47i.* ***Tuska*** *a(p)-17, 20, 24, 26, 28, 29, 36, 47. Painted c-75, 100.*

POWER OF PRIME
Malibu Comics (Ultraverse): July, 1995 - No. 4, Nov, 1995 ($2.50, lim. series)

1-4 — 2.50

POWER OF SHAZAM!, THE (See SHAZAM!)
DC Comics: 1994 (Painted graphic novel) (Prequel to new series)

Hardcover-($19.95)-New origin of Shazam!; Ordway painted-c/a & script

Powerpuff Girls #1 © Cartoon Network

Powers #1 © Brian Michael Bendis & Mike Oeming

Preacher #65 © Garth Ennis & Steve Dillon

GD2.0 FN6.0 NM9.4

2.50 7.50 25.00
Softcover-($7.50), Softcover-($9.95)-New-c. 1.50 4.50 12.00

POWER OF SHAZAM!, THE
DC Comics: Mar, 1995 - No. 47, Mar, 1999 ($1.50/$1.75/$1.95/$2.50)

1-Jerry Ordway scripts begin 4.00
2-20: 4-Begin $1.75-c. 6:Re-intro of Capt. Nazi. 8-Re-intro of Spy Smasher, Bulletman & Minuteman; Swan-a (7 pgs.). 11-Re-intro of Ibis,Swan-a(2 pgs.). 14-Gil Kane-a(p). 20-Superman-c/app.; "Final Night" 3.00
21-47: 21-Plastic Man-c/app. 22-Batman-c/app. 35,36-X-over w/Starman #39,40. 38-41-Mr. Mind. 43-Bulletman app. 45-JLA-c/app. 2.50
#1,000,000 (11/98) 853rd Century x-over; Ordway-c/s/a 3.00
Annual 1 (1996, $2.95)-Legends of the Dead Earth story; Jerry Ordway-c; Mike Manley-a 4.00

POWER OF STRONGMAN, THE (Also see Strongman)
AC Comics: 1989 ($2.95)

1-Powell G.A.-r 3.00

POWER OF THE ATOM (See Secret Origins #29)
DC Comics: Aug, 1988 - No. 18, Nov, 1989 ($1.00)

1-18: 6-Chronos returns; Byrne-p. 9-JLI app. 2.00

POWER PACHYDERMS
Marvel Comics: Sept, 1989 ($1.25, one-shot)

1-Elephant super-heroes; parody of X-Men, Elektra, & 3 Stooges 2.00

POWER PACK
Marvel Comics Group: Aug, 1984 - No. 62, Feb, 1991

1-($1.00, 52 pgs.)-Origin & 1st app. Power Pack 3.00
2-18,20-26,28,30-45,47-62 2.00
19-(52 pgs.)-Cloak & Dagger, Wolverine app. 3.00
27-Mutant massacre; Wolverine & Sabretooth app. 5.00
29,46: 29-Spider-Man & Hobgoblin app. 46-Punisher app. 2.50
Graphic Novel: Power Pack & Cloak & Dagger: Shelter From the Storm ('89, SC, $7.95) Velluto/Farmer-a 10.00
...Holiday Special 1 (2/92, $2.25, 68 pgs.) 2.25
NOTE: ***Austin** scripts-53. **Mignola** c-20. **Morrow** a-51. **Spiegle** a-55i. **Williamson** a(i)-43, 50, 52.*

POWER PACK (Volume 2)
Marvel Comics: Aug, 2000 - No. 4, Nov, 2000 ($2.99, limited series)

1-4-Doran & Austin-c/a 3.00

POWERPUFF GIRLS, THE (Also see Cartoon Network Starring... #1)
DC Comics: May, 2000 - Present ($1.99)

1 4.00
2-11 2.00
...Double Whammy (12/00, $3.95) r/#1,2 & a Dexter's Lab story 4.00

POWER RANGERS ZEO (TV)(Saban's...)(Also see Saban's Mighty Morphin Power Rangers)
Image Comics (Extreme Studios): Aug, 1996 ($2.50)

1-Based on TV show 2.50

POWERS
Image Comics: 2000 - Present ($2.95)

1-Bendis-s/Oeming-a; murder of Retro Girl 3.50
2-8: 6-End of Retro Girl arc. 7-Warren Ellis app. 3.00
...: Who Killed Retro Girl TPB (2000, $21.95) r/#1-6; sketchbook, cover gallery, and promotional strips from Comic Shop News 22.00

POWERS THAT BE (Becomes Star Seed No.7 on)
Broadway Comics: Nov, 1995 - No. 6, June, 1996 ($2.50)

1-6: 1-Intro of Fatale & Star Seed. 6-Begin $2.95-c. 3.00
Preview Editions 1-3 (9/95 - 11/95, B&W) 2.50

POW MAGAZINE (Bob Sproul's) (Satire Magazine)
Humor-Vision: Aug, 1966 - No. 3, Feb, 1967 (30¢)

1,2: 2-Jones-a 3.20 9.60 35.00
3-Wrightson-a 4.10 12.30 45.00

PREACHER
DC Comics (Vertigo): Apr, 1995 - No. 66, Oct, 2000 ($2.50, mature)

GD2.0 FN6.0 NM9.4

nn-Preview 2.50 7.50 25.00
1 ($2.95)-Ennis scripts, Dillon-a & Fabry-c in all; 1st app. Jesse, Tulip, & Cassidy 1.85 5.50 15.00
2,3: 2-1st app. Saint of Killers. 1.25 3.75 10.00
4,5 1.00 3.00 8.00
6-10 2.40 6.00
11-20: 12-Polybagged w/videogame w/Ennis text. 13-Hunters storyline begins; ends #17. 19-Saint of Killers app.; begin "Crusaders", ends #24 5.00
21-25: 21-24-Saint of Killers app. 25-Origin of Cassidy. 3.50
26-49,51-64: 51,52-Tulip origin 2.50
50-($3.75) Pin-ups by Jim Lee, Bradstreet, Quesada and Palmiotti 3.75
65,66-($3.75) 65-Almost everyone dies. 66-Final issue 3.75
All Hell's a-Coming (2000, $17.95, TPB)-r/#51-58, ...:Tall in the Saddle 18.00
...: Dead or Alive HC (2000, $29.95) Gallery of Glenn Fabry's cover paintings for every Preacher issue; commentary by Fabry & Ennis 30.00
Dixie Fried (1998, $14.95, TPB)-r/#27-33, Special: Cassidy 15.00
Gone To Texas (1996, $14.95, TPB)-r/#1-7; Fabry-c 15.00
Proud Americans (1997, $14.95, TPB)-r/#18-26; Fabry-c 15.00
Salvation (1999, $14.95, TPB)-r/#41-50; Fabry-c 15.00
Until the End of the World (1996, $14.95, TPB)-r/#8-17; Fabry-c 15.00
War in the Sun (1999, $14.95, TPB)-r/#34-40 15.00

PREACHER SPECIAL: CASSIDY: BLOOD & WHISKEY
DC Comics (Vertigo): 1998 ($5.95, one-shot)

1-Ennis-scripts/Fabry-c /Dillon-a 6.00

PREACHER SPECIAL: ONE MAN'S WAR
DC Comics (Vertigo): Mar, 1998 ($4.95, one-shot)

1-Ennis-scripts/Fabry-c /Snejbjerg-a 5.00

PREACHER SPECIAL: SAINT OF KILLERS
DC Comics (Vertigo): Aug, 1996 - No. 4, Nov, 1996 ($2.50, lim. series, mature)

1-4: Ennis-scripts/Fabry-c. 1,2-Pugh-a. 3,4-Ezquerra-a 3.00
1-Signed & numbered 20.00

PREACHER SPECIAL: THE GOOD OLD BOYS
DC Comics (Vertigo): Aug, 1997 ($4.95, one-shot, mature)

1-Ennis-scripts/Fabry-c /Esquerra-a 5.00

PREACHER SPECIAL: THE STORY OF YOU-KNOW-WHO
DC Comics (Vertigo): Dec, 1996 ($4.95, one-shot, mature)

1-Ennis-scripts/Fabry-c/Case-a 5.00

PREACHER: TALL IN THE SADDLE
DC Comics (Vertigo): 2000 ($5.95, one-shot)

1-Ennis-scripts/Fabry-c/Dillon-a; early romance of Tulip and Jesse 6.00

PREDATOR (Also see Aliens Vs. ..., Batman vs. ..., Dark Horse Comics, & Dark Horse Presents)
Dark Horse Comics: June, 1989 - No. 4, Mar, 1990 ($2.25, limited series)

1-Based on movie; 1st app. Predator 2.40 6.00
1-2nd printing 3.00
2 5.00
3,4 4.00
Trade paperback (1990, $12.95)-r/#1-4 13.00

PREDATOR: (title series) **Dark Horse Comics**

--BAD BLOOD, 12/93 - No. 4, 1994 ($2.50) 1-4 3.00
--BIG GAME, 3/91 - No. 4, 6/91 ($2.50) 1-4: 1-3-Contain 2 Dark Horse trading cards 3.00
--BLOODY SANDS OF TIME, 2/92 - No. 2, 2/92 ($2.50\) 1,2-Dan Barry-c/a(p)/scripts 3.00
--CAPTIVE, 4/98 ($2.95, one-shot) 1 3.00
--COLD WAR, 9/91 - No. 4, 12/91 ($2.50) 1-4: All have painted-c 3.00
--DARK RIVER, 7/96 - No.4, 10/96 ($2.95)1-4: Miran Kim-c 3.00
--HELL & HOT WATER, 4/97 - No. 3, 6/97 ($2.95) 1-3 3.00
--HELL COME A WALKIN', 2/98 - No. 2, 3/98 ($2.95) 1,2-In the Civil War 3.00
--HOMEWORLD, 3/99 - No. 4, 6/99 ($2.95) 1-4 3.00
--INVADERS FROM THE FOURTH DIMENSION, 7/94 ($3.95, one-shot,

Predator Kindred #1 © 20th Century Fox

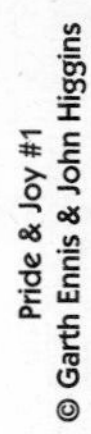
Pride & Joy #1 © Garth Ennis & John Higgins

Primer #6 © Comico

52 pgs.) 1 — 4.00

--JUNGLE TALES. 3/95 ($2.95t) 1-r/Dark Horse Comics — 3.00

--KINDRED, 12/96 - No. 4, 3/97 ($2.50) 1-4 — 3.00

--NEMESIS, 12/97 - No. 2, 1/98 ($2.95) 1,2-Predator in Victorian England; Taggart-c — 3.00

--PRIMAL, 7/97 - No. 2, 8/97 ($2.95) 1,2 — 3.00

--RACE WAR (See Dark Horse Presents #67), 2/93 - No. 4,10/93 ($2.50, color) 1-4,0: 1-4-Dorman painted-c #1-4, 0(4/930 — 3.00

--STRANGE ROUX, 11/96 ($2.95, one-shot) 1 — 3.00

--XENOGENESIS (Also see Aliens Xenogenesis), 8/99 - No. 4, 11/99 ($2.95) 1,2-Edginton-s — 3.00

PREDATOR 2
Dark Horse Comics: Feb, 1991 - No. 2, June, 1991 ($2.50, limited series)

1,2: 1-Adapts movie; both w/trading cards & photo-c — 3.00

PREDATOR VS. JUDGE DREDD
Dark Horse Comics: Oct, 1997 - No. 3 ($2.50, limited series)

1-3-Wagner-s/Alcatena-a/Bolland-c — 3.00

PREDATOR VS. MAGNUS ROBOT FIGHTER
Dark Horse/Valiant: Oct, 1992 - No. 2, 1993 ($2.95, limited series)
(1st Dark Horse/Valiant x-over)

1,2: (Reg.)-Barry Smith-c; Lee Weeks-a. 2-w/trading cards — 3.00
1 (Platinum edition, 11/92)-Barry Smith-c — 5.00

PREHISTORIC WORLD (See Classics Illustrated Special Issue)

PREMIERE (See Charlton Premiere)

PRESTO KID, THE (See Red Mask)

PRETTY BOY FLOYD (See On the Spot)

PREZ (See Cancelled Comic Cavalcade, Sandman #54 & Supergirl #10)
National Periodical Publications: Aug-Sept, 1973 - No. 4, Feb-Mar, 1974

	GD	FN	NM
1-Origin; Joe Simon scripts	2.30	7.00	20.00
2-4	1.50	4.50	12.00

PRICE, THE (See Eclipse Graphic Album Series)

PRIDE & JOY
DC Comics (Vertigo): July, 1997 - No. 4, Oct, 1997 (2.50, limited series)

1-4-Ennis-s — 2.50

PRIDE AND THE PASSION, THE
Dell Publishing Co.: No. 824, Aug, 1957

	GD	FN	NM
Four Color 824-Movie, Frank Sinatra & Cary Grant photo-c	8.35	25.00	100.00

PRIDE OF THE YANKEES, THE (See Real Heroes & Sport Comics)
Magazine Enterprises: 1949 (The Life of Lou Gehrig)

	GD	FN	NM
nn-Photo-c; Ogden Whitney-a	79.00	237.00	750.00

PRIEST (Also see Asylum)
Maximum Press: Aug, 1996 - No. 2, Oct, 1996 ($2.99)

1,2 — 3.00

PRIMAL FORCE
DC Comics: No. 0, Oct, 1994 - No. 14, Dec, 1995 ($1.95/$2.25)

0-14: 0- Teams Red Tornado, Golem, Jack O'Lantern, Meridian & Silver Dragon. 9-begin $2.25-c — 2.25

PRIMAL MAN (See The Crusaders)

PRIMAL RAGE
Sirius Entertainment: 1996 ($2.95)

1-Dark One-c; based of video game — 3.00

PRIME (See Break-Thru, Flood Relief & Ultraforce)
Malibu Comics (Ultraverse): June, 1993 - No. 26, Aug, 1995 ($1.95/$2.50)

1-1st app. Prime; has coupon for Ultraverse Premiere #0 — 3.00
1-With coupon missing — 2.00
1-Full cover holographic edition; 1st of kind w/Hardcase #1 & Strangers #1 — 2.40 — 6.00
1-Ultra 5,000 edition w/silver ink-c — 4.00
2-11,14-26: 2-Polybagged w/card & coupon for U. Premiere #0. 3,4-Prototype app. 4-Direct sale w/o card.4-($2.50)-Newsstand ed. polybagged w/card 5-($2.50, 48 pgs.)-Rune flip-c/story part B by Barry Smith; see Sludge #1 for 1st app. Rune; 3-pg. Night Man preview. 6-Bill & Chelsea Clinton app. 7-Break-Thru x-over. 8-Mantra app.; 2-pg. origin Freex by Simonson. 10-Firearm app.15-Intro Papa Verite; Perez-c/a. 16-Intro Turbo Charge — 2.50
12-($3.50, 68 pgs.)-Flip book w/Ultraverse Premiere #3; silver foil logo — 3.50
13-($2.95, 52 pgs.)-Variant covers — 3.00
...: Gross and Disgusting 1 (10/94, $3.95)-Boris-c; "Annual" on cover, published monthly in indicia — 4.00
...Month "Ashcan" (8/94, 75¢)-Boris-c — 2.00
... Time: A Prime Collection (1994, $9.95)-r/1-4 — 10.00
...Vs. The Incredible Hulk (1995)-mail away limited edition — 10.00
...Vs. The Incredible Hulk Premium edition — 10.00
...Vs. The Incredible Hulk Super Premium edition — 15.00

NOTE: *Perez a-15; c-15, 16.*

PRIME (Also see Black September)
Malibu Comics (Ultraverse): Infinity, Sept, 1995 - V2#15, Dec, 1996 ($1.50)

Infinity, V2#1-8: Post Black September storyline. 6-8-Solitaire app. 9-Breyfogle-c/a. 10-12-Ramos-c. 15-Lord Pumpkin app. — 2.00
Infinity Signed Edition (2,000 printed) — 5.00

PRIME/CAPTAIN AMERICA
Malibu Comics: Mar, 1996 ($3.95, one-shot)

1-Norm Breyfogle-a — 4.00

PRIMER (Comico...)
Comico: Oct (no month), 1982 - No. 6, Feb, 1984 (B&W)

	GD	FN	NM
1 (52 pgs.)	1.25	3.75	10.00
2-1st app. Grendel & Argent by Wagner	9.00	27.00	100.00
3,4	1.00	3.00	8.00
5-1st Sam Kieth art in comics ('83) & 1st The Maxx	3.00	9.00	30.00
6-Intro & 1st app. Evangeline	1.50	4.50	12.00

PRIMORTALS (Leonard Nimoy's...)

PRIMUS (TV)
Charlton Comics: Feb, 1972 - No. 7, Oct, 1972

	GD	FN	NM
1-Staton-a in all	1.85	5.50	15.00
2-7: 6-Drug propaganda story	1.25	3.75	10.00

PRINCE NAMOR, THE SUB-MARINER (Also see Namor ...)
Marvel Comics Group: Sept, 1984 - No. 4, Dec, 1984 (Limited-series)

1-4 — 2.50

PRINCE VALIANT (See Ace Comics, Comics Reading Libraries, & King Comics #146, 147)
David McKay Publ./Dell: No. 26, 1941; No. 67, June, 1954 - No. 900, May, 1958

	GD	FN	NM
Feature Books 26 ('41)-Harold Foster-c/a; newspaper strips reprinted, pgs. 1-28,30-63; color & 68 pgs; Foster cover is only original comic book artwork by him	75.00	225.00	900.00
Four Color 567 ((6/54)(#1)-By Bob Fuje-Movie, photo-c	11.00	33.00	130.00
Four Color 650 (9/55), 699 (4/56), 719 (8/56),-Fuje-a	6.30	19.00	75.00
Four Color 788 (4/57), 849 (1/58), 900-Fuje-a	6.30	19.00	75.00

PRINCE VALIANT
Marvel Comics: Dec, 1994 - No. 4, Mar, 1995 ($3.95, limited series)

1-4; Kaluta-c in all. — 4.00

PRINCE VANDAL
Triumphant Comics: Nov, 1993 - Apr?, 1994 ($2.50)

1-6: 1,2-Triumphant Unleashed x-over — 2.50

PRINCESS SALLY (Video game)
Archie Publications: Apr, 1995 - No. 3, June, 1995 ($1.50, limited series)

1-3: Spin-off from Sonic the Hedgehog — 3.00

PRIORITY: WHITE HEAT
AC Comics: 1986 - No. 2, 1986 ($1.75, mini-series)

1,2-Bill Black-a — 2.00

PRISCILLA'S POP

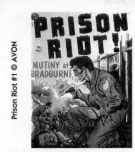

Prison Riot #1 © AVON

Prize Comics #5 © PRIZE

Professor Xavier and the X-Men #5 © MAR

GD2.0 FN6.0 NM9.4

Dell Publishing Co.: No. 569, June, 1954 - No. 799, May, 1957

Four Color 569 (#1), 630 (5/55), 704 (5/56),799 3.20 9.60 35.00

PRISON BARS (See Behind...)

PRISON BREAK!
Avon Per./Realistic No. 3 on: Sept, 1951 - No. 5, Sept, 1952 (Painted c-3)

1-Wood-c & 1 pg.; has-r/Saint #7 retitled Michael Strong Private Eye 41.00 123.00 370.00
2-Wood-c; Kubert-a; Kinstler inside front-c 31.00 94.00 250.00
3-Orlando, Check-a; c-/Avon paperback 179 26.00 79.00 210.00
4,5: 4-Kinstler-c & inside f/c; Lawrence, Lazarus-a. 5-Kinstler-c; Infantino-a 23.00 69.00 185.00

PRISONER, THE (TV)
DC Comics: 1988 - No. 4, 1989 ($3.50, squarebound, mini-series)

1-4 (Books a-d) 3.50

PRISON RIOT
Avon Periodicals: 1952

1-Marijuana Murders-1 pg. text; Kinstler-c; 2 Kubert illos on text pages 29.00 86.00 230.00

PRISON TO PRAISE
Logos International: 1974 (35¢) (Religious, Christian)

nn-True Story of Merlin R. Carothers 1.10 3.30 9.00

PRIVATE BUCK
Dell Publishing Co.: No. 21, 1941 - No. 12, 1942

Large Feature Comic 21 (#1)(1941)(Series I), 22 (1941)(Series I), 12 (1942)(Series II) 10.50 31.00 125.00

PRIVATEERS
Vanguard Graphics: Aug, 1987 - No. 2, 1987 ($1.50)

1,2 2.00

PRIVATE EYE (Cover title: Rocky Jorden...#6-8)
Atlas Comics (MCI): Jan, 1951 - No. 8, March, 1952

1-Cover title: Crime Cases... #1-5 21.00 66.00 175.00
2,3-Tuska c/a(3) 12.50 37.50 100.00
4-8 10.00 30.00 80.00

NOTE: ***Henkel*** *a-6(3), 7; c-7.* ***Sinnott*** *a-6.*

PRIVATE EYE (See Mike Shayne...)

PRIVATE SECRETARY
Dell Publishing Co.: Dec-Feb, 1962-63 - No. 2, Mar-May, 1963

1 3.00 9.00 30.00
2 2.50 7.50 24.00

PRIVATE STRONG (See The Double Life of...)

PRIZE COMICS (...Western #69 on) (Also see Treasure Comics)
Prize Publications: March, 1940 - No. 68, Feb-Mar, 1948

1-Origin Power Nelson, The Futureman & Jupiter, Master Magician; Ted O'Neil, Secret Agent M-11, Jaxon of the Jungle, Bucky Brady & Storm Curtis begin (1st app. of each) 232.00 695.00 2200.00
2-The Black Owl begins (1st app.) 105.00 316.00 1000.00
3,4: 4-Robot-c 89.00 268.00 850.00
5,6: Dr. Dekkar, Master of Monsters app. in each 82.00 245.00 775.00
7-(Scarce)-Black Owl by S&K; origin/1st app. Dr. Frost & Frankenstein; The Green Lama, Capt. Gallant, The Great Voodini & Twist Turner begin; 1st app. The Green Lama (12/40) 179.00 537.00 1700.00
8,9-Black Owl & Ted O'Neil by S&K 92.00 276.00 875.00
10-12,14-20: 11-Origin Bulldog Denny. 16-Spike Mason begins 63.00 189.00 600.00
13-Yank & Doodle begin (8/41, origin/1st app.) 71.00 213.00 675.00
21-24 47.00 140.00 420.00
25-30 30.00 90.00 240.00
31-33 25.00 75.00 200.00
34-Origin Airmale, Yank & Doodle; The Black Owl joins army, Yank & Doodle's father assumes Black Owl's role 30.00 90.00 240.00
35-36,38-40: 35-Flying Fist & Bingo begin 21.00 64.00 170.00
37-Intro. Stampy, Airmale's sidekick; Hitler-c 35.00 105.00 280.00
41-50: 45-Yank & Doodle learn Black Owl's I.D. (their father). 48-Prince Ra begins 16.00 48.00 125.00
51-62,64,67,68: 53-Transvestism story. 55-No Frankenstein. 57-X-Mas-c. 64-Black Owl retires 13.00 39.00 105.00
63-Simon & Kirby c/a 17.00 51.00 135.00
65,66-Frankenstein-c by Briefer 14.00 43.00 115.00

NOTE: ***Briefer*** *a 7-on; c-65, 66.* ***J. Binder*** *a-16; c-21-29.* ***Guardineer*** *a-62.* ***Kiefer*** *c-62.* ***Palais*** *c-68.* ***Simon & Kirby*** *c-63, 75, 83.*

GD2.0 FN6.0 NM9.4

PRIZE COMICS WESTERN (Formerly Prize Comics #1-68)
Prize Publications (Feature): No. 69(V7#2), Apr-May, 1948 - No. 119, Nov-Dec, 1956 (No. 69-84: 52 pgs.)

69(V7#2) 14.00 41.00 110.00
70-75: 74-Kurtzman-a (8 pgs.) 12.00 36.00 95.00
76-Randolph Scott photo-c; "Canadian Pacific" movie adaptation 13.00 39.00 105.00
77-Photo-c; Severin/Elder, Mart Bailey-a; "Streets of Laredo" movie adaptation 12.00 36.00 95.00
78-Photo-c; S&K-a, 10 pgs.; Severin, Mart Bailey-a; "Bullet Code", & "Roughshod" movie adaptations 18.00 53.00 140.00
79-Photo-c; Kurtzman-a, 8 pgs.; Severin/Elder, Severin, Mart Bailey-a; "Stage To Chino" movie adaptation w/George O'Brien 18.00 53.00 140.00
80-82-Photo-c; 80,81-Severin/Elder-a(2). 82-1st app. The Preacher by Mart Bailey; Severin/Elder-a(3) 12.50 37.50 100.00
83,84 10.00 30.00 80.00
85-1st app. American Eagle by John Severin & begins (V9#6, 1-2/51) 24.00 73.00 195.00
86,101-105, 109-Severin/Williamson-a 12.00 36.00 95.00
87-99,110,111-Severin/Elder-a(2-3) each 12.50 37.50 100.00
100 14.00 41.00 110.00
106-108,112 10.00 30.00 70.00
113-Williamson/Severin-a(2)/Frazetta? 12.50 37.50 100.00
114-119: Drifter series in all; by Mort Meskin #114-118 8.65 26.00 60.00

NOTE: ***Fass*** *a-81.* ***Severin*** *&* ***Elder*** *c-84-99.* ***Severin*** *a-72, 75, 77-79, 83-86, 96, 97, 100-105; c-92,100-109(most), 110-119.* ***Simon*** *&* ***Kirby*** *c-75, 83.*

PRIZE MYSTERY
Key Publications: May, 1955 - No. 3, Sept, 1955

1 10.00 30.00 75.00
2,3 7.85 23.50 55.00

PROFESSIONAL FOOTBALL (See Charlton Sport Library)

PROFESSOR COFFIN
Charlton Comics: No. 19, Oct, 1985 - No. 21, Feb, 1986

19-21: Wayne Howard-a(r) 5.00

PROFESSOR OM
Innovation Publishing: May, 1990 - No. 2, 1990 ($2.50, limited series)

1,2-East Meets West spin-off 2.50

PROFESSOR XAVIER AND THE X-MEN (Also see X-Men, 1st series)
Marvel Comics: Nov, 1995 - No. 18 (99¢)

1-18: Stories featuring the Original X-Men. 2-vs. The Blob. 5-Vs. the Original Brotherhood of Evil Mutants. 10-Vs The Avengers 2.00

PROJECT, THE
DC Comics (Paradox Press): No. 1,2, 1998? ($5.59)

1,2 6.00

PROJECT A-KO (Manga)
Malibu Comics: Mar, 1994 - No. 4, June, 1994 ($2.95)

1-4-Based on anime film 3.00

PROJECT A-KO 2 (Manga)
CPM Comics: May, 1995 - No. 3, Aug, 1995 ($2.95, limited series)

1-3 3.00

PROJECT A-KO VERSUS THE UNIVERSE (Manga)
CPM Comics: Oct, 1995 - No. 5, June, 1996 ($2.95, limited series, bi-monthly)

1-5 3.00

PROJECT: HERO

Promethea #5 © ABC

Proposition Player #3 © William Willingham

Pryde and Wisdom #3 © MAR

GD2.0 FN6.0 NM9.4

Vanguard Graphics (Canadian): Aug, 1987 ($1.50)

1 — 2.00

PROMETHEA
America's Best Comics: Aug, 1999 - Present ($3.50/$2.95)

1-Moore-s/Williams III & Gray-a; Alex Ross painted-c — 3.50
1-Variant-c by Williams III & Gray — 3.50
2-13-($2.95) — 3.00
Book 1 Hardcover ($24.95, dust jacket) r/#1-7 — 24.95

PROMETHEUS (VILLAINS) (Leads into JLA #16,17)
DC Comics: Feb, 1998 ($1.95, one-shot)

1-Origin & 1st app.; Morrison-s/Pearson-c — 3.00

PROPELLERMAN
Dark Horse Comics: Jan, 1993 - No. 8, Mar, 1994 ($2.95, limited series)

1-8: 2,4,8-Contain 2 trading cards — 3.00

PROPHET (See Youngblood #2)
Image Comics (Extreme Studios): Oct, 1993 - No. 10, 1995 ($1.95)

1-($2.50)-Liefeld/Panosian-c/a; 1st app. Mary McCormick; Liefeld scripts in 1-4; #1-3 contain coupons for Prophet #0 — 2.50
1-Gold foil embossed-c edition rationed to dealers — 4.00
2-10: 2-Liefeld-c(p). 3-1st app. Judas. 4-1st app. Omen; Black and White Pt. 3 by Thibert. 4-Alternate-c by Stephen Platt. 5,6-Platt-c/a. 7-(9/94, $2.50)-Platt-c/a. 8-Bloodstrike app. 10-Polybagged w/trading card; Platt-c. — 2.50
0-(7/94, $2.50)-San Diego Comic Con ed. (2200 copies) — 3.00

PROPHET
Image Comics (Extreme Studios): V2#1, Aug, 1995 - No. 8 ($3.50)

V2#1-8: Dixon scripts in all. 1-4-Platt-a. 1-Boris-c; F. Miller variant-c. 4-Newmen app. 5,6-Wraparound-c — 2.50
Annual 1 (9/95, $2.50)-Bagged w/Youngblood gaming card; Quesada-c — 2.50
Babewatch Special 1 (12/95, $2.50)-Babewatch tie-in — 2.50
1995 San Diego Edition-B&W preview of V2#1. — 3.00
TPB-(1996, $12.95) r/#1-7 — 13.00

PROPHET (Volume 3)
Awesome Comics: Mar, 2000 ($2.99)

1-Flip-c by Jim Lee and Liefeld — 3.00

PROPHET/CABLE
Image Comics (Extreme): Jan, 1997 - No. 2, Mar, 1997 ($3.50, limited series)

1,2-Liefeld-c/a: 2-#1 listed on cover — 3.50

PROPHET/CHAPEL: SUPER SOLDIERS
Image Comics (Extreme): May, 1996 - No. 2, June, 1996 ($2.50, limited series)

1,2: 1-Two covers exist — 2.50
1-San Diego Edition; B&W-c — 2.50

PROPOSITION PLAYER
DC Comics (Vertigo): Dec, 1999 - No. 6, May, 2000 ($2.50, limited series)

1-6-Willingham-s/Guinan-a/Bolton-c — 2.50

PROTECTORS (Also see The Ferret)
Malibu Comics: Sept, 1992 - No. 20, May, 1994 ($1.95-$2.95)

1-20 ($2.50, direct sale)-With poster & diff-c: 1-Origin; has 3/4 outer-c. 3-Polybagged w/Skycap — 2.50
1-12 ($1.95, newsstand)-Without poster — 2.00

PROTOTYPE (Also see Flood Relief & Ultraforce)
Malibu Comics (Ultraverse): Aug, 1993 - No. 18, Feb, 1995 ($1.95/$2.50)

1-Holo-c — 6.00
1-Ultra Limited silver foil-c — 4.00
1-12,0,14-18: 3-($2.50, 48 pgs.)-Rune flip-c/story by B. Smith (3 pgs.). 4-Intro Wrath. 5-Break-Thru & Strangers x-over. 6-Arena cameo. 7,8-Arena-c/story. 12-(7/94). 0-(8/94,$ 2.50, 44 pgs.), 14(10/94) — 2.50
13 (8/94, $3.50)-Flip book(Ultraverse Premiere #6) — 3.50
Giant Size 1 (10/94, $2.50, 44 pgs.) — 2.50

PROWLER (Also see Revenge of the…)
Eclipse Comics: July, 1987 - No. 4, Oct, 1987 ($1.75)

1-4: Snyder-c/a. 3,4-Origin — 2.00

PROWLER, THE
Marvel Comics: Nov, 1994 ($1.75)

1-4: 1-Spider-Man app. — 2.00

PROWLER IN "WHITE ZOMBIE", THE
Eclipse Comics: Oct, 1988 ($2.00, B&W, Baxter paper)

1-Adapts Bela Lugosi movie White Zombie — 2.00

PRUDENCE & CAUTION (Also see Dogs of War & Warriors of Plasm)
Defiant: May, 1994 - No. 2, June, 1994 ($3.50/$2.50)(Spanish versions exist)

1-($3.50, 52 pgs.)-Chris Claremont scripts in all — 3.50
2-($2.50) — 2.50

PRYDE AND WISDOM (Also see Excalibur)
Marvel Comics: Sept, 1996 - No. 3, Nov, 1996 ($1.95, limited series)

1-3: Warren Ellis scripts; Terry Dodson & Karl Story-c/a — 2.00

PSI-FORCE
Marvel Comics Group: Nov, 1986 - No. 32, June, 1989 (75¢/$1.50)

1-25: 11-13-Williamson-i — 2.00
26-32-(Lower print run) — 2.50
Annual 1 (10/87) — 2.00

PSI-JUDGE ANDERSON
Fleetway Publications (Quality): 1989 - No. 15, 1990 ($1.95, B&W)

1-15 — 2.50

PSI-LORDS
Valiant: Sept, 1994 - No. 10, June, 1995 ($2.25)

1-($3.50)-Chromium wraparound-c — 3.50
1-Gold — 5.00
2-10: 3-Chaos Effect Epsilon Pt. 2 — 2.25

PSYBA-RATS (Also see Showcase '94 #3,4)
DC Comics: Apr, 1995-No. 3, June, 1995 ($2.50, limited series)

1-3 — 2.50

PSYCHO (Magazine)
Skywald Publ. Corp.: Jan, 1971 - No. 24, Mar, 1975 (68 pgs.; B&W) (No #22?)

	GD2.0	FN6.0	NM9.4
1-All reprints	5.00	15.00	55.00
2-Origin & 1st app. The Heap, & Frankenstein series by Adkins	3.65	11.00	40.00
3-10	2.80	8.40	28.00
11-20: 13-Cannabalism; 3 pgs of Christopher Lee as Dracula photos. 18-Injury to eye-c. 20-Severed Head-c	2.50	7.50	24.00
21-24: 24-1975 Winter Special	2.80	8.40	28.00
Annual 1 (1972)(68 pgs.)	3.00	9.00	30.00
Fall Special (1974)-Reese, Wildey-a(r)	2.60	7.80	26.00
Winter Special 1 (1975)-Dave Sim scripts	2.60	7.80	26.00
Yearbook (1974-nn)-Everett, Reese-a	2.60	7.80	26.00

NOTE: ***Boris** c-3, 5. **Buckler** a-2, 4, 5. **Gene Day** a-24. **Everett** a-3-6. **B. Jones** a-4. **Jeff Jones** a-6, 7, 9; c-12. **Kaluta** a-13. **Katz/Buckler** a-3. **Kim** a-24. **Morrow** a-1. **Reese** a-5. **Dave Sim** a-24. **Sutton** a-3. **Wildey** a-5.*

PSYCHOANALYSIS
E. C. Comics: Mar-Apr, 1955 - No. 4, Sept-Oct, 1955

	GD2.0	FN6.0	NM9.4
1-All Kamen-c/a; not approved by code	16.00	49.00	180.00
2-4-Kamen-c/a in all	11.35	34.00	125.00

PSYCHOANALYSIS
Gemstone Publishing: Oct, 1999 - No. 4, Jan, 2000 ($2.50)

1-4-Reprints E.C. series — 2.50
Annual 1 (2000, $10.95) r/#1-4 — 10.95

PSYCHOBLAST
First Comics: Nov, 1987 - No. 9, July, 19898 ($1.75)

1-9 — 2.00

PSYCHONAUTS
Marvel Comics (Epic Comics): Oct, 1993 - No. 4, Jan, 1994 ($4.95, lim. series)

1-4: American/Japanese co-produced comic — 5.00

PSYLOCKE & ARCHANGEL CRIMSON DAWN
Marvel Comics: Aug, 1997 - No. 4, Nov, 1997 ($2.50, limited series)

Pulp Fantastic #1
© Howard Chaykin Inc.

Punch Comics #9 © CHES

Punisher #94 © MAR

1-4-Raab-s/Larroca-a(p) 2.50

P.T. 109 (See Movie Comics)

PUBLIC DEFENDER IN ACTION (Formerly Police Trap)
Charlton Comics: No. 7, Mar, 1956 - No. 12, Oct, 1957

7 10.00 30.00 75.00
8-12 6.40 19.25 45.00

PUBLIC ENEMIES
D. S. Publishing Co.: 1948 - No. 9, June-July, 1949

1-True Crime Stories 25.00 75.00 200.00
2-Used in **SOTI**, pg. 95 22.00 66.00 175.00
3-5: 5-Arrival date of 10/1/48 14.00 41.00 110.00
6,8,9 13.00 39.00 105.00
7-McWilliams-a; injury to eye panel 14.00 41.00 110.00

PUDGY PIG
Charlton Comics: Sept, 1958 - No. 2, Nov, 1958

1,2 2.50 7.50 25.00

PULP FANTASTIC (Vertigo V2K)
DC Comics (Vertigo): Feb, 2000 - No. 3, Apr, 2000 ($2.50, limited series)

1-3-Chaykin & Tischman-s/Burchett-a 2.50

PULP FICTION LIBRARY: MYSTERY IN SPACE
DC Comics: 1999 ($19.95, TPB)

nn-Reprints classic sci-fi stories from Mystery in Space, Strange Adventures, Real Fact Comics and My Greatest Adventure 19.95

PUMA BLUES
Aardvark One International/Mirage Studios #21 on: 1986 - No. 26, 1990 ($1.70-$1.75, B&W)

1-19, 21-26: 1-1st & 2nd printings. 25,26-$1.75-c 2.00
20 ($2.25)-By Alan Moore, Miller, Grell, others 3.00
Trade Paperback (12/88, $14.95) 15.00

PUMPKINHEAD: THE RITES OF EXORCISM (Movie)
Dark Horse Comics: 1993 - No. 2, 1993 ($2.50, limited series)

1,2: Based on movie; painted-c by McManus 2.50

PUNCH & JUDY COMICS
Hillman Per.: 1944; No. 2, Fall, 1944 - V3#2, 12/47; V3#3, 6/51 - V3#9, 12/51

V1#1-(60 pgs.) 21.00 64.00 170.00
2 12.00 36.00 95.00
3-12(7/46) 10.00 30.00 70.00
V2#1(8/49),3-9 6.40 19.25 45.00
V2#2,10-12, V3#1-Kirby-a(2) each 23.00 68.00 180.00
V3#2-Kirby-a 21.00 64.00 170.00
3-9 6.40 19.25 45.00

PUNCH COMICS
Harry 'A' Chesler: 12/41; #2, 2/42; #9, 7/44 - #19, 10/46; #20, 7/47 - #23, 1/48

1-Mr. E, The Sky Chief, Hale the Magician, Kitty Kelly begin 126.00 379.00 1200.00
2-Captain Glory app. 84.00 253.00 800.00
9-Rocketman & Rocket Girl & The Master Key begin 79.00 237.00 750.00
10-Sky Chief app.; J. Cole-a; Master Key-r/Scoop #3 61.00 182.00 575.00
11-Origin Master Key-r/Scoop #1; Sky Chief, Little Nemo app.; Jack Cole-a; Fineish art by Sultan 55.00 165.00 525.00
12-Rocket Boy & Capt. Glory app; classic Skull-c 190.00 570.00 1800.00
13-Cover has list of 4 Chesler artists' names on tombstone 61.00 182.00 575.00
14,15,19,21: 21-Hypo needle story 53.00 160.00 480.00
16,17-Gag-c 51.00 153.00 460.00
18-Bondage-c; hypodermic panels 66.00 197.00 625.00
20-Unique cover with bare-breasted women. Rocket Girl-c 95.00 285.00 900.00
22,23-Little Nemo-not by McCay. 22-Intro Baxter (teenage)(68 pgs.) 28.00 83.00 220.00

PUNCHY AND THE BLACK CROW
Charlton Comics: No. 10, Oct, 1985 - No. 12, Feb, 1986

10-12: Al Fago funny animal-r 3.00

PUNISHER (See Amazing Spider-Man #129, Blood and Glory, Captain America #241, Classic Punisher, Daredevil #182-184, 257, Daredevil and the..., Ghost Rider V2#5, 6, Marc Spector #8 & 9, Marvel Preview #2, Marvel Super Action, Marvel Tales, Power Pack #46, Spectacular Spider-Man #81-83, 140, 141, 143 & new Strange Tales #13 & 14)

PUNISHER (The...)
Marvel Comics Group: Jan, 1986 - No. 5, May, 1986 (Limited series)

1-Double size 1.50 4.50 12.00
2-5 2.40 6.00
Trade Paperback (1988)-r/#1-5 11.00
NOTE: ***Zeck** a-1-4; c-1-5.*

PUNISHER (The...) (Volume 2)
Marvel Comics: July, 1987 - No. 104, July, 1995

1 2.40 6.00
2-9: 8-Portacio/Williams-c/a begins, ends #18. 9-Scarcer, low dist. 3.00
10-Daredevil app; ties in w/Daredevil #257 5.00
11-74,76-85,87-89: 13-18-Kingpin app. 19-Stroman-c/a. 20-Portacio-c(p). 24-1st app. Shadowmasters. 25,50:($1.50,52 pgs.). 25-Shadowmasters app. 57-Photo-c; came w/outer-c (newsstand ed. w/o outer-c). 59-Punisher is severely cut & has skin grafts (has black skin). 60-62-Luke Cage app. 62-Punisher back to white skin. 68-Tarantula-c/story. 85-Prequel to Suicide Run Pt. 0. 87,88-Suicide Run Pt. 6 & 9 2.50
75-($2.75, 52 pgs.)-Embossed silver foil-c 3.00
86-($2.95, 52 pgs.)-Embossed & foil stamped-c; Suicide Run part 3 3.00
90-99, 101-103: 90-bound-in cards. 99-Cringe app. 102-Bullseye. 2.00
100,104: 100-($2.95, 68 pgs.). 104-Last issue 3.00
100-($3.95, 68 pgs.)-Foil cover 4.00
"Ashcan" edition (75¢)-Joe Kubert-c 2.00
Annual 1-7 ('88-'94, 68 pgs.)-1-Evolutionary War x-over. 2 -Atlantis Attacks x-over; Jim Lee-a(p) (back-up story, 6 pgs.); Moon Knight app. 4-Golden-c(p). 6-Bagged w/card. 7-Rapido app. 3.00
...: A Man Named Frank (1994, $6.95, TPB) 7.00
...and Wolverine in African Saga nn (1989, $5.95, 52 pgs.)-Reprints Punisher War Journal #6 & 7; Jim Lee-c/a(r) 6.00
... Assassin Guild ('88, $6.95, graphic novel) 10.00
Back to School Special 1-3 (11/92-10/94, $2.95, 68 pgs.) 3.00
.../Batman: Deadly Knights (10/94, $4.95) 5.00
.../Black Widow: Spinning Doomsday's Web (1992, $9.95, graphic novel) 12.00
...Bloodlines nn (1991, $5.95, 68 pgs.) 6.00
...: Die Hard in the Big Easy nn ('92, $4.95, 52 pgs.) 5.00
...: Empty Quarter nn ('94, $6.95) 7.00
...G-Force nn (1992, $4.95, 52 pgs.)-Painted-c 5.00
...Holiday Special 1-3 (1/93-1/95,, 52 pgs.,68pgs.)-1-Foil-c 3.00
...Intruder Graphic Novel (1989, $14.95, hardcover) 20.00
...Intruder Graphic Novel (1991, $9.95, softcover) 12.00
...Invades the 'Nam: Final Invasion nn (2/94, $6.95)-J. Kubert-c & chapter break art; reprints The 'Nam #84 & unpublished #85,86 7.00
...Kingdom Gone Graphic Novel (1990, $16.95, hardcover) 20.00
...Meets Archie (8/94, $3.95, 52 pgs.)-Die cut-c; no ads; same contents as Archie Meets The Punisher 5.00
...Movie Special 1 (6/90, $5.95, 68 pgs.) 6.00
...: No Escape nn (1990, $4.95, 52 pgs.)-New-a 5.00
...Return to Big Nothing Graphic Novel (Epic, 1989, $16.95, hardcover) 25.00
...Return to Big Nothing Graphic Novel (Marvel, 1989, $12.95, softcover) 15.00
...The Prize nn (1990, $4.95, 68 pgs.)-New-a 5.00
Summer Special 1-4(8/91-7/94, 52 pgs.):1-No ads. 2-Bisley painted-c; Austin-a(i). 3-No ads 3.00
NOTE: ***Austin** c(i)-47, 48. **Cowan** c-39. **Golden** c-50, 85, 86, 100. **Heath** a-26, 27, 89, 90; c-26, 27. **Quesada** c-56p, 62p. **Sienkiewicz** c-Back to School 1.**Stroman** a-76p(9 pgs.). **Williamson** a(i)-25, 60-62i, 64-70, 74, Annual 5; c(i)-62, 65-68.*

PUNISHER (Also see Double Edge)
Marvel Comics: Nov, 1995 - No. 18, Apr, 1997 ($2.95/$1.95/$1.50)

1 ($2.95)-Ostrander scripts begin; foil-c. 3.00
2-18: 7-Vs. S.H.I.E.L.D. 11-"Onslaught." 12-17-X-Cutioner-c/app. 17-Daredevil, Spider-Man-c/app. 2.00

PUNISHER (Marvel Knights)

Punisher V3 #1 © MAR

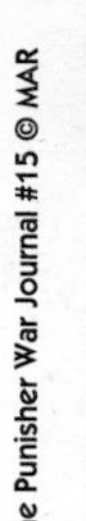
The Punisher War Journal #15 © MAR

Purgatori #5 © Chaos!

GD2.0 FN6.0 NM9.4

Marvel Comics: Nov, 1998 - No. 4, Feb, 1999 ($2.99, limited series)

1-4: 1-Wrightson-a; Wrightson & Jusko-c 3.00
1-($6.95) DF Edition; Jae Lee variant-c 7.00

PUNISHER (Marvel Knights) (Volume 3)
Marvel Comics: Apr, 2000 - No. 12, Mar, 2001 ($2.99, limited series)

1-Ennis-s/Dillon & Palmiotti-a/Bradstreet-c 5.00
1-Bradstreet white variant-c 10.00
1-($6.95) DF Edition; Jurgens & Ordway variant-c 7.00
2-Two covers by Bradstreet & Dillon 3.00
3-($3.99) Bagged with Marvel Knights Genesis Edition; Daredevil app. 4.00
4-12: 9-11-The Russian app. 3.00
.../Painkiller Jane (1/01, $3.50) Jusko-c; Ennis-s/Jusko and Dave Ross-a(p) 3.50

PUNISHER AND WOLVERINE: DAMAGING EVIDENCE (See Wolverine and...)

PUNISHER ARMORY, THE
Marvel Comics: 7/90 ($1.50); No. 2, 6/91; No. 3, 4/92 - 10/94($1.75/$2.00)

1-10: 1-r/weapons pgs. from War Journal. 1,2-Jim Lee-c. 3-10- All new material. 3-Jusko painted-c 2.00

PUNISHER KILLS THE MARVEL UNIVERSE
Marvel Comics: Nov, 1995 ($5.95, one-shot)

1-Garth Ennis script/Doug Braithwaite-a 7.00
1-2nd printing (3/00) Steve Dillon-c 5.95

PUNISHER MAGAZINE, THE
Marvel Comics: Oct, 1989 - No. 16, Nov, 1990 ($2.25, B&W, Magazine, 52 pgs.)

1-16: 1-r/Punisher #1('86). 2,3-r/Punisher 2-5. 4-16: 4-7-r/Punisher V2#1-8. 4-Chiodo-c. 8-r/Punisher #10 & Daredevil #257; Portacio & Lee-r. 14-r/Punisher War Journal #1,2 w/new Lee-c. 16-r/Punisher W. J. #3,8 3.00

NOTE: ***Chiodo*** *painted c-4, 7, 16.* ***Jusko*** *painted c-6, 8.* ***Jim Lee*** *r-8, 14-16; c-14.* ***Portacio/ Williams*** *r-7-12.*

PUNISHER MOVIE COMIC
Marvel Comics: Nov, 1989 - No. 3, Dec, 1989 ($1.00, limited series)

1-3: Movie adaptation 2.00
1 (1989, $4.95, squarebound)-contains #1-3 5.00

PUNISHER: ORIGIN OF MICRO CHIP, THE
Marvel Comics: July, 1993 - No. 2, Aug, 1993 ($1.75, limited series)

1,2 2.00

PUNISHER: P.O.V.
Marvel Comics: 1991 - No. 4, 1991 ($4.95, painted, limited series, 52 pgs.)

1-4: Starlin scripts & Wrightson painted-c/a in all. 2-Nick Fury app. 5.00

PUNISHER: THE GHOSTS OF INNOCENTS
Marvel Comics: Jan, 1993 - No. 2, Jan, 1993 ($5.95, 52 pgs.)

1,2-Starlin scripts 6.00

PUNISHER 2099 (See Punisher War Journal #50)
Marvel Comics: Feb, 1993 - No. 34, Nov, 1995 ($1.25/$1.50/$1.95)

1-24,26-34: 1-Foil stamped-c. 1-Second printing. 13-Spider-Man 2099 x-over; Ron Lim-c(p). 16-bound-in card sheet 2.00
25 ($2.95, 52 pgs.)-Deluxe edition; embossed foil-cover 3.00
25 ($2.25, 52 pgs.) 2.25

PUNISHER VS. DAREDEVIL
Marvel Comics: Jun, 2000 ($3.50, one-shot)

1-Reprints Daredevil #183,#184 & #257 3.50

PUNISHER WAR JOURNAL, THE
Marvel Comics: Nov, 1988 - No. 80, July, 1995 ($1.50/$1.75/$1.95)

1-Origin The Punisher; Matt Murdock cameo; Jim Lee inks begin 5.00
2-7: 2,3-Daredevil x-over; Jim Lee-c(i). 4-Jim Lee c/a begins. 6-Two part Wolverine story begins. 7-Wolverine-c, story ends 4.00
8-49,51-60,62,63,65: 13-16,20-22: No Jim Lee-a. 13-Lee-c only. 13-15-Heath-i. 14,15-Spider-Man x-over. 19-Last Jim Lee-c/a.29,30-Ghost Rider app. 31-Andy & Joe Kubert art. 36-Photo-c. 47,48-Nomad/Daredevil-c/stories; see Nomad. 57,58-Daredevil & Ghost Rider-c/stories. 62,63-Suicide Run Pt. 4 & 7. 3.00
50,61,64($2.95, 52 pgs.): 50-Preview of Punisher 2099 (1st app.); embossed-c. 61-Embossed foil cover; Suicide Run Pt. 1. 64-Die-cut-c; Suicide Run Pt. 10 3.00
64-($2.25, 52 pgs.)-Regular cover edition 2.25
66-74,76-80: 66-Bound-in card sheet 2.00
75 ($2.50, 52 pgs.) 2.50

NOTE: ***Golden*** *c-25-30, 40, 61, 62.* ***Jusko*** *painted c-31, 32.* ***Jim Lee*** *a-1i-3i, 4p-13p, 17p-19p; c-2i, 3i, 4p-15p, 17p, 18p, 19p. Painted c-40.*

PUNISHER: WAR ZONE, THE
Marvel Comics: Mar, 1992 - No. 41, July, 1995 ($1.75/$1.95)

1-($2.25, 40 pgs.)-Die cut-c; Romita, Jr.-c/a begins 3.00
2-22,24,26,27-41: 8-Last Romita, Jr.-c/a. 19-Wolverine app. 24-Suicide Run Pt. 5. 27-Bound-in card sheet 2.00
23-($2.95, 52 pgs.)-Enbossed foil-c; Suicide Run part 2; Buscema-a(part) 3.00
25-($2.25, 52 pgs.)-Suicide Run part 8; painted-c 2.25
Annual 1,2 ('93, 94, $2.95, 68 pgs.)-1-Bagged w/card; John Buscema-a 3.00

NOTE: ***Golden*** *c-23.* ***Romita, Jr.*** *c/a-1-8.*

PUNISHER: YEAR ONE
Marvel Comics: Dec, 1994 - No. 4, Apr, 1995 ($2.50, limited series)

1-4 2.50

PUNX
Acclaim (Valiant): Nov, 1995 - No. 3, Jan, 1996 ($2.50, unfinished lim. series)

1-3: Giffen story & art in all. 2-Satirizes Scott McCloud's Understanding Comics 2.50
(Manga) Special 1 (3/96, $2.50)-Giffen scripts 2.50

PUPPET COMICS
George W. Dougherty Co.: Spring, 1946 - No. 2, Summer, 1946

1,2-Funny animal 10.00 30.00 80.00

PUPPETOONS (See George Pal's...)

PUREHEART (See Archie as...)

PURGATORI
Chaos! Comics: Prelude #-1, 5/96 ($1.50, 16 pgs.); 1996 - No. 3 Dec, 1996 ($3.50/$2.95, limited series)

Prelude #-1-Pulido story; Balent-c/a; contains sketches & interviews 2.00
1/2 (12/00, $2.95) Al Rio-c/a 3.00
1-($3.50)-Wraparound cover; red foil embossed-c; Jim Balent-a 5.00
1-($19.95)-Premium Edition (1000 print run) 20.00
2-($3.00)-Wraparound-c 3.00
2-Variant-c 5.00
...The Dracula Gambit-($2.95) 3.00
...The Dracula Gambit Sketchbook-($2.95) 3.00
...The Vampire's Myth 1-($19.95) Premium Ed. (10,000) 20.00
...Vs. Chastity (7/00. $2.95) Two versions (Alpha and Omega) with different endings; Al Rio-a 2.95
...Vs. Lady Death (1/01, $2.95) Kaminski-s 2.95
...Vs. Vampirella (4/00, $2.95) Zanier-a; Chastity app. 2.95

PURGATORI
Chaos! Comics: Oct, 1998 - No. 7, Apr, 1999 ($2.95)

1-7-Quinn-s/Rio-c/a. 2-Lady Death-c 3.00

PURGATORI: EMPIRE
Chaos! Comics: May, 2000 - No. 3, July, 2000 ($2.95, limited series)

1-3-Cleavenger-c 3.00

PURGATORI: GODDESS RISING
Chaos! Comics: July, 1999 - No. 4, Oct, 1999 ($2.95, limited series)

1-4-Deodato-c/a 3.00

PURGE
ANIA/U.P. Comics: Aug, 1993 ($1.95, unfinished limited series)

1 2.00

PURPLE CLAW, THE (Also see Tales of Horror)
Minoan Publishing Co./Toby Press: Jan, 1953 - No. 3, May, 1953

1-Origin; horror/weird stories in all 31.00 92.00 245.00
2,3: 1-3 r-in Tales of Horror #9-11 23.00 68.00 180.00
I.W. Reprint #8-Reprints #1 2.80 8.40 28.00

PUSSYCAT (Magazine)

Quantum & Woody #18 © Acclaim

The Question #1 © DC

Quicksilver #13 © MAR

GD2.0 FN6.0 NM9.4 GD2.0 FN6.0 NM9.4

Marvel Comics Group: Oct, 1968 (B&W reprints from Men's magazines)
1-(Scarce)-Ward, Everett, Wood-a; Everett-c 17.50 70.00 190.00

PUZZLE FUN COMICS (Also see Jingle Jangle)
George W. Dougherty Co.: Spring, 1946 - No. 2, Summer, 1946 (52 pgs.)
1-Gustavson-a 23.00 68.00 180.00
2 15.00 45.00 120.00
NOTE: *#1 & 2('46) each contain a* ***George Carlson*** *cover plus a 6 pg. story "Alec in Fumbleland"; also many puzzles in each.*

QUACK!
Star Reach Productions: July, 1976 - No. 6, 1977? ($1.25, B&W)
1-Brunner-c/a on Duckaneer (Howard the Duck clone); Dave Stevens, Gilbert, Shaw-a 1.50 4.50 12.00
1-2nd printing (10/76) 3.00
2-6: 2-Newton the Rabbit Wonder by Aragones/Leialoha; Gilbert, Shaw-a; Leialoha-c. 3-The Beavers by Dave Sim begin, end #5; Gilbert, Shaw-a; Sim/Leialoha-c. 6-Brunner-a (Duckeneer); Gilbert-a 1.00 2.80 7.00

QUADRANT
Quadrant Publications: 1983 - No. 8, 1986 (B&W, nudity, adults)
1-Peter Hsu-c/a in all 2.40 6.00
2-8 3.00

QUANTUM & WOODY
Acclaim Comics: June, 1997 - No. 17, No. 32 (9/99), No. 18 - Present ($2.50)
1-17: 1-1st app.; two covers. 6-Copycat-c. 9-Troublemakers app. 2.50
32-(9/99); 18-(10/99),19-21 2.50
The Director's Cut TPB ('97, $7.95) r/#1-4 plus extra pages 8.00

QUANTUM LEAP (TV) (See A Nightmare on Elm Street)
Innovation Publishing: Sept, 1991 - No. 12, Jun, 1993 ($2.50, painted-c)
1-12: Based on TV show; all have painted-c. 8-Has photo gallery 3.00
Special Edition 1 (10/92)-r/#1 w/8 extra pgs. of photos & articles 3.00
Time and Space Special 1 (#13) ($2.95)-Foil logo 3.00

QUASAR (See Avengers #302, Captain America #217, Incredible Hulk #234, Marvel Team-Up #113 & Marvel Two-in-One #53)
Marvel Comics: Oct, 1989 - No. 60, Jul, 1994 ($1.00/$1.25, Direct sales #17 on)
1-Origin; formerly Marvel Boy/Marvel Man 3.00
2-49,51-60: 3-Human Torch app. 6-Venom cameo (2 pgs.). 7-Cosmic Spidey. 11-Excalibur x-over. 14-McFarlane-c. 16-($1.50, 52 pgs.). 17-Flash parody (Buried Alien). 20-Fantastic Four app. 23-Ghost Rider x-over. 25-($1.50, 52 pgs.)-New costume Quasar. 26-Infinity Gauntlet x-over; Thanos-c/story. 27-Infinity Gauntlet x-over. 30-Thanos cameo in flashback; last $1.00-c. 31-Begin $1.25-c; D.P. 7 guest stars. 38-40-Infinity War x-overs. 38-Battles Warlock. 39-Thanos-c & cameo. 40-Thanos app. 42-Punisher-c/story. 53-Warlock & Moondragon app. 58-w/bound-in card sheet 2.00
50-($2.95, 52 pgs.)-Holo-grafx foil-c; Silver Surfer, Man-Thing, Ren & Stimpy app. 3.00
Special #1-3 ($1.25, newsstand)-Same as #32-34 2.00

QUEEN OF THE WEST, DALE EVANS (TV)(See Dale Evans Comics, Roy Rogers & Western Roundup under Dell Giants)
Dell Publ. Co.: No. 479, 7/53 - No. 22, 1-3/59 (All photo-c; photo back c-4-8,15)
Four Color 479(#1, '53) 22.00 65.00 260.00
Four Color 528(#2, '54) 10.00 30.00 120.00
3,4: 3(4-6/54)-Toth-a. 4-Toth, Manning-a 8.00 24.00 95.00
5-10-Manning-a. 5-Marsh-a 6.70 20.00 80.00
11,19,21-No Manning 21-Tufts-a 4.60 13.75 55.00
12-18,20,22-Manning-a 5.35 16.00 65.00

QUENTIN DURWARD
Dell Publishing Co.: No. 672, Jan, 1956
Four Color 672-Movie, photo-c 6.30 19.00 75.00

QUESTAR ILLUSTRATED SCIENCE FICTION CLASSICS
Golden Press: 1977 (224 pgs.) ($1.95)
11197-Stories by Asimov, Sturgeon, Silverberg & Niven; Starstream-r 3.00 9.00 30.00

QUEST FOR CAMELOT
DC Comics: July, 1998 ($4.95)
1-Movie adaption 5.00

QUEST FOR DREAMS LOST (Also see Word Warriors)
Literacy Volunteers of Chicago: July 4, 1987 ($2.00, B&W, 52 pgs.)(Proceeds donated to help illiteracy)
1-Teenage Mutant Ninja Turtles by Eastman/Laird, Trollords, Silent Invasion, The Realm, Wordsmith, Reacto Man, Eb'nn, Aniverse 2.00

QUESTION, THE (See Americomics, Blue Beetle (1967), Charlton Bullseye & Mysterious Suspense)

QUESTION, THE (Also see Showcase '95 #3)
DC Comics: Feb, 1987 - No. 36, Mar, 1990 ($1.50)
1-36: Denny O'Neil scripts in all 2.00
Annual 1 (1988, $2.50) 2.50
Annual 2 (1989, $3.50) 3.50

QUESTION QUARTERLY, THE
DC Comics: Summer, 1990 - No. 5, Spring, 1992 ($2.50, 52pgs.)
1-5 2.50
NOTE: ***Cowan*** *a-1, 2, 4, 5; c-1-3, 5.* ***Mignola*** *a-5i.* ***Quesada*** *a-3-5.*

QUESTION RETURNS, THE
DC Comics: Feb, 1997 ($3.50, one-shot)
1-Brereton-c 3.50

QUESTPROBE
Marvel Comics: 8/84; No. 2, 1/85; No. 3, 11/85 (lim. series)
1-3: 1-The Hulk app. by Romita. 2-Spider-Man; Mooney-a(i). 3-Human Torch & Thing 3.00

QUICK DRAW McGRAW (TV) (Hanna-Barbera)(See Whitman Comic Books)
Dell Publishing Co./Gold Key No. 12 on: No. 1040, 12-2/59-60 - No. 11, 7-9/62; No. 12, 11/62; No. 13, 2/63; No. 14, 4/63; No. 15, 6/69
(1st show aired 9/29/59)
Four Color 1040(#1) 1st app. Quick Draw & Baba Looey, Augie Doggie & Doggie Daddy and Snooper & Blabber 13.00 40.00 160.00
2(4-6/60)-4,6: 2-Augie Doggie & Snooper & Blabber stories (8 pgs. each); pre-dates both of their #1 issues. 4-Augie Doggie & Snooper & Blabber stories. 7.00 21.00 85.00
5-1st Snagglepuss app.; last 10¢ issue 8.00 24.00 95.00
7-11 5.00 15.00 60.00
12,13-Title change to ...Fun-Type Roundup (84pgs.) 8.00 24.00 95.00
14,15: 15-Reprints 4.55 13.65 50.00

QUICK DRAW McGRAW (TV)(See Spotlight #2)
Charlton Comics: Nov, 1970 - No. 8, Jan, 1972 (Hanna-Barbera)
1 4.55 13.65 50.00
2-8 2.80 8.40 28.00

QUICKSILVER (See Avengers)
Marvel Comics: Nov, 1997 - No. 13, Nov, 1998 ($2.99/$1.99)
1-($2.99)-Peyer-s/Casey Jones-a; wraparound-c 3.00
2-11: 2-Two covers-variant by Golden. 4-6-Inhumans app. 2.00
12-($2.99) Siege of Wundagore pt. 4 3.00
13-Magneto-c/app.; last issue 2.00

QUICK-TRIGGER WESTERN (...Action #12; Cowboy Action #5-11)
Atlas Comics (ACI #12/WPI #13-19): No. 12, May, 1956 - No. 19, Sept, 1957
12-Baker-a 16.00 49.00 130.00
13-Williamson-a, 5 pgs. 15.00 45.00 120.00
14-Everett, Crandall, Torres-a; Heath-c 14.00 41.00 110.00
15,16: 15-Torres, Crandall-a. 16-Orlando, Kirby-a 10.50 32.00 85.00
17,18: 18-Baker-a 10.00 30.00 75.00
19 8.65 26.00 60.00
NOTE: ***Ayers*** *a-17.* ***Colan*** *a-16.* ***Maneely*** *a-15, 17; c-15, 18.* ***Morrow*** *a-18.* ***Powell*** *a-14.* ***Severin*** *a-19; c-12, 13, 16, 17, 19.* ***Shores*** *a-16.* ***Tuska*** *a-17.*

QUINCY (See Comics Reading Libraries)

Q-UNIT
Harris Comics: Dec, 1993 ($2.95)
1-($2.95)-Polybagged w/trading card version 1.2 3.00

RABID

Racer X #1 © Speed Racer Enterprises

Radioactive Man #100 © Bongo Entertainment

Raggedy Ann and Andy #5 © Bobbs & Merrill Co.

GD2.0 FN6.0 NM9.4

FantaCo Enterprises: 1994 ($5.95, B&W)

1 6.00

RACCOON KIDS, THE (Formerly Movietown Animal Antics)
National Periodical Publications (Arleigh No. 63,64): No. 52, Sept-Oct, 1954 - No. 62, Oct-Nov, 1956; No. 63, Sept, 1957; No. 64, Nov, 1957

52-Doodles Duck by Mayer 14.00 43.00 115.00
53-64: 53-62-Doodles Duck by Mayer 10.00 30.00 80.00

RACE FOR THE MOON
Harvey Publications: Mar, 1958 - No. 3, Nov, 1958

1-Powell-a(5); 1/2-pg. S&K-a; cover redrawn from Galaxy Science Fiction pulp (5/53) 14.00 41.00 110.00
2-Kirby/Williamson-c(r)/a(3); Kirby-p 7 more stys 26.00 79.00 210.00
3-Kirby/Williamson-c/a(4); Kirby-p 6 more stys 28.00 83.00 220.00

RACE OF SCORPIONS
Dark Horse Comics: 1990 - No. 2, 1990 ($4.50/$4.95, 52pgs.)

1,2: 1-r/stories from Dark Horse Presents #23-27. 2-($4.95-c) 5.00

RACER-X
Now Comics: 8/88 - No. 11, 8/89; V2#1, 9/89 - V2#10, 1990 ($1.75)

0-Deluxe ($3.50) 3.50
1 (9/88) - 11, V2#1-10 2.00

RACER X (See Speed Racer)
DC Comics (WildStorm): Oct, 2000 - No. 3, Dec, 2000 ($2.95, limited series)

1-3: 1-Tommy Yune-s/Jo Chen-a; 2 covers by Yune. 2,3-Kabala app. 3.50

RACING PETTYS
STP Corp.: 1980 ($2.50, 68 pgs., 10 1/8" x 13 1/4")

1-Bob Kane-a. Kane bio on inside back-c. 10.00

RACK & PAIN
Dark Horse Comics: Mar, 1994 - No. 4, June, 1994 ($2.50, limited series)

1-4: Brian Pulido scripts in all. 1-Greg Capullo-c 3.00

RACK & PAIN: KILLERS
Chaos! Comics: Sept, 1996 - No. 4, Jan, 1997 ($2.95, limited series)

1-4: Reprints Dark Horse series; Jae Lee-c 3.00

RACKET SQUAD IN ACTION
Capitol Stories/Charlton Comics: May-June, 1952 - No. 29, Mar, 1958

1 28.00 84.00 225.00
2-4,6: 3,4,6-Dr. Neff, Ghost Breaker app. 14.00 43.00 115.00
5-Dr. Neff, Ghost Breaker app; headlights-c 22.00 66.00 175.00
7-10: 10-Explosion-c 12.50 37.50 100.00
11-Ditko-c/a 30.00 90.00 240.00
12-Ditko explosion-c (classic); Shuster-a(2) 47.00 140.00 420.00
13-Shuster-c(p)/a. 10.00 30.00 80.00
14-Marijuana story "Shakedown" 12.50 37.50 100.00
15-28 10.00 30.00 75.00
29-(15¢, 68 pgs.) 10.50 32.00 85.00

RADIANT LOVE (Formerly Daring Love #1)
Gilmor Magazines: No. 2, Dec, 1953 - No. 6, Aug, 1954

2 7.85 23.50 55.00
3-6 5.00 15.00 32.00

RADICAL DREAMER
Blackball Comics: No. 0, May, 1994 - No. 4, Nov, 1994 ($1.99, bi-monthly) (1st poster format comic)

0-4: 0-2-($1.99, poster format): 0-1st app. Max Wrighter. 3,4-($2.50-c) 3.00

RADICAL DREAMER
Mark's Giant Economy Size Comics: V2#1, June, 1995 - V2#6, Feb, 1996 ($2.95, B&W, limited series)

V2#1-6 3.00
Prime (5/96, $2.95) 3.00
Dreams Cannot Die!-(1996, $20.00, softcover)-Collects V1#0-4 & V2#1-6; intro by Kurt Busiek; afterward by Mark Waid 20.00
Dreams Cannot Die!-(1996, $60.00, hardcover)-Signed & limited edition; collects V1#0-4 & V2#1-6; intro by Kurt Busiek; afterward by Mark Waid 60.00

GD2.0 FN6.0 NM9.4

RADIOACTIVE MAN (Simpsons TV show)
Bongo Comics: 1993 - No. 6, 1994 ($1.95/$2.25, limited series)

1-($2.95)-Glow-in-the-dark-c; bound-in jumbo poster; origin Radioactive Man; (cover dated Nov. 1952) 4.00
2-6: 2-Says #88 on-c & inside & dated May 1962; cover parody of Atlas Kirby monster-c; Superior Squad app.; origin Fallout Boy. 3-($1.95)-Cover "dated" Aug 1972 #216. 4-($2.25)-Cover "dated" Oct 1980 #412; w/trading card. 5-Cover "dated" Jan 1986 #679; w/trading card. 6-(Jan 1995 #1000) 3.00
Colossal #1-($4.95) 2.40 6.00
#100 (2000, $2.50) Comic Book Guy-c/app.; faux 1963 issue inside 2.50

RAGAMUFFINS
Eclipse Comics: Jan, 1985 ($1.75, one shot)

1-Eclipse Magazine-r, w/color 2.00

RAGGEDY ANN AND ANDY (See Dell Giants, March of Comics #23 & New Funnies)
Dell Publishing Co.: No. 5, 1942 - No. 533, 2/54; 10-12/64 - No. 4, 3/66

Four Color 5(1942) 50.00 150.00 600.00
Four Color 23(1943) 37.00 110.00 440.00
Four Color 45(1943) 30.00 90.00 360.00
Four Color 72(1945) 25.00 75.00 300.00
1(6/46)-Billy & Bonnie Bee by Frank Thomas 26.00 78.00 310.00
2,3: 3-Egbert Elephant by Dan Noonan begins 13.00 40.00 160.00
4-Kelly-a, 16 pgs. 14.00 42.00 170.00
5-10: 7-Little Black Sambo, Black Mumbo & Black Jumbo only app; Christmas-c 10.50 31.00 125.00
11-21: 21-Alice In Wonderland cover/story 8.35 25.00 100.00
22-27,29-39(8/49), Four Color 262(1/50): 34-"...In Candyland" 6.70 20.00 80.00
28-Kelly-c 7.50 22.50 90.00
Four Color 306,354,380,452,533 4.60 13.75 55.00
1(10-12/64-Dell) 3.40 10.35 38.00
2,3(10-12/65), 4(3/66) 2.50 7.50 24.00

NOTE: ***Kelly** art ("Animal Mother Goose")-#1-34, 36, 37; c-28. Peterkin Pottle by **John Stanley** in 32-38.*

RAGGEDY ANN AND ANDY
Gold Key: Dec, 1971 - No. 6, Sept, 1973

1 2.80 8.40 28.00
2-6 2.00 6.00 18.00

RAGGEDY ANN & THE CAMEL WITH THE WRINKLED KNEES (See Dell Jr. Treasury #8)

RAGMAN (See Batman Family #20, The Brave & The Bold #196 & Cancelled Comic Cavalcade)
National Per. Publ./DC Comics No. 5: Aug-Sept, 1976 - No. 5, Jun-Jul, 1977

1-Origin & 1st app. 1.25 3.75 10.00
2-5: 2-Origin ends; Kubert-c. 4-Drug use story 2.40 6.00

NOTE: ***Kubert** a-4, 5; c-1-5. **Redondo** studios a-1-4.*

RAGMAN (2nd Series)
DC Comics: Oct, 1991 - No. 8, May, 1992 ($1.50, limited series)

1-8: 1-Giffen plots/breakdowns. 3-Origin. 8-Batman-c/story 2.00

RAGMAN: CRY OF THE DEAD
DC Comics: Aug, 1993 - No. 6, Jan, 1994 ($1.75, limited series)

1-6: Joe Kubert-c 3.00

RAGMOP
Image Comics: Sept, 1997 - Present ($2.95, B&W)

1,2-Rob Walton-c/s/a 3.00

RAGS RABBIT (Formerly Babe Ruth Sports #10 or Little Max #10?; also see Harvey Hits #2, Harvey Wiseguys & Tastee Freez)
Harvey Publications: No. 11, June, 1951 - No. 18, March, 1954 (Written & drawn for little folks)

11-(See Nutty Comics #5 for 1st app.) 5.00 15.00 30.00
12-18 4.00 12.00 24.00

RAI (Rai and the Future Force #9-23) (See Magnus #5-8)
Valiant: Mar, 1992 - No. 0, Oct, 1992; No. 9, May, 1993 - No. 33, Jun, 1995 ($1.95/$2.25)

Rampaging Hulk (2nd series) #2 © MAR

Rangers Comics #44 © FH

Rat Patrol #3 © DELL

GD2.0 FN6.0 NM9.4

1-Valiant's 1st original character 2.40 6.00
2-4,0: 4-Low print run. 0-(11/92)-Origin/1st app. new Rai (Rising Spirit) & 1st full app. & partial origin Bloodshot; also see Eternal Warrior #4; tells future of all characters 5.00
5-33: 6,7-Unity x-overs. 7-Death of Rai. 9-($2.50)-Gatefold-c; story cont'd from Magnus #24; Magnus, Eternal Warrior & X-O app. 15-Manowar Armor app. 17-19-Magnus x-over. 21-1st app. The Starwatchers (cameo); trading card. 22-Death of Rai. 26-Chaos Effect Epsilon Pt. 3 2.50
NOTE: *Layton c-2i, 9i. Miller c-6. Simonson c-7.*

RAIDERS OF THE LOST ARK (Movie)
Marvel Comics Group: Sept, 1981 - No. 3, Nov, 1981 (Movie adaptation)
1-3: 1-r/Marvel Comics Super Special #18 3.00
NOTE: ***Buscema** a(p)-1-3; c(p)-1. **Simonson** a-3i; scripts-1-3.*

RAINBOW BRITE AND THE STAR STEALER
DC Comics: 1985
nn-Movie adaptation 1.00 3.00 8.00

RALPH KINER, HOME RUN KING
Fawcett Publications: 1950 (Pittsburgh Pirates)
nn-Photo-c; life story 58.00 174.00 550.00

RALPH SNART ADVENTURES
Now Comics: June, 1986 - V2#9, 1987; V3#1 - #26, Feb, 1991; V4#1, 1992 - #4, 1992
1-3, V2#1-7,V3#1-23,25,26:1-($1.00, B&W)-1(B&W),V2#1(11/86), B&W), 8,9-color. V3#1(9/88)-Color begins 2.50
V3#24-($2.50)-3-D issue, V4#1-3-Direct sale versions w/cards 2.50
V4#1-3-Newsstand versions w/random cards 2.50
Book 1 1.00 3.00 8.00
3-D Special (11/92, $3.50)-Complete 12-card set w/3-D glasses 3.50

RAMAR OF THE JUNGLE (TV)
Toby Press No. 1/Charlton No. 2 on: 1954 (no month); No. 2, Sept, 1955 - No. 5, Sept, 1956
1-Jon Hall photo-c; last pre-code issue 20.00 60.00 160.00
2-5: 2-Jon Hall photo-c 14.00 41.00 110.00

RAMM
Megaton Comics: May, 1987 - No. 2, Sept, 1987 ($1.50, B&W)
1,2-Both have 1 pg. Youngblood ad by Liefeld 2.00

RAMPAGING HULK (The Hulk #10 on; also see Marvel Treasury Edition)
Marvel Comics Group: Jan, 1977 - No. 9, June, 1978 ($1.00, B&W magazine)
1-Bloodstone story w/Buscema & Nebres-a. Origin re-cap w/Simonson-a; Gargoyle, UFO story; Ken Barr-c 1.75 5.25 14.00
2-Old X-Men app; origin old w/Simonson-a & new X-Men in text w/Cockrum illos; Bloodstone story w/Brown & Nebres-a 1.50 4.50 12.00
3-9: 3-Iron Man app. 4-Gallery of villains w/Giffen-a. 5,6-Hulk vs. Sub-Mariner. 7-Man-Thing story. 8-Original Avengers app. 9-Thor vs. Hulk battle; Shanna the She-Devil story w/DeZuniga-a 1.10 3.30 9.00
NOTE: ***Alcala** a-1-3i, 5i, 8i. **Buscema** a-1. **Giffen** a-4. **Nino** a-4i. **Simonson** a-1-3p. **Starlin** a-4(w/**Nino**), 7; c-4, 5, 7.*

RAMPAGING HULK
Marvel Comics: Aug, 1998 - No. 6, Jan, 1999 ($2.99/$1.99)
1-($2.99) Flashback stories of Savage Hulk; Leonardi-a 3.00
2-6-($1.99): 2-Two covers 2.00

RANDOLPH SCOTT (Movie star)(See Crack Western #67, Prize Comics Western #76, Western Hearts #8, Western Love #1 & Western Winners #7)

RANGE BUSTERS
Fox Features Syndicate: Sept, 1950 (One shot)
1 19.00 56.00 150.00

RANGE BUSTERS (Formerly Cowboy Love?; Wyatt Earp, Frontier Marshall #11 on)
Charlton Comics: No. 8, May, 1955 - No. 10, Sept, 1955
8 7.85 23.50 55.00
9,10 5.00 15.00 35.00

RANGELAND LOVE
Atlas Comics (CDS): Dec, 1949 - No. 2, Mar, 1950 (52 pgs.)

GD2.0 FN6.0 NM9.4

1-Robert Taylor & Arlene Dahl photo-c 16.00 49.00 130.00
2-Photo-c 13.00 39.00 105.00

RANGER, THE (See Zane Grey, Four Color #255)

RANGE RIDER, THE (TV)(See Flying A's...)

RANGE ROMANCES
Comic Magazines (Quality Comics): Dec, 1949 - No. 5, Aug, 1950 (#5: 52 pg)
1-Gustavson-c/a 26.00 79.00 210.00
2-Crandall-c/a; "spanking" scene 31.00 94.00 250.00
3-Crandall, Gustavson-a; photo-c 22.00 66.00 175.00
4-Crandall-a; photo-c 19.00 56.00 150.00
5-Gustavson-a; Crandall-a(p); photo-c 19.00 56.00 150.00

RANGERS COMICS (...of Freedom #1-7)
Fiction House Magazines: 10/41 - No. 67, 10/52; No. 68, Fall, 1952; No. 69, Winter, 1952-53 (Flying stories)
1-Intro. Ranger Girl & The Rangers of Freedom; ends #7, cover app. only #5 232.00 695.00 2200.00
2 79.00 237.00 750.00
3 63.00 189.00 600.00
4,5 58.00 174.00 550.00
6-10: 8-U.S. Rangers begin 47.00 140.00 420.00
11,12-Commando Rangers app. 42.00 125.00 375.00
13-Commando Ranger begins-not same as Commando Rangers 40.00 120.00 350.00
14-20 38.00 113.00 300.00
21-Intro/origin Firehair (begins, 2/45) 40.00 120.00 350.00
22-30: 23-Kazanda begins, ends #28. 28-Tiger Man begins (origin/1st app., 4/46), ends #46. 30-Crusoe Island begins, ends #40 28.00 84.00 225.00
31-40: 33-Hypodermic panels 24.00 71.00 190.00
41-46: 41-Last Werewolf Hunter 19.00 56.00 150.00
47-56- "Eisnerish" Dr. Drew by Grandenetti. 48-Last Glory Forbes. 53-Last 52 pg. issue. 55-Last Sky Rangers 19.00 56.00 150.00
57-60-Straight Dr. Drew by Grandenetti 14.00 41.00 110.00
61-69: 64-Suicide Smith begins. 63-Used in **POP**, pgs. 85, 99. 67-Space Rangers begin, end #69 12.00 36.00 95.00
NOTE: *Bondage, discipline covers, lingerie panels are common. Crusoe Island by **Larsen**-#30-36. Firehair by **Lubbers**-#30-49. Glory Forbes by **Baker**-#36-45, 47; by **Whitman**-#34, 35. I Confess in #41-53. Jan of the Jungle in #42-58. King of the Congo in #49-53. Tiger Man by **Celardo**-#30-39. **M. Anderson** a-30? **Baker** a-36-38, 42, 44. **John Celardo** a-34, 36-39. **Lee Elias** a-21-28. **Evans** a-19, 38-46, 48-52. **Hopper** a-25, 26. **Ingels** a-13-16. **Larsen** a-34. **Bob Lubbers** a-30-38, 40-44; c-40-45. **Moreira** a-41-47. **Tuska** a-16, 17, 19, 22. **M. Whitman** c-61-66. **Zolnerwich** c-1-17.*

RANGO (TV)
Dell Publishing Co.: Aug, 1967
1-Photo-c of comedian Tim Conway 2.50 7.50 25.00

RAPHAEL (See Teenage Mutant Ninja Turtles)
Mirage Studios: 1985 ($1.50, 7-1/2x11", B&W w/2 color cover, one-shot)
1-1st Turtles one-shot spin-off; contains 1st drawing of the Turtles as a group from 1983 4.00
1-2nd printing (11/87); new-c & 8 pgs. art 2.00

RASCALS IN PARADISE
Dark Horse Comics: Aug, 1994 - No. 3, Dec, 1994 ($3.95, magazine size)
1-3-Jim Silke-a/story 4.00
Trade paperback-($16.95)-r/#1-3 17.00

RATFINK (See Frantic, Zany, & Ed "Big Daddy" Roth's Ratfink Comix)
Canrom, Inc.: Oct, 1964
1-Woodbridge-a 4.55 13.65 50.00

RAT PATROL, THE (TV)
Dell Publishing Co.: Mar, 1967 - No. 5, Nov, 1967; No. 6, Oct, 1969
1-Christopher George photo-c 6.00 18.00 72.00
2-6: 3-6-Photo-c 3.65 11.00 40.00

RAVAGE 2099 (See Marvel Comics Presents #117)
Marvel Comics: Dec, 1992 - No. 33, Aug, 1995($1.25/$1.50)
1-($1.75)-Gold foil stamped-c; Stan Lee scripts 3.00

Ravage 2099 #32 © MAR

Rawhide Kid #1 © MAR

The Ray #0 © DC

GD2.0 FN6.0 NM9.4

1-($1.75)-2nd printing 2.00
2-24,26-33: 5-Last Ryan-c. 6-Last Ryan-a. 14-Punisher 2099 x-over. 15-Ron Lim-c(p). 18-Bound-in card sheet 2.00
25 ($2.25, 52 pgs.) 2.25
25 ($2.95, 52 pgs.)-Silver foil embossed-c 3.00

RAVEN, THE (See Movie Classics)

RAVEN CHRONICLES
Caliber (New Worlds): 1995 - Present ($2.95, B&W)
1-15: 10-Flip book w/Wordsmith #6. 15-Flip book w/High Caliber #4 3.00

RAVENING, THE
Avatar Press: June, 1997 - No. 2 ($3.00, B&W, limited series)
1,2 3.00

RAVENS AND RAINBOWS
Pacific Comics: Dec, 1983 (Baxter paper)(Reprints fanzine work in color)
1-Jeff Jones-c/a(r); nudity scenes 3.00

RAWHIDE (TV)
Dell Publishing Co./Gold Key: Sept-Nov, 1959 - June-Aug, 1962; July, 1963 - No. 2, Jan, 1964

	GD2.0	FN6.0	NM9.4
Four Color 1028 (#1)	23.00	68.00	270.00
Four Color 1097,1160,1202,1261,1269	14.00	41.00	165.00
01-684-208 (8/62, Dell)	12.00	35.00	145.00
1(10071-307) (7/63, Gold Key)	12.00	35.00	145.00
2-(12¢)	11.30	34.00	135.00

NOTE: *All have Clint Eastwood photo-c.* ***Tufts*** *a-1028.*

RAWHIDE KID
Atlas/Marvel Comics (CnPC No. 1-16/AMI No. 17-30): 3/55 - No. 16, 9/57; No. 17, 8/60 - No. 151, 5/79

	GD2.0	FN6.0	NM9.4
1-Rawhide Kid, his horse Apache & sidekick Randy begin; Wyatt Earp app.; #1 was not code approved; Maneely splash pg.	84.00	253.00	800.00
2	40.00	120.00	325.00
3-5	28.00	84.00	225.00
6-10: 7-Williamson-a (4 pgs.)	22.00	66.00	175.00
11-16: 16-Torres-a	19.00	56.00	150.00
17-Origin by Jack Kirby; Kirby-a begins	31.00	93.00	350.00
18-21,24-30	12.50	37.00	135.00
22-Monster-c/story by Kirby/Ayers	15.50	46.50	170.00
23-Origin retold by Jack Kirby	19.00	57.00	210.00
31-35,40: 31,32-Kirby-a. 33-35-Davis-a. 34-Kirby-a. 35-Intro & death of The Raven. 40-Two-Gun Kid x-over.	9.00	27.00	100.00
36,37,39,41,42-No Kirby. 42-1st Larry Lieber issue	8.15	24.50	90.00
38-Red Raven-c/story; Kirby-c (2/64).	11.50	34.00	125.00
43-Kirby-a (beware: pin-up often missing)	10.50	31.50	115.00
44,46: 46-Toth-a. 46-Doc Holliday-c/s	7.25	21.75	80.00
45-Origin retold, 17 pgs.	10.00	30.00	110.00
47-49,51-60	4.10	12.30	45.00
50-Kid Colt x-over; vs. Rawhide Kid	4.55	13.65	50.00
61-70: 64-Kid Colt story. 66-Two-Gun Kid story. 67-Kid Colt story. 70-Last 12¢ issue	3.20	9.60	35.00
71-78,80-83,85	2.30	7.00	20.00
79,84,86,95: 79-Williamson-a(r). 84,86: Kirby-a. 86-Origin-r; Williamson-r/Ringo Kid #13 (4 pgs.)	2.50	7.50	23.00
87-91: 90-Kid Colt app. 91-Last 15¢ issue	2.00	6.00	18.00
92,93 (52 pg.Giants). 92-Kirby-a	3.00	9.00	30.00
94,96-99	2.00	6.00	18.00
100 (6/72)-Origin retold & expanded	2.50	7.50	25.00
101-120: 115-Last new story	1.85	5.50	15.00
121-151	1.25	3.75	10.00
Special 1(9/71, 25¢, 68 pgs.)-All Kirby/Ayers-r	3.20	9.60	35.00

NOTE: ***Ayers*** *a-13, 14, 16.* ***Colan*** *a-5, 35, 37; c-145p, 148p, 149p.* ***Davis*** *a-125r.* ***Everett*** *a-54i, 65, 66, 88, 96i, 148i(r).* ***Gulacy*** *c-147.* ***Heath*** *c-4.* ***G. Kane*** *c-101, 144.* ***Keller*** *a-5, 144r.* ***Kirby*** *a-17-32, 34, 42, 43, 84, 86, 92, 109r, 112r, 137r, Spec. 1; c-17-35, 37, 38, 40, 41, 43-47, 137r.* ***Maneely*** *c-1, 2, 5, 6, 14.* ***Morisi*** *a-13.* ***Morrow/Williamson*** *r-111.* ***Roussos*** *r-146i, 147i, 149-151i.* ***Severin*** *a-16; c-8, 13.* ***Sutton*** *a-93.* ***Torres*** *a-99r.* ***Tuska*** *a-14.* ***Wildey*** *r-146-151(Outlaw Kid).* ***Williamson*** *r-79, 86, 95.*

RAWHIDE KID
Marvel Comics Group: Aug, 1985 - No. 4, Nov, 1985 (Mini-series)

GD2.0 FN6.0 NM9.

1-4 5.00

RAY, THE (See Freedom Fighters & Smash Comics #14)
DC Comics: Feb, 1992 - No. 6, July, 1992 ($1.00, mini-series)
1-Sienkiewicz-c; Joe Quesada-a(p) in 1-5 5.00
2-6: 3-6-Quesada-c(p). 6-Quesada layouts only 3.00
...In a Blaze of Power (1994, $12.95)-r/#1-6 w/new Quesada-c 13.00

RAY, THE
DC Comics: May, 1994 - No. 28, Oct, 1996 ($1.75/$1.95/$2.25)
1-Quesada-c(p); Superboy app. 3.00
1-($2.95)-Collectors Edition w/diff. Quesada-c; embossed foil-c 4.00
2-5,0,6-24,26-28: 2-Quesada-c(p); Superboy app. 5-(9/94). 0-(10/94) 2.25
25-($3.50)-Future Flash (Bart Allen)-c/app; double size 3.50
Annual 1 ($3.95, 68 pgs.)-Superman app. 4.00

RAY BRADBURY COMICS
Topps Comics: Feb, 1993 - V4#1, June, 1994 ($2.95)
1-5-Polybagged w/3 trading cards each. 1-All dinosaur issue; Corben-a; Williamson/Torres/Krenkel-r/Weird Science-Fantasy #25. 3-All dinosaur issue; Steacy painted-c; Stout-a 3.00
Special Edition 1 (1994, $2.95)-The Illustrated Man 3.00
...Special: Tales of Horror #1 ($2.50), ...Trilogy of Terror V3#1 (5/94, $2.50), ...Martian Chronicles V4#1 (6/94, $2.50)-Steranko-c 2.50

NOTE: ***Kelley Jones*** *a-Trilogy of Terror V3#1.* ***Kaluta*** *a-Martian Chronicles V4#1.* ***Kurtzman/Matt Wagner*** *c-2.* ***McKean*** *c-4.* ***Mignola*** *a-4.* ***Wood*** *a-Trilogy of Terror V3#1r.*

RAZOR
London Night Studios: May, 1992 - No. 51, Apr, 1999 ($3.95/$3.00, B&W)

	GD2.0	FN6.0	NM9.4
0 (5/92, $3.95)-Direct market	1.50	4.50	12.00
0 (4/95, $3.00)-London Night edition			3.50
1/2 (4/95, mail-in offer)-1st Poizon; Linsner-c			5.00
1 (8/92, $2.50)-Fathom Press	1.50	4.50	12.00
1-2nd printing			3.50
2 ($2.95)-J. O'Barr-c	1.25	3.75	10.00
2-Limited edi. in red & blue, 2-Platinum; no c-price	1.50	4.50	12.00
3-($3.95)-Jim Balent-c			5.00
3-w/poster insert		2.40	6.00
4-Vigil-c			4.00
4-w/poster insert			5.00
5-Linsner-c		2.40	6.00
5-Platinum	1.25	3.75	10.00
6-31,33,34:10-1st app. Stryke. 1,12 -Rituals Pt. 1 & 2. 21-Rose & Gunn app. 25-Photo-c			3.00
25-Uncut ($10.00)-Nude Edition; double-c			10.00
32-($3.50)			3.50
32-($5.00)-Nude Edition; Nude-c			5.00
35-49,51			3.00
40-Uncut ($6.00)-Nude Edition			6.00
50-Uncut-Four covers incl. Tony Dainel			3.00
Annual 1 (1993, $2.95)-1st app. Shi	2.50	7.50	20.00
Annual 1-Gold (1200 printed)	2.50	7.50	25.00
Annual 2 (Late 1994, $3.00)			3.00
.../Cry No More 1-($3.95)-Origin Razor; variant-c exists			4.00
.../Embrace nn-($3.00)-Variant photo-c(Carmen Electra)			3.00
...Pictorial 1-(10/97, $5.00)			5.00
.../Shi Special 1 (7/94, $3.00)		2.40	6.00
.../Switchblade Symphony 1-($3.95)-Hartsoe-s			4.00
...: Swimsuit Special-painted-c			3.00
...: The Darkest Night 1,2 ($4.95)-painted-c			5.00
.../Warrior Nun Areala-Faith-(5/96, $3.95)			4.00
.../Warrior Nun Areala-Faith-(5/96, $3.95)-Virgin-c			5.00

RAZOR AND THE LADIES OF LONDON NIGHT
London Night Studios: March, 1997 ($3.95, one-shot, mature)
1-Photo-c & insides 4.00

RAZOR: ARCHIVES
London Night Studios: May, 1997 - Present ($3.95/$5.00, mature)
1-($3.95). 2-5-($5.00) 5.00

RAZOR: BURN

Real Fact Comics #13 © DC

Realistic Romances #4 © AVON

Real Life Comics #4 © STD

GD2.0 FN6.0 NM9.4

ondon Night Studios: 1994 - No. 5, 1994 ($3.00, limited series, mature)
-5 3.00
PB-($14.95) r/ #1-5 15.00

AZOR/DARK ANGEL: THE FINAL NAIL
oneyard Press #1/London Night Studios #2: June, 1994 -No. 2, June, 1994
2.95, B&W, limited series, mature)
,2 3.00

AZOR• DEEP CUTS
ondon Night Studios: Sept, 1997 ($5.00, one-shot, mature)
-Photo-c & insides 5.00

AZOR/MORBID ANGEL: SOUL SEARCH
ondon Night Studios: Sept, 1996 - No. 3, 1997 ($3.00, limited series, mature)
-3 3.00

AZOR: THE SUFFERING
ondon Night Studios: 1994 - No. 3, 1995 ($2.95, limited series, mature)
-3 ($2.95): 2-(9/94), 1-($3.00)-Director's Cut 3.00
-Platinum 5.00
ade paperback-($12.95) 13.00

AZOR: TORTURE
ondon Night Studios: 1995 - No. 6, 1995 ($3.00, limited series, mature)
-($3.95)-Wraparound, chromium-c; polybagged w/card; alternate-c exists? 4.00
-6 ($3.00): 3-Error & corrected issues exist 3.00

AZOR: VOLUME TWO
ondon Night Studios: Oct, 1996 - No. 7, June, 1997 ($3.95/$3.00, mature)
-Wraparound foil-c; Quinn-s 4.00
-7-($3.00): 3-Error & corrected issues exist 3.00

AZORLINE
arvel Comics: Sept, 1993 (75¢, one-shot)
-Clive Barker super-heroes: Ectokid, Hokum & Hex, Hyperkind & Saint Sinner (all 1st app.) 2.00

EAL ADVENTURE COMICS (Action Adventure #2 on)
illmor Magazines: Apr, 1955
5.70 17.00 40.00

EAL ADVENTURES OF JONNY QUEST, THE
ark Horse Comics: Sept, 1996 - No. 12, Sept, 1997 ($2.95)
-12 3.00

EAL CLUE CRIME STORIES (Formerly Clue Comics)
illman Periodicals: V2#4, June, 1947 - V8#3, May, 1953
2#4(#1)-S&K c/a(3); Dan Barry-a 46.00 137.00 410.00
5-7-S&K c/a(3-4). 7-Iron Lady app. 38.00 113.00 300.00
8-12 10.00 30.00 80.00
3#1-8,10-12, V4#1-3,5-8,11,12 9.30 28.00 65.00
3#9-Used in **SOTI**, pg. 102 12.00 36.00 95.00
4#4-S&K-a 12.50 37.50 100.00
4#9,10-Krigstein-a 10.00 30.00 75.00
5#1-5,7,8,10,12 7.15 21.50 50.00
6,9,11(1/54)-Krigstein-a 10.00 30.00 70.00
6#1-5,8,9,11 6.40 19.25 45.00
6,7,10,12-Krigstein-a. 10-Bondage-c 9.30 28.00 65.00
7#1-3,5-11, V8#1-3: V7#6-1 pg. Frazetta ad "Prayer" - 1st app.? 6.40 19.25 45.00
4,12-Krigstein-a 9.30 28.00 65.00
OTE: *Barry a-9, 10; c-V2#8. Briefer a-V6#6. Fuje a- V2#7(2), 8, 11. Infantino a-V2#8; V2#11. Lawrence a-V3#8, V5#7. Powell a-V4#11, 12. V5#4, 5, 7 are 68 pgs.*

EAL EXPERIENCES (Formerly Tiny Tessie)
tlas Comics (20CC): No. 25, Jan, 1950
5-Virginia Mayo photo-c from movie "Red Light" 7.00 21.00 48.00

EAL FACT COMICS
ational Periodical Publications: Mar-Apr, 1946 - No. 21, July-Aug, 1949
-S&K-c/a; Harry Houdini story; Just Imagine begins (not by Finlay); Fred Ray-a 58.00 174.00 550.00
2-S&K-a; Rin-Tin-Tin & P. T. Barnum stories 40.00 120.00 340.00
3-H.G. Wells, Lon Chaney stories; 1st DC letter column 36.00 108.00 290.00
4-Virgil Finlay-a on 'Just Imagine' begins, ends #12 (2 pgs. each); Jimmy Stewart & Jack London stories; Joe DiMaggio 1 pg. biography 40.00 120.00 340.00
5-Batman/Robin-c taken from cover of Batman #9; 5 pg. story about creation of Batman & Robin; Tom Mix story 179.00 537.00 1700.00
6-Origin & 1st app. Tommy Tomorrow by Weisinger and Sherman (1-2/47); Flag-c; 1st writing by Harlan Ellison (letter column, non-professional); "First Man to Reach Mars" epic-c/story 111.00 332.00 1050.00
7-(No. 6 on inside)-Roussos-a; D. Fairbanks sty. 19.00 56.00 150.00
8-2nd app. Tommy Tomorrow by Finlay (5-6/47) 61.00 182.00 575.00
9-S&K-a; Glenn Miller, Indianapolis 500 stories 29.00 86.00 230.00
10-Vigilante by Meskin (based on movie serial); 4 pg. Finlay s/f story 28.00 83.00 220.00
11,12: 11-Annie Oakley, G-Men stories; Kinstler-a 15.00 45.00 120.00
13-Dale Evans and Tommy Tomorrow-c/stories 50.00 150.00 450.00
14,17,18: 14-Will Rogers story 14.00 41.00 110.00
15-Nuclear explosion part-c ("Last War on Earth" story); Clyde Beatty story 19.00 56.00 150.00
16-Tommy Tomorrow app.; 1st Planeteers? 44.00 133.00 400.00
19-Sir Arthur Conan Doyle story 16.00 49.00 130.00
20-Kubert-a, 4 pgs; Daniel Boone story 18.00 53.00 140.00
21-Kubert-a, 2 pgs; Kit Carson story 14.00 41.00 110.00
NOTE: *Barry c-16. Virgil Finlay c-6, 8. Meskin c-10. Roussos a-1-4, 6.*

REAL FUNNIES
Nedor Publishing Co.: Jan, 1943 - No. 3, June, 1943
1-Funny animal, humor; Black Terrier app. (clone of The Black Terror) 33.00 98.00 260.00
2,3 16.00 49.00 130.00

REAL GHOSTBUSTERS, THE (Also see Slimer)
Now Comics: Aug, 1988 - No. 32, 1991 ($1.75/$1.95)
1-32: 1-Based on Ghostbusters movie. #29-32 exist? 3.00

REAL HEROES COMICS
Parents' Magazine Institute: Sept, 1941 - No. 16, Oct, 1946
1-Roosevelt-c/story 33.00 98.00 260.00
2-J. Edgar Hoover-c/story 14.00 41.00 110.00
3-5,7-10: 4-Churchill, Roosevelt stories 12.00 36.00 95.00
6-Lou Gehrig-c/story 20.00 60.00 160.00
11-16: 13-Kiefer-a 8.65 26.00 60.00

REALISTIC ROMANCES
Realistic Comics/Avon Periodicals: July-Aug, 1951 - No. 17, Aug-Sept, 1954 (No #9-14)
1-Kinstler-a; c-/Avon paperback #211 21.00 64.00 170.00
2 10.00 30.00 75.00
3,4 9.30 28.00 65.00
5,8-Kinstler-a 10.00 30.00 70.00
6-c-/Diversey Prize Novels #6; Kinstler-a 10.00 30.00 75.00
7-Evans-a?; c-/Avon paperback #360 10.00 30.00 75.00
15,17: 17-Kinstler-c 8.65 26.00 60.00
16-Kinstler marijuana story-r/Romantic Love #6 10.00 30.00 75.00
I.W. Reprint #1,8,9: #1-r/Realistic Romances #4; Astarita-a. 9-r/Women To Love #1 1.75 5.25 14.00
NOTE: *Astarita a-2-4, 7, 8, 17. Photo c-1, 2. Painted c-3, 4.*

REAL LIFE COMICS
Nedor/Better/Standard Publ./Pictorial Magazine No. 13: Sept, 1941 - No. 59, Sept, 1952
1-Uncle Sam-c/story; Daniel Boone story 50.00 150.00 450.00
2 25.00 75.00 200.00
3-Hitler cover 63.00 189.00 600.00
4,5: 4-Story of American flag "Old Glory" 15.00 45.00 120.00
6-10: 6-Wild Bill Hickok story 14.00 43.00 115.00
11-20: 17-Albert Einstein story 12.50 37.50 100.00
21-23,25,26,28-30: 29-A-Bomb story 10.00 30.00 80.00

Real Screen Comics #3 © DC

Realworlds: Batman © DC

R.E.B.E.L.S. '95 #4 © DC

24-Story of Baseball (Babe Ruth) 18.00 53.00 140.00
27-Schomburg A-Bomb-c; story of A-Bomb 17.00 51.00 135.00
31-33,35,36,42-44,48,49: 49-Baseball issue 8.65 26.00 60.00
34,37-41,45-47: 34-Jimmy Stewart story. 37-Story of motion pictures; Bing Crosby story. 38-Jane Froman story. 39- "1,000,000 A.D." story. 40-Bob Feller story. 41-Jimmie Foxx story; "Home Run" Baker story. 45-Story of Olympic games; Burl Ives & Kit Carson story. 46-Douglas Fairbanks Jr. & Sr. story. 47-George Gershwin story 10.00 30.00 80.00
50-Frazetta-a (5 pgs.) 28.00 83.00 220.00
51-Jules Verne "Journey to the Moon" by Evans 19.00 56.00 150.00
52-Frazetta-a (4 pgs.); Severin/Elder-a(2); Evans-a 30.00 90.00 240.00
53-57-Severin/Elder-a. 54-Bat Masterson-c/story 12.50 37.50 100.00
58-Severin/Elder-a(2) 13.00 39.00 105.00
59-1 pg. Frazetta; Severin/Elder-a 12.50 37.50 100.00

NOTE: *Some issues had two titles.* ***Guardineer*** *a-40(2), 44.* ***Meskin*** *a-52.* ***Roussos*** *a-50.* ***Schomburg*** *c-1, 2, 4, 5, 7, 11, 13-21, 23, 24, 26, 28, 30-32, 34-40, 42, 44-47, 55.* ***Tuska*** *a-53. Photo-c 5, 6.*

REAL LIFE SECRETS (Real Secrets #2 on)
Ace Periodicals: Sept, 1949 (one-shot)

1-Painted-c 10.00 30.00 80.00

REAL LIFE STORY OF FESS PARKER (Magazine)
Dell Publishing Co.: 1955

1 9.00 27.00 110.00

REAL LIFE TALES OF SUSPENSE (See Suspense)

REAL LOVE (Formerly Hap Hazard)
Ace Periodicals (A. A. Wyn): No. 25, April, 1949 - No. 76, Nov, 1956

25 11.00 33.00 90.00
26 7.15 21.50 50.00
27-L. B. Cole-a 10.00 30.00 80.00
28-35 5.00 15.00 35.00
36-66: 66-Last pre-code (2/55) 5.00 15.00 32.00
67-76 4.15 12.50 25.00

NOTE: *Photo c-50-76. Painted c-46.*

REALM, THE
Arrow Comics/WeeBee Comics #13/Caliber Press #14 on: Feb, 1986 - No. 21, 1991 ($1.50/$1.95/$2.50, B&W)

1-21: 4-1st app. Deadworld (9/86) 2.50
Book 1 ($4.95, B&W) 5.00

REAL McCOYS, THE (TV)
Dell Publ. Co.: No. 1071, 1-3/60 - 5-7/1962 (All have Walter Brennan photo-c)

Four Color 1071,1134-Toth-a in both 9.00 27.00 110.00
Four Color 1193,1265 8.35 25.00 100.00
01-689-207 (5-7/62) 7.50 22.50 90.00

REAL SCREEN COMICS (#1 titled Real Screen Funnies; TV Screen Cartoons #129-138)
National Periodical Publications: Spring, 1945 - No. 128, May-June, 1959 (#1-40: 52 pgs.)

1-The Fox & the Crow, Flippity & Flop, Tito & His Burrito begin 100.00 300.00 950.00
2 47.00 141.00 425.00
3-5 33.00 98.00 260.00
6-10 (2-3/47) 21.00 64.00 170.00
11-20 (10-11/48): 13-The Crow x-over in Flippity & Flop 16.00 49.00 130.00
21-30 (6-7/50) 12.00 36.00 95.00
31-50 10.00 30.00 80.00
51-99 9.30 28.00 65.00
100 10.00 30.00 70.00
101-128 7.15 21.50 50.00

REAL SECRETS (Formerly Real Life Secrets)
Ace Periodicals: No. 2, Nov, 1950 - No. 5, May, 1950

2-Painted-c 9.30 28.00 65.00
3-5: 3-Photo-c 6.00 18.00 42.00

REAL SPORTS COMICS (All Sports Comics #2 on)
Hillman Periodicals: Oct-Nov, 1948 (52 pgs.)

1-Powell-a (12 pgs.) 40.00 120.00 320.0

REAL WAR STORIES
Eclipse Comics: July, 1987; No. 2, Jan, 1991 ($2.00, 52 pgs.)

1-Bolland-a(p), Bissette-a, Totleben-a(i); Alan Moore scripts (2nd printing exists, 2/88) 2.0
2-($4.95) 5.0

REAL WESTERN HERO (Formerly Wow #1-69; Western Hero #76 on)
Fawcett Publications: No. 70, Sept, 1948 - No. 75, Feb, 1949 (All 52 pgs.)

70(#1)-Tom Mix, Monte Hale, Hopalong Cassidy, Young Falcon begin 35.00 105.00 280.0
71-75: 71-Gabby Hayes begins. 71,72-Captain Tootsie by Beck. 75-Big Bow and Little Arrow app. 22.00 66.00 175.0

NOTE: *Painted/photo c-70-73; painted c-74, 75.*

REAL WEST ROMANCES
Crestwood Publishing Co./Prize Publ.: 4-5/49 - V1#6, 3/50; V2#1, Apr-May, 1950 (All 52 pgs. & photo-c)

V1#1-S&K-a(p) 25.00 75.00 200.0
2 12.00 36.00 95.0
3-Kirby-a(p) only 12.50 37.50 100.0
4-S&K-a; Whip Wilson, Reno Browne photo-c 19.00 56.00 150.0
5-Audie Murphy, Gale Storm photo-c; S&K-a 17.00 51.00 135.0
6-Produced by S&K, no S&K-a; Robert Preston & Cathy Downs photo-c 12.50 37.50 100.0
V2#1-Kirby-a(p) 10.00 30.00 80.0

NOTE: ***Meskin*** *a-V1#5, 6.* ***Severin/Elder*** *a-V1#3-6, V2#1.* ***Meskin*** *a-V1#6.* ***Leonard Starr*** *a-1. Photo-c V1#1-6, V2#1.*

REALWORLDS :...
DC Comics: 2000 ($5.95, one-shots, prestige format)

Batman - Marshall Rogers-a/Golden & Sniegoski-s; Justice League of America Dematteis-s/ Barr-painted art; Superman - Vance-s/García-López & Rubenstein-a; Wonder Woman - Hanson & Neuwirth-s/Sam-a 5.9

RE-ANIMATOR IN FULL COLOR
Adventure Comics: Oct, 1991 - No. 3, 1992 ($2.95, mini-series)

1-3: Adapts horror movie. 1-Dorman painted-c 3.0

REAP THE WILD WIND (See Cinema Comics Herald)

REBEL, THE (TV)
Dell Publishing Co.: No. 1076, Feb-Apr, 1960 - No. 1262, Dec-Feb, 1961-62

Four Color 1076 (#1)-Sekowsky-a, photo-c 10.00 30.00 120.0
Four Color 1138 (9-11/60), 1207 (9-11/61), 1262-Photo-c 8.35 25.00 100.0

R.E.B.E.L.S. '94 (Becomes R.E.B.E.L.S. '95 & R.E.B.E.L.S. '96)
DC Comics: No. 0, Oct, 1994 - No. 17, Mar, 1996 ($1.95/$2.25)

0-17: 8-$2.25-c begins. 15-R.E.B.E.L.S '96 begins. 2.2

REBEL SWORD (Manga)
Dark Horse Comics: Oct, 1994 - No. 6, Feb, 1995 ($2.50, B&W)

1-6 2.5

RECORD BOOK OF FAMOUS POLICE CASES
St. John Publishing Co.: 1949 (25¢, 132 pgs.)

nn-Kubert-a(3); r/Son of Sinbad; Baker-c 38.00 113.00 300.0

RED ARROW
P. L. Publishing Co.: May-June, 1951 - No. 3, Oct, 1951

1 10.00 30.00 75.0
2,3 8.65 26.00 60.0

RED BAND COMICS
Enwil Associates: Feb, 1945 - No. 4, May, 1945

1 38.00 113.00 300.0
2-Origin Bogeyman & Santanas; c-reprint/#1 28.00 84.00 225.0
3,4-Captain Wizard app. in both (1st app.); each has identical contents/cover 26.00 77.00 205.0

REDBLADE
Dark Horse Comics: Apr, 1993 - No. 3, July, 1993 ($2.50, mini-series)

Red Dragon Comics (2nd series) #7
© Condé Nast

Red Rabbit Comics #1 © Dearfield

Red Ryder Comics #6
© Lasswell & Slesinger

GD2.0 FN6.0 NM9.4

-3: 1-Double gatefold-c 3.00

ED CIRCLE COMICS (Also see Blazing Comics & Blue Circle Comics)
ural Home Publications (Enwil): Jan, 1945 - No. 4, April, 1945

-The Prankster & Red Riot begin 36.00 108.00 290.00
-Starr-a; The Judge (costumed hero) app. 29.00 86.00 230.00
,4-Starr-c/a. 3-The Prankster not in costume 22.00 66.00 175.00
-(Dated 4/45)-Leftover covers to #4 were later restapled over early 1950s coverless comics; variations in the coverless comics used are endless; Woman Outlaws, Dorothy Lamour, Crime Does Not Pay, Sabu, Diary Loves, Love Confessions & Young Love V3#3 known 16.00 48.00 125.00

ED CIRCLE SORCERY (Chilling Adventures in Sorcery #1-5)
ed Circle Prod. (Archie): No. 6, Apr, 1974 - No. 11, Feb, 1975 (All 25¢ iss.)

,8,9,11: 6-Early Chaykin-a. 7-Pino-a. 8-Only app. The Cobra 1.10 3.30 9.00
-Bruce Jones-a with Wrightson, Kaluta, Jeff Jones 1.50 4.50 12.00
0-Wood-a(i) 1.25 3.75 10.00
TE: ***Chaykin*** *a-6, 10.* ***McWilliams*** *a-10(2 & 3 pgs.).* ***Mooney*** *a-11p.* ***Morrow*** *a-6-8, 9(text s), 10, 11i; c-6-11.* ***Thorne*** *a-8, 10.* ***Toth*** *a-8, 9.*

ED DOG (See Night Music #7)

ED DRAGON
omico: June, 1996 ($2.95)

-Bisley-c 3.00

ED DRAGON COMICS (1st Series) (Formerly Trail Blazers; see Super agician V5#7, 8)
reet & Smith Publications: No. 5, Jan, 1943 - No. 9, Jan, 1944

-Origin Red Rover, the Crimson Crimebuster; Rex King, Man of Adventure, Captain Jack Commando, & The Minute Man begin; text origin Red Dragon; Binder-c 100.00 300.00 950.00
-Origin The Black Crusader & Red Dragon (3/43); 1st story app. Red Dragon & 1st cover (classic-c) 211.00 633.00 2000.00
-Classic-c 147.00 442.00 1400.00
-The Red Knight app. 71.00 213.00 675.00
-Origin Chuck Magnon, Immortal Man 71.00 213.00 675.00

ED DRAGON COMICS (2nd Series)(See Super Magician V2#8)
reet & Smith Publications: Nov, 1947 - No. 6, Jan, 1949; No. 7, July, 1949

-Red Dragon begins; Elliman, Nigel app.; Edd Cartier-c/a 90.00 268.00 850.00
-Cartier-c 63.00 189.00 600.00
-1st app. Dr. Neff Ghost Breaker by Powell; Elliman, Nigel app. 55.00 165.00 500.00
-Cartier c/a 71.00 213.00 675.00
-7 40.00 120.00 350.00
TE: ***Maneely*** *a-5, 7.* ***Powell*** *a-2-7; c-3, 5, 7.*

ED EAGLE
avid McKay Publications: No. 16, Aug, 1938

eature Books 16 17.00 50.00 200.00

EDEYE (See Comics Reading Libraries)

ED FOX (Formerly Manhunt! #1-14; also see Extra Comics)
agazine Enterprises: No. 15, 1954

5(A-1 #108)-Undercover Girl story; L.B. Cole-c/a (Red Fox); r-from Manhunt; Powell-a 19.00 56.00 150.00

ED FURY
gh Impact Entertainment: 1997 ($2.95, B&W)

3.00

ED GOOSE COMIC SELECTIONS (See Comic Selections)

ED HAWK (See A-1 Comics, Bobby Benson's ..#14-16 & Straight Arrow #2)
agazine Enterprises: No. 90, 1953

1 90-Powell-c/a 12.00 36.00 95.00

ED MASK (Formerly Tim Holt; see Best Comics, Blazing Six-Guns)
agazine Enterprises No. 42-53/Sussex No. 54 (M.E. on-c): No. 42, June-ly, 1954 - No. 53, May, 1956; No. 54, Sept, 1957

2-Ghost Rider by Ayers continues, ends #50; Black Phantom continues; 3-D effect c/stories begin 21.00 64.00 170.00
43- 3-D effect-c/stories 19.00 56.00 150.00
44-52: 3-D effect stories only. 47-Last pre-code issue. 50-Last Ghost Rider. 51-The Presto Kid begins by Ayers (1st app.); Presto Kid-c begins; last 3-D effect story. 52-Origin The Presto Kid 17.00 51.00 135.00
53,54-Last Black Phantom; last Presto Kid-c 13.00 39.00 105.00
I.W. Reprint #1 (r-/#52). 2 (nd, r/#51 w/diff.-c). 3, 8 (nd; Kinstler-c); 8-r/Red Mask #52 2.50 7.50 23.00
NOTE: ***Ayers*** *art on Ghost Rider & Presto Kid.* ***Bolle*** *art in all (Red Mask); c-43, 44, 49.* ***Guardineer*** *a-52. Black Phantom in #42-44, 47-50, 53, 54.*

REDMASK OF THE RIO GRANDE
AC Comics: 1990 ($2.50, 28pgs.)(Has photos of movie posters)

1-Bolle-c/a(r); photo inside-c 2.50

RED MOUNTAIN FEATURING QUANTRELL'S RAIDERS (Movie)(Also see Jesse James #28)
Avon Periodicals: 1952

nn-Alan Ladd; Kinstler-c 28.00 84.00 225.00

"RED" RABBIT COMICS
Dearfield Comic/J. Charles Laue Publ. Co.: Jan, 1947 - No. 22, Aug-Sep, 1951

1 12.50 37.50 100.00
2 7.15 21.50 50.00
3-10 5.70 17.00 40.00
11-17,19-22 5.00 15.00 35.00
18-Flying Saucer-c (1/51) 7.15 21.50 50.00

RED RAVEN COMICS (Human Torch #2 on)(Also see X-Men #44 & Sub-Mariner #26, 2nd series)
Timely Comics: August, 1940 GD2.0 FN6.0 VF8.0 NM9.4

1-Origin & 1st app. Red Raven; Comet Pierce & Mercury by Kirby, The Human Top & The Eternal Brain; intro. Magar, the Mystic & only app.; Kirby-c (his 1st signed work) 1000.00 3000.00 6250.00 12,000.00

RED ROCKET 7
Dark Horse Comics: Aug, 1997 - No. 7, June, 1998 ($3.95, square format, limited series)

1-7-Mike Allred-c/s/a 4.00

RED RYDER COMICS (Hi Spot #2)(Movies, radio)(See Crackajack Funnies & Super Book of Comics)
Hawley Publ. No. 1/Dell Publishing Co.(K.K.) No. 3 on: 9/40; No. 3, 8/41 - No. 5, 12/41; No. 6, 4/42 - No. 151, 4-6/57 GD2.0 FN6.0 NM9.4

1-Red Ryder, his horse Thunder, Little Beaver & his horse Papoose strip reprints begin by Fred Harman; 1st meeting of Red & Little Beaver; Harman line-drawn-c #1-85 272.00 818.00 3000.00
3-(Scarce)-Alley Oop, King of the Royal Mtd., Capt. Easy, Freckles & His Friends, Myra North, Dan Dunn strip-r begin 92.00 275.00 1100.00
4-6: 6-1st Dell issue (4/42) 42.00 125.00 500.00
7-10 33.00 100.00 400.00
11-20 23.00 69.00 275.00
21-32-Last Alley Oop, Dan Dunn, Capt. Easy, Freckles 15.00 45.00 175.00
33-40 (52 pgs.) 10.00 30.00 120.00
41 (52 pgs.)-Rocky Lane photo back-c; photo back-c begin, end #57 10.50 31.00 125.00
42-46 (52 pgs.): 46-Last Red Ryder strip-r 8.35 25.00 100.00
47-53 (52 pgs.): 47-New stories on Red Ryder begin. 49,52-Harmon photo back-c 7.00 21.00 85.00
54-92: 54-73 (36 pgs.). 59-Harmon photo back-c. 73-Last King of the Royal Mtd; strip-r by Jim Gary. 74-85,93 (52 pgs.)-Harman line-drawn-c. 86-92 (52 pgs.)-Harman painted-c 5.35 16.00 65.00
94-99,101-106: 94-96 (36 pgs.)-Harman painted-c. 97,98,107,108 (36 pgs.)-Harman line-drawn-c. 99,101-106 (36 pgs.)-Jim Bannon Photo-c 4.55 13.65 50.00
100 (36 pgs.)-Bannon photo-c 4.60 13.75 55.00
109-118 (52 pgs.)-Harman line-drawn-c 4.10 12.30 45.00
119-129 (52 pgs.): 119-Painted-c begin, not by Harman, end #151 3.65 11.00 40.00
130-151 (36 pgs.): 145-Title change to Red Ryder Ranch Mag. 149-Title change to R.R. Ranch Comics 3.20 9.60 35.00

Red Seal Comics #18 © SUPR

Red Sonja #10 © MAR

Reggie's Wise Guys Jokes #1 © AP

Four Color 916 (7/58) 3.45 10.35 38.00
NOTE: *Fred Harman a-1-99; c-1-98, 107-118. Don Red Barry, Allan Rocky Lane, Wild Bill Elliott & Jim Bannon starred as Red Ryder in the movies. Robert Blake starred as Little Beaver.*

RED RYDER PAINT BOOK
Whitman Publishing Co.: 1941 (8-1/2x11-1/2", 148 pgs.)

nn-Reprints 1940 daily strips 76.00 229.00 725.00

RED SEAL COMICS (Formerly Carnival Comics, and/or Spotlight Comics?)
Harry 'A' Chesler/Superior Publ. No. 19 on: No. 14, 10/45 - No. 18, 10/46; No. 19, 6/47 - No. 22, 12/47

14-The Black Dwarf begins (continued from Spotlight?); Little Nemo app; bondage/hypo-c; Tuska-a 71.00 213.00 675.00
15-Torture story; funny-c 47.00 140.00 420.00
16-Used in **SOTI**, pg. 181, illo "Outside the forbidden pages of de Sade, you find draining a girl's blood only in children's comics;" drug club story r-later in Crime Reporter #1; Veiled Avenger & Barry Kuda app; Tuska-a; funny-c 62.00 185.00 585.00
17,18,20: Lady Satan, Yankee Girl & Sky Chief app; 17-Tuska-a 47.00 142.00 425.00
19-No Black Dwarf (on-c only); Zor, El Tigre app. 42.00 125.00 375.00
21-Lady Satan & Black Dwarf app. 36.00 107.00 285.00
22-Zor, Rocketman app. (68 pgs.) 36.00 107.00 285.00

REDSKIN (Thrilling Indian Stories)(Famous Western Badmen #13 on)
Youthful Magazines: Sept, 1950 - No. 12, Oct, 1952

1-Walter Johnson-a (7 pgs.) 15.00 45.00 120.00
2 10.00 30.00 75.00
3-12: 3-Daniel Boone story. 6-Geronimo story 9.30 28.00 65.00
NOTE: ***Walter Johnson** c-3, 4. **Palais** a-11. **Wildey** a-5, 11. Bondage c-6, 12.*

RED SONJA (Also see Conan #23, Kull & The Barbarians, Marvel Feature & Savage Sword Of Conan #1)
Marvel Comics Group: 1/77 - No. 15, 5/79; V1#1, 2/83 - V2#2, 3/83; V3#1, 8/83 - V3#4, 2/84; V3#5, 1/85 - V3#13, 5/86

1-Created by Robert E. Howard 1.00 3.00 8.00
2-10: 5-Last 30¢ issue 5.00
11-15, V1#1,V2#2: 14-Last 35¢ issue 4.00
V3#1-13: #1-4 ($1.00, 52 pgs.) 3.00
NOTE: ***Brunner** c-12-14. **J. Buscema** a(p)-12, 13, 15; c-V#1. **Nebres** a-V3#3i(part). **N. Redondo** a-8i, V3#2i, 3i. **Simonson** a-V3#1. **Thorne** c/a-1-11.*

RED SONJA: SCAVENGER HUNT
Marvel Comics: Dec, 1995 ($2.95, one-shot)

1 3.00

RED SONJA: THE MOVIE
Marvel Comics Group: Nov, 1985 - No. 2, Dec, 1985 (Limited series)

1,2-Movie adapt-r/Marvel Super Spec. #38 3.00

RED STAR, THE
Image Comics: June, 2000 - Present ($2.95)

1-4 2.95

RED TORNADO (See All-American #20 & Justice League of America #64)
DC Comics: July, 1985 - No. 4, Oct, 1985 (Limited series)

1-4: Kurt Busiek scripts in all. 1-3-Superman & Batman cameos 3.00

RED WARRIOR
Marvel/Atlas Comics (TCI): Jan, 1951 - No. 6, Dec, 1951

1-Red Warrior & his horse White Wing; Tuska-a 16.00 49.00 130.00
2-Tuska-c 10.00 30.00 70.00
3-6: 4-Origin White Wing. 6-Maneely-c 8.65 26.00 60.00

RED WOLF (See Avengers #80 & Marvel Spotlight #1)
Marvel Comics Group: May, 1972 - No. 9, Sept, 1973

1-(Western hero); Gil Kane/Severin-c; Shores-a 2.00 6.00 18.00
2-9: 2-Kane-c; Shores-a. 6-Tuska-r in back-up. 7-Red Wolf as super hero begins. 9-Origin sidekick, Lobo (wolf) 1.50 4.50 12.00

REESE'S PIECES
Eclipse Comics: Oct, 1985 - No.2, Oct, 1985 ($1.75, Baxter paper)

1,2-B&W-r in color 2.00

REFORM SCHOOL GIRL!
Realistic Comics: 1951

nn-Used in **SOTI**, pg. 358, & cover ill. with caption "Comic books are supposed to be like fairy tales" 147.00 442.00 1400.
(Prices vary widely on this book)
NOTE: *The cover and title originated from a digest-sized book published by Diversey Publish Co. of Chicago in 1948. The original book "House of Fury", Doubleday, came out in 1941. girl's real name which appears on the cover of the digest and comic is Marty Collins, Canad model and ice skating star who posed for this special color photograph for the Diversey novel.*

REGENTS ILLUSTRATED CLASSICS
Prentice Hall Regents, Englewood Cliffs, NJ 07632: 1981 (Plus more recent reprintings) (48 pgs., B&W-a with 14 pgs. of teaching helps)

NOTE: *This series contains Classics Ill. art, and was produced from the same illegal source as **Cassette Books.** But when Twin Circle sued to stop the sale of the Cassette Books, they deci to permit this series to continue. This series was produced as a teaching aid. The 20 title serie divided into four levels based upon number of basic words used therein. There is also a teache manual for each level. All of the titles are still available from the publisher for about $5 each re The number to call for mail order purchases is (201)767-5937. Almost all of the issues have covers taken from some interior art panel. Here is a list of the series by Regents ident. no. the Classics Ill. counterpart.*

16770(CI#24-A2)18333(CI#3-A2)21668(CI#13-A2)32224(CI#21)33051(CI#26)
35788(CI#84)37153(CI#16)44460(CI#19-A2)44808(CI#18-A2)52395(CI#4-A2)
58627(CI#5-A2)60067(CI#30)68405(CI#23-A1)70302(CI#29)78192(CI#7-A2)
78193(CI#10-A2)79679(CI#85)92046(CI#1-A2)93062(CI#64)93512(CI#25)

RE: GEX
Awesome-Hyperwerks: Jul, 1998 - No. 0, Dec, 1998; ($2.50)

Preview (7/98) Wizard Con Edition 3.0
0-(12/98) Loeb-s/Liefeld-a/Pat Lee-c, 1-(9/98) Loeb-s/Liefeld-a/c 2.5

REGGIE (Formerly Archie's Rival...; Reggie & Me #19 on)
Archie Publications: No. 15, Sept, 1963 - No. 18, Nov, 1965

15(9/63), 16(10/64), 17(8/65), 18(11/65) 4.10 12.30 45.0
NOTE: *Cover title No. 15 & 16 is Archie's Rival Reggie.*

REGGIE AND ME (Formerly Reggie)
Archie Publ.: No. 19, Aug, 1966 - No. 126, Sept, 1980 (No. 50-68: 52 pgs.)

19-Evilheart app. 3.00 9.00 32.0
20-23-Evilheart app.; with Pureheart #22 2.40 7.35 22.0
24-40(3/70) 1.75 5.25 14.0
41-49(7/71) 1.50 4.50 12.0
50(9/71)-68 (1/74, 52 pgs.) 2.00 6.00 16.0
69-99 1.00 2.80 7.0
100(10/77) 1.25 3.75 10.0
101-126 5.0

REGGIE'S JOKES (See Reggie's Wise Guy Jokes)

REGGIE'S REVENGE!
Archie Comic Publications, Inc.: Spring, 1994 - No. 3 ($2.00, 52 pgs.) (Published semi-annually)

1-Bound-in pull-out poster 3.0
2,3 2.0

REGGIE'S WISE GUY JOKES
Archie Publications: Aug, 1968 - No. 60, Jan, 1982 (#5-28 are Giants)

1 3.80 11.40 42.0
2-4 2.00 6.00 18.0
5-16 (1/71)(68 pg. Giants) 2.50 7.50 24.0
17-28 (52 pg. Giants) 2.00 6.00 16.0
29-40(1/77) 1.00 2.80 7.0
41-60 4.0

REGISTERED NURSE
Charlton Comics: Summer, 1963

1-r/Nurse Betsy Crane & Cynthia Doyle 2.40 7.35 22.0

REG'LAR FELLERS
Visual Editions (Standard): No. 5, Nov, 1947 - No. 6, Mar, 1948

5,6 8.65 26.00 60.0

REG'LAR FELLERS HEROIC (See Heroic Comics)

REGULATORS
Image Comics: June, 1995 - No. 3, Aug, 1995 ($2.50)

Relative Heroes #1 © Devin Grayson & Yves Guichet

Ren & Stimpy Show Special: Around the World in a Daze © Nickelodeon

Resurrection Man #23 © DC

GD2.0 FN6.0 NM9.4

-3: Kurt Busiek scripts 2.50

ID FLEMING, WORLD'S TOUGHEST MILKMAN
ipse Comics/ Deep Sea Comics: 8/86; V2#1, 12/86 - V2#3, 12/88; V2#4, 89; V2#5, 11/90 (B&W)

(3rd print, large size, 8/86, $2.50), 1-4th & 5th printings ($2.50) 2.50
#1 (10/86, regular size, $2.00), 1-2nd print, 3rd print ($2.00, 2/89) 2.00
2-8 , V2#2-2nd & 3rd printings, V2#4-2nd printing, V2#5 ($2.00) 2.00

LATIVE HEROES
Comics: Mar, 2000 - No. 6 ($2.50, limited series)

-6-Grayson-s/Guichet & Sowd-a. 6-Superman-c/app. 2.50

LUCTANT DRAGON, THE (Walt Disney's...)
ll Publishing Co.: No. 13, 1940

ur Color 13-Contains 2 pgs. of photos from film; 2 pg. foreword to Fantasia by Leopold Stokowski; Donald Duck, Goofy, Baby Weems & Mickey Mouse (as the Sorcerer's Apprentice) app. 158.00 475.00 1900.00

MARKABLE WORLDS OF PROFESSOR PHINEAS B. FUDDLE, THE
Comics (Paradox Press): 2000 - No. 4, 2000 ($5.95, limited series)

4-Boaz Yakin-s/Erez Yakin-a 5.95

MEMBER PEARL HARBOR
eet & Smith Publications: 1942 (68 pgs.) (Illustrated story of the battle)

Uncle Sam-c; Jack Binder-a 44.00 133.00 400.00

N & STIMPY SHOW, THE (TV) (Nicklodeon cartoon characters)
rvel Comics: Dec, 1992 - No. 44, July, 1996 ($1.75/$1.95)

($2.25)-Polybagged w/scratch & sniff Ren or Stimpy air fowler (equal amounts of each were made) 2.40 6.00
2nd & 3rd printing; different dialogue on-c 2.00
6: 4-Muddy Mudskipper back-up. 5-Bill Wray painted-c. 6-Spider-Man vs. Powdered Toast Man 4.00
-17: 12-1st solo back-up story w/Tank & Brenner 2.50
-44: 18-Powered Toast Man app. 2.00
($2.95) Deluxe edition w/die cut cover 3.00
Don't Try This at Home (3/94, $12.95, TPB)-r/#9-12 13.00
Eenteractive Special ('95, $2.95) 3.00
Holiday Special 1994 (2/95, $2.95, 52 pgs.) 3.00
Mini Comic (1995) 5.00
Pick of the Litter nn (1993, $12.95, TPB)-r/#1-4 13.00
Radio Daze (11/95, $1.95) 2.00
Running Joke nn (1993, $12.95, TPB)-r/#1-4 plus new-a 13.00
Seeck Little Monkeys (1/95, $12.95)-r/#17-20 13.00
Special 2 (7/94, $2.95, 52 pgs.), ...Special 3 (10/94, $2.95, 52 pgs.)-Choose adventure, ...Special: Around the World in a Daze ($2.95), ...Special: Four Swerks (1/95, $2.95, 52 pgs.)-FF #1 cover swipe; cover reads "Four Swerks w/5 pg. coloring book.", ...Special: Powdered Toast Man 1 (4/94, $2.95, 52 pgs.), ...Special: Powdered Toast Man's Cereal Serial (4/95, $2.95), ...Special: Sports (10/95, $2.95) 3.00
Tastes Like Chicken nn (11/93,$12.95,TPB)-r/#5-8 13.00
Your Pals (1994, $12.95, TPB)-r/#13-16 13.00

NFIELD
liber Press: 1994 - No. 3, 1995 ($2.95, B&W, limited series)

-3 3.00

NO BROWNE, HOLLYWOOD'S GREATEST COWGIRL (Formerly rgie Comics; Apache Kid #53 on; also see Western Hearts, Western Life mances & Western Love)
rvel Comics (MPC): No. 50, April, 1950 - No. 52, Sept, 1950 (52 pgs.)

-Reno Browne photo-c on all 33.00 98.00 260.00
,52 28.00 83.00 220.00

PLACEMENT GOD
naze Ink: June, 1995 - No. 8 ($2.95, B&W)

-8-Zander Cannon-s/a 3.00

PLACEMENT GOD
age Comics: May, 1997 - No. 5 ($2.95, B&W)

-5: 1-Flip book w/"Knute's Escapes", r/original series. 2-Flip book w/"Harris Thermidor". 3-5: 3-Flip book w/"Myth and Legend" 3.00

GD2.0 FN6.0 NM9.4

REPTILICUS (Becomes Reptisaurus #3 on)
Charlton Comics: Aug, 1961 - No. 2, Oct, 1961

1 (Movie) 18.00 54.00 200.00
2 9.00 27.00 100.00

REPTISAURUS (Reptilicus #1,2)
Charlton Comics: V2#3, Jan, 1962 - No. 8, Dec, 1962; Summer, 1963

V2#3-8: 8-Montes/Bache-c/a 6.35 19.00 70.00
Special Edition 1 (Summer, 1963) 5.90 17.75 65.00

REQUIEM FOR DRACULA
Marvel Comics: Feb, 1993 ($2.00, 52 pgs.)

nn-r/Tomb of Dracula #69,70 by Gene Colan 2.00

RESCUERS, THE (See Walt Disney Showcase #40)

RESIDENT EVIL (Based on video game)
Image Comics (WildStorm): Mar, 1998 - No. 5 ($4.95, quarterly magazine)

1 7.00
2-5 5.00
...Collection One ('99, $14.95, TPB) r/#1-4 14.95

RESIDENT EVIL: FIRE AND ICE
DC Comics (WildStorm): Dec, 2000 - No. 4 ($2.50, limited series)

1,2-Bermejo-c 2.50

RESTAURANT AT THE END OF THE UNIVERSE, THE (See Hitchhiker's Guide to the Galaxy & Life, the Universe & Everything)
DC Comics: 1994 - No. 3, 1994 ($6.95, limited series)

1-3 7.00

RESTLESS GUN (TV)
Dell Publishing Co.: No. 934, Sept, 1958 - No. 1146, Nov-Jan, 1960-61

Four Color 934 (#1)-Photo-c 11.30 34.00 135.00
Four Color 986 (5/59), 1045 (11-1/60), 1089 (3/60), 1146-Wildey-a; all photo-c 8.00 24.00 95.00

RESURRECTION MAN
DC Comics: May, 1997 - No. 27, Aug, 1999 ($2.50)

1-Lenticular disc on cover 5.00
2-5: 2-JLA app. 4.00
6-10: 6-Genesis-x-over. 7-Batman app. 10-Hitman-c/app. 3.00
11-27: 16,17-Supergirl x-over. 18-Deadman & Phantom Stranger-c/app. 21-JLA-c/app 2.50
#1,000,000 (11/98) 853rd Century x-over 2.50

RETIEF (Keith Laumer's)
Adventure Comics (Malibu): Dec, 1989 - Vol. 2, No.6, ($2.25, B&W)

1-6,Vol. 2, #1-6,Vol. 3 (...of The CDT) #1-6 2.50
...and The Warlords #1-6, ...: Diplomatic Immunity #1 (4/91)
...: Giant Killer #1 (9/91), ...: Crime & Punishment #1 (11/91) 2.50

RETURN FROM WITCH MOUNTAIN (See Walt Disney Showcase #44)

RETURN OF GORGO, THE (Formerly Gorgo's Revenge)
Charlton Comics: No. 2, Aug, 1963; No. 3, Fall, 1964 (12¢)

2,3-Ditko-c/a; based on M.G.M. movie 7.25 21.75 80.00

RETURN OF KONGA, THE (Konga's Revenge #2 on)
Charlton Comics: 1962

nn 6.80 20.50 75.00

RETURN OF MEGATON MAN
Kitchen Sink Press: July, 1988 - No. 3, 1988 ($2.00, limited series)

1-3: Simpson-c/a 2.00

RETURN OF THE OUTLAW
Toby Press (Minoan): Feb, 1953 - No. 11, 1955

1-Billy the Kid 10.00 30.00 75.00
2 5.70 17.00 40.00
3-11 5.00 15.00 32.00

RETURN TO JURASSIC PARK
Topps Comics: Apr, 1995 - No. 9, Feb, 1996 ($2.50/$2.95)

1-9: 3-Begin $2.95-c. 9-Artist's Jam issue 3.00

Rex Hart #8 © MAR

Richard Dragon, Kung-Fu Fighter #3 © DC

Richie Rich #77 © HARV

GD2.0 FN6.0 NM9.4

RETURN TO THE AMALGAM AGE OF COMICS: THE MARVEL COMICS COLLECTION
Marvel Comics: 1997 ($12.95, TPB)

nn-Reprints Amalgam one-shots: Challengers of the Fantastic #1, The Exciting X-Patrol #1, Iron Lantern #1, The Magnetic Men Featuring Magneto #1, Spider-Boy Team-Up #1 & Thorion of the New Asgods #1 — 13.00

REVEALING LOVE STORIES (See Fox Giants)

REVEALING ROMANCES
Ace Magazines: Sept, 1949 - No. 6, Aug, 1950

	GD2.0	FN6.0	NM9.4
1	10.00	30.00	70.00
2	5.00	15.00	35.00
3-6	5.00	15.00	30.00

REVENGE OF THE PROWLER (Also see The Prowler)
Eclipse Comics: Feb, 1988 - No. 4, June, 1988 ($1.75/$1.95)

1,3,4: 1-$1.75. 3,4-$1.95-c; Snyder III-a(p) — 2.00
2 ($2.50)-Contains flexi-disc — 2.50

REVENGERS FEATURING MEGALITH
Continuity Comics: Apr, 1985; 1987 - No. 6, 1989 ($2.00, Baxter paper)

1 (1985)-Origin; Neal Adams-c/a, scripts, 1-6 ('87-'89, newsstand) — 2.00

REX ALLEN COMICS (Movie star)(Also see Four Color #877 & Western Roundup under Dell Giants)
Dell Publ. Co.: No. 316, Feb, 1951 - No. 31, Dec-Feb, 1958-59 (All-photo-c)

	GD2.0	FN6.0	NM9.4
Four Color 316(#1)(52 pgs.)-Rex Allen & his horse Koko begin; Marsh-a	13.00	40.00	160.00
2 (9-11/51, 36 pgs.)	8.00	24.00	95.00
3-10	5.85	17.50	70.00
11-20	4.60	13.75	55.00
21-23,25-31	4.55	13.65	50.00
24-Toth-a	5.00	15.00	60.00

NOTE: *Manning a-20, 27-30. Photo back-c F.C. #316, 2-12, 20, 21.*

REX DEXTER OF MARS (See Mystery Men Comics)
Fox Features Syndicate: Fall, 1940 (68 pgs.)

	GD2.0	FN6.0	NM9.4
1-Rex Dexter, Patty O'Day, & Zanzibar (Tuska-a) app.; Briefer-c/a	190.00	570.00	1800.00

REX HART (Formerly Blaze Carson; Whip Wilson #9 on)
Timely/Marvel Comics (USA): No. 6, Aug, 1949 - No. 8, Feb, 1950 (All photo-c)

	GD2.0	FN6.0	NM9.4
6-Rex Hart & his horse Warrior begin; Black Rider app; Captain Tootsie by Beck	28.00	84.00	225.00
7,8: 18 pg. Thriller in each. 8-Blaze the Wonder Collie app. in text	19.00	56.00	150.00

REX MORGAN, M.D. (Also see Harvey Comics Library)
Argo Publ.: Dec, 1955 - No. 3, Apr?, 1956

	GD2.0	FN6.0	NM9.4
1-r/Rex Morgan daily newspaper strips & daily panel-r of "These Women" by D'Alessio & "Timeout" by Jeff Keate	12.50	37.50	100.00
2,3	9.30	28.00	65.00

REX THE WONDER DOG (See The Adventures of...)

RHUBARB, THE MILLIONAIRE CAT
Dell Publishing Co.: No. 423, Sept-Oct, 1952 - No. 563, June, 1954

	GD2.0	FN6.0	NM9.4
Four Color 423 (#1)	4.60	13.75	55.00
Four Color 466(5/53),563	4.10	12.30	45.00

RIB
Dilemma Productions: Oct, 1995 - April, 1996 ($1.95, B&W)

Ashcan, 1 — 2.00

RIB
Bookmark Productions: 1996 ($2.95, B&W)

1-Sakai-c; Andrew Ford-s/a — 3.00

RIB
Caliber Comics: May, 1997 - No. 5, 1998 ($2.95, B&W)

1-5: 1-"Beginnings" pts. 1 & 2 — 3.00

RIBIT!
Comico: Jan, 1989 - No. 4, April?, 1989 ($1.95, limited series)

1-4: Frank Thorne-c/a/scripts — 2.

RIBTICKLER (Also see Fox Giants)
Fox Feature Synd./Green Publ. (1957)/Norlen (1959): 1945 - No. 9, Aug, 19 1957; 1959

	GD2.0	FN6.0	NM9.4
1-Funny animal	15.00	45.00	120.
2-(1946)	8.65	26.00	60.
3-9: 3,7-Cosmo Cat app.	7.00	21.00	48.
3,7,8 (Green Publ.-1957), 3,7,8 (Norlen Mag.-1959)	2.30	7.00	20.

RICHARD DRAGON, KUNG-FU FIGHTER (See The Batman Chronicles #5, Brave & the Bold, & The Question)
National Periodical Publ./DC Comics: Apr-May, 1975 - No. 18, Nov-Dec, 19

	GD2.0	FN6.0	NM9.4
1-Intro Richard Dragon, Ben Stanley & O-Sensei; 1st app. Barney Ling; adaptation of Jim Dennis novel "Dragon's Fists" begins, ends #4	1.50	4.50	12.
2,3: 2-Intro Carolyn Woosan; Starlin/Weiss-c/a; bondage-c. 3-Kirby-a(p); Giordano bondage-c	1.00	3.00	8.
4-8-Wood inks. 4-Carolyn Woosan dies. 5-1st app. Lady Shiva	2.40		6.
9-13,15-18: 9-Ben Stanley becomes Ben Turner; intro Preying Mantis. 16-1st app. Prof Ojo. 18-1st app. Ben Turner as The Bronze Tiger		2.40	6.
14-"Spirit of Bruce Lee"	1.10	3.30	9.

NOTE: ***Buckler** a-14. c-15, 18. **Chua** c-13. **Estrada** a-9, 13-18. **Estrada/Abel** a-10-12. **Estrada/Wood** a-4-8. **Giordano** c-1, 3-11. **Weiss** a-2(partial) c-2i.*

RICHARD THE LION-HEARTED (See Ideal a Classical Comic)

RICHIE RICH (See Harvey Collectors Comics, Harvey Hits, Little Dot, Little Lotta, Little Sad Sack, Million Dollar Digest, Mutt & Jeff, Super Richie, and 3-D Dolly)

RICHIE RICH (...the Poor Little Rich Boy) (See Harvey Hits #3, 9)
Harvey Publ.: Nov, 1960 - #218, Oct, 1982; #219, Oct, 1986 - #254, Jan, 199

	GD2.0	FN6.0	NM9.4
1-(See Little Dot for 1st app.)	145.00	435.00	1600.
2	50.00	150.00	550.
3-5	29.00	87.00	320.
6-10: 8-Christmas-c	18.00	55.00	200.
11-20	11.00	33.00	120.
21-30	8.00	25.00	90.
31-40	6.70	20.00	75.
41-50: 42(10/67)-Flying saucer-c	5.00	15.00	55.
51-55,57-60: 59-Buck, prototype of Dollar the Dog	3.60	11.00	40.
56-1st app. Super Richie	4.50	13.50	50.
61-64,66-80: 71-Nixon & Robert Kennedy caricatures	2.50	7.50	25.
65-1st app. Dollar the Dog	3.20	9.60	35.
81-99	2.00	6.00	18.
100(12/70)-1st app. Irona the robot maid	2.40	7.35	22.
101-111,117-120	1.75	5.25	14.
112-116: All 52 pg. Giants	2.30	7.00	20.
121-140: 137-1st app. Mr. Cheepers	1.10	3.30	9.
141-160: 145-Infinity-c. 155-3rd app. The Money Monster	1.00	2.80	7.
161-180		2.40	6.
181-199			5.
200	1.00	2.80	7.
201-218: 210-Stone-Age Riches app			4.
219-254: 237-Last original material			3.

RICHIE RICH
Harvey Comics: Mar, 1991 - No. 28, Nov, 1994 ($1.00, bi-monthly)

1-28: Reprints best of Richie Rich — 2.
Giant Size 1-4 (10/91-10/93, $2.25, 68 pgs.) — 3.

RICHIE RICH ADVENTURE DIGEST MAGAZINE
Harvey Comics: 1992 - No. 7, Sept, 1994 ($1.25, quarterly, digest-size)

1-7 — 4.

RICHIE RICH AND...
Harvey Comics: Oct, 1987 - No. 11, May, 1990 ($1.00)

1-Professore Keenbean — 4.
2-11: 2-Casper. 3-Dollar the Dog. 4-Cadbury. 5 Mayda Munny. 6-Irona. 7-Littl Dot. 8-Professor Keenbean. 9-Little Audrey. 10-Mayda Munny. 11-Cadbury. — 2.

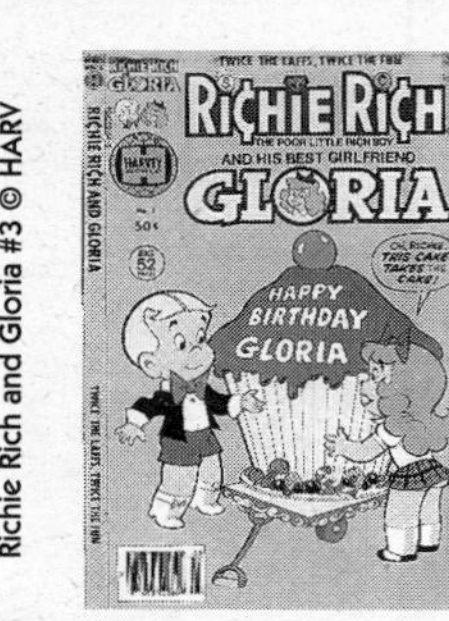

Richie Rich and Gloria #3 © HARV

Richie Rich Cash #14 © HARV

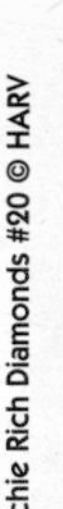
Richie Rich Diamonds #20 © HARV

RICHIE RICH AND BILLY BELLHOPS
Harvey Publications: Oct, 1977 (52 pgs., one-shot)

	GD2.0	FN6.0	NM9.4
1	1.50	4.50	12.00

RICHIE RICH AND CADBURY
Harvey Publ.: 10/77; #2, 9/78 - #23, 7/82; #24, 7/90 - #29, 1/91 (1-10: 52pgs.)

	GD2.0	FN6.0	NM9.4
1-(52 pg. Giant)	2.00	6.00	16.00
2-10-(52 pg. Giant)	1.25	3.75	10.00
11-23			5.00
24-29: 24-Begin $1.00-c			2.50

RICHIE RICH AND CASPER
Harvey Publications: Aug, 1974 - No. 45, Sept, 1982

	GD2.0	FN6.0	NM9.4
1	2.60	7.80	26.00
2-5	2.00	6.00	16.00
6-10: 10-Xmas-c	1.25	3.75	10.00
11-20		2.40	6.00
21-45: 22-Xmas-c			3.50

RICHIE RICH AND DOLLAR THE DOG (See Richie Rich #65)
Harvey Publications: Sept, 1977 - No. 24, Aug, 1982 (#1-10: 52 pgs.)

	GD2.0	FN6.0	NM9.4
1-(52 pg. Giant)	1.75	5.25	14.00
2-10-(52 pg. Giant)	1.10	3.30	9.00
11-24			4.00

RICHIE RICH AND DOT
Harvey Publications: Oct, 1974 (one-shot)

	GD2.0	FN6.0	NM9.4
1	2.30	7.00	20.00

RICHIE RICH AND GLORIA
Harvey Publications: Sept, 1977 - No. 25, Sept, 1982 (#1-11: 52 pgs.)

	GD2.0	FN6.0	NM9.4
1-(52 pg. Giant)	1.75	5.25	14.00
2-11-(52 pg. Giant)	1.10	3.30	9.00
12-25			4.00

RICHIE RICH AND HIS GIRLFRIENDS
Harvey Publications: April, 1979 - No. 16, Dec, 1982

	GD2.0	FN6.0	NM9.4
1-(52 pg. Giant)	1.75	5.25	14.00
2-(52 pg. Giant)	1.10	3.30	9.00
3-10		2.40	6.00
11-16			3.50

RICHIE RICH AND HIS MEAN COUSIN REGGIE
Harvey Publications: April, 1979 - No. 3, 1980 (50¢) (#1,2: 52 pgs.)

	GD2.0	FN6.0	NM9.4
1	1.50	4.50	12.00
2-3:	1.00	2.80	7.00

NOTE: *No. 4 was advertised, but never released.*

RICHIE RICH AND JACKIE JOKERS (Also see Jackie Jokers)
Harvey Publications: Nov, 1973 - No. 48, Dec, 1982

	GD2.0	FN6.0	NM9.4
1: 52 pg. Giant; contains material from unpublished Jackie Jokers #5	3.65	11.00	40.00
2,3-(52 pg. Giants). 2-R.R. & Jackie 1st meet	2.50	7.50	24.00
4,5	2.00	6.00	16.00
6-10	1.25	3.75	10.00
11-20,26: 11-1st app. Kool Katz. 26-Star Wars parody	1.00	3.00	8.00
21-25,27-40			5.00
41-48			3.50

RICHIE RICH AND PROFESSOR KEENBEAN
Harvey Comics: Sept, 1990 - No. 2, Nov, 1990 ($1.00)

	GD2.0	FN6.0	NM9.4
1,2			2.00

RICHIE RICH AND THE NEW KIDS ON THE BLOCK
Harvey Publications: Feb, 1991 - No. 3, June, 1991 ($1.25, bi-monthly)

	GD2.0	FN6.0	NM9.4
1-3: 1,2-New Richie Rich stories			2.00

RICHIE RICH AND TIMMY TIME
Harvey Publications: Sept, 1977 (50¢, 52 pgs, one-shot)

	GD2.0	FN6.0	NM9.4
1	1.25	3.75	10.00

RICHIE RICH BANK BOOKS
Harvey Publications: Oct, 1972 - No. 59, Sept, 1982

	GD2.0	FN6.0	NM9.4
1	4.10	12.30	45.00
2-5: 2-2nd app. The Money Monster	2.60	7.80	26.00
6-10	2.00	6.00	18.00
11-20: 18-Super Richie app.	1.50	4.50	12.00
21-30	1.00	3.00	8.00
31-40			5.00
41-59			3.50

RICHIE RICH BEST OF THE YEARS
Harvey Publications: Oct, 1977 - No. 6, June, 1980 (128 pgs., digest-size)

	GD2.0	FN6.0	NM9.4
1(10/77)-Reprints	1.75	5.25	14.00
2-6(11/79-6/80, 95¢). #2(10/78)-Rep.. #3(6/79, 75¢)	1.10	3.30	9.00

RICHIE RICH BIG BOOK
Harvey Publications: Nov, 1992 - No. 2, May, 1993 ($1.50, 52 pgs.)

	GD2.0	FN6.0	NM9.4
1,2			3.00

RICHIE RICH BIG BUCKS
Harvey Publications: Apr, 1991 - No. 8, July, 1992 ($1.00, bi-monthly)

	GD2.0	FN6.0	NM9.4
1-8			2.00

RICHIE RICH BILLIONS
Harvey Publications: Oct, 1974 - No. 48, Oct, 1982 (#1-33: 52 pgs.)

	GD2.0	FN6.0	NM9.4
1	3.20	9.60	35.00
2-5	2.30	7.00	20.00
6-10	1.75	5.25	14.00
11-20	1.25	3.75	10.00
21-33		2.40	6.00
34-48: 35-Onion app.			3.50

RICHIE RICH CASH
Harvey Publications: Sept, 1974 - No. 47, Aug, 1982

	GD2.0	FN6.0	NM9.4
1-1st app. Dr. N-R-Gee	3.20	9.60	35.00
2-5	2.30	7.00	20.00
6-10	1.85	5.50	15.00
11-20	1.25	3.75	10.00
21-30		2.40	6.00
31-47: 33-Dr. Blemish app.			3.50

RICHIE RICH CASH MONEY
Harvey Comics: May, 1992 - No. 2, Aug, 1992 ($1.25)

	GD2.0	FN6.0	NM9.4
1,2			2.00

RICHIE RICH COLLECTORS COMICS (See Harvey Collectors Comics)

RICHIE RICH DIAMONDS
Harvey Publications: Aug, 1972 - No. 59, Aug, 1982 (#1, 23-45: 52 pgs.)

	GD2.0	FN6.0	NM9.4
1-(52 pg. Giant)	5.00	15.00	55.00
2-5	2.50	7.50	24.00
6-10	1.85	5.50	15.00
11-22	1.10	3.30	9.00
23-30-(52 pg. Giants)	1.25	3.75	10.00
31-45: 39-r/Origin Little Dot		2.40	6.00
46-50			5.00
51-59			3.50

RICHIE RICH DIGEST
Harvey Publications: Oct, 1986 - No. 42, Oct, 1994 ($1.25/$1.75, digest-size)

	GD2.0	FN6.0	NM9.4
1	1.00	3.00	8.00
2-10			5.00
11-20			4.00
21-42			3.00

RICHIE RICH DIGEST STORIES (...Magazine #?-on)
Harvey Publications: Oct, 1977 - No., 17, Oct, 1982 (75¢/95¢, digest-size)

	GD2.0	FN6.0	NM9.4
1-Reprints	1.50	4.50	12.00
2-10: Reprints	1.00	2.80	7.00
11-17: Reprints			4.50

RICHIE RICH DIGEST WINNERS
Harvey Publications: Dec, 1977 - No. 16, Sept, 1982 (75¢/95¢, 132 pgs., digest-size)

	GD2.0	FN6.0	NM9.4
1	1.50	4.50	12.00
2-5	1.00	2.80	7.00

Richie Rich Dollars & Cents #67 © HARV

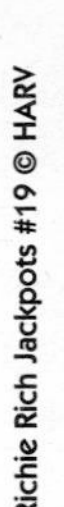

Richie Rich Jackpots #19 © HARV

Richie Rich Riches #20 © HARV

	GD2.0	FN6.0	NM9.4
6-16			4.50

RICHIE RICH DOLLARS & CENTS
Harvey Publications: Aug, 1963 - No. 109, Aug, 1982 (#1-43: 68 pgs.; 44-60, 71-94: 52 pgs.)

	GD2.0	FN6.0	NM9.4
1: (#1-64 are all reprint issues)	16.00	48.00	175.00
2	7.65	23.00	85.00
3-5: 5-r/1st app. of R.R. from Little Dot #1	5.00	15.00	55.00
6-10	3.20	9.60	35.00
11-20	3.00	9.00	30.00
21-30: 25-r/1st app. Nurse Jenny (Little Lotta #62)	2.40	7.35	22.00
31-43: 43-Last 68 pg. issue	2.00	6.00	18.00
44-60: All 52 pgs.	1.85	5.50	15.00
61-71	1.00	3.00	8.00
72-94: All 52 pgs.	1.50	4.50	12.00
95-99,101-109			5.00
100-Anniversary issue	1.00	2.80	7.00

RICHIE RICH FORTUNES
Harvey Publications: Sept, 1971 - No. 63, July, 1982 (#1-15: 52 pgs.)

	GD2.0	FN6.0	NM9.4
1	5.00	15.00	55.00
2-5	2.80	8.40	28.00
6-10	2.00	6.00	18.00
11-15: 11-r/1st app. The Onion	1.50	4.50	12.00
16-30	1.00	2.80	7.00
31-40			5.00
41-63: 62-Onion app.			3.50

RICHIE RICH GEMS
Harvey Publications: Sept, 1974 - No. 43, Sept, 1982

	GD2.0	FN6.0	NM9.4
1	3.20	9.60	35.00
2-5	2.00	6.00	18.00
6-10	1.20	3.60	12.00
11-20	1.00	2.80	7.00
21-30			5.00
31-43: 36-Dr. Blemish, Onion app. 38-1st app. Stone-Age Riches			3.50

RICHIE RICH GOLD AND SILVER
Harvey Publications: Sept, 1975 - No. 42, Oct, 1982 (#1-27: 52 pgs.)

	GD2.0	FN6.0	NM9.4
1	2.60	7.80	26.00
2-5	1.85	5.50	15.00
6-10	1.25	3.75	10.00
11-27	1.00	3.00	8.00
28-42: 34-Stone-Age Riches app.			4.00

RICHIE RICH GOLD NUGGETS DIGEST
Harvey Publications: Feb., 1991 - No. 4, June, 1991 ($1.75, digest-size)

	GD2.0	FN6.0	NM9.4
1			3.00
2-4			2.00

RICHIE RICH HOLIDAY DIGEST MAGAZINE (...Digest #4)
Harvey Publications: Jan, 1980 - #3, Jan, 1982; #4, 3/88; #5, 2/89 (annual)

	GD2.0	FN6.0	NM9.4
1-X-Mas-c	1.25	3.75	10.00
2-5: 2,3: All X-Mas-c. 4-(3/88, $1.25), 5-(2/89, $1.75)	1.00	2.80	7.00

RICHIE RICH INVENTIONS
Harvey Publications: Oct, 1977 - No. 26, Oct, 1982 (#1-11: 52 pgs.)

	GD2.0	FN6.0	NM9.4
1	1.50	4.50	12.00
2-5	1.00	3.00	8.00
6-11		2.40	6.00
12-26			4.00

RICHIE RICH JACKPOTS
Harvey Publications: Oct, 1972 - No. 58, Aug, 1982 (#41-43: 52 pgs.)

	GD2.0	FN6.0	NM9.4
1	5.00	15.00	55.00
2-5	2.50	7.50	24.00
6-10	2.00	6.00	16.00
11-15,17-20	1.25	3.75	10.00
16-Super Richie app.	1.50	4.50	12.00
21-30	1.00	2.80	7.00
31-40,44-50: 37-Caricatures of Frank Sinatra, Dean Martin, Sammy Davis, Jr. 45-Dr. Blemish app.		2.40	6.00
41-43 (52 pgs.)	1.10	3.30	9.00
51-58			4.00

RICHIE RICH MILLION DOLLAR DIGEST (...Magazine #?-on)(See Million Dollar Digest)
Harvey Publications: Oct, 1980 - No. 10, Oct, 1982 ($1.50)

	GD2.0	FN6.0	NM9.4
1	1.10	3.30	9.00
2-10			5.00

RICHIE RICH MILLIONS
Harvey Publ.: 9/61; #2, 9/62 - #113, 10/82 (#1-48: 68 pgs.; 49-64, 85-97: 52 pgs.)

	GD2.0	FN6.0	NM9.4
1: (#1-3 are all reprint issues)	19.00	57.00	210.00
2	10.00	30.00	110.00
3-10: All other giants are new & reprints. 5-1st 15 pg. Richie Rich story	8.15	24.50	90.00
11-20	4.10	12.30	45.00
21-30	3.20	9.60	35.00
31-48: 31-1st app. The Onion. 48-Last 68 pg. Giant	2.30	7.00	20.00
49-64: 52 pg. Giants	2.00	6.00	16.00
65-67,69-73,75-84	1.00	3.00	8.00
68-1st Super Richie-c (11/74)	2.00	6.00	16.00
74-1st app. Mr. Woody; Super Richie app.	1.25	3.75	10.00
85-97: 52 pg. Giants	1.25	3.75	10.00
98,99			5.00
100		2.40	6.00
101-113			3.50

RICHIE RICH MONEY WORLD
Harvey Publications: Sept, 1972 - No. 59, Sept, 1982

	GD2.0	FN6.0	NM9.4
1-(52 pg. Giant)-1st app. Mayda Munny	5.45	16.35	60.00
2-Super Richie app.	2.80	8.40	28.00
3-5	2.40	7.35	22.00
6-10: 9,10-Richie Rich mistakenly named Little Lotta on covers	1.85	5.50	15.00
11-20: 16,20-Dr. N-R-Gee	1.10	3.30	9.00
21-30	1.00	2.80	7.00
31-50			5.00
51-59			3.50
Digest 1 (2/91, $1.75)			4.00
2-8 (12/93, $1.75)			2.00

RICHIE RICH PROFITS
Harvey Publications: Oct, 1974 - No. 47, Sept, 1982

	GD2.0	FN6.0	NM9.4
1	3.65	11.00	40.00
2-5	2.00	6.00	18.00
6-10: 10-Origin of Dr. N-R-Gee	1.25	3.75	10.00
11-20: 15-Christmas-c	1.00	2.80	7.00
21-30			5.00
31-47			4.00

RICHIE RICH RELICS
Harvey Comics: Jan, 1988 - No.4, Feb, 1989 (75¢/$1.00, reprints)

	GD2.0	FN6.0	NM9.4
1-4			3.00

RICHIE RICH RICHES
Harvey Publications: July, 1972 - No. 59, Aug, 1982 (#1, 2, 41-45: 52 pgs.)

	GD2.0	FN6.0	NM9.4
1-(52 pg. Giant)-1st app. The Money Monster	5.00	15.00	55.00
2-(52 pg. Giant)	2.80	8.40	28.00
3-5	2.00	6.00	18.00
6-10	1.75	5.25	14.00
11-20: 17-Super Richie app. (3/75)	1.10	3.30	9.00
21-40	1.00	2.80	7.00
41-45: 52 pg. Giants	1.10	3.30	9.00
46-59: 56-Dr. Blemish app.			4.00

RICHIE RICH SUCCESS STORIES
Harvey Publications: Nov, 1964 - No. 105, Sept, 1982 (#1-38: 68 pgs., 39-55, 67-90: 52 pgs.)

	GD2.0	FN6.0	NM9.4
1	17.50	52.00	190.00
2-5	8.15	24.50	90.00
6-10	4.55	13.65	50.00
11-20	3.80	11.40	42.00

Richie Rich Success Stories #61 © HARV

The Rifleman #8 © DELL

Rin Tin Tin Four Color #476 © Lee Duncan

	GD2.0	FN6.0	NM9.4
21-30: 27-1st Penny Van Dough (8/69)	2.60	7.80	26.00
31-38: 38-Last 68 pg. Giant	2.40	7.35	22.00
39-55-(52 pgs.): 44-Super Richie app.	2.00	6.00	18.00
56-66	1.10	3.30	9.00
67-90: 52 pgs.	1.50	4.50	12.00
91-105: 91-Onion app. 101-Dr. Blemish app.			5.00

RICHIE RICH SUMMER BONANZA
Harvey Comics: Oct, 1991 ($1.95, one-shot, 68 pgs.)

1-Richie Rich, Little Dot, Little Lotta 3.00

RICHIE RICH TREASURE CHEST DIGEST (...Magazine #3)
Harvey Publications: Apr, 1982 - No. 3, Aug, 1982 (95¢, Digest Mag.) (#4 advertised but not publ.)

	GD2.0	FN6.0	NM9.4
1	1.00	3.00	8.00
2,3		2.40	6.00

RICHIE RICH VACATION DIGEST
Harvey Comics: Oct, 1991; Oct, 1992; Oct, 1993 ($1.75, digest-size)

1-(10/91), 1-(10/92), 1-(10/93) 4.00

RICHIE RICH VACATIONS DIGEST
Harvey Publ.: 11/77; No. 2, 10/78 - No. 7, 10/81; No. 8, 8/82; (Digest, 132 pgs.)

	GD2.0	FN6.0	NM9.4
1-Reprints	1.50	4.50	12.00
2-8	1.00	2.80	7.00

RICHIE RICH VAULT OF MYSTERY
Harvey Publications: Nov, 1974 - No. 47, Sept, 1982

	GD2.0	FN6.0	NM9.4
1	2.80	8.40	28.00
2-10	1.85	5.50	15.00
11-20	1.00	3.00	8.00
21-30			5.00
31-47			3.50

RICHIE RICH ZILLIONZ
Harvey Publ.: Oct, 1976 - No. 33, Sept, 1982 (#1-4: 68 pgs.; #5-18: 52 pgs.)

	GD2.0	FN6.0	NM9.4
1	3.00	9.00	30.00
2-4: 4-Last 68 pg. Giant	2.00	6.00	18.00
5-10	1.25	3.75	10.00
11-18: 18-Last 52 pg. Giant	1.00	2.80	7.00
19-33			3.50

RICK GEARY'S WONDERS AND ODDITIES
Dark Horse Comics: Dec, 1988 ($2.00, B&W, one-shot)

1 2.00

RICKY
Standard Comics (Visual Editions): No. 5, Sept, 1953

	GD2.0	FN6.0	NM9.4
5-Teenage humor	4.65	14.00	28.00

RICKY NELSON (TV)(See Sweethearts V2#42)
Dell Publishing Co.: No. 956, Dec, 1958 - No. 1192, June, 1961 (All photo-c)

	GD2.0	FN6.0	NM9.4
Four Color 956,998	18.35	55.00	220.00
Four Color 1115	14.00	41.00	165.00
Four Color 1192-Manning-a	14.00	41.00	165.00

RIDER, THE (Frontier Trail #6; also see Blazing Sixguns I.W. Reprint #10, 11)
Ajax/Farrell Publ. (Four Star Comic Corp.): Mar, 1957 - No. 5, 1958

	GD2.0	FN6.0	NM9.4
1-Swift Arrow, Lone Rider begin	11.00	33.00	90.00
2-5	6.40	19.25	45.00

RIDERS OF THE PURPLE SAGE (See Zane Grey & Four Color #372)

RIFLEMAN, THE (TV)
Dell Publ. Co./Gold Key No. 13 on: No. 1009, 7-9/59 - No. 12, 7-9/62; No. 13, 11/62 - No. 20, 10/64

	GD2.0	FN6.0	NM9.4
Four Color 1009 (#1)	23.00	70.00	280.00
2 (1-3/60)	11.70	35.00	140.00
3-Toth-a (4 pgs.)	11.70	35.00	140.00
4-10: 6-Toth-a (4 pgs.)	10.00	30.00	120.00
11-20	7.50	22.50	90.00

NOTE: ***Warren Tufts*** *a-2-9. All have Chuck Connors photo-c. Photo back c-13-15.*

RIMA, THE JUNGLE GIRL
National Periodical Publications: Apr-May, 1974 - No. 7, Apr-May, 1975

	GD2.0	FN6.0	NM9.4
1-Origin, part 1 (#1-5: 20¢; 6,7: 25¢)	1.25	3.75	10.00
2-7: 2-4-Origin, parts 2-4. 7-Origin & only app. Space Marshal		2.40	6.00

NOTE: ***Kubert*** *c-1-7.* ***Nino*** *a-1-7.* ***Redondo*** *a-1-7.*

RING OF BRIGHT WATER (See Movie Classics)

RING OF THE NIBELUNG, THE
DC Comics: 1989 - No. 4, 1990 ($4.95, squarebound, 52 pgs., mature readers)

1-4: Adapts novel, Gil Kane-c/a 5.00

RING OF THE NIBELUNG, THE
Dark Horse Comics: Feb, 2000 - Present ($2.95, limited series)

(The Rhinegold) 1-4: Adapts Wagner; P. Craig Russell-s/a 3.00
(The Valkyrie) 1-3: 1-(8/00) 2.95

RINGO KID, THE (2nd Series)
Marvel Comics Group: Jan, 1970 - No. 23, Nov, 1973; No. 24, Nov, 1975 - No. 30, Nov, 1976

	GD2.0	FN6.0	NM9.4
1-Williamson-a r-from #10, 1956.	2.80	8.40	28.00
2-11: 2-Severin-c. 11-Last 15¢ issue	2.00	6.00	16.00
12 (52 pg. Giant)	2.50	7.50	23.00
13-20: 13-Wildey-r. 20-Williamson-r/#1	1.50	4.50	12.00
21-30	1.10	3.30	9.00
27,28-(30¢-c variant, limited distribution)(5,7/76)	1.75	5.25	14.00

RINGO KID WESTERN, THE (1st Series) (See Wild Western & Western Trails)
Atlas Comics (HPC)/Marvel Comics: Aug, 1954 - No. 21, Sept, 1957

	GD2.0	FN6.0	NM9.4
1-Origin; The Ringo Kid begins	30.00	90.00	240.00
2-Black Rider app.; origin/1st app. Ringo's Horse Arab	15.00	45.00	120.00
3-5	10.00	30.00	80.00
6-8-Severin-a(3) each	11.00	33.00	90.00
9,11,12,14-21: 12-Orlando-a (4 pgs.)	8.65	26.00	60.00
10,13-Williamson-a (4 pgs.)	9.30	28.00	65.00

NOTE: ***Berg*** *a-8.* ***Maneely*** *a-1-5, 15, 16(text illos only), 17(4), 18, 20, 21; c-1-6, 8, 13, 15-18, 20.* ***J. Severin*** *c-10, 11.* ***Sinnott*** *a-1.* ***Wildey*** *a-16-18.*

RIN TIN TIN (See March of Comics #163,180,195)

RIN TIN TIN (TV) (...& Rusty #21 on; see Western Roundup under Dell Giants)
Dell Publishing Co./Gold Key: Nov, 1952 - No. 38, May-July, 1961; Nov, 1963 (All Photo-c)

	GD2.0	FN6.0	NM9.4
Four Color 434 (#1)	15.00	45.00	175.00
Four Color 476,523	7.50	22.50	90.00
4(3-5/54)-10	5.85	17.50	70.00
11-20	5.00	15.00	60.00
21-38: 36-Toth-a (4 pgs.)	4.10	12.30	45.00
... & Rusty 1 (11/63-Gold Key)	5.00	15.00	60.00

RIO (Also see Eclipse Monthly)
Comico: June, 1987 ($8.95, 64 pgs.)

1-Wildey-c/a 9.00

RIO AT BAY
Dark Horse Comics: July, 1992 - No. 2, Aug, 1992 ($2.95, limited series)

1,2-Wildey-c/a 3.00

RIO BRAVO (Movie) (See 4-Color #1018)
Dell Publishing Co.: June, 1959

	GD2.0	FN6.0	NM9.4
Four Color #1018-Toth-a; John Wayne, Dean Martin, & Ricky Nelson photo-c.	20.00	60.00	240.00

RIO CONCHOS (See Movie Comics)

RIOT (Satire)
Atlas Comics (ACI No. 1-5/WPI No. 6): Apr, 1954 - No. 3, Aug, 1954; No. 4, Feb, 1956 - No. 6, June, 1956

	GD2.0	FN6.0	NM9.4
1-Russ Heath-a	30.00	90.00	240.00
2-Li'l Abner satire by Post	22.00	66.00	175.00
3-Last precode (8/54)	19.00	56.00	150.00
4-Infinity-c; Marilyn Monroe "7 Year Itch" movie satire; Mad Rip-off ads	25.00	75.00	200.00
5-Marilyn Monroe, John Wayne parody; part photo-c	26.00	79.00	210.00

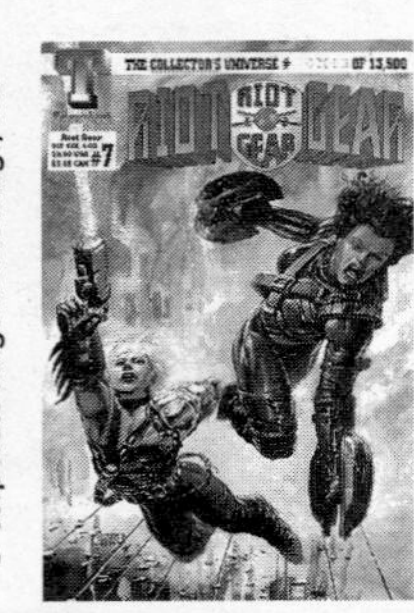

Riot Gear #7
© Corporate Kingdom Holdings, Inc.

Ripley's Believe It or Not #3 © HARV

Rising Stars #4 © J.M. Straczynski

6-Lorna of the Jungle satire by Everett; Dennis the Menace satire-c/story; part photo-c 19.00 56.00 150.00
NOTE: *Berg a-3. Burgos c-1, 2. Colan a-1. Everett a-1, 4, 6. Heath a-1. Maneely a-1, 2, 4-6; c-3, 4, 6. Post a-1-4. Reinman a-2. Severin a-4-6.*

RIOT GEAR
Triumphant Comics: Sept, 1993 - No. 11, July, 1994 ($2.50, serially numbered)
1-11: 1-2nd app. Riot Gear. 2-1st app. Rabin. 3,4-Triumphant Unleashed x-over. 3-1st app. Surzar. 4-Death of Captain Tich 2.50
Violent Past 1,2: 1-(2/94, $2.50) 2.50

R.I.P.
TSR, Inc.:1990 - No. 8, 1991 ($2.95, 44 pgs.)
1-8-Based on TSR game 3.00

RIPCLAW (See Cyberforce)
Image Comics (Top Cow Prod.): Apr, 1995 - No. 3, June, 1995 (Limited series)
1/2-Gold, 1/2-San Diego ed., 1/2-Chicago ed. 1.25 3.75 10.00
1-3: Brandon Peterson-a(p) 3.00
Special 1 (10/95, $2.50) 2.50

RIPCLAW
Image Comics (Top Cow Prod.): V2#1, Dec, 1995 - No. 6, June, 1996 ($2.50)
V2#1-6: 5-Medieval Spawn/Witchblade Preview 2.50

RIPCORD (TV)
Dell Publishing Co.: Mar-May, 1962
Four Color 1294 6.70 20.00 80.00

R.I.P.D.
Dark Horse Comics: Oct, 1999 - No. 4, Jan, 2000 ($2.95, limited series)
1-4 2.95

RIPFIRE
Malibu Comics (Ultraverse): No. 0, Apr, 1995 ($2.50, one-shot)
0 2.50

RIP HUNTER TIME MASTER (See Showcase #20, 21, 25, 26 & Time Masters)
National Periodical Publications: Mar-Apr, 1961 - No. 29, Nov-Dec, 1965
1-(3-4/61) 46.00 138.00 600.00
2 24.50 74.00 270.00
3-5: 5-Last 10¢ issue 14.50 43.50 160.00
6,7-Toth-a in each 10.00 30.00 110.00
8-15 7.25 21.75 80.00
16-20: 20-Hitler c/s 5.90 17.75 65.00
21-29: 29-Gil Kane-c 4.55 13.65 50.00

RIP IN TIME (Also see Teenage Mutant Ninja Turtles #5-7)
Fantagor Press: Aug, 1986 - No.5, 1987 ($1.50, B&W)
1-5: Corben-c/a in all 3.00

RIP KIRBY (Also see Harvey Comics Hits #57, & Street Comix)
David McKay Publications: 1948
Feature Books 51,54: Raymond-c; 51-Origin 34.00 101.00 270.00

RIPLEY'S BELIEVE IT OR NOT! (See Ace Comics, All-American Comics, Mystery Comics Digest #1, 4, 7, 10, 13, 16, 19, 22, 25)

RIPLEY'S BELIEVE IT OR NOT!
Harvey Publications: Sept, 1953 - No. 4, March, 1954
1-Powell-a 12.00 36.00 95.00
2-4 9.30 28.00 65.00

RIPLEY'S BELIEVE IT OR NOT! (Formerly ...True War Stories)
Gold Key: No. 4, April, 1967 - No. 94, Feb, 1980
4-Photo-c; McWilliams-a 3.00 9.00 30.00
5-Subtitled "True War Stories"; Evans-a; 1st Jeff Jones-a in comics? (2 pgs.) 3.00 9.00 30.00
6-10: 6-McWilliams-a. 10-Evans-a(2) 2.80 8.40 28.00
11-20: 15-Evans-a 2.40 7.35 22.00
21-30 2.00 6.00 16.00
31-38,40-60 1.50 4.50 12.00
39-Crandall-a 1.75 5.25 14.00
61-73 1.00 3.00 8.00
74,77-83-(52 pgs.) 1.25 3.75 10.00
75,76,84-94 2.40 6.00
Story Digest Mag. 1(6/70)-4-3/4x6-1/2", 148pp. 4.55 13.65 50.00
NOTE: *Evanish art by Luiz Dominguez #22-25, 27, 30, 31, 40. Jeff Jones a-5(2 pgs.). McWilliams a-65, 66, 70, 89. Orlando a-8. Sparling c-68. Reprints-74, 77-84, 87 (part); 91, 93 (all). Williamson, Wood a-80r/#1.*

RIPLEY'S BELIEVE IT OR NOT! TRUE GHOST STORIES (Becomes ...True War Stories) (See Dan Curtis)
Gold Key: June, 1965 - No. 2, Oct, 1966
1-Williamson, Wood & Evans-a; photo-c 5.45 16.35 60.00
2-Orlando, McWilliams-a; photo-c 3.20 9.60 35.00
Mini-Comic 1(1976-3-1/4x6-1/2") 1.25 3.75 10.00
11186(1977)-Golden Press; ($1.95, 224 pgs.)-All-r 3.00 9.00 30.00
11401(3/79)-Golden Press; ($1.00, 96 pgs.)-All-r 2.00 6.00 18.00

RIPLEY'S BELIEVE IT OR NOT! TRUE WAR STORIES (Formerly ...True Ghost Stories; becomes Ripley's Believe It or Not! #4 on)
Gold Key: Nov, 1966
1(#3)-No Williamson-a 3.00 9.00 32.00

RIPLEY'S BELIEVE IT OR NOT! TRUE WEIRD
Ripley Enterprises: June, 1966 - No. 2, Aug, 1966 (B&W Magazine)
1,2-Comic stories & text 2.50 7.50 24.00

RIPTIDE
Image Comics: Sep, 1995 - No. 2, Oct, 1995 ($2.50, limited series)
1,2: Rob Liefeld-c 2.50

RISE OF APOCALYPSE
Marvel Comics: Oct, 1996 - No. 4, Jan, 1997 ($1.95, limited series)
1-4: Adam Pollina-c/a 2.00

RISING STARS
Image Comics(Top Cow): Mar, 1999 - Present ($2.50)
Preview-(3/99, $5.00) Straczynski-s 2.40 6.00
0-(6/00, $2.50) Gary Frank-a/c 2.50
1-Four covers; Keu Cha-c/a 4.00
1-($10.00) Gold Editions-four covers 10.00
1-($50.00) Holofoil-c 50.00
2-4 3.00
5-12-Zanier & Lashley-a(p) 2.50
Born In Fire TPB (11/00, $19.95) r/#1-8; foreword by Neil Gaiman 20.00
Prelude-(10/00, $2.95) Cha-a/Lashley-c 3.00
Wizard #0-(3/99) Wizard supplement; Straczynski-s 2.00
Wizard #1/2 10.00

RIVERDALE HIGH (Archie's... #7,8)
Archie Comics: Aug, 1990 - No. 8, Oct, 1991 ($1.00, bi-monthly)
1-8 2.00

RIVER FEUD (See Zane Grey & Four Color #484)

RIVETS
Dell Publishing Co.: No. 518, Nov, 1953
Four Color 518 3.00 9.00 30.00

RIVETS (A dog)
Argo Publ.: Jan, 1956 - No. 3, May, 1956
1-Reprints Sunday & daily newspaper strips 5.00 15.00 32.00
2,3 4.00 11.00 22.00

ROACHMILL
Blackthorne Publ.: Dec, 1986 - No. 6, Oct, 1987 ($1.75, B&W)
1-6 2.00

ROACHMILL
Dark Horse Comics: May, 1988 - No. 10, Dec, 1990 ($1.75, B&W)
1-10: 10-Contains trading cards 2.00

ROAD RUNNER (See Beep Beep, the...)

ROAD TO PERDITION
DC Comics/Paradox Press: 1998? $13.95 (Paperback)
nn 14.00

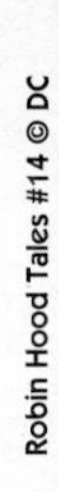
Robin #8 © DC

Robin Hood Tales #14 © DC

Robin II #3 © DC

GD2.0 FN6.0 NM9.4

ROADTRIP
Oni Press: Aug, 2000 ($2.95, B&W, one-shot)

1-Reprints Judd Winick's back-up stories from Oni Double Feature #9,10 2.95

ROADWAYS
Cult Press: May, 1994 ($2.75, B&W, limited series)

1 2.75

ROARIN' RICK'S RARE BIT FIENDS
King Hell Press: July, 1994 - No. 21, Aug, 1996 ($2.95, B&W, mature)

1-21: Rick Veitch-c/a/scripts in all. 20-(5/96). 21-(8/96)-Reads Subtleman #1 on cover 3.00
Rabid Eye: The Dream Art of Rick Veitch ($14.95, B&W, TPB)-r/#1-8 & the appendix from #12 15.00
Pocket Universe (6/96, $14.95, B&W, TPB)-Reprints 15.00

ROBERT E. HOWARD'S CONAN THE BARBARIAN
Marvel Comics: 1983 ($2.50, 68 pgs., Baxter paper)

1-r/Savage Tales #2,3 by Smith, c-r/Conan #21 by Smith. 4.00

ROBERT LOUIS STEVENSON'S KIDNAPPED (See Kidnapped)

ROBIN (See Aurora, Detective Comics #38, New Teen Titans, Robin II, Robin III, Robin 3000, Star Spangled Comics #65, Teen Titans & Young Justice)

ROBIN (See Batman #457)
DC Comics: Jan, 1991 - No. 5, May, 1991 ($1.00, limited series)

1-Free poster by N. Adams; Bolland-c on all 4.00
1-2nd & 3rd printings (without poster) 2.00
2-5 2.50
2-2nd printing 2.00
Annual 1,2 (1992-93, $2.50, 68 pgs.): 1-Grant/Wagner scripts; Sam Kieth-c. 2-Intro Razorsharp; Jim Balent-c(p) 2.50

ROBIN (See Detective #668)
DC Comics: Nov, 1993 - Present ($1.50/$1.95/$1.99/$2.25)

1-($2.95)-Collector's edition w/foil embossed-c; 1st app. Robin's car, The Redbird; Azrael as Batman app. 3.00
1-Newsstand ed. 2.00
0,2-49,51-66-Regular editions: 3-5-The Spoiler app. 6-The Huntress-c/story cont'd from Showcase '94 #5. 7-Knightquest: The Conclusion w/new Batman (Azrael) vs. Bruce Wayne. 8-KnightsEnd Pt. 5. 9-KnightsEnd Aftermath; Batman-c & app. 10-(9/94)-Zero Hour. 0-(10/94). 11-(11/94). 25-Green Arrow -c/app. 26-Batman app. 27-Contagion Pt. 3; Catwoman-c/app; Penguin & Azrael app. 28-Contagion Pt. 11. 29-Penguin app. 31-Wildcat-c/app. 32-Legacy Pt. 3. 33-Legacy Pt. 7. 35-Final Night. 46-Genesis. 52,53-Cataclysm pt. 7, conclusion. 55-Green Arrow app. 62-64-Flash-c/app. 2.00
14 ($2.50)-Embossed-c; Troika Pt. 4 2.50
50-($2.95)-Lady Shiva & King Snake app. 3.00
67-72-No Man's Land 2.00
73,74,76-78 2.00
75-($2.95) 2.95
79-86: 79-Begin $2.25-c; Green Arrow app. 86-Pander Bros.-a 2.25
#1,000,000 (11/98) 853rd Century x-over 2.00
Annual 3-5: 3-(1994, $2.95)-Elseworlds story. 4-(1995, $2.95)-Year One story. 5-(1996, $2.95)-Legends of the Dead Earth story 3.00
Annual 6 (1997, $3.95)-Pulp Heroes story. 4.00
.../Argent 1 (2/98, $1.95) Argent (Teen Titans) app. 2.00
...Eighty-Page Giant 1 (9/00, $5.95) Chuck Dixon-s/Diego Barreto-a 5.95
...: Flying Solo (2000, $12.95, TPB) r/#1-6, Showcase '94 #5,6 12.95
...Plus 1 (12/96, $2.95) Impulse-c/app.; Waid-s 3.00
...Plus 2 (12/97, $2.95) Fang (Scare Tactics) app. 3.00

ROBIN: A HERO REBORN
DC Comics: 1991 ($4.95, squarebound, trade paperback)

nn-r/Batman #455-457 & Robin #1-5; Bolland-c 5.00

ROBIN HOOD (See The Advs. of..., Brave and the Bold, Four Color #413, 669, King Classics, Movie Comics & Power Record Comics)

ROBIN HOOD (...& His Merry Men, The Illustrated Story of...) (See Classic Comics #7 & Classics Giveaways, 12/44)

ROBIN HOOD (Adventures of... #7, 8)
Magazine Enterprises (Sussex Pub. Co.): No. 52, Nov, 1955 - No. 6, Jun, 1957

GD2.0 FN6.0 NM9.4

52 (#1)-Origin Robin Hood & Sir Gallant of the Round Table 16.00 49.00 130.00
53 (#2), 3-6: 6-Richard Greene photo-c (TV) 12.00 36.00 95.00
I.W. Reprint #1,2,9: 1-r/#3. 2-r/#4. 9-r/#52 (1963) 2.00 6.00 18.00
Super Reprint #10,15: 10-r/#53. 15-r/#5 2.00 6.00 18.00
NOTE: ***Bolle** a-in all; c-52. **Powell** a-6.*

ROBIN HOOD (Not Disney)
Dell Publishing Co.: May-July, 1963 (one-shot)

1 2.50 7.50 24.00

ROBIN HOOD (Disney)
Western Publishing Co.: 1973 ($1.50, 8-1/2x11", 52 pgs., cardboard-c)

96151- "Robin Hood", based on movie, 96152- "The Mystery of Sherwood Forest", 96153- "In King Richard's Service", 96154- "The Wizard's Ring" each.... 2.30 7.00 20.00

ROBIN HOOD
Eclipse Comics: July, 1991 - No. 3, Dec, 1991 ($2.50, limited series)

1-3: Timothy Truman layouts 2.50

ROBIN HOOD AND HIS MERRY MEN (Formerly Danger & Adventure)
Charlton Comics: No. 28, Apr, 1956 - No. 38, Aug, 1958

28 9.30 28.00 65.00
29-37 7.15 21.50 50.00
38-Ditko-a (5 pgs.); Rocke-c 12.50 37.50 100.00

ROBIN HOOD TALES (Published by National Periodical #7 on)
Quality Comics Group (Comic Magazines): Feb, 1956 - No. 6, Nov-Dec, 1956

1-All have Baker/Cuidera-c 35.00 105.00 280.00
2-6-Matt Baker-a 34.00 101.00 270.00

ROBIN HOOD TALES (Cont'd from Quality series)(See Brave & the Bold #5)
National Periodical Publ.: No. 7, Jan-Feb, 1957 - No. 14, Mar-Apr, 1958

7-All have Andru/Esposito-c 40.00 120.00 320.00
8-14 34.00 101.00 270.00

ROBINSON CRUSOE (See King Classics & Power Record Comics)
Dell Publishing Co.: Nov-Jan, 1963-64

1 1.85 5.50 15.00

ROBIN II (The Joker's Wild)
DC Comics: Oct, 1991 - No. 4, Dec, 1991 ($1.50, mini-series)

1-(Direct sales, $1.50)-With 4 diff.-c; same hologram on each 2.50
1-(Newsstand, $1.00)-No hologram; 1 version 2.00
1-Collector's set ($10.00)-Contains all 5 versions bagged with hologram trading card inside 10.00
2-(Direct sales, $1.50)-With 3 different-c 2.50
2-4-(Newsstand, $1.00)-1 version of each 2.00
2-Collector's set ($8.00)-Contains all 4 versions bagged with hologram trading card inside 8.00
3-(Direct sale, $1.50)-With 2 different-c 2.50
3-Collector's set ($6.00)-Contains all 3 versions bagged with hologram trading card inside 6.00
4-(Direct sales, $1.50)-Only one version 2.50
4-Collector's set ($4.00)-Contains both versions bagged with Bat-Signal hologram trading card 4.00
Multi-pack (All four issues w/hologram sticker) 4.00
Deluxe Complete Set ($30.00)-Contains all 14 versions of #1-4 plus a new hologram trading card; numbered & limited to 25,000; comes with slipcase & 2 acid free backing boards 30.00

ROBIN III: CRY OF THE HUNTRESS
DC Comics: Dec, 1992 - No. 6, Mar, 1993 (Limited series)

1-6 ($2.50, collector's ed.)-Polybagged w/movement enhanced-c plus mini-poster of newsstand-c by Zeck 2.50
1-6 ($1.25, newsstand ed.): All have Zeck-c 2.00

ROBIN 3000
DC Comics (Elseworlds): 1992 - No. 2, 1992 ($4.95, mini-series, 52 pgs.)

1,2-Foil logo; Russell-c/a 5.00

ROBIN: YEAR ONE

Robocop #8 © Orion Pictures

Robotmen of the Lost Planet #1 © AVON

Rocket Comics #3 © HILL

DC Comics: 2000 - No. 4, 2001 ($4.95, square-bound, limited series)

1-4: Earliest days of Robin's career; Javier Pulido-c/a. 2,4-Two-Face app. 5.00

ROBOCOP
Marvel Comics: Oct, 1987 ($2.00, B&W, magazine, one-shot)

1-Movie adaptation 3.00

ROBOCOP (Also see Dark Horse Comics)
Marvel Comics: Mar, 1990 - No. 23, Jan, 1992 ($1.50)

1-Based on movie 3.00
2-23 2.00
nn (7/90, $4.95, 52 pgs.)-r/B&W magazine in color; adapts 1st movie 5.00

ROBOCOP: MORTAL COILS
Dark Horse Comics: Sept, 1993 - No. 4, Dec, 1993 ($2.50, limited series)

1-4: 1,2-Cago painted-c 2.50

ROBOCOP: PRIME SUSPECT
Dark Horse Comics: Oct, 1992 - No. 4, Jan, 1993 ($2.50, limited series)

1-4: 1,3-Nelson painted-c. 2,4-Bolton painted-c 2.50

ROBOCOP: ROULETTE
Dark Horse Comics: Dec, 1993 - No. 4, 1994 ($2.50, limited series)

1-4: 1,3-Nelson painted-c. 2,4-Bolton painted-c 2.50

ROBOCOP 2
Marvel Comics: Aug, 1990 ($2.25, B&W, magazine, 68 pgs.)

1-Adapts movie sequel 2.25

ROBOCOP 2
Marvel Comics: Aug, 1990; Late Aug, 1990 - #3, Late Sept, 1990 ($1.00, limited series)

nn-(8/90, $4.95, 68 pgs., color)-Same contents as B&W magazine 5.00
1: #1-3 reprint no number issue 3.00
2,3: 2-Guice-c(i) 2.00

ROBOCOP 3
Dark Horse Comics: July, 1993 - No. 3, Nov, 1993 ($2.50, limited series)

1-3: Nelson painted-c; Nguyen-a(p) 2.50

ROBOCOP VERSUS THE TERMINATOR
Dark Horse Comics: Sept, 1992 - No. 4, 1992 (Dec.) ($2.50, limited series)

1-4: Miller scripts & Simonson-c/a in all 2.50
1-Platinum Edition 6.00
NOTE: *All contain a different Robocop cardboard cut-out stand-up.*

ROBO-HUNTER (Also see Sam Slade...)
Eagle Comics: Apr, 1984 - No. 5, 1984 ($1.00)

1-5-2000 A.D. 2.00

R.O.B.O.T. BATTALION 2050
Eclipse Comics: Mar, 1988 ($2.00, B&W, one-shot)

1 2.00

ROBOT COMICS
Renegade Press: No. 0, June, 1987 ($2.00, B&W, one-shot)

0-Bob Burden story & art 2.00

ROBOTECH
Antarctic Press: Mar, 1997 - No. 11, Nov, 1998 ($2.95)

1-11, Annual 1 (4/98, $2.95) 3.00
...Class Reunion (12/98, $3.95, B&W) 4.00
...Escape (5/98, $2.95, B&W), ...Final Fire (12/98, $2.95, B&W) 3.00

ROBOTECH: COVERT-OPS
Antarctic Press: Aug, 1998 - No. 2, Sept, 1998 ($2.95, B&W, limited series)

1,2-Gregory Lane-s/a 3.00

ROBOTECH DEFENDERS
DC Comics: Mar, 1985 - No. 2, Apr, 1985 (Mini-series)

1,2 3.00

ROBOTECH IN 3-D (TV)
Comico: Aug, 1987 ($2.50)

1-Steacy painted-c 4.00

ROBOTECH MASTERS (TV)
Comico: July, 1985 - No. 23, Apr, 1988 ($1.50)

1-23 3.00

ROBOTECH: SENTINELS - RUBICON
Antarctic Press: July, 1998 - Present ($2.95, B&W)

1 3.00

ROBOTECH SPECIAL
Comico: May, 1988 ($2.50, one-shot, 44 pgs.)

1-Steacy wraparound-c; partial photo-c 4.00

ROBOTECH THE GRAPHIC NOVEL
Comico: Aug, 1986 ($5.95, 8-1/2x11", 52 pgs.)

1-Origin SDF-1; intro T.R. Edwards, Steacy-c/a; 2nd printing also exists (12/86). 7.00

ROBOTECH: THE MACROSS SAGA (TV)(Formerly Macross)
Comico: No. 2, Feb, 1985 - No. 36, Feb, 1989 ($1.50)

2-10 4.00
11-36: 12,17-Ken Steacy painted-c. 26-Begin $1.75-c. 35,36-($1.95) 3.00

ROBOTECH: THE NEW GENERATION
Comico: July, 1985 - No. 25, July, 1988

1-25 3.00

ROBOTECH: VERMILION
Antarctic Press: Mar, 1997 - No. 4, ($2.95, B&W, limited series)

1-4 3.00

ROBOTECH: WINGS OF GIBRALTAR
Antarctic Press: Aug, 1998 - No. 2, Sept, 1998 ($2.95, B&W, limited series)

1,2-Lee Duhig-s/a 3.00

ROBOTIX
Marvel Comics: Feb, 1986 (75¢, one-shot)

1-Based on toy 3.00

ROBOTMEN OF THE LOST PLANET (Also see Space Thrillers)
Avon Periodicals: 1952 (Also see Strange Worlds #19)

1-McCann-a (3 pgs.); Fawcette-a 103.00 308.00 975.00

ROB ROY
Dell Publishing Co.: 1954 (Disney-Movie)

Four Color 544-Manning-a, photo-c 7.50 22.50 90.00

ROCK & ROLL HIGH SCHOOL
Roger Corman's Cosmic Comics: Oct, 1995 ($2.50)

1-Bob Fingerman scripts 2.50

ROCK AND ROLLO (Formerly TV Teens)
Charlton Comics: V2#14, Oct, 1957 - No. 19, Sept, 1958

V2#14-19 5.00 15.00 32.00

ROCK COMICS
Landgraphic Publ.: Jul/Aug, 1979 ($1.25, tabloid size, 28 pgs.)

1-N. Adams-c; Thor(not Marvel's) story by Adams 2.00 6.00 16.00

ROCKET COMICS
Hillman Periodicals: Mar, 1940 - No. 3, May, 1940

1-Rocket Riley, Red Roberts the Electro Man (origin), The Phantom Ranger, The Steel Shark, The Defender, Buzzard Barnes and his Sky Devils, Lefty Larson, & The Defender, the Man with a Thousand Faces begin (1st app. of each); all have Rocket Riley-c 242.00 726.00 2300.00
2,3 121.00 363.00 1150.00

ROCKETEER, THE (See Eclipse Graphic Album Series, Pacific Presents & Starslayer)

ROCKETEER ADVENTURE MAGAZINE, THE
Comico/Dark Horse Comics No. 3: July, 1988 ($2.00); No. 2, July, 1989 ($2.75); No. 3, Jan, 1995 ($2.95)

1-(7/88, $2.00)-Dave Stevens-c/a in all; Kaluta back-up-a; 1st app. Jonas (character based on The Shadow) 1.10 3.30 9.00

Rocket to the Moon nn © AVON

Rocky and His Friends Four Color #1128 © Jay Ward

Rocky Lane Western #12 © FAW

	GD2.0	FN6.0	NM9.4
2-(7/89, $2.75)-Stevens/Dorman painted-c		2.40	6.00
3-(1/95, $2.95)-Includes pinups by Stevens, Gulacy, Plunkett, & Mignola			3.50
Volume 2-(9/96, $9.95, magazine size TPB)-Reprints #1-3			10.00

ROCKETEER SPECIAL EDITION, THE
Eclipse Comics: Nov, 1984 ($1.50, Baxter paper)(Chapter 5 of Rocketeer serial)

	GD2.0	FN6.0	NM9.4
1-Stevens-c/a; Kaluta back-c; pin-ups inside	1.50	4.50	12.00

NOTE: *Originally intended to be published in Pacific Presents.*

ROCKETEER: THE OFFICIAL MOVIE ADAPTATION, THE
W. D. Publications (Disney): 1991

	GD2.0	FN6.0	NM9.4
nn-($5.95, 68 pgs.)-Squarebound deluxe edition			6.00
nn-($2.95, 68 pgs.)-Stapled regular edition			3.00
3-D Comic Book (1991, $7.98, 52 pgs.)			8.00

ROCKET KELLY (See The Bouncer, Green Mask #10); becomes Li'l Pan #6)
Fox Feature Syndicate: 1944; Fall, 1945 - No. 5, Oct-Nov, 1946

	GD2.0	FN6.0	NM9.4
nn (1944), 1	33.00	98.00	260.00
2-The Puppeteer app. (costumed hero)	25.00	75.00	200.00
3-5: 5-(#5 on cover, #4 inside)	22.00	66.00	175.00

ROCKETMAN (Strange Fantasy #2 on) (See Hello Pal & Scoop Comics)
Ajax/Farrell Publications: June, 1952 (Strange Stories of the Future)

	GD2.0	FN6.0	NM9.4
1-Rocketman & Cosmo	40.00	120.00	350.00

ROCKET RACCOON
Marvel Comics: May, 1995 - No. 4, Aug, 1985 (color, limited series)

	GD2.0	FN6.0	NM9.4
1-4: Mignola-a			2.00

ROCKET SHIP X
Fox Features Syndicate: September, 1951; 1952

	GD2.0	FN6.0	NM9.4
1	61.00	182.00	575.00
1952 (nn, nd, no publ.)-Edited 1951-c	40.00	120.00	330.00

ROCKET TO ADVENTURE LAND (See Pixie Puzzle...)

ROCKET TO THE MOON
Avon Periodicals: 1951

	GD2.0	FN6.0	NM9.4
nn-Orlando-c/a; adapts Otis Aldebert Kline's "Maza of the Moon"	103.00	308.00	975.00

ROCK FANTASY COMICS
Rock Fantasy Comics: Dec, 1989 - No. 16?, 1991 ($2.25/$3.00, B&W)(No cover price)

	GD2.0	FN6.0	NM9.4
1-Pink Floyd part 1			4.00
1-2nd printing ($3.00-c)			3.00
2,3: 2-Rolling Stones #1. 3-Led Zeppelin #1			3.00
2,3: 2nd printings ($3.00-c, 1/90 & 2/90)			3.00
4-Stevie Nicks Not published			
5-Monstrosities of Rock #1; photo back-c			3.00
5-2nd printing ($3.00, 3/90 indicia, 2/90-c)			3.00
6-9,11-15,17,18: 6-Guns n' Roses #1 (1st & 2nd printings, 3/90)-Begin $3.00-c. 7-Sex Pistols #1. 8-Alice Cooper; not published. 9-Van Halen #1; photo back-c. 11-Jimi Hendrix #1; wraparound-c			3.00
10-Kiss #1; photo back-c	1.00	3.00	8.00
16-($5.00, 68 pgs.)-The Great Gig in the Sky(Floyd)			5.00

ROCK HAPPENING (See Bunny and Harvey Pop Comics:...)

ROCK N' ROLL COMICS
Revolutionary Comics: Jun, 1989 - No. 24, 1992 ($1.50/$1.95, B&W/col. #15 on)

	GD2.0	FN6.0	NM9.4
1-Guns N' Roses	1.00	3.00	8.00
1-2nd thru 7th printings. 7th printing (full color w/new-c/a)			2.00
2-Metallica	1.25	3.75	10.00
2-2nd thru 6th printings (6th in color)			2.00
3-Bon Jovi (no reprints)	1.00	3.00	8.00
4-8,10-24: 4-Motley Crue(2nd printing only, 1st destroyed). 5-Def Leppard (2 printings). 6-Rolling Stones(4 printings). 7-The Who(3 printings). 8-Skid Row; not published. 10-Warrant/Whitesnake(2 printings; 1st has 2 diff.-c). 11-Aerosmith (2 printings?). 12-New Kids on the Block(2 printings). 12-3rd printing; rewritten & titled NKOTB Hate Book. 13-Led Zeppelin. 14-Sex Pistols. 15-Poison; 1st color issue. 16-Van Halen. 17-Madonna. 18-Alice Cooper. 19-Public Enemy/2 Live Crew. 20-Queensryche/Tesla. 21-Prince? 22-AC/DC; begin $2.50-c. 23-Living Colour. 24-Anthrax			5.00
9-Kiss	1.50	4.50	12.00
9-2nd & 3rd printings			2.00

NOTE: *Most issues were reprinted except #3. Later reprints are in color. #8 was not released.*

ROCKO'S MODERN LIFE (TV)
Marvel Comics: June, 1994 - No. 7, Dec, 1994 ($1.95) (Nickelodeon cartoon)

	GD2.0	FN6.0	NM9.4
1-7			2.00

ROCKY AND HIS FIENDISH FRIENDS (TV)(Bullwinkle)
Gold Key: Oct, 1962 - No. 5, Sept, 1963 (Jay Ward)

	GD2.0	FN6.0	NM9.4
1 (25¢, 80 pgs.)	21.00	63.00	250.00
2,3 (25¢, 80 pgs.)	14.00	42.00	170.00
4,5 (Regular size, 12¢)	9.50	29.00	115.00

ROCKY AND HIS FRIENDS (See Kite Fun Book & March of Comics #216)

ROCKY AND HIS FRIENDS (TV)
Dell Publishing Co.: No. 1128, 8-10/60 - No.1311,1962 (Jay Ward)

	GD2.0	FN6.0	NM9.4
Four Color #1128 (#1) (8-10/60)	37.00	110.00	440.00
Four Color #1152 (12-2/61), 1166, 1208, 1275, 1311('62)	23.00	69.00	275.00

ROCKY HORROR PICTURE SHOW THE COMIC BOOK, THE
Caliber Press: Jul, 1990 - No. 3, Jan, 1991 ($2.95, mini-series, 52 pgs.)

	GD2.0	FN6.0	NM9.4
1-3: 1-Adapts cult film plus photos, etc., 1-2nd printing			3.00
...Collection ($4.95)			5.00

ROCKY JONES SPACE RANGER (See Space Adventures #15-18)

ROCKY JORDEN PRIVATE EYE (See Private Eye)

ROCKY LANE WESTERN (Allan Rocky Lane starred in Republic movies & TV for a short time as Allan Lane, Red Ryder & Rocky Lane) (See Black Jack Fawcett Movie Comics, Motion Picture Comics & Six-Gun Heroes)
Fawcett Publications/Charlton No. 56 on: May, 1949 - No. 87, Nov, 1959

	GD2.0	FN6.0	NM9.4
1 (36 pgs.)-Rocky, his stallion Black Jack, & Slim Pickens begin; photo-c begin, end #57; photo back-c	97.00	291.00	925.00
2 (36 pgs.)-Last photo back-c	40.00	120.00	360.00
3-5 (52 pgs.): 4-Captain Tootsie by Beck	30.00	90.00	240.00
6,10 (36 pgs.): 10-Complete western novelette "Badman's Reward"	21.00	64.00	170.00
7-9 (52 pgs.)	23.00	68.00	180.00
11-13,15-17 (52 pgs.): 15-Black Jack's Hitching Post begins, ends #25	17.00	51.00	135.00
14,18 (36 pgs.)	14.00	41.00	110.00
19-21,23,24 (52 pgs.): 20-Last Slim Pickens. 21-Dee Dickens begins, ends #55,57,65-68	14.00	41.00	110.00
22,25-28,30 (36 pgs. begin)	13.00	39.00	105.00
29-Classic complete novel "The Land of Missing Men" with hidden land of ancient temple ruins (r-in #65)	19.00	56.00	150.00
31-40	12.00	36.00	95.00
41-54	10.00	30.00	80.00
55-Last Fawcett issue (1/54)	11.00	33.00	90.00
56-1st Charlton issue (2/54)-Photo-c	19.00	56.00	150.00
57,60-Photo-c	11.00	33.00	90.00
58,59,61-64,66-78,80-86: 59-61-Young Falcon app. 64-Slim Pickens app. 66-68: Reprints #30,31,32	9.30	28.00	65.00
65-r/#29, "The Land of Missing Men"	10.00	30.00	75.00
79-Giant Edition (68 pgs.)	11.00	33.00	90.00
87-Last issue	10.00	30.00	80.00

NOTE: *Complete novels in #10, 14, 18, 22, 25, 30-32, 36, 38, 39, 49. Captain Tootsie in #4, 12, 20. Big Bow and Little Arrow in #11, 28, 63. Black Jack's Hitching Post in #15-25, 64, 73.*

ROCKY LANE WESTERN
AC Comics: 1989 ($2.50, B&W, one-shot?)

	GD2.0	FN6.0	NM9.4
1-Photo-c; Giordano reprints			4.00
Annual 1 (1991, $2.95, B&W, 44 pgs.)-photo front/back & inside-c; reprints.			4.00

ROD CAMERON WESTERN (Movie star)
Fawcett Publications: Feb, 1950 - No. 20, Apr, 1953

	GD2.0	FN6.0	NM9.4
1-Rod Cameron, his horse War Paint, & Sam The Sheriff begin; photo front/back-c begin	53.00	158.00	475.00
2	28.00	83.00	220.00

Rod Cameron Western #4 © FAW

Roly Poly Comic Book #12 © Green Pub. Co.

ROM #4 © Parker Brothers

3-Novel length story "The Mystery of the Seven Cities of Cibola"
23.00 68.00 180.00

4-10: 9-Last photo back-c 19.00 56.00 150.00

11-19 15.00 45.00 120.00

20-Last issue & photo-c 16.00 48.00 125.00

NOTE: *Novel length stories in No. 1-8, 12-14.*

RODEO RYAN (See A-1 Comics #8)

ROEL
Sirius: Feb, 1997 ($2.95, B&W, one-shot)

1 3.00

ROGAN GOSH
DC Comics (Vertigo): 1994 ($6.95, one-shot)

nn-Peter Milligan scripts 7.00

ROGER DODGER (Also in Exciting Comics #57 on)
Standard Comics: No. 5, Aug, 1952

5-Teen-age 5.00 15.00 30.00

ROGER RABBIT (Also see Marvel Graphic Novel)
Disney Comics: June, 1990 - No. 18, Nov, 1991 ($1.50)

1-18-All new stories 3.00

In 3-D 1 (1992, $2.50)-Sold at Wal-Mart?; w/glasses 4.00

ROGER RABBIT'S TOONTOWN
Disney Comics: Aug, 1991 - No. 5, Dec, 1991 ($1.50)

1-5 2.50

ROGER ZELAZNY'S AMBER: THE GUNS OF AVALON
DC Comics: 1996 - No. 3, 1996 ($6.95, limited series)

1-3: Based on novel 7.00

ROG 2000
Pacific Comics: June, 1982 ($2.95, 44 pgs., B&W, one-shot)

nn-Byrne-c/a (r) 1.25 3.75 10.00

2nd printing (7/82) 2.40 6.00

ROG 2000
Fantagraphics Books: 1987 - No. 2, 1987 ($2.00, limited series)

1,2-Byrne-r 3.00

ROGUE
Marvel Comics: Jan, 1995 - No. 4, Apr, 1995 ($2.95, limited series)

1-4: 1-Gold foil logo 4.00

TPB-($12.95) r/#1-4 13.00

ROGUES GALLERY
DC Comics: 1996 ($3.50, one-shot)

1-Pinups of DC villains by various artists 3.50

ROGUES, THE (VILLAINS) (See The Flash)
DC Comics: Feb, 1998 ($1.95, one-shot)

1-Augustyn-s/Pearson-c 2.00

ROGUE TROOPER
Quality Comics/Fleetway Quality #38-on : Oct, 1986 - No. 49, 1991 ($1.25/$1.50/$1.75)

1-49: 6-Double size. 21,22,25-27-Guice-c. 47,48-Alan Moore scripts 2.00

ROLLING STONES: VOODOO LOUNGE
Marvel Comics: 1995 ($6.95, Prestige format, one-shot)

nn-Dave McKean-script/design/art 7.00

ROLY POLY COMIC BOOK
Green Publishing Co.: 1945 - No. 15, 1946 (MLJ reprints)

1-Red Rube & Steel Sterling begin; Sahle-c 30.00 90.00 240.00

6-The Blue Circle & The Steel Fist app. 18.00 53.00 140.00

10-Origin Red Rube retold; Steel Sterling story (Zip #41)
26.00 79.00 210.00

11,12: The Black Hood app. in both 18.00 53.00 140.00

14-Classic decapitation-c; the Black Hood app. 38.00 113.00 300.00

15-The Blue Circle & The Steel Fist app.; cover exact swipe from Fox Blue Beetle #1 31.00 94.00 250.00

ROM (Based on the Parker Brothers toy)
Marvel Comics Group: Dec, 1979 - No. 75, Feb, 1986

1-Origin/1st app. 2.40 6.00

2-16,19-23,28-30: 5-Dr. Strange. 13-Saga of the Space Knights begins. 19-X-Men cameo. 23-Powerman & Iron Fist app. 3.00

17,18-X-Men app. 2.40 6.00

24-27: 24-F.F. cameo; Skrulls, Nova & The New Champions app. 25-Double size. 26,27-Galactus app. 3.50

31-49,51-60: 31,32-Brotherhood of Evil Mutants app. 32-X-Men cameo. 34,35-Sub-Mariner app. 41,42-Dr. Strange app. 56,57-Alpha Flight app. 58,59-Ant-Man app. 2.50

50-Skrulls app. (52 pgs.) Pin-ups by Konkle, Austin 4.00

61-74: 65-West Coast Avengers & Beta Ray Bill app. 65,66-X-Men app. 2.00

75-Last issue 2.40 6.00

Annual 1-4: (1982-85, 52 pgs.) 3.00

NOTE: ***Austin*** *c-3i, 18i, 61i.* ***Byrne*** *a-74i; c-56, 57, 74.* ***Ditko*** *a-59-75p, Annual 4.* ***Golden*** *c-7-12 19.* ***Guice*** *a-61i; c-55, 58, 60p, 70p.* ***Layton*** *a-59i, 72i; c-15, 59i, 69.* ***Miller*** *c-2p?, 3p, 17p, 18p.* ***Russell*** *a(i)-64, 65, 67, 69, 71, 75; c-64, 65i, 66, 71i, 75.* ***Severin*** *c-41p.* ***Sienkiewicz*** *a-53i; c-46 47, 52-54, 68, 71p, Annual 2.* ***Simonson*** *c-18.* ***P. Smith*** *c-59p.* ***Starlin*** *c-67.* ***Zeck*** *c-50.*

ROMANCE (See True Stories of...)

ROMANCE AND CONFESSION STORIES (See Giant Comics Edition)
St. John Publishing Co.: No date (1949) (25¢, 100 pgs.)

1-Baker-c/a; remaindered St. John love comics 40.00 120.00 340.00

ROMANCE DIARY
Marvel Comics (CDS)(CLDS): Dec, 1949 - No. 2, Mar, 1950

1,2 12.50 37.50 100.00

ROMANCE OF FLYING, THE
David McKay Publications: 1942

Feature Books 33 (nn)-WW II photos 14.00 41.00 110.00

ROMANCES OF MOLLY MANTON (See Molly Manton)

ROMANCES OF NURSE HELEN GRANT, THE
Atlas Comics (VPI): Aug, 1957

1 6.40 19.25 45.00

ROMANCES OF THE WEST (Becomes Romantic Affairs #3?)
Marvel Comics (SPC): Nov, 1949 - No. 2, Mar, 1950 (52 pgs.)

1-Movie photo-c of Yvonne DeCarlo & Howard Duff (Calamity Jane & Sam Bass) 22.00 66.00 175.00

2-Photo-c 14.00 43.00 115.00

ROMANCE STORIES OF TRUE LOVE (Formerly True Love Problems & Advice Illustrated)
Harvey Publications: No. 45, 5/57 - No. 50, 3/58; No. 51, 9/58 - No. 52, 11/58

45-51: 45,46,48-50-Powell-a 5.00 15.00 30.00

52-Matt Baker-a 7.85 23.50 55.00

ROMANCE TALES (Formerly Western Winners #6?)
Marvel Comics (CDS): No. 7, Oct, 1949 - No. 9, Mar, 1950 (7,8: photo-c)

7 12.50 37.50 100.00

8,9: 8-Everett-a 10.00 30.00 70.00

ROMANCE TRAIL
National Periodical Publications: July-Aug, 1949 - No. 6, May-June, 1950 (All photo-c & 52 pgs.)

1-Kinstler, Toth-a; Jimmy Wakely photo-c 58.00 174.00 550.00

2-Kinstler-a; Jim Bannon photo-c 32.00 96.00 255.00

3-Photo-c; Kinstler, Toth-a 35.00 105.00 280.00

4-Photo-c; Toth-a 25.00 75.00 200.00

5,6: Photo-c on both. 5-Kinstler-a 22.00 66.00 175.00

ROMAN HOLIDAYS, THE (TV)
Gold Key: Feb, 1973 - No. 4, Nov, 1973 (Hanna-Barbera)

1 3.65 11.00 40.00

2-4 2.50 7.50 25.00

ROMANTIC ADVENTURES (My... #49-67, covers only)
American Comics Group (B&I Publ. Co.): Mar-Apr, 1949 - No. 67, July, 1956 (Becomes My... #68 on)

Romantic Adventures #4 © ACG

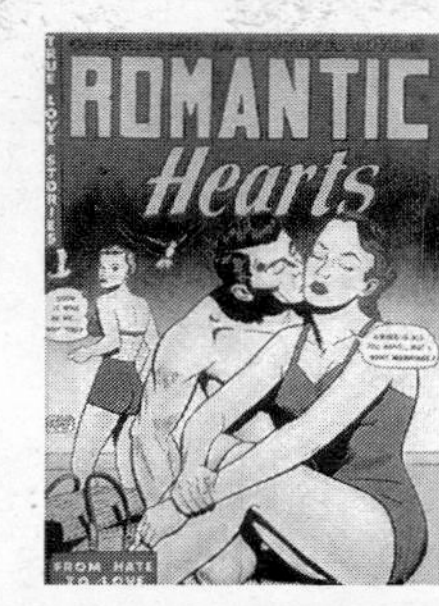

Romantic Hearts #3 © Story

Ronin #3 © Frank Miller

	GD2.0	FN6.0	NM9.4
1	16.00	49.00	130.00
2	9.30	28.00	65.00
3-10	6.00	18.00	42.00
11-20 (4/52)	5.00	15.00	32.00
21-45,49,51,52: 52-Last Pre-code (2/55)	4.65	14.00	28.00
46-48-3-D effect-c/stories (TrueVision)	10.00	30.00	80.00
50-Classic cover/story "Love of A Lunatic"	9.30	28.00	65.00
53-67	4.00	11.00	22.00

NOTE: *#1-23, 52 pgs.* ***Shelly*** *a-40. Whitney c/art in many issues.*

ROMANTIC AFFAIRS (Formerly Molly Manton's Romances #2 and/or Romances of the West #2 and/or Our Love #2?)
Marvel Comics (SPC): No. 3, Mar, 1950

	GD2.0	FN6.0	NM9.4
3-Photo-c from Molly Manton's Romances #2	8.65	26.00	60.00

ROMANTIC CONFESSIONS
Hillman Periodicals: Oct, 1949 - V3#1, Apr-May, 1953

	GD2.0	FN6.0	NM9.4
V1#1-McWilliams-a	15.00	45.00	120.00
2-Briefer-a; negligee panels	9.30	28.00	65.00
3-12	6.40	19.25	45.00
V2#1,2,4-8,10-12: 2-McWilliams-a	5.00	15.00	35.00
3-Krigstein-a	7.85	23.50	55.00
9-One pg. Frazetta ad	5.00	15.00	35.00
V3#1	5.00	15.00	32.00

ROMANTIC HEARTS
Story Comics/Master/Merit Pubs.: Mar, 1951 - No. 10, Oct, 1952; July, 1953 - No. 12, July, 1955

	GD2.0	FN6.0	NM9.4
1(3/51) (1st Series)	12.50	37.50	100.00
2	7.15	21.50	50.00
3-10: Cameron-a	5.70	17.00	40.00
1(7/53) (2nd Series)-Some say #11 on-c	8.65	26.00	60.00
2	5.00	15.00	35.00
3-12	4.65	14.00	28.00

ROMANTIC LOVE
Avon Periodicals/Realistic (No #14-19): 9-10/49 - #3, 1-2/50; #4, 2-3/51 - #13, 10/52; #20, 3-4/54 - #23, 9-10/54

	GD2.0	FN6.0	NM9.4
1-c-/Avon paperback #252	24.00	71.00	190.00
2-5: 3-c-/paperback Novel Library #12. 4-c-/paperback Diversey Prize Novel #5. 5-c-/paperback Novel Library #34	14.00	41.00	110.00
6- "Thrill Crazy" marijuana story; c-/Avon paperback #207; Kinstler-a	20.00	60.00	160.00
7,8: 8-Astarita-a(2)	12.50	37.50	100.00
9-12: 9-c-/paperback Novel Library #41; Kinstler-a. 10-c-/Avon paperback #212. 11-c-/paperback Novel Library #17; Kinstler-a. 12-c-/paperback Novel Library #13	14.00	41.00	110.00
13,21-23: 22,23-Kinstler-c	12.50	37.50	100.00
20-Kinstler-c/a	13.00	39.00	105.00
nn(1-3/53)(Realistic-r)	9.30	28.00	65.00

NOTE: ***Astarita*** *a-7, 10, 11, 21. Painted c-1-3, 5, 7-11, 13. Photo c-4, 6.*

ROMANTIC LOVE
Quality Comics Group: 1963-1964

	GD2.0	FN6.0	NM9.4
I.W. Reprint #2,3,8: 2-r/Romantic Love #2	1.50	4.50	12.00

ROMANTIC MARRIAGE (Cinderella Love #25 on)
Ziff-Davis/St. John No. 18 on (#1-8: 52 pgs.): #1-3 (1950, no months); #4, 5-6/51 - #17, 9/52; #18, 9/53 - #24, 9/54

	GD2.0	FN6.0	NM9.4
1-Photo-c; Cary Grant/Betsy Drake photo back-c.	19.00	56.00	150.00
2-Painted-c; Anderson-a (also #15)	12.00	36.00	95.00
3-9: 3,4,8,9-Painted-c; 5-7-Photo-c	10.00	30.00	70.00
10-Unusual format; front-c is a painted-c; back-c is a photo-c complete with logo, price, etc.	18.00	53.00	140.00
11-17 13-Photo-c. 15-Signed story by Anderson. 17-(9/52)-Last Z-D issue	9.30	28.00	65.00
18-22,24: 20-Photo-c	9.30	28.00	65.00
23-Baker-c; all stories are reprinted from #15	10.00	30.00	70.00

ROMANTIC PICTURE NOVELETTES
Magazine Enterprises: 1946

	GD2.0	FN6.0	NM9.4
1-Mary Worth-r; Creig Flessel-c	16.00	49.00	130.00

ROMANTIC SECRETS (Becomes Time For Love)
Fawcett/Charlton Comics No. 5 (10/55) on: Sept, 1949 - No. 39, 4/53; No. 5, 10/55 - No. 52, 11/64 (#1-5: photo-c)

	GD2.0	FN6.0	NM9.4
1-(52 pg. issues begin, end #?)	15.00	45.00	120.00
2,3	9.30	28.00	65.00
4,9-Evans-a	10.00	30.00	70.00
5-8,10	6.40	19.25	45.00
11-23	5.70	17.00	40.00
24-Evans-a	7.15	21.50	50.00
25-39('53)	5.00	15.00	35.00
5 (Charlton, 2nd Series)(10/55, formerly Negro Romances #4)	9.30	28.00	65.00
6-10	6.40	19.25	45.00
11-20	3.00	9.00	30.00
21-35: Last 10¢ issue?	2.40	7.35	22.00
36-52('64)	2.00	6.00	18.00

NOTE: ***Bailey*** *a-20.* ***Powell*** *a(1st series)-5, 7, 10, 12, 16, 17, 20, 26, 29, 33, 34, 36, 37.* ***Sekowsky*** *a-26. Photo c(1st series)-1-5, 16, 25, 27, 33.* ***Swayze*** *a(1st series)-16, 18, 19, 23, 26-28, 31, 32, 39.*

ROMANTIC STORY (Cowboy Love #28 on)
Fawcett/Charlton Comics No. 23 on: 11/49 - #22, Sum, 1953; #23, 5/54 - #27, 12/54; #28, 8/55 - #130, 11/73

	GD2.0	FN6.0	NM9.4
1-Photo-c begin, end #24; 52 pgs. begins	16.00	49.00	130.00
2	9.30	28.00	65.00
3-5	7.85	23.50	55.00
6-14	6.40	19.25	45.00
15-Evans-a	7.85	23.50	55.00
16-22(Sum, '53; last Fawcett issue). 21-Toth-a?	5.00	15.00	35.00
23-39: 26,29-Wood swipes	5.00	15.00	32.00
40-(100 pgs.)	10.00	30.00	80.00
41-50	2.50	7.50	24.00
51-80: 57-Hypo needle story	2.00	6.00	18.00
81-99	1.50	4.50	12.00
100	1.85	5.50	15.00
101-130	1.25	3.75	10.00

NOTE: ***Jim Aparo*** *a-94.* ***Powell*** *a-7, 8, 16, 20, 30.* ***Marcus Swayze*** *a-2, 12, 20, 32.*

ROMANTIC THRILLS (See Fox Giants)

ROMANTIC WESTERN
Fawcett Publications: Winter, 1949 - No. 3, June, 1950 (All Photo-c)

	GD2.0	FN6.0	NM9.4
1	21.00	64.00	170.00
2-(Spr/50)-Williamson, McWilliams-a	20.00	60.00	160.00
3	14.00	41.00	110.00

ROMEO TUBBS (...That Lovable Teenager; formerly My Secret Life)
Fox Feature Syndicate/Green Publ. Co. No. 27: No. 26, 5/50 - No. 28, 7/50; No. 1, 1950; No. 27, 12/52

	GD2.0	FN6.0	NM9.4
26-Teen-age	10.00	30.00	80.00
28 (7/50)	10.00	30.00	70.00
27 (12/52)-Contains Pedro on inside; Wood-a	15.00	45.00	120.00

RONALD McDONALD (TV)
Charlton Press (King Features Synd.): Sept, 1970 - No. 4, March, 1971

	GD2.0	FN6.0	NM9.4
1	6.80	20.50	75.00
2-4	3.65	11.00	40.00
V2#1,3-Special reprint for McDonald systems; "Not for resale" on cover	5.00	15.00	55.00

RONIN
DC Comics: July, 1983 - No. 6, Aug, 1984 ($2.50, limited series, 52 pgs.)

	GD2.0	FN6.0	NM9.4
1-5-Frank Miller-c/a/scripts in all			5.00
6-Scarcer; has fold-out poster.	1.00	3.00	8.00
Trade paperback (1987, $12.95)-Reprints #1-6			13.00

RONNA
Knight Press: Apr, 1997 ($2.95, B&W, one-shot)

	GD2.0	FN6.0	NM9.4
1-Beau Smith-s			3.00

ROOK (See Eerie Magazine & Warren Presents: The Rook)
Warren Publications: Oct, 1979 - No. 14, April, 1982

	GD2.0	FN6.0	NM9.4
1-Nino-a/Corben-c	1.85	5.50	15.00

Rose #1 © Jeff Smith

Roswell: Little Green Man #2 © Bongo Entertainment

Roy Rogers Comics #3 © DELL

GD2.0 FN6.0 NM9.4

2-14: 3,4-Toth-a 1.25 3.75 10.00

ROOK
Harris Comics: No. 0, Jun, 1995 - No. 4, 1995 ($2.95)
0-4: 0-short stories (3) w/preview. 4-Brereton-c. 3.00

ROOKIE COP (Formerly Crime and Justice?)
Charlton Comics: No. 27, Nov, 1955 - No. 33, Aug, 1957
27 8.65 26.00 60.00
28-33 6.00 18.00 42.00

ROOM 222 (TV)
Dell Publishing Co.: Jan, 1970; No. 2, May, 1970 - No. 4, Jan, 1971
1 4.55 13.65 50.00
2-4: 2,4-Photo-c. 3-Marijuana story. 4 r/#1 3.00 9.00 32.00

ROOTIE KAZOOTIE (TV)(See 3-D-ell)
Dell Publishing Co.: No. 415, Aug, 1952 - No. 6, Oct-Dec, 1954
Four Color 415 (#1) 10.00 30.00 120.00
Four Color 459,502(#2,3), 4(4-6/54)-6 6.70 20.00 80.00

ROOTS OF THE SWAMP THING
DC Comics: July, 1986 - No.5, Nov, 1986 ($2.00, Baxter paper, 52 pgs.)
1-5: r/Swamp Thing #1-10 by Wrightson & House of Mystery-r. 1-new Wrightson-c (2-5 reprinted covers). 4.00

ROSE (See Bone)
Cartoon Books: Nov, 2000 - No. 3 ($5.95, limited series, square-bound)
1-Jeff Smith-s/Charles Vess painted-a/c 5.95

ROSE N' GUNN
Bishop Press: Jan, 1995 - No. 6, May, 1996 ($2.95, B&W, mature)
1-6, Creator's Choice ($2.95)-reprints w/pin-ups 3.00

ROSE N'GUNN
London Night Studios: June, 1996 - Aug, 1996 ($3.00, B&W, mature)
1,2 3.00
1-($6.00)-Blood & Glory Edition 6.00

ROSWELL: LITTLE GREEN MAN (See Simpsons Comics #19-22)
Bongo Comics: 1996 - Present ($2.95, quarterly)
1-6 3.50
...Walks Among Us ('97, $12.95, TPB) r/ #1-3 & Simpsons flip books 13.00

ROUNDUP (...Western Crime Stories)
D. S. Publishing Co.: July-Aug, 1948 - No. 5, Mar-Apr, 1949 (All 52 pgs.)
1-Kiefer-a 20.00 60.00 160.00
2-5: 2-Marijuana drug mention story 14.00 41.00 110.00

ROYAL ROY
Marvel Comics (Star Comics): May, 1985 - No.6, Mar, 1986 (Children's book)
1-6 3.00

ROY CAMPANELLA, BASEBALL HERO
Fawcett Publications: 1950 (Brooklyn Dodgers)
nn-Photo-c; life story 58.00 174.00 550.00

ROY ROGERS (See March of Comics #17, 35, 47, 62, 68, 73, 77, 86, 91, 100, 105, 116, 121, 131, 136, 146, 151, 161, 167, 176, 191, 206, 221, 236, 250)

ROY ROGERS AND TRIGGER
Gold Key: Apr, 1967
1-Photo-c; reprints 4.55 13.65 50.00

ROY ROGERS ANNUAL
Wilson Publ. Co., Toronto/Dell: 1947 ("Giant Edition" on-c)(132 pgs., 50¢)
nn-(One known copy in VG/FN which sold in 1986 for $400, & 1996 for $1200 & 2000 for $1500)

ROY ROGERS COMICS (See Western Roundup under Dell Giants)
Dell Publishing Co.: No. 38, 4/44 - No. 177, 12/47 (#38-166: 52 pgs.)
Four Color 38 (1944)-49 pg. story; photo front/back-c on all 4-Color issues (1st western comic with photo-c) 217.00 650.00 2600.00
Four Color 63 (1945)-Color photos on all four-c 48.00 144.00 575.00
Four Color 86,95 (1945) 35.00 106.00 425.00
Four Color 109 (1946) 27.00 80.00 320.00
Four Color 117,124,137,144 21.00 63.00 250.00
Four Color 153,160,166: 166-48 pg. story 19.00 57.00 225.00
Four Color 177 (36 pgs.)-32 pg. story 19.00 57.00 225.00

ROY ROGERS COMICS (...& Trigger #92(8/55)-on)(Roy starred in Republic movies, radio & TV) (Singing cowboy) (Also see Dale Evans, It Really Happened #8, Queen of the West Dale Evans, & Roy Rogers' Trigger)
Dell Publishing Co.: Jan, 1948 - No. 145, Sept-Oct, 1961 (#1-19: 36 pgs.)
1-Roy, his horse Trigger, & Chuck Wagon Charley's Tales begin; photo-c begin, end #145 79.00 238.00 950.00
2 27.00 81.00 325.00
3-5 19.00 57.00 225.00
6-10 15.00 45.00 175.00
11-19: 19-Chuck Wagon Charley's Tales ends 11.30 34.00 135.00
20 (52 pgs.)-Trigger feature begins, ends #46 11.30 34.00 135.00
21-30 (52 pgs.) 9.50 29.00 115.00
31-46 (52 pgs.): 37-X-Mas-c 7.50 22.50 90.00
47-56 (36 pgs.): 47-Chuck Wagon Charley's Tales returns, ends #133. 49-X-mas-c. 55-Last photo back-c 5.35 16.00 65.00
57 (52 pgs.)-Heroin drug propaganda story 5.85 17.50 70.00
58-70 (52 pgs.): 58-Heroin drug use/dealing story. 61-X-Mas-c 5.35 16.00 65.00
71-80 (52 pgs.): 73-X-Mas-c 4.60 13.75 55.00
81-91 (36 pgs. #81-on): 85-X-Mas-c 4.55 13.65 50.00
92-99,101-110,112-118: 92-Title changed to Roy Rogers and Trigger (8/55) 4.35 13.00 48.00
100-Trigger feature returns, ends #131 5.35 16.00 65.00
111,119-124-Toth-a 5.85 17.50 70.00
125-131: 125-Toth-a (1 pg.) 3.65 11.00 40.00
132-144-Manning-a. 132-1st Dale Evans-sty by Russ Manning. 138,144-Dale Evans featured 4.60 13.75 55.00
145-Last issue 5.85 17.50 70.00
NOTE: ***Buscema** a-74-108(2 stories each). **Manning** a-123, 124, 132-144. **Marsh** a-110. Photo back-c No. 1-9, 11-35, 38-55.*

ROY ROGERS' TRIGGER (TV)
Dell Publishing Co.: No. 329, May, 1951 - No. 17, June-Aug, 1955
Four Color 329 (#1)-Painted-c 12.50 37.50 150.00
2 (9-11/51)-Photo-c 10.50 31.00 125.00
3-5: 3-Painted-c begin, end #17, most by S. Savitt 4.60 13.75 55.00
6-17: Title merges with Roy Rogers after #17 3.65 11.00 40.00

ROY ROGERS WESTERN CLASSICS
AC Comics: 1989 -No. 4 ($2.95/$3.95, 44pgs.) (24 pgs. color, 16 pgs. B&W)
1-4: 1-Dale Evans-r by Manning, Trigger-r by Buscema; photo covers & interior photos by Roy & Dale. 2-Buscema-r (3); photo-c & B&W photos inside. 3-Dale Evans-r by Manning; Trigger-r by Buscema plus other Buscema-r; photo-c. 4.00

RUDOLPH, THE RED-NOSED REINDEER
National Per. Publ.: 1950 - No. 13, Winter, 1962-63 (Issues are not numbered)
1950 issue (#1); Grossman-c/a begins 21.00 62.00 165.00
1951-53 issues (3 total) 12.00 36.00 95.00
1954/55, 55/56, 56/57 10.00 30.00 75.00
1957/58, 58/59, 59/60, 60/61, 61/62 5.90 17.75 65.00
1962/63 (rare) 10.00 30.00 110.00
NOTE: *The 1962-63 issue is 84 pages. 9? total issues published. Has games & puzzles also.*

RUDOLPH, THE RED-NOSED REINDEER (Also see Limited Collectors' Edition C-20, C-24, C-33, C-42, C-50; and All-New Collectors' Edition C-53 & C-60)
National Per. Publ.: Christmas 1972 (Treasury-size)
nn-Precursor to Limited Collectors' Edition title (scarce) (implied to be Lim. Coll .Ed.C-20) 25.00 75.00 275.00

RUFF AND REDDY (TV)
Dell Publ. Co.: No. 937, 9/58 - No. 12, 1-3/62 (Hanna-Barbera)(#9 on: 15¢)
Four Color 937(#1)(1st Hanna-Barbera comic book) 12.50 37.50 150.00
Four Color 981,1038 8.00 24.00 95.00
4(1-3/60)-12: 8-Last 10¢ issue 6.30 19.00 75.00

RUGGED ACTION (Strange Stories of Suspense #5 on)

Rulah Jungle Goddess #25 © FOX

Rune #5 © MAL

Rusty Comics #14 © MAR

GD2.0 FN6.0 NM9.4

Atlas Comics (CSI): Dec, 1954 - No. 4, June, 1955

1-Brodsky-c 12.50 37.50 100.00
2-4: 2-Last precode (2/55) 9.30 28.00 65.00
NOTE: *Ayers a-2, 3. **Maneely** c-2, 3. **Severin** a-2.*

RUGRATS COMIC ADVENTURES (TV)
Nickelodeon Magazines: 1999 - Present ($2.95, magazine size)

1-5 3.00
Volume 2: 1-6 2.95

RUINS
Marvel Comics (Alterniverse): July, 1995 - No. 2, Sept, 1995 ($5.00, painted, limited series)

1,2: Phil Sheldon from Marvels; Warren Ellis scripts; acetate-c 5.00

RULAH JUNGLE GODDESS (Formerly Zoot; I Loved #28 on) (Also see All Top Comics & Terrors of the Jungle)
Fox Features Syndicate: No. 17, Aug, 1948 - No. 27, June, 1949

17 92.00 276.00 875.00
18-Classic girl-fight interior splash 65.00 195.00 625.00
19,20 62.00 186.00 585.00
21-Used in **SOTI**, pg. 388,389 65.00 195.00 625.00
22-Used in **SOTI**, pg. 22,23 62.00 186.00 585.00
23-27 50.00 150.00 450.00
NOTE: ***Kamen** c-17-19, 21, 22.*

RUMBLE GIRLS: SILKY WARRIOR TANSIE
Image Comics: Apr, 2000 - Present ($3.50, B&W)

1-5-Lea Hernandez-s/a. 2-Adam Warren flip-c. 5-Warren Ellis short story 3.50

RUNAWAY, THE (See Movie Classics)

RUN BABY RUN
Logos International: 1974 (39¢, Christian religious)

nn-By Tony Tallarico from Nicky Cruz's book 1.00 2.80 7.00

RUN, BUDDY, RUN (TV)
Gold Key: June, 1967 (Photo-c)

1 (10204-706) 2.50 7.50 25.00

RUNE (See Curse of Rune, Sludge & all other Ultraverse titles for previews)
Malibu Comics (Ultraverse): 1994 - No. 9, Apr, 1995 ($1.95)

0-Obtained by sending coupons from 11 comics; came w/Solution #0, poster, temporary tattoo, card 1.00 3.00 8.00
1,2,4-9: 1-Barry Windsor-Smith-c/a/stories begin, ends #6. 5-1st app. of Gemini. 6-Prime & Mantra app. 2.00
1-(1/94)-"Ashcan" edition flip book w/Wrath #1 2.00
1-Ultra 5000 Limited silver foil edition 4.00
3-(3/94, $3.50, 68 pgs.)-Flip book w/Ultraverse Premiere #1 3.50
Giant Size 1 ($2.50, 44 pgs.)-B.Smith story & art. 2.50

RUNE (2nd Series)(Formerly Curse of Rune)(See Ultraverse Unlimited #1)
Malibu Comics (Ultraverse): Infinity, Sept, 1995 - V2#7, Apr, 1996 ($1.50)

Infinity, V2#1-7: Infinity-Black September tie-in; black-c & painted-c exist. 1,3-7-Marvel's Adam Warlock app; regular & painted-c exist. 2-Flip book w/ "Phoenix Resurrection" Pt. 6. 2.00
...Vs. Venom 1 (12/95, $3.95) 4.00

RUNE: HEARTS OF DARKNESS
Malibu Comics (Ultraverse): Sept, 1996 - No. 3, Nov, 1996 ($1.50, lim. series)

1-3: Doug Moench scripts & Kyle Hotz-c/a; flip books w/6 pg. Rune story by the Pander Bros. 2.00

RUNE/SILVER SURFER
Marvel Comics/Malibu Comics (Ultraverse): Apr, 1995 ($5.95/$2.95, one-shot)

1 ($5.95, direct market)-BWS-c 6.00
1 ($2.95, newstand)-BWS-c 3.00
1-Collector's limited edition 6.00

RUST
Now Comics: 7/87 - No. 15, 11/88; V2#1, 2/89 - No. 7, 1989 ($1.50/$1.75)

1-15,V2#1-7: 12-(8/88)-5 pg. preview of The Terminator (1st app.) 2.00

RUST
Caliber Comics: 1996/1997 ($2.95, B&W)

1,2 3.00

RUSTLERS, THE (See Zane Grey Four Color 532)

RUSTY, BOY DETECTIVE
Good Comics/Lev Gleason: Mar-April, 1955 - No. 5, Nov, 1955

1-Bob Wood, Carl Hubbell-a begins 8.65 26.00 60.00
2-5 5.00 15.00 35.00

RUSTY COMICS (Formerly Kid Movie Comics; Rusty and Her Family #21, 22; The Kelleys #23 on; see Millie The Model)
Marvel Comics (HPC): No. 12, Apr, 1947 - No. 22, Sept, 1949

12-Mitzi app. 19.00 56.00 150.00
13 10.00 30.00 75.00
14-Wolverton's Powerhouse Pepper (4 pgs.) plus Kurtzman's "Hey Look" 21.00 62.00 165.00
15-17-Kurtzman's "Hey Look" 15.00 45.00 120.00
18,19 9.30 28.00 65.00
20-Kurtzman-a (5 pgs.) 16.00 48.00 125.00
21,22-Kurtzman-a (17 & 22 pgs.) 21.00 62.00 165.00

RUSTY DUGAN (See Holyoke One-Shot #2)

RUSTY RILEY
Dell Publishing Co.: No. 418, Aug, 1952 - No. 554, April, 1954 (Frank Godwin strip reprints)

Four Color 418 (...a Boy, a Horse, and a Dog #1 4.10 12.30 45.00
Four Color #451(2/53), 486 ('53), 554 3.20 9.60 35.00

SAARI ("The Jungle Goddess")
P. L. Publishing Co.: November, 1951

1 42.00 125.00 375.00

SABAN POWERHOUSE (TV)
Acclaim Books: 1997 ($4.50, digest size)

1,2-Power Rangers, BeetleBorgs, and others 4.50

SABAN PRESENTS POWER RANGERS TURBO VS. BEETLEBORGS METALLIX (TV)
Acclaim Books: 1997 ($4.50, digest size, one-shot)

nn 4.50

SABAN'S MIGHTY MORPHIN POWER RANGERS
Hamilton Comics: Dec, 1994 - No. 6, May, 1995 ($1.95, limited series)

1-6: 1-w/bound-in Power Ranger Barcode Card 2.00

SABAN'S MIGHTY MORPHIN POWER RANGERS (TV)
Marvel Comics: 1995 - No. 8, 1996 ($1.75)

1-8 2.00

SABAN'S NINJA RANGERS
Hamilton Comics: Dec, 1995 - No. 4, Mar, 1995 ($1.95, limited series)

1-4: Flip book w/Saban's V.R. Troopers 2.00

SABAN'S V.R. TROOPERS (See Saban's Ninja Rangers)

SABLE (Formerly Jon Sable, Freelance; also see Mike Grell's...)
First Comics: Mar, 1988 - No. 27, May, 1990 ($1.75/$1.95)

1-27: 10-Begin $1.95-c 2.00

SABRE (See Eclipse Graphic Album Series)
Eclipse Comics: Aug, 1982 - No. 14, Aug, 1985 (Baxter paper #4 on)

1-14: 1-Sabre & Morrigan Tales begin. 4-6-Incredible Seven origin 2.00

SABRETOOTH (See Iron Fist, Power Man, X-Factor #10 & X-Men)
Marvel Comics: Aug, 1993 - No. 4, Nov, 1993 ($2.95, lim. series, coated paper)

1-4: 1-Die-cut-c. 3-Wolverine app. 4.00
...Special 1 "In the Red Zone"(1995, $4.95) Chromium wraparound-c 6.00
V2 #1 (1/98, $5.95, one-shot) Wildchild app. 6.00
Trade paperback (12/94, $12.95) r/#1-4 13.00

SABRETOOTH AND MYSTIQUE (See Mystique and Sabretooth)

SABRETOOTH CLASSIC
Marvel Comics: May, 1994 - No. 15, July, 1995 ($1.50)

Sabretooth Classic #5 © MAR

Sabrina the Teen-Age Witch #60 © AP

Saddle Romances #9 © WMG

1-15: 1-3-r/Power Man & Iron Fist #66,78,84. 4-r/Spec. S-M #116. 9-Uncanny X-Men #212, 10-r/Uncanny X-Men #213. 11-r/ Daredevil #238. 12-r/Classic X-Men #10 — 3.00

SABRINA (Volume 2) (Based on animated series)
Archie Publications: Jan, 2000 - Present ($1.79/$1.99)

	GD2.0	FN6.0	NM9.4
1-Teen-age Witch magically reverted to 12 years old			2.00
2-14: 4-Begin $1.99-c			2.00

SABRINA'S CHRISTMAS MAGIC (See Archie Giant Series Magazine #196, 207, 220, 231, 243, 455, 467, 479, 491, 503, 515)

SABRINA'S HALLOWEEN SPOOOKTACULAR
Archie Publications: 1993 - 1995 ($2.00, 52 pgs.)

	GD2.0	FN6.0	NM9.4
1-Neon orange ink-c; bound-in poster		2.40	6.00
2,3			4.00

SABRINA, THE TEEN-AGE WITCH (TV)(See Archie Giant Series, Archie's Madhouse 22, Archie's TV..., Chilling Advs. In Sorcery, Little Archie #59)
Archie Publications: April, 1971 - No. 77, Jan, 1983 (52 pg.Giants No. 1-17)

	GD2.0	FN6.0	NM9.4
1-52 pgs. begin, end #17	12.50	37.00	135.00
2-Archie's group x-over	5.90	17.75	65.00
3-5: 3,4-Archie's Group x-over	3.65	11.00	40.00
6-10	3.20	9.60	35.00
11-17(2/74)	2.80	8.40	28.00
18-30	2.30	7.00	20.00
31-40(8/77)	1.85	5.50	15.00
41-60(6/80)	1.25	3.75	10.00
61-70	1.00	3.00	8.00
71-76	1.10	3.30	9.00
77-Last issue; low print run	1.50	4.50	12.00

SABRINA, THE TEEN-AGE WITCH
Archie Publications: 1996 ($1.50, 32 pgs., one-shot)

	GD2.0	FN6.0	NM9.4
1-Updated origin			4.00

SABRINA, THE TEEN-AGE WITCH (Continues in Sabrina, Vol. 2)
Archie Publications: May, 1997 - No. 32, Dec, 1999 ($1.50/$1.75/$1.79)

	GD2.0	FN6.0	NM9.4
1-Photo-c with Melissa Joan Hart		2.40	6.00
2-10: 9-Begin $1.75-c			4.00
11-20			3.00
21-32: 24-Begin $1.79-c. 28-Sonic the Hedgehog-c/app.			2.50

SABU, "ELEPHANT BOY" (Movie; formerly My Secret Story)
Fox Features Syndicate: No. 30, June, 1950 - No. 2, Aug, 1950

	GD2.0	FN6.0	NM9.4
30(#1)-Wood-a; photo-c from movie	26.00	79.00	210.00
2-Photo-c from movie; Kamen-a	19.00	56.00	150.00

SACHS & VIOLENS
Marvel Comics (Epic Comics): Nov, 1993 - No. 4, July, 1994 ($2.25, limited series, mature)

	GD2.0	FN6.0	NM9.4
1-($2.75)-Embossed-c w/bound-in trading card			2.75
1-($3.50)-Platinum edition (1 for each 10 ordered)			4.00
2-4: Perez-c/a; bound-in trading card: 2-(5/94)			2.25

SACRAMENTS, THE
Catechetical Guild Educational Society: Oct, 1955 (25¢)

	GD2.0	FN6.0	NM9.4
304	4.00	11.00	22.00

SACRED AND THE PROFANE, THE (See Eclipse Graphic Album Series #9 & Epic Illustrated #20)

SADDLE JUSTICE (Happy Houlihans #1,2) (Saddle Romances #9 on)
E. C. Comics: No. 3, Spring, 1948 - No. 8, Sept-Oct, 1949

	GD2.0	FN6.0	NM9.4
3-The 1st E.C. by Bill Gaines to break away from M. C. Gaines' old Educational Comics format. Craig, Feldstein, H. C. Kiefer, & Stan Asch-a; mentioned in Love and Death	46.00	138.00	415.00
4-1st Graham Ingels-a for E.C.	42.00	125.00	375.00
5-8-Ingels-a in all	40.00	120.00	350.00

NOTE: *Craig and Feldstein art in most issues. Canadian reprints known; see Table of Contents.* ***Craig*** *c-3, 4.* ***Ingels*** *c-5-8. #4 contains a biography of* ***Craig.***

SADDLE ROMANCES (Saddle Justice #3-8; Weird Science #12 on)
E. C. Comics: No. 9, Nov-Dec, 1949 - No. 11, Mar-Apr, 1950

	GD2.0	FN6.0	NM9.4
9,11: 9-Ingels-c/a. 11-Ingels-a; Feldstein-c	42.00	125.00	375.00
10-Wood's 1st work at E. C.; Ingels-a; Feldstein-c	43.00	129.00	390.00

NOTE: *Canadian reprints known; see Table of Contents.* ***Wood/Harrison*** *a-10, 11.*

SADE
Bishop Press/London Night Studios: No. 0, May, 1995 - No. 2, 1996 ($2.95, B&W, mature)

	GD2.0	FN6.0	NM9.4
0-2: All Bishop Press issues. 1-Razor app; w/pin-ups			3.00
1($3.00)-London Night Studio's Encore Edition.			3.00
Special 1-Razor app.			3.00
Special 1 ($4.95, limited edition)-Razor app.			5.00

SADE
London Night Studios: June, 1996 - No. 4 ($3.00, B&W, mature)

	GD2.0	FN6.0	NM9.4
1-4, 1-Balance of Pain Edition			3.00

SADE AND ROSE & GUNN CONFEDERATE MISTS
Bishop Press: Mar, 1996 ($3.00, B&W, one-shot, mature)

	GD2.0	FN6.0	NM9.4
1-w/pin-ups.			3.00

SADIE SACK (See Harvey Hits #93)

SAD SACK AND THE SARGE
Harvey Publications: Sept, 1957 - No. 155, June, 1982

	GD2.0	FN6.0	NM9.4
1	12.50	37.00	135.00
2	5.90	17.75	65.00
3-10	4.10	12.30	45.00
11-20	3.65	11.00	40.00
21-30	2.50	7.50	25.00
31-50	2.00	6.00	16.00
51-70	1.50	4.50	12.00
71-90,97-99	1.00	3.00	8.00
91-96: All 52 pg. Giants	1.75	5.25	14.00
100	1.25	3.75	10.00
101-120		2.40	6.00
121-155			4.00

SAD SACK COMICS (See Harvey Collector's Comics #16, Little Sad Sack, Tastee Freez Comics #4 & True Comics #55)
Harvey Publications/Lorne-Harvey Publications (Recollections) #288 On: Sept, 1949 - No. 287, Oct, 1982; No. 288, 1992 - No. 293?, 1993

	GD2.0	FN6.0	NM9.4
1-Infinity-c; Little Dot begins (1st app.); civilian issues begin, end #21; based on comic strip	41.00	123.00	450.00
2-Flying Fool by Powell	20.50	61.00	225.00
3	11.50	34.00	125.00
4-10	8.15	24.50	90.00
11-21	5.90	17.75	65.00
22-("Back In The Army Again" on covers #22-36); "The Specialist" story about Sad Sack's return to Army	5.45	16.35	60.00
23-50	3.00	9.00	30.00
51-80,100: 62-"The Specialist" reprinted	2.50	7.50	24.00
81-99	2.30	7.00	20.00
101-140	2.00	6.00	16.00
141-170,200	1.75	5.25	14.00
171-199	1.50	4.50	12.00
201-207: 207-Last 12¢ issue	1.10	3.30	9.00
208-222	1.00	2.80	7.00
223-228 (25¢ Giants, 52 pgs.)	1.50	4.50	12.00
229-285			5.00
286,287-Limited distribution	1.00	2.80	7.00
288,289 ($2.75, 1992): 289-50th anniversary issue			5.00
290-293 ($1.00, 1993, B&W)			3.00
3-D 1 (1/54, 25¢)-Came with 2 pairs of glasses; titled "Harvey 3-D Hits"	17.00	51.00	185.00
...At Home for the Holidays 1 (1993, no-c price)-Publ. by Lorne-Harvey' X-Mas issue			2.00

NOTE: *The Sad Sack Comics comic book was a spin-off from a Sunday Newspaper strip launched through John Wheeler's Bell Syndicate. The previous Sunday page and the first 21 comics depicted the Sad Sack in civvies. Unpopularity caused the Sunday page to be discontinued in the early '50s. Meanwhile Sad Sack returned to the Army, by popular demand, in issue No. 22, remaining there ever since. Incidentally, relatively few of the first 21 issues were ever collected and remain scarce due to this.*

SAD SACK FUN AROUND THE WORLD

Saffire #1 © Image

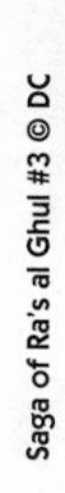
Saga of Ra's al Ghul #3 © DC

The Saint #5 © AVON

	GD2.0	FN6.0	NM9.4

Harvey Publications: 1974 (no month)

	GD2.0	FN6.0	NM9.4
1-About Great Britain	2.00	6.00	16.00

SAD SACK GOES HOME
Harvey Publications: 1951 (16 pgs. in color, no cover price)

	GD2.0	FN6.0	NM9.4
nn-By George Baker	4.55	13.65	50.00

SAD SACK LAUGH SPECIAL
Harvey Publications: Winter, 1958-59 - No. 93, Feb, 1977 (#1-9: 84 pgs.; #10-60: 68 pgs.; #61-76: 52 pgs.)

	GD2.0	FN6.0	NM9.4
1-Giant 25¢ issues begin	10.00	30.00	110.00
2	5.00	15.00	55.00
3-10	3.65	11.00	40.00
11-30	3.20	9.60	35.00
31-60: 31-1st app. Hi-Fi Tweeter. 60-Last 68 pg. Giant	2.30	7.00	20.00
61-76-(All 52 pg. issues)	2.00	6.00	16.00
77-93	1.00	2.80	7.00

SAD SACK NAVY, GOBS 'N' GALS
Harvey Publications: Aug, 1972 - No. 8, Oct, 1973

	GD2.0	FN6.0	NM9.4
1: 52 pg. Giant	2.30	7.00	20.00
2-8	1.50	4.50	12.00

SAD SACK'S ARMY LIFE (See Harvey Hits #8, 17, 22, 28, 32, 39, 43, 47, 51, 55, 58, 61, 64, 67, 70)

SAD SACK'S ARMY LIFE (...Parade #1-57, ...Today #58 on)
Harvey Publications: Oct, 1963 - No. 60, Nov, 1975; No. 61, May, 1976

	GD2.0	FN6.0	NM9.4
1-(68 pg. issues begin)	5.90	17.75	65.00
2-10	3.00	9.00	32.00
11-20	2.30	7.00	20.00
21-34: Last 68 pg. issue	2.00	6.00	16.00
35-51: All 52 pgs.	1.50	4.50	12.00
52-61	1.00	2.80	7.00

SAD SACK'S FUNNY FRIENDS (See Harvey Hits #75)
Harvey Publications: Dec, 1955 - No. 75, Oct, 1969

	GD2.0	FN6.0	NM9.4
1	9.00	27.00	100.00
2-10	4.55	13.65	50.00
11-20	2.50	7.50	25.00
21-30	2.00	6.00	18.00
31-50	1.85	5.50	15.00
51-75	1.50	4.50	12.00

SAD SACK'S MUTTSY (See Harvey Hits #74, 77, 80, 82, 84, 87, 89, 92, 96, 99, 102, 105, 108, 111, 113, 115, 117, 119, 121)

SAD SACK USA (...Vacation #8)
Harvey Publications: Nov, 1972 - No. 7, Nov, 1973; No. 8, Oct, 1974

	GD2.0	FN6.0	NM9.4
1	2.00	6.00	16.00
2-8	1.10	3.30	9.00

SAD SACK WITH SARGE & SADIE
Harvey Publications: Sept, 1972 - No. 8, Nov, 1973

	GD2.0	FN6.0	NM9.4
1-(52 pg. Giant)	2.30	7.00	20.00
2-8	1.10	3.30	9.00

SAD SAD SACK WORLD
Harvey Publ.: Oct, 1964 - No. 46, Dec, 1973 (#1-31: 68 pgs.; #32-38: 52 pgs.)

	GD2.0	FN6.0	NM9.4
1	5.00	15.00	55.00
2-10	2.80	8.40	28.00
11-20	2.40	7.35	22.00
21-31: 31-Last 68 pg. issue	2.30	7.00	20.00
32-39-(All 52 pgs)	1.75	5.25	14.00
40-46	1.00	3.00	8.00

SAFEST PLACE IN THE WORLD, THE
Dark Horse Comics: 1993 ($2.50, one-shot)

	GD2.0	FN6.0	NM9.4
1-Steve Ditko-c/a/scripts			2.50

SAFETY-BELT MAN
Sirius Entertainment: June, 1994 - No. 6, 1995 ($2.50, B&W)

	GD2.0	FN6.0	NM9.4
1-6: 1-Horan-s/Dark One-a/Sprouse-c. 2,3-Warren-c. 4-Linsner back-up story.			
5,6-Crilley-a			3.00

SAFETY-BELT MAN ALL HELL
Sirius Entertainment: June, 1996 - No. 6, Mar, 1997 ($2.95, color)

	GD2.0	FN6.0	NM9.4
1-6-Horan-s/Fillbach Bros.-a			3.00

SAFFIRE
Image Comics: Apr, 2000 - Present ($2.95)

	GD2.0	FN6.0	NM9.4
1-Broome-a(p)/c			3.00
Preview-Color & B&W pages			1.00

SAGA OF BIG RED, THE
Omaha World-Herald: Sept, 1976 ($1.25) (In color)

	GD2.0	FN6.0	NM9.4
nn-by Win Mumma; story of the Nebraska Cornhuskers (sports)			3.00

SAGA OF CRYSTAR, CRYSTAL WARRIOR, THE
Marvel Comics: May, 1983 - No. 11, Feb, 1985 (Remco toy tie-in)

	GD2.0	FN6.0	NM9.4
1 (Baxter paper)			4.00
2-11: 3-Dr. Strange app. 3-11-Golden-c (painted-4,5). 6-Nightcrawler app; Golden-c.11-Alpha Flight app.			3.00

SAGA OF RA'S AL GHUL, THE
DC Comics: Jan, 1988 - No. 4, Apr, 1988 ($2.50, limited series)

	GD2.0	FN6.0	NM9.4
1-4-r/N. Adams Batman		2.40	6.00

SAGA OF SABAN'S MIGHTY MORPHIN POWER RANGERS (Also see Saban's Mighty Morphin Power Rangers)
Hamilton Comics: 1995 - No. 4, 1995 ($1.95, limited series)

	GD2.0	FN6.0	NM9.4
1-4			2.00

SAGA OF THE SWAMP THING, THE (See Swamp Thing)

SAGA OF THE ORIGINAL HUMAN TORCH
Marvel Comics: Apr, 1990 - No. 4, July, 1990 ($1.50, limited series)

	GD2.0	FN6.0	NM9.4
1-4: 1-Origin; Buckler-c/a(p). 3-Hitler-c			2.00

SAGA OF THE SUB-MARINER, THE
Marvel Comics: Nov, 1988 - No. 12, Oct, 1989 ($1.25/$1.50 #5 on)

	GD2.0	FN6.0	NM9.4
1-12: 9-Original X-Men app.			3.00

SAILOR MOON (Manga)
Mixx Entertainment Inc.: 1998 - Present ($2.95)

	GD2.0	FN6.0	NM9.4
1	2.00	6.00	16.00
1-(San Diego edition)	2.00	6.00	16.00
2-5	1.25	3.75	10.00
6-16			4.00
... Rini's Moon Stick 1			15.00

SAILOR ON THE SEA OF FATE (See First Comics Graphic Novel #11)

SAILOR SWEENEY (Navy Action #1-11, 15 on)
Atlas Comics (CDS): No. 12, July, 1956 - No. 14, Nov, 1956

	GD2.0	FN6.0	NM9.4
12-14: 12-Shores-a. 13-Severin-c	8.65	26.00	60.00

SAINT, THE (Also see Movie Comics(DC) #2 & Silver Streak #18)
Avon Periodicals: Aug, 1947 - No. 12, Mar, 1952

	GD2.0	FN6.0	NM9.4
1-Kamen bondage-c/a	74.00	221.00	700.00
2	40.00	120.00	350.00
3-5: 4-Lingerie panels	35.00	105.00	280.00
6-Miss Fury app. by Tarpe Mills (14 pgs.)	42.00	125.00	375.00
7-c-/Avon paperback #118	27.00	81.00	215.00
8,9(12/50): Saint strip-r in #8-12; 9-Kinstler-c	24.00	71.00	190.00
10-Wood-a, 1 pg; c-/Avon paperback #289	24.00	71.00	190.00
11	17.00	51.00	135.00
12-c-/Avon paperback #123	20.00	60.00	160.00

NOTE: *Lucky Dale, Girl Detective in #1,2,4,6.* ***Hollingsworth*** *a-4, 6. Painted-c 7, 8, 10-12.*

SAINT ANGEL
Image Comics: Mar, 2000 - Present ($2.95/$3.95)

	GD2.0	FN6.0	NM9.4
0-Altstaetter & Napton-s/Altstaetter-a			3.00
1,2-($3.95) Flip book w/Deity. 1-(6/00). 2-(10/00)			3.95

ST. GEORGE
Marvel Comics (Epic Comics): June, 1988 - No.8, Oct, 1989 ($1.25,/$1.50)

	GD2.0	FN6.0	NM9.4
1-8: Sienkiewicz-c. 3-begin $1.50-c			2.00

Sam and Twitch #11 © TMP

Samson #14 © FOX

Sandman #49 © DC

SAINT GERMAINE
Caliber Comics: 1997 - Present ($2.95)

1-8: 1,5-Alternate covers 3.00

SAINT SINNER (See Razorline)
Marvel Comics (Razorline): Oct, 1993 - No. 7, Apr, 1994 ($1.75)

1-($2.50)-Foil embossed-c; created by Clive Barker 2.50

2-7: 5-Ectokid x-over 2.00

ST. SWITHIN'S DAY
Trident Comics: Apr, 1990 ($2.50, one-shot)

1-Grant Morrison scripts 3.00

ST. SWITHIN'S DAY
Oni Press: Mar, 1998 ($2.95, B&W, one-shot)

1-Grant Morrison-s/Paul Grist-a 3.00

SALOMÉ (See Night Music #6)

SAM AND MAX, FREELANCE POLICE SPECIAL
Fishwrap Prod./Comico: 1987 ($1.75, B&W); Jan, 1989 ($2.75, 44 pgs.)

1 ($1.75, B&W, Fishwrap) 2.00

2 ($2.75, color, Comico) 2.75

SAM AND TWITCH (See Spawn)
Image Comics (Todd McFarlane Prod.): Aug, 1999 - Present ($2.50)

1-16-Bendis-s. 1-14-Medina-a. 15,16-Maleev-a 2.50

SAM HILL PRIVATE EYE
Close-Up (Archie): 1950 - No. 7, 1951

1 16.00 49.00 130.00

2 10.00 30.00 75.00

3-7 9.30 28.00 65.00

SAM SLADE ROBOHUNTER
Quality Comics: Oct, 1986 - No. 31, 1989 ($1.25/$1.50)

1-31 2.00

SAMSON (1st Series) (Captain Aero #7 on; see Big 3 Comics)
Fox Features Syndicate: Fall, 1940 - No. 6, Sept, 1941 (See Fantastic Comics)

1-Samson begins, ends #6; Powell-a, signed 'Rensie;' Wing Turner by Tuska app; Fine-c? 253.00 758.00 2400.00

2-Dr. Fung by Powell; Fine-c? 87.00 261.00 825.00

3-Navy Jones app.; Joe Simon-c 68.00 205.00 650.00

4-Yarko the Great, Master Magician begins 58.00 174.00 550.00

5,6: 6-Origin The Topper 47.00 141.00 425.00

SAMSON (2nd Series) (Formerly Fantastic Comics #10, 11)
Ajax/Farrell Publications (Four Star): No. 12, April, 1955 - No. 14, Aug, 1955

12-Wonder Boy 30.00 90.00 240.00

13,14: 13-Wonder Boy, Rocket Man 26.00 79.00 210.00

SAMSON (See Mighty Samson)

SAMSON & DELILAH (See A Spectacular Feature Magazine)

SAM STORIES: LEGS
Image Comics: Dec, 1999 ($2.50, one-shot)

1-Sam Kieth-s/a 2.50

SAMUEL BRONSTON'S CIRCUS WORLD (See Circus World under Movie Classics)

SAMURAI (Also see Eclipse Graphic Album Series #14)
Aircel Publications: 1985 - No. 23, 1987 ($1.70, B&W)

1, 14-16-Dale Keown-a 3.00

1-(reprinted),2-12,17-23: 2 (reprinted issue exists) 2.00

13-Dale Keown's 1st published artwork (1987) 5.00

SAMURAI
Warp Graphics: May, 1997 ($2.95, B&W)

1 3.00

SAMURAI CAT
Marvel Comics (Epic Comics): June, 1991 - No. 3, Sept, 1991 ($2.25, limited series)

1-3: 3-Darth Vader-c/story parody 2.25

GD2.0 FN6.0 NM9.4

SAMUREE
Continuity Comics: May, 1987 - No. 9, Jan, 1991

1-9 3.00

SAMUREE
Continuity Comics: V2#1, May, 1993 - V2#4, Jan,1994 ($2.50)

V2#1-4-Embossed-c: 2,4-Adams plot, Nebres-i. 3-Nino-c(i) 2.50

SAMUREE
Acclaim Comics (Windjammer): Oct, 1995 - No. 2, Nov,1995 ($2.50, lim. series)

1,2 2.50

SAN DIEGO COMIC CON COMICS
Dark Horse Comics: 1992 - No.4, 1995 (B&W, promo comic for the San Diego Comic Con)

1-(1992)-Includes various characters published from Dark Horse including Concrete, The Mask, RoboCop and others; 1st app. of Sprint from John Byrne's Next Men; art by Quesada, Byrne, Rude, Burden, Moebius & others; pin-ups by Rude, Dorkin, Allred & others; Chadwick-c. 5.00

2-(1993)-Intro of Legend imprint; 1st app. of John Byrne's Danger Unlimited, Mike Mignola's Hellboy, Art Adams' Monkeyman & O'Brien; contains stories featuring Concrete, Sin City, Martha Washington & others; Grendel, Madman, & Big Guy pin-ups; Don Martin-c. 1.00 2.80 7.00

3-(1994)-Contains stories featuring Barb Wire, The Mask, The Dirty Pair, & Grendel by Matt Wagner; contains pin-ups of Ghost, Predator & Rascals In Paradise; The Mask-c. 5.00

4-(1995)-Contains Sin City story by Miller (3pg.), Star Wars, The Mask, Tarzan, Foot Soldiers; Sin City & Star Wars flip-c 5.00

SANDMAN, THE (1st Series) (Also see Adventure Comics #40, New York World's Fair & World's Finest #3)
National Periodical Publications: Winter, 1974; No. 2, Apr-May, 1975 - No. 6, Dec-Jan, 1975-76

1-1st app. Bronze Age Sandman by Simon & Kirby (last S&K collaboration) . 3.00 9.00 30.00

2-6: 6-Kirby/Wood-c/a 1.50 4.50 12.00

NOTE: *Kirby a-1p, 4-6p; c-1-5, 6p.*

SANDMAN (2nd Series) (See Books of Magic, Vertigo Jam & Vertigo Preview)
DC Comics (Vertigo imprint #47 on): Jan, 1989 - No. 75, Mar, 1996 ($1.50/$1.75/$2.50, mature)

1 ($2.00, 52 pgs.)-1st app. Modern Age Sandman (Morpheus); Neil Gaiman scripts begin; Sam Kieth-a(p) in #1-5; Wesley Dodds (G.A. Sandman) cameo. 3.00 9.00 30.00

2-Cain & Abel app. (from HOM & HOS) 1.50 4.50 12.00

3-5: 3-John Constantine app. 1.25 3.75 10.00

6,7 1.00 2.80 7.00

8-Death-c/story (1st app.)-Regular ed. has Jeanette Kahn publishorial & American Cancer Society ad w/no indicia on inside front-c 2.00 6.00 16.00

8-Limited ed. (600+ copies?); has Karen Berger editorial and next issue teaser on inside covers (has indicia) 5.00 15.00 55.00

9-14: 10-Has explaination about #8 mixup; has bound-in Shocker movie poster. 14-(52 pgs.)-Bound-in Nightbreed fold-out 1.00 3.00 8.00

15-20: 16-Photo-c. 17,18-Kelley Jones-a. 19-Vess-a. 2.40 6.00

18-Error version w/1st 3 panels on pg. 1 in blue ink 2.50 7.50 20.00

19-Error version w/pages 18 & 20 facing each other 1.85 5.50 15.00

21,23-27: Seasons of Mist storyline. 22-World Without End preview. 24-Kelley Jones/Russell-a 2.40 6.00

22-1st Daniel (Later becomes new Sandman) 1.10 3.30 9.00

28-30 5.00

31-49,51-74: 41,44-48-Metallic ink on-c. 48-Cerebus appears as a doll. 36-(52 pgs.). 54-Re-intro Prez; Death app.; Belushi, Nixon & Wildcat cameos. 57-Metallic ink on c. 65-w/bound-in trading card. 69-Death of Sandman. 70-73-Zulli-a. 74-Jon J. Muth-a. 4.00

50-($2.95, 52 pgs.)-Black-c w/metallic ink by McKean; Russell-a; McFarlane pin-up. 5.00

50-($2.95)-Signed & limited (5,000) Treasury Edition with sketch of Neil Gaiman 1.00 3.00 8.00

50-Platinum 20.00

75-($3.95)-Vess-a. 5.00

Sandman Mystery Theater #70 © DC

Sandman Presents: Love Street #1 © DC

Satan's Six #3 © Jack Kirby

Special 1 (1991, $3.50, 68 pgs.)-Glow-in-the-dark-c 5.00
...: A Gallery of Dreams ($2.95)-Intro by N. Gaiman 3.00
...: Preludes & Nocturnes ($29.95, HC)-r/#1-8. 30.00
...: The Doll's House (1990, $29.95, HC)-r/#8-16. 30.00
...: Dream Country ($29.95, HC)-r/#17-20. 30.00
...: Season of Mists ($29.95, Leatherbound HC)-r/#21-28. 50.00
...: A Game of You ($29.95, HC)-r/32-37, ...: Fables and Reflections ($29.95, HC)-r/Vertigo Preview #1, Sandman Special #1, #29-31, #38-40 & #50. ...: Brief Lives ($29.95, HC)-r/#41-49. ...: World's End ($29.95, HC)-r/#51-56. 30.00
...: The Kindly Ones (1996, $34.95, HC)-r/#57-69 & Vertigo Jam#1 35.00
...: The Wake ($29.95, HC)-r/#70-75. 30.00
NOTE: *A new set of hardcover printings with new covers was introduced in 1998-99. Multiple printings exist of softcover collections.* ***Bachalo*** *a-12;* ***Kelley Jones*** *a-17, 18, 22, 23, 26, 27.* ***Vess*** *a-19, 75.*

SANDMAN MIDNIGHT THEATRE
DC Comics (Vertigo): Sept, 1995 ($6.95, squarebound, one-shot)
nn-Modern Age Sandman (Morpheus) meets G.A. Sandman; Gaiman & Wagner story; McKean-c; Kristiansen-a 7.00

SANDMAN MYSTERY THEATRE (Also see Sandman (2nd Series) #1)
DC Comics (Vertigo): Apr, 1993 - No. 70, Feb, 1999 ($1.95/$2.25/$2.50)
1-G.A. Sandman advs. begin; Matt Wagner scripts begin 4.50
2-49: 5-Neon ink logo. 29-32-Hourman app. 38-Ted Knight (G.A. Starman) app. 42-Jim Corrigan (Spectre) app. 45-48-Blackhawk app. 2.50
50-($3.50, 48 pgs.) w/bonus story of S.A. Sandman, Torres-a 3.50
51-70 2.50
Annual 1 (10/94, $3.95, 68 pgs.)-Alex Ross, Bolton & others-a 5.00

SANDMAN PRESENTS: LOVE STREET
DC Comics (Vertigo): Jul, 1999 - No. 3, Sept, 1999 ($2.95, limited series)
1-3: Teenage Hellblazer in 1968 London; Zulli-a 3.00

SANDMAN PRESENTS: LUCIFER
DC Comics (Vertigo): Mar, 1999 - No. 3, May, 1999 ($2.95, limited series)
1-3: Scott Hampton painted-c/a 3.00

SANDMAN PRESENTS: PETREFAX
DC Comics (Vertigo): Mar, 2000 - No. 4, Jun, 2000 ($2.95, limited series)
1-4-Carey-s/Leialoha-a 3.00

SANDMAN, THE: THE DREAM HUNTERS
DC Comics (Vertigo): Oct, 1999 ($29.95/$19.95, one-shot)
Hardcover-Neil Gaiman-s/Yoshitaka Amano-painted art 30.00
Softcover-(2000, $19.95) new Amano-c 20.00

SANDS OF THE SOUTH PACIFIC
Toby Press: Jan, 1953
1 21.00 64.00 170.00

SANTA AND HIS REINDEER (See March of Comics #166)

SANTA AND THE ANGEL (See Dell Junior Treasury #7)
Dell Publishing Co.: Dec, 1949 (Combined w/Santa at the Zoo) (Gollub-a condensed from FC#128)
Four Color 259 4.10 12.30 45.00

SANTA AT THE ZOO (See Santa And The Angel)

SANTA CLAUS AROUND THE WORLD (See March of Comics #241 in Promotional Comics section)

SANTA CLAUS CONQUERS THE MARTIANS (See Movie Classics)

SANTA CLAUS FUNNIES (Also see Dell Giants)
Dell Publishing Co.: Dec?, 1942 - No. 1274, Dec, 1961
nn(#1)(1942)-Kelly-a 37.00 110.00 440.00
2(12/43)-Kelly-a 24.00 73.00 290.00
Four Color 61(1944)-Kelly-a 23.00 70.00 280.00
Four Color 91(1945)-Kelly-a 17.50 52.50 210.00
Four Color 128('46),175('47)-Kelly-a 14.00 41.00 165.00
Four Color 205,254-Kelly-a 12.50 37.50 150.00
Four Color 302,361,525,607,666,756,867 4.55 13.65 50.00
Four Color 958,1063,1154,1274 4.10 12.30 45.00
NOTE: *Most issues contain only one Kelly story.*

SANTA CLAUS PARADE
Ziff-Davis (Approved Comics)/St. John Publishing Co.: 1951; No. 2, Dec, 1952; No. 3, Jan, 1955 (25¢)
nn(1951-Ziff-Davis)-116 pgs. (Xmas Special 1,2) 28.00 84.00 225.00
2(12/52-Ziff-Davis)-100 pgs.; Dave Berg-a 22.00 66.00 175.00
V1#3(1/55-St. John)-100 pgs.; reprints-c/#1 19.00 56.00 150.00

SANTA CLAUS' WORKSHOP (See March of Comics #50,168 in Promotional Comics sect.)

SANTA IS COMING (See March of Comics #197 in Promotional Comics section)

SANTA IS HERE (See March of Comics #49 in Promotional Comics section)

SANTA'S BUSY CORNER (See March of Comics #31 in Promotional Comics section)

SANTA'S CANDY KITCHEN (See March of Comics #14 in Promotional Comics section)

SANTA'S CHRISTMAS BOOK (See March of Comics #123 in Promotional Comics sect.)

SANTA'S CHRISTMAS COMICS
Standard Comics (Best Books): Dec, 1952 (100 pgs.)
nn-Supermouse, Dizzy Duck, Happy Rabbit, etc. 18.00 53.00 140.00

SANTA'S CHRISTMAS LIST (See March of Comics #255 in Promotional Comics section)

SANTA'S HELPERS (See March of Comics #64, 106, 198 in Promotional Comics section)

SANTA'S LITTLE HELPERS (See March of Comics #270 in Promotional Comics section)

SANTA'S SHOW (See March of Comics #311 in Promotional Comics section)

SANTA'S SLEIGH (See March of Comics #298 in Promotional Comics section)

SANTA'S SURPRISE (See March of Comics #13 in Promotional Comics section)

SANTA'S TINKER TOTS
Charlton Comics: 1958
1-Based on "The Tinker Tots Keep Christmas" 2.50 7.50 25.00

SANTA'S TOYLAND (See March of Comics #242 in Promotional Comics section)

SANTA'S TOYS (See March of Comics #12 in Promotional Comics section)

SANTA'S VISIT (See March of Comics #283 in Promotional Comics section)

SANTA THE BARBARIAN
Maximum Press: Dec, 1996 ($2.99, one-shot)
1-Fraga/Mhan-s/a 3.00

SANTIAGO (Movie)
Dell Publishing Co.: Sept, 1956 (Alan Ladd photo-c)
Four Color 723-Kinstler-a 10.00 30.00 120.00

SARGE SNORKEL (Beetle Bailey)
Charlton Comics: Oct, 1973 - No. 17, Dec, 1976
1 2.00 6.00 16.00
2-10 1.25 3.75 10.00
11-17 1.00 3.00 8.00

SARGE STEEL (Becomes Secret Agent #9 on; also see Judomaster)
Charlton Comics: Dec, 1964 - No. 8, Mar-Apr, 1966 (All 12¢ issues)
1-Origin & 1st app. 3.00 9.00 30.00
2-5,7,8 2.00 6.00 18.00
6-2nd app. Judomaster 2.50 7.50 24.00

SATANIKA
Verotik: Jan, 1995 - No. 3, 1996 ($2.95, limited series, mature)
0-3: Danzig story in all. 0-(7/95)-Frazetta-c; 1-Bisley-c. 5.00
The Brimstone Trail (1996, $9.95, TPB)-r/#0-2. 10.00

SATANIKA
Verotik: Feb, 1996 - No. 11 ($2.95, mature)
1-11: Danzig story in all. 2-Igrat cameo; indicia reads "Satanika #1." 4,5-nudity-c. 8-Alternate-c 3.00

SATANIKA X
Verotik: Feb, 1996 ($4.95, one-shot, mature)
1-Embossed-c. 5.00

SATAN'S SIX
Topps Comics (Kirbyverse): Apr, 1993 - No. 4, July, 1993 ($2.95, lim. series)
1-4: 1-Polybagged w/Kirbychrome trading card; Kirby/McFarlane-c plus 8 pgs.

Savage Dragon #11 © Erik Larsen

Savage She-Hulk #3 © MAR

Savage Tales #1 © MAR

Kirby-a(p); has coupon for Kirbychrome ed. of Secret City Saga #0. 2-4-Polybagged w/3 cards. 4-Teenagents preview 3.00
NOTE: ***Ditko** a-1. **Miller** a-1.*

SATAN'S SIX: HELLSPAWN
Topps Comics (Kirbyverse): June, 1994 - No. 3, July, 1994 ($2.50, lim. series)

1-3: 1-(6/94)-Indicia incorrectly shows "Vol 1 #2". 2-(6/94) 2.50

SAVAGE COMBAT TALES
Atlas/Seaboard Publ.: Feb, 1975 - No. 3, July, 1975

1,3: 1-Sgt. Stryker's Death Squad begins (origin); Goodwin-s 2.40 6.00
2-Toth-a; only app. War Hawk; Goodwin-s 1.10 3.30 9.00
NOTE: ***Buckler** c-3. **McWilliams** a-1-3; c-1. **Sparling** a-1, 3.*

SAVAGE DRAGON, THE (See Megaton #3 & 4)
Image Comics (Highbrow Entertainment): July, 1992 - No. 3, Dec, 1992 ($1.95, limited series)

1-Erik Larsen-c/a/scripts & bound-in poster in all; 4 cover color variations w/4 different posters; 1st Highbrow Entertainment title 4.00
2-Intro SuperPatriot-c/story (10/92) 3.00
3-Contains coupon for Image Comics #0 3.00
3-With coupon missing 2.00
...Vs. Savage Megaton Man 1 (3/93, $1.95)-Larsen & Simpson-c/a. 2.00
TPB-('93, $9.95) r/#1-3 10.00

SAVAGE DRAGON, THE
Image Comics (Highbrow Entertainment): June, 1993 - Present ($1.95/$2.50)

1-Erik Larsen-c/a/scripts 3.00
2-30: 2-(Wondercon Exclusive): 2-($2.95, 52 pgs.)-Teenage Mutant Ninja Turtles-c/story; flip book features Vanguard #0 (See Megaton for 1st app.). 27 (Wondercon Exclusive)-new-c. 3-7: Erik Larsen-c/a/scripts. 3-Mighty Man back-up story w/Austin-a(i). 4-Flip book w/Ricochet. 5-Mighty Man flip-c & back-up plus poster. 6-Jae Lee poster. 7-Vanguard poster. 8-Deadly Duo poster by Larsen. 13A (10/94)-Jim Lee-c/a; 1st app. Max Cash (Condition Red).13B (6/95)-Larsen story. 15-Dragon poster by Larsen. 22-TMNT-c/a; Bisley pin-up. 28-Maxx-c/app. 29-Wildstar-c/app. 30-Spawn app. 2.50
25 ($3.95)-variant-c exists. 4.00
27-"Wondercon Exclusive" new-c 3.00
31-49,51-71: 31-God vs. The Devil; alternate version exists w/o expletives (has "God Is Good" inside Image logo) 33-Birth of Dragon/Rapture's baby. 34,35-Hellboy-c/app. 51-Origin of She-Dragon. 70-Ann Stevens killed 2.50
50-($5.95, 100 pgs.) Kaboom and Mighty Man app.; Matsuda back-c; pin-ups by McFarlane, Simonson, Capullo and others 6.00
72-74,76-81: 72-Begin $2.95-c. 76-New direction starts 2.95
75-($5.95) 5.95
The Fallen (11/97, $12.95, TPB) r/#7-11, ...Possessed (9/98, $12.95, TPB) r/#12-16, ...Revenge (1998, $12.95, TPB) r/#17-21 13.00
...Gang War (4/00, $16.95, TPB) r/#22-26 16.95
...Team-Ups (10/98, $19.95, TPB) r/team-ups 20.00

SAVAGE DRAGON ARCHIVES (See Dragon Archives, The)

SAVAGE DRAGON/DESTROYER DUCK, THE
Image Comics/ Highbrow Entertainment: Nov, 1996 ($3.95, one-shot)

1 4.00

SAVAGE DRAGON/MARSHALL LAW
Image Comics: July, 1997 - No. 2, Aug, 1997 ($2.95, B&W, limited series)

1,2-Pat Mills-s, Kevin O'Neill-a 3.00

SAVAGE DRAGON: SEX & VIOLENCE
Image Comics: Aug, 1997 - No. 2, Sept, 1997 ($2.50, limited series)

1,2-T&M Bierbaum-s, Mays, Lupka, Adam Hughes-a 2.50

SAVAGE DRAGON/TEENAGE MUTANT NINJA TURTLES CROSSOVER
Mirage Studios: Sept, 1993 ($2.75, one-shot)

1-Erik Larsen-c(i) only 2.75

SAVAGE DRAGON: THE RED HORIZON
Image Comics/ Highbrow Entertainment: Feb, 1997 - No. 3 ($2.50, lim. series)

1-3 2.50

SAVAGE FISTS OF KUNG FU
Marvel Comics Group: 1975 (Marvel Treasury)

1-Iron Fist, Shang Chi, Sons of Tiger; Adams, Starlin-a 2.30 7.00 20.00

SAVAGE HENRY
Vortex Comics: Jan, 1987 - No. 16?, 1990 ($1.75/$2.00, B&W, mature)

1-16 2.50

SAVAGE HULK, THE (Also see Incredible Hulk)
Marvel Comics: Jan, 1996 ($6.95, one-shot)

1-Bisley-c; David, Lobdell, Wagner, Loeb, Gibbons, Messner-Loebs scripts; McKone, Kieth, Ramos & Sale-a. 7.00

SAVAGE RAIDS OF GERONIMO (See Geronimo #4)

SAVAGE RANGE (See Luke Short, Four Color 807)

SAVAGE RETURN OF DRACULA
Marvel Comics: 1992 ($2.00, 52 pgs.)

1-r/Tomb of Dracula #1,2 by Gene Colan 2.00

SAVAGE SHE-HULK, THE (See The Avengers, Marvel Graphic Novel #18 & The Sensational She-Hulk)
Marvel Comics Group: Feb, 1980 - No. 25, Feb, 1982

1-Origin & 1st app. She-Hulk 1.25 3.75 10.00
2-5,25: 25-(52 pgs.) 5.00
6-24: 6-She-Hulk vs. Iron Man. 8-Vs. Man-Thing 4.00
NOTE: ***Austin** a-25i; c-23i-25i. **J. Buscema** a-1p; c-1, 2p. **Golden** c-8-11.*

SAVAGE SWORD OF CONAN (The... #41 on; ...The Barbarian #175 on)
Marvel Comics Group: Aug, 1974 - No. 235, July, 1995 ($1.00/$1.25/$2.25, B&W magazine, mature)

1-Smith-r; J. Buscema/N. Adams/Krenkel-a; origin Blackmark by Gil Kane (part 1, ends #3); Blackmark's 1st app. in magazine form-r/from paperback) & Red Sonja (3rd app.) 7.25 21.75 80.00
2-Neal Adams-c; Chaykin/N. Adams-a 3.00 9.00 32.00
3-Severin/B. Smith-a; N. Adams-a 2.30 7.00 20.00
4-Neal Adams/Kane-a(r) 2.00 6.00 18.00
5-10: 5-Jeff Jones frontispiece (r) 2.00 6.00 16.00
11-20 1.50 4.50 12.00
21-50: 34-3 pg. preview of Conan newspaper strip. 35-Cover similar to Savage Tales #1. 45-Red Sonja returns; begin $1.25-c 1.25 3.75 10.00
51-100: 63-Toth frontispiece. 65-Kane-a w/Chaykin/Miller/Simonson/Sherman finishes. 70-Article on movie. 83-Red Sonja-r by Neal Adams from #1 2.40 6.00
101-176: 163-Begin $2.25-c. 169-King Kull story. 171-Soloman Kane by Williamson (i). 172-Red Sonja story 4.00
177-220: 179,187,192-Red Sonja app. 190-193-4 part King Kull story. 196, 202-King Kull story. 200-New Buscema-a; Robert E. Howard app. with Conan in story. 204-60th anniversary (1932-92). 211-Rafael Kayanan's 1st Conan-a. 214-Sequel to Red Nails by Robert E. Howard 3.00
221-235 3.50
Special 1(1975, B&W)-B. Smith-r/Conan #10,13 2.00 6.00 18.00
NOTE: ***N. Adams** a-14p, 60, 83p(r). **Alcala** a-2 ,4, 7, 12, 15-20, 23, 24, 28, 59, 67, 69, 75, 76i, 80i, 82i, 83i, 89, 180i, 184i, 187i, 189i, 216p. **Austin** a-78i. **Boris** painted c-1, 4, 5, 7, 9, 10, 12, 15. **Brunner** a-30; c-8, 30. **Buscema** a-1-5, 7, 10-12, 15-24, 26-28, 31, 32, 36-43, 45, 47-58p, 60-67p, 70, 71-74p, 76-81p, 87-96p, 98, 99-101p, 190-204p; painted c-40. **Chaykin** c-31. **Chiodo** painted c-71, 76, 79, 81, 84, 85, 178. **Conrad** c-215, 217. **Corben** a-4, 16, 29. **Finlay** a-16. **Golden** a-98, 101; c-98, 101, 105, 106, 117, 124, 150. **Kaluta** a-11, 18; c-3, 91, 93. **Gil Kane** a-2, 3, 8, 13r, 29, 47, 64, 65, 67, 85p, 86p. **Rafael Kayanan** a-211-213, 215, 217. **Krenkel** a-9, 11, 14, 16, 24. **Morrow** a-7. **Nebres** a-93i, 101i, 107, 114. **Newton** a-6. **Nino** c/a-6. **Redondo** painted c-48-50, 52, 56, 57, 85i, 90, 96i. **Marie & John Severin** a-Special 1. **Simonson** a-7, 8, 12, 15-17. **Barry Smith** a-7, 16, 24, 82r, Special 1r. **Starlin** c-26. **Toth** a-64. **Williamson** a(i)-162, 171, 186. No. 8 , 10 & 16 contain a Robert E. Howard Conan adaptation.*

SAVAGE TALES (...Featuring Conan #4 on)(Magazine)
Marvel Comics Group: May, 1971; No. 2, 10/73; No. 3, 2/74 - No. 12, Summer, 1975 (B&W)

1-Origin/1st app. The Man-Thing by Morrow; Conan the Barbarian by Barry Smith (1st Conan x-over outside his own title); Femizons by Romita-r/in #3; Ka-Zar story by Buscema 13.50 40.00 150.00
2-B. Smith, Brunner, Morrow, Williamson-a; Wrightson King Kull reprint/ Creatures on the Loose #10 3.20 9.60 35.00
3-B. Smith, Brunner, Steranko, Williamson-a 2.50 7.50 25.00
4,5-N. Adams-c; last Conan (Smith-r/#4) plus Kane/N. Adams-a. 5-Brak the Barbarian begins, ends #8 2.30 7.00 20.00

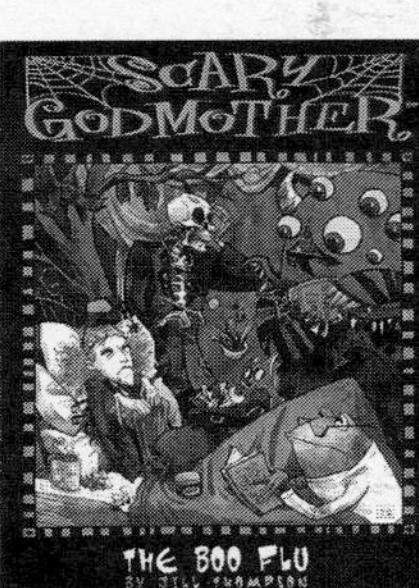

Scary Godmother - The Boo Flu © Jill Thompson

Scatterbrain #1 © DH

Scene of the Crime #3 © Ed Brubaker & Michael Lark

GD2.0 FN6.0 NM9.4

6-Ka-Zar begins; Williamson-r; N. Adams-c 1.50 4.50 12.00
7-N. Adams-i 1.10 3.30 9.00
8,9,11: 8-Shanna, the She-Devil app. thru #10; Williamson-r 1.00 3.00 8.00
10-Neal Adams-a(i), Williamson-r 1.25 3.75 10.00
...Featuring Ka-Zar Annual 1 (Summer, '75, B&W)(#12 on inside)-Ka-Zar origin by G. Kane; B. Smith-r/Astonishing Tales 1.75 5.25 14.00

NOTE: ***Boris** c-7, 10. **Buscema** a-5r, 6p, 8p; c-2. **Colan** a-1p. **Fabian** c-8. **Golden** a-1, 4; c-1. **Heath** a-10p, 11p. **Kaluta** c-9. **Maneely** r-2, 4(The Crusader in both). **Morrow** a-1, 2, Annual 1. **Reese** a-2. **Severin** a-1-7. **Starlin** a-5. Robert E. Howard adaptations-1-4.*

SAVAGE TALES
Marvel Comics Group: Nov, 1985 - No. 9, Mar, 1987 ($1.50, B&W, magazine, mature)

1-1st app. The Nam; Golden, Morrow-a 5.00
2-9: 2,7-Morrow-a. 4-2nd Nam story; Golden-a 3.00

SAVANT GARDE (Also see WildC.A.T.S...)
Image Comics/WildStorm Productions: Mar, 1997 - No. 7, Sept, 1997 ($2.50)

1-7 2.50

SAVED BY THE BELL (TV)
Harvey Comics: Mar, 1992 - No. 4, Aug, 1992? ($1.25, limited series)

1-4, Special 1 (9/92, $1.50)-photo-c 2.00

SCAMP (Walt Disney)(See Walt Disney's Comics & Stories #204)
Dell Publ. Co./Gold Key: No. 703, 5/56 - No. 1204, 8-10/61; 11/67 - No. 45, 1/79

Four Color 703(#1) 8.35 25.00 100.00
Four Color 777,806('57),833 5.85 17.50 70.00
5(3-5/58)-10(6-8/59) 4.60 13.75 55.00
11-16(12-2/60-61), Four Color 1204(1961) 3.65 11.00 40.00
1(12/67-Gold Key)-Reprints begin 3.65 11.00 40.00
2(3/69)-10 2.00 6.00 16.00
11-20 1.25 3.75 10.00
21-45 2.40 6.00

NOTE: *New stories-#20(in part), 22-25, 27, 29-31, 34, 36-40, 42-45. New covers-#11, 12, 14, 15, 17-25, 27, 29-31, 34, 36-38.*

SCARAB
DC Comics (Vertigo): Nov, 1993 - No. 8, June, 1994 ($1.95, limited series)

1-8-Glenn Fabry painted-c: 1-Silver ink-c. 2-Phantom Stranger app. 2.00

SCAR FACE (See The Crusaders)

SCARECROW OF ROMNEY MARSH, THE (See W. Disney Showcase #53)
Gold Key: April, 1964 - No. 3, Oct, 1965 (Disney TV Show)

10112-404 (#1) 3.20 9.60 35.00
2,3 2.50 7.50 25.00

SCARECROW (VILLAINS) (See Batman)
DC Comics: Feb, 1998 ($1.95, one-shot)

1-Fegredo-a/Milligan-s/Pearson-c 2.00

SCARE TACTICS
DC Comics: Dec, 1996 - No. 12, Mar, 1998 ($2.25)

1-12: 1-1st app. 2.25

SCARLET O'NEIL (See Harvey Comics Hits #59 & Invisible...)

SCARLET CRUSH
Awesome Entertainment: Jan, 1998 - No. 2, Feb, 1998 ($2.50)

1-Five covers by Liefeld, Stinsman(wraparound), Churchill, Skroce, and Sprouse; Stinsman-s/a(p) 2.50
1-American Entertainment Ed.; Stinsman-c 5.00
2-Three covers by Stinsman, McGuinness & Peterson 2.50

SCARLET SPIDER
Marvel Comics: Nov, 1995 - No. 2, Jan, 1996 ($1.95)

1,2: Replaces Spider-Man 2.00

SCARLET SPIDER UNLIMITED
Marvel Comics: Nov, 1995 ($3.95, one-shot)

1-Replaces Spider-Man Unlimited 4.00

SCARLETT
DC Comics: Jan, 1993 - No. 14, Feb, 1994 (1.75)

GD2.0 FN6.0 NM9.4

1-($2.95) 3.00
2-14 2.00

SCARLET THUNDER
Amaze Ink: Nov, 1995, - Present ($1.50, B&W)

1-3: 3-(5/96) 2.00

SCARLET WITCH (See Avengers #16, Vision &... & X-Men #4)
Marvel Comics: Jan, 1994 - No. 4, Apr, 1994 ($1.75, limited series)

1-4 2.00

SCARY GODMOTHER: ACTIVITY BOOK
Sirius: Dec, 2000 ($2.95, B&W, one-shot)

1-Jill Thompson-s/a 3.00

SCARY GODMOTHER: BLOODY VALENTINE SPECIAL
Sirius: Feb, 1998 ($3.95, B&W, one-shot)

1-Jill Thompson-s/a; pin-ups by Ross, Mignola, Russell 4.00

SCARY GODMOTHER: HOLIDAY SPOOKTAKULAR
Sirius: Nov, 1998 ($2.95, B&W, one-shot)

1-Thompson-s/a; pin-ups by Brereton, LaBan, Dorkin, Fingerman 3.00

SCARY GODMOTHER: THE BOO FLU
Sirius: Sept, 2000 ($19.95, hardcover with dust jacket, one-shot)

1-Jill Thompson-s/a 20.00

SCARY GODMOTHER: WILD ABOUT HARRY
Sirius: 2000 - No. 3 ($2.95, B&W, limited series)

1-3-Jill Thompson-s/a 3.00

SCARY TALES
Charlton Comics: 8/75 - #9, 1/77; #10, 9/77 - #20, 6/79; #21, 8/80 - #46, 10/84

1-Origin/1st app. Countess Von Bludd, not in #2 2.40 7.35 22.00
2,6,10 1.10 3.30 9.00
3-Sutton painted-c; Ditko-a 1.75 5.25 14.00
4,7,8: 4-Sutton-c. 7,8-Ditko-a 1.25 3.75 10.00
5,9,11: 5,11-Ditko-c/a. 9-Sutton-c/a 1.50 4.50 12.00
12,15,16,19,21,39-Ditko-a 1.00 3.00 8.00
13,17,20 1.00 2.80 7.00
14,18,30,32-Ditko-c/a 1.10 3.30 9.00
22-29,33-38,40: 37,38,40-New-a. 38-Mr. Jigsaw app. 2.40 6.00
31-Newton-c/a 1.10 3.30 9.00
41-46-(Low print): 41-45-New-a. 46-Reprints 1.00 2.80 7.00
1(Modern Comics reprint, 1977) 4.00

NOTE: ***Adkins** a-31i; c-31i. **Ditko** a-3, 5, 7, 8(2), 11, 12, 14-16r, 18(3)r, 19r, 21r, 30r, 32, 39r; c-5, 11, 14, 18, 30, 32. **Newton** a-31p; c-31p. **Powell** a-18r. **Staton** a-1(2 pgs.), 4, 20r; c-1, 20. **Sutton** a-9; c-4, 9.*

SCATTERBRAIN
Dark Horse Comics: Jun, 1998 - No. 4, Sept, 1998 ($2.95, limited series)

1-4-Humor anthology by Aragonés, Dorkin, Stevens and others 3.00

SCAVENGERS
Quality Comics: Feb, 1988 - No. 14, 1989 ($1.25/$1.50)

1-14: 9-13-Guice-c 2.00

SCAVENGERS
Triumphant Comics: 1993(nd, July) - No. 11, May, 1994 ($2.50, serially numbered)

1-9,0,10,11: 5,6-Triumphant Unleashed x-over. 9-(3/94). 0-Retail edition (3/94, $2.50, 36 pgs.). 0-Giveaway edition (3/94, 20 pgs.). 0-Coupon redemption edition. 10-(4/94) 2.50

SCENE OF THE CRIME (Also see Vertigo: Winter's Edge #2)
DC Comics (Vertigo): May, 1999 - No. 4, Aug, 1999 ($2.50, limited series)

1-4-Brubaker-s/Lark-a 2.50
...: A Little Piece of Goodnight TPB ('00, $12.95) r/#1-4; Winter's Edge #2 12.95

SCHOOL DAY ROMANCES (...of Teen-Agers #4; Popular Teen-Agers #5 on)
Star Publications: Nov-Dec, 1949 - No. 4, May-June, 1950 (Teenage)

1-Toni Gayle (later Toni Gay), Ginger Snapp, Midge Martin & Eve Adams begin 28.00 83.00 220.00
2,3: 3-Jane Powell photo on-c & true life story 20.00 60.00 160.00

Science Comics #5 © FOX

Scooby-Doo (DC) #36 © H-B

Scoop Comics #1 © CHES

4-Ronald Reagan photo on-c; L.B. Cole-c 30.00 90.00 240.00
NOTE: *All have **L. B. Cole** covers.*

SCHWINN BICYCLE BOOK (...Bike Thrills, 1959)
Schwinn Bicycle Co.: 1949; 1952; 1959 (10¢)

1949 5.00 15.00 35.00
1952-Believe It or Not facts; comic format; 36 pgs. 4.00 12.00 24.00
1959 2.40 6.00 12.00

SCIENCE COMICS (1st Series)
Fox Features Syndicate: Feb, 1940 - No. 8, Sept, 1940

1-Origin Dynamo (1st app., called Electro in #1), The Eagle (1st app.), & Navy Jones; Marga, The Panther Woman (1st app.), Cosmic Carson & Perisphere Payne, Dr. Doom begin; bondage/hypo-c; Electro-c 400.00 1200.00 4200.00
2-Classic Lou Fine Dynamo-c 211.00 633.00 2000.00
3-Classic Lou Fine Dynamo-c 174.00 521.00 1650.00
4-Kirby-a; Cosmic Carson-c by Joe Simon 153.00 458.00 1450.00
5-8: 5,8-Eagle-c. 6,7-Dynamo-c 90.00 268.00 850.00
NOTE: *Cosmic Carson by **Tuska**-#1-3; by **Kirby**-#4. **Lou Fine** c-1-3 only.*

SCIENCE COMICS (2nd Series)
Humor Publications (Ace Magazines?): Jan, 1946 - No. 5, 1946

1-Palais-c/a in #1-3; A-Bomb-c 18.00 53.00 140.00
2 10.00 30.00 77.00
3-Feldstein-a (6 pgs.) 15.00 45.00 120.00
4,5: 4-Palais-c 7.15 21.50 50.00

SCIENCE COMICS
Ziff-Davis Publ. Co.: May, 1947 (8 pgs. in color)

nn-Could be ordered by mail for 10¢; like the nn Amazing Adventures (1950) & Boy Cowboy (1950); used to test the market 38.00 113.00 300.00

SCIENCE COMICS (True Science Illustrated)
Export Publication Ent., Toronto, Canada: Mar, 1951
Distr. in U.S. by Kable News Co.

1-Science Adventure stories plus some true science features; man on moon story 10.00 30.00 70.00

SCIENCE FICTION SPACE ADVENTURES (See Space Adventures)

SCION (Also see CrossGen Chronicles)
CrossGeneration Comics: Jul, 2000 - Present ($2.95)

1-8: Marz-s/Cheung-a 3.00

SCI-TECH
DC Comics (WildStorm): Sept, 1999 - No. 4, Dec, 1999 ($2.50, limited series)

1-4-Benes-a/Choi & Peterson-s 2.50

SCOOBY DOO (TV)(...Where are you? #1-16,26; ...Mystery Comics #17-25, 27 on)(See March Of Comics #356, 368, 382, 391)
Gold Key: Mar, 1970 - No. 30, Feb, 1975 (Hanna-Barbera)

1 7.50 22.50 90.00
2-5 4.60 13.75 55.00
6-10 4.10 12.30 45.00
11-20: 11-Tufts-a 3.00 9.00 30.00
21-30 2.50 7.50 25.00

SCOOBY DOO (TV)
Charlton Comics: Apr, 1975 - No. 11, Dec, 1976 (Hanna-Barbera)

1 4.10 12.30 45.00
2-5 2.50 7.50 25.00
6-11 2.30 7.00 20.00

SCOOBY-DOO (TV) (Newsstand sales only)
Marvel Comics Group: Oct, 1977 - No. 9, Feb, 1979 (Hanna-Barbera)

1,6-9: 1-Dyno-Mutt begins 2.00 6.00 18.00
2-5 1.50 4.50 12.00

SCOOBY-DOO (TV)
Harvey Comics: Sept, 1992 - No. 3, May, 1993 ($1.25)

V2#1,2 3.00
Big Book 1,2 (11/92, 4/93, $1.95, 52 pgs.) 4.00
Giant Size 1,2 (10/92, 3/93, $2.25, 68 pgs.) 4.00

SCOOBY DOO (TV)
Archie Comics: Oct, 1995 -No. 21, June, 1997 ($1.50)

1-21: 12-Cover by Scooby Doo creative designer Iwao Takamoto 3.00

SCOOBY DOO (TV)
DC Comics: Aug, 1997 - Present ($1.75/$1.95/$1.99)

1-44: 5-Begin-$1.95-c. 14-Begin $1.99-c 2.50
...Spooky Spectacular 1 (10/99, $3.95) Comic Convention story 4.00
...Spooky Spectacular 2000 (10/00, $3.95) 4.00

SCOOP COMICS (Becomes Yankee Comics #4-7, a digest sized cartoon book not listed in this guide; becomes Snap #9)
Harry 'A' Chesler (Holyoke): November, 1941 - No. 3, Mar, 1943; No. 8, 1944

1-Intro. Rocketman & Rocketgirl & begins; origin The Master Key & begins; Dan Hastings begins; Charles Sultan-c/a 126.00 379.00 1200.00
2-Rocket Boy begins; injury to eye story (reprinted in Spotlight #3); classic-c 132.00 395.00 1250.00
3-Injury to eye story-r from #2; Rocket Boy 63.00 189.00 600.00
8-Formerly Yankee Comics; becomes Snap 42.00 125.00 375.00

SCOOTER (See Swing With...)

SCOOTER COMICS
Rucker Publ. Ltd. (Canadian): Apr, 1946

1-Teen-age/funny animal 10.00 30.00 80.00

SCORCHED EARTH
Tundra Publishing: Apr, 1991 - No. 6, 1991 ($2.95, stiff-c)

1-6 3.00

SCORE, THE
DC Comics (Piranha Press): 1989 - No. 4, 1990 ($4.95, 52 pgs, squarebound, mature)

Books One - Four 5.00

SCORPION
Atlas/Seaboard Publ.: Feb, 1975 - No. 3, July, 1975

1-Intro.; bondage-c by Chaykin 1.00 3.00 8.00
2-Chaykin-a w/Wrightson, Kaluta, Simonson assists(p) 1.00 3.00 8.00
3-Jim Craig-c/a 5.00
NOTE: ***Chaykin** a-1, 2; c-1. **Colon** c-2. **Craig** c/a-3.*

SCORPION CORPS
Dagger Comics Group: Nov, 1993 - No. 7, May, 1994? ($2.75/$2.50)

1,2-($2.75): 1-Intro Angel Dust, Shellcase, Tork, Feedback & Magnon 2.75
2-Bronze, 2-Gold, 2-Silver 2.75
3-7-($2.50) 2.50

SCORPIO ROSE
Eclipse Comics: Jan, 1983 - No. 2, Oct, 1983 ($1.25, Baxter paper)

1,2: Dr. Orient back-up story begins. 2-origin. 4.00

SCOTLAND YARD (Inspector Farnsworth of)(Texas Rangers in Action #5 on?)
Charlton Comics Group: June, 1955 - No. 4, Mar, 1956

1-Tothish-a 14.00 41.00 110.00
2-4: 2-Tothish-a 10.00 30.00 75.00

SCOUT (See Eclipse Graphic Album #16, New America & Swords of Texas)(Becomes Scout: War Shaman)
Eclipse Comics: Dec, 1985 - No. 24, Oct, 1987($1.75/$1.25, Baxter paper)

1-15,17,18,20-24: 19-Airboy preview. 10-Bissette-a. 11-Monday, the Eliminator begins. 15-Swords of Texas 2.00
16,19: 16-Scout 3-D Special ($2.50), 16-Scout 2-D Limited Edition, 19-contains flexidisk ($2.50) 2.50
...Handbook 1 (8/87, $1.75, B&W) 2.00
Mount Fire (1989, $14.95, TPB) r/#8-14 15.00

SCOUT: WAR SHAMAN (Formerly Scout)
Eclipse Comics: Mar, 1988 - No. 16, Dec, 1989 ($1.95)

1-16 2.00

SCREAM (...Comics) (Andy Comics #20 on)
Humor Publications/Current Books(Ace Magazines): Autumn, 1944 - No. 19, Apr, 1948

Scud: The Disposable Assassin #2 © Fireman Press

Sea Devils #3 © DC

Sea Hunt #11 © ZIV-UA Inc.

GD2.0 FN6.0 NM9.4

1-Teenage humor 15.00 45.00 120.00
2 9.30 28.00 65.00
3-16: 11-Racist humor (Indians). 16-Intro. Lily-Belle 7.15 21.50 50.00
17,19 5.70 17.00 40.00
18-Hypo needle story 7.15 21.50 50.00

SCREAM
Skywald Publ. Corp.: Aug, 1973 - No. 11, Feb, 1975 (68 pgs., B&W, magazine)
1 3.45 10.35 38.00
2-5: 2-Origin Lady Satan. 3 (12/73)-#3 found on pg. 22
2.50 7.50 24.00
6-8: 6-Origin The Victims 2.30 7.00 20.00
9-11: 9-Severed head-c. 11- "Mr. Poe and the Raven" story
2.80 8.40 28.00

SCREWBALL SQUIRREL
Dark Horse Comics: July, 1995 - No. 3, Sept, 1995 ($2.50, limited series)
1-3: Characters created by Tex Avery 2.50

SCRIBBLY (See All-American Comics, Buzzy, The Funnies, Leave It To Binky & Popular Comics)
National Periodical Publications: 8-9/48 - No. 13, 8-9/50; No. 14, 10-11/51 - No. 15, 12-1/51-52
1-Sheldon Mayer-c/a in all; 52 pgs. begin 95.00 285.00 900.00
2 61.00 184.00 580.00
3-5 50.00 150.00 450.00
6-10 38.00 113.00 300.00
11-15: 13-Last 52 pgs. 33.00 99.00 265.00

SCUD: TALES FROM THE VENDING MACHINE
Fireman Press: 1998 - No. 5 ($2.50, B&W)
1-5: 1-Kaniuga-a. 2-Ruben Martinez-a 2.50

SCUD: THE DISPOSABLE ASSASSIN
Fireman Press: Feb, 1994 - No. 19, 1997 ($2.95, B&W)
1 1.00 3.00 8.00
1-2nd printing in color 3.00
2,3 5.00
4-9 4.00
10-19 3.00
Heavy 3PO ($12.95, TPB) r/#1-4 13.00
Programmed For Damage ($14.95, TPB) r/#5-9 15.00
Solid Gold Bomb ($17.95, TPB) r/#10-15 18.00

SEA DEVILS (See Limited Collectors' Edition #39,45, & Showcase #27-29)
National Periodical Publications: Sept-Oct, 1961 - No. 35, May-June, 1967
1-(9-10/61) 50.00 150.00 650.00
2-Last 10¢ issue 27.50 82.00 300.00
3-Begin 12¢ issues thru #35 18.00 54.00 200.00
4,5 16.00 48.00 175.00
6-10 10.00 30.00 110.00
11,12,14-20 6.80 20.50 75.00
13-Kubert, Colan-a; Joe Kubert app. in story 7.25 21.75 80.00
21-35: 22-Intro. International Sea Devils; origin & 1st app. Capt. X & Man Fish 4.55 13.65 50.00
NOTE: *Heath a-B&B 27-29, 1-10; c-B&B 27-29, 1-10, 14-16.* ***Moldoff*** *a-16i.*

SEA DEVILS (See Tangent Comics/ Sea Devils)

SEADRAGON (Also see the Epsilion Wave)
Elite Comics: May, 1986 - No. 8, 1987 ($1.75)
1-8: 1-1st & 2nd printings exist 2.00

SEA HOUND, THE (Captain Silver's Log Of The...)
Avon Periodicals: 1945 (no month) - No. 2, Sept-Oct, 1945
nn (#1)-29 pg. novel length sty-"The Esmeralda's Treasure"
18.00 53.00 140.00
2 12.00 36.00 95.00

SEA HOUND, THE (Radio)
Capt. Silver Syndicate: No. 3, July, 1949 - No. 4, Sept, 1949
3,4 10.00 30.00 70.00

SEA HUNT (TV)
Dell Publishing Co.: No. 928, 8/58 - No. 1041, 10-12/59; No. 4, 1-3/60 - No. 13, 4-6/62 (All have Lloyd Bridges photo-c)
Four Color 928(#1) 11.70 35.00 140.00
Four Color 994(#2), 4-13: Manning-a #4-6,8-11,13 8.00 24.00 95.00
Four Color 1041(#3)-Toth-a 8.35 25.00 100.00

SEAQUEST (TV)
Nemesis Comics: Mar, 1994 ($2.25)
1-Has 2 diff-c stocks (slick & cardboard); Alcala-i 2.25

SEARCH FOR LOVE
American Comics Group: Feb-Mar, 1950 - No. 2, Apr-May, 1950 (52 pgs.)
1 11.00 33.00 90.00
2 8.65 26.00 60.00

SEARCHERS, THE (Movie)
Dell Publishing Co.: No. 709, 1956
Four Color 709-John Wayne photo-c 24.00 73.00 290.00

SEARCHERS, THE
Caliber Comics: 1996 - No. 4, 1996 ($2.95, B&W)
1-4 3.00

SEARCHERS, THE : APOSTLE OF MERCY
Caliber Comics: 1997 - No. 2, 1997 ($2.95/$3.95, B&W)
1-($2.95) 3.00
2-($3.95) 4.00

SEARS (See Merry Christmas From...)

SEASON'S GREETINGS
Hallmark (King Features): 1935 (6-1/4x5-1/4", 32 pgs. in color)
nn-Cover features Mickey Mouse, Popeye, Jiggs & Skippy. "The Night Before Christmas" told one panel per page, each panel by a famous artist featuring their character. Art by Alex Raymond, Gottfredson, Swinnerton, Segar, Chic Young, Milt Gross, Sullivan (Messmer), Herriman, McManus, Percy Crosby & others (22 artists in all)
Estimated value... 700.00

SEBASTION O
DC Comics (Vertigo): May, 1993 - No. 3, July, 1993 ($1.95, limited series)
1-3-Grant Morrison scripts 2.00

SECOND LIFE OF DOCTOR MIRAGE, THE (See Shadowman #16)
Valiant: Nov, 1993 - No. 18, May, 1995 ($2.50)
1-18: 1-With bound-in poster. 5-Shadowman x-over. 7-Bound-in trading card 2.50
1-Gold ink logo edition; no price on-c 3.00

SECRET AGENT (Formerly Sarge Steel)
Charlton Comics: V2#9, Oct, 1966; V2#10, Oct, 1967
V2#9-Sarge Steel part-r begins 2.50 7.50 24.00
10-Tiffany Sinn, CIA app. (from Career Girl Romances #39); Aparo-a
2.00 6.00 18.00

SECRET AGENT (TV) (See Four Color #1231)
Gold Key: Nov, 1966; No. 2, Jan, 1968
1-Photo-c 11.30 34.00 135.00
2-Photo-c 7.00 21.00 85.00

SECRET AGENT X-9 (See Flash Gordon #4 by King)
David McKay Publ.: 1934 (Book 1: 84 pgs.; Book 2: 124 pgs.) (8x7-1/2")
Book 1-Contains reprints of the first 13 weeks of the strip by Alex Raymond; complete except for 2 dailies 42.00 125.00 375.00
Book 2-Contains reprints immediately following contents of Book 1, for 20 weeks by Alex Raymond; complete except for two dailies. Note: Raymond mis-dated the last five strips from 6/34, and while the dating sequence is confusing, the continuity is correct 40.00 120.00 325.00

SECRET AGENT X-9 (See Magic Comics)
Dell Publishing Co.: Dec, 1937 (Not by Raymond)
Feature Books 8 38.00 113.00 450.00

SECRET AGENT Z-2 (See Holyoke One-Shot No. 7)

Secret Diary of Eerie Adventures nn © AVON

Secret Hearts #140 © DC

Secret Origins (3rd series) #20 © DC

SECRET CITY SAGA (See Jack Kirby's Secret City Saga)

SECRET DEFENDERS (Also see The Defenders & Fantastic Four #374)
Marvel Comics: Mar, 1993 - No. 25, Mar, 1995 ($1.75/$1.95)

1-($2.50)-Red foil stamped-c; Dr. Strange, Nomad, Wolverine, Spider Woman & Darkhawk begin 2.50
2-11,13-24: 9-New team w/Silver Surfer, Thunderstrike, Dr. Strange & War Machine. 13-Thanos replaces Dr. Strange as leader; leads into Cosmic Powers limited series; 14-Dr. Druid. 15-Bound in card sheet. 18-Giant Man & Iron Fist app. 2.00
12,25: 12-($2.50)-Prismatic foil-c. 25 ($2.50, 52 pgs.) 2.50

SECRET DIARY OF EERIE ADVENTURES
Avon Periodicals: 1953 (25¢ giant, 100 pgs., one-shot)

nn-(Rare)-Kubert-a; Hollingsworth-c; Sid Check back-c 168.00 505.00 1600.00

SECRET FILES & ORIGINS GUIDE TO THE DC UNIVERSE 2000
DC Comics: Mar, 2000 ($6.95, one-shot)

1-Overview of DC characters; profile pages by various 6.95

SECRET HEARTS
National Periodical Publications (Beverly)(Arleigh No. 50-113): 9-10/49 - No. 6, 7-8/50; No. 7, 12-1/51-52 - No. 153, 7/71

1-Kinstler-a; photo-c begin, end #6 53.00 158.00 475.00
2-Toth-a (1 pg.); Kinstler-a 28.00 84.00 225.00
3,6 (1950) 24.00 73.00 195.00
4,5-Toth-a 25.00 75.00 200.00
7(12-1/51-52) (Rare) 40.00 120.00 350.00
8-10 (1952) 18.00 53.00 140.00
11-20 14.00 41.00 110.00
21-26: 26-Last precode (2-3/55) 12.00 36.00 95.00
27-40 6.35 19.00 70.00
41-50 4.10 12.30 45.00
51-60 3.20 9.60 35.00
61-75,100: 75-Last 10¢ issue 3.00 9.00 30.00
76-99,101-109 2.50 7.50 25.00
110- "Reach for Happiness" serial begins, ends #138 2.50 7.50 25.00
111-119,121-126 2.30 7.00 20.00
120,134-Neal Adams-c 3.00 9.00 30.00
127 (4/68)-Beatles cameo 3.00 9.00 30.00
128-133,135-142: 141,142- "20 Miles to Heartbreak", Chapter 2 & 3 (see Young Love for Chapters 1 & 4); Toth, Colletta-a 2.00 6.00 18.00
143-148,150-152: 144-Morrow-a 1.75 5.25 14.00
149,153: 149-Toth-a. 153-Kirby-i 2.00 6.00 18.00

SECRET ISLAND OF OZ, THE (See First Comics Graphic Novel)

SECRET LOVE (See Fox Giants & Sinister House of...)

SECRET LOVE
Ajax-Farrell/Four Star Comic Corp. No. 2 on: 12/55 - No. 3, 8/56; 4/57 - No. 5, 2/58; No. 6, 6/58

1(12/55-Ajax, 1st series) 10.00 30.00 70.00
2,3 6.00 18.00 42.00
1(4/57-Ajax, 2nd series) 7.85 23.50 55.00
2-6: 5-Bakerish-a 5.00 15.00 35.00

SECRET LOVES
Comic Magazines/Quality Comics Group: Nov, 1949 - No. 6, Sept, 1950

1-Ward-c 23.00 69.00 185.00
2-Ward-c 20.00 60.00 160.00
3-Crandall-a 12.50 37.50 100.00
4,6 9.30 28.00 65.00
5-Suggestive art "Boom Town Babe"; photo-c 12.50 37.50 100.00

SECRET LOVE STORIES (See Fox Giants)

SECRET MISSIONS (Admiral Zacharia's...)
St. John Publishing Co.: February, 1950

1-Joe Kubert-c; stories of U.S. foreign agents 20.00 60.00 160.00

SECRET MYSTERIES (Formerly Crime Mysteries & Crime Smashers)
Ribage/Merit Publications No. 17 on: No. 16, Nov, 1954 - No. 19, July, 1955

16-Horror, Palais-a; Myron Fass-c 26.00 79.00 210.00
17-19-Horror. 17-Fass-c; mis-dated 3/54? 18.00 53.00 140.00

SECRET ORIGINS (1st Series) (See 80 Page Giant #8)
National Periodical Publications: Aug-Oct, 1961 (Annual) (Reprints)

1-Origin Adam Strange (Showcase #17), Green Lantern (Green Lantern #1), Challengers (partial-r/Showcase #6, 6 pgs. Kirby-a), J'onn J'onzz (Det. #225), The Flash (Showcase #4), Green Arrow (1 pg. text), Superman-Batman team (W. Finest #94), Wonder Woman (Wonder Woman #105) 46.00 138.00 600.00
Replica Edition (1998, $4.95) r/entire book and house ads 5.00

SECRET ORIGINS (2nd Series)
National Periodical Publications: Feb-Mar, 1973 - No. 6, Jan-Feb, 1974; No. 7, Oct-Nov, 1974 (All 20¢ issues) (All origin reprints)

1-Superman(r/1 pg. origin/Action #1, 1st time since G.A.), Batman(Det. #33), Ghost(Flash #88), The Flash(Showcase #4) 3.20 9.60 35.00
2-7: 2-Green Lantern & The Atom(Showcase #22 & 34), Supergirl(Action #252). 3-Wonder Woman(W.W. #1), Wildcat(Sensation #1). 4-Vigilante (Action #42) by Meskin, Kid Eternity(Hit #25). 5-The Spectre by Baily (More Fun #52,53). 6-Blackhawk(Military #1) & Legion of Super-Heroes(Superboy #147). 7-Robin (Detective #38), Aquaman (More Fun #73) 2.00 6.00 18.00

NOTE: ***Infantino** a-1. **Kane** a-2. **Kubert** a-1.*

SECRET ORIGINS (3rd Series)
DC Comics: 4/86 - No. 50, 8/90 (All origins)(52 pgs. #6 on)(#27 on: $1.50)

1-Origin Superman 5.00
2-6: 2-Blue Beetle. 3-Shazam. 4-Firestorm. 5-Crimson Avenger. 6-Halo/G.A. Batman 3.00
7-12,14-26: 7-Green Lantern(Guy Gardner)/G.A. Sandman. 8-Shadow Lass/Doll Man. 9-G.A. Flash/Skyman. 10-Phantom Stranger w/Alan Moore scripts; Legends spin-off. 11-G.A. Hawkman/Power Girl. 12-Challengers of Unknown/G.A. Fury (2nd modern app.). 14-Suicide Squad; Legends spin-off. 15-Spectre/Deadman. 16-G.A. Hourman/Warlord. 17-Adam Strange story by Carmine infantino; Dr. Occult. 18-G.A. Gr. Lantern/The Creeper. 19-Uncle Sam/The Guardian. 20-Batgirl/G.A. Dr. Mid-Nite. 21-Jonah Hex/Black Condor. 22-Manhunters. 23-Floronic Man/Guardians of the Universe. 24-Blue Devil/Dr. Fate. 25-LSH/Atom. 26-Black Lightning/Miss America 2.50
13-Origin Nightwing; Johnny Thunder app. 2.50
27-49: 27-Zatara/Zatanna. 28-Midnight/Nightshade. 29-Power of the Atom/Mr. America; new 3 pg. Red Tornado story by Mayer (last app. of Scribbly, 8/88). 30-Plastic Man/Elongated Man. 31-JSA. 32-JLA. 33-35-JLI. 36-Poison Ivy by Neil Gaiman & Mark Buckingham/Green Lantern. 37-Legion Of Substitute Heroes/Doctor Light. 38-Green Arrow/Speedy; Grell scripts. 39-Animal Man-c/story continued in Animal Man #10; Grant Morrison scripts;Batman app.40-All Ape issue. 41-Rogues Gallery of Flash. 42-Phantom Girl/GrimGhost. 43-Original Hawk & Dove/Cave Carson/Chris KL-99. 44-Batman app.;story based on Det. #40. 45-Blackhawk/El Diablo. 46-JLA/LSH/New Titans. 47-LSH. 48-Ambush Bug/Stanley & His Monster/Rex the Wonder Dog/Trigger Twins. 49-Newsboy Legion/Silent Knight/brief origin Bouncing Boy 2.00
50-($3.95, 100 pgs.)-Batman & Robin in text, Flash of Two Worlds, Johnny Thunder, Dolphin, Black Canary & Space Museum 5.00
Annual 1 (8/87)-Capt. Comet/Doom Patrol 3.00
Annual 2 ('88, $2.00)-Origin Flash II & Flash III 3.00
Annual 3 ('89, $2.95, 84 pgs.)-Teen Titans; 1st app. new Flamebird who replaces original Bat-Girl 3.50
Special 1 (10/89, $2.00)-Batman villains: Penguin, Riddler, & Two-Face; Bolland-c; Sam Kieth-a; Neil Gaiman scripts(2) 3.00

NOTE: ***Art Adams** a-33i(part). **M. Anderson** 8, 19, 21, 25i; c-19(part). **Aparo** c/a-10. **Bissette** c-23. **Bolland** c-7. **Byrne** c/a-Annual 1. **Colan** c/a-5p. **Forte** a-37. **Giffen** a-18p, 44p, 48. **Infantino** a-17, 50p. **Kaluta** c-39. **Gil Kane** a-2, 28; c-2p. **Kirby** c-19(part). **Erik Larsen** a-13. **Mayer** a-29. **Morrow** a-21. **Orlando** a-10. **Perez** a-50i, Annual 3i; c- Annual 3. **Rogers** a-6p. **Russell** a-27i. **Simonson** c-22. **Staton** a-36, 50p. **Steacy** a-35. **Tuska** a-4p, 9p.*

SECRET ORIGINS 80 PAGE GIANT (Young Justice)
DC Comics: Dec, 1998 ($4.95, one-shot)

1-Origin-s of Young Justice members; Ramos-a (Impulse) 5.00

SECRET ORIGINS FEATURING THE JLA
DC Comics: 1999 ($14.95, TPB)

1-Reprints recent origin-s of JLA members; Cassaday-c 15.00

Secret Society of Super-Villains #8 © DC

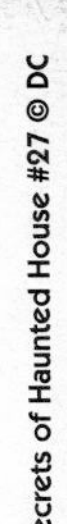
Secrets of Haunted House #27 © DC

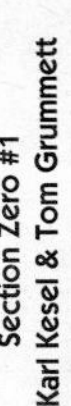
Section Zero #1 © Karl Kesel & Tom Grummett

GD2.0 FN6.0 NM9.4

SECRET ORIGINS OF SUPER-HEROES (See DC Special Series #10, 19)

SECRET ORIGINS OF SUPER-VILLAINS 80 PAGE GIANT
DC Comics: Dec, 1999 ($4.95, one-shot)

1-Origin-s of Sinestro, Amazo and others; Gibbons-c 5.00

SECRET ORIGINS OF THE WORLD'S GREATEST SUPER-HEROES
DC Comics: 1989 ($4.95, 148 pgs.)

nn-Reprints Superman, JLA origins; new Batman origin-s; Bolland-c 1.00 2.80 7.00

SECRET ROMANCE
Charlton Comics: Oct, 1968 - No. 41, Nov, 1976; No. 42, Mar, 1979 - No. 48, Feb, 1980

	GD2.0	FN6.0	NM9.4
1-Begin 12¢ issues, ends #?	2.00	6.00	18.00
2-10: 9-Reese-a	1.25	3.75	10.00
11-30	1.00	2.80	7.00
31-48			4.00

NOTE: *Beyond the Stars app.-No. 9, 11, 12, 14.*

SECRET ROMANCES (Exciting Love Stories)
Superior Publications Ltd.: Apr, 1951 - No. 27, July, 1955

	GD2.0	FN6.0	NM9.4
1	13.00	39.00	105.00
2	9.30	28.00	65.00
3-10	6.40	19.25	45.00
11-13,15-18,20-27	5.00	15.00	35.00
14,19-Lingerie panels	6.00	18.00	42.00

SECRET SERVICE (See Kent Blake of the...)

SECRET SIX (See Action Comics Weekly)
National Periodical Publications: Apr-May, 1968 - No. 7, Apr-May, 1969 (12¢)

	GD2.0	FN6.0	NM9.4
1-Origin/1st app.	5.40	16.35	60.00
2-7	3.20	9.60	35.00

SECRET SIX (See Tangent Comics/ Secret Six)

SECRET SOCIETY OF SUPER-VILLAINS
National Per. Publ./DC Comics: May-June, 1976 - No. 15, June-July, 1978

	GD2.0	FN6.0	NM9.4
1-Origin; JLA cameo & Capt. Cold app.	1.50	4.50	12.00
2-5,15: 2-Re-intro/origin Capt. Comet; Green Lantern x-over. 5-Green Lantern, Hawkman x-over; Darkseid app. 15-G.A. Atom, Dr. Midnite, & JSA app.	1.00	3.00	8.00
6-14: 9,10-Creeper x-over. 11-Capt. Comet; Orlando-i		2.40	6.00

SECRET SOCIETY OF SUPER-VILLAINS SPECIAL (See DC Special Series #6)

SECRETS OF HAUNTED HOUSE
National Periodical Publications/DC Comics: 4-5/75 - #5, 12-1/75-76; #6, 6-7/77 - #14, 10-11/78; #15, 8/79 - #46, 3/82

	GD2.0	FN6.0	NM9.4
1	3.20	9.60	35.00
2-4	2.00	6.00	16.00
5-Wrightson-c	2.00	6.00	18.00
6-14	1.25	3.75	10.00
15-30	1.00	3.00	8.00
31,44: 31-Mr. E series begins, ends #41. 44-Wrightson-c	1.00	3.00	8.00
32-43,45,46			5.00

NOTE: ***Aparo** c-7. **Aragones** a-1. **B. Bailey** a-8. **Bissette** a-46. **Buckler** c-32-40p. **Ditko** a-9, 12, 41, 45. **Golden** a-10. **Howard** a-13i. **Kaluta** c-8, 10, 11, 14, 16, 29. **Kubert** c-41, 42. **Sheldon Mayer** a-43p. **McWilliams** a-35. **Nasser** a-24. **Newton** a-30p. **Nino** a-1, 13, 19. **Orlando** c-13, 30, 43, 45i. **N. Redondo** a-4, 5, 29. **Rogers** c-26. **Spiegle** a-31-41. **Wrightson** c-5, 44.*

SECRETS OF HAUNTED HOUSE SPECIAL (See DC Special Series #12)

SECRETS OF LIFE (Movie)
Dell Publishing Co.: 1956 (Disney)

Four Color 749-Photo-c 4.55 13.65 5.00

SECRETS OF LOVE (See Popular Teen-Agers...)

SECRETS OF LOVE AND MARRIAGE
Charlton Comics: V2#1, Aug, 1956 - V2#25, June, 1961

	GD2.0	FN6.0	NM9.4
V2#1	3.80	11.40	42.00
V2#2-6	2.80	8.40	28.00
V2#7-9-(All 68 pgs.)	4.10	12.30	45.00
10-25	2.30	7.00	20.00

SECRETS OF MAGIC (See Wisco)

SECRETS OF SINISTER HOUSE (Sinister House of Secret Love #1-4)
National Periodical Publ.: No. 5, June-July, 1972 - No. 18, June-July, 1974

	GD2.0	FN6.0	NM9.4
5-(52 pgs.).	3.20	9.60	35.00
6-9: 7-Redondo-a	2.30	7.00	20.00
10-Neal Adams-a(i)	2.50	7.50	25.00
11-18: 15-Redondo-a. 17-Barry-a; early Chaykin 1 pg. strip	1.50	4.50	12.00

NOTE: ***Alcala** a-6, 13, 14. **Glanzman** a-7. **Kaluta** c-6, 7. **Nino** a-8, 11-13. Ambrose Bierce adapt.-#14.*

SECRETS OF THE LEGION OF SUPER-HEROES
DC Comics: Jan, 1981 - No. 3, Mar, 1981 (Limited series)

1-3: 1-Origin of the Legion. 2-Retells origins of Brainiac 5, Shrinking Violet, Sun-Boy, Bouncing Boy, Ultra-Boy, Matter-Eater Lad, Mon-El, Karate Kid, & Dream Girl 3.00

SECRETS OF TRUE LOVE
St. John Publishing Co.: Feb, 1958

1 5.00 15.00 32.00

SECRETS OF YOUNG BRIDES
Charlton Comics: No. 5, Sept, 1957 - No. 44, Oct, 1964; July, 1975 - No. 9, Nov, 1976

	GD2.0	FN6.0	NM9.4
5	3.65	11.00	40.00
6-10: 8-Negligee panel	2.80	8.40	28.00
11-20	2.50	7.50	24.00
21-30: Last 10¢ issue?	2.00	6.00	18.00
31-44(10/64)	1.75	5.25	14.00
1-(2nd series) (7/75)	1.85	5.50	15.00
2-9	1.00	3.00	8.00

SECRET SQUIRREL (TV)(See Kite Fun Book)
Gold Key: Oct, 1966 (12¢) (Hanna-Barbera)

1-1st Secret Squirrel and Morocco Mole, Squiddly Diddly, Winsome Witch 12.50 37.50 150.00

SECRET STORY ROMANCES (Becomes True Tales of Love)
Atlas Comics (TCI): Nov, 1953 - No. 21, Mar, 1956

	GD2.0	FN6.0	NM9.4
1-Everett-a; Jay Scott Pike-c	13.00	39.00	105.00
2	7.85	23.50	55.00
3-11: 11-Last pre-code (2/55)	6.00	18.00	42.00
12-21	5.00	15.00	35.00

NOTE: ***Colletta** a-10, 14, 15, 17, 21; c-10, 14, 17.*

SECRET VOICE, THE (See Great American Comics Presents...)

SECRET WARS II (Also see Marvel Super Heroes...)
Marvel Comics Group: July, 1985 - No. 9, Mar, 1986 (Maxi-series)

1,9: 9-(52 pgs.) X-Men app., Spider-Man app. 4.00
2-8: 2,8-X-Men app. 5-1st app. Boom Boom. 5,8-Spider-Man app. 3.00

SECRET WEAPONS
Valiant: Sept, 1993 - No. 21, May, 1995 ($2.25)

1-10,12-21: 3-Reese-a(i). 5-Ninjak app. 9-Bound-in trading card. 12-Bloodshot app. 2.50
11-(Sept. on envelope, Aug on-c, $2.50)-Enclosed in manilla envelope; Bloodshot app; intro new team. 2.50

SECTAURS
Marvel Comics: June, 1985 - No. 10?, 1986 (75¢) (Based on Coleco Toys)

1-10, 1-Coleco giveaway; different-c 3.00

SECTION ZERO
Image Comics (Gorilla): June, 2000 - Present ($2.50)

1-3-Kesel-s/Grummett-a 2.50

SEDUCTION OF THE INNOCENT (Also see New York State Joint Legislative Committee to Study...)
Rinehart & Co., Inc., N. Y.: 1953, 1954 (400 pgs.) (Hardback, $4.00)(Written by Fredric Wertham, M.D.)(Also printed in Canada by Clarke, Irwin & Co. Ltd.)

(1st Version)-with bibliographical note intact (pages 399 & 400)(several copies

Select Detective #2 © F.S. Publ.

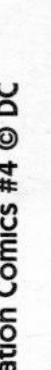
Sensational Spider-Man #27 (Sensational Hornet #1) © MAR

Sensation Comics #4 © DC

got out before the comic publishers forced the removal of this page) 53.00 158.00 475.00
Dust jacket only 30.00 90.00 240.00
(1st Version)-without bibliographical note 30.00 90.00 240.00
Dust jacket only 14.00 41.00 110.00
(2nd Version)-Published in England by Kennikat Press, 1954, 399 pgs. has bibliographical page 10.00 30.00 80.00
1972 r-/of 2nd version; 400 pgs. w/bibliography page; Kennikat Press 3.00 9.00 30.00

NOTE: *Material from this book appeared in the November, 1953(Vol.70, pp50-53,214) issue of the* ***Ladies' Home Journal*** *under the title "What Parents Don't Know About Comic Books". With the release of this book, Dr. Wertham reveals seven years of research attempting to link juvenile delinquency to comic books. Many illustrations showing excessive violence, sex, sadism, and torture are shown. This book was used at the Kefauver Senate hearings which led to the Comics Code Authority. Because of the influence this book had on the comic industry and the collector's interest in it, we feel this listing is justified. Also see* ***Parade of Pleasure.***

SEDUCTION OF THE INNOCENT! (Also see Halloween Horror)
Eclipse Comics: Nov, 1985 - 3-D#2, Apr, 1986 ($1.75)

1-6: Double listed under cover title from #7 on 3.00
3-D 1 (10/85, $2.25, 36 pgs.)-contains unpublished Advs. Into Darkness #15 (pre-code);Dave Stevens-c 4.00
2D 1 (100 copy limited signed & numbered edition)(B&W) 1.00 2.80 7.00
3-D 2 (4/86)-Baker, Toth, Wrightson-c 4.00
2-D 2 (100 copy limited signed & numbered edition)(B&W) 1.00 2.80 7.00

NOTE: ***Anderson*** *r-2, 3.* ***Crandall*** *c/a(r)-1.* ***Meskin*** *c/a(r)-3, 3-D 1.* ***Moreira*** *r-2.* ***Toth*** *a-1-6r; c-4r.* ***Tuska*** *r-6.*

SEEKER
Sky Comics: Apr, 1994 ($2.50, one-shot)

1 2.50

SEEKERS INTO THE MYSTERY
DC Comics (Vertigo): Jan, 1996 - No. 15, Apr, 1997 ($2.50)

1-14: J.M. DeMatteis scripts in all. 1-4-Glenn Barr-a. 5,10-Muth-c/a. 6-9-Zulli-c/a. 11-14-Bolton-c; Jill Thompson-a 2.50
15-($2.95)-Muth-c/a 3.00

SEEKER 3000 (See Marvel Premiere #41)
Marvel Comics: Jun, 1998 - No. 4, Sept, 1998 ($2.99/$2.50, limited series)

1-($2.99)-Set 25 years after 1st app.; wraparound-c 3.00
2-4-($2.50) 2.50
...Premiere 1 (6/98, $1.50) Reprints 1st app. from Marvel Premiere #41; wraparound-c 2.00

SELECT DETECTIVE (Exciting New Mystery Cases)
D. S. Publishing Co.: Aug-Sept, 1948 - No. 3, Dec-Jan, 1948-49

1-Matt Baker-a 27.00 81.00 215.00
2-Baker, McWilliams-a 18.00 53.00 140.00
3 15.00 45.00 120.00

SELF-LOATHING COMICS
Fantagraphics Books: Feb, 1995 ($2.95, B&W)

1,2-Crumb 3.00

SEMPER FI (Tales of the Marine Corp)
Marvel Comics: Dec, 1988- No.9, Aug, 1989 (75¢)

1-9: Severin-c/a 2.00

SENSATIONAL POLICE CASES (Becomes Captain Steve Savage, 2nd Series)
Avon Periodicals: 1952; No. 2, 1954 - No. 4, July-Aug, 1954

nn-(1952, 25¢, 100 pgs.)-Kubert-a?; Check, Larsen, Lawrence & McCann-a; Kinstler-c 40.00 120.00 330.00
2-4: 2-Kirbyish-a (3-4/54). 4-Reprint/Saint #5; spanking panel 13.00 39.00 105.00
I.W. Reprint #5-(1963?, nd)-Reprints Prison Break #5(1952-Realistic); Infantino-a 2.80 8.40 28.00

SENSATIONAL SHE-HULK, THE (She-Hulk #21-23) (See Savage She-Hulk)
Marvel Comics: V2#1, 5/89 - No. 60, Feb, 1994 ($1.50/$1.75, deluxe format)

V2#1-Byrne-c/a(p)/scripts begin, end #8 3.00
2,3,5-8: 3-Spider-Man app. 2.00
4,14-17,21-23: 4-Reintro G.A. Blonde Phantom. 14-17-Howard the Duck app. 21-23-Return of the Blonde Phantom. 22-All Winners Squad app. 2.50
9-13,18-20,24-49,51-60: 25-Thor app. 26-Excalibur app.;Guice-c. 29-Wolverine app. (3 pgs.). 30-Hobgoblin-c & cameo. 31-Byrne-c/a/scripts begin again. 35-Last $1.50-c. 37-Wolverine/Punisher/Spidey-c, but no app. 39-Thing app. 56-War Zone app.; Hulk cameo. 57-Vs. Hulk-c/story. 58-Electro-c/story. 59-Jack O'Lantern app. 2.00
50-($2.95, 52 pgs.)-Embossed green foil-c; Byrne app.; last Byrne-c/a; Austin, Chaykin, Simonson-a; Miller-a(2 pgs.) 3.00

NOTE: ***Dale Keown*** *a(p)-13, 15-22.*

SENSATIONAL SHE-HULK IN CEREMONY, THE
Marvel Comics: 1989 - No. 2, 1989 ($3.95, squarebound, 52 pgs.)

nn-Part 1, nn-Part 2 4.00

SENSATIONAL SPIDER-MAN
Marvel Comics: Apr, 1989 ($5.95, squarebound, 80 pgs.)

1-r/Amazing Spider-Man Annual #14,15 by Miller & Annual #8 by Kirby & Ditko. 6.00

SENSATIONAL SPIDER-MAN, THE
Marvel Comics: Jan, 1996 - No. 33, Nov, 1998 ($1.95/$1.99)

0 ($4.95)-Lenticular-c; Jurgens-a/scripts 5.00
1 5.00
1-($2.95) variant-c; polybagged w/cassette 1.00 3.00 8.00
2-5: 2-Kaine & Rhino app. 3-Giant-Man app. 4.00
6-18: 9-Onslaught tie-in; revealed that Peter & Mary Jane's unborn baby is a girl. 11-Revelations. 13-15-Ka-Zar app. 14,15-Hulk app. 3.00
19-24: Living Pharoah app. 22,23-Dr. Strange app. 2.50
25-($2.99) Spiderhunt pt. 1; Normie Osborne kidnapped 4.00
25-Variant-c 1.00 3.00 8.00
26-33: 26-Nauck-a. 27-Double-c with "The Sensational Hornet #1"; Vulture app. 28-Hornet vs. Vulture. 29,30-Black Cat-c/app. 33-Last issue; Gathering of Five concludes 2.50
#(-1) Flashback(7/97) Dezago-s/Wieringo-a 3.00
'96 Annual ($2.95) 3.00

SENSATION COMICS (Sensation Mystery #110 on)
National Per. Publ./All-American: Jan, 1942 - No. 109, May-June, 1952

	GD2.0	FN6.0	VF8.0	NM9.4
1-Origin Mr. Terrific(1st app.), Wildcat(1st app.), The Gay Ghost, & Little Boy Blue; Wonder Woman(cont'd from All Star #8), The Black Pirate begin; intro. Justice & Fair Play Club	2160.00	6480.00	14,000.00	27,000.00

1-Reprint, Oversize 13-1/2x10". WARNING: This comic is an exact duplicate reprint of the original except for its size. DC published it in 1974 with a second cover titling it as a Famous First Edition. There have been many reported cases of the outer cover being removed and the interior sold as the original edition. The reprint with the new outer cover removed is practically worthless. See Famous First Edition for value.

	GD2.0	FN6.0	NM9.4
2-Etta Candy begins	429.00	1285.00	4500.00
3-W. Woman gets secretary's job	253.00	758.00	2400.00
4-1st app. Stretch Skinner in Wildcat	179.00	537.00	1700.00
5-Intro. Justin, Black Pirate's son	142.00	426.00	1350.00
6-Origin/1st app. Wonder Woman's magic lasso	147.00	442.00	1400.00
7-10	103.00	308.00	975.00
11,12,14-20	95.00	285.00	900.00
13-Hitler, Tojo, Mussolini-c (as bowling pins)	126.00	379.00	1200.00
21-30	74.00	221.00	700.00
31-33	55.00	165.00	525.00
34-Sargon, the Sorcerer begins (10/44), ends #36; begins again #52	58.00	174.00	550.00
35-40: 38-X-Mas-c	50.00	150.00	450.00
41-50: 43-The Whip app.	43.00	130.00	390.00
51-67,69-80: 51-Last Black Pirate. 56,57-Sargon by Kubert. 63-Last Mr. Terrific. 66-Wildcat by Kubert	40.00	120.00	330.00
68-Origin & 1st app. Huntress (8/47)	40.00	120.00	360.00
81-Used in **SOTI**, pg. 33,34; Krigstein-a	40.00	120.00	350.00
82-93: 83-Last Sargon. 86-The Atom app. 90-Last Wildcat. 91-Streak begins by Alex Toth. 92-Toth-a (2 pgs.)	34.00	103.00	275.00
94-1st all girl issue	46.00	137.00	410.00
95-99,101-106: 95-Unmasking of Wonder Woman-c/story. 99-1st app. Astra, Girl of the Future, ends #106. 103-Robot-c. 105-Last 52 pgs. 106-Wonder Woman ends	42.00	125.00	375.00
100-(11-12/50)	55.00	165.00	525.00

Sentry #5 © MAR

Sgt. Fury #4 © MAR

Sgt. Rock #322 © DC

107-(Scarce, 1-2/52)-1st mystery issue; Johnny Peril by Toth(p), 8 pgs. & begins; continues from Danger Trail #5 (3-4/51)(see Comic Cavalcade #15 for 1st app.) 68.00 205.00 650.00
108-(Scarce)-Johnny Peril by Toth(p) 55.00 165.00 525.00
109-(Scarce)-Johnny Peril by Toth(p) 68.00 205.00 650.00
NOTE: ***Krigstein** a-(Wildcat)-81, 83, 84. **Moldoff** Black Pirate-1-25; Black Pirate not in 34-36, 43-48. **Oskner** c(i)-89-91, 94-106. Wonder Woman by **H. G. Peter**, all issues except #8, 17-19, 21; c-4-7, 9-18, 20-88, 92, 93. **Toth** a-91, 98; c-107. Wonder Woman c-1-106.*

SENSATION COMICS (Also see All Star Comics 1999 crossover titles)
DC Comics: May, 1999 ($1.99, one-shot)

1-Golden Age Wonder Woman and Hawkgirl; Robinson-s 2.00

SENSATION MYSTERY (Formerly Sensation Comics #1-109)
National Periodical Publ.: No. 110, July-Aug, 1952 - No. 116, July-Aug, 1953

110-Johnny Peril continues 42.00 125.00 375.00
111-116-Johnny Peril in all. 116-M. Anderson-a 42.00 125.00 375.00
NOTE: ***M. Anderson** c-110. **Colan** a-114p. **Giunta** a-112. **G. Kane** c(p)-108, 109, 111-115.*

SENTINELS OF JUSTICE, THE (See Americomics & Captain Paragon &...)

SENTRY
Marvel Comics: Sept, 2000 - No. 5, Jan, 2001 ($2.99, limited series)

1-5-Paul Jenkins-s/Jae Lee-a. 3-Spider-Man-c/app. 4-X-Men, FF app. 3.00
.../Fantastic Four (2/01, $2.99) Continues story from #5; Winslade-a 3.00
.../Spider-Man (2/01, $2.99) back story of the Sentry; Leonardi-a 3.00
.../X-Men (2/01, $2.99) Sentry and Archangel; Texeira-a 3.00

SENTRY SPECIAL
Innovation Publishing: 1991 ($2.75, one-shot)(Hero Alliance spin-off)

1-Lost in Space preview (3 pgs.) 2.75

SERAPHIM
Innovation Publishing: May, 1990 ($2.50, mature readers)

1 2.50

SERGEANT BARNEY BARKER (Becomes G. I. Tales #4 on)
Atlas Comics (MCI): Aug, 1956 - No. 3, Dec, 1956

1-Severin-c/a(4) 19.00 56.00 150.00
2,3: 2-Severin-c/a(4). 3-Severin-c/a(5) 13.00 39.00 105.00

SERGEANT BILKO (Phil Silvers Starring as...) (TV)
National Periodical Publications: May-June, 1957 - No. 18, Mar-Apr, 1960

1-All have Bob Oskner-c 71.00 213.00 675.00
2 40.00 120.00 325.00
3-5 34.00 103.00 275.00
6-18: 11,12,15,17-Photo-c 28.00 84.00 225.00

SGT. BILKO'S PVT. DOBERMAN (TV)
National Periodical Publications: June-July, 1958 - No. 11, Feb-Mar, 1960

1-Bob Oskner c-1-4,7,11 33.00 100.00 400.00
2 20.00 60.00 220.00
3-5: 5-Photo-c 14.00 42.00 155.00
6-11: 6,9-Photo-c 10.00 30.00 110.00

SGT. DICK CARTER OF THE U.S. BORDER PATROL (See Holyoke One-Shot)

SGT. FURY (& His Howling Commandos)(See Fury & Special Marvel Edition)
Marvel Comics Group (BPC earlier issues): May, 1963 - No. 167, Dec, 1981

1-1st app. Sgt. Nick Fury (becomes agent of Shield in Strange Tales #135); Kirby/Ayers-c/a; 1st Dum-Dum Dugan & the Howlers 100.00 300.00 1400.00
2-Kirby-a 31.00 94.00 375.00
3-5: 3-Reed Richards x-over. 4-Death of Junior Juniper. 5-1st Baron Strucker app.; Kirby-a 20.00 60.00 220.00
6-10: 8-Baron Zemo, 1st Percival Pinkerton app. 9-Hitler-c & app. 10-1st app. Capt. Savage (the Skipper)(9/64) 12.50 37.00 135.00
11,12,14-20: 14-1st Blitz Squad. 18-Death of Pamela Hawley 6.35 19.00 70.00
13-Captain America & Bucky app.(12/64); 2nd solo Capt. America x-over outside The Avengers; Kirby-a 31.00 93.00 360.00
21-30: 25-Red Skull app. 27-1st app. Eric Koenig; origin Fury's eye patch 4.55 13.65 50.00
31-50: 34-Origin Howling Commandos. 35-Eric Koenig joins Howlers. 43-Bob Hope, Glen Miller app. 44-Flashback on Howlers' 1st mission 2.80 8.40 28.00
51-60 2.40 7.35 22.00
61-67: 64-Capt. Savage & Raiders x-over. 67-Last 12¢ issue 2.30 7.00 20.00
68-80: 76-Fury's Father app. in WWI story 2.00 6.00 18.00
81-91: 91-Last 15¢ issue 2.00 6.00 16.00
92-(52 pgs.) 2.30 7.00 20.00
93-99: 98-Deadly Dozen x-over 1.75 5.25 14.00
100-Capt. America, Fantastic 4 cameos; Stan Lee, Martin Goodman & others app. 2.30 7.00 20.00
101-120: 101-Origin retold 1.50 4.50 12.00
121-130: 121-123-r/#19-21 1.10 3.30 9.00
131-167: 167-Reprints (from 1963) 1.00 3.00 8.00
133,134-(30¢-c variants, limited distribution)(5,7/76) 1.50 4.50 12.00
Annual 1(1965, 25¢, 72 pgs.)-r/#4,5 & new-a 13.50 40.00 150.00
Special 2(1966) 4.55 13.65 50.00
Special 3(1967) 3.00 9.00 30.00
Special 4(1968) 2.40 7.35 22.00
Special 5-7(1969-11/71) 1.85 5.50 15.00
NOTE: ***Ayers** a-8, Annual 1. **Ditko** a-15i. **Gil Kane** c-37, 96. **Kirby** a-1-7, 13p, 167p(r). Special 5; c-1-20, 25, 167p. **Severin** a-44-46, 48, 162, 164; inks-49-79, Special 4, 6; c-4i, 5, 6, 44, 46, 110, 149i, 155i, 162-166. **Sutton** a-57p. Reprints in #80, 82, 85, 87, 89, 91, 93, 95, 99, 101, 103, 105, 107, 109, 111, 121-123, 145-155, 167.*

SGT. FURY AND HIS HOWLING DEFENDERS (See The Defenders #147)

SERGEANT PRESTON OF THE YUKON (TV)
Dell Publishing Co.: No. 344, Aug, 1951 - No. 29, Nov-Jan, 1958-59

Four Color 344(#1)-Sergeant Preston & his dog Yukon King begin; painted-c begin, end #18 11.30 34.00 135.00
Four Color 373,397,419('52) 6.70 20.00 80.00
5(11-1/52-53)-10(2-4/54): 6-Bondage-c. 4.60 13.75 55.00
11,12,14-17 4.10 12.30 45.00
13-Origin Sgt. Preston 4.60 13.75 55.00
18-Origin Yukon King; last painted-c 4.60 13.75 55.00
19-29: All photo-c 6.30 19.00 75.00

SGT. ROCK (Formerly Our Army at War; see Brave & the Bold #52 & Showcase #45)
National Periodical Publications/DC Comics: No. 302, Mar, 1977 - No. 422, July, 1988 (See G.I. Combat #108)

302 3.00 9.00 30.00
303-310 2.00 6.00 18.00
311-320: 318-Reprints 1.50 4.50 12.00
321-350 1.10 3.30 9.00
351-399,401-421 2.40 6.00
400,422: 422-1st Joe, Adam, Andy Kubert-a team 1.00 3.00 8.00
Annual 2-4: 2(1982)-Formerly Sgt. Rock's Prize Battle Tales #1. 3(1983). 4(1984) 1.00 3.00 8.00
NOTE: ***Estrada** a-322, 327, 331, 336, 337, 341, 342i. **Glanzman** a-384, 421. **Kubert** a-302, 303, 305r, 306, 328, 351, 356, 368, 373, 422; c-317, 318r, 319-323, 325-333-on, Annual 2, 3. **Severin** a-347. **Spiegle** a-382, Annual 2, 3. **Thorne** a-384. **Toth** a-385r. **Wildey** a-307, 311, 313, 314.*

SGT. ROCK SPECIAL (Sgt. Rock #14 on; see DC Special Series #3)
DC Comics: Oct, 1988 - No. 21, Feb, 1992; No. 1, 1992; No. 2, 1994 ($2.00, quarterly/monthly, 52 pgs)

1-Reprint begin 1.00 3.00 8.00
2-21: All-r; 5-r/early Sgt. Rock/Our Army at War #81. 7-Tomahawk-r by Thorne. 9-Enemy Ace-r by Kubert. 10-All Rock issue. 11-r/1st Haunted Tank story. 12-All Kubert issue;begins monthly. 13-Dinosaur story by Heath(r). 14-Enemy Ace-r (22 pgs.) by Adams/Kubert. 15-Enemy Ace (22 pgs.) by Kubert. 16-Iron Major-c/story. 16,17-Enemy Ace-r. 19-r/Batman/Sgt. Rock team-up/B&B #108 by Aparo 2.40 6.00
1 (1992, $2.95, 68 pgs.)-Simonson-c; unpubbed Kubert-a; Glanzman, Russell, Pratt, & Wagner-a 5.00
2 (1994, $2.95) Brereton painted-c 4.00
NOTE: ***Neal Adams** r-1, 8, 14p. **Chaykin** a-2; r-3, 9(2pgs.); c-3. **Drucker** r-6. **Glanzman** r-20. **Golden** a-1. **Heath** a-2; r-5, 9-13, 16, 19, 21. **Krigstein** r-4, 8. **Kubert** r-1-17, 20, 21; c-1p, 2, 8, 14-21. **Miller** r-6p. **Severin** r-3, 6, 10. **Simonson** r-2, 4; c-4. **Thorne** r-7. **Toth** r-2, 8, 11. **Wood** r-4.*

SGT. ROCK SPECTACULAR (See DC Special Series #13)

Sergio Aragonés Stomps Star Wars #1 © DH & Lucasfilm Ltd.

Seven Seas Comics #4 © Universal Phoenix Features

Shade the Changing Man #4 © DC

GD2.0 FN6.0 NM9.4

SGT. ROCK'S PRIZE BATTLE TALES (Becomes Sgt. Rock Annual #2 on; see DC Special Series #18 & 80 Page Giant #7)
National Periodical Publications: Winter, 1964 (Giant - 80 pgs., one-shot)

1-Kubert, Heath-r; new Kubert-c 31.00 93.00 360.00
... Replica Edition (2000, $5.95) Reprints entire issue 5.95

SGT. STRYKER'S DEATH SQUAD (See Savage Combat Tales)

SERGIO ARAGONÉS' BLAIR WHICH?
Dark Horse Comics: Dec, 1999 ($2.95, B&W, one-shot)

nn-Aragonés-c/a; Evanier-s. Parody of "Blair Witch Project" movie 3.00

SERGIO ARAGONÉS' BOOGEYMAN
Dark Horse Comics: June, 1998 - No. 4, Sept, 1998 ($2.95, B&W, lim. series)

1-4-Aragonés-c/a 3.00

SERGIO ARAGONÉS DESTROYS DC
DC Comics: June, 1996 ($3.50, one-shot)

1-DC Superhero parody book; Aragonés-c/a; Evanier scripts 3.50

SERGIO ARAGONÉS' DIA DE LOS MUERTOS
Dark Horse Comics: Oct, 1998 ($2.95, one-shot)

1-Aragonés-c/a; Evanier scripts 3.00

SERGIO ARAGONÉS' GROO & RUFFERTO
Dark Horse Comics: Dec, 1998 - No. 4, Mar, 1999 ($2.95, lim. series)

1-3-Aragonés-c/a 3.00

SERGIO ARAGONÉS' GROO: MIGHTIER THAN THE SWORD
Dark Horse Comics: Jan, 2000 - No. 4, Apr, 2000 ($2.95, lim. series)

1-4-Aragonés-c/a; Evanier-s 3.00

SERGIO ARAGONÉS' GROO THE WANDERER (See Groo...)

SERGIO ARAGONÉS' LOUDER THAN WORDS
Dark Horse Comics: July, 1997 - No. 6, Dec, 1997 ($2.95, B&W, limited series)

1-6-Aragonés-c/a 3.00

SERGIO ARAGONÉS MASSACRES MARVEL
Marvel Comics: June, 1996 ($3.50, one-shot)

1-Marvel Superhero parody book; Aragonés-c/a; Evanier scripts 3.50

SERGIO ARAGONÉS STOMPS STAR WARS
Marvel Comics: Jan, 2000 ($2.95, one-shot)

1-Star Wars parody; Aragonés-c/a; Evanier scripts 2.95

SERRA ANGEL ON THE WORLDS OF MAGIC THE GATHERING
Acclaim Comics (Armada): Aug, 1996 ($5.95, one-shot)

1 6.00

SERINA
Antarctic Press: Mar, 1996 - No. 3, July, 1996 ($2.95)

1-3: Warrior Nun app. 3.00

SEVEN BLOCK
Marvel Comics (Epic Comics): 1990 ($4.50, one-shot, 52 pgs.)

1 4.50

SEVEN DEAD MEN (See Complete Mystery #1)

SEVEN DWARFS (Also see Snow White)
Dell Publishing Co.: No. 227, 1949 (Disney-Movie)

Four Color #227 10.00 30.00 120.00

SEVEN MILES A SECOND
DC Comics (Vertigo Verité): 1996 ($7.95, one-shot)

nn-Wojnarowicz-s/Romberg-a 8.00

SEVEN SAMUROID, THE (See Image Graphic Novel)

SEVEN SEAS COMICS
Universal Phoenix Features/Leader No. 6: Apr, 1946 - No. 6, 1947(no month)

1-South Sea Girl by Matt Baker, Capt. Cutlass begin; Tugboat Tessie by Baker app. 84.00 253.00 800.00
2-Swashbuckler-c 70.00 210.00 665.00
3,5,6: 3-Six pg. Feldstein-a 63.00 189.00 600.00
4-Classic Baker-c 67.00 202.00 640.00

NOTE: ***Baker** a-1-6; c-3-6.*

1776 (See Charlton Classic Library)

7TH VOYAGE OF SINBAD, THE (Movie)
Dell Publishing Co.: Sept, 1958 (photo-c)

Four Color 944-Buscema-a 12.50 37.50 150.00

77 SUNSET STRIP (TV)
Dell Publ. Co./Gold Key: No. 1066, Jan-Mar, 1960 - No. 2, Feb, 1963 (All photo-c)

Four Color 1066-Toth-a 11.30 34.00 135.00
Four Color 1106,1159-Toth-a 9.00 27.00 110.00
Four Color 1211,1263,1291, 01-742-209(7-9/62)-Manning-a in all 8.35 25.00 100.00
1,2: Manning-a. 1(11/62-G.K.) 9.00 27.00 110.00

77TH BENGAL LANCERS, THE (TV)
Dell Publishing Co.: May, 1957

Four Color 791-Photo-c 6.70 20.00 80.00

SEYMOUR, MY SON (See More Seymour)
Archie Publications (Radio Comics): Sept, 1963

1 2.80 8.40 28.00

SHADE, THE (See Starman)
DC Comics: Apr, 1997 - No. 4, July, 1997 ($2.25, limited series)

1-4-Robinson-s/Harris-c: 1-Gene Ha-a. 2-Williams/Gray-a 3-Blevins-a. 4-Zulli-a 3.00

SHADE, THE CHANGING MAN (See Cancelled Comic Cavalcade)
National Per. Publ./DC Comics: June-July, 1977 - No. 8, Aug-Sept, 1978

1-1st app. Shade; Ditko-c/a in all 1.25 3.75 10.00
2-8 2.40 6.00

SHADE, THE CHANGING MAN (2nd series) (Also see Suicide Squad #16)
DC Comics (Vertigo imprint #33 on): July, 1990 - No.70, Apr, 1996 ($1.50/$1.75/$1.95/$2.25, mature)

1-($2.50, 52 pgs.)-Peter Milligan scripts in all 4.00
2-41,45-49,51-59: 6-Preview of World Without End. 17-Begin $1.75-c. 33-Metallic ink on-c. 41-Begin $1.95-c 2.25
42-44-John Constantine app. 3.00
50-($2.95, 52 pgs.) 3.50
60-70: 60-begin $2.25-c 2.25

NOTE: ***Bachalo** a-1-9, 11-13, 15-21, 23-26, 33-39, 42-45, 47, 49, 50; c-30, 33-41.*

SHADO: SONG OF THE DRAGON (See Green Arrow #63-66)
DC Comics: 1992 - No. 4, 1992 ($4.95, limited series, 52 pgs.)

Book One - Four: Grell scripts; Morrow-a(i) 5.00

SHADOW, THE (See Batman #253, 259 & Marvel Graphic Novel #35)

SHADOW, THE (Pulp, radio)
Archie Comics (Radio Comics): Aug, 1964 - No. 8, Sept, 1965 (All 12¢)

1-Jerrry Siegel scripts in all; Shadow-c. 5.45 16.35 60.00
2-8: 2-App. in super-hero costume on-c only; Reinman-a(backup). 3-Superhero begins; Reinman-a (book-length novel). 3,4,6,7-The Fly 1 pg. strips. 4-8-Reinman-a. 5-8-Siegel scripts. 7-Shield app. 3.65 11.00 40.00

SHADOW, THE
National Periodical Publications: Oct-Nov, 1973 - No. 12, Aug-Sept, 1975

1-Kaluta-a begins 2.80 8.40 28.00
2 1.75 5.25 14.00
3-Kaluta/Wrightson-a 2.00 6.00 18.00
4,6-Kaluta-a ends. 4-Chaykin, Wrightson part-i 1.50 4.50 12.00
5,7-12: 11-The Avenger (pulp character) x-over 1.00 2.80 7.00

NOTE: ***Craig** a-10. **Cruz** a-10-12. **Kaluta** a-1, 2, 3p, 4, 6; c-1-4, 6, 10-12. **Kubert** c-9. **Robbins** a-5, 7-9; c-5, 7, 8.*

SHADOW, THE
DC Comics: May, 1986 - No. 4, Aug, 1986 (limited series)

1-4: Howard Chaykin art in all 3.00
Blood & Judgement ($12.95)-r/1-4 13.00

SHADOW, THE
DC Comics: Aug, 1987 - No. 19, Jan, 1989 ($1.50)

Shadow Cabinet #2 © Milestone Media

Shadow Comics V2 #2 © S&S

Shadow Lady #19 © Masaka Katsura

GD2.0 FN6.0 NM9.4

1-19: Andrew Helfer scripts in all. 3.00
Annual 1,2 (12/87, '88,)-2-The Shadow dies; origin retold (story inspired by the movie "Citizen Kane"). 4.00
NOTE: ***Kyle Baker** a-7i, 8-19, Annual 2. **Chaykin** c-Annual 1. **Helfer** scripts in all. **Orlando** a-Annual 1. **Rogers** c/a-7. **Sienkiewicz** c/a-1-6.*

SHADOW, THE (Movie)
Dark Horse Comics: June, 1994 - No. 2, July, 1994 ($2.50, limited series)
1,2-Adaptation from Universal Pictures film 3.00
NOTE: ***Kaluta** c/a-1, 2.*

SHADOW AND DOC SAVAGE, THE
Dark Horse Comics: July, 1995 - No. 2, Aug, 1995 ($2.95, limited series)
1,2 3.50

SHADOW AND THE MYSTERIOUS 3, THE
Dark Horse Comics: Sept, 1994 ($2.95, one-shot)
1-Kaluta co-scripts. 3.00
NOTE: ***Stevens** c-1.*

SHADOW CABINET (See Heroes)
DC Comics (Milestone): Jan, 1994 - No. 17, Oct, 1995 ($1.75/$2.50)
0,1-17: 0-($2.50, 52 pgs.)-Silver ink-c; Simonson-c. 1-Byrne-c 2.50

SHADOW COMICS (Pulp, radio)
Street & Smith Publications: Mar, 1940 - V9#5, Aug-Sept, 1949
NOTE: *The Shadow first appeared on radio in 1929 and was featured in pulps beginning in April, 1931, written by Walter Gibson. The early covers of this series were reprinted from the pulp covers.*

V1#1-Shadow, Doc Savage, Bill Barnes, Nick Carter (radio), Frank Merriwell, Iron Munro, the Astonishing Man begin 420.00 1260.00 4800.00
2-The Avenger begins, ends #6; Capt. Fury only app. 179.00 537.00 1700.00
3(nn-5/40)-Norgil the Magician app.; cover is exact swipe of Shadow pulp from 1/33 126.00 379.00 1200.00
4,5: 4-The Three Musketeers begins, ends #8. 5-Doc Savage ends 100.00 300.00 950.00
6,8,9: 9-Norgil the Magician app. 87.00 261.00 825.00
7-Origin/1st app. The Hooded Wasp & Wasplet (11/40); series ends V3#8; Hooded Wasp/Wasplet app. on-c thru #9 95.00 285.00 900.00
10-Origin The Iron Ghost, ends #11; The Dead End Kids begins, ends #14 87.00 261.00 825.00
11-Origin Hooded Wasp & Wasplet retold 87.00 261.00 825.00
12-Dead End Kids app. 68.00 205.00 650.00
V2#1,2(11/41): 2-Dead End Kids story 61.00 182.00 575.00
3-Origin & 1st app. Supersnipe (3/42); series begins; Little Nemo story 87.00 261.00 825.00
4,5: 4,8-Little Nemo story 55.00 165.00 500.00
6-9: 6-Blackstone the Magician story 50.00 150.00 450.00
10-12: 10-Supersnipe app. 50.00 150.00 450.00
V3#1-12: 10-Doc Savage begins, not in V5#5, V6#10-12, V8#4 47.00 140.00 420.00
V4#1-12 42.00 125.00 375.00
V5#1-12 40.00 120.00 340.00
V6#1-11: 9-Intro. Shadow, Jr. (12/46) 38.00 113.00 300.00
12-Powell-c/a; atom bomb panels 40.00 120.00 340.00
V7#1,2,5,7-9,12: 2,5-Shadow, Jr. app.; Powell-a 40.00 120.00 360.00
3,6,11-Powell-c/a 44.00 133.00 400.00
4-Powell-c/a; Atom bomb panels 47.00 142.00 425.00
10(1/48)-Flying Saucer-c/story (2nd of this theme; see The Spirit 9/28/47); Powell-c/a 55.00 165.00 500.00
V8#1-12-Powell-a. 8-Powell Spider-c/a 44.00 133.00 400.00
V9#1,5-Powell-a 42.00 125.00 375.00
2-4-Powell-c/a 44.00 133.00 400.00
NOTE: ***Binder** c-V3#1. **Powell** art in most issues beginning V6#12. Painted c-1-6.*

SHADOWDRAGON
DC Comics: 1995 ($3.50, annual)
Annual 1-Year One story 3.50

SHADOW EMPIRES: FAITH CONQUERS
Dark Horse Comics: Aug, 1994 - No. 4, Nov, 1994 ($2.95, limited series)
1-4 3.00

GD2.0 FN6.0 NM9.4

SHADOWHAWK (See Images of Shadowhawk, New Shadowhawk, Shadowhawk II, Shadowhawk III & Youngblood #2)
Image Comics (Shadowline Ink): Aug, 1992 - No. 4, Mar, 1993; No. 12, Aug, 1994 - No. 18, May, 1995 ($1.95/$2.50)
1-($2.50)-Embossed silver foil stamped-c; Valentino/Liefeld-c; Valentino-c/a/scripts in all; has coupon for Image #0; 1st Shadowline Ink title 4.00
1-With coupon missing 2.00
1-($1.95)-Newsstand version w/o foil stamp 2.00
2-13,0,1418: 2-Shadowhawk poster w/McFarlane-i; brief Spawn app.; wrap around-c w/silver ink highlights. 3-($2.50)-Glow-in-the-dark-c. 4-Savage Dragon-c/story; Valentino/Larsen-c. 5-11-(See Shadowhawk II and III). 12-Cont'd fromShadowhawk III; pull-out poster by Texeira.13-w/ShadowBone poster; WildC.A.T.s app. 0 (10/94)-Liefeld c/a/story; ShadowBart poster. 14-(10/94, $2.50)-The Others app. 16-Supreme app. 17-Spawn app.; story cont'd from Badrock & Co. #6. 18-Shadowhawk dies; Savage Dragon & Brigade app. 2.50
Special 1(12/94, $3.50, 52 pgs.)-Silver Age Shadowhawk flip book 3.50
Gallery (4/94, $1.95) 2.00
Out of the Shadows ($19.95)-r/Youngblood #2, Shadowhawk #1-4, Image Zero #0, Operation :Urban Storm (Never published) 20.00
.../Vampirella (2/95, $4.95)-Pt.2 of x-over (See Vampirella/Shadowhawk for Pt. 1) 5.00
NOTE: *Shadowhawk was originally a four issue limited series. The story continued in Shadowhawk II, Shadowhawk III & then became Shadowhawk again with issue #12.*

SHADOWHAWK II (Follows Shadowhawk #4)
Image Comics (Shadowline Ink): V2#1, May, 1993 - V2#3, Aug, 1993 ($3.50/$1.95/$2.95, limited series)
V2#1 ($3.50)-Cont'd from Shadowhawk #4; die-cut mirricard-c 3.50
2 ($1.95)-Foil embossed logo; reveals identity; gold-c variant exists 2.50
3 ($2.95)-Pop-up-c w/Pact ashcan insert 3.00

SHADOWHAWK III (Follows Shadowhawk II #3)
Image Comics (Shadowline Ink): V3#1, Nov, 1993 - V3#4, Mar, 1994 ($1.95, limited series);
V3#1-4: 1-Cont'd from Shadowhawk II; intro Valentine; gold foil & red foil stamped-c variations. 2-(52 pgs.)-Shadowhawk contracts HIV virus; U.S. Male by M. Anderson (p) in free 16 pg.insert. 4-Continues in Shadowhawk #12. 2.50

SHADOWHAWKS OF LEGEND
Image Comics (Shadowline Ink): Nov, 1995 ($4.95, one-shot)
nn-Stories of past Shadowhawks by Kurt Busiek, Beau Smith & Alan Moore. 5.00

SHADOW, THE: HELL'S HEAT WAVE (Movie, pulp, radio)
Dark Horse Comics: Apr, 1995 - No. 3, June, 1995 ($2.95, limited series)
1-3: Kaluta story 3.00

SHADOWHUNT SPECIAL
Image Comics (Extreme Studios): Apr, 1996 ($2.50)
1-Retells origin of past Shadowhawks; Valentino script; Chapel app. 2.50

SHADOW, THE: IN THE COILS OF THE LEVIATHAN (Movie, pulp, radio)
Dark Horse Comics: Oct, 1993 - No. 4, Apr, 1994 ($2.95, limited series)
1-4-Kaluta-c & co-scripter 3.00
Trade paperback (10/94, $13.95)-r/1-4 14.00

SHADOW LADY:... (Masakazu Katsura's...)
Dark Horse Comics ($2.50, B&W, limited series, Manga)
Dangerous Love: (Oct, 1998 - No. 7, Apr, 1999) 1-7-Katsura-s/a 2.50
TPB ($17.95) r/#1-7 17.95
The Eyes of a Stranger: (No. 8, May, 1999 - No. 12, Sept, 1999) 8-12 2.50
The Awakening: (No. 13, Oct, 1999 - No. 19, Apr, 2000) 13-19 2.50
Sudden Death: (No. 20, May, 2000 - No. 24) 20-23 2.50

SHADOWLINE SAGA: CRITICAL MASS, A
Marvel Comics (Epic): Jan, 1990 - No. 7, July, 1990 ($4.95, lim. series, 68 pgs)
1-6: Dr. Zero, Powerline, St. George 5.00
7 ($5.95, 84 pgs.)-Morrow-a, Williamson-c(i) 6.00

SHADOWMAN (See X-O Manowar #4)
Valiant/Acclaim Comics (Valiant): May, 1992 - No. 43, Dec, 1995 ($2.50)

Shadows Fall #6 © DC

Shaman's Tears #8 © Mike Grell

Sharky #1 © Dave Elliot

GD2.0 FN6.0 NM9.4

1-Partial origin 5.00
2-5: 3-1st app. Sousa the Soul Eater 4.00
6-43: 8-1st app. Master Darque. 16-1st app. Dr. Mirage (8/93). 15-Minor Turok app. 17,18-Archer & Armstrong x-over. 19-Aerosmith-c/story. 23-Dr. Mirage x-over. 24-(4/94). 25-Bound-in trading card. 29-Chaos Effect. 43-Shadowman jumps to his death 2.50
0-($2.50, 4/94)-Regular edition 2.50
0-($3.50)-Wraparound chromium-c edition 3.50
0-Gold 6.00
Yearbook 1 (12/94, $3.95) 4.00

SHADOWMAN (Volume 2)
Acclaim Comics (Valiant Heroes): Mar, 1997 - No. 20 ($2.50, mature)

1-20: 1-1st app. Zero; Garth Ennis scripts begin, end #4. 2-Zero becomes new Shadowman. 4-Origin; Jack Boniface (original Shadowman) rises from the grave. 5-Jamie Delano scripts begin. 9-Copycat-c 2.50
1-Variant painted cover 2.50

SHADOWMAN (Volume 3)
Acclaim Comics: July, 1999 - Present ($3.95/$2.50)

1-($3.95)-Abnett & Lanning-s/Broome & Benjamin-a 4.00
2-5-($2.50): 3,4-Flip book with Unity 2000 2.50

SHADOWMASTERS
Marvel Comics: Oct, 1989 - No.4, Jan, 1990 ($3.95, squarebound, 52 pgs.)

1-4: Heath-a(i). 1-Jim Lee-c; story cont'd from Punisher 4.00

SHADOW OF THE BATMAN
DC Comics: Dec, 1985 - No. 5, Apr, 1986 ($1.75, limited series)

	GD	FN	NM
1-Detective-r (all have wraparound-c)	1.00	2.80	7.00
2,3,5: 3-Penguin-c & cameo. 5-Clayface app.			5.00
4-Joker-c/story		2.40	6.00

NOTE: ***Austin** a(new)-2i, 3i; r-2-4i. **Rogers** a(new)-1, 2p, 3p, 4, 5; r-1-5p; c-1-5. **Simonson** a-1r.*

SHADOW OF THE TORTURER, THE
Innovation: July, 1991 - No. 3, 1992 ($2.50, limited series)

1-3: Based on Pocket Books novel 2.50

SHADOW ON THE TRAIL (See Zane Grey & Four Color #604)

SHADOW PLAY (Tales of the Supernatural)
Whitman Publications: June, 1982

1-Painted-c 5.00

SHADOW RIDERS
Marvel Comics UK, Ltd.: June, 1993 - No. 4, Sept, 1993 ($1.75, limited series)

1-($2.50)-Embossed-c; Cable-c/story 2.50
2-4-Cable app. 2-Ghost Rider app. 2.00

SHADOWS & LIGHT
Marvel Comics: Feb, 1998 - No. 3, July, 1998 ($2.99, B&W, quarterly)

1-3: 1-B&W anthology of Marvel characters; Black Widow art by Gene Ha, Hulk by Wrightson, Iron Man by Ditko & Daredevil by Stelfreeze; Stelfreeze painted-c. 2-Weeks, Sharp, Starlin, Thompson-a. 3-Buscema, Grindberg, Giffen, Layton-a 3.00

SHADOW'S FALL
DC Comics (Vertigo): Nov, 1994 - No. 6, Apr, 1995 ($2.95, limited series)

1-6: Van Fleet-c/a in all. 3.00

SHADOWS FROM BEYOND (Formerly Unusual Tales)
Charlton Comics: V2#50, October, 1966

	GD	FN	NM
V2#50-Ditko-c	2.50	7.50	25.00

SHADOW SLASHER
Pocket Change Comics: No. 0, 1994 - No. 6, 1995? ($2.50, B&W)

0-6 2.50

SHADOW STATE
Broadway Comics: Dec, 1995 - No. 5, Apr, 1996 ($2.50)

1-5: 1,2-Fatale back-up story; Cockrum-a(p) 2.50
Preview Edition 1,2 (10-11/95, $2.50, B&W) 2.50

SHADOW STRIKES!, THE (Pulp, radio)
DC Comics: Sept, 1989 - No.31, May, 1992 ($1.75)

GD2.0 FN6.0 NM9.4

1-31: 5,6-Doc Savage x-over. 31-Mignola-c. 2.50
Annual 1 (1989, $3.50, 68 pgs.)-Spiegle a; Kaluta-c 3.50

SHADOW WAR OF HAWKMAN
DC Comics: May, 1985 - No. 4, Aug, 1985 (limited series)

1-4 2.00

SHAGGY DOG & THE ABSENT-MINDED PROFESSOR (See Movie Comics & Walt Disney Showcase #46)(Disney-Movie)
Dell Publ. Co.: No. 985, May, 1959; No. 1199, Apr, 1961

	GD	FN	NM
Four Color #985,1199	6.70	20.00	80.00

SHALOMAN
Al Wiesner/ Mark 1 Comics: 1989 - Present (B&W)

V1#1-Al Wiesner-s/a in all 4.50
2-9 2.50
V2 #1(The New Adventures)-4,6-10, V3 (The Legend) #1-7 2.50
5 (Color)-Shows Vol 2, No. 4 in indicia 3.00

SHAMAN'S TEARS (Also see Maggie the Cat)
Image Comics (Creative Fire Studio): 5/93 - No. 2, 8/93; No. 3, 11/94 - No. 0, 1/96 ($2.50/$1.95)

0-2: 0-(DEC-c, 1/96)-Last Issue. 1-(5/93)-Embossed red foil-c; Grell-c/a & scripts in all. 2-Cover unfolds into poster (8/93-c, 7/93 inside) 2.50
3-12: 3-Begin $1.95-c. 5-Re-intro Jon Sable. 12-Re-intro Maggie the Cat (1 pg.) 2.00

SHANNA, THE SHE-DEVIL (See Savage Tales #8)
Marvel Comics Group: Dec, 1972 - No. 5, Aug, 1973 (All are 20¢ issues)

	GD	FN	NM
1-1st app. Shanna; Steranko-c; Tuska-a(p)	2.30	7.00	20.00
2-Steranko-c; heroin drug story	1.75	5.25	14.00
3-5	1.25	3.75	10.00

SHARDS
Ascension Comics: Apr, 1994 ($2.50, B&W, unfinished limited series)

1-Flip-c. 2.50

SHARK FIGHTERS, THE (Movie)
Dell Publishing Co.: Jan, 1957

	GD	FN	NM
Four Color 762-Buscema-a; photo-c	7.50	22.50	90.00

SHARKY
Image Comics: Feb, 1998 - No. 4, 1998 ($2.50, bi-monthly)

1-4: 1-Mask app.; Elliot-s/a. Horley painted-c. 3-Three covers by Horley, Bisley, & Horley/Elliot. 4-Two covers (swipe of Avengers #4 and wraparound) 2.50
1-($2.95) "$1,000,000" variant 3.00
2-($2.50) Savage Dragon variant-c 2.50

SHARP COMICS (Slightly large size)
H. C. Blackerby: Winter, 1945-46 - V1#2, Spring, 1946 (52 pgs.)

	GD	FN	NM
V1#1-Origin Dick Royce Planetarian	40.00	120.00	340.00
2-Origin The Pioneer; Michael Morgan, Dick Royce, Sir Gallagher, Planetarian, Steve Hagen, Weeny and Pop app.	38.00	113.00	300.00

SHARPY FOX (See Comic Capers & Funny Frolics)
I. W. Enterprises/Super Comics: 1958; 1963

	GD	FN	NM
1,2-I.W. Reprint (1958): 2-r/Kiddie Kapers #1	1.50	4.50	12.00
14-Super Reprint (1963)	1.50	4.50	12.00

SHATTER (See Jon Sable #25-30)
First Comics: June, 1985; Dec, 1985 - No. 14, Apr, 1988. ($1.75, Baxter paper/deluxe paper)

1 (6/85)-1st computer generated-a in a comic book (1st printing) 3.00
1-(2nd print.); 1(12/85)-14: computer generated-a & lettering in all 2.00
Special 1 (1988) 2.00

SHATTERED IMAGE
Image Comics (WildStorm Productions): Aug, 1996 - No. 4, Dec, 1996 ($2.50, limited series)

1-4: 1st Image company-wide x-over; Kurt Busiek scripts in all. 1-Tony Daniel-c/a(p). 2-Alex Ross-c/swipe (Kingdom Come) by Ryan Benjamin & Travis Charest 2.50

SHAZAM (See Giant Comics to Color, Limited Collectors' Edition & The Power Of Shazam!)

Shazam! #14 © DC

Sheena, Queen of the Jungle #14 © FH

Shi: Black, White and Red #1 © William Tucci

GD2.0 FN6.0 NM9.4

SHAZAM! (TV)(See World's Finest #253)
National Periodical Publ./DC Comics: Feb, 1973 - No. 35, May-June, 1978

1-1st revival of original Captain Marvel since G.A. (origin retold), by Beck; Captain Marvel Jr. & Mary Marvel x-over; Superman-c. 2.00 6.00 18.00
2-5: 2-Infinity photo-c.; re-intro Mr. Mind & Tawny. 3-Capt. Marvel-r. (10/46). 4-Origin retold; Capt. Marvel-r. (1949). 5-Capt. Marvel Jr. origin retold; Capt. Marvel-r. (1948, 7 pgs.) 1.10 3.30 9.00
6,7,9-11: 6-photo-c; Capt. Marvel-r (1950, 6 pgs.). 9-Mr. Mind app. 10-Last C.C. Beck issue. 11-Schaffenberger-a begins. 2.40 6.00
8 (100 pgs.) 8-r/Capt. Marvel Jr. by Raboy; origin/C.M. #80; origin Mary Marvel/C.M. #18; origin Mr. Tawny/C.M. #79 3.20 9.60 35.00
12-17-(All 100 pgs.). 15-vs. Lex Luthor & Mr. Mind. 2.50 7.50 25.00
18-24,26-30: 21-24-All reprints. 26-Sivana app. (10/76). 27-Kid Eternity teams up w/Capt. Marvel. 28-1st S.A. app. of Black Adam. 30-1st DC app. 3 Lt. Marvels. 1.00 3.00 8.00
25-1st app. Isis 1.25 3.75 10.00
31-35: 31-1st DC app. Minuteman. 34-Origin Capt. Nazi & Capt. Marvel Jr. retold 1.10 3.30 9.00

NOTE: *Reprints in #1-8, 10, 12-17, 21-24.* ***Beck*** *a-1-10, 12-17r, 21-24r; c-1, 3-9.* ***Nasser*** *c-35p.* ***Newton*** *a-35p.* ***Raboy*** *a-5r, 8r, 17r.* ***Schaffenberger*** *a-11, 14-20, 25, 26, 27p, 28, 29-31p, 33i, 35i; c-20, 22, 23, 25, 26i, 27i, 28-33.*

SHAZAM!: POWER OF HOPE
DC Comics: Nov, 2000 ($9.95, treasury size, one-shot)

nn-Painted art by Alex Ross; story by Alex Ross and Paul Dini 10.00

SHAZAM: THE NEW BEGINNING
DC Comics: Apr, 1987 - No. 4, July, 1987 (Legends spin-off) (Limited series)

1-4: 1-New origin & 1st modern app. Captain Marvel; Marvel Family cameo. 2-4-Sivana & Black Adam app. 3.00

SHEA THEATRE COMICS
Shea Theatre: No date (1940's) (32 pgs.)

nn-Contains Rocket Comics; MLJ cover in one color 10.00 30.00 70.00

SHE-BAT (See Murcielaga, She-Bat & Valeria the She-Bat)

SHEENA (Movie)
Marvel Comics: Dec, 1984 - No. 2, Feb, 1985 (limited series)

1,2-r/Marvel Comics Super Special #34; Tanya Roberts movie 3.00

SHEENA, QUEEN OF THE JUNGLE (See Jerry Iger's Classic..., Jumbo Comics, & 3-D Sheena)
Fiction House Magazines: Spr, 1942; No. 2, Wint, 1942-43; No. 3, Spr, 1943; No. 4, Fall, 1948; No. 5, Sum, 1949; No. 6, Spr, 1950; No. 7-10, 1950(nd); No. 11, Spr, 1951 - No. 18, Wint, 1952-53 (#1-3: 68 pgs.; #4-7: 52 pgs.)

1-Sheena begins 242.00 726.00 2300.00
2 (Winter, 1942-43) 105.00 316.00 1000.00
3 (Spring, 1943) 79.00 237.00 750.00
4,5 (Fall, 1948, Sum, 1949): 4-New logo; cover swipe from Jumbo #20 50.00 150.00 450.00
6,7 (Spring, 1950, 1950) 42.00 125.00 375.00
8-10(1950 - Win/50, 36 pgs.) 40.00 120.00 350.00
11-18: 15-Cover swipe from Jumbo #43. 18-Used in **POP**, pg. 98 34.00 103.00 275.00
I.W. Reprint #9-r/#18; c-r/White Princess #3 4.55 13.65 50.00

NOTE: ***Baker*** *c-5-10?* ***Whitman*** *c-11-18(most).*

SHEENA-QUEEN OF THE JUNGLE
London Night: Feb, 1998 - Present ($3.00)

0-($3.00)-Hartsoe-s/Sandoval-c 3.00
0-($5.00) Crocodile, Zebra, & Leopard editions 5.00
1-3-($3.00) 3.00
1-3-($5.00) Ministry Edition 5.00

SHEENA 3-D SPECIAL (Also see Blackthorne 3-D Series #1)
Eclipse Comics: Jan, 1985 ($2.00)

1-Dave Stevens-c 5.00

SHE-HULK (See The Savage She-Hulk & The Sensational She-Hulk)

SHERIFF BOB DIXON'S CHUCK WAGON (TV) (See Wild Bill Hickok #22)
Avon Periodicals: Nov, 1950

1-Kinstler-c/a(3) 13.00 39.00 105.00

SHERIFF OF TOMBSTONE
Charlton Comics: Nov, 1958 - No. 17, Sept, 1961

V1#1-Giordano-c; Severin-a 6.35 19.00 70.00
2 3.80 11.40 42.00
3-10 3.00 9.00 30.00
11-17 2.50 7.50 25.00

SHERLOCK HOLMES (See Marvel Preview, New Adventures of..., & Spectacular Stories)

SHERLOCK HOLMES (All New Baffling Adventures of...)(Young Eagle #3 on?)
Charlton Comics: Oct, 1955 - No. 2, Mar, 1956

1-Dr. Neff, Ghost Breaker app. 40.00 120.00 360.00
2 38.00 113.00 300.00

SHERLOCK HOLMES (Also see The Joker)
National Periodical Publications: Sept-Oct, 1975

1-Cruz-a; Simonson-c 2.50 7.50 23.00

SHERRY THE SHOWGIRL (Showgirls #4)
Atlas Comics: July, 1956 - No. 3, Dec, 1956; No. 5, Apr, 1957 - No. 7, Aug, 1957

1-Dan DeCarlo-c/a in all 14.00 43.00 115.00
2 10.00 30.00 80.00
3,5-7 7.85 23.50 55.00

SHE'S JOSIE (See Josie)

SHEVA'S WAR
DC Comics (Helix): Oct, 1998 - No. 5, Feb, 1999 ($2.95, mini-series)

1-5-Christopher Moeller-s/painted-a/c 3.00

SHI (See Razor Annual #1 for 1st app.)

SHI: BLACK, WHITE AND RED
Crusade Comics: Mar, 1998 - No. 2, May, 1998 ($2.95, B&W&Red, mini-series)

1,2-J.G. Jones-painted art 3.00
...- Year of the Dragon Collected Edition (2000, $5.95) r/#1&2 5.95

SHI/CYBLADE: THE BATTLE FOR THE INDEPENDENTS
Crusade Comics: Sept, 1995 ($2.95)

1-Tucci-c; features Cerebus, Bone, Hellboy, as well as others 4.00
1-Silvestri variant-c 2.40 6.00

SHI/DAREDEVIL: HONOR THY MOTHER (See Daredevil/Shi..)
Crusade Comics: Jan, 1997 ($2.95, one-shot)

1-Flip book 3.00

SHI: EAST WIND RAIN
Crusade Comics: Nov, 1997 - No. 2, Feb, 1998 ($3.50, limited series)

1,2-Shi at WW2 Pearl Harbor 3.50

SHI: FAN EDITIONS
Crusade Comics: 1997

1-3-Two covers polybagged in FAN #19-21 4.00
1-3-Gold editions 6.00

SHI: HEAVEN AND EARTH
Crusade Comics: June, 1997 - No. 4, Apr, 1998 ($2.95)

1-4 3.00
4-($4.95) Pencil-c variant 5.00
Rising Sun Edition-signed by Tucci in FanClub Starter Pack 4.00
"Tora No Shi" variant-c 3.00

SHI: JUDGMENT NIGHT
Crusade Comics: 2000 ($3.99, one-shot)

1-Wolverine app.; Battlebook card and pages included; Tucci-a 3.50

SHI: KAIDAN
Crusade Comics: Oct, 1996 ($2.95)

1-Two covers; Tucci-c; Jae Lee wraparound-c 3.00

SHI: MASQUERADE
Crusade Comics: Mar, 1998 ($3.50, one-shot)

1-Painted art by Lago, Texeira, and others 3.50

Shi: The Series #5 © William Tucci

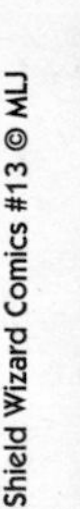
Shield Wizard Comics #13 © MLJ

Shock Illustrated #2 © WMG

GD2.0 FN6.0 NM9.4

SHI: NIGHTSTALKERS
Crusade Comics: Sept, 1997 ($3.50, one-shot)
1-Painted art by Val Mayerik 3.50

SHI: REKISHI
Crusade Comics: Jan, 1997 ($2.95)
1-Character bios and story summaries of Shi: The Way of the Warrior told in Detective Joe Labianca's point of view; Christopher Golden script; Tucci-c; J.G. Jones-a; flip book w/Shi: East Wind Rain preview 3.00

SHI: SENRYAKU
Crusade Comics: Aug, 1995 - No. 3, Nov, 1995 ($2.95, limited series)
1-3: 1-Tucci-c; Quesada, Darrow, Sim, Lee, Smith-a. 2-Tucci-c; Silvestri, Balent, Perez, Mack-a. 3-Jusko-c; Hughes, Ramos, Bell, Moore-a 4.00
1-variant-c (no logo) 2.40 6.00
Hardcover ($24.95)-r/#1-3; Frazetta-c. 25.00
Trade Paperback ($13.95)-r/#1-3; Frazetta-c. 14.00

SHI: THE ART OF WAR TOURBOOK
Crusade Comics: 1998 ($4.95, one-shot)
1-Blank cover for Convention sketches; early Tucci-a inside 5.00
1-Mexico Edition ($10.00) Mexican flag-c 10.00
1-U.K. Edition ($10.00) British flag-c 10.00

SHI: THE SERIES
Crusade Comics: Aug, 1997 - Present ($2.95, color #1-10, B&W #11)
1-10 3.00
11-13: 11-B&W. 12-Color; Lau-a 3.00

SHI: THE WAY OF THE WARRIOR
Crusade Comics: Mar, 1994 - No. 12, Apr, 1997 ($2.50/$2.95)
1/2 2.40 6.00
1 1.85 5.50 15.00
1-Commemorative ed., B&W, new-c; given out at 1994 San Diego Comic Con 2.40 7.35 22.00
1-Fan appreciation edition -r/#1 3.00
1-Fan appreciation edition (variant) 1.00 3.00 8.00
2 2.40 6.00
2-Commemorative edition (3,000) 2.00 6.00 18.00
2-Fan appreciation edition -r/#2 3.00
3 2.40 6.00
4-7: 4-Silvestri poster. 7-Tomoe app. 3.50
5,6: 5-Silvestri variant-c. 6-Tomoe #1 variant-c 5.00
5-Gold edition 20.00
6,8-12: 6-Fan appreciation edition 3.00
8-Signed Edition-(5000) 4.00
Trade paperback (1995, $12.95)-r/#1-4 13.00
Trade paperback (1995, $14.95)-r/#1-4 revised; Julie Bell-c 15.00

SHI/ VAMPIRELLA
Crusade Comics: Oct, 1997 ($2.95, one-shot)
1-Ellis-s/Lau-a 5.00

SHI VS. TOMOE
Crusade Comics: Aug, 1996 ($3.95, one-shot)
1-Tucci-a/scripts; wraparound foil-c 4.00
1-(6/96, $5.00. B&W)-Preview Ed.; sold at San Diego Comic Con 5.00

SHI: YEAR OF THE DRAGON
Crusade Comics: 2000 - No. 3 ($2.99, limited series)
1,2: 1-Two covers; Tucci-a/c; flashback to teen-aged Ana 3.00

S.H.I.E.L.D. (Nick Fury & His Agents of...) (Also see Nick Fury)
Marvel Comics Group: Feb, 1973 - No. 5, Oct, 1973 (All 20¢ issues)
1-All contain reprint stories from Strange Tales #146-155; new Steranko-c 1.85 5.50 15.00
2-New Steranko flag-c 1.50 4.50 12.00
3-5: 3-Kirby/Steranko-c(r). 4-Steranko-c(r) 1.00 3.00 8.00
NOTE: ***Buscema** a-3p(r). **Kirby** layouts 1-5; c-3 (w/**Steranko**). **Steranko** a-3r, 4r(2).*

SHIELD, THE (Becomes Shield-Steel Sterling #3; #1 titled Lancelot Strong; also see Advs. of the Fly, Double Life of Private Strong, Fly Man, Mighty Comics, The Mighty Crusaders, The Original... & Pep Comics #1)
Archie Enterprises, Inc.: June, 1983 - No. 2, Aug, 1983
1,2: Steel Sterling app. 2-Kanigher-s 3.00

SHIELD-STEEL STERLING (Formerly The Shield)
Archie Enterprises, Inc.: No. 3, Dec, 1983 (Becomes Steel Sterling No. 4)
3-Nino-a; Steel Sterling by Kanigher & Barreto 3.00

SHIELD WIZARD COMICS (Also see Pep Comics & Top-Notch Comics)
MLJ Magazines: Summer, 1940 - No. 13, Spring, 1944
1-(V1#5 on inside)-Origin The Shield by Irving Novick & The Wizard by Ed Ashe, Jr; Flag-c 420.00 1260.00 4800.00
2-(Winter/40)-Origin The Shield retold; Wizard's sidekick, Roy the Super Boy begins (see Top-Notch #8 for 1st app.) 211.00 633.00 2000.00
3,4 132.00 395.00 1250.00
5-Dusty, the Boy Detective begins 116.00 348.00 1100.00
6-8: 6-Roy the Super Boy begins. 7-Shield dons new costume (Summer, 1942) S & K-c? 8-Bondage-c; Hitler photo on-c 111.00 332.00 1050.00
9-13: 9,13-Bondage-c 82.00 245.00 775.00
NOTE: ***Bob Montana** c-13. **Novick** c-1-6,8-11. **Harry Sahle** c-12.*

SHINING KNIGHT (See Adventure Comics #66)

SHIP AHOY
Spotlight Publishers: Nov, 1944 (52 pgs.)
1-L. B. Cole-c 19.00 56.00 150.00

SHIP OF FOOLS
Image Comics: Aug, 1997 - Present ($2.95, B&W)
0-3-Glass-s/Oeming-a 3.00

SHIPWRECKED! (Disney-Movie)
Disney Comics: 1990 ($5.95, graphic novel, 68 pgs.)
nn-adaptation; Spiegle-a 6.00

SHMOO (See Al Capp's... & Washable Jones &...)

SHOCK (Magazine)
Stanley Publ.: May, 1969 - V3#4, Sept, 1971 (B&W reprints from horror comics, including some pre-code)
V1#1-Cover-r/Weird Tales of the Future #7 by Bernard Baily; r/Weird Chills #1 4.10 12.30 45.00
2-Wolverton-r/Weird Mysteries 5; r-Weird Mysteries #7 used in **SOTI**; cover reprints cover to Weird Chills #1 3.65 11.00 40.00
3,5,6 2.50 7.50 25.00
4-Harrison/Williamson-r/Forbid. Worlds #6 3.00 9.00 30.00
V2#2, V1#8, V2#4-6(1/71), V3#1-4: V2#4-Cover swipe from Weird Mysteries #6 2.40 7.35 22.00
NOTE: ***Disbrow** r-V2#4; Bondage c-V1#4, V2#6, V3#1.*

SHOCK DETECTIVE CASES (Formerly Crime Fighting Detective) (Becomes Spook Detective Cases No. 22)
Star Publications: No. 20, Sept, 1952 - No. 21, Nov, 1952
20,21-L.B. Cole-c; based on true crime cases 23.00 68.00 180.00
NOTE: ***Palais** a-20. No. 21-Fox-r.*

SHOCK ILLUSTRATED (...Adult Crime Stories; Magazine format)
E. C. Comics: Sept-Oct, 1955 - No. 3, Spring, 1956 (Adult Entertainment on-c #1,2)(All 25¢)
1-All by Kamen; drugs, prostitution, wife swapping 10.00 30.00 70.00
2-Williamson-a redrawn from Crime SuspenStories #13 plus Ingels, Crandall, Evans & part Torres-i; painted-c 10.00 30.00 80.00
3-Only 100 known copies bound & given away at E.C. office; Crandall, Evans-a; painted-c; shows May, 1956 on-c 90.00 268.00 850.00

SHOCKING MYSTERY CASES (Formerly Thrilling Crime Cases)
Star Publications: No. 50, Sept, 1952 - No. 60, Oct, 1954 (All crime reprints?)
50-Disbrow "Frankenstein" story 41.00 123.00 370.00
51-Disbrow-a 27.00 81.00 215.00
52-60: 56-Drug use story 25.00 75.00 200.00
NOTE: ***L. B. Cole** covers on all; a-60(2 pgs.). **Hollingsworth** a-52. **Morisi** a-55.*

SHOCKING TALES DIGEST MAGAZINE
Harvey Publications: Oct, 1981 (95¢)
1-1957-58-r; Powell, Kirby, Nostrand-a 1.50 4.50 12.00

Shock Rockets #1
© Kurt Busiek & Stuart Immonen

Shortstop Squad #1
© Ultimate Sports Ent. Inc.

Showcase #10 © DC

GD2.0 FN6.0 NM9.4

SHOCK ROCKETS
Image Comics (Gorilla): Apr, 2000 - Present ($2.50)

1-6-Busiek-s/Immonen & Grawbadger-a. 6-Flip book w/Superstar preview 2.50

SHOCK SUSPENSTORIES
E. C. Comics: Feb-Mar, 1952 - No. 18, Dec-Jan, 1954-55

1-Classic Feldstein electrocution-c 73.00 218.00 800.00
2 39.00 116.00 425.00
3,4: 4-Used in **SOTI**, pg. 387,388 28.00 84.00 310.00
5-Hanging-c 33.00 99.00 360.00
6-Classic hooded vigilante bondage-c 35.00 105.00 380.00
7-Classic face melting-c 36.00 109.00 400.00
8-Williamson-a 28.00 84.00 310.00
9-11: 9-Injury to eye panel. 10-Junkie story 23.00 69.00 250.00
12- "The Monkey" classic junkie cover/story; anti-drug propaganda issue
30.00 90.00 330.00
13-Frazetta's only solo story for E.C., 7 pgs. 33.00 99.00 360.00
14-Used in Senate Investigation hearings 18.00 55.00 200.00
15-Used in 1954 Reader's Digest article, "For the Kiddies to Read"; Bill Gaines stars in prose story "The EC Caper" 18.00 55.00 200.00
16-18: 16- "Red Dupe" editorial; rape story 16.00 48.00 175.00

NOTE: ***Ray Bradbury** adaptations-1, 7, 9. **Craig** a-11; c-11. **Crandall** a-9-13, 15-18. **Davis** a-1-5. **Evans** a-7, 8, 14-18; c-16-18. **Feldstein** c-1, 7-9, 12. **Ingels** a-1, 2, 6. **Kamen** a-in all; c-10, 13, 15. **Krigstein** a-14, 18. **Orlando** a-1, 3-7, 9, 10, 12, 16, 17. **Wood** a-2-15; c-2-6, 14.*

SHOCK SUSPENSTORIES
Russ Cochran/Gemstone Publishing: Sept, 1992 - No. 18, Dec, 1996 ($1.50/$2.00/$2.50, quarterly)

1-18: 1-3: Reprints with original-c. 17-r/HOF #17 2.50

SHOGUN WARRIORS
Marvel Comics Group: Feb, 1979 - No. 20, Sept, 1980 (Based on Mattel toys of the classic Japanese animation characters) (1-3: 35¢; 4-19: 40¢; 20: 50¢)

1-Raydeen, Combatra, & Dangard Ace begin; Trimpe-a 2.40 6.00
2-20: 2-Lord Maurkon & Elementals of Evil app.; Rok-Korr app. 6-Shogun vs. Shogun. 7,8-Cerberus. 9-Starchild. 11-Austin-c. 12-Simonson-c. 14-16-Doctor Demonicus. 17-Juggernaut. 19,20-FF x-over 4.00
1-3: Reprints 3.00

SHOOK UP (Magazine) (Satire)
Dodsworth Publ. Co.: Nov, 1958

V1#1 3.20 9.60 35.00

SHORT RIBS
Dell Publishing Co.: No. 1333, Apr - June, 1962

Four Color 1333 4.60 13.75 55.00

SHORTSTOP SQUAD (Baseball)
Ultimate Sports Ent. Inc.: 1999 ($3.95, one-shot)

1-Ripken Jr., Larkin, Jeter, Rodriguez app.; Edwards-c/a 4.00

SHORT STORY COMICS (See Hello Pal,...)

SHORTY SHINER (The Five-Foot Fighter in the Ten Gallon Hat)
Dandy Magazine (Charles Biro): June, 1956 - No. 3, Oct, 1956

1 5.70 17.00 40.00
2,3 4.65 14.00 28.00

SHOTGUN MARY
Antarctic Press: Sept, 1995 - No. 2; Mar, 1998 - No. 2, May, 1998 ($2.95)

1,2-w/pin-ups 3.00
1-($8.95)-Bagged w/CD 9.00
...Deviltown-(7/96, $2.95), ...Shooting Gallery-(6/96, $2.95), ...Son Of The Beast-(10/97, $2.95) Painted-a by Esad Ribic 3.00

SHOTGUN MARY: BLOOD LORE
Antarctic Press: Feb, 1997 - No.4, Aug, 1997 (2.95, mini-series)

1-4 3.00

SHOTGUN SLADE (TV)
Dell Publishing Co.: No. 1111, July-Sept, 1960

Four Color 1111-Photo-c 5.85 17.50 70.00

SHOWCASE (See Cancelled Comic Cavalcade & New Talent...)

GD2.0 FN6.0 NM9.4

National Per. Publ./DC Comics: 3-4/56 - No. 93, 9/70; No. 94, 8-9/77 - No. 104, 9/78

1-Fire Fighters; w/Fireman Farrell 238.00 713.00 3800.00
2-Kings of the Wild; Kubert-a (animal stories) 75.00 225.00 1050.00
3-The Frogmen by Russ Heath; Heath greytone-c (early DC example, 7-8/56)
71.00 214.00 1000.00

GD2.0 FN6.0 VF8.0 NM9.4

4-Origin/1st app. The Flash (1st DC S.A. hero, Sept-Oct, 1956) & The Turtle; Kubert-a; r/in Secret Origins #1 ('61 & '73); Flash shown reading G.A. Flash #13; Infantino/Kubert-c 1150.00 3450.00 12,500.00 32,000.00

GD2.0 FN6.0 NM9.4

5-Manhunters 75.00 225.00 1050.00

GD2.0 FN6.0 VF8.0 NM9.4

6-Origin/1st app. Challengers of the Unknown by Kirby, partly r/in Secret Origins #1 & Challengers #64,65 (1st S.A. hero team & 1st original concept S.A. series)(1-2/56) 263.00 790.00 2100.00 4200.00

GD2.0 FN6.0 NM9.4

7-Challengers of the Unknown by Kirby (2nd app.) reprinted in Challengers of the Unknown #75 136.00 407.00 1900.00

GD2.0 FN6.0 VF8.0 NM9.4

8-The Flash (5-6/57, 2nd app.); origin & 1st app. Capt. Cold
800.00 2400.00 6400.00 14,000.00
9-Lois Lane (Pre-#1, 7-8/57) (1st Showcase character to win own series) Superman app. on-c 600.00 1800.00 4200.00 8400.00

GD2.0 FN6.0 NM9.4

10-Lois Lane; Jor-el cameo; Superman app. on-c 200.00 600.00 3000.00
11-Challengers of the Unknown by Kirby (3rd) 129.00 386.00 1800.00
12-Challengers of the Unknown by Kirby (4th) 129.00 386.00 1800.00

GD2.0 FN6.0 VF8.0 NM9.4

13-The Flash (3rd app.); origin Mr. Element
300.00 900.00 2400.00 4800.00
14-The Flash (4th app.); origin Dr. Alchemy, former Mr. Element (rare in NM)
325.00 975.00 2600.00 5500.00

GD2.0 FN6.0 NM9.4

15-Space Ranger (7-8/58, 1st app.) 150.00 450.00 2100.00
16-Space Ranger (9-10/58, 2nd app.) 75.00 225.00 1050.00
17-(11-12/58)-Adventures on Other Worlds; origin/1st app. Adam Strange by Gardner Fox & Mike Sekowsky 173.00 520.00 2600.00
18-Adventures on Other Worlds (2nd A. Strange) 96.00 289.00 1350.00
19-Adam Strange; 1st Adam Strange logo 104.00 311.00 1450.00
20-Rip Hunter; origin & 1st app. (5-6/59); Moriera-a 75.00 225.00 1050.00
21-Rip Hunter (7-8/59, 2nd app.); Sekowsky-c/a 42.00 126.00 550.00

GD2.0 FN6.0 VF8.0 NM9.4

22-Origin & 1st app. Silver Age Green Lantern by Gil Kane (9-10/59); reprinted in Secret Origins #2 325.00 975.00 2600.00 5500.00

GD2.0 FN6.0 NM9.4

23-Green Lantern (11-12/59, 2nd app.); nuclear explosion-c
118.00 354.00 1650.00
24-Green Lantern (1-2/60, 3rd app.) 118.00 354.00 1650.00
25,26-Rip Hunter by Kubert. 25-Grey tone-c 31.00 93.00 350.00
27-Sea Devils (7-8/60, 1st app.); Heath-c/a 64.00 193.00 900.00
28-Sea Devils (9-10/60, 2nd app.); Heath-c/a 37.00 112.00 450.00
29-Sea Devils; Heath-c/a; grey tone c-27-29 37.00 110.00 440.00
30-Origin Silver Age Aquaman (1-2/61) (see Adventure #260 for 1st S.A. origin)
61.00 182.00 850.00
31,32-Aquaman 35.00 106.00 425.00
33-Aquaman 40.00 119.00 475.00
34-Origin & 1st app. Silver Age Atom by Kane & Anderson (9-10/61); reprinted in Secret Origins #2 107.00 321.00 1500.00
35-The Atom by Gil Kane (2nd); last 10¢ issue 61.00 182.00 850.00
36-The Atom by Gil Kane (1-2/62, 3rd app.) 50.00 150.00 650.00
37-Metal Men (3-4/62, 1st app.) 54.00 161.00 750.00
38-Metal Men (5-6/62, 2nd app.) 40.00 119.00 475.00
39-Metal Men (7-8/62, 3rd app.) 31.00 94.00 375.00
40-Metal Men (9-10/62, 4th app.) 29.00 88.00 325.00
41,42-Tommy Tomorrow (parts 1 & 2). 42-Origin 17.50 52.00 190.00
43-Dr. No (James Bond); Nodel-a; originally published as British Classics Illustrated #158A & as #6 in a European Detective series, all with diff. painted-c. This Showcase #43 version is actually censored, deleting all racial skin color

Showcase #45 © DC

Showcase #94 © DC

Sick V2 #4 © Feature Pub.

and dialogue thought to be racially demeaning (1st DC S.A. movie adaptation)(based on Ian Fleming novel & movie) 41.00 123.00 500.00
44-Tommy Tomorrow 12.00 36.00 130.00
45-Sgt. Rock (7-8/63); pre-dates B&B #52; origin retold; Heath-c 27.50 82.00 300.00
46,47-Tommy Tomorrow 10.00 30.00 110.00
48,49-Cave Carson (3rd tryout series; see B&B) 7.65 23.00 85.00
50,51-I Spy (Danger Trail-r by Infantino), King Farady story (#50 has new 4 pg. story) 7.65 23.00 85.00
52-Cave Carson 6.35 19.00 70.00
53,54-G.I. Joe (11-12/64, 1-2/65); Heath-a 11.00 33.00 120.00
55-Dr. Fate & Hourman (3-4/65); origin of each in text; 1st solo app. G.A. Green Lantern in Silver Age (pre-dates Gr. Lantern #40); 1st S.A. app. Solomon Grundy 25.00 75.00 275.00
56-Dr. Fate & Hourman 13.50 40.00 150.00
57-Enemy Ace by Kubert (7-8/65, 4th app. after Our Army at War #155) 20.50 61.00 225.00
58-Enemy Ace by Kubert (5th app.) 18.00 54.00 200.00
59-Teen Titans (11-12/65, 3rd app.) 11.00 33.00 120.00
60-1st S. A. app. The Spectre; Anderson-a (1-2/66); origin in text 29.00 88.00 325.00
61-The Spectre by Anderson (2nd app.) 14.50 43.50 160.00
62-Origin & 1st app. Inferior Five (5-6/66) 9.00 27.00 100.00
63,65-Inferior Five. 63-Hulk parody. 65-X-Men parody (11-12/66) 5.00 15.00 55.00
64-The Spectre by Anderson (5th app.) 13.50 40.00 150.00
66,67-B'wana Beast 3.20 9.60 35.00
68-Maniaks 3.20 9.60 35.00
69,71-Maniaks. 71-Woody Allen-c/app. 3.20 9.60 35.00
70-Binky (9-10/67)-Tryout issue 3.65 11.00 40.00
72-Top Gun (Johnny Thunder-r)-Toth-a 3.20 9.60 35.00
73-Origin/1st app. Creeper; Ditko-c/a (3-4/68) 12.50 37.00 135.00
74-Intro/1st app. Anthro; Post-c/a (5/68) 7.65 23.00 85.00
75-Origin/1st app. Hawk & the Dove; Ditko-c/a 10.00 30.00 110.00
76-1st app. Bat Lash (8/68) 5.45 16.35 60.00
77-1st app. Angel & The Ape (9/68) 5.45 16.35 60.00
78-1st app. Jonny Double (11/68) 3.20 9.60 35.00
79-1st app. Dolphin (12/68); Aqualad origin-r 5.00 15.00 55.00
80-1st S.A. app. Phantom Stranger (1/69); Neal Adams-c 5.45 16.35 60.00
81-Windy & Willy 3.65 11.00 40.00
82-1st app. Nightmaster (5/69) by Grandenetti & Giordano; Kubert-c 6.35 19.00 70.00
83,84-Nightmaster by Wrightson w/Jones/Kaluta ink assist in each; Kubert-c. 83-Last 12¢ issue 84-Origin retold; begin 15¢ 5.45 16.35 60.00
85-87-Firehair; Kubert-a 2.50 7.50 25.00
88-90-Jason's Quest: 90-Manhunter 2070 app. 2.00 6.00 18.00
91-93-Manhunter 2070: 92-Origin. 93-(9/70) Last 15¢ issue 2.00 6.00 18.00
94-Intro/origin new Doom Patrol & Robotman(8-9/77)1.50 4.50 12.00
95,96-The Doom Patrol. 95-Origin Celsius 1.10 3.30 9.00
97-99-Power Girl; origin-97,98; JSA cameos 1.10 3.30 9.00
100-(52 pgs.)-Most Showcase characters featured 1.50 4.50 12.00
101-103-Hawkman; Adam Strange x-over 1.00 3.00 8.00
104-(52 pgs.)-O.S.S. Spies at War 1.00 3.00 8.00

NOTE: ***Anderson** a-22-24i, 34-36i, 55, 56, 60, 61, 64, 101-103i; c-50i, 51i, 55, 56, 60, 61, 64. **Aparo** c-94-96. **Boring** c-10. **Estrada** a-104. **Fraden** c(p)-30, 31, 33. **Heath** c-3, 27-29. **Infantino** c/a(p)-4, 8, 13, 14; c-50p, 51p. **Gil Kane** a-22-24p, 34-36p; c-17-19, 22-24p(w/ **Giella**), 31. **Kane/Anderson** c-34-36. **Kirby** c-11, 12. **Kirby/Stein** c-6, 7. **Kubert** a-2, 4i, 25, 26, 45, 53, 54, 72; c-25, 26, 53, 54, 57, 58, 82-87, 101-104; c-2, 4i. **Moriera** c-5. **Orlando** a-62p, 63p, 97i; c-62, 63, 97i. **Sekowsky** a-65p. **Sparling** a-78. **Staton** a-94, 95-99p, 100; c-97-100p.*

SHOWCASE '93
DC Comics: Jan, 1993 - No. 12, Dec, 1993 ($1.95, limited series, 52 pgs.)

1-12: 1-Begin 4 part Catwoman story & 6 part Blue Devil story; begin Cyborg story; Art Adams/Austin-c. 3-Flash by Travis Charest (p). 6-Azrael in Bat-costume (2 pgs.). 7,8-Knightfall parts 13 & 14. 6-10-Deathstroke app. (6,10-cameo). 9,10-Austin-i. 10-Azrael as Batman in new costume app.; Gulacy-c. 11-Perez-c. 12-Creeper app.; Alan Grant scripts. 3.00

NOTE: ***Chaykin** c-9. **Fabry** c-8. **Giffen** a-12. **Golden** c-3. **Zeck** c-6.*

SHOWCASE '94
DC Comics: Jan, 1994 - No. 12, Dec, 1994 ($1.95, limited series, 52 pgs.)

1-12: 1,2-Joker & Gunfire stories. 1-New Gods. 4-Riddler story. 5-Huntress-c/story w/app. new Batman. 6-Huntress-c/story w/app. Robin; Atom story. 7-Penguin story by Peter David, P. Craig Russell, & Michael T. Gilbert; Penguin-c by Jae Lee. 8,9-Scarface origin story by Alan Grant, John Wagner,& Teddy Kristiansen; Prelude to Zero Hour. 10-Zero Hour tie-in story. 11-Man-Bat. 3.0

NOTE: ***Alan Grant** scripts-3, 4. **Kelley Jones** c-12. **Mignola** c-3. **Nebres** a(i)-2. **Quesada** c-1 **Russell** a-7p. **Simonson** c-5.*

SHOWCASE '95
DC Comics: Jan, 1995 - No. 12, Dec, 1995 ($2.50/$2.95, limited series)

1-4-Supergirl story. 3-Eradicator-c.; The Question story. 4-Thorn c/story 3.00
5-12: 5-Thorn-c/story; begin $2.95-c. 8-Spectre story. 12-The Shade story by James Robinson & Wade Von Grawbadger; Maitresse story by Chris Claremont & Alan Davis. 3.00

SHOWCASE '96
DC Comics: Jan, 1996 - No. 12, Dec, 1996 ($2.95, limited series)

1-12: 1-Steve Geppi cameo. 3-Black Canary & Lois Lane-c/story; Deadman story by Jamie Delano & Wade Von Grawbadger, Gary Frank-c. 4-Firebrand & Guardian-c/story; The Shade & Dr. Fate "Times Past" story by James Robinson & Matt Smith begins, ends #5. 6-Superboy-c/app.; Atom app.; Capt. Marvel (Mary Marvel)-c/app. 8-Supergirl by David & Dodson. 11-Scare Tactics app. 11,12-Legion of Super-Heroes vs. Brainiac. 12-Jesse Quick app. 3.00

SHOWGIRLS (Formerly Sherry the Showgirl #3)
Atlas Comics (MPC No. 2): No. 4, 2/57; June, 1957 - No. 2, Aug, 1957

4-Dan DeCarlo-c/a begins 9.30 28.00 65.00
1-Millie, Sherry, Chili, Pearl & Hazel begin 12.00 36.00 95.00
2 9.30 28.00 65.00

SHROUD, THE (See Super-Villain Team-Up #5)
Marvel Comics: Mar, 1994 - No. 4, June, 1994 ($1.75, mini-series)

1-4: 1,2,4-Spider-Man & Scorpion app. 2.00

SHROUD OF MYSTERY
Whitman Publications: June, 1982

1 5.00

SHUT UP AND DIE
Image Comics/Halloween: 1998 - Present ($2.95,B&W, bi-monthly)

1-3: Hudnall-s 3.00

SICK (Sick Special #131) (Magazine) (Satire)
Feature Publ./Headline Publ./Crestwood Publ. Co./Hewfred Publ./ Pyramid Comm./Charlton Publ. No. 109 (4/76) on: Aug, 1960 - No. 134, Fall, 1980

V1#1-Jack Paar photo on-c; Torres-a; Untouchables-s; Ben Hur movie photo-s 14.50 43.50 160.00
2-Torres-a; Elvis app.; Lenny Bruce app. 8.15 24.50 90.00
3-5-Torres-a in all. 3-Khruschev-c; Hitler-s. 4-Newhart-s; Castro-s; John Wayne 5-JFK/Castro-c; Elvis pin-up; Hitler. 6.80 20.50 75.00
6-Photo-s of Ricky Nelson & Marilyn Monroe; JFK 7.65 23.00 85.00
V2#1,2,4-8 (#7,8,10-14): 1-(#7) Hitler-s; Brando photo-s. 2-(#8) Dick Clark-s. 4-(#10) Untouchables-c; Candid Camera-s. 5-(#11) Nixon-c; Lone Ranger-s; JFK-s. 6-(#12) Beatnik-c/s. 8-(#14) Liz Taylor pin-up, JFK-s; Dobie Gillis-s; Sinatra & Dean Martin photo-s 5.90 17.75 65.00
3-(#9) Marilyn Monroe/JFK-c; Kingston Trio-s 6.80 20.50 75.00
V3#1-7(#15-21): 1-(#15) JFK app.; Liz Tayor/Richard Burton-s. 2-(#16) Ben Casey/ Frankenstein-c/s; Hitler photo-s. 5-(#19) Nixon back-c/s; Sinatra photo-s. 6-(#20) 1st Huckleberry Fink-c 3.65 11.00 40.00
8-(#22) Cassius Clay vs. Liston-s; 1st Civil War Blackouts-/Pvt. Bo Reargard w/ Jack Davis-a 4.55 13.65 50.00
V4#1-5 (#23-27): Civil War Blackouts-/Pvt. Bo Reargard w/ Jack Davis-a in all. 1-(#23) Smokey Bear-c; Tarzan-s. 2-(#24) Goldwater & Paar-s; Castro-s. 3-(#25) Frankenstein-c; Cleopatra/Liz Taylor-s; Steve Reeves photo-s. 4-(#26) James Bond-s; Hitler-s. 5-(#27) Taylor/Burton pin-up; Sinatra, Martin, Andress, Ekberg photo-s 3.00 9.00 32.00

Sideshow #1 © AVON

Sigil #1 © CRO

Silver Age: Green Lantern #1 © DC

8,31,36,39: 31-Pink Panther movie photo-s; Burke's Law-s. 39-Westerns; Elizabeth Montgomery photo-s; Beat mag-s 2.50 7.50 24.00
9,34,37,38: 29-Beatles-c by Jack Davis. 34-Two pg. Beatles-s & photo pin-up. 37-Playboy parody issue. 38-Addams Family-s 3.00 9.00 32.00
0,32,35,40: 30-Beatles photo pin-up; James Bond photo-s. 32-Ian Fleming-s; LBJ-s; Tarzan-s. 35-Beatles cameo; Three Stooges parody. 40-Tarzan-s; Crosby/Hope-s; Beatles parody 3.20 9.60 35.00
3-Ringo Starr photo-c & spoof on "A Hard Day's Night"; inside-c has Beatles photos 4.10 12.30 45.00
1,50,51,53,54,60: 41-Sports Illustrated parody-c/s. 50-Mod issue; flip-c w/1967 calendar w/Bob Taylor-a. 51-Get Smart-s. 53-Beatles cameo; nudity panels. 54-Monkees-c. 60-TV Daniel Boone-s 2.50 7.50 24.00
2-Fighting American-c revised from Simon/Kirby-c; "Good girl" art by Sparling; profile on Bob Powell; superhero parodies 4.55 13.65 50.00
3-49,52,55-59: 43-Sneaker set begins by Sparling. 45-Has #44 on-c & #45 on inside; TV Westerns-s; Beatles cameo. 46-Hell's Angels-s; NY Mets-s. 47-UFO/Space-c. 49-Men's Adventure mag. parody issue; nudity. 52-LBJ-s. 55-Underground culture special. 56-Alfred E. Neuman-c; inventors issue. 58-Hippie issue-c/s. 59-Hippie-s 2.30 7.00 20.00
1-64,66-69,71,73,75-80: 63-Tiny Tim-c & poster; Monkees-s. 64-Flip-c. 66-Flip-c; Mod Squad-s. 69-Beatles cameo; Peter Sellers photo-s. 71-Flip-c; Clint Eastwood0s. 76-Nixon-s; Marcus Welby-s. 78-Ma Barker-s; Courtship of Eddie's Father-s; Abbie Hoffman-s 2.00 6.00 18.00
5,70,74: 65-Cassius Clay/Brando/J. Wayne-c; Johnny Carson-s. 70-(9/69) John & Yoko-c,1/2 pg. story. 74-Clay,Agnew,Namath & others as superheroes-c/s; Easy Rider-s; Ghost and Mrs. Muir-s 2.30 7.00 20.00
'2-(84 pgs.) Xmas issue w/2 pg. slick color poster; Tarzan-s; 2 pg. Superman & superheroes-s 3.00 9.00 30.00
1-85,87-95,98,99: 81-(2/71) Woody Allen photo-s. 85 Monster Mag. parody-s; Nixon-s w/Ringo & John cameo. 88-Klute photo-s; Nixon paper dolls page. 92-Lily Tomlin; Archie Bunker pin-up. 93-Woody Allen 1.75 5.25 14.00
'6,96,97,100: 86-John & Yoko, Tiny Tim-c; Love Story movie photo-s. 96-Kung Fu-c; Mummy-s, Dracula & Frankenstein app. 97-Superman-s; 1974 Calendar; Charlie Brown & Snoopy pin-up. 100-Serpico-s; Cosell-s; J. Cousteau-s 2.00 6.00 18.00
01-103,105-114,116,119,120: 101-Three Musketeers-s; Dick Tracy-s. 102-Young Frankenstein-s. 103-Kojak-s; Evel Knievel-s. 105-Towering Inferno-s; Peanuts/Snoopy-s. 106-Cher-c/s. 107-Jaws-c/s. 108-Pink Panther-c/s; Archie-s. 109-Adam & Eve-s(nudity). 110-Welcome Back Kotter-s. 111-Sonny & Cher-s. 112-King Kong-c/s. 120-Star Trek-s 1.50 4.50 12.00
04,115,117,118: 104-Muhammad Ali-c/s. 115-Charlie's Angels-s. 117-Bionic Woman & Six Million $ Man-c/s; Cher D'Flower begins by Sparling (nudity). 118-Star Wars-s; Popeye-s 2.00 6.00 16.00
21-125,128,130: 122-Darth Vader-s. 123-Jaws II-s. 128-Superman-c/movie parody. 130-Alien movie-s 1.75 5.25 14.00
26,127: 126-(68 pgs.) Battlestar Galactica-c/s; Star Wars-s; Wonder Woman-s. 127-Mork & Mindy-s; Lord of the Rings-s 2.00 6.00 18.00
31-(1980 Special) Star Wars/Star Trek/Flash Gordon wraparound-c/s; Superman parody; Battlestar Galactica-s 2.30 7.00 20.00
32,133: 132-1980 Election-c/s; Apocalypse Now-s. 133-Star Trek-s; Chips-s; Superheroes page 2.00 6.00 18.00
34 (scarce)(68 pg. Giant)-Star Wars-c; Alien-s; WKRP-s; Mork & Mindy-s; Taxi-s; MASH-s 3.20 9.60 35.00
nnual 1- 7th Annual Yearbook (1967)-Davis-c, 2 pg. glossy poster insert 3.20 9.60 35.00
nnual 2- Birthday Annual (1967)-3 pg. Huckleberry Fink fold out 3.00 9.00 32.00
nnual 3 (1968) "Big Sick Laff-in" on-c (84 pgs.)-w/psychedelic posters; Frankenstein poster 3.00 9.00 30.00
nnual 1969, 1970, 1971 2.80 8.40 28.00
nnual 12,13-(1972,1973, 84 pgs.) 13-Monster-c 2.80 8.40 28.00
nnual 14 (1974, 84 pgs.) Hitler photo-s 2.80 8.40 28.00
nnual 2-4 (1980) 1.50 4.50 12.00
pecial 1 (1980) Buck Rogers-c/s; MASH-s 2.30 7.00 20.00
pecial 2 (1980) Wraparound Star Wars:Empire Strikes Back-c; Charlie's Angels/ Farrah-s; Rocky-s; plus reprints 2.30 7.00 20.00
'earbook 15(1975, 84 pgs.) Paul Revere-c 2.50 7.50 24.00
'OTE: ***Davis*** *a-42, 87; c-22, 23, 25, 29, 31, 32.* ***Powell*** *a-7, 31, 57.* ***Simon*** *a-1-3, 10, 41, 42, 87, 9; c-1, 47, 57, 59, 69, 91, 95-97, 99, 100, 102, 107, 112.* ***Torres*** *a-1-3, 29, 31, 47, 49.* ***Tuska*** *a-14, 41-43. Civil War Blackouts-23, 24. #42 has biography of Bob Powell.*

SIDESHOW
Avon Periodicals: 1949 (one-shot)
1-(Rare)-Similar to Bachelor's Diary 33.00 98.00 260.00

SIEGE
Image Comics (WildStorm Prod.): Jan, 1997 - No. 4, Apr, 1997 ($2.50)
1-4 2.50

SIEGEL AND SHUSTER: DATELINE 1930s
Eclipse Comics: Nov, 1984 - No. 2, Sept, 1985 ($1.50/$1.75, Baxter paper #1)
1,2: 1-Unpublished samples of strips from the '30s; includes 'Interplanetary Police'; Shuster-c. 2 ($1.75, B&W)-unpublished strips; Shuster-c 2.00

SIGIL (Also see CrossGen Chronicles)
CrossGeneration Comics: Jul, 2000 - Present ($2.95)
1-8: Barbara Kesel-s/Ben & Ray Lai-a 3.00

SIGMA
Image Comics (WildStorm Productions): March, 1996 - No. 3, June, 1996 ($2.50, limited series)
1-3: 1-"Fire From Heaven" prelude #2; Coker-a 2-"Fire From Heaven" pt. 6. 3-"Fire From Heaven" pt. 14. 2.50

SILENT INVASION, THE
Rengade Press: Apr, 1986 - No.12, Mar, 1988 ($1.70/$2.00, B&W)
1-12-UFO sightings of the '50's 3.00
Book 1- reprints ($7.95) 8.00

SILENT MOBIUS
Viz Select Comics: 1991 - No. 5, 1992 ($4.95, color, squarebound, 44 pgs.)
1-5: Japanese stories translated to English 5.00

SILENT RAPTURE
Avatar Press: Jan, 1997 - No.2, Apr, 1997 ($3.00, B&W, limited series)
1,2 3.00

SILENT SCREAMERS (Based on the Aztech Toys figures)
Image Comics: Oct, 2000 ($4.95)
Nosferatu Issue - Alex Ross front & back-c 5.00

SILLY PILLY (See Frank Luther's...)

SILLY SYMPHONIES (See Dell Giants)

SILLY TUNES
Timely Comics: Fall, 1945 - No. 7, June, 1947
1-Silly Seal, Ziggy Pig begin 20.00 60.00 160.00
2-(2/46) 10.50 32.00 85.00
3-7: 6-New logo 9.30 28.00 65.00

SILVER (See Lone Ranger's Famous Horse...)

SILVER AGE
DC Comics: July, 2000 ($3.95, limited series)
1-Waid-s/Dodson-a; "Silver Age" style x-over; JLA & villains switch bodies 3.95
...: Challengers of the Unknown ($2.50) Joe Kubert-c; vs. Chronos 2.50
...: Dial H For Hero ($2.50) Jim Mooney-c; vs. Martian Manhunter 2.50
...: Doom Patrol ($2.50) Ramona Fradon-c/Peyer-s 2.50
...: Flash ($2.50) Carmine Infantino-c; Kid Flash and Elongated Man app. 2.50
...: Green Lantern ($2.50) Gil Kane-c/Busiek-s/Anderson-a; vs. Sinestro 2.50
...: Justice League of America ($2.50) Ty Templeton-c 2.50
...: Showcase ($2.50) Dick Giordano-c/a; Batgirl, Adam Strange app. 2.50
... Secret Files ($4.95) Intro. Agamemno; short stories & profile pages 4.95
...: Teen Titans ($2.50) Nick Cardy-c; vs. Penguin, Mr. Element, Black Manta 2.50
...: The Brave and the Bold ($2.50) Jim Aparo-c; Batman & Metal Men 2.50
... 80-Page Giant ($5.95) Conclusion of x-over; "lost" Silver Age stories 5.95

SILVERBACK
Comico: 1989 - No. 3, 1990 ($2.50, color, limited series, mature readers)
1-3: Character from Grendel: Matt Wagner-a 3.00

SILVERBLADE
DC Comics: Sept, 1987 - No. 12, Sept, 1988
1-12: Colan -c/a in all 2.00

Silver Streak Comics #2 © LEV

Silver Surfer V1 #18 © MAR

Silver Surfer V3 #146 © MAR

SILVER CROSS (See Warrior Nun series)
Antarctic Press: Nov, 1997 - No. 3, Mar, 1998 ($2.95)

1-3-Ben Dunn-s/a 3.00

SILVERHAWKS
Star Comics/Marvel Comics #6: Aug, 1987 - No. 6, June, 1988 ($1.00)

1-6 3.00

SILVERHEELS
Pacific Comics: Dec, 1983 - No. 3, May, 1984 ($1.50)

1-3 2.00

SILVER KID WESTERN
Key/Stanmor Publications: Oct, 1954 - No. 5, July, 1955

1 10.00 30.00 75.00
2 5.70 17.00 40.00
3-5 5.00 15.00 35.00
I.W. Reprint #1,2-Severin-c: 1-r/#? 2-r/#1 1.75 5.25 14.00

SILVER SABLE AND THE WILD PACK (See Amazing Spider-Man #265)
Marvel Comics: June, 1992 - No. 35, Apr, 1995 ($1.25/$1.50

1-($2.00)-Embossed & foil stamped-c; Spider-Man app. 3.00
2-35: 4,5-Dr. Doom-c/story. 6,7-Deathlok-c/story. 9-Origin Silver Sable. 10-Punisher-c/s. 15-Capt. America-c/s. 16,17-Intruders app. 18,19-Venom-c/s. 19-Siege of Darkness x-over. 23-Daredevil (in new costume) & Deadpool app. 24-Bound-in card sheet. Li'l Sylvie backup story. 25-($2.00, 52 pgs.)-Li'l Sylvie backup story 2.00

SILVER STAR (Also see Jack Kirby's...)
Pacific Comics: Feb, 1983 - No. Jan, 1984 ($1.00)

1-6: 1-1st app. Last of the Viking Heroes. 1-5-Kirby-c/a. 2-Ditko-a 4.00

SILVER STREAK COMICS (Crime Does Not Pay #22 on)
Your Guide Publs. No. 1-7/New Friday Publs. No. 8-17/Comic House Publ./Newsbook Publ.: Dec, 1939 - No. 21, May, 1942; No. 23, 1946; No # 22 (Silver logo-#1-5)

GD2.0 FN6.0 VF8.0 NM9.4
1-(Scarce)-Intro The Claw by Cole (r-/in Daredevil #21), Red Reeves, Boy Magician, & Captain Fearless; The Wasp, Mister Midnight begin; Spirit Man app. Silver metallic-c begin, end #5; Claw c-1,2,6-8
1000.00 3000.00 6500.00 12,500.00

GD2.0 FN6.0 NM9.4
2-The Claw by Cole; Simon-c/a 381.00 1143.00 4000.00
3-1st app. & origin Silver Streak (2nd with lightning speed); Dickie Dean the Boy Inventor, Lance Hale, Ace Powers, Bill Wayne, & The Planet Patrol begin 324.00 971.00 3400.00
4-Sky Wolf begins; Silver Streak by Jack Cole (new costume); 1st app. Jackie, Lance Hale's sidekick 168.00 505.00 1600.00
5-Jack Cole c/a(2) 200.00 600.00 1900.00

GD2.0 FN6.0 VF8.0 NM9.4
6-(Scarce, 9/40)-Origin & 1st app. Daredevil (blue & yellow costume) by Jack Binder; The Claw returns; classic Cole Claw-c
1160.00 3480.00 7540.00 14,500.00
7-Claw vs. Daredevil (new costume-blue & red) by Jack Cole & 3 other Cole stories (38 pgs.) 716.00 2150.00 4475.00 8200.00

GD2.0 FN6.0 NM9.4
8-Claw vs. Daredevil by Cole; last Cole Silver Streak
305.00 915.00 3200.00
9-Claw vs. Daredevil by Cole 190.00 570.00 1800.00
10-Origin & 1st app. Captain Battle (5/41); Claw vs. Daredevil by Cole; Robot-c 168.00 505.00 1600.00
11-Intro. Mercury by Bob Wood, Silver Streak's sidekick; conclusion Claw vs. Daredevil by Rico; in 'Presto Martin,' 2nd pg., newspaper says 'Roussos does it again' 116.00 348.00 1100.00
12-14: 13-Origin Thun-Dohr 84.00 253.00 800.00
15, 17-Last Daredevil issue. 79.00 237.00 750.00
16-Hitler-c 89.00 268.00 850.00
18-The Saint begins (2/42, 1st app.) by Leslie Charteris (see Movie Comics #2 by DC); The Saint-c 68.00 205.00 650.00
19-21(1942): 20,21 have Wolverton's Scoop Scuttle. 21-Hitler app. in strip on cover 55.00 165.00 500.00
23(1946(An Atomic Comic)-Reprints; bondage-c 40.00 120.00 350.00

nn(11/46)(Newsbook Publ.)-R-/S.S. story from #4-7 plus 2 Captain Fearless stories, all in color; bondage/torture-c 50.00 150.00 450.00
NOTE: ***Binder*** *c-3, 4, 13-15, 17.* ***Jack Cole*** *a-(Daredevil)-#6-10, (Dickie Dean)-#3-10, (Pirate Prince)-#7, (Silver Streak)-#4-8, nn; c-5 (Silver Streak), 6 (Claw), 7, 8 (Daredevil).* ***Everett*** *Red Reed begins #20.* ***Guardineer*** *a-#8-13.* ***Don Rico*** *a-11-17 (Daredevil); c-11, 12, 16.* ***Simon*** *a-3 (Silver Streak).* ***Bob Wood*** *a-9 (Silver Streak); c-9, 10. Captain Battle c-11, 13-15, 17. Claw c-#1, 2, 6-8. Daredevil c-7, 8, 12. Dickie Dean c-19. Ned of the Navy c-20 (war). The Saint c-18. Silver Streak c-5, 9, 10, 16, 23.*

SILVER SURFER (See Fantastic Four, Fantasy Masterpieces V2#1, Fireside Book Series, Marvel Graphic Novel, Marvel Presents #8, Marvel's Greatest Comics & Tales To Astonish #92)

SILVER SURFER, THE (Also see Essential Silver Surfer)
Marvel Comics Group: Aug, 1968 - No. 18, Sept, 1970; June, 1982

1-More detailed origin by John Buscema (p); The Watcher back-up stories begin (origin), end #7; (No. 1-7: 25¢, 68 pgs.) 41.00 123.00 525.00
2 19.00 57.00 210.00
3-1st app. Mephisto 15.50 46.50 170.00
4-Low distribution; Thor & Loki app. 40.00 120.00 480.00
5-7-Last giant size. 5-The Stranger app.; Fantastic Four app. 6-Brunner inks. 7 (8/69)-1st app. Frankenstein's monster (cameo) 10.00 30.00 110.00
8-10: 8-18-(15¢ issues) 7.25 21.75 80.00
11-13,15-18: 15-Silver Surfer vs. Human Torch; Fantastic Four app. 17-Nick Fury app. 18-Vs. The Inhumans; Kirby-c/a 5.90 17.75 65.00
14-Spider-Man x-over 8.15 24.50 90.00
V2#1 (6/82, 52 pgs.)-Byrne-c/a 1.25 3.75 10.00
NOTE: ***Adkins*** *a-8-15i.* ***Brunner*** *a-6i.* ***J. Buscema*** *a-1-17p.* ***Colan*** *a-1-3p.* ***Reinman*** *a-1-4i. #1-14 were reprinted in Fantasy Masterpieces V2#1-14.*

SILVER SURFER (Volume 3) (See Marvel Graphic Novel #38)
Marvel Comics Group: V3#1, July, 1987 - No. 146, Nov, 1998

1-Double size ($1.25) 1.10 3.30 9.00
2-17: 15-Ron Lim-c/a begins (9/88) 4.00
18-33,39-43: 25,31 ($1.50, 52 pgs.). 25-Skrulls app. 32,39-No Ron Lim-c/a. 39-Alan Grant scripts 3.00
34-Thanos returns (cameo); Starlin scripts begin 5.00
35-38: 35-1st full Thanos app. in Silver Surfer (3/90); reintro Drax the Destroyer on last pg. (cameo). 36-Recaps history of Thanos; Capt. Marvel & Warlock app. in recap. 37-1st full app. Drax the Destroyer; Drax-c. 38-Silver Surfer battles Thanos 2.40 6.00
44,45,49-Thanos stories (c-44,45) 4.00
46-48: 46-Return of Adam Warlock (2/91); re-intro Gamora & Pip the Troll. 47-Warlock battles Drax. 48-Last Starlin scripts (also #50) 4.00
50-($1.50, 52 pgs.)-Embossed & silver foil-c; Silver Surfer has brief battle w/Thanos; story cont'd in Infinity Gauntlet #1 1.00 2.80 7.00
50-2nd & 3rd printings 2.00
51-59: 51-53: Infinity Gauntlet x-over . 54-57: Infinity Gauntlet x-overs. 54-Rhino app. 55,56-Thanos-c & app. 57-Thanos-c & cameo. 58,59-Infinity Gauntlet x-overs; 58-Ron Lim-c only. 59-Thanos battles Silver Surfer-c/story; Thanos joins 3.00
60-74,76-99,101-124,126-139: 63-Capt. Marvel app. 67-69-Infinity War x-overs. 76-78-Jack of Hearts-c/s. 83-85-Infinity Crusade x-over; 83,84-Thanos cameo. 85-Storm, Wonder Man x-over. 86-Thor-c/s. 87-Dr. Strange & Warlock app. 88-Thanos-c/s. 82 (52 pgs.). 101-Bound in card sheet. 5-FF app. 96-Hulk & FF app. 97-Terrax & Nova app. 106-Doc Doom app. 121-Quasar & Beta Ray Bill app. 123-w/card insert; begin Garney-a. 126-Dr. Strange-c/app. 128-Spider-Man & Daredevil-c/app. 138-Thing-c 2.00
75-($2.50, 52 pgs.)-Embossed foil-c; Lim-c/a 3.00
100 ($2.25, 52 pgs.)-Wraparound-c 2.25
100 ($3.95, 52 pgs.)-Enhanced-c 4.00
125 ($2.95)-Wraparound-c; Vs. Hulk-c/app. 3.00
140-146: 140-142,144,145-Muth-c/a. 143,146-Cowan-a. 146-Last issue 2.00
#(-1) Flashback (7/97) 2.00
Annual 1 (1988, $1.75)-Evolutionary War app.; 1st Ron Lim-a on Silver Surfer (20 pg. back-up story & pin-ups) 5.00
Annual 2-7 ('89-'94, 68 pgs.): 2-Atlantis Attacks. 4-3 pg. origin story; Silver Surfer battles Guardians of the Galaxy. 5-Return of the Defenders, part 3; Lim-c/a (3 pgs. of pin-ups only). 6-Polybagged w/trading card; 1st app. Legacy; card is by Lim/Austin 3.00
Annual '97 ($2.99), .../Thor Annual '98 ($2.99) 3.00
...Dangerous Artifacts-(1996, $3.95)-Ron Marz scripts; Galactus-c/app. 4.00
Graphic Novel (1988, Hardcover, $14.95) Judgment Day; Lee-s/Buscema-a 15.00

Simpsons Comics #28 © Bongo Entertainment

Sin City: The Big Fat Kill #2 © Frank Miller

Single Series #2 © UFS

GD2.0 FN6.0 NM9.4

The Enslavers Graphic Novel (1990, $16.95) 17.00
Homecoming Graphic Novel (1991, $12.95, softcover) Starlin-s 15.00
Inner Demons TPB (4/98, $3.50)r/#123,125,126 3.50
...: The First Coming of Galactus nn (11/92, $5.95, 68 pgs.)-Reprints Fantastic Four #48-50 with new Lim-c 2.40 6.00
Wizard 1/2 1.85 5.50 15.00

NOTE: ***Austin** c(i)-7, 8, 71, 73, 74, 76, 79. **Cowan** a-143,146. **Cully Hamner** a-83p. **Ron Lim** a(p)-15-31, 33-38, 40-55, (56, 57-part-p), 60-65, 73-82, Annual 2, 4; c(p)-15-31, 32-38, 40-84, 86-92, Annual 2, 4-6. **Muth** c/a-140-142,144,145. **M. Rogers** a-1-10, 12, 19, 21; c-1-9, 11, 12, 21.*

SILVER SURFER, THE
Marvel Comics (Epic): Dec, 1988 - No. 2, Jan, 1989 ($1.00, lim. series)
1,2: By Stan Lee scripts & Moebius-c/a 4.00
...: Parable ('98, $5.99) r/#1&2 6.00

SILVER SURFER: LOFTIER THAN MORTALS
Marvel Comics: Oct, 1999 - No. 2, Oct, 1999 ($2.50, limited series)
1,2-Remix of Fantastic Four #57-60; Velluto-a 2.50

SILVER SURFER/SUPERMAN
Marvel Comics: 1996 ($5.95,one-shot)
1-Perez-s/Lim-c/a(p) 6.00

SILVER SURFER VS. DRACULA
Marvel Comics: Feb, 1994 ($1.75, one-shot)
1-r/Tomb of Dracula #50; Everett Vampire-r/Venus #19; Howard the Duck back-up by Brunner; Lim-c(p) 2.00

SILVER SURFER/WARLOCK: RESURRECTION
Marvel Comics: Mar, 1993 - No. 4, June, 1993 ($2.50, limited series)
1-4: Starlin-c/a & scripts 2.50

SILVER SURFER/WEAPON ZERO
Marvel Comics: Apr, 1997 ($2.95,one-shot)
1-"Devil's Reign" pt. 8 3.00

SILVERTIP (Max Brand)
Dell Publishing Co.: No. 491, Aug, 1953 - No. 898, May, 1958
Four Color 491 (#1); all painted-c 7.50 22.50 90.00
Four Color 572,608,637,667,731,789,898-Kinstler-a 4.10 12.30 45.00
Four Color 835 4.10 12.30 45.00

SIMPSONS COMICS (See Bartman, Itchy & Scratchy & Radioactive Man)
Bongo Comics Group: 1993 - Present ($1.95, color)
1-($2.25)-FF#1-c swipe; pull-out poster; flip book 5.00
2-20: 2-Patty & Selma flip-c/sty. 3-Krusty, Agent of K.L.O.W.N. flip-c/story. 4-Infinity-c; flip-c of Busman #1; w/trading card. 5-Wraparound-c w/trading card. 6-40: All Flip books. 6-w/Chief Wiggum's "Crime Comics". 7-w/"McBain Comics". 8-w/"Edna, Queen of the Congo". 9-w/"Barney Gumble". 10-w/"Apu". 11-w/"Homer". 12-w/"White Knuckled War Stories". 13-w/"Jimbo Jones' Wedgie Comics". 14-w/"Grampa". 15-w/"Itchy & Scratchy". 16-w/"Bongo Grab Bag". 17-w/"Headlight Comics". 18-w/"Milhouse".19,20-w/"Roswell" 4.00
21-40: 21,22-w/"Roswell". 23-w/"Hellfire Comics". 24-w/"Lil' Homey". 36-39-Flip book w/Radioactive Man 3.00
41-49,51-53 ($2.50): 43-Flip book w/Poochie. 52-Paul Dini-s 2.50
50-($5.95) Wraparound-c; 80 pgs.; square-bound 5.95
... A Go-Go (1999, $11.95)-r/#32-35; ...Big Bonanza (1998, $11.95)-r/#28-31, ...Extravaganza (1994, $10.00)-r/#1-4; infinity-c, ...On Parade (1998, $11.95)-r/#24-27, ...Simpsorama (1996, $10.95)-r/#11-14 12.00

SIMPSONS COMICS AND STORIES
Welsh Publishing Group: 1993 ($2.95, one-shot)
1-(Direct Sale)-Polybagged w/Bartman poster 2.40 6.00
1-(Newsstand Edition)-Without poster 4.00

SIMPSONS COMICS PRESENTS BART SIMPSON
Bongo Comics Group: 2000 - Present ($2.50, quarterly)
1,2 2.50

SIMULATORS, THE
Neatly Chiseled Features: 1991 ($2.50, stiff-c)
1-Super hero group 2.50

SINBAD, JR (TV Cartoon)
Dell Publishing Co.: Sept-Nov, 1965 - No. 3, May, 1966
1 3.00 9.00 30.00
2,3 2.40 7.35 22.00

SIN CITY (See Dark Horse Presents, Decade of Dark Horse, A & San Diego Comic Con Comics #2,4)
Dark Horse Comics (Legend)
TPB ($15.00) Reprints early DHP stories 15.00
Booze, Broads & Bullets TPB ($15.00) 15.00

SIN CITY: A DAME TO KILL FOR
Dark Horse Comics (Legend): Nov, 1993 - No. 6, May, 1994 ($2.95, B&W, limited series)
1-6: Frank Miller-c/a & story in all. 1-1st app. Dwight. 5.00
Limited Edition Hardcover 85.00
Hardcover 25.00
TPB ($15.00) 15.00

SIN CITY: FAMILY VALUES
Dark Horse Comics (Legend): Oct, 1997 ($10.00, B&W, squarebound, one-shot)
nn-Miller-c/a & story 10.00
Limited Edition Hardcover 75.00

SIN CITY: HELL AND BACK
Dark Horse (Maverick): Jul, 1999 - No. 9 ($2.95/$4.95, B&W, limited series)
1-8-Miller-c/a & story. 7-Color 3.00
9-($4.95) 5.00

SIN CITY: JUST ANOTHER SATURDAY NIGHT
Dark Horse Comics (Legend): Aug, 1997 (Wizard 1/2 offer, B&W, one-shot)
1/2-Miller-c/a & story 1.00 3.00 8.00
nn (10/98, $2.50) r/#1/2 2.50

SIN CITY: LOST, LONELY & LETHAL
Dark Horse Comics (Legend): Dec, 1996 ($2.95, B&W and blue, one-shot)
nn-Miller-c/s/a; w/pin-ups 4.00

SIN CITY: SEX AND VIOLENCE
Dark Horse Comics (Legend): Mar, 1997 ($2.95, B&W and blue, one-shot)
nn-Miller-c/a & story 4.00

SIN CITY: SILENT NIGHT
Dark Horse Comics (Legend): Dec, 1995 ($2.95, B&W, one-shot)
1-Miller-c/a & story; Marv app. 4.00

SIN CITY: THAT YELLOW BASTARD
Dark Horse Comics (Legend): Feb, 1996 - No. 6, July, 1996 ($2.95/$3.50, B&W and yellow, limited series)
1-5: Miller-c/a & story in all. 1-1st app. Hartigan. 5.00
6-($3.50) Error & corrected 5.00
Limited Edition Hardcover 25.00
TPB ($15.00) 15.00

SIN CITY: THE BABE WORE RED AND OTHER STORIES
Dark Horse Comics (Legend): Nov, 1994 ($2.95, B&W and red, one-shot)
1-r/serial run in Previews as well as other stories; Miller-c/a & scripts; Dwight app. 3.00

SIN CITY: THE BIG FAT KILL
Dark Horse Comics (Legend): Nov, 1994 - No. 5, Mar, 1995 ($2.95, B&W, limited series)
1-5-Miller story & art in all; Dwight app. 4.00
Hardcover 25.00
TPB ($15.00) 15.00

SINDBAD (See Capt. Sindbad under Movie Comics, and Fantastic Voyages of Sindbad)

SINGING GUNS (See Fawcett Movie Comics)

SINGLE SERIES (Comics on Parade #30 on)(Also see John Hix...)
United Features Syndicate: 1938 - No. 28, 1942 (All 68 pgs.)

Note: See Individual Alphabetical Listings for prices

1-Captain and the Kids (#1)
2-Broncho Bill (1939) (#1)
3-Ella Cinders (1939)
4-Li'l Abner (1939) (#1)

Sinister House of Secret Love #2 © DC

Six-Gun Heroes #14 © FAW

Six Million Dollar Man (2nd series) #6 © CC

5-Fritzi Ritz (#1)
6-Jim Hardy by Dick Moores (#1)
7-Frankie Doodle
8-Peter Pat (On sale 7/14/39)
9-Strange As It Seems
10-Little Mary Mixup
11-Mr. and Mrs. Beans
12-Joe Jinks
13-Looy Dot Dope
14-Billy Make Believe
15-How It Began (1939)
16-Illustrated Gags (1940)-Has ad for Captain and the Kids #1 reprint listed below
17-Danny Dingle
18-Li'l Abner (#2 on-c)
19-Broncho Bill (#2 on-c)
20-Tarzan by Hal Foster
21-Ella Cinders (#2 on-c; on sale 3/19/40)
22-Iron Vic
23-Tailspin Tommy by Hal Forrest (#1)
24-Alice in Wonderland (#1)
25-Abbie and Slats
26-Little Mary Mixup (#2 on-c, 1940)
27-Jim Hardy by Dick Moores (1942)
28-Ella Cinders & Abbie and Slats (1942)
1-Captain and the Kids (1939 reprint)-2nd Edition
1-Fritzi Ritz (1939 reprint)-2nd ed.

NOTE: *Some issues given away at the 1939-40 New York World's Fair (#6).*

SINISTER HOUSE OF SECRET LOVE, THE (Becomes Secrets of Sinister House No. 5 on)
National Periodical Publ.: Oct-Nov, 1971 - No. 4, Apr-May, 1972

1 (all 52 pgs.) 13.50 40.00 150.00
2,4: 2-Jeff Jones-c 5.45 16.35 60.00
3-Toth-a 5.90 17.75 65.00

SINS OF YOUTH... (Also see Young Justice: Sins of Youth)
DC Comics: May 2000 ($4.95/$2.50, limited crossover series)

Secret Files 1 ($4.95) Short stories and profile pages; Nauck-c 4.95
...Aquaboy/Lagoon Man; Batboy and Robin; JLA Jr.; Kid Flash/Impulse; Starwoman and the JSA, Superman, Jr./Superboy, Sr.; The Secret/ Deadboy, Wonder Girls ($2.50-c) Old and young heroes switch ages 2.50

SIR CHARLES BARKLEY AND THE REFEREE MURDERS
Hamilton Comics: 1993 ($9.95, 8-1/2" x 11", 52 pgs.)

nn-Photo-c; Sports fantasy comic book fiction (uses real names of NBA super stars). Script by Alan Dean Foster, art by Joe Staton. Comes with bound-in sheet of 35 gummed "Moods of Charles Barkley" stamps. Photo/story on Barkley 1.25 3.75 10.00
Special Edition of 100 copies for charity signed on an affixed book plate by Barkley, Foster & Staton 150.00
Ashcan edition given away to dealers, distributors & promoters (low distribution). Four pages in color, balance of story in b&w 1.25 3.75 10.00

SIREN (Also see Eliminator & Ultraforce)
Malibu Comics (Ultraverse): Sept, 1995 - No. 3, Dec, 1995 ($1.50)

Infinity, 1-3: Infinity-Black-c & painted-c exists. 1-Regular-c & painted-c; War Machine app. 2-Flip book w/Phoenix Resurrection Pt. 3 2.00
Special 1-(2/96, $1.95, 28 pgs.)-Origin Siren; Marvel Comic's Juggernaut-c/app. 2.00

SIREN: SHAPES
Image Comics: May, 1998 - No. 3, Nov, 1998 ($2.95, B&W, limited series)

1-3-J. Torres -s 3.00

SIR LANCELOT (TV)
Dell Publishing Co.: No. 606, Dec, 1954 - No. 775, Mar, 1957

Four Color 606 (not TV) 6.70 20.00 80.00
Four Color 775(...and Brian)-Buscema-a; photo-c 8.35 25.00 100.00

SIR WALTER RALEIGH (Movie)
Dell Publishing Co.: May, 1955 (Based on movie "The Virgin Queen")

Four Color 644-Photo-c 6.30 19.00 75.00

SISTERHOOD OF STEEL (See Eclipse Graphic Adventure Novel #13)
Marvel Comics (Epic Comics): Dec, 1984 -No. 8, Feb, 1986 ($1.50, Baxter paper, mature)

1-8 3.00

SISTERS OF MERCY
Maximum Press/No Mercy Comics #3 on: Dec, 1995 - No. 5, Oct, 1996 ($2.50)

1-5: 1-Liefeld variant-c exists 2.50
V2#0-(3/97, $1.50) Liefeld-c 2.00

SISTERS OF MERCY: PARADISE LOST
London Night Studios/No Mercy Comics: Apr, 1997 - No. 4 ($2.50)

1-4 2.50

SISTERS OF MERCY: WHEN RAZORS CRY CRIMSON TEARS
No Mercy Comics: Oct, 1996 ($2.50, one-shot)

1 2.50

6, THE
Virtual Comics (Byron Preiss Multimedia): Oct, 1996 - No. 3, Dec, 1996 ($2.50, limited series)

1-3: L. Simonson-s 2.50

6 BLACK HORSES (See Movie Classics)

SIX FROM SIRIUS
Marvel Comics (Epic Comics): July, 1984 - No. 4, Oct, 1984 ($1.50, limited series, mature)

1-4: Moench scripts; Gulacy-c/a in all 2.00

SIX FROM SIRIUS II
Marvel Comics (Epic Comics): Feb, 1986 - No. 4, May, 1986 ($1.50, limited series, mature)

1-4: Moench scripts; Gulacy-c/a in all 2.00

SIX-GUN HEROES
Fawcett Publications: March, 1950 - No. 23, Nov, 1953 (Photo-c #1-23)

1-Rocky Lane, Hopalong Cassidy, Smiley Burnette begin (same date as Smiley Burnette #1) 44.00 133.00 400.00
2 28.00 83.00 220.00
3-5: 5-Lash LaRue begins 19.00 56.00 150.00
6-15 14.00 41.00 110.00
16-22: 17-Last Smiley Burnette. 18-Monte Hale begins 12.00 36.00 95.00
23-Last Fawcett issue 13.00 39.00 105.00

NOTE: *Hopalong Cassidy photo c-1-3. Monte Hale photo c-18. Rocky Lane photo c-4, 5, 7, 9, 11, 13, 15, 17, 20, 21, 23. Lash LaRue photo c-6, 8, 10, 12, 14, 16, 19, 22.*

SIX-GUN HEROES (Cont'd from Fawcett; Gunmasters #84 on) (See Blue Bird)
Charlton Comics: No. 24, Jan, 1954 - No. 83, Mar-Apr, 1965 (All Vol. 4)

24-Lash LaRue, Hopalong Cassidy, Rocky Lane & Tex Ritter begin; photo-c 20.00 60.00 160.00
25 10.00 30.00 75.00
26-30: 26-Rod Cameron story. 28-Tom Mix begins? 9.30 28.00 65.00
31-40: 38-Jingles & Wild Bill Hickok (TV) 8.65 26.00 60.00
41-46,48,50 7.85 23.50 55.00
47-Williamson-a, 2 pgs; Torres-a 8.65 26.00 60.00
49-Williamson-a (5 pgs.) 9.30 28.00 65.00
51-56,58-60: 58-Gunmaster app. 3.65 11.00 40.00
57-Origin & 1st app. Gunmaster 4.10 12.30 45.00
61,63-70 3.00 9.00 30.00
62-Origin Gunmaster 3.20 9.60 35.00
71-75,77,78,80-83 2.30 7.00 20.00
76,79: 76-Gunmaster begins. 79-1st app. & origin of Bullet, the Gun-Boy 2.50 7.50 23.00

SIXGUN RANCH (See Luke Short & Four Color #580)

SIX-GUN WESTERN
Atlas Comics (CDS): Jan, 1957 - No. 4, July, 1957

1-Crandall-a; two Williamson text illos 20.00 60.00 160.00
2,3-Williamson-a in both 14.00 43.00 115.00
4-Woodbridge-a 10.00 30.00 70.00

NOTE: ***Ayers** a-2, 3. **Maneely** a-1; c-2, 3. **Orlando** a-2. **Pakula** a-2. **Powell** a-3. **Romita** a-1, 4. **Severin** c-1, 4. **Shores** a-2.*

SIX MILLION DOLLAR MAN, THE (TV)
Charlton Comics: 6/76 - No. 4, 12/76; No. 5, 10/77; No. 6, 2/78 - No. 9, 6/78

1-Staton-c/a; Lee Majors photo on-c 1.50 4.50 12.00
2-9: 2-Neal Adams-c; Staton-a 1.00 3.00 8.00

SIX MILLION DOLLAR MAN, THE (TV)(Magazine)
Charlton Comics: July, 1976 - No. 7, Nov, 1977 (B&W)

1-Neal Adams-c/a 2.00 6.00 18.00
2-Neal Adams-c 1.75 5.25 14.00

Skeleton Key V2 #1 © Andrew Watson

Skypilot #10 © Z-D

Slam Bang Comics #4 © FAW

GD2.0 FN6.0 NM9.4

3-N. Adams part inks; Chaykin-a 1.75 5.25 14.00
4-7 1.50 4.50 12.00

SIX STRING SAMURAI
Awesome-Hyperwerks: Sept, 1998 ($2.95)

1-Stinsman & Fraga-a 3.00

67 SECONDS
Marvel Comics (Epic Comics): 1992 ($15.95, 54 pgs., graphic novel)

nn-James Robinson scripts; Steve Yeowell-c/a 2.00 6.00 18.00

SKATEMAN
Pacific Comics: Nov, 1983 (Baxter paper, one-shot)

1-Adams-c/a 4.00

SKELETON HAND (...In Secrets of the Supernatural)
American Comics Gr. (B&M Dist. Co.): Sept-Oct, 1952 - No. 6, Jul-Aug, 1953

1 42.00 125.00 375.00
2 31.00 94.00 250.00
3-6 26.00 79.00 210.00

SKELETON KEY
Amaze Ink: July, 1995 - No. 30, Jan, 1998 ($1.25/$1.50/$1.75, B&W)

1-30 2.00
Special #1 (2/98, $4.95) Unpublished short stories 5.00
Sugar Kat Special (10/98, $2.95) Halloween stories 3.00
Beyond The Threshold TPB (6/96. $11.95)-r/#1-6 12.00
Cats and Dogs TPB ($12.95)-r/#25-30 13.00
The Celestial Calendar TPB ($19.95)-r/#7-18 20.00
Telling Tales TPB ($12.95)-r/#19-24 13.00

SKELETON KEY (Volume 2)
Amaze Ink: 1999 - No. 4, 1999 ($2.95, B&W)

1-4-Andrew Watson-s/a 3.00

SKELETON WARRIORS
Marvel Comics: Apr, 1995 - No. 4, July, 1995 ($1.50)

1-4: Based on animated series. 2.00

SKIN GRAFT: THE ADVENTURES OF A TATTOOED MAN
DC Comics (Vertigo): July, 1993 - No. 4, Oct, 1993 ($2.50, lim. series, mature)

1-4 2.50

SKI PARTY (See Movie Classics)

SKREEMER
DC Comics: May, 1989 - No. 6, Oct, 1989 ($2.00, limited series, mature)

1-6: Contains graphic violence 2.00

SKRULL KILL KREW
Marvel Comics: Sept, 1995 - No. 5, Dec, 1995 ($2.95, limited series)

1-5: Grant Morrison scripts. 2,3-Cap America app. 3.00

SKUL, THE
Virtual Comics (Byron Preiss Multimedia): Oct, 1996 - No. 3, Dec, 1996 ($2.50, limited series)

1-3: Ron Lim & Jimmy Palmiotti-a 2.50

SKULL & BONES
DC Comics: 1992 - No. 3, 1992 ($4.95, limited series, 52 pgs.)

Book 1-3: 1-1st app. 5.00

SKULL, THE SLAYER
Marvel Comics Group: Aug, 1975 - No. 8, Nov, 1976 (20¢/25¢)

1-Origin & 1st app.; Gil Kane-c 1.25 3.75 10.00
2-8: 2-Gil Kane-c. 5,6-(Regular 25¢-c). 8-Kirby-c 2.40 6.00
5,6-(30¢-c variants, limited distribution)(5,7/76) 1.10 3.30 9.00

SKY BLAZERS (CBS Radio)
Hawley Publications: Sept, 1940 - No. 2, Nov, 1940

1-Sky Pirates, Ace Archer, Flying Aces begin 61.00 182.00 575.00
2-WWII aerial battle-c 40.00 120.00 350.00

SKYMAN (See Big Shot Comics & Sparky Watts)
Columbia Comics Gr.: Fall?, 1941 - No. 2, Fall?, 1942; No. 3, 1948 - No. 4, 1948

1-Origin Skyman, The Face, Sparky Watts app.; Whitney-c/a; 3rd story-r from Big Shot #1; Whitney c-1-4 116.00 348.00 1100.00
2 (1942)-Yankee Doodle 58.00 174.00 550.00
3,4 (1948) 40.00 120.00 325.00

SKYPILOT
Ziff-Davis Publ. Co.: No. 10, 1950(nd) - No. 11, Apr-May, 1951

10,11-Frank Borth-a; Saunders painted-c 14.00 43.00 115.00

SKY RANGER (See Johnny Law...)

SKYROCKET
Harry 'A' Chesler: 1944

nn-Alias the Dragon, Dr. Vampire, Skyrocket & The Desperado app.; WWII Jap zero-c 31.00 94.00 250.00

SKY SHERIFF (Breeze Lawson...) (Also see Exposed & Outlaws)
D. S. Publishing Co.: Summer, 1948

1-Edmond Good-c/a 12.50 37.50 100.00

SKY WOLF (Also see Airboy)
Eclipse Comics: Mar, 1988 - No. 3, Oct, 1988 ($1.25/$1.50/$1.95, lim. series)

1-3 2.00

SLACKER COMICS
Slave Labor Graphics: Aug, 1994 - Present ($2.95, B&W, quarterly)

1-18, 1 (2nd printing)-Reads "2nd print" in indicia 3.00

SLAINE, THE BERSERKER (Slaine the King #21 on)
Quality: July, 1987 - No. 28, 1989 ($1.25/$1.50)

1-28 2.00

SLAINE, THE HORNED GOD
Fleetway: 1998 - No. 3 ($6.99)

1-3-Reprints series from 2000 A.D.; Bisley-a 7.00

SLAM BANG COMICS (Western Desperado #8)
Fawcett Publications: Mar, 1940 - No. 7, Sept, 1940 (Combined with Master Comics #7)

1-Diamond Jack, Mark Swift & The Time Retarder, Lee Granger, Jungle King begin & continue in Master 211.00 633.00 2000.00
2 89.00 268.00 850.00
3-Classic-c 132.00 395.00 1250.00
4-7: 6-Intro Zoro, the Mystery Man (also in #7) 71.00 213.00 675.00

SLAPSTICK
Marvel Comics: Nov, 1992 - No. 4, Feb, 1993 ($1.25, limited series)

1-4: Fry/Austin-c/a. 4-Ghost Rider, D.D., F.F. app. 2.00

SLAPSTICK COMICS
Comic Magazines Distributors: nd (1946?) (36 pgs.)

nn-Firetop feature; Post-a(2) 24.00 71.00 190.00

SLASH-D DOUBLECROSS
St. John Publishing Co.: 1950 (Pocket-size, 132 pgs.)

nn-Western comics 22.00 66.00 175.00

SLASH MARAUD
DC Comics: Nov, 1987 - No. 6, Apr, 1988 ($1.75, limited series)

1-6 2.00

SLAUGHTERMAN
Comico: Feb, 1983 - No. 2, 1983 ($1.50, B&W)

1,2 3.00

SLAVE GIRL COMICS (See Malu... & White Princess of the Jungle #2)
Avon Periodicals/Eternity Comics (1989): Feb, 1949 - No. 2, Apr, 1949 (52 pgs.); Mar, 1989 (B&W, 44 pgs)

1-Larsen-c/a 87.00 261.00 825.00
2-Larsen-a 66.00 197.00 625.00
1-(3/89, $2.25, B&W, 44 pgs.)-r/#1 3.00

SLEDGE HAMMER (TV)
Marvel Comics: Feb, 1988 - No. 2, Mar,1988 ($1.00, limited series)

1,2 3.00

Sleepy Hollow #1 © Paramount/Mandalay

Slugger #1 © LEV

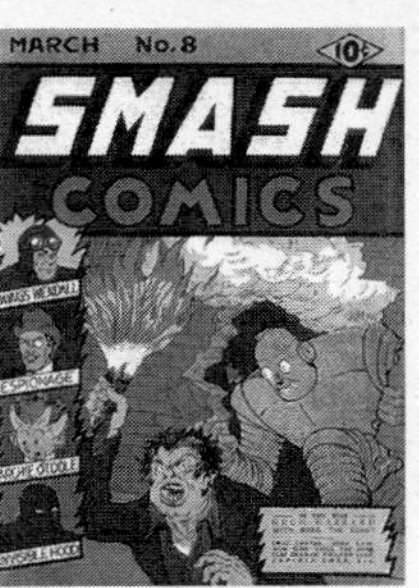

Smash Comics #8 © QUA

SLEEPING BEAUTY (See Dell Giants & Movie Comics)
Dell Publishing Co.: No. 973, May, 1959 - No. 984, June, 1959 (Disney)

Four Color 973 (...and the Prince) 11.30 34.00 135.00
Four Color 984 (...Fairy Godmother's) 8.35 25.00 100.00

SLEEPWALKER
Marvel Comics: June, 1991 - No. 33, Feb, 1994 ($1.00/$1.25)

1-1st app. Sleepwalker 3.00
2-33: 4-Williamson-i. 5-Spider-Man-c/stor. 7-Infinity Gauntlet x-over. 8-Vs. Deathlok-c/story. 11-Ghost Rider-c/story. 12-Quesada-c/a(p) 14-Intro Spectra. 15-F.F.-c/story. 17-Darkhawk & Spider-Man x-over. 18-Infinity War x-over; Quesada/Williamson-c. 21,22-Hobgoblin app. 19-($2.00)-Die-cut Sleepwalker mask-c 2.00
25-($2.95, 52 pgs.)-Holo-grafx foil-c; origin 3.00
Holiday Special 1 (1/93, $2.00, 52 pgs.)-Quesada-c(p) 2.00

SLEEPWALKING
Hall of Heroes: Jan, 1996 ($2.50, B&W)

1-Kelley Jones-c 2.50

SLEEPY HOLLOW (Movie Adaption)
DC Comics (Vertigo): 2000 ($7.95, one-shot)

1-Kelley Jones-a/Seagle-s 8.00

SLEEZE BROTHERS, THE
Marvel Comics (Epic Comics): Aug, 1989 - No. 6, Jan, 1990 ($1.75, mature)

1-6: 4-6 (9/89 - 11/89 indicia dates) 2.00
nn-(1991, $3.95, 52 pgs.) 4.00

SLICK CHICK COMICS
Leader Enterprises: 1947(nd) - No. 3, 1947(nd)

1-Teenage humor 11.00 33.00 90.00
2,3 8.65 26.00 60.00

SLIDERS (TV)
Acclaim Comics (Armada): June, 1996 - No. 2, July, 1996 ($2.50, lim. series)

1,2: D.G. Chichester scripts; Dick Giordano-a. 2.50

SLIDERS: DARKEST HOUR (TV)
Acclaim Comics (Armada): Oct, 1996 - No. 3, Dec, 1996 ($2.50, limited series)

1-3 2.50

SLIDERS SPECIAL
Acclaim Comics (Armada): Nov, 1996 - No 3, Mar, 1997 ($3.95, limited series)

1-3: 1-Narcotica-Jerry O'Connell-s. 2-Blood and Splendor. 3-Deadly Secrets 4.00

SLIDERS: ULTIMATUM (TV)
Acclaim Comics (Armada): Sept, 1996 - No. 2, Sept, 1996 ($2.50, lim. series)

1,2 2.50

SLIMER! (TV cartoon) (Also see the Real Ghostbusters)
Now Comics: 1989 - No. 19, Feb?, 1991 ($1.75)

1-19: Based on animated cartoon 3.00

SLIM MORGAN (See Wisco)

SLINGERS (See Spider-Man: Identity Crisis issues)
Marvel Comics: Dec, 1998 - No. 12, Nov, 1999 ($2.99/$1.99)

0-(Wizard #88 supplement) Prelude story 2.00
1-($2.99) Four editions w/different covers for each hero, 16 pages common to all, the other pages from each hero's perspective 3.00
2-12: 2-Two-c. 12-Saltares-a 2.00

SLUDGE
Malibu Comics (Ultraverse): Oct, 1993 - No. 12, Dec, 1994 ($2.50/$1.95)

1-($2.50, 48 pgs.)-Intro/1st app. Sludge; Rune flip-c/story Pt. 1 (1st app., 3 pgs.) by Barry Smith; The Night Man app. (3 pg. preview); The Mighty Magnor 1 pg strip begins by Aragones (cont. in other titles) 2.50
1-Ultra 5000 Limited silver foil 4.00
2-11: 3-Break-Thru x-over. 4-2 pg. Mantra origin. 8-Bloodstorm app. 2.00
12 ($3.50)-Ultraverse Premiere #8 flip book; Alex Ross poster 3.50
...:Red Xmas (12/94, $2.50, 44 pgs.) 2.50

SLUGGER (Little Wise Guys Starring...)(Also see Daredevil Comics)
Lev Gleason Publications: April, 1956

1-Biro-c 6.00 18.00 42.00

SMASH COMICS (Becomes Lady Luck #86 on)
Quality Comics Group: Aug, 1939 - No. 85, Oct, 1949

1-Origin Hugh Hazard & His Iron Man, Bozo the Robot, Espionage, Starring Black X by Eisner, & Hooded Justice (Invisible Justice #2 on); Chic Carter & Wings Wendall begin; 1st Robot on the cover of a comic book (Bozo) 295.00 885.00 2800.00
2-The Lone Star Rider app; Invisible Hood gains power of invisibility 100.00 300.00 950.00
3-Captain Cook & Eisner's John Law begin 63.00 189.00 600.00
4,5: 4-Flash Fulton begins 58.00 174.00 550.00
6-12: 12-One pg. Fine-a 50.00 150.00 450.00
13-Magno begins (8/40); last Eisner issue; The Ray app. in full page ad; The Purple Trio begins 53.00 158.00 475.00
14-Intro. The Ray (9/40) by Lou Fine & others 284.00 853.00 2700.00
15,16: 16-The Scarlet Seal begins 121.00 363.00 1150.00
17-Wun Cloo becomes plastic super-hero by Jack Cole (9-months before Plastic Man) 126.00 379.00 1200.00
18-Midnight by Jack Cole begins (origin & 1st app., 1/41) 158.00 474.00 1500.00
19-22: Last Ray by Fine; The Jester begins-#22 84.00 253.00 800.00
23,24: 24-The Sword app.; last Chic Carter; Wings Wendall dons new costume #24,25 66.00 197.00 625.00
25-Origin/1st app. Wildfire; Rookie Rankin begins 74.00 221.00 700.00
26-30: 28-Midnight-c begin, end #85 63.00 189.00 600.00
31,32,34: Ray by Rudy Palais; also #33 50.00 150.00 450.00
33-Origin The Marksman 61.00 182.00 575.00
35-37 50.00 150.00 450.00
38-The Yankee Eagle begins; last Midnight by Jack Cole 76.00 229.00 725.00
39,40-Last Ray issue 50.00 150.00 450.00
41,44-50 38.00 113.00 300.00
42-Lady Luck begins by Klaus Nordling 95.00 285.00 900.00
43-Lady Luck-c (1st & only in Smash) 40.00 120.00 350.00
51-60 26.00 79.00 210.00
61-70 22.00 66.00 175.00
71-85: 79-Midnight battles the Men from Mars-c/s 20.00 60.00 160.00

NOTE: ***Al Bryant*** *c-54, 63-68.* ***Cole*** *a-17-38, 68, 69, 72, 73, 78, 80, 83, 85; c-38, 60-62, 69-84.* ***Crandall*** *a-(Ray)-23-29, 35-38; c-36, 39, 40, 42-44, 46.* ***Fine*** *a(Ray)-14, 15, 16(w/**Tuska**), 17-22.* ***Fox*** *c-24-35.* ***Fuje*** *Ray-30.* ***Gil Fox*** *a-6-7, 9, 11-13.* ***Guardineer*** *a-(The Marksman)-39-?, 49, 52.* ***Gustavson*** *a-4-7, 9, 11-13 (The Jester)-22-46; (Magno)-13-21; (Midnight)-39(Cole inks), 49, 52, 63-65.* ***Kotzky*** *a-(Espionage)-33-38; c-45, 47-53.* ***Nordling*** *a-49, 52, 63-65.* ***Powell*** *a-11, 12, (Abdul the Arab)-13-24.Black X c-2, 6, 9, 11, 13, 16. Bozo the Robot c-1, 3, 5, 8, 10, 12, 14, 18, 20, 22, 24, 26. Midnight c-28-85. The Ray c-15, 17, 19, 21, 23, 25, 27. Wings Wendall c-4, 7.*

SMASH COMICS (Also see All Star Comics 1999 crossover titles)
DC Comics: May, 1999 ($1.99, one-shot)

1-Golden Age Doctor Mid-nite and Hourman 2.00

SMASH HIT SPORTS COMICS
Essankay Publications: V2#1, Jan, 1949

V2#1-L.B. Cole-c/a 30.00 90.00 240.00

SMILE COMICS (Also see Gay Comics, Tickle, & Whee)
Modern Store Publ.: 1955 (52 pgs.; 5x7-1/4") (7¢)

1 5.00 15.00 30.00

SMILEY BURNETTE WESTERN (Also see Patches #8 & Six-Gun Heroes)
Fawcett Publ.: March, 1950 - No. 4, Oct, 1950 (All photo front & back-c)

1-Red Eagle begins 44.00 133.00 400.00
2-4 34.00 101.00 270.00

SMILEY (THE PSYCHOTIC BUTTON) (See Evil Ernie)
Chaos! Comics: July, 1998 - Present ($2.95, one-shots)

1-Ivan Reis-a 3.00
... Holiday Special (1/99), ...'s Spring Break (4/99), ...Wrestling Special (5/99) 3.00

SMILIN' JACK (See Famous Feature Stories, Popular Comics, Super Book #1, 2, 7, 19 & Super Comics)

Smilin' Jack #2 © DELL

Sniffy the Pup #5 © STD

Snow White Four Color #382 © WDC

Dell Publishing Co.: No. 5, 1940 - No. 8, Oct-Dec, 1949

	GD2.0	FN6.0	NM9.4
Four Color 5	58.00	175.00	700.00
Four Color 10 (1940)	50.00	150.00	600.00
Large Feature Comic 12,14,25 (1941)	48.00	145.00	580.00
Four Color 4 (1942)	43.00	128.00	510.00
Four Color 14 (1943)	34.00	102.00	410.00
Four Color 36,58 (1943-44)	23.00	70.00	280.00
Four Color 80 (1945)	15.00	45.00	180.00
Four Color 149 (1947), 1 (1-3/48)	10.00	30.00	120.00
1 (1-3/48)	9.00	27.00	110.00
2	5.00	15.00	60.00
3-8 (10-12/49)	3.65	11.00	40.00

SMILING SPOOK SPUNKY (See Spunky)

SMITTY (See Popular Comics, Super Book #2, 4 & Super Comics)
Dell Publishing Co.: No. 11, 1940 - No. 7, Aug-Oct, 1949; No. 909, Apr, 1958

	GD2.0	FN6.0	NM9.4
Four Color 11 (1940)	35.00	105.00	425.00
Large Feature Comic 26 (1941)	25.00	75.00	300.00
Four Color 6 (1942)	22.00	65.00	260.00
Four Color 32 (1943)	16.00	48.00	190.00
Four Color 65 (1945)	12.50	37.50	150.00
Four Color 99 (1946)	10.50	31.00	125.00
Four Color 138 (1947)	9.00	27.00	110.00
1 (2-4/48)	8.35	25.00	100.00
2-(5-7/48)	4.55	13.65	50.00
3,4: 3-(8-10/48), 4-(11-1/48-49)	3.65	11.00	40.00
5-7, Four Color 909 (4/58)	3.00	9.00	30.00

SMOKEY BEAR (TV) (See March Of Comics #234, 362, 372, 383, 407)
Gold Key: Feb, 1970 - No. 13, Mar, 1973

	GD2.0	FN6.0	NM9.4
1	2.80	8.40	28.00
2-5	1.50	4.50	12.00
6-13	1.00	3.00	8.00

SMOKEY STOVER (See Popular Comics, Super Book #5,17,29 & Super Comics)
Dell Publishing Co.: No. 7, 1942 - No. 827, Aug, 1957

	GD2.0	FN6.0	NM9.4
Four Color 7 (1942)-Reprints	32.00	95.00	380.00
Four Color 35 (1943)	17.00	50.00	200.00
Four Color 64 (1944)	12.50	37.50	150.00
Four Color 229 (1949)	4.60	13.75	55.00
Four Color 730,827	3.80	11.40	42.00

SMOKEY THE BEAR (See Forest Fire for 1st app.)
Dell Publ. Co.: No. 653, 10/55 - No. 1214, 8/61 (See March of Comics #234)

	GD2.0	FN6.0	NM9.4
Four Color 653 (#1)	10.00	30.00	120.00
Four Color 708,754,818,932	5.00	15.00	60.00
Four Color 1016,1119,1214	3.20	9.60	35.00

SMOKY (See Movie Classics)

SMURFS (TV)
Marvel Comics: 1982 (Dec) - No. 3, 1983

	GD2.0	FN6.0	NM9.4
1-3	1.00	2.80	7.00
...Treasury Edition 1 (64 pgs.)-r/#1-3	2.80	8.40	28.00

SNAFU (Magazine)
Atlas Comics (RCM): Nov, 1955 - V2#2, Mar, 1956 (B&W)

	GD2.0	FN6.0	NM9.4
V1#1-Heath/Severin-a; Everett, Maneely-a	12.00	36.00	95.00
V2#1,2-Severin-a	10.00	30.00	70.00

SNAGGLEPUSS (TV)(See Hanna-Barbera Band Wagon, Quick Draw McGraw #5 & Spotlight #4)
Gold Key: Oct, 1962 - No. 4, Sept, 1963 (Hanna-Barbera)

	GD2.0	FN6.0	NM9.4
1	8.00	24.00	95.00
2-4	5.85	17.50	70.00

SNAP (Formerly Scoop #8; becomes Jest #10,11 & Komik Pages #10)
Harry 'A' Chesler: No. 9, 1944

	GD2.0	FN6.0	NM9.4
9-Manhunter, The Voice	19.00	56.00	150.00

SNAPPY COMICS
Cima Publ. Co. (Prize Publ.): 1945

	GD2.0	FN6.0	NM9.4
1-Airmale app.; 9 pg. Sorcerer's Apprentice adapt; Kiefer-a	33.00	98.00	260.00

SNARKY PARKER (See Life With...)

SNIFFY THE PUP
Standard Publ. (Animated Cartoons): No. 5, Nov, 1949 - No. 18, Sept, 1953

	GD2.0	FN6.0	NM9.4
5-Two Frazetta text illos	10.00	30.00	80.00
6-10	5.00	15.00	35.00
11-18	4.65	14.00	28.00

SNOOPER AND BLABBER DETECTIVES (TV) (See Whitman Comic Books)
Gold Key: Nov, 1962 - No. 3, May, 1963 (Hanna-Barbera)

	GD2.0	FN6.0	NM9.4
1	8.00	24.00	95.00
2,3	6.30	19.00	75.00

SNOWMAN
Hall of Heroes/Avatar Press: 1996 - Present ($2.50, B&W)

	GD2.0	FN6.0	NM9.4
1	1.25	3.75	10.00
1-Ltd. Ed.	1.85	5.50	15.00
2,3, 3-Chromium-c			4.00
2,3-Ltd. Ed.		2.40	6.00
0-(Avatar Press), 0-Alternate-c			4.00
0-Gold			8.00
0-Silver Foil			10.00
0-Black Leather			15.00
0-Blue Foil-c			30.00

SNOWMAN DEAD AND DYING
Avatar Press: Nov,1997 - No. 3, Apr, 1998 ($3.00, B&W, limited series)

	GD2.0	FN6.0	NM9.4
1-3			3.50
1-($4.95) Ltd. Edition, 3-($4.95) variant-c			5.00
3-($25.00) White velvet variant-c			25.00

SNOWMAN HORROR SHOW
Avatar Press: Mar, 1998 ($3.00, B&W, one-shot)

	GD2.0	FN6.0	NM9.4
1-Pin-ups by Matt Martin			3.00
1-($4.95) Frozen Fear Edition			5.00
1-Leather-c			25.00

SNOWMAN 1944
Entity Comics: Oct, 1996 - No. 4 ($2.75, B&W)

	GD2.0	FN6.0	NM9.4
1			3.00
1-Ltd. Ed.			5.00
2-4			3.00
3-Ltd. Ed.			3.00
...Special 1 (10/97, $3.95)			4.00

SNOWMAN SQUARED
Avatar Press: Sept, 1998 - No. 2 ($3.00, B&W, limited series)

	GD2.0	FN6.0	NM9.4
1-Matt Martin-s/a; Snowman vs. Snowman 1944			3.00
1-Commemorative Edition			5.00

SNOW WHITE (See Christmas With..., Mickey Mouse Mag., Movie Comics & Seven Dwarfs)
Dell Publishing Co.: No. 49, July, 1944 - No. 382, Mar, 1952 (Disney-Movie)

	GD2.0	FN6.0	NM9.4
Four Color 49 (...& the Seven Dwarfs)	60.00	181.00	725.00
Four Color 382 (1952)-origin; partial reprint of Four Color 49	10.00	30.00	120.00

SNOW WHITE
Marvel Comics: Jan, 1995 ($1.95, one-shot)

	GD2.0	FN6.0	NM9.4
1-r/1937 Sunday newspaper pages			2.00

SNOW WHITE AND THE SEVEN DWARFS
Whitman Publications: April, 1982 (60¢)

	GD2.0	FN6.0	NM9.4
nn-r/Four Color 49			5.00

SNOW WHITE AND THE SEVEN DWARFS GOLDEN ANNIVERSARY
Gladstone: Fall, 1987 ($2.95, magazine size, 52 pgs.)

	GD2.0	FN6.0	NM9.4
1-Contains poster	1.00	3.00	8.00

SOAP OPERA LOVE
Charlton Comics: Feb, 1983 - No. 3, June, 1983

Sock Monkey #2 © Tony Millionaire

Solar #23 © Voyager Comm.

Soldier Comics #7 © FAW

1-3 2.50 7.50 25.00

SOAP OPERA ROMANCES
Charlton Comics: July, 1982 - No. 5, March, 1983

1-5-Nurse Betsy Crane-r 2.50 7.50 25.00

SOCK MONKEY
Dark Horse Comics: Sept, 1998 - No. 2, Oct, 1998 ($2.95, B&W)

1,2-Tony Millionaire-s/a 3.00
Vol.2 -(Tony Millionaire's Sock Monkey) July, 1999 - Present
1,2 3.00

SO DARK THE ROSE
CFD Productions: Oct, 1995 ($2.95)

1-Wrightson-c 4.00

SOJOURN
White Cliffs Publ. Co.: Sept, 1977 - No. 2, 1978 ($1.50, B&W & color, full tabloid size)

1,2: 1-Tor by Kubert, Eagle by Severin, E. V. Race, Private Investigator by Doug Wildey, T. C. Mars by Aragones begin plus other strips 1.25 3.75 10.00
NOTE: Most copies came folded. Unfolded copies are worth 50% more.

SOLAR (...Man of the Atom) (Also see Doctor Solar)
Valiant/Acclaim Comics (Valiant): Sept, 1991 - No. 60, Apr, 1996 ($1.75/$1.95/$2.50, 44 pgs.)

1-Layton-a(i) on Solar; Barry Windsor-Smith-c/a 2.40 6.00
2-9: 2-Layton-a(i) on Solar, B. Smith-a. 3-1st app. Harada (11/91). 7-vs. X-O Armor 4.00
10-(6/92, $3.95)-1st app. Eternal Warrior (6 pgs.); black embossed-c; origin & 1st app. Geoff McHenry (Geomancer) 1.00 3.00 8.00
10-($3.95)-2nd printing 4.00
11-15: 11-1st full app. Eternal Warrior. 12,13-Unity x-overs. 14-1st app. Fred Bender (becomes Dr. Eclipse). 15-2nd Dr. Eclipse 3.00
16-60: 17-X-O Manowar app. 23-Solar splits. 29-1st Valiant Vision book. 33-Valiant Vision; bound-in trading card. 38-Chaos Effect Epsilion Pt.1. 46-52-Dan Jurgens-a(p)/scripts w/Giordano-i. 53,54-Jurgens scripts only. 60-Giffen scripts; Jeff Johnson-a(p) 2.50
0-($9.95, trade paperback)-r/Alpha and Omega origin story; polybagged w/poster 10.00
...:Second Death (1994, $9.95)-r/issues #1-4. 10.00
NOTE: *#1-10 all have free 8 pg. insert "Alpha and Omega" which is a 10 chapter Solar origin story. All 10 centerfolds can pieced together to show climax of story.* ***Ditko*** *a-11p, 14p.* ***Giordano*** *a-46, 47, 48, 49, 50, 51, 52i.* ***Johnson*** *a-60p.* ***Jurgens*** *a-46, 47, 48, 49, 50 , 51, 52p.* ***Layton*** *a-1-3i; c-2i, 11i, 17i, 25i.* ***Miller*** *c-12.* ***Quesada*** *c-17p, 20-23p, 29p.* ***Simonson*** *c-13.* ***B. Smith*** *a-1-10; c-1, 3, 5, 7, 19i.* ***Thibert*** *c-22i, 23i.*

SOLAR LORD
Image Comics: Mar, 1999 - No. 7, Sept, 1999 ($2.50)

1-7-Khoo Fuk Lung-s/a 2.50

SOLARMAN (See Pendulum Ill. Originals)
Marvel Comics: Jan, 1989 - No. 2, May, 1990 ($1.00, limited series)

1,2 2.00

SOLAR, MAN OF THE ATOM (Man of the Atom on cover)
Acclaim Comics (Valiant Heroes): Vol. 2, May, 1997 ($3.95, one-shot, 46 pgs) (1st Valiant Heroes Special Event)

Vol. 2-Reintro Solar; Ninjak cameo; Warren Ellis scripts; Darick Robertson-a 4.00

SOLAR, MAN OF THE ATOM: HELL ON EARTH
Acclaim Comics (Valiant Heroes): Jan, 1998 - No. 4 ($2.50, limited series)

1-4-Priest-s/ Zircher-a(p) 2.50

SOLAR, MAN OF THE ATOM: REVELATIONS
Acclaim Comics (Valiant Heroes): Nov, 1997 ($3.95, one-shot, 46 pgs.)

1-Krueger-s/ Zircher-a(p) 4.00

SOLDIER & MARINE COMICS (Fightin' Army #16 on)
Charlton Comics (Toby Press of Conn. V1#11): No. 11, Dec, 1954 - No. 15, Aug, 1955; V2#9, Dec, 1956

V1#11 (12/54)-Bob Powell-a 7.85 23.50 55.00
V1#12(2/55)-15: 12-Photo-c 5.00 15.00 32.00
V2#9(Formerly Never Again; Jerry Drummer V2#10 on) 4.65 14.00 28.00

SOLDIER COMICS
Fawcett Publications: Jan, 1952 - No. 11, Sept, 1953

1 11.00 33.00 90.00
2 6.40 19.25 45.00
3-5 5.70 17.00 40.00
6-11: 8-Illo. in **POP** 5.00 15.00 35.00

SOLDIERS OF FORTUNE
American Comics Group (Creston Publ. Corp.): Mar-Apr, 1951 - No. 13, Feb-Mar, 1953

1-Capt. Crossbones by Shelly, Ace Carter, Lance Larson begin 23.00 68.00 180.00
2 12.50 37.50 100.00
3-10: 6-Bondage-c 11.00 33.00 90.00
11-13 (War format) 6.40 19.25 45.00
NOTE: ***Shelly*** *a-1-3, 5.* ***Whitney*** *a-6, 8-11, 13; c-1-3, 5, 6.*

SOLDIERS OF FREEDOM
Americomics: 1987 - No. 2, 1987 ($1.75)

1,2 3.00

SOLITAIRE (Also See Prime V2#6-8)
Malibu Comics (Ultraverse): Nov, 1993 - No. 12, Dec, 1994 ($1.95)

1-($2.50)-Collector's edition bagged w/playing card 2.50
1-12: 1-Regular edition w/o playing card. 2,4-Break-Thru x-over. 3-2 pg. origin The Night Man. 4-Gatefold-c. 5-Two pg. origin the Strangers 2.00

SOLO
Marvel Comics: Sept, 1994 - No. 4, Dec, 1994 ($1.75, limited series)

1-4: Spider-Man app. 2.00

SOLO (Movie)
Dark Horse Comics: July, 1996 - No. 2, Aug, 1996 ($2.50, limited series)

1,2: Adaptation of film; photo-c 2.50

SOLO AVENGERS (Becomes Avenger Spotlight #21 on)
Marvel Comics: Dec, 1987 - No. 20, July, 1989 (75¢/$1.00)

1-Jim Lee-a on back-up story 3.00
2-20: 11-Intro Bobcat 2.00

SOLOMON AND SHEBA (Movie)
Dell Publishing Co.: No. 1070, Jan-Mar, 1960

Four Color 1070-Sekowsky-a; photo-c 9.00 27.00 110.00

SOLOMON KANE (Based on the Robert E. Howard character. Also see Blackthorne 3-D Series #60 & Marvel Premiere)
Marvel Comics: Sept, 1985 - No. 6, July, 1986 (Limited series)

1-6: 1-Double size. 3-6-Williamson-a(i) 3.00

SOLUTION, THE
Malibu Comics (Ultraverse): Sept, 1993 - No. 17, Feb, 1995 ($1.95)

1,3-15: 1-Intro Meathook, Deathdance, Black Tiger, Tech. 4-Break-Thru x-over; gatefold-c. 5-2 pg. origin The Strangers. 11-Brereton-c 2.00
1-($2.50)-Newsstand ed. polybagged w/trading card 2.50
1-Ultra 5000 Limited silver foil 4.00
0-Obtained w/Rune #0 by sending coupons from 11 comics 3.00
2-($2.50, 48 pgs.)-Rune flip-c/story by B. Smith; The Mighty Magnor 1 pg. strip by Aragones 2.50
16 ($3.50)-Flip-c Ultraverse Premiere #10 3.50
17 ($2.50) 2.50

SOMERSET HOLMES (See Eclipse Graphic Novel Series)
Pacific Comics/ Eclipse Comics No. 5, 6: Sept, 1983 - No. 6, Dec, 1984 ($1.50, Baxter paper)

1-6: 1-Brent Anderson-c/a. Cliff Hanger by Williams in all 3.00

SONG OF THE SOUTH (See Brer Rabbit)

SONIC & KNUCKLES
Archie Comics: Aug, 1995 ($2.00)

Sonic the Hedgehog #4 © SEGA

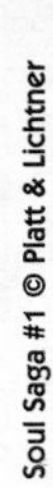
Soul Saga #1 © Platt & Lichtner

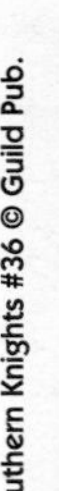
Southern Knights #36 © Guild Pub.

	GD2.0	FN6.0	NM9.4
1			5.00

SONIC DISRUPTORS
DC Comics: Dec, 1987 - No. 7, July, 1988 ($1.75, unfinished limited series)

	GD2.0	FN6.0	NM9.4
1-7			3.00

SONIC'S FRIENDLY NEMESIS KNUCKLES
Archie Publications: July, 1996 - No. 3, Sept, 1996 ($1.50, limited series)

	GD2.0	FN6.0	NM9.4
1-3			4.00

SONIC SUPER SPECIAL
Archie Publications: 1997 - Present ($2.00/$2.25/$2.29, 48 pgs)

	GD2.0	FN6.0	NM9.4
1-3			4.00
4-6,8-15: 10-Sabrina-c/app. 15-Sin City spoof			3.00
7-(w/Image) Spawn, Maxx, Savage Dragon-c/app.; Valentino-a			3.00

SONIC THE HEDGEHOG (TV, video game)
Archie Comics: Feb, 1993 - No. 3, May, 1993 ($1.25, mini-series)

	GD2.0	FN6.0	NM9.4
0(2/93),1: Shaw-a(p) & covers on all	2.30	7.00	20.00
2,3	1.50	4.50	12.00

SONIC THE HEDGEHOG (TV, video game)
Archie Comics: July, 1993 - Present ($1.25/$1.50/$1.75/$1.79/$1.99)

	GD2.0	FN6.0	NM9.4
1	2.50	7.50	25.00
2,3	1.85	5.50	15.00
4-10: 8-Neon ink-c.	1.50	4.50	12.00
11-20	1.25	3.75	10.00
21-30 ($1.50): 25-Silver ink-c	1.00	3.00	8.00
31-50		2.40	6.00
51-92			3.00
Triple Trouble Special (10/95, $2.00, 48 pgs.)			4.00

SONIC VS. KNUCKLES "BATTLE ROYAL" SPECIAL
Archie Publications: 1997 ($2.00, one-shot)

	GD2.0	FN6.0	NM9.4
1			4.00

SON OF AMBUSH BUG (See Ambush Bug)
DC Comics: July, 1986 - No. 6, Dec, 1986 (75¢)

	GD2.0	FN6.0	NM9.4
1-6: Giffen-c/a in all. 5-Bissette-a.			2.00

SON OF BLACK BEAUTY (Also see Black Beauty)
Dell Publishing Co.: No. 510, Oct, 1953 - No. 566, June, 1954

	GD2.0	FN6.0	NM9.4
Four Color 510, 566	3.20	9.60	35.00

SON OF FLUBBER (See Movie Comics)

SON OF MUTANT WORLD
Fantagor Press: 1990 - No. 5, 1990? ($2.00, bi-monthly)

	GD2.0	FN6.0	NM9.4
1-5: 1-3: Corben-c/a. 4,5 ($1.75, B&W)			3.00

SON OF ORIGINS OF MARVEL COMICS (See Fireside Book Series)

SON OF SATAN (Also see Ghost Rider #1 & Marvel Spotlight #12)
Marvel Comics Group: Dec, 1975 - No. 8, Feb, 1977 (25¢)

	GD2.0	FN6.0	NM9.4
1-Mooney-a; Kane-c(p), Starlin splash(p)	2.30	7.00	20.00
2,6-8: 2-Origin The Possessor. 8-Heath-a	1.50	4.50	12.00
3-5-(Regular 25¢ editions)(4-8/76): 5-Russell-p	1.50	4.50	12.00
3-5-(30¢-c variants, limited distribution)	2.00	6.00	18.00

SON OF SINBAD (Also see Abbott & Costello & Daring Adventures)
St. John Publishing Co.: Feb, 1950

	GD2.0	FN6.0	NM9.4
1-Kubert-c/a	40.00	120.00	350.00

SON OF SUPERMAN (Elseworlds)
DC Comics: 1999 ($14.95, prestige format, one-shot)

	GD2.0	FN6.0	NM9.4
nn-Chaykin & Tischman-s/Williams III & Gray-a			15.00

SON OF TOMAHAWK (See Tomahawk)

SON OF VULCAN (Formerly Mysteries of Unexplored Worlds #1-48; Thunderbolt V3#51 on)
Charlton Comics: V2#49, Nov, 1965 - V2#50, Jan, 1966

	GD2.0	FN6.0	NM9.4
V2#49,50: 50-Roy Thomas scripts (1st pro work)	2.50	7.50	25.00

SON OF YUPPIES FROM HELL (See Yuppies From Hell)
Marvel Comics: 1990 ($3.50, B&W, squarebound, 52 pgs.)

	GD2.0	FN6.0	NM9.4
nn			3.50

SONS OF KATIE ELDER (See Movie Classics)

SORCERY (See Chilling Adventures in... & Red Circle...)

SORORITY SECRETS
Toby Press: July, 1954

	GD2.0	FN6.0	NM9.4
1	8.65	26.00	60.00

SOULQUEST
Innovation: Apr, 1989 ($3.95, squarebound, 52 pgs.)

	GD2.0	FN6.0	NM9.4
1-Blackshard app.			4.00

SOUL SAGA
Image Comics (Top Cow): Feb, 2000 - Present ($2.50)

	GD2.0	FN6.0	NM9.4
1-4: 1-Madureira-c; Platt & Batt-a			2.50

SOULSEARCHERS AND COMPANY
Claypool Comics: June, 1995 - Present ($2.50, B&W)

	GD2.0	FN6.0	NM9.4
1-10: Peter David scripts			2.50
11-47			2.50

SOULWIND
Image Comics: Mar, 1997 - No. 8 ($2.95, B&W, limited series)

	GD2.0	FN6.0	NM9.4
1-8: 5-"The Day I Tried To Live" pt. 1			3.00
...The Kid From Planet Earth (1997, $9.95, TPB)			10.00
...The Kid From Planet Earth (Oni Press, 1/00, $8.50, TPB)			8.50
...The Day I Tried to Live (Oni Press, 4/00, $8.50, TPB)			8.50

SOUPY SALES COMIC BOOK (TV)(The Official...)
Archie Publications: 1965

	GD2.0	FN6.0	NM9.4
1	8.65	26.00	95.00

SOUTHERN KNIGHTS, THE (See Crusaders #1)
Guild Publ/Fictioneer Books: No. 2, 1983 - No. 41, 1993 (B&W)

	GD2.0	FN6.0	NM9.4
2-Magazine size		2.40	6.00
3-35, 37-41			3.00
36-($3.50-c)			3.50
Dread Halloween Special 1, Primer Special 1 (Spring, 1989, $2.25)			2.25
Graphic Novels #1-4			4.00

SOVEREIGN SEVEN (Also see Showcase '95 #12)
DC Comics: July, 1995 - No. 36, July, 1998 ($1.95) (1st creator-owned mainstream DC comic)

	GD2.0	FN6.0	NM9.4
1-1st app. Sovereign Seven (Reflex, Indigo, Cascade, Finale, Cruiser, Network & Rampart); 1st app. Maitresse; Darkseid app.; Chris Claremont scripts & Dwayne Turner-c/a begins.			3.00
1-Gold			8.00
1-Platinum			40.00
2-25: 2-Wolverine cameo. 4-Neil Gaiman cameo. 5,8-Batman app. 7-Ramirez cameo (from the movie Highlander). 9-Humphrey Bogart cameo from Casablanca. 10-Impulse app; Manoli Wetherell & Neal Conan cameo from Uncanny X-Men #226. 11-Robin app. 16-Final Night. 24-Superman app. 25-Power Girl app.			2.25
26-36: 26-Begin $2.25-c. 28-Impulse-c/app.			2.25
Annual 1 (1995, $3.95)-Year One story; Big Barda & Lobo app.; Jeff Johnson-c/a.			4.00
Annual 2 (1996, $2.95)-Legends of the Dead Earth; Leonardi-c/a			3.50
...Plus 1(2/97, $2.95)-Legion-c/app.			3.50
TPB-($12.95) r/#1-5, Annual #1 & Showcase '95 #12			13.00

SOVIET SUPER SOLDIERS
Marvel Comics: Nov, 1992 ($2.00, one-shot)

	GD2.0	FN6.0	NM9.4
1-Marvel's Russian characters; Median & Saltares-a			2.00

SPACE: ABOVE AND BEYOND (TV)
Topps Comics: Jan, 1996 - No. 3, Mar, 1996 ($2.95, limited series)

	GD2.0	FN6.0	NM9.4
1-3: Adaptation of pilot episode; Steacy-c.			3.00

SPACE: ABOVE AND BEYOND--THE GAUNTLET (TV)
Topps Comics: May, 1996 -No. 2, June, 1996 ($2.95, limited series)

	GD2.0	FN6.0	NM9.4
1,2			3.00

SPACE ACE (Also see Manhunt!)

Space Action #1 © ACE

Space Detective #4 © AVON

Spaceknights #2 © MAR

GD2.0 FN6.0 NM9.4

Magazine Enterprises: No. 5, 1952

5(A-1 #61)-Guardineer-a 50.00 150.00 450.00

SPACE ACTION
Ace Magazines (Junior Books): June, 1952 - No. 3, Oct, 1952

1-Cameron-a in all (1 story) 71.00 213.00 675.00
2,3 53.00 158.00 475.00

SPACE ADVENTURES (War At Sea #22 on)
Capitol Stories/Charlton Comics: 7/52 - No. 21, 8/56; No. 23, 5/58 - No. 59, 11/64; V3#60, 10/67; V1#2, 7/68 - V1#8, 7/69; No. 9, 5/78 - No. 13, 3/79

1 47.00 142.00 425.00
2 26.00 79.00 210.00
3-5: 4,6-Flying saucer-c/stories 21.00 62.00 165.00
6-9: 7-Sex change story "Transformation". 8-Robot-c. 9-A-Bomb panel 19.00 56.00 150.00
10,11-Ditko-c/a. 10-Robot-c. 11-Two Ditko stories 47.00 142.00 425.00
12-Ditko-c (classic) 55.00 165.00 525.00
13-(Fox-r, 10-11/54); Blue Beetle-c/story 15.00 45.00 120.00
14,15,17,18: 14-Blue Beetle-c/story; Fox-r (12-1/54-55, last pre-code). 15,17,18-Rocky Jones-c/s.(TV); 15-Part photo-c 20.00 60.00 160.00
16-Krigstein-a; Rocky Jones-c/story (TV) 22.00 66.00 175.00
19 13.00 39.00 105.00
20-Reprints Fawcett's "Destination Moon" 26.00 79.00 210.00
21-(8/56) (no #22)(Becomes War At Sea) 13.00 39.00 105.00
23-(5/58; formerly Nyoka, The Jungle Girl)-Reprints Fawcett's "Destination Moon" 23.00 68.00 180.00
24,25,31,32-Ditko-a. 24-Severin-a(signed "LePoer") 20.00 60.00 160.00
26,27-Ditko-a(4) each. 26,28-Flying saucer-c 21.00 64.00 170.00
28-30 9.30 28.00 65.00
33-Origin/1st app. Capt. Atom by Ditko (3/60) 37.00 112.00 450.00
34-40,42-All Captain Atom by Ditko 16.00 48.00 175.00
41,43,45-59: 45-Mercury Man app. 3.65 11.00 40.00
44-1st app. Mercury Man 4.10 12.30 45.00
V3#60(#1, 10/67)-Origin & 1st app. Paul Mann & The Saucers From the Future 4.10 12.30 45.00
2,5,6,8 (1968-69)-Ditko-a: 2-Aparo-c/a 2.50 7.50 25.00
3,4,7: 4-Aparo-c/a 2.30 7.00 20.00
9-13(1978-79)-Capt. Atom-r/Space Adventures by Ditko; 9-Reprints origin/1st app. Capt. Atom from #33 5.00

NOTE: ***Aparo** a-V3#60. c-V3#8. **Ditko** c-12, 31-42. **Giordano** c-3, 4, 7-9, 18p. **Krigstein** c-15. **Shuster** a-11. Issues 13 & 14 have Blue Beetle logos; #15-18 have Rocky Jones logos.*

SPACE ARK
Americomics (AC Comics)/ Apple Comics #3 on: June, 1985 - No. 5, Sept, 1987 ($1.75)

1-5: Funny animal (#1,2-color; #3-5-B&W) 2.00

SPACE BUSTERS
Ziff-Davis Publ. Co.: Spring, 1952 - No. 2, Fall, 1952

1-Krigstein-a(3); Painted-c by Norman Saunders 79.00 237.00 750.00
2-Kinstler-a(2 pgs.); Saunders painted-c 62.00 185.00 585.00

NOTE: ***Anderson** a-2. Bondage c-2.*

SPACE CADET (See Tom Corbett,...)

SPACE CIRCUS
Dark Horse Comics: July, 2000 - No. 4, Oct, 2000 ($2.95, limited series)

1-4-Aragonés-a/Evanier-s 2.95

SPACE COMICS (Formerly Funny Tunes)
Avon Periodicals: No. 4, Mar-Apr, 1954 - No. 5, May-June, 1954

4,5-Space Mouse, Peter Rabbit, Super Pup (formerly Spotty the Pup), & Merry Mouse continue from Funny Tunes 6.40 19.25 45.00
I.W. Reprint #8 (nd)-Space Mouse-r 1.25 3.75 10.00

SPACED
Anthony Smith Publ. #1,2/Unbridled Ambition/Eclipse Comics #10 on: 1982 - No. 13, 1988 ($1.25/$1.50, B&W, quarterly)

1-($1.25-c) 3.00
2-13, Special Edition (1983, Mimeo) 2.00

SPACE DETECTIVE
Avon Periodicals: July, 1951 - No. 4, July, 1952

1-Rod Hathway, Space Detective begins, ends #4; Wood-c/a(3)-23 pgs.; "Opium Smugglers of Venus" drug story; Lucky Dale-r/Saint #4 103.00 308.00 975.00
2-Tales from the Shadow Squad story; Wood/Orlando-c; Wood inside layouts; "Slave Ship of Saturn" story 74.00 221.00 700.00
3,4: 3-Kinstler-c. 4-Kinstlerish-a by McCann 40.00 120.00 350.00
I.W. Reprint #1(Reprints #2), 8(Reprints cover #1 & part Famous Funnies #191) 3.65 11.00 40.00
I.W. Reprint #9-Exist? 3.65 11.00 40.00

SPACE EXPLORER (See March of Comics #202)

SPACE FAMILY ROBINSON (TV)(...Lost in Space #15-37, ...Lost in Space On Space Station One #38 on)(See Gold Key Champion)
Gold Key: Dec, 1962 - No. 36, Oct, 1969; No. 37, 10/73 - No. 54, 11/78; No. 55, 3/81 - No. 59, 5/82 (All painted covers)

1-(Low distribution); Spiegle-a in all 23.00 70.00 280.00
2(3/63)-Family becomes lost in space 11.30 34.00 135.00
3-5 6.70 20.00 80.00
6-10: 6-Captain Venture back-up stories begin 5.85 17.50 70.00
11-20: 14-(10/65). 15-Title change (1/66) 4.10 12.30 45.00
21-36: 28-Last 12¢ issue. 36-Captain Venture ends 3.00 9.00 30.00
37-48: 37-Origin retold 1.25 3.75 10.00
49-59: Reprints #49,50,55-59 2.40 6.00

NOTE: *The TV show first aired on 9/15/65. Title changed after TV show debuted.*

SPACE FAMILY ROBINSON (See March of Comics #320, 328, 352, 404, 414)

SPACE GHOST (TV) (Also see Golden Comics Digest #2 & Hanna-Barbera Super TV Heroes #3-7)
Gold Key: March, 1967 (Hanna-Barbera) (TV debut was 9/10/66)

1 (10199-703)-Spiegle-a 33.00 100.00 400.00

SPACE GHOST (TV cartoon)
Comico: Mar, 1987 ($3.50, deluxe format, one-shot) (Hanna-Barbera)

1-Steve Rude-c/a 1.00 3.00 8.00

SPACE GIANTS, THE (TV cartoon)
FBN Publications: 1979 ($1.00, B&W, one-shots)

1-Based on Japanese TV series 1.25 3.75 10.00

SPACEHAWK
Dark Horse Comics: 1989 - No. 3, 1990 ($2.00, B&W)

1-3-Wolverton-c/a(r) plus new stories by others. 4.00

SPACE JAM
DC Comics: 1996 ($5.95, one-shot, movie adaption)

1-Wraparound photo cover of Michael Jordan 1.00 3.00 8.00

SPACE KAT-ETS (...in 3-D)
Power Publishing Co.: Dec, 1953 (25¢, came w/glasses)

1 33.00 98.00 260.00

SPACEKNIGHTS
Marvel Comics: Oct, 2000 - No. 5, Feb, 2001 ($2.99, limited series)

1-5-Starlin-s/Batista-a 3.00

SPACEMAN (Speed Carter...)
Atlas Comics (CnPC): Sept, 1953 - No. 6, July, 1954

1-Grey tone-c 65.00 195.00 615.00
2 42.00 126.00 375.00
3-6: 4-A-Bomb explosion-c 40.00 120.00 325.00

NOTE: ***Everett** c-1, 3. **Heath** a-1. **Maneely** a-1(3), 2(4), 3(3), 4-6; c-5, 6. **Romita** a-1. **Sekowsky** c-4. **Sekowsky/Abel** a-4(3). **Tuska** a-5(3).*

SPACE MAN
Dell Publ. Co.: No. 1253, 1-3/62 - No. 8, 3-5/64; No. 9, 7/72 - No. 10, 10/72

Four Color 1253 (#1)(1-3/62)(15¢-c) 6.70 20.00 80.00
2,3: 2-(15¢-c). 3-(12¢-c) 3.65 11.00 40.00
4-8-(12¢-c) 3.00 9.00 30.00
9,10-(15¢-c): 9-Reprints #1253. 10-Reprints #2 1.25 3.75 10.00

SPACE MOUSE (Also see Funny Tunes & Space Comics)
Avon Periodicals: April, 1953 - No. 5, Apr-May, 1954

Space Mouse #2 © AVON

Space Usagi V2 #1 © Stan Sakai

Sparkler Comics #37 © UFS

	GD2.0	FN6.0	NM9.4
1	10.00	30.00	70.00
2	6.00	18.00	42.00
3-5	5.00	15.00	30.00

SPACE MOUSE (Walter Lantz...#1; see Comic Album #17)
Dell Publishing Co./Gold Key: No. 1132, Aug-Oct, 1960 - No. 5, Nov, 1963 (Walter Lantz)

	GD2.0	FN6.0	NM9.4
Four Color 1132,1244, 1(11/62)(G.K.)	4.10	12.30	45.00
2-5	3.20	9.60	35.00

SPACE MYSTERIES
I.W. Enterprises: 1964 (Reprints)

	GD2.0	FN6.0	NM9.4
1-r/Journey Into Unknown Worlds #4 w/new-c	2.50	7.50	25.00
8,9: 9-r/Planet Comics #73	2.50	7.50	25.00

SPACE: 1999 (TV) (Also see Power Record Comics)
Charlton Comics: Nov, 1975 - No. 7, Nov, 1976

	GD2.0	FN6.0	NM9.4
1-Origin Moonbase Alpha; Staton-c/a	1.50	4.50	12.00
2,7: 2-Staton-a	1.00	3.00	8.00
3-6: All Byrne-a; c-3,5,6	1.50	4.50	12.00

SPACE: 1999 (TV)(Magazine)
Charlton Comics: Nov, 1975 - No. 8, Nov, 1976 (B&W) (#7 shows #6 inside)

	GD2.0	FN6.0	NM9.4
1-Origin Moonbase Alpha; Morrow-c/a	2.00	6.00	16.00
2-8: 2,3-Morrow-c/a. 4-6-Morrow-c. 5,8-Morrow-a	1.50	4.50	12.00

SPACE PATROL (TV)
Ziff-Davis Publishing Co. (Approved Comics): Summer, 1952 - No. 2, Oct-Nov, 1952 (Painted-c by Norman Saunders)

	GD2.0	FN6.0	NM9.4
1-Krigstein-a	87.00	261.00	825.00
2-Krigstein-a(3)	62.00	186.00	590.00

SPACE PIRATES (See Archie Giant Series #533)

SPACE RANGER (See Mystery in Space #92, Showcase #15 & Tales of the Unexpected)

SPACE SQUADRON (In the Days of the Rockets)(Becomes Space Worlds #6)
Marvel/Atlas Comics (ACI): June, 1951 - No. 5, Feb, 1952

	GD2.0	FN6.0	NM9.4
1-Space team; Brodsky c-1,5	65.00	194.00	615.00
2: Tuska c-2-4	55.00	165.00	525.00
3-5: 3-Capt. Jet Dixon by Tuska(3). 4-Weird advs. begin	45.00	135.00	405.00

SPACE THRILLERS
Avon Periodicals: 1954 (25¢ Giant)

	GD2.0	FN6.0	NM9.4
nn-(Scarce)-Robotmen of the Lost Planet; contains 3 rebound comics of The Saint & Strange Worlds. Contents could vary	111.00	332.00	1050.00

SPACE TRIP TO THE MOON (See Space Adventures #23)

SPACE USAGI
Mirage Studios: June, 1992 - No. 3, 1992 ($2.00, B&W, mini-series)
V2#1, Nov, 1993 - V2#3, Jan, 1994 ($2.75)

	GD2.0	FN6.0	NM9.4
1-3: Stan Sakai-c/a/scripts, V2#1-3			2.75

SPACE USAGI
Dark Horse Comics: Jan, 1996 - No. 3, Mar, 1996 ($2.95, B&W, limited series)

	GD2.0	FN6.0	NM9.4
1-3: Stan Sakai-c/a/scripts			2.00

SPACE WAR (Fightin' Five #28 on)
Charlton Comics: Oct, 1959 - No. 27, Mar, 1964; No. 28, Mar, 1978 - No. 34, 3/79

	GD2.0	FN6.0	NM9.4
V1#1-Giordano-c begin, end #3	13.50	40.00	150.00
2,3	6.80	20.50	75.00
4-6,8,10-Ditko-c/a	13.50	40.00	150.00
7,9,11-15: Last 10¢ issue?	4.10	12.30	45.00
16-27 (3/64): 18,19-Robot-c	3.65	11.00	40.00
28(3/78),29-31,33,34-Ditko-c/a(r): 30-Staton, Sutton/Wood-a. 31-Ditko-c/a(3); same-c as Strange Suspense Stories #2 (1968); atom blast-c	1.00	3.00	8.00
32-r/Charlton Premiere V2#2; Sutton-a			4.00

SPACE WESTERN (Formerly Cowboy Western Comics; becomes Cowboy Western Comics #46 on)
Charlton Comics (Capitol Stories): No. 40, Oct, 1952 - No. 45, Aug, 1953

	GD2.0	FN6.0	NM9.4
40-Intro Spurs Jackson & His Space Vigilantes; flying saucer story	57.00	171.00	540.00
41,43-45: 41-Flying saucer-c. 45-Hitler app.	42.00	126.00	375.00
42-Atom bomb explosion-c	45.00	135.00	405.00

SPACE WORLDS (Formerly Space Squadron #1-5)
Atlas Comics (Male): No. 6, April, 1952

	GD2.0	FN6.0	NM9.4
6-Sol Brodsky-c	42.00	126.00	375.00

SPANKY & ALFALFA & THE LITTLE RASCALS (See The Little Rascals)

SPANNER'S GALAXY
DC Comics: Dec, 1984 - No. 6, May, 1985 (limited series)

	GD2.0	FN6.0	NM9.4
1-6: Mandrake-c/a in all.			2.00

SPARKIE, RADIO PIXIE (Radio)(Becomes Big Jon & Sparkie #4)
Ziff-Davis Publ. Co.: Winter, 1951 - No. 3, July-Aug, 1952 (Painted-c)(Sparkie #2,3; #1?)

	GD2.0	FN6.0	NM9.4
1-Based on children's radio program	23.00	68.00	180.00
2,3: 3-Big Jon and Sparkie on-c only	16.00	49.00	130.00

SPARKLE COMICS
United Features Synd.: Oct-Nov, 1948 - No. 33, Dec-Jan, 1953-54

	GD2.0	FN6.0	NM9.4
1-Li'l Abner, Nancy, Captain & the Kids, Ella Cinders (#1-3: 52 pgs.)	14.00	41.00	110.00
2	7.85	23.50	55.00
3-10	6.00	18.00	42.00
11-20	5.00	15.00	35.00
21-33	4.65	14.00	28.00

SPARKLE PLENTY (See Harvey Comics Library #2 & Dick Tracy)

SPARKLER COMICS (1st series)
United Feature Comic Group: July, 1940 - No. 2, 1940

	GD2.0	FN6.0	NM9.4
1-Jim Hardy	40.00	120.00	325.00
2-Frankie Doodle	30.00	90.00	240.00

SPARKLER COMICS (2nd series)(Nancy & Sluggo #121 on)(Cover title becomes Nancy and Sluggo #101? on)
United Features Syndicate: July, 1941 - No. 120, Jan, 1955

	GD2.0	FN6.0	NM9.4
1-Origin 1st app. Sparkman; Tarzan (by Hogarth in all issues), Captain & the Kids, Ella Cinders, Danny Dingle, Dynamite Dunn, Nancy, Abbie & Slats, Broncho Bill, Frankie Doodle, begin; Spark Man c-1-9,11,12; Hap Hopper c-10,13	232.00	695.00	2200.00
2	79.00	237.00	750.00
3,4	63.00	189.00	600.00
5-9: 9-Spark Man's new costume	57.00	171.00	540.00
10-Origin Spark Man?	57.00	171.00	540.00
11,12-Spark Man war-c. 12-Spark Man's new costume (color change)	47.00	142.00	425.00
13-Hap Hopper war-c	42.00	125.00	375.00
14-Tarzan-c by Hogarth	53.00	158.00	475.00
15,17: 15-Capt & Kids-c. 17-Nancy & Sluggo-c	40.00	120.00	350.00
16,18-Spark Man war-c	43.00	128.00	385.00
19-1st Race Riley and the Commandos-c/s	42.00	125.00	375.00
20-Nancy war-c	40.00	120.00	360.00
21,25,28,31,34,37,39-Tarzan-c by Hogarth	44.00	133.00	400.00
22-24,26,27,29,30: 22-Race Riley & the Commandos strips begin, ends #44	34.00	101.00	270.00
32,33,35,36,38,40	20.00	60.00	160.00
41,43,45,46,48,49	14.00	41.00	110.00
42,44,47,50-Tarzan-c (42,47,50 by Hogarth)	28.00	84.00	225.00
51,52,54-70: 57-Li'l Abner begins (not in #58); Fearless Fosdick app. in #58	12.50	37.50	100.00
53-Tarzan-c by Hogarth	24.00	71.00	190.00
71-80	9.30	28.00	65.00
81,82,84-86: 86 Last Tarzan; lingerie panels	7.85	23.50	55.00
83-Tarzan-c; Li'l Abner ends	11.00	33.00	90.00
87-96,98-99	7.15	21.50	50.00
97-Origin Casey Ruggles by Warren Tufts	12.00	36.00	95.00
100	8.65	26.00	60.00
101-107,109-112,114-120	5.50	16.50	38.00
108,113-Toth-a	8.65	26.00	60.00

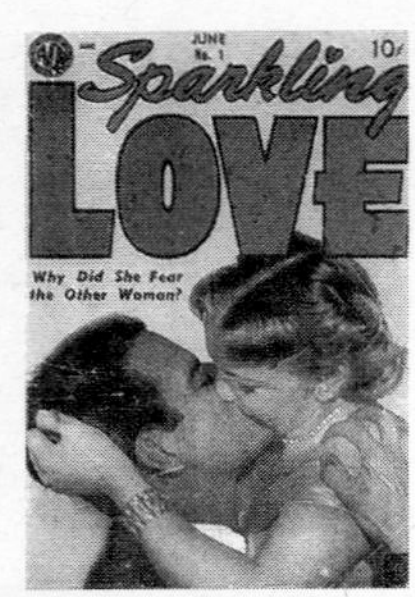

Sparkling Love #1 © AVON

Sparky Watts #5 © CCG

Spawn #70 © TMP

SPARKLING LOVE
Avon Periodicals/Realistic (1953): June, 1950; 1953

1(Avon)-Kubert-a; photo-c 23.00 68.00 180.00
nn(1953)-Reprint; Kubert-a 8.65 26.00 60.00

SPARKLING STARS
Holyoke Publishing Co.: June, 1944 - No. 33, March, 1948

1-Hell's Angels, FBI, Boxie Weaver, Petey & Pop, & Ali Baba begin 19.00 56.00 150.00
2-Speed Spaulding story 10.00 30.00 80.00
3-Actual FBI case photos & war photos 8.65 26.00 60.00
4-10: 7-X-Mas-c 7.15 21.50 50.00
11-19: 13-Origin/1st app. Jungo the Man-Beast-c/s 6.40 19.25 45.00
20-Intro Fangs the Wolf Boy 7.15 21.50 50.00
21-29,32,33: 29-Bondage-c 6.40 19.25 45.00
31-Sid Greene-a 7.00 21.00 48.00

SPARK MAN (See Sparkler Comics)
Frances M. McQueeny: 1945 (36 pgs., one-shot)

1-Origin Spark Man r/Sparkler #1-3; female torture story; cover redrawn from Sparkler #1 33.00 98.00 260.00

SPARKY WATTS (Also see Big Shot Comics & Columbia Comics)
Columbia Comic Corp.: Nov?, 1942 - No. 10, 1949

1(1942)-Skyman & The Face app; Hitler-c 50.00 150.00 450.00
2(1943) 26.00 79.00 210.00
3(1944) 19.00 56.00 150.00
4(1944)-Origin 18.00 53.00 140.00
5(1947)-Skyman app.; Boody Rogers-c/a 15.00 45.00 120.00
6,7,9,10: 6(1947),10(1949) 10.00 30.00 70.00
8(1948)-Surrealistic-c 13.00 39.00 105.00
NOTE: ***Boody Rogers** c-1-8.*

SPARTACUS (Movie)
Dell Publishing Co.: No. 1139, Nov, 1960 (Kirk Douglas photo-c)

Four Color 1139-Buscema-a 12.50 37.50 150.00

SPARTAN: WARRIOR SPIRIT (Also see WildC.A.T.S: Covert Action Teams)
Image Comics (WildStorm Productions): July, 1995 - No. 4, Nov, 1995 ($2.50, limited series)

1-4: Kurt Busiek scripts; Mike McKone-c/a 2.50

SPAWN (Also see Curse of the Spawn and Sam & Twitch)
Image Comics (Todd McFarlane Productions): May, 1992 - Present ($1.95)

1-1st app. Spawn; McFarlane-c/a begins; McFarlane/Steacy-c; 1st Todd McFarlane Productions title. 2.30 7.00 20.00
1-Black & white edition 3.00 9.00 30.00
2,3: 2-1st app. Violator; McFarlane/Steacy-c 1.85 5.50 15.00
4-Contains coupon for Image Comics #0 2.00 6.00 16.00
4-With coupon missing 4.00
4-Newsstand edition w/o poster or coupon 4.00
5-Cerebus cameo (1 pg.) as stuffed animal; Spawn mobile poster #1 1.25 3.75 10.00
6-8,10: 7-Spawn Mobile poster #2. 8-Alan Moore scripts; Miller poster. 10-Cerebus app.; Dave Sim scripts; 1 pg. cameo app. by Superman. 1.00 3.00 8.00
9-Neil Gaiman scripts; Jim Lee poster; 1st Angela. 1.25 3.75 10.00
11-17,19,20,22-30: 11-Miller script; Darrow poster. 12-Bloodwulf poster by Liefeld. 14,15-Violator app. 16,17-Grant Morrison scripts; Capullo-c/a(p). 23,24-McFarlane-a/stories. 25-(10/94). 19-(10/94). 20-(11/94) 2.40 6.00
18-Grant Morrison script, Capullo-c/a(p); low distr. 1.85 5.50 15.00
21-low distribution 1.85 5.50 15.00
31-49: 31-1st app. The Redeemer; new costume cameo. 32-1st full app. new costume. 38-40,42,44,46,48-Tony Daniel-c/a(p). 38-1st app. Cy-Gor. 40,41-Cy-Gor & Curse app. 3.00
50-($3.95, 48 pgs.) 4.00
51-66: 52-Savage Dragon app. 56-w/ Darkchylde preview. 57-Cy-Gor-c/app. 64-Polybagged w/McFarlane Toys catalog. 65-Photo-c of movie Spawn and McFarlane 3.00
67-97: 81-Billy Kincaid returns. 97-Angela-c/app. 2.00
98,99,101-($2.50): 98,99-Angela app. 2.50
100-($4.95) Angela dies; 6 covers by McFarlane, Ross, Miller, Capullo, Wood, Mignola 5.00
Annual 1-Blood & Shadows ('99, $4.95) Ashley Wood-c/a; Jenkins-s 5.00
...Bible-(8/96, $1.95)-Character bios 4.00
Book 1 TPB($9.95) r/#1-5; Book 2-r/#6-9,11; Book 3 -r/#12-15, Book 4- r/#16-20; Book 5-r/#21-25; Book 6- r/#26-30; Book 7-r/#31-34; Book 8-r/#35-38; Book 9-r/#39-42; Book 10-r/#43-47 10.00
Book 11 TPB ($10.95) r/#48-52 11.00
NOTE: ***Capullo** a-16p-18p; c-16p-18p. **Daniel** a-38-40, 42, 44, 46. **McFarlane** a-1-15; c-1-15. **Thibert** a-16i(part). Posters come with issues 1, 4, 7-9, 11, 12. #25 was released before #19 20.*

SPAWN-BATMAN (Also see Batman/Spawn: War Devil under Batman: One-Shots)
Image Comics (Todd McFarlane Productions): 1994 ($3.95, one-shot)

1-Miller scripts; McFarlane-c/a 2.40 6.00

SPAWN: BLOOD FEUD
Image Comics (Todd McFarlane Productions): June, 1995 - No. 4, Sept, 1995 ($2.25, limited series)

1-4-Alan Moore scripts, Tony Daniel-a 3.50

SPAWN FAN EDITION
Image Comics (Todd McFarlane Productions): Aug, 1996 - No. 3, Oct, 1996 (Giveaway, 12 pgs.) (Polybagged w/Overstreet's FAN)

1-3: Beau Smith scripts; Brad Gorby-a(p). 1-1st app. Nordik, the Norse Hellspawn. 2-1st app. McFallon, the Dragon Master. 3-1st app. Mercy 1.00 3.00 8.00
1-3-(Gold): All retailer incentives 16.00
1-3-Variant-c 1.00 3.00 8.00
2-(Platinum)-Retailer incentive 25.00

SPAWN: THE DARK AGES
Image Comics (Todd McFarlane Productions): Mar, 1999 - Present ($2.50)

1-Fabry-c; Holguin-s/Sharp-a; variant-c by McFarlane 2.50
2-21 2.50

SPAWN THE IMPALER
Image Comics (Todd McFarlane Productions): Oct, 1996 - No. 3, Dec, 1996 ($2.95, limited series)

1-3-Mike Grell scripts, painted-a 3.00

SPAWN: THE UNDEAD
Image Comics (Todd McFarlane Prod.): Jun, 1999 - No. 9, Feb, 2000 ($1.95/$2.25)

1-6-Dwayne Turner-c/a; Jenkins-s 1.95
7-9-($2.25) 2.25

SPAWN/WILDC.A.T.S
Image Comics (WildStorm): Jan, 1996 - No. 4, Apr, 1996 ($2.50, lim. series)

1-4: Alan Moore scripts in all. 3.00

SPECIAL AGENT (Steve Saunders...)(Also see True Comics #68)
Parents' Magazine Institute (Commended Comics No. 2): Dec, 1947 - No. 8, Sept, 1949 (Based on true FBI cases)

1-J. Edgar Hoover photo on-c 11.00 33.00 90.00
2 7.15 21.50 50.00
3-8 5.70 17.00 40.00

SPECIAL COLLECTORS' EDITION (See Savage Fists of Kung-Fu)

SPECIAL COMICS (Becomes Hangman #2 on)
MLJ Magazines: Winter, 1941-42

1-Origin The Boy Buddies (Shield & Wizard x-over); death of The Comet; origin The Hangman retold; Hangman-c 274.00 821.00 2600.00

SPECIAL EDITION (See Gorgo and Reptisaurus)

SPECIAL EDITION COMICS
Fawcett Publications: 1940 (August) (68 pgs., one-shot)

GD2.0 FN6.0 VF8.0 NM9.4
1-1st book devoted entirely to Captain Marvel; C.C. Beck-c/a; only app. of Capt. Marvel with belt buckle; Capt. Marvel appears with button-down flap; 1st story (came out before Captain Marvel #1) 800.00 2400.00 5000.00 9200.00

Special Edition X-Men #1 © MAR

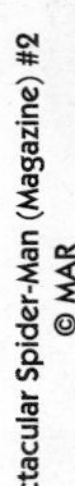

Spectacular Spider-Man (Magazine) #2 © MAR

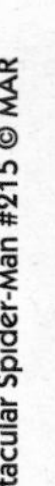

Spectacular Spider-Man #215 © MAR

GD2.0 FN6.0 NM9.4

GD2.0 FN6.0 NM9.4

NOTE: *Prices vary widely on this book. Since this book is all Captain Marvel stories, it is actually a pre-Captain Marvel #1. There is speculation that this book almost became* ***Captain Marvel*** *#1. After* ***Special Edition*** *was published, there was an editor change at Fawcett. The new editor commissioned Kirby to do a nn* ***Captain Marvel*** *book early in 1941. This book was followed by a 2nd book several months later. This 2nd book was advertised as a #3 (making Special Edition the #1, & the nn issue the #2). However, the 2nd book did come out as a #2.*

SPECIAL EDITION: SPIDER-MAN VS. THE HULK (See listing under The Amazing Spider-Man)

SPECIAL EDITION X-MEN
Marvel Comics Group: Feb, 1983 ($2.00, one-shot, Baxter paper)

	GD2.0	FN6.0	NM9.4
1-r/Giant-Size X-Men #1 plus one new story	1.50	4.50	12.00

SPECIAL MARVEL EDITION (Master of Kung Fu #17 on)
Marvel Comics Group: Jan, 1971 - No. 16, Feb, 1974 (#1-3: 25¢, 68 pgs.; #4: 52 pgs.; #5-16: 20¢, regular ed.)

1-Thor-r by Kirby; 68 pgs. 2.50 7.50 25.00
2-4: Thor-r by Kirby; 2,3-68 pg. Giant. 4-(52 pgs.) 2.00 6.00 16.00
5-14: Sgt. Fury-r; 11-r/Sgt. Fury #13 (Capt. America) 1.10 3.30 9.00
15-Master of Kung Fu (Shang-Chi) begins (1st app., 12/73); Starlin-a; origin/1st app. Nayland Smith & Dr. Petric 5.45 16.35 60.00
16-1st app. Midnight; Starlin-a (2nd Shang-Chi) 2.50 7.50 25.00
NOTE: ***Kirby*** *c-10-14.*

SPECIAL MISSIONS (See G.I. Joe...)

SPECIAL WAR SERIES (Attack V4#3 on?)
Charlton Comics: Aug, 1965 - No. 4, Nov, 1965

V4#1-D-Day (also see D-Day listing) 3.00 9.00 30.00
2-Attack! 2.00 6.00 18.00
3-War & Attack (also see War & Attack) 2.00 6.00 18.00
4-Judomaster (intro/1st app.; see Sarge Steel) 5.45 16.35 60.00

SPECIES (Movie)
Dark Horse Comics: June, 1995 - No. 4, Sept, 1995 ($2.50, limited series)

1-4: Adaptation of film 3.00

SPECIES: HUMAN RACE (Movie)
Dark Horse Comics: Nov, 1996 - No. 4, Feb, 1997 ($2.95, limited series)

1-4 3.00

SPECTACULAR ADVENTURES (See Adventures)

SPECTACULAR FEATURE MAGAZINE, A (Formerly My Confessions) (Spectacular Features Magazine #12)
Fox Feature Syndicate: No. 11, April, 1950

11 (#1)-Samson and Delilah 30.00 90.00 240.00

SPECTACULAR FEATURES MAGAZINE (Formerly A Spectacular Feature Magazine)
Fox Feature Syndicate: No. 12, June, 1950 - No. 3, Aug, 1950

12 (#2)-Iwo Jima; photo flag-c 30.00 90.00 240.00
3-True Crime Cases From Police Files 24.00 71.00 190.00

SPECTACULAR SCARLET SPIDER
Marvel Comics: Nov, 1995 - No. 2, Dec, 1995 ($1.95, limited series)

1,2: Replaces Spectacular Spider-Man 2.00

SPECTACULAR SPIDER-MAN, THE (See Marvel Special Edition and Marvel Treasury Edition)

SPECTACULAR SPIDER-MAN, THE (Magazine)
Marvel Comics Group: July, 1968 - No. 2, Nov, 1968 (35¢)

1-(B&W)-Romita/Mooney 52 pg. story plus updated origin story with Everett-a(i) 8.65 26.00 95.00
1-Variation w/single c-price of 40¢ 8.65 26.00 95.00
2-(Color)-Green Goblin-c & 58 pg. story; Romita painted-c (story reprinted in King Size Spider-Man #9); Romita/Mooney-a 11.00 33.00 120.00

SPECTACULAR SPIDER-MAN, THE (Peter Parker...#54-132, 134)
Marvel Comics Group: Dec, 1976 - No. 263, Nov, 1998

1-Origin recap in text; return of Tarantula 3.65 11.00 40.00
2-Kraven the Hunter app. 1.85 5.50 15.00
3-5: 3-Intro Lightmaster. 4-Vulture app. 1.25 3.75 10.00
6-8-Morbius app.; 6-r/Marvel Team-Up #3 w/Morbius 1.50 4.50 12.00
9-20: 9,10-White Tiger app. 11-Last 30¢-c. 17,18-Angel & Iceman app. (from Champions); Ghost Rider cameo in flashback 1.00 3.00 8.00
21,24-26: 21-Scorpion app. 26-Daredevil app. 1.00 2.80 7.00
22,23-Moon Knight app. 1.00 3.00 8.00
27-Miller's 1st art on Daredevil (2/79); also see Captain America #235 1.85 5.50 15.00
28-Miller Daredevil (p) 1.50 4.50 12.00
29-55,57,59: 33-Origin Iguana. 38-Morbius app. 5.00
56-2nd app. Jack O'Lantern (Macendale) & 1st Spidey/Jack O'Lantern battle (7/81) 2.40 6.00
58-Byrne-a(p) 5.00
60-Double size; origin retold with new facts revealed 2.40 6.00
61-63,65-68,71-74: 65-Kraven the Hunter app. 4.00
64-1st app. Cloak & Dagger (3/82) 1.10 3.30 9.00
69,70-Cloak & Dagger app. 2.40 6.00
75-Double size 5.00
76-82: 78,79-Punisher cameo. 81,82-Punisher, Cloak & Dagger app. 4.00
83-Origin Punisher retold (10/83) 1.00 2.80 7.00
84,86-99: 90-Spider-man's new black costume, last panel(ties w/Amazing Spider-Man #252 & Marvel Team-Up #141 for 1st app.). 94-96-Cloak & Dagger app. 98-Intro The Spot 3.00
85-Hobgoblin (Ned Leeds) app. (12/83); gains powers of original Green Goblin (see Amazing Spider-Man #238) 1.00 2.80 7.00
100-(3/85)-Double size 4.00
101-115,117,118,120-129: 107-110-Death of Jean DeWolff. 111-Secret Wars II tie-in. 128-Black Cat new costume 2.50
116,119-Sabretooth-c/story 5.00
130-132: 30-Hobgoblin app. 131-Six part Kraven tie-in. 132-Kraven tie-in 5.00
133-140: 138-1st full app. Tombstone (origin #139). 140-Punisher cameo app. 2.50
141-143-Punisher app. 3.00
144-146,148-157: 151-Tombstone returns 2.50
147-1st app. new Hobgoblin (Macendale) in 1 pg. cameo; continued in Web of Spider-Man #48 1.25 3.75 10.00
158-Spider-Man gets new powers (1st Cosmic Spidey, cont'd in Web of Spider-Man #59) 5.00
159-Cosmic Spider-Man app. 5.00
160-170: 161-163-Hobgoblin app. 168-170-Avengers x-over. 169-1st app. The Outlaws 2.50
171-188,190-199: 180,181,183,184-Green Goblin app. 197-199-Original X-Men-c/story 2.00
189-($2.95, 52 pgs.)-Silver hologram on-c; battles Green Goblin; origin Spidey retold; Vess poster w/Spidey & Hobgoblin 4.00
189-(2nd printing)-Gold hologram on-c 3.00
195-(Deluxe ed.)-Polybagged w/audio cassette 3.00
200-($2.95)-Holo-grafx foil-c; Green Goblin-c/story 3.00
201-219,221,222,224,226-228,230-247: 212-w/card sheet. 203-Maximum Carnage x-over. 204-Begin 4 part death of Tombstone story. 207,208-The Shroud-c/story. 208-Siege of Darkness x-over (#207 is a tie-in). 209-Black Cat back-up215,216-Scorpion app. 217-Power & Responsibility Pt. 4. 231-Return of Kaine; Spider-Man corpse discovered. 232-New Doc Octopus app. 233-Carnage-c/app. 235-Dragon Man cameo. 236-Dragon Man-c/app; Lizard app.; Peter Parker regains powers. 238,239-Lizard app. 239-w/card insert. 240-Revelations storyline begins. 241-Flashback 2.00
213-Collectors ed. polybagged w/16 pg. preview & animation cel; foil-c; 1st meeting Spidey & Typhoid Mary 3.00
213-Version polybagged w/Gamepro #7; no-c date, price 2.00
217,219 ($2.95)-Deluxe edition foil-c: flip book 3.00
220 ($2.25, 52 pgs.)-Flip book, Mary Jane reveals pregnancy 3.00
223,229: ($2.50) 229-Spidey quits 3.00
223,225: ($2.95)-223-Die Cut-c. 225-Newsstand ed. 3.00
225,229: ($3.95) 225-Direct Market Holodisk-c (Green Goblin). 229-Acetate-c, Spidey quits 4.00
240-Variant-c 3.00
248,249,251-254,256: 249-Return of Norman Osborne 256-1st app. Prodigy 2.00
250-($3.25) Double gatefold-c 3.25
255-($2.99) Spiderhunt pt. 4 3.00

Spectre (3rd series) #29 © DC

Speed Comics #2 © HARV

Speed Racer (DC) #2 © Speed Racer Ent.

257-262: 257-Double cover with "Spectacular Prodigy #1"; battles Jack O'Lantern. 258-Spidey is cleared. 259,260-Green Goblin & Hobgoblin app. 262-Byrne-s 2.00
263-Final issue; Byrne-c; Aunt May returns 3.00
#(-1) Flashback (7/97) 2.00
Annual 1 (1979)-Doc Octopus-c & 46 pg. story 1.00 3.00 8.00
Annual 2 (1980)-Origin/1st app. Rapier 5.00
Annual 3-14: 3('81-'94)-3-Last Man-Wolf. 8 ('88,$ 1.75)-Evolutionary War x-over; Daydreamer returns GwenStacy "clone" back to real self (not Gwen Stacy). 9 ('89, $2.00, 68 pgs.)-Atlantis Attacks. 10 ('90, $2.00, 68 pgs.)-McFarlane-a 11 ('91, $2.00, 68 pgs.)-Iron Man app. 12 ('92, $2.25, 68 pgs.)-Venom solo story cont'd from Amazing Spider-Man Annual #26. 13 ('93, $2.95, 68 pgs.)-Polybagged w/trading card; John Romita, Sr. back-up-a 3.00
Special 1 (1995, $3.95)-Flip book 4.00

NOTE: ***Austin*** *c-21i, Annual 11i.* ***Buckler*** *a-103, 107-111, 116, 117, 119, 122, Annual 1, Annual 10; c-103, 107-111, 113, 116-119, 122, Annual 1.* ***Buscema*** *a-121.* ***Byrne*** *c(p)-17, 43, 58, 101, 102.* ***Giffen*** *a-120p.* ***Hembeck*** *c/a-86p.* ***Larsen*** *c-Annual 11p.* ***Miller*** *c-46p, 48p, 50, 51p, 52p, 54p, 55, 56p, 57, 60.* ***Mooney*** *a-7i, 11i, 21p, 23p, 25p, 26p, 29-34p, 36p, 37p, 39i, 41, 42i, 49p, 50i, 51i, 53p, 54-57i, 59-66i, 68i, 71i, 73-79i, 81-83i, 85i, 87-99i, 102i, 125p, Annual 1i, 2p.* ***Nasser*** *c-37p.* ***Perez*** *c-10.* ***Simonson*** *c-54i.* ***Zeck*** *a-118, 131, 132; c-131, 132.*

SPECTACULAR STORIES MAGAZINE (Formerly A Star Presentation)
Fox Feature Syndicate (Hero Books): No. 4, July, 1950 - No. 3, Sept, 1950

4-Sherlock Holmes (true crime stories) 40.00 120.00 320.00
3-The St. Valentine's Day Massacre (true crime) 27.00 81.00 215.00

SPECTRE, THE (1st Series) (See Adventure Comics #431-440, More Fun & Showcase)
National Periodical Publ.: Nov-Dec, 1967 - No. 10, May-June, 1969 (All 12¢)

1-(11-12/67)-Anderson-c/a 11.00 33.00 120.00
2-5-Neal Adams-c/a; 3-Wildcat x-over 7.25 21.75 80.00
6-8,10: 6-8-Anderson inks. 7-Hourman app. 4.55 13.65 50.00
9-Wrightson-a 5.45 16.35 60.00

SPECTRE, THE (2nd Series) (See Saga of the Swamp Thing #58, Showcase '95 #8 & Wrath of the...)
DC Comics: Apr, 1987 - No. 31, Oct, 1989 ($1.00, new format)

1-31: 1-Colan-a begins. 9-Nudity panels. 10-Batman cameo. 10,11-Millennium tie-ins 3.00
Annual 1 (1988, $2.00)-Deadman app. 2.50

NOTE: ***Art Adams*** *c-Annual 1.* ***Colan*** *a-1-6.* ***Kaluta*** *c-1-3.* ***Mignola*** *c-7-9.* ***Morrow*** *a-9-15.* ***Sears*** *c/a-22.* ***Vess*** *c-13-15.*

SPECTRE, THE (3rd Series) (Also see Brave and the Bold #72, 75, 116, 180, 199 & Showcase '95 #8)
DC Comics: Dec, 1992 - No. 62, Feb, 1998 ($1.75/$1.95/$2.25/$2.50)

1-($1.95)-Glow-in-the-dark-c; Mandrake-a begins 5.00
2,3 3.00
4-7,9-12,14-20: 10-Kaluta-c. 11-Hildebrandt painted-c. 16-Aparo/K. Jones-a. 19-Snyder III-c. 20-Sienkiewicz-c 2.50
8,13-($2.50)-Glow-in-the-dark-c 3.00
21-62: 22-(9/94)-Superman-c & app. 23-(11/94). 43-Kent Williams-c. 44-Kaluta-c. 47-Final Night x-over. 49-Begin Bolton-c. 51-Batman-c/app. 52-Gianni-c. 54-Corben-c. 60-Harris-c 2.50
#0 (10/94) Released between #22 & #23 2.50
Annual 1 (1995, $3.95)-Year One story 4.00

NOTE: ***Bisley*** *c-27.* ***Fabry*** *c-2.* ***Kelley Jones*** *c-31.* ***Vess*** *c-5.*

SPECTRE, THE (4th Series) (Hal Jordan; also see Day of Judgment #5 and Legends of the DC Universe #33-36)
DC Comics: Mar, 2001 - Present ($2.50)

1-DeMatteis-s/Ryan Sook-c/a 2.50

SPEEDBALL (See Amazing Spider-Man Annual #12, Marvel Super-Heroes & The New Warriors)
Marvel Comics: Sept, 1988(10/88-inside) - No. 11, July, 1989 (75¢)

1-11: Ditko/Guice a-1-4, c-1; Ditko a-1-10; c-1-11p 2.00

SPEED BUGGY (TV)(Also see Fun-In #12, 15)
Charlton Comics: July, 1975 - No. 9, Nov, 1976 (Hanna-Barbera)

1 2.50 7.50 23.00
2-9 1.85 5.50 15.00

SPEED CARTER SPACEMAN (See Spaceman)

GD2.0 FN6.0 NM9.4

SPEED COMICS (New Speed)(Also see Double Up)
Brookwood Publ./Speed Publ./Harvey Publications No. 14 on:
10/39 - #11, 8/40; #12, 3/41 - #44, 1-2/47 (#14-16: pocket size, 100 pgs.)

1-Origin & 1st app. Shock Gibson; Ted Parrish, the Man with 1000 Faces begins; Powell-a; becomes Champion #2 on? 314.00 943.00 3300.00
2-Powell-a 105.00 316.00 1000.00
3 63.00 189.00 600.00
4,5: 4-Powell-a?5-Dinosaur-c 53.00 160.00 480.00
6-11: 7-Mars Mason begins, ends #11 47.00 140.00 420.00
12 (3/41; shows #11 in indicia)-The Wasp begins; Major Colt app. (Capt. Colt #12) 53.00 160.00 480.00
13-Intro. Captain Freedom & Young Defenders; Girl Commandos, Pat Parker (costumed heroine), War Nurse begins; Major Colt app. 58.00 174.00 550.00
14-16 (100 pg. pocket size, 1941): 14-2nd Harvey comic (See Pocket); Shock Gibson dons new costume. 15-Pat Parker dons costume, last in costume #23; no Girl Commandos 63.00 189.00 600.00
17-Black Cat begins (4/42, early app.; see Pocket #1); origin Black Cat-r/ Pocket #1; not in #40,41; S&K-c 71.00 213.00 675.00
18-20-S&K-c 55.00 165.00 500.00
21,22-Kirby-c. 21-Hitler, Tojo-c 55.00 165.00 500.00
23-Origin Girl Commandos; Kirby-c 55.00 165.00 520.00
24-Pat Parker team-up with Girl Commandos; Hitler, Tojo, & Mussolini-c 47.00 142.00 425.00
25-30: 26-Flag-c 42.00 125.00 375.00
31-Schomburg Hitler & Hirohito-c 58.00 174.00 550.00
32-36-Schomburg-c 50.00 150.00 450.00
37,39-42, 44 42.00 125.00 375.00
38-Iwo-Jima Flag-c 44.00 133.00 400.00
43-Robot-c 47.00 142.00 425.00

NOTE: ***Al Avison*** *c-14-16, 30, 43.* ***Briefer*** *a-6, 7.* ***Jon Henri*** *(Kirbyesque) c-17-20.* ***Kubert*** *a-7-11(Mars Mason), 37, 38, 42-44.* ***Kirby/Caseneuve*** *c-21-23.* ***Palais*** *c-37, 39-42.* ***Powell*** *a-1, 2, 4-7, 28, 31, 44.* ***Schomburg*** *c-31-36.* ***Tuska*** *a-3, 6, 7. Bondage c-18, 35. Captain Freedom c-16-24, 25(part), 26-44(w/Black Cat #27, 29, 31, 32-40). Shock Gibson c-1-15.*

SPEED DEMON (Also see Marvel Versus DC #3 & DC Versus Marvel #4)
Marvel Comics (Amalgam): Apr, 1996 ($1.95, one-shot)

1 2.00

SPEED DEMONS (Formerly Frank Merriwell at Yale #1-4?; Submarine Attack #11 on)
Charlton Comics: No. 5, Feb, 1957 - No. 10, 1958

5-10 5.70 17.00 40.00

SPEED FORCE (See The Flash 2nd Series #143-Cobalt Blue)
DC Comics: Nov, 1997 ($3.95, one-shot)

1-Flash & Kid Flash vs. Cobalt Blue; Waid-s/Aparo & Sienkiewicz-a; Flash family stories and pin-ups by various 4.00

SPEED RACER (Also see The New Adventures of...)
Now Comics: July, 1987 - No. 38, Nov, 1990 ($1.75)

1-38, 1-2nd printing 2.50
Special 1 (1988, $2.00) 2.50
Special 2 (1988, $3.50) 3.50

SPEED RACER (Also see Racer X)
DC Comics (WildStorm): Oct, 1999 - No. 3, Dec, 1999 ($2.50, limited series)

1-3-Tommy Yune-s/a; origin of Racer X; debut of the Mach 5 2.50
...: Born To Race (2000, $9.95, TPB) r/series & conceptual art 10.00
...: The Original Manga Vol. 1 ('00, $9.95, TPB) r/1950s B&W manga 9.95

SPEED RACER FEATURING NINJA HIGH SCHOOL
Now Comics: Aug, 1993 - No. 2, 1993 ($2.50, mini-series)

1,2: 1-Polybagged w/card. 2-Exists? 2.50

SPEED RACER: RETURN OF THE GRX
Now Comics: Mar, 1994 - No. 2, Apr, 1994 ($1.95, limited series)

1,2 2.50

SPEED SMITH-THE HOT ROD KING (Also see Hot Rod King)
Ziff-Davis Publishing Co.: Spring, 1952

1-Saunders painted-c 23.00 69.00 185.00

Spellbound #14 © MAR

Spider-Girl #17 © MAR

Spider-Man #91 © MAR

GD2.0 FN6.0 NM9.4

SPEEDY GONZALES
Dell Publishing Co.: No. 1084, Mar, 1960
Four Color 1084 4.55 13.65 50.00

SPEEDY RABBIT (See Television Puppet Show)
Realistic/I. W. Enterprises/Super Comics: nd (1953); 1963
nn (1953)-Realistic Reprint? 2.80 7.00 14.00
I.W. Reprint #1 (2 versions w/diff. c/stories exist)-Peter Cottontail #?
Super Reprint #14(1963) 1.25 3.75 10.00

SPELLBINDERS
Quality: Dec, 1986 - No. 12, Jan, 1988 ($1.25)
1-12: Nemesis the Warlock, Amadeus Wolf 2.00

SPELLBOUND (See The Crusaders)

SPELLBOUND (Tales to Hold You... #1, Stories to Hold You...)
Atlas Comics (ACI 1-15/Male 16-23/BPC 24-34): Mar, 1952 - #23, June, 1954; #24, Oct, 1955 - #34, June, 1957
1-Horror/weird stories in all 63.00 189.00 600.00
2-Edgar A. Poe app. 38.00 113.00 300.00
3-5: 3-Whitney-a; cannibalism story 33.00 98.00 260.00
6-Krigstein-a 33.00 98.00 260.00
7-10: 8-Ayers-a 28.00 83.00 220.00
11-16,18-20: 14-Ed Win-a 23.00 68.00 180.00
17-Krigstein-a 23.00 69.00 185.00
21-23: 23-Last precode (6/54) 19.00 56.00 150.00
24-28,30,31,34: 25-Orlando-a 17.00 51.00 135.00
29-Ditko-a (4 pgs.) 19.00 56.00 150.00
32,33-Torres-a 17.00 51.00 135.00
NOTE: ***Brodsky** a-5; c-1, 5-7, 10, 11, 13, 15, 25-27, 32. **Colan** a-17. **Everett** a-2, 5, 7, 10, 16, 28, 31; c-2, 8, 9, 14, 17-19, 28, 30. **Forgione/Abel** a-29. **Forte/Fox** a-16. **Al Hartley** a-2. **Heath** a-2, 4, 8, 9, 12, 14, 16; c-3, 4, 12, 16, 20, 21. **Infantino** a-15. **Keller** a-5. **Kida** a-2, 14. **Maneely** a-7, 14, 27; c-24, 29, 31. **Mooney** a-5, 13, 18. **Mac Pakula** a-22, 32. **Post** a-8. **Powell** a-19, 20, 32. **Robinson** a-1. **Romita** a-24, 26, 27. **R.Q. Sale** a-29. **Sekowsky** a-5. **Severin** c-29. **Sinnott** a-8, 16, 17.*

SPELLBOUND
Marvel Comics: Jan, 1988 - Apr, 1988 ($1.50, bi-weekly, Baxter paper)
1-5 2.00
6 ($2.25, 52 pgs.) 2.50

SPELLJAMMER (Also see TSR Worlds Comics Annual)
DC Comics: Sept, 1990 - No. 15, Nov, 1991 ($1.75)
1-15: Based on TSR game. 11-Heck-a. 2.00

SPENCER SPOOK (Formerly Giggle Comics; see Adventures of...)
American Comics Group: No. 100, Mar-Apr, 1955 - No. 101, May-June, 1955
100,101 6.40 19.25 45.00

SPIDER, THE
Eclipse Books: 1991 - Book 3, 1991 ($4.95, 52 pgs., limited series)
Book 1-3-Truman-c/a 5.00

SPIDER-BOY (Also see Marvel Versus DC #3)
Marvel Comics (Amalgam): Apr, 1996 ($1.95)
1-Mike Wieringo-c/a; Karl Kesel story; 1st app. of Bizarnage, Insect Queen, Challengers of the Fantastic, Sue Storm: Agent of S.H.I.E.L. D., & King Lizard. 2.00

SPIDER-BOY TEAM-UP
Marvel Comics (Amalgam): June, 1997 ($1.95, one-shot)
1-Karl Kesel & Roger Stern-s/Jo Ladronn-a(p) 2.00

SPIDER-GIRL (See What If #105)
Marvel Comics: Oct, 1998 - Present ($1.99/$2.25)
0-($2.99)-r/1st app. Peter Parker's daughter from What If #105; previews reg. series, Avengers-Next and J2 1.00 2.80 7.00
1-DeFalco-s/Olliffe & Williamson-s 1.00 2.80 7.00
2-Two covers 4.00
3-16,18-20: 3-Fantastic Five-c/app. 10,11-Spider-Girl time travels to meet teenaged Spider-Man 2.00
17-($2.99) Peter Parker suits up 3.00
21-24,26-29: 21-Begin $2.25-c 2.25
25-($2.99) Spider-Girl vs. the Savage Six 3.00
1999 Annual ($3.99) 4.00
... A Fresh Start (1/99,$5.99, TPB) r/#1&2 6.00

SPIDER-MAN (See Amazing..., Giant-Size..., Marvel Tales, Marvel Team-Up, Spectacular..., Spidey Super Stories, Venom, & Web Of...)

SPIDER-MAN
Marvel Comics: Aug, 1990 - No. 98, Nov, 1998 ($1.75/$1.95/ $1.99)
1-Silver edition, direct sale only (unbagged) 1.00 3.00 8.00
1-Silver bagged edition; direct sale, no price on comic, but $2.00 on plastic bag (125,000 print run) 20.00
1-Regular edition w/Spidey face in UPC area (unbagged); green-c 2.40 6.00
1-Regular bagged edition w/Spidey face in UPC area; green cover (125,000) 12.00
1-Newsstand bagged w/UPC code 10.00
1-Gold edition, 2nd printing (unbagged) with Spider-Man in box (400,000-450,000) 2.40 6.00
1-Gold 2nd printing w/UPC code; sold in Wal-Mart; not scarce 2.40 6.00
1-Platinum ed. mailed to retailers only (10,000 print run); has new McFarlane-a & editorial material instead of ads; stiff-c, no cover price 150.00
2-26: 2-McFarlane-c/a/scripts continue. 6,7-Ghost Rider & Hobgoblin app. 8-Wolverine cameo; Wolverine storyline begins. 12-Wolverine storyline ends. 13-Spidey's black costume returns; Morbius app. 14-Morbius app. 15-Erik Larsen-c/a; Beast c/s. 16-X-Force-c/story w/Liefeld assists; continues in X-Force #4; reads sideways; last McFarlane issue. 17-Thanos-c/story; Leonardi/Williamson-c/a. 13,14-Spidey in black costume. 18-Ghost Rider-c/story. 18-23-Sinister Six storyline w/Erik Larsen-c/a/scripts. 19-Hulk & Hobgoblin-c & app. 20-22-Deathlok app. 22,23-Ghost Rider, Hulk, Hobgoblin app. 23-Wrap-around gatefold-c. 24-Infinity War x-over w/Demogoblin & Hobgoblin-c/story. 24-Demogoblin dons new costume & battles Hobgoblin-c/story. 26-($3.50, 52 pgs.)-Silver hologram on-c w/gatefold poster by Ron Lim; Spidey retells his origin. 4.00
26-2nd printing; gold hologram on-c 3.50
27-45: 32-34-Punisher-c/story. 37-Maximum Carnage x-over. 39,40-Electro-c/s (cameo #38). 41-43-Iron Fist-c/stories w/Jae Lee-c/a. 42-Intro Platoon. 44-Hobgoblin app 2.50
46-49,51-53, 55, 56,58-74,76-81: 46-Begin $1.95-c; bound-in card sheet. 51-Power & Responsibility Pt. 3. 52,53-Venom app. 60-Kaine revealed. 61-Origin Kaine. 65-Mysterio app. 66-Kaine-c/app.; Peter Parker app. 67-Carnage-c/app. 68,69-Hobgoblin-c/app. 72-Onslaught x-over; Spidey vs. Sentinels. 74-Daredevil-c/app. 77-80-Morbius-c/app. 2.50
46-($2.95)-Polybagged; silver ink-c w/16 pg. preview of cartoon series & animation style print; bound-in trading card sheet 3.00
50-($2.50)-Newsstand edition 2.50
50-($3.95)-Collectors edition w/holographic-c 4.00
51-($2.95)-Deluxe edition foil-c; flip book 3.00
54 ($2.75, 52 pgs.)-Flip book 2.75
57 ($2.50) 2.50
57 ($2.95)-Die cut-c 3.00
65-($2.95)-Variant-c; polybagged w/cassette 3.00
75-($2.95)-Wraparound-c; return of the Green Goblin;death of Ben Reilly (who was the clone) 4.00
82-97: 84-Juggernaut app. 91-Double cover with "Dusk #1"; battles the Shocker. 93-Ghost Rider app. 2.00
98-Double cover; final issue 3.00
#(-1) Flashback (7/97) 2.00
Annual '97 ($2.99), '98 ($2.99)-Devil Dinosaur-c/app. 3.00
...and Batman ('95, $5.95) DeMatteis-s; Joker, Carnage app. 6.00
...and Daredevil ('84, $2.00) 1-r/Spectacular Spider-Man #26-28 by Miller 3.00
...: Carnage nn (6/93, $6.95, TPB)-r/Amazing S-M #344,345,359-363; spot varnish-c 7.00
.../Dr. Strange: "The Way to Dusty Death" nn (1992, $6.95, 68 pgs.) 7.00
.../Elektra '98-($2.99) vs. The Silencer 3.00
... Fear Itself Graphic Novel (2/92, $12.95) 18.00
Giant-Sized Spider-Man (12/98, $3.99) r/team-ups 4.00
Holiday Special 1995 ($2.95) 3.00
Identity Crisis (9/98, $19.95, TPB) 20.00
.../Marrow (2/01, $2.99) Garza-a 3.00
..., Punisher, Sabretooth: Designer Genes (1993, $8.95) 9.00

Spider-Man: Chapter One #1 © MAR

Spider-Man: Hobgoblin Lives #1 © MAR

Spider-Man Team-Up #1 © MAR

GD2.0 FN6.0 NM9.4

...Revelations ('97, $14.99, TPB) r/end of Clone Saga plus 14 new pages by Romita Jr. 15.00
Special Edition 1 (12/92-c, 11/92 inside)-The Trial of Venom; ordered thru mail with $5.00 donation or more to UNICEF; embossed metallic ink; came bagged w/bound-in poster; Daredevil app. 1.25 3.75 10.00
Super Special (7/95, $3.95)-Planet of the Symbiotes 4.00
The Death of Captain Stacy ($3.50) r/AS-M#88-90 3.50
The Death of Gwen Stacy ($14.95) r/AS-M#96-98,121,122 14.95
... Vs. Doctor Octopus ($17.95) reprints early battles; Sean Chen-c 17.95
... Vs. Punisher (7/00, $2.99) Michael Lopez-c/a 3.00
...Vs. Venom (1990, $8.95, TPB)-r/Amaz. S-M #300,315-317 w/new McFarlane-c 9.00
Wizard 1/2 ($10.00) Leonardi-a; Green Goblin app. 10.00
NOTE: ***Erik Larsen*** *c/a-15, 18-23.* ***M. Rogers/Keith Williams*** *c/a-27, 28.*

SPIDER-MAN ADVENTURES
Marvel Comics: Dec, 1994 - No. 15, Mar, 1996 ($1.50)
1-15 ($1.50)-Based on animated series 2.00
1-($2.95)-Foil embossed-c 3.00

SPIDER-MAN AND HIS AMAZING FRIENDS (See Marvel Action Universe)
Marvel Comics Group: Dec, 1981 (one-shot)
1-Adapted from NBC TV cartoon show; Green Goblin-c/story; 1st Spidey, Firestar, Iceman team-up; Spiegle-p 5.00

SPIDER-MAN AND THE INCREDIBLE HULK (See listing under Amazing...)

SPIDER-MAN AND THE UNCANNY X-MEN
Marvel Comics: Mar, 1996 ($16.95, trade paperback)
nn-r/Uncanny X-Men #27, Uncanny X-men #35, Amazing Spider-Man #92, Marvel Team-Up Annual #1, Marvel Team-Up #150, & Spectacular Spider-Man #197-199 17.00

SPIDER-MAN AND X-FACTOR
Marvel Comics: May, 1994 - No. 3, July, 1994 ($1.95, limited series)
1-3 2.00

SPIDER-MAN /BADROCK
Maximum Press: Mar, 1997 ($2.99, mini-series)
1A, 1B(#2)-Jurgens-s 3.00

SPIDER-MAN: CHAPTER ONE
Marvel Comics: Dec, 1998 - No. 12, Oct, 1999 ($2.50, limited series)
1-Retelling/updating of origin; John Byrne-s/c/a 2.50
1-($6.95) DF Edition w/variant-c by Jae Lee 7.00
2-11: 2-Two covers (one is swipe of ASM #1); Fantastic Four app. 9-Daredevil. 11-Giant-Man-c/app. 2.50
12-($3.50) Battles the Sandman 3.50
0-(5/99) Origins of Vulture, Lizard and Sandman 2.50

SPIDER-MAN CLASSICS
Marvel Comics: Apr, 1993 - No. 16, July, 1994 ($1.25)
1-14,16: 1-r/Amaz. Fantasy #15 & Strange Tales #115. 2-16-r/Amaz. Spider-Man #1-15. 6-Austin-c(i) 2.00
15-($2.95)-Polybagged w/16 pg. insert & animation style print; r/Amazing S-M #14 (1st Green Goblin) 3.00

SPIDER-MAN COLLECTOR'S PREVIEW
Marvel Comics: Dec, 1994 ($1.50, 100 pgs., one-shot)
1-wraparound-c; no comics 3.00

SPIDER-MAN COMICS MAGAZINE
Marvel Comics Group: Jan, 1987 - No. 13, 1988 ($1.50, digest-size)
1-13-Reprints 2.40 6.00

SPIDER-MAN: DEAD MAN'S HAND
Marvel Comics: Apr, 1997 ($2.99, one-shot)
1 3.00

SPIDER-MAN: DEATH AND DESTINY
Marvel Comics: Aug, 2000 - No. 3, Oct, 2000 ($2.99, limited series)
1-3-Aftermath of the death of Capt. Stacy 3.00

SPIDER-MAN: FRIENDS AND ENEMIES
Marvel Comics: Jan, 1995 - No. 4, Apr, 1995 ($1.95, limited series)
1-4-Darkhawk, Nova & Speedball app. 2.00

SPIDER-MAN: FUNERAL FOR AN OCTOPUS
Marvel Comics: Mar, 1995 - No. 3, May, 1995 ($1.50, limited series)
1-3 2.00

SPIDER-MAN/ GEN 13
Marvel Comics: Nov, 1996 ($4.95, one-shot)
nn-Peter David-s/Stuart Immonen-a 5.00

SPIDER-MAN: HOBGOBLIN LIVES
Marvel Comics: Jan, 1997 - No. 3, Mar, 1997 ($2.50, limited series)
1-3-Wraparound-c 2.50
TPB (1/98, $14.99) r/#1-3 plus timeline 15.00

SPIDER-MAN: HOT SHOTS
Marvel Comics: Jan, 1996 ($2.95, one-shot)
nn-fold out posters by various, inc. Vess and Ross 3.00

SPIDER-MAN: LEGACY OF EVIL
Marvel Comics: June, 1996 ($3.95, one-shot)
1-Kurt Busiek script & Mark Texeira-c/a 4.00

SPIDER-MAN: MADE MEN
Marvel Comics: Aug, 1998 ($5.99, one-shot)
1-Spider-Man & Daredevil vs. Kingpin 6.00

SPIDER-MAN MAGAZINE
Marvel Comics: 1994 - No. 3, 1994 ($1.95, magazine)
1-3: 1-Contains 4 S-M promo cards & 4 X-Men Ultra Fleer cards; Spider-Man story by Romita, Sr.; X-Men story; puzzles & games. 2-Doc Octopus & X-Men stories 3.00

SPIDER-MAN: MAXIMUM CLONAGE
Marvel Comics: 1995 ($4.95)
Alpha #1-Acetate-c, Omega #1-Chromium-c. 5.00

SPIDER-MAN MEGAZINE
Marvel Comics: Oct, 1994 - No. 6, Mar, 1995 ($2.95, 100 pgs.)
1-6: 1-r/ASM #16,224,225, Marvel Team-Up #1 3.00

SPIDER-MAN: POWER OF TERROR
Marvel Comics: Jan, 1995 - No. 4, Apr, 1995 ($1.95, limited series)
1-4-Silvermane & Deathlok app. 2.00

SPIDER-MAN/PUNISHER: FAMILY PLOT
Marvel Comics: Feb, 1996 - No. 2, Mar, 1996 ($2.95, limited series)
1,2 3.00

SPIDER-MAN: REDEMPTION
Marvel Comics: Sept, 1996 - No. 4, Dec, 1996 ($1.50, limited series)
1-4: DeMatteis scripts; Zeck-a 2.00

SPIDER-MAN: REVENGE OF THE GREEN GOBLIN
Marvel Comics: Oct, 2000 - No. 3, Dec, 2000 ($2.99, limited series)
1-3-Frenz & Olliffe-a; continues in AS-M #25 & PP:S-M #25 3.00

SPIDER-MAN SAGA
Marvel Comics: Nov, 1991 - No. 4, Feb, 1992 ($2.95, limited series)
1-4: Gives history of Spider-Man: text & illustrations 3.00

SPIDER-MAN TEAM-UP
Marvel Comics: Dec, 1995 - No. 7, June, 1996 ($2.95)
1-7: 1-w/ X-Men. 2-w/ Silver Surfer. 3-w/Fantastic Four. 4-w/Avengers. 5-Gambit & Howard the Duck-c/app. 7-Thunderbolts-c/app. 3.00

SPIDER-MAN: THE ARACHNIS PROJECT
Marvel Comics: Aug, 1994 - No. 6, Jan, 1995 ($1.75, limited series)
1-6-Venom, Styx, Stone & Jury app. 2.00

SPIDER-MAN: THE CLONE JOURNAL
Marvel Comics: Mar, 1995 ($2.95, one-shot)
1 3.00

Spider-Man Unlimited #1 © MAR

Spider-Woman #18 © MAR

Spidey Super Stories #31 © MAR

GD2.0 FN6.0 NM9.4

SPIDER-MAN: THE FINAL ADVENTURE
Marvel Comics: Nov, 1995 - No. 4, Feb, 1996 ($2.95, limited series)

1-4: 1-Nicieza scripts; foil-c 3.00

SPIDER-MAN: THE JACKAL FILES
Marvel Comics: Aug, 1995 ($1.95, one-shot)

1 2.00

SPIDER-MAN: THE LOST YEARS
Marvel Comics: Aug, 1995-No. 3, Oct, 1995; No. 0, 1996 ($2.95/$3.95,lim. series)

0-(1/96, $3.95)-Reprints. 4.00
1-3-DeMatteis scripts, Romita, Jr.-c/a 3.00
NOTE: ***Romita** c-0i. **Romita, Jr.** a-0r, 1-3p. c-0-3p. **Sharp** a-0r.*

SPIDER-MAN: THE MANGA
Marvel Comics: Dec, 1997 - No. 31, June, 1999 ($3.99/$2.99, B&W, bi-weekly)

1-($3.99)-English translation of Japanese Spider-Man 4.00
2-31-($2.99) 3.00

SPIDER-MAN: THE MUTANT AGENDA
Marvel Comics: No. 0, Feb, 1994; No. 1, Mar, 1994 - No. 3, May, 1994 ($1.75, limited series)

0-(2/94, $1.25, 52 pgs.)-Crosses over w/newspaper strip; has empty pages to paste in newspaper strips; gives origin of Spidey 2.00
1-3: Beast & Hobgoblin app. 1-X-Men app. 2.00

SPIDER-MAN: THE MYSTERIO MANIFESTO (Listed as "Spider-Man and Mysterio" in indicia)
Marvel Comics: Jan, 2001 - No. 3, Mar, 2001 ($2.99, limited series)

1-3-Daredevil-c/app.; Weeks & McLeod-a 3.00

SPIDER-MAN: THE PARKER YEARS
Marvel Comics: Nov, 1995 ($2.50, one-shot)

1 2.50

SPIDER-MAN 2099 (See Amazing Spider-Man #365)
Marvel Comics: Nov, 1992 - No. 46, Aug, 1996 ($1.25/$1.50/$1.95)

1-(stiff-c)-Red foil stamped-c; begins origin of Miguel O'Hara (Spider-Man 2099); Leonardi/Williamson-c/a begins 3.00
1-2nd printing, 2-24,26-46: 2-Origin continued, ends #3. 4-Doom 2099 app. 13-Extra 16 pg. insert on Midnight Sons. 19-Bound-in trading card sheet. 35-Variant-c. 36-Two-c; Jae Lee-a. 37,38-Two-c. 46-The Vulture app; Mike McKone-a(p) 2.00
25-($2.25, 52 pgs.)-Newsstand edition 2.25
25-($2.95, 52 pgs.)-Deluxe edition w/embossed foil-c 3.00
Annual 1 (1994, $2.95, 68 pgs.) 3.00
Special 1 (1995, $3.95) 4.00
NOTE: ***Chaykin** c-37. **Ron Lim** a(p)-18; c(p)-13, 16, 18. **Kelley Jones** c/a-9. **Leonardi/Williamson** a-1-8, 10-13, 15-17, 19, 20, 22-25; c-1-13, 15, 17-19, 20, 22-25, 35.*

SPIDER-MAN 2099 MEETS SPIDER-MAN
Marvel Comics: 1995 ($5.95, one-shot)

nn-Peter David script; Leonardi/Williamson-c/a. 6.00

SPIDER-MAN UNIVERSE
Marvel Comics: Mar, 2000 - Present ($4.95/$3.99, reprints)

1-5-Reprints recent issues from the various Spider-Man titles 5.00
6,7-($3.99) 4.00

SPIDER-MAN UNLIMITED
Marvel Comics: May, 1993 - No. 22, Nov, 1998 ($3.95, quarterly, 68 pgs.)

1-Begin Maximum Carnage storyline, ends; Carnage-c/story 5.00
2-12: 2-Venom & Carnage-c/story; Ron Lim-c/a(p) in #2-6. 10-Vulture app., McManus-a 4.00
13-22: 13-Begin $2.99-c; Scorpion-c/app. 15-Daniel-c; Puma-c/app. 19-Lizard-c/app. 20-Hannibal King and Lilith app. 21,22-Deodato-a 3.00

SPIDER-MAN UNLIMITED (Based on the TV animated series)
Marvel Comics: Dec, 1999 - No. 5, Apr, 2000 ($2.99/$1.99)

1-($2.99) Venom and Carnage app. 2.99
2-5: 2-($1.99) Green Goblin app. 2.00

SPIDER-MAN UNMASKED
Marvel Comics: Nov, 1996 ($5.95, one-shot)

nn-Art w/text 6.00

SPIDER-MAN: VENOM AGENDA
Marvel Comics: Jan, 1998 ($2.99, one-shot)

1-Hama-s/Lyle-c/a 3.00

SPIDER-MAN VS. DRACULA
Marvel Comics: Jan, 1994 ($1.75, 52 pgs., one-shot)

1-r/Giant-Size Spider-Man #1 plus new Matt Fox-a 2.00

SPIDER-MAN VS. WOLVERINE
Marvel Comics Group: Feb, 1987; V2#1, 1990 (68 pgs.)

1-Williamson-c/a(i); intro Charlemagne; death of Ned Leeds (old Hobgoblin) 2.30 7.00 20.00
V2#1 (1990, $4.95)-Reprints #1 (2/87) 5.00

SPIDER-MAN: WEB OF DOOM
Marvel Comics: Aug, 1994 - No. 3, Oct, 1994 ($1.75, limited series)

1-3 2.00

SPIDER-MAN: YEAR IN REVIEW
Marvel Comics: Feb, 2000 ($2.99)

1-Text recaps of 1999 issues 3.00

SPIDER REIGN OF THE VAMPIRE KING, THE (Also see The Spider)
Eclipse Books: 1992 - No. 3, 1992 ($4.95, limited series, coated stock, 52 pgs.)

Book One - Three: Truman scripts & painted-c 5.00

SPIDER'S WEB, THE (See G-8 and His Battle Aces)

SPIDER-WOMAN (Also see The Avengers #240, Marvel Spotlight #32, Marvel Super Heroes Secret Wars #7 & Marvel Two-In-One #29)
Marvel Comics Group: April, 1978 - No. 50, June, 1983 (New logo #47 on)

1-New complete origin & mask added 1.25 3.75 10.00
2-5,7-18,21-27,30,31,33-36,: 2-Excalibur app. 3,11,12-Brother Grimm app. 13,15-The Shroud-c/s. 16-Sienkiewicz-c 4.00
6,19,20,28,29,32: 6-Morgan LeFay app. 6,19,32-Werewolf by Night-c/s. 20,28,29-Spider-Man app. 32-Miller-c 5.00
37,38-X-Men x-over: 37-1st app. Siryn of X-Force; origin retold 2.40 6.00
39-49: 46-Kingpin app. 49-Tigra-c/story 4.00
50-(52 pgs.)-Death of Spider-Woman; photo-c 1.00 3.00 8.00
NOTE: ***Austin** a-37i. **Byrne** c-26p. **Infantino** a-1-19. **Layton** c-19. **Miller** c-32p.*

SPIDER-WOMAN
Marvel Comics: Nov, 1993 - No. 4, Feb, 1994 ($1.75, mini-series)

V2#1-4: 1,2-Origin; U.S. Agent app. 2.00

SPIDER-WOMAN
Marvel Comics: July, 1999 - No. 18, Dec, 2000 ($2.99/$1.99/$2.25)

1-($2.99) Byrne-s/Sears-a 3.00
2-11-($1.99): 2-Two covers 2.00
12-18: 12-Begin $2.25-c. 14-Nolan-a. 15-Capt. America-c/app. 2.25

SPIDEY SUPER STORIES (Spider-Man) (Also see Fireside Books)
Marvel/Children's TV Workshop: Oct, 1974 - No. 57, Mar, 1982 (35¢, no ads)

1-Origin (stories simplified) 3.20 9.60 35.00
2-Kraven 2.30 7.00 20.00
3-10,15: 6-Iceman. 15-Storm-c/sty 1.85 5.50 15.00
11-14,16-20: 19,20-Kirby-c 1.50 4.50 12.00
21-53: 24-Kirby-c. 31-Moondragon-c/story; Dr. Doom app. 33-Hulk. 34-Sub-Mariner. 38-F.F. 39-Thanos-c/story. 44-Vision. 45-Silver Surfer & Dr. Doom app. 1.25 3.75 10.00
54-57: 56-Battles Jack O'Lantern-c/sty (exactly one year after 1st app. in Machine Man #19) 1.85 5.50 15.00

SPIKE AND TYKE (See M.G.M.'s...)

SPIN & MARTY (TV) (Walt Disney's)(See Walt Disney Showcase #32)
Dell Publishing Co. (Mickey Mouse Club): No. 714, June, 1956 - No. 1082, Mar-May, 1960 (All photo-c)

Four Color 714 (#1) 11.70 35.00 140.00
Four Color 767,808 (#2,3) 9.00 27.00 110.00
Four Color 826 (#4)-Annette Funicello photo-c 23.00 70.00 280.00
5(3-5/58) - 9(6-8/59) 7.50 22.50 90.00

The Spirit (Fiction House) #5 © Will Eisner

The Spirit: The New Adventures #8 © Will Eisner

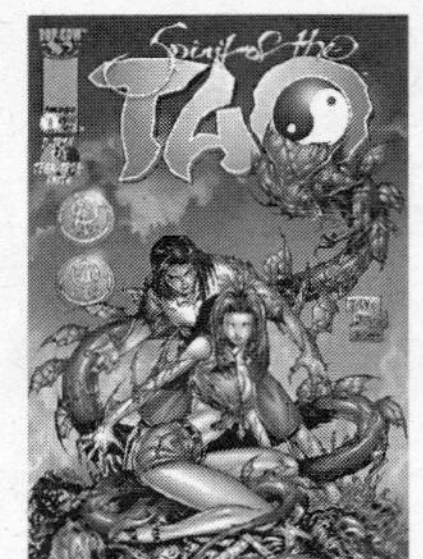
Spirit of the Tao #1 © Top Cow

GD2.0 FN6.0 NM9.4

Four Color 1026,1082 7.50 22.50 90.00

SPINE-TINGLING TALES (Doctor Spektor Presents...)
Gold Key: May, 1975 - No. 4, Jan, 1976 (All 25¢ issues)

1-1st Tragg-r/Mystery Comics Digest #3 1.25 3.75 10.00
2-4: 2-Origin Ra-Ka-Tep-r/Mystery Comics Digest #1; Dr. Spektor #12. 3-All Durak-r issue; 4-Baron Tibor's 1st app.-r/Mystery Comics Digest #4; painted-c 1.00 2.80 7.00

SPINWORLD
Amaze Ink (Slave Labor Graphics): July, 1997 - No. 4, Jan, 1998 ($2.95/$3.95, B&W, mini-series)

1-3-Brent Anderson-a(p) 3.00
4-($3.95) 4.00

SPIRAL PATH, THE
Eclipse Comics: July, 1986 - No. 2 ($1.75, Baxter paper, limited series)

1,2 2.00

SPIRAL ZONE
DC Comics: Feb, 1988 - No. 4, May, 1988 ($1.00, mini-series)

1-4-Based on Tonka toys 2.00

SPIRIT, THE (Newspaper comics - see Promotional Comics section)

SPIRIT, THE (1st Series)(Also see Police Comics #11)
Quality Comics Group (Vital): 1944 - No. 22, Aug, 1950

nn(#1)- "Wanted Dead or Alive" 74.00 221.00 700.00
nn(#2)- "Crime Doesn't Pay" 42.00 125.00 375.00
nn(#3)- "Murder Runs Wild" 38.00 113.00 300.00
4,5: 4-Flatfoot Burns begins, ends #22. 5-Wertham app. 30.00 90.00 240.00
6-10 25.00 75.00 200.00
11 22.00 66.00 175.00
12-17-Eisner-c. 19-Honeybun app. 34.00 103.00 275.00
18-21-Strip-r by Eisner; Eisner-c 40.00 120.00 350.00
22-Used by N.Y. Legis. Comm; classic Eisner-c 53.00 159.00 480.00
Super Reprint #11-r/Quality Spirit #19 by Eisner 3.00 9.00 32.00
Super Reprint #12-r/Spirit #17 by Fine; Sol Brodsky-c 3.00 9.00 32.00

SPIRIT, THE (2nd Series)
Fiction House Magazines: Spring, 1952 - No. 5, 1954

1-Not Eisner 40.00 120.00 350.00
2-Eisner-c/a(2) 40.00 120.00 325.00
3-Eisner/Grandenetti-c 31.00 94.00 250.00
4-Eisner/Grandenetti-c; Eisner-a 33.00 98.00 260.00
5-Eisner-c/a(4) 38.00 113.00 300.00

SPIRIT, THE
Harvey Publications: Oct, 1966 - No. 2, Mar, 1967 (Giant Size, 25¢, 68 pgs.)

1-Eisner-r plus 9 new pgs.(origin Denny Colt, Take 3, plus 2 filler pgs.) (#3 was advertised, but never published) 6.80 20.50 75.00
2-Eisner-r plus 9 new pgs.(origin of the Octopus) 5.90 17.75 65.00

SPIRIT, THE (Underground)
Kitchen Sink Enterprises (Krupp Comics): Jan, 1973 - No. 2, Sept, 1973 (Black & White)

1-New Eisner-c & 4 pgs. new Eisner-a plus-r (titled Crime Convention) 1.85 5.50 15.00
2-New Eisner-c & 4 pgs. new Eisner-a plus-r (titled Meets P'Gell) 2.30 7.00 20.00

SPIRIT, THE (Magazine)
Warren Publ. Co./Krupp Comic Works No. 17 on: 4/74 - No. 16, 10/76; No. 17, Winter, 1977 - No. 41, 6/83 (B&W w/color)

1-Eisner-r begin 3.00 9.00 30.00
2-5 2.30 7.00 20.00
6-9,11-15: 7-All Ebony issue. 8-Female Foes issue. 12-X-Mas issue 1.85 5.50 15.00
10-Giant Summer Special ($1.50)-Origin 2.40 7.35 22.00
16-Giant Summer Special ($1.50) 2.00 6.00 18.00
17,18(8/78): 17-Lady Luck-r 1.10 3.30 9.00
19-21-New Eisner-a. 20,21-Wood-r (#21-r/A DP on the Moon by Wood). 20-Outer Space-r 1.10 3.30 9.00
22-41: 22,23-Wood-r (#22-r/Mission the Moon by Wood). 28-r/last story (10/5/52). 30-(7/81)-Special Spirit Jam issue w/Caniff, Corben, Bolland, Byrne, Miller, Kurtzman, Rogers, Sienkiewicz-a & 40 others. 36-Begin Spirit Section-r; r/1st story (6/2/40) in color; new Eisner-c/a(18 pgs.)($2.95). 37-r/2nd story in color plus 18 pgs. new Eisner-a. 38-41: r/3rd - 6th stories in color. 41-Lady Luck Mr. Mystic in color 1.00 3.00 8.00
Special 1(1975)-All Eisner-a (mail only) 4.10 12.30 45.00

NOTE: *Covers pencilled/inked by* ***Eisner*** *only #1-9,12-16; painted by Eisner & Ken Kelly #10 & 11; painted by Eisner #17-up; one color story reprinted in #1-10.* ***Austin*** *a-30i.* ***Byrne*** *a-30p.* ***Miller*** *a-30p.*

GD2.0 FN6.0 NM9.4

SPIRIT, THE
Kitchen Sink Enterprises: Oct, 1983 - No. 87, Jan, 1992 ($2.00, Baxter paper)

1-60: 1-Origin-r/12/23/45 Spirit Section. 2-r/ 1/20/46-2/10/46. 3-r/2/17/46-3/10/46. 4-r/3/17/46-4/7/46. 11-Last color issue. 54-r/section 2/19/50 3.00
61-87: 85-87-Reprint the Outer Space Spirit stories by Wood. 86-r/A DP on the Moon by Wood from 1952 4.00

SPIRIT JAM
Kitchen Sink Press: Aug, 1998 ($5.95, B&W, oversized, square-bound)

nn-Reprints Spirit (Magazine) #30 by Eisner & 50 others; and "Cerebus Vs. The Spirit" from Cerebus Jam #1 6.00

SPIRIT, THE: THE NEW ADVENTURES
Kitchen Sink Press: 1997 - No. 8, Nov, 1998 ($3.50, anthology)

1-Moore-s/Gibbons-c/a 4.00
2-8: 2-Gaiman-s/Eisner-c. 3-Moore-s/Bolland-c/Moebius back-c. 4-Allred-s/a; Busiek-s/Anderson-a. 5-Chadwick-s/c/a(p); Nyberg-i. 6-S.Hampton & Mandrake-a 3.50

SPIRIT: THE ORIGIN YEARS
Kitchen Sink Press: May, 1992 - No. 10, Dec, 1993 ($2.95, B&W, high quality paper)

1-10: 1-r/sections 6/2/40(origin)-6/23/40 (all 1940s) 3.00

SPIRITMAN (Also see Three Comics)
No publisher listed: No date (1944) (10¢)
(Triangle Sales Co. ad on back cover)

1-Three 16pg. Spirit sections bound together, (1944, 10¢, 52 pgs.) 20.00 60.00 160.00
2-Two Spirit sections (3/26/44, 4/2/44) bound together; by Lou Fine 18.00 53.00 140.00

SPIRIT OF THE BORDER (See Zane Grey & Four Color #197)

SPIRIT OF THE TAO
Image Comics (Top Cow): Jun, 1998 - No. 15, May, 2000 ($2.50)

Preview 5.00
1-14: 1-D-Tron-s/Tan & D-Tron-a 2.50
15-($4.95) 4.95

SPIRIT OF WONDER (Manga)
Dark Horse Comics: Apr, 1996 - No. 5, Aug, 1996 ($2.95, B&W, limited series)

1-5 3.00

SPIRIT WORLD (Magazine)
National Periodical Publications: Fall, 1971 (B&W)

1-New Kirby-a; Neal Adams-c; poster inside 5.45 16.35 60.00
(1/2 price without poster)

SPITFIRE
Malverne Herald (Elliot)(J. R. Mahon): No. 132, 1944 (Aug) - No. 133, 1945 (Female undercover agent)

132,133: Both have Classics Gift Box ads on b/c with checklist to #20 25.00 75.00 200.00

SPITFIRE AND THE TROUBLESHOOTERS
Marvel Comics: Oct, 1986 - No. 9, June, 1987 (Codename: Spitfire #10 on)

1-3,5-9 2.00
4-McFarlane-a 3.00

SPITFIRE COMICS (Also see Double Up)
Harvey Publications: Aug, 1941 - No. 2, Oct, 1941 (Pocket size; 100 pgs.)

Spooky #3 © HARV

Sport Stars #3 © PMI

Spotlight Comics #1 © CHES

GD2.0 FN6.0 NM9.4

1-Origin The Clown, The Fly-Man, The Spitfire & The Magician From Bagdad 76.00 229.00 725.00
2-(Scarce) 68.00 205.00 650.00

SPLITTING IMAGE
Image Comics: Mar, 1993 - No. 2, 1993 ($1.95)
1,2-Simpson-c/a; parody comic 2.00

SPOOF
Marvel Comics Group: Oct, 1970; No. 2, Nov, 1972 - No. 5, May, 1973
1-Infinity-c; Dark Shadows-c & parody 2.00 6.00 18.00
2-5: 3-Beatles, Osmond's, Jackson 5, David Cassidy, Nixon & Agnew-c. 5-Rod Serling, Woody Allen, Ted Kennedy-c 1.50 4.50 12.00

SPOOK (Formerly Shock Detective Cases)
Star Publications: No. 22, Jan, 1953 - No. 30, Oct, 1954
22-Sgt. Spook-r; acid in face story; hanging-c 40.00 120.00 325.00
23,25,27: 25-Jungle Lil-r. 27-Two Sgt. Spook-r 28.00 83.00 220.00
24-Used in **SOTI**, pgs. 182,183-r/Inside Crime #2; Transvestism story 29.00 86.00 230.00
26,28-30: 26-Disbrow-a. 28,29-Rulah app. 29-Jo-Jo app. 30-Disbrow-c/a(2); only Star-c 28.00 83.00 220.00
NOTE: ***L. B. Cole** covers-all issues except #30; a-28(1 pg.). **Disbrow** a-26(2), 28, 29(2), 30(2); No. 30 r/Blue Bolt Weird Tales #114.*

SPOOK COMICS
Baily Publications/Star: 1946
1-Mr. Lucifer story 30.00 90.00 240.00

SPOOKY (The Tuff Little Ghost; see Casper The Friendly Ghost)
Harvey Publications: 11/55 - 139, 11/73; No. 140, 7/74 - No. 155, 3/77; No. 156, 12/77 - No. 158, 4/78; No. 159, 9/78; No. 160, 10/79; No. 161, 9/80
1-Nightmare begins (see Casper #19) 35.00 106.00 425.00
2 18.00 54.00 200.00
3-10(1956-57) 10.00 30.00 110.00
11-20(1957-58) 5.45 16.35 60.00
21-40(1958-59) 3.65 11.00 40.00
41-60 3.00 9.00 30.00
61-80,100 2.50 7.50 24.00
81-99 2.30 7.00 20.00
101-120 1.50 4.50 12.00
121-126,133-140 1.10 3.30 9.00
127-132: All 52 pg. Giants 1.85 5.50 15.00
141-161 2.40 6.00

SPOOKY
Harvey Comics: Nov, 1991 - No. 4, Sept, 1992 ($1.00/$1.25)
1 3.00
2-4: 3-Begin $1.25-c 2.00
...Digest 1-3 (10/92, 6/93, 10/93, $1.75, 100 pgs.)-Casper, Wendy, etc. 4.00

SPOOKY HAUNTED HOUSE
Harvey Publications: Oct, 1972 - No. 15, Feb, 1975
1 3.00 9.00 30.00
2-5 1.85 5.50 15.00
6-10 1.25 3.75 10.00
11-15 1.00 3.00 8.00

SPOOKY MYSTERIES
Your Guide Publ. Co.: No date (1946) (10¢)
1-Mr. Spooky, Super Snooper, Pinky, Girl Detective app. 19.00 56.00 150.00

SPOOKY SPOOKTOWN
Harvey Publ.: 9/61; No. 2, 9/62 - No. 52, 12/73; No. 53, 10/74 - No. 66, 12/76
1-Casper, Spooky; 68 pgs. begin 15.50 46.50 170.00
2 7.65 23.00 85.00
3-5 5.00 15.00 55.00
6-10 3.65 11.00 40.00
11-20 3.00 9.00 30.00
21-39: 39-Last 68 pg. issue 2.50 7.50 24.00
40-45: All 52 pgs. 2.00 6.00 16.00
46-66: 61-Hot Stuff/Spooky team-up story 1.00 3.00 8.00

GD2.0 FN6.0 NM9.4

SPORT COMICS (Becomes True Sport Picture Stories #5 on)
Street & Smith Publications: Oct, 1940 (No mo.) - No. 4, Nov, 1941
1-Life story of Lou Gehrig 53.00 158.00 475.00
2 30.00 90.00 240.00
3,4 26.00 79.00 210.00

SPORT LIBRARY (See Charlton Sport Library)

SPORTS ACTION (Formerly Sport Stars)
Marvel/Atlas Comics (ACI No. 2,3/SAI No. 4-14): No. 2, Feb, 1950 - No. 14, Sept, 1952
2-Powell painted-c; George Gipp life story 40.00 120.00 325.00
1-(nd,no price, no publ., 52pgs, #1 on-c; has same-c as #2; blank inside-c (giveaway?) 21.00 62.00 165.00
3-Everett-a 23.00 68.00 180.00
4-11,14: Weiss-a 21.00 62.00 165.00
12,13: 12-Everett-c. 13-Krigstein-a 23.00 68.00 180.00
NOTE: *Title may have changed after No. 3, to Crime Must Lose No. 4 on, due to publisher change. **Sol Brodsky** c-4-7, 13, 14. **Maneely** c-3, 8-11.*

SPORT STARS
Parents' Magazine Institute (Sport Stars): Feb-Mar, 1946 - No. 4, Aug-Sept, 1946 (Half comic, half photo magazine)
1- "How Tarzan Got That Way" story of Johnny Weissmuller 40.00 120.00 325.00
2-Baseball greats 26.00 79.00 210.00
3,4 23.00 68.00 180.00

SPORT STARS (Becomes Sports Action #2 on)
Marvel Comics (ACI): Nov, 1949 (52 pgs.)
1-Knute Rockne; painted-c 40.00 120.00 350.00

SPORT THRILLS (Formerly Dick Cole; becomes Jungle Thrills #16)
Star Publications: No. 11, Nov, 1950 - No. 15, Nov, 1951
11-Dick Cole begins, ends #13?; Ted Williams & Ty Cobb life stories 30.00 90.00 240.00
12-Joe DiMaggio, Phil Rizzuto stories & photos on-c; L.B. Cole-c/a 24.00 73.00 195.00
13-15-All L. B. Cole-c. 13-Jackie Robinson, Pee Wee Reese stories & photo on-c. 14-Johnny Weissmuler life story 24.00 73.00 195.00
Accepted Reprint #11 (#15 on-c, nd); L.B. Cole-c 8.65 26.00 60.00
Accepted Reprint #12 (nd); L.B. Cole-c; Joe DiMaggio & Phil Rizzuto life stories-r/#12 8.65 26.00 60.00

SPOTLIGHT (TV) (newsstand sales only)
Marvel Comics Group: Sept, 1978 - No. 4, Mar, 1979 (Hanna-Barbera)
1-Huckleberry Hound, Yogi Bear; Shaw-a 2.50 7.50 25.00
2,4: 2-Quick Draw McGraw, Augie Doggie, Snooper & Blabber. 4-Magilla Gorilla, Snagglepuss 2.00 6.00 18.00
3-The Jetsons; Yakky Doodle 2.50 7.50 25.00

SPOTLIGHT COMICS (Becomes Red Seal Comics #14 on?)
Harry 'A' Chesler (Our Army, Inc.): Nov, 1944 - No. 3, 1945
1-The Black Dwarf (cont'd in Red Seal?), The Veiled Avenger, & Barry Kuda begin; Tuska-c 63.00 189.00 600.00
2 55.00 165.00 500.00
3-Injury to eye story (reprinted from Scoop #3) 57.00 172.00 515.00

SPOTTY THE PUP (Becomes Super Pup #4, see Television Puppet Show)
Avon Periodicals/Realistic Comics: No. 2, Oct-Nov, 1953 - No. 3, Dec-Jan, 1953-54 (Also see Funny Tunes)
2,3 5.00 15.00 35.00
nn (1953, Realistic-r) 3.00 7.50 15.00

SPUNKY (...Junior Cowboy)(...Comics #2 on)
Standard Comics: April, 1949 - No. 7, Nov, 1951
1-Text illos by Frazetta 10.00 30.00 70.00
2-Text illos by Frazetta 8.65 26.00 60.00
3-7 5.00 15.00 32.00

SPUNKY THE SMILING SPOOK
Ajax/Farrell (World Famous Comics/Four Star Comic Corp.): Aug, 1957 - No. 4, May, 1958

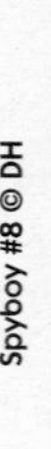

Spy Smasher #3 © FAW

Stalker #4 © DC

	GD2.0	FN6.0	NM9.4
1-Reprints from Frisky Fables	9.30	28.00	65.00
2-4	5.50	16.50	38.00

SPY AND COUNTERSPY (Becomes Spy Hunters #3 on)
American Comics Group: Aug-Sept, 1949 - No. 2, Oct-Nov, 1949 (52 pgs.)

	GD2.0	FN6.0	NM9.4
1-Origin, 1st app. Jonathan Kent, Counterspy	26.00	79.00	210.00
2	16.00	48.00	125.00

SPYBOY
Dark Horse Comics: Oct, 1999 - Present ($2.50/$2.95)

	GD2.0	FN6.0	NM9.4
1-6-Peter David-s/Pop Mhan-a			2.50
7-12-($2.95) 7,8-Meglia-a. 9-12-Mhan-a			2.95

SPY CASES (Formerly The Kellys)
Marvel/Atlas Comics (Hercules Publ.): No. 26, Sept, 1950 - No. 19, Oct, 1953

	GD2.0	FN6.0	NM9.4
26 (#1)	23.00	68.00	180.00
27(#2),28(#3, 2/51): 27-Everett-a; bondage-c	13.00	39.00	105.00
4(4/51) - 7,9,10	11.00	33.00	90.00
8-A-Bomb-c/story	12.50	37.50	100.00
11-19: 10-14-War format	10.00	30.00	70.00

NOTE: ***Sol Brodsky** c-1-5, 8, 9, 11-14, 17, 18. **Maneely** a-8; c-7, 10. **Tuska** a-7.*

SPY FIGHTERS
Marvel/Atlas Comics (CSI): March, 1951 - No. 15, July, 1953
(Cases from official records)

	GD2.0	FN6.0	NM9.4
1-Clark Mason begins; Tuska-a; Brodsky-c	24.00	71.00	190.00
2-Tuska-a	12.50	37.50	100.00
3-13: 3-5-Brodsky-c. 7-Heath-c	11.00	33.00	90.00
14,15-Pakula-a(3), Ed Win-a. 15-Brodsky-c	12.00	36.00	95.00

SPY-HUNTERS (Formerly Spy & Counterspy)
American Comics Group: No. 3, Dec-Jan, 1949-50 - No. 24, June-July, 1953
(#3-14: 52 pgs.)

	GD2.0	FN6.0	NM9.4
3-Jonathan Kent continues, ends #10	23.00	68.00	180.00
4-10: 4,8,10-Starr-a	12.50	37.50	100.00
11-15,17-22,24: 18-War-c begin. 21-War-c/stories begin	10.00	30.00	75.00
16-Williamson-a (9 pgs.)	15.00	45.00	120.00
23-Graphic torture, injury to eye panel	20.00	60.00	160.00

NOTE: ***Drucker** a-12. **Whitney** a-many issues; c-7, 8, 10-12, 15, 16.*

SPYMAN (Top Secret Adventures on cover)
Harvey Publications (Illustrated Humor): Sept, 1966 - No. 3, Feb, 1967 (12¢)

	GD2.0	FN6.0	NM9.4
1-Origin and 1st app. of Spyman. Steranko-a(p)-1st pro work; 1 pg. Neal Adams ad; Tuska-c/a, Crandall-a(i)	5.90	17.75	65.00
2-Simon-c; Steranko-a(p)	3.65	11.00	40.00
3-Simon-c	3.20	9.60	35.00

SPY SMASHER (See Mighty Midget, Whiz & Xmas Comics) (Also see Crime Smasher)
Fawcett Publications: Fall, 1941 - No. 11, Feb, 1943

	GD2.0	FN6.0	NM9.4
1-Spy Smasher begins; silver metallic-c	343.00	1030.00	3600.00
2-Raboy-c	163.00	490.00	1550.00
3,4: 3-Bondage-c. 4-Irvin Steinberg-c	111.00	332.00	1050.00
5-7: Raboy-a; 6-Raboy-c/a. 7-Part photo-c (movie).	100.00	300.00	950.00
8,11: War-c	79.00	237.00	750.00
9-Hitler, Tojo, Mussolini-c.	92.00	276.00	875.00
10-Hitler-c	87.00	261.00	825.00

SPY THRILLERS (Police Badge No. 479 #5)
Atlas Comics (PrPI): Nov, 1954 - No. 4, May, 1955

	GD2.0	FN6.0	NM9.4
1-Brodsky c-1,2	21.00	64.00	170.00
2-Last precode (1/55)	12.00	36.00	95.00
3,4	10.00	30.00	75.00

SQUADRON SUPREME (Also see Marvel Graphic Novel)
Marvel Comics Group: Aug, 1985 - No. 12, Aug, 1986 (Maxi-series)

	GD2.0	FN6.0	NM9.4
1-Double size			3.00
2-12			2.00
TPB ($24.99) r/#1-12; Alex Ross painted-c; printing inks contain some of the cremated remains of late writer Mark Gruenwald			25.00
TPB-2nd printing ($24.99): Inks contain no ashes			25.00

SQUADRON SUPREME: NEW WORLD ORDER
Marvel Comics: Sept, 1998 ($5.99, one-shot)

	GD2.0	FN6.0	NM9.4
1-Wraparound-c; Kaminski-s			6.00

SQUALOR
First Comics: Dec, 1989 - Aug, 1990 ($2.75, limited series)

	GD2.0	FN6.0	NM9.4
1-4: Sutton-a			2.75

SQUEE
Slave Labor Graphics: Apr, 1997 - No. 4, May, 1998 ($2.95, B&W)

	GD2.0	FN6.0	NM9.4
1-4: Jhonen Vasquez-s/a in all			3.00

SQUEEKS (Also see Boy Comics)
Lev Gleason Publications: Oct, 1953 - No. 5, June, 1954

	GD2.0	FN6.0	NM9.4
1-Funny animal; Biro-c; Crimebuster's pet monkey "Squeeks" begins	7.85	23.50	55.00
2-Biro-c	4.65	14.00	28.00
3-5: 3-Biro-c	4.00	12.00	24.00

S.R. BISSETTE'S SPIDERBABY COMIX
SpiderBaby Grafix: Aug, 1996 - No. 2 ($3.95, B&W, magazine size)

	GD2.0	FN6.0	NM9.4
Preview-(8/96, $3.95)-Graphic violence & nudity; Laurel & Hardy app.			4.00
1,2			4.00

S.R. BISSETTE'S TYRANT
SpiderBaby Grafix: Sept, 1994 - No. 4 ($2.95, B&W)

	GD2.0	FN6.0	NM9.4
1-4			4.00

STAINLESS STEEL RAT
Eagle Comics: Oct, 1985 - No. 6, Mar, 1986 (Limited series)

	GD2.0	FN6.0	NM9.4
1 (52 pgs.; $2.25-c)			2.50
2-6 ($1.50)			2.00

STALKER (Also see All Star Comics 1999 and crossover issues)
National Periodical Publications: June-July, 1975 - No. 4, Dec-Jan, 1975-76

	GD2.0	FN6.0	NM9.4
1-Origin & 1st app; Ditko/Wood-c/a	1.25	3.75	10.00
2-4-Ditko/Wood-c/a		2.40	6.00

STALKERS
Marvel Comics (Epic Comics): Apr, 1990 - No. 12, Mar, 1991 ($1.50)

	GD2.0	FN6.0	NM9.4
1-12: 1-Chadwick-c			2.00

STAMP COMICS (Stamps... on-c; Thrilling Adventures In...#8)
Youthful Magazines/Stamp Comics, Inc.: Oct, 1951 - No. 7, Oct, 1952

	GD2.0	FN6.0	NM9.4
1-(15¢) ('Stamps' on indicia No. 1-3,5,7)	29.00	86.00	230.00
2	16.00	49.00	130.00
3-6: 3,4-Kiefer, Wildey-a	14.00	43.00	115.00
7-Roy Krenkel (4 pgs.)	18.00	53.00	140.00

NOTE: *Promotes stamp collecting; gives stories behind various commemorative stamps. No. 2, 10¢ printed over 15¢ c-price. **Kiefer** a-1-7. **Kirkel** a-1-6. **Napoli** a-2-7. **Palais** a-2-4, 7.*

STANLEY & HIS MONSTER (Formerly The Fox & the Crow)
National Periodical Publ.: No. 109, Apr-May, 1968 - No. 112, Oct-Nov, 1968

	GD2.0	FN6.0	NM9.4
109-112	2.50	7.50	25.00

STANLEY & HIS MONSTER
DC Comics: Feb, 1993 - No. 4, May, 1993 ($1.50, limited series)

	GD2.0	FN6.0	NM9.4
1-4			2.00

STAN SHAW'S BEAUTY & THE BEAST
Dark Horse Comics: Nov, 1993 ($4.95, one-shot)

	GD2.0	FN6.0	NM9.4
1			5.00

STAR
Image Comics (Highbrow Entertainment): June, 1995 - No. 4, Oct, 1995 ($2.50, limited series)

	GD2.0	FN6.0	NM9.4
1-4			2.50

STARBLAST
Marvel Comics: Jan, 1994 - No. 4, Apr, 1994 ($1.75, limited series)

	GD2.0	FN6.0	NM9.4
1-4: 1-($2.00, 52 pgs.)-Nova, Quasar, Black Bolt; painted-c			2.00

STAR BLAZERS

Star Comics #13 © CEN

Starfire #3 © DC

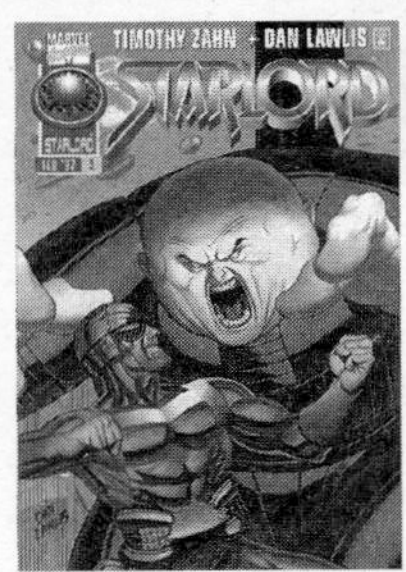

Starlord #3 © MAR

GD2.0 FN6.0 NM9.4

Comico: Apr, 1987 - No. 4, July, 1987 ($1.75, limited series)

1-4 3.00

STAR BLAZERS
Comico: 1989 ($1.95/$2.50, limited series)

1-5- Steacy wraparound painted-c on all 3.00

STAR BLAZERS (The Magazine of Space Battleship Yamato)
Argo Press: No. 0, Aug, 1995 - No. 3, Dec, 1995 ($2.95)

0-3 3.00

STAR BRAND
Marvel Comics (New Universe): Oct, 1986 - No. 19, May, 1989 (75¢/$1.25)

1-15: 14-begin $1.25-c 2.00
16-19-Byrne story & art. 3.00
Annual 1 (10/87) 2.00

STARCHILD
Tailspin Press: 1992 - No. 12($2.25/$2.50, B&W)

1,2-('92),0(4/93),3-12: 0-Illos by Chadwick, Eisner, Sim, M. Wagner. 3-(7/93). 4-(11/93). 6-(2/94) 3.00

STARCHILD: MYTHOPOLIS
Image Comics: No. 0, July, 1997 - No. 4, Apr, 1998 ($2.95, B&W, limited series)

0-4-James Owen-s/a 3.00

STAR COMICS
Ultem Publ. (Harry `A' Chesler)/Centaur Publications: Feb, 1937 - V2#7 (No. 23), Aug, 1939 (#1-6: large size)

V1#1-Dan Hastings (s/f) begins 168.00 505.00 1600.00
2 76.00 229.00 725.00
3-6 (#6, 9/37): 4,5-Little Nemo-c/stories 68.00 205.00 650.00
7-9: 8-Severed head centerspread; Impy & Little Nemo by Winsor McCay Jr, Popeye app. by Bob Wood; Mickey Mouse & Popeye app. as toys in Santa's bag on-c; X-Mas-c 61.00 182.00 575.00
10 (1st Centaur; 3/38)-Impy by Winsor McCay Jr; Don Marlow by Guardineer begins 84.00 253.00 800.00
11-1st Jack Cole comic-a, 1 pg. (4/38) 61.00 182.00 575.00
12-15: 12-Riders of the Golden West begins; Little Nemo app. 15-Speed Silvers by Gustavson & The Last Pirate by Burgos begins 55.00 165.00 500.00
16 (12/38)-The Phantom Rider & his horse Thunder begins, ends V2#6 55.00 165.00 520.00
V2#1(#17, 2/39)-Phantom Rider-c (only non-funny-c) 57.00 171.00 540.00
2-7(#18-23): 2-Diana Deane by Tarpe Mills app. 3-Drama of Hollywood by Mills begins. 7-Jungle Queen app. 49.00 147.00 440.00

NOTE: ***Biro** c-6, 9, 10. **Burgos** a-15, 16, V2#1-7. **Ken Ernst** a-10, 12, 14. **Filchock** c-15, 18, 22. **Gill Fox** c-14, 19. **Guardineer** a-6, 8-14. **Gustavson** a-13-16, V2#1-7. **Winsor McCay** c-4, 5. **Tarpe Mills** a-15, V2#1-7. **Schwab** c-20, 23. **Bob Wood** a-10, 12, 13; c-7, 8.*

STAR COMICS MAGAZINE
Marvel Comics (Star Comics): Dec, 1986 - No. 13, 1988 ($1.50, digest-size)

1,9-Spider-Man-c/s 1.25 3.75 10.00
2-8-Heathcliff, Ewoks, Top Dog, Madballs-r in #1-13 1.00 2.80 7.00
10-13 1.00 3.00 8.00

S.T.A.R. CORPS
DC Comics: Nov, 1993 - No. 6, Apr, 1994 ($1.50, limited series)

1-6: 1,2-Austin-c(i). 1-Superman app. 2.00

STAR CROSSED
DC Comics (Helix): June, 1997 - No. 3, Aug, 1997 ($2.50, limited series)

1-3-Matt Howarth-s/a 2.50

STARDUST (See Neil Gaiman and Charles Vess' Stardust)

STAR FEATURE COMICS
I. W. Enterprises: 1963

Reprint #9-Stunt-Man Stetson-r/Feat. Comics #141 1.50 4.50 12.00

STARFIRE (Not the Teen Titans character)
National Periodical Publ./DC Comics: Aug-Sept, 1976 - No. 8, Oct-Nov, 1977

1-Origin (CCA stamp fell off cover art; so it was approved by code) 1.25 3.75 10.00
2-8 2.40 6.00

STARGATE (Movie)
Entity Comics: July, 1996 - No. 4, Oct, 1996 ($2.95, limited series)

1-4: Based on film 3.00
1-4-($3.50): Special Edition foil-c 3.50

STARGATE: DOOMSDAY WORLD (Movie)
Entity Comics: Nov, 1996 - No. 3, Jan, 1997 ($2.95, limited series)

1-3 3.00
1-3-($3.50)-Foil-c 3.50

STARGATE: ONE NATION UNDER RA (Movie)
Entity Comics: Apr, 1997 ($2.75, B&W, one-shot)

1-($2.75) 3.00
1-($3.50)-Foil-c 3.50

STARGATE: REBELLION (Movie)
Entity Comics: May/June, 1997 - No. 3, Nov, 1997 ($2.75, B&W, limited series)

1-3 3.00
1-3-($3.50)-Gold foil-c 3.50

STARGATE: THE NEW ADVENTURES COLLECTION (Movie)
Entity Comics: Dec, 1997 ($5.95, B&W)

1-Regular and photo-c 6.00

STARGATE: UNDERWORLD (Movie)
Entity Comics: May, 1997 ($2.75, B&W, one-shot)

1 3.00

STAR HUNTERS (See DC Super Stars #16)
National Periodical Publ./DC Comics: Oct-Nov, 1977 - No. 7, Oct-Nov, 1978

1,7: 1-Newton-a(p). 7-44 pgs. 1.00 3.00 8.00
2-6 5.00

NOTE: ***Buckler** a-4-7p; c-1-7p. **Layton** a-1-5i; c-1-6i. **Nasser** a-3p. **Sutton** a-6i.*

STARJAMMERS (See X-Men Spotlight on Starjammers)

STARJAMMERS (Also see Uncanny X-Men)
Marvel Comics: Oct, 1995 - No. 4, Jan, 1996 ($2.95, limited series)

1-4: Foil-c; Ellis scripts 3.00

STARK TERROR
Stanley Publications: Dec, 1970 - No. 5, Aug, 1971 (B&W, magazine, 52 pgs.)

1-Bondage, torture-c 4.10 12.30 45.00
2-4 (Gillmor/Aragon-r) 2.80 8.40 28.00
5 (ACG-r) 2.50 7.50 24.00

STARLET O'HARA IN HOLLYWOOD (Teen-age) (Also see Cookie)
Standard Comics: Dec, 1948 - No. 4, Sept, 1949

1-Owen Fitzgerald-a in all 19.00 56.00 150.00
2 12.50 37.50 100.00
3,4 10.50 32.00 85.00

STAR-LORD THE SPECIAL EDITION (Also see Marvel Comics Super Special #10, Marvel Premiere & Preview & Marvel Spotlight V2#6,7)
Marvel Comics Group: Feb, 1982 (one-shot, direct sales)
(1st Baxter paper comic)

1-Byrne/Austin-a; Austin-c; 8 pgs. of new-a by Golden (p); Dr. Who story by Dave Gibbons; 1st deluxe format comic 2.40 6.00

STARLORD
Marvel Comics: Dec, 1996 - No. 3, Feb, 1997 ($2.50, limited series)

1-3-Timothy Zahn-s 2.50

STARLORD MEGAZINE
Marvel Comics: Nov, 1996 ($2.95, one-shot)

1-Reprints w/preview of new series 3.00

STARMAN (1st Series) (Also see Justice League & War of the Gods)
DC Comics: Oct, 1988 - No. 45, Apr, 1992 ($1.00)

1-25,29-45: 1-Origin. 4-Intro The Power Elite. 9,10,34-Batman app. 14-Superman app. 17-Power Girl app. 38-War of the Gods x-over. 42-Lobo cameo. 42-45-Eclipso-c/stories (#43,44 with Lobo) 2.50

Starman (2nd series) #72 © DC

Star Ranger Funnies (2nd series) #15 © CEN

Stars and S.T.R.I.P.E. #4 © DC

26-1st app. David Knight (G.A.Starman's son). 5.00
27,28: 27-Starman (David Knight) app. 28-Starman disguised as Superman; leads into Superman #50 4.00

STARMAN (2nd Series) (Also see The Golden Age, Showcase 95 #12, Showcase 96 #4,5)
DC Comics : No. 0, Oct, 1994 - No. 80, Aug, 2001 ($1.95/$2.25/$2.50)

0,1: 0-James Robinson scripts, Tony Harris-c/a(p) & Wade Von Grawbadger-a(i) begins; Sins of the Father storyline begins, ends #3; 1st app. new Starman (Jack Knight); reintro of the G.A. Mist & G.A. Shade; 1st app. Nash; David Knight dies 1.10 3.30 9.00
2-7: 2-Reintro Charity from Forbidden Tales of Dark Mansion. 3-Reintro/2nd app "Blue" Starman (1st app. in 1st Issue Special #12); Will Payton app. (both cameos). 5-David Knight app. 6-The Shade "Times Past" story; Teddy Kristiansen-a. 7-The Black Pirate cameo 1.00 2.80 7.00
8-17: 8-Begin $2.25-c. 10-1st app. new Mist (Nash). 11-JSA "Times Past" story; Matt Smith-a. 12-16-Sins of the Child. 17-The Black Pirate app. 4.00
18-37: 18-G.A. Starman "Times Past" story; Watkiss-a. 19-David Knight app. 20-23-G.A. Sandman app. 24-26-Demon Quest; all 3 covers make-up triptych. 33-36-Batman-c/app. 37-David Knight and deceased JSA members app. 3.00
38-49,51-56: 38-Nash vs. Justice League Europe. 39,40-Crossover w/ Power of Shazam! #35,36; Bulletman app. 42-Demon-c/app. 43-JLA-c/app. 44-Phantom Lady-c/app. 46-Gene Ha-a. 51-Jor-el app. 52,53-Adam Strange-c/app. 2.50
50-($3.95) Gold foil logo on-c; Star Boy (LSH) app. 4.00
57-76: 57-62-Painted covers by Harris and Alex Ross. 72-Death of Ted Knight. 73-Eulogy. 74-Scalphunter flashback; Heath-a. 75-Superman-c/app. 2.50
#1,000,000 (11/98) 853rd Century x-over; Snejbjerg-a 2.50
Annual 1 (1996, $3.50)-Legends of the Dead Earth story; Prince Gavyn & G.A. Starman stories; J.H. Williams III, Bret Blevins, Craig Hamilton-c/a(p) 4.00
Annual 2 (1997, $3.95)-Pulp Heroes story; 4.00
...80 Page Giant (1/99, $4.95) Harris-c 5.00
...Secret Files 1 (4/98, $4.95)-Origin stories and profile pages 5.00
...The Mist (6/98, $1.95) Girlfrenzy; Mary Marvel app. 2.00
Infernal Devices-($17.95, TPB) r/#29-35,37,38 18.00
Night and Day-($14.95, TPB)-r/#7-10,12-16 15.00
Sins of the Father-($12.95, TPB)-r/#0-5 13.00
Times Past-($17.95, TPB)-r/stories of other Starmen 18.00

STARMASTERS
Americomics: Mar, 1984 ($1.50, one-shot)

1-Origin The Women of W.O.S.P. & Breed 3.00

STAR PRESENTATION, A (Formerly My Secret Romance #1,2; Spectacular Stories #4 on) (Also see This Is Suspense)
Fox Features Syndicate (Hero Books): No. 3, May, 1950

3-Dr. Jekyll & Mr. Hyde by Wood & Harrison (reprinted in Startling Terror Tales #10); "The Repulsing Dwarf" by Wood; Wood-c 55.00 165.00 500.00

STAR QUEST COMIX (Warren Presents... on cover)
Warren Publications: Oct, 1978

1-Corben, Maroto, Neary-a; Ken Kelly-c 1.50 4.50 12.00

STAR RAIDERS (See DC Graphic Novel #1)

STAR RANGER (Cowboy Comics #13 on)
Ultem Publ./Centaur Publ.: Feb, 1937 - No. 12, May, 1938 (Large size: No. 1-6)

1-(1st Western comic)-Ace & Deuce, Air Plunder; Creig Flessel-a 174.00 521.00 1650.00
2 79.00 237.00 750.00
3-6 71.00 213.00 675.00
7-9: 8(12/37)-Christmas-c; Air Patrol, Gold coast app.; Guardineer centerfold 55.00 165.00 520.00
V2#10 (1st Centaur; 3/38) 84.00 253.00 800.00
11,12 63.00 189.00 600.00
NOTE: ***J. Cole*** *a-10, 12; c-12.* ***Ken Ernst*** *a-11.* ***Gill Fox*** *a-8(illo), 9, 10.* ***Guardineer*** *a-1, 3, 6, 7, 8(illos), 9, 10, 12.* ***Gustavson*** *a-8-10, 12.* ***Fred Schwab*** *c-2-11.* ***Bob Wood*** *a-8-10.*

STAR RANGER FUNNIES (Formerly Cowboy Comics)
Centaur Publications: V1#15, Oct, 1938 - V2#5, Oct, 1939

V1#15-Lyin Lou, Ermine, Wild West Junior, The Law of Caribou County by Eisner, Cowboy Jake, The Plugged Dummy, Spurs by Gustavson, Red Coat, Two Buckaroos & Trouble Hunters begin 97.00 292.00 925.00
V2#1 (1/39) 71.00 213.00 675.00
2-5: 2-Night Hawk by Gustavson. 4-Kit Carson app. 61.00 182.00 575.00
NOTE: ***Jack Cole*** *a-V2#1, 3; c-V2#1.* ***Filchock*** *c-V2#2, 3.* ***Guardineer*** *a-V2#3.* ***Gustavson*** *a-V2#2.* ***Pinajian*** *c/a-V2#5.*

STAR REACH
Star Reach Publ.: Apr, 1974 - No. 18 (B&W, #12-15 w/color)

1-(75¢, 52 pgs.) Art by Starlin, Simonson. Chaykin-c/a; origin Death. Cody Starbuck-sty 1.75 5.25 14.00
1-2nd, 3th, and 4th printings ($1.00-$1.50-c) 5.00
2-11: 2-Adams, Giordano-a; 1st Stephanie Starr-c/s. 3-1st Linda Lovecraft. 4-1st Sherlock Duck. 5-1st Gideon Faust by Chaykin. 6-Elric-c. 7-BWS-c. 9-14-Sacred & Profane-c/s by Steacy. 11-Samurai 1.00 2.80 7.00
2-2nd printing 4.00
12-15 (44 pgs.): 12-Zelazny-s. Nasser-a, Brunner-c 1.25 3.75 10.00
16-18-Magazine size: 17-Poe's Raven-c/s 1.00 3.00 8.00
NOTE: ***Adams*** *c-2.* ***Bonivert*** *a-17.* ***Brunner*** *a-3,5; c-3,10,12.* ***Chaykin*** *a-1,4,5; c-1(1st ed),4,5; back-c-1(2nd,3rd,4th ed).* ***Gene Day*** *a-6,8,9,11,15.* ***Friedrich*** *s-2,3,8,10.* ***Gasbarri*** *a-7.* ***Gilbert*** *a-9,12.* ***Giordano*** *a-2.* ***Gould*** *a-6.* ***Hirota/Mukaide*** *s/a-7.* ***Jones*** *c-6.* ***Konz*** *a-17.* ***Leialoha*** *a-3,4,6-i, 13,15; c-13,15.* ***Lyda*** *a-6,12-15.* ***Marrs*** *a-2-5,7,10,14,15,16,18; c-18; back-c-2.* ***Mukaide*** *a-18.* ***Nasser*** *a-12.* ***Nino*** *a-6;* ***Russell*** *a-8,10; c-8.* ***Dave Sim*** *s-7; lettering-9.* ***Simonson*** *a-1.* ***Skeates*** *a-1,2.* ***Starlin*** *a-1(x2), 2(x2); back-c-1(1st ed); c-1(2nd,3rd,4th ed).* ***Barry Smith*** *c-7.* ***Staton*** *a-5,6,7.* ***Steacy*** *a-8-14; c-9,11,14,16.* ***Vosburg*** *a-2-5,7,10.* ***Workman*** *a-2-5,8.*
Nudity panels in most. Wraparound-c: 3-5,7-11,13-16,18.

STAR REACH CLASSICS
Eclipse Comics: Mar, 1984 - No. 6, Aug, 1984 ($1.50, Baxter paper)

1-6: 1-Neal Adams-r/Star Reach #1 3.00
NOTE: ***Dave Sim*** *a-1.* ***Starlin*** *a-1.*

STARR FLAGG, UNDERCOVER GIRL (See Undercover...)

STARRIORS
Marvel Comics: Aug, 1984 - Feb, 1985 (Limited series) (Based on Tomy toys)

1-4 3.00

STARS AND S.T.R.I.P.E. (Also see JSA)
DC Comics: July, 1999 - No. 14, Sept, 2000 ($2.95/$2.50)

0-($2.95) Moder and Weston-a; Starman app. 3.00
1-Johns and Robinson-s/Moder-a; origin new Star Spangled Kid 2.50
2-14: 4-Marvel Family app. 9-Seven Soldiers of Victory-c/app. 2.50

STARS AND STRIPES COMICS
Centaur Publications: No. 2, May, 1941 - No. 6, Dec, 1941

2(#1)-The Shark, The Iron Skull, A-Man, The Amazing Man, Mighty Man, Minimidget begin; The Voice & Dash Dartwell, the Human Meteor, Reef Kinkaid app.; Gustavson Flag-c 221.00 663.00 2100.00
3-Origin Dr. Synthe; The Black Panther app. 124.00 371.00 1175.00
4-Origin/1st app. The Stars and Stripes; injury to eye-c 111.00 332.00 1050.00
5(#5 on cover & inside) 76.00 229.00 725.00
5(#6)-(#5 on cover, #6 on inside) 76.00 229.00 725.00
NOTE: ***Gustavson*** *c/a-3.* ***Myron Strauss*** *c-4, 5(#5), 5(#6).*

STAR SEED (Formerly Powers That Be)
Broadway Comics: No. 7, 1996 - No. 9 ($2.95)

7-9 3.00

STARSHIP TROOPERS
Dark Horse Comics: 1997 - No. 2, 1997 ($2.95, limited series)

1,2-Movie adaption 3.00

STARSHIP TROOPERS: BRUTE CREATIONS
Dark Horse Comics: 1997 ($2.95, one-shot)

1 3.00

STARSHIP TROOPERS: DOMINANT SPECIES
Dark Horse Comics: Aug, 1998 - No. 4, Nov, 1998 ($2.95, limited series)

1-4-Strnad-s/Bolton-c 3.00

STARSHIP TROOPERS: INSECT TOUCH
Dark Horse Comics: 1997 - No. 3, 1997 ($2.95, limited series)

Star Spangled Comics #25 © DC

Star Spangled Comics #116 © DC

Star Spangled War Stories #7 © DC

GD2.0 FN6.0 NM9.4

1-3 3.00

STAR SLAMMERS (See Marvel Graphic Novel #6)
Malibu Comics (Bravura): May, 1994 - No. 4, Aug, 1994 ($2.50, unfinished limited series)

1-4: W. Simonson-a/stories; contain Bravura stamps 2.50

STAR SLAMMERS SPECIAL
Dark Horse Comics (Legend): June, 1996 ($2.95, one-shot)

nn-Simonson-c/a/scripts; concludes Bravura limited series. 3.00

STARSLAYER
Pacific Comics/First Comics No. 7 on: Feb, 1982 - No. 6, Apr, 1983; No. 7, Aug, 1983 - No. 34, Nov, 1985

1-Origin & 1st app.; excessive blood & gore; 1 pg. Rocketeer cameo which continues in #2 5.00
2-Origin/1st full app. the Rocketeer (4/82) by Dave Stevens (Chapter 1 of Rocketeer saga; see Pacific Presents #1,2) 1.00 3.00 8.00
3-Chapter 2 of Rocketeer saga by Stevens 2.40 6.00
4,6,7: 7-Grell-a ends 3.00
5-2nd app. Groo the Wanderer by Aragones 1.00 2.80 7.00
8-34: 10-1st app. Grimjack (11/83, ends #17). 18-Starslayer meets Grimjack. 20-The Black Flame begins (9/84, 1st app.), ends #33. 27-Book length Black Flame story 2.00

NOTE: ***Grell** a-1-7; c-1-8. **Stevens** back c-2, 3. **Sutton** a-17p, 20-22p, 24-27p, 29-33p.*

STARSLAYER (The Director's Cut)
Acclaim Comics (Windjammer): June, 1994 - No. 8, Dec, 1995 ($2.50)

1-8: Mike Grell-c/a/scripts 2.50

STAR SPANGLED COMICS (Star Spangled War Stories #131 on)
National Periodical Publications: Oct, 1941 - No. 130, July, 1952

1-Origin/1st app. Tarantula; Captain X of the R.A.F., Star Spangled Kid (see Action #40), Armstrong of the Army begin; Robot-c 478.00 1435.00 5500.00
2 168.00 505.00 1600.00
3-5 105.00 316.00 1000.00
6-Last Armstrong/Army; Penniless Palmer begins 63.00 189.00 600.00
7-(4/42)-Origin/1st app. The Guardian by S&K, & Robotman (by Paul Cassidy & created by Siegel);The Newsboy Legion (1st app.), Robotman & TNT begin; last Captain X 626.00 1878.00 7200.00
8-Origin TNT & Dan the Dyna-Mite 232.00 695.00 2200.00
9,10 168.00 505.00 1600.00
11-17 126.00 379.00 1200.00
18-Origin Star Spangled Kid 158.00 474.00 1500.00
19-Last Tarantula 126.00 379.00 1200.00
20-Liberty Belle begins (5/43) 132.00 395.00 1250.00
21-29-Last S&K issue; 23-Last TNT. 25-Robotman by Jimmy Thompson begins. 29-Intro Robbie the Robotdog 103.00 308.00 975.00
30-40: 31-S&K-c 58.00 174.00 550.00
41-50: 41,49-Kirby-c 53.00 158.00 475.00
51-64: Last Newsboy Legion & The Guardian; last Liberty Belle? 51-Robot-c by Kirby. 53 by S&K 50.00 150.00 450.00
65-Robin begins with c/app. (2/47); Batman cameo in 1 panel; Robin-c begins, end #95 147.00 442.00 1400.00
66-Batman cameo in Robin story 84.00 253.00 800.00
67,68,70-80: 72-Burnley Robin-c 68.00 205.00 650.00
69-Origin/1st app. Tomahawk by F. Ray; atom bomb story & splash (6/47) 103.00 308.00 975.00
81-Origin Merry, Girl of 1000 Gimmicks in Star Spangled Kid story 53.00 160.00 480.00
82,85: 82-Last Robotman? 53.00 160.00 480.00
83-Tomahawk enters the lost valley, a land of dinosaurs; Capt. Compass begins, ends #130 53.00 160.00 480.00
84,87 (Rare): 87-Batman cameo in Robin 79.00 237.00 750.00
86-Batman cameo in Robin story; last Star Spangled Kid 58.00 174.00 550.00
88(1/49)-94: Batman-c/stories in all. 91-Federal Men begin, end #93. 94-Manhunters Around the World begin, end #121 61.00 182.00 575.00
95-Batman story; last Robin-c 55.00 165.00 525.00
96,98-Batman cameo in Robin stories. 96-1st Tomahawk-c (also #97-121) 40.00 120.00 340.00
97,99 35.00 105.00 280.00
100 (1/50)-Pre-Bat-Hound tryout in Robin story (pre-dates Batman #92). 40.00 120.00 350.00
101-109,118,119,121: 121-Last Tomahawk-c 33.00 98.00 260.00
110,111,120-Batman cameo in Robin stories. 120-Last 52 pg. issue 34.00 101.00 270.00
112-Batman & Robin story 36.00 108.00 290.00
113-Frazetta-a (10 pgs.) 42.00 125.00 375.00
114-Retells Robin's origin (3/51); Batman & Robin story 44.00 133.00 400.00
115,117-Batman app. in Robin stories 36.00 108.00 290.00
116-Flag-c 36.00 107.00 285.00
122-(11/51)-Ghost Breaker-c/stories begin (origin/1st app.), ends #130 (Ghost Breaker covers #122-130) 40.00 120.00 340.00
123-126,128,129 30.00 90.00 240.00
127-Batman cameo 31.00 94.00 250.00
130-Batman cameo in Robin story 34.00 101.00 270.00

NOTE: *Most all issues after #29 signed by Simon & Kirby are not by them. **Bill Ely** c-122-130. **Mortimer** c-65-74(most), 76-95(most). **Fred Ray** c-96-106, 109, 110, 112, 113, 115-120. **S&K** c-7-31, 33, 34, 36, 37, 39, 40, 48, 49, 50-54, 56-58. **Hal Sherman** c-1-6. **Dick Sprang** c-75.*

STAR SPANGLED COMICS (Also see All Star Comics 1999 crossover titles)
DC Comics: May, 1999 ($1.99, one-shot)

1-Golden Age Sandman and the Star Spangled Kid 2.00

STAR SPANGLED KID (See Action #40, Leading Comics & Star Spangled Comics)

STAR SPANGLED WAR STORIES (Formerly Star Spangled Comics #1-130; Becomes The Unknown Soldier #205 on) (See Showcase)
National Periodical Publications: No. 131, 8/52 - No. 133, 10/52; No. 3, 11/52 - No. 204, 2-3/77

131(#1) 84.00 252.00 925.00
132 59.00 177.00 650.00
133-Used in **POP**, pg. 94 50.00 150.00 550.00
3-6: 4-Devil Dog Dugan app. 6-Evans-a 29.00 87.00 320.00
7-10 23.50 71.00 260.00
11-20 20.00 60.00 220.00
21-30: 30-Last precode (2/55) 17.50 52.00 190.00
31-33,35-40 12.00 36.00 130.00
34-Krigstein-a 12.50 37.00 135.00
41-44,46-50: 50-1st S.A. issue 11.50 34.00 125.00
45-1st DC grey tone-c (5/56) 13.50 40.00 150.00
51,52,54-63,65,66, 68-83 7.65 23.00 85.00
53-"Rock Sergeant," 3rd Sgt. Rock prototype; inspired "P.I. & The Sand Fleas" in G.I. Combat #56 (1/57) 13.00 39.00 145.00
64-Pre-Sgt. Rock Easy Co. story (12/57) 11.00 33.00 120.00
67-2 Easy Co. stories without Sgt. Rock 12.00 36.00 130.00
84-Origin Mlle. Marie 16.50 49.00 180.00
85-89-Mlle. Marie in all 9.50 28.50 105.00
90-1st app. "War That Time Forgot" series; dinosaur issue-c/story (4-5/60) 33.00 100.00 400.00
91,93-No dinosaur stories 7.65 23.00 85.00
92-2nd dinosaur-c/s 12.50 37.00 135.00
94 (12/60)- "Ghost Ace" story; Baron Von Richter as The Enemy Ace (pre-dates Our Army... #151) 17.00 51.00 185.00
95-99: Dinosaur-c/s 11.50 34.00 125.00
100-Dinosaur-c/story. 13.50 40.00 150.00
101-115: All dinosaur issues 9.50 28.50 105.00
116-125,127-133,135-137-Last dinosaur story; Heath Birdman-#129,131 8.65 26.00 95.00
126-No dinosaur story 6.35 19.00 70.00
134-Dinosaur story; Neal Adams-a 10.00 30.00 110.00
138-New Enemy Ace-c/stories begin by Joe Kubert (4-5/68), end #150 (also see Our Army at War #151 and Showcase #57) 11.00 33.00 120.00
139-Origin Enemy Ace (7/68) 8.15 24.50 90.00
140-143,145: 145-Last 12¢ issue (6-7/69) 5.45 16.35 60.00
144-Neal Adams/Kubert-a 6.80 20.50 75.00
146-Enemy Ace-c only 3.45 10.35 38.00
147,148-New Enemy Ace stories 4.10 12.30 45.00
149,150-Last new Enemy Ace by Kubert. Viking Prince by Kubert

Startling Comics #3 © Nedor

Startling Terror Tales (2nd series) #5 © STAR

Star Trek #9 © Paramount

GD2.0 FN6.0 NM9.4

3.65 11.00 40.00
151-1st solo app. Unknown Soldier (6-7/70); Enemy Ace-r begin (from Our Army at War, Showcase & SSWS); end #161 13.50 40.00 150.00
152,153,155-Enemy Ace reprints 2.50 7.50 25.00
154-Origin Unknown Soldier 10.00 30.00 110.00
156-1st Battle Album; Unknown Soldier story; Kubert-c/a
2.50 7.50 25.00
157-Sgt. Rock x-over in Unknown Soldier story. 2.40 7.35 22.00
158-163-(52 pgs.): New Unknown Soldier stories; Kubert-c/a. 161-Last Enemy Ace-r 1.85 5.50 15.00
164-183,200: 181-183-Enemy Ace vs. Balloon Buster serial app; Frank Thorne-a. 200-Enemy Ace back-up 1.50 4.50 12.00
184-199,201-204 1.10 3.30 9.00

NOTE: ***Anderson** a-28. **Chaykin** a-167. **Drucker** a-59, 61, 64, 66, 67, 73-84. **Estrada** a-149. **John Giunta** a-72. **Glanzman** a-167, 171, 172, 174. **Heath** a-122, 132, 133; c-67, 122, 132-134. **Kaluta** a-197i; c-167. **G. Kane** a-169. **Kubert** a-6-163(most later issues), 200. **Maurer** a-160, 165. **Severin** a-65, 162. **S&K** c-7-31, 33, 34, 37, 40. **Simonson** a-170, 172, 174, 180. **Sutton** a-168. **Thorne** a-183. **Toth** a-164. **Wildey** a-161. Suicide Squad in 110, 116-118, 120, 121, 127.*

STARSTREAM (Adventures in Science Fiction)(See Questar illustrated)
Whitman/Western Publishing Co.: 1976 (79¢, 68 pgs, cardboard-c)

1-4: 1-Bolle-a. 2-4-McWilliams & Bolle-a 1.50 4.50 12.00

STARSTRUCK
Marvel Comics (Epic Comics): Feb, 1985 - No. 6, Feb, 1986 ($1.50, mature)

1-6: Kaluta-a 3.00

STARSTRUCK
Dark Horse Comics: Aug, 1990 - No. 4, Nov?, 1990 ($2.95, B&W, 52pgs.)

1-3:Kaluta-r/Epic series plus new-c/a in all 3.00
4 (68, pgs.)-contains 2 trading cards 3.00

STAR STUDDED
Cambridge House/Superior Publishers: 1945 (25¢, 132 pgs.); 1945 (196 pgs.)

nn-Captain Combat by Giunta, Ghost Woman, Commandette, & Red Rogue app.; Infantino-a 31.00 94.00 250.00
nn-The Cadet, Edison Bell, Hoot Gibson, Jungle Lil (196 pgs.); copies vary; Blue Beetle in some 26.00 79.00 210.00

STARTLING COMICS
Better Publications (Nedor): June, 1940 - No. 53, Sept, 1948

1-Origin Captain Future-Man Of Tomorrow, Mystico (By Eisner/Fine), The Wonder Man; The Masked Rider & his horse Pinto begins; Masked Rider formerly in pulps; drug use story 242.00 726.00 2300.00
2 -Don Davis, Espionage Ace begins 95.00 285.00 900.00
3 79.00 237.00 750.00
4 58.00 174.00 550.00
5-9 50.00 150.00 450.00
10-The Fighting Yank begins (9/41, origin/1st app.)
333.00 1000.00 3500.00
11-2nd app. Fighting Yank 105.00 316.00 1000.00
12-Hitler, Hirohito, Mussolini-c 84.00 253.00 800.00
13-15 58.00 174.00 550.00
16-Origin The Four Comrades; not in #32,35 63.00 189.00 600.00
17-Last Masked Rider & Mystico 47.00 142.00 425.00
18-Pyroman begins (12/42, origin)(also see America's Best Comics #3 for 1st app., 11/42) 95.00 285.00 900.00
19 47.00 142.00 425.00
20,21: 20-The Oracle begins (3/43); not in issues 26,28,33,34. 21-Origin The Ape, Oracle's enemy 50.00 150.00 450.00
22-34: 34-Origin The Scarab & only app. 47.00 142.00 425.00
35-Hypodermic syringe attacks Fighting Yank in drug story
50.00 150.00 450.00
36-43: 36-Last Four Comrades. 38-Bondage/torture-c. 40-Last Capt. Future & Oracle. 41-Front Page Peggy begins; A-Bomb-c. 43-Last Pyroman
40.00 120.00 360.00
44,45: 44-Lance Lewis, Space Detective begins; Ingels-c; sci/fi-c begin. 45-Tygra begins (intro/origin, 5/47); Ingels-c/a (splash pg. & inside f/c B&W ad
63.00 189.00 600.00
46-Classic Ingels-c; Ingels-a 95.00 285.00 900.00
47,48,50-53: 50,51-Sea-Eagle app. 58.00 174.00 550.00
49-Classic Schomburg Robot-c; last Fighting Yank

GD2.0 FN6.0 NM9.4

305.00 915.00 3200.00

NOTE: ***Ingels** a-44, 45; c-44, 45, 46(wash). **Schomburg** (**Xela**) c-21-43; 47-53 (airbrush). **Tuska** c-45? Bondage c-16, 21, 37, 46-49. Captain Future c-1-9, 13, 14. Fighting Yank c-10-12, 15-17, 21, 22, 24, 26, 28, 30, 32, 34, 36, 38, 40, 42. Pyroman c-18-20, 23, 25, 27, 29, 31, 33, 35, 37, 39, 41, 43.*

STARTLING TERROR TALES
Star Publications: No. 10, May, 1952 - No. 14, Feb, 1953; No. 4, Apr, 1953 - No. 11, 1954

10-(1st Series)-Wood/Harrison-a (r/A Star Presentation #3) Disbrow/Cole-c; becomes 4 different titles after #10; becomes Confessions of Love #11 on, The Horrors #11 on, Terrifying Tales #11 on, Terrors of the Jungle #11 on & continues w/Startling Terror #11 68.00 205.00 650.00
11-(8/52)-L. B. Cole Spider-c; r-Fox's "A Feature Presentation" #5 (blue-c)
105.00 316.00 1000.00
11-Black-c (variant; believed to be a pressrun change) (Unique)
126.00 379.00 1200.00
12,14 28.00 84.00 225.00
13-Jo-Jo-r; Disbrow-a 30.00 90.00 240.00
4-9,11(1953-54) (2nd Series): 11-New logo 25.00 75.00 200.00
10-Disbrow-a 31.00 94.00 250.00

NOTE: ***L. B. Cole** covers-all issues. **Palais** a-V2#8r, V2#11r.*

STAR TREK (TV) (See Dan Curtis Giveaways, Dynabrite Comics & Power Record Comics)
Gold Key: 7/67; No. 2, 6/68; No. 3, 12/68; No. 4, 6/69 - No. 61, 3/79

1-Photo-c begin, end #9 42.00 125.00 500.00
1 (rare variation w/photo back-c) 43.00 129.00 520.00
2 23.00 70.00 280.00
2 (rare variation w/photo back-c) 38.00 113.00 450.00
3-5 17.00 50.00 200.00
3 (rare variation w/photo back-c) 27.00 81.00 325.00
6-9 12.50 37.50 150.00
10-20 7.50 22.50 90.00
21-30 5.35 16.00 65.00
31-40 4.10 12.30 45.00
41-61: 52-Drug propaganda story 3.00 9.00 30.00
...the Enterprise Logs nn (8/76)-Golden Press, ($1.95, 224 pgs.)-r/#1-8 plus 7 pgs. by McWilliams (#11185)-Photo-c 3.65 11.00 40.00
...the Enterprise Logs Vol. 2 ('76)-r/#9-17 (#11187)-Photo-c
3.20 9.60 35.00
...the Enterprise Logs Vol. 3 ('77)-r/#18-26 (#11188); McWilliams-a (4 pgs.)-Photo-c 3.20 9.60 35.00
Star Trek Vol. 4 (Winter '77)-Reprints #27,28,30-34,36,38 (#11189) plus 3 pgs. new art 3.20 9.60 35.00

NOTE: ***McWilliams** a-38, 40-44, 46-61. #29 reprints #1; #35 reprints #4; #37 reprints #5; #45 reprints #7. The tabloids all have photo covers and blank inside covers. Painted covers #10-44, 46-59.*

STAR TREK
Marvel Comics Group: April, 1980 - No. 18, Feb, 1982

1: 1-3-r/Marvel Super Special; movie adapt. 1.25 3.75 10.00
2-16: 5-Miller-c 2.40 6.00
17-Low print run 1.25 3.75 10.00
18-Last issue; low print run 2.00 6.00 16.00

NOTE: ***Austin** c-18i. **Buscema** a-13. **Gil Kane** a-15. **Nasser** c/a-7. **Simonson** c-17.*

STAR TREK (Also see Who's Who In Star Trek)
DC Comics: Feb, 1984 - No. 56, Nov, 1988 (75¢, Mando paper)

1-Sutton-a(p) begins 1.25 3.75 10.00
2-5 2.40 6.00
6-10: 7-Origin Saavik 5.00
11-20: 19-Walter Koenig story 4.00
21-32 3.50
33-($1.25, 52 pgs.)-20th anniversary issue 4.00
34-49: 37-Painted-c 3.00
50-($1.50, 52 pgs.) 4.00
51-56, Annual 1-3: 1(1985). 2(1986). 3(1988, $1.50) 3.00

NOTE: ***Morrow** a-28, 35, 36, 56. **Orlando** c-8i. **Perez** c-1-3. **Spiegle** a-19. **Starlin** c-24, 25. **Sutton** a-1-6p, 8-18p, 20-27p, 29p, 31-34p, 39-52p, 55p; c-4-6p, 8-22p, 46p.*

STAR TREK
DC Comics: Oct, 1989 - No. 80, Jan, 1996 ($1.50/$1.75/$1.95/$2.50)

Star Trek: All of Me © Paramount

Star Trek: Deep Space Nine #13 © Paramount

Star Trek: The Next Generation #36 © Paramount

GD2.0 FN6.0 NM9.4

1-Capt. Kirk and crew 2.40 6.00
2,3 4.00
4-23,25-30: 10-12-The Trial of James T. Kirk. 21-Begin $1.75-c 2.50
24-($2.95, 68 pgs.)-40 pg. epic w/pin-ups 3.50
31-49,51-60 2.50
50-($3.50, 68 pgs.)-Painted-c 3.50
61-74,76-80 2.50
75 ($3.95) 4.00
Annual 1-6('90-'95, 68 pgs.): 1-Morrow-a. 3-Painted-c 4.00
Special 1-3 ('9-'95, 68 pgs.)-1-Sutton-a. 4.00
...: The Ashes of Eden (1995, $14.95, 100 pgs.)-Shatner story 15.00
...Generations (1994, $3.95, 68 pgs.)-Movie adaptation 4.00
...Generations (1994, $5.95, 68 pgs.)-Squarebound 6.00

STAR TREK...(TV)
DC Comics (WildStorm): one-shots
All of Me (4/00, $5.95, prestige format) Lopresti-a 5.95

STAR TREK: DEBT OF HONOR
DC Comics: 1992 ($24.95/$14.95, graphic novel)
Hardcover ($24.95) Claremont-s/Hughes-a(p) 25.00
Softvcover ($14.95) 15.00

STAR TREK: DEEP SPACE NINE (TV)
Malibu Comics: Aug, 1993 - No. 32, Jan, 1996 ($2.50)
1-Direct Sale Edition w/line drawn-c 2.50
1-Newsstand Edition with photo-c 2.50
0 (1/95, $2.95)-Terok Nor 3.00
2-30: 2-Polybagged w/trading card. 9-4 pg. prelude to Hearts & Minds 2.50
31-($3.95) 4.00
32-($3.50) 3.50
Annual 1 (1/95, $3.95, 68 pgs.) 4.00
Special 1 (1995, $3.50) 3.50
Ultimate Annual 1 (12/95, $5.95) 6.00
...:Lightstorm (12/94, $3.50) 3.50

STAR TREK: DEEP SPACE NINE (TV)
Marvel Comics (Paramount Comics): Nov, 1996 - No. 15, Mar, 1998 ($1.95/$1.99)
1-15: 12,13-"Telepathy War" pt. 2,3 2.00

STAR TREK: DEEP SPACE NINE -- N-VECTOR (TV)
DC Comics (WildStorm): Aug, 2000 - No. 4, Nov, 2000 ($2.50, limited series)
1-4-Cypress-a 2.50

STAR TREK DEEP SPACE NINE-THE CELEBRITY SERIES
Malibu Comics: May, 1995 ($2.95)
1-Blood and Honor; Mark Lenard script 3.00
1-Rules of Diplomacy; Aron Eisenberg script 3.00

STAR TREK: DEEP SPACE NINE HEARTS AND MINDS
Malibu Comics: June, 1994 - No. 4, Sept, 1994 ($2.50, limited series)
1-4 2.50
1-Holographic-c 4.00

STAR TREK: DEEP SPACE NINE, THE MAQUIS
Malibu Comics: Feb, 1995 - No. 3, Apr, 1995 ($2.50, limited series)
1-3-Newsstand-c, 1-Photo-c 2.50

STAR TREK: DEEP SPACE NINE/THE NEXT GENERATION
Malibu Comics: Oct, 1994 - No. 2, Nov, 1994 ($2.50, limited series)
1,2: Parts 2 & 4 of x-over with Star Trek: TNG/DS9 from DC Comics 2.50

STAR TREK: DEEP SPACE NINE WORF SPECIAL
Malibu Comics: Dec, 1995 ($3.95, one-shot)
1-Includes pinups 4.00

STAR TREK EARLY VOYAGES(TV)
Marvel Comics (Paramount Comics): Feb, 1997 - No. 17, Jun, 1998 ($2.95/$1.95/$1.99)
1-($2.95) 3.00
2-17 2.00

STAR TREK: FIRST CONTACT (Movie)
Marvel Comics (Paramount Comics): Nov, 1996 ($5.95, one-shot)
nn-Movie adaption 6.00

STAR TREK: MIRROR MIRROR
Marvel Comics (Paramount Comics): Feb, 1997 ($3.95, one-shot)
1-DeFalco-s 4.00

STAR TREK MOVIE SPECIAL
DC Comics: 1984 (June) - No. 2, 1987 ($1.50); No. 1, 1989 ($2.00, 52 pgs)
nn-(#1)-Adapts Star Trek III; Sutton-p (68 pgs.) 2.50
2-Adapts Star Trek IV; Sutton-a; Chaykin-c. (68 pgs.) 2.50
1 (1989)-Adapts Star Trek V; painted-c 2.50

STAR TREK: NEW FRONTIER - DOUBLE TIME
DC Comics (WildStorm): Nov, 2000 ($5.95, one-shot, prestige format)
nn-Captain Calhoun's USS Excalibur; Peter David-s; Stelfreeze-c 6.00

STAR TREK: OPERATION ASSIMILATION
Marvel Comics (Paramount Comics): Dec, 1996 ($2.95, one-shot)
1 3.00

STAR TREK VI: THE UNDISCOVERED COUNTRY (Movie)
DC Comics: 1992
1-($2.95, regular edition, 68 pgs.)-Adaptation of film 3.00
nn-($5.95, prestige edition)-Has photos of movie not included in regular edition; painted-c by Palmer; photo back-c 6.00

STAR TREK: STARFLEET ACADEMY
Marvel Comics (Paramount Comics): Dec, 1996 - No. 19, Jun, 1998 ($1.95/$1.99)
1-19: Begin new series. 12-"Telepathy War" pt. 1. 18-English and Klingon language editions 2.00

STAR TREK: TELEPATHY WAR
Marvel Comics (Paramount Comics): Nov, 1997 ($2.99, 48 pgs., one-shot)
1-"Telepathy War" x-over pt. 6 3.00

STAR TREK - THE MODALA IMPERATIVE
DC Comics: Late July, 1991 - No. 4, Late Sept, 1991 ($1.75, limited series)
1-4 2.50

STAR TREK: THE NEXT GENERATION (TV)
DC Comics: Feb, 1988 - No. 6, July, 1988 (limited series)
1 ($1.50, 52 pgs.)-Sienkiewicz painted-c 2.40 6.00
2-6 ($1.00) 4.00

STAR TREK: THE NEXT GENERATION (TV)
DC Comics: Oct, 1989 -No. 80, 1995 ($1.50/$1.75/$1.95)
1-Capt. Picard and crew from TV show 1.10 3.30 9.00
2,3 5.00
4-10 4.00
11-23,25-49,51-60 3.00
24,50: 24-($2.50, 52 pgs.). 50-($3.50, 68 pgs.)-Painted-c 5.00
61-74,76-80 2.50
75-($3.95, 50 pgs.) 4.00
Annual 1-6 ('90-'95, 68 pgs.) 4.00
Special 1 -3('93-'95, 68 pgs.)-1-Contains 3 stories 4.00
...-The Series Finale (1994, $3.95, 68 pgs.) 4.00

STAR TREK: THE NEXT GENERATION (TV)
DC Comics (WildStorm): one-shots
Embrace the Wolf (6/00, $5.95, prestige format) Golden & Sniegoski-s 6.00
The Gorn Crisis (1/01, $29.95, HC) Kordey painted-a/dust jacket-c 30.00

STAR TREK: THE NEXT GENERATION/DEEP SPACE NINE (TV)
DC Comics: Dec, 1994 - No. 2, Jan, 1995 ($2.50, limited series)
1,2-Parts 1 & 3 of x-over with Star Trek: DS9/TNG from Malibu Comics 2.50

STAR TREK: THE NEXT GENERATION - ILL WIND
DC Comics: Nov, 1995 - No. 4, Feb, 1996 ($2.50, limited series)
1-4: Hugh Fleming painted-c on all 2.50

STAR TREK: THE NEXT GENERATION - PERCHANCE TO DREAM
DC Comics/WildStorm: Feb, 2000 - No. 4, May, 2000 ($2.50, limited series)

Star Trek/ X-Men: Second Contact #1 © Paramount/MAR

Star Wars #15 © Lucasfilm Ltd.

Star Wars: Chewbacca #4 © Lucasfilm Ltd.

GD2.0 FN6.0 NM9.4

1-4-Bradstreet-c 2.50

STAR TREK: THE NEXT GENERATION - RIKER
Marvel Comics (Paramount Comics): July, 1998 ($3.50, one-shot)
1-Riker joins the Maquis 3.50

STAR TREK: THE NEXT GENERATION - SHADOWHEART
DC Comics: Dec, 1994 - No. 4, Mar, 1995 ($1.95, limited series)
1-4 2.00

STAR TREK: THE NEXT GENERATION - THE KILLING SHADOWS
DC Comics/WildStorm: Nov, 2000 - No. 4, Feb, 2001 ($2.50, limited series)
1-4-Scott Ciencin-s; Sela app. 2.50

STAR TREK: THE NEXT GENERATION - THE MODALA IMPERATIVE
DC Comics: Early Sept, 1991 - No. 4, Late Oct, 1991 ($1.75, limited series)
1-4 2.50

STAR TREK UNLIMITED
Marvel Comics (Paramount Comics): Nov, 1996 - No. 10, July, 1998 ($2.95/$2.99)
1,2-Stories from original series and Next Generation 4.00
3-10: 3-Begin $2.99-c. 6-"Telepathy War" pt. 4. 7-Q & Trelane swap Kirk & Picard 3.50

STAR TREK UNTOLD VOYAGES
Marvel Comics (Paramount Comics): May, 1998 - No. 5, July, 1998 ($2.50)
1-5-Kirk's crew after the 1st movie 2.50

STAR TREK: VOYAGER
Marvel Comics (Paramount Comics): Nov, 1996 - No. 15, Mar, 1998 ($1.95/$1.99)
1-15: 13-"Telepathy War" pt. 5. 14-Seven of Nine joins crew 3.00

STAR TREK: VOYAGER
DC Comics/WildStorm: one-shots
- Elite Force (7/00, $5.95) The Borg app.; Abnett & Lanning-s 6.00
- False Colors (1/00, $5.95) Photo-c and Jim Lee-c; Jeff Moy-a 6.00

STAR TREK: VOYAGER SPLASHDOWN
Marvel Comics (Paramount Comics): Apr, 1998 - No. 4, July, 1998 ($2.50, limited series)
1-4-Voyager crashes on a water planet 3.00

STAR TREK/ X-MEN
Marvel Comics (Paramount Comics): Dec, 1996 ($4.99, one-shot)
1-Kirk's crew & X-Men; art by Silvestri, Tan, Winn & Finch; Lobdell-s 5.00

STAR TREK/ X-MEN: 2ND CONTACT
Marvel Comics (Paramount Comics): May, 1998 ($4.99, 64 pgs., one-shot)
1-Next Gen. crew & X-Men battle Kang, Sentinels & Borg following First Contact movie 5.00
1-Painted wraparound variant cover 5.00

STAR WARS (Movie) (See Classic..., Contemporary Motivators, Dark Horse Comics, The Droids, The Ewoks, Marvel Movie Showcase, Marvel Special Ed.)
Marvel Comics Group: July, 1977 - No. 107, Sept, 1986
1-(Regular 30¢ edition)-Price in square w/UPC code; #1-6 adapt first movie 3.20 9.60 35.00
1-(35¢-c; limited distribution - 1500 copies?)- Price in square w/UPC code 46.00 138.00 600.00
NOTE: *The rare 35¢ edition has the cover price in a square box, and the UPC box in the lower left hand corner has the UPC code lines running through it.*
2-6: 2-4-30¢ issues. 4-Battle with Darth Vader. 6-Dave Stevens-a(i). 2.00 6.00 18.00
2-4-35¢ with UPC code; not reprints 4.10 12.30 45.00
7-20 1.50 4.50 12.00
21-70: 39-44-The Empire Strikes Back-r by Al Williamson in all. 68-Reintro Boba Fett. 1.10 3.30 9.00
71-80 1.25 3.75 10.00
81-90: 81-Boba Fett app. 1.50 4.50 12.00
91,93-99: 98-Williamson-a. 1.75 5.25 14.00
92,100-106: 92,100-($1.00, 52 pgs.). 2.00 6.00 16.00
107 (scarce); Portacio-a(i) 4.55 13.65 50.00
1-9: Reprints; has "reprint" in upper lefthand corner of cover or on inside or price and number inside a diamond with no date or UPC on cover; 30¢ and 35¢ issues published 4.00
Annual 1 (12/79, 52 pgs.)-Simonson-c 1.50 4.50 12.00
Annual 2 (11/82, 52 pgs.), 3(12/83, 52 pgs.) 1.25 3.75 10.00
***Austin** a-11-15i, 21i, 38; c-12-15i, 21i. **Byrne** c-13p. **Chaykin** a-1-10p; c-1. **Golden** c/a-38. **Miller** c-47p; pin-up-43. **Nebres** c/a-Annual 2i. **Portacio** a-107i. **Sienkiewicz** c-92i, 98. **Simonson** a-16p, 49p, 51-63p, 65p, 66p; c-16, 49-51, 52p, 53-62, Annual 1. **Steacy** painted a-105i, 106i; c-105. **Williamson** a-39-44p, 50p, 98; c-39, 40, 41-44p. Painted c-81, 87, 92, 95, 98, 100, 105.*

GD2.0 FN6.0 NM9.4

STAR WARS (Monthly series)
Dark Horse Comics: Dec, 1998 - Present ($2.50/$2.95, limited series)
1-12: 1-6-Prelude To Rebellion; Strnad-s. 4-Brereton-c. 7-12-Outlander 2.50
13, 17-18-($2.95): 13-18-Emissaries to Malastare; Truman-s 3.00
14-16-($2.50) Schultz-c 2.50
19-23: 19-22-Twilight; Duursema-a. 23-26-Infinity's End 2.95
#0 Another Universe.com Ed.($10.00) r/serialized pages from Pizzazz Magazine; new Dorman painted-c 10.00

STAR WARS: A NEW HOPE- THE SPECIAL EDITION
Dark Horse Comics: Jan, 1997 - No. 4, Apr, 1997 ($2.95, limited series)
1-4-Dorman-c 4.00

STAR WARS: BOBA FETT
Dark Horse Comics: Dec, 1995 - No. 3 ($3.95) (Originally intended as a one-shot)
1-Kennedy-c/a 2.40 6.00
2,3 5.00
Death, Lies, & Treachery TPB (1/98, $12.95) r/#1-3 13.00
Twin Engines of Destruction (1/97, $2.95) 3.00

STAR WARS: BOBA FETT: ENEMY OF THE EMPIRE
Dark Horse Comics: Jan, 1999 - No. 4, Apr, 1999 ($2.95, limited series)
1-4-Recalls 1st meeting of Fett and Vader 3.00

STAR WARS: CHEWBACCA
Dark Horse Comics: Jan, 2000 - No. 4, Apr, 2000 ($2.95, limited series)
1-4-Macan-s/art by various incl. Anderson, Kordey, Gibbons; Phillips-c 3.00

STAR WARS: CRIMSON EMPIRE
Dark Horse Comics: Dec, 1997 - No. 6, May, 1998 ($2.95, limited series)
1-Richardson-s/Gulacy-a 1.00 2.80 7.00
2-6 5.00

STAR WARS: CRIMSON EMPIRE II: COUNCIL OF BLOOD
Dark Horse Comics: Nov, 1998 - No. 6, Apr, 1999 ($2.95, limited series)
1-6-Richardson & Stradley-s/Gulacy-a 3.00

STAR WARS: DARK EMPIRE
Dark Horse Comics: Dec, 1991 - No. 6, Oct, 1992 ($2.95, limited series)
Preview-(99¢) 2.00
1-All have Dorman painted-c 1.10 3.30 9.00
1-3-2nd printing 4.00
2-Low print run 1.60 4.85 13.00
3 2.40 6.00
4-6 4.00
Gold Embossed Set (#1-6)-With gold embossed foil logo (price is for set) 65.00
Platinum Embossed Set (#1-6) 80.00
Trade paperback (4/93, 16.95) 17.00
Ltd. Ed. Hardcover ($99.95) Signed & numbered 100.00

STAR WARS: DARK EMPIRE II
Dark Horse Comics: Dec, 1994 - No. 6, May, 1995 ($2.95, limited series)
1-Dave Dorman painted-c 5.00
2-6: Dorman-c in all. 4.00
Platinum Embossed Set (#1-6) 35.00
Trade paperback ($17.95) 18.00

STAR WARS: DARK FORCE RISING
Dark Horse Comics: May, 1997 - No. 6, Oct, 1997 ($2.95, limited series)
1-6 4.00
TPB (2/98, $17.95) r/#1-6 18.00

STAR WARS: DARTH MAUL
Dark Horse Comics: Sept, 2000 - No. 4 ($2.95, limited series)

Star Wars: Darth Maul #3 © Lucasfilm Ltd.

Star Wars: Return of the Jedi #1 © Lucasfilm Ltd.

Star Wars: Union #4 © Lucasfilm Ltd.

GD2.0 FN6.0 NM9.4

1-3-Photo-c and Struzan painted-c; takes place 6 months before Ep. 1 3.00

STAR WARS: DROIDS (See Dark Horse Comics #17-19)
Dark Horse Comics: Apr, 1994 - #6, Sept, 1994; V2#1, Apr, 1995 - V2#8, Dec, 1995 ($2.50, limited series)

1-($2.95)-Embossed-c 4.00
2-6 , Special 1 (1/95, $2.50), V2#1-8 3.00

STAR WARS: EMPIRE'S END
Dark Horse Comics: Oct, 1995 - No. 2, Nov, 1995 ($2.95, limited series)

1,2-Dorman-c 3.00

STAR WARS: EPISODE 1 THE PHANTOM MENACE
Dark Horse Comics: May, 1999 - No. 4 ($2.95, movie adaption)

1-4-Regular and photo-c; Damaggio & Williamson-a 3.00
TPB ($12.95) r/#1-4 13.00
...Anakin Skywalker-Photo-c & Bradstreet-c, ...Obi-Wan Kenobi-Photo-c & Egeland-c, ...Queen Amidala-Photo-c & Bradstreet-c, ...Qui-Gon Jinn-Photo-c & Bradstreet-c 3.00
Gold foil covers; Wizard 1/2 10.00

STAR WARS HANDBOOK
Dark Horse Comics: July, 1998- Present ($2.95, one-shots)

...X-Wing Rogue Squadron (7/98)-Guidebook to characters and spacecraft 3.00
...Crimson Empire (7/99) Dorman-c 3.00
...Dark Empire (3/00) Dorman-c 3.00

STAR WARS : HEIR TO THE EMPIRE
Dark Horse Comics: Oct, 1995 - No.6, Apr, 1996 ($2.95, limited series)

1-6: Adaptation of Zahn novel 3.00

STAR WARS: JABBA THE HUTT
Dark Horse Comics: Apr, 1995 ($2.50, one-shots)

nn, ...The Betrayal, ...The Dynasty Trap, ...The Hunger of Princess Nampi 3.00

STAR WARS: JEDI ACADEMY - LEVIATHAN
Dark Horse Comics: Oct, 1998 - No. 4, Jan, 1999 ($2.95, limited series)

1-Lago-c. 2-4-Chadwick-c 3.00

STAR WARS: JEDI COUNCIL: ACTS OF WAR
Dark Horse Comics: Jun, 2000 - No. 4, ($2.95, limited series)

1-4-Stradley-s; set one year before Episode 1 3.00

STAR WARS: MARA JADE
Dark Horse Comics: Aug, 1998 - No. 6, Jan, 1999 ($2.95, limited series)

1-6-Ezquerra-a 3.00

STAR WARS: RETURN OF THE JEDI (Movie)
Marvel Comics Group: Oct, 1983 - No. 4, Jan, 1984 (limited series)

1-4-Williamson-p in all; r/Marvel Super Special #27 1.00 3.00 8.00
Oversized issue (1983, $2.95, 10-3/4x8-1/4", 68 pgs., cardboard-c)-r/#1-4 1.75 5.25 14.00

STAR WARS: RIVER OF CHAOS
Dark Horse Comics: June, 1995 - No. 4, Sept, 1995 ($2.95, limited series)

1-4: Louise Simonson scripts 3.00

STAR WARS: SHADOWS OF THE EMPIRE
Dark Horse Comics: May, 1996 - No. 6, Oct, 1996 ($2.95, limited series)

1-6: Story details events between The Empire Strikes Back & Return of the Jedi; Russell-a(i). 3.00

STAR WARS: SHADOWS OF THE EMPIRE - EVOLUTION
Dark Horse Comics: Feb, 1998 - No. 5, June, 1998 ($2.95, limited series)

1-5: Perry-s/Fegredo-c. 3.00

STAR WARS: SHADOW STALKER
Dark Horse Comics: Sept, 1997 ($2.95, one-shot)

nn-Windham-a. 3.00

STAR WARS: SPLINTER OF THE MIND'S EYE
Dark Horse Comics: Dec, 1995 - No. 4, June, 1996 ($2.50, limited series)

1-4: Adaption of Alan Dean Foster novel 3.00

STAR WARS TALES
Dark Horse Comics: Sept, 1999 - Present ($4.95, anthology)

1-5-Short stories by various 4.95

STAR WARS: TALES FROM MOS EISLEY
Dark Horse Comics: Mar, 1996 ($2.95, one-shot)

nn-Bret Blevins-a. 3.00

STAR WARS: TALES OF THE JEDI (See Dark Horse Comics #7)
Dark Horse Comics: Oct, 1993 - No. 5, Feb, 1994 ($2.50, limited series)

1-5: All have Dave Dorman painted-c. 3-r/Dark Horse Comics #7-9 w/new coloring & some panels redrawn 3.00
1-5-Gold foil embossed logo; limited # printed-7500 (set) 50.00

STAR WARS: TALES OF THE JEDI-DARK LORDS OF THE SITH
Dark Horse Comics: Oct, 1994 - No. 6, Mar, 1995 ($2.50, limited series)

1-6: 1-Polybagged w/trading card 3.00

STAR WARS: TALES OF THE JEDI-REDEMPTION
Dark Horse Comics: July, 1998 - No. 5, Nov, 1998 ($2.95, limited series)

1-5: 1-Kevin J. Anderson-s/Kordey-c 3.00

STAR WARS: TALES OF THE JEDI-THE FALL OF THE SITH
Dark Horse Comics: June, 1997 - No. 5, Oct, 1997 ($2.95, limited series)

1-5 3.00

STAR WARS: TALES OF THE JEDI-THE FREEDON NADD UPRISING
Dark Horse Comics: Aug, 1994 - No. 2, Nov, 1994 ($2.50, limited series)

1,2 3.00

STAR WARS: TALES OF THE JEDI-THE GOLDEN AGE OF THE SITH
Dark Horse Comics: July, 1996 - No. 5, Feb, 1997 (99¢/$2.95, limited series)

0-(99¢)-Anderson-s 2.00
1-5-Anderson-s 3.00

STAR WARS: TALES OF THE JEDI-THE SITH WAR
Dark Horse Comics: Aug, 1995 - No. 6, Jan, 1996 ($2.50, limited series)

1-6: Anderson scripts 3.00

STAR WARS: THE BOUNTY HUNTERS
Dark Horse Comics: July, 1999 - Present ($2.95, one-shots)

...Aurra Sing (7/99), ...Kenix Kil (10/99), ...Scoundrel's Wages (8/99) Lando Calrissian app. 3.00

STAR WARS: THE JABBA TAPE
Dark Horse Comics: Dec, 1998 ($2.95, one-shot)

nn-Wagner-s/Plunkett-a 3.00

STAR WARS: THE LAST COMMAND
Dark Horse Comics: Nov, 1997 - No. 6, July, 1998 ($2.95, limited series)

1-6:Based on the Timothy Zaun novel 4.00

STAR WARS: THE PROTOCOL OFFENSIVE
Dark Horse Comics: Sept, 1997 ($4.95, one-shot)

nn-Anthony Daniels & Ryder Windham-s 5.00

STAR WARS: UNION
Dark Horse Comics: Nov, 1999 - No. 4, Feb, 2000 ($2.95, limited series)

1-4-Wedding of Luke and Mara Jade; Teranishi-a/Stackpole-s 3.00

STAR WARS: VADER'S QUEST
Dark Horse Comics: Feb, 1999 - No. 4, May, 1999 ($2.95, limited series)

1-4-Follows destruction of 1st Death Star; Gibbons-a 3.00

STAR WARS: X-WING ROGUE SQUADRON (Star Wars: X-Wing Rogue Squadron-The Phantom Affair #5-8 appears on cover only)
Dark Horse Comics: July, 1995 - No. 35, Nov, 1998 ($2.95)

1/2 8.00
1-24,26-35: 1-4-Baron scripts. 5-20-Stackpole scripts 3.00
25-($3.95) 4.00
The Phantom Affair TPB ($12.95) r/#5-8 13.00

S.T.A.T.
Majestic Entertainment: Dec, 1993 ($2.25)

1 2.25

Static #1 © Milestone Media

Steampunk #1 © Chris Bachalo & Joe Kelly

Stone Cold #4 © Chaos!

GD2.0 FN6.0 NM9.4

STATIC (Also see Eclipse Monthly)
Charlton Comics: No, 11, Oct, 1985 - No. 12, Dec, 1985
11,12-Ditko-c/a 4.00

STATIC (See Heroes)
DC Comics (Milestone): June, 1993 - No. 45, Mar, 1997 ($1.50/$1.75/$2.50)
1-($2.95)-Collector's Edition; polybagged w/poster & trading card & backing board (direct sales only) 4.00
1-24,26-45: 2-Origin. 8-Shadow War; Simonson silver ink-c. 14-($2.50, 52 pgs.)-Worlds Collide Pt. 14. 27-Kent Williams-c 2.50
25 ($3.95) 4.00
...: Trial by Fire (2000, $9.95) r/#1-4; Leon-c 10.00

STATIC SHOCK!: REBIRTH OF THE COOL (TV)
DC Comics: Jan, 2001 - No. 4, April, 2001 ($2.50, limited series)
1-4: McDuffie-s/Leon-c/a 2.50

STEALTH SQUAD
Petra Comics: Sept, 1993 ($2.50, unfinished limited series)
1-Super hero team 2.50

STEAMPUNK
DC/WildStorm (Cliffhanger): Apr, 2000 - Present ($2.50)
Catechism (1/00) Prologue -Kelly-s/Bachalo-a 2.50
1-4,6,7: 4-Four covers by Bachalo, Madureira, Ramos, Campbell 2.50
5-($3.50) 3.50

STEED AND MRS. PEEL (TV)(Also see The Avengers)
Eclipse Books/ ACME Press: 1990 - No. 3, 1991 ($4.95, limited series)
Books One - Three: Grant Morrison scripts 5.00

STEEL (Also see JLA)
DC Comics: Feb, 1994 - No. 52, July, 1998 ($1.50/$1.95/$2.50)
1-8,0,9-52: 1-From Reign of the Supermen storyline. 6,7-Worlds Collide Pt. 5 & 12. 8-(9/94). 0-(10/94). 9-(11/94). 46-Superboy-c/app. 50-Millennium Giants x-over 2.50
Annual 1 (1994, $2.95)-Elseworlds story 3.00
Annual 2 (1995, $3.95)-Year One story 4.00
...Forging of a Hero TPB (1997, $19.95) r/ early app. 20.00

STEEL: THE OFFICIAL COMIC ADAPTION OF THE WARNER BROS. MOTION PICTURE
DC Comics: 1997 ($4.95, Prestige format, one-shot)
nn-Movie adaption; Bogdanove & Giordano-a 5.00

STEELGRIP STARKEY
Marvel Comics (Epic Comics): June, 1986 - No. 6, July, 1987 ($1.50, limited series, Baxter paper)
1-6 2.00

STEEL STERLING (Formerly Shield-Steel Sterling; see Blue Ribbon, Jackpot, Mighty Comics, Mighty Crusaders, Roly Poly & Zip Comics)
Archie Enterprises, Inc.: No. 4, Jan, 1984 - No. 7, July, 1984
4-7: 4-6-Kanigher-s; Barreto-a. 5,6-Infantino-a. 6-McWilliams-a 3.00

STEEL, THE INDESTRUCTIBLE MAN (See All-Star Squadron #8)
DC Comics: Mar, 1978 - No. 5, Oct-Nov, 1978
1 1.00 3.00 8.00
2-5: 5-44 pgs. 5.00

STEELTOWN ROCKERS
Marvel Comics: Apr, 1987 - No. 6, Sept, 1990 ($1.00, limited series)
1-6: Small town teens form rock band 2.00

STEVE AUSTIN (See Stone Cold Steve Austin)

STEVE CANYON (See Harvey Comics Hits #52)
Dell Publishing Co.: No. 519, 11/53 - No. No. 1033, 9/59 (All Milton Caniff-a except #519, 939, 1033)
Four Color 519 (1, '53) 8.35 25.00 100.00
Four Color 578 (8/54), 641 (7/55), 737 (10/56), 804 (5/57), 939 (10/58), 1033 (9/59) (photo-c) 4.60 13.75 55.00

STEVE CANYON
Grosset & Dunlap: 1959 (6-3/4x9", 96 pgs., B&W, no text, hardcover)
100100-Reprints 2 stories from strip (1953, 1957) 5.00 15.00 35.00
100100 (softcover edition) 4.65 14.00 28.00

STEVE CANYON COMICS
Harvey Publ.: Feb, 1948 - No. 6, Dec, 1948 (Strip reprints, No. 4,5: 52pgs.)
1-Origin; has biography of Milton Caniff; Powell-a, 2 pgs.; Caniff-a 23.00 68.00 180.00
2-Caniff, Powell-a in #2-6 14.00 41.00 110.00
3-6: 6-Intro Madame Lynx-c/story 12.50 37.50 100.00

STEVE CANYON IN 3-D
Kitchen Sink Press: June, 1986 ($2.25, one-shot)
1-Contains unpublished story from 1954 5.00

STEVE DITKO'S STRANGE AVENGING TALES
Fantagraphics Books: Feb, 1997 ($2.95, B&W)
1-Ditko-c/s/a 3.00

STEVE DONOVAN, WESTERN MARSHAL (TV)
Dell Publishing Co.: No. 675, Feb, 1956 - No. 880, Feb, 1958 (All photo-c)
Four Color 675-Kinstler-a 7.50 22.50 90.00
Four Color 768-Kinstler-a 5.85 17.50 70.00
Four Color 880 4.10 12.30 45.00

STEVE ROPER
Famous Funnies: Apr, 1948 - No. 5, Dec, 1948
1-Contains 1944 daily newspaper-r 11.00 33.00 90.00
2 7.15 21.50 50.00
3-5 5.70 17.00 40.00

STEVE SAUNDERS SPECIAL AGENT (See Special Agent)

STEVE SAVAGE (See Captain...)

STEVE ZODIAC & THE FIRE BALL XL-5 (TV)
Gold Key: Jan, 1964
10108-401 (#1) 8.00 24.00 95.00

STEVIE (Mazie's boy friend)(Also see Flat-Top, Mazie & Mortie)
Mazie (Magazine Publ.): Nov, 1952 - No. 6, Apr, 1954
1-Teenage humor; Stevie, Mortie & Mazie begin 7.15 21.50 50.00
2-6 5.00 15.00 30.00

STEVIE MAZIE'S BOY FRIEND (See Harvey Hits #5)

STEWART THE RAT (See Eclipse Graphic Album Series)

ST. GEORGE (See listing under Saint...)

STIG'S INFERNO
Vortex/Eclipse: 1985 - No. 7, Mar, 1987 ($1.95, B&W)
1-7 ($1.95) 2.00
Graphic Album (1988, $6.95, B&W, 100 pgs.) 7.00

STING OF THE GREEN HORNET (See The Green Hornet)
Now Comics: June, 1992 - No. 4, 1992 ($2.50, limited series)
1-4: Butler-c/a 2.50
1-4 ($2.75)-Collectors Ed.; polybagged w/poster 3.00

STONE
Avalon Studios: Aug, 1998 - No. 4, Apr, 1999 ($2.50, limited series)
1-4-Portacio-a/Haberlin-s 2.50
1-Alternate-c 5.00
2-($14.95) DF Stonechrome Edition 15.00

STONE (Volume 2)
Avalon Studios: Aug, 1999 - No. 4, May, 2000 ($2.50)
1-4-Portacio-a/Haberlin-s 2.50

STONE COLD STEVE AUSTIN (WWF Wrestling)
Chaos! Comics: Oct, 1999 - No. 4, Feb, 2000 ($2.95)
1-4-Reg. & photo-c; Steven Grant-s 3.00
1-Premium Ed. ($10.00) 10.00
Preview ($5.00) 5.00

STONEY BURKE (TV)

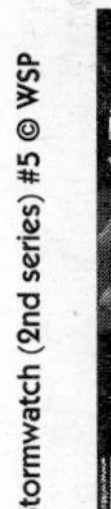

Storm #2 © MAR

Stormwatch (2nd series) #5 © WSP

Straight Arrow #8 © ME

ell Publishing Co.: June-Aug, 1963 - No. 2, Sept-Nov, 1963
,2-Jack Lord photo-c on both 2.30 7.00 20.00

TONY CRAIG
entagon Publishing Co.: 1946 (No #)
-Reprints Bell Syndicate's "Sgt. Stony Craig" newspaper strips
7.00 21.00 48.00

TORIES BY FAMOUS AUTHORS ILLUSTRATED (Fast Fiction #1-5)
eaboard Publ./Famous Authors Ill.: No. 6, Aug, 1950 - No. 13, Mar, 1951
-Scarlet Pimpernel-Baroness Orczy 35.00 105.00 280.00
-Capt. Blood-Raphael Sabatini 34.00 103.00 275.00
-She, by Haggard 40.00 120.00 340.00
-The 39 Steps-John Buchan 23.00 69.00 185.00
-Beau Geste-P. C. Wren 23.00 69.00 185.00
OTE: The above five issues are exact reprints of Fast Fiction #1-5 except for the title change nd new Kiefer covers on #1 and 2. Kiefer c(r)-3-5. The above 5 issues were released before amous Authors #6.
-Macbeth, by Shakespeare; Kiefer art (8/50); used in **SOTI**, pg. 22,143;
Kiefer-c; 36 pgs. 31.00 94.00 250.00
-The Window; Kiefer-c/a; 52 pgs. 23.00 68.00 180.00
-Hamlet, by Shakespeare; Kiefer-c/a; 36 pgs. 28.00 83.00 220.00
,10: 9-Nicholas Nickleby, by Dickens; G. Schrotter-a; 52 pgs. 10-Romeo &
Juliet, by Shakespeare; Kiefer-c/a; 36 pgs. 23.00 69.00 185.00
1-13: 11-Ben-Hur; Schrotter-a; 52 pgs. 12-La Svengali; Schrotter-a; 36 pgs.
13-Scaramouche; Kiefer-c/a; 36 pgs. 22.00 66.00 175.00
OTE: Artwork was prepared/advertised for #14, The Red Badge Of Courage. Gilberton bought ut Famous Authors, Ltd. and used that story as C.I. #98. Famous Authors, Ltd. then published e Classics Junior series. The Famous Authors titles were published as part of the regular lassics Ill. Series in Brazil starting in 1952.

TORIES FROM THE TWILIGHT ZONE
kylark Pub: Mar, 1979, 68pgs. (B&W comic digest, 5-1/4x7-5/8")
5405-2: Pfevfer-a, 56pgs, new comics 2.50 7.50 23.00

TORIES OF ROMANCE (Formerly Meet Miss Bliss)
tlas Comics (LMC): No. 5, Mar, 1956 - No. 13, Aug, 1957
5-Baker-a? 10.00 30.00 70.00
6-10,12,13 6.00 18.00 42.00
1-Baker, Romita-a; Colletta-c/a 7.15 21.50 50.00
OTE: ***Ann Brewster** a-13. **Colletta** a-9(2), 11; c-5, 11.*

TORM
arvel Comics: Feb, 1996 - No. 4, May, 1996 ($2.95, limited series)
1-4-Foil-c; Dodson-a(p); Ellis-s: 2-4-Callisto; 3.50

TORMQUEST
aliber Press (Sky Universe): Nov, 1994 - No. 6, Apr, 1995 ($1.95)
1-6 2.00

TORMWATCH (Also see The Authority)
nage Comics (WildStorm Prod.): May, 1993 - No. 50, Jul, 1997 ($1.95/$2.50)
1-8,0,9-36: 1-Intro StormWatch (Battalion, Diva, Winter, Fuji, & Hellstrike); 1st app. Weatherman; Jim Lee-c & part scripts; Lee plots in all. 1-Gold edition.1-3-Includes coupon for limited edition StormWatch trading card #00 by Lee. 3-1st app. Backlash (cameo). 0-($2.50)-Polybagged w/card; 1st full app. Backlash. 9-(4/94, $2.50)-Intro Defile. 10-(6/94), 11,12-Both (8/94). 13,14-(9/94). 15-(10/94). 21-Reads #1 on-c. 22-Direct Market; Wildstorm Rising Pt. 9, bound-in card. 23-Spartan joins team. 25-(6/94, June 1995 on-c, $2.50). 35-Fire From Heaven Pt. 5. 36-Fire From Heaven Pt. 12 2.50
0-Alternate Portacio-c, see Deathblow #5 4.00
2-($1.95)-Newsstand, Wildstorm Rising Pt. 9 2.50
7-(7/96, $3.50, 38 pgs.)-Weatherman forms new team; 1st app. Jenny Sparks, Jack Hawksmoor & Rose Tattoo; Warren Ellis scripts begin; Justice League #1-c/swipe 5.00
8-49: 44-Three covers. 3.00
0-($4.50) 5.00
pecial 1 ,2(1/94, 5/95, $3.50, 52 pgs.) 3.50
ourcebook 1 (1/94, $2.50) 2.50
orces of Nature ('99, $14.95, TPB) r/V1 #37-42 15.00
ightning Strikes ('00, $14.95, TPB) r/V1 #43-47 15.00

TORMWATCH (Also see The Authority)
Image Comics (WildStorm): Oct, 1997 - No. 11, Sept, 1998 ($2.50)
1-Ellis-s/Jimenez-a(p); two covers by Bennett 3.00
1-($3.50)-Voyager Pack bagged w/Gen 13 preview 4.00
2-9: 7,8-Freefall app. 9-Gen13 & DV8 app. 2.50
10,11-Not included in TPB reprint series 5.00
A Finer World ('99, $14.95, TPB) r/V2 #4-9 15.00
Change or Die ('99, $14.95, TPB) r/V1 #48-50 & V2 #1-3 15.00

STORMWATCHER
Eclipse Comics (Acme Press): Apr, 1989 - No. 4, Dec, 1989 ($2.00, B&W)
1-4 2.00

STORMY (Disney) (Movie)
Dell Publishing Co.: No. 537, Feb, 1954
Four Color 537 (...the Thoroughbred)-on top 2/3 of each page; Pluto story on bottom 1/3 3.20 9.60 35.00

STORY OF JESUS (See Classics Illustrated Special Issue)

STORY OF MANKIND, THE (Movie)
Dell Publishing Co.: No. 851, Jan, 1958
Four Color 851-Vincent Price/Hedy Lamarr photo-c 6.70 20.00 80.00

STORY OF MARTHA WAYNE, THE
Argo Publ.: April, 1956
1-Newspaper strip-r 5.00 15.00 35.00

STORY OF RUTH, THE
Dell Publishing Co.: No. 1144, Nov-Jan, 1961 (Movie)
Four Color #1144-Photo-c 9.00 27.00 110.00

STORY OF THE COMMANDOS, THE (Combined Operations)
Long Island Independent: 1943 (15¢, B&W, 68 pgs.) (Distr. by Gilberton)
nn-All text (no comics); photos & illustrations; ad for Classic Comics on back cover (Rare) 33.00 99.00 265.00

STORY OF THE GLOOMY BUNNY, THE (See March of Comics #9)

STRAIGHT ARROW (Radio)(See Best of the West & Great Western)
Magazine Enterprises: Feb-Mar, 1950 - No. 55, Mar, 1956 (All 36 pgs.)
1-Straight Arrow (alias Steve Adams) & his palomino Fury begin; 1st mention of Sundown Valley & the Secret Cave 44.00 133.00 400.00
2-Red Hawk begins (1st app?) by Powell (origin), ends #55
22.00 66.00 175.00
3-Frazetta-c 30.00 90.00 240.00
4,5: 4-Secret Cave-c 20.00 60.00 160.00
6-10 19.00 56.00 150.00
11-Classic story "The Valley of Time", with an ancient civilization made of gold
20.00 60.00 160.00
12-19 14.00 41.00 110.00
20-Origin Straight Arrow's Shield 16.00 49.00 130.00
21-Origin Fury 20.00 60.00 160.00
22-Frazetta-c 21.00 64.00 170.00
23,25-30: 25-Secret Cave-c. 28-Red Hawk meets The Vikings
9.30 28.00 65.00
24-Classic story "The Dragons of Doom!" with prehistoric pteradactyls
12.00 36.00 95.00
31-38: 36-Red Hawk drug story by Powell 7.15 21.50 50.00
39-Classic story "The Canyon Beast", with a dinosaur egg hatching a Tyranosaurus Rex 10.50 32.00 85.00
40-Classic story "Secret of The Spanish Specters", with Conquistadors' lost treasure 10.00 30.00 70.00
41,42,44-54: 45-Secret Cave-c 6.40 19.25 45.00
43-Intro & 1st app. Blaze, S. Arrow's Warrior dog 8.65 26.00 60.00
55-Last issue 10.00 30.00 70.00
NOTE: ***Fred Meagher** a 1-55; c-1, 2, 4-21, 23-55. **Powell** a 2-55. **Whitney** a-1. Many issues advertise the radio premiums associated with Straight Arrow.*

STRAIGHT ARROW'S FURY (Also see A-1 Comics)
Magazine Enterprises: No. 119, 1954 (one-shot)
A-1 119-Origin; Fred Meagher-c/a 15.00 45.00 120.00

STRANGE (Tales You'll Never Forget)
Ajax-Farrell Publ. (Four Star Comic Corp.): March, 1957 - No. 6, May, 1958

Strange Adventures #9 © DC

Strange Adventures ('99) #4 © DC

Strange Fantasy #2 © AJAX

	GD2.0	FN6.0	NM9.4
1	20.00	60.00	160.00
2-Censored r/Haunted Thrills	10.00	30.00	80.00
3-6	10.00	30.00	70.00

STRANGE ADVENTURES
National Periodical Publications: Aug-Sept, 1950 - No. 244, Oct-Nov, 1973 (No. 1-12: 52 pgs.)

	GD2.0	FN6.0	NM9.4
1-Adaptation of "Destination Moon"; preview of movie w/photo-c from movie (also see Fawcett Movie Comic #2); adapt. of Edmond Hamilton's "Chris KL-99" in #1-3; Darwin Jones begins	250.00	750.00	3500.00
2	111.00	332.00	1550.00
3,4	75.00	225.00	1050.00
5-8,10: 7-Origin Kris KL-99	64.00	193.00	900.00
9-(6/51)-Origin/1st app. Captain Comet (c/story).	154.00	462.00	2200.00
11-20: 12,13,17,18-Toth-a. 14-Robot-c	46.00	138.00	600.00
21-30: 28-Atomic explosion panel. 30-Robot-c	37.00	112.00	450.00
31,34-38	34.00	102.00	410.00
32,33-Krigstein-a	35.00	105.00	420.00
39-Ill. in **SOTI** "Treating police contemptuously" (top right)	38.00	114.00	460.00
40-49-Last Capt. Comet; not in 45,47,48	32.00	96.00	385.00
50-53-Last precode issue (2/55)	24.50	74.00	270.00
54-70	18.00	54.00	200.00
71-99	13.50	40.00	150.00
100	15.50	46.50	170.00
101-110: 104-Space Museum begins by Sekowsky.	10.00	30.00	110.00
111-116,118,119: 114-Star Hawkins begins, ends #185; Heath-a in Wood E.C. style	9.00	27.00	100.00
117-(6/60)-Origin/1st app. Atomic Knights.	50.00	150.00	650.00
120-2nd app. Atomic Knights	23.50	71.00	260.00
121,122,125,127,128,130,131,133,134: 134-Last 10¢ issue	7.25	21.75	80.00
123,126-3rd & 4th app. Atomic Knights	14.00	42.00	155.00
124-Intro/origin Faceless Creature	8.65	26.00	95.00
129,132,135,138,141,147-Atomic Knights app.	9.50	28.50	105.00
136,137,139,140,143,145,146,148,149,151,152,154,155,157-159: 159-Star Rovers app.; Gil Kane/Anderson-a.	5.45	16.35	60.00
142-2nd app. Faceless Creature	6.35	19.00	70.00
144-Only Atomic Knights-c (by M. Anderson)	11.00	33.00	120.00
150,153,156,160: Atomic Knights in each. 153-(6/63)-3rd app. Faceless Creature; atomic explosion-c. 160-Last Atomic Knights	6.80	20.50	75.00
161-179: 161-Last Space Museum. 163-Star Rovers app. 170-Infinity-c. 177-Intro/origin Immortal Man	3.65	11.00	40.00
180-Origin/1st app. Animal Man	19.00	57.00	210.00
181-183,185-189: 187-Intro/origin The Enchantress	3.00	9.00	30.00
184-2nd app. Animal Man by Gil Kane	12.00	36.00	130.00
190-1st app. Animal Man in costume	14.50	43.50	160.00
191-194,196-200,202-204	2.50	7.50	25.00
195-1st full app. Animal Man	7.65	23.00	85.00
201-Last Animal Man; 2nd full app.	4.10	12.30	45.00
205-(10/67)-Intro/origin Deadman by Infantino & begin series, ends #216	11.50	34.00	125.00
206-Neal Adams-a begins	6.80	20.50	75.00
207-210	5.45	16.35	60.00
211-216: 211-Space Museum-r. 216-(1-2/69)-Deadman story finally concludes in Brave & the Bold #86 (10-11/69); secret message panel by Neal Adams (pg. 13); tribute to Steranko	4.10	12.30	45.00
217-r/origin & 1st app. Adam Strange from Showcase #17, begin-r; Atomic Knights-r begin	2.00	6.00	16.00
218-221,223-225: 218-Last 12¢ issue. 225-Last 15¢ issue	1.75	5.25	14.00
222-New Adam Strange story; Kane/Anderson-a	3.00	9.00	30.00
226,227,230-236-(68-52 pgs.): 226, 227-New Adam Strange text story w/illos by Anderson (8,6 pgs.) 231-Last Atomic Knights-r. 235-JLA-c/s	2.00	6.00	16.00
228,229 (68 pgs.)	2.30	7.00	20.00
237-243	1.25	3.75	10.00
244-Last issue	1.50	4.50	12.00

NOTE: ***Neal Adams*** *a-206-216; c-207-216, 228, 235.* ***Anderson*** *a-8-52, 94, 96, 99, 115, 117, 119-163, 217r, 218r, 222, 223-225r, 226, 229r, 242i(r); c-18, 19, 21, 23, 24, 27, 30, 32-44(most), c/r-157i, 190i, 217-224, 228-231, 233, 235-239, 241-243.* ***Ditko*** *a-188, 189.* ***Drucker*** *a-42, 43,* ***Elias*** *a-212.* ***Finlay*** *a-2, 3, 6, 7, 210r, 229r.* ***Giunta*** *a-237r.* ***Heath*** *a-116.* ***Infantino*** *a-10-101, 106-151, 154, 157-163, 180, 190, 218-221r, 223-244p(r); c-50; c(r)-190p, 197, 199-211, 218-22 223-244.* ***Kaluta*** *c-238, 240.* ***Gil Kane*** *a-8-116, 124, 125, 130, 138, 146-157, 173-186, 204r, 222r, 227-231r; c(p)-11-17, 25, 154, 157.* ***Kubert*** *a-55(2 pgs.), 226; c-219, 220, 225-227, 232, 234.* ***Moriera*** *c-26, 28, 29, 71.* ***Morrow*** *c-230.* ***Mortimer*** *c-8.* ***Powell*** *a-4.* ***Sekowsky*** *a-71p, 97-162p, 217p(r), 218p(r); c-206, 217-219r.* ***Simon & Kirby*** *a-2r (2 pgs)* ***Sparling*** *a-201.* ***Toth*** *a-8, 12, 13, 17-19.* ***Wood*** *a-154i. Atomic Knights in #117, 120, 123, 126, 129, 132, 135, 138, 141, 144, 147, 150, 153, 156, 160. Atomic Knights reprints by* ***Anderson*** *in 217-221, 223-231. Chris KL99 in 1-3, 5, 7, 9, 11, 15. Capt. Comet covers-9-14, 17-19, 24, 26, 27, 32-44.*

STRANGE ADVENTURES
DC Comics (Vertigo): Nov, 1999 - No. 4 ($2.50, limited series)

1-3: 1-Bolland-c; art by Bolland, Gibbons, Quitely 2.5

STRANGE AS IT SEEMS (See Famous Funnies-A Carnival of Comics, Feature Funnies #1, The John Hix Scrap Book & Peanuts)

STRANGE AS IT SEEMS
United Features Syndicate: 1939

	GD2.0	FN6.0	NM9.4
Single Series 9, 1, 2	35.00	105.00	280.0

STRANGE ATTRACTORS
RetroGraphix: 1993 - No. 15, Feb, 1997 ($2.50, B&W)

1-15: 1-(5/93), 2-(8/93), 3-(11/93), 4-(2/94) 2.5
Volume One-($14.95, trade paperback)-r/#1-7 15.0

STRANGE ATTRACTORS: MOON FEVER
Caliber Comics: Feb, 1997 - No. 3, June, 1997 ($2.95, B&W, mini-series)

1-3 3.0

STRANGE COMBAT TALES
Marvel Comics (Epic Comics): Oct, 1993 - No. 4, Jan, 1994 ($2.50, limited series)

1-4 2.5

STRANGE CONFESSIONS
Ziff-Davis Publ. Co.: Jan-Mar (Spring on-c), 1952 - No. 4, Fall, 1952 (All have photo-c)

	GD2.0	FN6.0	NM9.4
1(Scarce)-Kinstler-a	47.00	142.00	425.0
2(Scarce, 7-8/52)	36.00	107.00	285.0
3(Scarce, 9-10/52)-#3 on-c, #2 on inside; Reformatory girl story; photo-c	36.00	107.00	285.0
4(Scarce)	36.00	107.00	285.0

STRANGE DAYS
Eclipse Comics: Oct, 1984 - No. 3, Apr, 1985 ($1.75, Baxter paper)

1-3: Freakwave, Johnny Nemo, & Paradax from Vanguard Illustrated; nudity, violence & strong language 2.0

STRANGE DAYS (Movie)
Marvel Comics: Dec, 1995 ($5.95, squarebound, one-shot)

1-Adaptation of film 6.0

STRANGE FANTASY (Eerie Tales of Suspense!)(Formerly Rocketman #1)
Ajax-Farrell: Aug, 1952 - No. 14, Oct-Nov, 1954

	GD2.0	FN6.0	NM9.4
2(#1, 8/52)-Jungle Princess story; Kamenish-a; reprinted from Ellery Queen #1	44.00	133.00	400.0
2(10/52)-No Black Cat or Rulah; Bakerish, Kamenish-a; hypo/meathook-c	40.00	120.00	325.0
3-Rulah story, called Pulah	39.00	118.00	315.0
4-Rocket Man app. (2/53)	36.00	107.00	285.0
5,6,8,10,12,14	25.00	75.00	200.0
7-Madam Satan/Slave story	36.00	107.00	285.0
9(w/Black Cat), 9(w/Boy's Ranch; S&K-a), 9(w/War)(A rebinding of Harvey interiors; not publ. by Ajax)	31.00	94.00	250.0
9-Regular issue; Steve Ditko's 3rd published work (tied with Captain 3D)	42.00	126.00	375.0
11-Jungle story	33.00	99.00	265.0
13-Bondage-c; Rulah (Kolah) story	33.00	99.00	265.0

STRANGE GALAXY
Eerie Publications: V1#8, Feb, 1971 - No. 11, Aug, 1971 (B&W, magazine)

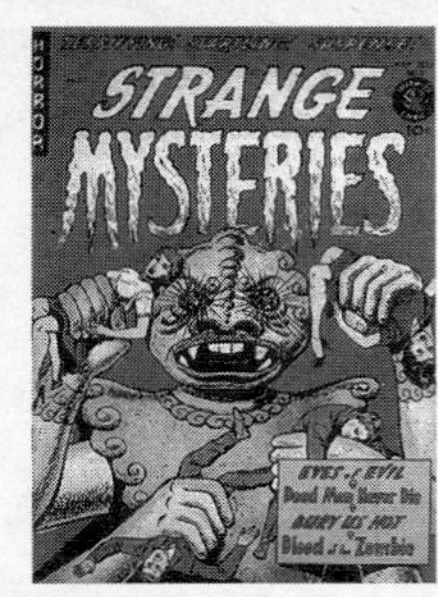

Strange Mysteries #5 © SUPR

Strangers in Paradise #10
© Terry Moore

Strange Stories From Another World #3
© FAW

GD2.0 FN6.0 NM9.4

	GD2.0	FN6.0	NM9.4
#8-Reprints-c/Fantastic V19#3 (2/70) (a pulp)	3.00	9.00	30.00
9-11	2.50	7.50	24.00

TRANGEHAVEN
iogenesis Press: June, 1995 - Present ($2.95, B&W)

-12			3.00

TRANGE JOURNEY
merica's Best (Steinway Publ.) (Ajax/Farrell): Sept, 1957 - No. 4, Jun, 1958 arrell reprints)

	19.00	56.00	150.00
-4: 2-Flying saucer-c	12.50	37.50	100.00

TRANGE KISS
vatar Press: Nov, 1999 - Present ($3.00, B&W)

-3-Warren Ellis-s			3.00

TRANGE LOVE (See Fox Giants)

TRANGELOVE
ntity Comics: 1995 ($2.50)

			2.50

TRANGE MYSTERIES
uperior/Dynamic Publications: Sept, 1951 - No. 21, Jan, 1955

-Kamenish-a & horror stories begin	58.00	174.00	550.00
	35.00	105.00	280.00
-5	31.00	92.00	245.00
-8	26.00	77.00	205.00
-Bondage 3-D effect-c	33.00	98.00	260.00
0-Used in **SOTI**, pg. 181	24.00	71.00	190.00
1-18	21.00	64.00	170.00
9-r/Journey Into Fear #1; cover is a splash from one story; Baker-r(2)	23.00	69.00	185.00
0,21-Reprints; 20-r/#1 with new-c	16.00	48.00	125.00

TRANGE MYSTERIES
W. Enterprises/Super Comics: 1963 - 1964

W. Reprint #9; Rulah-r/Spook #28; Disbrow-a	3.45	10.35	38.00
uper Reprint #10-12,15-17(1963-64): 10,11-r/Strange #2,1. 12-r/Tales of Horror #5 (3/53) less-c. 15-r/Dark Mysteries #23. 16-r/The Dead Who Walk. 17-r/Dark Mysteries #22	3.45	10.35	38.00
uper Reprint #18-r/Witchcraft #1; Kubert-a	3.45	10.35	38.00

TRANGE PLANETS
W. Enterprises/Super Comics: 1958; 1963-64

W. Reprint #1(nd)-Reprints E. C. Incredible S/F #30 plus-c/Strange Worlds #3	6.35	19.00	70.00
W. Reprint #9-Orlando/Wood-r/Strange Worlds #4; cover-r from Flying Saucers #1	8.15	24.50	90.00
uper Reprint #10-Wood-r (22 pg.) from Space Detective #1; cover-r/Attack on Planet Mars	8.15	24.50	90.00
uper Reprint #11-Wood-r (25 pg.) from An Earthman on Venus	9.50	28.50	105.00
uper Reprint #12-Orlando-r/Rocket to the Moon	8.15	24.50	90.00
uper Reprint #15-Reprints Journey Into Unknown Worlds #8; Heath, Colan-r	4.10	12.30	45.00
uper Reprint #16-Reprints Avon's Strange Worlds #6; Kinstler, Check-a	4.55	13.65	50.00
uper Reprint #18-r/Great Exploits #1 (Daring Adventures #6); Space Busters, Explorer Joe, The Son of Robin Hood; Krigstein-a	3.65	11.00	40.00

TRANGERS, THE
alibu Comics (Ultraverse): June, 1993 - No. 24, May, 1995 ($1.95/$2.50)

1-4,6-12,14-20: 1-1st app. The Strangers; has coupon for Ultraverse Premiere #0; 1st app. the Night Man (not in costume). 2-Polybagged w/trading card. 7-Break-Thru x-over. 8-2 pg. origin Solution. 12-Silver foil logo; wraparound-c. 17-Rafferty app.			2.50
1-With coupon missing			2.00
1-Full cover holographic edition, 1st of kind w/Hardcase #1 & Prime #1			6.00
1-Ultra 5000 limited silver foil			4.00
4-($2.50)-Newsstand edition bagged w/card			2.50
5-($2.50, 52 pgs.)-Rune flip-c/story by B. Smith (3 pgs.); The Mighty Magnor 1 pg. strip by Aragones; 3-pg. Night Man preview			2.50
13-($3.50, 68 pgs.)-Mantra app.; flip book w/Ultraverse Premiere #4			3.50
21-24 ($2.50)			2.50
...:The Pilgrim Conundrum Saga (1/95, $3.95, 68pgs.)			4.00

STRANGERS IN PARADISE
Antarctic Press: Nov, 1993 - No. 3, Feb, 1994 ($2.75, B&W, limited series)

1	5.45	16.35	60.00
1-2nd/3rd prints			5.00
2 (2300 printed)	4.10	12.30	45.00
3	3.00	9.00	30.00
Trade paperback (Antarctic Press, $6.95)-Red -c (5000 print run)			10.00
Trade paperback (Abstract Studios, $6.95)-Red-c (2000 print run)			15.00
Trade paperback (Abstract Studios, $6.95, 1st-4th printing)-Blue-			7.00
Hardcover ('98, $29.95) includes first draft pages			30.00
Gold Reprint Series ($2.75) 1-3-r/#1-3			2.75

STRANGERS IN PARADISE
Abstract Studios: Sept, 1994 - No. 14, July, 1996 ($2.75, B&W)

1	2.00	6.00	16.00
1,3- 2nd printings			4.00
2,3: 2-Color dream sequence	1.00	3.00	8.00
4-10			4.00
4-6-2nd printings			2.75
11-14: 14-The Letters of Molly & Poo			3.00
Gold Reprint Series ($2.75) 1-13-r/#1-13			2.75
I Dream Of You ($16.95, TPB) r/#1-9			17.00
It's a Good Life ($8.95, TPB) r/#10-13			9.00

STRANGERS IN PARADISE (Volume Three)
Homage Comics #1-8/Abstract Studios #9-on: Oct, 1996 - Present ($2.75, color #1-5, B&W #6-on)

1-Terry Moore-c/s/a in all; dream seq. by Jim Lee-a			4.00
1-Jim Lee variant-c	1.00	3.00	8.00
2-5			3.50
6-16: 6-Return to B&W. 13-15-High school flashback. 16-Xena Warrior Princess parody; two covers			3.00
17-35			2.75
...Lyrics and Poems (2/99)			2.75
High School ('98, $8.95, TPB) r/#13-16			9.00
Immortal ('98, $14.95, TPB) r/#6-12			15.00
Love Me Tender ($12.95, TPB) r/#1-5 in B&W w/ color Lee seq.			13.00
My Other Life ($14.95, TPB) r/#25-30			15.00

STRANGE SPORTS STORIES (See Brave & the Bold #45-49, DC Special, and DC Super Stars #10)
National Periodical Publications: Sept-Oct, 1973 - No. 6, July-Aug, 1974

1	2.80	8.40	28.00
2-6: 2-Swan/Anderson-a	2.00	6.00	16.00

STRANGE STORIES FROM ANOTHER WORLD (Unknown World #1)
Fawcett Publications: No. 2, Aug, 1952 - No. 5, Feb, 1953

2-Saunders painted-c	49.00	147.00	440.00
3-5-Saunders painted-c	40.00	120.00	320.00

STRANGE STORIES OF SUSPENSE (Rugged Action #1-4)
Atlas Comics (CSI): No. 5, Oct, 1955 - No. 16, Aug, 1957

5(#1)	39.00	118.00	315.00
6,9	24.00	71.00	190.00
7-E. C. swipe cover/Vault of Horror #32	24.00	73.00	195.00
8-Morrow/Williamson-a; Pakula-a	26.00	77.00	205.00
10-Crandall, Torres, Meskin-a	24.00	73.00	195.00
11-13: 12-Torres, Pakula-a. 13-E.C. art swipes	20.00	60.00	160.00
14-16: 14-Williamson/Mayo-a. 15-Krigstein-a. 16-Fox, Powell-a	22.00	66.00	175.00

NOTE: ***Everett** a-6, 7, 13; c-8, 9, 11-14. **Heath** a-5. **Maneely** c-5. **Morisi** a-11. **Morrow** a-13. **Powell** a-8. **Severin** c-7. **Wildey** a-14.*

STRANGE STORY (Also see Front Page)
Harvey Publications: June-July, 1946 (52 pgs.)

1-The Man in Black Called Fate by Powell	31.00	92.00	245.00

STRANGE SUSPENSE STORIES (Lawbreakers Suspense Stories #10-15;

Strange Suspense Stories #1 © FAW

Strange Tales #78 © MAR

Strange Tales #105 © MAR

This Is Suspense #23-26; Captain Atom V1#78 on)
Fawcett Publications/Charlton Comics No. 16 on: 6/52 - No. 5, 2/53; No. 16, 1/54 - No. 22, 11/54; No. 27, 10/55 - No. 77, 10/65; V3#1, 10/67 - V1#9, 9/69

1-(Fawcett)-Powell, Sekowsky-a 71.00 213.00 675.00
2-George Evans horror story 46.00 137.00 410.00
3-5 (2/53)-George Evans horror stories 40.00 120.00 350.00
16(1-2/54)-Formerly Lawbreakers S.S. 29.00 86.00 230.00
17,21: 21-Shuster-a 23.00 68.00 180.00
18-E.C. swipe/HOF 7; Ditko-c/a(2) 40.00 120.00 320.00
19-Ditko electric chair-c; Ditko-a 49.00 147.00 440.00
20-Ditko-c/a(2) 40.00 120.00 320.00
22(11/54)-Ditko-c, Shuster-a; last pre-code issue; becomes This Is Suspense 34.00 101.00 270.00
27(10/55)-(Formerly This Is Suspense #26) 14.00 41.00 110.00
28-30,38 10.00 30.00 75.00
31-33,35,37,40-Ditko-c/a(2-3 each) 21.00 64.00 170.00
34-Story of ruthless business man, Wm. B. Gaines; Ditko-c/a 42.00 125.00 375.00
36-(15¢, 68 pgs.); Ditko-a(4) 25.00 75.00 200.00
39,41,52,53-Ditko-a 17.00 51.00 135.00
42-44,46,49,54-60 4.10 12.30 45.00
45,47,48,50,51-Ditko-c/a 13.50 40.00 150.00
61-74 2.50 7.50 25.00
75(6/65)-Reprints origin/1st app. Captain Atom by Ditko from Space Advs. #33; r/Severin-a/Space Advs. #24 (75-77: 12¢ issues) 12.50 37.00 135.00
76,77-Captain Atom-r by Ditko/Space Advs. 5.45 16.35 60.00
V3#1(10/67): 12ç issues begin 2.80 8.40 28.00
V1#2-Ditko-c/a; atom bomb-c 2.50 7.50 25.00
V1#3-9: All 12¢ issues 1.85 5.50 15.00

NOTE: ***Alascia*** *a-19.* ***Aparo*** *a-60, V3#1, 2, 4; c-V1#4, 8.* ***Baily*** *a-1-3; c-2, 5.* ***Evans*** *c-3, 4.* ***Giordano*** *c-16, 17p, 24p, 25p.* ***Montes/Bache*** *c-66.* ***Powell*** *a-4.* ***Shuster*** *a-19, 21.* ***Marcus Swayze*** *a-27.*

STRANGE TALES (...Featuring Warlock #178-181; Doctor Strange #169 on)
Atlas (CCPC #1-67/ZPC #68-79/VPI #80-85)/Marvel #86(7/61) on:
June, 1951 - #168, May, 1968; #169, Sept, 1973 - #188, Nov, 1976

1-Horror/weird stories begin 300.00 900.00 3100.00
2 100.00 300.00 950.00
3,5: 3-Atom bomb panels 74.00 221.00 700.00
4-Cosmic eyeball story "The Evil Eye" 79.00 237.00 750.00
6-9: 6-Heath-c/a. 7-Colan-a 55.00 165.00 525.00
10-Krigstein-a 59.00 177.00 560.00
11-14,16-20 40.00 120.00 350.00
15-Krigstein-a 40.00 120.00 360.00
21,23-27,29-34: 27-Atom bomb panels. 33-Davis-a. 34-Last pre-code issue (2/55) 34.00 101.00 270.00
22-Krigstein, Forte/Fox-a 35.00 105.00 280.00
28-Jack Katz story used in Senate Investigation report, pgs. 7 & 169 35.00 105.00 280.00
35-41,43,44: 37-Vampire story by Colan 20.00 60.00 220.00
42,45,59,61-Krigstein-a; #61 (2/58) 20.50 61.00 225.00
46-57,60: 51-1st S.A. issue. 53,56-Crandall-a. 60-(8/57) 18.00 53.00 195.00
58,64-Williamson-a in each, with Mayo-#58 18.00 54.00 200.00
62,63,65,66: 62-Torres-a. 66-Crandall-a 16.50 49.00 180.00
67-Prototype ish. (Quicksilver) 19.00 57.00 210.00
68,71,72,74,77,80: Ditko/Kirby-a in #67-80 18.00 53.00 195.00
69,70,73,75,76,78,79: 69-Prototype ish. (Prof. X). 70-Prototype ish. (Giant Man). 73-Prototype ish. (Ant-Man). 75-Prototype ish. (Iron Man). 76-Prototype ish. (Human Torch). 78-Prototype ish. (Ant-Man). 79-Prototype ish. (Dr. Strange) (12/60) 23.00 68.00 250.00
81-83,85-88,90,91-Ditko/Kirby-a in all: 86-Robot-c. 90-(11/61)-Atom bomb blast panel 16.00 48.00 175.00
84-Prototype ish. (Magneto)(5/61); has powers like Magneto of X-Men, but two years earlier; Ditko/Kirby-a 20.50 61.00 225.00
89-1st app. Fin Fang Foom (10/61) by Kirby 41.00 123.00 500.00
92-Prototype ish. (Ancient One); last 10¢ issue 17.50 52.00 190.00
93,95,96,98-100: Kirby-a 14.50 43.50 160.00
94-Prototype ish. (The Thing); Kirby-a 17.50 52.00 190.00
97-1st app. Aunt May & Uncle Ben by Ditko (6/62), before Amazing Fantasy #15; (see Tales Of Suspense #7); Kirby-a 43.00 128.00 430.0
101-Human Torch begins by Kirby (10/62); origin recap Fantastic Four & Human Torch; H. Torch-c begin 79.00 236.00 1100.0
102-1st app. Wizard; robot-c 31.00 94.00 375.0
103-105: 104-1st app. Trapster. 105-2nd Wizard 27.50 82.00 300.0
106,108,109: 106-Fantastic Four guests (3/63) 18.00 54.00 200.0
107-(4/63)-Human Torch/Sub-Mariner battle; 4th S.A. Sub-Mariner app. & 1st x-over outside of Fantastic Four 23.00 68.00 250.0
110-(7/63)-Intro Doctor Strange, Ancient One & Wong by Ditko 100.00 300.00 1400.0
111-2nd Dr. Strange 31.00 94.00 375.0
112,113 12.50 37.00 135.0
114-Acrobat disguised as Captain America, 1st app. since the G.A.; intro. & 1st app. Victoria Bentley; 3rd Dr. Strange app. & begin series (11/63) 33.00 100.00 400.0
115-Origin Dr. Strange; Human Torch vs. Sandman (Spidey villain; 2nd app. & brief origin); early Spider-Man x-over, 12/63 41.00 123.00 500.0
116-(1/64)-Human Torch battles The Thing; 1st Thing x-over 11.00 33.00 120.0
117,118,120: 120-1st Iceman x-over (from X-Men) 7.25 21.75 80.0
119-Spider-Man x-over (2 panel cameo) 10.00 30.00 110.0
121,122,124,126-134: Thing/Torch team-up in 121-134. 126-Intro Clea. 128-Quicksilver & Scarlet Witch app. (1/65). 130-The Beatles cameo. 134-Last Human Torch; The Watcher-c/story; Wood-a(i) 5.00 15.00 55.0
123-1st app. The Beetle (see Amazing Spider-Man #21 for next app.); 1st Thor x-over (8/64); Loki app. 5.45 16.35 60.0
125-Torch & Thing battle Sub-Mariner (10/64) 5.45 16.35 60.0
135-Col. (formerly Sgt.) Nick Fury becomes Nick Fury Agent of Shield (origin/1st app.) by Kirby (8/65); series begins 11.00 33.00 120.0
136-140: 138-Intro Eternity 3.65 11.00 40.0
141-147,149: 145-Begins alternating-c features w/Nick Fury (odd #'s) & Dr. Strange (even #'s). 146-Last Ditko Dr. Strange who is in consecutive stories since #113; only full Ditko Dr. Strange-c this title. 147-Dr. Strange (by Everett #147-152) continues thru #168, then Dr. Strange #169 3.20 9.60 35.0
148-Origin Ancient One 5.90 17.75 65.0
150(11/66)-John Buscema's 1st work at Marvel 3.65 11.00 40.0
151-Kirby/Steranko-c/a; 1st Marvel work by Steranko 5.45 16.35 60.0
152,153-Kirby/Steranko-a 3.65 11.00 40.0
154-158-Steranko-a/script 3.65 11.00 40.0
159-Origin Nick Fury retold; Intro Val; Captain America-c/story; Steranko-a 4.10 12.30 45.0
160-162-Steranko-a/scripts; Capt. America app. 3.20 9.60 35.0
163-166,168-Steranko-a(p). 168-Last Nick Fury (gets own book next month) & last Dr. Strange who also gets own book 3.00 9.00 30.0
167-Steranko pen/script; classic flag-c; last 12¢-c 4.10 12.30 45.0
169-1st app. Brother Voodoo(origin in #169,170) & begin series, ends #173. 1.50 4.50 12.0
170-174: 174-Origin Golem 1.10 3.30 9.0
175-177: 177-Brunner-c 2.40 6.0
178-(2/75)-Warlock by Starlin begins; origin Warlock & Him retold; 1st app. Magus; Starlin-c/a/scripts in 178-181 (all before Warlock #9) 2.00 6.00 18.0
179-181-All Warlock. 179-Intro/1st app. Pip the Troll. 180-Intro Gamora. 181-(8/75)-Warlock story continued in Warlock #9 1.50 4.50 12.0
182-188: 185,186-(Regular 25¢ editions) 4.0
185,186-(30¢-c variants, limited distribution)(5,7/76) 2.40 6.0
Annual 1(1962)-Reprints from Strange Tales #73,76,78, Tales of Suspense #7,9, Tales to Astonish #1,6,7, & Journey Into Mystery #53,55,59; (1st Marve annual?) 44.00 133.00 575.0
Annual 2(7/63)-Reprints from Strange Tales #67, Strange Worlds (Atlas) #1-3, World of Fantasy #16; new Human Torch vs. Spider-Man story by Kirby/Ditko (1st Spidey x-over; 4th app.); Kirby-c 48.00 144.00 625.0

NOTE: ***Briefer*** *a-17.* ***Burgos*** *a-123p.* ***J. Buscema*** *a-174p.* ***Colan*** *a-7, 11, 20, 37, 53, 169-173p, 188p.* ***Davis*** *c-71.* ***Ditko*** *a-46, 50, 67-122, 123-125p, 126-146, 175r, 182-188r; c-51, 93, 115, 121, 146.* ***Everett*** *a-4, 21, 40-42, 73, 147-152, 164i; c-8, 10, 11, 13, 15, 24, 45, 49-54, 56, 58, 6 61, 63, 148, 150, 152, 158i.* ***Forte*** *a-27, 43, 50, 53, 54, 60.* ***Heath*** *a-2, 6; c-6, 18-20.* ***Kamen*** *a-4* ***G. Kane*** *c-170-173, 182p.* ***Kirby*** *Human Torch-101-105, 108, 109, 114, 120; Nick Fury-135p, 141-143p; (Layouts)-135-153; other* ***Kirby*** *a-67-100p; c-68-70, 72-74, 76-92, 94, 95, 101-114, 116-123, 125-130, 132-135, 136p, 138-145, 147, 149, 151p.* ***Kirby/Ayers*** *c-101-106, 108-110.* ***Kirby/Ditko*** *a-80, 88, 121; c-75, 93, 97, 100, 139.* ***Lawrence*** *a-29.* ***Leiber/ Fox*** *a-110-113.*

Strange Tales V2 #10 © MAR

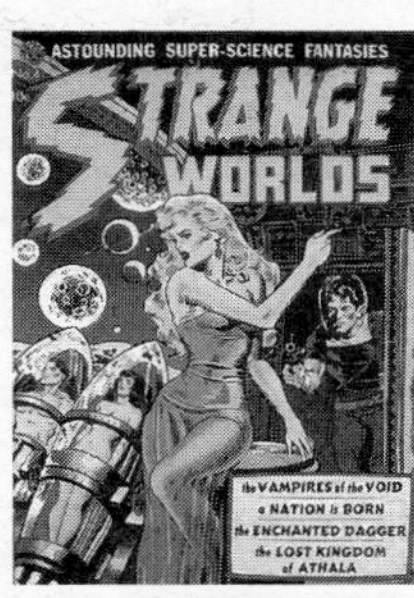

Strange Worlds #4 © AVON

Stray Bullets #18 © David Lapham

GD2.0 FN6.0 NM9.4

neely a-3, 7, 37, 42; c-33, 40. ***Moldoff*** *a-20.* ***Mooney*** *a-174i.* ***Morisi*** *a-53, 56.* ***Morrow*** *a-54.* ***ando*** *a-41, 44, 46, 49, 52.* ***Powell*** *a-42, 44, 49, 54, 130-134p; c-131p.* ***Reinman*** *a-11, 50, 74, 91, 95, 104, 106, 112i, 124-127i.* ***Robinson*** *a-17.* ***Romita*** *c-169.* ***Roussos*** *c-201i.* ***R.Q. Sale*** *6; c-16.* ***Sekowski*** *a-3, 11.* ***Severin*** *a(i)-136-138; c-137.* ***Starlin*** *a-178, 179, 180p, 181p; c--180, 181p.* ***Steranko*** *a-151-161, 162-168p; c-151i, 153, 155, 157, 159, 161, 163, 165, 167.* ***rres*** *a-53, 62.* ***Tuska*** *a-14, 166p.* ***Whitney*** *a-149.* ***Wildey*** *a-42, 56.* ***Woodbridge*** *a-59. ntastic Four cameos #101-134. Jack Katz app.-26.*

RANGE TALES
rvel Comics Group: Apr, 1987 - No. 19, Oct, 1988

#1-19 2.00

RANGE TALES
rvel Comics: Nov, 1994 ($6.95, one-shot)

#1-acetate-c 7.00

RANGE TALES (Anthology; continues stories from Man-Thing #8 and erewolf By Night #6)
rvel Comics: Sept, 1998 - No. 2, Oct, 1998 ($4.99)

2: 1-Silver Surfer app. 2-Two covers 5.00

RANGE TALES: DARK CORNERS
rvel Comics: May, 1998 ($3.99, one-shot)

-Anthology; stories by Baron & Maleev, McGregor & Dringenberg, DeMatteis & Badger; Estes painted-c 4.00

RANGE TALES OF THE UNUSUAL
as Comics (ACI No. 1-4/WPI No. 5-11): Dec, 1955 - No. 11, Aug, 1957

-Powell-a 42.00 125.00 375.00
28.00 83.00 220.00
Williamson-a (4 pgs.) 28.00 84.00 225.00
6,8,11 20.00 60.00 160.00
-Crandall, Ditko-a 25.00 75.00 200.00
9: 7-Kirby, Orlando-a. 9-Krigstein-a 22.00 66.00 175.00
-Torres, Morrow-a 20.00 60.00 160.00

TE: ***Baily*** *a-6.* ***Brodsky*** *c-2-4.* ***Everett*** *a-2, 6; c-6, 9, 11.* ***Heck*** *a-1.* ***Maneely*** *c-1.* ***Orlando*** *a-* ***Pakula*** *a-10.* ***Romita*** *a-1.* ***R.Q. Sale*** *a-3.* ***Wildey*** *a-3.*

RANGE TERRORS
John Publishing Co.: June, 1952 - No. 7, Mar, 1953

-Bondage-c; Zombies spelled Zoombies on-c; Fine-*esque* -a
50.00 150.00 450.00
30.00 90.00 240.00
-Kubert-a; painted-c 40.00 120.00 320.00
-Kubert-a (reprinted in Mystery Tales #18); Ekgren painted-c; Fine-*esque* -a; Jerry Iger caricature 47.00 142.00 425.00
-Kubert-a; painted-c 40.00 120.00 320.00
-Giant (25¢, 100 pgs.)(1/53); bondage-c 47.00 142.00 425.00
-Giant (25¢, 100 pgs.); Kubert-c/a 53.00 158.00 475.00

TE: ***Cameron*** *a-6, 7.* ***Morisi*** *a-6.*

RANGE WORLD OF YOUR DREAMS
ze Publications: Aug, 1952 - No. 4, Jan-Feb, 1953

-Simon & Kirby-a 61.00 182.00 575.00
3-Simon & Kirby-c/a. 2-Meskin-a 49.00 147.00 440.00
-S&K-c; Meskin-a 40.00 120.00 360.00

RANGE WORLDS (#18 continued from Avon's Eerie #1-17)
on Periodicals: 11/50 - No. 9, 11/52; No. 18, 10-11/54 - No. 22, 9-10/55 o #11-17)

-Kenton of the Star Patrol by Kubert (r/Eerie #1 from 1947); Crom the Barbarian by John Giunta 100.00 300.00 950.00
-Wood-a; Crom the Barbarian by Giunta; Dara of the Vikings app.; used in **SOTI**, pg. 112; injury to eye panel 95.00 285.00 900.00
-Wood/Orlando-a (Kenton), Wood/Williamson/Frazetta/Krenkel/Orlando-a (7 pgs.); Malu Slave Girl Princess app.; Kinstler-c
179.00 537.00 1700.00
-Wood-c/a (Kenton); Orlando-a; origin The Enchanted Daggar; Sultan-a; classic cover 100.00 300.00 950.00
-Orlando/Wood-a (Kenton); Wood-c 58.00 174.00 550.00
-Kinstler-a(2); Orlando/Wood-c; Check-a 42.00 125.00 375.00
-Fawcette & Becker/Alascia-a 40.00 120.00 320.00
-Kubert, Kinstler, Hollingsworth & Lazarus-a; Lazarus Robot-c
40.00 120.00 320.00

GD2.0 FN6.0 NM9.4

9-Kinstler, Fawcette, Alascia-a 38.00 113.00 300.00
18-(Formerly Eerie #17)-Reprints "Attack on Planet Mars" by Kubert
32.00 96.00 255.00
19-r/Avon's "Robotmen of the Lost Planet"; last pre-code issue; Robot-c
32.00 96.00 255.00
20-War-c/story; Wood-c(r)/U.S. Paratroops #1 10.00 30.00 70.00
21,22-War-c/stories. 22-New logo 7.15 21.50 50.00
I.W. Reprint #5-Kinstler-a(r)/Avon's #9 3.00 9.00 30.00

STRANGE WORLDS
Marvel Comics (MPI No. 1,2/Male No. 3,5): Dec, 1958 - No. 5, Aug, 1959

1-Kirby & Ditko-a; flying saucer issue 82.00 245.00 775.00
2-Ditko-c/a 49.00 147.00 440.00
3-Kirby-a(2) 40.00 120.00 330.00
4-Williamson-a 38.00 113.00 300.00
5-Ditko-a 33.00 98.00 260.00

NOTE: ***Buscema*** *a-3, 4.* ***Ditko*** *a-1-5; c-2..* ***Heck*** *a-2.* ***Kirby*** *a-1, 3.* ***Kirby/Brodsky*** *c-1, 3-5.*

STRAWBERRY SHORTCAKE
Marvel Comics (Star Comics): Jun, 1985 - No. 7, Apr, 1986 (Children's comic)

1-7: Howie Post-a (#7 exist?) 4.00

STRAY BULLETS
El Capitan Books: 1995 - Present ($2.95, B&W, mature readers)

1-David Lapham-c/a/scripts 1.50 4.50 12.00
2,3 2.40 6.00
4-8 3.50
9-21-($2.95) 3.00
22-($3.50) Includes preview to Murder Me Dead 3.50
Volume 1 ($29.95, hardcover) 30.00

NOTE: *Multiple printings of all issues exist & are worth cover price.*

STRAY TOASTERS
Marvel Comics (Epic Comics): Jan, 1988 - No. 4, April, 1989 ($3.50, square-bound, limited series)

1-4: Sienkiewicz-c/a/scripts 3.50

STREET COMIX
Street Enterprises/King Features: 1973 (50¢, B&W, 36 pgs.)(20,000 print run)

1-Rip Kirby 1.50 4.50 12.00
2-Flash Gordon 1.85 5.50 15.00

STREETFIGHTER
Ocean Comics: Aug, 1986 - No. 4, Spr, 1987 ($1.75, limited series)

1-4: 2-Origin begins 2.00

STREET FIGHTER
Malibu Comics: Sept, 1993 - No. 3, Nov, 1993 ($2.95)

1-3: 3-Includes poster; Ferret x-over 3.00

STREET FIGHTER: THE BATTLE FOR SHADALOO
DC Comics/CAP Co. Ltd.: 1995 ($3.95, one-shot)

1-polybagged w/trading card & Tattoo 4.00

STREET FIGHTER II
Tokuma Comics (Viz): Apr, 1994 - No. 8, Nov, 1994 ($2.95, limited series)

1-8 3.00

STREET POET RAY
Blackthorne Publ./Marvel Comics: Spring, 1989; 1990 - No. 4, 1990 ($2.95, B&W, squarebound)

1 (Blackthorne, $2.00) 3.00
1-4 (Marvel, $2.95, thick-c & paper) 3.00

STREETS
DC Comics: 1993 - No. 3, 1993 ($4.95, limited series, 52 pgs.)

Book 1-3-Estes painted-c 5.00

STREET SHARKS
Archie Publications: Jan, 1996 - No. 3, Mar, 1996 ($1.50, limited series)

1-3 2.00

STREET SHARKS
Archie Publications: May, 1996 - Present ($1.50, published 8 times a year)

Stumbo Tinytown #2 © HARV

Stupid, Stupid Rat Tails #1 © Jeff Smith

The Sub-Mariner #2 © MAR

1-6 2.00

STRICTLY PRIVATE (You're in the Army Now)
Eastern Color Printing Co.: July, 1942 (#1 on sale 6/15/42)

1,2: Private Peter Plink. 2-Says 128 pgs. on-c 23.00 68.00 180.00

STRIKE!
Eclipse Comics: Aug, 1987 - No. 6, Jan, 1988 ($1.75)

1-6, ...Vs. Sgt. Strike Special 1 (5/88, $1.95) 2.00

STRIKEBACK! (The Hunt For Nikita)
Malibu Comics (Bravura): Oct, 1994 - No. 3, Jan, 1995 ($2.95, unfinished limited series)

1-3: Jonathon Peterson script, Kevin Maguire-c/a 3.00
1-Gold foil embossed-c 5.00

STRIKEBACK!
Image Comics (WildStorm Productions): Jan, 1996 - No. 5, May, 1996 ($2.50, limited series)

1-5: Reprints original Bravura series w/additional story & art by Kevin Maguire & Jonathon Peterson; new Maguire-c in all. 4,5-New story & art 2.50

STRIKEFORCE: AMERICA
Comico: Dec, 1995 ($2.95)

V2#1-Polybagged w/gaming card; S. Clark-a(p) 3.00

STRIKEFORCE: MORITURI
Marvel Comics Group: Dec, 1986 - No. 31, July, 1989

1-24: 14-Williamson-i. 13-Double size 2.00
25-31-(Lower print run): 25-Heath-c 3.00

STRIKEFORCE MORITURI: ELECTRIC UNDERTOW
Marvel Comics: Dec, 1989 - No. 5, Mar, 1990 ($3.95, 52 pgs., limited series)

1-5 Squarebound 4.00

STRONG GUY REBORN (See X-Factor)
Marvel Comics: Sept, 1997 ($2.99, one-shot)

1-Dezago-s/Andy Smith, Art Thibert-a 3.00

STRONG MAN (Also see Complimentary Comics & Power of...)
Magazine Enterprises: Mar-Apr, 1955 - No. 4, Sept-Oct, 1955

1(A-1 #130)-Powell-c/a 22.00 66.00 175.00
2-4: (A-1 #132,134,139)-Powell-a. 2-Powell-c 18.00 53.00 140.00

STRONTIUM DOG
Eagle Comics: Dec, 1985 - No. 4, Mar, 1986 ($1.25, limited series)

1-4: 4-Moore script. 2.00
Special 1 (1986)-Moore script 2.00

STRYFE'S STRIKE FILE
Marvel Comics: Jan, 1993 ($1.75, one-shot, no ads)

1-Stroman, Capullo, Andy Kubert, Brandon Peterson-a; silver metallic ink-c; X-Men tie-in to X-Cutioner's Song 2.00
1-Gold metallic ink 2nd printing 2.00

STUCK RUBBER BABY
DC Comics (Paradox Press): 1998 (Graphic novel)

Hardcover ($24.95) 25.00
Softcover ($13.95) 14.00

STUMBO THE GIANT (See Harvey Hits #49,54,57,60,63,66,69,72,78,88 & Hot Stuff #2)

STUMBO TINYTOWN
Harvey Publications: Oct, 1963 - No. 13, Nov, 1966 (All 25¢ giants)

1-Stumbo, Hot Stuff & others begin 13.50 41.00 150.00
2 8.15 24.50 90.00
3-5 5.90 17.75 65.00
6-13 4.55 13.65 50.00

STUNT DAWGS
Harvey Comics: Mar, 1993 ($1.25, one-shot)

1 2.00

STUNTMAN COMICS (Also see Thrills Of Tomorrow)
Harvey Publ.: Apr-May, 1946 - No. 2, June-July, 1946; No. 3, Oct-Nov, 1946

1-Origin Stuntman by S&K reprinted in Black Cat #9; S&K-c
105.00 316.00 1000.0
2-S&K-c/a; The Duke of Broadway story 66.00 197.00 625.0
3-Small size (5-1/2x8-1/2"; B&W; 32 pgs.); distributed to mail subscribers only; S&K-a; Kid Adonis by S&K reprinted in Green Hornet #37
63.00 189.00 600.0
(Also see All-New #15, Boy Explorers #2, Flash Gordon #5 & Thrills of Tomorrow)

STUPID HEROES
Mirage Studios: Sept, 1993 - No. 3, Dec, 1994 ($2.75, unfinished limited serie

1-3-Laird-c/a & scripts; 2 trading cards bound in 2.7

STUPID, STUPID RAT TAILS (See Bone)
Cartoon Books: Dec, 1999 - No. 3, Feb, 2000 ($2.95, limited series)

1-3-Jeff Smith-a/Tom Sniegoski-s 3.0

STYGMATA
Entity Comics: No. 0, July, 1994 - No. 3, Oct, 1994 ($2.95, B&W, limited serie

0, 1-3: 0,1-Foil-c. 3-Silver foil logo 3.0
Yearbook 1 (1995, $2.95) 3.0

SUBHUMAN
Dark Horse Comics: Nov, 1998 - No. 4, Feb, 1999 ($2.95, limited series)

1-4-Mark Schultz-c 3.0

SUBMARINE ATTACK (Formerly Speed Demons)
Charlton Comics: No. 11, May, 1958 - No. 54, Feb-Mar, 1966

11 3.20 9.60 35.0
12-20 2.80 8.40 28.0
21-30 2.50 7.50 23.0
31-54 2.00 6.00 18.0
NOTE: *Glanzman c/a-25. Montes/Bache a-38, 40, 41.*

SUB-MARINER (See All-Select, All-Winners, Blonde Phantom, Daring, The Defenders, Fantastic Four #4, Human Torch, The Invaders, Iron Man &..., Marvel Mystery, Marvel Spotlight #27, Men's Adventures, Motion Picture Funnies Weekly, Namora, Namor, The..., Prince Namor, The Sub-Mariner, Saga Of The..., Tales to Astonish #70 & 2nd series, USA & Young Men)

SUB-MARINER, THE (2nd Series)(Sub-Mariner #31 on)
Marvel Comics Group: May, 1968 - No. 72, Sept, 1974 (No. 43: 52 pgs.)

1-Origin Sub-Mariner; story continued from Iron Man & Sub-Mariner #1
14.50 43.50 160.0
2-Triton app. 5.45 16.35 60.0
3-5: 5-1st Tiger Shark (9/68) 3.65 11.00 40.0
6,7,9,10: 6-Tiger Shark-c & 2nd app., cont'd from #5. 7-Photo-c. (1968). 9-1st app. Serpent Crown (origin in #10 & 12) 3.20 9.60 35.0
8-Sub-Mariner vs. Thing 3.65 11.00 40.0
11-13,15: 15-Last 12¢ issue 2.50 7.50 25.0
14-Sub-Mariner vs. G.A. Human Torch; death of Toro (1st modern app. & only app. Toro, 6/69) 3.20 9.60 35.0
16-20: 19-1st Sting Ray (11/69); Stan Lee, Romita, Heck, Thomas, Everett & Kirby cameos. 20-Dr. Doom app. 2.00 6.00 16.0
21,23-33,37-39,41,42: 25-Origin Atlantis. 30-Capt. Marvel x-over. 37-Death of Lady Dorma. 38-Origin retold. 42-Last 15¢ issue. 1.50 4.50 12.0
22,40: 22-Dr. Strange x-over. 40-Spider-Man x-over 1.85 5.50 15.0
34-Prelude (w/#35) to 1st Defenders story; Hulk & Silver Surfer x-over
4.10 12.30 45.0
35-Namor/Hulk/Silver Surfer team-up to battle The Avengers-c/story (3/71); hints at teaming up again 3.00 9.00 30.0
36-Wrightson-a(i) 2.30 7.00 20.0
43-King Size Special (52 pgs.) 1.85 5.50 15.0
44,45-Sub-Mariner vs. Human Torch 1.50 4.50 12.0
46-49,56,62,64-72: 47,48-Dr. Doom app. 49-Cosmic Cube story. 62-1st Tales of Atlantis, ends #66. 64-Hitler cameo. 67-New costume; F.F. x-over. 69-Spider-Man x-over (6 panels) 1.00 2.80 7.0
50-1st app. Nita, Namor's niece (later Namorita in New Warriors)
1.50 4.50 12.0
51-55,57,58,60,61,63-Everett issues: .61-Last artwork by Everett; 1st 4 pgs. completed by Mortimer; pgs. 5-20 by Mooney 1.00 3.00 8.0
59-1st battle with Thor; Everett-a 1.50 4.50 12.0
Special 1 (1/71)-r/Tales to Astonish #70-73 2.00 6.00 18.0
Special 2 (1/72)-(52 pgs.)-r/T.T.A. #74-76; Everett-a 1.50 4.50 12.0

Sub-Mariner Comics #1 © MAR

Sugar & Spike #3 © DC

Suicide Squad #14 © DC

NOTE: *Bolle a-67i. Buscema a(p)-1-8, 20, 24. Colan a(p)-10, 11, 40, 43, 46-49, Special 1, 2; c(p)-10, 11, 40. Craig a-17i, 19-23i. Everett a-45r, 50-55, 57, 58, 59-61(plot), 63(plot); c-47, 48i, 55, 57-59i, 61, Spec. 2. G. Kane c(p)-42-52, 58, 66, 70, 71. Mooney a-24i, 25i, 32-35i, 39i, 42i, 44i, 45i, 60i, 61i, 65p, 66p, 68i. Severin c/a-38i. Starlin c-59p. Tuska a-41p, 42p, 69-71p. Wrightson a-36i. #53, 54-r/stories Sub-Mariner Comics #41 & 39.*

SUB-MARINER COMICS (1st Series) (The Sub-Mariner #1, 2, 33-42)(Official True Crime Cases #24 on; Amazing Mysteries #32 on; Best Love #33 on)
Timely/Marvel Comics (TCI 1-7/SePI 8/MPI 9-32/Atlas Comics (CCC 33-42)): Spring, 1941 - No. 23, Sum, 1947; No. 24, Wint, 1947 - No. 31, 4/49; No. 32, 7/49; No. 33, 4/54 - No. 42, 10/55

	GD2.0	FN6.0	VF8.0	NM9.4
1-The Sub-Mariner by Everett & The Angel begin	2160.00	6480.00	14,040.00	27,000.00

	GD2.0	FN6.0	NM9.4
2-Everett-a	478.00	1435.00	5500.00
3-Churchill assassination-c; 40 pg. Sub-Mariner story	381.00	1143.00	4000.00
4-Everett-a, 40 pgs.; 1 pg. Wolverton-a	305.00	915.00	3200.00
5-Gabrielle/Klein-c	253.00	758.00	2400.00
6-10: 9-Wolverton-a, 3 pgs.; flag-c	211.00	633.00	2000.00
11-Classic Schomburg-c	200.00	600.00	1900.00
12-15	147.00	442.00	1400.00
16-20	126.00	379.00	1200.00
21-Last Angel; Everett-a	100.00	300.00	950.00
22-Young Allies app.	100.00	300.00	950.00
23-The Human Torch, Namora x-over (Sum/47); 2nd app. Namora after Marvel Mystery #82	111.00	332.00	1050.00
24-Namora x-over (3rd app.)	100.00	300.00	950.00
25-The Blonde Phantom begins (Spr/48), ends No. 31; Kurtzman-a; Namora x-over; last quarterly issue	121.00	363.00	1150.00
26-28: 28-Namora cover; Everett-a	100.00	300.00	950.00
29-31 (4/49): 29-The Human Torch app. 31-Capt. America app.	100.00	300.00	950.00
32 (7/49, Scarce)-Origin Sub-Mariner	153.00	458.00	1450.00
33 (4/54)-Origin Sub-Mariner; The Human Torch app.; Namora x-over in Sub-Mariner #33-42	95.00	285.00	900.00
34,35-Human Torch in each	74.00	221.00	700.00
36,37,39-41: 36,39-41-Namora app.	71.00	213.00	675.00
38-Origin Sub-Mariner's wings; Namora app.; last pre-code (2/55)	82.00	245.00	775.00
42-Last issue	84.00	253.00	800.00

NOTE: *Angel by Gustavson-#1, 8. Brodsky c-34-36, 42. Everett a-1-4, 22-24, 26-42; c-32, 33, 40. Maneely a-38; c-37, 39-41. Rico c-27-31. Schomburg c-1-4, 6, 8-18, 20. Sekowsky c-24, 25, 26(w/Rico). Shores c-21-23, 38. Bondage c-13, 22, 24, 25, 34.*

SUBSPECIES
Eternity Comics: May, 1991 - No. 4, Aug, 1991 ($2.50, limited series)

	GD2.0	FN6.0	NM9.4
1-4: New stories based on horror movie			2.50

SUBTLE VIOLENTS
CFD Productions: 1991 ($2.50, B&W, mature)

	GD2.0	FN6.0	NM9.4
1-Linsner-c & story	1.85	5.50	15.00
San Diego Limited Edition	6.80	20.50	75.00

SUE & SALLY SMITH (Formerly My Secret Life)
Charlton Comics: V2#48, Nov, 1962 - No. 54, Nov, 1963 (Flying Nurses)

	GD2.0	FN6.0	NM9.4
V2#48	2.50	7.50	23.00
49-54	2.00	6.00	16.00

SUGAR & SPIKE (Also see The Best of DC & DC Silver Age Classics)
National Periodical Publications: Apr-May, 1956 - No. 98, Oct-Nov, 1971

	GD2.0	FN6.0	NM9.4
1 (Scarce)	242.00	726.00	2300.00
2	84.00	253.00	800.00
3-5: 3-Letter column begins	61.00	182.00	575.00
6-10	40.00	120.00	350.00
11-20	36.00	108.00	290.00
21-29: 26-Christmas-c	24.00	73.00	195.00
30-Scribbly & Scribbly, Jr. x-over	25.00	75.00	200.00
31-40	14.50	43.00	160.00
41-60	8.65	26.00	95.00
61-80: 69-1st app. Tornado-Tot-c/story. 72-Origin & 1st app. Bernie the Brain	6.35	19.00	70.00
81-84,86-95: 84-Bernie the Brain apps. as Superman in 1 panel (9/69)	4.10	12.30	45.00
85 (68 pgs.)-r/#72	5.45	16.35	60.00
96 (68 pgs.)	6.35	19.00	70.00
97,98 (52 pgs.)	5.45	16.35	60.00

NOTE: *All written and drawn by Sheldon Mayer.*

SUGAR BOWL COMICS (Teen-age)
Famous Funnies: May, 1948 - No. 5, Jan, 1949

	GD2.0	FN6.0	NM9.4
1-Toth-c/a	14.00	43.00	115.00
2,4,5	7.15	21.50	50.00
3-Toth-a	10.00	30.00	75.00

SUGARFOOT (TV)
Dell Publishing Co.: No. 907, May, 1958 - No. 1209, Oct-Dec, 1961

	GD2.0	FN6.0	NM9.4
Four Color 907 (#1)-Toth-a, photo-c	12.50	37.50	150.00
Four Color 992 (5-7/59), Toth-a, photo-c	11.70	35.00	140.00
Four Color 1059 (11-1/60), 1098 (5-7/60), 1147 (11-1/61), 1209-all photo-c	8.35	25.00	100.00

SUICIDE SQUAD (See Brave & the Bold and Doom Patrol & Suicide Squad Spec., Legends #3 & note under Star Spangled War stories)
DC Comics: May, 1987 - No. 66, June, 1992 (Direct sales only #32 on)

	GD2.0	FN6.0	NM9.4
1-66: 9-Millennium x-over. 10-Batman-c/story. 13-JLI app. (Batman). 16-Re-intro Shade The Changing Man. 23-1st Oracle. 27-34-Snyder-a. 36,37-Snyder-a. 40-43-"The Phoenix Gambit" Batman storyline. 40-Free Batman/Suicide Squad poster			2.00
Annual 1 (1988, $1.50)-Manhunter x-over			2.00

NOTE: *Chaykin c-1.*

SUIT, THE
Virtual Comics (Byron Preiss Multimedia): Oct, 1996 - No. 3, Dec, 1996 ($2.50, limited series)

	GD2.0	FN6.0	NM9.4
1-3			2.50

SUMMER FUN (See Dell Giants)

SUMMER FUN (Formerly Li'l Genius; Holiday Surprise #55)
Charlton Comics: No. 54, Oct, 1966 (Giant)

	GD2.0	FN6.0	NM9.4
54	3.20	9.60	35.00

SUMMER FUN (Walt Disney's...)
Disney Comics: Summer, 1991 ($2.95, annual, 68 pgs.)

	GD2.0	FN6.0	NM9.4
1-D. Duck, M. Mouse, Brer Rabbit, Chip 'n' Dale & Pluto, Li'l Bad Wolf, Super Goof, Scamp stories			3.00

SUMMER LOVE (Formerly Brides in Love?)
Charlton Comics: V2#46, Oct, 1965; V2#47, Oct, 1966; V2#48, Nov, 1968

	GD2.0	FN6.0	NM9.4
V2#46-Beatles-c/story	12.50	37.00	135.00
47-Beatles story	10.00	30.00	110.00
48	1.50	4.50	12.00

SUMMER MAGIC (See Movie Comics)

SUNDANCE (See Hotel Deparee...)

SUNDANCE KID (Also see Blazing Six-Guns)
Skywald Publications: June, 1971 - No. 3, Sept, 1971 (52 pgs.)

	GD2.0	FN6.0	NM9.4
1-Durango Kid; Two Kirby Bullseye-r	1.85	5.50	15.00
2,3: 2-Swift Arrow, Durango Kid, Bullseye by S&K; Meskin plus 1 pg. origin. 3-Durango Kid, Billy the Kid, Red Hawk-r	1.50	4.50	12.00

SUN DEVILS
DC Comics: July, 1984 - No. 12, June, 1985 ($1.25, maxi series)

	GD2.0	FN6.0	NM9.4
1-12: 6-Death of Sun Devil			2.00

SUN FUN KOMIKS
Sun Publications: 1939 (15¢, B&W & red)

	GD2.0	FN6.0	NM9.4
1-Satire on comics	31.00	94.00	250.00

SUNFIRE & BIG HERO SIX (See Alpha Flight)
Marvel Comics: Sept, 1998 - No. 3, Nov, 1998 ($2.50, limited series)

	GD2.0	FN6.0	NM9.4
1-3-Lobdell-s			2.50

SUN GIRL (See The Human Torch & Marvel Mystery Comics #88)
Marvel Comics (CCC): Aug, 1948 - No. 3, Dec, 1948

Sunny, America's Sweetheart #11 © FOX

Superboy #98 © DC

Superboy #202 © DC

GD2.0 FN6.0 NM9.4

1-Sun Girl begins; Miss America app. 147.00 442.00 1400.00

2,3: 2-The Blonde Phantom begins 108.00 324.00 1025.00

SUNGLASSES
Verotik: Nov, 1995 - No. 6, Nov, 1996 ($2.95, limited series, mature)

1-5: Nancy Collins scripts; adapt. of "Sunglasses after Dark" 3.00

6-($3.95) 4.00

SUNNY, AMERICA'S SWEETHEART (Formerly Cosmo Cat #1-10)
Fox Features Syndicate: No. 11, Dec, 1947 - No. 14, June, 1948

11-Feldstein-c/a 74.00 221.00 700.00

12-14-Feldstein-c/a; 14-Lingerie panels 58.00 174.00 550.00

I.W. Reprint #8-Feldstein-a; r/Fox issue 12.00 36.00 130.00

SUN-RUNNERS (Also see Tales of the...)
Pacific Comics/Eclipse Comics/Amazing Comics: 2/84 - No. 3, 5/84; No. 4, 11/84 - No. 7, 1986 (Baxter paper)

1-7: P. Smith-a in #2-4 2.00

Christmas Special 1 (1987, $1.95)-By Amazing 2.00

SUNSET CARSON (Also see Cowboy Western)
Charlton Comics: Feb, 1951 - No. 4, 1951 (No month) (Photo-c on each)

1-Photo/retouched-c (Scarce, all issues) 84.00 253.00 800.00

2-Kit Carson story; adapts "Kansas Raiders" w/Brian Donlevy, Audie Murphy & Margaret Chapman 61.00 182.00 575.00

3,4 47.00 140.00 420.00

SUNSET PASS (See Zane Grey & 4-Color #230)

SUPER ANIMALS PRESENTS PIDGY & THE MAGIC GLASSES
Star Publications: Dec, 1953 (25¢, came w/glasses)

1-(3-D Comics)-L. B. Cole-c 41.00 122.00 365.00

SUPERBOY (See Adventure, Aurora, DC Comics Presents, DC 100 Page Super Spectacular #15, DC Super Stars, 80 Page Giant #10, More Fun Comics, The New Advs. of... & Superman Family #191, Young Justice)

SUPERBOY (1st Series)(...& the Legion of Super-Heroes with #231)(Becomes The Legion of Super-Heroes No. 259 on)
National Periodical Publications/DC Comics: Mar-Apr, 1949 - No. 258, Dec, 1979 (#1-16: 52 pgs.)

1-Superman cover; intro in More Fun #101 (1-2/45) 697.00 2090.00 8000.00

2-Used in **SOTI**, pg. 35-36,226 190.00 570.00 1800.00

3 147.00 442.00 1400.00

4,5: 5-1st pre-Supergirl tryout (c/story, 11-12/49) 100.00 300.00 950.00

6-10: 8-1st Superbaby. 10-1st app. Lana Lang 87.00 260.00 825.00

11-15 66.00 197.00 625.00

16-20: 20-2nd Jor-El cover 47.00 142.00 425.00

21-26,28-30: 21-Lana Lang app. 40.00 120.00 325.00

27-Low distribution 40.00 120.00 340.00

31-38: 38-Last pre-code issue (1/55) 31.00 94.00 250.00

39-48,50 (7/56) 26.00 78.00 230.00

49 (6/56)-1st app. Metallo (Jor-El's robot) 28.00 84.00 250.00

51-60: 52-1st S.A. issue 18.00 54.00 160.00

61-67 14.00 42.00 125.00

68-Origin/1st app. original Bizarro (10-11/58) 55.00 165.00 525.00

69-77,79: 76-1st Supermonkey 11.00 32.00 95.00

78-Origin Mr. Mxyzptlk & Superboy's costume 19.00 57.00 170.00

80-1st meeting Superboy/Supergirl (4/60) 16.00 47.00 140.00

81,83-85,87,88: 83-Origin/1st app. Kryptonite Kid 9.00 27.00 80.00

82-1st Bizarro Krypto 10.00 30.00 90.00

86-(1/61)-4th Legion app; Intro Pete Ross 17.00 50.00 150.00

89-(6/61)-1st app. Mon-el; 2nd Phantom Zone 31.00 93.00 280.00

90-92: 90-Pete Ross learns Superboy's I.D. 92-Last 10¢ issue 9.00 27.00 80.00

93-10th Legion app.(12/61); Chameleon Boy app. 8.15 24.50 90.00

94-97,99 5.45 16.35 60.00

98-(7/62)-18th Legion app; origin & 1st app. Ultra Boy; Pete Ross joins Legion 9.00 27.00 100.00

100-(10/62)-Ultra Boy app; 1st app. Phantom Zone villains, Dr. Xadu & Erndine. 2 pg. map of Krypton; origin Superboy retold; r-cover of Superman #1 18.00 54.00 200.00

101-120: 104-Origin Phantom Zone. 115-Atomic bomb-c. 117-Legion app. 4.55 13.65 50.00

121-128: 124-(10/65)-1st app. Insect Queen (Lana Lang). 125-Legion cameo. 126-Origin Krypto the Super Dog retold with new facts 4.10 12.30 45.00

129-(80-pg. Giant G-22)-Reprints origin Mon-el 5.45 16.35 60.00

130-137,139,140: 131-Legion statues cameo in Dog Legionnaires story. 132-1st app. Supremo. 133-Superboy meets Robin 3.00 9.00 30.00

138 (80-pg. Giant G-35) 4.55 13.65 50.00

141-146,148-155,157: 145-Superboy's parents regain their youth. 148-Legion app. 157-Last 12¢ issue 2.30 7.00 20.00

147(6/68)-Giant G-47; 1st origin of L.S.H. (Saturn Girl, Lightning Lad, Cosmic Boy); origin Legion of Super-Pets-r/Adv. #293 3.20 9.60 35.00

156,165,174 (Giants G-59,71,83): 165-r/1st app. Krypto the Superdog from Adventure Comics #210 2.50 7.50 25.00

158-164,166-171,175: 171-1st app. Aquaboy? 1.85 5.50 15.00

172,173,176-Legion app.: 172-Origin Yango (Super Ape). 176-Partial photo-c; last 15¢ issue 2.00 6.00 16.00

177-184,186,187 (All 52 pgs.): 182-All new origin of the classic World's Finest team (Superman & Batman) as teenagers (2/72, 22pgs). 184-Origin Dial H for Hero-r. 2.00 6.00 18.00

185-Also listed as DC 100 Pg. Super Spectacular #12; Legion-c/story; Teen Titans, Kid Eternity(r/Hit #46), Star Spangled Kid-r(S.S. #55) (see DC 100 Pg. Super Spectacular #12 for price)

188-190,192,194,196: 188-Origin Karkan. 196-Last Superboy solo story 1.00 3.00 8.00

191,193,195: 191-Origin Sunboy retold; Legion app. 193-Chameleon Boy & Shrinking Violet get new costumes. 195-1st app. Erg-1/Wildfire; Phantom Girl gets new costume. 1.25 3.75 10.00

197-Legion series begins; Lightning Lad's new costume 2.40 7.35 22.00

198,199: 198-Element Lad & Princess Projectra get new costumes 1.75 5.25 14.00

200-Bouncing Boy & Duo Damsel marry; J'onn J'onzz cameo 2.00 6.00 18.00

201,204,206,207,209: 201-Re-intro Erg-1 as Wildfire. 204-Supergirl resigns from Legion. 206-Ferro Lad & Invisible Kid app. 209-Karate Kid gets new costume 1.50 4.50 12.00

202,205-(100 pgs.): 202-Light Lass gets new costume; Mike Grell's 1st comic work-i (5-6/74) 3.20 9.60 35.00

203-Invisible Kid dies 2.00 6.00 16.00

208,210: 208-(68 pgs.). 208-Legion of Super-Villains app. 210-Origin Karate Kid 1.85 5.50 15.00

211-220: 212-Matter-Eater Lad resigns. 216-1st app. Tyroc, who joins the Legion in #218 1.25 3.75 10.00

221-230,246-249: 226-Intro. Dawnstar. 228-Death of Chemical King 1.00 3.00 8.00

231-245: (Giants). 240-Origin Dawnstar. 242-(52 pgs.). 243-Legion of Substitute Heroes app. 243-245-(44 pgs.). 1.25 3.75 10.00

250-258: 253-Intro Blok. 257-Return of Bouncing Boy & Duo Damsel by Ditko 5.00

Annual 1 (Sum/64, 84 pgs.)-Origin Krypto-r 17.50 52.00 190.00

Spectacular 1 (1980, Giant)-Distr. through comic stores; mostly-r 5.00

NOTE: ***Neal Adams*** *c-143, 145, 146, 148-155, 157-161, 163, 164, 166-168, 172, 173, 175, 176, 178.* ***M. Anderson*** *a-178,179, 245i.* ***Ditko*** *a-257p.* ***Grell*** *a-202i, 203-219, 220-224p, 235p; c-207-232, 235, 236p, 237, 239p, 240p, 243p, 246, 258.* ***Nasser*** *a(p)-222, 225, 226, 230, 231, 233, 236.* ***Simonson*** *a-237p.* ***Starlin*** *a(p)-239, 250, 251; c-238.* ***Staton*** *a-227p, 243-249p, 252-258p; c-247-251p.* ***Swan/Moldoff*** *c-109.* ***Tuska*** *a-172, 173, 176, 183, 235p.* ***Wood*** *inks-153-155, 157-161. Legion app.-172, 173, 176, 177, 183, 184, 188, 190, 191, 193, 195, 197-258.*

SUPERBOY (TV)(2nd Series)(The Adventures of...#19 on)
DC Comics: Feb, 1990 - No. 22, Dec, 1991 ($1.00/$1.25)

1-22: Mooney-a(p) in 1-8,18-20; 1-Photo-c from TV show. 8-Bizarro-c/story; Arthur Adams-a(i). 9-12,14-17-Swan-p 2.00

...Special 1 (1992, $1.75) Swan-a 2.50

SUPERBOY (3rd Series)
DC Comics: Feb, 1994 - Present ($1.50/$1.95/$1.99)

1-8,0,9-24,26-76: 1-Metropolis Kid from Reign of the Supermen. 6,7-Worlds Collide Pts. 3 & 8. 8-(9/94)-Zero Hour x-over. 0-(10/94). 9-(11/94)-King Shark app. 21-Legion app. 28-Supergirl-c/app. 33-Final Night. 38-41-"Meltdown". 45-

Superboy (3rd series) #59 © DC

Super Comics #4 © DELL

Super Duck Comics #45 © AP

GD2.0 FN6.0 NM9.4

Legion-c/app. 47-Green Lantern-c/app. 50-Last Boy on Earth begins. 60-Crosses Hypertime. 68-Demon-c/app. 2.00
25-($2.95)-New Gods & Female Furies app.; w/pin-ups 3.00
77-85: 77-Begin $2.25-c. 79-Superboy's powers return. 80,81-Titans app. 83-New costume. 85-Batgirl app. 2.25
#1,000,000 (11/98) 853rd Century x-over 2.00
Annual 1 (1994, $2.95, 68 pgs.)-Elseworlds story, Pt. 2 of The Super Seven (see Adventures Of Superman Annual #6) 3.00
Annual 2 (1995, $3.95)-Year One story 4.00
Annual 3 (1996, $2.95)-Legends of the Dead Earth 3.00
Annual 4 (1997, $3.95)-Pulp Heroes story 4.00
...Plus 1 (Jan, 1997, $2.95) w/Capt. Marvel Jr. 3.00
...Plus 2 (Fall, 1997, $2.95) w/Slither (Scare Tactics) 3.00
.../Risk Double-Shot 1 (Feb, 1998, $1.95) w/Risk (Teen Titans) 2.00

SUPERBOY & THE RAVERS
DC Comics: Sept, 1996 - No. 19, March, 1998 ($1.95)

1-19: 4-Adam Strange app. 7-Impulse-c/app. 9-Superman-c/app. 2.00

SUPERBOY/ROBIN: WORLD'S FINEST THREE
DC Comics: 1996 - No. 2, 1996 ($4.95, squarebound, limited series)

1,2: Superboy & Robin vs. Metallo & Poison Ivy; Karl Kesel & Chuck Dixon scripts; Tom Grummett-c(p)/a(p) 5.00

SUPER BRAT (Li'l Genius #5 on)
Toby Press: Jan, 1954 - No. 4, July, 1954

1 6.40 19.25 45.00
2-4: 4-Li'l Teevy by Mel Lazarus 4.65 14.00 28.00
I.W. Reprint #1,2,3,7,8('58): 1-r/#1 1.25 3.75 10.00
I.W. (Super) Reprint #10('63) 1.25 3.75 10.00

SUPERCAR (TV)
Gold Key: Nov, 1962 - No. 4, Aug, 1963 (All painted-c)

1 22.00 65.00 260.00
2,3 10.50 31.00 125.00
4-Last issue 15.00 45.00 175.00

SUPER CAT (Formerly Frisky Animals; also see Animal Crackers)
Star Publications #56-58/Ajax/Farrell Publ. (Four Star Comic Corp.): No. 56, Nov, 1953 - No. 58, May, 1954; Aug, 1957 - No. 4, May, 1958

56-58-L.B. Cole-c on all 20.00 60.00 160.00
1(1957-Ajax)- "The Adventures of..." c-only 9.30 28.00 65.00
2-4 5.70 17.00 40.00

SUPER CIRCUS (TV)
Cross Publishing Co.: Jan, 1951 - No. 5, Sept, 1951 (Mary Hartline)

1-(52 pgs.)-Cast photos on-c 12.50 37.50 100.00
2-Cast photos on-c 9.30 28.00 65.00
3-5 7.15 21.50 50.00

SUPER CIRCUS (TV)
Dell Publ. Co.: No. 542, Mar, 1954 - No. 694, Mar, 1956 (Mary Hartline)

Four Color 542: Mary Hartline photo-c 6.70 20.00 80.00
Four Color 592,694: Mary Hartline photo-c 5.85 17.50 70.00

SUPER COMICS
Dell Publishing Co.: May, 1938 - No. 121, Feb-Mar, 1949

1-Terry & The Pirates, The Gumps, Dick Tracy, Little Orphan Annie, Little Joe, Gasoline Alley, Smilin' Jack, Smokey Stover, Smitty, Tiny Tim, Moon Mullins, Harold Teen, Winnie Winkle begin 288.00 863.00 2300.00
2 103.00 309.00 825.00
3 94.00 281.00 750.00
4,5: 4-Dick Tracy-c; also #8-10,17,26(part),31 75.00 225.00 600.00
6-10 59.00 178.00 475.00
11-20: 20-Smilin' Jack-c (also #29,32) 47.00 141.00 375.00
21-29: 21-Magic Morro begins (origin & 1st app., 2/40). 22,27-Ken Ernst-c (also #25?); Magic Morro c-22,25,27,34 38.00 113.00 300.00
30- "Sea Hawk" movie adaptation-c/story with Errol Flynn 39.00 116.00 310.00
31-40: 34-Ken Ernst-c 31.00 94.00 250.00
41-50: 41-Intro Lightning Jim. 43-Terry & The Pirates ends 26.00 79.00 210.00
51-60 19.00 56.00 160.00
61-70: 62-Flag-c. 65-Brenda Starr-r begin? 67-X-Mas-c 18.00 53.00 140.00
71-80 13.00 39.00 105.00
81-99 11.00 33.00 90.00
100 12.50 37.50 100.00
101-115-Last Dick Tracy (moves to own title) 9.30 28.00 65.00
116-121: 116,118-All Smokey Stover. 117-All Gasoline Alley. 119-121-Terry & The Pirates app. in all 7.85 23.50 55.00

SUPER COPS, THE
Red Circle Productions (Archie): July, 1974 (one-shot)

1-Morrow-c/a; art by Pino, Hack, Thorne 1.00 2.80 7.00

SUPER COPS
Now Comics: Sept, 1990 - No. 4, Dec?, 1990 ($1.75)

1-($2.75, 52 pgs.)-Dave Dorman painted-c (both printings) 2.75
2-4 2.00

SUPER CRACKED (See Cracked)

SUPER DC GIANT (25-50¢, all 68-52 pg. Giants)
National Periodical Publications: No. 13, 9-10/70 - No. 26, 7-8/71; V3#27, Summer, 1976 (No #1-12)

S-13-Binky 9.50 28.50 105.00
S-14-Top Guns of the West; Kubert-c; Trigger Twins, Johnny Thunder, Wyoming Kid-r; Moreira-r (9-10/70) 3.20 9.60 35.00
S-15-Western Comics; Kubert-c; Pow Wow Smith, Vigilante, Buffalo Bill-r; new Gil Kane-a (9-10/70) 3.20 9.60 35.00
S-16-Best of the Brave & the Bold; Batman-r & Metamorpho origin-r from Brave & the Bold; Spectre pin-up. 3.00 9.00 30.00
S-17-Love 1970 (scarce) 23.00 68.00 250.00
S-18-Three Mouseketeers; Dizzy Dog, Doodles Duck, Bo Bunny-r; Sheldon Mayer-a 8.15 24.50 90.00
S-19-Jerry Lewis; Neal Adams pin-up 8.15 24.50 90.00
S-20-House of Mystery; N. Adams-c; Kirby-r(3) 5.00 15.00 55.00
S-21-Love 1971 (scarce) 25.50 76.00 280.00
S-22-Top Guns of the West; Kubert-c 2.50 7.50 25.00
S-23-The Unexpected 3.00 9.00 32.00
S-24-Supergirl 3.00 9.00 32.00
S-25-Challengers of the Unknown; all Kirby/Wood-r 2.50 7.50 25.00
S-26-Aquaman (1971)-r/S.A. Aquaman origin story from Showcase #30 2.50 7.50 25.00
27-Strange Flying Saucers Adventures (Sum, 1976) 2.30 7.00 20.00

NOTE: *Sid Greene r-27p(2), Heath r-27. G. Kane a-14r(2), 15, 27r(p). Kubert r-16.*

SUPER-DOOPER COMICS
Able Mfg. Co./Harvey: 1946 - No. 8, 1946 (10¢, 32 pgs., paper-c)

1-The Clock, Gangbuster app. 21.00 62.00 165.00
2 12.50 37.50 100.00
3,4,6 10.50 32.00 85.00
5-Capt. Freedom 12.50 37.50 100.00
7,8-Shock Gibson. 7-Where's Theres A Will by Ed Wheelan, Steve Case Crime Rover, Penny & Ullysses Jr. 8-Sam Hill app. 12.50 37.50 100.00

SUPER DUCK COMICS (The Cockeyed Wonder) (See Jolly Jingles)
MLJ Mag. No. 1-4(9/45)/Close-Up No. 5 on (Archie): Fall, 1944 - No. 94, Dec, 1960 (Also see Laugh #24)(#1-5 are quarterly)

1-Origin; Hitler & Hirohito-c 50.00 150.00 450.00
2-Bill Vigoda-c 23.00 68.00 180.00
3-5: 4-20-Al Fagaly-c (most) 15.00 45.00 120.00
6-10 12.00 36.00 95.00
11-20(6/48) 10.00 30.00 75.00
21,23-40 (10/51) 8.65 26.00 60.00
22-Used in **SOTI**, pg. 35,307,308 9.30 28.00 65.00
41-60 (2/55) 6.40 19.25 45.00
61-94 5.00 15.00 32.00

SUPER DUPER (Formerly Pocket Comics #1-4?)
Harvey Publications: No. 5, 1941 - No. 11, 1941

5-Captain Freedom & Shock Gibson app. 31.00 94.00 250.00
8,11 20.00 60.00 160.00

Super Friends #15 © DC

Supergirl #2 © DC

Supergirl (2nd series) #4 © DC

GD2.0 FN6.0 NM9.4

SUPER DUPER COMICS (Formerly Latest Comics?)
F. E. Howard Publ.: No. 3, May-June, 1947

3-1st app. Mr. Monster 12.50 37.50 100.00

SUPER FRIENDS (TV) (Also see Best of DC & Limited Collectors' Edition)
National Periodical Publications/DC Comics: Nov, 1976 - No. 47, Aug, 1981 (#14 is 44 pgs.)

1-Superman, Batman, Robin, Wonder Woman, Aquaman, Atom, Wendy, Marvin & Wonder Dog begin (1st Super Friends) 2.50 7.50 25.00
2-Penquin-c/sty 1.50 4.50 12.00
3-5 1.25 3.75 10.00
6-10,14: 7-1st app. Wonder Twins & The Seraph. 8-1st app. Jack O'Lantern. 9-1st app. Icemaiden. 14-Origin Wonder Twins 1.00 3.00 8.00
11-13,15-30: 13-1st app. Dr. Mist. 25-1st app. Fire as Green Fury. 28-Bizarro app. 1.00 2.80 7.00
31,47: 31-Black Orchid app. 47-Origin Fire & Green Fury 1.00 3.00 8.00
32-46: 36,43-Plastic Man app. 2.40 6.00
...Special 1 (1981, giveaway, no ads, no code or price)-r/Super Friends #19 & 36 1.25 3.75 10.00
NOTE: ***Estrada** a-1p, 2p. **Orlando** a-1p. **Staton** a-43, 45.*

SUPER FUN
Gillmor Magazines: Jan, 1956 (By A.W. Nugent)

1-Comics, puzzles, cut-outs by A.W. Nugent 4.15 12.50 25.00

SUPER FUNNIES (...Western Funnies #3,4)
Superior Comics Publishers Ltd. (Canada): Dec, 1953 - No. 4, Sept, 1954

1-(3-D, 10¢)-...Presents Dopey Duck; make your own 3-D glasses cut-out inside front-c; did not come w/glasses 40.00 120.00 320.00
2-Horror & crime satire 12.50 37.50 100.00
3-Phantom Ranger-c/s; Geronimo, Billy the Kid app. 7.15 21.50 50.00
4-Phantom Ranger-c/story 7.15 21.50 50.00

SUPERGIRL (See Action, Adventure #281, Brave & the Bold, Crisis on Infinite Earths #7, Daring New Advs. of..., Super DC Giant, Superman Family, & Super-Team Family)

SUPERGIRL
National Periodical Publ.: Nov, 1972 - No. 9, Dec-Jan, 1973-74; No. 10, Sept-Oct, 1974 (1st solo title)(20¢)

1-Zatanna back-up stories begin, end #5 3.20 9.60 35.00
2-4,6,7,9 1.85 5.50 15.00
5,8,10: 5-Zatanna origin-r. 8-JLA x-over; Batman cameo. 10-Prez 2.00 6.00 18.00
NOTE: *Zatanna in #1-5, 7(Guest); Prez app. in #10. #1-10 are 20¢ issues.*

SUPERGIRL (Formerly Daring New Adventures of...)
DC Comics: No. 14, Dec, 1983 - No. 23, Sept, 1984

14-23: 16-Ambush Bug app. 20-JLA & New Teen Titans app. 3.00
...Movie Special (1985)-Adapts movie; Morrow-a; photo back-c 4.00

SUPERGIRL
DC Comics: Feb, 1994 - No. 4, May, 1994 ($1.50, limited series)

1-4: Guice-a(i) 3.00

SUPERGIRL (See Showcase '96 #8)
DC Comics: Sept, 1996 - Present ($1.95/$1.99)

1-Peter David scripts & Gary Frank-c/a; DC cover logo in upper left is blue 1.00 3.00 8.00
1-2nd printing-DC cover logo in upper left is red 3.00
2,4-9: 4-Gorilla Grodd-c/app. 6-Superman-c/app. 9-Last Frank-a 4.00
3-Final Night, Gorilla Grodd app. 5.00
10-19: 14-Genesis x-over. 16-Power Girl app. 3.50
20-35: 20-Millennium Giants x-over; Superman app. 23-Steel-c/app. 24-Resurrection Man x-over. 25-Comet ID revealed; begin $1.99-c 3.00
36-46: 36,37-Young Justice x-over 2.00
47-49,51-54: 47-Begin $2.25-c. 51-Wears costume from animated series. 54-Green Lantern app. 2.25
50-($3.95) Supergirl's final battle with the Carnivore 4.00
#1,000,000 (11/98) 853rd Century x-over 3.00
Annual 1 (1996, $2.95)-Legends of the Dead Earth 3.00
Annual 2 (1997, $3.95)-Pulp Heroes; LSH app.; Chiodo-c 4.00
...Plus (2/97, $2.95) Capt.(Mary) Marvel-c/app.; David-s/Frank-a 3.00
.../Prysm Double-Shot 1 (Feb, 1998, $1.95) w/Prysm (Teen Titans) 2.00
TPB-('98, $14.95) r/Showcase '96 #8 & Supergirl #1-9 15.00

SUPERGIRL/LEX LUTHOR SPECIAL (Supergirl and Team Luthor on-c)
DC Comics: 1993 ($2.50, 68 pgs., one-shot)

1-Pin-ups by Byrne & Thibert 2.50

SUPER GOOF (Walt Disney) (See Dynabrite & The Phantom Blot)
Gold Key No. 1-57/Whitman No. 58 on: Oct, 1965 - No. 74, 1982

1 3.45 10.35 38.00
2-5 2.30 7.00 20.00
6-10 2.00 6.00 16.00
11-20 1.50 4.50 12.00
21-30 1.00 3.00 8.00
31-50 2.40 6.00
51-57 5.00
58,59 (Whitman) 2.40 6.00
60-62 (8/80-12/80, 3-pack?) 1.85 5.50 15.00
63-66('81) 1.00 2.80 7.00
67-69 5.00
70-74 (#90180 on-c; pre-pack? nd, nd code) 1.50 4.50 12.00
NOTE: *Reprints in #16, 24, 28, 29, 37, 38, 43, 45, 46, 54(1/2), 56-58, 65(1/2), 72(r-#2).*

SUPER GREEN BERET (Tod Holton...)
Lightning Comics (Milson Publ. Co.): Apr, 1967 - No. 2, Jun, 1967

1-(25¢, 68 pgs) 4.10 12.30 45.00
2-(25¢, 68 pgs) 3.20 9.60 35.00

SUPER HEROES (See Giant-Size... & Marvel...)

SUPER HEROES
Dell Publishing Co.: Jan, 1967 - No. 4, June, 1967

1-Origin & 1st app. Fab 4 3.20 9.60 35.00
2-4 2.50 7.50 24.00

SUPER-HEROES BATTLE SUPER-GORILLAS (See DC Special #16)
National Periodical Publications: Winter, 1976 (52 pgs., all reprints, one-shot)

1-Superman, Batman, Flash stories; Infantino-a(p) 1.50 4.50 12.00

SUPER HEROES VERSUS SUPER VILLAINS
Archie Publications (Radio Comics): July, 1966 (no month given)(68 pgs.)

1-Flyman, Black Hood, Web, Shield-r; Reinman-a 5.00 15.00 55.00

SUPERHERO WOMEN, THE - FEATURING THE FABULOUS FEMALES OF MARVEL COMICS (See Fireside Book Series)

SUPERICHIE (Formerly Super Richie)
Harvey Publications: No. 5, Oct, 1976 - No. 18, Jan, 1979 (52 pgs. giants)

5-Origin/1st app. new costumes for Rippy & Crashman 1.25 3.75 10.00
6-18 1.00 3.00 8.00

SUPERIOR STORIES
Nesbit Publishers, Inc.: May-June, 1955 - No. 4, Nov-Dec, 1955

1-The Invisible Man by H.G. Wells 23.00 68.00 180.00
2-4: 2-The Pirate of the Gulf by J.H. Ingrahams. 3-Wreck of the Grosvenor by William Clark Russell. 4-The Texas Rangers by O'Henry 10.00 30.00 80.00
NOTE: ***Morisi** c/a in all. Kiwanis stories in #3 & 4. #4 has photo of Gene Autry on-c.*

SUPER MAGIC (Super Magician Comics #2 on)
Street & Smith Publications: May, 1941

V1#1-Blackstone the Magician-c/story; origin/1st app. Rex King (Black Fury); Charles Sultan-c; Blackstone-c begin 147.00 442.00 1400.00

SUPER MAGICIAN COMICS (Super Magic #1)
Street & Smith Publications: No. 2, Sept, 1941 - V5#8, Feb-Mar, 1947

V1#2-Blackstone the Magician continues; Rex King, Man of Adventure app. 58.00 174.00 550.00
3-Tao-Anwar, Boy Magician begins 40.00 120.00 325.00
4-7,9-12: 4-Origin Transo. 11-Supersnipe app. 38.00 113.00 300.00
8-Abbott & Costello story (1st app?, 11/42) 40.00 120.00 325.00
V2#1-The Shadow app. 40.00 120.00 350.00
2-12: 5-Origin Tigerman. 8-Red Dragon begins 20.00 60.00 160.00

Super Magician Comics V4 #8 © Condé Nast

Superman #22 © DC

Superman #100 © DC

GD2.0 FN6.0 NM9.4

V3#1-12: 5-Origin Mr. Twilight 20.00 60.00 160.00
V4#1-12: 11-Nigel Elliman Ace of Magic begins (3/46), V5#1-6 16.00 48.00 125.00
7,8-Red Dragon by Edd Cartier-c/a 40.00 120.00 320.00

NOTE: *Jack Binder c-1-14(most). Red Dragon c-V5#7, 8.*

SUPERMAN (See Action Comics, Advs. of..., All-New Coll. Ed., All-Star Comics, Best of DC, Brave & the Bold, Cosmic Odyssey, DC Comics Presents, Heroes Against Hunger, JLA, The Kents, Krypton Chronicles, Limited Coll. Ed., Man of Steel, Phantom Zone, Power Record Comics, Special Edition, Steel, Super Friends, Superman: The Man of Steel, Superman: The Man of Tomorrow, Taylor's Christmas Tabloid, Three-Dimension Advs., World Of Krypton, World Of Metropolis, World Of Smallville & World's Finest)

SUPERMAN (Becomes Adventures of...#424 on)
National Periodical Publ./DC Comics: Summer, 1939 - No. 423, Sept, 1986 (#1-5 are quarterly)

GD2.0 FN6.0 VF8.0 NM9.4

1(nn)-1st four Action stories reprinted; origin Superman by Siegel & Shuster; has a new 2 pg. origin plus 4 pgs. omitted in Action story; see The Comics Magazine #1 & More Fun #14-17 for Superman proto-type app.; cover r/splash page from Action #10; 1st pin-up Superman on back-c - 1st pin-up in comics 14,000.00 42,000.00 91,000.00 175,000.00

1-Reprint, Oversize 13-1/2x10". **WARNING**: This comic is an exact duplicate reprint of the original except for its size. DC published it in 1978 with a second cover titling it as a Famous First Edition. There have been many reported cases of the outer cover being removed and the interior sold as the original edition. The reprint with the new outer cover removed is practically worthless. See Famous First Edition for value.

GD2.0 FN6.0 NM9.4

2-All daily strip-r; full pg. ad for N.Y. World's Fair 1020.00 3060.00 12,750.00
3-2nd story-r from Action #5; 3rd story-r from Action #6 697.00 2090.00 8000.00
4-2nd mention of Daily Planet (Spr/40); also see Action #23; 2nd & 3rd app. Luthor (red-headed; also see Action #23) 522.00 1565.00 6000.00
5-4th Luthor app. (red hair) 429.00 1286.00 4500.00
6,7: 6-1st splash pg. in a Superman comic. 7-1st Perry White? (11-12/40) 300.00 900.00 3000.00
8-10: 10-5th app. Luthor (1st bald Luthor, 5-6/41) 284.00 853.00 2700.00
11-13,15: 13-Jimmy Olsen & Luthor app. 211.00 633.00 2000.00
14-Patriotic Shield-c classic by Fred Ray 305.00 915.00 3200.00
16,18-20: 16-1st Lois Lane-c this title (5-6/42); 2nd Lois-c after Action #29 168.00 505.00 1600.00
17-Hitler, Hirohito-c 232.00 695.00 2200.00
21,22,25: 25-Clark Kent's only military service; Fred Ray's only super-hero story 126.00 379.00 1200.00
23-Classic periscope-c 147.00 442.00 1400.00
24-Classic Jack Burnley flag-c 190.00 570.00 1800.00
26-Classic war-c 158.00 474.00 1500.00
27-29: 27,29-Lois Lane-c. 28-Lois Lane Girl Reporter series begins, ends #40,42 116.00 348.00 1100.00
28-Overseas edition for Armed Forces; same as reg. #28 116.00 348.00 1100.00
30-Origin & 1st app. Mr. Mxyztplk (9-10/44)(pronounced "Mix-it-plk") in comic books; name later became Mxyzptlk ("Mix-yez-pit-l-ick"); the character was inspired by a combination of the name of Al Capp's Joe Blyfstyk (the little man with the black cloud over his head) & the devilish antics of Bugs Bunny; he 1st app. in newspapers 3/7/44 221.00 663.00 2100.00
31-40: 33-(3-4/45)-3rd app. Mxyztplk. 35,36-Lois Lane-c. 38-Atomic bomb story (1-2/46); delayed because of gov't censorship; Superman shown reading Batman #32 on cover. 40-Mxyztplk-c 100.00 300.00 950.00
41-50: 42-Lois Lane-c. 45-Lois Lane as Superwoman (see Action #60 for 1st app.). 46-(5-6/47)-1st app. Superboy this title? 48-1st time Superman travels thru time 79.00 237.00 750.00
51,52: 51-Lois Lane-c 63.00 189.00 600.00
53-Third telling of Superman origin; 10th anniversary issue ('48); classic origin-c by Boring 274.00 821.00 2600.00
54,56-60: 57-Lois Lane as Superwoman-c. 58-Intro Tiny Trix 63.00 189.00 600.00
55-Used in **SOTI**, pg. 33 66.00 197.00 625.00
61-Origin Superman retold; origin Green Kryptonite (1st Kryptonite story); Superman returns to Krypton for 1st time & sees his parents for 1st time since infancy, discovers he's not an Earth man 132.00 395.00 1250.00
62-70: 62-Orson Welles-c/story. 65-1st Krypton Foes: Mala, Kizo, & U-Ban. 66-2nd Superbaby story. 67-Perry Como-c/story. 68-1st Luthor-c this title (see Action Comics) 61.00 182.00 575.00
71-75: 74-2nd Luthor-c this title. 75-Some have #74 on-c 58.00 174.00 550.00
76-Batman x-over; Superman & Batman learn each other's I.D. for the 1st time (5-6/52)(also see World's Finest #71) 168.00 505.00 1600.00
77-81: 78-Last 52 pg. issue. 81-Used in **POP**, pg. 88 57.00 170.00 510.00
82-87,89,90: 89-1st Curt Swan-c in title 53.00 160.00 480.00
88-Prankster, Toyman & Luthor team-up 57.00 170.00 510.00
91-95: 95-Last precode issue (2/55) 47.00 140.00 420.00
96-99: 96-Mr. Mxyztplk-c/story 40.00 120.00 360.00
100 (9-10/55)-Shows cover to #1 on-c 200.00 600.00 1900.00
101-105,107-110: 109-1st S.A. issue 40.00 120.00 325.00
106 (7/56)-Retells origin 40.00 120.00 360.00
111-120 31.00 93.00 280.00
121,122,124-127,129: 127-Origin/1st app. Titano. 129-Intro/origin Lori Lemaris, The Mermaid 27.00 80.00 240.00
123-Pre-Supergirl tryout-c/story (8/58). 30.00 90.00 270.00
128-(4/59)-Red Kryptonite used. Bruce Wayne x-over who protects Superman's i.d. (3rd story) 28.00 83.00 250.00
130-(7/59)-1st app, Krypto, the Superdog with Superman (all previous app. w/Superboy 28.00 83.00 250.00
131-139: 135-2nd Lori Lemaris app. 139-Lori Lemaris app.; "Untold Lois Lane Story" back-up story 21.00 63.00 190.00
140-1st Blue Kryptonite & Bizarro Supergirl; origin Bizarro Jr. #1 22.00 67.00 200.00
141-145,148: 142-2nd Batman x-over 17.00 50.00 150.00
146-(7/61)-Superman's life story; back-up hints at Earth II. Classic-c 22.00 67.00 200.00
147(8/61)-7th Legion app; 1st app. Legion of Super-Villains; 1st app. Adult Legion; swipes-c to Adv. #247 20.00 60.00 180.00
149(11/61)-8th Legion app. (cameo); "The Death of Superman" imaginary story; last 10¢ issue 18.00 55.00 165.00
150,151,153,154,157,159,160: 157-Gold Kryptonite used (see Adv. #299); Mon-el app.; Lightning Lad cameo (11/62) 8.15 24.50 90.00
152,155,156,158,162: 152(4/62)-15th Legion app. 155-(8/62)-Legion app; Lightning Man & Cosmic Man, & Adult Legion app. 156,162-Legion app. 158-1st app. Flamebird & Nightwing & Nor-Kan of Kandor(12/62) 8.65 26.00 95.00
161-1st told death of Ma and Pa Kent 8.65 26.00 95.00
161-2nd printing (1987, $1.25)-New DC logo; sold thru So Much Fun Toy Stores (cover title: Superman Classic) 3.00
163-166,168-180: 166-XMas-c. 168-All Luthor issue; JFK tribute/memorial. 169-Bizarro Invasion of Earth-c/story; last Sally Selwyn. 170-Pres. Kennedy story is finally published after delay from #169 due to assassination. 172,173-Legion cameos. 174-Super-Mxyzptlk; Bizarro app. 6.35 19.00 70.00
167-New origin Brainiac & Brainiac 5; intro Tixarla (later Luthor's wife) 9.00 27.00 100.00
181,182,184-186,188-192,194-196,198,200: 181-1st 2965 story/series. 182-1st S.A. app. of The Toyman (1/66). 189-Origin/destruction of Krypton II. 5.00 15.00 55.00
183,187,193,197 (Giants G-18,G-23,G-31,G-36) 6.35 19.00 70.00
199-1st Superman/Flash race (8/67): also see Flash #175 & World's Finest #198,199 (r-in Limited Coll. Ed. #48) 23.00 68.00 250.00
201,203-206,208-211,213-216: 213-Brainiac-5 app. 216-Last 12¢ issue 3.65 11.00 40.00
202 (80-pg. Giant G-42)-All Bizarro issue 4.55 13.65 50.00
207,212,217,222,239 (Giants G-48,G-54,G-60,G-66,G-84): 207-30th anniversary Superman (6/68) 4.55 13.65 50.00
218-221,223-226,228-231 3.00 9.00 30.00
227,232(Giants, G-72,G-78)-All Krypton issues 4.10 12.30 45.00
233-2nd app. Morgan Edge; Clark Kent switches from newspaper reporter to TV newscaster; all Kryptonite on earth destroyed; classic Adams-c 4.55 13.65 50.00
234-238 2.50 7.50 24.00
240-Kaluta-a; last 15¢ issue 2.00 6.00 16.00
241-244 (All 52 pgs.): 241-New Wonder Woman app. 243-G.A.-r/#38 2.30 7.00 20.00
245-Also listed as DC 100 Pg. Super Spectacular #7; Air Wave, Kid Eternity,

Superman #388 © DC

Superman (2nd series) #33 © DC

Superman (2nd series) #135 © DC

GD2.0 FN6.0 NM9.4

Hawkman-r; Atom-r/Atom #3
(see DC 100 Pg. Super Spectacular #7 for price)
246-248,250,251,253 (All 52 pgs.): 246-G.A.-r/#40. 248-World of Krypton story. 251-G.A.-r/#45. 253-Finlay-a, 2 pgs., G.A.-r/#1 2.30 7.00 20.00
249,254-Neal Adams-a. 249-(52 pgs.); origin & 1st app. Terra-Man by Neal Adams (inks) 2.50 7.50 25.00
252-Also listed as DC 100 Pg. Super Spectacular #13; Ray(r/Smash #17), Black Condor, (r/Crack #18), Hawkman(r/Flash #24); Starman-r/Adv. #67; Dr. Fate & Spectre-r/More Fun #57; N. Adams-c
(see DC 100 Pg. Super Spectacular #13 for price)
255-271,273-277,279-283: 263-Photo-c. 264-1st app. Steve Lombard. 276-Intro Capt. Thunder. 279-Batman, Batgirl app. 1.25 3.75 10.00
272,278,284-All 100 pgs. G.A.-r in all. 272-r/2nd app. Mr. Mxyztplk from Action #80 2.80 8.40 28.00
285-299: 289-Partial photo-c. 292-Origin Lex Luthor retold 1.00 2.80 7.00
300-(6/76) Superman in the year 2001 2.30 7.00 20.00
301-350: 301,320-Solomon Grundy app. 323-Intro. Atomic Skull. 327-329-(44 pgs.). 330-More facts revealed about I. D. 338-The bottled city of Kandor enlarged. 344-Frankenstein & Dracula app. 4.00
351-399: 353-Brief origin. 354,355,357-Superman 2020 stories (354-Debut of Superman III). 356-World of Krypton story (also #360,367,375). 366-Fan letter by Todd McFarlane. 372-Superman 2021 story. 376-Free 16 pg. preview Daring New Advs. of Supergirl. 377-Free 16 pg. preview Masters of the Universe 3.00
400 (10/84, $1.50, 68 pgs.)-Many top artists featured; Chaykin painted cover, Miller back-c 5.00
401-422: 405-Super-Batman story. 408-Nuclear Holocaust-c/story. 411-Special Julius Schwartz tribute issue. 414,415-Crisis x-over. 422-Horror-c 3.00
423-Alan Moore scripts; Perez-a(i); last Earth I Superman story, cont'd in Action #583 1.00 3.00 8.00
Annual 1(10/60, 84 pgs.)-Reprints 1st Supergirl story/Action #252; r/Lois Lane #1; Krypto-r (1st Silver Age DC annual) 82.00 246.00 1150.00
Annual 2(Win, 1960-61)-Super-villain issue; Brainiac, Titano, Metallo, Bizarro origin-r 40.00 119.00 475.00
Annual 3(Sum, 1961)-Strange Lives of Superman 29.00 88.00 325.00
Annual 4(Win, 1961-62)-11th Legion app; 1st Legion origins (text & pictures); advs. in time, space & on alien worlds 23.50 71.00 260.00
Annual 5(Sum, 1962)-All Krypton issue 18.00 54.00 200.00
Annual 6(Win, 1962-63)-Legion-r/Adv. #247 17.00 51.00 185.00
Annual 7(Sum, 1963)-Origin-r/Superman-Batman team/Adv. 275; r/1955 Superman dailies 12.50 37.00 135.00
Annual 8(Win, 1963-64)-All origins issue 11.00 33.00 120.00
Annual 9(8/64)-Was advertised but came out as 80 Page Giant #1 instead
Annual 9(1983)-Toth/Austin-a 2.40 6.00
Annuals 10-12: 10(1984, $1.25)-M. Anderson inks. 11(1985)-Moore scripts. 12(1986)-Bolland-c 4.00
Special 1-3('83-'85): 1-G. Kane-c/a; contains German-r 4.00
The Amazing World of Superman "Official Metropolis Edition" (1973, $2.00, treasury-size)-Origin retold; Wood-r(i) from Superboy #153,161; poster incl. (half price if poster missing) 3.00 9.00 30.00
11195 (2/79, $1.95, 224 pgs.)-Golden Press 2.00 6.00 18.00

*NOTE: **N. Adams** a-249i, 254p; c-204-206, 210, 212-215, 219, 231i, 233-237, 240-243, 249-252, 254, 263, 307, 308, 313, 314, 317. **Adkins** a-323i. **Austin** c-368i. **Wayne Boring** art-late 1940's to early 1960's. **Buckler** a(p)-352, 363, 364, 369; c(p)-324-327, 356, 363, 368, 369, 373, 376, 378. **Burnley** a-252r; c-19-25, 30, 33, 34, 35p, 38p, 39p, 45p. **Fine** a-252r. **Kaluta** a-400. **Gil Kane** a-272r, 367, 372, 375, Special 2; c-374p, 375p, 377, 381, 382, 384-390, 392, Annual 9, Special 2. **Joe Kubert** c-216. **Morrow** a-238. **Mortimer** a-250r. **Perez** c-364p. **Fred Ray** a-25; c-6, 8-18. **Starlin** c-355. **Staton** a-354i, 355i. **Swan/Moldoff** c-149. **Williamson** a(i)-408-410, 412-416; c-408i, 409i. **Wrightson** a-400, 416.*

SUPERMAN (2nd Series)
DC Comics: Jan, 1987 - Present (75¢/$1.00/$1.25/$1.50/$1.95/$1.99)

0-(10/94) Zero Hour; released between #93 & #94 2.00
1-Byrne-c/a begins; intro new Metallo 4.00
2-8,10: 3-Legends x-over; Darkseid-c & app. 7-Origin/1st app. Rampage. 8-Legion app. 3.00
9-Joker-c 4.50
11-15,17-20,22-49,51,52,54-56,58-67: 11-1st new Mr. Mxyzptlk. 12-Lori Lemaris revived. 13-1st app. new Toyman. 13,14-Millennium x-over. 20-Doom Patrol app.; Supergirl cameo. 31-Mr. Mxyzptlk app. 37-Newsboy Legion app. 41-Lobo app. 44-Batman storyline, part 1. 45-Free extra 8 pgs. 54-Newsboy Legion story. 63-Aquaman x-over. 67-Last $1.00-c 2.50
16,21: 16-1st app. new Supergirl (4/88). 21-Supergirl-c/story; 1st app. Matrix who becomes new Supergirl 4.00
50-($1.50, 52 pgs.)-Clark Kent proposes to Lois 5.00
50-2nd printing 2.00
53-Clark reveals i.d. to Lois (Cont'd from Action #662) 3.00
53-2nd printing 2.00
57-($1.75, 52 pgs.) 3.00
68-72: 65,66,68-Deathstroke-c/stories. 70-Superman & Robin team-up 2.00
73-Doomsday cameo 5.00
74-Doomsday Pt. 2 (Cont'd from Justice League #69); Superman battles Doomsday 2.40 6.00
73,74-2nd printings 2.00
75-($2.50)-Collector's Ed.; Doomsday Pt. 6; Superman dies; polybagged w/poster of funeral, obituary from Daily Planet, postage stamp & armband premiums (direct sales only) 1.85 5.50 15.00
75-Direct sales copy (no upc code, 1st print) 2.40 6.00
75-Direct sales copy (no upc code, 2nd-4th prints) 2.00
75-Newsstand copy w/upc code 6.00
75-Platinum Edition; given away to retailers 40.00
76,77-Funeral For a Friend parts 4 & 8 3.00
78-($1.95)-Collector's Edition with die-cut outer-c & bound-in mini poster; Doomsday cameo 3.00
78-($1.50)-Newsstand Edition w/poster and different-c; Doomsday-c & cameo 2.00
79-81,83-89: 83-Funeral for a Friend epilogue; new Batman (Azrael) cameo. 87,88-Bizarro-c/story 2.00
82-($3.50)-Collector's Edition w/all chromium-c; real Superman revealed; Green Lantern x-over from G.L. #46; no ads 2.40 6.00
82-($2.00, 44 pgs.)-Regular Edition w/different-c 2.00
90-99: 93-(9/94)-Zero Hour. 94-(11/94). 95-Atom app. 96-Brainiac returns 2.00
100-Death of Clark Kent foil-c 4.00
100-Newsstand 3.00
101-122: 101-Begin $1.95-c; Black Adam app. 105-Green Lantern app. 110-Plastic Man-c/app. 114-Brainiac app; Dwyer-c. 115-Lois leaves Metropolis. 116-(10/96)-1st app. Teen Titans by Dan Jurgens & George Perez in 8 pg. preview. 117-Final Night. 118-Wonder Woman app. 119-Legion app. 122-New powers 2.00
123-Collector's Edition w/glow in the dark-c, new costume 2.40 6.00
123-Standard ed., new costume 4.00
124-149: 128-Cyborg-c/app. 131-Birth of Lena Luthor. 132-Superman Red/ Superman Blue. 134-Millenium Giants. 136,137-Superman 2999. 139-Starlin-a. 140-Grindberg-a 2.00
150-($2.95) Standard Ed.; Brainiac 2.0 app.; Jurgens-s 3.00
150-($3.95) Collector's Ed. w/holo-foil enhanced variant-c 4.00
151-158: 151-Loeb-s begins; Daily Planet reopens 2.00
159-167: 159-$2.25-c begin. 161-Joker-c/app. 162-Aquaman-c/app. 163-Young Justice app. 165-JLA app.; Ramos; Madureira, Liefeld, A. Adams, Wieringo, Churchill-a. 166-Collector's and reg. editions. 167-Return to Krypton 2.25
#1,000,000 (11/98) 853rd Century x-over; Gene Ha-c 2.00
Annual 1,2: 1 (1987)-No Byrne-a. 2 (1988)-Byrne-a; Newsboy Legion; return of the Guardian 4.00
Annual 3-6 ('91-'94 68 pgs.): 1-Armageddon 2001 x-over; Batman app.; Austin-c(i) & part inks. 4-Eclipso app. 6-Elseworlds sty 3.00
Annual 3-2nd & 3rd printings; 3rd has silver ink 2.00
Annual 7 (1995, $3.95, 69 pgs.)-Year One story 4.00
Annual 8 (1996, $2.95)-Legends of the Dead Earth story 3.00
Annual 9 (1997, $3.95)-Pulp Heroes story 4.00
Annual 10 (1998, $2.95)-Ghosts; Wrightson-c 3.00
Annual 11 (1999, $2.95)-JLApe; Art Adams-c 3.00
Annual 12 (2000, $3.50)-Planet DC 3.50
...: 80 Page Giant (2/99, $4.95) Jurgens-c 5.00
...: 80 Page Giant 2 (6/99, $4.95) Harris-c 5.00
...: 80 Page Giant 3 (11/00, $5.95) Nowlan-c; art by various 6.00
...: Eradication! The Origin of the Eradicator (1996, $12.95, TPB) 13.00
...: Exile (1998, $14.95, TPB)-Reprints space exile following execution of Kryptonian criminals; 1st Eradicator 15.00
... In the Seventies ('00, $19.95, TPB) Intro. by Christopher Reeve 20.00

Superman Adventures #42 © DC

Superman & Bugs Bunny #1 © DC/WB

Superman For All Seasons #3 © DC

GD2.0 FN6.0 NM9.4

.. No Limits ('00, $14.95, TPB) Reprints early 2000 stories 15.00
...Plus 1(2/97, $2.95)-Legion of Super-Heroes-c/app. 3.00
Special 1 (1992, $3.50, 68 pgs.)-Simonson-c/a 5.00
The Death of Clark Kent (1997, $19.95, TPB)-Reprints Man of Steel #43 (1 page), Superman #99 (1 page),#100-102, Action #709 (1 page), #710,711, Advs. of Superman #523-525, Superman:The Man of Tomorrow #1 20.00
The Death of Superman (1993, $4.95, TPB)-Reprints Man of Steel #17-19, Superman #73-75, Advs. of Superman #496,497, Action #683,684, & Justice League #69 1.00 3.00 8.00
The Death of Superman, 2nd & 3rd printings 5.00
The Death of Superman Platinum Edition 15.00
The Trial of Superman ('97, $14.95, TPB) reprints story arc 15.00
...: They Saved Luthor's Brain ('00, $14.95) r/ "death" and return of Luthor 14.95
...: Time and Time Again (1994, $7.50, TPB)-Reprints 8.00
...: Transformed ('98, $12.95, TPB) r/post Final Night powerless Superman to Electric Superman 13.00
... Vs. The Revenge Squad (1999, $12.95, TPB) 13.00
NOTE: ***Austin*** *a(i)-1-3.* ***Byrne*** *a-1-16p, 17, 19-21p, 22; c-1-17, 20-22; scripts-1-22.* ***Guice*** *c/a-64.* ***Kirby*** *c-37p.* ***Joe Quesada*** *c-Annual 4.* ***Russell*** *c/a-23i.* ***Simonson*** *c-69i. #19-21 2nd printings sold in multi-packs.*

SUPERMAN (one-shots)
Daily News Magazine Presents DC Comics' Superman
nn-(1987, 8 pgs.)-Supplement to New York Daily News; Perez-c/a 5.00
...: A Nation Divided (1999, $4.95)-Elseworlds Civil War story 5.00
... & Savage Dragon: Metropolis (11/99, $4.95) Bogdanove-a 5.00
...: At Earth's End (1995, $4.95)-Elseworlds story 5.00
...: Distant Fires (1998, $5.95)-Elseworlds; Chaykin-s 6.00
...: Emperor Joker (10/00, $3.50)-Follows Action #769 3.50
...: End of the Century (2/00, $24.95, HC)-Immonen-s/a 25.00
... For Earth (1991, $4.95, 52 pgs, printed on recycled paper)-Ordway wraparound-c. 5.00
...IV Movie Special (1987, $2.00)-Movie adaptation; Heck-a 3.00
...Gallery, The 1 (1993, $2.95)-Poster-a 3.00
..., Inc. (1999, $6.95)-Elseworlds Clark as a sports hero; Garcia-Lopez-a 7.00
...: Kal (1995, $5.95)-Elseworlds story 6.00
...: Lex 2000 (1/01, $3.50)-Election night for the Luthor Presidency 3.50
...: Monster (1999, $5.95)-Elseworlds story; Anthony Williams-a 6.00
...Movie Special-(9/83)-Adaptation of Superman III; other versions exist with store logos on bottom 1/3 of-c 4.00
...'s Metropolis-(1996, $5.95, prestige format)-Elseworlds; McKeever-c/a 6.00
...: Speeding Bullets-(1993, $4.95, 52 pgs.)-Elseworlds 5.00
.../Spider-Man-(1995, $3.95)-r/DC and Marvel Presents... 4.00
...: The Earth Stealers 1-(1988, $2.95, 52 pgs, prestige format) Byrne script; painted-c 4.00
...: The Earth Stealers 1-2nd printing 3.00
...: The Legacy of Superman #1 (3/93, $2.50, 68 pgs.)-Art Adams-c; Simonson-a 4.00
...: The Last God of Krypton ('99,$4.95) Hildebrandt Bros.-a/Simonson-s 5.00
...: The Odyssey ('99, $4.95) Clark Kent's post-Smallville journey 5.00
.../Toyman-(1996, $1.95) 2.00
...: 3-D (12/98, $3.95)-with glasses 4.00
...: Under A Yellow Sun (1994, $5.95, 68 pgs.)-A Novel by Clark Kent; embossed-c 6.00
...: War of the Worlds (1999, $5.95)-Battles Martians 6.00
...: Y2K (2/00, $4.95)-1st Brainiac 13 app.; Guice-c/a 5.00

SUPERMAN ADVENTURES, THE (TV)
DC Comics: Oct, 1996 - Present ($1.75/$1.95/$1.99)(Based on animated series)
1-Rick Burchett-c/a begins; Paul Dini script; Lex Luthor app.; silver ink, wraparound-c. 3.00
2-20,22: 2-Scott McCloud scripts begin; Metallo-c/app. 3-Brainiac-c/app. 6-Mxyzptlk-c/app. 2.50
21-($3.95) 1st animated Supergirl 5.00
23-53: 23-Begin $1.99-c; Livewire app. 25-Batgirl-c/app. 28-Manley-a 2.00
Annual 1 (1997, $3.95)-Zatanna and Bruce Wayne app. 4.00
Special 1 (2/98, $2.95) Superman vs. Lobo 3.00
TPB (1998, $7.95) r/#1-6 8.00

SUPERMAN & BATMAN: GENERATIONS (Elseworlds)
DC Comics: 1999 - No. 4, 1999 ($4.95, limited series)
1-4-Superman & Batman team-up from 1939 to the future; Byrne-c/s/a 5.00
TPB (2000, $14.95) r/series 14.95

SUPERMAN & BATMAN: WORLD'S FUNNEST (Elseworlds)
DC Comics: 2000 ($6.95, square-bound, one-shot)
nn-Mr. Mxyzptlk and Bat-Mite destroy each DC Universe; Dorkin-s/ art by various incl. Ross, Timm, Miller, Allred, Moldoff, Gibbons, Cho, Jimenez 2.50

SUPERMAN & BUGS BUNNY
DC Comics: Jul, 2000 - No. 4, Oct, 2000 ($2.50, limited series)
1-4-JLA & Looney Tunes characters meet 2.50

SUPERMAN/BATMAN: ALTERNATE HISTORIES
DC Comics: 1996 ($14.95, trade paperback)
nn-Reprints Detective Comics Annual #7, Action Comics Annual #6, Steel Annual #1, Legends of the Dark Knight Annual #4 15.00

SUPERMAN/DOOMSDAY: HUNTER/PREY
DC Comics: 1994 - No. 3, 1994 ($4.95, limited series, 52 pgs.)
1-3 5.00

SUPERMAN FAMILY, THE (Formerly Superman's Pal Jimmy Olsen)
National Per. Publ./DC Comics: No. 164, Apr-May, 1974 - No. 222, Sept, 1982
164-(100 pgs.) Jimmy Olsen, Supergirl, Lois Lane begin 3.20 9.60 35.00
165-169 (100 pgs.) 2.50 7.50 24.00
170-176 (68 pgs.) 2.00 6.00 16.00
177-190 (52 pgs.): 177-181-52 pgs. 182-Marshall Rogers-a; $1.00 issues begin; Krypto begins, ends #192. 183-Nightwing-Flamebird begins, ends #194. 189-Brainiac 5, Mon-el app. 1.25 3.75 10.00
191-193,195-199: 191-Superboy begins, ends #198 1.00 3.00 8.00
194,200: 194-Rogers-a. 200-Book length sty 1.10 3.30 9.00
201-222: 211-Earth II Batman & Catwoman marry 2.40 6.00
NOTE: ***N. Adams*** *c-182-185.* ***Anderson*** *a-186i.* ***Buckler*** *c(p)-190, 191, 209, 210, 215, 217, 220.* ***Jones*** *a-191-193.* ***Gil Kane*** *c(p)-221, 222.* ***Mortimer*** *a(p)-191-193, 199, 201-222.* ***Orlando*** *a(i)-186, 187.* ***Rogers*** *a-182, 194.* ***Staton*** *a-191-194, 196p.* ***Tuska*** *a(p)-203, 207-209.*

SUPERMAN/FANTASTIC FOUR
DC Comics/Marvel Comics: 1999 ($9.95, tabloid size, one-shot)
1-Battle Galactus and the Cyborg; wraparound-c by Alex Ross and Dan Jurgens; Jurgens-s/a; Thibert-a 10.00

SUPERMAN FOR ALL SEASONS
DC Comics: 1998 - No, 4, 1998 ($4.95, limited series, prestige format)
1-Loeb-s/Sale-a/c; Superman's first year in Metropolis 6.00
2-4 5.00
Hardcover (1999, $24.95) r/#1-4 25.00

SUPERMAN FOR EARTH (See Superman one-shots)

SUPERMAN FOREVER
DC Comics: Jun, 1998 ($5.95, one-shot)
1-($5.95)-Collector's Edition with a 7-image lenticular-c by Alex Ross; Superman returns to normal; s/a by various 7.00
1-($4.95) Standard Edition with single image Ross-c 5.00

SUPERMAN/GEN13
DC Comics (WildStorm): Jun, 2000 - No. 3, Aug, 2000 ($2.50, limited series)
1-3-Hughes-s/ Bermejo-a; Campbell variant-c for each 2.50

SUPERMAN: KING OF THE WORLD
DC Comics: June, 1999 ($3.95/$4.95, one-shot)
1-($3.95) Regular Ed. 4.00
1-($4.95) Collectors' Ed. with gold foil enhanced-c 5.00

SUPERMAN: LAST SON OF EARTH
DC Comics: 2000 - No. 2, 2000 ($5.95, limited series, prestige format)
1,2-Elseworlds; baby Clark rockets to Krypton; Gerber-s/Wheatley-a 5.95

SUPERMAN: LOIS LANE (Girlfrenzy)
DC Comics: Jun, 1998 ($1.95, one shot)
1-Connor & Palmiotti-a 2.00

SUPERMAN/MADMAN HULLABALOO!

Superman's Girlfriend Lois Lane #70 © DC

Superman's Girlfriend Lois Lane #122 © DC

Superman's Pal Jimmy Olsen #111 © DC

Dark Horse Comics: June, 1997 - No. 3, Aug, 1997 ($2.95, limited series)

1-3-Mike Allred-c/s/a 3.00
TPB (1997, $8.95) 9.00

SUPERMAN METROPOLIS SECRET FILES
DC Comics: Jun, 2000 ($4.95, one shot)

1-Short stories, pin-ups and profile pages; Hitch and Neary-c 4.95

SUPERMAN: PEACE ON EARTH
DC Comics: Jan, 1999 ($9.95, Treasury-sized, one-shot)

1-Alex Ross painted-c/a; Paul Dini-s 12.00

SUPERMAN RED/ SUPERMAN BLUE
DC Comics: Feb, 1998 ($4.95, one shot)

1-Polybagged w/3-D glasses and reprint of Superman 3-D (1955); Jurgens-plot/3-D cover; script and art by various 5.00
1-($3.95)-Standard Ed.; comic only, non 3-D cover 4.00

SUPERMAN: SAVE THE PLANET
DC Comics: Oct, 1998 ($2.95, one-shot)

1-($2.95) Regular Ed.; Luthor buys the Daily Planet 3.00
1-($3.95) Collector's Ed. with acetate cover 4.00

SUPERMAN SCRAPBOOK (Has blank pages; contains no comics)

SUPERMAN: SECRET FILES
DC Comics: Jan, 1998; May 1999 ($4.95)

1,2: 1-Retold origin story, "lost" pages & pin-ups 5.00

SUPERMAN'S GIRLFRIEND LOIS LANE (See Action Comics #1, 80 Page Giant #3, 14, Lois Lane, Showcase #9, 10, Superman #28 & Superman Family)

SUPERMAN'S GIRLFRIEND LOIS LANE (See Showcase #9,10)
National Periodical Publ.: Mar-Apr, 1958 - No. 136, Jan-Feb, 1974; No. 137, Sept-Oct, 1974

1-(3-4/58) 250.00 750.00 4000.00
2 70.00 210.00 975.00
3 50.00 150.00 650.00
4,5 41.00 123.00 525.00
6,7 33.00 100.00 400.00
8-10: 9-Pat Boone-c/story 29.00 88.00 325.00
11-13,15-19: 12-(10/59)-Aquaman app. 17.00 51.00 185.00
14-Supergirl x-over; Batman app. on-c only 17.50 52.00 190.00
20-Supergirl-c/sty 17.50 52.00 190.00
21-28: 23-1st app. Lena Thorul, Lex Luthor's sister. 27-Bizarro-c/story 12.75 38.00 140.00
29-Aquaman, Batman, Green Arrow cover app. and cameo; last 10¢ issue 13.50 40.00 150.00
30-32,34-46,48,49 6.80 20.50 75.00
33(5/62)-Mon-el app. 7.65 23.00 85.00
47-Legion app. 7.65 23.00 85.00
50(7/64)-Triplicate Girl, Phantom Girl & Shrinking Violet app. 7.25 21.75 80.00
51-55,57-67,69: 59-Jor-el app.; Batman back-up sty 5.00 15.00 55.00
56-Saturn Girl app. 5.45 16.35 60.00
68-(Giant G-26) 6.35 19.00 70.00
70-Penguin & Catwoman app. (1st S.A. Catwoman, 11/66; also see Detective #369 for 3rd app.); Batman & Robin cameo 23.00 68.00 250.00
71-Batman & Robin cameos (3 panels); Catwoman story cont'd from #70 (2nd app.); see Detective #369 for 3rd app 12.75 38.00 140.00
72,73,75,76,78 3.20 9.60 35.00
74-1st Bizarro Flash (5/67); JLA cameo 3.80 11.40 42.00
77-(Giant G-39) 5.00 15.00 55.00
79-Neal Adams-c or c(i) begin, end #95,108 3.45 10.35 38.00
80-85,87,88,90-92: 92-Last 12¢ issue 2.50 7.50 25.00
86,95 (Giants G-51,G-63)-Both have Neal Adams-c 4.10 12.30 45.00
89,93: 89-Batman x-over; all N. Adams-c. 93-Wonder Woman-c/story 2.80 8.40 28.00
94,96-99,101-103,107-110 2.30 7.00 20.00
100 2.50 7.50 25.00
104-(Giant G-75) 4.10 12.30 45.00
105-Origin/1st app. The Rose & the Thorn. 4.35 13.00 48.00
106-"Black Like Me" sty; Lois changes her color to black 2.50 7.50 25.00
111-Justice League-c/s; Morrow-a; last 15¢ issue 2.50 7.50 25.00
112,114-123 (52 pgs.): 122-G.A. Lois Lane-r/Superman #30. 123-G.A. Batman-r/Batman #35 (w/Catwoman) 2.40 7.35 22.00
113-(Giant G-87) Kubert-a (previously unpublished G.A. story)(scarce in NM) 4.55 13.65 50.00
124-135: 130-Last Rose & the Thorn. 132-New Zatanna story 1.50 4.50 12.00
136,137: 136-Wonder Woman x-over 1.85 5.50 15.00
Annual 1(Sum, 1962)-r/L. Lane #12; Aquaman app. 19.00 57.00 210.00
Annual 2(Sum, 1963) 12.50 37.00 135.00

NOTE: ***Buckler** a-117-121p. **Curt Swan or Kurt Schaffenberger** a-1-81(most); c(p)-1-15.*

SUPERMAN: SILVER BANSHEE
DC Comics: Dec, 1998 - No. 2, Jan, 1999 ($2.25, mini-series)

1,2-Brereton-s/c; Chin-a 2.25

SUPERMAN'S NEMESIS: LEX LUTHOR
DC Comics: Mar, 1999 - No. 4, Jun, 1999 ($2.50, mini-series)

1-4-Semeiks-a 2.50

SUPERMAN'S PAL JIMMY OLSEN (Superman Family #164 on)
(See Action Comics #6 for 1st app. & 80 Page Giant)
National Periodical Publ.: Sept-Oct, 1954 - No. 163, Feb-Mar, 1974 (Fourth World #133-148)

1 353.00 1060.00 6000.00
2 114.00 343.00 1600.00
3-Last pre-code issue 61.00 182.00 850.00
4,5 46.00 138.00 600.00
6-10 33.00 100.00 400.00
11-20: 15-1st S.A. issue 23.50 71.00 260.00
21-30: 29-1st app. Krypto in Jimmy Olsen 15.00 45.00 165.00
31-Origin & 1st app.Elastic Lad (Jimmy Olsen) 12.75 38.00 140.00
32-40: 33-One pg. biography of Jack Larson (TV Jimmy Olsen). 36-Intro Lucy Lane. 37-2nd app. Elastic Lad & 1st cover app. 10.50 31.50 115.00
41-50: 41-1st J.O. Robot. 48-Intro/origin Superman Emergency Squad 8.15 24.50 90.00
51-56: 56-Last 10¢ issue 6.80 20.50 75.00
57-62,64-70: 57-Olsen marries Supergirl. 62-Mon-el & Elastic Lad app. but not as Legionnaires. 70-Element Boy (Lad) app. 4.10 12.30 45.00
63(9/62)-Legion of Super-Villains app. 4.55 13.65 50.00
71,74,75,78,80-84,86,89,90: 86-Jimmy Olsen Robot becomes Congorilla 3.20 9.60 35.00
72,73,76,77,79,85,87,88: 72(10/63)-Legion app; Elastic Lad (Olsen) joins. 73-Ultra Boy app. 76,85-Legion app. 76-Legion app. 77-Olsen with Colossal Boy's powers & costume; origin Titano retold. 79-(9/64)-Titled The Red-head ed Beatle of 1000 B.C. 85-Legion app. 87-Legion of Super-Villains app. 88-Star Boy app. 3.45 10.35 38.00
91-94,96-98 2.80 8.40 28.00
95 (Giant G-25) 5.45 16.35 60.00
99-Olsen w/powers & costumes of Lightning Lad, Sun Boy & Element Lad 3.00 9.00 30.00
100-Legion cameo 3.65 11.00 40.00
101-103,105-112,114-120: 106-Legion app. 110-Infinity-c. 117-Batman & Legion cameo. 120-Last 12¢ issue 2.30 7.00 20.00
104 (Giant G-38) 4.55 13.65 50.00
113,122,131,140 (Giants G-50,G-62,G-74,G-86) 3.65 11.00 40.00
121,123-130,132 2.00 6.00 18.00
133-(10/70)-Re-intro Newsboy Legion; Kirby story & art begins; 1st app. Morgan Edge. 5.45 16.35 60.00
134-1st app. Darkseid (1 panel, 12/70) 6.80 20.50 75.00
135-2nd app. Darkseid (1 pg. cameo; see New Gods & Forever People); G.A. Guardian app. 3.20 9.60 35.00
136-139: 136-Origin new Guardian. 138-Partial photo-c. 139-Last 15¢ issue 2.80 8.40 28.00
141-150: (25¢,52 pgs.). 141-Photo-c; Newsboy Legion-r by S&K begin; full pg. self-portrait Kirby; Don Rickles cameo. 149,150-G.A. Plastic Man-r in both; 150-Newsboy Legion app. 2.50 7.50 25.00
151-163 1.75 5.25 14.00

NOTE: *Issues #141-148 contain **Simon & Kirby** Newsboy Legion reprints from Star Spangled #7*

Superman: The Man of Steel #80 © DC

Superman: The Man of Tomorrow #4 © DC

Superman Vs. the Terminator: Death to the Future #3 © DC/DH

8, 9, 10, 11, 12, 13, 14 in that order. ***N. Adams*** *c-109-112, 115, 117, 118, 120, 121, 132, 134-136, 147, 148.* ***Kirby*** *a-133-139p, 141-148p; c-133, 137, 139, 142, 145p.* ***Kirby/N. Adams*** *c-137, 138, 141-144, 146.* ***Curt Swan*** *c-1-14(most)., 140.*

SUPERMAN SPECTACULAR (Also see DC Special Series #5)
DC Comics: 1982 (Magazine size, 52 pgs., square binding)

1-Saga of Superman Red/ Superman Blue; Luthor and Terra-Man app.; Gonzales & Colletta-a 1.25 3.75 10.00

SUPERMAN: THE DARK SIDE
DC Comics: 1998 - No. 3, 1998 ($4.95, squarebound, mini-series)

1-3: Elseworlds; Kal-El lands on Apokolips 5.00

SUPERMAN: THE DOOMSDAY WARS
DC Comics: 1998 - No. 3, 1999 ($4.95, squarebound, mini-series)

1-3: Superman & JLA vs. Doomsday; Jurgens-s/a(p) 5.00

SUPERMAN: THE MAN OF STEEL (Also see Man of Steel, The)
DC Comics: July, 1991 - Present ($1.00/$1.25/$1.50/$1.95)

0-(10/94) Zero Hour; released between #37 & #38 2.00
1-($1.75, 52 pgs.)-Painted-c 4.00
2-16: 3-War of the Gods x-over. 5-Reads sideways. 10-Last $1.00-c. 14-Superman & Robin team-up 2.50
17-1st app. Doomsday (cameo) 1.00 2.80 7.00
17,18: 17-2nd printing. 18-2nd & 3rd printings 2.00
18-1st full app. Doomsday 1.10 3.30 9.00
19-Doomsday battle issue (c/story) 2.40 6.00
20-22: 20,21-Funeral for a Friend. 22-($1.95)-Collector's Edition w/die-cut outer-c & bound-in poster; Steel-c/story 2.50
22-($1.50)-Newsstand Ed. w/poster & different-c 2.00
23-49,51-99: 30-Regular edition. 32-Bizarro-c/story. 35,36-Worlds Collide Pt. 1 & 10. 37-(9/94)-Zero Hour x-over. 38-(11/94). 48-Aquaman app. 54-Spectre-c/app; Lex Luthor app. 56-Mxyzptlk-c/app. 57-G.A. Flash app. 58-Supergirl app. 59-Parasite-c/app.; Steel app. 60-Reintro Bottled City of Kandor. 62-Final Night. 64-New Gods app. 67-New powers. 75-"Death" of Mxyzptlk. 78,79-Millennium Giants. 80-Golden Age style. 92-JLA app. 98-Metal Men app. 2.00
30-($2.50)-Collector's Edition; polybagged with Superman & Lobo vinyl clings that stick to wraparound-c; Lobo-c/story 2.50
50 ($2.95)-The Trial of Superman 4.00
100-($2.99) New Fortress of Solitude revealed 3.00
100-($3.99) Special edition with fold out cardboard-c 4.00
101,102-101-Batman app. 2.00
103-111: 103-Begin $2.25. 105-Batman-c/app. 111-Return to Krypton 2.25
#1,000,000 (11/98) 853rd Century x-over; Gene Ha-c 2.00
Annual 1-5 ('92-'96,68 pgs.): 1-Eclipso app.; Joe Quesada-c(p). 2-Intro Edge. 3 -Elseworlds story; Mignola-c; Batman app. 4-Year One story. 5-Legends of the Dead Earth story 3.00
Annual 6 (1997, $3.95)-Pulp Heroes story 4.00
...Gallery (1995, $3.50) Pin-ups by various 3.50

SUPERMAN: THE MAN OF TOMORROW
DC Comics: 1995 - No. 15, Fall, 1999 ($1.95, quarterly)

1-15: 1-Lex Luthor app. 3-Lex Luthor-c/app; Joker app. 4-Shazam! app. 5-Wedding of Lex Luthor. 10-Maxima-c/app. 13-JLA-c/app. 2.00
#1,000,000 (11/98) 853rd Century x-over; Gene Ha-c 2.00

SUPERMAN: THE SECRET YEARS
DC Comics: Feb, 1985 - No. 4, May, 1985 (limited series)

1-4-Miller-c on all 3.00

SUPERMAN: THE WEDDING ALBUM
DC Comics: Dec, 1996 ($4.95, 96 pgs, one-shot)

1-Standard Edition-Story & art by past and present Superman creators; gatefold back-c. Byrne-c 5.00
1-Collector's Edition-Embossed cardstock variant-c w/ metallic silver ink and matte and gloss varnishes 5.00
TPB ('97, $14.95) r/Wedding and honeymoon stories 15.00

SUPERMAN 3-D (See Three-Dimension Adventures)

SUPERMAN VILLAINS SECRET FILES
DC Comics: Jun, 1998 ($4.95, one shot)

1-Origin stories, "lost" pages & pin-ups 5.00

SUPERMAN VS. ALIENS
DC Comics/Dark Horse Comics: July, 1995 - No. 3, Sept, 1995 ($4.95, limited series)

1-3: Jurgens/Nowlan-a 5.00

SUPERMAN VS. PREDATOR
DC Comics/Dark Horse Comics: 2000 - No. 3, ($4.95, limited series)

1-3-Micheline-s/Maleev-a 5.00

SUPERMAN VS. THE AMAZING SPIDER-MAN (Also see Marvel Treasury Edition No. 28)
National Periodical Publications/Marvel Comics Group: 1976 ($2.00, Treasury sized, 100 pgs.)

1-Andru/Giordano-a; 1st Marvel/DC x-over. 6.35 19.00 70.00
1-2nd printing; 5000 numbered copies signed by Stan Lee & Carmine Infantino on front cover & sold through mail 12.75 38.00 140.00
nn-(1995, $5.95)-r/#1 2.40 6.00

SUPERMAN VS. THE TERMINATOR: DEATH TO THE FUTURE
Dark Horse/DC Comics: Dec, 1999 - No. 4, Mar, 2000 ($2.95, limited series)

1-4-Grant-s/Pugh-a/c: Steel and Supergirl app. 2.95

SUPERMAN/WONDER WOMAN: WHOM GODS DESTROY
DC Comics: 1997 ($4.95, prestige format, limited series)

1-4-Elseworlds; Claremont-s 5.00

SUPERMAN WORKBOOK
National Periodical Publ./Juvenile Group Foundation: 1945 (B&W, one-shot, reprints, 68 pgs)

nn-Cover-r/Superman #14 147.00 442.00 1400.00

SUPER MANGA BLAST
Dark Horse Comics: Mar, 2000 - Present ($4.95, B&W, anthology)

1-4-Reprints Oh My Goddess, 3X3 Eyes, What's Michael and others 5.00

SUPER MARIO BROS. (Also see Adventures of the..., Blip, Gameboy, and Nintendo Comics System)
Valiant Comics: 1990 - No. 5?, 1991 ($1.95, slick-c) V2#1, 1991 - No. 5, 1991

1-Wildman-a 4.00
2-5, V2#1-5-($1.50) 3.00
Special Edition 1 (1990, $1.95)-Wildman-a 3.00

SUPERMEN OF AMERICA
DC Comics: Mar, 1999 ($3.95/$4.95, one-shot)

1-($3.95) Regular Ed.; Immonen-s/art by various 4.00
1-($4.95) Collectors' Ed. with membership kit 5.00

SUPERMEN OF AMERICA (Mini-series)
DC Comics: Mar, 2000 - No. 6, Aug, 2000 ($2.50)

1-6-Nicieza-s/Braithwaite-a 2.50

SUPERMOUSE (...the Big Cheese; see Coo Coo Comics)
Standard Comics/Pines No. 35 on (Literary Ent.): Dec, 1948 - No. 34, Sept, 1955; No. 35, Apr, 1956 - No. 45, Fall, 1958

1-Frazetta text illos (3) 29.00 86.00 230.00
2-Frazetta text illos 14.00 43.00 115.00
3,5,6-Text illos by Frazetta in all 12.00 36.00 95.00
4-Two pg. text illos by Frazetta 12.50 37.50 100.00
7-10 5.70 17.00 40.00
11-20: 13-Racist humor (Indians) 5.00 15.00 30.00
21-45 4.00 12.00 24.00
1-Summer Holiday issue (Summer, 1957, 25¢, 100 pgs.)-Pines 12.50 37.50 100.00
2-Giant Summer issue (Summer, 1958, 25¢, 100 pgs.)-Pines; has games, puzzles & stories 10.00 30.00 70.00

SUPER-MYSTERY COMICS
Ace Magazines (Periodical House): July, 1940 - V8#6, July, 1949

V1#1-Magno, the Magnetic Man & Vulcan begins (1st app.); Q-13, Corp. Flint, & Sky Smith begin 211.00 633.00 2000.00
2 84.00 253.00 800.00

Super-Mystery Comics #3 © ACE

Super Rabbit #1 © MAR

Supersnipe Comics #8 © S&S

3-The Black Spider begins (1st app.) 73.00 220.00 695.00
4-Origin Davy 55.00 165.00 500.00
5-Intro. The Clown & begin series (12/40) 58.00 174.00 550.00
6(2/41) 50.00 150.00 450.00
V2#1(4/41)-Origin Buckskin 47.00 142.00 425.00
2-6(2/42): 6-Vulcan begins again 44.00 133.00 400.00
V3#1(4/42),2: 1-Black Ace begins 40.00 120.00 350.00
3-Intro. The Lancer; Dr. Nemesis & The Sword begin; Kurtzman-c/a(2) (Mr. Risk & Paul Revere Jr.); Robot-c 51.00 153.00 460.00
4-Kurtzman-c/a 43.00 128.00 385.00
5-Kurtzman-a(2); L.B. Cole-a; Mr. Risk app. 50.00 150.00 450.00
6(10/43)-Mr. Risk app.; Kurtzman's Paul Revere Jr.; L.B. Cole-a 50.00 150.00 450.00
V4#1(1/44)-L.B. Cole-a 42.00 125.00 375.00
2-6(4/45): 2,5,6-Mr. Risk app. 31.00 94.00 250.00
V5#1(7/45)-6 31.00 94.00 250.00
V6#1-6: 3-Torture story. 4-Last Magno. Mr. Risk app. in #2,4-6. 6-New logo 25.00 75.00 200.00
V7#1-6, V8#1-4,6 23.00 69.00 185.00
V8#5-Meskin, Tuska, Sid Greene-a 23.00 69.00 185.00

*NOTE: **Sid Greene** a-V7#4. **Mooney** c-V1#5, 6, V2#1-6. **Palais** a-V5#3, 4; c-V4#6-V5#4, V6#2, V8#4. Bondage c-V2#5, 6, V3#2, 5. Magno c-V1#1-V3#6, V4#2-V5#5, V6#2. The Sword c-V4#1, 6(w/Magno).*

SUPERNATURAL LAW (Formerly Wolff & Byrd, Counselors of the Macabre)
Exhibit A Press: No. 24, Oct, 1999 - Present ($2.50, B&W)

24-28-Batton Lash-s/a 2.50

SUPERNATURALS
Marvel Comics: Dec, 1998 - No. 4, Dec, 1998 ($3.99, weekly limited series)

1-4-Pulido-s/Balent-c; bound-in Halloween masks 4.00
1-4-With bound-in Ghost Rider mask (1 in 10) 4.00

SUPERNATURAL THRILLERS
Marvel Comics Group: Dec, 1972 - No. 6, Nov, 1973; No. 7, Jul, 1974 - No. 15, Oct, 1975

1-It!; Sturgeon adap. (see Astonishing Tales #21). 2.30 7.00 20.00
2-4,6: 2-The Invisible Man; H.G. Wells adapt. 3-The Valley of the Worm; R.E. Howard adapt. 4-Dr. Jekyll & Mr. Hyde; R.L. Stevenson adapt.. 6-The Headless Horseman; last 20¢ issue 1.50 4.50 12.00
5-1st app. The Living Mummy 4.55 13.65 50.00
7-15: 7-The Living Mummy begins 1.85 5.50 15.00

*NOTE: **Brunner** c-11. **Buckler** a-5p. **Ditko** a-8r, 9r. **G. Kane** a-3p; c-3, 9p, 15p. **Mayerik** a-2p, 7, 8, 9p, 10p, 11. **McWilliams** a-14i. **Mortimer** a-4. **Steranko** c-1, 2. **Sutton** a-15. **Tuska** a-6p.*

SUPERPATRIOT (Also see Freak Force & Savage Dragon #2)
Image Comics (Highbrow Entertainment): July, 1993 - No. 4, Dec, 1993 ($1.95, limited series)

1-4: Dave Johnson-c/a; Larsen scripts; Giffen plots 2.50

SUPERPATRIOT: LIBERTY & JUSTICE
Image Comics (Highbrow Entertainment): July, 1995 - No. 4, Oct, 1995 ($2.50, limited series)

1-4: Dave Johnson-c/a. 1-1st app. Liberty & Justice 2.50

SUPER POWERS (1st Series)
DC Comics: July, 1984 - No. 5, Nov, 1984

1-5: 1-Joker/Penguin-c/story; Batman app.; all Kirby-c. 5-Kirby c/a 5.00

SUPER POWERS (2nd Series)
DC Comics: Sept, 1985 - No. 6, Feb, 1986

1-6: Kirby-c/a; Capt. Marvel & Firestorm join; Batman cameo; Darkseid storyline in all. 4-Batman cameo. 5,6-Batman app. 4.00

SUPER POWERS (3rd Series)
DC Comics: Sept, 1986 - No. 4, Dec, 1986

1-4: 1-Cyborg joins; 1st app. Samurai from Super Friends TV show. 1-4-Batman cameos; Darkseid storyline in #1-4 3.00

SUPER PUP (Formerly Spotty The Pup) (See Space Comics)
Avon Periodicals: No. 4, Mar-Apr, 1954 - No. 5, 1954

4,5: 5-Robot-c 5.00 15.00 35.00

SUPER RABBIT (See All Surprise, Animated Movie Tunes, Comedy Comics, Comic Capers, Ideal Comics, It's A Duck's Life, Movie Tunes & Wisco)
Timely Comics (CmPl): Fall, 1944 - No. 14, Nov, 1948

1-Hitler & Hirohito-c; war effort paper recycling PSA by S&K; Ziggy Pig & Silly begin? 66.00 197.00 625.00
2 35.00 105.00 280.00
3-5 22.00 66.00 175.00
6-Origin 24.00 71.00 190.00
7-10: 9-Infinity-c 13.00 39.00 105.00
11-Kurtzman's "Hey Look" 14.00 41.00 110.00
12-14 12.50 37.50 100.00
I.W. Reprint #1,2('58),7,10('63): 1-r/#13. 2-r/#10. 2.00 6.00 16.00

SUPER RICHIE (Superichie #5 on) (See Richie Rich Millions #68)
Harvey Publications: Sept, 1975 - No. 4, Mar, 1976 (All 52 pg. Giants)

1 2.00 6.00 18.00
2-4 1.50 4.50 12.00

SUPER SLUGGERS (Baseball)
Ultimate Sports Ent. Inc.: 1999 ($3.95, one-shot)

1-Bonds, Piazza, Caminiti, Griffey Jr. app.; Martinbrough-c/a 4.00

SUPERSNIPE COMICS (Formerly Army & Navy #1-5)
Street & Smith Publications: V1#6, Oct, 1942 - V5#1, Aug-Sept, 1949 (See Shadow Comics V2#3)

V1#6-Rex King - Man of Adventure (costumed hero, see Super Magic/ Magician) by Jack Binder begins; Supersnipe by George Marcoux continues from Army & Navy #5; Bill Ward-a 79.00 237.00 750.00
7,10-12: 10,11-Little Nemo app. 50.00 150.00 450.00
8-Hitler, Tojo, Mussolini in Hell with Devil-c 63.00 189.00 600.00
9-Doc Savage x-over in Supersnipe; Hitler-c 68.00 205.00 650.00
V2 #1: Both V2#1(2/44) & V2#2(4/44) have V2#1 on outside-c; Huck Finn by Clare Dwiggins begins, ends V3#5 (rare) 42.00 125.00 375.00
V2#2-12: V2#2 (4/44) has V2#1 on outside-c 40.00 120.00 325.00
V3#1-12: 8-Bobby Crusoe by Dwiggins begins, ends V3#12. 9-X-Mas-c 34.00 101.00 270.00
V4#1-12, V5#1: V4#10-X-Mas-c 24.00 73.00 195.00

*NOTE: **George Marcoux** c-V1#6-V3#4. Doc Savage app. in some issues.*

SUPER SOLDIER (See Marvel Versus DC #3)
DC Comics (Amalgam): Apr, 1996 ($1.95, one-shot)

1-Mark Waid script & Dave Gibbons-c/a. 2.00

SUPER SOLDIER: MAN OF WAR
DC Comics (Amalgam): June, 1997 ($1.95, one-shot)

1-Waid & Gibbons-s/Gibbons & Palmiotti-c/a. 2.00

SUPER SOLDIERS
Marvel Comics UK: Apr, 1993 - No. 8, Nov, 1993 ($1.75)

1-($2.50)-Embossed silver foil logo 2.50
2-8: 5-Capt. America app. 6-Origin; Nick Fury app.; neon ink-c 2.00

SUPERSPOOK (Formerly Frisky Animals on Parade)
Ajax/Farrell Publications: No. 4, June, 1958

4 7.85 23.50 55.00

SUPER SPY (See Wham Comics)
Centaur Publications: Oct, 1940 - No. 2, Nov, 1940 (Reprints)

1-Origin The Sparkler 111.00 332.00 1050.00
2-The Inner Circle, Dean Denton, Tim Blain, The Drew Ghost, The Night Hawk by Gustavson, & S.S. Swanson by Glanz app. 68.00 205.00 650.00

SUPER STAR HOLIDAY SPECIAL (See DC Special Series #21)

SUPER-TEAM FAMILY
National Periodical Publ./DC Comics: Oct-Nov, 1975 - No. 15, Mar-Apr, 1978

1-Reprints by Neal Adams & Kane/Wood; 68 pgs. begin, ends #4. New Gods app. 2.00 6.00 16.00
2,3: New stories 1.25 3.75 10.00
4-7: Reprints. 4-G.A. JSA-r & Superman/Batman/Robin-r from World's Finest. 5-52 pgs. begin 1.25 3.75 10.00
8-14: 8-10-New Challengers of the Unknown stories. 9-Kirby-a. 11-14: New stories 1.50 4.50 12.00
15-New Gods app. New stories 1.85 5.50 15.00

Super-Villain Team-Up #12 © MAR

Supreme the Return #6 © Awesome

Suspense Comics #2 © Continental Magazines

GD2.0 FN6.0 NM9.4

NOTE: ***Neal Adams*** *r-1-3.* ***Brunner*** *c-3.* ***Buckler*** *c-8p.* ***Tuska*** *a-7r.* ***Wood*** *a-1i(r), 3.*

SUPER TV HEROES (See Hanna-Barbera...)

SUPER-VILLAIN CLASSICS
Marvel Comics Group: May, 1983

1-Galactus -The Origin; Kirby-a 5.00

SUPER-VILLAIN TEAM-UP (See Fantastic Four #6 & Giant-Size...)
Marvel Comics Group: 8/75 - No. 14, 10/77; No. 15, 11/78; No. 16, 5/79; No. 17, 6/80

1-Giant-Size Super-Villian Team-Up #2; Sub-Mariner & Dr. Doom begin, end #10 2.00 6.00 18.00
2-5: 5-1st app. The Shroud 1.25 3.75 10.00
6,7-(25¢ editions) 6-(6/76)-F.F., Shroud app. 7-Origin Shroud 1.00 2.80 7.00
6,7-(30¢-c, limited distribution) 1.25 3.75 10.00
8-17: 9-Avengers app. 11-15-Dr. Doom & Red Skull app. 1.00 2.80 7.00

NOTE: ***Buckler*** *c-4p, 5p, 7p.* ***Buscema*** *c-1.* ***Byrne/Austin*** *c-14.* ***Evans*** *a-1p, 3p.* ***Everett*** *a-1p.* ***Giffen*** *a-8p, 13p; c-13p.* ***Kane*** *c-2p, 9p.* ***Mooney*** *a-4i.* ***Starlin*** *c-6.* ***Tuska*** *r-1p, 15p.* ***Wood*** *r-15p.*

SUPER WESTERN COMICS (Also see Buffalo Bill)
Youthful Magazines: Aug, 1950 (One shot)

1-Buffalo Bill begins; Wyatt Earp, Calamity Jane & Sam Slade app; Powell-c/a 13.00 39.00 105.00

SUPER WESTERN FUNNIES (See Super Funnies)

SUPERWORLD COMICS
Hugo Gernsback (Komos Publ.): Apr, 1940 - No. 3, Aug, 1940 (68 pgs.)

1-Origin & 1st app. Hip Knox, Super Hypnotist; Mitey Powers & Buzz Allen, the Invisible Avenger, Little Nemo begin; cover by Frank R. Paul (all have sci/fi-c)(Scarce) 565.00 1695.00 6500.00
2-Marvo 1-2 Go+, the Super Boy of the Year 2680 (1st app.); Paul-c (Scarce) 343.00 1029.00 3600.00
3 (Scarce) 263.00 790.00 2500.00

SUPREME (Becomes ...The New Adventures #43-48)(See Youngblood #3) (Also see Bloodwulf Special, Legend of Supreme, & Trencher #3)
Image Comics (Extreme Studios)/ Awesome Entertainment #49 on: V2#1, Nov, 1992 - V2#42, Sept, 1996; V3#49 - No. 56, Feb, 1998

V2#1-Liefeld-a(i) & scripts; embossed foil logo 4.00
1-Gold Edition 6.00
2-(3/93)-Liefeld co-plots & inks; 1st app. Grizlock 3.00
3-42: 3-Intro Bloodstrike; 1st app. Khrome. 5-1st app. Thor. 6-The Starguard cameo. 7-1st full app. The Starguard. 10-Black and White Pt 1 (1st app.) by Art Thibert (2 pgs. ea. installment). 25-(5/94)-Platt-c. 11-Coupon #4 for Extreme Prejudice #0; Black and White Pt. 7 by Thibert. 12-(4/94)-Platt-c. 13,14-(6/94). 15 (7/94). 16 (7/94)-Stormwatch app. 18-Kid Supreme Sneak Preview; Pitt app.19,20-Polybagged w/trading card. 20-1st app. Woden & Loki (as a dog); Overkill app. 21-1st app. Loki (in true form). 21-23-Poly-bagged trading card. 32-Lady Supreme cameo. 33-Origin & 1st full app. of Lady Supreme (Probe from the Starguard); Babewatch! tie-in. 37-Intro Loki; Fraga-c. 40-Retells Supreme's past advs. 41-Alan Moore scripts begin; Supreme revised; intro The Supremacy; Jerry Ordway-c (Joe Bennett vari ant-c exists). 42-New origin w/Rick Veitch-a; intro Radar, The Hound Supreme & The League of Infinity 3.00
28-Variant-c by Quesada & Palmiotti 3.00
(#43-48-**See Supreme: The New Adventures**)
V3#49,51: 49-Begin $2.99-c 3.00
50-($3.95)-Double sized, 2 covers, pin-up gallery 4.00
52a,52b-($3.50) 3.50
53-56: 53-Sprouse-a begins. 56-McGuinness-c 3.00
Annual 1-(1995, $2.95) 3.00

NOTE: ***Rob Liefeld*** *a(i)-1, 2; co-plots-2-4; scripts-1, 5, 6.* ***Ordway*** *c-41.* ***Platt*** *c-12, 25.* ***Thibert*** *c(i)-7-9.*

SUPREME: GLORY DAYS
Image Comics (Extreme Studios): Oct, 1994 - No. 2, Dec, 1994 ($2.95/$2.50, limited series)

1,2: 2-Diehard, Roman, Superpatriot, & Glory app. 3.00

SUPREME: THE NEW ADVENTURES (Formerly Supreme)
Maximum Press: V3#43, Oct, 1996 - V3#48, May, 1997 ($2.50)

V3#43-48: 43-Alan Moore scripts begin; Joe Bennett-a; Rick Veitch-a (8 pgs.); Dan Jurgens-a (1 pg.); intro Citadel Supreme & Suprematons; 1st app. Allied Supermen of America 3.00

SUPREME: THE RETURN
Awesome Entertainment: May, 1999 - Present ($2.99)

1-6: Alan Moore-s. 1,2-Sprouse & Gordon-a/c. 2,4-Liefeld-c. 6-Kirby app. 3.00

SURE-FIRE COMICS (Lightning Comics #4 on)
Ace Magazines: June, 1940 - No. 4, Oct, 1940 (Two No. 3's)

V1#1-Origin Flash Lightning & begins; X-The Phantom Fed, Ace McCoy, Buck Steele, Marvo the Magician, The Raven, Whiz Wilson (Time Traveler) begin (all 1st app.); Flash Lightning c-1-4 158.00 474.00 1500.00
2 76.00 229.00 725.00
3(9/40), 3(#4)(10/40)-nn on-c, #3 on inside 58.00 174.00 550.00

SURF 'N' WHEELS
Charlton Comics: Nov, 1969 - No. 6, Sept, 1970

1 3.00 9.00 30.00
2-6 2.30 7.00 20.00

SURGE
Eclipse Comics: July, 1984 - No. 4, Jan, 1985 ($1.50, lim. series, Baxter paper)

1-4 Ties into DNAgents series 2.00

SURPRISE ADVENTURES (Formerly Tormented)
Sterling Comic Group: No. 3, Mar, 1955 - No. 5, July, 1955

3-5: 3,5-Sekowsky-a 6.40 19.25 45.00

SUSIE Q. SMITH
Dell Publishing Co.: No. 323, Mar, 1951 - No. 553, Apr, 1954

Four Color 323 (#1) 3.65 11.00 40.00
Four Color 377, 453 (2/53), 553 3.20 9.60 35.00

SUSPENSE (Radio/TV issues #1-11; Real Life Tales of... #1-4) (Amazing Detective Cases #3 on?)
Marvel/Atlas Comics (CnPC No. 1-10/BFP No. 11-29): Dec, 1949 - No. 29, Apr, 1953 (#1-8,17-23: 52 pgs.)

1-Powell-a; Peter Lorre, Sidney Greenstreet photo-c from Hammett's "The Verdict" 58.00 174.00 550.00
2-Crime stories; Dennis O'Keefe & Gale Storm photo-c from Universal movie "Abandoned" 34.00 103.00 275.00
3-Change to horror 38.00 113.00 300.00
4,7-10: 7-Dracula-sty 28.00 84.00 225.00
5-Krigstein, Tuska, Everett-a 30.00 90.00 240.00
6-Tuska, Everett, Morisi-a 29.00 87.00 235.00
11-13,15-17,19,20 22.00 66.00 175.00
14-Clasic Heath Hypo-c; A-Bomb panels 31.00 94.00 250.00
18,22-Krigstein-a 24.00 73.00 195.00
21,23,24,26-29: 24-Tuska-a 21.00 62.00 165.00
25-Electric chair-c/story 29.00 87.00 235.00

NOTE: ***Ayers*** *a-20.* ***Briefer*** *a-5, 7, 27.* ***Brodsky*** *c-4, 6-9, 11, 16, 17, 25.* ***Colan*** *a-8(2), 9.* ***Everett*** *a-5, 6(2), 19, 23, 28; c-21-23, 26.* ***Fuje*** *a-29.* ***Heath*** *a-5, 6, 8, 10, 12, 14; c-14, 19, 24.* ***Maneely*** *a-12, 23, 24, 28, 29; c-5, 6p, 10, 13, 15, 18.* ***Mooney*** *a-24, 28.* ***Morisi*** *a-6, 12.* ***Palais*** *a-10.* ***Rico*** *a-7-9.* ***Robinson*** *a-29.* ***Romita*** *a-20(2), 25.* ***Sekowsky*** *a-11, 13, 14.* ***Sinnott*** *a-23, 25.* ***Tuska*** *a-5, 6(2), 12; c-12.* ***Whitney*** *a-15, 16, 22.* ***Ed Win*** *a-27.*

SUSPENSE COMICS
Continental Magazines: Dec, 1943 - No. 12, Sept, 1946

1-The Grey Mask begins; bondage/torture-c; L. B. Cole-a (7 pgs.) 400.00 1200.00 4200.00
2-Intro. The Mask; Rico, Giunta, L. B. Cole-a (7 pgs.) 295.00 885.00 2800.00
3-L.B. Cole-a; classic Schomburg-c (Scarce) 1500.00 4500.00 14,000.00
4-6: 5-L. B. Cole-c begin 221.00 663.00 2100.00
7,9,10,12: 9-L.B. Cole eyeball-c 168.00 505.00 1600.00
8-Classic L. B. Cole spider-c 400.00 1200.00 4200.00
11-Classic Devil-c 314.00 943.00 3300.00

NOTE: ***L. B. Cole*** *c-5-12.* ***Fuje*** *a-8.* ***Larsen*** *a-11.* ***Palais*** *a-10, 11. Bondage c-1, 3, 4.*

SUSPENSE DETECTIVE
Fawcett Publications: June, 1952 - No. 5, Mar, 1953

Suspense Detective #1 © FAW

Swamp Thing #169 © DC

Swamp Thing (3rd series) #1 © DC

GD2.0 FN6.0 NM9.4

1-Evans-a (11 pgs); Baily-c/a 42.00 125.00 375.00
2-Evans-a (10 pgs.) 28.00 83.00 220.00
3-5 23.00 68.00 180.00
NOTE: *Baily a-4, 5; c-1-3.* ***Sekowsky*** *a-2, 4, 5; c-5.*

SUSPENSE STORIES (See Strange Suspense Stories)

SUSPIRA: THE GREAT WORKING
Chaos! Comics: Apr, 1997 - No. 4, Aug, 1997 ($2.95, limited series)

1-4 3.00

SUSSEX VAMPIRE, THE (Sherlock Holmes)
Caliber Comics: 1996 ($2.95, 32 pgs., B&W, one-shot)

nn-Adapts Sir Arthur Conan Doyle's story; Warren Ellis scripts 3.00

SUZIE COMICS (Formerly Laugh Comix; see Laugh Comics, Liberty Comics #10, Pep Comics & Top-Notch Comics #28)
Close-Up No. 49,50/MLJ Mag./Archie No. 51 on: No. 49, Spring, 1945 - No. 100, Aug, 1954

49-Ginger begins 23.00 69.00 185.00
50-55: 54-Transvestism story 14.00 43.00 115.00
56-Katy Keene begins by Woggon 13.00 39.00 105.00
57-65 10.00 30.00 75.00
66-80 10.00 30.00 70.00
81-87,89-99 9.15 27.00 65.00
88,100: 88-Used in **POP**, pgs. 76,77; Bill Woggon draws himself in story. 100-Last Katy Keene 10.00 30.00 70.00
NOTE: ***Al Fagaly*** *c-49-67. Katy Keene app. in 53-82, 85-100.*

SWAMP FOX, THE (TV, Disney)(See Walt Disney Presents #2)
Dell Publishing Co.: No. 1179, Dec, 1960

Four Color 1179-Leslie Nielson photo-c 8.35 25.00 100.00

SWAMP THING (See Brave & the Bold, Challengers of the Unknown #82, DC Comics Presents #8 & 85, DC Special Series #2, 14, 17, 20, House of Secrets #92, Limited Collectors' Edition C-59, & Roots of the...)

SWAMP THING
National Per. Publ./DC Comics: Oct-Nov, 1972 - No. 24, Aug-Sept, 1976

1-Wrightson-c/a begins; origin 11.00 33.00 120.00
2-1st app. Patchwork Man (1 panel cameo) 4.10 12.30 45.00
3-1st full app. Patchwork Man (see House of Secrets #140) 3.00 9.00 30.00
4-6,8-10: 10-Last Wrightson issue 2.50 7.50 25.00
7-Batman-c/story 3.00 9.00 30.00
11-20: 11-19-Redondo-a. 13-Origin retold (1 pg.) 1.25 3.75 10.00
21-24: 23,24-Swamp Thing reverts back to Dr. Holland. 23-New logo 1.25 3.75 10.00
NOTE: ***J. Jones*** *a-9i(assist).* ***Kaluta*** *a-9i.* ***Redondo*** *c-12-19, 21.* ***Wrightson*** *issues (#1-10) reprinted in DC Special Series #2, 14, 17, 20 & Roots of the Swampthing.*

SWAMP THING (Saga Of The... #1-38,42-45) (See Essential Vertigo:...)
DC Comics (Vertigo imprint #129 on): May, 1982 - No. 171, Oct, 1996 (Direct sales #65 on)

1-Origin retold; Phantom Stranger series begins; ends #13; Yeates-c/a begins 5.00
2-15: 2-Photo-c from movie. 13-Last Yeates-a 3.00
16-19: Bissette-a. 4.00
20-1st Alan Moore issue 2.00 6.00 18.00
21-New origin 1.85 5.50 15.00
22,23,25: 25-John Constantine 1-panel cameo 1.10 3.30 9.00
24-JLA x-over; Last Yeates-c. 1.50 4.50 12.00
26-30 2.40 6.00
31-33,35,36: 33-r/1st app. from House of Secrets #92 5.00
34 1.00 3.00 8.00
37-1st app. John Constantine (Hellblazer) (6/85) 1.85 5.50 15.00
38-40: John Constantine app. 1.00 3.00 8.00
41-52,54-64: 44-Batman cameo. 44-51-John Constantine app. 46-Crisis x-over; Batman cameo. 49-Spectre app. 50-($1.25, 52 pgs.)-Deadman, Dr. Fate, Demon. 52-Arkham Asylum-c/story; Joker-c/cameo. 58-Spectre preview. 64-Last Moore issue 3.50
53-($1.25, 52 pgs.)-Arkham Asylum; Batman-c/story 4.50
65-83,85-99,101-124,126-149,151-153: 65-Direct sales only begins. 66-Batman & Arkham Asylum story. 70,76-John Constantine x-over; 76-X-over w/Hellblazer #9. 79-Superman-c/story. 85-Jonah Hex app. 102-Preview of World Without End. 116-Photo-c. 129-Metallic ink on-c. 140-Millar scripts begin, end #171. 3.00
84-Sandman (Morpheus) cameo. 4.00
100,125,150: 100 ($2.50, 52 pgs.). 125-($2.95, 52 pgs.)-20th anniversary issue. 150 (52 pgs.)-Anniversary issue 3.00
154-171: 154-$2.25-c begins. 165-Curt Swan-a(p). 166,169,171-John Constantine & Phantom Stranger app. 168-Arcane returns 2.50
Annual 1,3-6('82-91): 1-Movie Adaptation; painted-c. 3-New format; Bolland-c. 4-Batman-c/story. 5-Batman cameo; re-intro Brother Power (Geek),1st app. since 1968 4.00
Annual 2 (1985)-Moore scripts; Bissette-a(p); Deadman, Spectre app. 7.00
Annual 7(1993, $3.95)-Children's Crusade 4.00
...: Roots (1998, $7.95) Jon J Muth-s/painted-a/c 8.00
Saga of the Swamp Thing ('87, '89)-r/#21-27 (1st & 2nd print) 13.00
...Love and Death (1990, $17.95)-r/#28-34 & Annual #2; Totleben painted-c 18.00
NOTE: ***Bissette*** *a(p)-16-19, 21-27, 29, 30, 34-36, 39-42, 44, 46, 50, 64; c-17i, 24-32p, 35-37p, 40p, 44p, 46-50p, 51-58, 61, 62, 63p.* ***Kaluta*** *c/a-74.* ***Spiegle*** *a-1-3, 6.* ***Sutton*** *a-98p.* ***Totleben*** *a(i)-10, 16-27, 29, 31, 34-40, 42, 44, 46, 48, 50, 53, 55i; c-25-32i, 33, 35-40i, 42i, 44i, 46-50i, 53, 55i, 59p, 64, 65, 68, 73, 76, 80, 82, 84, 89, 91-100, Annual 4, 5.* ***Vess*** *painted c-121, 129-139, Annual 7.* ***Williamson*** *86i.* ***Wrightson*** *a-18i(r), 33r. John Constantine appears in #37-40, 44-51, 65-67, 70-77, 80-90, 99, 114, 115, 130, 134-138.*

SWAMP THING
DC Comics (Vertigo): May, 2000 - Present ($2.50)

1-11-Tefé Holland's return; Vaughan-s/Petersen-a. 1-3-Hale painted-c. 7-9-Bisley-c. 10-John Constantine-c/app. 10,11-Fabry-c 2.50
Preview-16 pg. flip book w/Lucifer Preview 1.00

SWARM (See Futuretech)
Mushroom Comics: Jan, 1996 ($2.50, limited series)

1-Flip book w/Futuretech #1 2.50

SWAT MALONE (America's Home Run King)
Swat Malone Enterprises: Sept, 1955

V1#1-Hy Fleishman-a 10.00 30.00 80.00

SWEENEY (Formerly Buz Sawyer)
Standard Comics: No. 4, June, 1949 - No. 5, Sept, 1949

4,5: 5-Crane-a 8.65 26.00 60.00

SWEE'PEA (Also see Popeye #46)
Dell Publishing Co.: No. 219, Mar, 1949

Four Color 219 8.35 25.00 100.00

SWEET CHILDE
Advantage Graphics Press: 1995 - No. 2, 1995 ($2.95, B&W, mature)

1,2 3.00

SWEETHEART DIARY (Cynthia Doyle #66-on)
Fawcett Publications/Charlton Comics No. 32 on: Wint, 1949; #2, Spr, 1950; #3, 6/50 - #5, 10/50; #6, 1951(nd); #7, 9/51 - #14, 1/53; #32, 10/55; #33, 4/56 - #65, 8/62 (#1-14: photo-c)

1 15.00 45.00 120.00
2 8.65 26.00 60.00
3,4-Wood-a 14.00 43.00 115.00
5-10: 8-Bailey-a 7.15 21.50 50.00
11-14: 13-Swayze-a. 14-Last Fawcett issue 5.00 15.00 35.00
32 (10/55; 1st Charlton issue)(Formerly Cowboy Love #31) 6.00 18.00 42.00
33-40: 34-Swayze-a 4.00 12.00 24.00
41-(68 pgs.) 4.30 13.00 26.00
42-60 2.00 6.00 18.00
61-65 2.00 6.00 16.00

SWEETHEARTS (Formerly Captain Midnight)
Fawcett Publications/Charlton No. 122 on: #68, 10/48 - #121, 5/53; #122, 3/54; V2#23, 5/54 - #137, 12/73

68-Photo-c begin 15.00 45.00 120.00
69-80 6.40 19.25 45.00
81-84,86-93,95-99,105 5.00 15.00 35.00

Sweet Sixteen #1 © PMI

Sword of Damocles #1 © WSP

Sword of the Atom #1 © DC

GD2.0 FN6.0 NM9.4

85,94,103,110,117-George Evans-a 7.15 21.50 50.00
100 6.00 18.00 42.00
101,107-Powell-a 5.50 16.50 38.00
102,104,106,108,109,112-116,118 5.00 15.00 30.00
111-1 pg. Ronald Reagan biography 7.85 23.50 55.00
119-Marilyn Monroe & Richard Widmark photo-c (1/54?); also appears in story; part Wood-a 40.00 120.00 325.00
120-Atom Bomb story 9.30 28.00 65.00
121-Liz Taylor/Fernanado Lamas photo-c 10.00 30.00 75.00
122-(1st Charlton? 3/54)-Marijuana story 9.30 28.00 65.00
V2#23 (5/54)-28: 28-Last precode issue (2/55) 5.00 15.00 30.00
29-39,41,43-45,47-50 2.50 7.50 24.00
40-Photo-c; Tommy Sands story 3.00 9.00 30.00
42-Ricky Nelson photo-c/story 6.80 20.50 75.00
46-Jimmy Rodgers photo-c/story 3.00 9.00 30.00
51-60 2.40 7.35 22.00
61-80,100 2.30 7.00 20.00
81-99 2.00 6.00 18.00
101-110 1.50 4.50 12.00
111-137 1.25 3.75 10.00

NOTE: *Photo c-68-121(Fawcett), 40, 42, 46(Charlton).* **Swayze** *a(Fawcett)-70-118(most).*

SWEETHEART SCANDALS (See Fox Giants)

SWEETIE PIE
Dell Publishing Co.: No. 1185, May-July, 1961 - No. 1241, Nov-Jan, 1961/62

Four Color 1185 (#1) 3.45 10.35 38.00
Four Color 1241 3.00 9.00 32.00

SWEETIE PIE
Ajax-Farrell/Pines (Literary Ent.): Dec, 1955 - No. 15, Fall, 1957

1-By Nadine Seltzer 7.15 21.50 50.00
2 (5/56; last Ajax?) 5.00 15.00 30.00
3-15 4.00 10.00 20.00

SWEET LOVE
Home Comics (Harvey): Sept, 1949 - No. 5, May, 1950 (All photo-c)

1 10.00 30.00 70.00
2 5.50 16.50 38.00
3,4: 3-Powell-a 5.00 15.00 30.00
5-Kamen, Powell-a 7.85 23.50 55.00

SWEET ROMANCE
Charlton Comics: Oct, 1968

1 1.75 5.25 14.00

SWEET SIXTEEN (...Comics and Stories for Girls)
Parents' Magazine Institute: Aug-Sept, 1946 - No. 13, Jan, 1948 (All have movie stars photos on covers)

1-Van Johnson's life story; Dorothy Dare, Queen of Hollywood Stunt Artists begins (in all issues); part photo-c 19.00 56.00 150.00
2-Jane Powell, Roddy McDowall "Holiday in Mexico" photo on-c; Alan Ladd story 12.50 37.50 100.00
3,5,6,8-11: 5-Ann Francis photo on-c; Gregory Peck story. 6-Dick Haymes story. 8-Shirley Jones photo on-c. 10-Jean Simmons photo on-c; James Stewart story 10.00 30.00 70.00
4-Elizabeth Taylor photo on-c 14.00 41.00 110.00
7-Ronald Reagan's life story 19.00 56.00 150.00
12-Bob Cummings, Vic Damone story 10.00 30.00 75.00
13-Robert Mitchum's life story 10.00 30.00 80.00

SWEET XVI
Marvel Comics: May, 1991 - No. 5, Sept, 1991($1.00, color)

1-5: Barbara Slate story & art 2.00

SWIFT ARROW (Also see Lone Rider & The Rider)
Ajax/Farrell Publications: Feb-Mar, 1954 - No. 5, Oct-Nov, 1954; Apr, 1957 - No. 3, Sept, 1957

1(1954) (1st Series) 15.00 45.00 120.00
2 8.65 26.00 60.00
3-5: 5-Lone Rider story 6.40 19.25 45.00
1 (2nd Series) (Swift Arrow's Gunfighters #4) 7.15 21.50 50.00
2,3: 2-Lone Rider begins 5.75 17.00 40.00

SWIFT ARROW'S GUNFIGHTERS (Formerly Swift Arrow)
Ajax/Farrell Publ. (Four Star Comic Corp.): No. 4, Nov, 1957

4 5.70 17.00 40.00

SWING WITH SCOOTER
National Periodical Publications: June-July, 1966 - No. 35, Aug-Sept, 1971; No. 36, Oct-Nov, 1972

1 6.80 20.50 75.00
2,6-10: 9-Alfred E. Newman swipe in last panel 3.00 9.00 30.00
3-5: 3-Batman cameo on-c. 4-Batman cameo inside. 5-JLA cameo 3.20 9.60 35.00
11-13,15-19: 18-Wildcat of JSA 1pg. text. 19-Last 12¢-c 2.40 7.35 22.00
14-Alfred E. Neuman cameo 2.50 7.50 25.00
20 (68 pgs.) 3.20 9.60 35.00
21-23,25-31 2.00 6.00 16.00
24-Frankenstein-c. 2.30 7.00 20.00
32-34 (68 pgs.). 32-Batman cameo. 33-Interview with David Cassidy. 34-Interview with Ron Ely (Doc Savage) 3.20 9.60 35.00
35-(52 pgs.). 1 pg. app. Clark Kent and 4 full pgs. of Superman 6.80 20.50 75.00
36-Bat-signal refererence to Batman 2.50 7.50 25.00

NOTE: **Aragonés** a-13 (1pg.), 18(1pg.), 30(2pgs.) **Orlando** *a-1-11; c-1-11, 13. #20, 33, 34: 68 pgs.; #35: 52 pgs.*

SWISS FAMILY ROBINSON (Walt Disney's..; see King Classics & Movie Comics)
Dell Publishing Co.: No. 1156, Dec, 1960

Four Color 1156-Movie-photo-c 6.70 20.00 80.00

SWORD & THE DRAGON, THE
Dell Publishing Co.: No. 1118, June, 1960

Four Color 1118-Movie, photo-c 7.50 22.50 90.00

SWORD & THE ROSE, THE (Disney)
Dell Publishing Co.: No. 505, Oct, 1953 - No. 682, Feb, 1956

Four Color 505-Movie, photo-c 8.35 25.00 100.00
Four Color 682-When Knighthood Was in Flower-Movie, reprint of #505; Renamed the Sword & the Rose for the novel; photo-c 6.70 20.00 80.00

SWORD IN THE STONE, THE (See March of Comics #258 & Movie Comics & Wart and the Wizard)

SWORD OF DAMOCLES
Image Comics (WildStorm Productions): Mar, 1996 - No. 2, Apr, 1996 ($2.50, limited series)

1,2: Warren Ellis scripts. 1-Prelude to "Fire From Heaven" x-over; 1st app. Sword 2.50

SWORD OF SORCERY
National Periodical Publications: Feb-Mar, 1973 - No. 5, Nov-Dec, 1973 (20¢)

1-Leiber Fafhrd & The Grey Mouser; Chaykin/Neal Adams (Crusty Bunkers) art; Kaluta-c 2.00 6.00 18.00
2,3: 2-Wrightson-c(i); Adams-a(i). 3-Wrightson-i(5 pgs.) 1.25 3.75 10.00
4,5: 5-Starlin-a(p); Conan cameo 1.00 3.00 8.00

NOTE: **Chaykin** *a-1-4p; c-2p, 3-5.* **Kaluta** *a-3i.* **Simonson** *a-3i, 4i, 5p; c-5.*

SWORD OF THE ATOM
DC Comics: Sept, 1983 - No. 4, Dec, 1983 (Limited series)

1-4: Kane-c/a in all, Special 1-3('84, '85, '88): 1,2-Kane-c/a each 3.00

SWORDS OF TEXAS (See Scout #15)
Eclipse Comics: Oct, 1987 - No. 4, Jan, 1988 ($1.75, color, Baxter paper)

1-4: Scout app. 2.00

SWORDS OF THE SWASHBUCKLERS (See Marvel Graphic Novel)
Marvel Comics (Epic Comics): May, 1985 - No. 12, Jun, 1987 ($1.50; mature)

1-12-Butch Guice-c/a (Cont'd from Marvel G.N.) 2.00

SWORN TO PROTECT
Marvel Comics: Sept, 1995 ($1.95) (Based on card game)

Taffy Comics #6 © Orbit Pub.

Tales Calculated to Drive You Bats #2 © AP

Tales From the Crypt #23 © WMG

nn-Overpower Game Guide; Jubilee story 2.00

SYPHONS
Now Comics: V2#1, May, 1994 - V2#3, 1994 ($2.50, limited series)
V2#1-3: 1-Stardancer, Knightfire, Raze & Brigade begin 2.50

SYSTEM, THE
DC Comics (Vertigo Verite): May, 1996 - No. 3, July, 1996 ($2.95, lim. series)
1-3: Kuper-c/a 3.00
TPB (1997, $12.95) r/#1-3 13.00

TAFFY COMICS
Rural Home/Orbit Publ.: Mar-Apr, 1945 - No. 12, 1948
1-L.B. Cole-c; origin & 1st app. of Wiggles The Wonderworm plus 7 chapter WWII funny animal adventures 55.00 165.00 500.00
2-L.B. Cole-c; Wiggles-c/stories in #1-4 28.00 84.00 225.00
3,4,6-12: 6-Perry Como-c/story. 7-Duke Ellington, 2 pgs. 8-Glenn Ford-c/story. 9-Lon McCallister part photo-c & story. 10-Mort Leav-c. 11-Mickey Rooney-c/story 12.00 36.00 95.00
5-L.B. Cole-c; Van Johnson-c/story 20.00 60.00 160.00

TAILGUNNER JO
DC Comics: Sept, 1988 - No. 6, Jan, 1989 ($1.25)
1-6 2.00

TAILS
Archie Publications; Dec, 1995 - No. 3, Feb, 1996 ($1.50, limited series)
1-3: Based on Sonic, the Hedgehog video game 3.00

TAILSPIN
Spotlight Publishers: November, 1944
nn-Firebird app.; L.B. Cole-c 28.00 83.00 220.00

TAILSPIN TOMMY (Also see Popular Comics)
United Features Syndicate/Service Publ. Co.: 1940; 1946
Single Series 23(1940) 40.00 120.00 350.00
Best Seller (nd, 1946)-Service Publ. Co. 14.00 41.00 110.00

TAINTED
DC Comics (Vertigo): Jan, 1995 ($4.95, one-shot)
1-Jamie Delano scripts; Al Davison-c/a; reads February '95 on-c 5.00

TAKION
DC Comics: June, 1996 - No. 7, Dec, 1996 ($1.75)
1-7: Lopresti-c/a(p). 1-Origin; Green Lantern app. 6-Final Night x-over 2.50

TALENT SHOWCASE (See New Talent Showcase)

TALE OF ONE BAD RAT, THE
Dark Horse Comics: Oct, 1994 - No. 4, Jan, 1995 ($2.95, limited series)
1-4: Bryan Talbot-c/a/scripts 3.00
HC ($69.95, signed and numbered) R/#1-4 70.00

TALES CALCULATED TO DRIVE YOU BATS
Archie Publications: Nov, 1961 - No. 7, Nov, 1962; 1966 (Satire)
1-Only 10¢ issue; has cut-out Werewolf mask (price includes mask) 11.00 33.00 120.00
2-Begin 12¢ issues 5.45 16.35 60.00
3-6: 3-UFO cover 4.10 12.30 45.00
7-Storyline change 3.65 11.00 40.00
1(1966, 25¢, 44 pg. Giant)-r/#1; UFO cover 4.55 13.65 50.00

TALES CALCULATED TO DRIVE YOU MAD
E.C. Publications: Summer, 1997 - No. 8, Winter, 1999 ($3.99/$4.99, satire)
1-6-Full color reprints of Mad: 1-(#1-3), 2-(#4-6), 3-(#7-9), 4-(#10-12) 5-(#13-15), 6-(#16-18) 4.00
7,8-($4.99-c): 7-(#19-21), 8-(#22,23) 5.00

TALES FROM THE AGE OF APOCALYPSE
Marvel Comics: 1996 ($5.95, prestige format, one-shots)
1, ...: Sinister Bloodlines (1997, $5.95) 6.00

TALES FROM THE BOG
Aberration Press: Nov, 1995 - No. 7, Nov, 1997 ($2.95/$3.95, B&W)
1-7 4.00

TALES FROM THE CRYPT (Formerly The Crypt Of Terror; see Three Dimensional...)
E.C. Comics: No. 20, Oct-Nov, 1950 - No. 46, Feb-Mar, 1955
20-See Crime Patrol #15 for 1st Crypt Keeper 105.00 315.00 1150.00
21-Kurtzman-r/Haunt of Fear #15(#1) 86.00 259.00 950.00
22-Moon Girl costume at costume party, one panel 67.00 200.00 735.00
23-25: 24-E. A. Poe adaptation 51.00 153.00 560.00
26-30 40.00 120.00 440.00
31-Williamson-a(1st at E.C.); B&W and color illos. in **POP**; Kamen draws himself, Gaines & Feldstein; Ingels, Craig & Davis draw themselves in his story 42.00 126.00 460.00
32,35-39: 38-Censored-c 36.00 109.00 400.00
33-Origin The Crypt Keeper 58.00 174.00 640.00
34-Used in **POP**, pg. 83; lingerie panels 36.00 109.00 400.00
40-Used in Senate hearings & in Hartford Cournat anti-comics editorials-1954 36.00 109.00 400.00
41-45: 45-2 pgs. showing E.C. staff 35.00 105.00 385.00
46-Low distribution; pre-advertised cover for unpublished 4th horror title "Crypt of Terror" used on this book 39.00 116.00 425.00
NOTE: ***Ray Bradbury*** *adaptations-34, 36.* ***Craig*** *a-20, 22-24; c-20.* ***Crandall*** *a-38, 44.* ***Davis*** *a-24-46; c-29-46.* ***Elder*** *a-37, 38.* ***Evans*** *a-32-34, 36, 40, 41, 43, 46.* ***Feldstein*** *a-20-23; c-21-25, 28. Ingels a-in all.* ***Kamen*** *a-20, 22, 25, 27-31, 33-36, 39, 41-45.* ***Krigstein*** *a-40, 42, 45.* ***Kurtzman*** *a-21.* ***Orlando*** *a-27-30, 35, 37, 39, 41-45.* ***Wood*** *a-21, 24, 25; c-26, 27. Canadian reprints known; see Table of Contents.*

TALES FROM THE CRYPT (Magazine)
Eerie Publications: No. 10, July, 1968 (35¢, B&W)
10-Contains Farrell reprints from 1950s 3.00 9.00 32.00

TALES FROM THE CRYPT
Gladstone Publishing: July, 1990 - No. 6, May, 1991 ($1.95/$2.00, 68 pgs.)
1-r/TFTC #33 & Crime S.S. #17; Davis-c(r) 2.50
2-6: 2,3,5,6-Davis-c(r). 4-Begin $2.00-c; Craig-c(r) 2.50

TALES FROM THE CRYPT
Extra-Large Comics (Russ Cochran)/Gemstone Publishing: Jul, 1991 - No. 6 ($3.95, 10 1/4 x13 1/4", 68 pgs.)
1-Davis-c(r); Craig back-c(r); E.C. reprints 4.00
2-6 ($2.00, comic sized) 2.50

TALES FROM THE CRYPT
Russ Cochran: Sept, 1991 - No. 7, July, 1992 ($2.00, 64 pgs.)
1-7 2.50

TALES FROM THE CRYPT
Russ Cochran/Gemstone: Sept, 1992 - No. 30, Dec, 1999 ($1.50, quarterly)
1-4-r/Crypt of Terror #17-19, TFTC #20 w/original-c 2.50
5-30: 5-15 ($2.00)-r/TFTC #21-23 w/original-c. 16-30 ($2.50) 2.50
Annual 1-6('93-'99) 1-r/#1-5. 2- r/#6-10. 3- r/#11-15. 4- r/#16-20. 5-r/#21-25. 6- r/#26-30 14.00

TALES FROM THE GREAT BOOK
Famous Funnies: Feb, 1955 - No. 4, Jan, 1956 (Religious themes)
1-Story of Samson; John Lehti-a in all 8.65 26.00 60.00
2-4: 2-Joshua. 3-Joash the Boy King. 4-David 5.00 15.00 35.00

TALES FROM THE HEART OF AFRICA (The Temporary Natives)
Marvel Comics (Epic Comics): Aug, 1990 ($3.95, 52 pgs.)
1 4.00

TALES FROM THE TOMB (Also see Dell Giants)
Dell Publishing Co.: Oct, 1962 (25¢ giant)

	GD2.0	FN6.0	VF8.0	NM9.4
1(02-810-210)-All stories written by John Stanley	10.00	30.00	80.00	200.00

TALES FROM THE TOMB (Magazine)
Eerie Publications: V1#6, July, 1969 - V7#3, 1975 (52 pgs.)
V1#6-8 5.00 15.00 55.00
V2#1-6: 4-LSD story-r/Weird V3#5. 6-Rulah-r 3.65 11.00 40.00
V3#1-Rulah-r 3.65 11.00 40.00
2-6('70),V4#1-5('72),V5#1-6('73),V6#1-6('74),V7#1-3('75) 3.20 9.60 35.00

Tales of Horror #4 © Minoan Publ.

Tales of Suspense #2 © MAR

Tales of Terror #2 © WMG

GD2.0 FN6.0 NM9.4

TALES OF ASGARD
Marvel Comics Group: Oct, 1968 (25¢, 68 pgs.); Feb, 1984 ($1.25, 52 pgs.)

1-Reprints Tales of Asgard (Thor) back-up stories from Journey into Mystery #97-106; new Kirby-c; Kirby-a 3.65 11.00 40.00
V2#1 (2/84)-Thor-r; Simonson-c 3.00

TALES OF EVIL
Atlas/Seaboard Publ.: Feb, 1975 - No. 3, July, 1975 (All 25¢ issues)

1-3: 1-Werewolf w/Sekowsky-a. 2-Intro. The Bog Beast; Sparling-a. 3-Origin The Man-Monster; Buckler-a(p) 2.40 6.00
NOTE: *Grandenetti a-1, 2. Lieber c-1. Sekowsky a-1. Sutton a-2. Thorne c-2.*

TALES OF GHOST CASTLE
National Periodical Publications: May-June, 1975 - No. 3, Sept-Oct, 1975 (All 25¢ issues)

1-Redondo-a 2.30 7.00 20.00
2,3: 2-Nino-a. 3-Redondo-a. 1.50 4.50 12.00

TALES OF G.I. JOE
Marvel Comics: Jan, 1988 - No. 15, Mar, 1989

1 ($2.25, 52 pgs.) 3.00
2-15 ($1.50): 1-15-r/G.I. Joe #1-15 2.00

TALES OF HORROR
Toby Press/Minoan Publ. Corp.: June, 1952 - No. 13, Oct, 1954

1 40.00 120.00 325.00
2-Torture scenes 33.00 98.00 260.00
3-13: 9-11-Reprints Purple Claw #1-3 21.00 62.00 165.00
12-Myron Fass-c/a; torture scenes 22.00 66.00 175.00
NOTE: *Andru a-5. Baily a-5. Myron Fass a-2, 3, 12; c-1-3, 12. Hollingsworth a-2. Sparling a-6, 9; c-9.*

TALES OF JUSTICE
Atlas Comics(MjMC No. 53-66/Male No. 67): No. 53, May, 1955 - No. 67, Aug, 1957

53 15.00 45.00 120.00
54-57: 54-Powell-a 10.00 30.00 80.00
58,59-Krigstein-a 11.00 33.00 90.00
60-63,65: 60-Powell-a 10.00 30.00 70.00
64,66,67: 64,67-Crandall-a. 66-Torres, Orlando-a 10.00 30.00 75.00
NOTE: *Everett a-53, 60. Orlando a-65, 66. Severin a-64; c-58, 60, 65. Wildey a-64, 67.*

TALES OF SUSPENSE (Becomes Captain America #100 on)
Atlas (WPI No. 1,2/Male No. 3-12/VPI No. 13-18)/Marvel No. 19 on: Jan, 1959 - No. 99, Mar, 1968

1-Williamson-a (5 pgs.); Heck-c; #1-4 have sci/fi-c 129.00 386.00 1800.00
2,3: 2-Robot-c. 3-Flying saucer-c/story 50.00 150.00 650.00
4-Williamson-a (4 pgs.); Kirby/Everett-c/a 42.00 126.00 550.00
5,6,8,10: 5-Kirby monster-c begin 31.00 94.00 375.00
7-Prototype ish. (Lava Man); 1 panel app. Aunt May (see Str. Tales #97) 35.00 105.00 420.00
9-Prototype ish. (Iron Man) 37.00 112.00 450.00
11,12,15,17-19: 12-Crandall-a. 26.50 79.00 290.00
13-Elektro-c/story 27.50 82.00 300.00
14-Intro/1st app. Colossus-c/sty 31.00 93.00 360.00
16-1st Metallo-c/story (4/61, Iron Man prototype) 31.00 93.00 360.00
20-Colossus-c/story (2nd app.) 27.50 82.00 300.00
21-25: 25-Last 10¢ issue 20.50 61.00 225.00
26,27,29,30,33,34,36-38: 33-(9/62)-Hulk 1st x-over cameo (picture on wall) 17.50 52.00 190.00
28-Prototype ish. (Stone Men) 18.00 53.00 195.00
31-Prototype ish. (Dr. Doom) 22.00 65.00 240.00
32-Prototype ish. (Dr. Strange)(8/62)-Sazzik The Sorcerer app.; "The Man and the Beehive" story, 1 month before TTA #35 (2nd Antman), came out after "The Man in the Ant Hill" in TTA #27 (1/62) (1st Antman)-Characters from both stories were tested to see which got best fan response 31.00 94.00 375.00
35-Prototype issue (The Watcher) 22.00 65.00 240.00

GD2.0 FN6.0 VF8.0 NM9.4

39 (3/63)-Origin/1st app. Iron Man & begin series; 1st Iron Man story has Kirby layouts 310.00 930.00 2480.00 5200.00

GD2.0 FN6.0 NM9.4

40-2nd app. Iron Man (in new armor) 104.00 311.00 1450.00
41-3rd app. Iron Man; Dr. Strange (villain) app. 57.00 171.00 800.00
42-45: 45-Intro. & 1st app. Happy & Pepper 33.00 100.00 400.00
46,47: 46-1st app. Crimson Dynamo 23.00 68.00 250.00
48-New Iron Man armor by Ditko 29.00 88.00 325.00
49-1st X-Men x-over (same date as X-Men #3, 1/64); also 1st Avengers x-over (w/o Captain America); 1st Tales of the Watcher back-up story & begins (2nd app. Watcher; see F.F. #13) 21.50 64.00 235.00
50-1st app. Mandarin 14.50 43.50 160.00
51-1st Scarecrow 11.50 34.00 125.00
52-1st app. The Black Widow (4/64) 15.50 46.50 170.00
53-Origin The Watcher; 2nd Black Widow app. 13.50 40.00 150.00
54-56: 56-1st app. Unicorn 7.65 23.00 85.00
57-Origin/1st app. Hawkeye (9/64) 18.00 53.00 195.00
58-Captain America battles Iron Man (10/64)-Classic-c; 2nd Kraven app. (Cap's 1st app. in this title) 27.50 82.00 300.00
59-Iron Man plus Captain America double feature begins (11/64); 1st S.A. Captain America solo story; intro Jarvis, Avenger's butler; classic-c 27.50 82.00 300.00
60-2nd app. Hawkeye (#64 is 3rd app.) 12.75 38.00 140.00
61,62,64: 62-Origin Mandarin (2/65) 7.65 23.00 85.00
63-1st Silver Age origin Captain America (3/65) 22.00 65.00 240.00
65,66-G.A. Red Skull in WWII stories: 65-1st Silver-Age Red Skull (5/65). 66-Origin Red Skull 14.50 43.50 160.00
67-70: 69-1st app. Titanium Man. 70-Begin alternating-c features w/Capt. America (even #'s) & Iron Man (odd #'s) 4.55 13.65 50.00
71-78,81-98: 75-1st app. Agent 13 later named Sharon Carter. 76-Intro Batroc & Sharon Carter, Agent 13 of Shield. 78-Col. Nick Fury app. 81-Intro the Adaptoid by Kirby (also in #82-84). 88-Mole Man app. in Iron Man story. 92-1st Nick Fury x-over (cameo, as Agent of Shield, 8/67). 94-Intro Modok. 95-Capt. America's i.d. revealed. 98-1st app. new Zemo (son?) in cameo (#99 is 1st full app.) 4.10 12.30 45.00
79-Begin 3 part Iron Man Sub-Mariner battle story; Sub-Mariner-c & cameo; 1st app. Cosmic Cube; 1st modern Red Skull 5.90 17.75 65.00
80-Iron Man battles Sub-Mariner story cont'd in Tales to Astonish #82; classic Red Skull-c 5.45 16.35 60.00
99-Captain America story cont'd in Captain America #100; Iron Man story cont'd in Iron Man & Sub-Mariner #1 6.35 19.00 70.00
NOTE: *Abel a-73-81i(as Gary Michaels), J. Buscema a-1; c-3. Colan a-39, 73-99p; c(p)-73, 75, 77, 79, 81, 83, 85-87, 89, 91, 93, 95, 97, 99. Crandall a-12. Davis a-38. Ditko a-1-15, 17-44, 46, 47-49p; c-2, 10i, 13i, 23i. Kirby/Ditko a-7; c-10, 13, 22, 28, 34. Everett a-8. Forte a-5, 9. Giacoia a-82. Heath a-2, 10. Gil Kane a-88p, 89-91; c-88, 89-91p. Kirby a(p)-2-4, 6-35, 40, 41, 43, 59-75, 77-86, 92-99; layouts-69-75, 77; c(p)4-28(most), 29-56, 58-72, 74, 76, 78, 80, 82, 84, 86, 92, 94, 96, 98. Leiber/Fox a-42, 43, 45, 51. Reinman a-26, 44i, 49i, 52i, 53i. Tuska a-58, 70-74. Wood c/a-71i.*

TALES OF SUSPENSE
Marvel Comics: V2#1, Jan, 1995 ($6.95, one-shot)

V2#1-James Robinson script; acetate-c. 7.00

TALES OF SWORD & SORCERY (See Dagar)

TALES OF TERROR
Toby Press Publications: 1952 (no month)

1-Fawcette-c; Ravielli-a 25.00 75.00 200.00
NOTE: *This title was cancelled due to similarity to the E.C. title.*

TALES OF TERROR (See Movie Classics)

TALES OF TERROR (Magazine)
Eerie Publications: Summer, 1964

1 3.65 11.00 40.00

TALES OF TERROR
Eclipse Comics: July, 1985 - No. 13, July, 1987 ($2.00, Baxter paper, mature)

1-13: 5-1st Lee Weeks-a. 7-Sam Kieth-a. 10-Snyder-a. 12-Vampire story 2.00

TALES OF TERROR ANNUAL
E.C. Comics: 1951 - No. 3, 1953 (25¢, 132 pgs., 16 stories each)

GD2.0 FN6.0 VF8.0

nn(1951)(Scarce)-Feldstein infinity-c 425.00 1275.00 3400.00

GD2.0 FN6.0 NM9.4

2(1952)-Feldstein-c 159.00 477.00 1750.00
3(1953)-Feldstein bondage/torture-c 127.00 382.00 1400.00

Tales of the Darkness #2 © Top Cow

Tales of the Mysterious Traveller #3 © CC

Tales of the Unexpected #4 © DC

GD2.0 FN6.0 NM9.4

NOTE: No. 1 contains three horror and one science fiction comic which came out in 1950. No. 2 contains a horror, crime, and science fiction book which generally had cover dates in 1951, and No. 3 had horror, crime, and shock books that generally appeared in 1952. All E.C. annuals contain four complete books that did not sell on the stands which were rebound in the annual format, minus the covers, and sold from the E.C. office and on the stands in key cities. The contents of each annual may vary in the same year. Crypt Keeper, Vault Keeper, Old Witch app. on all-c.

TALES OF TERROR ILLUSTRATED (See Terror Illustrated)

TALES OF TEXAS JOHN SLAUGHTER (See Walt Disney Presents, 4-Color #997)

TALES OF THE BEANWORLD
Beanworld Press/Eclipse Comics: Feb, 1985 - No. 19, 1991; No. 20, 1993 - No. 21, 1993 ($1.50/$2.00, B&W)

1-21 — 3.00

TALES OF THE BIZARRO WORLD
DC Comics: 2000 ($14.95, TPB)

nn-Reprints early Bizarro stories; new Jaime Hernandez-c — 15.00

TALES OF THE DARKNESS
Image Comics (Top Cow): Apr, 1998 - Present ($2.95)

1-4: 1,2-Portacio-c/a(p). 3,4-Lansing & Nocon-a(p) — 3.00
1-American Entertainment Ed. — 3.00
#1/2 (1/01, $2.95)

TALES OF THE GREEN BERET
Dell Publishing Co.: Jan, 1967 - No. 5, Oct, 1969

1-Glanzman-a in 1-4 & 5r — 3.00 9.00 30.00
2-5: 5-Reprints #1 — 2.40 7.35 22.00

TALES OF THE GREEN HORNET
Now Comics: Sept, 1990 - No. 2, 1990; V2#1, Jan, 1992 - No.4, Apr, 1992; V3#1, Sept, 1992 - No. 3, Nov, 1992

1,2 — 2.00
V2#1-4 ($1.95) — 2.00
V3#1 ($2.75)-Polybagged w/hologram trading card — 3.00
V3#2,3 ($2.50) — 2.50

TALES OF THE GREEN LANTERN CORPS (See Green Lantern #107)
DC Comics: May, 1981 - No. 3, July, 1981 (Limited series)

1-3: 1-Origin of G.L. & the Guardians, Annual 1 (1/85)-Gil Kane-c/a — 3.00

TALES OF THE INVISIBLE SCARLET O'NEIL (See Harvey Comics Hits #59)

TALES OF THE KILLERS (Magazine)
World Famous Periodicals: V1#10, Dec, 1970 - V1#11, Feb, 1971 (B&W, 52 pg)

V1#10-One pg. Frazetta; r/Crime Does Not Pay — 3.25 9.75 36.00
11-similar-c to Crime Does Not Pay #47; contains r/Crime Does Not Pay — 3.00 9.00 30.00

TALES OF THE LEGION (Formerly Legion of Super-Heroes)
DC Comics: No. 314, Aug, 1984 - No. 354, Dec, 1987

314-354: 326-r-begin — 2.50
Annual 4,5 (1986, 1987)-Formerly LSH Annual — 3.50

TALES OF THE MARINES (Formerly Devil-Dog Dugan #1-3)
Atlas Comics (OPI): No. 4, Feb, 1957 (Marines At War #5 on)

4-Powell-a; Severin-c — 6.40 19.25 45.00

TALES OF THE MARVELS
Marvel Comics: 1995/1996 (all acetate, painted-c)

...Blockbuster 1 (1995, $5.95, one-shot), ...Inner Demons 1 (1996, $5.95, one shot), ...Wonder Years 1,2 (1995, $4.95, limited series) — 6.00

TALES OF THE MARVEL UNIVERSE
Marvel Comics: Feb, 1997 ($2.95, one-shot)

1-Anthology; wraparound-c; Thunderbolts, Ka-Zar app. — 3.00

TALES OF THE MYSTERIOUS TRAVELER (See Mysterious…)
Charlton Comics: Aug, 1956 - No. 13, June, 1959; V2#14, Oct, 1985 - No. 15, Dec, 1985

1-No Ditko-a; Giordano/Alascia-c — 44.00 133.00 400.00
2-Ditko-a(1) — 40.00 120.00 350.00
3-Ditko-c/a(1) — 40.00 120.00 350.00
4-6-Ditko-c/a(3-4 stories each) — 44.00 133.00 400.00
7-9-Ditko-a(1-2 each). 8-Rocke-c — 40.00 120.00 325.00
10,11-Ditko-c/a(3-4 each) — 40.00 120.00 360.00
12 — 16.00 48.00 125.00
13-Baker-a (r?) — 18.00 53.00 140.00
V2#14,15 (1985)-Ditko-c/a — 5.00

TALES OF THE NEW TEEN TITANS
DC Comics: June, 1982 - No. 4, Sept, 1982 (Limited series)

1-4 — 4.00

TALES OF THE PONY EXPRESS (TV)
Dell Publishing Co.: No. 829, Aug, 1957 - No. 942, Oct, 1958

Four Color 829 (#1)--Painted-c — 4.10 12.30 45.00
Four Color 942-Title -Pony Express — 4.10 12.30 45.00

TALES OF THE SUN RUNNERS
Sirius Comics/Amazing Comics No. 3: V2#1, July, 1986 - V2#3, 1986? ($1.50)

V2#1-3, Christmas Special 1(12/86) — 2.00

TALES OF THE TEENAGE MUTANT NINJA TURTLES
Mirage Studios: May, 1987 - No. 7, Aug (Apr-c), 1989 (B&W, $1.50) (See Teenage Mutant…)

1-7: 2-Title merges w/Teenage Mutant Ninja… — 2.00

TALES OF THE TEEN TITANS (Formerly The New Teen Titans)
DC Comics: No. 41, Apr, 1984 - No. 91, July, 1988 (75¢)

41,45-49: 46-Aqualad & Aquagirl join — 3.00
42-44: The Judas Contract part 1-3 with Deathstroke the Terminator in all; concludes in Annual #3. 44-Dick Grayson becomes Nightwing (3rd to be Nightwing) & joins Titans; Jericho (Deathstroke's son) joins; origin Deathstroke — 3.50
50,53-55: 50-Double size; app. Betty Kane (Bat-Girl) out of costume. 53-1st full app. Azrael; Deathstroke cameo. 54,55-Deathstroke-c/stories — 3.50
51,52,56-91: 52-1st app. Azrael in cameo (not same as newer character). 56-Intro Jinx. 57-Neutron app. 59-r/DC Comics Presents #26. 60-91-r/New Teen Titans Baxter series. 68-B. Smith-c. 70-Origin Kole — 2.00
Annual 3(1984, $1.25)-Part 4 of The Judas Contract; Deathstroke-c/story; Death of Terra; indicia says Teen Titans Annual; previous annuals listed as New Teen Titans Annual #1,2 — 4.00
Annual 4,5: 4-(1986, $1.25)-Reprints. 5-(1987) — 2.50

TALES OF THE TEXAS RANGERS (See Jace Pearson…)

TALES OF THE UNEXPECTED (Becomes The Unexpected #105 on)(See Adventure #75, Super DC Giant)
National Periodical Publications: Feb-Mar, 1956 - No. 104, Dec-Jan, 1967-68

1 — 89.00 268.00 1250.00
2 — 44.00 133.00 575.00
3-5 — 31.00 94.00 375.00
6-10: 6-1st Silver Age issue — 26.50 79.00 290.00
11,14,19,20 — 16.50 49.00 180.00
12,13,15-18,21-24: All have Kirby-a. 15,17-Grey tone-c. 16-Character named 'Thor' with a magic hammer by Kirby (8/57, not like later Thor) — 23.00 68.00 250.00
25-30 — 15.00 45.00 165.00
31-39 — 12.75 38.00 140.00
40-Space Ranger begins (8/59, 3rd ap.), ends #82 — 79.00 236.00 1100.00
41,42-Space Ranger stories — 31.00 93.00 350.00
43-1st Space Ranger-c this title; grey tone-c — 61.00 182.00 850.00
44-46 — 24.50 74.00 270.00
47-50 — 17.50 52.00 190.00
51-60: 54-Dinosaur-c/story — 15.00 45.00 165.00
61-67: 67-Last 10¢ issue — 12.50 37.00 135.00
68-82: 82-Last Space Ranger — 6.80 20.50 75.00
83-90,92-99 — 4.10 12.30 45.00
91,100: 91-1st Automan (also in #94,97) — 4.55 13.65 50.00
101-104 — 3.65 11.00 40.00

*NOTE: **Neal Adams** c-104. **Anderson** a-50. **Brown** a-50-82(Space Ranger); c-19, 40, & many Space Ranger-c. **Cameron** a-24, 27, 29; c-24. **Heath** a-49. **Bob Kane** a-24, 48. **Kirby** a-12, 13, 15-18, 21-24; c-13, 18, 22. **Meskin** a-15, 18, 26, 27, 35, 66. **Moreira** a-16, 20, 29, 38, 44, 62, 71; c-38. **Roussos** c-10. **Wildey** a-31.*

TALES OF THE WEST (See 3-D…)

Tales of the Witchblade #7 © Top Cow

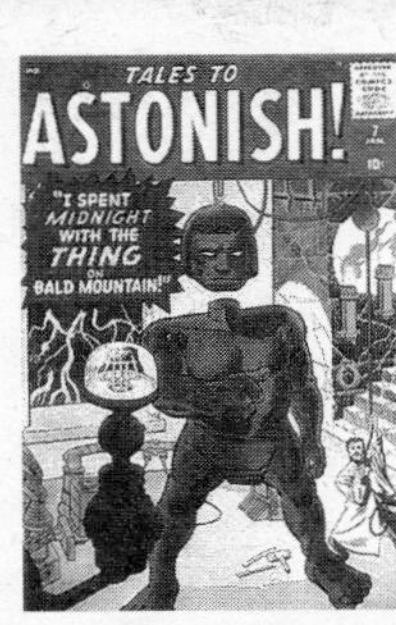

Tales to Astonish #7 © MAR

Tally-Ho Comics nn © Baily Pub. Co.

GD2.0 FN6.0 NM9.4

TALES OF THE WITCHBLADE
Image Comics (Top Cow Productions): Nov, 1996 - Present ($2.95)

1/2 1.10 3.30 9.00
1/2 Gold 15.00
1-Daniel-c/a(p) 1.25 3.75 10.00
1-Variant-c by Turner 1.85 5.50 15.00
1-Platinum Edition 30.00
2,3 2.40 6.00
4-6: 6-Green-c 5.00
7-9: 9-Lara Croft-c 3.00
7-Variant-c by Turner 1.00 3.00 8.00

TALES OF THE WITCHBLADE COLLECTED EDITION
Image Comics (Top Cow): May, 1998 - Present ($4.95/$5.95, square-bound)

1,2: 1-r/#1,2. 2-($5.95) r/#3,4 6.00

TALES OF THE WIZARD OF OZ (See Wizard of OZ, 4-Color #1308)

TALES OF THE ZOMBIE (Magazine)
Marvel Comics Group: Aug, 1973 - No. 10, Mar, 1975 (75¢, B&W)

V1#1-Reprint/Menace #5; origin 2.50 7.50 25.00
2,3: 2-Everett biog. & memorial 2.00 6.00 18.00
V2#1(#4)-Photos & text of James Bond movie "Live & Let Die"
2.00 6.00 18.00
5-10: 8-Kaluta-a 1.75 5.25 14.00
Annual 1(Summer,'75)(#11)-B&W; Everett, Buscema-a
2.30 7.00 20.00

NOTE: Brother Voodoo app. 2, 5, 6, 10. ***Alcala*** *a-7-9.* ***Boris*** *c-1-4.* ***Colan*** *a-2r, 6.* ***Heath*** *a-5r.* ***Reese*** *a-2.* ***Tuska*** *a-2r.*

TALES OF THUNDER
Deluxe Comics: Mar, 1985

1-Dynamo, Iron Maiden, Menthor app.; Giffen-a 2.00

TALES OF VOODOO
Eerie Publications: V1#11, Nov, 1968 - V7#6, Nov, 1974 (Magazine)

V1#11 4.10 12.30 45.00
V2#1(3/69)-V2#4(9/69) 3.20 9.60 35.00
V3#1-6('70): 4- "Claws of the Cat" redrawn from Climax #1
2.80 8.40 28.00
V4#1-6('71), V5#1-7('72), V6#1-6('73), V7#1-6('74) 2.80 8.40 28.00
Annual 1 3.00 9.00 30.00

NOTE: *Bondage-c-V1#10, V2#4, V3#4.*

TALES OF WELLS FARGO (TV)(See Western Roundup under Dell Giants)
Dell Publishing Co.: No. 876, Feb, 1958 - No. 1215, Oct-Dec, 1961

Four Color 876 (#1)-Photo-c 9.00 27.00 110.00
Four Color 968 (2/59), 1023, 1075 (3/60), 1113 (7-9/60)-All photo-c
8.35 25.00 100.00
Four Color 1167 (3-5/61), 1215-Photo-c 7.50 22.50 90.00

TALESPIN (Also see Cartoon Tales & Disney's Talespin Limited Series)
Disney Comics: June, 1991 - No. 7, Dec, 1991 ($1.50)

1-7 2.00

TALES TO ASTONISH (Becomes The Incredible Hulk #102 on)
Atlas (MAP No. 1/ZPC No. 2-14/VPI No. 15-21/Marvel No. 22 on: Jan, 1959 - No. 101, Mar, 1968

1-Jack Davis-a; monster-c. 129.00 386.00 1800.00
2-Ditko flying saucer-c (Martians); #2-4 have sci/fi-c.
54.00 161.00 750.00
3,4 41.00 123.00 500.00
5-Prototype issue (Stone Men); Williamson-a (4 pgs.); Kirby monster-c begin
42.00 126.00 550.00
6-Prototype issue (Stone Men) 35.00 106.00 425.00
7-Prototype issue (Toad Men) 35.00 106.00 425.00
8-10 31.00 94.00 375.00
11-14,17-20: 13-Swipes story from Menace #8 25.50 76.00 280.00
15-Prototype issue (Electro) 33.00 100.00 400.00
16-Prototype issue (Stone Men) 29.00 87.00 320.00
21-(7/61)-Hulk prototype 29.00 87.00 320.00
22-26,28-34 19.00 57.00 210.00
27-1st Ant-Man app. (1/62); last 10¢ issue (see Strange Tales #73,78 & Tales of Suspense #32) 263.00 788.00 4200.00
35-(9/62)-2nd app. Ant-Man, 1st in costume; begin series & Ant-Man-c
121.00 364.00 1700.00
36-3rd app. Ant-Man 52.00 156.00 675.00
37-40: 38-1st app. Egghead 35.00 106.00 425.00
41-43 25.00 75.00 275.00
44-Origin & 1st app. The Wasp (6/63) 31.00 93.00 350.00
45-48: Origin & 1st app. The Porcupine. 16.00 48.00 175.00
49-Ant-Man becomes Giant Man (11/63) 20.50 61.00 225.00
50,51,53-56,58: 50-Origin/1st app. Human Top (alias Whirlwind). 53-Origin Colossus 10.00 30.00 110.00
52-Origin/1st app. Black Knight (2/64) 11.50 34.00 125.00
57-Early Spider-Man app. (7/64) 14.50 43.50 160.00
59-Giant Man vs. Hulk feature story (9/64); Hulk's 1st app. this title
16.50 49.00 180.00
60-Giant Man & Hulk double feature begins 18.00 54.00 200.00
61-69: 61-All Ditko issue; 1st mailbag. 62-1st app./origin The Leader; new Wasp costume. 63-Origin Leader; 65-New Giant Man costume. 68-New Human Top costume. 69-Last Giant Man. 6.35 19.00 70.00
70-Sub-Mariner & Incredible Hulk begins (8/65) 8.15 24.50 90.00
71-81,83-91,94-99: 72-Begin alternating-c features w/Sub-Mariner (even #'s) & Hulk (odd #'s). 79-Hulk vs. Hercules-c/story. 81-1st app. Boomerang. 90-1st app. The Abomination. 97-X-Men cameo (brief) 4.55 13.65 50.00
82-Iron Man battles Sub-Mariner (1st Iron Man x-over outside The Avengers & TOS); story cont'd from Tales of Suspense #80 5.00 15.00 55.00
92-1st Silver Surfer x-over (outside of Fantastic Four, 6/67); 1 panel cameo only 5.00 15.00 55.00
93-Hulk battles Silver Surfer-c/story (1st full x-over) 6.35 19.00 70.00
100-Hulk battles Sub-Mariner full-length story 5.45 16.35 60.00
101-Hulk story cont'd in Incredible Hulk #102; Sub-Mariner story continued in Iron Man & Sub-Mariner #1 6.80 20.50 75.00

NOTE: ***Ayers*** *c(i)-9-12, 16, 18, 19.* ***Berg*** *a-1.* ***Burgos*** *a-62-64p.* ***Buscema*** *a-85-87p.* ***Colan*** *a(p)-70-76, 78-82, 84, 85, 101; c(p)-71-76, 78, 80, 82, 84, 86, 88, 90.* ***Ditko*** *a-1, 3-48, 50i, 60-67p; c-2, 7i, 8i, 14i, 17i.* ***Everett*** *a-78, 79i, 80-84, 85-90i, 94i, 95, 96; c(i)-79-81, 83, 86, 88.* ***Forte*** *a-6.* ***Kane*** *a-76, 88-91; c-89, 91.* ***Kirby*** *a(p)-1, 5-34-40, 44, 49-51, 68-70, 82, 83; layouts-71-84; c(p)-1, 3-48, 50-70, 72, 73, 75, 77, 78, 79, 81, 85, 90.* ***Kirby/Ditko*** *a-7, 8, 12, 13, 50; c-7, 8, 10, 13.* ***Leiber/Fox*** *a-47, 48, 50, 51.* ***Powell*** *a-65-69p, 73, 74.* ***Reinman*** *a-6, 36, 45, 46, 54i, 56-60i.*

TALES TO ASTONISH (2nd Series)
Marvel Comics Group: Dec, 1979 - No. 14, Jan, 1981

V1#1-Reprints Sub-Mariner #1 by Buscema 5.00
2-14: Reprints Sub-Mariner #2-14 3.00

TALES TO ASTONISH
Marvel Comics: V3#1, Oct, 1994 ($6.95, one-shot)

V3#1-Peter David scripts; acetate, painted-c 7.00

TALES TO HOLD YOU SPELLBOUND (See Spellbound)

TALES TO OFFEND
Dark Horse Comics: July, 1997 ($2.95, one-shot)

1-Frank Miller-s/a, EC-style cover 3.50

TALKING KOMICS
Belda Record & Publ. Co.: 1947 (20 pgs, slick-c)

Each comic contained a record that followed the story - much like the Golden Record sets. Known titles: Chirpy Cricket, Lonesome Octopus, Sleepy Santa, Grumpy Shark, Flying Turtle, Happy Grasshopper
with records... 3.20 7.00 20.00

TALLY-HO COMICS
Swappers Quarterly (Baily Publ. Co.): Dec, 1944

nn-Frazetta's 1st work as Giunta's assistant; Man in Black horror story; violence; Giunta-c 40.00 102.00 360.00

TALOS OF THE WILDERNESS SEA
DC Comics: Aug, 1987 ($2.00, one-shot)

1 2.00

TALULLAH (See Comic Books Series I)

TAMMY, TELL ME TRUE
Dell Publishing Co.: No. 1233, 1961

Four Color 1233-Movie 5.85 17.50 70.00

Tangent Comics/ The Flash #1 © DC

Target Comics V9 #6 © NOVP

Tarot: Witch of the Black Rose #4 © Jim Balent

GD2.0 FN6.0 NM9.4 GD2.0 FN6.0 NM9.4

TANGENT COMICS

.../ THE ATOM, DC Comics: Dec, 1997 ($2.95, one-shot)
1-Dan Jurgens-s/Jurgens & Paul Ryan-a 3.00

.../ THE BATMAN, DC Comics: Sept, 1998 ($1.95, one-shot)
1-Dan Jurgens-s/Klaus Janson-a 2.00

.../ DOOM PATROL, DC Comics: Dec, 1997 ($2.95, one-shot)
1- Dan Jurgens-s/Sean Chen & Kevin Conrad-a 3.00

.../ THE FLASH, DC Comics: Dec, 1997 ($2.95, one-shot)
1-Todd Dezago-s/Gary Frank & Cam Smith-a 3.00

.../ GREEN LANTERN, DC Comics: Dec, '97 ($2.95, one-shot)
1-James Robinson-s/J.H. Williams III & Mick Gray-a 3.00

.../ JLA, DC Comics: Sept, 1998 ($1.95, one-shot)
1-Dan Jurgens-s/Banks & Rapmund-a 2.00

.../ THE JOKER, DC Comics: Dec, 1997 ($2.95, one-shot)
1-Karl Kesel-s/Matt Haley & Tom Simmons-a 3.00

.../ THE JOKER'S WILD, DC Comics: Sept, 1998 ($1.95, one-shot)
1-Kesel & Simmons-s/Phillips & Rodriguez-a 2.00

.../ METAL MEN, DC Comics: Dec, 1997 ($2.95, one-shot)
1-Ron Marz-s/Mike McKone & Mark McKenna-a 3.00

.../ NIGHTWING, DC Comics: Dec, 1997 ($2.95, one-shot)
1-John Ostrander-s/Jan Duursema-a 3.00

.../ NIGHTWING: NIGHTFORCE, DC Comics: Sept, 1998 ($1.95, one-shot)
1-John Ostrander-s/Jan Duursema-a 2.00

.../ POWERGIRL, DC Comics: Sept, 1998 ($1.95, one-shot)
1-Marz-s/Abell & Vines-a 2.00

.../ SEA DEVILS, DC Comics: Dec, 1997 ($2.95, one-shot)
1-Kurt Busiek-s/Vince Giarrano & Tom Palmer-a 3.00

.../ SECRET SIX, DC Comics: Dec, 1997 ($2.95, one-shot)
1-Chuck Dixon-s/Tom Grummett & Lary Stucker-a 3.00

.../ THE SUPERMAN, DC Comics: Sept, 1998 ($1.95, one-shot)
1-Millar-s/Guice-a 2.00

.../ TALES OF THE GREEN LANTERN, DC Comics: Sept, 1998 ($1.95, one-shot)
1-Story & art by various 2.00

.../ THE TRIALS OF THE FLASH, DC Comics: Sept, 1998 ($1.95, one-shot)
1-Dezago-s/Pelletier & Lanning-a 2.00

.../ WONDER WOMAN DC Comics: Sept, 1998 ($1.95, one-shot),
1-Peter David-s/Unzueta & Mendoza-a 2.00

TANK GIRL
Dark Horse Comics: May, 1991 - No. 4, Aug, 1991 ($2.25, B&W, mini-series)
1-4: 1-Contains Dark Horse trading cards 4.00

TANK GIRL: APOCALYPSE
DC Comics: Nov, 1995 - No. 4, Feb, 1996 ($2.25, limited series)
1-4 3.00

TANK GIRL: MOVIE ADAPTATION
DC Comics: 1995 ($5.95, 68 pgs., one-shot)
nn-Peter Milligan scripts 6.00

TANK GIRL: THE ODYSSEY
DC Comics: May, 1995 - No.4, Oct, 1995 ($2.25, limited series)
1-4: Peter Milligan scripts; Hewlett-a 3.00

TANK GIRL 2
Dark Horse Comics: June, 1993 - No. 4, Sept, 1993 ($2.50, lim. series, mature)
1-4: Jamie Hewlett & Alan Martin-s/a 2.50
TPB (2/95, $17.95) r/#1-4 18.00

TAPPAN'S BURRO (See Zane Grey & 4-Color #449)

TAPPING THE VEIN (Clive Barker's...)
Eclipse Comics: 1989 - No. 5, 1992 ($6.95, squarebound, mature, 68 pgs.)
Book 1-5: 1-Russell-a, Bolton-c. 2-Bolton-a. 4-Die-cut-c 7.00

TARANTULA (See Weird Suspense)

TARGET: AIRBOY
Eclipse Comics: Mar, 1988 ($1.95)
1 2.00

TARGET COMICS (...Western Romances #106 on)
Funnies, Inc./Novelty Publications/Star Publications: Feb, 1940 - V10#3 (#105), Aug-Sept, 1949

V1#1-Origin & 1st app. Manowar, The White Streak by Burgos, & Bulls-Eye Bill by Everett; City Editor (ends #5), High Grass Twins by Jack Cole (ends #4), T-Men by Joe Simon(ends #9), Rip Rory (ends #4), Fantastic Feature Films by Tarpe Mills (ends #39), & Calling 2-R (ends #14) begin; marijuana use story 435.00 1305.00 5000.00
2 232.00 695.00 2200.00
3,4 132.00 395.00 1250.00
5-Origin The White Streak in text; Space Hawk by Wolverton begins (6/40) (see Blue Bolt & Circus) 400.00 1200.00 4200.00
6-The Chameleon by Everett begins (7/40, 1st app.); White Streak origin cont'd. in text; early mention of comic collecting in letter column; 1st letter column in comics? (7/40) 168.00 505.00 1600.00
7-Wolverton Spacehawk-c/story (Scarce) 435.00 1305.00 5000.00
8,9,12: 12-(1/41) 126.00 379.00 1200.00
10-Intro/1st app. The Target (11/40); Simon-c 169.00 505.00 1600.00
11-Origin The Target & The Targeteers 158.00 474.00 1500.00
V2#1-Target by Bob Wood; Uncle Sam flag-c 79.00 237.00 750.00
2-Ten part Treasure Island serial begins; Harold Delay-a; reprinted in Catholic Comics V3#1-10 (see Key Comics #5) 71.00 213.00 675.00
3-5: 4-Kit Carter, The Cadet begins 55.00 165.00 500.00
6-9: Red Seal with White Streak in #6-10 55.00 165.00 500.00
10-Classic-c 92.00 277.00 875.00
11,12: 12-10-part Last of the Mohicans serial begins; Delay-a 53.00 158.00 475.00
V3#1-7,9,10: 10-Last Wolverton issue 53.00 158.00 475.00
8-Hitler, Tojo, Flag-c; 6-part Gulliver Travels serial begins; Delay-a. 63.00 189.00 600.00
11,12 14.00 41.00 110.00
V4#1-12: 6-Targetoons by Wolverton. 8-X-Mas-c 10.50 32.00 85.00
V5#1-8 10.00 30.00 75.00
V6#1-10, V7#1-12 10.00 30.00 70.00
V8#1,3-5,8,9,11,12 9.30 28.00 65.00
2,6,7-Krigstein-a 10.00 30.00 70.00
10-L.B. Cole-c 33.00 98.00 260.00
V9#1,4,6,8,10,12, V10#2,3-L.B. Cole-c 33.00 98.00 260.00
V9#2,3,5,7,9,11, V10#1 9.30 28.00 65.00

NOTE: ***Certa*** *c-V8#9, 11, 12, V9#5, 9, 11, V10#1.* ***Jack Cole*** *a-1-8.* ***Everett*** *a-1-9; c(signed Blake)-1, 2.* ***Al Fago*** *c-V6#8.* ***Sid Greene*** *c-V2#9, 12, V3#3.* ***Walter Johnson*** *c-V5#6, V6#4.* ***Tarpe Mills*** *a-1-4, 6, 8, 11, V3#1.* ***Rico*** *a-V7#4, 10, V8#5, 6, V9#3; c-V7#6, 8, 10, V8#2, 4, 6, 7.* ***Simon*** *a-1, 2.* ***Bob Wood*** *c-V2#2, 3, 5, 6.*

TARGET: THE CORRUPTORS (TV)
Dell Publishing Co.: No. 1306, Mar-May, 1962 - No. 3, Oct-Dec, 1962
(All have photo-c)
Four Color 1306(#1), #2,3 5.00 15.00 60.00

TARGET WESTERN ROMANCES (Formerly Target Comics; becomes Flaming Western Romances #3)
Star Publications: No. 106, Oct-Nov, 1949 - No. 107, Dec-Jan, 1949-50
106(#1)-Silhouette nudity panel; L.B. Cole-c 38.00 113.00 300.00
107(#2)-L.B. Cole-c; lingerie panels 32.00 96.00 255.00

TARGITT
Atlas/Seaboard Publ.: March, 1975 - No. 3, July, 1975
1-3: 1-Origin; Nostrand-a in all. 2-1st in costume. 3-Becomes Man-Stalker 5.00

TAROT: WITCH OF THE BLACK ROSE
Broadsword Comics: Mar, 2000 - Present ($2.95)
1-5-Jim Balent-s/c/a; two covers for each issue 2.95

TARZAN (See Aurora, Comics on Parade, Crackajack, DC 100-Page Super Spec., Edgar Rice Burroughs'..., Famous Feature Stories #1, Golden Comics Digest #4, 9, Jeep Comics #1-29, Jungle Tales of..., Limited Collectors' Edition, Popular, Sparkler, Sport Stars #1, Tip Top & Top Comics)

TARZAN
Dell Publishing Co./United Features Synd.: No. 5, 1939 - No. 161, Aug, 1947

Tarzan #17 © ERB

Tarzan #210 © ERB

Tarzan #24 © ERB

GD2.0 FN6.0 NM9.4

Large Feature Comic 5('39)-(Scarce)-By Hal Foster; reprints 1st dailies from 1929 125.00 375.00 1500.00
Single Series 20(:40)-By Hal Foster 96.00 288.00 1150.00
Four Color 134(2/47)-Marsh-c/a 63.00 188.00 750.00
Four Color 161(8/47)-Marsh-c/a 54.00 163.00 650.00

TARZAN (...of the Apes #138 on)
Dell Publishing Co./Gold Key No. 132 on: 1-2/48 - No. 131, 7-8/62; No. 132, 11/62 - No. 206, 2/72

1-Jesse Marsh-a begins 100.00 300.00 1200.00
2 48.00 144.00 575.00
3-5 33.00 100.00 400.00
6-10: 6-1st Tantor the Elephant. 7-1st Valley of the Monsters 27.00 80.00 320.00
11-15: 11-Two Against the Jungle begins, ends #24. 13-Lex Barker photo-c begin 22.00 65.00 260.00
16-20 17.00 50.00 200.00
21-24,26-30 13.00 40.00 160.00
25-1st "Brothers of the Spear" episode; series ends #156,160,161,196-206 15.00 46.00 185.00
31-40 9.00 27.00 110.00
41-54: Last Barker photo-c 6.30 19.00 75.00
55-60: 56-Eight pg. Boy story 4.60 13.75 55.00
61,62,64-70 4.10 12.30 45.00
63-Two Tarzan stories, 1 by Manning 4.35 13.00 48.00
71-79 3.45 10.35 38.00
80-99: 80-Gordon Scott photo-c begin 3.20 9.60 35.00
100 4.10 12.30 45.00
101-109 3.00 9.00 32.00
110 (Scarce)-Last photo-c 3.65 11.00 40.00
111-120 3.00 9.00 30.00
121-131: Last Dell issue 2.80 8.40 28.00
132-1st Gold Key issue 3.80 11.40 42.00
133-138,140-154 2.80 8.40 28.00
139-(12/63)-1st app. Korak (Boy); leaves Tarzan & gets own book (1/64) 3.65 11.00 40.00
155-Origin Tarzan 3.20 9.60 35.00
156-161: 157-Banlu, Dog of the Arande begins, ends #159, 195. 169-Leopard Girl app. 2.50 7.50 25.00
162,165,168,171 (TV)-Ron Ely photo covers 3.00 9.00 30.00
163,164,166,167,169,170: 169-Leopard Girl app. 2.40 7.35 22.00
172-199,201-206: 178-Tarzan origin-r/#155; Leopard Girl app., also in #179, 190-193 2.30 7.00 20.00
200 2.50 7.50 25.00
Story Digest 1-(6/70, G.K., 148pp.)(scarce) 7.25 21.75 80.00

*NOTE: #162, 165, 168, 171 are TV issues. #1-153 all have **Marsh** art on Tarzan. #154-161, 163, 164, 166, 167, 172-177 all have **Manning** art on Tarzan. #178, 202 have **Manning** Tarzan reprints. No "Brothers of the Spear" in #1-24, 157-159, 162-195. #39-126, 128-156 all have **Russ Manning** art on "Brothers of the Spear". #196-201, 203-205 all have **Manning** B.O.T.S. reprints; #25-38, 127 all have Jesse **Marsh** art on B.O.T.S. #206 has a Marsh B.O.T.S. reprint. **Gollub** c-8-12. **Marsh** c-1-7. **Doug Wildey** a-162, 179-187. Many issues have front and back photo covers.*

TARZAN (Continuation of Gold Key series)
National Periodical Publications: No. 207, Apr, 1972 - No. 258, Feb, 1977

207-Origin Tarzan by Joe Kubert, part 1; John Carter begins (origin); 52 pg. issues thru #209 3.00 9.00 30.00
208,209-(52 pgs.): 208-210-Parts 2-4 of origin. 209-Last John Carter 2.00 6.00 18.00
210-220: 210-Kubert-a. 211-Hogarth, Kubert-a. 212-214: Adaptations from "Jungle Tales of Tarzan". 213-Beyond the Farthest Star begins, ends #218. 215-218,224,225-All by Kubert. 215-part Foster-r. 219-223: Adapts "The Return of Tarzan" by Kubert. 1.75 5.25 14.00
221-229: 221-223-Continues adaptation of "The Return of Tarzan". 226-Manning-a 1.50 4.50 12.00
230-DC 100 Page Super Spectacular; Kubert, Kaluta-a(p); Korak begins, ends #234; Carson of Venus app. 2.50 7.50 25.00
231-235-New Kubert-a.: 231-234-(All 100 pgs.)-Adapts "Tarzan and the Lion Man"; Rex, the Wonder Dog r-#232, 233. 235-(100 pgs.)-Last Kubert issue. 2.40 7.35 22.00
236,237,239-258: 240-243 adapts "Tarzan & the Castaways". 250-256 adapts "Tarzan the Untamed." 252,253-r/#213 1.25 3.75 10.00
238-(68 pgs.) 2.00 6.00 16.00
Comic Digest 1-(Fall, 1972, 50¢, 164 pgs.)(DC)-Digest size; Kubert-c; Manning-a 5.00 15.00 55.00

*NOTE: **Anderson** a-207, 209, 217, 218. **Chaykin** a-216. **Finlay** a(r)-212. **Foster** strip-r #207-209, 211, 212, 221. **Heath** a-230i. **G. Kane** a(r)-232p, 233p. **Kubert** a-207-225, 227-235, 257r, 258r; c-207-249, 253. **Lopez** a-250-255p; c-250p, 251, 252, 254. **Manning** strip-r 230-235, 238. **Morrow** a-208. **Nino** a-231-234. **Sparling** a-230, 231. **Starr** a-233r.*

TARZAN (Lord of the Jungle)
Marvel Comics Group: June, 1977 - No. 29, Oct, 1979

1-New adaptions of Edgar Rice Burrough stories; Buscema-a 2.40 6.00
2-29: 2-Origin by John Buscema. 9-Young Tarzan. 12-14-Jungle Tales of Tarzan. 25-29-New stories 4.00
Annual 1-3: 1-(1977). 2-(1978). 3-(1979) 4.00

*NOTE: **N. Adams** c-11i, 12i. **Alcala** a-9i, 10i; c-8i, 9i. **Buckler** c-25-27p, Annual 3p. **John Buscema** a-1-3, 4-18p, Annual 1; c-1-7, 8p, 9p, 10, 11p, 12p, 13, 14-19p, 21p, 22, 23p, 24p, 28p, Annual 1. **Mooney** a-22i. **Nebres** a-22i. **Russell** a-29i.*

TARZAN
Dark Horse Comics: July, 1996 - No. 20, Mar, 1998 ($2.95)

1-20: 1-6-Suydam-c 3.00

TARZAN / CARSON OF VENUS
Dark Horse Comics: May, 1998 - No. 4, Aug, 1998 ($2.95, limited series)

1-4-Darko Macan-s/Igor Korday-a 3.00

TARZAN FAMILY, THE (Formerly Korak, Son of Tarzan)
National Periodical Publications: No. 60, Nov-Dec, 1975 - No. 66, Nov-Dec, 1976

60-62-(68 pgs.): 60-Korak begins; Kaluta-r 1.75 5.25 14.00
63-66 (52 pgs.) 1.25 3.75 10.00

*NOTE: Carson of Venus-r 60-65. New John Carter-62-64, 65r, 66r. New Korak-60-66. Pellucidar feature-66. Foster strip r-60(9/4/32-10/16/32), 62(6/29/32-7/31/32), 63(10/11/31-12/13/31). **Kaluta** Carson of Venus-60-65. **Kubert** a-61, 64; c-60-64. **Manning** strip-r 60-62, 64. **Morrow** a-66r.*

TARZAN/JOHN CARTER: WARLORDS OF MARS
Dark Horse Comics: Jan, 1996 - No. 4, June, 1996 ($2.50, limited series)

1-4: Bruce Jones scripts in all. 1,2,4-Bret Blevins-c/a. 2-(4/96)-Indicia reads #3 2.50

TARZAN KING OF THE JUNGLE (See Dell Giant #37, 51)

TARZAN, LORD OF THE JUNGLE
Gold Key: Sept, 1965 (Giant) (25¢, soft paper-c)

1-Marsh-r 7.00 21.00 85.00

TARZAN: LOVE, LIES AND THE LOST CITY (See Tarzan the Warrior)
Malibu Comics: Aug. 10, 1992 - No. 3, Sept, 1992 ($2.50, limited series)

1-($3.95, 68 pgs.)-Flip book format; Simonson & Wagner scripts 4.00
2,3-No Simonson or Wagner scripts 2.50

TARZAN MARCH OF COMICS (See March of Comics #82, 98, 114, 125, 144, 155, 172, 185, 204, 223, 240, 252, 262, 272, 286, 300, 332, 342, 354, 366)

TARZAN OF THE APES
Metropolitan Newspaper Service: 1934? (Hardcover, 4x12", 68 pgs.)

1-Strip reprints 23.00 68.00 180.00

TARZAN OF THE APES
Marvel Comics Group: July, 1984 - No. 2, Aug, 1984 (Movie adaptation)

1,2: Origin-r/Marvel Super Spec. 3.00

TARZAN'S JUNGLE ANNUAL (See Dell Giants)

TARZAN'S JUNGLE WORLD (See Dell Giant #25)

TARZAN: THE LOST ADVENTURE (See Edgar Rice Burroughs' ...)

TARZAN-THE RIVERS OF BLOOD
Dark Horse Comics: Nov, 1999 - No. 8 ($2.95, limited series)

1-4: Korday-c/a 3.00

TARZAN THE SAVAGE HEART
Dark Horse Comics: Apr, 1999 - No. 4, July, 1999 ($2.95, limited series)

1-4: Grell-c/a 3.00

TARZAN THE WARRIOR (Also see Tarzan: Love, Lies and the Lost City)
Malibu Comics: Mar, 19, 1992 - No. 5, 1992 ($2.50, limited series)

Team America #11 © MAR

Team 7 #2 © WSP

Team Superman #1 © DC

GD2.0 FN6.0 NM9.4

1-5: 1-Bisley painted pack-c (flip book format-c) 3.00
1-2nd printing w/o flip-c by Bisley 2.50

TARZAN VS. PREDATOR AT THE EARTH'S CORE
Dark Horse Comics: Jan, 1996 - No. 4, June, 1996 ($2.50, limited series)

1-4: Lee Weeks-c/a; Walt Simonson scripts 2.50

TASMANIAN DEVIL & HIS TASTY FRIENDS
Gold Key: Nov, 1962 (12¢)

1-Bugs Bunny & Elmer Fudd x-over 12.00 36.00 145.00

TATTERED BANNERS
DC Comics (Vertigo): Nov, 1998 - No. 4, Feb, 1999 ($2.95, limited series)

1-4-Grant & Giffen-s/McMahon-a 3.00

TEAM AMERICA (See Captain America #269)
Marvel Comics Group: June, 1982 - No. 12, May, 1983

1-12:1-Origin; Ideal Toy motorcycle characters. 9-Iron Man app. 11-Ghost Rider app. 12-Double size 2.00

TEAM ANARCHY
Dagger Comics: Oct, 1993 - No.8, 1994? ($2.50)

1-($2.75)-Red foil logo; intro Team Anarchy 2.75
1-Platinum, 2,3,3-Bronze,3-Gold,3-Silver,4-8 2.75

TEAM HELIX
Marvel Comics: Jan, 1993 - No. 4, Apr, 1993 ($1.75, limited series)

1-4: Teen Super Group. 1,2-Wolverine app. 2.00

TEAM ONE: STORMWATCH (Also see StormWatch)
Image Comics (WildStorm Productions): June, 1995 - No. 2, Aug, 1995 ($2.50, limited series)

1,2: Steven T. Seagle scripts 2.50

TEAM ONE: WILDC.A.T.S (Also see WildC.A.T.S)
Image Comics (WildStorm Productions): July, 1995 - No. 2, Aug, 1995 ($2.50, limited series)

1,2: James Robinson scripts 2.50

TEAM 7
Image Comics (WildStorm Productions): Oct, 1994 - No.4, Feb, 1995 ($2.50, limited series)

1-4: Dixon scripts in all, 1-Portacio variant-c 2.50

TEAM 7-DEAD RECKONING
Image Comics (WildStorm Productions): Jan, 1996 - No. 4, Apr, 1996 ($2.50, limited series)

1-4: Dixon scripts in all 2.50

TEAM 7-OBJECTIVE HELL
Image Comics (WildStorm Productions): May, 1995 - No. 3, July, 1995 ($1.95/$2.50, limited series)

1-($1.95)-Newstand; Dixon scripts in all; Barry Smith-c 2.00
1-3: 1-($2.50)-Direct Market; Barry Smith-c, bound-in card 2.50

TEAM SUPERMAN
DC Comics: May, 1998 ($4.95, one-shot)

1-Origin-s and pin-ups of Superboy, Supergirl and Steel 5.00

TEAM TITANS (See Deathstroke & New Titans Annual #7)
DC Comics: Sept, 1992 - No. 24, Sept, 1994 ($1.75/$1.95)

1-Five different #1s exist w/origins in 1st half & the same 2nd story in each: Kilowat, Mirage, Nightrider w/Netzer/Perez-a, Redwing, & Terra w/part Perez-p; Total Chaos Pt. 3 3.00
2-24: 2-Total Chaos Pt 6. 11-Metallik app. 24-Zero Hour x-over 2.00
Annual 1,2 ('93, '94, $3.50, 68 pgs.): 2-Elseworlds tory 3.50

TEAM X/TEAM 7
Marvel Comics: Nov, 1996 ($4.95, one-shot)

1 5.00

TEAM X 2000
Marvel Comics: Feb, 1999 ($3.50, one-shot)

1-Kevin Lau-a; Bishop vs. Shi'ar Empire 3.50

GD2.0 FN6.0 NM9.4

TEAM YANKEE
First Comics: Jan, 1989 - No. 6, Feb, 1989 ($1.95, weekly limited series)

1-6 2.00

TEAM YOUNGBLOOD (Also see Youngblood)
Image Comics (Extreme Studios): Sept, 1993 - No. 22, Sept, 1995 ($1.95/$2.50)

1-22: 1-9-Liefeld scripts in all: 1,2,4-6,8-Thibert-c(i). 1-1st app. Dutch & Masada. 3-Spawn cameo. 5-1st app. Lynx. 7,8-Coupons 1 & 4 for Extreme Prejudice #0; Black and White Pt. 4 & 8 by Thibert. 8-Coupon #4 for E. P. #0. 9-Liefeld wraparound-c(p)/a(p) on Pt. I. 10-Liefeld-c(p). 16-Polybagged w/trading card 17-Polybagged w/trading card. 18-Extreme 3000 Prelude. 19-Cruz-a. 21-Angela & Glory-app. 22-Shadowhawk-c/app 2.50

TEDDY ROOSEVELT & HIS ROUGH RIDERS (See Real Heroes #1)
Avon Periodicals: 1950

1-Kinstler-c; Palais-a; Flag-c 18.00 53.00 140.00

TEDDY ROOSEVELT ROUGH RIDER (See Battlefield #22 & Classics Illustrated Special Issue)

TED MCKEEVER'S METROPOL
Marvel Comics (Epic Comics): Mar, 1991 - No. 12, Mar, 1992 ($2.95, limited series)

V1#1-12: Ted McKeever-c/a/scripts 3.50

TED MCKEEVER'S METROPOL A.D.
Marvel Comics (Epic Comics): Oct, 1992 - No. 3, Dec, 1992 ($3.50, limited series)

V2#1-3: Ted McKeever-c/a/scripts 3.50

TEENA
Magazine Enterprises/Standard Comics No. 20 on: No. 11, 1948 - No. 15, 1948; No. 20, Aug, 1949 - No. 22, Oct, 1950

A-1 #11-Teen-age; Ogden Whitney-c 7.85 23.50 55.00
A-1 #12, 15 7.15 21.50 50.00
20-22 (Standard) 5.00 15.00 30.00

TEEN-AGE BRIDES (True Bride's Experiences #8 on)
Harvey/Home Comics: Aug, 1953 - No. 7, Aug, 1954

1-Powell-a 10.00 30.00 80.00
2-Powell-a 7.85 23.50 55.00
3-7: 3,6-Powell-a 6.40 19.25 45.00

TEEN-AGE CONFESSIONS (See Teen Confessions)

TEEN-AGE CONFIDENTIAL CONFESSIONS
Charlton Comics: July, 1960 - No. 22, 1964

1 3.20 9.60 35.00
2-10 2.50 7.50 24.00
11-22 2.00 6.00 16.00

TEEN-AGE DIARY SECRETS (Formerly Blue Ribbon Comics; becomes Diary Secrets #10 on)
St. John Publishing Co.: No. 4, 9/49; nn (#5), 9/49 - No. 7, 11/49; No. 8, 2/50; No. 9, 8/50

4(9/49)-Oversized; part mag., part comic 27.00 81.00 215.00
nn(#5)(no indicia)-Oversized, all comics; contains sty "I Gave Boys the Green Light." 23.00 68.00 180.00
6,8: (Reg. size) -Photo-c; Baker-a(2-3) in each 23.00 68.00 180.00
7,9-Digest size (Pocket Comics); Baker-a(5); photo-c; both have same contents; diff.-c 25.00 75.00 200.00

TEEN-AGE DOPE SLAVES (See Harvey Comics Library #1)

TEENAGE HOTRODDERS (Top Eliminator #25 on; see Blue Bird)
Charlton Comics: Apr, 1963 - No. 24, July, 1967

1 5.00 15.00 55.00
2-10 3.00 9.00 30.00
11-24 2.50 7.50 24.00

TEEN-AGE LOVE (See Fox Giants)

TEEN-AGE LOVE (Formerly Intimate)
Charlton Comics: V2#4, July, 1958 - No. 96, Dec, 1973

Teenage Mutant Ninja Turtles #23 © MS

Teenage Mutant Ninja Turtles Adventures #4 © MS

Teenage Mutant Ninja Turtles Presents Donatello & Leatherhead #2 © MS

	GD2.0	FN6.0	NM9.4
V2#4	3.65	11.00	40.00
5-9	3.00	9.00	30.00
10(9/59)-20	2.50	7.50	24.00
21-35	2.30	7.00	20.00
36-70	1.85	5.50	15.00
71-96: 61&62-Jonnie Love begins (origin)	1.25	3.75	10.00

TEENAGE MUTANT NINJA TURTLES (Also see Anything Goes, Donatello, First Comics Graphic Novel, Gobbledygook, Grimjack #26, Leonardo, Michaelangelo, Raphael & Tales Of The...)
Mirage Studios: 1984 - No. 62, Aug, 1993 ($1.50/$1.75, B&W; all 44-52 pgs.)

	GD2.0	FN6.0	NM9.4
1-1st printing (3000 copies)-Only printing to have ad for Gobbledygook #1 & 2; Shredder app. (#1-4: 7-1/2x11")	18.00	54.00	200.00
1-2nd printing (6/84)(15,000 copies)	1.85	5.50	15.00
1-3rd printing (2/85)(36,000 copies)	1.25	3.75	10.00
1-4th printing, new-c (50,000 copies)			5.00
1-5th printing, new-c (8/88-c, 11/88 inside)			4.00
1-Counterfeit. **Note**: Most counterfeit copies have a half inch wide white streak or scratch marks across the center of back cover. Black part of cover is a bluish black instead of a deep black. Inside paper is very white & inside cover is bright white. These counterfeit the 1st printings (no value).			
2-1st printing (1984; 15,000 copies)	4.55	13.65	50.00
2-2nd printing	1.25	3.75	10.00
2-3rd printing; new Corben-c/a (2/85)			5.00
2-Counterfeit with glossy cover stock (no value).			
3-1st printing (1985, 44 pgs.)	3.20	9.60	35.00
3-Variant, 500 copies, given away in NYC. Has 'Laird's Photo' in white rather than light blue	6.80	20.50	75.00
3-2nd printing; contains new back-up story			3.00
4-1st printing (1985, 44 pgs.)	2.50	7.50	25.00
4,5-2nd printing (5/87, 11/87)			2.00
5-Fugitoid begins, ends #7; 1st full color-c (1985)	1.25	3.75	10.00
6-1st printing (1986)	1.00	3.00	8.00
6-2nd printing (4/88-c, 5/88 inside)			2.00
7-4 pg. Eastman/Corben color insert; 1st color TMNT (1986, $1.75-c); Bade Biker back-up story	1.00	2.80	7.00
7-2nd printing (1/89) w/o color insert			2.00
8-Cerebus-c/story with Dave Sim-a (1986)		2.40	6.00
9,10: 9 (9/86)-Rip In Time by Corben			5.00
11-15			4.00
16-18: 18-Mark Bode'-a			3.00
18-2nd printing ($2.25, color, 44 pgs.)-New-c			2.50
19-34: 19-Begin $1.75-c. 24-26-Veitch-c/a.			2.50
32-2nd printing ($2.75, 52 pgs., full color)			3.00
35-49,51: 35-Begin $2.00-c.			2.50
50-Features pin-ups by Larsen, McFarlane, Simonson, etc.			3.00
52-62: 52-Begin $2.25-c			2.50
nn (1990, $5.95, B&W)-Movie adaptation			6.00
Book 1,2($1.50, B&W): 2-Corben-c			2.50
...Christmas Special 1 (12/90, $1.75, B&W, 52 pgs.)-Cover title: Michaelangelo Christmas Special; r/Michaelangelo one-shot plus new Raphael story			2.50
...Special (The Maltese Turtle) nn (1/93, $2.95, color, 44 pgs.)			3.00
...Special: "Times" Pipeline nn (9/92, $2.95, color, 44 pgs.)-Mark Bode-c/a			3.00
Hardcover ($100)-r/#1-10 plus one-shots w/dust jackets - limited to 1000 w/letter of authenticity			100.00
Softcover ($40)-r/#1-10			40.00

TEENAGE MUTANT NINJA TURTLES
Mirage Studios: V2#1, Oct, 1993 - V2#13, Oct, 1995 ($2.75)

V2#1-13: 1-Wraparound-c 2.75

TEENAGE MUTANT NINJA TURTLES
Image Comics (Highbrow Ent.): June, 1996 - No. 23, Oct, 1999 ($1.95)

1-23: 1-8: Eric Larsen-c(i) on all. 10-Savage Dragon-c/app. 3.00

TEENAGE MUTANT NINJA TURTLES (Adventures)
Archie Publications: Jan, 1996 - No. 3, Mar, 1996 ($1.50, limited series)

1-3 2.00

TEENAGE MUTANT NINJA TURTLES ADVENTURES (TV)
Archie Comics: 8/88 - No. 3, 12/88; 3/89 - No. 72, Oct, 1995 ($1.00/$1.25/$1.50/$1.75)

	GD2.0	FN6.0	NM9.4
1-Adapts TV cartoon; not by Eastman/Laird			3.00
2,3,1-5: 2,3 (Mini-series). 1 (2nd on-going series). 5-Begins original stories not based on TV			2.00
1-11: 2nd printings			2.00
6-72: 14-Simpson-a(p). 19-1st Mighty Mutanimals (also in #20, 51-54). 22-Gene Colan-c/a. 50-Poster by Eastman/Laird. 62-w/poster			2.00
nn (1990, $2.50)-Movie adaptation			2.50
nn (Spring, 1991, $2.50, 68 pgs.)-(Meet Archie)			2.50
nn (Sum, 1991, $2.50, 68 pgs.)-(Movie II)-Adapts movie sequel			2.50
...Meet the Conservation Corps 1 (1992, $2.50, 68 pgs.)			2.50
...III The Movie: The Turtles are Back...In Time (1993, $2.50, 68 pgs.)			2.50
Special 1,4,5 (Sum/92, Spr/93, sum/93, 68 pgs.)-1-Bill Wray-c			2.50
Giant Size Special 6 (Fall/93, $1.95, 52 pgs.)			2.50
Special 7-10 (Win/93-Fall//94, 52 pgs.): 9-Jeff Smith-c			2.50

NOTE: *There are 2nd printings of #1-11 w/B&W inside covers. Originals are color.*

TEENAGE MUTANT NINJA TURTLES CLASSICS DIGEST (TV)
Archie Comics: Aug, 1993 - No. 8, Mar, 1995? ($1.75)

1-8: Reprints TMNT Advs. 2.00

TEENAGE MUTANT NINJA TURTLES/FLAMING CARROT CROSSOVER
Mirage Publishing: Nov, 1993 - No. 4, Feb, 1994 ($2.75, limited series)

1-4: Bob Burden story 2.75

TEENAGE MUTANT NINJA TURTLES PRESENTS: APRIL O'NEIL
Archie Comics: Mar, 1993 - No. 3, June, 1993 ($1.25, limited series)

1-3 2.00

TEENAGE MUTANT NINJA TURTLES PRESENTS: DONATELLO AND LEATHERHEAD
Archie Comics: July, 1993 - No. 3, Sept, 1993 ($1.25, limited series)

1-3 2.00

TEENAGE MUTANT NINJA TURTLES PRESENTS: MERDUDE
Archie Comics: Oct, 1993 - No. 3, Dec, 1993 ($1.25, limited series)

1-3-See Mighty Mutanimals #7 for 1st app. Merdude 2.00

TEENAGE MUTANT NINJA TURTLES/SAVAGE DRAGON CROSSOVER
Mirage Studios: Aug, 1995 ($2.75, one-shot)

1 3.00

TEEN-AGE ROMANCE (Formerly My Own Romance)
Marvel Comics (ZPC): No. 77, Sept, 1960 - No. 86, Mar, 1962

	GD2.0	FN6.0	NM9.4
77-83	2.50	7.50	25.00
84-86-Kirby-c. 84-Kirby-a(2 pgs.). 85,86-(3 pgs.)	3.25	9.75	36.00

TEEN-AGE ROMANCES
St. John Publ. Co. (Approved Comics): Jan, 1949 - No. 45, Dec, 1955

	GD2.0	FN6.0	NM9.4
1-Baker-c/a(1)	40.00	120.00	340.00
2,3: 2-Baker-c/a. 3-Baker-c/a(3)	24.00	71.00	190.00
4,5,7,8-Photo-c; Baker-a(2-3) each	20.00	60.00	160.00
6-Slightly large size; photo-c; part magazine; Baker-a (10/49)	22.00	66.00	175.00
9-Baker-c/a; Kubert-a	26.00	77.00	205.00
10-12,20-Baker-c/a(2-3) each	19.00	56.00	150.00
13-19,21,22-Complete issues by Baker	26.00	77.00	205.00
23-25-Baker-c/a(2-3) each	18.00	53.00	140.00
26,27,33,34,36-40,42: Baker-c/a. 33,40-Signed story by Estrada. 38-Suggestive-c. 42-r/Cinderella Love #9; Last pre-code (3/55)	11.00	33.00	90.00
28-30-No Baker-a	5.70	17.00	40.00
31,32-Baker-c	9.30	28.00	65.00
35-Baker-c/a (16 pgs.)	11.00	33.00	90.00
41-Baker-c; Infantino-a(r); all stories are Ziff-Davis-r	10.00	30.00	70.00
43-45-Baker-c/a	10.00	30.00	70.00

TEEN-AGE TALK
I.W. Enterprises: 1964

	GD2.0	FN6.0	NM9.4
Reprint #1	2.00	6.00	16.00
Reprint #5,8,9: 5-r/Hector #? 9-Punch Comics #?; L.B. Cole-c reprint from School Day Romances #1	1.75	5.25	14.00

Teen Confessions #90 © CC

Teen Love Stories #1 © WP

Teen Titans #43 © DC

GD2.0 FN6.0 NM9.4

TEEN-AGE TEMPTATIONS (Going Steady #10 on)(See True Love Pictorial)
St. John Publishing Co.: Oct, 1952 - No. 9, Aug, 1954

1-Baker-c/a; has story "Reform School Girl" by Estrada 43.00 130.00 390.00
2,4-Baker-c 16.00 49.00 130.00
3,5-7,9-Baker-c/a 24.00 71.00 190.00
8-Teenagers smoke reefers; Baker-c/a 24.00 71.00 190.00
NOTE: ***Estrada*** *a-1, 3-5.*

TEEN BEAM (Formerly Teen Beat #1)
National Periodical Publications: No. 2, Jan-Feb, 1968

2-Superman cameo; Herman's Hermits, Yardbirds, Simon & Garfunkel, Lovin Spoonful, Young Rascals app.; Orlando, Drucker-a(r); Monkees photo-c; 6.35 19.00 70.00

TEEN BEAT (Becomes Teen Beam #2)
National Periodical Publications: Nov-Dec, 1967

1-Photos & text only; Monkees photo-c; Beatles, Herman's Hermits, Animals, Supremes, Byrds app. 7.65 23.00 85.00

TEEN COMICS (Formerly All Teen; Journey Into Unknown Worlds #36 on)
Marvel Comics (WFP): No. 21, Apr, 1947 - No. 35, May, 1950

21-Kurtzman's "Hey Look"; Patsy Walker, Cindy (1st app.?), Georgie, Margie app.; Syd Shores-a begins, end #23 14.00 41.00 110.00
22,23,25,27,29,31-35: 22-(6/47)-Becomes Hedy Devine #22 (8/47) on? 10.00 30.00 75.00
24,26,28,30-Kurtzman's "Hey Look" 11.00 33.00 90.00

TEEN CONFESSIONS
Charlton Comics: Aug, 1959 - No. 97, Nov, 1976

1 6.80 20.50 75.00
2 3.45 10.35 38.00
3-10 2.80 8.40 28.00
11-30 2.40 7.35 22.00
31-Beatles-c 11.50 34.00 125.00
32-36,38-55 2.00 6.00 16.00
37 (1/66)-Beatles Fan Club story; Beatles-c 11.50 34.00 125.00
56-58,60-97: 89,90-Newton-c 1.25 3.75 10.00
59-Kaluta's 1st pro work? (12/69) 2.30 7.00 20.00

TEENIE WEENIES, THE (America's Favorite Kiddie Comic)
Ziff-Davis Publishing Co.: No. 10, 1950 - No. 11, Apr-May, 1951 (Newspaper reprints)

10,11-Painted-c 19.00 56.00 150.00

TEEN-IN (Tippy Teen)
Tower Comics: Summer, 1968 - No. 4, Fall, 1969

nn(#1, Summer, 1968) 4.55 13.65 50.00
nn(#2, Spring, 1969),3,4 3.20 9.60 35.00

TEEN LIFE (Formerly Young Life)
New Age/Quality Comics Group: No. 3, Winter, 1945 - No. 5, Fall, 1945 (Teenage magazine)

3-June Allyson photo on-c & story 11.00 33.00 90.00
4-Duke Ellington photo on-c & story 9.30 28.00 65.00
5-Van Johnson, Woody Herman & Jackie Robinson articles; Van Johnson & Woody Herman photos on-c 12.00 36.00 95.00

TEEN LOVE STORIES (Magazine)
Warren Publ. Co.: Sept, 1969 - No. 3, Jan, 1970 (68 pgs., photo covers, B&W)

1-3: Photos & articles plus 36-42 pgs. new comic stories. 1-Frazetta-a. 2-Anti-marijuana story 3.65 11.00 40.00

TEEN ROMANCES
Super Comics: 1964

10,11,15-17-Reprints 1.25 3.75 10.00

TEEN SECRET DIARY (Nurse Betsy Crane #12 on)
Charlton Comics: Oct, 1959 - No. 11, June, 1961; No. 1, 1972

1 3.65 11.00 40.00
2 2.80 8.40 28.00
3-11 2.40 7.35 22.00
1 (1972)(exist?) 2.00 6.00 18.00

TEEN TALK (See Teen)

TEEN TITANS (See Brave & the Bold #54,60, DC Super-Stars #1, Marvel & DC Present, New Teen Titans, New Titans, Official...Index and Showcase #59)
National Periodical Publications/DC Comics: 1-2/66 - No. 43, 1-2/73; No. 44, 11/76 - No. 53, 2/78

1-(1-2/66)-Titans join Peace Corps; Batman, Flash, Aquaman, Wonder Woman cameos 23.00 68.00 250.00
2 10.00 30.00 110.00
3-5: 4-Speedy app. 5.45 16.35 60.00
6-10: 6-Doom Patrol app.; Beast Boy x-over; readers polled on him joining Titans 4.55 13.65 50.00
11-18: 11-Speedy app. 13-X-Mas-c 3.80 11.40 42.00
19-Wood-i; Speedy begins as regular 4.10 12.30 45.00
20-22: All Neal Adams-a. 21-Hawk & Dove app.; last 12¢ issue. 22-Origin Wonder Girl 4.55 13.65 50.00
23-31: 23-Wonder Girl dons new costume. 25-Flash, Aquaman, Batman, Green Arrow, Green Lantern, Superman, & Hawk & Dove guests; 1st app. Lilith who joins T.T. West in #50. 29-Hawk & Dove & Ocean Master app. 30-Aquagirl app. 31-Hawk & Dove app.; last 15¢ issue 2.50 7.50 25.00
32-34,40-43 1.85 5.50 15.00
35-39-(52 pgs.): 36,37-Superboy-r. 38-Green Arrow/Speedy-r; Aquaman/Aqualad story. 39-Hawk & Dove-r. 2.00 6.00 18.00
44,45,47,49,51,52: 44-Mal becomes the Guardian 1.25 3.75 10.00
46,48: 46-Joker's daughter begins (see Batman Family). 48-Intro Bumblebee; Joker's daughter becomes Harlequin 1.85 5.50 15.00
50-1st revival original Bat-Girl; intro. Teen Titans West 2.00 6.00 18.00
53-Origin retold 1.25 3.75 10.00
NOTE: ***Aparo*** *a-36.* ***Buckler*** *c-46-53.* ***Cardy*** *c-1-16.* ***Kane*** *a(p)-19, 22-24, 39r.* ***Tuska*** *a(p)-31, 36, 38, 39. DC Super-Stars #1 (3/76) was released before #44.*

TEEN TITANS (Also see Titans Beat in the Promotional Comics section)
DC Comics: Oct, 1996 - No. 24, Sept, 1998 ($1.95)

1-Dan Jurgens-c/a(p)/scripts & George Pérez-c/a(i) begin; Atom forms new team (Risk, Argent, Prysm, & Joto); 1st app. Loren Jupiter & Omen; no indicia. 1-3-Origin. 4.00
2-24: 4,5-Robin, Nightwing, Supergirl, Capt. Marvel Jr. app. 12-"Then and Now" begins w/original Teen Titans-c/app. 15-Death of Joto. 17-Capt. Marvel Jr. and Fringe join. 19-Millennium Giants x-over. 23,24-Superman app. 3.00
Annual 1 (1997, $3.95)-Pulp Heroes story 4.00

TEEN TITANS SPOTLIGHT
DC Comics: Aug, 1986 - No. 21, Apr, 1988

1-21: 7-Guice's 1st work at DC. 14-Nightwing; Batman app. 15-Austin-c(i). 18,19-Millennium x-over. 21-($1.00-c)-Original Teen Titans; Spiegle-a 3.00
Note: ***Guice*** *a-7p, 8p; c-7,8.* ***Orlando*** *c/a-11p.* ***Perez*** *c-1, 17i, 19.* ***Sienkiewicz*** *c-10*

TEEPEE TIM (...Heap Funny Indian Boy)(Formerly Ha Ha Comics)
American Comics Group: No. 100, Feb-Mar, 1955 - No. 102, June-July, 1955

100-102 4.65 14.00 28.00

TEGRA JUNGLE EMPRESS (Zegra Jungle Empress #2 on)
Fox Features Syndicate: August, 1948

1-Blue Beetle, Rocket Kelly app.; used in **SOTI**, pg. 31 55.00 165.00 500.00

TEKNO COMIX HANDBOOK
Tekno Comix: May, 1996 ($3.95, one-shot)

1-Guide to the Tekno Universe 4.00

TEKNOPHAGE (See Neil Gaiman's...)

TEKNOPHAGE VERSUS ZEERUS
BIG Entertainment: July, 1996 ($3.25, one-shot)

1-Paul Jenkins script 3.25

TEKWORLD (William Shatner's... on-c only)
Epic Comics (Marvel): Sept, 1992 - Aug, 1994 ($1.75)

1-Based on Shatner's novel, TekWar, set in L.A. in the year 2120 2.50
2-24 2.00

Tellos #9 © Todd Dezago & Mike Wieringo

10th Muse #1 © Tidal Wave Studios

Terminal City #7 © Dean Motter

GD2.0 FN6.0 NM9.4

TELEVISION (See TV)

TELEVISION COMICS (Early TV comic)
Standard Comics (Animated Cartoons): No. 5, Feb, 1950 - No. 8, Nov, 1950

5-1st app. Willy Nilly 10.00 30.00 70.00
6-8: 6 has #2 on inside 7.85 23.50 55.00

TELEVISION PUPPET SHOW (Early TV comic) (See Spotty the Pup)
Avon Periodicals: 1950 - No. 2, Nov, 1950

1-1st app. Speedy Rabbit, Spotty The Pup 18.00 53.00 140.00
2 13.00 39.00 105.00

TELEVISION TEENS MOPSY (See TV Teens)

TELL IT TO THE MARINES
Toby Press Publications: Mar, 1952 - No. 15, July, 1955

1-Lover O'Leary and His Liberty Belles (with pin-ups), ends #6; Spike & Bat begin, end #6 19.00 56.00 150.00
2-Madame Cobra-c/story 10.00 30.00 80.00
3-5 7.85 23.50 55.00
6-12,14,15: 7-9,14,15-Photo-c 5.70 17.00 40.00
13-John Wayne photo-c 11.00 33.00 90.00
I.W. Reprint #9-r/#1 above 1.50 4.50 12.00
Super Reprint #16(1964)-r/#4 above 1.50 4.50 12.00

TELLOS
Image Comics: May, 1999 - Present ($2.50)

1-Dezago-s/Wieringo-a 3.00
1-Variant-c ($7.95) 8.00
2-10: 4-Four covers 2.50
Prelude ($5.00) 5.00
...Collected Edition 1 (12/99, $8.95) r/#1-3 8.95

TEMPEST (See Aquaman, 3rd Series)
DC Comics: Nov, 1996 - No. 4, Feb, 1997 ($1.75, limited series)

1-4: Formerly Aqualad; Phil Jimenez-c/a/scripts in all 2.00

TEMPUS FUGITIVE
DC Comics: 1990 - No. 4, 1991 ($4.95, squarebound, 52 pgs.)

Book 1,2: Ken Steacy painted-c/a & scripts 2.40 6.00
Book 3,4-($5.95-c) 2.40 6.00
TPB (Dark Horse Comics, 1/97, $17.95) 18.00

TEN COMMANDMENTS (See Moses & the... and Classics Illustrated Special)

TENDER LOVE STORIES
Skywald Publ. Corp.: Feb, 1971 - No. 4, July, 1971

1 (All 25¢, 52 pgs.) 2.40 7.35 22.00
2-4 2.00 6.00 16.00

TENDER ROMANCE (Ideal Romance #3 on)
Key Publications (Gilmour Magazines): Dec, 1953 - No. 2, Feb, 1954

1-Headlight & lingerie panels; B. Baily-c 17.00 51.00 135.00
2-Bernard Baily-c 10.00 30.00 75.00

TENSE SUSPENSE
Fago Publications: Dec, 1958 - No. 2, Feb, 1959

1 9.30 28.00 65.00
2 8.00 24.00 56.00

TEN STORY LOVE (Formerly a pulp magazine with same title)
Ace Periodicals: V29#3, June-July, 1951 - V36#5(#209), Sept, 1956 (#3-6: 52 pgs.)

V29#3(#177)-Part comic, part text; painted-c 10.00 30.00 80.00
4-6(1/52) 6.00 18.00 42.00
V30#1(3/52)-6(1/53) 5.00 15.00 35.00
V31#1(2/53),V32#2(4/53)-6(12/53) 4.65 14.00 28.00
V33#1(1/54)-3(5#54, #195), V34#4(7/54, #196)-6(10/54, #198) 4.65 14.00 28.00
V35#1(12/54, #199)-3(4/55, #201)-Last precode 4.00 11.00 22.00
V35#4-6(9/55, #201-204), V36#1(11/55, #205)-3, 5(9/56, #209) 4.00 10.00 20.00
V36#4-L.B. Cole-a 8.65 26.00 60.00

TENTH, THE
Image Comics: Jan, 1997 - No. 4, June, 1997 ($2.50, limited series)

1-4-Tony Daniel-c/a, Beau Smith-s 5.00
Abuse of Humanity TPB ($10.95) r/#1-4 11.00
Abuse of Humanity TPB (10/98, $11.95) r/#1-4 & 0(8/97) 12.00

TENTH, THE
Image Comics: Sept, 1997 - No. 14, Jan, 1999 ($2.50)

0-(8/97, $5.00) American Ent. Ed. 2.40 6.00
1-Tony Daniel-c/a, Beau Smith-s 2.40 6.00
2-9: 3,7-Variant-c 4.00
10-14 3.00
...Configuration (8/98) Re-cap and pin-ups 2.50
...Collected Edition 1 ('98, $4.95, square-bound) r/#1,2 5.00
...Special (4/00, $2.95) r/#0 and Wizard #1/2 2.95
Wizard #1/2-Daniel-s/Steve Scott-a 10.00

TENTH, THE (Volume 2) (The Black Embrace)
Image Comics: Mar, 1999 - No. 4, June, 1999 ($2.95)

1-4-Daniel-c/a 3.00
TPB (1/00, $12.95) r/#1-4 12.95

TENTH, THE (Volume 4) (Evil's Child)
Image Comics: Sept, 1999 - No. 4, Mar, 2000 ($2.95, limited series)

1-4-Daniel-c/a 3.00

10th MUSE
Image Comics (TidalWave Studios): Nov, 2000 - Present ($2.95)

1-Character based on wrestling's Rena Mero; regular & photo covers 3.00

TEN WHO DARED (Disney)
Dell Publishing Co.: No. 1178, Dec, 1960

Four Color 1178-Movie, painted-c; cast member photo on back-c 6.70 20.00 80.00

TERMINAL CITY
DC Comics (Vertigo): July, 1996 - No. 9, Mar, 1997 ($2.50, limited series)

1-9: Dean Motter scripts, 7,8-Matt Wagner-c 2.50
TPB ('97, $19.95) r/series 20.00

TERMINAL CITY: AERIAL GRAFFITI
DC Comics (Vertigo): Nov, 1997 - No. 5, Mar, 1998 ($2.50, limited series)

1-5: Dean Motter-s/Lark-a/Chiarello-c 2.50

TERMINATOR, THE (See Robocop vs. ... & Rust #12 for 1st app.)
Now Comics: Sept, 1988 - No. 17, 1989 ($1.75, Baxter paper)

1-Based on movie 2.40 6.00
2-5 4.50
6-17: 12-($2.95, 52 pgs.)-Intro. John Connor 3.00
Trade paperback (1989, $9.95) 10.00

TERMINATOR, THE
Dark Horse Comics: Aug, 1990 - No. 4, Nov, 1990 ($2.50, limited series)

1-Set 39 years later than the movie 4.00
2-4 3.00

TERMINATOR, THE
Dark Horse Comics: 1998 - No. 4, Dec, 1998 ($2.95, limited series)

1-4-Alan Grant-s/Steve Pugh-a/c 3.00
...Special (1998, $2.95) Darrow-c/Grant-s 3.00

TERMINATOR, THE: ALL MY FUTURES PAST
Now Comics: V3#1, Aug, 1990 - V3#2, Sept, 1990 ($1.75, limited series)

V3#1,2 3.00

TERMINATOR, THE: ENDGAME
Dark Horse Comics: Sept, 1992 - No. 3, Nov, 1992 ($2.50, limited series)

1-3: Guice-a(p); painted-c 3.00

TERMINATOR, THE: HUNTERS AND KILLERS
Dark Horse Comics: Mar, 1992 - No. 3, May, 1992 ($2.50, limited series)

1-3 3.00

TERMINATOR, THE: ONE SHOT
Dark Horse Comics: July, 1991 ($5.95, 56 pgs.)

The Terminator: Secondary Objectives #4 © DH

Terrific Comics #5 © Continental Magazines

Terry and the Pirates #5 © NY News Syndicate

nn-Matt Wagner-a; contains stiff pop-up inside 6.00

TERMINATOR, THE: SECONDARY OBJECTIVES
Dark Horse Comics: July, 1991 - No. 4, Oct, 1991 ($2.50, limited series)

1-4: Gulacy-c/a(p) in all 3.00

TERMINATOR, THE: THE BURNING EARTH
Now Comics: V2#1, Mar, 1990 - V2#5, July, 1990 ($1.75, limited series)

V2#1: Alex Ross painted art (1st published work) 1.50 4.50 12.00
2-5: Ross-c/a in all 1.00 3.00 8.00
Trade paperback (1990, $9.95)-Reprints V2#1-5 12.00

TERMINATOR, THE: THE DARK YEARS
Dark Horse Comics: Aug, 1999 - No. 4, Dec, 1999 ($2.95, limited series)

1-4-Alan Grant-s/Mel Rubi-a; Jae Lee-c 3.00

TERMINATOR: THE ENEMY FROM WITHIN, THE
Dark Horse Comics: Nov, 1991 - No. 4, Feb, 1992 ($2.50, limited series)

1-4: All have Simon Bisley painted-c 2.50

TERMINATOR 2: CYBERNETIC DAWN
Malibu: Nov, 1995 - No.4, Feb, 1996; No. 0. Apr, 1996 ($2.50, lim. series)

0 (4/96, $2.95)-Erskine-c/a; flip book w/Terminator 2: Nuclear Twilight 3.00
1-4: Continuation of film. 2.50

TERMINATOR 2: JUDGEMENT DAY
Marvel Comics: Early Sept, 1991 - No. 3, Early Oct, 1991 ($1.00, lim. series)

1-3: Based on movie sequel; 1-3-Same as nn issues 2.00
nn (1991, $4.95, squarebound, 68 pgs.)-Photo-c 5.00
nn (1991, $2.25, B&W, magazine, 68 pgs.) 2.25

TERMINATOR 2: NUCLEAR TWILIGHT
Malibu: Nov, 1995 - No.4, Feb, 1996; No. 0, Apr, 1996 ($2.50, lim. series)

0 (4/96, $2.95)-Erskine-c/a; flip book w/Terminator 2: Cybernetic Dawn 3.00
1-4:Continuation of film. 2.50

TERRAFORMERS
Wonder Color Comics: April, 1987 - No. 2, 1987 ($1.95, limited series)

1,2-Kelley Jones-a 2.00

TERRANAUTS
Fantasy General Comics: Aug, 1986 - No. 2, 1986 ($1.75, limited series)

1,2 2.00

TERRARISTS
Marvel Comics (Epic): Nov, 1993 - No. 4, Feb, 1994 ($2.50, lim. series)

1-4-Bound-in trading cards in all 2.50

TERRIFIC COMICS (Also see Suspense Comics)
Continental Magazines: Jan, 1944 - No. 6, Nov, 1944

1-Kid Terrific; opium story 333.00 1000.00 3500.00
2-1st app. The Boomerang by L.B. Cole & Ed Wheelan's "Comics" McCormick, called the world's #1 comic book fan begins 242.00 726.00 2300.00
3-Diana becomes Boomerang's costumed aide; L.B. Cole-c 242.00 726.00 2300.00
4-Classic war-c (Scarce) 400.00 1200.00 4200.00
5-The Reckoner begins; Boomerang & Diana by L.B. Cole; Classic Schomburg bondage & hooded vigilante-c (Scarce) 667.00 2000.00 6000.00
6-L.B. Cole-c/a 221.00 663.00 2100.00
NOTE: ***L.B. Cole** a-1, 2(2), 3-6. **Fuje** a-5, 6. **Rico** a-2; c-1. **Schomburg** c-2, 5.*

TERRIFIC COMICS (Formerly Horrific; Wonder Boy #17 on)
Mystery Publ.(Comic Media)/(Ajax/Farrell): No. 14, Dec, 1954; No. 16, Mar, 1955 (No #15)

14-Art swipe/Advs. into the Unknown #37; injury-to-eye-c; pg. 2, panel 5 swiped from Phantom Stranger #4; surrealistic Palais-a; Human Cross story; classic-c 42.00 125.00 375.00
16-Wonder Boy-c/story (last pre-code) 22.00 66.00 175.00

TERRIFYING TALES (Formerly Startling Terror Tales #10)
Star Publications: No. 11, Jan, 1953 - No. 15, Apr, 1954

11-Used in **POP**, pgs. 99,100; all Jo-Jo-r 49.00 147.00 440.00
12-Reprints Jo-Jo #19 entirely; L.B. Cole splash 47.00 142.00 425.00
13-All Rulah-r; classic devil-c 53.00 158.00 475.00
14-All Rulah reprints 42.00 125.00 375.00
15-Rulah, Zago-r; used in **SOTI**-r/Rulah #22 42.00 125.00 375.00
NOTE: *All issues have **L.B. Cole** covers; bondage covers-No. 12-14.*

TERRITORY, THE
Dark Horse Comics: Jan, 1999 - No. 4, Apr, 1999 ($2.95, limited series)

1-4-Delano-s/David Lloyd-c/a 3.00

TERROR ILLUSTRATED (Adult Tales of...)
E.C. Comics: Nov-Dec, 1955 - No. 2, Spring (April on-c), 1956 (Magazine, 25¢)

1-Adult Entertainment on-c 15.00 45.00 120.00
2-Charles Sultan-a 11.00 33.00 90.00
NOTE: ***Craig, Evans, Ingels, Orlando** art in each. **Crandall** c-1, 2.*

TERROR INC. (See A Shadowline Saga #3)
Marvel Comics: July, 1992 - No. 13, July, 1993 ($1.75)

1-8,11-13: 6,7-Punisher-c/story. 13-Ghost Rider app. 2.00
9,10-Wolverine-c/story 3.00

TERRORS OF THE JUNGLE (Formerly Jungle Thrills)
Star Publications: No. 17, 5/52 - No. 21, 2/53; No. 4, 4/53 - No. 10, 9/54

17-Reprints Rulah #21, used in **SOTI**; L.B. Cole bondage-c 47.00 142.00 425.00
18-Jo-Jo-r 36.00 108.00 290.00
19,20(1952)-Jo-Jo-r; Disbrow-a 34.00 103.00 275.00
21-Jungle Jo, Tangi-r; used in **POP**, pg. 100 & color illos.; shrunken heads on-c 38.00 113.00 300.00
4-10: All Disbrow-a. 5-Jo-Jo-r. 8-Rulah, Jo-Jo-r. 9-Jo-Jo-r; Disbrow-a; Tangi by Orlando10-Rulah-r 34.00 103.00 275.00
NOTE: ***L.B. Cole** c-all; bondage c-17, 19, 21, 5, 7.*

TERROR TALES (See Beware Terror Tales)

TERROR TALES (Magazine)
Eerie Publications: V1#7, 1969 - V6#6, Dec, 1974; V7#1, Apr, 1976 - V10, 1979? (V1-V6: 52 pgs.; V7 on: 68 pgs.)

V1#7 4.35 13.00 48.00
V1#8-11('69): 9-Bondage-c 3.20 9.60 35.00
V2#1-6('70), V3#1-6('71), V4#1-7('72), V5#1-6('73), V6#1-6('74), V7#1,4(no V7#2), V8#1-3('77) 3.00 9.00 30.00
V7#3-LSD story-r/Weird V3#5 3.00 9.00 30.00
V9#2-4, V10 3.00 9.00 32.00

TERRY AND THE PIRATES (See Famous Feature Stories, Merry Christmas From Sears Toyland, Popular Comics, Super Book #3,5,9,16,28, & Super Comics)

TERRY AND THE PIRATES
Dell Publishing Co.: 1939 - 1953 (By Milton Caniff)

Large Feature Comic 2(1939) 67.00 200.00 800.00
Large Feature Comic 6(1938)-r/1936 dailies 60.00 181.00 725.00
Four Color 9(1940) 58.00 175.00 700.00
Large Feature Comic 27('41), 6('42) 50.00 150.00 600.00
Four Color 44('43) 40.00 119.00 475.00
Four Color 101('45) 26.00 78.00 310.00
Family Album(1942) 20.00 60.00 160.00

TERRY AND THE PIRATES (Formerly Boy Explorers; Long John Silver & the Pirates #30 on) (Daily strip-r) (Two #26's)
Harvey Publications/Charlton No. 26-28: No. 3, 4/47 - No. 26, 4/51; No. 26, 6/55 - No. 28, 10/55

3(#1)-Boy Explorers by S&K; Terry & the Pirates begin by Caniff; 1st app. The Dragon Lady 40.00 120.00 325.00
4-S&K Boy Explorers 23.00 68.00 180.00
5-11: 11-Man in Black app. by Powell 11.00 33.00 90.00
12-20: 16-Girl threatened with red hot poker 10.00 30.00 70.00
21-26(4/51)-Last Caniff issue & last pre-code issue 9.30 28.00 65.00
26-28('55)(Formerly This Is Suspense)-No Caniff-a 7.15 21.50 50.00
NOTE: ***Powell** a (Tommy Tween)-5-10, 12, 14; 15-17(1/2 to 2 pgs. each).*

TERRY BEARS COMICS (TerryToons, The... #4)
St. John Publishing Co.: June, 1952 - No. 3, Mar, 1953

1-By Paul Terry 8.65 26.00 60.00
2,3 5.70 17.00 40.00

TERRY-TOONS ALBUM (See Giant Comics Edition)

Tessie the Typist #7 © MAR

The Texan #11 © STJ

Tex Ritter Western #3 © FAW

GD2.0 FN6.0 NM9.4

TERRY-TOONS COMICS (1st Series) (Becomes Paul Terry's Comics #85 on; later issues titled "Paul Terry's...")
Timely/Marvel No. 1-59 (8/47)(Becomes Best Western No. 58 on?, Marvel)/ St. John No. 60 (9/47) on: Oct, 1942 - No. 86, May, 1951

1 (Scarce)-Features characters that 1st app. on movie screen; Gandy Goose & Sourpuss begin; war-c; Gandy Goose c-1-37 158.00 474.00 1500.00
2 61.00 182.00 575.00
3-5 42.00 125.00 375.00
6,8-10 34.00 101.00 270.00
7-Hitler, Hirohito, Mussolini-c 42.00 125.00 375.00
11-20 21.00 64.00 170.00
21-37 14.00 43.00 115.00
38-Mighty Mouse begins (1st app., 11/45); Mighty Mouse-c begin, end #86; Gandy, Sourpuss welcome Mighty Mouse on-c 111.00 332.00 1050.00
39-2nd app. Mighty Mouse 38.00 113.00 300.00
40-49: 43-Infinity-c 17.00 51.00 135.00
50-1st app. Heckle & Jeckle (11/46) 38.00 113.00 300.00
51-60: 55-Infinity-c. 60-(9/47)-Atomic explosion panel; 1st St. John issue 11.00 33.00 90.00
61-86: 85,86-Same book as Paul Terry's Comics #85,86 with only a title change; published at same time? 10.00 30.00 75.00

TERRY-TOONS COMICS (2nd Series)
St. John Publishing Co./Pines: June, 1952 - No. 9, Nov, 1953; 1957; 1958

1-Gandy Goose & Sourpuss begin by Paul Terry 19.00 56.00 150.00
2 10.00 30.00 70.00
3-9 8.65 26.00 60.00
Giant Summer Fun Book 101,102-(Sum, 1957, Sum, 1958, 25¢, Pines)(TV) CBS Television Presents...; Tom Terrific, Mighty Mouse, Heckle & Jeckle Gandy Goose app. 12.50 37.50 100.00

TERRYTOONS, THE TERRY BEARS (Formerly Terry Bears Comics)
Pines Comics: No. 4, Summer, 1958 (CBS Television Presents...)

4 5.00 15.00 35.00

TESSIE THE TYPIST (Tiny Tessie #24; see Comedy Comics, Gay Comics & Joker Comics)
Timely/Marvel Comics (20CC): Summer, 1944 - No. 23, Aug, 1949

1-Doc Rockblock & others by Wolverton 61.00 182.00 575.00
2-Wolverton's Powerhouse Pepper 38.00 113.00 300.00
3-(3/45)-No Wolverton 13.00 39.00 105.00
4,5,7,8-Wolverton-a. 4-(Fall/45) 26.00 79.00 210.00
6-Kurtzman's "Hey Look", 2 pgs. Wolverton-a 26.00 79.00 210.00
9-Wolverton's Powerhouse Pepper (8 pgs.) & 1 pg. Kurtzman's "Hey Look" 29.00 87.00 235.00
10-Wolverton's Powerhouse Pepper (4 pgs.) 28.00 83.00 220.00
11-Wolverton's Powerhouse Pepper (8 pgs.) 29.00 87.00 235.00
12-Wolverton's Powerhouse Pepper (4 pgs.) & 1 pg. Kurtzman's "Hey Look" 28.00 83.00 220.00
13-Wolverton's Powerhouse Pepper (4 pgs.) 28.00 83.00 220.00
14,15: 14-Wolverton's Dr. Whackyhack (1 pg.); 1-1/2 pgs. Kurtzman's "Hey Look". 15-Kurtzman's "Hey Look" (3 pgs.) & 3 pgs. Giggles 'n' Grins 21.00 62.00 165.00
16-18-Kurtzman's "Hey Look" (?, 2 & 1 pg.) 14.00 41.00 110.00
19-Annie Oakley story (8 pgs.) 10.00 30.00 80.00
20-23: 20-Anti-Wertham editorial (2/49) 10.00 30.00 70.00
NOTE: *Lana app.-21. Millie The Model app.-13, 15, 17, 21. Rusty app.-10, 11, 13, 15, 17.*

TEXAN, THE (Fightin' Marines #15 on; Fightin' Texan #16 on)
St. John Publishing Co.: Aug, 1948 - No. 15, Oct, 1951

1-Buckskin Belle 15.00 45.00 120.00
2 9.30 28.00 65.00
3,10: 10-Oversized issue 8.65 26.00 60.00
4,5,7,15-Baker-c/a 16.00 49.00 130.00
6,9-Baker-c 10.00 30.00 80.00
8,11,13,14-Baker-c/a(2-3) each 17.00 51.00 135.00
12-All Matt Baker-c/a; Peyote story 23.00 69.00 185.00
NOTE: ***Matt Baker** c-4-9, 11-15. **Larsen** a-4-6, 8-10, 15. **Tuska** a-1, 2, 7-9.*

TEXAN, THE (TV)
Dell Publishing Co.: No. 1027, Sept-Nov, 1959 - No. 1096, May-July, 1960

Four Color 1027 (#1)-Photo-c 8.35 25.00 100.00
Four Color 1096-Rory Calhoun photo-c 7.50 22.50 90.00

TEXAS JOHN SLAUGHTER (See Walt Disney Presents, 4-Color #997, 1181 & #2)

TEXAS KID (See Two-Gun Western, Wild Western)
Marvel/Atlas Comics (LMC): Jan, 1951 - No. 10, July, 1952

1-Origin; Texas Kid (alias Lance Temple) & his horse Thunder begin; Tuska-a 24.00 71.00 190.00
2 12.00 36.00 95.00
3-10 10.00 30.00 75.00
NOTE: ***Maneely** a-1-4; c-1, 3, 5-10.*

TEXAS RANGERS, THE (See Jace Pearson of... and Superior Stories #4)

TEXAS RANGERS IN ACTION (Formerly Captain Gallant or Scotland Yard?)
Charlton Comics: No. 5, Jul, 1956 - No. 79, Aug, 1970 (See Blue Bird Comics)

5 7.85 23.50 55.00
6,7,9,10 5.00 15.00 30.00
8-Ditko-a (signed) 9.35 28.00 65.00
11-Williamson-a(5&8 pgs.); Torres/Williamson-a (5 pgs.) 9.30 28.00 65.00
12,14-20 4.30 13.00 26.00
13-Williamson-a (5 pgs); Torres, Morisi-a 7.15 21.50 50.00
21-30 2.40 7.35 22.00
31-59: 32-Last 10¢ issue? 2.00 6.00 18.00
60-Riley's Rangers begin 2.30 7.00 20.00
61-65,68-70 1.75 5.25 14.00
66,67: 66-1st app. The Man Called Loco. 67-Origin 2.00 6.00 16.00
71-79 1.25 3.75 10.00
76 (Modern Comics-r, 1977) 4.00

TEXAS SLIM (Also see A-1 Comics)
Magazine Enterprises: No. 2, 1947 - No.10, 1948

A-1 2-8,10: Texas Slim & Dirty Dalton, The Corsair, Teddy Rich, Dotty Dripple, Inca Iinca, Tommy Tinker, Little Mexico & Tugboat Tim, The Masqu'rader & others. 7-Corsair-c/s. 8-Intro Rodeo Ryan 6.40 19.25 45.00
A-1 9-All Texas Slim 7.15 21.50 50.00

TEX DAWSON, GUN-SLINGER (Gunslinger #2 on)
Marvel Comics Group: Jan, 1973 (20¢)(Also see Western Kid, 1st series)

1-Steranko-c; Williamson-r (4 pgs.); Tex Dawson-r by Romita(3) from 1955; Tuska-r 2.30 7.00 20.00

TEX FARNUM (See Wisco)

TEX FARRELL (...Pride of the Wild West)
D. S. Publishing Co.: Mar-Apr, 1948

1-Tex Farrell & his horse Lightning; Shelly-c 12.50 37.50 100.00

TEX GRANGER (Formerly Calling All Boys; see True Comics)
Parents' Magazine Inst./Commended: No. 18, Jun, 1948 - No. 24, Sept, 1949

18-Tex Granger & his horse Bullet begin 11.00 33.00 90.00
19 9.30 28.00 65.00
20-24: 22-Wild Bill Hickok story. 23-Vs. Billy the Kid; Tim Holt app. 7.15 21.50 50.00

TEX MORGAN (See Blaze Carson and Wild Western)
Marvel Comics (CCC): Aug, 1948 - No. 9, Feb, 1950

1-Tex Morgan, his horse Lightning & sidekick Lobo begin 28.00 84.00 225.00
2 19.00 56.00 150.00
3-6: 3,4-Arizona Annie app. 12.00 36.00 95.00
7-9: All photo-c. 7-Captain Tootsie by Beck. 8-18 pg. story "The Terror of Rimrock Valley"; Diablo app. 19.00 56.00 150.00
NOTE: *Tex Taylor app.-6, 7, 9. **Brodsky** c-6. **Syd Shores** c-2, 5.*

TEX RITTER WESTERN (Movie star; singing cowboy; see Six-Gun Heroes and Western Hero)
Fawcett No. 1-20 (1/54)/Charlton No. 21 on: Oct, 1950 - No. 46, May, 1959 (Photo-c: 1-21)

1-Tex Ritter, his stallion White Flash & dog Fury begin; photo front/back-c begin 68.00 205.00 650.00
2 33.00 98.00 260.00

THB #6A © Paul Pope

The Thing! #2 © CC

The Thing #1 © MAR

	GD2.0	FN6.0	NM9.4
3-5: 5-Last photo back-c	25.00	75.00	200.00
6-10	19.00	56.00	150.00
11-19	13.00	39.00	105.00
20-Last Fawcett issue (1/54)	14.00	43.00	115.00
21-1st Charlton issue; photo-c (3/54)	18.00	53.00	140.00
22-B&W photo back-c begin, end #32	10.00	30.00	80.00
23-30: 23-25-Young Falcon app.	10.00	30.00	70.00
31-38,40-45	8.65	26.00	60.00
39-Williamson-a; Whitman-c (1/58)	10.00	30.00	75.00
46-Last issue	10.00	30.00	70.00

TEX TAYLOR (...The Fighting Cowboy on-c #1, 2)(See Blaze Carson, Kid Colt, Tex Morgan, Wild West, Wild Western, & Wisco)
Marvel Comics (HPC): Sept, 1948 - No. 9, March, 1950

	GD2.0	FN6.0	NM9.4
1-Tex Taylor & his horse Fury begin	30.00	90.00	240.00
2	16.00	49.00	130.00
3	14.00	43.00	115.00
4-6: All photo-c. 4-Anti-Wertham editorial. 5,6-Blaze Carson app.	17.00	51.00	135.00
7-9: 7-Photo-c;18 pg. Movie-Length Thriller "Trapped in Time's Lost Land!" with sabre toothed tigers, dinosaurs; Diablo app. 8-Photo-c; 18 pg. Movie-Length Thriller "The Mystery of Devil-Tree Plateau!" with dwarf horses, dwarf people & a lost miniature Inca type village; Diablo app. 9-Photo-c; 18 pg. Movie-Length Thriller "Guns Along the Border!" Captain Tootsie by Schreiber; Nimo the Mountain Lion app.	20.00	60.00	160.00

NOTE: ***Syd Shores** c-1-3.*

THANE OF BAGARTH (Also see Hercules, 1967 series)
Charlton Comics: No. 24, Oct, 1985 - No. 25, Dec, 1985

	GD2.0	FN6.0	NM9.4
24,25			4.00

THANOS QUEST, THE (See Capt. Marvel #25, Infinity Gauntlet, Iron Man #55, Logan's Run, Marvel Feature #12, Silver Surfer #34 & Warlock #9)
Marvel Comics: 1990 - No. 2, 1990 ($4.95, squarebound, 52 pgs.)

	GD2.0	FN6.0	NM9.4
1,2-Both have Starlin scripts & covers (both printings)	1.00	2.80	7.00
1-(3/2000, $3.99) r/material from #1&2			4.00

THAT CHEMICAL REFLEX
CFD Productions: 1994 - No. 3 ($2.50, B&W, mature)

	GD2.0	FN6.0	NM9.4
1-3: 1-Dan Brereton-c/a			2.50

THAT DARN CAT (See Movie Comics & Walt Disney Showcase #19)

THAT'S MY POP! GOES NUTS FOR FAIR
Bystander Press: 1939 (76 pgs., B&W)

	GD2.0	FN6.0	NM9.4
nn-by Milt Gross	28.00	83.00	220.00

THAT WILKIN BOY (Meet Bingo...)
Archie Publications: Jan, 1969 - No. 52, Oct, 1982

	GD2.0	FN6.0	NM9.4
1-1st app. Bingo's Band, Samantha & Tough Teddy	3.25	9.75	36.00
2-5	2.00	6.00	18.00
6-11	1.75	5.25	14.00
12-26-Giants. 12-No # on-c	2.00	6.00	16.00
27-40(1/77)	1.00	2.80	7.00
41-52			4.00

THB
Horse Press: Oct, 1994 - Present ($5.50/$2.50/$2.95, B&W)

	GD2.0	FN6.0	NM9.4
1 ($5.50)	1.00	3.00	8.00
1 (2nd Printing)-r/#1 w/new material			3.00
2 ($2.50)			5.00
3-5			4.00
69 (1995, no price, low distribution, 12 pgs.)-story reprinted in #1 (2nd Printing).			3.00
Giant THB-($4.95)			5.00
...M3/THB: Mars' Mightiest Mek #1 (2000, $3.95)			3.95
...6A: Mek-Power #1 (2000, $3.95)			3.95

T.H.E. CAT (TV)
Dell Publishing Co.: Mar, 1967 - No. 4, Oct, 1967 (All have photo-c)

	GD2.0	FN6.0	NM9.4
1	3.00	9.00	30.00
2-4	2.50	7.50	23.00

THERE'S A NEW WORLD COMING
Spire Christian Comics/Fleming H. Revell Co.: 1973 (35/49¢)

	GD2.0	FN6.0	NM9.4
nn		2.40	6.00

THEY ALL KISSED THE BRIDE (See Cinema Comics Herald)

THEY RING THE BELL
Fox Feature Syndicate: 1946

	GD2.0	FN6.0	NM9.4
1 (exist?)	12.00	36.00	95.00

THIEF OF BAGHDAD
Dell Publishing Co.: No. 1229, Oct-Dec, 1961 (one-shot)

	GD2.0	FN6.0	NM9.4
Four Color 1229-Movie, Crandall/Evans-a, photo-c	6.30	19.00	75.00

THIEVES & KINGS
I Box: 1994 - Present ($2.35, B&W, bi-monthly)

	GD2.0	FN6.0	NM9.4
1			4.00
1-(2nd printing), 2-26			2.50

THIMK (Magazine) (Satire)
Counterpoint: May, 1958 - No. 6, May, 1959

	GD2.0	FN6.0	NM9.4
1	8.65	26.00	60.00
2-6	5.70	17.00	40.00

THING!, THE (Blue Beetle #18 on)
Song Hits No. 1,2/Capitol Stories/Charlton: Feb, 1952 - No. 17, Nov, 1954

	GD2.0	FN6.0	NM9.4
1-Weird/horror stories in all; shrunken head-c	79.00	237.00	750.00
2,3	55.00	165.00	525.00
4-6,8,10: 5-Severed head-c; headlights	50.00	150.00	450.00
7-Injury to eye-c & inside panel	68.00	205.00	650.00
9-Used in **SOTI**, pg. 388 & illo "Stomping on the face is a form of brutality which modern children learn early"	76.00	228.00	725.00
11-Necronomicon story; Hansel & Gretel parody; Injury-to-eye panel; Check-a	61.00	182.00	575.00
12-1st published Ditko-c; "Cinderella" parody; lingerie panels. Ditko-a	80.00	240.00	760.00
13,15-Ditko-c/a(3 & 5)	80.00	240.00	760.00
14-Extreme violence/torture; Rumpelstiltskin story; Ditko-c/a(4)	82.00	246.00	775.00
16-Injury to eye panel	30.00	90.00	240.00
17-Ditko-c; classic parody "Through the Looking Glass"; Powell-r/Beware Terror Tales #1 & recolored	71.00	213.00	675.00

NOTE: *Excessive violence, severed heads, injury to eye are common No. 5 on. **Al Fago** c-4. **Forgione** c-1i, 2, 6, 8, 9. All **Ditko** issues #14, 15.*

THING, THE (See Fantastic Four, Marvel Fanfare, Marvel Feature #11, 12 & Marvel Two-In-One)
Marvel Comics Group: July, 1983 - No. 36, June, 1986

	GD2.0	FN6.0	NM9.4
1-Life story of Ben Grimm; Byrne scripts begin			3.00
2-36: 5-Spider-Man, She-Hulk app.			2.00

NOTE: ***Byrne** a-2i, 7; c-1, 7, 36i; scripts-1-13, 19-22. **Sienkiewicz** c-13i.*

THING, THE (From Another World)
Dark Horse Comics: 1991 - No. 2, 1992 ($2.95, mini-series, stiff-c)

	GD2.0	FN6.0	NM9.4
1,2-Based on Universal movie; painted-c/a			3.00

THING FROM ANOTHER WORLD: CLIMATE OF FEAR, THE
Dark Horse Comics: July, 1992 - No. 4, Dec, 1992 ($2.50, mini-series)

	GD2.0	FN6.0	NM9.4
1-4: Painted-c			3.00

THING FROM ANOTHER WORLD: ETERNAL VOWS
Dark Horse Comics: Dec, 1993 - No. 4, 1994 ($2.50, mini-series)

	GD2.0	FN6.0	NM9.4
1-4-Gulacy-c/a			3.00

THIRD WORLD WAR
Fleetway Publ. (Quality): 1990 - No. 6, 1991 ($2.50, thick-c, mature)

	GD2.0	FN6.0	NM9.4
1-6			2.50

THIRTEEN (...Going on 18)
Dell Publishing Co.: 11-1/61-62 - No. 25, 12/67; No. 26, 7/69 - No. 29, 1/71

	GD2.0	FN6.0	NM9.4
1	5.45	16.35	60.00
2-10	4.10	12.30	45.00
11-29: 26-29-r	3.20	9.60	35.00

NOTE: ***John Stanley** script-No. 3-29; art?*

This Magazine is Haunted #7 © FAW

Thor #270 © MAR

Thor #478 © MAR

GD2.0 FN6.0 NM9.4

: ASSASSIN
SR, Inc.: 1990 - No. 8, 1991 ($2.95, 44 pgs.)
-8: Agent 13; Alcala-a(i); Springer back-up-a 3.00

HIRTY SECONDS OVER TOKYO (See American Library)

HIS IS SUSPENSE! (Formerly Strange Suspense Stories; Strange Suspense Stories #27 on)
harlton Comics: No. 23, Feb, 1955 - No. 26, Aug, 1955
3-Wood-a(r)/A Star Presentation #3 "Dr. Jekyll & Mr. Hyde"; last pre-code issue 27.00 81.00 215.00
4-Censored Fawcett-r; Evans-a (r/Suspense Detective #1) 14.00 43.00 115.00
5,26: 26-Marcus Swayze-a 10.00 30.00 70.00

HIS IS THE PAYOFF (See Pay-Off)

HIS IS WAR
andard Comics: No. 5, July, 1952 - No. 9, May, 1953
-Toth-a 12.50 37.50 100.00
,9-Toth-a 10.00 30.00 80.00
,8: 8-Ross Andru-c 6.40 19.25 45.00

HIS IS YOUR LIFE, DONALD DUCK (See Donald Duck..., Four Color #1109)

HIS MAGAZINE IS CRAZY (Crazy #? on)
harlton Publ. (Humor Magazines): V3#2, July, 1957 - V4#8, Feb, 1959 (25¢, agazine, 68 pgs.)
3#2-V4#7: V4#5-Russian Sputnik-c parody 7.15 21.50 50.00
4#8-Davis-a (8 pgs.) 8.65 26.00 60.00

HIS MAGAZINE IS HAUNTED (Danger and Adventure #22 on)
awcett Publications/Charlton No. 15(2/54) on: Oct, 1951 - No. 14, 12/53; o. 15, 2/54 - V3#21, Nov, 1954
-Evans-a; Dr. Death as host begins 60.00 178.00 565.00
,5-Evans-a 42.00 125.00 375.00
,4: 3-Vampire-c/story 33.00 98.00 260.00
-9,11,12,14 23.00 68.00 180.00
0-Severed head-c 38.00 113.00 300.00
3-Severed head-c/story 36.00 107.00 285.00
5,20: 15-Dick Giordano-c. 20-Cover is swiped from panel in The Thing #16 19.00 56.00 150.00
6,19-Ditko-c. 19-Injury-to-eye panel; story-r/#1 39.00 118.00 315.00
7-Ditko-c/a(4); blood drainage story 43.00 128.00 385.00
8-Ditko-c/a(1 story); E.C. swipe/Haunt of Fear #5; injury-to-eye panel; reprints "Caretaker of the Dead" from Beware Terror Tales & recolored 40.00 120.00 335.00
1-Ditko-c, Evans-r/This Magazine Is Haunted #1 36.00 108.00 290.00
OTE: ***Baily*** *a-1, 3, 4, 21r/#1.* ***Moldoff*** *c/a-1-13.* ***Powell*** *a-3-5, 11, 12, 17.* ***Shuster*** *a-18-20. sues 19-21 have reprints which have been recolored from This Magazine is Haunted #1.*

HIS MAGAZINE IS HAUNTED (2nd Series) (Formerly Zaza the Mystic; uter Space #17 on)
harlton Comics: V2#12, July, 1957 - V2#16, May, 1958
2#12-14-Ditko-c/a in all 40.00 120.00 325.00
15-No Ditko-c/a 8.65 26.00 60.00
16-Ditko-a 25.00 75.00 200.00

HIS MAGAZINE IS WILD (See Wild)

HIS WAS YOUR LIFE (Religious)
ack T. Chick Publ.: 1964 (3 1/2 x 5 1/2", 40 pgs., B&W and red)
, Another version (5x2 3/4", 26 pgs.) 1.25 3.75 10.00

HOR (See Avengers #1, Giant-Size..., Marvel Collectors Item Classics, Marvel Graphic ovel #33, Marvel Preview, Marvel Spectacular, Marvel Treasury Edition, Special Marvel Edition Tales of Asgard)

HOR (Journey Into Mystery #1-125, 503-on)(The Mighty Thor #413-490)
arvel Comics Group: No. 126, Mar, 1966 - No. 502, Sept, 1996
26-Thor continues (#125-130 Thor vs. Hercules) 15.50 46.50 170.00
27-130: 127-1st app. Pluto 5.90 17.75 65.00
31-133,135-140 5.00 15.00 55.00
34-Intro High Evolutionary 5.45 16.35 60.00
41-150: 146-Inhumans begin (early app.), end #151 (see Fantastic Four #45 for 1st app.). 146,147-Origin The Inhumans. 148,149-Origin Black Bolt in each. 149-Origin Medusa, Crystal, Maximus, Gorgon, Kornak 4.10 12.30 45.00
151-157,159,160 3.20 9.60 35.00
158-Origin-r/#83; 158,159-Origin Dr. Blake (Thor) 6.80 20.50 75.00
161,167,170-179: 179-Last Kirby issue 2.80 8.40 28.00
162,168,169-Origin Galactus; Kirby-a 3.65 11.00 40.00
163,164-2nd & 3th brief cameo Warlock (Him) 2.80 8.40 28.00
165-1st full app. Warlock (Him) (6/69, see Fantastic Four #67); last 12¢ issue; Kirby-a 5.90 17.75 65.00
166-2nd full app. Warlock (Him); battles Thor 5.00 15.00 55.00
180,181-Neal Adams-a 3.00 9.00 32.00
182-192: 192-Last 15¢ issue 2.00 6.00 16.00
193-(25¢, 52 pgs.); Silver Surfer x-over 4.55 13.65 50.00
194-199 1.50 4.50 12.00
200 2.00 6.00 16.00
201-224 1.00 3.00 8.00
225-Intro. Firelord 1.25 3.75 10.00
226-245 2.40 6.00
246-250-(Regular 25¢ editions)(4-8/76) 2.40 6.00
246-250-(30¢-c variants, limited distribution) 1.10 3.30 9.00
251-280: 271-Iron Man x-over. 274-Death of Balder the Brave 4.00
281-299: 294-Origin Asgard & Odin 3.50
300-(12/80)-End of Asgard; origin of Odin & The Destroyer 2.40 6.00
301-336,338-373,375-381,383: 316-Iron Man x-over. 340-Donald Blake returns as Thor. 341-Clark Kent & Lois Lane cameo. 373-X-Factor tie-in 3.00
337-Simonson-c/a begins, ends #382; Beta Ray Bill becomes new Thor 2.40 6.00
374-Mutant Massacre; X-Factor app. 4.00
382-($1.25)-Anniversary issue; last Simonson-a 3.50
384-Intro. new Thor 3.00
385-399,401-410,413-428: 385-Hulk x-over. 391-Spider-Man x-over; 1st Eric Masterson. 395-Intro Earth Force. 408-Eric Masterson becomes Thor. 427, 428-Excalibur x-over 2.50
400,411: 400-($1.75, 68 pgs.)-Origin Loki. 411-Intro New Warriors (appears in costume in last panel); Juggernaut-c/story 4.00
412-1st full app. New Warriors (Marvel Boy, Kid Nova, Namorita, Night Thrasher, Firestar & Speedball) 5.00
429-431,434-443: 429,430-Ghost Rider x-over. 434-Capt. America x-over. 437-Thor vs. Quasar; Hercules app.;Tales of Asgard back-up stories begin. 443-Dr. Strange & Silver Surfer x-over; last $1.00-c 2.00
432,433: 432-(52 pgs.)-Thor's 300th app. (vs. Loki); reprints origin & 1st app. from Journey into Mystery #83. 433-Intro new Thor 3.00
444-449,451-473: 448-Spider-Man-c/story. 455,456-Dr. Strange back-up. 457-Old Thor returns (3 pgs.). 459-Intro Thunderstrike. 460-Starlin scripts begin. 465-Super Skrull app. 466-Drax app. 469,470-Infinity Watch x-over. 472-Intro the Godlings 2.00
450-($2.50, 68 pgs.)-Flip-book format; r/story JIM #87 (1st Loki) plus-c plus a gallery of past-c; gatefold-c 3.00
474,476-481,483-499: 474-Begin $1.50-c; bound-in trading card sheet. 459-Intro Thunderstrike, 460-Starlin scripts begin. 472-Intro the Godlings. 490-The Absorbing Man app. 491-Warren Ellis scripts begins, ends #494; Deodato-c/a begins. 492-Reintro The Enchantress; Beta Ray Bill dies. 495-Wm. Messner-Loebs scripts begin; Isherwood-c/a. 2.00
475 ($2.00, 52 pgs.)-Regular edition 2.00
475 ($2.50, 52 pgs.)-Collectors edition w/foil embossed-c 3.00
482 ($2.95, 84 pgs.)-400th issue 3.00
500 ($2.50)-Double-size; wraparound-c; Deodato-c/a; Dr. Strange app. 5.00
501-Reintro Red Norvell 3.00
502-Onslaught tie-in; Red Norvell, Jane Foster & Hela app. 3.50
Special 2(9/66)-See Journey Into Mystery for 1st annual 5.90 17.75 65.00
King Size Special 3(1/71) 2.30 7.00 20.00
Special 4(12/71)-r/Thor #131,132 & JIM #113 1.85 5.50 15.00
Annual 5,6: 5(11/76). 6(10/77)-Guardians of the Galaxy app. 1.25 3.75 10.00
Annual 7,8: 7(1978). 8(1979)-Thor vs. Zeus-c/story 1.00 2.80 7.00
Annual 9-12: 9('81). 10('82). 11('83). 12('84) 5.00
Annual 13-19('85-'94, 68 pgs.):14-Atlantis Attacks. 16-3 pg. origin; Guardians of

Thor V2 #3 © MAR

3-D Action #1 © MAR

3-D Alien Terror #1 © ECL

the Galaxy x-over.18-Polybagged w/card 3.00
...Alone Against the Celestials nn (6/92, $5.95)-r/Thor #387-389 6.00
...: Worldengine (8/96, $9.95)-r/#491-494; Deodato-c/a; story & new intermission by Warren Ellis 10.00

NOTE: ***Neal Adams*** *a-180,181; c-179-181.* ***Austin*** *a-342i, 346i; c-312i.* ***Buscema*** *a(p)-178, 182-213, 215-226, 231-238, 241-253, 254r, 256-259, 272-278, 283-285, 370, Annual 6, 8, 11i; c(p)-175, 182-196, 198-200, 202-204, 206, 211, 212, 215, 219, 221, 226, 256, 259, 261, 262, 272-278, 283, 289, 370, Annual 6.* ***Everett*** *a(i)-143, 170-175; c(i)-171, 172, 174, 176, 241.* ***Gil Kane*** *a-318p; c(p)-201, 205, 207-210, 216, 220, 222, 223, 231, 233-240, 242, 243, 318.* ***Kirby*** *a(p)-126-177, 179, 194r, 254r; c(p)-126-169, 171-174, 176-178, 249-253, 255, 257, 258, Annual 5, Special 2-4.* ***Mooney*** *a(i)-201, 204, 214-216, 218, 322i, 324i, 325i, 327i.* ***Sienkiewicz*** *c-332, 333, 335.* ***Simonson*** *a-260-271p, 337-354, 357-367, 380, Annual 7p; c-260, 263-271, 337-355, 357-369, 371, 373-382, Annual 7.* ***Starlin*** *c-213.*

THOR (Volume 2)
Marvel Comics: July, 1998 - Present ($2.99/$1.99)

1-($2.99)-Follows Heroes Return; Jurgens-s/Romita Jr. & Janson-a; wraparound-c; battles the Destroyer 4.00
1-Variant-c 1.00 3.00 8.00
1-Rough Cut-($2.99) Features original script and pencil pages 3.00
2-($1.99) Two covers; Avengers app. 3.00
3-11,13-23: 3-Assumes Jake Olson ID. 4-Namor-c/app. 8-Spider-Man-c/app. 14-Iron Man c/app. 17-Juggernaut-c 2.00
12-($2.99) Wraparound-c; Hercules appears 3.00
12-($10.00) Variant-c by Jusko 10.00
24,26-31,33: 24-Begin $2.25-c. 26-Mignola-c/Larsen-a. 29-Andy Kubert-a. 30-Maximum Security x-over; Beta Ray Bill-c/app. 33-Immonen-a 2.25
25-($2.99) 3.00
25-($3.99) Gold foil enhanced cover 4.00
32-($3.50, 100 pgs.) new story plus reprints w/Kirby-a; Simonson-a 3.50
...1999 Annual ($3.50) Jurgens-s/a(p) 3.50
...2000 Annual ($3.50) Jurgens-s/Ordway-a(p); back-up stories 3.50
...Resurrection ($5.99, TPB) r/#1,2 6.00
...: The Dark Gods (7/00, $15.95, TPB) r/#9-13 15.95

THOR CORPS
Marvel Comics: Sept, 1993 - No. 4, Jan, 1994 ($1.75, limited series)

1-4: 1-Invaders cameo. 2-Invaders app. 3-Spider-Man 2099, Rawhide Kid, Two-Gun Kid & Kid Colt app. 4-Painted-c 2.00

THORION OF THE NEW ASGODS
Marvel Comics (Amalgam): June, 1997 ($1.95, one-shot)

1-Keith Giffen-s/John Romita Jr.-c/a 2.00

THOR: THE LEGEND
Marvel Comics: Sept, 1996 ($3.95, one-shot)

nn-Tribute issue 4.00

THOSE MAGNIFICENT MEN IN THEIR FLYING MACHINES (See Movie Comics)

THRAX
Event Comics: Nov, 1996 ($2.95, one-shot)

1 3.00

THREE CABALLEROS (Walt Disney's...)
Dell Publishing Co.: No. 71, 1945

Four Color 71-by Walt Kelly, c/a 79.00 238.00 950.00

THREE CHIPMUNKS, THE (TV)
Dell Publishing Co.: No. 1042, Oct-Dec, 1959

Four Color 1042 (#1)-(Alvin, Simon & Theodore) 5.35 16.00 65.00

THREE COMICS (Also see Spiritman)
The Penny King Co.: 1944 (10¢, 52 pgs.) (2 different covers exist)

1,3,4-Lady Luck, Mr. Mystic, The Spirit app. (3 Spirit sections bound together); Lou Fine-a 25.00 75.00 200.00

NOTE: *No. 1 contains Spirit Sections 4/9/44 - 4/23/44, and No. 4 is also from 4/44.*

3-D (NOTE: The prices of all the 3-D comics listed include glasses. Deduct 40-50 percent if glasses are missing, and reduce slightly if glasses are loose.)

3-D ACTION
Atlas Comics (ACI): Jan, 1954 (Oversized, 15¢)(2 pairs of glasses included)

1-Battle Brady; Sol Brodsky-c 39.00 116.00 310.00

3-D ADVENTURE COMICS
Stats, Etc.: Aug, 1986 (one shot)

1-Promo material 4.0

3-D ALIEN TERROR
Eclipse Comics: June, 1986 ($2.50)

1-Old Witch, Crypt-Keeper, Vault Keeper cameo; Morrow, John Pound-a, Yeates-c 2.40 6.0
...in 2-D: 100 copies signed, numbered(B&W) 1.00 3.00 8.0

3-D ANIMAL FUN (See Animal Fun)

3-D BATMAN (Also see Batman 3-D)
National Periodical Publications: 1953 (Reprinted in 1966)

1953-(25¢)-Reprints Batman #42 & 48 (Penguin-c/story); Tommy Tomorrow story; came with pair of 3-D Bat glasses 111.00 332.00 1050.0
1966-Reprints 1953 issue; new cover by Infantino/Anderson; has inside-c photos of Batman & Robin from TV show (50¢) 38.00 113.00 300.0

3-D CIRCUS
Fiction House Magazines (Real Adventures Publ.): 1953 (25¢, w/glasses)

1 40.00 120.00 320.0

3-D COMICS (See Mighty Mouse, Tor and Western Fighters)

3-D DOLLY
Harvey Publications: December, 1953 (25¢, came with 2 pairs of glasses)

1-Richie Rich story redrawn from his 1st app. in Little Dot #1; shows cover in 3-D on inside 24.00 71.00 190.0

3-D-ELL
Dell Publishing Co.: No. 1, 1953; No. 3, 1953 (3-D comics) (25¢, came w/glasses)

1-Rootie Kazootie (#2 does not exist) 40.00 120.00 330.0
3-Flukey Luke 38.00 113.00 300.0

3-D EXOTIC BEAUTIES
The 3-D Zone: Nov, 1990 ($2.95, 28 pgs.)

1-L.B. Cole-c 5.0

3-D FEATURES PRESENTS JET PUP
Dimensions Publications: Oct-Dec (Winter on-c), 1953 (25¢, came w/glasses)

1-Irving Spector-a(2) 40.00 120.00 320.0

3-D FUNNY MOVIES
Comic Media: 1953 (25¢, came w/glasses)

1-Bugsey Bear & Paddy Pelican 40.00 120.00 320.0

THREE-DIMENSION ADVENTURES (Superman)
National Periodical Publications: 1953 (25¢, large size, came w/glasses)

nn-Origin Superman (new art) 111.00 332.00 1050.0

THREE DIMENSIONAL ALIEN WORLDS (See Alien Worlds)
Pacific Comics: July, 1984 (1st Ray Zone 3-D book)(one-shot)

1-Bolton-a(p); Stevens-a(i); Art Adams 1st published-a(p) 2.40 6.0

THREE DIMENSIONAL DNAGENTS (See New DNAgents)

THREE DIMENSIONAL E. C. CLASSICS (Three Dimensional Tales From the Crypt No. 2)
E. C. Comics: Spring, 1954 (Prices include glasses; came with 2 pair)

1-Stories by Wood (Mad #3), Krigstein (W.S. #7), Evans (F.C. #13), & Ingels (CSS #5); Kurtzman-c (rare in high grade due to unstable paper) 84.00 253.00 800.0

NOTE: *Stories redrawn to 3-D format. Original stories not necessarily by artists listed. CSS: Crime SuspenStories; F.C.: Frontline Combat; W.S.: Weird Science.*

THREE DIMENSIONAL TALES FROM THE CRYPT (Formerly Three Dimensional E. C. Classics)(Cover title: ...From the Crypt of Terror)
E. C. Comics: No. 2, Spring, 1954 (Prices include glasses; came with 2 pair)

2-Davis (TFTC #25), Elder (VOH #14), Craig (TFTC #24), & Orlando (TFTC #22) stories; Feldstein-c (rare in high grade) 84.00 253.00 800.0

NOTE: *Stories redrawn to 3-D format. Original stories not necessarily by artists listed. TFTC: Tales From the Crypt; VOH: Vault of Horror.*

3-D LOVE
Steriographic Publ. (Mikeross Publ.): Dec, 1953 (25¢, came w/glasses)

3 Geeks #10 © 3 Finger Prints

Three Mouseketeers #3 © DC

Three Stooges #1 © Norman Maurer

40.00 120.00 320.00

D NOODNICK (See Noodnick)

D ROMANCE
eriographic Publ. (Mikeross Publ.): Jan, 1954 (25¢, came w/glasses)
40.00 120.00 320.00

D SHEENA, JUNGLE QUEEN (Also see Sheena 3-D)
ction House Magazines: 1953 (25¢, came w/glasses)
-Maurice Whitman-c 71.00 213.00 675.00

D SUBSTANCE
e 3-D Zone: July, 1990 ($2.95, 28 pgs.)
-Ditko-c/a(r) 4.00

D TALES OF THE WEST
las Comics (CPS): Jan, 1954 (Oversized) (15¢, came with 2 pair of glasses)
(3-D)-Sol Brodsky-c 40.00 120.00 325.00

D THREE STOOGES (Also see Three Stooges)
:lipse Comics: Sept, 1986 - No. 2, Nov, 1986; No. 3, Oct, 1987; No. 4, 1989
2.50)
-4: 3-Maurer-r. 4-r-/"Three Missing Links" 5.00
-3 (2-D) 5.00

D WHACK (See Whack)

D ZONE, THE
e 3-D Zone (Renegade Press)/Ray Zone: Feb, 1987 - No. 20, 1989 ($2.50)
,3,4,7-9,11,12,14,15,17,19,20: 1-r/A Star Presentation. 3-Picture Scope Jungle Advs. 4-Electric Fear. 7-Hollywood 3-D Jayne Mansfield photo-c. 8-High Seas 3-D, 9-Redmask-r. 11-Danse Macabre; Matt Fox c/a(r). 12-3-D Presidents. 14-Tyranostar. 15-3-Dementia Comics; Kurtzman-c, Kubert, Maurer-a. 17-Thrilling Love. 19-Cracked Classics. 20-Commander Battle and His Atomic Submarine 2.40 6.00
,5,6,10,13,16,18: 2-Wolverton-r. 5-Krazy Kat-r. 6-Ratfink. 10-Jet 3-D; Powell & Williamson-r. 13-Flash Gordon. 16-Space Vixens; Dave Stevens-c/a. 18-Spacehawk; Wolverton-r 2.40 6.00
*TE: **Davis** r-19. **Ditko** r-19. **Elder** r-19. **Everett** r-19. **Feldstein** r-17. **Frazetta** r-17. **Heath** r-. **Kamen** r-17. **Severin** r-19. **Ward** r-17,19. **Wolverton** r-2,18,19. **Wood** r-1,17. Photo c-12*

GEEKS, THE (Also see Geeksville)
Finger Prints: 1996 - No. 11, Jun, 1999 (B&W)
,2 -Rich Koslowski-s/a in all 1.00 3.00 8.00
-(2nd printing) 2.50
-7, 9-11 2.50
-(48 pgs.) 4.00
0-Variant-c 3.50
ow to Pick Up Girls If You're a Comic Book Geek (color)(7/97) 4.00

0
rk Horse Comics: May, 1998 - No. 5 ($2.95, limited series)
,5: 1-Frank Miller-s/c/a; Spartans vs. Persians war 4.00
-Second printing, 2-4 3.00

LITTLE PIGS (Disney)(...and the Wonderful Magic Lamp)
ell Publishing Co.: No. 218, Mar, 1949
our Color 218 (#1) 11.30 34.00 135.00

LITTLE PIGS, THE (See Walt Disney Showcase #15 & 21)
old Key: May, 1964; No. 2, Sept, 1968 (Walt Disney)
-Reprints Four Color #218 3.00 9.00 30.00
2.00 6.00 18.00

HREE MOUSEKETEERS, THE (1st Series)(See Funny Stuff #1)
ational Per. Publ.: 3-4/56 - No. 24, 9-10/59; No. 25, 8-9/60 - No. 26, 10-12/60
18.00 54.00 200.00
9.00 27.00 100.00
-10: 6,8-Grey tone-c 7.25 21.75 80.00
1-26: 24-Cover says 11/59, inside says 9-10/59 5.90 17.75 65.00
*TE: **Rube Grossman** a-1-26. **Sheldon Mayer** a-1-8; c-1-7.*

HREE MOUSEKETEERS, THE (2nd Series) (See Super DC Giant)
ational Periodical Publications: May-June, 1970 - No. 7, May-June, 1971
(#5-7: 68 pgs.)
1-Mayer-r in all 4.55 13.65 50.00
2-4: 4-Doodles Duck begins (1st app.) 2.80 8.40 28.00
5-7: (68 pgs.). 5-Dodo & the Frog, Bo Bunny begin
4.10 12.30 45.00

THREE MUSKETEERS, THE (See Disney's The Three Musketeers)

THREE NURSES (Confidential Diary #12-17; Career Girl Romances #24 on)
Charlton Comics: V3#18, May, 1963 - V3#23, Mar, 1964
V3#18-23 2.40 7.35 22.00

THREE RASCALS
I. W. Enterprises: 1958; 1963
I.W. Reprint #1,2,10: 1-(Says Super Comics on inside)-(M.E.'s Clubhouse Rascals). #2-(1958). 10-(1963)-r/#1 1.50 4.50 12.00

THREE RING COMICS
Spotlight Publishers: March, 1945
1-Funny animal 15.00 45.00 120.00

THREE RING COMICS (Also see Captain Wizard & Meteor Comics)
Century Publications: April, 1946
1-Prankster-c; Captain Wizard, Impossible Man, Race Wilkins, King O'Leary, & Dr. Mercy app. 34.00 103.00 275.00

THREE ROCKETEERS (See Blast-Off)

THREE STOOGES (See Comic Album #18, Top Comics, The Little Stooges, March of Comics #232, 248, 268, 280, 292, 304, 316, 336, 373, Movie Classics & Comics & 3-D Three Stooges)

THREE STOOGES
Jubilee No. 1/St. John No. 1 (9/53) on: Feb, 1949 - No. 2, May, 1949; Sept, 1953 - No. 7, Oct, 1954
1-(Scarce, 1949)-Kubert-a; infinity-c 111.00 332.00 1050.00
2-(Scarce)-Kubert, Maurer-a 76.00 229.00 725.00
1(9/53)-Hollywood Stunt Girl by Kubert (7 pgs.) 68.00 205.00 650.00
2(3-D, 10/53, 25¢)-Came w/glasses; Stunt Girl story by Kubert
50.00 150.00 450.00
3(3-D, 10/53, 25¢)-Came w/glasses; has 3-D-c 46.00 137.00 410.00
4(3/54)-7(10/54): 4-1st app. Li'l Stooge? 39.00 116.00 310.00
NOTE: *All issues have **Kubert-Maurer** art & **Maurer** covers. 6, 7-Partial photo-c.*

THREE STOOGES
Dell Publishing Co./Gold Key No. 10 (10/62) on: No. 1043, Oct-Dec, 1959 - No. 55, June, 1972
Four Color 1043 (#1) 19.00 56.00 225.00
Four Color 1078,1127,1170,1187 10.00 30.00 120.00
6(9-11/61) - 10: 6-Professor Putter begins; ends #16
8.35 25.00 100.00
11-14,16,18-20 6.70 20.00 80.00
15-Go Around the World in a Daze (movie scenes) 7.50 22.50 90.00
17-The Little Monsters begin (5/64)(1st app.?) 7.50 22.50 90.00
21,23-30 5.85 17.50 70.00
22-Movie scenes from "The Outlaws Is Coming" 6.70 20.00 80.00
31-55 4.60 13.75 55.00
NOTE: *All Four Colors, 6-50, 52-55 have photo-c.*

THREE STOOGES IN 3-D, THE
Eternity Comics: 1991 ($3.95, high quality paper, w/glasses)
1-Reprints Three Stooges by Gold Key; photo-c 5.00

3 WORLDS OF GULLIVER
Dell Publishing Co.: No. 1158, July, 1961 (2 issues exist with diff. covers)
Four Color 1158-Movie, photo-c 6.30 19.00 75.00

THRILL COMICS (See Flash Comics, Fawcett)

THRILLER
DC Comics: Nov, 1983 - No. 12, Nov, 1984 ($1.25, Baxter paper)
1-12: 1-Intro Seven Seconds; Von Eeden-c/a begins. 2-Origin. 5,6-Elvis satire
2.00

THRILLING ADVENTURES IN STAMPS COMICS (Formerly Stamp Comics)
Stamp Comics, Inc. (Very Rare): V1#8, Jan, 1953 (25¢, 100 pgs.)

Thrilling Comics #70 © BP

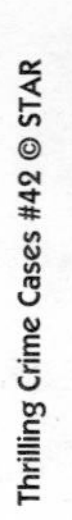
Thrilling Crime Cases #42 © STAR

Thrillkiller #1 © DC

V1#8-Harrison, Wildey, Kiefer, Napoli-a 71.00 213.00 675.00

THRILLING ADVENTURE STORIES (See Tigerman)
Atlas/Seaboard Publ.: Feb, 1975 - No. 2, Aug, 1975 (B&W, 68 pgs.)

1-Tigerman, Kromag the Killer begin; Heath, Thorne-a; Doc Savage movie photos of Ron Ely 2.00 6.00 16.00
2-Heath, Toth, Severin, Simonson-a; Adams-c 2.50 7.50 24.00

THRILLING COMICS
Better Publ./Nedor/Standard Comics: Feb, 1940 - No. 80, April, 1951

1-Origin & 1st app. Dr. Strange (37 pgs.), ends #?; Nickie Norton of the Secret Service begins 284.00 853.00 2700.00
2-The Rio Kid, The Woman in Red, Pinocchio begins 126.00 379.00 1200.00
3-The Ghost & Lone Eagle begin 79.00 237.00 750.00
4-6,8-10: 5-Dr. Strange changed to Doc Strange 61.00 182.00 575.00
7-Classic-c 74.00 221.00 700.00
11-18,20 53.00 158.00 475.00
19-Origin & 1st app. The American Crusader (8/41), ends #39,41 61.00 182.00 575.00
21-30: 24-Intro. Mike, Doc Strange's sidekick (1/42). 27-Robot-c. 29-Last Rio Kid 47.00 142.00 425.00
31-40: 36-Commando Cubs begin (7/43, 1st app.) 40.00 120.00 350.00
41-Hitler & Mussolini-c 63.00 189.00 600.00
42,43,45-52: 52-The Ghost ends. 45-Hitler pict. on-c 34.00 103.00 275.00
44-Hitler-c 58.00 174.00 550.00
53-The Phantom Detective begins; The Cavalier app.; no Commando Cubs 30.00 90.00 240.00
54-The Cavalier app.; no Commando Cubs 30.00 90.00 240.00
55-Lone Eagle ends 30.00 90.00 240.00
56-Princess Pantha begins (10/46, 1st app.) 46.00 137.00 410.00
57-66: 61-Ingels-a; The Lone Eagle app. 65-Last Phantom Detective & Commando Cubs. 66-Frazetta text illo 40.00 120.00 320.00
67,70-73: Frazetta-a(5-7 pgs.) in each. 72-Sea Eagle app.; Buck Ranger, Cowboy Detective begins 44.00 133.00 400.00
68,69-Frazetta-a(2), 8 & 6 pgs.; 9 & 7 pgs. 47.00 140.00 420.00
74-Last Princess Pantha; Tara app. 30.00 90.00 240.00
75-78: 75-All western format begins 14.00 43.00 115.00
79-Krigstein-a 15.00 45.00 120.00
80-Severin & Elder, Celardo, Moreira-a 15.00 45.00 120.00

NOTE: *Bondage c-5, 9, 13, 20, 22, 27-30, 38, 41, 52, 54, 70.* ***Kinstler*** *a-45.* ***Leo Morey*** *a-7.* ***Schomburg*** *(sometimes signed as* ***Xela****) c-7, 9-19, 36-80 (airbrush 62-71).* ***Tuska*** *a-62, 63. Woman in Red not in #19, 23, 31-33, 39-45. No. 45 exists as a Canadian reprint but numbered #48. No. 72 exists as a Canadian reprint with no* ***Frazetta*** *story.American Crusader c-20-24. Buck Ranger c-72-80. Commando Cubs c-37, 39, 41, 43, 45, 47, 49, 51. Doc Strange c-1-19, 25-36, 38, 40, 42, 44, 46, 48, 50, 52-57, 59. Princess Pantha c-58, 60-71.*

THRILLING COMICS (Also see All Star Comics 1999 crossover titles)
DC Comics: May, 1999 ($1.99, one-shot)

1-Golden Age Hawkman and Wildcat; Russ Heath-a 2.00

THRILLING CRIME CASES (Formerly 4Most; becomes Shocking Mystery Cases #50 on)
Star Publications: No. 41, June-July, 1950 - No. 49, July, 1952

41 28.00 84.00 225.00
42-45: 42-L. B. Cole-c/a (1); Chameleon story (Fox-r) 25.00 75.00 200.00
46-48: 47-Used in **POP**, pg. 84 24.00 71.00 190.00
49-(7/52)-Classic L. B. Cole-c 42.00 125.00 375.00

NOTE: ***L. B. Cole*** *c-all; a-43p, 45p, 46p, 49(2 pgs.).* ***Disbrow*** *a-48.* ***Hollingsworth*** *a-48.*

THRILLING ROMANCES
Standard Comics: No. 5, Dec, 1949 - No. 26, June, 1954

5 11.00 33.00 90.00
6,8 6.40 19.25 45.00
7-Severin/Elder-a (7 pgs.) 9.30 28.00 65.00
9,10-Severin/Elder-a; photo-c 7.85 23.50 55.00
11,14-21,26: 12-Tyrone Power/ Susan Hayward photo-c.14-Gene Tierney & Danny Kaye photo-c from movie "On the Riviera". 15-Tony Martin/Janet Leigh photo-c 5.00 15.00 35.00
12-Wood-a (2 pgs.) 10.00 30.00 75.00
13-Severin-a 6.40 19.25 45.0
22-25-Toth-a 8.65 26.00 60.0

NOTE: *All photo-c.* ***Celardo*** *a-9, 16.* ***Colletta*** *a-23, 24(2).* ***Toth*** *text illos-19.* ***Tuska*** *a-9.*

THRILLING SCIENCE TALES
AC Comics: 1989 - No. 2 ($3.50, 2/3 color, 52 pgs.)

1,2: 1-r/Bob Colt #6(saucer); Frazetta, Guardineer (Space Ace), Wood, Krenkel, Orlando, WIlliamson-r; Kaluta-c. 2-Capt. Video-r by Evans, Capt. Science-r by Wood, Star Pirate-r by Whitman & Mysta of the Moon-r by Moreira 4.0

THRILLING TRUE STORY OF THE BASEBALL...
Fawcett Publications: 1952 (Photo-c, each)

...Giants-photo-c; has Willie Mays rookie photo-biography; Willie Mays, Eddie Stanky & others photos on-c 66.00 197.00 625.0
...Yankees-photo-c; Yogi Berra, Joe DiMaggio, Mickey Mantle & others photos on-c 61.00 182.00 575.0

THRILLING WONDER TALES
AC Comics : 1991 ($2.95, B&W)

1-Includes a Bob Powell Thun'da story 3.0

THRILLKILLER
DC Comics : Jan, 1997 - No. 3, Mar, 1997($2.50, limited series)

1-3-Elseworlds Robin & Batgirl; Chaykin-s/Brereton-c/a 3.0
...'62 ('98, $4.95, one-shot) Sequel; Chaykin-s/Brereton-c/a 5.0
TPB-(See Batman: Thrillkiller)

THRILLOGY
Pacific Comics: Jan, 1984 (One-shot, color)

1-Conrad-c/a 3.0

THRILL-O-RAMA
Harvey Publications (Fun Films): Oct, 1965 - No. 3, Dec, 1966

1-Fate (Man in Black) by Powell app.; Doug Wildey-a(2); Simon-c 4.10 12.30 45.0
2-Pirana begins (see Phantom #46); Williamson 2 pgs.; Fate (Man in Black) app.; Tuska/Simon-c 3.00 9.00 30.0
3-Fate (Man in Black) app.; Sparling-c 2.50 7.50 25.0

THRILLS OF TOMORROW (Formerly Tomb of Terror)
Harvey Publications: No. 17, Oct, 1954 - No. 20, April, 1955

17-Powell-a (horror); r/Witches Tales #7 13.00 39.00 105.0
18-Powell-a (horror); r/Tomb of Terror #1 10.50 32.00 85.0
19,20-Stuntman-c/stories by S&K (r/from Stuntman #1 & 2); 19 has origin & is last pre-code (2/55) 33.00 98.00 260.0

NOTE: ***Kirby*** *c-19, 20.* ***Palais*** *a-17.* ***Simon*** *c-18?*

THROBBING LOVE (See Fox Giants)

THROUGH GATES OF SPLENDOR
Spire Christian Comics (Flemming H. Revell Co.): 1973, 1974 (36 pages) (3 49 cents)

nn 1.00 2.80 7.0

THUMPER (Disney)
Dell Publishing Co.: No, 19, 1942 - No. 243, Sept, 1949

Four Color 19-Walt Disney's...Meets the Seven Dwarfs; reprinted in Silly Symphonies 54.00 163.00 650.0
Four Color 243-...Follows His Nose 10.00 30.00 120.0

THUN'DA (...King of the Congo)
Magazine Enterprises: 1952 - No. 6, 1953

1(A-1 #47)-Origin; Frazetta c/a; only comic done entirely by Frazetta; all Thun'da stories, no Cave Girl 132.00 395.00 1250.0
2(A-1 #56)-Powell-c/a begins, ends #6; Intro/1st app. Cave Girl in filler strip (also app. in 3-6) 22.00 66.00 175.0
3(A-1 #73), 4(A-1 #78) 15.00 45.00 120.0
5(A-1 #83), 6(A-1 #86) 14.00 41.00 110.0

THUN'DA TALES (See Frank Frazetta's...)

THUNDER AGENTS (See Dynamo, Noman & Tales Of Thunder)
Tower Comics: 11/65 - No. 17, 12/67; No. 18, 9/68, No. 19, 11/68, No. 20, 11/69 (No. 1-16: 68 pgs.; No. 17 on: 52 pgs.)(All are 25¢)

Thunderbolts #2 © MAR

Thunderstrike #10 © MAR

The Tick #10 © Ben Edlund

GD2.0 FN6.0 NM9.4

Origin & 1st app. Dynamo, Noman, Menthor, & The Thunder Squad; 1st app. The Iron Maiden 18.00 54.00 200.00
Death of Egghead; A-bomb blast panel 10.00 30.00 110.00
5: 4-Guy Gilbert becomes Lightning who joins Thunder Squad; Iron Maiden app. 6.35 19.00 70.00
10: 7-Death of Menthor. 8-Origin & 1st app. The Raven 5.00 15.00 55.00
-15: 13-Undersea Agent app.; no Raven story 3.65 11.00 40.00
-19 3.65 11.00 40.00
-Special Collectors Edition; all reprints 2.50 7.50 25.00
TE: ***Crandall** a-1, 4p, 5p, 18, 20r; c-18. **Ditko** a-6, 7p, 12p, 13?, 14p, 16, 18. **Giunta** a-6. ne a-1, 5p, 6p?, 14, 16p; c-14, 15. **Reinman** a-13. **Sekowsky** a-6. **Tuska** a-1p, 7, 8, 10, 13-19. **Whitney** a-9p, 10, 13, 15, 17, 18; c-17. **Wood** a-1-11, 15(w/**Ditko**-12, 18), (inks-#9, 13, 16, 17), 19i, 20r; c-1-8, 9i, 10-13(#10 w/**Williamson**(p)), 16.*

.U.N.D.E.R. AGENTS (See Blue Ribbon Comics, Hall of Fame aturing the..., JCP Features & Wally Wood's...)
Comics (Archie Publications): May, 1983 - No. 2, Jan, 1984
2: 1-New Manna/Blyberg-c/a. 2-Blyberg-c 5.00

UNDER BIRDS (See Cinema Comics Herald)

UNDERBOLT (See The Atomic...)

UNDERBOLT (Peter Cannon...; see Crisis on Infinite Earths & Peter...)
arlton Comics: Jan, 1966; No. 51, Mar-Apr, 1966 - No. 60, Nov, 1967
-Origin & 1st app. Thunderbolt 3.00 9.00 32.00
-(Formerly Son of Vulcan #50) 2.40 7.35 22.00
-59: 54-Sentinels begin. 59-Last Thunderbolt & Sentinels (back-up story) 1.75 5.25 14.00
-Prankster app. 2.00 6.00 16.00
',58 ('77)-Modern Comics-r 4.00
TE: ***Aparo** a-60. **Morisi** a-1, 51-56, 58; c-1, 51-56, 58, 59.*

UNDERBOLTS (Also see Incredible Hulk #449)
rvel Comics: Apr, 1997 - Present ($1.95-$2.99)
-($2.99)-Busiek-s/Bagley-c/a 1.10 3.30 9.00
2nd printing; new cover colors 2.50
-4: 2-Two covers. 4-Intro. Jolt 2.40 6.00
-11: 9-Avengers app. 3.50
-($2.99)-Avengers and Fantastic Four-c/app. 4.00
-24: 14-Thunderbolts return to Earth. 21-Hawkeye app. 2.50
-($2.99) Wraparound-c 3.00
-38: 26-Manco-a 2.00
-($2.99) 100 Page Monster; Iron Man reprints 3.00
-47: 40-Begin $2.25-c; Sandman-c/app. 44-Avengers app. 47-Captain Marvel app. 2.25
nual '97 ($2.99)-Wraparound-c 3.00
nual 2000 ($3.50) Breyfogle-a 3.50
Distant Rumblings (#-1) (7/97, $1.95) Busiek-s 5.00
st Strikes (1997, $4.99,TPB) r/#1,2 5.00
Marvel's Most Wanted TPB ('98, $16.99) r/origin stories of original Masters of Evil 17.00
zard #0 (bagged with Wizard #89) 2.00

UNDERBUNNY (Also see Blue Ribbon Comics #13, Charlton Bullseye & Pep mics #393)
d Circle Comics: Jan, 1984 (Direct sale only)
aRP Graphics: Second series No. 1, 1985 - No. 6, 1985
ple Comics: No. 7, 1986 - No. 12, 1987
-Humor/parody; originThunderbunny; 2 page pin-up by Anderson 5.00
nd series) 1-12: 1,2-Magazine size 2.00

UNDERCATS (TV)
rvel Comics (Star Comics)/Marvel #22 on: Dec, 1985 - No. 24, June, 1988 5¢)
-Mooney-c/a begins 1.00 3.00 8.00
-20: 2-(65¢ & 75¢ cover exists). 12-Begin $1.00-c. 18-20-Williamson-i 2.40 6.00
-24: 23-Williamson-c(i) 1.00 2.80 7.00

UNDERGOD
usade Entertainment: July, 1996 - No. 3 ($2.95, B&W)
1-3: Christopher Golden scripts; painted-c 3.00

THUNDERGOD
Caliber Comics: 1997 ($2.95, B&W, one-shot)
1 3.00

THUNDER MOUNTAIN (See Zane Grey, Four Color #246)

THUNDERSTRIKE (See Thor #459)
Marvel Comics: June, 1993 - No. 24, July, 1995 ($1.25)
1-($2.95, 52 pgs.)-Holo-grafx lightning patterned foil-c; Bloodaxe returns 3.00
2-24: 2-Juggernaut-c/s. 4-Capt. America app. 4-6-Spider-Man app. 8-bound-in trading card sheet. 18-Bloodaxe app. 24-Death of Thunderstrike. 2.00
Marvel Double Feature...Thunderstrike/Code Blue #13 ($2.50)-Same as Thunderstrike #13 w/Code Blue flip book 2.50

TICK, THE (Also see The Chroma-Tick)
New England Comics Press: Jun, 1988 - No. 12, May, 1993 ($1.75/$1.95/$2.25; B&W, over-sized)
Special Edition 1-1st comic book app. serially numbered & limited to 5,000 copies 4.10 12.30 45.00
Special Edition 1-(5/96, $5.95)-Double-c; foil-c; serially numbered (5,001 thru 14,000) & limited to 9,000 copies 2.40 6.00
Special Edition 2-Serially numbered and limited to 3000 copies 3.65 11.00 40.00
Special Edition 2-(8/96, $5.95)-Double-c; foil-c; serially numbered (5,001 thru 14,000) & limited to 9,000 copies 1.00 3.00 8.00
1-Regular Edition 1st printing; reprints Special Ed. 1 w/minor changes 3.20 9.60 35.00
1-2nd printing 2.40 6.00
1-3rd-5th printing 3.00
2-Reprints Special Ed. 2 w/minor changes 2.00 6.00 16.00
2-8-All reprints 3.00
3-5 ($1.95): 4-1st app. Paul the Samurai 1.00 3.00 8.00
6,8 ($2.25) 4.00
7-1st app. Man-Eating Cow. 5.00
8-Variant with no logo, price, issue number or company logos. 2.00 6.00 16.00
9-12 ($2.75) 3.00
12-Special Edition; card-stock, virgin foil-c; numbered edition 2.30 7.00 20.00
Pseudo-Tick #13 (11/00, $3.50) Continues story from #12 (1993) 3.50
Promo Sampler-(1990)-Tick-c/story 1.00 3.00 8.00

TICK, THE (One shots)
--BIG BACK TO SCHOOL SPECIAL
1-(10/98, $3.50, B&W) Tick and Arthur undercover in high school 3.50
--BIG CRUISE SHIP VACATION SPECIAL
1-(9/00, $3.50, B&W) 3.50
--BIG FATHER'S DAY SPECIAL
1-(6/00, $3.50, B&W) 3.50
--BIG HALLOWEEN SPECIAL
1-(10/99, $3.50, B&W) 3.50
...2000 (10/00, $3.50) 3.50
--BIG MOTHER'S DAY SPECIAL
1-(4/00, $3.50, B&W) 3.50
--BIG SUMMER ANNUAL
1-(7/99, $3.50, B&W) Chainsaw Vigilante vs. Barry 3.50
--BIG SUMMER FUN SPECIAL
1-(8/98, $3.50, B&W) Tick and Arthur at summer camp 3.50
--BIG TAX TIME TERROR
1-(4/00, $3.50, B&W) 3.50
--BIG YEAR 2000 SPECTACLE
1-(3/00, $3.50, B&W) 3.50
--BIG YULE LOG SPECIAL
2001-(12/00, $3.50, B&W) 3.50
--MASSIVE SUMMER DOUBLE SPECTACLE
1,2-(7,8/00, $3.50, B&W) 3.50

Tick-Tock Tales #5 © ME

Timber Wolf #2 © DC

Timely Presents: Human Torch #1 © MAR

TICK'S BACK, THE
0-(8/97, $2.95, B&W) 3.00

TICK'S BIG ROMANTIC ADVENTURE, THE
1-(2/98, $2.95, B&W) Candy box cover with candy map on back 3.00

TICK AND ARTHUR, THE
New England Comics: Feb, 1999 - Present ($3.50, B&W)

1-6-Sean Wang-s/a 3.50

TICK BIG BLUE DESTINY, THE
New England Comics: Oct, 1997 - Present ($2.95)

1-4: 1-"Keen" Ed. 2-Two covers 3.00
1-($4.95) "Wicked Keen" Ed. w/die cut-c 5.00
5-($3.50) 3.50
6-Luny Bin Trilogy Preview #0 (7/98, $1.50) 2.00
7-9: 7-Luny Bin Trilogy begins 3.50

TICK BIG BLUE YULE LOG SPECIAL, THE
New England Comics: Dec, 1997; 1999 ($2.95, B&W)

1-"Jolly" and "Traditional" covers; flip book w/"Arthur Teaches the Tick About Hanukkah" 3.00
...1999 ($3.50) 3.50

TICK, THE : CIRCUS MAXIMUS
New England Comics: Mar, 2000 - No. 4, Jun, 2000 ($3.50, B&W)

1-4-Encyclopedia of characters from Tick comics 3.50

TICK, THE - HEROES OF THE CITY
New England Comics: Feb, 1999 - Present ($3.50, B&W)

1-6-Short stories by various 3.50

TICK KARMA TORNADO (The...)
New England Comics Press: Oct, 1993 - No. 9, Mar, 1995 ($2.75, B&W)

1-($3.25) 3.50
2-9: 2-$2.75-c begins 3.00

TICK'S GIANT CIRCUS OF THE MIGHTY, THE
New England Comics: Summer, 1992 - No. 3, Fall, 1993 ($2.75, B&W, magazine size)

1-(A-O). 2-(P-Z). 3-1993 Update 3.50

TICKLE COMICS (Also see Gay, Smile, & Whee Comics)
Modern Store Publ.: 1955 (7¢, 5x7-1/4", 52 pgs)

1 4.15 12.50 25.00

TICK TOCK TALES
Magazine Enterprises: Jan, 1946 - V3#33, Jan-Feb, 1951

1-Koko & Kola begin 12.50 37.50 100.00
2 7.15 21.50 50.00
3-10 6.00 18.00 42.00
11-33: 19-Flag-c. 23-Muggsy Mouse, The Pixies & Tom-Tom the Jungle Boy app. 25-The Pixies & Tom-Tom app. 5.00 15.00 35.00

TIGER (Also see Comics Reading Libraries)
Charlton Press (King Features): Mar, 1970 - No. 6, Jan, 1971 (15¢)

1 2.30 7.00 20.00
2-6 1.25 3.75 10.00

TIGER BOY (See Unearthly Spectaculars)

TIGER GIRL
Gold Key: Sept, 1968 (15¢)

1(10227-809)-Sparling-c/a; Jerry Siegel scripts 3.20 9.60 35.00

TIGERMAN (Also see Thrilling Adventure Stories)
Seaboard Periodicals (Atlas): Apr, 1975 - No. 3, Sept, 1975 (All 25¢ issues)

1-3: 1-Origin; Colan-c. 2,3-Ditko-p in each 2.40 6.00

TIGER WALKS, A (See Movie Comics)

TIGRESS, THE
Hero Graphics: Aug, 1992 - No. 6?, June, 1993 ($3.95/$2.95/$3.95, B&W)

1,6: 1-Tigress vs. Flare. 6-44 pgs. 4.00
2-5: 2-$2.95-c begins 3.00

TILLIE THE TOILER (See Comic Monthly)
Dell Publishing Co.: No. 15, 1941 - No. 237, July, 1949

Four Color 15(1941) 34.00 102.00 410.
Large Feature Comic 30(1941) 23.00 68.00 270.
Four Color 8(1942) 23.00 68.00 270.
Four Color 22(1943) 17.50 52.50 210.
Four Color 55(1944), 89(1945) 13.00 40.00 160.
Four Color 106('45),132('46): 132-New stories begin 9.50 29.00 115.
Four Color 150,176,184 8.75 26.25 105.
Four Color 195,213,237 6.30 19.00 75.

TIMBER WOLF (See Action Comics #372, & Legion of Super-Heroes)
DC Comics: Nov, 1992 - No. 5, Mar, 1993 ($1.25, limited series)

1-5 2.

TIME BANDITS
Marvel Comics Group: Feb, 1982 (one-shot, Giant)

1-Movie adaptation 4.

TIME BEAVERS (See First Comics Graphic Novel #2)

TIME BREAKERS
DC Comics (Helix): Jan, 1997 - No. 5, May, 1997 ($2.25, limited series)

1-5-Pollack-s 2.

TIMECOP (Movie)
Dark Horse Comics: Sept, 1994 - No. 2, Nov, 1994 ($2.50, limited series)

1,2-Adaptation of film 2.

TIME FOR LOVE (Formerly Romantic Secrets)
Charlton Comics: V2#53, Oct, 1966; Oct, 1967 - No. 47, May, 1976

V2#53(10/66) 2.00 6.00 18.
1(10/67) 3.00 9.00 32.
2(12/67)-10 2.40 7.35 22.
11-20 2.00 6.00 16.
21-29 1.50 4.50 12.
30-(10/72)-Full-length portrait of David Cassidy 2.40 7.35 22.
31-47 1.10 3.30 9.

TIMELESS TOPIX (See Topix)

TIMELY PRESENTS: ALL WINNERS
Marvel Comics: Dec, 1999 ($3.99)

1-Reprints All Winners Comics #19 (Fall 1946); new Lago-c 4.

TIMELY PRESENTS: HUMAN TORCH
Marvel Comics: Feb, 1999 ($3.99)

1-Reprints Human Torch Comics #5 (Fall 1941); new Lago-c 4.

TIME MACHINE, THE
Dell Publishing Co.: No. 1085, Mar, 1960 (H.G. Wells)

Four Color 1085-Movie, Alex Toth-a; Rod Taylor photo-c 15.00 45.00 175.

TIME MASTERS
DC Comics: Feb, 1990 - No. 8, Sept, 1990 ($1.75, mini-series)

1-8: New Rip Hunter series. 5-Cave Carson, Viking Prince app. 6-Dr. Fate app. 2.

TIMESLIP COLLECTION
Marvel Comics: Nov, 1998 ($2.99, one-shot)

1-Pin-ups reprinted from Marvel Vision magazine 3.

TIMESLIP SPECIAL (The Coming of the Avengers)
Marvel Comics: Oct, 1998 ($5.99, one-shot)

1-Alternate world Avengers vs. Odin 6.

TIMESPIRITS
Marvel Comics (Epic Comics): Oct, 1984 - No. 8, Mar, 1986 ($1.50, Baxter paper, direct sales)

1-8: 4-Williamson-a 2.

TIME TUNNEL, THE (TV)
Gold Key: Feb, 1967 - No. 2, July, 1967 (12¢)

1-Photo back-c on both issues 5.35 16.00 65.

Tim Holt #21 © ME

Tim Tyler Cowboy #13 © KFS

Tiny Tot Comics #3 © EC

GD2.0 FN6.0 NM9.4

2 4.60 13.75 55.00

TIME TWISTERS
Quality Comics: Sept, 1987 - No. 21, 1989 ($1.25/$1.50)

1-21: Alan Moore scripts in 1-4, 6-9, 14 (2 pg.). 14-Bolland-a (2 pg.). 15,16 Guice-c 2.00

TIME 2: THE EPIPHANY (See First Comics Graphic Novel #9)

TIMEWALKER (Also see Archer & Armstrong)
Valiant: Jan, 1994 - No. 15, Oct, 1995 ($2.50)

1-15,0(3/96): 2-"JAN" on-c, February, 1995 in indicia. 2.50
Yearbook 1 (5/95, $2.95) 3.00

TIME WARP (See The Unexpected #210)
DC Comics, Inc.: Oct-Nov, 1979 - No. 5, June-July, 1980 ($1.00, 68 pgs.)

1 1.25 3.75 10.00
2-5 1.00 3.00 8.00
NOTE: ***Aparo** a-1. **Buckler** a-1p. **Chaykin** a-2. **Ditko** a-1-4. **Kaluta** c-1-5. **G. Kane** a-2. **Nasser** a-4. **Newton** a-1-5p. **Orlando** a-2. **Sutton** a-1-3.*

TIME WARRIORS: THE BEGINNING
Fantasy General Comics: 1986 (Aug) - No. 2, 1986? ($1.50)

1,2-Alpha Track/Skellon Empire 2.00

TIM HOLT (Movie star) (Becomes Red Mask #42 on; also see Crack Western #72, & Great Western)
Magazine Enterprises: 1948 - No. 41, April-May, 1954 (All 36 pgs.)

1-(A-1 #14)-Line drawn-c w/Tim Holt photo on-c; Tim Holt, His horse Lightning & sidekick Chito begin 63.00 189.00 600.00
2-(A-1 #17)(9-10/48)-Photo-c begin, end #18 36.00 108.00 290.00
3-(A-1 #19)-Photo back-c 28.00 83.00 220.00
4(1-2/49),5: 5-Photo front/back-c 20.00 60.00 160.00
6-(5/49)-1st app. The Calico Kid (alias Rex Fury), his horse Ebony & Sidekick Sing-Song (begin series); photo back-c 34.00 101.00 270.00
7-10: 7-Calico Kid by Ayers. 8-Calico Kid by Guardineer (r-in/Great Western #10). 9-Map of Tim's Home Range 17.00 51.00 135.00
11-The Calico Kid becomes The Ghost Rider (origin & 1st app.) by Dick Ayers (r-in/Great Western I.W. #8); his horse Spectre & sidekick Sing-Song begin series 41.00 122.00 365.00
12-16,18-Last photo-c 12.50 37.50 100.00
17-Frazetta Ghost Rider-c 38.00 113.00 300.00
19,22,24: 19-Last Tim Holt-c; Bolle line-drawn-c begin; Tim Holt photo on covers #19-28,30-41. 22-interior photo-c 11.00 33.00 90.00
20-Tim Holt becomes Redmask (origin); begin series; Redmask-c #20-on 17.00 51.00 135.00
21-Frazetta Ghost Rider/Redmask-c 33.00 98.00 260.00
23-Frazetta Redmask-c 28.00 84.00 225.00
25-1st app. Black Phantom 20.00 60.00 160.00
26-30: 28-Wild Bill Hickok, Bat Masterson team up with Redmask. 29-B&W photo-c 10.00 30.00 75.00
31-33-Ghost Rider ends 10.00 30.00 70.00
34-Tales of the Ghost Rider begins (horror)-Classic "The Flower Women" & "Hard Boiled Harry!" 12.00 36.00 95.00
35-Last Tales of the Ghost Rider 10.00 30.00 75.00
36-The Ghost Rider returns, ends #41; liquid hallucinogenic drug story 11.00 33.00 90.00
37-Ghost Rider classic "To Touch Is to Die!", about Inca treasure 11.00 33.00 90.00
38-The Black Phantom begins (not in #39); classic Ghost Rider "The Phantom Guns of Feather Gap!" 11.00 33.00 90.00
39-41: All 3-D effect c/stories 14.00 41.00 110.00
NOTE: ***Dick Ayers** a-7, 9-41. **Bolle** a-1-41; c-19, 20, 22, 24-28, 30-41.*

TIM McCOY (Formerly Zoo Funnies; Pictorial Love Stories #22 on)
Charlton Comics: No. 16, Oct, 1948 - No. 21, Aug, 1949 (Western Movie Stories)

16-John Wayne, Montgomery Clift app. in "Red River"; photo back-c 42.00 125.00 375.00
17-21: 17-Allan "Rocky" Lane guest stars. 18-Rod Cameron guest stars. 19-Whip Wilson, Andy Clyde guest star; Jesse James story. 20-Jimmy Wakely guest stars. 21-Johnny Mack Brown guest stars 40.00 120.00 325.00

GD2.0 FN6.0 NM9.4

TIMMY
Dell Publishing Co.: No. 715, Aug, 1956 - No. 1022, Aug-Oct, 1959

Four Color 715 (#1) 3.20 9.60 35.00
Four Color 823 (8/57), 923 (8/58), 1022 2.50 7.50 24.00

TIMMY THE TIMID GHOST (Formerly Win-A-Prize?; see Blue Bird)
Charlton Comics: No. 3, 2/56 - No. 44, 10/64; No. 45, 9/66; 10/67 - No. 23, 7/71; V4#24, 9/85 - No. 26, 1/86

3(1956) (1st Series) 10.00 30.00 70.00
4,5 5.00 15.00 35.00
6-10 2.50 7.50 24.00
11,12(4/58,10/58)(100 pgs.) 5.90 17.75 65.00
13-20 2.30 7.00 20.00
21-45(1966) 1.85 5.50 15.00
1(10/67, 2nd series) 2.00 6.00 18.00
2-10 1.50 4.50 12.00
11-23 1.10 3.30 9.00
24-26 (1985-86): Fago-r 4.00

TIM TYLER (See Harvey Comics Hits #54)

TIM TYLER (Also see Comics Reading Libraries)
Better Publications: 1942

1 12.50 37.50 100.00

TIM TYLER COWBOY
Standard Comics (King Features Synd.): No. 11, Nov, 1948 - No. 18, 1950

11-By Lyman Young 8.65 26.00 60.00
12-18: 13-15-Full length western adventures 6.00 18.00 42.00

TINCAN MAN
Image Comics: Jan, 2000 - No. 3, Mar, 2000 ($2.95, limited series)

1-3-Thornton-s/Dietrich Smith & Pierre Andre-Dery-a 2.95

TINKER BELL (Disney, TV)(See Walt Disney Showcase #37)
Dell Publishing Co.: No. 896, Mar, 1958 - No. 982, Apr-June, 1959

Four Color 896 (#1)-The Adventures of... 8.00 24.00 95.00
Four Color 982-The New Advs. of... 7.50 22.50 90.00

TINY FOLKS FUNNIES
Dell Publishing Co.: No. 60, 1944

Four Color 60 15.00 45.00 180.00

TINY TESSIE (Tessie #1-23; Real Experiences #25)
Marvel Comics (20CC): No. 24, Oct, 1949 (52 pgs.)

24 9.30 28.00 65.00

TINY TIM (Also see Super Comics)
Dell Publishing Co.: No. 4, 1941 - No. 235, July, 1949

Large Feature Comic 4('41) 31.00 94.00 375.00
Four Color 20(1941) 28.00 85.00 340.00
Four Color 42(1943) 17.00 50.00 200.00
Four Color 235 4.10 12.30 45.00

TINY TOT COMICS
E. C. Comics: Mar, 1946 - No. 10, Nov-Dec, 1947 (For younger readers)

1(nn)-52 pg. issues begin, end #4 36.00 108.00 290.00
2 (5/46) 21.00 64.00 170.00
3-10: 10-Christmas-c 19.00 56.00 150.00

TINY TOT FUNNIES (Formerly Family Funnies; becomes Junior Funnies)
Harvey Publ. (King Features Synd.): No. 9, June, 1951

9-Flash Gordon, Mandrake, Dagwood, Daisy, etc. 6.40 19.25 45.00

TINY TOTS COMICS
Dell Publishing Co.: 1943 (Not reprints)

1-Kelly-a(2); fairy tales 40.00 120.00 350.00

TIPPY & CAP STUBBS (See Popular Comics)
Dell Publishing Co.: No. 210, Jan, 1949 - No. 242, Aug, 1949

Four Color 210 (#1) 4.10 12.30 45.00
Four Color 242 3.20 9.60 35.00

TIPPY'S FRIENDS GO-GO & ANIMAL

Tip Top Comics #34 © UFS

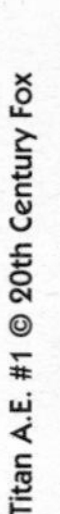

Titan A.E. #1 © 20th Century Fox

Titans #2 © DC

Tower Comics: July, 1966 - No. 15, Oct, 1969 (25¢)

	GD2.0	FN6.0	NM9.4
1	5.45	16.35	60.00
2-5,7,9-15: 12-15 titled "Tippy's Friend Go-Go"	3.00	9.00	30.00
6-The Monkees photo-c	5.45	16.35	60.00
8-Beatles app. on front/back-c	9.00	27.00	100.00

TIPPY TEEN (See Vicki)
Tower Comics: Nov, 1965 - No. 27, Feb, 1970 (25¢)

	GD2.0	FN6.0	NM9.4
1	5.45	16.35	60.00
2-4,6-10	3.20	9.60	35.00
5-1 pg. Beatles pin-up	3.65	11.00	40.00
11-20: 16-Twiggy photo-c	3.00	9.00	30.00
21-27	2.50	7.50	24.00
Special Collectors' Editions nn-(1969, 25¢)	3.20	9.60	35.00

TIPPY TERRY
Super/I. W. Enterprises: 1963

	GD2.0	FN6.0	NM9.4
Super Reprint #14('63)-r/Little Groucho #1	1.50	4.50	12.00
I.W. Reprint #1 (nd)-r/Little Groucho #1	1.50	4.50	12.00

TIP TOP COMICS
United Features #1-187/St. John #188-210/Dell Publishing Co. #211 on: 4/36 - No. 210, 1957; No. 211, 11-1/57-58 - No. 225, 5-7/61

	GD2.0	FN6.0	NM9.4
1-Tarzan by Hal Foster, Li'l Abner, Broncho Bill, Fritzi Ritz, Ella Cinders, Capt. & The Kids begin; strip-r (1st comic book app. of each)	938.00	2813.00	7500.00
2	213.00	638.00	1700.00
3-Tarzan-c	200.00	600.00	1600.00
4	113.00	338.00	900.00
5-8,10: 7-Photo & biography of Edgar Rice Burroughs. 8-Christmas-c	81.00	244.00	650.00
9-Tarzan-c	103.00	309.00	825.00
11,13,16,18-Tarzan-c: 11-Has Tarzan pin-up	80.00	240.00	640.00
12,14,15,17,19,20: 20-Christmas-c	65.00	195.00	520.00
21,24,27,30-(10/38)-Tarzan-c	65.00	195.00	520.00
22,23,25,26,28,29	44.00	131.00	350.00
31,35,38,40	40.00	120.00	320.00
32,36-Tarzan-c: 32-1st published Jack Davis-a (cartoon). 36-Kurtzman panel (1st published comic work)	53.00	158.00	475.00
33,34,37,39-Tarzan-c	50.00	150.00	450.00
41-Reprints 1st Tarzan Sunday; Tarzan-c	53.00	158.00	475.00
42,44,46,48,49	34.00	103.00	275.00
43,45,47,50,52-Tarzan-c. 43-Mort Walker panel	40.00	120.00	340.00
51,53	33.00	99.00	265.00
54-Origin Mirror Man & Triple Terror, also featured on cover	40.00	120.00	320.00
55,56,58,60: Last Tarzan by Foster	26.00	79.00	210.00
57,59,61,62-Tarzan by Hogarth	33.00	99.00	265.00
63-80: 65,67-70,72-74,77,78-No Tarzan	16.00	49.00	130.00
81-90	14.00	41.00	110.00
91-99	12.00	36.00	95.00
100	13.00	39.00	105.00
101-140: 110-Gordo story. 111-Li'l Abner app. 118, 132-No Tarzan. 137-Sadie Hawkins Day story	8.65	26.00	60.00
141-170: 145,151-Gordo stories. 157-Last Li'l Abner; lingerie panels	6.00	18.00	42.00
171-188-Tarzan reprints by B. Lubbers in all. 177-Peanuts by Schulz begins?; no Peanuts in #178,179,181-183	6.40	19.25	45.00
189-225	5.00	15.00	30.00
Bound Volumes (Very Rare) sold at 1939 World's Fair; bound by publisher in pictorial comic boards (also see Comics on Parade)			
Bound issues 1-12	253.00	758.00	2400.00
Bound issues 13-24	132.00	395.00	1250.00
Bound issues 25-36	116.00	348.00	1100.00

NOTE: *Tarzan by* ***Foster***-*#1-40, 44-50; by* ***Rex Maxon***-*#41-43; by* ***Burne Hogarth***-*#57, 59, 62.*

TIP TOPPER COMICS
United Features Syndicate: Oct-Nov, 1949 - No. 28, 1954

	GD2.0	FN6.0	NM9.4
1-Li'l Abner, Abbie & Slats	10.00	30.00	70.00
2	6.00	18.00	42.00
3-5: 5-Fearless Fosdick app.	5.00	15.00	35.00
6-10: 6-Fearless Fosdick app.	5.00	15.00	30.00
11-25: 17-22,24,26-Peanuts app. (2 pgs.)	4.00	12.00	24.00
26-28-Twin Earths	5.00	15.00	35.00

NOTE: *Many lingerie panels in Fritzi Ritz stories.*

TITAN A.E.
Dark Horse Comics: May, 2000 - No. 3, July, 2000 ($2.95, limited series)

	GD2.0	FN6.0	NM9.4
1-3-Movie prequel; Al Rio-a			3.00

TITANS (Also see Teen Titans, New Teen Titans and New Titans)
DC Comics: Mar, 1999 - Present ($2.50)

	GD2.0	FN6.0	NM9.4
1-Titans re-form; Grayson-s; 2 covers			2.50
2-11,13-24: 2-Superman-c/app. 9,10,21,22-Deathstroke app. 24-Titans from "Kingdom Come" app.			2.50
12-($3.50, 48 pages)			3.50
25-($3.95) Titans from "Kingdom Come" app.; Wolfman & Faerber-s; art by Pérez, Cardy, Grummett, Jimenez, Dodson, Pelletier			4.00
Annual 1 ('00, $3.50) Planet DC; intro Bushido			3.50
...Secret Files 1,2 (3/99, 10/00; $4.95) Profile pages & short stories			5.00

TITANS/ LEGION OF SUPER-HEROES: UNIVERSE ABLAZE
DC Comics: 2000 - No. 4, 2000 ($4.95, prestige format, limited series)

	GD2.0	FN6.0	NM9.4
1-4-Jurgens-s/a; P. Jimenez-a; teams battle Universo			5.00

TITAN SPECIAL
Dark Horse Comics: June, 1994 ($3.95, one-shot)

	GD2.0	FN6.0	NM9.4
1-($3.95, 52 pgs.)			4.00

TITANS: SCISSORS, PAPER, STONE
DC Comics: 1997 ($4.95, one-shot)

	GD2.0	FN6.0	NM9.4
1-Manga style Elseworlds; Adam Warren-s/a(p)			5.00

TITANS SELL-OUT SPECIAL
DC Comics: Nov, 1992 ($3.50, 52 pgs., one-shot)

	GD2.0	FN6.0	NM9.4
1-Fold-out Nightwing poster; 1st Teeny Titans			3.50

T-MAN (Also see Police Comics #103)
Quality Comics Group: Sept, 1951 - No. 38, Dec, 1956

	GD2.0	FN6.0	NM9.4
1-Pete Trask, T-Man begins; Jack Cole-a	40.00	120.00	320.00
2-Crandall-c	21.00	64.00	170.00
3,7,8: All Crandall-c	19.00	56.00	150.00
4,5-Crandall-c/a each	20.00	60.00	160.00
6-"The Man Who Could Be Hitler" c/story; Crandall-c.	21.00	64.00	170.00
9,10-Crandall-c	16.00	49.00	130.00
11-Used in **POP**, pg. 95 & color illo.	12.00	36.00	95.00
12,13,15-19,21,22-26: 21- "The Return of Mussolini" c/story. 23-H-Bomb panel. 24-Last pre-code issue (4/55). 25-Not Crandall-a	10.00	30.00	75.00
14-Hitler-c	12.00	36.00	95.00
20-H-Bomb explosion-c/story	13.00	39.00	105.00
27-38	10.00	30.00	70.00

NOTE: *Anti-communist stories common.* ***Crandall*** *c-2-10p.* ***Cuidera*** *c(i)-1-38. Bondage c-15.*

TMNT MUTANT UNIVERSE SOURCEBOOK
Archie Comics: 1992 - No. 3, 1992? ($1.95, 52 pgs.)(Lists characters from A-Z)

	GD2.0	FN6.0	NM9.4
1-3: 3-New characters; fold-out poster			2.00

TNT COMICS
Charles Publishing Co.: Feb, 1946 (36 pgs.)

	GD2.0	FN6.0	NM9.4
1-Yellowjacket app.	30.00	90.00	240.00

TOBY TYLER (Disney, see Movie Comics)
Dell Publishing Co.: No. 1092, Apr-June, 1960

	GD2.0	FN6.0	NM9.4
Four Color 1092-Movie, photo-c	5.85	17.50	70.00

TODAY'S BRIDES
Ajax/Farrell Publishing Co.: Nov, 1955; No. 2, Feb, 1956; No. 3, Sept, 1956; No. 4, Nov, 1956

	GD2.0	FN6.0	NM9.4
1	7.85	23.50	55.00
2-4	5.00	15.00	35.00

TODAY'S ROMANCE
Standard Comics: No. 5, March, 1952 - No. 8, Sept, 1952 (All photo-c?)

Today's Romance #5 © STD

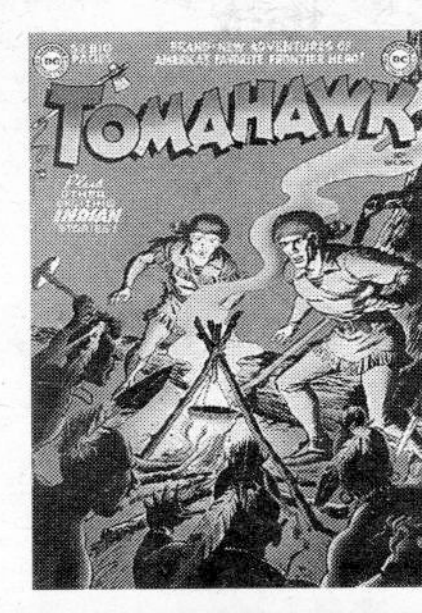

Tomahawk #1 © DC

Tomb of Dracula #66 © MAR

GD2.0 FN6.0 NM9.4

5-Photo-c 7.85 23.50 55.00
6-Photo-c; Toth-a 8.65 26.00 60.00
7,8 5.00 15.00 35.00

TOKA (Jungle King)
Dell Publishing Co.: Aug-Oct, 1964 - No. 10, Jan, 1967 (Painted-c #1,2)

1 3.20 9.60 35.00
2 2.30 7.00 20.00
3-10 2.00 6.00 16.00

TOMAHAWK (Son of... on-c of #131-140; see Star Spangled Comics #69 & World's Finest Comics #65)
National Periodical Publications: Sept-Oct, 1950 - No. 140, May-June, 1972

1-Tomahawk & boy sidekick Dan Hunter begin by Fred Ray
158.00 474.00 1500.00
2-Frazetta/Williamson-a (4 pgs.) 63.00 189.00 600.00
3-5 40.00 120.00 360.00
6-10: 7-Last 52 pg. issue 31.00 94.00 250.00
11-20 23.00 69.00 185.00
21-27,30: 30-Last precode (2/55) 19.00 56.00 150.00
28-1st app. Lord Shilling (arch-foe) 20.00 60.00 160.00
29-Frazetta-r/Jimmy Wakely #3 (3 pgs.) 25.00 75.00 200.00
31-40 11.00 33.00 120.00
41-50 8.65 26.00 95.00
51-56,58-60 6.35 19.00 70.00
57-Frazetta-r/Jimmy Wakely #6 (3 pgs.) 9.50 28.50 105.00
61-77: 77-Last 10¢ issue 5.00 15.00 55.00
78-85: 81-1st app. Miss Liberty. 83-Origin Tomahawk's Rangers
3.65 11.00 40.00
86-99: 96-Origin/1st app. The Hood, alias Lady Shilling
2.80 8.40 28.00
100 3.00 9.00 32.00
101-110: 107-Origin/1st app. Thunder-Man 2.40 7.35 22.00
111-115,120,122: 122-Last 12¢ issue 2.30 7.00 20.00
116-119,121,123-130-Neal Adams-c 2.40 7.35 22.00
131-Frazetta-r/Jimmy Wakely #7 (3 pgs.); origin Firehair retold
2.50 7.50 23.00
132-135: 135-Last 15¢ issue 1.85 5.50 15.00
136-138,140 (52 pg. Giants) 2.30 7.00 20.00
139-Frazetta-r/Star Spangled #113 2.50 7.50 23.00

NOTE: ***Fred Ray*** *c-1, 2, 8, 11, 30, 34, 35, 40-43, 45, 46, 82. Firehair by* ***Kubert****-131-134, 136.* ***Maurer*** *a-138.* ***Severin*** *a-135.* ***Starr*** *a-5.* ***Thorne*** *a-137, 140.*

TOM AND JERRY (See Comic Album #4, 8, 12, Dell Giant #21, Dell Giants, Golden Comics Digest #1, 5, 8, 13, 15, 18, 22, 25, 28, 35, Kite fun Book & March of Comics #21, 46, 61, 70, 88, 103, 119, 128, 145, 154, 173, 190, 207, 224, 281, 295, 305, 321,333, 345, 361, 365, 388, 400, 444, 451, 463, 480)

TOM AND JERRY (...Comics, early issues) (M.G.M.)
(Formerly Our Gang No. 1-59) (See Dell Giants for annuals)
Dell Publishing Co./Gold Key No. 213-327/Whitman No. 328 on:
No. 193, 6/48; No. 60, 7/49 - No. 212, 7-9/62; No. 213, 11/62 - No. 291, 2/75; No. 292, 3/77 - No. 342, 5/82 - No. 344, 4/83

Four Color 193 (#1)-Titled "M.G.M. Presents..." 15.00 45.00 180.00
60-Barney Bear, Benny Burro cont. from Our Gang; Droopy begins
7.50 22.50 90.00
61 6.70 20.00 80.00
62-70: 66-X-Mas-c 5.00 15.00 60.00
71-80: 77,90-X-Mas-c. 79-Spike & Tyke begin 4.55 13.65 50.00
81-99 3.60 11.00 40.00
100 4.10 12.30 45.00
101-120 3.20 9.60 35.00
121-140: 126-X-Mas-c 3.00 9.00 32.00
141-160 2.80 8.40 28.00
161-200 2.50 7.50 25.00
201-212(7-9/62)(Last Dell issue) 2.40 7.35 22.00
213,214-(84 pgs.)-Titled "...Funhouse" 5.00 15.00 60.00
215-240: 215-Titled "...Funhouse" 2.30 7.00 20.00
241-270 2.00 6.00 16.00
271-300: 286- "Tom & Jerry" 1.25 3.75 10.00
301-327 (Gold Key) 2.40 6.00
328,329 (Whitman) 1.00 2.80 7.00

GD2.0 FN6.0 NM9.4

330(8/80),331(10/80), 332-(3-pack?) 1.75 5.25 14.00
333-341 1.00 3.00 8.00
342-344-All #90058, no date or date code (3-pack?) 1.25 3.75 10.00
Mouse From T.R.A.P. 1(7/66)-Giant, G. K. 3.65 11.00 40.00
Summer Fun 1(7/67, 68 pgs.)(Gold Key)-Reprints Barks' Droopy from Summer Fun #1 3.65 11.00 40.00

NOTE: *#60-87, 98-121, 268, 277, 289, 302 are 52 pgs.. Reprints-#225, 241, 245, 247, 252, 254, 266, 268, 270, 292-327, 329-342, 344.*

TOM & JERRY
Harvey Comics: Sept, 1991 - No. 4, 1992 ($1.25)

1-4: 1-Tom & Jerry, Barney Bear-r by Carl Barks 3.00
50th Anniversary Special 1 (10/91, $2.50, 68 pgs.)-Benny the Lonesome Burro-r by Barks (story/a)/Our Gang #9 3.00

TOMB OF DARKNESS (Formerly Beware)
Marvel Comics Group: No. 9, July, 1974 - No. 23, Nov, 1976

9 2.30 7.00 20.00
10-23: 11,16,18-21-Kirby-a. 15,19-Ditko-r. 17-Woodbridge-r/Astonishing #62; Powell-r. 20-Everett Venus-r/Venus #19. 22-r/Tales To Astonish #27; 1st Hank Pym. 23-Everett-r 1.50 4.50 12.00
20,21-(30¢-c variants, limited distribution)(5,7/76) 2.00 6.00 16.00

TOMB OF DRACULA (See Giant-Size Dracula, Dracula Lives, Nightstalkers, Power Record Comics & Requiem for Dracula)
Marvel Comics Group: Apr, 1972 - No. 70, Aug, 1979

1-1st app. Dracula & Frank Drake; Colan-p in all 11.00 33.00 120.00
2 4.55 13.65 50.00
3-5: 3-Intro. Dr. Rachel Van Helsing & Inspector Chelm
3.20 9.60 35.00
6-9 2.80 8.40 28.00
10-1st app. Blade the Vampire Slayer 4.55 13.65 50.00
11,12,14-20: 12-Brunner-c(p) 2.00 6.00 18.00
13-Origin Blade 2.80 8.40 28.00
21-24,26-40 1.75 5.25 14.00
25-1st app. & origin Hannibal King 2.00 6.00 16.00
41,42,48,49,51-60 1.10 3.30 9.00
43-47-(Regular 25¢ editions)(4-8/76) 1.10 3.30 9.00
43-47-(30¢-c variants, limited distribution) 1.75 5.25 14.00
50-Silver Surfer app. 1.75 5.25 14.00
61-69 1.10 3.30 9.00
70-Double size 1.50 4.50 12.00

NOTE: ***N. Adams*** *c-1, 6.* ***Colan*** *a-1-70p; c(p)-8, 38-42, 44-56, 58-70.* ***Wrightson*** *c-43.*

TOMB OF DRACULA, THE (Magazine)
Marvel Comics Group: Oct, 1979 - No. 6, Aug, 1980 (B&W)

1,3: 1-Colan-a; features on movies "Dracula" and "Love at First Bite" w/photos. 3-Good girl cover-a; Miller-a (2 pg. sketch) 1.00 2.80 7.00
2,6: 2-Ditko-a (36 pgs.); Nosferatu movie feature. 6-Lilith story w/Sienkiewicz-a 5.00
4,5: Stephen King interview 1.10 3.30 9.00

NOTE: ***Buscema*** *a-4p, 5p.* ***Chaykin*** *c-5, 6.* ***Colan*** *a(p)-1, 3-6.* ***Miller*** *a-3.* ***Romita*** *a-2p.*

TOMB OF DRACULA
Marvel Comics (Epic Comics): 1991 - No. 4, 1992 ($4.95, 52 pgs., squarebound, mini-series)

Book 1-4: Colan/Williamson-a; Colan painted-c 5.00

TOMB OF LEGEIA (See Movie Classics)

TOMB OF TERROR (Thrills of Tomorrow #17 on)
Harvey Publications: June, 1952 - No. 16, July, 1954

1 40.00 120.00 360.00
2 24.00 71.00 190.00
3-Bondage-c; atomic disaster story 25.00 75.00 200.00
4-12: 4-Heart ripped out. 8-12-Nostrand-a 23.00 69.00 185.00
13,14-Special S/F issues. 14-Check-a 30.00 90.00 240.00
15-S/F issue; c-shows face exploding 43.00 128.00 385.00
16-Special S/F issue; Nostrand-a 28.00 84.00 225.00

NOTE: ***Edd Cartier*** *a-13?* ***Elias*** *c-2, 5-16.* ***Kremer*** *a-1, 7; c-1.* ***Nostrand*** *a-8-12, 15r 16.* ***Palais*** *a-2, 3, 5-7.* ***Powell*** *a-1, 3, 5, 9-16.* ***Sparling*** *a-12, 13, 15.*

TOMB RAIDER: THE SERIES (Also see Witchblade/Tomb Raider)
Image Comics (Top Cow Prod.): Dec, 1999 - Present ($2.50)

Tomb Raider: The Series #2 © Eidos

Tom Mix Western #20 © FAW

Tom Strong #6 © ABC

GD2.0 FN6.0 NM9.4

1-Jurgens-s/Park-a; 3 covers by Park, Finch, Turner 3.00
2-10 2.50
...Gallery (12/00, $2.95) Pin-ups & previous covers by various 3.00
...: Saga of the Medusa Mask (9/00, $9.95, TPB) r/#1-4; new Park-c 10.00

TOMB RAIDER/WITCHBLADE SPECIAL (Also see Witchblade/Tomb Raider)
Top Cow Prod.: Dec, 1997 (mail-in offer, one-shot)

1-Turner-s/a(p); green background cover 1.25 3.75 10.00
1-Variant-c with orange sun background 1.25 3.75 10.00
1-Variant-c with black sides 1.25 3.75 10.00
1-Revisited (12/98, $2.95) reprints #1, Turner-c 3.00

TOMBSTONE TERRITORY (See Four Color #1123)

TOM CAT (Formerly Bo; Atom The Cat #9 on)
Charlton Comics: No. 4, Apr, 1956 - No. 8, July, 1957

4-Al Fago-c/a 7.15 21.50 50.00
5-8 5.00 15.00 35.00

TOM CORBETT, SPACE CADET (TV)
Dell Publishing Co.: No. 378, Jan-Feb, 1952 - No. 11, Sept-Nov, 1954
(All painted covers)

Four Color 378 (#1)-McWilliams-a 17.00 50.00 200.00
Four Color 400,421-McWilliams-a 9.00 27.00 110.00
4(11-1/53) - 11 6.70 20.00 80.00

TOM CORBETT SPACE CADET (See March of Comics #102)

TOM CORBETT SPACE CADET (TV)
Prize Publications: V2#1, May-June, 1955 - V2#3, Sept-Oct, 1955

V2#1-Robot-c 31.00 94.00 250.00
2,3-Meskin-c 25.00 75.00 200.00

TOM, DICK & HARRIET (See Gold Key Spotlight)

TOM LANDRY AND THE DALLAS COWBOYS
Spire Christian Comics/Fleming H. Revell Co.: 1973 (35/49¢)

nn-35¢ edition 1.50 4.50 12.00
nn-49¢ edition 1.00 3.00 8.00

TOM MIX WESTERN (Movie, radio star) (Also see The Comics, Crackajack Funnies, Master Comics, 100 Pages Of Comics, Popular Comics, Real Western Hero, Six Gun Heroes, Western Hero & XMas Comics)
Fawcett Publications: Jan, 1948 - No. 61, May, 1953 (1-17: 52 pgs.)

1 (Photo-c, 52 pgs.)-Tom Mix & his horse Tony begin; Tumbleweed Jr. begins, ends #52,54,55 100.00 300.00 950.00
2 (Photo-c) 42.00 125.00 375.00
3-5 (Painted/photo-c): 5-Billy the Kid & Oscar app. 34.00 103.00 275.00
6-8: 6,7 (Painted/photo-c). 8-Kinstler tempera-c 29.00 86.00 230.00
9,10 (Painted/photo-c)-Used in **SOTI**, pgs. 323-325 28.00 83.00 220.00
11-Kinstler oil-c 24.00 71.00 190.00
12 (Painted/photo-c) 21.00 64.00 170.00
13-17 (Painted-c, 52 pgs.) 21.00 64.00 170.00
18,22 (Painted-c, 36 pgs.) 18.00 53.00 140.00
19 (Photo-c, 52 pgs.) 19.00 56.00 150.00
20,21,23 (Painted-c, 52 pgs.) 18.00 53.00 140.00
24,25,27-29 (52 pgs.): 24-Photo-c begin, end #61. 29-Slim Pickens app. 14.00 43.00 115.00
26,30 (36 pgs.) 13.00 39.00 105.00
31-33,35-37,39,40,42 (52 pgs.): 39-Red Eagle app. 12.50 37.50 100.00
34,38 (36 pgs. begin) 11.00 33.00 90.00
41,43-60: 57-(9/52)-Dope smuggling story 9.30 28.00 65.00
61-Last issue 10.00 30.00 80.00

NOTE: *Photo-c from 1930s Tom Mix movies (he died in 1940). Many issues contain ads for Tom Mix, Rocky Lane, Space Patrol and other premiums. Captain Tootsie by* **C.C. Beck** *in #6-11, 20.*

TOM MIX WESTERN
AC Comics: 1988 - No. 2, 1989? ($2.95, B&W w/16 pgs. color, 44 pgs.)

1-Tom Mix-r/Master #124,128,131,102 plus Billy the Kid-r by Severin; photo front/back/inside-c 3.50
2-($2.50, B&W)-Gabby Hayes-r; photo covers 3.00
...Holiday Album 1 (1990, $3.50, B&W, one-shot, 44 pgs.)-Contains photos & 1950s Tom Mix-r; photo inside-c 4.00

TOMMY OF THE BIG TOP (Thrilling Circus Adventures)
King Features Synd./Standard Comics: No. 10, Sep, 1948 - No. 12, Mar, 1949

10-By John Lehti 7.15 21.50 50.00
11,12 5.00 15.00 30.00

TOMMY TOMORROW (See Action Comics #127, Real Fact #6, Showcase #41,42,44,46,47 & World's Finest #102)

TOMOE (Also see Shi: The Way Of the Warrior #6)
Crusade Comics: July, 1995 - No. 3, June, 1996($2.95)

0-3: 2-B&W Dogs o' War preview. 3-B&W Demon Gun preview 3.00
0 (3/96, $2.95)-variant-c. 3.00
0-Commemorative edition (5,000) 1.50 4.50 12.00
1-Commemorative edition (5,000) 1.85 5.50 15.00
1-($2.95)-FAN Appreciation edition 3.00
TPB (1997, $14.95) r/#0-3 15.00

TOMOE: UNFORGETTABLE FIRE
Crusade Comics: June, 1997 ($2.95, one-shot)

1-Prequel to Shi: The Series 3.00

TOMOE-WITCHBLADE/FIRE SERMON
Crusade Comics: Sept, 1996 ($3.95, one-shot)

1-Tucci-c 5.00
1-($9.95)-Avalon Ed. w/gold foil-c 10.00

TOMOE-WITCHBLADE/MANGA SHI PREVIEW EDITION
Crusade Comics: July, 1996 ($5.00, B&W)

nn-San Diego Preview Edition 5.00

TOMORROW KNIGHTS
Marvel Comics (Epic Comics): June, 1990 - No. 6, Mar, 1991 ($1.50)

1-6: 1-($1.95, 52 pgs.) 2.00

TOMORROW STORIES
America's Best Comics: Oct, 1999 - Present ($3.50/$2.95)

1-Two covers by Ross and Nowlan; Moore-s 3.50
2-10-($2.95) 3.00

TOM SAWYER (See Adventures of... & Famous Stories)

TOM SKINNER-UP FROM HARLEM (See Up From Harlem)

TOM STRONG
America's Best Comics: June, 1999 - Present ($3.50/$2.95)

1-Two covers by Ross and Sprouse; Moore-s/Sprouse-a 4.00
2-10-($2.95): 4-Art Adams-a (8 pgs.) 3.00

TOM TERRIFIC! (TV)(See Mighty Mouse Fun Club Magazine #1)
Pines Comics (Paul Terry): Summer, 1957 - No. 6, Fall, 1958
(See Terry Toons Giant Summer Fun Book)

1-1st app.?; CBS Television Presents... 22.00 66.00 175.00
2-6-(scarce) 16.00 49.00 130.00

TOM THUMB
Dell Publishing Co.: No. 972, Jan, 1959

Four Color 972-Movie, George Pal 9.00 27.00 110.00

TOM-TOM, THE JUNGLE BOY (See A-1 Comics & Tick Tock Tales)
Magazine Enterprises: 1947 - No. 3, 1947; Nov, 1957 - No. 3, Mar, 1958

1-Funny animal 10.00 30.00 70.00
2,3(1947): 3-Christmas issue 7.15 21.50 50.00
Tom-Tom & Itchi the Monk 1(11/57) - 3(3/58) 2.30 7.00 20.00
I.W. Reprint No. 1,2,8,10: 1,2,8-r/Koko & Kola #? 1.25 3.75 10.00

TONGUE LASH
Dark Horse Comics: Aug, 1996 - No. 2, Sept, 1996 ($2.95, lim. series, mature)

1,2: Taylor-c/a 3.00

TONGUE LASH II
Dark Horse Comics: Feb, 1999 - No. 2, Mar, 1999 ($2.95, lim. series, mature)

1,2: Taylor-c/a 3.00

TONKA (Disney)
Dell Publishing Co.: No. 966, Jan, 1959

Four Color 966-Movie (Starring Sal Mineo)-photo-c 7.50 22.50 90.00

Too Much Coffee Man Special © Shannon Wheeler

Top Cat #17 © H-B

Topix V5 #1 © Catechetical Guild

TONTO (See The Lone Ranger's Companion…)

TONY TRENT (The Face #1,2)
Big Shot/Columbia Comics Group: No. 3, 1948 - No. 4, 1949

3,4: 3-The Face app. by Mart Bailey 18.00 53.00 140.00

TOODLES, THE (The Toodle Twins with #1)
Ziff-Davis (Approved Comics)/Argo: No. 10, July-Aug, 1951; Mar, 1956 (Newspaper-r)

10-Painted-c, some newspaper-r by The Baers 10.00 30.00 70.00
…Twins 1(Argo, 3/56)-Reprints by The Baers 7.15 21.50 50.00

TOO MUCH COFFEE MAN
Adhesive Comics: July, 1993 - Present ($2.50, B&W)

1-Shannon Wheeler story & art 1.85 5.50 15.00
2,3 1.10 3.30 9.00
4,5 2.40 6.00
6-9 3.00
Full Color Special-nn($2.95),2-(7/97, $3.95) 4.00

TOO MUCH COFFEE MAN SPECIAL
Dark Horse Comics: July, 1997 ($2.95, B&W)

nn-Reprints Dark Horse Presents #92-95 3.00

TOOTH AND CLAW
Image Comics: Aug, 1999 - No. 3, Oct, 1999 ($2.95, limited series)

1-3-Mark Pacella-s/a 3.00

TOOTS & CASPER
Dell Publishing Co.: No. 5, 1942

Large Feature Comic 5 11.70 35.00 140.00

TOP ADVENTURE COMICS
I. W. Enterprises: 1964 (Reprints)

1-r/High Adv. (Explorer Joe #2); Krigstein-r 2.30 7.00 20.00
2-Black Dwarf-r/Red Seal #22; Kinstler-c 2.40 7.35 22.00

TOP CAT (TV) (Hanna-Barbera)(See Kite Fun Book)
Dell Publishing Co./Gold Key No. 4 on: 12-2/61-62 - No. 3, 6-8/62; No. 4, 10/62 - No. 31, 9/70

1 (TV show debuted 9/27/61) 16.00 48.00 175.00
2-Augie Doggie back-ups in #1-4 8.15 24.50 90.00
3-5: 3-Last 15¢ issue. 4-Begin 12¢ issues; Yakky Doodle app. in 1 pg. strip. 5-Touché Turtle app. 6.35 19.00 70.00
6-10 4.10 12.30 45.00
11-20 3.20 9.60 35.00
21-31-Reprints 2.50 7.50 25.00

TOP CAT (TV) (Hanna-Barbera)(See TV Stars #4)
Charlton Comics: Nov, 1970 - No. 20, Nov, 1973

1 5.00 15.00 55.00
2-10 2.80 8.40 28.00
11-20 2.40 7.35 22.00

NOTE: *#8 (1/72) went on sale late in 1972 between #14 and #15 with the 1/73 issues.*

TOP COMICS
K. K. Publications/Gold Key: July, 1967 (All reprints)

nn-The Gnome-Mobile (Disney-movie) 1.50 4.50 12.00
1-Beagle Boys (#7), Beep Beep the Road Runner (#5), Bugs Bunny, Chip 'n' Dale, Daffy Duck (#50), Flipper, Huey, Dewey & Louie, Gnome-Mobile, Junior Woodchucks, Lassie, The Little Monsters (#71), Moby Duck, Porky Pig (has Gold Key label - says Top Comics on inside), Scamp, Super Goof, Tom & Jerry, Top Cat (#21), Tweety & Sylvester (#7), Walt Disney C&S (#322), Woody Woodpecker known issues; each character given own book 1.25 3.75 10.00
1-Donald Duck (not Barks), Mickey Mouse 2.00 6.00 16.00
1-Flintstones 3.00 9.00 30.00
1-Huckleberry Hound, Three Stooges (#35), Yogi Bear (#30) 2.00 6.00 18.00
1-The Jetsons 3.65 11.00 40.00
1-Tarzan of the Apes (#169) 2.00 6.00 18.00
1-Uncle Scrooge (#70) 2.30 7.00 20.00
1-Zorro (r/G.K. Zorro #7 w/Toth-a; says 2nd printing) 2.00 6.00 18.00
2-Bugs Bunny, Daffy Duck, Mickey Mouse (#114), Porky Pig, Super Goof, Tom & Jerry, Tweety & Sylvester, Walt Disney's C&S (r/#325), Woody Woodpecker 1.25 3.75 10.00
2-Donald Duck (not Barks), Three Stooges, Uncle Scrooge (#71)-Barks-c, Yogi Bear (#30), Zorro (r/#8; Toth-a) 1.75 5.25 14.00
2-Snow White & 7 Dwarfs(6/67)(1944-r) 1.50 4.50 12.00
3-Donald Duck 1.75 5.25 14.00
3-Uncle Scrooge (#72) 2.00 6.00 16.00
3,4-The Flintstones 3.00 9.00 30.00
3,4: 3-Mickey Mouse (r/#115), Tom & Jerry, Woody Woodpecker, Yogi Bear. 4-Mickey Mouse, Woody Woodpecker 1.25 3.75 10.00

NOTE: *Each book in this series is identical to its counterpart except for cover, and came out at same time. The number in parentheses is the original issue it contains.*

TOP COW CLASSICS IN BLACK AND WHITE
Image Comics (Top Cow): Feb, 2000 - Present ($2.95, B&W reprints)

…: Ascension #1(4/00) B&W reprint plus time-line of series 2.95
…: Darkness #1(3/00) B&W reprint plus time-line of series 2.95
…: Fathom #1(5/00) B&W reprint 2.95
…: Midnight Nation #1(9/00) B&W preview 2.95
…: Rising Stars #1(7/00) B&W reprint plus cover gallery 2.95
…: Tomb Raider #1(12/00) B&W reprint plus back-story 2.95
…: Witchblade #1(2/00) B&W reprint plus back-story 2.95

TOP COW PRODUCTIONS, INC./BALLISTIC STUDIOS SWIMSUIT SPECIAL
Image Comics (Top Cow Productions): May, 1995 ($2.95, one-shot)

1 4.00

TOP COW SECRETS:SPECIAL WINTER LINGERIE EDITION
Image Comics (Top Cow Productions): Jan, 1996 ($2.95, one-shot)

1-Pin-ups 3.00

TOP DETECTIVE COMICS
I. W. Enterprises: 1964 (Reprints)

9-r/Young King Cole #14; Dr. Drew (not Grandenetti) 1.85 5.50 15.00

TOP DOG (See Star Comics Magazine, 75¢)
Star Comics (Marvel): Apr, 1985 - No. 14, June, 1987 (Children's book)

1-14: 10-Peter Parker & J. Jonah Jameson cameo 3.00

TOP ELIMINATOR (Teenage Hotrodders #1-24; Drag 'n' Wheels #30 on)
Charlton Comics: No. 25, Sept, 1967 - No. 29, July, 1968

25-29 2.00 6.00 18.00

TOP FLIGHT COMICS: Four Star Publ.: 1947 (Advertised, not published)

TOP FLIGHT COMICS
St. John Publishing Co.: July, 1949

1(7/49, St. John)-Hector the Inspector; funny animal 8.65 26.00 60.00

TOP GUN (See Luke Short, 4-Color #927 & Showcase #72)

TOP GUNS OF THE WEST (See Super DC Giant)

TOPIX (…Comics) (Timeless Topix-early issues) (Also see Men of Battle, Men of Courage & Treasure Chest)(V1-V5#1,V7#1-20-paper-c)
Catechetical Guild Educational Society: 11/42 - V10#15, 1/28/52 (Weekly - later issues)

V1#1(8 pgs.,8x11") 24.00 71.00 190.00
2,3(8 pgs.,8x11") 13.00 39.00 105.00
4-8(16 pgs.,8x11") 10.00 30.00 80.00
V2#1-10(16 pgs.,8x11"): V2#8-Pope Pius XII 10.00 30.00 70.00
V3#1-10(16 pgs.,8x11") 10.00 30.00 70.00
V4#1-10 7.85 23.50 55.00
V5#1(10/46,52 pgs.)-9,12-15(12/47): 13-Lists V5#4 6.00 18.00 42.00
10,11-Life of Christ editions 9.30 28.00 65.00
V6#1-14 5.00 15.00 35.00
V7#1(9/1/48)-20(6/15/49), 32 pgs. 5.00 15.00 30.00
V8#1(9/19/49)-3,5-11,13-30(5/15/50) 5.00 15.00 30.00
4-Dagwood Splits the Atom(10/10/49)-Magazine format 5.70 17.00 40.00
12-Ingels-a 9.30 28.00 65.00
V9#1(9/25/50)-11,13-30(5/14/51) 4.65 14.00 28.00
12-Special 36 pg. Xmas issue, text illos format 5.00 15.00 30.00

Top Love Stories #3 © STAR

Top-Notch Comics #1 © AP

Top Secrets #8 © S&S

V10#1(10/1/51)-15: 14-Hollingsworth-a 4.65 14.00 28.00

TOP JUNGLE COMICS
I. W. Enterprises: 1964 (Reprint)

1(nd)-Reprints White Princess of the Jungle #3, minus cover; Kintsler-a
2.60 7.80 26.00

TOP LOVE STORIES (Formerly Gasoline Alley #2)
Star Publications: No. 3, 5/51 - No. 19, 3/54

3(#1) 23.00 68.00 180.00
4,5,7-9: 8-Wood story 18.00 54.00 145.00
6-Wood-a 24.00 71.00 190.00
10-16,18,19-Disbrow-a 18.00 53.00 140.00
17-Wood art (Fox-r) 19.00 58.00 155.00
NOTE: *All have **L. B. Cole** covers.*

TOP-NOTCH COMICS (...Laugh #28-45; Laugh Comix #46 on)
MLJ Magazines: Dec, 1939 - No. 45, June, 1944

1-Origin/1st app. The Wizard; Kardak the Mystic Magician, Swift of the Secret Service (ends #3), Air Patrol, The Westpointer, Manhunters (by J. Cole), Mystic (ends #2) & Scott Rand (ends #3) begin; Wizard covers begin, end #8
565.00 1695.00 6500.00
2-Dick Storm (ends #8), Stacy Knight M.D. (ends #4) begin; Jack Cole-a
232.00 695.00 2200.00
3-Bob Phantom, Scott Rand on Mars begin; J. Cole-a
158.00 474.00 1500.00
4-Origin/1st app. Streak Chandler on Mars; Moore of the Mounted only app.; J. Cole-a 132.00 395.00 1250.00
5-Flag-c; origin/1st app. Galahad; Shanghai Sheridan begins (ends #8); Shield cameo; Novick-a; classic-c 147.00 442.00 1400.00
6-Meskin-a 103.00 308.00 975.00
7-The Shield x-over in Wizard; The Wizard dons new costume
126.00 379.00 1200.00
8-Origin/1st app. The Firefly & Roy, the Super Boy (9/40, 2nd costumed boy hero after Robin?; also see Toro in Human Torch #1 (Fall/40)
147.00 442.00 1400.00
9-Origin & 1st app. The Black Hood; 1st Black Hood-c & logo (10/40); Fran Frazier begins (Scarce) 522.00 1565.00 6000.00
10-2nd app. Black Hood 168.00 505.00 1600.00
11-15 100.00 300.00 950.00
16-20 90.00 268.00 850.00
21-30: 23-26-Roy app. 24-No Wizard. 25-Last Bob Phantom. 27-Last Firefly. 28-Suzie, Pokey Oakey begin. 29-Last Kardak 68.00 205.00 650.00
31-44: 33-Dotty & Ditto by Woggon begins (2/43, 1st app.). 44-Black Hood series ends 40.00 120.00 350.00
45-Last issue 44.00 133.00 400.00
NOTE: ***J. Binder** a-1-3. **Meskin** a-2, 3, 6, 15. **Bob Montana** a-30; c-28-31. **Harry Sahle** c-42-45. **Woggon** a-33-40, 42. Bondage c-17, 19. Black Hood also appeared on radio in 1944.Black Hood app. on c-9-34, 41-44. Roy the Super Boy app. on c-8, 9, 11-27. The Wizard app. on c-1-8, 11-13, 15-22, 24, 25, 27. Pokey Oakey app. on c-28-43. Suzie app. on c-44-on.*

TOPPER & NEIL (TV)
Dell Publishing Co.: No. 859, Nov, 1957

Four Color 859 4.10 12.30 45.00

TOPPS COMICS: Four Star Publications: 1947 (Advertised, not published)

TOPS
July, 1949 - No. 2, Sept, 1949 (25¢, 10-1/4x13-1/4", 68 pgs.)
Tops Magazine, Inc. (Lev Gleason): (Large size-magazine format; for the adult reader)

1 (Rare)-Story by Dashiell Hammett; Crandall/Lubbers, Tuska, Dan Barry, Fuje-a; Biro painted-c 111.00 442.00 1050.00
2 (Rare)-Crandall/Lubbers, Biro, Kida, Fuje, Guardineer-a
103.00 410.00 975.00

TOPS COMICS
Consolidated Book Publishers: 1944 (10¢, 132 pgs.)

2000-(Color-c, inside in red shade & some in full color)-Ace Kelly by Rick Yager, Black Orchid, Don on the Farm, Dinky Dinkerton (Rare)
26.00 79.00 210.00
NOTE: *This book is printed in such a way that when the staple is removed, the strips on the left side of the book correspond with the same strips on the right side. Therefore, if strips are removed from the book, each strip can be folded into a complete comic section of its own.*

GD2.0 FN6.0 NM9.4

TOPS COMICS (See Tops in Humor)
Consolidated Book (Lev Gleason): 1944 (7-1/4x5", 32 pgs.)

2001-The Jack of Spades (costumed hero) 15.00 45.00 120.00
2002-Rip Raider 9.30 28.00 65.00
2003-Red Birch (gag cartoons) 3.00 7.50 15.00

TOP SECRET
Hillman Publ.: Jan, 1952

1 20.00 60.00 160.00

TOP SECRET ADVENTURES (See Spyman)

TOP SECRETS (...of the F.B.I.)
Street & Smith Publications: Nov, 1947 - No. 10, July-Aug, 1949

1-Powell-c/a 34.00 103.00 275.00
2-Powell-c/a 25.00 75.00 200.00
3-6,8,10-Powell-a 22.00 66.00 175.00
9-Powell-c/a 23.00 69.00 185.00
7-Used in **SOTI**, pg. 90 & illo. "How to hurt people"; used by N.Y. Legis. Comm.; Powell-c/a 34.00 103.00 275.00
NOTE: ***Powell** c-1-3, 5-10.*

TOPS IN ADVENTURE
Ziff-Davis Publishing Co.: Fall, 1952 (25¢, 132 pgs.)

1-Crusader from Mars, The Hawk, Football Thrills, He-Man; Powell-a; painted-c 44.00 133.00 400.00

TOPS IN HUMOR (See Tops Comics?)
Consolidated Book Publ. (Lev Gleason): 1944 (7-1/4x5")

2001(#1)-Origin The Jack of Spades, Ace Kelly by Rick Yager, Black Orchid (female crime fighter) app. 16.00 49.00 130.00
2 10.00 30.00 80.00

TOP SPOT COMICS
Top Spot Publ. Co.: 1945

1-The Menace, Duke of Darkness app. 33.00 99.00 265.00

TOPSY-TURVY (Teenage)
R. B. Leffingwell Publ.: Apr, 1945

1-1st app. Cookie 10.00 30.00 80.00

TOP TEN
America's Best Comics: Sept, 1999 - Present ($3.50/$2.95)

1-Two covers by Ross and Ha/Cannon; Alan Moore-s/Gene Ha-a 3.50
2-11-($2.95) 3.00
Hardcover ('00, $24.94) Dust jacket with Gene Ha-a; r/#1-7 25.00

TOR (Prehistoric Life on Earth) (Formerly One Million Years Ago)
St. John Publ. Co.: No. 2, Oct, 1953; No. 3, May, 1954 - No. 5, Oct, 1954

3-D 2(10/53)-Kubert-c/a 12.50 37.50 100.00
3-D 2(10/53)-Oversized, otherwise same contents 11.00 33.00 90.00
3-D 2(11/53)-Kubert-c/a; has 3-D cover 11.00 33.00 90.00
3-5-Kubert-c/a: 3-Danny Dreams by Toth; Kubert 1 pg. story (w/self portrait)
13.00 39.00 105.00
NOTE: *The two October 3-D's have same contents and **Powell** art; the October & November issues are titled 3-D Comics. All 3-D issues are 25¢ and came with 3-D glasses.*

TOR (See Sojourn)
National Periodical Publications: May-June, 1975 - No. 6, Mar-Apr, 1976

1-New origin by Kubert 1.25 3.75 10.00
2-6: 2-Origin-r/St. John #1 2.40 6.00
NOTE: ***Kubert** a-1, 2-6r; c-1-6. **Toth** a(p)-3r.*

TOR (3-D)
Eclipse Comics: July, 1986 - No. 2, Aug, 1987 ($2.50)

1,2: 1-r/One Million Years Ago. 2-r/Tor 3-D #2 5.00
...2-D: 1,2-Limited signed & numbered editions 2.40 6.00

TOR
Marvel Comics (Epic Comics/Heavy Hitters): June, 1993 - No. 4, 1993 ($5.95, limited series)

1-4: Joe Kubert-c/a/scripts 6.00

Torchy #6 © QUA

Tough Kid Squad Comics #1 © MAR

Toy Town Comics #1 © Toytown

GD2.0 FN6.0 NM9.4

TORCH OF LIBERTY SPECIAL
Dark Horse Comics (Legend): Jan, 1995 ($2.50, one-shot)
1-Byrne scripts 2.50

TORCHY (...Blonde Bombshell) (See Dollman, Military, & Modern)
Quality Comics Group: Nov, 1949 - No. 6, Sept, 1950
1-Bill Ward-c, Gil Fox-a 147.00 442.00 1400.00
2,3-Fox-c/a 63.00 189.00 600.00
4-Fox-c/a(3), Ward-a (9 pgs.) 79.00 237.00 750.00
5,6-Ward-c/a, 9 pgs; Fox-a(3) each 100.00 300.00 950.00
Super Reprint #16(1964)-r/#4 with new-c 8.15 24.50 90.00

TO RIVERDALE AND BACK AGAIN (Archie Comics Presents...)
Archie Comics: 1990 ($2.50, 68 pgs.)
nn-Byrne-c, Colan-a(p); adapts NBC TV movie 4.00

TORMENTED, THE (Becomes Surprise Adventures #3 on)
Sterling Comics: July, 1954 - No. 2, Sept, 1954
1,2: Weird/horror stories 24.00 71.00 190.00

TORNADO TOM (See Mighty Midget Comics)

TORSO (See Jinx: Torso)

TOTAL ECLIPSE
Eclipse Comics: May, 1988 - No. 5, Apr, 1989 ($3.95, 52 pgs., deluxe size)
Book 1-5: 3-Intro/1st app. new Black Terror 4.00

TOTAL ECLIPSE
Image Comics: July, 1998 (one-shot)
1-McFarlane-c; Eclipse Comics character pin-ups by Image artists 2.00

TOTAL ECLIPSE: THE SERAPHIM OBJECTIVE
Eclipse Comics: Nov, 1988 ($1.95, one-shot, Baxter paper)
1-Airboy, Valkyrie, The Heap app. 3.00

TOTAL JUSTICE
DC Comics: Oct, 1996 - No. 3, Nov, 1996 ($2.25, bi-weekly limited series)
(Based on toyline)
1-3 2.25

TOTAL RECALL (Movie)
DC Comics: 1990 ($2.95, 68 pgs., movie adaptation, one-shot)
1-Arnold Schwarzenegger photo-c 3.00

TOTAL WAR (M.A.R.S. Patrol #3 on)
Gold Key: July, 1965 - No. 2, Oct, 1965 (Painted-c)
1-Wood-a in both issues 5.35 16.00 65.00
2 4.60 13.65 55.00

TOTEMS (Vertigo V2K)
DC Comics (Vertigo): Feb, 2000 ($5.95, one-shot)
1-Swamp Thing, Animal Man, Zatanna, Shade app.; Fegredo-c 5.95

TO THE HEART OF THE STORM
Kitchen Sink Press: 1991 (B&W, graphic novel)
Softcover-Will Eisner-s/a/c 15.00
Hardcover ($24.95) 25.00
TPB-(DC Comics, 9/00, $14.95) reprints 1991 edition 15.00

TO THE LAST MAN (See Zane Grey Four Color #616)

TOUCH OF SILVER, A
Image Comics: Jan, 1997 - Present ($2.95, B&W, bi-monthly)
1-7-Valentino-s/a; photo-c: 5-color pgs. w/Round Table 3.00

TOUGH KID SQUAD COMICS
Timely Comics (TCI): Mar, 1942
1-(Scarce)-Origin & 1st app.The Human Top & The Tough Kid Squad; The Flying Flame app. 870.00 2610.00 10,000.00

TOUR OF TORTURE
London Night Studios: June, 1996 ($10.00, one-shot)
nn-Photo-c 10.00

TOWER OF SHADOWS (Creatures on the Loose #10 on)
Marvel Comics Group: Sept, 1969 - No. 9, Jan, 1971
1-Steranko, Craig-a(p) 5.00 15.00 55.00
2,3: 2-Neal Adams-a. 3-Barry Smith, Tuska-a 3.00 9.00 32.00
4,6: 4-Marie Severin-c. 6-Wood-a 2.40 7.35 22.00
5-B. Smith-a(p), Wood-a; Wood draws himself (1st pg., 1st panel) 2.50 7.50 24.00
7-9: 7-B. Smith-a(p), Wood-a. 8-Wood-a; Wrightson-c. 9-Wrightson-c; Roy Thomas app. 3.00 9.00 32.00
Special 1(12/71, 52 pgs.)-Neal Adams-a 2.50 7.50 24.00
NOTE: ***J. Buscema** a-1p, 2p, Special 1r. **Colan** a-3p, 6p, Special 1. **J. Craig** a(r)-1p. **Ditko** a-6, 8, 9r, Special 1. **Everett** a-9(i)r; c-5i. **Kirby** a-9(p)r. **Severin** c-5p, 6. **Steranko** a-1p. **Tuska** a-3. **Wood** a-5-8. Issues 1-9 contain new stories with some pre-Marvel age reprints in 6-9. **H. P. Lovecraft** adaptation-9.*

TOWN & COUNTRY
Publisher?: May, 1940
nn-Origin The Falcon 44.00 133.00 400.00

TOXIC AVENGER (Movie)
Marvel Comics: Apr, 1991 - No. 11, Feb, 1992 ($1.50)
1-11: Based on movie character. 3,10-Photo-c 2.00

TOXIC CRUSADERS (TV)
Marvel Comics: May, 1992 - No. 8, Dec, 1992 ($1.25)
1-8: 1-3,8-Sam Kieth-c; based on USA network cartoon 2.00

TOXIC GUMBO
DC Comics (Vertigo): 1998 ($5.95, one-shot, mature)
1-McKeever-a/Lydia Lunch-s 6.00

TOYBOY
Continuity Comics: Oct, 1986 - No. 7, Mar, 1989 ($2.00, Baxter paper)
1-7 3.00
NOTE: ***N. Adams** a-1; c-1, 2,5. **Golden** a-7p; c-6,7. **Nebres** a(i)-1,2.*

TOYLAND COMICS
Fiction House Magazines: Jan, 1947 - No. 2, Mar, 1947; No. 3, July, 1947
1-Wizard of the Moon begins 28.00 83.00 220.00
2,3-Bob Lubbers-c. 3-Tuska-a 16.00 49.00 130.00
NOTE: *All above contain strips by **Al Walker.***

TOY TOWN COMICS
Toytown/Orbit Publ./B. Antin/Swapper Quarterly: 1945 - No. 7, May, 1947
1-Mertie Mouse; L. B. Cole-c/a; funny animal 38.00 113.00 300.00
2-L. B. Cole-a 23.00 68.00 180.00
3-7-L. B. Cole-a. 5-Wiggles the Wonderworm-c 19.00 56.00 150.00

TRAGG AND THE SKY GODS (See Gold Key Spotlight, Mystery Comics Digest #3,9 & Spine Tingling Tales)
Gold Key/Whitman No. 9: June, 1975 - No. 8, Feb, 1977; No. 9, May, 1982
(Painted-c #3-8)
1-Origin 1.25 3.75 10.00
2-9: 4-Sabre-Fang app. 8-Ostellon app.; 9-r/#1 2.40 6.00
NOTE: ***Santos** a-1, 2, 9r; c-3-7. **Spiegel** a-3-8.*

TRAIL BLAZERS (Red Dragon #5 on)
Street & Smith Publications: 1941; No. 2, Apr, 1942 - No. 4, Oct, 1942
(True stories of American heroes)
1-Life story of Jack Dempsey & Wright Brothers 34.00 103.00 275.00
2-Brooklyn Dodgers-c/story; Ben Franklin story 22.00 66.00 175.00
3,4: 3-Fred Allen, Red Barber, Yankees stories 20.00 60.00 160.00

TRAIL COLT (Also see Extra Comics & Manhunt!)
Magazine Enterprises: 1949 - No. 2, 1949
nn(A-1 #24)-7 pg. Frazetta-a r-in Manhunt #13; Undercover Girl app.; The Red Fox by L. B. Cole; Ingels-c; Whitney-a (Scarce) 40.00 120.00 320.00
2(A-1 #26)-Undercover Girl; Ingels-c; L. B. Cole-a (6 pgs.) 33.00 98.00 260.00

TRANSFORMERS, THE (TV)(See G.I. Joe and...)
Marvel Comics Group: Sept, 1984 - No. 80, July, 1991 (75¢/$1.00)
1-Based on Hasbro Toys 1.50 4.50 12.00
2-5 1.00 3.00 8.00
6-10 5.00

Transformers #80 © Hasbro

Transmetropolitan #9 © Warren Ellis & Darick Robertson

Treasure Chest #1 © George A. Pflaum

	GD2.0	FN6.0	NM9.4
11-49: 21-Intro Aerialbots			3.00
50-60: 54-Intro Micromasters			4.00
61-70			6.00
71-77: 75-($1.50, 52 pgs.) (Low print run)	1.25	3.75	10.00
78,79 (Low print run)	1.85	5.50	15.00
80-Last issue	2.30	7.00	20.00

NOTE: Second and third printings of all issues exist and are worth less than originals. Was originally planned as a four issue mini-series. ***Wrightson*** *a-64i(4 pgs.).*

TRANSFORMERS DIGEST
Marvel Comics: Jan, 1987 - No. 9, May, 1988

	GD2.0	FN6.0	NM9.4
1,2-Spider-Man-c/s	1.50	4.50	12.00
3-9	1.10	3.30	9.00

TRANSFORMERS: GENERATION 2
Marvel Comics: Nov, 1993 - No. 12, Oct, 1994 ($1.75)

	GD2.0	FN6.0	NM9.4
1-($2.95, 68 pgs.)-Collector's ed. w/bi-fold metallic-c	1.00	2.80	7.00
1-11: 1-Newsstand edition (68 pgs.)			5.00
12-($2.25, 52 pgs.)	1.00	2.80	7.00

TRANSMETROPOLITAN
DC Comics (Vertigo): Sept, 1997 - Present ($2.50)

	GD2.0	FN6.0	NM9.4
1-Warren Ellis-s/Darick Robertson-a(p)	1.50	4.50	12.00
2 ,3	1.00	2.80	7.00
4-8			4.00
9-42: 15-Jae Lee-c. 25-27-Jim Lee-c. 37-39-Bradstreet-c			2.50
Back on the Street ('97, $7.95) r/#1-3			8.00
I Hate It Here ('00, $5.95) Spider's columns with pin-up art by various			6.00
Lust For Life ('98, $14.95) r/#4-12			15.00
The New Scum ('00, $12.95) r/#19-24 & Vertigo: Winter's Edge #3			13.00
Year of the Bastard ('99, $12.95) r/#13-18			13.00

TRANSMUTATION OF IKE GARUDA, THE
Marvel Comics (Epic Comics): July, 1991 - No. 2, 1991 ($3.95, 52 pgs.)

	GD2.0	FN6.0	NM9.4
1,2			4.00

TRAPMAN
Phantom Comics: June, 1994 - No. 2, 1994? ($2.95, quarterly, unfinished limited series)

	GD2.0	FN6.0	NM9.4
1,2			3.00

TRAPPED!
Periodical House Magazines (Ace): Oct, 1954 - No. 4, April, 1955

	GD2.0	FN6.0	NM9.4
1 (All reprints)	10.00	30.00	70.00
2-4: 4-r/Men Against Crime #4 in its entirety	6.40	19.25	45.00

NOTE: ***Colan*** *a-1, 4.* ***Sekowsky*** *a-1.*

TRASH
Trash Publ. Co.: Mar, 1978 - No. 4, Oct, 1978 (B&W, magazine, 52 pgs.)

	GD2.0	FN6.0	NM9.4
1,2: 1-Star Wars parody. 2-UFO-c	1.75	5.25	14.00
3-Parodies of KISS, the Beatles, and monsters	2.30	7.00	20.00
4-(84 pgs.)-Parodies of Happy Days, Rocky movies	2.50	7.50	24.00

TRAVELS OF JAIMIE McPHEETERS, THE (TV)
Gold Key: Dec, 1963

	GD2.0	FN6.0	NM9.4
1-Kurt Russell photo on-c plus photo back-c	3.20	9.60	35.00

TREASURE CHEST (Catholic Guild; also see Topix)
George A. Pflaum: 3/12/46 - V27#8, July, 1972 (Educational comics) (Not published during Summer)

	GD2.0	FN6.0	NM9.4
V1#1	25.00	75.00	200.00
2-6 (5/21/46): 5-Dr. Styx app. by Baily	11.00	33.00	90.00
V2#1-20 (9/3/46-5/27/47)	10.00	30.00	70.00
V3#1-5,7-20 (1st slick cover)	8.65	26.00	60.00
V3#6-Jules Verne's "Voyage to the Moon"	10.00	30.00	80.00
V4#1-20 (9/9/48-5/31/49)	7.15	21.50	50.00
V5#1-20 (9/6/49-5/31/50)	6.40	19.25	45.00
V6#1-20 (9/14/50-5/31/51)	6.40	19.25	45.00
V7#1-20 (9/13/51-6/5/52)	5.00	15.00	35.00
V8#1-20 (9/11/52-6/4/53)	5.00	15.00	32.00
V9#1-20 ('53-'54), V10#1-20 ('54-'55)	5.00	15.00	30.00
V11('55-'56), V12('56-'57)	4.65	14.00	28.00
V13#1,3-5,7,9-V17#1 ('57-'63)	4.15	12.50	25.00
V13#2,6,8-Ingels-a	5.90	17.75	65.00
V17#2- "This Godless Communism" series begins(not in odd #'d issues); cover shows hammer & sickle over Statue of Liberty; 8 pg. Crandall-a of family life under communism	17.50	52.00	190.00
V17#3,5,7,9,11,13,15,17,19	2.00	6.00	18.00
V17#4,6,14- "This Godless Communism" stories	11.50	34.00	125.00
V17#8-Shows red octopus encompassing Earth, firing squad; 8 pgs. Crandall-a	14.50	43.50	160.00
V17#10- "This Godless Communism" - how Stalin came to power, part I; Crandall-a	13.50	40.00	150.00
V17#12-Stalin in WWII, forced labor, death by exhaustion; Crandall-a	13.50	40.00	150.00
V17#16-Kruschev takes over; de-Stalinization	13.50	40.00	150.00
V17#18-Kruschev's control; murder of revolters, brainwash, space race by Crandall	13.50	40.00	150.00
V17#20-End of series; Kruschev-people are puppets, firing squads hammer & sickle over Statue of Liberty, snake around communist manifesto by Crandall	15.50	46.50	170.00
V18#1-20, V19#11-20, V20#1-20(1964-65): V18#11-Crandall draws himself & 13 other artists on cover	2.00	6.00	18.00
V18#5- "What About Red China?" - describes how communists took over China	5.45	16.35	60.00
V19#1-10- "Red Victim" anti-communist series in all	5.45	16.35	60.00
V21-V25(1965-70)-(two V24#5's 11/7/68 & 11/21/68) (no V24#6)	2.00	6.00	16.00
V26, V27#1-8 (V26,27-68 pgs.)	2.00	6.00	18.00
Summer Edition V1#1-6('66)(exist?), V2#1-6('67)	2.30	7.00	20.00

NOTE: ***Anderson*** *a-V18#13.* ***Borth*** *a-V7#10-19 (serial), V8#8-17 (serial), V9#1-10 (serial), V13#2, 6, 11, V14-V25 (except V22#1-3, 11-13), Summer Ed. V1#3-6.* ***Crandall*** *a-V16#7, 9, 12 14, 16-18, 20; V17#1, 2, 4-6, 10, 12, 14, 16-18, 20; V18#1, 2, 3(2 pg.), 7, 9-20; V19#4, 11, 13, 1 19, 20; V20#1, 2, 4, 6, 8-10, 12, 14-16, 18, 20; V21#1-5, 8-11, 13, 16-18; V22#3, 7, 9-11, 14; V23#3, 6, 9, 16, 18; V24#7, 8, 10, 13, 16; V25#8, 16; V27#1-7r, 8r(2 pg.), Summer Ed. V1#3-5, V2#3; c-V16#7, V18#2(part), 7, 11, V19#4, 19, 20, V20#15, V21#5, 9, V22#3, 7, 9, 11, V23#9, 16, V24#13, 16, V25#8, Summer Ed. V1#2 (back c-V1#2-5).* ***Powell*** *a-V10#11. V19#11, 15, V10#13, V13#6, 8 all have wraparound covers.*

TREASURE CHEST OF THE WORLD'S BEST COMICS
Superior, Toronto, Canada: 1945 (500 pgs., hard-c)

	GD2.0	FN6.0	NM9.4
Contains Blue Beetle, Captain Combat, John Wayne, Dynamic Man, Nemo, Li'l Abner; contents can vary - represents random binding of extra books; Capt. America on-c	84.00	253.00	800.00

TREASURE COMICS
Prize Publications? (no publisher listed): No date (1943) (50¢, 324 pgs., cardboard-c)

	GD2.0	FN6.0	NM9.4
1-(Rare)-Contains rebound Prize Comics #7-11 from 1942 (blank inside-c)	211.00	633.00	2000.00

TREASURE COMICS
Prize Publ. (American Boys' Comics): June-July, 1945 - No. 12, Fall, 1947

	GD2.0	FN6.0	NM9.4
1-Paul Bunyan & Marco Polo begin; Highwayman & Carrot Topp only app.; Kiefer-a	33.00	98.00	260.00
2-Arabian Knight, Gorilla King, Dr. Styx begin	16.00	49.00	130.00
3,4,9,12: 9-Kiefer-a	12.00	36.00	95.00
5-Marco Polo-c; Krigstein-a	20.00	60.00	160.00
6,11-Krigstein-a; 11-Krigstein-c	18.00	53.00	140.00
7,8-Frazetta-a (5 pgs. each). 7-Capt. Kidd Jr. app.	38.00	113.00	300.00
10-Simon & Kirby-c/a	31.00	94.00	250.00

NOTE: ***Barry*** *a-9-11; c-12.* ***Kiefer*** *a-3, 5, 7; c-2, 6, 7.* ***Roussos*** *a-11.*

TREASURE ISLAND (See Classics Illustrated #64, Doc Savage Comics #1, King Classics, Movie Classics & Movie Comics)
Dell Publishing Co.: No. 624, Apr, 1955 (Disney)

	GD2.0	FN6.0	NM9.4
Four Color 624-Movie, photo-c	8.35	25.00	100.00

TREASURY OF COMICS
St. John Publishing Co.: 1947; No. 2, July, 1947 - No. 4, Sept, 1947; No. 5, Jan, 1948

	GD2.0	FN6.0	NM9.4
nn(#1)-Abbie an' Slats (nn on-c, #1 on inside)	14.00	43.00	115.00
2-Jim Hardy Comics; featuring Windy & Paddles	10.00	30.00	80.00
3-Bill Bumlin	8.65	26.00	60.00
4-Abbie an' Slats	10.00	30.00	80.00

Treasury of Comics #4 © STJ

Trenchcoat Brigade #3 © DC

Trouble Magnet #1 © Ryder Windham & Kilian Plunkett

GD2.0 FN6.0 NM9.4

5-Jim Hardy Comics #1 10.00 30.00 80.00

TREASURY OF COMICS
St. John Publishing Co.: Mar, 1948 - No. 5, 1948 (Reg. size); 1948-1950 (Over 500 pgs., $1.00)

1 19.00 56.00 150.00
2(#2 on-c, #1 on inside) 10.00 30.00 80.00
3-5 10.00 30.00 70.00
1-(1948, 500 pgs., hard-c)-Abbie & Slats, Abbott & Costello, Casper, Little Annie Rooney, Little Audrey, Jim Hardy, Ella Cinders (16 books bound together) (Rare) 100.00 300.00 950.00
1(1949, 500 pgs.)-Same format as above 100.00 300.00 950.00
1(1950, 500 pgs.)-Same format as above; different-c; (also see Little Audrey Yearbook) (Rare) 100.00 300.00 950.00

TREASURY OF DOGS, A (See Dell Giants)

TREASURY OF HORSES, A (See Dell Giants)

TREEHOUSE OF HORROR (Bart Simpson's...)
Bongo Comics: 1995 - Present ($2.95/$2.50/$3.50/$4.50, annual)

1-(1995, $2.95)-Groening-c; Allred, Robinson & Smith stories. 3.00
2-(1996, $2.50)-Stories by Dini & Bagge; infinity-c by Groening 2.50
3-(1997, $2.50)-Dorkin-s/Groening-c 2.50
4-(1998, $2.50)-Lash & Dixon-s/Groening-c 2.50
5-(1999, $3.50)-Thompson-s; Shaw & Aragonés-s/a; TenNapel-s/a 3.50
6-(2000, $4.50)-Mahfood-s/a; DeCarlo-a; Morse-s/a; Kuper-s/a 4.50

TREKKER (See Dark Horse Presents #6)
Dark Horse Comics: May, 1987 - No. 6, Mar,1988 ($1.50, B&W)

1-6: Sci/Fi stories 2.00
Color Special 1 (1989, $2.95, 52 pgs.) 3.00
Collection ($5.95, B&W) 6.00
Special 1 (6/99, $2.95, color) 3.00

TRENCHCOAT BRIGADE, THE
DC Comics (Vertigo): Mar, 1999 - No. 4, Jun, 1999 ($2.50, limited series)

1-4: Hellblazer, Phantom Stranger, Mister E, Dr. Occult app. 2.50

TRENCHER (See Blackball Comics)
Image Comics: May, 1993 - No. 4, Oct, 1993 ($1.95, unfinished limited series)

1-4: Keith Giffen-c/a/scripts. 3-Supreme-c/story 2.00

TRIBAL FORCE
Mystic Comics: Aug, 1996 ($2.50)

1-Reads "Special Edition" on-c 2.50

TRIB COMIC BOOK, THE
Winnipeg Tribune: Sept. 24, 1977 - Vol. 4, #36, 1980 (8-1/2"x11", 24 pgs., weekly) (155 total issues)

V1# 1-Color pages (Sunday strips)-Spiderman, Asterix, Disney's Scamp, Wizard of Id, Doonesbury, Inside Woody Allen, Mary Worth, & others (similar to Spirit sections) 1.75 5.25 14.00
V1#2-15, V2#1-52, V3#1-52, V4#1-33 1.25 3.75 10.00
V4#34-36 (not distributed) 2.30 7.00 20.00

Note: All issues have Spider-Man. Later issues contain Star Trek and Star Wars. 20 strips in ea. The first newspaper to put Sunday pages into a comic book format.

TRIBE (See WildC.A.T.S #4)
Image Comics/Axis Comics No. 2 on: Apr, 1993; No. 2, Sept, 1993 - No. 3, 1994 ($2.50/$1.95)

1-By Johnson & Stroman; gold foil & embossed on black-c 2.50
1-($2.50)-Ivory Edition; gold foil & embossed on white-c; available only through the creators 2.50
2,3: 2-1st Axis Comics issue. 3-Savage Dragon app. 2.00

TRIBUTE TO STEVEN HUGHES, A
Chaos! Comics: Sept, 2000 ($6.95)

1-Lady Death & Evil Ernie pin-ups by various artists; testimonials 7.00

TRIGGER (See Roy Rogers'...)

TRIGGER TWINS
National Periodical Publications: Mar-Apr, 1973 (20¢, one-shot)

1-Trigger Twins & Pow Wow Smith-r/All-Star Western #94,103 & Western Comics #81; Infantino-r(p) 2.30 7.00 20.00

TRINITY (See DC Universe: Trinity)

TRINITY ANGELS
Acclaim Comics (Valiant Heroes): July, 1997 - No. 12, June, 1998 ($2.50)

1-12-Maguire-s/a(p):4-Copycat-c 3.00

TRIPLE GIANT COMICS (See Archie All-Star Specials under Archie Comics)

TRIPLE THREAT
Special Action/Holyoke/Gerona Publ.: Winter, 1945

1-Duke of Darkness, King O'Leary 28.00 84.00 225.00

TRIPLE-X
Dark Horse Comics: Dec, 1994 - No. 7, June, 1995 ($3.95, B&W, limited series)

1-7 4.00

TRIUMPH (Also see JLA #28-30, Justice League Task Force & Zero Hour)
DC Comics: June, 1995 - No. 4, Sept, 1995 ($1.75, limited series)

1-4: 3-Hourman, JLA app. 2.00

TRIUMPHANT UNLEASHED
Triumphant Comics: No. 0, Nov, 1993 - No. 1, Nov, 1993 ($2.50, lim. series)

0-Serially numbered, 0-Red logo, 0-White logo (no cover price; giveaway), 1-Cover is negative & reverse of #0-c 2.50

TROLL (Also see Brigade)
Image Comics (Extreme Studios): Dec, 1993 ($2.50, one-shot, 44 pgs.)

1-1st app. Troll; Liefeld scripts; Matsuda-c/a(p) 2.50
Halloween Special (1994, $2.95)-Maxx app. 3.00
...Once A Hero (8/94, $2.50) 2.50

TROLLORDS
Tru Studios/Comico V2#1 on: 2/86 - No. 15, 1988; V2#1, 11/88 - V2#4, 1989 (1-15: $1.50, B&W)

1-15: 1-Both printings. 6-Christmas issue; silver logo 2.50
V2#1-4 ($1.75, color, Comico) 2.50
Special 1 ($1.75, 2/87, color)-Jerry's Big Fun Bk. 2.50

TROLLORDS
Apple Comics: July, 1989 - No. 6, 1990 ($2.25, B&W, limited series)

1-6: 1-"The Big Batman Movie Parody" 2.50

TROLL PATROL
Harvey Comics: Jan, 1993 ($1.95, 52 pgs.)

1 2.00

TROLL II (Also see Brigade)
Image Comics (Extreme Studios): July, 1994 ($3.95, one-shot)

1 4.00

TROUBLED SOULS
Fleetway: 1990 ($9.95, trade paperback)

nn-Garth Ennis scripts & John McCrea painted-c/a. 10.00

TROUBLE MAGNET
DC Comics: Feb, 2000 - No. 4, May, 2000 ($2.50, limited series)

1-4-Windham-s/Plunkett-a 2.50

TROUBLEMAKERS
Acclaim Comics (Valiant Heroes): Apr, 1997 - No. 19, June, 1998 ($2.50)

1-19: Fabian Nicieza scripts in all. 1-1st app. XL, Rebound & Blur. 8-Copycat-c. 12-Shooting of Parker 2.50

TROUBLEMAN
Image Comics (Motown Machineworks): June, 1996 - No. 3, Aug, 1996 ($2.25, limited series)

1-3 2.25

TROUBLE SHOOTERS, THE (TV)
Dell Publishing Co.: No. 1108, Jun-Aug, 1960

Four Color 1108-Keenan Wynn photo-c 4.60 13.75 55.00

TROUBLE WITH GIRLS, THE
Malibu Comics (Eternity Comics) #7-14/Comico V2#1-4/Eternity V2#5 on:

True Aviation Picture Stories #10 © PMI

True Comics #8 © PMI

True Confidences #1 © FAW

8/87 - #14, 1988; V2#1, 2/89 - V2#23, 1991? ($1.95, B&W/color)

1-14 ($1.95, B&W, Eternity)-Gerard Jones scripts & Tim Hamilton-c/a in all. 2.00
V2#1-23-Jones scripts, Hamilton-c/a. 2.00
Annual 1 (1988, $2.95) 3.00
Christmas Special 1 (12/91, $2.95, B&W, Eternity)-Jones scripts, Hamilton-c/a. 3.00
Graphic Novel 1,2 (7/88, B&W)-r/#1-3 & #4-6 8.00

TROUBLE WITH GIRLS, THE: NIGHT OF THE LIZARD
Marvel Comics (Epic Comics/Heavy Hitters): 1993 - No. 4, 1993 ($2.50/$1.95, limited series)

1-Embossed-c; Gerard Jones scripts & Bret Blevins-c/a in all 2.50
2-4: 2-Begin $1.95-c. 2.00

TRUE ADVENTURES (Formerly True Western)(Men's Adventures #4 on)
Marvel Comics (CCC): No. 3, May, 1950 (52 pgs.)

3-Powell, Sekowsky-a; Brodsky-c 16.00 48.00 125.00

TRUE ANIMAL PICTURE STORIES
True Comics Press: Winter, 1947 - No. 2, Spring-Summer, 1947

1,2 10.00 30.00 70.00

TRUE AVIATION PICTURE STORIES (Becomes Aviation Adventures & Model Building #16 on)
Parents' Mag. Institute: 1942; No. 2, Jan-Feb, 1943 - No. 15, Sept-Oct, 1946

1-(#1 & 2 titled ...Aviation Comics Digest)(not digest size) 14.00 41.00 110.00
2 9.30 28.00 65.00
3-14: 3-10-Plane photos on-c. 11,13-Photo-c 8.65 26.00 60.00
15-(Titled "True Aviation Adventures & Model Building") 7.85 23.50 55.00

TRUE BRIDE'S EXPERIENCES (Formerly Teen-Age Brides)
(True Bride-To-Be Romances No. 17 on)
True Love (Harvey Publications): No. 8, Oct, 1954 - No. 16, Feb, 1956

8 7.85 23.50 55.00
9,10: 10-Last pre-code (2/55) 5.00 15.00 35.00
11-15 5.00 15.00 30.00
16-Spanking panels (3) 6.00 18.00 42.00
NOTE: *Powell a-8-10, 12, 13.*

TRUE BRIDE-TO-BE ROMANCES (Formerly True Bride's Experiences)
Home Comics/True Love (Harvey): No. 17, Apr, 1956 - No. 30, Nov, 1958

17-S&K-c, Powell-a 10.00 30.00 70.00
18-20,22,25-28,30 5.00 15.00 30.00
21,23,24,29-Powell-a. 29-Baker-a (1 pg.) 5.00 15.00 35.00

TRUE COMICS (Also see Outstanding American War Heroes)
True Comics/Parents' Magazine Press: April, 1941 - No. 84, Aug, 1950

1-Marathon run story; life story Winston Churchill 31.00 94.00 250.00
2-Red Cross story; Everett-a 14.00 43.00 115.00
3-Baseball Hall of Fame story; Chiang Kai-Shek-c/s 17.00 51.00 135.00
4,5: 4-Story of American flag "Old Glory". 5-Life story of Joe Louis 12.00 36.00 95.00
6-Baseball World Series story 16.00 49.00 130.00
7-10: 7-Buffalo Bill story. 10,11-Teddy Roosevelt 9.30 28.00 65.00
11-14,16,18-20: 11-Thomas Edison, Douglas MacArthur stories. 13-Harry Houdini story. 14-Charlie McCarthy story. 18-Story of America begins, ends #26. 19-Eisenhower-c/s 8.65 26.00 60.00
15-Flag-c; Bob Feller story 10.00 30.00 70.00
17-Brooklyn Dodgers story 10.00 30.00 80.00
21-30: 24-Marco Polo story. 28-Origin of Uncle Sam. 29-Beethoven story 30-Cooper Brothers baseball story 7.15 21.50 50.00
31-Red Grange "Galloping Ghost" story 5.00 15.00 35.00
32-46: 33-Origin/1st app. Steve Saunders, Special Agent of the FBI, series begins. 35-Mark Twain story. 38-General Bradley-c/s. 39-FDR story. 44-Truman story. 46-George Gershwin story 5.00 15.00 30.00
47-Atomic bomb issue (c/story, 3/46) 9.30 28.00 65.00
48-54,56-65: 49-1st app. Secret Warriors. 53-Bobby Riggs story. 58-Jim Jeffries (boxer) story; Harry Houdini story. 59-Bob Hope story; pirates-c/s.

GD2.0 FN6.0 NM9.4

60-Speedway Speed Demon-c/story. 4.65 14.00 28.00
55-(12/46)-1st app. Sad Sack by Baker (1/2 pg.) 5.70 17.00 40.00
66-Will Rogers-c/story 5.00 15.00 32.00
67-1st oversized issue (12/47); Steve Saunders, Special Agent begins 6.00 18.00 42.00
68-70,74-77,79: 68-70,74-77-Features Steve Sanders True FBI advs. 68-Oversized; Admiral Byrd-c/s. 69-Jack Benny story. 74-Amos 'n' Andy story 4.65 14.00 28.00
71-Joe DiMaggio-c/story. 7.15 21.50 50.00
72-Jackie Robinson story; True FBI advs. 5.00 15.00 35.00
73-Walt Disney's life story 7.15 21.50 50.00
78-Stan Musial-c/story; True FBI advs. 5.00 15.00 35.00
80-84 (Scarce)-All distr. to subscribers through mail only; paper-c. 80-Rocket trip to the moon story. 81-Red Grange story 16.00 49.00 130.00
(Prices vary widely on issues 80-84)
NOTE: ***Bob Kane** a-7. **Palais** a-80. **Powell** c/a-80. #80-84 have soft covers and combined with Tex Granger, Jack Armstrong, and Calling All Kids. #68-78 featured true FBI adventures.*

TRUE COMICS AND ADVENTURE STORIES
Parents' Magazine Institute: 1965 (Giant) (25¢)

1,2: 1-Fighting Hero of Viet Nam; LBJ on-c 2.30 7.00 20.00

TRUE COMPLETE MYSTERY (Formerly Complete Mystery)
Marvel Comics (PrPl): No. 5, Apr, 1949 - No. 8, Oct, 1949

5 26.00 79.00 210.00
6-8: 6-8-Photo-c 20.00 60.00 160.00

TRUE CONFIDENCES
Fawcett Publications: 1949 (Fall) - No. 4, June, 1950 (All photo-c)

1-Has ad for Fawcett Love Adventures #1, but publ. as Love Memoirs #1 as Marvel published the title first; Swayze-a 16.00 49.00 130.00
2-4: 3-Swayze-a. 4-Powell-a 10.00 30.00 80.00

TRUE CRIME CASES (...From Official Police Files)
St. John Publishing Co.: 1944 (25¢, 100 pg. Giant)

nn-Matt Baker-c 41.00 123.00 370.00

TRUE CRIME COMICS (Also see Complete Book of...)
Magazine Village: No. 2, May, 1947; No. 3, July-Aug, 1948 - No. 6, June-July, 1949; V2#1, Aug-Sept, 1949 (52 pgs.)

2-Jack Cole-c/a; used in **SOTI**, pgs. 81,82 plus illo. "A sample of the injury-to-eye motif" & illo. "Dragging living people to death"; used in **POP**, pg. 105; "Murder, Morphine and Me" classic drug propaganda story used by N.Y. Legis. Comm. 137.00 411.00 1300.00
3-Classic Cole-c/a; drug story with hypo, opium den & with drawing addict 103.00 308.00 975.00
4-Jack Cole-c/a; c-taken from a story panel in #3 (r-(2) **SOTI** & **POP** stories/#2?) 92.00 276.00 875.00
5-Jack Cole-c, Marijuana racket story (Canadian ed. w/cover similar to #3 exists w/out drug story) 61.00 182.00 575.00
6-Not a reprint, original story (Canadian ed. reprints #4 w/different coloring on-c) 48.00 145.00 435.00
V2#1-Used in **SOTI**, pgs. 81,82 & illo. "Dragging living people to death"; Toth, Wood (3 pgs.), Roussos-a; Cole-r from #2 82.00 245.00 775.00
NOTE: *V2#1 was reprinted in Canada as V2#9 (12/49); same-c & contents minus Wood-a.*

TRUE FAITH
Fleetway: 1990 ($9.95, graphic novel)

nn-Garth Ennis scripts 2.30 7.00 20.00
Reprinted by DC/Vertigo ('97, $12.95) 13.00

TRUE GHOST STORIES (See Ripley's...)

TRUE LIFE ROMANCES (...Romance on cover)
Ajax/Farrell Publications: Dec, 1955 - No. 3, Aug, 1956

1 10.00 30.00 70.00
2 6.00 18.00 42.00
3-Disbrow-a 7.15 21.50 50.00

TRUE LIFE SECRETS
Romantic Love Stories/Charlton: Mar-April, 1951 - No. 28, Sept, 1955; No. 29, Jan, 1956

1-Photo-c begin, end #3? 11.00 33.00 90.00

True Love Pictorial #2 © STJ

True Sport Picture Stories #11 © S&S

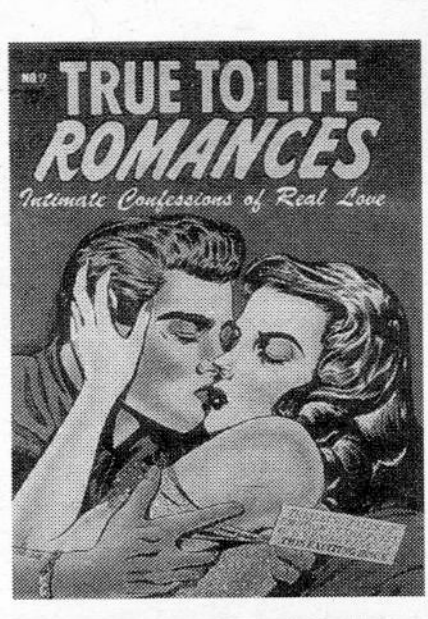

True-To-Life Romances #9 © STAR

GD2.0 FN6.0 NM9.4

2 6.40 19.25 45.00
3-19: 12-"I Was An Escort Girl" story 5.00 15.00 32.00
20-29: 25-Last precode(3/55) 4.65 14.00 28.00

RUE LIFE TALES (Formerly Mitzi's Romances #8?)
larvel Comics (CCC): No. 8, Oct, 1949 - No. 2, Jan, 1950 (52 pgs.)
8(#1, 10/49), 2-Both have photo-c 10.00 30.00 70.00

'RUE LOVE
:clipse Comics: Jan, 1986 - No. 2, Jan, 1986 ($2.00, Baxter paper)
1,2-Love stories reprinted from pre-code Standard Comics; Toth-a(p) in both; 1-Dave Stevens-c. 2-Mayo-a 3.00

'RUE LOVE CONFESSIONS
'remier Magazines: May, 1954 - No. 11, Jan, 1956
1-Marijuana story 10.00 30.00 75.00
2 5.00 15.00 35.00
3-11 5.00 15.00 30.00

'RUE LOVE PICTORIAL
t. John Publishing Co.: 1952 - No. 11, Aug, 1954
1-Only photo-c 15.00 45.00 120.00
2-Baker-c/a 20.00 60.00 160.00
3-5(All 25¢, 100 pgs.): 4-Signed story by Estrada. 5-(4/53)-Formerly Teen-Age Temptations; Kubert-a in #3; Baker-a in #3-5 34.00 101.00 270.00
6,7: Baker-c/a. 7-Signed story by Estrada 18.00 54.00 145.00
8,10,11-Baker-c/a 18.00 53.00 140.00
9-Baker-c 12.50 37.50 100.00

TRUE LOVE PROBLEMS AND ADVICE ILLUSTRATED (Becomes Romance Stories of True Love No. 45 on)
McCombs/Harvey Publ./Home Comics: June, 1949 - No. 6, Apr, 1950; No. 7, Jan, 1951 - No. 44, Mar, 1957
V1#1 14.00 43.00 115.00
2 8.65 26.00 60.00
3-10: 7-9-Elias-c 6.00 18.00 42.00
11-13,15-23,25-31: 31-Last pre-code (1/55) 5.00 15.00 30.00
14,24-Rape scene 5.70 17.00 40.00
32-37,39-44 4.30 13.00 26.00
38-S&K-c 7.85 23.50 55.00
NOTE: *Powell a-1, 2, 7-14, 17-25, 28, 29, 33, 40, 41. #3 has True Love... on inside.*

TRUE MOVIE AND TELEVISION (Part teenage magazine)
Toby Press: Aug, 1950 - No. 3, Nov, 1950; No. 4, Mar, 1951 (52 pgs.)(1-3: 10¢)
1-Elizabeth Taylor photo-c; Gene Autry, Shirley Temple, Li'l Abner app. 42.00 125.00 375.00
2-(9/50)-Janet Leigh/Liz Taylor/Ava Gardner & others photo-c; Frazetta John Wayne illo from J.Wayne Adv. Comics #2 (4/50) 34.00 103.00 275.00
3-June Allyson photo-c; Montgomery Cliff, Esther Williams, Andrews Sisters app; Li'l Abner featured; Sadie Hawkins' Day 28.00 84.00 225.00
4-Jane Powell photo-c (15¢) 14.00 41.00 110.00
NOTE: *16 pgs. in color, rest movie material in black & white.*

TRUE SECRETS (Formerly Our Love?)
Marvel (IPS)/Atlas Comics (MPI) #4 on: No. 3, Mar, 1950; No. 4, Feb, 1951 - No. 40, Sept, 1956
3 (52 pgs.)(IPS one-shot)` 12.00 36.00 95.00
4,5,7-10 7.15 21.50 50.00
6,22-Everett-a 9.30 28.00 65.00
11-20 6.00 18.00 42.00
21,23-28: 24-Colletta-c. 28-Last pre-code (2/55) 5.00 15.00 30.00
29-40: 34,36-Colletta-a 4.65 14.00 28.00

TRUE SPORT PICTURE STORIES (Formerly Sport Comics)
Street & Smith Publications: V1#5, Feb, 1942 - V5#2, July-Aug, 1949
V1#5-Joe DiMaggio-c/story 34.00 103.00 275.00
6-12 (1942-43): 12-Jack Dempsey story 20.00 60.00 160.00
V2#1-12 (1944-45): 7-Stan Musial-c/story; photo story of the New York Yankees 19.00 56.00 150.00
V3#1-12 (1946-47): 7-Joe DiMaggio, Stan Musial, Bob Feller & others back from the armed service story. 8-Billy Conn vs. Joe Louis-c/story 16.00 49.00 130.00
V4#1-12 (1948-49), V5#1,2 14.00 43.00 115.00
NOTE: ***Powell** a-V3#10, V4#1-4, 6-8, 10-12; V5#1, 2; c-V3#11, V4#3-7, 9-12. **Ravielli** c-V5#2.*

TRUE STORIES OF ROMANCE
Fawcett Publications: Jan, 1950 - No. 3, May, 1950 (All photo-c)
1 12.00 36.00 95.00
2,3: 3-Marcus Swayze-a 8.65 26.00 60.00

TRUE STORY OF JESSE JAMES, THE (See Jesse James, Four Color 757)

TRUE SWEETHEART SECRETS
Fawcett Publications: 5/50; No. 2, 7/50; No. 3, 1951(nd); No. 4, 9/51 - No. 11, 1/53 (All photo-c)
1-Photo-c; Debbie Reynolds? 12.50 37.50 100.00
2-Wood-a (11 pgs.) 17.00 51.00 135.00
3-11: 4,5-Powell-a. 8-Marcus Swayze-a. 11-Evans-a 10.00 30.00 70.00

TRUE TALES OF LOVE (Formerly Secret Story Romances)
Atlas Comics (TCI): No. 22, April, 1956 - No. 31, Sept, 1957
22 7.85 23.50 55.00
23-24,26-31-Colletta-a in most: 5.00 15.00 32.00
25-Everett-a; Colletta-a 5.70 17.00 40.00

TRUE TALES OF ROMANCE
Fawcett Publications: No. 4, June, 1950
4-Photo-c 8.65 26.00 60.00

TRUE 3-D
Harvey Publications: Dec, 1953 - No. 2, Feb, 1954 (25¢)(Both came with 2 pair of glasses)
1-Nostrand, Powell-a 5.45 16.35 60.00
2-Powell-a 5.90 17.75 65.00
NOTE: *Many copies of #1 surfaced in 1984.*

TRUE-TO-LIFE ROMANCES (Formerly Guns Against Gangsters)
Star Publ.: #8, 11-12/49; #9, 1-2/50; #3, 4/50 - #5, 9/50; #6, 1/51 - #23, 10/54
8(#1, 1949) 24.00 71.00 190.00
9(#2),4-10 17.00 51.00 135.00
3-Janet Leigh/Glenn Ford photo on-c plus true life story of each 19.00 56.00 150.00
11,22,23 14.00 41.00 110.00
12-14,17-21-Disbrow-a 16.00 49.00 130.00
15,16-Wood & Disbrow-a in each 19.00 56.00 150.00
NOTE: ***Kamen** a-13. **Kamen/Feldstein** a-14. All have **L.B. Cole** covers.*

TRUE WAR EXPERIENCES
Harvey Publications: Aug, 1952 - No. 4, Dec, 1952
1 8.15 24.50 90.00
2-4 4.55 13.65 50.00

TRUE WAR ROMANCES (Becomes Exotic Romances #22 on)
Quality Comics Group: Sept, 1952 - No. 21, June, 1955
1-Photo-c 12.50 37.50 100.00
2 7.15 21.50 50.00
3-10: 9-Whitney-a 5.70 17.00 40.00
11-21: 20-Last precode (4/55). 14-Whitney-a 5.00 15.00 35.00

TRUE WAR STORIES (See Ripley's...)

TRUE WESTERN (True Adventures #3)
Marvel Comics (MMC): Dec, 1949 - No. 2, March, 1950
1-Photo-c; Billy The Kid story 16.00 48.00 125.00
2: Alan Ladd photo-c 20.00 60.00 160.00

TRUMP
HMH Publishing Co.: Jan, 1957 - No. 2, Mar, 1957 (50¢, magazine)
1-Harvey Kurtzman satire 23.00 68.00 180.00
2-Harvey Kurtzman satire 19.00 56.00 150.00
NOTE: ***Davis, Elder, Heath, Jaffee** art-#1,2; **Wood** a-1. Article by Mel Brooks in #2.*

TRUMPETS WEST (See Luke Short, Four Color #875)

TRUTH ABOUT CRIME (See Fox Giants)

TRUTH ABOUT MOTHER GOOSE (See Mother Goose, Four Color #862)

TRUTH BEHIND THE TRIAL OF CARDINAL MINDSZENTY, THE (See

Tuffy #8 © STD

Turok, Dinosaur Hunter #4 © Acclaim

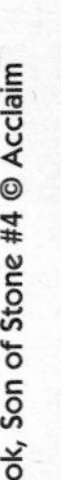
Turok, Son of Stone #4 © Acclaim

Cardinal Mindszenty)

TRUTHFUL LOVE (Formerly Youthful Love)
Youthful Magazines: No. 2, July, 1950

2-Ingrid Bergman's true life story 10.00 30.00 70.00

TRY-OUT WINNER BOOK
Marvel Comics: Mar, 1988

1-Spider-Man vs. Doc Octopus 3.00

TSR WORLD (...Annual on cover only)
DC Comics: 1990 ($3.95, 84 pgs.)

1-Advanced D&D, ForgottenRealms, Dragonlance & 1st app. Spelljammer 4.00

TSUNAMI GIRL
Image Comics: 1999 - No. 3, 1999 ($2.95)

1-3-Sorayama-c/Paniccia-s/a 3.00

TUBBY (See Marge's...)

TUFF GHOSTS STARRING SPOOKY
Harvey Publications: July, 1962 - No. 39, Nov, 1970; No. 40, Sept, 1971 - No. 43, Oct, 1972

	GD	FN	NM
1-12¢ issues begin	12.00	36.00	130.00
2-5	5.90	17.75	65.00
6-10	3.65	11.00	40.00
11-20	3.20	9.60	35.00
21-30: 29-Hot Stuff/Spooky team-up story	2.40	7.35	22.00
31-39,43	1.85	5.50	15.00
40-42: 52 pg. Giants	2.30	7.00	20.00

TUFFY
Standard Comics: No. 5, July, 1949 - No. 9, Oct, 1950

	GD	FN	NM
5-All by Sid Hoff	5.00	15.00	35.00
6-9	4.00	12.00	24.00

TUFFY TURTLE
I. W. Enterprises: No date

1-Reprint 1.50 4.50 12.00

TUG & BUSTER
Art & Soul Comics: Nov, 1995 - No. 7, Feb, 1998 ($2.95, B&W, bi-monthly)

1-7: Marc Hempel-c/a/scripts 3.00

TUG & BUSTER
Image Comics: Aug, 1998 - Present ($2.95, B&W)

1-Marc Hempel-s/a 3.00

TUROK
Acclaim Comics: Mar, 1998 - No. 4, Jun, 1998 ($2.50)

1-4-Nicieza-s/Kayanan-a 2.50

TUROK, CHILD OF BLOOD
Acclaim Comics (Valiant): Jan, 1998 ($3.95, one-shot)

1-Nicieza-s/Kayanan-a 4.00

TUROK, DINOSAUR HUNTER (See Magnus Robot Fighter #12 & Archer & Armstrong #2)
Valiant/Acclaim Comics: June, 1993 - No. 47, Aug, 1996 ($2.50)

1-($3.50)-Chromium & foil-c 3.50
1-Gold foil-c variant 5.00
0, 2-47: 4-Andar app. 5-Death of Andar. 7-9-Truman/Glanzman-a. 11-Bound-in trading card. 16-Chaos Effect 2.50
Yearbook 1 (1994, $3.95, 52 pgs.) 4.00

TUROK, REDPATH
Acclaim Comics (Valiant): Oct, 1997 ($3.95, one-shot)

1-Nicieza-s/Kayanan-a 4.00

TUROK /SHADOWMAN
Acclaim Comics: Feb, 1999 ($3.95, one-shot)

1-Priest-s/Broome & Jimenez-a 4.00

TUROK, SON OF STONE (See Dan Curtis, Golden Comics Digest #31 & March of Comics #378, 399, 408)
Dell Publ. Co. #1-29(9/62)/Gold Key #30(12/62)-85(7/73)/Gold Key or Whitman #86(9/73)-125(1/80)/Whitman #126(3/81) on: No. 596, 12/54 - No. 29, 9/62; No. 30, 12/62 - No. 91, 7/74; No. 92, 9/74 - No. 125, 1/80; No. 126, 3/81 - No. 130, 4/82

	GD	FN	NM
Four Color 596 (12/54)(#1)-1st app./origin Turok & Andar; dinosaur-c. Created by Matthew H. Murphy; written by Alberto Giolitti	58.00	175.00	700.0
Four Color 656 (10/55)(#2)-1st mention of Lanok	33.00	100.00	400.0
3(3-5/56)-5: 3-Cave men	20.00	60.00	240.0
6-10: 8-Dinosaur of the deep; Turok enters Lost Valley; series begins. 9-Paul S. Newman-s (most issues thru end)	13.00	40.00	160.0
11-20: 17-Prehistoric Pygmies	8.35	25.00	100.0
21-29	5.85	17.50	70.0
30-1st Gold Key. 30-33-Painted back-c.	6.30	19.00	75.0
31-Drug use story	5.85	17.50	70.0
32-40	4.55	13.65	50.0
41-50	3.20	9.60	35.0
51-57,59,60	3.00	9.00	30.0
58-Flying Saucer c/story	3.20	9.60	35.0
61-70: 62-12¢ & 15¢ covers. 63-Only line drawn-c	2.50	7.50	25.0
71-84: 84-Origin & 1st app. Hutec	2.00	6.00	18.0
85-99: 93-r-c/#19 w/changes. 94-r-c/#28 w/changes. 97-r-c/#31 w/changes. 98-r/#58 w/o spaceship & spacemen on-c. 99-r-c/#52 w/changes.	1.75	5.25	14.0
100	2.30	7.00	20.0
101-129: 114,115-(52 pgs.)	2.00	6.00	18.0
130-Last issue	2.40	7.35	22.0
Giant 1(30031-611) (11/66)-Slick-c; r/#10-12 & 16 plus cover to #11	9.50	28.50	105.0
Giant 1-Same as above but with paper-c	11.00	33.00	120.0

NOTE: *Most painted-c; line-drawn #63 & 130.* ***Alberto Gioletti*** *a-24-27, 30-119, 123; painted-c No. 30-129.* ***Sparling*** *a-117, 120-130. Reprints-#36, 54, 57, 75, 112, 114(1/3), 115(1/3), 118, 121, 125, 127(1/3), 128, 129(1/3), 130(1/3), Giant 1. Cover r-93, 94, 97-99, 126(all different from original covers.*

TUROK: SPRING BREAK IN THE LOST LAND
Acclaim Comics (Valiant): July, 1997 ($3.95, one-shot)

1-Nicieza-s/Kayanan-a 4.0

TUROK: TALES OF THE LOST LAND
Acclaim Comics (Valiant): Apr, 1998 ($3.95, one-shot)

1 4.0

TUROK: THE EMPTY SOULS
Acclaim Comics (Valiant): Apr, 1997 ($3.95, one-shot)

1-Nicieza-s/Kayanan-a; variant-c 4.0

TUROK THE HUNTED
Valiant/Acclaim Comics: Mar, 1995 - No. 2, Apr, 1995 ($2.50, limited series)

1,2-Mike Deodato-a(p); price omitted on #1 2.5

TUROK THE HUNTED
Acclaim Comics (Valiant): Feb, 1996 - No. 2, Mar, 1996 ($2.50, limited series)

1,2-Mike Grell story 2.5

TUROK, TIMEWALKER
Acclaim Comics (Valiant): Aug, 1997 - No. 2, Sept, 1997 ($2.50, limited series

1,2-Nicieza story 2.5

TUROK 2 (Magazine)
Acclaim Comics: Oct, 1998 ($4.99, magazine size)

...Seeds of Evil-Nicieza-s/Broome & Benjamin-a; origin back-up story 5.0
#2 Adon's Curse -Mack painted-c/Broome & Benjamin-a; origin pt. 2 5.0

TUROK 3: SHADOW OF OBLIVION
Acclaim Comics: Sept, 2000 ($4.95, one-shot)

1-Includes pin-up gallery 5.0

TURTLE SOUP
Mirage Studios: Sept, 1987 ($2.00, 76 pgs., B&W, one-shot)

1-Featuring Teenage Mutant Ninja Turtles 4.0

TURTLE SOUP
Mirage Studios: Nov, 1991 - No. 4, 1992 ($2.50, limited series, coated paper)

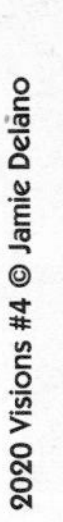
2099 Unlimited #9 © MAR

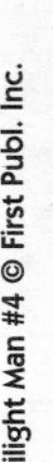
2020 Visions #4 © Jamie Delano

Twilight Man #4 © First Publ. Inc.

	GD2.0	FN6.0	NM9.4
1-4: Features the Teenage Mutant Ninja Turtles			2.50

TV CASPER & COMPANY
Harvey Publications: Aug, 1963 - No. 46, April, 1974 (25¢ Giants)

1: 68 pg. Giants begin; Casper, Little Audrey, Baby Huey, Herman & Catnip, Buzzy the Crow begin	11.50	34.00	125.00
2-5	5.00	15.00	55.00
6-10	3.80	11.40	42.00
11-20	2.80	8.40	28.00
21-31: 31-Last 68 pg. issue	2.30	7.00	20.00
32-46: All 52 pgs.	2.00	6.00	16.00

NOTE: *Many issues contain reprints.*

TV FUNDAY FUNNIES (See Famous TV...)

TV FUNNIES (See New Funnies)

TV FUNTIME (See Little Audrey)

TV LAUGHOUT (See Archie's...)

TV SCREEN CARTOONS (Formerly Real Screen)
National Periodical Publ.: No. 129, July-Aug, 1959 - No. 138, Jan-Feb, 1961

129-138 (Scarce)	7.25	21.75	80.00

TV STARS (TV) (Newsstand sales only)
Marvel Comics Group: Aug, 1978 - No. 4, Feb, 1979 (Hanna-Barbera)

1-Great Grape Ape app.	2.50	7.50	24.00
2,4: 4-Top Cat app.	2.00	6.00	18.00
3-Toth-c/a; Dave Stevens inks	2.50	7.50	23.00

TV TEENS (Formerly Ozzie & Babs; Rock and Rollo #14 on)
Charlton Comics: V1#14, Feb, 1954 - V2#13, July, 1956

V1#14 (#1)-Ozzie & Babs	8.65	26.00	60.00
15 (#2)	5.00	15.00	32.00
V2#3(6/54) - 6-Don Winslow	5.00	15.00	35.00
7-13-Mopsy. 8(7/55)	5.00	15.00	32.00

TWEETY AND SYLVESTER (1st Series) (TV)
Dell Publishing Co.: No. 406, June, 1952 - No. 37, June-Aug, 1962

Four Color 406 (#1)-1st app.?	8.00	24.00	95.00
Four Color 489,524	4.10	12.30	45.00
4 (3-5/54) - 20	3.00	9.00	32.00
21-37	2.40	7.35	22.00

(See March of Comics #421, 433, 445, 457, 469, 481)

TWEETY AND SYLVESTER (2nd Series)(See Kite Fun Book)
Gold Key No. 1-102/Whitman No. 103 on: Nov, 1963; No. 2, Nov, 1965 - No. 121, July, 1984

1	3.00	9.00	32.00
2-10	2.30	7.00	20.00
11-30	2.00	6.00	16.00
31-50	1.25	3.75	10.00
51-70	1.00	2.80	7.00
71-102			5.00
103,104 (Whitman)		2.40	6.00
105(9/80),106(10/80),107(12/80) 3-pack?	1.75	5.25	14.00
108-116	1.00	3.00	8.00
117-121: (All # 90094 on-c; nd, nd code). 119-r(1/3)	1.50	4.50	12.00
Mini Comic No. 1(1976, 3-1/4x6-1/2")	1.00	3.00	8.00

12 O'CLOCK HIGH (TV)
Dell Publishing Co.: Jan-Mar, 1965 - No. 2, Apr-June, 1965 (Photo-c)

1	5.45	16.35	60.00
2	4.10	12.30	45.00

2099 A.D.
Marvel Comics: May, 1995 ($3.95, one-shot)

1-Acetate-c by Quesada & Palmiotti.			4.00

2099 APOCALYPSE
Marvel Comics: Dec, 1995 ($4.95, one-shot)

1-Chromium wraparound-c; Ellis script			5.00

2099 GENESIS
Marvel Comics: Jan, 1996 ($4.95, one-shot)

1-Chromium wraparound-c; Ellis script			5.00

2099 MANIFEST DESTINY
Marvel Comics: Mar, 1998 ($5.99, one-shot)

1-Origin of Fantastic Four 2099; intro Moon Knight 2099			6.00

2099 UNLIMITED
Marvel Comics: Sept, 1993 - No. 10, 1996 ($3.95, 68 pgs.)

1-10: 1-1st app. Hulk 2099 & begins. 1-3-Spider-Man 2099 app. 9-Joe Kubert-c; Len Wein & Nancy Collins scripts			4.00

2099 WORLD OF DOOM SPECIAL
Marvel Comics: May, 1995 ($2.25, one-shot)

1-Doom's "Contract w/America"			2.25

2099 WORLD OF TOMORROW
Marvel Comics: Sept, 1996 - No. 8, Apr, 1997 ($2.50) (Replaces 2099 titles)

1-8: 1-Wraparound-c. 2-w/bound-in card. 4,5-Phalanx			2.50

21
Image Comics (Top Cow Productions): Feb, 1996 - No. 3, Apr, 1996 ($2.50)

1-3: Len Wein scripts			2.50
1-Variant-c			2.50

2020 VISIONS
DC Comics (Vertigo): May, 1997 - No. 12, Apr, 1998 ($2.25, limited series)

1-12-Delano-s: 1-3-Quitely-a. 4-"la tormenta"-Pleece-a			2.25

20,000 LEAGUES UNDER THE SEA (Movie)(See King Classics, Movie Comics & Power Record Comics)
Dell Publishing Co.: No. 614, Feb, 1955 (Disney)

Four Color 614-Movie, painted-c	9.00	27.00	110.00

22 BRIDES (See Ash/)
Event Comics: Mar, 1996 - No. 4, Jan, 1997 ($2.95)

1-4: Fabian Nicieza scripts			3.00
2,3-Variant-c			3.00

TWICE TOLD TALES (See Movie Classics)

TWILIGHT
DC Comics: 1990 - No. 3, 1991 ($4.95, 52 pgs, lim. series, squarebound, mature)

1-3: Tommy Tomorrow app; Chaykin scripts, Garcia-Lopez-c/a.			5.00

TWILIGHT AVENGER, THE
Elite Comics: July, 1986 - No. 4, 1987 ($1.75, 28 pgs, limited series)

1-4			2.00

TWILIGHT MAN
First Publishing: June, 1989 - No. 4, Sept, 1989 ($2.75, limited series)

1-4			2.75

TWILIGHT ZONE, THE (TV) (See Dan Curtis & Stories From...)
Dell Publishing Co./Gold Key/Whitman No. 92: No. 1173, 3-5/61 - No. 91, 4/79; No. 92, 5/82

Four Color 1173 (#1)-Crandall-c/a	20.00	60.00	240.00
Four Color 1288-Crandall/Evans-c/a	11.00	33.00	130.00
01-860-207 (5-7/62-Dell, 15¢)	7.50	22.50	90.00
12-860-210 on-c; 01-860-210 on inside(8-10/62-Dell)-Evans-c/a (3 stories)	7.50	22.50	90.00
1(11/62-Gold Key)-Crandall/Frazetta-a (10 & 11 pgs.); Evans-a	11.00	33.00	130.00
2	6.70	20.00	80.00
3-11: 3(11 pgs.),4(10 pgs.),9-Toth-a	4.55	13.65	50.00
12-15: 12-Williamson-a. 13,15-Crandall-a. 14-Orlando/Crandall/Torres-a	3.65	11.00	40.00
16-20	2.80	8.40	28.00
21-25: 21-Crandall-a(r). 25-Evans/Crandall-a(r); Toth-r/#4; last 12¢ issue	2.40	7.35	22.00
26,27: 26-Flying Saucer-c/story; Crandall, Evans-a(r). 27-Evans-r(2)	2.40	7.35	22.00
28-32: 32-Evans-a(r)	2.00	6.00	18.00
33-51: 43-Celardo-a. 51-Williamson-a	1.50	4.50	12.00
52-70	1.25	3.75	10.00

The Twilight Zone V3 #4 © Now Comics

Two-Fisted Tales #30 © WMG

Two-Gun Kid #6 © MAR

	GD2.0	FN6.0	NM9.4
71-82,85-91: 71-Reprint		2.40	6.00
83-(52 pgs.)	1.50	4.50	12.00
84-(52 pgs.) Frank Miller's 1st comic book work	2.00	6.00	18.00
92-Last issue; r/#1.	1.00	3.00	8.00
Mini Comic #1(1976, 3-1/4x6-1/2")	1.10	3.30	9.00

NOTE: ***Bolle** a-13(w/**McWilliams**), 50, 55, 57, 59, 77, 78, 80, 83, 84. **McWilliams** a-59, 78, 80, 82, 84. **Miller** a-84, 85. **Orlando** a-15, 19, 20, 22, 23. **Sekowsky** a-3. **Simonson** a-50, 54, 55, 83r. **Weiss** a-39, 79r(#39). (See Mystery Comics Digest 3, 6, 9, 12, 15, 18, 21, 24). Reprints-26(1/3), 71, 73, 79, 83, 84, 86, 92. Painted c-1-91.*

TWILIGHT ZONE, THE (TV)
Now Comics: Nov, 1990 ($2.95); Oct, 1991; V2#1, Nov, 1991 - No. 11, Oct, 1992 ($1.95); V3#1, 1993 - No. 4, 1993 ($2.50)

	GD2.0	FN6.0	NM9.4
1-(11/90, $2.95, 52 pgs.)-Direct sale edition; Neal Adams-a, Sienkiewicz-c; Harlan Ellison scripts			3.00
1-(11/90, $1.75)-Newsstand ed. w/N. Adams-c			2.00
1-Prestige Format (10/91, $4.95)-Reprints above with extra Harlan Ellison short story			5.00
1-Collector's Edition (10/91, $2.50)-Non-code approved and polybagged; reprints 11/90 issue; gold logo, 1-Reprint ($2.50)-r/direct sale 11/90 version			
1-Reprint ($2.50)-r/newsstand 11/90 version			2.50
V2#1-Direct sale & newsstand ed. w/different-c			2.50
V2#2-8,10-11			2.50
V2#9-($2.95)-3-D Special; polybagged w/glasses & hologram on-c			3.00
V2#9-($4.95)-Prestige Edition; contains 2 extra stories & a different hologram on-c; polybagged w/glasses			5.00
V3#1-4, Anniversary Special 1 (1992, $2.50)			2.50
Annual 1 (4/93, $2.50)-No ads			2.50
...Science Fiction Special (3/93, $3.50)			3.50

TWINKLE COMICS
Spotlight Publishers: May, 1945

	GD2.0	FN6.0	NM9.4
1	24.00	71.00	190.00

TWIST, THE
Dell Publishing Co.: July-Sept, 1962

	GD2.0	FN6.0	NM9.4
01-864-209-Painted-c	3.65	11.00	40.00

TWISTED TALES (See Eclipse Graphic Album Series #15)
Pacific Comics/Independent Comics Group (Eclipse) #9,10: 11/82 - No. 8, 5/84; No. 9, 11/84; No. 10, 12/84 (Baxter paper)

	GD2.0	FN6.0	NM9.4
1-9: 1-B. Jones/Corben-c; Alcala-a; nudity/violence in al. 2-Wrightson-c; Ploog-a			4.00
10-Wrightson painted art; Morrow-a			6.00

NOTE: ***Bolton** painted c-4, 6, 7; a-7. **Conrad** a-1, 3, 5; c-1i, 3, 5. **Guice** a-8. **Wildey** a-3.*

TWO BIT THE WACKY WOODPECKER (See Wacky...)
Toby Press: 1951 - No. 3, May, 1953

	GD2.0	FN6.0	NM9.4
1	9.30	28.00	65.00
2,3	5.00	15.00	35.00

TWO FACES OF TOMORROW, THE
Dark Horse: Aug, 1997 - No. 13, Aug, 1998 ($2.95/$3.95, B&W, lim. series)

	GD2.0	FN6.0	NM9.4
1-13: 1-Manga			4.00

TWO-FISTED TALES (Formerly Haunt of Fear #15-17)
E. C. Comics: No. 18, Nov-Dec, 1950 - No. 41, Feb-Mar, 1955

	GD2.0	FN6.0	NM9.4
18(#1)-Kurtzman-c	78.00	235.00	860.00
19-Kurtzman-c	63.00	190.00	695.00
20-Kurtzman-c	38.00	115.00	420.00
21,22-Kurtzman-c	29.00	87.00	320.00
23-25-Kurtzman-c	23.00	70.00	255.00
26-35: 33- "Atom Bomb" by Wood	16.00	48.00	175.00
36-41	13.00	40.00	145.00
Two-Fisted Annual (1952, 25¢, 132 pgs.)	68.00	205.00	750.00
Two-Fisted Annual (1953, 25¢, 132 pgs.)	51.00	153.00	560.00

NOTE: ***Berg** a-29. **Colan** a-39p. **Craig** a-18, 19, 32. **Crandall** a-35, 36. **Davis** a-20-36, 40; c-30, 34, 35, 41, Annual 2. **Evans** a-34, 40, 41; c-40. **Feldstein** a-18. **Krigstein** a-41. **Kubert** a-32, 33. **Kurtzman** a-18-25; c-18-29, 31, Annual 1. **Severin** a-26, 28, 29, 31, 34-41 (No. 37-39 are all-Severin issues); c-36-39. **Severin/Elder** a-19-29, 31, 33, 36. **Wood** a-18-28, 30-35, 41; c-32, 33. Special issues: #26 (ChanJin Reservoir), 31 (Civil War), 35 (Civil War). Canadian reprints known; see Table of Contents. #25-Davis biog. #27-Wood biog. #28-Kurtzman biog.*

TWO-FISTED TALES
Russ Cochran/Gemstone Publishing: Oct, 1992 - No. 24, May, 1998 ($1.50/$2.00/$2.50)

	GD2.0	FN6.0	NM9.4
1-24: 1-4r/Two-Fisted Tales #18-21 w/original-c			2.50

TWO-GUN KID (Also see All Western Winners, Best Western, Black Rider, Blaze Carson, Kid Colt, Western Winners, Wild West, & Wild Western)
Marvel/Atlas (MCI No. 1-10/HPC No. 11-59/Marvel No. 60 on): 3/48(No mo.) - No. 10, 11/49; No. 11, 12/53 - No. 59, 4/61; No. 60, 11/62 - No. 92, 3/68; No. 93, 7/70 - No. 136, 4/77

	GD2.0	FN6.0	NM9.4
1-Two-Gun Kid & his horse Cyclone begin; The Sheriff begins	103.00	308.00	975.00
2	42.00	125.00	375.00
3,4: 3-Annie Oakley app.	35.00	105.00	280.00
5-Pre-Black Rider app. (Wint. 48/49); spanking panel; Anti-Wertham editorial (1st?)	40.00	120.00	340.00
6-10(11/49): 8-Blaze Carson app. 9-Black Rider app.	28.00	83.00	220.00
11(12/53)-Black Rider app.; 1st to have Atlas globe on-c; explains how Kid Colt became an outlaw	21.00	64.00	170.00
12-Black Rider app.	21.00	64.00	170.00
13-20: 14-Opium story	15.00	45.00	120.00
21-24,26-29	14.00	41.00	110.00
25,30: 25-Williamson-a (5 pgs.). 30-Williamson/Torres-a (4 pgs.)	15.00	45.00	120.00
31-33,35,37-40	7.25	21.75	80.00
34-Crandall-a	7.65	23.00	85.00
36,41,42,48-Origin in all	7.65	23.00	85.00
43,44,47	5.45	16.35	60.00
45,46-Davis-a	6.35	19.00	70.00
49,50,52,53-Severin-a(2/3) in each	5.00	15.00	55.00
51-Williamson-a (5 pgs.)	6.35	19.00	70.00
54,55,57,59-Severin-a(3) in each. 59-Kirby-a; last 10¢ issue (4/61)	4.55	13.65	50.00
56	3.65	11.00	40.00
58,60-New origin. 58-Kirby/Ayers-c/a "The Monster of Hidden Valley" cover/story (Kirby monster-c)	4.55	13.65	50.00
60-Edition w/handwritten issue number on cover	6.80	20.50	75.00
61,62-Kirby-a	4.10	12.30	45.00
63-74: 64-Intro. Boom-Boom	2.50	7.50	25.00
75-77-Kirby-a	3.20	9.60	35.00
78-89	2.40	7.35	22.00
90,95-Kirby-a	3.00	9.00	30.00
91,92: 92-Last new story; last 12¢ issue	2.30	7.00	20.00
93,94,96-99	1.85	5.50	15.00
100-Last 15¢-c	2.00	6.00	18.00
101-Origin retold/#58; Kirby-a	2.00	6.00	18.00
102-120-reprints	1.50	4.50	12.00
121-136-reprints. 129-131-(Regular 25¢ editions)	1.10	3.30	9.00
129-131-(30¢-c variants, limited distribution)(4-8/76)	1.75	5.25	14.00

NOTE: ***Ayers** a-26, 27. **Davis** c-45-47. **Drucker** a-23. **Everett** a-82, 91. **Fuje** a-13. **Heath** a-3(2), 4(3), 5(2), 7; c-13, 21, 23, 53. **Keller** a-16, 19, 28. **Kirby** a-54, 55, 57-62, 75-77, 90, 95, 101, 119, 120, 129; c-10, 52, 54-65, 67-72, 74-76, 116. **Maneely** a-20; c-11, 12, 16, 19, 20, 25-28, 35, 49. **Powell** a-38, 102, 104. **Severin** a-9, 29, 51, 55, 57, 99r(3); c-9, 51, 99. **Shores** c-1-8, 11. **Tuska** a-11, 12. **Whitney** a-87, 89-91, 98-113, 124, 129; c-87, 89, 91, 113. **Wildey** a-21. **Williamson** a-110r. Kid Colt in #13, 14, 16-21.*

TWO GUN KID:SUNSET RIDERS
Marvel Comics: Nov, 1995 - No. 2, Dec, 1995 ($6.95, squarebound, lim. series)

	GD2.0	FN6.0	NM9.4
1,2: Fabian Nicieza scripts in all. 1-painted-c.			7.00

TWO GUN WESTERN (1st Series) (Formerly Casey Crime Photographer #1-4? or My Love #1-4?)
Marvel/Atlas Comics (MPC): No. 5, Nov, 1950 - No. 14, June, 1952

	GD2.0	FN6.0	NM9.4
5-The Apache Kid (Intro & origin) & his horse Nightwind begin by Buscema	26.00	79.00	210.00
6-10: 8-Kid Colt, The Texas Kid & his horse Thunder begin?	19.00	56.00	150.00
11-14: 13-Black Rider app.	13.00	39.00	105.00

NOTE: ***Maneely** a-6, 7, 9; c-6, 11-13. **Morrow** a-9. **Romita** a-8. **Wildey** a-8.*

2-GUN WESTERN (2nd Series) (Formerly Billy Buckskin #1-3; Two-Gun Western #5 on)

2001, A Space Odyssey #7 © MAR

Ultimate Spider-Man #1 © MAR

Ultimate X-Men #1 © MAR

GD2.0 FN6.0 NM9.4

Atlas Comics (MgPC): No. 4, May, 1956

4-Colan, Ditko, Severin, Sinnott-a; Maneely-c 16.00 49.00 130.00

TWO-GUN WESTERN (Formerly 2-Gun Western)
Atlas Comics (MgPC): No. 5, July, 1956 - No. 12, Sept, 1957

5-Return of the Gun-Hawk-c/story; Black Rider app. 15.00 45.00 120.00
6,7 10.50 32.00 85.00
8,10,12-Crandall-a 12.00 36.00 95.00
9,11-Williamson-a in both (5 pgs. each) 12.00 36.00 95.00
NOTE: ***Ayers** a-9. **Colan** a-5. **Everett** c-12. **Forgione** a-5, 6. **Kirby** a-12. **Maneely** a-6, 8, 12; c-5, 6, 8, 11. **Morrow** a-9, 10. **Powell** a-7, 11. **Severin** c-10. **Sinnott** a-5. **Wildey** a-9.*

TWO MINUTE WARNING
Ultimate Sports Ent.: 2000 - No. 3 ($3.95, cardstock covers)

1,2-NFL players & Teddy Roosevelt battle evil 4.00

TWO MOUSEKETEERS, THE (See 4-Color #475, 603, 642 under M.G.M.'s...;

TWO ON A GUILLOTINE (See Movie Classics)

2000 A.D. MONTHLY/PRESENTS (Showcase #25 on)
Eagle Comics/Quality Comics No. 5 on: 4/85 - #6, 9/85; 4/86 - #54, 1991 ($1.25-$1.50, Mando paper)

1-6,1-25:1-4 r/British series featuring Judge Dredd; Alan Moore scripts begin.
1-25 ($1.25)-Reprints from British 2000 AD 2.00
26,27/28, 29/30, 31-54: 27/28, 29/30,31-Guice-c 2.00

2001, A SPACE ODYSSEY (Movie)
Marvel Comics Group: Dec, 1976 - No. 10, Sept, 1977 (30¢)

1,8: 1-Adaptation of film; Kirby-c/a in all. 8-Original/1st app. Machine Man (called Mr. Machine) 1.00 3.00 8.00
2-7,9,10 5.00
...Treasury 1 ('76, 84 pgs.)-All new Kirby-a 2.00 6.00 16.00

2001 NIGHTS
Viz Premiere Comics: 1990 - No. 10, 1991 ($3.75, B&W, limited series, mature readers, 84 pgs.)

1-10: Japanese sci-fi. 1-Wraparound-c 4.25

2010 (Movie)
Marvel Comics Group: Apr, 1985 - No. 2, May, 1985

1,2-r/Marvel Super Special movie adaptation. 2.00

TYPHOID (Also see Daredevil)
Marvel Comics: Nov, 1995 - No. 4, Feb, 1996 ($3.95, squarebound, lim. series)

1-4: Van Fleet-c/a 4.00

UFO & ALIEN COMIX
Warren Publishing Co.: Jan, 1978 (one-shot)

nn-Toth, Severin-a(r) 1.75 5.25 14.00

UFO & OUTER SPACE (Formerly UFO Flying Saucers)
Gold Key: No. 14, June, 1978 - No. 25, Feb, 1980 (All painted covers)

14-Reprints UFO Flying Saucers #3 1.00 3.00 8.00
15,16-Reprints 1.00 3.00 8.00
17-25: 17-20-New material. 23-McWilliams-a. 24-(3 pg.-r). 25-Reprints UFO Flying Saucers #2 w/cover 1.00 2.80 7.00

UFO ENCOUNTERS
Western Publishing Co.: May, 1978 ($1.95, 228 pgs.)

11192-Reprints UFO Flying Saucers 2.80 8.40 28.00
11404-Vol.1 (128 pgs.)-See UFO Mysteries for Vol.2 2.50 7.50 23.00

UFO FLYING SAUCERS (UFO & Outer Space #14 on)
Gold Key: Oct, 1968 - No. 13, Jan, 1977 (No. 2 on, 36 pgs.)

1(30035-810) (68 pgs.) 3.00 9.00 30.00
2(11/70), 3(11/72), 4(11/74) 2.00 6.00 16.00
5(2/75)-13: Bolle-a #4 on 1.50 4.50 12.00

UFO MYSTERIES
Western Publishing Co.: 1978 ($1.00, reprints, 96 pgs.)

11400-(Vol.2)-Cont'd from UFO Encounters, pgs. 129-224 2.00 6.00 18.00

ULTIMATE... (Collects 4-issue alternate titles from X-Men Age of Apocalypse crossovers)
Marvel Comics: May, 1995 ($8.95, trade paperbacks, gold foil covers)

Amazing X-Men, Astonishing X-Men, Factor-X, Gambit & the X-Ternals, Generation Next, X-Calibre, X-Man 9.00
Weapon X 10.00

ULTIMATE SPIDER-MAN
Marvel Comics: Oct, 2000 - Present ($2.99/$2.50)

1-Bendis-s/Bagley & Thibert-a; cardstock-c; introduces revised origin and cast separate from regular Spider-continuity 8.00
1-Variant white-c (Retailer incentive) 25.00
1-DF Edition 15.00
2-Two covers 5.00
3-5: 4-Uncle Ben dies 2.50

ULTIMATE X-MEN
Marvel Comics: Feb, 2001 - Present ($2.99/$2.50)

1-Millar-s/Adam Kubert & Thibert-a; cardstock-c; introduces revised origin and cast separate from regular X-Men continuity 3.00
1-DF Edition 10.00

ULTRACYBERNETIC DOLPHINDROIDS, THE
Polestar Comics: Dec, 1993 ($2.50, unfinished limited series)

1 2.50

ULTRAFORCE (1st Series) (Also see Avengers/Ultraforce #1)
Malibu Comics (Ultraverse): Aug, 1994 - No. 10, Aug, 1995 ($1.95/$2.50)

0 (9/94, $2.50)-Perez-c/a. 2.50
1-($2.50, 44 pgs.)-Bound-in trading card; team consisting of Prime, Prototype, Hardcase, Pixx, Ghoul, Contrary & Topaz; Gerard Jones scripts begin, ends #6; Perez-c/a begins. 2.50
1-Ultra 5000 Limited Silver Foil Edition 4.00
1-Holographic-c, no price 6.00
2-5: Perez-c/a in all. 2 (10/94, $1.95)-Prime quits, Strangers cameo. 3-Origin of Topaz; Prime rejoins. 5-Pixx dies. 2.50
2 ($2.50)-Florescent logo; limited edition stamp on-c 3.00
6-10: 6-Begin $2.50-c, Perez-c/a. 7-Ghoul story, Steve Erwin-a. 8-Marvel's Black Knight enters the Ultraverse (last seen in Avengers #375); Perez-c/a. 9,10-Black Knight app.; Perez-c. 10-Leads into Ultraforce/Avengers Prelude. 2.50
Malibu "Ashcan ": Ultraforce #0A (6/94) 2.00
.../Avengers Prelude 1 (8/95, $2.50)-Perez-c. 2.50
.../Avengers 1 (8/95, $3.95)-Warren Ellis script; Perez-c/a; foil-c 4.00

ULTRAFORCE (2nd Series)(Also see Black September)
Malibu Comics (Ultraverse): Infinity, Sept, 1995 - V2#15, Dec, 1996 ($1.50)

Infinity, V2#1-15: Infinity-Team consists of Marvel's Black Knight, Ghoul, Topaz, Prime & redesigned Prototype; Warren Ellis scripts begin, ends #3; variant-c exists. 1-1st app.Cromwell, Lament & Wreckage. 2-Contains free encore presentation of Ultraforce #1; flip book "Phoenix Resurrection" Pt. 7. 7-Darick Robertson, Jeff Johnson & others-a. 8,9-Intro. Future Ultraforce (Prime, Hellblade, Angel of Destruction, Painkiller & Whipslash); Gary Erskine-c/a. 9-Foxfire app. 10-Len Wein scripts & Deodato Studios-c/a begin. 10-Lament back-up story. 11-Ghoul back-up story by Pander Bros. 12-Ultraforce vs. Maxis (cont'd in Ultraverse Unlimited #2); Exiles & Iron Clad app. 13-Prime leaves; Hardcase returns 2.00
Infinity (2000 signed) 4.00
.../Spider-Man ($3.95)-Marv Wolfman script; Green Goblin app; 2 covers exist. 4.00

ULTRAGIRL
Marvel Comics: Nov, 1996 - No. 3 Mar, 1997($1.50, limited series)

1-3: 1-1st app. 2.00

ULTRA KLUTZ
Onward Comics: 1981; 6/86 - #27, 1/89, #28, 4/90 - #31, 1990? ($1.50/$1.75/$2.00, B&W)

1 (1981)-Re-released after 2nd #1 2.00
1-30: 1-(6/86). 27-Photo back-c 2.00
31-($2.95, 52 pgs.) 3.00

Ultraverse Double Feature #1 © MAL

Uncanny Tales #17 © MAR

Uncle Sam Quarterly #5 © QUA

GD2.0 FN6.0 NM9.4 — GD2.0 FN6.0 NM9.4

ULTRAMAN
Nemesis Comics: Mar, 1994 - No. 4, 1995? ($1.75/$1.95)

1-($2.25)-Collector's edition; foil-c; special 3/4 wraparound-c 3.00
1-($1.75)-Newsstand edition 2.50
2-4: 3-$1.95-c begins 2.50

ULTRAVERSE DOUBLE FEATURE
Malibu Comics (Ultraverse): Jan, 1995 ($3.95, one-shot, 68 pgs.)

1-Flip-c featuring Prime & Solitaire. 4.00

ULTRAVERSE ORIGINS
Malibu Comics (Ultraverse): Jan, 1994 (99¢, one-shot)

1-Gatefold-c; 2 pg. origins all characters 2.00
1-Newsstand edition; different-c, no gatefold 2.00

ULTRAVERSE PREMIERE
Malibu Comics (Ultraverse): 1994 (one-shot)

0-Ordered thru mail w/coupons 5.00

ULTRAVERSE UNLIMITED
Malibu Comics (Ultraverse): June, 1996; No. 2, Sept, 1996 ($2.50)

1,2: 1-Adam Warlock returns to the Marvel Universe; Rune-c/app. 2-Black Knight, Reaper & Sierra Blaze return to the Marvel Universe 2.50

ULTRAVERSE YEAR ONE
Malibu Comics (Ultraverse): 1994 ($4.95, one-shot)

nn-In-depth synopsis of the first year's titles & stories. 5.00

ULTRAVERSE YEAR TWO
Malibu Comics (Ultraverse): Aug, 1995 ($4.95, one-shot)

nn-In-depth synopsis of second year's titles & stories 5.00

ULTRAVERSE YEAR ZERO: THE DEATH OF THE SQUAD
Malibu Comics (Ultraverse): Apr, 1995 - No. 4, July, 1995 ($2.95, lim. series)

1-4: 3-Codename: Firearm back-up story. 3.00

UNBIRTHDAY PARTY WITH ALICE IN WONDERLAND (See Alice In Wonderland, Four Color #341)

UNBOUND
Image Comics (Desperado): Jan, 1998 - Present ($2.95, B&W)

1-Pruett-s/Peters-a 3.00

UNCANNY ORIGINS
Marvel Comics: Sept, 1996 - No. 14, Oct, 1997 (99¢)

1-14: 1-Cyclops. 2-Quicksilver. 3-Archangel. 4-Firelord. 5-Hulk. 6-Beast 7-Venom. 8-Nightcrawler. 9-Storm. 10-Black Cat. 11-Black Knight. 12-Dr. Strange. 13-Daredevil. 14-Iron Fist 2.00

UNCANNY TALES
Atlas Comics (PrPI/PPI): June, 1952 - No. 56, Sept, 1957

Issue	GD2.0	FN6.0	NM9.4
1-Heath-a; horror/weird stories begin	84.00	253.00	800.00
2	47.00	142.00	425.00
3-5	40.00	120.00	350.00
6-Wolvertonish-a by Matt Fox	41.00	123.00	370.00
7-10: 8-Atom bomb story; Tothish-a (by Sekowsky?). 9-Crandall-a	38.00	113.00	300.00
11-20: 17-Atom bomb panels; anti-communist story; Hitler story. 19-Krenkel-a. 20-Robert Q. Sale-c	28.00	84.00	225.00
21-25,27: 25-Nostrand-a?	24.00	71.00	190.00
26-Spider-Man prototype c/story	34.00	103.00	275.00
28-Last precode issue (1/55); Kubert-a; #1-28 contain 2-3 sci/fi stories each	25.00	75.00	200.00
29-41,43-49,51	16.00	48.00	125.00
42,54,56-Krigstein-a	17.00	51.00	135.00
50,53,55-Torres-a	16.00	48.00	125.00
52-Oldest? Iron Man prototype (2/57)	19.00	56.00	150.00

NOTE: ***Andru** a-15, 27. **Ayers** a-22. **Bailey** a-51. **Briefer** a-19, 20. **Brodsky** c-1, 3, 4, 6, 8, 12-16, 19. **Brodsky/Everett** c-9. **Cameron** a-47. **Colan** a-11, 16, 17, 52. **Drucker** a-37, 42, 45. **Everett** a-2, 9, 12, 32, 36, 39, 48; c-7, 11, 17, 39, 41, 50, 52, 53. **Fass** a-9, 10, 15, 24. Forte a-18, 27, 34, 52, 53. **Heath** a-13, 14; c-5, 10, 18. **Keller** a-3. **Lawrence** a-14, 17, 19, 23, 27, 28, 35. **Maneely** a-4, 8, 10, 16, 29, 35; c-2, 22, 26, 33, 38. **Moldoff** a-23. **Morisi** a-48, 52. **Morrow** a-46, 51. **Orlando** a-49, 50, 53. **Powell** a-12, 18, 34, 36, 38, 43, 50, 56. **Robinson** a-3, 13. **Reinman** a-12. **Romita** a-10. **Roussos** a-8. **Sale** a-47, 53; c-20. **Sekowsky** a-25. **Sinnott** a-15, 52. **Torres** a-53. **Tothish**-a by **Andru**-27. **Wildey** a-22, 48.*

UNCANNY TALES
Marvel Comics Group: Dec, 1973 - No. 12, Oct, 1975

Issue	GD2.0	FN6.0	NM9.4
1-Crandall-r/Uncanny Tales #9('50s)	2.30	7.00	20.00
2-12: 7,12-Kirby-a	1.50	4.50	12.00

NOTE: ***Ditko** reprints-#4, 6-8, 10-12.*

UNCANNY X-MEN, THE (See **X-Men, The**, 1st series, #142-on)

UNCANNY X-MEN AND THE NEW TEEN TITANS (See Marvel and DC Present...)

UNCENSORED MOUSE, THE
Eternity Comics: Apr, 1989 - No. 2, Apr, 1989 ($1.95, B&W)(Came sealed in plastic bag)(Both contain racial stereotyping & violence)

Issue	GD2.0	FN6.0	NM9.4
1,2-Early Gottfredson strip-r in each	1.10	3.30	9.00

NOTE: *Both issues contain unauthorized reprints. Series was cancelled. **Win Smith** r-1, 2.*

UNCLE CHARLIE'S FABLES
Lev Gleason Publ.: Jan, 1952 - No. 5, Sept, 1952 (All have Biro painted-c)

Issue	GD2.0	FN6.0	NM9.4
1-Norman Maurer-a; has Biro's picture	14.00	41.00	110.00
2-Fuje-a; Biro photo	9.30	28.00	65.00
3-5	7.85	23.50	55.00

UNCLE DONALD & HIS NEPHEWS DUDE RANCH (See Dell Giant #52)

UNCLE DONALD & HIS NEPHEWS FAMILY FUN (See Dell Giant #38)

UNCLE JOE'S FUNNIES
Centaur Publications: 1938 (B&W)

Issue	GD2.0	FN6.0	NM9.4
1-Games, puzzles & magic tricks, some interior art; Bill Everett-c	50.00	150.00	450.00

UNCLE MILTY (TV)
Victoria Publications/True Cross: Dec, 1950 - No. 4, July, 1951 (52 pgs.)(Early TV comic)

Issue	GD2.0	FN6.0	NM9.4
1-Milton Berle photo on-c of #1,2	50.00	150.00	450.00
2	33.00	98.00	260.00
3,4	28.00	83.00	220.00

UNCLE REMUS & HIS TALES OF BRER RABBIT (See Brer Rabbit, 4-Color #129, 208, 693)

UNCLE SAM
DC Comics (Vertigo): 1997 - No. 2, 1997 ($4.95, limited series)

1,2-Alex Ross painted c/a. Story by Ross and Steve Darnell 5.00
Hardcover (1998, $17.95) 18.00
Softcover (2000, $9.95) 10.00

UNCLE SAM QUARTERLY (Blackhawk #9 on)(See Freedom Fighters)
Quality Comics Group: Autumn, 1941 - No. 8, Fall, 1943 (see National Comics)

Issue	GD2.0	FN6.0	NM9.4
1-Origin Uncle Sam; Fine/Eisner-c, chapter headings, 2 pgs. by Eisner; (2 versions: dark cover, no price; light cover with price sticker); Jack Cole-a	333.00	1000.00	3500.00
2-Cameos by The Ray, Black Condor, Quicksilver, The Red Bee, Alias the Spider, Hercules & Neon the Unknown; Eisner, Fine-c/a	126.00	379.00	1200.00
3-Tuska-c/a; Eisner-a(2)	95.00	285.00	900.00
4	84.00	253.00	800.00
5,7-Hitler, Mussolini & Tojo-c	95.00	285.00	900.00
6,8	68.00	205.00	650.00

NOTE: ***Kotzky** (or **Tuska**) a-3-8.*

UNCLE SCROOGE (Disney) (Becomes Walt Disney's... #210 on) (See Cartoon Tales, Dell Giants #33, 55, Disney Comic Album, Donald and Scrooge, Dynabrite, Four Color #178, Gladstone Comic Album, Walt Disney's Comics & Stories #98, Walt Disney's ...)
Dell #1-39/Gold Key #40-173/Whitman #174-209: No. 386, 3/52 - No. 39, 8-10/62; No. 40, 12/62 - No. 209, 1984

Issue	GD2.0	FN6.0	NM9.4
Four Color 386(#1)-in "Only a Poor Old Man" by Carl Barks; r-in Uncle Scrooge & Donald Duck #1('65) & The Best of Walt Disney Comics (1974). The very 1st cover app. of Uncle Scrooge	96.00	275.00	1100.00

1-(1986)-Reprints F.C. #386; given away with lithograph "Dam Disaster at Money Lake" & as a subscription offer giveaway to Gladstone subscribers

Uncle Scrooge #13 © WDC

Underdog #2 © Leonardo T.T.V.

Undertaker #5 © Chaos!

GD2.0 FN6.0 NM9.4

GD2.0 FN6.0 NM9.4

2.30 7.00 20.00

Four Color 456(#2)-in "Back to the Klondike" by Carl Barks; r-in Best of U.S. & D.D. #1('66) & Gladstone C.A. #4 58.00 175.00 700.00

Four Color 495(#3)-r-in #105 44.00 131.00 525.00

4(12-2/53-54)-r-in Gladstone Comic Album #11 32.00 96.00 385.00

5-r-in Gladstone Special #2 & Walt Disney Digest #1 27.00 80.00 320.00

6-r-in U.S. #106,165,233 & Best of U.S. & D.D. #1('66) 20.00 60.00 240.00

7-The Seven Cities of Cibola by Barks; r-in #217 & Best of D.D. & U.S. #2 ('67) 18.35 55.00 220.00

8-10: 8-r-in #111,222. 9-r-in #104,214. 10-r-in #67 15.00 45.00 180.00

11-20: 11-r-in #237. 17-r-in #215. 19-r-in Gladstone C.A. #1. 20-r-in #213 14.00 41.00 165.00

21-30: 24-X-Mas-c. 26-r-in #211 11.70 35.00 140.00

31-35,37-40: 34-r-in #228. 40-X-Mas-c 9.50 29.00 115.00

36-1st app. Magica De Spell; Number one dime 1st identified by name 11.00 33. 00 130.00

41-60: 48-Magica De Spell-c/story (3/64). 49-Sci/fi-c. 51-Beagle Boys-c/story (8/64) 8.00 24.00 95.00

61-63,65,66,68-71:71-Last Barks issue w/original story (#71-he only storyboarded the script) 6.70 20.00 80.00

64-Barks Vietnam War story "Treasure of Marco Polo" banned for reprints by Disney since the 1970s because of its third world revolutionary war theme 9.00 27.00 110.00

67,72,73: 67,72,73-Barks-r 6.70 20.00 80.00

74-84: 74-Barks-r(1pg.). 75-81,83-Not by Barks. 82,84-Barks-r begin 4.55 13.65 50.00

85-110 3.65 11.00 40.00

111-120 2.50 7.50 25.00

121-141,143-152,154-157 2.40 7.35 22.00

142-Reprints Four Color #456 with-c 2.50 7.50 25.00

153,158,162-164,166,168-170,178,180: No Barks 1.50 4.50 12.00

159-160,165,167 1.75 5.25 14.00

161(r/#14), 171(r/#11), 177(r/#16),183(r/#6)-Barks-r 1.75 5.25 14.00

172(1/80),173(2/80)-Gold Key. Barks-a 2.00 6.00 18.00

174(3/80),175(4/80),176(5/80)-Whitman. Barks-a 2.40 7.35 22.00

177(6/80),178(7/80) 2.80 8.40 28.00

179(9/80)(4/#9)-(Very low distribution) 37.00 112.00 450.00

180(11/80),181(12/80, r/4-Color #495) pre-pack? 3.20 9.60 35.00

182-195: 184,185,187,188-Barks-a. 182,186,191-194-No Barks. 189(r/#5), 190(r/#4), 195(r/4-Color #386) 1.75 5.25 14.00

196(4/82),197(5/82): 196(r/#13) 2.00 6.00 18.00

198-209 (All #90038 on-c; pre-pack?; no date or date code)
198-202,204-206: No Barks. 203(r/#12), 207(r/#93,92), 208(r/U.S. #18), 209(r/U.S. #21)-Barks-r 2.30 7.00 20.00

Uncle Scrooge & Money(G.K.)-Barks-r/from WDC&S #130 (3/67) 3.65 11.00 40.00

Mini Comic #1(1976)(3-1/4x6-1/2")-r/U.S. #115; Barks-c 1.10 3.30 9.00

NOTE: ***Barks** c-Four Color 386, 456, 495, #4-37, 39, 40, 43-71.*

UNCLE SCROOGE & DONALD DUCK
Gold Key: June, 1965 (25¢, paper cover)

1-Reprint of Four Color #386(#1) & lead story from Four Color #29 6.70 20.00 80.00

UNCLE SCROOGE COMICS DIGEST
Gladstone Publishing: Dec, 1986 - No. 5, Aug, 1987 ($1.25, Digest-size)

1,3 1.00 2.80 7.00
2,4 5.00
5 (low print run) 1.00 3.00 8.00

UNCLE SCROOGE GOES TO DISNEYLAND (See Dell Giants)
Gladstone Publishing Ltd.: Aug, 1985 ($2.50)

1-Reprints Dell Giant w/new-c by Mel Crawford, based on old cover 1.50 4.50 12.00

...Comics Digest 1 ($1.50, digest size) 1.75 5.25 14.00

UNCLE SCROOGE IN COLOR
Gladstone Publishing: 1987 ($29.95, Hardcover, 9-1/4"X12-1/4", 96 Pgs.)

nn-Reprints "Christmas on Bear Mountain" from Four Color 178 by Barks; Uncle Scrooge's Christmas Carol (published as Donald Duck & the Christmas Carol, A Little Golden Book), reproduced from the original art as adapted by Norman McGary from pencils by Barks; and Uncle Scrooge the Lemonade King, reproduced from the original art, plus Barks' original pencils 4.55 13.65 50.00

nn-Slipcase edition of 750, signed by Barks, issued at $79.95 90.00 300.00

UNCLE SCROOGE THE LEMONADE KING
Whitman Publishing Co.: 1960 (A Top Top Tales Book, 6-3/8"x7-5/8", 32 pgs.)

2465-Storybook pencilled by Carl Barks, finished art adapted by Norman McGary 40.00 119.00 475.00

UNCLE WIGGILY (See March of Comics #19)
Dell Publishing Co.: No. 179, Dec, 1947 - No. 543, Mar, 1954

Four Color 179 (#1)-Walt Kelly-c 15.00 45.00 180.00
Four Color 221 (3/49)-Part Kelly-c 9.00 27.00 110.00
Four Color 276 (5/50), 320 (#1, 3/51) 7.50 22.50 90.00
Four Color 349 (9-10/51), 391 (4-5/52) 5.85 17.50 70.00
Four Color 428 (10/52), 503 (10/53), 543 4.55 13.65 50.00

UNDERCOVER GIRL (Starr Flagg) (See Extra Comics & Manhunt!)
Magazine Enterprises: No. 5, 1952 - No. 7, 1954

5(#1)(A-1 #62)-Fallon of the F.B.I. in all 40.00 120.00 320.00
6(A-1 #98), 7(A-1 #118)-All have Starr Flagg 38.00 113.00 300.00

NOTE: ***Powell** c-6, 7. **Whitney** a-5-7.*

UNDERDOG (TV)(See Kite Fun Book, March of Comics #426, 438, 467, 479)
Charlton Comics/Gold Key: July, 1970 - No. 10, Jan, 1972; Mar, 1975 - No. 23, Feb, 1979

1 (1st series, Charlton)-1st app. Underdog 7.00 21.00 85.00
2-10 4.10 12.30 45.00
1 (2nd series, Gold Key) 5.00 15.00 60.00
2-10 3.00 9.00 32.00
11-20: 13-1st app. Shack of Solitude 2.30 7.00 20.00
21-23 2.50 7.50 24.00

UNDERDOG
Spotlight Comics: 1987 - No. 3?, 1987 ($1.50)

1-3 4.00

UNDERDOG SUMMER SPECIAL (TV)
Harvey Comics: Oct, 1993 ($2.25, 68 pgs.)

1 3.00

UNDERSEA AGENT
Tower Comics: Jan, 1966 - No. 6, Mar, 1967 (25¢, 68 pgs.)

1-Davy Jones, Undersea Agent begins 6.80 20.50 75.00
2-6: 2-Jones gains magnetic powers. 5-Origin & 1st app. of Merman. 6-Kane/Wood-c(r) 4.55 13.65 50.00

NOTE: ***Gil Kane** a-3-6; c-4, 5. **Moldoff** a-2i.*

UNDERSEA FIGHTING COMMANDOS (See Fighting Undersea...)
I.W. Enterprises: 1964

I.W. Reprint #1,2('64): 1-r/#? 2-r/#1; Severin-c 1.75 5.25 14.00

UNDERTAKER (World Wrestling Federation)
Chaos! Comics: Feb, 1999 - Present ($2.50/$2.95)

Preview (2/99) 2.50
1-10: Reg. and photo covers for each. 1-(4/99) 3.00
1-($6.95) DF Ed.; Brereton painted-c 7.00
...Halloween Special (10/99, $2.95) Reg. & photo-c 3.00
Wizard #0 2.00

UNDERWATER CITY, THE
Dell Publishing Co.: No. 1328, 1961

Four Color 1328-Movie, Evans-a 6.70 20.00 80.00

UNDERWORLD (...True Crime Stories)
D. S. Publishing Co.: Feb-Mar, 1948 - No. 9, June-July, 1949 (52 pgs.)

1-Moldoff (Shelly)-c; excessive violence 42.00 125.00 375.00
2-Moldoff (Shelly)-c; Ma Barker story used in **SOTI**, pg. 95; female

The Underworld Story nn © AVON

The Unexpected #191 © DC

Unity 2000 #1 © Acclaim

GD2.0 FN6.0 NM9.4

electrocution panel; lingerie art 40.00 120.00 360.00
3-McWilliams-c/a; extreme violence, mutilation 38.00 113.00 300.00
4-Used in Love and Death by Legman; Ingels-a 31.00 92.00 245.00
5-Ingels-a 23.00 69.00 185.00
6-9: 8-Ravielli-a 18.00 54.00 145.00

UNDERWORLD
DC Comics: Dec, 1987 - No. 4, Mar, 1988 ($1.00, limited series, mature)

1-4 2.00

UNDERWORLD CRIME
Fawcett Publications: June, 1952 - No. 9, Oct, 1953

1 31.00 94.00 250.00
2 20.00 60.00 160.00
3-6,8,9 (8,9-exist?) 18.00 53.00 140.00
7-(6/53)-Bondage/torture-c 28.00 83.00 220.00

UNDERWORLD STORY, THE (Movie)
Avon Periodicals: 1950

nn-(Scarce)-Ravielli-c 29.00 87.00 235.00

UNDERWORLD UNLEASHED
DC Comics: Nov, 1995 - No. 3, Jan, 1996 ($2.95, limited series)

1-3: Mark Waid scripts & Howard Porter-c/a(p) 3.50
...: Abyss: Hell's Sentinel 1-($2.95)-Alan Scott, Phantom Stranger, Zatanna app. 3.00
...: Apokolips-Dark Uprising 1 ($1.95) 2.00
...: Batman-Devil's Asylum 1-($2.95)-Batman app. 3.00
...: Patterns of Fear-($2.95) 3.00
TPB (1998, $17.95) r/#1-3 & Abyss-Hell's Sentinel 18.00

UNEARTHLY SPECTACULARS
Harvey Publications: Oct, 1965 - No. 3, Mar, 1967

1-(12¢)-Tiger Boy; Simon-c 3.20 9.60 35.00
2-(25¢ giants)-Jack Q. Frost, Tiger Boy & Three Rocketeers app.; Williamson, Wood, Kane-a; r-1 story/Thrill-O-Rama #2 3.65 11.00 40.00
3-(25¢ giants)-Jack Q. Frost app.; Williamson/Crandall-a; r-from Alarming Advs. #1,1962 3.65 11.00 40.00

NOTE: ***Crandall** a-3r. **G. Kane** a-2. **Orlando** a-3. **Simon, Sparling, Wood** c-2. **Simon/Kirby** a-3r. **Torres** a-1?. **Wildey** a-1(3). **Williamson** a-2, 3r. **Wood** a-2(2).*

UNEXPECTED, THE (Formerly Tales of the...)
National Per. Publ./DC Comics: No. 105, Feb-Mar, 1968 - No. 222, May, 1982

105-Begin 12¢ cover price 4.10 12.30 45.00
106-113: 113-Last 12¢ issue (6-7/69) 2.80 8.40 28.00
114,115,117,118,120-125 2.40 7.35 22.00
116 (36 pgs.)-Wrightson-a? 2.80 8.40 28.00
119-Wrightson-a, 8pgs.(36 pgs.) 3.20 9.60 35.00
126,127,129-136-(52 pgs.) 2.40 7.35 22.00
128(52 pgs.)-Wrightson-a 3.20 9.60 35.00
137-156 1.75 5.25 14.00
157-162-(100 pgs.) 3.00 9.00 30.00
163-188: 187,188-(44 pgs.) 1.10 3.30 9.00
189,190,192-195 ($1.00, 68 pgs.): 189 on are combined with House of Secrets & The Witching Hour 1.25 3.75 10.00
191-Rogers-a(p) ($1.00, 68 pgs.) 1.50 4.50 12.00
196-222: 200-Return of Johhny Peril by Tuska. 205-213-Johnny Peril app. 210-Time Warp story 1.00 2.80 7.00

NOTE: ***Neal Adams** c-110, 112-115, 118, 121, 124. **J. Craig** a-195. **Ditko** a-189, 221p, 222p; c-222. **Drucker** a-107r, 132r. **Giffen** a-219, 222. **Kaluta** c-203, 212. **Kirby** a-127r, 162. **Kubert** c-204, 214-216, 219-221. **Mayer** a-217p, 220, 221p. **Moldoff** a-136r. **Moreira** a-133. **Mortimer** a-212p. **Newton** a-204p. **Orlando** a-202; c-191. **Perez** a-217p. **Redondo** a-155, 166, 195. **Reese** a-145. **Sparling** a-107, 205-209p, 212p. **Spiegle** a-217. **Starlin** c-198. **Toth** a-126r, 127r. **Tuska** a-127, 132, 134, 136, 139, 152, 180, 200p. **Wildey** a-128r, 193. **Wood** a-122i, 133i, 137i, 138i. **Wrightson** a-161r(2 pgs.). Johnny Peril in #106-114, 116, 117, 200, 205-213.*

UNEXPECTED ANNUAL, THE (See DC Special Series #4)

UNIDENTIFIED FLYING ODDBALL (See Walt Disney Showcase #52)

UNION
Image Comics (WildStorm Productions): June, 1993 - No. 0, July, 1994 ($1.95, limited series)

0-(7/94, $2.50) 2.50
0-Alternate Portacio-c (See Deathblow #5) 5.00
1-($2.50)-Embossed foil-c; Texeira-c/a in all 2.50
1-($1.95)-Newsstand edition w/o foil-c 2.00
2-4: 4-(7/94) 2.50

UNION
Image Comics (WildStorm Prod.): Feb, 1995 - No. 9, Dec, 1995 ($2.50)

1-3,5-9: 3-Savage Dragon app. 6-Fairchild from Gen 13 app. 2.50
4-($1.95, Newsstand)-WildStorm Rising Pt. 3 2.00
4-($2.50, Direct Market)-WildStorm Rising Pt. 3, bound-in card 2.50

UNION: FINAL VENGEANCE
Image Comics (WildStorm Productions): Oct, 1997 ($2.50)

1-Golden-c/Heisler-s 2.50

UNION JACK
Marvel Comics: Dec, 1998 - No. 3, Feb, 1999 ($2.99, limited series)

1-3-Raab-s/Cassaday-s/a 3.00

UNITED COMICS (Formerly Fritzi Ritz #7; has Fritzi Ritz logo)
United Features Syndicate: Aug, 1940; No. 8, 1950 - No. 26, Jan-Feb, 1953

1(68 pgs.)-Fritzi Ritz & Phil Fumble 23.00 69.00 185.00
8-Fritzi Ritz, Abbie & Slats 5.00 15.00 35.00
9-21,23,24,26: 20-Strange As It Seems; Russell Patterson Cheesecake-a 5.00 15.00 30.00
22,25-Peanuts app. 5.00 15.00 35.00

NOTE: *Abbie & Slats reprinted from Tip Top.*

UNITED NATIONS, THE (See Classics Illustrated Special Issue)

UNITED STATES AIR FORCE PRESENTS: THE HIDDEN CREW
U.S. Air Force: 1964 (36 pgs.)

nn-Schaffenberger-a 2.40 6.00

UNITED STATES FIGHTING AIR FORCE (Also see U.S. Fighting Air Force)
Superior Comics Ltd.: Sept, 1952 - No. 29, Oct, 1956

1 10.00 30.00 80.00
2 5.70 17.00 40.00
3-10 4.65 14.00 28.00
11-29 4.15 12.50 25.00

UNITED STATES MARINES
William H. Wise/Life's Romances Publ. Co./Magazine Ent. #5-8/Toby Press #7-11: 1943 - No. 4, 1944; No. 5, 1952 - No. 8, 1952; No. 7 - No. 11, 1953

nn-Mart Bailey-a 14.00 41.00 110.00
2-Bailey-a; Tojo classic-c 30.00 90.00 240.00
3-Tojo-c 21.00 62.00 165.00
4 10.00 30.00 70.00
5(A-1 #55)-Bailey-a, 6(A-1 #60), 7(A-1 #68), 8(A-1 #72) 7.15 21.50 50.00
7-11 (Toby) 5.00 15.00 30.00

NOTE: ***Powell** a-5-7.*

UNITY
Valiant: No. 0, Aug, 1992 - No. 1, 1992 (Free comics w/limited dist., 20 pgs.)

0 (Blue)-Prequel to Unity x-overs in all Valiant titles; B. Smith-c/a. (Free to everyone that bought all 8 titles that month.) 2.00
0 (Red)-Same as above, but w/red logo (5,000). 4.00
0 (Gold)-Promotional copy. 3.00
1-Epilogue to Unity x-overs; B. Smith-c/a. (1 copy available for every 8 Valiant books ordered by dealers.) 2.00
1 (Gold)-Promotional copy. 3.00
1 (Platinum)-Promotional copy. 4.00
Yearbook 1 (2/95, $3.95)-"1994" in indicia. 4.00

UNITY 2000 (See preludes in Shadowman #3,4 flipbooks)
Acclaim Comics: Nov, 1999 - No. 6 ($2.50, limited series)

Preview -B&W plot preview and cover art; paper cover 1.00
1,2-Starlin-a/Shooter-s 2.50

UNIVERSAL MONSTERS
Dark Horse Comics: 1993 ($4.95/$5.95, 52 pgs.)(All adapt original movies)

Creature From the Black Lagoon nn-($4.95)-Art Adams/Austin-c/a, Dracula nn-($4.95), Frankenstein nn-($3.95)-Painted-c/a, The Mummy nn-($4.95)-

Universe X - Spidey © MAR

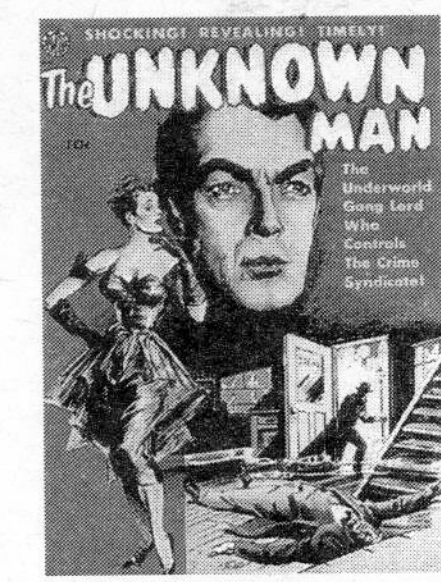

Unknown Man nn © AVON

Untold Tales of Purgatori #1 © Chaos!

Painted-c 1.00 2.80 7.00

UNIVERSAL PRESENTS DRACULA-THE MUMMY& OTHER STORIES
Dell Publishing Co.: Sept-Nov, 1963 (one-shot, 84 pgs.) (Also see Dell Giants)
GD2.0 FN6.0 VF8.0 NM9.4
02-530-311-r/Dracula 12-231-212, The Mummy 12-437-211 & part of Ghost Stories No. 1 12.50 37.50 100.00 250.00

UNIVERSAL SOLDIER (Movie)
Now Comics: Sept, 1992 - No. 3, Nov, 1992 (Limited series, polybagged, mature)
1-3 ($2.50, Direct Sales) 1-Movie adapatation; hologram on-c (all direct sales editions have painted-c) 2.50
1-3 ($1.95, Newsstand)-Rewritten & redrawn code approved version; all newsstand editions have photo-c 2.00

UNIVERSE X (See Earth X)
Marvel Comics: Sept, 2000 - No. 12 ($3.99/$3.50, limited series)
0-Ross-c/Braithwaite-a/Ross & Krueger-s 4.00
1-5: 5-Funeral of Captain America 3.50
...Cap (Capt. America) (2/01, $3.99) Yeates & Totleben-a/Ross-c; Cap dies 4.00
...4 (Fantastic 4) (10/00, $3.99) Brent Anderson-a/Ross-c 4.00
...Spidey (1/01, $3.99) Romita Sr. flashback-a/Guice-a/Ross-c 4.00
Sketchbook- Wizard supplement; B&W character sketches and bios 1.00

UNKNOWN MAN, THE (Movie)
Avon Periodicals: 1951
nn-Kinstler-c 28.00 84.00 225.00

UNKNOWN SOLDIER (Formerly Star-Spangled War Stories)
National Periodical Publications/DC Comics: No. 205, Apr-May, 1977 - No. 268, Oct, 1982 (See Our Army at War #168 for 1st app.)
205 1.85 5.50 15.00
206-210,220,221,251: 220,221 (44pgs.). 251-Enemy Ace begins 1.25 3.75 10.00
211-218,222-247,250,252-264 1.00 3.00 8.00
219-Miller-a (44 pgs.) 1.75 5.25 14.00
248,249,265-267: 248,249-Origin. 265-267-Enemy Ace vs. Balloon Buster. 1.10 3.30 9.00
268-Death of Unknown Soldier 1.85 5.50 15.00
NOTE: ***Chaykin*** *a-234.* ***Evans*** *a-265-267; c-235.* ***Kubert*** *c-Most.* ***Miller*** *a-219p.* ***Severin*** *a-251-253, 260, 261, 265-267.* ***Simonson*** *a-254-256.* ***Spiegle*** *a-258, 259, 262-264.*

UNKNOWN SOLDIER, THE (Also see Brave &the Bold #146)
DC Comics: Winter, 1988-'89 - No. 12, Dec, 1989 ($1.50, maxi-series, mature)
1-12: 8-Begin $1.75-c 3.00

UNKNOWN SOLDIER
DC Comics (Vertigo): Apr, 1997 - No 4, July, 1997 ($2.50, mini-series)
1-Ennis-s/Plunkett-a/Bradstreet-c in all 2.40 6.00
2 -4 4.00
TPB (1998, $12.95) r/#1-4 13.00

UNKNOWN WORLD (Strange Stories From Another World #2 on)
Fawcett Publications: June, 1952
1-Norman Saunders painted-c 40.00 120.00 320.00

UNKNOWN WORLDS (See Journey Into...)

UNKNOWN WORLDS
American Comics Group/Best Synd. Features: Aug, 1960 - No. 57, Aug, 1967
1-Schaffenberger-c 20.50 61.00 225.00
2-Dinosaur-c/story 12.50 37.00 135.00
3-5 10.00 30.00 110.00
6-11: 9-Dinosaur-c/story. 11-Last 10¢ issue 8.15 24.50 90.00
12-19: 12-Begin 12¢ issues?; ends #57 6.35 19.00 70.00
20-Herbie cameo (12-1/62-63) 6.80 20.50 75.00
21-35 4.10 12.30 45.00
36- "The People vs. Hendricks" by Craig; most popular ACG story ever 4.55 13.65 50.00
37-46 3.65 11.00 40.00
47-Williamson-a r-from Adventures Into the Unknown #96, 3 pgs.; Craig-a 4.10 12.30 45.00
48-57: 53-Frankenstein app. 3.20 9.60 35.00
NOTE: ***Ditko*** *a-49, 50p, 54.* ***Forte*** *a-3, 6, 11.* ***Landau*** *a-56(2).* ***Reinman*** *a-3, 9, 13, 20, 22, 23, 36, 38, 54.* ***Whitney*** *c/a-most issues. John Force, Magic Agent app.-35, 36, 48, 50, 52, 54, 56.*

UNKNOWN WORLDS OF FRANK BRUNNER
Eclipse Comics: Aug, 1985 - No. 2, Aug, 1985 ($1.75)
1,2-B&W-r in color 3.00

UNKNOWN WORLDS OF SCIENCE FICTION
Marvel Comics: Jan, 1975 - No. 6, Nov, 1975; 1976 ($1.00, B&W Magazine)
1-Williamson/Krenkel/Torres/Frazetta-r/Witzend #1, Neal Adams-r/Phase 1; Brunner & Kaluta-r; Freas/Romita-c 1.75 5.25 14.00
2-6: 5-Kaluta text illos 1.25 3.75 10.00
Special 1(1976,100 pgs.)-Newton painted-c 1.75 5.25 14.00
NOTE: ***Brunner*** *a-2; c-4, 6.* ***Buscema*** *a-Special 1p.* ***Chaykin*** *a-5.* ***Colan*** *a(p)-1, 3, 5, 6.* ***Corben*** *a-4.* ***Kaluta*** *a-2, Special 1(ext illos); c-2.* ***Morrow*** *a-3, 5.* ***Nino*** *a-3, 6, Special 1.* ***Perez*** *a-2, 3. Ray Bradbury interview in #1.*

UNLIMITED ACCESS (Also see Marvel Vs. DC))
Marvel Comics: Dec, 1997 - No. 4, Mar, 1998 ($2.99/$1.99, limited series)
1-Spider-Man, Wonder Woman, Green Lantern & Hulk app. 3.50
2,3-($1.99): 2-X-Men, Legion of Super-Heroes app. 3-Original Avengers vs. original Justice League 2.00
4-($2.99) Amalgam Legion vs. Darkseid & Magneto 3.00

UNSANE (Formerly Mighty Bear #13, 14? or The Outlaws #10-14?)(Satire)
Star Publications: No. 15, June, 1954
15-Disbrow-a(2); L. B. Cole-c 38.00 113.00 300.00

UNSEEN, THE
Visual Editions/Standard Comics: No. 5, 1952 - No. 15, July, 1954
5-Horror stories in all; Toth-a 40.00 120.00 325.00
6,7,9,10-Jack Katz-a 29.00 87.00 235.00
8,11,13,14 21.00 62.00 165.00
12,15-Toth-a. 12-Tuska-a 29.00 86.00 230.00
NOTE: ***Nick Cardy*** *c-12.* ***Fawcette*** *a-13, 14.* ***Sekowsky*** *a-7, 8(2), 10, 13, 15.*

UNTAMED
Marvel Comics (Epic Comics/Heavy Hitters): June, 1993 - No. 3, Aug, 1993 ($1.95, limited series)
1-($2.50)-Embossed-c 2.50
2,3 2.00

UNTAMED LOVE (Also see Frank Frazetta's Untamed Love)
Quality Comics Group (Comic Magazines): Jan, 1950 - No. 5, Sept, 1950
1-Ward-c, Gustavson-a 25.00 75.00 200.00
2,4: 2-5-Photo-c 15.00 45.00 120.00
3,5-Gustavson-a 17.00 51.00 135.00

UNTOLD LEGEND OF CAPTAIN MARVEL, THE
Marvel Comics: Apr, 1997 - No. 3, June, 1997 ($2.50, limited series)
1-3 2.50

UNTOLD LEGEND OF THE BATMAN, THE (Also see Promotional section)
DC Comics: July, 1980 - No. 3, Sept, 1980 (Limited series)
1-Origin; Joker-c; Byrne's 1st work at DC 5.00
2,3 4.00
NOTE: ***Aparo*** *a-1i, 2, 3.* ***Byrne*** *a-1p.*

UNTOLD ORIGIN OF THE FEMFORCE, THE (Also see Femforce)
AC Comics: 1989 ($4.95, 68 pgs.)
1-Origin Femforce; Bill Black-a(i) & scripts 2.40 6.00

UNTOLD TALES OF CHASTITY
Chaos! Comics: Nov, 2000 ($2.95, one-shot)
1-Origin; Steven Grant-s/Peter Vale-c/a 2.95
1-Premium Edition with glow in the dark cover 12.95

UNTOLD TALES OF LADY DEATH
Chaos! Comics: Nov, 2000 ($2.95, one-shot)
1-Origin of Lady Death; Cremator app.; Kaminski-s 2.95
1-Premium Edition with glow in the dark cover by Steven Hughes 12.95

UNTOLD TALES OF PURGATORI
Chaos! Comics: Nov, 2000 ($2.95, one-shot)

Untold Tales of Spider-Man #6 © MAR

USA Comics #4 © MAR

Usagi Yojimbo V3 #23 © Stan Sakai

GD2.0 FN6.0 NM9.4

1-Purgatori in 57 B.C.; Rio-a/Grant-s 2.95
1-Premium Edition with glow in the dark cover 12.95

UNTOLD TALES OF SPIDER-MAN (Also see Amazing Fantasy #16-18)
Marvel Comics: Sept, 1995 - No. 25, Sept, 1997 (99¢)

1-Kurt Busiek scripts begin; Pat Olliffe-c/a in all (except #9). 2.00
2-22, -1(7/97), 23-25: 2-1st app. Batwing. 4-1st app. The Spacemen (Gantry, Orbit, Satellite & Vacuum). 8-1st app. The Headsman; The Enforcers (The Big Man, Montana, The Ox & Fancy Dan) app. 9-Ron Frenz-a. 10-1st app. Commanda. 16-Reintro Mary Jane Watson. 21-X-Men-c/app. 25-Green Goblin 2.00
...'96-(1996, $1.95, 46 pgs.)-Kurt Busiek scripts; Mike Allred-c/a; Kurt Busiek & Pat Olliffe app. in back-up story; contains pin-ups 2.00
...'97-(1997, $1.95)-Wraparound-c 2.00
...: Strange Encounters ('98, $5.99) Dr. Strange app. 6.00

UNTOUCHABLES, THE (TV)
Dell Publishing Co.: No. 1237, 10-12/61 - No. 4, 8-10/62
(All have Robert Stack photo-c)

	GD2.0	FN6.0	NM9.4
Four Color 1237(#1)	23.00	68.00	270.00
Four Color 1286	16.00	48.00	190.00
01-879-207, 12-879-210(01879-210 on inside)	8.35	25.00	100.00

UNTOUCHABLES
Caliber Comics: Aug, 1997 - No. 4 ($2.95, B&W)

1-4: 1-Pruett-s; variant covers by Kaluta & Showman 3.00

UNUSUAL TALES (Blue Beetle & Shadows From Beyond #50 on)
Charlton Comics: Nov, 1955 - No. 49, Mar-Apr, 1965

	GD2.0	FN6.0	NM9.4
1	28.00	83.00	220.00
2	14.00	41.00	110.00
3-5	10.00	30.00	75.00
6-Ditko-c only	12.50	37.50	100.00
7,8-Ditko-c/a. 8-Robot-c	25.00	75.00	200.00
9-Ditko-c/a (20 pgs.)	28.00	83.00	220.00
10-Ditko-c/a(4)	30.00	90.00	240.00
11-(3/58, 68 pgs.)-Ditko-a(4)	28.00	84.00	225.00
12,14-Ditko-a	18.00	53.00	140.00
13,16-20	5.00	15.00	55.00
15-Ditko-c/a	15.00	45.00	165.00
21,24,28	3.65	11.00	40.00
22,23,25-27,29-Ditko-a	9.00	27.00	100.00
30-49	3.00	9.00	30.00

NOTE: *Colan a-11. **Ditko** c-22, 23, 25-27, 31(part).*

UP FROM HARLEM (Tom Skinner...)
Spire Christian Comics (Fleming H. Revell Co.): 1973 (35/49¢)

nn 1.00 2.80 7.00

UP-TO-DATE COMICS
King Features Syndicate: No date (1938) (36 pgs.; B&W cover) (10¢)

nn-Popeye & Henry cover; The Phantom, Jungle Jim & Flash Gordon by Raymond, The Katzenjammer Kids, Curley Harper & others. Note: Variations in content exist. 25.00 75.00 200.00

UP YOUR NOSE AND OUT YOUR EAR (Satire)
Klevart Enterprises: Apr, 1972 - No. 2, June, 1972 (52 pgs., magazine)

V1#1,2 1.50 4.50 12.00

URBAN
Moving Target Entertainment: 1994 ($1.75, B&W)

1 2.00

URTH 4 (Also see Earth 4)
Continuity Comics: May, 1989 - No. 4, Dec, 1990 ($2.00, deluxe format)

1-4: Ms. Mystic characters. 2-Neal Adams-c(i) 2.00

URZA-MISHRA WAR ON THE WORLD OF MAGIC THE GATHERING
Acclaim Comics (Armada): 1996 - No. 2, 1996 ($5.95, limited series)

1,2 6.00

U.S. (See Uncle Sam)

USA COMICS

GD2.0 FN6.0 NM9.4

Timely Comics (USA): Aug, 1941 - No. 17, Fall, 1945

	GD2.0	FN6.0	VF8.0	NM9.4
1-Origin Major Liberty (called Mr. Liberty #1), Rockman by Wolverton, & The Whizzer by Avison; The Defender with sidekick Rusty & Jack Frost begin; The Young Avenger only app.; S&K-c plus 1 pg. art	1000.00	3000.00	6500.00	12,500.00

	GD2.0	FN6.0	NM9.4
2-Origin Captain Terror & The Vagabond; last Wolverton Rockman; Hitler-c	333.00	1000.00	3500.00
3-No Whizzer	274.00	821.00	2600.00
4-Last Rockman, Major Liberty, Defender, Jack Frost, & Capt. Terror; Corporal Dix app.	232.00	695.00	2200.00
5-Origin American Avenger & Roko the Amazing; The Blue Blade, The Black Widow & Victory Boys, Gypo the Gypsy Giant & Hills of Horror only app.; Sergeant Dix begins; no Whizzer; Hitler, Mussolini & Tojo-c	221.00	663.00	2100.00
6-Captain America (ends #17), The Destroyer, Jap Buster Johnson, Jeep Jones begin; Terror Squad only app.	284.00	853.00	2700.00
7-Captain Daring, Disk-Eyes the Detective by Wolverton app.; origin & only app. Marvel Boy (3/43); Secret Stamp begins; no Whizzer, Sergeant Dix	263.00	790.00	2500.00
8,10: 10-The Thunderbird only app.	184.00	553.00	1750.00
9-Last Secret Stamp; Hitler-c; classic-c	195.00	585.00	1850.00
11,12: 11-No Jeep Jones	147.00	442.00	1400.00
13-17: 13-No Whizzer; Jeep Jones ends. 15-No Destroyer; Jap Buster Johnson ends	105.00	316.00	1000.00

NOTE: ***Brodsky** c-14. **Gabrielle** c-4. **Schomburg** c-6, 7, 10, 12, 13, 15-17. **Shores** a-1, 4; c-9, 11. **Ed Win** a-4. Cover features: 1-The Defender; 2, 3-Captain Terror; 4-Major Liberty; 5-Victory Boys; 6-17-Captain America & Bucky.*

U.S. AGENT (See Jeff Jordan...)

U.S. AGENT (See Captain America #354)
Marvel Comics: June, 1993 - No. 4, Sept, 1993 ($1.75, limited series)

1-4 2.00

USAGI YOJIMBO (See Albedo, Doomsday Squad #3 & Space Usagi)
Fantagraphics Books: July, 1987 - No. 38 ($2.00/$2.25, B&W)

1 1.00 2.80 7.00
1,8,10-2nd printings 2.00
2-9 4.00
10,11: 10-Leonardo app. (TMNT). 11-Aragonés-a 5.00
12-29 3.00
30-39: 30-Begin $2.25-c 3.00
Color Special 1 (11/89, $2.95, 68 pgs.)-new & r 3.50
Color Special 2 (10/91, $3.50) 3.50
Color Special #3 (10/92, $3.50)-Jeff Smith's Bone promo on inside-c 3.50
Summer Special 1 (1986, B&W, $2.75)-r/early Albedo issues 3.00

USAGI YOJIMBO
Mirage Studios: V2#1, Mar, 1993 - No. 16, 1994 ($2.75)

V2#1-16: 1-Teenage Mutant Ninja Turtles app. 3.00

USAGI YOJIMBO
Dark Horse Comics: V3#1, Apr, 1996 - Present ($2.95, B&W)

V3#1-38: Stan Sakai-c/a 3.00
Color Special #4 (7/97, $2.95) "Green Persimmon" 3.00

U.S. AIR FORCE COMICS (Army Attack #38 on)
Charlton Comics: Oct, 1958 - No. 37, Mar-Apr, 1965

	GD2.0	FN6.0	NM9.4
1	5.00	15.00	55.00
2	3.00	9.00	30.00
3-10	2.50	7.50	24.00
11-20	2.40	7.35	22.00
21-37	2.30	7.00	20.00

NOTE: ***Glanzman** c/a-9, 10, 12. **Montes/Bache** a-33.*

USA IS READY
Dell Publishing Co.: 1941 (68 pgs., one-shot)

1-War propaganda 40.00 120.00 350.00

U.S. BORDER PATROL COMICS (Sgt. Dick Carter of the...) (See Holyoke One Shot)

U.S. FIGHTING AIR FORCE (Also see United States Fighting Air Force)

U.S. 1 #4 © MAR

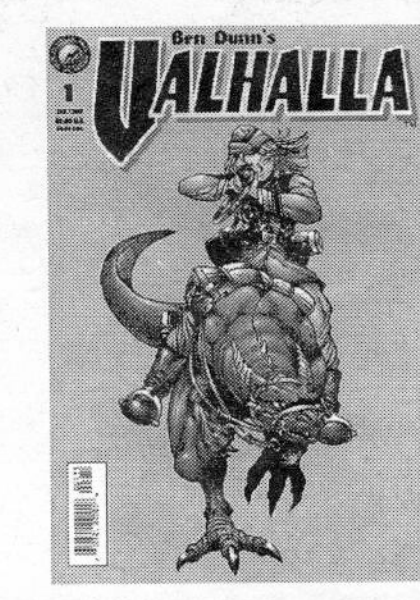

Valhalla #1 © Ben Dunn

Vampi #1 © Harris Pub.

I. W. Enterprises: No date (1960s?)

1,9(nd): 1-r/United States Fighting...#?. 9-r/#1 — 1.50 — 4.50 — 12.00

U.S. FIGHTING MEN
Super Comics: 1963 - 1964 (Reprints)

10-r/With the U.S. Paratroops #4(Avon) — 1.75 — 5.25 — 14.00
11,12,15-18: 11-r/Monty Hall #10. 12,16,17,18-r/U.S. Fighting Air Force #10,3,?&? 15-r/Man Comics #11 — 1.75 — 5.25 — 14.00

U.S. JONES (Also see Wonderworld Comics #28)
Fox Features Syndicate: Nov, 1941 - No. 2, Jan, 1942

1-U.S. Jones & The Topper begin; Nazi-c — 126.00 — 379.00 — 1200.00
2-Nazi-c — 87.00 — 261.00 — 825.00

U.S. MARINES
Charlton Comics: Fall, 1964 (12¢, one-shot)

1-1st app. Capt. Dude; Glanzman-a — 2.50 — 7.50 — 25.00

U.S. MARINES IN ACTION
Avon Periodicals: Aug, 1952 - No. 3, Dec, 1952

1-Louis Ravielli-c/a — 8.65 — 26.00 — 60.00
2,3: 3-Kinstler-c — 5.00 — 15.00 — 35.00

U.S. 1
Marvel Comics Group: May, 1983 - No. 12, Oct, 1984 (7,8: painted-c)

1-12: 2-Sienkiewicz-c. 3-12-Michael Golden-c — 2.00

U.S. PARATROOPS (See With the...)

U.S. PARATROOPS
I. W. Enterprises: 1964?

1,8: 1-r/With the U.S. Paratroops #1; Wood-c. 8-r/With the U.S. Paratroops #6; Kinstler-c — 1.75 — 5.25 — 14.00

U.S. TANK COMMANDOS
Avon Periodicals: June, 1952 - No. 4, Mar, 1953

1-Kinstler-c — 9.30 — 28.00 — 65.00
2-4: Kinstler-c — 6.40 — 19.25 — 45.00
I.W. Reprint #1,8: 1-r/#1. 8-r/#3 — 1.75 — 5.25 — 14.00
NOTE: ***Kinstler** a-I.W. #1; c-1-4, I.W. #1, 8.*

"V" (TV)
DC Comics: Feb, 1985 - No. 18, July, 1986

1-Based on TV movie & series (Sci/Fi) — 3.00
2-18: 17,18-Denys Cowan-c/a — 2.00

VACATION COMICS (Also see A-1 Comics)
Magazine Enterprises: No. 16, 1948 (one-shot)

A-1 16-The Pixies, Tom Tom, Flying Fredd & Koko & Kola — 4.65 — 14.00 — 28.00

VACATION DIGEST
Harvey Comics: Sept, 1987 ($1.25, digest size)

1 — 2.40 — 6.00

VACATION IN DISNEYLAND (Also see Dell Giants)
Dell Publishing Co./Gold Key (1965): Aug-Oct, 1959; May, 1965 (Walt Disney)

Four Color 1025-Barks-a — 18.35 — 55.00 — 220.00
1(30024-508)(G.K., 5/65, 25¢)-r/Dell Giant #30 & cover to #1 ('58); celebrates Disneyland's 10th anniversary — 4.55 — 13.65 — 50.00

VACATION PARADE (See Dell Giants)

VAGABOND
Image Comics: Aug, 2000 - Present ($2.95)

1-Benjamin-a/Ruffner-s — 2.95

VALERIA THE SHE BAT
Continuity Comics: May, 1993 - No. 5, Nov, 1993

1-Premium; acetate-c; N. Adams-a/scripts; given as gift to retailers — 5.00
5 (11/93)-Embossed-c; N. Adams-a/scripts — 2.50
NOTE: *Due to lack of continuity, #2-4 do not exist.*

VALERIA THE SHE BAT
Acclaim Comics (Windjammer): Sept, 1995 - No.2, Oct, 1995 ($2.50, limited series)

1,2 — 2.50

VALHALLA
Antarctic Press: Feb, 1999 ($2.99)

1-Ben Dunn-s/a/c — 3.00

VALKYRIE (See Airboy)
Eclipse Comics: May,1987 - No. 3, July, 1987 ($1.75, limited series)

1-3: 2-Holly becomes new Black Angel — 2.50

VALKYRIE
Marvel Comics: Jan, 1997 ($2.95, one-shot)

1-w/pin-ups — 3.00

VALKYRIE!
Eclipse Comics: July, 1988 - No. 3, Sept, 1988 ($1.95, limited series)

1-3 — 2.00

VALLEY OF THE DINOSAURS (TV)
Charlton Comics: Apr, 1975 - No. 11, Dec, 1976 (Hanna-Barbara)

1,3: 3-Byrne text illos (early work, 7/75) — 1.85 — 5.50 — 15.00
2,4-11: 1,2-W. Howard-i — 1.25 — 3.75 — 10.00

VALLEY OF THE DINOSAURS (TV)
Harvey Comics: Oct, 1992 ($1.50, giant-sized)

1-Reprints — 3.00

VALLEY OF GWANGI (See Movie Classics)

VALOR
E. C. Comics: Mar-Apr, 1955 - No. 5, Nov-Dec, 1955

1-Williamson/Torres-a; Wood-c/a — 24.00 — 71.00 — 260.00
2-Williamson-c/a; Wood-a — 20.00 — 60.00 — 220.00
3,4: 3-Williamson, Crandall-a. 4-Wood-c — 14.00 — 41.00 — 150.00
5-Wood-c/a; Williamson/Evans-a — 13.00 — 38.00 — 140.00
NOTE: ***Crandall** a-3, 4. **Ingels** a-1, 2, 4, 5. **Krigstein** a-1-5. **Orlando** a-3, 4; c-3. **Wood** a-1, 2, 5; c-1, 4, 5.*

VALOR
Gemstone Publishing: Oct, 1998 - No. 5, Feb, 1999 ($2.50)

1-5-Reprints — 2.50

VALOR (Also see Legion of Super-Heroes & Legionnaires)
DC Comics: Nov, 1992 - No. 23, Sept, 1994 ($1.25/$1.50)

1-23: 1-Eclipso The Darkness Within aftermath. 2-Vs. Supergirl. 4-Vs. Lobo. 12-Lobo cameo. 14-Legionnaires, JLA app. 17-Austin-c(i); death of Valor. 18-22-Build-up to Zero Hour. 23-Zero Hour tie-in — 2.00

VALOR THUNDERSTAR AND HIS FIREFLIES
Now Comics: Dec, 1986 ($1.50)

1-Ordway-c(p) — 2.00

VAMPI (Vampirella's...)
Harris Publications: Aug, 2000 - Present ($2.95)

Limited Edition Preview Book (5/00) Preview pages & sketchbook — 2.95
1-(8/00, $2.95) Lau-a(p)/Conway-s — 2.95
1-Platinum Edition — 20.00
2,3 — 2.95

VAMPIRE BITES
Brainstorm Comics: May, 1995 - No. 2, Sept, 1996 ($2.95, B&W)

1,2:1-Color pin-up — 3.00

VAMPIRE LESTAT, THE
Innovation Publishing: Jan, 1990 - No. 12, 1991 ($2.50, painted limited series)

1-Adapts novel; Bolton painted-c on all — 2.00 — 6.00 — 18.00
1-2nd printing (has UPC code, 1st prints don't) — 3.00
1-3rd & 4th printings — 2.50
2-1st printing — 1.00 — 3.00 — 8.00
2-2nd & 3rd printings — 2.50
3-5 — 5.00
3-6,9-2nd printings — 2.50
6-12 — 3.00

VAMPIRELLA (Magazine)(See Warren Presents)
Warren Publishing Co./Harris Publications #113: Sept, 1969 - No. 112, Feb,

Vampirella #12 © WP

Vampirella (The Monthly) #20 © Harris Pub.

Vampirella & The Blood Red Queen of Hearts © Harris Pub.

1983; No. 113, Jan, 1988? (B&W)

1-Intro. Vampirella 37.00 112.00 450.00
2-Amazonia series begins, ends #12 13.50 40.00 150.00
3 (Low distribution) 33.00 100.00 400.00
4-7 8.65 26.00 95.00
8-Vampi begins by Tom Sutton as serious strip (early issues-gag line) 9.50 28.50 105.00
9-Barry Smith-a; Boris-c 8.65 26.00 95.00
10-No Vampi story 4.10 12.30 45.00
11-15: 11-Origin & 1st app. Pendragon. 12-Vampi by Gonzales begins 5.45 16.35 60.00
16-18,20-25: 17-Tomb of the Gods begins, ends #22. 25-Begin partial color issues 4.55 13.65 50.00
19 (1973 Annual) 6.35 19.00 70.00
26,28-36,38-40: 30-Intro. Pantha; Corben-a(color). 31-Origin Luana, the Beast Girl. 33-Pantha ends 3.00 9.00 32.00
27 (1974 Annual) 3.65 11.00 40.00
37 (1975 Annual) 3.20 9.60 35.00
41-45,47-50: 49-1st app. The Blood Red Queen of Hearts. 50-Spirit cameo by Eisner 2.50 7.50 25.00
46-Origin retold (10/75) 3.00 9.00 32.00
51-66,68,70,72,73,75,79-89: 60-62,65,66-The Blood Red Queen of Hearts app. 2.30 7.00 20.00
67,69,71,74,76-78-photo-c 2.80 8.40 28.00
91-99: 93-Cassandra St. Knight begins, ends #103; new Pantha series begins, ends #108 2.40 7.35 22.00
100 (96 pg. r-special)-Origin reprinted; Vampirella appears topless 6.35 19.00 70.00
101-110,112: 101,102-The Blood Red Queen of Hearts app. 108-Torpedo series by Toth begins 3.65 11.00 40.00
111-Giant Collector's Edition ($2.50) 5.00 15.00 55.00
113 (1988)-1st Harris Issue 27.50 82.00 300.00
Annual 1(1972)-New origin Vampirella by Gonzales; reprints by Neal Adams (from #1), Wood (from #9) 26.50 79.00 290.00
Special 1 (1977) Softcover (color, large-square bound)(only available thru mail order) 15.00 45.00 165.00
Special 1 (1977) Hardcover (color, large-square bound)-Only available through mail order (scarce)(500 produced, signed & #'d) 33.00 100.00 400.00

NOTE: ***Neal Adams** a-1, 10p, 19p(r/#10). **Alcala** a-90, 93i. **Bode'/Todd** c-3. **Bode'/Jones** c-4. **Boris** c-9. **Brunner** a-10, 12(1 pg.). **Corben** a-30, 31, 33, 54. **Crandall** a-1, 19(r/#1). **Frazetta** c-1, 5, 7, 11, 31. **Heath** a-76-78, 83. **Jones** a-5, 9, 12, 27, 32, 33(2 pg.), 34, 50i, 83r. **Nino** a-59i, 61i, 67, 76, 85, 90. **Ploog** a-14. **Barry Smith** a-9. **Starlin** a-78. **Sutton** a-11. **Toth** a-90i, 108, 110. **Wood** a-9, 10, 12, 19(r/#12), 27r; c-9. **Wrightson** a-33(w/**Jones**), 63r. All reprint issues-37, 74, 83, 87, 91, 105, 107, 109, 111. Annuals from 1973 on are included in regular numbering. Later annuals are same format as regular issues.*

VAMPIRELLA (Also see Cain/… & Vengeance of…)
Harris Publications: Nov, 1992 - No. 5, Nov, 1993 ($2.95)

0 5.00
0-Gold 3.00 9.00 30.00
1-Jim Balent inks in #1-3; Adam Hughes c-1-3 2.30 7.00 20.00
1-2nd printing 5.00
1-(11/97) Commemorative Edition 3.00
2 1.85 5.50 15.00
3-5: 4-Snyder III-c. 5-Brereton painted-c 1.00 3.00 8.00
Trade paperback nn (10/93, $5.95)-r/#1-4; Jusko-c 6.00

NOTE: *Issues 1-5 contain certificates for free **Dave Stevens** Vampirella poster.*

VAMPIRELLA (THE NEW MONTHLY)
Harris Publications: Nov, 1997 - No. 26, Apr, 2000 ($2.95)

1-3-"Ascending Evil" -Morrison & Millar-s/Conner &Palmiotti-a. 1-Three covers by Quesada/Palmiotti, Conner, and Conner/Palmiotti 3.00
1-3-($9.95) Jae Lee variant covers 10.00
1-($24.95) Platinum Ed.w/Quesada-c 25.00
4-6-"Holy War"-Small & Stull-a, 4-Linsner variant-c 3.00
7-9-"Queen's Gambit"-Shi app. 7-Two covers. 8-Pantha-c/app. 3.00
7-($9.95) Conner variant-c 10.00
10-12-"Hell on Earth"; Small-a/Coney-s. 12-New costume 3.00
10-Jae Lee variant-c 1.25 3.75 10.00
13-15-"World's End" Zircher-p; Pantha back-up, Texeira-a 3.00
16,17: 16-Pantha-c;Texeira-a; Vampi back-up story. 17-(Pantha #2) 3.00
18-20-"Rebirth": Jae Lee-c on all. 18-Loeb-s/Sale-a. 19-Alan Davis-a. 20-Bruce Timm-a 3.00
18-20-($9.95) Variant covers: 18-Sale. 19-Davis. 20-Timm 10.00
21-26: 21,22-Dangerous Games; Small-a. 23-Lady Death-c/app.; Cleavenger-a. 24,25-Lau-a. 26-Lady Death & Pantha-c/app.; Cleavenger-a. 2.95
0-(1/99) also variant-c with Pantha #0; same contents 3.00
TPB ($7.50) r/#1-3 "Ascending Evil" 8.00
Ascending Evil Ashcan (8/97, $1.00) 2.00
Hell on Earth Ashcan (7/98, $1.00) 2.00
The End Ashcan (3/00, $6.00) 6.00
...30th Anniversary Celebration Preview (7/99) B&W preview of #18-20 9.95

VAMPIRELLA & PANTHA SHOWCASE
Harris Publications: Jan, 1997 ($1.50, one-shot)

1-Millar-s/Texeira-c/a; flip book w/"Blood Lust"; Robinson-s/Jusko-c/a 2.00

VAMPIRELLA & THE BLOOD RED QUEEN OF HEARTS
Harris Publications: Sept, 1996 ($9.95, 96 pgs., B&W, squarebound, one-shot)

nn-r/Vampirella #49,60-62,65,66,101,102; John Bolton-c; Michael Bair back-c 1.25 3.75 10.00

VAMPIRELLA: BLOODLUST
Harris Publications: July, 1997 - No. 2, Aug, 1997 ($4.95, limited series)

1,2-Robinson-s/Jusko-painted c/a 5.00

VAMPIRELLA CLASSICS
Harris Publications: Feb, 1995 - No. 5, Nov, 1995 ($2.95, limited series)

1-5: Reprints Archie Goodwin stories. 3.00

VAMPIRELLA: CROSSOVER GALLERY
Harris Publications: Sept, 1997 ($2.95, one-shot)

1-Wraparound-c by Campbell, pinups by Jae Lee, Mack, Allred, Art Adams, Quesada & Palmiotti and others 3.00

VAMPIRELLA: DEATH & DESTRUCTION
Harris Publications: July, 1996 - No. 3, Sept, 1996 ($2.95, limited series)

1-3: Amanda Conner-a(p) in all. 1-Tucci-c. 2-Hughes-c. 3-Jusko-c 3.00
1-($9.95)-Limited Edition; Beachum-c 10.00

VAMPIRELLA/DRACULA & PANTHA SHOWCASE
Harris Publications: Aug, 1997 ($1.50, one-shot)

1-Ellis, Robinson, and Moore-s; flip book w/"Pantha" 2.00

VAMPIRELLA/DRACULA: THE CENTENNIAL
Harris Publications: Oct, 1997 ($5.95, one-shot)

1-Ellis, Robinson, and Moore-s; Beachum, Frank/Smith, and Mack/Mays-a Bolton-painted-c 6.00

VAMPIRELLA: JULIE STRAIN SPECIAL
Harris Publications: Sept, 2000 ($3.95, one-shot)

1-Photo-c w/yellow background; interview and photo gallery 3.95
1-Limited Edition ($9.95); cover photo w/black background 10.00

VAMPIRELLA/LADY DEATH (Also see Lady Death/Vampirella)
Harris Publications: Feb, 1999 ($3.50, one-shot)

1-Small-a/Nelson painted-c 3.50
1-Valentine Edition ($9.95); pencil-c by Small 10.00

VAMPIRELLA: LEGENDARY TALES
Harris Publications: May, 2000 - No. 2, June, 2000 ($2.95, B&W)

1,2-Reprints from magazine; Cleavenger painted-c 2.95
1,2-($9.95) Variant painted-c by Mike Mayhew 9.95

VAMPIRELLA LIVES
Harris Publications: Dec, 1996 - No. 3, Feb, 1997 ($3.50/$2.95, limited series)

1-Die cut-c; Quesada & Palmiotti-c, Ellis-s/Conner-a 3.50
1-Deluxe Ed.-photo-c 3.50
2,3-($2.95)-Two editions (1 photo-c): 3-J. Scott Campbell-c 3.00

VAMPIRELLA: MORNING IN AMERICA
Harris Publications/Dark Horse Comics: 1991 - No. 4, 1992 ($3.95, B&W, limited series, 52 pgs.)

1,2-All have Kaluta painted-c 1.00 3.00 8.00
3,4 1.25 3.75 10.00

Vampirella of Drakulon #5 © Harris Pub.

Vamps #3 © Elaine Lee & Will Simpson

Vandala #1 © Chaos!

GD2.0 FN6.0 NM9.4

VAMPIRELLA OF DRAKULON
Harris Publications: Jan, 1996 - No. 5, Sept, 1996 ($2.95)
0-5: All reprints. 0-Jim Silke-c. 3-Polybagged w/card. 4-Texiera-c 3.00

VAMPIRELLA/PAINKILLER JANE
Harris Publications: May, 1998 ($3.50, one-shot)
1-Waid & Augustyn-s/Leonardi & Palmiotti-a 3.50
1-($9.95) Variant-c 10.00

VAMPIRELLA PIN-UP SPECIAL
Harris Publications: Oct, 1995 ($2.95, one-shot)
1-Hughes-c, pin-ups by various 5.00
1-Variant-c 5.00

VAMPIRELLA: RETRO
Harris Publications: Mar, 1998 - No. 3, May, 1998 ($2.50, B&W, limited series)
1-3: Reprints; Silke painted covers 3.00

VAMPIRELLA: SAD WINGS OF DESTINY
Harris Publications: Sept, 1996 ($3.95, one-shot)
1-Jusko-c 4.00

VAMPIRELLA/SHADOWHAWK: CREATURES OF THE NIGHT (Also see Shadowhawk)
Harris Publications: 1995 ($4.95, one-shot)
1 5.00

VAMPIRELLA/SHI (See Shi/Vampirella)
Harris Publications: Oct, 1997 ($2.95, one-shot)
1-Ellis-s 3.00
1-Chromium-c 6.00

VAMPIRELLA: SILVER ANNIVERSARY COLLECTION
Harris Publications: Jan, 1997 - No. 4 Apr, 1997 ($2.50, limited series)
1-4: Two editions: Bad Girl by Beachum, Good Girl by Silke 2.50

VAMPIRELLA'S SUMMER NIGHTS
Harris Publications: 1992 (one-shot)
1-Art Adams infinity cover; centerfold by Stelfreeze 3.20 9.60 35.00

VAMPIRELLA STRIKES
Harris Publications: Sept, 1995 - No. 8, Dec, 1996 ($2.95, limited series)
1-8: 1-Photo-c. 2-Deodato-c; polybagged w/card. 5-Eudaemon-c/app; wraparound-c; alternate-c exists. 6-(6/96)-Mark Millar script; Texeira-c; alternate-c exists. 7-Flip book 3.00
1-Newsstand Edition; diff. photo-c., 1-Limited Edi.; diff. photo-c 3.00
Annual 1-(12/96, $2.95) Delano-s; two covers 3.00

VAMPIRELLA: 25TH ANNIVERSARY SPECIAL
Harris Publications: Oct, 1996 ($5.95, squarebound, one-shot)
nn-Reintro The Blood Red Queen of Hearts; James Robinson, Grant Morrison & Warren Ellis scripts; Mark Texeira, Michael Bair & Amanda Conner-a(p); Frank Frazetta-c 6.00
nn-($6.95)-Silver Edition 7.00

VAMPIRELLA VS. HEMORRHAGE
Harris Publications: Apr, 1997($3.50)
1 3.50

VAMPIRELLA VS. PANTHA
Harris Publications: Mar, 1997 ($3.50)
1-Two covers; Millar-s/Texiera-c/a 3.50

VAMPIRELLA/WETWORKS (See Wetworks/Vampirella)
Harris Publications: June, 1997 ($2.95, one-shot)
1 3.00
1-($9.95) Alternate Edition; cardstock-c 10.00

VAMPIRE TALES
Marvel Comics Group: Aug, 1973 - No. 11, June, 1975 (75¢, B&W, magazine)
1-Morbius, the Living Vampire begins by Pablo Marcos (1st solo Morbius series & 5th Morbius app.) 3.65 11.00 40.00
2-Intro. Satana; Steranko-r 3.20 9.60 35.00
3,5,6,8: 3-Satana app. 5-Origin Morbius. 6-1st Lilith app. 8-Blade app. (see Tomb of Dracula) 2.50 7.50 25.00
4,7 2.30 7.00 20.00
9-11: 9-Blade app. 2.30 7.00 20.00
Annual 1(10/75)-Heath-r/#9 2.30 7.00 20.00
NOTE: *Alcala a-6, 8, 9i.* ***Boris*** *c-4, 6.* ***Chaykin*** *a-7.* ***Everett*** *a-1r.* ***Gulacy*** *a-7p.* ***Heath*** *a-9.* ***Infantino*** *a-3r.* ***Gil Kane*** *a-4, 5r.*

VAMPIRE VERSES, THE
CFD Productions: Aug, 1995 - No. 4, 1995 ($2.95, B&W, mature)
1-4 3.00

VAMPRESS LUXURA, THE
Brainstorm Comics: Feb, 1996 ($2.95)
1-Lindo-c/a/scripts 3.00
1-($10.00, Gold edition)-Gold foil logo 10.00
Leather Special-(3/96, $2.95) 3.00

VAMPS
DC Comics (Vertigo): Aug, 1994 - No. 6, Jan, 1995 ($1.95, lim. series, mature)
1-6-Bolland-c 3.00
Trade paperback ($9.95)-r/#1-6 10.00

VAMPS: HOLLYWOOD & VEIN
DC Comics (Vertigo): Feb, 1996 - No. 6, July, 1996 ($2.25, lim. series, mature)
1-6: Winslade-c 2.50

VAMPS: PUMPKIN TIME
DC Comics (Vertigo): Dec, 1998 - No. 3, Feb, 1999 ($2.50, lim. series, mature)
1-3: Quitely-c 2.50

VANDALA
Chaos! Comics: Aug, 2000 - Present ($2.95)
1-Cleavenger-c 3.00
1-($9.95) Premium Edition 9.95

VANGUARD (...Outpost: Earth) (See Megaton)
Megaton Comics: 1987 ($1.50)
1-Erik Larsen-c(p) 3.00

VANGUARD (See Savage Dragon #2)
Image Comics (Highbrow Entertainment): Oct, 1993 - No.6, 1994 ($1.95)
1-6: 1-Wraparound gatefold-c; Erik Larsen back-up-a; Supreme x-over. 3-(12/93)-Indicia says December 1994. 4-Berzerker back-up. 5-Angel Medina-a(p). 3.00

VANGUARD (See Savage Dragon #2)
Image Comics: Aug, 1996 - No.4, Feb, 1997 ($2.95, B&W, limited series)
1-4 3.00

VANGUARD: ETHEREAL WARRIORS
Image Comics: Aug, 2000 ($5.95, B&W)
1-Fosco & Larsen-a 6.00

VANGUARD ILLUSTRATED
Pacific Comics: Nov, 1983 - No. 11, Oct, 1984 (Baxter paper)(Direct sales only)
1-6,8-11: 1,7-Nudity scenes. 2-1st app. Stargrazers (see Legends of the Stargrazers; Dave Stevens-c 3.00
7-1st app. Mr. Monster (r-in Mr. Monster #1) 5.00
NOTE: ***Evans*** *a-7.* ***Kaluta*** *c-5, 7p.* ***Perez*** *a-6; c-6.* ***Rude*** *a-1-4; c-4.* ***Williamson*** *c-3.*

VANGUARD: STRANGE VISITORS
Image Comics: Oct, 1996 - No.4, Feb, 1997 ($2.95, B&W, limited series)
1-4: 3-Supreme-c/app. 3.00

VANITY (See Pacific Presents #3)
Pacific Comics: Jun, 1984 - No. 2, Aug, 1984 ($1.50, direct sales)
1,2: Origin 2.00

VARIETY COMICS (The Spice of Comics)
Rural Home Publ./Croyden Publ. Co.: 1944 - No. 2, 1945; No. 3, 1946
1-Origin Captain Valiant 21.00 64.00 170.00
2-Captain Valiant 12.00 36.00 95.00
3(1946-Croyden)-Captain Valiant 10.00 30.00 80.00

VARIETY COMICS (See Fox Giants)

Vault of Horror #35 © WMG

Venom on Trial #3 © MAR

VENUS
10¢
THE MOST BEAUTIFUL GIRL IN THE WORLD!

Venus #1 © MAR

GD2.0 FN6.0 NM9.4

VARIOGENESIS
Dagger Comics Group: June, 1994 ($3.50)

0 — 3.50

VARSITY
Parents' Magazine Institute: 1945

1 — 7.15 21.50 50.00

VAULT OF EVIL
Marvel Comics Group: Feb, 1973 - No. 23, Nov, 1975

1 (1950s reprints begin) — 2.00 6.00 18.00
2-23: 3,4-Brunner-c. 11-Kirby-a — 1.50 4.50 12.00

NOTE: ***Ditko** a-14r, 15r, 20-22r. **Drucker** a-10r(Mystic #52), 13r(Uncanny Tales #42). **Everett** a-11r(Menace #2), 13r(Menace #4); c-10. **Heath** a-5r. **Gil Kane** c-1, 6. **Kirby** a-11. **Krigstein** a-20r(Uncanny Tales #54). **Reinman** r-1. **Tuska** a-6r.*

VAULT OF HORROR (Formerly War Against Crime #1-11)
E. C. Comics: No. 12, Apr-May, 1950 - No. 40, Dec-Jan, 1954-55

12 (Scarce)-ties w/Crypt Of Terror as 1st horror comic — 420.00 1260.00 4600.00
13-Morphine story — 92.00 277.00 1015.00
14 — 82.00 246.00 900.00
15- "Terror in the Swamp" is same story w/minor changes as "The Thing in the Swamp" from Haunt of Fear #15 — 70.00 210.00 770.00
16 — 53.00 160.00 585.00
17-19 — 41.00 123.00 450.00
20-25: 22-Frankenstein-c & adaptation. 23-Used in **POP**, pg. 84; Davis-a(2). 24-Craig biography — 33.00 100.00 365.00
26-B&W & color illos in **POP** — 33.00 100.00 365.00
27-37: 30-Dismemberment-c. 31-Ray Bradbury biog. 32-Censored-c. 35-X-Mas-c. 36- "Pipe Dream" classic opium addict story by Krigstein; "Twin Bill" cited in articles by T.E. Murphy, Wertham. 37-1st app. Drusilla, a Vampirella look alike; Williamson-a — 26.00 78.00 285.00
38-39: 39-Bondage-c — 22.00 66.00 240.00
40-Low distribution — 28.00 86.00 310.00

NOTE: ***Craig** art in all but No. 13 & 33; c-12-40. **Crandall** a-33, 34, 39. **Davis** a-17-38. **Evans** a-27, 28, 30, 32, 33. **Feldstein** a-12-16. **Ingels** a-13-20, 22-40. **Kamen** a-15-22, 25, 29, 35. **Krigstein** a-36, 38-40. **Kurtzman** a-12, 13. **Orlando** a-24, 31, 40. **Wood** a-12-14. #22, 29 & 31 have Ray Bradbury adaptations. #16 & 17 have H. P. Lovecraft adaptations.*

VAULT OF HORROR, THE
Gladstone Publ.: Aug, 1990 - No. 6, June, 1991 ($1.95, 68 pgs.)(#4 on: $2.00)

1-Craig-c(r); all contain EC reprints — 4.00
2-6: 2,4-6-Craig-c(r). 3-Ingels-c(r) — 3.00

VAULT OF HORROR
Russ Cochran/Gemstone Publishing: Sept, 1991 - No. 5, May, 1992 ($2.00); Oct, 1992 - No. 29, Oct, 1999 ($1.50/$2.00/$2.50)

1-29: E.C reprints. 1-4r/VOH #12-15 w/original-c — 2.50

V...-COMICS (Morse code for "V" - 3 dots, 1 dash)
Fox Features Syndicate: Jan, 1942 - No. 2, Mar-Apr, 1942

1-Origin V-Man & the Boys; The Banshee & The Black Fury, The Queen of Evil, & V-Agents begin; Nazi-c — 126.00 379.00 1200.00
2-Nazi bondage/torture-c — 92.00 276.00 875.00

VECTOR
Now Comics: 1986 - No. 4, 1986? ($1.50, 1st color comic by Now Comics)

1-4: Computer-generated art — 2.00

VEGAS KNIGHTS
Pioneer Comics: 1989 ($1.95, one-shot)

1 — 2.00

VEILS
DC Comics (Vertigo): 1999 ($24.95, one-shot)

Hardcover-($24.95) Painted art and photography; McGreal-s — 24.95
Softcover ($14.95) — 14.95

VELOCITY (Also see Cyberforce)
Image Comics (Top Cow Productions): Nov, 1995 - No. 3, Jan, 1996 ($2.50, limited series)

1-3: Kurt Busiek scripts in all. 2-Savage Dragon-c/app. — 3.00

GD2.0 FN6.0 NM9.4

VENGEANCE OF VAMPIRELLA (Becomes Vampirella: Death & Destruction)
Harris Comics: Apr, 1994 - No. 25, Apr, 1996 ($2.95)

1-($3.50)-Quesada/Palmiotti "bloodfoil" wraparound-c — 5.00
1-2nd printing; blue foil-c — 3.00
1-Gold — 15.00
2-25: 8-Polybagged w/trading card; 10-w/coupon for Hyde -25 poster. 11,19-Polybagged w/ trading card. 25-Quesada & Palmiotti red foil-c. — 3.00
...: Bloodshed (1995, $6.95) — 7.00

VENGEANCE OF VAMPIRELLA: THE MYSTERY WALK
Harris Comics: Nov, 1995 ($2.95, one-shot)

0 — 3.00

VENGEANCE SQUAD
Charlton Comics: July, 1975 - No. 6, May, 1976 (#1-3 are 25¢ issues)

1-Mike Mauser, Private Eye begins by Staton — 1.00 3.00 8.00
2-6: Morisi-a in all — 5.00
5,6(Modern Comics-r, 1977) — 3.00

VENOM: Marvel Comics (Also see Amazing Spider-Man #298-300)

... ALONG CAME A SPIDER, 1/96 - No. 4, 4/96 ($2.95)-Spider-Man & Carnage app. — 3.00
... CARNAGE UNLEASHED, 4/95 - No. 4, 7/95 ($2.95) — 3.00
... FINALE, 11/97 - No. 3, 1/98 ($1.99) — 2.00
... FUNERAL PYRE, 8/93- No. 3, 10/93 ($2.95)-#1-Holo-grafx foil-c; Punisher app. in all — 3.00

VENOM: LETHAL PROTECTOR
Marvel Comics: Feb, 1993 - No. 6, July, 1993 ($2.95, limited series)

1-Red holo-grafx foil-c; Bagley-c/a in all — 5.00
1-Gold variant sold to retailers — 15.00
1-Black-c (**counterfeit**, valueless) — -
2-6: Spider-Man app. in all — 3.00

... LICENSE TO KILL,6/97 - No. 3, 8/97 ($1.95) — 2.00
... NIGHTS OF VENGEANCE, 8/94 - No. 4, 11/94 ($2.95), #1-Red foil-c — 3.00
... ON TRIAL, 3/97 - No. 3, 5/97 ($1.95) — 2.00
... SEED OF DARKNESS, 7/97 ($1.95) #(-1) Flashback — 2.00
... SEPARATION ANXIETY,12/94- No. 4, 3/95 ($2.95) #1-Embossed-c — 3.00
... SIGN OF THE BOSS,3/97 - No. 2, 10/97 ($1.99) — 2.00
... SINNER TAKES ALL, 8/95 - No. 5, 10/95 ($2.95) — 3.00
... SUPER SPECIAL, 8/95($3.95) #1-Flip book — 4.00
... THE ENEMY WITHIN, 2/94 - No. 3, 4/94 ($2.95)-Demogoblin & Morbius app. 1-Glow-in-the-dark-c — 3.00
... THE HUNGER, 8/96- No. 4, 11/96 ($1.95) — 2.00
... THE HUNTED, 5/96-No. 3, 7/96 ($2.95) — 3.00
... THE MACE, 5/94 - No. 3, 7/94 ($2.95)-#1-Embossed-c — 3.00
... THE MADNESS, 11/93- No. 3, 1/94 ($2.95)-Kelley Jones-c/a(p). 1-Embossed-c; Juggernaut app. — 3.00
... TOOTH AND CLAW, 12/96 - No. 3, 2/97 ($1.95)-Wolverine-c/app. — 2.00

VENTURE
AC Comics (Americomics): Aug, 1986 - No. 3, 1986? ($1.75)

1-3: 1-3-Bolt. 1-Astron. 2-Femforce. 3-Fazers — 2.00

VENUS (See Marvel Spotlight #2 & Weird Wonder Tales)
Marvel/Atlas Comics (CMC 1-9/LCC 10-19): Aug, 1948 - No. 19, Apr, 1952 (Also see Marvel Mystery #91)

1-Venus & Hedy Devine begin; 1st app. Venus; Kurtzman's "Hey Look" — 121.00 363.00 1150.00
2 — 70.00 210.00 665.00
3,5 — 58.00 174.00 550.00
4-Kurtzman's "Hey Look" — 59.00 177.00 560.00
6-9: 6-Loki app. 7,8-Painted-c. 9-Begin 52 pgs.; book-length feature "Whom the Gods Destroy!" — 54.00 162.00 485.00
10-S/F-horror issues begin (7/50) — 72.00 216.00 685.00
11-S/F end of the world (11/50) — 84.00 253.00 800.00

Venus Wars #5 © DH

Veronica #41 © AP

Vext #1 © DC

12-Colan-a 48.00 145.00 435.00
13-19-Venus by Everett, 2-3 stories each; covers-#13,15-19; 14-Everett part cover (Venus). 17-Bondage-c 73.00 220.00 695.00
NOTE: ***Berg*** *s/f story-13.* ***Everett*** *c-13, 14(part; Venus only), 15-19.* ***Heath*** *s/f story-11.* ***Maneely*** *s/f story-10(3pg.), 16.* ***Morisi*** *a-19.* ***Syd Shores*** *c-6.*

VENUS WARS, THE (Manga)
Dark Horse Comics: Apr, 1991 - No.14, May, 1992 ($2.25, B&W)
1-14: 1-3 Contain 2 Dark Horse trading cards. 1,3,7,10-(44 pgs.) 2.50

VERI BEST SURE FIRE COMICS
Holyoke Publishing Co.: No date (circa 1945) (Reprints Holyoke one-shots)
1-Captain Aero, Alias X, Miss Victory, Commandos of the Devil Dogs, Red Cross, Hammerhead Hawley, Capt. Aero's Sky Scouts, Flagman app.; same-c as Veri Best Sure Shot #1 39.00 116.00 310.00

VERI BEST SURE SHOT COMICS
Holyoke Publishing Co.: No date (circa 1945) (Reprints Holyoke one-shots)
1-Capt. Aero, Miss Victory by Quinlan, Alias X, The Red Cross, Flagman, Commandos of the Devil Dogs, Hammerhead Hawley, Capt. Aero's Sky Scouts; same-c as Veri Best Sure Fire #1 39.00 116.00 310.00

VERMILLION
DC Comics (Helix): Oct, 1996 - No. 12, Sept, 1997 ($2.25/$2.50)
1-12: 1-4: Lucius Shepard scripts. 4,12-Kaluta-c 2.50

VERONICA (Also see Archie's Girls, Betty &...)
Archie Comics: Apr, 1989 - Present
1-(75¢-c) 2.40 6.00
2-10: 2-(75¢-c) 4.00
11-38 3.00
39-Love Showdown pt. 4, Cheryl Blossom 5.00
40-109: 34-Neon ink-c 2.00

VERONICA'S PASSPORT DIGEST MAGAZINE (Becomes Veronica's Digest Magazine #3 on)
Archie Comics: Nov, 1992 - Present ($1.50/$1.79, digest size)
1 5.00
2-6 3.00

VERONICA'S SUMMER SPECIAL (See Archie Giant Series Magazine #615, 625)

VERTIGO GALLERY, THE: DREAMS AND NIGHTMARES
DC Comics (Vertgo): 1995 ($3.50, one-shot)
1-Pin-ups of Vertigo characters by Sienkiewicz, Toth, Van Fleet & others; Dave McKean-c 4.00

VERTIGO JAM
DC Comics (Vertigo): Aug, 1993 ($3.95, one-shot, 68 pgs.)(Painted-c by Fabry)
1-Sandman by Neil Gaiman, Hellblazer, Animal Man, Doom Patrol, Swamp Thing, Kid Eternity & Shade the Changing Man 5.00

VERTIGO PREVIEW
DC Comics (Vertigo): 1992 (75¢, one-shot, 36 pgs.)
1-Vertigo previews; Sandman story by Neil Gaiman 2.00

VERTIGO RAVE
DC Comics (Vertigo): Fall, 1994 (99¢, one-shot)
1-Vertigo previews 2.00

VERTIGO SECRET FILES
DC Comics (Vertigo): Aug, 2000 ($4.95)
...: Hellblazer 1 (8/00, $4.95) Background info and story summaries 4.95
...: Swamp Thing 1 (11/00, $4.95) Backstories and origins; Hale-c 4.95

VERTIGO VERITE: THE UNSEEN HAND
DC Comics (Vertigo): Sept, 1996 - No. 4, Dec, 1996 ($2.50, limited series)
1-4: Terry LaBan scripts in all 2.50

VERTIGO VISIONS
DC Comics (Vertigo): June, 1993 - Present (one-shots)
Dr. Occult 1 (7/94, $3.95) 4.00
Dr. Thirteen 1 (9/98, $5.95) Howarth-s 6.00
Prez 1 (7/95, $3.95) 4.00
The Geek 1 (6/93, $3.95) 4.00
The Eaters ($4.95, 1995)-Milligan story. 5.00
The Phantom Stranger 1 (10/93, $3.50) 3.50
Tomahawk 1 (7/98, $4.95) Pollack-s 5.00

VERTIGO WINTER'S EDGE
DC Comics (Vertigo): 1998, 1999 ($7.95/$6.95, square-bound, annual)
1-Winter stories by Vertigo creators; Desire story by Gaiman/Bolton; Bolland wraparound-c 8.00
2,3-($6.95)-Winter stories: 2-Allred-c. 3-Bond-c; Desire by Gaiman/Zulli 7.00

VERY BEST OF DENNIS THE MENACE, THE
Fawcett Publ.: July, 1979 - No. 2, Apr, 1980 (95¢/$1.00, digest-size, 132 pgs.)
1,2-Reprints 1.25 3.75 10.00

VERY BEST OF DENNIS THE MENACE, THE
Marvel Comics Group: Apr, 1982 - No. 3, Aug, 1982 ($1.25, digest-size)
1-3: Reprints 1.10 3.30 9.00
1,2-Mistakenly printed with DC logo on cover 1.75 5.25 14.00
NOTE: ***Hank Ketcham*** *c-all. A few thousand of #1 & 2 were printed with DC emblem.*

VERY VICKY
Meet Danny Ocean: 1993? - No. 8, 1995 ($2.50, B&W)
1-8, ...: Calling All Hillbillies (1995, $2.50) 2.50

VEXT
DC Comics: Mar, 1999 - No. 6, Aug, 1999 ($2.50, limited series)
1-6-Giffen-s. 1-Superman app. 2.50

V FOR VENDETTA
DC Comics: Sept, 1988 - No. 10, May, 1989 ($2.00, maxi-series)
1-10: Alan Moore scripts in all 3.00
Trade paperback (1990, $14.95) 15.00

VIC BRIDGES FAZERS SKETCHBOOK AND FACT FILE
AC Comics: Nov, 1986 ($1.75)
1 3.00

VIC FLINT(Crime Buster...)(See Authentic Police Cases #10-14 & Fugitives From Justice #2)
St. John Publ. Co.: Aug, 1948 - No. 5, Apr, 1949 (Newspaper reprints; NEA Service)
1 12.50 37.50 100.00
2 10.00 30.00 70.00
3-5 7.85 23.50 55.00

VIC FLINT (Crime Buster...)
Argo Publ.: Feb, 1956 - No. 2, May, 1956 (Newspaper reprints)
1,2 8.65 26.00 60.00

VIC JORDAN (Also see Big Shot Comics #32)
Civil Service Publ.: April, 1945
1-1944 daily newspaper-r 12.50 37.50 100.00

VICKI (Humor)
Atlas/Seaboard Publ.: Feb, 1975 - No. 4, Aug, 1975 (No. 1,2: 68 pgs.)
1,2-(68 pgs.)-Reprints Tippy Teen; Good Girl art 2.50 7.50 23.00
3,4 (Low print) 2.30 7.00 20.00

VICKI VALENTINE (...Summer Special #1)
Renegade Press: July, 1985 - No. 4, July, 1986 ($1.70, B&W)
1-4: Woggon, Rausch-a; all have paper dolls. 2-Christmas issue 3.00

VICKY
Ace Magazine: Oct, 1948 - No. 5, June, 1949
nn(10/48)-Teenage humor 6.00 18.00 42.00
4(12/48), nn(2/49), 4(4/49), 5(6/49): 5-Dotty app. 5.00 15.00 32.00

VIC TORRY & HIS FLYING SAUCER (Also see Mr. Monster's...#5)
Fawcett Publications: 1950 (one-shot)
nn-Book-length saucer story by Powell; photo/painted-c 61.00 182.00 575.00

VICTORY
Topps Comics: June, 1994 ($2.50, unfinished limited series)
1-Kurt Busiek script; Giffen-c/a; Rob Liefeld variant-c exists 2.50

Vietnam Journal #7 © Don Lomax

The Vigilante #4 © DC

VIP #1 © Columbia Tri-Star TV Dist.

GD2.0 FN6.0 NM9.4

VICTORY COMICS
Hillman Periodicals: Aug, 1941 - No. 4, Dec, 1941 (#1 by Funnies, Inc.)
1-The Conqueror by Bill Everett, The Crusader, & Bomber Burns begin; Conqueror's origin in text; Everett-c 295.00 885.00 2800.00
2-Everett-c/a 126.00 379.00 1200.00
3,4 84.00 253.00 800.00

VIC VERITY MAGAZINE
Vic Verity Publ: 1945; No. 2, Jan?, 1947 - No. 7, Sept, 1946 (A comic book)
1-C. C. Beck-c/a 20.00 60.00 160.00
2-Beck-c 10.50 32.00 85.00
3-7: 6-Beck-a. 7-Beck-c 10.00 30.00 75.00

VIDEO JACK
Marvel Comics (Epic Comics): Nov, 1987 - No. 6, Nov, 1988 ($1.25)
1-5 2.00
6-Neal Adams, Keith Giffen, Wrightson, others-a 4.00

VIETNAM JOURNAL
Apple Comics: Nov, 1987 - No. 16, Apr, 1991 ($1.75/$1.95, B&W)
1-16: Don Lomax-c/a/scripts in all, 1-2nd print 3.00
...: Indian Country Vol. 1 (1990, $12.95)-r/#1-4 plus one new story 13.00

VIETNAM JOURNAL: VALLEY OF DEATH
Apple Comics: June, 1994 - No. 2, Aug, 1994 ($2.75, B&W, limited series)
1,2: By Don Lomax 2.75

VIGILANTE, THE (Also see New Teen Titans #23 & Annual V2#2)
DC Comics: Oct, 1983 - No. 50, Feb, 1988 ($1.25, Baxter paper)
1-Origin 3.00
2-16,19-49: 3-Cyborg app. 4-1st app. The Exterminator; Newton-a(p). 6,7-Origin. 20,21-Nightwing app. 35-Origin Mad Bomber. 47-Batman-c/s 2.50
17,18,50: 17,18-Alan Moore scripts. 50-Ken Steacy painted-c 3.00
Annual nn, 2 ('85, '86) 2.50

VIGILANTE: CITY LIGHTS, PRAIRIE JUSTICE (Also see Action Comics #42, Justice League of America #78, Leading Comics & World's Finest #244)
DC Comics: Nov, 1995 - No. 4, Feb, 1996 ($2.50, limited series)
1-4: James Robinson scripts in all 2.50

VIGILANTES, THE
Dell Publishing Co.: No. 839, Sept, 1957
Four Color 839-Movie 6.70 20.00 80.00

VIGILANTE 8: SECOND OFFENSE
Chaos! Comics: Dec, 1999 ($2.95, one-shot)
1-Based on video game 2.95

VIKINGS, THE (Movie)
Dell Publishing Co.: No. 910, May, 1958
Four Color 910-Buscema-a, Kirk Douglas photo-c 8.35 25.00 100.00

VILLAINS AND VIGILANTES
Eclipse Comics: Dec, 1986 - No. 4, May, 1987 ($1.50/$1.75, limited series, Baxter paper)
1-4: Based on role-playing game. 2-4 ($1.75-c) 2.00

VILLAINY OF DOCTOR DOOM, THE
Marvel Comics: 1999 ($17.95, TPB)
nn-Reprints early battle with the Fantastic Four 17.95

VINTAGE MAGNUS (...Robot Fighter)
Valiant: Jan, 1992 - No. 4, Apr, 1992 ($2.25, limited series)
1-4: 1-Layton-c; r/origin from Magnus R.F. #22 2.25

VIOLATOR (Also see Spawn #2)
Image Comics (Todd McFarlane Productions): May, 1994 - No. 3, Aug, 1994 ($1.95, limited series)
1-Alan Moore scripts in all 5.00
2,3: Bart Sears-c(p)/a(p) 4.00

VIOLATOR VS. BADROCK
Image Comics (Extreme Studios): May, 1995 - No. 4, Aug, 1995 ($2.50, limited series)
1-4: Alan Moore scripts in all. 1-1st app Celestine; variant-c (3?) 2.50

VIOLENT MESSIAHS
Image Comics: June, 2000 - Present ($2.95)
1-Two covers by Travis Smith and Medina 3.50
1-Tower Records variant edition 3.50
2-4 3.00

VIP (TV)
TV Comics: 2000 - No. 3 ($2.95)
1-Based on the Pamela Lee TV show; photo-c 2.95

VIPER (TV)
DC Comics: Aug, 1994 - No. 4, Nov, 1994 ($1.95, limited series)
1-4-Adaptation of television show 2.00

VIRGINIAN, THE (TV)
Gold Key: June, 1963
1(10060-306)-Part photo-c of James Drury plus photo back-c 3.80 11.40 42.00

VIRTUA FIGHTER (Video Game)
Marvel Comics: Aug, 1995 (2.95, one-shot)
1-Sega Saturn game 3.00

VIRUS
Dark Horse Comics: 1993 - No. 4, 1993 ($2.50, limited series)
1-4: Ploog-c 2.50

VISION, THE
Marvel Comics: Nov, 1994 - No. 4, Feb, 1995 ($1.75, limited series)
1-4 2.00

VISION AND THE SCARLET WITCH, THE (See Marvel Fanfare)
Marvel Comics Group: Nov, 1982 - No. 4, Feb, 1983 (Limited series)
1-4: 2-Nuklo & Future Man app. 3.00

VISION AND THE SCARLET WITCH, THE
Marvel Comics Group: Oct, 1985 - No. 12, Sept, 1986 (Maxi-series)
V2#1-12: 1-Origin; 1st app. in Avengers #57. 2-West Coast Avengers x-over 2.50

VISIONARIES
Marvel Comics (Star)/Marvel Comics #3 on: Nov, 1987 - No. 6, Sept, 1988
1-6 2.50

VISIONS
Vision Publications: 1979 - No. 5, 1983 (B&W, fanzine)
1-Flaming Carrot begins(1st app?); N. Adams-c 3.65 11.00 40.00
2-N. Adams, Rogers-a; Gulacy back-c; signed & numbered to 2000 3.00 9.00 30.00
3-Williamson-c(p); Steranko back-c 2.30 7.00 20.00
4-Flaming Carrot-c & info. 2.30 7.00 20.00
5-1 pg. Flaming Carrot 1.10 3.30 9.00
NOTE: ***Eisner** a-4. **Miller** a-4. **Starlin** a-3. **Williamson** a-5. After #4, Visions became an annual publication of The Atlanta Fantasy Fair.*

VISITOR, THE
Valiant/Acclaim Comics (Valiant): Apr, 1995 - No. 13, Nov, 1995 ($2.50)
1-13: 8-Harbinger revealed. 13-Visitor revealed to be Sting from Harbinger. 2.50

VISITOR, VS. THE VALIANT UNIVERSE, THE
Valiant: Feb, 1995 - No. 2, Mar, 1995 ($2.95, limited series)
1,2 3.00

VOGUE (Also see Youngblood)
Image Comics (Extreme Studios): Oct, 1995 - No.3, Jan, 1996 ($2.50, limited series)
1-3: 1-Liefeld-c, 1-Variant-c 2.50

VOID INDIGO (Also see Marvel Graphic Novel)
Marvel Comics (Epic Comics): 11/84 - No. 2, 3/85 ($1.50, direct sales, unfinished series, mature)
1,2: Cont'd from Marvel G.N.; graphic sex & violence 2.00

Voodoo #18 © AJAX

Wagon Train #7 © DELL

Wahoo Morris #1 © Craig Taillefer

GD2.0 FN6.0 NM9.4

)LCANIC REVOLVER)
ni Press: Dec, 1998 - No. 3, Mar, 1999 ($2.95, B&W, limited series)

-3: Scott Morse-s/a			3.00
'B (12/99, $9.95, digest size) r/#1-3 and Oni Double Feature #7 prologue			9.95

)LTRON (TV)
odern Publishing: 1985 - No. 3, 1985 (75¢, limited series)

-3: Ayers-a in all			4.00

)ODA (Jungle Princess) (Formerly Voodoo)
ax-Farrell (Four Star Publications): No. 20, April, 1955 - No. 22, Aug, 1955

)-Baker-c/a (r/Seven Seas #6)	39.00	118.00	315.00
,22-Baker-a plus Kamen/Baker story, Kimbo Boy of Jungle, & Baker-c (p) in all. 22-Censored Jo-Jo-r (name Powaa)	34.00	103.00	275.00

)TE: *#20-22 each contain one heavily censored-r of South Sea Girl by **Baker** from Seven Seas mics with name changed to Vooda. #20-r/Seven Seas #6; #21-r/#4; #22-r/#3.*

)ODOO (Weird Fantastic Tales) (Vooda #20 on)
ax-Farrell (Four Star Publ.): May, 1952 - No. 19, Jan-Feb, 1955

-South Sea Girl-r by Baker	55.00	165.00	500.00
-Rulah story-r plus South Sea Girl from Seven Seas #2 by Baker (name changed from Alani to El'nee)	44.00	133.00	400.00
-Bakerish-a; man stabbed in face	38.00	113.00	300.00
,8-Baker-r. 8-Severed head panels	38.00	113.00	300.00
-7,9,10: 5-Nazi death camp story (flaying alive). 6-Severed head panels	30.00	90.00	240.00
1-18: 14-Zombies take over America. 15-Opium drug story-r/Ellery Queen #3. 16-Post nuclear world story.17-Electric chair panels	26.00	79.00	210.00
9-Bondage-c; Baker-r(2)/Seven Seas #5 w/minor changes & #1, heavily modified; last pre-code; contents & covers change to jungle theme	34.00	103.00	275.00
nual 1(1952, 25¢, 100 pgs.)-Baker-a (scarce)	84.00	253.00	800.00

)ODOO
age Comics (WildStorm): Nov, 1997 - No. 4, Mar, 1998 ($2.50, lim. series)

-4:Alan Moore-s in all; Hughes-c. 2-4-Rio-a			2.50
-Platinum Ed			10.00
ancing on the Dark TPB ('99, $9.95) r/#1-4			10.00
-Zealot: Skin Trade (8/95, $4.95)			5.00

)ODOO (See Tales of...)

)ODOOM
ni Press: June, 2000 ($4.95, B&W)

-Scott Morse-s/Jim Mahfood-a			5.00

)RTEX
ortex Publs.: Nov, 1982 - No. 15, 1988 (No month) ($1.50/$1.75, B&W)

($1.95)-Peter Hsu-a; Ken Steacy-c; nudity			5.00
,12: 2-1st app. Mister X (on-c only). 12-Sam Kieth-a			4.00
-11,13-15			2.00

)RTEX
omico: 1991 - No. 2? ($2.50, limited series)

,2: Heroes from The Elementals			2.50

)RTEX
ntity Comics: 1996 ($2.95)

,1b: 1b-Kaniuga-c			3.00

)YAGE TO THE BOTTOM OF THE SEA (Movie, TV)
ell Publishing Co./Gold Key: No. 1230, Sept-Nov, 1961; Dec, 1964 - #16, Apr, 70 (Painted-c)

our Color 1230 (1961)	10.00	30.00	120.00
)133-412(#1, 12/64)(Gold Key)	6.30	19.00	75.00
(7/65) - 5: Photo back-c, 1-5	4.60	13.75	55.00
-14	3.65	11.00	40.00
5,16-Reprints	2.50	7.50	25.00

)YAGE TO THE DEEP
ell Publishing Co.: Sept-Nov, 1962 - No. 4, Nov-Jan, 1964 (Painted-c)

	4.55	13.65	50.00
-4	3.20	9.60	35.00

GD2.0 FN6.0 NM9.4

WACKO
Ideal Publ. Corp.: Sept, 1980 - No. 3, Oct, 1981 (84 pgs., B&W, magazine)

1-3	1.25	3.75	10.00

WACKY ADVENTURES OF CRACKY (Also see Gold Key Spotlight)
Gold Key: Dec, 1972 - No. 12, Sept, 1975

1	2.00	6.00	16.00
2	1.10	3.30	9.00
3-12	1.00	2.80	7.00

(See March of Comics #405, 424, 436, 448)

WACKY DUCK (...Comics #3-6; formerly Dopey Duck; Justice Comics #7 on) (See Film Funnies)
Marvel Comics (NPP): No. 3, Fall, 1946 - No. 6, Summer, 1947; Aug, 1948 - No. 2, Oct, 1948

3	20.00	60.00	160.00
4-Infinity-c	19.00	56.00	150.00
5,6(1947)-Becomes Justice comics	15.00	45.00	120.00
1,2(1948)	10.00	30.00	80.00
I.W. Reprint #1,2,7('58): 1-r/Wacky Duck #6	1.75	5.25	14.00
Super Reprint #10(I.W. on-c, Super-inside)	1.75	5.25	14.00

WACKY QUACKY (See Wisco)

WACKY RACES (TV)
Gold Key: Aug, 1969 - No. 7, Apr, 1972 (Hanna-Barbera)

1	4.55	13.65	50.00
2-7	3.00	9.00	30.00

WACKY SQUIRREL (Also see Dark Horse Presents)
Dark Horse Comics: Oct, 1987 - No. 4, 1988 ($1.75, B&W)

1-4: 4-Superman parody			2.00
Halloween Adventure Special 1 (1987, $2.00)			2.00
Summer Fun Special 1 (1988, $2.00)			2.00

WACKY WITCH (Also see Gold Key Spotlight)
Gold Key: March, 1971 - No. 21, Dec, 1975

1	3.00	9.00	30.00
2	1.85	5.50	15.00
3-10	1.50	4.50	12.00
11-21	1.00	3.00	8.00

(See March of Comics #374, 398, 410, 422, 434, 446, 458, 470, 482)

WACKY WOODPECKER (See Two Bit the...)
I. W. Enterprises/Super Comics: 1958; 1963

I.W. Reprint #1,2,7 (nd-reprints Two Bit...): 7-r/Two-Bit, the Wacky Woodpecker #1.	1.50	4.50	12.00
Super Reprint #10('63): 10-r/Two-Bit, The Wacky Woodpecker #?	1.50	4.50	12.00

WAGON TRAIN (1st Series) (TV) (See Western Roundup under Dell Giants)
Dell Publishing Co.: No. 895, Mar, 1958 - No. 13, Apr-June, 1962 (All photo-c)

Four Color 895 (#1)	11.30	34.00	135.00
Four Color 971(#2),1019(#3)	6.30	19.00	75.00
4(1-3/60),6-13	5.00	15.00	60.00
5-Toth-a	5.85	17.50	70.00

WAGON TRAIN (2nd Series)(TV)
Gold Key: Jan, 1964 - No. 4, Oct, 1964 (All front & back photo-c)

1-Tufts-a in all	5.00	15.00	60.00
2-4	3.80	11.40	42.00

WAHOO MORRIS
Image Comics: Mar, 2000 - Present ($3.50, B&W)

1-Craig Taillefer-s/a			3.50

WAITING PLACE, THE
Slave Labor Graphics: Apr, 1997 - No. 6, Sept, 1997 ($2.95)

1-6-Sean McKeever-s			3.00
Vol. 2- 1(11/99), 2-6			2.95

WAITING ROOM WILLIE (See Sad Case of...)

WALLY (Teen-age)
Gold Key: Dec, 1962 - No. 4, Sept, 1963

Walt Disney's Comics Digest #30 © WDC

Walt Disney's Comics and Stories #22 © WDC

Walt Disney's Comics and Stories #36 © WDC

1 — 3.00 — 9.00 — 30.00
2-4 — 2.50 — 7.50 — 23.00

WALLY THE WIZARD
Marvel Comics (Star Comics): Apr, 1985 - No. 12, Mar, 1986 (Children's comic)
1-12: Bob Bolling a-1,3; c-1,9,11,12 — 3.00

WALLY WOOD'S T.H.U.N.D.E.R. AGENTS (See Thunder Agents)
Deluxe Comics: Nov, 1984 - No. 5, Oct, 1986 ($2.00, 52 pgs.)
1-5: 5-Jerry Ordway-c/a in Wood style — 5.00
NOTE: ***Anderson** a-2i, 3i. **Buckler** a-4. **Ditko** a-3, 4. **Giffen** a-1p-4p. **Perez** a-1p, 2, 4; c-1-4.*

WALT DISNEY CHRISTMAS PARADE (Also see Christmas Parade)
Whitman Publ. Co. (Golden Press): Wint, 1977 ($1.95, cardboard-c, 224 pgs.)
11191-Barks-r/Christmas in Disneyland #1, Dell Christmas Parade #9 & Dell Giant #53 — 2.50 — 7.50 — 25.00

WALT DISNEY COMICS DIGEST
Gold Key: June, 1968 - No. 57, Feb, 1976 (50¢, digest size)
1-Reprints Uncle Scrooge #5; 192 pgs. — 7.50 — 22.50 — 90.00
2-4-Barks-r — 4.60 — 13.75 — 55.00
5-Daisy Duck by Barks (8 pgs.); last published story by Barks (art only) plus 21 pg. Scrooge-r by Barks — 8.00 — 24.00 — 95.00
6-13-All Barks-r — 3.45 — 10.35 — 38.00
14,15 — 2.40 — 7.35 — 22.00
16-Reprints Donald Duck #26 by Barks — 3.20 — 9.60 — 35.00
17-20-Barks-r — 2.80 — 8.40 — 28.00
21-31,33,35-37-Barks-r; 24-Toth Zorro — 2.50 — 7.50 — 24.00
32,41,45,47-49 — 2.00 — 6.00 — 16.00
34,38,39: 34-Reprints 4-Color #318. 38-Reprints Christmas in Disneyland #1. 39-Two Barks-r/WDC&S #272, 4-Color #1073 plus Toth Zorro-r — 2.50 — 7.50 — 24.00
40-Mickey Mouse-r by Gottfredson — 2.00 — 6.00 — 18.00
42,43-Barks-r — 2.00 — 6.00 — 18.00
44-(Has Gold Key emblem, 50¢)-Reprints 1st story of 4-Color #29,256,275,282 — 4.55 — 13.65 — 50.00
44-Republished in 1976 by Whitman; not identical to original; a bit smaller, blank back-c, 69¢ — 2.50 — 7.50 — 24.00
46,50,52-Barks-r. 52-Barks-r/WDC&S #161,132 — 2.00 — 6.00 — 16.00
51-Reprints 4-Color #71 — 2.50 — 7.50 — 24.00
53-55: 53-Reprints Dell Giant #30. 54-Reprints Donald Duck Beach Party #2. 55-Reprints Dell Giant #49 — 1.75 — 5.25 — 14.00
56-r/Uncle Scrooge #32 (Barks) — 2.00 — 6.00 — 18.00
57-r/Mickey Mouse Almanac('57) & two Barks stories — 2.00 — 6.00 — 16.00
NOTE: *Toth a-52r. #1-10, 196 pgs.; #11-41, 164 pgs.; #42 on, 132 pgs. Old issues were being reprinted & distributed by Whitman in 1976.*

WALT DISNEY GIANT (Disney)
Bruce Hamilton Company (Gladstone): Sept, 1995 - No. 7, Sept, 1996 ($2.25, bi-monthly, 48 pgs.)
1-7: 1-Scrooge McDuck in the Yukon; Rosa-c/a/scripts plus r/F.C. #218. 2-Uncle Scrooge-r by Barks plus 17 pg. text story. 3-Donald the Mighty Duck; Rosa-c; Barks & Rosa-r. 4-Mickey and Goofy; new-a (story actually stars Goofy. Mickey Mouse by Caesar Ferioli; Donald Duck by Giorgio Cavazzano (1st in U.S.). 6-Uncle Scrooge & the Jr. Woodchucks; new-a and Barks-r. 7-Uncle Scrooge-r by Barks plus new-a — 2.50
NOTE: *Series was initially solicited as Uncle Walt's Collectory. Issue #8 was advertised, but later cancelled.*

WALT DISNEY PAINT BOOK SERIES
Whitman Publ. Co.: No dates; circa 1975 (Beware! Has 1930s copyright dates) (79¢-c, 52pgs. B&W, treasury-sized) (Coloring books, text stories & comics-r)
#2052 (Whitman #886-r) Mickey Mouse & Donald Duck Gag Book — 3.00 — 9.00 — 30.00
#2053 (Whitman #677-r) — 3.00 — 9.00 — 30.00
#2054 (Whitman #670-r) Donald-c — 3.20 — 9.60 — 35.00
#2055 (Whitman #627-r) Mickey-c — 3.00 — 9.00 — 30.00
#2056 (Whitman #660-r) Buckey Bug-c — 2.50 — 7.50 — 25.00
#2057 (Whitman #887-r) Mickey & Donald-c — 3.00 — 9.00 — 30.00

WALT DISNEY PRESENTS (TV)(Disney)
Dell Publishing Co.: No. 997, 6-8/59 - No. 6, 12-2/1960-61; No. 1181, 4-5/61 (All photo-c)
Four Color 997 (#1) — 6.70 — 20.00 — 80.0
2(12-2/60)-The Swamp Fox(origin), Elfego Baca, Texas John Slaughter (Disney TV show) begin — 4.55 — 13.65 — 50.0
3-6: 5-Swamp Fox by Warren Tufts — 4.10 — 12.30 — 45.0
Four Color 1181-Texas John Slaughter — 6.70 — 20.00 — 80.0

WALT DISNEY'S CHRISTMAS PARADE (Also see Christmas Parade)
Gladstone: Winter, 1988; No. 2, Winter, 1989 ($2.95, 100 pgs.)
1-Barks-r/painted-c — 1.50 — 4.50 — 12.0
2-Barks-r — 1.10 — 3.30 — 9.0

WALT DISNEY'S COMICS AND STORIES (Cont. of Mickey Mouse Magazine) (#1-30 contain Donald Duck newspaper reprints) (Titled "Comics And Stories" #264 to #?; titled "Walt Disney's Comics And Stories" #511 on)
Dell Publishing Co./Gold Key #264-473/Whitman #474-510/Gladstone #511-547(4/90)/Disney Comics #548(6/90)-#585/Gladstone #586(8/93) on: 10/40 - #263, 8/62; #264, 10/62 - #510, 1984; #511, 10/86 - #633, 2/99
NOTE: The whole number can always be found at the bottom of the title page in the lower left-hand or right hand panel.

GD2.0 — FN6.0 — VF8.0 — NM9.
1(V1#1-c; V2#1-indicia)-Donald Duck strip-r by Al Taliaferro & Gottfredson's Mickey Mouse begin — 1520.00 — 4560.00 — 9880.00 — 19,000.0

GD2.0 — FN6.0 — NM9.
2 — 550.00 — 1650.00 — 6600.0
3 — 191.00 — 573.00 — 2100.0
4-X-Mas-c; 1st Huey, Dewey & Louie-c this title (See Mickey Mouse Magazine V4#2 for 1st-c ever) — 136.00 — 409.00 — 1500.0
4-Special promotional, complimentary issue; cover same except one corner was blanked out & boxed in to identify the giveaway (not a paste-over). This special pressing was probably sent out to former subscribers to Mickey Mouse Mag. whose subscriptions had expired. (Very rare-5 known copies) — 227.00 — 682.00 — 2500.0
5-Goofy-c — 105.00 — 315.00 — 1150.0
6-10: 8-Only Clarabelle Cow-c. 9-Taliaferro-c (1st) — 86.00 — 259.00 — 950.0
11-14: 11-Huey, Dewey & Louie-c/app. — 70.00 — 210.00 — 775.0
15-17: 15-The 3 Little Kittens (17 pgs.). 16-The 3 Little Pigs (29 pgs.); X-Mas-c. 17-The Ugly Duckling (4 pgs.) — 66.00 — 198.00 — 725.0
18-21 — 55.00 — 164.00 — 600.0
22-30: 22-Flag-c. 24-The Flying Gauchito (1st original comic book story done for WDC&S). 27-Jose Carioca by Carl Buettner (2nd original story in WDC&S) — 46.00 — 136.00 — 500.0
31-New Donald Duck stories by Carl Barks begin (See F.C. #9 for 1st Barks Donald Duck) — 291.00 — 873.00 — 3200.0
32-Barks-a — 127.00 — 382.00 — 1400.0
33-Barks-a; infinity-c — 91.00 — 273.00 — 1000.0
34-Gremlins by Walt Kelly begin, end #41; Barks-a — 75.00 — 225.00 — 825.0
35,36-Barks-a — 68.00 — 205.00 — 750.0
37-Donald Duck by Jack Hannah — 34.00 — 102.00 — 375.0
38-40-Barks-a. 39-X-Mas-c. 40,41-Gremlins by Kelly — 46.00 — 136.00 — 500.0
41-50-Barks-a. 43-Seven Dwarfs-c app. (4/44). 45-50-Nazis in Gottfredson's Mickey Mouse Stories — 36.00 — 109.00 — 400.0
51-60-Barks-a. 51-X-Mas-c. 52-Li'l Bad Wolf begins, ends #203 (not in #55). 58-Kelly flag-c — 25.00 — 75.00 — 275.0
61-70: Barks-a. 61-Dumbo story. 63,64-Pinocchio stories. 63-Cover swipe from New Funnies #94. 64-X-Mas-c. 65-Pluto story. 66-Infinity-c. 67,68-Mickey Mouse Sunday-r by Bill Wright — 22.00 — 65.00 — 240.0
71-80: Barks-a. 75-77-Brer Rabbit stories, no Mickey Mouse. 76-X-Mas-c — 16.00 — 48.00 — 175.0
81-87,89,90: Barks-a. 82-Goofy-c. 82-84-Bongo stories. 86-90-Goofy & Agnes app. 89-Chip 'n' Dale story — 14.50 — 43.50 — 160.0
88-1st app. Gladstone Gander by Barks (1/48) — 19.00 — 57.00 — 210.0
91-97,99: Barks-a. 95-1st WDC&S Barks-c. 96-No Mickey Mouse; Little Toot begins, ends #97. 99-X-Mas-c — 12.50 — 37.00 — 135.0
98-1st Uncle Scrooge app. in WDC&S (11/48) — 24.50 — 74.00 — 270.0
100-(1/49)-Barks-a — 15.00 — 45.00 — 165.0
101-110-Barks-a. 107-Taliaferro-c; Donald acquires super powers — 11.50 — 34.00 — 125.0
111,114,117-All Barks-a — 8.65 — 26.00 — 95.0
112-Drug (ether) issue (Donald Duck) — 8.65 — 26.00 — 95.0

Walt Disney's Comics and Stories #122 © WDC

Walt Disney's Comics and Stories #546 © WDC

Walt Disney's Donald and Mickey #29 © WDC

GD2.0 FN6.0 NM9.4

3,115,116,118-123: No Barks. 116-Dumbo x-over. 121-Grandma Duck begins, ends #168; not in #135,142,146,155 4.55 13.65 50.00
4,126-130-All Barks-a. 124-X-Mas-c 7.25 21.75 80.00
5-1st app. Junior Woodchucks (2/51); Barks-a 11.00 33.00 120.00
1,133,135-137,139-All Barks-a 7.25 21.75 80.00
2-Barks-a(2) (D. Duck & Grandma Duck) 7.65 23.00 85.00
4-Intro. & 1st app. The Beagle Boys (11/51) 16.50 49.00 180.00
8-Classic Scrooge money story 12.50 37.00 135.00
0-(5/52)-1st app. Gyro Gearloose by Barks; 2nd Barks Uncle Scrooge-c; 3rd Uncle Scrooge-c app. 16.50 49.00 180.00
1-150-All Barks-a. 143-Little Hiawatha begins, ends #151,159 5.45 16.35 60.00
1-170-All Barks-a 4.55 13.65 50.00
1-199-All Barks-a 4.10 12.30 45.00
0 5.00 15.00 55.00
1-240: All Barks-a. 204-Chip 'n' Dale & Scamp begin 3.65 11.00 40.00
1-283: Barks-a. 241-Dumbo x-over. 247-Gyro Gearloose begins, ends #274. 256-Ludwig Von Drake begins, ends #274 3.20 9.60 35.00
4,285,287,290,295,296,309-311-Not by Barks 2.00 6.00 16.00
6,288,289,291-294,297,298,308-All Barks stories; 293-Grandma Duck's Farm Friends. 297-Gyro Gearloose. 298-Daisy Duck's Diary-r 2.30 7.00 20.00
9-307-All contain early Barks-r (#43-117). 305-Gyro Gearloose 2.40 7.35 22.00
2-Last Barks issue with original story 2.40 7.35 22.00
3-315,317-327,329-334,336-341 1.75 5.25 14.00
6-Last issue published during life of Walt Disney 1.75 5.25 14.00
28,335,342-350-Barks-r 1.75 5.25 14.00
51-360-With posters inside; Barks reprints (2 versions of each with & without posters)-without posters... 2.30 7.00 20.00
51-360-With posters... 3.00 9.00 30.00
61-400-Barks-r 1.75 5.25 14.00
01-429-Barks-r 1.75 5.25 14.00
30,433,437,438,441,444,445,466-No Barks 1.00 2.80 7.00
31,432,434-436,439,440,442,443-Barks-r 1.00 3.00 8.00
46-465,467-473-Barks-r 1.00 2.80 7.00
74(3/80),475-478 (Whitman) 1.50 4.50 12.00
79(8/80),481(10/80)-484(1/81) pre-pack? 2.50 7.50 24.00
80 (8-12/80)-(Very low distribution) 6.80 20.50 75.00
85-499: 494-r/WDC&S #98 1.50 4.50 12.00
00-510 (All #90011 on-c; pre-packs?): 506-No Barks 1.75 5.25 14.00
11-Donald Duck by Daan Jippes (1st in U.S.; in all through #518); Gyro Gearloose Barks-r begins (in most through #547); Wuzzles by Disney studio (1st by Gladstone) 2.50 7.50 23.00
12,513 1.75 5.25 14.00
14-516,520 1.00 3.00 8.00
17-519,521,522,525,527,529,530,532-546: 518-Infinity-c. 522-r/1st app. Huey, Dewey & Louie from D. Duck Sunday. 535-546-Barks-r. 537-1st Donald Duck by William Van Horn in WDC&S. 541-545-52 pgs. 546,547-68 pgs. 546-Kelly-r. 547-Rosa-a 4.00
23,524,526,528,531,547: Rosa-s/a in all. 523-1st Rosa 10 pager 1.50 4.50 12.00
48-($1.50, 6/90)-1st Disney issue; new-a; no M. Mouse 5.00
49,551-570,572,573,577-579,581,584 ($1.50): 549-Barks-r begin, ends #585, not in #555, 556, & 564. 551-r/1 story from F.C. #29. 556,578-r/Mickey Mouse Cheerios Premium by Dick Moores. 562,563,568-570, 572, 581-Gottfredson strip-r. 570-Valentine issue; has Mickey/Minnie centerfold. 584-Taliaferro strip-r 3.00
50 ($2.25, 52 pgs.)-Donald Duck by Barks; previously printed only in The Netherlands (1st time in U.S.); r/Chip 'n Dale & Scamp from #204 4.00
71-($2.95, 68 pgs)-r/Donald Duck's Atomic Bomb by Barks from 1947 Cheerios premium 5.00
74-576,580,582,583 ($2.95, 68 pgs.): 574-r/1st Pinocchio Sunday strip (1939-40). 575-Gottfredson-r, Pinocchio-r/WDC&S #64. 580-r/Donald Duck's 1st app. from Silly Symphony strip 12/16/34 by Taliaferro; Gottfredson strip-r begin; not in #584 & 600. 582,583-r/Mickey Mouse on Sky Island from WDC&S #1,2 3.50
585 ($2.50, 52 pgs.)-r/#140; Barks-r/WDC&S #140 3.50
586,587: 586-Gladstone issues begin again; begin $1.50-c; Gottfredson-r begins (not in #600). 587-Donald Duck by William Van Horn begins 3.00
588-597: 588,591-599-Donald Duck by William Van Horn 3.00
598,599 ($1.95, 36 pgs.): 598-r/1st drawings of Mickey Mouse by Ub Iwerks 3.00
600 ($2.95, 48 pgs.)-L.B. Cole-c(r)/WDC&S #1; Barks-r/WDC&S #32 plus Rosa, Jippes, Van Horn-r and new Rosa centerspread 4.00
601-611 ($5.95, 64 pgs., squarebound, bi-monthly): 601-Barks-c, r/Mickey Mouse V1#1, Rosa-a/scripts. 602-Rosa-c. 604-Taliaferro strip-r/1st Silly Symphony Sundays from 1932. 604,605-Jippes-a. 605-Walt Kelly-c; Gottfredson "Mickey Mouse Outwits the Phantom Blot" r/F.C. #16 6.00
612-633 ($6.95) 7.00

NOTE: *(#1-38, 68 pgs.; #39-42, 60 pgs.; #43-57, 61-134, 143-168, 446, 447, 52 pgs.; #58-60, 135-142, 169-540, 36 pgs.)*

NOTE: ***Barks*** *art in all issues #31 on, except where noted; c-95, 96, 104, 108, 109, 130-172, 174-178, 183, 198-200, 204, 206-209, 212-216, 218, 220, 226, 228-233, 235-238, 240-243, 247, 250, 253, 256, 260, 261, 276-283, 288-292, 295-298, 301, 303, 304, 306, 307, 309, 310, 313-316, 319, 321, 322, 324, 326, 328, 329, 331, 332, 334, 341, 342, 350, 351, 527r, 530r, 540(never before published), 546r, 557-586r(most), 596p, 601p.* **Kelly** *a-24p, 34-41, 43; r-522-524, 546, 547, 582, 583; covers(most)-34-118, 531r, 537r, 541r-543r, 562r, 571r, 605r. Walt Disney's Comics & Stories featured Mickey Mouse serials which were in practically every issue from #1 through #394 and #511 to date. The titles of the serials, along with the issues they are in, are listed in previous editions of this price guide.* **Floyd Gottfredson** *Mickey Mouse serials in issues #1-14, 18-66, 69-74, 78-100, 128, 562, 563, 568-572, 582, 583, 586-599 , 601-603 , 605-present , plus "Service with a Smile" in #13; "Mickey Mouse in a Warplant" (3 pgs.), and "Pluto Catches a Nazi Spy" (4 pgs.) in #62; "Mystery Next Door", #93; "Sunken Treasure", #94; "Aunt Marissa", #95 (r in #575); "Gangland", #98 (r in #562); "Thanksgiving Dinner", #99 (r in #567); and "The Talking Dog", #100 (r in #563); "Morty's Escapade," #128. "The Brave Little Tailor", #580; "Introducing Mickey Mouse Movies ", #581; Circus Roustabout, #585; "Rumplewatt the Giant", #604. Mickey Mouse by* **Paul Murry** *#152-547 except 155-57 (***Dick Moore***), 327-29 (***Tony Strobl***), 348-50 (***Jack Manning***), 533 (***Bill Wright***).* **Don Rosa** *story/a-523, 524, 526, 528, 531, 547, 601-present.* **Al Taliaferro** *Silly Symphonies in #5-"Three Little Pigs"; #13-"Birds of a Feather"; #14-"The Boarding School Mystery"; #15-"Cookieland" and "Three Little Kittens"; #16-"The Practical Pig"; #17-"The Ugly Duckling"; "The Wise Little Hen" in #580; and "Ambrose the Robber Kitten"; #19-"Penguin Isle"; and "Bucky Bug" in #20-23, 25, 26, 28 (one continuous story from 1932-34; first 2 pgs. not Taliaferro).* **Gottfredson** *strip r-562, 563, 568-572, 581, 585, 586, 590.* **Taliaferro** *strip r-584, 580.* **Van Horn** *a-537, 545, 561, 574, 587, 588, 591-present.*

WALT DISNEY'S COMICS DIGEST
Gladstone: Dec, 1986 - No. 7, Sept, 1987

1 1.00 3.00 8.00
2-7 2.40 6.00

WALT DISNEY'S COMICS PENNY PINCHER
Gladstone: May, 1997 - No. 4, Aug, 1997 (99¢, limited series)

1-4 2.00

WALT DISNEY'S DONALD AND MICKEY (Formerly Walt Disney's Mickey and Donald)
Gladstone (Bruce Hamilton Company): No. 19, Sept, 1993 - No. 30, 1995 ($1.50, 36 & 68 pgs.)

19,21-24,26-30: New & reprints. 19,21,23,24-Barks-r. 19,26-Murry-r. 22-Barks "Omelet" story r/WDC&S #146. 27-Mickey Mouse story by Caesar Ferioli (1st U.S work). 29-Rosa-c; Mickey Mouse story actually starring Goofy (does not include Mickey except on title page.) 4.00
20,25-($2.95, 68 pgs.): 20-Barks, Gottfredson-r 5.00

NOTE: *Donald Duck stories were all reprints.*

WALT DISNEY'S DONALD DUCK ADVENTURES (D.D. Adv. #1-3)
Gladstone: 11/87-No. 20, 4/90 (1st Series); No. 21,8/93-No. 48, 2/98(3rd Series)

1 1.00 2.80 7.00
2-r/F.C. #308 3.00
3,4,6,7,9-11,13,15-18: 3-r/F.C. #223. 4-r/F.C. #62. 9-r/F.C. #159, "Ghost of the Grotto". 11-r/F.C. #159, "Adventure Down Under." 16-r/F.C. #291; Rosa-c. 18-r/FC #318; Rosa-c 3.00
5,8-Don Rosa-c/a 5.00
12($1.50, 52pgs)-Rosa-c/a w/Barks poster 2.40 6.00
14-r/F.C. #29, "Mummy's Ring" 4.00
19($1.95, 68 pgs.)-Barks-r/F.C. #199 (1 pg.) 3.00
20($1.95, 68 pgs.)-Barks-r/F.C. #189 & cover-r; William Van Horn-a 3.00
21,22: 21-r/D.D. #46. 22-r/F.C. #282 3.00
23-25,27,29,31,32-($1.50, 36 pgs.): 21,23,29-Rosa-c. 23-Intro/1st app. Andold Wild Duck by Marco Rota. 24-Van Horn-a. 27-1st Pat Block-a, "Mystery of Widow's Gap." 31,32-Block-c. 2.00
26,28,33($2.95, 68 pgs.): 26-Barks-r/F.C. #108, "Terror of the River". 28-Barks-r/F.C. #199, "Sheriff of Bullet Valley" 4.00

Walt Disney's Donald Duck Adventures #1 © WDC

Walt Disney Showcase #30 © WDC

Walt Disney's Uncle Scrooge #218 © WDC

30($2.95, 68 pgs.)-r/F.C. #367, Barks' "Christmas for Shacktown" 4.00
34-43: 34-Resume $1.50-c. 34,35,37-Block-a/scripts. 38-Van Horn-c/a 2.00
44-48-($1.95-c) 2.00
NOTE: ***Barks*** *a-1-22r, 26r, 28r, 33r, 36r; c-10r, 14r, 20r.* ***Block*** *a-27, 30, 34, 35, 37; c-27, 30-32, 34, 35, 37; c-27, 30, 31, 32, 34, 35, 37.* ***Rosa*** *a-5, 8, 12; c-13, 16-18, 21, 23.*

WALT DISNEY'S DONALD DUCK ADVENTURES (2nd Series)
Disney Comics: June, 1990 - No. 38, July, 1993 ($1.50)

1-Rosa-a & scripts 5.00
2-21,23,25,27-33,35,36,38: 2-Barks-r/WDC&S #35; William Van Horn-a begins, ends #20. 9-Barks-r/F.C. #178. 9,11,14,17-No Van Horn-a. 11-Mad #1 cover parody. 14-Barks-r. 17-Barks-r. 21-r/FC #203 by Barks. 29-r/MOC #20 by Barks 3.00
22,24,26,34,37: 22-Rosa-a (10 pgs.) & scripts. 24-Rosa-a & scripts. 26-r/March of Comics #41 by Barks. 34-Rosa-c/a. 37-Rosa-a; Barks-r 4.00
NOTE: ***Barks*** *r-2, 4, 9(F.C. #178), 14(D.D. #45), 17, 21, 26, 27, 29 , 35, 36(D.D #60)-38.* ***Taliaferro*** *a-34r, 36r.*

WALT DISNEY'S DONALD DUCK AND MICKEY MOUSE (Formerly Walt Disney's Donald and Mickey)
Gladstone (Bruce Hamilton Company): Sept, 1995 - No. 7, Sept, 1996 ($1.50, 32 pgs.)

1-7: 1-Barks-r and new Mickey Mouse stories in all. 5,6-Mickey Mouse stories by Caesar Ferioli. 7-New Donald Duck and Mickey Mouse x-over story; Barks-r/WDC&S #51 2.00
NOTE: *Issue #8 was advertised, but cancelled.*

WALT DISNEY SHOWCASE
Gold Key: Oct, 1970 - No. 54, Jan, 1980 (No. 44-48: 68pgs., 49-54: 52pgs.)

	GD2.0	FN6.0	NM9.4
1-Boatniks (Movie)-Photo-c	2.80	8.40	28.00
2-Moby Duck	2.00	6.00	18.00
3,4,7: 3-Bongo & Lumpjaw-r. 4,7-Pluto-r	1.75	5.25	14.00
5-$1,000,000 Duck (Movie)-Photo-c	2.30	7.00	20.00
6-Bedknobs & Broomsticks (Movie)	2.30	7.00	20.00
8-Daisy & Donald	1.75	5.25	14.00
9- 101 Dalmatians (cartoon feat.); r/F.C. #1183	2.30	7.00	20.00
10-Napoleon & Samantha (Movie)-Photo-c	2.30	7.00	20.00
11-Moby Duck-r	1.50	4.50	12.00
12-Dumbo-r/Four Color #668	1.75	5.25	14.00
13-Pluto-r	1.50	4.50	12.00
14-World's Greatest Athlete (Movie)-Photo-c	2.30	7.00	20.00
15- 3 Little Pigs-r	1.75	5.25	14.00
16-Aristocats (cartoon feature); r/Aristocats #1	2.30	7.00	20.00
17-Mary Poppins; r/M.P. #10136-501-Photo-c	2.30	7.00	20.00
18-Gyro Gearloose; Barks-r/F.C. #1047,1184	2.60	7.80	26.00
19-That Darn Cat; r/That Darn Cat #10171-602-Hayley Mills photo-c	2.30	7.00	20.00
20,23-Pluto-r	1.75	5.25	14.00
21-Li'l Bad Wolf & The Three Little Pigs	1.50	4.50	12.00
22-Unbirthday Party with Alice in Wonderland; r/Four Color #341	2.00	6.00	18.00
24-26: 24-Herbie Rides Again (Movie); sequel to "The Love Bug"; photo-c. 25-Old Yeller (Movie); r/F.C. #869; Photo-c. 26-Lt. Robin Crusoe USN (Movie); r/Lt. Robin Crusoe USN #10191-601; photo-c	1.75	5.25	14.00
27-Island at the Top of the World (Movie)-Photo-c	2.00	6.00	18.00
28-Brer Rabbit, Bucky Bug-r/WDC&S #58	1.75	5.25	14.00
29-Escape to Witch Mountain (Movie)-Photo-c	2.00	6.00	18.00
30-Magica De Spell; Barks-r/Uncle Scrooge #36 & WDC&S #258	3.00	9.00	30.00
31-Bambi (cartoon feature); r/Four Color #186	2.00	6.00	18.00
32-Spin & Marty-r/F.C. #1026; Mickey Mouse Club (TV)-Photo-c	2.30	7.00	20.00
33-40: 33-Pluto-r/F.C. #1143. 34-Paul Revere's Ride with Johnny Tremain (TV); r/F.C. #822. 35-Goofy-r/F.C. #952. 36-Peter Pan-r/F.C. #442. 37-Tinker Bell & Jiminy Cricket-r/F.C. #982,989. 38,39-Mickey & the Sleuth, Parts 1 & 2. 40-The Rescuers (cartoon feature)	1.50	4.50	12.00
41-Herbie Goes to Monte Carlo (Movie); sequel to "Herbie Rides Again"; photo-c	1.75	5.25	14.00
42-Mickey & the Sleuth	1.50	4.50	12.00
43-Pete's Dragon (Movie)-Photo-c	2.00	6.00	18.00
44-Return From Witch Mountain (new) & In Search of the Castaways-r (Movies)-Photo-c; 68 pg. giants begin	2.30	7.00	20.0
45-The Jungle Book (Movie); r/#30033-803	2.30	7.00	20.0
46-48: 46-The Cat From Outer Space (Movie)(new), & The Shaggy Dog (Movi r/F.C. #985; photo-c. 47-Mickey Mouse Surprise Party-r. 48-The Wonderful Advs. of Pinocchio-r/F.C. #1203; last 68 pg. issue	1.75	5.25	14.0
49-54: 49-North Avenue Irregulars (Movie); Zorro-r/Zorro #11; 52 pgs. begin; photo-c. 50-Bedknobs & Broomsticks-r/#6; Mooncussers-r/World of Adv. #1 photo-c. 51-101 Dalmatians-r. 52-Unidentified Flying Oddball (Movie); r/Picnic Party #8; photo-c. 53-The Scarecrow-r (TV). 54-The Black Hole (Movie)-Photo-c (predates Black Hole #1)	1.50	4.50	12.0

WALT DISNEY'S MAGAZINE (TV)(Formerly Walt Disney's Mickey Mouse Club Magazine) (50¢, bi-monthly)
Western Publishing Co.: V2#4, June, 1957 - V4#6, Oct, 1959

V2#4-Stories & articles on the Mouseketeers, Zorro, & Goofy and other Disney characters & people	4.60	13.75	55.0
V2#5, V2#6(10/57)	4.10	12.30	45.0
V3#1(12/57), V3#3-5	3.20	9.60	35.0
V3#2-Annette Funicello photo-c	9.00	27.00	110.0
V3#6(10/58)-TV Zorro photo-c	6.30	19.00	75.0
V4#1(12/58) - V4#2-4,6(10/59)	3.20	9.60	35.0
V4#5-Annette Funicello photo-c, w/ 2-photo articles	9.00	27.00	110.0

NOTE: *V2#4-V3#6 were 11-1/2x8-1/2", 48 pgs.; V4#1 on were 10x8", 52 pgs. (Peak circulation 400,000).*

WALT DISNEY'S MERRY CHRISTMAS (See Dell Giant #39)

WALT DISNEY'S MICKEY AND DONALD(M & D #1,2)(Becomes Walt Disney Donald & Mickey #19 on)
Gladstone: Mar, 1988 - No. 18, May, 1990 (95¢)

1-Don Rosa-a; r/1949 Firestone giveaway		2.40	6.0
2-8: 3-Infinity-c. 4-8-Barks-r			3.0
9-15: 9-r/1948 Firestone giveaway; X-Mas-c			3.0
16($1.50, 52 pgs.)-r/FC #157			5.0
17-(68 pgs.) Barks M.M.-r/FC #79 plus Barks D.D.-r; Rosa-a; x-mas-c			6.0
18($1.95, 68 pgs.)-Gottfredson-r/WDC&S #13,72-74; Kelly-c(r); Barks-r			5.0

NOTE: ***Barks*** *reprints in 1-15, 17, 18.* ***Kelly*** *c-13r, 14 (r/Walt Disney's C&S #58), 18r.*

WALT DISNEY'S MICKEY MOUSE CLUB MAGAZINE (TV)(Becomes Walt Disney's Magazine)
Western Publishing Co.: Winter, 1956 - V2#3, Apr, 1957 (11-1/2x8-1/2", quarterly, 48 pgs.)

V1#1	12.00	36.00	145.
2-4	6.30	19.00	75.
V2#1,2	4.60	13.75	55.
3-Annette photo-c	10.50	31.00	125.0
Annual(1956)-Two different issues; ($1.50-Whitman); 120 pgs., cardboard covers, 11-3/4x8-3/4"; reprints	13.00	40.00	160.0
Annual(1957)-Same as above	11.00	33.00	130.0

WALT DISNEY'S PINOCCHIO SPECIAL
Gladstone: Spring, 1990 ($1.00)

1-50th anniversary edition; Kelly-r/F.C. #92 3.0

WALT DISNEY'S THE JUNGLE BOOK
W.D. Publications (Disney Comics): 1990 ($5.95, graphic novel, 68 pgs.)

nn-Movie adaptation; movie rereleased in 1990 6.0
nn-($2.95, 68 pgs.)-Comic edition; wraparound-c 3.0

WALT DISNEY'S UNCLE SCROOGE (Formerly Uncle Scrooge #1-209)
Gladstone #210-242/Disney Comics #243-280/Gladstone #281 on: No. 210, 10/86 - No. 242, 4/90; No. 243, 6/90 - No. 318, 2/99

210-1st Gladstone issue; r/WDC&S #134 (1st Beagle Boys)	1.85	5.50	15.0
211-218: 216-New story ("Go Slowly Sands of Time") plotted and partly scripted by Barks. 217-r/U.S. #7, "Seven Cities of Cibola"	1.85	5.50	15.0
219-"Son Of The Sun" by Rosa	2.50	7.50	25.0
220-Don Rosa-a/scripts	1.00	3.00	8.0
221-223,225,228-234,236-240			3.0
224,226,227,235: 224-Rosa-c/a. 226,227-Rosa-a. 235-Rosa-a/scripts			5.0
241-($1.95, 68 pgs.)-Rosa finishes over Barks-r		2.40	6.0
242-($1.95, 68 pgs.)-Barks-r; Rosa-a(1 pg.)		2.40	6.0

Walt Disney's Uncle Scrooge Adventures #28 © WDC

Wanted Comics #30 © Toytown Publ.

Wanted, The World's Most Dangerous Villains #8 © DC

-249,251-260,264-275,277-280,282-284-($1.50): 243-1st by Disney Comics.
274-All Barks issue. 275-Contains poster by Rosa. 283-r/WDC&S #98 2.25
-($2.25, 52 pgs.)-Barks-r; wraparound-c 3.00
-263,276-Don Rosa-c/a 4.00
-Gladstone issues start again; Rosa-c 2.40 6.00
-The Life and Times of Scrooge McDuck Pt. 1; Rosa-c/a/scripts
1.25 3.75 10.00
-293: The Life and Times of Scrooge McDuck Pt. 2-8; Rosa-c/a/scripts.
293-($1.95, 36 pgs.)-The Life and Times of Scrooge McDuck Pt. 9
2.40 6.00
-299, 301-308-($1.50, 32 pgs.): 294-296-The Life and Times of Scrooge McDuck Pt. 10-12. 297-The Life and Times of Uncle Scrooge Pt. 0; Rosa-c/a/scripts 2.50
-($2.25, 48 pgs.)-Rosa-c; Barks-r/WDC&S #104 and U.S. #216; r/U.S. #220; includes new centerfold. 3.00
-318-($6.95) 7.00
E: *Barks r-210-218, 220-223, 224(2pg.), 225-234, 236-242, 245, 246, 250-253, 255, 256, 261(2 pg.), 265, 267, 268, 270(2), 272-284, 299-present; c(r)-210, 212, 221, 228, 229, 232, 284. scripts-287, 293. Rosa a-219, 220, 224, 226, 227, 235, 261-263, 268, 275-277, 285-; c-219, 224, 231, 261-263, 276, 278-281, 285-289; scripts-219, 220, 224, 235, 261-263, 268, 285-289.*

LT DISNEY'S UNCLE SCROOGE ADVENTURES (U. Scrooge Advs. #1-3)
dstone Publishing: Nov, 1987 - No. 21, May, 1990; No. 22, Sept, 1993 - 55

Barks-r begin, ends #26 1.00 3.00 8.00
4 4.00
9,14: 5-Rosa-c/a; no Barks-r. 9,14-Rosa-a 5.00
8,10-13,15-19: 10-r/U.S. #18(all Barks) 3.00
21 ($1.95, 68 pgs.) 20-Rosa-c/a. 21-Rosa-a 5.00
($1.50)-Rosa-c; r/U.S. #26 5.00
-($2.95, 68 pgs.)-Vs. The Phantom Blot-r/P.B. #3; Barks-r 4.00
-26,29,31,32,34-36: 24,25,29,31,32-Rosa-c. 25-r/U.S. #21 2.00
-Guardians of the Lost Library - Rosa-c/a/story; origin of Junior Woodchuck Guidebook 3.00
-($2.95, 68 pgs.)-r/U.S. #13 w/restored missing panels 4.00
-($2.95, 68 pgs.)-r/U.S. #12; Rosa-c 4.00
-($2.95, 64 pgs.)-New Barks story 3.00
-55 2.00
E: *Barks r-1-4, 6-8, 10-13, 15-21, 23, 22, 24; c(r)-15, 16, 17, 21. Rosa a-5, 9, 14, 20, 21, 27; 13, 14, 17(finishes), 20, 22, 24, 25, 27, 28; scripts-5, 9, 14, 27.*

LT DISNEY'S UNCLE SCROOGE ADVENTURES IN COLOR
dstone Publ.: Dec, 1995 - Present ($8.95/$9.95, squarebound, 56 issue lim- series) (Polybagged w/card) (Series chronologically reprints all the stories ten & drawn by Carl Barks)

56: 1-(12/95)-r/FC #386. 15-(12/96)-r/US #15. 16-(12/96)-r/US #16. 18-(1/97)-r/US #18 10.00

LT DISNEY'S WHEATIES PREMIUMS (See Wheaties in the Promotional section)

LTER (Campaign of Terror) (Also see The Mask)
k Horse Comics: Feb, 1996 - No. 4, May, 1996 ($2.50, limited series)

4 2.50

LTER LANTZ ANDY PANDA (Also see Andy Panda)
d Key: Aug, 1973 - No. 23, Jan, 1978 (Walter Lantz)

Reprints 2.00 6.00 16.00
10-All reprints 1.10 3.30 9.00
-23: 15,17-19,22-Reprints 2.40 6.00

LT KELLY'S...
ipse Comics: Dec, 1987; Apr, 1988 ($1.75/$2.50, Baxter paper)

Christmas Classics 1 (12/87)-Kelly-r/Peter Wheat & Santa Claus Funnies, ...Springtime Tales 1 (4/88, $2.50)-Kelly-r 2.50

LTONS, THE (See Kite Fun Book)

LT SCOTT (See Little People)

LT SCOTT'S CHRISTMAS STORIES (See Christmas Stories, 4-Color #959, 1062)

MBI, JUNGLE BOY (See Jungle Comics)
tion House Magazines: Spr, 1942; No. 2, Win, 1942-43; No. 3, Spr, 1943; 4, Fall, 1948; No. 5, Sum, 1949; No. 6, Spr, 1950; No. 7-10, 1950(nd); No. Spr, 1951 - No. 18, Win, 1952-53 (#1-3: 68 pgs.)

1-Wambi, the Jungle Boy begins 89.00 268.00 850.00
2 (1942)-Kiefer-c 50.00 150.00 450.00
3 (1943)-Kiefer-c/a 35.00 105.00 280.00
4 (1948)-Origin in text 22.00 66.00 175.00
5 (Fall, 1949, 36 pgs.)-Kiefer-c/a 19.00 56.00 150.00
6-10: 7-(52 pgs.)-New logo 18.00 53.00 140.00
11-18 12.00 36.00 95.00
I.W. Reprint #8('64)-r/#12 with new-c 2.50 7.50 24.00
NOTE: ***Alex Blum** c-8. **Kiefer** c-1-5. **Whitman** c-11-18.*

WANDERERS (See Adventure Comics #375, 376)
DC Comics: June, 1988 - No. 13, Apr, 1989 ($1.25) (Legion of Super-Heroes spin off)

1-13: 1,2-Steacy-c. 3-Legion app. 2.00

WANDERING STAR
Pen & Ink Comics/Sirius Entertainment No. 12 on: 1993 - No. 21, Mar, 1997 ($2.50/$2.75, B&W)

1-1st printing; Teri Sue Wood c/a/scripts in all 1.00 3.00 8.00
1-2nd and 3rd printings 2.75
2-1st printing. 4.00
2-21: 2-2nd printing. 12-(1/96)-1st Sirius issue 2.75
Trade paperback ($11.95)-r/1-7; 1st printing of 1000, signed and #'d 18.00
Trade paperback-2nd printing, 2000 signed 15.00
TPB Volume 2,3 (11/98, 12/98, $14.95) 2-r/#8-14, 3-r/#15-21 15.00

WANTED COMICS
Toytown Publications/Patches/Orbit Publ.: No. 9, Sept-Oct, 1947 - No. 53, April, 1953 (#9-33: 52 pgs.)

9-True crime cases; radio's Mr. D. A. app. 21.00 62.00 165.00
10,11: 10-Giunta-a; radio's Mr. D. A. app. 12.50 37.50 100.00
12-Used in **SOTI**, pg. 277 12.50 37.50 100.00
13-Heroin drug propaganda story 11.00 33.00 90.00
14-Marijuana drug mention story (2 pgs.) 10.00 30.00 75.00
15-17,19,20 9.30 28.00 65.00
18-Marijuana story, "Satan's Cigarettes"; r-in #45 & retitled
23.00 68.00 180.00
21,22: 21-Krigstein-a. 22-Extreme violence 10.00 30.00 70.00
23,25-34,36-38,40-44,46-48,53 6.40 19.25 45.00
24-Krigstein-a; "The Dope King", marijuana mention story
10.00 30.00 75.00
35-Used in **SOTI**, pg. 160 10.00 30.00 70.00
39-Drug propaganda story "The Horror Weed" 14.00 43.00 115.00
45-Marijuana story from #18 9.30 28.00 65.00
49-Has unstable pink-c that fades easily; rare in mint condition
7.85 23.50 55.00
50-Has unstable pink-c like #49; surrealist-c by Buscema; horror stories
13.00 39.00 105.00
51- "Holiday of Horror" junkie story; drug-c 10.00 30.00 80.00
52-Classic "Cult of Killers" opium use story 10.00 30.00 80.00
NOTE: ***Buscema** c-50, 51. **Lawrence** and **Leav** c/a most issues. **Syd Shores** c/a-48; c-37. Issues 9-46 have wanted criminals with their descriptions & drawn picture on cover.*

WANTED: DEAD OR ALIVE (TV)
Dell Publishing Co.: No. 1102, May-July, 1960 - No. 1164, Mar-May, 1961

Four Color 1102 (#1)-Steve McQueen photo-c 12.00 35.00 145.00
Four Color 1164-Steve McQueen photo-c 9.00 27.00 110.00

WANTED, THE WORLD'S MOST DANGEROUS VILLAINS (See DC Special)
National Periodical Publications: July-Aug, 1972 - No. 9, Aug-Sept, 1973 (All reprints & 20¢ issues)

1-Batman, Green Lantern (story r-from G.L. #1), & Green Arrow
3.00 9.00 30.00
2-Batman/Joker/Penguin-c/story r-from Batman #25; plus Flash story (r-from Flash #121) 2.50 7.50 24.00
3-9: 3-Dr. Fate(r/More Fun #65), Hawkman(r/Flash #100), & Vigilante(r/Action #69). 4-Gr. Lantern(r/All-American #61) & Kid Eternity(r/Kid Eternity #15). 5-Dollman/Green Lantern. 6-Burnley Starman; Wildcat/Sargon. 7-Johnny Quick(r/More fun #76), Hawkman(r/Flash #90), Hourman by Baily(r/Adv. #72). 8-Dr. Fate/Flash(r/Flash #114). 9-S&K Sandman/Superman
2.00 6.00 18.00
NOTE: ***B. Bailey** a-7r. **Infantino** a-2r. **Kane** r-1, 5. **Kubert** r-3i, 6, 7. **Meskin** r-3, 7. **Reinman** r-4, 6.*

War Action #6 © ATLAS

War Battles #4 © HARV

War Dogs of the U.S. Army #1 © AVON

	GD2.0	FN6.0	NM9.4

WAR (See Fightin' Marines #122)
Charlton Comics: Jul, 1975 - No. 9, Nov, 1976; No. 10, Sept, 1978 - No. 49, 1984

	GD2.0	FN6.0	NM9.4
1-Boyette painted-c	1.75	5.25	14.00
2-10	1.00	3.00	8.00
11-20		2.40	6.00
21-40			5.00
41-49 (lower print run): 47-Reprints		2.40	6.00
7,9 (Modern Comics-r, 1977)			3.00

WAR, THE (See The Draft & The Pitt)
Marvel Comics: 1989 - No. 4, 1990 ($3.50, squarebound, 52 pgs.)

	GD2.0	FN6.0	NM9.4
1-4: Characters from New Universe			3.50

WAR ACTION (Korean War)
Atlas Comics (CPS): April, 1952 - No. 14, June, 1953

	GD2.0	FN6.0	NM9.4
1	19.00	56.00	150.00
2	10.00	30.00	75.00
3-10,14: 7-Pakula-a	8.65	26.00	60.00
11-13-Krigstein-a	10.00	30.00	70.00

NOTE: ***Brodsky** c-1-4. **Heath** a-1; c-7, 14. **Keller** a-6. **Maneely** a-1. **Tuska** a-2, 8.*

WAR ADVENTURES
Atlas Comics (HPC): Jan, 1952 - No. 13, Feb, 1953

	GD2.0	FN6.0	NM9.4
1-Tuska-a	16.00	49.00	130.00
2	9.30	28.00	65.00
3-7,9-13: 3-Pakula-a. 7-Maneely-c	7.15	21.50	50.00
8-Krigstein-a	10.00	30.00	70.00

NOTE: ***Brodsky** c-1-3, 6, 8, 11, 12. **Heath** a-5, 7, 10; c-4, 5, 9, 13. **Robinson** a-3; c-10.*

WAR ADVENTURES ON THE BATTLEFIELD (See Battlefield)

WAR AGAINST CRIME! (Becomes Vault of Horror #12 on)
E. C. Comics: Spring, 1948 - No. 11, Feb-Mar, 1950

	GD2.0	FN6.0	NM9.4
1-Real Stories From Police Records on-c #1-9	68.00	205.00	650.00
2,3	40.00	120.00	360.00
4-9	40.00	120.00	325.00
10-1st Vault Keeper app. & 1st Vault of Horror	182.00	545.00	2000.00
11-2nd Vault Keeper app.; 1st horror-c	105.00	315.00	1155.00

NOTE: *All have **Johnny Craig** covers. **Feldstein** a-4, 7-9. **Harrison/Wood** a-11. **Ingels** a-1, 2, 8. **Palais** a-8. Changes to horror with #10.*

WAR AGAINST CRIME
Gemstone Publishing: Apr, 2000 - No. 11, Feb, 2001 ($2.50)

	GD2.0	FN6.0	NM9.4
1-11: E.C. reprints			2.50

WAR AND ATTACK (Also see Special War Series #3)
Charlton Comics: Fall, 1964; V2#54, June, 1966 - V2#63, Dec, 1967

	GD2.0	FN6.0	NM9.4
1-Wood-a (25 pgs.)	3.80	11.40	42.00
V2#54(6/66)-#63 (Formerly Fightin' Air Force)	2.00	6.00	18.00

NOTE: ***Montes/Bache** a-55, 56, 60, 63.*

WAR AT SEA (Formerly Space Adventures)
Charlton Comics: No. 22, Nov, 1957 - No. 42, June, 1961

	GD2.0	FN6.0	NM9.4
22	5.00	15.00	32.00
23-30	4.00	12.00	24.00
31-42	2.00	6.00	18.00

WAR BATTLES
Harvey Publications: Feb, 1952 - No. 9, Dec, 1953

	GD2.0	FN6.0	NM9.4
1-Powell-a; Elias-c	10.00	30.00	110.00
2-Powell-a	5.00	15.00	55.00
3-5,7-9: 3,7-Powell-a	4.55	13.65	50.00
6-Nostrand-a	5.90	17.75	65.00

WAR BIRDS
Fiction House Magazines: 1952(nd) - No. 3, Winter, 1952-53

	GD2.0	FN6.0	NM9.4
1	14.00	43.00	115.00
2,3	8.65	26.00	60.00

WARBLADE: ENDANGERED SPECIES (Also see WildC.A.T.S: Covert Action Teams)
Image Comics (WildStorm Productions): Jan, 1995 - No. 4, Apr, 1995 ($2.50, limited series)

	GD2.0	FN6.0	NM9.4
1-4: 1-Gatefold wraparound-c			2.50

WARCHILD
Maximum Press: Jan. 1995 - No. 4, Aug, 1995 ($2.50)

	GD2.0	FN6.0	NM9.4
1-4-Rob Liefeld-c/a/scripts			2.5
1-4: Variant-c			3.0
Trade paperback (1/96, $12.95)-r/#1-4.			13.0

WAR COMBAT (Becomes Combat Casey #6 on)
Atlas Comics (LBI No. 1/SAI No. 2-5): March, 1952 - No. 5, Nov, 1952

	GD2.0	FN6.0	NM9.4
1	14.00	43.00	115.0
2	8.65	26.00	60.0
3-5	6.40	19.25	45.0

NOTE: ***Berg** a-2, 4, 5. **Brodsky** c-1, 2, 4, 5. **Henkel** a-5. **Maneely** a-1, 4; c-3.*

WAR COMICS (War Stories #5 on)(See Key Ring Comics)
Dell Publishing Co.: May, 1940 (No month given) - No. 4, Sept, 1941?

	GD2.0	FN6.0	NM9.4
1-Sikandur the Robot Master, Sky Hawk, Scoop Mason, War Correspondent begin; McWilliams-c; 1st war comic	55.00	165.00	500.0
2-Origin Greg Gilday (5/41)	34.00	101.00	270.0
3-Joan becomes Greg Gilday's aide	21.00	64.00	170.0
4-Origin Night Devils	24.00	71.00	190.0

WAR COMICS
Marvel/Atlas (USA No. 1-41/JPI No. 42-49): Dec, 1950 - No. 49, Sept, 1957

	GD2.0	FN6.0	NM9.4
1	25.00	75.00	200.0
2	12.50	37.50	100.0
3-10	10.00	30.00	80.0
11-Flame thrower w/burning bodies on-c	11.00	33.00	90.0
12-20	10.00	30.00	70.0
21,23-32: 26-Valley Forge story. 32-Last precode issue (2/55)	7.15	21.50	50.0
22-Krigstein-a	9.30	28.00	65.0
33-37,39-42,44,45,47,48	7.15	21.50	50.0
38-Kubert/Moskowitz-a	8.65	26.00	60.0
43,49-Torres-a. 43-Severin/Elder E.C. swipe from Two-Fisted Tales #31	8.65	26.00	60.0
46-Crandall-a	8.65	26.00	60.0

NOTE: ***Colan** a-4, 36, 48, 49. **Drucker** a-37, 43, 48. **Everett** a-17. **Heath** a-7-9, 16, 19, 25, 36; 11, 16, 19, 25, 26, 29-31, 36. **G. Kane** a-19. **Lawrence** a-36. **Maneely** a-7, 9; c-6, 27, 37. **Orlando** a-42, 48. **Pakula** a-26. **Ravielli** a-27. **Reinman** a-26. **Robinson** a-15; c-13. **Severin** a 26, 27; c-48.*

WAR DANCER (Also see Charlemagne, Doctor Chaos #2 & Warriors of Plasm)
Defiant: Feb, 1994 - No. 6, July, 1994 ($2.50)

	GD2.0	FN6.0	NM9.4
1-3,5,6: 1-Intro War Dancer; Weiss-c/a begins. 1-3-Weiss-a(p). 6-Pre-Schism issue			2.5
4-($3.25, 52 pgs.)-Charlemagne app.			3.2

WAR DOGS OF THE U.S. ARMY
Avon Periodicals: 1952

	GD2.0	FN6.0	NM9.4
1-Kinstler-c/a	14.00	41.00	110.0

WARFRONT
Harvey Publications: 9/51 - #35, 11/58; #36, 10/65; #39, 2/67

	GD2.0	FN6.0	NM9.4
1-Korean War	10.50	31.50	115.0
2	5.45	16.35	60.0
3-10	4.10	12.30	45.0
11,12,14,16-20	3.20	9.60	35.0
13,15,22-Nostrand-a	5.45	16.35	60.0
21,23-27,31-33,35	3.20	9.60	35.0
28-30,34-Kirby-c	5.90	17.75	65.0
36-(12/66)-Dynamite Joe begins, ends #39; Williamson-a	4.10	12.30	45.0
37-Wood-a (17 pgs.)	4.10	12.30	45.0
38,39-Wood-a, 2-3 pgs.; Lone Tiger app.	3.20	9.60	35.0

NOTE: ***Powell** a-1-6, 9-11, 14, 17, 20, 23, 25-28, 30, 31, 34, 36. **Powell/Nostrand** a-12, 13, 15. **Simon** c-36?, 38.*

WAR FURY
Comic Media/Harwell (Allen Hardy Assoc.): Sept, 1952 - No. 4, Mar, 1953

	GD2.0	FN6.0	NM9.4
1-Heck-c/a in all; Palais-a; bullet hole in forehead-c; all issues are very violent; soldier using flame thrower on enemy	19.00	56.00	150.0
2-4: 4-Morisi-a	10.00	30.00	75.0

Warlands #1 © Dreamwave Productions

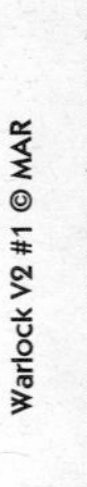

Warlock V2 #1 © MAR

Warlord #47 © DC

GD2.0 FN6.0 NM9.4

VAR GODS OF THE DEEP (See Movie Classics)

VARHAWKS
'SR, Inc.: 1990 - No. 10, 1991 ($2.95, 44 pgs.)

1-10-Based on TSR game, Spiegle a-1-6 3.00

VARHEADS
Iarvel Comics UK: June, 1992 - No. 14, Aug, 1993 ($1.75)

1-Wolverine-c/story; indicia says #2 by mistake 3.00
2-14: 2-Nick Fury app. 3-Iron Man-c/story. 4,5-X-Force. 5-Liger vs. Cable. 6,7-Death's Head II app. (#6 is cameo) 2.00

VAR HEROES (See Marine War Heroes)

VAR HEROES
Iell Publishing Co.: 7-9/42 (no month); No. 2, 10-12/42 - No. 11, 3/45 Published quarterly)

1-General Douglas MacArthur-c 23.00 69.00 185.00
2 12.50 37.50 100.00
3,5: 3-Pro-Russian back-c 10.00 30.00 75.00
4-Disney's Gremlins app. 17.00 51.00 135.00
6-11: 6-Tothish-a by Discount 9.30 28.00 65.00
IOTE: *No. 1 was to be released in July, but was delayed. Painted c-4, 6-9.*

VAR HEROES
Ace Magazines: May, 1952 - No. 8, Apr, 1953

1 10.00 30.00 75.00
2-Lou Cameron-a 6.40 19.25 45.00
3-8: 6,7-Cameron-a 5.00 15.00 35.00

VAR HEROES (Also see Blue Bird Comics)
Charlton Comics: Feb, 1963 - No. 27, Nov, 1967

1,2: 2-John F. Kennedy story 3.00 9.00 30.00
3-10 2.30 7.00 20.00
11-26 1.85 5.50 15.00
27-1st Devils Brigade by Glanzman 2.40 7.35 22.00
IOTE: ***Montes/Bache** a-3-7, 21, 25, 27; c-3-7.*

VAR IS HELL
Iarvel Comics Group: Jan, 1973 - No. 15, Oct, 1975

1-Williamson-a(r), 5 pgs.; Ayers-a 2.40 7.35 22.00
2-8-Reprints. 7,8-Kirby-a 1.50 4.50 12.00
9-Intro Death 3.20 9.60 35.00
10-15-Death app. 1.85 5.50 15.00
NOTE: ***Bolle** a-3r. **Powell** a-1. **Woodbridge** a-1. Sgt. Fury reprints-7, 8.*

WARLANDS
Image Comics: Aug, 1999 - Present ($2.50)

1-9,11-Pat Lee-a(p)/Adrian Tsang-s 2.50
10-($2.95) Flip book w/Shidima preview 3.00
... Chronicles 1 (2/00, $7.95) r/#1-3 7.95
... Chronicles 2 (7/00, $7.95) r/#4-6 7.95

WARLOCK (The Power of...)(Also see Fantastic Four #66, 67, Incredible Hulk #178, Infinity Crusade, Infinity Gauntlet, Infinity War, Marvel Premiere #1, Silver Surfer V3#46, Strange Tales #178-181 & Thor #165)
Marvel Comics Group: Aug, 1972 - No. 8, Oct, 1973; No. 9, Oct, 1975 - No. 15, Nov, 1976

1-Origin by Kane 3.20 9.60 35.00
2,3 2.00 6.00 18.00
4-8: 4-Death of Eddie Roberts 1.50 4.50 12.00
9-Starlin's 2nd Thanos saga begins, ends #15; new costume Warlock; Thanos cameo only; story cont'd from Strange Tales #178-181; Starlin-c/a in #9-15 2.00 6.00 16.00
10-Origin Thanos & Gamora; recaps events from Capt. Marvel #25-34. Thanos vs.The Magus-c/story 2.30 7.00 20.00
11-Thanos app.; Warlock dies 2.00 6.00 16.00
12-14: (Regular 25¢ edition) 14-Origin Star Thief; last 25¢ issue 1.25 3.75 10.00
12-14-(30¢-c, limited distribution) 1.85 5.50 15.00
15-Thanos-c/story 1.50 4.50 12.00
NOTE: ***Buscema** a-2p; c-8p. **G. Kane** a-1p, 3-5p; c-1p, 2, 3, 4p, 5p, 7p. **Starlin** a-9-14p, 15; c-9, 10, 11p, 12p, 13-15. **Sutton** a-1-8i.*

GD2.0 FN6.0 NM9.4

WARLOCK (...Special Edition on-c)
Marvel Comics Group: Dec, 1982 - No. 6, May, 1983 ($2.00, slick paper, 52 pgs.)

1-Warlock-r/Strange Tales #178-180. 4.00
2-6: 2-r/Str. Tales #180,181 & Warlock #9. 3-r/Warlock #10-12(Thanos origin recap). 4-r/Warlock #12-15. 5-r/Warlock #15, Marvel Team-Up #55 & Avengers Ann. #7. 6-r/2nd half Avengers Annual #7 & Marvel Two-in-One Annual #2 4.00
Special Edition #1(12/83) 4.00
NOTE: ***Byrne** a-5r. **Starlin** a-1-6r; c-1-6(new). Direct sale only.*

WARLOCK
Marvel Comics: V2#1, May, 1992 - No. 6, Oct, 1992 ($2.50, limited series)

V2#1-6: 1-Reprints 1982 reprint series w/Thanos 2.50

WARLOCK
Marvel Comics: Nov, 1998 - No. 4, Feb, 1999 ($2.99, limited series)

1-4-Warlock vs. Drax 3.00

WARLOCK (M-Tech)
Marvel Comics: Oct, 1999 - No. 9, June, 2000 ($1.99/$2.50)

1-5: 1-Quesada-c. 2-Two covers 2.00
6-9: 6-Begin $2.50-c. 8-Avengers app. 2.50

WARLOCK AND THE INFINITY WATCH (Also see Infinity Gauntlet)
Marvel Comics: Feb, 1992 - No. 42, July, 1995 ($1.75) (Sequel to Infinity Gauntlet)

1-Starlin-scripts begin; brief origin recap; sequel to Infinity Gauntlet 3.00
2,3: 2-Reintro Moondragon 2.00
4-24,26: 7-Reintro The Magus; Moondragon app.; Thanos cameo on last 2 pgs. 8,9-Thanos battles Gamora-c/story. 8-Magus & Moondragon app. 10-Thanos-c/story; Magus app. 13-Hulk x-over. 21-Drax vs. Thor 2.00
25-($2.95, 52 pgs.)-Die-cut & embossed double-c; Thor & Thanos app. 3.00
28-42: 28-$1.95-c begins; bound-in card sheet 2.00
NOTE: ***Austin** c/a-1-4i, 7i. **Leonardi** a(p)-3, 4. **Medina** c/a(p)-1, 2, 5; 6, 9, 10, 14, 15, 20. **Williams** a(i)-8, 12, 13, 16-19.*

WARLOCK CHRONICLES
Marvel Comics: June, 1993 - No. 8, Feb, 1994 ($2.00, limited series)

1-($2.95)-Holo-grafx foil & embossed-c; origin retold; Starlin scripts begin; Keith Williams-a(i) in all 3.00
2-8: 3-Thanos & Mephisto-c/story. 4-Vs. Magus-c/s. 8-Contains free 16 pg. Razorline insert 2.00

WARLOCK 5
Aircel Pub.: 11/86 - No. 22, 5/89; V2#1, June, 1989 - V2#5, 1989 ($1.70, B&W)

1-5,7-11-Gordon Derry-s/Denis Beauvais-a thru #11. 5-Green Cyborg on-c. 5-Misnumbered as #6 (no #6); Blue Girl on-c. 2.00
12-22-Barry Blair-s/a. 18-$1.95-c begins 3.00
V2#1-5 ($2.00, B&W)-All issues by Barry Blair 2.00
Compilation 1,2: 1-r/#1-5 (1988, $5.95); 2-r/#6-9 6.00

WARLORD (See 1st Issue Special #8)
National Periodical Publications/DC Comics #123 on: 1-2/76; No.2, 3-4/76; No.3, 10-11/76 - No. 133, Win, 1988-89

1-Story cont'd. from 1st Issue Special #8 2.30 7.00 20.00
2-Intro. Machiste 1.10 3.30 9.00
3-5 7.00
6-10: 6-Intro Mariah. 7-Origin Machiste. 9-Dons new costume 5.00
11-20: 11-Origin-r. 12-Intro Aton. 15-Tara returns; Warlord has son 4.00
21-36,40,41: 27-New facts about origin. 28-1st app. Wizard World. 32-Intro Shakira. 40-Warlord gets new costume 3.00
37-39: 37,38-Origin Omac by Starlin. 38-Intro Jennifer Morgan, Warlord's daughter. 39-Omac ends. 4.00
42-48: 42-47-Omac back-up series. 48-(52 pgs.)-1st app. Arak; contains free 14 pg. Arak Son of Thunder; Claw The Unconquered app. 3.00
49-62,64-99,101-130,132: 49-Claw The Unconquered app. 50-Death of Aton. 51-Reprints #1. 55-Arion Lord of Atlantis begins, ends #62. 91-Origin w/new facts. 114,115-Legends x-over. 125-Death of Tara 2.00
63-The Barren Earth begins; free 16pg. Masters of the Universe preview 3.00
100-($1.25, 52 pgs.). 3.00
131-1st DC work by Rob Liefeld (9/88) 4.00
133-($1.50, 52 pgs.) 3.00

War Machine #4 © MAR

Warp #7 © FC

Warrior Nun Areala/Razor #1 © Antarctic Press

GD2.0 FN6.0 NM9.4

Remco Toy Giveaway (2-3/4x4") 5.00
Annual 1('82-'87): 1-Grell-c,/a(p). 6-New Gods app. 3.00
NOTE: ***Grell*** *a-1-15, 16-50p, 51r, 52p, 59p, Annual 1p; c-1-70, 100-104, 112, 116, 117, Annual 1, 5.* ***Wayne Howard*** *a-64i.* ***Starlin*** *a-37-39p.*

WARLORD
DC Comics: Jan, 1992 - No. 6, June, 1992 ($1.75, limited series)
1-6: Grell-c & scripts in all 2.00

WARLORDS (See DC Graphic Novel #2)

WAR MAN
Marvel Comics (Epic Comics): Nov, 1993 - No. 2, Dec, 1993 ($2.50, lim. series)
1,2 2.50

WAR MACHINE (Also see Iron Man #281,282 & Marvel Comics Presents #152)
Marvel Comics: Apr, 1994 - No. 25, Apr, 1996 ($1.50)
"Ashcan" edition (nd, 75¢, B&W, 16 pgs.) 2.00
1-($2.00, 52 pgs.)-Newsstand edition; Cable app. 2.00
1-($2.95, 52 pgs.)-Collectors ed.; embossed foil-c 3.00
2-14, 16-25: 2-Bound-in trading card sheet; Cable app. 2,3-Deathlok app. 8-red logo 2.00
8-($2.95)-Polybagged w/16 pg. Marvel Action Hour preview & acetate print; yellow logo 3.00
15 ($2.50)-Flip book 2.50

WAR OF THE GODS
DC Comics: Sept, 1991 - No. 4, Dec, 1991 ($1.75, limited series)
1-4: Perez layouts, scripts & covers. 1-Contains free mini posters (Robin, Deathstroke). 2-4-Direct sale versions include 4 pin-ups printed on cover stock plus different-c 2.00

WAR OF THE WORLDS, THE
Caliber: 1996 - Present ($2.95, B&W, 32 pgs.)(Based on H. G. Wells novel)
1-Randy Zimmerman scripts begin 3.00

WARP
First Comics: Mar, 1983 - No. 19, Feb, 1985 ($1.00/$1.25, Mando paper)
1-Sargon-Mistress of War app. 2.00
2-19: 2-Faceless Ones begin. 10-New Warp advs., & Outrider begin 2.00
Special 1-3: 1(7/83, 36 pgs.)-Origin Chaos-Prince of Madness; origin of Warp Universe begins, ends #3. 2(1/84)-Lord Cumulus vs. Sargon Mistress of War ($1.00). 3(6/84)-Chaos-Prince of Madness 2.00

WAR PARTY
Lightning Comics: Oct, 1994 (2.95, B&W)
1-1st app. Deathmark 3.00

WARPED
Empire Entertainment (Solson): Jun, 1990 - No. 2, Oct-Nov, 1990 (B&W mag)
1,2 2.00

WARPATH (Indians on the...)
Key Publications/Stanmor: Nov, 1954 - No. 3, Apr, 1955
1 10.00 30.00 75.00
2,3 6.40 19.25 45.00

WARP GRAPHICS ANNUAL
WaRP Graphics: Dec, 1985; 1988 ($2.50)
1-Elfquest, Blood of the Innocent, Thunderbunny & Myth Adventures app. 5.00
1 (1988) 4.00

WARREN PRESENTS
Warren Publications: Jan, 1979 - No. 14, Nov, 1981
1-Eerie, Creepy, & Vampirella-r 2.00 6.00 16.00
2-6 10/79): 2-The Rook 1.50 4.50 12.00
8(10/80)-r/1st app. Pantha from Vamp. #30 2.00 6.00 16.00
9(11/80) 1.75 5.25 14.00
13(10/81),14(11/81) 2.30 7.00 20.00
(#7,10,11,12 may not exist, or may be a Special below)
Special-Alien Collectors Edition (1979) 2.30 7.00 20.00
Special-Close Encounters of the Third Kind (1978) 1.50 4.50 12.00
Special-Lord of the Rings (6/79) 2.30 7.00 20.00
Special-Meteor (1/80) 1.50 4.50 12.00
Special-Moonraker (10/79) 1.50 4.50 12.00
Special-Star Wars (1977) 2.50 7.50 24.00

WAR REPORT
Ajax/Farrell Publications (Excellent Publ.): Sept, 1952 - No. 5, May, 1953
1 10.00 30.00 75.00
2-Flame thrower w/burning bodies on-c 6.40 19.25 45.00
3-5: 4-Used in **POP**, pg. 94 5.70 17.00 40.00

WARRIOR (Wrestling star)
Ultimate Creations: May, 1996 - No. 4, 1997 ($2.95)
1-4: Warrior scripts; Callahan-c/a. 3-Wraparound-c. 4-Warrior #3 in indicia; pin-ups 3.00
1-Variant-c. 5.00

WARRIOR COMICS
H.C. Blackerby: 1945 (1930s DC reprints)
1-Wing Brady, The Iron Man, Mark Markon 22.00 66.00 175.00

WARRIOR NUN AREALA
Antarctic Press: Dec, 1994 - No. 3, Apr, 1995 ($2.95, limited series)
1 2.40 6.00
1-Special Edition (5000) 1.25 3.75 10.00
2-3, 3-Bagged w/CD 4.00

WARRIOR NUN AREALA
Antarctic Press: July, 1997 - No. 6, May, 1998 ($2.95)
1-6-Lyga-s 3.00

WARRIOR NUN AREALA (Volume 3)
Antarctic Press: July, 1999 - Present ($2.50)
1-4 2.50

WARRIOR NUN AREALA AND AVENGELYNE 1996 (See Avengelyne/...)
Antarctic Press: Dec, 1996 ($2.95)
1 3.00

WARRIOR NUN AREALA AND GLORY,
Antarctic Press: Sept, 1997
1-Ben Dunn-s/a ($2.95, color) 3.00
1-($5.95) Ltd. Poster Edition w/pin-ups 6.00

WARRIOR NUN AREALA: HAMMER AND THE HOLOCAUST
Antarctic Press: June, 1997- Present ($2.95)
1,2 3.00

WARRIOR NUN AREALA: PORTRAITS,
Antarctic Press: Mar, 1996 ($3.95, one-shot)
1-Pin-ups 4.00

WARRIOR NUN AREALA/RAZOR
Antarctic Press: Jan, 1999 ($2.99, one-shot)
1-Dunn-c/a 3.00
1-($5.99)-Deluxe Ed. with painted-c 6.00

WARRIOR NUN AREALA: RESURRECTION
Antarctic Press: Nov, 1998 - No. 3, Mar, 1999 ($2.95)
1-3 3.00
1-($5.95)-Special Ed. with poster 6.00

WARRIOR NUN AREALA: RITUALS,
Antarctic Press: July, 1995 - No. 6, June, 1996 ($2.95/$3.50)
1-5 3.00
6-($3.50) 3.50

WARRIOR NUN AREALA: SCORPIO ROSE
Antarctic Press: Sept, 1996 - No. 4, Mar, 1997 ($2.95, color)
1-4 3.00

WARRIOR NUN AREALA VS. RAZOR (See Razor/...)
Antarctic Press: May, 1996 ($3.95, one-shot)
1-Dunn-c/a 4.00
1-($9.95)-Comic polybagged w/CD 10.00

Warrior Nun: Frenzy #1 © Ben Y. Dunn

Wartime Romances #7 © STJ

Watchmen #3 © DC

GD2.0 FN6.0 NM9.4

WARRIOR NUN: BLACK AND WHITE,
Antarctic Press: Feb, 1997 - Present ($2.95//$2.99/$2.50, B&W)

1-20 3.00
21-($2.50) 2.50

WARRIOR NUN DEI: AFTERTIME
Antarctic Press: Jan, 1997 - No. 2, ($2.95)

1-2-Patrick Thornton-s/a 3.00

WARRIOR NUN: FRENZY
Antarctic Press: Jan, 1998 - No. 2, Jun, 1998 ($2.95)

1,2: 1-Ribic painted-c/a. 2-Horvatic-s/a 3.00

WARRIOR NUN: RHEINTÖCHTER
Antarctic Press: Dec, 1997 - No. 2, Apr, 1998 ($2.95, B&W, limited series)

1,2-Set in medieval Europe; Paquette & Lacombe-s/a 3.00

WARRIOR OF WAVERLY STREET, THE
Dark Horse Comics: Nov, 1996 - No. 2, Dec, 1996 ($2.95, mini-series)

1,2-Darrow-c 3.00

WARRIORS
CFD Productions: 1993 (B&W, one-shot)

1-Linsner, Dark One-a 1.85 5.50 15.00

WARRIORS OF PLASM (Also see Plasm)
Defiant: Aug, 1993 - No. 13, Aug, 1995 ($2.95/$2.50)

1-4: Shooter-scripts; Lapham-c/a: 1-1st app. Glory. 4-Bound-in fold-out poster 3.00
5-7,10-13: 5-Begin $2.50-c. 13-Schism issue 2.50
8,9-($2.75, 44 pgs.) 2.75
The Collected Edition (2/94, $9.95)-r/Plasm #0, WOP #1-4 & Splatterball 10.00

WAR ROMANCES (See True...)

WAR SHIPS
Dell Publishing Co.: 1942 (36 pgs.)(Similar to Large Feature Comics)

nn-Cover by McWilliams; contains photos & drawings of U.S. war ships 16.00 49.00 130.00

WAR STORIES (Formerly War Comics)
Dell Publ. Co.: No. 5, 1942(nd); No. 6, Aug-Oct, 1942 - No. 8, Feb-Apr, 1943

5-Origin The Whistler 25.00 75.00 200.00
6-8: 6-8-Night Devils app. 8-Painted-c 19.00 56.00 150.00

WAR STORIES (Korea)
Ajax/Farrell Publications (Excellent Publ.): Sept, 1952 - No. 5, May, 1953

1 10.00 30.00 70.00
2 5.00 15.00 35.00
3-5 5.00 15.00 30.00

WAR STORIES (See Star Spangled...)

WARSTRIKE
Malibu Comics (Ultraverse): May, 1994 - No. 7, Nov, 1995 ($1.95)

1-7: 1-Simonson-c 2.00
1-Ultra 5000 Limited silver foil 4.00
Giant Size 1 (12/94, 2.50, 44pgs.)-Prelude to Godwheel 2.50

WART AND THE WIZARD (See The Sword & the Stone under Movie Comics)
Gold Key: Feb, 1964 (Walt Disney)(Characters from Sword in the Stone movie)

1 (10102-402) 3.80 11.40 42.00

WARTIME ROMANCES
St. John Publishing Co.: July, 1951 - No. 18, Nov, 1953

1-All Baker-c/a 33.00 99.00 265.00
2-All Baker-c/a 23.00 69.00 185.00
3,4-All Baker-c/a 21.00 62.00 165.00
5-8-Baker-c/a(2-3) each 19.00 58.00 155.00
9,11,12,16,18: Baker-c/a each. 9-Two signed stories by Estrada 14.00 41.00 110.00
10,13-15,17-Baker-c only 8.65 26.00 60.00

WAR VICTORY ADVENTURES (#1 titled War Victory Comics)
U.S. Treasury Dept./War Victory/Harvey Publ.: Summer, 1942 - No. 3, Winter, 1943-44 (5¢)

1-(Promotion of Savings Bonds)-Featuring America's greatest comic art by top syndicated cartoonists; Blondie, Joe Palooka, Green Hornet, Dick Tracy, Superman, Gumps, etc.; (36 pgs.); all profits were contributed to U.S.O. & Army/Navy relief funds 40.00 120.00 325.00
2-Battle of Stalingrad story; Powell-a (8/43); flag-c 21.00 62.00 165.00
3-Capt. Red Cross-c & text only; Powell-a 19.00 56.00 150.00

WAR WAGON, THE (See Movie Classics)

WAR WINGS
Charlton Comics: Oct, 1968

1 2.00 6.00 18.00

WARWORLD!
Dark Horse Comics: Feb, 1989 ($1.75, B&W, one-shot)

1-Gary Davis sci/fi art in Moebius style 2.00

WARZONE
Entity Comics: 1995 ($2.95, B&W)

1-3 3.00

WASHABLE JONES AND THE SHMOO (Also see Al Capp's Shmoo)
Toby Press: June, 1953

1- "Super-Shmoo" 20.00 60.00 160.00

WASH TUBBS (See The Comics, Crackajack Funnies)
Dell Publishing Co.: No. 11, 1942 - No. 53, 1944

Four Color 11 (#1) 29.00 88.00 350.00
Four Color 28 (1943) 21.00 63.00 250.00
Four Color 53 15.00 46.00 185.00

WASTELAND
DC Comics: Dec, 1987 - No. 18, May, 1989 ($1.75-$2.00 #13 on, mature)

1-5(4/88), 5(5/88), 6(5/88)-18: 13,15-Orlando-a 2.00
NOTE: ***Orlando** a-12, 13, 15. **Truman** a-10; c-13.*

WATCHMEN
DC Comics: Sept, 1986 - No. 12, Oct, 1987 (maxi-series)

1-Alan Moore scripts & Dave Gibbons-c/a in all 1.00 2.80 7.00
2-12 5.00
Hardcover Collection-Slip-cased-r/#1-12 w/new material; produced by Graphitti Designs 70.00
Trade paperback (1987, $14.95)-r/#1-12 18.00

WATER BIRDS AND THE OLYMPIC ELK (Disney)
Dell Publishing Co.: No. 700, Apr, 1956

Four Color 700-Movie 4.60 13.75 55.00

WATERWORLD: CHILDREN OF LEVIATHAN
Acclaim Comics: Aug, 1997 - No. 4, Nov, 1997 ($2.50, mini-series)

1-4 2.50

WEAPON X
Marvel Comics: Apr, 1994 ($12.95, one-shot)

nn-r/Marvel Comics Presents #72-84 13.00

WEAPON X
Marvel Comics: Mar, 1995 - No. 4, June, 1995 ($1.95)

1-Age of Apocalypse 4.00
2-4 2.00

WEAPON ZERO
Image Comics (Top Cow Productions): No. T-4(#1), June, 1995 - No. T-0(#5), Dec, 1995 ($2.50, limited series)

T-4(#1): Walt Simonson scripts in all. 5.00
T-3(#2) - T-1(#4) 4.00
T-0(#5) 3.00

WEAPON ZERO
Image Comics (Top Cow Productions): V2#1, Mar, 1996 - No. 15, Dec, 1997 ($2.50)

V2#1-Walt Simonson scripts. 3.00
2-14: 8-Begin Top Cow. 10-Devil's Reign 2.50

Weasel Guy: Road Trip #2 © Steve Buccellato

Web of Spider-Man #12 © MAR

Webspinners: Tales of Spider-Man #11 © MAR

15-($3.50) Benitez-a 3.50

WEAPON ZERO/SILVER SURFER
Image Comics/Marvel Comics: Jan, 1997($2.95, one-shot)

1-Devil's Reign Pt. 1 3.00

WEASELGUY: ROAD TRIP
Image Comics: Sept, 1999 - No. 2 ($3.50, limited series)

1,2-Steve Buccellato-s/a 3.50
1-Variant-c by Bachalo 5.00

WEASELGUY/WITCHBLADE
Hyperwerks: July, 1998 ($2.95, one-shot)

1-Steve Buccellato-s/a; covers by Matsuda and Altstaetter. 3.00

WEASEL PATROL SPECIAL, THE (Also see Fusion #17)
Eclipse Comics: Apr, 1989 ($2.00, B&W, one-shot)

1-Funny animal 2.00

WEAVEWORLD
Marvel Comics (Epic): Dec, 1991 - No. 3, 1992 ($4.95, lim. series, 68 pgs.)

1-3: Clive Barker adaptation 5.00

WEB, THE (Also see Mighty Comics & Mighty Crusaders)
DC Comics (Impact Comics): Sept, 1991 - No. 14, Oct, 1992 ($1.00)

1-14: 5-The Fly x-over 9-Trading card inside 2.00
Annual 1 (1992, $2.50, 68 pgs.)-With Trading card 2.50

NOTE: ***Gil Kane*** *c-5, 9, 10, 12-14.* ***Bill Wray*** *a(i)-1-9, 10(part).*

WEB OF EVIL
Comic Magazines/Quality Comics Group: Nov, 1952 - No. 21, Dec, 1954

	GD2.0	FN6.0	NM9.4
1-Used in **SOTI**, pg. 388. Jack Cole-a; morphine use story	55.00	165.00	525.00
2-4,6,7: 2,3-Jack Cole-a. 4,6,7-Jack Cole-c/a	40.00	120.00	350.00
5-Electrocution-c/story; Jack Cole-c/a	44.00	133.00	400.00
8-11-Jack Cole-a	38.00	113.00	300.00
12,13,15,16,19-21	23.00	68.00	180.00
14-Part Crandall-c; Old Witch swipe	24.00	71.00	190.00
17-Opium drug propaganda story	23.00	68.00	180.00
18-Acid-in-face story	24.00	71.00	190.00

NOTE: ***Jack Cole*** *a(2 each)-2, 6, 8, 9.* ***Cuidera*** *c-1-21i.* ***Ravielli*** *a-13.*

WEB OF HORROR
Major Magazines: Dec, 1969 - No. 3, Apr, 1970 (Magazine)

	GD2.0	FN6.0	NM9.4
1-Jeff Jones painted-c; Wrightson-a, Kaluta-a	8.65	26.00	95.00
2-Jones painted-c; Wrightson-a(2), Kaluta-a	6.35	19.00	70.00
3-Wrightson-c/a (1st published-c); Brunner, Kaluta, Bruce Jones-a	6.35	19.00	70.00

WEB OF MYSTERY
Ace Magazines (A. A. Wyn): Feb, 1951 - No. 29, Sept, 1955

	GD2.0	FN6.0	NM9.4
1	50.00	150.00	450.00
2-Bakerish-a	28.00	83.00	220.00
3-10: 4-Colan-a	26.00	79.00	210.00
11-18,20-26: 12-John Chilly's 1st cover art. 13-Surrealistic-c. 20-r/The Beyond #1	23.00	68.00	180.00
19-Reprints Challenge of the Unknown #6 used in N.Y. Legislative Committee	23.00	68.00	180.00
27-Bakerish-a(r/The Beyond #2); last pre-code ish	21.00	64.00	170.00
28,29: 28-All-r	16.00	49.00	130.00

NOTE: *This series was to appear as "Creepy Stories", but title was changed before publication.* ***Cameron*** *a-6, 8, 11-13, 17-20, 22, 24, 25, 27; c-8, 13, 17.* ***Palais*** *a-28r.* ***Sekowsky*** *a-1-3, 7, 8, 11, 14, 21, 29.* ***Tothish*** *a-by* ***Bill Discount*** *#16. 29-all-r, 19-28-partial-r.*

WEB OF SCARLET SPIDER
Marvel Comics: Oct, 1995 - No. 4, Jan, 1996 ($1.95, limited series)

1-4: Replaces "Web of Spider-Man" 2.00

WEB OF SPIDER-MAN (Replaces Marvel Team-Up)
Marvel Comics Group: Apr, 1985 - No. 129, Sept, 1995

	GD2.0	FN6.0	NM9.4
1-Painted-c (5th app. black costume?)	1.85	5.50	15.00
2,3		2.40	6.00
4-8: 7-Hulk x-over; Wolverine splash			5.00
9-13: 10-Dominic Fortune guest stars; painted-c			4.00
14-17,19-28: 19-Intro Humbug & Solo			3.00
18-1st app. Venom (behind the scenes, 9/86)			3.00
29-Wolverine, new Hobgoblin (Macendale) app.	1.00	3.00	8.00
30-Origin recap The Rose & Hobgoblin I (entire book is flashback story); Punisher & Wolverine cameo			4.00
31,32-Six part Kraven storyline begins			5.00
33-37,39-47,49: 36-1st app. Tombstone (cameo)			2.50
38-Hobgoblin app.; begin $1.00-c			4.00
48-Origin Hobgoblin II(Demogoblin) cont'd from Spectacular Spider-Man #147; Kingpin app.	1.10	3.30	9.00
50-($1.50, 52 pgs.)			3.00
51-58			2.00
59-Cosmic Spidey cont'd from Spect. Spider-Man			3.00
60-89,91-99,101-106: 66,67-Green Goblin (Norman Osborn) app. as a super-hero. 69,70-Hulk x-over. 74-76-Austin-c(i). 76-Fantastic Four x-over. 78-Cloa & Dagger app. 81-Origin/1st app. Bloodshed. 84-Begin 6 part Rose & Hobgoblin II storyline; last $1.00-c. 86-Demon leaves Hobgoblin; 1st Demo-goblin. 93-Gives brief history of obgoblin. 93,94-Hobgoblin (Macendale) Reborn-c/story, parts 1,2; MoonKnight app. 94-Venom cameo.95-Begin 4 pa x-over w/Spirits of Venom w/Ghost Rider/Blaze/Spidey vs. Venom & Demo-goblin (cont'd in Ghost Rider/Blaze #5,6). 96-Spirits of Venom part 3; painted c. 101,103-Maximum Carnage x-over. 103-Venom & Carnage app. 104-106-Nightwatch back-up stories			2.00
90-($2.95, 52 pgs.)-Polybagged w/silver hologram-c, gatefold poster showing Spider-Man & Spider-Man 2099 (Williamson-i)			3.00
90-2nd printing; gold hologram-c			2.00
100-($2.95, 52 pgs.)-Holo-grafx foil-c; intro new Spider-Armor			4.00
107-111: 107-Intro Sandstorm; Sand & Quicksand app.			2.00
112-116, 118, 119, 121-124, 126-128: 112-Begin $1.50-c; bound-in trading card sheet. 113-Regular Ed.; Gambit & Black Cat app. 118-1st solo clone story; Venom app			2.00
113 ($2.95)-Collector's ed. polybagged w/foil-c; 16 pg. preview of Spider-Man cartoon & animation cel			3.00
117 ($1.50)-Flip book; Power & Responsibility Pt.1			2.00
117 ($2.95)-Collector's edition; foil-c; flip book			3.00
119 ($6.45)-Direct market edition; polybagged w/ Marvel Milestone Amazing Spider-Man #150 & coupon for Amazing Spider-Man #396, Spider-Man #53, & Spectacular Spider-Man #219.			7.00
120 ($2.25)-Flip book w/ preview of the Ultimate Spider-Man			2.25
125 ($3.95)-Holodisk-c; Gwen Stacy clone			4.00
125,129: 25 ($2.95)-Newsstand. 129-Last issue			3.00
Annual 1 (1985)			3.00
Annual 2 (1986)-New Mutants; Art Adams-a	1.00	3.00	8.00
Annual 3-10 ('87-'94, 68 pgs.): 4-Evolutionary War x-over. 5-Atlantis Attacks; Captain Universe by Ditko (p) & Silver Sable stories; F.F. app. 6-Punisher back-up plus Capt. Universe by Ditko; G. Kane-a. 7-Origins of Hobgoblin I, Hobgoblin II, Green Goblin I & II & Venom; Larsen/Austin-c. 8-Part 3 of Venom story; New Warriors x-over;Black Cat back-up sty. 9-Bagged w/card			3.00
Super Special 1 (1995, $3.95)-flip book			4.00

NOTE: ***Art Adams*** *a-Annual 2.* ***Byrne*** *c-3-6.* ***Chaykin*** *c-10.* ***Mignola*** *a-Annual 2.* ***Vess*** *c-1, 8, Annual 1, 2.* ***Zeck*** *a-6i, 31, 32; c-31, 32.*

WEBSPINNERS: TALES OF SPIDER-MAN
Marvel Comics: Jan, 1999 - No. 18, Jun, 2000 ($2.99/$2.50)

1-DeMatteis-s/Zulli-a; back-up story w/Romita Sr. art 3.00
1-($6.95) DF Edition 7.00
2,3: 2-Two covers 2.50
4-11,13-18: 4,5-Giffen-a; Silver Surfer-c/app. 7-9-Kelly-s/Sears and Smith-a. 10,11-Jenkins-s/Sean Phillips-a 2.50
12-($3.50) J.G. Jones-c/a; Jenkins-s 3.50

WEDDING BELLS
Quality Comics Group: Feb, 1954 - No. 19, Nov, 1956

	GD2.0	FN6.0	NM9.4
1-Whitney-a	14.00	41.00	110.00
2	9.30	28.00	65.00
3-9: 8-Last precode (4/55)	5.70	17.00	40.00
10-Ward-a (9 pgs.)	12.50	37.50	100.00
11-14,17	5.00	15.00	30.00
15-Baker-c	5.75	17.00	40.00
16-Baker-c/a	9.30	28.00	65.00

Weekender V2 #1 © Rucker Pub. Co.

Weird Fantasy #13 © WMG

Weird Mysteries #1 © Gilmore Publ.

GD2.0 FN6.0 NM9.4

8,19-Baker-a each 7.15 21.50 50.00

EDDING OF DRACULA
arvel Comics: Jan, 1993 ($2.00, 52 pgs.)

-Reprints Tomb of Dracula #30,45,46 2.00

EEKENDER, THE (Illustrated...)
ucker Pub. Co.: V1#1, Sept, 1945? - V1#4, Nov, 1945; V2#1, Jan, 1946 - V2#3, ıg, 1946 (52 pgs.)

1#1-4: 1-Same-c as Zip Comics #45, inside-c and back-c blank; Steel Sterling, Senor Banana, Red Rube and Ginger. 2-Capt. Victory on-c. 3-Super hero-c; Mr. E, Dan Hastings, Sky Chief and the Echo. 4-Same-c as Punch Comics #10 (9/44); r/Hale the Magician (7 pgs.) & r/Mr. E (8 pgs.-Lou Fine? or Gustavson?) plus 3 humor strips & many B&W photos & r/newspaper articles plus cheesecake photos of Hollywood stars 15.00 45.00 120.00

2#1-Same-c as Dynamic Comics #11; 36 pgs. comics, 16 in newspaper format with photos; partial Dynamic Comics reprints; 4 pgs. of cels from the Disney film Pinocchio; Little Nemo story by Winsor McCay, Jr.; Jack Cole-a; 18.00 53.00 140.00

2#2,3: 2-Same-c as Dynamic Comics #9 by Raboy; Dan Hastings (Tuska), Rocket Boy, The Echo, Lucky Coyne. 3-Humor-c by Boddington?; Dynamic Man, Ima Slooth, Master Key, Dynamic Boy, Captain Glory 15.00 45.00 120.00

EEKLY COMIC MAGAZINE
ox Publications: May 12, 1940 (16 pgs.) (Others exist w/o super-heroes)

st Version)-8 pg. Blue Beetle story, 7 pg. Patty O'Day story; two copies known to exist. Estimated value... 600.00

nd Version)-7 two-pg. adventures of Blue Beetle, Patty O'Day, Yarko, Dr. Fung, Green Mask, Spark Stevens, & Rex Dexter; one copy known to exist. Estimated value... 500.00

scovered with business papers, letters and exploitation material promoting **Weekly Comic agazine** for use by newspapers in the same manner of **The Spirit** weeklies. Interesting note: ese are dated three weeks before the first Spirit comic. Letters indicate that samples may have en sent to a few newspapers. These sections were actually 15-1/2x22" pages which will fold wn to an approximate 8x10" comic booklet. Other various comic sections were found with the ove, but were more like the Sunday comic sections in format.

EIRD
erie Publications: V1#10, 1/66 - V8#6, 12/74; V9#1, 1/75 - V11#4, Dec, 1978 lagazine) (V1-V8: 52 pgs.; V9 on: 68 pgs.)

1#10(#1)-Intro. Morris the Caretaker of Weird (ends V2#10); Burgos-a 5.90 17.75 65.00
11,12 3.65 11.00 40.00
2#1-4(10/67), V3#1(1/68), V2#6(4/68)-V2#7,9,10(12/68) 3.80 11.40 42.00
2#8-r/Ditko's 1st story/Fantastic Fears #5 4.55 13.65 50.00
3#1(2/69)-V3#4 3.20 9.60 35.00
3#5(12/69)-Rulah reprint; "Rulah" changed to "Pulah", LSD story reprinted in Horror Tales V4#4, Tales From the Tomb V2#4, & 20 3.20 9.60 35.00
4#1-6('70), V5#1-6('71), V6#1-7('72), V7#1-7('73), V8#1-6('74), V9#1-4 (1/75-'76), V10#1-3('77), V11#1-4 3.20 9.60 35.00

OTE: V9#4 (12/76) has a cover swipe from Horror Tales V5#1 (2/73).

EIRD
C Comics (Paradox Press): Sum, 1997 - Present ($2.99, B&W, magazine)

1-4: 4-Mike Tyson-c 3.00

EIRD, THE
C Comics: Apr, 1988 - No. 4, July, 1988 ($1.50, limited series)

1-4: Wrightson-c/a in all 3.00

EIRD ADVENTURES
. L. Publishing Co. (Canada): May-June, 1951 - No. 3, Sept-Oct, 1951

1- "The She-Wolf Killer" by Matt Baker (6 pgs.) 53.00 158.00 475.00
2-Bondage/hypodermic panel 42.00 125.00 375.00
3-Male bondage/torture-c; severed head story 40.00 120.00 325.00

EIRD ADVENTURES
ff-Davis Publishing Co.: No. 10, July-Aug, 1951

0-Painted-c 40.00 120.00 325.00

EIRD CHILLS
Key Publications: July, 1954 - No. 3, Nov, 1954

1-Wolverton-r/Weird Mysteries No. 4; blood transfusion-c by Baily 74.00 221.00 700.00
2-Extremely violent injury to eye-c by Baily; Hitler story 68.00 205.00 650.00
3-Bondage E.C. swipe-c by Baily 44.00 133.00 400.00

WEIRD COMICS
Fox Features Syndicate: Apr, 1940 - No. 20, Jan, 1942

1-The Birdman, Thor, God of Thunder (ends #5), The Sorceress of Zoom, Blast Bennett, Typhon, Voodoo Man, & Dr. Mortal begin; Lou Fine bondage-c 435.00 1305.00 5000.00
2-Lou Fine-c 211.00 633.00 2000.00
3,4: 3-Simon-c. 4-Torture-c 116.00 348.00 1100.00
5-Intro. Dart & sidekick Ace (8/40) (ends #20); bondage/hypo-c 121.00 363.00 1150.00
6,7-Dynamite Thor app. in each. 6-Super hero covers begin 95.00 285.00 900.00
8-Dynamo, the Eagle (11/40, early app.; see Science #1) & sidekick Buddy & Marga, the Panther Woman begin 92.00 276.00 875.00
9,10: 10-Navy Jones app. 76.00 229.00 725.00
11-19: 16-Flag-c. 17-Origin The Black Rider. 58.00 174.00 550.00
20-Origin The Rapier; Swoop Curtis app; Churchill & Hitler-c 68.00 205.00 650.00

NOTE *Cover features: Sorceress of Zoom-4; Dr. Mortal-5; Dart & Ace-6-13, 15; Eagle-14, 16-20.*

WEIRD FANTASY (Formerly A Moon, A Girl, Romance; becomes Weird Science-Fantasy #23 on)
E. C. Comics: No. 13, May-June, 1950 - No. 22, Nov-Dec, 1953

13(#1) (1950) 182.00 545.00 2000.00
14-Necronomicon story; Cosmic Ray Bomb explosion-c/story by Feldstein; Feldstein & Gaines star 82.00 246.00 900.00
15,16: 16-Used in **SOTI**, pg. 144 55.00 164.00 600.00
17 (1951) 46.00 136.00 500.00
6-10: 6-Robot-c 37.00 112.00 410.00
11-13 (1952): 12-E.C. artists cameo. 13-Anti-Wertham "Cosmic Correspondence" 30.00 90.00 330.00
14-Frazetta/Williamson(1st team-up at E.C.)/Krenkel-a (7 pgs.); Orlando draws E.C. staff 43.00 130.00 475.00
15-Williamson/Evans-a(3), 4,3,&7 pgs. 30.00 90.00 330.00
16-19-Williamson/Krenkel-a in all. 18-Williamson/Feldstein-c 28.00 84.00 310.00
20-Frazetta/Williamson-a (7 pgs.) 30.00 90.00 330.00
21-Frazetta/Williamson-c & Williamson/Krenkel-a 43.00 130.00 475.00
22-Bradbury adaptation 21.00 61.00 225.00

NOTE: ***Ray Bradbury** adaptations-13, 17-20, 22. **Crandall** a-22. **Elder** a-17. **Feldstein** a-13(#1)-8; c-13(#1)-18 (#18 w/**Williamson**), 20. **Harrison/Wood** a-13. **Kamen** a-13(#1)-16, 18-22. **Krigstein** a-22. **Kurtzman** a-13(#1)-17(#5), 6. **Orlando** a-9-22 (2 stories in #16); c-19, 22. **Severin/Elder** a-18-21. **Wood** a-13(#1)-14, 17(2 stories ea. in #10-13). Ray Bradbury adaptations in #17-19, 22. Canadian reprints exist; see Table of Contents.*

WEIRD FANTASY
Russ Cochran/Gemstone Publ.: Oct, 1992 - No. 22, Jan, 1998 ($1.50/$2.00/$2.50)

1-22: 1,2: 1,2-r/Weird Fantasy #13,14; Feldstein-c. 3-5-r/Weird Fantasy #15-17 2.50

WEIRD HORRORS (Nightmare #10 on)
St. John Publishing Co.: June, 1952 - No. 9, Oct, 1953

1-Tuska-a 53.00 158.00 475.00
2,3: 3-Hashish story 34.00 101.00 270.00
4,5 28.00 84.00 225.00
6-Ekgren-c; atomic bomb story 44.00 133.00 400.00
7-Ekgren-c; Kubert, Cameron-a 50.00 150.00 450.00
8,9-Kubert-c/a 40.00 120.00 340.00

NOTE: ***Cameron** a-7, 9. **Finesque** a-1-5. **Forgione** a-6. **Morisi** a-3. Bondage c-8.*

WEIRD MYSTERIES
Gillmore Publications: Oct, 1952 - No. 12, Sept, 1954

1-Partial Wolverton-c swiped from splash page "Flight to the Future" in Weird Tales of the Future #2; "Eternity" has an Ingels swipe 74.00 221.00 700.00

Weird Science #6 © WMG

Weird Science Fantasy Annual 1953 © WMG

Weird Tales of the Future #3 © Aragon

2- "Robot Woman" by Wolverton; Bernard Baily-c reprinted in Mister Mystery #18; acid in face panel 103.00 308.00 975.00
3,6: Both have decapitation-c 53.00 158.00 475.00
4- "The Man Who Never Smiled" (3 pgs.) by Wolverton; Classic B. Baily skull-c 92.00 276.00 875.00
5-Wolverton story "Swamp Monster" (6 pgs.). Classic exposed brain-c 95.00 285.00 900.00
7-Used in **SOTI**, illo "Indeed", illo "Sex and blood" 74.00 221.00 700.00
8-Wolverton-c panel-r/#5; used in a '54 Readers Digest anti-comics article by T. E. Murphy entitled "For the Kiddies to Read" 53.00 158.00 475.00
9-Excessive violence, gore & torture 50.00 150.00 450.00
10-Silhouetted nudity panel 43.00 130.00 390.00
11,12: 12-r/Mr. Mystery #8(2), Weird Mysteries #3 & Weird Tales of the Future #6 40.00 120.00 350.00

NOTE: ***Baily** c-2-12. Anti-Wertham column in #5. #1-12 all have 'The Ghoul Teacher' (host).*

WEIRD MYSTERIES (Magazine)
Pastime Publications: Mar-Apr, 1959 (35¢, B&W, 68 pgs.)

1-Torres-a; E. C. swipe from Tales From the Crypt #46 by Tuska "The Ragman" 6.70 20.00 50.00

WEIRD MYSTERY TALES (See DC 100 Page Super Spectacular)

WEIRD MYSTERY TALES (See Cancelled Comic Cavalcade)
National Periodical Publications: July-Aug, 1972 - No. 24, Nov, 1975

1-Kirby-a; Wrightson splash pg. 4.10 12.30 45.00
2-Titanic-c/s 2.80 8.40 28.00
3,21: 21-Wrightson-c 2.30 7.00 20.00
4-10 1.85 5.50 15.00
11-20,22-24 1.50 4.50 12.00

NOTE: ***Alcala** a-5, 10, 13, 14. **Aparo** c-4. **Bailey** a-8. **Bolle** a-8?. **Howard** a-4. **Kaluta** a-4, 24; c-1. **G. Kane** a-10. **Kirby** a-1, 2p, 3p. **Nino** a-5, 6, 9, 13, 16, 21. **Redondo** a-9, 17. **Sparling** c-6. **Starlin** a-3?, 4. **Wood** a-23.*

WEIRD ROMANCE (Seduction of the Innocent #9)
Eclipse Comics: Feb, 1988 ($2.00, B&W)

1-Pre-code horror-r; Lou Cameron-r(2) 2.00

WEIRD SCIENCE (Formerly Saddle Romances) (Becomes Weird Science-Fantasy #23 on)
E. C. Comics: No. 12, May-June, 1950 - No. 22, Nov-Dec, 1953

12(#1) (1950)-"Lost in the Microcosm" classic-c/story by Kurtzman; "Dream of Doom" stars Gaines & E.C. artists 182.00 545.00 2000.00
13-Flying saucers over Washington-c/story, 2 years before the actual event 82.00 246.00 900.00
14-Robot, End of the World-c/story by Feldstein 77.00 232.00 850.00
15-War of Worlds-c/story (1950) 73.00 218.00 800.00
5-Atomic explosion-c 55.00 165.00 600.00
6-10 44.00 132.00 485.00
11-14 (1952) 30.00 90.00 330.00
15-18-Williamson/Krenkel-a in each; 15-Williamson-a. 17-Used in **POP**, pgs. 81,82. 18-Bill Gaines doll app. in story 32.00 97.00 355.00
19,20-Williamson/Frazetta-a (7 pgs. each). 19-Used in **SOTI**, illo "A young girl on her wedding night stabs her sleeping husband to death with a hatpin..." 42.00 127.00 465.00
21-Williamson/Frazetta-a (6 pgs.); Wood draws E.C. staff; Gaines & Feldstein app. in story 42.00 127.00 465.00
22-Williamson/Frazetta/Krenkel/Krigstein-a (8 pgs.); Wood draws himself in his story (last pg. & panel) 42.00 127.00 465.00

NOTE: ***Elder** a-14, 19. **Evans** a-22. **Feldstein** a-12(#1)-8; c-12(#1)-8, 11. **Ingels** a-15. **Kamen** a-12(#1)-13, 15-18, 20, 21. **Kurtzman** a-12(#1)-7. **Orlando** a-10-22. **Wood** a-12(#1), 13(#2), 5-22 (#9, 10, 12, 13 all have 2 **Wood** stories); c-9, 10, 12-22. Canadian reprints exist; see Table of Contents. Ray Bradbury adaptations in #17-20.*

WEIRD SCIENCE
Gladstone Publishing: Sept, 1990 - No. 4, Mar, 1991 ($1.95/$2.00, 68 pgs.)

1-4: Wood-c(r); all reprints in each 3.00

WEIRD SCIENCE
Russ Cochran/Gemstone Publishing: Sept, 1992 - No. 22, Dec, 1997 ($1.50/$2.00/$2.50)

1-22: 1,2: r/Weird Science #12,13 w/original-c. ,4-r/#14,15. 5-7-w/original-c 2.50

WEIRD SCIENCE-FANTASY (Formerly Weird Science & Weird Fantasy) (Becomes Incredible Science Fiction #30)
E. C. Comics: No. 23 Mar, 1954 - No. 29, May-June, 1955 (#23,24: 15¢)

23-Williamson, Wood-a; Bradbury adaptation 29.00 87.00 320.00
24-Williamson & Wood-a; Harlan Ellison's 1st professional story, "Upheaval!", later adapted into a short story as "Mealtime", and then into a TV episode of Voyage to the Bottom of the Sea as "The Price of Doom" 29.00 87.00 320.00
25-Williamson-c; Williamson/Torres/Krenkel-a plus Wood-a; Bradbury adaptation; cover price back to 10¢ 32.00 96.00 350.00
26-Flying Saucer Report; Wood, Crandall-a; A-bomb panels 29.00 87.00 320.00
27-Adam Link/I Robot series begins? 29.00 87.00 320.00
28-Williamson/Krenkel/Torres-a; Wood-a 31.00 93.00 340.00
29-Frazetta-c; Williamson/Krenkel & Wood-a; last pre-code issue; new logo 50.00 150.00 550.00

NOTE: ***Crandall** a-26, 27, 29. **Evans** a-26. **Feldstein** c-24, 26, 28. **Kamen** a-27, 28. **Krigstein** a-23-25. **Orlando** a-in all. **Wood** a-in all; c-23, 27. The cover to #29 was originally intended for Famous Funnies #217 (Buck Rogers), but was rejected for being "too violent."*

WEIRD SCIENCE-FANTASY
Russ Cochran/Gemstone Publishing: Nov, 1992 - No. 7, May , 1994 ($1.50/$2.00/$2.50)

1-7: 1,2: r/Weird Science-Fantasy #23,24. 3-7 r/#25-29 2.50

WEIRD SCIENCE-FANTASY ANNUAL
E. C. Comics: 1952, 1953 (Sold thru the E. C. office & on the stands in some major cities) (25¢, 132 pgs.)

1952-Feldstein-c 164.00 491.00 1800.00
1953-Feldstein-c 105.00 315.00 1150.00

NOTE: *The 1952 annual contains books cover-dated in 1951 & 1952, and the 1953 annual from 1952 & 1953. Contents of each annual may vary in same year.*

WEIRD SUSPENSE
Atlas/Seaboard Publ.: Feb, 1975 - No. 3, July, 1975

1-3: 1-Tarantula begins. 3-Freidrich-s 2.40 6.00

NOTE: ***Boyette** a-1-3. **Buckler** c-1, 3.*

WEIRD SUSPENSE STORIES (Canadian reprint of Crime SuspenStories #1-3; see Table of Contents)

WEIRD TALES ILLUSTRATED
Millennium Publications: 1992 - No. 2, 1992 ($2.95, high quality paper)

1,2-Bolton painted-c. 1-Adapts E.A. Poe & Harlan Ellison stories. 2-E.A. Poe & H.P. Lovecraft adaptations 3.50
1-($4.95, 52 pgs.)-Deluxe edition w/Tim Vigil-a not in regular #1; stiff-c; Bolton painted-c 5.00

WEIRD TALES OF THE FUTURE
S.P.M. Publ. No. 1-4/Aragon Publ. No. 5-8: Mar, 1952 - No. 8, July-Aug, 1953

1-Andru-a(2); Wolverton partial-c 95.00 285.00 900.00
2,3-Wolverton-c/a(3) each. 2- "Jumpin Jupiter" satire by Wolverton begins, ends #5 121.00 363.00 1150.00
4- "Jumpin Jupiter" satire & "The Man From the Moon" by Wolverton; partial Wolverton-c 103.00 308.00 975.00
5-Wolverton-c/a(2); "Jumpin Jupiter" satire 121.00 363.00 1150.00
6-Bernard Baily-c 52.00 155.00 465.00
7- "The Mind Movers" from the art to Wolverton's "Brain Bats of Venus" from Mr. Mystery #7 which was cut apart, pasted up, partially redrawn, and rewritten by Harry Kantor, the editor; Baily-c 100.00 300.00 950.00
8-Reprints Weird Mysteries #1(10/52) minus cover; gory cover showing heart ripped out by B. Baily 63.00 189.00 600.00

WEIRD TALES OF THE MACABRE (Magazine)
Atlas/Seaboard Publ.: Jan, 1975 - No. 2, Mar, 1975 (75¢, B&W)

1-Jeff Jones painted-c; Boyette-a 2.00 6.00 16.00
2-Boris Vallejo painted-c; Severin-a 2.50 7.50 23.00

WEIRD TERROR (Also see Horrific)
Allen Hardy Associates (Comic Media): Sept, 1952 - No. 13, Sept, 1954

1- "Portrait of Death", adapted from Lovecraft's "Pickman's Model"; lingerie panels, Hitler story 50.00 150.00 450.00
2,3: 2-Text on Marquis DeSade, Torture, Demonology, & St. Elmo's Fire. 3-

Weird War Tales #111 © DC

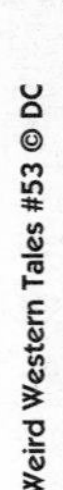
Weird Western Tales #53 © DC

Weird Worlds #3 © ERB

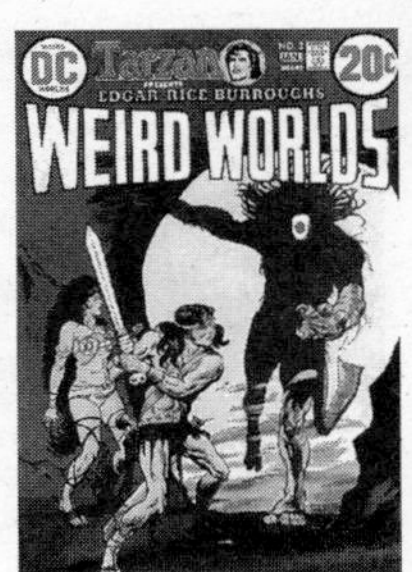

GD2.0 FN6.0 NM9.4

Extreme violence, whipping, torture; article on sin eating, dowsing 41.00 122.00 365.00
4-Dismemberment, decapitation, article on human flesh for sale, Devil, whipping 41.00 122.00 365.00
5-Article on body snatching, mutilation; cannibalism story 38.00 113.00 300.00
6-Dismemberment, decapitation, man hit by lightning 40.00 120.00 325.00
7-Body burning in fireplace-c 38.00 113.00 300.00
8,11: 8-Decapitation story; Ambrose Bierce adapt.. 11-End of the world story w/atomic blast panels; Tothish-a by Bill Discount 40.00 120.00 320.00
9,10,13: 13-Severed head panels 31.00 94.00 250.00
2-Discount-a 30.00 90.00 240.00
OTE: ***Don Heck*** *a-most issues; c-1-13.* ***Landau*** *a-6.* ***Morisi*** *a-2-5, 7, 9, 12.* ***Palais*** *a-1, 5, 6, '2), 10, 12.* ***Powell*** *a-10.* ***Ravielli*** *a-11, 20.*

/EIRD THRILLERS
iff-Davis Publ. Co. (Approved Comics): Sept-Oct, 1951 - No. 5, Oct-Nov, 952 (#2-5: painted-c)

1-Rondo Hatton photo-c 79.00 237.00 750.00
2-Toth, Anderson, Colan-a 58.00 174.00 550.00
3-Two Powell, Tuska-a; classic-c 76.00 229.00 725.00
4-Kubert, Tuska-a 55.00 165.00 500.00
5-Powell-a 50.00 150.00 450.00
OTE: ***M. Anderson*** *a-2, 3.* ***Roussos*** *a-4. #2, 3 reprinted in Nightmare #10 & 13; #4, 5 reprinted Amazing Ghost Stories #16 & #15.*

/EIRD WAR TALES
ational Periodical Publications/DC Comics: Sept-Oct, 1971 - No. 124, June, 983 (#1-5: 52 pgs.)

1-Kubert-a in #1-4,7; c-1-7 20.50 61.00 225.00
2,3-Drucker-a: 2-Crandall-a. 3-Heath-a 7.25 21.75 80.00
4,5: 5-Toth-a; Heath-a 5.45 16.35 60.00
6,7,9,10: 6,10-Toth-a. 7-Heath-a 3.20 9.60 35.00
8-Neal Adams-c/a(i) 4.55 13.65 50.00
11-20 2.30 7.00 20.00
21-35 1.85 5.50 15.00
36-(68 pgs.)-Crandall & Kubert-r/#2; Heath-r/#3; Kubert-c 2.30 7.00 20.00
37-63: 38-Kubert-c 1.00 3.00 8.00
64,68-Frank Miller-a in both. 64-Miller's 1st DC work 2.00 6.00 16.00
65-67,69-92,95-99,102-124: 97-2nd Creature Commandos; series begins 5.00
93,94,100,101: 93-Intro/origin Creature Commandos. 94,99-Return of War that time forgot-Dinosaur-c/s. 101-Intro/origin G.I. Robot 2.40 6.00

/EIRD WAR TALES
)C Comics (Vertigo): June, 1997 - No. 4, Sept, 1997 ($2.50)

1-4-Anthology by various 3.00

/EIRD WAR TALES
)C Comics (Vertigo): April, 2000 ($4.95, one-shot)

1-Anthology by various; last Biukovic-a 5.00

/EIRD WESTERN TALES (Formerly All-Star Western)
lational Per. Publ./DC Comics: No. 12, June-July, 1972 - No. 70, Aug, 1980

12-(52 pgs.)-3rd app. Jonah Hex; Bat Lash, Pow Wow Smith reprints; El Diablo by Neal Adams/Wrightson 8.15 24.50 90.00
13-Jonah Hex-c (1st?) & 4th app.; Neal Adams-a 4.55 13.65 50.00
14,15: 14-Toth-a. 15-Adams-c/a; no Jonah Hex 3.00 9.00 30.00
16,17,19,20 2.30 7.00 20.00
18,29: 18-1st all Jonah Hex issue (7-8/73) & begins. 29-Origin Jonah Hex 3.00 9.00 30.00
21-28,30-38: Jonah Hex in all. 38-Last Jonah Hex 1.50 4.50 12.00
39-Origin/1st app. Scalphunter & begins 1.50 4.50 12.00
40-47,50-69: 64-Bat Lash-c/story 1.00 3.00 8.00
48,49: (44 pgs.)-1st & 2nd app. Cinnamon 1.00 3.00 8.00
70-Last issue 1.25 3.75 10.00
NOTE: ***Alcala*** *a-16, 17.* ***Evans*** *inks-39-48; c-39i, 40, 47.* ***G. Kane*** *a-15, 20.* ***Kubert*** *c-12, 33.* ***Starlin*** *c-44, 45.* ***Wildey*** *a-26. 48 & 49 are 44 pgs..*

WEIRD WONDER TALES
Marvel Comics Group: Dec, 1973 - No. 22, May, 1977

GD2.0 FN6.0 NM9.4

1-Wolverton-r/Mystic #6 (Eye of Doom) 2.30 7.00 20.00
2-10 1.50 4.50 12.00
11-22: 16-18-Venus-r by Everett from Venus #19,18 & 17. 19-22-Dr. Druid (Droom)-r 1.25 3.75 10.00
15-17-(30¢-c variants, limited distribution)(4-8/76) 1.85 5.50 15.00
NOTE: *All 1950s & early 1960s reprints.* ***Check*** *r-1.* ***Colan*** *r-17.* ***Ditko*** *r-4, 5, 10-13, 19-21.* ***Drucker*** *r-12, 20.* ***Everett*** *r-3(Spellbound #16), 6(Astonishing #10), 9(Adv. Into Mystery #5).* ***Heath*** *a-13r.* ***Heck*** *a-1or, 14r.* ***Gil Kane*** *c-1, 2, 10.* ***Kirby*** *r-4, 6, 10, 11, 13, 15-22; c-17, 19, 20.* ***Krigstein*** *r-19.* ***Kubert*** *r-22.* ***Maneely*** *r-8.* ***Mooney*** *r-7p.* ***Powell*** *r-3, 7.* ***Torres*** *r-7.* ***Wildey*** *r-2, 7.*

WEIRD WORLDS (See Adventures Into...)

WEIRD WORLDS (Magazine)
Eerie Publications: V1#10(12/70), V2#1(2/71) - No. 4, Aug, 1971 (52 pgs.)

V1#10-Sci-fi/horror 3.25 9.75 36.00
V2#1-4 2.80 8.40 28.00

WEIRD WORLDS (Also see Ironwolf: Fires of the Revolution)
National Periodical Publications: Aug-Sept, 1972 - No. 9, Jan-Feb, 1974; No. 10, Oct-Nov, 1974 (All 20¢ issues)

1-Edgar Rice Burrough's John Carter Warlord of Mars & David Innes begin (1st DC app.); Kubert-c 2.00 6.00 18.00
2-4: 2-Infantino/Orlando-c. 3-Murphy Anderson-c. 4-Kaluta-a 1.50 4.50 12.00
5-7: .5-Kaluta-c. 7-Last John Carter. 1.10 3.30 9.00
8-10: 8-Iron Wolf begins by Chaykin (1st app.) 1.00 3.00 8.00
NOTE: ***Neal Adams*** *a-2i, 3i. John Carter by* ***Andersonin*** *#1-3.* ***Chaykin*** *c-7, 8.* ***Kaluta*** *a-4; c-4-6, 10.* ***Orlando*** *a-4i; c-2, 3, 4i.* ***Wrightson*** *a-2i, 4i.*

WELCOME BACK, KOTTER (TV) (See Limited Collectors' Edition #57)
National Periodical Publ./DC Comics: Nov, 1976 - No. 10, Mar-Apr, 1978

1-Sparling-a(p) 2.30 7.00 20.00
2-10: 3-Estrada-a 1.50 4.50 12.00

WELCOME SANTA (See March of Comics #63,183)

WELCOME TO THE LITTLE SHOP OF HORRORS
Roger Corman's Cosmic Comics: May, 1995 -No. 3, July, 1995 ($2.50, limited series)

1-3 2.50

WELLS FARGO (See Tales of...)

WENDY AND THE NEW KIDS ON THE BLOCK
Harvey Comics: Mar, 1991 - No. 3, July, 1991 ($1.25)

1-3 2.00

WENDY DIGEST
Harvey Comics: Oct, 1990 - No. 5, Mar, 1992 ($1.75, digest size)

1-5 4.00

WENDY PARKER COMICS
Atlas Comics (OMC): July, 1953 - No. 8, July, 1954

1 10.00 30.00 75.00
2 6.40 19.25 45.00
3-8 5.70 17.00 40.00

WENDY, THE GOOD LITTLE WITCH (TV)
Harvey Publ.: 8/60 - #82, 11/73; #83, 8/74 - #93, 4/76; #94, 9/90 - #97, 12/90

1-Wendy & Casper the Friendly Ghost begin 18.00 54.00 200.00
2 8.15 24.50 90.00
3-5 5.90 17.75 65.00
6-10 4.55 13.65 50.00
11-20 3.20 9.60 35.00
21-30 2.80 8.40 28.00
31-50 2.30 7.00 20.00
51-64,66-69 1.85 5.50 15.00
65 (2/71)-Wendy origin. 2.40 7.35 22.00
70-74: All 52 pg. Giants 2.30 7.00 20.00
75-93 1.10 3.30 9.00
94-97 (1990, $1.00-c): 94-Has #194 on-c 4.00
(See Casper the Friendly Ghost #20 & Harvey Hits #7, 16, 21, 23, 27, 30, 33)

WENDY THE GOOD LITTLE WITCH (2nd Series)
Harvey Comics: Apr, 1991 - No. 15, Aug, 1994 ($1.00/$1.25 #7-11/$1.50 #12-15)

1-15-Reprints Wendy & Casper stories. 12-Bunny app. 3.00

Werewolf By Night V2 #4 © MAR

Western Action #1 © Atlas/Seaboard Pub.

Western Comics #2 © DC

GD2.0 FN6.0 NM9

WENDY WITCH WORLD
Harvey Publications: 10/61; No. 2, 9/62 - No. 52, 12/73; No. 53, 9/74

1-(25¢, 68 pg. Giants begin) 12.00 36.00 130.00
2-5 5.90 17.75 65.00
6-10 3.65 11.00 40.00
11-20 3.00 9.00 32.00
21-30 2.50 7.50 25.00
31-39: 39-Last 68 pg. issue 2.30 7.00 20.00
40-45: 52 pg. issues 1.85 5.50 15.00
46-53 1.10 3.30 9.00

WEREWOLF (Super Hero) (Also see Dracula & Frankenstein)
Dell Publishing Co.: Dec, 1966 - No. 3, April, 1967

1-1st app. 2.50 7.50 25.00
2,3 2.00 6.00 16.00

WEREWOLF BY NIGHT (See Giant-Size..., Marvel Spotlight #2-4 & Power Record Comics)
Marvel Comics Group: Sept, 1972 - No. 43, Mar, 1977

1-Ploog-a cont'd. from Marvel Spotlight #4 7.25 21.75 80.00
2 3.00 9.00 32.00
3-5 2.50 7.50 25.00
6-10 2.00 6.00 16.00
11-14,16-20 1.50 4.50 12.00
15-New origin Werewolf; Dracula-c/story cont'd from Tomb of Dracula #18 2.00 6.00 18.00
21-31 1.00 3.00 8.00
32-Origin & 1st app. Moon Knight (8/75) 8.15 24.50 90.00
33-2nd app. Moon Knight 3.65 11.00 40.00
34-43: 35-Starlin/Wrightson-c. 37-Moon Knight app; part Wrightson-c 1.00 3.00 8.00
38,39-(30¢-c variants, limited distribution)(5,7/76) 1.50 4.50 12.00

NOTE: ***Bolle** a-6i. **G. Kane** a-11p, 12p; c-21, 22, 24-30, 34p. **Mooney** a-7i. **Ploog** 1-4p, 5, 6p, 7p, 13-16p; c-5-8, 13-16. **Reinman** a-8i. **Sutton** a(i)-9, 11, 16, 35.*

WEREWOLF BY NIGHT (Vol. 2, continues in Strange Tales #1 (9/98))
Marvel Comics Group: Feb, 1998 - No. 6, July, 1998 ($2.99)

1-6-Manco-a: 2-Two covers. 6-Ghost Rider-c/app. 3.00

WEREWOLVES & VAMPIRES (Magazine)
Charlton Comics: 1962 (One Shot)

1 7.65 23.00 85.00

WEST COAST AVENGERS
Marvel Comics Group: Sept, 1984 - No. 4, Dec, 1984 (lim. series, Mando paper)

1-Origin & 1st app. W.C. Avengers (Hawkeye, Iron Man, Mockingbird & Tigra) 4.00
2-4 3.00

WEST COAST AVENGERS (Becomes Avengers West Coast #48 on)
Marvel Comics Group: Oct, 1985 - No. 47, Aug, 1989

V2#1-41 2.00
42-47: 42-Byrne-a(p)/scripts begin. 46-Byrne-c; 1st app. Great Lakes Avengers 3.00
Annual 1-3 (1986-1988): 3-Evolutionary War app. 3.00
Annual 4 (1989, $2.00)-Atlantis Attacks; Byrne/Austin-a 3.00

WESTERN ACTION
I. W. Enterprises: No. 7, 1964

7-Reprints Cow Puncher #? by Avon 1.50 4.50 12.00

WESTERN ACTION
Atlas/Seaboard Publ.: Feb, 1975

1-Kid Cody by Wildey & The Comanche Kid stories; intro. The Renegade 2.40 6.00

WESTERN ACTION THRILLERS
Dell Publishers: Apr, 1937 (10¢, square binding; 100 pgs.)

1-Buffalo Bill, The Texas Kid, Laramie Joe, Two-Gun Thompson, & Wild West Bill app. 84.00 253.00 800.00

WESTERN ADVENTURES COMICS (Western Love Trails #7 on)
Ace Magazines: Oct, 1948 - No. 6, Aug, 1949

nn(#1)-Sheriff Sal, The Cross-Draw Kid, Sam Bass begin 22.00 66.00 175.0
nn(#2)(12/48) 11.00 33.00 90.0
nn(#3)(2/49)-Used in **SOTI**, pgs. 30,31 12.00 36.00 95.0
4-6 10.00 30.00 75.0

WESTERN BANDITS
Avon Periodicals: 1952 (Painted-c)

1-Butch Cassidy, The Daltons by Larsen; Kinstler-a; c-part-r/paperback Avon Western Novel #1 16.00 49.00 130.0

WESTERN BANDIT TRAILS (See Approved Comics)
St. John Publishing Co.: Jan, 1949 - No. 3, July, 1949

1-Tuska-a; Baker-c; Blue Monk, Ventrilo app. 25.00 75.00 200.0
2-Baker-c 19.00 56.00 150.0
3-Baker-c/a; Tuska-a 23.00 69.00 185.0

WESTERN COMICS (See Super DC Giant #15)
National Per. Publ: Jan-Feb, 1948 - No. 85, Jan-Feb, 1961 (1-27: 52pgs.)

1-Wyoming Kid & his horse Racer, The Vigilante in "Jesse James Rides Agair (Meskin-a), Cowboy Marshal, Rodeo Rick begin 79.00 237.00 750.0
2 40.00 120.00 350.0
3,4-Last Vigilante 36.00 108.00 290.0
5-Nighthawk & his horse Nightwind begin (not in #6); Captain Tootsie by Beck 30.00 90.00 240.0
6,7,9,10 23.00 69.00 185.0
8-Origin Wyoming Kid; 2 pg. pin-ups of rodeo queens 35.00 105.00 280.0
11-20 19.00 56.00 150.0
21-40: 24-Starr-a. 27-Last 52 pgs. 28-Flag-c 14.00 41.00 110.0
41,42,44-49: 49-Last precode issue (2/55) 12.50 37.50 100.0
43-Pow Wow Smith begins, ends #85 12.50 37.50 100.0
50-60 11.00 33.00 90.0
61-85-Last Wyoming Kid. 77-Origin Matt Savage Trail Boss. 82-1st app. Fleetfoot, Pow Wow's girlfriend 10.00 30.00 75.0

NOTE: ***G. Kane**, **Infantino** art in most. **Meskin** a-1-4. **Moreira** a-28-39. **Post** a-3-5.*

WESTERN CRIME BUSTERS
Trojan Magazines: Sept, 1950 - No. 10, Mar-Apr, 1952

1-Six-Gun Smith, Wilma West, K-Bar-Kate, & Fighting Bob Dale begin; headlight-a 35.00 105.00 280.0
2 18.00 54.00 145.0
3-5: 3-Myron Fass-c 18.00 53.00 140.0
6-Wood-a 34.00 101.00 270.0
7-Six-Gun Smith by Wood 34.00 101.00 270.0
8 18.00 53.00 140.0
9-Tex Gordon & Wilma West by Wood; Lariat Lucy app. 33.00 98.00 260.0
10-Wood-a 30.00 90.00 240.0

WESTERN CRIME CASES (Formerly Indian Warriors #7,8; becomes The Outlaws #10 on)
Star Publications: No. 9, Dec, 1951

9-White Rider & Super Horse; L. B. Cole-c 21.00 62.00 165.0

WESTERNER, THE (Wild Bill Pecos)
"Wanted" Comic Group/Toytown/Patches: No. 14, June, 1948 - No. 41, Dec 1951 (#14-31: 52 pgs.)

14 12.50 37.50 100.0
15-17,19-21: 19-Meskin-a 7.15 21.50 50.0
18,22-25-Krigstein-a 10.00 30.00 75.0
26(4/50)-Origin & 1st app. Calamity Kate, series ends #32; Krigstein-a 12.50 37.50 100.0
27-Krigstein-a(2) 12.00 36.00 95.0
28-41: 33-Quest app. 37-Lobo, the Wolf Boy begins 5.00 15.00 35.0

NOTE: ***Mort Lawrence** a-20-27, 29, 37, 39; c-19, 22-24, 26, 27. **Leav** c-14-18, 20, 31. **Syd Shores** a-39; c-34, 35, 37-41.*

WESTERNER, THE
Super Comics: 1964

Super Reprint 15-17: 15-r/Oklahoma Kid #? 16-r/Crack West. #65; Severin-c; Crandall-r. 17-r/Blazing Western #2; Severin-c 1.25 3.75 10.0

Western Fighters #4 © HILL

Western Hearts #3 © STD

Western Killers #64 © FOX

GD2.0 FN6.0 NM9.4

WESTERN FIGHTERS
Hillman Periodicals/Star Publ.: Apr-May, 1948 - V4#7, Mar-Apr, 1953 (#1-V3#2: 52 pgs.)

V1#1-Simon & Kirby-c 35.00 105.00 280.00
2-Not Kirby-a 10.00 30.00 70.00
3-Fuje-c 9.30 28.00 65.00
4-Krigstein, Ingels, Fuje-a 10.00 30.00 75.00
5,6,8,9,12 6.40 19.25 45.00
7,10-Krigstein-a 10.00 30.00 70.00
11-Williamson/Frazetta-a 30.00 90.00 240.00
V2#1-Krigstein-a 10.00 30.00 70.00
2-12: 4-Berg-a 5.00 15.00 32.00
V3#1-11,V4#1,4-7 5.00 15.00 30.00
12,V4#2,3-Krigstein-a 9.30 28.00 65.00
3-D 1(12/53, 25¢, Star Publ.)-Came w/glasses; L. B. Cole-c 38.00 113.00 300.00

NOTE: ***Kinstlerish*** *a-V2#6, 8, 9, 12; V3#2, 5-7, 11, 12; V4#1(plus cover).* ***McWilliams*** *a-11.* ***Powell*** *a-V2#2.* ***Reinman*** *a-1-12, V4#3.* ***Rowich*** *c-5, 6i.* ***Starr*** *a-5.*

WESTERN FRONTIER
P. L. Publishers: Apr-May, 1951 - No. 7, 1952

1 12.00 36.00 95.00
2 7.15 21.50 50.00
3-7 5.70 17.00 40.00

WESTERN GUNFIGHTERS (1st Series) (Apache Kid #11-19)
Atlas Comics (CPS): No. 20, June, 1956 - No. 27, Aug, 1957

20 12.00 36.00 95.00
21-Crandall-a 12.00 36.00 95.00
22-Wood & Powell-a 18.00 53.00 140.00
23,24: 23-Williamson-a. 24-Toth-a 12.00 36.00 95.00
25-27 10.00 30.00 70.00

NOTE: ***Berg*** *a-20.* ***Colan*** *a-20, 26, 27.* ***Crandall*** *a-21.* ***Heath*** *a-25.* ***Maneely*** *a-24, 25; c-22, 23, 25.* ***Morisi*** *a-24.* ***Morrow*** *a-26.* ***Pakula*** *a-23.* ***Severin*** *c-20, 27.* ***Torres*** *a-26.* ***Woodbridge*** *a-27.*

WESTERN GUNFIGHTERS (2nd Series)
Marvel Comics Group: Aug, 1970 - No. 33, Nov, 1975 (#1-6: 25¢, 68 pgs.)

1-Ghost Rider begins; Fort Rango, Renegades & Gunhawk app. 3.65 11.00 40.00
2-6: 2-Origin Nightwind (Apache Kid's horse) 2.50 7.50 24.00
7-(52 pgs) Origin Ghost Rider retold 2.40 7.35 22.00
8-14: 10-Origin Black Rider. 12-Origin Matt Slade 2.00 6.00 18.00
15-20 1.50 4.50 12.00
21-33 1.25 3.75 10.00

NOTE: ***Baker*** *r-2, 3.* ***Colan*** *r-2.* ***Drucker*** *r-3.* ***Everett*** *a-6i.* ***G. Kane*** *c-29, 31.* ***Kirby*** *a-1p(r), 5, 10-12; c-19, 21.* ***Kubert*** *r-2.* ***Maneely*** *r-2, 10.* ***Morrow*** *r-29.* ***Severin*** *c-10.* ***Shores*** *a-3, 4.* ***Barry Smith*** *a-4.* ***Steranko*** *c-14.* ***Sutton*** *a-1, 2i, 5, 4.* ***Torres*** *r-26('57).* ***Wildey*** *r-8, 9.* ***Williamson*** *r-2, 18.* ***Woodbridge*** *r-27('57). Renegades in #4, 5; Ghost Rider in #1-7.*

WESTERN HEARTS
Standard Comics: Dec, 1949 - No. 10, Mar, 1952 (All photo-c)

1-Severin-a; Whip Wilson & Reno Browne photo-c 21.00 62.00 165.00
2-Beverly Tyler & Jerome Courtland photo-c from movie "Palomino"; Williamson/Frazetta-a (2 pgs.) 20.00 60.00 160.00
3-Rex Allen photo-c 11.00 33.00 90.00
4-7,10-Severin & Elder, Al Carreno-a. 5-Ray Milland & Hedy Lamarr photo-c from movie "Copper Canyon". 6-Fred MacMurray & Irene Dunn photo-c from movie "Never a Dull Moment". 7-Jock Mahoney photo-c. 10-Bill Williams & Jane Nigh photo-c 11.00 33.00 90.00
8-Randolph Scott & Janis Carter photo-c from "Santa Fe"; Severin & Elder-a 11.00 33.00 90.00
9-Whip Wilson & Reno Browne photo-c; Severin & Elder-a 12.50 37.50 100.00

WESTERN HERO (Wow Comics #1-69; Real Western Hero #70-75)
Fawcett Publications: No. 76, Mar, 1949 - No. 112, Mar, 1952

76(#1, 52 pgs.)-Tom Mix, Hopalong Cassidy, Monte Hale, Gabby Hayes, Young Falcon (ends #78,80), & Big Bow and Little Arrow (ends #102,105) begin; painted-c begin 30.00 90.00 240.00
77 (52 pgs.) 16.00 49.00 130.00
78,80-82 (52 pgs.): 81-Capt. Tootsie by Beck 16.00 49.00 130.00
79,83 (36 pgs.): 83-Last painted-c 13.00 39.00 105.00
84-86,88-90 (52 pgs.): 84-Photo-c begin, end #112. 86-Last Hopalong Cassidy 14.00 41.00 110.00
87,91,95,99 (36 pgs.): 87-Bill Boyd begins, ends #95 12.00 36.00 95.00
92-94,96-98,101 (52 pgs.): 96-Tex Ritter begins. 101-Red Eagle app. 13.00 39.00 105.00
100 (52 pgs.) 14.00 41.00 110.00
102-111: 102-Begin 36 pg. issues 12.00 36.00 95.00
112-Last issue 13.00 39.00 105.00

NOTE: *1/2 to 1 pg. Rocky Lane (Carnation) in 80-83, 86, 88, 97. Photo covers feature Hopalong Cassidy #84, 86, 89; Tom Mix #85, 87, 90, 92, 94, 97; Monte Hale #88, 91, 93, 95, 98, 100, 104, 107, 110; Tex Ritter #96, 99, 101, 105, 108, 111; Gabby Hayes #103.*

WESTERN KID (1st Series)
Atlas Comics (CPC): Dec, 1954 - No. 17, Aug, 1957

1-Origin; The Western Kid (Tex Dawson), his stallion Whirlwind & dog Lightning begin 20.00 60.00 160.00
2 (2/55)-Last pre-code 10.00 30.00 80.00
3-8 10.00 30.00 70.00
9,10-Williamson-a in both (4 pgs. each) 10.00 30.00 75.00
11-17 7.15 21.50 50.00

NOTE: ***Ayers*** *a-6, 7.* ***Maneely*** *c-2-7, 10, 14.* ***Romita*** *a-1-17; c-1, 12.* ***Severin*** *c-17.*

WESTERN KID, THE (2nd Series)
Marvel Comics Group: Dec, 1971 - No. 5, Aug, 1972 (All 20¢ issues)

1-Reprints; Romita-c/a(3) 2.50 7.50 25.00
2,4,5: 2-Romita-a; Severin-c. 4-Everett-r 2.00 6.00 16.00
3-Williamson-a 2.30 7.00 20.00

WESTERN KILLERS
Fox Features Syndicate: nn, July?, 1948; No. 60, Sept, 1948 - No. 64, May, 1949; No. 6, July, 1949

nn(#59?)(nd, F&J Trading Co.)-Range Busters; formerly Blue Beetle #57? 24.00 71.00 190.00
60 (#1, 9/48)-Extreme violence; lingerie panel 26.00 79.00 210.00
61-Jack Cole, Starr-a 21.00 64.00 170.00
62-64, 6 19.00 56.00 150.00

WESTERN LIFE ROMANCES (My Friend Irma #3 on?)
Marvel Comics (IPP): Dec, 1949 - No. 2, Mar, 1950 (52 pgs.)

1-Whip Wilson & Reno Browne photo-c 19.00 56.00 150.00
2-Audie Murphy & Gale Storm photo-c; spanking scene 16.00 49.00 130.00

WESTERN LOVE
Prize Publ.: July-Aug, 1949 - No. 5, Mar-Apr, 1950 (All photo-c & 52 pgs.)

1-S&K-a; Randolph Scott photo-c from movie "Canadian Pacific" (see Prize Comics #76) 30.00 90.00 240.00
2,5-S&K-a: 2-Whip Wilson & Reno Browne photo-c. 5-Dale Robertson photo-c 23.00 69.00 185.00
3,4: 3-Reno Browne? photo-c 14.00 43.00 115.00

NOTE: ***Meskin & Severin/Elder*** *a-2-5.*

WESTERN LOVE TRAILS (Formerly Western Adventures)
Ace Magazines (A. A. Wyn): No. 7, Nov, 1949 - No. 9, Mar, 1950

7 11.00 33.00 90.00
8,9 10.00 30.00 70.00

WESTERN MARSHAL (See Steve Donovan…)
Dell Publishing Co.: No. 534, 2-4/54 - No. 640, 7/55 (Based on Ernest Haycox's "Trailtown")

Four Color 534 (#1)-Kinstler-a 5.00 15.00 60.00
Four Color 591 (10/54), 613 (2/55), 640-All Kinstler-a 4.60 13.75 55.00

WESTERN OUTLAWS (Junior Comics #9-16; My Secret Life #22 on)
Fox Features Syndicate: No. 17, Sept, 1948 - No. 21, May, 1949

17-Kamen-a; Iger shop-a in all; 1 pg. "Death and the Devil Pills" r-in Ghostly Weird #122 35.00 105.00 280.00
18-21 20.00 60.00 160.00

WESTERN OUTLAWS
Atlas Comics (ACI No. 1-14/WPI No. 15-21): Feb, 1954 - No. 21, Aug, 1957

1-Heath, Powell-a; Maneely hanging-c 21.00 62.00 165.00

Western Outlaws (2nd series) #3 © MAR

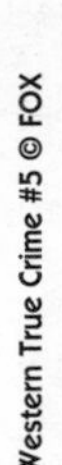
Western True Crime #5 © FOX

Wetworks #10 © WSP

GD2.0 FN6.0 NM9.4

2 11.00 33.00 90.00
3-10: 7-Violent-a by R.Q. Sale 9.30 28.00 65.00
11,14-Williamson-a in both (6 pgs. each) 10.00 30.00 80.00
12,18,20,21: Severin covers 8.65 26.00 60.00
13,15: 13-Baker-a. 15-Torres-a 9.30 28.00 65.00
16-Williamson text illo 8.65 26.00 60.00
17,19-Crandall-a. 17-Williamson text illo 9.30 28.00 65.00
NOTE: ***Ayers** a-7, 10, 18, 20. **Bolle** a-21. **Colan** a-5, 10, 11, 17. **Drucker** a-11. **Everett** a-9, 10. **Heath** a-1; c-3, 4, 8, 16. **Kubert** a-9p. **Maneely** a-13, 16, 17, 19; c-1, 5, 7, 9, 10, 12, 13. **Morisi** a-18. **Powell** a-3, 16. **Romita** a-7, 13. **Severin** a-8, 16, 19; c-17, 18, 20, 21. **Tuska** a-6, 15.*

WESTERN OUTLAWS & SHERIFFS (Formerly Best Western)
Marvel/Atlas Comics (IPC): No. 60, Dec, 1949 - No. 73, June, 1952
60 (52 pgs.) 22.00 66.00 175.00
61-65: 61-Photo-c 18.00 53.00 140.00
66-Story contains 5 hangings 18.00 53.00 140.00
68-72 13.00 39.00 105.00
67-Cannibalism story 18.00 53.00 140.00
73-Black Rider story; Everett-c 14.00 41.00 110.00
NOTE: ***Maneely** a-62, 67; c-62, 69-73. **Robinson** a-68. **Sinnott** a-70. **Tuska** a-69-71.*

WESTERN PICTURE STORIES (1st Western comic)
Comics Magazine Company: Feb, 1937 - No. 4, June, 1937
1-Will Eisner-a 168.00 505.00 1600.00
2-Will Eisner-a 100.00 300.00 950.00
3,4: 3-Eisner-a. 4-Caveman Cowboy story 79.00 237.00 750.00

WESTERN PICTURE STORIES (See Giant Comics Edition #6, 11)

WESTERN ROMANCES (See Target...)

WESTERN ROUGH RIDERS
Gillmor Magazines No. 1,4 (Stanmor Publ.): Nov, 1954 - No. 4, May, 1955
1 8.65 26.00 60.00
2-4 5.70 17.00 40.00

WESTERN ROUNDUP (See Dell Giants & Fox Giants)

WESTERN TALES (Formerly Witches...)
Harvey Publications: No. 31, Oct, 1955 - No. 33, July-Sept, 1956
31,32-All S&K-a; Davy Crockett app. in each 19.00 56.00 150.00
33-S&K-a; Jim Bowie app. 19.00 56.00 150.00
NOTE: *#32 & 33 contain Boy's Ranch reprints. **Kirby** c-31.*

WESTERN TALES OF BLACK RIDER (Formerly Black Rider; Gunsmoke Western #32 on)
Atlas Comics (CPS): No. 28, May, 1955 - No. 31, Nov, 1955
28 (#1): The Spider (a villain) dies 19.00 56.00 150.00
29-31 12.50 37.50 100.00
NOTE: ***Lawrence** a-30. **Maneely** c-28-30. **Severin** a-28. **Shores** c-31.*

WESTERN TEAM-UP
Marvel Comics Group: Nov, 1973 (20¢)
1-Origin & 1st app. The Dakota Kid; Rawhide Kid-r; Gunsmoke Kid-r by Jack Davis 3.00 9.00 30.00

WESTERN THRILLERS (My Past Confessions #7 on)
Fox Features Syndicate/M.S. Distr. No. 52: Aug, 1948 - No. 6, June, 1949; No. 52, 1954?
1- "Velvet Rose" (Kamenish-a); "Two-Gun Sal", "Striker Sisters" (all women outlaws issue); Brodsky-c 47.00 142.00 425.00
2 21.00 62.00 165.00
3,6 19.00 58.00 155.00
4,5-Bakerish-a; 5-Butch Cassidy app. 21.00 62.00 165.00
52-(Reprint, M.S. Dist.)-1954? No date given (becomes My Love Secret #53) 7.85 23.50 55.00

WESTERN THRILLERS (Cowboy Action #5 on)
Atlas Comics (ACI): Nov, 1954 - No. 4, Feb, 1955 (All-r/Western Outlaws & Sheriffs)
1 15.00 45.00 120.00
2-4 9.30 28.00 65.00
NOTE: ***Heath** c-3. **Maneely** a-1; c-2. **Powell** a-4. **Robinson** a-4. **Romita** c-4. **Tuska** a-2.*

WESTERN TRAILS (Ringo Kid Starring in...)
Atlas Comics (SAI): May, 1957 - No. 2, July, 1957

GD2.0 FN6.0 NM9.4

1-Ringo Kid app.; Severin-c 12.50 37.50 100.00
2-Severin-c 8.65 26.00 60.00
NOTE: ***Bolle** a-1, 2. **Maneely** a-1, 2. **Severin** c-1, 2.*

WESTERN TRUE CRIME (Becomes My Confessions)
Fox Features Syndicate: No. 15, Aug, 1948 - No. 6, June, 1949
15(#1)-Kamen-a; formerly Zoot #14 (5/48)? 31.00 94.00 250.00
16(#2)-Kamenish-a; headlight panels, violence 22.00 66.00 175.00
3-Kamen-a 24.00 73.00 195.00
4-6: 4-Johnny Craig-a 15.00 45.00 120.00

WESTERN WINNERS (Formerly All-Western Winners; becomes Black Rider #8 on & Romance Tales #7 on?)
Marvel Comics (CDS): No. 5, June, 1949 - No. 7, Dec, 1949
5-Two-Gun Kid, Kid Colt, Black Rider; Shores-c 33.00 98.00 260.00
6-Two-Gun Kid, Black Rider, Heath Kid Colt story; Captain Tootsie by C.C. Beck 28.00 83.00 220.00
7-Randolph Scott Photo-c w/true stories about the West 28.00 83.00 220.00

WEST OF THE PECOS (See Zane Grey, 4-Color #222)

WESTWARD HO, THE WAGONS (Disney)
Dell Publishing Co.: No. 738, Sept, 1956 (Movie)
Four Color 738-Fess Parker photo-c 8.35 25.00 100.00

WETWORKS (See WildC.A.T.S: Covert Action Teams #2)
Image Comics (WildStorm): June, 1994 - No. 43, Aug, 1998 ($1.95/$2.50)
1-"July" on-c; gatefold wraparound-c; Portacio/Williams-c/a 3.00
1-Chicago Comicon edition 2.40 6.00
1-(2/98, $4.95) "3-D Edition" w/glasses 5.00
2-4 2.50
2-Alternate Portacio-c, see Deathblow #5 2.40 6.00
5-7,9-24: 5-($2.50). 13-Portacio-c. 16-Fire From Heaven Pt. 4. 17-Fire From Heaven Pt. 11 2.50
8 ($1.95)-Newstand, Wildstorm Rising Pt. 7 2.00
8 ($2.50)-Direct Market, Wildstorm Rising Pt. 7 2.50
25-($3.95) 4.00
26-43: 32-Variant-c by Pat Lee & Charest. 39,40-Stormwatch app. 42-Gen 13 app. 2.50
Sourcebook 1 (10/94, $2.50)-Text & illustrations (no comics) 2.50
Voyager Pack (8/97, $3.50)- #32 w/Phantom Guard preview 3.50

WETWORKS/VAMPIRELLA (See Vampirella/Wetworks)
Image Comics (WildStorm Productions): July, 1997 ($2.95, one-shot)
1-Gil Kane-c 3.00

WHACK (Satire)
St. John Publishing Co. (Jubilee Publ.): Oct, 1953 - No. 3, May, 1954
1-(3-D, 25¢)-Kubert-a; Maurer-c; came w/glasses 31.00 94.00 250.00
2,3-Kubert-a in each. 2-Bing Crosby on-c; Mighty Mouse & Steve Canyon parodies. 3-Li'l Orphan Annie parody; Maurer-c 16.00 49.00 130.00

WHACKY (See Wacky)

WHAM COMICS (See Super Spy)
Centaur Publications: Nov, 1940 - No. 2, Dec, 1940
1-The Sparkler, The Phantom Rider, Craig Carter and his Magic Ring, Detecto, Copper Slug, Speed Silvers by Gustavson, Speed Centaur & Jon Linton (s/f) begin 158.00 474.00 1500.00
2-Origin Blue Fire & Solarman; The Buzzard app. 105.00 316.00 1000.00

WHAM-O GIANT COMICS
Wham-O Mfg. Co. : April, 1967 (98¢, newspaper size, one-shot)(Six issue subscription was advertised)
1-Radian & Goody Bumpkin by Wood; 1 pg. Stanley-a; Fine, Tufts-a; flying saucer reports; wraparound-c 6.30 19.00 75.00

WHAT IF? (1st Series) (What If? Featuring... #13 & #?-33)
Marvel Comics Group: Feb, 1977 - No. 47, Oct, 1984; June, 1988 (All 52 pgs.)
1-Brief origin Spider-Man, Fantastic Four 2.30 7.00 20.00
2-Origin The Hulk retold 1.25 3.75 10.00
3-5: 3-Avengers. 4-Invaders. 5-Capt. America 1.00 3.00 8.00
6-10,13,17: 8-Daredevil; Spidey parody. 9-Origins Venus, Marvel Boy, Human

What If...? (1st series) #42 © MAR

Whisper #14 © FC

White Chief of the Pawnee Indians nn © AVON

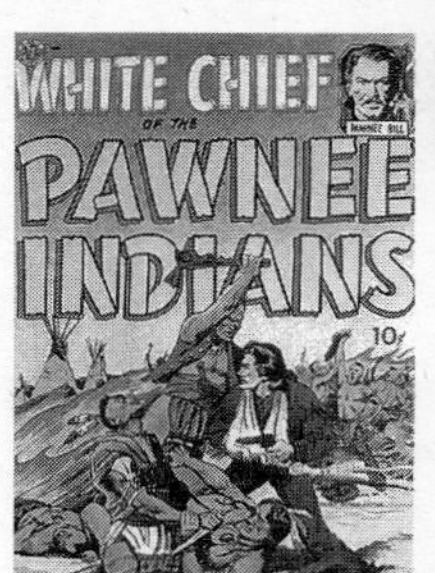

GD2.0 FN6.0 NM9.4

Robot, 3-D Man. 13-Conan app.; John Buscema-c/a(p). 17-Ghost Rider & Son of Satan app. 1.00 2.80 7.00
11,12,14-16: 11-Marvel Bullpen as F.F. 5.00
18-26,29: 18-Dr. Strange. 19-Spider-Man. 22-Origin Dr. Doom retold 4.00
27-X-Men app.; Miller-c 1.25 3.75 10.00
28-Daredevil by Miller; Ghost Rider app. 1.00 3.00 8.00
30-"What If...Spider-Man's Clone Had Lived?" 1.00 3.00 8.00
31-Begin $1.00-c; featuring Wolverine & the Hulk; X-Men app.; death of Hulk, Wolverine & Magneto 1.85 5.50 15.00
32-34,36-47: 32,36-Byrne-a. 34-Marvel crew each draw themselves. 37-Old X-Men & Silver Surfer app. 39-Thor battles Conan 4.00
35-What if Elektra had lived?; Miller/Austin-a. 5.00
Special 1 ($1.50, 6/88)-Iron Man, F.F., Thor app. 3.00

NOTE: ***Austin*** *a-27p, 32i, 34, 35i; c-35i, 36i.* ***J. Buscema*** *a-13p, 15p; c-10, 13p, 23p.* ***Byrne*** *a-32i, 36; c-36p.* ***Colan*** *a-21p; c-17p, 18p, 21p.* ***Ditko*** *a-35, Special 1.* ***Golden*** *c-29, 40-42.* ***Guice*** *a-40p.* ***Gil Kane*** *a-3p, 24p; c(p)-2-4, 7, 8.* ***Kirby*** *a-11p; c-9p, 11p.* ***Layton*** *a-32i, 33i; c-30, 32p, 33i, 34.* ***Mignola*** *c-39i.* ***Miller*** *a-28p, 32i, 34(1), 35p; c-27, 28p.* ***Mooney*** *a-8i, 30i.* ***Perez*** *a-15p.* ***Robbins*** *a-4p.* ***Sienkiewicz*** *c-43-46.* ***Simonson*** *a-15p, 32i.* ***Starlin*** *a-32i.* ***Stevens*** *a-8, 16i(part).* ***Sutton*** *a-2i, 18p, 28.* ***Tuska*** *a-5p.* ***Weiss*** *a-37p.*

WHAT IF...? (2nd Series)
Marvel Comics: V2#1, July, 1989 - No. 114, Nov, 1998 ($1.25/$1.50)

V2#1-...The Avengers Had Lost the Evol. War 4.00
2-5: 2-Daredevil, Punisher app. 3.00
6-X-Men app. 4.00
7-Wolverine app.; Liefeld-c/a(1st on Wolvie?) 5.00
8,10,11,13-15,17-30: 10-Punisher app. 11-Fantastic Four app.; McFarlane-c(i).13-Prof. X; Jim Lee-c. 14-Capt. Marvel; Lim/Austin-c.15-F.F.; Capullo-c/a(p). 17-Spider-Man/Kraven. 18-F.F. 19-Vision. 20,21-Spider-Man. 22-Silver Surfer by Lim/Austin-c/a 23-X-Men. 24-Wolverine; Punisher app. 25-(52 pgs.)-Wolverine app. 26-Punisher app. 27-Namor/F.F. 28,29-Capt. America. 29-Swipes cover to Avengers #4. 30-(52 pgs.)-Sue Richards/F.F. 3.00
9,12-X-Men 3.50
16-Wolverine battles Conan; Red Sonja app.; X-Men cameo 4.00
31-104: 31-Cosmic Spider-Man & Venom app.; Hobgoblin cameo. 32,33-Phoenix; X-Men app. 35-Fantastic Five (w/Spidey). 36-Avengers vs. Guardians of the Galaxy. 37-Wolverine; Thibert-c(i). 38-Thor; Rogers-p (part). 40-Storm; X-Men app. 41-(52 pgs.)-Avengers vs. Galactus. 42-Spider-Man. 43-Wolverine. 44-Venom/Punisher. 45-Ghost Rider. 46-Cable. 47-Magneto. 49-Infinity Gauntlet w/Silver Surfer & Thanos. 50-(52 pgs.)-Foil embossed-c; "What If Hulk Had Killed Wolverine" 52-Dr. Doom. 54-Death's Head. 57-Punisher as Shield. 58-"What if Punisher Had Killed Spider-Man" w/cover similar to Amazing S-M #129. 59-...Wolverine led Alpha Flight. 60-X-Men Wedding Album. 61-bound-in card sheet. 61,86,88-Spider-Man. 74,77,81,84,85-X-Men. 76-Last app. Watcher in title. 78-Bisley-c. 80-Hulk. 87-Sabretooth. 89-Fantastic Four. 90-Cyclops & Havok. 91-The Hulk. 93-Wolverine. 94-Juggernaut. 95-Ghost Rider. 97-Black Knight. 100-($2.99, double-sized) Gambit and Rogue, Fantastic Four 3.00
105-Spider-Girl debut; Sienkiewicz-a 2.50 7.50 20.00
106-114: 106-Gambit. 108-Avengers. 111-Wolverine. 114-Secret Wars 2.00
#(-1) Flashback(7/97) 3.00

WHAT'S NEW? - THE COLLECTED ADVENTURES OF PHIL & DIXIE'
Palliard Press: Oct, 1991 - No. 2, 1991 ($5.95, mostly color, sq.-bound, 52 pgs.)

1,2-By Phil Foglio 6.00

WHAT THE- -?!
Marvel Comics: Aug, 1988 - No. 26, 1993 ($1.25/$1.50/$2.50, semi-annual #5 on)

1-All contain parodies 3.00
2-24: 3-X-Men parody; Todd McFarlane-a. 5-Punisher/Wolverine parody; Jim Lee-a. 6-Punisher, Wolverine, Alpha Flight. 9-Wolverine. 16-EC back-c parody. 17-Wolverine/Punisher parody. 18-Star Trek parody w/Wolverine. 19-Punisher, Wolverine, Ghost Rider. 21-Weapon X parody. 22-Punisher/Wolverine parody 2.00
25-Summer Special 1 (1993, $2.50)-X-Men parody 2.50
26-Fall Special ($2.50, 68 pgs.)-Spider-Ham 2099-c/story; origin Silver Surfer; Hulk & Doomsday parody; indica reads "Winter Special." 2.50

NOTE: ***Austin*** *a-6i.* ***Byrne*** *a-2, 6, 10; c-2, 6-8, 10, 12, 13.* ***Golden*** *a-22.* ***Dale Keown*** *a-8p(8 pgs.).* ***McFarlane*** *a-3.* ***Rogers*** *c-15i, 16p.* ***Severin*** *a-2.* ***Staton*** *a-21p.* ***Williamson*** *a-2i.*

WHEE COMICS (Also see Gay, Smile & Tickle Comics)
Modern Store Publications: 1955 (7¢, 5x7-1/4", 52 pgs.)

GD2.0 FN6.0 NM9.4

1-Funny animal 4.15 12.50 25.00

WHEEDIES (See Panic #11 -EC Comics)

WHEELIE AND THE CHOPPER BUNCH (TV)
Charlton Comics: July, 1975 - No. 7, July, 1976 (Hanna-Barbera)

1-3: 1-Byrne text illo (see Nightmare for 1st art); Staton-a. 2-Byrne-a. 2,3-Mike Zeck text illos. 3-Staton-a; Byrne-c/a 2.40 7.35 22.00
4-7-Staton-a 1.75 5.25 14.00

WHEN KNIGHTHOOD WAS IN FLOWER (See The Sword & the Rose, 4-Color #505, 682)

WHEN SCHOOL IS OUT (See Wisco in Promotional Comics section)

WHERE CREATURES ROAM
Marvel Comics Group: July, 1970 - No. 8, Sept, 1971

1-Kirby/Ayers-c/a(r) 2.80 8.40 28.00
2-8-Kirby-c/a(r) 2.00 6.00 18.00

NOTE: ***Ditko*** *r-1-6, 7.* ***Heck*** *r-2, 5. All contain pre super-hero reprints.*

WHERE IN THE WORLD IS CARMEN SANDIEGO (TV)
DC Comics: June, 1996 - No. 4, Dec, 1996 ($1.75)

1-4: Adaptation of TV show 2.00

WHERE MONSTERS DWELL
Marvel Comics Group: Jan, 1970 - No. 38, Oct, 1975

1-Kirby/Ditko-r; all contain pre super-hero-r 3.00 9.00 30.00
2-10: 4-Crandall-a(r) 2.00 6.00 18.00
11,13-20: 11-Last 15¢ issue. 18,20-Starlin-c 1.75 5.25 14.00
12-Giant issue (52 pgs.) 2.50 7.50 24.00
21-37 1.50 4.50 12.00
38-Williamson-r/World of Suspense #3 1.75 5.25 14.00

NOTE: ***Colan*** *r-12.* ***Ditko*** *a(r)-4, 6, 8, 10, 12, 17-19, 23-25, 37.* ***Kirby*** *r-1-3, 5-16, 18-27, 30-32, 34-36, 38; c-12?* ***Reinman*** *a-3r, 4r, 12r.* ***Severin*** *c-15.*

WHERE'S HUDDLES? (TV) (See Fun-In #9)
Gold Key: Jan, 1971 - No. 3, Dec, 1971 (Hanna-Barbera)

1 2.80 8.40 28.00
2,3: 3-r/most #1 2.00 6.00 16.00

WHIP WILSON (Movie star) (Formerly Rex Hart; Gunhawk #12 on; see Western Hearts, Western Life Romances, Western Love)
Marvel Comics: No. 9, April, 1950 - No. 11, Sept, 1950 (#9,10: 52 pgs.)

9-Photo-c; Whip Wilson & his horse Bullet begin; origin Bullet; issue #23 listed on splash page; cover changed to #9 58.00 174.00 550.00
10,11: Both have photo-c. 11-36 pgs. 36.00 108.00 290.00
I.W. Reprint #1(1964)-Kinstler-c; r-Marvel #11 2.80 8.40 28.00

WHIRLWIND COMICS (Also see Cyclone Comics)
Nita Publication: June, 1940 - No. 3, Sept, 1940

1-Origin & 1st app. Cyclone; Cyclone-c 158.00 474.00 1500.00
2,3: Cyclone-c 100.00 300.00 950.00

WHIRLYBIRDS (TV)
Dell Publishing Co.: No. 1124, Aug, 1960 - No. 1216, Oct-Dec, 1961

Four Color 1124 (#1)-Photo-c 8.35 25.00 100.00
Four Color 1216-Photo-c 7.50 22.50 90.00

WHISPER (Female Ninja)
Capital Comics: Dec, 1983 - No. 2, 1984 ($1.75, Baxter paper)

1,2: 1-Origin; Golden-c, Special (11/85, $2.50) 2.50

WHISPER (Vol. 2)
First Comics: Jun, 1986 - No. 37, June, 1990 ($1.25/$1.75/$1.95)

1-37 2.00

WHITE CHIEF OF THE PAWNEE INDIANS
Avon Periodicals: 1951

nn-Kit West app.; Kinstler-c 16.00 48.00 125.00

WHITE EAGLE INDIAN CHIEF (See Indian Chief)

WHITE FANG
Disney Comics: 1990 ($5.95, 68 pgs.)

nn-Graphic novel adapting new Disney movie 6.00

WHITE INDIAN

White Princess of the Jungle #2 © AVON

Whiz Comics #48 © FAW

Who's Who in Star Trek #1 © Paramount

GD2.0 FN6.0 NM9.4 GD2.0 FN6.0 NM9.4

Magazine Enterprises: No. 11, July, 1953 - No. 15, 1954

11(A-1 94), 12(A-1 101), 13(A-1 104)-Frazetta-r(Dan Brand) in all from Durango Kid. 11-Powell-c 23.00 68.00 180.00
14(A-1 117), 15(A-1 135)-Check-a; Torres-a-#15 11.00 33.00 90.00

NOTE: *#11 contains reprints from Durango Kid #1-4; #12 from #5, 9, 10, 11; #13 from #7, 12, 13, 16. #14 & 15 contain all new stories.*

WHITEOUT
Oni Press: July, 1998 - No. 4, Nov, 1998 ($2.95, B&W, limited series)

1-4: 1-Matt Wagner-c. 2-Mignola-c. 3-Gibbons-c 3.00
TPB (5/99, $10.95) r/#1-4; Miller-c 11.00

WHITEOUT: MELT
Oni Press: Sept, 1999 - No. 4, Feb, 2000 ($2.95, B&W, limited series)

1-4-Greg Rucka-s/Steve Lieber-a 3.00

WHITE PRINCESS OF THE JUNGLE (Also see Jungle Adventures & Top Jungle Comics)
Avon Periodicals: July, 1951 - No. 5, Nov, 1952

1-Origin of White Princess (Taanda) & Capt'n Courage (r); Kinstler-c 53.00 160.00 480.00
2-Reprints origin of Malu, Slave Girl Princess from Avon's Slave Girl Comics #1 w/Malu changed to Zora; Kinstler-c/a(2) 40.00 120.00 350.00
3-Origin Blue Gorilla; Kinstler-c/a 36.00 108.00 290.00
4-Jack Barnum, White Hunter app.; r/Sheena #9 30.00 90.00 240.00
5-Blue Gorilla by McCann?; Kinstler inside-c; Fawcette/Alascia-a(3) 33.00 98.00 260.00

WHITE RIDER AND SUPER HORSE (Formerly Humdinger V2#2; Indian Warriors #7 on; also see Blue Bolt #1, 4Most & Western Crime Cases)
Novelty-Star Publications/Accepted Publ.: No. 4, 9/50 - No. 6, 3/51

4-6-Adapts "The Last of the Mohicans". 4(#1)-(9/50)-Says #11 on inside 16.00 49.00 130.00
Accepted Reprint #5(r/#5),6 (nd); L.B. Cole-c 8.65 26.00 60.00

NOTE: *All have **L. B. Cole** covers.*

WHITE WILDERNESS (Disney)
Dell Publishing Co.: No. 943, Oct, 1958

Four Color 943-Movie 5.85 17.50 70.00

WHITMAN COMIC BOOK, A
Whitman Publishing Co.: Sept., 1962 (136 pgs.; 7-3/4x5-3/4; hardcover) (B&W)

1-3,5,7: 1-Yogi Bear. 2-Huckleberry Hound. 3-Mr. Jinks and Pixie & Dixie. 5-Augie Doggie & Loopy de Loop. 7-Bugs Bunny-r from #47,51,53,54 & 55 6.35 19.00 70.00
4,6: 4-The Flintstones. 6-Snooper & Blabber Fearless Detectives/ Quick Draw McGraw of the Wild West 7.25 21.75 80.00
8-Donald Duck-reprints most of WDC&S #209-213. Includes 5 Barks stories, 1 complete Mickey Mouse serial by Paul Murry & 1 Mickey Mouse serial missing the 1st episode 8.15 24.50 90.00

NOTE: *Hanna-Barbera #1-6(TV), reprints of British tabloid comics. Dell reprints-#7,8.*

WHIZ COMICS (Formerly Flash & Thrill Comics #1)(See 5 Cent Comics)
Fawcett Publications: No. 2, Feb, 1940 - No. 155, June, 1953

GD2.0 FN6.0 VF8.0 NM9.4

1-(nn on cover, #2 inside)-Origin & 1st newsstand app. Captain Marvel (formerly Captain Thunder) by C. C. Beck (created by Bill Parker), Spy Smasher, Golden Arrow, Ibis the Invincible, Dan Dare, Scoop Smith, Sivana, & Lance O'Casey begin 7,000.00 21,000.00 38,500.00 72,000.00
(The only Mint copy sold in 1995 for $176,000 cash)

1-Reprint, oversize 13-1/2x10". **WARNING**: This comic is an exact duplicate reprint (except for dropping "Gangway for Captain Marvel" from-c) of the original except for its size. DC published it in 1974 with a second cover titling it as a Famous First Edition. There have been many reported cases of the outer cover being removed and the interior sold as the original edition. The reprint with the new outer cover removed is practically worthless. See Famous First Edition for value.

GD2.0 FN6.0 NM9.4

2-(3/40, nn on cover, #3 inside); cover to Flash #1 redrawn, pg. 12, panel 4; Spy Smasher reveals I.D. to Eve 435.00 1305.00 5000.00
3-(4/40, #3 on-c, #4 inside)-1st app. Beautia 305.00 915.00 3200.00
4-(5/40, #4 on cover, #5 inside)-Brief origin Capt. Marvel retold 284.00 853.00 2700.00
5-Captain Marvel wears button-down flap on splash page only 232.00 695.00 2200.00
6-10: 7-Dr. Voodoo begins (by Raboy-#9-22) 174.00 521.00 1650.00
11-14: 12-Capt. Marvel does not wear cape 121.00 363.00 1150.00
15-Origin Sivana; Dr. Voodoo by Raboy 132.00 395.00 1250.00
16-18-Spy Smasher battles Captain Marvel 126.00 379.00 1200.00
19,20 84.00 253.00 800.00
21-(9/41)-Origin & 1st cover app. Lt. Marvels, the 1st team in Fawcett comics. In this issue, Capt. Death similar to Ditko's later Dr. Strange 89.00 268.00 850.00
22-24: 23-Only Dr. Voodoo by Tuska 68.00 205.00 650.00
25-(12/41)-Captain Nazi jumps from Master Comics #21 to take on Capt. Marvel solo after being beaten by Capt. Marvel/Bulletman team, causing the creation of Capt. Marvel Jr.; 1st app./origin of Capt. Marvel Jr. (part II of trilogy origin by CC. Beck & Mac Raboy); Captain Marvel sends Jr. back to Master #22 to aid Bulletman against Capt. Nazi; origin Old Shazam in text. 522.00 1565.00 6000.00
26-30 61.00 182.00 575.00
31,32: 32-1st app. The Trolls; Hitler/Mussolini satire by Beck 53.00 158.00 475.00
33-Spy Smasher, Captain Marvel x-over on cover and inside 61.00 182.00 575.00
34,36-40: 37-The Trolls app. by Swayze 40.00 120.00 340.00
35-Captain Marvel & Spy Smasher-c 50.00 150.00 450.00
41-50: 43-Spy Smasher, Ibis, Golden Arrow x-over in Capt. Marvel. 44-Flag-c. 47-Origin recap (1 pg.) 35.00 105.00 280.00
51-60: 52-Capt. Marvel x-over in Ibis. 57-Spy Smasher, Golden Arrow, Ibis cameo 29.00 86.00 230.00
61-70 26.00 79.00 210.00
71,77-80 24.00 71.00 190.00
72-76-Two Captain Marvel stories in each; 76-Spy Smasher becomes Crime Smasher 24.00 73.00 195.00
81-99: 86-Captain Marvel battles Sivana Family; robot-c. 91-Infinity-c 24.00 71.00 190.00
100-(8/48)-Anniversary issue 28.00 84.00 225.00
101-106: 102-Commando Yank app. 106-Bulletman app. 23.00 68.00 180.00
107-152: 107-Capitol Building photo-c. 108-Brooklyn Bridge photo-c. 112-Photo-c. 139-Infinity-c. 140-Flag-c. 142-Used in **POP**, pg. 89 23.00 68.00 180.00
153-155-(Scarce):154,155-1st/2nd Dr. Death stories 33.00 98.00 260.00

NOTE: ***C.C. Beck** Captain Marvel-No. 25(part). **Krigstein** Golden Arrow-No. 75, 78, 91, 95, 96, 98-100. **Mac Raboy** Dr. Voodoo-No. 9-22. Captain Marvel-No. 25(part). **M.Swayze** a-37, 38, 59; c-38. **Schaffenberger** c-138-158(most). **Wolverton** 1/2 pg. "Culture Corner"-No. 65-67, 68(2 1/2 pgs), 70-85, 87-96, 98-100, 102-109, 112-121, 123, 125, 126, 128-131, 133, 134, 136, 142, 143, 146.*

WHOA, NELLIE (Also see Love & Rockets)
Fantagraphics Books: July, 1996 - No. 3, Sept, 1996 ($2.95, B&W, lim. series)

1-3: Jamie Hernandez-c/a/scripts 3.00

WHODUNIT
D.S. Publishing Co.: Aug-Sept, 1948 - No. 3, Dec-Jan, 1948-49 (#1,2: 52 pgs.)

1-Baker-a (7 pgs.) 25.00 75.00 200.00
2,3-Detective mysteries 12.00 36.00 95.00

WHODUNNIT?
Eclipse Comics: June, 1986 - No. 3, Apr, 1987 ($2.00, limited series)

1-3: Spiegle-a. 2-Gulacy-c 2.00

WHO FRAMED ROGER RABBIT (See Marvel Graphic Novel)

WHO IS NEXT?
Standard Comics: No. 5, Jan, 1953

5-Toth, Sekowsky, Andru-a; crime stories 20.00 60.00 160.00

WHO IS THE CROOKED MAN?
Crusade: Sept, 1996 ($3.50, B&W, 40 pgs.)

1-Intro The Martyr, Scarlet 7 & Garrison 3.50

WHO'S MINDING THE MINT? (See Movie Classics)

WHO'S WHO IN STAR TREK
DC Comics: Mar, 1987 - #2, Apr, 1987 ($1.50, limited series)

1,2 2.40 6.00

The Wicked #1 © Avalon Studios

Wild Animals #1 © Pacific Comics

Wild Boy of the Congo #9 © Z-D

GD2.0 FN6.0 NM9.4

NOTE: **Byrne** *a-1, 2.* **Chaykin** *c-1, 2.* **Morrow** *a-1, 2.* **McFarlane** *a-2.* **Perez** *a-1, 2.* **Sutton** *a-1, 2.*

WHO'S WHO IN THE LEGION OF SUPER-HEROES
DC Comics: Apr, 1987 - No. 7, Nov, 1988 ($1.25, limited series)
1-7 4.00

WHO'S WHO: THE DEFINITIVE DIRECTORY OF THE DC UNIVERSE
DC Comics: Mar, 1985 - No. 26, Apr, 1987 (Maxi-series, no ads)
1-DC heroes from A-Z 4.00
2-26: All have 1-2 pgs-a by most DC artists 4.00
NOTE: **Art Adams** *a-4, 11, 18, 20.* **Anderson** *a-1-5, 7-12, 14, 15, 19, 21, 23-25.* **Aparo** *a-2, 3, 9, 10, 12, 13, 14, 15, 17, 18, 21, 23.* **Byrne** *a-4, 7, 14, 16, 18i, 19, 22i, 24; c-22.* **Cowan** *a-3-5, 8, 10-13, 16-18, 22-25.* **Ditko** *a-19-22.* **Evans** *a-20.* **Giffen** *a-1, 3,-6, 8, 13, 15, 17, 18, 23.* **Grell** *a-6, 9, 14, 20, 23, 25, 26.* **Infantino** *a-1-10, 12, 15, 17-22, 24, 25.* **Kaluta** *a-14, 21.* **Gil Kane** *a-1-11, 13, 14, 16, 19, 21-23, 25.* **Kirby** *a-2-6, 8-18, 20, 22, 25.* **Kubert** *a-2, 3, 7-11, 19, 20, 25.* **Erik Larsen** *a-24.* **McFarlane** *a-10-12, 17, 19, 25, 26.* **Morrow** *a-4, 7, 25, 26.* **Orlando** *a-1, 4, 10, 11, 21i.* **Perez** *a-1-5, 8-19, 22-26; c-1-4, 13-18.* **Rogers** *a-1, 2, 5-7, 11, 12, 15, 24.* **Starlin** *a-13, 14, 16.* **Stevens** *a-4, 7, 18.*

WHO'S WHO UPDATE '87
DC Comics: Aug, 1987 - No. 5, Dec, 1987 ($1.25, limited series)
1-5: Contains art by most DC artists 3.00
NOTE: **Giffen** *a-1.* **McFarlane** *a-1-4; c-4.* **Perez** *a-1-4.*

WHO'S WHO UPDATE '88
DC Comics: Aug, 1988 - No. 4, Nov, 1988 ($1.25, limited series)
1-4: Contains art by most DC artists 3.00
NOTE: **Giffen** *a-1.* **Erik Larsen** *a-1.*

WICKED, THE
Avalon Studios: Dec, 1999 - No. 7, Aug, 2000 ($2.95)
Preview-(7/99, $5.00, B&W) 5.00
1-7-Anacleto-c/Martinez-a 2.95
...: Medusa's Tale (11/00, $3.95, one shot) story plus pin-up gallery 3.95

WILBUR COMICS (Teen-age) (Also see Laugh Comics, Laugh Comix, Liberty Comics #10 & Zip Comics)
MLJ Magazines/Archie Publ. No. 8, Spring, 1946 on: Sum', 1944 - No. 87, 11/59; No. 88, 9/63; No. 89, 10/64; No. 90, 10/65 (No. 1-46: 52 pgs.) (#1-11 are quarterly)
1 50.00 150.00 450.00
2(Fall, 1944) 28.00 84.00 225.00
3,4(Wint, '44-45; Spr, '45) 20.00 60.00 160.00
5-1st app. Katy Keene (Sum, '45) & begin series; Wilbur story same as Archie story in Archie #1 except Wilbur replaces Archie 74.00 221.00 700.00
6-10: 10-(Fall, 1946) 19.00 56.00 150.00
11-20 11.00 33.00 90.00
21-30: 30-(4/50) 8.65 26.00 60.00
31-50 6.40 19.25 45.00
51-70 5.00 15.00 35.00
71-90: 88-Last 10¢ issue (9/63) 2.50 7.50 25.00
NOTE: *Katy Keene in No. 5-56, 58-69.* **Al Fagaly** *c-6-9, 12-24 at least.* **Vigoda** *c-2.*

WILD
Atlas Comics (IPC): Feb, 1954 - No. 5, Aug, 1954
1 26.00 79.00 210.00
2 15.00 45.00 120.00
3-5 12.50 37.50 100.00
NOTE: **Berg** *a-5; c-4.* **Burgos** *c-3.* **Colan** *a-4.* **Everett** *a-1-3.* **Heath** *a-2, 3, 5.* **Maneely** *a-1-3, 5; c-1, 5.* **Post** *a-2, 5.* **Ed Win** *a-1, 3.*

WILD (This Magazine Is...) (Satire)
Dell Publishing Co.: Jan, 1968 - No. 3, 1968 (Magazine, 52 pgs.)
1-3 2.00 6.00 18.00

WILD ANIMALS
Pacific Comics: Dec, 1982 ($1.00, one-shot, direct sales)
1-Funny animal; Sergio Aragones-a; Shaw-c/a 4.00

WILD BILL ELLIOTT (Also see Western Roundup under Dell Giants)
Dell Publishing Co.: No. 278, 5/50 - No. 643, 7/55 (No #11,12) (All photo-c)
Four Color 278(#1, 52pgs.)-Titled "Bill Elliott"; Bill & his horse Stormy begin; photo front/back-c begin 12.50 37.50 150.00
2 (11/50), 3 (52 pgs.) 6.70 20.00 80.00
4-10(10-12/52) 4.60 13.75 55.00
Four Color 472(6/53),520(12/53)-Last photo back-c 4.10 12.30 45.00
13(4-6/54) - 17(4-6/55) 3.65 11.00 40.00
Four Color 643 (7/55) 3.20 9.60 35.00

WILD BILL HICKOK (Also see Blazing Sixguns)
Avon Periodicals: Sept-Oct, 1949 - No. 28, May-June, 1956
1-Ingels-c 23.00 69.00 185.00
2-Painted-c; Kit West app. 11.00 33.00 90.00
3-5-Painted-c (4-Cover by Howard Winfield) 8.65 26.00 60.00
6-10,12: 8-10-Painted-c. 12-Kinsler-c? 8.65 26.00 60.00
11,13,14-Kinstler-c/a (#11-c & inside-f/c art only) 9.30 28.00 65.00
15,17,18,20: 18-Kit West story. 20-Kit West by Larsen 6.40 19.25 45.00
16-Kamen-a; r-3 stories/King of the Badmen of Deadwood 7.15 21.50 50.00
19-Meskin-a 6.40 19.25 45.00
21-Reprints 2 stories/Chief Crazy Horse 5.70 17.00 40.00
22-McCann-a?; r/Sheriff Bob Dixon's... 5.70 17.00 40.00
23-27: 23-Kinstler-c. 24-27-Kinstler-c/a(r) (24,25-r?) 6.00 18.00 42.00
28-Kinstler-c/a (new); r-/Last of the Comanches 6.00 18.00 42.00
I.W. Reprint #1-r/#2; Kinstler-c 1.75 5.25 14.00
Super Reprint #10-12: 10-r/#18. 11-r/#?. 12-r/#8 1.75 5.25 14.00
NOTE: *#23, 25 contain numerous editing deletions in both art and script due to code.* **Kinstler** *c-6, 7, 11-14, 17, 18, 20-22, 24-28.* **Howard Larsen** *a-1, 2, 4, 5, 6(3), 7-9, 11, 12, 17, 18, 20-24, 26.* **Meskin** *a-7.* **Reinman** *a-6, 17.*

WILD BILL HICKOK AND JINGLES (TV)(Formerly Cowboy Western) (Also see Blue Bird)
Charlton Comics: No. 68, Aug, 1958 - No. 75, Dec, 1959
68,69-Williamson-a (all are 10¢ issues) 10.00 30.00 75.00
70-Two pgs. Williamson-a 7.15 21.50 50.00
71-75 (#76, exist?) 5.00 15.00 30.00

WILD BILL PECOS WESTERN (Also see The Westerner)
AC Comics: 1989 ($3.50, 1/2 color/1/2 B&W, 52 pgs.)
1-Syd Shores-c/a(r)/Westerner; photo back-c 4.00

WILD BOY OF THE CONGO (Also see Approved Comics)
Ziff-Davis No. 10-12,4-8/St. John No. 9,11 on: No. 10, 2-3/51 - No. 12, 8-9/51; No. 4, 10-11/51 - No. 9, 10/53; No. 11-#15,6/55 (No #10, 1953)
10(#1)(2-3/51)-Origin; bondage-c by Saunders (painted); used in **SOTI**, pg. 189; painted-c begin, end #9 22.00 66.00 175.00
11(4-5/51),12(8-9/51)-Norman Saunders painted-c 12.00 36.00 95.00
4(10-11/51)-Saunders painted bondage-c 12.00 36.00 95.00
5(Winter,'51)-Saunders painted-c 10.00 30.00 80.00
6,8,9(10/53): 6-Saunders-c. 6-9-Painted-c 10.00 30.00 80.00
7(8-9/52)-Kinstler-a 12.00 36.00 95.00
11-13-Baker-c. 11-r/#7 w/new Baker-c; Kinstler-a (2 pgs.) 12.50 37.50 100.00
14(4/55)-Baker-c; r-#12('51) 12.50 37.50 100.00
15(6/55) 10.00 30.00 70.00

WILDCAT (See Sensation Comics #1)

WILDC.A.T.S ADVENTURES (TV cartoon)
Image Comics (WildStorm): Sept, 1994 - No. 10, June, 1995 ($1.95/$2.50)
1-10 2.50
Sourcebook 1 (1/95, $2.95) 3.00

WILDC.A.T.S: COVERT ACTION TEAMS
Image Comics (WildStorm Productions): Aug, 1992 - No. 4, Mar, 1993; No. 5, Nov, 1993 - No. 50, June, 1998 ($1.95/$2.50)
1-1st app; Jim Lee/Williams-c/a & Lee scripts begin; contains 2 trading cards (Two diff versions of cards inside); 1st WildStorm Productions title 4.50
1-All gold foil signed edition 12.00
1-All gold foil unsigned edition 8.00
1-Newsstand edition w/o cards 3.00
1-"3-D Special"(8/97, $4.95) w/3-D glasses; variant-c by Jim Lee 5.00
2-($2.50)-Prism foil stamped-c; contains coupon for Image Comics #0 & 4 pg. preview to Portacio's Wetworks (back-up) 4.50
2-With coupon missing 2.00
2-Direct sale misprint w/o foil-c 3.00

Wildcats V2 #8 © WSP

Wildcore #2 © WSP

Wild Frontier #1 © CC

GD2.0 FN6.0 NM9.4

2-Newsstand ed., no prism or coupon 2.00
3-Lee/Liefeld-c (1/93-c, 12/92 inside) 3.50
4-($2.50)-Polybagged w/Topps trading card; 1st app. Tribe by Johnson & Stroman; Youngblood cameo 3.50
4-Variant w/red card 2.40 6.00
5-7-Jim Lee/Williams-c/a; Lee script 3.00
8-X-Men's Jean Grey & Scott Summers cameos 4.00
9-12: 10-1st app. Huntsman & Soldier; Claremont scripts begin, ends #13. 11-1st app. Savant, Tapestry & Mr. Majestic. 3.00
11-Alternate Portacio-c, see Deathblow #5 5.00
13-19,21-24: 15-James Robinson scripts begin, ends #20. 15,16-Black Razor story. 21-Alan Moore scripts begin, end #34; intro Tao & Ladytron; new WildC.A.T.S team forms (Mr. Majestic, Savant, Condition Red (Max Cash), Tao & Ladytron). 22-Maguire-a 3.00
20-($2.50)-Direct Market, WildStorm Rising Pt. 2 w/bound-in card 3.00
20-($1.95)-Newsstand, WildStorm Rising Part 2 2.00
25-($4.95)-Alan Moore script; wraparound foil-c. 5.00
26-49: 29-(5/96)-Fire From Heaven Pt 7; reads Apr on-c. 30-(6/96)-Fire From Heaven Pt. 13; Spartan revealed to have transplanted personality of John Colt (from Team One: WildC.A.T.S). 31-(9/96)-Grifter rejoins team; Ladytron dies 2.50
40-($3.50)Voyager Pack bagged w/Divine Right preview 2.40 6.00
50-($3.50) Stories by Robinson/Lee, Choi & Peterson/Benes, and Moore/Charest; Charest sketchbook; Lee wraparound-c 4.00
50-Chromium cover 6.00
Annual 1 (2/98, $2.95) Robinson-s 3.00
Compendium (1993, $9.95)-r/#1-4; bagged w/#0 10.00
Sourcebook 1 (9/93, $2.50)-Foil embossed-c 2.50
Sourcebook 1-($1.95)-Newsstand ed. w/o foil embossed-c 2.00
Sourcebook 2 (11/94, $2.50)-wraparound-c 2.50
Special 1 (11/93, $3.50, 52 pgs.)-1st Travis Charest WildC.A.T.S-a 3.50
...A Gathering of Eagles (5/97, $9.95, TPB) r/#10-12 10.00
...Gang War ('98, $16.95, TPB) r/#28-34 17.00
...Homecoming (8/98, $19.95, TPB) r/#21-27 20.00

WILDCATS
DC Comics (WildStorm Productions): Mar, 1999 - Present ($2.50, bi-monthly)

1-Charest-a; six covers by Lee, Adams, Bisley, Campbell, Madureira and, Ramos; Lobdell-s 3.00
1-($6.95) DF Edition; variant cover by Ramos 7.00
2-19: 2-Voodoo cover. 3-Bachalo variant-c. 5-Hitch-a. 7-Meglia-a. 8-Phillips-a begins. 17,19-J.G. Jones-c. 18-Jim Lee-c 2.50
Annual 2000 (12/00, $3.50) Bermejo-a; Devil's Night x-over 3.50
... Ladytron (10/00, $5.95) Origin; Casey-s/Canete-a 5.95
... Mosaic (2/00, $3.95) Tuska-a (10 pg. back-up story) 3.95
...: Street Smart ('00, $24.95, HC) r/#1-6; Charest-c 24.95

WILDC.A.T.S/ ALIENS
Image Comics/Dark Horse: Aug, 1998 ($4.95, one-shot)

1-Ellis-s/Sprouse-a/c; Aliens invade Skywatch; Stormwatch app.; death of Winter; destruction of Skywatch 1.00 3.00 8.00
1-Variant-c by Gil Kane 1.25 3.75 10.00

WILDC.A.T.S: SAVANT GARDE FAN EDITION
Image Comics/WildStorm Productions: Feb, 1997 - No. 3, Apr, 1997 (Giveaway, 8 pgs.) (Polybagged w/Overstreet's FAN)

1-3: Barbara Kesel-s/Christian Uche-a(p) 3.00
1-3-(Gold): All retailer incentives 10.00

WILDC.A.T.S TRILOGY
Image Comics (WildStorm Productions): June, 1993 - No. 3, Dec, 1993 ($1.95, limited series)

1-($2.50)-1st app. Gen 13 (Fairchild, Burnout, Grunge, Freefall) Multi-color foil-c; Jae Lee-c/a in all 5.00
1-($1.95)-Newsstand ed. w/o foil-c 2.00
2,3-($1.95)-Jae Lee-c/a 2.00

WILDC.A.T.S/ X-MEN: THE GOLDEN AGE
Image Comics (WildStorm Productions): Feb, 1997 ($4.50, one-shot)

1-Lobdell-s/Charest-a; Two covers(Charest, Jim Lee) 5.00
1-"3-D" Edition ($6.50) w/glasses 7.00

GD2.0 FN6.0 NM9.4

WILDC.A.T.S/ X-MEN: THE MODERN AGE
Image Comics (WildStorm Productions): Aug, 1997 ($4.50, one-shot)

1-Robinson-s/Hughes-a; Two covers(Hughes, Paul Smith) 5.00
1-"3-D" Edition ($6.50) w/glasses 7.00

WILDC.A.T.S/ X-MEN: THE SILVER AGE
Image Comics (WildStorm Productions): June, 1997 ($4.50, one-shot)

1-Lobdell-s/Jim Lee-a; Two covers(Neal Adams, Jim Lee) 5.00
1-"3-D" Edition ($6.50) w/glasses 7.00

WILDCORE
Image Comics (WildStorm Prods.): Nov, 1997 - No. 10, Dec, 1998 ($2.50)

1-10: 1-Two covers (Booth/McWeeney, Charest) 2.50
1-($3.50)-Voyager Pack w/DV8 preview 3.50
1-Chromium-c 5.00

WILD DOG
DC Comics: Sept, 1987 - No. 4, Dec, 1987 (75¢, limited series)

1-4 2.50
Special 1 (1989, $2.50, 52 pgs.) 2.50

WILDERNESS TREK (See Zane Grey, Four Color 333)

WILDFIRE (See Zane Grey, FourColor 433)

WILD FRONTIER (Cheyenne Kid #8 on)
Charlton Comics: Oct, 1955 - No. 7, Apr, 1957

1-Davy Crockett 9.30 28.00 65.00
2-6-Davy Crockett in all 5.70 17.00 40.00
7-Origin & 1st app. Cheyenne Kid 6.40 19.25 45.00

WILDSTAR (Also see The Dragon & The Savage Dragon)
Image Comics (Highbrow Entertainment): Sept, 1995 - No. 3, Jan, 1996 ($2.50, limited series)

1-3: Al Gordon scripts; Jerry Ordway-c/a 2.50

WILDSTAR: SKY ZERO
Image Comics (Highbrow Entertainment): Mar, 1993 - No. 4, Nov, 1993 ($1.95, limited series)

1-4: 1-($2.50)-Embossed-c w/silver ink; Ordway-c/a in all 2.50
1-($1.95)-Newsstand ed. w/silver ink-c, not embossed 2.50
1-Gold variant 6.00

WILDSTORM
Image Comics (WildStorm Publishing): 1994-2000 (one-shots)

...Annual 2000 (12/00, $3.50) Devil's Night x-over; Moy-a 3.50
...Chamber of Horrors (10/95, $3.50)-Bisley-c 3.50
...Fine Arts: The Gallery Collection (12/98, $19.95) Lee-c 20.00
...Halloween 1 (10/97, $2.50) Warner-c 2.50
...Rarities 1(12/94, $4.95, 52 pgs.)-r/Gen 13 1/2 & other stories 5.00
...Swimsuit Special 1 (12/94, $2.95), ...Swimsuit Special 2 (1995, $2.50) 3.00
...Swimsuit Special '97 #1 (7/97, $2.50) 2.50
...Thunderbook 1 (10/00, $6.95) Short stories by various incl. Hughes, Moy 7.00
...Ultimate Sports 1 (8/97, $2.50) 2.50
...Universe Sourcebook (5/95, $2.50) 2.50

WILDSTORM!
Image Comics (WildStorm Publishing): Aug, 1995 - No. 4, Nov, 1995 ($2.50, B&W/color, anthology)

1-4: 1-Simonson-a 2.50

WILDSTORM RISING
Image Comics (WildStorm Publishing): May, 1995 - No.2, June, 1995 ($1.95/$2.50)

1 ($2.50)-Direct Market, WildStorm Rising Pt. 1 w/bound-in card 2.50
1 ($1.95)-Newstand, WildStorm Rising Pt. 1 2.00
2 ($2.50)-Direct Market, WildStorm Rising Pt. 10 w/bound-in card; continues in WildC.A.T.S #21. 2.50
2 ($1.95)-Newstand, WildStorm Rising Pt. 10 2.00
Trade paperback (1996, $19.95)-Collects x-over; B. Smith-c 20.00

WILDSTORM SPOTLIGHT
Image Comics (WildStorm Publishing): Feb, 1997 - No. 4 ($2.50)

1-4: 1-Alan Moore-s 2.50

Wild Thing #1 © MAR

Wild West #1 © MAR

Willie the Penguin #6 © STD

GD2.0 FN6.0 NM9.4

WILDSTORM UNIVERSE '97
Image Comics (WildStorm Publishing): Dec, 1996 - No. 3 ($2.50, limited series)
1-3: 1-Wraparound-c. 3-Gary Frank-c 2.50

WILDTHING
Marvel Comics UK: Apr, 1993 - No. 7, Oct, 1993 ($1.75)
1-($2.50)-Embossed-c; Venom & Carnage cameo 2.50
2-7: 2-Spider-Man & Venom. 6-Mysterio app. 2.00

WILD THING (Wolverine's daughter in the M2 universe)
Marvel Comics: Oct, 1999 - No. 5, Feb, 2000 ($1.99)
1-5: 1-Lim-a in all. 2-Two covers 2.00
Wizard #0 supplement; battles the Hulk 1.00

WILDTIMES
DC Comics (WildStorm Productions): Aug, 1999 ($2.50, one-shots)
...Deathblow #1 -set in 1899; Edwards-a; Jonah Hex app., ...DV8 #1 -set in 1944; Altieri-s/p; Sgt. Rock app., ...Gen13 #1 -set in 1969; Casey-s/Johnson-a;, Teen Titans app., ...Grifter #1 -set in 1923; Paul Smith-a, ...Wetworks #1 - Waid-s/Lopresti-a; Superman app. 2.50
...WildC.A.T.s #0 -Wizard supplement; Charest-c 2.00

WILD WEST (Wild Western #3 on)
Marvel Comics (WFP): Spring, 1948 - No. 2, July, 1948
1-Two-Gun Kid, Arizona Annie, & Tex Taylor begin; Shores-c 35.00 105.00 280.00
2-Captain Tootsie by Beck; Shores-c 23.00 69.00 185.00

WILD WEST (Black Fury #1-57)
Charlton Comics: V2#58, Nov, 1966
V2#58 2.00 6.00 16.00

WILD WEST C.O.W.-BOYS OF MOO MESA (TV)
Archie Comics: Dec, 1992 - No. 3, Feb, 1993 (limited series)
V2#1, Mar, 1993 - No. 3, July, 1993 ($1.25)
1-3,V2#1-3 2.00

WILD WESTERN (Formerly Wild West #1,2)
Marvel/Atlas (WFP): No. 3, 9/48 - No. 57, 9/57 (3-11: 52 pgs, 12-on: 36 pgs)
3(#1)-Tex Morgan begins; Two-Gun Kid, Tex Taylor, & Arizona Annie continue from Wild West 28.00 83.00 220.00
4-Last Arizona Annie; Captain Tootsie by Beck; Kid Colt app. 20.00 60.00 160.00
5-2nd app. Black Rider (1/49); Blaze Carson, Captain Tootsie (by Beck) app. 23.00 69.00 185.00
6-8: 6-Blaze Carson app; anti-Wertham editorial 14.00 41.00 110.00
9-Photo-c; Black Rider begins, ends #19 19.00 56.00 150.00
10-Charles Starrett photo-c 22.00 66.00 175.00
11-(Last 52 pg. issue) 14.00 41.00 110.00
12-14,16-19: All Black Rider-c/stories. 12-14-The Prairie Kid & his horse Fury app. 12.50 37.50 100.00
15-Red Larabee, Gunhawk (origin), his horse Blaze, & Apache Kid begin, end #22; Black Rider-c/story 13.00 39.00 105.00
20-30: 20-Kid Colt-c begin. 24-Has 2 Kid Colt stories. 26-1st app. The Ringo Kid? (2/53); 4 pg. story. 30-Katz-a 11.00 33.00 90.00
31-40 9.30 28.00 65.00
41-47,49-51,53,57 7.85 23.50 55.00
48-Williamson/Torres-a (4 pgs); Drucker-a 10.00 30.00 75.00
52-Crandall-a 10.00 30.00 75.00
54,55-Williamson-a in both (5 & 4 pgs.), #54 with Mayo plus 2 text illos 10.00 30.00 75.00
56-Baker-a? 7.85 23.50 55.00
NOTE: *Annie Oakley in #46, 47. Apache Kid in #15-22, 39. Arizona Kid in #21, 23. Arrowhead in #34-39. Black Rider in #5, 9-19, 33-44. Fighting Texan in #17. Kid Colt in #4-6, 9-11, 20-47, 52, 54-56. Outlaw Kid in #43. Red Hawkins in #13, 14. Ringo Kid in #26, 39, 41, 43, 44, 46, 47, 50, 52-56. Tex Morgan in #3, 4, 6, 9, 11. Tex Taylor in #3-6, 9, 11. Texas Kid in #23-25. Two-Gun Kid in #3-6, 9, 11, 12, 33-39, 41. Wyatt Earp in #47.* ***Ayers*** *a-41, 42.* ***Berg*** *a-26; c-24.* ***Colan*** *a-49.* ***Forte*** *a-28, 30.* ***Al Hartley*** *a-16.* ***Heath*** *a-4, 5, 8; c-34, 44.* ***Keller*** *a-24, 26(2), 29-40, 44-46, 48, 52.* ***Maneely*** *a-10, 12, 15, 16, 28, 35, 38, 40-45; c-18-22, 33, 35, 36, 38, 39, 41, 42, 45.* ***Morisi*** *a-23, 52.* ***Pakula*** *a-42, 52.* ***Powell*** *a-51.* ***Romita*** *a-24(2).* ***Severin*** *a-46, 47; c-48.* ***Shores*** *a-3, 5, 30, 31, 33, 35, 36, 38, 41; c-3-5.* ***Sinnott*** *a-34-39.* ***Wildey*** *a-43. Bondage c-19.*

WILD WESTERN ACTION (Also see The Bravados)
Skywald Publ. Corp.: Mar, 1971 - No. 3, June, 1971 (25¢, reprints, 52 pgs.)
1-Durango Kid, Straight Arrow-r; with all references to "Straight" in story relettered to "Swift"; Bravados begin; Shores-a (new) 1.85 5.50 15.00
2,3: 2-Billy Nevada, Durango Kid. 3-Red Mask, Durango Kid 1.25 3.75 10.00

WILD WESTERN ROUNDUP
Red Top/Decker Publications/I. W. Enterprises: Oct, 1957; 1960-'61
1(1957)-Kid Cowboy-r 4.00 12.00 24.00
I.W. Reprint #1('60-61)-r/#1 by Red Top 1.50 4.50 12.00

WILD WEST RODEO
Star Publications: 1953 (15¢)
1-A comic book coloring book with regular full color cover & B&W inside 6.40 19.25 45.00

WILD WILD WEST, THE (TV)
Gold Key: June, 1966 - No. 7, Oct, 1969 (Robert Conrad photo-c)
1-McWilliams-a; photo back-c 11.70 35.00 140.00
2-McWilliams-a; photo back-c 9.00 27.00 110.00
3-7 6.70 20.00 80.00

WILD, WILD WEST, THE (TV)
Millennium Publications: Oct, 1990 - No. 4, Jan?, 1991 ($2.95, limited series)
1-4-Based on TV show 3.00

WILKIN BOY (See That...)

WILL EISNER READER
Kitchen Sink Press: 1991 ($9.95, B&W, 8 1/2" x 11", TPB)
nn-Reprints stories from Will Eisner's Quarterly; Eisner-s/a/c 10.00
nn-(DC Comics, 10/00, $9.95) 10.00

WILLIE COMICS (Formerly Ideal #1-4; Crime Cases #24 on; Li'l Willie #20 & 21) (See Gay Comics, Laugh, Millie The Model & Wisco)
Marvel Comics (MgPC): #5, Fall, 1946 - #19, 4/49; #22, 1/50 - #23, 5/50 (No #20 & 21)
5(#1)-George, Margie, Nellie the Nurse & Willie begin 18.00 53.00 140.00
6,8,9 10.00 30.00 75.00
7(1),10,11-Kurtzman's "Hey Look" 10.00 30.00 80.00
12,14-18,22,23 9.30 28.00 65.00
13,19-Kurtzman's "Hey Look" (#19-last by Kurtzman?) 10.00 30.00 70.00
NOTE: *Cindy app. in #17. Jeanie app. in #17. Little Lizzie app. in #22.*

WILLIE MAYS (See The Amazing...)

WILLIE THE PENGUIN
Standard Comics: Apr, 1951 - No. 6, Apr, 1952
1-Funny animal 8.65 26.00 60.00
2-6 5.00 15.00 30.00

WILLIE THE WISE-GUY (Also see Cartoon Kids)
Atlas Comics (NPP): Sept, 1957
1-Kida, Maneely-a 8.65 26.00 60.00

WILLOW
Marvel Comics: Aug, 1988 - No. 3, Oct, 1988 ($1.00)
1-3-R/Marvel Graphic Novel #36 (movie adaptation) 3.00

WILL ROGERS WESTERN (Formerly My Great Love #1-4; see Blazing & True Comics #66)
Fox Features Syndicate: No. 5, June, 1950 - No. 2, Aug, 1950
5(#1) 34.00 101.00 270.00
2: Photo-c 29.00 86.00 230.00

WILL TO POWER (Also see Comic's Greatest World)
Dark Horse Comics: June, 1994 - No. 12, Aug, 1994 ($1.00, weekly limited series, 20 pgs.)
1-12: 12-Vortex kills Titan. 2.00
NOTE: ***Mignola*** *c-10-12.* ***Sears*** *c-1-3.*

WILL-YUM!

Wings Comics #79 © FH

THE WISE LITTLE HEN
WRITTEN AND ILLUSTRATED BY THE STAFF OF THE WALT DISNEY STUDIOS

Wise Little Hen nn © WDC

Witchblade #40 © Top Cow

GD2.0 FN6.0 NM9.4

Dell Publishing Co.: No. 676, Feb, 1956 - No. 902, May, 1958
Four Color 676 (#1), 765 (1/57), 902 2.50 7.50 25.00

WIN A PRIZE COMICS (Timmy The Timid Ghost #3 on?)
Charlton Comics: Feb, 1955 - No. 2, Apr, 1955
V1#1-S&K-a; Poe adapt; E.C. War swipe 68.00 205.00 650.00
2-S&K-a 50.00 150.00 450.00

WINDY & WILLY
National Periodical Publications: May-June, 1969 - No. 4, Nov-Dec, 1969
1- r/Dobie Gillis with some art changes begin 3.20 9.60 35.00
2-4 2.30 7.00 20.00

WINGS COMICS
Fiction House Mag.: 9/40 - No. 109, 9/49; No. 110, Wint, 1949-50; No. 111, Spring, 1950; No. 112, 1950(nd); No. 113 - No. 115, 1950(nd); No. 116, 1952(nd); No. 117, Fall, 1952 - No. 122, Wint, 1953-54; No. 123 - No. 124, 1954(nd)
1-Skull Squad, Clipper Kirk, Suicide Smith, Jane Martin, War Nurse, Phantom Falcons, Greasemonkey Griffin, Parachute Patrol & Powder Burns begin
232.00 695.00 2200.00
2 95.00 285.00 900.00
3-5 63.00 189.00 600.00
6-10: 8-Indicia shows #7 (#8 on cover) 55.00 165.00 500.00
11-15 47.00 140.00 420.00
16-Origin & 1st app. Captain Wings & begin series 53.00 158.00 475.00
17-20 40.00 120.00 340.00
21-30 38.00 113.00 300.00
31-40 31.00 94.00 250.00
41-50 25.00 75.00 200.00
51-60: 60-Last Skull Squad 22.00 66.00 175.00
61-67: 66-Ghost Patrol begins (becomes Ghost Squadron #71 on); ends #112?
20.00 60.00 160.00
68,69: 68-Clipper Kirk becomes The Phantom Falcon-origin, Part 1; part 2 in #69 20.00 60.00 160.00
70-72: 70-1st app. The Phantom Falcon in costume, origin-Part 3; Capt. Wings battles Col. Kamikaze in all 19.00 56.00 150.00
73-99: 80-Phantom Falcon by Larsen. 99-King of the Congo begins?
19.00 56.00 150.00
100-(12/48) 20.00 60.00 160.00
101-124: 111-Last Jane Martin. 112-Flying Saucer-c/story (1950). 115-Used in **POP**, pg. 89 16.00 49.00 130.00

NOTE: *Bondage covers are common. Captain Wings battles Sky Hag-#75, 76; ...Mr. Atlantis-#85-92; ...Mr. Pupin(Red Agent)-#98-103. Capt. Wings by* ***Elias****-#52-64, 68, 69; by* ***Lubbers****-#29-32, 70-111; by* ***Renee****-#33-46.* ***Evans*** *a-85-106, 108-111(Jane Martin); text illos-72-84.* ***Larsen*** *a-52, 59, 64, 73-77. Jane Martin by* ***Fran Hopper****-#68-84; Suicide Smith by* ***John Celardo****-#72, 74, 76, 80-104; by* ***Hollingsworth****-#68-70, 105-109, 111; Ghost Squadron by* ***Astarita****-#67-79; by* ***Maurice Whitman****-#80-111. King of the Congo by* ***Moreira****-#99, 100. Skull Squad by* ***M. Baker****-#52-60; Clipper Kirk by* ***Baker****-#60, 61; by* ***Colan****-#53; by* ***Ingels****-(some issues?). Phantom Falcon by* ***Larsen****-#73-84.* ***Elias*** *c-58-72.* ***Fawcette*** *c-3-12, 16, 17, 19, 22-33.* ***Lubbers*** *c-74-109.* ***Tuska*** *a-5.* ***Whitman*** *c-110-124.* ***Zolnerwich*** *c-15, 21.*

WINGS OF THE EAGLES, THE
Dell Publishing Co.: No. 790, Apr, 1957 (10¢ & 15¢ editions exist)
Four Color 790-Movie; John Wayne photo-c; Toth-a 15.00 45.00 175.00

WINKY DINK (Adventures of...)
Pines Comics: No. 75, Mar, 1957 (one-shot)
75-Marv Levy-c/a 4.65 14.00 28.00

WINKY DINK (TV)
Dell Publishing Co.: No. 663, Nov, 1955
Four Color 663 (#1) 7.50 22.50 90.00

WINNIE-THE-POOH (Also see Dynabrite Comics)
Gold Key No. 1-17/Whitman No. 18 on: January, 1977 - No. 33, 1984 (Walt Disney) (Winnie-The-Pooh began as Edward Bear in 1926 by Milne)
1-New art 1.85 5.50 15.00
2-5: 5-New material 1.00 3.00 8.00
6-17: 12-up-New material 2.40 6.00
18,19(Whitman) 1.00 3.00 8.00
20-22('80) pre-pack? 1.50 4.50 12.00
23-28 1.00 3.00 8.00
29-33 (#90299 on-c, no date or date code; pre-pack) 1.50 4.50 12.00

GD2.0 FN6.0 NM9.4

WINNIE WINKLE (See Popular Comics & Super Comics)
Dell Publishing Co.: 1941 - No. 7, Sept-Nov, 1949
Large Feature Comic 2 (1941) 17.50 52.50 210.00
Four Color 94 (1945) 11.70 35.00 140.00
Four Color 174 7.00 21.00 85.00
1(3-5/48)-Contains daily & Sunday newspaper-r from 1939-1941
6.30 19.00 75.00
2 (6-8/48) 4.10 12.30 45.00
3-7 3.00 9.00 30.00

WINTERWORLD
Eclipse Comics: Sept, 1987 - No. 3, Mar, 1988 ($1.75, limited series)
1-3 2.00

WISE GUYS (See Harvey...)

WISE LITTLE HEN, THE
David McKay Publ./Whitman: 1934 ,1935(48 pgs.); 1937 (Story book)
nn-(1934 edition w/dust jacket)(48 pgs. with color, 8-3/4x9-3/4") -Debut of Donald Duck (see Advs. of Mickey Mouse); Donald app. on cover with Wise Little Hen & Practical Pig; painted cover; same artist as the B&W's from Silly Symphony Cartoon, The Wise Little Hen (1934) (McKay)
Book w/dust jacket 225.00 675.00 1800.00
Dust jacket only 43.00 129.00 325.00
nn.(1935 edition w/dust jacket), same as 1934 ed. 138.00 413.00 1100.00
888(1937)(9-1/2x13", 12 pgs.)(Whitman) Donald Duck app.
30.00 90.00 240.00

WISE SON: THE WHITE WOLF
DC Comics (Milestone): Nov, 1996 - No. 4, Feb, 1997 ($2.50, limited series)
1-4: Ho Che Anderson-c/a 2.50

WIT AND WISDOM OF WATERGATE (Humor magazine)
Marvel Comics: 1973, 76 pgs., squarebound
1 2.80 8.40 28.00

WITCHBLADE (Also see Cyblade/Shi, Tales Of The..., & Top Cow Classics)
Image Comics (Top Cow Productions): Nov, 1995 - Present ($2.50)
0 1.00 3.00 8.00
1/2-Mike Turner/Marc Silvestri-c. 4.55 13.65 50.00
1/2 Gold Ed., 1/2 Chromium-c 4.55 13.65 50.00
1-Mike Turner-a(p) 4.00 12.00 40.00
1,2-American Ent. Encore Ed. 1.00 3.00 7.00
2,3 2.50 7.50 25.00
4,5 2.00 6.00 18.00
6-9: 8-Wraparound-c. 9-Tony Daniel-a(p) 1.25 3.75 10.00
9-Sunset variant-c 1.50 4.50 12.00
10-Flip book w/Darkness #0, 1st app. the Darkness 1.50 4.50 12.00
10-Variant-c 1.85 5.50 15.00
10-($3.95) Dynamic Forces alternate-c 1.00 3.00 8.00
11-15 5.00
16-19: 18,19-"Family Ties" Darkness x-over pt. 1,4 4.00
18-Face to face variant-c, 18-American Ent. Ed., 19-AE Gold Ed.
1.00 3.00 8.00
20-25: 24-Pearson, Green-a. 25-($2.95) Turner-a(p) 3.00
25 (prism variant) 40.00
25 (Special) 20.00
26-39: 26-Green-a begins 2.50
27 (Variant) 10.00
40-44: 40-Begin Jenkins & Veitch-s/Keu Cha-a 2.50
40-Pittsburgh Convention Preview edition; B&W preview of #40 3.00
41-eWanted Chrome-c edition 5.00
.../Darkchylde (7/00, $2.50) Green-s/a(p) 2.50
.../Darkness: Family Ties Collected Edition (10/98, $9.95) r/#18,19 and Darkness #9,10 10.00
.../Darkness Special (12/99, $3.95) Green-c/a 3.95
... Gallery (11/00, $2.95) Profile pages and pin-ups by various; Turner-c 2.95
Infinity (5/99, $3.50) Lobdell-s/Pollina-c/a 3.50
...: Prevailing TPB (2000, $14.95) r/#20-25; new Turner-c 14.95
...: Revelations TPB (2000, $24.95) r/#9-17; new Turner-c 24.95
.../Tomb Raider #1/2 (7/00, $2.95) Covers by Turner and Cha 3.00
Wizard #500 10.00

Witches Tales #3 © HARV

Witching Hour #34 © DC

The Witching Hour #3 © Jeph Loeb & Chris Bachalo

GD2.0 FN6.0 NM9.4

/ITCHBLADE COLLECTED EDITION
nage Comics (Top Cow Productions): July, 1996 - Present ($4.95/$6.95, quarebound, limited series)

1-7-($4.95): Two issues reprinted in each 5.00
3-($6.95) r/#15-17 7.00
Slipcase (10/96, $10.95)-Packaged w/ Coll. Ed. #1-4 11.00

/ITCHBLADE: DESTINY'S CHILD
nage Comics (Top Cow): Jun, 2000 - No. 3, Sept, 2000 ($2.95, lim. series)

1-3: 1-Boller-a/Keu Cha-c 3.00

/ITCHBLADE/ ELEKTRA
nage Comics (Top Cow Productions): Mar, 1997 ($2.95)

1-Devil's Reign Pt. 6 3.00

/ITCHBLADE/ TOMB RAIDER SPECIAL (Also see Tomb Raider/...)
nage Comics (Top Cow Productions): Dec, 1998 ($2.95)

1-Based on video game character; Turner-a(p) 3.00
1-Silvestri variant-c 5.00
1-Turner bikini variant-c 10.00
/izard 1/2 -Turner-s 10.00

/ITCHCRAFT (See Strange Mysteries, Super Reprint #18)
von Periodicals: Mar-Apr, 1952 - No. 6, Mar, 1953

	GD2.0	FN6.0	NM9.4
1-Kubert-a; 1 pg. Check-a	64.00	193.00	610.00
2-Kubert & Check-a	50.00	150.00	450.00
3,6: 3-Lawrence-a; Kinstler inside-c	40.00	120.00	320.00
4-People cooked alive c/story	41.00	123.00	370.00
5-Kelly Freas painted-c	46.00	137.00	410.00

OTE: *Hollingsworth a-4-6; c-4, 6. McCann a-3?*

/ITCHCRAFT
C Comics (Vertigo): June, 1994 - No. 3, Aug, 1994 ($2.95, limited series)

1-3: James Robinson scripts & Kaluta-c in all 4.00
1-Platinum Edition 8.00
'rade paperback-(1996, $14.95)-r/#1-3; Kaluta-c 15.00

/ITCHCRAFT: LA TERREUR
C Comics (Vertigo): Apr, 1998 - No. 3, Jun, 1998 ($2.50, limited series)

1-3: Robinson-s/Zulli & Locke-a; interlocking cover images 2.50

/ITCHES TALES (Witches Western Tales #29,30)
/itches Tales/Harvey Publications: Jan, 1951 - No. 28, Dec, 1954 (date misrinted as 4/55)

	GD2.0	FN6.0	NM9.4
1-Powell-a (1 pg.)	53.00	158.00	475.00
2-Eye injury panel	31.00	94.00	250.00
3-7,9,10	21.00	64.00	170.00
8-Eye injury panels	23.00	69.00	185.00
11-13,15,16: 12-Acid in face story	21.00	62.00	165.00
14,17-Powell/Nostrand-a. 17-Atomic disaster story	23.00	68.00	180.00
8-Nostrand-a; E.C. swipe/Shock S.S.	23.00	68.00	180.00
9-Nostrand-a; E.C. swipe/ "Glutton"; Devil-c	24.00	73.00	195.00
'0-24-Nostrand-a. 21-E.C. swipe; rape story. 23-Wood E.C. swipes/Two-Fisted Tales #34	23.00	68.00	180.00
5-Nostrand-a; E.C. swipe/Mad Barber; decapitation-c	28.00	83.00	220.00
:6-28: 27-r/#6 with diff.-c. 28-r/#8 with diff.-c	16.00	48.00	125.00

IOTE: *Check a-24. Elias c-8, 10, 16-27. Kremer a-18; c-25. Nostrand a-17-25; 14, 7(w/Powell). Palais a-1, 2, 4(2), 5(2), 7-9, 12, 14, 15, 17. Powell a-3-7, 10, 11, 19-27. Bondage-1, 3, 5, 6, 8, 9.*

VITCHES TALES (Magazine)
:erie Publications: V1#7, July, 1969 - V7#1, Feb, 1975 (B&W, 52 pgs.)

	GD2.0	FN6.0	NM9.4
/1#7(7/69) - 9(11/69)	4.55	13.65	50.00
/2#1-6('70), V3#1-6('71)	3.20	9.60	35.00
/4#1-6('72), V5#1-6('73), V6#1-6('74), V7#1	3.00	9.00	30.00

IOTE: *Ajax/Farrell reprints in early issues.*

VITCHES' WESTERN TALES (Formerly Witches Tales)(Western Tales #31on)
Harvey Publications: No. 29, Feb, 1955 - No. 30, Apr, 1955

	GD2.0	FN6.0	NM9.4
29,30-Featuring Clay Duncan & Boys' Ranch; S&K-r/from Boys' Ranch including-c. 29-Last pre-code	20.00	60.00	160.00

VITCHFINDER, THE
Image Comics (Liar): Sept, 1999 - No. 3, Jan, 2000 ($2.95)

1-3-Romano-a/Sharon & Matthew Scott-plot 3.00

WITCH HUNTER
Malibu Comics (Ultraverse): Apr, 1996 ($2.50, one-shot)

1 2.50

WITCHING HOUR ("The ..." in later issues)
National Periodical Publ./DC Comics: Feb-Mar, 1969 - No. 85, Oct, 1978

	GD2.0	FN6.0	NM9.4
1-Toth-a, plus Neal Adams-a (2 pgs.)	11.00	33.00	120.00
2,6: 6-Toth-a	4.10	12.30	45.00
3,5-Wrightson-a; Toth-p. 3-Last 12¢ issue	4.55	13.65	50.00
4,7-12: Toth-a in all. 8-Toth, Neal Adams-a	2.50	7.50	25.00
13-Neal Adams-c/a, 2pgs.	3.00	9.00	30.00
14-Williamson/Garzon, Jones-a; N. Adams-c	3.20	9.60	35.00
15	1.85	5.50	15.00
16-21-(52 pg. Giants)	2.30	7.00	20.00
22-37,39,40	1.50	4.50	12.00
38-(100 pgs.)	3.80	11.40	42.00
41-60	1.25	3.75	10.00
61-83,85	1.00	3.00	8.00
84-(44 pgs.)	1.25	3.75	10.00

NOTE: *Combined with The Unexpected with #189.* ***Neal Adams*** *c-7-11, 13, 14.* ***Alcala*** *a-24, 27, 33, 41, 43.* ***Anderson*** *a-9, 38.* ***Cardy*** *c-4, 5.* ***Kaluta*** *a-7.* ***Kane*** *a-12p.* ***Morrow*** *a-10, 13, 15, 16.* ***Nino*** *a-31, 40, 45, 47.* ***Redondo*** *a-20, 23, 24, 34, 65; c-53.* ***Reese*** *a-23.* ***Sparling*** *a-1.* ***Toth*** *a-1, 3-12, 38r.* ***Tuska*** *a-11, 12.* ***Wood*** *a-15.*

WITCHING HOUR, THE
DC Comics (Vertigo): 1999 - No. 3, 2000 ($5.95, limited series)

1-3-Bachalo & Thibert-c/a; Loeb & Bachalo-s 6.00
Hardcover (2000, $29.95) r/#1-3; embossed cover 30.00

WITHIN OUR REACH
Star Reach Productions: 1991 ($7.95, 84 pgs.)

nn-Spider-Man, Concrete by Chadwick, Gift of the Magi by Russell; X-mas stories; Chadwick-c; Spidey back-c 8.00

WITH THE MARINES ON THE BATTLEFRONTS OF THE WORLD
Toby Press: 1953 (no month) - No. 2, Mar, 1954 (Photo covers)

	GD2.0	FN6.0	NM9.4
1-John Wayne story	29.00	86.00	230.00
2-Monty Hall in #1,2	8.65	26.00	60.00

WITH THE U.S. PARATROOPS BEHIND ENEMY LINES (Also see U.S. Paratroops...; #2-6 titled U.S. Paratroops...)
Avon Periodicals: 1951 - No. 6, Dec, 1952

	GD2.0	FN6.0	NM9.4
1-Wood-c & inside f/c	16.00	48.00	125.00
2-Kinstler-c & inside f/c only	9.30	28.00	65.00
3-6: 6-Kinstler-c & inside f/c only	8.65	26.00	60.00

NOTE: *Kinstler c-2, 4-6.*

WITNESS, THE (Also see Amazing Mysteries, Captain America #71, Ideal #4, Marvel Mystery #92 & Mystic #7)
Marvel Comics (MjMe): Sept, 1948

	GD2.0	FN6.0	NM9.4
1(Scarce)-Rico-c?	168.00	505.00	1600.00

WITTY COMICS
Irwin H. Rubin Publ./Chicago Nite Life News No. 2: 1945 - No. 2, 1945

	GD2.0	FN6.0	NM9.4
1-The Pioneer, Junior Patrol; Jap war-c	25.00	75.00	200.00
2-The Pioneer, Junior Patrol	12.00	36.00	95.00

WIZARD OF FOURTH STREET, THE
Dark Horse Comics: Dec, 1987 - No. 2, 1988 ($1.75, B&W, limited series)

1,2: Adapts novel by S/F author Simon Hawke 2.00

WIZARD OF OZ (See Classics Illustrated Jr. 535, Dell Jr. Treasury No. 5, First Comics Graphic Novel, Marvelous..., & Marvel Treasury of Oz)
Dell Publishing Co.: No. 1308, Mar-May, 1962 (TV)

	GD2.0	FN6.0	NM9.4
Four Color 1308	11.00	33.00	130.00

WIZARD'S TALE, THE
Image Comics (Homage Comics): 1997 ($19.95, squarebound, one-shot)

nn-Kurt Busiek-s/David Wenzel-painted-a/c 20.00

WOLF & RED

Wolff & Byrd, Counselors of the Macabre #2 © Batton Lash

Wolverine #124 © MAR

Wolverine: Days of Future Past #3 © MAR

GD2.0 FN6.0 NM9.4

Dark Horse Comics: Apr, 1995 - No. 3, June, 1995 ($2.50, limited series)
1-3: Characters created by Tex Avery 2.50

WOLFF & BYRD, COUNSELORS OF THE MACABRE (Becomes Supernatural Law with issue #24)
Exhibit A Press: May, 1994 - No. 23, Aug, 1999 ($2.50, B&W)
1-23-Batton Lash-s/a 2.50

WOLF GAL (See Al Capp's...)

WOLFMAN, THE (See Movie Classics)

WOLFPACK
Marvel Comics: Feb, 1988 ($7.95); Aug, 1988 - No. 12, July, 1989 (Lim. series)
1-1st app./origin (Marvel Graphic Novel #31) 8.00
1-12 2.00

WOLVERINE (See Alpha Flight, Daredevil #196, 249, Ghost Rider; Wolverine; Punisher, Havok &..., Incredible Hulk #180, Incredible Hulk &..., Kitty Pryde And..., Marvel Comics Presents, Power Pack, Punisher and..., Spider-Man vs... & X-Men #94)

WOLVERINE (See Incredible Hulk #180 for 1st app.)
Marvel Comics Group: Sept, 1982 - No. 4, Dec, 1982 (limited series)
1-Frank Miller-c/a(p) in all 3.65 11.00 40.00
2-4 3.00 9.00 30.00
Trade paperback 1(7/87, $4.95)-Reprints #1-4 with new Miller-c. 1.75 5.25 14.00
Trade paperback nn (2nd printing, $9.95)-r/#1-4 1.50 4.50 12.00

WOLVERINE
Marvel Comics: Nov, 1988 - Present ($1.50/$1.75/$1.95/$1.99, Baxter paper)
1 3.00 9.00 30.00
2 1.85 5.50 15.00
3-5: 4-BWS back-c 1.50 4.50 12.00
6-9: 6-McFarlane back-c. 7,8-Hulk app. 1.10 3.30 9.00
10-1st battle with Sabretooth (before Wolverine had his claws) 2.50 7.50 25.00
11-16: 11-New costume 1.00 2.80 7.00
17-20: 17-Byrne-c/a(p) begins, ends #23 1.00 2.80 7.00
21-30: 24,25,27-Jim Lee-c. 26-Begin $1.75-c 5.00
31-40,44,47 4.00
41-Sabretooth claims to be Wolverine's father; Cable cameo 5.00
41-Gold 2nd printing ($1.75) 2.00
42-Sabretooth, Cable & Nick Fury app.; Sabretooth proven not to be Wolverine's father 5.00
42-Gold ink 2nd printing ($1.75) 2.00
43-Sabretooth cameo (2 panels); saga ends 5.00
45,46-Sabretooth-c/stories 5.00
48-51: 48,49-Sabretooth app. 48-Begin 3 part Weapon X sequel. 50-(64 pgs.)-Die cut-c; Wolverine back to old yellow costume; Forge, Cyclops, Jubilee, Jean Grey & Nick Fury app.51-Sabretooth-c & app. 5.00
52-74,76-80: 54-Shatterstar (from X-Force) app. 55-Gambit, Jubilee, Sunfire-c/story. 55-57,73-Gambit app. 57-Mariko Yashida dies (Late 7/92). 58,59-Terror, Inc. x-over. 60-64-Sabretooth storyline (60,62,64-c) 3.00
75-($3.95, 68 pgs.)-Wolverine hologram on-c 1.00 3.00 8.00
81-84,86: 81-bound-in card sheet 3.00
85-($2.50)-Newsstand edition 3.00
85-($3.50)-Collectors edition 4.00
87-90 ($1.95)-Deluxe edition 3.00
87-90 ($1.50)-Regular edition 2.50
91-99,101-114: 91-Return from "Age of Apocalypse," 93-Juggernaut app. 94-Gen X app. 101-104-Elektra app. 104-Origin of Onslaught. 105-Onslaught x-over. 110-Shaman-c/app. 114-Alternate-c 2.50
100 ($3.95)-Hologram-c; Wolverine loses humanity 1.00 3.00 8.00
100 ($2.95)-Regular-c. 4.00
115-124: 115- Operation Zero Tolerance 2.00
125-($2.99) Wraparound-c; Viper secret 3.00
125-($6.95) Jae Lee variant-c 7.00
126-144: 126,127-Sabretooth-c/app. 128-Sabretooth & Shadowcat app.;Platt-a. 129-Wendigo-c/app. 131-Initial printing contained lettering error. 133-Begin Larsen-s/Matsuda-a. 138-Galactus-c/app. 139-Cable app.; Yu-a. 142,143-Alpha Flight app. 2.00
145-($2.99) 25th Anniversary issue; Hulk and Sabretooth app. 3.00
145-($3.99) Foil enhanced cover 4.00
146-149: 147-Apocalypse: The Twelve; Angel-c/app. 149-Nova-c/app. 1.99
150-($2.99) Steve Skroce-s/a 2.99
151-159: 151-Begin $2.25-c. 154,155-Liefeld-s/a. 156-Churchill-a. 159-Chen-a 2.25
#(-1) Flashback (7/97) Logan meets Col. Fury; Nord-a 2.50
Annual nn (1990, $4.50, squarebound, 52 pgs.)-The Jungle Adventure; Simonson scripts; Mignola-c/a 5.00
Annual 2 (12/90, $4.95, squarebound, 52 pgs.)-Bloodlust 5.00
Annual nn (#3, 8/91, $5.95, 68 pgs.)-Rahne of Terror; Cable & The New Mutants app.; Andy Kubert-c/a (2nd print exists) 6.00
Annual '95 (1995, $3.95) 4.00
Annual '96 (1996, $2.95)- Wraparound-c; Silver Samurai, Yukio, and Red Ronin app. 3.00
Annual '97 (1997, $2.99)- Wraparound-c 3.00
Annual 1999, 2000 ($3.50) : 1999-Deadpool app. 3.50
...Battles The Incredible Hulk nn (1989, $4.95, squarebound, 52 pg.) r/Incredible Hulk #180,181 5.00
...Black Rio (11/98, $5.99)-Casey-s/Oscar Jimenez-a 6.00
...Blood Hungry nn (1993, $6.95, 68 pgs.)-Kieth-r/Marvel Comics Presents #85-92 w/ new Kieth-c 7.00
...: Bloody Choices nn (1993, $7.95, 68 pgs.)-r/Graphic Novel; Nick Fury app. 8.00
... Cable Guts and Glory (10/99, $5.99) Platt-a 6.00
... Doombringer (11/97, $5.99)-Silver Samurai-c/app. 6.00
... Evilution (9/94, $5.95) 6.00
...: Global Jeopardy 1 (12/93, $2.95, one-shot)-Embossed-c; Sub-Mariner, Zabu, Ka-Zar, Shanna & Wolverine app.; produced in cooperation with World Wildlife Fund 3.00
...:Inner Fury nn (1992, $5.95, 52 pgs.)-Sienkiewicz-c/a 6.00
...: Judgment Night (2000, $3.99) Shi app.; Battlebook 4.00
...: Killing (9/93)-Kent Williams-a 6.00
...: Knight of Terra (1995, $6.95)-Ostrander script 7.00
.../ Nick Fury: The Scorpio Connection Hardcover (1989, $16.95) 25.00
.../ Nick Fury: The Scorpio Connection Softcover(1990, $12.95) 15.00
...: Not Dead Yet (12/98, $14.95, TPB)-r/#119-122 15.00
...: Save The Tiger 1 (7/92, $2.95, 84 pgs.)-Reprints Wolverine stories from Marvel Comics Presents #1-10 w/new Kieth-c 3.00
...Scorpio Rising ($5.95, prestige format, one-shot) 6.00
.../Shi: Dark Night of Judgment (Crusade Comics, 2000, $2.99) Tucci-a 3.00
...Triumphs And Tragedies-(1995, $16.95, trade paperback)-r/Uncanny X-Men #109,172,173, Wolverine limited series #4, & Wolverine #41,42,75 17.00
...Typhoid's Kiss (6/94, $6.95)-r/Wolverine stories from Marvel Comics Presents #109-116 7.00
...Vs. Spider-Man 1 (3/95, $2.50) -r/Marvel Comics Presents #48-50 2.50
.../Witchblade 1 (3/97, $2.95) Devil's Reign Pt. 5 4.00
Wizard #1/2 (1997) Joe Phillips-a(p) 10.00
NOTE: ***Austin*** *c-3i.* ***Bolton*** *c(back)-5.* ***Buscema*** *a-1-16,25,27p; c-1-10.* ***Byrne*** *a-17-22p, 23; c-1(back), 17-22, 23p.* ***Colan*** *a-24.* ***Andy Kubert*** *c/a-51.* ***Jim Lee*** *c-24, 25, 27.* ***Silvestri*** *a(p)-31-43, 45, 46, 48-50, 52, 53, 55-57; c-31-42p, 43, 45p, 46p, 48, 49p, 50p, 52p, 53p, 55-57p.* ***Stroman*** *a-44p; c-60p.* ***Williamson*** *a-1i, 3-8i; c(i)-1, 3-6.*

WOLVERINE AND THE PUNISHER: DAMAGING EVIDENCE
Marvel Comics: Oct, 1993 - No. 3, Dec, 1993 ($2.00, limited series)
1-3: 2,3-Indicia says "The Punisher and Wolverine..." 2.50

WOLVERINE: DAYS OF FUTURE PAST
Marvel Comics: Dec, 1997 - No. 3, Feb, 1998 ($2.50, limited series)
1-3: J.F. Moore-s/Bennett-a 2.50

WOLVERINE/GAMBIT: VICTIMS
Marvel Comics: Sept, 1995 - No. 4, Dec, 1995 ($2.95, limited series)
1-4: Jeph Loeb scripts & Tim Sale-a; foil-c 4.00

WOLVERINE/PUNISHER REVELATIONS (Marvel Knights)
Marvel Comics: Jun, 1999 - No. 4, Sept, 1999 ($2.95, limited series)
1-4: Pat Lee-a(p) 4.00
...: Revelation (4/00, $14.95, TPB) r/#1-4 14.95

WOLVERINE SAGA
Marvel Comics: Sept, 1989 - No. 4, Mid-Dec, 1989 ($3.95, lim. series, 52 pgs.)

Women Outlaws #8 © FOX

Wonder Comics #13 © BP

Wonder Woman #12 © DC

GD2.0 FN6.0 NM9.4

-Gives history; Liefeld/Austin-c (front & back) 5.00
-4: 2-Romita, Jr./Austin-c. 4-Kaluta-c 5.00

OMEN IN LOVE (A Feature Presentation #5)
ox Features Synd./Hero Books: Aug, 1949 - No. 4, Feb, 1950

 30.00 90.00 240.00
-Kamen/Feldstein-c 25.00 75.00 200.00
 17.00 51.00 135.00
-Wood-a 20.00 60.00 160.00

OMEN IN LOVE (Thrilling Romances for Adults)
ff-Davis Publishing Co.: Winter, 1952 (25¢, 100 pgs.)

-(Scarce)-Kinstler-a; painted-c 52.00 155.00 465.00

OMEN OUTLAWS (My Love Memories #9 on)(Also see Red Circle)
ox Features Syndicate: July, 1948 - No. 8, Sept, 1949

-Used in **SOTI**, illo "Giving children an image of American womanhood"; negligee panels 72.00 216.00 685.00
,3: 3-Kamenish-a 57.00 171.00 540.00
-8 46.00 137.00 410.00
(nd)-Contains Cody of the Pony Express; same cover as #7
 34.00 102.00 270.00

OMEN TO LOVE
ealistic: No date (1953)

-(Scarce)-Reprints Complete Romance #1; c-/Avon paperback #165
 40.00 120.00 325.00

ONDER BOY (Formerly Terrific Comics) (See Blue Bolt, Bomber Comics Samson)
ax/Farrell Publ.: No. 17, May, 1955 - No. 18, July, 1955 (Code approved)

7-Phantom Lady app. Bakerish-c/a 44.00 133.00 400.00
8-Phantom Lady app. 40.00 120.00 350.00
OTE: *Phantom Lady not by Matt Baker.*

ONDER COMICS (Wonderworld #3 on)
ox Features Syndicate: May, 1939 - No. 2, June, 1939 (68 pgs.)

GD2.0 FN6.0 VF8.0 NM9.4
-(Scarce)-Wonder Man only app. by Will Eisner; Dr. Fung (by Powell), K-51 begins; Bob Kane-a; Eisner-c 1280.00 3840.00 8320.00 16,000.00

GD2.0 FN6.0 NM9.4
-(Scarce)-Yarko the Great, Master Magician (see Samson) by Eisner begins; 'Spark' Stevens by Bob Kane, Patty O'Day, Tex Mason app. Lou Fine's 1st-c; Fine-a (2 pgs.); Yarko-c (Wonder Man-c #1) 435.00 1305.00 5000.00

ONDER COMICS
reat/Nedor/Better Publications: May, 1944 - No. 20, Oct, 1948

1-The Grim Reaper & Spectro, the Mind Reader begin; Hitler/Hirohito bondage-c 132.00 395.00 1250.00
2-Origin The Grim Reaper; Super Sleuths begin, end #8,17
 66.00 197.00 625.00
3-5 60.00 180.00 570.00
6-10: 6-Flag-c. 8-Last Spectro. 9-Wonderman begins
 50.00 150.00 450.00
1-14: 11-Dick Devens, King of Futuria begins, ends #14. 11,12-Ingels-c & splash pg. 14-Bondage-c 57.00 171.00 540.00
5-Tara begins (origin), ends #20 67.00 201.00 635.00
6,18: 16-Spectro app.; last Grim Reaper. 18-The Silver Knight begins
 57.00 171.00 540.00
7-Wonderman with Frazetta panels; Jill Trent with all Frazetta inks
 60.00 180.00 570.00
9-Frazetta panels 57.00 171.00 540.00
0-Most of Silver Knight by Frazetta 69.00 207.00 655.00
OTE: ***Ingels** c-11, 12. **Roussos** a-19. **Schomburg (Xela)** c-1-10; (airbrush)-13-20. Bondage c-2, 13, 15. Cover features: Grim Reaper #1-8; Wonder Man #9-15; Tara #16-20.*

ONDER DUCK (See Wisco)
arvel Comics (CDS): Sept, 1949 - No. 3, Mar, 1950

1-Funny animal 15.00 45.00 120.00
2,3 10.00 30.00 75.00

ONDERFUL ADVENTURES OF PINOCCHIO, THE (See Movie Comics & alt Disney Showcase #48)
hitman Publishing Co.: April, 1982 (Walt Disney)

GD2.0 FN6.0 NM9.4

nn-(Continuation of Movie Comics?); r/FC #92 2.40 6.00

WONDERFUL WORLD OF DISNEY, THE (Walt Disney)
Whitman Publishing Co.: 1978 (Digest, 116 pgs.)

1-Barks-a (reprints) 2.60 7.80 26.00
2 (no date) 2.00 6.00 18.00

WONDERFUL WORLD OF THE BROTHERS GRIMM (See Movie Comics)

WONDERLAND COMICS
Feature Publications/Prize: Summer, 1945 - No. 9, Feb-Mar, 1947

1-Alex in Wonderland begins; Howard Post-c 15.00 45.00 120.00
2-Howard Post-c/a(2) 8.65 26.00 60.00
3-9: 3,4-Post-c 7.15 21.50 50.00

WONDERLANDERS
Oktomica Ent: Jan, 1999 - Present ($2.50)

1,2 2.50

WONDER MAN (See The Avengers #9, 151)
Marvel Comics Group: Mar, 1986 ($1.25, one-shot, 52 pgs.)

1 3.00

WONDER MAN
Marvel Comics Group: Sept, 1991 - No. 29, Jan, 1994 ($1.00)

1-29: 1-Free fold out poster by Johnson/Austin. 1-3-Johnson/Austin-c/a. 2-Avengers West Coast x-over. 4 Austin-c(i) 2.00
Annual 1 (1992, $2.25)-Immonen-a (10 pgs.) 2.50
Annual 2 (1993, $2.25)-Bagged w/trading card 2.50

WONDERS OF ALADDIN, THE
Dell Publishing Co.: No. 1255, Feb-Apr, 1962

Four Color 1255-Movie 5.85 17.50 70.00

WONDER WOMAN (See Adventure Comics #459, All-Star Comics, Brave & the Bold, DC Comics Presents, JLA, Justice League of America, Legend of..., Power Record Comics, Sensation Comics, Super Friends and World's Finest Comics #244)

WONDER WOMAN
National Periodical Publications/All-American Publ./DC Comics: Summer, 1942 - No. 329, Feb, 1986

GD2.0 FN6.0 VF8.0 NM9.4
1-Origin Wonder Woman retold (more detailed than All-Star #8); H. G. Peter-c/a begins 1760.00 5280.00 11,400.00 22,000.00

1-Reprint, Oversize 13-1/2x10". **WARNING:** This comic is an exact reprint of the original except for its size. DC published it in 1974 with a second cover titling it as a Famous First Edition. There have been many reported cases of the outer cover being removed and the interior sold as the original edition. The reprint with the new outer cover removed is practically worthless. See Famous First Edition for value.

GD2.0 FN6.0 NM9.4
2-Origin/1st app. Mars; Duke of Deception app. 300.00 900.00 3000.00
3 200.00 600.00 1900.00
4,5: 5-1st Dr. Psycho app. 158.00 474.00 1500.00
6-10: 6-1st Cheetah app. 10-Invasion from Saturn 126.00 379.00 1200.00
11-20 100.00 300.00 950.00
21-30: 23-Story from Wonder Woman's childhood 84.00 253.00 800.00
31-40: 34-Robot-c. 38-Last H.G. Peter-c 58.00 174.00 550.00
41-44,46-49: 49-Used in **SOTI**, pgs. 234,236; last 52 pg. issue
 47.00 140.00 420.00
45-Origin retold 89.00 268.00 850.00
50-(44 pgs.)-Used in **POP**, pg. 97 47.00 140.00 420.00
51-60: 60-New logo 34.00 103.00 275.00
61-72: 62-Origin of W.W. i.d. 64-Story about 3-D movies. 70-1st Angle Man app. 72-Last pre-code (2/55) 30.00 90.00 240.00
73-90: 80-Origin The Invisible Plane. 85-1st S.A. issue. 89-Flying saucer-c/story 28.00 84.00 225.00
91-94,96,97,99: 97-Last H. G. Peter-a 21.00 62.00 165.00
95-A-Bomb-c 22.00 66.00 175.00
98-New origin & new art team (Andru & Esposito) begin (5/58); origin W.W. id w/new facts 23.00 69.00 185.00
100-(8/58) 24.00 73.00 195.00
101-104,106,108-110 19.00 56.00 150.00
105-(Scarce, 4/59)-W. W.'s secret origin; W. W. appears as girl (no costume yet) (called Wonder Girl - see DC Super-Stars #1) 79.00 237.00 750.00
107-1st advs. of Wonder Girl; 1st Merboy; tells how Wonder Woman won her

Wonder Woman #200 © DC

Wonder Woman (2nd series) #131 © DC

Wonderworld Comics #7 © FOX

costume 22.00 66.00 175.00
111-120 15.00 45.00 120.00
121-126: 122-1st app. Wonder Tot. 124-1st app. Wonder Woman Family. 126-Last 10¢ issue 11.00 33.00 90.00
127-130: 128-Origin The Invisible Plane retold. 129-2nd app. Wonder Woman Family (#133 is 3rd app.) 6.35 19.00 70.00
131-150: 132-Flying saucer-c 5.00 15.00 55.00
151-155,157,158,160-170 (1967): 151-Wonder Girl solo issue 4.10 12.30 45.00
156-(8/65)-Early mention of a comic book shop & comic collecting; mentions DCs selling for $100 a copy 4.10 12.30 45.00
159-Origin retold (1/66); 1st S.A. origin? 6.80 20.50 75.00
171-176 3.00 9.00 30.00
177-W. Woman/Supergirl battle 5.00 15.00 55.00
178-1st new W. Woman 5.00 15.00 55.00
179-Wears no costume to issue #203. 3.65 11.00 40.00
180-195: 180-Death of Steve Trevor. 195-Wood inks 2.50 7.50 24.00
196 (52 pgs.)-Origin-r/All-Star #8 (6 out of 9 pgs.) 2.80 8.40 28.00
197,198 (52 pgs.)-Reprints 2.80 8.40 28.00
199-Jeff Jones painted-c; 52 pgs. 3.50 9.60 35.00
200 (5-6/72)-Jeff Jones-c; 52 pgs. 4.10 12.30 45.00
201,202-Catwoman app. 202-Fafhrd & The Grey Mouser debut. 2.30 7.00 20.00
203,205-210,212: 212-The Cavalier app. 1.75 5.25 14.00
204-Return to old costume; death of I Ching. 2.00 6.00 18.00
211,214-(100 pgs.) 3.65 11.00 40.00
213,215,216,218-220: 220-N. Adams assist 1.50 4.50 12.00
217: (68 pgs.) 2.30 7.00 20.00
221,222,224-227,229,230,233-236,238-240 1.00 3.00 8.00
223,228,231,232,237,241,248: 223-Steve Trevor revived as Steve Howard & learns W.W.'s I.D. 228-Both Wonder Women team up & new World War II stories begin, end #243. 231,232: JSA app. 237-Origin retold. 241-Intro Bouncer; Spectre app. 248-Steve Trevor Howard dies (44 pgs.) 1.00 3.00 8.00
242-246,252-266,269,270: 243-Both W. Women team-up again. 269-Last Wood a(i) for DC? (7/80) 5.00
247,249-251,271: 247,249 (44 pgs.). 249-Hawkgirl app. 250-Origin/1st app. Orana, the new W. Woman. 251-Orana dies. 271-Huntress & 3rd Life of Steve Trevor begin 2.40 6.00
267,268-Re-intro Animal Man (5/80 & 6/80) 1.25 3.75 10.00
272-280,284-286,289,290,294-299,301-325 4.00
281-283: Joker-c/stories in Huntress back-ups 2.40 6.00
287,288,291-293: 287-New Teen Titans x-over. 288-New costume & logo. 291-293-Three part epic with Super-Heroines 4.00
300-($1.50, 76 pgs.)-Anniv. issue; Giffen-a; New Teen Titans, Bronze Age Sandman, JLA & G.A. Wonder Woman app.; 1st app. Lyta Trevor who becomes Fury in All-Star Squadron #25; G.A. W.W. & Steve Trevor revealed as married. 5.00
326-328 4.00
329 (Double size)-S.A. W.W. & Steve Trevor wed 1.00 3.00 8.00
NOTE: ***Andru/Esposito** c-66-160(most). **Buckler** a-300. **Colan** a-288-305p; c-288-290p. **Giffen** a-300p. **Grell** c-217. **Kaluta** c-297. **Gil Kane** c-294p, 303-305, 307, 312, 314. **Miller** c-298p. **Morrow** c-233. **Nasser** a-232p; c-231p, 232p. **Bob Oskner** c(i)-39-65(most). **Perez** c-283p, 284p. **Spiegle** a-312. **Staton** a(p)-241, 271-287, 289, 290, 294-299; c(p)-241, 245, 246. Huntress back-up stories 271-287, 289, 290, 294-299, 301-321.*

WONDER WOMAN
DC Comics: Feb, 1987 - Present (75¢/$1.00/$1.25/$1.95/$1.99)

0-(10/94) Zero Hour; released between #90 & #91 1.00 3.00 8.00
1-New origin; Perez-c/a begins 5.00
2-5 4.00
6-20: 9-Origin Cheetah. 12,13-Millennium x-over. 18,26-Free 16 pg. story 3.00
21-49,51-62: 24-Last Perez-a; scripts continue thru #62. 60-Vs. Lobo; last Perez-c. 62-Last $1.00-c 2.50
50-($1.50, 52 pgs.)-New Titans, Justice League 3.00
63-New direction & Bolland-c begin; Deathstroke story continued from Wonder Woman Special #1 3.00
64-84 2.00
85-1st Deodato-a; ends #100 1.50 4.50 12.00
86-88: 88-Superman-c & app. 5.00
89-97: 90-(9/94)-1st Artemis. 91-(11/94). 93-Hawkman app. 96-Joker-c 4.0
98,99 3.0
100 ($2.95, Newsstand)-Death of Artemis; Bolland-c ends. 4.0
100 ($3.95, Direct Market)-Death of Artemis; foil-c. 2.40 6.0
101-119, 121-125: 101-Begin $1.95-c; Byrne-c/a/scripts begin. 101-104-Darkseid app. 105-Phantom Stranger cameo. 106-108-Phantom Stranger & Demon app. 107,108-Arion app. 111-1st app. new Wonder Girl. 111,112-Vs.Doomsday. 112-Superman app. 113-Wonder Girl-c/app; Sugar & Spike app. 2.0
120 ($2.95)-Perez-c 3.0
126-149: 128-Hippolyta becomes new W.W. 130-133-Flash (Jay Garrick) & JSA app. 136-Diana returns to W.W. role; last Byrne issue. 137-Priest-s. 139-Luke-s/Paquette-a begin; Hughes-c thru #146 2.0
150-($2.95) Hughes-c/Clark-a; Zauriel app. 3.0
151-158-Hughes-c. 153-Superboy app. 2.0
159-163: 159-Begin $2.25-c. 160,161-Clayface app. 162,163-Aquaman app. 2.2
164-167: Phil Jimenez-s/a begin; Hughes-c; Batman app. 2.2
#1,000,000 (11/98) 853rd Century x-over; Deodato-c 3.0
Annual 1,2: 1 ('88, $1.50)-Art Adams-a. 2 ('89, $2.00, 68 pgs.)-All women artists issue; Perez-c(i)/a. 4.0
Annual 3 (1992, $2.50, 68 pgs.)-Quesada-c(p) 3.0
Annual 4 (1995, $3.50)-Year One 3.5
Annual 5 (1996, $2.95)-Legends of the Dead Earth story; Byrne scripts; Cockrum-a 3.0
Annual 6 (1997, $3.95)-Pulp Heroes 4.0
Annual 7,8 ('98,'99, $2.95)-7-Ghosts; Wrightson-c. 8-JLApe, A.Adams-c 3.0
...Donna Troy (6/98, $1.95) Girlfrenzy; Jimenez-a 2.0
Gallery (1996, $3.50)-Bolland-c; pin-ups by various 4.0
Lifelines TPB ('98, $9.95) r/#106-112; Byrne-c/a 10.0
Plus 1 (1/97, $2.95)-Jesse Quick-c/app. 3.0
Second Genesis TPB (1997, $9.95)-r/#101-105 10.0
Secret Files 1,2 (3/98, 7/99; $4.95) 5.0
Special 1 (1992, $1.75, 52 pgs.)-Deathstroke-c/story continued in Wonder Woman #63 3.0
The Challenge Of Artemis TPB (1996, $9.95)-r/#94-100; Deodato-c/a 10.0
NOTE: ***Art Adams** a-Annual 1. **Byrne** c/a 101-107. **Bolton** a-Annual 1. **Deodato** a-85-100. **Perez** a-Annual 1; c-Annual 1(i). **Quesada** c(p)-Annual 3.*

WONDER WOMAN: AMAZONIA
DC Comics: 1997 ($7.95, Graphic Album format, one shot)

1-Elseworlds; Messner-Loebs-s/Winslade-a 8.0

WONDER WOMAN SPECTACULAR (See DC Special Series #9)

WONDER WOMAN: THE ONCE AND FUTURE STORY
DC Comics: 1998 ($4.95, one-shot)

1-Trina Robbins-s/Doran & Guice-a 5.0

WONDERWORLD COMICS (Formerly Wonder Comics)
Fox Features Syndicate: No. 3, July, 1939 - No. 33, Jan, 1942

3-Intro The Flame by Fine; Dr. Fung (Powell-a), K-51 (Powell-a?), & Yarko the Great, Master Magician (Eisner-a) continues; Eisner/Fine-c 626.00 1878.00 7200.0
4-Lou Fine-c 305.00 915.00 3200.0
5,6,9,10: Lou Fine-c 174.00 521.00 1650.0
7-Classic Lou Fine-c 295.00 885.00 2800.0
8-Classic Lou Fine-c 242.00 726.00 2300.0
11-Origin The Flame 132.00 395.00 1250.0
12-15:13-Dr. Fung ends; last Fine-c 111.00 332.00 1050.0
16-20 82.00 245.00 775.0
21-Origin The Black Lion & Cub 74.00 221.00 700.0
22-27: 22,25-Dr. Fung app. 61.00 182.00 575.0
28-Origin & 1st app. U.S. Jones (8/41); Lu-Nar, the Moon Man begins 82.00 245.00 775.0
29,31,33 50.00 150.00 450.0
30-Intro & Origin Flame Girl 89.00 268.00 850.0
32-Hitler-c 66.00 197.00 625.0
NOTE: *Spies at War by **Eisner** in #13, 17. Yarko by **Eisner** in #3-11. **Eisner** text illos-3. **Lou Fi**[ne] a-3-11; c-3-13, 15; text illos-4. **Nordling** a-4-14. **Powell** a-3-12. **Tuska** a-5-9. Bondage-c 14, 15, 28, 31, 32. Cover features: The Flame-#3, 5-31; U.S. Jones-#32, 33.*

WONDERWORLDS
Innovation Publishing: 1992 ($3.50, squarebound, 100 pgs.)

Woody Woodpecker #34 © Walter Lantz

The World Around Us #24 © GIL

The World Below #3 © Paul Chadwick

GD2.0 FN6.0 NM9.4

1-Rebound super-hero comics, contents may vary; Hero Alliance, Terraformers, etc. 3.50

/OODSY OWL (See March of Comics #395)
old Key: Nov, 1973 - No. 10, Feb, 1976

1 2.00 6.00 16.00
2-10 1.25 3.75 10.00

/OODY WOODPECKER (Walter Lantz... #73 on?)(See Dell Giants for nnuals)(Also see The Funnies, Jolly Jingles, Kite Fun Book, New Funnies)
ell Publishing Co./Gold Key No. 73-187/Whitman No. 188 on:
o. 169, 10/47 - No. 72, 5-7/62; No. 73, 10/62 - No. 201, 4/84 (nn 192)

our Color 169(#1)-Drug turns Woody into a Mr. Hyde
15.00 45.00 180.00
our Color 188 10.00 30.00 120.00
our Color 202,232,249,264,288 6.30 19.00 75.00
our Color 305,336,350 4.10 12.30 45.00
our Color 364,374,390,405,416,431('52) 3.65 11.00 40.00
6 (12-1/52-53) - 30('55) 2.50 7.50 25.00
31-50 2.40 7.35 22.00
51-72 (Last Dell) 2.00 6.00 18.00
'3-75 (Giants, 84 pgs., Gold Key) 4.10 12.30 45.00
'6-80 2.00 6.00 18.00
31-103: 103-Last 12¢ issue 1.75 5.25 14.00
04-120 1.50 4.50 12.00
21-140 1.10 3.30 9.00
41-160 1.00 2.80 7.00
61-187 2.40 6.00
88,189 (Whitman) 1.00 3.00 8.00
90(9/80),191(11/80)-pre-pack? 1.75 5.25 14.00
No #192)
93-197 1.25 3.75 10.00
98-201 (All #90062 on-c, no date or date code, pre-pack?)
1.50 4.50 12.00
Christmas Parade 1(11/68-Giant)(G.K.) 3.20 9.60 35.00
Summer Fun 1(6/66-G.K.)(84 pgs.) 4.10 12.30 45.00
OTE: *15¢ Canadian editions of the 12¢ issues exist. Reprints-No. 92, 102, 103, 105, 106, 124, 25, 152, 153, 157, 162, 165, 194(1/3)-200(1/3).*

/OODY WOODPECKER (See Comic Album #5,9,13, Dell Giant #24, 40, 54, Dell Giants, he Funnies, Golden Comics Digest #1, 3, 5, 8, 15, 16, 20, 24, 32, 37, 44, March of Comics #16, 4, 85, 93, 109, 124, 139, 158, 177, 184, 203, 222, 239, 249, 261, 420, 454, 466, 478, New unnies & Super Book #12, 24)

/OODY WOODPECKER
Harvey Comics: Sept, 1991 - No. 7, 1993 ($1.25)

1-7: 1-r/W.W. #53 2.00
0th Anniversary Special 1 (10/91, $2.50, 68 pgs.) 3.00

/OODY WOODPECKER AND FRIENDS
Harvey Comics: Dec, 1991 - No. 4, 1992 ($1.25)

1-4 2.00

/ORDSMITH (1st Series)
Renegade Press: Aug, 1985 - No. 12, Jan, 1988 ($1.70/$2.00, B&W, bi-monthly)

1-12: R. G. Taylor-c/a 3.00

/ORDSMITH (2nd Series)
Caliber: 1996 - No. 9, 1997 ($2.95, B&W, limited series)

1-9: Reprints in all. 1-Contains 3 pg. sketchbook. 6-Flip book w/Raven Chronicles #10 3.00

/ORD WARRIORS (Also see Quest for Dreams Lost)
Literacy Volunteers of Chicago: 1987 ($1.50, B&W)(Proceeds donated to help iteracy)

1-Jon Sable by Grell, Ms. Tree, Streetwolf; Chaykin-c 3.00

/ORLD AROUND US, THE (Illustrated Story of...)
Gilberton Publishers (Classics Illustrated): Sep, 1958 -No. 36, Oct, 1961 25¢)

1-Dogs; Evans-a 7.15 21.50 50.00
2-4: 2-Indians; Check-a. 3-Horses; L. B. Cole-c. 4-Railroads; L. B. Cole-a (5 pgs.) 7.15 21.50 50.00
5-Space; Ingels-a 9.30 28.00 65.00
6-The F.B.I.; Disbrow, Evans, Ingels-a 9.30 28.00 65.00
7-Pirates; Disbrow, Ingels, Kinstler-a 8.65 26.00 60.00
8-Flight; Evans, Ingels, Crandall-a 8.65 26.00 60.00
9-Army; Disbrow, Ingels, Orlando-a 7.15 21.50 50.00
10-13: 10-Navy; Disbrow, Kinstler-a. 11-Marine Corps. 12-Coast Guard; Ingels-a (9 pgs.). 13-Air Force; L.B. Cole-c 7.15 21.50 50.00
14-French Revolution; Crandall, Evans, Kinstler-a 9.30 28.00 65.00
15-Prehistoric Animals; Al Williamson-a, 6 & 10 pgs. plus Morrow-a
10.00 30.00 70.00
16-18: 16-Crusades; Kinstler-a. 17-Festivals; Evans, Crandall-a. 18-Great Scientists; Crandall, Evans, Torres, Williamson, Morrow-a
8.65 26.00 60.00
19-Jungle; Crandall, Williamson, Morrow-a 10.00 30.00 70.00
20-Communications; Crandall, Evans, Torres-a 9.30 28.00 65.00
21-American Presidents; Crandall/Evans, Morrow-a 9.30 28.00 65.00
22-Boating; Morrow-a 6.40 19.25 45.00
23-Great Explorers; Crandall, Evans-a 8.65 26.00 60.00
24-Ghosts; Morrow, Evans-a 9.30 28.00 65.00
25-Magic; Evans, Morrow-a 9.30 28.00 65.00
26-The Civil War 10.00 30.00 80.00
27-Mountains (High Advs.); Crandall/Evans, Morrow, Torres-a
8.65 26.00 60.00
28-Whaling; Crandall, Evans, Morrow, Torres, Wildey-a; L.B. Cole-c
8.65 26.00 60.00
29-Vikings; Crandall, Evans, Torres, Morrow-a 10.00 30.00 70.00
30-Undersea Adventure; Crandall/Evans, Kirby, Morrow, Torres-a
9.30 28.00 65.00
31-Hunting; Crandall/Evans, Ingels, Kinstler, Kirby-a 8.65 26.00 60.00
32,33: 32-For Gold & Glory; Morrow, Kirby, Crandall, Evans-a. 33-Famous Teens; Torres, Crandall, Evans-a 8.65 26.00 60.00
34-36: 34-Fishing; Crandall/Evans-a. 35-Spies; Kirby, Morrow?, Evans-a. 36-Fight for Life (Medicine); Kirby-a 8.65 26.00 60.00
NOTE: See Classics Illustrated Special Edition. Another *World Around Us* issue entitled *The Sea* had been prepared in 1962 but was never published in the U.S. It was published in the British/European *World Around Us* series. Those series then continued with seven additional WAU titles not in the U.S. series.

WORLD BELOW, THE
Dark Horse Comics: Mar, 1999 - No. 4, Jun, 1999 ($2.50, limited series)

1-4-Paul Chadwick-s/c/a 2.50

WORLD BELOW, THE: DEEPER AND STRANGER
Dark Horse Comics: Dec, 1999 - No. 4, Mar, 2000 ($2.95, B&W)

1-4-Paul Chadwick-s/c/a 2.95

WORLD FAMOUS HEROES MAGAZINE
Comic Corp. of America (Centaur): Oct, 1941 - No. 4, Apr, 1942 (comic book)

1-Gustavson-c; Lubbers, Glanzman-a; Davy Crockett, Paul Revere, Lewis & Clark, John Paul Jones stories; Flag-c 116.00 348.00 1100.00
2-Lou Gehrig life story; Lubbers-a 50.00 150.00 450.00
3,4-Lubbers-a. 4-Wild Bill Hickok story; 2 pg. Marlene Dietrich story
44.00 133.00 400.00

WORLD FAMOUS STORIES
Croyden Publishers: 1945

1-Ali Baba, Hansel & Gretel, Rip Van Winkle, Mid-Summer Night's Dream
12.50 37.50 100.00

WORLD IS HIS PARISH, THE
George A. Pflaum: 1953 (15¢)

nn-The story of Pope Pius XII 5.00 15.00 30.00

WORLD OF ADVENTURE (Walt Disney's...)(TV)
Gold Key: Apr, 1963 - No. 3, Oct, 1963 (12¢)

1-Disney TV characters; Savage Sam, Johnny Shiloh, Capt. Nemo, The Mooncussers 3.00 9.00 30.00
2,3 2.00 6.00 18.00

WORLD OF ARCHIE, THE (See Archie Giant Series Mag. #148, 151, 156, 160, 165, 171, 177, 182, 188, 193, 200, 208, 213, 225, 232, 237, 244, 249, 456, 461, 468, 473, 480, 485, 492, 497, 504, 509, 516, 521, 532, 543, 554, 565, 574, 587, 599, 612, 627)

WORLD OF ARCHIE
Archie Comics: Aug, 1992 - No. 26 ($1.25/$1.50)

World of Fantasy #6 © MAR

World of Mystery #5 © MAR

World's Finest Comics #8 © DC

GD2.0 FN6.0 NM9.4

1 3.00
2-15: 9-Neon ink-c 2.50
16-26 2.00

WORLD OF FANTASY
Atlas Comics (CPC No. 1-15/ZPC No. 16-19): May, 1956 - No. 19, Aug, 1959

	GD2.0	FN6.0	NM9.4
1	44.00	133.00	400.00
2-Williamson-a (4 pgs.)	31.00	94.00	250.00
3-Sid Check, Roussos-a	28.00	83.00	220.00
4-7	21.00	64.00	170.00
8-Matt Fox, Orlando, Berg-a	22.00	66.00	175.00
9-Krigstein-a	21.00	64.00	170.00
10-15: 11-Torres-a	17.00	51.00	135.00
16-Williamson-a (4 pgs.); Ditko, Kirby-a	24.00	71.00	190.00
17-19-Ditko, Kirby-a	24.00	71.00	190.00

NOTE: ***Ayers** a-3. **B. Baily** a-4. **Berg** a-5, 6, 8. **Brodsky** c-3. **Check** a-3. **Ditko** a-17, 19. **Everett** a-2; c-4-7, 9, 12, 13. **Forte** a-4. **Infantino** a-14. **Kirby** c-15, 17-19. **Krigstein** a-9. **Maneely** c-2, 14. **Mooney** a-14. **Morrow** a-7. **Orlando** a-8, 13, 14. **Pakula** a-9. **Powell** a-4, 6. **R.Q. Sale** a-3, 9. **Severin** c-1.*

WORLD OF GIANT COMICS, THE (See Archie All-Star Specials under Archie Comics)

WORLD OF GINGER FOX, THE (Also see Ginger Fox)
Comico: Nov, 1986 ($6.95, 8 1/2 x 11", 68 pgs., mature)

Graphic Novel ($6.95) 7.00
Hardcover ($27.95) 28.00

WORLD OF JUGHEAD, THE (See Archie Giant Series Mag. #9, 14, 19, 24, 30, 136, 143, 149, 152, 157, 161, 166, 172, 178, 183, 189, 194, 202, 209, 215, 227, 233, 239, 245, 251, 457, 463, 469, 475, 481, 487, 493, 499, 505, 511, 517, 523, 531, 542, 553, 564, 577, 590, 602)

WORLD OF KRYPTON, THE (World of...#3) (See Superman #248)
DC Comics, Inc.: 7/79 - No. 3, 9/79; 12/87 - No. 4, 3/88 (Both are lim. series)

1-3 (1979, 40¢; 1st comic book mini-series): 1-Jor-El marries Lara. 3-Baby Superman sent to Earth; Krypton explodes; Mon-el app. 4.00
1-4 (75¢)-Byrne scripts; Byrne/Simonson-c 3.00

WORLD OF METROPOLIS, THE
DC Comics: Aug, 1988 - No. 4, July, 1988 ($1.00, limited series)

1-4: Byrne scripts 3.00

WORLD OF MYSTERY
Atlas Comics (GPI): June, 1956 - No. 7, July, 1957

	GD2.0	FN6.0	NM9.4
1-Torres, Orlando-a; Powell-a?	44.00	133.00	400.00
2-Woodish-a	19.00	56.00	150.00
3-Torres, Davis, Ditko-a	24.00	71.00	190.00
4-Pakula, Powell-a	24.00	71.00	190.00
5,7: 5-Orlando-a	19.00	56.00	150.00
6-Williamson/Mayo-a (4 pgs.); Ditko-a; Crandall text illo	24.00	71.00	190.00

NOTE: ***Brodsky** c-2. **Colan** a-7. **Everett** c-1, 3. **Pakula** a-4, 6. **Romita** a-2. **Severin** c-7.*

WORLD OF SMALLVILLE
DC Comics: Apr, 1988 - No. 4, July, 1988 (75¢, limited series)

1-4: Byrne scripts 3.00

WORLD OF SUSPENSE
Atlas News Co.: Apr, 1956 - No. 8, July, 1957

	GD2.0	FN6.0	NM9.4
1	40.00	120.00	320.00
2-Ditko-a (4 pgs.)	23.00	69.00	185.00
3,7-Williamson-a in both (4 pgs.); #7-with Mayo	23.00	69.00	185.00
4-6,8	19.00	56.00	150.00

NOTE: ***Berg** a-6. **Cameron** a-2. **Ditko** a-2. **Drucker** a-1. **Everett** a-1, 5; c-6. **Heck** a-5. **Maneely** a-1; c-1-3. **Orlando** a-5. **Powell** a-6. **Reinman** a-4. **Roussos** a-6. **Shores** a-1.*

WORLD OF WHEELS (Formerly Dragstrip Hotrodders)
Charlton Comics: No. 17, Oct, 1967 - No. 32, June, 1970

	GD2.0	FN6.0	NM9.4
17-20-Features Ken King	2.50	7.50	25.00
21-32-Features Ken King	2.30	7.00	20.00
Modern Comics Reprint 23(1978)			5.00

WORLD OF WOOD
Eclipse Comics: 1986 - No. 4, 1987; No. 5, 2/89 ($1.75, limited series)

1-4:1-Dave Stevens-c. 2-Wood/Stevens-c 3.00
5 ($2.00, B&W)-r/Avon's Flying Saucers 4.00

WORLD'S BEST COMICS (World's Finest Comics #2 on)
National Per. Publications (100 pgs.): Spring, 1941 (Cardboard-c)(DC's 6th annual format comic)

	GD2.0	FN6.0	VF8.0	NM9.4
1-The Batman, Superman, Crimson Avenger, Johnny Thunder, The King, Young Dr. Davis, Zatara, Lando, Man of Magic, & Red, White & Blue begin; Superman, Batman & Robin covers begin (inside-c is blank); Fred Ray-c; 15¢ cover price	1360.00	4080.00	8840.00	17,000.00

WORLDS BEYOND (Stories of Weird Adventure)(Worlds of Fear #2 on)
Fawcett Publications: Nov, 1951

	GD2.0	FN6.0	NM9.4
1-Powell, Bailey-a; Moldoff-c	42.00	125.00	375.00

WORLDS COLLIDE
DC Comics: July, 1994 ($2.50, one-shot)

1-($2.50, 52 pgs.)-Milestone & Superman titles x-over 2.50
1-($3.95, 52 pgs.)-Polybagged w/vinyl clings 4.00

WORLD'S FAIR COMICS (See New York...)

WORLD'S FINEST (Also see Legends of World Finest
DC Comics: 1990 - No. 3, 1990 ($3.95, squarebound, limited series, 52 pgs.)

1-3: Batman & Superman team-up against The Joker and Lex Luthor; Dave Gibbons scripts & Steve Rude-c/a. 2,3-Joker/Luthor painted-c by Steve Rude 5.00
TPB-($19.95) r/#1-3 20.00

WORLD'S FINEST COMICS (Formerly World's Best Comics #1)
National Periodical Publ./DC Comics: No. 2, Sum, 1941 - No. 323, Jan, 1986 (#1-17 have cardboard covers) (#2-9 have 100 pgs.)

	GD2.0	FN6.0	NM9.4
2 (100 pgs.)-Superman, Batman & Robin covers continue from World's Best; (cover price 15¢ #2-70)	420.00	1260.00	4800.00
3-The Sandman begins; last Johnny Thunder; origin & 1st app. The Scarecrow	314.00	943.00	3300.00
4-Hop Harrigan app.; last Young Dr. Davis	253.00	758.00	2400.00
5-Intro. TNT & Dan the Dyna-Mite; last King & Crimson Avenger	253.00	758.00	2400.00
6-Star Spangled Kid begins (Sum/42); Aquaman app.; S&K Sandman with Sandy in new costume begins, ends #7	190.00	570.00	1800.00
7-Green Arrow begins (Fall/42); last Lando & Red, White & Blue; S&K art	190.00	570.00	1800.00
8-Boy Commandos begin (by Simon(p) #12); last The King	174.00	521.00	1650.00
9-Batman cameo in Star Spangled Kid; S&K-a; last 100 pg. issue; Hitler, Mussolini, Tojo-c	200.00	600.00	1900.00
10-S&K-a; 76 pg. issues begin	158.00	474.00	1500.00
11-17: 17-Last cardboard cover issue	157.00	411.00	1300.00
18-20: 18-Paper covers begin; last Star Spangled Kid. 20-Last quarterly issue	116.00	348.00	1100.00
21-30: 21-Begin bi-monthly. 30-Johnny Everyman app.	84.00	253.00	800.00
31-40: 33-35-Tomahawk app.	74.00	221.00	700.00
41-50: 41-Boy Commandos end. 42-Intro The Wyoming Kid & begins (9-10/49), ends #63. 43-Full Steam Foley begins, ends #48. 48-Last square binding. 49-Tom Sparks, Boy Inventor begins; robot-c	55.00	165.00	525.00
51-60: 51-Zatara ends. 54-Last 76 pg. issue. 59-Manhunters Around the World begins (7-8/52), ends #62	55.00	165.00	525.00
61-64: 61-Joker story. 63-Capt. Compass app.	55.00	165.00	500.00
65-Origin Superman; Tomahawk begins (7-8/53), ends #101	76.00	229.00	725.00
66-70-(15¢ issues, scarce)-Last 15¢, 68pg. issue	55.00	165.00	500.00
71-(10¢ issue, scarce)-Superman & Batman begin as team (7-8/54); were in separate stories until now; Superman & Batman exchange identities; 10¢ issues begin	88.00	264.00	1050.00
72-(10¢ issue, scarce)	60.00	180.00	725.00
73-(10¢ issue, scarce)	60.00	180.00	725.00
74-Last pre-code issue	48.00	144.00	575.00
75-(1st code approved, 3-4/55)	44.00	132.00	525.00
76-80: 77-Superman loses powers & Batman obtains them this issue only	35.00	105.00	350.00

81-90: 84-1st S.A. issue. 88-1st Joker/Luthor team-up. 89-2nd Batmen of All Nations (aka Club of Heroes). 90-Batwoman's 1st app. in World's Finest

World's Finest Comics #180 © DC

World's Finest Comics #323 © DC

Worlds of Fear #9 © FAW

(10/57, 3rd app. anywhere) plus-c app. 28.00 85.00 280.00
1-93,95-99: 96-99-Kirby Green Arrow. 99-Robot-c 21.00 63.00 210.00
4-Origin Superman/Batman team retold 53.00 159.00 635.00
)0 (3/59) 35.00 105.00 350.00
)1-110: 102-Tommy Tomorrow begins, ends #124 15.00 45.00 150.00
1-121: 111-1st app. The Clock King. 113-Intro. Miss Arrowette in Green Arrow; 1st Bat-Mite/Mr. Mxyzptlk team-up (11/60). 117-Batwoman-c. 121-Last 10¢ issue 12.00 36.00 120.00
2-128,130-142: 123-2nd Bat-Mite/Mr. Mxyzptlk team-up (2/62). 125-Aquaman begins (5/62), ends #139 (Aquaman #1 is dated 1-2/62). 135-Last Dick Sprang story. 140-Last Green Arrow; last Clayface until Action #443. 142-Origin The Composite Superman (villain); Legion app. 6.35 19.00 70.00
29-Joker/Luthor team-up-c/story 8.15 24.50 90.00
43-150: 143-1st Mailbag 4.55 13.65 50.00
51-153,155,157-160: 156-Intro of Bizarro Batman. 157-2nd Super Sons story; last app. Kathy Kane (Bat-woman) until Batman Family #10 3.65 11.00 40.00
54-1st Super Sons story; last Bat-Woman in costume until Batman Family #10. 4.55 13.65 50.00
56-1st Bizarro Batman; Joker-c/story 10.00 30.00 110.00
61,170 (80-Pg. Giants G-28,G-40) 4.55 13.65 50.00
62-165,167-169,171,172: 168,172-Adult Legion app. 169-3rd app. new Batgirl(9/67)(cover and 1 panel cameo); 3rd Bat-Mite/Mr. Mxyzptlk team-up. 3.00 9.00 30.00
66-Joker-c/story 3.20 9.60 35.00
73-('68)-1st S.A. app. Two-Face as Batman becomes Two-Face in story 7.65 23.00 85.00
74-Adams-c 3.00 9.00 32.00
75,176-Neal Adams-c/a; both reprint J'onn J'onzz origin/Detective #225,226 3.20 9.60 35.00
77-Joker/Luthor team-up-c/story 3.00 9.00 30.00
78,180,182,183,185,186: Adams-c on all. 182-Silent Knight-r/Brave & Bold #6. 185-Last 12¢ issue. 186-Johnny Quick-r 2.50 7.50 25.00
79-(80 Page Giant G-52) -Adams-c; r/#94 3.65 11.00 40.00
81,184,187: 187-Green Arrow origin-r by Kirby (Adv. #256) 2.40 7.35 22.00
88,197:(Giants G-64,G-76; 64 pages) 3.65 11.00 40.00
89-196: 190-193-Robin-r 2.00 6.00 18.00
98,199-3rd Superman/Flash race (see Flash #175 & Superman #199) 199-Adams-c 7.35 21.75 80.00
00-Adams-c 2.50 7.50 25.00
01-203: 203-Last 15¢ issue. 2.00 6.00 16.00
04,205-(48 pgs.) Adams-c: 204-Wonder Woman app. 205-Shining Knight-r (6 pgs.) by Frazetta/Adv. #153; Teen Titans x-over 2.40 7.35 22.00
06 (Giant G-88, 64 pgs.) 3.20 9.60 35.00
07,212: 207-(48 pgs.). 212-(25¢, 52 pgs.) 2.30 7.00 20.00
08-211(25¢-c) Adams-c: 208-(48 pgs.) Origin Robotman-r/Det. #138. 209-211-(52 pgs.) 2.00 6.00 18.00
13,214,216-222,229: 217-Metamorpho begins, ends #220; Batman/Superman team-ups resume. 229-r/origin Superman-Batman team 1.50 4.50 12.00
15-Intro. Batman Jr. & Superman Jr. 2.40 7.35 22.00
23-228-(100 pgs.). 223-N. Adams-r. 223-Deadman origin. 226-N. Adams, S&K, Toth-r; Manhunter part origin-r/Det. #225,226. 227-Deadman app. 2.50 7.50 25.00
30-(68 pgs.) 2.00 6.00 16.00
31-243,247,248: 242-Super Sons. 248-Last Vigilante 1.25 3.75 10.00
44-246-Adams-c: 244-$1.00, 84 pg. issues begin; Green Arrow, Black Canary, Wonder Woman, Vigilante begin; 246-Death of Stuff in Vigilante; origin Vigilante retold 1.50 4.50 12.00
49-252 (84 pgs.) Ditko-a: 249-The Creeper begins by Ditko, 84 pgs. 250-The Creeper origin retold by Ditko. 252-Last 84 pg. issue 1.50 4.50 12.00
53-257,259-265: 253-Capt. Marvel begins; 68 pgs. begin, end #265. 255-Last Creeper. 256-Hawkman begins. 257-Black Lightning begins. 263-Super Sons. 264-Clay Face app. 1.00 2.80 7.00
58-Adams-c 1.00 3.00 8.00
66-270,272-282-(52 pgs.). 267-Challengers of the Unknown app. 268-Capt. Marvel Jr. origin retold. 274-Zatanna begins. 279, 280-Capt. Marvel Jr. & Kid Eternity learn they are brothers. 5.00
271-(52pgs.) Origin Superman/Batman team retold 2.40 6.00
283-299: 284-Legion app. 4.00
300-($1.25, 52pgs.)-Justice League of America, New Teen Titans & The Outsiders app.; Perez-a (3 pgs.) 4.00
301-322: 304-Origin Null and Void. 309,319-Free 16 pg. story in each (309-Flash Force 2000, 319-Mask preview) 3.00
323-Last issue 5.00

NOTE: ***Neal Adams** a-230ir; c-174-176, 178-180, 182, 183, 185, 186, 199-205, 208-211, 244-246, 258. **Austin** a-244-246i. **Burnley** a-8, 10; c-7-9, 11-14, 15p?, 16-18p, 20-31p. **Colan** a-274p, 297, 299. **Ditko** a-249-255. **Giffen** a-322; c-284p, 322. **G. Kane** a-38, 174r, 282, 283; c-281, 282, 289. **Kirby** a-187. **Kubert** Zatara-40-44. **Miller** c-285p. **Mooney** c-134. **Morrow** a-245-248. **Mortimer** c-16-21, 26-71. **Nasser** a(p)-244-246, 259, 260. **Newton** a-253-281p. **Orlando** a-224r. **Perez** a-300i; c-271, 276, 277p, 278p. **Fred Ray** c-1-5. **Fred Ray/Robinson** c-13-16. **Robinson** a-2, 9, 13-15; c-6. **Rogers** a-259p. **Roussos** a-212r. **Simonson** c-291. **Spiegle** a-275-278, 284. **Staton** a-262p, 273p. **Swan/Moldoff** c-126. **Swan/Mortimer** c-79-82. **Toth** a-228r. **Tuska** a-230r, 250p, 252p, 254p, 257p, 283p, 284p, 308p. Boy Commandos by **Infantino** #39-41.*

WORLD'S FINEST COMICS DIGEST (See DC Special Series #23)

WORLD'S GREATEST ATHLETE (See Walt Disney Showcase #14)

WORLD'S GREATEST SONGS
Atlas Comics (Male): Sept, 1954

1-(Scarce)-Heath & Harry Anderson-a; Eddie Fisher life story plus-c; gives lyrics to Frank Sinatra song "Young at Heart" 40.00 120.00 325.00

WORLD'S GREATEST STORIES
Jubilee Publications: Jan, 1949 - No. 2, May, 1949

1-Alice in Wonderland; Lewis Carroll adapt. 33.00 98.00 260.00
2-Pinocchio 31.00 94.00 250.00

WORLDS OF FEAR (Stories of Weird Adventure)(Formerly Worlds Beyond #1)
Fawcett Publications: V1#2, Jan, 1952 - V2#10, June, 1953

V1#2 42.00 125.00 375.00
3-Evans-a 40.00 120.00 325.00
4-6(9/52) 34.00 103.00 275.00
V2#7-9 30.00 90.00 240.00
10-Saunders painted-c; man with no eyes surrounded by eyeballs-c plus eyes ripped out story 63.00 189.00 600.00

NOTE: ***Moldoff** c-2-8. **Powell** a-2, 4, 5. **Sekowsky** a-4, 5.*

WORLDS UNKNOWN
Marvel Comics Group: May, 1973 - No. 8, Aug, 1974

1-r/from Astonishing #54; Torres, Reese-a 2.00 6.00 16.00
2-8 1.25 3.75 10.00

NOTE: ***Adkins/Mooney** a-5. **Buscema** c/a-4p. **W. Howard** c/a-3i. **Kane** a(p)-1,2; c(p)-5, 6, 8. **Sutton** a-2. **Tuska** a(p)-7, 8; c-7p. No. 7, 8 has Golden Voyage of Sinbad movie adaptation.*

WORLD WAR STORIES
Dell Publishing Co.: Apr-June, 1965 - No. 3, Dec, 1965

1-Glanzman-a in all 3.20 9.60 35.00
2,3 2.50 7.50 24.00

WORLD WAR II (See Classics Illustrated Special Issue)

WORLD WAR II: 1946
Antarctic Press: Oct, 1998 - No. 2 ($3.95, B&W)

1,2-Nomura-s/a 4.00

WORLD WAR III
Ace Periodicals: Mar, 1953 - No. 2, May, 1953

1-(Scarce)-Atomic bomb blast-c; Cameron-a 58.00 174.00 550.00
2-Used in **POP**, pg. 78 & B&W & color illos; Cameron-a 55.00 165.00 500.00

WORLD WITHOUT END
DC Comics: 1990 - No. 6, 1991 ($2.50, limited series, mature, stiff-c)

1-6: Horror/fantasy; all painted-c/a 2.50

WORLD WRESTLING FEDERATION BATTLEMANIA
Valiant: 1991 - No. 5?, 1991 ($2.50, magazine size, 68 pgs.)

1-5: 5-Includes 2 free pull-out posters 4.00

WORST FROM MAD, THE (Annual)
E. C. Comics: 1958 - No. 12, 1969 (Each annual cover is reprinted from the

Wow Comics #4 © Henle Publ.

Wow Comics #32 © FAW

Wyatt Earp #2 © MAR

cover of the Mad issues being reprinted)(Value is 1/2 if bonus is missing)
nn(1958)-Bonus; record labels & travel stickers; 1st Mad annual; r/Mad #29-34 — 40.00 120.00 320.00
2(1959)-Bonus is small 33[1]/3 rpm record entitled "Meet the Staff of Mad"; r/Mad #35-40 — 40.00 120.00 360.00
3(1960)-Has 20x30" campaign poster "Alfred E. Neuman for President"; r/Mad #41-46 — 19.00 57.00 210.00
4(1961)-Sunday comics section; r/Mad #47-54 — 17.50 52.00 190.00
5(1962)-Has 33-1/3 record; r/Mad #55-62 — 27.50 82.00 300.00
6(1963)-Has 33-1/3 record; r/Mad #63-70 — 28.00 85.00 310.00
7(1964)-Mad protest signs; r/Mad #71-76 — 9.50 28.50 105.00
8(1965)-Build a Mad Zeppelin — 12.50 37.00 135.00
9(1966)-33-1/3 rpm record; Beatles on-c — 19.00 57.00 210.00
10(1967)-Mad bumper sticker — 6.35 19.00 70.00
11(1968)-Mad cover window stickers — 5.90 17.75 65.00
12(1969)-Mad picture postcards; Orlando-a — 5.90 17.75 65.00
NOTE: *Covers: **Bob Clarke**-#8. **Mingo**-#7, 9-12.*

WOTALIFE COMICS (Formerly Nutty Life #2; Phantom Lady #13 on)
Fox Features Syndicate/Norlen Mag.: No. 3, Aug-Sept, 1946 - No. 12, July, 1947; 1959

3-Cosmo Cat, Li'l Pan, others begin — 10.00 30.00 75.00
4-12-Cosmo Cat, Li'l Pan in all — 7.85 23.50 55.00
1(1959-Norlen)-Atomic Rabbit, Atomic Mouse; reprints cover to #6; reprints entire book? — 6.40 19.25 45.00

WOTALIFE COMICS
Green Publications: 1957 - No. 5, 1957

1 — 5.70 17.00 40.00
2-5 — 4.65 14.00 28.00

WOW COMICS
Henle Publishing Co.: July, 1936 - No. 4, Nov, 1936 (52 pgs., magazine size)

1-Buck Jones in "The Phantom Rider" (1st app. in comics), Fu Manchu; Capt. Scott Dalton begins; Eisner-a; Briefer-c — 263.00 790.00 2500.00
2-Ken Maynard, Fu Manchu, Popeye by Segar plus article on Popeye; Eisner-a — 200.00 600.00 1900.00
3-Eisner-c/a(3); Popeye by Segar, Fu Manchu, Hiram Hick by Bob Kane, Space Limited app.; Jimmy Dempsey talks about Popeye's punch; Bob Ripley Believe it or Not begins; Briefer-a — 179.00 537.00 1700.00
4-Flash Gordon by Raymond, Mandrake, Popeye by Segar, Tillie The Toiler, Fu Manchu, Hiram Hick by Bob Kane; Eisner-a(3); Briefer-c/a — 221.00 663.00 2100.00

WOW COMICS (Real Western Hero #70 on)(See XMas Comics)
Fawcett Publ.: Winter, 1940-41; No. 2, Summer, 1941 - No. 69, Fall, 1948

GD2.0 FN6.0 VF8.0 NM9.4
nn(#1)-Origin Mr. Scarlet by S&K; Atom Blake, Boy Wizard, Jim Dolan, & Rick O'Shay begin; Diamond Jack, The White Rajah, & Shipwreck Roberts, only app.; 1st mention of Gotham City in comics; the cover was printed on unstable paper stock and is rarely found in fine or mint condition; blank inside-c; bondage-c by Beck — 1200.00 3600.00 7800.00 15,000.00

GD2.0 FN6.0 NM9.4
2 (Scarce)-The Hunchback begins — 232.00 695.00 2200.00
3 (Fall, 1941) — 111.00 332.00 1050.00
4-Origin & 1st app. Pinky — 116.00 348.00 1100.00
5 — 74.00 221.00 700.00
6-Origin & 1st app. The Phantom Eagle (7/15/42); Commando Yank begins — 74.00 221.00 700.00
7,8,10: 10-Swayze-c/a on Mary Marvel — 58.00 174.00 550.00
9 (1/6/43)-Capt. Marvel, Capt. Marvel Jr., Shazam app.; Scarlet & Pinky x-over; Mary Marvel-c/stories begin (cameo #9) — 126.00 379.00 1200.00
11-17,19,20: 15-Flag-c — 44.00 133.00 400.00
18-1st app. Uncle Marvel (10/43); infinity-c — 47.00 140.00 420.00
21-30: 23-Robot-c. 28-Pinky x-over in Mary Marvel — 28.00 84.00 225.00
31-40: 32-68-Phantom Eagle by Swayze — 19.00 56.00 150.00
41-50 — 18.00 53.00 140.00
51-58: Last Mary Marvel — 16.00 48.00 125.00
59-69: 59-Ozzie (teenage) begins. 62-Flying Saucer gag-c (1/48). 65-69-Tom Mix stories (cont'd in Real Western Hero) — 14.00 41.00 110.00
NOTE: *Cover features: Mr. Scarlet-#1-5; Commando Yank-#6, 7, (w/Mr. Scarlet #8); Mary Marvel-#9-56, (w/Commando Yank-#46-50), (w/Mr. Scarlet & Commando Yank-#51), (w/ Scarlet & Pinky #53), (w/Phantom Eagle #54, 56), (w/Commando Yank & Phantom Eagle #5 Ozzie-#59-69.*

WRATH (Also see Prototype #4)
Malibu Comics: Jan, 1994 - No. 9, Nov, 1995 ($1.95)

1-9: 2-Mantra x-over. 3-Intro/1st app. Slayer. 4,5-Freex app. 8-Mantra & Warstrike app. 9-Prime app. — 2.0
1-Ultra 5000 Limited silver foil — 4.0
Giant Size 1 (2.50, 44 pgs.) — 2.5

WRATH OF THE SPECTRE, THE
DC Comics: May, 1988 - No. 4, Aug, 1988 ($2.50, limited series)

1-3: Aparo-r/Adventure #431-440 — 4.0
4-New stories — 5.0

WRECK OF GROSVENOR (See Superior Stories #3)

WRETCH, THE
Caliber: 1996 ($2.95, B&W)

1-Phillip Hester-a/scripts — 3.0

WRETCH, THE
Amaze Ink: 1997 - Present ($2.95, B&W)

1-4-Phillip Hester-a/scripts — 3.0

WRINGLE WRANGLE (Disney)
Dell Publishing Co.: No. 821, July, 1957

Four Color 821-Based on movie "Westward Ho, the Wagons"; Marsh-a; Fess Parker photo-c — 7.50 22.50 90.0

WULF THE BARBARIAN
Atlas/Seaboard Publ.: Feb, 1975 - No. 4, Sept, 1975

1,2: 1-Origin; Janson-a. 2-Intro. Berithe the Swordswoman; Janson-a w/Neal Adams, Wood, Reese-a assists — 2.40 6.0
3,4: 3-Skeates-s. 4-Friedrich-s — 5.0

WYATT EARP
Atlas Comics/Marvel No. 23 on (IPC): Nov, 1955 - #29, June, 1960; #30, Oct, 1972 - #34, June, 1973

1 — 21.00 64.00 170.0
2-Williamson-a (4 pgs.) — 12.50 37.50 100.0
3-6,8-11: 3-Black Bart app. 8-Wild Bill Hickok app — 10.00 30.00 80.0
7,12-Williamson-a, 4 pgs. ea.; #12 with Mayo — 10.00 30.00 80.0
13-20: 17-1st app. Wyatt's deputy, Grizzly Grant — 10.00 30.00 70.0
21-Davis-c — 8.65 26.00 60.0
22-24,26-29: 22-Ringo Kid app. 23-Kid From Texas app. 29-Last 10¢ issue — 6.40 19.25 45.0
25-Davis-a — 7.15 21.50 50.0
30-Williamson-r (1972) — 2.00 6.00 18.0
31-34-Reprints. 32-Torres-a(r) — 1.85 5.50 15.0
NOTE: ***Ayers** a-8, 10(2), 17, 20(4). **Berg** a-9. **Everett** c-6. **Kirby** c-25, 29. **Maneely** a-1; c-1-4, 8, 12, 17, 20. **Maurer** a-2(2), 3(4), 4(4), 8(4). **Severin** a-4, 9(4), 10; c-2, 9, 10, 14. **Wildey** a-5, 17, 24, 28.*

WYATT EARP (TV) (Hugh O'Brian Famous Marshal)
Dell Publishing Co.: No. 860, Nov, 1957 - No. 13, Dec-Feb, 1960-61 (Hugh O'Brian photo-c)

Four Color 860 (#1)-Manning-a — 10.00 30.00 120.0
Four Color 890,921(6/58)-All Manning-a — 7.00 21.00 85.0
4 (9-11/58) - 12-Manning-a. 5-Photo back-c — 4.60 13.75 55.0
13-Toth-a — 5.00 15.00 60.0

WYATT EARP FRONTIER MARSHAL (Formerly Range Busters) (Also see Blue Bird)
Charlton Comics: No. 12, Jan, 1956 - No. 72, Dec, 1967

12 — 8.65 26.00 60.00
13-19 — 5.00 15.00 35.00
20-(68 pgs.)-Williamson-a(4), 8,5,5,& 7 pgs. — 10.00 30.00 75.00
21-30 — 2.50 7.50 24.00
31-50 — 2.00 6.00 16.00
51-72 — 1.10 3.30 9.00

WYNONNA EARP
Image Comics (WildStorm Productions): Dec, 1996 - No. 5, Apr, 1997 ($2.50)

Xena: Warrior Princess #10 © 2000 Studios USA

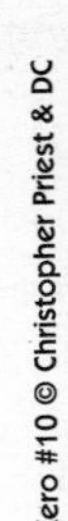
Xero #10 © Christopher Priest & DC

X-Factor #106 © MAR

GD2.0 FN6.0 NM9.4

1-5-Smith-s/Chin-a 2.50

X (Comics' Greatest World: X #1 only) (Also see Comics' Greatest World & Dark Horse Comics #8)
Dark Horse Comics: Feb, 1994 - No. 25, Apr, 1996 ($2.00/$2.50)

1-25: 3-Pit Bulls x-over. 8 -Ghost-c & app. 18-Miller-c.; Predator app. 19-22-Miller-c. 2.50
Hero Illustrated Special #1,2 (1994, $1.00, 20 pgs.) 2.00
One Shot to the Head (1994, $2.50, 36 pgs.)-Miller-c. 2.50
NOTE: ***Miller** c-18-22. **Quesada** c-6. **Russell** a-6.*

XANADU COLOR SPECIAL
Eclipse Comics: Dec, 1988 ($2.00, one-shot)

1-Continued from Thoughts & Images 2.00

XAVIER INSTITUTE ALUMNI YEARBOOK (See X-Men titles)
Marvel Comics: Dec, 1996 ($5.95, square-bound, one-shot)

1-Text w/art by various 6.00

X-BABIES
Marvel Comics: (one-shots)

...: Murderama (8/98, $2.95) J.J. Kirby-a 3.00
...: Reborn (1/00, $3.50) J.J. Kirby-a 3.00

X-CALIBRE
Marvel Comics: Mar, 1995 - No. 4, July, 1995 ($1.95, limited series)

1-4-Age of Apocalypse 2.00

XENA: WARRIOR PRINCESS (TV)
Topps Comics: Aug, 1997 - No. 0, Oct, 1997 ($2.95)

	GD2.0	FN6.0	NM9.4
1-Two stories by various; J. Scott Campbell-c	1.25	3.75	10.00
1,2-Photo-c	1.25	3.75	10.00
2-Stevens-c		2.40	6.00
0-(10/97)-Lopresti-c, 0-(10/97)-Photo-c	1.00	3.00	8.00
...First Appearance Collection ('97, $9.95) r/Hercules the Legendary Journeys #3-5 and 5-page story from TV Guide			10.00

XENA: WARRIOR PRINCESS (TV)
Dark Horse Comics: Sept, 1999 - No. 14, Oct, 2000 ($2.95/$2.99)

1-14: 1-Mignola-c and photo-c. 2,3-Bradstreet-c & photo-c 3.00

XENA: WARRIOR PRINCESS AND THE ORIGINAL OLYMPICS (TV)
Topps Comics: Jun, 1998 - No. 3, Aug, 1998 ($2.95, limited series)

1-3-Regular and Photo-c; Lim-a/T&M Bierbaum-s 3.00

XENA: WARRIOR PRINCESS-BLOODLINES (TV)
Topps Comics: May, 1998 - No. 2, June, 1998 ($2.95, limited series)

1,2-Lopresti-s/c/a. 2-Reg. and photo-c 3.00
1-Bath photo-c, 1-American Ent. Ed 4.00

XENA: WARRIOR PRINCESS / JOXER: WARRIOR PRINCE (TV)
Topps Comics: Nov, 1997 - No. 3, Jan, 1998 ($2.95, limited series)

1-3-Regular and Photo-c; Lim-a/T&M Bierbaum-s 3.00

XENA: WARRIOR PRINCESS-THE DRAGON'S TEETH (TV)
Topps Comics: Dec, 1997 - No. 3, Feb, 1998 ($2.95, limited series)

1-3-Regular and Photo-c; Teranishi-a/Thomas-s 3.00

XENA: WARRIOR PRINCESS-THE ORPHEUS TRILOGY (TV)
Topps Comics: Mar, 1998 - No. 3, May, 1998 ($2.95, limited series)

1-3-Regular and Photo-c; Teranishi-a/T&M Bierbaum-s. 3.00

XENA: WARRIOR PRINCESS VS. CALLISTO (TV)
Topps Comics: Feb, 1998 - No. 3, Apr, 1998 ($2.95, limited series)

1-3-Regular and Photo-c; Morgan-a/Thomas-s 3.00

XENOBROOD
DC Comics: No. 0, Oct, 1994 - No. 6, Apr, 1995 ($1.50, limited series)

0-6: 0-Indicia says "Xenobroods" 2.00

XENON
Eclipse Comics: Dec, 1987 - No. 23, Nov. 1, 1988 ($1.50, B&W, bi-weekly)

1-23 2.00

XENOTECH
Mirage Studios: Sept, 1993 - No. 3, Dec, 1994 ($2.75)

1-3: Bound with 2 trading cards. 2-(10/94) 2.75

XENOZOIC TALES (Also see Cadillacs & Dinosaurs, Death Rattle #8)
Kitchen Sink Press: Feb, 1986 - No. 14, Oct, 1996

	GD2.0	FN6.0	NM9.4
1	1.00	2.80	7.00
1(2nd printing)(1/89)			3.00
2-14			5.00

XENYA
Sanctuary Press: Apr, 1994 - No. 3 ($2.95)

1-3: 1-Hildebrandt-c; intro Xenya 3.00

XERO
DC Comics: May, 1997 - No. 12, Apr, 1998 ($1.75)

1-7 2.50
8-12 2.00

X-FACTOR (Also see The Avengers #263, Fantastic Four #286 and Mutant X)
Marvel Comics Group: Feb, 1986 - No. 149, Sept, 1998

	GD2.0	FN6.0	NM9.4
1-($1.25, 52 pgs)-Story recaps 1st app. from Avengers #263; story cont'd from F.F. #286; return of original X-Men (now X-Factor); Guice/Layton-a; Baby Nathan app. (2nd after X-Men #201)		2.40	6.00
2-4			4.00
5-1st app. Apocalypse (2-pg. cameo)			4.00
6-1st full app. Apocalypse	1.25	3.75	10.00
7-10: 10-Sabretooth app. (11/86, 3 pgs.) cont'd in X-Men #212; 1st app. in an X-Men comic book			4.00
11-22: 13-Baby Nathan app. in flashback. 14-Cyclops vs. The Master Mold. 15-Intro wingless Angel			3.00
23-1st app. Archangel (2 pg. cameo)	1.00	2.80	7.00
24-1st full app. Archangel (now in Uncanny X-Men); Fall Of The Mutants begins; origin Apocalypse	1.10	3.30	9.00
25,26: Fall Of The Mutants; 26-New outfits			3.00
27-39,41-83,87-91,93-99,101: 35-Origin Cyclops. 38,50-(52 pgs.): 50-Liefeld /Mc-Farlane-c. 51-53-Sabretooth app. 52-Liefeld-c(p). 54-Intro Crimson; Silvestri-c/a(p). 60-X-Tinction Agenda x-over; New Mutants (w/Cable) x-over in #60-62; Wolverine in #62. 60-Gold ink 2nd printing. 61,62-X-Tinction Agenda. 62-Jim Lee-c. 63-Portacio/Thibert-c/a(p) begins, ends #69. 65-68-Lee co-plots. 65-The Apocalypse Files begins, ends #68.66,67-Baby Nathan app. 67-nhumans app. 68-Baby Nathan is sent into future to save his life. 69,70-X-Men(w/Wolve rine) x-over. 71-New team begins (Havok, Polaris, Strong Guy, Wolfsbane & Madrox); Stroman-c/a begins. 71-2nd printing ($1.25). 75-(52 pgs.). 77-Cannonball (of X-Force) app. 87-Quesada-c/a(p) in monthly comic begins,ends #92. 88-1st app. Random			2.00
40-Rob Liefield-c/a (4/89, 1st at Marvel?)			3.00
84-86 -Jae Lee a(p); 85,86-Jae Lee-c. Polybagged with trading card in each; X-Cutioner's Song x-overs.			3.00
92-($3.50, 68 pgs.)-Wraparound-c by Quesada w/Havok hologram on-c; begin X-Men 30th anniversary issues; Quesada-a.			5.00
92-2nd printing			2.00
100-($2.95, 52 pgs.)-Embossed foil-c; Multiple Man dies.			5.00
100-($1.75, 52 pgs.)-Regular edition			2.00
102-105,107: 102-bound-in card sheet			2.00
106-($2.00)-Newsstand edition			2.00
106-($2.95)-Collectors edition			3.00
108-124,126-148: 112-Return from Age of Apocalypse. 115-card insert. 119-123-Sabretooth app. 123-Hound app. 124-w/Onslaught Update. 126-Onslaught x-over; Beast vs. Dark Beast 128-w/card insert; return of Multiple Man. 130-Assassination of Grayson Creed. 146,148-Moder-a			2.00
125-($2.95)-"Onslaught"; Post app.; return of Havok			4.00
149-Last issue			3.00
#(-1) Flashback (7/97) Matsuda-a			2.00
Annual 1-9: 1-(10/86-'94, 68 pgs.) 3-Evolutionary War x-over. 4-Atlantis Attacks; Byrne/Simonson-a;Byrne-c. 5-Fantastic Four, New Mutants x-over;Keown 2 pg. pin-up. 6-New Warriors app.; 5th app. X-Force cont'd from X-Men Annual #15. 7-1st Quesada-a(p) on X-Factor plus-c(p). 8-Bagged w/trading card. 9-Austin-a(i)			3.00
...Prisoner of Love (1990, $4.95, 52 pgs.)-Starlin scripts; Guice-a			5.00

NOTE: ***Art Adams** a-41p, 42p. **Buckler** a-50p. **Liefeld** a-40; c-40, 50i, 52p. **McFarlane** c-50i. **Mignola** c-70. **Brandon Peterson** a-78p(part). **Whilce Portacio** c/a(p)-63-69. **Quesada** a(p)-87-*

X-51 #1 © MAR

X-Force #76 © MAR

X-Man #66 © MAR

GD2.0 FN6.0 NM9.4

92, Annual 7. c(p)-78, 79, 82, Annual 7. ***Simonson*** *c/a-10, 11, 13-15, 17-19, 21, 23-31, 33, 34, 36-39; c-12, 16.* ***Paul Smith*** *a-44-48; c-43.* ***Stroman*** *a(p)-71-75, 77, 78(part), 80, 81; c(p)-71-77, 80, 81, 84.* ***Zeck*** *c-2.*

X-51 (Machine Man)
Marvel Comics: Sept, 1999 - No. 12, Jul, 2000 ($1.99/$2.50)

1-7: 1-Joe Bennett-a. 2-Two covers 2.00
8-12: 8-Begin $2.50-c 2.50
Wizard #0 1.00

X-FILES, THE (TV)
Topps Comics: Jan, 1995 - No. 41, July, 1998 ($2.50)

-2(9/96)-Black-c; r/X-Files Magazine #1&2 1.25 3.75 10.00
-1(9/96)-Silver-c; r/Hero Illustrated Giveaway 1.25 3.75 10.00
0-($3.95)-Adapts pilot episode 4.00
0-"Mulder" variant-c 1.00 3.00 8.00
0-"Scully" variant-c 1.00 3.00 8.00
1/2-W/certificate 2.50 7.50 25.00
1-New stories based on the TV show; direct market & newsstand editions; Miran Kim-c on all 3.50 10.50 35.00
2 2.50 7.50 20.00
3,4 1.25 3.75 10.00
5-10 5.00
11-41: 11-Begin $2.95-c. 21-W/bound-in card. 40,41-Reg. & photo-c 3.00
Annual 1,2 ($3.95) 4.00
Afterflight TPB ($5.95) Art by Thompson, Saviuk, Kim 6.00
Collection 1 TPB ($19.95)-r/#1-6. 20.00
Collection 2 TPB ($19.95)-r/#7-12, Annual #1. 20.00
...Fight the Future ('98, $5.95) Movie adaption 6.00
Hero Illustrated Giveaway 1.85 5.50 15.00
Special Edition 1-5 ($4.95)-r/#1-3, 4-6, 7-9, 10-12, 13, Annual 1 5.00
Star Wars Galaxy Magazine Giveaway (B&W) 1.25 3.75 10.00
Trade paperback ($19.95) 20.00

X-FILES COMICS DIGEST, THE
Topps Comics: Dec, 1995 - No. 3 ($3.50, quarterly, digest-size)

1-3: 1,2: New X-Files stories w/Ray Bradbury Comics-r 4.00
NOTE: ***Adlard*** *a-1, 2.* ***Jack Davis*** *a-2r.* ***Russell*** *a-1r.*

X-FILES, THE: GROUND ZERO (TV)
Topps Comics: Nov, 1997 - No. 4, March, 1998 ($2.95, limited series)

1-4-Adaption of the Kevin J. Anderson novel 3.00

X-FILES, THE: SEASON ONE (TV)
Topps Comics: July, 1997 - Present ($4.95, adaptions of TV episodes)

1,2,Squeeze, Conduit, Ice, Space, Fire, Beyond the Sea, Shadows 5.00

X-FORCE (Also see The New Mutants #100 & 1992 X-Men Annuals)
Marvel Comics: Aug, 1991 - Present ($1.00/$1.25/$1.50/$1.95/$1.99/$2.25)

1-($1.50, 52 pgs.)-Polybagged with 1 of 5 diff. Marvel Universe trading cards inside (1 each); 6th app. of X-Force; Liefeld-c/a begins 4.00
1-1st printing with Cable trading card inside 5.00
1-2nd printing; metallic ink-c (no bag or card) 2.00
2-4: 2-Deadpool-c/story. 3-New Brotherhood of Evil Mutants app. 4-Spider-Man x-over; cont'd from Spider-Man #16; reads sideways 3.00
5-10: 6-Last $1.00-c. 7,9-Weapon X back-ups. 8-Intro The Wild Pack (Cable, Kane, Domino, Hammer, G.W. Bridge, & Grizzly); Liefeld-c/a (4); Mignola-a. 10-Weapon X full-length story (part 3). 11-1st Weapon Prime (cameo); Deadpool-c/story. 3.00
11-15,19-24,26-33: 15-Cable leaves X-Force 2.00
16-18-Polybagged w/trading card in each; X-Cutioner's Song x-overs 3.00
25-($3.50, 52 pgs.)-Wraparound-c w/Cable hologram on-c; Cable returns 4.00
34-37,39-45: 34-bound-in card sheet 2.00
38,40-43: 38-($2.00)-Newsstand edition. 40-43 (1.95)-Deluxe edition 2.00
38-($2.95)-Collectors edition 5.00
44-49,51-67: 44-Return from Age of Apocalypse. 45-Sabretooth app. 49-Sebastian Shaw app. 52-Blob app., Onslaught cameo. 55-Vs. S.H.I.E.L.D. 56-Deadpool app. 57-Mr. Sinister & X-Man-c/app. 57,58-Onslaught x-over. 59-W/card insert; return of Longshot. 60-Dr. Strange 2.00
50 ($3.95)-Gatefold wrap-around foil-c 4.00
50 ($3.95)-Liefeld variant-c 5.00
68-74: 68-Operation Zero Tolerance 2.00
75,100-($2.99): 75-Cannonball-c/app. 3.00
76-99,101,102: 81-Pollina poster. 95-Magneto-c. 102-Ellis-s/Portacio-a 2.00
103-110: 103-Begin $2.25-c; Portacio-a thru #106 2.25
#(-1) Flashback (7/97) story of John Proudstar; Pollina-a 2.00
Annual 1-3 ('92-'94, 68 pgs.)-1-1st Greg Capullo-a(p) on X-Force. 2-Polybagged w/trading card; intro X-Treme & Neurtap 3.00
...And Cable '95 (12/95, $3.95)-Impossible Man app. 4.00
...And Cable '96, ...'97 ('96, 7/97) -'96-Wraparound-c 3.00
...And Spider-Man: Sabotage nn (11/92, $6.95)-Reprints X-Force #3,4 & Spider-Man #16 7.00
.../ Champions '98 ($3.50) 3.50
Annual 99 ($3.50) 3.50
...Rough Cut ($2.99) Pencil pages and script for #102 3.00
...Youngblood (8/96, $4.95)-Platt-c 5.00
NOTE: ***Capullo*** *a(p)-15-25, Annual 1; c(p)-14-27.* ***Rob Liefeld*** *a-1-7, 9p; c-1-9, 11p; plots-1-12.* ***Mignola*** *a-8p.*

X-FORCE MEGAZINE
Marvel Comics: Nov, 1996 ($3.95, one-shot)

1-Reprints 4.00

XIMOS: VIOLENT PAST
Triumphant Comics: Mar, 1994 - No. 2, Mar, 1994 ($2.50, limited series)

1,2 2.50

X-MAN (Also see X-Men Omega & X-Men Prime)
Marvel Comics: Mar, 1995 - No. 75, May, 2001 ($1.95/$1.99/$2.25)

1-Age of Apocalypse 5.00
1-2nd print 2.00
2-4,25: 25-($2.99)-Wraparound-c 3.00
5-24, 26-28: 5-Post Age of Apocalypse stories begin. 5-7-Madelyne Pryor app. 10-Professor X app. 12-vs. Excalibur. 13-Marauders, Cable app. 14-Vs. Cable; Onslaught app. 15-17-Vs. Holocaust. 17-w/Onslaught Update. 18-Onslaught x-over; X-Force-c/app; Marauders app. 19-Onslaught x-over. 20-Abomination-c/app.; w/card insert. 23-Bishop-c/app. 24-Spider-Man Morbius-c/app. 27-Re-appearance of Aurora(Alpha Flight) 2.00
29-49,51-62: 29-Operation Zero Tolerance. 37,38-Spider-Man-c/app. 56-Spider-Man app. 2.00
50-($2.99) Crossover with Generation X #50 3.00
63-72: 63-Ellis & Grant-s/Olivetti-a begins. 64-Begin $2.25-c 2.25
#(-1) Flashback (7/97) 2.00
...'96, ...'97-($2.95)-Wraparound-c; '96-Age of Apocalypse 3.00
...: All Saints' Day ('97, $5.99) Dodson-a 6.00
.../Hulk '98 ($2.99) Wraparound-c; Thanos app. 3.00

XMAS COMICS
Fawcett Publications: 12?/1941 - No. 2, 12?/1942; (50¢, 324 pgs.)
No. 7, 12?/1947 (25¢, 132 pgs.)(#3-6 do not exist)

1-Contains Whiz #21, Capt. Marvel #3, Bulletman #2, Wow #3, & Master #18; Raboy back-c. Not rebound, remaindered comics; printed at same time as originals 381.00 1143.00 4000.00
2-Capt. Marvel, Bulletman, Spy Smasher 147.00 442.00 1400.00
7-Funny animals (Hoppy, Billy the Kid & Oscar) 58.00 174.00 550.00

XMAS COMICS
Fawcett Publications: No. 4, Dec, 1949 - No. 7, Dec, 1952 (50¢, 196 pgs.)

4-Contains Whiz, Master, Tom Mix, Captain Marvel, Nyoka, Capt. Video, Bob Colt, Monte Hale, Hot Rod Comics, & Battle Stories. Not rebound, remaindered comics; printed at the same time as originals 63.00 189.00 600.00
5-7-Same as above. 7-Bill Boyd app.; stocking on cover is made of green felt (novelty cover) 50.00 150.00 450.00

X-MEN, THE (See Adventures of Cyclops and Phoenix, Amazing Adventures, Archangel, Capt. America #172, Classic X-Men, Further Adventures of Cyclops & Phoenix, Gambit, Giant-Size..., Heroes For Hope..., Kitty Pryde & Wolverine, Marvel & DC Present, Marvel Collector's Edition:..., Marvel Fanfare, Marvel Graphic Novel, Marvel Super Heroes, Marvel Team-Up, Marvel Triple Action, The Marvel X-Men Collection, New Mutants, Nightcrawler, Official Marvel Index To..., Rogue, Special Edition..., The Uncanny..., Wolverine, X-Factor, X-Force, X-Terminators)

X-MEN, THE (1st series)(Becomes Uncanny X-Men at #142)(The X-Men #1-93; X-Men #94-141) (The Uncanny X-Men on-c only #114-141)
Marvel Comics Group: Sept, 1963 - No. 66, Mar, 1970; No. 67, Dec, 1970 - No.

The X-Men #7 © MAR

The X-Men #139 © MAR

The Uncanny X-Men #207 © MAR

-1, Jan, 1981

	GD2.0	FN6.0	VF8.0	NM9.4
-Origin/1st app. X-Men (Angel, Beast, Cyclops, Iceman & Marvel Girl); 1st app. Magneto & Professor X	559.00	1675.00	3915.00	9500.00

	GD2.0	FN6.0	NM9.4
:-1st app. The Vanisher	143.00	429.00	2000.00
3-1st app. The Blob (1/64)	55.00	166.00	775.00
4-1st Quick Silver & Scarlet Witch & Brotherhood of the Evil Mutants (3/64); 1st app. Toad; 2nd app. Magneto	59.00	177.00	825.00
5-Magneto & Evil Mutants-c/story	41.00	123.00	525.00
6-9: 6-Sub-Mariner app. 7-Magneto app. 8-1st Unus the Untouchable. 9-Early Avengers app. (1/65); 1st Lucifer	31.00	94.00	375.00
0-1st S.A. app. Ka-Zar & Zabu the sabertooth (3/65)	33.00	100.00	375.00
1,13-15: 11-1st app. The Stranger. 14-1st app. Sentinels. 15-Origin Beast	27.50	82.00	300.00
2-Origin Prof. X; Origin/1st app. Juggernaut	33.00	100.00	400.00
6-20: 19-1st app. The Mimic (4/66)	14.50	43.50	160.00
1-27,29,30: 27-Re-enter The Mimic (r-in #75); Spider-Man cameo	11.50	34.00	125.00
8-1st app. The Banshee (1/67)(r-in #76)	16.50	49.00	180.00
1-34,36,37,39,40: 34-Adkins-c/a. 39-New costumes	7.65	23.00	85.00
5-Spider-Man x-over (8/67)(r-in #83); 1st app. Changeling	12.75	38.00	140.00
8-Origins of the X-Men series begins, ends #57	10.00	30.00	110.00
1-49: 42-Death of Prof. X (Changeling disguised as). 44-1st S.A. app. G.A. Red Raven. 49-Steranko-c; 1st Polaris	7.25	21.75	80.00
0,51-Steranko-c/a	7.65	23.00	85.00
2	5.45	16.35	60.00
3-Barry Smith-c/a (his 1st comic book work)	7.65	23.00	85.00
4,55-B. Smith-c. 54-1st app. Alex Summers who later becomes Havok. 55-Summers discovers he has mutant powers	8.15	24.50	90.00
6,57,59-63,65-Neal Adams-a(p). 56-Intro Havok w/o costume. 60-1st Sauron. 65-Return of Professor X.	6.80	20.50	75.00
8-1st app. Havok in costume; N. Adams-a(p)	10.00	30.00	110.00
4-1st app. Sunfire	7.25	21.75	80.00
6-Last new story w/original X-Men; battles Hulk	6.80	20.50	75.00
7-70,72: (52 pgs.). 67-Reprints begin, end #93	3.65	11.00	40.00
1,73-93: 71-Last 15¢ issue. 73-86-r/#25-38 w/new-c. 83-Spider-Man-c/story. 87-93-r/#39-45 with covers	3.20	9.60	35.00
4 (8/75)-New X-Men begin (see Giant-Size X-Men for 1st app.); Colossus, Nightcrawler, Thunderbird, Storm, Wolverine, & Banshee join; Angel, Marvel Girl, & Iceman resign	54.00	161.00	750.00
5-Death of Thunderbird	13.50	40.00	150.00
6,97	9.00	27.00	100.00
8,99-(Regular 25¢ edition)(4,6/76)	9.00	27.00	100.00
8,99-(30¢-c variants, limited distribution)	13.50	40.00	150.00
00-Old vs. New X-Men; part origin Phoenix; last 25¢ issue (8/76)	9.00	27.00	100.00
00-(30¢-c variant, limited distribution)	13.50	40.00	150.00
01-Phoenix origin concludes	8.15	24.50	90.00
02-104,107: 102-Origin Storm. 104-1st app. Starjammers (brief cameo); Magneto-c/story. 107-1st full app. Starjammers; last 30¢ issue	4.55	13.65	50.00
05,106-(Regular 30¢ editions). 106-(8/77)Old vs. New X-Men	4.55	13.65	50.00
05,106-(35¢-c variants, limited distribution)	6.80	20.50	75.00
08-Byrne-a begins (see Marvel Team-Up #53)	8.15	24.50	90.00
09-1st app. Weapon Alpha (becomes Vindicator)	6.35	19.00	70.00
10,111: 110-Phoenix joins	4.55	13.65	50.00
12-119: 117-Origin Professor X	4.10	12.30	45.00
20-1st app. Alpha Flight (cameo), story line begins (4/79); 1st app. Vindicator (formerly Weapon Alpha); last 35¢ issue	6.35	19.00	70.00
21-1st full Alpha Flight story	6.80	20.50	75.00
22-128: 123-Spider-Man x-over. 124-Colossus becomes Proletarian	3.20	9.60	35.00
29-Intro Kitty Pryde (1/80); last Banshee; Dark Phoenix saga begins	4.10	12.30	45.00
30-1st app. The Dazzler by Byrne (2/80)	3.65	11.00	40.00
31-135: 131-Dazzler app. 132-1st White Queen. 133-Wolverine app.			
134-Phoenix becomes Dark Phoenix	3.00	9.00	30.00
136,138: 138-Dazzler app.; Cyclops leaves	2.50	7.50	25.00
137-Giant; death of Phoenix	3.00	9.00	30.00
139-Alpha Flight app.; Kitty Pryde joins; new costume for Wolverine	3.80	11.40	42.00
140-Alpha Flight app.	3.65	11.00	40.00
141-Intro Future X-Men & The New Brotherhood of Evil Mutants; 1st app. Rachel (Phoenix II); Death of Franklin Richards	3.80	11.40	42.00

X-MEN: Titled THE UNCANNY X-MEN #142, Feb, 1981 - Present

	GD2.0	FN6.0	NM9.4
142-Rachel app.; deaths of alt. future Wolverine, Storm & Colossus	3.20	9.60	35.00
143-Last Byrne issue	2.00	6.00	18.00
144-150: 144-Man-Thing app. 145-Old X-Men app. 148-Spider-Woman, Dazzler app. 150-Double size	1.00	3.00	8.00
151-157,159-161,163,164: 161-Origin Magneto. 163-Origin Binary. 164-1st app. Binary as Carol Danvers		2.40	6.00
158-1st app. Rogue in X-Men (6/82, see Avengers Annual #10)	1.25	3.75	10.00
162-Wolverine solo story	1.00	3.00	8.00
165-Paul Smith-c/a begins, ends #175	1.00	2.80	7.00
166-170: 166-Double size; Paul Smith-a. 167-New Mutants app. (3/83); same date as New Mutants #1; 1st meeting w/X-Men; ties into N.M. #3,4; Starjammers app.; contains skin "Tattooz" decals. 168-1st app. Madelyne Pryor (last pg. cameo) in X-Men (see Avengers Annual #10)		2.40	6.00
171-Rogue joins X-Men; Simonson-c/a	1.25	3.75	10.00
172-174: 172,173-Two part Wolverine solo story. 173-Two cover variations, blue & black. 174-Phoenix cameo		2.40	6.00
175-(52 pgs.)-Anniversary issue; Phoenix returns	1.00	3.00	8.00
176-185,187-192,194-199: 181-Sunfire app. 182-Rogue solo story. 184-1st app. Forge (8/84). 190,191-Spider-Man & Avengers x-over. 195-Power Pack x-over			5.00
186,193: 186-Double-size; Barry Smith/Austin-a. 193-Double size; 100th app. New X-Men; 1st app. Warpath in costume (see New Mutants #16)		2.40	6.00
200-(12/85, $1.25, 52 pgs.)	1.00	2.80	7.00
201-(1/86)-1st app. Cable? (as baby Nathan; see X-Factor #1); 1st Whilce Portacio-c/a(i) on X-Men (guest artist)	1.85	5.50	15.00
202-204,206-209: 204-Nightcrawler solo story; 2nd Portacio-a(i) on X-Men. 207-Wolverine/Phoenix story			5.00
205-Wolverine solo story by Barry Smith	1.25	3.75	10.00
210,211-Mutant Massacre begins	1.85	5.50	15.00
212,213-Wolverine vs. Sabretooth (Mutant Mass.)	2.00	6.00	18.00
214-221,223,224: 219-Havok joins (7/87); brief app. Sabretooth			5.00
222-Wolverine battles Sabretooth-c/story	1.85	5.50	15.00
225-242: 225-227: Fall Of The Mutants. 226-Double size. 240-Sabretooth app. 242-Double size, X-Factor app., Inferno tie-in			5.00
243,245-247: 245-Rob Liefeld-a(p)			5.00
244-1st app. Jubilee	2.30	7.00	20.00
248-1st Jim Lee art on X-Men (1989)	2.00	6.00	18.00
248-2nd printing (1992, $1.25)			2.00
249-252: 252-Lee-c			5.00
253-255: 253-All new X-Men begin. 254-Lee-c			5.00
256,257-Jim Lee-c/a begins	1.00	2.80	7.00
258-Wolverine solo story; Lee-c/a	1.00	2.80	7.00
259-Silvestri-c/a; no Lee-a			5.00
260-265-No Lee-a. 260,261,264-Lee-c			5.00
266-1st full app. Gambit (see Ann. #14)-No Lee-a	3.00	9.00	30.00
267-Jim Lee-c/a resumes; 2nd full Gambit app.	1.50	4.50	12.00
268-Capt. America, Black Widow & Wolverine team-up; Lee-a	1.75	5.25	14.00
268,270: 268-2nd printing. 270-Gold 2nd printing			2.00
269,273-275: 269-Lee-a. 273-New Mutants (Cable) & X-Factor x-over; Golden, Byrne & Lee part pencils. 275-(52 pgs.)-Tri-fold-c by Jim Lee (p); Prof. X.			5.00
270-X-Tinction Agenda begins		2.40	6.00
271,272-X-Tinction Agenda		2.40	6.00
275-Gold 2nd printing			2.50
276-280: 277-Last Lee-c/a. 280-X-Factor x-over			4.00
281-(10/91)-New team begins (Storm, Archangel, Colossus, Iceman & Marvel			

The Uncanny X-Men #361 © MAR

X-Men #24 © MAR

X-Men #72 © MAR

Girl); Whilce Portacio-c/a begins; Byrne scripts begin; wraparound-c (white logo) 5.00
281-2nd printing with red metallic ink logo w/o UPC box ($1.00-c); does not say 2nd printing inside 2.00
282-1st app. Bishop (cover & 1 pg. cameo) 1.25 3.75 10.00
282-Gold ink 2nd printing ($1.00-c) 2.00
283-1st full app. Bishop (12/91) 1.25 3.75 10.00
284-299: 284-Last $1.00-c. 286,287-Lee plots. 287-Bishop joins team. 288-Lee/Portacio plots. 290-Last Portacio-c/a. 294-Brandon Peterson-a(p) begins (#292 is 1st Peterson-c). 294-296 ($1.50)-Polybagged w/trading card in each; X-Cutioner's Song x-overs; all have Peterson/Austin-c/a 3.00
300-($3.95, 68 pgs.)-Holo-grafx foil-c; Magneto app. 2.40 6.00
301-303,305-309,311 2.50
303,307-Gold Edition 2.40 6.00
304-($3.95, 68 pgs.)-Wraparound-c with Magneto hologram on-c; 30th anniversary issue; Jae Lee-a (4 pgs.) 2.40 6.00
310-($1.95)-Bound-in trading card sheet 2.50
312-$1.50-c begins; bound-in card sheet; 1st Madureira 4.00
313-321 2.50
316,317-($2.95)-Foil enhanced editions 3.50
318-321-($1.95)-Deluxe editions 2.50
322-Onslaught 5.00
323,324,326-346: 323-Return from Age of Apocalypse. 328-Sabretooth-c. 329,330-Dr. Strange app. 331-White Queen-c/app. 334-Juggernaut app.; w/Onslaught Update. 335-Onslaught, Avengers, Apocalypse, & X-Man app. 336-Onslaught. 338-Archangel's wings return to normal. 339-Havok vs. Cyclops; Spider-Man app. 341-Gladiator-c/app. 342-Deathbird cameo; two covers. 343,344-Phalanx 2.50
325-($3.95)-Anniversary issue; gatefold-c 5.00
342-Variant-c 1.10 3.30 9.00
347-349:347-Begin $1.99-c. 349-"Operation Zero Tolerance" 2.50
350-($3.99, 48 pgs.) Prismatic etched foil gatefold wraparound-c; Trial of Gambit; Seagle-s begin 1.00 3.00 8.00
351-359: 353-Bachalo-a begins. 354-Regular-c. 355-Alpha Flight-c/app. 356-Original X-Men-c 2.00
354-Dark Phoenix variant-c 3.00
360-($2.99) 35th Anniv. issue; Pacheco-c 3.00
360-($3.99) Etched Holo-foil enhanced-c 4.00
360-($6.95) DF Edition with Jae Lee variant-c 7.00
361-374: 361-Gambit returns; Skroce-a. 362-Hunt for Xavier pt. 1; Bachelo-a. 364-Yu-a. 366-Magneto-c.369-Juggernaut-c 2.00
375-($2.99) Autopsy of Wolverine 3.00
376-379: 376,377-Apocalypse: The Twelve 2.00
380-($2.99) Polybagged with X-Men Revolution Genesis Edition preview 3.00
381,382,384-389: 381-Begin $2.25-c; Claremont-s. 387-Maximum Security x-over 2.25
383-($2.99) 2.99
#(-1) Flashback (7/97) Ladronn-c/Hitch & Neary-a 2.50
Special 1(12/70)-Kirby-c/a; origin The Stranger 7.25 21.75 80.00
Special 2(11/71, 52 pgs.) 5.45 16.35 60.00
Annual 3(1979, 52 pgs.)-New story; Miller/Austin-c; Wolverine still in old yellow costume 2.50 7.50 25.00
Annual 4(1980, 52 pgs.)-Dr. Strange guest stars 1.25 3.75 10.00
Annual 5(1981, 52 pgs.) 1.00 3.00 8.00
Annual 6-8('82-'84 52 pgs.)-6-Dracula app. 2.40 6.00
Annual 9,10('85, '86)-9-New Mutants x-over cont'd from New Mutants Special Ed. #1;Art Adams-a. 10-Art Adams-a 1.00 3.00 8.00
Annual 11-13:('87-'89, 68 pgs.): 12-Evolutionary War; A.Adams-a(p). 13-Atlantis Attacks 4.00
Annual 14(1990, $2.00, 68 pgs.)-1st app. Gambit (minor app., 5 pgs.);Fantastic Four, New Mutants (Cable) & X-Factor x-over; Art Adams-c/a(p) 2.30 7.00 20.00
Annual 15 (1991, $2.00, 68 pgs.)-4 pg. origin; New Mutants x-over; 4 pg. Wolverine solo back-up story; 4th app. X-Force cont'd from New Warriors Annual #1 4.00
Annual 16-18 ('92-'94, 68 pgs.)-16-Jae Lee-c/a(p). 17-Bagged w/card 3.00
Annual '95-(11/95, $3.95)-Wraparound-c 4.00
Annual '96,'97-Wraparound-c 3.00
.../Fantastic Four Annual '98 ($2.99) Casey-s 3.00
Annual '99 ($3.50) Jubilee app. 3.50

...At The State Fair of Texas (1983, 36 pgs., one-shot); Supplement to the Dallas Times Herald 1.50 4.50 12.00
...: The Dark Phoenix Saga (1990, $12.95, trade paperback) 13.00
...From The Ashes (1990, $14.95, trade paperback) r/#168-176 15.00
...:God Loves, Man Kills ($6.95)-r/Marvel Graphic Novel #5 7.00
...In The Days of Future Past (1989, $3.95, trade paperback, 52 pgs.) 4.00

NOTE: ***Art Adams** a-Annual 9, 10p, 12p, 14p; c-218p. **Neal Adams** a-56-63p, 65p; c-56-63. **Adkins** a-34, 35p; c-31, 34, 35. **Austin** a-108i, 109i, 111-117i, 119-143i, 186i, 204i, 228i, 294-297i, Annual 3i, 7i, 9i, 13; c-109-111i, 114-122i, 123, 124-141i, 142, 143, 196i, 204i, 228i, 294-297i, Annual 3i. **J. Buscema** c-42, 43, 45. **Buscema/Tuska** a-45. **Byrne** a(p)-108, 109, 111-143 273; c(p)-113-116, 127, 129, 131-141. **Capullo** c-14. **Ditko** r-86, 89-91, 93. **Everett** c-73. **Golde** a-273, Annual 7p. **Guice** a-216p, 217p. **G. Kane** c(p)-33, 74-76, 79, 80, 94, 95. **Kirby** a(p)-1-17 (#12-17, 67r-layouts); c(p)-1-17, 25, 30 (18, 26-parts). **Layton** a-105i; c-112i, 113i. **Jim Lee** a(p)- 248, 256-258, 267-277; c(p)-252, 254, 256-261, 264, 267, 270, 275-277, 286. **Perez** a-Annual 3p c(p)-112, 128, Annual 3. **Peterson** a(p)-294-300, 304(part); c(p)-294-299. **Whilce Portacio** a(p)- 281-286, 289, 290; a(i)-267; c-281-285p, 289p, 290; c(i)-267. **Romita, Jr.** a-300; c-300. **Rousso** a-84i. **Simonson** a-171p; c-171, 217. **B. Smith** a-53, 186p, 198p, 205, 214; c-53-55, 186p, 198, 205, 212, 214, 216. **Paul Smith** a(p)-165-170, 172-175, 278; c-165-170, 172-175, 278. **Sparling** a-78p. **Steranko** a-50p, 51p; c-49-51. **Sutton** a-106i. **Art Thibert** a(i)-281-286; c(i)-281, 282, 28- 285. **Toth** a-12p, 67p(r). **Tuska** a-40-42i, 43-46p, 88i(r); c-39-41, 77p, 78p. **Williamson** a-202i, 203i, 211i; c-202i, 203i, 206i. **Wood** c-14i.*

UNCANNY X-MEN AND THE NEW TEEN TITANS (See Marvel and DC Present...)

X-MEN (2nd Series)
Marvel Comics: Oct, 1991 - Present ($1.00/$1.25/$1.95/$1.99)

1 a-d ($1.50, 52 pgs.)-Jim Lee-c/a begins, ends #11; new team begins (Cyclops, Beast, Wolverine, Gambit, Psylocke & Rogue); new Uncanny X-Men & Magneto app.; four different covers exist 4.00
1 e ($3.95)-Double gate-fold-c consisting of all four covers from 1a-d by Jim Lee; contains all pin-ups from #1a-d plus inside-c foldout poster; no ads; printed on coated stock 5.00
2-7: 4-Wolverine back to old yellow costume (same date as Wolverine #50); last $1.00-c. 5-Byrne scripts. 6-Sabretooth-c/story 5.00
8-10: 8-Gambit vs. Bishop-c/story; last Lee-a; Ghost Rider cameo cont'd in Ghost Rider #26. 9-Wolverine vs. Ghost Rider; cont'd/G.R. #26. 10-Return of Longshot 4.00
11-13,17-24,26-29,31: 12,13-Art Thibert-c/a. 28,29-Sabretooth app. 3.00
11-Silver ink 2nd printing; came with X-Men board game 1.85 5.50 15.00
14-16-($1.50)-Polybagged with trading card in each; X-Cutioner's Song x-overs; 14-Andy Kubert-c/a begins 3.00
25-($3.50, 52 pgs.)-Wraparound-c with Gambit hologram on-c; Professor X erases Magneto's mind 1.50 4.50 12.00
25-30th anniversary issue w/B&W-c with Magneto in color & Magneto hologram & no price on-c 1.85 5.50 15.00
25-Gold 30.00
30-($1.95)-Wedding issue w/bound-in trading card sheet 5.00
32-37: 32-Begin $1.50-c; bound-in card sheet. 33-Gambit & Sabretooth-c/story 3.00
36,37-($2.95)-Collectors editions 5.00
38-44,46-49,51-53, 55-65: 42,43- Paul Smith-a. 46,49,53-56-Onslaught app. 51-Waid scripts begin, end #56. 54-(Reg. edition)-Onslaught revealed as Professor X. 55, 56-Onslaught x-over; Avengers, FF & Sentinels app. 56-Dr. Doom app. 57-Xavier taken into custody; Byrne-c/swipe (X-Men,1st Series #138). 59-Hercules-c/app. 61-Juggernaut-c/app. 62-Re-intro. Shang Chi; two covers. 63-Kingpin cameo. 64- Kingpin app. 2.50
45 ($3.95)-Annual issue; gatefold-c 5.00
50 ($2.95)-Vs. Onslaught, wraparound-c. 4.00
50 ($3.95)-Vs. Onslaught, wraparound foil-c. 5.00
50 ($2.95)-Variant-c. 1.00 3.00 8.00
54-(Limited edition)-Embossed variant-c; Onslaught revealed as Professor X 3.00 9.00 30.00
66-69,71-74,76-79: 66-Operation Zero Tolerance. 76-Origin of Maggott 2.00
70-($2.99, 48 pgs.)-Joe Kelly-s begin, new members join 3.00
75-($2.99, 48 pgs.) vs. N'Garai; wraparound-c 3.00
80-($3.99) 35th Anniv. issue; holo-foil-c 5.00
80-($2.99) Regular-c 3.00
80-($6.95) Dynamic Forces Ed.; Quesada-c 7.00
81-93,95: 82-Hunt for Xavier pt. 2. 85-Davis-a. 86-Origin of Joseph. 87-Magneto War ends. 88-Juggernaut app. 2.00
94-($2.99) Contains preview of X-Men: Hidden Years 3.00
96-99: 96,97-Apocalypse: The Twelve 2.00

X-Men #103 © MAR

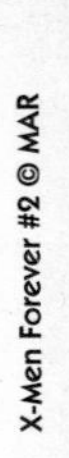

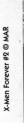

X-Men Forever #2 © MAR

X-Men: Hidden Years #8 © MAR

GD2.0 FN6.0 NM9.4

)0-($2.99) Art Adams-c; begin Claremont-s/Yu-a 3.00
)1-105,107,108: 101-Begin $2.25-c. 107-Maximum Security x-over; Bishop-c/app. 108-Moira MacTaggart dies; Senator Kelly shot 2.25
)6-($2.99) X-Men battle Domina 3.00
)9-($3.50, 100 pgs.) new and reprinted Christmas-themed stories 3.50
-1) Flashback (7/97); origin of Magneto 2.50
nnual 1-3 ('92-'94, $2.25-$2.95, 68 pgs.) 1-Lee-c & layouts; #2-Bagged w/card 4.00
nnual 2000 ($3.50) Art Adams-c/Claremont-s/Eaton-a 3.50
nimation Special Graphic Novel (12/90, $10.95) adapted animated series 11.00
shcan #1 (1994, 75¢) Introduces new team members 2.00
shcan (75¢ Ashcan Edition) (1994) 2.00
pecial '95 ($3.95) 4.00
'96,...'97-Wraparound-c 3.00
/ Dr. Doom '98 Annual ($2.99) Lopresti-a 3.00
. Annual '99 ($3.50) Adam Kubert-c 3.50
. Archives Sketchbook (12/00, $2.99) Early B&W character design sketches by various incl. Lee, Davis, Yu, Pacheco, BWS, Art Adams, Liefeld 3.00
.: Declassified (10/00, $3.50) Profile pin-ups by various; Jae Lee-c 3.50
.:Fatal Attractions ('94, $17.95)-r/x-Factor #92, X-Force #25, Uncanny X-Men #304, X-Men #25, Wolverine #75, & Excalibur #71 18.00
.Millennial Visions (8/00, $3.99) Various artists interpret future X-Men 4.00
.Pizza Hut Mini-comics-(See Marvel Collector's Edition: X-Men in Promotional Comics section)
.Premium Edition #1 (1993)-Cover says "Toys 'R' Us Limited Edition X-Men" 2.00
.:Rarities (1995, $5.95)-Reprints 6.00
.:Road Trippin' ('99, $24.95, TPB) r/X-Men road trips 25.00
.:The Coming of Bishop ('95, $12.95)-r/Uncanny X-Men #282-285, 287,288 13.00
..:The Magneto War (3/99, $2.99) Davis-a 3.00
..:The Rise of Apocalypse ('98, $16.99)-r/Rise Of Apocalypse #1-4, X-Factor #5,6 17.00
.. Visionaries: Chris Claremont ('98, $24.95)-r/Claremont-s; art by Byrne, Barry Smith, and Jim Lee 25.00
.. Visionaries: Joe Madureira (7/00, $17.95)-r/Uncanny X-Men #325,326,329, 330,341-343; new Madureira-c 18.00
..: Zero Tolerance ('00, $24.95, TPB) r/crossover series 25.00

IOTE: ***Jim Lee** a-1-11p; c-1-6p, 7, 8, 9p, 10, 11p. **Art Thibert** a-6-9i, 12, 13; c-6i, 12, 13.*

X-MEN ADVENTURES (TV)
Marvel Comics: Nov, 1992 - No. 15, Jan, 1994 ($1.25)(Based on animated series)

1-Wolverine, Cyclops, Jubilee, Rogue, Gambit 3.00
2-15: 3-Magneto-c/story. 6-Sabretooth-c/story. 7-Cable-c/story. 10-Archangel guest star. 11-Cable-c/story. 15-($1.75, 52 pgs.) 2.00

X-MEN ADVENTURES II (TV)
Marvel Comics: Feb, 1994 - No. 13, Feb, 1995 ($1.25/$1.50)(Based on 2nd TV season)

1-13: 4-Bound-in trading card sheet. 5-Alpha Flight app. 2.00
...Captive Hearts/Slave Island (TPB, $4.95)-r/X-Men Adventures #5-8 5.00
...The Irresistible Force, The Muir Island Saga (5.95, 10/94, TPB) r/X-Men Adventures #9-12 6.00

X-MEN ADVENTURES III (TV)(See Adventures of the X-Men)
Marvel Comics: Mar, 1995 - No. 13, Mar, 1996 ($1.50) (Based on 3rd TV season)

1-13 2.00

X-MEN ALPHA
Marvel Comics: 1994 ($3.95, one-shot)

nn-Age of Apocalypse; wraparound chromium-c 1.00 3.00 8.00
nn ($49.95)-Gold logo 50.00

X-MEN/ALPHA FLIGHT
Marvel Comics Group: Dec, 1985 - No. 2, Dec, 1985 ($1.50, limited series)

1,2: 1-Intro The Berserkers; Paul Smith-a 5.00

X-MEN/ALPHA FLIGHT
Marvel Comics Group: May, 1998 - No. 2, June, 1998 ($2.99, limited series)

1,2-Flashback to early meeting; Raab-s/Cassaday-s/a 3.00

X-MEN AND THE MICRONAUTS, THE
Marvel Comics Group: Jan, 1984 - No. 4, Apr, 1984 (Limited series)

1-4: Guice-c/a(p) in all 4.00

X-MEN ARCHIVES
Marvel Comics: Jan, 1995 - No. 4, Apr, 1995 ($2.25, limited series)

1-4: Reprints Legion stories from New Mutants. 4-Magneto app. 2.25

X-MEN ARCHIVES FEATURING CAPTAIN BRITAIN
Marvel Comics: July, 1995 - No. 7, 1996 ($2.95, limited series)

1-7: Reprints early Capt. Britain stories 3.00

X-MEN BLACK SUN (See Black Sun:...)

X-MEN BOOKS OF ASKANI
Marvel Comics: 1995 ($2.95, one-shot)

1-Painted pin-ups w/text 3.00

X-MEN CHRONICLES
Marvel Comics: Mar, 1995 - No. 2, June, 1995 ($3.95, limited series)

1,2: Age of Apocalypse x-over. 1-wraparound-c 5.00

X-MEN: CHILDREN OF THE ATOM
Marvel Comics: Nov, 1999 - No. 6 ($2.99, limited series)

1-6-Casey-s; X-Men before issue #1. 1-3-Rude-c/a. 4-Paul Smith-a/Rude-c. 5,6-Essad Ribic-c/a 3.00

X-MEN: CLANDESTINE
Marvel Comics: Oct, 1996 - No. 2, Nov, 1996 ($2.95, limited series, 48 pgs.)

1,2: Alan Davis-c(p)/a(p)/scripts & Mark Farmer-c(i)/a(i) in all; wraparound-c 3.00

X-MEN CLASSIC (Formerly Classic X-Men)
Marvel Comics: No. 46, Apr, 1990 - No. 110, Aug, 1995 ($1.25/$1.50)

46-110: Reprints from X-Men. 54-(52 pgs.). 57,60-63,65-Russell-c(i); 62-r/X-Men #158(Rogue). 66-r/#162(Wolverine). 69-Begins-r of Paul Smith issues (#165 on). 70,79,90,97(52 pgs.). 70-r/X-Men #166. 90-r/#186. 100-($1.50). 104-r/X-Men #200 2.00

X-MEN CLASSICS
Marvel Comics Group: Dec, 1983 - No. 3, Feb, 1984 ($2.00, Baxter paper)

1-3: X-Men-r by Neal Adams 2.40 6.00

NOTE: ***Zeck** c-1-3.*

X-MEN: EARTHFALL
Marvel Comics: Sept, 1996 ($2.95, one-shot)

1-r/Uncanny X-Men #232-234; wraparound-c 3.00

X-MEN FIRSTS
Marvel Comics: Feb, 1996 ($4.95, one-shot)

1-r/Avengers Annual #10, Uncanny X-Men #266, #221; Incredible Hulk #181 5.00

X-MEN FOREVER
Marvel Comics: Jan, 2001 - No. 6 ($3.50, limited series)

1,2-Jean Grey, Iceman, Mystique, Toad, Juggernaut app.; Maguire-a 3.50

X-MEN: HELLFIRE CLUB
Marvel Comics: Jan, 2000 - No. 4, Apr, 2000 ($2.50, limited series)

1-4-Origin of the Hellfire Club 2.50

X-MEN: HIDDEN YEARS
Marvel Comics: Dec, 1999 - No. 22, Sept. 2001 ($3.50/$2.50)

1-New adventures from pre-#94 era; Byrne-s/a(p) 3.50
2-4,6-11,13-16-($2.50): 2-Two covers. 3-Ka-Zar app. 8,9-FF-c/app. 2.50
5-($2.75) 2.75
12-($3.50) Magneto-c/app. 3.50

X-MEN: LIBERATORS
Marvel Comics: Nov, 1998 - No. 4, Feb, 1999 ($2.99, limited series)

1-4-Wolverine, Nightcrawler & Colossus; P. Jimenez 3.00

X-MEN LOST TALES
Marvel Comics: 1997 ($2.99)

1,2-r/Classic X-Men back-up stories 3.00

X-MEN OMEGA

X-Men The Movie Adaption © MAR

X-Men: The Manga #2 © MAR

X-Men Unlimited #3 © MAR

Marvel Comics: June, 1995 ($3.95, one-shot)

nn-Age of Apocalypse finale 1.25 3.75 10.00
nn-($49.95)-Gold edition 50.00

X-MEN: PHOENIX
Marvel Comics: Dec, 1999 - No. 3, Mar, 2000 ($2.50, limited series)

1-3: 1-Apocalypse app. 2.50

X-MEN PRIME
Marvel Comics: July, 1995 ($4.95, one-shot)

nn-Post Age of Apocalyse begins 1.25 3.75 10.00

X-MEN RARITIES
Marvel Comics: 1995 ($5.95, one-shot)

nn-Reprints hard-to-find stories 6.00

X-MEN ROAD TO ONSLAUGHT
Marvel Comics: Oct, 1996 ($2.50, one-shot)

nn-Retells Onslaught Saga 2.50

X-MEN: SEARCH FOR CYCLOPS
Marvel Comics: Oct, 2000 - No. 4 ($2.99, limited series)

1,2-Two covers (Raney,Pollina); Raney-a 3.00

X-MEN SPOTLIGHT ON... STARJAMMERS (Also see X-Men #104)
Marvel Comics: 1990 - No. 2, 1990 ($4.50, 52 pgs.)

1,2: Features Starjammers 4.50

X-MEN SURVIVAL GUIDE TO THE MANSION
Marvel Comics: Aug, 1993 ($6.95, spiralbound)

1 7.00

X-MEN: THE EARLY YEARS
Marvel Comics: May, 1994 - No. 17, Sept, 1995 ($1.50/$2.50)

1-16: r/X-Men #1-8 w/new-c 2.00
17-$2.50-c; r/X-Men #17,18 2.50

X-MEN: THE MANGA
Marvel Comics: Mar, 1998 - No. 26, June, 1999 ($2.99, B&W)

1-26-English version of Japanese X-Men comics: 23,24-Randy Green-c 3.00

X-MEN: THE MOVIE
Marvel Comics: Aug, 2000; Sept, 2000

Adaption (9/00, $5.95) Macchio-s/Williams & Lanning-a 5.95
Adaption TPB (9/00, $14.95) Movie adaption and key reprints of main characters; four photo covers (movie X, Magneto, Rogue, Wolverine) 14.95
Prequel: Magneto (8/00, $5.95) Texeira & Palmiotti-a; art & photo covers 5.95
Prequel: Rogue (8/00, $5.95) Evans & Nikolakakis-a; art & photo covers 5.95
Prequel: Wolverine (8/00, $5.95) Waller & McKenna-a; art & photo covers 5.95
TPB X-Men: Beginnings (8/00, $14.95) reprints 3 prequels w/photo-c 14.95

X-MEN: THE ULTRA COLLECTION
Marvel Comics: Dec, 1994 - No. 5, Apr, 1995 ($2.95, limited series)

1-5: Pin-ups; no scripts 3.00

X-MEN: THE WEDDING ALBUM
Marvel Comics: 1994 ($2.95, magazine size, one-shot)

1-Wedding of Scott Summers & Jean Grey 3.00

X-MEN TRUE FRIENDS
Marvel Comics: Sept, 1999 - No. 3, Nov, 1999 ($2.99, limited series)

1-3-Claremont-s/Leonardi-a 3.00

X-MEN 2099 (Also see 2099: World of Tomorrow)
Marvel Comics: Oct, 1993 - No. 35, Aug, 1996 ($1.25/$1.50/$1.95)

1-($1.75)-Foil-c; Ron Lim/Adam Kubert-a begins 3.00
1-2nd printing ($1.75) 2.00
1-Gold edition (15,000 made); sold thru Diamond for $19.40 20.00
2-24,26-35: 3-Death of Tina; Lim-c/a(p) in #1-8. 8-Bound-in trading card sheet. 35-Nostromo (from X-Nation) app; storyline cont'd in 2099: World of Tomorrow. 2.00
25 ($2.50)-Double sized 2.50
Special 1 ($3.95) 4.00
...: Oasis ($5.95, one-shot) -Hildebrandt Bros.-c/a 6.00

X-MEN ULTRA III PREVIEW
Marvel Comics: 1995 ($2.95)

nn-Kubert-a 3.0

X-MEN UNIVERSE
Marvel Comics: Dec, 1999 - Present ($4.99/$3.99)

1-8-Reprints stories from recent X-Men titles 5.0
9-15-($3.99) 4.0

X-MEN UNIVERSE: PAST, PRESENT AND FUTURE
Marvel Comics: Feb, 1999 ($2.99, one-shot)

1-Previews 1999 X-Men events; background info 3.0

X-MEN UNLIMITED
Marvel Comics: 1993 - Present ($3.95/$2.99, 68 pgs.)

1-Chris Bachalo-c/a; Quesada-a. 5.0
2-11: 3-Sabretooth-c/story. 2-Origin of Magneto script. 10-Dark Beast vs. Bea Mark Waid script. 11-Magneto & Rogue 4.0
12-29: 12-Begin $2.99-c; Onslaught x-over; Juggernaut-c/app. 19-Caliafore-a 20-Generation X app. 27-Origin Thunderbird. 29-Maximum Security x-over; Bishop-c/app. 3.0
NOTE: ***Bachalo** c/a-1. **Quesada** a-1. **Waid** scripts-10*

X-MEN VS. DRACULA
Marvel Comics: Dec, 1993 ($1.75)

1-r/X-Men Annual #6; Austin-c(i) 2.0

X-MEN VS. THE AVENGERS, THE
Marvel Comics Group: Apr, 1987 - No. 4, July, 1987 ($1.50, limited series, Baxter paper)

1 4.0
2-4 3.0

X-MEN VS. THE BROOD, THE
Marvel Comics Group: Sept, 1996 - No. 2, Oct, 1996 ($2.95, limited series)

1,2-Wraparound-c; Ostrander-s/Hitch-a(p) 3.0
TPB('97, $16.99) reprints X-Men/Brood: Day of Wrath #1,2 & Uncanny X-Men #232-234 17.0

X-MEN VISIONARIES
Marvel Comics: 1995 ($8.95, trade paperback)

nn-Reprints X-Men stories; Adam & Andy Kubert-a 9.0

X-MEN/WILDC.A.T.S.: THE DARK AGE (See also WildC.A.T.S./X-Men...)
Marvel Comics: 1998 ($4.50, one-shot)

1-Two covers (Broome & Golden); Ellis-s 4.5

X-NATION 2099
Marvel Comics: Mar, 1996 - No. 6, Aug, 1996 ($1.95)

1-($3.95)-Humberto Ramos-a(p); wraparound, foil-c 4.0
2-6: 2,3-Ramos-a. 4-Exodus-c/app. 5-Exodus cameo. 6-Reed Richards app 2.0

X-O MANOWAR (1st Series)
Valiant/Acclaim Comics (Valiant) No. 43 on: Feb, 1992 - No. 68, Sept, 1996 ($1.95/$2.25/$2.50, high quality)

0-(8/93, $3.50)-Wraparound embossed chromium-c by Quesada; Solar app.; origin Aric (X-O Manowar) 3.5
0-Gold variant 5.0
1-Intro/1st app. & partial origin of Aric (X-O Manowar); Barry Smith/Layton-a 1.00 3.00 8.0
2-4: 2-B. Smith/Layton-c; Layton part inks. 3-Layton-c(i). 4-1st app. Shadowman (cameo) 2.40 6.0
5-14: 5-B. Smith-c. 6-Begin $2.25-c; Ditko-a(p). 7,8-Unity x-overs. 7-Miller-c. 8-Simonson-c. 12-1st app. Randy Calder. 14,15-Turok-c/stories 3.0
15-Hot pink logo variant; came with Ultra Pro Rigid Comic Sleeves box; no pric on cover 4.0
16-24,26-43: 20-Serial number contest insert. 27-29-Turok x-over. 28-Bound-in trading card. 30-1st app. new "good skin"; Solar app. 33-Chaos Effect Delta Pt. 3. 42-Shadowman app.; includes X-O Manowar Birthquake! Prequel 2.5
25-($3.50)-Has 16 pg. Armorines #0 bound-in w/origin 3.5
44-68: 44-Begin $2.50-c. 50-X, 50-O, 51, 52, 63-Bart Sears-c/a/scripts.

Xombi #0 © Milestone Media

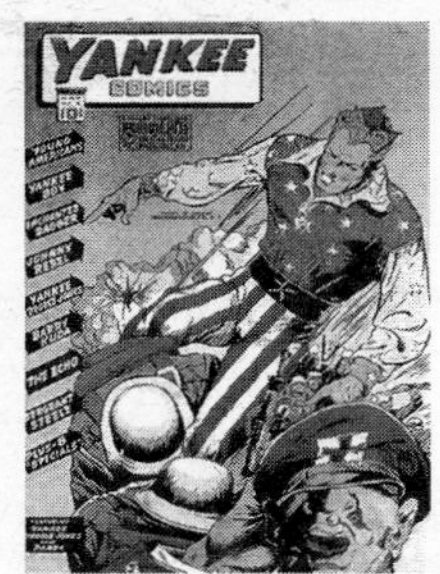

Yankee Comics #4 © CHES

Yeah! #1 © Peter Bagge & DC

GD2.0 FN6.0 NM9.4

68-Revealed that Aric's past stories were premonitions of his future 2.50
de paperback nn (1993, $9.95)-Polybagged with copy of X-O Database #1
nside 10.00
ırbook 1 (4/95, $2.95) 3.00
'E: *Layton* a-1i, 2i(part); c-1, 2i, 3i, 6i, 21i. *Reese* a-4i(part); c-26i.

MANOWAR (2nd Series)(Also see Iron Man/X-O Manowar: Heavy Metal)
:laim Comics (Valiant Heroes): V2#1, Oct, 1996 - No. 21, Jun, 1998 ($2.50)

‡1-21: 1-Mark Waid & Brian Augustyn scripts begin; 1st app. Donavon Wylie;
Rand Banion dies; painted variant-c exists. 2-Donavon Wylie becomes new
X-O Manowar. 7-9-Augustyn-s. 10-Copycat-c 2.50

MANOWAR FAN EDITION
:laim Comics (Valiant Heroes): Feb, 1997 (Overstreet's FAN giveaway)

Reintro the Armorines & the Hard Corps; 1st app. Citadel; Augustyn scripts;
McKone-c/a 4.00

MANOWAR/IRON MAN: IN HEAVY METAL (See Iron Man/X-O Manowar:
ıvy Metal)
:laim Comics (Valiant Heroes): Sept, 1996 ($2.50, one-shot)
' Marvel/Valiant x-over)

Pt 1 of X-O Manowar/Iron Man x-over; Arnim Zola app.; Fabian Nicieza
scripts; Andy Smith-a 2.50

MBI
Comics (Milestone): Jan, 1994 - No. 21, Feb, 1996 ($1.75/$2.50)

($1.95)-Shadow War x-over; Simonson silver ink varnish-c 2.50
21: 1-John Byrne-c 2.50
Platinum 8.00

'ATROL
rvel Comics (Amalgam): Apr, 1996 ($1.95, one-shot)

Cruz-a(p) 2.00

E
rvel Comics: Nov, 1996 - No. 4, Feb, 1997 ($1.95, limited series)

4: 1-Bishop & Shard app. 2.00
Variant-c 3.00

'ERMINATORS
rvel Comics: Oct, 1988 - No. 4, Jan, 1989 ($1.00, limited series)

1st app.; X-Men/X-Factor tie-in; Williamson-i 3.00
4 2.00

THE MAN WITH THE X-RAY EYES (See Movie Comics)

INIVERSE
rvel Comics: May, 1995 - No. 2, June, 1995 ($3.50, limited series)

2: Age of Apocalypse 5.00

'ENTURE (Super Heroes)
tory Magazines Corp.: July, 1947 - No. 2, Nov, 1947

Atom Wizard, Mystery Shadow, Lester Trumble begin
95.00 285.00 900.00
55.00 165.00 500.00

R (See Eclipse Graphic Album Series #21)

K YAK
l Publishing Co.: No. 1186, May-July, 1961 - No. 1348, Apr-June, 1962

ır Color 1186 (#1)- Jack Davis-c/a; 2 versions, one minus 3pgs.
7.50 22.50 90.00
ır Color 1348 (#2)-Davis c/a 7.50 22.50 90.00

KKY DOODLE & CHOPPER (TV) (See Dell Giant #44)
ld Key: Dec, 1962 (Hanna-Barbera)

7.00 21.00 85.00

NG (See House of Yang)
arlton Comics: Nov, 1973 - No. 13, May, 1976; V14#15, Sept, 1985 - No. 17,
ı, 1986 (No V14#14, series resumes with #15)

Origin; Sattler-a begins; slavery-s 1.50 4.50 12.00
13(1976) 1.00 2.80 7.00
-17(1986): 15-Reprints #1 (Low print run) 5.00
10,11(Modern Comics-r, 1977) 3.00

GD2.0 FN6.0 NM9.4

YANKEE COMICS
Harry 'A' Chesler: Sept, 1941 - No. 7, 1942?

1-Origin The Echo, The Enchanted Dagger, Yankee Doodle Jones, The
Firebrand, & The Scarlet Sentry; Black Satan app.; Yankee Doodle Jones
app. on all covers 158.00 474.00 1500.00
2-Origin Johnny Rebel; Major Victory app.; Barry Kuda begins
76.00 229.00 725.00
3,4: 4-(3/42) 58.00 174.00 550.00
4 (nd, 1940s; 7-1/4x5", 68 pgs, distr. to the service)-Foxy Grandpa, Tom, Dick
& Harry, Impy, Ace & Deuce, Dot & Dash, Ima Slooth by Jack Cole
(Remington Morse publ.) 6.40 19.25 45.00
5-7 (nd; 10¢, 7-1/4x5", 68 pgs.)(Remington Morse publ.)-urges readers to send
their copies to servicemen. 5.00 15.00 35.00

YANKEE DOODLE THE SPIRIT OF LIBERTY
Spire Publications: 1984 (no price, 36 pgs)

nn-Al Hartley-s/c/a 8.00

YANKS IN BATTLE
Quality Comics Group: Sept, 1956 - No. 4, Dec, 1956; 1963

1-Cuidera-c(i) 9.30 28.00 65.00
2-4: Cuidera-c(i) 5.70 17.00 40.00
I.W. Reprint #3(1963)-r/#?; exist? 1.75 5.25 14.00

YARDBIRDS, THE (G. I. Joe's Sidekicks)
Ziff-Davis Publishing Co.: Summer, 1952

1-By Bob Oskner 10.00 30.00 75.00

YARN MAN (See Megaton Man)
Kitchen Sink : Oct, 1989 ($2.00, B&W, one-shot)

1-Donald Simpson-c/a/scripts 2.00

YARNS OF YELLOWSTONE
World Color Press: 1972 (50¢, 36 pgs.)

nn-Illustrated by Bill Chapman 1.25 3.75 10.00

YEAH!
DC Comics (Homage): Oct, 1999 - No. 9, Jun, 2000 ($2.95)

1-Bagge-s/Hernandez-a 3.00
2-9: 2-Editorial page contains adult language 3.00

YELLOW CLAW (Also see Giant Size Master of Kung Fu)
Atlas Comics (MjMC): Oct, 1956 - No. 4, Apr, 1957

1-Origin by Joe Maneely 92.00 276.00 875.00
2-Kirby-a 75.00 225.00 715.00
3,4-Kirby-a; 4-Kirby/Severin-a 71.00 213.00 675.00
NOTE: *Everett* c-3. *Maneely* c-1. *Reinman* a-2i, 3. *Severin* c-2, 4.

YELLOWJACKET COMICS (Jack in the Box #11 on)(See TNT Comics)
E. Levy/Frank Comunale/Charlton: Sept, 1944 - No. 10, June, 1946

1-Intro & origin Yellowjacket; Diana, the Huntress begins; E.A. Poe's "The
Black Cat" adaptation 63.00 189.00 600.00
2-Yellowjacket-c begin, end #10 40.00 120.00 320.00
3,5 38.00 113.00 300.00
4-E.A. Poe's "Fall of the House Of Usher" adaptation; Palais-a
40.00 120.00 320.00
6,8-10: 1,3,4,6-10-Have stories narrated by old witch in "Tales of Terror"
(1st horror series?) 40.00 120.00 350.00
7-Classic skull-c 63.00 189.00 600.00

YELLOWSTONE KELLY (Movie)
Dell Publishing Co.: No. 1056, Nov-Jan, 1959/60

Four Color 1056-Clint Walker photo-c 5.00 15.00 60.00

YELLOW SUBMARINE (See Movie Comics)

YIN FEI THE CHINESE NINJA
Leung's Publications: 1988 - No. 8, 1990 ($1.80/$2.00, 52 pgs.)

1-8 2.00

YOGI BEAR (See Dell Giant #41, Golden Comics Digest, Kite Fun Book, March of Comics #253, 265, 279, 291, 309, 319, 337, 344, Movie Comics under "Hey There It's..." & Whitman Comic Books)

YOGI BEAR (TV) (Hanna-Barbera) (See Four Color #990)

Young Allies Comics #2 © MAR

Youngblood #6 © Awesome Ent.

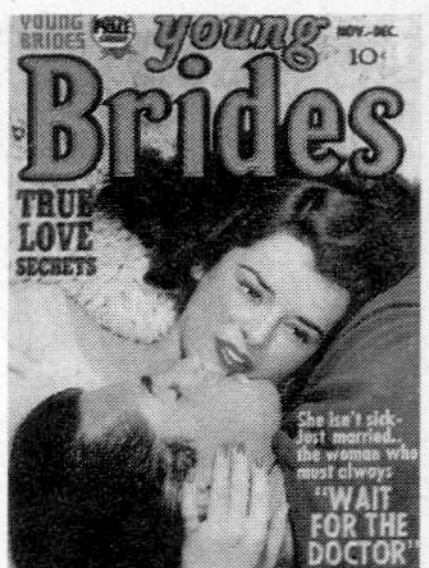

Young Brides #2 © PRIZE

GD2.0 FN6.0 NM9

Dell Publishing Co./Gold Key No. 10 on: No. 1067, 12-2/59-60 - No. 9, 7-9/62; No. 10, 10/62 - No. 42, 10/70

Four Color 1067 (#1)-TV show debuted 1/30/61 11.00 33.00 130.00
Four Color 1104,1162 (5-7/61) 7.00 21.00 85.00
4(8-9/61) - 6(12-1/61-62) 4.60 13.75 55.00
Four Color 1271(11/61) 4.60 13.75 55.00
Four Color 1349(1/62)-Photo-c 9.00 27.00 110.00
7(2-3/62) - 9(7-9/62)-Last Dell 4.60 13.75 55.00
10(10/62-G.K.), 11(1/63)-titled "Yogi Bear Jellystone Jollies" (80 pgs.);
11-X-Mas-c 6.70 20.00 80.00
12(4/63), 14-20 4.10 12.30 45.00
13(7/63, 68 pgs.)-Surprise Party 7.25 21.75 80.00
21-30 3.00 9.00 30.00
31-42 2.50 7.50 25.00

YOGI BEAR (TV)
Charlton Comics: Nov, 1970 - No. 35, Jan, 1976 (Hanna-Barbera)

1 3.65 11.00 40.00
2-6,8-10 2.50 7.50 24.00
7-Summer Fun (Giant, 52 pgs.) 4.10 12.30 45.00
11-20 2.30 7.00 20.00
21-35: 28-31-partial-r 1.85 5.50 15.00

YOGI BEAR (TV)(See The Flintstones, 3rd series & Spotlight #1)
Marvel Comics Group: Nov, 1977 - No. 9, Mar, 1979 (Hanna-Barbera)

1,7-9: 1-Flintstones begin (Newsstand sales only) 2.00 6.00 18.00
2-6 1.50 4.50 12.00

YOGI BEAR (TV)
Harvey Comics: Sept, 1992 - No. 6, Mar, 1994 ($1.25/$1.50) (Hanna-Barbera)

V2#1-6 2.00
...Big Book V2#1,2 ($1.95, 52 pgs): 1-(11/92). 2-(3/93) 2.50
...Giant Size V2#1,2 ($2.25, 68 pgs.): 1-(10/92). 2-(4/93) 2.50

YOGI BEAR'S EASTER PARADE (See The Funtastic World of Hanna-Barbera #2)

YOGI BERRA (Baseball hero)
Fawcett Publications: 1951 (Yankee catcher)

nn-Photo-c (scarce) 68.00 205.00 650.00

YOSEMITE SAM (...& Bugs Bunny) (TV)
Gold Key/Whitman: Dec, 1970 - No. 81, Feb, 1984

1 3.20 9.60 35.00
2-10 2.00 6.00 18.00
11-20 1.50 4.50 12.00
21-30 1.25 3.75 10.00
31-50 1.00 3.00 8.00
51-65 (Gold Key) 5.00
66,67 (Whitman) 1.00 3.00 8.00
68(9/80), 69(10/80), 70(12/80) 3-pack? 1.85 5.50 15.00
71-78 1.25 3.75 10.00
79-81 (All #90263 on-c, no date or date code; 3-pack?): 81-(1/3-r)
1.50 4.50 12.00
(See March of Comics #363, 380, 392)

YOUNG ALLIES COMICS (All-Winners #21; see Kid Komics #2)
Timely Comics (USA 1-7/NPI 8,9/YAI 10-20): Sum, 1941 - No. 20, Oct, 1946

GD2.0 FN6.0 VF8.0 NM9.4
1-Origin/1st app. The Young Allies (Bucky, Toro, others); 1st meeting of Captain America & Human Torch; Red Skull-c & app.; S&K-c/splash; Hitler-c
1000.00 3000.00 6500.00 12,500.00
GD2.0 FN6.0 NM9.4
2-(Winter, 1941)-Captain America & Human Torch app.; Simon & Kirby-c
305.00 915.00 3200.00
3-Fathertime, Captain America & Human Torch app.; Remember Pearl Harbor issue (Spring, 1942); Stan Lee scripts; Vs. Japs-c/full-length story
253.00 758.00 2400.00
4-The Vagabond & Red Skull, Capt. America, Human Torch app. Classic Red Skull-c 343.00 1029.00 3600.00
5-Captain America & Human Torch app. 168.00 505.00 1600.00
6-8,10: 10-Origin Tommy Tyme & Clock of Ages; ends #19
116.00 348.00 1100.00
9-Hitler, Tojo, Mussolini-c. 132.00 395.00 1250.(
11-20: 12-Classic decapitation story 92.00 276.00 875.(

NOTE: ***Brodsky** c-15. **Gabrielle** a-3; c-3, 4. **S&K** c-1, 2. **Schomburg** c-5-14, 16-19. **Shores** c-20.*

YOUNG ALL-STARS
DC Comics: June, 1987 - No. 31, Nov, 1989 ($1.00, deluxe format)

1-31: 1-1st app. Iron Munro & The Flying Fox. 8,9-Millennium tie-ins 2.0
Annual 1 (1988, $2.00) 2.0

YOUNGBLOOD (See Brigade #4, Megaton Explosion & Team Youngblood)
Image Comics (Extreme Studios): Apr, 1992 - No. 4, Feb, 1993 ($2.50, lim. series); No. 6, June, 1994 (No #5) - No. 10, Dec, 1994 ($1.95/$2.50)

1-Liefeld-c/a/scripts in all; flip book format with 2 trading cards; 1st Image/Extreme Studios title. 5.(
1-2nd printing 2.(
2-(JUN-c, July 1992 indicia)-1st app. Shadowhawk in solo back-up story; 2 trading cards inside; flip book format; 1st app. Prophet, Kirby, Berzerkers, Darkthorn 2.5
2-2nd printing (1.95) 2.5
3,0,4,5: 3-(OCT-c, August 1992 indicia)-Contains 2 trading cards inside (flip book); 1st app. Supreme in back-up story; 1st app. Showdown. 0-(12/92, $1.95)-Contains 2 trading cards; 2 cover variations exist, green or beige log w/Image #0 coupon. 4-(2/93)-Glow-in-the-dark-c w/2 trading cards; 2nd app Dale Keown's The Pitt; Bloodstrike app. 5-Flip book w/Brigade #4 2.5
6-($3.50, 52 pgs.)-Wraparound-c 3.5
7-10: 7, 8-Liefeld-c(p)/a(p)/story. 8,9-(9/94) 9-Valentino story & art 2.5
Battlezone 1 (May-c, 4/93 inside, $1.95)-Arsenal book; Liefeld-c(p) 2.5
Battlezone 2 (7/94, $2.95)-Wraparound-c 3.0
Yearbook 1 (7/93, $2.50)-Fold out panel; 1st app. Tyrax & Kanan 2.5
...Super Special (Winter '97, $2.99) Sprouse -a 3.0
TPB (1996, $16.95)-r/Team Youngblood #8-10 & Youngblood #6-8,10 17.0

YOUNGBLOOD
Image Comics (Extreme Studios)/Maximum Press No. 14: V2#1, Sept, 1995 No. 14, Dec, 1996 ($2.50)

V2#1-10,14: Roger Cruz-a in all. 4-Extreme Destroyer Pt. 4 w/gaming card. 5-Variant-c exists. 6-Angela & Glory. 7-Shadowhunt Pt. 3; Shadowhawk ap 8,10-Thor (from Supreme) app. 10-(7/96). 14-(12/96)-1st Maximum Press issue 2.5

YOUNGBLOOD (Volume 3)
Awesome/ Awesome-Hyperwerks #2 on: Feb, 1998 - Present ($2.50)

1-Alan Moore-s/Skroce & Stucker-a; 12 diff. covers 2.5
1-Gold foil-c 5.0
1-Blue foil-c Orlando Con Ed. 10.0
1+ Alter Ego Gold Foil 5.0
2-(8/98) Skroce & Liefeld covers 2.5

YOUNGBLOOD: STRIKEFILE
Image Comics (Extreme Studios): Apr, 1993 - No. 11, Feb, 1995 ($1.95/$2.50/$2.95)

1-10: 1-($1.95)-Flip book w/Jae Lee-c/a & Liefeld-c/a in #1-3; 1st app. The Allies,Giger, & Glory. 3-Thibert-i asisst. 4-Liefeld-c(p); no Lee-a. 5-Liefeld-c(p). 8-Platt-c 3.0

NOTE: *Youngblood: Strikefile began as a four issue limited series.*

YOUNGBLOOD/X-FORCE
Image Comics (Extreme Studios): July, 1996 ($4.95, one-shot)

1-Cruz-a(p); two covers exist 5.0

YOUNG BRIDES (True Love Secrets)
Feature/Prize Publ.: Sept-Oct, 1952 - No. 30, Nov-Dec, 1956 (Photo-c: 1-4)

V1#1-Simon & Kirby-a 31.00 94.00 250.0
2-S&K-a 16.00 49.00 130.0
3-6-S&K-a 15.00 45.00 120.0
V2#1,3-7,10-12 (#7-18)-S&K-a 14.00 41.00 110.0
2,8,9-No S&K-a 5.00 15.00 32.0
V3#1-3(#19-21)-Last precode (3-4/55) 4.65 14.00 28.0
4,6(#22,24), V4#1,3(#25,27) 4.00 11.00 22.0
V3#5(#23)-Meskin-c 5.00 15.00 30.0
V4#2(#26)-All S&K issue 11.00 33.00 90.0

Young Heroes in Love #5 © Dan Raspler & Dev Madan

Young Justice #1 © DC

Young Love #3 © PRIZE

	GD2.0	FN6.0	NM9.4
V4#4(#28)-S&K-a	10.00	30.00	75.00
V4#5,6(#29,30)	5.00	15.00	35.00

YOUNG DR. MASTERS (See The Adventures of Young Dr. Masters)

YOUNG DOCTORS, THE
Charlton Comics: Jan, 1963 - No. 6, Nov, 1963

	GD2.0	FN6.0	NM9.4
V1#1	3.00	9.00	30.00
2-6	2.30	7.00	20.00

YOUNG EAGLE
Fawcett Publications/Charlton: 12/50 - No. 10, 6/52; No. 3, 7/56 - No. 5, 4/57 (Photo-c: 1-10)

	GD2.0	FN6.0	NM9.4
1-Intro Young Eagle	16.00	49.00	130.00
2-Complete picture novelette "The Mystery of Thunder Canyon"	9.30	28.00	65.00
3-9	8.65	26.00	60.00
10-Origin Thunder, Young Eagle's Horse	7.15	21.50	50.00
3-5(Charlton)-Formerly Sherlock Holmes?	5.00	15.00	30.00

YOUNG HEARTS
Marvel Comics (SPC): Nov, 1949 - No. 2, Feb, 1950

	GD2.0	FN6.0	NM9.4
1-Photo-c	11.00	33.00	90.00
2-Colleen Townsend photo-c from movie	7.85	23.50	55.00

YOUNG HEARTS IN LOVE
Super Comics: 1964

	GD2.0	FN6.0	NM9.4
17,18: 17-r/Young Love V5#6 (4-5/62)	1.85	5.50	15.00

YOUNG HEROES (Formerly Forbidden Worlds #34)
American Comics Group (Titan): No. 35, Feb-Mar, 1955 - No. 37, Jun-Jul, 1955

	GD2.0	FN6.0	NM9.4
35-37-Frontier Scout	10.00	30.00	70.00

YOUNG HEROES IN LOVE
DC Comics: June, 1997 - No. 17; #1,000,000, Nov, 1998 ($1.75/$1.95/$2.50)

	GD2.0	FN6.0	NM9.4
1-1st app. Young Heroes; Madan-a			3.00
2-17: 3-Superman-c/app. 7-Begin $1.95-c			2.00
#1,000,000 (11/98, $2.50) 853 Century x-over			2.50

YOUNG INDIANA JONES CHRONICLES, THE
Dark Horse Comics: Feb, 1992 - No. 12, Feb, 1993 ($2.50)

	GD2.0	FN6.0	NM9.4
1-12: Dan Barry scripts in all			2.50

NOTE: ***Dan Barry*** *a(p)-1, 2, 5, 6, 10; c-1-10.* ***Morrow*** *a-3, 4, 5p, 6p.* ***Springer*** *a-1i, 2i.*

YOUNG INDIANA JONES CHRONICLES, THE
Hollywood Comics (Disney): 1992 ($3.95, squarebound, 68 pgs.)

	GD2.0	FN6.0	NM9.4
1-3: 1-r/YIJC #1,2 by D. Horse. 2-r/#3,4. 3-r/#5,6			4.00

YOUNG JUSTICE
DC Comics: Sept, 1998 - Present ($2.50)

	GD2.0	FN6.0	NM9.4
1-Robin, Superboy & Impulse team-up; David-s/Nauck-a			4.00
2,3: 3-Mxyzptlk app.			3.00
4-20: 4-Wonder Girl, Arrowette and the Secret join. 6-JLA app. 13-Supergirl x-over. 20-Sins of Youth aftermath			3.00
21-30: 25-Empress ID revealed. 28,29-Forever People app.			2.50
#1,000,000 (11/98) 853 Century x-over			2.50
...: A League of Their Own (2000, $14.95, TPB) r/#1-7, Secret Files #1			15.00
...: 80-Page Giant (5/99, $4.95) Ramos-c; stories and art by various			5.00
...: In No Man's Land (7/99, $3.95) McDaniel-c			4.00
...: Secret Files (1/99, $4.95) Origin-s & pin-ups			5.00
...: The Secret (6/98, $1.95) Girlfrenzy; Nauck-a			2.00

YOUNG JUSTICE: SINS OF YOUTH (See Sins of Youth x-over issues)
DC Comics: May, 2000 - No. 2, May, 2000 ($3.95, limited series)

	GD2.0	FN6.0	NM9.4
1,2-Young Justice, JLA & JSA swap ages; David-s/Nauck-a			4.00
TPB (2000, $19.95) r/#1,2 & all x-over issues)			20.00

YOUNG KING COLE (...Detective Tales)(Becomes Criminals on the Run)
Premium Group/Novelty Press: Fall, 1945 - V3#12, July, 1948

	GD2.0	FN6.0	NM9.4
V1#1-Toni Gayle begins	30.00	90.00	240.00
2	13.00	39.00	105.00
3-4	12.00	36.00	95.00
V2#1-7(8-9/46-7/47): 6,7-Certa-c	10.00	30.00	70.00
V3#1,3-6,8,9,12: 3-Certa-c. 5-McWilliams-c/a. 8,9-Harmon-c	9.30	28.00	65.00
2-L.B. Cole-a; Certa-c	15.00	45.00	120.00
7-L.B. Cole-c/a	21.00	62.00	165.00
10,11-L.B. Cole-c	18.00	53.00	140.00

YOUNG LAWYERS, THE (TV)
Dell Publishing Co.: Jan, 1971 - No. 2, Apr, 1971

	GD2.0	FN6.0	NM9.4
1	2.30	7.00	20.00
2	2.00	6.00	16.00

YOUNG LIFE (Teen Life #3 on)
New Age Publ./Quality Comics Group: Summer, 1945 - No. 2, Fall, 1945

	GD2.0	FN6.0	NM9.4
1-Skip Homeier, Louis Prima stories	14.00	41.00	110.00
2-Frank Sinatra photo on-c plus story	14.00	41.00	110.00

YOUNG LOVE (Sister title to Young Romance)
Prize(Feature)Publ.(Crestwood): 2-3/49 - No. 73, 12-1/56-57; V3#5, 2-3/60 - V7#1, 6-7/63

	GD2.0	FN6.0	NM9.4
V1#1-S&K-c/a(2)	41.00	122.00	365.00
2-Photo-c begin; S&K-a	24.00	71.00	190.00
3-S&K-a	18.00	53.00	140.00
4-5-Minor S&K-a	10.00	30.00	80.00
V2#1(#7)-S&K-a(2)	18.00	53.00	140.00
2-5(#8-11)-Minor S&K-a	9.30	28.00	65.00
6,8(#12,14)-S&K-c only. 14-S&K 1 pg. art	10.00	30.00	80.00
7,9-12(#13,15-18)-S&K-c/a	16.00	49.00	130.00
V3#1-4(#19-22)-S&K-c/a	14.00	43.00	115.00
5-7,9-12(#23-25,27-30)-Photo-c resume; S&K-a	12.50	37.50	100.00
8(#26)-No S&K-a	5.00	15.00	30.00
V4#1,6(#31,36)-S&K-a	12.00	36.00	95.00
2-5,7-12(#32-35,37-42)-Minor S&K-a	9.30	28.00	65.00
V5#1-12(#43-54), V6#1-9(#55-63)-Last precode; S&K-a in some	5.00	15.00	32.00
V6#10-12(#64-66)	2.50	7.50	24.00
V7#1-7(#67-73)	2.40	7.35	22.00
V3#5(2-3/60),6(4-5/60)(Formerly All For Love)	2.30	7.00	20.00
V4#1(6-7/60)-6(4-5/61)	2.00	6.00	18.00
V5#1(6-7/61)-6(4-5/62)	2.00	6.00	18.00
V6#1(6-7/62)-6(4-5/63), V7#1	1.75	5.25	14.00

NOTE: ***Meskin*** *a-14(2), 27, 42.* ***Powell*** *a-V4#6.* ***Severin/Elder*** *a-V1#3. S&K art not in #53, 57, 58, 61, 63-65. Photo c-V3#5-V5#11.*

YOUNG LOVE
National Periodical Publ.(Arleigh Publ. Corp #49-61)/DC Comics: #39, 9-10/63 - #120, Wint./75-76; #121, 10/76 - #126, 7/77

	GD2.0	FN6.0	NM9.4
39	3.80	11.40	42.00
40-50	2.80	8.40	28.00
51-68,70	2.50	7.50	25.00
69-(80 pg. Giant)(8-9/68)	4.55	13.65	50.00
71,72,74-77,80	2.50	7.50	23.00
73,78,79-Toth-a	2.30	7.00	20.00
81-99: 88-96-(52 pg. Giants)	2.00	6.00	18.00
100	2.50	7.50	23.00
101-106,115-122	1.50	4.50	12.00
107 (100 pgs.)	6.80	20.50	75.00
108-114 (100 pgs.)	5.45	16.35	60.00
121-126 (52 pgs.)	3.00	9.00	30.00

NOTE: ***Bolle*** *a-117.* ***Colan*** *a-107r.* ***Nasser*** *a-123, 124.* ***Orlando*** *a-122.* ***Simonson*** *c-125.* ***Toth*** *a-73, 78, 79, 122-125r.* ***Wood*** *a-109r(4 pgs.).*

YOUNG LOVER ROMANCES (Formerly & becomes Great Lover...)
Toby Press: No. 4, June, 1952 - No. 5, Aug, 1952

	GD2.0	FN6.0	NM9.4
4,5-Photo-c	5.70	17.00	40.00

YOUNG LOVERS (My Secret Life #19 on)(Formerly Brenda Starr?)
Charlton Comics: No. 16, July, 1956 - No. 18, May, 1957

	GD2.0	FN6.0	NM9.4
16,17('56): 16-Marcus Swayze-a	6.40	19.25	45.00
18-Elvis Presley picture-c, text story (biography)(Scarce)	58.00	174.00	550.00

YOUNG MARRIAGE
Fawcett Publications: June, 1950

	GD2.0	FN6.0	NM9.4
1-Powell-a; photo-c	11.00	33.00	90.00

Young Men #24 © MAR

Young Romance Comics #1 © DC

Youthful Romances #18 © Ribage

YOUNG MEN (Formerly Cowboy Romances)(...on the Battlefield #12-20 (4/53); ...In Action #21)
Marvel/Atlas Comics (IPC): No. 4, 6/50 - No. 11, 10/51; No. 12, 12/51 - No. 28, 6/54

4-(52 pgs.) 19.00 56.00 150.00
5-11 11.00 33.00 90.00
12-23: 12-20-War format. 21-23-Hot Rod issues starring Flash Foster 10.50 32.00 85.00
24-(12/53)-Origin Captain America, Human Torch, & Sub-Mariner which are revived thru #28; Red Skull app. 274.00 821.00 2600.00
25-28: 25-Romita-c/a (see Men's Advs.) 105.00 316.00 1000.00

*NOTE: **Berg** a-7, 14, 17, 18, 20; c-17? **Brodsky** c-4-9, 13, 14, 16, 17, 21-25. **Burgos** c-26-28. **Colan** a-14, 15. **Everett** a-18-20. **Heath** a-13, 14. **Maneely** c-10, 12, 15. **Pakula** a-14, 15. **Robinson** c-18. Captain America by **Romita**-#24?, 25, 26?, 27, 28. Human Torch by **Burgos**-#25, 27, 28. Sub-Mariner by **Everett**-#24-28.*

YOUNG REBELS, THE (TV)
Dell Publishing Co.: Jan, 1971

1-Photo-c 2.00 6.00 16.00

YOUNG ROMANCE COMICS (The 1st romance comic)
Prize/Headline (Feature Publ.) (Crestwood): Sept-Oct, 1947 - V16#4, June-July, 1963 (#1-33: 52 pgs.)

V1#1-S&K-c/a(2) 14.00 133.00 400.00
2-S&K-c/a(2-3) 30.00 90.00 240.00
3-6-S&K-c/a(2-3) each 26.00 79.00 210.00
V2#1-6(#7-12)-S&K-c/a(2-3) each 23.00 69.00 185.00
V3#1-3(#13-15): V3#1-Photo-c begin; S&K-a 15.00 45.00 120.00
4-12(#16-24)-Photo-c; S&K-a 15.00 45.00 120.00
V4#1-11(#25-35)-S&K-a 14.00 41.00 110.00
12(#36)-S&K, Toth-a 16.00 49.00 130.00
V5#1-12(#37-48), V6#4-12(#52-60)-S&K-a 14.00 41.00 110.00
V6#1-3(#49-51)-No S&K-a 6.40 19.25 45.00
V7#1-11(#61-71)-S&K-a in most 11.00 33.00 90.00
V7#12(#72), V8#1-3(#73-75)-Last precode (12-1/54-55)-No S&K-a 5.00 15.00 30.00
V8#4(#76, 4-5/55), 5(#77)-No S&K-a 4.65 14.00 28.00
V8#6-8(#78-80, 12-1/55-56)-S&K-a 9.30 28.00 65.00
V9#3,5,6(#81, 2-3/56, 83,84)-S&K-a 9.30 28.00 65.00
4, V10#1(#82,85)-All S&K-a 10.00 30.00 75.00
V10#2-6(#86-90, 10-11/57)-S&K-a 5.90 17.75 65.00
V11#1,2,5,6(#91,92,95,96)-S&K-a 5.90 17.75 65.00
3,4(#93,94), V12#2,4,5(#98,100,101)-No S&K 2.40 7.35 22.00
V12#1,3,6(#97,99,102)-S&K-a 5.90 17.75 65.00
V13#1(#103)-Powell-a; S&K's last-a for Crestwood 5.90 17.75 65.00
2,4-6(#104-108) 1.85 5.50 15.00
V13#3(#105, 4-5/60)-Elvis Presley-c app. only 3.20 9.60 35.00
V14#1-6, V15#1-6, V16#1-4(#109-124) 1.50 4.50 12.00

*NOTE: **Meskin** a-16, 24(2), 33, 47, 50. **Robinson/Meskin** a-6. **Leonard Starr** a-11. Photo c-13-32, 34-65. Issues 1-3 say "Designed for the More **Adult** Readers of **Comics**" on cover.*

YOUNG ROMANCE COMICS (Continued from Prize series)
National Periodical Publ.(Arleigh Publ. Corp. No. 127): No. 125, Aug-Sept, 1963 - No. 208, Nov-Dec, 1975

125 6.80 20.50 75.00
126-140 3.20 9.60 35.00
141-153,156-162,165-169 3.00 9.00 30.00
155-1st publ. Aragonés-s (no art) 3.20 9.60 35.00
154-Neal Adams-c 3.65 11.00 40.00
163,164-Toth-a 3.00 9.00 30.00
170-172 (68 pg. Giants): 170-Michell from Young Love ends; Lily Martin, the Swinger begins 3.20 9.60 35.00
173-183 (52 pgs.) 2.80 8.40 28.00
184-196 2.00 6.00 18.00
197-204-(100 pgs.) 5.45 16.35 60.00
205-208 1.50 4.50 12.00

YOUNG ZEN: CITY OF DEATH
Entity Comics: Late 1994 ($3.25, B&W)

1 3.25

YOUNG ZEN INTERGALACTIC NINJA (Also see Zen...)
Entity Comics: 1993 - No. 3, 1994 ($3.50/$2.95, B&W)

1-($3.50)-Polybagged w/Sam Kieth chromium trading card; gold foil logo 3.50
2,3-($2.95)-Gold foil logo 3.00

YOUR DREAMS (See Strange World of...)

YOU'RE UNDER ARREST (Manga)
Dark Horse Comics: Dec, 1995 - No. 8, July, 1996 ($2.95, limited series)

1-8 3.00

YOUR UNITED STATES
Lloyd Jacquet Studios: 1946

nn-Used in **SOTI**, pg. 309,310; Sid Greene-a 23.00 69.00 185.00

YOUTHFUL HEARTS (Daring Confessions #4 on)
Youthful Magazines: May, 1952 - No. 3, Sept, 1952

1- "Monkey on Her Back" swipes E.C. drug story/Shock SuspenStories #12; Frankie Laine photo on-c; Doug Wildey-a in all 28.00 83.00 220.00
2,3: 2-Vic Damone photo on-c. 3-Johnny Raye photo on-c 20.00 60.00 160.00

YOUTHFUL LOVE (Truthful Love #2)
Youthful Magazines: May, 1950

1 10.50 32.00 85.00

YOUTHFUL ROMANCES
Pix-Parade #1-14/Ribage #15 on: 8-9/49 - No. 5, 4/50; No. 6, 2/51; No. 7, 5/51 - #14, 10/52; #15, 1/53 - #18, 7/53; No. 5, 9/53 - No. 9, 8/54

1-(1st series)-Titled Youthful Love-Romances 25.00 75.00 200.00
2-Walter Johnson c-1-4 15.00 45.00 120.00
3-5 11.00 33.00 90.00
6,7,9-14(10/52, Pix-Parade; becomes Daring Love #15). 10(1/52)-Mel Torme photo-c/story. 12-Tony Bennett photo-c, 8pg. story & text bio.13-Richard Hayes (singer) photo-c/story; Bob & Ray photo/text story. 10.00 30.00 75.00
8-Frank Sinatra photo/text story; Wood-c/a 17.00 51.00 135.00
15-18 (Ribage)-All have photos on-c. 15-Spike Jones photo-c/story. 16-Tony Bavaar photo-c 9.30 28.00 65.00
5(9/53, Ribage)-Les Paul & Mary Ford photo-c/story; Charlton Heston photo/text story 8.65 26.00 60.00
6-9: 6-Bobby Wayne (singer) photo-c/story; Debbie Reynolds photo/text story 7(2/54)-Tony Martin photo-c/story; Cyd Charise photo/text story. 8(5/54)-Gordon McCrae photo-c/story. 9(8/54)-Ralph Flanagan (band leader) photo-c/story; Audrey Hepburn photo/text story. 6.40 19.25 45.00

Y2K: THE COMIC
New England Comics Press: Oct, 1999 ($3.95, one-shot)

1-Y2K scenarios and survival tips 3.95

YUPPIES FROM HELL (Also see Son of...)
Marvel Comics: 1989 ($2.95, B&W, one-shot, direct sales, 52 pgs.)

1-Satire 3.00

ZAGO, JUNGLE PRINCE (My Story #5 on)
Fox Features Syndicate: Sept, 1948 - No. 4, Mar, 1949

1-Blue Beetle app.; partial-r/Atomic #4 (Toni Luck) 58.00 174.00 550.00
2,3-Kamen-a 47.00 142.00 425.00
4-Baker-c 40.00 120.00 350.00

ZANE GREY'S STORIES OF THE WEST
Dell Publishing Co./Gold Key 11/64: No. 197, 9/48 - No. 996, 5-7/59; 11/64 (All painted-c)

Four Color 197(#1)(9/48) 11.00 33.00 130.00
Four Color 222,230,236('49) 5.85 17.50 70.00
Four Color 246,255,270,301,314,333,346 4.10 12.30 45.00
Four Color 357,372,395,412,433,449,467,484 3.20 9.60 35.00
Four Color 511-Kinstler-a; Kubert-a 4.10 12.30 45.00
Four Color 532,555,583,604,616,632(5/55) 3.20 9.60 35.00
27(9-11/55) - 39(9-11/58) 3.20 9.60 35.00
Four Color 996(5-7/59) 3.20 9.60 35.00
10131-411-(11/64-G.K.)-Nevada; r/4-Color #996 2.50 7.50 25.00

ZANY (Magazine)(Satire)(See Frantic & Ratfink)

Zegra, Jungle Empress #3 © FOX

Zero Girl #1 © I Before E, Inc.

Zip Comics #13 © MLJ

:andor Publ. Co.: Sept, 1958 - No. 4, May, 1959
1-Bill Everett-c 10.00 30.00 70.00
2-4: 4-Everett-c 7.85 23.50 55.00

:ATANNA (See Adv. Comics #413, JLA #161, Supergirl #1, World's Finest :omics #274)
)C Comics: July, 1993 - No. 4, Oct, 1993 ($1.95, limited series)
1-4 2.00
;pecial 1(1987, $2.00)-Gray Morrow-c/a 3.00

:AZA, THE MYSTIC (Formerly Charlie Chan; This Magazine Is Haunted /2#12 on)
:harlton Comics: No. 10, Apr, 1956 - No. 11, Sept, 1956
10,11 11.00 33.00 90.00

:EALOT (Also see WildC.A.T.S: Covert Action Teams)
mage Comics: Aug, 1995 - No. 3, Nov, 1995 ($2.50, limited series)
1-3 2.50

ZEGRA JUNGLE EMPRESS (Formerly Tegra)(My Love Life #6 on)
:ox Features Syndicate: No. 2, Oct, 1948 - No. 5, April, 1949
2 61.00 182.00 575.00
3-5 47.00 140.00 420.00

ZEN INTERGALACTIC NINJA
No Publisher: 1987 -1993 ($1.75/$2.00, B&W)
1-(scarce) 1.85 5.50 15.00
2-6: Copyright-Stern & Cote 1.00 3.00 8.00
V2#1-4-($2.00) 3.00
V3#1-5-($2.95) 3.00
... :Christmas Special 1 (1992, $2.95) 3.00
... :Earth Day Special 1 (1993, $2.95) 3.00

ZEN, INTERGALACTIC NINJA (mini-series)
Zen Comics/Archie Comics: Sept, 1992 - No. 3, 1992 ($1.25)(Formerly a B&W comic by Zen Comics)
1-3: 1-Origin Zen; contains mini-poster 2.00

ZEN INTERGALACTIC NINJA
Entity Comics: No. 0, June-July, 1993 - No. 3, 1994 ($2.95, B&W, limited series)
0-Gold foil stamped-c; photo-c of Zen model 3.00
1-3: Gold foil stamped-c; Bill Maus-c/a 3.00
0-(1993, $3.50, color)-Chromium-c by Jae Lee 3.50
...Sourcebook 1-(1993, $3.50) 3.50
...Sourcebook '94-(1994, $3.50) 3.50

ZEN INTERGALACTIC NINJA: APRIL FOOL'S SPECIAL
Parody Press: 1994 ($2.50, B&W)
1-w/flip story of Renn Intergalactic Chihuahua 2.50

ZEN INTERGALACTIC NINJA COLOR
Entity Comics: 1994 - No. 7, 1995 ($2.25)
1-($3.95)-Chromium die cut-c 4.00
1, 0-($2.25)-Newsstand; Jae Lee-c; r/...All New Color Special #0 3.00
2-($2.50)-Flip book 3.00
2-($3.50)-Flip book, polybagged w/chromium trading card 3.50
3-7 3.00
Summer Special (1994, $2.95) 3.00
Yearbook: Hazardous Duty 1 (1995) 3.00
Zen-isms 1 (1995, 2.95) 3.00
Ashcan-Tour of the Universe-(no price) w/flip cover 2.00

ZEN INTERGALACTIC NINJA COMMEMORATIVE EDITION
Zen Comics Publishing: 1997 ($5.95, color)
1-Stern-s/Cote-a 6.00

ZEN INTERGALACTIC NINJA MILESTONE
Entity Comics: 1994 - No. 3, 1994 ($2.95, limited series)
1-3: Gold foil logo; r/Defend the Earth 3.00

ZEN INTERGALATIC NINJA SPRING SPECTACULAR
Entity Comics: 1994 ($2.95, B&W, one-shot)
1-Gold foil logo 3.00

ZEN INTERGALACTIC NINJA STARQUEST
Entity Comics: 1994 - No. 6, 1995 ($2.95, B&W)
1-6: Gold foil logo 3.00

ZEN, INTERGALACTIC NINJA: THE HUNTED
Entity Comics: 1993 - No. 3, 1994 ($2.95, B&W, limited series)
1-3: Newsstand Edition; foil logo 3.00
1-($3.50)-Polybagged w/chromium card by Kieth; foil logo 3.50

ZERO GIRL
DC Comics (Homage): Feb, 2001 - No. 5, Jun, 2001 ($2.95, limited series)
1-5-Sam Kieth-s/a 3.00

ZERO HOUR: CRISIS IN TIME (Also see Showcase '94 #8-10)
DC Comics: No. 4(#1), Sept, 1994 - No. 0(#5), Oct, 1994 ($1.50, limited series)
4(#1)-0(#5) 4.00
"Ashcan"-(1994, free, B&W, 8 pgs.) several versions exist 2.00
TPB ('94, $9.95) 10.00

ZERO PATROL, THE
Continuity Comics: Nov, 1984 - No. 2 ($1.50); 1987 - No. 5, May, 1989 ($2.00)
1,2: Neal Adams-c/a; Megalith begins 4.00
1-5 (#1,2-reprints above, 1987) 3.00

ZERO TOLERANCE
First Comics: Oct, 1990 - No. 4, Jan, 1991 ($2.25, limited series)
1-4: Tim Vigil-c/a(p) (his 1st color limited series) 3.00

ZERO ZERO
Fantagraphics: Mar, 1995 -No. 27 ($3.95/$4.95, B&W, anthology, mature)
1-7,9-15,17-25 4.00
8,16 6.00
26-($4.95) Bagge-c 5.00

ZIGGY PIG-SILLY SEAL COMICS (See Animal Fun, Animated Movie-Tunes, Comic Capers, Krazy Komics, Silly Tunes & Super Rabbit)
Timely Comics (CmPL): Fall, 1944 - No. 6, Fall, 1946
1-Vs. the Japs 24.00 71.00 190.00
2 12.00 36.00 95.00
3-5 10.00 30.00 80.00
6-Infinity-c 12.50 37.50 100.00
I.W. Reprint #1(1958)-r/Krazy Komics 1.75 5.25 14.00
I.W. Reprint #2,7,8 1.75 5.25 14.00

ZIP COMICS
MLJ Magazines: Feb, 1940 - No. 47, Summer, 1944 (#1-7?: 68 pgs.)
1-Origin Kalathar the Giant Man, The Scarlet Avenger, & Steel Sterling; Mr. Satan (by Edd Ashe), Nevada Jones (masked hero) & Zambini, the Miracle Man, War Eagle, Captain Valor begins 435.00 1305.00 5000.00
2-Nevada Jones adds mask & horse Blaze 211.00 633.00 2000.00
3 158.00 474.00 1500.00
4,5 126.00 379.00 1200.00
6-8 111.00 332.00 1050.00
9-Last Kalathar & Mr. Satan; classic-c 126.00 379.00 1200.00
10-Inferno, the Flame Breather begins, ends #13 116.00 348.00 1100.00
11,12: 11-Inferno without costume 92.00 276.00 875.00
13,14,16,17,19: 17-Last Scarlet Avenger 89.00 268.00 850.00
15-Classic spider-c 100.00 300.00 950.00
18-Wilbur begins (9/41, 1st app.) 95.00 285.00 900.00
20-Origin & 1st app. Black Jack (11/41); Hitler-c 147.00 442.00 1400.00
21,23-26: 25-Last Nevada Jones. 26-Black Witch begins; last Captain Valor 82.00 245.00 775.00
22-Classic-c 103.00 308.00 975.00
27-Intro. Web (7/42) plus-c app. 124.00 371.00 1175.00
28-Origin Web 113.00 340.00 1075.00
29,30: 29-The Hyena app. 55.00 165.00 552.00
31-38: 34-1st Applejack app. 35-Last Zambini, Black Jack. 38-Last Web issue 47.00 142.00 425.00
39-Red Rube begins (origin, 8/43) 47.00 142.00 425.00
40-47: 45-Wilbur ends 40.00 120.00 350.00

*NOTE: **Biro** a-5, 9, 17; c-3-17. **Meskin** a-1-3, 5-7, 9, 10, 12, 13, 15, 16 at least. **Montana** c-29, 30, 32-35. **Novick** c-18-28, 31. **Sahle** c-37, 38, 40-46. Bondage c-8, 9, 33, 34. Cover features:*

Zombie World: Eat Your Heart Out © DH

Zone Continuum #1 © Caliber

Zoot #11 © FOX

Steel Sterling-1-43, 47; (w/Blackjack-20-27 & Web-27-35), 28-39; (w/Red Rube-40-43); Red Rube-44-47.

ZIP-JET (Hero)
St. John Publishing Co.: Feb, 1953 - No. 2, Apr-May, 1953

1-Rocketman-r from Punch Comics; #1-c from splash in Punch #10 71.00 213.00 675.00
2 50.00 150.00 450.00

ZIPPY THE CHIMP (CBS TV Presents...)
Pines (Literary Ent.): No. 50, March, 1957; No. 51, Aug, 1957

50,51 6.40 19.25 45.00

ZODY, THE MOD ROB
Gold Key: July, 1970

1 2.30 7.00 20.00

ZOMBIE WORLD (one-shots)
Dark Horse Comics

... :Eat Your Heart Out (4/98, $2.95) Kelley Jones-c/s/a 3.00
... :Home For The Holidays (12/97, $2.95) 3.00

ZOMBIE WORLD: CHAMPION OF THE WORMS
Dark Horse Comics: Sept, 1997 - No. 3, Nov, 1997 ($2.95, limited series)

1-3-Mignola & McEown-c/s/a 3.00

ZOMBIE WORLD: DEAD END
Dark Horse Comics: Jan, 1998 - No. 2, Feb, 1998 ($2.95, limited series)

1,2-Stephen Blue-c/s/a 3.00

ZOMBIE WORLD: TREE OF DEATH
Dark Horse Comics: Jun, 1999 - No. 4, Oct, 1999 ($2.95, limited series)

1-4-Mills-s/Deadstock-a 3.00

ZOMBIE WORLD: WINTER'S DREGS
Dark Horse Comics: May, 1998 - No. 4, Aug, 1998 ($2.95, limited series)

1-4-Fingerman-s/Edwards-a 3.00

ZONE (Also see Dark Horse Presents)
Dark Horse Comics: 1990 ($1.95, B&W)

1-Character from Dark Horse Presents 2.00

ZONE CONTINUUM, THE
Caliber Press: 1994 ($2.95, B&W)

1 3.00

ZOO ANIMALS
Star Publications: No. 8, 1954 (15¢, 36 pgs.)

8-(B&W for coloring) 5.00 15.00 30.00

ZOO FUNNIES (Tim McCoy #16 on)
Charlton Comics/Children Comics Publ.: Nov, 1945 - No. 15, 1947

101(#1)(11/45, 1st Charlton comic book)-Funny animal; Al Fago-c 19.00 56.00 150.00
2(12/45, 52 pgs.) 10.00 30.00 75.00
3-5 9.30 28.00 65.00
6-15: 8-Diana the Huntress app. 7.15 21.50 50.00

ZOO FUNNIES (Becomes Nyoka, The Jungle Girl #14 on?)
Capitol Stories/Charlton Comics: July, 1953 - No. 13, Sept, 1955; Dec, 1984

1-1st app.? Timothy The Ghost; Fago-c/a 10.00 30.00 75.00
2 6.40 19.25 45.00
3-7 5.00 15.00 35.00
8-13-Nyoka app. 8.65 26.00 60.00
1(1984) (Low print run) 5.00

ZOONIVERSE
Eclipse Comics: 8/86 - No. 6, 6/87 ($1.25/$1.75, limited series, Mando paper)

1-6 2.00

ZOO PARADE (TV)
Dell Publishing Co.: #662, 1955 (Marlin Perkins)

Four Color 662 4.55 13.65 50.00

ZOOM COMICS
Carlton Publishing Co.: Dec, 1945 (one-shot)

nn-Dr. Mercy, Satannas, from Red Band Comics; Capt. Milksop origin retold 40.00 120.00 360.0

ZOOT (Rulah Jungle Goddess #17 on)
Fox Features Syndicate: nd (1946) - No. 16, July, 1948 (Two #13s & 14s)

nn-Funny animal only 20.00 60.00 160.0
2-The Jaguar app. 19.00 56.00 150.0
3(Fall, 1946) - 6-Funny animals & teen-age 10.00 30.00 80.0
7-(6/47)-Rulah, Jungle Goddess (origin/1st app.) 95.00 285.00 900.0
8-10 63.00 189.00 600.0
11-Kamen bondage-c 68.00 205.00 650.0
12-Injury-to-eye panels, torture scene 47.00 140.00 420.0
13(2/48) 47.00 140.00 420.0
14(3/48)-Used in **SOTI**, pg. 104, "One picture showing a girl nailed by her wrists to trees with blood flowing from the wounds, might be taken straight from an ill. ed. of the Marquis deSade" 61.00 182.00 575.0
13(4/48),14(5/48)-Western True Crime #15 on? 47.00 140.00 420.0
15,16 47.00 140.00 420.0

ZORRO (Walt Disney with #882)(TV)(See Eclipse Graphic Album)
Dell Publishing Co.: May, 1949 - No. 15, Sept-Nov, 1961 (Photo-c 882 on)
(Zorro first appeared in a pulp story Aug 19, 1919)

Four Color 228 (#1) 21.00 63.00 250.0
Four Color 425,617,732 11.70 35.00 140.0
Four Color 497,538,574-Kinstler-a 12.50 37.50 150.0
Four Color 882-Photo-c begin;1st TV Disney; Toth-a 17.00 50.00 200.0
Four Color 920,933,960,976-Toth-a in all 11.70 35.00 140.0
Four Color 1003('59)-Toth-a 11.70 35.00 140.0
Four Color 1037-Annette Funicello photo-c 15.00 45.00 175.0
8(12-2/59-60) 7.50 22.50 90.0
9-Toth-a 8.00 24.00 95.0
10,11,13-15-Last photo-c 6.70 20.00 80.0
12-Toth-a; last 10¢ issue 8.00 24.00 95.0
NOTE: ***Warren Tufts** a-4-Color 1037, 8, 9, 10, 13.*

ZORRO (Walt Disney)(TV)
Gold Key: Jan, 1966 - No. 9, Mar, 1968 (All photo-c)

1-Toth-a 7.00 21.00 85.0
2,4,5,7-9-Toth-a. 5-r/F.C. #1003 by Toth 4.10 12.30 45.0
3,6-Tufts-a 3.65 11.00 40.0
NOTE: *#1-9 are reprinted from Dell issues.* ***Tufts** a-3, 4. #1-r/F.C. #882. #2-r/F.C. #960. #3-r/#1 c & #8 inside. #4-r/#9-c & insides. #6-r/#11(all); #7-r/#14-c. #8-r/F.C. #933 inside & back-c & #976-c. #9-r/F.C. #920.*

ZORRO (TV)
Marvel Comics: Dec, 1990 - No. 12, Nov, 1991 ($1.00)

1-12: Based on TV show. 12-Toth-c 2.0

ZORRO (Also see Mask of Zorro)
Topps Comics: Nov, 1993 - No. 11, Nov, 1994 ($2.50/$2.95)

0-(11/93, $1.00, 20 pgs.)-Painted-c; collector's ed. 2.0
1,4,6-9,11: 1-Miller-c. 4-Mike Grell-c. 6-Mignola-c. 7-Lady Rawhide-c by Gulacy. 8-Perez-c. 10-Julie Bell-c. 11-Lady Rawhide-c 3.0
2-Lady Rawhide-app. (not in costume) 5.0
3-1st app. Lady Rawhide in costume, 3-Lady Rawhide-c by Adam Hughes 1.00 3.00 8.0
5-Lady Rawhide app. 4.0
10 ($2.95)-Lady Rawhide-c/app. 3.0
The Lady Wears Red (12/98, $12.95, TPB) r/#1-3 13.0
Zorro's Renegades (2/99, $14.95, TPB) r/#4-8 15.0

ZOT!
Eclipse Comics: 4/84 - No. 10, 7/85; No. 11, 1/87 - No. 36 7/91 ($1.50, Baxter-p

1 5.0
2,3 4.0
4-10: 4-Origin. 10-Last color issue 3.0
10 1/2 (6/86, 25¢, Not Available Comics) Ashcan; art by Feazell & McCloud 4.0
11-14,15-35-($2.00-c) B&W issues 3.0
14 1/2 (Adventures of Zot! in Dimension 10 1/2)(7/87) Antisocialman app. 3.0
36-($2.95-c) B&W 3.0

Z-2 COMICS (Secret Agent...)(See Holyoke One-Shot #7)

ZULU (See Movie Classics)

HEARD THESE LINES BEFORE?

1. WE WILL OUTBID ANYONE, ANYWHERE, ANYTIME!
2. QUICK, IMMEDIATE, UNLIMITED CASH!
3. WE SPEND MORE THAN ANYONE!
4. TOP PRICES PAID!
5. NO ONE PAYS MORE!

THE TRUTH IS:

Almost every comic book dealer advertising in this guide has probably made one or more of the above claims at one time or another. **We have too.** After being involved in this business since 1972 and having dealt frequently with most of the major dealers/companies advertising in this guide, we have come to the **"startling conclusion"** that no person or company (including us) **ever always** pays the most. **We have bid against the other big guys and have won some and lost some.** Often times, it's not who has (or claims to have) the most money that counts, it's who **has** the most established customers **looking anxiously** for comic books to buy. This is precisely why we at WANT LIST COMICS can be **EXTREMELY COMPETITIVE** when we purchase individual books or collections. Because we have **many** want list customers waiting in line for books that we purchase, (*please note our other ads in this guide) we can usually expect a quick return on our money invested, and therefore justify buying books at **very, very** high percentages of current Overstreet. We have purchased some books at **OVER 250% Guide** because of customer demand!

In the past few years, we have purchased books in **All** grades (some for **WORLD RECORD PRICES**) like **Action 1**, **Detective 27**, **Marvel 1**, **Superman 1**, **Captain America 1**, **All American 16**, **New Fun 2**, and **Batman 1** plus every "key" **Marvel** and **DC Silver Age** issue imaginable! We must be doing something right! SINCE WE ARE LOCATED IN THE MIDWEST, we can easily and quickly come to you to compete against the local stores or dealers for your books.

ALL WE ASK FOR IS A CHANCE TO BID AGAINST THE OTHER GUYS (ESPECIALLY THE "TOO GOOD TO BE TRUE" ADS)

We don't mind the competition. We **ESPECIALLY** want **Golden Age** and **Silver Age books** with 10¢ and 12¢ covers. We will buy both large and small collections and aren't interested in just "cherry picking" certain issues · · we will take all you want to sell. **We also pay generous finder's fees for any information leading to the purchase of collections.** For a fast reply, just call, FAX or mail us a list of what you have for sale. References are always gladly given upon request.

Our office/warehouse # is:

1-918-299-0440

Call us anytime between 1 pm and 8 pm, CST
Please ask for our private FAX #

WANT LIST COMICS

COMICS GUARANTY, LLC
Charter
Member Dealer

BOX 701932
TULSA, OK 74170-1932

Senior Advisor to the Overstreet Comic Price Guide
CBG Customer Service Award
References gladly provided!

Charter
Member Dealer

MOTOR CITY COMICS
Gold & Silver Age
BUYING:
• Top Prices Paid !!! •
• We Pay 50%-150% of Guide for pre-1970 Comics •
• Will Travel Anywhere to View Large Collections •
• Senior Overstreet Advisor •
• Consignment Sales •
& SELLING:
• Over 25,000 Gold & Silver Age Comics In Stock •
• Accurate Grading • Competitive Pricing •
• Pulps & Original Art • Want List Service •
• Free Catalogs: call or write for your copy •
NOW OPEN
Come Visit Our Warehouse
by appointment only
MOTOR CITY COMICS
19785 W. 12 MILE RD. • PMB 231 • SOUTHFIELD, MI 48076
PHONE: (248) 426-8059 • FAX: (248) 426-8064
www.motorcitycomics.com
Buying & Selling Premium Comics & Collectibles Since 1986
Fantastic Four © Marvel Comics; Superman © DC Comics

BUYING ALL COMICS

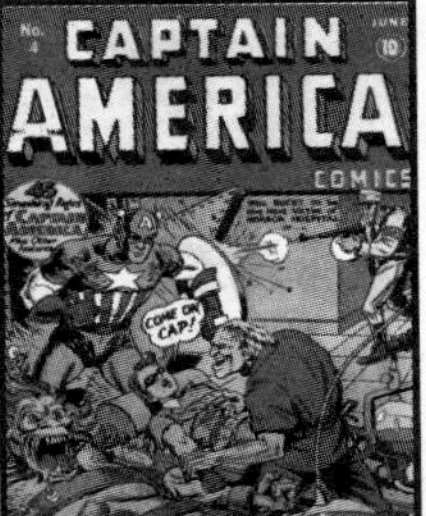

with 10 and 12¢ cover prices

TOP PRICES PAID!

IMMEDIATE CASH PAYMENT

Stop Throwing Away
Those Old Comic Books!

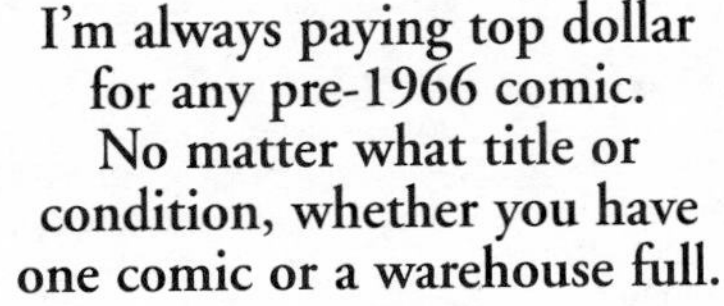
I'm always paying top dollar
for any pre-1966 comic.
No matter what title or
condition, whether you have
one comic or a warehouse full.

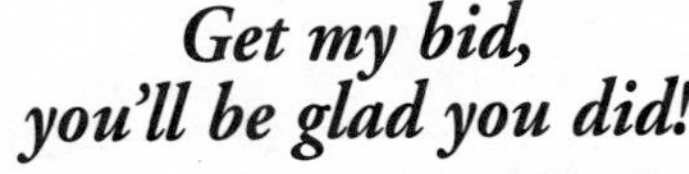
Get my bid,
you'll be glad you did!

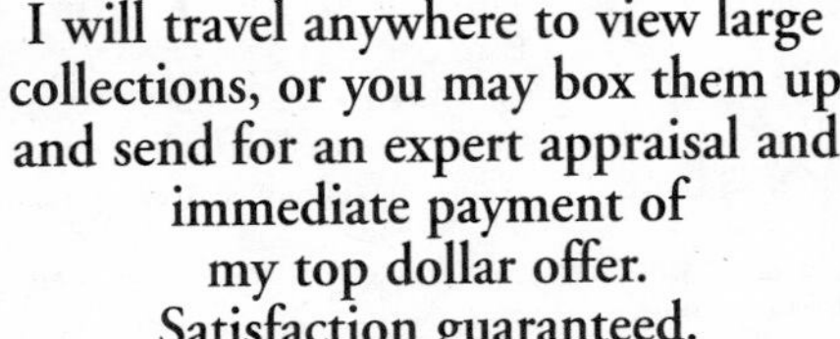
I will travel anywhere to view large
collections, or you may box them up
and send for an expert appraisal and
immediate payment of
my top dollar offer.
Satisfaction guaranteed.

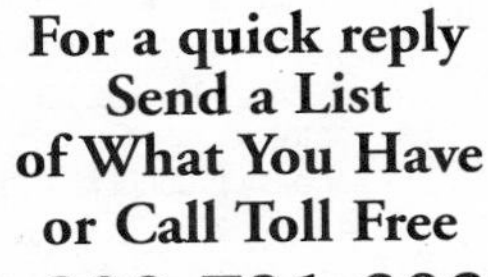
For a quick reply
Send a List
of What You Have
or Call Toll Free

1-800-791-3037

or

1-608-277-8750

or write

Jef Hinds
P.O. Box 44803
Madison, WI 53744-4803

Also available for
Insurance & Estate Appraisals, Strictly Confidential.

Follow the Leader in Golden and Silver Age Comics with
BEDROCK CITY
COMIC COMPANY
TM
6517 Westheimer
(at Hillcroft)
Houston, Texas 77057
(713) 780-0675
2204-D FM 1960 W.
(at Kuykendahl)
Houston, Texas 77090
(281) 444-9763
fax (713) 780-2366
www.bedrockcity.com
Captain America © 1997 Marvel Entertainment Group

Our 29th Continuous Year In Business
"VIEWING A COLLECTION"
TOMORROWS TREASURES
BUYING/SELLING:
Golden Age & Silver Age • DC • Timely • EC• Disney • Early Marvel • Fox • Quality • Fiction House • Horror • Sci-Fi • Movie • TV • Romance • Western • Coverless & Incomplete Comics (1933-1969)
Original Comic Art & Pulps
PO Box 925
Commack, NY 11725
24 hr. Phone/Fax 631-543-5737
Email:
comics@tomorrowstreasures.com
Web Site:
www.tomorrowstreasures.com
Send $2.00 for our 100 page illustrated comic catalog.
Steve Lowenthal

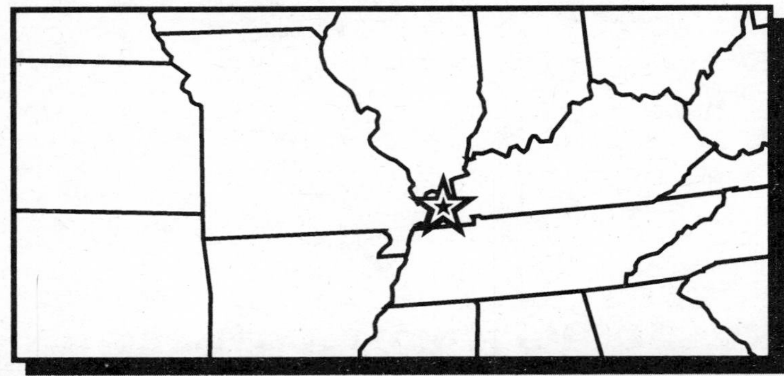

Comics 10¢
APRIL
PHANTOM LADY
"The SODA MINT KILLER!"
DEC.-JAN.
No. 27
64 PAGES OF ACTION!
Detect
COMIC
STARTING THIS ISSUE: THE AMAZING AND UNIQUE ADVENTURES OF THE BATMAN!
SUB-MARINER
COMICS
HITLER'S BERCHTESGADEN
DEATH'S BRIGHT FINGER

DIAMOND
INTERNATIONAL GALLERIES

ether you're buying or selling, Diamond International
eries is dedicated to giving you the best deal, backed
nparalleled customer service from one of the industry's
most responsible and knowledgeable staffs!

Send us your list by fax at (410) 560-7143

Diamond International Galleries
1966 Greenspring Drive, Suite 401
Timonium, MD 21093
Please call for appointment.

Buying CGC Certified and other comics

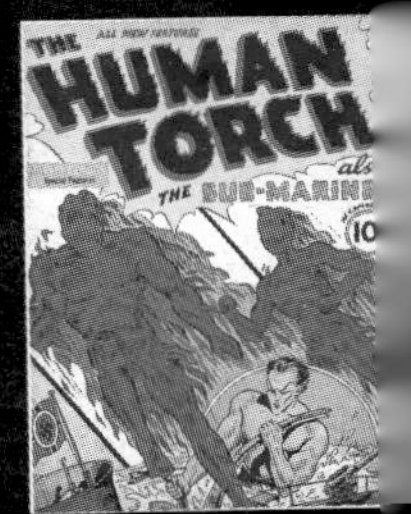

WANTED

We are actively purchasing comics and related memorabilia. We buy one item or entire collections. If you are looking for a friendly approach to buying or selling contact us. We also sell what we buy and have many items available.

Buying

Comics 1897-1969 All grades, Character Collectibles, premiums, buttons, statues, rings, etc. Disney Memorabilia, Original Comic Art, Pulp Magazines, Superman Collectibles, Vintage Star Wars and Transformer toys, And much more!!

The following is a sample of a few of the items we are purchasing:

-PAYING 100% of Hake's Guide for Superman of Canada Patch

-Adventures of Detective Ace King Comic

-Low grade examples of rare premium rings Spider, Operator #5, and others

Contact: Tom Gordon III
Monumental Collectibles
P.O. Box 295
Reisterstown, MD 21136
410-848-0275
www.monumentalcollectibles.com
want@monumentalcollectibles.com

LEE'S
COMICS

TOMORROWS
Our 29th Continuous Year In Business
·TREASURES'
BUYING

* Missoula

THE OVERSTREET COMIC BOOK PRICE GUIDE BUSINESS CARD ADS are a great way to advertise in the Guide! Simply send us your business card and we'll reduce it and run it as is. Have your ad seen by thousands of serious comic book collectors for an entire year! If you are a comic book or collectible dealer, retail establishment, mail-order house, etc., you can reach potential customers throughout the United States and around the world in our **BUSINESS CARDS ADS**!

For more information, contact our Advertising Dept.
Gemstone Publishing, Inc. 1966 Greenspring Drive, Suite LL3, Timonium, MD 21093.
Call (888) 375-9800 Ext. 249, or fax (410) 560-7143, or e-mail **ads@gemstonepub.com**.

- Buy and Sell: Gold and Silver Age Comics
- Discount Sales of Back Issues and Supplies
- New Comics, Paper Back Books and Toys

8280 Clairemont Mesa Blvd. #124, San Diego, CA 92111
email: SoCalCom@aol.com Ph (858)715-8669
www.SoCalComics.com Fax (858)715-8669#

James F. Payette
Rare Books & Comics
P.O. Box 750
Bethlehem, NH 03574
Dealing in Old & New Rare Comic Books
Big Little Books • 1st Ed. Books • Pulp Magazines
Sci-Fi Fantasy Material • Old Coins • Baseball Cards
TELEPHONE: (603) 869-2097

The Collector's Slave

BUY • SELL • TRADE • CONSIGN
Specializing in
SERIOUS COLLECTOR'S WANT LISTS
DELL • GOLD KEY • CHARLTON • DC
MARVEL • CLASSICS • MAGAZINES
FANZINES • POCKET BOOKS & MORE!
256 Imperial Ave. Winnipeg MB R2M 0K8
GREG HARDER **204 • 237 • 4428**
FAX 204•947•2944

COMIC BOOKS
BASEBALL CARDS
MEMORABILIA
256 E. 89TH ST.
N Y C
212-831-CARD

4th Annual Virginia VINTAGE COMICS & Collectibles Show
July 28, 2001
Salem Civic Center
Salem, VA 1000 Blvd.
Interstate-81, Exit 141
1-540-789-7056

WE BUY EVERYTHING!

Send correspondence
to: NEAT STUFF

PO BOX 3069
FORT LEE, NJ 07024-3069
PHONE 1-800-903-7246
FAX 1-201-224-8722

SPECIAL OFFER!
While supplies last!
Order both **Hake's Price Guide To Character Toys 1st and 2nd Editions and get $5.00 off!**
Both volumes include highly informative articles about the history of collectibles.
Huge color sections.
$44.90 (+S&H) **/ Save $5.00!**
Call Toll Free (888) 375-9800 ext. 249

JIM BROUGHTON www.jimscomics.com

Comics On the Side
"The Best Deals Around"

Phone: 937-839-4258
Fax: 937-839-8006
E-Mail: jtb@infinet.com
8039 Pyrmont Road
Lewisburg, OH 45338

RTS UNLIMITED, INC.

Tim Collins
PO Box 150412
Lakewood, CO 80215-0412
e-mail: rtsunlimited@earthlink.net
Voice: (303)-403-1840
FAX: (303)-403-1837
We do mail order right!
Buy ~Sell~Trade
Specializing in Pre-1990 Comics

CBG Customer Service Award - 1999

Over 100,000 Different Comics in Stock!!

Platinum, Gold, Silver, Bronze, & Modern Age Comics, Supplies & More!
Authorized Fortress Dealer, Bill Cole Products, Mylar, Acid - Free Boards, and Gerber's Photo-Journal Guide to Comic Books.

Geoffrey's Comics

Tops in hot, old & discount comics

15900 Crenshaw Blvd. 'B'
Gardena, CA 90249
(310) 538-3198
(310) 538-1114 fax

Business Hours:
10am—8pm Sat-Tues
10am—9pm Wed-Fri
12pm—5pm holidays

We Buy Comics!!!

Open everyday of the year!
geoffreyscomics.com

A & G Comics

We buy comics and collectibles from the 1930s to the 1970s. Thousands of discounted comics available. Please send your want list.

Alan Rutledge
611 S. Newhope St. #C
Santa Ana, CA 92704
714-839-4993
AlanRutledge@compuserve.com

Gary Burke
720 E. 8th St. #2
Long Beach, CA 90813
562-435-1065

JOHN ROMITA SPIDER-MAN ART WANTED!

• BY COLLECTOR •

• AS-M INTERIOR PAGES •
• SKETCHES • STRIP ART •

Jeff Sharpe 920-426-2849
jsharpe@vbe.com
www.vbe.com/~jsharpe/asf.html

* * * * * * * * * * *

NEW and RARE COMICS and PAPER COLLECTIBLES

* * * * * * * * * * *

Since 1979

- RETAIL
- MAIL-ORDER
- WHOLESALE

2009 EASTERN S.E.
GRAND RAPIDS, MI 49507
(616) 247-7828
FAX (616) 247-0245
E-mail tcorner@iserv.net

Don't Miss These Two Great Shows!

Novi, Michigan

MOTOR CITY COMIC CON

Friday 11-8 Saturday 10-7 Sunday 10-5 **MAY 18, 19 & 20, 2001**

And

Saturday 11-5 Sunday 11-5 **NOVEMBER 17 & 18, 2001**

MOTOR CITY CONVENTIONS
19785 W. 12 Mile Rd., PMB 231, Southfield, MI 48076
For Dealer, Publisher, & Guest Information Call **(248) 426-8059**

POP CULTURE FOR THE MILLENNIUM!

COMIC BOOKS, STAR TREK, STAR WARS, ANIME, GAMING, TV & SCREEN STARS
Visit Us On the Web! www.motorcityconventions.com

(Buy-Sell-Trade) **WWW.BUNKYBROTHERS.COM** (Buy-Sell-Trade)

Comic Books : Golden Age, Atomic Age, Silver Age, Bronze Age
(1930-1980) All Superhero, Horror, Crime, Sci-Fi, Original Art, Monster Mags-Famous Monsters Etc.
Toys/Model Kits : Monsters, Superhero, Movies, TV, Sci-Fi
(1950-1980) Aurora-Mego-Ahi-Matt Mason-Billiken, Colorforms Outer Space Men-Rat Fink, Captain Action-Planet Of The Apes, Micronauts-Thingmakers-GI Joe -Big Jim, Pirates Of The Caribbean-Don Post Masks
Bubble Gum Cards : Wacky Packages, Mars Attacks, Movie/TV, Monsters/Sci-Fi, Superhero, Sports
(1950-1980) Unopened Material, Uncut Sheets, Original Artwork
Autographs/Movie Related Paper : Universal Horror, Notorious/Unusual

VISIT US ON THE WEB: WWW.BUNKYBROTHERS.COM KEN HUNT: PHONE 909.941.6402 / EMAIL: NUPHINAAAA@AOL.COM
BRIAN FORNESI: FAX 650.347.2305 / 1243 BROADWAY BURLINGAME, CA 94010 USA / EMAIL: BFORNESI@MSN.COM
(ALL RELATED ITEMS WANTED - ITEMS LISTED ARE JUST SOME EXAMPLES)

CASH for Walt Disney autographs,
Disney animation art, & Golden Age
comics and collections.
FOR SALE: thousands of comics-all kinds-
at 25 % OFF 2000 OVERSTREET. Will trade.
I GUARANTEE SATISFACTION.
Enclose a stamp & want list. Dave Yaruss,
7916 Blue Lake Dr., San Diego, CA 92119.
619-465-3090. Remember: want list required.

65,000 COMIC BOOKS FOR SALE!!!
All listed on the internet at
www.comicbookwarehouse.com
We also buy comics. Phone: 607-648-4025
Rick Semowich, 56 John Smith Rd.
Binghamton, New York 13901

ORIGINAL ART WANTED!
1960s-80s Marvel/DC pages/covers.
Contact: Aaron Sultan 919-954-7111

1960s MARVEL MEMORABILIA WANTED!
Fan Club, Buttons, MMMS, Marvelmania.
Contact: Aaron Sultan 919-954-7111

AMAZING SPIDER-MAN ORIGINAL ART WANTED!
Any Page, Any Issue 1-400.
Romita, Ditko, Frenz, Andru, etc.
Contact: Aaron Sultan 919-954-7111

$*$*SUPERMAN COLLECTIBLES WANTED!*$*$
BUYING ALL SUPERMAN ITEMS FROM 1938-1966:
TOYS, GAMES, FIGURES, BUTTONS, RINGS,
PREMIUMS, ADV. MATERIALS,...ANYTHING!!!!
DANNY FUCHS, 209-80p 18th AVE., BAYSIDE, NY
11360. 718-225-9030 superdf62@aol.com
"AMERICA'S FOREMOST SUPERMAN COLLECTOR"

Newer comics @ 50% O.P.G. (G.A. @ 75% & up).
Send a SASE plus 50¢ per list. Indicate desired
lists. Comic Book * BLB * N.P. Comic Strip *
Pulp * Paperback * Movie TV Items * Life, Look,
Post, Misc. Magazines. Above also bought.
G. A. Rauch, 3500 Manila Dr., Westerville, OH 43081.

1000's of Comics for sale 1947-95.
Send $1 for catalogues.
D.E. Kerksiek, P.O. Box 231, Stover, MO 65078

COMIC BOOKS FOR SALE
One of the world's largest catalogues selling
Golden Age, DC, Marvel, Dell, Classic Illustrated,
plus BLBs, Sunday pages, original art.
We supply Canadians with all types of
plastic bags, acid free boxes and boards, etc.
Send $2.00 for catalogue
COMIC BOOKS WANTED
Highest prices paid for comic books, BLBs,
newspaper comics before 1959. 41 years as a
collector and dealer. Contact us before selling.

INTERNATIONAL COMIC BOOK COMPANY
CALVIN AND ELEANOR SLOBODIAN
74 WATERLOO CRES., BRANDON,
MANITOBA CANADA R7B3W7
PHONE 204-728-4337

1/4 MILLION COMICS FOR SALE
Our 40-page catalog contains Silver
& Bronze Age books in low to high grades
w/ key issues! Comics from 1960-2000,
with runs of Horror, Suspense, War, Westerns,
& Super-Heroes. 100 Different Publishers.
Send $1.00, refundable w/ first order to:
High-Quality Comics,
1106 2nd St., #110, Encinitas, CA 92024,
(1-800-682-3936), E-Mail: hqcom@utm.net,
Website: www.highqualitycomics.com

FREE PREVIEWS CATALOG
Low Prices on New Comics - Marvel, DC,
Image, Dark Horse, etc. Card, Toys, Signed
Comics, Videos, and Back Issues Also Available.
Send Name & Address to:
Steve Tafuni, POB 43, Valrico, FL 33595
813-651-0352 Email: SSTCMX@AOL.COM

COMIC BOOKS
Buying and Selling 1930's to 1970's
Original Art Wanted:
Marshall Rogers (Batman), DC Special #29
+1970's DC Superhero Items Wanted
JOHN F. EL-HAJJEH 905-668-4370
E-Mail: captain_blood2000@yahoo.ca

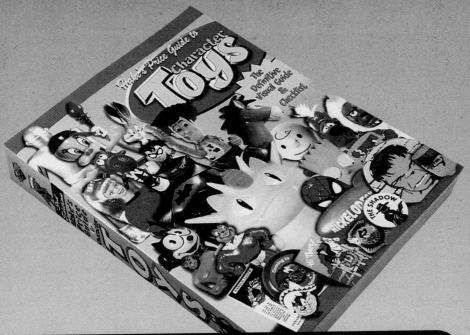

SHOP DIRECTORY

(PAID ADVERTISING - STORE LISTINGS)

You can have your store listed here for very reasonable rates. Send for details for next year's Guide. The following list of stores have paid to be included in this list. We cannot assume any responsibility in your dealings with these shops. This list is provided for your information only. When planning trips, it would be advisable to make appointments in advance. Remember, to get your shop included in the next edition, contact us for rates. **Gemstone Publishing, Inc., 1966 Greenspring Dr., Suite LL3, Timonium, MD 21093. PH 888-375-9800 or 410-560-5806, FAX 410-560-6107.**

Items stocked by these shops are noted at the end of each listing and are coded as follows:

(a) Golden Age Comics
(b) Silver Age Comics
(c) New Comics, Magazines
(d) Pulps
(e) Paperbacks
(f) Big Little Books
(g) Magazines
(h) Books (old)
(i) Movie Posters
(j) Original Art
(k) Toys
(l) Records/CDs,Videos,DVD
(m) Trading Cards
(n) Underground Comics
(o) Premiums (Rings, Decoders, etc.)
(p) Comic Related Posters
(q) Comic Supplies
(r) Role Playing Games
(s) Star Trek Items
(t) Doctor Who Items
(u) Japanimation/Manga
(v) Collectible Card Games

ALABAMA

Sincere Comics
4667 Airport Blvd.
Mobile, AL 36608
PH: (334) 342-2603
FAX: (334) 342-2659
E-Mail:
sincerecmx@aol.com
Web:
www.sincerecomics.com
(a-c,e,m,p-s,u)

ARIZONA

Atomic Comics Chandler
5965 W. Ray Rd. #19
Chandler, AZ 85226
PH: (480) 940-6061
E-Mail: mail@
atomiccomics.com
Web: www.
atomiccomics.com
(a-c,e,g,j-v)

Atomic Comics Mesa
1310 W. Southern Ave. #3
Mesa, AZ 85202
PH: (480) 649-0807
E-Mail: mail@
atomiccomics.com
Web: www.
atomiccomics.com
(a-c,e,g,j-v)

Key Comics: Discount Back-Issues
P.O. Box 5035
Mesa, AZ 85211
PH: (480) 890-0055
FAX: (480) 890-0220
E-Mail: keycomics@
hotmail.com
(a-c,j)

All About Books & Comics III
4022 E. Greenway
Phoenix, AZ 85032
PH: (602) 494-1976
(c,g,k,l,m,p-s,u,v)

All About Books & Comics
5060 N. Central
Phoenix, AZ 85012
PH: (602) 277-0757
Web:
www.allaboutcomics.com
(a-g,i-v)

Atomic Comics Phoenix
10215 N. 28th Dr. #A-1
Phoenix, AZ 85051
E-Mail: mail@
atomiccomics.com
Web: www.
atomiccomics.com
(a-c,e,g,j-v)

All About Books & Comics V
810 S. Ash
Tempe, AZ 85281
PH: (480) 858-9447
(c,g,k,m,p-s,u,v)

ARKANSAS

Alternate Worlds Cards & Comics
3812 Central Ave. Suite G
Hot Springs, AR 71913
PH: (501) 525-8999
(b,c,e,g,k,l,m,q,r,s,u,v)

The Comic Book Store
9307 Treasure Hill
Little Rock, AR 72227
PH: (501) 227-9777
(a-d,g,k,m,p-s,u,v)

Collector's Edition
3217 John F. Kennedy Blvd.
North Little Rock, AR 72116
PH: (501) 791-4222
(a-d,g,k,m,p,q,r,s,u,v)

CALIFORNIA

Jeff Thomas
Buying all types of comic books, wacky packages, record albums, and movie posters
Atwater Village, CA 90039
PH: (818) 763-5734
(a,b,i,l,m)

Terry's Comics
P.O. Box 471
Atwood, CA 92811
PH: (714) 288-8993
FAX: (714) 288-8992
E-Mail: terryscomics
@earthlink.net
Web: www.terryscomics.com
(a,b,d-h,m,n,q)

Crush Comics & Cards
2869 Castro Valley Blvd.
Castro Valley, CA 94546
PH: (510) 581-4779
(b,c,g,k,m,p,q,v)

Collectors Ink
2593 Highway 32
Chico, CA 95973
PH: (530) 345-0958
E-Mail: collink@cmc.net
Web:
www.cmc.net/~collink/
(a-c,e,g,k-n,p-v)

Comic Bookie
415 W. Foothill #318
Claremont, CA 91711
PH: (909) 399-0228
E-mail: comicbookie
@prodigy.net
Web:
www.comicbookie.net
(b,c,g,k,l,m,p,q,s,u,v)

Flying Colors Comics & Other Cool Stuff
2980 Treat Blvd.,
Oak Grove Plaza
Concord, CA 94518
PH: (925) 825-5410
Web: www.
flyingcolorscomics.com
(a-c,j,k,m,p,q,u,v)

High-Quality Comics
1106 2nd St., #110
Encinitas, CA 92024
PH: (800) 682-3936
FAX: (760) 723-7269
E-Mail: hqcom@utm.net
Web: www.
highqualitycomics.com
(b,c,e,g,h,n,p,s)

21st Century Comics
124 W. Commonwealth Ave.
Fullerton, CA 92832
PH: (714) 992-6649
Web: www.
21stcenturycomics.com
(a-c,e-g,k,m,n,p,q,u,v)

Geoffrey's Comics
15900 Crenshaw Blvd.; Ste. B
Gardena, CA 90249
PH: (888) 538-3198 (toll free)
FAX: (310) 538-1114
E-mail:
info@geoffreyscomics.com
Web:
www.geoffreyscomics.com
(a,b,c,g,i,k,m,n,p,q,s,u,v)

Back Issue Comics
695 E. Lewelling
Hayward, CA 94541
PH: (510) 276-5262
(b,e,g,k,l,m)

Treasures Of Youth
1201 C St.
Hayward, CA 94541
PH: (510) 888-9675
FAX: (510) 888-9675
E-Mail:
smcatoyguy@aol.com
Web:
www.treasuresofyouth.com
(a,b,d-g,j,k,m,n,o)

Ambrosia Books, Comics & Collectibles
10679 West Pico Blvd.
Los Angeles, CA 90064
PH: (310) 475-5825
PH: (888) 47-DRWHO
E-Mail: knb1138@msn.com
Web: www.
gallifreyone.com
(b,c,e,g,h,k-n,p-u)

Another World Comics & Books
1615 Colorado Blvd.
Los Angeles, CA 90041
PH: (213) 257-7757
E-Mail: bob
@anotherworld.com
Web: www.
anotherworld.com
(a-g,i,m,p,t,u)

Golden Apple Comics
7711 Melrose Ave.
Los Angeles, CA 90046
PH: (323) 658-6047
Web: www.
goldenapplecomics.com
(a-c,l-n,p,q,t)

Brian's Books
73 North Milpitas Blvd.
Milpitas, CA 95035
PH: (408) 942-6903
(a-c,g,m,p,q,s,u)

Lee's Comics
1040 N. Rengstorff Ave.
Mountain View, CA 94043
PH: (650) 493-3957
E-Mail: lee@lcomics.com
Web: www.lcomics.com
(a-v)

The Big Guy's Comics
167 El Camino East
Mountain View, CA 94040
PH: (650) 965-8272
(a-d,f,g,k,m,n,p,q,s,u,v)

Golden Apple Comics
8962 Reseda Blvd.
Northridge, CA 91324
PH: (818) 993-7804
Web: www.
goldenapplecomics.com
(a-c,e,l-n,p,q,u)

Pacific Comic Exchange, Inc.
(By Appointment Only)
P. O. Box 2629
Palos Verdes Peninsula,
CA 90274
PH: (310) 544-4936
FAX: (310) 544-4900
E-Mail: sales@pcei.com
Web: www.pcei.com/
(a, b)

A-1 Comics
5800 Madison Ave.
Sacramento, CA 95841
PH: (916) 331-9203
(a-m,p-s,u,v)

San Diego Comics
6937 El Cajon Blvd.
San Diego, CA 92115
PH: (619) 698-1177
(a,b,c,g)

Captain Nemo's Comics & Games
779 Marsh St.
San Luis Obispo, CA 93401
PH: (805) 544-NEMO
FAX: (805) 543-3938
E-Mail: Nemoslo@aol.com
(b,c,e,g,i,k-s,v)

Lee's Comics
2222 S. El Camino Real
San Mateo, CA 94403
PH: (650) 571-1489
(a-v)

Metro Entertainment
6 West Anapamu
Santa Barbara, CA 93101
PH: (805) 963-2168
(a-c,e,g,i,k-n,p-s,u,v)

Brian's Books
2767 El Camino
Santa Clara, CA 95051
PH: (408) 985-7481
(a-c,g,m,p,q,s,u)

Hi De Ho Comics & Books With Pictures
525 Santa Monica Blvd.
Santa Monica, CA 90401-2401
PH: (310) 394-2820
Web: www.hideho.com
(a-n,p-v)

Cisco's Graded Comics
By Appointment Only
Upland, CA 91786
PH: (909) 870-6633
E-Mail: cgcit@x-men.com
Web: www.cgcit.com
(a,b)

Comic Goblin and Collectibles
1042 N. Mountain Ave. #B-322
Upland, CA 91786-3430
PH: (909) 870-6633
E-Mail:
sales@comicgoblin.com
(a,b,m)

A Collector's Dream
21222 Venture Blvd.
Woodland Hills, CA 91364
PH: (818) 992-1636
(a-c,e,g,j,k,m,n,p,q,s,v)

COLORADO

All C's Collectibles, Inc.
1113 So. Abilene St. #104
Aurora, CO 80012
PH: (303) 751-6882
(a-d,g,k,m-p,s,u,v)

Castaway Comics
778 Peoria St.
Aurora, CO 80011
PH: (303) 341-0806
(a-c,g,i-n,p,q,u)

Time Warp Comics & Cards, Inc.
1631 28th St.
Boulder, CO 80301
PH: (303) 443-4500
E-Mail: timewarp
@earthlink.net
Web: www.time-warp.com
(a-c,g,n,q-s)

Bargain Comics
21 E. Bijou St.
Colorado Springs, CO 80903
PH: (719) 578-8847
E-Mail: bargaincom
@aol.com
(a-c,g,k,n,q,v)

Blue Coyote Comics
P. O. Box 2163
Evergreen, CO 80437-2163
PH: (303) 670-8386
(a,b,n)

J. R. R. Comix
P. O. Box 2163
Evergreen, CO 80437-2163
PH: (303) 670-8386
(a-e,g,k-n,p-u)

RTS Unlimited Inc.
P. O. Box 150412
Lakewood, CO 80215-0412
PH: (303) 403-1840
FAX: (303) 403-1837
E-Mail:
rtsunlimited@earthlink.net
(a,b,c,q)

CONNECTICUT

The Bookie
155 Burnside Ave.
E. Hartford, CT 06108
PH: (860) 289-1208
(a-h,j,k,m,n,p,q-s,u,v)

D.J.'s Comics, Cards, Games
303 East Main St.
Meriden, CT 06450
PH: (203) 235-7300
(a-c,e,g,h,j-n,p-v)

Sarge's Megastore
124 State Street
New London, CT 06320
PH: (860) 443-2004
Web:
www.sarges-online.com
(a-c,e,g,i,k-n,p-s,u,v)

D-J Cards & Comics
1 Lincoln Street,
Corner Washington Ave.
North Haven, CT 06473
PH: (203) 234-2989
FAX: (203) 234-2989
E-mail:
dj.sports.cllctbls@snet.net
Web: www.
agelesscollectibles.com
(a-c,e,k,m,q,r,s,u,v)

Legends of Superheros
1269 West Main St.
Waterbury, CT 06708
PH: (203) 756-2440
FAX: (203) 757-1909
E-Mail: legends@
legendsofsuperheros.com
Web: www.legendsof
superheros.com
(b,c,e,g,k,l,p,q,v)

DELAWARE

Captain Blue Hen Comics & Cards
280 E. Main St. #101
Newark, DE 19711
PH: (302) 737-3434
FAX: (302) 737-6201
E-Mail: cbhcomic@dca.net
Web: www.
captainbluehen.com
(a-c,g,k-n,p,q,u,v)

FLORIDA

Lost Realms, Inc.
23066 Sandlefoot Plaza Dr.
Boca Raton, FL 33428
PH: (561) 470-5700
(b,c,e,g,j,k,m,n,p-s,u)

Emerald City Too Comics
& Collectables, Inc.
2475-L McMullen Booth Rd.
Clearwater, FL 33759
PH: (727) 797-0664
E-Mail: CowardlyLion
@emeraldcitycomics.com
Web: www.
emeraldcitycomics.com
(a-c,g,j-u,v)

Borderlands
Comics and Games
10230-11 Atlantic Blvd.
Jacksonville, FL 32225
PH: (904) 720-0774
(b,c,m,p,q,u,v)

Phil's Comic Shoppe
6512 W. Atlantic Blvd.
Margate, FL 33063
PH: (888) 977-6947
(a,b,c,g,k,m,p,q)

Emerald City
Comics & Collectibles, Inc.
9249 Seminole Blvd.
Seminole, FL 33772
PH: (727) 398-2665
E-Mail: CowardlyLion
@emeraldcitycomics.com
Web: www.
emeraldcitycomics.com
(a-c,e,g,j-v)

GEORGIA

Oxford Comics & Games
2855 Piedmont Rd.
Atlanta, GA 30305
PH: (404) 233-8682
(a-v)

Titan Games & Comics
5436 Riverdale Rd.
College Park, GA 30349
PH: (770) 996-9129
(a-c,e,g,k-m,p-u)

Comic Company
1058 Mistletoe Rd.
Decatur, GA 30033
PH: (404) 248-9846
FAX: (404) 325-2334
E-Mail: mail
@comiccompany.com
Web: www.
comiccompany.com
(a-c,g,k,m,p-r,u,v)

Titan Games & Comics IV
2131 Pleasant Hill Rd.
Duluth, GA 30136
PH: (770) 497-0202
(a-c,e,g,k-m,p-u)

Heroes Ink
2500 Cobb Pkwy. NW
Kennesaw, GA 30152
Ph: (770) 428-3033
(a-c,e,g,k,m,p,q,s,u,v)

Odin's Cosmic Bookshelf
Killian Hill Crossing
4760 Hwy. 29, Suite A-1
Lilburn, GA 30047
PH: (770) 923-0123
E-Mail: odins@aol.com
(a-c,e-g,j,k,m-r,u,v)

Titan Games & Comics III
2585 Spring Rd.
Smyrna, GA 30080
PH: (770) 433-8223
(a-c,e,g,k-m,p-u)

Titan Games & Comics II
3853 Lawrenceville Hwy.
Tucker, GA 30084
PH: (770) 491-8067
(a-c,k-m,q-u)

ILLINOIS

Chicago Comics
3244 North Clark St.
Chicago, IL 60657
PH: (773) 528-1983
PH: 1-(800)-509-0333
Web: www.
chicagocomics.com
(a-c,g,k,m,n,p,q,u)

Independence Comics,
Comic Book Art/
Collectibles
3955 West Irving Park Rd.
Chicago, IL 60618
PH: (773) 539-6720
FAX: (773) 588-1628
E-Mail: spawnski@aol.com
Web: www.independence
comics.com
(a-c,j-m,p,q,s,u,v)

Yesterday
1143 West Addison St.
Chicago, IL 60613
PH: (773) 248-8087
(a,b,d-i,k-n,p,q,s)

The Paper Escape
205 West First St.
Dixon, IL 61021
PH: (815) 284-7567
(c,e,g,k,m,p-s,v)

GEM Comics
125 W. First St.
Elmhurst, IL 60126
PH: (630) 833-8787
(b,c,g,k,m,p-r,v)

Comix Revolution
606 Davis Street
Evanston, IL 60201
PH: (847) 866-2800
(c,g,i,k,m,n,p,q,u,v)

Comix Revolution
999 N. Elmhurst Road
Mt. Prospect, IL 60056
PH: (847) 506-0800
(c,g,i,k,m,n,p,q,u,v)

M & M Comic Service
13617 Southwest Hwy.
Orland Park, IL 60462
PH: (888) 662-6642
Web: www.mmcomics.com
(b,c,g,i,k,o,p,q,u)

Tomorrow is Yesterday,
Inc.
5600 N. 2nd St.
Rockford, IL 61111
PH: (815) 633-0330
E-mail: info@
tomorrowisyesterday.com
(a-n,p-v)

Comic Cavalcade
9 Triumph Dr.
Urbana, IL 61802
PH: (217) 384-2211
Web: www.comcav.com
(a,b,c,j)

Unicorn Comics & Cards
216 S. Villa Ave.
Villa Park, IL 60181
PH: (630) 279-5777
(a-g,k-m,p,q,s,v)

INDIANA

Comic Cave
3221 17th Street
Columbus, IN 47201
PH: (812) 372-8430
E-Mail: comiccav
@reliable-net.net
(b,c,g,k-m,p-s,u,v)

The Book Broker
2717 Covert Avenue
Evansville, IN 47714
PH: (812) 479-3677
(a-h,l-n,p-v)

Books, Comics & Things
2212 Maplecrest Rd.
Fort Wayne, IN 46815
PH: (219) 446-0025
FAX: (219) 446-0030
E-mail:
bct@bctcomics.com
Web: www.bctcomics.com
(a-c,k,p-s,v)

Comic Carnival
6265 North Carrollton Ave.
Indianapolis, IN 46220
PH: (317) 253-8882
(a-v)

Comic Carnival
7311 U.S. 31 South
Indianapolis, IN 46227
PH: (317) 889-8899
(a-v)

Comic Carnival
3837 N. High School Rd.
Indianapolis, IN 46254
PH: (317) 293-4386
(a-v)

Comic Carnival
9729 East Washington St.
Indianapolis, IN 46229
PH: (317) 898-5010
(a-v)

Downtown Comics
137 E. Ohio St.
Indianapolis, IN 46204
PH: (317) 237-0397
E-Mail: dtc@indy.net
Web: www.dtcomics.com
(a-u)

Downtown
Comics - Carmel
13682 N. Meridian St.
Indianapolis, IN 46032
PH: (317) 848-2305
(a-u)

Downtown
Comics - Castleton
5767 E. 86th St.
Indianapolis, IN 46258
PH: (317) 845-9991
(a-u)

Downtown
Comics - Greenwood
8925 S. Meridian St.
Indianapolis, IN 46227
PH: (317) 885-6395
(a-u)

Downtown Comics - West
8336 W. 10th St.
Indianapolis, IN 46234
PH: (317) 271-7610
(a-u)

Galactic Greg's
1407 E. Lincolnway
Valparaiso, IN 46383
PH: (219) 464-0119
(b,c,k,p-r,u,v)

IOWA

Oak Leaf Comics
23-5th St. S.W.
Mason City, IA 50401
PH: (614) 424-0333
Web: www.dustcatchers.com
(a-c,f,i,k-s,u)

KANSAS

Prairie Dog Comics
Main Store
7130 W. Maple, Suite 150
Wichita, KS 67209
PH: (316) 942-3456
(a-v)

KENTUCKY

The Great Escape
1051 Bryant Way
Bowling Green, KY 42103
PH: (270) 782-8092
E-Mail: pacrats@blue.net
(a-c,e,g,k,l,m,p,q,r,u,v)

Comic Book World
7130 Turfway Rd.
Florence, KY 41042
PH: (859) 371-9562
E-Mail: cbwinfo@one.net
Web: www.
comicbookworld.com
(a-c,k,m,n,p-v)

Comic Book World
6905 Shepherdsville Rd.
Louisville, KY 40219
PH: (502) 964-5500
E-Mail: cbwinfo@one.net
Web: www.
comicbookworld.com

The Great Escape
2433 Bardstown Road
Louisville, KY 40205
PH: (502) 456-2216
(a-c,e,g,i,k-n,p-s,u,v)

LOUISIANA

B.T. & W.D. Giles
P.O. Box 271
Keithville, LA 71047
PH: (318) 925-6654
(a,b,d-f,h,l)

MAINE

Top Shelf Comics
25 Central Street
Bangor, ME 04401
PH: (207) 947-4939
E-Mail: topshelf
@tcomics.com
Web: www.tcomics.com
(a-c,m,p,r,v

MARYLAND

Geppi's Comic World
Security
1722 N. Rolling Road
Baltimore, MD 21244
PH: (410) 298-1758
(a-c,k-m,q,s,t,v)

Big Planet Comics, Inc.
4908 Fairmont Ave.
Bethesda, MD 20814

Alternate Worlds
72 Cranbrook Road
Cockeysville, MD 21030
PH: (410) 666-3290
(b,c,g,k-n,p-v)

The Closet of Comics
7315 Baltimore Ave. (US.1)
College Park, MD 20740
PH: (301) 699-0498
E-Mail: closetofcomics
@hotmail.com
(a-e,g,h,m,n,p,q)

Comics To Astonish
9400 Snowden River Pkwy.
Columbia, MD 21045
PH: (410) 381-2732
E-Mail: comics2u@aol.com
Web:
www.comicstoastonish.com
(a-c,k,m,p,q,u,v)

Cards, Comics &
Collectibles
100-A Chartley Drive
Reisterstown, MD 21136
PH: (410) 526-7410
FAX: (410) 526-4006
E-Mail:
cardscomicscollectibles
@yahoo.com
(a-c,f,g,j,k,m,n,p,q,s,u,v)

Geppi's Comic World
Silver Spring
8317 Fenton St.
Silver Spring, MD 20910
PH: (301) 588-2546
(a-c,k-m,q,s,t,v)

MASSACHUSETTS

New England Comics
131 Harvard Avenue
Allston, MA 02134
PH: (617) 783-1848
Web: www.
newenglandcomics.com
(a-c,e,g,k-n,p-v)

New England Comics
744 Crescent St.
East Crossing Plaza
Brockton, MA 02402
PH: (508) 559-5068
Web: www.
newenglandcomics.com
(a-c,e,g,k-n,p-v)

New England Comics
316 Harvard St.
Coolidge Corner
Brookline, MA 02146
PH: (617) 566-0115
Web: www.
newenglandcomics.com
(a-c,e,g,k-n,p-v)

New England Comics
14A Eliot Street
Harvard Square
Cambridge, MA 02138
PH: (617) 354-5352
Web: www.
newenglandcomics.com
(a-c,e,g,k-n,p-v)

That's Entertainment II
371 John Fitch Hwy.
Fitchburg, MA 01420
PH: (978) 342-8607
Web: www.thatse.com
(a-v)

Jams Comic Connection
435 King St. (Rt. 110/2A)
Littleton, MA 01460
PH: (978) 486-1099
(c,d,g,k,q,r,s,v)

New England Comics
18 Pleasant St.
Malden Center
Malden, MA 02148
PH: (781) 322-2404
Web: www.
newenglandcomics.com
(a-c,e,g,k-n,p-v)

New England Comics
732 Washington Street
Norwood Center
Norwood, MA 02062
PH: (781) 769-4552
Web: www.
newenglandcomics.com
(a-c,e,g,k-n,p-v)

New England Comics
1511 Hancock St.
Quincy Center
Quincy, MA 02169
PH: (617) 770-1848
Web: www.
newenglandcomics.com
(a-c,e,g,k-n,p-v)

New England Comics
FFAST New Comic Service
(Mail Order Only)
P.O. Box 690346
Quincy, MA 02269
PH: (617) 774-1745
Web: www.ffast.com
(a-c,e,g,k-n,p-v)

The Outer Limits
463 Moody St.
Waltham, MA 02453
PH: (781) 891-0444
(a-v)

That's Entertainment
244 Park Ave. (Rte. 9)
Worcester, MA 01609-1927
PH: (508) 755-4207
Web: www.thatse.com
(a-v)

MICHIGAN

Cashman's Comics
1018 S. Madison Ave.
Bay City, MI 48708-7261
PH: (517) 895-1113
E-Mail: cashmanscomics
@aol.com
(a-c,f,g,j,k-v)

Comics North!
425 N. Main Street
Cheboygan, MI 49721-1546
PH: (231) 627-3740
(b,c,g,i,k,l,p,q,r,s,u)

Amazing Book Store, Inc.
3718 Richfield Rd.
Flint, MI 48506
PH: (810) 736-3025
(a-c,n,q)

Tardy's Collector's
Corner, Inc.
2009 Eastern Ave. S.E.
Grand Rapids, MI 49507
PH: (616) 247-7828
(a-g,j,m,n)

MINNESOTA

Comic Book College
3151 Hennepin Av. S
Minneapolis, MN 55408
PH: (612) 822-2309
Web: www.comicopolis.com
(a,b,c,j,k,q)

Nostalgia Zone
3149 1/2 Hennepin Av. S
Minneapolis, MN
55408-2620
PH: (612) 822-2806
Web:
www.nostalgiazone.com
(a,b,d-g,j,m,n)

Midway Book & Comic
1579 University Ave.
St Paul, MN 55104
PH: (651) 644-7605
(a-h,n,q)

MISSOURI

Antiquarium
504 East High St.
Jefferson City, MO 65101
PH: (573) 636-8995
E-Mail: Antiquarium
@prodigy.net
Web: members.
tripod.com/~antiquarium
(a-n,p-v)

B•Bop
3940 Main
Kansas City, MO 64111
PH: (816) 753-BBOP(2267)
(a-c,g,k-m,p-s,u,v)

Friendly Frank's Comic Cavern
5404 NW 64th St.
Kansas City, MO 64151
PH: (816) 746-4569
(a-g,j-n,p-v)

MONTANA

The Book Exchange
Butte Plaza Mall
3100 Harrison Ave.
Butte, MT 59701
PH: (406) 494-7788
(c,e,h,q,s)

The Book Exchange
2335 Brooks St.
Missoula, MT 59801
PH: (406) 728-6342
(a,b,e,h,q-s)

NEVADA

Silver Cactus Comics
480 N. Nellis Blvd. #C1A
Las Vegas, NV 89110
PH: (702) 438-4408
FAX: (702) 438-5208
(b,c,e,g,k,l,m,p-s,u)

NEW HAMPSHIRE

Rare Books & Comics
James F. Payette
P.O. Box 750
Bethlehem, NH 03574
PH: (603) 869-2097
(a,b,d-h)

NEW JERSEY

ZAPP! Comics
3710 Route 9 South
Freehold Raceway Mall
Freehold, NJ 07728
PH: (732) 866-6655
(a-c,e,g,k,m,n,p,q,s,u,v)

Frontline Comics
By Appointment Only
P.O. Box 203
Hazlet, NJ 07730
PH: (732) 495-0184
E-Mail: dford@netlabs.net
(a,b,q)

J.C. Comics
579 Route 22 West
North Plainfield, NJ 07060
PH: (908) 756-1212
FAX: (908) 756-5606
E-Mail: JoeConzolo
@msn.com
Web: www.jccomics.com
(a-c,e,g,i,k-m,o-q,s,u)

Comic Explosion
339 Franklin Ave.
Nutley, NJ 07110
PH: (973) 235-1336
(c,g,m,n,p,q,u)

Fat Jack's Comicrypt
521 White Horse Pike
Oaklyn, NJ 08107
PH: (856) 858-3877
(a-c,g,k,m,n,p-r,u,v)

ZAPP! Comics
574 Valley Road-A&P Center
Wayne, NJ 07470
PH: (973) 628-4500
FAX: (973) 628-1771
E-Mail:
ZAPPComics@aol.com
Web: www.zappcomics.com
(a-c,e,g,k,m,n,p,q,s,u,v)

Frankenstein Comics
845 Mantua Pike, Rt. 45
Woodbury, NJ 08096
PH: (856) 848-6347
E-Mail:
Frankenbill@snip.net

JHV Associates
By Appointment Only
P. O. Box 317
Woodbury Hghts, NJ 08097
PH: (856) 845-4010
FAX: (856) 845-3977
E-Mail: DJVERENEAULT
@MAINSITE.COM
(a,b,d)

NEW YORK

Silver Age Comics
22-55 31 St.
Astoria, NY 11105
PH: (718) 721-9691
PH: (800) 278-9691
FAX: (718) 728-9691
E-Mail: gus
@silveragecomics.com
Web: www.
silveragecomics.com
(a-c,f,g,k,m,n,p-s,u)

Excellent Adventures
110 Milton Ave. (Rte. 50)
Ballston SPA, NY 12020
PH: (518) 884-9498
E-Mail: jbelskis37@aol.com
(a-d,f,g,j,k,m,o,q-s,u)

Wow Comics
1491 Williams Bridge Road
Bronx, NY 10461
PH: (718) 829-0461
FAX: (718) 828-1700
E-Mail:
wowcomics@aol.com
Web:
www.wowcomics.com
(a-c,e,k,m,o-s,u)

Comic Quest
51-49 Simonson Street
Elmhurst, NY 11373
PH: (718) 205-8174
E-Mail:
thequestcomics@aol.com
(a-e,g,k,m,n,q,r,v)

Comic Box Productions
74-05 Metropolitan Ave.
Middle Village, NY 11379
PH: (718) 326-2248
FAX: (718) 326-2248
E-Mail:
bigapplecon@earthlink.net
Web:
www.bigapplecon.com
(a-p,s-v)

Alex's MVP Cards & Comics
256 East 89th St.
New York, NY 10128
PH: (212) 831-2273
E-Mail: mvpalex@aol.com
(a-c,k,m,n,q,v)

Gotham City Comics
800 Lexington Ave.
New York, NY 10021
PH: (212) 980-0009
E-Mail:GothamCT@aol.com
(b,c,g,k,l,m,p,u,v)

Jerry Ohlinger's Movie Material Store, Inc.
242 West 14 Street
New York, NY 10011
PH: (212) 989-0869
E-Mail: jomms@aol.com
(g,i)

Amazing Comics
12 Gillette Ave.
Sayville, NY 11782
PH: (631) 567-8069
Web: www.amazingco.com
(a-c,e,g,j,k,m,q,v)

One if By Cards, Two if By Comics, Inc.
1107 Central Ave.
Scarsdale, NY 10583
PH: (914) 725-2225
Web: www.1ifbycards.com
(a,b,c,k,m,q,s,v)

Electric City Comics
1704 Van Vranken Ave.
Schenectady, NY 12308
(518) 377-1500
(a-c,g,k,n,p,q,u)

NORTH CAROLINA

Super Giant Comics
697 Brevard Rd.
Asheville, NC 28806
PH: (828) 665-2800
(a-c,j,l,n,q)

Acme Comics
2150 Lawndale Dr.
Greensboro, NC 27408
PH: (336) 574-2263
(a-c,g,i,k,p,q)

The Nostalgia Newstand
919 Dickinson Ave.
Greenville, NC 27834
PH: (252) 758-6909
(b,c,e,g,m,n,p,q,u)

NORTH DAKOTA

Tom's Coin Stamp Gem Baseball & Comic Shop
#2 1st Street S.W.
Minot, ND 58701
PH: (701) 852-4522
E-Mail: tomscoin@minot.com
Web: www.minot.com/
~tomscoin
(a-q,s-u)

OHIO

Comic Book World, Inc.
4016 Harrison Avenue
Cincinnati, OH 45211
PH: (513) 661-6300
E-Mail: cbwinfo@one.net
Web: www.
comicbookworld.com
(a-c,k,m,n,p-v)

Bookery Fantasy
16 W. Main St.
Fairborn, OH 45324
PH: (937) 879-1408
FAX: (937) 879-9327
Web: www.
bookeryfantasy.com
(a-n,p-v)

Parker's Records & Comics
1222 Suite C Route 28
Milford, OH 45150
PH: (513) 575-3665
FAX: (513) 575-3665
(a-c,g,l,p-r,v)

Funnie Farm Bookstore
328 N. Dixie Drive
Vandalia, OH 45377
PH: (937) 898-2794
E-Mail: pdbroida@
earthlink.net
(a-c,m,p-s,v)

OKLAHOMA

New World Comics & Games
6219 N. Meridian
Oklahoma City, OK 73112
PH: (405) 721-7634
(a-c,g,i,k,m-v)

New World Comics & Games
4420 SE 44th St.
Oklahoma City, OK 73135
PH: (405) 677-2559
(c,g,k,m,p-v)

Comic Empire of Tulsa
3122 S. Mingo
Tulsa, OK 74146
PH: (918) 664-5808
(a-c,g,m,n,p,q,s,t)

OREGON

Emerald City Comics
770 E. 13th
Eugene, OR 97401
PH: (541) 345-2568
(c,e,g,k-n,p,q,r,u,v)

Nostalgia Collectibles
527 Willamette Street
Eugene, OR 97401
PH: (541) 484-9202
(a-g,k-o,r,s,u,v)

Beyond Comics
322 East Main
Medford, OR 97501
PH: 1 (800) 428-9543
Web: www.
beyondcomics.com
(a,b,c,p,q,r,v)

Heroes Haven
635 S.E. Jackson St.
Roseburg, OR 97470
PH: (541) 673-5004
E-Mail:
grendel@rosenet.net
(a-c,e,g,k,m,p-s,u,v)

PENNSYLVANIA

Dreamscape Comics
310 W. Broad St.
Bethlehem, PA 18018
PH: (610) 867-1178
(a-c,m,n,p-r)

New Dimension Comics
20550 Route 19,
Piazza Plaza
Cranberry Township, PA
16066-7520
PH: (724) 776-0433
E-Mail: ndc@sgi.net
Web: www.ndcomics.com
(a-d,f,g,k-n,q-s,u,v)

New Dimension Comics
508 Lawrence Ave.
Ellwood City, PA 16117
PH: (724) 758-2324
E-Mail: ec@ndcomics.com
(a-d,f,g,k-n,q-s,u,v)

Comic Collection
931 Bustleton Pike
Feasterville, PA 19053
PH: (215) 357-3332
(a-c,e,g,i-s,u,v)

The Comic Store
28 McGovern Ave.
Station Square
Lancaster, PA 17602
PH: (717) 397-8737
FAX: (717) 397-8903
E-Mail:
comicstore@juno.com
Web:
www.comicstorepa.com
(a-c,e,g,m,n,p-s,u)

Fat Jack's Comicrypt
2006 Sansom St.
Philadelphia, PA 19103
PH: (215) 963-0788
(a-c,g,k,m,n,p-r,u,v)

Duncan Comics, Books, and Accessories
1047 Perry Highway
Pittsburgh (North Hills),
PA 15237
PH: (412) 635-0886
Web: www.
duncancomics.ohgolly.com
(a-e,g,h,k-m,p-s,v)

Eide's Entertainment
1111 Penn Ave.
Pittsburgh, PA 15222
PH: (412) 261-0900
FAX: (412) 261-3102
E-Mail: eides@eides.com
Web: www.eides.com
(a-q,s-v)

Collectible Dreams
12 N. Market Street
Selinsgrove, PA 17870
PH: (570) 372-0824
E-Mail:
cdreams@sunlink.net
(a-c,i,k,m,q-v)

Comic Swap
110 South Fraser Street
State College, PA 16801
PH: (814) 234-6005
E-Mail:
comicswap@home.com
(c,g,k,m,n,p,q,r,u,v)

Comic Store West
984 Loucks Rd.
Maple Village 2
York, PA 17474
PH: (717) 845-9198
E-Mail:
comicswest@aol.com
(c,m,q,r)

RHODE ISLAND

The Annex
314 Broadway
Newport, RI 02840
PH: (401) 847-4607
E-Mail: annexcomics
@prodigy.net
(b,c,k,l,q,u,v)

SOUTH CAROLINA

Planet Comics
3448 Cinema Center
Anderson, SC 29621-4141
PH: (864) 261-3578
Web:
www.planetcomics.net
(a-c,e,g,k-v)

TENNESSEE

The Great Escape
111-B North Gallatin Rd.
Madison, TN 37115
PH: (615) 865-8052
(a-c, e-i, k-v)

The Great Escape
1925 Broadway
Nashville, TN 37203
PH: (615) 327-0646
E-Mail: tge@bellsouth.net
Web: www.
comicsandrecords.com
(a-u)

TEXAS

Lone Star Comics Books & Games
504 East Abram St.
Arlington, TX 76010
PH: (817) Metro 265-0491
(a-c,e,g,k,m,p-v)

Lone Star Comics
5720 Forest Bend Dr.,
Suite 101
Arlington, TX 76017
PH: (817) 563-2550
(b,c,e,g,k,m,p-v)

Austin Books
5002 N. Lamar
Austin, TX 78751
PH: (512) 454-4197
E-Mail:
info@austinbooks.com
(a-i,k,m,n,p,q,s-v)

Lone Star Comics Books & Games
11661 Preston Rd. #151
Dallas, TX 75230
PH: (214) 373-0934
(b,c,e,g,k,m,p-v)

Remember When
2431 Valwood Pkwy.
Dallas, TX 75234
PH: (972) 243-3439
Web: www.
rememberwhenshop.com
(a-d,g,i,j,m,n,p,q,s,t)

Titan Comics
3701 W. Northwest Hwy
#125
Dallas, TX 75220
PH: (214) 350-4420
FAX: (214) 956-0560
E-Mail: info@titancomics.com
Web: www.titancomics.com
(a,b,c,n,p,q)

Lone Star Comics Books & Games
6312 Hulen Bend Blvd.
Ft. Worth, TX 76132
PH: (817) 346-7773
(b,c,e,g,k,m,p-v)

Third Planet Sci-Fi Super Store
2718 Southwest Freeway
Houston, TX 77098
PH: (713) 528-1067
E-Mail: 3planet
@third-planet.com
Web: www.third-planet.com
(a-v)

Third Planet Sci-Fi Super Store
in Willowbrook Mall
Houston, TX 77077
PH: (281) 477-8555
(a-v)

Lone Star Comics Books & Games
931 Melbourne
Hurst, TX 76053
PH: (817) 595-4375
(b,c,e,g,k,m,p-v)

Lone Star Comics Books & Games
2550 N. Beltine Rd.
Irving, TX 75062
PH: (972) 659-0317
(b,c,e,g,k,m,p-v)

Lone Star Comics Books & Games
3600 Gus Thomasson,
Suite 107
Mesquite, TX 75150
PH: (972) 681-2040
(b,c,e,g,k,m,p-v)

Lone Star Comics Books & Games
3100 Independence
Pkwy., Suite 219
Plano, TX 75075
PH: (972) 985-1593
(b,c,e,g,k,m,p-v)

Ground Zero Comics
1700 SSE Loop 323, #302
Tyler, TX 75701
PH: (903) 566-1185
Web: www.
groundzerocomics.com
(c,e,g,k-m,p-s,u,v)

Bankston's
1321 S. Valley Mills Dr.
Waco, TX 76711
PH: (254) 755-0070
E-Mail:
banks1@iamerica.net
(b,c,f,g,i,k,m,p,q,s,u,v)

VIRGINIA

Geppi's Comic World Crystal City
1606 Crystal Square Arcade
Arlington, VA 22202
PH: (703) 413-0618
(a-c,k-m,q,s,t,v)

Atlas Comics
222 Albemarle Square
Charlottesville, VA 22901
PH: (804) 974-7512
(b,c,g,k,l,m,p,q,r,u,v)

Hole in the Wall Books
905 West Broad Street
Falls Church, VA 22046
PH: (703) 536-2511
(b-e,g,h,l,n,p,q,s,t,u)

Trilogy Shop #2
700 E. Little Creek Rd.
Norfolk, VA 23518
PH: (757) 587-2540
FAX: (757) 587-5637
E-Mail: trilogy2
@trilogycomics.com
Web: www.
trilogycomics.com
(c,l,m,q,r,s,u,v)

B & D Comic Shop
802 Elm Avenue S.W.
Roanoke, VA 24016
PH: (540) 342-6642
(c,g,l,m,p,q,r,s,v)

Comics & Things
4406 Holland Rd.
Virginia Beach, VA 23452
PH: (757) 486-5870
Web: www.
comicsandthings.com
(b,c,g,i,k,l,m,q,s,u,v)

Trilogy Shop #1
5773 Princess Anne Rd.
Virginia Beach, VA 23462
PH: (757) 490-2205
FAX: (757) 671-7721
E-Mail: trilogy1
@trilogycomics.com
Web: www.
trilogycomics.com
(a-i,k,m,p-r,u,v)

WASHINGTON

Fantasy Illustrated
P.O. Box 30183
Seattle, WA 98103
PH: (425) 750-4513
E-Mail: rocket@jetcity.com
(a,b,d,e,f,g)

Golden Age Collectables
1501 Pike Place Market 401
Lower Level
Seattle, WA 98101
PH: (206) 622-9799
(a-g,i-v)

WEST VIRGINIA

Comic Castle
233 Second St.
Beckley, WV 25801
PH: (304) 253-1974
(b,c,k,p,q)

Comic World
1204 - 4th Avenue
Huntington, WV 25701
PH: (304) 522-3923
(a-c,m,p,q)

CANADA

ALBERTA

Another Dimension
130-10th Street N.W.
Calgary, Alberta T2N 1V3
PH: (403) 283-7078
E-Mail: another@
cadvision.com
Web: www.
another-dimension.com
(a-c,e,g,k,n,p,q,s,u)

Redd Skull Comics & CDs
720 A Edmonton Trail N.E.
Calgary, Alberta T2E 3J4
PH: (403) 230-2716
E-Mail:
reddskul@cadvision.com
Web: www.reddskull.com
(a-c,j-r,u,v)

MANITOBA

The Collector's Slave
156 Imperial Ave.
WPG., MB., R2M 0K8
PH: (204) 237-4428
FAX: (204) 237-5047
(a-c,e-g,m,n,s)

ONTARIO

The Comic Cave
25 Perth Street
Brockville, ONT K6V 5C3
613-345-4349
PH: (613) 345-4349
E-Mail:
thunder1@recorder.ca
(a-c,g,i-k,n,p,q,r,v)

3RD Quadrant
226 Queen St. W.
Toronto, ON M5V 1Z6
PH: (416) 974-9211
CGC Dealer
E-Mail:
idamahn@hotmail.com
(b,c,e,g,j,k,m,p,q,s,v)

The Final Stop...
381 McArthur Avenue
Vanier, ON K1L 6N5
PH: (613) 749-1247
E-Mail: comics
@thefinalstop.com
(c,g,k,m,n,p,q)

QUEBEC

Heroes Comics
1116 Cure LaBelle
Laval, QC H7V 2V5
PH: (450) 686-9155
(a-c,e,g,k,m,o,p-s,u,v)

FAN WEB SPOTLIGHT - SEQUENTIAL TART

by Jennifer M. Contino (with a little help from sister Tarts Marcia Allass, Danielle Fletcher & Karon Flage)

Editor's note: *Sequential Tart was one of the first comics advocacy groups to make effective use of the Internet.* ***The Overstreet Comic Book Price Guide*** *is proud to offer them the first website spotlight in the Guide by way of introduction to our fan website directory.*

The Internet is a vast and far-reaching means of communication and for an increasing number of people it has become a source of information and a place to exchange ideas and discover new interests. It is also a great opportunity for people to meet, create, and perhaps produce something wonderful - and often with only a fraction of the expenses or complications that are attached to projects in the "real" world. Online you can produce your own magazine, fanzine, webcomic, and so much more without the need to invest in a printer, publisher, or distributor. Through the magic of e-mail, banner exchanges, link exchanges, and word of mouth, a small online enterprise can grow into something extraordinary. No more waiting months for the latest entertainment news; with the convenience of online services you can know what you want in hours, minutes, or, sometimes, even seconds.

Where else but on the World Wide Web could a group of women from all over the world (many of whom have never even spoken on the phone, let alone met face-to-face) come together to create an award-winning monthly e-zine? Where else but in cyberspace would one have the chance to make a dream a reality without much personal or financial risk?

Having a website about comics seems as natural to me as having a website about baseball, cooking, TV, movies, or any other number of hobbies, pastimes or special interests. Comic books are a unique and amazing form of entertainment. Combining elements of both books and film, contained within the covers are great adventures, fun ideas, poignant tales, or any number of other stories that are only confined by a creator's imagination. Almost anyone can relate to comics on some level, and what better way to express opinions, foster discussions, and learn about the books and the people whose work we enjoy than to write about them monthly?

However, in 1998, when the founders of Sequential Tart looked around at the existing sources of comics' journalism, we found that nothing quite had exactly what we were looking for. Sure, there were interesting sources of information, but there weren't a lot of women writing for these places. Nor were there many topics that would hold the interest of most women already reading comics - let alone those newcomers who might be considering sampling the medium. I mean seriously, what did the top ten "Chick Pick Up Lines" polls hold for most of us? Certainly it was interesting reading about the men doing comics, but what about the women? Most online and offline 'zines seemed to avoid female creators altogether or just focus on a few. And they almost wholly ignored the female audience that we knew was out there, and had money to spend. Obviously there was a lack in this area of journalism and something needed to be formed to fill this void. But what?

The founding members of Sequential Tart were already acquaintances from an online, all-female Garth Ennis mailing list. Over time, they had come to realize that they did not fit the cookie-cutter mould of what women who read comics were supposed to read and enjoy. Conversation turned to other creators, other books, and also to their collective dissatisfaction in what both online and offline comics magazines had to offer - none as a whole appealed to them. They talked about their disappointment in the lack of coverage of female creators and independent creators, the lack of coverage in some subjects, the overexposure of certain other areas, and a particularly sexist tone in one publication really lit the fuse. And then they began discussing what they would like to see in a publication, and what they would do if they had their own resource. Someone suggested that rather than spend time complaining, they should utilize their resources, talent, and "net sense" and create their own. Thus, at Comicon International: San Diego in August 1998, the core of the e-zine was formed, a domain name was purchased, creators approached for interviews, and the following month the first issue of Sequential Tart went live on the net.

The benefits to having a monthly e-zine that is run by women but is intended for all readers are enormous. Most people assume that women are not interested in comics at all and that if we do read comics the only genres that might interest us are romance or slice-of-life, erroneously believing that sci-fi, superhero, horror, adventure or a multitude of other genres are beyond our liking. However, that couldn't be further from the truth. There are tons of stereotypes associated with female creators and readers and one of the things that Sequential Tart is trying to accomplish is to shatter the myths that surround the female readership. Women make up a considerable percentage of the prose reading community, and they read books of all styles and genres. The same applies to the medium of comics. Women read comics. Women collect comics. Women create comics. Women like comics - not just one type, but a variety of genres. With Sequential Tart we can raise the awareness of both the comics industry and the general public to that fact and also show just how much women are influencing comics. And not just as readers, but as active participants in discussions with creators, publishers, and the independents struggling to survive in this mainstream world.

Yet, Sequential Tart isn't just about women - although it's true to say that it's produced solely by an eclectic band of women each month and excepting our monthly Redirected Male column, all the contributors are female. Our goal is to be accessible to anyone who likes comics, manga, music, anime, or more. We're trying to present a different point of view, and provide a platform for women such as ourselves, long ignored by the industry and who have previously had no involvement in or opportunity to speak via the established publications. Sequential Tart advocates increasing the awareness of the many contributions women are making to this trade, but we aren't about belittling, quashing, or ignoring the contributions of our male counterparts. Which is why in a given month you might find an interview with Mark Millar side-by-side with an interview of Elizabeth Watasin; or Ron Marz and Ramona Fradon; or the like. Monthly, Sequential Tart offers detailed, in-depth interviews, articles, and news and our message boards encourage a free-exchange of opinion and comment from our readership.

Being involved with Sequential Tart as a Staff Member or Contributor makes you a part of a large family. Sequential Tart is a labor of love. No one involved with makes a profit from the site. All of us are volunteers working our hardest because we want to. All of us have careers, partners, children, academic studies - or a combination of these - and Sequential Tart is something that we do over and above all those because we enjoy it and the medium that we focus on. With Sequential Tart you can be assured that every word we write is sincere. We're not out to get rich. We're not associated with comic book stores or with existing publications and we answer only to ourselves and our audience. Sequential Tart isn't a job, it's a community, and we encourage other women to contribute whatever they can to our magazine and make themselves heard about the medium that they love.

In the two-plus years that Sequential Tart has been in existence, we have gradually built up a large and loyal readership, whose support gained us the 2000 Eagle Award for Best Fan-Organized Comics-Related Website, and who have made our panels at Mid-Ohio-Con and Comicon International a rousing success. We have gained the support of retailers, creators and professional comics journalists, and seemingly filled a niche in the industry that amazingly, had never previously been addressed. However, the greatest benefit is being able to share your love of comics. There are few things better than to receive email or read a post on a message board from someone who was turned on to a new title thanks to your efforts.

FAN WEBSITE DIRECTORY

The world of comics and the world of cyberspace have collided rather dramatically at the end of the millennium. New websites are springing up all the time, providing more and more information on various publishers, creators, titles and characters in the vast universe of comics.

The following is a brief list of fan-created comic book websites. If you have a website you'd like to see listed, e-mail us with the name, URL, and description, and maybe you'll see YOUR site listed here in the **Overstreet Fan Website Directory**!

ALEN YEN'S TOYBOXDX
www.ToyboxDX.com
Fan-powered site celebrating the coolness of Japanese comic and animation-related character collectibles. Featuring open-access BBS and Cafe Chogokin weekly chats. Massive link resource list, and over 40 MB of images and AVIs.

ALEX HORLEY ONLINE ART GALLERY
horley.redsectorart.com
The Alex Horley website.

AMAZON ARCHIVES - HOME OF THE WONDER WOMAN COMIC BOOK REFERENCE GUIDE
www.amazon-archives.com
A great resource for fans and collectors of DC's "Wonder Woman."

THE ARGGH!!! CHRONICLES
www.arggh.com
Online comics chock-full of superhero humor and spoofs! Plus, NIHILIST-MAN, LIBRA, and KID COCKROACH!!!

THE ART OF JAMES STERANKO
www.geocities.com/Area51/Nebula/8650
On-line gallery of Steranko art.

THE ATTACK OF THE SECOND STRINGERS
www.flash.net/~jeanneb
Bios of those obscure good guys who turn up in trivia contests.

AVENGERS ASSEMBLE!
www.avengersassemble.com
The first and greatest Avengers site on the Web—news, files, art, bios, chat room, and the infamous Avengers Mailing List!

THE BATTLECHASERS REALM
www.geocities.com/~bladeshadow
This site has everything for your Battle Chasers needs. Images, reviews, games, you name it and it's here

BEEK'S BOOKS
www.RZero.com/books/
A guide to many favorite graphic novels and comicbook series, including in-depth reviews of a diverse variety of genres.

BIGBOT.COM - TRANSFORMERS/ BEAST WARS/BEASTIES
www.bigbot.com/
Your gateway to BeastWars/ Transformers info on the Web!

BIRDWATCHING: BLACK CANARY & ORACLE: BIRDS OF PREY
www.canarynoir.com
Perhaps the first and only site devoted to DC's Birds of Prey.

BRING ON THE BAD GUYS: THE VILLAINS OF MARVEL COMICS
www.sigma.net/burch
A salute to the villains—if not for them, the heroes wouldn't have anything to do!

CARTOOZINE
www.CartooZine.com
Online comic magazine in which new., talented people can publish their work. CZ also features articles, news and a discussion page.

THE CAT DRAGGED IN
www.geocities.com/Area51/Dimension/9064/index.html
The zine, Judas Goat Quarterly, also featuring a "musical" with Topps Xena cards and a top ten list of the world's greatest comic book bad guys. Assorted weirdness too.

COLLECTING-COMICS.COM
www.collecting-comics.com
For everyone that loves comic books. We have everything from creator interviews, comic news, comic reviews, message boards, and a Comic Book Museum showcasing the best comics ever made.

COMIC ART
www.geocities.com/soho/cafe/6707
Original comic art, including Neal Adams, Carl Barks, John Byrne, Bruce Timm, and more!

COMIC BOOK AWARDS ALMANAC
www.enteract.com/~aardy/comics/awards/
An attempt to list, in one place, all awards ever given to comic books.

COMIC BOOK NETWORK
members.aol.com/ComicBkNet
Home of the weekly Comic Book Net Electronic Magazine—cutting edge news, reviews, opinions, and a trivia contest—free online or by e-mail. PLUS links, convention lists and more!

COMIC BOOK RESOURCES
www.comicbookresources.com/
The resource for comic fans on the web. Industry news, message boards, interviews, huge links database, calendars and much more.

THE COMIC PAGE—YOUR GUIDE TO THE HISTORY OF COMICS
www.dereksantos.com/comicpage/
Dedicated to the history and details of the 100+ year American comic book medium. Also features message boards, polls, free giveaways, and a giant link directory.

COMICFAN
www.comicfanmag.com
A comic book information center featuring news, reviews, previews, interviews, and a monthly drawing contest with prizes!

COMICPOINT.COM
www.comicpoint.com
Featuring an online database of comics and a directory of comic-related web sites.

COMICOGRAPHY OF RICHARD CORBEN
www.saunalahti.fi/~sidi/Corben-pg/Lista.html
Complete Site of Richard Corben Comics, including descriptions of separated stories.

COMICS KOSMOS
www.comicskosmos.com

Here you'll find info and images on all your favorite comics and artists from America, Europe, Scandinavia and Japan!

COMICS RESEARCH BIBLIOGRAPHY
www.rpi.edu/~bulloj/comixbib.html
This is an international bibliography of comic books, comic strips, animation, caricature, cartoons, bandes dessinees, and related topics.

COMICS2FILM
www.comics2film.com
Comics 2 Film tracks the development of comics into movies. Updated with news several times a week. Free e-mail newsletter!

CRAWLSPACE
www.crawlspace.com/
News and info on WildStorm books, links to WildStorm & CliffHanger fan-sites.

DANGER GIRL BY CRAWLSPACE
www.dangergirl.com/
Newly relaunched home of the most dangerous girls in comics. Featuring polls, enormous image gallery, fan fiction, downloads, bios, summaries and comprehensive news coverage.

THE DAREDEVIL RESOURCE
www.geocities.com/Area51/1257/
All about Marvel's Man Without Fear. Issue listings, cover thumbnails, issues summaries, character descriptions, appearance index, and much, MUCH more.

DAREDEVIL:THE MAN WITHOUT FEAR
www.manwithoutfear.com
Site devoted to the Marvel Comics super-hero, with news, interviews and much more.

DC HQ! YOUR GUIDE TO THE DC UNIVERSE.
www.comic-store.com/DCHQ/
The site for information on the DC Universe. Previews, Reviews, Newsletters, and much more!

DCU: NEXT GENERATION
members.aol.com/teens-dc
For all the latest news and info on DC's teen heroes! Featuring: live creator chats, creator interviews, pro art, newsroom, character bios, fan fic, fan art, discussion board, reviews, upcoming comics, free classifieds, DC teens quiz, and more!

DISABLED COMIC COLLECTOR'S CLUB
www.airnet.net/kenj/dclub.html
Free Pen-Pal Club for Disabled/Challenged People who collect comic books and want to meet new friends who are just like them, and understand about being disabled.

DITKO LOOKED UP
www.interlog.com/~ditko37/ditko.html
Unofficial site for Steve Ditko, including three-tiered checklist, scans and original articles.

DIVINE RIGHT BY CRAWLSPACE
www.maxfaraday.com/
A huge fan site for Jim Lee's Divine Right—and he's even on the mailing list!

DR. STRANGE: SANCTUM SANCTORUM
www.DocStrange.com
Dedicated to Marvel's Master of the Mystic Arts. Featuring the latest news on Dr. Strange appearances, series chronologies, character profiles, discussion forum, and mystical links.

DV8 BY CRAWLSPACE
dv8.crawlspace.com/
DV8 images, message board, mad libs and reader reviews!

EC COMICS FROM THE FIFTIES
www.sci.fi/~karielk/eccomics.htm
EC titles, issues, genres and reprints. Lists of selected readings about EC Comics and EC artists.

EMERALD DAWN DOT COM
www.emeralddawn.com
A site that is devoted to the greatest of all Green Lanterns: The Many Faces of Hal Jordan. Here you can keep up to date with all things related to Hal Jordan, including his upcoming series The Spectre. Also on this site, I have Green Lantern News, a checklist of Green Lantern items coming out, the Mall of Oa: an online store that specializes in selling GL related products, toys and costumes! There is an online gallery of custom made action figures as well as a GL forum to discuss all things GL.

FANDOM DIRECTORY
www.fandata.com
Your on-line link to Fandom around the world! Science Fiction, Star Trek, Comics, Trading Cards, Gaming and More! Point and click access to thousands of fan, collector, dealer, store, publisher, club and convention email addresses and web sites. Listings are FREE!

FLASH: THOSE WHO RIDE THE LIGHTNING
www.hyperborea.org/flash
A "Who's Who" of DC's speedsters, plus supporting characters, allies, and enemies.

4-COLOR REVIEW
4colorreview.simplenet.com
Regularly updated reviews, news, previews of and columns on comic books, from the biggest publishers to the smallest indies.

4 FREEDOMS PLAZA
welcome.to/ffplaza
Dedicated to the Fantastic Four, this site covers all aspects of the "World's Greatest Comic Magazine!"

GEN13 BY CRAWLSPACE
www.gen13.com/
A comprehensive Gen13 site with daily image additions—over 800 images in the gallery.

GENE COLAN COLLECTION & TRIBUTE
members.aol.com/genecolan
Dedicated to showing the art of Silver Age Master Gene Colan.

GHENT'S STAR WARS COMICS REPORT
theforce.net/comics
Up-to-date news and reviews of all Star Wars comics, new and old.

GOLD KEY RESEARCH DATABASE
www.oz.net/~fur/comics/gk.htm
A complete list of all Gold Key Comics in a searchable page formatted for IE 4+ browsers. Text-only, also available.

GOLDEN AGE BATMAN SITE
www.ocsonline.com/~bjourdain
Devoted to the Golden Age Batman and contains cover reprints, index of stories, reprint index and other helpful information.

THE GOOD GUYS & GALS OF THE GOLDEN-AGE
goldenage.cjb.net
Come explore the past with us on this exciting journey into the Who's Who of the Golden Age of Comics. See the way it really was, with concise biographies of heroes and heroines as they truly happened. See pictures of those

great Good Guys and Gals from the Glorious Golden Age of Comics.

GOTHIK APA
members.tripod.com/~gothikapa
An Amateur Press Association devoted to comics which push the boundaries of what comics can be. Such as: Bone, Castle Waiting, Hate, Love & Rockets, Preacher, Sandman, etc.

THE GRAND COMIC-BOOK DATABASE
www.comics.org
The Grand Comic-Book Database Project is an ongoing, fan-based, non-commercial, international effort to index, catalog, preserve, and exchange history and knowledge of every comic book ever made all over the world. Also, our chat reflectors have some of the greatest historians, fans, collectors, scholars and dealers who are sharing their knowledge of comic book history, comic book creators, and much scholarly research into many aspects of the hobby.

GREEN LANTERN CORPS WEB PAGE
www.glcorps.org/glcorps.html
Huge resource site with profiles and pictures of nearly every Green Lantern ever known.

HEROES: THE FANFICTION FAN MAGAZINE
victorian.fortunecity.com/belvedere/223
The fanfiction group's fan magazine, HEROES is devoted to covering the web's continuity-based fanfic groups.

THE HOUSE OF VERTIGO
vertigo.vurt.net/
A central guide to DC's Mature Readers imprint, featuring the Vertigo Discussion List, fan fiction, and fan art.

THE HULK LIBRARY
io.spaceports.com/~hulk
Large incredible Hulk web site with hundreds of comic book summaries, usually unknown info about Ol'Greenskin, his victories and defeats, etc.

INCOMPLETE COMICBOOK ARTIST CHECKLIST
www.casema.net/~pafrankn/
This site contains checklists of some of the greatest artists in world of comics.

INCREDIBLE HULK—EARTH'S MIGHTIEST MORTAL
www.hulk-emm.com
An incredible resource for information about the Hulk's powers history, various incarnations, merchandise, friends, foes and much more.

JAAG: COMICDOM'S FINEST
www.comicxone.50megs.com
Gives detailed character bios, comic book reviews, and info about the creators, artists, etc.

JAY'S COMIC BOOK COMPENDIUM
www.geocities.com/Area51/Rampart/1434/
Thor/Avengers compendium.

JAZMA UNIVERSE ONLINE
www.jazmaonline.com
New URL! Same stuff! We promote amateur and professional comic book artwork, scripts, storylines, unpublished comic books! We carry professional interviews, fan art pages, reviews, message board, promotional information, link page, and more! Home of the online comic book - The Legendary Dark Silhouette!

THE JLA WATCHTOWER/ USTICE LEAGUE GALLERY
members.nbci.com/can3boy
A gallery dedicated to the JLA. Witness the Justice League of America at their best.

MARVEL CHRONOLOGY PROJECT
www.chronologyproject.com
Listing every appearance of every Marvel character...in chronological order.

THE MARVEL FAMILY WEB
shazam.imginc.com
The Marvel Family Web is devoted to the original Captain Marvel and members of his family as well as all the other great Fawcett characters!

MEXICO COMIC BOOK GUIDE
esquizofrenia.8m.com
The most complete comic guide in Mexico. Events, news, discusion boards and more.

MINICOMIC.COM
www.minicomic.com/
minicomics, old and new; with attention to culture and history of minicomics

THE MUSEUM OF BLACK SUPERHEROES
www.blacksuperhero.com
A well-designed museum with exhibits and articles about black superheroes past and present.

THE MUTANT PAGE
www.santarosa.edu/~sthoemke/x/x.html
Marvel's Merry Mutant X-Men Universe

MUTATIS MUTANDIS
members.nbci.com/charleyx
One of the largest X-Men information sites around! Mutatis Mutandis has over 390 character and team profiles, weekly reviews of each title, lots of original logo graphics, a message board, chat room, links, a Panel of the Week section and much more! Check out the Fan Art section and the Mutant Powers theory too. Coming soon, Games in the Danger Room and a Fan Fiction section! Whether you're a dedicated X-Fan or know nothing about mutants at all, MM has something to capture your interest.

THE NORWEGIAN GROO PAGE
norwgroo.cjb.net
Site devoted to Sergio Aragones' Groo the Wanderer.
Collects lots of info about Groo; Hidden messages, Reviews, Quotes, etc.

THE OFFICIAL BRYAN TALBOT FANPAGE
www.bryan-talbot.com/
The definitive place for all information on Bryan Talbot (author of One Bad Rat and The Adventures of Luther Arkwright), including biographies, stripographies, image galleries and more.

PHOENIX APA WEB SITE
www.eaze.net/~oz/phoenix
This is the official site of Phoenix APA, which is dedicated to comics, science fiction, writing and art.

PLANET OF THE APES INTERNATIONAL FAN CLUB
www.dlcwest.com/~comicsape/ape.htm
Website devoted to the movies, memorabilia, and Marvel & Adventure Comics products!

POP IMAGE
www.popimage.com
A webzine "Where Comics Come First"... the very best in interviews, reviews, original features and comic book commentary every month.

THE POWER OF IRON MAN
www.geocities.com/Area51/Meteor/5627/im_index.htm
Documenting the adventures of Iron Man. Synopsis and covers of Iron Man issues. Polls to vote, and Iron Man-related items.

PSYCOMIC! THE FINAL WORD ON COMICS
www.psycomic.com
Weekly reviews of new comics, with additional reviews added daily.

ROGUE STAR
www.rogue-star.com
Science Fiction Online Comic book

SDTV COMIC BOOK PUBLISHERS CHANNEL LIST
www.SmartDigitalTelevision.com/comicbooks.html
A complete guide to comic book publisher websites on the World Wide Web.

SEQUENTIAL ELLISON: THE HARLAN ELLISON COMIC BOOK BIBLIOGRAPHY
www.enteract.com/~chrisday/Ellison/
Sequential Ellison is a disgustingly detailed listing, organization, and bibliographic reference exploring the comic book and comic book related work of the award-winning writer Harlan Ellison.

SEQUENTIAL TART
www.sequentialtart.com
sequential tart (si-kwen'shel tart) n.—1. a Web Zine about the comics industry published by an eclectic band of women; 2. a publication dedicated to providing exclusive interviews, in-depth articles and news, while working towards raising the awareness of women's influence in the comics industry and other realms.

SILVER LANTERN
members.tripod.com/~Red1962/index.html
A tribute to the Silver Age superheroes of DC Comics, featuring Green Lantern.

THE SOURCE
www.geocities.com/Area51/Stargate/3999/
Dedicated to the Fourth World works of Jack Kirby.

SUPERBOY & WONDER GIRL'S PAGE OF LOVE!
fly.to/superboy
Dedicated to the relationship between DC's modern Superboy (Kon-El) and modern Wonder Girl (Cassandra Sandsmark)

THIRD MILLENNIUM ENTERTAINMENT
www.teako170.com
Something different. Features comic book info, DD live-action script, storyboarding, screenwriting, filmmaking & more.

THOUGHTFUL MAN COMICS
www.thoughtfulman.com
Tired of all those insane, tights-wearing, over-the-top superheroes you just can't relate to? Then pick up Thoughtful Man comics. Thoughtful Man: He's a hero you can settle for.

THE ULTIMATE ERIK LARSEN FAN PAGE
members.tripod.com/fantom_dragonfan/index.html
A very comprehensive site that has almost everything you need to know about the creator of the Savage Dragon, Erik Larsen.

THE ULTIMATE HELLBLAZER INDEX
www.qusoor.com/hellblazer
A site which catalogs all the appearances of John Constantine both in his own comic, Hellblazer, and in other titles.

THE UNOFFICIAL AQUAMAN SITE
www.eskimo.com/~tegan/aqua/index.html
A page that covers Aquaman in all his incarnations.

THE UNOFFICIAL FORGOTTEN HEROES WEB SITE
omega.animefringe.com/forgottenheroes/
The Immortal Man brought them together from obscurity to be remembered as heroes once again. Featuring: in-depth annotations, character bios, and much more.

THE UNOFFICIAL GUIDE TO THE DC UNIVERSE
welcome.to/the.DC.Guide/
A web-based encyclopedia of the DC Universe, including Who's Who profiles, issue-by-issue indexes, and a history of the DC Universe.

THE UNOFFICIAL HYPERTIME WEBSITE
travel.to/hypertime
The UHWS strives to document the concept of Hypertime in DC Comics, and its effects on DC Comics characters and readers.

THE UNOFFICIAL IMPULSE SITE
www.geocities.com/Athens/Troy/7023
One of the best fan sites about Impulse, the coolest of DC characters. Here you will find a lot about our little friend and his world.

THE UNOFFICIAL SPIDER-MAN HOME PAGE
www.spiderfan.org
The most complete Spider-Man reference site on the Internet, incorporating Peter Parker's Pad, a monthly e-zine featuring reviews of the latest Spider-Man comics, plus news and editorials on everything in the Spider-Verse. Reviews, Quizzes, Images, Icons, Sounds, Themes, History, Profiles, Games, Books, Fan Fiction—has to be seen to be believed.

THE UNOFFICIAL TEEN TITANS HOMEPAGE
titans.simplenet.com/titan.htm
A detailed listing of the Titans past and present including synopsis of every book they've appeared in along with character bios, cover scans, and much, much more.

VERTIGO SITES ON THE WWW
www.ionet.net/~hodge/vertigo
A collection of links to Vertigo comics related sites.

WAHOO! THE COMIC BOOK WEBSITE DIRECTORY
www.dereksantos.com/wahoo/
Contains hundreds of quality links to comic-related websites, organized into dozens of easy-to-use categories.

WISDOMS WEB
katryn.future.easyspace.com
Everything you ever wanted to know about Pete Wisdom and his partners in crime - Excalibur and Kitty Pryde. With extensive links to other sites.

WOMAN OF WONDER
members.nbci.com/wonderthing/thingvall.html
Joel Thingvall's Woman of Wonder Gallery features more than 400 illustrations of Wonder Woman by the top talents in the field. Visit the "About This Venture" page to find out the story behind the gallery, and take a moment to sign the guest book. A "wonder"ful site.

YOUNG JUSTICE: THE HANGOUT
www.geocities.com/Area51/Nebula/9376/
This site is dedicated to Young Justice, DC Comic's superteen team and is home to the Young Justice Experience Webring.

A Chronology of the Development of the American Comic Book by M. Thomas Inge

Precursors: The facsimile newspaper strip reprint collections constitute the earliest "comic books." The first of these was a collection of Richard Outcault's **Yellow Kid** from the **Hearst New York American** in March 1897. Commercial and promotional reprint collections, usually in cardboard covers, appeared through the 1920s and featured such newspaper strips as **Mutt and Jeff**, **Foxy Grandpa**, **Buster Brown**, and **Barney Google**. During 1922 a reprint magazine, **Comic Monthly**, appeared with each issue devoted to a separate strip, and from 1929 to 1930 George Delacorte published 36 issues of **The Funnies** in tabloid format with original comic pages in color, becoming the first four-color comic newsstand publication.

1933: The Ledger syndicate published a small broadside of their Sunday comics on 7" by 9" plates. Employees of Eastern Color Printing Company in New York, sales manager Harry I. Wildenberg and salesman Max C. Gaines, saw it and figured that two such plates would fit a tabloid page, which would produce a book about 7-1/2" x 10" when folded. Thus 10,000 copies of **Funnies on Parade**, containing 32 pages of Sunday newspaper reprints, was published for Proctor and Gamble to be given away as premiums. Some of the strips included were: **Joe Palooka**, **Mutt and Jeff**, **Hairbreadth Harry**, and **Reg'lar Fellas**. M. C. Gaines was very impressed with this book and convinced Eastern Color that he could sell a lot of them to such big advertisers as Milk-O-Malt, Wheatena, Kinney Shoe Stores, and others to be used as premiums and radio give-aways. So, Eastern Color printed **Famous Funnies: A Carnival of Comics**, and then **Century of Comics**, both as before, containing Sunday newspaper reprints. Mr. Gaines sold these books in quantities of 100,000 to 250,000. Although slightly larger in size than **Famous Funnies**, Humor Publications produced two one-issue magazines, **Detective Dan** and **The Adventures of Detective Ace King**, which contained original comic art and sold for ten cents per copy.

1934: The give-away comics were so successful that Mr. Gaines believed that youngsters would buy comic books for ten cents like the "Big Little Books" coming out at that time. So, early in 1934, Eastern Color ran off 35,000 copies of **Famous Funnies, Series 1**, 64 pages of reprints for Dell Publishing Company to be sold for ten cents in chain stores. Since it sold out promptly on the stands, Eastern Color, in May 1934, issued **Famous Funnies** No. 1 (dated July 1934) which became, with issue No. 2 in July, the first monthly comic magazine. The title continued for over 20 years through 218 issues, reaching a circulation peak of over 400,000 copies a month. At the same time, Mr. Gaines went to the sponsors of Percy Crosby's *Skippy*, which was on the radio, and convinced them to put out a Skippy book, advertise it on the air, and give away a free copy to anyone who bought a tube of Phillip's toothpaste. Thus 500,000 copies of **Skippy's Own Book of Comics** was run off and distributed through drug stores everywhere. This was the first four-color comic book of reprints devoted to a single character.

1935: Major Malcolm Wheeler-Nicholson's National Periodical Publications issued in February a tabloid-sized comic publication called **New Fun**, which became **More Fun** after the sixth issue and was converted to the normal comic-book size after issue eight. **More Fun** was the first comic book of a standard size to publish original material, and it continued publication until 1947. **Mickey Mouse Magazine** began in the summer, to become **Walt Disney's Comics and Stories** in 1940, and combined original material with reprinted newspaper strips in most issues.

1936: In the wake of the success of **Famous Funnies**, other publishers, in conjunction with the major newspaper strip syndicates, inaugurated more reprint comic books: **Popular Comics** (News Tribune, February), **Tip Top Comics** (United Features, April), **King Comics** (King Features, April), and **The Funnies** (new series, NEA, October). Four issues of **Wow Comics**, from David McKay and Henle Publications, appeared, edited by S. M. Iger and including early art by Will Eisner, Bob Kane, and Alex Raymond. The first non-reprint comic book devoted to a single theme was **Detective Picture Stories** issued in December by The Comics Magazine Company.

1937: The second single theme title, **Western Picture Stories**, came in February from The Comics

Magazine Company, and the third was **Detective Comics**, an offshoot of **More Fun**, which began in March to be published to the present. The book's initials, "D.C.," have long served to refer to National Periodical Publications, which was purchased from Major Nicholson by Harry Donenfeld late this year.

1938: "DC" copped a lion's share of the comic book market with the publication of **Action Comics** #1 in June which contained the first appearance of Superman by writer Jerry Siegel and artist Joe Shuster, a discovery of Max C. Gaines. The "man of steel" inaugurated the "Golden Era" in comic book history. Fiction House, a pulp publisher, entered the comic book field in September with **Jumbo Comics**, featuring Sheena, Queen of the Jungle, and appearing in over-sized format for the first eight issues.

1939: The continued success of "DC" was assured in May with the publication of **Detective Comics** #27 containing the first episode of Batman by artist Bob Kane and writer Bill Finger. **Superman Comics** appeared in the summer. Also, during the summer, a black and white premium comic titled **Motion Picture Funnies Weekly** was published to be given away at motion picture theatres. The plan was to issue it weekly and to have continued stories so that the kids would come back week after week not to miss an episode. Four issues were planned but only one came out. This book contains the first appearance and origin of the Sub-Mariner by Bill Everett (8 pages) which was later reprinted in **Marvel Comics**. In November, the first issue of **Marvel Comics** came out, featuring the Human Torch by Carl Burgos and the Sub-Mariner reprint with color added.

1940: The April issue of **Detective Comics** #38 introduced Robin the Boy Wonder as a sidekick to Batman, thus establishing the "Dynamic Duo" and a major precedent for later costumed heroes who would also have boy companions. **Batman Comics** began in the spring. Over 60 different comic book titles were being issued, including **Whiz Comics** begun in February by Fawcett Publications. A creation of writer Bill Parker and artist C. C. Beck, Whiz's Captain Marvel was the only superhero ever to surpass Superman in comic book sales. Drawing on their own popular pulp magazine heroes, Street and Smith Publications introduced **Shadow Comics** in March and **Doc Savage Comics** in May. A second trend was established with the summer appearance of the first issue of **All Star Comics**, which brought several superheroes together in one story and in its third issue that winter would announce the establishment of the Justice Society of America.

1941: Wonder Woman was introduced in the spring issue of **All Star Comics** #8, the creation of psychologist William Moulton Marston and artist Harry Peter. **Captain Marvel Adventures** began this year. By the end of 1941, over 160 titles were being published, including **Captain America** by Jack Kirby and Joe Simon, **Police Comics** with Jack Cole's Plastic Man and later Will Eisner's Spirit, **Military Comics** with Blackhawk by Eisner and Charles Cuidera, **Daredevil Comics** with the original character by Charles Biro, **Air Fighters** with Airboy also by Biro, and **Looney Tunes & Merrie Melodies** with Porky Pig, Bugs Bunny, and Elmer Fudd, reportedly created by Bob Clampett for the Leon Schlesinger Productions animated films and drawn for the comics by Chase Craig. Also, Albert Kanter's Gilberton Company initiated the **Classics Illustrated** series with **The Three Musketeers**.

1942: Crime Does Not Pay by editor Charles Biro and publisher Lev Gleason, devoted to factual accounts of criminals' lives, began a different trend in realistic crime stories. **Wonder Woman** appeared in the summer. John Goldwater's character Archie, drawn by Bob Montana, first published in **Pep Comics**, was given his own magazine **Archie Comics**, which has remained popular over 40 years. The first issue of **Animal Comics** contained Walt Kelly's "Albert Takes the Cake," featuring the new character of Pogo. In mid-1942, the undated Dell Four Color title, #9, **Donald Duck Finds Pirate Gold**, appeared with art by Carl Barks and Jack Hannah. Barks, also featured in **Walt Disney's Comics and Stories**, remained the most popular delineator of Donald Duck and later introduced his greatest creation, Uncle Scrooge, in **Christmas on Bear Mountain** (Dell Four Color #178). The fantasy work of George Carlson appeared in the first issue of **Jingle Jangle Comics**, one of the most imaginative titles for children ever to be published.

1945: The first issue of **Real Screen Comics** introduced the Fox and the Crow by James F. Davis, and John Stanley began drawing the **Little Lulu** comic book based on a popular feature in the **Saturday Evening Post** by Marjorie Henderson Buell from 1935 to 1944. Bill Woggon's Katy Keene appears in #5 of **Wilbur Comics** to be followed by appearances in **Laugh, Pep, Suzie** and her own comic book in 1950. The popularity of Dick Briefer's satiric version of the Frankenstein monster, originally drawn for **Prize Comics** in 1941, led to the publication of **Frankenstein Comics** by Prize publications.

1950: The son of Max C. Gaines, William M. Gaines,

who earlier had inherited his father's firm Educational Comics (later Entertaining Comics), began publication of a series of well-written and masterfully drawn titles which would establish a "New Trend" in comics magazines: **Crypt of Terror** (later **Tales from the Crypt**, April), **The Vault of Horror** (April), **The Haunt of Fear** (May), **Weird Science** (May), **Weird Fantasy** (May), **Crime SuspenStories** (October), and **Two Fisted Tales** (November), the latter stunningly edited by Harvey Kurtzman.

1952: In October EC published the first number of **Mad** under Kurtzman's creative editorship, thus establishing a style of humor which would inspire other publications and powerfully influence the underground comic book movement of the 1960s.

1953: All Fawcett titles featuring Captain Marvel were ceased after many years of litigation in the courts during which National Periodical Publications claimed that the superhero was an infringement on the copyrighted Superman. In December, Captain America, Human Torch, and Sub-Mariner were revived by Atlas Comics. The first 3-D comic book, **Three Dimension Comics**, featuring **Mighty Mouse** and created by Joe Kubert and Norman Maurer, was issued in September by St. John Publishing Co.

1954: The appearance of Fredric Wertham's book **Seduction of the Innocent** in the spring was the culmination of a continuing war against comic books fought by those who believed they corrupted youth and debased culture. The U. S. Senate Subcommittee on Juvenile Delinquency investigated comic books and in response the major publishers banded together in October to create the Comics Code Authority and adopted, in their own words, "the most stringent code in existence for any communications media." Before the Code took effect, more than 1,000,000,000 issues of comic books were being sold annually.

1955: In an effort to avoid the Code, EC launched a "New Direction" series of titles, such as **Impact**, **Valor**, **Aces High**, **Extra, M.D.**, and **Psychoanalysis**, none of which lasted beyond the year. **Mad** was changed into a larger magazine format with #24 in July to escape the Comics Code entirely, and EC closed down its line of comic books altogether.

1956: Beginning with the Flash in **Showcase** #4, Julius Schwartz began a popular revival of DC superheroes which would lead to the Silver Age in comic book history.

1957: Atlas reduced the number of titles published by two-thirds, with **Journey into Mystery** and **Strange Tales** surviving, while other publishers did the same or went out of business. Atlas would survive as a part of the Marvel Comics Group.

1960: After several efforts at new satire magazines (**Trump** and **Humbug**), Harvey Kurtzman, no longer with Gaines, issued in August the first number of another abortive effort, **Help!**, where the early work of underground cartoonists Jay Lynch, Skip Williamson, Gilbert Shelton, and Robert Crumb appeared.

1961: Stan Lee edited in November the first **Fantastic Four**, featuring Mr. Fantastic, the Human Torch, the Thing, and the Invisible Girl, and inaugurated an enormously popular line of titles from Marvel Comics featuring a more contemporary style of superhero.

1962: Lee introduced **The Amazing Spider-Man** in August, with art by Steve Ditko, **The Hulk** in May and **Thor** in August, the last two produced by Dick Ayers and Jack Kirby.

1963: Marvel's **The X-Men**, with art by Jack Kirby, began a successful run in November, but the title would experience a revival and have an even more popular reception in the 1980s.

1965: James Warren issued **Creepy**, a larger black and white comic book, outside Comics Code's control, which emulated the EC horror comic line. Warren's **Eerie** began in September and **Vampirella** in September 1969.

1968: Robert Crumb's **Zap** #1 appeared in February, the first underground comic book to achieve wide popularity, although counterculture precursors included **Adventures of Jesus** by Foolbert Sturgeon (Frank Stack) in 1962 and **God Nose** by Jack Jackson in 1964.

1970: Editor Roy Thomas at Marvel begins **Conan the Barbarian** based on fiction by Robert E. Howard with art by Barry Smith, and Neal Adams began to draw for DC a series of **Green Lantern/Green Arrow** stories which would deal with relevant social issues such as racism, urban poverty, and drugs. The publication of the first edition of **The Overstreet Comic Book Price Guide** in November served to stabilize the rapidly developing market for comic book collectors and provided the first dependable publication data and history for research.

1972: **The Swamp Thing** by Berni Wrightson begins in November from DC.

1973: In February, DC revived the original **Captain Marvel** with new art by C. C. Beck and reprints in the first issue of **Shazam** and in October **The Shadow** with scripts by Denny O'Neil and art by Mike Kaluta.

1974: DC began publication in the spring of a series of over-sized facsimile reprints of the most valued comic books of the past under the general title of "Famous First Editions," beginning with a reprint of **Action** #1 and including afterwards **Detective Comics** #27, **Sensation Comics** #1, **Whiz Comics** #2, **Batman** #1, **Wonder Woman** #1, **All-Star Comics** #3, **Flash Comics** #1, and **Superman** #1. Mike Friedrich, an independent publisher, released **Star-Reach** with work by Jim Starlin, Neal Adams, and Dick Giordano, with ownership of the characters and stories invested in the creators themselves.

1975: In the first collaborative effort between the two major comic book publishers of the previous decade, Marvel and DC produced together an over-sized comic book version of MGM's **Marvelous Wizard of Oz** in the fall, and then the following year, in an unprecedented crossover, produced **Superman vs. the Amazing Spider-Man**, written by Gerry Conway, drawn by Ross Andru, and inked by Dick Giordano.

1976: Frank Brunner's Howard the Duck, who had appeared earlier in Marvel's **Fear** and **Man-Thing**, was given his own book in January, which because of distribution problems became an overnight collector's item. After decades of litigation, Jerry Siegel and Joe Shuster were given financial recompense and recognition by National Periodical Publications for their creation of Superman, after several friends of the team made a public issue of the case.

1977: Stan Lee's **Spider-Man** was given a second birth, fifteen years after his first, through a highly successful newspaper comic strip, which began syndication on January 3 with art by John Romita. This invasion of the comic strip by comic book characters continued with the appearance on June 6 of Marvel's **Howard the Duck**, with story by Steve Gerber and visuals by Gene Colan. In an unusually successful collaborative effort, Marvel began publication of the comic book adaption of the George Lucas film **Star Wars**, with script by Roy Thomas and art by Howard Chaykin, at least three months before the film was released nationally on May 25. The demand was so great that all six issues of **Star Wars** were reprinted at least seven times, and the installments were reprinted in two volumes of an over-sized Marvel Special Edition and a single paperback volume for the book trade. Dave Sim, with an issue dated December, began self-publication of his **Cerebus the Aardvark**, the success of which would help establish the independent market for non-traditional black-and-white comics.

1978: In an effort to halt declining sales, Warner Communications drastically cut back on the number of DC titles and overhauled its distribution process in June. The interest of the visual media in comic book characters reached a new high with the Hulk, Spider-Man, and Doctor Strange, the subjects of television shows; with various film versions produced of Flash Gordon, Dick Tracy, Popeye, Conan, The Phantom, and Buck Rogers; and with the movement reaching an outlandish peak of publicity with the release of **Superman** in December. Two significant applications of the comic book format to traditional fiction appeared this year: **A Contract with God and Other Tenement Stories** by Will Eisner and **The Silver Surfer** by Stan Lee and Jack Kirby. Eclipse Enterprises published Don McGregor and Paul Gulacy's **Sabre**, the first graphic album produced for the direct sales market, and initiated a policy of paying royalties and granting copyrights to comic book creators. Wendy and Richard Pini's **Elfquest**, a self-publishing project begun this year, eventually became so popular that it achieved bookstore distribution. The magazine **Heavy Metal** brought to American attention the avant-garde comic book work of European artists.

1980: Publication of the November premiere issue of **The New Teen Titans**, with art by George Perez and story by Marv Wolfman, brought back to widespread popularity a title originally published by DC in 1966.

1981: Distributor Pacific Comics began publishing titles for direct sales through comic shops with the first issue of Jack Kirby's **Captain Victory and the Galactic Rangers** and offered royalties to artists and writers on the basis of sales. DC would do the same for regular newsstand comics in November (with payments retroactive to July 1981), and Marvel followed suit by the end of the year. The first issue of **Raw**, irregularly published by Art Spiegelman and Francoise Mouly, carried comic book art into new extremes of experimentation and innovation with work by European and American artists. With #158, Frank Miller began to write and draw Marvel's **Daredevil** and brought a vigorous style of violent action to comic book pages.

1982: The first slick format comic book in regular size appeared, **Marvel Fanfare** #1, with a March date. Fantagraphics Books began publication in July of **Love and Rockets** by Mario, Gilbert, and Jaime Hernandez and brought a new ethnic sensibility and sophistication in style and content to comic book narratives for adults.

1983: More comic book publishers, aside from Marvel and DC, issued more titles than had existed in the past 40 years, most small independent publishers relying on direct sales, such as Americomics, Capital, Eagle, Eclipse, First, Pacific, and Red Circle, and with Archie, Charlton, and Whitman publishing on a limited scale. Frank Miller's mini-series **Ronin** demonstrated a striking use of sword play and martial arts typical of Japanese comic book art, and Howard Chaykin's stylish but controversial **American Flagg** appeared with an October date on its first issue.

1984: A publishing, media, film, and merchandising phenomenon began with the first issue of **Teenage Mutant Ninja Turtles** from Mirage Studios by Kevin Eastman and Peter Laird.

1985: Ohio State University's Library of Communication and Graphic Arts hosted the first major exhibition devoted to the comic book May 19 through August 2. In what was billed as an irreversible decision, the Silver Age superheroine Supergirl was killed in the seventh (October) issue of **Crisis on Infinite Earths**, a limited series intended to reorganize and simplify the DC universe on the occasion of their 50th anniversary.

1986: In recognition of its twenty-fifth anniversary, Marvel began publishing several new ongoing titles comprising Marvel's "New Universe", a self-contained fictional world. DC attracted extensive publicity and media coverage with its revisions of the character of **Superman** by John Byrne and of **Batman** in the **Dark Knight** series by Frank Miller. **Watchmen**, a limited-series graphic novel by Alan Moore and artist Dave Gibbons, began publication with a September issue from DC and Marvel's **The `Nam**, written by Vietnam veteran Doug Murray and penciled by Michael Golden, began with its December issue. DC issued guidelines in December for labelling their titles either for mature readers or for readers of all ages; in response, many artists and writers publicly objected or threatened to resign.

1987: Art Spiegelman's **Maus: A Survivor's Tale** was nominated for the National Book Critics Circle Award in biography, the first comic book to be so honored. A celebration of Superman's fiftieth Birthday began with the opening of an exhibition on his history at the Smithsonian's Museum of American History in Washington, D.C., in June and a symposium on "The Superhero in America" in October.

1988: Superman's birthday celebration continued with a public party in New York and a CBS television special in February, a cover story in **Time Magazine** in March (the first comic book character to appear on the cover), and an international exposition in Cleveland in June. With issue number 601 for May 24, **Action Comics** became the first modern weekly comic book, which ceased publication after 42 issues with the December 13 issue. In August, DC initiated a new policy of allowing creators of new characters to retain ownership of them rather than rely solely on work-for-hire.

1989: The fiftieth anniversary of Batman was marked by the release of the film **Batman**, starring Michael Keaton as Bruce Wayne and Jack Nicholson as the Joker; it grossed more money in its opening weekend than any other motion picture in film history to that time.

1990: The publication of a new **Classics Illustrated** series began in January from Berkley/First with adaptations of Poe's **The Raven and Other Poems** by Gahan Wilson, Dickens' **Great Expectations** by Rick Geary, Carroll's **Through the Looking Glass** by Kyle Baker, and Melville's **Moby Dick** by Bill Sienkiewicz, with extensive media attention. The adaptation of characters to film continued with the most successful in terms of popularity and box office receipts being **Teenage Mutant Ninja Turtles** and Warren Beatty's **Dick Tracy**. In November, the engagement of Clark Kent and Lois Lane was announced in **Superman** #50 which brought public fanfare about the planned marriage.

1991: One of the first modern comic books to appear in the former Soviet Union was a Russian version of **Mickey Mouse** published in Moscow on May 16 in a printing of 200,000 copies which were sold out within hours. The first issue of **Bone**, written, drawn, and published by Jeff Smith, appeared with a July cover date. Issue number one of a new series of Marvel's **X-Men**, with story and art by Chris Claremont and Jim Lee, was published in October in five different editions with a print run of eight million copies, the highest number in the history of the comic book. On December 18, Sotheby's of New York held its first auction of comic book material.

1992: In April, Image Comics debuted with **Youngblood** #1, changing the comic book industry by widening the playing field and legitimizing independent comics. Image Comics began publication of the first Todd McFarlane Productions title, **Spawn**, with a May cover date. The opening weekend for **Batman Returns** in June was the biggest in film box office history, bringing in over 46 million dollars, exceeding the record set by **Batman** in 1989, and not to be topped until the release of **Jurassic Park** a year later. At the second Sotheby auction in September, **Action Comics** #1 brought $82,500, a world record for a single comic book sold at auction. In November the death of Superman generated considerable media attention, with **Superman** #75 selling in excess of 4 million copies, the second best-selling issue in comic book history. A record number of over one hundred publishers of comic books and graphic albums issued titles this year.

1993: In April, for the first time since 1987, DC Comics surpassed Marvel in sales, primarily because of interest in the titles devoted to the return of Superman.

1994: Overproduction, changes in marketing practices, and publisher mergers and collapses triggered an apparent crisis in comic book publishing–which some have read as a sign of its influence and presence in American commerce and culture.

1995: Batman Forever, released in June with Val Kilmer in the lead role, grossed in its opening weekend over $53 million, the largest return in film box office history, exceeding the similar records set by the first two Batman films in 1989 and 1992. Writer Neil Gaiman decided after seven years to retire his popular and literate version of **Sandman**, the second revival of a Golden Age DC superhero first created in 1939.

1996: The longest-running give-away title ended after #467 of **The Adventures of the Big Boy** in September. In a long anticipated event coordinated between several comic book titles, the ABC television series **Lois & Clark**: **The New Adventures of Superman**, and the publication of **Superman: The Wedding Album**, Lois Lane and Clark Kent were married in October.

1997: Several Marvel Universe titles (**Fantastic Four**, **Avengers**, **Captain America**, **Iron Man**) ended their long runs and started over with new #1 issues under the umbrella title **Heroes Reborn**, a separate universe under the creative direction of Rob Liefeld and Jim Lee. They later returned, again with new #1s, in the **Heroes Return** crossover. Superman went through a startling metamorphosis at DC, complete with new powers and a new costume, eventually splitting into two beings, Superman Red & Superman Blue. The latest Batman film, **Batman & Robin**, was released to a tepid response, while the movie adaptation of Todd McFarlane's **Spawn** movie was moderately well received.

1998: Marvel continued to relaunch their popular titles, and Spider-Man was the focus. His titles were restarted with #1 issues, and John Byrne updated his origins with the start of the **Spider-Man: Chapter One** mini-series. Movie director Kevin Smith took over the reigns of **Daredevil**, and other titles were restarted under the **Marvel Knights** banner. DC bought Jim Lee's WildStorm properties, bringing into the fold popular titles like **Gen13**, **WildCATS**, and the highly successful new **Cliffhanger** titles **Battle Chasers**, **Danger Girl** and **Crimson**. The 20th anniversary of the publication of **A Contract with God** was observed by a conference "The Graphic Novel: An Emerging Literary and Artistic Medium" held in honor of Will Eisner at the University of Massachusetts in Amherst.

1999: The manga/anime influx reached gargantuan proportions with the runaway success of **Pokémon** on TV, in theaters, and most especially in comics, trading cards and toys. Other titles like **Sailor Moon** and **DragonballZ** were also prominent this year. The JSA returned to regular publication. **Marvel Knights** continued to garner praise with titles like **The Inhumans**, **Black Widow**, **Black Panther**, **Daredevil**, **Antman**, and **Punisher**. Gladstone ceased publication of Disney titles in February. That month also celebrated **The Wedding of Popeye and Olive** from Ocean Comics. Alex Ross followed up the tabloid-sized painted **Superman** adventure, **Peace on Earth**, with a **Batman** tabloid titled **War on Crime.**

2000: Marvel began to issue an **Ultimate Marvel** series designed to feature their superheroes as 21st century teenagers, beginning in September with the best-selling **Ultimate Spider-Man** #1. Film interest in comic book properties and ideas continued with the successful and faithful version of **X-Men** in July and the comic book themed movie **Unbreakable** in November. The graphic novel garnered praise and attention in the nation's literary media with the publication of such works as **From Hell** by Alan Moore and Eddie Campbell, **Jimmy Corrigan: The Smartest Kid on Earth** by Chris Ware, and **David Boring** by Daniel Clowes.

HISTORIC FIRSTS

(First comic book of a genre, publisher, theme or type, etc.)

AVIATION COMIC–Wings Comics #1, 9/40
COMIC BOOK ANNUAL–Big Book of Fun Comics #1, Spr, 1936
COMIC BOOK–Funnies On Parade nn, 1933
COMIC BOOK TO GO INTO ENDLESS REPRINTS–Classic Comics #1, 10/41
COMIC BOOK TO KILL OFF A SUPERHERO–Pep Comics #17, 7/41 (The Comet)
COMIC BOOK WITH METALLIC LOGO–Silver Streak #1, 12/39
COMIC BOOK WITH ORIGINAL MATERIAL–New Fun Comics #1, 2/35
COSTUMED HERO BATTLE COMIC–Marvel Mystery #9, 7/40
COSTUMED HERO COMIC (STRIP)–Ace Comics #11, 2/38 (The Phantom)
COSTUMED HERO COMIC (Original material)–Funny Pages V2/10 9/38 (The Arrow) (3 months after Superman)
COSTUMED HERO SIDEKICK COMIC– Detective Comics #38, 4/40 (Robin)
CRIME–Crime Does Not Pay #22, 6/42
DETECTIVE COMIC–Detective Picture Stories #1, 12/36
DISNEY SINGLE CHARACTER COMIC BOOK–Donald Duck nn, 1938
DISNEY SINGLE CHARACTER COMIC BOOK IN COLOR–Donald Duck 4-Color #4, 3/40
EDUCATIONAL THEME COMIC–Classic Comics #1, 10/41
5 CENT COMIC–Nickel Comics #1, 1938
15 CENT COMIC–New York World's Fair, 1940
FLYING SAUCER COMIC–Spirit Section 9/28/47 (3 months after 1st alleged sighting in Idaho on 6/25/47)
FUNNY ANIMAL SERIES–Walt Disney's Comics & Stories #1, 10/40
FUNNY ANIMAL SINGLE CHARACTER COMIC–Donald Duck nn, 1938
GIVEAWAY COMIC–Funnies on Parade nn, 1933
GOLDEN AGE COMIC–Action Comics #1, 6/38
HEROINE SINGLE THEME COMIC–Sheena, Queen of the Jungle #1, Spr, 1942
HORROR COMIC (ONE SHOT)–Eerie Comics #1, 1/47
HORROR COMIC (SERIES)–Adventures into the Unknown #1, Fall, 1948
JUNGLE COMIC–Jumbo Comics #1, 9/38
LARGE SIZED COMIC–New Fun Comics #1, 2/35
LOVE COMIC (ONE SHOT)–Romantic Picture Novelettes #1, 1946 (Mary Worth strip-r)
LOVE COMIC (SERIES)–Young Romance Comics #1, 10/47
MAGICIAN COMIC–Super Magic Comics #1, 5/41
MAGICIAN COMIC SERIES–Super Magician Comics #2, 9/41
MASKED HERO–Funny Pages #6, 11/36 (The Clock)
MOVIE COMIC–Movie Comics #1, 4/39
NEGRO COMIC–Negro Heroes, Spr, 1947
NEWSSTAND COMIC–Famous Funnies #1, 7/34
#2 IN COMICS–Famous Funnies #2, 8/34
100 PAGE COMIC–Century of Comics nn, 1933
100TH ISSUE–Famous Funnies #100, 11/42
ONE SHOT SERIES–Feature Book nn, 1937
PATRIOTIC HERO COMIC–Pep Comics #1, 1/40 (The Shield)
PROTOTYPE COMIC–The Comics Magazine #1, 5/36 (Superman)
PUBLIC EVENT COMIC–New York World's Fair 1939
RELIGIOUS THEME SERIES–Topix Comics #1, 11/42

The Spirit #1 (6/2/40) © QUA
1st Weekly Comic Book

REPRINT COMIC–Funnies on Parade nn, 1933
SATIRE COMIC–Mad #1, 10-11/52
SCIENCE FICTION COMIC–Planet Comics #1, 1/40
SIDEKICK GROUP COMIC–Young Allies #1, Sum, 1941
SILVER AGE ARCHIE COMIC–Double Life of Private Strong #1, 6/59
SILVER AGE COMIC–Showcase #4, 9-10/56
SILVER AGE DC ANNUAL–Superman Annual #1, 10/60
SILVER AGE MARVEL ANNUAL–Strange Tales Annual #1, 1962
SILVER AGE MARVEL COMIC–Fantastic Four #1, 11/61
SINGLE CHARACTER COMIC–Skippy's Own Book of Comics, 1934
SINGLE ORIGINAL CHARACTER COMIC–Superman #1, Sum, 1939
SINGLE STRIP REPRINT CHARACTER COMIC–Mutt and Jeff #1, Sum, 1939
SINGLE THEME COMIC–Detective Picture Stories #1, 12/36
SINGLE THEME COMIC, THE FIRST IMPORTANT–Detective Comics #1, 3/37
SINGLE THEME REPRINT STRIP COMIC–Mutt and Jeff #1, Sum, 1939
SMALL-SIZED COMIC–Little Giant Comics #1, 7/38
SPORTS COMIC–Champion Comics #2, 12/39
SQUAREBOUND COMIC–New Book of Comics #1, 1937
SQUAREBOUND SERIES–World's Best #1, Spr, 1941
SUPER HERO COMIC–Action Comics #1, 6/38 (Superman)
SUPER HERO TEAM–All Star Comics #3, Wint, 1940-41
SUPER HEROINE COMIC–All Star Comics #8, 11-12/41
SUPER HEROINE COMIC SERIES–Sensation Comics #1, 1/42
SUPERMAN IMITATOR–Wonder Comics #1, 5/39 (Wonder Man)
TEEN-AGE COMIC–Pep Comics #22, 12/41
TEEN-AGE COMIC SERIES–Archie Comics #1, Wint, 1942-43
10 CENT COMIC–Famous Funnies Series 1, 3-5/34
3-D COMIC–Mighty Mouse 3-D #1, 9/53
T.V. COMIC–Howdy Doody #1, 1/50
25 CENT COMIC–New York World's Fair, 1939
TRUE LIFE COMIC–Sport Comics #1, 10/40
VILLAIN COVER (FU MANCHU)–Detective Comics #1, 3/37
VILLAIN STORY (FU MANCHU)–Detective Comics #17, 7/38
VILLAIN COVER/STORY (ORIGINAL TO COMICS)– Silver Streak #1, 12/39 (The Claw)
WAR COMIC–War Comics #1, 5/40
WEEKLY COMIC BOOK–The Spirit #1, 6/2/40
WESTERN COMIC–Western Picture Stories #1, 2/37 & Star Ranger #1, 2/37
WESTERN OF ONE CHARACTER–The Lone Ranger Comics nn, 1939
WESTERN RUN OF ONE CHARACTER (GIVEAWAY)–Tom Mix #1, 9/40
WESTERN NEWSSTAND RUN OF ONE CHARACTER–Red Ryder Comics #1, 8/41
WESTERN WITH PHOTO COVER–Roy Rogers Four Color #38, 4/44
X-OVER COMIC–Marvel Mystery #9, 7/40

A-Man the Amazing Man - Amazing-Man Comics #5, 9/39
Adam Strange - Showcase #17, 11-12/58
Adult Legion - Superman #147, 8/61
Agent Liberty - Superman #60 (2nd Series), 10/91
Air Man - (Hawkman imitator) Keen Detective Funnies #23, 8/40
Air Wave - Detective Comics #60, 2/42
Air Wave II - Green Lantern #100, 1/78
Airboy - Air Fighters Comics V1#2, 11/42
Airwave I - Detective Comics #60, 2/42
Alex Summers - (becomes Havok) X-Men #54, 3/69
Alfred - Batman #16 4-5/43; (1st skinny Alfred) Detective Comics #83, 1/44
Alice Cooper - Marvel Premiere #50, 10/79
Alicia Masters - Fantastic Four #8, 11/62
Aliens - Aliens #1 May '88; Magnus, Robot Fighter #1, 2/63
Alley Oop - Funnies #1, 10/36
Alpha Flight - X-Men #120, 4/78
Amazing Man - All Star Squadron #23, 7/83
American Ace - (1st newsstand app.) Marvel Mystery Comics #2, 12/39
American Crusader - Thrilling Comics #19, 8/41
American Eagle - Marvel Two-In-One Annual #6, 1981; (1st pub lished app.) Motion Picture Funnies Weekly #1, 1939
Ancient One - Strange Tales #110, 7/63
Andy Panda - Crackajack Funnies #39, 9/41
Angel - Marvel Comics #1, 10-11/39
Angel (now Archangel) - X-Men #1, 9/63
Angel & the Ape - Showcase #77, 9/68
Animal Man - (in costume) Strange Adventures #190, 7/66; (no cos tume) Strange Adventures #180, 9/65; (re-intro) Wonder Woman #267, 5/80
Ant-Man - (costume) Tales to Astonish #35, 9/62; (new) Marvel Premiere #47, 4/79; (no costume) Tales to Astonish #27, 1/62; (re-intro) Avengers #46, 11/67
Anthro - Showcase #74, 5/68
Apache Kid - Two Gun Western #5, 11/50
Ape, The - Startling Comics #21, 5/43
Aqua-Girl - Aquaman #33, 5-6/67
Aquababy - Aquaman #23, 9-10/65
Aquaboy - Superboy #171
Aquagirl - (try out, not same as other) Adventure Comics #266, 11/59
Aquagirl - Aquaman #33, 5-6/67
Aqualad - Adventure Comics #269, 2/60
Aquarian (Wundarr) - Adventure Into Fear #17, '73
Aquaman - More Fun Comics #73, 11/41
Arak - Warlord #48, 8/81
Archangel - (cameo) (formerly Angel) X-Factor #23, 12/87; (full app.) X-Factor #24, 1/88
Archie Andrews - Pep Comics #22, 12/41
Arion - Warlord #55
Arrow - Funny Pages V2#10, 9/38
Arthur Stacy - Amazing Spider-Man #93, 2/71
Asbestos Lady - Captain America Comics #63, 7/47
Astro Boy - Astro Boy #1, 8/65
Atom - All-American Comics #19, 10/40; (S.A.) Showcase #34, 9-10/61
Atoman - Atoman #1, 2/46
Atomaster - Comic Books #1, 1950
Atomic Mouse - Atomic Mouse #1, 3/53
Atomic Rabbit - Atomic Rabbit #1, 8/55
Atomic Thunderbolt - Atomic Thunderbolt #1, 2/46
Aunt May - Amazing Fantasy #15, 8-9/62; (prototype) Strange Tales #92, 6/62
Aurora - X-Men #120
Avenger - Shadow Comics #2, 4/40
Azrael - (cameo) Tales of the Teen Titans #52, 4/85; (full app.) Tales of the Teen Titans #53, 5/85
Baby Huey - Casper, the Friendly Ghost #1, 9/49; (1st Harvey app.) Harvey Comics Hits #60, 9/52
Badger - Badger #1, 12/83
Balbo, the Boy Magician - Master Comics #32, 11/42
Bamm Bamm - (Flintstones) Flintstones #16, 1/64
Barker - National Comics #42, 5/44
Barney Bear - Our Gang Comics #1, 9-10/42
Baron Strucker - Sgt. Fury #5, 1/64
Bat Lash - Showcase #76, 8/68
Bat-Girl - Batman #139, 4/61; (new) Detective #359, 1/67
Batgirl - Detective Comics #359, 1/67
Batman - Detective Comics #27, May '39; (new look w/new costume) Detective Comics #327, 5/64
Batman, Jr. - World's Finest Comics #215, 10/72
Batmite - Detective Comics #267, 5/59
Batwoman - Detective Comics #233, 7/56; (1st modern app. G.A. Batwoman) Brave and the Bold #182, 1/82; (new) Detective Comics #624, 12/90; (re-intro) Batman Family #10, 3-4/77
Beast - X-Men #1, 9/63; (new) (1st in mutated form) Amazing Adventures #11, 3/72
Beast Boy - (becomes Changeling) Doom Patrol #99, 11/65
Belit - Giant-Size Conan #1, 9/74
Bennett Brant - Amazing Spider-Man #11, 4/64
Bernie the Brain - Sugar & Spike #72, ?, '68
Berserkers, The - X-Men/Alpha Flight #1, 12/85
Betty - Pep Comics #22, 12/41
Betty Brant - Amazing Spider-Man #4, 9/63
Bill Barnes - (Air Ace) Shadow Comics #1, 3/40
Binary - (formerly Ms. Marvel) X-Men #164, 12/82
Birdman, The - Weird Comics #1, 4/40
Bishop - (cameo) X-Men #282, 11/91; (full app.) X-Men #283, 12/91
Bizarro Jimmy Olsen - Adventure Comics #287, 8/61
Bizarro Lana Lang - Adventure Comics #292, 1/62
Bizarro Lois Lane - Action Comics #255, 8/59
Bizarro Lucy Lane - Adventure Comics #292, 1/62
Bizarro Marilyn Monroe - Adventure Comics #294, 3/62
Bizarro Perry White - Adventure Comics #287, 8/61
Bizarro President Kennedy - Adventure Comics #294, 3/62
Black Bolt - (1st full app.) Fantastic Four #46, 1/66 (cameo) (from Inhumans) Fantastic Four #45, 12/65
Black Canary - Flash Comics #86, 8/47; (Silver Age) Justice League of America #73; (1st modern app.) Detective Comics #554, 9/85; (1st solo story) Flash Comics #92, 2/48
Black Cat - Pocket Comics #1, 8/41
Black Cobra - Captain Flight Comics #8 ?, '46
Black Condor - Crack Comics #1, 5/40
Black Dwarf - Spotlight Comics #1, 11/44
Black Flame - Starslayer #20 9/84; Action Comics #304, 9/63
Black Fury - Fantastic Comics #18, 5/41
Black Goliath - Black Goliath #1, 2/76
BlackHawk - Military Comics #1, 8/41
Black Hood - Top-Notch Comics #9, 10/40; (S.A.) Adventures of the Fly #7, 7/60
Black Jack - Zip Comics #20, 11/41
Black Knight - Black Knight #1, 5/55
Black Knight - Tales to Astonish #52, 2/64
Black Knight II - Avengers #48, 1/68
Black Lightning - Black Lightning #1, 4/77
Black Marvel - Mystic Comics #5, 3/41
Black Orchid - Adventure Comics #428, 6-7/73; (new) Black Orchid #1, 12/88
Black Owl - Prize Comics #2, 4/40
Black Panther - Stars & Stripes #3, 7/41
Black Panther - Fantastic Four #52, 7/66
Black Phantom - Tim Holt #25, 9/51
Black Pirate - Sensation Comics #1, 1/42
Black Rider - All Western Winners #2, Win '48-49
Black Spider - Super-Mystery Comics V1#3, 10/40
Black Terror - Exciting Comics #9, 5/41
Black Widow - Mystic Comics #4, 7-8/40
Black Widow - Tales of Suspense #52, 4/64
Blackie the Hawk - Blackhawk #75, 4/54
Blackie the Hawk - (re-intro) Blackhawk #108, 1/57
Blade the Vampire Slayer - Tomb of Dracula #10, ?/73?
Blok - (Legion) Superboy #253, 7/79
Blonde Phantom - All-Select Comics #11, Fall '46; (re-intro) Sensational She-Hulk #4, 8/89
Blondie - Ace Comics #1, 4/37
Bloodshot - (cameo) Eternal Warrior #4, 11/92; (1st full app.) Rai #0, 11/92
Bloodstone - Marvel Presents #1, 10/75
Blue Beetle - (G.A.) Mystery Men Comics #1, 8/39; (Charlton) Blue Beetle #18, 2/55; (Ted Kord) Captain Atom #83, 11/66; (1st DC app.) Crisis on Infinite Earths #1, 4/85
Blue Blade - USA Comics #5, Sum '42
Blue Blaze - Mystic Comics #1, 3/40
Blue Bolt - Blue Bolt #1, 6/40
Blue Circle - Blue Circle Comics #1, 6/44
Blue Devil - Fury of Firestorm #24, 6/84
Blue Streak - Crash Comics #1, 5/40
Bo Bunny - Funny Stuff #70, 1-2?/53
Bobby Benson - Bobby Benson's B-Bar-B Riders #1, 5-6/50
Boboes - Marvel Mystery Comics #32, 6/42
Bomba - Bomba, the Jungle Boy #1, 9-10/67
Bombshell - Boy Comics #3, 4/42
Booster Gold - Booster Gold #1, 2/86
Bouncer - Bouncer nn, 1944
Bouncing Boy - (Legion) Action Comics #276, 5/61
Boy Commandos - Detective Comics #64, 6/42
Bozo the Robot - Smash Comics #1, 8/39
Brainiac 5 - Action Comics #276, 5/61
Brick Bradford - King Comics #1, 4/36
Broncho Bill - Tip Top Comics #1, 4/36
Brother Power - Brother Power, the Geek #1, 9-10/68; (re-intro) Saga of Swamp Thing Annual #5, 1989
Buck Rogers - (in comics) Famous Funnies #3, 9/34
Buckskin - Super Mystery V2#1, 4/41
Bucky - (Captain America's sidekick) Captain America Comics #1, 3/41; (Silver Age) Avengers #4, 3/64
Bugs Bunny - Looney Tunes & Merrie Melodies #1, 1941
Bullet - Amazing Mystery Funnies V3#1, 1/40
Bulletboy - Master Comics #48, 3/44
Bulletman - Nickel Comics #1, 5/40
Bumblebee - Teen Titans (1st series) #48, 1977
Buzzy - All Funny Comics #1, Win '43-44
Buzzy the Crow - Harvey Comics Hits #60, 9/52
B'Wanna Beast - Showcase #66
Cable - (1st full app.) New Mutants #87, 3/90; (cameo) New Mutants #86, 2/90
Cain - (House of Mystery host) House of Mystery #176, 10/67
Calico Kid - (becomes Ghost Rider) Tim Holt #6, 5/49
Camilla - Jungle Comics #1, 1/40
Candy - Police Comics #37, 12/44
Captain & the Kids - Famous Comics Cartoon Books #1200, 1934; Tip Top Comics #1, 4/36
Captain Action - Captain Action & Action Boy nn, 1967
Captain Aero - Captain Aero Comics V1#7, 12/41
Captain America - Captain America Comics #1, 3/41; (Silver Age) Strange Tales #114, 11/63; (Acrobat disguised as) Avengers #4, 3/64; (fomerly Super Patriot) Captain America #333, 9/87; (new) Captain America #181, 1/75; (new) (formerly Nomad) Captain America #183, 3/75
Captain Atom - (1st DC app.) Crisis on Infinite Earths #6, 9/85; (new) Captain Atom #84, 1/67; (new) Captain Atom #1 3/87; (S.A.) Space Adventures #33, 3/60
Captain Battle - Silver Streak

Comics #10, 5/41
Captain Britain - Captain Britain #1, 3/87; (1st U.S. app.) Marvel Team-Up #65, 1/78
Captain Comet - Strange Adventures #9, 6/51; (re-intro) Secret Society of Super-Villains #2, 7-8/76
Captain Commando - Pep Comics #30, 8/42
Captain Courageous - Banner Comics #3, 9/41
Captain Daring - Buccaneers #19, 1/50; Daring Mystery Comics #7, 4/41
Captain Desmo - Adventure Comics #32, 11/38
Captain Easy - Funnies #1, 10/36; Famous Comics Cartoon Books #1202, 1934
Captain Fearless - Silver Streak Comics #1, 12/39
Captain Fight - Fight Comics #16, 12/41
Captain Flag - Blue Ribbon Comics #16, 9/41
Captain Flash - Captain Flash #1, 11/54
Captain Freedom - Speed Comics #13, 5/41
Captain Future - Man of Tomorrow - Startling Comics #1, 6/40
Captain George Stacy - Amazing Spider-Man #56, 1/68
Captain Marvel (Shazam) - Whiz Comics #1, 2/40; (M.F.Enterprises) Captain Marvel #1, 4/66; (mod ern) Shazam: the New Beginning #1, 4/87; (new) Legends #1, 11/86; (re-intro) Shazam! #1, 2/73
Captain Marvel (female) - Amazing Spider-Man Annual #16, 1982
Captain Marvel of the Kree - Marvel Super-Heroes #12, 12/67
Captain Marvel, Jr. - Whiz Comics #25, 12/41
Captain Midnight - Funnies #57, 7/41
Captain Savage - Mystery Men Comics #4, 11/39
Captain Storm - Captain Storm #1, 5-6/64
Captain Strong - Action Comics #421, 3/73
Captain Terror - U.S.A. #2, 11/41
Captain Terry Thunder - Jungle Comics #1, 1/40
Captain Thunder - Flash Comics (Fawcett) #1, 1/40
Captain Thunder - Superman #276, ?'74
Captain Triumph - Crack Comics #27, 1/43
Captain Universe - Micronauts #8, 8/79
Captain Victory - Our Flag Comics #1, 8/41
Captain Wizard - Red Band Comics #3, ?'45
Captain Wonder - Kid Komics #1, 2/43
Captain Yank - Big Shot Comics #29, 11/42
Casper the Friendly Ghost - (1st Harvey app.) Harvey Comics Hits #60, 9/52; Casper #1, 9/49
Cat - The Cat #1, 11/72
Cat Girl - Adventures of the Fly #9, 11/60
Catman - Crash Comics #5, 11/40
Cave Carson - Brave and the Bold #31, 8-9/60
Cerebus - Cerebus the Aardvark #1, 12/77
Challenger - Mystic Comics #6, 10/41
Chameleon - Target Comics V1#6, 7/40
Chameleon Boy - (Legion) Action Comics #267, 8/60
Champ - Champion Comics #2, 12/39
Changeling - (formerly Beast Boy) New Teen Titans #1, 11/80; (X-Men) X-Men #35, 8/67
Charlie Chan - Feature Comics #23, 8/39
Charlie-27 - Marvel Super Heroes #18, 1/69
Checkmate - Action Comics #598, 3/88
Chemical King - (Legion) Adventure Comics #371, 8/68
Chlorophyll Kid - (Legion) Adventure Comics #306, 2/63
Chop Chop - (Blackhawk's sidekick) Military Comics #3, 10/41
Chuck - (Black Fury's aide) Fantastic Comics #18, 5/41
Cisco Kid - Cisco Kid Comics #1, Win '44
Claw the Unconquered - Claw the Unconquered #1, 5-6/75
Clea - Strange Tales #126, 11/64
Cletus Kasady - (1st full app.) Amazing Spider-Man #345, 3/91; (cameo; becomes Carnage) Amazing Spider-Man #344, 2/91
Clip Carson - Action Comics #14, 7/39
Cloak - (Spy Master) Big Shot Comics #1, 5/40
Cloak & Dagger - Spec. Spider-Man #64, 3/82
Clock - Crack Comics #1, 5/40
Clock - Funny Pages V1#6, 11/36
Clown - Super-Mystery Comics V1#5, 12/40
Clown - Spitfire Comics #1, 8/41
Cobra Kid - (Black Cobra's sidekick) Captain Flight Comics #8, ?'46
Colossal Boy - (Legion) Action Comics #267, 8/60
Colossus - Tales of Suspense #14, 2/61; Giant-Size X-Men #1, Sum '75
Combat Kelly - Combat Kelly #1, 11/51; (new) Combat Kelly #1, 6/72
Comet - Pep Comics #1, 1/40; (re-intro) Comet #1, 10/83; (S.A.) Advent. of the Fly #30, 10/64
Commando Yank - Wow Comics #6, 7/15/42
Commissioner Gordon - Detective Comics #27, 5/39
Conan, the Barbarian - (1st in comics) Conan, the Barbarian #1, 10/70
Concrete - Dark Horse Presents #1, 7/86
Congo Bill - More Fun Comics #56, 6/40
Congorilla - Action Comics #248, 1/59
Conqueror, The - Victory Comics #1, 8/41
Cookie - Topsy-Turvy #1, 4/45
Corporal Collins - Blue Ribbon Comics #2, 12/39
Cosmic Boy - (Legion) Adventure Comics #247, 4/58
Cosmo Cat - All Top Comics #1, 1945
Cosmo Mann - Bang-Up Comics #1, 12/41
Cosmo, the Phantom of Disguise - Detective Comics #1, 3/37
Cotton Carver - Adventure Comics #50, 5/40
Cougar - The Cougar #1, 4/75
Creeper - Showcase #73, 3-4/67
Crimebuster - Boy Comics #3, 4/42
Crimson Avenger - Detective Comics #20, 10/38
Crusader - Aquaman #56, 3-4/71; (formerly old Marvel Boy) Fantastic Four #164, 11/75
Crypt Keeper - Crime Patrol #15, 12-1/49-50
Crystal - Fantastic Four #45, 12/65
Cyborg - (New Teen Titans) DC Comics Presents #26, 10/80
Cyclone - Whirlwind Comics #1, 6/40
Cyclops - X-Men #1, 9/63
Cyclotronic Man - Black Lightning #4, 7/77
D-Man - Captain America #328, 4/86
Daffy Duck - Looney Tunes & Merrie Melodies #1, 1941
Daimon Hellstrom - (1st full app.) Ghost Rider #2, 10/73; (cameo) (Son of Satan) Ghost Rider #1, 9/73
Daisy Duck - (back cover only) Large Feature Comic #16, 6/41
Dale Daring - Adventure Comics #32, 11/38
Dan Hastings - Star Comics #1, 2/37
Danny Chase - New Teen Titans Annual #3, 1987
Daredevil - Silver Streak Comics #6, 9/40 (blue & yellow costume)
Daredevil - Daredevil #1, 4/64
Darkhawk - Darkhawk #1, 3/91
Darklon the Mystic - Eerie #79, 11/76
Dart & sidekick Ace - Weird Comics #5, 8/40
David - (Samson's aide) Fantastic Comics #10, 9/40
David Marshall - (as himself) Adventure; (as Electra Man) Electra Man #1 , 1980s
Dawnstar - (Legion) Superboy #226, 4/77
Dazzler - X-Men #130, 2/80
Deadman - Strange Adventures #205, 10/67
Deadpool - New Mutants #98, 2/91
Death - Sandman #8, 1990
Death's Head - (new) (1 pg. strip on back-c) Dragon's Claws #3, 9/88; (new) (1st full app.) Dragon's Claws #5, 11?/88
Deathlok the Demolisher - Astonishing Tales #25, 8/74
Deathstroke the Terminator - New Teen Titans #2, 12/80; (1st solo story) New Titans #70, 10/90
Demon - Demon #1, 8-9/72
Dennis the Menace - Dennis the Menace #1, 8/53
Deputy Dawg - New Terrytoons #1, 6-8/60
Destroyer, The - USA Comics #6, 12/42
Destroyer - Invaders #16, 5/77; Mystic Comics #6, 10/41
Destroyer Duck - Destroyer Duck #1, 1982
Destructor - The Destructor #1, 2/75
Devil-Slayer - Marvel Spotlight #33, 4/77
Dial "H" for Hero - (Robby Reed) House of Mystery #156, 11-12/65
Dick Cole - Blue Bolt #1, 6/40
Dick Tracy - (1st comic book app.) Popular Comics #1, 2/36
Dixie Dugan - Feature Funnies #1, 10/37
Doc Samson - Incredible Hulk #141, 7/71
Doc Savage - (1st in comics) Shadow Comics #1, 3/40; (pulp-1st app.) 3/33
Doc Strong - Blue Ribbon Comics #4, 6/40
Doctor (Dr. Who) - (American debut) Marvel Premiere #57, 12/80
Doctor Fate - (female) Doctor Fate #25, 2/91
Doctor Midnight - (new) Infinity, Inc. #21, 12/85
Doctor Solar - Doctor Solar #1, 10/62; (1st in costume) Doctor Solar #5, ?'63
Doctor Strange - Strange Tales #110, 7/63
Dodo & the Frog - Funny Stuff #18, 2/47
Doiby Dickles - (Green Lantern's side-kick) All-American Comics #27, 6/41
Doll Man - Feature Comics #27, 12/39
Dolphin - (of Forgotten Heroes) Showcase #79, 12/68
Dominic Fortune - Marvel Preview #2, 1975; (1st color app.) Marvel Premiere #56, 10/80; (new) Iron Man #213, 12/86
Domino - New Mutants #98, 2/91
Donald Duck - The Wise Little Hen, 1934
Don Winslow - Popular Comics #1, 2/36
Doodles Duck - Dodo & the Frog #80, 9-10/54
Dotty & Ditto - Top-Notch Comics #33, 2/43
Dr. Fate - More Fun Comics #55, 5/40; (Silver Age) Justice League of America #21
Dr. Hypno - Amazing-Man Comics #14, 7/40
Dr. Mid-Nite - (1st story app.) All-American Comics #25, 4/41; (text only) All-American Comics #24, 3/41
Dr. Mystic - (Superman prototype) Comics Magazine #1, 5/36
Dr. Neff, Ghost Breaker - Red Dragon Comics #3, 5/48
Dr. Occult - New Fun Comics #6, 10/35; (1st in color & 1st DC app.) More Fun Comics #14, 10/36
Dr. Specktor - Mystery Comics Digest #5, 7/72
Dr. Strange - Thrilling Comics #1, 2/40
Dr. Strange - Strange Tales #110, 7/63
Dracula - Tomb of Dracula #1, 4/72; Dracula #2, 11/66
Dragon - (1st full app.) Megaton #3, 2/86; (cameo)(later Savage Dragon) Megaton #2, 10/85
Drax the Destroyer - Iron Man #55, 2/73
Dreadstar - Epic Illustrated #15, 12/82
Dream Girl - (Legion) Adventure Comics #317, 2/64
Duo Damsel - (Legion)(formerly Triplicate Girl) Adventure Comics #341, 2/66
Duplicate Boy - Adventure Comics #324
Dusty - (Shield's sidekick) Pep Comics #11, 1/41
Dynamic Man - Mystic Comics #1, 3/40
Dynamite Thor - Blue Beetle #6, 3-4/41
Dynamo - Thunder Agents #1, 11/65; (Electro #1 only) Science Comics #1, 2/40
Dynamo, The Eagle - Weird Comics #8, 11/40
Eagle - Science Comics #1, 2/40
Ebony - Police Comics #12, 10/42
Echo, The - All-New Comics #1, 1/43
Eclipso - House of Secrets #61, 7-8/63
Eddie Brock - (becomes Venom) Amazing Spider-Man #298, 3/88
Egbert - Egbert #1, Spr '46
El Diablo - All Star Western #2, 10-11/70
Elasti-Girl - My Greatest Adventure #80, 6/63
Elastic Lad - (Jimmy Olsen) Superman's Pal Jimmy Olsen #31, ?/62
Electro, the Marvel of the Age - Marvel Mystery Comics #4, 2/40

Elektra - Daredevil #168, ? /81?
Element Girl - Metamorpho #10, 1-2/67
Element Lad - (Legion) Adventure Comics #307, 4/63
Elfquest - Fantasty Quarterly #1, Spr '78
Ella Cinders - Famous Comics Cartoon Books #1203, 1934; Tip Top Comics #1, 4/36
Ellery Queen - (1st app. in comics) Crackajack Funnies #23, 5/40
Elmer Fudd - Looney Tunes & Merrie Melodies #1, 1941
Elongated Man - Flash #112, 4-5/60
E-Man - E-Man #1, 10/73
Enchantress - Journey Into Mystery #103, 4/64
Enemy Ace - Our Army at War #151, 2/65
Erg -1 (becomes Wildfire) Superboy #195,6/73
Eternal Warrior - (cameo) Solar #10, 6/92; (full app.) Solar #11, 7/92
Evangeline - Primer #6, 2/84
Everyman - Captain America #267, 3/82
Face - (Tony Trent) Big Shot Comics #1, 5/40
Faceless Creature - Strange Adv. #124, 1/61
Falcon - Pep Comics #1, 1/40
Falcon - Captain America #117, 9/69; Daring Mystery Comics #5, 6/40
Fantomah, Mystery Woman - Jungle Comics #1, 1/40
Fatman - Fatman the Human Flying Saucer #1, 4/67
Fearless Flint, the Flint Man - Famous Funnies #89, 12/42
Feral - (of X-Force) New Mutants #99, 3/91
Ferret - Man of War #2, 1/42
Ferret, Mystery Detective - Marvel Mystery Comics #4, 2/40
Ferris - (becomes Star Sapphire) Showcase #22, 9-10/59
Ferro Lad - (Legion) Adventure Comics #346, 7/66
Fiery Mask - Daring Mystery Comics #1, 1/40
Fighting American - Fighting American #1, 4-5/54
Fighting Yank - Startling Comics #10, 9/41
Fin - Daring Mystery Comics #7, 4/41
Fin Fang Foom - Strange Tales #89, 10/61
Fire - Super Friends #25
Fireball - Pep Comics #12, 2/41; (S.A.) Mighty Crusaders #4, 5?/66
Firebrand - Police Comics #1, 8/41
Firefist - Blue Beetle #1, 6/86
Firefly - Top-Notch Comics #8, 9/40
Firehair - Rangers Comics #21, 2/45
Firehawk - Fury of Firestorm #17, 10/83
Fire Lad - Adventure Comics #306, 2/63
Firelord - Thor #225, 7/74
FireStar - X-Men #193, 4/85
Firestorm - Firestorm,the Nuclear Man #1, 3/78; (new) Firestorm, the Nuclear Man Annual #5, 10/87
Flag, The - Our Flag Comics #2, 10/41
Flame, The - Wonderworld Comics #3, 7/39
Flamebird - (Jimmy Olsen as) Superman #158, 12/62; (new) Secret Origins Annual #3, 1989
Flaming Carrot - Visions #1, 1979
Flash (Jay Garrick)- Flash Comics #1, 1/40; (1st app. in S.A.) Flash #123, 9/61
Flash (Barry Allen)- Showcase #4, 9-10/56
Flash (Wally West) (former Kid Flash) Flash #110, 12-1/59-60; (as Flash) Crisis on Infinite Earths #12, 3/86
Flash Gordon - King Comics #1, 4/36
Flash Lightning - (becomes Lash Lightning) Sure-Fire Comics #1, 6/40
Flash Rabbit - All Top Comics #1, 1945
Flexo the Rubber Man - Mystic Comics #1, 3/40
Flintstones - Dell Giant #48, 7/61
Fly - Double Life of Private Strong #1, 6/59
Fly Girl - (1st in costume) Adventures of the Fly #14, 9?/61; (w/o costume) Adventures of the Fly #13, 7?/61
Fly-Man, The - Spitfire Comics #1, 8/41
Forbush Man - Not Brand Echh #5, 12/67
Forge - (X-Force) X-Men #184, 8/84
Fox - Blue Ribbon Comics #4, 6/40; (new) Black Hood #11, 11/92
Frankenstein - Prize Comics #7, 12/40; Frankenstein #2, 9/66
Frankenstein's monster - (cameo) Silver Surfer #7, 8/69
Freckles & His Friends - Famous Comics Cartoon Books #1204, 1934
Fred Bender - (becomes Dr. Eclipse) Solar #14, 10/92
Freezum - Blue Bolt V2#5, 10/41
Fritzi Ritz - Tip Top Comics #1, 4/36
Fu Manchu - (1st in Detective) Detective Comics #17, 7/38; (1st cvr.) Det. #1, 3/37
G. I. Robot - Weird War Tales #101, 7/81
Gambit - (cameo) X-Men Annual #14, 1990; (full app.) X-Men #266, 8/90
Gandy Goose - Terry-Toons Comics #1, 10/42
Gangbuster - Adventures of Superman #434, 11/87
Gargoyle - Defenders #94, 4/80
Gary Concord - (Ultra Man) All-American Comics #8, 11/39
Gay Ghost - Sensation Comics #1, 1/42
Genius Jones - All Funny Comics #1, Win '43-44
Gentleman Ghost - Atom & Hawkman #43, 6-7/69
Ghost Breaker - Star Spangled Comics #122, 11/51
Ghost Patrol - Flash Comics #29, 5/42
Ghost Patrol - Wings #66, 2/46
Ghost Rider - (formerly Calico Kid) Tim Holt #11, ?/49
Ghost Rider - (western) Ghost Rider #1, 2/67; (Johnny Blaze) Marvel Spotlight #5, 8/72; (new-Daniel Ketch) Ghost Rider V2#1, 5/90
Giant-Man - (formerly Ant-Man) Tales to Astonish #49, 11/63
Gideon - New Mutants #98, 2/91
Gladstone Gander - Walt Disney's Comics and Stories #88, 1/48
Glory Grant - Amazing Spider-Man #140, 1/75
Gnort - Justice League International #10
God Of Thunder, The - Weird Comics #1, 4/40
Godiva - New Teen Titans Annual #3, 11/87
Golden Arrow - Whiz Comics #1, 2/40
Golden Dragon - Adventure Comics #32, 11/38
Golden Girl - Golden Lad #5, 6/46
Golden Gladiator - Brave and the Bold #1, 8-9/55
Golden Gorilla - Action Comics #224, 1/57
Golden Lad - Golden Lad #1, 7/45
Golem - Strange Tales #174, 2/74
Goliath - (formerly Giant-Man) Avengers #28, 5/66 (formerly Hawkeye) Avengers #63, 4/69
Grandma Duck - Donald and Mickey Merry Christmas nn, 1945
Great Gazoo - (Flintstones) Flintstones #34
Green Arrow - More Fun Comics #73, 11/41
Green Falcon - Blue Ribbon Comics #4, 6/40
Green Flame - Super Friends #42, 3/81
Green Fury - (formerly Green Flame) Infinity, Inc. #32, 11/86
Green Hornet - (1st in comics) Green Hornet Comics #1, 12/40; (Silver Age) Green Hornet #1, 2/67
Green Lama - Prize Comics #7, 12/40
Green Lantern (Alan Scott)- (G.A) All-American Comics #16, 7/40
Green Lantern (Hal Jordan)- (S.A.) Showcase #22, 9-10/59
Green Lantern (Kyle Rayner)- (Mod.) Green Lantern #50 (3rd series), 3/94
Green Mask - Mystery Men Comics #1, 8/39
Green Turtle - Blazing Comics #1, 6/44
Grendel - Primer #2, 2/83
Grey Mask - Suspense Comics #1, 12/43
Grimjack - Starslayer #10, 11/83
Grim Reaper, The - Wonder Comics #1, 5/44
Groo the Wanderer - Destroyer Duck #1, 1982
Gruesomes - (Flintstones) Flintstones #24
Guardian - Star Spangled Comics #7, 4/42; (formerly Vindicator) Alpha Flight #2, 9/83
Guardian Angel - (formerly Hop Harrigan) All-American Comics #25, 4/41
Guardsman I - Iron Man #43, 11?/71?
Guardsman II - Iron Man #96, 3/77
Gunner & Sarge - All-American Men of War #57, ? '58?; Our Fighting Forces #45, 5/59
Guy Gardner - (later a Green Lantern)Green Lantern #59, 3/68; (1st app. as a Green Lantern) Green Lantern #116, 5/79
Gwen Stacy - Amazing Spider-Man #31, 12/65
Gyro Gearloose - Walt Disney's Comics and Stories #140, 5/52
Halo - Blue Beetle #24, 8/43
Hangman - Pep Comics #17, 7/41
Hangman - (re-intro) Comet #6, 12/91; (S.A.) Fly Man #33, 9/65
Happy Houlihans - Blackstone, the Magician Detective #1, Fall '47
Harada - Solar #3, 11/91
Harbinger - Harbinger #1, 1/92
Harlequin - (Joker's Daughter) Teen Titans #48, '77
Harry Osborn - (later becomes Green Goblin II) Amazing Spider-Man #31, 12/65
Harvey Bullock - Batman #361, 7/83
Havok - (no costume) X-Men #56, 5/69; (with costume) X-Men #58, 7/69
Hawk & Dove - Showcase #75, 7-8/67
Hawkeye - Tales of Suspense #57, 9/64; (formerly Goliath) Avengers #98, 4/72
Hawkgirl - (formerly Shiera Sanders) All Star Comics #5, 6-7/41; (Silver Age) Brave & the Bold #34, 2-3/61
Hawkman - Flash Comics #1, 1/40; (S.A.) Brave and the Bold #34, 2-3/61; (modern) Hawkworld: Book #1, 1989
Heap - Air Fighters Comics V1#3, 12/42
Heckle & Jeckle - Terry-Toons Comics #50, 11/46
Hedy Devine - Hedy Devine Comics #22, 8/47
Hedy Wolfe - Miss America Magazine #2, 11/44
Heimdall - Journey Into Mystery #85, 10/62
Hellblazer - (John Constantine) Saga of Swamp Thing #37, 6/85
Hellboy - John Byrne's Next Men #21
Hellcat - Avengers #144, 2/76
Her - (formerly Paragon) Marvel Two-In-One #61, 3/80
Herbie - Forbidden Worlds #73, '59?
Hercules - Blue Ribbon Comics #4, 6/40; Incredible Hulk #3, 9/62; Hit Comics #1 7/40; Mystic Comics #3, 6/40
Herman & Catnip - Harvey Comics Hits #60, 9/52
High Evolutionary - Thor #134, 11/66
Him - (Warlock) (cameo) Fantastic Four #67, 10/67 (Warlock) (full app.) Thor #165, 6/69
Hocus & Pocus - Action Comics #83, 4/45
Hooded Horseman - Blazing West #14, 11-12/50
Hooded Wasp - Shadow Comics #7, 11/40
Hop Harrigan - All-American Comics #1, 4/39
Hoppy the Marvel Bunny - Fawcett's Funny Animals #1, 12/42
Hourman - Adventure Comics #48, 3/40; (1st app. in S.A.) Justice League of America #21, 8/63
Hourman -(new) Infinity, Inc. #21, 12/85
Hourman - (future) JLA #12, 11/97
Howard the Duck - Fear #19, 12/73
Huey, Dewey and Louie - Donald Duck nn (bubble pipe cover)
Hulk - (green skin) Incredible Hulk #2, 7/62; (grey skin) Incredible Hulk #1, 5/62; (new) Incredible Hulk #377, 1/91; (re-intro with grey skin) Incredible Hulk #324, 10/86
Hulk 2099 - 2099 Unlimited #1, 9/93
Human Target - Action Comics #419, 1/73
Human Top - Red Raven Comics #1, 8/40; Tough Kid Squad #1, 3/42
Human Torch - Marvel Comics #1, 10-11/39; (Johnny Storm) Fantastic Four #1, 11/61; (re-intro G.A.) Avengers West Coast #50, 9?/89
Humphrey - Joe Palooka #15, 12/47
Hunchback, The - Wow Comics #2, Spr, 1941
Huntress - (G.A.) Sensation Comics #68, 8/47; (1st S.A. app. of G.A. Huntress) Brave and the Bold #62, 10-11/65; (modern) All Star Comics #69, 11-12/77
Hurricane - Captain America Comics #1, 3/41
Hydroman - Heroic Comics #1, 8/40
Hyper, the Phenomenal - Hyper Mystery Comics #1, 5/40
Ibis the Invincible - Whiz Comics #1, 2/40
Ice - Super Friends #9
Ice Cream Soldier - Our Army at War #85, 8/59
Iceman - X-Men #1, 9/63
Imp - Captain America Comics #12, 3/42
Impossible Man - Fantastic Four #11, 2/63; (re-intro) Fantastic Four #176, 11/76

Impossible Woman - Marvel Two-In-One #60, 2/80
Impulse - Flash #92 (2nd series), 7/94
Inferno - (S.A.) Mighty Crusaders #4, 5?/66
Inferno, the Flame Breather - Zip Comics #10, 1/41
Insect Queen - (Lana Lang) (Legion) Superboy #124, 10/65
Invisible Girl - (Sue Storm) Fantastic Four #1, 11/61
Invisible Kid - (Legion) Action Comics #267, 8/60 (new) Legion of Super-Heroes Annual #1, 1982
Invisible Scarlett O'Neil - Famous Funnies #81, 4/42
Iron Fist - Marvel Premiere #15, 5/74; (re-intro, cameo) Namor, the Sub-Mariner #8, 11/90; (re-intro, full app.) Namor, the Sub-Mariner #10, 1/91
Iron Major - Our Army at War #158, 9/65
Iron Man - (Tony Starks) Tales of Suspense #39, 3/63; (new armor) Tales of Suspense #40, 4/63; (new) (Jim Rhodes) Iron Man #231, 6/88
Iron Wolf - Weird Worlds #8, 11-12/73
Isis - Shazam! #25, ?'76
Jack Monroe - (1st full app.) Captain America #154, 10/72; (cameo) Captain America #153, 9/72
Jack of Hearts - Deadly Hands of Kung-Fu #22, 4?/76; (1st solo book) Marvel Premiere #44, 10/78
Jack Q. Frost - Unearthly Spectaculars #1, 10/65
Jack Woods - Adventure Comics #39, 1/39
Jaguar - Adventures of the Jaguar #1, 9/61
Jarella (Hulk's love) - The Incredible Hulk #140, 6/71
Jason Bard - (becomes Robin) Detective Comics #392, 10/69
Jason Todd - Batman #357, 3/83; (1st in Robin costume) Batman #366, 12/83
Jean DeWolf - Marvel Team Up #48, 8/76
Jester - Smash Comics #22, 5/41
Jigsaw - Jigsaw #1, 9/66
Jiminy Cricket - Mickey Mouse Magazine V5#3, 12/39
Jimmy "Minuteman" Martin - Adventure Comics #53, 8/40
Jimmy Martin as Hourman's aide - Adventure Comics #71, 2/42
Jimmy Olsen - Action Comics #6, 11/38; (new) Man of Steel #2, 10/86
Jo-Jo, Congo King - Jo-Jo Comics #7, 7/47
Joe Palooka - Joe Palooka nn, 1933; (1st in comic book format) Feature Funnies #1, 10/37
Joe Robertson - Amazing Spider-Man #52, 9/67
John Carter of Mars - Funnies #30, 4/39
John Carter, Warlord of Mars - Weird Worlds #1, 8-9/72
John Connor - Terminator #12, ?/89
John Constantine - (Hellblazer) Saga of Swamp Thing #37, 6/85
John Force - (Magic Agent) Magic Agent #1, 1-2/62
John Jameson - Amazing Spider-Man #1, 3/63
John Law - Smash Comics #3, 10/39
John Stewart - (later a Green Lantern) Green Lantern #87, 12-1/71-72
Johnny Blaze - (re-intro) Ghost Rider V2#10, 2/91; (Ghost Rider) Marvel Spotlight #5, 8/72
Johnny Cloud - All-American Men of War #82
Johnny Dynamite - Dynamite #3, 9/53
Johnny Peril - Comic Cavalcade #15, 6-7/46
Johnny Quick - More Fun Comics #71, 9/41
Johnny Thunder - All-American Comics #100, 8/48; Flash Comics #1, 1/40; (1st S.A. app.) Flash #137, ?/63
Jon Linton - Amazing Mystery Funnies V2#11, 11/39
Jonah Hex - All Star Western #10, 2-3/72
J'onn J'onzz (See Martian Manhunter)
Jonni Thunder - (Thunderbolt) Jonni Thunder #1, 2/85
Jonny Double - Showcase #78, 11/68
Jordan Brothers - Green Lantern #9, 11-12/61
Jose Delgado - (becomes Gangbuster) Adventures of Superman #432, 9/87
Jubilee - X-Men #244, 2?/89
Judomaster - Special War Series V4#4, 11/65; (1st DC app.) Crisis on Infinite Earths #6, 9/85
Jughead Jones - Pep Comics #22, 12/41
Julie Madison - Detective Comics #31, 9/39
Jungle Jim - Ace Comics #1, 4/37
Junior Woodchucks - Walt Disney's Comics and Stories #125, 2/51
Kaanga, Lord of the Jungle - Jungle Comics #1, 1/40
Kamandi - Kamandi, the Last Boy on Earth #1, 10-11/72
Karate Kid - (Legion) Adventure Comics #346, 7/66
Karma - (New Mutants) Marvel Team-Up #100, 12/80
Katy Keene - Wilbur Comics #5, Sum '45
Kazar the Great - Marvel Comics #1, 10-11/39; (Silver Age) X-Men #10, 6/64
Ken Shannon - Police Comics #103, 12/50
Kid Eternity - Hit Comics #25, 12/42
Kid Flash - (later becomes Flash) Flash #110, 12-1/59-60
Killer Frost - Firestorm, the Nuclear Man #3, 6-7/78
King Kull - Creatures on the Loose #10, 3/71
Kit - (Black Cat's sidekick) Black Cat Comics #28, 4/51
Kitty Pryde - (Ariel) (X-Men) X-Men #129, 1/80
Kobra - Kobra #1, 2-3/76
Kole - (New Teen Titan) New Teen Titans #8, 5?/85
Kong the Untamed - Kong the Untamed #1, 6-7/75
Kraven - (War of the Worlds) Amazing Adventures #18, 5/73
Krazy Kat - Ace Comics #1, 4/37
Krypto - Adventure Comics #210, 3/55
Kryptonite (Blue) - Superman #128, 4/59
Kryptonite (Gold) - Superman #140, 4/60
Kryptonite (Red) - Adventure #299, 8/62
Kryptonite Kid - Superboy #83, ?/60
Lady Blackhawk - Blackhawk #133, 2/58
Lady Luck - Spirit nn, 6/2/40
Lana Lang - (becomes Insect Queen) Superboy #10, 9-10/50
Lance Hale - Silver Streak Comics #3, 3/40
Lance O'Casey - Whiz Comics #1, 2/40
Lancer - Super-Mystery Comics V3#3, 1/43
Lash Lightning - (formerly Flash Lightning) Lightning Comics V2#2, 8/41
Lassie - Adventures of Lassie nn, ?/49
Lemonade Kid - Bobby Benson's B-Bar-B Riders #15, 6/50
Leopard Girl - Jungle Action #1, 10/54
Li'l Abner - Tip Top Comics #1, 4/36
Li'l Jinx - Pep Comics #62, 7/47
Liberator - Exciting Comics #15, 12/41
Liberty Belle - Star Spangled #20, 5/43
Light Lass - (formerly Lightning Lass) Adventure Comics #317, 2/64
Lightning - Thunder Agents #4, 4/66
Lightning - (cover only) Jumbo Comics #14, 4/40; (1st story app.) Jumbo Comics #15, 5/40
Lightning Boy - (Legion) Adventure Comics #247, 4/58
Lightning Girl - Lightning Comics V3#1, 6/42
Lightning Lad - (formerly Lightning Boy) Adventure Comics #267, 12/59
Lightning Lass - (Legion) Adventure Comics #308, 5/63
Lilith - Vampire Tales #6, ?/74; (Dracula's daughter) Giant-Size Chillers #1, 6/74; (re-intro) New Teen Titans #2, 9/84; (Teen Titans) Teen Titans #25, 1-2/70
Little Audrey - LIttle Audrey #1, 4/48
Little Dot - Sad Sack Comics #1, 9/49
Little Dynamite - Boy Comics #6, 10/42
Little Lotta - LIttle Dot #1, 9/53
Little Lulu - Marge's Little Lulu 4-Color #74, 6/45; (as text illo) King Comics #46, 2/40
Little Max - Joe Palooka #27, 12/48
Little Orphan Annie - Popular Comics #1, 2/36
Little Wise Guys - Daredevil Comics #13, 10/42
LIving Mummy - Supernatural Thrillers #5, 8/73
Liz Allen - Amazing Spider-Man #4, 9/63
Lobo - (1st full story) Omega Men #10, 1/84; (1st solo story, back-up) Omega Men #37, 4/86; (cameo) Omega Men #3, 6/83
Lockheed - X-Men #166, 2/83
Lois Lane - Action Comics #1, 6/38; (new) Man of Steel #2, 10/86
Lois Lane as Superwoman - Action Comics #60, 5/43
Lone Warrior - Banner Comics #3, 9/41
Longshot - Longshot #1, 9/85
Lori Lemaris the Mermaid - Superman #129, 5/59
Lt. Marvels - Whiz Comics #21, 9/41
Lucy Lane - Superman's Pal Jimmy Olsen #36, ?/62
Luke Cage - (Hero for Hire) Hero For Hire #1, 6/72
Lynx & sidekick Blackie - Mystery Men Comics #13, 8/40
Mad Hatter - Mad Hatter #1, 1-2/46
Madame Satan - Pep Comics #16, 6/41
Madame Web - Amazing Spider-Man #210, 11/80
Madelyne Pryor - (of X-Men) Avengers Annual #10, 1981
Madrox - Giant-Size Fantastic Four #4, 2/75
Mage - (re-intro) Grendel #16, 1/88
Magic Morro - Super Comics #21, 2/40
Magician from Mars - Amazing-Man Comics #7, 11/39
Magicman - Forbidden Worlds #125
Magma - New Mutants #10, 12/83
Magno the Magnetic Man & Davey - Super-Mystery Comics V1#1, 7/40
Magnus, Robot Fighter - Magnus, Robot Fighter #1, 2/63
Major Mynah - Atom #37, 6-7/68
Man Bat - Detective #400, 6/70
Man in Black - Front Page Comic Book #1, 1945
Man of War - Man of War #1, 11/41
Manowar - Target Comics #1, 2/40
Man-Thing - Savage Tales #1, 5/71; (1st full story) Fear #15, 8/73
Mandrake the Magician - King Comics #1, 4/36
Manhunter - Police Comics #8, 3/42; (1st in new costume) Detective Comics #437, 10-11/73; (Paul Kirk) Adventure Comics #58, 1/41; (new) Adventure Comics #73, 4/42
Mantis - Avengers #112, 6/73
Margie - Comedy Comics #34, Fall '46
Mark Merlin - House of Secrets #23, 8/59
Marshal Law - Marshal Law #1, 10/87
Martan, the Marvel Man - Popular Comics #46, 12/39
Martian Manhunter - (J'onn J'onzz) Detective Comics #225, 11/55; (re-intro) Justice League of America #228, 7/84
Marvel Boy - (1st & only app.) Daring Mystery Comics #6, 9/40
Marvel Girl - (becomes Phoenix) X-Men #1, 9/63
Marvel Man - (later Quasar) Captain America #217, 1/78
Mary Jane & Sniffles - Looney Tunes & Merrie Melodies #1, 1941
Mary Jane Watson - (1st mention) Amazing Spider-Man #15, 8/64; (cameo, face not shown) Amazing Spider-Man #25, 6/65; (cameo, face shown) Amazing Spider-Man #42, 11/66; (cameo, not shown) Amazing Spider-Man #38, 7/66; (re-intro) Amazing Spider-Man #243, 8/83
Mary Marvel - Captain Marvel Adventures #18, 12/42
Mask, The - Exciting Comics #1, 4/40
Mask, The - Suspense Comics #2, 1944
Masked Marvel - Keen Detective Funnies V2#7, 7/39
Masked Raider - Marvel Comics #1, 10-11/39
Master Key - Scoop Comics #1, 11/41
Master Man - Master Comics #1, 3/40
Master of Kung-Fu - (Shang-Chi) Special Marvel Edition #15, 12/73
Matter-Eater Lad - (Legion) Adventure Comics #303, 12/62
Maximillian O'Leary - (Sargon's aide) All-American Comics #70, 1-2/46
Maya - Atom #1, 6-7/62
Megaton - Megaton #1, 11/83
Menthor - Thunder Agents #1, 11/65
Mento - (non-member) Doom Patrol #91, 11/64
Mentor - Iron Man #55, 2/73
Mera - Aquaman #11, 9-10/63
Merboy - Wonder Woman #107
Mercury - (Silver Streak's sidekick) Silver Streak Comics #11, 6/41
Mercury Man - Space Adventures #44, ?/61?
Metal Men - Showcase #37, 3-4/62
Metallo - (Jor-El's robot) Superboy #49, 6/56
Metamorpho - Brave and the Bold #57, 12-1/64-65

Mickey Finn - (1st comic book app.) Feature Funnies #1, 10/37
Mickey Mouse - Mickey Mouse Book nn, '30
Midnight - Smash Comics #18, 1/41
Mighty Girl - Adventure Comics #453,9-10/77
Mighty Mouse - Terry-Toons Comics #38, 11/45
Mighty Samson - Mighty Samson #1, 7/64
Millie the Model - Gay Comics #1, 3/44
Milton Berle - Uncle Milty #1, 12/50
Minnie Mouse - Mickey Mouse Book nn, 1930
Minute Man - Master Comics #11, 2/41
Minuteman - (re-intro) Shazam! #31,9-10/77
Miss Arrowette - World's Finest #113, 4/60
Miss America - (modern) Giant-Size Avengers #1, 8/74
Miss Masque - Exciting Comics #51, 9/46; America's Best Comics #23, 9/47
Miss Patriot - Marvel Mystery Comics #50, 12/43
Miss Victory - Captain Fearless Comics #1, 8/41
Mister Miracle - Mister Miracle #1, 3-4/71
Mister X - (on cover only) Vortex #2
Moby Duck - Donald Duck #112
Mockingbird - Marvel Team-Up #95, 7/80
Modred the Mystic - Marvel Chillers #1, 10/75
Molly O'Day - Molly O'Day #1, 2/45
Mon-El - (Legion) Superboy #89, 6/61
Monarch Starstalker - Marvel Premiere #32, 10/76
Moon Girl - Happy Houlihans #1, Fall '47; Moon Girl and the Prince #1, Fall '47
Moon Knight - Werewolf by Night #32, 8/75; (1st solo book) Marvel Spotlight #28, 6/76
Moondragon - Iron Man #54, 1/73; (re-intro) Warlock and the Infinity Watch #2, 3/92
Morbius - Amaz. Spider-Man #101, 10/71
Morgan Edge - (cameo) Superman's Pal Jimmy Olsen #133, 10/70
Morlock 2001 - Morlock 2001 #1, 2/75
Morty and Ferdie - (Mickey Mouse's nephews) Mickey Mouse #3, 1933
Moth Man - Mystery Men Comics #9, 4/40
Mr. America - (formerly Tex Thompson) Action Comics #33, 2/41
Mr. Fantastic - (Reed Richards) Fantastic Four #1, 11/61
Mr. Justice - Blue Ribbon Comics #9, 2/41
Mr. Miracle - Captain Fearless Comics #1, 8/41
Mr. Monster - Super Duper Comics #3, 5-6/47; (new) Vanguard Illustrated #7, 5/84
Mr. Mystic - Spirit nn, 6/2/40
Mr. Satan - Zip Comics #1, 2/40
Mr. Scarlet - Wow Comics #1, Win '40-41
Mr. Tawny - Captain Marvel #79, 12/47; (Silver Age) Shazam! #2, 4/73
Mr. Terrific - Sensation Comics #1, 1/42; (1st app. in S.A.) Justice League of America #37, 8?/65
Ms. Marvel - (becomes Binary) Ms. Marvel #1, 1/77
Ms. Victory - Femforce Special #1, Fall '84; (new) Femforce #25
Mutt & Jeff- (1st in comic book format) Funnies #1, 10/36
Mutt & Jeff - Mutt & Jeff #1, 1910
Mystery Men of Mars - All-American Comics #1, 4/39
Nam - Savage Tales #1, 11/85
Namora - Marvel Mystery Comics #82, 5/47
Ned Leeds - (later becomes Hobgoblin) Amazing Spider-Man #18, 11/64
Negative Man - My Greatest Adventure #80, 6/63
Neil the Horse - Charlton Bullseye #2, 8?/81
Nemesis - Adventures into the Unknown #154, ?/66?
Nemesis Kid - (Legion) Adventure Comics #346, 7/66
Neon the Unknown - Hit Comics #1, 7/40
Neuman, Alfred E. - (cover only, fake ad) Mad #21, 3/55
Nevada Jones - Zip Comics #1, 2/40
New Gods - New Gods #1, 2-3/71
Nick Fury - (formerly Sgt. Fury) Strange Tales #135, 8/65
Night Hawk - All-New Comics #1, 1/43
Nightcrawler - Giant-Size X-Men #1, Sum '75
Nightgirl - Adventure Comics #306, 11/63
Nighthawk - Avengers #71, 12/69
Nightmare - (Casper's horse) Casper, the Friendly Ghost #19, 4/54
Nightmaster - Showcase #82, 5/69
Nightshade - Amazing-Man Comics #24, 10/41; Captain Atom #82, 9/66; (1st DC app.) Crisis on Infinite Earths #6, 9/85
Night Thrasher - Thor #412
Nightwing - (Dick Grayson) Tales of the Teen Titans #44, 7/84; (Superman as) Superman #158, 12/62; (Van-Zee) Superman Family #183, 5-6/77
Nita - (later Namorita in New Warriors) Sub-Mariner #50
Nomad - (formerly Steve Rogers) Captain America #180, 12/74
Noman - Thunder Agents #1, 11/65
Norman Osborn - (Green Goblin I) Amazing Spider-Man #37, 6/66
Nova - E-Man #8, 1975
Nth Man - Marvel Comics Presents #25, ?/89
Nukla - Nukla #1, 10-12/65
Nutsy Squirrel - Funny Folks #1, 4-5/46
Nyoka, the Jungle Girl - Jungle Girl #1, Fall/42 (movie serial adaption)
Ocean Master - Aquaman #25, 1-2/66
Odin - (1st full app.) Journey Into Myst. #86, 11/62; (cameo) Journey Into Mystery #85,10/62
Omac - Omac #1, 9-10/74
Omega - Omega the Unknown #1, 3/76
Oracle, The - Startling Comics #20, 2/43
Orion - (New Gods) New Gods #1, 2-3/71; (of New Gods) (1st new costume) First Issue Special #13, 4/76
Oswald the Rabbit - New Fun Comics #1, 2/35
Outlaw Kid - Outlaw Kid #1, 9/54
Owl - Crackajack Funnies #25, 7/40
Pantha - (New Titan) New Titans #74, 3/91
Paragon - (becomes Her) Incredible Hulk Annual #6, 1977
Pat Parker - (in costume) Speed Comics #15, 11/41; (no costume) Speed Comics #13, 5/41
Pat, Patsy & Pete - Looney Tunes & Merrie Melodies #1, 1941
Patchwork Man - (cameo) Swamp Thing #2, 12-1/72-73; (full app.) Swamp Thing #3, 2-3/73
Patriot - Marvel Mystery Comics #21, 7/41; (modern age) Marvel Premiere #29, 4/76
Patsy Walker - Miss America Magazine #2, 11/44
Peacemaker - Fightin' Five V2#40, ?/66; (1st DC app.) Crisis on Infinite Earths #6, 9/85
Pebbles - (Flintstones) Flintstones #11, 6/63
Perry White - Superman #7, 11-12/40
Pete Ross - (Legion) Superboy #86, 1/61; (tryout only) Superboy #77, 9?/59
Peter Parker's parents - Amazing Spider-Man Special #5, 11/68; (re-intro) Amazing Spider-Man #365, 8/92
Peter Porkchops - Leading Comics #23, 2-3/47
Phantasmo, Master of the World -Funnies #45, 7/40
Phantom - Ace Comics #11, 2/38
Phantom Eagle - (S.A.) Marvel Super-Heroes #16, 9/68; (G.A.) Wow Comics #6, 7/42
Phantom Falcon - Wings #68, 4/46
Phantom Girl - (Legion) Action Comics #276, 5/61
Phantom Lady - Police Comics #1, 8/41
Phantom Lady - Phantom Lady #13, 8/47
Phantom of the Fair - Amazing Mystery Funnies V2#7, 7/39
Phantom Rider - Star Comics #16, 12/38
Phantom Stranger - Phantom Stranger #1, 5-6/69
Phoenix - (formerly Marvel Girl) X-Men #101, 10/76
Phoenix II - (Rachel) X-Men #141, 1/81
Pinocchio - (cameo) Mickey Mouse Mag. V5#2, 11/39; (full app.) Mickey Mouse Magazine V5#3, 12/39
Pip the Troll - Strange Tales #179, 4/75
Plastic Man - Police Comics #1, 8/41; (S.A. tryout) House of Mystery #160, 7/66; (S.A.) Plastic Man #1, 11-12/66
Pluto - Thor #127, 4/66
Pluto - (Disney) Mickey Mouse #2, 1932
Pogo - Animal Comics #1, 12-1/41-42
Polar Boy - Adventure #306, 11/63
Polaris - (X-Men) X-Men #44, 5/68
Popsicle Pete - All-American Comics #6, 9/39
Porky Pig - Looney Tunes & Merrie Melodies #1, '41
Pow Wow Smith - Detective Comics #151, 9/49
Power Girl - All Star Comics #58, 1-2/76
Power Man - (Rip Regan) Fight Comics #3, 3/40
Power Nelson the Future Man - Prize Comics #1, 3/40
Powerhouse Pepper - Joker Comics #1, 4/42
Predator - Predator #1, 6/89
Presto Kid - Red Mask #51, 9/55
Prince Ra-Man - (formerly Mark Merlin) House of Secrets #73, 7-8/65
Prince Valiant - Ace Comics #26, 5/39
Princess Pantha - Thrilling Comics #56, 10/46
Princess Projectra - (Legion) Adventure Comics #346, 7/66
Professor Supermind & Son - Popular Comics #60, 2/41
Professor Warren - Amazing Spider-Man #31, 12/65
Professor X - X-Men #1, 9/63
Psylocke - New Mutants Annual #2, 10/86
Punisher - Amaz. Spider-Man #129, 2/74
Punisher 2099 - Punisher War Journal #50, 1/93
Pureheart the Powerful - Archie as Pureheart the Powerful #1, 9/66
Purple Mask - Daring Mystery Comics #3, 4/40
Pyroman - America's Best Comics #3, 11/42; Startling Comics #18, 12/42
Quantum Queen - Adventure Comics #375, 12/68
Quasar - (formerly Marvel Man) Incredible Hulk #234, Apr '79; (re-intro) Avengers #302, 4/89
Question - Captain Atom #83, 11/66; (1st DC app.) Crisis on Infinite Earths #6, 9/85
Quicksilver - National Comics #5, 11/40; X-Men #4, 3/64
Quislet - (Legion) Legion of Super-Heroes #14, 9/85
Quisp - Aquaman #1, 1-2/62
Rachel - (Pheonix II) X-Men #141, 1/81
Radar - Captain Marvel Adventures #35, 5/44; Master Comics #50, 5/44
Rage - Avengers #326, 11/90
Ragman - Ragman #1, 8-9/76
Rags Rabbit - Nutty Comics #5, ?/46
Rai - Magnus Robot Fighter #5, 10/91; (new) Rai #0, 11/92
Rainbow Boy - Heroic Comics #14, 9/42
Randy Robertson - Amazing Spider-Man #67, 12/68
Ravage 2099 - Marvel Comics Presents #117, '92
Raven, The - Sure-Fire Comics #1, 6/40
Raven - Thunder Agents #8, 9?/66; (New Teen Titans) DC Comics Presents #26, 10/80
Rawhide Kid - Rawhide Kid #1, 3/55
Ray - Smash Comics #14, 9/40
Ray O'Light - All-New Comics #1, 1/43
Red Bee - Hit Comics #1, 7/40
Red Blazer - Pocket Comics #1, 8/41; All-New Comics #6, 1/44
Red Demon - Black Cat Comics #4, 2-3/47
Red Dragon - (1st story app.) Red Dragon Comics #6, 3/43; (text app. only) Red Dragon Comics #5, 1/43
Red Guardian - Avengers #43, 8/67; (new) Defenders #3, 5/76
Red Hawk - Blazing Comics #1, 6/44
Red Hawk - Straight Arrow #2, 4-5/50
Red Mask - Best Comics #1, 11/39
Red Raven - Red Raven Comics #1, 8/40; (1st modern app. G.A. Red Raven) X-Men #44, 5/69
Red Rocket - Captain Flight Comics #5, 11/44
Red Rube - Zip Comics #39, 8/43
Red Ryder - (1st app. in comics, strip-r) Crackajack Funnies #9, 3/39
Red Sonja - (1st full app.) Conan, the Barbarian #24, 3/73; (cameo) Conan #23, 2/73
Red Tornado - (formerly Ma Hunkle) All-American Comics #20, 11/40; (S.A.) Justice League of America #64, 8/68
Red White & Blue - All-American Comics #1, 4/39

Red Wolf - Avengers #80, 9/70; (1st solo book) Marvel Spotlight #1, 11/71
Reflecto - (Legion) Legion of Super-Heroes #277, 7/81
Rex Dexter of Mars - Mystery Men Comics #1, 8/39
Rex King - Supersnipe #6, 10/42
Rex The Wonder Dog - Rex the Wonder Dog #1, 1-2/52
Richie Rich - LIttle Dot #1, 9/53
Richy the Amazing Boy - Blue Ribbon Comics #1, 11/39
Rip Hunter - Showcase #20, 5-6/59
Robby Reed - (Dial "H" for Hero) House of Mystery #156, 11-12/65
Robin - (1st app. in S.A.) Justice League of America #55, ?/67; (Batman's sidekick) Detective Comics #38, 4/40; (Jason Todd) Batman #368, 2/84; (Carrie Kelly) Batman: The Dark Knight #2, 4/86; (Timothy Drake) Batman #442 (1st), #457 (official) 12/90
Robin Hood - (DC) Brave and the Bold #5, 4-4/56
Robocop - Robocop #1, 10/87
Robotman - Star Spangled Comics #7, 4/42; (new) Showcase #94, Aug-Sept '77; (S.A.) My Greatest Adventure #80, 6/63
Rocket Girl - Hello Pal Comics #1, 1/43
Rocket Man - Hello Pal Comics #1, 1/43
Rocketeer - (cameo) Starslayer #1, 2/82; (full app.) Starslayer #2, 4/82
Rocketgirl - Scoop Comics #1, 11/41
Rocketman - Scoop Comics #1, 11/41
Rocky X of the Rocketeers - Boy Comics #80
Rogue - (of X-Men) Avengers Annual #10, 1981 (see X-Men #158)
Roh Kar, the Man Hunter from Mars - Batman #78, 8-9/53
Rom - Rom #1, 12/79
Rond Vidar - (Universo's son, Legion) Adventure Comics #349, 10/66
Rose And The Thorn - Superman's Girlfriend Lois Lane #105, 1968
Roy Raymond - Detective Comics #153, 11/49
Roy the Super Boy - Top-Notch Comics #8, 9/40
Rudolph the Red Nosed Reindeer - Rudolph the Red Nosed Reindeer nn, 1939
Ruff and Reddy - Four Color #937, 9/58
Rulah, Jungle Goddess - Zoot #7, 6/47
Rusty & His Pals - Adventure Comics #32, 11/38
Sabre - Eclipse Graphic Album Series #1, 10/78
Sabrina the Teen-age Witch - Archie's Madhouse #22, 10/62
Sad Sack - True Comics #55, 12/46
Saint, The - Silver Streak Comics #18, 2/42
Samson - Fantastic Comics #1, 12/39
Sandman - (1st published app.) New York World's Fair nn, 1939; (1st app. in S.A.) Justice League of America #46, 8/66; (1st conceived story) Adventure Comics #40, 7/39; (modern) Sandman (2nd Series) #1, 1/89
Sandy the Golden Boy - Adventure Comics #69, 12/41
Sarge Steel - Sarge Steel #1, 12/64
Sargon The Sorcerer - All American Comics #26, 5/41
Sasquatch - X-Men #120
Satana - Vampire Tales #2, ?/73
Saturn Girl - Adventure Comics #247, 4/58
Scalphunter - Weird Western Tales #39, 3-4/77
Scarlet Avenger - Zip Comics #1, 2/40
Scarlet Witch - X-Men #4, 3/64
Scorpion - Scorpion #1, 2/75
Scribbly - Funnies #2, 11/36
Sensor Girl - (Legion) Legion of Super-Heroes #14, 9/85
Sergeant Spook - Blue Bolt #1, 6/40
Sgt. Bilko - Sgt. Bilko #1, 5-6/57
Sgt. Fury - (becomes Nick Fury of Shield) Sgt. Fury #1, 5/63
Sgt. Rock - Our Army at War #81, 4/59
Sgt. Rock (by Kubert & Kanigher) - Our Army at War #83, 6/59
Shade the Changing Man - Shade #1, 6-7/77
Shadow - (1st in comics) Shadow Comics #1, 3/40; (DC) The Shadow #1, 10-11/73
Shadowcat - X-Men #129
Shadow Lass - (Legion) Adventure Comics #365, 2/68
Shadow, Jr. - Shadow Comics V6#9, 12/46
Shadowhawk - Youngblood #2, 6/92
Shadowman - Shadowman #1, 5/92; (cameo) X-O Manowar #4, 5/92
Shang-Chi - (Master of Kung-Fu) Special Marvel Edition #15, 12/73
Shanna, the She-Devil - Shanna, the She-Devil #1, 12/72
Shakira - Warlord #32
Sharon Carter - Tales of Suspense #76 (formerly Agent 13), 1966
Shatterstar - (of X-Force) (cameo) New Mutants Annual #6, 1990
Shazam (Captain Marvel) - Shazam #1, 2/73
She-Bat - Detective Comics #424, 6?/72
She-Hulk - Savage She-Hulk #1, 2/80
Sheena - Jumbo Comics #1, 9/38
Sherlock Holmes - Classic Comics #33, 1/47
Shield - Pep Comics #1, 1/40; (S.A.) Adventures of the Fly #8, 9/60
Shiera Sanders - (later becomes Hawkgirl) Flash Comics #1, 1/40
Shining Knight - Adventure Comics #66, 9/41
Shock Gibson - Speed Comics #1, 10/39
Shrinking Violet - (Legion) Action Comics #276, 5/61
Sif - Journey Into Mystery #102, 3/64
Silent Knight - Brave and the Bold #1, 8-9/55
Silly Seal - Krazy Komics #1, 7/42
Silver Fox - Blue Ribbon Comics #2, 12/39
Silver Knight - Wonder Comics #18, 6/48
Silver Sable - Amazing Spider-Man #265, 6/85
Silver Streak - Silver Streak Comics #3, 3/40
Silver Surfer - Fantastic Four #48, 3/66
Siryn - (of X-Force) Spider-Woman #37, 4/81
Skippy - Skippy's Own Book Of Comics, 1934
Skull the Slayer - Skull, the Slayer #1, 8/75
Sky Wizard - Miracle Comics #1, 2/40
Skyman - Big Shot Comics #1, 5/40; (formerly Star Spangled Kid) Infinity, Inc. #31, 10/86
Skywolf - Air Fighters Comics V1#2, 11/42
Slam Bradley - Detective Comics #1, 3/37
Sleepwalker - Sleepwalker #1, 6/91
Snapper Carr - Brave and the Bold #28, 2-3/60
Snow White & the Seven Dwarfs - Mickey Mouse Magazine V3#3, 12/37
Socko Strong - Adventure Comics #40, 7/39
Solomon Kane - (1st color app.) Marvel Premiere #33, 12/76
Son Of Satan (Daimon Hellstrom) - (cameo) Ghost Rider #1, 9/73; (full app.) #2, 10/73
Son of Vulcan - Mysteries of Unexplored Worlds #46, 5/65
Space Ace - Manhunt! #1, 10/47
Space Cabbie - Mystery In Space #21, 8-9/54
Space Museum - Strange Adventures #104, 5/59
Space Ranger - Showcase #15, 7-8/58
Sparkler, The - Super Spy #1, 10/40
Sparkman - Sparkler Comics #1, 7/41
Sparky - (Blue Beetle's sidekick) Blue Beetle #14, 9/42; (Red Blazer's sidekick) All-New Comics #6, 1/44
Sparky Watts - Big Shot Comics #14, 6/41
Spawn - Spawn #1, 5/92
Spectre - (1st full app. in costume) More Fun Comics #54, 4/40; (in costume splash panel) More Fun Comics #52, 2/40; (S.A.) Showcase #60, 1-2/66; (in costume in one panel ad) More Fun Comics #51, 1/40
Speed Centaur - Amazing Mystery Funnies V2#8, 8/39
Speed Saunders - Detective Comics #1, 3/37
Speed Spaulding - Famous Funnies #72, 7/40
Speedball - Amazing Spider-Man Annual #22, '88
Speedboy - (Fighting America's side kick) Fighting American #1, 4-5/54
Speedy - (Green Arrow's sidekick) More Fun Comics #73, 11/41
Spencer Smythe - Amazing Spider-Man #25, 6/65
Spider-Girl - What If...? #105, 2/98
Spider-Man - Amazing Fantasy #15, 8-9/62; (cosmic) Spectacular Spider-Man #158, 12/89
Spider-Man - (black costume) Amazing Spider-Man #252, 5/84
Spider-Man 2099 - Amazing Spider-Man #365, 8/92
Spider-Woman - Marvel Spotlight #32, 2/77; (new) Marvel Super Heroes Secret Wars #7, 11/84
Spirit - Spirit nn, 6/40; (1st comic book app.) Police Comics #11, 9/42
Spooky - Casper, the Friendly Ghost #10, 6/53
Spy Smasher - Whiz Comics #1, 2/40
Stalker - Stalker #1, 6-7/75
Stanley & His Monster - Fox and the Crow #95, 12-1?/65-66
Star Boy - (Legion) Adventure Comics #282, 3/61
Starfire - (Teen Titans) Teen Titans #18, 11-12/68; (new) (New Teen Titans) DC Comics Presents #26, 10/80
Starfox - Iron Man #55, 2/73
Starhawk - (1st full app.) Defenders #28, 10/75; (cameo) Defenders #27, 9/75; (re-intro) Guardians of the Galaxy #22, 3/92
Star-Lord - Marvel Preview #4, 11/75
Starman - Adventure Comics #61, 4/41; (1st app. in S.A.) Justice League of America #29, 8/64; (new) First Issue Special #12, 3/76
Star Sapphire - All-Flash #32, 12-1/47-48; (formerly Ferris) Green Lantern #16, 10/62; (re-intro, 1st full app.) Green Lantern #191, 8/85; (re-intro, cameo) Green Lantern #191, 8/85
Starslayer - Starslayer #1, 2/82
Star Spangled Kid - Action Comics #40, 9/41
Stars and Stripes - Stars and Stripes Comics #4, 9/41
Star Spangled Kid - Star Spangled Comics #1, 10/41
Steel Fist - Blue Circle Comics #1, 6/44
Steel Sterling - Zip Comics #1, 2/40; (Silver Age) Fly Man #39, 9/66
Steel the Indestructable Man - Steel #1, 3/78; (re-intro) All Star Squadron #8, 4/82
Steve Conrad Adventurer - Adventure Comics #47, 2/40
Stone Boy - Adventure Comics #306, 2/63
Storm - Giant-Size X-Men #1, Sum '75
Stormy Foster, the Great Defender - Hit Comics #18, 12/41
Straight Arrow - Straight Arrow #1, 2-3/50
Stranger - X-Men #11, 5/65
Stratosphere Jim - Crackajack Funnies #18, 12/39
Stripesy - Action Comics #40, 9/41
Strongman - Crash Comics #1, 5/40
Stuff - (Vigilante sidekick) Action Comics #45, 2/42
Stumbo the Giant - Hot Stuff, the Little Devil #2, 12/57
Stuntman - Stuntman #1, 4-5/46
Stuntman Stetson - Feature Comics #140, 11/49
Sub-Mariner - (1st newsstand app.) Marvel Comics #1, 10-11/39; (1st published app.?) Motion Pic. Funnies Weekly #1, 1939; (Silver Age) FantasticFour #4, 5/62; (new) Namor, the Sub-Mariner #26, 5/92
Sub-Zero Man - Blue Bolt #1, 6/40
Sun Boy - (Legion) Action Comics #276, 5/61
Sunfire - (X-Men) X-Men #64, 1/70
Super American - Fight Comics #15, 10/41
Superbaby - Superboy #8, 5-6/50
Superboy - More Fun Comics #101, 1-2/45
Super Cat - Animal Crackers #1, 1946
Super Duck - Jolly Jingles #10, Sum '43; (re-intro) Laugh #24, ?/90
Supergirl - Action Comics #252, 5/59; (re-intro) Action Comics #674, 2/92; (tryout only) Superboy #5, 11-12/49
Super Goof - Phantom Blot #2, ?/65
Super Mouse - Coo Coo Comics #1, 10/42
Super Patriot - Nick Fury Agent of Shield #13, 6?/69; (new) Captain America #323, 11/86
Super Rabbit - Comedy Comics #14, 3/43
Super Richie - Richie Rich Millions #68, 11/74
Superichie - Superichie #5, 10/76
Superkatt - Giggle #9, 6/44
Superman - Action Comics #1, 6/38
Superman, Jr. - World's Finest Comics #215, 10/72
Supersnipe - Shadow Comics V2#3, 3/42
Superwoman - DC Comics Presents Annual #2, 7/83
Supreme - Youngblood #3, 10/92
Swamp Thing - House of Secrets #92, 6-7/71

Swift Deer - (J. Thunder's sidekick) All-American Western #113, 4-5/50
Sword - Captain Courageous Comics #6, 3/42; Super-Mystery Comics V3#3, 1/43
T-Man - Police Comics #103, 12/50
Tailspin Tommy - Tailspin Tommy Story & Picture Book #266, 1931; (1st in comic book format) Funnies #1, 10/36
Tank Killer - G. I. Combat #67, 12?/58
Tarantula - All-Star Comics #1, 10/41
Target - Target Comics V1#10, 11/40
Targitt - (in costume) Targitt #2, 6/75; (no costume) Targitt #1, 3/75
Tarzan - Tarzan Book #1, 1929; (1st comic book app.) Tip Top Comics #1, 4/36
Teenage Mutant Ninja Turtles - Teenage Mutant Ninja Turtles #1, 1984
Tellus - (Legion) Legion of Super-Heroes #14, 9/85
Terminator - Rust #12, 8/88
Terra - (New Teen Titan) New Teen Titans #26, 12/82
Terra-Man - Superman #249, 12/71
Terry & The Pirates - Popular Comics #1, 2/36
Tessie the Typist - Joker Comics #2, 6/42
Tex Thompson - (becomes Mr. America) Action Comics #1, 6/38
Thing - (Ben Grimm) Fantastic Four #1, 11/61
Thongor - Creatures On The Loose #22, 1973
Thor - (Beta Ray Bill) Thor #337, 11/83; (Dargo) Thor #384, 10/87; (Donald Blake) Journey Into Mystery #83, 8/62; (Eric Masterson) Thor #433, 6/91
Thorndike - (becomes Hourman's aide)Adventure Comics #74, 5/42
Three Lt. Marvels - Whiz # 21, 9/41; (re-intro) Shazam! #30, 7-8/77
Three-D Man - Marvel Premiere #35, 4/77
Thunderbird - Giant-Size X-Men #1, Sum '75
Thunderbolt - Power Man #41, 10/76; (1st DC app.) Crisis on Infinite Earths #6, 9/85; (Jonni Thunder) Jonni Thunder #1, 2/85; (Peter Cannon) Thunderbolt #1, 1/66
Thunderbunny - Charlton Bullseye #6, 12?/81
Thunderstrike - (Eric Masterson) Thor #459, 2/93
Tick - Tick #1, 6/88
Tiger Girl - Fight Comics #32, 6/44
Tigra - Startling Comics #45, 5/47
Tigra - (formerly The Cat) Giant-Size Creatures #1, 5/75
Tim - (Black Terror's sidekick) Exciting Comics #9, 5/41
Timber Wolf - (Legion) Adventure Comics #327, 12/64
Timecop -Dark Horse Comics #1, 8/82
Timothy Drake - Batman #436, 8/89; (1st in Robin costume) Batman #442, 1990
Timothy the Ghost - Zoo Funnies #1, 7/53
TNT & Dan the Dyna-Mite - World's Finest Comics #5, Spr '42
Todd Hunter - Adventure Comics #32, 11/38
Tom & Jerry - Our Gang Comics #1, 9-10/42
Tom Brent - Adventure Comics #32, 11/38
Tom Mix - The Comics #1, 3/37
Tomahawk - Star Spangled Comics #69, 6/47
Tommy the Amazing Kid - Amazing-Man Comics #23, 8/41
Tommy Tomorrow - Real Fact Comics #6, 1-2/47
Tony Trent - (The Face) Big Shot Comics #1, 5/40
Tor - One Million Years Ago #1, 9/53
Torchy - Doll Man Quarterly #8, Spr '46
Toro - (Human Torch's sidekick) Human Torch #2(#1), Fall '40; (modern) Sub-Mariner #14, 6/69
Torpedo - (new) Daredevil #126, 9/75
Tragg - Mystery Comics Digest #3, ?/72
Trail Colt - Manhunt! #8, 5/48
Triplicate Girl - (Legion) Action Comics #276, 5/61
Tubby - King Comics #46, 2/40; Marge's Little Lulu Four Color #74, ? '45
Tuk the Cave Boy - Captain America Comics #1, 3/41
Turbo - New Warriors #28, 10/92
Turok - Turok Four Color #596, 12/54; (re-intro in Valiant Universe) Magnus Robot Fighter #12, 5/92
Two Gun Kid - Two Gun Kid #1, 3/48
Ty-Gor, Son of the Tiger - Blue Ribbon Comics #4, 6/40
Tygra - Startling Comics #45, 5/47
Tyroc - (Legion) Superboy #216
U.S. Agent - Captain America #354, 6/89
Ultra Boy - (Legion) Superboy #98, 7/62
Ultra Man - (Gary Concord) All-American Comics #8, 11/9
Uncle Ben - Amazing Fantasy #15, 8-9/62
Uncle Marvel - Wow Comics #18, 10/43
Uncle Sam - National Comics #1, 7/40
Uncle Scrooge - Donald Duck 4-Color #178, 12/47
Underdog - Underdog #1, 7/70
Union Jack I - Invaders #7, 7/76
Union Jack II - Invaders #20, 9/77
Union Jack III - Captain America #254, 2/81
Unknown Soldier - Star Spangled War Stories #151, 6-7/70
Untouchables - Four Color 1237, 10-12/61
Usagi Yojimbo - Albedo #1, 4/85
U.S. Jones - Wonderworld #28, 8/41
Val - Strange Tales #159, 8/67
V-Man - Big-3 #7, 1/42; V...- Comics #1, 1/42
Valkyrie - Air Fighters Comics V2#2, 11/43
Vampirella - Vampirella #1, 9/69
Vanessa - (Kingpin's wife) Amazing Spider-Man #83, 4/70
Vanguard - New Teen Titans Annual #1, 1985; Iron Man #109, Apr '78; Megaton #1, 11/83
Vault Keeper - War Against Crime #10, 12-1/49-50
Veiled Avenger - Spotlight Comics #1, 11/44
Venus - Venus #1, 8/48
Veronica Lodge - Pep Comics #26, 4/42
Vicki Vale - Batman #45, 2-3/48
Victoria Bentley - Strange Tales #114, 11/63
Victory Boys - USA Comics #5, Sum '42
Vigilante - Action Comics #42, 11/41; (female) (1st full app.) Deathstroke: the Terminator #10, 5/92; (female) (cameo) Deathstroke: the Terminator #9, 4/92; (modern, in costume) New Teen Titans Annual #2, 1985; (modern, not in costume) New Teen Titans #23, 9/82; (S.A.) Justice League of America #78, 2/70
Viking Prince - Brave and the Bold #1, 8-9/55
Vindicator - (formerly Weapon Alpha) (becomes Guardian) X-Men #120, 4/79
Vision - (G.A.) Marvel Mystery Comics #13, 11/40; (S.A.) Avengers #57, 10/68
Vixen - Action Comics #521, 7/81
Voice, The - Popular Comics #51, 5/40
Voltage, Man of Lightning - Fat & Slat #1, Sum '47
Vulcan - Super-Mystery Comics V1#1, 7/40
Wagon Train - Four Color #895, 3/58
Wambi, Jungle Boy - Jungle Comics #1, 1/40
Warlock - (Him) (cameo) Fantastic Four #67, 10/67; (Him) (full app.) Thor #165, 6/69; (new) New Mutants #18, 8/84; (re-intro) Silver Surfer #46, 2/91
Warlord - First Issue Special #8, 11/75
Warpath - (with costume) X-Men #193, 5/85; (without costume) New Mutants #16, 6/84
Wash Tubbs - Famous Comics Cartoon Books #1202, 1934
Wasp, The - Speed Comics #12, 3/41
Wasp - Tales to Astonish #44, 6/63
Wasplet - (Hooded Wasp's sidekick) Shadow Comics #7, 11/40
Watcher - Fantastic Four #13, 4/63
Waverider - Armageddon 2001 #1, 5/91
Weapon Alpha - (becomes Vindicator) X-Men #109, 2/78
Web - Zip Comics #27, 7/42; (S.A.) Fly Man #36, 3/66
Wendigo - Incredible Hulk #162, 4/73
Wendy the Good Little Witch - Casper, the Friendly Ghost #20, ?/54
Werewolf - Werewolf #1, 12/66
Werewolf by Night - Marvel Spotlight #2, 1?/72
Whirlybats - Detective Comics #257, 7/58
White Rider & Super Horse - Blue Bolt #1, 6/40
White Streak - Target Comics V1#1, 2/40
White Tiger - Deadly Hands of Kung-Fu #19, 1?/76
White Witch - (Legion) Adventure Comics #351, 12/66
Whizzer, The - USA Comics #1, 8/41; (modern) Giant-Size Avengers #1, 8/74
Whizzer McGee - (Phantasmo's side kick) Funnies #45, 7/40
Wiggles the Wonderworm - Taffy Comics #1, 3/45
Wilbur - Zip Comics #18, 9/41
Wild Bill Elliott - Four Color #278, 5/50
Wildcat - Sensation Comics #1, 1/42; (S.A.) Brave and the Bold #62, 10-11/65
Wildfire - (formerly Erg-1) Superboy #201, 4/74
Will O' the Wisp - Amazing Spider-Man #167, 4/77
Willie - Gay Comics #1, Mar '44
Winky, Blinky & Noddy - All-Flash #5, Sum '42
Witchblade - Cyblade/ Shi #1, 1995
Witch Hazel - Marge's Little Lulu #39, 9/51
Witness - Mystic Comics #7, 12/40
Wizard - Top-Notch Comics #1, 12/39; (S.A.) Fly Man #33, 9/65
Wizard - Strange Tales #102, 11/62
Wolverine - (1st full app.) Incredible Hulk #181, 11/74; (cameo) Incredible Hulk #180, 10/74
Wonder Boy - Blue Bolt #1, 6/40; National Comics #1, 7/40
Wonder Boy - Bomber Comics #1, 3/44
Wonder Duck - Wonder Duck #1, 9/49
Wonder Girl - Wonder Woman #107, 7/61; (new) (Teen Titan) Brave and the Bold #60, 6-7/65
Wonder Man - Startling Comics #1, 6/40
Wonderman - Wonder Comics #9, 1945
Wonder Man - Avengers #9, 10/64; Wonder Comics #1, 5/39; (re-intro) Avengers #151, 9/76
Wonder Tot - Wonder Woman #122
Wonder Woman - All Star Comics #8, 12-1/41-42; (Orana) Wonder Woman #250, 12/78
Wonder Woman Family - Wonder Woman #124, 12/62
Wonderman - (Brad Spencer) Mystery Comics #1, 1944
Wong - Strange Tales #110, 7/63
Woodgod - Marvel Premiere #31, 8/76
Woody Woodpecker - Funnies #64, 5/42
Woozy Winks - Police Comics #13, 11/42
X-O Manowar - X-O Manowar #1, 2/92
XS - (Legion) Legionnaires #0, 10/94
X-Terminators - X-Terminators #1, 10/88
Yank and Doodle - Prize Comics #13, 8/41
Yankee Doodle Jones - Yankee Comics #1, 9/41
Yarko the Great, Master Magician - Wonder Comics #2, 6/39
Yellow Claw - Yellow Claw #1, 10/56
Yellowjacket - Yellowjacket #1, 9/44
Yellowjacket - Avengers #59, 12/68; (formerly Goliath) Avengers #63, 4/69
Yogi Bear - Four Color #1067, 12-2/59-60
Yosemite Sam - Yosemite Sam #1, 12/70
Zanzibar - Mystery Men Comics #1, 8/39
Zardi, the Eternal Man - Amazing-Man Comics #11, 4/40
Zatanna - Hawkman #4, 10-11/64
Zatara - Action Comics #1, 6/38
Zebra - All-New Comics #7, 3/44; Pocket Comics #1, 8/41
Zegra, Jungle Empress - Zegra #2, 10/48
Ziggy Pig - Krazy Komics #1, 7/42
Zombie - Menace #5, 7/53
Zorro - Zorro Four Color #228, 5/49

FIRST APPEARANCES: VILLAINS

Abomination - Tales to Astonish #90, 4/67
Abra Kadabra - Flash #128, 2?/62
Absorbing Man - Journey Into Mystery #114, 3/65
Amazo The Android - Brave & The Bold #30, 6-7/60
Angle Man - Wonder Woman #70, 11/54
Annihilus - Fantastic Four Annual #6, 11/68
Apocalypse - (cameo) X-Factor #5, 6/86; (full app.) X-Factor #6, 7/86
Arcade - Marvel Team-Up #66, 2/78
Atomic Skull - Superman #323, 5/78; (modern) Action Comics #670, 10/91
Attuma - Fantastic Four #33, 12/64
Bane - Batman: Vengeance of Bane Special #1, '92
Banshee - X-Men #28, 1/67
Baron Blood - Invaders #7, 7/76
Baron Mordo - Strange Tales #111, 8/63
Baron Strucker - Sgt. Fury #5, 1963
Baron Zemo - Captain America #276
Batmite - Detective #267, 5/59
Batroc - Tales of Suspense #76, 4/66
Beetle - Strange Tales #123, 8/64
Bengal - Daredevil #258, 9/88
Beyonder - Marvel Two-In-One #63, 1986
Big Man - Amazing Spider-Man #10, 3/64
Bizarro - Superboy #68, 10-11/56
Bizarro Batman - World's Finest Comics #156
Bizarro Flash - Superman's Girlfriend Lois Lane #74, 5/67
Bizarro Krypto - Superboy #82, ?/60
Bizarro Lana Lang - Adventure Comics #292, 1/62
Bizarro Lucy Lane -Adventure Comics #292, 1/62
Bizarro Lex Luthor - Adventure Comics #293, 2/62
Bizarro Lois Lane - Action Comics #255, 8/59
Bizarro Mxyzptlk - Adventure Comics #286, 7/61
Bizarro Supergirl - Superman #140, 10/60
Bizarro Titano - Adventure Comics #295, 4/62
Black Cat - Amazing Spider-Man #194, 7/79
Black Mask - Batman #386, 8/85
Blackout - Ghost Rider #2, 6/90
Black Racer - New Gods #3, 6-7/71
Black Spider - Detective Comics #463
Blastarr - Fantastic Four #62, 5/67
Blizzard - Iron Man #86, ?/76?
Blob - X-Men #3, 1/64
Blockbuster - Detective Comics #345, 11/65
Boomerang - Tales to Astonish #81, 7/66
Brain Storm - Justice League of America #32, 12/64
Brain Wave - All Star Comics #15, 2-3/43
Brainiac - Action Comics #242, 7/58; (modern) Adventures of Superman #438, 2/88
Brainwasher - (Kingpin) Amazing Spider-Man #59, 4/68
Brother Blood - New Teen Titans #21, 7/82
Brother Voodoo - Strange Tales #169, 9/73
Bullet - Daredevil #250, 12/88
Bullseye - Nick Fury Agent of Shield #15, 11/69
Calypso - Amazing Spider-Man #209, 10/80
Captain Boomerang - Flash #117, 12/60
Captain Cold - Showcase #8, 5-6/57
Captain Fear - Adventure Comics #425, 12-1/72-73
Captain Nazi - Master Comics #21, 12/41
Cardinal - New Warriors #28, 10/92
Carnage - (1st full app.) Amazing Spider-Man #361, 4/92; (cameo) Amazing Spider-Man #360, 3/92
Carrion - Spectacular Spider-Man #25, 12/78
Cat-Man - Detective Comics #311, 1/63
Catwoman - (1st in costume) Batman #3, Fall '40; (1st time called Catwoman) Batman #2, Sum '40; (modern, Selina Kyle) Batman #404, 2/87; (new costume w/o cat-head mask) Batman #35, 5-6/46; (new) Detective Comics #624, 12/90; (S.A.) Superman's Girlfriend Lois Lane #70, 11/66; (The Cat) Batman #1, Spr '40
Cavalier - Detective Comics #81, 11/43
Chameleon - Amazing Spider-Man #1, 3/63
Changeling - X-Men #35, 8/67
Cheetah - Wonder Woman #6, Fall '43; (new) (cameo) Wonder Woman #274, 12/80; (new) (full app.) Wonder Woman #275, 1/81
Chronos - Atom #3, 10-11/62
Chunk - Flash #9, 2/88
Claw - Silver Streak Comics #1, 12/39
Clayface I - (Basil Karlo) Detective Comics #40, 6/40
Clayface II - (Matt Hagen) Detective Comics #298, 12/61
Clayface III - (Preston Payne) Detective Comics #478, 7-8/78
Clock King - World's Finest Comics #111, 8/60
Clown - Flash #270, 2/79
Cobra (see Human Cobra)
Colonel Computron - Flash #304, 12/81
Composite Superman - World's Finest #142
Computo - Adventure Comics #340, 1/66
Constrictor - Incredible Hulk #212, 6/77
Copperhead - Daredevil #124, 6?/75
Crime Master - Amazing Spider-Man #26, 7/65
Crimson Dynamo - (Anton Vanko) Tales of Suspense #46, 10/63
Crimson Dynamo II - (Boris Turgenov) Tales of Suspense #52, 4/64
Crimson Dynamo III - (Alex Nevsky) Iron Man #21, 3/78
Crimson Dynamo IV - (Yuri Petrovich) Champions #8, 10/76
Crimson Dynamo V - (Dimitri Bukharin) Iron Man #109, 4/78
Cyborg - (Superman impersonator) Adventures of Superman #466, 5/90
Cyclone - Amazing Spider-Man #143, 4/75
Dark Phoenix - X-Men #134
Darkseid - (1st full app.) Forever People #1, 2-3/71; (cameo) Superman's Pal Jimmy Olsen #134, 12/70
Deadshot - Batman #59, 6-7/50; (1st modern app.) Detective Comics #474, 11-12/77
Death's Head - Daredevil #56, 9/69
Deathstalker - (formerly Death's Head) Daredevil #114, 7/?/74
Demogoblin - Web of Spider-Man #86, 3/92
Despero - Justice League of America #1, 10-11/60
Destroyer - Journey Into Mystery #118, 7/65
Dev-Em, the Knave from Krypton - Adventure Comics #287, 8/61
Diablo - Fantastic Four #30, 9/64
Doctor Destiny - Justice League of America #5, 6-7/61
Doctor Doom - Fantastic Four #5, 6/62
Doctor Light I - Justice League of America #12, 6/62
Doctor Light II - Crisis on Infinite Earths #4, 6/85
Doctor Octopus - Amazing Spider-Man #3, 6/63
Doctor Polaris - Green Lantern #21, 6/63
Doctor Regulus - Adventure Comics #348, 9/66
Doom 2099 - Marvel Comics Presents #118, '92
Doomsday - (cameo) Superman: The Man of Steel #17, 11/92; (full app.) Superman: The Man of Steel #18, 12/92
Dormammu - Strange Tales #126, 11/64
Dr. Death - (modern) Batman #345, 3/82
Dr. Doom - Fantastic Four #5, 6/62
Dr. Double X - Detective Comics #261, 11/58
Dr Light - Justice League of America #12, '62
Dr. Octopus - Amazing Spider-Man #3, 5/63
Dr. Phosphorous - Detective Comics #469
Dr. Psycho - Wonder Woman #5, 6-7/43
Dr. Spectro - Captain Atom #78, 12/65; (new) Captain Atom #6, 8/87; (1st DC app.) Crisis on Infinite Earths #9, 12/85
Dragon Man - Fantastic Four #35, 2/65
Drax the Destroyer - (re-intro) (cameo) Silver Surfer #35, 3/90; (re-intro) (full app.) Silver Surfer #37, 5/90
Dreadknight - Iron Man #101, 8/77
Dragon Man - Fantastic Four #35, 2/65
Dummy - (Vigilante villain) Leading Comics #1, Win '41-42
Electro - Amazing Spider-Man #9, 2/64
Enchantress - Journey Into Mystery #103, 4/64
Enchantress - Strange Adventures #187
Enforcer - Ghost Rider #22, ?/77
Evil Star - Green Lantern #37, 7/65
Exterminator - (becomes Death-Stalker) Daredevil #39, 4/68
Fatal Five - Adventure Comics #352, 1/67
Fatman - Batman #113, 2/58
Felix Faust - Justice League of America #10, 3/62
Fiddler - All-Flash #32, 12-1/47-48
Fin Fang Foom - Strange Tales #89, 10/61
Firelord - Thor #225
Foolkiller - (1st) Man-Thing #3, 3/74
Foolkiller II - (Greg Salinger) (cameo) Omega the Unknown #8, 5/77; (Greg Salinger) (full app.) Omega the Unknown #9, 7/77
Galactus - Fantastic Four #48, 3/66
Gambler - Green Lantern #12, Sum '44
Gamora - Strange Tales #180, 6/75; (re-intro) Silver Surfer #46, 2/91
Gentleman Ghost - (modern) Batman #310, 4/79
Gibbon - Amazing Spider-Man #110, 7/72
Gladiator - Daredevil #18, 7/66
Golden Glider - Flash #250, 6/77
Gorgon - Fantastic Four #44, 11/65
Gorilla Grodd, the Super Gorilla - Flash #106, 4-5/59
Green Goblin I - (Norman Osborn) Amazing Spider-Man #14, 7/64
Green Goblin II - (Harry Osborn) Amazing Spider-Man #136, 9/74
Grey Gargoyle - Journey Into Mystery #107, 8/64
Grim Reaper - Avengers #52, 5/68
Grizzly - Amazing Spider-Man #139, 12/74
Hammerhead - Amazing Spider-Man #113, 10/72
Harlequin - All-American Comics #89, 9/47
Hate Monger - Fantastic Four #21, 12/63
Havoc - (not in costume) X-Men #56; (in costume) #58
Heat Wave - Flash #140, 6/63
Hector Hammond - Green Lantern #5, 3-4/61
Hela - Journey Into Mystery #102, 3/64
High Evolutionary - Thor #134, 11/66
Hobgoblin - (new) (Macendale) Spectacular Spider-Man #147, 2/89
Hobgoblin I - (Ned Leeds) Amazing Spider-Man #238, 3/83
Hobgoblin II - (Macendale/Jack O'Lantern) Amazing Spider-Man #289, 6/87
Hugo Strange - (1st modern app.) Detective Comics #470, 3-4/77
Human Cobra - Journey Into Mystery #98, 11/63
Human Top - (Whirlwind) Tales to Astonish #50, 12/63
Humbug - Web of Spider-Man #19, 10/86
Hydro Man - Amazing Spider-Man #212, 12/81
Hyena - Firestorm #4, 8-9/78
Icicle - All-American Comics #90, 10/47
Insect Queen - (Lana Lang) Superboy #124, 10/65
Iron Jaw - Boy Comics #3, 4/42
Jack O'Lantern - (Macendale) Machine Man #19, 2/81; (new) Captain America #396, 1/92
Jackal - Amazing Spider-Man #129,

2/74
Jester - Daredevil #42 ,7/68
Jigsaw - Amazing Spider-Man #188, 1/79
Joker - Batman #1, Spr '40
Joker's Daughter - Batman Family #6, 7-8/76
Juggernaut - X-Men #12, 7/65
Kang - Avengers #8, 9/64
Kanjar Ro - Justice League of America #3, 2-3/61
Key, The - Justice League of America #41, 12/65
Killer Croc - Batman #357, 3/83
Killer Shark - Blackhawk #50, 3/52
Kingpin - Amazing Spider-Man #50, 7/67
Klaw - Fantastic Four #53, 8/66
Kraven the Hunter - Amazing Spider-Man #15, 8/64
Kurgo - Fantastic Four #7, 10/62
Leader - Tales to Astonish #62, 12/64
Legion of Super Villains - Superman #147, 8/61
Lex Luthor - (bald) Superman #10, 5-6/41; (new) Man of Steel #4, 12/86; (red hair) Action Comics #23, 5/40; (Silver Age) Adventure Comics #271, 4/60
Lightmaster - Spectacular Spider-Man #3, 2/77
Living Monolith - X-Men #56
Lizard - Amazing Spider-Man #6, 11/63
Loki - Journey Into Mystery #85, 10/62
Looter - Amazing Spider-Man #36, 5/66
Lord Shilling - (Tomahawk foe) Tomahawk #28, 11/54
Lunatik - (1st full app.) Defenders #56, 2/78; (cameo) Defenders #53, 11/77
Mad Hatter - Batman #49, 10-11/48; Detective Comics #230, 4/56
Mad Thinker - Fantastic Four #15, 6/63
Madame Medusa - Fantastic Four #36, 3/65
Maelstrom - Marvel Two-In-One #71, 1/81
Magica de Spell-Uncle Scrooge #36, 12/62
Magneto - X-Men #1, 9/63
Magpie - (new) Man of Steel #3, 11/86
Magus - Strange Tales #178, 2/75; (re-intro) Warlock and the Infinity Watch #7, 8/92
Malevolence - (Mephisto's daugh ter) Guardians of the Galaxy #7, 12/90
Man-Ape - Avengers #62
Man-Bat - Detective Comics #400, 6/70
Man-Wolf - Amazing Spider-Man #124, 9/73
Mandarin - Tales of Suspense #50, 2/64
Manhunters - 1st Issue Special #5, 8/75
Mephisto - Silver Surfer #3, 12/68
Metallo (Jor-El's robot) - (1st app.) Superboy #49, 6/56; (new) Superman #310, 4/77; (new) Superman #1, 1/87; (re-intro) Action Comics #252, 5/59; (re-intro, 3rd app.) Adventure Comics #276, 9/60
Microwave Man - Action Comics #487, 9/78
Mime - Batman #412, 10/87
Mimic - X-Men #19, 4/66
Mirror Master - Flash #105, 2-3/59
Mist - Adventure Comics #67, 10/41
Mister Element - Showcase #13, 3-4/58
Mister Sinister - X-Men #221
Modok - Tales of Suspense #94, 10/67
Modred the Mystic - (re-intro) Darkhold #3, 12/92
Mole Man- Fantastic Four #1, 11/61
Molecule Man - Fantastic Four #20, 11/63
Molten Man - Amazing Spider-Man #28, 9/65
Morbius the Living Vampire - Amazing Spider-Man #101, 10/71
Mordru - Adventure Comics #369, 6/68
Mortan - (Adam Strange foe) Mystery In Space #62
Mr. Atom - Captain Marvel Adventures #78, 11/47
Mr. Baffle - Detective Comics #63, 5/42
Mr. Freeze - Batman #121, 2/59
Mr. Hyde - Journey Into Mystery #99,12/63
Mr. Mind - Captain Marvel Adventures #22, 3/43; (re-intro) Shazam! #2, 4/73
Mr. Mxyzptlk - Superman #131, 8/59; (new) Superman #11, 11/87; Superman #30, 10/44
Mr. Tawny - Captain Marvel Adventures #79, 12/47
Multi-Man - Challengers of the Unknown #14, 12-1/59-60
Mysterio - Amazing Spider-Man #13, 6/64
Nightmare - Strange Tales #110, 7/63
Nightshade - Captain America #164, 8/73
Nitro - Captain Marvel #34, 9/74
Ocean Master - Aquaman #29
Outsider - Detective Comics #334, 12/64
Owl - Daredevil #3, 8/64
Paladin - Daredevil #150, 2/78
Parasite - Action Comics #340, 8/66; Fury of Firestorm #58, 4/87
Peg-leg Pete - Mickey Mouse #3, 1933
Penguin - Detective Comics #58, 12/41; (S.A.) Batman #155, 4/63
Pied Piper - Flash #106, 4-5/59
Pieface - Green Lantern #2, 9-10/60
Plant-Master - Atom #1, 6-7/62
Plunderer - Daredevil #12, 1/66
Poison Ivy - Batman #181, 6/66
Porcupine - Tales To Astonish #48, 10/63
Prankster - Action Comics #51, 8/42
Princess Python - Amazing Spider-Man #22, 3/65
Professor Amos Fortune - Justice League of America #6, 8-9/61
Professor Zoom - Flash #139, ?/63
Prowler - Amazing Spider-Man #78, 11/69
Psycho Pirate - All Star Comics #23, Win '44-45
Psycho-Man - Fantastic Four Annual #5, 11/67
Puma - Amazing Spider-Man #256, 9/84
Punisher - Amazing Spider-Man #129, 2/74
Puppet Master - Batman #3, Fall '40; Fantastic Four #8, 11/62
Rainbow Raider - Flash #286, 6/80
Rama-Tut - Fantastic Four #19, 10/63
Rampage - Superman #7, 7/87
Rancor - (1st full app.) Guardians of the Galaxy #9, 2/91; (cameo) (descendant of Wolverine) Guardians of the Galaxy #8, 1/91
Ras Al Ghul - Batman #232, 7/71
Reaper - Batman #237, 12/71
Red Ghost - Fantastic Four #13, 4/63
Red Skull - Captain America Comics #1, 3/41; (S.A.) Tales of Suspense #65, 5/65
Rhino - Amazing Spider-Man #41, 10/66
Riddler - Detective Comics #140, 10/48; (S.A.) Batman #171, 5/65
Ringmaster - Incredible Hulk #3, 9/62
Rose - Amazing Spider-Man #253, 6/84
Rose and the Thorn - Flash Comics #89, 11/47; (new) Superman's Girlfriend Lois Lane #105
Saber-Tooth - Flash #291, 11/80
Sabretooth - Iron Fist #14, 8/77
Sandman - Amazing Spider-Man #4, 9/63
Sandstorm - Web of Spider-Man #107, 12/93
Sargon - (re-intro) Flash #186, 8?/69
Sargon the Sorcerer - (1st story app.) All-American Comics #26, 5/41; (text only) All-American Comics #24, 3/41
Sauron - X-Men #60
Scarecrow - Tales of Suspense #51, 3/64; World's Finest Comics #3, Fall '41; Dead of Night #11, 8/75; (S.A.) Batman #189, ? '67?
Schemer - Amazing Spider-Man #83, 4/70
Scorpion - Amazing Spider-Man #20, 1/65
Serpent Crown - Sub-Mariner #9, 1/69
Sha-Shan - Amazing Spider-Man #108, 5/72
Shade - (modern) Flash #298, 6/81
Shadow Thief - Brave and the Bold #36,6-7/61
Shaper - Incredible Hulk #155, 9/72
Shark - Amazing-Man Comics #6, 10/39; Green Lantern #24, 10/63
Shocker - Amazing Spider-Man #46, 3/67
Shotgun - Daredevil #272, 9?/89
Shroud - Super-Villain Team-Up #5, 4/76
Signalman - Batman #112, 12/57; (S.A.) Detective Comics #466
Silver Banshee - Action Comics #495, 12/87
Silvermane - Amazing Spider-Man #73, 6/69
Silver Samurai - Daredevil #111, 6/74
Sinestro - Green Lantern #7, 7-8/61
Sivana - Whiz Comics #1, 2/40
Sivana, Jr. - Captain Marvel Adventures #52, 1/46
Sky Pirate - Green Lantern #27, 8-9/47
Solarr - Captain America #160, 4/73
Solo - Web of Spider-Man #19, 10/86
Solomon Grundy - All-American Comics #61, 11/44; (S.A.) Showcase #55, 3-4/65
Sonar - Green Lantern #14, 7/62
Sorcerer - Alpha Flight #71, 5/89
Speed McGee - Flash #5, 10/87
Spirit of Vengeance - (futuristic Ghost Rider) Guardians of the Galaxy #13, 6/91
Spyder - New Mutants #68, 10/88
Star Thief - Warlock #14, 10/76
Stilt-Man - Daredevil #8, 6/65
Sting Ray - Sub-Mariner #19, 11/69
Stranger - X-Men #11, 5/65
Sub-Mariner - (S.A) Fantastic Four #4, 5/62
Sunburst - New Adventures of Superboy #45, 9/83
Super Skrull - Fantastic Four #18, 9/63
Supremo - Superboy #132, ?/66
Swordsman - Avengers #19, 8/65
Tantrum - Night Thrasher: Four Control #2, 11/92
Tarantula - Amazing Spider-Man #134, 7/74
Taskmaster - Avengers #119, 1/80
Tattooed Man - Green Lantern #23, 9?/63
Terra-Man - Superman #249, 4/72
Terrax - Fantastic Four #211, 10/79
Terrible Tinkerer - Amazing Spider-Man #2, 5/63
Thanos - Iron Man #55, 2/73; (re-intro) (cameo) Silver Surfer #34, 2/90; (re-intro) (full app.) Silver Surfer #35, 3/90
Thinker - All-Flash #12, Fall '43
Thundra - Fantastic Four #129, 12/72
Tiger Shark - (new) Namor, the Sub-Mariner #35, 2/93; (S.A.) Sub-Mariner #5, 9/68
Time Trapper - Adventure Comics #321, 6/64
Titanium Man - Tales of Suspense #69, 9/65
Titano - Superman #127, 2/59
Toad - X-Men #4, 3/64
Tombstone - Web of Spider-Man #36, 3/88; (full app.) Spectacular Spider-Man #138, 5/88
Top - Flash #122, 6-7?/61
Torpedo - Daredevil #126, 8?/75
Toyman - Action Comics #64, 9/43; (new) Superman #13, 1/88; (S.A.) Action Comics #432, 2/74
Trapster - Strange Tales #104, 1/63
Trauma - Incredible Hulk #394, 6/92
Trickster - Flash #113, 6-7/60
Turtle - Showcase #4, 9-10/56
Tweedledum & Tweedledee - Detective Comics #74, 4/43
Two-Face - Detective Comics #66, 8/42; (S.A) World's Finest #173, 1/68
Typhoid Mary - Daredevil #254, 5/88
Ulik - Thor #137
Ultron - Avengers #54
Ulthoon - (Adam Strange foe) Mystery In Space #61,
Umar - Strange Tales #150, 11/66
Unicorn - Tales of Suspense #56, 8/64
Universo - Adventure Comics #349, 10/66
Unus the Untouchable - X-Men #8, 11/64
U. S. Jones - Wonderworld Comics #28, 8/41
Vandall Savage - Green Lantern #10 ,Win '43; (S.A.) Flash #137, ?/63
Vanisher - X-Men #2, 11/63
Venom - (1st full app.) Amazing Spider-Man #300, 5/88; (cameo w/costume) Amazing Spider-Man #298; (cameo, no costume), #299, 4/88
Vindicator - X-Men #109, 5/78
Viper - Captain America #110, 2/69
Vulture - Amazing Spider-Man #2, 5/63
Warpath - X-Men #193, 5/85
Watcher - Fantastic Four #13, 4/63
Weapon Omega - Alpha Flight #102, 11/81
Weather Wizard - Flash #110, 12-1/59-60
Whirlwind - (Human Top) Tales to Astonish #50, 12/63
White Queen - X-Men #132, 4/80
Wizard - Strange Tales #102, 11/62
Zemo - Avengers #6, 7/64
Zzzax - Incredible Hulk #166, 8/73

FIRST APPEARANCES: GROUPS

Adult Legion - Superman #147, 8/61
All Star Squadron - Justice League of America #193, 8/81
All Winners Squad - All Winners Comics #19, Fall, 1946
Alpha Flight -(cameo) X-Men #120, 4/79; (full app.) X-Men #121, 5/79
Atari Force - New Teen Titans #27, 1/83
Atomic Knights - Strange Adventures #117, 6/60
Avengers - Avengers #1, 9/63
Avengers new line up - Avengers #16, 5/65; Avengers #150, 8/76; Avengers #181, 3/79; Avengers #211, 9/81
Avengers West Coast - West Coast Avengers #1, 9/84
Big-3 - (Blue Beetle/Flame/ Samson) Big-3 #1, Fall, 1940
Bizarro Legionnaires - Adventure Comics #329, 2/65
Boy Commandos - Detective Comics #64, 6/42
Challengers of the Unknown - Showcase #6, 1-2/57
Champions - Champions #1, 10/75
Creature Commandos - Weird War Tales #93, 11/80
Damage Control - Marvel Comics Presents #19, 5/89
Darkstars - Dark Stars #1, 10/92
Defenders - Marvel Feature #1, 12/71; (new) Defenders #125, 11/83; (pre-lude) Sub-Mariner #34, 2/71
Doom Patrol - My Greatest Adventure #80, 6/63; (new) Showcase #94, 8-9/77
Easy Company - Our Army At War #81, 4/59
Elementals, The - Justice Machine Annual #1, 1/84
Eternals - Eternals #1, 7/76
Excalibur - Excalibur Special Edition nn, 1987
Explorers - Boy Explorers #1, 5-6/46
Fab 4 - Super Heroes #1, 1/67
Fantastic Four - Fantastic Four #1, 11/61; (1st in costumes) Fantastic Four #3, 3/62; (new team) Fantastic Four #306, 9/87
Federal Men - New Comics #2, 1/36
Femforce - Femforce Special #1, Fall, 1984
Fightin' Five - Fightin' Five V2#28, 7/64
Forever People - Forever People #1,2-3/71
Freedom Fighters - Justice League of America #107, 1975
Frightful Four - Fantastic Four #36, 10/64
Future X-Men - X-Men #141, 1/81
Gen13 - WildC.A.T.S Trilogy #1, 6/93
Ghost Patrol - Flash Comics #29, 5/42
Girl Commandos - Speed Comics #13, 4/41
Great Lakes Avengers - West Coast Avengers #46, 7/89
Green Lantern Corp. - Green Lantern #130
Guardians of the Galaxy - Marvel Super-Heroes #18, 1/69; (1st solo book) Marvel Presents #3, 2/76
Guardians of the Universe - Green Lantern #1, 7-8/60
H.A.R.D. Corps - Harbinger #10, 10/92
Inferior Five - Showcase #62, 5-6/66
Infinity, Inc. - All Star Squadron #25,9/83
Inhumans - Fantastic Four #45, 12/65
Injustice Society Of The World - All Star Comics #37, 10-11/47
Intergalactic Vigilante Squadron - Adventure Comics #237, 6/57
International Sea Devils - Sea Devils #22, 3-4/66
Invaders - Avengers #71, 12/69; (re-intro) Namor, the Sub-Mariner #12, 3/91
Justice League Europe - Justice League International #24, 2/89; (new) Justice League Spectacular #1, 1992
Justice League International - (new) Justice League Spectacular #1, 1992
Justice League of America - Brave and the Bold #28, 2-3/60; Legends #6, 4/87; (new team) Justice Leagueof America Annual #2, 1984
Justice Legion A - JLA #23, 10/98
Justice Society of America - All Star Comics #3, Win, '40-41; (1st S.A. cameo) Flash #137, ?/63
Kiss - (1st full app.) Howard the Duck #13, 6/77; (cameo) Howard the Duck #12, 3/77
Knights of the Galaxy - Mystery In Space #1, 4-5/51
Legion of Monsters - (Ghost Rider, Man-Thing, Morbius, Werewolf) Marvel Premiere #28, 1975
Legion of Substitute Heroes - Adventure Comics #306, 3/63
Legion of Super Heroes - Adventure Comics #247, 4/58
Legion Of Super Pets - Adventure Comics #293, 2/62
Liberators - Avengers #83, 12/70
Liberty Legion - Marvel Premiere #29, 1975
Losers - (Storm/Gunner/Sarge/J. Cloud) G. I. Combat #138, 10-11/69
Lt. Marvels - Whiz Comics #21, 9/41
Marvel Family - Captain Marvel Adventures #18, 12/42
Masters Of Evil - Avengers #6, 2/64
Masters of the Universe - New Teen Titans #25, 11/82
Mercenaries - G.I. Combat #244, 1982
Metal Men - Showcase #37, 3-4/62
Mighty Crusaders - Mighty Crusaders #1, 11/65
New Gods - New Gods #1, 2-3/71
New Mutants - Marvel Graphic Novel #4, 1982
New Teen Titans - DC Comics Presents #26, 10/80
New Warriors - (cameo) Thor #411, 12/89; (full app.) Thor #412, 12/89
Newsboy Legion - Star Spangled Comics #7, 4/42; (re-intro) Superman's Pal Jimmy Olsen #133, 10/70
Next Men - Dark Horse Presents #54, 9/91
Night Force - New Teen Titans #21, 7/82
Omega Men - Green Lantern #141, 6/81
Our Gang - Our Gang Comics #1, 9-10/42
Outsiders - Brave and the Bold #200, 7/83
Planeteers - Real Fact Comics #16, 9-10/48
Power Elite - Starman #4, Win '88
Power Pack - Power Pack #1, 8/84
Sea Devils - Showcase #27, 7-8/60
Secret Six - Secret Six #1, 4-5/68; (re-intro) Action Comics #601, 6/88
Sentinels - X-Men #14, 11/65
Seven Soldiers of Victory - Leading Comics #1, Wint, '41-42
Shadowmaster - Punisher #24, ?/89
S.H.I.E.L.D. - Nick Fury Agent of Shield #1, 6/68
Stargazers - Vanguard Ill. #2, 12/83
Starjammers - (cameo) X-Men #104, 4/77; (full app.) X-Men #107, 10/77
Star Rovers - Mystery In Space #66, 1961
Stargrazers - Vanguard Illustrated #2, 12/83
Suicide Squad - Brave and the Bold #25, 8-9/59; (new) Legends #3, 1/87
Super Friends - Super Friends #1, 11/76
Team America - Captain America #269, 5/82
Team Titans - (Teen Titans) New Titans Annual #7, 1991
Teenage Mutant Ninja Turtles - Gobbledygook #1, 1984
Teen Titans - Brave and the Bold #54, 6-7/64
Terrific Three - (Jaguar, Mr. Justice, Steel Sterling) Mighty Crusaders #5, 9/66
Three Mouseketeers - Funny Stuff #1, Sum '44
Thunder Agents - Thunder Agents #1, 11/65
Tiger Squadron - Blue Beetle #20, 4/43
Toxic Crusaders - Toxic Crusaders #1, 5/92
Tough Kid Squad - Tough Kid Squad #1, 3/42
Transformers - Transformers #1, 9/84
Tribe - WILDC.A.T.s: Covert Action Teams #4, 3/93
Ultra-Men - (Fox, Web, Capt. Flag) Mighty Crusaders #5, 9/66
Wanderers - Adventure Comics #375, 12/68
West Coast Avengers - West Coast Avengers #1, 9/84
Wildcats - WILDC.A.T.s: Covert Action Teams #1, 8/92
X-Factor - Avengers #263, 1/86; (new team) X-Factor #71, 10/91
X-Force - (cameo) New Mutants #100, 4/91
X-Men - X-Men #1, 9/63; X-Men #1, 10/91; (new team) X-Men #253, 1989; (new team) X-Men #281, 10/91; (new) Giant-Size X-Men #1, Sum, '75
X-Terminators - X-Terminators #1, 10/88
Young Allies - Young Allies #1, Sum '41
Youngblood - (1 pg. ad) Megaton #8, 8/87; (2pgs.) Megaton Explosion nn, 6/87
Young Justice - Young Justice: The Secret #1, 6/98

FIRST APPEARANCES: VILLAIN GROUPS

Beagle Boys - Walt Disney's Comics and Stories #134, 11/51
Blue Trinity - Flash #7, 12/87
Brotherhood of Evil - (new) New Teen Titans #15, 1/82
Brotherhood of Evil Mutants - X-Men #4, 3/64; (new) X-Men #141, 1/81
Citadel - Green Lantern #136, 1/81
Enforcers - Amazing Spider-Man #10, 3/64
Fearsome Five - New Teen Titans #3, 1/81
Frightful Four - (Sandman/Wizard/P.P. Pete) Fantastic Four #36, 3/65
Injustice Society - All Star Comics #37, 10-11/47
Krypton Foes - Superman #65, 7-8/50
Legion of Super-Villains - Superman #147, 8/61
Masters of Evil - Avengers #6, 7/64; (new) Avengers #54, 7/68
Phantom Zone Villains (Dr. Zadu & Emdine) - Superboy #100, 10/62
Royal Flush Gang - Justice League of America #43, ?/66; (new) Justice League of America #203, 6/82
Secret Society of Super-Villains - Secret Society of Super-Villains #1, 5-6/76
Sinister Six - Amazing Spider-Man Annual #1, 1964
Skrulls - Fantastic Four #2, 1/62
Toad Men - Incredible Hulk #2, 7/62

CROSSOVERS

Ant-Man - Fantastic Four #16, 7/63
Avengers - Tales of Suspense #49, 1/64
Capt. America - (outside of Avengers) Sgt. Fury #13
Conan - Savage Tales #1, 5/71
Daredevil - Amazing Spider-Man #16, 9/64
Doctor Strange - Fantastic Four #27, 6/64
Fantastic Four - Amazing Spider-Man #1, 3/63
Hulk - Fantastic Four #12, 3/63
G.A. Green Lantern x-over in S.A. - Showcase #55, 3-4/65
Iceman - Strange Tales #120, 5/64
Iron Man - (x-over outside Avengers) Tales to Astonish #82, 8/66
Magneto - Journey Into Mystery #109, 10/64
Nick Fury - (as agent of Shield) Tales of Suspense #92, 8/67
S.A. Captain America - Sgt. Fury #13, 12/64
Sgt. Fury - Fantastic Four #21, 12/63
Silver Surfer - (cameo) Tales to Astonish #92, 6/67; (full app.) Tales to Astonish #93, 7/67
Spider-Man - Strange Tales Annual #2, 7/63
Sub-Mariner - (outside Fantastic Four) Strange Tales #107, (4/63)
Thing - Strange Tales #116, 1/64
Thor - Strange Tales #123, 8/64
X-Men - Tales of Suspense #49, 1/64

FIRST SUPERPETS

Ace the Bat-Hound - Star Spangled Comics #100 (1/50); Batman #92, 6/55
Beppo the Supermonkey - Superboy #76, 8/59
Captain Carrot - New Teen Titans #16, 2/82
Comet the Superhorse - Adventure Comics #293, 2/62
Cosmo - (Challengers Spacepet) Challengers of the Unknown #18, 9-10/60
Krypto the Super Dog - Adventure Comics #210, 3/55
Legion of Super Pets - Adventure Comics #293, 2/62
Proty II - Adventure Comics #316 , 1/64
Rang-A-Tang the Wonder Dog - Blue Ribbon Comics #1, 11/39
Streak the Wonder Dog - Green Lantern #30, 2-3/48
Streaky the Super Cat - Action Comics #261, 2/60
Wolf - (Boy Commandos mascot) Boy Commandos #34, 7-8/49

FIRST PROTOTYPES

Some of today's popular super hero characters were developed from or after earlier forms or prototypes. These prototype characters sometimes were introduced to test new ideas and concepts which later developed into full fledged super heroes, or old material sometimes would inspire new characters. Below is a list of all known prototypes. The Marvel/Atlas issues have been verified by Stan Lee, Steve Ditko and Jack Kirby.

Ancient One - Strange Tales #92, 1/62
Ant-Man - Strange Tales #73, 2/60; Strange Tales #78, 11/60
Aunt May - Strange Tales #97, 6/62
Doctor Doom - Tales of Suspense #31, 7/62
Doctor Strange - Journey Into Mystery #78, 3/62; Strange Tales #79, 12/60; Tales of Suspense #32, 8/62
Electro - Tales To Astonish #15, 1/61
Giant-Man - Strange Tales #70, 8/59
Hulk - Journey Into Mystery #62, 11/60; Journey Into Mystery #66, 3/61
Human Torch - Strange Tales #76, 8/60
Iron Man - Strange Tales #75, 6/60; Tales of Suspense #9, 5/60; Tales of Suspense #16, 4/61
Kamandi - Alarming Tales #1, 9/57
Lava Men - Tales of Suspense #7, 1/60
Magneto - Strange Tales #84, 5/61
Mr. Hyde - Journey Into Mystery #79, 4/62
Professor X - Amazing Adult Fantasy #14, 7/62; Strange Tales #69, 6/59
Quicksilver - Strange Tales #67, 2/59
Red Tornado - House Of Mystery #155, 9-10/65
Sandman - Journey Into Mystery #70, 7/61
Savage Dragon - Marvel Comics Presents #50, 1990
Spider-Man - Journey Into Mystery #73, 10/61
Stone Men - Tales of Suspense #28, 4/62; Tales to Astonish #5, 9/59; Tales to Astonish #16, 2/61
Superman - (Dr. Mystic) Comics Magazine #1, 5/36; More Fun Comics #14, 10/36; New Book of Comics #2, Spr '38
Toad Men - Tales to Astonish #7, 1/60
Uncle Ben - Strange Tales #97, 6/62
Watcher - Tales of Suspense #35, 11/62

FIRST OF A PUBLISHER

Ace Magazines - Sure-Fire #1, 6/40
American Comics Group - Giggle #1 & Ha Ha #1, 10/43
Atlas Comics - All Winners #11, Wint.'43/44
Avon Comics -Molly O'Day #1, 2/45
Better Publications (Standard) - Best Comics #1, 11/39
Bilbara Publishing Co. - Cyclone #1, 6/40
Brookwood Publications - Speed Comics #1, 10/39
Carlton Publishing Co. - Zoom Comics #1, 12/45
Catechetical Guild - Topix #1, 11/42
Centaur Publications -Funny Pages V2#6, 3/38; Funny Picture Stories V2#6, 3/38; Star Comics #10, 3/38; Star Ranger V2#10, 3/38
Charlton Comics -Zoo Funnies #1, 11/45
Columbia Comics Group - Big Shot #1, 5/40
Comico - Primer #1, 10/82
Comics Magazine - Comics Magazine #1, 5/36
Dark Horse - Dark Horse Presents #1, 7/86
David McKay Publ. - King Comics #1, 4/36
DC Comics - New Fun Comics #1, 2/35
Defiant Comics - Warriors Of Plasm #1, 8/93
Dell Publishing Co. - Popular Comics #1, 2/36
Eastern Color - Funnies On Parade nn, 1933
Elliot Publications - Double Comics, 1940
Fawcett Publications - Whiz Comics #2 (#1), 2/40
Fiction House - Jumbo Comics #1, 9/38
Flying Cadet - Flying Cadet #1, 1/43
Fox Features Syndicate - Wonder Comics #1, 5/39
Funnies, Inc. - Motion Picture Funnies Weekly #1, 1939
Gilberton Publ. - Classic Comics #1, 10/41
Gladstone - Disneyland Birthday Party, 8/85; Uncle Scrooge Goes To Disneyland, 8/85
Globe Syndicate - Circus Comics #1, 6/38
Great Publications - Great Comics #1, 11/41
Harry 'A' Chesler - Star Comics #1, 2/37
Harvey Comics - Pocket Comics #1, 8/41
Hawley Publications - Captain Easy nn, 1939
Hillman Periodicals - Miracle Comics #1, 2/40
Holyoke (Continental) - Crash Comics #1, 5/40
Hugo Gernsback - Superworld #1, 4/40
Hyper Publications - Hyper Mystery #1, 5/40
Image Comics - Youngblood #1, 4/92
K.K. Publications - Mickey Mouse Magazine #1, Sum, 1935
Lev Gleason - Silver Streak #1, 12/39
Mirage Studios - Gobbledygook #1, no month '84
MLJ Magazines - Blue Ribbon Comics #1, 11/39
Nita Publications - Whirlwind Comics #1, 6/40
Novelty Publications - Target Comics #1, 6/40
Parents' Magazine Institute - True Comics #1, 4/41
Prize Publications - Prize Comics #1, 3/40
Progressive Publishers - Feature Comics #21, 6/39
Quality Comics Group - Feature Comics #21, 6/39
Ralston-Purina Co. - Tom Mix #1, 9/40
Standard Comics (Better Publ.) - Best Comics #1, 11/39
Street and Smith Publications - Shadow Comics #1, 3/40
Sun Publications - Colossus Comics #1, 3/40
Timely Comics - Marvel Mystery #1, 11/39
United Features Syndicate - Tip Top Comics #1, 4/36
Valiant Comics - (hero) Magnus Robot Fighter, 5/91
Warren all comics magazine - Creepy #1, no month '64
Whitman Publishing Co. - Mammoth Comics #1, 1937
Will Eisner - Spirit #1, 6/2/40
William H. Wise - Columbia Comics #1, 1943

a-Story art; **a(i)**-Story art inks; **a(p)**-Story art pencils; **a(r)**-Story art reprint.

adult material–Contains story and/or art for "mature" readers. Re: sex, violence, strong language.

adzine-A magazine primarily devoted to the advertising of comic books and collectibles as its first publishing priority as opposed to written articles.

annual-A book that is published yearly.

arrival date-Markings on a comic book cover (usually in pencil) made by either the newsstand dealer or the distributor. These markings denote the date the book was placed on the newsstand. Usually the arrival date is one to two months prior to the cover date.

ashcan-A prepublication facsimile or dummy issue of an intended title usually prepared to show advertisers. Part or all of the pages may be blank or from a different book with a new cover. Black and white ashcans are common.

Atom Age- The period beginning in 1946 after the dropping of the first Atom bomb, continuing until the start of the Silver Age in 1956

B&W-Black and white art.

bad girl art (BGA)-A term coined in 1993 to describe an attitude as well as a style of art that portrays women in a sexually implicit way.

Baxter paper–A high quality, white, heavy paper used in the printing of some comic books.

bi-monthly-Published every two months.

bi-weekly-Published every two weeks.

bondage cover-Usually denotes a female in restraints.

brittleness-The final stage of paper deterioration.

Bronze Age–(1) Non-specific term not in general acceptance by collectors which denotes comics published from approximately 1970 through 1980, (2) Term which describes "the Age" of comic books after the Silver Age.

browning-Paper aging between tanning and brittleness.

c-Cover art; **c(i)**-Cover inks; **c(p)**-Cover pencils; **c(r)**-Cover reprint.

cameo-When a character appears briefly.

CCA-Comics Code Authority.

CCA seal-An emblem that was placed on the cover of all CCA approved comics beginning in April-May, 1955.

center crease– (see Subscription Crease)

centerfold-The stapled, four page middle sheet of a comic or magazine.

CFO–Abbreviation for "Centerfold out."

chromium cover–A special Chromium foil used on covers

Church, Edgar collection-A large high grade comic book collection discovered by Mile High Comics in Colorado (over 22,000 books).

classic cover–A cover highly prized by collectors as a prime or matchless example of its kind.

cleaning–A process in which dirt and dust is removed.

color touch–A restoration process by which colored ink is used to hide color flecks, flakes and larger areas

colorist-An artist who paints the color guides for comics. Many modern colorists use computer technology.

comic book dealer–(1) A seller of comic books. (2) One who makes a living buying and selling comic books.

comic book repair-When a tear, loose staple or centerfold has been mended without changing or adding to the original finish of the book. Repair may involve tape, glue or nylon gossamer and is easily detected. It is considered a defect

comic book restoration-Any attempt, whether professional or amateur, to enhance the appearance of a comic book. These procedures may include any or all of the following techniques: recoloring, adding missing paper, stain, ink, dirt, tape removal, whitening, pressing out wrinkles, staple replacement, trimming, re-glossing, etc. Note: Unprofessional work can lower the value of a book. In all cases, except for some simple cleaning procedures, a restored book can never be worth the same as an unrestored book in the same condition.

Comics Code Authority-In 1954 the major publishers joined together and formed a committee which set up guidelines for acceptable comic contents. It was their task to approve the contents of comics before publication.

complete run–All issues of a given title.

con-A Convention or public gathering of fans.

condition–The state of preservation of a comic book.

Cosmic Aeroplane-Refers to a large collectionof 1930s-1940s comics discovered by Cosmic Aeroplane Books.

costumed hero–A costumed crime fighter with "developed" powers instead of "super" powers.

coupon cut–Comic book missing a coupon.

cover loose–Cover is detached from staple or staples

cover trimmed–Cover has been reduced in size through trimming.

crease–A paper fold that occurs in comic books from misuse

crossover–When one character or characters appears briefly in another character's story.

deacidification–The process of reducing acid in paper.

debut-The first time that a character appears anywhere.

defect–Any fault or flaw that detracts from perfection.

Denver collection–A collection of early '40s high grade #1s bought at auction in Pennsylvania by a Denver, Colorado dealer.

die-cut cover–When areas of a cover are precut by a printer to a special shape or to create a desired effect.

distributor painted stripes–Color brushed or sprayed

on the edges of comic book stacks as special coding by distributors (not a defect).
double–A duplicate copy.
double cover-An error in the binding process which results in two or more covers being bound to a single book. Multiple covers are not considered a defect.
drug propaganda story-Where comic makes an editorial stand about drug abuse.
drug use story-Shows the actual use of drugs: shooting, taking a trip, harmful effects, etc.
dust shadow–Usually the fore-edge of a comic cover exposed to the gathering of dust creating a dark stripe.
embossed cover–When a pattern is embossed onto the cover creating a raised area.
eye appeal–A term used to describe the overall appeal of a comic's apparent condition.
fanzine-An amateur fan publication.
file copy-A comic originating from the publisher's file. Not all file copies are in pristine condition. **Note:** An arrival date on the cover of a comic indicates that it is not a file copy though a copyright date may.
first app.-Same as debut.
flashback-When a previous story is being recalled.
foil cover–A thin metallic foil that is hot stamped on comic covers.
four color-A printing process in which the three primary colors plus black are used. Also refers to the Four Color series published by Dell.
foxing-Tiny orange-brown spots on the cover or pages of a comic book caused by mold growth.
G. A.-Golden Age period.
gatefold cover–A double cover folded in itself.
genre–Categories of comic book subject matter grouped as to type.
giveaway–Type of comic book used as a premium for promotional purposes.
Golden Age (G.A.)-The period beginning with **Action** #1 (June, 1938) and ending with World War II in 1945.
good girl art (GGA)-A term coined in 1977 to describe a style of art that portrays women in a sexually implicit way.
headlights-Women's breasts, usually provocative.
hologram cover–True 3-D holograms are prepared and affixed to comic book covers and cards for special effect.
hot stamping–The process of pressing foil, prism paper and inks on cover stock.
i-Art inks.
indicia-Publishers title, issue number, date, copyright and general information statement usually located on the inside front facing pages or inside back cover.
infinity cover-Shows the same scene within a scene repeated into infinity.
inker-Artist that does the inking.
intro-Same as debut.
JLA-Justice League of America.
JLI-Justice League International.
JSA-Justice Society of America.
key issue–An important issue in a run.
Lamont Larson-Refers to a large high grade collection of 1940s comics. Many of the books have Lamont or Larson written on the cover.
lenticular covers (aka flicker covers)– Images move when viewed at different angles specially prepared and affixed to cover.
logo-The title of a strip or comic book as it appears on the cover or title page.
LSH-Legion of Super-Heroes.
Marvel chipping-A defect that occurred during the trimming process of 1950s and 1960s Marvels which produced a ragged edge around the comic cover. Usually takes the form of a tiny chip or chips along the right hand edge of the cover.
Mile High-Refers to a large NM-Mint collection of comics originating from Denver, Colorado (Edgar Church collection of 20,000+ copies).
Modern Age–Period from 1980 to the present.
Mylar ™–An inert, very hard, space age plastic used to make high quality protective bags and sleeves used for comic storage. Mylar ™ is a trademark of the DuPont Company.
nd-No date.
nn-No number.
N. Y. Legis. Comm.-New York Legislative Committee to Study the Publication of Comics (1951).
one-shot-When only one issue is published of a title or the title is published on an infrequent or irregular schedule, whether or not as part of a numbered series (such as Dell's Four Color).
origin-When the story of the character's creation is given.
over Guide-When a comic book is priced at a value over Guide list.
p-Art pencils.
painted cover–Cover taken from an actual painting instead of a line drawing.
paper cover–Comic book cover made from the same newsprint as interior pages (self cover). These books are extremely rare in high grade.
pedigree-A book from a famous collection, e.g. Allentown, Larson, Church/Mile High, Denver, San Francisco, Cosmic Aeroplane, etc. Note: Beware of non-pedigree collections being promoted as pedigree books. Only outstanding high grade collections similar to those listed qualify.
penciler-Artist that does the pencils.
photo cover–Made from a photograph instead of a line drawing or painting.
Platinum Age-First age of comics, beginning with newspaper strip reprint collections (**The Yellow Kid**) in 1897, and ending with 1933's **Detective Dan**, which contained original material.
POP-Parade of Pleasure, book about the censorship of comics.

post-Code-Comic books published with the CCA seal.
post-Golden Age-Comic books published between 1945 and 1950.
post-Silver Age-Comic books published from 1969 to present.
Poughkeepsie-Refers to a large collection of Dell Comics' "file copies" believed to have originated from the warehouse of Western Publishing in Poughkeepsie, N.Y.
pre-Code-Comic books published before the CCA seal.
pre-Golden Age-Comic books published prior to **Action** #1 (June, 1938).
pre-hero–A term that describes the issues in a run prior to a superhero entering the run.
pre-Silver Age-Comic books published between 1950 and **Showcase** #4 (1956).
printing defect-A defect caused by the printing process. Examples would include paper wrinkling, miscut edges, misfolded spine, untrimmed pages, off-registered color, off-centered trimming, misfolded and misbound pages. It should be noted that these are defects that lower the grade of the book.
prism cover–Special reflective foil material with 3-dimensional repeated designs. Used for special effect.
provenance-When the owner of a book is known and is stated for the purpose of authenticating and documenting the history of the book. Example: A book from the Stan Lee or Forrest Ackerman collection would be an example of a value-adding provenance.
quarterly-Published every three months (four times a year).
R or r-Reprint.
rare-10 to 20 copies estimated to exist.
rat chew–Damage caused by gnawing rats or mice.
reprint comics-Comic books that contain newspaper strip reprints.
restoration–The fine art of repairing a comic book to look as close as possible to its original condition.
rice paper-A thin, transparent paper commonly used by restorers to repair tears and replace small pieces on covers and pages of comic books.
Reilly, Tom–A large high grade collection of 1939-1945 comics with 5000+ books.
rolled spine–A spine condition caused by folding back pages while reading.
S. A.-Silver Age.
Rockford–A high grade collection of 1940s comics with 2000+ books from Rockford, IL.
saddle stitch–The staple binding of comic books.
San Francisco Collection–(see Reilly, Tom)
S&K-Joe Simon and Jack Kirby (artists).
scarce-20 to 100 copies estimated to exist.
semi-monthly-Published twice a month, as distinguished from biweekly.
Silver Age-Officially begins with **Showcase** #4 in 1956 and ends in 1969.
silver proof-A black & white actual size print on thick glossy paper hand painted by an artist to indicate colors to the engraver.
SOTI-Seduction of the Innocent, book about the censorship of comics. Refer to listing in this Guide.
spine-The area representing the folded and stapled part of a comic book.
spine roll-A defect caused by improper storage which results in uneven pages and the shifting or bowing of the spine.
splash panel-A large panel that usually appears at the front of a comic story.
squarebound-A comic book gluebound with a square spined cover, aka perfect bound.
store stamp–Store name stamped in ink on cover.
stress lines-Light, tiny wrinkles occuring along the spine, projecting from the staples or appearing anywhere on the covers of a comic book.
subscription crease-A center crease caused by the folding of comic books for mailing to subscribers. This is considered a defect.
sun shadow–A darkened strip along the fore-edge of a comic cover caused by prolonged exposure to light, unlike the dust shadow which can often be removed. A serious defect.
superhero–A costumed hero crime fighter with powers beyond those of mortal man.
supervillain–A costumed criminal with powers beyond those of mortal man.
swipe–A panel, sequence, or story obviously stolen or copied from previously published material.
3-D comic-Comic art that is drawn and printed in two mismatched colors, producing a 3-D effect when viewed through special glasses.
3-D effect comic-Comic art that is drawn to appear 3-D, but isn't.
title page–The first page showing the title of a story.
under Guide-When a comic book is priced at a value less than Guide list.
variant cover-a different cover image used on the same issue of a comic title.
very rare-1 to 10 copies estimated to exist.
warehouse copy-Originating from a publisher's warehouse; similar to file copy.
White Mountain–A large high grade collection of 1950s-1960s comics from New England.
x-over-When one character crosses over into another's strip.
zine-See Fanzine

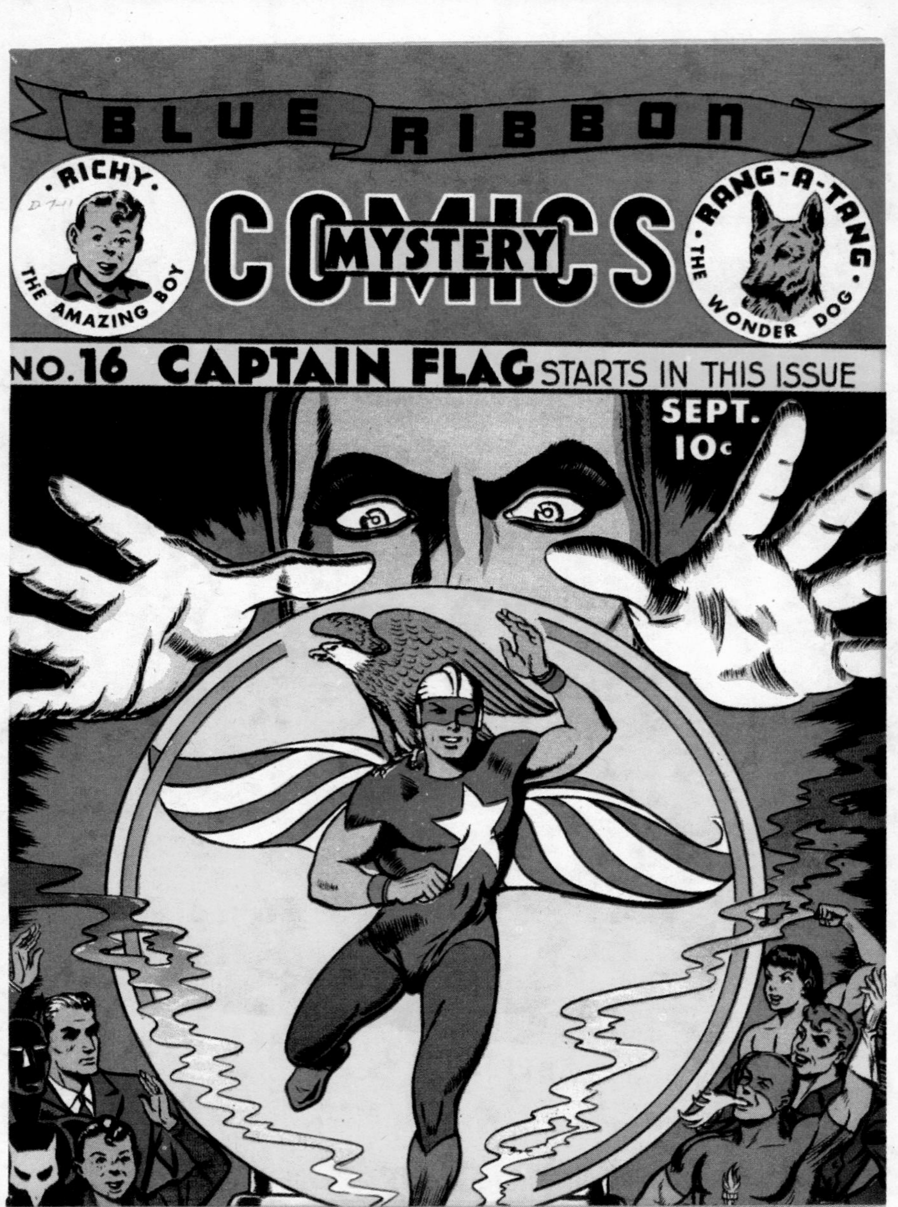

BLUE RIBBON COMICS #16
September 1941. Captain Flag's first appearance. From the Mile High collection. ©MLJ

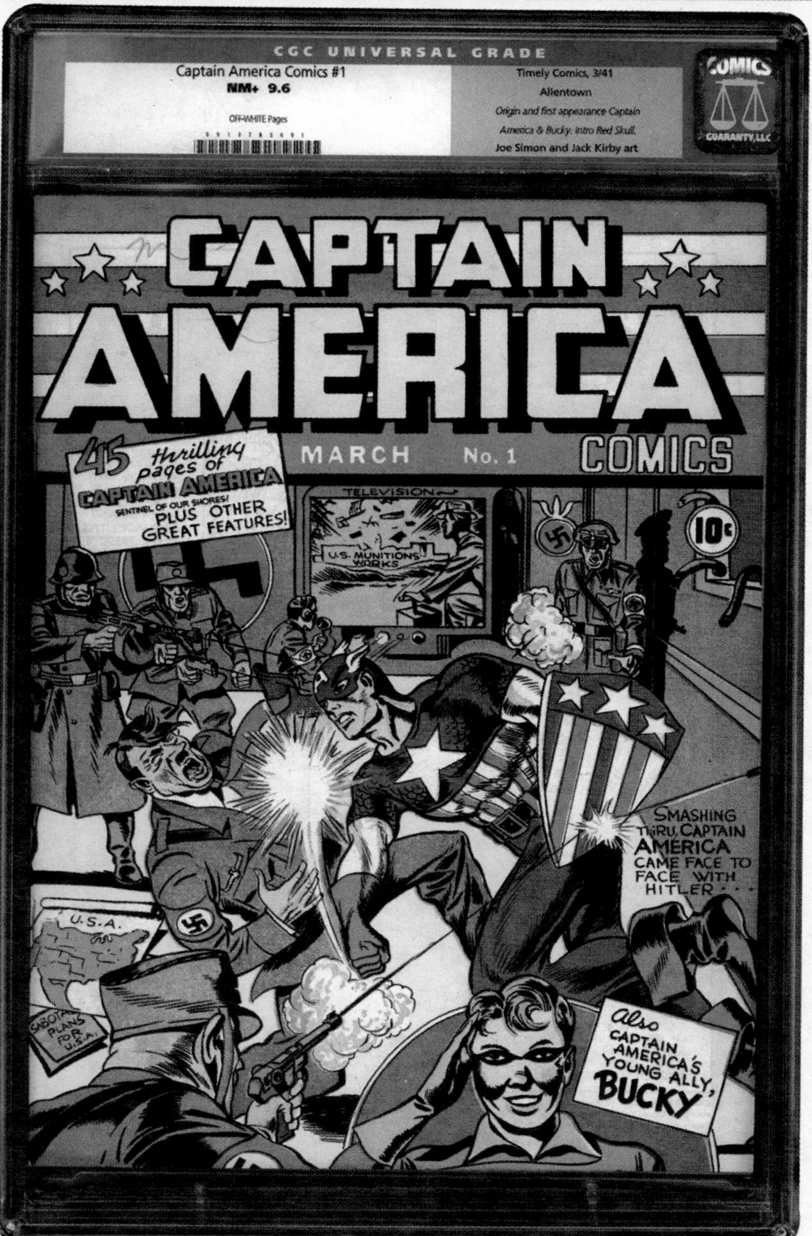

CAPTAIN AMERICA COMICS #1
March 1941. The best known copy. From the Allentown collection, graded CGC 9.6. Sold for a world record price of $265,000. ©MAR

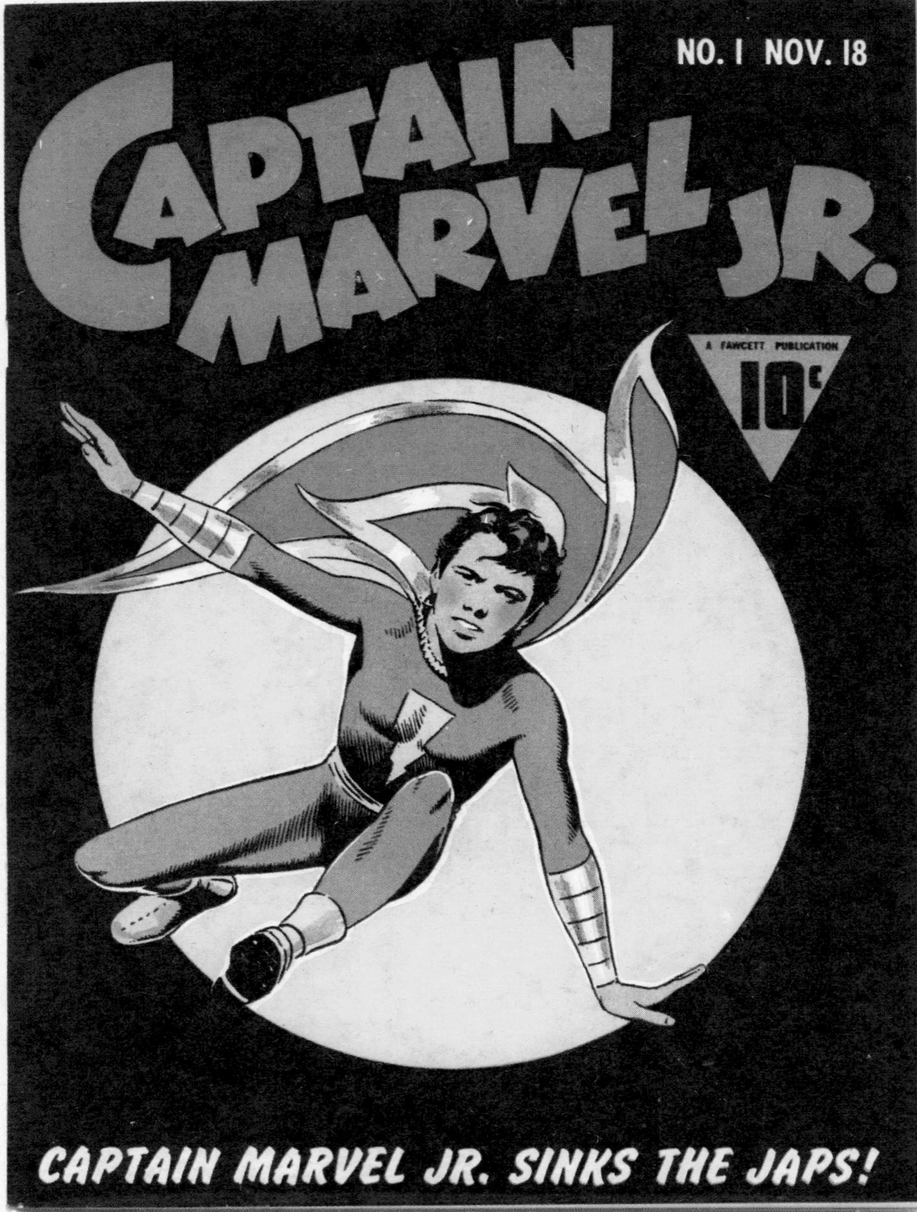

NO. 1 NOV. 18
CAPTAIN MARVEL JR.
A FAWCETT PUBLICATION
10¢
CAPTAIN MARVEL JR. SINKS THE JAPS!

CAPTAIN MARVEL JR. #1
November 1942. From the Mile High collection. Classic Mac Raboy art. ©FAW

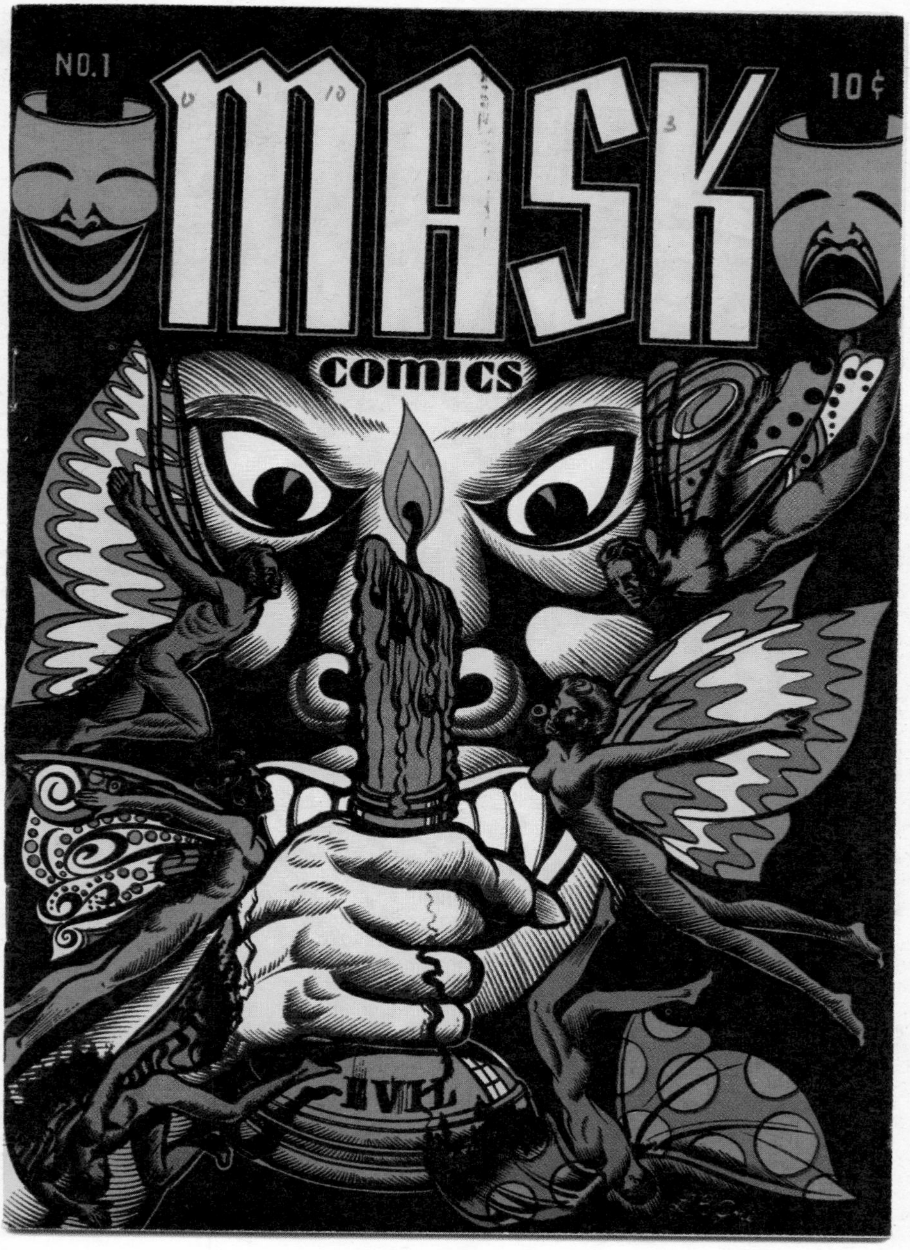

MASK COMICS #1

February-March 1945. From the Mile High Collection. Classic L.B. Cole art. ©RH

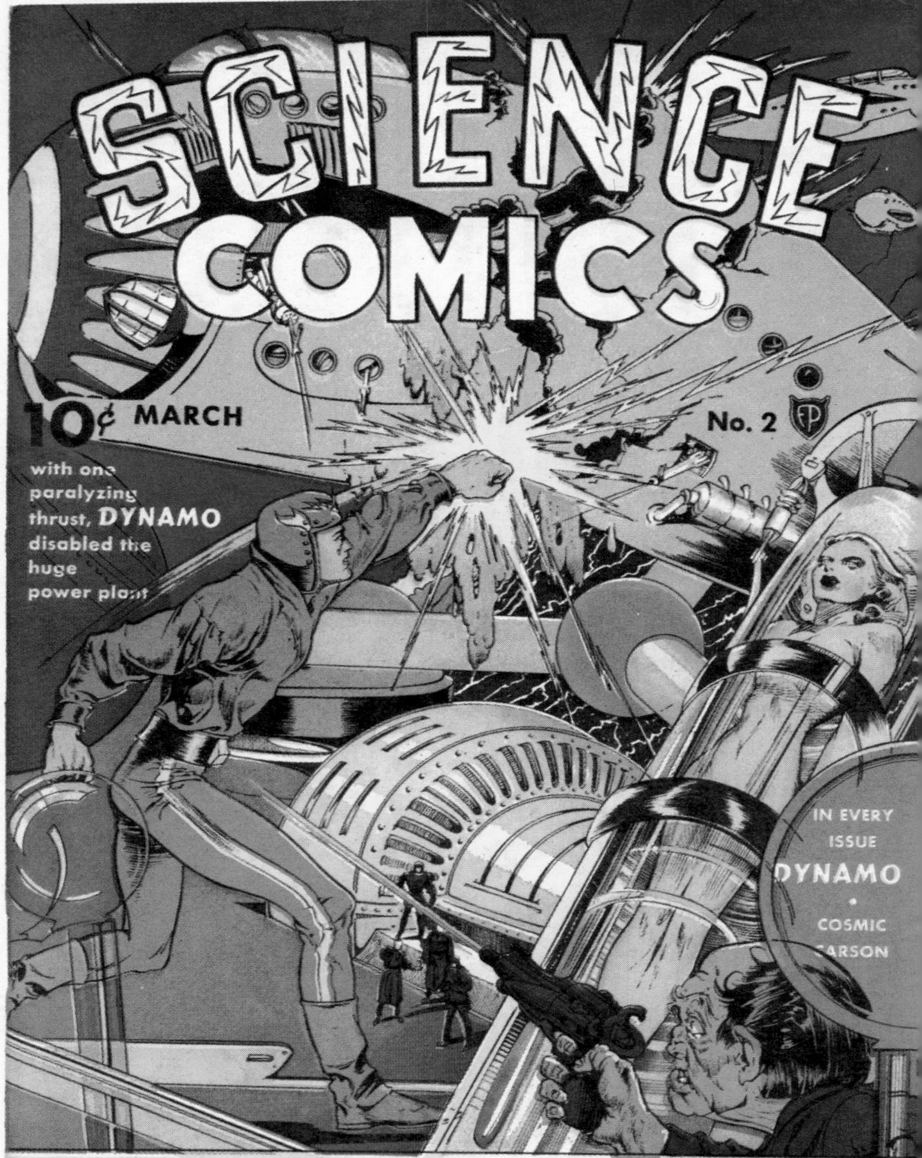

SCIENCE COMICS #2
March 1940. Classic cover art by Lou Fine. From the Mile High collection. ©FOX

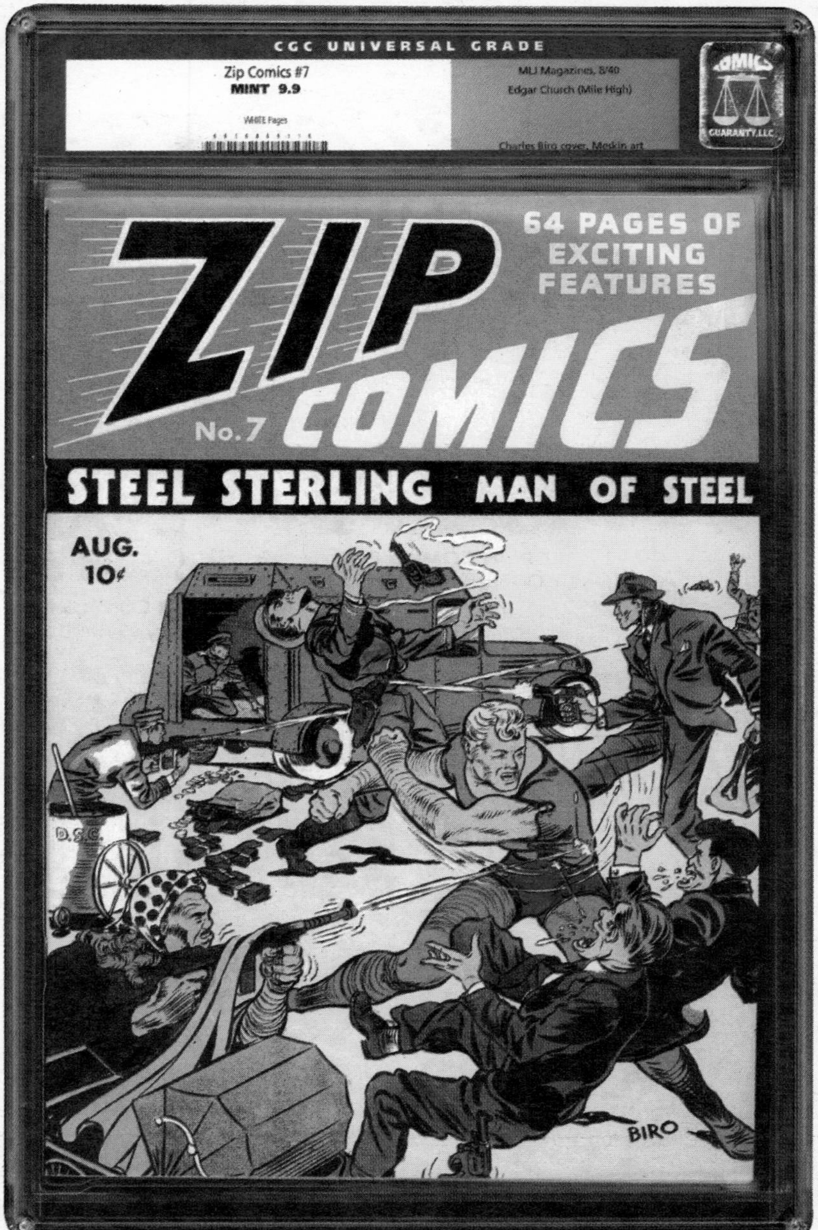

ZIP COMICS #7
August 1940. The first Golden Age comic graded Mint 9.9 by CGC.
From the Mile High collection. ©MLJ

ACTION COMICS #23
April 1940 ©DC

ACTION COMICS #29
October 1940 ©DC

ACTION COMICS #32
January 1941 ©DC

ADVENTURE COMICS #40
July 1939 ©DC

ADVENTURE COMICS #46
January 1940 ©DC

ALL-AMERICAN COMICS #22
January 1941 ©DC

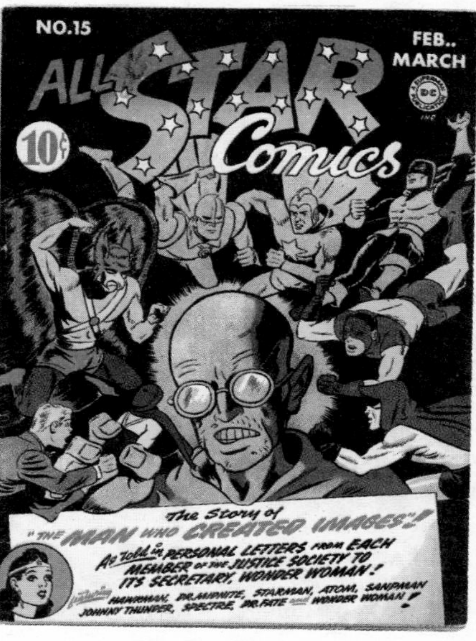

ALL STAR COMICS #15
February-March 1943 ©DC

ALL TOP COMICS #8
November 1947. Kamen cover art.
©FOX

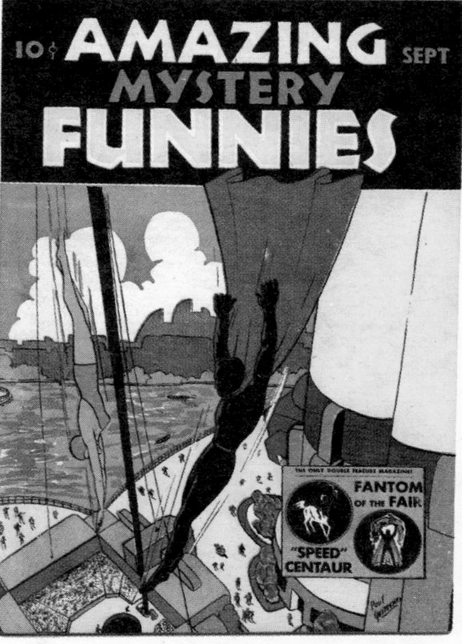

AMAZING MYSTERY FUNNIES V2#9
September 1939. Paul Gustavson cover art.
©CEN

C O V E R

AMAZING-MAN COMICS #24
October 1941. From the Mile High collection.
©CEN

AVENGERS #1
September 1963 ©MAR

BATMAN #8
December-January 1942
©DC

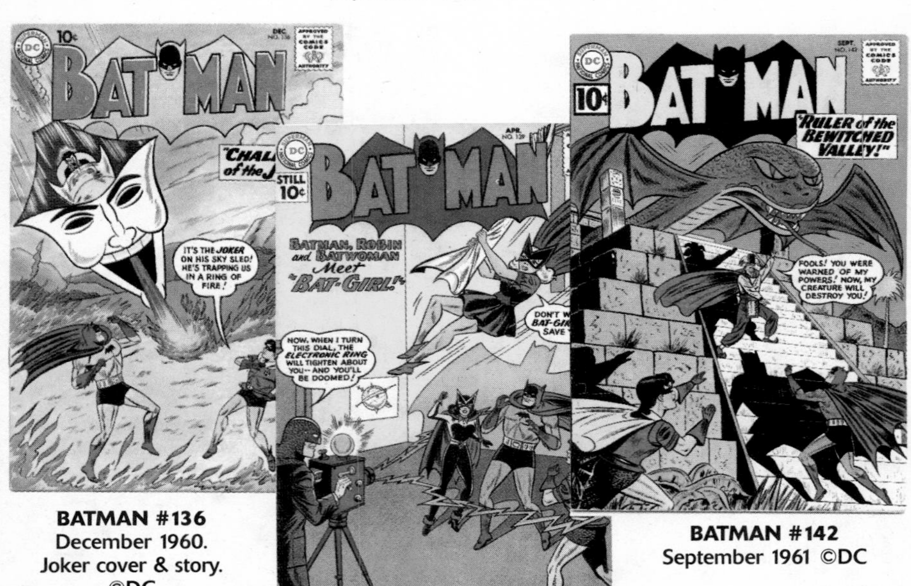

BATMAN #136
December 1960.
Joker cover & story.
©DC

BATMAN #139
April 1961. Introduction of Bat-Girl.
©DC

BATMAN #142
September 1961 ©DC

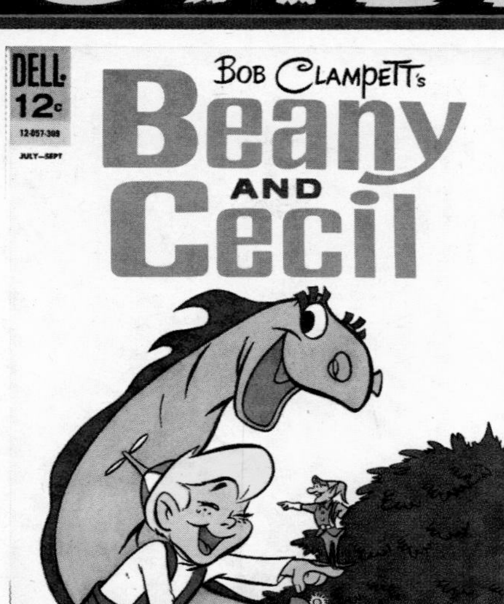

BEANY & CECIL #5
September 1963 ©Bob Clampett

BLACKHAWK #9 (#1)
Winter 1944 ©DC

BLACKHAWK #81
October 1954 ©DC

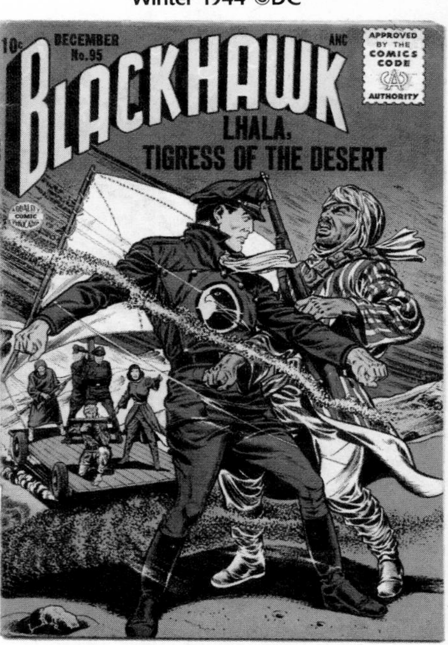

BLACKHAWK #95
December 1955 ©DC

BLACKHAWK #114
July 1957 ©DC

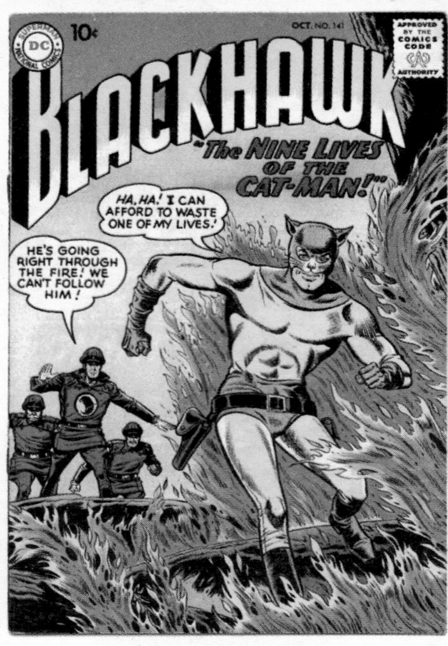

BLACKHAWK #141
October 1959. Catman appears. ©DC

BRAVE & THE BOLD #23
May 1959 ©DC

BRAVE & THE BOLD #51
January 1964 ©DC

BRAVE & THE BOLD #41
May 1962 ©DC

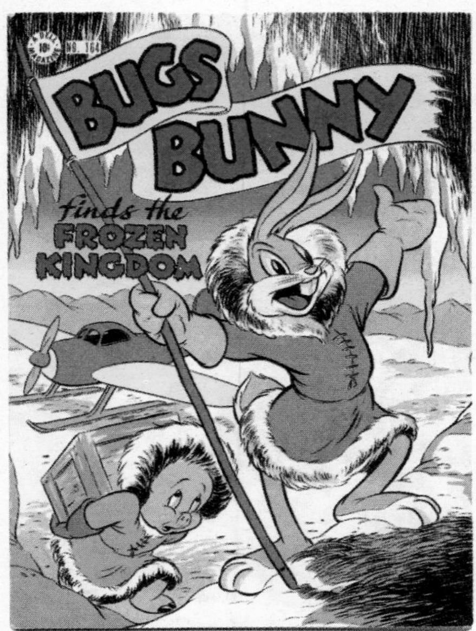

BUGS BUNNY FOUR COLOR #164
September 1947 ©Warner Bros.

BULLETMAN #6
July 1942. Mac Raboy cover art.
From the Mile High collection. ©FAW

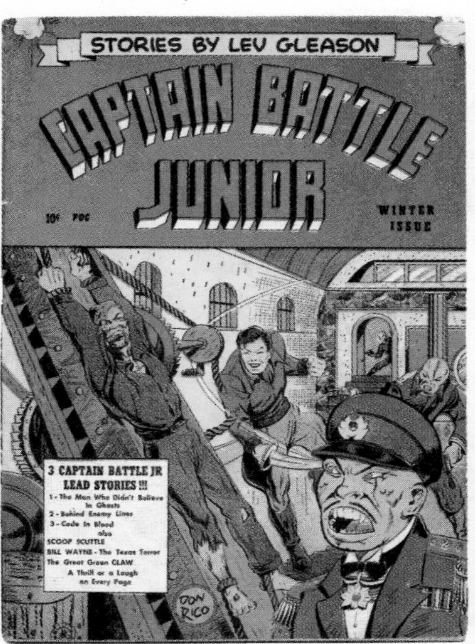

CAPTAIN BATTLE JR. #2
Winter 1943 ©LEV

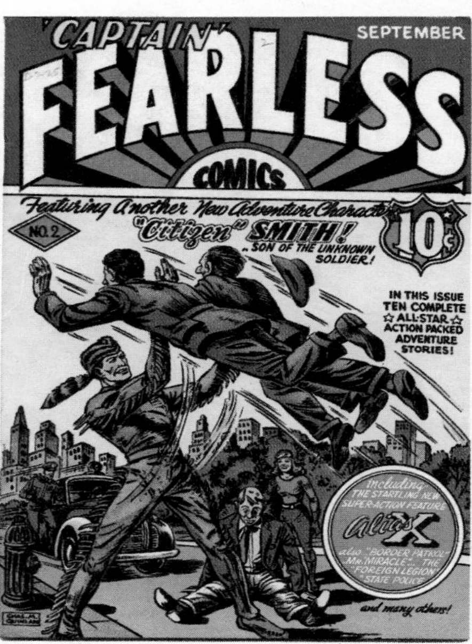

CAPTAIN FEARLESS COMICS #2
September 1941.
From the Mile High collection. ©HOKE

CAPTAIN MARVEL JR. #3
January 1943. From the Mile High collection. ©FAW

CAPTAIN MARVEL JR. #4
February 1943. From the Mile High collection. ©FAW

CAPTAIN MARVEL JR. #5
March 1943. From the Mile High collection. ©FAW

CAPTAIN MARVEL JR. #17
March 1944. From the Mile High collection. ©FAW

CAPTAIN MARVEL JR. #18
April 1944. From the Mile High collection. ©FAW

CAPTAIN MARVEL JR. #19
May 1944. From the Mile High collection. ©FAW

GALLERY

COMMANDER BATTLE AND THE ATOMIC SUB #5
March-April 1955
©ACG

CRUSADER RABBIT FOUR COLOR #805
August 1957
©MAR

THE CRYPT OF TERROR #17 (#1)
April-May 1950 ©WMG

DAREDEVIL COMICS #12
August 1942 ©LEV

DAREDEVIL #1
April 1964 ©MAR

DETECTIVE COMICS #85
March 1944. Joker cover appearance. ©DC

DETECTIVE COMICS #357
November 1966 ©DC

DETECTIVE COMICS #359
January 1967.
Intro and origin new Batgirl.
©DC

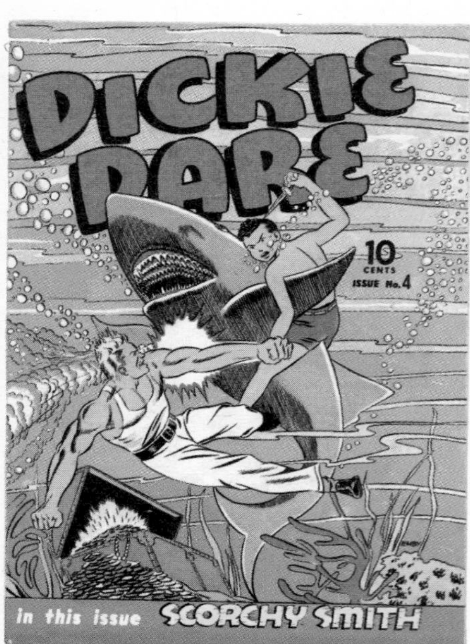

DICKIE DARE #4
1942 ©EAS

DR. KILDARE FOUR COLOR #1337 (#1)
June 1962 ©DELL

THE EAGLE #1
July 1941. From the Mile High collection.
©FOX

THE EAGLE #3
November 1941.
From the Mile High collection.
©FOX

THE EAGLE #4
January 1942. From the Mile High collection.
©FOX

FEATURE COMICS #60
September 1942 ©QUA

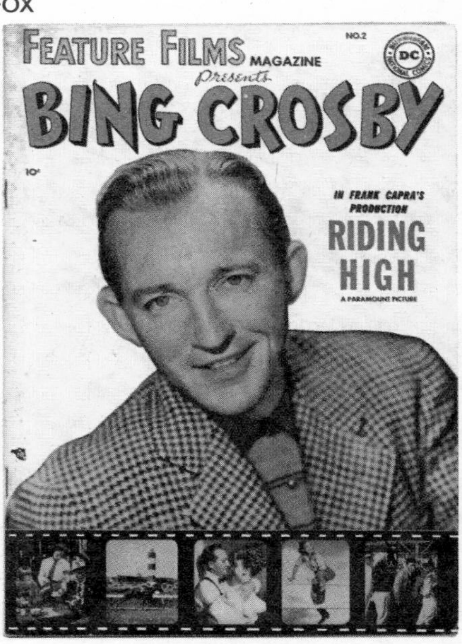

FEATURE FILMS #2
May-June 1950 ©DC

FLASH COMICS #3
March 1940 ©DC

FLASH COMICS #17
May 1941 ©DC

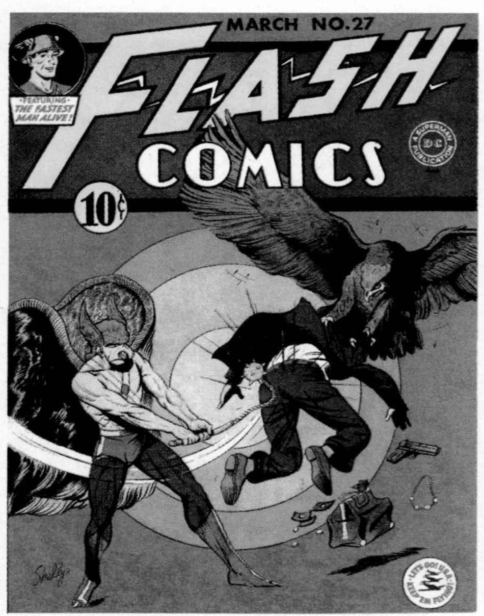

FLASH COMICS #27
March 1942 ©DC

THE FLASH #122
August 1961 ©DC

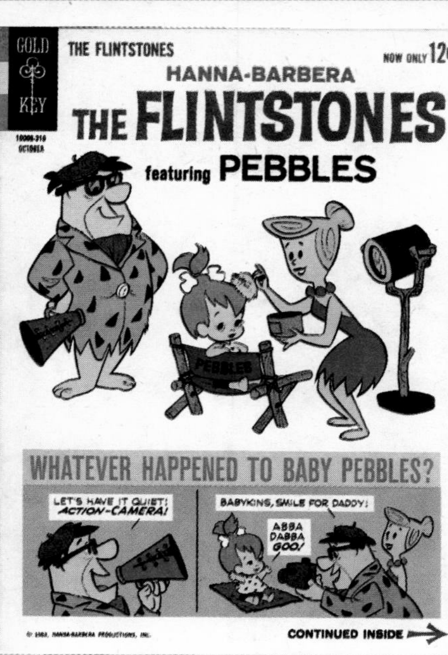

THE FLINTSTONES #14
October 1963 ©HANNA-BARBERA

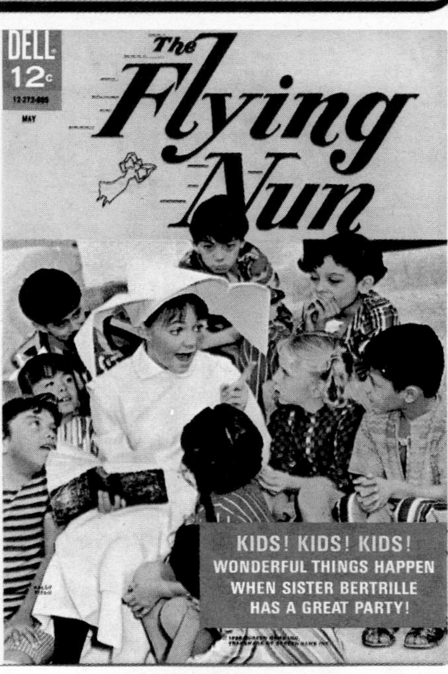

THE FLYING NUN #2
May 1968. Sally Field photo cover. ©DELL

FRONTLINE COMBAT #8
September-October 1952.
Gaines file copy. ©WMG

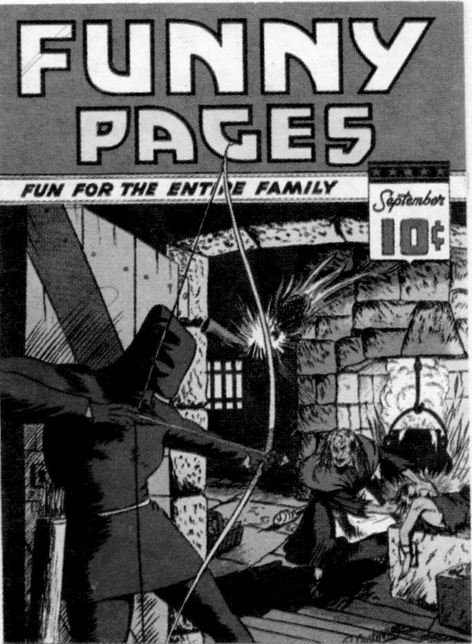

FUNNY PAGES V3 #7
September 1939. From the
Mile High collection. ©CEN

GET SMART #5
March 1967 ©DELL

GOLDEN LAD #5
June 1946 ©SPARK PUBL.

GREEN HORNET COMICS #1
December 1940 ©HARV

GREEN HORNET COMICS #9
October 1942. Cover by Jack Kirby.
©HARV

GALLERY

GREEN LAMA #4
April 1945.
Mac Raboy cover art.
©SPARK PUBL.

GREEN LAMA #6
August 1945.
Mac Raboy cover art.
©SPARK PUBL.

GREEN LAMA #8
March 1946.
Mac Raboy cover art.
©SPARK PUBL.

HAUNT OF FEAR #17
February 1953 ©WMG

HOWDY DOODY #11
Nov 1951 ©California Ntl. Publ.

IBIS THE INVINCIBLE #1, 1942. From the Mile High collection. ©FAW

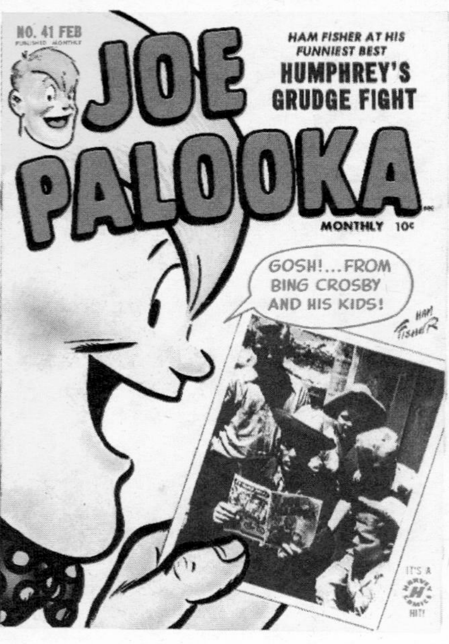

JOE PALOOKA #41
February 1950 ©HARV

JUNGLE COMICS #1
January 1940. Cover by Lou Fine.
©FH

KEEN DETECTIVE FUNNIES #8 (#1)
July 1938 ©CEN

KEEN DETECTIVE FUNNIES V2#4
April 1939.
From the Mile High collection.
©CEN

KEEN DETECTIVE FUNNIES #24
September 1940. From the Mile High collection.
©CEN

LEADING COMICS #5
Winter 1942. From the Mile High collection.
©DC

THE LONE RANGER #105
March 1957 ©Lone Ranger Inc.

MARY MARVEL #1
December 1945 ©FAW

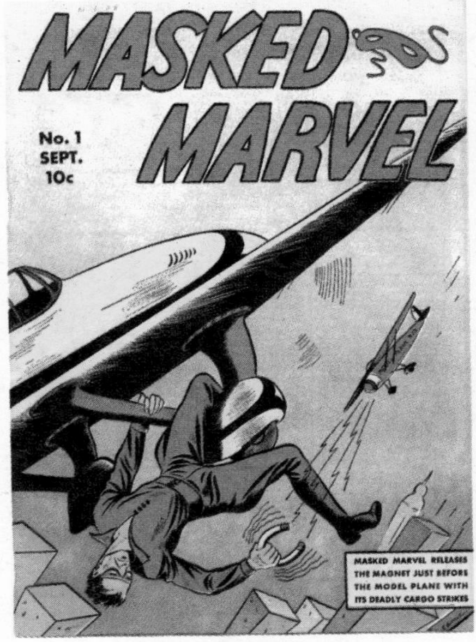

MASKED MARVEL #1
September 1940.
From the Mile High collection. ©CEN

MASTER COMICS #12
March 1941 ©FAW

MASTER COMICS #30
September 1942. Mac Raboy cover art.
©FAW

MASTER COMICS #31
October 1942. Mac Raboy cover art.
©FAW

MASTER COMICS #33
December 1942. Mac Raboy cover art.
©FAW

MOON GIRL #3
1948. Shelly Moldoff cover art. ©WMG

MY GREATEST ADVENTURE #25
November 1957 ©DC

MY SECRET MARRIAGE #9
1960s. IW reprint. ©SUPR

NATIONAL COMICS #16
October 1941. Lou Fine cover art. ©BP

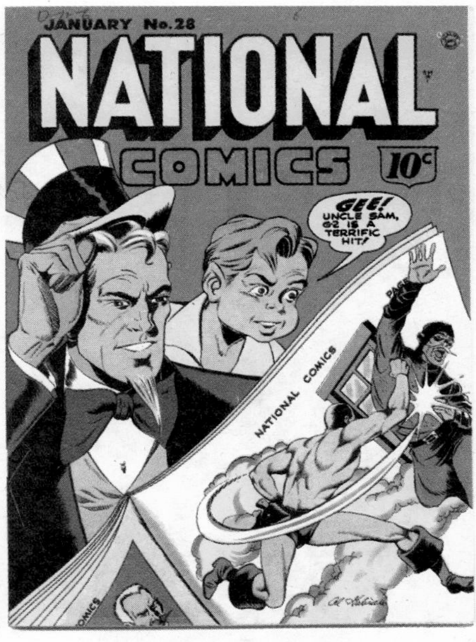

NATIONAL COMICS #28
January 1943. From the Mile High collection. ©BP

NICKEL COMICS #3
June 1940. Jack Binder cover art. From the Mile High collection. ©FAW

NICKEL COMICS #4
June 1940. Jack Binder cover art. Mile High copy. ©FAW

NICKEL COMICS #8
August 1940. C.C. Beck cover art. From the Mile High collection. ©FAW

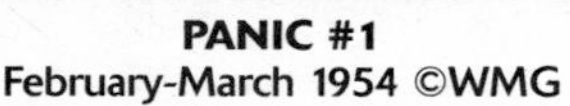

PANIC #1
February-March 1954 ©WMG

PLANET COMICS #44
September 1946 ©FH

PRIZE COMICS #19
February 1942.
From the Mile High collection. ©PRIZE

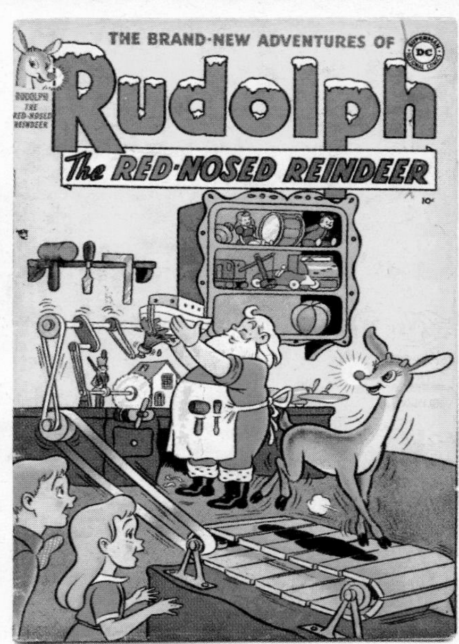

RUDOLPH THE RED-NOSED REINDEER
December 1950 (#1).
Grossman cover art. ©DC

SCIENCE COMICS #3
April 1940.
From the Mile High collection. ©FOX

SCIENCE COMICS #6
July 1940.
From the Mile High collection. ©FOX

SCIENCE COMICS #8
September 1940.
From the Mile High collection. ©FOX

SHOCK SUSPENSTORIES #7
February-March 1953.
Classic Feldstein face melting cover. ©WMG

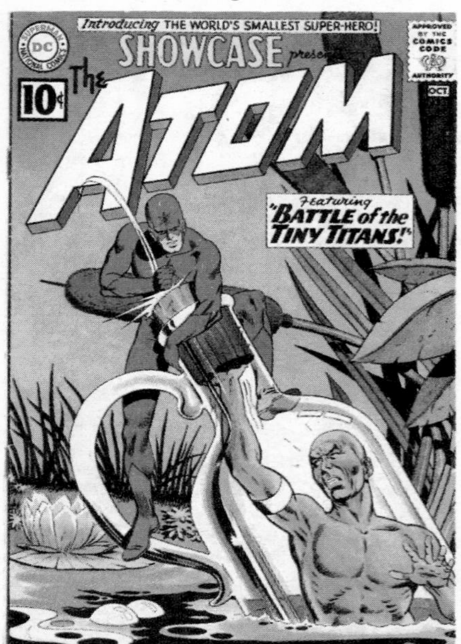

SHOWCASE #34
October 1961.
First appearance Silver Age Atom. ©DC

SILVER STREAK COMICS #23
1946 ©LEV

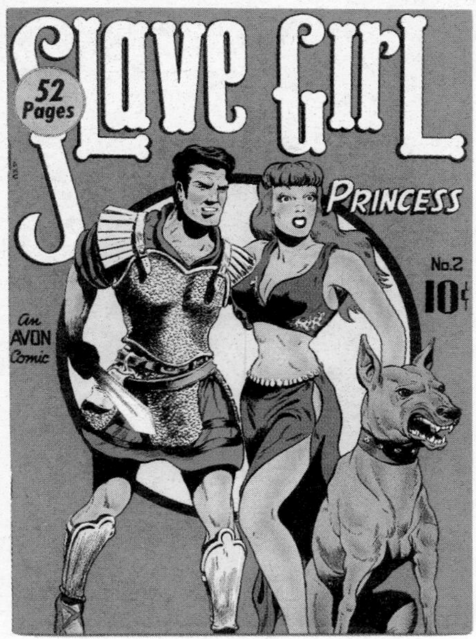

SLAVE GIRL #2
April 1949.
From the Mile High collection. ©AVON

STAR SPANGLED COMICS #24
September 1943. Simon & Kirby cover art.
From the Mile High collection. ©DC

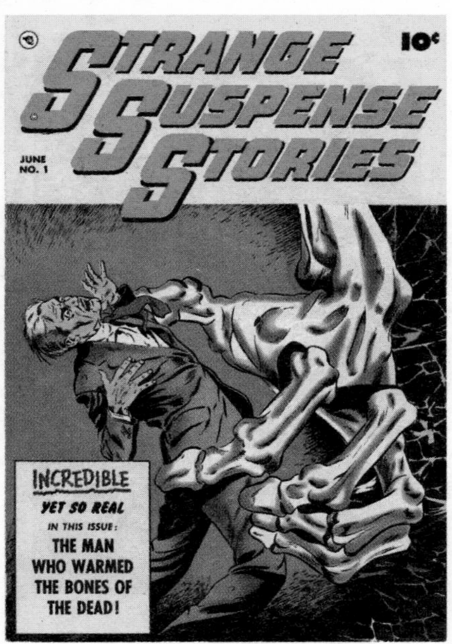

STRANGE SUSPENSE STORIES #1
June 1952 ©FAW

SUPER COMICS #74
July 1944 ©DELL

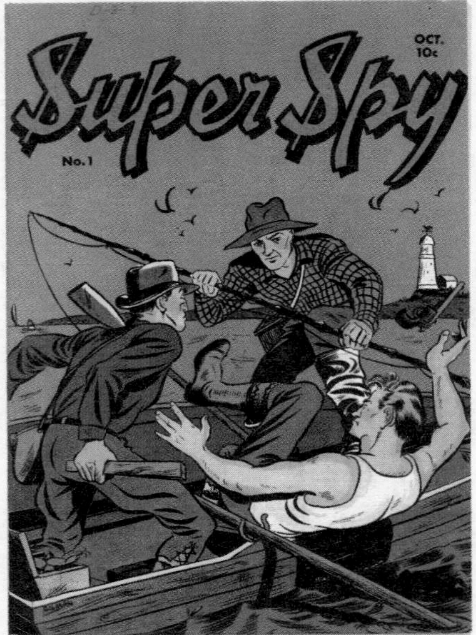

SUPER SPY #1
October 1940.
From the Mile High collection. ©CEN

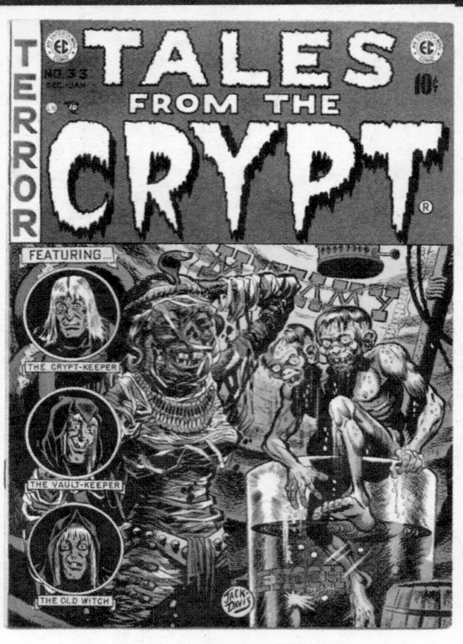

TALES FROM THE CRYPT #33
December-January 1953.
Origin of The Crypt Keeper. ©WMG

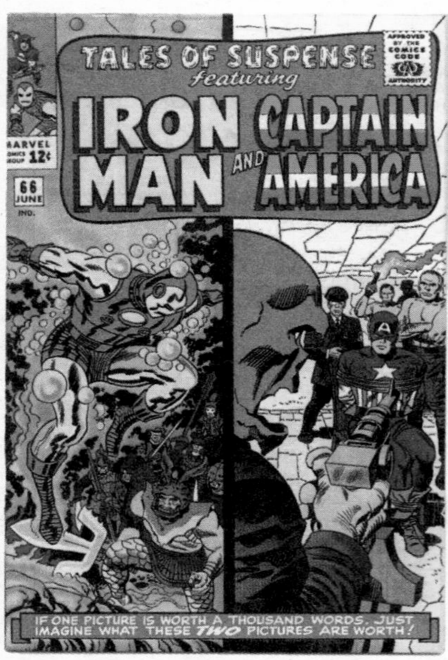

TALES OF SUSPENSE #66
June 1966. Origin of The Red Skull.
©MAR

TALLY-HO COMICS #1
December 1944. Frazetta's first comic work inside. ©Swappers Quart.

TARGET COMICS VOL. 1 #7
August 1940.
From the Mile High collection. ©NOVP

TARGET COMICS VOL. 2 #1
March 1941.
From the Mile High collection. ©NOVP

TARGET COMICS VOL. 9 #8
November 1943. From the Mile High collection. L.B. Cole cover art. ©NOVP

TARGET COMICS VOL. 2 #10
December 1941.
From the Mile High collection. ©NOVP

TARGET COMICS VOL. 3 #8
October 1948.
From the Mile High collection. ©NOVP

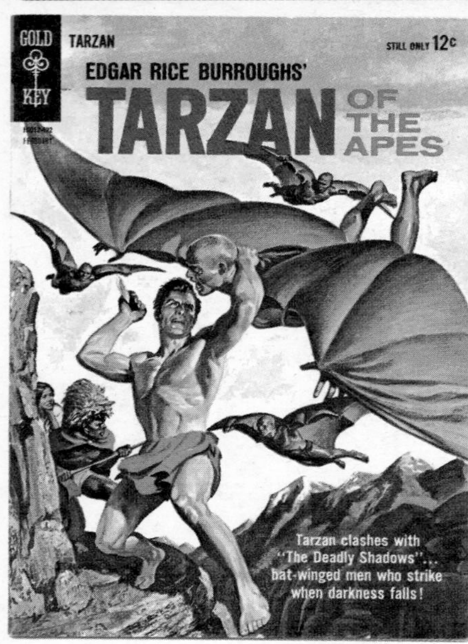

TARZAN #140
February 1964 ©ERB

TEX FARRELL #1
March-April 1948 ©DS

THIS MAGAZINE IS HAUNTED #10
April 1953.
Decapitation cover. ©FAW

THIS MAGAZINE IS HAUNTED #13
October 1953.
Decapitation cover. ©FAW

TIM HOLT #3
November-December 1948 ©ME

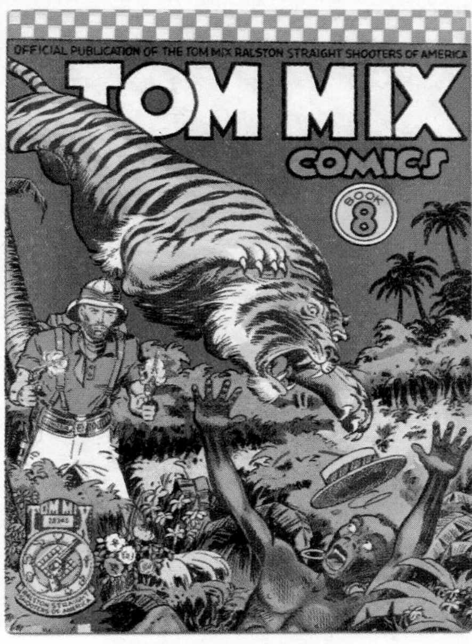

TOM MIX RALSTON #8
1941 ©FAW

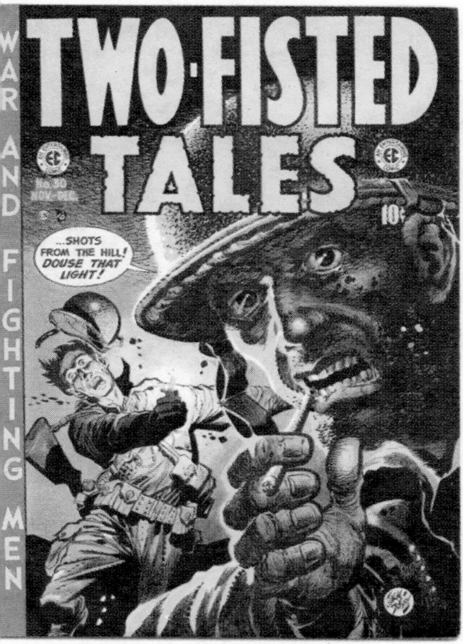

TWO FISTED TALES #30
November-December 1952 ©WMG

UNDERWORLD #1
February-March 1948 ©D.S. Publ.

UNUSUAL TALES #32
February 1962 ©CC

THE VAULT OF HORROR #35
March 1954 ©WMG

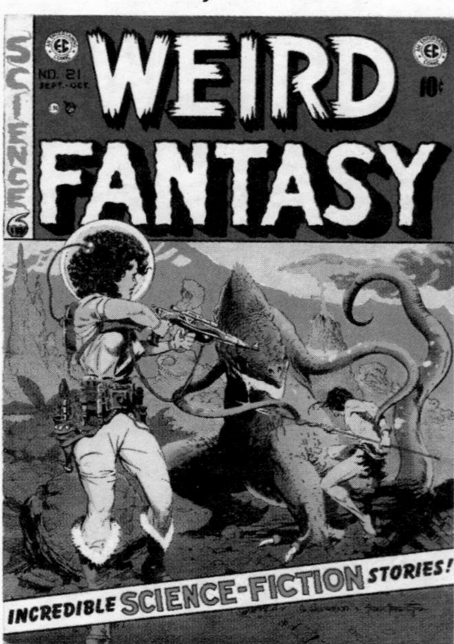

WEIRD FANTASY #21
September-October 1953.
Frazetta/Williamson cover art. ©WMG

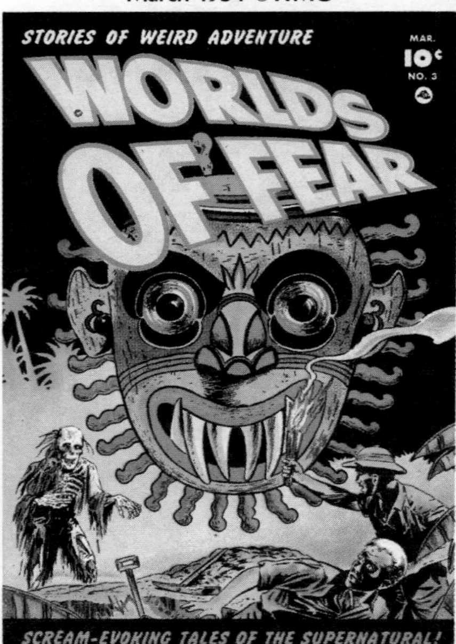

WORLDS OF FEAR #3
March 1952 ©FAW

WOW COMICS #16
August 1943.
From the Mile High collection. ©FAW

WOW COMICS #19
November 1943.
From the Mile High collection. ©FAW

WOW COMICS #35
April 1945.
From the Mile High collection. ©FAW

WOW COMICS #44
June 1946.
From the Mile High collection. ©FAW

OVERSTREET HALL OF FAME

For decades, historians, collectors and bibliofiles have tried to identify, list and document all the important, trend-setting comic books of the past century. This interesting topic continues to be debated and discussed by experts everywhere. In an attempt to answer these questions, Overstreet would like to nominate the following books to Overstreet's Hall Of Fame. The author invites your comments and ideas concerning the accuracy of this list for future editions. Remember, only the very top books will be considered for inclusion.

PLATINUM AGE 1897-1932

Yellow Kid in McFadden's Flats, The, 1897, Dillingham Co. (1st comic book)
Funny Folk, 1899, E.P. Dutton (2nd comic book)
Vaudeville and Other Things, 1900, Blandiard Co. (3rd comic book)
Blackberries, The, 1901, R.H. Russell (Ties as 4th comic book)
Foxy Grandpa, 1901, F.A. Stokes Co. (Ties as 4th comic book)
Pore Li'l Mose, 1902, Cupples & Leon (1st satire book) (1st Cupples & Leon book)
Alphonse & Gaston & Leon, 1903, Hearst's New York American
Buster Brown and His Resolutions, 1903, F.A. Stokes Co. (1st nationally distr. comic)
Happy Hooligan, 1903, Hearst's New York American (1st comic book app.)
Katzenjammer Kids, 1903, Hearst's New York American (1st comic book app.)
Brown's Blue Ribbon Book of Jokes and Jingles, 1904, Brown Shoe Co. (1st comic book premium)
Dreams of the Rarebit Fiend, 1905, Doffield & Co. (Ties as 1st Winsor McCay book)
Little Sammy Sneeze, 1905, New York Herald Co. (Ties as 1st Winsor McCay book)
Buster Brown, 1906, Cupples & Leon (1st C&L series comic)
Little Nemo, 1906, Doffield & Co. by Winsor McCay
3 Funmakers, 1908, Stokes (1st comic to feature more than one character)
Mutt & Jeff, 1910, Ball Publ. (1st comic book app.)
Comic Monthly, 1922, Embee Dist. Co. (1st monthly newsstand comic)
Funnies, The, 1929, Dell Publ. Co. (1st four-color comic newsstand publ.)
Mickey Mouse Book, 1930, Bibo & Lang (1st Disney licensed book)
Thimble Theatre Starring Popeye, 1931, Sonnet Publ. Co. (1st Popeye book)
Detective Dan, 1933, Humor Publ. Co. (1st comic w/original art & 1st on newsstand)
Adventures of Detective Ace King, 1933, Humor Publ. Co. (along with **Detective Dan**, helped bridge the gap between the PA and GA)

PRE-GOLDEN AGE 1933-May 1938

Funnies On Parade #nn, 1933, Eastern Color (1st GA comic book)
Century Of Comics #nn, 1933, Eastern Color (2nd GA comic book, 1st 100 pgs.)
Famous Funnies-Carnival Of Comics, nn, 1933, Eastern Color, (3rd GA comic book)
Famous Funnies-Series 1, 1934, Eastern Color, (1st 10 cent comic)
Famous Funnies #1, 7/34, Eastern Color (1st newsstand comic book)
New Fun Comics #1, 2/35, DC (1st DC comic book)
Big Book Of Fun Comics #1, Spr/35, DC, (1st annual in comics)
New Fun Comics #6, 10/35, DC (1st Siegel & Shuster work in comics)
More Fun Comics #14, 10/36, DC (1st Superman prototype at DC, 1st in color)
Detective Comics #1, 3/37, DC (1st issue of title that launched Batman)

GOLDEN AGE June 1938-1945

Action Comics #1, 6/38, DC (1st Superman and Lois Lane)
Funny Pages #V2#10, 9/38, Centaur (1st Arrow, 1st costumed hero)
Jumbo Comics #1, 9/38, Fiction House (1st Sheena, 1st Fiction House comic book)
Motion Picture Funnies Weekly #1, 1939, First Funnies Inc. (1st printed app. Sub-Mariner)
Movie Comics #1, 4/39, DC (1st movie comic)
New York World's Fair 1939, 4/39, DC (1st published Sandman story)
Detective Comics #27, 5/39, DC (1st Batman)
Wonder Comics #1, 5/39, Fox (1st Wonderman, 1st Superman imitator)
Superman nn (#1), Summer/39, DC (1st issue, 1st hero to get his own book)
Adventure Comics #40, 7/39, DC (1st conceived Sandman story)
Marvel Comics #1, 10/39, Timely (1st newsstand Sub-Mariner, 1st Human Torch, 1st Marvel comic)
Silver Streak #1, 12/39, Lev Gleason (1st Gleason comic book, 1st Claw)
Flash Comics #1, 1/40, DC (1st Flash, Hawkman, & Johnny Thunder)
Pep Comics #1, 1/40, MLJ/Archie (1st app. Shield, 1st patriotic hero)
Planet Comics #1, 1/40, Fiction House (1st all science fiction comic book)
More Fun Comics #52, 2/40, DC (1st Spectre)
Whiz Comics #2 (#1), 2/40, Fawcett (1st Captain Marvel & Spy Smasher, 1st Fawcett comic book)

Mutt & Jeff #1 © Ball Publ.

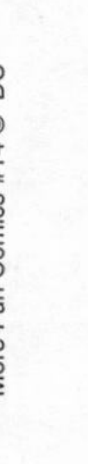

More Fun Comics #14 © DC

Pep Comics #1 © MLJ

Batman #1 © DC

All-Flash #1 © DC

Four Color #9 (Donald Duck) © WDC

Adventure Comics #48, 3/40, DC (1st Hourman)
More Fun Comics #53, 3/40, DC (Part II of 1st Spectre story)
Four Color Ser. 1 #4 (Donald Duck), 3?/40, (1st four color Donald Duck)
Action Comics #23, 4/40, DC (1st Lex Luthor)
Detective Comics #38, 4/40, DC (1st Robin)
Batman #1, Spring/40, DC (1st issue of DC's 2nd most important character; 1st 2 Joker stories; 1st Catwoman)
More Fun Comics #55, 5/40, DC (1st Dr. Fate)
The Spirit #1, 6/2/40, Will Eisner (1st Spirit app. in weekly newspaper strip)
All American Comics #16, 7/40, DC (1st Green Lantern)
Blue Bolt #3, 7/40, Fox (1st Simon & Kirby story art)
Marvel Mystery Comics #9, 7/40, Timely (1st superhero battle; key battle issue)
Red Raven #1, 8/40, Timely (Early Kirby art)
Special Edition Comics #1, 8/40, Fawcett (1st comic book devoted to Captain Marvel)
Silver Streak #6, 9/40, Lev Gleason (1st Daredevil)
Batman #3, Fall/40, DC (1st Catwoman in costume)
Human Torch #2 (#1), Fall/40, Timely (1st issue of early Marvel star)
Walt Disney's Comics & Stories #1, 10/40, Dell (1st funny animal comic book series)
All American Comics #19, 10/40, DC (1st Atom)
All Star Comics #3, Winter/40-41, DC (1st superhero group)
Adventure Comics #72, 3/41, DC (1st Simon & Kirby Sandman)

Captain America Comics #1, 3/41, Timely (1st Captain America)
Captain Marvel Adventures #1, 3/41, Fawcett (1st issue of Fawcett's top character)
Sub-Mariner Comics #1, Spring/41, Timely (1st issue of Marvel's important character)
Adventure Comics #61, 4/41, DC (1st Starman)
All Flash #1, Summer/41, DC (1st issue of top DC character)
Daredevil #1, 7/41, Lev Gleason (1st issue of top character)
Military Comics #1, 8/41, Quality (1st Blackhawk)
Famous Funnies #100, 10/41, Eastern (1st comic book to reach issue #100)
Green Lantern #1, Fall/41, DC (1st issue of top DC character)
Looney Tunes #1, Fall/41, Dell (1st Bugs Bunny, Porky Pig & Elmer Fudd in comics)
More Fun Comics #73, 11/41, DC (1st Aquaman; 1st Green Arrow and Speedy)
Pep Comics #22, 12/41, MLJ/Archie (1st Archie)
Whiz Comics #25, 12/41, Fawcett (1st Captain Marvel Jr.)
Four Color Ser. 1 (Mickey Mouse) #16, 1941, (1st comic book devoted to Mickey Mouse)
All Star Comics #8, 12-1/41-42, DC (1st Wonder Woman)
Animal Comics #1, 12-1/41-42, Dell (1st Pogo by Walt Kelly)
Sensation Comics #1, 1/42, DC (1st series to star Wonder Woman)
Crime Does Not Pay #22, 6/42, Gleason (1st Crime comic series)
Sensation #6, June, 1942, DC, (1st app. Wonder Woman's magic lasso)
Wonder Woman #1, Summer/42, DC (1st issue of top DC character)

Four Color (Donald Duck) #9, 8/42 Dell (1st Barks work on Donald Duck)
Air Fighters Comics V1 #3, 12/42, Hillman, (1st app. of the Heap, 1st swamp creature in comics)
Archie Comics #1, Winter/42-43, MLJ/ Archie, (1st Teenage comic)
Capt Marvel Adventures #22, 3/43, Fawcett, (Begins Mr. Mind serial)
Plastic Man #1, Summer/43, Quality (1st issue of top Quality character)
Big All-American Comic Book #1, 1944, DC, (1st annual of **All-American Comics**)
More Fun Comics #101, 1/2/45, DC (1st Superboy)
Molly O'Day #1, 2/45, Avon (1st Avon comic)
Terry Toones #38, 11/45, Timely (1st Mighty Mouse)

ATOM AGE 1946-1956

Romantic Picture Novelette #1, 1946, ME (one shot)(1st love comic theme)
All Winners #19, Fall/46, Timely (1st All Winners Squad, 1st Marvel group)
All Winners #21, Winter/46-47, Timely (2nd All Winners Squad)
Eerie #1, 1/47, Avon (1st horror comic)
Young Romance Comics #1, 9-10/47, Prize (1st romance series)
Four Color (Uncle Scrooge) #178, 12/47, Dell (1st Uncle Scrooge)
Phantom Lady #17, 4/48, Fox (Classic cover issue–good girl art)
Adventures Into The Unknown #1, Fall/48, ACG (1st horror series)
Moon Girl #5, Winter/48, EC (1st EC horror story)
Casper #1, 9/49, St John (1st Baby Huey)
Crime Patrol #15, 12-1/49-50, EC

Red Raven Comics #1 © MAR

Crime Does Not Pay #22 © LEV

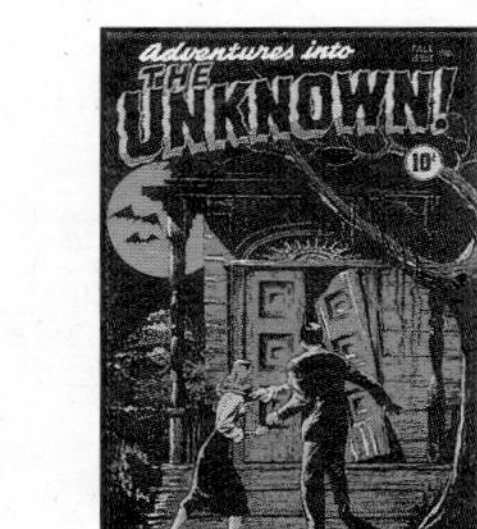

Adventures into the Unknown #1 © ACG

Crypt of Terror #17 © WMG

House of Secrets #1 © DC

Amazing Adventures #1 © MAR

(1st Crypt Keeper)
War Against Crime #10, 12-1/49-50, EC (1st Vault Keeper)
Howdy Doody #1, 1/50, Dell (1st TV comic book)
Archie Annual #1, 1950, Archie (1st **Archie** annual)
Crypt Of Terror #17, 4-5/50, EC (1st issue of Crypt Keeper tales, EC horror)
Haunt Of Fear #15 (#1), 5-6/50, EC (1st issue of EC horror, trend-setting)
Weird Fantasy #13 (#1), 5-6/50, EC (1st issue of EC science fiction, trend-setting)
Weird Science #12 (#1), 5-6/50, EC (1st issue of EC science fiction)
Strange Tales #1, 6/51, Marvel (1st issue of top Marvel title)
Mad #1, 10-11/52, EC (1st satire comic)
Journey Into Mystery #1, 6/52, Marvel (1st issue of top Marvel title)
Little Dot #1, 9/53, Harvey (1st Richie Rich)
Young Men #24, 12/53, Marvel (Revival of Capt. America, Human Torch & Sub-Mariner)
World's Finest Comics #71, 7-8/54, DC (1st Superman/Batman team issue)
Superman's Pal, Jimmy Olsen #1, 9-10/54, DC, (1st issue of top DC title)
My Greatest Adventure #1, 1-2/55, DC (1st issue of top DC fantasy title)
Brave And The Bold #1, 8-9/55, DC (1st issue of top DC showcase title)
Superman #100, 9-10/55, DC (Landmark issue)
Detective Comics #225, 11/55, DC (1st Martian Manhunter)
Tales Of The Unexpected #1, 2-3/56, DC (1st issue of top DC fantasy title)
Showcase #1, 3-4/56, DC (1st issue of top DC title)
Sugar & Spike #1, 4-5/56, DC (1st issue of top title by Sheldon Mayer)
Batman #100, 6/56, DC (Landmark issue)
Detective Comics #233, 7/56, DC (1st Batwoman)

SILVER AGE Sept. 1956-1969

Showcase #4, 9-10/56, DC (1st Silver Age book) (The Flash)
House Of Secrets #1, 11-12/56, DC (1st issue of top DC horror title)
Showcase #6, 1-2/57, DC (1st Silver Age group)(Challengers)
Showcase #9, 7-8/57, DC (1st Lois Lane book)
Superman's Girl Friend, Lois Lane #1, 3-4/58, DC (1st issue of top character)
Adventure Comics #247, 4/58, DC (1st Legion of Superheroes)
Challengers Of The Unknown #1, 4-5/58, DC, (1st issue of 1st Silver Age group)
Showcase #15, 7-8/58, DC (1st Space Ranger)
Showcase #17, 11-12/58, DC (1st Adam Strange)
Tales Of Suspense #1, 1/59, Marvel (1st issue of top fantasy title)
Tales To Astonish #1, 1/59, Marvel (1st issue of top fantasy title)
Flash #105 (#1), 2-3/59, DC (1st issue of top DC title)
Our Army At War #83, 6/59, DC (1st Sgt. Rock by Kubert/Kanigher)
Action Comics #252, 5/59, DC (1st Supergirl)
Showcase #20, 5-6/59, DC (1st Rip Hunter)
Double Life Of Private Strong #1, 6/59, Archie (1st Silver Age Shield, 1st Fly)
Mystery In Space #53, 8/59, DC (1st Adam Strange)
Tales Of The Unexpected #40, 8/59, DC (1st Space Ranger in own title)
Adventures of the Fly #1, 8/59, Archie (1st issue of top Archie title)
Showcase #22, 9-10/59, DC (1st Silver Age Green Lantern)
Flash #110, 12-1/59/60, DC (1st Kid Flash)
Brave And The Bold #28, 2/3/60, DC (1st Justice League of America)
Green Lantern #1, 7-8/60, DC (1st issue of top DC character)
Showcase #27, 7-8/60, DC (1st Sea Devils)
Brave And The Bold #31, 8-9/60, DC (1st Cave Carson)
Justice League Of America #1, 10-11/60, DC (1st issue of top DC title)
Showcase #30, 1-2/61, DC (Spotlights Silver Age Aquaman)
Brave And The Bold #34, 2-3/61, DC (1st Silver Age Hawkman)
Amazing Adventures #1, 6/61, Marvel (1st Dr. Droom, the 1st Marvel-Age superhero)
Flash #123, 9/61, DC (1st G.A. Flash in Silver Age)
Showcase #34, 9-10/61, DC (1st Silver Age Atom)
Fantastic Four #1, 11/61, Marvel (1st Fantastic Four)
Amazing Adult Fantasy #7, 12/61, Marvel (1st issue of title that leads to Spider-Man)
Tales To Astonish #27, 1/62, Marvel (1st Antman)
Showcase #37, 3-4/62, DC (1st Metal Men)
Fantastic Four #4, 5/62, Marvel (1st Silver Age Sub-Mariner)
Incredible Hulk #1, 5/62, Marvel (1st Hulk)

Little Dot #1 © HARV

Adventure Comics #247 © DC

Showcase #34 © DC

Green Lantern #76 © DC

Incredible Hulk #181 © MAR

Batman The Dark Knight #1 © DC

Mystery In Space #75, 5/62, DC (Early JLA cross-over in Adam Strange story)
Fantastic Four #5, 7/62, Marvel (1st Dr. Doom)
Journey Into Mystery #83, 8/62, Marvel (1st Thor)
Amazing Fantasy #15, 8-9/62, Marvel (1st Spider-Man)
Tales To Astonish #35, 9/62, Marvel (2nd Antman, 1st in costume)
Strange Tales #101, 10/62, Marvel (1st S.A. Human Torch solo story)
Amazing Spider-Man #1, 3/63, Marvel (1st Spider-Man in own title)
Tales Of Suspense #39, 3/63, Marvel (1st Iron Man)
Strange Tales #110, 7/63, Marvel (1st Dr. Strange)
Justice League of America #21, 8/63, DC (1st JLA/JSA crossover)
Avengers #1, 9/63, Marvel (1st Avengers)
X-Men #1, 9/63, Marvel (1st X-Men)
Mystery In Space #87, 11/63, DC (1st Hawkman in title)
Avengers #4, 3/64, Marvel (1st Silver Age Captain America)
Daredevil #1, 4/64, Marvel (1st Daredevil)
Detective Comics #327, 5/64, DC (New Batman) (Silver Age/ Bronze)
Brave and the Bold #54, 6-7/64, DC (1st Teen Titans)
Amazing Spider-Man #14, 7/64, Marvel (1st Green Goblin)
Strange Tales #135, 7/65, Marvel (Origin & 1st app. Nick Fury)
Fantastic Four #48, 3/66, Marvel (1st Silver Surfer)
Our Army at War #168, 6/66, DC (1st Unknown Soldier)
Strange Adventures #205, 10/67, DC (1st Deadman)
Zap Comix#1, 11/67, Apex (Underground comic which instigated the direct sales market)

BRONZE AGE 1970-1979

Green Lantern #76, 4/70, DC (Begins Green Lantern/Green Arrow series by Denny O'Neil & Neal Adams)
Detective Comics #400, 6/70, DC (1st Man-Bat)
Superman's Pal, Jimmy Olsen #133, 10/70, DC (1st Silver Age Newsboy Legion)
Forever People #1, 2-3/71, DC (1st Forever People)
New Gods #1, 3/71, DC (1st New Gods)
Mister Miracle #1, 3/71, DC (1st Mister Miracle)
Savage Tales #1, 5/71, Marvel (1st Man-Thing)
House of Secrets #92, 6/71, DC (1st app. Swamp Thing by Bernie Wrightson)
Amazing Spider-Man #101, 10/71, Marvel (1st Morbius the Living Vampire)
Marvel Feature #1, 12/71, Marvel (Origin and 1st app. Defenders)
All Star Western #10, 2-3/72, DC (1st Jonah Hex)
Tomb of Dracula #1, 4/72, Marvel (1st app. Dracula)
Marvel Spotlight #2, 6/72, Marvel (1st app. Werewolf by Night)
Marvel Spotlight #5, 8/72, Marvel (Origin and 1st app. new Ghost Rider)
Kamandi: The Last Boy on Earth #1, 10/72, DC (Origin/1st Kamandi)
Iron Man #55, 2/73, Marvel (1st. app. Thanos & Drax the Destroyer)
Shazam #1, 2/73, DC (1st revival of Captain Marvel since mid 50s)
Amazing Spider-Man #121, 6/73 Marvel (Death of Gwen Stacy)
Amazing Spider-Man #122, 7/73, Marvel (Death of Green Goblin I)
Marvel Spotlight #12, 10/73, Marvel (1st solo Son of Satan)
Marvel Special Edition #15, 12/73, Marvel (1st Master of Kung Fu)
Amazing Spider-Man #129, 2/74, Marvel (1st Punisher)
Astonishing Tales #25, 8/74, Marvel (1st Deathlok)
Incredible Hulk #181, 11/74, Marvel (1st story app. of Wolverine)
Giant Size X-Men #1, Summer/75, Marvel (1st New X-Men; intro Nightcrawler, Storm, Colossus & Thunderbird)
X-Men #94, 8/75, Marvel (New X-Men team begins)
All Star Comics #58, 1-2/76, DC (1st Power Girl)
Marvel Spotlight #32, 2/77, Marvel (1st Spider-Woman)
Black Lightning #1, 4/77, DC (1st Black Lightning)
Cerebus #1, 12/77, Aardvark-Vanaheim (1st app. Cerebus)(B&W)
X-Men #108, 12/77, Marvel (1st important Byrne work)
Daredevil #158, 5/79, Marvel (Frank Miller begins work on Daredevil; his 1st important work)

MODERN AGE 1980-Present

X-Men #137, 9/80, Marvel (The story that started comicdom's "Death Craze")
Daredevil #168, 1/81, Marvel (1st Elektra)
Gobbledygook #1, pre 6/84; Mirage, (1st app. Teenage Mutant Ninja Turtles)
Crisis on Infinite Earths #1-12, 85/86, DC (1st appearance of revamped Modern Age DC universe) (#7, Death of Supergirl) (#8, Death of the Barry Allen Flash)
Batman: The Dark Knight #1, 3/86, DC (Beginning of Frank Miller's landmark revision of Batman)
Maus, 1986, Pantheon Books (1st comic book to win the Pulitzer Prize) (depicts the horrors of the Holocaust through the eyes of artist Art Spiegelman's father)
The Man of Steel #1, 6/86, DC (Beginning of John Byrne's update of the Superman mythos)
Watchmen #1, 10/87, DC (Beginning of Alan Moore's revisionist look at superheroes)
Batman: The Killing Joke, 1988, DC (Batgirl Barbara Gordon is crippled by the Joker)
Amazing Spider-Man #300, 5/88, Marvel (1st Venom) (full app & story)
Sandman #1, 1/89, DC (1st app. new Sandman)
X-Men #1, 10/91, Marvel (1st comic to reach a print run of 8 million copies)
Youngblood #1, 4/92, Image (1st Image comic)
Spawn #1, 5/92, Image (1st app. Spawn)
Superman (2nd Series) #75, 1/93, DC (Death of Superman) (Huge Media Coverage)
Deathmate Black, 9/93, Valiant/ Image (1st Gen13 story)
Starman #0, 10/94, DC (1st app. of Modern Age Starman)
Strangers in Paradise #1, 11/94, Antarctic (1st issue of Terry Moore's series)
DC Vs. Marvel #1, 1996, DC (1st issue of landmark company crossover)
Kingdom Come #1-4, 1996, DC (Fully painted Elseworlds series about the future DC universe)
Superman: The Wedding Album, 12/96, DC (Marriage of Clark Kent and Lois Lane)

OVERSTREET PRICE GUIDE BACK ISSUES

The Overstreet® Comic Book Price Guide has held the record for being the longest running annual comic book publication. We are now celebrating our 31st anniversary and comic book collectors are as interested in putting together complete sets of these books as they are in collecting the old comics. The demand for the Overstreet® price guides is very strong and the collectors have created a legitimate market for them. They continue to bring record prices each year. Besides the price consideration, collectors also have a record of comic book prices going back further than any other source in comic fandom. The prices listed below are for near mint condition only. The other grades can be determined as follows: Good - 25% and Fine - 50% of the near mint value. Canadian editions exist for a couple of the early issues. Special thanks is given to Robert Rogovin of Four Color Comics for his assistance in researching the prices listed in this section.

Abbreviations used: SC = soft cover; HC = hard cover, L = leather bound.

1970
#1 White Soft cover
$1700.00

1970
#1 Blue Soft cover
(2nd Printing)
$1400.00

1972
#2 SC $600.00
#2 HC $1000.00

1973
#3 SC $275.00
#3 HC $900.00

1974
#4 SC $150.00
#4 HC $450.00

1975
#5 SC $150.00
#5 HC $250.00

1976
#6 SC $100.00
#6 HC $150.00

1977
#7 SC $140.00
#7 HC $225.00

1978
#8 SC $125.00
#8 HC $175.00

1979
#9 SC $125.00
#9 HC $175.00

1980
#10 SC $125.00
#10 HC $175.00

1981
#11 SC $80.00
#11 HC $110.00

1982
#12 SC $80.00
#12 HC $110.00

1983
#13 SC $80.00
#13 HC $110.00

1984
#14 SC $55.00
#14 HC $110.00
#14 L $170.00

1985
#15 SC $55.00
#15 HC $80.00
#15 L $160.00
1986
#16 SC $55.00
#16 HC $80.00
#16 L $160.00
1987
#17 SC $55.00
#17 HC $110.00
#17 L $160.00
1988
#18 SC $45.00
#18 HC $65.00
#18 L $160.00
1989
#19 SC $45.00
#19 HC $55.00
#19 L $160.00
1990
#20 SC $32.00
#20 HC $50.00
#20 L $135.00
1991
#21 SC $32.00
#21 HC $50.00
#21 L $135.00
1992
#22 SC $32.00
#22 HC $50.00
1993
#23 SC $32.00
#23 HC $50.00
1994
#24 SC $24.00
#24 HC $34.00
1995
#25 SC $24.00
#25 HC $34.00
#25 L $100.00
1996
#26 SC $20.00
#26 HC $30.00
#26 L $100.00
1997
#27 SC $22.00
#27 HC $38.00
#27 L $125.00
1997
#27 SC $22.00
#27 HC $38.00
#27 L $125.00
1998
#28 SC $20.00
#28 HC $35.00
1998
#28 SC $20.00
#28 HC $35.00
1999
#29 SC $20.00
#29 HC $35.00
1999
#29 SC $20.00
#29 HC $35.00
2000
#30 SC $22.00
#30 HC $32.00
2000
#30 SC $22.00
#30 HC $32.00

FEATURE ARTICLE INDEX

Over the years, the **Overstreet Comic Book Price Guide** has grown into much more than a simple catalog of values. Almost since the very beginning, Bob has worked hard to make sure that the book reflects the latest information about the hobby, and this has resulted in some fascinating in-depth articles about aspects of the industry and the rich history of comics. Sadly, many of you may never have read a lot of these articles, or even knew they existed...until now.

Now, for the first time, we present a comprehensive index to every feature article ever published in the **Overstreet Comic Book Price Guide**. From interviews with legendary creators to exhaustively researched retrospectives, it's all here. Enjoy this look back at the Overstreet legacy, and remember, many of these editions are still available through Gemstone and your local comic book dealer.

Note: The first three editions of the Guide had no feature articles, but from #4 on, a tradition was born that has carried through to the very volume you hold in your hands. This index begins with the 4th edition and lists all articles published up to and including last year's 30th edition of the guide.

ED.	YR.	TITLE	AUTHOR(S)	PGS.
#4	1974	Secrets Behind ALL-STAR COMICS(More Than You May Want to Know)	Jerry Bails	26-37
#5	1975	Edgar Rice Burroughs and the Comics	Kevin B. Hancer	33-38
#6	1976	An Interview with Will Eisner, Creator of the Spirit	Jerry DeFuccio	31-37
		Good Girl Art - An Introduction: Why it Was and What it WasAmerican Comic Book Co.	produced by the (Carl Macek)	38-43
		The Archives of the Comic Book Price Guide	Landon Chesney (comic strip)	44-45
#7	1977	Esoteric Comics: The Ultimate Collectable	prod. by the American Comic Book Co. (Carl Macek in consultation with Scott Shaw)	A-30-35
		Carl Barks - From Burbank to Calisota	E. B. Boatner	A-37-57
#8	1978	Confessions of a Former Comic Book Artist	Jay Disbrow	A-31-38
		The Man Behind Torchy	Bill Ward	A-40-53
		Women in Comics	Carl Macek in collaboration with Art Amsie	A-54-75
		Tarpe Mills - An Appreciation	Trina Robbins	A-76
#9	1979	For Those Who Know How to Look	Carl Macek	A-35-42
		Good Lord! choke... gasp... It's EC!	E. B. Boatner	A-43-76
#10	1980	The Origin of Marvel Comics	George Olshevsky	A-46-73
#11	1981	Anaglyphs	Ray Zone	A-44-53
		A Survey of the 3-D Comic Books		
		L. B. Cole: The Man Behind the Mask: (and Captain Aero and Catman and...)	E. B. Boatner	A-55-72
#12	1982	Norman Mingo and Alfred: The World's Greatest Facelift	Jerry DeFuccio	A-45-57
		The Pop Hollinger Story: The First Comic Book Collector/Dealer	Tim Hessee	A-58-66
#13	1983	Great Old Time Radio Premiums	"Little" Jimmy Dempsey	A-62-63
		Reminiscences of a Comic Book Editor	Jack Schiff and Gene Reed	A-64-70
		DC Before Superman	Gary M. Carter and Ken Lane Carter	A-72-86
#14	1984	Katy WHO?...Never Heard of it...	Barbara A. Rausch	A-52-56
		Congratulations Katy Keene (various comic book and cartoon creators and their character)		A-57-59
		Katy Keene - The Overstreet Connection	Craig Leavitt	A-67-78
#15	1985	Charles Clarence Beck: The World's Second Mightiest Mortal	Jerry DeFuccio	A-78-88
		Mr. Mind and the Monster Society of Evil	C. C. Beck	A-89-93
#16	1986	Twenty-Five Years? I Don't Believe It!	Stan Lee	A-82-84
		Marvel and Me	Jim Shooter	A-85-96
#17	1987	The Man Behind the Cover - Ron Dias	staff	A-84
		The Enduring Magic of Disney Comics	Thomas Andrae (with Bruce Hamilton)	A-85-99
		Walt Disney's Snow White and the Seven: Dwarfs - Fifty Years of Collectibles	Terry Taylor	A-101-111
#18	1988	The Man Behind the Cover - L. B. Cole	Christopher Irons	A-77
		Of Supermen and Kids With Dreams:	Thomas Andrae	A-79-98

		An Interview with Jerry Seigel and Joe Shuster		
#19	1989	Origins of the Dark Knight: A Conversation with Batman Artists	Thomas Andrae, Bob Kane and Jerry Robinson	A-72-93
#20	1990	In a League of Their Own !	Harry B. Thomas	A-77-93
		The Silver Age...The Beginning: A Comparative Chronology of the First Silver Age Comic Books	Gary M. Carter	A-94-107
#21	1991	Archie Comic Publications: The Mirth of a Legend	Scott D. Fulop	A-77-78
		1941: Comic Books Go To War!: Those fabulous comics of World War II	Harry B. Thomas and Gary M. Carter	A-79-98
#22	1992	Spider-Man - An Amazing Success Story	Steve Saffel	A-77-86
		Journey Into the Unknown World of Atlas Fantasy	Gary M. Carter and Pat S. Calhoun	A-87-103
#23	1993	Green Lantern's Light! A History by...	Thomas Andrae with Keif Fromm	A-71-79
		Silver Sagas of the Scarlet Speedster: Whirlwind Adventures of the Fastest Man Alive! 1956-1960	Gary M. Carter	A-80-86
#24	1994	Three Uncanny Decades of X-Men!	John Townsend, Ph.D.	A-146-156
		Living on Borrowed Time! Pat S. Calhoun and A Nostalgic Look at the Early Years of DC's Challengers of the Unknown!	Gary M. Carter	A-157-164
#25	1995	The Mystery of the 12 Missing ECs	Bruce Hamilton	A-99-106
		100 Years - A Century of Comics	Pat S. Calhoun	A-107-123
#26	1996	The American Comic Book: 1897-1932 The Formative Years - The Platinum Age	Richard D. Olson, Ph.D.	pp. 1-2
		The American Comic Book: 1933-Present The Modern Comic Book The Golden Age and Beyond	Richard D. Olson, Ph.D.	pp. 10-11
		A Short History of Comic Book Fandom & Comic Book Collecting in America	Jerry Weist Sotheby's Comic Book Consultant	652-667
#27	1997	Gotham Knights - A Conversation	Arnold T. Blumberg with Jerry Robinson	A-25-27
		Strange Adventures - A Conversation with Murphy Anderson	Scott Braden	A-30-32
		The American Comic Book: 1897-1932 The Beginning: The Platinum Age	Robert L. Beerbohm	pp. 1-15
		The American Comic Book: 1933-Present The Golden Age and Beyond: The Modern Comic Book	Richard D. Olson, Ph.D.	23-24
#28	1998	Friends of Lulu Sounds Off on Comics	Jackie Estrada	79-81
		The World of Tomorrow : How Comics of the Past Portrayed the 1990s	Arnold T. Blumberg	82-88
		Invasion of the Giant (and Not So Giant) Robots!	Arnold T. Blumberg	83-87
		Built to Last	J. C. Vaughn and Scott Braden	89-102
		The American Comic Book: 1897-1932 In the Beginning: The Platinum Age:	J. C. Vaughn	201-203
		The American Comic Book: 1933-Present The Golden Age & Beyond: The Modern Comic Book (Revised)	Richard D. Olson, Ph.D.	211-212
#29	1999	Special Feature: Grading The Next Revolution for Comic Books	Bruce Hamilton	17-21
		Avenues of Collecting: A Walk Through the Comic Book Neighborhood	J. C. Vaughn	91-94
		Just Another Justice League?	J. C. Vaughn	95-100
		Legiondary Adventures	Mark Huesman	101-106
		One For All and All For One:	Arnold T. Blumberg	107-112
		A Brief History of Super-Teams: Top Ten Greatest Super-Teams	Benn Ray	108-112
		The American Comic Book: 1897-1932 In the Beginning: The Platinum Age (Rev.)	Robert L. Beerbohm & Richard D. Olson, PhD	211-218
		The American Comic Book: 1933-Present The Golden Age & Beyond & The Origin of the Modern Comic Book	Robert L. Beerbohm Richard D. Olson, PhD	226-233
#30	2000	History with a Twist	Arnold T. Blumberg	18-22
		EC, MAD and Beyond: Al Feldstein	J. C. Vaughn	24-28
		Flights to EC and Beyond with Al Williamson	J. C. Vaughn	36-39
		Bob's Bizarre Tales	Bob Overstreet	42-63
		The Marketing of a Medium	Arnold T. Blumberg	195-198
		New Discoveries Beyond the Platinum Age	Beerbohm & Olson	226-234
		The Golden Age & Beyond: Origins of the Modern Comic Book	Beerbohm & Olson	242-249

OVERSTREET ADVISORS

DAVID T. ALEXANDER
David Alexander Comics
Tampa, FL

DAVE ANDERSON
Want List Comics
Tulsa, OK

STEPHEN BARRINGTON
Collector
Chickasaw, AL

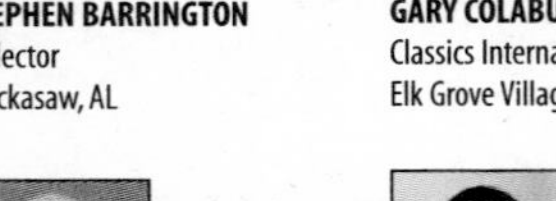

ROBERT BEERBOHM
Robert Beerbohm Comic Art
Fremont, NE

JON BERK
Collector
Hartford, CT

STEVE BOROCK
Primary Grader
Comics Guaranty, LLC

ERICK CARTER
Tropic Comics
Plantation, FL

GARY CARTER
Editor, CBM
Coronado, CA

JOHN CHRUSCINSKI
Grader
Comics Guaranty, LLC

GARY COLABUONO
Classics International Ent.
Elk Grove Village, IL

BILL COLE
Bill Cole Enterprises, Inc.
Randolph, MA

LARRY CURCIO
Avalon Comics
Los Angeles, CA

GARY DOLGOFF
Gary Dolgoff Comics
Easthampton, MA

BRUCE ELLSWORTH
Tropic Comics
Plantation, FL

CONRAD ESCHENBERG
Collector/Dealer
Cold Spring, NY

RICHARD EVANS
Bedrock City Comics
Houston, TX

STEPHEN FISHLER
Metropolis Collectibles, Inc.
New York, NY

STEVEN GENTNER
Golden Age Specialist
Portland, OR

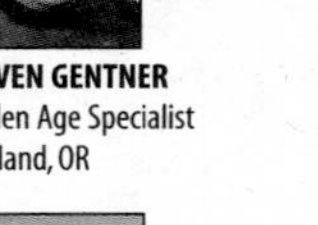

MICHAEL GOLDMAN
Motor City Comics
Southfield, MI

JAMIE GRAHAM
Graham Crackers
Chicago, IL

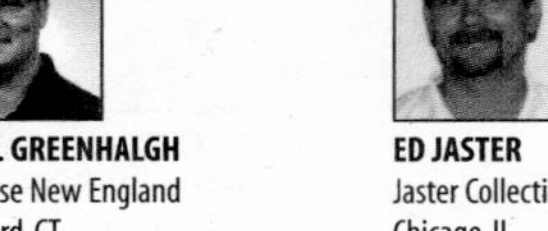

DANIEL GREENHALGH
Showcase New England
Northford, CT

ERIC J. GROVES
Dealer/Collector
Oklahoma City, OK

ROBERT HALL
Collector
Harrisburg, PA

BRUCE HAMILTON
Hamilton Comics
Prescott, AZ

MARK HASPEL
Grader
Comics Guaranty, LLC

JOHN HAUSER
Dealer/Collector
New Berlin, WI

BILL HUGHES
Greg Manning Auctions, Inc.
West Caldwell, NJ

ROB HUGHES
Arch Angels
Manhattan Beach, CA

ED JASTER
Jaster Collectibles
Chicago, IL

JOSEPH KOCH
Dealer/Collector
Brooklyn, NY

PHIL LEVINE
Dealer/Collector
Three Bridges, NJ

HARRY MATETSKY
Collector
Middletown, NJ

JON McCLURE
Dealer/Collector
Newport, OR

MIKE McKENZIE
Alternate Worlds
Cockeysville, MD

JASON McKIBBIN
Clarence Road, Inc.
Tacoma, WA

PETER MEROLO
Collector
Sedona, AZ

DALE MOORE
Clarence Road, Inc.
Tacoma, WA

MICHAEL NAIMAN
Silver Age Specialist
San Diego, CA

JOSHUA NATHANSON
ComicLink
Little Neck, NY

MATT NELSON
Classic Conservations
New Orleans, LA

RICHARD OLSON
Collector/Academician
Slidell, LA

JIM PAYETTE
Golden Age Specialist
Bethlehem, NH

CHRIS PEDRIN
Pedrin Conservatory
Redwood City, CA

RON PUSSELL
Redbeard's Book Den
Crystal Bay, NV

TODD REZNIK
Pacific Comic Exchange
Palos Verdes Peninsula, CA

ROBERT ROGOVIN
Four Color Comics
New York, NY

RORY ROOT
Comic Relief
Berkeley, CA

MARNIN ROSENBERG
Collectors Assemble
Great Neck, NY

ROBERT ROTER
Pacific Comic Exchange
Palos Verdes Peninsula, CA

CHUCK ROZANSKI
Mile High Comics
Denver, CO

MATT SCHIFFMAN
Bronze Age Specialist
Aloha, OR

DAVID SMITH
Fantasy Illustrated/Rocket Comics
Seattle, WA

JOHN SNYDER
Diamond Int. Galleries
Timonium, MD

TONY STARKS
Silver Age Specialist
Evansville, IN

TERRY STROUD
Dealer/Collector
Santa Monica, CA

DOUG SULIPA
"Everything 1960-1996"
Manitoba, Canada

MICHAEL TIERNEY
The Comic Book Store
Little Rock, AR

JOE VERENEAULT
JHV Associates
Woodbury Heights, NJ

JERRY WEIST
Sotheby's
New York, NY

JODI WOLFRUM
Collector
Durham, NH

HARLEY YEE
Dealer/Collector
Detroit, MI

VINCENT ZURZOLO, JR.
Metropolis Collectibles, Inc.
New York, NY

OVERSTREET ADVISORS

A-1 Comics
Brian Peets
5800 Madison Ave.
Sacramento, CA 95841
916.331.9203
a1comics@a-1comics.com

All About Books & Comics
Phil Mateer
517 East Camelback Road
Phoenix, AZ 85012
602.277.0757
phil@all-about-comics.com

Alternate Worlds
Michael McKenzie
72 Cranbrook Rd.
Cockeysville, MD 21030
410.666.3290
altworld@aol.com

Amazing Comics
Bob Nastasi
12 Gillette Ave
Sayville, NY 11782-3123
631.567.8069
info@amazingco.com

The American Comic Book Co.
Terry Stroud
P.O.Box 23
Santa Monica, CA 90406
310.399.4352

Arch Angels
Rob Hughes
1116 8th Street #106
Manhattan, CA 90266
310.335.1359
rhughes@archangels.com

Avalon Comics
Larry Curcio
P.O. Box 481251
Los Angeles, CA 90048-1251
323.571.2424
avalon-curcio@mediaone.net

Bedrock City Comic Co.
Richard Evans
6517 Westheimer
Houston, TX 77057
713.780.0675
bedrock@flash.net

Jon Berk
JBComicbox@aol.com

Bill Cole Enterprises
Bill Cole
P.O. Box 60
Randolph, MA 02368-0060
781.986.2653
bcemylar@cwbusiness.com

CB Comics Plus
Brian and Carol Morris
P.O. Box 3792
Champaign, IL 61826-3792
217.398.0155
bkmorris@prairienet.org

Clarence Road, Inc.
Dale & Sheri Moore/ Jason McKibbin
631 N. Trafton #2
Tacoma, WA 98403
253.383.7173
crinc6@qwest.net

Classic Comics/Illustrated
Phil Gaudino
49 Park Ave.
Port Washington, NY 11050
516.883.5659
prospect19@aol.com

Classic Conservations
Matt Nelson
P.O. Box 2335
Slidell, LA 70459
504.639.0621
spectre52@aol.com

Collectors Assemble
Marnin Rosenberg
P.O. Box 222047
Great Neck, NY 11022-9998
516.466.8147
www.collectorsassemble.com

The Comic Art Foundation
Eric Groves
P.O. Box 1414
Oklahoma City, OK 73101
405.236.5303

The Comic Book Store
Michael Tierney
9307 Treasure Hill
Little Rock, AR 72227
501.227.9777
cbsrock@swbell.net

Comic Detectives
Dan & Kim Fogel/Jim Pitts/Rick Calou
P.O. Box 20474
El Sobrante, CA 94820
510.758.0688
fogelcomix@aol.com

Comic Heaven
John Verzyl
P.O. Box 900
Big Sandy, TX 75755
903.636.5555

ComicLink
Joshua Nathanson
4842 Glenwood St.
Little Neck, NY 11362
718.423.6079
buysell@comiclink.com

Comics Guaranty, LLC
Steven Borock
Mark Haspel, John Chruscinski
P.O. Box 1938
Parsippany, NJ 07054-0237
1-877-NM-COMIC
www.cgccomics.com

Comics Ina Flash!
Tony Starks
P.O. Box 3611
Evansville, IN 47735
866.671.2146
comicflash@aol.com

David T. Alexander's Comics
David T. Alexander
P. O. Box 273086
Tampa, FL 33618
813.968.1805
dtacoll@tampa.mindspring.com

Doc Robinson's Comics
Doc Robinson
687 N. High St.; Suite 3A
Columbus, OH 43215
888.266.9362

Doug Sulipa's Comic World
Doug Sulipa
#10 Herscheld, Box #21986
Steinbach, Manitoba Canada R5G 1B5
204.346.3674
cworld@mb.sympatico.ca

Eldorado Comics
Austin Flinn
2110 E. Rt. 70
Cherry Hill, NJ 08034
609.489.1199
eldorado@uscom.com

Emerald City
Chad Rivard
9249 Seminole Blvd.
Seminole, FL 33772
727.797.0664
Cowardlylion@emeraldcitycomics.com

Conrad Eschenberg
108 Hustis Rd.
Cold Spring, NY 10516
914.265.2649
comicart@pcrealm.net

Fantasy Illustrated
David Smith
P.O. Box 30183
Seattle, WA 98103
206.784.7300
rocket@jetcity.com

Flying Color Comics
Joe Field
2980 Treat Blvd.
Concord, CA 94518
925.825.5410
flyingcolorscomics@compuserve.com

Four Color Comics
Robert Rogovin
115 W. 27th St.
New York, NY 10001
212.675.6990
Keybooks@aol.com

Funny Business Comics Ltd.
Dr. Roger Smyth
660B Amsterdam Ave.
New York, NY 10025
212.799.9477

Gary Dolgoff Comics
Gary Dolgoff
116 Pleasant St.
Easthampton, MA 01027
413.529.0326
gdcomics@javanet.com

Steven Gentner
2430 SW 83rd Avenue
Portland, OR 97225
503.228.7221

Geoffrey's Comics
Geoffrey Patterson
15900 Crenshaw Blvd.; Suite B
Gardena, CA 90249
888.538.3198

Golden Age Collectables Ltd.
Tony Morigi
1501 Pike Place Marketplace #401
Seattle, WA 98101
206.622.9799
GACollect@aol.com

Graham Crackers
Jamie Graham
1271 Rickert Dr., Suite 135
Naperville, IL 60540
630.355.4310
JamieGram@aol.com

Greg Manning Auctions, Inc.
Bill Hughes
775 Passaic Avenue
West Caldwell, NJ 07006
800.221.0243
info@gregmanning.com

John M. Hauser
P.O. Box 510673
New Berlin, WI 53151-0673
262.789.1863
JMHComics@aol.com

HighGradeComics.com
Robert C. Storms
333 Bronx River Rd., Apt. 727
Yonkers, NY 10704
914.237.6699
BobStorms@HighGradeComics.com

Jaster Collectibles
Ed Jaster
P.O. Box 30
St. Charles, IL 60174
630.762.9350
info@nearmint.com

JHV Associates
Joe Vereneault
P.O. Box 317
Woodbury Hts., NJ 08097
856.845.4010
jhvassoc@hotmail.com

Key Comics
Robert Letscher II
1318 N. Emerson
Mesa, AZ 85201
480.890.0055
keycomics@hotmail.com

Lee's Comics, Inc.
Lee Hester & Mark Crane
2222 S. El Camino Real
San Mateo, CA 94403
650.571.1489
lee@lcomics.com

Jon McClure
P.O. Box 2406
Newport, OR 97365
541.574.9376
MCCL@newportnet.com

Metro Entertainment
Bob Ficarra
6 W. Anapamu
Santa Barbara, CA 93101
805.963.2168
metrocomix@aol.com

Metropolis Collectibles, Inc.
Stephen Fishler & Vincent Zurzolo, Jr.
873 Broadway #201
New York, NY 10003
212.260.4147
buying@metropoliscomics.com

Mile High Comics
Chuck Rozanski
2151 West 56th Avenue
Denver, CO 80221
303.455.2659
chuck@milehighcomics.com

John Mlachnik
410 Second St. SW
Chisholm, MN 55719
218.254.3763

Motor City Comics
Michael Goldman & Gary Bishop
19785 W. 12 Mile Rd, Ste. 231
Southfield, MI 48076
248.426.8059
mccomics@earthlink.net

Michael Naiman
P.O. Box 151029
San Diego, CA 92175-1029
619.698.6666
mnaiman1@aol.com

New Dimension Comics
Todd McDevitt
20550 Route 19
Cranberry Township, PA 16066-7520
724.776.0433
NDC@SGI.NET

Pacific Comic Exchange
Robert Roter & Todd Reznik
P.O. Box 2629
Palos Verdes Peninsula, CA 90274
310.544.4936
info@pcei.com

Pedrin Conservatory
Chris Pedrin
P.O. Box 219
Redwood City, CA 94064
415.730.1569

Pegasus Hobbies
John Franco
5505 Moreno Blvd.
Montclair, CA 91763
909.931.4872

Pop Culture Resources
Gary Colabuono
P.O. Box 117
Elk Grove Village, IL 60009
800.344.6060
moondog100@home.com

Quantum Comics/ Marketing
Kevin J. Cleary
2490 Black Rock Tpk #290
Fairfield, CT 06430
203.336.9511
quantumcomics@juno.com

Quasar Comics and Collectibles
Bruce Edwards
P.O. Box 2227
Louisville, KY 40201-2227
502.451.4852
bruce@quasarcomics.com

Rare Books & Comics
Jim Payette
P.O. Box 750
Bethlehem, NH 03574-0750
603.869.2097

Redbeard's Book Den
Ron Pussell
P.O. Box 217
Crystal Bay, NV 89402-0217
775.831.4848
sales@redbeardsbookden

Robert Beerbohm Comic Art
Robert Beerbohm
P.O. Box 507
Fremont, NE 68026
402.727.4071
beerbohm@teknetwork.com

RTS Unlimited Inc.
Tim Collins
P.O. Box 150412
Lakewood, CO 80215-0412
303.403.1840
rtsunlimited@earthlink.net

San Diego Comics & Collectibles
Greg Pharis
6937 El Cajon
San Diego, CA 92115
619.698.1177

Matt Schiffman
310 SW 4th Ave. Suite #800
Portland, OR 97204
503.223.5784

Showcase New England
Dan Greenhalgh
67 Gail Dr.
Northford, CT 06472
203.484.4579

Sincere Comics
David Sincere
4667 Airport Blvd.
Regency Square
Mobile, AL 36608
334.342.2603
sincerecmx@aol.com

Terry's Comics
Terry O'Neill
P.O. Box 2232
Orange, CA 92859
714.288.8993
terryscomics@earthlink.net

Tropic Comics
Bruce Ellsworth
Erick Carter
P.O. Box 15428
Plantation, FL 33318
954.587.8878
sales@tropiccomics.com

Want List Comics
Dave Anderson
P.O. Box 701932
Tulsa, OK 74170-1932
918.299.0440

Warp 9
Lauren Becker
21 W. 14 Mile Rd.
Clawson, MI 48017
248.288.5699
Comiclord@aol.com

Harley Yee
P.O. Box 51758
Livonia, MI 48151-5758
800.731.1029

ADVERTISERS' INDEX

A

B

C

D

E

F

G

H

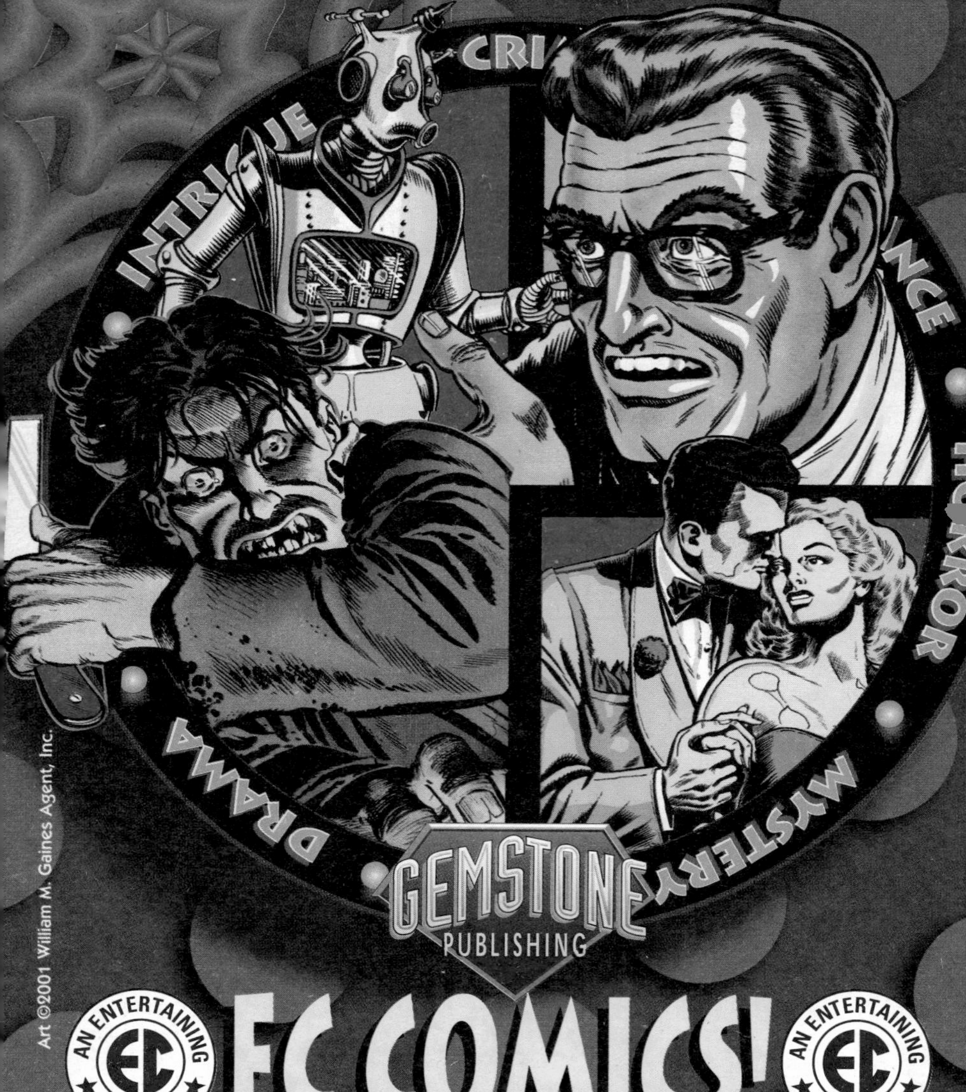
DRAMA
MYSTERY
GEMSTONE
PUBLISHING
Art ©2001 William M. Gaines Agent, Inc.

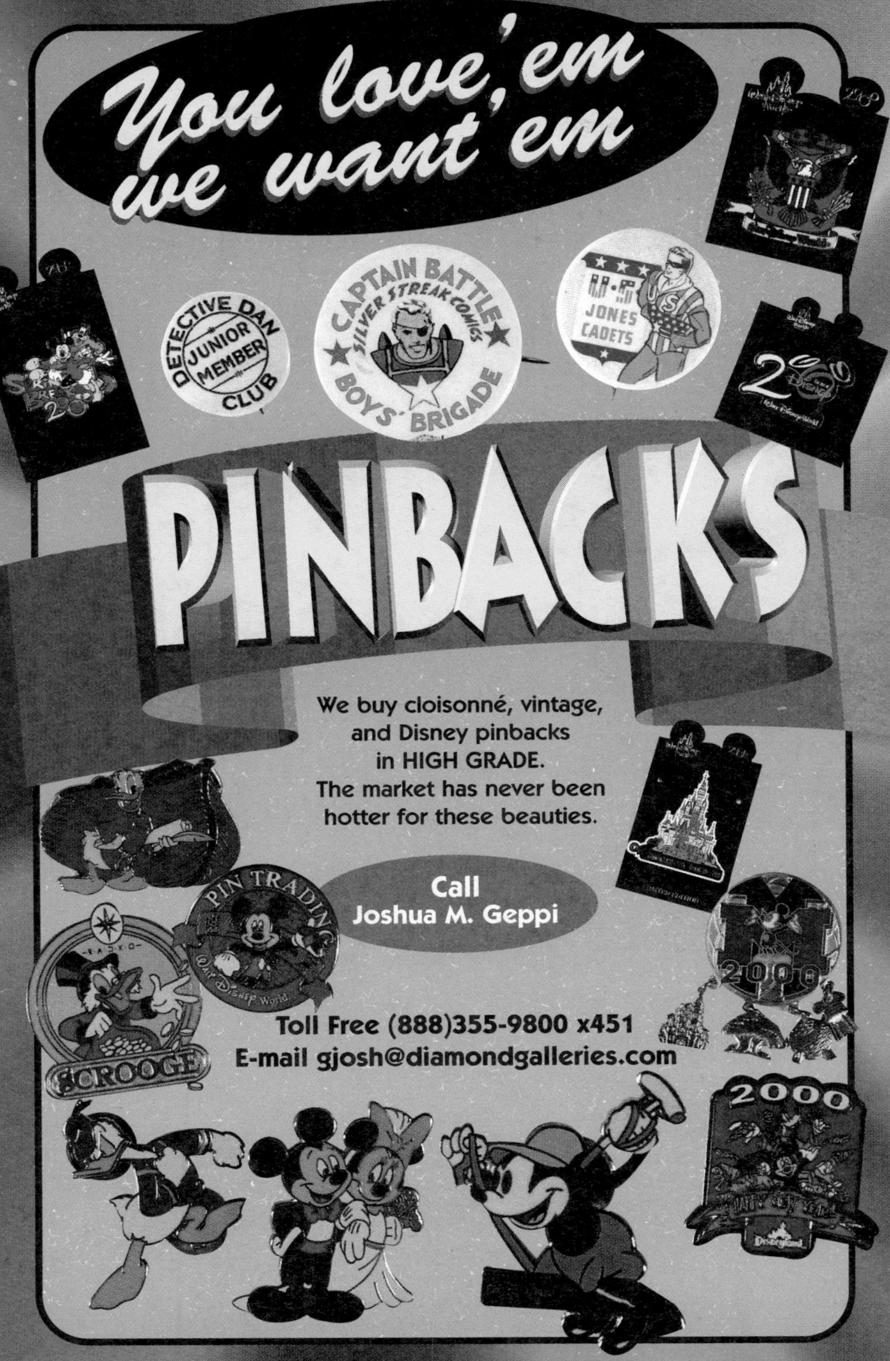
You love 'em
we want 'em
DETECTIVE DAN
JUNIOR MEMBER
CLUB
CAPTAIN BATTLE
SILVER STREAK COMICS
BOYS' BRIGADE
JONES CADETS
PINBACKS
We buy cloisonné, vintage,
and Disney pinbacks
in HIGH GRADE.
The market has never been
hotter for these beauties.
Call
Joshua M. Geppi
PIN TRADING
SCROOGE
2000
Toll Free (888)355-9800 x451
E-mail gjosh@diamondgalleries.com
2000

COLLECTOR BUYING PRE-1965 COMIC BOOKS

& RELATED COLLECTIBLES

COMIC BOOKS

CLUB KITS • PREMIUMS • OTHER CHARACTER COLLECTIBLES

I am the most serious collector you'll ever find…I LOVE THIS STUFF!

SEND YOUR SALE LIST!

Stephen A. Geppi
1966 Greenspring Drive, Suite 300
Timonium, MD 21093
Tel (888) 375-9800 ext. 271
Fax (410) 560-7143
gsteve@diamondcomics.com